American Casebook Series
Hornbook Series and Basic Legal Texts
Nutshell Series

of

WEST PUBLISHING COMPANY
P.O. Box 64526
St. Paul, Minnesota 55164–0526

ACCOUNTING

Faris' Accounting and Law in a Nutshell, 377 pages, 1984 (Text)

Fiflis, Kripke and Foster's Teaching Materials on Accounting for Business Lawyers, 3rd Ed., 838 pages, 1984 (Casebook)

Siegel and Siegel's Accounting and Financial Disclosure: A Guide to Basic Concepts, 259 pages, 1983 (Text)

ADMINISTRATIVE LAW

Davis' Cases, Text and Problems on Administrative Law, 6th Ed., 683 pages, 1977 (Casebook)

Davis' Basic Text on Administrative Law, 3rd Ed., 617 pages, 1972 (Text)

Gellhorn and Boyer's Administrative Law and Process in a Nutshell, 2nd Ed., 445 pages, 1981 (Text)

Mashaw and Merrill's Cases and Materials on Administrative Law–The American Public Law System, 2nd Ed., 976 pages, 1985 (Casebook)

Robinson, Gellhorn and Bruff's The Administrative Process, 3rd Ed., approximately 950 pages, 1986 (Casebook)

ADMIRALTY

Healy and Sharpe's Cases and Materials on Admiralty, 2nd Ed., approximately 900 pages, 1986 (Casebook)

Maraist's Admiralty in a Nutshell, 390 pages, 1983 (Text)

Sohn and Gustafson's Law of the Sea in a Nutshell, 264 pages, 1984 (Text)

AGENCY—PARTNERSHIP

Fessler's Alternatives to Incorporation for Persons in Quest of Profit, 2nd Ed., approximately 300 pages, 1986 (Casebook)

AGENCY—PARTNERSHIP—Continued

Henn's Cases and Materials on Agency, Partnership and Other Unincorporated Business Enterprises, 2nd Ed., 733 pages, 1985 (Casebook)

Reuschlein and Gregory's Hornbook on the Law of Agency and Partnership, 625 pages, 1979, with 1981 pocket part (Text)

Seavey, Reuschlein and Hall's Cases on Agency and Partnership, 599 pages, 1962 (Casebook)

Selected Corporation and Partnership Statutes and Forms, 555 pages, 1985

Steffen and Kerr's Cases and Materials on Agency-Partnership, 4th Ed., 859 pages, 1980 (Casebook)

Steffen's Agency-Partnership in a Nutshell, 364 pages, 1977 (Text)

AGRICULTURAL LAW

Meyer, Pedersen, Thorson and Davidson's Agricultural Law: Cases and Materials, 931 pages, 1985 (Casebook)

ALTERNATIVE DISPUTE RESOLUTION

Kanowitz' Cases and Materials on Alternative Dispute Resolution, 1024 pages, 1986 (Casebook)

AMERICAN INDIAN LAW

Canby's American Indian Law in a Nutshell, 288 pages, 1981 (Text)

Getches and Wilkinson's Cases on Federal Indian Law, 2nd Ed., approximately 750 pages, 1986 (Casebook)

ANTITRUST LAW

Gellhorn's Antitrust Law and Economics in a Nutshell, 2nd Ed., 425 pages, 1981 (Text)

Gifford and Raskind's Cases and Materials on Antitrust, 694 pages, 1983 with 1985 Supplement (Casebook)

List current as of January, 1986

T7202—1g

I

LAW SCHOOL PUBLICATIONS—Continued

ANTITRUST LAW—Continued

Hovenkamp's Economics and Federal Antitrust Law, Student Ed., 414 pages, 1985 (Text)

Oppenheim, Weston and McCarthy's Cases and Comments on Federal Antitrust Laws, 4th Ed., 1168 pages, 1981 with 1985 Supplement (Casebook)

Posner and Easterbrook's Cases and Economic Notes on Antitrust, 2nd Ed., 1077 pages, 1981, with 1984–85 Supplement (Casebook)

Sullivan's Hornbook of the Law of Antitrust, 886 pages, 1977 (Text)

See also Regulated Industries, Trade Regulation

ART LAW

DuBoff's Art Law in a Nutshell, 335 pages, 1984 (Text)

BANKING LAW

Lovett's Banking and Financial Institutions in a Nutshell, 409 pages, 1984 (Text)

Symons and White's Teaching Materials on Banking Law, 2nd Ed., 993 pages, 1984 (Casebook)

BUSINESS PLANNING

Epstein and Scheinfeld's Teaching Materials on Business Reorganization Under the Bankruptcy Code, 216 pages, 1980 (Casebook)

Painter's Problems and Materials in Business Planning, 2nd Ed., 1008 pages, 1984 (Casebook)

Selected Securities and Business Planning Statutes, Rules and Forms, 470 pages, 1985

CIVIL PROCEDURE

Casad's Res Judicata in a Nutshell, 310 pages, 1976 (text)

Cound, Friedenthal, Miller and Sexton's Cases and Materials on Civil Procedure, 4th Ed., 1202 pages, 1985 with 1985 Supplement (Casebook)

Ehrenzweig, Louisell and Hazard's Jurisdiction in a Nutshell, 4th Ed., 232 pages, 1980 (Text)

Federal Rules of Civil-Appellate-Criminal Procedure—West Law School Edition, 852 pages, 1985

Friedenthal, Kane and Miller's Hornbook on Civil Procedure, 876 pages, 1985 (Text)

Kane's Civil Procedure in a Nutshell, 2nd Ed., 306 pages, 1986 (Text)

Karlen, Meisenholder, Stevens and Vestal's Cases on Civil Procedure, 923 pages, 1975 (Casebook)

Koffler and Reppy's Hornbook on Common Law Pleading, 663 pages, 1969 (Text)

CIVIL PROCEDURE—Continued

Marcus and Sherman's Complex Litigation—Cases and Materials on Advanced Civil Procedure, 846 pages, 1985 (Casebook)

Park's Computer-Aided Exercises on Civil Procedure, 2nd Ed., 167 pages, 1983 (Coursebook)

Siegel's Hornbook on New York Practice, 1011 pages, 1978 with 1985 Pocket Part (Text)

See also Federal Jurisdiction and Procedure

CIVIL RIGHTS

Abernathy's Cases and Materials on Civil Rights, 660 pages, 1980 (Casebook)

Cohen's Cases on the Law of Deprivation of Liberty: A Study in Social Control, 755 pages, 1980 (Casebook)

Lockhart, Kamisar and Choper's Cases on Constitutional Rights and Liberties, 5th Ed., 1298 pages plus Appendix, 1981, with 1985 Supplement (Casebook)—reprint from Lockhart, et al. Cases on Constitutional Law, 5th Ed., 1980

Vieira's Civil Rights in a Nutshell, 279 pages, 1978 (Text)

COMMERCIAL LAW

Bailey's Secured Transactions in a Nutshell, 2nd Ed., 391 pages, 1981 (Text)

Epstein and Martin's Basic Uniform Commercial Code Teaching Materials, 2nd Ed., 667 pages, 1983 (Casebook)

Henson's Hornbook on Secured Transactions Under the U.C.C., 2nd Ed., 504 pages, 1979 with 1979 P.P. (Text)

Murray's Commercial Law, Problems and Materials, 366 pages, 1975 (Coursebook)

Nordstrom and Clovis' Problems and Materials on Commercial Paper, 458 pages, 1972 (Casebook)

Nordstrom and Lattin's Problems and Materials on Sales and Secured Transactions, 809 pages, 1968 (Casebook)

Nordstrom, Murray and Clovis' Problems and Materials on Sales, 515 pages, 1982 (Casebook)

Selected Commercial Statutes, 1389 pages, 1985

Speidel, Summers and White's Teaching Materials on Commercial and Consumer Law, 3rd Ed., 1490 pages, 1981 (Casebook)

Stockton's Sales in a Nutshell, 2nd Ed., 370 pages, 1981 (Text)

Stone's Uniform Commercial Code in a Nutshell, 2nd Ed., 516 pages, 1984 (Text)

Uniform Commercial Code, Official Text with Comments, 994 pages, 1978

UCC Article 9, Reprint from 1962 Code, 128 pages, 1976

UCC Article 9, 1972 Amendments, 304 pages, 1978

COMMERCIAL LAW—Continued

Weber and Speidel's Commercial Paper in a Nutshell, 3rd Ed., 404 pages, 1982 (Text)

White and Summers' Hornbook on the Uniform Commercial Code, 2nd Ed., 1250 pages, 1980 (Text)

COMMUNITY PROPERTY

Mennell's Community Property in a Nutshell, 447 pages, 1982 (Text)

Verrall and Bird's Cases and Materials on California Community Property, 4th Ed., 549 pages, 1983 (Casebook)

COMPARATIVE LAW

Barton, Gibbs, Li and Merryman's Law in Radically Different Cultures, 960 pages, 1983 (Casebook)

Glendon, Gordon and Osakive's Comparative Legal Traditions: Text, Materials and Cases on the Civil Law, Common Law, and Socialist Law Traditions, 1091 pages, 1985 (Casebook)

Glendon, Gordon, and Osakwe's Comparative Legal Traditions in a Nutshell, 402 pages, 1982 (Text)

Langbein's Comparative Criminal Procedure: Germany, 172 pages, 1977 (Casebook)

COMPUTERS AND LAW

Mason's An Introduction to the Use of Computers in Law, 223 pages, 1984 (Text)

CONFLICT OF LAWS

Cramton, Currie and Kay's Cases-Comments-Questions on Conflict of Laws, 3rd Ed., 1026 pages, 1981 (Casebook)

Scoles and Hay's Hornbook on Conflict of Laws, Student Ed., 1085 pages, 1982 (Text)

Scoles and Weintraub's Cases and Materials on Conflict of Laws, 2nd Ed., 966 pages, 1972, with 1978 Supplement (Casebook)

Siegel's Conflicts in a Nutshell, 469 pages, 1982 (Text)

CONSTITUTIONAL LAW

Engdahl's Constitutional Power in a Nutshell: Federal and State, 411 pages, 1974 (Text)

Lockhart, Kamisar, Choper and Shiffrin's Cases-Comments-Questions on Constitutional Law, 6th Ed., approximately 1590 pages, 1986 (Casebook)

Lockhart, Kamisar and Choper's Cases-Comments-Questions on the American Constitution, 5th Ed., 1185 pages plus Appendix, 1981, with 1985 Supplement (Casebook)—abridgment of Lockhart, et al. Cases on Constitutional Law, 5th Ed., 1980

CONSTITUTIONAL LAW—Continued

Manning's The Law of Church-State Relations in a Nutshell, 305 pages, 1981 (Text)

Miller's Presidential Power in a Nutshell, 328 pages, 1977 (Text)

Nowak, Rotunda and Young's Hornbook on Constitutional Law, 3rd Ed., Student Ed., approximately 1100 pages, 1986 (Text)

Rotunda's Modern Constitutional Law: Cases and Notes, 2nd Ed., 1004 pages, 1985, with 1985 Supplement (Casebook)

Williams' Constitutional Analysis in a Nutshell, 388 pages, 1979 (Text)

See also Civil Rights

CONSUMER LAW

Epstein and Nickles' Consumer Law in a Nutshell, 2nd Ed., 418 pages, 1981 (Text)

McCall's Consumer Protection, Cases, Notes and Materials, 594 pages, 1977, with 1977 Statutory Supplement (Casebook)

Selected Commercial Statutes, 1389 pages, 1985

Spanogle and Rohner's Cases and Materials on Consumer Law, 693 pages, 1979, with 1982 Supplement (Casebook)

See also Commercial Law

CONTRACTS

Calamari & Perillo's Cases and Problems on Contracts, 1061 pages, 1978 (Casebook)

Calamari and Perillo's Hornbook on Contracts, 2nd Ed., 878 pages, 1977 (Text)

Corbin's Text on Contracts, One Volume Student Edition, 1224 pages, 1952 (Text)

Fessler and Loiseaux's Cases and Materials on Contracts, 837 pages, 1982 (Casebook)

Freedman's Cases and Materials on Contracts, 658 pages, 1973 (Casebook)

Friedman's Contract Remedies in a Nutshell, 323 pages, 1981 (Text)

Fuller and Eisenberg's Cases on Basic Contract Law, 4th Ed., 1203 pages, 1981 (Casebook)

Hamilton, Rau and Weintraub's Cases and Materials on Contracts, 830 pages, 1984 (Casebook)

Jackson and Bollinger's Cases on Contract Law in Modern Society, 2nd Ed., 1329 pages, 1980 (Casebook)

Keyes' Government Contracts in a Nutshell, 423 pages, 1979 (Text)

Reitz's Cases on Contracts as Basic Commercial Law, 763 pages, 1975 (Casebook)

Schaber and Rohwer's Contracts in a Nutshell, 2nd Ed., 425 pages, 1984 (Text)

COPYRIGHT

See Patent and Copyright Law

LAW SCHOOL PUBLICATIONS—Continued

CORPORATIONS

Hamilton's Cases on Corporations—Including Partnerships and Limited Partnerships, 3rd Ed., approximately 1223 pages, 1986 with 1986 Statutory Supplement (Casebook)

Hamilton's Law of Corporations in a Nutshell, 379 pages, 1980 (Text)

Henn's Cases on Corporations, 1279 pages, 1974, with 1980 Supplement (Casebook)

Henn and Alexander's Hornbook on Corporations, 3rd Ed., Student Ed., 1371 pages, 1983 (Text)

Jennings and Buxbaum's Cases and Materials on Corporations, 5th Ed., 1180 pages, 1979 (Casebook)

Selected Corporation and Partnership Statutes, Regulations and Forms, 555 pages, 1985

Solomon, Stevenson and Schwartz' Materials and Problems on Corporations: Law and Policy, 1172 pages, 1982 with 1984 Supplement (Casebook)

CORPORATE FINANCE

Hamilton's Cases and Materials on Corporate Finance, 895 pages, 1984 (Casebook)

CORRECTIONS

Krantz's Cases and Materials on the Law of Corrections and Prisoners' Rights, 3rd Ed., approximately 760 pages, 1986 (Casebook)

Krantz's Law of Corrections and Prisoners' Rights in a Nutshell, 2nd Ed., 384 pages, 1983 (Text)

Popper's Post-Conviction Remedies in a Nutshell, 360 pages, 1978 (Text)

Robbins' Cases and Materials on Post Conviction Remedies, 506 pages, 1982 (Casebook)

CREDITOR'S RIGHTS

Bankruptcy Code, Rules and Forms, Law School and C.L.E. Ed., 602 pages, 1984

Epstein's Debtor-Creditor Law in a Nutshell, 3rd Ed., 383 pages, 1986 (Text)

Epstein and Landers' Debtors and Creditors: Cases and Materials, 2nd Ed., 689 pages, 1982 (Casebook)

Epstein and Sheinfeld's Teaching Materials on Business Reorganization Under the Bankruptcy Code, 216 pages, 1980 (Casebook)

LoPucki's Player's Manual for the Debtor-Creditor Game, 123 pages, 1985 (Coursebook)

Riesenfeld's Cases and Materials on Creditors' Remedies and Debtors' Protection, 3rd Ed., 810 pages, 1979 with 1979 Statutory Supplement and 1981 Case Supplement (Casebook)

CREDITOR'S RIGHTS—Continued

White's Bankruptcy and Creditor's Rights: Cases and Materials, 812 pages, 1985 (Casebook)

CRIMINAL LAW AND CRIMINAL PROCEDURE

Abrams', Federal Criminal Law and its Enforcement, approximately 978 pages, 1986 (Casebook)

Cohen and Gobert's Problems in Criminal Law, 297 pages, 1976 (Problem book)

Dix and Sharlot's Cases and Materials on Criminal Law, 2nd Ed., 771 pages, 1979 (Casebook)

Federal Rules of Civil-Appellate-Criminal Procedure—West Law School Edition, 852 pages, 1985

Grano's Problems in Criminal Procedure, 2nd Ed., 176 pages, 1981 (Problem book)

Israel and LaFave's Criminal Procedure in a Nutshell, 3rd Ed., 438 pages, 1980 (Text)

Johnson's Cases, Materials and Text on Criminal Law, 3rd Ed., 783 pages, 1985 (Casebook)

Kamisar, LaFave and Israel's Cases, Comments and Questions on Modern Criminal Procedure, 5th ed., 1635 pages plus Appendix, 1980 with 1985 Supplement (Casebook)

Kamisar, LaFave and Israel's Cases, Comments and Questions on Basic Criminal Procedure, 5th Ed., 869 pages, 1980 with 1985 Supplement (Casebook)—reprint from Kamisar, et al. Modern Criminal Procedure, 5th ed., 1980

LaFave's Modern Criminal Law: Cases, Comments and Questions, 789 pages, 1978 (Casebook)

LaFave and Israel's Hornbook on Criminal Procedure, Student Ed., 1142 pages, 1985 with 1985 P.P. (Text)

LaFave and Scott's Hornbook on Criminal Law, 2nd Ed., approximately 800 pages, 1986 (Text)

Langbein's Comparative Criminal Procedure: Germany, 172 pages, 1977 (Casebook)

Loewy's Criminal Law in a Nutshell, 302 pages, 1975 (Text)

Saltzburg's American Criminal Procedure, Cases and Commentary, 2nd Ed., 1193 pages, 1985 with 1985 Supplement (Casebook)

Uviller's The Processes of Criminal Justice: Investigation and Adjudication, 2nd Ed., 1384 pages, 1979 with 1979 Statutory Supplement and 1983 Update (Casebook)

LAW SCHOOL PUBLICATIONS—Continued

CRIMINAL LAW AND CRIMINAL PROCEDURE—Continued

Uviller's The Processes of Criminal Justice: Adjudication, 2nd Ed., 730 pages, 1979. Soft-cover reprint from Uviller's The Processes of Criminal Justice: Investigation and Adjudication, 2nd Ed. (Casebook)

Uviller's The Processes of Criminal Justice: Investigation, 2nd Ed., 655 pages, 1979. Soft-cover reprint from Uviller's The Processes of Criminal Justice: Investigation and Adjudication, 2nd Ed. (Casebook)

Vorenberg's Cases on Criminal Law and Procedure, 2nd Ed., 1088 pages, 1981 with 1985 Supplement (Casebook)

See also Corrections, Juvenile Justice

DECEDENTS ESTATES

See Trusts and Estates

DOMESTIC RELATIONS

Clark's Cases and Problems on Domestic Relations, 3rd Ed., 1153 pages, 1980 (Casebook)

Clark's Hornbook on Domestic Relations, 754 pages, 1968 (Text)

Krause's Cases and Materials on Family Law, 2nd Ed., 1221 pages, 1983 with 1986 Supplement (Casebook)

Krause's Family Law in a Nutshell, 2nd Ed., approximately 420 pages, 1986 (Text)

Krauskopf's Cases on Property Division at Marriage Dissolution, 250 pages, 1984 (Casebook)

ECONOMICS, LAW AND

Goetz' Cases and Materials on Law and Economics, 547 pages, 1984 (Casebook)

See also Antitrust, Regulated Industries

EDUCATION LAW

Alexander and Alexander's The Law of Schools, Students and Teachers in a Nutshell, 409 pages, 1984 (Text)

Morris' The Constitution and American Education, 2nd Ed., 992 pages, 1980 (Casebook)

EMPLOYMENT DISCRIMINATION

Player's Cases and Materials on Employment Discrimination Law, 2nd Ed., 782 pages, 1984 (Casebook)

Player's Federal Law of Employment Discrimination in a Nutshell, 2nd Ed., 402 pages, 1981 (Text)

See also Women and the Law

ENERGY AND NATURAL RESOURCES LAW

Laitos' Cases and Materials on Natural Resources Law, 938 pages, 1985 (Casebook)

ENERGY AND NATURAL RESOURCES LAW—Continued

Rodgers' Cases and Materials on Energy and Natural Resources Law, 2nd Ed., 877 pages, 1983 (Casebook)

Selected Environmental Law Statutes, 786 pages, 1985

Tomain's Energy Law in a Nutshell, 338 pages, 1981 (Text)

See also Environmental Law, Oil and Gas, Water Law

ENVIRONMENTAL LAW

Bonine and McGarity's Cases and Materials on the Law of Environment and Pollution, 1076 pages, 1984 (Casebook)

Findley and Farber's Cases and Materials on Environmental Law, 2nd Ed., 813 pages, 1985 (Casebook)

Findley and Farber's Environmental Law in a Nutshell, 343 pages, 1983 (Text)

Rodgers' Hornbook on Environmental Law, 956 pages, 1977 with 1984 pocket part (Text)

Selected Environmental Law Statutes, 786 pages, 1985

See also Energy Law, Natural Resources Law, Water Law

EQUITY

See Remedies

ESTATES

See Trusts and Estates

ESTATE PLANNING

Kurtz' Cases, Materials and Problems on Family Estate Planning, 853 pages, 1983 (Casebook)

Lynn's Introduction to Estate Planning, in a Nutshell, 3rd Ed., 370 pages, 1983 (Text)

See also Taxation

EVIDENCE

Broun and Meisenholder's Problems in Evidence, 2nd Ed., 304 pages, 1981 (Problem book)

Cleary and Strong's Cases, Materials and Problems on Evidence, 3rd Ed., 1143 pages, 1981 (Casebook)

Federal Rules of Evidence for United States Courts and Magistrates, 337 pages, 1984

Graham's Federal Rules of Evidence in a Nutshell, 429 pages, 1981 (Text)

Kimball's Programmed Materials on Problems in Evidence, 380 pages, 1978 (Problem book)

Lempert and Saltzburg's A Modern Approach to Evidence: Text, Problems, Transcripts and Cases, 2nd Ed., 1296 pages, 1983 (Casebook)

Lilly's Introduction to the Law of Evidence, 486 pages, 1978 (Text)

LAW SCHOOL PUBLICATIONS—Continued

EVIDENCE—Continued

McCormick, Elliott and Sutton's Cases and Materials on Evidence, 5th Ed., 1212 pages, 1981 (Casebook)

McCormick's Hornbook on Evidence, 3rd Ed., Student Ed., 1155 pages, 1984 (Text)

Rothstein's Evidence, State and Federal Rules in a Nutshell, 2nd Ed., 514 pages, 1981 (Text)

Saltzburg's Evidence Supplement: Rules, Statutes, Commentary, 245 pages, 1980 (Casebook Supplement)

FEDERAL JURISDICTION AND PROCEDURE

Currie's Cases and Materials on Federal Courts, 3rd Ed., 1042 pages, 1982 with 1985 Supplement (Casebook)

Currie's Federal Jurisdiction in a Nutshell, 2nd Ed., 258 pages, 1981 (Text)

Federal Rules of Civil-Appellate-Criminal Procedure—West Law School Edition, 852 pages, 1985

Forrester and Moye's Cases and Materials on Federal Jurisdiction and Procedure, 3rd Ed., 917 pages, 1977 with 1985 Supplement (Casebook)

Redish's Cases, Comments and Questions on Federal Courts, 878 pages, 1983 with 1986 Supplement (Casebook)

Vetri and Merrill's Federal Courts, Problems and Materials, 2nd Ed., 232 pages, 1984 (Problem Book)

Wright's Hornbook on Federal Courts, 4th Ed., Student Ed., 870 pages, 1983 (Text)

FUTURE INTERESTS

See Trusts and Estates

IMMIGRATION LAW

Aleinikoff and Martin's Immigration Process and Policy, 1042 pages, 1985 (Casebook)

Weissbrodt's Immigration Law and Procedure in a Nutshell, 345 pages, 1984 (Text)

INDIAN LAW

See American Indian Law

INSURANCE

Dobbyn's Insurance Law in a Nutshell, 281 pages, 1981 (Text)

Keeton's Cases on Basic Insurance Law, 2nd Ed., 1086 pages, 1977

Keeton's Basic Text on Insurance Law, 712 pages, 1971 (Text)

Keeton's Case Supplement to Keeton's Basic Text on Insurance Law, 334 pages, 1978 (Casebook)

Keeton's Programmed Problems in Insurance Law, 243 pages, 1972 (Text Supplement)

INSURANCE—Continued

York and Whelan's Cases, Materials and Problems on Insurance Law, 715 pages, 1982, with 1985 Supplement (Casebook)

INTERNATIONAL LAW

Buergenthal and Maier's Public International Law in a Nutshell, 262 pages, 1985 (Text)

Folsom, Gordon and Spanogle's International Business Transactions – a Problem-Oriented Coursebook, 1160 pages, 1986 (Casebook)

Henkin, Pugh, Schachter and Smit's Cases and Materials on International Law, 2nd Ed., 1152 pages, 1980, with Documents Supplement (Casebook)

Jackson's Legal Problems of International Economic Relations, 1097 pages, 1977, with Documents Supplement (Casebook)

Kirgis' International Organizations in Their Legal Setting, 1016 pages, 1977, with 1981 Supplement (Casebook)

Weston, Falk and D'Amato's International Law and World Order—A Problem Oriented Coursebook, 1195 pages, 1980, with Documents Supplement (Casebook)

Wilson's International Business Transactions in a Nutshell, 2nd Ed., 476 pages, 1984 (Text)

INTERVIEWING AND COUNSELING

Binder and Price's Interviewing and Counseling, 232 pages, 1977 (Text)

Shaffer's Interviewing and Counseling in a Nutshell, 353 pages, 1976 (Text)

INTRODUCTION TO LAW STUDY

Dobbyn's So You Want to go to Law School, Revised First Edition, 206 pages, 1976 (Text)

Hegland's Introduction to the Study and Practice of Law in a Nutshell, 418 pages, 1983 (Text)

Kinyon's Introduction to Law Study and Law Examinations in a Nutshell, 389 pages, 1971 (Text)

See also Legal Method and Legal System

JUDICIAL ADMINISTRATION

Nelson's Cases and Materials on Judicial Administration and the Administration of Justice, 1032 pages, 1974 (Casebook)

JURISPRUDENCE

Christie's Text and Readings on Jurisprudence—The Philosophy of Law, 1056 pages, 1973 (Casebook)

JUVENILE JUSTICE

Fox's Cases and Materials on Modern Juvenile Justice, 2nd Ed., 960 pages, 1981 (Casebook)

JUVENILE JUSTICE—Continued

Fox's Juvenile Courts in a Nutshell, 3rd Ed., 291 pages, 1984 (Text)

LABOR LAW

Gorman's Basic Text on Labor Law—Unionization and Collective Bargaining, 914 pages, 1976 (Text)

Leslie's Labor Law in a Nutshell, 2nd Ed., 397 pages, 1986 (Text)

Nolan's Labor Arbitration Law and Practice in a Nutshell, 358 pages, 1979 (Text)

Oberer, Hanslowe and Andersen's Cases and Materials on Labor Law—Collective Bargaining in a Free Society, 2nd Ed., 1168 pages, 1979, with 1979 Statutory Supplement and 1982 Case Supplement (Casebook)

See also Employment Discrimination, Social Legislation

LAND FINANCE

See Real Estate Transactions

LAND USE

Callies and Freilich's Cases and Materials on Land Use, approximately 1250 pages, 1986 (Casebook)

Hagman's Cases on Public Planning and Control of Urban and Land Development, 2nd Ed., 1301 pages, 1980 (Casebook)

Hagman and Juergensmeyer's Hornbook on Urban Planning and Land Development Control Law, 2nd Ed., Student Edition, approximately 580 pages, 1986 (Text)

Wright and Gitelman's Cases and Materials on Land Use, 3rd Ed., 1300 pages, 1982 (Casebook)

Wright and Wright's Land Use in a Nutshell, 2nd Ed., 356 pages (Text)

LEGAL HISTORY

Presser and Zainaldin's Cases on Law and American History, 855 pages, 1980 (Casebook)

See also Legal Method and Legal System

LEGAL METHOD AND LEGAL SYSTEM

Aldisert's Readings, Materials and Cases in the Judicial Process, 948 pages, 1976 (Casebook)

Berch and Berch's Introduction to Legal Method and Process, 550 pages, 1985 (Casebook)

Bodenheimer, Oakley and Love's Readings and Cases on an Introduction to the Anglo-American Legal System, 161 pages, 1980 (Casebook)

Davies and Lawry's Institutions and Methods of the Law—Introductory Teaching Materials, 547 pages, 1982 (Casebook)

LEGAL METHOD AND LEGAL SYSTEM—Continued

Dvorkin, Himmelstein and Lesnick's Becoming a Lawyer: A Humanistic Perspective on Legal Education and Professionalism, 211 pages, 1981 (Text)

Fryer and Orentlicher's Cases and Materials on Legal Method and Legal System, 1043 pages, 1967 (Casebook)

Greenberg's Judicial Process and Social Change, 666 pages, 1977 (Casebook)

Kelso and Kelso's Studying Law: An Introduction, 587 pages, 1984 (Coursebook)

Kempin's Historical Introduction to Anglo-American Law in a Nutshell, 2nd Ed., 280 pages, 1973 (Text)

Kimball's Historical Introduction to the Legal System, 610 pages, 1966 (Casebook)

Murphy's Cases and Materials on Introduction to Law—Legal Process and Procedure, 772 pages, 1977 (Casebook)

Reynolds' Judicial Process in a Nutshell, 292 pages, 1980 (Text)

See also Legal Research and Writing

LEGAL PROFESSION

Aronson, Devine and Fisch's Problems, Cases and Materials on Professional Responsibility, 745 pages, 1985 (Casebook)

Aronson and Weckstein's Professional Responsibility in a Nutshell, 399 pages, 1980 (Text)

Mellinkoff's The Conscience of a Lawyer, 304 pages, 1973 (Text)

Mellinkoff's Lawyers and the System of Justice, 983 pages, 1976 (Casebook)

Pirsig and Kirwin's Cases and Materials on Professional Responsibility, 4th Ed., 603 pages, 1984 (Casebook)

Schwartz and Wydick's Problems in Legal Ethics, 285 pages, 1983 (Casebook)

Selected Statutes, Rules and Standards on the Legal Profession, 276 pages, Revised 1984

Smith's Preventing Legal Malpractice, 142 pages, 1981 (Text)

Wolfram's Hornbook on Modern Legal Ethics, Student Edition, approximately 950 pages, 1986 (Text)

LEGAL RESEARCH AND WRITING

Cohen's Legal Research in a Nutshell, 4th Ed., 450 pages, 1985 (Text)

Cohen and Berring's How to Find the Law, 8th Ed., 790 pages, 1983. Problem book by Foster and Kelly available (Casebook)

Cohen and Berring's Finding the Law, 8th Ed., Abridged Ed., 556 pages, 1984 (Casebook)

Dickerson's Materials on Legal Drafting, 425 pages, 1981 (Casebook)

Felsenfeld and Siegel's Writing Contracts in Plain English, 290 pages, 1981 (Text)

LAW SCHOOL PUBLICATIONS—Continued

LEGAL RESEARCH AND WRITING—
Continued

Gopen's Writing From a Legal Perspective, 225 pages, 1981 (Text)

Mellinkoff's Legal Writing—Sense and Nonsense, 242 pages, 1982 (Text)

Rombauer's Legal Problem Solving—Analysis, Research and Writing, 4th Ed., 424 pages, 1983 (Coursebook)

Squires and Rombauer's Legal Writing in a Nutshell, 294 pages, 1982 (Text)

Statsky's Legal Research, Writing and Analysis, 2nd Ed., 167 pages, 1982 (Coursebook)

Statsky and Wernet's Case Analysis and Fundamentals of Legal Writing, 2nd Ed., 441 pages, 1984 (Text)

Teply's Programmed Materials on Legal Research and Citation, 334 pages, 1982. Student Library Exercises available (Coursebook)

Weihofen's Legal Writing Style, 2nd Ed., 332 pages, 1980 (Text)

LEGISLATION

Davies' Legislative Law and Process in a Nutshell, 2nd Ed., approximately 300 pages, 1986 (Text)

Nutting and Dickerson's Cases and Materials on Legislation, 5th Ed., 744 pages, 1978 (Casebook)

Statsky's Legislative Analysis: How to Use Statutes and Regulations, 2nd Ed., 217 pages, 1984 (Text)

LOCAL GOVERNMENT

McCarthy's Local Government Law in a Nutshell, 2nd Ed., 404 pages, 1983 (Text)

Michelman and Sandalow's Cases-Comments-Questions on Government in Urban Areas, 1216 pages, 1970, with 1972 Supplement (Casebook)

Reynolds' Hornbook on Local Government Law, 860 pages, 1982 (Text)

Valente's Cases and Materials on Local Government Law, 2nd Ed., 980 pages, 1980 with 1982 Supplement (Casebook)

MASS COMMUNICATION LAW

Gillmor and Barron's Cases and Comment on Mass Communication Law, 4th Ed., 1076 pages, 1984 (Casebook)

Ginsburg's Regulation of Broadcasting: Law and Policy Towards Radio, Television and Cable Communications, 741 pages, 1979, with 1983 Supplement (Casebook)

Zuckman and Gayne's Mass Communications Law in a Nutshell, 2nd Ed., 473 pages, 1983 (Text)

MEDICINE, LAW AND

King's The Law of Medical Malpractice in a Nutshell, 340 pages, 1977 (Text)

MEDICINE, LAW AND—Continued

Shapiro and Spece's Problems, Cases and Materials on Bioethics and Law, 892 pages, 1981 (Casebook)

Sharpe, Fiscina and Head's Cases on Law and Medicine, 882 pages, 1978 (Casebook)

MILITARY LAW

Shanor and Terrell's Military Law in a Nutshell, 378 pages, 1980 (Text)

MORTGAGES

See Real Estate Transactions

NATURAL RESOURCES LAW

See Energy and Natural Resources Law

NEGOTIATION

Edwards and White's Problems, Readings and Materials on the Lawyer as a Negotiator, 484 pages, 1977 (Casebook)

Williams' Legal Negotiation and Settlement, 207 pages, 1983 (Coursebook)

OFFICE PRACTICE

Hegland's Trial and Practice Skills in a Nutshell, 346 pages, 1978 (Text)

Strong and Clark's Law Office Management, 424 pages, 1974 (Casebook)

See also Computers and Law, Interviewing and Counseling, Negotiation

OIL AND GAS

Hemingway's Hornbook on Oil and Gas, 2nd Ed., Student Ed., 543 pages, 1983 (Text)

Huie, Woodward and Smith's Cases and Materials on Oil and Gas, 2nd Ed., 955 pages, 1972 (Casebook)

Kuntz, Lowe, Anderson and Smith's Cases and Materials on Oil and Gas Law, approximately 805 pages, 1986 (Casebook)

Lowe's Oil and Gas Law in a Nutshell, 443 pages, 1983 (Text)

See also Energy and Natural Resources Law

PARTNERSHIP

See Agency—Partnership

PATENT AND COPYRIGHT LAW

Choate and Francis' Cases and Materials on Patent Law, 2nd Ed., 1110 pages, 1981 (Casebook)

Miller and Davis' Intellectual Property—Patents, Trademarks and Copyright in a Nutshell, 428 pages, 1983 (Text)

Nimmer's Cases on Copyright and Other Aspects of Entertainment Litigation, 3rd Ed., 1025 pages, 1985 (Casebook)

LAW SCHOOL PUBLICATIONS—Continued

POVERTY LAW

Brudno's Poverty, Inequality, and the Law: Cases-Commentary-Analysis, 934 pages, 1976 (Casebook)

LaFrance, Schroeder, Bennett and Boyd's Hornbook on Law of the Poor, 558 pages, 1973 (Text)

See also Social Legislation

PRODUCTS LIABILITY

Noel and Phillips' Cases on Products Liability, 2nd Ed., 821 pages, 1982 (Casebook)

Noel and Phillips' Products Liability in a Nutshell, 2nd Ed., 341 pages, 1981 (Text)

PROPERTY

Aigler, Smith and Tefft's Cases on Property, 2 volumes, 1339 pages, 1960 (Casebook)

Bernhardt's Real Property in a Nutshell, 2nd Ed., 448 pages, 1981 (Text)

Boyer's Survey of the Law of Property, 766 pages, 1981 (Text)

Browder, Cunningham and Smith's Cases on Basic Property Law, 4th Ed., 1431 pages, 1984 (Casebook)

Bruce, Ely and Bostick's Cases and Materials on Modern Property Law, 1004 pages, 1984 (Casebook)

Burby's Hornbook on Real Property, 3rd Ed., 490 pages, 1965 (Text)

Burke's Personal Property in a Nutshell, 322 pages, 1983 (Text)

Chused's A Modern Approach to Property: Cases-Notes-Materials, 1069 pages, 1978 with 1980 Supplement (Casebook)

Cohen's Materials for a Basic Course in Property, 526 pages, 1978 (Casebook)

Cunningham, Stoebuck and Whitman's Hornbook on the Law of Property, Student Ed., 916 pages, 1984 (Text)

Donahue, Kauper and Martin's Cases on Property, 2nd Ed., 1362 pages, 1983 (Casebook)

Hill's Landlord and Tenant Law in a Nutshell, 2nd Ed., approximately 353 pages, 1986 (Text)

Moynihan's Introduction to Real Property, 254 pages, 1962 (Text)

Uniform Land Transactions Act, Uniform Simplification of Land Transfers Act, Uniform Condominium Act, 1977 Official Text with Comments, 462 pages, 1978

See also Real Estate Transactions, Land Use

PSYCHIATRY, LAW AND

Reisner's Law and the Mental Health System, Civil and Criminal Aspects, 696 pages, 1985 (Casebooks)

REAL ESTATE TRANSACTIONS

Bruce's Real Estate Finance in a Nutshell, 2nd Ed., 262 pages, 1985 (Text)

REAL ESTATE TRANSACTIONS—Continued

Maxwell, Riesenfeld, Hetland and Warren's Cases on California Security Transactions in Land, 3rd Ed., 728 pages, 1984 (Casebook)

Nelson and Whitman's Cases on Real Estate Transfer, Finance and Development, 2nd Ed., 1114 pages, 1981, with 1986 Supplement (Casebook)

Nelson and Whitman's Hornbook on Real Estate Finance Law, 2nd Ed., Student Ed., 941 pages, 1985 (Text)

Osborne's Cases and Materials on Secured Transactions, 559 pages, 1967 (Casebook)

REGULATED INDUSTRIES

Gellhorn and Pierce's Regulated Industries in a Nutshell, 394 pages, 1982 (Text)

Morgan, Harrison and Verkuil's Cases and Materials on Economic Regulation of Business, 2nd Ed., 666 pages, 1985 (Casebook)

Pozen's Financial Institutions: Cases, Materials and Problems on Investment Management, 844 pages, 1978 (Casebook)

See also Mass Communication Law, Banking Law

REMEDIES

Dobbs' Hornbook on Remedies, 1067 pages, 1973 (Text)

Dobbs' Problems in Remedies, 137 pages, 1974 (Problem book)

Dobbyn's Injunctions in a Nutshell, 264 pages, 1974 (Text)

Friedman's Contract Remedies in a Nutshell, 323 pages, 1981 (Text)

Leavell, Love and Nelson's Cases and Materials on Equitable Remedies and Restitution, 4th Ed., approximately 900 pages, 1986 (Casebook)

McCormick's Hornbook on Damages, 811 pages, 1935 (Text)

O'Connell's Remedies in a Nutshell, 2nd Ed., 325 pages, 1985 (Text)

York, Bauman and Rendleman's Cases and Materials on Remedies, 4th Ed., 1029 pages, 1985 (Casebook)

REVIEW MATERIALS

Ballantine's Problems

Black Letter Series

Smith's Review Series

West's Review Covering Multistate Subjects

SECURITIES REGULATION

Hazen's Hornbook on The Law of Securities Regulation, Student Ed., 739 pages, 1985 (Text)

Ratner's Securities Regulation: Materials for a Basic Course, 3rd Ed., 1000 pages, 1986 (Casebook)

LAW SCHOOL PUBLICATIONS—Continued

SECURITIES REGULATION—Continued

Ratner's Securities Regulation in a Nutshell, 2nd Ed., 322 pages, 1982 (Text)

Selected Securities and Business Planning Statutes, Rules and Forms, 470 pages, 1985

SOCIAL LEGISLATION

Hood and Hardy's Workers' Compensation and Employee Protection Laws in a Nutshell, 274 pages, 1984 (Text)

LaFrance's Welfare Law: Structure and Entitlement in a Nutshell, 455 pages, 1979 (Text)

Malone, Plant and Little's Cases on Workers' Compensation and Employment Rights, 2nd Ed., 951 pages, 1980 (Casebook)

See also Poverty Law

SPORTS LAW

Schubert, Smith and Trentadue's Sports Law, approximately 400 pages, 1986 (Text)

TAXATION

Dodge's Cases and Materials on Federal Income Taxation, 820 pages, 1985 (Casebook)

Dodge's Federal Taxation of Estates, Trusts and Gifts: Principles and Planning, 771 pages, 1981 with 1982 Supplement (Casebook)

Garbis and Struntz' Cases and Materials on Tax Procedure and Tax Fraud, 829 pages, 1982 with 1984 Supplement (Casebook)

Gelfand and Salsich's State and Local Taxation and Finance in a Nutshell, 309 pages, 1986 (Text)

Gunn's Cases and Materials on Federal Income Taxation of Individuals, 785 pages, 1981 with 1985 Supplement (Casebook)

Hellerstein and Hellerstein's Cases on State and Local Taxation, 4th Ed., 1041 pages, 1978 with 1982 Supplement (Casebook)

Kahn and Gann's Corporate Taxation and Taxation of Partnerships and Partners, 2nd Ed., 1204 pages, 1985 (Casebook)

Kragen and McNulty's Cases and Materials on Federal Income Taxation: Individuals, Corporations, Partnerships, 4th Ed., 1287 pages, 1985 (Casebook)

McNulty's Federal Estate and Gift Taxation in a Nutshell, 3rd Ed., 509 pages, 1983 (Text)

McNulty's Federal Income Taxation of Individuals in a Nutshell, 3rd Ed., 487 pages, 1983 (Text)

Posin's Hornbook on Federal Income Taxation of Individuals, Student Ed., 491 pages, 1983 with 1985 pocket part (Text)

Rose and Raskind's Advanced Federal Income Taxation: Corporate Transactions—Cases, Materials and Problems, 955 pages, 1978 (Casebook)

TAXATION—Continued

Selected Federal Taxation Statutes and Regulations, 1402 pages, 1985

Soboloff and Weidenbruch's Federal Income Taxation of Corporations and Stockholders in a Nutshell, 362 pages, 1981 (Text)

TORTS

Christie's Cases and Materials on the Law of Torts, 1264 pages, 1983 (Casebook)

Dobbs' Torts and Compensation—Personal Accountability and Social Responsibility for Injury, 955 pages, 1985 (Casebook)

Green, Pedrick, Rahl, Thode, Hawkins, Smith and Treece's Cases and Materials on Torts, 2nd Ed., 1360 pages, 1977 (Casebook)

Green, Pedrick, Rahl, Thode, Hawkins, Smith, and Treece's Advanced Torts: Injuries to Business, Political and Family Interests, 2nd Ed., 544 pages, 1977 (Casebook)—reprint from Green, et al. Cases and Materials on Torts, 2nd Ed., 1977

Keeton, Keeton, Sargentich and Steiner's Cases and Materials on Torts, and Accident Law, 1360 pages, 1983 (Casebook)

Kionka's Torts in a Nutshell: Injuries to Persons and Property, 434 pages, 1977 (Text)

Malone's Torts in a Nutshell: Injuries to Family, Social and Trade Relations, 358 pages, 1979 (Text)

Prosser and Keeton's Hornbook on Torts, 5th Ed., Student Ed., 1286 pages, 1984 (Text)

Shapo's Cases on Tort and Compensation Law, 1244 pages, 1976 (Casebook)

See also Products Liability

TRADE REGULATION

McManis' Unfair Trade Practices in a Nutshell, 444 pages, 1982 (Text)

Oppenheim, Weston, Maggs and Schechter's Cases and Materials on Unfair Trade Practices and Consumer Protection, 4th Ed., 1038 pages, 1983 with 1986 Supplement (Casebook)

See also Antitrust, Regulated Industries

TRIAL AND APPELLATE ADVOCACY

Appellate Advocacy, Handbook of, 2nd Ed., approximately 250 pages, 1986 (Text)

Bergman's Trial Advocacy in a Nutshell, 402 pages, 1979 (Text)

Binder and Bergman's Fact Investigation: From Hypothesis to Proof, 354 pages, 1984 (Coursebook)

Goldberg's The First Trial (Where Do I Sit?, What Do I Say?) in a Nutshell, 396 pages, 1982 (Text)

Haydock, Herr and Stempel's, Fundamentals of Pre-Trial Litigation, 768 pages, 1985 (Casebook)

Hegland's Trial and Practice Skills in a Nutshell, 346 pages, 1978 (Text)

TRIAL AND APPELLATE ADVOCACY— Continued

Hornstein's Appellate Advocacy in a Nutshell, 325 pages, 1984 (Text)

Jeans' Handbook on Trial Advocacy, Student Ed., 473 pages, 1975 (Text)

McElhaney's Effective Litigation, 457 pages, 1974 (Casebook)

Nolan's Cases and Materials on Trial Practice, 518 pages, 1981 (Casebook)

Parnell and Shellhaas' Cases, Exercises and Problems for Trial Advocacy, 171 pages, 1982 (Coursebook)

Sonsteng, Haydock and Boyd's The Trialbook: A Total System for Preparation and Presentation of a Case, Student Ed., 404 pages, 1984 (Coursebook)

TRUSTS AND ESTATES

Atkinson's Hornbook on Wills, 2nd Ed., 975 pages, 1953 (Text)

Averill's Uniform Probate Code in a Nutshell, 425 pages, 1978 (Text)

Bogert's Hornbook on Trusts, 5th Ed., 726 pages, 1973 (Text)

Clark, Lusky and Murphy's Cases and Materials on Gratuitous Transfers, 3rd Ed., 970 pages, 1985 (Casebook)

Gulliver's Cases and Materials on Future Interests, 624 pages, 1959 (Casebook)

Gulliver's Introduction to the Law of Future Interests, 87 pages, 1959 (Casebook)— reprint from Gulliver's Cases and Materials on Future Interests, 1959

McGovern's Cases and Materials on Wills, Trusts and Future Interests: An Introduction to Estate Planning, 750 pages, 1983 (Casebook)

Mennell's Cases and Materials on California Decedent's Estates, 566 pages, 1973 (Casebook)

Mennell's Wills and Trusts in a Nutshell, 392 pages, 1979 (Text)

Powell's The Law of Future Interests in California, 91 pages, 1980 (Text)

TRUSTS AND ESTATES—Continued

Simes' Hornbook on Future Interests, 2nd Ed., 355 pages, 1966 (Text)

Turano and Radigan's Hornbook on New York Estate Administration, approximately 575 pages, 1986 (Text)

Uniform Probate Code, 5th Ed., Official Text With Comments, 384 pages, 1977

Waggoner's Future Interests in a Nutshell, 361 pages, 1981 (Text)

Waterbury's Materials on Trusts and Estates, approximately 1100 pages, 1986 (Casebook)

WATER LAW

Getches' Water Law in a Nutshell, 439 pages, 1984 (Text)

Sax and Abram's Cases and Materials on Legal Control of Water Resources in the United States, 941 pages, 1986 (Casebook)

Trelease and Gould's Cases and Materials on Water Law, 4th Ed., approximately 758 pages, 1986 (Casebook)

See also Energy and Natural Resources Law, Environmental Law

WILLS

See Trusts and Estates

WOMEN AND THE LAW

Kay's Text, Cases and Materials on Sex-Based Discrimination, 2nd Ed., 1045 pages, 1981, with 1986 Supplement (Casebook)

Thomas' Sex Discrimination in a Nutshell, 399 pages, 1982 (Text)

See also Employment Discrimination

WORKERS' COMPENSATION

See Social Legislation

BASIC
PROPERTY LAW
Fourth Edition

By

Olin L. Browder, Jr.
James V. Campbell, Professor of Law, Emeritus,
University of Michigan

Roger A. Cunningham
Professor of Law, University of Michigan

Allan F. Smith
Professor of Law, Emeritus, University of Michigan

AMERICAN CASEBOOK SERIES

WEST PUBLISHING CO.
ST. PAUL, MINN., 1984

COPYRIGHT © 1984 By WEST PUBLISHING CO.
50 West Kellogg Boulevard
P.O. Box 43526
St. Paul, Minnesota 55164

Library of Congress Cataloging in Publication Data

Browder, Olin L.
    Basic property law.

    (American casebook series)
    Rev. ed. of: Basic property law / by Olin L.
Browder, Jr. ... [et al.]. 1979.
    Includes index.
    1. Property—United States—Cases. 2. City planning
and redevelopment law—United States—Cases.
I. Cunningham, Roger A., 1921–   . II. Smith, Allan F.
III. Basic property law. IV. Title. V. Series.
KF560.B7 1984   346.7304   84–5223
                347.3064

ISBN 0–314–80501–X

Preface

This Fourth Edition of BASIC PROPERTY LAW involves some rearrangement of the materials in the Third Edition, although it does not reflect any major shifts in emphasis. Chapter 1 has been substantially revised to include an expanded historical and jurisprudential introduction to the study of property law and to provide a more comprehensive view of the statutes of limitation which underlie the law of adverse possession. Minor revisions have been made in Chapters 2 through 12: some new cases have been added, some old cases have been dropped, and the Notes following the principal cases have been substantially revised and expanded. The most significant changes in these chapters are in Sections 4 and 5 of Chapter 4, which are concerned with the "fitness" of leased premises. In Part 3 (Government Control of Land Use), there has been a significant rearrangement of materials: Chapter 13 has been thoroughly revised to provide an overview of the police power basis of government land use controls and the regulatory "taking" problem; Chapter 14 now covers the zoning "process," previously included in Chapter 13; suburban growth control and "exclusionary" land use controls are now grouped together in Chapter 16; and "environmental" land use controls are no longer allotted a separate chapter, although some of the materials on that topic contained in the Third Edition are included elsewhere in Part 3 of the Fourth Edition. The many important cases on government control of land use decided since early 1979—e.g., Agins v. City of Tiburon, San Diego Gas & Electric Co. v. City of San Diego, the second *Mount Laurel Township* case—will be found in the revised Part 3.

We who have produced this Fourth Edition of BASIC PROPERTY LAW are reasonably satisfied with the choice, arrangement, and emphasis of the materials herein, although we may have some differences of opinion on these matters. We are aware, however, that others who may use the Fourth Edition may be less well-satisfied. We believe that persons who prefer a different order of topics, or a greater or lesser emphasis on certain topics, may, without great inconvenience, make the necessary adjustments. In fact, one or more of us occasionally varies the order of, or emphasis on, some topics included in this book. This is made possible, we hope, by adherence to our original objective: to present materials constituting a survey of most of the Property Law not traditionally reserved for courses on non-commercial property transactions such as Trusts, Wills, and Estate Planning. In preserving such breadth of coverage, we reiterate our acknowledgment that BASIC PROPERTY LAW may be too long to be covered in its entirety by many Property

Law teachers, since the length and scope of basic property law courses obviously varies considerably. But we continue to hope that the scope of BASIC PROPERTY LAW is such as to allow selection and omission where that is necessary.

Although one of our former co-editors, Professor Joseph R. Julin, did not participate in the preparation of either the Third or Fourth Edition of BASIC PROPERTY LAW, we wish to acknowledge his continuing contribution to this book.

O.L.B.
R.A.C.
A.F.S.

March, 1984

Acknowledgments

A number of publishers and authors have granted us permission to reproduce their copyrighted materials. Such materials are clearly identified where they appear in this book by source and date of publication. In several instances, we were asked to note additional information about the materials reproduced or to acknowledge permission to reprint in a specified form. We now gratefully acknowledge permission to reproduce the following materials.

American Law Institute, Restatement of Property, Introductory Note to Chapter 1 and portions of Sections 1–5, 9, 10, 450, and 476, copyright 1936 and 1944 by The American Law Institute; Restatement (Second) of Torts, Section 858A, copyright 1979 by The American Law Institute; Model Land Development Code, Sections 2–103(3), 2–210, 2–312(4), and Reporter's Note to Section 2–312, copyright 1976 by The American Law Institute. All reprinted with permission of The American Law Institute.

Ballentine, When Are Deeds Testamentary, 18 Michigan Law Review 470, at 478–479. Copyright 1920 by the Michigan Law Review Association.

Barnett, Marketable Title Acts—Panacea or Pandemonium?, 53 Cornell Law Review 45, at 84–87, 89–91 (1967). © Copyright by Cornell University. All rights reserved.

Berle, Property, Production and Revolution. Copyright © 1965 by the Directors for the Columbia Law Review Association, Inc. All rights reserved. This article originally appeared in 65 Columbia Law Reivew 1 (1965). Material reprinted is drawn from pp. 5, 8, 12, 16, and 17. Reprinted by permission.

Bonderman, Comment on San Diego Gas & Electric Co. v. City of San Diego, 33 Land Use Law & Zoning Digest, No. 5, p. 10, at p. 11 (1981). Copyright 1981 by American Planning Association.

Cribbet, Conveyancing Reform, 35 N.Y.U. Law Review 1291, at 1300 (1960). Copyright 1960 by the New York University Law Review.

Friedman, The Law of the Living and the Dead: Property, Succession, and Society, 1966 Wisconsin Law Review 340, at 344–347. Copyright 1966 by the University of Wisconsin.

Haar, In Accordance With a Comprehensive Plan, 68 Harvard Law Review 1154, at 1156, 1173 (1955). Copyright 1955 by the Harvard Law Review Association.

Hohfeld, FUNDAMENTAL LEGAL CONCEPTIONS (Cook ed. 1928), at pp. 96–97. Copyright 1928 by the Yale University Press.

Manuel, Ramapo's Managed Growth Program, 4 PLANNER'S NOTEBOOK, No. 5, p. 5. Copyright 1974 by the American Planning Association.

North & Van Buren, REAL ESTATE, TITLES AND CONVEYANCING (rev. ed. 1940), at p. 131. Copyright 1940 by Prentice-Hall, Inc.

PLANNING, Vol. 49 (June 1983), at pp. 8–9. Copyright 1983 by the American Planning Association.

Reich, The New Property, 73 Yale Law Journal 733 (1964). Reprinted by permission of the Yale Law Journal and Fred B. Rothman & Company from the Yale Law Journal, Vol. 73, pp. 734–737, 739–741, 744, and 785–786.

Rose, The *Mount Laurel II* Decision: Is It Based on Wishful Thinking, 12 Real Estate Law Journal 115, at 130, 136 (1983). Copyright 1983 by Jerome G. Rose.

Sax, Takings, Private and Public Rights, 81 Yale Law Journal 149 (1971). Reprinted by permission of the Yale Law Journal and Fred B. Rothman & Company from the Yale Law Journal, Vol. 73, pp. 159–171.

Simpson, Equity, 1946 Annual Survey of American Law 829, at 844. Copyright 1946 by New York University School of Law.

Thompson, ABSTRACTS AND TITLES (1930), at pp. 26–67. Copyright 1930 by Michie/Bobbs-Merrill Company.

Tiffany, REAL PROPERTY (3d ed. 1939), Section 756. Copyright 1939 by Callaghan & Company, 3201 Old Glenview Rd., Wilmette, IL. 60091.

Yelen, Lawyers' Title Guaranty Funds: The Florida Experience, 51 American Bar Association Journal 1070, at pp. 1070, 1072–1074 (1965). Reprinted with permission from the American Bar Association Journal.

Summary of Contents

*

Table of Contents

*

Table of Cases

The principal cases are in Italic type. Cases cited or discussed are in Roman type. References are to Pages.

Table of Abbreviations

A.L.P.   American Law of Property (1952, Supp.1977)

Cunningham   Cunningham, Stoebuck & Whitman, Law of
                        Property (1984)

Powell   Powell, Real Property (rev. Rohan)

Restatement   Restatement, Property (1936, 1940, 1944)

Rest.2d (L. & T.)   Restatement, Property 2d, Landlord & Tenant
                        (1977)

Tiffany   Tiffany, Real Property (3d ed. 1939)

URLTA   Uniform Residential Landlord and Tenant Act
                        (1972)

*

BASIC
PROPERTY LAW

Fourth Edition

*

Part One

THE NATURE AND DIVISION OF OWNERSHIP

Chapter 1

PROPERTY, POSSESSION AND OWNERSHIP

SECTION 1. THE CONCEPT OF PROPERTY

A. IN GENERAL

When a layman is asked to define "property," he is likely to say that "property" is something tangible "owned" by a natural person (or persons), a corporation, or a unit of government. But such a response is inaccurate from a lawyer's viewpoint for at least two reasons: (1) it confuses "property" with the various *subjects* of "property," and (2) it fails to recognize that even the subjects of "property" may be intangible.

For the lawyer, "property" is not a "thing" at all, although "things" are the subject of property. Rather, as Jeremy Bentham asserted,[1] property is a legally protected "expectation * * * of being able to draw such or such an advantage from the thing" in question, "according to the nature of the case." Although Bentham conceded that [2] "[t]here have been from the beginning, and there always will be, circumstances in which a man may secure himself, by his own means, in the enjoyment of certain things," Bentham correctly noted that "the catalogue of these cases is very limited" and that "a strong and permanent expectation" of being able to draw an advantage from the thing in question "can result only from law." In this book, we shall adopt Bentham's view of the nature of property, more recently summarized as follows by Felix Cohen:[3]

"That is property to which the following label can be attached. To the world: Keep off unless you have my permission, which I may grant or withhold. Signed: Private citizen. Endorsed: The state."

Cohen's statement, just quoted, obviously assumes that "private" property is the norm. Although two or more persons may have "undivided" interests in a thing, the Anglo-American legal system views these interests as divisible though not currently divided. In other societies, however, it is common to recognize ownership by social collectives such as the "family" or the "clan." Such collective ownership generally insures automatic succession to property rights by members of the col-

---

1. J. Bentham, Theory of Legislation 68 (Oceana Pub. Inc. 1975).

2. Id. 69.

3. F. Cohen, Dialogue on Private Property, 9 Rutgers L.Rev. 357, 374 (1954).

lective, in contrast to our private property system where individuals have the power to transfer property either during their lives or at death. "A collectivity can be immortal though the members are not. An extended family need never die; its property can serve new masters in each generation without any formal transfer from individual owner to individual owner."[4]

The institution of "private" property, which has existed in most of Western Europe since the end of the Middle Ages and in the United States since its founding, has long been a subject of controversy among philosophers, political scientists, and economists. At least five different theories have been advanced to justify the institution of "private" property. These theories, briefly stated, are as follows:[5] (1) the "occupation" theory—that the simple fact of occupation or possession of a thing justifies legal protection of the occupier's or possessor's claim to the thing; (2) the "labor" theory—that a person has a moral right to the ownership and control of things he produces or acquires through his or her labor; (3) the "contract" theory—that "private" property is the result of a contract between individuals and the community; (4) the "natural rights" theory—that the "natural law" dictates the recognition of "private" property; and (5) the "social utility" theory—that the law should promote the maximum fulfillment of human needs and aspirations, and that legal protection of "private" property does, in fact promote such fulfillment.

The institution of "private" property has, of course, been the subject of vigorous criticism in the Western world from very early times. Such eminent philosophers as Plato[6] and Sir Thomas More[7] rejected "private" property and argued for "communal" property. More recently, Marx[8] and Engels proposed the abolition of "private" property in the "means of production" and transfer of the ownership of the "means of production" to the State.[9] Despite important modifications, the doctrines of Marx and Engels still provide the philosophical basis for the widespread transfer of ownership of the "means of production" to the State in the Soviet Union, most of Eastern Europe, China, Viet Nam, and other "Communist" nations. But even in the "Communist" nations "private" property has not been completely abolished. In the Soviet Union, e.g., "personal ownership" is permitted with respect to certain "property which is intended for the satisfaction of * * * [citizens'] material and cultural needs."[10] Thus, "[each] citizen may personally

4. Friedman, The Law of the Living, The Law of the Dead: Property, Succession, and Society, 1966 Wis.L.Rev. 340, 343.

5. For discussion of these theories, see the Rational Basis of Legal Institutions 387–400, 195–200, 167–184, 315–344 (H. Wigmore and A. Kocourek ed. 1923), reprinting excerpts from works by H. Rashdall, J. Locke, E. de Laveleye, L. Duguit, and R. Tawney; F. Cohen, Property and Sovereignty, 13 Cornell L.J. 15–16, (1927); J. Stone, The Province and Function of Law 529 (1950).

6. Plato, Republic.

7. T. More, Utopia.

8. K. Marx, Das Kapital.

9. For discussion of socialist theories of property, see 2 W. Lecky, Democracy and Liberty 224–361 (1896), excerpts from which are reprinted in The Rational Basis of Legal Institutions 232–254 (H. Wigmore and A. Kocourek ed. 1923).

10. Civil Code of the Russian Soviet Federated Socialist Republic, Art. 105 (transl. W. Gray and R. Stults 1965).

own his income from work, and his savings, a house (or part of a house) and subsidiary household production, and household articles of personal use and convenience."[11]   But "[p]roperty under the personal ownership of citizens may not be used to derive non-labor income."[12]

In recent years a number of American scholars have advanced an economic theory of property.   Posner,[13] e.g., asserts that "the legal protection of property rights has an important economic function: to create incentives to use resources efficiently," and that there are three criteria of an efficient system of property rights:

1.   Universality—i.e., "all resources should be owned, or ownable, by someone, except resources so plentiful that everybody can consume as much of them as he wants without reducing consumption by anyone else   *   *   *.''

2.   Exclusivity—to give owners an incentive to incur the costs required to make efficient use of resources owned by them.

3.   Transferability—because, "[i]f a property right cannot be transferred, there is no way of shifting a resource from a less productive to a more productive use through voluntary exchange."

Posner's assertion that the legal protection of property rights performs the economic function of creating incentives to use resources efficiently is, of course, a normative proposition rather than a factual description of the way in which the rules of property law actually operate at any given time in a particular legal system.   But—although neither the courts nor the legislatures have consistently been articulate on the point—it seems clear that the Anglo-American law of property has rarely lost sight of this normative proposition.   Moreover, it seems likely that the future development of the Anglo-American law of property will be more explicitly based on that proposition.[14]

It should be noted that much of the "private" property in the United States and Western Europe is held, at the present time, not by individuals directly, but by "legal entities" such as business corporations and religious corporations.   Moreover, a good many things—both land and things other than land—are owned by governments.

B.   REAL AND PERSONAL PROPERTY

The subject matter of "property" may be land, chattels, or intangible things.   In general, property in land (and things attached thereto) is classified as "real property," and the land itself (with the things attached thereto, such as buildings and other structures) is often termed "real estate" or "realty."   "Real property" in Anglo-American law corresponds substantially with "immoveable property" in the European civil law.   Property in chattels and in intangible things is classified as

---

11.   Ibid.

12.   Ibid.

13.   R. Posner, Economic Analysis of Law 10–13 (1972).

14.   See id. 13–39; R. Coase, The Problem of Social Cost, 3 J. Law & Econ. 1 (1960); H. Demsetz, Toward a Theory of Property Rights, 57 Am.Econ.Rev. Papers and Proceedings 347 (1967).

"personal property" in Anglo-American law, and corresponds substantially with "moveable property" in the European civil law.

The term "chattel" requires no explanation. The list of "intangible" things that may form the subject matter of "personal property" is long, including claims represented by bank accounts, promissory notes, corporate and government bonds, shares of corporate stock, life insurance policies and annuities, patents, copyrights, trademarks, and even the "good will" of business enterprises. These intangible subjects of property are often called "choses in action."

The classification of property as "real" or "personal" makes little sense in the modern world and can be understood only by reference to the historical development of legal remedies for the protection of property in land and chattels in English law. In the medieval period, property in land was protected by the "real" actions—i.e., actions in which possession of the land itself—the *res*—could be recovered from a wrongful possessor. Property in chattels, however, was generally protected only by various "personal" actions in which the successful plaintiff recovered a personal judgment for damages against a defendant who had wrongfully appropriated the plaintiff's chattel. Hence property in land came to be called "real property" and property in chattels came to be called "personal property."

Classification of property on the basis of the common law actions available for their protection in England prior to the middle of the fifteenth century makes little sense today. In the United States, as a general rule, chattels may be recovered *in specie* from a defendant wrongfully in possession by means of a modern version of the common law action called "replevin." And when land is leased for a limited period of time the lessee may recover possession of the land from one who wrongfully acquires or withholds possession by a means of a modern version of the common law action called "ejectment."[15] Yet (for many purposes) the lessee's property interest is still classified as "personal property" because, prior to the evolution of "ejectment" at the end of the fifteenth century a lessee had no action by which he could recover possession of the leased land. The classification of leasehold interests in land as "personal property" continues to be significant in states where the intestate succession laws still distinguish between "real property" and "personal property" owned by a decedent.

As previously indicated, "real property" includes interests in things attached to land as well as land itself. Substantial structures and all natural vegetation (trees and perennial shrubs and grasses, sometimes called *fructus naturales*) are treated as "real property" for practically all purposes. Interests in cultivated crops (sometimes called *emblements* or *fructus industriales*), however, are sometimes treated as "real property" and sometimes as "personal property," depending upon the circumstances.

---

15. "Trespass," "ejectment," and other common law remedies for interference with property rights are discussed briefly in Section 2, which deals with Possession and Ownership.

Chattels placed on or affixed to land or structures attached to land by the landowner for the purpose of "improving" the land are called *fixtures* and are treated as "real property" for most purposes.[16] If such a fixture is temporarily severed from the land by accident, mistake, or "act of God" without the consent of the landowner, the landowner's interest in the fixture is still considered to be "real property."[17] But life tenants and lessees are generally privileged to remove fixtures installed by them for trade, domestic, or ornamental purposes.[18] And when the vendor of a chattel which becomes a fixture retains a chattel security interest therein, the vendor is frequently privileged to remove the fixture if the purchaser fails to pay the full purchase price, as against both the purchaser and third parties such as mortgagees of the real property.[19] If a fixture is lawfully removed by a tenant or by one who has a security interest therein, it becomes and remains a chattel unless it is again affixed to land or a structure attached to land.

C. "LEGAL" AND "EQUITABLE" PROPERTY

As a result of the peculiar development of English law prior to the founding of the United States, we still have separate bodies of law based, respectively, on the "common law" and "equity jurisprudence" of England despite the procedural reforms of the nineteenth and twentieth centuries which have effected a substantial "merger" of "law" and "equity."[20] One consequence of the continuing distinction between "law" and "equity" is that in many cases "equitable" property interests may be recognized and protected in persons who have no "legal" property interests. "Equitable" property interests arise, in most cases, as a result of (1) the creation of a trust or (2) the making of a specifically enforceable contract.

A "trust" is created whenever "legal" ownership of land, chattels, or intangibles is transferred to or retained by one person—the "trustee"—to be held for the benefit of another—the "cestui que trust" or beneficiary.[21] Protection of the beneficiary's interest under the trust is provided on the "equity side of the court" in accordance with "equitable" principles by virtue of which the court will compel the trustee to deal fairly with the beneficiary and to manage the trust *res* or *corpus* honestly and

---

16. See 5 A.L.P. §§ 19.1 through 19.14; 5 Powell ¶¶ 651–660.

17. E.g., Rogers v. Gilinger, 30 Pa. 185 (1853). Contra: Buckout v. Swift, 27 Cal. 433 (1865).

18. 5 A.L.P. § 19.11; Cunningham § 6.46; 5 Powell ¶¶ 656, 657.

19. 5 A.L.P. § 19.12; 5 Powell ¶ 659.

20. On the historical development of "common law" and "equity" jurisprudence in England, with primary emphasis on "common law," see T: Plucknett, Concise History of the Common Law (4th ed.). For a more detailed treatment of the historical development of "equity," see 1 J. Pomeroy, Equity Jurisprudence 14–117 (5th ed. S. Symons 1941); H. McClintock, Equity 1–19 (2d ed. 1948); W. Walsh, Equity 1–36 (1930). McClintock defines "equity" as follows: "In Anglo-American law, equity means the system of legal materials developed and applied by the court of chancery in England and the courts succeeding to its powers in the British Empire and the United States." H. McClintock, Equity 1 (2d ed. 1948).

21. The law of trusts will be considered only incidentally in this book. The principal multi-volume treatises on the law of trusts are A. Scott, Trusts (3d ed. 1967, 6 vols.); G. Bogert, Trusts and Trustees (2d ed. 1965–69, 18 vols.). The best single-volume textbook is G. & T. Bogert, Trusts (5th ed. 1973).

prudently. The beneficiary of a trust is generally described as the "equitable" owner of the *res* or *corpus*, although his or her interest was historically regarded as a claim *in personam* against the trustee rather than a claim *in rem* against the world. In litigation between the beneficiary and trustee, in the absence of statutory authority, a court does not enforce the beneficiary's rights directly against the *res* (e.g., by awarding the right to possession to the beneficiary), but merely orders the trustee to perform his duties in accordance with the terms of the trust and the applicable "equitable" principles. Moreover, the trustee as "legal" owner of the *res*, is the proper party to sue third persons in order to protect the *res*. But the "equitable" interest of the trust beneficiary is protected against unauthorized transfers of trust property by the trustee except in cases where the transferee acquires a legal interest for value and without notice of the trust. A donee or a purchaser with notice of the trust will acquire the legal interest subject to all the trustee's duties to the beneficiary with respect to the trust property.

The "trust" concept has been extended to many situations where there is no real trust—e.g., where courts impose a "constructive" or "resulting" trust or an "equitable" lien on specific land, chattels, or intangibles in order to prevent "unjust enrichment" of a wrongdoer.[22] When a "constructive" or "resulting" trust is imposed, the "legal" owner will be treated like a trustee and ordered to transfer "legal" ownership to the person who is "equitably" entitled to ownership. Similar relief may be granted where a plaintiff is entitled to the "equitable" remedy of rescission or reformation of a contract or conveyance.[23] Hence a person with an "equitable" right to rescission or reformation can be described in some cases as the "equitable" owner of land, chattels, or intangibles "legally" owned by another.

Because land is generally deemed to be unique, "equity" courts will ordinarily order specific performance of an enforceable contract for the sale of land in favor of either party to the contract.[24] The purchaser's "equitable" right to specific performance is said to make him the "equitable" owner of the land in question, although the vendor remains the "legal" owner until he executes an effective conveyance in favor of the purchaser.[25] Like the beneficiary of a trust, the purchaser as "equitable" owner is protected against a subsequent unauthorized transfer "legal" ownership of the land except in cases where the transferee is a bona fide purchaser for value without notice of the prior land sale contract.

22. For an extended discussion, see A. Scott, Trusts §§ 404–552 (3d ed. 1967); 1 G. Palmer, Restitution 9–21, § 6.7 (1978); H. McClintock, Equity §§ 85, 120 (2d ed. 1948).

23. See H. McClintock, Equity §§ 84, 86, 94–104 (2d ed. 1948); W. Walsh, Equity §§ 106, 110, 111 (1930); 2 G. Palmer, Restitution §§ 12.6, 13.8 through 13.19, 14.25, 14.26 (1978).

24. See 4 J. Pomeroy, Equity Jurisprudence §§ 1400–1410 (5th ed. S. Symons 1941); H. McClintock, Equity §§ 53–78 (2d ed. 1948); W. Walsh, Equity §§ 58–85 (1930).

25. See H. McClintock, Equity §§ 106–117 (2d ed. 1948); W. Walsh, Equity §§ 86–98 (1930). See also post Chapter 12.

Under the recording system established in all jurisdictions in the United States,[26] the recording of a written trust instrument or land sale contract will ordinarily charge any subsequent transferee of the land in question with notice of the trust or contract, as the case may be. Moreover, the American recording statutes, in force in all states, in substance prevent any unrecorded conveyance (or other instrument affecting land ownership) from transferring more than an "equitable" interest because these statutes declare the unrecorded instrument to be void as against any subsequent bona fide purchaser for value without notice of the unrecorded instrument. Hence the distinction between "legal" and "equitable" property interests in land is substantially lessened, although it is not entirely eliminated.

The making of an enforceable contract for the sale of land does more than make the purchaser the "equitable" owner of the land so that his interest under the contract is deemed to be "real" property "in equity." In most states, the contract also effects an "equitable conversion" of the vendor's "legal" ownership of the land into "personal" property for certain purposes.[27] Thus, if the vendor dies before the contract is performed, the vendor's claim to the purchase money passes to his or her next-of-kin or legatees as "personal" property; and if the purchaser dies before the contract is performed, the purchaser's claim to the land passes to his or her heirs or devisees as "real" property. The doctrine of "equitable conversion" is also applied in cases where land is devised by will to a trustee with a direction to sell it and distribute the proceeds, or where a marriage settlement directs the conversion of land into money or vice versa. But the importance of the doctrine has been much reduced by the general enactment of intestate succession laws providing that a decedent's "real" and "personal" property shall pass to the same persons.

D. THE MODERN CORPORATION AND "PRODUCTIVE PROPERTY"

Reference has already been made to "personal property" in "intangibles" such as stock and bonds issued by business corporations, bank accounts, money market funds, life insurance policies, and the like. Corporate stocks and bonds represent property in productive assets of business corporations. Bank accounts, money market funds, and life insurance policies represent claims against intermediate financial institutions whose assets include large amounts of corporate stocks and bonds. In the aggregate, property in such "intangibles" as stocks, bonds, bank accounts, money market funds, and life insurance policies amounts to well over one-half of the individually owned wealth of the United States. This has led such distinguished legal scholars as Adolph A. Berle to argue that a new classification of property should be superimposed on the old classification of property as "real" or "personal," so that property is divided into two categories: "(a) consumption property

---

26. The recording system is considered in detail post Chapter 10.

27. See H. McClintock, Equity § 106 (2d ed. 1948); W. Walsh, Equity § 86 (1930); Cunningham § 10.13.

on the one hand and (b) productive property on the other—property devoted to production, manufacture, service or commerce, and designed to offer, for a price, goods or services to the public from which a holder expects to derive a return." [28]   Berle further observes that, "As a corollary, productive property has been divided into two layers: (1) that fraction which, though not managed by active owners, is administered to yield a return by way of interest, dividends or distribution of profit, and (2) that layer dominated and controlled by the representatives or delegates of the passive owners whose decisions are now subject to the political process   *   *   *." [29]   Berle further develops his thesis in the following passage from the article from which the preceding quotations are drawn. [30]

"We must note an enormous expansion of the scope of the term 'property' in this connection. Not only is it divorced from the decision-making power of its supposedly beneficial holders (stockholders and their various removes), but it has come to encompass a set of conceptions superimposed upon the central reality of domination over tangible things. Businessmen describe an enterprise, great or small, as 'the property.' They do not mean merely the physical plant. They include access to all the facilities necessary to produce, transport, distribute and sell. They mean an entire organization of personnel without which the physical plant would be junk; they mean a hierarchy of executives, technical experts, sales managers and men; as well as the dealer organization and the labor relations habits. These relationships are increasingly protected, not merely by the law of contract, but by an increasing body of law imposing upon individuals a measure of loyalty to the central enterprise. For example, they may not acquire and sell to others as part of their personal capacity or equipment, confidential technical information, data on sales, or customer goodwill. Underlying this extension of the property concept to management relationships is recognition of the fact that the 'capital' has been projected far into the realm of intangibles., The central enterprise is spending good money—often in immense amounts—building this organization, this technical information, these relationships; it is entitled to be protected against their appropriation by individuals.   *   *   *

A shift in attitude toward corporate property arises in part from the changed origin of finance-capital. The property of corporations is dedicated to production, not to personal consumption; but, even more significant, that property is no longer the result of individual effort or choice. This change has come silently. Its implications even yet are not understood.

"Corporations were originally groups of investors pooling their individual contributions of risk capital to organize and carry on an enterprise. Since they had saved their earnings or gains and had risked them in the undertaking, they were assimilated to the owner of land, who cleared and cultivated it, and sold its products. As the economics

28. Berle, Property, Production and Revolution, 65 Colum.L.Rev. 1, 4 (1965).

29. Id. at 5.

30. Id. at 5, 8, 12, 14, 16, 17. Copyright 1965 by Directors of the Columbia Law Review Association, Inc. Author's footnotes have been omitted.

of the time went, this was justifiable. They had sacrificed, risked and, to some extent, worked at the development of the product. Presumably they had done something useful for the community, since it was prepared to pay for the product.

"A mature corporation typically does not call for investor-supplied capital. It charges a price for its products from which it can pay taxation, costs, depreciation allowances, and can realize a profit over and above all these expenses. Of this profit item, approximately half goes as income taxes to the federal government, and sixty percent of the remaining half is distributed to its shareholders. It accumulates for capital purposes the undistributed forty percent and its depreciation charges. This is a phenomenon not of 'investment,' but of market power. Since corporations legally have perpetual life, this process can continue indefinitely. The result has been that more than sixty percent of capital entering a particular industry is 'internally generated' or, more accurately, 'price-generated' because it is collected from the customers. Another twenty percent of the capital the corporation uses is borrowed from banks chiefly in anticipation of this accumulative process. The corporations in aggregate do indeed tap individual 'savings,' but for only a little less than twenty percent of their capital, and mainly through the issuance of bonds to intermediate savings-collecting institutions (life insurance companies, trust funds, pension trusts and savings banks).

"The corporation becomes the legal 'owner' of the capital thus collected and has complete decision-making power over it; the corporation runs on its own economic steam. On the other hand, its stockholders, by now grandsons or great-grandsons of the original 'investor' or (far more often) transferees of their transferees at thousands of removes, have and expect to have through their stock the 'beneficial ownership' of the assets and profits thus accumulated and realized, after taxes, by the corporate enterprise. Management thus becomes, in an odd sort of way, the uncontrolled administrator of a kind of trust having the privilege of perpetual accumulation. The stockholder is the passive beneficiary, not only of the original 'trust,' but of the compounded annual accretions to it.

"Not surprisingly, therefore, we discover a body of law building up to protect and deal with this remarkable phenomenon. To that fact itself perhaps is due a continuing tendency: subjection of property devoted to *production*—that is, chiefly in managerial hands—to legal rules requiring a use of it, more or less corresponding to the evolving expectations of American civilization. * * *

"Increased size and domination of the American corporation has automatically split the package of rights and privileges comprising the old conception of property. Specifically, it splits the personality of the individual beneficial owner away from the enterprise manager. The 'things' themselves—including the intangible elements noted earlier in this essay—'belong' to the corporation which holds legal title to them. The ultimate beneficial interest embodied in a share of stock represents an expectation that a portion of the profits remaining after taxes will be declared as dividends, and that in the relatively unlikely event of liquidation each share will get its allocable part of the assets. The former expectation is vivid; the latter so remote that it plays little part in giving market value to shares. Stockholders do have a right to vote which is of diminishing importance as the number of shareholders in each corporation increases—diminishing in fact to negligible importance as the corporations become giants. As the number of stockholders increases, the capacity of each to express opinions is extremely limited. No one is bound to take notice of them, though they may have quasi-political importance, similar to that of constituents who write letters to their congressman. Finally, they have a right, difficult to put into operation, to bring a stockholders' action against the corporation and its management, demanding that the corporation be made whole from any damage it may have suffered in case of theft, fraud, or wrongdoing by directors or administrators. Such actions are common, though few stockholders are involved in them. They are a useful deterrent to dishonesty and disloyalty on the part of management.

"These shares nevertheless have become so desirable that they are now the dominant form of personal wealth-holding because, through the device of stock exchanges, they have acquired 'liquidity'—that is, the capability of being sold for ready cash within days or hours. The stockholder, though no longer the sole residuary legatee of all profits, is the residuary legatee of about half of them, and that is a vast stake. (Sophisticated estimates indicate that dividends combined with increase in market value of shares have yielded better than eight percent per annum during the generation past.) The package of passive property rights and expectations has proved sufficiently satisfactory to have induced an increasing number of Americans to place their savings in this form of property. * * *

"Yet this is only the 'top level' of passive property-holding. A very large number of shares are not held by individuals, but by intermediate fiduciary institutions which in turn distribute the benefits of shareholding to participating individuals. One of the two largest groups of such intermediary institutions is that of the pension trust funds maintained by corporations or groups of corporations for the benefit of employees; these collect savings in regular installments from employers to be held in trust for their employees and subsequently paid to them as old age or other similar benefits. The second is the relatively smaller group of institutions known as mutual funds; these buy a portfolio of assorted stocks and sell participations in the portfolio to individuals desiring to hold an interest in diversified groups of stock instead of directly holding shares in one or more companies. * * *

"In addition to these two categories there are other intermediate institutions which are also holders (though less significant) of stocks— namely, life insurance companies which invest about three percent of their assets in stocks, and fire and casualty companies which invest a considerably larger percentage. * * *

"The significance of the intermediate institutions is twofold. First, they vastly increase the number of citizens who, to some degree, rely on the stockholding form of wealth. Second, they remove the individual still further from connection with or impact on the management and administration of the productive corporations themselves. * * *

"Now, clearly, this wealth cannot be justified by the old economic maxims, despite passionate and sentimental arguments of neoclassic economists who would have us believe the old system has not changed. The purchaser of stock does not contribute savings to an enterprise, thus enabling it to increase its plant or operations. He does not take the "risk" of a new or increased economic operation; he merely estimates the chance of the corporation's shares increasing in value. The contribution his purchase makes to anyone other than himself is the maintenance of liquidity for other shareholders who may wish to convert their holdings into cash. Clearly he can not and does not intend to contribute managerial or entrepreneurial effort or service.

"This raises a problem of social ethics that is bound to push its way into the legal scene in the next generation. Why have stockholders? What contribution do they make, entitling them to heirship of half the profits of the industrial system, receivable partly in the form of dividends, and partly in the form of increased market values resulting from undistributed corporate gains? Stockholders toil not, neither do they spin, to earn that reward. They are beneficiaries by position only. Justification for their inheritance must be sought outside classic economic reasoning.

"It can be founded only upon social grounds. There is—and in American social economy, there always has been—a value attached to individual life, individual development, individual solution of personal problems, individual choice of consumption and activity. Wealth unquestionably does add to an individual's capacity and range in pursuit of happiness and self-development. There is certainly advantage to the community when men take care of themselves. But that justification turns on the distribution as well as the existence of wealth. Its force exists only in direct ratio to the number of individuals who hold such wealth. Justification for the stockholder's existence thus depends on increasing distribution within the American population. Ideally, the stockholder's position will be impregnable only when every American family has its fragment of that position and of the wealth by which the opportunity to develop individuality becomes fully actualized. * * *

"One would expect therefore that the law would increasingly encourage an ever wider distribution of stocks—whether through tax policy or some other device. It would encourage pension trust or social security trust entry into stockholder position. The time may well come when the government social security funds are invested, not wholly in government bonds as at present but in a broadening list of American stocks. As social security and pension trusts increasingly cover the entire working population of the United States, the stockholder position, though having lost its ancient justification, could become a vehicle for rationalized wealth distribution corresponding to and serving the American ideal of a just civilization. The institution of passive property has an advantage which, so far as we know, is new to history in that distribution and redistribution of wealth-holding can take place without interruption of the productive process. Ancient Hebrew law required redistribution of land every half-century through the institution of the 'Jubilee Year,' but ran into operational difficulties, as might have been expected. The great revolutionary movements of 1848 and, in our time, in Russia, China and Cuba, involved extreme productive losses, none of which has yet been recouped (though after nearly half a century the Soviet Union may finally be at the point of doing so). The corporate system, accompanied by reasonably enlightened tax policies and aided by continuously growing productivity, can achieve whatever redistribution the American people want. *   *   * ''

E. THE EMERGING "NEW PROPERTY": JOBS, PENSION RIGHTS, AND GOVERNMENT LARGESS

According to traditional notions as to what may constitute "property," one's interest in his or her job and in perquisites associated with that job, such as pensions, is not property. This is so for a variety of reasons. Generally such interests are not transferable, and they are often given relatively little legal protection. Such interests have become more and more "property-like" in recent years, as Professor Lawrence M. Friedman pointed out in his article, The Law of the Living, The Law of the Dead: Property, Succession, and Society,[31] from which the following excerpt is drawn.[32]

"In public offices, rules of succession are laid down by positive law (that is, by statute and judicial rule). Office is not to be bought, sold, or inherited. Life tenure is a rarity, though federal judges do have it. Private positions, offices, and jobs have their own rules of succession. These rules are far too diverse for a summary statement. Consider, for example, the complexity of succession to jobs in a factory, an office, a university, a hospital; consider the various retirement provisions (mandatory and permissive) in institutions, the rules of seniority and of severance; consider the different modes of succession to executive offices in large corporations, small shops, and charitable foundations. Mostly, rules of succession to positions in private organizations are provided for by contract or by custom, rather than by positive law. But there have been important legal interventions. Through law, the power of unions has been solidified or at least ratified; and this means that for many workers a principle of seniority has replaced a principle of succession in which full discretion is in the hands of the employer.

"The seniority system in industrial jobs is one of many recent changes in the direction of regularizing and standardizing job succession and hence job tenure. The right to a particular job is increasingly under legal protection, or the protection of strong occupational groups. Job tenure seems closely related, historically, to the permanence and stability of the employing institution. Extremely stable organizations may even be able and willing to guarantee life rights and security to some of their employees. The Roman Catholic Church, for example,

---

31. 1966 Wis.L.Rev. 340.

32. Id. at 344–347. Copyright 1966 by the University of Wisconsin. The author's footnotes have been omitted.

does this for priests and members of religious orders. The civil service, the armed forces, and the tenured staffs of universities (public and private) provide examples of similar commitments, somewhat less sweeping. Business corporations have resisted the notion of granting tenure to industrial workers, but they have made more and more concessions to the unions which tend in this direction. The major corporate employers are profitable, vast, and economically stable. They approach, in other words, the permanence of a government or a church. Tenure within such bureaucratic organizations is feasible, though small, shaky businesses would find it impossible to grant firm rights of tenure and succession.

"Job tenure is like a property right in that it is legally secured from adverse action. But in other senses it is not property. Our legal system closely associates the concept of property with economic risk. Maximum freedom to 'initiate economic decision' with regard to a valuable right means the power to make economic gambles on the basis of that right; tenure in a job usually means a limitation on both risk and opportunity. Job tenure rights are nontransferable, are at most life interests, and give rise to no conventional problems of succession at death because they cannot be inherited.

"There are, however, certain perquisites of office and job which more closely resemble transferable assets, in the sense that they are money claims that arise out of the employment contract and, like bank accounts, draw interest and increase with the passage of time. Pension rights, both public and private, are among the most valuable fringe benefits in many jobs. We need not concern ourselves with the question whether and under what circumstances pension rights are 'property' in the sense that they cannot be taken away from their holder without his consent, or at least without compensation. Pension rights, by and large, are *not* property in the sense of marketable assets. They are nontransferable. Though many pension plans include death benefits for the worker's survivors, they reject the principle of freedom of testation and limit inheritance to the immediate family circle of the deceased. A study by Professor Dunham found sixty systems of succession operative in Illinois—forty under state statutes and twenty under federal laws. These special laws were mostly pension laws—for firemen, teachers, policemen. They differed somewhat among themselves, but agreed in rejecting free testation in favor of the claims of widows and children and in bypassing the ordinary procedures for handling estates at death. Perhaps the most familiar of the sixty is the federal program of old-age insurance benefits. Under this program, a worker and his employer both make contributions. Payments are made to qualifying workers when they retire or become unable to work. If the worker dies, a little money is paid to his estate to cover burial expenses, and his widow and small children are entitled to benefits. Payments go no further. The worker may not, under social security, select his beneficiaries; and if he dies young, leaving no close surviving relatives, his contributions will be forfeited to the system. We may, if we wish, call this a program of 'social insurance' but it is proper to bear in mind how different it is from ordinary insurance. Ordinary insurance, for example, is an economic asset; it is property in every sense of the word. Social insurance has been boldly and frankly removed from the property system.

"In fact, social security rights, like some private pension rights, are not 'property' even in the sense that the rights of contributors are safe from the risk of government encroachment. In theory, Congress retains the right to abolish the whole social security system and use the amounts contributed to build rockets. In practice, even the mention of such a possibility is political suicide. In 1964 Senator Goldwater did his cause grievous harm merely by suggesting a change in the nature of the program. In Flemming v. Nestor * the Supreme Court upheld the right of Congress to take away the social security benefits of a former Communist. The Court held that Nestor's rights in the social security program were matters of legislative grace; they were not property rights. The Social Security Act clearly reserves to Congress power to abolish the program and clearly implies that individuals' rights are not vested. This does not mean that Flemming v. Nestor was correct. It can be strenuously argued, as a matter of constitutional doctrine, that Congress may not use its powers in so discriminatory a manner. It is certain, too, that the significance of the decision is limited. Congress is not likely to fall into the Goldwater trap and seriously interfere with accrued rights under social security. The doctrine is likely to be applied only to a numerically small and highly unpopular class of beneficiaries. But the principle is valuable to Congress and the Social Security Agency, if only for reasons of administrative convenience. Flemming v. Nestor and its background underscore the complexity of the decisions—implicit and explicit—which decide whether rights are to be treated as 'property' in any of the various senses of the word. The case also illustrates the use of nonproperty interests for purposes of preserving the formal freedom of action supposed to be essential to the administrative state. But those who demand an end to the tyranny of *Nestor* and who demand the vesting of pensions go no further; they do not seek to return these payments to the laws which govern the succession of marketable goods."

Social security rights are simply one example of what Professor Charles A. Reich, in his famous article entitled The New Property,[33] called "government-created wealth" or "government largess," which he catalogued as follows:[34]

"**Income and Benefits.** For a large number of people, government is a direct source of income although they hold no public job. Their eligibility arises from legal status. Examples are Social Security benefits, unemployment compensation, aid to dependent children, veterans benefits, and the whole scheme of state and local welfare. These represent a principal source of income to a substantial segment of the community. * * *

* 363 U.S. 603, 80 S.Ct. 1367, 4 L.Ed.2d 1435 (1960), rehearing denied 364 U.S. 854, 81 S.Ct. 29.

33. 73 Yale L.J. 733 (1964).

34. Id. at 734–737. Reprinted by permission of the Yale Law Journal Company and Fred B. Rothman & Company. The author's footnotes have been omitted.

"**Jobs.** More than nine million persons receive income from public funds because they are directly employed by federal, state, or local government. The size of the publicly employed working force has increased steadily since the founding of the United States, and seems likely to keep on increasing. If the three to four million persons employed in defense industries, which exist mainly on government funds, are added to the nine million directly employed, it may be estimated that fifteen to twenty percent of the labor force receives its primary income from government.

"**Occupational Licenses.** Licenses are required before one may engage in many kinds of work, from practicing medicine to guiding hunters through the woods. Even occupations which require little education or training, like that of longshoremen, often are subject to strict licensing. Such licenses, which are dispensed by government, make it possible for their holders to receive what is ordinarily their chief source of income.

"**Franchises.** A franchise, which may be held by an individual or by a company, is a partial monopoly created and handed out by government. Its value depends largely upon governmental power; by limiting the number of franchises, government can make them extremely remunerative. A New York City taxi medallion, which costs very little when originally obtained from the city, can be sold for over twenty thousand dollars. The reason for this high price is that the city has not issued new transferable medallions despite the rise in population and traffic. A television channel, handed out free, can often be sold for many millions. Government distributes wealth when it dispenses route permits to truckers, charters to bus lines, routes to air carriers, certificates to oil and gas pipelines, licenses to liquor stores, allotments to growers of cotton or wheat, and concessions in national parks.

"**Contracts.** Many individuals and many more businesses enjoy public generosity in the form of government contracts. Fifty billion dollars annually flows from the federal government in the form of defense spending. These contracts often resemble subsidies; it is virtually impossible to lose money on them. Businesses sometimes make the government their principal source of income, and many 'free enterprises' are set up primarily to do business with the government.

"**Subsidies.** Analogous to welfare payments for individuals who cannot manage independently in the economy are subsidies to business. Agriculture is subsidized to help it survive against better organized (and less competitive) sectors of the economy, and the shipping industry is given a dole because of its inability to compete with foreign lines. Local airlines are also on the dole. So are other major industries, notably housing. Still others, such as the railroads, are eagerly seeking help. Government also supports many non-business activities, in such areas as scientific research, health, and education. Total federal subsidies for 1964 were expected to be just under eight and a half billion dollars.

"**Use of Public Resources.** A very large part of the American economy is publicly owned. Government owns or controls hundreds of millions of acres of public lands valuable for mining, grazing, lumbering, and recreation; sources of energy such as the hydroelectric power of all major rivers, the tidelands reservoirs of oil, and the infant giant of nuclear power; routes of travel and commerce such as the airways, highways, and rivers; the radio-television spectrum which is the avenue for all broadcasting; hoards of surplus crops and materials; public buildings and facilities; and much more. These resources are available for utilization by private businesses and individuals; such use is often equivalent to a subsidy. The radio-television industry uses the scarce channels of the air, free of charge; electric companies use publicly-owned water power; stockmen graze sheep and cattle on public lands at nominal cost; ships and airplanes arrive and depart from publicly-owned docks and airports; the atomic energy industry uses government materials, facilities, and know-how, and all are entitled to make a profit.

"**Services.** Like resources, government services are a source of wealth. Some of these are plainly of commercial value: postal service for periodicals, newspapers, advertisers, and mail-order houses; insurance for home builders and savings banks; technical information for agriculture. Other services dispensed by government include sewage, sanitation, police and fire protection, and public transportation. The Communications Satellite represents an unusual type of subsidy through service: the turning over of government research and know-how to a quasi-private organization. The most important public service of all, education, is one of the greatest sources of value to the individual. *   *   *"

Professor Reich then went on to discuss in some detail "the unique legal system that is emerging" with respect to "government largess." The entire article will repay careful reading. We reprint here only a few short extracts from Professor Reich's discussion.[35]

"As government largess has grown in importance, quite naturally there has been pressure for the protection of individual interests in it. The holder of a broadcast license or a motor carrier permit or a grazing permit for the public lands tends to consider this wealth his 'own,' and to seek legal protection against interference with his enjoyment. The development of individual interests has been substantial, but it has not come easily.

"From the beginning, individual rights in largess have been greatly affected by several traditional legal concepts, each of which has had lasting significance:

"**Right vs. Privilege.** The early law is marked by courts' attempts to distinguish which forms of largess were 'rights' and which were 'privileges.' Legal protection of the former was by far the greater. If the holder of a license had a 'right,' he might be entitled to a hearing before the license could be revoked; a 'mere privilege' might be revoked without notice or hearing.

"**The Gratuity Principle.** Government largess has often been considered a 'gratuity' furnished by the state. Hence it is said that the state can withhold, grant, or revoke the largess at its pleasure. Under

35.   Id. at 739–741, 744, 785–786.

this theory, government is considered to be in somewhat the same position as a private giver.

"**The Whole and the Parts.** Related to the gratuity theory is the idea that, since government may completely withhold a benefit, it may grant it subject to any terms or conditions whatever. This theory is essentially an exercise in logic: the whole power must include all of its parts.

"**Internal Management.** Particularly in relation to its own contracts, government has been permitted extensive power on the theory that it should have control over its own housekeeping or internal management functions. Under this theory, government is treated like a private business. In its dealings with outsiders it is permitted much of the freedom to grant contracts and licenses that a private business would have. * * *

"These sentiments are often voiced in the law of government largess, but individual interests have grown up nevertheless. The most common forms of protection are procedural, coupled with an insistence that government action be based on standards that are not 'arbitrary' or unauthorized. Development has varied mainly according to the particular type of wealth involved. The courts have most readily granted protection to those types which are intimately bound up with the individual's freedom to earn a living. They have been reluctant to grant individual rights in those types of largess which seem to be exercises of the managerial functions of government, such as subsidies and government contracts. * * *

"In all of the cases concerning individual rights in largess the exact nature of the government action which precipitates the controversy makes a great difference. A controversy over government largess may arise from such diverse situations as denial of the right to apply, denial of an application, attaching of conditions to a grant, modification of a grant already made, suspension or revocation of a grant, or some other sanction. In general, courts tend to afford the greatest measure of protection in revocation or suspension cases. The theory seems to be that here some sort of rights have 'vested' which may not be taken away without proper procedure. On the other hand, an applicant for largess is thought to have less at stake, and is therefore entitled to less protection. The mere fact that a particular form of largess is protected in one context does not mean that it will be protected in all others.

"While individual interests in largess have developed along the lines of procedural protection and restraint upon arbitrary official action, substantive rights to possess and use largess have remained very limited. In the first place, largess does not 'vest' in a recipient; it almost always remains revocable. * * *

"Eventually those forms of largess which are closely linked to status must be deemed to be held as of right. Like property, such largess could be governed by a system of regulation plus civil or criminal sanctions, rather than a system based upon denial, suspension and revocation. As things now stand, violations lead to forfeitures—outright confiscation of wealth and status. But there is surely no need for these drastic results. Confiscation, if used at all, should be the ultimate, not the most common and convenient penalty. The presumption should be that the professional man will keep his license, and the welfare recipient his pension. These interests should be 'vested.' If revocation is necessary, not by reason of the fault of the individual holder, but by reason of overriding demands of public policy, perhaps payment of just compensation would be appropriate. The individual should not bear the entire loss for a remedy primarily intended to benefit the community.

"The concept of right is most urgently needed with respect to benefits like unemployment compensation, public assistance, and old age insurance. These benefits are based upon a recognition that misfortune and deprivation are often caused by forces far beyond the control of the individual, such as technological change, variations in demand for goods, depressions, or wars. The aim of these benefits is to preserve the self-sufficiency of the individual, to rehabilitate him where necessary, and to allow him to be a valuable member of a family and a community; in theory they represent part of the individual's rightful share in the commonwealth. Only by making such benefits into rights can the welfare state achieve its goal of providing a secure minimum basis for individual well-being and dignity in a society where each man cannot be wholly the master of his own destiny."

Since the publication of Professor Reich's article, the United States Supreme Court has decided a series of so-called "entitlement" cases in which government action was challenged as violating the "due process" clause of the Fifth or Fourteenth Amendment.[36] All these cases were decided since 1970.

In Board of Regents v. Roth, 408 U.S. 564, 92 S.Ct. 2701, 33 L.Ed.2d 548 (1972), an untenured assistant professor, hired for a probationary one-year term, had no Fourteenth Amendment due process procedural right to a hearing when his contract was not renewed at the end of the year. The Court said that the Fourteenth Amendment does not require opportunity for a hearing prior to nonrenewal of a non-tenured state teacher's contract unless he can show that the nonrenewal deprived him of an interest in "liberty" or that he had a "property" interest in continued employment despite his lack of tenure. The Court held that the probationary one-year employment contract created no "property" interest protected by procedural due process.

In Perry v. Sinderman, 408 U.S. 593, 92 S.Ct. 2694, 33 L.Ed.2d 570 (1972), decided at the same time as *Roth*, however, where a junior college failed to renew the contract of a professor who had been employed in the state college system for ten years and at the junior college in question for four years under a series of one-year contracts, the Court held that the teacher was entitled to an opportunity to show that the renewal of his contract was denied in retaliation for his exercise of the

---

36. The Fifth Amendment of the United States Constitution provides in part that "No person shall * * * be deprived of life, liberty, or property without due process of law * * *." The Fourteenth Amendment provides in part, " * * * nor shall any state deprive any person of life, liberty, or property without due process of law * * *."

right of free speech as he alleged. The Court said that the teacher must be allowed to prove a claim to an "entitlement" protected under the procedural due process requirement imposed by the Fourteenth Amendment. The Court went on to say (408 U.S. at 601, 92 S.Ct. at 2699),

> "We have made clear   *   *   *   that 'property' interests subject to procedural due process are not limited by a few rigid, technical forms. Rather, 'property' denotes a broad range of interests that are secured by 'existing rules or understandings.'   *   *   *   A person's interest in a benefit is a 'property' interest for due process purposes if there are such rules or mutually explicit understandings that support his claim of entitlement to the benefit and that he may invoke at a hearing." Thus, the Court said, the respondent need not prove that he was entitled to any formal tenure status, but might prove, after having held his position for a number of years, "from the circumstances of this service—and from other relevant facts— that he has a legitimate claim of entitlement to job tenure."

Four years later, in Bishop v. Wood, 426 U.S. 341, 96 S.Ct. 2074, 48 L.Ed.2d 684 (1976), the Court held that there was no Fourteenth Amendment right to procedural due process where a policeman was discharged without a hearing, pursuant to a local ordinance providing that he "held his position at the will and pleasure of the city." The Court indicated that the policeman did not have a protected property interest since under the ordinance his employment was terminable at will.

Compare the cases discussed above, dealing with a person's interest in his or her job, with Goldberg v. Kelly, 397 U.S. 254, 90 S.Ct. 1011, 25 L.Ed.2d 287 (1970), and Goss v. Lopez, 419 U.S. 565, 95 S.Ct. 729, 42 L.Ed.2d 726 (1975).

In Goldberg v. Kelly, New York City residents receiving financial aid under a federally-assisted Aid to Families with Dependent Children program brought a suit challenging the adequacy of the provisions for notice and hearing when such aid was terminated by the City. The Court held that the procedures followed by the City in terminating such aid denied due process of law in violation of the Fourteenth Amendment because they failed to allow recipients to appear personally, with or without counsel, before the official who finally made the determination as to continued eligibility for such aid, and because they failed to permit recipients to present oral evidence to that official and to confront or cross-examine adverse witnesses. The Court did not say in so many words that recipients were denied either "liberty" or "property" without due process of law. Instead, the Court said,

> "Appellant does not contend that procedural due process is not applicable to the termination of welfare benefits. Such benefits are a matter of statutory entitlement for persons qualified to receive them. Their termination involves state action that adjudicates important rights. The constitutional challenge cannot be answered by an argument that public assistance benefits are a 'privilege' and not a 'right'."

A footnote is added which says, "It may be realistic today to regard welfare entitlements as more like 'property' than a 'gratuity'" (citing the Reich article).

In Goss v. Lopez, students in a public high school brought a class action contesting their temporary suspension from school for misconduct without a hearing. Judgment for the students was affirmed. Conceding that the state was not obligated to maintain a public school system, the court observed that it had nevertheless done so and had made attendance compulsory. On the basis of state law therefore, "appellees plainly had legitimate claims of entitlement to a public education * * * as a property interest which is protected by the Due Process Clause."

What do you make of this series of cases? Some commentators think that these cases indicate a rejection by the Supreme Court of traditional ideas as the distinction between property rights and personal rights, thus seriously undercutting the holdings of earlier cases such as Flemming v. Nestor, discussed above in the excerpt from Professor Friedman's article. Professor Tribe, for example says,[37]

> [t]he body of rules determining which expectations constitute compensable property interests and which do not, see, e.g., Flemming v. Nestor * * * plainly requires reconsideration in light of the broader definition of property interests now employed in the procedural law of due process.

And Professor Michelman has argued that the "entitlement" doctrine, conditioning procedural due process rights on the existence of some entitlement rooted in positive law, has been weakened by the cases in which procedural due process rights have been recognized even though no positive entitlement of the sort required by the *Roth* case, supra, was present.[38]

Cf. the discussion of "entitlements," "property," and procedural due process in Professor Alexander's recent article entitled The Concept of Property in Private and Constitutional Law: The Ideology of the Scientific Turn in Legal Analysis.[39]

SECTION 2.   POSSESSION AND OWNERSHIP

A. JUDICIAL REMEDIES FOR PROTECTION OF PROPERTY

Although "property" law determines what "expectations of being able to draw such or such an advantage" from particular "things" will be legally protected, the mode of protection is largely determined, in the Anglo-American legal system, by the historical evolution of "common law" civil remedies in England between the twelfth and the sixteenth centuries. These remedies were mainly designed to protect those in possession of land or chattels from unauthorized interference with their possession.

37. L. Tribe, American Constitutional Law 459 n. 11 (1978).

38. Michelman, Formal and Associational Aims in Procedural Due Process, in Nomos XVIII, Due Process 126 (J. Pennock & J. Chapman eds. 1977), at 147.

39. 82 Colum.L.Rev. 1545, 1550–1552, 1583–1587 (1982).

Common law actions for recovery of land *in specie* developed in England as early as the reign of Henry II. Ultimately, a wide variety of "real" actions became available to a plaintiff who alleged that he was entitled to possession (*seisin*) of land presently in the defendant's possession.[1] But these "real" actions, collectively, did not provide a fully satisfactory set of judicial remedies for plaintiffs who sought to recover possession of land wrongfully taken or withheld by a defendant. When the action of "ejectment" became generally available in the sixteenth century as a specific remedy for plaintiffs seeking to recover possession of land wrongfully withheld from them, the older "real" actions gradually fell into disuse and had become practically obsolete by the end of the seventeenth century.[2]

"Ejectment," which provided a relatively expeditious method for recovering possession of land and carried with it a right to jury trial, was an offshoot of the ancient action of "trespass," which was a "personal" rather than a "real action" because it resulted in a judgment—if the plaintiff was successful—for money damages rather than for restitution *in specie*.[3] The action of "trespass" originally provided a damage remedy for any direct and tortious interference with the actual possession of either land or chattels. But "trespass" produced many offshoots, including "ejectment," that became separate forms of action. Among these other offshoots were "case" (or "trespass on the case"), which provided a damage remedy for indirect or consequential injury to land or chattels resulting from the wrongful act (intended or negligent) of the defendant,[4] and "trover," which provided a damage remedy in cases where the defendant had "converted" the plaintiff's chattel(s) to his own use by wrongful seizure, withholding, or disposition.[5]

Money damages was the usual remedy for wrongful interference with a plaintiff's right to possession of chattels. In certain cases the plaintiff could recover possession of chattels by means of an action of "replevin"[6] or "detinue."[7] Replevin originated as a remedy for the tenant whose chattels had been wrongfully "distrained" by his landlord for nonpayment of rent or other breach of duty. In England the courts seem never to have expanded the scope of replevin to cover wrongful

---

1. S. Milsom, Historical Foundations of the Common Law 106–124 (1969); T. Plucknett, Concise History of the Common Law 335–343 (4th ed. 1948); E. Morgan, The Study of Law 83–88 (2d ed. 1948); W. Maitland, The Forms of Action at Common Law 21–48 (1936).

2. S. Milsom, supra note 1, at 127–138; T. Plucknett, supra note 1, at 354; E. Morgan, supra note 1, at 112–115; W. Maitland, supra note 1, at 56–61. For more detailed discussion, see P. Bordwell, Ejectment Takes Over, 55 Iowa L.Rev. 1089 (1970).

3. S. Milsom, supra note 1, at 244–256; T. Plucknett, supra note 1, at 349–352; E. Morgan, supra note 1, at 102–105; W. Maitland, supra note 1, at 48–50, 53–55, 65.

4. S. Milsom, supra note 1, at 256–270; T. Plucknett, supra note 1, at 352–353; E. Morgan, supra note 1, at 105–107; W. Maitland, supra note 1, at 65–68.

5. T. Plucknett, supra note 1, 354–356; E. Morgan, supra note 1, at 111–112; W. Maitland, supra note 1, at 71. See also S. Milsom, supra note 1, at 321–332.

6. T. Plucknett, supra note 1, at 348–349; E. Morgan, supra note 1, at 88–92; W. Maitland, supra note 1, at 48, 61.

7. S. Milsom, supra note 1, at 219–223, 227–235; T. Plucknett, supra note 1, at 345–346; E. Morgan, supra note 1, at 96–99; W. Maitland, note 1, at 61–63.

seizures other than seizures by way of distraint,[8] and replevin clearly did not provide a remedy for the mere wrongful withholding of possession.[9] The latter was the function of detinue, where the defendant, if found to have wrongfully withheld possession of the plaintiff's chattel(s), had the option of returning the chattel(s) or paying their value as damages.[10] If the defendant in detinue chose to pay damages, the outcome of the action was similar to the outcome of a successful trover action.

In most American jurisdictions, from an early date, the common law action of ejectment was available to plaintiffs seeking to recover possession of land.[11] The other forms of action mentioned above were also available for protection of property interests in land and chattels. In most jurisdictions the scope of replevin was broadened so that it could be used to recover chattels *in specie* in any case where the defendant was wrongfully withholding them,[12] and to recover damages in cases where the defendant had wrongfully disposed of the plaintiff's chattel(s).[13] Since a plaintiff could recover either possession or damages by means of an action of replevin or an action of trover, detinue fell into disuse in most American jurisdictions. Where chattels were damaged but not converted to the defendant's use, trespass and case were available in all American jurisdictions to provide a damage remedy.[14] Trespass also provided the possessor of land with a damage remedy when his right to possession was invaded but he was not dispossessed;[15] and an action on the case for nuisance gave him a remedy for non-trespassory interference with the use and enjoyment of his land.[16]

The forms of action mentioned above, along with others designed to protect personal and contract rights, evolved in the English "common law" courts. But the English Court of Chancery also developed distinctive "equitable" remedies for the protection of property interests—e.g., injunctions against interference with such interests, rescission of property transactions, reformation of instruments, and removal of "clouds" on title to land.[17] In some cases Chancery only provided a better reme-

8. S. Milsom, supra note 1, at 95 ("never much widened in England"); T. Plucknett, supra note 1, at 349; W. Maitland, supra note 1, at 61 ("A few instances of replevin used to recover goods though not taken by distress * * * occur late in the day, and are not important in relation to general theory."). But cf. J. Ames, Lectures on Legal History 69–70 (1913).

9. Mennie v. Blake, 6 E. & B. 842 (1856).

10. W. Maitland, supra note 1, at 62; E. Morgan, supra note 1, at 98. Damages for the detention (loss of use) in addition to the value were awarded.

11. In the New England states, the action for possession of realty was called a "writ of entry" but it was substantially the same as "ejectment" and was quite different from the old English "writ of entry."

12. T. Plucknett, supra note 1, at 349. But cf. E. Morgan, supra note 1, at 91 (orthodox rule in U.S. allowed replevin only where there was a wrongful taking, but Pennsylvania and Massachusetts extended replevin to all cases of wrongful detention in early cases).

13. Although the early English cases allowed recovery of damages in such cases, the American cases were in conflict in the absence of a governing statute. E. Morgan, supra note 1, at 91. Such statutes have been enacted in most jurisdictions.

14. Generally, see Prosser, Torts §§ 7, 14 (4th ed. 1971).

15. See post Chapter 2, Section 2.

16. See post Chapter 2, Section 1.

17. Generally as to the origin of "equity" and "equitable remedies," see H. Mc-

dy for protection of "legal" property interests; in other cases, Chancery protected property interests not recognized in the "common law" courts.[18] Although not all American jurisdictions established separate "equity" courts, "equitable" as well as "legal" remedies were generally available in America from an early date.[19]

At the present time, the "common law" forms of action have been abolished in almost all American jurisdictions, and in most of them all forms of "legal" and "equitable" relief are now available in a single form of civil action.[20] But the "common law" forms of action and the "equitable" remedies for protection of property that evolved in England continue to have a profound influence on modern property law.

B. PROPERTY RIGHTS BASED ON POSSESSION

YOUNG v. HICHENS

Queen's Bench.
1 Dav. & Mer. 592, 6 Q.B. 606, 115 Eng.Rep. 228 (1844).

[Action in trespass. The first count of the declaration charged that after the plaintiff had enclosed 2,000,000 mackerel worth £2,000 with his net and had thereby taken them into its possession, the defendant by force, for twenty days prevented plaintiff from taking the fish out, drove many away, and killed or injured the rest so that all were lost to the plaintiff; that the defendant caused damage to plaintiff's sean; and finally that the defendant caused plaintiff to hire fifty men to watch, protect, and save the fish. The second count charged that defendant seized the 2,000,000 fish of the plaintiff and converted and disposed of them to its own use. The defendant pleaded (1) not guilty, (2) that the fish did not belong to plaintiff, and (3) that defendant's actions were justified in that plaintiff was in violation of certain statutes regulating fishing in the Bay of St. Ives.

[At the trial, before Atcherley, Serjt., at the Cornwall Spring Assizes, 1843, it appeared that on the day in question a large shoal of mackerel had come into the Bay of St. Ives. Plaintiff's boat, the Wesley, put out and shot her sean. The sean nearly 140 fathoms long, was drawn in a semicircle completely around the shoal, with the exception of a space five or seven fathoms wide (there was a dispute as to the number) which was about to be closed with a stop net and in which plaintiff's fishermen were splashing their oars and creating a disturbance such that the fish would be frightened to pass through. But before the plaintiff could completely enclose the fish, the defendant's boat, the Ellen, rowed through the gap, shot her sean, enclosed the fish and captured the whole of them.

Clintock, Equity §§ 1–7 (2d ed. 1948); W. Walsh, Equity chaps. 1–83 (1930).

18. E.g., the rights of a trust beneficiary in the trust property.

19. McClintock, Equity § 5 (2d ed. 1948).

20. McClintock, Equity § 6 (2d ed. 1948); W. Walsh, Equity § 7 (1930); C. Clark, Code Pleading §§ 6–10, 15 (2d ed. 1947); F. James and G. Hazard, Civil Procedure 18–22 (2d ed. 1977).

[It was argued at the trial that the plaintiff did not have possession sufficient to entitle him to maintain trespass and that even if he did defendant could justify his interposition in consequence of the plaintiff's violation of the statutes. The Serjeant left these questions to the jury, and the jury returned a verdict for the plaintiff. The Serjeant then directed a verdict be entered for plaintiff for £569 (£568 for the value of the fish and £1 for damages to the net). Leave was given defendant to move to have the verdict entered for him if the Court of Queen's Bench should be of the opinion that the fish were not in plaintiff's possession or if they were of the opinion that defendant's acts were justified. Counsel for defendant obtained a rule nisi for entering a verdict for defendant on all the issues or for reducing the damages to 20s. and entering a verdict for defendant on the first possession issue.]

*   *   *   [Counsel for plaintiff argued:] The jury were justified in finding as they did, unless it be legally impossible for a man to have possession of a wild animal which is not in his actual occupation. It appears that a strong probability of complete capture is enough to give a right of possession against a party preventing the capture. If the net here had been completely closed, but there had been a fracture in it, a party could not have acquired a right to the fish by enticing it out of the net through the fracture, and then taking it. (They also argued on the statutes.)   *   *   *

*   *   *   [Counsel for defendant:] The question really is, whether nearly catching a fish amounts to the same thing, as regards the acquisition of property, as actually catching it. No English law book at all events admits the position that property can be acquired unless the taking is complete. The language of Bracton is "Nec sola persecutio facit rem esse meam. Nam etsi feram bestiam vulneraverim ita ut capi possit, non tamen est mea nisi eam cepero, imo erit potius occupantis, *quia multa accidere solent ne capias.*" If an animal, once taken, escapes, the property having once vested is not lost, nor acquired by a subsequent taker. But this is quite a different proposition from that contended for, which is, that where an animal *nearly* taken escapes, the subsequent taker does not gain the property. In Churchward v. Studdy the fact that on which the decision turned was, that the labourer had taken up the hare to assist the hunters "as an associate of them." But Lord Ellenborough continues, "If, indeed, he had taken it up for the defendant before it was caught by the dogs, that would have been different; or, even if he had taken it as an indifferent person, in the nature of a stakeholder." The opinion of his lordship may, therefore, be taken as an authority against the plaintiff in this case.   *   *   *

DENMAN, C.J. It does appear almost certain that the plaintiff would have had possession of the fish but for the act of the defendant: but it is quite certain that he had not possession. Whatever interpretation may be put upon such terms as "custody" and "possession," the question will be whether any custody or possession has been obtained here. I think it is impossible to say that it had, until the party had actual power over the fish. It may be that the defendant acted unjustifiably in preventing the plaintiff from obtaining such power: but that would only shew a wrongful act, for which he might be liable in a proper form of action.

PATTESON, J. I do not see how we could support the affirmative of these issues upon the present evidence, unless we were prepared to hold that all but reducing into possession is the same as reducing into possession. Whether the plaintiff has any cause of action at all is not clear: possibly there may be a remedy under the statutes.

WIGHTMAN, J. I am of the same opinion. If the property in the fish was vested in the plaintiff by his partially inclosing them but leaving an opening in the nets, he would be entitled to maintain trover for fish which escaped through that very opening.

(COLERIDGE, J., was absent.)

Rule absolute for reducing the damages to 20s., and entering the verdict for defendant on * * * [his second plea.]

In Trinity term (June 1st) 1844, [counsel for plaintiff] obtained a rule to shew cause why a nonsuit should not be entered, or the action discontinued on payment of costs by the plaintiff. The ground of application was that the action had been brought to try rights under the Fishery Acts; and that the fish had been sold, and the proceeds, amounting to £700, deposited with bankers to abide the result; but the decision on the second and third issues left the rights undetermined, and another action was necessary to ascertain them. * * *

DENMAN, C.J. There are some peculiar circumstances in this case, but for which a rule to shew cause would not have been granted. The application to enter a nonsuit seems to be given up. And it does not appear that leave to discontinue has ever been granted in a case like the present. A special verdict is distinguishable from a general one, as my brother Coleridge has pointed out; and here the verdict entered for the defendant is general. However, the proceedings being such as they are in this case, we might, perhaps, under some circumstances, have granted a rule to discontinue. But I think that the plaintiff is himself to blame for the situation in which he stands as to the money deposited. And, if he wished for an opportunity to try the real question of right, he should have stated his views on that subject in last Hilary vacation when the case was decided. The delay is not satisfactorily accounted for; and, if we granted this rule, we should encourage the making of similar applications at any distance of time. I regret the consequences; but we cannot go so far out of our way to protect parties against the result of their own acts.

WILLIAMS, COLERIDGE, and WIGHTMAN, JJ., concurred.

Rule discharged.

Notes and Questions

1. The Court of Queen's Bench which decided Young v. Hichens, originally traveled with the English King, but as the judiciary became more specialized the Court took up permanent quarters at Westminster Hall in London, as did the other two superior courts of common law, Common Pleas (or Common

Bench) and Exchequer. Litigants had to come to file their cases in Westminster Hall, and originally the cases had to be tried there. Because of the inconvenience this entailed, however, the superior courts evolved the practice of traveling around England to conduct jury trials during the recesses between their terms of court at Westminster Hall. These trials were presided over either by a single justice of one of the superior courts or, in some cases, by a highly qualified barrister (a "serjeant at law"). The trial sessions conducted during court recesses had a variety of names, depending on how they were authorized. Most commonly, the trial sessions were called either "assizes" or "nisi prius" sessions. All pleadings and most motions, however, still had to be heard at Westminster Hall either by the full bench of the appropriate superior court or by a single justice in chambers during one of the regular terms of court. (These terms were called, respectively, Hilary, Easter, Trinity, and Michaelmas, and were—obviously—based on the Christian calendar.) See T. Plucknett, Concise History of the Common Law 111–112, 165–167 (5th ed. 1956). Generally, for a brief introduction to the history of the English courts, see id. 177–289. 1 W. Holdsworth, History of English Law (7th ed. 1956) contains a fuller account of that topic.

2. Young v. Hichens was tried at "the Cornwall Spring Assizes" before Serjeant Atcherley. A "serjeant" was a member of the highest class of barristers-at-law in England. Until the Judicature Act (1873), only serjeants could be appointed to serve as judges in the superior courts of common law. The title and rank of "serjeant" have now disappeared.

3. In the principal case, counsel for plaintiff relied heavily on the "custom" of the Greenland whale fishery, which he stated as follows: "the first striker of a whale does not acquire the property if the line break; and another party may then take the whale; but   *   *   * if the fish remained entangled in the line, and the line in the power of the striker, although the harpoon was detached, the whale was still in the possession of the striker." Plaintiff's counsel also argued that, "without reference to custom,   *   *   * if the fish be harpooned and the line attached, a party who causes the liberation of the fish cannot appropriate it," citing several cases in support of this rule. Counsel for plaintiff concluded by quoting a treatise to the effect that, "It is the first seizure that introduceth property, and not the first attempt   *   *   *; as he who pursueth or woundeth a wild beast, a fowl or fish, is not thereby proprietor, unless he had brought it within his power, as if he had killed it or wounded it to death, or otherwise given the effectual cause whereby it cannot use its native freedom, as at the whale-fishing at Greenland, he that woundeth a whale so that she cannot keep the sea for the smart of her wound, and so must needs come to land, is proprietor, and not he that lays hand on her at land." Do you think this quotation was helpful to the plaintiff's case?

4. In Churchward v. Studdy, 14 East 249, 104 Eng.Rep. 596 (K.B.1811), cited in the principal case, a hare was chased by plaintiff and his dogs onto the land of defendant. Exhausted, the hare ran between the legs of a laborer employed by defendant, where one of plaintiff's dogs caught it. The laborer picked it up alive, whereupon defendant immediately took the hare, killed it, and refused to give it to plaintiff, who arrived a few moments later and demanded it. The court held for plaintiff, saying that plaintiff through his dogs had reduced the hare to possession, and that the laborer had picked it up "for the benefit of the hunter; as an associate of them [as his testimony had indicated]; which is the same as if it had been taken by one of the dogs." Id. at 251, 104 Eng.Rep. at 597. It is not clear why plaintiff's counsel (in an omitted portion of his argument) cited Churchward in the principal case, since both he and defen-

dant's counsel agreed that the decision in *Churchward* did not turn on the question when possession of the hare was complete.

5. On the question what constitutes possession of fish in the water, compare Young v. Hichens with State v. Shaw, 67 Ohio 157, 65 N.E. 875 (1902). In the *Shaw* case, the court held that possession had been acquired by the owners of "trap nets" set out in Lake Erie. The court concluded as follows:

" * * * [T]he fish were not at large in Lake Erie. They were confined in nets, from which it was not absolutely impossible for them to escape, yet it was practically so impossible; for it seems that under ordinary circumstances few if any, of the fish escape. The fish that were taken [by defendants from the aforesaid trap nets] had not escaped, and it does not appear that they would have escaped, or even that they probably would have escaped. They were so safely secured that the owners of the nets could have taken them out of the water at will as readily as the defendants did. The possession of the owners of the nets was so complete and certain that the defendants went to the nets and raised them with absolute assurance that they could get the fish that were in them. We think, therefore, that the owners of the nets, having captured and confined the fish, had acquired such a property in them that the taking of them was larceny."

6. In Young v. Hichens, the court held that the plaintiff could not recover the value of the fish in a trespass action because he failed to show that he ever had possession of the fish. In order to argue the defendant was liable for the value of the fish because of a violation of the "Fishery Acts," plaintiff would have to resort to a different form of action—trespass on the case. But if he allowed the judgment in the principal case to stand, a second action might be barred by the doctrines of *res judicata* or collateral estoppel. The doctrine of *res judicata* precludes re-litigation of the same claim after it has been litigated to final judgment. The doctrine of collateral estoppel provides that, if a material fact is established in an action that is litigated to final judgment, that fact must be considered established in any subsequent action between the same parties, even if the later action involves a different claim for relief. This is presumably the reason why plaintiff in the principal case asked the court to grant a nonsuit.

Although the court denied plaintiff's motion for a nonsuit or discontinuance, plaintiff did, as indicated in the court's last footnote, begin a second action against defendant to recover the value of the fish on the ground that defendant had violated plaintiff's "rights under the Fishery Acts." The latter contained elaborate regulations as to the manner of fishing in the Bay of St. Ives. See 16 Geo. III, c. 36, and 4 & 5 Vict., c. 57. These statutes imposed criminal sanctions for violation of the regulations, but contained no mention of civil liability. How do you suppose plaintiff expected to recover damages on the basis of a violation of "the Fishery Acts"?

7. We begin our consideration of property law with a case involving possession of wild animals, not because acquisition of ownership by acquiring possession is of great importance in modern times, but because possession is one of the most primitive concepts in the law of property. In the beginning, it was hardly distinguishable from ownership. Only the needs of a more sophisticated society forced the separation of the concepts of possession and ownership. You may have assumed that so primitive a concept as possession is relatively simple. In fact, however, possession is itself a very subtle concept which has received much attention down through centuries from Roman jurists and from medieval and modern philosophers. In modern times, commentaries on the concept of possession have sought to escape the dogmatic and abstract approach of the

older writers and to concentrate on how courts have, or should have, used the possession concept in dealing with concrete legal problems. The analysis of possession by Holmes in his famous book, The Common Law, is a good example of this approach. Holmes asserted that possession requires (1) "a relation of manifested power" in relation to the object in question and (2) "an intent to exclude others" from interfering with the object. In Young v. Hichens and other cases involving attempts to capture wild animals, the second requirement for possession as stated by Holmes is clearly present in all the claimants, and the real issue is which of the competing claimants first established "a relation of manifested power" in relation to the animals in question. As to the concept of possession generally, see Holmes, The Common Law, Lecture VI (1881, 1946 ed.)

8. Once possession of a wild animal is lawfully obtained, the possessor acquires "ownership" of, or "complete property in," the animal. Similarly, one who obtains possession of an "abandoned" thing in a lawful manner—i.e., without committing a tort—acquires "ownership" of, or "complete property" in, the thing. See R. Brown, Personal Property § 2.1 (3d ed. Raushenbush 1976).

CLARK v. MALONEY

Superior Court of Delaware, 1840.
3 Har. 68.

Action of trover to recover the value of ten white pine logs. The logs in question were found by plaintiff floating in the Delaware bay after a great freshet, were taken up and moored with ropes in the mouth of Mispillion creek. They were afterwards in the possession of defendants, who refused to give them up, alleging that they had found them adrift and floating up the creek.

BAYARD, Chief Justice, charged the jury. The plaintiff must show first, that the logs were his property; and secondly, that they were converted by the defendants to their own use. In support of his right of property, the plaintiff relies upon the fact of his possession of the logs. They were taken up by him, adrift in the Delaware bay, and secured by a stake at the mouth of Mispillion creek. Possession is certainly prima facie evidence of property. It is called prima facie evidence because it may be rebutted by evidence of better title, but in the absence of better title it is as effective a support of title as the most conclusive evidence could be. It is for this reason, that *the finder of a chattel, though he does not acquire an absolute property in it, yet has such a property, as will enable him to keep it against all but the rightful owner.* * The defence consists, not in showing that the defendants are the rightful owners, or claim under the rightful owner; but that the logs were found by them adrift in Mispillion creek, having been loosened from their fastening either by accident or design, and they insist that their title is as good as that of the plaintiff. But it is a well settled rule of law that the loss of a chattel does not change the right of property; and for the same reason that the original loss of these logs by the rightful owner,

---

* This proposition was first declared in the leading and much-cited English case, Armory v. Delamirie, 1 Strange 505, 93 Eng.Rep. 664 (1722). In that case plaintiff, a chimney sweeper's boy, found a jewel and delivered it to an apprentice in defendant's shop for appraisal. The stones were removed and the socket delivered back to plaintiff, who sued in trover and recovered the value of the stones.

did not change his absolute property in them, but he might have maintained trover against the plaintiff upon refusal to deliver them, so the subsequent loss did not divest the special property of the plaintiff. It follows, therefore, that as the plaintiff has shown a special property in these logs, which he never abandoned, and which enabled him to keep them against all the world but the rightful owner, he is entitled to a verdict.

Verdict for the plaintiff.

Notes and Questions

1. Why do you suppose the charge of a trial judge to the jury is reported, in light of the usual practice of reporting only appellate court opinions? Why do you suppose that Clark v. Maloney was tried before the Chief Justice of the Delaware Court of Errors and Appeals?

2. Although "finders keepers, losers weepers" is part of the folk-wisdom, it is not true. As against the "true owner," a finder of "lost" goods does not acquire ownership. But as to almost all other persons the finder's rights are tantamount to ownership; the finder has the right, above all, to have his possession of the goods legally protected against interference by anyone who cannot show a better legal right to possession. As to the "true owner" (or one with a better legal right to possession), the finder is often said to be a "bailee" or "quasi-bailee." We shall explore the implication of attaching such a label to a finder post in Section 3. If a finder knows or has reasonable means of discovering the identity of the "true owner" (or one with a better legal right to possession) but nevertheless appropriates the "lost" goods to his own use, he is guilty both of the tort of "conversion" and the crime of "larceny." Generally, as to the rights and duties of finders, see R. Brown, Personal Property ch. 3 (3d ed. Raushenbush 1975).

3. The right of a finder to "possess and hold the found goods" is generally thought to rest upon the fact that his possession is prior in time to that of one who, without right, deprives him of possession in some manner. But why should mere possession, acquired by finding, be given legal protection? The answer given by Holmes in his classic book, The Common Law, is as follows:

"Law, being a practical thing, must found itself on actual forces. It is quite enough, therefore, for the law, that man, by an instinct which he shares with the domestic dog, and of which the seal gives a most striking example, will not allow himself to be dispossessed, either by force or fraud, of what he holds, without trying to get it back again., Philosophy may find a hundred reasons to justify the instinct, but it would be totally immaterial if it should condemn it and bid us surrender without a murmur. As long as the instinct remains, it will be more comfortable for the law to satisfy it in an orderly manner, than to leave people to themselves. If it should do otherwise, it would become a matter for pedagogues, wholly devoid of reality." (The Common Law 213 (1881).)

4. If the finder's right to possession is based upon his having acquired possession, does it logically follow that, when he subsequently loses possession, he still has a better legal right to possession than does a subsequent finder? Clark v. Baker assumes the answer is affirmative, but provides no rationale. Compare Holmes, The Common Law 235 (1881):

"We are led, in this connection, to the subject of the continuance of the rights acquired by gaining possession. To gain possession, it has been seen, there must be certain physical relations, as explained, and a certain intent. It remains to be inquired, how far these facts must continue to be presently true of a person in order that he may keep the rights which follow from their presence. The prevailing view is that of Savigny. He thinks that there must be always the same *animus* as at the moment of acquisition, and a constant power to reproduce at will the original physical relations to the object. Every one agrees that it is not necessary to have always a present power over the thing, otherwise one could only possess what was under his hand. But it is a question whether we cannot dispense with even more. The facts which constitute possession are in their nature capable of continuing presently true for a lifetime. Hence there has arisen an ambiguity of language which has led to much confusion of thought. We use the word 'possession,' indifferently, to signify the presence of all the facts needful to gain it, and also the condition of him who, although some of them no longer exist, is still protected as if they did. Consequently it has been only too easy to treat the cessation of the facts as the loss of the right, as some German writers very nearly do.

"But it no more follows, from the single circumstance that certain facts must concur in order to create the rights incident to possession, that they must continue in order to keep those rights alive, than it does, from the necessity of a consideration and a promise to create a right *ex contractu*, that the consideration and promise must continue moving between the parties until the moment of performance. When certain facts have once been made manifest which confer a right, there is no general ground on which the law need hold the right at an end except the manifestation of some fact inconsistent with its continuance, although the reasons for conferring the particular right may have great weight in determining what facts shall be deemed to be so. Cessation of the original physical relations to the object might be treated as such a fact; but it never has been, unless in times of more ungoverned violence than the present. On the same principle, it is only a question of tradition or policy whether a cessation of the power to reproduce the original physical relations shall affect the continuance of the rights. It does not stand on the same ground as a new possession adversely taken by another. We have adopted the Roman law as to animals *ferae naturae*, but the general tendency of our law is to favor appropriation. It abhors the absence of proprietary or possessory rights as a kind of vacuum. Accordingly, it has been expressly decided, where a man found logs afloat and moored them, but they again broke loose and floated away, and were found by another, that the first finder retained the rights which sprung from his having taken possession, and that he could maintain trover against the second finder, who refused to give them up."

Do you find Holmes' argument for the rule applied in Clark v. Maloney persuasive?

SOUTH STAFFORDSHIRE WATER CO. v. SHARMAN

Queen's Bench Division, 1896.
[1896] 2 Q.B. 44.

LORD RUSSELL of Killowen, C.J.   *   *   *   The action was brought in detinue to recover the possession of two gold rings from the defendant. The defendant did not deny that he had possession of the rings, but he denied the plaintiffs' title to recover them from him. Under those circumstances the burden of proof is cast upon the plaintiffs to make out that they have, as against the defendant, the right to the possession of the rings.

Now, the plaintiffs, under a conveyance from the corporation of Lichfield, are the owners in fee simple of some land on which is situate a pool known as the Minster Pool. For purposes of their own the plaintiffs employed the defendant, among others, to clean out that pool. In the course of that operation several articles of interest were found, and amongst others the two gold rings in question were found by the defendant in the mud at the bottom of the pool.

The plaintiffs are the freeholders of the locus in quo, and as such they have the right to forbid anybody coming on their land or in any way interfering with it. They had the right to say that their pool should be cleaned out in any way that they thought fit, and to direct what should be done with anything found in the pool in the course of such cleaning out. It is no doubt right, as the counsel for the defendant contended, to say that the plaintiffs must shew that they had actual control over the locus in quo and the things in it; but under the circumstances, can it be said that the Minster Pool and whatever might be in that pool were not under the control of the plaintiffs? In my opinion, they were. The case is like the case, of which several illustrations were put in the course of the argument, where an article is found on private property, although the owners of that property are ignorant that it is there.

The principle on which this case must be decided, and the distinction which must be drawn between this case and that of Bridges v. Hawkesworth, 21 L.J., Q.B., 75, is to be found in a passage in Pollock and Wright's Essay on Possession in the Common Law, p. 41: "The possession of land carries with it in general, by our law, possession of everything which is attached to or under that land, and, in the absence of a better title elsewhere, the right to possess it also. And it makes no difference that the possessor is not aware of the thing's existence.
* * *

"It is free to any one who requires a specific intention as part of a de facto possession to treat this as a positive rule of law. But it seems preferable to say that the legal possession rests on a real de facto possession constituted by the occupier's general power and intent to exclude unauthorized interference."

The case of Bridges v. Hawkesworth [21 L.J. (Q.B.) 75] stands by itself, and on special grounds; and on those grounds it seems to me that the decision in that case was right. Some one had accidentally dropped a bundle of bank-notes in a public shop. The shopkeeper did not know they had been dropped, and did not in any sense exercise control over them. The shop was open to the public, and they were invited to come there. A customer picked up the notes and gave them to the shopkeeper in order that he might advertise them. The owner of the notes was not found, and the finder then sought to recover them from the shopkeeper. It was held that he was entitled to do so, the ground of the decision being, as was pointed out by Patteson, J., that the notes, being dropped in the public part of the shop, were never in the custody of the shopkeeper, or "within the protection of his house."

It is somewhat strange that there is no more direct authority on the question; but the general principle seems to me to be that where a person has possession of house or land, with a manifest intention to exercise control over it and the things which may be upon or in it, then, if something is found on that land, whether by an employee of the owner or by a stranger, the presumption is that the possession of that thing is in the owner of the locus in quo. *   *   *

Appeal allowed; judgment for the plaintiff.

Note

This was an appeal from a judgment rendered by a County Court. County Courts were established in 1846. The appeal was heard and decided by the Queen's Bench Division of the High Court of Justice, which is the successor of the old common law Court of Queen's Bench which heard and decided Young v. Hichens, ante. The High Court of Justice is the lower half of the Supreme Court of Judicature established in 1873 to take the place of the old courts of common law and equity, and other courts of special jurisdiction. The High Court of Justice consists of three divisions, the Queen's (or King's) Bench Division, which combines the jurisdiction and functions of the common law Courts of Queen's (or King's) Bench, Common Pleas, and Exchequer; the Chancery Division, which exercises the jurisdiction of the old Court of Chancery; and the Probate, Divorce, and Admiralty Division, whose name clearly indicates its jurisdiction. The upper half of the Supreme Court of Judicature is called the Court of Appeal, which since 1934 has heard appeals from both the High Court of Justice and the County Courts. With the permission of the Court of Appeal or the Judicial Committee of the House of Lords, further appeals may be taken from the former to the latter. For a good discussion of the development and current operation of the English court system, see H. Hanbury, English Courts of Law (1944).

Note on Finders and the Concept of Possession

It is not expected that your study of two cases is sufficient to explore the full extent or depth of the problems involved in determining the rights of finders of lost chattels. We are engaged in the pursuit of the meaning and significance of possession. Obviously the study of problems involving the finding of lost chattels is relevant to that inquiry. A finder by discovering a chattel and taking possession of it, acquires rights that are superior to those of most other persons. But they are subject to the rights of the person whose chattel has been lost. The Sharman case indicates that a finder's rights may also be subject to the claims of still another person: the owner of the land upon which the chattel was found. In fact, most of the finders cases involve contests between those two persons.

It would appear from the opinion in South Staffordshire Water Co. v. Sharman that the issue in such cases can be framed in terms of the proper dimensions of the possession of land. What are we saying about the possession of land when we hold that an owner of land has a claim to chattels left on his land that is prior in time and so prior in right to the claim of a finder? Since the landowner usually has no knowledge of the presence of the chattel until it has been found by some one else, what significance can or should be given to such "unconscious possession"? In fact, what does such possession really mean? Is it helpful to speak, as does the court in the *Sharman* case, of "the occupier's general power and intent to exclude unauthorized interference"? (This statement is a quotation from Pollock & Wright, Essay on Possession in the Common Law, which, in turn relies upon the second requirement—"intent to exclude"—set out in Holmes' discussion of possession in The Common Law.)

Would you agree that, in Bridges v. Hawkesworth, the proprietor of the shop had no "general intent to exclude unauthorized interference" with "lost" articles found on the floor of the shop, and that the water company did have such a general intent with respect to articles found at the bottom of its reservoir?

You may be led to suspect that courts, in deciding between finders and landowners, are really moved by considerations other than conceptual regularity. Some unstated values may be at work which are too elusive and variable to be articulated. The statement of the issues in possessory terms may be a disguise of the real issues or an imperfect expression of them. Judging by the inconclusive results of the cases, the law on finders is a good example of an apparently simple factual situation for which there is no single or obvious solution. Small differences in fact appear to have greater significance than an uninformed or superficial examination of them would suggest. What significance, for example, should be attached to the place where a chattel is found as bearing on the priority between a finder and a landlowner?

What about the difference between a place open to the public and a private place, in the light of the obvious difficulties of degree implicit in such a distinction? What about a chattel buried in the ground or hidden within a certain structure as against a chattel lying loose upon some surface? Is buried "treasure" to be treated differently from other chattels which have been buried or left lying upon the ground? Of what importance are the circumstances under which a chattel has been "lost," if in fact it has been lost at all, in the light of the difficulty of proving what those circumstances were? Is a court justified in inferring the manner in which a chattel was lost from proof as to the place where it was found? Some courts have distinguished "mislaid" from "lost" chattels, holding that the possessor of the place of finding is entitled to possession of the former and the finder is entitled to possession of the latter. Looking ahead to the Section on bailments, the question might be raised whether a preference for the possessor of the place of finding reflects a judgment that he owes a duty of care to the owner of the "mislaid" or "lost" goods.

Of what significance is the fact that a finder may have found a chattel in the course of his employment, in the light of the further question whether such a finding was a normal incident of his employment or only an unexpected coincidence? If any or all of these matters are significant, of what value is any attempt to explain a decision in terms of the prior possession of the chattel? In addition to disagreements upon the relevance of these factors, courts are not in agreement upon the relative weight to be given to the several factors.

A series of cases in the Supreme Court of Oregon offers a fascinating sort of laboratory in which one can follow the painful efforts of one court to thread its way through almost all of these variations. See Danielson v. Roberts, 44 Or. 108, 74 Pac. 913 (1904).; Ferguson v. Ray, 44 Or. 557, 77 Pac. 600 (1904); Roberson v. Ellis, 58 Or. 219, 114 Pac. 100 (1911); and Jackson v. Steinberg, 186 Or. 129, 200 P.2d 376, rehearing denied, 186 Or. 140, 205 P.2d 562 (1948). The English courts have fared little better. Compare South Staffordshire Water Co. v. Sharman, supra, with Bridges v. Hawkesworth, 21 L.J.N.S. 75 (Q.B.1851); Elwes v. Briggs Gas Co., 33 Ch.Div. 562 (1886); and Hannah v. Peel, [1945] K.B. 509.

Statutes exist in a number of states. In general they impose a duty on a finder of giving specified notice of his finding for the purpose of discovering the owner. Upon failure of the owner to appear within a prescribed time, the finder is usually left with the right to keep the chattel only upon payment of half or all of its appraised value to certain state or local officials. See Riesman, Possession and the Law of Finders, 52 Harv.L.Rev. 1105, 1123 (1939).

ANDERSON v. GOULDBERG

Supreme Court of Minnesota, 1892.
51 Minn. 294, 53 N.W. 636.

Appeal by defendants, Hans J. Gouldberg and D.O. Anderson, from an order of the District Court of Isanti County, Lochren, J., made November 14, 1892, refusing a new trial.

This action was brought by the plaintiff, Sigfrid Anderson, against the defendants, partners as Gouldberg & Anderson, to recover the possession of ninety-three pine logs, marked LSX, or for the value thereof. Plaintiff claimed to have cut the logs on section 22, township 27, range 25, Isanti County, in the winter of 1889–1890, and to have hauled them to a mill on section 6, from which place defendants took them. The title to section 22 was in strangers, and plaintiff showed no authority from the owners to cut logs thereon. Defendants claimed that the logs were cut on section 26, in the adjoining township, on land belonging to the Ann River Logging Company, and that they took the logs by direction of the Logging Company, who were the owners. The court charged that even if plaintiff got possession of the logs as a trespasser, his title would be good as against any one except the real owner or some one who had authority from the owner to take them, and left the case to the jury on the question as to whether the logs were cut on the land of the Logging Company, and taken by defendants under its authority. The jury found a verdict for the plaintiff and assessed his damages at $153.45. From an order denying their motion for a new trial, defendants appeal.

MITCHELL, J. It is settled by the verdict of the jury that the logs in controversy were not cut upon the land of the defendants, and consequently that they were entire strangers to the property.

For the purposes of this appeal, we must also assume the fact to be (as there was evidence from which the jury might have so found) that the plaintiffs obtained possession of the logs in the first instance by trespassing upon the land of some third party.

Therefore the only question is whether bare possession of property, though wrongfully obtained is sufficient title to enable the party enjoying it to maintain replevin against a mere stranger, who takes it from him. We had supposed that this was settled in the affirmative as long ago, at least, as the early case of Armory v. Delamirie, 1 Strange 505, so often cited on that point.

When it is said that to maintain replevin the plaintiff's possession must have been lawful, it means merely that it must have been lawful as against the person who deprived him of it; and possession is good title against all the world except those having a better title.

Counsel says that possession only raises a presumption of title, which, however, may be rebutted. Rightly understood, this is correct; but counsel misapplies it. One who takes property from the possession of another can only rebut this presumption by showing a superior title in himself, or in some way connecting himself with one who has. One who has acquired the possession of property, whether by finding, bailment, or by mere tort, has a right to retain that possession as against a mere wrongdoer who is a stranger to the property. Any other rule would lead to an endless series of unlawful seizures and reprisals in every case where property had once passed out of the possession of the rightful owner.

Order affirmed.

Notes

1. The opinion in *Anderson* refers to the action as "replevin" but the action was, in fact, one "to recover the possession of ninety-three pine logs * * * or for the value thereof," and the plaintiff obtained a verdict for damages amounting to $153.45. The explanation lies in the fact that Minnesota, while it was a territory, had adopted and, upon admission to the Union in 1857, had re-enacted a statutory provision (based on New York's Code of 1848) establishing a statutory form of replevin, called "claim and delivery." This statute provided that the plaintiff must by affidavit show (a) that the plaintiff is the owner of the property claimed or has special property therein; (b) that the property is wrongfully detained by defendant; (c) that the property had not been seized to satisfy a tax claim, fine, or judgment or, if seized for such purpose, that the seizure was not in conformity with the enabling statute; (d) the actual value of the property claimed. In addition, the statute provided that a defendant willing to post a bond in the amount of the property's value may retain possession of the property until the action is completed, and that the judgment in the "claim and delivery action," if for the plaintiff, shall be for the return of the property or, if the defendant no longer has the property, for the value thereof. These statutory provisions were in force when the principal case was decided and remained in force without substantial change until 1979. See Minn. Stat.Ann. §§ 548.04, 565.01 through 565.11 (1947). In 1979, §§ 565.01 through 565.11 were repealed and replaced by Minn.Laws 1979, ch. 18, now codified as Minn.Stat.Ann. §§ 565.21 through 565.29 (Supp.1983).

2. Are you satisfied with the rationale of the decision in Anderson v. Gouldberg—i.e., that a rule allowing "a mere wrongdoer who is a stranger to the property" to prove that a third party (not the plaintiff) is the owner "would lead to an endless series of unlawful seizures and reprisals in every case where property had once passed out of the possession of the rightful owner"? This rationale is adopted in 1 F. Harper & F. James, Torts 118 (1956), although it is conceded that the rule "may occasionally permit a thief or other wrongdoer to obtain protection designed for the rightful owner." Cf. W. Prosser, Torts 94 (4th ed. 1971), asserting that in every case where a wrongful possessor was allowed to recover the full value of chattels in a conversion action, "the plaintiff has been in possession under some colorable claim of title," and that "[n]o court has allowed an admitted, or even a clearly proved, thief without claim of right to recover, and it seems improbable that one ever will." But if the general rule disallows any plea of *jus tertii*, how can a defendant ever prove that the plaintiff is a "thief without claim of right"? In Anderson v. Gouldberg, it is clear that (for purposes of the appeal, at least) the plaintiff was a "wrongdoer." He may have had a "colorable claim of title," although the jury's verdict indicated that this claim was not valid. It is not clear that the plaintiff was a "thief"—i.e., one who took another's property knowing that it did not belong to the taker.

3. In Anderson v. Gouldberg the court says that "title to section 22 was in strangers, and plaintiff showed no authority from the owners to cut logs thereon." Although it is not expressly stated, it may be inferred that the identity of the owners of section 22 was, or could have been, established, since ownership of section 22 was undoubtedly a matter of public record. The case was thus quite different from the usual case involving the finder of a chattel who sues one who wrongfully takes the chattel from him, where the "true owner" of the chattel is rarely known and generally cannot be determined.

4. The rule enunciated in Anderson v. Gouldberg has generally been applied in similar cases, although such cases are quite rare. A contrary rule has been laid down in North Carolina, however, at least where the identity of the "true owner" is established. In Barwick v. Barwick, 33 N.C. 80 (1850) (involving slaves), the court allowed the defendant in a trover action to plead and prove that a third person was the owner of the chattels and concluded its opinion with the following language:

"There are cases in the English books, and in the reports of some of our sister states to the contrary; but we must be allowed to say, that the doctrine of our Courts is fully sustained by the reason of the thing, and is most consonant with the peculiar principles of this action. The cases differing from our decision, are all based upon a misapprehension of the principle laid down in the leading case, Delimere v. Armory. In that case the jewel was lost, and was found by the plaintiff, a chimney sweeper. He had a right to take it into possession, and became the owner by the title of occupancy, except in the event of the true owner becoming known. The former owner of the jewel was not known, and it was properly decided that the finder might maintain trover against the defendant, to whom he had handed it for inspection, and who refused to restore it.

"But the result of that case would have been very different, if the owner had been known. The defendant could then have said to the plaintiff, you have no right to make me pay you the value, when I must forthwith deliver up the property to the owner, or else pay him the value a second time.

"The distinction between that case, when the possessor was the only known owner, and the ordinary case of one, who himself has the possession wrongfully and sues another wrong doer for interfering with his possession, the true owner being known and standing by, ready to sue for the property, is as clear as day-light.

"In this case, for instance, as the facts appeared on the trial, the plaintiff was in wrongful possession, which was disturbed by the defendant, and for that injury he had a right to recover in trespass. But Sarah Sutton was known as the true owner, and had a right to demand her property of the defendants, or else to recover its value, and they could not protect themselves by showing that they had paid the full value to the plaintiff, under the coercion of a judgment and execution. This result would seem by the *reductio ad absurdum*, to show that the inference from the case of Delimere v. Armory, that trover can be maintained against a wrongdoer by one not having [more than] a naked possession, when the true owner is known, is contrary to good sense. That which is not good sense, is not good law."

Relying on Barwick v. Barwick, the North Carolina court reached the same result in Russell v. Hill, 125 N.C. 470, 34 S.E. 640 (1900), where the facts were similar to those in Anderson v. Gouldberg. One Mrs. McCoy sold plaintiff timber standing on land she claimed to own. Plaintiff cut the timber and placed the logs in a stream. Defendant took the logs, without any claim of right, and sold them. Plaintiff then sued for the value of the logs. Upon failure to prove that Mrs. McCoy owned the land from which the logs were taken, the plaintiff was denied recovery. The court said:

"The present action is in the nature of the old action of trover, and, before the plaintiff could recover in an action of that nature, he had to show both title and possession, or the right to possession."

The court (as did the *Barwick* court) distinguished Armory v. Delamire on the ground that in *Armory* the owner of the chattel was not known. In Russell, however, the evidence established the identity of the owner of the land on which the timber was cut. Is this a sufficient basis for distinguishing *Barwick* and *Russell* from Armory and from Clark v. Maloney?

See, generally, Annot., 150 A.L.R. 163 (1944).

5. What do you think of the *Barwick* court's statement that, if the defendant were compelled to pay the full value of the chattels to the plaintiff in an action for conversion, the true owner could nevertheless later compel the defendant to "deliver up the property   *   *   *   or else pay him the value a second time"? See 1 Harper & James, Torts 100, 121 (1956):

"Whether, if a possessor who has wrongfully obtained the chattel recovers from a second converter on the strength of his possession, the person entitled to possession is precluded from recovering from the second converter seems not settled. It is unlikely however, that he would be so barred.   *   *   *   In such a case, the burden of double payment by the second wrongdoer seems preferable to the hardship of remitting the owner to the first of two wrongdoers. Since the owner is the only innocent one of the three, he should be protected at the expense of whichever wrongdoer he can catch, and indeed it seems not too much if his protection comes at the double expense of one of them. The only alternative to this solution is to deprive the first wrongdoer of his remedy against the second."

However, if the second wrongdoer can identify the rightful owner and join him as a party in the conversion action, it seems clear that the first wrongdoer's claim should be dismissed. The rightful owner would still be entitled to judgment against both of the wrongdoers for the conversion of the chattels in question, but would be entitled to only one full satisfaction of the judgment for the value of the chattels.

6. In the case of a bailment, where the plaintiff received possession of chattels from or with the consent of the owner, a recovery of judgment for the full value of the chattels against a wrongdoer will bar any action by the owner (bailor) against the same wrongdoer. But the rule has been vigorously criticized. See, e.g., W. Prosser, Torts 95 (4th ed. 1971):

"Such a rule may result in considerable hardship where the possessor mishandles the suit, or is not to be trusted with the proceeds. For these reasons it has been suggested that the possessor's right to recover more than the value of his interest in the chattel should be limited to cases where he has the express or implied consent of the owner to bring the action, or the owner cannot be found *   *   *."

7. One might suppose that in actions of replevin the courts would consistently deny to the defendant the right to prove the *jus tertii* and allow a possessor to recover. In fact the courts in this country are substantially divided on the question, although the apparent division may not disclose the existence in some cases of circumstances which vary from the simple norm. Annot. 150 A.L.R. 163, 192 (1944); Shipman, Common Law Pleading 126 (3d ed. 1923). Some courts have even stated that, while trover can be maintained by one who had mere possession, replevin cannot be maintained except by one who has "the

property, either general or special." The reason for such a requirement may be found in some states in applicable statutes. Otherwise the reason is not clear. It may have something to do with the fact that upon the filing of an action in replevin the sheriff seizes the property in the hands of the defendant before any proof is offered of the plaintiff's allegations. It may turn on the fact that, while trespass and trover are remedies for a tort, the recovery of specific property is the aim of replevin. In other words, perhaps the proprietary nature of replevin is emphasized, which may have led some courts to insist that a plaintiff prove his proprietary right. Such a view, of course, produces the opposite result, both in trover and replevin, from what one would expect on the basis of the policy asserted in Barwick.

The traditional procedure in replevin by which a sheriff is directed to seize the chattel and deliver it to the plaintiff upon the plaintiff's giving a bond to prosecute the action and return the chattel if the action goes against him, but before any hearing on the merits, has encountered constitutional obstacles. See Fuentes v. Shevin, 407 U.S. 67, 92 S.Ct. 1983 (1972).

TAPSCOTT v. COBBS

Court of Appeals of Virginia, 1854.
52 Va. (11 Grat.) 172.

This was an action of ejectment in the Circuit court of Buckingham county, brought in February 1846, by the lessee of Elizabeth A. Cobbs and others against William H. Tapscott. Upon the trial the defendant demurred to the evidence. It appears that Thomas Anderson died in 1800, having made a will, by which he appointed several persons his executors, of whom John Harris, Robert Rives and Nathaniel Anderson qualified as such. By his will his executors were authorized to sell his real estate.

At the time of Thomas Anderson's death the land in controversy had been surveyed for him, and in 1802 a patent was issued therefor to Harris, Rives and N. Anderson as executors. Some time between the years 1820 and 1825, the executors sold the land at public auction, when it was knocked off to Robert Rives; though it appears from a contract between Rives and Sarah Lewis, dated in September 1825, that the land had, prior to that date, been sold by the executors to Mrs. Lewis for three hundred and sixty-seven dollars and fifty cents. This contract was for the sale by Mrs. Lewis to Rives of her dower interest in another tract of land, for which Rives was to pay to the executors of Thomas Anderson the sum of two hundred and seventeen dollars and fifty cents in part of her purchase. In a short time after her purchase she moved upon the land, built upon and improved it, and continued in possession until 1835, when she died. In 1825 the executor Harris was dead, and Nathaniel Anderson died in 1831, leaving Rives surviving him. And it appears that in an account settled by a commissioner in a suit by the devisees and legatees of Thomas Anderson against the executors of Robert Rives, there was an item under date of the 28th of August 1826, charging Rives with the whole amount of the purchase money, in which it is said, "The whole not yet collected, but Robert Rives assumes the liability."

There is no evidence that the heirs of Mrs. Lewis were in possession of the land after her death, except as it may be inferred from the fact that she had been living upon the land from the time of her purchase until her death, and that she died upon it.

The proof was that [Tapscott] took possession of the land about the year 1842, without, so far as appears, any pretense of title. He made an entry with the surveyor of the county in December 1844, with a view to obtain a patent for it.

The court gave a judgment upon the demurrer for the plaintiffs, and Tapscott thereupon applied to this court for a *supersedeas*, which was allowed.

DANIEL, J. It is no doubt true, as a general rule, that the right of a plaintiff in ejectment to recover, rests on the strength of his own title, and is not established by the exhibition of defects in the title of the defendant, and that the defendant may maintain his defence by simply showing that the title is not in the plaintiff, but in some one else. And the rule is usually thus broadly stated by the authorities, without qualification. There are, however, exceptions to the rule as thus announced, as well established as the rule itself. As when the defendant has entered under the title of the plaintiff he cannot set up a title in a third person in contradiction to that under which he entered. Other instances might be cited in which it is equally as well settled that the defendant would be estopped from showing defects in the title of the plaintiff. In such cases, the plaintiff may, and often does recover, not by the exhibition of a title good in itself, but by showing that the relations between himself and the defendant are such that the latter cannot question it.
* * *

Whether the case of an intrusion by a stranger without title, on a peaceable possession, is not one to meet the exigencies of which the courts will recognize a still further qualification or explanation of the rule requiring the plaintiff to recover only on the strength of his own title, is a question which, I believe, has not as yet been decided by this court. And it is somewhat remarkable that there are but few cases to be found in the English reporters in which the precise question has been decided or considered by the courts.

The cases of Read & Morpeth v. Erington, Croke Eliz. 321; Bateman v. Allen, Ibid. 437; and Allen v. Rivington, 2 Saund.R. 111, were each decided on special verdicts, in which the facts with respect to the title were stated. In each case it was shown that the plaintiff was in possession, and that the defendant entered without title or authority; and the court held that it was not necessary to decide upon the title of the plaintiff, and gave judgment for him. In the report of Bateman v. Allen it is said that Williams Sergeant moved, "that for as much as in all the verdict it is not found that the defendant had the *primer* possession, nor that he entered in the right or by the command of any who had title, but that he entered on the possession of the plaintiff without title, his entry is not lawful"; and so the court held.

And in Read & Morpeth v. Erington it was insisted that for a portion of the premises the judgment ought to be for the defendant, in as much as it appeared from the verdict that the title to such portion was outstanding in a third party; but the court said it did not matter, as it was shown that the plaintiff had entered, and the defendant had entered on him. * * *

In this country the cases are numerous, and to some extent conflicting, yet I think that the larger number will be found to be in accordance with the earlier English decisions. I have found no case in which the question seems to have been more fully examined or maturely considered than in Sowden, &c. v. McMillan's Heirs, 4 Dana's R. 456. The views of the learned judge (Marshall) who delivered the opinion, in which the whole court concurred, are rested on the authority of several cases in Kentucky, previously decided, on a series of decisions made by the Supreme court of New York, and on the three British cases of Bateman v. Allen, Allen v. Rivington, and Read & Morpeth v. Erington, before mentioned. * * *

"It is a natural principle of justice, that he who is in possession has the right to maintain it, and if wrongfully expelled, to regain it by entry on the wrongdoer. When titles are acknowledged as separate and distinct from the possession, this right of maintaining and regaining the possession is, of course, subject to the exception that it cannot be exercised against the real owner, in competition with whose title it wholly fails. But surely it is not accordant with the principles of justice, that he who ousts a previous possession should be permitted to defend his wrongful possession against the claim of restitution merely by showing that a stranger, and not the previous possessor whom he has ousted, was entitled to the possession. The law protects a peaceable possession against all except him who has the actual right to the possession, and no other can rightfully disturb or intrude upon it. While the peaceable possession continues, it is protected against a claimant in the action of ejectment, by permitting the defendant to show that a third person and not the claimant has the right. But if the claimant, instead of resorting to his action, attempt to gain the possession by entering upon and ousting the existing peaceable possession, he does not thereby acquire a rightful or a peaceable possession. The law does not protect him against the prior possessor. Neither does it indulge any presumption in his favor, nor permit him to gain any advantage by his own wrongful act." * * *

In Delaware, North Carolina, South Carolina, Indiana, and perhaps in other states of the Union, the opposite doctrine has been held.

In this state of the law, untrammeled as we are by any decisions of our own courts, I feel free to adopt that rule which seems to be best calculated to attain the ends of justice. The explanation of the law (as usually announced) given by Judge Marshall, in the portions of his opinion which I have cited, seems to me to be founded on just and correct reasoning; and I am disposed to follow those decisions which uphold a peaceable possession for the protection as well of a plaintiff as of a defendant in ejectment, rather than those which invite disorderly scrambles for the possession, and clothe a mere trespasser with the means of maintaining his wrong, by showing defects, however slight, in the title of him on whose peaceable possession he has intruded without shadow of authority or title.

The authorities in support of the maintenance of ejectment upon the force of a mere prior possession, however, hold it essential that the prior possession must have been removed by the entry or intrusion of the defendant; and that the entry under which the defendant holds the possession must have been a trespass upon the prior possession.   *   *   * And it is also said that constructive possession is not sufficient to maintain trespass to real property; that actual possession is required, and hence that where the injury is done to an heir or devisee by an abator, before he has entered, he cannot maintain trespass until his re-entry *   *   *. An apparent difficulty, therefore, in the way of a recovery by the plaintiffs, arises from the absence of *positive* proof of their possession at the time of the defendant's entry. It is to be observed, however, that there is no proof to the contrary. Mrs. Lewis died in possession of the premises, and there is no proof that they were vacant at the time of the defendant's entry. And in Gilbert's Tenures 37 (in note,) it is stated, as the law, that as the heir has the right to the hereditaments descending, the law presumes that he has the possession also. The presumption may indeed, like all other presumptions, be rebutted: but if the possession be not shown to be in another, the law concludes it to be in the heir.

The presumption is but a fair and reasonable one; and does, I think, arise here; and as the only evidence tending to show that the defendant sets up any pretense of right to the land, is the certificate of the surveyor of Buckingham, of an entry by the defendant, for the same, in his office, in December 1844; and his possession of the land must, according to the evidence, have commenced at least as early as some time in the year 1842; it seems to me that he must be regarded as standing in the attitude of a mere intruder on the possession of the plaintiffs.

Whether we might not in this case presume the whole of the purchase money to be paid, and regard the plaintiffs as having a perfect equitable title to the premises, and in that view as entitled to recover by force of such title; or whether we might not resort to the still further presumption in their favor, of a conveyance of the legal title, are questions which I have not thought it necessary to consider; the view, which I have already taken of the case, being sufficient, in my opinion, to justify us in affirming the judgment.

ALLEN, MONCURE and SAMUELS, Js. concurred in the opinion of DANIEL, J.

LEE, J. dissented.

Judgment affirmed.

Notes

1. From the statement of facts you should assume the following: (a) When Thomas Anderson died he had not yet obtained legal ownership of the land in

question, but in 1802 his executors did obtain legal ownership by virtue of the "patent * * * issued therefor" by the State of Virginia; (b) Mrs. Lewis had contracted to buy the land in question from Mr. Anderson's executors for $367.50, and had subsequently sold "her dower interest in another tract of land" to Rives in consideration of his paying $217.50 to the executors as part of the purchase price for the land involved in Tapscott v. Cobbs for which Mrs. Lewis was liable by virtue of her contract with the executors; (c) the subsequent "sale" of the land in question to Rives "at public auction" would not deprive Mrs. Lewis of her rights as purchaser under her prior contract with the executors; (d) there was no evidence as to how much, if any, of the $367.50 purchase price was ever, in fact, paid either by Mrs. Lewis or by Rives; (e) there was no evidence that the executors had ever transferred legal ownership of the land in question to Mrs. Lewis by delivering a deed of conveyance to her; (f) when Mrs. Lewis took possession of the land in question, most courts would consider her to be the "equitable owner" of the land, even if some, or even all, of the purchase price was never paid; (g) up to the time of her death, Mrs. Lewis had an equitable right to pay the unpaid balance of the purchase price (if any) and obtain a deed of conveyance from Anderson's executors.

2. Why do you suppose the Virginia court relied upon decisions in other American jurisdictions with respect to the rights of a mere "prior possessor" of land, in light of the following resolution adopted by the Virginia General Convention in May, 1776:

"That the common law of England, all statutes or acts of Parliament made in aid of the common law prior to the fourth year of the reign of King James the first, and which are of a general nature, not local to that kingdom, together with the several acts of the general assembly of this colony now in force, so far as the same may consist with the several ordinances, declarations, and resolutions of the general convention, shall be the rule of decision, and shall be considered as in full force, until the same shall be altered by the legislative power of this colony."

This resolution was similar to resolutions or declarations adopted in many other states at the time of the American Revolution. It was in effect in Virginia at the time Tapscott v. Cobbs was decided. It is still in effect, so far as the English common law is concerned. See Va.Code §§ 1–10, 1–11 (1979).

3. The rule that ejectment may be maintained "upon the force of a mere prior possession" seems to be the majority rule in the United States, although in some states it is apparently not applicable if the defendant has acquired possession peaceably and in good faith under claim of title. See 28 C.J.S. Ejectment § 18(a). The rule is consistent with the concept underlying the old English "assize of novel disseisin" in which, however, the defendant was not permitted to show a "superior right to possession" as a defense but was required to bring another action to establish his "superior right" and recover seisin (possession). In ejectment, however, the defendant was always permitted to prove a "superior right to possession" based on ownership of a fee simple or any lesser estate in the land, or based simply on the fact that the defendant had an even earlier possession than the plaintiff and was wrongfully dispossessed by the plaintiff. But most of the American cases deny the defendant any defense on the basis of proving a *jus tertii*—i.e., showing that a third person has a right to possession superior to that of the plaintiff. In such cases, there is no possibility of double liability for the value of the land, since there is no action analogous to an action for conversion of chattels in which the rightful owner of land may recover its value from a wrongful possessor.

4.   In most cases like Tapscott v. Cobbs, the defendant is unlikely to be able
to prove that a third party has a better right to possession than the plaintiff,
but may be able, as the court suggests, to show "defects * * * in the title
of him on whose peaceable possession he has intruded." As used in this context, "title" refers to to the chain of written instruments—or the recorded copies thereof—by which the plaintiff ordinarily seeks to prove ownership of the
land in question. The "defects" to which the *Tapscott* court adverted might be
"missing links" in the chain of title—i.e., instruments that are entirely missing
or instruments that are defectively executed in some respect so that they are
not admissible as evidence of the transfer of ownership from the grantor to the
grantee named therein. In *Tapscott*, plaintiff was unable to produce any written instruments transferring ownership from Anderson's executors to Mrs.
Lewis and then to plaintiff.

5.   What do you think of the court's holding that Mrs. Cobbs was entitled to
the benefit of a presumption, in the absence of proof to the contrary, that Mrs.
Cobbs was actually in possession of the land in question as heir of Mrs. Lewis,
who "died in possession of the premises"? Is there any rational basis for such
a presumption in absence of any evidence as to whether Mrs. Cobbs was in
possession after the death of Mrs. Lewis? The court said that "[t]he presumption is but a fair and reasonable one," but seems to have relied mainly on the
supposed authority of Gilbert's Treatise on Tenures. An inspection of Gilbert's
Treatise, page 37 note, however, discloses nothing that would support the presumption recognized by the *Tapscott* court. Instead, the cited note in Gilbert's
Treatise discusses the rights of the heir of a "disseizor" (i.e., one who wrongfully dispossesses another) against the "disseizee" (the one who is wrongfully dispossessed) when the "disseizor" dies in possession of the land in question, and
states that the disseizor's heir has the right to possession (*jus possessionis*);
the note does not say that the disseizor's heir is presumed to have actual possession of the land. But there is some American case authority in support of
the rule that an heir (or devisee) of one who, although not the rightful owner,
was in possession of the land at the date of his death under a "bona fide claim
of right," may recover on the strength of his ancestor's possession, as against
one who subsequently takes possession of the land without right. See 28 C.J.S.
Ejectment § 18(f). See also Restatement, Second, Torts § 157. Cases so holding go further than Tapscott v. Cobbs, since they recognize a legal right to
possession rather than a mere rebuttable presumption of actual possession in
the heir of the former possessor.

6.   If, in fact, Mrs. Cobbs was actually in possession of the land in question
after Mrs. Lewis' death, and retained possession until Tapscott took possession,
what do you think of the competence of Mrs. Cobb's attorney in Tapscott v.
Cobbs?

7.   It has been held and is often asserted that a mere possessor of land can
recover in trespass against one who, without right, enters on the land without
the possessor's consent. See 1 F. Harper & F. James, Torts § 1.2 (1956); W.
Prosser, Torts 68 (4th ed. 1971). But in Winchester v. City of Stevens Point, 58
Wis. 350, 17 N.W. 3 (1883), the plaintiff, who sought damages for injury to land
resulting from flooding caused by defendant's damming of a stream, was denied damages for the "permanent" reduction in the value of the land because
the plaintiff, although she alleged ownership of the land, was only able to prove
possession of the land at the time of the flooding. The court laid emphasis on
the fact that the plaintiff attempted to prove a "good paper title" but failed to
do so because of the defective execution of certain deeds of conveyance in the
plaintiff's "chain of title." This raises the question whether the plaintiff might
have recovered damages for the "permanent" reduction in the value of the land

if she had merely relied on her possession of the land. It seems that she could not have done so. The court said, "if she were not the owner of the premises, why should she recover damages for a permanent injury to them? She saw fit to put her title in issue, to rely upon it, and sought to recover as owner. The case is much like condemnation proceedings, and should be governed by the same rule as to proof of title. Since the early case of Robbins v. Milwaukee & Horicon Railroad Co., 6 Wis. 636 (1858), it has been understood that the plaintiff [in such proceedings] must show title, and that title will not be presumed from evidence of possession under claim of title."

Cf. the dissenting opinion of Taylor, J., in *Winchester*, which contained the following arguments:

"If, in an action like the one at bar, the plaintiff cannot recover for her permanent damages to the premises, there is no one who can, and the wrong-doer will escape all liability, except for such as affect the rights of a mere occupant who claims no title. * * * The only cases which are relied upon as supporting the opinion of the court in this case are * * * both cases under the statute to have assessed the plaintiff's damages for lands taken by a railroad company under the statute. The railroad company was not a wrong-doer in any sense. It was taking the plaintiff's land as it had the right to do; and in such case it might be very just to compel the plaintiff to show his title before he should be entitled to charge the company with the price of the lands taken. The rule established in such cases ought to have no application where the plaintiff is proceeding against a mere trespasser who makes no claim of right as against the plaintiff."

See also Frisbee v. Town of Marshall, 122 N.C. 760, 30 S.E. 21 (1898).

Is it more or less objectionable to permit a mere possessor of land to recover from a subsequent trespasser to the full extent of the injury done to the land than to permit a mere possessor to recover full value in an action for conversion of a chattel?

8. The courts are divided as to whether a tenant for life or for years in possession of land may recover full damages for "permanent" injury to the land by a trespasser. See 1 F. Harper & F. James, Torts § 1.9 (1956); McCormick, Damages 516 (1935). Rest., Prop. § 118 takes the position that a life tenant may recover, as damages, only "the difference between the value of the estate for life before and its value after the violation of" his "right that his possession be not disturbed." For a suggestion that, if a life tenant seeks to recover damages for "an injury both to the possession and to the inheritance," the trespasser-defendant's proper course is to have the remaindermen (who are entitled to the inheritance) joined as parties by order of the court, on defendant's motion, see Schell v. Rice, 37 N.C.App. 377, 246 S.E.2d 61 (1978).

C. FROM ADVERSE POSSESSION TO OWNERSHIP

The medieval common law of England focussed on "seisin"—i.e., possession of land as tenant of a feudal lord—rather than ownership in the modern sense. Before the action of ejectment developed, all the common law "real actions" (such as "novel disseisin") were designed to determine whether the plaintiff or the defendant had the better (i.e., older) seisin. But proof of the date when a plaintiff (or his ancestor) was last seized of the land became more and more difficult as time passed. In early times, numerous English statutes limited the time within which an action could be brought to recover seisin by designating a certain year back of which the plaintiff could not go. Thus, in an assize of novel disseisin the seisin on which the plaintiff relied must have existed in the year 1242 or later (a maximum of 33 years when the statute was enacted); in an assize of mort d'ancestor, the limiting date was 1216; and in a writ of right the date was 1189. From time to time a later date was fixed for all these real actions. This method of limiting the proof of a prior seisin to a fixed date was discontinued when the statute of Henry VIII, c. 2 (1540) established a flat period of 60 years for a writ of right and of 50 years for the other real actions. This statute did not apply to the new action of ejectment, which was rapidly displacing the older real actions in the sixteenth century. Finally, in 1623, the Statute of Limitations, 21 James I, c. 16, was enacted, "for quieting men's estates, and avoiding of suits." The 1623 statute provided that designated actions for the recovery of lands "shall be sued and taken within twenty years next after the title and cause of action first descended or fallen, and at no time after the said twenty years," and that "no person or persons shall at any time hereafter make any entry into any lands, tenements, or hereditaments, but within twenty years next after his or their right or title shall hereafter first descend or accrue to the same." Although the 1623 statute did not specifically refer to the action of ejectment, it was held that its effect was to bar ejectment after twenty years because it expressly barred the right of entry on which the plaintiff's right to maintain ejectment depended. See 3 A.L.P. 756.

In the United States statutes of limitation modelled on the English statute of 1623 were enacted very early in all jurisdictions. With the passage of time, there was a tendency in the eastern and midwestern states to amend the original statutes to shorten the limitation period; and as the line of settlement moved westward in the nineteenth century the original statutes of limitations tended to specify periods much shorter than the 20 year period of the English statute of 1623. In addition, there was a marked tendency in the United States to make the statutes of limitation more detailed and complex. Consider the following examples:

Massachusetts General Laws Annotated ch. 260, § 21 (1980): An action for the recovery of land shall be commenced, or an entry made thereupon, only within twenty years after the right of action or of entry first accrued, or within twenty years after the demandant [plaintiff] or the person making the entry, or those under whom they claim, have been seized or possessed of the premises, except as hereinafter provided.

Michigan Compiled Laws Annotated § 600.5801 (1968): No person may bring * * * any action for the recovery of possession * * * or make any entry upon any lands unless after the claim or right to make the entry first accrued to himself or to someone through whom he claims, he commences the action or makes the entry within the periods of time prescribed by this section.

(1) When the defendant claims title to the land in question by or through some deed made upon the sale of the premises by an executor, administrator, guardian, or testamentary trustee; or by a sheriff or other proper ministerial officer under the order, judgment, process, or decree of a court or

legal tribunal of competent jurisdiction within this state, or by a sheriff upon a mortgage foreclosure sale the period of limitation is 5 years.

(2) When the defendant claims title under some deed made by an officer of this state or the United States who is authorized to make deeds upon the sale of lands for taxes assessed and levied within this state the period of limitation is 10 years.

(3) When the defendant claims title through a devise in any will, the period of limitation is 15 years after the probate of the will in this state.

(4) In all other cases under this section, the period of limitation is 15 years.

New York Consolidated Laws:

Civil Practice Act and Rules § 212(a) (1972). An action to recover real property or its possession cannot be commenced unless the plaintiff, or his predecessor in interest, was seized or possessed of the premises within ten years before the commencement of the action.

Real Property Actions and Proceedings Law § 511 (1979). Where the occupant or those under whom he claims entered into possession of the premises under claim of title, exclusive of any other right, founding the claim upon a written instrument, as being a conveyance of the premises in question, or upon the decree or judgment of a competent court, and there has been a continued occupation of the premises included in the instrument, decree or judgment, or of some part thereof, for ten years, under the same claim, the premises so included are deemed to have been held adversely; except that when they they consist of a tract divided into lots, the possession of one lot is not deemed a possession of any other lot.

Real Property Actions and Proceedings Law § 512 (1979). For the purpose of constituting an adverse possession by a person claiming a title founded upon a written instrument or a judgment or decree, land is deemed to have been possession and occupied in either of the following cases:

1.   Where it has been usually cultivated or improved.

2.   Where it has been protected by a substantial inclosure.

3.   Where, although not inclosed, it has been used for the supply of fuel, or of fencing timber, either for the purposes of husbandry or for the ordinary use of the occupant.

Where a known farm or a single lot has been partly improved, the portion of the farm or lot that has been left not cleared or not inclosed, according to the usual course and custom of the adjoining country, is deemed to have been occupied for the same length of time as the part improved and cultivated.

Real Property Actions and Proceedings Law § 521 (1979). Where there has been an actual continued occupation of premises under a claim of title, exclusive of any other right, but not founded upon a written instrument or a judgment or decree, the premises so actually occupied, and no others, are deemed to have been held adversely.

Real Property Actions and Proceedings Law § 522 (1979). For the purpose of constituting an adverse possession by a person claiming title not founded on a written instrument or a judgment or decree, land is deemed to have been possessed in either of the following cases, and no others:

1.   Where it has been usually cultivated or improved.

2.   Where it has been protected by a substantial inclosure.

The Massachusetts statute set out above is obviously closer in its form and language to the original English statute of 1623 than either the Michigan or New York statute of limitations. Subsections 1 and 2 of the Michigan statute and N.Y. Actions and Proceedings Law §§ 511 and 512 deal with situations where the defendant in an action to recover possession of land is in possession under a deed of conveyance or under the judgment or decree of a court. Such possession is generally referred to as being "under color of title." In general, "color of title" refers to a written instrument or other document which purports and appears to transfer ownership to a designated person but which fails for any of a number of reasons to have that effect. Under most statutes of limitation "color of title" is not required, but it is frequently present. In a few states "color of title" is required in order that the period of limitation may run in favor of a possessor of land. See 3 Am. L.Prop. § 15.4(c). Note that "color of title" under the Michigan statute reduces the limitation period from 15 to either 5 or 10 years; but under the New York statute there is no reduction in the period of limitation.

The New York statute of limitations can be traced back to the extensive revision of New York real property law enacted in 1829. The New York statutory provision set out above may be found, with only one substantial change, in Calif.Code of Civ.Proc.Ann. §§ 322–325. The one substantial change is that the limitation period in all cases is only five years in California.

Since statutes of limitations are designed to bar a cause of action after a designated lapse of time, it is obvious that a statute of limitations cannot operate unless one party has a cause of action against another. Consequently, the mere fact that one person is in possession of another's land will not cause the statutory period to run against the owner when the possession is rightful—i.e., with the owner's permission, express or implied—as is the case when a tenant is in possession under a lease or an informal agreement of some sort. A landlord does not have a right to recover possession from his tenant unless and until the tenancy has been terminated by one of the several means which the law provides. And for a similar, though somewhat different reason, if L has been given only a life interest in land by deed or by will, with a provision that upon L's death the land shall go to R, possession of the land by A during L's lifetime cannot be wrongful (and therefore "adverse") so as to create a cause of action in R, since L, not R, is the one rightfully entitled to possession during L's lifetime.

It is strongly arguable that whenever A is in possession of O's land without the permission of O, the owner, O has a cause of action against which the applicable statute of limitations will run because A's possession is wrongful. But the judicially developed law surrounding the statutes of limitations does not really focus on the question whether the owner (or other person legally entitled to possession) had a cause of action. Instead, the courts have evolved a body of legal doctrine known as the law of "adverse possession" which focusses on the characteristics of the wrongful possession and imposes a variety of requirements in order that the possession may be deemed "adverse." Thus there are literally hundreds of judicial opinions stating the requirements for "adverse possession" substantially as follows:

"There are five essential elements necessary to constitute an effective adverse possession: *first,* the possession must be hostile and *under claim of right; second,* it must be actual; *third,* it must be open and notorious; *fourth,* it must be exclusive; and *fifth,* it must be continuous." Belotti v. Bickhardt, 228 N.Y. 296, 302, 127 N.E. 239, 241 (1920).

No doubt the phrase "claim of right" was intended by the *Belotti* court to be synonymous with the statutory phrase "claim of title," which is found in the New York statute of limitations provisions set out above. But neither the Massachusetts nor the Michigan statute includes either phrase; and none of the three statutes set out above contains any of the other langauge from the *Belotti* case quoted above. This language, in fact, is a judicial gloss on the statutes of limitations in force in the various American jurisdictions.

The requirement that possession must be "actual" before it can be "adverse" (i.e., cause the limitation period to run) is both logically and practically necessary. But, as we shall see, it is not always easy to determine when a person is "actually" in possession of land; and, in some circumstances, a mere "constructive" possession of land may have the same legal effect as "actual" possession in the law of adverse possession. See Monroe v. Rawlings, infra. The requirement that possession be "open and notorious" is obviously designed to safeguard the rights of the owner or other person legally entitled to possession of land against claims of adverse possession that he could not reasonably have discovered through regular surveillance of his land. But it is not clear whether this requirement really does more than describe one of the normal characteristics of an "actual" possession of land. In exceptional cases, however, the "open and notorious" requirement may have independent significance. See e.g., Marengo Cave Co. v. Ross, 212 Ind. 624, 10 N.E.2d 917 (1937) (possession of a cave extending beneath the surface into plaintiff's land was not "adverse" where the only entrance was on the defendant's land). See also Manillo v. Gorski, reprinted infra as a principal case.

The reason for the stated requirement that adverse possession must be "continuous" in order to bar the true owner's cause of action is clear. If an adverse possessor, A, ceases to maintain his possession of O's land before the statutory period has run, O's cause of action is terminated and, if A again wrongfully takes possession at a later time, O will have a new cause of action and the statutory period will start to run all over again. And the reason for the requirement that adverse possession must be "exclusive" is also clear. Unless A's possession is "exclusive" of O, it will not, as a general rule, be wrongful.

The stated requirements that, to be "adverse," a wrongful possession must be "hostile and under claim of right" have resulted in considerable confusion. Most of the cases in this part of the book are concerned with the question whether, and to what extent these requirements add anything to the basic requirement that the defendant's possession be wrongful so as to create a cause of action.

For a concise treatment of the doctrine of "adverse possession," see Cunningham § 11.7.

MONROE v. RAWLINGS

Supreme Court of Michigan, 1951.
331 Mich. 49, 49 N.W.2d 55.

DETHMERS, Justice. This is ejectment, brought in 1949, to recover possession of a section of land in Kalkaska county. Plaintiff relies on what she claims to be an unbroken chain of title tracing back to government patent. Defendants deny that plaintiff ever had title, and claim (1) title in themselves under a tax deed, (2) title by adverse possession, and (3) that plaintiff's action is barred by C.L.1948, § 609.1(2), Stat.Ann. § 27.593(2). A finding favorable to defendants on any one of these theories requires affirmance of the judgment in their favor from which plaintiff appeals. We think defendants established title by adverse possession. Accordingly, we need not pass on the other questions.

The land is wild, undeveloped, covered with scrub oak and some pine, not suitable for farming or the production of crops, but there are some deer there, and it is suitable for hunting and fishing and recreational purposes, not "worth leaving outdoors * * * unless it has some value for oil leasing purposes", but at one time pulpwood on parts of it was of some value.

In 1926 some of defendants built a hunting cabin on the land and used the premises for hunting and fishing. In 1928 they bought the tax title to the entire section for the 1924 taxes, recorded the tax deed, and in 1929 attempted service of notice to redeem upon the person whom defendants claim to have been the one then appearing to be the owner of record (and recorded a copy with sheriff's return of service), as provided in C.L.1948, § 211.140, Stat.Ann. § 7.198, which procedure plaintiff claims to have been a nullity for failure to make service upon the proper persons. Defendants have paid the taxes on the premises for every year from 1924 until date of trial in 1949, except for the year 1945, when it was paid by an undisclosed person. After the hunting season in 1932 the cabin was destroyed and in 1933 defendants built a new one upon the premises, at a cost for materials of $300, placed it on a cement foundation, painted it, cleared the brush and planted grass around it and erected a sign at the crossroads bearing the name of the camp. This cabin remained to the time of trial and it, together with the land, has been used by defendants every year for hunting, fishing and vacations. Defendants kept a register of camp guests which showed the visits of defendants and their guests from 1934 to 1949, indicating occupancy of the cabin by them for such purposes on an average of six times each year, including each of the hunting seasons. In 1939 defendants sold the pulpwood on the entire section for $2,150, the purchaser having thereafter engaged in cutting and removing it over a period of five years, during which time his loggers occupied temporary cabins and camps on the land visible from the road. From 1907 until 1948, when plaintiff acquired a deed to the premises, only one conveyance was recorded by plaintiff's predecessors in chain of title, which was a deed recorded shortly after the above mentioned service of notice to redeem. During the entire period from 1926 to 1949 defendants used the property as above indicated with no one challenging or questioning their use or possession thereof, nor insofar as shown by the record, did plaintiff or her predecessors in title ever enter upon or pay any attention to the premises or assert title or right to possession, offer to pay taxes, or in any way indicate anything other than abandonment of their rights. During that time defendants sold a portion of the land to the county road commission for road purposes and executed and had recorded a number of oil leases and mortgages and also certain conveyances between themselves, all covering the land in question.

Plaintiff stresses that defendants have never improved the land, fenced it, posted it, attempted to keep off others, or lived on it. She relies on cases holding that mere payment of taxes for years, removal of timber and gravel, cutting of hay, and occasional squatting on the premises, do not suffice to establish title by adverse possession, viz., Lasley v. Kniskern, 152 Mich. 244, 115 N.W. 971; Duck v. McQueen, 263 Mich. 325, 248 N.W. 637; Doctor v. Turner, 251 Mich. 175, 231 N.W. 115; McVannel v. Pure Oil Co., 262 Mich. 518, 247 N.W. 735, and others.

In Whitaker v. Erie Shooting Club, 102 Mich. 454, 60 N.W. 983, 984, defendant had a tax deed to premises "valuable for little else than shooting". He occasionally cut hay on the premises, planted trees and rented the land for hunting to a hunting club which posted the premises and undertook to keep off others. In holding that defendant had acquired title by adverse possession this court said: "The established rule of this court is, 'It is sufficient if the acts of ownership are of such a character as to openly and publicly indicate an assumed control or use such as are consistent with the character of the premises in question.' Murray v. Hudson, 65 Mich. 670 [673], 32 N.W. 889. * * * *Pedes possessio* is not indispensable. The land need not be fenced. Buildings are not necessary. Where the possession claimed was by cutting grass and pasturing cattle each year during the season, and planting trees, it was held to be evidence of a practically continuous, exclusive, and hostile possession. Sauers v. Giddings, 90 Mich. 50, 51 N.W. 265. Openly and notoriously claiming and using land in the only way it could be used without fencing or cultivation was held to establish adverse possession. Curtis v. Campbell, 54 Mich. 340, 20 N.W. 69."

In Corby v. Thompson, 196 Mich. 706, 163 N.W. 80, 81, this court said: "An examination of this record is convincing that there is abundant evidence of adverse possession on the part of the plaintiffs in this suit. The occupation of the land by the plaintiffs, the payment of the taxes, the transfer by warranty deeds, the leasing, inventorying and listing of this property as their own, were outward acts of exclusive ownership of an unequivocal character, overt, and notorious."

Appropriate here is the following from Burns v. Curran, 282 Ill. 476, 118 N.E. 750, 752: "Neither actual occupancy, cultivation, nor residence is necessary to constitute actual possession of land. Where property is so situated as not to admit of permanent useful improvements, the continued claim of the party, evidenced by public acts of ownership such as he would exercise over property which he claimed in his own right and would not exercise over property which he did not claim, may constitute actual possession."

A recent expression of the applicable test is to be found in Fractional School District No. 4 v. Hedlund, 330 Mich. 73, 47 N.W.2d 19, 22, as follows:

"In order to claim title by adverse possession the acts of possession must be open and of a hostile character.

"In Murray v. Hudson, 65 Mich. 670, 32 N.W. 889, 890, we approved the following: 'To constitute possession it is not necessary that the land should be enclosed with a fence, or that the same should be cultivated or resided upon, or that buildings should be erected thereon. It is sufficient if the acts of ownership are of such a character as to openly and publicly indicate an assumed control or use such as are consistent with the character of the premises in question.'"

Application of the above leads to the conclusion that defendants acquired title by adverse possession for over 15 years consisting of such open and public use, acts of ownership and assumption of control as were consistent with the character of the premises and to which alone the land was adapted.

That the title thus acquired by defendants extends to the entire section of land in question follows from the fact that they went into possession under color and claim of title (tax deed) to the entire section and paid the taxes on the whole of it continuously thereafter. Lang v. Osceola Consolidated Mining Co., 145 Mich. 370, 108 N.W. 678; 1 Am.Jur., Adverse Possession, §§ 201, 205. See also, Gardner v. Gardner, 257 Mich. 172, 241 N.W. 179.

Affirmed, with costs to defendants.

Notes

1. The term "adverse possession" is universally employed by American courts to describe the kind of possession that will cause the applicable statute of limitations to "run." The court's statement, in the principal case, that defendants claimed "title by adverse possession" clearly means that defendants were claiming title under what is now Mich.Comp.Laws Ann. § 600.5801(4), on the basis of 15 or more years of "adverse possession." In addition, defendants claimed they had acquired title under what is now Mich.Comp.Laws Ann. § 600.5801(2), on the basis of 10 years of "adverse possession" in reliance on the 1928 tax deed. (Mich.Comp.Laws § 600.5801 was formerly § 609.1, the section referred to in the court's opinion.) But what language in the Michigan statute set out above either states or suggests that the continuance of an "adverse possession" for the statutory period will confer "title" upon the adverse possessor? It is clear that the running of the statute, by its express provision, will bar either an action by the "true owner" to recover possession or an "entry"—i.e., recovery of possession by self-help. But the statute says nothing about a transfer of title to the adverse possessor. That consequence has evolved almost entirely through judicial decisions in the United States. The right to exclusive possession of land is such a central attribute of ownership

that the courts have decided the loss of that right should have the effect of extinguishing all the other rights, privileges and powers of a landowner who has allowed another person to maintain an adverse possession of the land for the statutory period. Simultaneously with the extinguishment of the former owner's interest, the adverse possessor acquires substantially identical rights, privileges and powers, and is thereafter deemed to be the "owner" of the land in question.

2. Monroe v. Rawlings turned on the question whether the defendants had maintained "actual" possession of the land in question for the requisite statutory period. When one seeks to apply to land the ideas about possession which have evolved in cases involving chattels, an obvious difference and difficulty appears which virtually reduces the term to a figure of speech. An intent element surely remains; and maybe the Holmes' requirement of an intent to exclude others will do. As for the physical relation, no thought can survive of any real control as one might control a chattel. For this one would have to go back to feudal times and discover a possessor protecting his claim by walls and moats with armed men posted to insure their inviolability. For us, in regard to land, possession as implying control obviously will not work. But this does not mean abandoning a requirement of a physical relation between possessor and the land. The nature of this relation is explained and applied by the court in Monroe v. Rawlings, supra. The standard announced there would be considered adequate by most courts. Compare the court's statement in Russo v. Stearns Farms Realty Co., 117 R.I. 387, 367 A.2d 714, 717 (1977): "Essentially, the test is whether the use to which the land has been put is similar to that which would ordinarily be made of like land by the owners thereof."

3. Why didn't the court simply decide the principal case on the ground that the defendants had acquired ownership of the land in question by virtue of their purchase of the "tax deed" in 1928 and their subsequent actions designed to perfect their "tax title" in 1929? If the court thought defendants' attempt to perfect their "tax title" in 1929 was ineffective because the "notice to redeem" was not served on the proper persons, why did the court assume that the doctrine of adverse possession was applicable? Is it clear that defendants' possession after 1928 was wrongful as against the true owner? If so, why didn't the court decide the case under section 2 of the Michigan statute which provides for a limitation period of only 10 years, rather than section 4 which provides for a 15 year period? Was it not clearer by 1939 than it was in 1934 that the defendants were, in fact, claiming and dealing with the entire section of land "as owners"?

4. What do you make of the court's concluding statement in the principal case that the title acquired by defendants "extends to the entire section of land in question [one square mile]" because "they went into possession under color and claim of title (tax deed) to the entire section and paid the taxes on the whole of it continuously thereafter"? The usual explanation is that, when an adverse possessor holds under "color of title," he is deemed to have "constructive" possession of the entire tract described in the instrument or document constituting his "color of title" although he has been in "actual" possession of only part of that tract. This doctrine is limited to cases where the adverse possessor has actual possession of part (some cases require the part to be a substantial fraction) of a single tract which is adequately described in the written instrument or document upon which the adverse possessor relies. The doctrine is generally applied even if the applicable statute of limitations does not provide for a reduced limitation period when there is "color of title." The underlying theory seems to be that possession under "color of title" makes clear to the "true owner" the extent of the adverse possessor's claim, and puts him on notice that

failure to bring an action to recover possession within the statutory period will result in extinguishment of his title to the entire tract. Many courts refuse to apply the "color of title" doctrine in favor of an adverse possessor unless the adverse possessor believes in good faith that the instrument or document constituting his "color of title" actually gives him ownership of the land in question.

5. In its application to concrete cases the "constructive" adverse possession doctrine may raise difficult issues. In part this is because the owner (or other person legally entitled to possession) is always deemed to have "constructive" possession of his land even though he is not in "actual" possession of any part of it, provided no other person is actually in wrongful possession of any part of the land. Suppose, for example, that A takes a deed of conveyance covering a tract of land from B, but that the deed for some reason is invalid; that A moves into a house on the tract and farms part of it; and that the rest of the tract is timberland on which A performs no acts of ownership. As between A and B the "color of title" doctrine would apply, and at the end of the statutory period A would acquire ownership of the entire tract. But if B, before the limitation period ran against him, took possession of any of the timberland, A's "constructive" possession thereof would be wholly vitiated. If, on the other hand, C, a stranger, took possession of any of the timberland, A's constructive possession would continue as to all the timberland not actually possessed by C. Moreover, if two "overlapping" constructive adverse possessions are established, the first in time is not supplanted by the second. But where the title deeds of two rival claimants overlap and one claimant has possession of part of the "lappage" and the other does not, the former is deemed to have possession of the whole of the "lappage." Price v. Tomrich Corp., 3 N.C.App. 402, 165 S.E.2d 22 (1969). Generally, see 3. A.L.P. § 15.11.

6. Although payment of taxes by the adverse possessor tends to establish his "claim of right" and to identify the land when actually he occupies only part of the land, it is not generally held to be essential to make a wrongful possession "adverse." But some statutes of limitations require payment of taxes. See, e.g., Cal.Code Civ.Proc. § 325, which requires that, when there is no "color of title," there is no "adverse possession" unless the possessor and his predecessors has "paid all the taxes, state, county, or municipal which have been levied and assessed upon such land."

NEVELLS v. CARTER

Supreme Court of Maine, 1922.
122 Me. 81, 119 A. 62.

MORRILL, J. Real action to recover $^{19}/_{21}$ of certain real estate to which demandant claims title as an heir of Coleman Carter, who died March 15, 1906, and as grantee of the widow and five other heirs of said Carter. The tenants are the widow and next of kin of Edbert E. Carter, the remaining heir of Coleman Carter, who died April 27, 1907. They claim title by an oral grant of the demanded premises by Coleman to his son, Edbert, in the year 1885, in consideration that Edbert would make needed repairs and reconstruction of the buildings on the premises. They contend that Edbert entered into possession in the fall of 1885, made the repairs and reconstruction as he had agreed to do, assumed the control and management of the farm at that time, and continued that possession and control under claim of right until his death in 1907, and that such possession and control has since been continued by his son Myron.

Under instructions to which no exceptions were taken, the jury found for defendants, and the case is before us upon a general motion for a new trial.

It must be considered as settled law that, where one enters upon land claiming title, though under a parol grant only, and holds open, exclusive, adverse, and uninterrupted possession thereof for 20 years, he thereby acquires title. Sumner v. Stevens, 6 Metc. (Mass.) 337; Webster v. Holland, 58 Me. 168, 169; Jewett v. Hussey, 70 Me. 433, 436; Shirley v. Lancaster, 6 Allen (Mass.) 31, 32. An occupation of land under a parol gift from the owner is an occupation as of right. Stearns v. Janes, 12 Allen (Mass.) 582, 584. Possession under a claim of title with or without deed is adverse. Ashley v. Ashley, 4 Gray (Mass.) 197, 200.

The principle is thus stated by Chief Justice Shaw in Sumner v. Stevens, supra, and we here quote his language because the quotation in Jewett v. Hussey, supra, contains typographical errors which confuse the meaning:

"A grant, sale, or gift of land by parol is void by the statute. But, when accompanied by an actual entry and possession, it manifests the intent of the donee to enter and take as owner, and not as tenant; and it equally proves an admission on the part of the donor that the possession is so taken. Such a possession is adverse. It would be the same if the grantee should enter under a deed not executed conformably to the statute, but which the parties, by mistake, believe good. The possession of such grantee or donee cannot, in strictness, be said to be held in subordination to the title of the legal owner; but the possession is taken by the donee, as owner, and because he claims to be owner; and the grantor or donor admits that he is owner, and yields the possession because he is owner. He may reclaim and reassert his title, because he has not conveyed his estate according to law, and thus regain the possession; but until he does this, by entry or action, the possession is adverse. Such adverse possession, continued 20 years, takes away the owner's right of entry."

It is thus clear that a parol grant of real estate is ineffectual to change the ownership of the property; the tenants must rest then their claim of title upon an actual entry as of right and adverse possession. The evidence in relation to the grant is immaterial, except as it bears on the character of Edbert's occupation. The testimony as to his subsequent acts and the acts of the present tenants must be examined to determine whether they constitute actual, open, exclusive, and adverse possession of the real estate by Edbert and his widow and heirs for 20 years or more. Duff v. Leary, 146 Mass. 533, 540, 16 N.E. 417.

If the jury believed the witnesses who testified in behalf of the tenants, they were clearly warranted in finding that in the year 1885 Coleman Carter made a parol grant of the disputed premises to his son, Edbert, upon Edbert's agreement to make necessary repairs and reconstruction of the buildings; that Edbert in September and October of that year assumed possession and control of the property, and made the promised repairs and reconstruction of the buildings, expending approximately as much as the property without the buildings was worth; that he continued in control and possession of the demanded premises until his death in 1907, notwithstanding his business and residence was in Cambridge, Mass.; that his family spent their summers there, and that Edbert paid the taxes and furnished any money needed on the place; that in June 1904, he sent his son, Myron, to live on the place; and that since the death of Edbert in 1907 Myron has occupied the place and had actual possession thereof for the present tenants.

But it is urged that upon this theory Edbert permitted his father and mother to live on the place until Coleman's death in 1906, thus, it is said, constituting the owner "the agent for the disseizor in thus acquiring title against himself by adverse possession." We think, however, that the jury was warranted in finding that at all times after 1885 Coleman Carter recognized Edbert's claim of right and possession, and occupied in subordination to it. The statements of Coleman Carter to the effect that "The place belongs to Bert and Annie," "Bert owns the place," "I am glad I gave Bert my place," "I hope that I shall never be sorry that I gave Bert my place," and his statement that he could not give security for an old debt because he had transferred his property to his son, were competent evidence as bearing upon the question of adverse possession in Edbert under a claim of right. They tended to establish such adverse possession with the knowledge of Coleman, to whom knowledge must be brought home (Motte v. Alger, 15 Gray [Mass.] 322, 325), and to show his acquiescence in such adverse claim (Stearns v. Hendersass, 9 Cush. [Mass.] 497, 503, 57 Am.Dec. 65). The jury were warranted in finding and must have found that from 1885 to his death in 1906 Coleman was the tenant of Edbert, and recognized the latter's claim as of right to the place. Coleman's possession was therefore Edbert's possession, and is available to the latter, and to his heirs, for the purpose of creating a prescriptive title in Edbert against Coleman, and his heirs other than Edbert; the period of 20 years having fully expired in the lifetime of Coleman. Cobb v. Robertson, 99 Tex. 138, 86 S.W. 746, 87 S.W. 1148, 122 Am.St.Rep. 609. Having once become Edbert's tenant, before Coleman could dispute the former's title, he must have at least repudiated the tenancy. Davis v. Williams, 130 Ala. 530, 30 So. 488, 54 L.R.A. 749, 89 Am.St.Rep. 55, note pp. 73, 87; Carson v. Broady, 56 Neb. 648, 77 N.W. 80, 71 Am.St.Rep. 691; Saunders v. Moore, 14 Bush (Ky.) 97, 100. In some states it is held that he must first surrender the premises, or there must be an eviction or something equivalent thereto, and such has been recognized in this state as the law. Ryder v. Mansell, 66 Me. 167, 170. There is no evidence that from September or October 1885, until his death in March, 1906, Coleman ever surrendered or disavowed his tenancy under Edbert or his occupancy under him. Although Edbert's claim was equitable under an oral grant, of which the consideration was fully performed by him, it thus ripened into a legal title before Coleman's death. Wheeler v. Laird, 147 Mass. 421, 18 N.E. 212.

Motion overruled.

Notes and Questions

1. The statute which made the gift of land by parol "void" was the Statute of Frauds. As originally enacted in England in 1677, the relevant provision of the statute declared that all estates in land "made or created by livery and seisin only, or by parol, and not put in writing, and signed by the parties so making or creating the same, or by their agents thereunto lawfully authorized by writing, shall have the force and effect of leases at will only." Massachusetts and all other American jurisdictions have statutes containing substantially the same provision. The effect of the statute in the principal case, therefore, was to cause the attempted "oral grant of the demanded premises by Coleman to his son, Edbert, in the year 1885," to create only an "estate at will" in Edbert. Such an estate will continue only until either the owner or the tenant indicates that he wishes to terminate the estate or dies, or the owner transfers the property.

2. In the principal case, was Edbert's possession wrongful, so as to give Coleman a cause of action against him? How could Edbert's possession be wrongful in view of the fact that Coleman obviously consented to Edbert's taking and retaining possession of the land? Do you understand the following statement from Pendley v. Pendley, 338 So.2d 405, 407 (Ala.1976) (also involving possession by a son under an attempted oral gift of land by his father):

> "The possession must be adverse and cannot be permissive. 'Permissive' denotes retention of title by the owner. If the title holder (the father), although *permitting* another's (the son's) use of the property, intended to surrender title, the son's exclusive possession is hostile and constitutes adverse possession to the father. In this context, 'permissive use' is not used in the sense of a licensed possession in subordination to another's title." Does this make sense?

Cf. the following statement from Fisher v. Hagstrom, 35 Wn.2d 632, 645, 214 P.2d 654, 662 (1950):

> "Appellants argue that there is no evidence of 'hostile intent' on the part of the respondents. Apparently appellants have misconstrued the legal meaning of the term 'hostile intent' for, as we said in Young v. Newbro, 32 Wash.2d 141, 200 P.2d 975 (1949), the term 'hostile' does not import enmity or ill-will, but rather imports that the claimant is in possession as owner, in contradistinction to possession of real property in recognition of or subordination to the title of the true owner."

3. What does the court mean, at the end of the principal case, when it says "Edbert's claim was equitable under an oral grant, of which the consideration was fully performed by him"? What was the "consideration" that was "fully performed"? Did Coleman intend to make a gift to Edbert or to enter into a contract with him? Was the contract "bilateral" or "unilateral"? In any case, how could an oral contract be enforced in light of the fact that the Statute of Frauds also precludes enforcement of a contract for the sale of an interest in land unless the contract or a memorandum thereof is "signed by the party to be charged"?

.. In Newells v. Carter, Edbert seems to have claimed full ownership of the land in "good faith," although the court does not discuss the point. If he did, his "good faith" must have been based on his ignorance of the writing requirement imposed by the Statute of Frauds. But suppose Edbert claimed ownership in "bad faith," knowing that the "oral grant" was legally ineffective. Should this prevent his possession from being deemed "adverse" to Coleman?

The next case deals with the problem of wrongful possession taken and maintained in "bad faith."

WARREN v. BOWDRAN

Supreme Judicial Court of Massachusetts, 1892.
156 Mass. 280, 31 N.E. 300.

LATHROP, J. This is a writ of entry, dated April 9, 1890, to recover a strip of land on Maple street, in Somerville. The demanded premises and the adjoining lands were in 1866 owned by one Hadley. In May of that year, Hadley conveyed to the tenant a lot of land on Maple street, which did not include the demanded premises. In May, 1868, Hadley conveyed to one Lane, the demandant's predecessor in title, a lot of land on Maple street, by a deed which described the land as bounded on one side by the land of the tenant, and on the opposite side by the land of one Connors. It was admitted that in 1868, and soon after the conveyance to Lane, the tenant built a fence extending from Maple street along the southeasterly line of the demanded premises to the boundary line in the rear, and thence along the rear line and the rear line of the land conveyed to him by Hadley. This fence was maintained by the tenant from that time until the bringing of writ in this case,—a period of more than 20 years. There was evidence that, before Hadley conveyed to Lane, he pointed out to the tenant the line on which the fence was afterwards built. But this evidence was contradicted, and we must assume, for the purposes of this decision that by building the fence the tenant inclosed land which had been conveyed to Lane. At the time the fence was built, Lane was the owner and occupant of the land conveyed to him by Hadley, and he testified that he objected to the line upon which the tenant put the fence; that "there was a wordy dispute over the matter, but the tenant insisted, and put the fence on the line where it has ever since been maintained." This testimony was uncontradicted. The jury returned a general verdict for the tenant, but found specially that, at the time the tenant built the fence, he did not honestly believe that, by the deed of Hadley, he acquired a title to the land up to the line of the fence.

The principal question which has been argued is that involved in the special finding of the jury, namely, whether the taking possession of another man's land, with intent to make it the taker's land by 20 years' possession will constitute a claim of title. Under the instructions of the court the jury must have found by their general verdict that the tenant's possession of the demanded premises was adverse, and not permissive; that it was actual; that it was visible, notorious, and exclusive; that it was continuous, and was under a claim of title. These terms were also fully explained to the jury. It is difficult to see how the fact that the tenant did not honestly believe that he had title to the land inclosed has any material bearing on the case. Pub.St. c. 196, § 1, provides that "no person shall commence an action for the recovery of lands, nor make an entry thereon, unless within twenty years after the right to bring such action or to make such entry first accrued, or within twenty years after he, or those from, by, or under whom he claims have been seised or possessed of the premises, except as is hereinafter provided." The subsequent sections contain various exceptions to this general rule, but none of them applies to the case at bar. Neither the demandant nor his predecessor in title was seised or possessed of the premises within 20 years from the date of the writ. The principal case on which the demandant relies is Livingston v. Iron Co., 9 Wend. 511. But this was not a case under the statute of limitations, but under the New York champerty act, which provides that "every grant of lands shall be absolutely void if, at the time of the delivery thereof, such lands shall be in possession of a person claiming under a title adverse to that of the grantor." In that case the defendant claimed to be in adverse possession of land under a deed, and contended that, while his possession continued, his grantor could not convey the land to the plaintiff. The defendant had no actual possession, and the deed to him was proved to have been obtained by fraud. The point decided was that no such constructive possession in the defendant had been established as disqualified his grantor from conveying the land to the plaintiff. On the other hand, it was expressly decided in the case of Humbert v. Trinity Church, 24 Wend. 587, that neither fraud in obtaining or continuing possession of land, or knowledge on the part of the tenant that his claim is unfounded, wrongful and fraudulent, will excuse the not bringing an action within the time allowed by the statute of limitations. See, also, Crary v. Goodman, 22 N.Y. 170.

Hadley, who was called as a witness by the demandant, testified that in 1884 or 1885 he first learned that the tenant had inclosed by the fence land which did not pass to him by his deed; that he then notified the tenant to remove the fence, and had negotiations with him in regard to selling the demanded premises to the tenant; and that the tenant offered to buy the land, and made no claim of title thereto. The tenant admitted that he had a conversation with Hadley about the land, and that Hadley offered to sell it, but denied that he made any offer to buy the land, or that Hadley notified him to remove the fence. The demandant asked the judge to instruct the jury that, if they believed that the tenant offered to purchase said strip, this was fatal to the tenant's claim of title. The judge left to the jury the question what the conversation was, and instructed them that, if the tenant did attempt to buy the land of Hadley, it would not be decisive against the claim he now asserted; that it might be that, having some doubt as to the validity of his title, he was willing to pay something for the land to avoid litigation; and if that was his motive, and he made an offer for the land, that fact would not conclusively show that he had not a title upon which he could stand in this action; but if the conversation was in fact an admission by the tenant that he had no title to the land, and that he claimed no lawful title, then it was evidence of great importance, as tending to show that his possession during the 20 years was not an adverse possession. These instructions were certainly sufficiently favorable to the demandant. In 1884 and 1885, Hadley had no title to the premises. There was no evidence of any offer made to the demandant, or to his immediate predecessor in title. A person in possession of land, claiming ownership, may purchase an outstanding claim of title from a third person without abandoning or impairing his own title by adverse possession. Blight v. Rochester, 7 Wheat. 535; Jackson v. Given, 8 Johns. 107; Jackson v. Smith, 13 Johns. 406; Chapin v. Hunt, 40 Mich. 595.

We find nothing else in the demandant's exceptions which requires any comment.

Exceptions overruled.

Notes and Questions

1. Is the decision in Warren v. Bowdran consistent with the frequent assertion that a wrongful possession is "adverse" only if the possessor holds under a "claim of right" (or "claim of title")? There is some authority in support of the view that a bona fide belief that the possessor has title, or some legal right to possession, is an essential element of adverse possession. Thus in Jasperson v. Scharnikow, 150 F. 571 (9th Cir.1907), the court said,

"These facts fully justified, we think, the trial court in saying at the close of the evidence that the entry of Bryant and his wife was without any pretense of 'having a right as owner of the property at the inception of their entry, which is necessary to make out a title by adverse possession. This idea of acquiring title by larceny does not go in this country. A man must have a bona fide claim, or believe in his own mind that he has got a right as owner, when he goes upon land that does not belong to him, in order to acquire title by occupation and possession.'" Creel v. Hammans, 234 Iowa 532, 13 N.W.2d 305 (1944), contains a dictum in accord with *Jasperson*. Ga.Code Ann. § 85–402 provides that an adverse possession "must not have originated in fraud." For an application of this statute, see Hannah v. Kenny, 210 Ga. 824, 83 S.E.2d 1 (1954), where the court said,

"Before prescription can arise under an asserted claim of right, the claim must be honestly entertained. * * * A person entering upon lands, not claiming in good faith the right to do so by virtue of any title of his own or by virtue of some agreement with someone else he believes to hold the title, is called a squatter. A squatter can never gain prescriptive title to land no matter how long he holds the possession. His possession is never deemed adverse."

See also Roy v. Elmer, 153 So.2d 209 (La.App.1963), where the court said that parties who enclosed the land of another by a fence and used it for 30 years but did not pay taxes on the land, and who had no "indicia of written title," were mere trespassers in bad faith who could not acquire "title by prescription" under La.Stat.Civ.Code art. 3499 (providing for acquisition of a prescriptive title by 30 years' possession).

None of these cases explains why an intentionally tortious possession of the land of another does not create a cause of action in the true owner, and thus start the statutory period running. In any event, the *Jasperson* case probably has no value as a precedent in view of Erie Railroad Co. v. Tompkins, 304 U.S. 64, 58 S.Ct. 817, 82 L.Ed. 1188 (1938). Warren v. Bowdran seems to be in accord with the substantial weight of authority. But see the contrary assertion in Helmholz, Adverse Possession and Subjective Intent, 61 Wash.U.L.Q. 331, 341–349 (1983).

2. A number of cases have arisen in which persons have taken possession of land believed to be "homestead" land and subject to being acquired by procedures established by law, which include possession of the land by the claimant. It turns out that the land is not government land at all, but is owned by private parties. After possession for the statutory period, title is claimed by adverse

possession. The authorities are divided on whether this sort of possession is adverse. Compare Roach v. Knappenberger, 172 Ark. 417, 288 S.W. 912 (1926) with Smith v. Jones, 103 Tex. 632, 132 S.W. 469 (1910). In the latter case the court said "The difficulty with the cases in which there is evidence of no further facts than those in this, as we view it, is that it is not made to appear that the possession was adverse and hostile to anyone; for the mere holding of it under the belief that the land is the state's and with the purpose of acquiring it lawfully at some future time does not define the attitude of the possessor as hostile to the claim of an owner of whose existence he is ignorant. * * * " What do you think of this view? See 3 A.L.P. 781 (1952).

3. In Warren v. Bowdran, suppose that Bowdran had offered to buy the disputed strip of land from Warren in 1884 or 1885. What legal consequences, if any, should result from the making of such an offer? What do you think of the following statement from 4 Tiffany § 1164?

"Whether, in a particular case, there was such a recognition of the rightful title as to change the character of the possession, would seem ordinarily to be a question of fact, but the courts have tended to discuss it as a matter of law, particularly with reference to the question whether the person in possession may offer to purchase from the rightful owner, without thereby recognizing the latter's title. The proper distinction would seem to be that between an offer to purchase the land and an offer to purchase immunity from litigation, and that such is the distinction is recognized in a number of cases. In some cases, on the other hand, such a distinction appears to be ignored, and an offer to purchase from the rightful owner is regarded as necessarily involving a recognition of the latter's title."

Do you understand the distinction suggested by Tiffany? If the possessor's "offer to purchase" is "regarded as necessarily involving a recognition of the latter's title," what is the legal consequence, so far as the possessor's claim that he is an adverse possessor is concerned?

PATTERSON v. REIGLE

Supreme Court of Pennsylvania, 1846.
4 Pa. 201, 45 Am.Dec. 684.

The plaintiffs in this ejectment claimed title to one-half of a donation tract as acquired by the statute of limitations under an entry by Reigle, their father, in 1806, and possession continued for upwards of twenty-one years. The defendants had the title of the original owner of the tract, and obtained possession by agreement with the widow of Reigle and her second husband in 1833. The question was, whether there had been an adverse possession by Reigle, who with one Shingledecker entered on the whole tract in 1806, and occupied it jointly until 1815 or 1816, when a partition was made. After Reigle had been in possession some time, the evidence of the plaintiff showed that he claimed the land as his own, and paid the taxes until his death, in 1825, when his widow continued in possession until the sale by her to the defendant, mentioned above. To show the character of the possession, plaintiffs read the deposition of Shingledecker, who stated, "We intended to leave when the real owner, with a good deed, that is, the old soldier, who had a good deed, should come for it, but not till then. We settled it to hold it until a better owner came for it, and then to give it up."

A witness who had purchased Shingledecker's moiety stated that Reigle had endeavoured to find the real owner, and obtain compensation for his improvements, and that both Reigle and Shingledecker had told him they settled the land "to buy it, or get pay for the improvements." Another witness stated he had known Reigle since 1810; that in frequent conversations, Reigle totally disclaimed holding any interest in the land whatever, and said, if the owner came and gave him anything as a compensation for his improvements it would be well, if not, he would have to move off the land. This witness was in the same situation as Reigle, the owners of neither tract being then known. Another witness stated that he was employed by Reigle a few years before his death, to make rails, and was refused permission to use the green timber, Reigle giving as a reason that the land was not his own, and he might be put to trouble by the owner for destroying the timber, and that he had frequently heard Reigle say he wished to purchase the land from the owner when he came.

The defendant's points were, 1. If R., when he entered, did so intending to hold it only until the owner should come, and then give it up, and so continued until 1816 (the time of the partition), the plaintiff could not recover, the possession having been changed in 1834.

2. If the evidence of the two witnesses lastly stated above was true, the plaintiffs could not recover.

On the first point, the court (Bredin, P.J.) having stated the requisites to a possession to entitle a party to the benefit of the statute, instructed the jury, that to prevent the party availing himself of the statute of limitations, the evidence must be such as would amount to an agreement to hold under, and not against the title of defendants, or subject to the control of the person having such title, so that it would be a fraud on that title, if afterwards the statute of limitations was set up. The second point was answered in the negative.

The errors assigned were: In so instructing the jury as to lead them to believe that an express agreement with the owner himself, or some one on his behalf, to hold under him, was necessary, and consequently that declarations, on entering and while in possession, of an intention to hold under, or subject to an unknown owner, were not sufficient to take the case out of the statute; and in the answer to the second point.

GIBSON, C.J. It would perhaps be too much to say that a trespasser entering on vacant land may not preclude himself from claiming to hold it adversely, by a general declaration of intention to hold it in subjection to whomsoever may hold the title. It has been held that possession, taken by mistake, and continued with no view to acquire title by it, is not adverse, because not hostile. It may therefore well be, as was said in Criswell v. Altemus, 7 Watts, Pa., 581, though it was not exactly the point decided, that it is sufficient to prevent the possession from being adverse, that the party taking it intends to hold subject to the will of the owner. It has been determined that one already in possession estops himself by declarations of submission addressed to the owner; and it would seem he might do so by a general declaration explanatory of the nature of his entry. But there is a presumption which lasts till it is rebutted, that an intruder enters to hold for himself; and it is not to be doubted that a trespasser entering to gain a title, though conscious that he is a wrongdoer, will accomplish his object, if the owner do not enter or prosecute his claim within the prescribed period. But to do so, it is necessary that his possession be adverse from the first; and to infer that he intended it to be otherwise, would impute to him an inconsistency of purpose. Was there evidence to rebut the presumption that the entry and possession of Reigle and Shingledecker were adverse to the title? No declaration by them was inconsistent with an intention to hold the land as long as they could, or evincive of a design to give it up before they should be compelled to do so by the appearance of a claimant whom they could not resist. They were conscious they had no title themselves, and they said so; they were conscious they could not resist him who had it, and they said so; but they did not say that they meant not to acquire a title to it for themselves. Whatever they did say was predicated on the expected appearance of the owner while he continued to be so; for they certainly did not mean to purchase the land from any one else. Shingledecker himself testified that he and Reigle settled on the land "to hold it till a better owner came for it;" but the holder of the title would lose it, and cease to be the better owner at the end of one-and-twenty years. They intended to hold adversely to all the world till the title should be produced to them, and consequently as adversely to the owner before he disclosed himself as to any one else. The sum of the evidence is that they entered to hold the land as long as they could; and they consequently gained the title to it by the statute of limitations.

Judgment affirmed.

Notes and Questions

1. In Ottavia v. Savarese, 338 Mass. 330, 333, 155 N.E.2d 432, 434 (1959), the court said:

"* * * It is well established in this Commonwealth that an adverse possessor, to gain title, must hold under a claim of right and with an intention to 'hold the same as owner, and to the exclusion, right or wrongfully, of every one else.' * * * This rule has been severely criticized. It has been said that apart from two situations, namely the situation where a disclaimer by the user to the true owner of any purpose to gain rights by adverse possession lulls the latter into inaction, and the situation involving a 'mere squatter' where the possession is doubtful and equivocal in fact, 'there seems to be no justification for requiring a claim of right or title as essential to an adverse possession.' Am. Law of Property, § 15.4, p. 776 et seq. 'The great majority of the cases establish convincingly that the alleged requirements of claim of title and of hostility of possession mean only that the possessor must use and enjoy the property continuously for the required period as the average owner would use it, without the consent of the true owner and therefore in actual hostility to him irrespective of the possessor's actual state of mind or intent.' Am.Law of Property, § 15.4, pp. 776–777. From the standpoint of the true owner, the purpose of the various requirements of adverse possession—that the nonpermissive use by another be actual, open, notorious, exclusive and adverse—is to put him on notice of the hostile activity of the possessor so that he, the owner, may have an opportunity to take steps to vindicate his rights by legal action. Where a claim of right is made or where an intention to oust exists and is communicated or is open and notorious, the purpose of notice is satisfied, for it is likely that the encroachment and the fact of its hostility will come to the attention of the true owner. The nonexistence of a claim of right or intent to oust does not, however, necessarily preclude notice. Where the user has acted, without license or permission of the true owner, in a manner inconsistent with the true owner's rights, the acts alone (without any explicit claim of right or intent to dispossess) may be sufficient to put the true owner on notice of the nonpermissive use. See Am.Law of Property, § 15.4, pp. 771–785; Restatement: Property, § 458, comment a and comment d. Acts undeniably may evidence an intent to claim as of right, * * * and the physical facts of entry and continued possession may themselves evidence an intent to occupy and to hold as of right sufficient in law to support the acquisition of rights by prescription. * * * That the uncommunicated mental attitude of the possessor is irrelevant where his acts import an adverse character to his holding is shown by cases involving disputed boundaries where the possessor intends to hold without intending to deprive any other of what is rightfully his. In Van Allen v. Sweet, 239 Mass. 571, 132 N.E. 348, 349, a boundary case, the possessor was held to have acquired rights by prescription to a strip of land despite his statement to the plaintiff 'I do not want anything not belonging to me.' See also Ridgely v. Lewis, 204 Md. 563, 105 A.2d 212; Am.Law of Property, § 15.5, pp. 785–791."

2. Where "the possession is * * * doubtful and equivocal in fact," it has been suggested that "the failure of the owner to act against the squatter may well have been induced by his acquiescence in a use of his property which is not that of a person claiming as owner." 3 Am.L.Prop. 776 (1952). In such a case, "[n]o doubt the owner may at his election maintain ejectment to recover the property, and the squatter could not set up lack of possession as a defense. Nevertheless the equivocal character of the possession accompanied by affirmative evidence of lack of claim may well be the cause of the owner's failure to take action." Ibid. The thrust of these suggestions seems to be that the "squatter" should be "estopped" to assert that his possession was "adverse," although it was clearly "wrongful," even if the owner did not, either expressly or by clear implication, consent to that possession. But what of the court's statement, in Patterson v. Reigle, that a wrongful possessor "by a general declaration of intention to hold it [the land] in subjection to whomsoever may hold the title" might "preclude himself from claiming to hold it adversely." Surely there could be no basis for an estoppel unless there is evidence that the possessor's "general declaration" was communicated to the owner of the land in some way.

3. Cf. the late Professor Bordwell's view on the need for a "claim of title" as a basis for adverse possession:

"The requirement that the possessor have the mind of the owner, the intention to hold as owner or to acquire ownership, in order that his possession ripen into ownership by the lapse of time seems so natural from the point of view of affirmative prescription and the substantive law of property that once adverse possession is recognized as primarily affirmative prescription, rather than as a special phase of the limitation actions, some such requirement as claim of title seems inevitable." Bordwell, Disseisin and Adverse Possession, 33 Yale L.J. 1, 150 (1923).*

4. The materials presented above should demonstrate the subtlety and elusiveness of any requirement of a mental element in adverse possession, and the

* Reprinted by permission of the Yale Law Journal Company and Fred B. Rothman & Company.

difficulty of putting any clear idea of what is meant by a "claim of right" or even "the mind of the owner." But if the courts are going to insist on such a requirement, what is to be done about the case where there is no evidence which reveals the possessor's "claim" or belief? Compare the quotations which follow.

(a) "The adverse claimant must prove by clear, positive and unequivocal evidence that he acquired a good title by limitation. No presumption is indulged in his favor. * * * Possession by one other than the holder of the record title is presumed to be subordinate to the record holder." Jacobi v. Jacobi, 345 Ill. 518, 521, 178 N.E. 88, 90 (1931).

(b) "Plaintiff argues that the proof is deficient because it fails to disclose that defendants' possession was under a claim of ownership. Proof of oral claims is not essential. It is enough that the claimant prove he so acted that it showed he claimed the title. Leonard v. Leonard, 369 Ill. 572, 17 N.E.2d 553. Using and controlling property as an owner is the ordinary mode of asserting a claim of title, and it is the only way a claim of title could be proved in many cases." Hauer v. Van Straaten Chemical Co., 415 Ill. 268, 273, 112 N.E.2d 623, 625 (1953).

(c) "While it is necessary for an adverse claimant to 'unfurl his flag on the land' in order to apprise the owner of the claim upon the land, * * * it is not necessary that the claimant verbally state to the owner that he has 'planted his standard of conquest.' Quite to the contrary, his 'use, or acts, may declare that they are done under a claim of right as effectively as the words of the claimant.' * * *

"From the record, it is apparent that the Quero family openly used the disputed property for various purposes from 1929 to 1976. Such use was such that 'a man reasonably attentive to his own interests would have known that an adverse right was being asserted.' * * * Absent evidence of permission, open and notorious use for the statutorily prescribed period of time gives rise to a prima facie claim of right." Zuanich v. Quero, 135 Vt. 332, 376 A.2d 763 (1977).

5. There is at least one situation where the alleged "adverse possessor" must clearly assert a right to possession exclusive of any right in those against whom the adverse possession is asserted: where one co-owner seeks to establish a title by adverse possession against the other co-owners. See, e.g., Johnson v. James, 237 Ark. 900, 377 S.W.2d 44 (1964), where the court said, "It is well settled that possession by a tenant in common is presumed to be possession by all cotenants"—i.e., possession by one cotenant is presumed to be "nonadverse" and thus not wrongful as against his cotenants. The court also said that "knowledge of adverse possession must be made known to other cotenants directly or by notorious acts of such an unequivocal character that notice may be presumed and * * * acts of possession, payment of taxes, enjoyment of rents and profits, and the making of improvements are consistent with a cotenancy and do not necessarily amount to disseisin." In view of this statement, what do you make of the court's ultimate holding that the occupying cotenant had acquired complete ownership (in "fee simple") by adverse possession, because he "lived on and had exclusive possession of the property * * * for thirty-six years exercising such acts of ownership as payment of taxes, enjoyment of rents and profits, payment of insurance made payable to him, together with possession of an unprobated will giving him the property [absolutely]," and because, according to him, the other cotenants had "direct knowledge of the will"? Since the other cotenants claimed that they thought the unprobated will gave the occupying cotenant only a life estate, it seems that the court's

holding must really have been based on an implicit conclusion that the trial judge could properly disbelieve the claim of the other cotenants as to the will.

In Johnson v. James, there was no evidence that any of the other co-tenants ever sought to share the occupying co-tenant's possession of the land and were excluded. An actual exclusion or ouster of the other co-tenants would, of course, have made it clear that the occupying co-tenant was asserting an "adverse" claim of some sort. But if the testimony of the other co-tenants as to their belief that the occupying co-tenant had only a life estate had been believed, the "adverse" claim would presumably have been only a claim to a life estate, not to complete ownership of the land.

6. Suppose a life tenant of land who also holds an undivided half interest in the "remainder" files an affidavit claiming to have complete ownership in "fee simple" and then purports to convey complete ownership of the land to her brother, who takes possession, and that the life tenant dies eleven years later. When does the statute of limitations begin to run against the holder of the other undivided half interest in the land? See Piel v. DeWitt, 170 Ind.App. 63, 351 N.E.2d 48 (1976).

MANNILLO v. GORSKI

Supreme Court of New Jersey, 1969.
54 N.J. 378, 255 A.2d 258.

The opinion of the court was delivered by HANEMAN, J. Plaintiffs filed a complaint in the Chancery Division seeking a mandatory and prohibitory injunction against an alleged trespass upon their lands. Defendant counterclaimed for a declaratory judgment which would adjudicate that she had gained title to the disputed premises by adverse possession under N.J.S. 2A:14–6 which provides:

> "Every person having any right or title of entry into real estate shall make such entry within 20 years next after the accrual of such right or title of entry, or be barred therefrom thereafter."

After plenary trial, judgment was entered for plaintiffs. Mannillo v. Gorski, 100 N.J.Super. 140, 241 A.2d 276 (Ch.Div.1968). Defendant appealed to the Appellate Division. Before argument there, this Court granted defendant's motion for certification. R.R. 1:10–1A.

The facts are as follows: In 1946, defendant and her husband entered into possession of premises in Keansburg known as Lot No. 1007 in Block 42, under an agreement to purchase. Upon compliance with the terms of said agreement, the seller conveyed said lands to them on April 16, 1952. Defendant's husband thereafter died. The property consisted of a rectangular lot with a frontage of 25 feet and a depth of 100 feet. Plaintiffs are the owners of the adjacent Lot 1008 in Block 42 of like dimensions, to which they acquired title in 1953.

In the summer of 1946 Chester Gorski, one of the defendant's sons, made certain additions and changes to the defendant's house. He extended two rooms at the rear of the structure, enclosed a screened porch on the front, and put a concrete platform with steps on the west side thereof for use in connection with a side door. These steps were built to replace existing wooden steps. In addition, a concrete walk was installed from the steps to the end of the house. In 1953, defendant raised the house. In order to compensate for the resulting added height from the ground, she modified the design of the steps by extending them toward both the front and the rear of the property. She did not change their width.

Defendant admits that the steps and concrete walk encroach upon plaintiffs' lands to the extent of 15 inches. She contends, however, that she has title to said land by adverse possession. N.J.S.A. 2A:14–6, quoted above. Plaintiffs assert contrawise that defendant did not obtain title by adverse possession as her possession was not of the requisite hostile nature. They argue that to establish title by adverse possession, the entry into and continuance of possession must be accompanied by an intention to invade the rights of another in the lands, i.e., a knowing wrongful taking. They assert that, as defendant's encroachment was not accompanied by an intention to invade plaintiffs' rights in the land, but rather by the mistaken belief that she owned the land, and that therefore an essential requisite to establish title by adverse possession, i.e., an intentional tortious taking, is lacking.

The trial court concluded that defendant had clearly and convincingly proved that her possession of the 15-inch encroachment had existed for more than 20 years before the institution of this suit and that such possession was "exclusive, continuous, uninterrupted, visible, notorious and against the right and interest of the true owner." There is ample evidence to sustain this finding except as to its visible and notorious nature, of which more hereafter. However, the judge felt impelled by existing New Jersey case law, holding as argued by plaintiffs above, to deny defendant's claim and entered judgment for plaintiffs. 100 N.J. Super, at 150, 241 A.2d 276. The first issue before this Court is, therefore, whether an entry and continuance of possession under the mistaken belief that the possessor has title to the lands involved, exhibits the requisite hostile possession to sustain the obtaining of title by adverse possession.

The first detailed statement and acceptance by our then highest court, of the principle that possession as an element of title by adverse possession cannot be bottomed on mistake, is found in Folkman v. Myers, 93 N.J.Eq. 208, 115 A. 615 (E. & A.1921), which embraced and followed that thesis as expressed in Myers v. Folkman, 89 N.J.L. 390 (Sup. Ct.1916). It is not at all clear that this was the common law of this State prior to the latter case. An earlier opinion, Davok v. Nealon, 58 N.J.L. 21, 32 A. 675 (Sup.Ct.1895), held for an adverse possessor who had entered under the mistaken belief that he had title without any discussion of his hostile intent. However, the court in Myers v. Folkman, supra, at p. 393, 99 A. at p. 98 distinguished *Davock* from the case then under consideration by referring to the fact that "Charles R. Myers *disclaims* any intent to claim what did not belong to him and apparently never asserted a right to land outside the bounds of his title * * *." (Emphasis supplied) The factual distinction between the two cases, according to *Myers*, is that in the later case there was not only an entry by mistake but also an articulated disclaimer of an intent by the entrant to claim title to lands beyond his actual boundary. *Folkman*, although apparently relying on *Myers*, eliminated the requirement of that decision that there be expressed an affirmative disclaimer, and expanded the doctrine to exclude from the category of hostile possessors those whose entry and continued possession was under a mistaken belief that the lands taken were embraced within the description of the possessor's deed. In so doing, the former Court of Errors and Appeals aligned this State with that branch of a dichotomy which traces its genesis to Preble v. Main Cent. R. Co., 85 Me. 260, 27 A. 149, 21 L.R.A. 829 (Sup.Jud.Ct. Me.1893) and has become known as the Maine doctrine. In *Preble*, the court said at 27 A. at p. 150:

> "There is every presumption that the occupancy is in subordination to the true title, and, if the possession is claimed to be adverse, the act of the wrongdoer must be strictly construed, and the character of the possession clearly shown. Roberts v. Richards, 84 Me. 1, 24 A. 425, and authorities cited. 'The intention of the possessor to claim adversely,' says Mellen, C.J., in Ross v. Gould, supra, [5 Me. 204], 'is an essential ingredient in disseisin.' And in Worcester v. Lord, supra [56 Me. 266], the court says: 'To make a disseisin in fact, there must be an intention on the part of the party assuming possession to assert title in himself.' Indeed, the authorities all agree that this intention of the occupant to claim the ownership of land not embraced in his title is a necessary element of adverse possession; and in case of occupancy by mistake beyond a line capable of being ascertained this intention to claim title to the extent of the occupancy must appear to be absolute, and not conditional; otherwise the possession will not be deemed adverse to the true owner. It must be an intention to claim title to all land within a certain boundary on the face of the earth, whether it shall eventually be found to be the correct one or not. If, for instance, one in ignorance of his actual boundaries takes and holds possession by mistake up to a certain fence beyond his limits, upon the claim and in the belief that it is the true line, with the intention to claim title, and thus, if necessary, to acquire 'title by possession' up to that fence, such possession, having the requisite duration and continuity, will ripen into title. Hitchings v. Morrison, 72 Me. 331, is a pertinent illustration of this principle. See, also, Abbott v. Abbott, 51 Me. 575; Ricker v. Hibbard, 73 Me. 105.

> "If, on the other hand, a party through ignorance, inadvertence, or mistake occupies up to a given fence beyond his actual boundary, because he believes it to be the true line, but has no intention to claim title to that extent if it should be ascertained that the fence was on his neighbor's land, an indispensable element of adverse possession is wanting. In such a case the intent to claim title exists only upon the condition that the fence is on the true line. The intention is not absolute, but provisional, and the possession is not adverse."

This thesis, it is evident, rewards the possessor who entered with a premeditated and predesigned "hostility"—the intentional wrongdoer and disfavors an honest, mistaken entrant. 3 American Law of Property

(Casner ed. 1952), § 104, pp. 773, 785; Bordwell, "Disseisin and Adverse Possession," 33 Yale L.J. 1, 154 (1923); Darling, "Adverse Possession in Boundary Cases," 19 Ore.L.Rev. 117 (1940); Sternberg, "The Element of Hostility in Adverse Possession," 6 Temp.L.Q. 206 (1932); Annotation, "Adverse possession involving ignorance or mistake as to boundaries—modern views," 80 A.L.R.2d 1171 (1961).

The other branch of the dichotomy relies upon French v. Pearce, 8 Conn. 439 (Sup.Ct.Conn.1831). The court said in *Pearce* on the question of the subjective hostility of a possessor, at pp. 442, 445–446:

"Into the recesses of his [the adverse claimant's] mind, his motives or purposes, his guilt or innocence, no enquiry is made.
* * *

* * *

* * * The very nature of the act [entry and possession] is an assertion of his own title, and the denial of the title of all others. It matters not that the possessor was mistaken, and had he been better informed would not have entered on the land." 8 Conn. at 442, 445–46.

The Maine doctrine has been the subject of much criticism in requiring a knowing wrongful taking. The criticism of the Maine and the justification of the Connecticut branch of the dichotomy is well stated in 6 Powell, Real Property (1969) ¶ 1015, pp. 725–728:

"Do the facts of his possession, and of his conduct as if he were the owner, make immaterial his mistake, or does such a mistake prevent the existence of the prerequisite claim of right. The leading case holding the mistake to be of no importance was French v. Pearce, decided in Connecticut in 1831. * * * This viewpoint has gained increasingly widespread acceptance. The more subjectively oriented view regards the 'mistake' as necessarily preventing the existence of the required claim of right. The leading case on this position is Preble v. Maine Central R.R., decided in 1893. This position is still followed in a few states. It has been strongly criticized as unsound historically, inexpedient practically, and as resulting in better treatment for a ruthless wrongdoer than for the honest landowner. * * * On the whole the law is simplified, in the direction of real justice, by a following of the Connecticut leadership on this point."

Again, 4 Tiffany, Real Property (3d ed. 1939), § 1159, pp. 474–475, criticizes the employment of mistake as negating hostility as follows:

" * * * Adopting this view, it is only in so far as the courts, which assert the possible materiality of the mistake, recognize a contrary presumption, of an intention on the part of the wrongful possessor not to claim title if he is mistaken as to the boundary, that the assertion of the materiality of mistake as to boundary becomes of substantial importance. That the presumption is properly in favor of the adverse or hostile character of the possession rather than against it has been previously argued, but whatever presumption in this regard may be recognized, the introduction of the element of mistake in the discussion of the question of adverse possession is, it is submitted, unnecessary and undesirable. In no case except in that of a mistake as to boundary has the element of mistake been regarded as having any significance, and there is no reason for attributing greater weight thereto when the mistake is as to the proper location of a boundary than when it is a mistake as to the title to all the land wrongfully possessed. And to introduce the element of mistake, and then limit its significance by an inquiry as to the intention which the possessor may have as to his course of action in case there should be a mistake, an intention which has ordinarily no existence whatsoever, is calculated only to cause confusion without, it is conceived, any compensating advantage."

Our Appellate Division in Predham v. Holfester, 32 N.J.Super. 419, 108 A.2d 458 (App.Div.1954) although acknowledging that the Maine doctrine had been severely criticized felt obliged because of *stare decisis* to adhere thereto. See also Rullis v. Jacobi, 79 N.J.Super. 525, 528, 192 A.2d 186 (Ch.Div.1963).

We are in accord with the criticism of the Maine doctrine and favor the Connecticut doctrine for the above quoted reasons. As far as can be seen, overruling the former rule will not result in undermining any of the values which *stare decisis* is intended to foster. The theory of reliance, a cornerstone of *stare decisis*, is not here apt, as the problem is which of two mistaken parties is entitled to land. Realistically, the true owner does not rely upon entry of the possessor by mistake as a reason for not seeking to recover possession. Whether or not the entry is caused by mistake or intent, the same result eventuates—the true owner is ousted from possession. In either event his neglect to seek recovery of possession, within the requisite time, is in all probability the result of a lack of knowledge that he is being deprived of possession of lands to which he has title.

Accordingly, we discard the requirement that the entry and continued possession must be accompanied by a knowing intentional hostility and hold that any entry and possession for the required time which is exclusive, continuous, uninterrupted, visible and notorious, even though under mistaken claim of title, is sufficient to support a claim of title by adverse possession.

However, this conclusion is not dispositive of the matter *sub judice*. Of equal importance under the present factual complex, is the question of whether defendant's acts meet the necessary standard of "open and notorious" possession. It must not be forgotten that the foundation of so-called "title by adverse possession" is the failure of the true owner to commence an action for the recovery of the land involved, within the period designated by the statute of limitations. The justifications for the doctrine are aptly stated in 4 Tiffany, Real Property (3d ed. 1939) § 1134, p. 406 as follows:

"The desirability of fixing, by law, a definite period within which claims to land must be asserted has been generally recognized, among the practical considerations in favor of such a policy being the prevention of the making of illegal claims after the evidence necessary to defeat them has been lost, and the interest which the community as the whole has in the security, of title. The moral justification of the policy lies in the consideration that one who has reason to know that land belonging to him is in the possession of another, and neglects, for a considerable period of time, to assert his right thereto, may properly be penalized by his preclusion from thereafter asserting such right. It is, apparently, by reason of the demerit of the true owner, rather than any supposed merit in the person who has acquired wrongful possession of the land, that this possession, if continued for the statutory period, operates to debar the former owner of all right to recover the land."

See also 5 Thompson, Real Property (1957 Replacement), 497.

In order to afford the true owner the opportunity to learn of the adverse claim and to protect his rights by legal action within the time specified by the statute, the adverse possession must be visible and notorious. In 4 Tiffany, supra (Supp.1969, at 291), the character of possession for that purpose, is stated to be as follows:

" * * * it must be public and based on physical facts, including known and visible lines and boundaries. Acts of dominion over the land must be so open and notorious as to put an ordinarily prudent person on notice that the land is in actual possession of another. Hence, title may never be acquired by mere possession, however long continued, which is surreptitious or secret or which is not such as will give unmistakable notice of the nature of the occupant's claim."

See also 5 Thompson, supra, § 2546; 6 Powell, Real Property, ¶ 1013 (1969).

Generally, where possession of the land is clear and unequivocal and to such an extent as to be immediately visible, the owner may be presumed to have knowledge of the adverse occupancy. In *Foulke v. Bond*, 41 N.J.L. 527, 545 (E. & A.1879), the court said:

"Notoriety of the adverse claim under which possession is held, is a necessary constituent of title by adverse possession, and therefore the occupation or possession must be of that nature that the real owner is *presumed to have known* that there was a possession adverse to his title, under which it was intended to make title against him." (Emphasis supplied)

However, when the encroachment of an adjoining owner is of a small area and the fact of an intrusion is not clearly and self-evidently apparent to the naked eye but requires an on-site survey for certain disclosure as in urban sections where the division line is only infrequently delineated by any monuments, natural or artificial, such a presumption is fallacious and unjustified. See concurring opinion of Judge (now Justice) Francis in Predham v. Holfester, 32 N.J.Super. 419, 428–429, 108 A.2d 458 (App.Div.1954). The precise location of the dividing line is then ordinarily unknown to either adjacent owner and there is nothing on the land itself to show by visual observation that a hedge, fence, wall or other structure encroaches on the neighboring land to a minor extent. Therefore, to permit a presumption of notice to arise in the case of minor border encroachments not exceeding several feet would fly in the face of reality and require the true owner to be on constant alert for possible small encroachments. The only method of certain determination would be by obtaining a survey each time the adjacent owner undertook any improvement at or near the boundary, and this would place an undue and inequitable burden upon the true owner. Accordingly we hereby hold that no presumption of knowledge arises from a minor encroachment along a common boundary. In such a case, only where the true owner has actual knowledge thereof may it be said that the possession is open and notorious.

It is conceivable that the application of the foregoing rule may in some cases result in undue hardship to the adverse possessor who under an innocent and mistaken belief of title has undertaken an extensive improvement which to some extent encroaches on an adjoining property. In that event the situation falls within the category of those cases of which Riggle v. Skill, 9 N.J.Super. 372, 74 A.2d 424 (Ch.Div.1950), affirmed 7 N.J. 268, 81 A.2d 364 (1951), is typical and equity may furnish relief. Then, if the innocent trespasser of a small portion of land adjoining a boundary line cannot without great expense remove or eliminate the encroachment, or such removal or elimination is impractical or could be accomplished only with great hardship, the true owner may be forced to convey the land so occupied upon payment of the fair value thereof without regard to whether the true owner had notice of the encroachment at its inception. Of course, such a result should eventuate only under appropriate circumstances and where no serious damage would be done to the remaining land as, for instance, by rendering the balance of the parcel unusable or no longer capable of being built upon by reason of zoning or other restrictions.

We remand the case for trial of the issues (1) whether the true owner had actual knowledge of the encroachment, (2) if not, whether plaintiffs should be obliged to convey the disputed tract to defendant, and (3) if the answer to the latter question is in the affirmative, what consideration should be paid for the conveyance. The remand, of course, contemplates further discovery and a new pretrial.

Remanded for trial in accordance with the foregoing.

For remandment—Chief Justice WEINTRAUB and Justices JACOBS, FRANCIS, PROCTOR, HALL and HANEMAN—6.

Opposed—None.

Notes

1. The most common form of adverse possession is one in which the possessor believes that he is the owner of an entire tract of land with known boundaries by virtue of a written instrument that turns out to be void for some reason. Monroe v. Rawlings, supra, is such a case. As the *Monroe* case makes clear, the claim of adverse possession is not defeated in such cases by proof that the wrongful possessor mistakenly believed that he was the true owner of the land in question. Instead, his "color of title" will generally enable him to acquire ownership of the entire tract described in the instrument or document constituting his "color of title" even though he has actually been in possession of only

part of that tract.   Moreover, no cases have been found in which a wrongful possession of an entire tract without "color of title" but in the mistaken belief that the possessor is actually the owner of the tract has been held not to be "adverse."   The "Maine doctrine" discussed in Mannillo v. Gorski, in short, has been applied only in cases involving a relatively small "encroachment" by the owner of one tract onto an adjacent tract as a result of his mistake in locating the boundary.

2.   That the decision in Mannillo v. Gorski is in accord with the present weight of authority as to the effect of a boundary mistake, see 3 A.L.P. 786, 789.   Do you prefer the "Connecticut doctrine" adopted in *Mannillo*, or the contrary "Maine doctrine"?   In deciding your preference, consider the following testimony in two cases involving the same issue as *Mannillo:*

(a) Plaintiff and defendant owned adjacent lots.   Plaintiff landscaped his lot and a three-foot strip of defendant's lot after a surveyor employed by plaintiff had run a boundary line which included the strip.   In a suit over whether plaintiff had acquired title to the strip by adverse possession, the following testimony of the plaintiff was received in evidence:

"Q.   Did you receive this property by deed?   A.   I did.

"Q.   And you are claiming then up to the boundaries of lot 16, is that your testimony, that you received by deed?   A.   Well I wouldn't say that exactly, if there was a mistake made in the survey and I have owned the property 25 years, I don't know.

"Q.   What property are you claiming, lot 16?   A.   That's right.

"Q.   Are you claiming any additional property?   A.   Wait a minute.

"Q.   How do you claim any property you don't have a deed to?   A.   Well we have been there that long.   We have never been disputed there before.

"Q.   When you went into possession, Mr. Burns, was it your intention to claim more than lot 16?   A.   No, that is why we had it surveyed.

"Q.   Then really all you claim or intended to claim was lot 16, is that right?   A.   At that time, yes.

"Q.   Are you claiming it now?   A.   That is for my attorney to say.

"Q.   That is for you to decide, Mr. Burns?   A.   I don't know."

Burns v. Foster, 348 Mich. 8, 81 N.W.2d 386 (1957).

(b) Compare the following line of questioning:

"Q.   How did you happen to build it [the fence] on the line on which you did build it?   A.   Well, I didn't know where the line was, nor did Chapman know, so we just decided to build it and whenever the survey was made why that survey would be the line. There was an agreement between Mr. Chapman and I.   *   *   *   It was agreed between Chapman and I when I bought it that whenever a correct survey was made that would be our line, so there was no question about it after we had already built the fence.   *   *   *

"Q.   And this fence that you made, this rail fence, neither you nor Mr. Chapman agreed that that was to be the boundary line?   A.   No.   *   *   *

"Q.   You never intended to claim then up to the fence, did you?   A.   Certainly not.

"Q.   As I gather, you only intended to claim to wherever the true boundary line actually was?   A.   Certainly.

"Q.   Now when you built your buildings did you realize they might be over the line?   A.   [Objection overruled]   A.   There was a possibility that it would be, yes.   *   *   *

"Q. In other words, it was with your permission if he was using your land or it was with his permission if you were using his? A. Absolutely our agreement."

Beck v. Loveland, 37 Wash.2d 249, 222 P.2d 1066 (1950).

BRAND v. PRINCE

New York Supreme Court, Appellate Division, 1973.
43 App.Div.2d 638, 349 N.Y.S.2d 222.

MEMORANDUM DECISION. * * *

In this action brought to establish title to realty pursuant to article 15 of the Real Property Actions and Proceedings Law, plaintiffs claim title to a 10-acre parcel of land on the northerly side of Mapes Road in the Town of Deposit, County of Delaware, under and by virtue of a deed from Elmer C. Romer and Cecilia L. Romer dated October 16, 1961, and recorded in the Delaware County Clerk's Office on November 2, 1961 in Liber 430 of Deeds at page 256, and by adverse possession thereof.

Defendant, by way of counterclaim, also claims title to the 10-acre parcel under and by virtue of a deed from Ruth E. Millspaugh as Administratrix of the Estate of Stanley Millspaugh, recorded November 13, 1959 in the Delaware County Clerk's Office in Liber 409 of Deeds at page 51, and by adverse possession.

The County Court, after a trial without a jury, determined that neither party had established title by written instrument; and that plaintiffs failed to establish title by adverse possession; and implicitly that defendant was entitled to possession.

Title to the disputed 10-acre parcel is traced from a deed in 1873 by Mary L. Baker and James Baker to Betsy L. Coon, which conveyed a 40-acre parcel. In 1876, Betsy L. Coon conveyed the disputed 10 acres to Christina C. Turner, who thereafter in 1878, conveyed the same to Charles M. Putnam and James S. Minor.

In 1879, they reconveyed the 10 acres to Christina C. Turner. In 1890, she conveyed the 10 acres to John H. Coon, who owned adjoining lands. John H. Coon died in 1908, and by his last will and testament which was admitted to probate on April 4, 1908, he devised all of his property to his sister, Sarah E. Coon. In 1916, Sarah E. Coon conveyed a parcel of land to Nettie Surine which is recorded in Liber 176 of Deeds at page 263 containing the following recital: "The said premises being the same premises owned and occupied by the said John H. Coon in his lifetime." The description of the parcel conveyed, however, did not include the 10-acre parcel in dispute.

On September 30, 1956, Minerva Brokaw, as administratrix of the estate of Nettie Surine conveyed the premises acquired by Nettie Surine from Sarah E. Coon to Elmer C. Romer. This deed was recorded on October 29, 1956 in Liber 378 of Deeds at page 127, and contained the same recital. Elmer C. Romer and Cecilia L. Romer, his wife, on October 16, 1961, conveyed this parcel to Arthur Brand, the plaintiff. This deed was recorded on November 2, 1961 in Liber 430 of Deeds at page 256, and contained the same recital.

Defendant's chain of title also starts with the 1873 deed to Betsy L. Coon. She died intestate on April 12, 1898, survived by Christina Turner, Louisa Loucks, David H. Coon, Sarah E. Coon, and John H. Turner. In 1916, they conveyed the 40-acre parcel to Bertha Huyck Bresee, excepting and reserving therefrom "the 10-acre parcel sold heretofore to Christina Turner, and now owned or occupied by one Schultz." In 1935, the heirs of Bertha Huyck Bresee conveyed, by the same description, that parcel to Albert Papenmeyer. This deed is recorded in Liber 236 of Deeds at page 572. After several conveyances containing the same description and exception, title is found in 1951 in Colvin Clapper. The next deed in the chain is a deed from the Delaware County Treasurer to Ruth E. Millspaugh, as administratrix of the estate of Stanley Millspaugh, recorded in Liber 398 of Deeds at page 223 wherein the parcel is described as follows: "School District 8, bounded north by Surine, east by Clapper, south by Romer, west by Surine, 30 acres." On November 13, 1959, Ruth C. Millspaugh, by administrator's deed, conveyed the parcel by the same description as in the deed to her, to Richard T. Prince, the defendant. This deed was recorded on November 13, 1959 in Liber 409 of Deeds at page 41.

"A grant or devise of real property passes all the estate or interest of the grantor or testator unless the intent to pass a less estate or interest appears by the express terms of such grant or devise or by necessary implication therefrom." (Real Property Law, § 245.) The description in plaintiff's deed admittedly does not cover the 10 acres in question. The recital "Being the same premises owned and occupied by the said John H. Coon in his lifetime" is as consistent with the parcel conveyed as it is to the entire parcel.

The description in defendant's deed might be considered as including the 10-acre parcel, since the western boundary is stated to be Surine, and it appears that Nettie Surine did not acquire title to the 10-acre parcel by her deed. The description, however, limits the amount conveyed to 30 acres, the same acreage as owned by the assessed owner under his deed. By implication then this deed expresses the intent to convey only the 30 acres owned by Colvin Clapper, the assessed owner. It thus appears that neither party established title to the 10 acres in question by written instrument, and that record title to the 10 acres remains in Sarah E. Coon, and her descendants.

Plaintiffs, however, produced Cecilia Romer who testified that at the time her husband, Elmer C. Romer, purchased the parcel adjoining the 10 acres from the administratrix of the estate of Nettie Surine, a Mr. Schultz, who ran a store for Nettie Surine, pointed out the boundary lines of the property, and that the 10-acre parcel was within the boundaries so pointed out. She also believed that the description in the deed included the 10-acre parcel. She also testified that they had rented the Surine farm from Nettie Surine from 1945 to the time of the purchase, and had pastured cows on the 10-acre parcel all the time the land had been rented, and after the purchase until about two years before the sale to plaintiffs when her husband became ill. Thereafter, the 10 acres were used to pasture cows by others until the property was sold to the defendant. She also testified that the parcel was fenced; that she became acquainted with defendant after he purchased the 30 acres from Ruth Millspaugh, who was her daughter-in-law; that defendant never questioned the location of the fence on the easterly line of the 10-acre parcel; that he made no effort to utilize the 10 acres on her side of the fence; and that no one else contested her right to use the 10-acre parcel. She further testified that this fence line was shown by her to plaintiff at the time he bought, as the boundary line.

J. Leland Rickard testified on behalf of plaintiffs that he was the attorney for the Surine Estate; that he had known Mr. Schultz; that Schultz had at one time occupied a cabin on the 10-acre parcel which he believed to be on the Surine lands; that, at the time he settled the Surine Estate, it was his understanding that the parcel owned by Nettie Surine extended to Mapes Road, thus including the 10-acre parcel.

Plaintiff also testified to his use and occupancy of the parcel including leasing the same to one Friend Decker who cut hay and pastured young stock there until about 1968; the renting of the land to a hunting club starting in 1962 and the posting of the land along the boundary against hunting and fishing; that the boundaries were pointed out to him when he purchased; and that he believed that the 10 acres in dispute were included in the description of the parcel conveyed to him. Two members of the hunting club testified to the renting of the property including the 10 acres from the plaintiffs, and to their use thereof which included posting along the fence lines of the 10-acre parcel since 1962. They stated that they had no trouble until 1970 when defendant began taking down their no hunting posters, but that defendant made no effort to stop their use.

Defendant offered contradictory testimony as to his own use of the property. His witnesses stated that they were children at the time they were familiar with the property, and the time of their occupancy was prior to 1955 and, therefore, of little value. The testimony of defendant and of his witnesses was in direct conflict with that of the plaintiffs and their witnesses and for the most part is unconvincing.

"There are five essential elements necessary to constitute an effective adverse possession: *First*, the possession must be hostile and *under claim of right; second*, it must be actual; *third*, it must be open and notorious; *fourth*, it must be exclusive; and *fifth*, it must be continuous. If any of these constituents is wanting, the possession will not effect a bar of the legal title." (Belotti v. Bickhardt, 228 N.Y. 296, 302, 127 N.E. 239, 241 [italics in original]; Bradt v. Giovannone, 35 A.D.2d 322, 315 N.Y.S.2d 961.)

The fact that plaintiffs claim more land than their deed specifies is not controlling, since "adverse possession, even when held by mistake or through inadvertence, may ripen into a prescriptive right." (Belotti v. Bickhardt, supra; West v. Tilley, 33 A.D.2d 228, 306 N.Y.S.2d 591, mot. for lv. to app. den., 27 N.Y.2d 481, 312 N.Y.S.2d 1025, 260 N.E.2d 874.)

Plaintiffs' evidence indicates that they and their predecessors in interest were in possession of the 10-acre parcel under claim of right, albeit under mistaken belief that their deeds included that parcel; that they actually possessed the land openly and notoriously to the exclusion of all others. Their possession was also continuous for more than 15 years. Although plaintiffs did not acquire their title until 1961, they are entitled to the benefits of the use and occupation by their predecessors, since the record clearly establishes their intent to convey what they mistakenly thought was theirs and had been using and occupying. Privity may be established by parol, and here there is ample evidence of the intent to hold and convey more than the land which the deed to plaintiff specifically conveyed. (See Belotti v. Bickhardt, supra.) Since the evidence indicates the intent of plaintiffs' predecessors to include the 10-acre parcel in the conveyance, they are permitted to "tack" their adverse uses onto their predecessors' use to make up the required prescriptive period of 15 years under section 34 of the former Civil Practice Act which is the governing statute. (See Reiter v. Landon Homes, 31 A.D.2d 538, 295 N.Y.S.2d 103, mot. for lv. to app. den., 24 N.Y.2d 738, 300 N.Y.S.2d 1025, 248 N.E.2d 452.)

We have concluded that the judgment should be reversed to give effect to the credible evidence so as to grant judgment to plaintiffs and dismiss the counterclaim. (See CPLR 5522; Hacker v. City of New York, 26 A.D.2d 400, 403, 275 N.Y.S.2d 146, 150.)

Judgment reversed, on the law and the facts, insofar as it adjudged defendant to be the owner of the 10 acres of real property described in the complaint herein, and judgment directed to be entered in favor of plaintiffs adjudging them to be the owners and seized and possessed of said real property, and dismissing defendant's counterclaim, with costs.

Notes and Questions

1. The Appellate Division's decision in the principal case was affirmed by the Court of Appeals, 35 N.Y.2d 634, 364 N.Y.S.2d 826, 324 N.E.2d 314 (1974), with an opinion that omits most of the relevant facts and concludes with the following language:

> The rule is that successive adverse possessions of property omitted from a deed description, especially contiguous property, may be tacked if it appears that the adverse possessor intended to and actually turned over possession of the undescribed part with the portion of the land included in the deed. (Belotti v. Bickhardt, 228 N.Y. 296, 303, 308, 127 N.E. 239, 241, 243, supra; Adverse Possession—Tacking, Ann., 17 A.L.R.2d 1128, 1131–1132; 3 American Law of Property, § 15.10.) Because the possessory title is entirely an incident of the adverse holder's possession, transfer of that possession, even by parol, effects a transfer of the possessory interest. (3 American Law of Property, § 15.10.) The circumstances of this case are entirely consistent with a finding that plaintiff's predecessors intended to and actually turned over their possessory interest in the 10-acre parcel. Hence, the tacking was proper.

2. Note that the principal case did not involve an action to recover possession of land. Plaintiff (through his lessee, the hunting club) was in possession, and brought an "action to compel the determination of a claim to real property"

as authorized by N.Y. Real Property Actions & Proceedings Law § 1501. Most states have statutory authorization for such actions, which are commonly referred to as "quiet title actions." The statutory actions have evolved from earlier equity proceedings to "remove a cloud on the title" of a plaintiff in possession of the land. Both equity and statutory proceedings of this type enable one who has acquired ownership of land by adverse possession for the statutory period to establish a "record title" to the land and to preclude any subsequent action by the former owner to recover possession of the land.

3.   For other recent cases in accord on the "tacking" problem, see Carpenter v. Huffman, 294 Ala. 189, 314 So.2d 65 (1975); Alukonis v. Kashulines, 96 N.Y. 107, 70 A.2d 202 (1950). The ability of one adverse possessor to "tack" his possession to that of a prior adverse possessor may seem inconsistent with the purposes of a statute of limitation. If a cause of action arises against the first possessor, why does not that cause of action end and a new one arise upon the shifting of possession to the second taker? How can anyone have a cause of action to recover land except against some person who is holding the land? What sense does it make to say that the first possessor transfers his liability to be sued to his successor? In any event, tacking of successive adverse possessions is universally recognized and in adverse possession cases is relied on as often as not. This corollary to the doctrine of adverse possession may tend to prove the proposition previously mentioned that the modern doctrine emphasizes the positive notion that an adverse possessor by his conduct builds a title for himself rather than the negative feature of penalizing an owner who defaults on his rights. If one can really be thought of as building some sort of inchoate interest during the statutory period, it may make sense to say that he can transfer this interest to another. In fact, an adverse possessor does have a possessory title, good as against anyone who cannot show a better title, and in the process called tacking, he can be said to transfer that title.

The indispensable requirement for tacking is "privity" between the successive possessors. Privity is one of those weasel words whose meaning shifts with the problem involved. It has been held that privity cannot be established by a deed between one possessor and another if the deed did not cover the land in question. This may seem rather obvious, but privity does not require a formal transaction or a written instrument. Then what does privity mean?

"Possession and voluntary transfer thereof are physical facts provable by the testimony of an eye or ear witness or any other evidentiary fact or conduct. The only qualification to the possession is that it must be such as to exclude the true owner; not derived from or in subordination to him. The only essential of the transfer is that the predecessor passes it to the successor by mutual consent, as distinguished from the case where a possessor abandons possession generally, and another, finding the premises unoccupied, enters without contact or relation with the former.   *   *   *"   Illinois Steel Co. v. Paczocha, 139 Wis. 23, 28, 119 N.W. 550, 552 (1909).

4.   Since the plaintiffs had been in possession of the disputed tract from 1961 to 1972 before bringing their quiet title action, and since the statutory period of limitation was reduced to 10 years in 1962, why did the plaintiffs have to resort to the "tacking" doctrine to establish their title by adverse possession? See N.Y. Civil Practice Law & Rules § 218(b), which provides as follows: "Where a cause of action accrued before and is not barred when this article [reducing, *inter alia*, the period from fifteen to ten years] becomes effective, the time within which an action must be commenced shall be the time which would have been applicable apart from the provisions of this article, or the time which would have been applicable if the provisions of this article had been in

effect when the cause of action accrued, whichever is longer." The Commentary on § 218(b) states that it "is needed to avoid any constitutional problems that might arise if the statute of limitations on existing causes of action were suddenly abbreviated." But see Scurlock, Retroactive Legislation Affecting Interests in Land 42 (1953), stating that "the owner has no constitutionally protected right that the particular statute of limitations in effect when his cause of action first arose should remain in effect," and that the period of limitation applicable to actions to recover possession of land "may be shortened retroactively, provided a reasonable time is allowed after the [new period] goes into effect to bring actions not yet barred under the old period."

5. Does the Appellate Division's opinion contain an adequate analysis of the "tacking" problem in the principal case? *Suppose* that Nettie Surine took possession of the disputed tract in 1916 in the mistaken belief that Sarah Coon had conveyed it to her along with the 30-acre parcel. If so, and if Nettie Surine's possession continued at least until 1931, Nettie Surine would have acquired title by adverse possession in 1931, and her administratrix could not have transferred title to the disputed parcel without a written conveyance describing that tract. (As we have previously seen, the Statute of Frauds requires a written conveyance to transfer anything more than an estate at will.) The 15-year limitation period would then have started to run in favor of the Romers in 1956, when they took possession of the disputed tract in the mistaken belief that it was included in the deed conveying the adjacent 30-acre parcel to them; and Nettie Surine's heirs would have been barred only in 1971, in which case the plaintiffs would have to "tack" the Romers' 5 years of adverse possession from 1956 to 1961 to the plaintiffs' subsequent period of adverse possession in order to satisfy the 15-year statute of limitations. *But suppose*, on the other hand, that Nettie Surine did not begin her own adverse possession of the disputed strip until sometime between 1942 and 1946. In that case, the Romers would have acquired title, with the aid of the "tacking" doctrine, sometime between 1957 and 1961; the attempted parol transfer of the disputed strip to the plaintiffs in 1961 would have been ineffective; and the adverse possession of the plaintiffs from 1961 to 1972 would have been insufficient to give them title by adverse possession as against the Romers!

6. A takes possession of Lot 3 of a certain block in the certain subdivision under a tax deed which is void. A also possesses a three-foot strip of Lot 4, which is owned by O. After the period of the statute has run A conveys Lot 3 to B. B takes possession of Lot 3 and the three-foot strip. Who has title to the strip? Can O recover it from B? See Hughes v. Graves, 39 Vt. 359 (1867); Du Val v. Miller, 183 Or. 287, 192 P.2d 249, rehearing denied 192 P.2d 992 (1948). Can A recover it from B?

7. Suppose A possesses land for a period short of the statute of limitations and is ousted by B. Can B gain any benefit from A's possession? Suppose A promptly sues and recovers the land from B. Has A's possession been interrupted? See Powell ¶ 1014.

8. Do you see any reason why tacking should not be allowed between an heir and his ancestor, or between a devisee and his testator? Accepting without further explanation here that land can be conveyed to L for life, then to R, and accepting also that a deed which appears to be good on its face may be void for one of several reasons, suppose a void deed purports to convey in the above way. L enters believing the deed is good. Later upon his death R enters. Should it be possible to tack these two periods? Hanson v. Johnson, 62 Md. 25 (1884).

9.   Suppose land is conveyed to L for life, then to R. A adversely possesses the land for the statutory period during L's life. What sort of interest should A get? Should it make any difference that A's adverse possession began when the land was owned by O who later conveyed to L for life, then to R? See 3 A.L.P. § 15.8.

10.   An inverse sort of tacking question is presented where A takes adverse possession of B's land under a 15-year statute and continues in possession for 5 years, and then B conveys the land to C, after which A continues his adverse possession for 10 years. Has A now acquired title? This is a common situation, and the result is taken for granted in A's favor. B had a cause of action against A, but no longer has it when he conveys to C. Does C gain a new cause of action, or has B's cause of action simply passed to him? If it is the latter, the statute has been shortened as to him to 10 years. Conceivably C might have bought the land one month or even one day before the statute runs. Why should C's right to sue be so fore-shortened? See the Michigan statute supra. As a practical matter, such extreme cases seldom occur. In fact rules exist in a few states restricting the power of a landowner to convey land which is adversely possessed by someone else. See 3 A.L.P. § 12.69.

O'KEEFFE v. SNYDER

Supreme Court of New Jersey, 1980.
83 N.J. 478, 416 A.2d 862.

POLLOCK, J. This is an appeal from an order of the Appellate Division granting summary judgment to plaintiff, Georgia O'Keeffe, against defendant, Barry Snyder, d/b/a Princeton Gallery of Fine Art, for replevin of three small pictures painted by O'Keeffe. O'Keeffe v. Snyder, 170 N.J.Super. 75, 405 A.2d 840 (1979). In her complaint, filed in March, 1976, O'Keeffe alleged she was the owner of the paintings and that they were stolen from a New York art gallery in 1946. Snyder asserted he was a purchaser for value of the paintings, he had title by adverse possession, and O'Keeffe's action was barred by the expiration of the six-year period of limitations provided by N.J.S.A. 2A:14-1 pertaining to an action in replevin. Snyder impleaded third party defendant, Ulrich A. Frank, from whom Snyder purchased the paintings in 1975 for $35,000.

The trial court granted summary judgment for Snyder on the ground that O'Keeffe's action was barred because it was not commenced within six years of the alleged theft. The Appellate Division reversed and entered judgment for O'Keeffe. O'Keeffe, supra, 170 N.J.Super. at 92, 405 A.2d 840. A majority of that court concluded that the paintings were stolen, the defenses of expiration of the statute of limitations and title by adverse possession were identical, and Snyder had not proved the elements of adverse possession. Consequently, the majority ruled that O'Keeffe could still enforce her right to possession of the paintings.

The dissenting judge stated that the appropriate measurement of the period of limitation was not by analogy to adverse possession, but by application of the "discovery rule" pertaining to some statutes of limitation. He concluded that the six-year period of limitations commenced when O'Keeffe knew or should have known who unlawfully possessed the paintings, and that the matter should be remanded to determine if and when that event had occurred. Id. at 96–97, 405 A.2d 840.

We granted certification to consider not only the issues raised in the dissenting opinion, but all other issues. 81 N.J. 406, 408 A.2d 800 (1979). We reverse and remand the matter for a plenary hearing in accordance with this opinion.

I

The record, limited to pleadings, affidavits, answers to interrogatories, and depositions, is fraught with factual conflict. Apart from the creation of the paintings by O'Keeffe and their discovery in Snyder's gallery in 1976, the parties agree on little else.

O'Keeffe contended the paintings were stolen in 1946 from a gallery, An American Place. The gallery was operated by her late husband, the famous photographer Alfred Stieglitz.

An American Place was a cooperative undertaking of O'Keeffe and some other American artists identified by her as Marin, Hardin, Dove, Andema, and Stevens. In 1946, Stieglitz arranged an exhibit which included an O'Keeffe painting, identified as Cliffs. According to O'Keeffe, one day in March, 1946, she and Stieglitz discovered Cliffs was missing from the wall of the exhibit. O'Keeffe estimates the value of the painting at the time of the alleged theft to have been about $150.

About two weeks later, O'Keeffe noticed that two other paintings, Seaweed and Fragments, were missing from a storage room at An American Place. She did not tell anyone, even Stieglitz, about the missing paintings, since she did not want to upset him.

Before the date when O'Keeffe discovered the disappearance of Seaweed, she had already sold it (apparently for a string of amber beads) to a Mrs. Weiner, now deceased. Following the grant of the motion for summary judgment by the trial court in favor of Snyder, O'Keeffe submitted a release from the legatees of Mrs. Weiner purportedly assigning to O'Keeffe their interest in the sale.

O'Keeffe testified on depositions that at about the same time as the disappearance of her paintings, 12 or 13 miniature paintings by Marin also were stolen from An American Place. According to O'Keeffe, a man named Estrick took the Marin paintings and "maybe a few other things." Estrick distributed the Marin paintings to members of the theater world who, when confronted by Stieglitz, returned them. However, neither Stieglitz nor O'Keeffe confronted Estrick with the loss of any of the O'Keeffe paintings.

There was no evidence of a break and entry at An American Place on the dates when O'Keeffe discovered the disappearance of her paintings. Neither Stieglitz nor O'Keeffe reported them missing to the New York Police Department or any other law enforcement agency. Apparently the paintings were uninsured, and O'Keeffe did not seek reimbursement from an insurance company. Similarly, neither O'Keeffe nor Stieglitz advertised the loss of the paintings in Art News or any other publication. Nonetheless, they discussed it with associates in the art world and later O'Keeffe mentioned the loss to the director of the Art Institute of Chicago, but she did not ask him to do anything because "it wouldn't have been my way." O'Keeffe does not contend that Frank or Snyder had actual knowledge of the alleged theft.

Stieglitz died in the summer of 1946, and O'Keeffe explains she did not pursue her efforts to locate the paintings because she was settling his estate. In 1947, she retained the services of Doris Bry to help settle the estate. Bry urged O'Keeffe to report the loss of the paintings, but O'Keeffe declined because "they never got anything back by reporting it." Finally, in 1972, O'Keeffe authorized Bry to report the theft to the Art Dealers Association of America, Inc., which maintains for its members a registry of stolen paintings. The record does not indicate whether such a registry existed at the time the paintings disappeared.

In September, 1975, O'Keeffe learned that the paintings were in the Andrew Crispo Gallery in New York on consignment from Bernard Danenberg Galleries. On February 11, 1976, O'Keeffe discovered that Ulrich A. Frank had sold the paintings to Barry Snyder, d/b/a Princeton Gallery of Fine Art. She demanded their return and, following Snyder's refusal, instituted this action for replevin.

Frank traces his possession of the paintings to his father, Dr. Frank, who died in 1968. He claims there is a family relationship by marriage between his family and the Stieglitz family, a contention that O'Keeffe disputes. Frank does not know how his father acquired the paintings, but he recalls seeing them in his father's apartment in New Hampshire as early as 1941–1943, a period that precedes the alleged theft. Consequently, Frank's factual contentions are inconsistent with O'Keeffe's allegation of theft. Until 1965, Dr. Frank occasionally lent the paintings to Ulrich Frank. In 1965, Dr. and Mrs. Frank formally gave the paintings to Ulrich Frank, who kept them in his residences in Yardley, Pennsylvania and Princeton, New Jersey. In 1968, he exhibited anonymously Cliffs and Fragments in a one day art show in the Jewish Community Center in Trenton. All of these events precede O'Keeffe's listing of the paintings as stolen with the Art Dealers Association of America, Inc. in 1972.

Frank claims continuous possession of the paintings through his father for over thirty years and admits selling the paintings to Snyder. Snyder and Frank do not trace their provenance, or history of possession of the paintings, back to O'Keeffe.

As indicated, Snyder moved for summary judgment on the theory that O'Keeffe's action was barred by the statute of limitations and title had vested in Frank by adverse possession. For purposes of his motion, Snyder conceded that the paintings had been stolen. On her cross motion, O'Keeffe urged that the paintings were stolen, the statute of limitations had not run, and title to the paintings remained in her.

II

In general, cross motions for summary judgment do not "obviate a plenary trial of disputed issues of fact, where such exists; nor do cross-

motions constitute a waiver by the litigants to such a trial." *   *   *
Cross motions do not warrant granting summary judgment unless one
of the moving parties is entitled to judgment as a matter of law.
*   *   *   Cross motions for summary judgment do not preclude the existence of issues of fact. Id. at 345. Although a defendant may assert
that, according to his theory of the case, the material facts are undisputed, he must be allowed to show that if plaintiff's theory is adopted
there remains a genuine issue of material fact. *   *   *   Where there
are cross motions for summary judgment, a party may make concessions for the purposes of his motion that do not carry over and support
the motion of his adversary. *   *   *

The Appellate Division accepted O'Keeffe's contention that the paintings had been stolen. However, in his deposition, Ulrich Frank traces
possession of the paintings to his father in the early 1940's, a date that
precedes the alleged theft by several years. The factual dispute about
the loss of the paintings by O'Keeffe and their acquisition by Frank, as
well as the other subsequently described factual issues, warrant a remand for a plenary hearing. *   *   *

In reversing the cross motions for summary judgment, the Appellate
Division erred in accepting one of two conflicting versions of material
fact: the theft of the paintings in March, 1946 as asserted by O'Keeffe
as against the possession of the paintings by the Frank family since the
early 1940's. Instead of recognizing the existence of this controversy,
the Appellate Division misconstrued Snyder's concession that the paintings had been stolen. That concession was made to enable the trial
court to determine Snyder's motion for summary judgment that title
had passed by adverse possession. The concession was not available to
resolve O'Keeffe's cross motion for summary judgment. Hence, there
is an issue of material fact, whether the paintings were stolen, that compels remand for trial.

Without purporting to limit the scope of the trial, other factual issues include whether (1) O'Keeffe acquired title to Seaweed by obtaining releases from the legatees of Mrs. Weiner; (2) the paintings
were not stolen but sold, lent, consigned, or given by Stieglitz to Dr.
Frank or someone else without O'Keeffe's knowledge before he died;
and (3) there was any business or family relationship between Stieglitz
and Dr. Frank so that the original possession of the paintings by the
Frank family may have been under claim of right.

III

On the limited record before us, we cannot determine now who has
title to the paintings. That determination will depend on the evidence
adduced at trial. Nonetheless, we believe it may aid the trial court and
the parties to resolve questions of law that may become relevant at
trial.

Our decision begins with the principle that, generally speaking, if the
paintings were stolen, the thief acquired no title and could not transfer
good title to others regardless of their good faith and ignorance of the
theft. *   *   *   Proof of theft would advance O'Keeffe's right to pos-

session of the paintings absent other considerations such as expiration of the statute of limitations.

*   *   *

The trial court found that O'Keefe's cause of action accrued on the date of the alleged theft, March, 1946, and concluded that her action was barred. The Appellate Division found that an action might have accrued more than six years before the date of suit if possession by the defendant or his predecessors satisfied the elements of adverse possession. As indicated, the Appellate Division concluded that Snyder had not established those elements and that the O'Keefe action was not barred by the statute of limitations.

Since the alleged theft occurred in New York, a preliminary question is whether the statute of limitations of New York or New Jersey applies. The New York statute, N.Y.Civ.Prac. Law § 214 (McKinney), has been interpreted so that the statute of limitations on a cause of action for replevin does not begin to run until after refusal upon demand for the return of the goods. * * * Here, O'Keeffe demanded return of the paintings in February, 1976. If the New York statute applied, her action would have been commenced within the period of limitations.

* * * In the present case, none of the parties resides in New York and the paintings are located in New Jersey. On the facts before us, it would appear that the appropriate statute of limitations is the law of the forum, N.J.S.A. 2A:14–1. On remand, the trial court may reconsider this issue if the parties present other relevant facts.

IV

On the assumption that New Jersey law will apply, we shall consider significant questions raised about the interpretation of N.J.S.A. 2A:14–1. The purpose of a statute of limitations is to "stimulate to activity and punish negligence" and "promote repose by giving security and stability to human affairs". Wood v. Carpenter, 101 U.S. 135, 139, 25 L.Ed. 807, 808 (1879); Tevis v. Tevis, 79 N.J. 422, 430–431, 400 A.2d 1189 (1979); Fernandi v. Strully, 35 N.J. 434, 438, 173 A.2d 277 (1961). A statute of limitations achieves those purposes by barring a cause of action after the statutory period. In certain instances, this Court has ruled that the literal language of a statute of limitations should yield to other considerations. * * *

To avoid harsh results from the mechanical application of the statute, the courts have developed a concept known as the discovery rule. Lopez v. Swyer, 62 N.J. 267, 273–275, 300 A.2d 563 (1973); Prosser, The Law of Torts (4 ed. 1971), § 30 at 144–145; 51 Am.Jur.2d, Limitation of Actions, § 146 at 716. The discovery rule provides that, in an appropriate case, a cause of action will not accrue until the injured party discovers, or by exercise of reasonable diligence and intelligence should have discovered, facts which form the basis of a cause of action. * * * The rule is essentially a principle of equity, the purpose of which is to mitigate unjust results that otherwise might flow from strict adherence to a rule of law. * * *

This Court first announced the discovery rule in *Fernandi*, supra, 35 N.J. at 434, 173 A.2d 277. In *Fernandi*, a wing nut was left in a patient's abdomen following surgery and was not discovered for three years. Id. at 450–451, 173 A.2d 277. The majority held that fairness and justice mandated that the statute of limitations should not have commenced running until the plaintiff knew or had reason to know of the presence of the foreign object in her body. The discovery rule has since been extended to other areas of medical malpractice. See, e.g., *Lopez*, supra (alleged negligent radiation therapy following a radical mastectomy for breast cancer); Yerzy v. Levine, 108 N.J.Super. 222, 260 A.2d 533 (App.Div.), aff'd per curiam as modified, 57 N.J. 234, 271 A.2d 425 (1970) (negligent severance by surgeon of bile duct).

Increasing acceptance of the principle of the discovery rule has extended the doctrine to contexts unrelated to medical malpractice.
* * *

The statute of limitations before us, N.J.S.A. 2A:14–1, has been held subject to the discovery rule in an action for wrongful detention of shares of stock. * * *

Similarly, we conclude that the discovery rule applies to an action for replevin of a painting under N.J.S.A. 2A:14–1. O'Keeffe's cause of action accrued when she first knew, or reasonably should have known through the exercise of due diligence, of the cause of action, including the identity of the possessor of the paintings. See N. Ward, Adverse Possession of Loaned or Stolen Objects—Is Possession Still $^9/_{10}$ths of the Law?, published in Legal Problems of Museum Administration (ALI–ABA 1980) at 89–90.

* * *

In determining whether O'Keeffe is entitled to the benefit of the discovery rule, the trial court should consider, among others, the following issues: (1) whether O'Keeffe used due diligence to recover the paintings at the time of the alleged theft and thereafter; (2) whether at the time of the alleged theft there was an effective method, other than talking to her colleagues, for O'Keeffe to alert the art world; and (3) whether registering paintings with the Art Dealers Association of America, Inc. or any other organization would put a reasonably prudent purchaser of art on constructive notice that someone other than the possessor was the true owner.

V

The acquisition of title to real and personal property by adverse possession is based on the expiration of a statute of limitations. R. Brown, The Law of Personal Property (3d ed. 1975), § 4.1 at 33 (Brown). Adverse possession does not create title by prescription apart from the statute of limitations. Walsh, Title by Adverse Possession, 17 N.Y.U.L.Q.Rev. 44, 82 (1939) (Walsh); see Developments in the Law— Statutes of Limitations, 63 Harv.L.Rev. 1177 (1950) (Developments).

To establish title by adverse possession to chattels, the rule of law has been that the possession must be hostile, actual, visible, exclusive, and continuous. Redmond v. New Jersey Historical Society, 132 N.J. Eq. 464, 474, 28 A.2d 189 (E. & A.1942); 54 C.J.S. Limitations of Actions § 119 at 23. *Redmond* involved a portrait of Captain James Lawrence by Gilbert Stuart, which was bequeathed by its owner to her son with a provision that if he should die leaving no descendants, it should go to the New Jersey Historical Society. The owner died in 1887, when her son was 14, and her executors delivered the painting to the Historical Society. The painting remained in the possession of the Historical Society for over 50 years, until 1938, when the son died and his children, the legatees under his will, demanded its return. The Historical Society refused, and the legatees instituted a replevin action.

The Historical Society argued that the applicable statute of limitations, the predecessor of N.J.S.A. 2A:14–1, had run and that plaintiffs' action was barred. The Court of Errors and Appeals held that the doctrine of adverse possession applied to chattels as well as to real property, *Redmond*, supra, 132 N.J.Eq. at 473, 28 A.2d 189, and that the statute of limitations would not begin to run against the true owner until possession became adverse. Id. at 475, 28 A.2d 189. The Court found that the Historical Society had done nothing inconsistent with the theory that the painting was a "voluntary bailment or gratuitous loan" and had "utterly failed to prove that its possession of the portrait was 'adversary', 'hostile'." Id. at 474–475, 28 A.2d at 195. The Court found further that the Historical Society had not asserted ownership until 1938, when it refused to deliver the painting to plaintiff, and that the statute did not begin to run until that date. Consequently, the Court ordered the painting to be returned to plaintiffs.

The only other New Jersey case applying adverse possession to chattels is Joseph v. Lesnevich, 56 N.J.Super. 340, 153 A.2d 349 (App.Div. 1949). In *Lesnevich*, several negotiable bearer bonds were stolen from plaintiff in 1951. In October, 1951, Lesnevich received an envelope containing the bonds. On October 21, 1951, Lesnevich and his business partner pledged the bonds with a credit company. They failed to pay the loan secured by the bonds and requested the credit company to sell the bonds to pay the loan. On August 1, 1952, the president of the credit company purchased the bonds and sold them to his son. In 1958, within one day of the expiration of six years from the date of the purchase, the owner of the bonds sued the credit company and its president, among others, for conversion of the bonds. The Appellate Division found that the credit company and its president held the bonds "as openly and notoriously as the nature of the property would permit". *Lesnevich*, supra, 56 N.J.Super. at 355, 153 A.2d at 357. The pledge of the bonds with the credit company was considered to be open possession.

As *Lesnevich* demonstrates, there is an inherent problem with many kinds of personal property that will raise questions whether their possession has been open, visible, and notorious. In *Lesnevich*, the court strained to conclude that in holding bonds as collateral, a credit company satisfied the requirement of open, visible, and notorious possession.

Other problems with the requirement of visible, open, and notorious possession readily come to mind. For example, if jewelry is stolen from a municipality in one county in New Jersey, it is unlikely that the owner would learn that someone is openly wearing that jewelry in another county or even in the same municipality. Open and visible possession of personal property, such as jewelry, may not be sufficient to put the original owner on actual or constructive notice of the identity of the possessor.

The problem is even more acute with works of art. Like many kinds of personal property, works of art are readily moved and easily concealed. O'Keeffe argues that nothing short of public display should be sufficient to alert the true owner and start the statute running. Although there is merit in that contention from the perspective of the original owner, the effect is to impose a heavy burden on the purchasers of paintings who wish to enjoy the paintings in the privacy of their homes.

In the present case, the trial court and Appellate Division concluded that the paintings, which allegedly had been kept in the private residences of the Frank family, had not been held visibly, openly, and notoriously. Notwithstanding that conclusion, the trial court ruled that the statute of limitations began to run at the time of the theft and had expired before the commencement of suit. The Appellate Division determined it was bound by the rules in *Redmond* and reversed the trial court on the theory that the defenses of adverse possession and expiration of the statute of limitations were identical. Nonetheless, for different reasons, the majority and dissenting judges in the Appellate Division acknowledged deficiencies in identifying the statute of limitations with adverse possession. The majority stated that, as a practical matter, requiring compliance with adverse possession would preclude barring stale claims and acquiring title to personal property. *O'Keeffe*, supra, 170 N.J.Super. at 86, 405 A.2d 840. The dissenting judge feared that identifying the statutes of limitations with adverse possession would lead to a "handbook for larceny". Id. at 96, 405 A.2d 840. The divergent conclusions of the lower courts suggest that the doctrine of adverse possession no longer provides a fair and reasonable means of resolving this kind of dispute.

The problem is serious. According to an affidavit submitted in this matter by the president of the International Foundation for Art Research, there has been an "explosion in art thefts" and there is a "worldwide phenomenon of art theft which has reached epidemic proportions".

The limited record before us provides a brief glimpse into the arcane world of sales of art, where paintings worth vast sums of money sometimes are bought without inquiry about their provenance. There does not appear to be a reasonably available method for an owner of art to record the ownership or theft of paintings. Similarly, there are no reasonable means readily available to a purchaser to ascertain the provenance of a painting. It may be time for the art world to establish a means by which a good faith purchaser may reasonably obtain the provenance of a painting. An efficient registry of original works of art might better serve the interests of artists, owners of art, and bona fide purchasers than the law of adverse possession with all of its uncertainties. * * * Although we cannot mandate the initiation of a registration system, we can develop a rule for the commencement and running of the statute of limitations that is more responsive to the needs of the art world than the doctrine of adverse possession.

We are persuaded that the introduction of equitable considerations through the discovery rule provides a more satisfactory response than the doctrine of adverse possession. The discovery rule shifts the emphasis from the conduct of the possessor to the conduct of the owner. The focus of the inquiry will no longer be whether the possessor has met the tests of adverse possession, but whether the owner has acted with due diligence in pursuing his or her personal property.

For example, under the discovery rule, if an artist diligently seeks the recovery of a lost or stolen painting, but cannot find it or discover the identity of the possessor, the statute of limitations will not begin to run. The rule permits an artist who uses reasonable efforts to report, investigate, and recover a painting to preserve the rights of title and possession.

Properly interpreted, the discovery rule becomes a vehicle for transporting equitable considerations into the statute of limitations for replevin, N.J.S.A. 2A:14–1. In determining whether the discovery rule should apply, a court should identify, evaluate, and weigh the equitable claims of all parties. *Lopez*, supra, 62 N.J. at 274, 300 A.2d 563. If a chattel is concealed from the true owner, fairness compels tolling the statute during the period of concealment. * * * That conclusion is consistent with tolling the statute of limitations in a medical malpractice action where the physician is guilty of fraudulent concealment. * * *

It is consistent also with the law of replevin as it has developed apart from the discovery rule. In an action for replevin, the period of limitations ordinarily will run against the owner of lost or stolen property from the time of the wrongful taking, absent fraud or concealment. Where the chattel is fraudulently concealed, the general rule is that the statute is tolled. * * * Annotation, "When statute of limitations commences to run against action to recover, or for conversion of, property stolen or otherwise wrongfully taken," 136 A.L.R. 658, 661–665 (1942); See Dawson, Fraudulent Concealment and Statutes of Limitation, 31 Mich.L.Rev. 875 (1933); Annotation, "What constitutes concealment which will prevent running of statutes of limitations," 173 A.L.R. 576 (1948); Annotation, "When statute of limitations begins to run against action for conversion of property by theft," 79 A.L.R.3d 847, § 3 at 853 (1975); see also Dawson, Estoppel and Statutes of Limitation, 34 Mich.L.Rev. 1, 23–24 (1935).

A purchaser from a private party would be well-advised to inquire whether a work of art has been reported as lost or stolen. However, a bona fide purchaser who purchases in the ordinary course of business a painting entrusted to an art dealer should be able to acquire good title against the true owner. Under the U.C.C. entrusting possession of goods to a merchant who deals in that kind of goods gives the merchant the power to transfer all the rights of the entruster to a buyer in the ordinary course of business. N.J.S.A. 12A:2–403(2). In a transaction under that statute, a merchant may vest good title in the buyer as against the original owner. See *Anderson*, supra § 2–403:17 et seq. The interplay between the statute of limitations as modified by the discovery rule and the U.C.C. should encourage good faith purchases from legitimate art dealers and discourage trafficking in stolen art without frustrating an artist's ability to recover stolen art works.

The discovery rule will fulfill the purposes of a statute of limitations and accord greater protection to the innocent owner of personal property whose goods are lost or stolen. Accordingly, we overrule Redmond v. New Jersey Historical Society, supra, and Joseph v. Lesnevich, supra, to the extent that they hold that the doctrine of adverse possession applies to chattels.

By diligently pursuing their goods, owners may prevent the statute of limitations from running. The meaning of due diligence will vary with the facts of each case, including the nature and value of the personal property. For example, with respect to jewelry of moderate value, it may be sufficient if the owner reports the theft to the police. With respect to art work of greater value, it may be reasonable to expect an owner to do more. In practice, our ruling should contribute to more careful practices concerning the purchase of art.

The considerations are different with real estate, and there is no reason to disturb the application of the doctrine of adverse possession to real estate. Real estate is fixed and cannot be moved or concealed. The owner of real property knows or should know where his property is located and reasonably can be expected to be aware of open, notorious, visible, hostile, continuous acts of possession on it.

Our ruling not only changes the requirements for acquiring title to personal property after an alleged unlawful taking, but also shifts the burden of proof at trial. Under the doctrine of adverse possession, the burden is on the possessor to prove the elements of adverse possession. * * * Under the discovery rule, the burden is on the owner as the one seeking the benefit of the rule to establish facts that would justify deferring the beginning of the period of limitations. See *Lopez*, supra, 62 N.J. at 276, 300 A.2d 563.

VI

Read literally, the effect of the expiration of the statute of limitations under N.J.S.A. 2A:14–1 is to bar an action such as replevin. The statute does not speak of divesting the original owner of title. By its terms the statute cuts off the remedy, but not the right of title. Nonetheless, the effect of the expiration of the statute of limitations, albeit on the theory of adverse possession, has been not only to bar an action for possession, but also to vest title in the possessor. There is no reason to change that result although the discovery rule has replaced adverse possession. History, reason, and common sense support the conclusion that the expiration of the statute of limitations bars the remedy to recover possession and also vests title in the possessor.

Professor Brown explains the historical reason for construing the statute of limitations as barring the right of title as well as an action for possession:

> The metamorphosis of statutes simply limiting the time in which an action may be commenced into instrumentalities for the transfer of title may be explained perhaps by the historical doctrine of disseisin which, though more customarily applied to land, was probably originally controlling as to chattels also. By this doctrine the wrongful possessor as long as his possession continued, was treated as the owner and the dispossessed occupant considered merely to have a personal right to recapture his property if he could. [Brown, supra, § 4.1 at 34]   *   *   *.

Before the expiration of the statute, the possessor has both the chattel and the right to keep it except as against the true owner. The only imperfection in the possessor's right to retain the chattel is the original owner's right to repossess it. Once that imperfection is removed, the possessor should have good title for all purposes. Ames, The Disseisin of Chattels, 3 Harv.L.Rev. 313, 321 (1890) (Ames). As Dean Ames wrote: "An immortal right to bring an eternally prohibited action is a metaphysical subtlety that the present writer cannot pretend to understand." Id. at 319.

Recognizing a metaphysical notion of title in the owner would be of little benefit to him or her and would create potential problems for the possessor and third parties. The expiration of the six-year period of N.J.S.A. 2A:14–1 should vest title as effectively under the discovery rule as under the doctrine of adverse possession.

Our construction of N.J.S.A. 2A:14–1 is consistent with the construction of N.J.S.A. 2A:14–6, one of the statutes pertaining to title by adverse possession of real estate. That statute recites that one with right or title of entry into real estate shall make such entry within 20 years after the accrual of the right or be barred. It does not expressly state that the expiration of 20 years vests title in the possessor. Two other statutes pertaining to the adverse possession of real estate, N.J.S.A. 2A:14–30 and 31, expressly state that adverse possession for the statutory period shall vest title in the possessor. Notwithstanding the difference in wording between N.J.S.A. 2A:14–6 and N.J.S.A. 2A:14–30 and 31, the former statute has always been construed as vesting title in the adverse possessor at the end of the statutory period. See, e.g., Braue v. Fleck, 23 N.J. 1, 16, 127 A.2d 1 (1956).

To summarize, the operative fact that divests the original owner of title to either personal or real property is the expiration of the period of limitations. In the past, adverse possession has described the nature of the conduct that will vest title of a chattel at the end of the statutory period. Our adoption of the discovery rule does not change the conclusion that at the end of the statutory period title will vest in the possessor.

VII

We next consider the effect of transfers of a chattel from one possessor to another during the period of limitation under the discovery rule. Under the discovery rule, the statute of limitations on an action for replevin begins to run when the owner knows or reasonably should know of his cause of action and the identity of the possessor of the chattel. Subsequent transfers of the chattel are part of the continuous dispossession of the chattel from the original owner. The important point is not that there has been a substitution of possessors, but that there has been a continuous dispossession of the former owner.

Professor Ballantine explains:

Where the same claim of title has been consistently asserted for the statutory period by persons in privity with each other, there is the same reason to quiet and establish the title as where one person has held. The same flag has been kept flying for the whole period. It is the same ouster and disseisin. If the statute runs, it quiets a title which has been consistently asserted and exercised as against the true owner, and the possession of the prior holder justly enures to the benefit of the last. [H. Ballantine, Title by Adverse Possession, 32 Harv.L.Rev. 135, 158 (1919)]

The same principle appears in the Restatement (Second) of Torts:

In some cases, the statute of limitations begins to run before the defendant took possession as when a previous taker converted the chattel and later transferred possession to the defendant. [Restatement (Second) of Torts 2d § 899 at 442 (1977)]

For the purpose of evaluating the due diligence of an owner, the dispossession of his chattel is a continuum not susceptible to separation into distinct acts. Nonetheless, subsequent transfers of the chattel may affect the degree of difficulty encountered by a diligent owner seeking to recover his goods. To that extent, subsequent transfers and their potential for frustrating diligence are relevant in applying the discovery rule. An owner who diligently seeks his chattel should be entitled to the benefit of the discovery rule although it may have passed through many hands. Conversely an owner who sleeps on his rights may be denied the benefit of the discovery rule although the chattel may have been possessed by only one person.

We reject the alternative of treating subsequent transfers of a chattel as separate acts of conversion that would start the statute of limitations running anew. At common law, apart from the statute of limitations, a subsequent transfer of a converted chattel was considered to be a separate act of conversion. In his dissent, Justice Handler seeks to extend the rule so that it would apply even if the period of limitations had expired before the subsequent transfer. Nonetheless, the dissent does not cite any authority that supports the position that the statute of limitations should run anew on an act of conversion already barred by the statute of limitations. Adoption of that alternative would tend to undermine the purpose of the statute in quieting titles and protecting against stale claims. Brown, supra, § 4.3 at 38.

The majority and better view is to permit tacking, the accumulation of consecutive periods of possession by parties in privity with each other. * * *

As explained by Professor Walsh:

The doctrine of tacking applies as in corresponding cases of successive adverse possessions of land where privity exists between such possessors. Uncertainty is created by cases which hold that each successive purchaser is subject to a new cause of action against which the statute begins to run from that time, in this way indefinitely extending the time when the title will be quieted by operation of the statute. It should be entirely clear that the purposes of statutes of limitation are the same whether they relate to land or chattels, and therefore the same reasons exist for tacking successive possessions as the prevailing cases hold. Nevertheless, under the cases, new actions in conversion arise against successive purchases of the converted property, and there is strong reason back of the argument that the statute runs anew against each succeeding cause of action. No doubt the prevailing rule recognizing privity in these cases may be based upon the argument that the possessory title is transferred on each successive sale of the converted chattel, subject to the owner's action to recover the property, and the action of replevin which is his proprietory action, continues in effect against succeeding possessors so that the statute bars the action after the successive possessions amount to the statutory period. [Walsh, supra, at 83–84]

In New Jersey tacking is firmly embedded in the law of real property. O'Brien v. Bilow, 121 N.J.L. 576, 578–579, 3 A.2d 641 (E. & A. 1938). The rule has been applied also to personal property. *Lesnevich*, supra, 56 N.J.Super. at 357, 153 A.2d 349. In *Lesnevich*, the pledge of the bonds with the credit company and the subsequent purchase by the company's president were separate acts of conversion. The pledge was beyond the period of the statute of limitations and the purchase was within the period. Id. at 353. The Appellate Division permitted tacking of the two periods, with the result that the second act of conversion did not alter the running of the period. Id. at 357, 153 A.2d 349.

The dissent by our colleague Justice Handler seeks to distinguish *Lesnevich* because it involved negotiable instruments. However, the law of negotiable instruments was irrelevant to the decision since the court held the credit company and its president were not holders in due course. *Lesnevich*, supra, 56 N.J.Super. at 352, 153 A.2d 349.

Treating subsequent transfers as separate acts of conversion could lead to absurd results. As explained by Dean Ames:

The decisions in the case of chattels are few. As a matter of principle, it is submitted this rule of tacking is as applicable to chattels as to land. A denial of the right to tack would, furthermore, lead to this result. If a converter were to sell the chattel, five years after its conversion, to one ignorant of the seller's tort, the disposed owner's right to recover the chattel from the purchaser would continue five years longer than his right to recover from the converter would have lasted if there had been no sale. In other words, an innocent purchaser from a wrong-doer would be in a worse position than the wrong-doer himself,—a conclusion as shocking in point of justice as it would be anomalous in law. [Ames, supra at 323, footnotes omitted]

It is more sensible to recognize that on expiration of the period of limitations, title passes from the former owner by operation of the statute. Needless uncertainty would result from starting the statute running anew merely because of a subsequent transfer. 3 American Law of Property, § 15.16 at 837. It is not necessary to strain equitable principles, as suggested by the dissent, to arrive at a just and reasonable determination of the rights of the parties. The discovery rule permits an equitable accommodation of the rights of the parties without establishing a rule of law fraught with uncertainty.

* * *

[The dissenting opinions of Sullivan and Handler, JJ., are omitted. Eds.]

Notes

1. The court's statement that "a bona fide purchaser who purchases in the ordinary course of business a painting entrusted to an art dealer should be able to acquire good title against the true owner" must be read together with the following sentence in the opinion: "Under the U.C.C. entrusting possession of goods to a merchant who deals in that kind of goods gives the merchant power to transfer all the rights of the entruster to a buyer in the ordinary course of business." Thus "a bona fide purchaser" in "the ordinary course of business" acquires "good title against the true owner" *only if the true owner has entrusted the goods to the merchant.*

2. The dissenting opinion of Handler, J., asserts that the "discovery rule" makes "it relatively more easy for the receiver or possessor of an artwork with a 'checkered background' to gain security and title than for the artist or true owner to reacquire it," because—although the owner can prevent the statute of limitations from running against him by showing "due diligence" in making efforts to find and retrieve the stolen artwork—"[n]o similar duty of diligence or vigilance is placed upon the subsequent receiver or possessor, who, innocent or not, has actually trafficked in stolen art." Sullivan, J., also argues that the majority is incorrect in taking "the view that a subsequent transfer of stolen property does not, in effect, constitute a separate conversionary act" which will start the statute of limitations running anew against the transferee, no matter how long a time has elapsed since the first conversionary act. Thus Sullivan, J., rejects the majority's holding that the "tacking" doctrine is generally applicable in replevin actions, although he concedes that it does apply to negotiable instruments, "a long-established exception to the general rule."

3. Compare the principal case with Kunstsammlungen zu Weimar v. Elicofon, 678 F.2d 1150 (2d Cir.1982), holding (*inter alia*) that under New York law an innocent purchaser of stolen goods becomes a wrongdoer only after refusing the owner's demand for their return, and hence that a cause of action for return of stolen Duerer paintings held by an innocent purchaser did not

accrue until the purchaser refused to comply with the owner's demand for return of the paintings. See 678 F.2d at 1160–1164. The result was that the owner was able to recover the stolen paintings despite the fact that Elicofon, the defendant, proved "his uninterrupted possession of the Duerer paintings from the time of his good faith purchase of them in 1946 from an American serviceman in Brooklyn to his discovery in 1966 of the identity of the paintings." The owner made no demand until 1966, after learning of the location of the paintings.

4. See Comment, The Recovery of Lost Art: Of Paintings, Statues, and Statutes of Limitations, 27 U.C.L.A.L.Rev. 1122 (1980).

DISABILITY PROVISIONS IN STATUTES OF LIMITATIONS

The American statutes of limitations generally include provisions extending the time within which actions to recover possession may be brought if the owner (or other person entitled to possession) is under a "disability."

The Michigan statute of limitations partly set out above (Mich.Comp. Laws Ann. § 600.5801) also includes the following provision (id. § 600.5851):

(1) If the person first entitled to make an entry or bring an action is under 18 years of age, insane or imprisoned at the time his claim accrues, he or those claiming under him shall have 1 year after his disability is removed through death or otherwise to make the entry or bring the action although the period of limitations has run.   *   *   *

(2) The term insane as employed in this chapter means a condition of mental derangement such as to prevent the sufferer from comprehending rights he is otherwise bound to know and is not dependent on whether or not the person has been judicially declared to be insane.

(3) To be deemed a disability, the infancy, insanity or imprisonment must exist at the time the claim accrues. If it comes into existence after the claim has accrued it shall not be recognized under this section for the purpose of modifying the period of limitations.

(4) Successive disabilities shall not be tacked. That is, only those disabilities which exist at the time the claim first accrues and which disable the person to whom the claim first accrues shall be recognized under this section for the purpose of modifying the period of limitations.

(5) All of the disabilities of infancy, insanity and imprisonment which disable the person to whom the claim first accrues at the time the claim first accrues shall be recognized. That is, the year of grace provided in this section shall be counted from the termination of the last disability to the person to whom the claim originally accrued which has continued from the time the claim accrued, whether this disability terminates because of the death of the person disabled or for some other reason.

(6) With respect to a claim accruing before the effective date of Act No. 79 of the Public Acts of 1971, being sections 722.51 to 722.55 of the Compiled Laws of 1948, disability of infancy shall be considered removed as of the effective date of Act No. 79 as to persons who were at least 18 years of age but less than 21 years of age on January 1, 1972 and shall be considered removed as of the eighteenth birthday of a person who was under 18 years of age on January 1, 1972.

The New York statute of limitations partly set out above (Real Property Actions and Proceedings Law §§ 511 et seq., and Civil Practice Law and Rules § 212(a)) also includes the following section (Civil Practice Law and Rules § 208):

> If a person entitled to commence an action is under a disability because of infancy or insanity at the time the cause of action accrues, and the time otherwise limited for commencing the action is three years or more and expires no later than three years after the disability ceases, or the person under the disability dies, the time within which the action must be commenced shall be extended to three years after the disability ceases or the person under disability dies, whichever event first occurs; * * * The time within which the action must be commenced shall not be extended by this provision beyond ten years after the cause of action accrued except * * * where the person was under a disability due to infancy. * * *

New Jersey seems to be unique in having two different statutory limitation periods for actions to recover possession of land. N.J.Stat. Ann. §§ 2A:14–6 and 2A:14–7 (1952) provide that actions must be brought or rights of entry asserted within 20 years. N.J.Stat.Ann. §§ 2A:14–30 and 2A:14–31 (1952) provide that possession for 30 years "excepting woodlands or uncultivated lands" shall bar all claims or actions brought by any person. When a litigant relies on the 20-year limitation period, he is subject to N.J.Stat.Ann. § 2A:14–21, which provides as follows:

> If any person entitled to any of the actions or proceedings specified in sections 2A:14–1 to 2A:14–8 or to a right or title of entry under section 2A:14–6 of this title is or shall be, at the time of any such cause of action or right or title accruing, under the age of 21 years, or insane, such person may commence such action or make such entry, within such time as limited by said sections, after his coming to or being of full age or of sane mind.

But when a litigant relies on the 30-year limitation period, he is subject to N.J.Stat.Ann. § 2A:14–32, which provides as follows:

> If any person having a right or title to real estate shall, at the time such right or title first accrued or descended, be either not of sound mind or under the age of 21 years, or without the United States, he, and his heirs, may, notwithstanding the fact that the periods of time mentioned in sections 2A:14–30 and 2A:14–31 of this title have expired, bring his or their action to enforce his or their right or title, if such action shall be commenced within 5 years after his disability is removed or he comes within the United States, but not thereafter.

Problems

In what year would A's title by adverse possession ripen under each of the above statutes in the following cases:

1. In 1950 A goes into adverse possession of land owned by O, who has been adjudged mentally incompetent. In 1969 O is adjudged mentally competent.

2. In 1950 A goes into adverse possession of land owned by O, who is an adult. In 1965 O dies devising the land to B, who is 15 years old.

3. In 1950 A goes into adverse possession of land owned by O, who is 16 years of age. In 1964 O dies, and title to the land passes by intestacy to his brother, B, who is 12 years of age.

4. In 1950 A goes into adverse possession of land owned by O, who is 18 years of age. O attains his majority in 1953.

SECTION 3. THE DUTIES OF POSSESSORS: A LOOK AT BAILMENT

PEET v. ROTH HOTEL CO.

Supreme Court of Minnesota, 1934.
191 Minn. 151, 253 N.W. 546.

Action in the district court for Ramsey county to recover judgment against defendant for the value of a ring belonging to plaintiff, valued at $2,500, which became lost after plaintiff had left it with defendant's cashier to be delivered to a guest in its hotel. The case was tried before Richard A. Walsh, Judge, and a jury. Plaintiff recovered a verdict of $2,140.66. Defendant appealed from an order denying its alternative motion for judgment or a new trial. Affirmed.

STONE, J. After an adverse verdict, defendant moved in the alternative for judgment notwithstanding or a new trial. That motion denied, defendant appeals.

The record is the story of a ring. Defendant operates the St. Paul Hotel in St. Paul. Mr. Ferdinand Hotz is a manufacturing jeweler. For 20 years or more he has visited St. Paul periodically on business, making his local headquarters at the St. Paul Hotel. He has long been one of its regular patrons, personally known to the management. Plaintiff's engagement ring, a platinum piece set with a large cabochon sapphire surrounded by diamonds, was made to order by Mr. Hotz. One of its small diamonds lost, plaintiff had arranged with him to have it replaced and for that purpose was to leave it for him at the St. Paul Hotel. November 17, 1931, he was a guest there on one of his seasonal visits. About four p.m. of that day plaintiff went to the cashier's desk of the hotel, wearing the ring. The cashier on duty was a Miss Edwards. At this point plaintiff may as well tell her own story, for upon it is based the jury's verdict. She thus testified:

"I had it [the ring] on my finger and took if off my finger. The cashier—I told the cashier that it was for Mr. Ferdinand Hotz. She took out an envelope and wrote 'Ferdinand Hotz.' I remember spelling it to her, and then I left. * * * I handed the ring to the cashier, and she wrote on the envelope. * * * The only instructions I remember are telling her that it was for Mr. Ferdinand Hotz, who was stopping at the hotel."

Plaintiff's best recollection is that Miss Edwards told her that Mr. Hotz was registered but was not in at the moment. Miss Edwards frankly admitted, as a witness, that the ring had been delivered to her. It is conceded that it was immediately lost, doubtless stolen, probably by an outsider. Miss Edwards herself is beyond suspicion. But the ring, where she placed it upon its delivery to her by plaintiff, was on her desk or counter and within easy reach of anyone standing or passing just outside her cashier's window.

The loss was not then reported either to plaintiff or Mr. Hotz. About a month later he was again in St. Paul, and then plaintiff was advised for the first time that her ring had never reached him. Upon inquiry at the hotel office, it was learned that it had been lost. The purpose of this action is to recover from defendant, as bailee of the ring, its reasonable value, fixed by the jury at $2,140.66. The reasonableness of that figure is not questioned.

1. The jury took the case under a charge that there was a bailment as a matter of law. Error is assigned upon the supposition that there was at least a question of fact whether the evidence showed the mutual assent prerequisite to the contract of bailment which is the sine qua non of plaintiff's case. The supporting argument is put upon the cases holding that where the presence or identity of the article claimed to have been bailed is concealed from the bailee he has not assented to assume that position with its attendant obligation, and so there is no bailment. Samples v. Geary, Mo.App., 292 S.W. 1066 (fur piece concealed in coat checked in parcel room); U.S. v. Atlantic Coast Line R. Co., 206 F. 190 (cut diamonds in mail package with nothing to indicate nature of contents); Riggs v. Bank of Camas Prairie, 34 Idaho 176, 200 P. 118, 18 A.L.R. 83 (bailee of locked box supposed to contain only "papers and other valuables" not liable for money therein of which it had no knowledge).

The claim here is not that plaintiff perpetrated fraud upon defendant but that she failed to divulge the unusual value of her ring when she left it with Miss Edwards. The latter testified that at the moment she did not realize its value. Taking both facts and their implications as favorably as we may for defendant, the stubborn truth remains that plaintiff delivered and defendant accepted the ring with its identity and at least its outward character perfectly obvious.

The mutual assent necessary to a contract may be expressed as well by conduct as by words; or it may be manifested by both. Restatement, Contracts, § 21. The latter is the case here. The expression of mutual assent is found in what passed between plaintiff and Miss Edwards. The former delivered and the latter accepted the ring to be delivered to Mr. Hotz. Below that irreducible minimum the case cannot be lowered. No decision has been cited and probably none can be found where the bailee of an article of jewelry, undeceived as to its identity, was relieved of liability because of its own erroneous underestimate of its value.

If there was mistake with legal effect worth while to defendant, it must have been of such character as to show no mutual assent and so no contract. There was no such error here. Identity of the property and all its attributes, except only its value, were as well known to defendant as to plaintiff. The case is identical in principle with Wood v. Boynton, 64 Wis. 265, 25 N.W. 42, 54 Am.R. 610. There the plaintiff had sold to defendant, for one dollar, a stone which she supposed was at best a topaz. It turned out to be an uncut diamond worth $700. Neither its true character nor value were known to either buyer or seller at the time of the sale. There being neither fraud nor mistake as to identity, the mutual mistake as to value was held no obstacle to completion of the contract. Plaintiff was denied recovery. * * *

2. The jury was instructed also that defendant was a "non-gratuitous" bailee. By that it is doubtless intended to say that the bailment was "reciprocally beneficial to both parties." 1 Dunnell, Minn.Dig., 2 Ed. & Supp., § 782. Clearly, that was a correct interpretation of the proof. The ring was accepted in the ordinary course of business by defendant in rendering a usual service for a guest, and so, plainly, it was for defendant's advantage, enough so, at least, to make the bailment as matter of law one for the benefit of both bailor and bailee.

3. The jury was charged also that the bailment, being for the reciprocal benefit of the parties, defendant as bailee was under duty of exercising, in respect to the subject matter, ordinary care, that is, the degree of care which an ordinarily prudent man would have exercised in the same or similar circumstances. The instruction was correct. 1 Dunnell, Minn.Dig., 2 Ed. & Supp., § 732. The former distinction between bailments for the sole benefit of the bailor; those for the mutual benefit of both bailor and bailee; and those for the sole benefit of the latter, in respect to the degree of care required of the bailee in order to protect him from liability for negligence, has long since been pretty much discarded here as elsewhere. "It is evident that the so-called distinctions between slight, ordinary and gross negligence over which courts have perhaps somewhat quibbled for a hundred years, can furnish no assistance." Elon College v. Elon Banking & Trust Co., 182 N.C. 298, 303, 109 S.E. 6, 17 A.L.R. 1205.

Defendant's liability, if any, is for negligence. In that field generally the legal norm is a care commensurate to the hazard, i.e., the amount and kind of care that would be exercised by an ordinarily prudent person in the same or similar circumstances. The character and amount of risk go far, either to decrease or increase the degree of care required. The value of the property, its attractiveness to light-fingered gentry, and the ease or difficulty of its theft have much to say with triers of fact in determining whether there has been exercised a degree of care commensurate to the risk, whether the bailment be gratuitous or otherwise. However unsatisfactory it may be, until legal acumen has developed and formulated a more satisfactory criterion, that of ordinary care should be followed in every case without regard to former distinctions between slight, ordinary, and great care. Even the courts which adhere to the former distinctions will be found in most cases to be demanding no other degree of care than one commensurate to the risk and other relevant circumstances; e.g., in Ridenour v. Woodward, 132 Tenn. 620, 179 S.W. 148, 149, 4 A.L.R. 1192, it was held that a gratuitous bailee was answerable only for his gross negligence or bad faith. But, as the court proceeded to say, the care to be taken was [132 Tenn. 623, 179 S.W. 149] "to be measured however, with reference to the nature of the thing placed in his keeping." The defendant was relieved of liability because it was held as matter of law that he had [132 Tenn. 628, 179 S.W. 150] "acted with a fairly commensurate discretion" in handling the bailed property.   See annotation of that case, "Propriety of distinction between degrees of negligence."   4 A.L.R. 1201.

As long ago as 1887, this court, speaking through Mr. Chief Justice Gilfillan, observed that "it is not easy, nor generally profitable, to define or point out the somewhat hazy distinction between these several degrees of diligence."   Cannon River Mfg'rs Assn. v. First Nat. Bank, 37 Minn. 394, 398, 34 N.W. 741, 742.   "The doctrine that there are three degrees of negligence—slight, ordinary, and gross—does not prevail in this state."   4 Dunnell, Minn.Dig., 2 Ed., § 6971.

4.   The rule of our decision law (Hoel v. Flour City Fuel & Transfer Co., 144 Minn. 280, 175 N.W. 300, following Rustad v. G.N. Ry. Co., 122 Minn. 453, 142 N.W. 727) puts upon the bailee the burden of proving that the loss did not result from his negligence.   This burden, in the language of the late Mr. Justice Dibell [144 Minn. 281, 175 N.W. 300], is "not merely the burden of going forward with proofs, nor a shifting burden, but a burden of establishing before the jury that its negligence did not cause the loss."   That proposition we adopted as "the practical working rule."   We are not disposed to depart from it.

5.   With the foregoing statement concerning the burden of proof, we go to an assignment of error questioning an instruction that "it makes no difference what care the defendant may have taken of its own property, that being its own concern, and the care it may give to its own property is of no importance in the determination of this case."   That instruction was given in connection with and in explanation of the rule concerning the due or ordinary care required of defendant.

Because the care required was that of the ordinary person in the same or similar circumstances, it is but obvious that, whatever defendant's care of its own property may have been, it would not alter the standard of care applicable to plaintiff's property in its hands as bailee. It may have been too much to say that defendant's care of its own property "is of no importance."   There may be cases where the care of his own property exercised by a defendant bailee would have some relevancy as evidence.   But if in that respect the charge went a bit too far, and was pro tanto error, no prejudice could have resulted to defendant, for no issue was made as to the quantum of care exercised by it, concerning its own property, if any, of a kind and value comparable to those of plaintiff's "cabochon sapphire."   *   *   *

Order affirmed.

Notes and Questions

1.   In the principal case, the court assumed that "bailment" is a matter of "contract" requiring "mutual assent" which may be "expressed as well by conduct as by words."   Compare the following statements from other cases:

(a) "A bailment is a delivery of personal property by one person to another in trust for a specific purpose, with an express or implied contract that the property will be returned or accounted for when the specific purpose has been accomplished or when the bailor reclaims the property.   *   *   *   No agreement is necessary; a bailment may be created by operation of law. Thus, where a person comes into lawful possession of the personal property of another, even though there is no formal agreement between the property's owner and its possessor, the possessor will become a constructive bailee when justice so requires." Christenson v. Hoover, 643 P.2d 525, 528–529 (Colo.1982).

(b) "It is the element of lawful possession, however created, and duty to account for the thing as the property of another that creates the bailment, regardless of whether or not such possession is based on contract in the ordinary sense." K–B Corp. v. Gallagher, 218 Va. 381, 384, 237 S.E.2d 183, 185 (1977).

Does it really matter whether courts find "an implied contract that the property will be returned or accounted for when the specific purpose [of the bailment] has been accomplished or when the bailor reclaims the property," or simply hold that the law imposes on the bailee a duty to return or account for the subject matter of the bailment? As the principal case indicates, a bailee is also subject to a duty to exercise care to prevent loss of or damage to the subject matter of the bailment. Does it matter whether this duty is based on an "implied contract" or is simply imposed by law?

2. In cases "where the presence or identity of the article claimed to have been bailed is concealed from the bailee," would you prefer to say, as did the court in the *Peet* case, that the bailee "has not assented to assume that position with its attendant obligation, and so there is no bailment," or simply to say that, under such circumstances, the law does not impose a duty of care with respect to an article the presence or identity of which is concealed from the bailee? In most such cases, the article in question is contained within another article the presence and identity of which is known to the bailee. Sometimes the "unknown" contents are of a type that might be expected to be contained in the other article—e.g., the "fur piece concealed in" the coat in Samples v. Geary, 292 S.W. 1066 (Mo.App.1927). In other cases, the contrary is true—e.g., the "cut diamonds" in the mail package "with nothing to indicate the nature of" the contents in United States v. Atlantic Coast Line Railroad Co., 206 F. 190 (E.D.N.C.1913). Should the liability or nonliability of the bailee turn on this factual difference?

3. The concept of "bailment" is very broad, and it is of considerable significance in the modern business world. Thus, e.g., common carriers, private carriers, warehouses, are bailees of the goods they carry or store. On the other hand, companies that lease automobiles, excavating and construction equipment, or furniture are bailors. The rights of such bailees and bailors are, of course, usually regulated by express written contracts. But bailments may also arise from very informal transactions, such as the loaning of a book by one person to another. Bailments may be classified in several ways. For example, bailments may be classified as either "gratuitous" or "compensated" ("for hire"); or as "for the sole benefit of the bailee," "for the sole benefit of the bailor," or "for mutual benefit." The first classification can be equated with the second if "gratuitous" is treated as identical with "for the sole benefit of the bailor" and "for hire" is considered to include both "for the sole benefit of the bailee" and "mutual benefit."

4. The analytical classifications set out in the preceding Note were useful primarily as a basis, in nineteenth century Anglo-American law, for the rule that when the bailment was for the sole benefit of the bailor, the bailee was liable for loss or damage only if it was the result of the bailee's "gross negligence"; that when the bailment was for mutual benefit, the bailee was liable

for loss or damage caused by his "ordinary negligence"; and that when the bailment was for the sole benefit of the bailee, he was liable for loss or damage caused even by his "slight negligence." The Minnesota court, as indicated in the *Peet* case, abandoned this rule as early as 1887 and adopted the rule that all bailees have a duty to exercise "care commensurate to the hazard"—i.e., that the standard of care is always the same—although the actual degree of care will vary with the circumstances—whether the bailment is for mutual benefit or for the sole benefit of one party or the other. But a majority of the courts seems to adhere to the old doctrine that there are three different standards of care (and three different degrees of negligence) depending on which type of bailment is found to have been created. For a recent case holding that a "gratuitous bailee"—i.e., for the sole benefit of the bailor—is not liable for the loss of the bailed article unless proved guilty of "gross negligence," see Morris v. Hamilton, 302 S.E.2d 51 (Va.1983). But see Christensen v. Hoover, 643 P.2d 525 (Colo.1982), holding that "even a gratuitous bailee must exercise reasonable care to protect the bailor's property, i.e., that which a person of common prudence would use under the circumstances," and hence that it was error for the lower court to hold a gratuitous bailee only for "malicious, willful, or grossly negligent" conduct.

5. Finders are often referred to as "gratuitous bailees," "quasi-bailees," or "constructive bailees." The finder seems, generally, to be treated as a gratuitous bailee with respect to the care he must exercise while in possession of lost chattels. See R. Brown, Personal Property § 3.5 (3d ed. Raushenbush 1975). Where the duty of a gratuitous bailee is only to exercise "slight care," the finder's duty will also be limited to "slight care," and he will be liable for loss or damage only if it is caused by his "gross negligence."

6. Mention is sometimes made of an "involuntary bailee," although this certainly sounds like a contradiction in terms. Consider the landowner in South Staffordshire Water Co. v. Sharman, ante, which was held to have a "prior possession" of the rings later found by Sharman. Was the landowner a bailee of the rings? Surely no duty should be imposed on one who is unaware of the presence of a chattel on his land, and there is apparently no case imposing any duty of care on such a person even after he learned of the presence of such a chattel. Compare the situation of such a person with that of the defendant in Cowen v. Pressprich, 202 App.Div. 796, 194 N.Y.S. 926 (1922). In the *Cowen* case, B ordered a negotiable bond of the X Company from A. By mistake A sent a negotiable bond of the Y Company. A's messenger boy dropped the bond through the door slot in B's office. Immediately afterward a member of B's firm came out, called to a boy in the office whom he assumed to be A's messenger, and told him to take the bond back to A's office and correct the error. The boy was not A's messenger and the bond disappeared. The trial court held that B was strictly liable for the value of the bond as an involuntary bailee who was guilty of the tort of conversion. On appeal, the Appellate Division reversed and dismissed A's complaint, relying on the dissenting opinion of Lehman, J., in the trial court. Lehman had argued that there was no such exercise of dominion on B's part as to make applicable the rule that a converter is strictly liable, and pointed out that "the complaint does not allege any negligence on the part of the defendants."

7. The presumptions, if any, arising when the bailor simply proves the creation of a bailment and the failure of the bailee to redeliver the goods when a proper demand is made, and the related issue of burden of proof, are discussed in the Notes following the next principal case.

JOSEPH H. REINFELD, INC. v. GRISWOLD & BATEMAN

Superior Court of New Jersey, Law Division, 1983.
189 N.J.Super. 141, 458 A.2d 1341.

GRIFFIN, J.S.C. While the product involved in this case is not unique in New Jersey, the legal issue is.

Three hundred and thirty-seven cases of Chivas Regal Scotch Whiskey were stored for plaintiff Reinfeld by defendant Griswold and Bateman in its bonded warehouse. A proper warehouse receipt was issued. After complying with governmental tax and duty requirements, Reinfeld sent its truck to pick up the merchandise. Forty cases were missing. Plaintiff sued in both negligence and conversion for the wholesale market value of the whiskey, $6,417.60. Plaintiff presented evidence of his delivery, demand and the subsequent failure by defendant to return the bailed goods. Plaintiff then claimed that the burden of producing evidence shifted to defendant to explain the disappearance. Defendant claimed that plaintiff's prima facie case had only raised the presumption of negligence. Defendant admitted liability for negligence and asserted a limit by contract to 250 times the monthly storage rate, a total of $1,925.

N.J.S.A. 12A:7-204(2) permits a warehouseman to limit his liability for negligent "loss or damage" to the bailed goods if stated in the storage agreement. The statute reads: "No such limitation is effective with respect to the warehouseman's liability for *conversion to his own use*." (Emphasis supplied). Since plaintiff had sued in both negligence and conversion, plaintiff argued that without an explanation of the disappearance of the goods by defendant, plaintiff's prima facie case raised a presumption of both negligence and conversion. Therefore, the contractual limitation on liability would not apply.

As hereinafter set forth, an inadvertent misdelivery is a conversion. Can a bailee simply refuse to explain a disappearance and then have his liability limited by N.J.S.A. 12A:7-204? If so, what will prevent a dishonest warehouseman from stealing the goods entrusted to his care and then saying, "I don't know what happened but I admit my negligence." He would then pay only the amount limited by contract and pocket the difference.

A bailee who accepts responsibility for goods should have the burden of producing evidence as to the fate of those goods. To hold otherwise would place an impossible burden on a plaintiff. How is a plaintiff to present sufficient evidence of conversion when knowledge of the fate of the goods is available only to defendant? This court holds that plaintiff has presented a prima facie case of conversion and the burden of going forward or producing evidence as to what happened to the whiskey shifts to defendant.

This position is supported by language in Mueller v. Technical Devices Corp., 8 N.J. 201, 207, 84 A.2d 620 (1951): "A demand and refusal do not of themselves amount to a conversion, but are evidence from which a jury may find that a conversion had been committed."

This issue was addressed by the New York Court of Appeals in I.C.C. Metals, Inc. v. Municipal Warehouse Co., 431 N.Y.S.2d 372, 50 N.Y.2d 657, 409 N.E.2d 849 (1980).

In I.C.C. plaintiff delivered metal to be stored by defendant. The storage contract contained a limitation on liability. Upon demand, defendant informed plaintiff that the metal had been stolen "through no fault of defendants," 431 N.Y.S.2d at 375, 50 N.Y.2d at 662, 409 N.E.2d at 852, so liability was limited by the contract terms. The court held that unless a bailee can "make a sufficient showing in support of its suggested explanation of the loss," the bailee is liable for conversion and the contractual limitation does not apply. 431 N.Y.S.2d at 376–77, 50 N.Y.2d at 665, 409 N.E.2d at 853–54. The explanation proffered by the warehouse in such a case must be supported by sufficient evidence and cannot be merely the product of speculation and conjecture. "It is not enough to show that defendant bailee used reasonable care in its system of custody if mysterious disappearance is the only 'explanation' given." Footnote 3, 431 N.Y.S.2d at 377, 50 N.Y.2d at 665, 409 N.E.2d at 854. (citation omitted). This ruling by the court was predicated on "practical necessity" since it is the bailee who is in the best position to explain the loss of the property. 431 N.Y.S.2d at 377, 50 N.Y.2d at 665, 409 N.E.2d at 854.

Thus, the burden of producing evidence is shifted to defendant, but the burden of proof that the bailee is at fault or that conversion or negligence exist remains on the bailor. 431 N.Y.S.2d at 379, 50 N.Y.2d at 668, 409 N.E.2d at 856. As the New York court stated, the holding of I.C.C. does not indicate "that proof of negligence will support a recovery in conversion." Footnote 4, 431 N.Y.S.2d at 377, 50 N.Y.2d at 665, 409 N.E.2d at 854. Rather, once the bailee has produced evidence, plaintiff must then prove "all the traditional elements of conversion." Id.

This position finds support in other jurisdictions as well. In McCallister v. Cord Moving & Storage Co., 301 S.W.2d 852, 855 (Mo.App.Div. 1957), the court held that delivery by the bailee of 25 television sets to a third party constituted conversion. The court stated that the burden of proof was on the bailor to show title and right to possession. Then the burden shifted to the bailee to justify or excuse his failure to return the bailed goods. When the bailee failed to meet this burden, he was held for conversion.

The Arkansas Supreme Court in American Express Field Warehousing Corp. v. First National Bank, 233 Ark. 666, 346 S.W.2d 518, 521–522 (1961), stated:

When the bailor sues the bailee for *conversion* of the bailment, the bailor has the duty of proving (a) that the bailment was delivered to the bailee, (b) that due and seasonable demand was made on the bailee for the return of the bailment and (c) that the bailee could not or would not return the bailment. When the bailor proves these three points, the law says that the bailee had converted the bailment unless the bailee goes forward with the proof and shows either (1) that the bailment was destroyed by fire without the negligence of the bailee, or (2) that the bailment was lost or stolen from the bailee without the negligence of the bailee.

The Supreme Court of California held that the bailor presents a prima facie case of conversion when he proves a bailment and subsequent refusal to return the bailed goods on demand. The burden of proving the fate of the goods and that the bailee had exercised due care is on the bailee. George v. Bekins Van & Storage, 33 Cal.2d 834, 205 P.2d 1037 (1949). In that case the defendant proved that the goods were destroyed by fire and the court found the bailee was negligent, but did not convert. Accord, Allen v. Line, 72 S.D. 392, 34 N.W.2d 835 (S.D.Sup.Ct.1948); 26 A.L.R., Bailment-Theft, § 223 at 243. See, also, 8 Am.Jur.2d, § 328 at 1065–1066.

* * *

Thus, this court holds that to earn the protection of N.J.S.A. 12A:7–204(2), defendant must meet his burden of explaining the disappearance or be held liable for conversion. If defendant meets this burden, then the burden of proof that conversion or negligence exists shifts back to plaintiff.

After the court's ruling defendant produced evidence of three possible explanations: United States Customs officials had been convicted of theft from the warehouse; some goods had been confiscated by the United States Customs Department, and there had been misdeliveries by warehouse employees.

The court, as trier of the fact, found that misdelivery was the most probable.

Misdelivery due to negligence is conversion. Restatement, Torts 2d, § 234, provides:

Conversion as Against Bailor by Misdelivery.

A bailee, agent, or servant who makes an unauthorized delivery of a chattel is subject to liability for conversion to his bailor, principal, or master unless he delivers to one who is entitled to immediate possession of the chattel.

Comment "a" applies this section to bailees who make unauthorized delivery by "mistake or otherwise." Therefore, under the Restatement, mere misdelivery does constitute conversion. New Jersey follows this well settled law. See Winkler v. Hartford Acc. & Ind. Co., 66 N.J. Super. 22, 27, 168 A.2d 418 (App.Div.1961), and Mueller v. Technical Devices Corp., supra.

Plaintiff's proofs of delivery, demand and failure to return the goods raised a prima facie case of conversion. The evidence which defendant then produced not only failed to meet this case, but established that there was a prior misdelivery. Defendant falls within the exception to the limitation of liability contained in N.J.S.A. 12A:7–204(2) because the property was converted by misdelivery. Hence, plaintiff is entitled to the market value of the whiskey, which is $6,417.60 together with interest and costs.

Notes and Questions

1. This is a commercial bailment case governed by the Uniform Commercial Code as adopted in New Jersey. UCC § 7–204(1), N.J.S.A. 12A:7–204(1), provides as follows: "A warehouseman is liable for damages for loss of or injury to the goods caused by his failure to exercise such care in regard to them as a reasonably careful man would exercise under like circumstances but unless otherwise agreed he is not liable for damages which could not have been avoided by the exercise of such care." This provision adopts the rule as to duty of care recognized and applied in the *Peet* case, ante. As indicated in Reinfeld, Inc. v. Griswold & Bateman, UCC § 7–204(2), N.J.S.A. 12A:7–204(2), permits a warehouseman to limit his liability for negligent "loss or damage" to the goods, but not for conversion of the goods, by an appropriate provision in the storage agreement.

2. A deliberate misdelivery of the subject matter of a bailment to someone not authorized to take possession—e.g., by an unauthorized sale—is, of course an act of conversion which exposes the bailee to strict liability for the full value of the goods. And a deliberate refusal by the bailee to return the goods to the bailor when there is a proper demand for return amounts to a conversion, whether the bailee acts in good faith or in bad faith. But there is considerable difference of judicial opinion as to when a "deviation" from the terms of the bailment will make the bailee liable for conversion. See R. Brown, Personal Property § 11.9 (3d ed. Raushenbush 1975).

3. As both the *Peet* and the *Reinfeld* cases indicate, when a bailor introduces credible evidence of the creation of a bailment and the bailee's failure to return the goods when a proper demand is made, the bailor is generally held to have established a *prima facie* case, which, if not rebutted, will entitle the bailor to recover the full value of the goods. As indicated in the *Reinfeld* case, the rationale of this rule is that "[a] bailee who accepts responsibility for goods should have the burden of producing evidence as to the fate of those goods" because "[t]o hold otherwise would place an impossible burden on a plaintiff" and "it is the bailee who is in the best position to explain the loss of the property." But in *Peet* the court said the bailee's "liability, if any, is for negligence," while in *Reinfeld* the court said that the bailee's liability is for "conversion," if the *prima facie* case is not rebutted. How do you explain this difference? Does it make any difference, in most cases, whether liability is predicated on "negligence" or on "conversion." What difference, if any, did it make in *Reinfeld*? Would it be preferable simply to say that proof of the bailment and the bailee's failure to return the goods on demand creates a presumption that the bailee's failure to return is caused by some violation of his duty to the bailor? See R. Brown, Personal Property § 11.8 nn. 4, 5 (3d ed. Raushenbush 1975), for cases holding, respectively that the presumption is one of "negligence" or one of "conversion."

4. There has been much controversy as to the procedural effect of the presumption, in bailment cases, that the bailee's failure to return the goods to the bailor is caused by some breach of duty on the bailee's part. One view, adopted by the Minnesota court in the *Peet* case, is that the presumption in favor of the bailor not only enables him to make a *prima facie* case by introducing evidence that a bailment was created and that the bailee failed to return the goods, but also shifts the ultimate burden of persuasion to the bailee. The opposing view, apparently adopted by the court in the *Reinfeld* case, is that the effect of the presumption is to enable the bailor to avert the risk that his case will be dismissed for lack of evidence and to place upon the bailee the burden of introduc-

ing evidence to rebut the presumption, but not to shift the ultimate burden of persuasion to the bailee. Under this view, if the bailee fails to introduce any evidence, the case will be submitted to the jury (if there is a jury) with an instruction to find for the bailor if the jury believes the bailor's evidence as to creation of a bailment and the bailee's failure to return the goods. But if the bailee introduces some evidence to show that the goods were lost or stolen without any negligence on the part of the bailee, the case will be submitted to the jury with an instruction that the bailor, as plaintiff, has the burden of persuasion. In cases where the trier of fact is unable to decide whether the bailee was at fault or not, it must find for the bailee if the ultimate burden of persuasion is on the bailor; but it must find for the bailor if the burden has been shifted to the bailee.

5. In the *Peet* case, the bailor's action was clearly based on a tort (negligence) theory, and the court held that the burden of persuasion shifted to the bailee when the making of the bailment and failure to return the goods to the bailor were proved. In some cases, however, it has been asserted that the burden shifts to the bailee if the bailor sues on the theory that failure to return the goods is a breach of contract, but not if the bailee sues on a tort (negligence) theory. E.g., Broadview Leasing Co. v. Cape Central Airways, Inc., 539 S.W.2d 553 (Mo.App.1976); Scruggs v. Dennis, 222 Tenn. 714, 440 S.W.2d 20 (1969) (semble).

6. Whatever the rule in a given state as to placement of the ultimate burden of persuasion in bailment cases, there is also some difference of judicial opinion as to what kind of evidence is sufficient to rebut the bailor's *prima facie* case. Suppose the bailee proves by credible evidence that loss of (or damage to) the goods resulted from fire, windstorm, or some similar casualty. It seems clear that this will rebut any presumption of "misdelivery"; but will it rebut a presumption of "negligence"? The trend in recent cases is to hold that such proof is not enough, and that the bailee must also introduce evidence to show that the casualty was not causally related to negligence on his part. See R. Brown, Personal Property § 11.8 (3d ed. Raushenbush 1975).

7. Suppose A bails a chattel to B, and B, within the scope of his authority, delivers possession of the chattel to C. If C then converts the chattel to his own use by a wrongful sale or a wrongful refusal to return the chattel to A, what remedies, if any, do A and B, respectively, have against C? Suppose both A and B demand return of the chattel from C, who has not otherwise done anything wrongful. To whom must C then deliver the chattel? Compare Anderson v. Gouldberg, ante. See also Seaboard Sand & Gravel Corp. v. Moran Towing Corp., 154 F.2d 399 (2d Cir.1946); R. Brown, Personal Property §§ 11.7, 11.11 (3d ed. Raushenbush 1975).

WALL v. AIRPORT PARKING COMPANY OF CHICAGO

Supreme Court of Illinois, 1969.
41 Ill.2d 506, 244 N.E.2d 190.

Action by insurer as subrogee to recover amount paid by it to its insured for damage to automobile stolen from parking lot operated by defendant.

HOUSE, Justice. Defendant, Airport Parking Company of Chicago, operator of a self-parking lot at O'Hare Airport as lessee of the city of Chicago, appealed to the Appellate Court, First District, from a judgment against it in favor of the insurer of an automobile stolen from the lot. The Appellate Court reversed, (88 Ill.App.2d 108, 232 N.E.2d 38) and we granted leave to appeal.

The cause was submitted on an agreed statement of facts. The lot is wholly enclosed, well lighted, paved and marked into parking spaces. Motorists enter through automatic gates and there receive a ticket bearing the date and time of arrival. They park in any available parking space, lock their automobiles, and retain the keys. When ready to depart they walk into the lot, pick up their vehicle and leave via an exit where the ticket is handed to an attendant to compute and collect the parking charges.

This is a case of first impression in this court although there is a great variety of holdings in the area of the liability of operators of parking-lot facilities, mostly by courts of intermediate jurisdiction. From this welter of decisions there emerge two principal classes of relationship between the automobile owner and the lot operator. One is that of the leasing of a parking space with no bailment being created. The other is a delivery of the vehicle into the possession and control of the lot operator thereby creating a bailment.

Typical of the first class of cases is where the owner parks his own car either at a place designated by an attendant or chosen by himself, retains the keys, and does not actually deliver the car to the lot operator. In the second class of cases, a bailment is usually created where the keys are left in the parked vehicle (at the request of the parking-lot attendant to permit moving it for the entrance or exit of other vehicles on the lot) and where tickets are issued identifying the car for redelivery. (See 38 Am.Jur.2d, Garages and Filling and Parking Stations, sec. 28; 7 A.L.R.3d, pp. 927–991, Annotations, Liability for Loss or Damage to Automobile Left in Parking Lot or Garage; 8 C.J.S. Bailments § 1(2).) In final analysis, however, parking-lot cases do not readily lend themselves to precise categorization of whether the motorist is leasing space on the one hand, or whether delivery of the vehicle onto a parking lot creates a *prima facie* bailment. As was said by the Court of Appeals of New York in Osborn v. Cline, 263 N.Y. 434, 189 N.E. 483, 484: "Whether a person simply hires a place to put his car or whether he has turned its possession over to the care and custody of another depends on the place, the conditions and the nature of the transaction." In a case very similar to this, except that parking was in an enclosed parking garage and valuables in the car rather than the car itself were stolen, the Pennsylvania Supreme Court said: "Since here plaintiffs reserved possession of the car at all times by retaining the keys thereto, defendant acquired no dominion over the vehicle nor any right to control removal of it; hence there was no bailment." Taylor v. Philadelphia Parking Authority, 398 Pa. 9, 156 A.2d 525, 527.

In recent years a new type of self-service vehicular parking lot has developed, particularly at the larger airports of this country. The one here involved is typical. A motorist gains admission to the lot through one or more automatic entrance gates, which open when he takes a machine dispensed ticket from an automatic dispenser. The ticket is stamped with the day and hour of arrival, but it does not identify any particular automobile or owner. No attendant is present nor is the motorist directed where to park, except that he is expected to park within the lines marking individual parking spaces. The motorist retains the keys. There is nothing to prevent him from moving the car from place to place within the confines of the lot as often as he chooses. He may not have (and probably has not) seen an attendant until he re-enters his car and proceeds to an exit where an attendant computes and collects the charges for the period of time the vehicle has been on the lot. This checking-out process is his only necessary contact with the lot operator or attendants.

In order to establish a bailor-bailee relationship there must be either an express agreement (there is none here) or an agreement by implication, which may be gathered from the circumstances surrounding the transaction, such as the benefits to be received by the parties, their intentions, the kind of property involved, and the opportunities of each to exercise control over the property. There must not only be a delivery of possession, but there must also be an acceptance, either actual or constructive, before there can be a bailment. (8 Am.Jur.2d, Bailments, §§ 56, 57.) Applying these criteria to the facts here we find that the self-parking-lot operator primarily offers spaces for parking with a minimum amount of labor, which presumably is reflected in the fees charged for use of the facilities. There undoubtedly is more protection to the users of the facilities than is afforded by street parking in that the parking lot is fenced, well lighted, attended around the clock by one to five attendants, and is patrolled by the Chicago police squad cars from time to time. But space rather than security is the primary purpose of a self-service parking lot. The motorist, is, of course, benefited by having parking space reasonably close to the airport.

By its very nature a self-service parking lot must be open at all times to the public and the operator has no control over who uses the lot. True, temporary possession in the sense that the motorist leaves a vehicle on the lot may be said to have been given up, but actual control is retained by the act of locking the vehicle and taking the keys, thereby preventing its movement. There is no acceptance of the vehicle by the lot owner. Plaintiff asserts that National Safe Deposit Co. v. Stead, 250 Ill. 584, 95 N.E. 973, is analogous. There, the safe deposit company held itself out as safeguarding valuables, and security was that which was being bought by the public. Valuables were stored in vaults and entry was through iron gates manned by armed guards. It was inherent in the nature of the service offered that the primary objective was to safeguard customers. That case is not persuasive.

We are of the opinion that use of self-service parking lots, such as the one here involved, does not create a bailor-bailee relationship and the lot operator is not subject to the liability imposed by the rules relating to bailments.

Plaintiff infers that a *prima facie* case of negligence was made against the defendant, but the cases cited in support are all bailment cases. It is fundamental that where plaintiff is an invitee, as here, and a lease relationship is established, the lot operator owes the duty of rea-

sonable care in the operation of the parking lot. But, it is just as fundamental in the common law of negligence that the plaintiff has the burden of proving negligence on the part of defendant and that defendant's
negligence was the cause of the loss. There is no proof of negligence in
this case under the agreed statement of facts and plaintiff is not entitled to recover.

The judgment of the Appellate Court, First District, is accordingly,
affirmed.

Judgment affirmed.

Notes and Questions

1. In Scruggs v. Dennis, 222 Tenn. 714, 440 S.W.2d 20 (1969), on facts similar to those in the principal case, the court found a bailment, without discussing
the facts upon which the finding was based, and imposed liability on the bailee
on a "contractual" basis.

2. In Nargi v. Parking Associates Corp., 36 Misc.2d 836, 234 N.Y.S.2d 42
(N.Y.City Ct.1962), a parking lot operator was held liable for loss of a car from
a lot which had not been fully enclosed by a fence, as required by municipal
regulations. Among other things, the court said, "Defendant argues that the
fact that the car was locked and plaintiff took the key absolves defendant of
any responsibility as bailee. * * * The fact that plaintiff's car was locked
and he took the key does not require a finding, on the facts of this case, that
the car was not turned over to the defendant's care." The court also quoted
the following from an opinion of a court of the Appellate Division:

"While the burden remains at all times upon the plaintiff to establish the
defendant's negligence, that does not mean that he is required to adduce
evidence pointing out the precise negligent act or omission. The surrounding facts and circumstances may be such as to permit an inference of negligence. Where the situation is such that in the ordinary course of events the
theft would not have occurred but for want of proper care on the part of the
bailee, his failure to show that he had taken such precautions as ordinary
prudence would dictate, where the proof, if it existed, would be within his
power to produce, may subject him to the inference that such precautions
were omitted."

The rule mentioned in the quoted excerpt is generally called the rule of *res ipsa
loquitur*. It is not clear whether the court would have held the parking lot
operator liable in *Nargi* on the basis of *res ipsa loquitur* even if the court had
not found that a bailment was created. What precautions against theft should
any parking lot operator take in order to protect his patrons, whether or not
patrons retain the keys to their cars? Generally, as to *res ipsa loquitur*, see
Prosser, Torts § 39 (4th ed. 1971). See also Equity Mutual Insurance Co v.
Affiliated Parking, Inc., 448 S.W.2d 909 (Mo.App.1969); Continental Insurance
Co. v. Meyers Brothers Operations, Inc., 56 Misc.2d 435, 288 N.Y.S.2d 756 (N.Y.
City Ct.1968).

3. Compare the principal case, supra, with Pinto v. Bridgeport Mack
Trucks, Inc., 38 Conn.Super. 639, 458 A.2d 696 (1983), where a "diesel mechanic" sued his employer to recover the fair value of his work tools, which were
stolen from the employer's premises. The plaintiff claimed that his employer
was negligent in failing to lock the front door, leaving the work place unattended during periods when employees took their lunch and supper breaks, and in
failing to secure his employee's tools by padlocking or chaining them or provid-

ing an enclosed area for their storage. The plaintiff's 500-pound tool box was stolen either during the night after the repair shop was closed or during the supper break of the evening shift. The court held that there was no bailment with respect to plaintiff's tool box, because "there was no delivery of the plaintiff's tools to the defendant nor receipt of them in a sense that could serve as a basis for concluding that the defendant had assumed control over them. Delivery connotes a handing over or surrender of possession to another. * * * Locking the tools in a box and leaving the box wherever one chooses in the work area of the employer's premises, pursuant to a trade custom, is not consistent with a handing over or surrender of either the tools or the box to the employer within the meaning of a bailment." However, the court went on to observe that "[a] conclusion that there was no bailment is not necessarily dispositive of the ultimate issue, as the existence of a bailment does nothing more than create a presumption of negligence." The court then concluded as follows:

> The defendant did not know, nor did its employees have any knowledge of facts which would charge it with knowledge that thieves would steal an employee's 500 pound tool chest. There was no evidence of prior thefts. On the contrary, there was evidence that there had been no thefts in the preceding nine years. A chain link fence surrounding the sides and rear of this commercial building were secured by the day shift. The sole night access to the 39,000 square foot building was through a single door leading into the show room. The tool chests, meanwhile, were in a maintenance area in the rear of the building. Employees were in and out of this area constantly. The totality of the facts and the circumstances militating against such a thing occurring remove the theft from the realm of what was reasonably foreseeable. The strongest evidence on the issue of foreseeability was the fact that the theft itself occurred. This isolated instance is not enough to impose upon the defendant the duty to exercise due care in preventing its occurrence.

Chapter 2

SOME FURTHER DIMENSIONS OF PROPERTY IN LAND

SECTION 1. THE RIGHT OF REASONABLE USE: NUISANCE

BOVE v. DONNER–HANNA COKE CORP.

Supreme Court of New York, Appellate Division, 1932.
236 App.Div. 37, 258 N.Y.S. 229.

EDGCOMB, J. The question involved upon this appeal is whether the use to which the defendant has recently put its property constitutes a private nuisance, which a court of equity should abate.

In 1910 plaintiff purchased two vacant lots at the corner of Abby and Baraga streets in the city of Buffalo, and two years later built a house thereon. The front of the building was converted into a grocery store, and plaintiff occupied the rear as a dwelling. She rented the two apartments on the second floor.

Defendant operates a large coke oven on the opposite side of Abby street. The plant runs twenty-four hours in the day, and three hundred and sixty-five days in the year. Of necessity, the operation has to be continuous, because the ovens would be ruined if they were allowed to cool off. The coke is heated to a temperature of around 2,000 degrees F., and is taken out of the ovens and run under a "quencher," where 500 or 600 gallons of water are poured onto it at one time. This is a necessary operation in the manufacture of coke. The result is a tremendous cloud of steam, which rises in a shaft and escapes into the air, carrying with it minute portions of coke, and more or less gas. This steam and the accompanying particles of dirt, as well as the dust which comes from a huge coal pile necessarily kept on the premises, and the gases and odors which emanate from the plant, are carried by the wind in various directions, and frequently find their way onto the plaintiff's premises and into her house and store. According to the plaintiff this results in an unusual amount of dirt and soot accumulating in her house, and prevents her opening the windows on the street side; she also claims that she suffers severe headaches by breathing the impure air occasioned by this dust and these offensive odors, and that her health and that of her family has been impaired, all to her very great discomfort and annoyance; she also asserts that this condition has lessened the rental value of her property, and has made it impossible at times to rent her apartments.

Claiming that such use of its plant by the defendant deprives her of the full enjoyment of her home, invades her property rights, and consti-

111

tutes a private nuisance, plaintiff brings this action in equity to enjoin the defendant from the further maintenance of said nuisance, and to recover the damages which she asserts she has already sustained.

As a general rule, an owner is at liberty to use his property as he sees fit, without objection or interference from his neighbor, provided such use does not violate an ordinance or statute. There is, however, a limitation to this rule; one made necessary by the intricate, complex and changing life of to-day. The old and familiar maxim, that one must so use his property as not to injure that of another (*sic utere tuo ut alienum non laedas*) is deeply imbedded in our law. An owner will not be permitted to make an unreasonable use of his premises to the material annoyance of his neighbor if the latter's enjoyment of life or property is materially lessened thereby. This principle is aptly stated by Andrews, Ch. J., in Booth v. R., W. & O.T.R.R. Co. (140 N.Y. 267, 274, 35 N.E. 592, 594) as follows: "The general rule that no one has absolute freedom in the use of his property, but is restrained by the co-existence of equal rights in his neighbor to the use of his property, so that each in exercising his right must do no act which causes injury to his neighbor, is so well understood, is so universally recognized, and stands so impregnably in the necessities of the social state, that its vindication by argument would be superfluous. The maxim which embodies it is sometimes loosely interpreted as forbidding all use by one of his own property, which annoys or disturbs his neighbor in the enjoyment of his property. The real meaning of the rule is that one may not use his own property to the injury of any legal right of another."

Such a rule is imperative, or life to-day in our congested centers would be intolerable and unbearable. If a citizen was given no protection against unjust harassment arising from the use to which the property of his neighbor was put, the comfort and value of his home could easily be destroyed by any one who chose to erect an annoyance nearby, and no one would be safe, unless he was rich enough to buy sufficient land about his home to render such disturbance impossible. When conflicting rights arise, a general rule must be worked out which, so far as possible, will preserve to each party that to which he has a just claim.

While the law will not permit a person to be driven from his home, or to be compelled to live in it in positive distress or discomfort because of the use to which other property nearby has been put, it is not every annoyance connected with business which will be enjoined. Many a loss arises from acts or conditions which do not create a ground for legal redress. *Damnum absque injuria* is a familiar maxim. Factories, stores and mercantile establishments are essential to the prosperity of the nation. They necessarily invade our cities, and interfere more or less with the peace and tranquillity of the neighborhood in which they are located.

One who chooses to live in the large centers of population cannot expect the quiet of the country. Congested centers are seldom free from smoke, odors and other pollution from houses, shops and factories, and one who moves into such a region cannot hope to find the pure air of the village or outlying district. A person who prefers the advantages of community life must expect to experience some of the resulting inconveniences. Residents of industrial centers must endure without redress a certain amount of annoyance and discomfiture which is incident to life in such a locality. Such inconvenience is of minor importance compared with the general good of the community.   *   *   *

Whether the particular use to which one puts his property constitutes a nuisance or not is generally a question of fact, and depends upon whether such use is reasonable under all the surrounding circumstances. What would distress and annoy one person would have little or no effect upon another; what would be deemed a disturbance and a torment in one locality would be unnoticed in some other place; a condition which would cause little or no vexation in a business, manufacturing or industrial district might be extremely tantalizing to those living in a restricted and beautiful residential zone; what would be unreasonable under one set of circumstances would be deemed fair and just under another. Each case is unique. No hard and fast rule can be laid down which will apply in all instances.   *   *   *

The inconvenience, if such it be, must not be fanciful, slight or theoretical but certain and substantial, and must interfere with the physical comfort of the ordinarily reasonable person.   *   *   *

Applying these general rules to the facts before us it is apparent that defendant's plant is not a nuisance *per se*, and that the court was amply justified in holding that it had not become one by reason of the manner in which it had been conducted. Any annoyance to plaintiff is due to the nature of the business which the defendant conducts, and not to any defect in the mill, machinery or apparatus. The plant is modern and up to date in every particular. It was built under a contract with the Federal government, the details of which are not important here. The plans were drawn by the Kopperas Construction Company, one of the largest and best known manufacturers of coke plants in the world, and the work was done under the supervision of the War Department. No reasonable change or improvement in the property can be made which will eliminate any of the things complained of. If coke is made, coal must be used. Gas always follows the burning of coal, and steam is occasioned by throwing cold water on red hot coals.

The cases are legion in this and other States where a defendant has been held guilty of maintaining a nuisance because of the annoyance which he has caused his neighbor by reason of noise, smoke, dust, noxious gases and disagreeable smells which have emanated from his property. But smoke and noisome odors do not always constitute a nuisance. I find none of these cases controlling here; they all differ in some particular from the facts in the case at bar.

It is true that the appellant was a resident of this locality for several years before the defendant came on the scene of action, and that, when the plaintiff built her house, the land on which these coke ovens now stand was a hickory grove. But in a growing community changes are inevitable. This region was never fitted for a residential district; for years it has been peculiarly adapted for factory sites. This was apparent when plaintiff bought her lots and when she built her house. The land is low and lies adjacent to the Buffalo river, a navigable stream connecting with Lake Erie. Seven different railroads run through this area. Freight tracks and yards can be seen in every direction. Railroads naturally follow the low levels in passing through a city. Cheap transportation is an attraction which always draws factories and industrial plants to a locality. It is common knowledge that a combination of rail and water terminal facilities will stamp a section as a site suitable for industries of the heavier type, rather than for residential purposes. In 1910 there were at least eight industrial plants, with a total assessed valuation of over a million dollars, within a radius of a mile from plaintiff's house.

With all the dirt, smoke and gas which necessarily come from factory chimneys, trains and boats, and with full knowledge that this region was especially adapted for industrial rather than residential purposes, and that factories would increase in the future, plaintiff selected this locality as the site of her future home. She voluntarily moved into this district, fully aware of the fact that the atmosphere would constantly be contaminated by dirt, gas and foul odors; and that she could not hope to find in this locality the pure air of a strictly residential zone. She evidently saw certain advantages in living in this congested center. This is not the case of an industry, with its attendant noise and dirt, invading a quiet, residential district. It is just the opposite. Here a residence is built in an area naturally adapted for industrial purposes and already dedicated to that use. Plaintiff can hardly be heard to complain at this late date that her peace and comfort have been disturbed by a situation which existed, to some extent at least, at the very time she bought her property, and which condition she must have known would grow worse rather than better as the years went by.

To-day there are twenty industrial plants within a radius of less than a mile and three-quarters from appellant's house, with more than sixty-five smokestacks rising in the air, and belching forth clouds of smoke; every day there are 148 passenger trains, and 225 freight trains, to say nothing of switch engines, passing over these various railroad tracks near to the plaintiff's property; over 10,000 boats, a large portion of which burn soft coal, pass up and down the Buffalo river every season. Across the street, and within 300 feet from plaintiff's house, is a large tank of the Iroquois Gas Company which is used for the storage of gas.

The utter abandonment of this locality for residential purposes, and its universal use as an industrial center, becomes manifest when one considers that in 1929 the assessed valuation of the twenty industrial plants above referred to aggregated over $20,000,000, and that the city in 1925 passed a zoning ordinance putting this area in the third industrial district, a zone in which stockyards, glue factories, coke ovens, steel furnaces, rolling mills and other similar enterprises were permitted to be located.

One has only to mention these facts to visualize the condition of the atmosphere in this locality. It is quite easy to imagine that many of the things of which the plaintiff complains are due to causes over which the defendant has no control. At any rate, if appellant is immune from the annoyance occasioned by the smoke and odor which must necessarily come from these various sources, it would hardly seem that she could consistently claim that her health has been impaired, and that the use and enjoyment of her home have been seriously interfered with solely because of the dirt, gas and stench which have reached her from defendant's plant.

It is very true that the law is no respecter of persons, and that the most humble citizen in the land is entitled to identically the same protection accorded to the master of the most gorgeous palace. However, the fact that the plaintiff has voluntarily chosen to live in the smoke and turmoil of this industrial zone is some evidence, at least, that any annoyance which she has suffered from the dirt, gas and odor which have emanated from defendant's plant is more imaginary and theoretical than it is real and substantial.

I think that the trial court was amply justified in refusing to interfere with the operation of the defendant's coke ovens. No consideration of public policy or private rights demands any such sacrifice of this industry.

Plaintiff is not entitled to the relief which she seeks for another reason.

Subdivision 25 of section 20 of the General City Law (added by Laws of 1917, chap. 483) gives to the cities of this State authority to regulate the location of industries and to district the city for that purpose. Pursuant to such authority the common council of the city of Buffalo adopted an ordinance setting aside the particular area in which defendant's plant is situated as a zone in which coke ovens might lawfully be located.

After years of study and agitation it has been found that development in conformity with some well-considered and comprehensive plan is necessary to the welfare of any growing municipality. The larger the community the greater becomes the need of such plan. Haphazard city building is ruinous to any city. Certain areas must be given over to industry, without which the country cannot long exist. Other sections must be kept free from the intrusion of trade and the distraction of business, and be set aside for homes, where one may live in a wholesome environment. Property owners, as well as the public, have come to recognize the absolute necessity of reasonable regulations of this character in the interest of public health, safety and general welfare, as well as for the conservation of property values. Such is the purpose of our zoning laws.

After due consideration the common council of Buffalo decreed that an enterprise similar to that carried on by the defendant might properly be located at the site of this particular coke oven. It is not for the court to step in and override such decision, and condemn as a nuisance a business which is being conducted in an approved and expert manner, at the very spot where the council said that it might be located. A court of equity will not ordinarily assume to set itself above officials to whom the law commits a decision, and reverse their discretion and judgment, unless bad faith is involved. No such charge is made here. * * *

I see no good reason why the decision of the Special Term should be disturbed. I think that the judgment appealed from should be affirmed.

All concur.

Judgment affirmed, with costs.

Note

The term "nuisance" has been used indiscriminately to denote certain kinds of tortious activity for which, at common law, the appropriate remedy was an action on the case for nuisance, and a rather nondescript group of minor criminal offenses characterized, at common law, as "common nuisances." Thus the term "nuisance" has from an early date been applied to conduct which invades two different types of legally protected interest: (1) The interest of a landowner, tenant, or other possessor of land in freedom from any unreasonable nontrespassory interference with his use and enjoyment of the land or his use of the land of another which is subject to an easement or other servitude in his favor. (2) The public interest in freedom from activity which endangers the health or safety or property of a considerable number of persons, offends public morals, or interferes with the comfort or convenience of a considerable number of people. Invasion of the former is said to constitute a "private" nuisance; invasion of the latter is said to constitute a "public" nuisance.

Prosser declares that the two types of nuisance "have almost nothing in common except that each causes inconvenience to some one, and [that] it would have been fortunate if they had been called from the beginning by different names."[1] Beuscher and Morrison, however, have concluded that the public-private dichotomy has little significance when recent nuisance cases are approached in terms of the extent to which the courts are meeting demands for protection against discordant land uses in unzoned areas.[2] This is mainly because the same activity may invade both private and public interests of the types which are protected under the nuisance rubric. Indeed, as Beuscher and Morrison point out, many nuisances are "public" merely because they have adverse effects on the use or enjoyment of a considerable number of privately owned parcels of land, in which case the "public" nuisance is "merely a composite of numerous private nuisances."[3] Moreover, an individual can maintain a tort action to recover for "special damage" which he may suffer as a consequence of a "public" nuisance even if there is no invasion of his interest in the reasonable use or enjoyment of land—although there would seem to be few cases where an individual could show "special damage" unless there was an invasion of that interest.

As a matter of fact, it appears that a large majority of the nuisance suits in recent years have been brought either by multiple plaintiffs, usually organized in committees, or by the attorney for some local governmental unit—in which case the courts tend to speak in terms of "public" nuisance. Only a minority of the suits were of the single-plaintiff type which traditionally falls under the "private" nuisance rubric, and most of these suits involved relatively minor invasions of the plaintiff's interest in the reasonable use or enjoyment of land.

1. Prosser, Torts 573 at n. 18 (4th ed. 1971).

2. Beuscher & Morrison, Judicial Zoning Through Recent Nuisance Cases, 1955 Wis.L.Rev. 440.

3. Beuscher & Morrison, supra note 2.

In most private nuisance cases, the plaintiff is the owner of the land subject to the nontrespassory interference of which he complains. But a nuisance action may be maintained by a plaintiff who has only a limited possessory interest in the land—e.g., a life tenant or a lessee, or even a mere possessor, at least if the possessor is holding "adversely." See 6A Am.L.Prop. 87 at n. 6; Rest., Torts 2d § 821E and Comment c thereto (1979). At least where an "adverse possessor" is the plaintiff, the defendant will not be able to defend on the basis of *jus tertii*. Any qualified plaintiff who is successful in proving the existence of a nuisance can recover damages for the interference with his use and enjoyment. In appropriate cases the plaintiff may also enjoin the continued maintenance of the nuisance.

When the focus is placed upon nuisance as a tool for land use control, those activities which interfere substantially and unreasonably with the interest of substantial numbers of landholders in the use or enjoyment of their land are most significant, whether considered to fall under the heading of "public" or of "private" nuisance. Interference with the plaintiffs' interest in the use or enjoyment of their land may occur in myriad ways—e.g., nontrespassory interference with the physical condition of the land itself, through blasting, vibrations caused by industrial operations, flooding, raising the water table, polluting a stream, or causing destruction of crops by the emission of dust, soot, or fumes; or interference with the health, comfort, or convenience of the plaintiffs by the emission of unpleasant odors, dust, soot, fumes, loud noises, excessive light or heat, and the like. If there is an interference with the physical condition of the land itself, there will often, though not always, be an interference with the health, comfort, or convenience of the occupant. If there is no interference with the physical condition of the land, the interference with the health, comfort, or convenience of the occupant must normally affect his "physical" senses, not merely his mental state. But this rule has been relaxed in a few instances—e.g., maintenance of a bawdy house, an undertaking establishment or a tuberculosis hospital near the plaintiffs' residences. And a threat of future interference with the physical condition of the plaintiffs' land, or with their health, comfort, or convenience, may be such a substantial and unreasonable interference with their present use or enjoyment of the land as to constitute a nuisance.

Absent an interference with the physical condition of the land, an activity which reduces the value of the plaintiff's land is generally not a nuisance unless it "physically" affects the plaintiffs' health, comfort, or convenience. Of course, the value of the plaintiffs' land is not likely to be reduced unless there is some "physical" interference with the condition of the land or with the plaintiffs' health, comfort, or safety. But the maintenance of a structure or the carrying on of an activity which offends the plaintiffs' aesthetic sense may in fact reduce the value of their property as well as cause "mental" discomfort. In such cases, most courts have refused to find a nuisance because of the difficulty of establishing generally acceptable aesthetic standards.

Most nuisance cases involve recurrent activity rather than an isolated wrongful act. This has led some courts and writers to say that a nuisance necessarily involves continuance or recurrence over an appreciable period of time. In many cases, of course, continuance or recurrence is required in order to meet the substantial interference test. In other cases, it is necessary before injunctive relief can be obtained by the plaintiff. And if the harm was neither foreseeable in the first instance or a result of ultra-hazardous activity some continuance of the defendant's activity is necessary to establish his fault and consequent liability. Moreover, the duration or frequency of the invasion of the plaintiff's interest certainly has a bearing on the reasonableness of his conduct. But there are undoubtedly cases where the plaintiff has recovered damages on the ground of nuisance because of substantial but instantaneous harm resulting from the defendant's conduct. It would seem therefore, that the duration or recurrence of the interference with the plaintiff's interest is only one factor, not necessarily conclusive in determining whether the harm is substantial enough to constitute a nuisance.

Most nuisance litigation has focussed on the reasonableness of the defendant's conduct. Since all landholders are equally entitled to the reasonable use and enjoyment of their lands, some balance must be struck between the conflicting interests of different landholders in different, and often discordant, uses of their lands. As Prosser has pointed out,[4] "The plaintiff must be expected to endure some inconvenience rather than curtail the defendant's freedom of action, and the defendant must so use his own property that he causes no unreasonable harm to the plaintiff. The law of private nuisance is very largely a series of adjustments to limit the reciprocal rights and privileges of both. In every case the court must make a comparative evaluation of the conflicting interests according to objective legal standards, and the gravity of the harm to the plaintiff must be weighed against the utility of the defendant's conduct."

The gravity of the harm to the plaintiff depends upon both the extent and the duration of the interference and the character of the harm. If there is physical injury to the property, courts have generally been more willing to find a nuisance than where there is only an interference with the plaintiff's comfort or convenience. The utility of the defendant's conduct depends, of course, upon the social value which the courts attach to its ultimate purpose. Modern society requires factories, smelters, oil refineries, chemical plants, power stations, and use of explosives for blasting. Such activities may not be nuisances even though they cause substantial discomfort or inconvenience to neighboring landholders, if they are carried on in suitable localities and the adverse impact upon neighboring landholders is avoidable only at prohibitive expense. But if the defendant's conduct has little or no social value, or is a result of pure malice or spite, the defendant may be liable for causing a nuisance although the harm to the plaintiff is relatively slight.

In the process of balancing the conflicting interests of the plaintiff and the defendant in the reasonable use and enjoyment of their lands, courts also give weight to the social value of the use or enjoyment invaded and the cost to the plaintiff of avoiding the harm caused by the defendant's conduct.

Once the existence of a nuisance is established, the traditional judicial remedies include (1) an award of monetary damages, and (2) equitable relief by way of injunction. Damages will always be awarded, and sometimes an injunction will also be granted. For more on judicial remedies, see the next two principal cases.

For a concise discussion of "nuisance" law, see Cunningham § 7.2.

BOOMER v. ATLANTIC CEMENT CO.

Court of Appeals of New York, 1970.
26 N.Y.2d 219, 309 N.Y.S.2d 312, 257 N.E.2d 870.

BERGAN, Judge. Defendant operates a large cement plant near Albany. These are actions for injunction and damages by neighboring land owners alleging injury to property from dirt, smoke and vibration emanating from the plant. A nuisance has been found after trial, temporary damages have been allowed; but an injunction has been denied.

The public concern with air pollution arising from many sources in industry and in transportation is currently accorded ever wider recognition accompanied by a growing sense of responsibility in State and Federal Governments to control it. Cement plants are obvious sources of air pollution in the neighborhoods where they operate.

But there is now before the court private litigation in which individual property owners have sought specific relief from a single plant operation. The threshold question raised by the division of view on this appeal is whether the court should resolve the litigation between the parties now before it as equitably as seems possible; or whether, seeking promotion of the general public welfare, it should channel private litigation into broad public objectives.

A court performs its essential function when it decides the rights of parties before it. Its decision of private controversies may sometimes greatly affect public issues. Large questions of law are often resolved by the manner in which private litigation is decided. But this is normally an incident to the court's main function to settle controversy. It is a rare exercise of judicial power to use a decision in private litigation as a purposeful mechanism to achieve direct public objectives greatly beyond the rights and interests before the court.

Effective control of air pollution is a problem presently far from solution even with the full public and financial powers of government. In large measure adequate technical procedures are yet to be developed and some that appear possible may be economically impracticable.

It seems apparent that the amelioration of air pollution will depend on technical research in great depth; on a carefully balanced consideration of the economic impact of close regulation; and of the actual effect on public health. It is likely to require massive public expenditure and to demand more than any local community can accomplish and to depend on regional and interstate controls.

A court should not try to do this on its own as a by-product of private litigation and it seems manifest that the judicial establishment is neither equipped in the limited nature of any judgment it can pronounce nor prepared to lay down and implement an effective policy for the elimination of air pollution. This is an area beyond the circumference of one private lawsuit. It is a direct responsibility for government and should not thus be undertaken as an incident to solving a dispute between property owners and a single cement plant—one of many—in the Hudson River valley.

The cement making operations of defendant have been found by the court at Special Term to have damaged the nearby properties of plaintiffs in these two actions. That court, as it has been noted, accordingly found defendant maintained a nuisance and this has been affirmed at the Appellate Division. The total damage to plaintiffs' properties is, however, relatively small in comparison with the value of defendant's operation and with the consequences of the injunction which plaintiffs seek.

The ground for the denial of injunction, notwithstanding the finding both that there is a nuisance and that plaintiffs have been damaged substantially, is the large disparity in economic consequences of the nuisance and of the injunction. This theory cannot, however, be sustained without overruling a doctrine which has been consistently reaffirmed in several leading cases in this court and which has never been disavowed here, namely that where a nuisance has been found and where there has been any substantial damage shown by the party complaining an injunction will be granted.

The rule in New York has been that such a nuisance will be enjoined although marked disparity be shown in economic consequence between the effect of the injunction and the effect of the nuisance.

The problem of disparity in economic consequence was sharply in focus in Whalen v. Union Bag & Paper Co., 208 N.Y. 1, 101 N.E. 805. A pulp mill entailing an investment of more than a million dollars polluted a stream in which plaintiff, who owned a farm, was "a lower riparian owner". The economic loss to plaintiff from this pollution was small. This court, reversing the Appellate Division, reinstated the injunction granted by the Special Term against the argument of the mill owner that in view of "the slight advantage to plaintiff and the great loss that will be inflicted on defendant" an injunction should not be granted (p. 2, 101 N.E. p. 805). "Such a balancing of injuries cannot be justified by the circumstances of this case", Judge Werner noted (p. 4, 101 N.E. p. 805). He continued: "Although the damage to the plaintiff may be slight as compared with the defendant's expense of abating the condition, that is not a good reason for refusing an injunction" (p. 5, 101 N.E. p. 806).

Thus the unconditional injunction granted at Special Term was reinstated. The rule laid down in that case, then, is that whenever the damage resulting from a nuisance is found not "unsubstantial", viz., $100 a year, injunction would follow. This states a rule that had been followed in this court with marked consistency (McCarty v. Natural Carbonic Gas Co., 189 N.Y. 40, 81 N.E. 549; Strobel v. Kerr Salt Co., 164 N.Y. 303, 58 N.E. 142; Campbell v. Seaman, 63 N.Y. 568).

There are cases where injunction has been denied. McCann v. Chasm Power Co., 211 N.Y. 301, 105 N.E. 416 is one of them. There, however, the damage shown by plaintiffs was not only unsubstantial, it was non-existent. Plaintiffs owned a rocky bank of the stream in which defendant had raised the level of the water. This had no economic or other adverse consequence to plaintiffs, and thus injunctive relief was denied. Similar is the basis for denial of injunction in Forstmann v. Joray Holding Co., 244 N.Y. 22, 154 N.E. 652 where no benefit to plaintiffs could be seen from the injunction sought (p. 32, 154 N.E. 655). Thus if, within Whalen v. Union Bag & Paper Co., supra which authoritatively states the rule in New York, the damage to plaintiffs in these present cases from defendant's cement plant is "not unsubstantial", an injunction should follow.

Although the court at Special Term and the Appellate Division held that injunction should be denied, it was found that plaintiffs had been damaged in various specific amounts up to the time of the trial and damages to the respective plaintiffs were awarded for those amounts. The effect of this was, injunction having been denied, plaintiffs could maintain successive actions at law for damages thereafter as further damage was incurred.

The court at Special Term also found the amount of permanent damage attributable to each plaintiff, for the guidance of the parties in the event both sides stipulated to the payment and acceptance of such permanent damage as a settlement of all the controversies among the parties. The total of permanent damages to all plaintiffs thus found was $185,000. This basis of adjustment has not resulted in any stipulation by the parties.

This result at Special Term and at the Appellate Division is a departure from a rule that has become settled; but to follow the rule literally in these cases would be to close down the plant at once. This court is fully agreed to avoid that immediately drastic remedy; the difference in view is how best to avoid it.[*]

One alternative is to grant the injunction but postpone its effect to a specified future date to give opportunity for technical advances to permit defendant to eliminate the nuisance; another is to grant the injunction conditioned on the payment of permanent damages to plaintiffs which would compensate them for the total economic loss to their property present and future caused by defendant's operations. For reasons which will be developed the court chooses the latter alternative.

If the injunction were to be granted unless within a short period—e.g., 18 months—the nuisance be abated by improved methods, there would be no assurance that any significant technical improvement would occur.

The parties could settle this private litigation at any time if defendant paid enough money and the imminent threat of closing the plant would build up the pressure on defendant. If there were no improved techniques found, there would inevitably be applications to the court at Special Term for extensions of time to perform on showing of good faith efforts to find such techniques.

Moreover, techniques to eliminate dust and other annoying by-products of cement making are unlikely to be developed by any research the defendant can undertake within any short period, but will depend on the total resources of the cement industry nationwide and throughout the world. The problem is universal wherever cement is made.

For obvious reasons the rate of the research is beyond control of defendant. If at the end of 18 months the whole industry has not found

[*] Respondent's investment in the plant is in excess of $45,000,000. There are over 300 people employed there.

a technical solution a court would be hard put to close down this one cement plant if due regard be given to equitable principles.

On the other hand, to grant the injunction unless defendant pays plaintiffs such permanent damages as may be fixed by the court seems to do justice between the contending parties. All of the attributions of economic loss to the properties on which plaintiffs' complaints are based will have been redressed.

The nuisance complained of by these plaintiffs may have other public or private consequences, but these particular parties are the only ones who have sought remedies and the judgment proposed will fully redress them. The limitation of relief granted is a limitation only within the four corners of these actions and does not foreclose public health or other public agencies from seeking proper relief in a proper court.

It seems reasonable to think that the risk of being required to pay permanent damages to injured property owners by cement plant owners would itself be a reasonable effective spur to research for improved techniques to minimize nuisance.

The power of the court to condition on equitable grounds the continuance of an injunction on the payment of permanent damages seems undoubted. (See, e.g., the alternatives considered in McCarty v. Natural Carbonic Gas Co., supra, as well as Strobel v. Kerr Salt Co., supra.)

The damage base here suggested is consistent with the general rule in those nuisance cases where damages are allowed. "Where a nuisance is of such a permanent and unabatable character that a single recovery can be had, including the whole damage past and future resulting therefrom, there can be but one recovery" (66 C.J.S. Nuisances § 140, p. 947). It has been said that permanent damages are allowed where the loss recoverable would obviously be small as compared with the cost of removal of the nuisance (Kentucky-Ohio Gas Co. v. Bowling, 264 Ky. 470, 477, 95 S.W.2d 1).

The present cases and the remedy here proposed are in a number of other respects rather similar to Northern Indiana Public Service Co. v. W.J. & M.S. Vesey, 210 Ind. 338, 200 N.E. 620 decided by the Supreme Court of Indiana. The gases, odors, ammonia and smoke from the Northern Indiana company's gas plant damaged the nearby Vesey greenhouse operation. An injunction and damages were sought, but an injunction was denied and the relief granted was limited to permanent damages "present, past, and future" (p. 371, 200 N.E. 620).

Denial of injunction was grounded on a public interest in the operation of the gas plant and on the court's conclusion "that less injury would be occasioned by requiring the appellant [Public Service] to pay the appellee [Vesey] all damages suffered by it * * * than by enjoining the operation of the gas plant; and that the maintenance and operation of the gas plant should not be enjoined" (p. 349, 200 N.E. p. 625).

The Indiana Supreme Court opinion continued: "When the trial court refused injunctive relief to the appellee upon the ground of public interest in the continuance of the gas plant, it properly retained jurisdiction of the case and awarded full compensation to the appellee. This is upon the general equitable principle that equity will give full relief in one action and prevent a multiplicity of suits" (pp. 353–354, 200 N.E. p. 627).

It was held that in this type of continuing and recurrent nuisance permanent damages were appropriate. See, also, City of Amarillo v. Ware, 120 Tex. 456, 40 S.W.2d 57 where recurring overflows from a system of storm sewers were treated as the kind of nuisance for which permanent depreciation of value of affected property would be recoverable.

There is some parallel to the conditioning of an injunction on the payment of permanent damages in the noted "elevated railway cases" (Pappenheim v. Metropolitan El. Ry. Co., 128 N.Y. 436, 28 N.E. 518 and others which followed). Decisions in these cases were based on the finding that the railways created a nuisance as to adjacent property owners, but in lieu of enjoining their operation, the court allowed permanent damages.

Judge Finch, reviewing these cases in Ferguson v. Village of Hamburg, 272 N.Y. 234, 239–240, 5 N.E.2d 801, 803, said: "The courts decided that the plaintiffs had a valuable right which was being impaired, but did not grant an absolute injunction or require the railway companies to resort to separate condemnation proceedings. Instead they held that a court of equity could ascertain the damages and grant an injunction which was not to be effective unless the defendant failed to pay the amount fixed as damages for the past and permanent injury inflicted." (See, also, Lynch v. Metropolitan El. Ry. Co., 129 N.Y. 274, 29 N.E. 315; Van Allen v. New York El. R.R. Co., 144 N.Y. 174, 38 N.E. 997; Cox v. City of New York, 265 N.Y. 411, 193 N.E. 251, and similarly, Westphal v. City of New York, 177 N.Y. 140, 69 N.E. 369.)

Thus it seems fair to both sides to grant permanent damages to plaintiffs which will terminate this private litigation. The theory of damage is the "servitude on land" of plaintiffs imposed by defendant's nuisance. (See United States v. Causby, 328 U.S. 256, 261, 262, 267, 66 S.Ct. 1062, 90 L.Ed. 1206, where the term "servitude" addressed to the land was used by Justice Douglas relating to the effect of airplane noise on property near an airport.)

The judgment, by allowance of permanent damages imposing a servitude on land, which is the basis of the actions, would preclude future recovery by plaintiffs or their grantees (see Northern Indiana Public Serv. Co. v. W.J. & M.S. Vesey, supra, p. 351, 200 N.E. 620).

This should be placed beyond debate by a provision of the judgment that the payment by defendant and the acceptance by plaintiffs of permanent damages found by the court shall be in compensation for a servitude on the land.

Although the Trial Term has found permanent damages as a possible basis of settlement of the litigation, on remission the court should be entirely free to re-examine this subject. It may again find the permanent damage already found; or make new findings.

The orders should be reversed, without costs, and the cases remitted to Supreme Court, Albany County to grant an injunction which shall be vacated upon payment by defendant of such amounts of permanent damage to the respective plaintiffs as shall for this purpose be determined by the court.

JASEN, Judge (dissenting).

I agree with the majority that a reversal is required here, but I do not subscribe to the newly enunciated doctrine of assessment of permanent damages, in lieu of an injunction, where substantial property rights have been impaired by the creation of a nuisance.

It has long been the rule in this State, as the majority acknowledges, that a nuisance which results in substantial continuing damage to neighbors must be enjoined. (Whalen v. Union Bag & Paper Co., 208 N.Y. 1, 101 N.E. 805; Campbell v. Seaman, 63 N.Y. 568; see, also, Kennedy v. Moog Servocontrols, 21 N.Y.2d 966, 290 N.Y.S.2d 193, 237 N.E.2d 356.) To now change the rule to permit the cement company to continue polluting the air indefinitely upon the payment of permanent damages is, in my opinion, compounding the magnitude of a very serious problem in our State and Nation today.

In recognition of this problem, the Legislature of this State has enacted the Air Pollution Control Act (Public Health Law, Consol. Laws, c. 45, §§ 1264 to 1299–m) declaring that it is the State policy to require the use of all available and reasonable methods to prevent and control air pollution (Public Health Law § 1265 [4]).

The harmful nature and widespread occurrence of air pollution have been extensively documented. Congressional hearings have revealed that air pollution causes substantial property damage, as well as being a contributing factor to a rising incidence of lung cancer, emphysema, bronchitis and asthma.[5]

The specific problem faced here is known as particulate contamination because of the fine dust particles emanating from defendant's cement plant. The particular type of nuisance is not new, having appeared in many cases for at least the past 60 years. (See Hulbert v. California Portland Cement Co., 161 Cal. 239, 118 P. 928 [1911].) It is interesting to note that cement production has recently been identified as a significant source of particulate contamination in the Hudson Valley.[6] This type of pollution, wherein very small particles escape and stay in the atmosphere, has been denominated as the type of air pollution which produces the greatest hazard to human health.[7] We have

4. See also, Air Quality Act of 1967, 81 U.S.Stat. 485 (1967).

5. See U.S.Cong., Senate Comm. on Public Works, Special Subcomm. on Air and Water Pollution, Air Pollution 1966, 89th Cong., 2d Sess., 1966, at pp. 22–24; U.S.Cong., Senate Comm. on Public Works, Special Subcomm. on Air and Water Pollution, Air Pollution 1968, 90th Cong., 2d Sess., 1968, at pp. 850, 1084.

6. New York State Bureau of Air Pollution Control Services, Air Pollution Capital District, 1968, at p. 8.

7. J. Ludwig, Air Pollution Control Technology: Research and Development on New and Improved Systems, 33 Law & Contemp.Prob., 217, 219 (1968).

thus a nuisance which not only is damaging to the plaintiffs,[8] but also is decidedly harmful to the general public.

I see grave dangers in overruling our long-established rule of granting an injunction where a nuisance results in substantial continuing damage. In permitting the injunction to become inoperative upon the payment of permanent damages, the majority is, in effect, licensing a continuing wrong. It is the same as saying to the cement company, you may continue to do harm to your neighbors so long as you pay a fee for it. Furthermore, once such permanent damages are assessed and paid, the incentive to alleviate the wrong would be eliminated, thereby continuing air pollution of an area without abatement.

It is true that some courts have sanctioned the remedy here proposed by the majority in a number of cases,[9] but none of the authorities relied upon by the majority are analogous to the situation before us. In those cases, the courts, in denying an injunction and awarding money damages, grounded their decision on a showing that the use to which the property was intended to be put was primarily for the public benefit. Here, on the other hand, it is clearly established that the cement company is creating a continuing air pollution nuisance primarily for its own private interest with no public benefit.

This kind of inverse condemnation (Ferguson v. Village of Hamburg, 272 N.Y. 234, 5 N.E.2d 801) may not be invoked by a private person or corporation for private gain or advantage. Inverse condemnation should only be permitted when the public is primarily served in the taking or impairment of property. (Matter of New York City Housing Auth. v. Muller, 270 N.Y. 333, 343, 1 N.E.2d 153, 156; Pocantico Water Works Co. v. Bird, 130 N.Y. 249, 258, 29 N.E. 246, 248.) The promotion of the interests of the polluting cement company has, in my opinion, no public use or benefit.

Nor is it constitutionally permissible to impose servitude on land, without consent of the owner, by payment of permanent damages where the continuing impairment of the land is for a private use. (See Fifth Ave. Coach Lines v. City of New York, 11 N.Y.2d 342, 347, 229 N.Y.S.2d 400, 403, 183 N.E.2d 684, 686; Walker v. City of Hutchinson, 352 U.S. 112, 77 S.Ct. 200, 1 L.Ed.2d 178.) This is made clear by the State Constitution (art. I, § 7, subd. [a]) which provides that "[p]rivate property shall not be taken for *public use* without just compensation" (emphasis added). It is, of course, significant that the section makes no mention of taking for a *private* use.

In sum, then, by constitutional mandate as well as by judicial pronouncement, the permanent impairment of private property for private

---

8. There are seven plaintiffs here who have been substantially damaged by the maintenance of this nuisance. The trial court found their total permanent damages to equal $185,000.

9. See United States v. Causby, 328 U.S. 256, 66 S.Ct. 1062, 90 L.Ed. 1206; Kentucky-Ohio Gas Co. v. Bowling, 264 Ky. 470, 477, 95 S.W.2d 1; Northern Indiana Public Service Co. v. W.J. & M.S. Vesey, 210 Ind. 338, 200 N.E. 620; City of Amarillo v. Ware, 120 Tex. 456, 40 S.W.2d 57; Pappenheim v. Metropolitan El. Ry. Co., 128 N.Y. 436, 28 N.E. 518; Ferguson v. Village of Hamburg, 272 N.Y. 234, 5 N.E.2d 801.

purposes is not authorized in the absence of clearly demonstrated public benefit and use.

I would enjoin the defendant cement company from continuing the discharge of dust particles upon its neighbors' properties unless, within 18 months, the cement company abated this nuisance.[10]

It is not my intention to cause the removal of the cement plant from the Albany area, but to recognize the urgency of the problem stemming from this stationary source of air pollution, and to allow the company a specified period of time to develop a means to alleviate this nuisance.

I am aware that the trial court found that the most modern dust control devices available have been installed in defendant's plant, but, I submit, this does not mean that *better* and more effective dust control devices could not be developed within the time allowed to abate the pollution.

Moreover, I believe it is incumbent upon the defendant to develop such devices, since the cement company, at the time the plant commenced production (1962), was well aware of the plaintiffs' presence in the area, as well as the probable consequences of its contemplated operation. Yet, it still chose to build and operate the plant at this site.

In a day when there is a growing concern for clean air, highly developed industry should not expect acquiescence by the courts, but should, instead, plan its operations to eliminate contamination of our air and damage to its neighbors.

Accordingly, the orders of the Appellate Division, insofar as they denied the injunction, should be reversed, and the actions remitted to Supreme Court, Albany County to grant an injunction to take effect 18 months hence, unless the nuisance is abated by improved techniques prior to said date.

FULD, C.J., and BURKE and SCILEPPI, JJ., concur with BERGAN, J.

JASEN, J., dissents in part and votes to reverse in a separate opinion.

BREITEL and GIBSON, JJ., taking no part.

In each action: Order reversed, without costs, and the case remitted to Supreme Court, Albany County, for further proceedings in accordance with the opinion herein.

Notes

1. In terms of the law of private nuisance, the requirement that interferences with the use and enjoyment of land must be "unreasonable" before they are actionable admits of a variety of considerations which are relevant to so broad a standard. As indicated in the *Bove* case, it is difficult for a court to escape balancing the extent of the harm done to a plaintiff against the public

---

10. The issuance of an injunction to become effective in the future is not an entirely new concept. For instance, in Schwarzenbach v. Onconta Light & Power Co., 207 N.Y. 671, 100 N.E. 1134, an injunction against the maintenance of a dam spilling water on plaintiff's property was issued to become effective one year hence.

benefit of the defendant's operations. Although the law of nuisance is one application of the old maxim that one may not so use his property as to injure another in the use and enjoyment of his property, courts are fond of saying that a person must suffer some annoyance and inconvenience in living in proximity to others. The court in the *Bove* case laid some emphasis on the fact that the defendant could make no reasonable change or improvement in his plant which would eliminate any of the conditions complained of. In contrast the trial court in the *Boomer* case, although conceding that the defendant had at great expense installed the most efficient devices to prevent air pollution, nevertheless found that the emission of dust and excessive vibrations from blasting did constitute a nuisance. See 55 Misc.2d 1023, 287 N.Y.S.2d 112 (1967). No further relevant facts were recited by the court, and the *Bove* case was not cited.

Most plaintiffs in nuisance cases seek injunctive relief. In such cases, if a nuisance is found, the question arises whether a court will balance the equities or interests of the parties once more, but with a different frame of reference, and with the possible consequence of confining a plaintiff to the recovery of damages. As you can tell from the *Boomer* opinion, this is not a new problem, and the courts have not been in agreement in dealing with it. Consistency is not to be found either in deciding whether a court has power to balance the equities, or if it does, in deciding what degree of imbalance in favor of the defendant will justify the denial of equitable relief. In fact, is it entirely clear that the court in the *Bove* case was holding that the defendant's conduct did not constitute a nuisance, or merely that the plaintiff was not entitled to an injunction? The New York court was candid in conceding that its judgment in the *Boomer* case was a departure from prior authority. You should try to sense the real reason for its holding, whether and to what extent, for example, it reflected the court's response to the complexities of the pollution problem.

2. What do you think of the plaintiffs' argument, in *Boomer*, that refusal of an injunction would result in an unconstitutional "taking" of plaintiffs' property to achieve a purely "private" purpose? Should judicial refusal to grant an injunction be conceptualized as conferring on defendant an "easement to pollute" the airspace above plaintiffs' land rather than simply an exercise of judicial discretion as to the appropriate remedy for the nuisance defendant was found to be causing? The *Boomer* case has produced adverse comment in the law reviews. See, e.g., 19 Kan.L.Rev. 142 (1970); 45 N.Y.U.L.Rev. 919 (1970); 1971 Utah L.Rev. 142. For a collection of cases on the doctrine of balancing the equities in nuisance cases, see 40 A.L.R.3d 601 (1971).

3. What should be the measure of damages in a case like *Boomer* if the plaintiff is not the owner but only an "adverse possessor"? If the plaintiff is only a life tenant or a long-term lessee?

4. After the *Boomer* case was remanded for further proceedings, two of the plaintiffs (including Boomer) settled with the defendant and the trial court proceeded to determine the "permanent damages" of the remaining plaintiff, Kinley, who owned a 238 acre dairy farm. The trial court received testimony that the defendant had converted the primary fuel of its cement plant from coal to oil, had put an additional "spray system" in the conveying apparatus from the quarry to the stockpiles at the plant site, and had replaced the "multiclone dust collectors on the clinker cooler" with a "fiberglass bag type collector," all at a cost of $1,600,000. The trial court determined Kinley's "permanent damages" to be $140,000 after finding that the value of his farm without the nuisance would be $265,000 and that its value with the nuisance was $125,000. 340 N.Y.S.2d 97 (1972). On appeal from this decision, the trial court judgment was affirmed. The majority of the Appellate Division panel held that the prop-

er measure of "permanent damages" in a nuisance case was "the difference between the market value of the property before and after the nuisance." One judge, in a concurring opinion, took a different view, asserting that, although the "before and after" measure of damages is proper in eminent domain cases it is not necessarily appropriate in private nuisance cases where "it would be unrealistic to assume that the defendant could acquire a servitude of the present nature simply by paying the price which a willing seller would accept. * * * While the public interest may dictate that the defendant be afforded an opportunity to acquire a servitude, there is no apparent reason to assume that the purchase is being made either by or on behalf of the public and, accordingly, the value of the servitude should reflect the private interest of the parties to this lawsuit." The concurring judge then concluded that defendants in such cases should be required to pay the "holdup" price required to persuade an "unwilling" landowner to sell the "easement to pollute." See 42 A.D.2d 496, 349 N.Y.S.2d 199.

5. Suppose that the defendant paid Kinley the "permanent" damages of $140,000 and that the defendant was later able to reduce or eliminate the air pollution found to constitute a nuisance, or that a state or federal air pollution control agency later closes down or substantially curtails the operation of the defendant's cement plant. Would the defendant then be entitled to restitution of some part of the "permanent damages" it paid to Kinley. Could the problem of determining the amount of restitution be avoided by awarding Kinley, instead of "permanent damages," a right to recover on a periodic basis all damages up to the time of suit? The latter would result, in substance, in the defendant's being required to pay a periodic "rent" for its "easement to pollute."

6. Another possible alternative in cases like *Boomer* would be to enjoin the nuisance and require the plaintiff to compensate the defendant for its financial loss by paying money damages. The court adopted this remedy in the next principal case.

SPUR INDUSTRIES, INC. v. DEL E. WEBB DEVELOPMENT CO.

Supreme Court of Arizona, 1972.
108 Ariz. 178, 494 P.2d 700.

CAMERON, Vice Chief Justice. From a judgment permanently enjoining the defendant, Spur Industries, Inc., from operating a cattle feedlot near the plaintiff Del E. Webb Development Company's Sun City, Spur appeals. Webb cross-appeals. Although numerous issues are raised, we feel that it is necessary to answer only two questions. They are:

1. Where the operation of a business, such as a cattle feedlot is lawful in the first instance, but becomes a nuisance by reason of a nearby residential area, may the feedlot operation be enjoined in an action brought by the developer of the residential area?

2. Assuming that the nuisance may be enjoined, may the developer of a completely new town or urban area in a previously agricultural area be required to indemnify the operator of the feedlot who must move or cease operation because of the presence of the residential area created by the developer?

The facts necessary for a determination of this matter on appeal are as follows. The area in question is located in Maricopa County, Arizona, some 14 to 15 miles west of the urban area of Phoenix, on the Phoenix-Wickenburg Highway, also known as Grand Avenue. About two miles south of Grand Avenue is Olive Avenue which runs east and west. 111th Avenue runs north and south as does the Agua Fria River immediately to the west. See Exhibits A and B below.

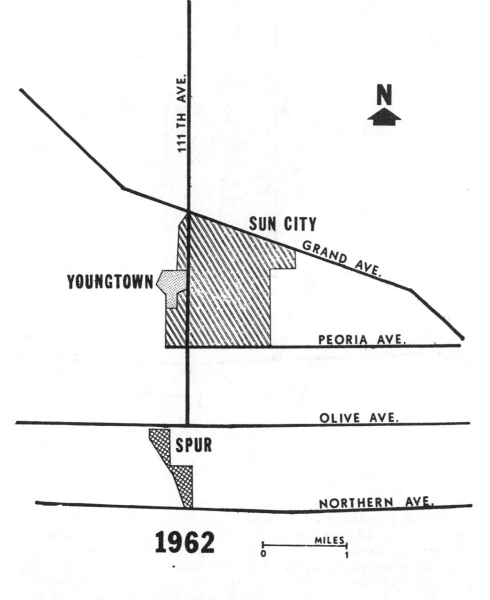

EXHIBIT A

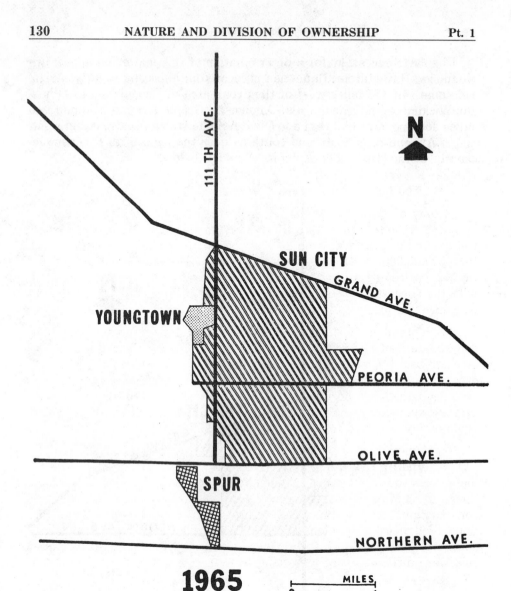

EXHIBIT B

Farming started in this area about 1911. In 1929, with the completion of the Carl Pleasant Dam, gravity flow water became available to the property located to the west of the Agua Fria River, though land to the east remained dependent upon well water for irrigation. By 1950, the only urban areas in the vicinity were the agriculturally related communities of Peoria, El Mirage, and Surprise located along Grand Avenue. Along 111th Avenue, approximately one mile south of Grand Avenue and 1½ miles north of Olive Avenue, the community of Youngtown was commenced in 1954. Youngtown is a retirement community appealing primarily to senior citizens.

In 1956, Spur's predecessors in interest, H. Marion Welborn and the Northside Hay Mill and Trading Company, developed feedlots, about ½ mile south of Olive Avenue, in an area between the confluence of the usually dry Agua Fria and New Rivers. The area is well suited for cattle feeding and in 1959, there were 25 cattle feeding pens or dairy operations within a 7 mile radius of the location developed by Spur's predecessors. In April and May of 1959, the Northside Hay Mill was feeding between 6,000 and 7,000 head of cattle and Welborn approximately 1,500 head on a combined area of 35 acres.

In May of 1959, Del Webb began to plan the development of an urban area to be known as Sun City. For this purpose, the Marinette and the Santa Fe Ranches, some 20,000 acres of farmland, were purchased for $15,000,000 or $750.00 per acre. This price was considerably less than the price of land located near the urban area of Phoenix, and along with the success of Youngtown was a factor influencing the decision to purchase the property in question.

By September 1959, Del Webb had started construction of a golf course south of Grand Avenue and Spur's predecessors had started to level ground for more feedlot area. In 1960, Spur purchased the property in question and began a rebuilding and expansion program extending both to the north and south of the original facilities. By 1962, Spur's expansion program was completed and had expanded from approximately 35 acres to 114 acres. See Exhibit A above.

Accompanied by an extensive advertising campaign, homes were first offered by Del Webb in January 1960 and the first unit to be completed was south of Grand Avenue and approximately 2½ miles north of Spur. By 2 May 1960, there were 450 to 500 houses completed or under construction. At this time, Del Webb did not consider odors from the Spur feed pens a problem and Del Webb continued to develop in a southerly direction, until sales resistance became so great that the parcels were difficult if not impossible to sell.

*   *   *

By December 1967, Del Webb's property had extended south to Olive Avenue and Spur was within 500 feet of Olive Avenue to the north. See Exhibit B above. Del Webb filed its original complaint alleging that in excess of 1,300 lots in the southwest portion were unfit for development for sale as residential lots because of the operation of the Spur feedlot.

Del Webb's suit complained that the Spur feeding operation was a public nuisance because of the flies and the odor which were drifting or being blown by the prevailing south to north wind over the southern portion of Sun City. At the time of the suit, Spur was feeding between 20,000 and 30,000 head of cattle, and the facts amply support the finding of the trial court that the feed pens had become a nuisance to the people who resided in the southern part of Del Webb's development. The testimony indicated that cattle in a commercial feedlot will produce 35 to 40 pounds of wet manure per day, per head, or over a million pounds of wet manure per day for 30,000 head of cattle, and that despite the admittedly good feedlot management and good housekeeping practices by Spur, the resulting odor and flies produced an annoying if not unhealthy situation as far as the senior citizens of southern Sun City were concerned. There is no doubt that some of the citizens of Sun City were unable to enjoy the outdoor living which Del Webb had advertised and that Del Webb was faced with sales resistance from prospective purchasers as well as strong and persistent complaints from the people who had purchased homes in that area.

Trial was commenced before the court with an advisory jury. The advisory jury was later discharged and the trial was continued before the court alone. Findings of fact and conclusions of law were requested and given. The case was vigorously contested, including special actions in this court on some of the matters. In one of the special actions before this court, Spur agreed to, and did, shut down its operation without prejudice to a determination of the matter on appeal. On appeal the many questions raised were extensively briefed.

It is noted, however, that neither the citizens of Sun City nor Youngtown are represented in this lawsuit and the suit is solely between Del E. Webb Development Company and Spur Industries, Inc.

MAY SPUR BE ENJOINED?

The difference between a private nuisance and a public nuisance is generally one of degree. A private nuisance is one affecting a single individual or a definite small number of persons in the enjoyment of private rights not common to the public, while a public nuisance is one affecting the rights enjoyed by citizens as a part of the public. To constitute a public nuisance, the nuisance must affect a considerable number of people or an entire community or neighborhood. City of Phoenix v. Johnson, 51 Ariz. 115, 75 P.2d 30 (1938).

Where the injury is slight, the remedy for minor inconveniences lies in an action for damages rather than in one for an injunction. Kubby v. Hammond, 68 Ariz. 17, 198 P.2d 134 (1948). Moreover, some courts have held, in the "balancing of conveniences" cases, that damages may be the sole remedy. See Boomer v. Atlantic Cement Co., 26 N.Y.2d 219, 309 N.Y.S.2d 312, 257 N.E.2d 870, 40 A.L.R.3d 590 (1970), and annotation comments, 40 A.L.R.3d 601.

Thus, it would appear from the admittedly incomplete record as developed in the trial court, that, at most, residents of Youngtown would be entitled to damages rather than injunctive relief.

We have no difficulty, however, in agreeing with the conclusion of the trial court that Spur's operation was an enjoinable public nuisance as far as the people in the southern portion of Del Webb's Sun City were concerned.

§ 36–601, subsec. A reads as follows:

"§ 36–601. Public nuisances dangerous to public health

"A. The following conditions are specifically declared public nuisances dangerous to the public health:

"1. Any condition or place in populous areas which constitutes a breeding place for flies, rodents, mosquitoes and other insects which are capable of carrying and transmitting disease-causing organisms to any person or persons."

By this statute, before an otherwise lawful (and necessary) business may be declared a public nuisance, there must be a "populous" area in which people are injured:

" * * * [I]t hardly admits a doubt that, in determining the question as to whether a lawful occupation is so conducted as to constitute a nuisance as a matter of fact, the locality and surroundings are of the first importance. (citations omitted) A business which is not per se a public nuisance may become such by being carried on at a place where the health, comfort, or convenience of a populous neighborhood is affected. * * * What might amount to a serious nuisance in one locality by reason of the density of the population, or character of the neighborhood affected, may in another place and under different surroundings be deemed proper and unobjectionable. * * *." MacDonald v. Perry, 32 Ariz. 39, 49–50, 255 P. 494, 497 (1927).

It is clear that as to the citizens of Sun City, the operation of Spur's feedlot was both a public and a private nuisance. They could have successfully maintained an action to abate the nuisance. Del Webb, having shown a special injury in the loss of sales, had a standing to bring suit to enjoin the nuisance. Engle v. Clark, 53 Ariz. 472, 90 P.2d 994 (1939); City of Phoenix v. Johnson, supra. The judgment of the trial court permanently enjoining the operation of the feedlot is affirmed.

MUST DEL WEBB INDEMNIFY SPUR?

A suit to enjoin a nuisance sounds in equity and the courts have long recognized a special responsibility to the public when acting as a court of equity:

§ 104. Where public interest is involved.

"Courts of equity may, and frequently do, go much further both to give and withhold relief in furtherance of the public interest than they are accustomed to go when only private interests are involved. Accordingly, the granting or withholding of relief may properly be dependent upon considerations of public interest. * * *." 27 Am.Jur.2d, Equity, page 626.

In addition to protecting the public interest, however, courts of equity are concerned with protecting the operator of a lawfully, albeit noxious, business from the result of a knowing and willful encroachment by others near his business.

In the so-called "coming to the nuisance" cases, the courts have held that the residential landowner may not have relief if he knowingly came into a neighborhood reserved for industrial or agricultural endeavors and has been damaged thereby:

"Plaintiffs chose to live in an area uncontrolled by zoning laws or restrictive covenants and remote from urban development. In such an area plaintiffs cannot complain that legitimate agricultural pursuits are being carried on in the vicinity, nor can plaintiffs, having chosen to build in an agricultural area, complain that the agricultural pursuits carried on in the area depreciate the value of their homes. The area being *primarily agricultural*, any opinion reflecting the value of such property must take this factor into account. The standards affecting the value of residence property in an urban setting, subject to zoning controls and controlled planning techniques, cannot be the standards by which agricultural properties are judged.

"People employed in a city who build their homes in suburban areas of the county beyond the limits of a city and zoning regulations do so for a reason. Some do so to avoid the high taxation rate imposed by cities, or to avoid special assessments for street, sewer and water projects. They usually build on improved or hard surface highways, which have been built either at state or county expense and thereby avoid special assessments for these improvements. It may be that they desire to get away from the congestion of traffic, smoke, noise, foul air and the many other annoyances of city life. But with all these advantages in going beyond the area which is zoned and restricted to protect them in their homes, they must be prepared to take the disadvantages." Dill v. Excel Packing Company, 183 Kan. 513, 525, 526, 331 P.2d 539, 548, 549 (1958). See also East St. Johns Shingle Co. v. City of Portland, 195 Or. 505, 246 P.2d 554, 560–562 (1952).

And:

" * * * a party cannot justly call upon the law to make that place suitable for his residence which was not so when he selected it. * * *." Gilbert v. Showerman, 23 Mich. 448, 455, 2 Brown 158 (1871).

Were Webb the only party injured, we would feel justified in holding that the doctrine of "coming to the nuisance" would have been a bar to the relief asked by Webb, and, on the other hand, had Spur located the feedlot near the outskirts of a city and had the city grown toward the feedlot, Spur would have to suffer the cost of abating the nuisance as to those people locating within the growth pattern of the expanding city:

"The case affords, perhaps, an example where a business established at a place remote from population is gradually surrounded and becomes part of a populous center, so that a business which formerly was not an interference with the rights of others has become so by the encroachment of the population * * *." City of Ft. Smith v. Western Hide & Fur Co., 153 Ark. 99, 103, 239 S.W. 724, 726 (1922).

We agree, however, with the Massachusetts court that:

"The law of nuisance affords no rigid rule to be applied in all instances. It is elastic. It undertakes to require only that which is fair and reasonable under all the circumstances. In a common-wealth like this, which depends for its material prosperity so largely on the continued growth and enlargement of manufacturing of diverse varieties, 'extreme rights' cannot be enforced. * * *." Stevens v. Rockport Granite Co., 216 Mass. 486, 488, 104 N.E. 371, 373 (1914).

There was no indication in the instant case at the time Spur and its predecessors located in western Maricopa County that a new city would spring up, full-blown, alongside the feeding operation and that the developer of that city would ask the court to order Spur to move because of the new city. Spur is required to move not because of any wrongdoing on the part of Spur, but because of a proper and legitimate regard of the courts for the rights and interests of the public.

Del Webb, on the other hand, is entitled to the relief prayed for (a permanent injunction), not because Webb is blameless, but because of the damage to the people who have been encouraged to purchase homes in Sun City. It does not equitably or legally follow, however, that Webb, being entitled to the injunction, is then free of any liability to Spur if Webb has in fact been the cause of the damage Spur has sustained. It does not seem harsh to require a developer, who has taken advantage of the lesser land values in a rural area as well as the availability of large tracts of land on which to build and develop a new town or city in the area, to indemnify those who are forced to leave as a result.

Having brought people to the nuisance to the foreseeable detriment of Spur, Webb must indemnify Spur for a reasonable amount of the cost of moving or shutting down. It should be noted that this relief to Spur is limited to a case wherein a developer has, with foreseeability, brought into a previously agricultural or industrial area the population which makes necessary the granting of an injunction against a lawful business and for which the business has no adequate relief.

It is therefore the decision of this court that the matter be remanded to the trial court for a hearing upon the damages sustained by the defendant Spur as a reasonable and direct result of the granting of the permanent injunction. Since the result of the appeal may appear novel and both sides have obtained a measure of relief, it is ordered that each side will bear its own costs.

Affirmed in part, reversed in part, and remanded for further proceedings consistent with this opinion.

HAYS, C.J., STRUCKMEYER and LOCKWOOD, JJ., and UDALL, Retired Justice.

Notes and Questions

1. Do you agree with the court in the principal case that the only cases in which a "compensated injunction" is the appropriate remedy are those "wherein a developer has, with foreseeability, brought into a previously agricultural or industrial area the population which makes necessary the granting of an injunc-

tion against a lawful business and for which the business has no adequate relief"?

2.   How do you think the court would have handled the principal case if the action to enjoin the nuisance had been brought by the Sun City municipal attorney?   If it had been a class action by a substantial number of the residents of Sun City?

3.   Upon remand in the principal case, how should the trial court frame its judgment?   Should the injunction be conditioned upon tender of the damages assessed by the court to Spur Industries, or should the payment of the damages be conditioned upon compliance with the injunction against continued operation of its feed lot?

4.   Although the unorthodox remedy adopted in the *Spur Industries* case does not cite and presumably is not based on it, an article published in the Harvard Law Review at about the same time proposed the same remedial alternative in the course of developing a model for dealing with nuisance cases. The authors, Calabresi and Melamed, worked out a model based on the theory that an entitlement (i.e., a property right) to use a natural resource (e.g., clean air) may be allocated either to the plaintiff or the defendant in a nuisance case, and that this entitlement may be protected either by an injunction (a "property rule") so that the entitlement may be taken away only by one who obtains the permission of the owner of the entitlement, or by an award of damages (a "liability rule") so that the entitlement may be taken away by one who pays judicially determined compensatory damages. The authors reasoned that, since an entitlement may initially be located in either of the parties and can be protected either by an injunction or by an award of damages, there must be four possible outcomes in nuisance cases, rather than only the three traditionally found in court decisions. Thus, in addition to finding "no nuisance," or finding "nuisance" and granting an injunction, or finding "nuisance" and awarding only damages, Calabresi and Melamed argued that courts should be free to grant an injunction and require the plaintiff to pay damages to compensate the defendant for the loss caused by the injunction. See Calabresi & Melamed, Property Rules, Liability Rules, and Inalienability; One View of the Cathedral, 85 Harv. L.Rev. 1089 (1972), arguing that through choice among all four possible outcomes, courts can do a better job in achieving both economic efficiency and fairness that is possible when they limit themselves to the three traditional outcomes. For commentary on the thesis advanced by Calabresi and Melamed, see Rabin, Nuisance Law: Rethinking Fundamental Assumptions, 63 Va.L.Rev. 1299 (1977); Ellickson, Alternatives to Zoning: Covenants, Nuisance Rules, and Fines as Land Use Controls, 40 U.Chi.L.Rev. 681 (1973); Polinsky, Resolving Nuisance Disputes: The Simple Economics of Injunctive and Damages Remedies, 32 Stan.L.Rev. 1075 (1980). See also Michelman, Norms and Normativity in the Economic Theory of Law, 62 Minn.L.Rev. 1015, 1028 and passim (1978).

Note on Nuisance Law and Environmental Protection

By means of the *Boomer* case, we not only savor the dimensions of the modern law on private nuisance, but also dip our toes into deep and troubled waters: the protection of our environment in general, air and water pollution in particular. This problem is so vast that we cannot here attempt even to outline its scope or the possible legal responses to it. It is obvious to anyone who is awake to the news media that massive efforts are needed, and are being made, to discover the presence of pollutants and their effect upon human and other life, to measure and decide upon their tolerable limits, and to discover and improve methods to abate or alleviate pollution. Equally overwhelming is the problem how best to fashion or apply inducements or coercive measures to those whose activities cause pollution. Implicit in this problem are the complexities of the American political and legal structure, and the question as to how authority is best distributed for this purpose within the limitations of our constitutional system.

During the past decade and a half, the major impetus for environmental protection has come from the federal government. Among the principal federal statutes concerned with environmental protection are the Clean Air Act, 42 U.S. C.A. §§ 7401 et seq., the Water Pollution Control Act, 33 U.S.C.A. §§ 1251 et seq., and the National Environmental Policy Act, 42 U.S.C.A. §§ 4321 et seq. (establishing the Environmental Protection Agency at the federal level). Both the Clean Air Act and the Water Pollution Control Act have as their main objective the attainment of statutory air and water quality standards which are to be met within time periods prescribed by the legislation or by regulations adopted by the Environmental Protection Agency. Program implementation under both statutes is initially the responsibility of the Environmental Protection Agency, but EPA may delegate program enforcement responsibilities to state and local agencies if these agencies meet the detailed requirements contained in the federal statutes. Most (if not all) the states have, in fact, established air and water pollution control agencies, and the EPA has delegated substantial authority to these agencies.

There is a natural disposition on the part of both courts and administrative agencies to proceed with caution in applying legal sanctions against polluters. This is strikingly illustrated in the *Boomer* case, supra. It is further illustrated by the experience of the Dundee Cement Company, which operates a cement plant at Dundee, Michigan. Dundee's plant was built in 1959 and was apparently built to substantially the same specifications as was the cement plant of the Atlantic Cement Company involved in the *Boomer* case. To travelers on nearby U.S. Highway 23, the tall Dundee Cement Company smoke stack has for many years been a landmark, and its "plume" of smoke has also served as an unintended weather vane. For a long time, when the wind was right, travelers also sensed an acrid odor even inside automobiles with their windows closed. The plant is located in sparsely inhabited farm land with only one small community, Dundee, Michigan, nearby, which is located on the lee side of the prevailing wind directions. At any rate, we know of no private lawsuits against the company on account of the effluent from the plant. But apparently there have been numerous complaints over the years.

With the coming of the federal Clean Air Act and related state legislative and administrative machinery, the Company apparently saw the handwriting on the wall. At any rate, in 1971 they voluntarily applied to the Michigan Air Pollution Control Commission for permission to install electrostatic precipitator dust collectors in two cement kilns. Permission was granted and this equipment was installed at a cost of over $4 million. Thereafter inspection by the Commission revealed that these changes had not sufficiently reduced the pollution problem. Whereupon, in 1975 the Company proposed and the Commission directed the installation of two additional electric fields designed to increase the collection area by 33.3% and also to increase the current (power) capability by 25%. Apparently these changes were undertaken by the vendor of the equipment in an effort to meet its warranty. The same year the Company, upon permission and direction of the Commission, also installed two gravel bed dust collectors. Altogether the company has spent $40 million on air pollution control equipment.

Since then the only proceeding by the Commission was the approval in 1977 of a petition by the Company to burn a petroleum and coal mixture in its cement kilns instead of coal. The result of such a change, in the Commission's staff analysis, would be to increase the ground level concentration of sulfur dioxide. Tentative approval was nevertheless given because the Commission was studying new sulfur dioxide emission limits and the staff did not believe that the change would have a significant impact on attaining air quality standards for sulfur dioxide.

Altogether it may be that the Company's compliance with the Commission's applicable air quality specifications is still only "marginal," particularly in respect to "opacity" requirements. An officer of the Company has stated that the Company's vendor has not completely met the specifications of its warranty. A staff member of the Commission has stated that the Company is still making certain efforts to improve the quality of its electrostatic precipitators. These efforts were delayed by a long strike of company workers throughout the summer of 1978.

It seems that in the light of this history and the Company's efforts, the Commission is unwilling to take any further action against the Company at this time. In addition to the geographical circumstances mentioned above, it may be relevant that the cement plant is located on 1700 acres of land owned by the Company, which may mean that the most concentrated area of emission fall-out occurs on the Company's own land. These factors may at least be a partial explanation of the absence of any action against the Company other than the administrative action of the Michigan Air Pollution Control Commission.

The formulation of effective and fair legal remedies depends not only upon the accumulation of scientific and technological data, but also upon no less attention to economic factors. If dangerous pollution is duly proved, it may seem that adequate procedures have been established for decreeing its abatement, even if this means the closing of a plant operated by an offender. In the great new re-ordering of our scheme of values which the urgency of our pollution problem has forced upon us, there are those among us who would so weigh the "equities" as to to accept the hard economic consequences of drastic injunctive relief. There are undoubtedly many instances where, by any reasonable assessment of values, such remedies are even now in order. But in other circumstances, fairness to particular defendants, as well as the ultimate public interest, indicates some temporizing in an effort to cushion or distribute economic losses. Indeed there may be those in authority who would strive to reserve any judgment until all the returns are in.

Such responses, together with the inevitable delays inherent in our bureaucratic and political processes, have created the fear in some quarters that in the unprecedented strain of confronting problems of such immensity and complexity, the surge of forces for purifying our environment will be frustrated and vitiated. The idea has emerged that the private citizen should be given a direct hand in this business. This does not mean a redefinition of the law of private nuisance. The new Michigan statute set out below is a response to this idea. Without trying to cope with all the implications of these new proposals, you should try at least to discover whether or how they escape the obstacles which deterred the New York court in the *Boomer* case. It is one thing to fashion remedies so as to constitute private parties as instruments for enforcing the public interest. In permitting a private party to short-circuit the full panoply of administrative investigations, rules, and decrees, however, courts may be left to formulate in particular law suits the standards of conduct which private parties are to be permitted to enforce in the public interest. Is there any assurance that the Michigan courts, if the new statute is invoked, will be induced to assume the full responsibilities which that statute seems to confer?

MICHIGAN COMPILED LAWS ANNOTATED

691.1201 Short Title

Sec. 1. This act, shall be known and may be cited as the "Thomas J. Anderson, Gordon Rockwell environmental protection act of 1970".

691.1202 Actions for Declaratory and Equitable Relief; Standards for Pollution or Anti-Pollution Devices or Procedure

Sec. 2. (1) The attorney general, any political subdivision of the state, any instrumentality or agency of the state or of a political subdivision thereof, any person, partnership, corporation, association, organization or other legal entity may maintain an action in the circuit court having jurisdiction where the alleged violation occurred or is likely to occur for declaratory and equitable relief against the state, any political subdivision thereof, any instrumentality or agency of the state or of a political subdivision thereof, any person, partnership, corporation, association, organization or other legal entity for the protection of the air, water and other natural resources and the public trust therein from pollution, impairment or destruction.

(2) In granting relief provided by subsection (1) where there is involved a standard for pollution or for an anti-pollution device or procedure, fixed by rule or otherwise, by an instrumentality or agency of the state or a political subdivision thereof, the court may:

(a) Determine the validity, applicability and reasonableness of the standard.

(b) When a court finds a standard to be deficient, direct the adoption of a standard approved and specified by the court.

691.1202a Surety Bonds or Cash, Posting to Secure Costs or Judgments

Sec. 2a. If the court has reasonable ground to doubt the solvency of the plaintiff or the plaintiff's ability to pay any cost or judgment which might be rendered against him in an action brought under this act the court may order the plaintiff to post a surety bond or cash not to exceed $500.00.

691.1203 Prima Facie Showing of Pollution, Rebuttal; Affirmative Defenses; Burden of Proof; Weight of Evidence; Masters or Referees; Costs, Apportionment

Sec. 3. (1) When the plaintiff in the action has made a prima facie showing that the conduct of the defendant has, or is likely to pollute, impair or destroy the air, water or other natural resources or the public trust therein, the defendant may rebut the prima facie showing by the submission of evidence to the contrary. The defendant may also show, by way of an affirmative defense, that there is no feasible and prudent alternative to defendant's conduct and that such conduct is consistent with the promotion of the public health, safety and welfare in light of the state's paramount concern for the protection of its natural resources from pollution, impairment or destruction. Except as to the affirmative defense, the principles of burden of proof and weight of the evidence generally applicable in civil actions in the circuit courts shall apply to actions brought under this act.

(2) The court may appoint a master or referee, who shall be a disinterested person and technically qualified, to take testimony and make a record and a report of his findings to the court in the action.

(3) Costs may be apportioned to the parties if the interests of justice require.

691.1204 Granting Equitable Relief; Imposition of Conditions; Remitting Parties to Other Proceedings; Review

Sec. 4. (1) The court may grant temporary and permanent equitable relief, or may impose conditions on the defendant that are required to protect the air, water and other natural resources or the public trust therein from pollution, impairment or destruction.

(2) If administrative, licensing or other proceedings are required or available to determine the legality of the defendant's conduct, the court may remit the parties to such proceedings, which proceedings shall be conducted in accordance with and subject to the provisions of Act No. 306 of the Public Acts of 1969, being sections 24.201 to 24.313 of the Compiled Laws of 1948. In so remitting the court may grant temporary equitable relief where necessary for the protection of the air, water and other natural resources or the public trust therein from pollution, impairment or destruction. In so remitting the court shall retain jurisdiction of the action pending completion thereof for the purpose of determining whether adequate protection from pollution, impairment or destruction has been afforded.

(3) Upon completion of such proceedings, the court shall adjuciate the impact of the defendant's conduct on the air, water or other natural resources and on the public trust therein in accordance with this act. In such adjudication the court may order that additional evidence be taken to the extent necessary to protect the rights recognized in this act.

(4) Where, as to any administrative, licensing or other proceeding, judicial review thereof is available, notwithstanding the provisions to the contrary of Act No. 306 of the Public Acts of 1969, pertaining to judicial review, the court originally taking jurisdiction shall maintain jurisdiction for purposes of judicial review.

691.1205 Intervention; Determination as to Pollution; Collateral Estoppel; Res Judicata

Sec. 5. (1) Whenever administrative, licensing or other proceedings, and judicial review thereof are available by law, the agency or the court may permit the attorney general, any political subdivision of the state, any instrumentality or agency of the state or of a political subdivision thereof, any person, partnership, corporation, association, organization or other legal entity to intervene as a party on the filing of a pleading asserting that the proceeding or action for judicial review involves conduct which has, or which is likely to have, the effect of polluting, impairing or destroying the air, water or other natural resources or the public trust therein.

(2) In any such administrative, licensing or other proceedings, and in any judicial review thereof, any alleged pollution, impairment or destruction of the air, water or other natural resources or the public trust therein, shall be determined, and no conduct shall be authorized or approved which does, or is likely to have such effect so long as there is a feasible and prudent alternative consistent with the reasonable requirements of the public health, safety and welfare.

(3) The doctrines of collateral estoppel and res judicata may be applied by the court to prevent multiplicity of suits.

691.1206   Supplementary to Existing Administrative and Regulatory Procedures

Sec. 6. This act shall be supplementary to existing administrative and regulatory procedures provided by law.

691.1207   Effective Date

Sec. 7. This act shall take effect October 1, 1970.

For some insight into the thinking that underlies the Michigan statute set out above, see, Sax, Defending the Environment (1970); Sax, The Public Trust Doctrine in Natural Resource Law: Effective Judicial Intervention, 68 Mich.L. Rev. 471 (1970). For a study of the first two years of experience with the Michigan statute, see Sax, Michigan's Environmental Protection Act of 1970: A Progress Report, 70 Mich.L.Rev. 1104 (1972).

For discussion of the role that nuisance law may continue to play in environmental protection, see Stewart & Krier, Environmental Law and Policy, 255–324 (1978); Krier, The Pollution Problem and Legal Institutions: A Conceptual Overview, 18 U.C.L.A.L.Rev. 429, 459–475 (1971); Michelman, Pollution as a Tort: A Non-Accidental Perspective of Calabresi's *Costs*, 80 Yale L.J. 647, 666–683 (1971).

SECTION 2.   RIGHTS ABOVE AND BELOW THE SURFACE

EDWARDS v. SIMS

Court of Appeals of Kentucky, 1929.
232 Ky. 791, 24 S.W.2d 619.

STANLEY, C. This case presents a novel question.

In the recent case of Edwards v. Lee, 230 Ky. 375, 19 S.W.2d 992, an appeal was dismissed which sought a review and reversal of an order of the Edmonson circuit court directing surveyors to enter upon and under the lands of Edwards and others and survey the Great Onyx Cave for the purpose of securing evidence on an issue as to whether or not a part of the cave being exploited and shown by the appellants runs under the ground of Lee. The nature of the litigation is stated in the opinion and the order set forth in full. It was held that the order was interlocutory and consequently one from which no appeal would lie.

Following that decision, this original proceeding was filed in this court by the appellants in that case (who were defendants below) against Hon. N.P. Sims, judge of the Edmonson circuit court, seeking a writ of prohibition to prevent him enforcing the order and punishing the petitioners for contempt for any disobedience of it. It is alleged by the petitioners that the lower court was without jurisdiction or authority to make the order, and that their cave property and their right of possession and privacy will be wrongfully and illegally invaded, and that they will be greatly and irreparably injured and damaged without having an adequate remedy, since the damage will have been suffered before there can be an adjudication of their rights on a final appeal. It will thus be seen that there are submitted the two grounds upon which this court will prohibit inferior courts from proceeding, under the provisions of section 110 of the Constitution, namely: (1) Where it is a matter in which it has no jurisdiction and there is no remedy through appeal, and (2) where the court possesses jurisdiction but is exercising or about to exercise its power erroneously, and which would result in great injustice and irreparable injury to the applicant, and there is no adequate remedy by appeal or otherwise. Duffin v. Field, Judge, 208 Ky. 543, 271 S.W. 596; Potter v. Gardner, 222 Ky. 487, 1 S.W.2d 537; Litteral v. Woods, 223 Ky. 582, 4 S.W.2d 395.

1. There is no question as to the jurisdiction of the parties and the subject-matter. It is only whether the court is proceeding erroneously within its jurisdiction in entering and enforcing the order directing the survey of the subterranean premises of the petitioners. There is but little authority of particular and special application to caves and cave rights. In few places, if any, can be found similar works of nature of such grandeur and of such unique and marvelous character as to give to caves a commercial value sufficient to cause litigation as those peculiar to Edmonson and other counties in Kentucky. The reader will find of interest the address on "The Legal Story of Mammoth Cave" by Hon. John B. Rodes, of Bowling Green, before the 1929 Session of the Kentucky State Bar Association, published in its proceedings. In Cox v. Colossal Cavern Co., 210 Ky. 612, 276 S.W. 540, the subject of cave rights was considered, and this court held there may be a severance of the estate in the property, that is, that one may own the surface and another the cave rights, the conditions being quite similar to but not exactly like those of mineral lands. But there is no such severance involved in this case, as it appears that the defendants are the owners of the land and have in it an absolute right.

Cujus est solum, ejus est usque ad coelum ad infernos (to whomsoever the soil belongs, he owns also to the sky and to the depths), is an old maxim and rule. It is that the owner of realty, unless there has been a division of the estate, is entitled to the free and unfettered control of his own land above, upon, and beneath the surface. So whatever is in a direct line between the surface of the land and the center of the earth belongs to the owner of the surface. Ordinarily that ownership cannot be interfered with or infringed by third persons. 17 C.J. 391; 22 R.C.L. 56; Langhorne v. Turman, 141 Ky. 809, 133 S.W. 1008, 34 L.R.A.,N.S., 211. There are, however, certain limitations on the right of enjoyment of possession of all property, such as its use to the detriment or interference with a neighbor and burdens which it must bear in common with property of a like kind. 22 R.C.L. 77.

With this doctrine of ownership in mind, we approach the question as to whether a court of equity has a transcendent power to invade that right through its agents for the purpose of ascertaining the truth of a matter before it, which fact thus disclosed will determine certainly whether or not the owner is trespassing upon his neighbor's property.

Our attention has not been called to any domestic case, nor have we found one, in which the question was determined either directly or by analogy. It seems to the court, however, that there can be little differentiation, so far as the matter now before us is concerned, between caves and mines. And as declared in 40 C.J. 947: "A court of equity, however, has the inherent power, independent of statute, to compel a mine owner to permit an inspection of his works at the suit of a party who can show reasonable ground for suspicion that his lands are being trespassed upon through them, and may issue an injunction to permit such inspection."

There is some limitation upon this inherent power, such as that the person applying for such an inspection must show a bona fide claim and allege facts showing a necessity for the inspection and examination of the adverse party's property; and, of course, the party whose property is to be inspected must have had an opportunity to be heard in relation thereto. In the instant case it appears that these conditions were met.

* * *

We can see no difference in principle between the invasion of a mine on adjoining property to ascertain whether or not the minerals are being extracted from under the applicant's property and an inspection of this respondent's property through his cave to ascertain whether or not be is trespassing under this applicant's property.

It appears that before making this order the court had before him surveys of the surface of both properties and the conflicting opinions of witnesses as to whether or not the Great Onyx Cave extended under the surface of the plaintiff's land. This opinion evidence was of comparatively little value, and as the chancellor (now respondent) suggested, the controversy can be quickly and accurately settled by surveying the cave; and "if defendants are correct in their contention this survey will establish it beyond all doubt and their title to this cave will be forever quieted. If the survey shows the Great Onyx Cave extends under the lands of plaintiffs, defendants should be glad to know this fact and should be just as glad to cease trespassing upon plaintiff's lands, if they are in fact doing so." The peculiar nature of these conditions, it seems to us, makes it imperative and necessary in the administration of justice that the survey should have been ordered and should be made.

It appearing that the circuit court is not exceeding its jurisdiction or proceeding errroneously, the claim of irreparable injury need not be given consideration. It is only when the inferior court is acting erroneously, *and* great or irreparable damage will result, *and* there is no adequate remedy by appeal, that a writ of prohibition will issue restraining the other tribunal, as held by authorities cited above.

The writ of prohibition is therefore denied.

Whole court sitting.

LOGAN, J. (dissenting). The majority opinion allows that to be done which will prove of incalculable injury to Edwards without benefiting Lee, who is asking that this injury be done. I must dissent from the majority opinion, confessing that I may not be able to show, by any legal precedent, that the opinion is wrong, yet having an abiding faith in my own judgment that it is wrong.

It deprives Edwards of rights which are valuable, and perhaps destroys the value of his property, upon the motion of one who may have no interest in that which it takes away, and who could not subject it to his dominion or make any use of it, if he should establish that which he seeks to establish in the new suit wherein the survey is sought.

It sounds well in the majority opinion to tritely say that he who owns the surface of real estate, without reservation, owns from the center of the earth to the outmost sentinel of the solar system. The age-old statement, adhered to in the majority opinion as the law, in truth and fact, is not true now and never has been. I can subscribe to no doctrine which makes the owner of the surface also the owner of the atmosphere filling illimitable space. Neither can I subscribe to the doctrine that he who owns the surface is also the owner of the vacant spaces in the bowels of the earth.

The rule should be that he who owns the surface is the owner of everything that may be taken from the earth and used for his profit or happiness. Anything which he may take is thereby subjected to his dominion, and it may be well said that it belongs to him. I concede the soundness of that rule, which is supported by the cases cited in the majority opinion; but they have no application to the question before the court in this case. They relate mainly to mining rights; that is, to substances under the surface which the owner may subject to his dominion. But no man can bring up from the depths of the earth the Stygian darkness and make it serve his purposes; neither can he subject to his dominion the bottom of the ways in the caves on which visitors tread, and for these reasons the owner of the surface has no right in such a cave which the law should, or can, protect because he has nothing of value therein, unless, perchance, he owns an entrance into it and has subjected the subterranean passages to his dominion.

A cave or cavern should belong absolutely to him who owns its entrance, and this ownership should extend even to its utmost reaches if he has explored and connected these reaches with the entrance. When the surface owner has discovered a cave and prepared it for purposes of exhibition, no one ought to be allowed to disturb him in his dominion over that which he has conquered and subjected to his uses.

It is well enough to hang to our theories and ideas, but when there is an effort to apply old principles to present-day conditions, and they will not fit, then it becomes necessary for a readjustment; and principles and facts as they exist in this age must be made conformable. For these reasons the old sophistry that the owner of the surface of land is the owner of everything from zenith to nadir must be reformed, and the reason why a reformation is necessary is because the theory was never true in the past, but no occasion arose that required the testing of it. Man had no dominion over the air until recently, and, prior to his conquering the air, no one had any occasion to question the claim of the surface owner that the air above him was subject to his dominion. Naturally the air above him should be subject to his dominion in so far as the use of the space is necessary for his proper enjoyment of the surface, but further than that he has no right in it separate from that of the public at large. The true principle should be announced to the effect that a man who owns the surface, without reservation, owns not only the land itself, but everything upon, above, or under it which he may use for his profit or pleasure, and which he may subject to his dominion and control. But further than this his ownership cannot extend. It should not be held that he owns that which he cannot use and which is of no benefit to him, and which may be of benefit to others.

Shall a man be allowed to stop airplanes flying above his land because he owns the surface? He cannot subject the atmosphere through which they fly to his profit or pleasure; therefore, so long as airplanes do not injure him, or interfere with the use of his property, he should be helpless to prevent their flying above his dominion. Should the waves that transmit intelligible sound through the atmosphere be allowed to pass over the lands of surface-owners? If they take nothing from him and in no way interfere with his profit or pleasure, he should be powerless to prevent their passage.

If it be a trespass to enter on the premises of the landowner, ownership meaning what the majority opinion holds that it means, the aviator who flies over the land of one who owns the surface, without his consent, is guilty of a trespass as defined by the common law and is subject to fine or imprisonment, or both, in the discretion of a jury.

If he who owns the surface does not own and control the atmosphere above him, he does not own and control vacuity beneath the surface. He owns everything beneath the surface that he can subject to his profit or pleasure, but he owns nothing more. Therefore, let it be written that a man who owns land does, in truth and in fact, own everything from zenith to nadir, but only for the use that he can make of it for his profit or pleasure. He owns nothing which he cannot subject to his dominion.

In the light of these unannounced principles which ought to be the law in this modern age, let us give thought to the petitioner Edwards, his rights and his predicament, if that is done to him which the circuit judge has directed to be done. Edwards owns this cave through right of discovery, exploration, development, advertising, exhibition, and conquest. Men fought their way through the eternal darkness, into the mysterious and abysmal depths of the bowels of a groaning world to discover the theretofore unseen splendors of unknown natural scenic wonders. They were conquerors of fear, although now and then one of them, as did Floyd Collins, paid with his life, for his hardihood in adventuring into the regions where Charon with his boat had never before seen any but the spirits of the departed. They let themselves down by flimsy ropes into pits that seemed bottomless; they clung to scanty handholds as they skirted the brinks of precipices while the flickering flare of their flaming flambeaux disclosed no bottom to the yawning gulf beneath them; they waded through rushing torrents, not knowing what awaited them on the farther side; they climbed slippery steps to find other levels; they wounded their bodies on stalagmites and stalactites and other curious and weird formations; they found chambers, star-studded and filled with scintillating light reflected by a phantasmagoria revealing fancied phantoms, and tapestry woven by the toiling gods in the dominion of Erebus; hunger and thirst, danger and deprivation could not stop them. Through days, weeks, months, and years— ever linking chamber with chamber, disclosing an underground land of enchantment, they continued their explorations; through the years they toiled connecting these wonders with the outside world through the entrance on the land of Edwards which he had discovered; through the years they toiled finding safe ways for those who might come to view what they had found and placed their seal upon. They knew nothing, and cared less, of who owned the surface above; they were in another world where no law forbade their footsteps. They created an underground kingdom where Gulliver's people may have lived or where Ayesha may have found the revolving column of fire in which to bathe meant eternal youth.

When the wonders were unfolded and the ways were made safe, then Edwards patiently, and again through the years, commenced the advertisement of his cave. First came one to see, then another, then two together, then small groups, then small crowds, then large crowds, and then the multitudes. Edwards had seen his faith justiifed. The cave was his because he had made it what it was, and without what he had done it was nothing of value. The value is not in the black vacuum that the uninitiated call a cave. That which Edwards owns is something intangible and indefinable. It is his vision translated into a reality.

Then came the horse leach's daughters crying: "Give me," "give me." Then came the "surface men" crying, "I think this cave may run under my lands." They do not know they only "guess," but they seek to discover the secrets of Edwards so that they may harass him and take from him that which he has made his own. They have come to a court of equity and have asked that Edwards be forced to open his doors and his ways to them so that they may go in and despoil him; that they may lay his secrets bare so that others may follow their example and dig into the wonders which Edwards has made his own. What may be the result if they stop his ways? They destroy the cave, because those who visit it are they who give it value, and none will visit it when the ways are barred so that it may not be exhibited as a whole.

It may be that the law is as stated in the majority opinion of the court, but equity, according to my judgment, should not destroy that which belongs to one man when he at whose behest the destruction is visited, although with some legal right, is not benefited thereby. Any ruling by a court which brings great and irreparable injury to a party is erroneous.

For these reasons I dissent from the majority opinion.

Notes and Questions

1. Dean Prosser has called the decision in the *Edwards* case "dog-in-the-manger law." Prosser, Torts 73 (4th ed. 1971).

In Boehringer v. Montalto, 142 Misc. 560, 254 N.Y.S. 276 (1931), it was held that a sewer acquired by condemnation at a depth of over 150 feet was not an encumbrance upon the title of the owner of the surface. After referring to the limitations on landowners' ownership of air space (considered in the cases below), the court said, "By analogy, the title of an owner of the soil will not be extended to a depth below ground beyond which the owner may not reasonably make use thereof."

In Marengo Cave Co. v. Ross, 212 Ind. 624, 10 N.E.2d 917 (1937), on facts similar to those in the *Edwards* case, the court assumed the same law that was declared in the *Edwards* case in holding that the defendant-cave exhibitor had not acquired title to the plaintiff's part of the cave by adverse possession. Assuming that the statutory period had run since the time the defendant began his cave operations, and that neither party knew until just prior to the suit that the cave extended under the plaintiff's land, do you perceive the reason why the court held that the requirements for adverse possession had not been met?

2. If we were to accept Judge Logan's dissenting view that rejects ownership of land to the center of the earth and substitutes "everything that may be taken from the earth and used for his profit and happiness," an obvious difficulty exists in any attempt to define the landowner's ownership of the subsurface of his land. Judge Logan does not say "everything that he has in fact taken," but "everything that may be taken." What is the meaning of this? He seems to distinguish mineral rights from a cave. Does this mean that a landowner owns a vein of coal in place, but not a cave, even though they both may be the same distance below the surface? When a vein of coal has been removed, who owns the vacant space? All this certainly presents some difficulty in arriving at any spatial definition of the extent of ownership of land.

3. Under the traditional view, adopted by the majority in the principal case, the occupation of that portion of the cave owned by Lee was an interference with his "constructive" possession of the cave, and amounted to an ouster or continuing trespass. But suppose that Lee had not been the owner of any portion of the surface above the cave, only a wrongful possessor. Would the court have decided the case the same as it did on the actual facts? It would seem that, as a wrongful possessor of some part of the surface, Lee could not show either possession or a right to possession of that part of the cave beneath the surface area wrongfully in his possession. However, suppose Lee had been an adverse possessor with "color of title." Would he then be deemed to have "constructive" possession of that part of the cave lying beneath the surface area described in the instrument constituting his "color of title"?

4. Most of the problems raising the extent of ownership of land below the surface in fact involve mineral rights. The old *ad coelum* doctrine has been accepted generally by the courts in respect to solid minerals. It is not difficult to see why the nature of the "fugitive" minerals like oil and gas present special problems which strain the normal concepts of ownership and which have produced rules which are theoretically inconsistent.

Some courts hold that a landowner owns oil and gas in place ("title in place" theory). Others hold that a landowner does not have such ownership, but only the exclusive right to reduce them to possession (non-ownership theory). One may ask if this verbal difference is a real one. The practical consequences of the two theories cannot be explored here, but they are not very great, as you might guess. In both types of jurisdictions, and with an obvious inconsistency in a "title in place" jurisdiction, the generally accepted "rule of capture" holds that a landowner may drill for oil or gas on his land without limit in amount and without regard to the fact that he may have in the process drawn oil and gas from under the land of someone else. Such a rule must stand more on a practical than a theoretical foundation. It has in fact been much qualified by legislation, which in turn has been produced more by policy than theoretical considerations. It has been generally held, on the other hand, that "whip-stocking" or crooked-hole or slant drilling across a neighbor's boundary is a trespass. This sort of thing has been much in the news in recent times and poses some difficult problems. One is the technological problem of determining when such a trespass has occurred as much as a mile below the surface. See Alphonzo E. Bell Corp. v. Bell View Oil Syndicate, 24 Cal.App.2d 587, 76 P.2d 167 (1938). Another is the problem of measuring the damages due in such a case. Ibid.

It is well settled that oil and gas rights may by conveyance be separated from surface rights. In a title-in-place state this has been described as resulting in a division "into two tracts as if the division had been made by superficial lines, or had been severed vertically by horizontal planes."

See generally 2 A.L.P. §§ 10.5, 10.6.

5. Subsequently to the decision in Edwards v. Sims a further proceeding resulted in the establishment of the boundary between the parties' tracts of land and consequently a finding as to that part of the cave which lay under Lee's land. In a still further proceeding brought by Lee's administrator the court held that the plaintiff was entitled to an injunction against further trespasses and to a proportionate amount of the net profits earned by the defendant in exhibiting the cave. Since that part of the cave under Lee's land was 2040 feet out of the total footage of 6449 feet, the plaintiff was awarded a judgment for the same proportion of the net profits over a period of five years plus interest at 6% from the beginning of that period, which amounted to $17,240. The court concluded that a restitution principle was applicable that a wrongdoer shall not profit from his wrong, and that the present case was a proper extension of cases allowing the recovery of mesne profits in an action of ejectment to recover possession. Edwards v. Lee's Adm'r, 265 Ky. 418, 96 S.W. 2d 1028 (1936).

"Restitution" is a term which can be used to characterize a miscellany of legal remedies. We cannot here even begin to outline the dimensions of this law, to which entire courses in law schools are devoted. For the present purposes it can be observed that restitutionary remedies include those which render a defendant accountable for profits realized by a wrong done to the plaintiff or where he has otherwise been unjustly enriched at the plaintiff's expense. The common-law actions of replevin and ejectment are essentially restitutionary. More often resort is had to remedies designed as alternatives to traditional actions for damages or for injunctive relief. Some of these were adaptions of the common-law remedy of assumpsit. The action called "special assumpsit" came to be the standard remedy to recover damages for breach of an express contract not under seal. The action of "general assumpsit" was developed to give restitutionary relief by use of the fiction of an implied promise by the defendant to restore to the plaintiff benefits which constituted an unjust enrichment of the defendant at the plaintiff's expense. In fact the law of restitution is sometimes called the law of quasi-contract. This remedy was applied in certain cases in which not only was there no express contract, but where the defendant's conduct was tortious. A plaintiff who resorted to this remedy in such a case was said to have "waived the tort and sued in assumpsit".

Where the tort consisted of the wrongful possession of another's chattels, the latter could resort to an action of assumpsit, in which he could recover the value of the chattels, or if they had been restored to him, their reasonable rental value for the period of their detention. Restatement, Restitution § 128 (1937).

Where a person tortiously severed and took possession of anything in or upon the land of another, a restitutionary remedy for the value of the things taken was allowed. Id. § 129(3).

In cases where the wrong consisted of the unlawful possession of land, a plaintiff could recover "mesne profits" as an incident to an action of ejectment. In fact the measure of recovery in such cases was the reasonable rental value of the property for the period of the defendant's possession, in addition to the recovery of possession of the land itself. Traditionally, however, the former was merely an incident of the latter, and could not be recovered apart from an action of ejectment.

The *Edwards* case does not fit under any of these categories. But the plaintiff was allowed to recover in an action which the court said was essentially *ex contractu*. Apart from this case there is little authority for such a recovery. Since actions based on trespass to land frequently involve title questions, it was thought that an action of assumpsit was inconvenient and inappropriate for determining such questions. Id., comment a.

There may seem to be little reason under modern civil procedure for adhering to the restrictive aspect of these historical distinctions. But to the extent that the court in the *Edwards* case was extending the recovery of mesne profits to a case not involving the recovery of possession in ejectment, should not the plaintiff be limited to the recovery of the reasonable rental value of his property? The court recognized the difficulty in applying such a standard in this case for the reason that there had been no continuous occupation of the cave by the defendant. But the court said that rental value has been adopted "as a convenient yardstick by which to measure the proportionate profit derived by the trespasser directly from the use of the land itself," and that profits rather than rent can form the basis of recovery.

Apart from the historical deficiencies of traditional legal remedies, a difficult legal and economic problem is presented by the question: what is a fair measure of the plaintiff's rights in such a case? Does the use of the old maxim that a defendant should not profit by his wrong require him to account for his net profits to the extent allowed in the *Edwards* case, even though the result places the plaintiff in a better position than he would have been in had there been no trespass? Does the effect amount to the imposition of a penalty? Is this the sort of situation in which penal remedies are in order? Note that the plaintiff's recovery is of profits which he could not have earned if there had been no trespass. Should not the defendant at least be entitled to some consideration for his outlays in fitting the cave for commercial use? Does the result in the *Edwards* case mean that in many cases the value of caves cannot be exploited by anyone? If the parties are left to bargain for the continuation of the defendant's operations, it is not likely that the defendant would be willing to pay for his use of the plaintiff's part of the land the entire net profits of such use. Maybe in furtherance of his own economic interests, a person in the plaintiff's position would be willing to accept less rather than accept the consequences of the defendant's withdrawal to his own subsurface. But as a result of this case, he may be fortified in his bargaining position to an extent that may seem excessive. See Note, 37 Colum.L.Rev. 503 (1937).

If the full utilization of such a natural resource for the public benefit is to be encouraged, Judge Logan's dissent in the principal case may gain an added appeal, with the result of course that the plaintiff would have no remedy at all.

GUITH v. CONSUMERS POWER CO.

District Court, E.D. Michigan, N.D. (1940).
36 F.Supp. 21.

TUTTLE, District Judge. The plaintiffs are operators of the Grand Blanc Airport, situated about four miles south of Flint, Michigan. The defendant owns in fee land adjacent to the airport upon which it is about to erect an electric transmission line consisting of pole structures and wires. The plaintiffs filed a bill of complaint for an injunction restraining the defendant from erecting said line.

The defendant filed a motion to dismiss the bill of complaint, alleging that the same failed to state a claim against the defendant upon which relief could be granted, stating, among other reasons, that:

(a) The plaintiffs have no right, title or interest in the defendant's land or the air space above it for a reasonable and useful altitude.

(b) That the electric transmission line is a lawful, reasonable and necessary use of the defendant's land and the overlying air space; and

(c) That the flight of airplanes over the defendant's land at such low altitude as to interfere with the use of said land by defendant for said transmission line is unlawful.

The fundamental issue involved in this case is: Does the landowner own the air space above the land to a height necessary for occupancy of an electric transmission line to the exclusion of airplanes using an adjacent airport?

The bill of complaint does not allege any right in the plaintiffs to use the air space over the defendant's land for low altitude flying incident to the take-off and landing of airplanes at the airport, which is superior to the right of the defendant to use its land for said transmission line. Neither have the plaintiffs cited any authority establishing such right, and the court believes no authority can be cited therefor.

In the Restatement of the Law of Torts by The American Law Institute, the common law on the relative rights of the landowner and the aviator to the use of air space above the surface of the earth is stated as follows:

"Section 159, Comment e:

"An unprivileged intrusion in the space above the surface of the earth, at whatever height above the surface, is a trespass."

"Section 194—Travel Through Air Space.

"An entry above the surface of the earth, in the air space in the possession of another, by a person who is traveling in an aircraft, is privileged if the flight is conducted:

"(a) for the purpose of travel through the air space or for any other legitimate purpose,

"(b) in a reasonable manner,

"(c) at such a height as not to interfere unreasonably with the possessor's enjoyment of the surface of the earth and the air space above it, and

"(d) in conformity with such regulations of the State and federal aeronautical authorities as are in force in the particular State."

Act 224 of the Public Acts of Michigan for 1923, being Sections 4811–4821, Compiled Laws of 1929, and Sections 10.21 to 10.29, Michigan Statutes Annotated, pertains to aeronautics over land and water, Sections 3 and 4 of said Act are as follows:

"Sec. 3. The ownership of the space above the lands and waters of this state is declared to be vested in the several owners of the surface beneath, subject to the right of flight described in section four [4]. [C.L. '29, Sec. 4813.]

"Sec. 4. Flight in aircraft over the lands and waters of this state is lawful, unless at such low altitude as to interfere with the then existing use to which the land or water, or the space over the land or water, is put by the owner, or unless so conducted as to be imminently dangerous to persons or property lawfully on the land or water beneath. The landing of an aircraft on the lands or waters of another, without his consent, is unlawful, except in the case of a forced landing. For damages caused by a forced landing, however, the owner or lessee of the aircraft or the aeronaut shall be liable, as provided in section five [5]. [C.L. '29, Sec. 4814.]"

The State of Indiana has the identical statutory provisions above mentioned and the same were construed by the Supreme Court of Indiana in the case of Capitol Airways, Inc. v. Indianapolis Power & Light Company, 215 Ind. 462, 18 N.E.2d 776, 778.

In the *Capitol Airways* case, supra, the airport operator brought a suit against the defendant public utility to recover damages resulting from the destruction of the usefulness of the airport. From an adverse judgment, the plaintiff appealed and the judgment of the lower court was affirmed. In this case, the public utility had acquired a right of way for the construction of an electric transmission line upon property across the highway from the airport of the plaintiff. The transmission line consisted of steel towers ninety feet in height carrying 130,000 volts. Plaintiff contended that its flying field was so small that airplanes could not land or leave the field without flying over the adjacent land and that the transmission line obstructed the approach of airplanes to the airport, and created a flying hazard which would result in discontinuing the use of the plaintiff's airport and would destroy plaintiff's business. A demurrer to the complaint was sustained. The court, after quoting the sections of the Uniform Aeronautics Law hereinabove set forth, stated:

"The word 'then' must be interpreted as referring to the existing use of the land at the time of the flight. The establishment of an airport upon the appellant's land in no way affected or limited the right of adjacent landowners to use their land in any manner and for any purpose for which they might have used it before. Had the appellee chosen to erect flagpoles, factory chimneys, or tall buildings across the whole of its land, and several times as high as its power line, it was within its rights notwithstanding it might have entirely prevented the landing of airplanes at appellant's airport. It cannot be said that the appellee might reasonably have anticipated that the general public was liable to come in contact with its high tension wires upon its power line. The flight of an airplane across its land at such a low altitude as to interfere with the land for the purpose of maintaining a power line is expressly made unlawful by the statute, and the statute cannot be construed as requiring the appellee to guard against this unlawfulness any more than to guard against the unlawfulness of a trespasser who climbs its towers and thus comes in contact with the wires. * * *

"The appellee's power line interferes with none of the appellant's rights. It owes no duty to protect the public against dangers that cannot reasonably be anticipated. The owner of property is under no duty to keep the premises safe for a trespasser, who comes without enticement, allurement, or invitation. * * *"

The common law as set forth in the Restatement of the Law of Torts and the statutory law of Michigan recognize air space ownership in the landowner subject to a public right or privilege of flight. This, however, does not mean indiscriminate flight at any altitude irrespective of the use of the land by the landowner, but only such flights are privileged and lawful as do not interfere with the lawful use and possession made and to be made by the landowner of the surface and the air space above it. Any use of the air space over land which is injurious to the land or impairs or interferes with the possession or enjoyment thereof is unlawful.

The coming of the airplane has not taken away any of the rights of the landowner to the use and enjoyment of his land and the air space above it. The privilege or right of airplanes to fly through the air space recognized by the common law and in the statutory law of Michigan is limited to that portion of the air space which the landowner does not need or want and the use of which does not interfere with the use, occupation or enjoyment of the land or the air space above it by the landowner.

The motion to dismiss the bill of complaint is granted.

Notes

1. The American Law Institute has changed the rule of the Restatement of Torts §§ 159 and 194, which were cited by the court in *Guith*. See note 5.

2. In Burnham v. Beverly Airways, Inc., 311 Mass. 628, 42 N.E.2d 575 (1942), the plaintiffs sued to enjoin the nuisance and trespasses alleged to result from the maintenance of the defendant's airport and the flying of aircraft over the plaintiff's land, and for damages. The court affirmed a decree granting an injunction against the operation of aircraft below 500 feet except when necessary for a safe emergency landing, and granting damages in the amount of one dollar. The court referred to a state statute and to regulations by the Secretary of Commerce (under an act of Congress) fixing 500 feet as a minimum altitude for the operation of aircraft over thickly settled or business districts,

defining "navigable air space" as being above that level, and declaring such space as subject to a public right of air navigation as limited by prescribed regulations. The court said that the provisions defining navigable air space served not only as a regulation upon the operation of aircraft, but also to establish the property rights of landowners. But in further explanation of the rights of such parties, the court said that the statutory authorization of certain flights below 500 feet were not limitations on the property rights of landowners, that such flights, even for the purpose of taking off or landing "might amount to trespass," but that when such flights caused no actual damage or material discomfort, injunctive relief will not be granted. The court did not make it entirely clear whether such low level flights were at least a technical trespass or whether in certain circumstances they would not constitute a trespass at all. The court also left open the question whether or when flights above 500 feet might be an invasion of a landowner's right.

3. In Swetland v. Curtiss Airports Corp., 55 F.2d 201 (6th Cir.1932), the court ordered that a decree be entered enjoining the defendant from the use and development of certain land as an airport, on the ground that it constituted a nuisance with respect to the plaintiffs as adjacent landowners. The court spoke of a "lower stratum" and "upper stratum" of air space and said that a landowner has a "dominant right of occupancy" of the former, but can prevent the use of the upper stratum by others only to the extent that it constitutes an unreasonable interference with his complete enjoyment so as to constitute a nuisance. The court refused to fix a definite and unvarying height for the lower stratum, but said that a landowner's right of occupancy must be incidental to his use and enjoyment of the surface, and spoke of this as his "zone of expected use". The court also said that this definition was not affected by the 500 feet restriction prescribed by the Department of Commerce and adopted by statute in Ohio. In conclusion the court said that the flying of the defendants over the plaintiff's land was not within the restricted zone, but that it would deprive the plaintiffs of the use and enjoyment of their property, and so should be enjoined as a nuisance. It is of further interest that in decreeing an injunction rather than remitting plaintiffs to their remedy at law, the court said that the "balance of conveniences" favored the plaintiffs, despite the asserted public interest, since the defendants had already acquired another site on which their operations could be conducted.

See also Vanderslice v. Shawn, 26 Del.Ch. 225, 27 A.2d 87 (1942), where the court enjoined as a nuisance flights by the defendant under 500 feet, in taking off and landing, upon proof of the effects of the noise upon the use and enjoyment of the plaintiff's land.

On the flight of aircraft as a nuisance, see Annotation, 79 A.L.R.3d 253 (1977).

4. In Hinman v. Pacific Air Transport, 84 F.2d 755 (9th Cir.1936), plaintiff alleged "that defendants are engaged in the business of operating a commercial air line, and that at all times 'after the month of May, 1929, defendants daily, repeatedly and upon numerous occasions have disturbed, invaded and trespassed upon the ownership and possession of plaintiffs' tract'; that at said times defendants have operated aircraft in, across, and through said airspace at altitudes less than 100 feet above the surface; that plaintiffs notified defendants to desist from trespassing on said airspace; and that defendants have disregarded said notice, unlawfully and against the will of plaintiffs, and continue and threaten to continue such trespasses."

Alleging that the remedy at law was inadequate, the plaintiff sought injunctive relief. The suit was dismissed by the trial court. On appeal the judgment was affirmed. In part the court said:

"We own so much of the space above the ground as we can occupy or make use of, in connection with the enjoyment of our land. This right is not fixed. It varies with our varying needs and is coextensive with them. The owner of land owns as much of the space above him as he uses, but only so long as he uses it. All that lies beyond belongs to the world.

"When it is said that man owns, or may own, to the heavens, that merely means that no one can acquire a right to the space above him that will limit him in whatever use he can make of it as a part of his enjoyment of the land. To this extent his title to the air is paramount. No other person can acquire any title or exclusive right to any space above him.

"Any use of such air or space by others which is injurious to his land, or which constitutes an actual interference with his possession or his beneficial use thereof, would be a trespass for which he would have remedy. But any claim of the landowner beyond this cannot find a precedent in law, nor support in reason.

"It would be, and is, utterly impracticable and would lead to endless confusion, if the law should uphold attempts of landowners to stake out, or assert claims to definite, unused spaces in the air in order to protect some contemplated future use of it. Such a rule, if adopted, would constitute a departure never before attempted by mankind, and utterly at variance with the reason of the law. If such a rule were conceivable, how will courts protect the various landowners in their varying claims of portions of the sky? How enforce a right of ejectment or restitution? Such a rule is not necessary for the protection of the landowner in any right guaranteed him by the Constitution in the enjoyment of his property. If a right like this were recognized and upheld by the courts, it would cause confusion worse confounded. It is opposed to common sense and to all human experience.

"We cannot shut our eyes to the practical result of legal recognition of the asserted claims of appellants herein, for it leads to a legal implication to the effect that any use of airspace above the surface owner of land, without his consent would be a trespass either by the operator of an airplane or a radio operator. We will not foist any such chimerical concept of property rights upon the jurisprudence of this country. * * *

"Appellants are not entitled to injunctive relief upon the bill filed here, because no facts are alleged with respect to circumstances of appellants' use of the premises which will enable this court to infer that any actual or substantial damage will accrue from the acts of the appellees complained of.

"The case differs from the usual case of enjoining a trespass. Ordinarily, if a trespass is committed upon land, the plaintiff is entitled to at least nominal damages without proving or alleging any actual damage. In the instant case, traversing the airspace above appellants' land is not, of itself, a trespass at all, but it is a lawful act unless it is done under circumstances which will cause injury to appellants' possession.

"Appellants do not, therefore, in their bill state a case of trespass, unless they allege a case of actual and substantial damage. The bill fails to do this. It merely draws a naked conclusion as to damages without facts or circumstances to support it. It follows that the complaint does not state a case for injunctive relief."

5. The American Law Institute has announced a different rule from the Restatement of Torts §§ 159 and 194, which were cited by the court in *Guith.* It is now provided that a flight by aircraft in the air space above the land of another is a trespass only if

> "(a) it enters into the immediate reaches of the air space next to the land, and

> "(b) it interferes substantially with the other's use and enjoyment of his land."

Immediate reaches are not defined other than by the statement that ordinarily a flight above 500 feet is not within the immediate reaches, a flight within 50 feet that interferes with actual use is, and that a flight between the two figures presents a question of fact. Considerable reliance was placed on United States v. Causby, the opinion in which appears infra. It is stated further that a flight not within the immediate reaches may still unreasonably interfere with the use and enjoyment of land and so be actionable as a nuisance.ı Restatement, Second, Torts § 159 (1965).

6. How many different theories concerning a landowner's ownership of air space do you discover in the materials appearing above? What differences in result do you think turn upon the particular theory adopted?

Most of the cases in which landowners complain of the operation of aircraft involve the use of airports. And many of the large airports are operated under some sort of governmental authority. To the extent that a government agency can be held responsible for the flights of aircraft in and out of airports, the rights of landowners gain a constitutional dimension, as revealed by the two cases which follow.

UNITED STATES v. CAUSBY

Supreme Court of the United States, 1946.
328 U.S. 256, 66 S.Ct. 1062, 90 L.Ed. 1206.

Mr. Justice DOUGLAS delivered the opinion of the Court.

This is a case of first impression. The problem presented is whether respondents' property was taken within the meaning of the Fifth Amendment by frequent and regular flights of army and navy aircraft over respondents' land at low altitudes. The Court of Claims held that there was a taking and entered judgment for respondent, one judge dissenting. 60 F.Supp. 751. The case is here on a petition for a writ of certiorari which we granted because of the importance of the question presented.

Respondents own 2.8 acres near an airport outside of Greensboro, North Carolina. It has on it a dwelling house, and also various outbuildings which were mainly used for raising chickens. The end of the airport's northwest-southeast runway is 2,220 feet from respondents' barn and 2,275 feet from their house. The path of glide to this runway passes directly over the property—which is 100 feet wide and 1,200 feet long. The 30 to 1 safe glide angle approved by the Civil Aeronautics Authority passes over this property at 83 feet, which is 67 feet above the house, 63 feet above the barn and 18 feet above the highest tree. The use by the United States of this airport is pursuant to a lease executed in May, 1942, for a term commencing June 1, 1942 and ending June 30, 1942, with a provision for renewals until June 30, 1967, or six months after the end of the national emergency, whichever is the earlier.

Various aircraft of the United States use this airport—bombers, transports and fighters. The direction of the prevailing wind determines when a particular runway is used. The northwest-southeast runway in question is used about four per cent of the time in taking off and about seven per cent of the time in landing. Since the United States began operations in May, 1942, its four-motored heavy bombers, other planes of the heavier type, and its fighter planes have frequently passed over respondents' land and buildings in considerable numbers and rather close together. They come close enough at times to appear barely to miss the tops of the trees and at times so close to the tops of the trees as to blow the old leaves off. The noise is startling. And at night the glare from the planes brightly lights up the place. As a result of the noise, respondents had to give up their chicken business. As many as six to ten of their chickens were killed in one day by flying into the walls from fright. The total chickens lost in that manner was about 150. Production also fell off. The result was the destruction of the use of the property as a commercial chicken farm. Respondents are frequently deprived of their sleep and the family has become nervous and frightened. Although there have been no airplane accidents on respondents' property, there have been several accidents near the airport and close to respondents' place. These are the essential facts found by the Court of Claims. On the basis of these facts, it found that respondents' property had depreciated in value. It held that the United States had taken an easement over the property on June 1, 1942, and that the value of the property destroyed and the easement taken was $2,000.

The United States relies on the Air Commerce Act of 1926, 44 Stat. 568, 49 U.S.C. § 171 et seq., 49 U.S.C.A. § 171 et seq., as amended by the Civil Aeronautics Act of 1938, 52 Stat. 973, 49 U.S.C. § 401 et seq., 49 U.S.C.A. § 401 et seq. * * * It is argued that since these flights were within the minimum safe altitudes of flight which had been prescribed, they were an exercise of the declared right of travel through the airspace. The United States concludes that when flights are made within the navigable airspace without any physical invasion of the property of the landowners, there has been no taking of property. It says that at most there was merely incidental damage occurring as a consequence of authorized air navigation. It also argues that the landowner does not own superadjacent airspace which he has not subjected to possession by the erection of structures or other occupancy. Moreover, it is argued that even if the United States took airspace owned by respondents, no compensable damage was shown. Any damages are said to be merely consequential for which no compensation may be obtained under the Fifth Amendment.

It is ancient doctrine that at common law ownership of the land extended to the periphery of the universe—*Cujus est solum ejus est usque ad coelum.* But that doctrine has no place in the modern world. The air is a public highway, as Congress has declared. Were that not true, every transcontinental flight would subject the operator to countless trespass suits. Common sense revolts at the idea. To recognize such private claims to the airspace would clog these highways, seriously interfere with their control and development in the public interest, and transfer into private ownership that to which only the public has a just claim.

But that general principle does not control the present case. For the United States conceded on oral argument that if the flights over respondents' property rendered it uninhabitable, there would be a taking compensable under the Fifth Amendment. * * * If, by reason of the frequency and altitude of the flights, respondents could not use this land for any purpose, their loss would be complete. It would be as complete as if the United States had entered upon the surface of the land and taken exclusive possession of it.

We agree that in those circumstances there would be a taking. Though it would be only an easement of flight which was taken, that easement, if permanent and not merely temporary, normally would be the equivalent of a fee interest. It would be a definite exercise of complete dominion and control over the surface of the land. The fact that the planes never touched the surface would be as irrelevant as the absence in this day of the feudal livery of seisin on the transfer of real estate. The owner's right to possess and exploit the land—that is to say, his beneficial ownership of it—would be destroyed. It would not be a case of incidental damages arising from a legalized nuisance such as was involved in Richards v. Washington Terminal Co., 233 U.S. 546, 34 S.Ct. 654, 58 L.Ed. 1088, L.R.A.1915A, 887. In that case property owners whose lands adjoined a railroad line were denied recovery for damages resulting from the noise, vibrations, smoke and the like, incidental to the operations of the trains. In the supposed case the line of flight is over the land. And the land is appropriated as directly and completely as if it were used for the runways themselves.

There is no material difference between the supposed case and the present one, except that here enjoyment and use of the land are not completely destroyed. But that does not seem to us to be controlling. The path of glide for airplanes might reduce a valuable factory site to grazing land, an orchard to a vegetable patch, a residential section to a wheat field. Some value would remain. But the use of the airspace immediately above the land would limit the utility of the land and cause a diminution in its value. * * *

The fact that the path of glide taken by the planes was that approved by the Civil Aeronautics Authority does not change the result. The navigable airspace which Congress has placed in the public domain is "airspace above the minimum safe altitudes of flight prescribed by the Civil Aeronautics Authority." 49 U.S.C. § 180, 49 U.S.C.A. § 180. If that agency prescribed 83 feet as the minimum safe altitude, then we would have presented the question of the validity of the regulation. But nothing of the sort has been done. The path of glide governs the method of operating—of landing or taking off. The altitude required for that operation is not the minimum safe altitude of flight which is the downward reach of the navigable airspace. The minimum prescribed by the authority is 500 feet during the day and 1000 feet at night for air carriers (Civil Air Regulations, Pt. 61, §§ 61.7400, 61.7401, Code Fed. Reg.Cum.Supp., Tit. 14, ch. 1) and from 300 to 1000 feet for other aircraft depending on the type of plane and the character of the terrain. Id., Pt. 60, §§ 60.350–60.3505, Fed.Reg.Cum.Supp., supra. Hence, the flights in question were not within the navigable airspace which Congress placed within the public domain. If any airspace needed for landing or taking off were included, flights which were so close to the land as to render it uninhabitable would be immune. But the United States concedes, as we have said, that in that event there would be a taking. Thus, it is apparent that the path of glide is not the minimum safe altitude of flight within the meaning of the statute. The Civil Aeronautics Authority has, of course, the power to prescribe air traffic rules. But Congress has defined navigable airspace only in terms of one of them— the minimum safe altitudes of flight.

We have said that the airspace is a public highway. Yet it is obvious that if the landowner is to have full enjoyment of the land, he must have exclusive control of the immediate reaches of the enveloping atmosphere. Otherwise buildings could not be erected, trees could not be planted, and even fences could not be run. The principle is recognized when the law gives a remedy in case overhanging structures are erected on adjoining land. The landowner owns at least as much of the space above the ground as he can occupy or use in connection with the land. See Hinman v. Pacific Air Transport, 9 Cir., 84 F.2d 755. The fact that he does not occupy it in a physical sense—by the erection of buildings and the like—is not material. As we have said, the flight of airplanes, which skim the surface but do not touch it, is as much an appropriation of the use of the land as a more conventional entry upon it. We would not doubt that if the United States erected an elevated railway over respondents' land at the precise altitude where its planes now fly, there would be a partial taking, even though none of the supports of the structure rested on the land. The reason is that there would be an intrusion so immediate and direct as to subtract from the owner's full enjoyment of the property and to limit his exploitation of it. While the owner does not in any physical manner occupy that stratum of airspace or make use of it in the conventional sense, he does use it in somewhat the same sense that space left between buildings for the purpose of light and air is used. The superadjacent airspace at this low altitude is so close to the land that continuous invasions of it affect the use of the surface of the land itself. We think that the landowner, as an incident to his ownership, has a claim to it and that invasions of it are in the same category as invasions of the surface.   *   *   *

The airplane is part of the modern environment of life, and the inconveniences which it causes are normally not compensable under the Fifth Amendment. The airspace, apart from the immediate reaches above the land, is part of the public domain. We need not determine at this time what those precise limits are. Flights over private land are not a taking, unless they are so low and so frequent as to be a direct and immediate interference with the enjoyment and use of the land. We need not speculate on that phase of the present case. For the findings of the Court of Claims plainly establish that there was a diminution in value of the property and that the frequent, low-level flights were the direct and immediate cause. We agree with the Court of Claims that a servitude has been imposed upon the land.   * * *

The Court of Claims held, as we have noted, that an easement was taken. But the findings of fact contain no precise description as to its nature. It is not described in terms of frequency of flight, permissible altitude, or type of airplane. Nor is there a finding as to whether the easement taken was temporary or permanent. Yet an accurate description of the property taken is essential, since that interest vests in the United States. United States v. Cress, supra, 243 U.S. 328, 329, 37 S.Ct. 385, 386, 61 L.Ed. 746, and cases cited.   * * *

Since on this record it is not clear whether the easement taken is a permanent or a temporary one, it would be premature for us to consider whether the amount of the award made by the Court of Claims was proper.

The judgment is reversed and the cause is remanded to the Court of Claims so that it may make the necessary findings in conformity with this opinion.

Reversed.

Mr. Justice BLACK, dissenting.

The Fifth Amendment provides that "private property" shall not "be taken for public use, without just compensation." The Court holds today that the Government has "taken" respondents' property by repeatedly flying Army bombers directly above respondents' land at a height of eighty-three feet where the light and noise from these planes caused respondents to lose sleep and their chickens to be killed. Since the effect of the Court's decision is to limit, by the imposition of relatively absolute Constitutional barriers, possible future adjustments through legislation and regulation which might become necessary with the growth of air transportation, and since in my view the Constitution does not contain such barriers, I dissent.

* * * It is inconceivable to me that the Constitution guarantees that the airspace of this Nation needed for air navigation, is owned by the particular persons who happen to own the land beneath to the same degree as they own the surface below. No rigid Constitutional rule, in my judgment, commands that the air must be considered as marked off into separate compartments by imaginary metes and bounds in order to synchronize air ownership with land ownership. * * * Old concepts of private ownership of land should not be introduced into the field of air regulation. I have no doubt that Congress will, if not handicapped by judicial interpretations of the Constitution, preserve the freedom of the air, and at the same time, satisfy the just claims of aggrieved per-

sons. The noise of newer, larger, and more powerful planes may grow louder and louder and disturb people more and more. But the solution of the problems precipitated by these technological advances and new ways of living cannot come about through the application of rigid Constitutional restraints formulated and enforced by the courts. What adjustments may have to be made, only the future can reveal. It seems certain, however, that courts do not possess the techniques or the personnel to consider and act upon the complex combinations of factors entering into the problems. The contribution of courts must be made through the awarding of damages for injuries suffered from the flying of planes, or by the granting of injunctions to prohibit their flying. When these two simple remedial devices are elevated to a Constitutional level under the Fifth Amendment, as the Court today seems to have done, they can stand as obstacles to better adapted techniques that might be offered by experienced experts and accepted by Congress. Today's opinion is, I fear, an opening wedge for an unwarranted judicial interference with the power of Congress to develop solutions for new and vital and national problems. In my opinion this case should be reversed on the ground that there has been no "taking" in the Constitutional sense.

Mr. Justice BURTON joins in this dissent.

Notes and Questions

1. As was suggested by the materials preceding United States v. Causby, to the extent that one's property rights in land include rights in the superadjacent air space, any unprivileged entry into that air space is a trespass; and an unreasonable interference with one's use and enjoyment of his land by conduct which does not involve a "physical" invasion is a nuisance. Both trespass and nuisance are tortious when caused by a private person, and the injured party may recover damages and/or, in some circumstances, obtain injunctive relief against the tort. So why did the plaintiff in United States v. Causby sue to recover compensation for a "taking" of property for public use rather bring a tort action? The answer lies in the traditional rule of sovereign immunity against tort liability.

2. Where action which would be a trespass or a nuisance if taken by a private person is engaged in by or under governmental authority, no tort liability is incurred unless the sovereign by legislation submits itself thereto. But under federal and state constitutions, an arm of government may not take private property without paying just compensation therefor. On this foundation rests the power of eminent domain or condemnation. Normally what constitutes a "taking" of one's property presents no problem. The usual processes of condemnation make clear that the government is seeking a possessory estate in the land, usually in fee simple absolute, or a nonpossessory restricted right of use which we normally call an easement.

The problem of what constitutes a taking of a person's land, or some interest therein, becomes more critical when the governmental agency does not proceed in condemnation but rather, through its officers or agents, engages in conduct which in one way or another would be tortious if engaged in by a private party. Obviously if the government takes land in fact, its failure to follow the procedure of condemnation does not rob the injured party of a remedy guaranteed him by the applicable constitutional provision. As is indicated in the next principal case, this remedy is obtained by what is now generally called an "inverse condemnation" action.

3. In the principal case, do you think the court based its finding that the United States "took" the plaintiffs' land for a public use because (a) United States military aircraft repeatedly "trespassed" on the plaintiff's superadjacent air space at low levels, or (b) the low level flights of the military aircraft interfered substantially and unreasonably with the plaintiffs' use and enjoyment of their land? In short, is the court's "taking" holding based on a "trespass" or a "nuisance" theory?

4. In *Griggs v. Allegheny County*, 369 U.S. 84, 82 S.Ct. 531, 7 L.Ed.2d 585 (1962), rehearing denied 369 U.S. 857, 82 S.Ct. 931, 8 L.Ed.2d 16, respondent owned and operated the Greater Pittsburgh Airport. The airlines that used the airport were lessees of the respondent under leases which gave them, among other things, the right to land and take off. No flights were in violation of the regulations of the C.A.A. and no flights were lower than necessary for safe landing or take-off. But the noise of these operations rendered the plaintiff's property unusable as a place of residence. Plaintiff sought to recover damages from the respondent on the basis that an easement of flight had been taken. The Pennsylvania Supreme Court held that if there had been a "taking" of the plaintiff's property in the constitutional sense, respondent was not responsible for it. On certiorari, this judgment was reversed. The rule of the *Causby* case was held applicable to impose liability for a taking upon the respondent in its capacity as promoter, owner, and lessor of the airport. The right of access of aircraft to the airport was a necessary appurtenance to the real estate acquired for such purpose, and proper acquisition of such appurtenance was the responsibility of the respondent.

The Court in *Causby* said that low-level flights for take-offs and landings were not within the "navigable airspace" as defined by Congress. After *Causby* Congress redefined that airspace to include airspace needed to insure safety in take-off and landing of aircraft. With respect to the effect of this change, the Court in *Griggs* said merely, "But as we said in *Causby* the use of land presupposes the use of some of the airspace above it. * * * Otherwise no home could be built, no tree planted, no fence constructed, no chimney erected. An invasion of the 'superjacent airspace' will often 'affect the use of the surface of the land itself.'"

5. In cases like *Causby* and *Griggs*, how should the compensation be determined if the plaintiff is only a life tenant or a long-term lessee? If the plaintiff is only an "adverse possessor"?

THORNBURG v. PORT OF PORTLAND

Supreme Court of Oregon, 1962.
233 Or. 178, 376 P.2d 100.

GOODWIN, Justice. A trial jury denied plaintiffs the compensation which they sought in an action for "inverse condemnation".[1] In so do-

1. Inverse condemnation is the popular description of a cause of action against a governmental defendant to recover the value of property which has been taken in fact by the governmental defendant, even though nor formal exercise of the power of eminent domain has been attempted by the taking agency. See, e.g., State by and through State Highway Comm. v. Stumbo et al., 222 Or. 62, 66, 352 P.2d 478, 480 (1960); Tomasek v. State Highway Comm., 196 Or. 120, 248 P.2d 703 (1952). [Footnotes are the court's. Some have been omitted and some have been renumbered. Ed.]

ing, the jury necessarily found that the Port of Portland had not taken the plaintiffs' property. The plaintiffs appeal.

The issues in their broadest sense concern the rights of landowners adjacent to airports and the rights of the public in the airspace near the ground. Specifically, we must decide whether a noise-nuisance can amount to a taking.

The Port of Portland owns and operates the Portland International Airport. It has the power of eminent domain. It has used this power to surround itself with a substantial curtilage, but its formal acquisition stopped short of the land of the plaintiffs. For the purposes of this case, the parties have assumed that the Port is immune from ordinary tort liability. Further, it is conceded that injunctive relief would not be in the public interest. Aircraft are not ordinarily operated by the Port itself, but by third parties which use its facilities. Air navigation and other related operations are, for all practical purposes, regulated by a federal agency. The Port merely holds the airport open to the flying public.

The plaintiffs own and reside in a dwelling house located about 6,000 feet beyond the end of one runway and directly under the glide path of aircraft using it. Their land lies about 1,500 feet beyond the end of a second runway, but about 1,000 feet to one side of the glide path of aircraft using that runway.

The plaintiffs contend that flights from both runways have resulted in a taking of their property. Their principal complaint is that the noise from jet aircraft makes their land unusable. The jets use a runway the center line of which, if extended, would pass about 1,000 feet to one side of the plaintiffs' land. Some planes pass directly over the plaintiffs' land, but these are not, for the most part, the civilian and military jets which cause the most noise.

The plaintiffs' case proceeded on two theories: (1) Systematic flights directly over their land cause a substantial interference with their use and enjoyment of that land. This interference constitutes a nuisance. Such a nuisance, if persisted in by a private party, could ripen into a prescription. Such a continuing nuisance, when maintained by government, amounts to the taking of an easement, or, more precisely, presents a jury question whether there is a taking. (2) Systematic flights which pass close to their land, even though not directly overhead, likewise constitute the taking of an easement, for the same reasons, and upon the same authority.

The Port of Portland contends that its activities do not constitute the taking of easements in the plaintiffs' land. The Port argues: (1) The plaintiffs have no right to exclude or protest flights directly over their land, if such flights are so high as to be in the public domain, i.e., within navigable airspace as defined by federal law.[2] (2) The plaintiffs have no

---

2. The Air Commerce Act of 1926, as amended by the Civil Aeronautics Act of 1938, provided that the Civil Aeronautics Authority could prescribe air traffic rules. See 49 U.S.C.A. § 551(a)(7). One of these rules fixed 500 feet as the minimum safe altitude over persons, vehicles, and structures. 14 CFR 60.107 (1947 Supp.). There can be no doubt that Congress has, during all material times, denominated the airspace 500 feet above any person, vessel, vehicle or structure in other than con-

right to protest flights which do not cross the airspace above their land, since these could commit no trespass in any event. Accordingly, the Port contends, there is no interference with any legally protected interest of the plaintiffs and thus no taking of any property for which the plaintiffs are entitled to compensation. In short, the Port's theory is that the plaintiffs must endure the noise of the nearby airport with the same forbearance that is required of those who live near highways and railroads. The Port's arguments, supported as they are by substantial authority, prevailed in the lower court, even though they were not entirely responsive to the plaintiffs' case. (The plaintiffs founded their case upon a nuisance theory; the defendant answered that there was no trespass.)

The trial court proceeded as if the rights of the plaintiffs were limited by the imaginary lines that would describe a cube of airspace exactly 500 feet high and bounded on four sides by perpendicular extensions of the surface boundaries of their land. The trial court thus in effect adapted the law of trespass to the issues presented in this case, and held that unless there was a continuing trespass within the described cube of space there could be no recovery. The trial court accordingly adopted the view that even if there was a nuisance, a nuisance could not give rise to a taking.

This appeal requires us to decide whether, under the circumstances of this case, the landowner has a right to have the jury pass upon his claim. If we so hold, then we have necessarily decided that the owner's interest in the use of his land free from the inconvenience of noise coming in upon him from outside his boundaries is an interest for the taking of which the government must pay. It would, of course, remain for the jury, under proper instructions, to decide when such a taking has occurred.

There is no doubt that noise can be a nuisance. See cases collected in Annotation, 44 A.L.R.2d 1381, 1394 (1953) (dance halls); Lloyd, Noise As a Nuisance, 82 Pa.L.Rev. 567 (1934); de Funiak, Equitable Relief Against Nuisances, 38 Ky.L.J. 223 (1949); and Notes, 15 Or.L.Rev. 268 (1936). At common law, one could obtain a prescriptive right to impose an unreasonable noise upon one's neighbor, and hence an easement for a nuisance. Sturges v. Bridgman, L.R. 11 Ch.D. 852 (1879); Restatement, Property, § 451, Comment *a*. (The authorities do not all agree about when the prescriptive period begins to run,[3] but that problem is

gested areas as navigable airspace which is subject to a public right of transit. The authority of Congress to pass such legislation is bottomed on the commerce power, and the validity of the legislation is not in question. See Braniff Airways v. Nebraska State Board, 347 U.S. 590, 596, 74 S.Ct. 757, 98 L.Ed. 967 (1954); Smith v. New England Aircraft Co., Inc., 270 Mass. 511, 525, 526, 170 N.E. 385, 69 A.L.R. 300 (1930).

3. Where a slaughterhouse had maintained a stench for 20 years, held: it had acquired a prescriptive right to continue the nuisance. Dana v. Valentine, 5 Metc. 8, 46 Mass. 8 (1842). See other cases collected in Annotation, 152 A.L.R. 343 (1944), and notes, 13 Harv.L.Rev. 142 (1899); 21 Notre Dame Lawyers 358 (1946); 2 Wash. & Lee L.Rev. 159 (1940). The Oregon Court has recognized (dictum) that a prescriptive right to maintain a private nuisance could be created by continuous conduct for the statutory time, although the case under study involved a trespassory invasion (drainage). Laurance et al. v. Tucker, 160 Or. 474, 85 P.2d 374 (1939).

not before us now.) It is clear that freedom from unreasonable noise is a right which, in a proper case, the law will protect. On similar principles, offensive smells are treated as nuisances for which a remedy will lie. See cases collected in Annotation, 18 A.L.R.2d 1033 (1950) (slaughterhouse). It is equally clear that a reasonable volume of noise (like a reasonable olfactory insult from industrial odors) must be endured as the price of living in a modern industrial society. See generally Restatement, Torts, §§ 822–831. Freedom from noise can be a legally protected right.

We come then to the facts of the case at bar. At the outset the parties concede that because of the wording of the Oregon Constitution, Art. I, § 18 (eminent domain), a plaintiff aggrieved by a public activity must show that there has been a taking of his property. There must be more than merely the suffering of some damage. See, e. g., Moeller et ux. v. Multnomah County, 218 Or. 413, 424, 430, 345 P.2d 813 (1959) (See Note, 40 Or.L.Rev. 241 (1961)); Tomasek v. Oregon State Highway Comm., supra note 1.

A taking within the meaning of Oregon Constitution, Art. I, § 18, had been defined as "any destruction, restriction, or interruption of the common and necessary use and enjoyment of the property of a person for a public purpose * * *." Morrison v. Clackamas County, 141 Or. 564, 568, 18 P.2d 814, 816 (1933). See Note, 16 Or.L.Rev. 155 (1937). The definition from Morrison v. Clackamas County, supra, is broad enough to cover a continuing nuisance, and hence the plaintiffs' case unless there is some policy reason for limiting its application.

Since United States v. Causby, 328 U.S. 256, 66 S.Ct. 1062, 90 L.Ed. 1206 (1946), and particularly since Griggs v. Allegheny County, 369 U.S. 84, 82 S.Ct. 531, 7 L.Ed.2d 585 (1962), we know that easements can be taken by repeated low-level flights over private land. Such easements have been found in actions against the federal government (Causby) and in actions against municipal corporations (Griggs). When such easements are said to have been taken, compensation must be paid to the owners of the lands thus burdened. This much appears to be settled.

It is not so well settled, however, that the easements discussed in the Causby and Griggs cases are easements to impose upon lands near an airport a servitude of noise. Courts operating upon the theory that repeated trespasses form the basis of the easement have not found it necessary to decide whether a repeated nuisance, which may or may not have been an accompaniment of a trespass, could equally give rise to a servitude upon neighboring land. It must be remembered that in both the Causby and Griggs cases the flights were virtually at tree-top level. Accordingly, both decisions could perhaps be supported on trespass theories exclusively. Following the Causby case, several federal district courts held that while repeated flights at low levels directly over private land may amount to a taking for which compensation must be paid, repeated flights nearby but not directly overhead must be endured as mere "damages" which, for various reasons, may not be compensable. See, e.g., Moore v. United States, 185 F.Supp. 399 (N.D.Tex.1960); Freeman v. United States, 167 F.Supp. 541 (W.D.Okl.1958); and see Cheskov

v. Port of Seattle, 55 Wash.2d 416, 348 P.2d 673 (1960), where the court found no taking, but held that damages might be recoverable in a proper case under the Washington constitution.[4]

After the case at bar had been argued and submitted, the United States Court of Appeals for the Tenth Circuit, which had previously held in Batten v. United States, 292 F.2d 144 (10th Cir.1961), that a complaint sounding substantially in nuisance stated a cause of action under circumstances very like those now before us, held, on the merits in the same case, that the interference with the use and enjoyment of the land complained of was a consequential damage not amounting to a taking, and adopted the rule that there must be a trespass before there can be a taking. Batten v. United States, 306 F.2d 580 (10th Cir.1962). As pointed out in a dissent by Murrah, Chief Judge, the interference proven was substantial enough to impose a servitude upon the lands of the plaintiffs, and under the Causby and Griggs cases equally could have constituted a taking. 306 F.2d at 585. In view of the importance of the question presented in the Batten case, and in view of the strong dissent by the chief judge, it would be premature to speculate now upon the final direction the federal courts will take. We believe the dissenting view in the Batten case presents the better-reasoned analysis of the legal principles involved, and that if the majority view in the Batten case can be defended it must be defended frankly upon the ground that considerations of public policy justify the result: i.e., that private rights must yield to public convenience in this class of cases. The rationale of the case is circular. The majority said in effect that there is no taking because the damages are consequential, and the damages are consequential because there is no taking.

As we noted in a recent case which involved a different aspect of the airport problem,[5] some of the decisions reveal internal ambivalence with reference to the theory upon which they proceed. In perhaps the leading case, United States v. Causby, supra, the court used language appropriate to the law of trespass more or less interchangeably with language appropriate to the law of nuisance.[6] It appears that the majority in the Batten case accepted the rule that only a trespass in the airspace

---

4. Unlike ours, the constitutions of several states permit the recovery of compensation for property "taken or damaged" for a public purpose. The significance of these constitutional provisions was fully discussed in Moeller v. Multnomah County, supra. Compare Oregon Constitution, Art. I, § 18, and Washington Constitution, Art. I, § 16. See also Tomasek v. Oregon State Highway Comm., supra note 1; Metzger v. City of Gresham, 152 Or. 682, 54 P.2d 311 (1936); Morrison v. Clackamas County, supra. Compare Levene et ux. v. City of Salem, 191 Or. 182, 197, 229 P.2d 255 (1951), where we talked as if a trespass could be either a "mere nuisance" (presumably a noncompensable one) or a "taking".

5. Atkinson et al. v. Bernard, Inc., 223 Or. 624, 355 P.2d 229 (1960).

6. The case says that the landowner owns at least as much of the space above the ground as he can occupy or use in connection with the land, and that the landowner as an incident of ownership has a claim to it and invasions of it are in the same category as invasions of the surface. 328 U.S. at 264, 265, 66 S.Ct. 1062. In the same opinion, the court also says that "[f]lights over private land are not a taking, unless they are so low and so frequent as to be a direct and immediate interference with the enjoyment and use of the land. * * *" 328 U.S. at 266, 66 S.Ct. at 1068. The commingling of trespass and nuisance language has been noted elsewhere. See 51 Northw.U.L.Rev. 346 (1962).

directly overhead can give rise to an action for a taking, and that nuisance principles ought not to be applied in actions against the government. This may be a cogent policy argument, but does violence to the law of servitudes.

The fact that the defendant in the case at bar is a governmental agency is of obvious importance, but, before we can decide whether to adopt one rule for governmental defendants and another for private parties, we need to know what the alternatives are. We need to know what the constitutional protection of private property means when balanced against those policy considerations which arise out of the governmental character of the defendant. In other words, as is frequently the case, we must balance apparently conflicting principles before we can tell whether or not this particular case is one for the jury.

While not every wrong committed by government will amount to a taking of private property, there are some wrongs which do constitute a taking. See, e.g., Cereghino et al. v. State by and through State Hwy. Comm., 230 Or. 439, 370 P.2d 694 (1962), and Moeller et ux. v. Multnomah County, supra. Many of these wrongs involve trespassory activities. The inquiry must not beg the question, however, whether a nuisance can also amount to a taking. Whether a nuisance has, in fact, produced the results alleged by the plaintiff in this case is another matter; first we must decide whether a nuisance can ever constitute a taking. If there is a taking, then what is taken must be paid for. Armstrong v. United States, 364 U.S. 40, 48, 80 S.Ct. 1563, 4 L.Ed.2d 1554 (1960). And see Annotation, 84 A.L.R.2d 348, Eminent Domain—View—Interference (1962).

The subject matter of inverse condemnation is always private property. Narrowed down to a meaningful definition for the purposes of this case, however, the only "property" right of the possessor of land which has any value is his ability to use and enjoy his land. This is true whatever estate the possessor holds, whether in fee, or for life, or for years, or merely an incorporeal interest such as an easement or profit. See Ackerman v. Port of Seattle, 55 Wash.2d 400, 348 P.2d 664, 77 A.L.R.2d 1344 (1960). If the government substantially deprives the owner of the use of his land, such deprivation is a taking for which the government must pay. Cereghino et al. v. State Hwy. Comm., supra; Ackerman v. Port of Seattle, supra. If, on the other hand, the government merely commits some tort which does not deprive the owner of the use of his land, then there is no taking.

Therefore, unless there is some reason of public policy which bars compensation in cases of governmental nuisance as a matter of law, there is a question, in each case, as a matter of fact, whether or not the governmental activity complained of has resulted in so substantial an interference with use and enjoyment of one's land as to amount to a taking of private property for public use. This factual question, again barring some rule which says we may not ask it, is equally relevant whether the taking is trespassory or by a nuisance. A nuisance can be such an invasion of the rights of a possessor as to amount to a taking, in theory at least, any time a possessor is in fact ousted from the enjoyment of his land.

It now becomes relevant to consider whether a jury ought to be permitted to find that a given nuisance is so aggravated as to be a taking when the perpetrator of the nuisance happens to be the government. The Port argues that the plight of the plaintiffs in this case is indistinguishable from that of thousands of their fellow countrymen whose homes abut highways and railroads and who endure the noise without complaint. Granting the similarity, it must be noted, however, that the matter is one of degree.[7] We do not decide that the positions of the parties are the same. The Port points to our previous decisions in support of the proposition that nuisance (nontrespassory) invasions by government are not compensable. The cases cited by the Port did not, however, hold that a nuisance so aggravated as to amount to a complete ouster or deprivation of the beneficial use of property was not a taking. That question does not appear to have been passed upon by our court. But cf. Wilson v. City of Portland, 132 Or. 509, 514, 285 P. 1030 (1930), where there is *dictum* to the effect that nontrespassory incursions give rise to no liability. There are cases elsewhere which tend to support the Port's theory that nuisances, when committed by government, are "legal" and therefore can never be a taking in the constitutional sense, but must always be endured with fortitude. Indeed, some authorities hold that the king can do no wrong and that the government never perpetrates a nuisance. See cases noted in 66 C.J.S. Nuisances § 17, p. 761. Again, "lawful" nuisances have been held to be of such public desirability (utility) that only those portions of the invasion that could be severed from the whole and characterized as trespass could be considered in an action for damages. See, e.g., Richards v. Washington Terminal Co., 233 U.S. 546, 34 S.Ct. 654, 58 L.Ed. 1088, L.R.A.1915A, 887 (1914), holding that railroad noises and smoke (but not soot) must be endured where the conduct that created the nuisance is in the public interest and has been encouraged by law. The reason for assigning mystical power to trespass *quare clausum fregit* is elusive. But Richards v. Washington Terminal Co. did not say that the public interest demands that all governmentally approved activities (except trespass) be endured without compensation. We have found no case which goes that far, and we doubt that the constitutional right to compensation can be so construed.

The plaintiffs concede that single-instance torts, as torts, are not compensable. Inverse condemnation, however, provides the remedy where an injunction would not be in the public interest, and where the continued interference amounts to a taking for which the constitution demands a remedy. In summary, a taking occurs whenever government acts in such a way as substantially to deprive an owner of the useful possession of that which he owns, either by repeated trespasses or by repeated nontrespassory invasions called "nuisance". If reparations are to be denied, they should be denied for reasons of policy which are themselves strong enough to counterbalance the constitutional de-

---

7. " * * * The law is not indifferent to considerations of degree." Cardozo, J., concurring in Schechter Poultry Corp. v. United States, 295 U.S. 495, 554, 55 S.Ct. 837, 853, 79 L.Ed. 1570, 97 A.L.R. 947.

mand that reparations be paid. None has been pointed out to us in this case.

If we accept, as we must upon established principles of the law of servitudes, the validity of the propositions that a noise can be a nuisance; that a nuisance can give rise to an easement; and that a noise coming straight down from above one's land can ripen into a taking if it is persistent enough and aggravated enough, then logically the same kind and degree of interference with the use and enjoyment of one's land can also be a taking even though the noise vector may come from some direction other than the perpendicular.

If a landowner has a right to be free from unreasonable interference caused by noise, as we hold that he has, then when does the noise burden become so unreasonable that the government must pay for the privilege of being permitted to continue to make the noise? Logically, the answer has to be given by the trier of fact (subject to the usual exercise of the proper function of the court in screening the evidence). See Restatement, Torts, § 826, Comment d. It may be contended that the jury is an imperfect instrument in these cases, but such an argument raises constitutional and legislative questions that are not now before us. See Holden v. Pioneer Broadcasting Co., 228 Or. 405, 365 P.2d 845.

While it is no doubt anticipatory to advert to the problem of instructing the jury in cases of this kind, it is relevant to point out that the nuisance theory provides the jury a useful method for balancing the gravity of the harm to the plaintiff against the social utility of the airport's conduct, in a way that would not be available if the trespass theory were used. In Restatement, Torts, §§ 826–831, we find principles for balancing gravity against utility which can be adapted to jury instruction so that the question of reasonableness need not be any more mysterious to the jury in this type of case than it is in an automobile accident case. The balancing of private rights and public necessity is not a novel problem.[8]

Whether expressed in so many words or not, the principle found in the Causby, Griggs, and Ackerman cases is that when the government conducts an activity upon its own land, which after balancing the question of reasonableness, is sufficiently disturbing to the use and enjoyment of neighboring lands to amount to a taking thereof, then the public, and not the subservient landowner, should bear the cost of such public benefit. Under this principle, it was error to exclude the plaintiffs' proffered testimony concerning the jet flights near his land. The real question was not one of perpendicular extension of surface boundaries into the airspace, but a question of reasonableness based upon nuisance theories. In effect, the inquiry should have been whether the

8. See Madison v. Copper Co. [Madison v. Ducktown Sulphur, Copper & Iron Co., 113 Tenn. 331, 83 S.W. 658], supra, where damages were allowed and the injunction was refused. And see the related case of State of Georgia v. Tennessee Copper Co., 206 U.S. 230, 27 S.Ct. 618, 51 L.Ed. 1038, 11 Ann.Cas. 488 (1907); 237 U.S. 474, 35 S.Ct. 631, 59 L.Ed. 1054 (1915); 240 U.S. 650, 36 S.Ct. 465, 60 L.Ed. 846 (1916). Similar considerations are discussed in Booth-Kelly Lumber Co. v. City of Eugene, 67 Or. 381, 136 P. 29 (1913) and York et ux. v. Stallings et al., 217 Or. 13, 341 P.2d 529 (1959).

government had undertaken a course of conduct on its own land which, in simple fairness to its neighbors, required it to obtain more land so that the substantial burdens of the activity would fall upon public land, rather than upon that of involuntary contributors who happen to lie in the path of progress.

As noted above, this court has expressed a policy against allowing compensation in several situations where there was no actual physical injury to the real property. The cases used terms such as "consequential damages",[9] or "damages which do not amount to a 'taking' ",[10] or *"damnum absque injuria."* [11] Such expressions describe conclusions that the court reached when it had decided that the facts involved did not measure up to the standard necessary for a "taking". Such injuries were then held to be noncompensable as a matter of law, under the policy against allowing compensation for mere "damages". Such decisions, which were no doubt right in cases of single-instance wrongs, prove too much when applied to continuing and substantial interference with the use and enjoyment of property. Ordinarily, in a case of a continuing interference, whether it is substantial enough to constitute a taking will be for the jury to determine.

Another assignment of error in the case at bar challenges the failure of the court to give a requested instruction with respect to low-level flights directly over plaintiffs' land. The court instead instructed the jury that only such flights as were conducted over the land at altitudes of less than 500 feet could constitute a taking.

The challenged instruction requires us to decide when, if ever, an airport can be liable for taking property because it permits flights to and from it over private land, but within "navigable airspace". On this point, there is no doubt that a taking of private property can occur even though the flights are within navigable airspace as defined by law if the flights are below 500 feet. Matson v. United States, 171 F.Supp. 283, 145 Ct.Cl. 225 (1959), held that the plaintiff should recover for a taking, even though the court recognized that the taking was accomplished in what today would be navigable airspace.[12] Griggs v. Allegheny County, supra, is a square holding that taking of private property can be accomplished by planes taking off and landing within navigable airspace. 369 U.S. 84, 82 S.Ct. 531, 533, 7 L.Ed.2d 585, 588. There is, therefore, no merit in the defense argument that all flights within the navigable air-

---

9. Brand v. Multnomah County, 38 Or. at 92, 60 P. 390, 62 P. 209, 50 L.R.A. 389.

10. Moeller et ux. v. Multnomah County, 218 Or. supra, at 427, 345 P.2d at 820.

11. Barrett et al. v. Union Bridge Co., (on merits) 117 Or. 220, 243 P. 93, 45 A.L.R. 521, (on petition for rehearing) 117 Or. 566, 578, 245 P. 308, 45 A.L.R. 527 (1926), quoting with approval Less v. City of Butte, 28 Mont. 27, 31, 72 P. 140, 61 L.R.A. 601, 98 Am.St.Rep. 545 (1903).

12. In Matson v. United States, supra, the court said:

" * * * We do not think, however, that the change in the definition of navigable airspace affects plaintiffs' causes of action. The Government's easement over plaintiffs' property may be perpetual. Although today navigable airspace with its public rights of transit * * * includes the glide, its use by the United States or other aeroplane operators at heights below the minimum altitudes of flight except where necessary for take-off or landing may require compensation. * * * " 171 F.Supp. at 285.

space are automatically free from liability.[13] The debate centers on the legal effect of the 500-foot rule.

The Port's argument that flights above 500 feet are immune from private litigation seems to be based on two grounds:

1. As a result of the legislation by Congress in denominating navigable airspace and declaring a public right of transit through it, the landowner cannot claim there has been a "trespass" through a column of air which he does not own.[14] Ownership of the navigable airspace is said to be in the public.[15]

2. As a result of the same legislation, the landowner is in a position analogous to that of a person abutting a highway or a railroad right-of-way who must be content with the incidental inconveniences that are unavoidably attendant upon those operations.[16]

The instruction given below forces a choice between consistency, which is on the side of the plaintiffs, and public convenience, which is on the side of the Port. Logically, it makes no difference to a plaintiff disturbed in the use of his property whether the disturbing flights pass 501 feet or 499 feet above his land. If he is in fact ousted from the legitimate enjoyment of his land, it is to him an academic matter that the planes which have ousted him did not fly below 500 feet.[17] The rule adopted by the majority of the state and federal courts is, then, an arbitrary one. The barring of actions when the flights are above 500 feet is also difficult to reconcile with the theory that recovery should be based upon nuisance concepts rather than upon the trespass theory which we have rejected. Whether a plaintiff is entitled to recover should depend upon the fact of a taking, and not upon an arbitrary rule. The ultimate

13. Since navigable airspace now includes both the cruising altitudes and the space needed for the glide, it is meaningless to say that flights in the navigable airspace cannot constitute a servitude on land. It is necessary to know how the flights affect the land. See Griggs v. Allegheny County, supra.

14. Title 49 U.S.C.A.:

§ 176(a). "The United States of America is declared to possess and exercise complete and exclusive national sovereignty in the airspace above the United States * * *."

§ 403. "There is recognized and declared to exist in behalf of any citizen of the United States a public right of freedom of transit in air commerce through the navigable airspace of the United States."

§ 180. "As used in sections 171, 174–177, and 179–184 of this title, the term 'navigable airspace' means airspace above the minimum safe altitudes of flight prescribed by the Civil Aeronautics Authority, and such navigable airspace shall be subject to a public right of freedom of interstate and foreign air navigation in conformity with the requirements of said sections."

15. We need not here consider whether such ownership of the airspace is in the United States or in the individual states. See 57 Mich.L.Rev. 1214, 1223 (1959).

16. Brand v. Multnomah County, supra note 7; Richards v. Washington Terminal Co., 233 U.S. 546, 34 S.Ct. 654, 58 L.Ed. 1088, supra; and Matson v. United States, 171 F.Supp. 283, 145 Ct.Cl. 225, supra.

17. See 14 J.Air L. & Com. 112, 116, discussing a decision to the effect that "[t]he height at which an airplane operator may pass above the surface without trespassing is a question depending for solution on the facts in the particular case, and this question is unaffected by the regulations promulgated by the Department of Commerce, under the Air Commerce Act of 1926 * * *." Cory v. Physical Culture Hotel, 14 F.Supp. 977, 982 (W.D.N.Y. 1936). In any event, unless experts, equipped with the necessary instruments, have measured each flight, it is highly unlikely that trustworthy evidence would be produced to prove the exact altitude of flights over private land.

question is whether there was a sufficient interference with the land-owner's use and enjoyment to be a taking.

It is sterile formality to say that the government takes an easement in private property when it repeatedly sends aircraft directly over the land at altitudes so low as to render the land unusable by its owner, but does not take an easement when it sends aircraft a few feet to the right or left of the perpendicular boundaries (thereby rendering the same land equally unusable). The line on the ground which marks the land-owner's right to deflect surface invaders has no particular relevance when the invasion is a noise nuisance. Neither is a 500-foot ceiling relevant, desirable though it may be as an administrative device. If the interest to be protected is worth protecting at all, it is necessary to employ a system of rules that will meet the problem. Whatever virtue the establishment of a 500-foot floor under the cruising flight of aircraft may have as a matter of public safety, there can be only one sound reason to make it a rule of the law of real property. That reason ought to be the knowledge, derived from factual data, that flights above 500 feet do not disturb the ordinary, reasonable landowner. This may be true. We do not know that it is. It may well be that only the most sensitive are offended by such flights. It may equally be true that some of the aircraft now in use are so disturbing to those on the ground that 500 feet of air will not provide protection to the landowner below. We are not justified in adopting the 500-foot rule as a rule of property law in cases of this character merely because to do so might make our work easier. The trier of fact in each case is best able to work out the solution. The difficulty was foreseen in the Causby case.[18] Congress may very properly declare certain airspace to be in the public domain for navigational purposes, but it does not necessarily follow that rights of navigation may be exercised unreasonably. The power to invade the rights of servient landowners no doubt reposes in the federal government, but there is a point beyond which such power may not be exercised without compensation. United States v. Causby, supra. The same limitation applies to lesser governmental agencies.[19] See Griggs v. Allegheny County, supra.

Unfortunately for trial judges trying to formulate instructions for juries, the cases have not dealt with the instructions to be given to the

18. "The airplane is part of the modern environment of life, and the inconveniences which it causes are normally not compensable under the Fifth Amendment. The airspace, apart from the immediate reaches above the land, is part of the public domain. We need not determine at this time what those precise limits are. Flights over private land are not a taking, unless they are so low and so frequent as to be a direct and immediate interference with the enjoyment and use of the land. We need not speculate on that phase of the present case. For the findings of the Court of Claims plainly established that there was a diminution in value of the property and that the frequent, low-level flights were the direct and immediate cause. We agree with the Court of Claims that a servitude has been imposed upon the land." United States v. Causby, supra, 328 U.S. at 266, 267, 66 S.Ct. at 1068.

19. The question of who, under the current Federal definition of navigable airspace, ought to be liable for the taking is discussed in Comment, 57 Mich.L.Rev. 1214, 1225 (1959), and the possibility is suggested that suits could be brought against the United States. See also Harvey, Landowners' Rights in the Air Age: The Airport Dilemma. 56 Mich.L.Rev. 1313, 1326 (1958).

laymen who must work out the answer under Oregon law. In submitting to a jury a case such as we have before us, the trial court is confronted with the need to verbalize rules as abstract as any to be found in the law, but, as we have said before,[20] the ingenuity of trial judges in formulating meaningful instructions to juries is usually equal to the task.

The idea that must be expressed to the jury is that before the plaintiff may recover for a taking of his property he must show by the necessary proof that the activities of the government are unreasonably interfering with his use of his property, and in so substantial a way as to deprive him of the practical enjoyment of his land. This loss must then be translated factually by the jury into a reduction in the market value of the land.

We cannot say, as a matter of law, that jet or rocket or some other kind of noise within 500 feet, or within some other number of feet, of private land might not in a particular case cause a taking for public use. The question in each case must be decided by an appropriate tribunal. Our present constitution places this duty upon the jury. If the jury proves unequal to the task, that, as noted above, is a legislative problem. If the case should arise when it is claimed that insufficient evidence was placed before the jury to support a verdict, then will be time enough to pass upon the amount of evidence necessary to get to the jury. In the case at bar, much of the evidence was excluded. As we have noted, this exclusion was error.

Other assignments of error challenge various rulings which were made in a logical and consistent pattern which followed from the able trial court's view of the case as one controlled essentially by trespass concepts. On another trial, these rulings are not likely to be repeated, and need not detain us further now.

Reversed and remanded.

[The dissenting opinion of PERRY, J., is omitted.]

Notes

1. Upon remand of the Thornburg case, a further trial resulted in a jury verdict for the defendant. The plaintiff appealed again, assigning errors in the instructions to the jury. Without setting out the instructions, the court found that they were in error, and again reversed and remanded. The court's opinion in part is as follows:

"The proper test to determine whether there has been a compensable invasion of the individual's property rights in a case of this kind is whether the interference with use and enjoyment is sufficiently direct, sufficiently peculiar, and of sufficient magnitude to support a conclusion that the interference has reduced the fair market value of the plaintiff's land by a sum certain in money. If so, justice as between the state and the citizen requires the burden imposed to be borne by the public and not by the individual alone. See Murrah, C.J., dissenting, Batten v. United States, 306 F.2d 580, 587 (10th Cir.1962). * * *

20. Williamson v. McKenna, 223 Or. 366, 401, 354 P.2d 56 (1960).

"The jury will decide, if the court finds that there is a jury question, what the facts are. If the jury finds an interference with the plaintiff's use and enjoyment of his land, substantial enough to result in a loss of market value, there is a taking. If the jury determines that there has been a taking, its only concern thereafter is to fix the monetary compensation therefor.

"The court can tell the jury by way of special instruction in this type of case that there is a difference between negligible, or inconsequential, interferences which all property owners must share and the direct, peculiar, and substantial interferences which result in a loss of market value to the extent that a disinterested observer would characterize the loss as a taking. It is then for the jury to decide from all the evidence upon which side of the line a particular controverted nuisance falls. The error below was in telling the jury in effect to consider the utility of the airport in deciding whether the plaintiff's property had been depreciated in value by the defendant's activities. This notion is wholly inconsistent with the law of eminent domain, and had no place in the jury's consideration of a decrease in fair market value." Thornburg v. Port of Portland, 244 Or. 69, 415 P.2d 750 (1966). See also Aaron v. City of Los Angeles, 40 Cal.App.3d 471, 115 Cal.Rptr. 162 (1974).

2. As indicated in the principal case, the federal courts have generally been unwilling to find a "taking" unless there are repeated low-level overflights of the plaintiff's land by aircraft owned and operated by the United States. In Batten v. United States, 306 F.2d 580 (10th Cir.1962), operation of an Air Force base in Topeka, Kansas, produced sound and shock waves which caused windows and dishes in the plaintiff's house to rattle and made conversation and sleep virtually impossible in the plaintiff's house when aircraft were taking off and landing. At times the smoke from take-offs left an oily black deposit on the plaintiffs' houses and personal property. The court found that there was no "taking" of the plaintiffs' property, despite a finding that "plaintiffs have suffered a substantial interference with the use and enjoyment of their properties," because (1) there was no actual physical invasion of their properties and (2) the interference with use and enjoyment was not "so complete" as to deprive the plaintiffs of "all or most" of their interest in their properties. The court also stressed that the Fifth Amendment's "taking" clause does not require payment of compensation when private property is only "damaged" (unlike many state constitutions), and said that the distinction between "taking" and mere "damaging" would be blurred if compensation were awarded when, as in *Batten*, there is only an interference with the use and enjoyment of land. Judge Murrah dissented, on grounds set forth in the *Thornburg* case.

3. In Aaron v. United States, 311 F.2d 798 (Ct.Cl.1963), several land owners, some of whom owned land subject to direct overflights by aircraft owned and operated by the United States and some of whom owned land not subject to direct overflights, sought to recover compensation on an inverse condemnation theory. Some of the plaintiffs owned land affected by flights at altitudes below 500 feet, and some of the plaintiffs owned land affected only by flights at altitudes above 500 feet. The court not only followed *Batten* in allowing compensation only where there were direct overflights, but also held that compensation was not payable for the interference with use and enjoyment caused even by direct overflights at altitudes above 500 feet on the ground that "flights above 500 feet over noncongested areas are in the navigable air space in which there is a public right of freedom of transit." Although the court conceded that there might be a case where flights above the lower limit of the navigable air space might result in practical destruction of the property interest of a land owner, the court found that this had not occurred in the *Aaron* case. The Court of Claims followed its prior decision in the *Aaron* case in Avery v.

United States, 330 F.2d 640 (Ct.Cl.1964), and once again refused to award compensation unless a plaintiff proved that his air space was invaded by direct overflights at levels below 500 feet. But in Branning v. United States, 654 F.2d 88 (Ct.Cl.1981), the Court of Claims found that there was a "taking" as a result of direct overflights above the 500 foot limit because of the severity of the interference with the plaintiff's use and enjoyment of its land, located close to the Marine Air Corps Station near Beaufort, South Carolina. This airbase was used in part to train pilots for landings on aircraft carriers and "heavy jet aircraft followed one another almost nose to tail in an unvarying loop over plaintiff's land." The court said that this flight pattern, in fact, "reduced or destroyed the value of the property for its highest and best use, namely, for single family residential use and development." The *Branning* court referred with approval to the *Thornburg* court's holding that it is the quality of the interference with the use and enjoyment of land, and not the physical locus of the interfering agency, that determines whether there is a compensable "taking." While the *Branning* court did not accept the *Thornburg* court's holding that it makes no difference whether there are direct overflights or not, it did concede that the basis for finding a "taking" in *Branning* was the real injury caused by the noise rather than the technical injury caused by invasion of the air space over the plaintiff's land. The court met the argument that flights above 500 feet are absolutely privileged by stating that "the navigational servitude [created by federal regulations] does not preclude application of the taking clause [of the Fifth Amendment] when Congress in acting to regulate aviation exceeds its reasonable power to regulate."

4. Early state court cases which follow *Thornburg* in allowing recovery of compensation in airport cases in the absence of proof of direct overflights include City of Jacksonville v. Schumann, 167 So.2d 95 (Fla.1964); City of Charlotte v. Pratt, 263 N.C. 656, 140 S.E.2d 341 (1965); State ex rel. Royal v. City of Columbus, 3 Ohio St.2d 154, 209 N.E.2d 405 (1965); Henthorn v. Oklahoma City, 453 P.2d 1013 (Okl.1969); Johnson v. City of Greeneville, 222 Tenn. 260, 435 S.W.2d 476 (1968); Martin v. Port of Seattle, 64 Wn.2d 309, 391 P.2d 540 (1964). More recently, the highest courts of New Hampshire and Pennsylvania have adopted the rule that direct overflights need not be shown. Sundell v. Town of New London, 119 N.H. 839, 409 A.2d 1315 (1979); Philadelphia v. Keyser, 45 Pa.Cmwlth. 271, 407 A.2d 55 (1979). See also Aaron v. City of Los Angeles, 40 Cal.App.3d 471, 115 Cal.Rptr. 162 (1974) (plaintiff must prove measurable reduction in market value and that the injury inflicted on him is "special and peculiar," and not simply incidental damage suffered by the general public). In some of these states—e.g., California and Washington—the state constitution requires compensation to be paid whenever private property is either "taken" or "damaged" for public use.

5. Nothing in the Fourteenth Amendment to the United States Constitution prohibits state courts from adopting a more liberal definition of "taking" when they interpret their own state constitutional provisions requiring compensation when private property is "taken" for public use. Hence the state courts are free to disregard the restrictive definitions of "taking" adopted by the federal courts, pursuant to the Fifth Amendment, in airport cases like *Batten, Aaron, Avery,* and *Branning,* supra Note 2. *Sed quaere* whether more liberal state court decisions like *Thornburg* might be deemed to conflict with the constitutional power of the Congress to regulate interstate commerce.

Note on the Subject Matter of Property in Land

It may not be amiss at this point to put the following question: what is the nature of the "thing" or "things" to which property in land relates? No similar problem exists in respect to personal property except in the case of intangibles. In the case of chattels, it is easy to identify the physical extent of the "thing" in which the property inheres; so easy, in fact, that rarely do we need to define its extent. In the case of land, however, we invariably have to carve out by lines which are at least imaginary the substance of any landowner's interest, so as to distinguish it from the similar interests of his neighbors. This takes us into the problem of boundaries, which is a subject specifically treated later in this course. For the most part we deal in such cases more or less with a horizontal plane, and seek to divide such plane into segments.

But we have seen that land, like any physical thing, is three-dimensional. Hence we have encountered problems in the vertical delineation of the extent of ownership, which began with the unrealistic *ad coelum* doctrine, which has had to be much modified in dealing with minerals and air space. As for subsurface rights, we have, as a practical matter, never faced the necessity for drawing imaginary lines below the surface of land to separate property in the surface from property in the subsurface. Yet the recognition of property in minerals in place presupposes the existence of separate horizontal planes, the boundary between which can, as a practical matter, be left without precise delineation. (Descriptions in deeds of surface boundaries, if left similarly vague, would render the deeds void for uncertainty).

We have seen a similar problem in defining property interests in air space. Here, too, it is necessary to recognize the division of space into horizontal planes, and here, too, we have not often had to face the problem of defining with precision the boundary between the planes.

This in turn gives particular point to our initial question: What is the nature of the "thing" or "things" to which property in land relates? It cannot be said to be merely a segment of the soil, for it extends above the soil. Could it ever be merely air space unconnected with the soil? If property in land extends above the surface, is it possible to separate a plane above the surface of land from the surface and make it the subject of separate ownership just as we suppose we may do with a subjacent section of the soil itself? If so, does this mean that property in land in some cases relates to no "thing" at all (for an owner of air space is interested in the space, not the air), but only to a conception of space?

One distinguished jurisprudential writer has made the paradoxical statement that for the purpose of establishing jural relations land is no more nor less than "tri-dimensional space". Kocourek, Jural Relations 336 (1927). He says that the "soil and the substances in the earth and the structures built upon the surface are merely chattels which go with the land by conveyance and inheritance." Although this may be a useful concept for some purposes, we may find some difficulty with it in dealing with the traditional distinction which the law makes between land and chattels, particularly in relation to the law of fixtures, a subject which we consider later in this course.

If Kocourek's definition is too broadly put, we are left with the problem of finding a substitute, or we may conclude that no precise concept of this sort is possible, or if possible, it is without practical utility. Before we dismiss any efforts in this direction, we should recognize that problems can arise, the solution of which seems to presuppose a basic premise or assumption of the sort we are seeking.

Note on the Condominium Concept

You probably have heard of the new development in housing projects called "condominiums." Statutes in all the states now permit the separate conveyance and ownership in fee simple absolute of individual apartments or units in such projects, instead of the traditional practice of leasing such units to tenants. But the only thing that is individually owned (owned "in severalty") is the space within the walls, ceiling, and floor of a particular unit. The walls and other portions of the structure such as roof, basement, hallways and other common areas within the structure, and the exterior grounds associated with the structure are owned by all the unit owners as tenants in common. Although condominiums could probably have been created in the United States under the common law, utilization of the condominium concept has generally proceeded on the basis of special state enabling legislation.

We shall return to the topic of condominiums later in this book in connection with our consideration of concurrent ownership and covenants relating to land use. It should be pointed out that, in addition to these traditional topics in the law of real property, the condominium form of ownership also implicates the law of business organizations and other fields of law not directly concerned with the nature and extent of property in land.

SECTION 3.   WATER RIGHTS

A. COMMON LAW RIGHTS AS TO STREAMS AND SURFACE WATER

PENDERGRAST v. AIKEN

Supreme Court of North Carolina, 1977.
293 N.C. 201, 236 S.E.2d 787.

Plaintiffs' evidence tends to establish the following:

Plaintiffs are the owners of a tract of land which borders U.S. Highway 25 in Buncombe County in an area of commercial development known as Skyland. On this tract plaintiffs own a brick and concrete-block building consisting of an upper floor and a basement with a dirt floor. The building measures approximately 50 by 50 feet. At the time of the incidents which precipitated this lawsuit, plaintiffs maintained a laundry and dry-cleaning business in part of the building and leased the remaining area to a hardware company and a beauty salon.

A small branch entered plaintiffs' property from the north through a corrugated iron culvert 30 inches in diameter. A second, smaller branch joined the first branch at the upper end of the property after entering through two 15-inch culverts. The resulting small creek drained a watershed of approximately 90 acres and maintained a continuous flow throughout the year, even during dry spells. The creek flowed in a southerly direction about 30 feet from the rear of the building.

The property immediately to the south, which also adjoins U.S. 25, was undeveloped at the time of this lawsuit and belonged to defendants Aiken. The southern boundary of the Aiken property was Allen Avenue. The stream flowed through this property in a natural drainage ditch or depression and exited through two 24-inch culverts under Allen Avenue.

In 1972 the State Highway Commission began a project to widen U.S. 25 in that area from two lanes to five. Charles Smith was the general superintendent of defendant Perry M. Alexander Construction Company, the general contractor for the road work. After work began on U.S. 25, Smith contacted defendants and asked them if they would like to have their land filled with excess dirt from the highway project. At the time, the Aiken property was between four and six feet below the level of the road. The Aikens replied that they did not want dirt containing trash, which Smith was offering at no charge, but that they would pay to have "good dirt," free from debris, dumped on their land. Smith pointed out that they would need to have a pipe laid to carry the stream, which otherwise would be filled in. After some negotiation, the Aikens and Smith agreed that Smith would order 274 feet of 36-inch iron corrugated pipe, would place the pipe in the creek and would then fill up the creek and the property with "good dirt." Smith maintains that the Aikens specified 36-inch diameter pipe, while the Aikens testified that Smith recommended that size. In any event, in February 1973 the pipe was installed and the land filled.

Thereafter on 15 or 16 March 1973 there was a rainfall of substantial but apparently normal volume. For the first time since plaintiffs moved onto their property in 1962, the creek backed up and flooded the basement of plaintiffs' building to a depth of approximately 13 inches. Two other rains in April and May 1973 caused similar flooding. On 27 May 1973 Buncombe County experienced an exceptionally heavy rain which exceeded 4 inches in a 12-hour period. Some witnesses testified that was the heaviest rain they had ever seen in the area. According to plaintiffs' expert witness, a civil engineer, that amount of rain "is an extraordinary unexpected downfall of water." The creek again backed up and flooded plaintiffs' basement, this time to a depth of over five feet. Subsequent heavy rains also resulted in flooding. In all, plaintiffs' complaint alleges six separate flooding incidents.

Concerning the drainage at the two properties, plaintiffs testified that before the pipe was installed on the Aikens' land, "[o]ccasionally, the stream would back up behind Allen Avenue [on defendants' property]. There would be a big puddle of water down there, but it just dispersed over that property below me. It never did back up on my property at all." Plaintiffs enlisted the services of Walter C. Bearden, a civil engineer, to study and report on his property's drainage problems. Bearden testified that sound engineering practices required the installation of drainage facilities capable of handling a "twenty-five year flood," that is, the greatest amount of rainfall in a single twenty-four hour period that, according to National Weather Service statistics, one might expect in a twenty-five year period. In Asheville, that figure is seven inches of rain. According to Bearden's calculations, the ninety-acre watershed which drained into the small creek would produce a flow of 800 gallons of water per minute during a "twenty-five year flood." According to his calculations, the 36-inch culvert on the Aiken property has a maximum capacity of 260 gallons per minute. Thus, in his opinion, "the culvert, the thirty-six inch culvert, was completely inadequate to carry the water."

Bearden also testified that a single 36-inch culvert carried more water than two 24-inch culverts and that "[g]enerally speaking, it is bad engineering practice to run a pipe with capacity of thirty-six inches into two twenty-four inch pipes." Thus, in Bearden's opinion, the 36-inch pipe was too large to be connected to the 24-inch pipes and yet was too small to drain the Pendergrast property.

Sometime in the fall of 1974 the State Highway Commission installed two 60-inch culverts underneath Allen Avenue. These culverts each have a capacity of 1,120 gallons per minute. However, the installation of these large diameter culverts did not stop the flooding on plaintiffs' land.

Bearden also inspected plaintiffs' building. "I found two water marks obviously made at two different times. The highest water mark was five and four-tenths feet above the basement floor. The lowest water mark was three and two-tenths feet above the basement floor. These water marks were obviously made at different times. The floor was very wet and covered with mud. * * * I examined the basement wall. North wall was very badly cracked. There were cracks also in the two other walls." In his opinion, the building "had been badly flooded two different times." The cause of this flooding was the "completely inadequate" capacity of the Aikens' 36-inch culvert to carry the expected run-off from the watershed into the creek.

Immediately before this action came to trial, defendants Aiken sold the property to a third party who promptly dug up the buried culvert. Although the pipe was left in place, the net effect was to restore the original drainage conditions to the Pendergrast property.

Defendants offered no evidence.

Perry Alexander Construction Company's motion for a directed verdict was allowed and plaintiffs did not appeal that decision.

The following issues were submitted to the jury: (1) Did the defendants Aiken create a nuisance by installing and covering a 36-inch drain across their property? (2) If so, did defendants Aiken thereby cause damage to plaintiffs' property? (3) What amount of damages, if any, are plaintiffs entitled to recover of the defendants Aiken? The jury answered the first issue "Yes," the second issue "No" and did not answer the third issue. Judgment on the verdict was entered for defendants and plaintiffs appealed to the Court of Appeals which upheld the judgment, Judge Martin dissenting. Plaintiffs thereupon appealed to this Court as of right assigning errors noted in the opinion.

HUSKINS, Justice. Plaintiffs assign as error the failure of the trial judge to instruct the jury correctly on the law arising from the evidence. By this assignment plaintiffs present three questions for consideration: (1) Did the court err in its original charge by framing its instructions in terms of nuisance? (2) Did the court err in its instruction to the jury that it must first determine whether defendant created a nuisance and then decide whether plaintiffs were harmed thereby? (3) Did the court err in its supplemental instructions regarding the effect of the two 24-inch culverts installed by the City under Allen Avenue? We shall consider these questions seriatim. Since their resolution lies in determination of applicable law, we commence by examining the development and status of the law governing drainage of surface waters. In that connection we first delineate the scope of the term "surface water," a term which has caused some confusion in the past.

Many jurisdictions have classified drainage problems according to whether the water drained (1) is composed of spring water, rain or snow melt spreading over the land without pattern or order, i.e., "diffused surface water," or (2) travels a clearly defined channel and hence is a watercourse. See e.g., Garbarino v. Van Cleave, 214 Or. 554, 330 P.2d 28 (1958). Based on such classification some courts have applied different rules of law. 5 R. Clark, Waters and Water Rights § 450.5 (1972). We see no basis for such a distinction. "What difference does it make, in principle, whether the water comes directly upon the field from the clouds above, or has fallen upon remote hills, and comes thence in a running stream upon the surface, or rises in a spring upon the upper field and flows upon the lower." Gormley v. Sanford, 52 Ill. 158 (1869).

Such technical distinctions have unnecessarily complicated the analysis of drainage problems, masking the truly critical issues. Hence, in the past this Court, for purposes of analyzing drainage problems, has combined diffuse surface waters, watercourses and overflow waters from the ocean into the broader category of *surface waters*. Compare Davis v. R.R., 227 N.C. 561, 42 S.E.2d 905 (1947), with City of Kings Mountain v. Goforth, 283 N.C. 316, 196 S.E.2d 231 (1973), and Midgett v. Highway Commission, 260 N.C. 241, 132 S.E.2d 599 (1963); accord, Clark, supra § 450.5. We approve of this method of analysis and adhere to it. With this definition of "surface waters" in mind, we now discuss the various legal rules applicable to surface water drainage.

American courts have developed three distinct doctrines governing the disposal of surface waters. The first, *the common enemy rule*, states substantially that "[s]urface water is recognized as a common enemy, which each proprietor may fight off or control as he will or is able either by retention, diversion, repulsion, or altered transmission; so that no cause of action arises from such interference, even if some injury occurs, causing damage." Borchsenius v. Chicago, St. P., M. & O. Ry. Co., 96 Wis. 448, 71 N.W. 884 (1897); Clark, supra § 450.6; see Annot., 59 A.L.R.2d 421 (1958). Grounded in the maxim *cujus est solum, ejus est usque ad coelum et ad inferos* (whose is the soil, his is even to the skies and to the depths below), the doctrine is based on two concepts: "(1) the necessity for improving lands with the recognition that some injury results from even minor improvements, and (2) philosophical preference for freedom of each landowner to deal with his own land essentially as he sees fit." Clark, supra § 451.1. Despite these laudable goals the rule created many problems. In the words of one commentator: " * * * landowners are encouraged to engage in contests of hydraulic engineering in which might makes right, and breach of the peace is often inevitable." Maloney and Plager, Diffused Surface Water: Scourge or Bounty?, 8 Nat.Res.J. 73 (1968); accord, Butler v. Bruno, 115 R.I. 264, 341 A.2d 735 (1975). The extreme consequences occasioned by strict application of the common enemy rule soon led many courts to adopt modifications based upon concepts of reasonable use or negligence. Note, Disposition of Diffused Surface Waters in North Carolina, 47 N.C.L.Rev. 205 (1968); e.g., Stacy v. Walker, 222 Ark. 819, 262 S.W.2d 889 (1953); Mason v. Lamb, 189 Va. 348, 53 S.E.2d 7 (1949). While courts have couched modifications of the common enemy rule in different language, the principle in substance is that a landowner is privileged to use and improve his land for proper purposes even though the natural flow of surface water is thereby altered so long as he uses reasonable care to avoid causing unnecessary harm to others. Kinyon and McClure, Interferences with Surface Waters, 24 Minn.L.Rev. 891 (1940), and cases cited.

The second doctrine, commonly called the *civil law rule*, is, in its purest form, opposed to the common enemy rule. Based on the quoted maxim *aqua currit et debet currere, ut currere solebat* (water flows and as it flows so it ought to flow), the civil law rule subjects a landowner to liability whenever he interferes with the *natural flow* of surface waters to the detriment of another in the use and enjoyment of his land. Kinyon and McClure, supra. Various rationales have been advanced in support of this rule. Many courts have simply felt that, as it was necessary to have some rule establishing rights and duties in regard to surface water disputes, it was reasonable and just to follow the law of nature. It was said early in Gormley v. Sanford, supra, that "[a]s water must flow, and some rule in regard to it must be established where land is held under the artificial titles created by human law, there can clearly be no other rule at once so equitable and so easy of application as that which enforces nature's laws. There is no surprise or hardship in this, for each successive owner takes whatever advantages or inconveniences nature has stamped upon his land." Other courts have chosen the civil law rule in order to avoid the element of contest or force inherent in the common enemy rule. Mayor of Albany v. Sikes, 94 Ga. 30, 20 S.E. 257 (1894).

Nevertheless, since almost any use of land involves some change in drainage and water flow, courts have found that a strict application of civil law principles discourages proper improvement and utilization of land. Thus courts have modified the rule to permit the reasonable use of land. See Annot., 59 A.L.R.2d 421 (1958). For the most part such changes have been piece-meal responses to specialized situations. One modification frequently found in civil law jurisdictions arises when one owner discharges surface waters on the lands of another by artificial means. Faced with this situation courts have often held, with minor variations, that the upper owner may deposit surface water by artificial means into a natural drainway even though the amount of water flowing into adjoining land is thereby increased. E.g., Lambert v. Alcorn, 144 Ill. 313, 33 N.E. 53 (1893); Miller v. Hester, 167 Iowa 180, 149 N.W. 93 (1914); Mizell v. McGowan, 120 N.C. 134, 26 S.E. 783 (1897).

Some courts, however, have announced more general modifications. The Maryland court at one time fashioned a special hardship rule, stating: "[A] strict application of [the civil law rule] also might result in very great hardship on the lower land owner, who would thereby be prevented from improving his land or using it as he would otherwise have a right to use it. In cases where such hardship would necessarily ensue to one or the other of the owners, courts have sometimes adopted what may be called a 'reasonableness of use' rule. * * * The case before us presents a state of facts in which the rule of reasonableness of use is applicable." Whitman v. Forney, 181 Md. 652, 31 A.2d 630 (1943).

Perhaps the most comprehensive modification of the civil law rule was undertaken in the California case of Keys v. Romley, 64 Cal.2d 396, 50 Cal.Rptr. 273, 412 P.2d 529 (1966). There the court noted that California traditionally adheres to the civil law rule, yet observed that:

" * * * [N]o rule can be applied by a court of justice with utter disregard for the peculiar facts and circumstances of the parties and properties involved. No party, whether an upper or a lower landowner, may act arbitrarily and unreasonably in his relations with other land-owners and still be immunized from all liability.

"It is therefore incumbent upon every person to take reasonable care in using his property to avoid injury to adjacent property through the flow of surface waters. Failure to exercise reasonable care may result in liability by an upper to a lower landowner. It is equally the duty of any person threatened with injury to his property by the flow of surface waters to take reasonable precautions to avoid or reduce any actual or potential injury.

"If the actions of both the upper and lower landowners are reasonable, necessary, and generally in accord with the foregoing, then the injury must necessarily be borne by the upper landowner who changes a natural system of drainage, in accordance with our traditional civil law rule."

The third doctrine of surface water disposition is known as the *reasonable use rule*. Briefly, this rule allows each landowner to make reasonable use of his land even though, by doing so, he alters in some way the flow of surface water thereby harming other landowners. Liability is incurred only when this harmful interference is found to be unreasonable. City of Franklin v. Durgee, 71 N.H. 186, 51 A. 911 (1901); Armstrong v. Francis Corp., 20 N.J. 320, 120 A.2d 4 (1956); Enderson v. Kelehan, 226 Minn. 163, 32 N.W.2d 286 (1948); see generally, Clark supra § 453. Reasonableness is a question of fact for the jury. Kinyon and McClure, supra.

Although sometimes denominated as a "new" or "emerging" doctrine, the rule of reasonable use traces its origin to the mid-nineteenth century. In Basset v. Company, 43 N.H. 569 (1862), the New Hampshire Supreme Court first took note of conflicts inherent in any rigid inflexible system of rules applied to drainage issues. The court there said:

> "No land-owner has an absolute and unqualified right to the unaltered natural drainage or percolation to or from his neighbor's land. In general it would be impossible for a land-owner to avoid disturbing the natural percolation or drainage, without a practical abandonment of all improvement or beneficial enjoyment of his land. Any doctrine that would forbid all action of a landowner, affecting the relations as to percolation or drainage between his own and his neighbors' land, would in effect deprive him of his property. * * *"

For this reason the court held that " * * * in the drainage a man may exercise his own right on his own land as he pleases, provided he does not interfere with the rights of others. The rights are correlative, and from the necessity of the case, the right of each is only to a reasonable user or management. * * *"

After considerable struggle the Minnesota court adopted a similar rule. See Sheehan v. Flynn, 59 Minn. 436, 61 N.W. 462 (1894); Enderson v. Kelehan, supra. Although these jurisdictions were for many years the sole adherents to the reasonable use rule, a growing number have recently adopted the rule fully, e.g., Weinberg v. Northern Alaska Development Corp., 384 P.2d 450 (Alaska, 1963); Rodrigues v. State, 52 Haw. 156, 472 P.2d 509 (1970); Armstrong v. Francis Corp., supra; Jones v. Boeing Company, 153 N.W.2d 897 (N.D.1967); Butler v. Bruno, supra; Sanford v. University of Utah, 26 Utah 2d 285, 488 P.2d 741 (1971); State v. Deetz, 66 Wis.2d 1, 224 N.W.2d 407 (1974), or in part, Lunsford v. Stewart, 95 Ohio App. 383, 120 N.E.2d 136 (1953); Mulder v. Tague, 85 S.D. 544, 186 N.W.2d 884 (1971); City of Houston v. Renault, Inc., 431 S.W.2d 322 (Tex.1968). In addition, several states have approved modifications of the common enemy or the civil law rule approaching actual adoption of the reasonable use rule. See Keys v. Romley, supra; Templeton v. Huss, 57 Ill.2d 134, 311 N.E.2d 141 (1974); Commonwealth, Dept. of Hwys. v. S & M Land Co., Inc., 503 S.W.2d 495 (Ky.1972); Baer v. Board of County Com'rs of Washington Co., 255 Md. 163, 257 A.2d 201 (1969); Morris v. McNicol, 83 Wash.2d 491, 519 P.2d 7 (1974).

The rising prominence of the reasonable use rule is seemingly attributable to the increasing industrialization and urbanization of the nation. Where people are forced by social and demographic pressures to live in close proximity with each other and with commercial and industrial development, there will be, of necessity, increased conflict over the proper utilization of land. Long and Long, Surface Waters and the Civil Law Rule, 23 Emory L.J. 1015 (1974). It is no longer simply a matter of balancing the interests of individual landowners; the interests of society must be considered. On the whole the rigid solutions offered by the common enemy and civil law rules no longer provide an adequate vehicle by which drainage problems may be properly resolved. For this reason courts have responded, first with modifications of existing rules and then, when those proved unwieldy, by the adoption of the rule of reasonable use.

North Carolina has long adhered to the civil law rule. See Note, Disposition of Diffused Surface Waters in North Carolina, 47 N.C.L. Rev. 205 (1968). In Porter v. Durham, 74 N.C. 767 (1876), this Court held:

"* * * [A]n owner of lower land is obliged to receive upon it the surface-water which falls on adjoining higher land, and which naturally flows on the lower land. Of course, when the water reaches his land the lower owner can collect it in a ditch and carry it to a proper outlet so that it will not damage him. He cannot, however, raise any dike or barrier by which it will be intercepted and thrown back on the land of the higher owner."

As we have noted, this rule applies whether the drainage technically involves diffused surface water, Phillips v. Chesson, 231 N.C. 566, 58 S.E.2d 343 (1950); Davis v. R.R., supra; Winchester v. Byers, 196 N.C. 383, 145 S.E. 774 (1928); Staton v. R.R., 109 N.C. 337, 13 S.E. 933 (1891); or a natural watercourse, City of Kings Mountain v. Goforth, supra; Midgett v. Highway Commission, supra; Clark v. Guano Co., 144 N.C. 64, 56 S.E. 858 (1907); Mizell v. McGowan, 120 N.C. 134, 26 S.E. 783 (1897); Porter v. Durham, supra; accord, Jones v. Loan Association, 252 N.C. 626, 114 S.E.2d 638 (1960).

Nevertheless, North Carolina has found, like other states, that in a changing society dogmatic adherence to this rule is unfeasible and unwise. Thus the Court early committed itself to a policy of flexible application of the civil law rule. Note, Disposition of Diffused Surface Waters in North Carolina, 47 N.C.L.Rev. 205 (1968). This policy was stated clearly and succinctly by Chief Justice Faircloth in Mizell v. McGowan, supra:

"The upper owner can not divert and throw water on his neighbor, nor the latter back water on the other with impunity. *Sic utere tuo, ut alienum non laedas* [Use your own property in such a manner as not to injure that of another]. This rule, however, can not be enforced in its strict letter, without impeding rightful progress and without hindering industrial enterprise. Minor individual interest must sometimes yield to the paramount good. Otherwise the benefits of discovery and progress in all the enterprises of life would be withheld from activity in life's affairs. 'The rough outline of natural right or liberty must submit to the chisel of the mason that it may enter symmetrically into the social structure.' Under this principle the defendants are permitted not to divert, but to drain their lands, having due regard to their neighbor, provided they do no more than concentrate the water and cause it to flow more rapidly and in greater volume down the natural streams through or by the lands of the plaintiff."

Another example of this Court's flexible approach to water law problems is found in Yowmans v. Hendersonville, 175 N.C. 574, 96 S.E. 45 (1918). In that case there was evidence tending to show that, by the grading and paving of streets, the City of Hendersonville diverted water onto plaintiff's lot causing damage. The trial court charged the jury that plaintiff should recover if the jury found that defendant had "diverted upon plaintiff's property more water than would naturally flow there, causing damage. * * * " This Court noted that the charge adequately stated the law as between private owners or public service corporations, but pointed out that:

" * * * in regard to the flow and disposal of surface water incident to the grading and pavement of streets, a different rule is recognized, and a municipality, acting pursuant to legislative authority, is not ordinarily responsible for the increase in the flow of water upon abutting owners unless there has been negligence on their part causing the damage. The right to change the grade of the streets and to improve the same, according to modern and generally approved methods, passed to the municipality in the original dedication and may be exercised by the authorities as the good of the public may require. It is held in this jurisdiction, however, that the right referred to is not absolute, but is on condition that the same is exercised with proper skill and caution. * * * "

As these decisions illustrate, this Court has generally adhered to the civil law rule yet has not hesitated to modify that rule where time and circumstance so required.

A similar situation, demonstrating the Court's willingness to modify water law in response to social change, arose during the development of the law of riparian rights. See generally Aycock, Introduction to Water Use Law in North Carolina, 46 N.C.L.Rev. 1 (1967). Like the laws of drainage riparian rights were early expressed in terms of the "natural flow" rule. By this rule an owner of lands abutting a stream had the right to have the flow continue through his land undiminished in quantity or quality except for such "natural uses" as drinking, bathing, watering farm animals and irrigation of home supportive gardens. Industrial use was permitted only insofar as the water was returned to the stream without substantial diminution in quality or quantity. Although adequate early in our history, this rule was soon outmoded by the needs of a growing urban and industrial society. This Court therefore adopted the "American rule" or rule of reasonable use that a "riparian proprietor is entitled to the natural flow of a stream running through or along his land in its accustomed channel, undiminished in quantity and unimpaired in quality, except as may be occasioned by the reasonable use of the water by other like proprietors." Smith v. Morganton, 187 N.C. 801, 123 S.E. 88 (1924); accord, Pugh v. Wheeler, 19 N.C. 50 (1836).

This rule was expounded upon in Dunlap v. Light Co., 212 N.C. 814, 195 S.E. 43 (1938). There the Court said:

"The right of a riparian proprietor to the natural flow of a stream running through or along his land in its accustomed channel undiminished in quantity and unimpaired in quality, is qualified by the right of other riparian owners to make a reasonable use of such water as it passes through or along their lands. In determining the rights of a lower riparian owner, the question is whether the upper riparian proprietor is engaged in a reasonable exercise of his right to use the stream as it flows by or through his land, whether with or without retaining the water for a time, or obstructing temporarily the accustomed flow. * * *

* * * The rights of riparian owners in a running stream above and below are equal; each has a right to the reasonable use and enjoyment of the water, and each has a right to the natural flow of the stream subject to such disturbance and consequent inconvenience and annoyance as may result to him from a reasonable use of the waters by others. There may be a diminution in quantity or a retardation or acceleration of the natural flow indispensable for the general valuable use of the water perfectly consistent with the existence of the common right and this may be done so long as the retardation and acceleration is reasonably necessary in the lawful and beneficial use of the stream. * * *

"What constitutes a reasonable use is a question of fact having regard to the subject matter and the use; the occasion and manner of its application; its object and extent and necessity; the nature and size of the stream; the kind of business to which it is subservient; and the importance and necessity of the use claimed by one party and the extent of the injury caused by it to the other."

Thus our Court adopted a flexible rule of reasonable use with regard to the rights and duties of riparian owners where such a position was mandated by basic long-term change in the social and economic structure of society.

With this background of the law, we now turn to plaintiffs' first contention, to wit, that the court erred by instructing the jury on the law of nuisance rather than restricting its instructions to the duties of a lower landowner to receive water from the upper owner.

By his charge the judge instructed the jury to determine whether defendants engaged in tortious conduct amounting to a private nuisance. In substance, this part of the charge amounts to an instruction in accord with the rule of reasonable use. As noted previously, North Carolina has traditionally adhered to a modified civil law doctrine. Midgett v. Highway Commission, supra. Thus, on its face the charge of the trial judge, with emphasis on the reasonableness of the defendants' actions, is an incorrect statement of the law. Defendants, however, argue that a nuisance analysis is "useful in situations such as this case presents because it requires of the fact finder a consideration of the reasonableness of the defendant's conduct in light of all the circumstances." In effect, defendants argue that this Court should abandon the civil law rule in favor of the rule of reasonable use. For the reasons which follow, we agree.

In this jurisdiction, as already noted, various modifications of the strict civil law doctrine have been made, case by case, to permit the reasonable use of land. Doubtless the evolution of the law could continue in such piecemeal fashion. This method of change, however, has left a legacy of contradiction and confusion in our law regarding the drainage of surface water.

The nature of this confusion and its cause are revealed by examination of the methods by which drainage law problems have been analyzed. The civil law doctrine has historically been regarded as a species of property law. Thus most courts have articulated the doctrine through property law concepts such as rights, servitudes, easements, and so forth. E.g., Clark v. Guano Co., supra; see Comment, The Application of Surface Water Rules in Urban Areas, 42 Mo.L.Rev. 76 (1977). These property concepts are rigid and absolute in nature and, while they are appropriate where the civil law doctrine is strictly applied, they serve as an impediment where it becomes necessary to modify the doctrine to accommodate changing social and economic needs. Kinyon and McClure, Interference with Surface Waters, 24 Minn.L.Rev. 891 (1940).

The resulting inflexibility presents a particularly difficult problem in drainage cases. In an era of increasing urbanization and suburbanization, drainage of surface water most often becomes a subordinate feature of the more general problem of proper land use—a problem acutely sensitive to social change. Since property concepts do not easily admit of modification, many courts, *ours included*, have responded by making exceptions to the rule on a case-by-case basis, e.g., Mizell v. McGowan, supra, or by adjusting the theory of the action in a particular case to achieve a just result, compare City of Kings Mountain v. Goforth, supra, with Midgett v. Highway Commission, supra; Davis v. R.R., supra, and Johnson v. Winston-Salem, 239 N.C. 697, 81 S.E.2d 153 (1954).

The adoption of exceptions, most of which incorporate some element of reasonable use, has resulted in uncertainty of the law and reduced predictability which is a chief virtue of the civil law rule. Butler v. Bruno, supra. Adjustments in the theory of the action tend to cause confusion when courts are required to pass on the applicability of statutes of limitation or the availability of other defenses such as contributory negligence or easement by prescription. Maloney and Plager, Diffused Surface Water: Scourge or Bounty?, 8 Nat.Res.J. 72 (1968). Our decisions seem to provide clear guidance to attorneys and trial courts only in a case where the facts are on "all fours" with the facts of a previously decided case. Hence it is understandable that, as later appears, the able trial judge in the case before us charged on both the civil law rule and the reasonable use rule!

We believe the reasonable use doctrine affords a sounder approach to the problems presented by surface water drainage. It can be applied effectively, fairly and consistently in any factual setting, Butler v. Bruno, supra, and thus has the capacity to accommodate changing social needs without occasioning the unpredictable disruptions in the law associated with our civil law rule.

Other advantages of the reasonable use rule, particularly those relating to evidentiary aspects, are less obvious though no less important. Under the civil law rule it is crucial to determine the "natural flow" of the surface water. The continual process of construction and reconstruction, a hallmark of our age, has made it increasingly difficult to determine accurately how surface waters flowed "when untouched and undirected by the hand of man." City of Houston v. Renault, Inc., supra. Adoption of the reasonable use rule obviates the necessity of making such a finding. See Comment, The Application of Surface Water Rules in Urban Areas, 42 Mo.L.Rev. 76 (1977). In sum, we think the reasonable use rule is more in line with the realities of modern life and that consistency, fairness and justice are better served through the flexibility afforded by that rule.

Accordingly, we now formally adopt the rule of reasonable use with respect to *surface water drainage*. That rule is expressed as follows: Each possessor is legally privileged to make a reasonable use of his land, even though the flow of surface water is altered thereby and causes some harm to others, but liability is incurred when his harmful interference with the flow of surface waters is unreasonable and causes substantial damage. Armstrong v. Francis Corp., supra; accord, Weinberg v. Northern Alaska Development Corp., supra.

Analytically, a cause of action for unreasonable interference with the flow of surface water causing substantial damage is a private nuisance action, with liability arising where the conduct of the landowner making the alterations in the flow of surface water is either (1) intentional and unreasonable or (2) negligent, reckless or in the course of an abnormally dangerous activity. See Restatement of Torts § 833 (1939); Restatement (Second) of Torts § 822 (Tent. Draft No. 17, 1971); accord, Watts v. Manufacturing Co., 256 N.C. 611, 124 S.E.2d 809 (1962); Morgan v. Oil Co., 238 N.C. 185, 77 S.E.2d 682 (1953); City of Houston v. Renault, Inc., supra; Sanford v. University of Utah, supra; State v. Deetz, supra.

Most nuisances of this kind are intentional, usually in the sense that "the defendant has *created or continued* the condition causing the nuisance with full knowledge that the harm to the plaintiff's interests is substantially certain to follow." (Emphasis added.) W. Prosser, Law of Torts § 87 (4th Ed. 1971). Other nuisances may arise from negligence as, for example, where the defendant negligently permits otherwise adequate culverts replacing natural drainways to become obstructed, Johnson v. City of Winson-Salem, 239 N.C. 697, 81 S.E.2d 153 (1954); Price v. R.R., 179 N.C. 279, 102 S.E. 308 (1920).

Regardless of the category into which the defendant's actions fall, the reasonable use rule explicitly, as in the case of intentional acts, or implicitly, as in the case of negligent acts, requires a finding that the conduct of the defendant was unreasonable. This is the essential inquiry in any nuisance action. See Watts v. Manufacturing Co., supra; Morgan v. Oil Co., supra.

Reasonableness is a question of fact to be determined in each case by weighing the gravity of the harm to the plaintiff against the utility of the conduct of the defendant. Armstrong v. Francis Corp., supra; State v. Deetz, supra; Restatement (Second) of Torts § 826 (Tent. Draft No. 18, 1972). Determination of the gravity of the harm involves consideration of the extent and character of the harm to the plaintiff, the social value which the law attaches to the type of use which is invaded, the suitability of the locality for that use, the burden on plaintiff to minimize the harm, and other relevant considerations arising upon the evidence. Determination of the utility of the conduct of the defendant involves consideration of the purpose of the defendant's conduct, the social value which the law attaches to that purpose, the suitability of the locality for the use defendant makes of the property, and other relevant considerations arising upon the evidence. Rodrigues v. State, supra; Armstrong v. Francis Corp., supra; Watts v. Manufacturing Co., supra; Jones v. Boeing, supra; Restatement of Torts §§ 829–831 (1939); Restatement (Second) of Torts §§ 827, 828 (Tent.Draft No. 17, 1971); Restatement (Second) of Torts § 829A (Tent.Draft No. 18, 1972); Note, 50 Ky.L.J. 254 (1961–62).

We emphasize that, even should alteration of the water flow by the defendant be "reasonable" in the sense that the social utility arising from the alteration outweighs the harm to the plaintiff, defendant may nevertheless be liable for damages for a private nuisance "if the resulting interference with another's use and enjoyment of land is greater than it is reasonable to require the other to bear under the circumstances without compensation." See Restatement (Second) of Torts (Tent.Draft No. 17, 1971); Restatement (Second) of Torts §§ 826, 829A (Tent.Draft No. 18, 1972). The gravity of the harm may be found to be so significant that it requires compensation regardless of the utility of the conduct of the defendant.

As the New Jersey court perceptively noted in Armstrong v. Francis Corp., supra:

"* * * [W]hile today's mass home building projects * * * are assuredly in the social good, no reason suggests itself why in justice, the economic costs incident to the expulsion of surface waters in the transformation of the rural or semi-rural areas of our State into urban or suburban communities should be borne in every case by adjoining landowners rather than by those who engage in such projects for profit. Social progress and the common wellbeing are in actuality better served by a just and right balancing of the competing interests according to the general principles of fairness and common sense which attend the application of the rule of reason."

* * *

We now consider the charge of the trial judge to determine whether he correctly instructed the jury. In relevant part the judge instructed as follows:

"Now, the first issue: did the defendants Aiken create a nuisance by installing and covering a 36-inch drain across their property. In order to answer that issue with any intelligent approach to it, you must know what is meant by the use of the word 'nuisance' as applied in that issue. Now I instruct you that the law provides that every owner of land has a right to be free from interference with the use and enjoyment of his land. When one person by the improper use of his land does injury to the land, property, or rights of another, although he does not actually physically trespass upon such property, that conduct constitutes a private nuisance. In order for the plaintiff in this case to recover for a private nuisance, the conduct complained of, that is, the conduct that the plaintiffs say that the Aikens did, that conduct must be unreasonable, and there must be a substantial invasion of the plaintiffs' interest in the private use and enjoyment of their property although the defendants did not actually trespass upon the plaintiffs' property. It must work some substantial injury to the plaintiffs' property. The law of private nuisance rests upon the concept that every person should use his own property as not to injure the property of another.

"As a consequence, a private nuisance exists in a legal sense when one person makes an improper use of his own property and in that way injures the land or property of his neighbor. An invasion of another's interest in the use and enjoyment of his land is intentional in the law of private nuisance when the person whose conduct is in question has a basis for liability actionable in the purpose in causing it, or knows that it is resulting from his conduct, or knows that it is substantially certain to result from his conduct. A person who intentionally creates or maintains a private nuisance is liable for the resulting injury to others regardless of the degree of care or skill exercised by him to avoid such injury.

"Now, members of the jury, conduct may be a nuisance by reason of its location or the manner in which it is constructed, maintained, or operated. For there to be liability, the defendants Aikens' conduct must have been unreasonable, and such unreasonable conduct must have caused substantial injury to the plaintiffs Pendergrasts' property. In determining if the defendants Aikens' conduct was unreasonable, you are to consider all of the circumstances of this case. The question is not whether a reasonable person in the plaintiffs' or the defendants' position would regard the conduct as unreasonable, but whether reasonable persons in general looking at the whole situation impartially and objectively would consider it unreasonable. Some of the circumstances which you should consider on the question of the reasonableness of the defendants' conduct include the defendants' conduct itself, the character of the neighborhood, the relationship of the properties in question, the nature, utility and social value of both plaintiffs' and defendants' use of their land, the extent, nature and frequency of the alleged harm to the plaintiffs' interest. All of the circumstances in the case must be considered."

To this point the instruction, though somewhat rough, is substantially in accord with the rule of reasonable use as applied to the facts of this case. The trial judge went on, however, to state:

"Now one of the circumstances existing from the evidence in the case is the relationship of the two pieces of property; one being that of the plaintiffs, being an upper property, and that of the defendants being a lower property in speaking of the flow of the water. The water first comes to Mr. Pendergrast's property and then goes to the Aikens' property. So the Pendergrasts own what is known as the upper estate, and the Aikens own the lower estate.

"Now the law confers on the owner of an upper estate of land an easement, or servitude, in the lower estate for the drainage of surface waters flowing in its natural course and manner without obstruction or interruption by the owners of the lower estate to the detriment or injury of the upper estate. Each of the lower parcels along the drainway are servient to those on the higher level to the extent that each is required to receive and allow passage of the natural flow of surface water from the higher land. As servient to the upper estate, the defendants are not permitted by law to interrupt or prevent the natural passage of the water in the event it causes damage to the upper estate. Where a lower estate, such as the Aikens' in this case, presumably for their own convenience and for the better enjoyment of their property closed the natural depression and channel through which the water from the upper dominant tenement had been accustomed to flow and installed in lieu thereof an underground culvert or conduit, the law imposed upon the defendants' ownership the burden of installing a pipe of sufficient size to accommodate the natural flow of surface water from the upper tenement across the defendants' land without injury to the upper tenement's property."

By this latter statement the trial judge departed from the reasonable use rule and, using such property terms as easement and servitude, reverted to the civil law rule. The juxtaposition of reasonable use and civil law concepts placed contradictory instructions before the jury and could have no other effect than to confuse and mislead it. In that respect there was error in the charge. See Hardee v. York, 262 N.C. 237, 136 S.E.2d 582 (1964); Hubbard v. Southern R. Co., 203 N.C. 675, 166 S.E. 802 (1932).

We now turn to the second issue raised by plaintiffs' assignment of error, that is, did the court err in instructing the jury that it must first determine whether defendant created a nuisance, and then separately decide whether plaintiffs were harmed thereby.

In his original charge the trial judge instructed the jury that it must determine whether defendants created a nuisance. The court then told the jury that, should it answer that issue yes, it would "take up and consider the second issue, that issue being: if so, did the defendants Aiken thereby cause damage to the plaintiffs' property. Another way of saying that issue is: if you find that a nuisance was created, did the nuisance damage the plaintiffs' property." Later, in reply to a direct question from the foreman of the jury, the trial judge stated that the jury could answer the first issue yes and the second issue no.

The court erred in these instructions. The jury could not find that a nuisance existed at all without a finding of substantial damage to plaintiffs. Midgett v. Highway Commission, 265 N.C. 373, 144 S.E.2d 121 (1965); Watts v. Manufacturing Co., supra. This is so because "[e]ach individual in a community must put up with a certain amount of annoyance, inconvenience or interference, and must take a certain amount of risk in order that all may get on together." Watts v. Manufacturing Co., supra. Indeed the judge in one part of his charge instructed the jury that a finding of substantial injury to the plaintiff was a necessary element of a finding that a private nuisance existed.

Thus it was error to instruct the jury that it might answer the first issue yes and the second no. When the jury returned such a verdict it was hopelessly contradictory and its true meaning could not be determined. See Cody v. England, 216 N.C. 604, 5 S.E.2d 833 (1939). Because of the possibility of such a meaningless verdict, this Court has previously noted in *obiter dictum* that a submission of the second issue, in a private nuisance case, is itself error. Watts v. Manufacturing Co., supra.

The third issue raised by plaintiffs' assignment of error concerns the court's supplemental instructions on the effect of the two 24-inch culverts under Allen Avenue. These instructions arose from the following colloquy:

"FOREMAN: * * * Our question really concerns the release of the water from the Aiken property onto Allen Street versus—in other words, if the release of the water onto Allen Street is limited beyond the limitation placed by the Aiken property, how that would affect it.

COURT: Now let me see if I can answer your question. Is your question this: if there is more water coming off of the Aiken property than the Allen Street culverts can handle, how does that affect the lawsuit?

FOREMAN: Yes, sir.

COURT: Speaking about the two twenty-four inch culverts going under Allen Street.

FOREMAN: If the thirty-six inch culvert releases more water than the two twenty-fours will handle, therefore it's backed up because of that, how does that affect it?

COURT: Well, let me say this: now the plaintiffs have the burden of proof on each issue, and the plaintiffs have the burden to prove that by the installation and covering of the thirty-six inch culvert the defendants created a nuisance, and that the creation of that nuisance is what caused the damage to their property.

COURT: Now, if the jury finds that the plaintiffs have failed to prove that the creation—well, first of all they've got to prove there's a nuisance. If you find that they do prove that there's a nuisance, now then if you fail to find that the plaintiffs have satisfied you that they were damaged as a result of the creation of the nuisance, then the plaintiffs cannot prevail. Now if the jury finds that the plaintiffs' damage is not caused by the creation of a nuisance by the defendant, assuming that you find they have created a nuisance—I don't mean to infer what your verdict should be on that issue, but if you find that the damage was not caused by the creation of a nuisance, but was caused by something further downstream, then the plaintiffs could not recover."

In passing we note the trial judge again erred in instructing the jury that it must determine substantial damages apart from its determination of the existence of a nuisance. Of more immediate concern, however, is that part of the instruction stating " * * * but if you find that the damage was not caused by the creation of a nuisance, but was caused by something further downstream, then the plaintiffs could not recover."

As an abstract concept of law this statement is correct and, were there some evidence that the downstream 24-inch culverts caused the water to back onto plaintiffs' land, the instruction would have been entirely proper.   Here, however, there was neither allegation nor proof that the 24-inch culverts under Allen Avenue caused the flooding of plaintiffs' land.   In fact, all evidence is to the contrary.   John Pendergrast, a named plaintiff, testified that the water had never before backed up on plaintiffs' land although it had flooded the southern part of defendants' land.   Numerous witnesses confirmed this testimony. Walter Bearden, an expert in the field of civil engineering, testified that the 36-inch culvert emplaced by the defendant was "completely inadequate to carry the water."   Moreover, there is evidence that water continued to back onto the plaintiffs' land after the 24-inch culverts had been replaced by 60-inch culverts.

A court errs in charging upon a principle of law which is not presented by the pleadings and which does not arise from the evidence.   Textile Motor Freight v. DuBose, 260 N.C. 497, 133 S.E.2d 129 (1963).   Under the pleadings and evidence in this case the effect, if any, of the two 24-inch culverts had no legal significance relative to the dispute between the plaintiffs and defendants and the court erred in instructing the jury that it might consider the inadequate drainage from the Aikens land.

The judge had a positive duty to instruct the jury on all substantial matters arising from the evidence, whether or not requested to do so. See generally 7 N.C.Index 2d, Trial § 33.   As applied to this case, this principle obligated the court, upon the jury's inquiry, to instruct it not to consider the inadequacies of the Allen Avenue drainage in deciding whether defendants had wrongfully diverted the flow of surface waters upon plaintiffs' land.   This the court did not do.

For errors committed, there must be a *new trial*.

Notes and Questions

1.   Although the court in the principal case draws an analogy between the historical development of the American common law of riparian rights and the American common law of surface water drainage, it should be recognized that the two bodies of law deal with fundamentally different issues.   In litigation as to the respective rights of riparian landowners, the parties are always asserting conflicting claims to use or appropriate water from the stream to which their lands are riparian.   In litigation with respect to surface water drainage, however, the issue is whether one landowner has violated the legal rights of the other by adopting a particular means of ridding himself of unwanted surface water. We know of no case where a landowner complained that his neighbor was appropriating all or too much of the surface water that drained across the neighbor's land.

2.   At one point in its opinion in the principal case, the court states the "reasonable use" rule as to interference with surface drainage as follows: "this rule allows each landowner to make a reasonable use of his land even though, by doing so, he alters in some way the flow of surface water thereby harming other landowners.   Liability is incurred only when this harmful interference is found to be unreasonable."   Does this make sense?   What relation, if any, does the "reasonableness" of a particular use of land—e.g., for residence, for agri-

culture, for retail business, or for manufacturing—have to the "reasonableness" of *the particular method adopted by the landowner to rid himself of unwanted surface water?* If the latter causes substantial harm and is found "unreasonable," what significance does the "reasonableness" or "unreasonableness" of the use of the land from which the water is drained? And what of the court's statement that "reasonableness is a question of fact to be determined in each case by weighing the gravity of the harm to the plaintiff against the utility of the conduct of the defendant"? Can a judgment as to "reasonableness" based on such a weighing process realistically be described as involving "a question of fact"? And how does the trier of fact reach a conclusion that "even should alteration of the water flow by the defendant be 'reasonable' in the sense that the social utility arising from the alteration outweighs the harm to the plaintiff," the defendant should nevertheless be liable for damages to the plaintiff because the resulting interference with the plaintiff's use and enjoyment of land "is greater than it is reasonable to require the other [the plaintiff] to bear under the circumstances without compensation"? Does this mean that factors other than "social utility" and "gravity of harm"—such as "the suitability of the locality for the use defendant makes of the property"—may require imposition of liability on the defendant?

3. In the principal case, the court equates the "reasonable use" doctrine as to surface water drainage with the broader doctrine of "nuisance." This reflects the position taken in Rest., Torts 2d § 833 (1979) and presumably means that an "adverse possessor" of land, as well as an owner is protected against a nuisance-causing interference with the natural flow of surface water. But why is the intrusion of water on the plaintiff's land viewed as a "nuisance" rather than as a "trespass"? Surely an intentional diversion of water onto the plaintiff's land in such a way as to cause substantial and "unreasonable" harm seems to be a "trespassory" invasion. Moreover, as the court points out, most such invasions "are intentional in * * * the sense that "the defendant has *created or continued* the condition causing the nuisance with full knowledge that the harm to the plaintiff's interests is substantially certain to follow."

4. Although a substantial group of American states has now formally adopted the "reasonable use" doctrine as to surface water drainage, these states are still in the minority. But "substantially all of the jurisdictions which purport to follow the civil law or common enemy rules have engrafted upon them numerous qualifications and exceptions which, in actual result, produce decisions which are not as conflicting as would be expected, and which would generally be reached under the reasonable use rule." Kinyon & McClure, Interferences with Surface Waters, 24 Minn.L.Rev. 891, 913 (1940). In connection with pleading and jury instructions, however, the rule formally accepted in a particular jurisdiction makes a big difference. Even a modified civil law or common enemy rule will require quite different pleadings and instructions than will the reasonable use rule.

5. For a concise discussion of the rights of possessors of land with respect to diffuse surface water, see Cunningham § 7.6.

Note on Rights of Riparian Owners at Common Law

Natural flow vs. reasonable use. The English "natural flow" rule as to the rights of riparian owners in streams is said to remain in force in Georgia, New Jersey, Pennsylvania, West Virginia, and, possibly in Maine. But it is clear that, in fact, the "natural flow" rule has everywhere been modified in order to allow all riparian owners some use of the water in the stream to which their lands are riparian. A thoroughgoing application of the "natural flow" rule would deny any riparian use that would alter the stream's purity, volume, or rate of flow—i.e., would preclude any use whatever. Of course, no such rule was ever applied even in England, where the "natural flow" rule originated. In the great majority of the American states, the "reasonable use" rule has been formally substituted for the "natural flow" rule. For a statement of the "reasonable use" rule, see the last principal case. The major impetus to development of the "reasonable use" rule was undoubtedly the need for a rule that would permit construction of a series of mills along the rivers, creeks and streams of the eastern and midwestern states. As was said by Woodworth, J., in Merrit v. Brinkerhoff, 17 Johns. 306, 321 (1829).

"The common use of the water of a stream by persons having mills above, is frequently if not generally attended with damage and loss to the mills below; but that is incident to that common use, and for the most part unavoidable. * * * The person owning an upper mill on the same stream has a lawful right to use the water, and may apply it in order to work his mills to the best advantage, subject, however, to this limitation: that if in the exercise of this right, and in consequence of it, the mills lower down the stream are rendered useless and unproductive, the law in that case will interpose and limit this common right so that the owners of the lower mills shall enjoy a fair participation." (Cited with approval in Dumont v. Kellogg, 29 Mich. 420 (1874).)

It has been held that a lower court's decree awarding "100 miner's inches" of water from a stream could not be sustained under the reasonable use doctrine. The court believed that the right to a reasonable amount of water could not be declared in quantitative terms, but must continually vary with the amount of water in the stream, the amount of land requiring water, and the varying extent of ordinary use needs. Lone Tree Ditch Co. v. Cyclone Ditch Co., 26 S.D. 307, 128 N.W. 596 (1910).

On the other hand, in Hoover v. Crane, 362 Mich. 36, 106 N.W.2d 563 (1960), plaintiffs were cottage and resort owners of land on a lake who complained of defendant's use of lake water to irrigate his fruit orchard on land that also abutted on the lake. The evidence was not clear on whether or to what extent the reduced lake level was caused by defendant's operations rather than natural causes. In the light of such evidence the trial court decreed that defendant could take water without limit so long as the lake level remained above the one natural outlet of the lake. When the lake level fell below that level the court decreed that defendant could take ¼ inch of water from the entire lake area, to be measured by a meter to be installed at defendant's pump, and that jurisdiction was retained to entertain further petitions in the event of changed conditions. On appeal, the court, in purporting to follow the reasonable use rule, affirmed. Is this result consistent with the *Lone Tree Ditch* case?

Ordinary v. Extraordinary Uses. It has been part of the American law from the beginning and continues as a qualification of the reasonable use rule on riparian rights that a riparian owner has an unlimited right to take water from a stream for "ordinary" or "natural" uses, that is, for domestic purposes and for watering livestock, even though such taking consumed all available water. The correlative rights implied by the notion of reasonable use is applicable to "artificial" or "extraordinary" uses, such as for industrial purposes or irrigation.

A strain is put on this distinction when a municipality erects a plant on riparian land to supply water to its inhabitants. Can this use be justified as natural or ordinary or domestic? Compare City of Canton v. Shock, 66 Ohio St. 19, 63 N.E. 600 (1902), with City of Emporia v. Soden, 25 Kan. 588 (1881).

Non-riparian Use. It is clear that the rule of reasonable use is applicable as between riparian owners. One who owns no riparian land has no rights as against riparian owners whose use is interfered with by his appropriation of water. A riparian owner may grant an easement to take water to a non-riparian owner, which is valid as against the grantor, but binds no other riparian owner.

Suppose a riparian owner takes water for use on nonriparian land. It is usually held that such use is an invasion of the rights of riparian owners who are injured thereby in their use of water. In other words, a nonriparian use of water is not protected by the doctrine of reasonable use. Or one may say that a nonriparian use is per se unreasonable. See e.g. Stratton v. Mt. Hermon Boys' School, 216 Mass. 83, 103 N.E. 87 (1913). In a few cases, however, courts seem to have held that a nonriparian use can be sustained as reasonable. See Gillis v. Chase, 67 N.H. 161, 31 A. 18 (1892); Smith v. Stanolind Oil & Gas Co., 197 Okl. 499, 172 P.2d 1002 (1946). But in these cases it also appears that there may have been insufficient evidence that the plaintiffs were injured by the defendants' operations. As stated in *Pendergrast*, under the reasonable use doctrine, no one has a cause of action for a taking of water that does not injure him. The recovery of nominal damages in such a case was granted in early cases that followed the old "natural flow" theory of riparian rights.

It is a normal assumption that for land to be riparian, it must abut a stream. Sometimes an additional requirement has been declared: land is not riparian if it is outside the watershed drained by the stream. Stratton v. Mt. Hermon Boys' School, supra.

The "reasonable use" rule is applicable to lakes as well as to flowing streams, and the term "riparian" is commonly used in connection with both, although technically one who owns land along a lake is a "littoral" owner. The relative rights of the various "littoral" owners to the "flow" of the lake is rarely, if ever, a matter of controversy, however. Instead controversies are likely to involve the respective privileges of "littoral" owners to boat, fish, or swim over the surface of the entire lake. A number of courts have held that such privileges exist, along with the privilege of using the lake for access to land adjacent to the lake.

A "riparian proprietor" entitled to assert "riparian rights" includes any person who is in possession of riparian land or who owns an estate in it. See Rest., Torts 2d § 844 (1979).

See Horwitz, The Transformation of the Concept of Property in American Law, 1780–1860, 40 U.Chi.L.Rev. 248 (1973), for a commentary on the history of the development of water law in this country.

B. STREAMS—THE DOCTRINE OF PRIOR APPROPRIATION

In the western states a doctrine regulating private rights in the waters of streams and lakes has been evolved which is strikingly different from the law of the eastern states which we call the doctrine of riparian rights. This is the doctrine of appropriation or prior appropriation. The name suggests its basic thesis, that is, it is an adaptation of the maxim "prior in time is prior in right."

The doctrine is said to have originated during the California gold rush in the middle of the nineteenth century. The most significant features of that phenomenon were the rapid influx of large numbers of miners seeking gold, and the fact that virtually all the land on which the mining was done still lay in the public domain. Unlike the waves of homesteaders who came later, these men sought gold, not land. By the same token they sought water only because it was necessary to mine gold. But in view of the circumstances, the miners had no standing as riparian owners to claim water rights. In fact the mining itself would have been chaotic if the miners' only rights were to the minerals actually extracted. Some sort of interest in the land itself was necessary. Such interests came to be established by custom.

"These rules * * * all recognized discovery, followed by appropriation, as the foundation of the possessor's title, and development by working as the condition of its retention. And they were so framed as to secure to all comers, within practicable limits, absolute equality of right and privilege in working the mines. Nothing but such equality would have been tolerated by the miners, who were emphatically the lawmakers, as respects mining, upon the public lands in the State."

Field, J., in Jennison v. Kirk, 98 U.S. 453, 457, 25 L.Ed. 240 (1878).

Since water was necessary to mining, the "ownership of all the water in the streams and lakes was—like that of the mines—in the government, and the miners proceeded to use it in connection with the mines under the same rules, customs and regulations, so far as applicable." Clayberg, The Genesis and Development of the Law of Waters in the Far West, 1 Mich.L.Rev. 91, 95 (1902). So it developed that the "one who first appropriated water, and afterwards diverted and used it, obtained the prior and exclusive right to the use of such water." Id. at 96.

By an act of Congress in 1866 these practices were acknowledged and approved upon public lands, and by a later statute, all homestead rights were made subject to any water rights which were vested and accrued under the prior statute. The customary rights were further vindicated by judicial decisions in the several states. In this developing law, the rights of appropriation came to be recognized also in respect to the operation of saw-mills, which were another incident of the elaboration of mining processes. The most important development for our time was the extension of this indigenous water law to embrace the use of water for irrigation. Today this system has general application to the various uses of water in streams and lakes, and is usually justified on the ground that it is more suitable for arid regions than the doctrine of riparian rights.

This law was in due course formalized by statutes, which among other things, interposed administrative machinery for the establishment and protection of private water rights. The selected sections of the California Water Code set out below are illustrative of the basic outlines of a statutory prior appropriation system. It cannot be our purpose to examine in detail the operation of this system in any state. You should read these sections primarily to discover in particular the differences between it and the doctrine of riparian rights. You should also note that priority of appropriation is not the only standard governing the distribution of water rights. Your reading of these sections may raise certain questions to which you will not find an answer in these limited materials. On these you may refer to the statutes and decisions in one or more of the states or to general commentaries on the subject. See for example Weil, Water Rights in the Western States (3d ed. 1911); Hutchins, Selected Problems in the law of Water Rights in the West (1942); 5 Powell c. 68.

CALIFORNIA WATER CODE ANNOTATED (West)

§ 1201. Public Water of State; Appropriation

All water flowing in any natural channel, excepting so far as it has been or is being applied to useful and beneficial purposes upon, or in so far as it is or may be reasonably needed for useful and beneficial purposes upon lands riparian thereto, or otherwise appropriated, is hereby declared to be public water of the state and subject to appropriation in accordance with the provisions of this code.

§ 1202. Unappropriated Water

The following are hereby declared to constitute unappropriated water:

(a) All water which has never been appropriated.

(b) All water appropriated prior to December 19, 1914, which has not been in process, from the date of the initial act of appropriation, of being put, with due diligence in proportion to the magnitude of the work necessary properly to utilize it for the purpose of the appropriation, or which has not been put, or which has ceased to be put to some useful or beneficial purpose.

(c) All water appropriated pursuant to the Water Commission Act or this code which has ceased to be put to the useful or beneficial purpose for which it was appropriated, or which has been or may be or may have been appropriated and is not or has not been in the process of being put, from the date of the initial act of appropriation, to the useful or beneficial purpose for which it was appropriated, with due diligence in proportion to the magnitude of the work necessary properly to utilize it for the purpose of the appropriation.

(d) Water which having been appropriated or used flows back into a stream, lake or other body of water.

§ 1225. Compliance With Division Provisions

No right to appropriate or use water subject to appropriation shall be initiated or acquired except upon compliance with the provisions of this division.

§ 1250. Action of Board

The board [State Water Resources Control Board] shall consider an act upon all applications for permits to appropriate water and shall do all things required or proper relating to such applications.

§ 1252. Persons Who May Apply

Any person may apply for and secure from the board, in conformity with this part and in conformity with reasonable rules and regulations adopted from time to time by it, a permit for any unappropriated water.

§ 1253. Terms and Conditions of Appropriation

The board shall allow the appropriation for beneficial purposes of unappropriated water under such terms and conditions as in its judgment will best develop, conserve, and utilize in the public interest the water sought to be appropriated.

§ 1254. Policy Guiding Action on Applications

In acting upon applications to appropriate water the board shall be guided by the policy that domestic use is the highest use and irrigation is the next highest use of water.

§ 1255. Rejection of Application

The board shall reject an application when in its judgment the proposed appropriation would not best conserve the public interest.

§ 1257. Consideration of Relative Benefit

In acting upon applications to appropriate water, the board shall consider the relative benefit to be derived from (1) all beneficial uses of the water concerned including, but not limited to, use for domestic, irrigation, municipal, industrial, preservation and enhancement of fish and wildlife, recreational, mining and power purposes, and any uses specified to be protected in any relevant water quality control plan, and (2) the reuse or reclamation of the water sought to be appropriated, as proposed by the applicant. The board may subject such appropriations to such terms and conditions as in its judgment will best develop, conserve, and utilize in the public interest, the water sought to be appropriated.

§ 1260. Required Contents

Every application for a permit to appropriate water shall set forth all of the following:

(a) The name and post office address of the applicant.

(b) The source of water supply.

(c) The nature and amount of the proposed use.

(d) The location and description of the proposed headworks, ditch, canal, and other works.

(e) The proposed place of diversion.

(f) The place where it is intended to use the water.

(g) The time within which it is proposed to begin construction.

(h) The time required for completion of the construction.

(i) The time for the complete application of the water to the proposed use.

(j) All data and information reasonably available to applicant or that can be obtained from the Department of Fish and Game concerning the extent, if any, to which fish and wildlife would be affected by the appropriation, and a statement of any measures proposed to be taken for the protection of fish and wildlife in connection with the appropriation.

§ 1300. Issuance of Notice; Delivery

As soon as practicable after the receipt of an application for a permit to appropriate water which conforms to the rules and regulations of the board and to law, the board shall issue and deliver a notice of the application (a) to the applicant, (b) to the district attorney of each county wherein the applicant proposes to divert water under the application, and (c) to the board of supervisors of each county wherein the applicant proposes to divert water under the application.

§ 1304. Contents of Protest

The notice shall contain appropriate general information as to what protests against the approval of the application shall contain in order to accord with the requirements of law and the rules and regulations of the board.

§ 1310. Requirement

If the application is for more than three cubic feet per second or for more than 200 acre-feet per annum of storage the notice of application shall be published in accordance with this article.

§ 1320. Requirement

Notice of an application for three cubic feet or less per second or for 200 acre-feet or less per annum of storage shall be given by posting and mailing in accordance with this article.

§ 1330. Time for Filing

Any person interested may, within the time allowed in the notice of application or within such further time as may, for good cause shown, be allowed by the board, file with it a written protest against the approval of an application.

§ 1340. Protested Application

Notice of hearing on a protested application shall be given by mailing notice not less than 20 days before the date of hearing to both the applicant and protestant by registered mail.

§ 1350. Powers of Board

The board may grant, or refuse to grant a permit and may reject any application, after hearing.

§ 1351. Hearing Unnecessary

No hearing is necessary in order to issue a permit upon an unprotested application or in order to reject a defective application after notice, unless the board elects to hold a hearing.

§ 1360. Petition for Writ of Mandate; Filing in Superior Court; Time

Any person interested in any application may, within 30 days after final action by the board, file a petition for a writ of mandate in the superior court in and for the county in which the applicant seeks to divert water to inquire into the validity of the action of the board. If the applicant seeks to divert water in more than one county, the petition may be filed in any one of the counties. The right to petition shall not be affected by the failure to seek reconsideration before the board.

§ 1375. Essential Conditions

As prerequisite to the issuance of a permit to appropriate water the following facts must exist:

(a) There must be an applicant.

(b) The application must contain the matter and information prescribed by this division and be in the form required by the board.

(c) The intended use must be beneficial.

(d) There must be unappropriated water available to supply the applicant.

(e) All fees due must be paid.

§ 1380. Issuance on Approval of Application

Upon the approval of an application the board shall issue a permit.

§ 1381. Right Conferred

The issuance of a permit gives the right to take and use water only to the extent and for the purpose allowed in the permit.

§ 1395. Time for Commencing Construction

Actual construction work upon any project shall begin within the time specified in the permit, which time shall not be less than 60 days from the date of the permit.

§ 1396. Prosecution of Work

The construction of the work thereafter and the utilization of water for beneficial purposes shall be prosecuted with due diligence in accordance with this division, the terms of the permit, and the rules and regulations of the board.

§ 1397. Completion of Work; Use of Water

The work shall be completed and the water applied to beneficial use in accordance with this division, the rules and regulations of the board, and the terms of the permit and within the period specified in the permit.

§ 1410. Hearing; Notice; Grounds for Revocation

If the work is not commenced, prosecuted, and completed, or the water applied to beneficial use as contemplated in the permit and in accordance with this division and the rules and regulations of the board, the board shall, after notice in writing and mailed in a sealed, postage prepaid and registered letter addressed to the permittee at his last-known address, and after a hearing, revoke the permit and declare the water subject to further appropriation.

§ 1450. Application Date; Continuance of Priority

Any application properly made gives to the applicant a priority of right as of the date of the application until such application is approved or rejected. Such priority continues only so long as the provisions of law and the rules and regulations of the board are followed by the applicant.

§ 1455. Continuance of Priority; Right Conferred

The issuance of a permit continues in effect the priority of right as of the date of the application and gives the right to take and use the amount of water specified in the permit until the issuance of a license for the use of the water or until the permit is revoked.

§ 1600. Permit Holder's Report

Immediately upon completion of the construction of works and application of the water to beneficial use the permitee shall report the completion to the board.

§ 1605. Duties of Board

The board shall as soon as practicable after receiving the report of completion cause to be made a full inspection and examination of the works constructed and the use of water therefrom. The permittee shall furnish the board with such records, data, and information as may be required to enable the board to determine the amount of water that has been applied to beneficial use and whether the construction of the works and the use of the water therefrom is in conformity with law, the rules and regulations of the board, and the permit.

§ 1610. Issuance of License

If the determination of the board as to completion is favorable to the permittee, the board shall issue a license which confirms the right to the appropriation of such an amount of water as has been determined to have been applied to beneficial use.

§ 1627. Duration

A license shall be effective for such time as the water actually appropriated under it is used for a useful and beneficial purpose in conformity with this division but no longer.

§ 1650. Time and Place of Recording

A true copy of each license issued or of each order modifying or changing a license shall within 30 days after issuance thereof be recorded by the board in the office of the recorder of the county in which the point of diversion specified in the license lies or in case there are points of diversion lying in more than one county then in each of those counties in which a point of diversion lies and in case the place or places of use specified in the license are in different counties than the point or points of diversion also in the county or counties in which the place or places of use lie.

§ 1675. Grounds; Hearing; Licensee Defined

If it appears to the board at any time after a license is issued that the licensee has not put the water granted under the license to a useful or beneficial purpose in conformity with this division or that the licensee has ceased to put the water to such useful or beneficial purpose, or that the licensee has failed to observe any of the terms and conditions in the license, the board, after due notice to the licensee and after a hearing, may revoke the license and declare the water to be subject to appropriation in accordance with this part. As used in this section "licensee" includes the heirs, successors, or assigns of the licensee.

Note

Special problems exist by reason of the fact that in some states the doctrine of prior appropriation has not entirely supplanted the common-law doctrine. The tier of Pacific coast states (Washington, Oregon, and California) so hold. In the same category is the western tier of plains states (North Dakota, South

Dakota, Nebraska, Kansas, Oklahoma, and Texas). This position has been referred to as the "California Doctrine." This does not mean, however, that the co-existence of the prior appropriation and common-law doctrines is managed on the same basis in all of these states. The statutes and decisions in the several states should be consulted in this regard. Between these two tiers of western states lies a third group of mountain and desert states (Arizona, Colorado, Idaho, Montana, Nevada, New Mexico, Utah, and Wyoming) in which the common-law doctrine is treated as unsuited to arid regions and has therefore been entirely superseded by the doctrine of prior appropriation. This has been called the "Colorado Doctrine." You may infer that there is some significance in this respect in the geographical distribution of these several groups of states. See 5 Powell ¶¶ 739–742; 6A A.L.P. § 28.58.

For a concise discussion of the rights of possessors of land with respect to streams and lakes, see Cunningham § 7.4.

C. UNDERGROUND WATER

FINLEY v. TEETER STONE, INC.

Court of Appeals of Maryland, 1968.
251 Md. 428, 248 A.2d 106.

BARNES, Judge. This appeal involves a claim for damages alleged to have resulted to at least 35 acres (and possibly 57 acres) of improved farmland in Carroll County. The land in question is owned and occupied by the appellants, George M. Finley and Elizabeth Englar Finley, his wife, (Finleys), who claim that the quarrying operations of the appellee, Teeter Stone, Inc. (Teeter) on adjacent land has resulted in the Finleys' land being dewatered, thereby causing damage by reason of substantial subsidence. The Circuit Court for Carroll County (Macgill, C.J.), at the end of the case presented by the plaintiffs, the Finleys, directed a verdict for the defendant, Teeter, and granted a judgment for costs in Teeter's favor. From this decision, the Finleys have taken a timely appeal.

The facts are presented by an agreed statement of the case pursuant to Maryland Rule 826g and are not in dispute.

The Finleys own and occupy a farm of 282.44 acres located on Stone Chapel Road in the Wakefield Valley in the New Windsor and Westminster Election District of Carroll County. Teeter owns a large tract of land located immediately adjacent to the southwest line of the Finley land. Since 1958 Teeter has operated a stone quarry on its land and conducts stone crushing operations and other related activities directly connected with the mining and refining of stone. Teeter's land consists of approximately 100 acres and is roughly rectangular in size. Since beginning its quarrying operations in 1958 it has gradually enlarged its quarry pit so that it now extends virtually from border to border of its tract and to a depth of some 80 feet. In the course of conducting its quarrying operations it is necessary for Teeter to keep its excavation dry by continually pumping out the water that accumulates in its quarry pit.

The testimony of James A. Humphreyville, a well qualified consulting geologist, was presented on behalf of the Finleys and is not contradicted in this case.　His testimony established that the rock formation into which the quarry pit was sunk was limestone which has been named Wakefield Marble.　The stone which is quarried is used for road stone and other purposes.

By boring operations on the Finley property, the consideration of other data and the exposure in the Teeter quarry, the extreme differential solution and erosion in the form of irregularly shaped pinnacles and spires is demonstrated.　In the area under consideration the striking dipping nature of the rock formation has also contributed to the saw-toothed top of the rock profile.　In addition, the rock mass is characterized by jointing, fracturing, faulting and voids resulting from the saw-toothed top of the rock profile.

The geologist observed that sink holes related to limestone areas generally and to the Wakefield Valley specifically are not unusual.　He demonstrated, however, that the likelihood of the occurrence of sink holes in the 35 acres of the Finley land, now subject to subsidence, in the absence of the removal of water, was negligible.　This area was approximately five feet superior to the level of the natural water table. Inasmuch as the land in question was at the low point of the local portion of the Valley, the movement of ground water in its natural state was slow but the excavation of the quarry and the pumping of water by Teeter caused the velocity of the flow toward the quarry sump to be substantially increased.　This action resulted in the dislodging of soils forming the roofs of the solution channels as well as causing soils from the clay mantel to be removed by percolation and flow, thus leaving voids causing subterranean and surface collapse.

The rock, itself, is impervious, but because of the cracks, solution channels (most of them interconnected), cavities, joints and fractures, the formation as a whole is highly permeable by water.　The pumping from the quarry has resulted in a "draw-down" of the water table so that there is a shallow "cone of depression" reaching under the Finley land.　This lowering of the water table causes the water support for the saturated clay to be removed so that the clay in the plugs on the solution channels begins to move out and is carried away by the water into lower positions on the solution channels.　In other situations the dropping of the water table may not directly wash away the clay plugs but allows the clay plugs to desiccate as they are no longer in contact with water.　As the overlying mantle of soils over the bed rock in this area varies from 17 to 30 feet, a vault, unsupported by earth, is then formed and may be three, four or even ten feet high.　The diameter may be up to 15 feet and when the rain comes in the late winter or early spring, the sudden rush of water infiltrates and saturates this clay and precipitates a series of collapses.　These propagate upwards until the surface of the land caves in and causes sink holes.　This has resulted in the sink holes on the 35 acres of the Finley land which were the basis of the study and principal testimony of the geologist in this case.　The photographs introduced into evidence indicated the severe nature of the sink holes which had occurred on the 35 acre tract.　There was evidence of a qualified real estate appraiser that the land of the Finleys had been substantially damaged as a result of the sink holes.

There was no contention by the Finleys that Teeter interfered with any underground bodies or streams of water flowing in known and defined or ascertainable channels or courses as opposed to percolating waters. Nor was there any contention by the Finleys that Teeter had acted in a negligent manner in the operation of its quarry, including the necessary pumping of water from it. All of the subsidence occurred entirely on the Finley land. Teeter's excavations did not cause any loss of lateral support of any of the Finley land immediately adjacent to the line of the quarry property. As already indicated, the trial court upon Teeter's motion, and after considering trial memoranda of the parties, directed a verdict for Teeter at the end of the Finleys' case because in its opinion the Finleys were not entitled to recover damages from Teeter as a matter of law. The trial court filed a well considered written opinion in denying the motion of the Finleys for a new trial, stating the reasons for its action. We agree with the conclusions of Chief Judge Macgill and will affirm the judgment for Teeter for costs.

As the present case involves the use of subterranean water, we will now consider the law applicable to such waters.

Subterranean waters are generally considered to be of two distinct types: (1) underground streams and (2) percolating waters. To be classified as an underground stream, the water must flow in a definite and fixed channel whose existence and location is either known or may be ascertained from indications on the surface of the land or by other means without subsurface excavations to determine such existence and location. * * *

Percolating waters, on the other hand, are those "which ooze, seep or filter through soil beneath the surface, without a defined channel, or in a course that is unknown and not discoverable from surface indications without excavation for that purpose. The fact that they may, in their underground course, at places come together so as to form veins or rivulets does not destroy their character as percolating waters."
* * *

Unless it can be shown that the "underground water flows in a defined and known channel, it will be presumed to be percolating water." Clinchfield Coal Corp. v. Compton, supra, 148 Va. at 448, 139 S.E. at 311–312, 55 A.L.R. at 1381–1382. Accord, Western Maryland R.R. Co. v. Martin, 110 Md. 554, 566–567, 73 A. 267, 272 (1909). See generally, McGowan v. United States, 206 F.Supp. 439, 442 (D.Mont.1962); Canada v. City of Shawnee, supra, 179 Okl. at 54, 64 P.2d at 696; 93 C.J.S. Waters § 87 at 762 (1956). While normally the use of underground streams is governed by the same law as applies to those waters flowing in defined and fixed channels above the surface, see e.g., Sycamore Coal Co. v. Stanley, 292 Ky. 168, 166 S.W.2d 293 (1942); McGowan v. United States, supra, 206 F.Supp. at 442; see generally 93 C.J.S. Waters § 89 at 763 (1956); 56 Am.Jur. Waters § 109 at 591 (1945), a separate and distinct body of law has developed governing the use of percolating waters.

In view of the agreed statement of facts, already mentioned, as well as the answers to interrogatories by the Finleys, together with the evidence in the lower court, it is clear that there has been no suggestion that the waters with which we are concerned are anything other than percolating.

There are two basic lines of authority applicable to the use of percolating waters. The first is known as the English Rule, and was first firmly established in England by the decision in Acton v. Blundell, 12 Messon and Welsby's Report, 324, 152 Eng.Rep. 1223 (1843). This case involved an action for damages by a landowner whose well had allegedly been made dry as a result of the activities of an adjoining landowner (the defendant) who in the normal operation of his mine drained away percolating water. Cowling, as counsel for the plaintiff, urged the Court to apply the maxim, *sic utere tuo ut alienum non laedas*, but the Court held that since the water involved was not a river or flowing stream, but percolating water, the landowner could apply it for any purpose he pleased. Lord Chief Justice Tindal stated, for the Court:

"[W]e think the present case, for the reasons above given, is not to be governed by the law which applied to rivers and flowing streams, but that it rather falls within that principle, which gives to the owner of the soil all that lies beneath his surface; that the land immediately below is his property, whether it is solid rock, or porous ground, or venous earth, or part soil, part water; that the person who owns the surface may dig therein, and apply all that is there found to his own purposes at his free will and pleasure; and that if, in the exercise of such right, he intercepts or drains off the water collected from underground springs in his neighbour's well, this inconvenience to his neighbour falls within the description of damnum absque injuria, which cannot become the ground of an action." (12 Messon and Welsby's Report at 354, 152 Eng.Rep. at 1235.)

Thus, under the English Rule, the owner of the freehold was deemed to own all of the percolating waters beneath the surface of the land as he owned the soil and minerals beneath the surface of the land and the air and sky above the surface—an application of the maxim *cujus est solum, ejus est usque ad coelum et ad inferos*. The English Rule is sometimes referred to as the "Absolute Ownership Rule," as the owner of the surface of the land had the absolute right to intercept underground percolating water before it left his property for whatever purpose he pleased and without regard to the effect of such interception on the owner of neighboring land.

* * *

In Coulson & Forbes, Law of Waters, 221 (6th Ed.1952), the English Rule is stated to be as follows:

"[It is] now established on the highest authority that the owner of land containing underground water which percolates by undefined channels and flows to the land of a neighbor has the right to divert or appropriate the percolating water within his own land so as to deprive the neighbor of it; and his right is the same whatever his motive may be, whether *bona fide* to improve his own land, or maliciously to injure his neighbor, or to induce his neighbor to buy him out." [1]

The other line of authority is known as the American Rule, and was developed in this country more recently, probably as a reaction to the harshness and abuses possible under the English Rule. Under it, in order for a landowner, who, in the course of using his own land, obstructs, diverts, or removes percolating water to the injury of his neighbor, to escape liability, the activity or conduct causing such obstruction, diversion or removal must be a reasonable exercise of his proprietary right, i.e., such an exercise as may be reasonably necessary for some useful or beneficial purpose, generally relating to the land in which the waters are found.[2] See e.g., Gallerani v. United States, 41 F.Supp. 293 (D.Mass.1941) (U.S. gov't held to same duty as a private individual); Sycamore Coal Co. v. Stanley, supra; N.M. Long & Co. v. Cannon-Papanikolas Constr. Co., 9 Utah 2d 307, 343 P.2d 1100 (1959). The American Rule is based upon the concept that the surface owner's right to obstruct, divert or remove the percolating waters under the surface of his land shall be exercised in such a way that will not unreasonably injure the exercise of a similar right by the owner of neighboring land— an application of the maxim *sic utere tuo ut alienum non laedas.* The American Rule is sometimes referred to as the "Reasonable Use Rule" or the "Correlative Rights Rule." [3]

There are three excellent and comprehensive annotations in the American Law Reports which consider the English and American decisions applying the two rules, viz., Subterranean and Percolating Waters; Springs; Wells, 55 A.L.R. 1385 to 1566 (1928), a supplement to that annotation, 109 A.L.R.2d 395 to 422 (1937) and Liability for Obstruction or Diversion of Subterranean Waters in Use of Land, 29 A.L.R.2d 1354 to 1379 (1953). It appears from these annotations and from an analysis of the various cases that while many of the early American decisions fol-

---

1. [The court's first footnote has been omitted. Ed.]

2. Possibly the first case to hold that a rule of reasonable use should apply was Bassett v. Salisbury Mfg. Co., 43 N.H. 569 (1862).

3. The terms "Reasonable Use Rule" and "Correlative Rights Rule" are often used interchangeably as synonymous for the "American Rule," but as pointed out in Bristor v. Cheatham, 75 Ariz. 227, 236, 255 P.2d 173, 178 (1953), the doctrines may be considered as distinct.

It would appear, however, that the interpretation given the phrase "Correlative Rights" in California where water, both surface and underground, is of great importance, both public and private, has been construed to include the concept of the use of a "fair share" of the percolating water in a common basin, underground reservoir, or a saturated strata, see City of San Bernardino v. City of Riverside, 186 Cal. 7, 15,

198 P. 784, 787 (1921), whereas in States in which the use of water is not of such vital importance the unlimited use of percolating water by the surface owner for some useful or beneficial purpose relating to his land is considered a "reasonable use." In short, the "Correlative Rights Rule" when used in judicial opinions in California appears to be a refinement or possibly an extension of the scope of the reasonableness of the use rather than a departure from the basic principle of reasonable use underlying the American Rule. For an interesting case reviewing the decisions of the Supreme Court of Utah seemingly applying the two rules at various times, see Snake Creek Mining & Tunnel Co. v. Midway Irrigation Co., 260 U.S. 596, 43 S.Ct. 215, 67 L.Ed. 423 (1923), which eventually concluded that the American Rule controlled, giving great weight to the conditions of the area, i.e., the scarcity of water and need for irrigation.

lowed the English Rule and that a slight majority of the jurisdictions in the United States may still follow this rule, the adoption of the American Rule appears to represent the trend in the American authorities.

Our predecessors, in 1909, considered the two rules in Western Maryland R.R. Co. v. Martin, supra, which involved an action at law by a plaintiff landowner against the defendant railroad company which it was claimed had caused a stream to overflow and deposit mud in the plaintiff's spring which, in turn, prevented the normal seepage of underground water into the spring, so that springs appeared in the plaintiff's meadow thereby injuring it. The railroad company requested an instruction that the jury in considering damages should exclude from its consideration any injury from the appearance of springs or water on that part of the plaintiff's land that was not actually submerged by the flooded stream. The trial court declined to grant the instruction. On appeal, in reversing the judgment for the plaintiff, this Court held that the instruction should have been granted. * * *

Although the language of the opinion in *Martin* rather indicates that the Court inclined to the American Rule [4] we will, like our predecessors in that case, assume without deciding, that the American Rule does apply, as under either the English Rule or the American Rule, the Finleys cannot recover in this case. It is apparent that under the English Rule, Teeter would have the absolute right to use the percolating waters under its land for any purpose without regard to the effect of that use on the Finley land.

Under the American Rule, Teeter would have the right to use the percolating waters under its land for any purpose connected with the legitimate use of its land. It is manifest that the conducting of quarrying operations is normally a legitimate and reasonable use of land, and certainly, in this case, there is no suggestion that such a use is unreasonable or inappropriate, considering all of the circumstances. See Sycamore Coal Co. v. Stanley; C & W Coal Corp. v. Salyer; Clinchfield Coal Corp. v. Compton, all supra; Sloss-Sheffield Steel & Iron Co. v. Wilkes, 231 Ala. 511, 165 So. 764, 109 A.L.R. 385 (1936), reaffirmed on subsequent appeal, 236 Ala. 173, 181 So. 276 (1938); Dickey v. Honeycutt, 39 Ala.App. 606, 106 So.2d 665 (1958), cert. denied, 268 Ala. 696, 106 So.2d 671 (1958). Moreover, it is established that the pumping of large quantities of water, incident to mining or quarrying operations, is both reasonable and necessary. Bayer v. Nello L. Teer Co., 256 N.C. 509, 124 S.E.2d 552 (1962); Evans v. City of Seattle, supra. See also Associated Contractors Stone Co. v. Pewee Valley Sanitarium & Hospital, 376 S.W.2d 316 (Ky.1963); Wheatley v. Baugh, 25 Pa. 528, 64 Am.Dec. 721 (1855); Behrens v. Scharringhausen, 22 Ill.App.2d 326, 161 N.E.2d 44 (1959). Indeed, the evidence in the present case, as in the above cases, makes inescapable the conclusion that such procedures are accepted

---

4. It may be observed that this Court has adopted a "reasonableness of use" rule on a case to case basis as a modification of the strict civil law rule in regard to surface waters. See Sainato v. Potter, 222 Md. 263, 267–268, 159 A.2d 632, 634 (1960) noted in 21 Md.L.Rev. 88–89 (1961); see also Maryland Surface Waters—A Critical Analysis, 18 Md.L.Rev. 61 (1958) and Note, Drainage of Surface Waters Under the Civil Law Rule as Applied in Maryland, 11 Md.L.Rev. 58 (1950).

practice in the industry, and strongly suggests that without them, it would be economically, if not absolutely unfeasible for the landowner to put his property to such use. * * *

The general rule is that a landowner engaged in ordinary and usual mining operations is not responsible for damages resulting from the diversion or destruction of the flow of percolating waters. In addition to Bayer v. Nello L. Teer Co., see Clinchfield Coal Corp. v. Compton; Sycamore Coal Co. v. Stanley and Sloss-Sheffield Steel & Iron Co. v. Wilkes, Dickey v. Honeycutt, C & W Coal Corp. v. Salyer, all supra.

As it is prima facie established that Teeter's use of the percolating waters on its land is a legitimate and reasonable one, it is incumbent upon the Finleys to show that such was unreasonable. There are cases which have indicated that the diversion or destruction of the flow of percolating waters may be unreasonable if the water is being sold for commercial purposes, see e.g., Koch v. Wick, 87 So.2d 47 (Fla.1956); Rothrauff v. Sinking Spring Water Co., 339 Pa. 129, 14 A.2d 87 (1940); Canada v. City of Shawnee, supra, or if the water is being unreasonably wasted, see e.g., City of Pasadena v. City of Alhambra, 33 Cal.2d 908, 207 P.2d 17 (1949); Southwest Engineering Co. v. Ernst, 79 Ariz. 403, 291 P.2d 764 (1955) (these cases relied primarily upon the legislative intent expressed in statutes prohibiting the wasting of water). In addition, there are numerous cases which have established that a malicious or negligent use of percolating waters is unreasonable. See generally 93 C.J.S. Waters § 93 at 767–772, § 94 at 773 (1956); 56 Am.Jur. Waters § 114 at 596–599, § 117 at 599–601 (1947). The cases of Cabot v. Kingman, 166 Mass. 403, 44 N.E. 344, 33 L.R.A. 45 (1896); New York Cent. R.R. Co. v. Marinucci Bros. & Co., Inc., 337 Mass. 469, 149 N.E.2d 680 (1958); Gamer v. Town of Milton, 346 Mass. 617, 195 N.E.2d 65 (1964), relied upon by the appellants, are examples of a negligent use as the basis of liability.[5]

Inasmuch as there is no contention or proof by the Finleys that there was any negligence by Teeter in its excavation of its quarry or of any waste, malice or sale of percolating waters, or other unreasonable use, Teeter has no liability to the Finleys for damages resulting from Teeter's pumping or percolating waters from its quarry. The injury to the Finleys is *damnum absque injuria.*

The Finleys have argued both to the court below, and before us, that the law relating to the use of percolating waters should not apply, and because the eventual result of Teeter's activities was subsidence of the Finley land, the law relating to the support of land should be dispositive.

In considering the cases relied on by the Finleys, it is important to keep in mind the distinction between *lateral* support and *subjacent* support. "Lateral support" is "the right which soil in its natural state has to support *from land adjoining it.*" 1 Am.Jur.2d Adjoining Landowners § 37 at 717 (1962) (emphasis supplied)." "Subjacent support," on

---

5. We will assume that these cases are to be treated as resting on the law of percolating waters, even though there was evidence in all of them that the defendants were draining out solid matter from under the plaintiffs' land as well as water.

the other hand, is "the support of the surface *by the underlying strata* of the earth (emphasis supplied)." Id. § 77 at 746. The evidence established that the sink holes on the Finley land resulted from the *downward* movement of the earth. There was no sidewise movement of soil or rock from the Finley land into the Teeter quarry. It is clear that the cases involving the impairment of *lateral* support, relied on by the Finleys, are not apposite. These cases include Levi v. Schwartz, 201 Md. 575, 95 A.2d 322, 36 A.L.R.2d 1241 (1953); Mullan v. Hacker, 187 Md. 261, 49 A.2d 640 (1946); and Baltimore & Potomac R.R. Co. v. Reaney, 42 Md. 117 (1875).

Farnandis v. Great Northern Ry. Co., 41 Wash. 486, 84 P. 18, 5 L.R.A., N.S., 1086 (1906), although principally concerned with cracks in the earth resulting from blasting, also involved some evidence that the cracks had resulted from the tapping of an underground stream which caused the soil to be carried away, rather than from the diversion of percolating waters.

In Rouse v. City of Kinston, 188 N.C. 1, 123 S.E. 482, 35 A.L.R. 1203 (1924), the Supreme Court of North Carolina adopted the American Rule for North Carolina and held that the removal of percolating waters for sale was not a reasonable use of those waters. It is clear, however, that the pumping of percolating waters by a quarry owner is considered to be a reasonable use of percolating waters in North Carolina. See Bayer v. Nello L. Teer Co., supra.

The cases involving the removal of barriers to a stratum of quicksand or of sand also involved a deprivation of lateral support. See Prete v. Cray, 49 R.I. 209, 141 A. 609, 59 A.L.R. 1241 (1928) and Muskatell v. City of Seattle, 10 Wash.2d 221, 116 P.2d 363 (1941).[6]

It is our opinion that there is a vital distinction between all of the cases of lateral support where some substance, which in its natural position is stationary and provides a foundation for the overlying land, is caused to be removed from its position of rest and the present case where a body of naturally moving water is diverted or affected. The fact that some of the cases involved quicksand or other liquid or semi-liquid substances is not persuasive, as it may be assumed that such substances are not normally flowing, shifting, or changing position in response to the vagaries of weather and climatic conditions. Water, on the other hand, whether in defined streams or percolating, is known to flow or move in response to virtually every change in conditions, both natural and man-made. It is primarily because of this dynamic quality that we cannot hold that interference with the support provided by water is subject to the same rules of absolute liability that are imposed on a landowner who deprives his neighbor of the natural support provided by soils and other more solid materials. See Restatement of Torts § 818 (1939) which provides: "To the extent that a person is not liable for withdrawing subterranean waters from the land of another, he is

---

6. It should be observed that the *Farnandis* and *Muskatell* cases also involved a provision of the Constitution of the State of Washington which prohibited the taking or damaging of private property for public use without the payment of just compensation.

not liable for a subsidence of the other's land which is caused by the withdrawal." In Comment b to that section, it is explained: "The freedom from liability stated in this Section is restricted to the withdrawal of fluids of which the constituents are preponderantly water, and does not extend to fluids of which the constituents are preponderantly solid matter." We emphasize that we need not decide here whether the result might be different if, in the course of its operations, the defendant had caused substantial amounts of soil or clay to be drawn out from under the plaintiffs' land, or if there had been any evidence of lateral movement of supporting materials from the plaintiffs' land to the defendant's land.

Nor do we believe that there is any issue of subjacent support, within the legal definition of that term, involved in this case. Both Black's Law Dictionary and Bouvier's Law Dictionary define subjacent support as "the right of land to be supported by the *land* which lies under it." Black's Law Dictionary 1593 (4th Ed.1951); 3 Bouvier's Law Dictionary 3189 (3rd Revision 1914). (Emphasis supplied.) Similarly, the Introductory Note to the Restatement of Torts, Ch. 39 (1939) defines subjacent support as the situation where "the supported land is above and the supporting land is beneath it." It is our opinion that the right should be so limited, and in the absence of the type of situation where the surface ownership is separated from the subsoil ownership, or where there is an actual encroachment on the land underlying that which is allegedly deprived of support, we do not think there is any question of deprivation of subjacent support. Thus, it has been stated:

> "[A]lthough there may be an absolute duty to the surface owners of the same land in which mining operations are conducted not to cause falls and sinks or cracks in the surface, such duty arises as an incident to that of subjacent support * * *, which does not exist as to adjoining surface landowners. As to them there is no difference between the duty to avoid surface disturbances and that to avoid drainage of percolating water, since the duty of subjacent support is not existent so long as lateral support is not interfered with." (Sloss-Sheffield Steel & Iron Co. v. Wilkes, supra, 231 Ala. at 518, 165 So. at 770, 109 A.L.R. at 392.)

See generally 1 Am.Jur.2d Adjoining Landowners § 77 at 746 (1962); Restatement of Torts § 818, supra.

It was suggested at the argument by counsel for the Finleys that because of the increase of knowledge in regard to geology and the action and reaction of soil and percolating waters, and in view of the serious and extensive damage suffered by the Finleys by the appearance of the sink holes on their land, an expanded "American Rule" should be adopted by us. There is little question that the Finleys have been gravely injured by the sink holes, and although we are sympathetic with their plight, we are of the opinion that we must adhere to the authorities we have cited. If the public interest requires a change of the law in regard to percolating waters, a remedy lies with the General Assembly where the rights, duties and opinions of those concerned could be fully considered and evaluated.

Judgment affirmed, the costs to be paid by the appellants.

Notes

1. In State v. Michels Pipeline Construction, Inc., 63 Wis.2d 278, 217 N.W.2d 339, 219 N.W.2d 308 (1973), the defendant contracted to build a deep sewer, which required pumping from wells to lower the water level to a point that would permit tunnelling. The result was the drying up of private wells of a number of neighboring residents. The suit alleged a public nuisance and sought a decree that the defendants conduct operations so as not to create a nuisance. A demurrer was sustained on the basis that a prior case had established that there is no cause of action for interference with ground water. This decree was reversed on appeal. The court held that a sufficiently large number of persons were affected to sustain the allegation of a public nuisance. The case relied on by the trial court was overruled. The court reviewed the various rules relating to percolating waters and decided to accept the rule proposed in the Restatement, Torts Second § 858 (1979) which provides:

> "A possessor of land or his grantee who withdraws ground water from the land and uses it for a beneficial purpose is not subject to liability for interference with the use of water by another, unless

> "(a) The withdrawal of water causes unreasonable harm through lowering the water table or reducing artesian pressure   *   *   *."

As is the case with riparian rights in streams, a possessor of land who is not the owner will be protected against or compensated for unreasonable harm caused by withdrawal of ground water. See Rest., Torts 2d, Topic 4 Scope Note preceding § 858.

2. Smith-Southwest Industries v. Friendswood Dev. Co., 546 S.W.2d 890 (Tex.Civ.App.1977) is also similar to the *Finley* case in that the plaintiffs complained of subsidence of their land resulting from the withdrawal of large quantities of underground water by the defendants. Texas had previously committed itself to the English rule. Here the plaintiffs alleged both a nuisance and negligence. The court reversed the trial court's order granting a summary judgment for the defendants, concluding that the plaintiffs did not fail to state a cause of action on either the nuisance or the negligence issues. Little light was shed upon the proof necessary to sustain either allegation. The court asserted the principle "that imposes upon all persons a duty to use due care in the use of their property or the conduct of their business to avoid injury to others." The court also said that "if the landowner is negligent in the manner by which he produces the water" he may be liable for his negligent conduct. The only allegations relevant to negligence, other than the amount of water taken, was that the defendants had spaced their wells in too tight a pattern, thus concentrating the subsidence.

The ruling on negligence may seem analogous to some courts' treatment of the common-law right of lateral support of an owner's land. As stated in *Finley*, that right is limited to support of land in its natural state and does not include the right to the support of land that bears the weight of buildings. A number of courts, however, in cases involving damage to buildings, have held defendants liable for negligence. See 6A A.L.P. § 28.40. It should seem obvious that unless the meaning of negligence is carefully limited in such a context, such a result amounts to recognizing the right of support of buildings in the guise of the law of negligence. In other words, if negligence rests merely on the foreseeability of harm resulting from an excavation, how is that different from a duty not to withdraw support?

If this sort of analysis is really applicable to the *Smith-Southwest* case, one notes the striking consequence that in a jurisdiction adhering to the English rule about underground water, a defendant may be more limited in withdrawing water than in the *Finley* case, where the court purported to follow the rule of reasonable use.

An appeal in the *Smith-Southwest* case is pending in the Texas Supreme Court.

See Note, 15 Hous.L.Rev. 454 (1978).

3. About half the states which have the doctrine of prior appropriation apply this doctrine with some variations to ground water. In respect to the others, there is some question about the constitutionality of such extension of the appropriation doctrine to the extent that there has been a prior commitment to a different doctrine. See 6A A.L.P. § 28.67. In some states the control of ground water use in application of certain conservation measures should be noted. Such statutes exist both in appropriation and non-appropriation states. Some questions remain here also about the constitutionality of some of these statutes. 5 Powell ¶ 728.

4. For a concise discussion of the rights of possessors of land with respect to underground water see Cunningham § 7.5.

Note on Water Law and the Public Interest

The water law doctrines introduced in the preceding cases and notes are concerned primarily with the rights of one owner or possessor of land against another. But it is clear that these legal doctrines are totally inadequate to deal with the water supply problems which now confront the United States as a result of the population explosion, the growth of heavy industry, and the increasing reliance of American agriculture on the heavy use of chemical fertilizers. All of this has produced an enormous increase in the demand for water at a time when ground water in some parts of the country is becoming seriously depleted and both surface and ground waters are polluted by sewage, industrial and mining wastes, and run-off from agricultural lands. In fact, water pollution is now recognized as one of the most important problems facing the United States. Yet none of the cases in this chapter deals with water pollution. This is rather surprising, for it would seem that in states where the "reasonable use" or "natural flow" doctrine of riparian rights is recognized any land use that causes substantial pollution of a stream or lake would violate the riparian rights of downstream landowners.

In some cases, of course, riparian owners have alleged that water pollution by upstream landowners violates their rights. Most of these are cases in which the plaintiff alleged interference with a commercial use of his land—e.g., alleging injury to a farmer's livestock that drink from a stream. A riparian owner who uses a stream or lake only for swimming, boating, or fishing may not find it worthwhile to bring a suit against a polluter unless he can join with other landowners who are similarly affected. See, e.g., White Lake Improvement Association v. City of Whitehall, 22 Mich.App. 262, 177 N.W.2d 473 (1970), where the plaintiffs alleged that the defendants were creating a public nuisance dumping industrial waste and municipal sewage into a lake in a recreational area.

Governmental regulation of water use at the national, state, and local levels has been present to some degree for more than a century, but until recently it has been limited and sporadic. The situation has fundamentally changed, however, since enactment of the federal Water Pollution Control Act, 33 U.S.C.A. §§ 1251 et seq., which establishes water quality standards that are to be met within statutorily prescribed periods. The Environmental Protection Agency (EPA), established by the National Environmental Policy Act, 42 U.S.C.A. §§ 4321 et seq. (NEPA), has been assigned the basic responsibility for drafting and promulgating detailed regulations as to water quality. The EPA is also assigned the basic responsibility for enforcing water quality standards, but it has delegated this authority, to a considerable extent, to state and local agencies which meet requirements contained in the Water Pollution Control Act. At present, however, there is still no national policy—let alone any detailed regulations or enforcement procedures—with respect to conservation of the nation's water and its allocation to the uses that will best serve the nation's long-run interests.

In contrast to the elaborate administrative machinery established under the federal Water Pollution Control Act, in Michigan and other states with legislation modelled on the Michigan Environmental Protection Act of 1970, there has been a recent enlargement of the rights of private citizens to bring lawsuits in order to impose sanctions on those who "pollute, impair, or destroy" natural resources, including, of course, "water." Under such statutes, the right to bring suit is not limited to riparian owners in cases of stream pollution or diversion, nor is it limited to owners of overlying land in cases of underground water pollution or excessive pumping.

Underlying the legal problems arising in connection with large-scale attempts to deal with the nation's water use problems are difficult scientific and technological problems. And when scientific and technological data suggest adoption of specific legal rules, complex social and economic problems may remain. For example, what criteria should determine priorities as to use where water supplies are inadequate? To what extent can industry absorb the costs of eliminating water pollution and to what extent should governmental subsidies be provided?

Jurisprudential Note: Property, Ownership, and Interests Less Than Ownership

If, as Bentham asserted, *property* is a legally protected *expectation* of deriving certain advantages from a *thing*, it follows that *property* is comprised of *legal relations* between *persons* with respect to *things*. These legal relations may be of varying types, as we have seen in considering the materials in this and the preceding chapter of this book. One of the most important of these legal relations arises from actual possession of land or chattels, which as a general rule gives the possessor a legally protected right to possession as against anyone who cannot show a better right to possession. This principle provides the major theme of Chapter 1, Section 2 of this book. But a legally protected right to possession would in most cases not be worth very much unless the possessor could also legally make some beneficial use of the land or chattels in his possession. And, as the materials in the present chapter of this book indicate, the right of a possessor of land to make a "reasonable" use of the land in his possession, including the immediately superadjacent airspace, along with the water in streams flowing through and percolating beneath his land, is legally protected against interference by other persons.

It is thus clear, on the basis of the materials in the first two chapters of this book, that possession of land or chattels creates substantial property rights. Indeed, possession of the requisite "adverse" character, if continued for the statutory period of limitation applicable to actions for recovery of the possession of land or chattels, has the effect of extinguishing all the former owner's rights with respect to the land or chattels in question and of conferring on the adverse possessor the "ownership" thereof. This unusual way of acquiring ownership was considered in the first chapter of this book not because it is, at the present time, an important mode of acquisition—we know that a person normally acquires ownership of land or chattels by a consensual transfer from the former owner or by intestate succession upon the death of the former owner—but because it helps to convey an idea of what it is that the adverse possessor acquires when he becomes an "owner" of land or chattels.

One who acquires "ownership" of land or chattels in any way recognized by law obtains—as the materials in the first two chapters of this book clearly show—the rights to exclusive possession and beneficial use of the subject matter. In addition, the "owner" of land or chattels obtains the power to transfer ownership to any other person.[7] In the case of land, however, since ownership is generally evidenced by a public record that contains a written "history" of the ownership of particular tracts, one who acquires ownership of land by adverse possession cannot, as a practical matter, transfer his ownership in a commercial transaction unless or until he makes his ownership a matter of public record in some legally authorized way such as recording a favorable judgment in an action to recover possession of the land or to "quiet title" to the land.

The concept of "ownership" as consisting essentially of exclusive rights to possession and beneficial use which are legally protected against "the whole world," coupled with a power to transfer all the "owner's" rights and powers to any other person, is clearly central to "property" law both in the Anglo-American legal "common law" system and in the "civil law" system that prevails in western continental Europe and in Latin America. Hence the "owner" may transfer a variety of "nonpossessory" or "incorporeal" interests to other persons without ceasing to be the owner.[8] In the case of land, for example, the owner may transfer a variety of rights to make a limited use of his land—called "easements" or "servitudes"—which do not carry with them either a present or future right of possession. In such case, the landowner is deemd to retain "ownership" because the interests he retains are much more substantial than the interests transferred; the landowner is said to retain the right to possession, although the limited rights of user transferred to others do, in fact, interfere to some extent with the owner's possession. Of course, a landowner who has transferred "easements" to several persons may limit his own rights to the point that he would seem to retain no substantial right either to possession or beneficial use. He does, however, even in such a case, retain the residual right to make any otherwise lawful use of the land that does not interfere with the "easements" he has transferred to others. As a matter of practical convenience in dealing with land transfers and in fashioning a scheme of legal remedies to protect all the interests in a given parcel of land, it is useful to treat the transferor in such a case as retaining "ownership" of the land.

Our tentative definition of "ownership" as consisting of legally protected rights of possession and beneficial use coupled with a power to transfer all the "owner's" rights suggests the possibility of a concept of property and a mode of analysis quite different from that which we have developed up to this point. This alternative concept and mode of analysis—originated by Wesley Hohfeld[9]

7. The law relating to transfer of "ownership" is considered mainly in Part 2 of this book.

8. The law relating to such "nonpossessory" or "incorporeal" interests is considered mainly in Chapters 5 and 6 of this book.

9. See W. Hohfeld, Fundamental Legal Conceptions 23–124 (1928). See also L. Becker, Property Rights ch. 2 (1977);

and adopted by the first Restatement of Property [10]—postulates four basic legal relations, represented by four sets of correlative terms: (1) right—duty, (2) privilege—no right, (3) power—liability," and (4) immunity—disability.

In the Hohfeldian scheme, "right" is defined as "a legally enforceable claim of one person against another, that the other shall do a given act or * * * not do a given act." Any person against whom a "right" exists has a correlative "duty." "Privilege" is defined as "a legal freedom on the part of one person as against other to do a given act or * * * not to do a given act." Any person against whom the "privilege" exists has a correlative absence of right ("no right") that the person enjoying the "privilege" shall do or not do the act in question. "Power" is defined as "an ability on the part of a person to produce a change in a given legal relation by doing or not doing a given act." Any person against whom a "power" exists has a correlative "liability" to have the given legal relation changed by the doing or omission of the given act. "Immunity" is defined as a freedom on the part of one person against having a given legal relation altered by a given act or omission on the part of another person." A person against whom the "immunity" exists is under a correlative "disability" to alter the given legal relation by the doing or omission of the given act.[11]

The first Property Restatement, following common usage, employs the term "interest" to designate any single, right, privilege, power, or immunity, or, generically, "varying aggregates of rights, privileges, powers and immunities," [12] and further states that the totality of "interests" which it is legally possible for a person to have with respect to a "thing," other than those interests which a person has merely because he is a member of society, constitutes "complete property" in the thing.[13]

> This totality varies from time to time, and from place to place, either because of changes in the common law, or because of alterations by statute.
> * * * At any one time and place, however, there is a maximum combination of rights, privileges, powers and immunities * * * that is legally possible, and which constitutes complete property in * * * land or [a] thing other than land.[14]

It thus appears that "complete property," as the term is used in the first Property Restatement, corresponds to the layman's concept of "absolute, unencumbered ownership."

All this is pretty abstract, however, The Hohfeldian analytical scheme adopted in the Property Restatement can be made more concrete by considering Hohfeld's own application of his analytical scheme to interests in land: [15]

> Suppose * * * that A is * * * owner of Blackacre. His "legal interest" or property relating to the tangible object that we call *land* consists of a complex aggregate of rights (or claims), privileges, powers, and immunities. First, A has multital legal rights [rights in rem], or claims that *others*, respectively, shall *not* enter on the land, that they shall not cause physical harm to the land, etc., such others being under respective correlative legal duties. Second, A has an indefinite number of legal privileges of entering on the land, using the land, harming the land, etc., that is, within the limits fixed by law on grounds of social and economic policy, he has privileges of doing on or to the land what he pleases; and correlative to all

Kocourek, The Hohfeld System of Fundamental Legal Concepts, 15 Ill.L.Rev. 24 (1920); Corbin, Legal Analysis and Terminology, 29 Yale L.J. 163 (1919).

10. Rest., Prop. §§ 1–5, 10.

11. Id. §§ 1–4.

12. Id. § 5.

13. Id. § 5, Comment e. Also see id. § 10.

14. Ibid.

15. W. Hohfeld, supra note 9, at 96–97.

such legal privileges are respective legal no-rights of other persons. Third, A has the legal power to alienate his legal interest to another, i.e., to extinguish his complex aggregate of jural relations and create a new and similar aggregate in the other person; * * * also the legal power to create a privilege of entrance in any other person by giving "leave and license"; and so on indefinitely. Correlative to all such legal powers are the legal liabilities in other persons—this meaning that the latter are subject *nolens volens* to the changes of jural relations involved in the exercise of A's powers. Fourth, A has an indefinite number of legal immunities, using the term "immunity" in the very specific sense of non-liability, or non-subjection to a power on the part of another person. Thus A has the immunity that no ordinary person can alienate A's legal interest or aggregate of legal relations to another person; the immunity that no ordinary person can extinguish A's own privileges of using the land; the immunity that no ordinary person can extinguish A's right that another person, X, shall not enter on the land, or, in other words, create in X a privilege of entering on the land. Correlative to all these immunities are the respective legal disabilities of other persons in general.

Hohfeld's analysis of legal relations has been subjected to severe criticism by a number of writers.[16] Thus it has been said that there is an apparent overlap between the concepts of "privilege" and "power" which Hohfeld does not adequately explain; that "no right" is no more entitled to be considered *the* correlative of "privilege" than is "liability"; and that a person may be under a "disability" because of the existence of a "duty" as well as because of the absence of a "power." Moreover, when the Hohfeldian analysis is applied to property, it is not useful in explaining how the "owner" of land or chattels can transfer his property therein to another, since the "owner" has both the "power" and the correlative "disability" with respect to any transfer. However, the concepts of "power" and "disability" are useful in dealing with a case where O, the owner of land or chattels, creates in his agent, A, a "power of sale" or "power of appointment" relating to the land or chattels. In such a case, A (together with a consenting transferee) has a Hohfeldian "power" to transfer O's property to the transferee, and O is under a Hohfeldian "disability" with respect to continued ownership of the land or chattels.

The Hohfeldian analysis is also useful in connection with those "nonpossessory" or "incorporeal" property interests in land called "easements," "real covenants," and "equitable servitudes" in Anglo-American law. Most "easements" consist of a single "privilege" to make a limited use of the land of another, buttressed with a "right" to enjoy that use without interference from either the "owner" of the land or any other person, coupled with a power to transfer the "easement" to any other person. Most "equitable servitudes" and some "real covenants" transfer to another landowner a right to prevent the owner of the "servient" land from making specified uses of his land—uses that he would otherwise be privileged to make as "owner." And some "equitable servitudes" and "real covenants transfer to another landowner the right to require the performance of specified affirmative acts by the owner of the "servient" land—acts that he would otherwise have no duty to perform.

"Nonpossessory" of "incorporeal" interests illustrate the meaning of the term "interest" in property law—each of these interests comprises a characteristic bundle of rights, privileges, powers, and immunities, but does not include a right to possession either presently or at any future time. In the Anglo-American legal system, however, the "owner" of land (and the owner of certain kinds

16. E.g., Kocourek, supra note 9.

of personal property) may divide his ownership into two or more smaller segments or "interests" each of which includes either a present or a future right to possession and substantial present or future privileges of use or enjoyment. Interests that include a present right to possession may differ from each other with respect to the temporal duration of the interest—e.g., a "present interest" might endure for the life of the holder of that interest, or for a fixed period of time. Those "interests" that include only a future right to possession may differ from each other with respect to the time and manner in which the right to possession and the privileges of use or enjoyment accrue to the owner of each type of "future interest." The ability of the "owner" of land (or certain kinds of personal property) to divide his ownership into two or more "interests"—one of which will include a present right to possession and the rest of which will include a future right to possession—is perhaps the most distinctive feature of Anglo-American property law.[17] The "civil law" system treats "ownership" as basically unitary and recognizes only to a very limited extent the power of the "owner" to divide his ownership into smaller present and future interests.[18]

17. The law relating to "present" and "future" interests—called "estates" when the subject matter is land—are considered mainly in Chapter 3 of this book. "The word 'estate,' as it is used in this Restatement, means an interest in land which (a) is or may become possessory; and (b) is ownership measured in terms of duration." Rest., Prop. § 9 (1936).

18. As previously noted, the "civil law" system is in force in western continental Europe and most of Latin America. This legal system is, in many of its fundamental features, derived from Roman law. Legislative codification of legal doctrine is a characteristic feature of the civil-law system. This is in contrast to the English common law, under which a large portion of basic legal doctrine was evolved from judicial decisions. The common law prevails throughout the English speaking world. We cannot here pursue any general comparative study of these two legal systems, even in respect to the institution of property. But the following selected portions of the Louisiana Civil Code are set out as an example of the systematic statement of fundamental property concepts which is characteristic of the "civil law" system. Louisiana is the only jurisdiction in the United States which received the "civil law" rather than the "common law" as the basis for judicial decisions.

Art. 448. Ownership, Definition

Art. 488. Ownership is the right by which a thing belongs to some one in particular, to the exclusion of all other persons.

Art. 489. Dominion as Element of Ownership

Art. 489. The ownership of a thing is vested in him who has the immediate dominion of it, and not in him who has a mere beneficiary right in it.

Art. 490. Perfect and Imperfect Ownership; Naked Ownership

Art. 490. Ownership is divided into perfect and imperfect.

Ownership is perfect, when it is perpetual, and when the thing is unincumbered with any real right towards any other person than the owner.

On the contrary, ownership is imperfect, when it is to terminate at a certain time or on a condition, or if the thing, which is the object of it, being an immovable, is charged with any real right towards a third person; as a usufruct, use or servitude.

When an immovable is subject to a usufruct, the owner of it is said to possess the naked ownership.

Art. 491. Perfect Ownership

Art. 491. Perfect ownership gives the right to use, to enjoy and to dispose of one's property in the most unlimited manner, provided it is not used in any way prohibited by laws or ordinances.

*　*　*

Art. 533. Usufruct, Definition

Art. 533. Usufruct is the right of enjoying a thing, the property of which is vested in another, and to draw from the same all the profit, utility and advantages which it may produce, provided it be without altering the substance of the thing.

*　*　*

Art. 606. Death of Usufructuary

Art. 606. The right of the usufruct expires at the death of the usufructuary.

*　*　*

The Hohfeldian analysis adopted in the first Property Restatement is applicable to "personal" interests—so-called interests *in personam*—as well as to "property" interests—often called interests *in rem*. What distinguishes "property" interests from "personal" interests is that the former (1) relate to things—land, chattels, and "intangible" things—and (2) are usually protected by law against an indefinitely large number of persons—as many writers put it, "against the world." Some "personal" interests, which do not relate to things, are nevertheless given legal protection against an indefinitely large number of persons—e.g., the interest of each person in freedom from personal injury caused by the intentional or negligent conduct of others (protected under rubrics such as "assault," "battery," "false imprisonment," and "negligence." [19] Other "personal" interests may or may not relate to things but are—initially, at least—protected as against only one or a few persons. An example of the latter kind of "personal" interest would be the interest of one contracting party in securing the performance of promises made by the other party to the contract.[20]

Suppose A, for a legally adequate consideration, promises to pay a sum of money to B. B's right to receive payment from A is a "personal" right, and is ordinarily enforced, if A fails to perform his promise, by obtaining a court judgment requiring A to pay the money to B. But it has been settled for almost two centuries that B's "personal" right against A can be transferred ("assigned") to someone else, C, who then becomes A's creditor and has the right to enforce A's promise to pay the agreed sum of money. Since transferability is one of the principal hallmarks of "property," we have come to think of contract rights as a kind of "property"—especially when the contract right is represented by or embodied in a formal writing such as a promissory note, bond, or insurance policy. Moreover, when A for a legally adequate consideration promises to transfer ownership of a tract of land to B, B normally has a right to specific performance of the contract; and this, as we have already seen, is now generally deemed to give B an "equitable" property interest in the land that is the subject matter of the contract.[21]

Art. 646. Kinds of Servitudes: Personal; Real or Predial

Art. 646. All servitudes which affect lands may be divided into two kinds, personal and real.

Personal servitudes are those attached to the person for whose benefit they are established, and terminate with his life. This kind of servitude is of three sorts: usufruct, use and habitation.

[Definitions of "use" and "habitation" are omitted. Ed.]

Real servitudes, which are also called *predial or landed servitudes*, are those which the owner of an estate enjoys on a neighboring estate for the benefit of his own estate.

They are called *predial or landed servitudes*, because, being established for the benefit of an estate, they are rather due to the estate than to the ownership personally.

Under the Louisiana Civil Code, it is apparent that a "usufruct" is, in general,

similar to a "life interest" in the Anglo-American legal system, and that a "predial or landed servitude" is, in general, similar to an "easement" in the Anglo-American legal system. The application of these concepts requires extensive elaboration, which is to be found in the full text of the code and the judicial interpretation of its various sections. Our objective is to explore the meaning of property in our own legal system. This may imply the need to inquire whether there are basic ideas concerning property which are common to all legal systems.

19. Such interests are dealt with in the law school course in Torts.

20. This interest is the subject matter of the law school course in Contracts.

21. Some of the special legal rules applicable to contracts for the sale of an interest in land are explored in Chapter 12 of this book.

The law of property is closely related to the law of torts as well as to the law of contracts. Property interests always include both rights and privileges, which tend to occur in pairs. Thus, e.g., if one has a privilege to use the land of another in a particular way—an "easement"—he also has a right that no one shall interfere with his exercise of that privilege. In such a case the right and the privilege are two sides of the same coin. In the law of property, the usual emphasis is upon the privileges included in the particular property interest that is under consideration. But when we shift our attention to remedies for invasion of the rights comprised in a property interest, we become involved with the law of torts because the acts which invade the property interest of another— e.g., trespass, conversion, wrongful ouster from land, nuisance, interference with water rights, and the like —are all "torts."

Chapter 3

ESTATES

SECTION 1. PRESENT AND FUTURE ESTATES [1]

A. THE THEORY OF ESTATES

The concept of an "estate" has its origin in England's feudal society, and the study of that society is itself a fascinating experience. Regrettably, we shall here have to confine our pursuit of history to that minimum which is required for a functional understanding of modern law. But such an understanding does require some reference to history, and some of the terminology, which is technical (it is something like learning a foreign language), is derived from early English law. That vocabulary simply must be mastered as part of the process of understanding. We will study the estate concept with reference to interests in land, because it was developed in that connection. But we will eventually learn that much of the same classification is applicable to personal property.

It may help to stimulate and maintain your interest in this subject matter if you are told now that the law of estates is of great importance to understanding the many options available to one contemplating either an inter vivos or a testamentary disposition of property. By utilizing the power to create present and future estates (to fragment ownership) an individual can provide that one or more persons shall have the benefit of his accumulated wealth for a period of time, e.g., their respective lives, and simultaneously create future rights of enjoyment in a subsequent generation. Moreover, the system permits private control over land use in a variety of ways. These factors have immense practical significance today.

Now a bit of history.

The feudal society that began after the Norman Conquest of 1066 was founded on an assumption that all land in England belonged to the King. The King parcelled out large pieces to his principal subordinates (let's call them barons), in return for their promise to perform certain services for the King. The most important practical service was to furnish a number of knights for the King's army. Land was power, and

---

1. You will find the following text materials helpful in studying this chapter: Bergin and Haskell, Preface to Estates in Land and Future Interests (1966); Cunningham chs. 2–5 (1983); Moynihan, Introduction to the Law of Real Property (1962); Simes, Handbook of the Law of Future Interests (2d ed. 1966); Simpson, Introduction to the History of the Land Law (1961); Merryman, Ownership and Estate (Variations on a Theme by Lawson), 48 Tulane L.Rev. 916 (1974).

220

the feudal system developed not as an abstract system of ownership but because it worked to meet the perceived needs of the established order. These barons exercised rights and enjoyed many of the benefits which we associate with ownership. But, as to the King, they were tenants, and deemed to "hold the land" of the King. In turn, the barons would often parcel out portions of their land to smaller holders in return for promised or obligated services which would help meet the obligation to the King and also the needs of the baron. This process might be repeated several times with each link creating a "lord" and a "tenant," held together by the tenurial obligations. This process of creating a new tier of tenants was known as subinfeudation. Each tenant "held" the land from his lord, and thus each parcel of land might be perceived as being "owned" by several persons at the same time, in the sense that each was entitled to some benefit from the relationship in accordance with the form and conditions of his tenure. Indeed, the overlord was said to be "seized in services," while the last tenant in line was said to be "seized in possession." Divided ownership is thus not new to the Anglo-American system. The modern landlord-tenant relationship bears some resemblance to the feudal tenure.

The feudal structure began to break down after the statute Quia Emptores in 1290. This statute essentially prohibited the process of subinfeudation but, in turn, allowed a person to transfer his interest in the land freely to another. The result was that he could substitute a new person in his place, but could not interpose himself as a lord between the one from whom he held the land and the new transferee. Over a period of centuries, the feudal hierarchy disappeared, and only the relationship between King and owner remains, but the "estate" concept which developed in the same centuries, is still retained in our modern law.

One of the fundamental notions of the concept was, and still is, that a person does not "own" a piece of land. Rather, he owns an "estate" in land. And, if a legal system permits the creation of various "estates" (each of which can be owned by a different person), then we can organize and distribute the benefits flowing from the land over a substantial period of time and among any number of persons. One judge put it this way:

> "[T]he land itself is one thing and the estate in the land is another thing, for an estate in land is a time in the land, or land for a time, and there are diversities of estates which are no more than diversities of time, for he who has a fee simple has a time in the land without end. * * * " Walshingham's Case, 2 Plowd. 517, 555, 75 Eng. Rep. 805, 816 (1579).

The Restatement of Property defines an "estate" as "an interest in land which

(a) is or may become possessory; and

(b) is ownership measured in terms of duration."

If we look first at the requirement that the interest "is or may become possessory," it seems clear that we are eliminating some interests which may be very important and very valuable. A nonpossessory interest in land, such as a right of way or other easement, may be created, but it is not an estate. Nor is such an interest viewed as part of "ownership." It is viewed as a burden on the land—an interest which subjects the ownership to a "servitude." Such interests will clearly restrict the possessor-owner in the use of the land, but they are still not part of ownership. Restrictions imposed on land use to serve the public interest (such as zoning laws), or restrictions imposed by enforceable private agreements are also viewed as burdening, but not dividing, ownership.

The second requirement—an estate is ownership measured in terms of duration—is a product of the brief history set out above and is a notion which is basic to understanding the estate concept.

Accordingly we must now talk about interests in land (estates) in durational terms. We will talk about estates which are "inheritable," and about interests in land which are "potentially durable forever" (of infinite duration). The idea that ownership may be of infinite duration (which necessarily includes the idea of inheritability) did not arise instantaneously. Rather, it developed slowly over the centuries following William's conquest of England. But assuming that the idea is accepted, what do these terms mean today? Suppose we conceive that one person, O, has *all* of the interests (rights, powers, privileges) that are legally recognized concerning a piece of land. He owns Blackacre. He dies. What happens? Are his heirs entitled to take possession of Blackacre? Do they take a "new" ownership? Or do they succeed to the interest of O? In the United States we are very much accustomed to "inheritability", and we would say that of course O's interest is "inheritable", and, if we conceive that the heirs don't have a "new" ownership, but rather they succeed as takers of the interest which O had, then we are conceiving of O's interest (estate) as one that goes on and on, forever.

Originally under the feudal system it seems that land was held under tenures that were limited in duration to the holder's lifetime. The idea that one's ownership could descend to his heirs was the earliest development that led to our modern idea of ownership. But at first this idea did not leave any room for an owner to prevent such inheritance by conveying the land to some one else. In other words, the inheritability of land was a feature that limited its alienability. Alienability, however, was not long in coming, and when it came, it produced a drastic restriction on inheritability. In other words, if A conveyed land to to B, B was the one who had the estate, which would descend to his heirs unless he too conveyed it before his death. Much later it became possible for one who had an inheritable estate to devise it by will. This also would permit the estate to go to the devisee at the testator's death rather than to the latter's heirs. And so all the components of a modern inheritable estate were finally provided. These elements formed a kind of hierarchy of values, in the sense that alienation inter vivos would prevent any later devise or inheritance, and a devise by will would prevent any inheritance. These features must be kept in mind in our notion of an estate that is potentially durable forever.

We have already noted that technically a person does not "own" a piece of land, but rather owns an "estate" in land. Still, we know that it is common to say that "O owns Blackacre," and we know what that means. It means O has the right to possess, to use, to enjoy, to exploit a given piece of land. Ownership is thus a possessory matter as indicated above. But the idea we deal with here is that ownership is divisible. O's ownership can by a proper conveyance be divided into segments. Thus, suppose that O made a conveyance of Blackacre (by some legally effective method) "To A for life, and then to B and his heirs." What effect would you expect to follow? Of course, one would say that A can possess, use, enjoy Blackacre for his lifetime, and then B will be entitled to possess, use, and enjoy the benefits of Blackacre. Both A and B acquire segments of ownership in the sense that each of the interests carries the right to possession and most of the elements of ownership *for a period of time*. Both segments are called estates. A acquires an immediate right to possession, and so we say he has a "present" estate. Neither A nor B is the "owner" in the sense that O was the owner. Both A and B are owners in the sense that each of them acquires an interest that is or will become possessory. And, when A has died so that his time segment has ended, B will be left as the sole "owner" and will be "owner" in the same sense that O was before he made the conveyance.

At the risk of repetition, be careful that you understand the terms "present" estate and "future" estate. Suppose we ask in the above case: When did B become an owner? Did he become an owner at the time O made the conveyance? Or did B become an owner only when A died and he (B) became entitled to possession? You must understand that B acquired his segment of ownership at the time of the conveyance. At that time, he is immediately the owner of a future estate. It is called "future" only because his right to possession will be in the future. In many ways, he has a protectable interest *now*. For example, suppose A started to tear down a valuable building, or to strip the land of a valuable redwood forest. Would you think B is owner enough that he should get some immediate protection of his "future" estate? Of course he should.

Or, look at the notion a bit further. Suppose B dies before A does. What happens to B's interest (estate)? Is he an owner of an inheritable interest? We would have to know how long B's interest was to last. The conveyance says "to B and his heirs." It sounds as though that ownership was to be inheritable by B's heirs, and go on and on. If it is of potentially infinite duration, then of course B's interest (estate) survives his death and would now be owned by B's heirs. On the facts given, that would be the case and it is inheritable. Or, if B left a will, giving all his real property to X, his interest would be and is devisable by will and would be owned by X. (Or, if B conveyed the land to Y, his interest would be owned by Y.) In a few pages you will understand how we decide that B has an interest which is so durable, and which is alienable, devisable, and inheritable.

We need to take into account one more notion that is fundamental to the estate concept. It is this: When we start with an owner who has complete (unitary) ownership, then if that owner conveys an interest of a lesser duration (a smaller estate), he has something left and it doesn't disappear. He has the interest left whether the conveyance says so or not. We can see this easily and in a familiar setting if we consider the owner who leases a farm to T (tenant) for five years. The landlord still is a land owner (only now we know that he owns a *future* estate because he is not presently entitled to possession), and T owns a newly created possessory estate for five years. We would say that the landlord still has that part of ownership which he has not transferred to the tenant. And at the end of five years, T's estate comes to an end, and the landlord resumes possession. The same notion applies whenever the interest conveyed is deemed lesser (potentially smaller) than the one which the conveyor owned. For example, an owner conveys to A for life. The owner still retains that part of ownership not given to A. At A's death, O resumes possession. We will find that the various estates are ranked in a hierarchy so that it is usually easy to tell when the estate conveyed is a "lesser" estate.

We must now recognize another of the important aspects of our system of estates. The person who starts with unitary, undivided ownership is not free to fashion segments of ownership in any way that he pleases. He may only divide his ownership into the kinds of segments that the courts have come to recognize. Put it another way: There are only certain "estates" that can be created, and each of them has a name, and each different name carries with it different characteristics. One author [2] has said:

> It is conceivable that, in a matured system of law, interests in land could be created without models and with an infinite variety of legal consequences, somewhat as contracts are formed. In other words, a legal system could exist in which each grantor would make his own provisions applicable only to the individual grant—as to inheritance, whether in male or female line or alternately; as to privileges of enjoyment, whether absolute or limited according to the whims of the conveyor; as to powers of alienation, if any, whether they are to be broad or narrow. In fact the Anglo-American land law has not developed in this way. Interests are created in accordance with more or less fixed types, known as estates. Each one is differentiated from the others as to mode of creation and as to legal consequences. If the estate created is once found to be in one of these fixed categories, then the legal consequences of that type of estate follow as a matter of course. Thus, where a grantor attempted to devise land in such a way that it would pass by intestacy to heirs general on the father's side only, we have no less a jurist than Mr. Justice Holmes declaring, on the authority of Lord Coke, that 'a man cannot create a new kind of inheritance.' No doubt it is extremely useful to have these ready-made patterns from which one

2.   Simes, The Law of Future Interests,
§ 36 (1st ed. 1936).

may select the type best fitted to his needs; for it is unlikely that the man who provides for an estate of a given duration, such as an estate for life or an estate in fee, considers any of the legal consequences other than the extent of enjoyment. Yet one legal category having been selected, legal consequences, such as liability for waste, right to prevent trespasses, and power of alienation, necessarily follow.

Here are the present (possessory) estates which are recognized:

Freehold Estates

Fee Simple Absolute

Defeasible Fee

       1. Fee simple determinable

       2. Fee simple on condition subsequent

       3. Fee simple subject to an executory limitation

Fee Tail (and its predecessor, the Fee Simple Conditional)

Life Estate

Non-Freehold Estates

Term of Years

Periodic (e.g. from month to month)

At Will

At Sufferance

The above listing introduces a new classification which should be part of our vocabulary—the difference between freehold estates and non-freehold estates. History can explain the distinction, and at one time the consequences of this distinction were of major significance. The common law was for centuries very much concerned with "seisin," an incident of feudal tenure. "Seisin" finally came to mean possession under claim of an estate of freehold, and the person who was seized (who held seisin) was the person who was responsible for the feudal services owed to the lord. For this reason, the common law insisted that seisin be continuous, never in abeyance, so that one could always ascertain the person who owed the feudal services. This notion had a marked effect on some of the rules relating to remainders which we will explore later. In any event, as indicated above, only the various "fee" estates (fee simple, fee tail, etc.) and the life estate are called freehold estates, and they are distinguished from the interests that arise in the landlord-tenant relationship which are called non-freehold. These interests of a tenant may be referred to as estates, but are very likely to be called *tenancies,* e.g. a "tenancy for years," a "periodic tenancy." This difference in common terminology should not obscure the fact that when an owner (landlord) has leased land to a tenant for a term of 20 years, we look upon the tenant as owner of an estate—owner of an interest in land that is possessory and is ownership measured in terms of duration. At common law such a non-freehold tenant did not have "seisin" even though he was in possession.

These enumerated estates are distinguished from each other by the difference in duration, and we are now ready to turn specifically to each of those estates. We need to know: (1) what language will create the estate; and (2) what are its characteristics in terms of duration, alienability and inheritability. For convenience, we will also take note of the future estates which may exist in connection with each possessory estate, although detailed study of the future estates is postponed.

B. THE PRESENT ESTATES

(1) Fee Simple Absolute

Future Estate—None

Language Creating—

        (a) to "A and his heirs"

        (b) to "A, his heirs and assigns"

        (c) to "A"

Duration—Unlimited

Transferability—By deed, will or intestacy.

This is the estate which represents our form of unitary undivided ownership. The typical sale of residential property involves a transfer of the fee simple absolute from seller to buyer. It is the largest estate known to the law, and we understand "largest" to mean unlimited in duration. In turn, that means the estate can be inherited, can be devised by will, and is freely alienable by the present holder of the estate. Notice that if an estate in fee simple absolute is conveyed by A to B, in a sense A's estate has ended. But properly speaking it has not ended, it has been transferred to B. Even if the owner of a fee simple absolute dies intestate and no heirs (direct descendants or collateral relatives) can be found, our modern statutes provide that the estate passes to the state.

Look now at the language which is used to create this estate in the transferee. "To A and his heirs." What person or persons acquire any interest (estate) in the land? Only A. It is A who holds the fee simple estate. At the moment of the conveyance, his prospective heirs have nothing—not even a future interest. They do not now have any part of the ownership. The prospective heirs may, perhaps, expect that they will inherit the estate, but if A decides to sell the land or give it away, they cannot interfere, and a deed from A will give the transferee the full estate in fee simple.

Another way of expressing this idea lies in the distinction between "words of purchase" and "words of limitation." The former are the words in a conveyance which describe and identify the person or persons who take the estate. The latter—words of limitation—are the words which describe or limit the estate which is transferred. Thus, in our conveyance "To A and his heirs," the word "A" is a word of purchase, but the words "and his heirs" are words of limitation which describe the estate conveyed.

History does not conclusively indicate just why the courts came to decide that the words "and his heirs" were words of limitation (not words of purchase). Indeed, it is likely that in very early feudal times such was not the case. But whatever the reason, it eventually became firmly established that the presumptive heirs took nothing by such a conveyance. We may note that by so holding, the courts took a huge step in making land freely alienable. The owner A could transfer by himself. There was no need to get any presumptive heirs to join him in the conveyance.

Words of limitation can also consist of other language by which the estate conveyed is described so as to designate something less than a fee simple absolute. For example, if a conveyance is made "To A for life," the words "for life" are the words of limitation, describing a life estate.

Not only did the words "and his heirs" come to be words of limitation, they came to be for all practical purposes, the *only* words which would create the fee simple estate by conveyance. At the common law, a conveyance "To A" with nothing more, created only a life estate in A. This formalism was not applied to transfers by will after the English Statute of Wills (1540) made it possible to transfer estates in land by that means. And today, by virtue of statutory changes, this formalism is no longer required when the conveyance is by deed. A deed "To A" will give A the full estate. The statutes usually provide in effect that any conveyance will be presumed to pass the entire estate of the grantor unless the contrary intent is expressed in the document. It is up to grantor, if he wants to convey a lesser estate, to make that intention clear. It is still common practice, however, at least in conveyances by deed, to convey land to one "and his heirs." The formalism by which the words "and his heirs" have controlling effect as to the estate created may still be encountered today. For example, in Wayburn v. Smith, 270 S.C. 38, 239 S.E.2d 890 (1977), the court had to construe a deed in which the grantor rather clearly expressed an intention to give a grantee a life estate, but in one part of the deed (the habendum) used the language "to A and her heirs and assigns forever." The court gave A a fee simple estate and went so far as to say that intention is unavailing to overcome the fixed meaning of the words in the habendum.

A Vocabulary Note: When we say that the words "To A" are words of purchase, we do not necessarily mean that A bought the land or paid for it. The transfer may have been a gift transaction, without consideration. Taking "by purchase" is contrasted with taking "by inheritance."

Another Vocabulary Note: The word "heirs" has a technical meaning. It is used to mean the person or persons who, according to the statutes of descent and distribution in the particular state, are to inherit the real property owned by an intestate decedent. This means that a living person does not technically have any heirs. He or she may have presumptive heirs, but the persons who are actually "heirs" cannot be determined until the moment of the ancestor's death. This notion has some practical impact later when we discuss the future interest known as a contingent remainder.

One More Vocabulary Note: Not only are the words "and his heirs" called words of limitation. They are also technically known as words of inheritance. By that we mean that they describe an *inheritable* estate—one which does not end at the holder's death, but which can be inherited if held at the moment of death. As we have seen, inheritability is a primary characteristic in any estate in fee simple.

It should be emphasized again that when a grantee, devisee, or intestate taker, has acquired fee simple absolute, it does not follow that he alone has interests in the land which the law recognizes and protects. He does have the largest estate known to the law. He does have an estate entitling him to possession presently. But the grantee's right of use and enjoyment may be encumbered by interests in land held by one having no right to possession, but having an easement, a mortgage, or other interest which restricts the manner in which the subject parcel may be used. Furthermore, as we have seen, adjoining landowners may under the doctrine of private nuisance take steps to curb uses by a landowner which unreasonably interfere with the use and enjoyment of their land. A state, through the exercise of the police power, may restrict uses which offend or jeopardize the health, safety, morals and general welfare of the public generally. These restrictions on user are of course equally applicable to other possessory estates described below.

(2) Defeasible Fee Estates

Early in the development of the law of estates, it became necessary to decide whether an owner in fee simple absolute could transfer an estate in fee simple but still keep a string attached so that if a certain event occurred the estate might come back to him (or, if he were dead, to his successors). The answer was "Yes." In fact, as matters developed, he could make such provision in two different ways. First, he could use language which would cause the estate to revest in the grantor *automatically* upon the happening of the event. Second, he could use language which did not *automatically* terminate the grantee's estate, but gave the grantor the power to terminate the grantee's estate. Actual termination occurred only when the grantor made an election and exercised that power.

Obviously, when we have two estates with such different characteristics, we need a separate name for each. We have them. The estate which ends automatically upon the happening event is called a *determinable estate*. The estate which only becomes vulnerable to being terminated at the grantor's election is called an *estate on condition subsequent*.

Vocabulary Note: The courts are not always as precise in their terminology as the above discussion might lead you to believe. The fee simple determinable is also sometimes called "qualified fee," "fee on special limitation," or "base fee." On occasion it is even called fee on conditional limitation (see the next case), but this is unusual, and is sure-ly to be avoided because such language is misleading and confusing. The fee simple on condition subsequent does not have so many different names, but it may be called simply a fee on condition or a fee subject to a condition subsequent or subject to a power of termination.

Vocabulary Note: The heading of this section is "defeasible fee es-tates." Both of the estates we have met (the fee simple determinable and the fee simple on condition subsequent) have one common charac-teristic: they may not last as long as a fee simple absolute will last. (The fee simple absolute is of unlimited duration.) The fee simple deter-minable may expire if the event occurs, and the fee on condition subse-quent may be cut short by the exercise of the power of termination. The word "defeasible" is thus used to describe estates that have that characteristic.

Vocabulary Note: We also need names for the two kinds of inter-ests which are left in the grantor who transfers one or the other of these defeasible estates. The interest left in a grantor after transfer-ring a fee simple determinable is called a possibility of reverter. The interest left after transfer of a fee on condition subsequent is called a "right of entry" or "power of termination." We will come back to these interests when we get to our detailed consideration of future estates.

There is a third kind of "defeasible fee." It arises when the grantor uses language which requires the estate to shift over to a third party upon the happening of an event rather than coming back to the grantor. E.g. "To A and his heirs, but if B marries C, over to B and his heirs." For the time being, we will merely make these observations: (1) this kind of legal estate could not be created before the 16th century; (2) the interest in the third party has its own name—executory interest; and (3) the defeasible estate is (quite consistently) known as a fee simple sub-ject to an executory limitation. We will explore this further a bit later, and right now we will concentrate on the other two defeasible estates.

Substantive Note: All of these defeasible estates in fee simple are transferable in the same way that a fee simple absolute is transfera-ble—by deed, by will, by intestacy. It goes without saying, however, that the transferee takes only the defeasible estate which his grantor had. Do you understand that statement?

Problem

O, owner in fee simple absolute, conveys Blackacre "To A and his heirs so long as the premises are used for residential purposes only, and if not so used, the land to revert to O and his heirs." A makes a deed "To B and his heirs," with no other language. B conveys "To C in fee simple absolute." C leases the land to "T for ten years." T starts to use the premises commercially. Who is entitled to possession? What estate did C own?

A Further Substantive Note: We have been talking about defeasi-ble estates in fee simple. The same kinds of defeasibility can be at-tached to other estates such as an estate for life. Thus, a conveyance "To my wife for her life so long as she does not remarry" creates a determinable life estate.

In Summary:

Defeasible Fee	Future Estate	Duration	Transferability
Fee simple determinable	Possibility of Reverter	Potentially infinite, so long as event does not occur	By deed, will or intestacy
Fee Simple on condition subsequent	Right of Entry or Power of Termination	Potentially infinite, so long as the condition is not breached and, thereafter, until the holder of the right of entry timely exercises the power of termination	Same
Fee Simple subject to an Executory Limitation	Executory Interest	Potentially infinite, so long as stated contingency does not occur	Same

We are now ready to discuss some other matters or problems associated with defeasible estates, and the first relates to the language which will effectively create them. An attorney should be able (1) to draft an instrument which will produce the legal effect the parties desire; and (2) to advise a client concerning the legal effect of previous instruments drawn by others. Fortunately, the first part of the job is comparatively easy for the well trained attorney who understands estates and the essential difference between a determinable estate and an estate on condition subsequent. If he wants deliberately to create a determinable fee he will use language of duration ("so long as," "until", "during the time that") and will specifically provide for automatic termination upon the happening of the stated contingency and revesting in the grantor. Thus language "To A so long as the premises are not used for commercial purposes, and if so used the estate will terminate and automatically revest in the grantor and his heirs" would leave little doubt that the grantor intended to create a fee simple determinable. Conversely, if the draftsman wants an estate on condition subsequent, he will use language of condition ("on condition that," "provided that,") and will expressly provide for a right of entry upon breach of the condition. Thus language "To A on condition that the premises are not used for commercial purposes, but if the premises are ever used for such purposes the grantor or his heirs shall have the right to re-enter and take possession" would hardly be capable of any construction other than as creating a fee on condition subsequent.

But suppose one encounters instruments which contain only these provisions:

1. To A so long as the land is used for church purposes.

2. To A School District on condition that the premises be used for school purposes.

3. To A City, to revert to the grantor if used for anything but park purposes.

4. To A City for the purpose of creating a public park.

5. To B, and B covenants and agrees that the land will be used only for single family residential purposes.

If we look at the first example, we have some language appropriate to creating a determinable fee, but have no express provision for reverter. Authority can be found that it will still create a determinable fee, since the words of special limitation may suffice. Occasionally a careless draftsman may use a reverter clause without initial words of limitation. (See example 3 above.) This, too should suffice, but the result cannot be predicted with confidence.

The second example shows words of condition without express provision for reentry. In theory, these words alone might be sufficient to create the defeasible estate, and this was the rule in England. There are a few such decisions in the United States. But there is also substantial authority that words of condition are not enough and an express reservation of a right of entry is required. This result is understandable because there are many instances where words of condition are used where there is no intention to provide for forfeiture. Such words of condition are thus, at best, ambiguous. If the court finds that no defeasible estate is created, then the language may be held either (a) to have no effect as a mere expression of purpose (see example 4) or (b) to create a covenant which can be enforced in ways other than forfeiture (see example 5).

Example 4 shows an instrument which recites the purpose of the conveyance. One cannot tell why the language was used. Perhaps the city can only acquire land for specific purposes, and the language is designed to make a record that the purchase is legitimate. Such a declaration of purpose does not prevent the estate transferred from being a fee simple absolute, and if the court decides that the language means only that, then no defeasibility attaches.

Frequently, as in example 5, a transferee may "agree and covenant" to use the property in question for a stated purpose, e.g., for residential purposes, for a single-family dwelling, or to improve the premises in a stated manner. Here the right of the transferor is based upon the contractual undertaking of the purchaser, the appropriate remedy for breach being an action for damages or an action seeking injunctive relief. The consequence of breach is neither automatic termination of the estate nor forfeiture by the assertion of a right of entry. Since parties are often careless in stating the terms of their agreement, and often use words of condition where they really mean only to create a contractual obligation, we here discover one of the reasons why words of condition alone have been held not to create a fee simple on a condition subsequent.

It has been noted above that where the possessor has a fee on condition subsequent, his estate does not automatically end when the stated condition is breached. The conveyor, or his successor in interest must elect to terminate. It was held at one time that the holder of the future interest must actually re-enter the land. Literally, he could not maintain an action to recover possession until he had reentered. Today, this is not necessary, and the usual method for terminating the possessory estate is by bringing an action at law for the recovery of possession.

Whenever total ownership is divided between one presently entitled to possession and one who definitely is or may be entitled to possession in the future, the holder of the future estate is likely to have a good deal of interest in the way in which the possessor cares for or exploits the property. In certain circumstances, the law will protect the holder of the future interest against conduct which results in injury to the land. These matters constitute the law of Waste.

" * * * [Waste] is conduct (including in this word both acts of commission and of omission) on the part of the person in possession which is actionable at the behest of, and for the protection of the reasonable expectations of, another owner of an interest in the same land. * * * thus, waste is, functionally, a part of the law which keeps in balance the conflicting desires of persons having interests in the same land." Powell and Rohan, Powell on Real Property 679 (Ab.Ed.1968).

Waste is most obviously a problem in the relations of landlord and tenant and those between life tenants and the holders of succeeding interests. The latter problem is considered below under the head "Protection of Future Interests." Unlike a life tenant, the holder of a determinable fee has an estate which is like a fee simple absolute except for the stated limitation. For this reason, there is some question whether he is accountable for his use of the land at all, if he observes the limitation. There are some cases, however, which do indicate that such a fee holder will be liable for conduct which is "unconscionable" if there is some reasonable prospect that his estate will end by an occurrence of the contingency.

There are some important policy matters which must be noted in connection with defeasible estates. First, the existence of a possibility of reverter or a power of termination detracts substantially from the marketability of the estate of the possessor. Second, if the condition or limitation is associated with the land use, it may severely restrict that use. At common law there was no limit to the duration of these future interests, and it seems obvious that long-continued unmarketability or long-continued use restrictions create conditions which current owners do not like, and which society can perhaps ill afford. Accordingly, proposals for reform have been made and acted upon. A number of statutes limit the life of the possibility of reverter or the power of termination to a stated number of years.[3] Once this period has expired without a forfeiture having occurred, the defeasible fee (whether determinable or on condition subsequent) becomes a fee simple absolute. Another type of statute provides for the disregarding of any "condition" which

---

3. Ill.Stat.Ann. (Smith-Hurd) c. 30 § 37e. The Uniform Simplification of Land Transfers Act (1977) proposes, in § 3–409: "A possibility of reverter, a right of entry for condition broken (power of termination), or a resulting trust that restricts a fee simple estate in land is extinguished by the passage of 30 years after it or a notice of intent to preserve the interest was most recently recorded."

has become merely nominal and is of no actual or substantial benefit to those in whose favor the condition or user is to be enforced.[4]

A Florida statute provides for a 21-year limitation on possibilities of reverter and rights of entry. Thereafter the limitation on user can be enforced only as a contractual obligation of the possessor.[5]

There is another point of distinction between these two defeasible estates which is operationally important. It has to do with the enforcement of the legal consequences upon breach of the stated contingency. One might suppose that if the stated contingency has in fact happened, it would not make much difference whether the future interest was a possibility of reverter or a power of termination—that in either case the holder could, by appropriate action, get the land back. Our law is actually not quite that way. If the estate is a fee simple determinable, it ends automatically upon the happening of the event. The holder of the future interest (the possibility of reverter) immediately becomes the holder of the fee simple absolute. When he brings an action to oust the erstwhile possessor, the only defense may be to prove that the event had not occurred. But because a breach of the condition does not automatically terminate the estate on condition subsequent, our courts have permitted a number of defenses in this case which are not available against the owner of a fee simple determinable. Thus, if the holder of the power of termination, *before* breach of the condition, has by word or conduct led the holder of the possessory estate to believe that no forfeiture will be enforced, he will not later be allowed to do so. He may have "waived" the condition. Or, the court may find that he is "estopped" from asserting the forfeiture. Notice that this "waiver" may mean merely that the one breach cannot be enforced or, more broadly, it may mean that the whole condition is gone, destroying the power of termination. Another defense sometimes recognized arises from conduct *after* the breach. If the holder of the power of termination waits too long to elect his forfeiture, particularly where conditions have changed, the court may declare that he is guilty of *laches*, and deny the power to forfeit the estate.

The following case illustrates how some of these problems may arise, and how the court may respond.

STORKE v. PENN MUTUAL LIFE INSURANCE CO.

Supreme Court of Illinois, 1945.
390 Ill. 619, 61 N.E.2d 552.

GUNN, Justice. Appellants, as plaintiffs, prosecuted this action in the circuit court of Cook county as heirs-at-law of Jay E. Storke. Jay E.

---

4. Mich.Comp.Laws Ann. § 544.46 (1967).

5. Fla.Stat.Ann. § 689.18. The statute was sustained in Vereen & Sons, Inc. v. City of Miami, 397 So.2d 979 (Fla.App. 1981). The retroactive application of statutes limiting reverters and rights of entry to a stated number of years has been upheld: Cline v. Johnson City Board of Education, 548 S.W.2d 507 (Ky.1977); Hiddles-ton v. Nebraska Jewish Education, 186 Neb. 786, 186 N.W.2d 904 (1971); Trustees of Schools of Township No. 1 v. Batdorf, 6 Ill.2d 486, 130 N.E.2d 111 (1955); and denied: Biltmore Village Inc. v. Royal, 71 So. 2d 727 (Fla.1954); Board of Education of Central School District No. 1 v. Miles, 15 N.Y.2d 364, 259 N.Y.S.2d 129, 207 N.E.2d 181 (1965).

Storke and Bernard Timmerman, now both deceased in 1889 subdivided approximately forty acres of land into lots. At that time the property was outside the limits of the city of Chicago. It is now located in the neighborhood of Halsted street between Seventy-fifth and Seventy-ninth streets. Part of the property involved was conveyed by deed containing the following covenant:

"And the party of the second part [the grantee in said deed], his heirs and assigns hereby covenant and agree that no saloon shall be kept and no intoxicating liquors be sold or permitted to be sold on said premises herein conveyed or in any building erected upon said premises; and that in case of breach in these covenants or any of them said premises shall immediately revert to the grantors, and the said party of the second part shall forfeit all right, title and interest in and to said premises."

It was agreed to be binding upon the heirs, executors, administrators and assigns of the respective parties. The balance of the premises involved had a covenant of substantially the same wording and with like effect. There was also one providing that the building erected upon the premises should cost at least $2500, but no question is raised as to the value of the building upon the premises.

By mesne conveyances, appellee Penn Mutual Life Insurance Company, on November 19, 1934, acquired title to the premises involved herein by quitclaim deed, which did not contain the covenant prohibiting the use of saloons upon the premises. The premises have been occupied by Edward Walsh as tenant of Penn Mutual Life Insurance Company since 1934, and have been operated during all of that period as a saloon or tavern. The plaintiffs are the heirs-at-law of Jay E. Storke. The heirs of Bernard Timmerman are unknown. There are 491 lots in the sixteen blocks embraced in the subdivision, which are covered by the same restrictions as to the use of the premises.

The facts disclose this subdivision has become a built up business section of the city of Chicago, and located in various parts of it are saloons or taverns, with at least sixteen saloons in the neighborhood of the property involved or in the adjoining blocks, and liquor has been almost continuously sold in this subdivision since 1933, the date of the repeal of the prohibition amendment. There have been numerous instances where the heirs-at-law of Timmerman or Storke have released and waived the restriction contained in the deed, from as far back as 1904 to as late as 1924.

In 1926, appellee Penn Mutual Life Insurance Company purchased a first mortgage on the premises herein involved for the sum of $42,500, and in November, 1934, it purchased the title to said property and released said mortgage lien and the personal liability of the mortgagor in reliance upon the abandonment of the possible right of reverter by the heirs of Jay E. Storke, and by their waiver of the restriction by acquiescing in the use of the said premises in said subdivision for saloon purposes and by releasing and relinquishing any possible right of reverter therein.

December 29, 1942, plaintiffs filed their complaint asking that the court establish title in the plaintiffs and the unknown heirs of Timmerman, and that defendant and appellee insurance company be decreed to have no right or title in the premises; that the interest of the plaintiffs and the heirs of Timmerman be ascertained; that partition be had of the premises; that the defendant Walsh be perpetually enjoined from maintaining a tavern, and that plaintiffs have further relief, etc. The case was tried upon a stipulation of facts, and anything not pointed out above, necessary to a decision of this case, will be referred to hereafter.

To reach a proper conclusion under the disclosed facts, it is necessary to determine the character of the condition, covenant, or reservation contained in the deed from the original grantors. Appellants say they do not deem it necessary to classify their supposed reversionary interests as either based upon a conditional limitation or as a condition subsequent, but assert that they rely upon the decision of Pure Oil Co. v. Miller-McFarland Drilling Co., Inc., 376 Ill. 486, 34 N.E.2d 854, 135 A.L.R. 567. Since the reversionary right in that case was held to arise from a deed containing a conditional limitation, we must infer that such is the basis of appellants' case. Appellee insurance company, however, contends the provisions in the deed upon which appellants seek to recover constitute conditions subsequent. Such different results follow from these different contentions that resolving the character of the restrictions contained in the deed will be determinative of the case.

The distinction between a conditional limitation and a condition subsequent is sometimes very refined, because of the language used under the different situations under which the question arises. Many distinctions are to be found in the books whether from the words used there is created a condition subsequent making the estate voidable, or words of limitation causing the estate to cease. The term "conditional limitation" in this State has been applied both where, upon the happening of certain events, the estate goes to third persons, and where a determinable or base fee is granted to the first taker followed by a possibility of reverter upon the happening of a contingency. (Tiffany, 2d, sec. 90.) The term will be used herein in the latter sense.

The basic difference between estates upon a conditional limitation and those upon condition subsequent is ascertained by the fact that, in the latter case, the entire estate has passed to another, but can be returned to the grantor upon the subsequent happening of a described event; while in the case of a conditional limitation, the estate passed to another contains within itself the ground for its return to the grantor. The common-law writers witness the distinction as follows: In Preston on Estates, pages 40–45, it is said: "Every limitation which is to vest an interest on condition, or rather a contingency, (for that is the correct phrase,) in other words, an event which may or *may not* happen is a conditional limitation. * * * Between a limitation and a condition there is this important difference: A limitation marks the *utmost* time of *continuance;* a condition marks some event, which if it takes place in the course of that time, will defeat the *estate.*" In Kent's Commentaries, vol. 4, p. 127, it is stated: "Words of *limitation* mark the period which is to determine the estate; but words of *condition* render the estate liable to be defeated in the intermediate time, if the event expressed in the condition arises before the determination of the estate, or completion of the period described by the limitation. The one specifies the utmost time of continuance, and the other marks some event, which, if it takes place in the course of that time, will defeat the estate." So, in Touchstone, page 121, it is said: "So that howsoever a limitation hath much affinity and agreement with a condition, and therefore it is sometimes called a condition in law, both of them do determine an estate in being before; and a limitation cannot make an estate to be void as to one person, and good as to another; * * * yet herein they differ: 1. A stranger may take advantage of an estate determined by limitation, and so he cannot upon a condition. 2. A limitation doth always determine the estate, without entry or claim, and so doth not a condition."

The accepted authorities of the common law are collected and aptly condensed with the following statement: "A condition determines an estate after breach, upon entry or claim by the grantor or his heirs, or the heirs of the devisor. A limitation marks the period which determines the estate, without any act on the part of him who has the next expectant interest. Upon the happening of the prescribed contingency, the estate first limited comes at once to an end, and the subsequent estate arises. * * * A conditional limitation is therefore of a mixed nature, partaking both of a condition and of a limitation; of a condition because it defeats the estate previously limited; and of a limitation, because, upon the happening of the contingency, the estate passes to the person having the next expectant interest, without entry or claim." (Proprietors of the Church in Brattle Square v. Grant, 69 Mass. 142, 3 Gray 142, 63 Am.Dec. 725.) To the same effect is Smith v. Smith, 23 Wis. 176, 99 Am.Dec. 153.

Illustrations from our own decisions show these distinctions have been observed and followed. Thus, a conveyance to a grantee for so long as the property is used for church purposes may be forever, but if it ceased to be used for church purposes the condition upon which the grant is made ends, (Pure Oil Co. v. Miller-McFarland Drilling Co., Inc., 376 Ill. 486, 34 N.E.2d 854, 135 A.L.R. 567; North v. Graham, 235 Ill. 178, 85 N.E. 267;) or a grant upon condition that if said grantee herein shall die before the age of twenty-one years then the land shall revert to others, (Roberts v. Dazey, 284 Ill. 241, 119 N.E. 910;) or a deed to a grantee, and upon the death of grantee leaving no widow or children to another, (Cutler v. Garber, 289 Ill. 200, 124 N.E. 441,) are all grants of estates upon conditional limitation. On the other hand, a deed for premises to be used as a church, and in case of failure of such use, grantee to pay a sum to grantors, (Board of Education v. Trustees of Baptist Church, 63 Ill. 204;) premises conveyed on condition to pay the debts of another, (Koch v. Streuter, 232 Ill. 594, 83 N.E. 1072;) or in consideration of support, (Phillips v. Gannon, 246 Ill. 98, 92 N.E. 616;) or a condition that grantee pay grantor's children $500 each, (Nowak v. Dombrowski, 267 Ill. 103, 107 N.E. 807;) or a conveyance to a village on condition that a town hall be erected, with a provision for reverter, (Village of Peoria Heights v. Keithley, 299 Ill. 427, 132 N.E. 532;) or a deed made subject to the payment of an annuity for the life of the grantor, with provision for reverter, (Powell v. Powell, 335 Ill. 533, 167 N.E. 802; Plummer v. Worthington, 321 Ill. 450, 152 N.E. 133,) are all illustrations of conditions subsequent.

Courts prefer to construe provisions that terminate an estate as conditions subsequent rather than conditional limitations, and in doubtful cases will so construe them. (Rooks Creek Evangelical Lutheran Church v. First Lutheran Church, 290 Ill. 133, 124 N.E. 793, 7 A.L.R. 1422.) Conditions subsequent which destroy an estate are not favored and will not be enlarged. (McElvain v. Dorris, 298 Ill. 377, 131 N.E. 608.) Such covenants are to be strictly construed. (Dodd v. Rotterman, 330 Ill. 362, 161 N.E. 756.) If the parties intended the estate to vest and the grantee to perform acts or refrain from certain acts after taking possession, it is a condition subsequent. Hooper v. Haas, 332 Ill. 561, 164 N.E. 23, 63 A.L.R. 658.

The foregoing cases clearly show the line of cleavage between an estate upon conditional limitation and a conveyance subject to a condition subsequent. If the deed contains language which purports to pass immediate title, but limits its duration by some event which may or may not happen, a conditional limitation is created, because there is always a possibility of reverter to the grantor. The estate fails upon the happening of the event by its own terms, because it comes within the condition which limits it, and it is self-operative.

On the other hand, a breach of a condition subsequent does not revest title in the original grantor or his heirs. (Newton v. Village of Glen Ellyn, 343 Ill. 489, 175 N.E. 770; Powell v. Powell, 335 Ill. 533, 167 N.E. 802; McElvain v. Dorris, 298 Ill. 377, 131 N.E. 608.) Reentry is necessary to revest title, (Powell v. Powell, 335 Ill. 533, 167 N.E. 802;) and a court of equity will not aid a forfeiture where no right of re-entry is provided in the covenant. (Newton v. Village of Glen Ellyn, 374 Ill. 50, 27 N.E.2d 821.) The deeds in question did not contain a right of re-entry. Under the authorities, the restrictions in the deed did not constitute a conditional limitation.

The action brought by the plaintiffs was partition. In order to maintain partition, it is requisite that the plaintiffs have title. (Hart v. Lake, 273 Ill. 60, 112 N.E. 286; Harris v. Ingleside Building Corp., 370 Ill. 617, 19 N.E.2d 585; Webster v. Hall, 388 Ill. 401, 58 N.E.2d 575.) Appellants rely upon the Ingleside case, which, among other things, held that an equitable title could, in the same proceeding, be converted into a legal title sufficient to support partition. Here, however, re-entry being necessary to effect the forfeiture, and there being no reservation of a right of re-entry, it was not within the power of equity to make the legal estate necessary to maintain a suit in partition. (Newton v. Village of Glen Ellyn, 374 Ill. 50, 27 N.E.2d 821.) There being no title in the plaintiffs, and there having been no reentry, or provision for re-entry, the case was properly dismissed, as lacking in the elements necessary to maintain a partition suit.

We have indicated above that there was not a conditional limitation which would terminate the estate of its own force, and that the plaintiffs have not established that they are entitled to a forfeiture under a condition subsequent. There is a finding by the court that the plaintiffs had actually a constructive knowledge of the sale of liquor, for a period of time, which would render it highly unjust and contrary to the doctrines of equity for them to divest the defendant of title purchased for a valuable consideration and in good faith.

The court also found that release had been given to other owners in the subdivision by the plaintiffs, and by John W. Ellis, one of the plaintiffs' attorneys, which had created a change in the neighborhood from that contemplated in the original grant. If the provisions in the deed were construed as a restrictive covenant, they could not be enforced by the plaintiffs because the stipulation of facts and findings of the court show that the change in the circumstances and use of the property in the subdivision has been brought about by the acts of the grantors or their assigns. Under such circumstances, they cannot be enforced. Cuneo v. Chicago Title and Trust Co., 337 Ill. 589, 169 N.E. 760; Ewertsen v. Gerstenberg, 186 Ill. 344, 57 N.E. 1051; Star Brewery Co. v. Primas, 163 Ill. 652, 45 N.E. 145.

If the contention of appellants were correct, that the deed in question contained a conditional limitation, it would not aid them. In such case, as pointed out, no re-entry would be necessary and the estate would terminate immediately upon breach without action or re-entry. That being the case, the fourth paragraph of section 3 of the Limitations Act (Ill.Rev.Stat.1943, chap. 83, par. 3,) would apply. The statute provides that if a person claims an estate by reason of a forfeiture or breach of condition, his right shall be deemed to have accrued when the forfeiture occurred or the condition was broken. This section must be construed in connection with section 6 of the same act. The use of said premises as a saloon commenced before appellee obtained a deed therefor. The deed to appellee purporting to convey the entire estate constituted color of title in good faith, and taxes were paid for more than seven years. This would give appellee a good title, even if the position assumed by appellants was correct. Under either construction, the facts and the law bar the plaintiffs from recovery.

The deed to the original grantors cannot be construed as creating a conditional limitation. As a condition subsequent, appellants are not entitled to recover. Considered as a restrictive covenant, all rights of enforcement have been waived. And assuming appellants' contention that the estate was terminated by breach of condition, they are barred from recovery by the Statute of Limitations.

The decree denying the plaintiffs' right to recover, and confirming the title of the appellee, was correct, and is hereby affirmed.

Decree affirmed.

Questions

1. Does the Illinois court recognize the two different kinds of defeasible estates—one that terminates automatically upon happening of the condition, and one that requires election?

2. What name does the court give to the estate which our text has called a determinable estate?

3. Do you see the pronounced difference between the two estates, at common law, when it becomes necessary to determine when a cause of action accrued which might start the running of the statute of limitations?

4. Under Ill.Rev.Stat. ch. 83, para. 3, did it really make any difference which kind of defeasible estate was created by the original 1889 deed?

5. Do you agree with the court that "[t]he deed to appellee purporting to convey the entire estate constituted color of title in good faith," so that appellee was entitled to the benefit of a seven-year statutory period of limitation? How could the "deed to appellee" constitute "color of title in good faith" when the original 1889 deed containing the defeasance clause was duly recorded and undoubtedly was shown in the abstract of title provided to appellee when it "purchased a first mortgage on the premises" in 1926?

(3) Fee Tail and (Its Predecessor) The Fee Simple Conditional

Future Interest—*Reversion* in conveyor, his heirs or devisees, or *Remainder* in a grantee or devisee other than the taker of the fee tail.

Language Creating—(a) To "A and the heirs of his body" (b) To "A and the heirs of his body, remainder to B."

Duration—For the life of the first taker (commonly called "tenant") in tail and thereafter through succeeding generations so long as there are any living lineal descendants of the first tenant in tail.

Transferability—By deed, but the transferee acquired an estate which would end at the transferor's death in favor of the latter's bodily heirs. Descent limited to heirs of body. Not devisable by will.

The English courts evolved a fictitious kind of judicial proceeding whereby a tenant in tail could "bar the entail," the effect of which was a transfer to a designated transferee in fee simple absolute.

In 1834 an English statute permitted a tenant in tail to convey in fee simple by deed. In most of the American states which still recognize the fee tail there are statutes to the same effect.

The fee tail estate and its predecessor, the fee simple conditional, have relatively little contemporary significance, and our purposes are served with a very limited history. Prior to 1285, if one owning land in fee simple absolute made a conveyance "To A and the heirs of his body," it seems likely that he wanted to create an estate which would descend through successive generations in direct line of descent (children, grandchildren, etc.) and not go to collateral relatives. It may also be supposed that the grantor wanted the land to come back to him or his successors if that line of descent ran out. Part of this desire was recognized and enforced by the courts. They did hold that the words "heirs of the body" were words of limitation, not words of purchase. They did hold that the estate was inheritable, and that the inheritance was restricted to direct lineal descendants. But they also treated the estate as if it were a fee simple on condition that A have heirs of the body. The courts held that once an heir was born to A, he could alienate a fee simple, thus destroying the expectancy of his descendants, and frustrating the grantor's intent that the land come back to him if the grantee's line of descent ran out. The compensating gain, of course, was that land was made more freely alienable. This estate was known as the fee simple conditional (not to be confused with the defeasible estate already encountered, known as the fee on condition subsequent.)

But the grantors in these conveyances were often powerful people. And, when they found the courts frustrating their intention, they did what powerful people often do: they went to parliament and secured the passage of a statute which reversed the courts: the Statute De Donis Conditionalibus, 13 Edw. 1, c. 1 (1285).

The language of the statute is interesting. Stripped of much complicated verbiage, and translated into modern idiom, it might be said to read something like this:

> Land is often given to a person and the heirs of his body with the condition expressed that if the same person dies without issue the land shall revert to the giver or his heir. Now it seems to the giver that his will being expressed it ought to be enforced, but it is not being enforced. The courts have held that as soon as the grantee has issue born he can alienate in fee simple and disinherit his issue. He can also cut off the reversion to the original grantor. Now, therefore, the King declares that from now on the will of the giver, according to the form of the gift, shall be observed. Specifically, the person to whom the land is given shall have no power to alien the land. Instead, the land will descend to the issue or, if issue fail, it shall revert to the giver.

The result of that statute was to create a new estate, which we now know as the fee tail estate. A conveyance "to A and the heirs of his body" created an estate which would indeed pass through direct descendants only, and, if the estate ended by failure of direct descendants, the land would revert to the grantor. The holder of the fee tail estate (A) could no longer alienate an estate in fee simple. His grantee got an interest which lasted only for A's life, and then the land would go back to the heirs of A's body. To that extent, it was a "smaller" estate than the fee simple absolute, and the estate remaining in the grantor was a reversion.

This estate was very popular in England for many years, and a large part of the land was "entailed" for many generations. The estate can be understood against the early English law of descent, which embraced the principle of primogeniture. Land held in fee simple descended to the holder's eldest son, but if he had no sons, to his daughters equally. The fee tail estate was one of the devices for perpetuating and preserving English landed estates. But the search for free alienability of land remained a powerful force. In the fifteenth century, the English courts developed a fictitious kind of judicial proceeding known as a common recovery. The whole purpose of the proceeding was to permit the holder of the fee tail estate to "bar the entail," i.e., to convey an interest which would cut off the right of the bodily heirs to take the land. Before long, the fictitious proceeding was also allowed to bar the reversion in the grantor. When we reach that point, we are in a position where we still can create a fee tail estate (because if the holder of the estate did not "bar the entail," the land was still inheritable only by direct descendants) but it can be turned into a fee simple if proper steps are taken. In 1834 an English statute permitted a tenant in tail to convey in fee simple by deed.

What has happened to this estate in the United States? What is the result of a conveyance "To A and the heirs of his body"?

1. In three states, South Carolina, Iowa, and Oregon, it still creates a fee simple conditional, because the Statute De Donis is not regarded as being in force in the jurisdiction. Only in South Carolina are there many decisions concerning the estate.[6]

2. In Delaware, Maine, Massachusetts, and Rhode Island (as to deeds only), the fee tail estate is recognized, but it is not in modern use, and the entail can be barred by a simple conveyance by deed.[7]

3. In Ohio, Connecticut and Rhode Island (as to devises) there are statutes which give the first taker a fee tail estate, but when the estate passes to his issue it becomes a fee simple. Thus, a fee tail exists for only one generation, and then enlarges to a fee simple.[8]

4. Six states (Arkansas, Colorado, Florida, Georgia, Illinois, and Kansas) have statutes which convert the estate in the first taker to a life estate with a remainder in fee simple in the issue.[9]

5. Some states have simply passed statutes which abolish the fee tail.[10]

6. About half the states convert the estate into a fee simple in the designated first taker. (The first taker's fee simple may, by statute, be subject to an executory interest to take effect, if at all, upon the death of the first taker without a lineal descendant surviving him.)[11]

No competent draftsman today uses language which would create a fee tail at common law. Uninformed grantors occasionally still use such language, presumably to serve some vague notion about keeping property within family blood lines.

One technical matter should be noted. At early common law, when the fee simple conditional was the estate created by a conveyance "To A and the heirs of his body," the interest left in the transferror would properly be called a possibility of reverter. After the fee tail estate, the interest left in the grantor is properly called a reversion.

(4) Life Estate

Future Interest—*Reversion* in grantor, his heirs, or devisees, or *Remainder* in grantee or devisee other than the life tenant.

6. 2 Powell § 195.

7. Id., § 196.

8. Id., § 198[1].

9. Id., § 198[2]. E.g., 2 Fla.Stat. (1971) § 689.14.

10. Id., § 197.

11. Id., § 198[3]. E.g. Mich.Comp. Laws Ann. §§ 554.3, 554.4 (1967).

Language Creating—

    (a) To "A for life"

    (b) To "A for and during his natural life"

    (c) To "A until he dies"

    (d) To A for the life of B

    Also created by the operation of law. (See marital estates infra).

Duration—For the life or lives of the person or persons indicated by the conveyor as the measuring life or lives. Usually the estate will be created for the life of the transferee. (An estate in one person for the life of another as in (d) above is a life estate *pur autre vie.*)

Transferability—By deed only. An estate *pur autre vie* held by the decedent at the time of his death will in most states pass by will or intestacy of the life tenant.

The life estate is an essential part of most plans by which persons who have accumulated substantial property distribute their wealth among the desired objects of their bounty. A gift of an interest for the life of the beneficiary (usually followed by a remainder in favor of a group of persons within a succeeding generation) is essentially a gift of the use and enjoyment of property intended ultimately to pass in fee simple to others. In many ways, it is analogous to a gift of income from an invested sum of money, the principal of which is to remain intact and undiminished in value.

The practical problems inherent in a dispositive plan which calls for successive rights of enjoyment are here and most pronounced. A conflict of interest between a life tenant and those awaiting possession is almost inevitable. Questions of maintenance, payment of taxes and other charges such as interest and principal on any existing mortgage, as well as exploitation of mineral resources and other use of the property which may enhance the value of the current possessor's estate at the expense of the future estate, can easily lead to unpleasant relationships as well as costly litigation. For a consideration of a life tenant's liability for waste, see "Protection of Future Interests" below.

For these reasons and others, such as providing for flexibility in investment, the life estate-future estate pattern of disposition may be implemented through use of the trust device. Here, in addition to a chronological division of ownership, there is a separation of legal and equitable ownership. The legal title is given to a trustee who, upon acceptance of the trust, assumes an obligation to preserve and manage the trust property, to distribute net income resulting from investments, and ultimately to pay over the corpus of the trust as directed by the donor. For example, an owner of property might provide in his will:

    All the rest, residue and remainder of my property, real and personal, I leave to Trust Company to hold, manage, invest and reinvest, in trust to pay the net income to my wife, Sarah, during her lifetime, and then to divide the trust property among my children.

This would produce a division of the fee simple into legal and equitable estates as well as a division of the equitable ownership between an income beneficiary for life and those entitled to the corpus. The Trust Company has the full *legal* ownership. Sarah has an equitable life estate, and the children (assuming there are some) have an equitable estate in fee simple.[12]

A life estate may be made defeasible by words of limitation or condition, so as to create a determinable life estate, a life estate subject to a condition subsequent, or subject to an executory limitation. A devise "to my wife Sarah for her life or so long as she remains unmarried" creates a determinable life estate. Suppose a conveyor provides that should the life tenant "fail or neglect to pay the taxes, keep up the insurance or keep the buildings in repair * * * then his estate and interest therein shall terminate on such default." This language has been construed to create a life estate "on special limitation in that, by its terms, it terminates automatically if a specified event occurs before the time at which the estate would otherwise terminate." A second life tenant was held entitled to possession. Conger v. Conger, 208 Kan. 823, 494 P.2d 1081, 1086 (1972).

(5) Leasehold Estates

Estate for Years

Periodic Tenancy (year-to-year, month-to-month, etc.)

Tenancy at Will

Tenancy at Sufferance

We have already noted that these several interests in land are the so-called nonfreehold estates, a characterization of historical origin which distinguishes a tenant's interest under the landlord-tenant relationship from rights under a freehold estate, i.e., fee simple, fee tail or life estate. The landlord-tenant relation results only from the creation of one of the nonfreehold estates. In addition, the nonfreehold estates are technically called "chattels real," which means that, while they are interests in land, they are regarded for some purposes as personal, not real, property. This is significant in states where the statutes of descent and distribution of intestate estates provide separately and somewhat differently for real and personal property. The main conse-

---

12. The Uniform Principal and Income Act was adopted by the National Conference of Commissioners on Uniform State Laws in 1931. Among other matters covered, it deals with the allocation of income and expenses between life tenant and remainderman where the instrument creating the interests is silent on the subject. The act is applicable to both succesive legal interests and successive interests under trusts.

In 1962, a Revised Act was adopted by the Commissioners. Contrary to the 1931 Act, the Revised Act sets forth rules of administration for successive interests under trusts only. One reason for this limitation is that trusts to a large extent consist of

securities while successive legal estates are for the most part in land. The local statutes should be examined with care whenever one faces questions such as those discussed here before one concludes the common law controls.

It is also possible for the instrument creating the successive estates to enlarge the rights of the life tenant beyond those normally enjoyed. The life tenant may be given the "power to consume" or may take a life estate without impeachment for waste. In such instance, the life tenant cannot be held liable for decreasing the value of the future estate unless his acts have been wanton or malicious.

quence, the creation of the landlord-tenant relation, is treated in some detail in Chapter 4. Included in that chapter is a consideration of the distinctions between the four types of nonfreehold estates listed above.

For present purposes we may note here that the leasehold estates may also be made defeasible by words of limitation or words of condition. As a practical matter, because the landlord always wants to maintain as much control as possible over the termination of the estate, and would not want the tenant to be able to bring about automatic termination by violating a limitation, defeasible leasehold estates are routinely created as estates on condition subsequent.

C. THE FUTURE ESTATES

(Further Description and Characteristics)

You have already encountered some "future estates", and you already know that they are "future" only in the sense that they are to become possessory only in the future. Just as we can create only certain kinds of present estate, so, too, there are only 5 kinds of future estates (with some subdivisions) which are recognized. Here is the complete system of classification which we must master:

I. Interests which *remain* in a grantor after he has conveyed away a lesser estate than the one he owns.

    A. Reversion

    B. Possibility of Reverter

    C. Right of Entry or Power of Termination.

II. Interests which are created in a third party other than the grantor.

    A. Remainder

        1. Vested Remainders

            a. Indefeasibly vested

            b. Vested subject to open

            c. Vested subject to complete defeasance.

        2. Contingent Remainders

    B. Executory Interest

Notice that for purposes of classification, we have different names for those interests which *remain in a grantor* after he has conveyed away a lesser interest than the one he owns, and those which are created in a third party other than the grantor. This difference is illustrated in its simplest form by comparing two conveyances. Assume that O is owner in fee simple absolute. O conveys:

    (1) To A for life

    (2) To A for life, then to B and his heirs

In the first case the grantor O has *retained* a future interest and will be entitled to possession when A's life estate terminates. O's interest would be called a reversion. In the second, the grantor has retained nothing, but has *created a future interest in a third party*, B. The interest of B is a remainder.

For classification purposes, there are three future interests which are created because the grantor has conveyed away a lesser estate than he owns. We look now at these and take note of their characteristics.

(1) Reversion

According to Restatement § 154, a reversionary interest is any future interest left in a transferor or his successor in interest. A reversion is one kind of reversionary interest. Most commonly, it is retained by a grantor when he conveys without more a fee tail, a life estate, or for a definite period of time, however long or short (term of years). If the grantor had a fee simple absolute before his conveyance, his reversion is in fee simple absolute. If one who has a leasehold interest for the term of 10 years sublets to another for 5 years, he retains a reversion for the balance of the original term.

If a testator who has a fee simple absolute devises by will to another for life without more, the testator's heirs have a reversion in fee simple absolute.

As you will understand more fully after Remainders have been discussed below, if a grantor, having a fee simple absolute, conveys "to A for his life, then to B if B survives A," B takes a contingent remainder, and the grantor here also retains a reversion in fee simple absolute.

Reversions are freely alienable, devisable, and descendible.

(2) Possibility of Reverter

This also is a reversionary interest. According to Restatement § 154, it is different from a reversion because it is subject to a condition precedent. Such is the interest retained by the transferor of a fee simple determinable. It is subject to a condition precedent in that it can be become possessory only upon the happening of the contingency which terminates the possessory estate.

Example: *Conveyance "to A and his heirs so long as the land hereby conveyed is used for residence purposes only."*

The grantor has a possibility of reverter.

If a grantor conveys "to A for life, then to B so long as the premises are used for residence purposes only," here too the grantor retains a possibility of reverter.

A difficult question of classification can arise from a conveyance such as this: "To W for life, so long as she remains unmarried." Should we say that the grantor retains a reversion because only a life estate is conveyed? A possibility of reverter because W's remarriage constitutes a contingency which will terminate the possessory estate? Both? Probably the retained estate would simply be termed a reversion, even though it would become possessory whether W's life estate terminated by death or by remarriage.

Possibilities of reverter are generally held to be devisable and descendible. The trend is to hold them alienable inter vivos, although this is not a uniform rule. In Illinois by statute, such interests are neither alienable nor devisable, but are descendible. Statutes in a number of other states make them alienable inter vivos.

Reference is made again to statutes in several states which limit the period of time during which fee simple estates can be made determinable. Under such statutes, upon the expiration of the prescribed period, a possibility of reverter terminates, and the possessory estate becomes indefeasible.

Problem

O is the owner of Blackacre in fee simple absolute. He makes an effective conveyance "To A and his heirs so long as the premises are not used for commercial purposes." Thereafter O dies leaving a will devising all his real property to X. Thereafter A dies intestate, leaving Y as his sole heir. Y consults you and asks your advice as to whether he may erect a shopping center on Blackacre, and, if not, what steps could be taken to permit him to do so. How would you advise him, and what characteristics of a possibility of reverter are involved?

(3) Right of Entry (Power of Termination)

This future interest is not classified by the Restatement as a reversionary interest. This may be a way of emphasizing that it cannot become possessory automatically upon the happening of a contingency. It is rather a right or power in a conveyor to take certain action which will terminate a possessory estate which he has conveyed. It is like a reversionary interest in that it can be reserved only by a conveyor for himself or his successors; it cannot be created in any other person. It is created by a conveyance which transfers a possessory estate (almost always a fee simple or a term of years) on a condition subsequent.

Examples:

(a) *Conveyance "to the Plymouth School District on condition that the described premises shall always be maintained and used solely for school purposes, and upon breach of this condition, the grantor, his heirs, successors or assigns shall have the right to enter and take possession."*

(b) *Lease by an owner in fee simple "to Lessee for the term of five years at a monthly rental of $150, payable on the first day of each month of the term. Lessee agrees that if default shall be made in the payment of the rent when due, Lessor shall be entitled immediately to re-enter and take possession."* (In this case the lessor also retains a reversion.)

As indicated by the above examples, and as stated in the discussion of the fee simple on a condition subsequent, it is not wise to rely on words of condition alone to create a right of entry. Words of reentry or their equivalent should also be included. It should also be noted again that a right of entry today is usually exercised by bringing an action for the recovery of possession.

Rights of entry are generally held to be devisable and descendible, but at common law they are not transferable inter vivos except by release to the holder of the possessory estate. There is some authority, now much discredited, that an attempt to transfer a right of entry destroys it. An exception to the rule of inalienability is a right of entry which is incident to a reversion. In such a case a conveyance of the reversion will carry with it the right of entry. In a number of states, statutes make rights of entry transferable inter vivos.

Reference is made again to statutes in several states which limit the period of time during which fee estates can remain subject to conditions subsequent. Under such statutes, upon the expiration of the prescribed period, a right of entry terminates and the possessory estate becomes indefeasible.

Problems

(1) O is the owner of Blackacre in fee simple absolute. He makes an effective conveyance "To the city of A on condition that the land be used solely for park purposes, and if not so used, the grantor or his heirs may re-enter and take possession." What characteristics of the power of termination would you be interested in if you had the following case?

O dies leaving a will devising all his real property to X. Thereafter X executes a deed conveying all his real property to Y. The City of A starts using using Blackare as a parking lot. Y brings an action to recover possession.

(2) Suppose O is owner of Blackacre and leases it to T for 20 years. Then T sublets to X for 10 years. There is a provision in the sublease that if X does not continuously use the premises for grocery store purposes, T may re-enter and retake possession. Thereafter T assigns all his right, title and interest in Blackacre to A. Would A be entitled to re-enter if X ceased to maintain a grocery store? How would you describe the interests created and conveyed?

(4) Remainders

Future estates created in third persons are either remainders (of which there are several varieties) or executory interests, and to these we now turn our attention. We deal first with remainders.

There are several distinctions which we now approach, and it will perhaps be helpful if we identify in advance the points of distinction which we must make in order to complete our understanding of the classification of future estates.

1. We must distinguish the *vested* remainder (of which there are three kinds) from the *contingent* remainder.

2. We must distinguish the three kinds of vested remainders from each other.

3. We must distinguish *all* remainders from executory interests, and particularly we must distinguish the contingent remainder from the executory interest.

Let us start with what is an elaborate, but perhaps a helpful definition of a remainder:

A remainder is a future interest created in someone other than a transferor which, according to the terms of its creation, will become a present estate (if ever) immediately upon and no sooner than the expiration of all prior estates created simultaneously with it.[13]

Suppose we translate that with an example. Suppose O makes a conveyance

"to A for life, then to B"

"to A for life, remainder to B"

In each case B has a remainder. It meets our definition. The future interest is in B, not the transferor. According to the language it becomes possessory immediately upon A's death and no sooner than A's death. (It does not cut off A's interest, and there is no gap between A's death and B's right to a present estate.) And, A's estate is the only prior estate created simultaneously with B's interest. We observe that B acquires his remainder at the same time that A acquires his life estate; but since it is a future estate, his right to possession accrues on A's death. During A's lifetime he had the rights of a remainderman, which include the right to hold A accountable for waste, and usually the power to transfer his estate to some one else.

A remainder can be created to follow, not only a life estate, but any possessory estate other than a fee simple (absolute or defeasible); that is, a remainder can be limited after a fee tail (where that estate is still recognized) or a term of years.

In the above examples, under the rule dispensing with the necessity of words of inheritance, B's estate is a remainder in fee simple absolute. The liberality and flexibility of our law of estates permits remainders which are limited in duration in all the ways in which the possessory estates can be limited. Remainders can be for life, in fee tail, or for a term of years, and can be made defeasible. This panoply of possibilities permits a succession of remainders. Unless such a succession ends with a remainder in fee simple absolute, the conveyor will have retained a future interest: a reversionary interest or a right of entry. But as soon as a provision appears for a remainder in fee simple absolute, no further remainders can be included, for nothing more remains.

It is equally important to our understanding of the function of remainders to consider another way in which remainders can be differentiated and classified. This requires more extended analysis, but before moving on, try your hand at describing the interests created by these conveyances:

1. O, owner in fee simple absolute, conveys "To A for life, then to B, for life, then to C and the heirs of his body."

2. O, owner in fee simple absolute, conveys to A for life, remainder to B for life, remainder to C.

---

13. Compare Restatement of Property § 156 (1936).

(a) The Distinction Between Vested Remainders and Contingent Remainders

Let us now attack the difference between a *vested* remainder and a contingent remainder. Obviously, unless they have different legal characteristics, there would be little use in having two names, and it may help if you know in advance that:

Contingent remainders are at common law destructible. Vested remainders are not. More later on the meaning of "destructible."

Contingent remainders may not be alienable inter vivos. All vested remainders are fully alienable.

Contingent remainders are subject to a condition precedent before they can become possessory. Vested remainders are not.

If you want to know whether the distinction makes any practical difference today, look at the case of In Re Estate of Houston, infra p. 273, Problem 13, where it made a difference of several million dollars to some of the litigants.

So, we should learn to tell the difference when we read a deed or will which creates one or the other.

Compare these conveyances:

1. *To A for life, remainder to B.*

2. *To A for life, and if B has reached 21, remainder to B.*

3. *To A for life, remainder to those children of B who survive A.*

If we were back in feudal times, we would ask some question such as: who will have the seisin at A's death? Today, we might only ask: who is entitled to possession at A's death?

In the first conveyance, we can say with assurance that B is so entitled. According to our definition B's estate "will become a present estate immediately upon and no sooner than the expiration of all prior estates created simultaneously with it." It is a remainder. And for our present concern, it is vested. When we say it is vested, we mean that there is no condition which must be met other than the expiration of A's life estate before B's estate becomes a present estate. Indeed, A's death is not regarded as a condition upon B's right to possession. The existence of the life estate merely *postpones* the right of enjoyment, which is certain to accrue upon A's death. We know there is no condition because none is expressed or can reasonably be implied. Moreover, there is no condition expressed which will ever cut off B's interest. The essence of the vested remainder is that we have an ascertained taker, and he is ready, so long as his estate continues, to take possession whenever and however the preceding estate ends.

In the second conveyance, suppose we ask: is B entitled to possession when A dies? We must answer that we don't know. The conveyance says he gets possession only if he has reached the age of 21. Thus, there is an express condition (other than the expiration of all preceding estates) which must be met before B is entitled to possession. His remainder is contingent. (We may note, of course, that if B reaches

21 while A is still alive, then B's remainder will change to a vested remainder.)

In the third conveyance, can we identify with certainty the person or persons who will be entitled to possession at A's death? Certainly not. If B doesn't have any children at the time of the conveyance, there are no ascertained persons to take. Such a remainder is contingent. But even if B has children, we cannot identify the remaindermen because according to the conveyance the interest goes *only to those children who survive A*. And, a remainder to unascertained persons is contingent. You may also look upon survival as a condition precedent, which renders the remainder contingent.

To repeat: the vested remainder is one which is held by an ascertained person which is ready to become a present estate when all preceding estates come to an end (i.e, there is nothing else required to occur.) By contrast, the remainder is contingent if it is either:

(a) to unascertained persons; or

(b) to ascertained persons but subject to an express condition precedent.

You may find it helpful to think of these as two different kinds of contingent remainders, or you may think of them as two kinds of uncertainty, either of which makes the remainder contingent. The Restatement of Property adopts the second view.[14]

Here are some other examples of contingent remainders:

(4) *To A for life, remainder to the heirs of B* (a living person). This remainder is contingent because a person is not regarded as having heirs until his death, and is therefore to unascertained persons. The grantor retains a reversion.

(5) *To A for life, remainder to such of A's children as reach the age of 21.* (Assuming A has no child aged 21 or more.)

The children of A have a contingent remainder. The contingency or condition is inherent in the description of the future interest takers. Although A may have children alive, no such child is described as taking under the gift until he reaches 21. So long as the remainder is contingent, the grantor retains a reversion.

(6) *To A for life, remainder to such of A's children as survive A, and if none survive A then to the children of B.*

The children of A have a contingent remainder. The children of B are considered as having an alternative contingent remainder, which is subject to the condition precedent that A die without leaving children. During A's life estate and even if B has living children, the grantor retains a reversion. Why?

(7) *To A for life, remainder to the first son of A to obtain a college degree.*

If A has no son at the creation of the interest or at least no son with a college degree, the remainder is contingent, since a condition prece-

14. Restatement of Property § 157.

dent to the future interest becoming possessory is some son of A obtaining a college degree. So long as the remainder is contingent the grantor retains a reversion.

You should pay particular attention to cases such as example (6) above. The language here creates *alternative contingent* remainders, since there is an express condition precedent for both possible takers. And this leaves a reversion in the grantor. You can see why there is a reversion: What if A dies leaving no children, and also there are no children of B? The conveyance does not make any provision for this, and so the grantor must be said not to have disposed of that part of ownership. You must also recognize that even if B should have living children, there is still a reversion for reasons indicated in the following example.

Let's put one more case:

(8) *To A for life, and if C survives A, then to C and his heirs, but if C does not survive A, then to D and his heirs.*

Again, there is an express condition precedent to both C's interest and to D's interest. Hence, there are alternative contingent remainders. But there is a difference here, because the two alternatives seem to exhaust all possibilities, that is, it seems that either C or D will surely take and there are no other possibilities. Can we still say there is a reversion? This presents a difficulty, but the answer is yes, for reasons which are technical and historical, and which you will understand shortly when we discuss the destructibility of contingent remainders.

We assume that by now you should be well along toward being able to identify a contingent remainder, and for the moment we can just say that all remainders which are not contingent are vested. But remember we must still learn to distinguish the various kinds of vested remainders and we must still learn to distinguish all remainders from executory interests. We will do that but, before we go on, we must look at the problems that arise because contingent remainders are destructible. What does that mean, and why should it be?

Go back to the second example above.

To A for life, and if B has reached 21, remainder to B.

We have called B's remainder contingent and we have said that if A dies before B has reached 21, then B is not entitled to possession. Who is entitled to possession? There seems only one answer: O, the transferror, has not provided for this, so he must still own that part of our divided ownership and must be entitled to take possession. That is exactly the right answer, and we would know that O's interest would be called a reversion.

Here we want to emphasize this important bit of learning that has been mentioned above: whenever a conveyance leaves a contingent remainder in fee as the final disposition, there is always a reversion in the grantor, and that reversion persists until the condition precedent is satisfied. In our case then, if B reaches 21 while A is still alive, his remainder will cease to be contingent. It will become a vested remainder in fee, and O's reversion will be divested. O will no longer have any interest.

It must also occur to you to ask: What happens if B has not reached age 21 when A dies, so that O takes possession under his reversion, and then later B does reach age 21? Will B then be entitled to oust O? At common law, the answer was "no." Why? Because B no longer had any interest. His contingent interest was destroyed.

To find out why such an answer was reached, we must again go back to brief history. The requirements of feudal tenure and the primitive nature of conveyancing in feudal times were reflected in several hard and fast rules of conveyancing. One of such rules was the following:

1. A freehold estate could not be created to commence *in futuro*. Thus A could not convey land to B to be effective 10 years from date. In other words, freehold estates could not be created so as to *spring up* automatically at some future date. In those times, a conveyance consisted of the owner of land putting another person into possession thereof with intent to pass the ownership to him. In this view, you either put the conveyee into possession, or you did not. The thought that you might vest him with the seisin by a present act which, however, would not become effective until some future time was a refinement which simply would not have occurred to most people; and when it was thought of, it was rejected as a kind of heresy. This rule is sometimes spoken of as the rule against *springing* freehold interests.

Related to the above rule was another:

2. An estate in fee simple could not be created in one person with the provision that it should automatically shift to another person at some future date, or upon the happening of a future event.

This rule was founded on much the same policy expressed above. If you undertook to invest one person with the seisin how could it be possible that seisin would go automatically out of him and into another? This was called the rule against *shifting* interests in fee.

Neither of these rules is the law today; nor have they been since the Statute of Uses (1536); but they form the background of the rule of the destructibility of contingent remainders, which, oddly enough, is still the common law today. That rule may be stated as follows:

A contingent remainder must vest on or before the termination of the preceding estate; if it does not, it is destroyed.

So, going back to our simple case, "To A for life, and if B has reached 21, remainder to B," if B had not reached 21 when A died, his contingent remainder was destroyed. It did not vest before the termination of the preceding estate. If it were asked why B could not take when he later reached 21, the answer would be there there could not be any intervening gap in the seisin. Of course, such a gap could be prevented by allowing the grantor to take his reversion until B reached 21 at which time the fee would vest in him; but this would violate the rule against springing freehold interests. So, in our case, B's contingent remainder would be destroyed for failure to vest upon or before the expiration of the preceding freehold estate.

As if this were not enough, we must also note that contingent remainders could be destroyed by failure to vest before an *artificial* termination of the preceding estate. The preceding estate could be so terminated in one of two ways: by *forfeiture* or by *merger*. Forfeiture might occur whenever the life tenant failed to perform his feudal obligations or attempted to convey a fee, the latter being called a tortious feoffment. Merger would occur in the following situation. Suppose land was conveyed to A for life, remainder to the heirs of B (a living person). Thereafter the grantor dies leaving A as his only heir. The grantor's reversion in fee descends to A and A's life estate merges with it and disappears. There being no estate of freehold left to support the contingent remainder, it is destroyed if it is not then vested. This may seem by modern lights to be a highly questionable way of squeezing out a contingent remainderman, but it became settled law.

Here is another way that the notion of merger could be used to destroy a contingent remainder. Suppose we have a conveyance from O: "To A for life, remainder to those children of B who survive A." We know that even if B has some children, their remainder interest is contingent upon survival of A. We also know that O therefore has a reversion. Now suppose O dies and his reversion passes to X. And suppose that X and A decide they want to cut out B's children. If X conveys to A, or if A conveys to X, or if both X and A convey to some other party, E, it will produce a situation in which *both* the life estate and the reversion in fee would be owned by one person. The two estates merge, and again there is no life estate left to support the contingent remainder. It is destroyed.

Now you can see why in example (8) above, it was important in the early law to recognize that there was a reversion in the grantor when there are alternative contingent remainders, even though the alternatives seem to exhaust all possibilities. Merger of the life estate with the reversion could destroy *both* of the contingent remainders. And the reversion had substantial value because this was so. If there were no reversion, neither could be destroyed. This recognition of a reversion after contingent remainders was probably based upon a policy under which it was thought desirable to get rid of contingent remainders. There was as yet no Rule against Perpetuities to prevent remote vesting, and the perpetuation of contingent interests was not to be encouraged. Thus, the destructibility rule was consistent with a negative attitude toward contingent remainders, and it is not surprising that the courts were willing to accept the recognition of a reversion even when alternative contingent remainders exhausted all possibilities.

An exception to this sort of destruction of a contingent remainder should be noted. Where all the interests are created simultaneously, the vested estates will not merge so as to destroy the contingent remainder. For example, if an owner in fee simple devises by will "to my sole heir, A, for life, remainder to B if he attains 21," A will upon the testator's death receive a life estate by will and the reversion by inheritance as the testator's heir. This was held not to destroy the contingent remainder in B at the very moment of its creation. If, however, A transfers both his life estate and his reversion to C before B reaches 21, the vested estates so transferred will then merge, and B's contingent remainder will be destroyed.

In addition to this exception to the destructibility rule, you should also note that the rule was not applied where the contingent remainder was in the form of a beneficial interest under a trust. Suppose property were conveyed to T in trust, to pay the income to A for life, then to convey the property to B if he attained the age of 21. Although B would not be entitled to the property if he died under 21, his interest could not be destroyed prior to his attaining that age, because the rules about shifting interests in fee simple were applicable only to "legal" estates. Here the only legal estate was in the trustee.

The destructibility of contingent remainders was so firmly established that it has endured into our time. It is recognized as the law in some American states. In about half the states it has been abolished by statute or by judicial decision. In some states the courts have not had occasion to rule on the question. In those states where the destructibility rule has been abolished, contingent remainders can now take effect after the ending of life estates, not as contingent remainders, but as executory interests, which are considered below. You should not, however, misconstrue the effect of the abolition of the destructibility rule. A contingent remainder will still fail if the condition precedent which makes it contingent is not satisfied.

Unless a contingent remainder is so limited that it will terminate on or before the death of the remainderman, it is devisable and descendible. In the early common law, contingent remainders were inalienable inter vivos. They were originally regarded as such tenuous property interests that they seem to have been treated like choses in action, which were not assignable, lest they become devices for stiring up litigation. Contingent remainders are still inalienable inter vivos in a few states; in other states some kinds of contingent remainders are alienable, others are not. In some states contingent remainders have been declared alienable by courts without statutes, and in other states statutes make then alienable. On the whole, contingent remainders are alienable inter vivos in all but a few states. One must not forget, however, that the successor takes the contingent remainder exactly as it was—it is still contingent, and it will fail if the condition is not fulfilled.

While these ideas are fresh in your mind, let us emphasize and anticipate the distinction between a contingent remainder and an executory interest. We noted that the common law would not permit *springing* legal interests or *shifting* legal interests. We have noted that those rules did not apply to *equitable* interests. The chancellor permitted those kinds of interest in equity. In 1536, after the Statute of Uses, it became possible to create such interests as *legal* interests, and when created as legal interests they are known as executory interests. These interests have been recognized for some 450 years, but legal historians may think of them as relative newcomers to the hierarchy of future interests. Their recognition brought some other developments in their wake. We will look at them in more detail later.

(b) Kinds of Vested Remainders

We have already examined the concept of a "vested" remainder. We have seen that the significant element is that it is a remainder which, throughout its continuance, is ready to take effect as a present estate immediately upon the expiration of the preceding estate. There is no condition precedent. But we must now separate three types of "vested" remainders:

Indefeasibly vested remainders

Remainders vested subject to complete defeasance

Remainders vested subject to open

Look at these conveyances:

(1) *To A for life, remainder to B.*

(2) *To A for life, remainder to B, but if B should die under the age of 25, then remainder to C.*

(3) *To A for life, remainder to his children.*

(4) *To A for life, remainder to B for life.*

In (1) B has an indefeasibly vested remainder.

In (2) B has a vested remainder subject to complete defeasance.

In (3), A's children have a vested remainder subject to open.

The first point we must note is that not every *vested* remainder is certain to become a present interest at some time in the future. Some "vested" remainders may expire by their own terms before the time comes for it to become possessory. In example (4) all authorities agree that B has a vested remainder. There is an identified taker, and no condition precedent which must be met other than the termination of A's preceding life estate. However, since B may die before A does, it is possible that B's life estate will never become possessory. This fact gives rise to some question as to the further classification of the remainder. Is it "indefeasibly vested" or "vested subject to complete defeasance"? The Restatement of Property § 157, comment f, restricts the term "indefeasibly vested" remainder to those interests which are certain to become possessory, and therefore treats B's interest as vested subject to complete defeasance.

The second point is that some "vested" remainders may be able to become possessory, and may in fact become possessory but still be subject to a condition which will prematurely cut off the interest. (See example (2).) And some "vested" remainders may get cut down in size because they have to be shared with other persons in a class. (See example (3) above and the discussion below.)

By elimination, then, it is only the *indefeasibly vested* remainder which is both certain to become possessory at some future time and also certain not to be prematurely cut off or cut down in size. Here are typical examples:

(5) *To A for life, remainder to C.*

(6) *To A for life, then to B for life, remainder to C.*

In both cases, C has an indefeasibly vested remainder.

But we must now deal with the vested remainder subject to complete defeasance. The name implies that this kind of remainder is one which may come to an end prematurely. The hardest part of recognizing and classifying this remainder lies in cases where it must be distinguished from a contingent remainder. This involves distinguishing a *condition precedent* from a *condition subsequent.*

Note again a typical example of an indefeasibly vested remainder:

(7) *To A for life, remainder to B.*

Consider also an example of a contingent remainder:

(8) *To A for life, and if B has reached the age of 25, then to B.*

Suppose, however, the conveyance is as follows:

(9) *To A for life, remainder to B, provided, however, if B dies under the age of 25, then to C.*

Is example (9) comparable to (7) or (8)? It seems more like (8) because under both (8) and (9) B's interest is subject to what appear to be conditions requiring him to attain the age of 25. But there is a difference. What do these conveyances say about the right to possession? What if, at A's death, B is still under 25. Under (8) he is not entitled to possession because the conveyor appears to have expressed the intention that B is to have possession only upon his attaining 25. The condition is a condition precedent. But under (9) there seems to be nothing to prevent B from taking possession on A's death. In this respect (9) is like (7): neither is subject to a condition precedent, and so both remainders are vested. Upon A's death, in example (7), B will have a fee simple absolute. Under (9), if B is still under 25 at A's death, he will also have a possessory estate. But if the apparent intention of the conveyor is to be followed, B should still be subject to the possibility of losing his estate if he dies under 25. He will have one of those "defeasible" fee estates previously considered: a fee simple subject to an executory limitation. The condition about B's dying under 25 is, in other words, regarded as a condition subsequent, or a condition of defeasance. All these possibilities are implicit when the conveyance under example (9) takes effect. B acquires at that time a remainder vested subject to complete defeasance. And his estate in fee may be cut off even after it becomes a possessory estate upon A's death, if B is still under 25. If B attains 25 in A's lifetime, the condition of defeasance has been satisfied, and his remainder becomes indefeasibly vested. If B dies under 25 in A's lifetime, his interest is defeated or divested in favor of C. C's interest is, at the time of its creation, an executory interest, because it will take effect by cutting short B's vested remainder if B dies under 25 either before or after A's death. We may note that if B dies under 25 while A is still living, C's interest will become an indefeasibly vested remainder.

The above examples indicate there is some substance to the distinction between a condition precedent and a condition of defeasance. Consider now the following two examples:

(10) *To A for life, and if B survives A, remainder to B.*

(11) *To A for life, remainder to B, but if B dies in A's lifetime, then to C.*

Traditionally, the remainder to B in (10) is contingent, but in (11) it is vested subject to complete defeasance. What is the difference? In (10) if B fails to survive A, the conveyor's reversion will come into possession. In (11) if B fails to survive A, C will take. But suppose (10) were changed to read: "To A for life, and if B survives A, remainder to B, but if B fails to survive A, then to C." Here there are alternative contingent remainders in B and C. Is there now any difference in substance between these provisions and those in (11)? There are significant differences in the legal consequences of labelling an interest contingent rather than vested subject to complete defeasance. For example, remainders vested subject to complete defeasance, since they are not contingent, are not destructible under the rule making contingent remainders destructible. Can we let such important consequences turn on the way the grantor expressed himself? You may think that it is wrong to do so. Yet, if we concede that there may be times when a grantor *wants* one result and not the other, our law should permit the widest range of dispositive choice. And, if we recognize that a court will enforce a clearly expressed intent, then we reach a point where we must find some way to decide which of the two consequences the particular grantor wanted and we can only try to reach a conclusion from the way in which the language is used. Did he intend a condition precedent or a condition subsequent?

We cannot at this point examine all the rules of construction which courts have developed to help resolve specific cases, but we should note three matters: (1) mechanically, if the conditional language comes *after* the language which would otherwise create a vested remainder, it will likely be said to create a condition subsequent (see example (11) above); (2) if the conditional language comes *before* the language creating the remainder, or if it appears to be part of the description of the taker, it will likely be said to be a condition precedent (see example (10) above); and (3) when there is substantial doubt, the courts express a preference for a vested construction.

Here are some other examples of remainders which are vested subject to complete defeasance:

(12) *To A for life, remainder to B in fee so long as a grocery store is operated thereon.*

(13) *To A for life, remainder to such persons as A may appoint, but in default of, and until appointment to B and his heirs.*

B's interest in (12) may never become possessory if A were to breach the special limitation causing the grantor's possibility of reverter to take effect and automatically revest the land in the grantor.

B's interest in (13) is vested (it is ready to take effect in possession) but it can be cut off (divested) by the exercise of the power of appointment which A has been given.

The third type of "vested" remainder is one which is "vested subject to open." It is sometimes called a remainder "vested subject to partial defeasance." It is a label given to only one kind of remainder—a remainder in favor of a class of persons which is capable of increasing in membership. A typical example is the one given earlier:

To A for life, remainder to his children

If A has no children when this gift is made, the remainder is contingent upon A's having his first child. (This would be a typical case of a remainder which is contingent because it is to an unascertained person.) But, upon the birth of A's first child, C–1, (or if A has a child at the time of the gift) that child has a remainder vested subject to open. It is vested because it is subject to no condition precedent. But it is subject to partial defeasance by the birth of other children of A. Upon the birth of another child, C–2, the remainder in C–1 is partially divested, but is otherwise unchanged. C–1 and C–2 have undivided one-half interests in the remainder, which is still vested subject to open. And so on, if and when A has more children. Not until A's death will the fractional share of each child be indefeasibly ascertained.

Suppose after A has had three children, C–1 dies in A's lifetime. Since C–1's interest is vested subject only to open, but not subject to any condition of survivorship, his interest will pass to his heirs unless he has otherwise transferred it in his lifetime or by his will.

If a gift is made "to A for life, then to the children of A who survive him," we have said that the remainder is contingent. In fact, it is also subject to open, because it is a remainder to a class. But traditional terminology does not differentiate between kinds of contingent remainders in this respect. This remainder is simply called contingent.

Be careful of the class gift which is not capable of increasing in membership. For example, suppose a gift "To A for life, remainder to the children of B"; and suppose further that B is dead at the time of the gift. There can be no more children. Hence, the remainder to the children of B is indefeasibly vested.

Be careful also about how long the class may keep on increasing in size. Suppose a conveyance "To A for life, remainder to the children of B." B is alive, and assume that B has two children at the time of the gift. We know the children have a remainder vested subject to open. Now suppose that A dies very shortly afterward. At that time, of course the two children would take possession. What if two years later B has a third child? Would that child share? Probably not. The class would close at the time the interest became possessory (at A's death). The full development of doctrines relating to class gifts must await another course.

Remainders vested subject to open are not destructible. It has also been held that, if there are living members of a designated class, the potential interests of unborn members are also not destructible; that is, all the vested interests cannot be merged so as to defeat the right of unborn class members to take upon their birth.

All vested remainders are alienable, devisable and descendible. But, one must note that remainders which are vested subject to open remain subject to open in the hands of a successor in interest. And, a remainder which is subject to complete defeasance remains subject to complete defeasance in the hands of a successor in interest. If the condition is violated at the remainderman's death, no interest remains which can descend or be devised.

Examples

1.   O conveys "to A for life, remainder to the children of A." At the time of the conveyance, A has two children, C–1 and C–2. Child C–1 conveys all his interest in the land to X. Child C–2 dies before A does, leaving a will which devises all his real property to Y. Thereafter A has a third child, C–3. The remainder created in "the children of A" is vested subject to open. The interest of C–1 is alienable, and is now owned by X. The interest of C–2 is devisable and is now owned by Y. But both X and Y have interests still "subject to open" so they now share the remainder with C–3. Each of them (X, Y and C–3) owns an undivided one-third interest.

2.   O conveys "to A for life, remainder to B and his heirs, but if B dies without any children surviving him, then to C and his heirs." Thereafter A dies. Thereafter B conveys the land to X and his heirs. Thereafter B dies without any surviving children. The remainder to B was vested subject to complete defeasance. When A dies B is entitled to possession. B's interest is alienable and X becomes the owner of B's interest. But the interest in X's hands is still subject to complete defeasance should B die without surviving children. Thus when that condition happens, X's interest ends and C becomes owner of a present estate in fee simple absolute. What was B's interest after A died?

3.   O conveys "to A for life, remainder to B and his heirs, but if B dies without surviving children, then to C and his heirs." Thereafter B dies without surviving children, leaving a will which devises all his real property to X. B's vested remainder was subject to complete defeasance and even though such interests are devisable, the condition was violated at his death so there was no interest remaining to be devised. X takes nothing, and C has an indefeasibly vested remainder.

(5)   Executory Interests

We have already said enough about executory interests so that you have some notion as to what they are. You know that historically they were the last additions to the company of future interests. You know that they became possible only after 1536 when the Statute of Uses eliminated the obstacles which had prevented their creation as legal interests. You know those obstacles were (1) that you could not create legal freehold estates which would "spring" up in the future; and (2) that you could not create legal freehold estates which would automatically "shift" over from one person to another upon the happening of a condition or event. If you put that knowledge to work, you have this perception: an executory interest is a future interest created in a third party which is not a remainder, and which takes effect by "springing" into possession or by "shifting" from one person to another. The important point is that *remainders* take effect in possession at the *expiration* of the preceding estates whereas *executory interests* take effect in possession by divesting (cutting off prematurely) the preceding estate.

Let's go over it again: A *remainder* is a future interest given to a transferee after interests *less* than a fee simple have been given to others and it becomes possessory upon the *expiration* of preceding estates. You will also recall that if, after a life estate, a remainder in fee simple absolute is given, nothing more remains of the divided fee simple to be given to anyone else. But you must now also recognize that a present or future estate in fee simple can be given subject to a condition which will divest it. If such an estate is divested in favor of a person other than the conveyor, that person's interest is an executory interest. In other words, every interest that takes effect in possession by way of divesting a prior vested estate is an executory interest.

There is one exception to this proposition that you must recall. That is, we can have one kind of *remainder* which does divest a prior *vested* estate. You remember this one: Suppose a conveyance from O "To A for life and if B reaches 21 years of age, remainder to B." B has a contingent remainder and O has a *reversion* (a prior vested estate). But we know that if B reaches age 21 before A dies, so that the condition precedent is met, his remainder ceases to be contingent and becomes indefeasibly vested. In so doing, it divests (cuts off) the reversion of O.

On the other hand, there is one kind of executory interest that does not divest a prior interest. An executory interest can be given after a fee simple determinable. Suppose, for example we have a conveyance "To A and his heirs so long as the premises are used during A's lifetime for residential purposes, and if not so used then to B and his heirs." Clearly, A has a determinable fee simple. What is the natural *expiration* of that estate? Well, one could say that it will last forever (as a fee simple) or until the premises are used for other than residential purposes. We know that the fee simple determinable ends automatically upon the happening of the special limitation. One could say, therefore, that B's estate will take effect (if ever) at the *expiration* of A's estate and ought to be called a remainder. But, it is called an executory interest because one could not at common law create a remainder after a fee simple (even a determinable one).

So, we may say that, with one exception, executory interests *must* take effect by way of automatically divesting either a possessory estate or a vested future estate, and, with one exception, *only* executory interests can so operate. Executory interests appear in a profuse variety. Following are examples of several types which, for the sake of clarity, can be differentiated.

(1) *To A, but if he should die without leaving issue, to B.*

A takes a fee simple subject to an executory limitation; B takes an executory interest in fee simple absolute. Like remainders, executory interests can be limited to create interests other than those in fee simple absolute. For example, property may be given "to A, but if he should die without leaving issue, to B for life, then to C." B takes an executory interest for life, and we can say that C takes an interest which is in one respect an executory interest, and in another respect a remainder; that is, we may say that C takes a remainder in an executory interest. The type of executory interest involved here is sometimes called a *shifting* executory interest, which means that it divests an estate in some one other than the conveyor.

(2) *Devise to A upon his marriage.*

If upon the testator's death, A is not married, A gets a future interest only, which means that a possessory estate passes to the testator's heirs, unless by some other provision of his will it was given to some one else. That possessory estate is a fee simple subject to an executory limitation. A takes an executory interest which divests the possessory estate if and when he is married. This is sometimes called a *springing* executory interest, which means that it divests a possessory estate in the conveyor or his heirs.

The above two examples contain executory interests which divest possessory estates. More often executory interests divest future estates, as in the following example:

(3) *To A for life, remainder to B, but if B dies in A's lifetime, then to C.*

This of course is example (11) under "Kinds of Vested Remainders," as an illustration of a "remainder subject to complete defeasance." B has a remainder subject to complete defeasance; C has an executory interest. This, too, is a shifting type of executory interest.

Suppose a conveyance "to A for life, then to B if he attains 21." As we learned, if B is alive but under 21 at A's death, his remainder is destroyed under the destructibility rule. If that rule has been abolished, the conveyor's reversion becomes possessory upon A's death, subject to defeasance if B later attains 21. B's remainder has become an executory interest. Why? Because now it will take effect by *divesting* the conveyor's vested reversion rather than at the *expiration* of the life estate.

Most executory interests are contingent. The condition which operates as a condition of defeasance on the prior estate operates as a condition precedent to the succeeding executory interest. It is arguable whether an executory interest can be created which is subject to no conditions. Suppose a conveyance is made "to A and his heirs, but at the end of 20 years, to B." Is this a term of years in A, with a remainder in B, or is it a defeasible fee simple in A, with an executory interest in B? If B has an executory interest, is it contingent or vested? In the absence of any condition precedent, it would seem to be vested. But it has been argued, upon historical grounds, that the only future interests capable of being vested are reversions and remainders. There are no conclusive answers to these questions.

Although executory interests are much like contingent remainders, they were never held to be destructible.

Where the destructibility rule has been abolished, little difference in legal effect remains between contingent remainders and executory interests. In fact some states have statutes which define remainders in such a way that they have been construed to include executory interests. You should be prepared to find courts which use the two terms interchangeably. It is still important to distinguish both contingent remainders and executory interests from vested remainders. Whatever terminology is employed, it is useful to remember that the presence of a traditional executory interest signifies the presence of a prior vested estate rather than one which is contingent. In other words, the identification of executory interests is part of the important process, when a succession of present and future estates has been created, of differentiating conditions precedent from conditions subsequent, contingency from defeasance.

Executory interests, or at least those which are subject to conditions precedent, are subject to the same rules on transferability as are noted above for contingent remainders.

We may note here, that England has long since abolished all *legal* estates except the fee simple and the estate for years. The other interests may be created as equitable interests. It has been argued that we should follow the example. See Bostick, Loosening the Grip of the Dead Hand: Shall We Abolish Legal Future Interests in Land?, 32 Vanderbilt L.Rev. 1061 (1979).

D. TWO RULES RELATING TO REMAINDERS: ONE DEAD—ONE REVIVED

(1) The Rule in Shelley's Case

> *"To A for life, remainder to the heirs of A."*
> *"To A for life, remainder to the heirs of the body of A."*

In medieval England it was all-important to the perpetuation of those feudal governmental revenues dependent on the incidents of tenure, that an heir took by descent from his ancestor and not by purchase from his ancestor's grantor. Take the simple conveyance to A for life, remainder to the heirs of A. One not particularly versed in the rule in Shelley's case might hastily, logically, but erroneously, conclude the interests created to be—

1. A life estate in A

2. A contingent remainder in the unascertained heirs of A subject to the doctrine of destructibility and

3. A reversion in the grantor.

Assuming the validity of the analysis, at the termination of A's estate, if termination resulted from A's death and not prior to that time, the heirs of A—at common law under primogeniture, the heir of A—would take not from A by descent but as purchasers from the grantor of A. The incidents of tenure accompanying inheritance would not arise. But if we conclude, as did the common law, that the language "remainder to the heirs of A" described no interest to be taken by the heirs from the grantor at the termination of his freehold, but a remainder in fee simple to be taken by the purchaser A, the heirs of A will take if at all not from the grantor as purchasers under a contingent remainder but by descent or inheritance from A. The words seemingly describing an interest in the heirs of A are not words of purchase but words of limitation defining the estate in A by way of remainder.

There have been various reasons offered for treating the words "to the heirs of A" as words of limitation. One suggests that the conveyance

"To A for life remainder to the heirs of A"

is really quite the same as a gift

"To A and his heirs."

In an age when conveyancing was not common and legal estates in land were not devisable, the practical consequence in terms of the ultimate taker of the fee would be the same. On A's death, the property would next be enjoyed by the heir of A assuming A's estate to be one of inheritance. Describing A's fee simple as being an estate which A first enjoyed for life and which then remained in favor of A's heirs was, in fact, an accurate statement of the normal course of events. This reason for the rule, of course, disappeared at an early date.

A second somewhat different explanation for this historical development causing the words "remainder to the heirs of A" to be construed as words of limitation describing the limit of A's estate rather than as words of purchase describing a contingent remainder in the heirs of A is founded solely on feudal fiscal policy. It was important to the protection of the feudal revenues that heirs took by inheritance from the ancestor rather than as purchasers from the ancestor's grantor.

Whatever the true explanation, the rule became a rule of property not a rule of construction. This means it was to be applied whether or not it coincided with the intention of the grantor.

In order for the rule in Shelley's case to apply—

1. There must be an estate of freehold in the ancestor, e.g., "To A for life".

2. There must be a remainder in the heirs or the heirs of the body of the ancestor, e.g., "To A for life, remainder to the heirs (or heirs of the body) of A."

3. The estates must be created in the same gift or conveyance, e.g., A conveyance to A for life without more, followed by a devise of the reversion retained by the grantor to the heirs of A would not call for the rule.

4. The limitations in favor of heir and ancestor must be of the same quality, i.e., both legal or both equitable.

Proper analysis under the doctrine of the rule in Shelley's Case of a gift to A for life remainder to the heirs of A indicates the interests created were—

1. A life estate in A.

2. A vested remainder in A in fee simple absolute.

The two successive estates in A then merged to leave A with a fee simple.

If the language describing the remainder was to the heirs of the body of A, A's future estate would be a remainder in fee tail, which again by merger would leave A with an estate in fee tail.

This then is the rule in Shelley's case:

"If in a conveyance or a will a freehold estate is given to a person and in the same conveyance or will a remainder is limited to the heirs or to the heirs of the body of that person that person takes both the freehold estate and the remainder."

Since it would defy reason to suppose the rule, which in most instances gives A the fee instead of a life estate as the grantor obviously intended, effectuates intention or is grounded in any overriding contemporary public policy, all but a few jurisdictions have abolished it. Generally, the legislation is not retroactive.

Where abolished, the ancestor A takes a life estate and the heirs or heirs of the body of the ancestor take a remainder contingent until the death of A when his heirs will be ascertained. And that's what the transferor clearly stated as his intention in the first instance.

Because the Rule is practically a dead issue in the United States, there is no reason to explore all the learning which surrounded its application. But one thing should perhaps be noted. The rule applied only if the remainder was to "heirs" or "heirs of the body" *as such*. If the conveyance was "To A for life, remainder to B the eldest child of A," the rule did not apply, even though B was the heir expectant of A. This would produce an indefeasibly vested remainder in B.

The fact that legislation abolishing the rule is not retroactive means that questions may still arise today. For example, in Evans v. Giles, 83 Ill.2d 448, 47 Ill.Dec. 349, 415 N.E.2d 354 (1980) the court was faced with a devise which took the form "To Daughter for life, remainder to her heirs of the body, and in the event she dies without issue, then" to another. Testator had died before the rule had been abolished, and under the rule the daughter would take a fee tail estate. Interestingly, there was also a statute abolishing the fee tail estate and converting it into a life estate in the first taker with a fee simple in the person to whom it would first pass at common law. Thus, if the daughter had left issue, we might have had a circular operation of the rule and the statute. The case is noted in 1982 So.Ill.U.L.J. 313.

(2) The Doctrine of Worthier Title

"To A for life remainder to the heirs of the grantor."

This common law rule of property is deceptively similar to the rule in Shelley's case. It is not the same, however, since it concerns a conveyance or devise by the landowner to his own heirs, not the heirs of the grantee tenant for life.

The doctrine of worthier title as applied to an *inter vivos* transfer holds that the seeming remainder in favor of the heirs of the grantor is a nullity. This leaves the grantor with a reversion which will become possessory at the termination of the life estate. As in the case of the rule in Shelley's case, it is likely that the inspiration for this was the feudal preoccupation with the desirability of heirs taking by descent rather than purchase.

In the case of a devise to the heirs of the testator, the doctrine causes the devisees to take by descent the estate which the decedent intended to pass to his heirs by purchase. In any event, the heirs take. Today it is of little consequence whether an heir takes from his deceased ancestor by descent or purchase.

In most instances, the rule, like the rule in Shelley's case, frustrates intention. It nullifies an interest which the grantor plainly intended to create—a remainder contingent until the grantor's death.

Even so, the contemporary significance of this rule is much greater than in the rule in Shelley's case, although certain jurisdictions have abolished both. Its impact on *inter vivos* transfers has been tempered somewhat by its transformation from a rule of property, i.e. a rule which applies even if contrary to manifested intention of the grantor, into a rule of construction, i.e., a court may find that the grantor really intended to create a remainder. If so the force of the rule is overcome.

Where the rule in Shelley's case is still in force, it is a rule of property but applies only to transfers of real property whereas the doctrine of worthier title is applicable to transfers of real and personal property alike.

E. ESTATES IN PERSONAL PROPERTY

Although the system of estates developed in connection with real property, the ability to create equitable future interests in chattels or personal property has long been recognized. It is now generally assumed that the law of estates and future interests governing the disposition of real property is equally applicable to personal property. Indeed, the modern law of future interests is largely concerned with trusts, with personal property as the corpus. Statutory provisions may be relevant.[15]

Chattels Personal

A gift of a jug of wine to A for life with remainder to B would logically create little more than a remote expectancy for B. In legal terminology, the intention of the grantor would seem to be that A takes not only a possessory interest but an absolute power of consumption as well. Is not the interest of B repugnant to that previously given A? The sense of the decisions on this point supports the conclusion that a

---

15. For example, in 1953, the North Carolina legislature enacted a statute providing that "Any interest or estate in personal property which may be created by last will and testament may also be created by a written instrument of transfer." Gen.Stat.N.C. § 39–6.2.

gift of a consumable does not admit of division between present and future interests, a proposition not applicable to the case of a gift of a chattel personal other than a consumable. There seems no reason today why in the case of tangible personal property, other than consumables, and intangibles one could not create possessory and future interests comparable to those described in the case of real property except for the fee tail. The Statute De Donis was not applicable to chattels. For a full consideration of this general subject consult Simes and Smith, Ch. 12 (1956).

Chattels Real

It was most difficult for the common law to concede this chattel, the nonfreehold estate, so inferior in terms of status, could be divided into a life estate, an interest qualitatively greater than the chattel real itself, and remainder. So it was to be expected that initially a devise of an interest in a chattel real to A for life and then to B left nothing for the supposed remainderman. The future interest was soon recognized, however, but considered an executory interest rather than a remainder. It would be surprising indeed if a contemporary court would decree the future interest as other than a vested remainder. Presumably it would follow that reversions, possibilities of reverter, rights of entry, and true executory interests could also be carved out of a chattel real.

F. THE RULE AGAINST PERPETUITIES

> *"No interest is good unless it must vest, if at all, not later than twenty-one years after some life in being at the creation of the interest."* [16]

This apparently simple statement has plagued students, lawyers, and judges perhaps more than any other rule of property.

"[F]ew, if any, areas of the law have been fraught with more confusion or concealed more traps for the unwary draftsman; * * * members of the bar, probate courts, and title insurance companies make errors in these matters." Lucas v. Hamm, 56 Cal.2d 583, 15 Cal.Rptr. 821, 826, 364 P.2d 685 (1962).

The conflict between the individual landowner's desire for freedom to carve a fee simple into successive estates, one or more of which is contingent upon the happening of an uncertain event, and the practical necessity to assure land will be alienable and not removed for unreasonable periods from the stream of commerce, has been compromised in the judge-made Rule Against Perpetuities. It is a rule of property and public policy, and where violated defeats the intention of the grantor.

Consider the following gift.

> To my wife for life and then to such of my lineal descendants as are alive 100 years after the date of my wife's death.

---

16. Gray, The Rule Against Perpetuities 191 (4th ed. 1942).

The donor's wife has a part of the fee—a life estate. At the termination of the life estate, the donor will have a right to possession by way of a reversion. This reversion will last for 100 years at which time it will be cut short in favor of the executory interest in favor of certain persons whose identity remains unknown for the life of the wife and one century thereafter. For all practical purposes the parcel in question has been taken off the market for a very substantial period of time.

The basic question of policy with which the law must come to grips is whether this form of restraint is acceptable. The answer is the Rule Against Perpetuities, first announced in the seventeenth century. Unlike the Rule in Shelley's case and the Doctrine of Worthier Title, the Rule "is not of feudal origin; it has its support in the practical needs of the modern times."

In a very real sense the rule is directed at the same problem raised by a gift in fee tail. The creator of the fee tail sought to impose a course of descent upon the subject parcel until failure of lineal descendants. The common law, in recognizing remedies whereby the present tenant in tail could effectively alienate the total fee and destroy outstanding future interests, avoided the perpetual indirect restraint on alienation otherwise resulting.

The legal contingent remainder had to vest or be destroyed at the termination of the preceding supporting estate of freehold. Again, the indirect restraint on alienation created by the existence of contingent remainders was limited as a practical matter.

Subsequent to the Statute of Uses there must have been considerable doubt as to the destructibility of the newly recognized legal executory interests. It was not until 1620 that in Pells v. Brown [17] the court decided executory interests were indestructible. Had the decision of the court been consistent with treatment of the estate tail, so that the holder of the possessory estate could alienate the fee simple by resort to an appropriate legal proceeding, the course of development of our land law would be very different.

The courts were, however, equal to the task of preserving alienability. In the Duke of Norfolk's case, decided in 1682,[18] the rule limiting the period of time during which the executory interests could remain contingent was first announced. The modern rule evolved during the succeeding two centuries.

The rule as finally developed applies generally to contingent future interests, with some exceptions. It was first applied to executory interests, since most if not all of them are regarded as contingent. It also applies to contingent remainders except in certain limited circumstances where the destructibility of the remainder may save it from the rule. For reasons which are open to objection, possibilities of reverter and rights of entry, at least in this country, are exempt from the rule, but legislation in some states has imposed special restrictions on their duration.

17.　Cro.Jac. 590, 79 Eng.Rep. 504.　　　　18.　3 Ch.Ca. 1, 22 Eng.Rep. 931.

The rule today is most frequently stated in the form set forth at the outset of this section.

The rule does not require that all future interests become possessory within the period prescribed. It simply requires that all interests be certain to "vest" *or fail to vest* within the technical meaning of that term within the period prescribed by the rule.

If it is possible at the time of the creation of the contingent future interest and under any imaginable set of facts that the future interest will not vest or fail within the stated period, it is void. That an interest does in fact vest within the period of the rule is not relevant.

Here are examples of future interests which may not vest or fail within the appropriate period:

1. *To A so long as the property is used for church purposes and then to B.*

B has an executory interest which may not vest or fail within the period prescribed. A has a determinable fee. B's executory interest is void. The grantor retains a possibility of reverter, an interest which in this country is not subject to the Rule.

2. *To A on the condition that the property is used for church purposes and upon breach of said condition to B.*

Again B has an interest which may not vest or fail within the period prescribed. B's executory interest is void. A's fee on a condition probably becomes absolute, the grantor not having reserved a right of entry.

3. *To A for life, remainder to the first son of A whenever born who becomes a clergyman.*

Assuming at the date on which the interests are created A has no son then a clergyman, the future interest may not vest or fail within the period prescribed. If indestructible, by statute, the contingent remainder in the prospective clergyman is void. On termination of A's life estate, the grantor's reversion will become possessory. Where the remainder is destructible, it is valid.

4. *To A for life, remainder to the first son of A to reach 25.*

Assuming at the date on which the interests are created A is alive but none of his children has attained 25, the future interest may not vest or fail within the period prescribed. If indestructible, by statute, the contingent remainder in the unknown first son to reach 25 is void. On termination of A's life estate, the grantor's reversion will become possessory. Where the remainder is destructible, it is valid.

5. *To A for life, remainder to the children of A for life, and upon the death of the last surviving child of A, to such of A's grandchildren as may be then living.*

Assuming at the date on which the interests are created A is alive, the future interest in A's grandchildren may not vest or fail within the period prescribed. The life estates in A and his children, including children of A not born at the creation of these interests are good. On termination of the last life estate, the grantor's reversion will become possessory.

6. *To A for life and then to such of A's lineal descendants as are alive January 1, 1990.*

Assuming the instrument of disposition is effective before January 1, 1969, the interests in favor of A's descendants may not vest or fail within the period prescribed. Upon termination of A's life estate, the transferor's reversion will become possessory.

It should be noted that all of the above answers are predicated on the assumption that the common law rule, stated above, is in effect. A number of states have adopted statutes which adopt a "wait and see" approach, under which the court does not declare the interest void *ab initio*, but waits to see whether the interest does in fact vest within the prescribed limit. Thus, in example number 4, above, if A had a 24-year old son at the time of the creation of the interest, and that son lived another year, the interest would be valid. The Restatement (Second) of Property has adopted this approach. § 1.4, Comment f, at 73 (Tent. Draft No. 2 1979). See Casner, Restatement (Second) of Property as an Instrument of Law Reform, 67 Ia.L.Rev. 87 (1981). See also, Chaffin, The Rule Against Perpetuities as Applied to Georgia Wills and Trusts: A Survey and Suggestions for Reform, 16 Ga.L.Rev. 235 (1982).

The Restatement has been criticized. Comment, Rule Against Perpetuities: The Second Restatement Adopts Wait and See, 19 Santa Clara L.Rev. 1063 (1979).

It has recently been suggested that possible malpractice suits against lawyers may stimulate greater efforts by them to meet their obligation to reform some dreary, technical, and sometimes meaningless laws. Dukeminier, Cleansing The Stables of Property: A River Found at Last, 65 Ia.L.Rev. 151 (1979).

An adequate knowledge of the Rule against perpetuities cannot be gained by a study of these pages. A thorough coverage of the subject is usually provided in courses on future interests or on Wills and Trusts.

G. DIRECT RESTRAINTS ON ALIENATION

"To A and his heirs, but A shall have no right to alienate said estate"

*" * * * but upon the condition that A does not alienate and upon an attempt to alienate said estate, it shall be forfeited in favor of Grantor and his heirs or assigns"*

*" * * * but said grantee covenants for himself his heirs and assigns that no alienation of said estate shall be made."*

It must be obvious that any division of the fee simple absolute has a practical effect on the alienability of a given parcel of land. A society which recognizes a system of disposition permitting estate planning involving present and future interests as does ours, is committed to whatever cost is to be paid for this type of indirect restraint on alienation. To the extent that the rule against perpetuities and like common law or statutory restrictions limit the creation of interests contingent in nature, we admit that the cost for total freedom of alienation is too great.

Direct restraints are another matter. There must be a reasonable distinction if only in degree between a gift

(1) To A so long as the property is not used for the sale of liquor and

(2) To A so long as A and his heirs or devisees do not alienate said property.

Direct restraints, as in example numbered (2), may be divided into three categories: disabling, forfeiture, and promissory.

In the case of the so-called disabling restraint, the grantor seeks to make a given estate in land totally inalienable for the duration of the estate whether limited or indefinite in duration. One might suggest the property which is the subject of the conveyance has been pretty well taken out of the stream of commerce.

In the case of the so-called forfeiture restraint, the grantor seeks to create an estate in the grantee which either automatically terminates upon an attempt to alienate or which is subject to a power of termination held by the grantor in such event. This then involves a present estate in the grantee and a future interest in the nature of a possibility of reverter or right of entry in the grantor.

An unlimited restraint of either type, when imposed on a fee estate, is void. Where a forfeiture restraint is limited in time or scope, one can find limited authority for upholding it.

Where a disabling restraint is imposed on a life estate, it is void. Where the restraint on a life estate is of the forfeiture type, there is authority supporting its validity. A special rule should be noted in relation to the so-called "spendthrift trust." Here the equitable interest of a trust beneficiary is made inalienable by him and inaccessible to his creditors. Within certain limitations, spendthrift trusts, at least to the extent of a right to receive income, have been upheld in most states which have passed on the matter.

Forfeiture and promissory restraints on the alienation of leasehold interests are valid. Covenants by a lessee not to assign without consent of the lessor are common. Disabling restraints may be invalid unless they can be construed as promissory.

In the case of the so-called promissory restraint, the grantor seeks to create a contract right against a grantee conveying an interest in land which the grantee has agreed he will not transfer. The practical effect of the restraint is quite like that in the case of the forfeiture restraint. If unlimited in time and scope in the conveyance of the fee simple absolute, the restraint is likely to be held of no effect. As the restraint shades away from this exacting position, the chances for it being upheld increase.

For a full consideration of this general subject consult Simes and Smith §§ 1101–1171.

Note on Options to Purchase and Rights of First Refusal

Although the rule against perpetuities is a rule of property law not a rule of contract law, an option to purchase real (or personal property in some cases) may be specifically enforceable and thus create a contingent equitable future interest in the property. It has generally been held in the United States that an option "in gross" to purchase land—i.e., an option not appendant to a leasehold or other property interest—is subject to the rule against perpetuities and is void if it could be exercised at a time beyond the perpetuities period. And an option to purchase personal property which is specifically enforceable because of the unique character of the personal property is also void if it could be exercised at a time beyond the perpetuities period. But the better view is that options appendant to a leasehold or other interest in land are not subject to the rule against perpetuities because alienability is not fettered and improvement of the land is promoted by the existence of the option to purchase. Thus an option to purchase in a lease is valid even though it might be exercised at a time beyond the period of perpetuities.

Land is sometimes conveyed in fee simple subject to a "right of first refusal," requiring that, before the land can be sold to another person, it must first be offered to the transferor or his heirs, or to some designated person. A provision creating a right of first refusal may set a fixed price at which the land may be purchased by the one entitled to exercise the right. In such a case, there is a substantial indirect restraint upon alienation because the price is usually fixed at the value of the land when the right of first refusal is created and the secular trend of land values has been upward. A right of refusal of this type, if unlimited in duration, is generally held void either as a violation of the rule against perpetuities or as a violation of the rule against restraints on alienation. Even where the right of first refusal is limited to the period of a life or lives, the better reasoned cases have held it void as a restraint on alienation. In cases where the right of first refusal may be exercised at a price set by the owner, or at the market price, or "at the best bona fide price offered by responsible third parties," however, the right of first refusal does not substantially restrain alienation. Where the right of first refusal is limited to a life or lives, it seems clearly to be valid since it does not violate the rule against perpetuities and does not effect any significant restraint upon alienation. Even if the right of first refusal is unlimited in duration, it should not be deemed to violate the rule against restraints upon alienation, although it technically violates the rule against perpetuities because it creates a contingent future interest in favor of the person who may become entitled to exercise the right. It would seem that the right of refusal should be held valid in such case, but the cases are divided.

In order to control the ownership of condominium units without violating the rule against restraints on alienation, most condominium association by-laws provide that the association shall have a pre-emptive right of first refusal whenever a unit owner wishes to sell or lease his unit. Since the right of first refusal generally allows the association to purchase "at the best bona fide price offered by responsible third parties," there ordinarily will be no violation of the rule against restraints on alienation. However, if the association's pre-emptive right is considered to be an option in gross it will be subject to the rule against perpetuities and will be void if it can be exercised at a date beyond the perpetuities period. But if such pre-emptive rights are considered to be analogous to options to purchase appendant to a leasehold estate, the rule against perpetuities is generally held to be inapplicable. And in some states the condominium enabling acts expressly provide that neither the rule against perpetuities nor the rule against direct restraints on alienation shall defeat any of the provisions of the act. This is highly desirable since it clearly validates pre-emptive rights of first refusal which are exercisable at a date beyond the perpetuities period— e.g., at any time during the continuance of the condominium regime.

Statutory provisions for termination of the interests of unit owners in their individual units upon destruction of their building may also run afoul of the rule against perpetuities. If the interest of each unit owner is a fee simple, a statutory provision divesting the unit owner's title and vesting it in all the property owners as tenants in common after destruction of their building has the effect of creating an executory interest in all the property owners. Since the statutory executory interest is contingent upon an event that is uncertain either to occur or become impossible of occurrence within the perpetuities period, it is void *ab initio* unless the statutory provision for creation of such an executory interest is expressly exempted from the operation of the rule against perpetuities or is construed as exempting them.

Problems on Present and Future Estates

In the following problems, assume that A owns Blackacre in fee simple absolute. The common law is in force except as modified by statutes providing that every conveyance of land shall be deemed to convey the entire estate or interest of the grantor unless an intent to convey a lesser estate or interest is expressed in the instrument of conveyance. In each of the following problems, determine the type of interest given to or retained by each of the parties.

1. A conveys to B for life, remainder to C for life.

2. A conveys to the X church forever, provided that if the land shall ever cease to be used for church purposes, the conveyance shall be null and void.

3. A conveys to B for life, remainder to B's surviving children.

4. A conveys to B for life, remainder to the children of B.

5. A conveys to B for life, remainder to such of B's children as attain 21. Two years later B dies survived by 3 children, none of whom has attained 21.

6. A conveys to B for life, remainder to B's surviving children, but if B should die without leaving any children him surviving, remainder to C.

Consider the following possibilities:

(a) B has no children.

(b) B has six children.

(c) B dies without leaving any children him surviving.

(d) B dies leaving six children him surviving.

7. A conveys to B for life, then to the children of B, but if any child of B dies under 21, that child's share to C.

8. A conveys to B for life, remainder to the children of C, but if C dies without children him surviving, then to the children of D.

Suppose that at successive periods the facts are as follows:

(a) Neither C nor D has children.

(b) C gives birth to a child, E.

(c) E being still alive, D dies without ever having had any children.

(d) E being still alive and D having died as stated, C gives birth to a second child, F.

(e) E and F predecease C, both dying intestate; then C dies intestate.

9. A conveys to B for life, remainder to B's children if B pays $10,000 to A.

Consider the following possibilities:

(a) B pays A $10,000 but has no children. A later makes a further conveyance to B of all his "right, title, and interest" in Blackacre.

(b) B has 3 children but does not pay A the $10,000. A later conveys to X all his "right, title, and interest" in Blackacre. Thereafter B dies without having paid the $10,000, leaving the 3 children him surviving.

(c) B pays A $10,000 and has 3 children. Thereafter all 3 children die intestate during B's lifetime. Later A makes a further conveyance of all his "right, title, and interest" in Blackacre to B.

10. A conveys to B for life, remainder to A's heirs. A later conveys to X, all his "right, title, and interest" in Blackacre. Thereafter both A and B die intestate.

11. A conveys to B and his heirs, but if B should die without issue, remainder to C and his heirs.

12. Try a problem arising when the dispositive instrument is phrased in more elaborate terms: O, by his will devised certain described land "to my wife, W, for life so long as she remains my widow; then to my children, A, B, and C, in equal shares; but if any of my said children should die in the lifetime of my said wife leaving a child or children him or her surviving, such child's share shall go to his or her children in equal shares; or if any of my said children should die in the lifetime of my said wife, without leaving any children him or her surviving, the deceased child's share shall go to such of my children as survive my said wife. If all of my said children shall die in the lifetime of my wife, W, without leaving any children them surviving, I devise the above described land to D." Now suppose that all of the named devisees survived O. Also, at O's death, one child of C was living. How would you answer the following questions? (You may ignore the concurrent nature of any of the interests).

(a) What is W's interest?

(b) What interests does A have?

(c) What is the interest of C's child?

(d) What is D's interest?

(e) What is the interest of O's heirs?

13. If you wonder whether all these distinctions have any significance in modern times, consider the problem which the court faced in In re Houston, 414 Pa. 579, 201 A.2d 592 (1964). A testator died in 1892, leaving a widow, three children and six living grandchildren. Six other grandchildren were born after his death. The will was an elaborate one, but among other things it created a trust of the residuary estate with the widow and each of three children to get one-fourth of the income for their respective lives. Other provisions disposed of the income up to the time that the last surviving child died. It then provided: "On the death of my last surviving child I direct that the whole of the principal of the trust estate shall be distributed in equal portions to and among my grand-children, the children of any deceased grand-child taking their deceased parents share."

One of the testator's children lived 69 years more, until 1961. At her death, there were eight living grandchildren. Of the four deceased grandchildren, only one left any surviving children. The residuary estate was allegedly worth $145,000,000. The court framed the issue which it had to decide as follows:

"If the remainders for testator's *grandchildren* were vested at testator's death, or became vested on birth after testator's death, subject in both cases to being *divested in favor of their children* if any such grandchild predeceased testator's last surviving child, the principal of the residuary trust * * * will be divided into *12 equal parts*—eight of such parts being for testator's eight living grandchildren; three of such parts for the heirs (or personal representatives) of testator's three grandchildren who died after testator's death but before the death of testator's last surviving child (Mrs. Woodward), intestate and unmarried; and one such part for the two (living) daughters of testator's deceased grandson, T. Charlton Henry.

"If, however, the remainders were contingent upon testator's grandchildren or their children living at the death of testator's last surviving child (Mrs. Woodward), testator's remainder estate would be divided into and distributed in nine *equal* parts—eight such parts to testator's eight living grandchildren, and the ninth part to the two living daughters per stirpes of testator's deceased grandchild, T. Charlton Henry."

Thus, for the living grandchildren, a decision that their remainders were contingent upon survival would increase the value of each legacy by about $4,000,000. How would you decide the case? Would you think the State of Pennsylvania would have any interest in the outcome?

H. PROTECTION OF FUTURE INTERESTS

(Some comments on the Law of Waste)

The owner of a possessory interest in land may find that his use and enjoyment is restricted in a number of ways. Zoning laws, building codes, environmental protection laws, laws prohibiting public nuisances and the like, put limits on his use. These regulations are promulgated under the sovereign police power, presumably to benefit the public generally. We have already seen that the law of private nuisance limits a possessor in his use to that which will not infringe upon the rights of his neighbor. We are here to consider the law of waste which operates to restrict a possessor in his use if his possessory estate is limited, i.e., less than a fee simple absolute. These restrictions really involve a determination of the extent to which the holder of a future estate may protect the value of that estate by limiting the diminution in value which the owner of the possessory freehold, i.e., life estate, fee tail or defeasible fee may cause. (The rights of a landlord *vis-a-vis* his tenant are separately treated.)

In essence, waste, as that term is used here, is unreasonable use of the property by the owner of the possessory estate which reduces the value of a future estate. A life tenant who razes a building and thereby decreases the value of the property in question decreases the value not only of his own limited interest, but the value of the reversion or remainder as well. The same is true even though the possessor may own a fee simple which is defeasible in favor of the holder of a reverter, right of entry, or executory interest upon the happening of a stated contingency.

There are occasional statements that it is not necessary to prove loss of value in order to prove a case for waste if the wrongful acts consist of actual removal of the substance of the soil. E.g., Berns Construction Co. v. Highley, 332 F.2d 240 (C.A.Ind.1964). Such a statement usually means that such removal is per se waste, and may mean, in addition, that the damages to be awarded will be measured in some way other than by determining the value of the land before and after the wrongful acts. Thus the removal of 10,000 cubic yards of sand from a large farm would probably not produce measurable change in the market value of the farm, but the value of the sand could readily be ascertained.

The nature of the future estate has a significant bearing both on the extent of user considered to be reasonable and the remedy which the holder of the future estate may pursue in the event of actual or threatened waste. The owner of a life estate obviously has an estate less in quantum than the owner of a fee simple who may lose his estate "if liquor is ever sold on the premises" or "if he dies without children surviving him." In similar fashion, a distinction can easily be drawn between the holder of a vested future estate and the holder of a contingent future estate which may never take effect in possession.

A life tenant is entitled to the use of property ultimately to be enjoyed by the reversioner or remainderman, provided the use does not unreasonably reduce the value of the future estate. It is as if a sum of money has been invested. The life tenant is entitled to income but has no right to encroach upon the principal. The corpus is owned by the holder of the future estate whose right to possession is deferred to permit interim enjoyment by the life tenant. In effect, the holder of the future estate is entitled to the corpus intact. With certain exceptions, this means that the life tenant may not commit acts which will decrease the value of the future estate, i.e. commit *voluntary* waste, and may not permit the property as a whole to decrease in value for want of those day-to-day repairs a reasonable man would make to maintain his property. If the life tenant breaches this obligation of repair, he has committed *permissive* waste. This does not mean he must rebuild in the event the property is destroyed or substantially damaged by fires or other casualty. Nor is the life tenant liable for a diminution in value resulting from ordinary wear and tear, except to the extent failure of maintenance will result in greater deterioration than one would expect from reasonable use. Failure to repair a leaky roof, which omission will result in more than ordinary wear and tear, would be permissive waste.

The notion that the life tenant owes a fiduciary obligation to the remainderman may affect decisions in areas other than actions for waste. For example, suppose a life tenant of a fund of money also has a power to dispose of the assets. Suppose further that he commingles the assets with his own money, and spends from combined fund. Because of the fiduciary relationship, the court may raise a presumption that he spent his own money first, and thus give the remainderman access to what is left. See Note, Effect of Life Tenant With Power of Disposition Commingling Life Estate and Personal Funds, 19 Washburn L.J. 633 (1980).

There are situations in which the life tenant may adversely affect the value of the future estate without thereby committing voluntary waste. The common-law under a doctrine of estovers permitted the life tenant to cut timber needed for his reasonable use of the premises. Wood for fires or fencing or other repairs could come from timber on the premises. Then too under a so-called open mines policy, a life tenant could continue removing minerals from mines or wells already open. For similar reasons, if the land has no use other than as a lumber-producing forest, the life tenant may be allowed to harvest timber for profit if he acts in accordance with approved forestry practices.

The owner of a fee simple estate, even though it may be subject to defeasance, has been given an interest which may last forever. One might expect, therefore, that his privileges of use would be broader than those of a life tenant. Conversely, one might expect the holder of a possibility of reverter, a power of termination, or a contingent executory interest to receive less protection than that given to a vested remainder following a life estate. By analogy, the holder of the defeasible fee receives not only the income from a sum of money properly invested, but the principal as well, subject to the possibility that his ownership of the whole will come to an end. This possibility is enough to call for some limitation on his acts if they may reduce or destroy the value of the property in question and coincidentally any value of the future estate. As previously indicated, the owner of a defeasible fee estate is chargeable for waste only in limited circumstances. See Restatement § 193. These include the requirement that such owner's conduct be "unconscionable," and that a reasonable probability exists that the future interest will become a present interest.

Suppose the owner of the limited or defeasible estate threatens or does in fact act to the damage of the future estate. What remedy does the owner of the threatened interest have? This depends on the nature of the future estate.

If the future interest is indefeasibly vested, i.e. it will take effect in possession at some date in the future, the owner of the future estate, is entitled to damages for injuries sustained and, under various statutory provisions, multiple damages. He may also be entitled to a prohibitory injunction; or, if it is a case of the life tenant failing to protect the property as he is required to do, a mandatory injunction. In some states, there are statutes which provide a very drastic remedy: that the estate will be forfeited.[19] As one might expect, such a remedy is often restricted to extreme cases (e.g., where the waste is "wanton" or where defendant has failed to pay damages awarded), and its availability is curtailed by strict judicial construction.

---

19. 5 Powell ¶ 650 lists 20 jurisdictions with statutes permitting forfeiture as a remedy in some limited circumstances.

Where the future estate is contingent or vested but subject to defeasance the holder of the future estate should be able to enjoin threatened waste, unless the probability of the future estate ever vesting in possession is extremely remote. It is doubtful that damages should be awarded before it is clear the future estate will in fact become possessory. There is authority for damages to be assessed in this situation with the amount collected on the judgment being impounded until it is determined who in fact acquires the future estate which suffered damage. Watson v. Wolff-Goldman Realty Co., 95 Ark. 18, 128 S.W. 581 (1910).

For a concise but fairly detailed discussion of the legal relations between owners of present and future estates in the same realty or personalty, including the law of "waste" and the law as to payment of carrying charges, rights to insurance proceeds, apportionment of rents, and rights as to "emblements" and "fixtures," see Cunningham, ch. 4.

What does and does not constitute actionable waste is not always easy to determine. The case which follows deals with that question.

BROKAW v. FAIRCHILD

Supreme Court, Special Term, New York County, 1929.
135 Misc. 70, 237 N.Y.S. 6.

HAMMER, J. This is an action under section 473 of the Civil Practice Act and Rules of Civil Practice 210 to 212, in which plaintiff asks that it be declared and adjudged that the plaintiff, upon giving such security as the court may direct, has the right and is authorized to remove the present structures and improvements on or affecting the real property No. 1 East Seventy-Ninth street, or any part thereof, except the party wall, and to erect new structures and improvements thereon in accordance with certain proposed plans and specifications.

*   *   *

In the year 1886 the late Isaac V. Brokaw bought for $199,000 a plot of ground in the borough of Manhattan, city of New York, opposite Central Park, having a frontage of 102 feet 2 inches on the easterly side of Fifth avenue and a depth of 150 feet on the northerly side of Seventy-Ninth street. Opposite there is an entrance to the park and Seventy-Ninth street is a wide crosstown street running through the park. Upon the corner portion, a plot of ground 51 feet 2 inches on Fifth avenue and a depth of 110 feet on Seventy-Ninth street, Mr. Brokaw erected in the year 1887, for his own occupancy, a residence known as No. 1 East Seventy-Ninth street, at a cost of over $300,000. That residence and corner plot is the subject-matter of this action. The residence, a three-story, mansard and basement granite front building, occupies the entire width of the lot. The mansard roof is of tile. On the first floor are two large drawing rooms on the Fifth avenue side, and there are also a large hallway running through from south to north, a reception room, dining room, and pantry. The dining room is paneled with carved wood. The hallway is in Italian marble and mosaic. There are murals and ceiling panels. There is a small elevator to the upper portion of the house.

On the second floor are a large library, a large bedroom with bath on the Fifth avenue side, and there are also four other bedrooms and baths. The third floor has bedrooms and baths. The fourth floor has servants' quarters, bath, and storage rooms. The building has steam heat installed by the plaintiff, electric light and current, hardwood floors, and all usual conveniences. It is an exceedingly fine house, in construction and general condition as fine as anything in New York. It is contended by plaintiff that the decorations are heavy, not of a type now required by similar residences, and did not appeal to the people to whom it was endeavored to rent the building. It is "a masonry house of the old-fashioned type with very thick walls and heavy reveals in the windows, very high ceilings, monumental staircase and large rooms." (S.M. p. 53): "Such as has not been built for probably twenty-five years." (S.M. p. 54): "Utterly impractical to remodel for occupancy by more than one family." It "was offered to a great many people for rental at $25,000 with the statement that a lower figure might be considered and no offer of rental was obtained (S.M. p. 27). Mr. Brokaw (the plaintiff) directed that the asking rental be $30,000 to start and finally reduced to $20,000. There is no demand for rental of private houses. There is a sporadic demand for purchase and sale on Fifth avenue for use as private homes. Once in a while somebody will want a private house." The taxes are $16,881, upkeep for repairs $750, and watchman $300. The taxes for 1913 were $8,950.77 (S.M. p. 92).

Since 1913, the year of the death of Isaac V. Brokaw and the commencement of the life estate of plaintiff, there has been a change of circumstances and conditions in connection with Fifth avenue properties. Apartments were erected with great rapidity and the building of private residences has practically ceased. Forty-four apartments and only 2 private residences have been erected on Fifth avenue from Fifty-Ninth street to 110th street. There are to-day but 8 of these 51 blocks devoted exclusively to private residences (Exhibits 11 and 12). Plaintiff's expert testified: "It is not possible to get an adequate return on the value of that land by any type of improvement other than an apartment house. The structure proposed in the plans of plaintiff is proper and suitable for the site and show 172 rooms which would rent for $1,000 per room. There is an excellent demand for such apartments. * * * There is no corner in the City of New York as fine for an apartment house as that particular corner."

The plaintiff testified also that his expenses in operating the residence which is unproductive would be at least $70,542 greater than if he resided in an apartment. He claims such difference constitutes a loss and contends that the erected apartment house would change this loss into an income or profit of $30,000. Plaintiff claims that under the facts and changed conditions shown the demolition of the building and erection of the proposed apartment is for the best interests of himself as life tenant, the inheritance, and the remaindermen. The defendants deny these contentions and assert certain affirmative defenses: (1) That the proposed demolition of the residence is waste, which against the objection of the adult defendant remaindermen plaintiff cannot be permitted to accomplish. * * *

Defendants claim that: (3) Severance of the premises in question from the rest of the original plot would impair the plottage value of the other parcels and reduce the value of the buildings, (4) the proposed plan of erecting such apartment on the premises is unsound because of the diminutive size of the lot in question in comparison with what is needed for a successful apartment and the increasing tendency to overbuild. * * *

Since the four life estates of the parties are separate and there is no testamentary scheme, it follows that the properties not being in a common ownership can have no plottage value, and such contention by defendants is entirely without merit. The claim of the unsoundness of the venture is also without merit. Indeed, defendants made little effort by proof to uphold such defense. If permissible, it would be sound.

* * *

Coming, therefore, to plaintiff's claimed right to demolish the present residence and to erect in its place the proposed apartment, I am of the opinion that such demolition would result in such an injury to the inheritance as under the authorities would constitute waste. The life estate given to plaintiff under the terms of the will and codicil is not merely in the corner plot of ground with improvements thereon, but, without question, in the residence of the testator. Four times in the devising clause the testator used the words "my residence." This emphasis makes misunderstanding impossible. The identical building which was erected and occupied by the testator in his lifetime and the plot of ground upon which it was built constitute that residence. By no stretch of the imagination could "my residence" be in existence at the end of the life tenancy were the present building demolished and any other structure, even the proposed 13-story apartment, erected on the site.

It has been generally recognized that any act of the life tenant which does permanent injury to the inheritance is waste. The law intends that the life tenant shall enjoy his estate in such a reasonable manner that the land shall pass to the reversioner or remainderman as nearly as practicable unimpaired in its nature, character, and improvements. The general rule in this country is that the life tenant may do whatever is required for the general use and enjoyment of his estate as he received it. The use of the estate he received is contemplated, and not the exercise of an act of dominion or ownership. What the life tenant may do in the future in the way of improving or adding value to the estate is not the test of what constitutes waste. The act of the tenant in changing the estate, and whether or not such act is lawful or unlawful, i.e., whether the estate is so changed as to be an injury to the inheritance, is the sole question involved. The tenant has no right to exercise an act of ownership. In the instant case the inheritance was the residence of the testator—"my residence"—consisting of the present building on a plot of ground 51 feet 2 inches on Fifth avenue by 110 feet on Seventy-Ninth

street. "My residence," such is what the plaintiff under the testator's will has the use of for life. He is entitled to use the building and plot reasonably for his own convenience or profit. To demolish that building and erect upon the land another building, even one such as the contemplated 13-story apartment house, would be the exercise of an act of ownership and dominion. It would change the inheritance or thing, the use of which was given to the plaintiff as tenant for life, so that the inheritance or thing could not be delivered to the remaindermen or reversioners at the end of the life estate. The receipt by them at the end of the life estate of a 13-story $900,000 apartment house might be more beneficial to them. Financially, the objecting adults may be unwise in not consenting to the proposed change. They may be selfish and unmindful that in the normal course of time and events they probably will not receive the fee. With motives and purposes the court is not concerned. In Matter of Brokaw's Will, 219 App.Div. 337, 219 N.Y.S. 734; Id., 245 N.Y. 614, 157 N.E. 880, their right to object to a proposed building loan and mortgage for the erection of the proposed apartment was established by decision. They have the same right of objection in this action. To tear down and demolish the present building, which cost at least $300,000 to erect and would cost at least as much to replace, under the facts in this case, is clearly and beyond question an act of waste.
* * *

The cases given by plaintiff are either cases where a prohibitory injunction against future waste has been sought and the parties have been refused the injunction and relegated to an action for damages for waste, or where, in condemnation proceedings or actions in equity, it appears that the equities between the parties are such that the technical waste committed has been ameliorated. The three cases upon which the plaintiff principally relies are Melms v. Pabst Brewing Co., 104 Wis. 7, 79 N.W. 738, 46 L.R.A. 478, and New York, O. & W.R. Co. v. Livingston, 238 N.Y. 300, 144 N.E. 589, 34 A.L.R. 1078, and Doherty v. Allman, 3 L.R.App.Cas. 709, 717, 721. These are readily distinguishable from the case at bar. In Melms v. Pabst Brewing Co., supra, there was a large expensive brick dwelling house built by one Melms in the year 1864. He also owned the adjoining real estate and a brewery upon part of the premises. He died in 1869. The brewery and dwelling were sold and conveyed to Pabst Brewing Company. The Pabst Company used the brewery part of the premises. About the year 1890 the neighborhood about the dwelling house had so changed in character that it was situated on an isolated lot standing from 20 to 30 feet above the level of the street, the balance of the property having been graded down to fit it for business purposes. It was surrounded by business property, factories, and railroad tracks with no other dwellings in the neighborhood. Pabst Brewing Company, in good faith regarding itself as the owner, tore down the building and graded down the ground for business purposes. Thereafter it was held, in the action of Melms v. Pabst Brewing Co., 93 Wis. 140, 66 N.W. 244, that the brewing company had only acquired a life estate in the homestead, although in another action between the same parties (93 Wis. 153, 66 N.W. 518, 57 Am.St.Rep. 899) it was held that as to the other property the brewing company had acquired full title in fee. The action for waste in which the decision of 104 Wis. was delivered was brought and decided after the decisions in the other actions. We find it there said at page 9 (79 N.W. 738): "The action was tried before the court without a jury, and the court found, in addition to the facts above stated, that the removal of the building and the grading down of the earth was done by the defendant in 1891 and 1892, believing itself to be the owner in fee simple of the property, and that by the said acts the estate of the plaintiffs in the property was substantially increased, and that the plaintiffs have been in no way injured thereby."

Again, it was stated at page 13 of 104 Wis., 79 N.W. 740, 46 L.R.A. 478: "There are no contract relations in the present case. The defendants are the grantees of a life estate, and their rights may continue for a number of years. The evidence shows that the property became valueless for the purpose of residence property as the result of the growth and development of a great city. Business and manufacturing interests advanced and surrounded the once elegant mansion, until it stood isolated and alone, standing upon just enough ground to support it, and surrounded by factories and railroad tracks, absolutely undesirable as a residence, and incapable of any use as business property. Here was a complete change of conditions, not produced by the tenant, but resulting from causes which none could control. Can it be reasonably or logically said that this entire change of condition is to be completely ignored, and the ironclad rule applied that the tenant can make no change in the uses of the property because he will destroy its identity? Must the tenant stand by, and preserve the useless dwelling house, so that he may at some future time turn it over to the reversioner, equally useless?"

The facts in the above case are clearly not analogous to the facts here. Especially is this recognized from the fact that the plaintiff's dwelling house is far from being "isolated and alone, standing upon just enough ground to support it, surrounded by factories and railroad tracks, absolutely undesirable as a residence." It is located on the northeast corner of Fifth avenue and Seventy-Ninth street. Across the avenue to the west is Central Park. To the south across Seventy-Ninth street the block Seventy-Eighth to Seventy-Ninth streets is restricted to private dwellings. The residence itself is surrounded by the three other palatial Brokaw dwellings, forming a magnificent residential layout of the four plots (Exhibit B). It may, of course, be that the situation will change in the future. The decision here is concerned only with the present.

*   *   *

From the foregoing I am of the opinion, and it will accordingly be adjudged and declared, that upon the present facts, circumstances, and conditions as they exist and are shown in this case, regardless of the proposed security and the expressed purpose of erecting the proposed 13-story apartment, or any other structure, the plaintiff has no right

and is not authorized to remove the present structures on or affecting
the real estate in question.

* * *

Note

The decision was affirmed in 231 App.Div. 704, 245 N.Y.S. 402 (1930), with
Judge Finch filing a dissenting opinion, in part of which he wrote:

" * * * (T)his plaintiff has received a plain, unconditional life estate and
* * * the entire remainder is now vested in his daughter, subject only to a
contingent remainder in the three other children of the testator and their issue
who will be living at the death of the life tenant, provided his young daughter
should predecease him. The dwelling house in question was built by the testator many years ago and is of the old-fashioned type. In addition, it appears
that obsolescence generally has fallen upon large dwelling houses such as this
in the city of New York, due to the disinclination of dwellers to burden themselves with the care and expense of a large dwelling house, particularly when
the same is not completely modern. As a practical matter, the upkeep of this
dwelling costs the life tenant approximately $70,000 annually, and the greatest
amount of rent which he apparently can obtain is $20,000 annually, provided it
can be rented at all. He proposes to erect in place of this dwelling house a
modern apartment house, for which the site is exceptionally adapted and which
the evidence upon this record shows will produce a net income of approximately
$100,000 a year. The contingent remaindermen object to this improvement and
seek a declaration that equity will restrain what they allege is waste.

"It is obvious that the opposition to the application of the plaintiff is not
based upon any fear of actual damage to the inheritance, but is actuated solely
by ulterior motives, namely, because of its effect upon the light and air of the
adjoining property, and the very remote possibility of the entire plottage occupied by the aforesaid four dwellings, being developed as a unit at some future
time. These considerations have no bearing upon the question presented,
namely, whether the particular inheritance will be damaged by the act proposed
by the plaintiff.

"Certain it is that there will be no waste in the sense that there will be no
devastavit, but instead a very substantial benefit. Clearly, from a monetary
point of view, a deficit of some $50,000 in annual income is to be turned into a
profit of some $100,000 a year, or a net difference of $150,000 a year. The
adjoining owners are therefore forced to rest upon the objection that this inheritance is being changed from this particular form of dwelling house to a dwelling in apartment form. If the application were to convert the dwelling into a
commercial building, the objection would be stronger, but here at the most the
change is from one form of dwelling house to another. For such damage as the
contingent remaindermen may show, they have an adequate remedy in an action at law for damages for waste.

"The only question which is now presented before us is whether equity will
restrain this act. There is a dearth of authority in this country upon this subject. In England, however, the question has arisen more frequently and has
given rise to a principle which is connoted under the term "meliorating waste,"
where, as here, a situation is presented showing, not a devastavit, but a real
benefit to the inheritance. In other words, there is a change in the inheritance,
but a change which really benefits the inheritance rather than one which causes
a wasting thereof. The leading case on the subject in England is that of Doher-

ty v. Allman, 3 App.Cas. 709, decided by the House of Lords in 1878. A lessee under a lease for 999 years sought to convert into six dwelling houses a store which was on the premises at the beginning of the lease and which the lessee had covenanted to keep in good order and repair, and so to yield the same up at the end of the term. It appeared that the store had become obsolete and that dwelling houses upon the plot in question would be profitable. It was unanimously held that the lessor was not entitled to an injunction to prevent the tenant from making the proposed replacement. * * *

"Equity never acts where the facts are such as in the case at bar. It is inhibited by the fundamental principle that no injunction will issue where the damage to the one seeking the injunction is small as against a large damage to the adverse party. In the case at bar, not only will the damage, if any, to the defendants by reason of the change, be small, as compared to great damage to the plaintiff if the change be forbidden, but in addition there is present the remoteness of any actual damage to those opposed to the change, in view of the contingent nature of their interest.

"It follows that the judgment, in so far as appealed from by the plaintiff and by defendants Ann Brokaw, Margot McNair Fairchild, and Elvira Brokaw Hutchinson, should be reversed, and the relief prayed for in the complaint granted."

I. UNPRODUCTIVE PROPERTY

As the preceding case indicates, the division of ownership between the holder of a present possessory life estate and the holder of a future estate can work great hardship. The life tenant is restricted in his exploitation of the property by the law of waste. At the same time, he is obligated to pay real estate taxes and other carrying charges to the extent these payments do not exceed income derived from the property or the fair rental value if the life tenant occupies the property himself. His position is a far cry from that of the beneficiary of a trust entitled to income from investment of a corpus managed by a trustee. And what if the land in question has no rental value, given the uncertainty as to the duration of the life tenant's possessory right or the lack of improvements on the land?

In the preceding case there was every likelihood that the remainder interest would vest in the daughter of the life tenant, and so the willingness of the life tenant to make a large investment in new construction was understandable. In the usual case involving a legal life estate, it is not likely that the life tenant is going to make a substantial investment, faced as he is with the possibility that the holder of the future interest will be the only one to derive a net benefit. Why not have the property sold, the net proceeds of sale invested, and the income paid to the life tenant until the end of his estate, at which time the principal would be delivered to the holder of the future estate? As logical as this solution may seem, it may be difficult to accomplish, either because the identifiable remainderman or reversioner may not agree to this course of action or because certain of the persons intended to take the future estate in possession are unidentifiable or not in being. (E.g., "To my wife for life and then to such of my grandchildren as reach the age of 21.") The matter is a complicated one, as the following opinion indicates.

BAKER v. WEEDON

Supreme Court of Mississippi, 1972.
262 So.2d 641.

PATTERSON, Justice. This is an appeal from a decree of the Chancery Court of Alcorn County. It directs a sale of land affected by a life estate and future interests with provision for the investment of the proceeds. The interest therefrom is to be paid to the life tenant for her maintenance. We reverse and remand.

John Harrison Weedon was born in High Point, North Carolina. He lived throughout the South and was married twice prior to establishing his final residence in Alcorn County. His first marriage to Lula Edwards resulted in two siblings, Mrs. Florence Weedon Baker and Mrs. Delette Weedon Jones. Mrs. Baker was the mother of three children, Henry Baker, Sarah Baker Lyman and Louise Virginia Baker Heck, the appellants herein. Mrs. Delette Weedon Jones adopted a daughter, Dorothy Jean Jones, who has not been heard from for a number of years and whose whereabouts are presently unknown.

John Weedon was next married to Ella Howell and to this union there was born one child, Rachel. Both Ella and Rachel are now deceased.

Subsequent to these marriages John Weedon bought Oakland Farm in 1905 and engaged himself in its operation. In 1915 John, who was then 55 years of age, married Anna Plaxco, 17 years of age. This marriage, though resulting in no children, was a compatible relationship. John and Anna worked side by side in farming this 152.95-acre tract of land in Alcorn County. There can be no doubt that Anna's contribution to the development and existence of Oakland Farm was significant. The record discloses that during the monetarily difficult years following World War I she hoed, picked cotton and milked an average of fifteen cows per day to protect the farm from financial ruin.

While the relationship of John and Anna was close and amiable, that between John and his daughters of his first marriage was distant and strained. He had no contact with Florence, who was reared by Mr. Weedon's sister in North Carolina, during the seventeen years preceding his death. An even more unfortunate relationship existed between John and his second daughter, Delette Weedon Jones. She is portrayed by the record as being a nomadic person who only contacted her father for money, threatening on several occasions to bring suit against him.

With an obvious intent to exclude his daughters and provide for his wife Anna, John executed his last will and testament in 1925. It provided in part:

> Second; I give and bequeath to my beloved wife, Anna Plaxco Weedon all of my property both real, personal and mixed during her natural life and upon her death to her children, if she has any, and in

the event she dies without issue then at the death of my wife Anna Plaxco Weedon I give, bequeath and devise all of my property to my grandchildren, each grandchild sharing equally with the other.

Third; In this will I have not provided for my daughters, Mrs. Florence Baker and Mrs. Delette Weedon Jones, the reason is, I have given them their share of my property and they have not looked after and cared for me in the latter part of my life.

Subsequent to John Weedon's death in 1932 and the probate of his will, Anna continued to live on Oakland Farm. In 1933 Anna, who had been urged by John to remarry in the event of his death, wed J.E. Myers. This union lasted some twenty years and produced no offspring which might terminate the contingent remainder vested in Weedon's grandchildren by the will.

There was no contact between Anna and John Weedon's children or grandchildren from 1932 until 1964. Anna ceased to operate the farm in 1955 due to her age and it has been rented since that time. Anna's only income is $1000 annually from the farm rental, $300 per year from sign rental and $50 per month by way of social security payments. Without contradiction Anna's income is presently insufficient and places a severe burden upon her ability to live comfortably in view of her age and the infirmities therefrom.

In 1964 the growth of the city of Corinth was approaching Oakland Farm. A right-of-way through the property was sought by the Mississippi State Highway Department for the construction of U.S. Highway 45 bypass. The highway department located Florence Baker's three children, the contingent remaindermen by the will of John Weedon, to negotiate with them for the purchase of the right-of-way. Dorothy Jean Jones, the adopted daughter of Delette Weedon Jones, was not located and due to the long passage of years, is presumably dead. A decree pro confesso was entered against her.

Until the notice afforded by the highway department the grandchildren were unaware of their possible inheritance. Henry Baker, a native of New Jersey, journeyed to Mississippi to supervise their interests. He appears, as was true of the other grandchildren, to have been totally sympathetic to the conditions surrounding Anna's existence as a life tenant. A settlement of $20,000 was completed for the right-of-way bypass of which Anna received $7500 with which to construct a new home. It is significant that all legal and administrative fees were deducted from the shares of the three grandchildren and not taxed to the life tenant. A contract was executed in 1970 for the sale of soil from the property for $2500. Anna received $1000 of this sum which went toward completion of payments for the home.

There was substantial evidence introduced to indicate the value of the property is appreciating significantly with the nearing completion of U.S. Highway 45 bypass plus the growth of the city of Corinth. While the commercial value of the property is appreciating, it is notable that the rental value for agricultural purposes is not. It is apparent that the land can bring no more for agricultural rental purposes than the $1000 per year now received.

The value of the property for commercial purposes at the time of trial was $168,500. Its estimated value within the ensuing four years is placed at $336,000, reflecting the great influence of the interstate construction upon the land. Mr. Baker, for himself and other remaindermen, appears to have made numerous honest and sincere efforts to sell the property at a favorable price. However, his endeavors have been hindered by the slowness of the construction of the bypass.

Anna, the life tenant and appellee here, is 73 years of age and although now living in a new home, has brought this suit due to her economic distress. She prays that the property, less the house site, be sold by a commissioner and that the proceeds be invested to provide her with an adequate income resulting from interest on the trust investment. She prays also that the sale and investment management be under the direction of the chancery court.

The chancellor granted the relief prayed by Anna under the theory of economic waste. His opinion reflects:

> * * * [T]he change of the economy in this area, the change in farming conditions, the equipment required for farming, and the age of this complainant leaves the real estate where it is to all intents and purposes unproductive when viewed in light of its capacity and that a continuing use under the present conditions would result in economic waste.

The contingent remaindermen by the will, appellants here, were granted an interlocutory appeal to settle the issue of the propriety of the chancellor's decree in divesting the contingency title of the remaindermen by ordering a sale of the property.

The weight of authority reflects a tendency to afford a court of equity the power to order the sale of land in which there are future interests. Simes, Law of Future Interest, section 53 (2d ed. 1966), states:

> By the weight of authority, it is held that a court of equity has the power to order a judicial sale of land affected with a future interest and an investment of the proceeds, where this is necessary for the preservation of all interests in the land. When the power is exercised, the proceeds of the sale are held in a judicially created trust. The beneficiaries of the trust are the persons who held interests in the land, and the beneficial interests are of the same character as the legal interests which they formally held in the land.

See also Simes and Smith, The Law of Future Interest, § 1941 (2d ed. 1956).

This Court has long recognized that chancery courts do have jurisdiction to order the sale of land for the prevention of waste. Kelly v. Neville, 136 Miss. 429, 101 So. 565 (1924). In Riley v. Norfleet, 167

Miss. 420, 436–437, 148 So. 777, 781 (1933), Justice Cook, speaking for the Court and citing *Kelly*, supra, stated:

> * * * The power of a court of equity on a plenary bill, with adversary interest properly represented, to sell contingent remainders in land, under some circumstances, though the contingent remaindermen are not then ascertained or in being, as, for instance, to preserve the estate from complete or partial destruction, is well established.

While Mississippi and most jurisdictions recognize the inherent power of a court of equity to direct a judicial sale of land which is subject to a future interest, nevertheless the scope of this power has not been clearly defined. It is difficult to determine the facts and circumstances which will merit such a sale.

It is apparent that there must be "necessity" before the chancery court can order a judicial sale. It is also beyond cavil that the power should be exercised with caution and only when the need is evident. Lambdin v. Lambdin, 209 Miss. 672, 48 So.2d 341 (1950). These cases, *Kelly*, *Riley* and *Lambdin*, supra, are all illustrative of situations where the freehold estate was deteriorating and the income therefrom was insufficient to pay taxes and maintain the property. In each of these this Court approved a judicial sale to preserve and maintain the estate. The appellants argue, therefore, that since Oakland Farm is not deteriorating and since there is sufficient income from rental to pay taxes, a judicial sale by direction of the court was not proper.

The unusual circumstances of this case persuade us to the contrary. We are of the opinion that deterioration and waste of the property is not the exclusive and ultimate test to be used in determining whether a sale of land affected by future interest is proper, but also that consideration should be given to the question of whether a sale is necessary for the best interest of all the parties, that is, the life tenant and the contingent remaindermen. This "necessary for the best interest of all parties" rule is gleaned from Rogers, Removal of Future Interest Encumbrances—Sale of the Fee Simple Estate, 17 Vanderbilt L.Rev. 1437 (1964); Simes, Law of Future Interest, supra; Simes and Smith, The Law of Future Interest, § 1941 (1956); and appears to have the necessary flexibility to meet the requirements of unusual and unique situations which demand in justice an equitable solution.

Our decision to reverse the chancellor and remand the case for his further consideration is couched in our belief that the best interest of all the parties would not be served by a judicial sale of the entirety of the property at this time. While true that such a sale would provide immediate relief to the life tenant who is worthy of this aid in equity, admitted by the remaindermen, it would nevertheless under the circumstances before us cause great financial loss to the remaindermen.

We therefore reverse and remand this cause to the chancery court, which shall have continuing jurisdiction thereof, for determination upon motion of the life tenant, if she so desires, for relief by way of sale of a part of the burdened land sufficient to provide for her reasonable needs from interest derived from the investment of the proceeds. The sale, however, is to be made only in the event the parties cannot unite to hypothecate the land for sufficient funds for the life tenant's reasonable needs. By affording the options above we do not mean to suggest that other remedies suitable to the parties which will provide economic relief to the aging life tenant are not open to them if approved by the chancellor. It is our opinion, shared by the chancellor and acknowledged by the appellants, that the facts suggest an equitable remedy. However, it is our further opinion that this equity does not warrant the remedy of sale of all of the property since this would unjustly impinge upon the vested rights of the remaindermen.

Reversed and remanded.

RODGERS, P.J., and JONES, INZER, and ROBERTSON, JJ., concur.

Note

"In approximately one-half of the states there are statutes which under specified conditions authorize the court to order a sale of the complete ownership of the land for reinvestment. Moynihan, Introduction to the Law of Real Property 61 (1962). See also Rest., Prop. § 179, Note; Cunningham § 4.10.

SECTION 2.   MARITAL ESTATES

Certain legal life estates arise by operation of law as opposed to creation by deed or will. These are derivative interests of husband and wife and are now for the most part defined by statute, although the precise character of the particular marital estate is often determined or affected by its common law counterpart.[1]

A.   HUSBAND'S INTEREST IN WIFE'S REALTY

The legal position of the married woman was, at common law, a lowly one, and it was not until the nineteenth century that significant changes in status took place. The lowly position is reflected in the relationship of the parties with respect to land owned by a married woman. If a man married a woman who was seised of an estate of freehold in land, or if, during coverture the wife acquired such an estate, he became entitled to the use of the land (i.e., the occupancy and profits), for the time of the marriage. Since the English law had not until comparatively recently recognized absolute divorce, except by special act of Parliament, the husband's right was in effect a right to the land during the joint lives of the spouses. This estate was known as *jure uxoris*, and since its duration was measured by human life, it is classed with the life estates. It was a genuine, possessory estate. A husband might convey this interest or encumber it by mortgage or otherwise.

---

1. For a thorough treatment of estates arising from the marriage relationship and their characteristics see 1 A.L.P. §§ 5.1–5.120, pp. 615–911.

It was liable for his debts and could be sold on execution against him. He could, of course, sue for any injury to his interest. The above statements applied, not only to an inheritable freehold owned by the wife, but also to a life estate either for her own, or the life of another. Upon the death of either spouse, or after absolute divorce became possible, upon such divorce, the husband's right terminated, and the wife, if the husband had died, or the wife's heirs, if the wife had died, became entitled to the land, unaffected by any conveyance or encumbrance of it by the husband.

If, in addition to the marriage, there was the birth of issue of the marriage, the estate *jure uxoris* merged into another and different estate for the husband—the estate by the curtesy.

"Tenant by the curtesy of England, is where a man marries a woman seised of an estate of inheritance, that is, of lands and tenements in fee simple or fee tail; and has by her issue, born alive, which was capable of inheriting her estate. In this case he shall, on the death of his wife, hold the lands for his life, as tenant by the curtesy of England. * * *." II Blackstone's Commentaries 126.

Notice that this estate is measured by the husband's own life and thus persists beyond the wife's death, whereas the estate *jure uxoris* would terminate at the wife's death.

The husband had, at common law, no curtesy in a reversion or remainder if the present, possessory estate was a freehold. In such instances the wife had neither seisin nor a right to seisin.[2] There was one case where the wife had seisin but where the husband would not have curtesy. This was the result when the wife's seisin was for the benefit of others, as where she was a trustee or a mortgagee. On the other hand, there was one case where the wife did not have seisin but curtesy was allowed. This was the result when the wife owned an equitable estate in fee. Seisin in such a case was, of course, in the holder of the legal estate.

The life estate that is curtesy is a subtraction from the inheritable estate of the wife. Her heirs or devisees, then, assuming that the husband survives her, succeed merely to what she had at her death. This was true whether her estate was in fee simple or fee tail.

The enactment of the Married Women's Laws in the nineteenth century removed a married woman's disability of coverture and permitted her to dispose of her property during marriage. This had the effect of abrogating any right of the husband to manage or dispose of his wife's land, and thus effectively destroyed the estate *jure uxoris*. In some jurisdictions this was also held, by implication, to have abolished the estate of curtesy altogether. In other states it left the estate to take ef-

---

2. In the early history of the English land law, when the distinction between ownership and possession had not fully matured, "seisin" meant possession under a claim of a freehold (one of the fee estates or a life estate). It was not said that a man owned land in fee simple, but that he was seised in fee simple. To explore all the consequences of seisin or disseisin would require elaborate explanation. It may be noted here merely that if one held a future estate, he was not seised so long as his estate remained nonpossessory.

fect in land held by a wife at her death, but without claim to any land she might have conveyed in her lifetime.   In still other states a husband is recognized as having an inchoate interest in his wife's land during her lifetime, which she cannot defeat by her sole act.   In the last category, the husband's interest in this respect is similar to the wife's dower interest in her husband's land.

B.   WIFE'S INTEREST IN HUSBAND'S REALTY

Unlike the husband who under the common law has an "estate" in his wife's freeholds, either for their joint lives, *"jure uxoris,"* or for his own life, "by the curtesy of England," the wife has no "estate" in her husband's lands during his lifetime.   She may, however, have an "interest" therein.   This is "dower," which during the husband's life-time is commonly referred to as "inchoate dower."   Upon death of the husband, assuming the essential elements were present for inchoate dower, she is entitled under the common law to a life estate in one-third of his lands in which her inchoate dower then existed, such third to be set off to her by the heirs or by appropriate court proceedings.   Until such assignment her interest is not a possessory one; she has no conveyable interest, except by way of release, and it is not subject to claims of her creditors.

We must now notice the elements necessary for the existence of such interest.   First, only an actual wife of the deceased at the time of his decease can have dower.   A woman who has been completely divorced, as distinguished from a divorce "a mensa et thoro," is not entitled to dower.   By the common law, as said by Mr. Justice Brandeis, "dower is not barred even by misconduct during marriage."   But an early English statute declared that "if a wife willingly leave her husband and go away, and continue with her advouterer," she should lose her dower unless her husband should take her back.   This statute is, of course, early enough to be a possible part of the common law of our states.   Comparable legislation, in varying terms, is not uncommon in the United States.

As to what lands the wife's dower applies, Blackstone says:

"We are next to inquire, of what may a wife be endowed?   And she is now by law entitled to be endowed of all lands and tenements, of which her husband was seised in fee simple or fee tail, at any time during the coverture; and of which issue, which she might have had, might by possibility have been heir.   *   *   *   A seisin in law of the husband will be as effectual as a seisin in deed, in order to render the wife dowable; for it is not in the wife's power to bring the husband's title to an actual seisin, as it is in the husband's power to do with regard to the wife's lands: which is one reason why he shall not be tenant by the curtesy, but of such lands whereof the wife, or he himself in her right, was actually seized in deed.   *   *   *"

When, for the purposes of dower, may it be said that the husband was "seised"?

In an interesting New Jersey case a widow whose husband was at one time the sole stockholder in a corporation which owned land, claimed dower in that land. The corporation was formed before the marriage and there was nothing indicating a purpose to defraud the wife. In an opinion by Vanderbilt, C.J., it was concluded that the claim should be denied; he said that on the facts it could not be said that the deceased husband, "or another to his use was seized of an estate of inheritance at any time during coverture" as required for dower by the statute.[3]

It seems clear that the widow of one who has inherited an estate in fee is entitled to dower though he never actually entered upon the land.[4] In other words, a seisin in law, as distinguished from a seisin in fact, suffices.

The owner of a remainder or reversion subject to an outstanding possessory freehold estate cannot properly be said to be seised, nor is he entitled to possession until the termination of the preceding estate, hence such estates are not subject to dower at the common law. Here, too, however, legislation has effected changes in many states. Until repealed by the Probate Code, the Ohio statute, for example, provided as follows:

"A widow or widower who has not relinquished [relinquished] or been barred of it, shall be endowed of an estate for life in one-third of all the real property of which the deceased consort was seized as an estate of inheritance at any time during the marriage, in one-third of all the real property of which the deceased consort, at decease, held the fee simple in reversion or remainder, and in one-third of all the title or interest that the deceased consort had at decease, in any real property held by article, bond, or other evidence of claim."[5]

By statute, dower has occasionally been allowed in terms of years. For example, in Missouri "dower in leasehold estate for a term of twenty years or more shall be granted and assigned as in real estate,"[6] and in Massachusetts, "If land is demised for the term of one hundred years or more, the term shall, so long as fifty years thereof remain unexpired, be regarded as an estate in fee simple as to everything concerning the descent and devise thereof * * * the right of dower * * * therein," etc.[7] In Ralston Steel Car Co. v. Ralston,[8] the Ohio court held that the

3. Frank v. Franks, Inc., 9 N.J. 218, 87 A.2d 724, 32 A.L.R.2d 700 (1952).

4. On the death intestate of an owner in fee of land, the ownership instantly vests in his heirs subject to be divested by sale to pay debts of the deceased. In Pfaff v. Heizman, 218 Ark. 201, 235 S.W.2d 551, 23 A.L.R.2d 957 (1951), it was held that on the death of a husband's father the ownership and "seisin" of lands owned by the father passed immediately to the son, the heir, and his wife became entitled to dower despite the fact that the administrator would have power to divest the hus-band's ownership by sale, as necessary to pay the debts of the deceased. In that case the debts were paid out of personalty.

5. Gen.Code, § 8606. The applicable section of the repealing statute is Ohio Rev.Code Ann. § 2103.02.

6. See Orchard v. Wright-Dalton-Bell-Anchor Store Co., 225 Mo. 414, 125 S.W. 486, 20 Ann.Cas. 1072 (1909).

7. Mass.Ann.Laws c. 186, § 1.

8. 112 Ohio St. 306, 147 N.E. 513, 39 A.L.R. 334 (1925).

widow of a lessee under a lease for ninety-nine years, renewable forever, was entitled to dower.

At common law the owner of a freehold equitable estate was not deemed seised. Hence, as said in Mayburry v. Brien,[9] "By the common law, dower does not attach to an equity of redemption. The fee is vested in the mortgagee, and the wife is not dowable of an equitable seisin."

Though technically the wife of a trustee may seem entitled to dower, it will not be allowed, for his seisin is nonbeneficial.

In many states, the matter of dower is covered by statute. Even when the statute appears, in its terms, merely to state the common law, the door is open to construction and equitable estates may be deemed to be subject to dower.

Under 3 & 4 Wm. IV, c. 105, a wife is dowable in equity of all lands in which her husband possessed a beneficial interest at the time of his death. Statutes may limit the dower in equitable estates to those owned by the husband at death.[10]

The question of dower in equitable estates arises most frequently in cases of land purchase contracts, and it is to be noted that a general readiness by the courts to allow dower to the wife of the purchaser when the contract has been fully performed on the part of her husband may not extend to situations in which, at the time of his death, he has not fully performed.

That a widow, under the common law, may have dower (or a husband, curtesy) in inheritable estates of the spouse as against the heirs or devisees of the deceased seems clear. The right to dower (or curtesy) as against those whose rights are not based upon inheritance or devise is in a considerable measure of confusion.

One may, at the outset, set aside those situations in which the estate of the deceased spouse was subject to a collateral limitation, as "to H and his heirs so long as the premises are used for" a designated purpose, or "to H and his heirs, but on condition, however," etc., in short, an effective condition subsequent, with a right of reentry (or power of termination) in case the premises cease to be used for the designated purpose. Here the nonowning spouse's interest or estate is subject to be ended by the same event or act that ends the owner's estate, and it makes no difference whether the terminating event or act occurs before or after the death of the owning spouse.

When the inheritable estate of the husband (or wife, in the case of curtesy) was an estate in fee tail which reverted at his death, because of his death without lineal heirs, the English cases clearly recognize dower (or curtesy) in the surviving spouse. This may have been due, as suggested in the Appendix to the Restatement's discussion of freehold estates, to the fact that over a long period of English history so much land

9.   40 U.S. 21, 15 Pet. 21, 10 L.Ed. 646 (1841).

10.   1 A.L.P. § 5.23.

there was entailed, a condition which has not prevailed in the United States.

The real confusion is found in those situations in which the estate of the first-dying spouse comes to an end before, at, or after such death by reason of the taking effect of an executory limitation or devise over to a third party. If the husband's estate ends during his lifetime upon the happening of a specified event, there is no basis for reviving his estate at his death for the benefit of his widow. If his estate has not ended at his death, there is no reason why his widow should not have dower. There appears to be no case on the question of the effect of the occurrence of the divesting contingency during the period of the widow's estate. A number of cases have arisen in which the divesting contingency occurs at the husband's death. For example, suppose the land has been conveyed "to Husband in fee simple, but if Husband dies without issue him surviving, then to X in fee simple." Now suppose Husband dies without surviving issue. Can the surviving wife claim dower as against X, whose executory interest takes effect immediately? If we think about dower as a derivative estate (coming out of the husband's estate) then it would seem that if the husband's estate is divested at his death, no estate is left in which dower can be claimed. This is the position of Section 54 of the Restatement of Property. But it appears that most of the cases in England and this country hold that dower is preserved in such situations.[11] The basis for such decisions is not clear. It may be the similarity between these circumstances and the case of a husband who has a fee tail and dies without leaving issue. See 1 A.L.P. § 5.60.

In addition to the effect of divorce, dower may be barred by antenuptial or postnuptial contracts between husband and wife respecting each other's property rights, provided such agreements are fair and supported by adequate consideration. A husband may make a testamentary disposition to his wife in lieu of dower, which means that she is put to an election either to claim dower or to take under the will. In many states she is put to such an election by a testamentary provision in her favor which is not expressly made in lieu of dower. See 1 A.L.P. §§ 5.39, 5.40.

Problem

In 1958, the Massachusetts legislature considered Senate Bill 388,[12] which contained this provision: "A husband shall upon the death of his wife hold for his life one third of all land owned by her at the time of her death. Such estate shall be known as his tenancy by curtesy, and the law relative to dower shall be applicable to curtesy. A wife shall, upon the death of her husband, hold her dower at common law in land owned by him at the time of his death. Such estate shall be known as her tenancy by dower. Any encumbrances on land at the time of the owner's death shall have precedence over curtesy or dower. To be entitled to such curtesy or dower the surviving husband or wife shall file his or her election and claim therefor in the registry of probate within six months

---

11. 1 A.L.P. § 5.29.

12. This section is now to be found in Mass.Ann.Laws, c. 189, § 1. Ed.

after the date of the approval of the bond of the executor or administrator of the deceased, and shall thereupon hold instead of the interest in real property given in section one of chapter one hundred and ninety, curtesy or dower, respectively, otherwise such estate shall be held to be waived. Such curtesy and dower may be assigned by the probate court in the same manner as dower is now assigned, and the tenant by curtesy or dower shall be entitled to the possession and profits of one undivided third of the real estate of the deceased from her or his death until the assignment of curtesy or dower and to all remedies therefor which the heirs of the deceased have in the residue of the estate. Except as preserved herein dower and curtesy are abolished."

What changes would this statute make concerning dower and curtesy? Could it be retroactively applied? See Opinion of the Justices, 337 Mass. 786, 151 N.E.2d 475 (1958).

C. MODERN MODIFICATION OF MARITAL ESTATES AND MARITAL PROPERTY

In a society where land was the major form of wealth, and where the marital unity was defined in terms of the husband's dominance, the concepts of dower and curtesy are understandable. The widow's dower interest would in many cases provide adequate maintenance during her lifetime. But today large portions of wealth are likely to be in stocks, bonds and other assets, and the notion of husband's dominance is rapidly being replaced with a notion of equality within the marital union. As a result there have been many statutory modifications of the law, and if one seeks to determine the rights of either spouse in the property owned by the other during the marriage or at the death of the first to die, or in property jointly or separately acquired, he will necessarily examine these modifications. A detailed consideration of all these changes is beyond the scope of a first-year course, but it seems useful to sketch the outlines of the major changes. For convenience, we look first at the changes which have occurred with respect to rights at the death of the first to die, and then at rights which may be adjudicated while both spouses are alive. The latter controversy most commonly arises when the marital union is being broken by divorce.

At common law, the wife was not an "heir" of her husband. That is, she did not share in the property owned by the husband who died intestate, except for her dower interest. If all the husband's wealth was in forms other than land, dower was, of course, no help. As early as late 17th century, England provided that the wife shared in the intestate succession to personal property. And in this country one major change has been in the statute of descent and distribution. Today the surviving spouse (husband or wife) is declared to be an "heir" who is entitled to share in the intestate distribution of both real and personal property. Moreover, this intestate share comes to the surviving spouse as absolute ownership rather than as a life estate. In making this change, some states have taken occasion simultaneously to abolish the estates of dower and curtesy. If that is not done so that both dower and an intestate share are available in a given state, the surviving widow may be required to elect which she will take.

Dower, if it is more than a name for a wife's intestate share, gave some protection against disinheritance by will. But if dower is abolished, then even though she is an "heir" the possibility existed that the wife could be disinherited by will. Even if dower persisted, the decline in the relative importance of land as wealth made it possible to bring about virtual disinheritance by will. This possibility moved legislators to take another step which would provide protection. These statutes provide that if a spouse is omitted from a decedent's will, the spouse is given the right to claim a share (usually a third) of the decedent's estate. If the decedent's will makes some provision for the testator's spouse, the spouse may elect to "take against the will"—i.e., renounce whatever is given by the will and take the intestate share which would have been received had there been no will. So we say that a surviving spouse is a "forced heir" of the decedent. In a few states where dower and/or curtesy persist, the surviving spouse may have an election among three alternatives: to take under the will; to take the intestate share; or to take dower or curtesy.

The above-described statutes were the first generation of dower substitutes. They left open two undesirable possibilities. On one side the use of certain "will substitutes" could still deplete the estate and render the "forced heirship" valueless. For example, the husband could put assets into life insurance policies payable to third parties, or could create joint tenancies between himself and a third person. On the other side, the surviving spouse who had been well provided for by inter vivos arrangements could nevertheless elect her prescribed share of the probate estate, and thus get excessive recognition. A new statutory generation is developing as a result of the Uniform Probate Code, promulgated by the Conference of Commissioners on Uniform Laws, now adopted (sometimes with local modifications) in some fourteen states and pending in many more. This Code goes further in adjusting property rights on the occasion of the death of one spouse, and attacks both of these concerns. It does so through Sections 2–201 and 2–202 which create the concept of the "augmented estate" and provide that a surviving spouse has a right to an elective share of one-third of the value of the augmented estate. The basic idea of the "augmented" estate is not complicated. In part it is just an extension of the "forced heir" concept. The surviving spouse should not be disinherited and should receive a "fair share" of the estate. But for this purpose the "estate" is to include not only the usual property (i.e., property owned by the decedent at death and thus subject to probate) but also the value of property which the decedent has disposed of during his lifetime (and during the marriage) in a way that is really a substitute for a will. This would include the value of revocable trusts, gratuitous transfers to children, transfers from the decedent to himself and another as joint tenants, transfers over which the decedent held a power of appointment, and so on. Of course the value of property transferred to purchasers for value would not be included in the augmented estate, nor would any transfer in which the surviving spouse had joined or to which such survivor had consented in writing. By thus "augmenting" the estate, the law assures the surviving spouse of the "fair share" of all the property which has passed through the marriage union, and prevents disinheritance by means of will substitutes.

There is also a provision, however, which precludes "over recognition," by virtue of which the "fair share" must include property which the surviving spouse owns which has been derived from the decedent during the marriage. For example, if the decedent had, during the marriage, placed substantial assets in a trust for the sole benefit of the surviving spouse the value of this trust property, though not in the probate estate, should be included in the total computation and its entire value would count against the one third elective share which the statute gives the surviving spouse.

It should be noted that the surviving spouse may take the elective share without taking against the will. If the will gives less than she is entitled to under the statute, she takes that provided in the will and also the balance due. The will is otherwise fully operative.

Despite the uncomplicated nature of the idea, the statutory provisions which are required to implement it are complex (Section 2–202 covers two printed pages), and it is probable that not all states which can be expected to adopt the Uniform Probate Code will include this idea. The comment to this section of the Code does suggest some of the consequences which would follow if the "augmented estate" concept is accepted:

> "Depending on the circumstances it is obvious that this section will operate in the long run to decrease substantially the number of elections. This is because the statute will encourage and provide a legal base for counseling of testators against schemes to disinherit the spouse, and because the spouse can no longer elect in cases where substantial provision is made by joint tenancy, life insurance, lifetime gifts, living trusts set up by the decedent, and the other numerous nonprobate arrangements by which wealth is today transferred. On the other hand the section should provide realistic protection against disinheritance of the spouse in the rare case where decedent tries to achieve that purpose by depleting his probate estate."

When we turn to the changes applicable to marital property rights while the parties are still alive, we find recent developments which seem of considerable significance. These are changes which have occurred as a result of statutes which are ostensibly related only to divorce law, but which, as interpreted and applied, produce varying species of "marital property" which do not fit comfortably under any common law title, and whose characteristics are not necessarily presently predictable.

We have seen that the wife's dower interest, during marriage, was regarded as "inchoate" and did not rise to the dignity of an estate or "property". One would normally suppose in a common law state, that if a husband inherited Blackacre from his father, and title was in his name, the wife's only interest during his lifetime would be inchoate dower. And if dower were abolished (as it often is) it would be thought that she has no present "property interest" in Blackacre other than a possible assurance of some right at death which could not be blocked by a will. Or, if the wife inherited a $10,000 diamond ring from her mother, one would scarcely think of the husband having any property interest in it, or any part of its ownership. But consider these developments.

We may take as an example the New Jersey statute which, following an amendment in 1971,[13] provides in part as follows:

"In all actions where a judgment of divorce   *   *   *   is entered the court may make such award or awards to the parties, in addition to alimony and maintenance, to effectuate an equitable distribution of the property, both real and personal, which was legally and beneficially acquired by them or either of them during the marriage."

In dealing with this statute, the New Jersey Supreme Court has declared:

"The statutory provision for equitable distribution of property is merely the recognition that each spouse contributes something to the establishment of the marital estate even though one or the other may actually acquire the particular property. Therefore, when the parties become divorced, each spouse should receive his or her fair share of what has been accumulated during the marriage. The concept of fault is not relevant to such distribution since all that is being effected is the allocation to each party of what really belongs to him or her." [14]

This sounds very much as though the form in which "title" or "ownership" of property is taken or recorded by either party is quite immaterial in deciding the "right" thereto when the parties are divorced. It sounds also as though the marital assets somehow "belong" to both parties while they are married, which may mean that there is some form of present interest which, at the time of divorce, will be recognized in the property settlement. Later cases confirm this suspicion. The operation of the statute, in New Jersey, requires that the trial judge engage in a 3-step process:

" *   *   *   he must first decide what specific property of each spouse is eligible for distribution. Secondly, he must determine its value for purposes of such distribution. Thirdly, he must decide how such allocation can most equitably be made." [15]

The New Jersey court has already decided that although the statute by its terms excludes property which was separately owned by either spouse at the time of the marriage [16] any property acquired by either party between the date of the marriage and the date the divorce action is begun is eligible for inclusion in the "equitable distribution." [17]

---

13. N.J.S.A. 2A:34–23, as amended by L.1971, c. 212.

14. Chalmers v. Chalmers, 65 N.J. 186, 320 A.2d 478 (1974).

15. Rothman v. Rothman, 65 N.J. 219, 320 A.2d 496 (1974).

16. Painter v. Painter, 65 N.J. 196, 320 A.2d 484 (1974). Not all states which have equitable distribution statutes reach this result.

17. Painter v. Painter, supra, n. 16.

Specifically, it has held that property acquired during the marriage by gift, devise or inheritance is to be included in the calculation.[18] And, it has held that property acquired by a husband after he had separated from his wife because of her admitted adultery was to be included (up to the time the divorce action was begun).[19] Moreover, the fact that one party's "fault" was the basis of the divorce action does not preclude that party from entitlement to an "equitable" division.[20] One should not suppose, however, that the court has decided upon any fixed share as in the inheritance cases. The court has expressly refrained [21] from requiring that the distributing judge start from an assumption that a "half and half" distribution is the starting point of equity. It is thus not like the community property concept. (See infra at page 330.) Instead, it concedes that each case is to be decided on its own facts, with reference to such criteria as: (1) respective age, background and earning ability of the parties; (2) duration of the marriage; (3) the standard of living of the parties during the marriage; (4) what money or property each brought into the marriage; (5) the present income of the parties; (6) the property acquired during the marriage by either or both parties; (7) the source of acquisition; (8) the current value and income producing capacity of the property; (9) the debts and liabilities of the parties to the marriage; (10) the present mental and physical health of the parties; (11) the probability of continuing present employment at present earnings or better in the future; (12) effect of distribution of assets on the ability to pay alimony and support, and (13) gifts from one spouse to the other during marriage.[22]

The New Jersey statute has survived a barrage of constitutional attacks,[23] and the public policy is described by the New Jersey

18. Id. This result is not followed in all states having similar statutes.

19. Chalmers v. Chalmers, supra n. 14.

20. Id.

21. Rothman v. Rothman, supra n. 15.

22. Painter v. Painter, supra n. 36. Compare § 307 of the Uniform Marriage and Divorce Act, 60 A.B.A.J. 446, 451 (Apr. 1974).

23. It does not violate the constitutional requirement that the purpose of the act be expressed in the title Chalmers v. Chalmers, supra, n. 14. The standard which requires "equitable distribution" is sufficiently precise to escape a charge of being "vague." Painter v. Painter, supra, n. 22. Nor is it unconstitutionally vague merely because it fails to describe with precision the property which is to be included in the distribution. Id. The statute does apply to marriages and to separate estates which were created prior to its passage, Scalingi v. Scalingi, 65 N.J. 180, 320 A.2d 475 (1974). But this fact does not mean that it is operating retroactively. It operates only at the time of the divorce decree rendered after the act, and that is a prospective operation. Rothman v. Rothman,

supra, n. 15. And merely because the "equitable distribution" may result in having property owned in the name of one spouse assigned to the other spouse does not mean that there is any deprivation of property without due process or any denial of equal protection. Id. All property is held subject to reasonable exercise of the police power of the state, and the management of divorce is a legitimate area for its exercise. Id.

The New Jersey court has drawn a distinction between statutes which operate directly to affect property interests and this statute which only authorizes an equitable distribution. Thus, it has held that a statute which purports to change a dower interest from one-third to one-half would be constitutionally invalid if applied to pre-existing inchoate dower interests. Gerhardt v. Sullivan, 107 N.J.Eq. 374, 152 A. 663 (Ch. 1930).

It has held that a statute which would under some circumstances permit partition of land held as tenants by the entireties could not constitutionally be applied to such estates created prior to its enactment. Mueller v. Mueller, 95 N.J.Super. 244, 230 A.2d 534 (1967). To do so would destroy

court [24] as follows: "The public policy sought to be served is at least twofold. Hitherto future financial support for a divorced wife has been available only by grant of alimony. Such support has always been inherently precarious. It ceases upon the death of the former husband and will cease or falter upon his experiencing financial misfortune disabling him from continuing his regular payments. This may result in serious misfortune to the wife and in some cases will compel her to become a public charge. An allocation of property to the wife at the time of the divorce is at least some protection against such an eventuality. In the second place the enactment seeks to right what many have felt to be a grave wrong. It gives recognition to the essential supportive role played by the wife in the home, acknowledging that as homemaker, wife and mother she should clearly be entitled to a share of family assets accumulated during the marriage. Thus the division of property upon divorce is responsive to the concept that marriage is a shared enterprise, a joint undertaking, that in many ways it is akin to a partnership. Only if it is clearly understood that far more than economic factors are involved, will the resulting distribution be equitable within the true intent and meaning of the statute."

With many variations as to the property which is included, as to the criteria for "equitable distribution," and as to the role of "fault" by one party, well over half the states have experienced the same developments as those in New Jersey. These holdings present an interesting comparison with the law in the eight "community property" states, which is briefly noted infra, p. 330. In those states it is clear that property owned by each spouse at the time of marriage is "separate." It is clear that property received by one spouse by gift, devise, or inheritance is "separate" property. And it is clear that as to the "community property" each spouse owns one-half rather than any sliding scale. Current litigation frequently raises questions about non-vested pension rights of a spouse. Do they constitute marital property which is subject to equitable division upon divorce? An affirmative answer is given in a well-written opinion in Kalinoski v. Kalinoski, Pa.Ct. Common Pleas, printed in 9 Family Law Reporter 3033 (1983).

A third statutory generation which will move the common law states closer to the community property concept [25] may be anticipated. The Conference of Commissioners on Uniform Laws has approved (in 1983) and promulgated a Uniform Marital Property Act (UMPA). This Act is designed to move further toward making legal reality out of the common perception that economic sharing should be the "property" mode for the marital union. It fills a gap left by the Probate Code and by the "equitable distribution" provisions of divorce laws. Those acts protect the "non-owning" spouse only upon dissolution or if the "owning" spouse is the first to die. UMPA operates to create present shared property rights *during* the marriage, and thus make economic divisions

---

the right of survivorship. Yet it would appear that in making an "equitable distribution", the court may do what it will with property held by the entirety and destroy the right of survivorship.

24. Rothman v. Rothman, supra, n. 15.

25. The community property system is given brief consideration post at the end of Section 3 (Concurrent Estates).

at death or dissolution more predictable and less a product of adversary process. The clear trend of social change toward recognition of equality of contributions by both spouses makes it likely that the Act will receive prompt and favorable attention by state legislatures. The Act carefully separates questions of management from ownership, and provides fully for the protection of purchasers. Recent publications on the matter include: Donahue, What Causes Fundamental Legal Ideas? Marital Property in England and France in the Thirteenth Century, 78 Mich.L.Rev. (1979); Younger, Marital Regimes: A Story of Compromise and Demoralization, Together with Criticism and Suggestions for Reform, 67 Cornell L.Rev. 45 (1981); Cheadle, The Development of Sharing Principles in Common Law Marital Property States, 28 U.C.L.A.L. Rev. 1269 (1982); Fellows, Simon & Rau, Public Attitudes About Distribution at Death and Intestate Succession Laws in the United States, 1978 American Bar Foundation Research J. 319; Gregory, Marital Property in Illinois: The Complexities Wrought by the Presumption of Gift, Transmutation and Commingling, 1982 So.Ill.U.L.J. No. 2 159 (1982). And see Stokes v. Stokes, 271 Ark. 300, 613 S.W.2d 372 (1981), noted in 4 U.Ark. Little Rock L.J. 361 (1981). The case struck down a number of Arkansas statutes which had applied to widows, on the ground that they constituted impermissible gender-based discrimination.

D. HOMESTEAD RIGHTS

The right of homestead, sometimes established by a state constitution and sometimes by statute, is intended to protect certain property from the claims of various creditors and from alienation by the owner without the consent of his or her spouse. The purpose is to assure a home for the family both during the lifetime of the owner and for the lifetime of the surviving spouse.

The laws creating a right of homestead vary greatly. There are, however, a number of common factors. It is usually required that the owner have a family. A typical statute provides that a homestead shall consist of a dwelling and the land upon which it is situated. In respect to the exemption of a homestead from creditors' claims, homestead rights are usually limited to a stated value or area or both.

Upon the death of an owner, the homestead interest continues in a surviving spouse for his or her lifetime. In some states such protection is afforded to minor children during their minority. A spouse's interest may not be defeated by the decedent's will, although in some states the spouse may be put to an election between claiming the homestead or taking under the will. Subject to these rights, homestead property passes by will or descent like other property.

SECTION 3. CONCURRENT ESTATES

The term "concurrent estates" suggests a division of ownership of a very different sort from the division into present and future estates. The term in fact suggests that, whatever may be divided, the right to possession is to be enjoyed concurrently. Although the idea of concurrent ownership is difficult to define, the notion is easy to understand without definition, for it is very common in ordinary human experience. Two or more persons own land together. Their rights are equal in quality and are usually equal in quantity. Our main problem in dealing with these estates is that there are several kinds of concurrent ownership.

A. COMMON LAW CONCURRENT ESTATES

The common law recognized a "joint tenancy," a "tenancy by the entirety," and a "tenancy in common". We must understand the differences between them. Another group of problems arises from the very fact that the owners' rights to possession are concurrent. How does one owner enjoy his rights without invading the rights of his co-owner or co-owners? These are the problems involved in fixing the rights and duties of the parties *inter se*.

Joint Tenancy

To A and B, not as tenants in common, but as joint tenants with right of survivorship

At common law, a conveyance to two or more persons was presumed to create a joint tenancy. The principal characteristic of a joint tenancy is the right of survivorship. Upon the death of one of two or more joint tenants, the number of co-owners is reduced by one, the ownership of the survivors being increased proportionately. The last survivor, of course, ceases to be a concurrent owner, for he has the whole. He will own in fee simple absolute unless the joint tenancy was created with a limited duration, such as for life or in defeasible fee simple.

By a traditional dogma, it was held that a joint tenancy depends upon "four unities": the unities of time, title, interest, and possession. Unity of time means the interests of the joint tenants must arise at the same time. Unity of title is present only if the interests are acquired by the same instrument. Unity of interest means that the tenants acquired identical interests, that is, in fee simple absolute or otherwise. Unity of possession means a common right of possession and enjoyment. Lack of any of the unities in a conveyance resulted in the creation of a tenancy in common. In most situations the four-fold requirement has little practical significance; and courts today are tending to discount the significance or necessity of these technical ingredients. One important remnant of the old dogma is the rule that if one joint tenant conveys his interest to a third party, the latter acquires an interest as tenant in common with the remaining joint tenant or tenants, who, if more than one, continue as joint tenants among themselves. Such a conveyance is said to "sever" the joint tenancy by removing the unities of time and title. The important consequence of a severance is that the right of survivorship is destroyed between the old tenant or tenants and the new. There is some uncertainty about other acts which may be held to work a severance. For example, there are decisions that if one joint tenant mortgages his interest or enters into a binding contract to sell it (thereby creating a specifically enforceable right in the buyer and making him the equitable owner of the seller's interest), the joint tenancy is severed. It has been argued, however, that severance should not be automatic when one joint tenant mortgages his interest, and that there are alternative ways to protect the expectations of all parties. Mattis, Severance of Joint Tenancies by Mortgages: A Contextual Approach, 1977 So.Ill.U.L.J. 27. A recent Illinois decision has held that a joint tenant can unilaterally sever the joint tenancy by conveying her interest to herself as a tenant in common. Minonk State Bank, Adm'r v. Grassman, 95 Ill.2d 392, 69 Ill.Dec. 387, 447 N.E.2d 822 (1983). In a recent California case, however, one joint tenant had leased the property for a term of years and died during that term. The court held that the giving of the lease did not sever the joint tenancy, and that accordingly the surviving joint tenant was entitled to have the lease declared invalid. Tenhet v. Boswell, 19 Cal.3d 150, 133 Cal.Rptr. 10, 554 P.2d 330 (1976).

As the rule on severance implies, the interest of any joint tenant is freely alienable inter vivos. Under the rules against restraints on alienation, there is no way to prevent any joint tenant from conveying his interest and severing the joint tenancy. Anyone who desires to create a property arrangement between two or more persons so as to be assured that a right of survivorship will remain intact should keep this point in mind. Creation of a joint tenancy gives no such assurance.

It is equally clear, however, that a joint tenant's interest cannot be devised by will or pass by descent, for the right of survivorship operates immediately on the decedent's death.

The concurrent right to possession of joint tenants means that their possessory rights are "undivided." Each has the right to possess the whole, subject to the same right in his fellows. The undivided interests, however, can be divided, which of course ends the joint tenancy. This is what is called partition, which means a physical division of the land into separately owned parts. Partition may be voluntary, that is, by mutual conveyances. But any joint tenant (or tenant in common) has a right to partition which he can enforce by a judicial proceeding. The result is either a physical division of the land involved, a partition in kind, or a sale of the land and a division of the proceeds.

The right to partition is not absolute, however, and a court may deny partition when it would be inequitable to allow it. See Greco v. Greco, 160 N.J.Super. 98, 388 A.2d 1308 (1978). Moreover, a transferor of land in joint tenancy may use language which purports to restrain partition, and despite the fact that this involves some restraint on alienation, such a provision is generally upheld if it is reasonable and is limited to the period of perpetuities. This is especially important to the unit owners in a condominium development, because the condominium enabling legislation usually prohibits any action by individual unit owners to compel partition of the common elements of the condominium, which are held by the unit owners as tenants in common.

Joint tenancy was the favorite of the common law. A conveyance by deed or will "to A and B" created a joint tenancy. Most states now have statutes which reverse the common-law preference and create a preference for the tenancy in common. Typically the statute will provide that "any grant or devise, other than to executors and trustees, to two or more persons shall create a tenancy in common unless the intention of the grantor to create a joint tenancy and not a tenancy in common is clearly expressed." Under such a statute a conveyance "to A and B" creates a tenancy in common. Courts differ on the language required under the modern statutes to create a joint tenancy. The answers in part reflect differences in the statutes. In some states the statutes in fact purport to abolish joint tenancy. In such states, where the intention to create concurrent interests with right of survivorship is expressed, some courts declare that such an intention should not be frustrated. The result may be a holding that leaves co-tenants with life estates and a future interest in the survivor. In other states the statutes are construed to create a presumption against joint tenancy. Courts differ on the force of the presumption. A court may require merely that the language of a conveyance indicate an intent to create a joint tenancy, by words declaring a right of survivorship or otherwise. A conveyance to two or more persons "jointly" may not be enough. A conveyance to them "as joint tenants" may be. It has actually been held by some courts that an intention not to create a tenancy in common must be expressly stated, in the manner of the example first set out above. That is the safest language to use in any jurisdiction.

The four-unities requirement has had a further troublesome effect. A sole owner cannot convey to himself and another as joint tenants or convey an undivided half interest so as to make himself and his grantee joint tenants. Attempts to do so resulted in tenancies in common. See Note, Creation of Joint Tenancies—Common Law Technicalities v. The Grantor's Intent, 82 W.Va.L.Rev. 335 (1979). Persons desiring to achieve this result utilize a third-party grantee (called a "straw man") who in turn conveys so as to create the desired joint tenancy. Some courts have managed to circumvent the rule by a construction which in effect leaves life estates in the grantees with one or more future interests in the survivor or survivors. Some courts have reached the point of brushing aside the technical relic altogether. Statutes in a number of states are designed to resolve this difficulty. One such statute is as follows:

> "Whenever a grant or conveyance of lands * * * shall be made * * * [declaring] that the estate created be not in tenancy in common but in joint tenancy, the estate so created shall be an estate with right of survivorship notwithstanding the fact that the grantor is * * * a grantee * * * in said instrument of grant * * *." (Ill.Ann.Stat. c. 76, § 1b (Smith-Hurd 1966).

It is generally held that joint tenancies can be created in personal property. One should note, however, the existence of legislation respecting joint bank accounts and joint accounts in savings and loan associations which may control the incidents of such relationships.

The above summary does not sufficiently indicate the variations in the laws of the several states on the requirements and incidents of joint tenancy. In any particular case the statutes and decisions of the state whose law governs the case should be consulted.

Tenancy by the Entirety

To H and W, husband and wife

To H and W, husband and wife, and the survivor

To H and W, husband and wife, as tenants by the entirety

A tenancy by the entirety is a concurrent estate that can exist only between husband and wife. At common law this was the preferred estate for married persons, and any conveyance to husband and wife was presumed to create an estate by the entirety. It was similar to a joint tenancy in having a right of survivorship and the four unities were required. But it was unlike the joint tenancy in that it was not severable. The common law perceived of husband and wife as a unit, with the result that each person was not considered to have an undivided half interest. The wife's disability of coverture of course robbed her of all power over the estate or her interest therein. Because of the nature of the estate, the husband also could not convey or encumber his separate interest, nor subject it to the claims of his creditors. But since the common-law unity of husband and wife implied the predominance of the husband, he had the full powers of management of the property and could convey or encumber the entire estate, and his creditors could levy on it, but subject to the wife's right of survivorship; that is, a grantee's interest would be perfected only if the husband survived the wife.

The enactment of the married women's laws in the nineteenth century abrogated the disability of coverture. In a majority of American states these laws were held to be inconsistent with the conception of the tenancy by the entirety, and the estate was held to be abolished altogether. It has been urged that this result be reexamined in Illinois, the author arguing that the early decisions are not really binding, and that the estate by the entireties represents a desirable alternative mode of land ownership. Note, Tenancy by the Entirety in Illinois: A Reexamination, 1980 So. Ill.U.L.J. 83. In most states in which the estate was held not to have been abolished, the predominance of the husband was abrogated. The result was to establish an equality between the parties, but to preserve the special qualities of the estate, so that it remains nonseverable, and neither husband nor wife can separately convey or encumber any interest in the estate, nor subject it to the claims of creditors. In a few jurisdictions the predominance of the husband and its consequences remain as an ingredient of the estate. This anachronism has produced considerable litigation over its proper extent.

Originally a conveyance to a husband and wife necessarily created a tenancy by the entirety, even if the conveyance expressed an intention to create a joint tenancy or a tenancy in common. Today, where the tenancy by the entirety exists, any of the three concurrent estates can be created in a husband and wife, depending on the expressed intention of the conveyor. The rub comes in determining what language is required or sufficient. Statutes creating a preference for the tenancy in common were held not to apply to tenancies by the entirety, so that a conveyance "to H and W, husband and wife" still creates a tenancy by the entirety. The effect of a conveyance "to H and W, husband and wife, as joint tenants" has been to create a joint tenancy in some states, a tenancy by the entirety in others. Where the language required has not been settled, a conveyor should expressly designate that the estate conveyed is a tenancy by the entirety. See generally, Annotation, 161 A.L.R. 457 (1946).

If a conveyance declares a tenancy by the entirety, but the grantees are not in fact husband and wife, some decisions declare that a joint tenancy results, others a tenancy in common. The latter result may derive from the statutory preference for the tenancy in common, but the former result seems preferable because it is closer to the expressed intention of the conveyor. The same question is presented by the divorce of tenants by the entirety. The estate is converted into either a joint tenancy or a tenancy in common.

At common law a tenancy by the entirety could not be created in personal property because the disability of coverture prevented ownership of chattels by a married woman. After the married women's laws, most of the courts which recognize the tenancy at all extended it to personal property. Some courts, however, have held that personal property can be held only in joint tenancy or tenancy in common. Joint bank deposits in the name of husband and wife present a special problem. It has been held that the nature of such an account, where either is authorized to draw on the account, is inconsistent with the nature of a tenancy by the entirety.

As in the case of joint tenancy, considerable litigation has resulted from attempts by an owner to convey to himself and his wife as tenants by the entirety, or to convey an undivided interest to his wife with the same effect. The four unities are an obstacle which have been held to prevent it except by means of two conveyances through an intermediate grantee (straw man). Some courts have escaped this result. At least one court held that a conveyance by a husband to himself and his wife was a conveyance to a separate entity consisting of husband and wife. See Matter of Klatzel, 216 N.Y. 83, 110 N.E. 181 (1915). Other courts have circumvented the problem by finding that such a conveyance created in effect a tenancy in common for life with a "remainder" in the survivor. See Annotation, 1 A.L.R.2d 242 (1948). Statutes permitting an owner to convey to himself and another as joint tenants leave at least a doubt about whether they were intended to apply to tenancies by the entirety. There are decisions that they do not apply. Later statutes or later amendments to older statutes have been more carefully framed to produce the desired result. A recent Florida decision, reversing earlier law, validated a conveyance by a sole owner to himself and his wife as tenants by the entirety. Jameson v. Jameson, 387 So.2d 351 (Fla.1980), noted in 33 U.Fla.L.Rev. 289 (1981).

There are even greater variations and divergencies among the states respecting the creation and incidents of the tenancy by the entirety than in the case of joint tenancy. In particular controversies or in drafting instruments, the statutes and decisions of the particular state must be consulted.

Tenancy in Common

To A and B

To A and B as tenants in common

Most of the features of this tenancy have become apparent in the description above of the joint tenancy. There is no right of survivorship in a tenancy in common. The interest of a tenant in common is freely alienable inter vivos, and if not conveyed in his lifetime, passes at his death to his devisees or heirs. Only one of the "four unities" is required, the unity of possession. A tenant in common is the owner of an undivided fractional part of the whole.

Modern statutes create a preference for the tenancy in common, so that unless the intention to create a joint tenancy is properly expressed, a tenancy in common will result. So also, as previously explained, where a conveyance does not meet the four unities for a joint tenancy; and also where a joint tenancy is "severed" by a conveyance by one joint tenant of his interest. When a sole owner dies without devising the property by will, his heirs, if more than one, take as tenants in common. A husband and wife can take as tenants in common if, under the law of the applicable jurisdiction, the intention to create that estate is properly expressed.

The interests of tenants in common, like those of joint tenants, can be partitioned, either voluntarily by appropriate conveyances, or by a judicial proceeding for partition.

Problems

1. Suppose, in a jurisdiction which recognizes both joint tenancies and tenancies by the entirety, a grantor conveys land "to H[1] and W[1], husband and wife; and H[2] and W[2], husband and wife, all as joint tenants with the right of survivorship in all four, and not as tenants in common." What share would W[1] own after these events take place in the order stated:

   a. H[1] and W[1] are divorced.

   b. H[1] conveys his interest to W[2] and H[2], husband and wife.

   c. H[2] dies intestate.

See Nelson v. Hotchkiss, 601 S.W.2d 14 (Mo.1980), noted in 46 Mo.L.Rev. 439 (1981). Cf. Fekkes v. Hughes, 354 Mass. 303, 237 N.E.2d 19 (1968).

2. O, owning Blackacre in fee simple absolute, made a conveyance "to A, B and C in fee simple." Thereafter A conveyed "all my interest in Blackacre to X and his heirs." Thereafter B died, leaving a will in which he devised "all my real property" to Y. Thereafter C conveyed all his interest in Blackacre "to H and W, husband and wife." Thereafter H conveyed "all my interest in Blackacre to Z." Thereafter H died, survived by W.

In what shares, and by whom is Blackacre now owned (a) at common law? (b) under a statute which reversed the common law presumption in favor of joint tenancies?

3. O, owning Blackacre in fee simple absolute, made a conveyance "to A and B as joint tenants and not as tenants in common." Thereafter A entered into a lease of Blackacre to Tenant for a term of four years. What would be the result if A died at the end of two years? What would be the result if A survived until after the four year lease had expired, and then died leaving a will devising his real property to X? See Tenhet v. Boswell, 19 Cal.3d 150, 133 Cal. Rptr. 10, 554 P.2d 330 (1976), noted in 66 Cal.L.Rev. 69 (1978).

MILLER v. RIEGLER

Supreme Court of Arkansas, 1967.
243 Ark. 251, 419 S.W.2d 599.

HARRIS, Chief Justice.[1] Marjorie Miller, appellant herein, and Mary Jane Riegler, appellee, are sisters, and reside in Little Rock. Minnie Wagar, who died in Little Rock, testate, on August 8, 1963, was an aunt of these two sisters. In March, 1957, Mrs. Wagar lived in Long Beach, California. She had been ill, and Mrs. Riegler and her mother went to California and brought Mrs. Wagar back to this city. The latter lived with appellee, paying $100.00 per month for room, and board, until January, 1958, when she went to a nursing home, staying there until her death. A joint checking account was opened with Mrs. Wagar's funds in the names of Minnie M. Wagar and Mary Jane Riegler, and a joint safe deposit box was taken in their names and Mrs. Wagar's property was placed there. On July 23, 1957, Mrs. Wagar, then 81 years of age, executed her last will and testament, and on July 25, she caused several hundred shares of stocks of the approximate value of $45,000.00 (representing about one-half of stocks owned by Mrs. Wagar) to be transferred to the joint names of Mrs. Riegler and herself. The new stock certificates reflected the owners of the stock to be "Mrs. Minnie W. Wagar and Mrs. Mary Jane Riegler, as joint tenants with right of survivorship and not as tenants in common." It was agreed that the aunt would receive the dividends for the balance of her life. Subsequently, the dividends from these stocks were placed in the joint checking account, and these dividends were reported on the Federal Income Tax returns of Mrs. Wagar. As previously stated, Mrs. Wagar departed this life in August, 1963, and her will was duly admitted to probate in Pulaski County. Mrs. Riegler, the executrix of the estate, recognized that the money in the joint checking account was a part of the estate, but she claimed absolute ownership of the stock as the survivor of the joint tenancy. Thereupon, Mrs. Miller instituted suit, asserting that the stocks that were still held in the joint names at date of Mrs. Wagar's death actually belonged solely to the deceased (and accordingly were a part of her estate), and should be administered as such. Appellant asked for judgment for one-half of the stocks and one-half of the value of any that had been converted. Mrs. Riegler answered, denying that the transfer of the stock was for the convenience of Mrs. Wagar, asserted that it was a gift to Mrs. Riegler, and that Mrs. Miller accordingly had no interest. On trial, the Pulaski Chancery Court (1st Division) held:

1. The court's footnotes are omitted. Ed.

"That all of the stock certificates involved in this suit (including all stock certificates sold by Mary Jane Riegler prior to the institution of this suit and all stock certificates held by Mary Jane Riegler at the commencement of this suit which had been reissued in her name individually) were originally issued in the name of the testatrix and Mary Jane Riegler as joint tenants with right of survivorship and not as tenants in common, and all of said stocks are the sole property in fee simple absolute of Mary Jane Riegler, individually, and all dividends received from this stock are the sole property in fee simple absolute of Mary Jane Riegler, individually."

From the decree so entered, appellant brings this appeal. For reversal, it is asserted that the stocks involved in this case, which were held in the joint names of Minnie M. Wagar and Mary Jane Riegler at the time of the death of Mrs. Wagar, were the property of Minnie M. Wagar, and the 1957 transfer of the stocks into the joint names of Minnie M. Wagar and Mary Jane Riegler did not constitute or create a true joint tenancy or gift, or otherwise vest any ownership rights in Mrs. Riegler.

It is first argued that the circumstances surrounding the transfer of the stocks clearly show that there was no intention by the aunt of making a gift to her niece. It is pointed out that, though reissued in the joint names of the two women, the stocks were returned to a joint safe deposit box (which had been acquired in their names on May 27, 1957), and that all other property in the box belonged to Mrs. Wagar. It is likewise pointed out that all of the dividends from all stocks including those held jointly, and those simply in Mrs. Wagar's name, were placed in the joint bank account at the Worthen Bank. Further, it is mentioned that the dividends from the joint stocks were reported solely on the federal income tax return of the aunt. Mrs. Wagar also received a $65.00 per month pension, which was placed in the joint bank account. No separate monies or funds of Mrs. Riegler were deposited in this account and all checks written on it were solely for the debts or expenditures of Mrs. Wagar. The checks were all written by appellee, with the exception of five or six of $100.00 each, which were given to Mrs. Riegler, and signed by Mrs. Wagar in payment of room and board. These facts are all argued by appellant as evidence that Mrs. Wagar had no intention, in creating the joint tenancy, of giving an interest in the transferred stock to Mrs. Riegler, but only made the transfer for the purpose of convenience, i.e., to enable Mrs. Riegler to handle financial transactions for the aunt with handiness. Appellant also calls attention to the fact that Mrs. Riegler recognized that funds in the joint bank account (with her aunt) were properly a part of the estate, and such funds were listed as assets. It is also argued that it simply isn't reasonable that Mrs. Wagar would give this amount of stock to a person (Mrs. Riegler) that she had only seen three or four times in her life before moving to Little Rock. Mention is made of the fact that the deceased was apparently very devoted to her brother, and that it was her principal intent, as evidenced by her will, that he be taken care of the rest of his life; that the will provided that, upon his death, the two daughters should take the residue of the estate. We see little, if any, significance to the fact that Mrs. Wagar held a high regard for her brother, as expressed in her will. The proof reflects that Mr. Miller had an income of over $200.00 per month, was older than Mrs. Wagar, and certainly the income, or even the principal, if needed, of the remaining $45,000.00 worth of stock (still held by Mrs. Wagar) would have been considered adequate to take care of his needs. For that matter, however affectionately Mrs. Wagar might have felt toward her brother, she had made no provision for him until the will of July, 1957, was executed. At any rate, appellant's arguments, heretofore quoted, are all based on surmise and speculation. It is sometimes difficult to ascertain people's motives, but it is generally true, even with relatives, that a decedent feels closer to, or likes, one relative more than another. Here, one fact instantly stands out, viz., that Mrs. Wagar lived with Mrs. Riegler for nearly a year, and at the time of making the stock transfer, evidently planned to live with appellee for the balance of her life, this plan being altered because of illness suffered by the aunt following a fall in November of 1957. Not only that, but the very fact that the aunt would pick Mrs. Riegler to handle her business for her (which is not disputed) indicates that she had more confidence in, or closer ties with, appellee than with appellant. Still again, Mrs. Riegler was named Executrix of the Wagar estate, as well as Trustee. Of course, if the transfer was only made for convenience, one immediately wonders why all stocks were not transferred, instead of only half.

Be that as it may, litigation cannot be decided on surmise, or what someone else might have done under similar circumstances. It can only be decided on the evidence presented in court. The testimony heavily preponderates to the effect that the transfer was made at a time when Mrs. Wagar was fully possessed of all her faculties, and understood exactly what was being done. Only three people testified, Mrs. Riegler, Mrs. Miller, and Warren Bass, a certified public accountant of Little Rock, who handled tax matters for Mrs. Wagar.

Mrs. Miller testified that it was her "understanding" from a conversation with her sister that the latter was going to take care of the aunt's affairs, and the transfer of stock had been made for convenience only; she also stated that her sister said that, though part of the estate was in her (appellee's) name, everything would be divided "50–50." Mrs. Riegler denied making these statements, and said that she had informed Mrs. Miller that everything *in the estate* would be divided "50–50."

The strongest evidence introduced was that of Mr. Bass, who testified as follows: Mrs. Wagar was a small lady, quite bright, alert, knowledgeable, and very interesting to talk to. She knew the property she owned, and planned a transfer of stock along with executing the will. She stated that she intended to make her home with Mrs. Riegler the rest of her life; she also said that there were two people she cared for, one being Mrs. Riegler, and the other being the brother.

The witness made a list of the stocks which were to be transferred, such list being offered as an exhibit at the trial. He discussed the matter with Mrs. Wagar several times. Bass was very emphatic in stating that Mrs. Wager knew exactly what she was doing, and that it was her intention to transfer the $45,000.00 worth of stock to Mrs. Riegler as a joint tenant. We think it was clearly established that the aunt, of her own free will and accord, made the transfer with full knowledge that the stocks transferred would not be a part of her estate, and the survivor of the joint tenancy created would take the full amount.

It is next contended that the requisites of a joint tenancy were not met, and accordingly, the gift must fail. It is first pointed out that there is no statutory provision here involved, such as those which cover savings and loan associations and banks; that accordingly, when a joint tenancy is created, the four "unities" must exist. These are set out in the case of Stewart v. Tucker, 208 Ark. 612, 188 S.W.2d 125, and are listed, in a quote from 33 C.J. 907, as follows:

"(1) Unity of interest. (2) Unity of title. (3) Unity of time. (4) Unity of possession. That is, each of the owners must have one and the same interest, conveyed by the same act or instrument to vest at one and the same time * * * and each must have the entire possession of every parcel of the property held in joint tenancy as well as of the whole."

Let it first be said that we have already, to some degree, departed from the rule of the four unities. In Ebrite v. Brookhyser, 219 Ark. 676, 244 S.W.2d 625, 44 A.L.R.2d 587, George Brookhyser conveyed real property, which he owned, from himself to his wife and himself as tenants by the entirety. The trial court held that an estate by the entirety had been created, and Ebrite appealed to this court. There too, Stewart v. Tucker, supra, was principally relied upon, and it was contended that essential requirements to create the estate had not been complied with, the wife's undivided half interest not having been acquired at the same time as the interest retained by her husband; that the husband could not convey to himself, and therefore could have acquired no new title by virtue of his own deed. In upholding the trial court, we stated that there was no reason why parties should not be able to do directly that which they could undoubtedly do indirectly through the device of a strawman. The late Justice J.S. Holt, writing for this court stated:

"We cannot agree with this reasoning. A complete answer is given in what is now the leading case of In re Klatzl's Estate, 216 N.Y. 83, 110 N.E. 181, 185. There a majority of the judges, Bartlett, Collin, Hiscock, and Cardozo, agreed that under modern married women's property acts a husband may create a tenancy by the entirety by a conveyance to himself and his wife. The same argument as to the unity of time was presented there as here, but Judge Collin answered: 'The husband did not convey to himself but to a legal unity or entity which was the consolidation of himself and another.'"

This decision certainly has not been viewed as unsound for there can be no logic in preventing a spouse from directly giving to his or her marriage partner equal rights in property that is owned, when the same result was permitted by creating the estate through a third party who really held no interest in the property at all.

Likewise, it also appears that the same view is being widely followed with reference to joint tenancy. The landmark case is probably that of Colson v. Baker, et al., 42 Misc. 407, 87 N.Y.S. 238. The issue was stated in the opening line of the opinion, as follows:

"The question to be determined on this motion is whether a person seised in fee of an estate can, by a direct grant, deed the property to another and himself in joint tenancy, instead of tenancy in common, without the intervention of a third party."

A part of the logic used by the court is interesting. It is pointed out that the unity of time refers to joint parties becoming joint tenants at the same time. As stated:

" * * * When, therefore, he attempts to create for himself and his grantee an estate in joint tenancy out of his fee by a direct deed to the grantee, why does not the joint tenancy arise at the same time and by the same act? I think it does. Of course, each joint tenant has the same interest by such a deed, and each is in possession of the whole like tenants in common.

"In all references to the 'four unities' requisite to create a joint tenancy, I find nothing that prevents their existence or creation by the act of the grantor for himself and another as well as by his act for two other persons."

In the case of Kleemann v. Sheridan, 75 Ariz. 311, 256 P.2d 553, there is a succinct discussion of the issue with which we are here concerned. There, the question was whether a joint tenancy in personal property had been created by two sisters who, in leasing a safe deposit box, recited in writing that all property theretofore or thereafter placed in the box was the joint property of both and would pass to the survivor. The Arizona Supreme Court discussed the history of joint tenancy, saying:

"Before entering upon a discussion of the points raised by appellant it will perhaps be pertinent to briefly recount the common-law essentials to create a joint tenancy. They are unity of time, unity of title, unity of interest, unity of possession. Such tenancy could not arise by descent or other operation of the law but may arise by grant, devise or contract. Of course the right of survivorship is inherent in the joint tenancy estate and without which joint tenancy does not exist. At first joint tenancy under the common law involved only interest in land but at an early date it was recognized as applying to personal property as well. At common law a person could not make a conveyance to himself. An attempt to convey land to himself and to another resulted in a conveyance of only one-half of the property to the other and the grantor still held his moiety under his original title, thus destroying two essentials of joint tenancy, unity of time and of title. The result of such attempt was to create a tenancy in common.

"The same rule would seem to logically apply to personal property and is the rule of law relating to both real and personal property in many of the states of the Union including Maine, Illinois, Wisconsin and Nebraska but the majority of the state courts have held that common-law concept of the four unity essentials should give way to the intention of the parties and that a joint tenancy may be created by a conveyance from one to himself and another as joint tenants. California has passed a law making the rule applicable to husband and wife.

"We have apparently aligned ourselves with the majority rule insofar as personal property, the title to which passes by delivery, is concerned. * * *

"Another characteristic of joint tenancy is that it is not testamentary but 'is a present estate in which both joint tenants are seized in the case of real estate, and possession in case of personal property, per my et per tout,' that is, such joint tenant is seized by the half as well as by the whole. The right of survivorship in a joint tenancy therefore does not pass anything from the deceased to the surviving joint tenant. Inasmuch as both cotenants in a joint tenancy are possessors and owners per tout, i.e., of the whole, the title of the first joint tenant who dies merely terminates and the survivor continues to possess and own the whole of the estate as before."

The court, mentioning that it was holding in line with the majority rule, and that it was the intention of the sisters to create a joint tenancy, held that that estate had been created. Numerous other cases also hold that the intention of the parties is controlling, rather than the common law concept of the four unities.

Here, we think the intention of Mrs. Wagar is established, i.e., to create a joint tenancy, and we can see no more reason to hold to the old premise that the four unities must exist, than the jurisdictions (and numerous others) just quoted, particularly when we have already, as earlier pointed out, to some extent discarded that concept of the law.

However, appellant also relies upon the fact that Mrs. Wagar and Mrs. Riegler agreed that Mrs. Wagar was to retain—and did retain— the dividends from the stocks jointly transferred. This, says appellant, is fatal to the creation of a joint tenancy for the reason that the two parties did not have equal rights to share in the enjoyment of the property during their lifetime. In connection with this argument, it is also urged that the retaining of the dividends from the transferred stock prevents the transfer from acquiring the status of a gift. We do not agree with these arguments. Joint tenants may agree between (or among) themselves as to the use to be made of the property. In 48 C.J.S. under Joint Tenancy § 10, page 933, we find:

"Joint tenants may contract with each other concerning the use of the common property, as for the exclusive use of the property by one of them, or the division of the income from the property."

In Tindall, et al. v. Yeats, et al., 392 Ill. 502, 64 N.E.2d 903, the question was whether a Mrs. Adams and Mrs. Yeats were joint tenants or tenants in common. The trial court held that they were joint tenants, and this holding was appealed to the Supreme Court. One of the points argued by appellant was that Mrs. Yeats had agreed that Mrs. Adams should have all rents from the land, as well as the possession thereof during the life of Mrs. Adams, and this, said appellant, prevented the estate from being one of joint tenancy. The Illinois Supreme Court disagreed, holding that it was clear that it was the intention of the parties that Mrs. Adams should enjoy the possession of the entire estate; that this was done with the permission and consent of Mrs. Yeats, and that the parties had the right to make this agreement. And why should this not be permissible? Why should owners of property, real or personal, be prohibited from doing as they desire with that property, so long as the disposition is not for an immoral purpose, or against public policy?

Nor do we agree with appellant's argument with reference to the invalidity of the gift. Appellant states in her reply brief:

"We submit it cannot be that there is any difference in the presumptions applicable to or the basic rules essential to the creation of a gift, whether in the form of outright ownership, joint tenancy, or otherwise, except such as might be inherent in the nature of the particular estate created. * * * If there is a retention of a right to income or principal, or both, inconsistent with the estate ostensibly donated, so that it is not made 'beyond recall,' then we submit it is incomplete and ineffectual as between the parties. * * * And, as pointed out in our brief in main, to permit a joint tenancy with retention of all income is nothing more than a void testamentary arrangement."

This stock was given to Mrs. Riegler, and placed in the lock box. We have shown, in the citations mentioned, that the joint tenancy was not affected, even though Mrs. Riegler was not to share in the dividends. We here point out that, in the creation of the joint tenancy, Mrs. Riegler did not first become possessed of her interest or rights in the property when Mrs. Wagar died; rather, she acquired a *present* interest when the estate was created, i.e., her rights as a joint tenant had already vested before her aunt's death. This fact, of course, silences the argument that a joint tenancy with retention of income is nothing but a void testamentary arrangement.

Affirmed.

HOLBROOK v. HOLBROOK

Supreme Court of Oregon, 1965.
240 Or. 567, 403 P.2d 12.

O'CONNELL, Justice.[2] Plaintiff seeks a declaratory decree declaring her to be the sole owner of a certain parcel of land. Defendant appeals from a decree for plaintiff.

Plaintiff, Bertha Clyde Holbrook, was the wife of William H. Holbrook. In contemplation of divorce they entered into a property settlement agreement which made provision for the disposition of the land in question which, at the time of the agreement, was owned by William and Bertha. The agreement provided in part that "the parties shall be and become joint tenants with right of survivorship in the property." The agreement contained the following paragraphs:

2. Footnotes of the court have been omitted. Ed.

"It is further agreed that the said joint tenancy shall be accomplished by the parties executing a deed to their entire present estates in said property to Eleanor L. Anderson with instructions that she convey the same to the parties herein as joint tenants and not as tenants in common or as tenants by the entirety, but with right of survivorship between them, which right of survivorship shall continue without regard to whether or not a divorce shall be granted to one or the other of the parties.

"It is further understood and agreed that during the lifetime of the husband, he shall be entitled to have and receive all rents, issues and profits of the property above described in this paragraph with the duty to maintain the same and to pay all lawful taxes, liens and other charges and assessments on the same which shall accrue during his lifetime.

"At anytime during his lifetime the husband shall have the right to make a bonafide sale of the property at a reasonable price to any third person or party, and in event of such sale the wife shall join with him in such conveyance and shall be entitled to receive as her own property, one-half of the net principal and interests, if any, to be received from such sale."

On October 22, 1958, William and Bertha executed a quitclaim deed to Eleanor L. Anderson and two months thereafter, William and Bertha were divorced. The following January, Eleanor L. Anderson quitclaimed to William and Bertha, describing them, "as joint tenants with right of survivorship and not as tenants in common." Subsequently, on January 8, 1963, William conveyed to his nephew James W. Holbrook, an undivided one-half interest in the land in question. William died on November 3, 1963.

It is defendant's position that the deed from Eleanor Anderson to William H. Holbrook and Bertha Clyde Holbrook created a common law joint tenancy which was subject to severance. It is contended that the deed from William Holbrook to defendant, James W. Holbrook, effected a severance as a consequence of which James Holbrook and Bertha Holbrook held as tenants in common.

If, as defendant contends, the estate held by William and Bertha was a common law joint tenancy, then, of course, William's conveyance to James would convert the joint estate into a tenancy in common. But we have held that ORS 93.180 abolishes the common law joint tenancy in this state. Halleck v. Halleck et al., 216 Or. 23, 337 P.2d 330 (1959). In the Halleck case we recognized that a right of survivorship can be created in co-grantees but that unlike the concurrent interest of joint tenants, the interest created by a conveyance to co-grantees with a right of survivorship could not be destroyed by severance.

We see no essential difference between the language in the deed from Eleanor Anderson to William and Bertha Holbrook and the language in the deed construed in the Halleck case. Since we regard the Halleck case as controlling, it follows that William and Bertha were not vested with a joint tenancy as the same was known at common law and that there was, therefore, no power of severance in either of them.

As in Halleck (216 Or. at 40, 337 P.2d 330) we read the language, "as joint tenants with right of survivorship and not as tenants in common," as creating concurrent estates for life with contingent remainders in the life tenants, the remainder to vest in the survivor. The effect of that language in a conveyance creates the equivalent of a common law joint tenancy except for the power of severance.

It is argued that the bulk revision of the Oregon Statutes in 1953 had the effect of removing from the statutes the prohibition against the creation of a common law joint tenancy. In the 1953 revision the statutes relating to the creation of joint tenancies were brought together into one section, but the revised section retained the language "joint tenancy is abolished." It is apparent that this revision was in form only and was not intended to change the substantive statute law. This was our assumption in deciding the Halleck case.

There seems to be no reason for forbidding the creation of the common law form of joint tenancy. However, the legislature has seen fit to abolish it and we have found no way to read out of the statute (ORS 93.180) the express declaration that "joint tenancy is abolished." It would appear that there is need for legislation on the subject.

The decree of the trial court is affirmed.

Notes

1. The Oregon statute which was involved reads as follows: "Every conveyance or devise of lands, or interest therein, made to two or more persons, other than executors and trustees, creates a tenancy in common unless it is expressly declared in the conveyance or devise that the grantees or devisees take the land as joint tenants. Joint tenancy is abolished and all persons having an undivided interest in real property are deemed and considered tenants in common." Ore.Rev.Stat. § 93.180 (1973). Would you consider the statute a model of clarity? And does this help explain the court's decision?

2. A Michigan statute provides: "All grants and devises of lands, made to two (2) or more persons, except as provided in the following section, shall be construed to create estates in common, and not in joint tenancy, unless expressly declared to be in joint tenancy." M.C.L.A. § 554.44.

Suppose, under such statute, there is a conveyance "To A and B *as joint tenants with the right of survivorship.*" The normal judicial response might be that the italicized words were merely the expression of intention to create a joint tenancy which is required to rebut the statutory presumption in favor of a tenancy in common. The Michigan court has reached a different result. It seems to hold that the words "as joint tenants" would by themselves be enough to rebut the statutory presumption. The court then felt it must give some added meaning to the words "with the right of survivorship." This it did by holding that the estate created by such a conveyance, unlike the common law joint tenancy, could not be severed by means of an inter vivos conveyance by one of the cotenants. The "right of survivorship" is thus not destructible by one cotenant, and the grantee of one conveying cotenant does not become a tenant in common with the other non-conveying cotenants. The practical result is much the same as that reached in Oregon. See annotations to the above statute.

Note on Rights and Duties Inter Se

Where two or more persons have "undivided" ownership interests in the same land at the same time, it is obvious that problems will arise and decisions will have to be made about their rights and duties between or among themselves. We may note immediately that if the parties cannot agree on management, use or possession, the law provides any cotenant the remedy of partition. They can, as noted above, change common ownership of the whole into separate ownership of separate parts by voluntary conveyance, or, by court order if partition in kind is possible. Or, if partition is by sale, they can get the value of their separate shares from the sale proceeds. We may note also that the notion of concurrent rights carries with it the idea that no cotenant is entitled to make unilateral decisions which adversely affect his cotenants nor to try to make unilateral decisions which impose obligations upon his cotenants. The problems which most frequently give rise to controversy are those which involve (1) the right of one cotenant to occupy the whole property or, conversely, his obligation to account for the value of his possession or profits derived from that possession; (2) the right of one cotenant to compel contribution for repairs which he alone has paid for; (3) the obligation of each cotenant to pay taxes, or to make mortgage payments to prevent loss of the property, and the right of one cotenant to compel contribution if he alone makes such payments; (4) the rights of one cotenant who makes improvements on his own initiative; and (5) the right of one cotenant to acquire a superior title to that of a cotenancy without being under a duty to hold that superior title for the benefit of his cotenants.

With respect to the first problem, each cotenant (tenant in common or joint tenant) clearly has a right to possession, use and enjoyment of the whole property so long as he does not exclude his cotenants. It logically follows that he owes his cotenants nothing merely because he exercises that right. Moreover, it would seem to follow that he might lease the property and receive rent without accounting to his cotenants. Apparently this was the view of the common law prior to the English Statute of Anne in 1705. The statute provides for an accounting to other cotenants by one who receives more than his share of rents received from third persons. The statute was construed so as not to require him to account for the rental value of his use of the land, nor for profits derived from his own use. In a number of states, the Statute of Anne is considered as part of the common law. In others similar statutes have been enacted. In a minority of states, these statutes have been construed to require a cotenant to account for all profits, whatever the source.

With respect to the second problem, it is generally held that a cotenant in possession has no right to contribution for the cost of repairs, although if he is compelled to account for rents and profits, credit will be given for the costs of repairs. Credit will also be given in a final accounting in an action of partition.

It is generally held that a cotenant who pays taxes on the property can compel contribution, since it can be said that he is not acting as a volunteer but on behalf of all cotenants to save the property. It is not so clear that he has any right of contribution when he has made mortgage payments on mortgages upon which his cotenants had no personal liability, though he may get relief in connection with a judgment in partition.

It is quite clear that if one cotenant makes improvements without an agreement that costs will be shared, he cannot compel contribution from his cotenants. He may, however, get some reimbursement if he is later called upon to account for rents and profits and he can show that some of such rents or profits are attributable to his improvements. So, also, if the land is later partitioned in kind, the court may reward the improver by allocating the improved part of the premises to him. If partition is by sale, the improver may be entitled to credit if his improvements increased the sale value.

The cases which follow are concerned with some of these problems and with the fiduciary obligation between cotenants.

For a discussion of all these problems, see 2 A.L.P. §§ 6.13–6.18, and for an excellent summary of the general rules relating to taxes, repairs and improvements, and the apportionment thereof as among cotenants, see Burby, Real Property 228 (3d Ed.1965).

GIVENS v. GIVENS

Court of Appeals of Kentucky, 1965.
387 S.W.2d 851.

CLAY, Commissioner. This is a suit for a declaration of rights, the principal objective of which was to have declared void a long term coal lease appellee obtained from his mother. The Chancellor adjudged the lease valid. Appellants contend this was error, and in the alternative contend that the lease, if valid, should inure to their benefit.

In 1948 W.M. Givens deeded the real estate involved to his wife, Willa Givens, and the deed provided in part:

"To have and to hold to her in during her natural life, then the lands of whatever the parties have not transferred shall belong to the heirs of the party of the second part * * *."

The grantor had in 1937 conveyed the same property to his wife under somewhat similar terms, but the parties claim their rights under the last deed from which we have quoted. The grantee life tenant, Willa Givens, is dead and the appellants and appellee are her heirs and now own as cotenants the fee in the property.

The parties agree that Willa Givens had a life estate with a power to encroach upon the corpus. Nine days before her death she executed a coal mining lease to appellee, her son. This lease had a term of 40 years.

Appellants' first contention is that a life tenant has no authority to execute a lease for a term longer than her lifetime. This is the accepted general rule. 31 C.J.S. Estates § 54, p. 115; Pikeville Oil & Tire Company v. Deavors, Ky., 320 S.W.2d 782, 785. It is also recognized that a life tenant can make no oil and gas lease. Summers Oil and Gas, Permanent Edition, Vol. 2, section 223 (page 70); Union Gas & Oil Co. v. Wiedemann Oil Co., 211 Ky. 361, 277 S.W. 323; Rowe v. Bird, Ky., 304 S.W.2d 775. Since the reason for the rule is that this would permit the life tenant to deplete or waste the estate of the remaindermen, the same principle would apply to a coal lease. This seems to be recognized by KRS 353.300, which provides for the appointment of a trustee to execute an oil, gas, coal or other mineral lease where present and future interests are involved.

It is the position of the appellee that the right of the life tenant to encroach upon the corpus authorized her to execute a long term mineral lease. The argument is that if the life tenant could convey the property, she could lease it. There is merit in this argument. The only authority we have been able to discover on the point is Holland v. Bogardus-Hill Drug Co., 314 Mo. 214, 284 S.W. 121. Therein the court upheld a lease of business property which extended beyond the lifetime of the life tenant who had a power of disposition. Even though the lease in the present case is of a different kind and will result in the depletion of the estate of the remaindermen, it seems that the life tenant's power to encroach (which is admitted) would authorize her to transfer in this manner an interest in the devised property. We so decide. It may be observed that the remaindermen will benefit from this lease.

Appellee relied upon a judgment in another case involving leases executed by both the grantor and the life tenant, in which suit appellants and appellee were parties. We do not think the matter is res adjudicata because the judgment did not decide the question we have here or involve the same lease. However, the result is the same on this phase of the case.

The next question is whether this lease inures to the benefit of appellee's cotenants. It is clear that after the death of the life tenant, when the remainder estates matured into a fee simple and the coremaindermen had become cotenants, appellee could not have acquired an outstanding interest against the property for his exclusive benefit. The accepted principle is thus stated in 54 A.L.R. 874, at page 875:

"Tenants in common and joint tenants are said to stand in confidential relations to each other in respect to their interests in the common property and the common title under which they hold; and the courts generally assert that it would be inequitable to permit one, without the consent of the others, to buy in an outstanding adversary claim to the common estate and assert it for his exclusive benefit to the injury or prejudice of his coowners; and, if one cotenant actually does acquire such claim, he is regarded as holding it in trust for the benefit of all his cotenants, in proportion to their respective interests in the common property, who seasonably contribute their share of his necessary expenditures; the courts will not, ordinarily, permit one cotenant to acquire and set up for his exclusive benefit any claim adverse to the common rights; at least, where all the cotenants derive title from a common ancestor by descent, or from a common grantor by a single conveyance."

See also Thompson on Real Property (1961), section 1801, page 136, specifying the fiduciary duties of cotenants.

That rule is not specifically applicable here because appellee acquired his interest *prior* to the time the cotenancy relationship came into being. As a general rule the fiduciary duties of joint tenants or tenants in common [3] are coextensive with the cotenancy. Sneed's Heirs

---

3. A distinction is recognized between "joint tenants" and "tenants in common" for some purposes, but the fiduciary duties are the same. See 48 C.J.S. Joint Tenancy § 11, p. 933; 86 C.J.S. Tenancy in Common § 17, p. 376; Thompson on Real Property (1961), section 1801 (page 136). [This footnote is the court's. Ed.]

v. Atherton, 6 Dana 276, 32 Am.Dec. 70; Ford v. Jellico Grocery Co., 194 Ky. 552, 240 S.W. 65, 54 A.L.R. 884.

As we have before noted, at the time appellee acquired this lease from his mother, the life tenant, she had a power of disposition of the corpus of the property. At that time appellants and appellee were not cotenants (because lacking the right to possession). They were, however, jointly vested with a defeasible remainder. Restatement of the Law, Vol. 2, section 157 (page 54). It could be argued that when the life tenant executed the lease she thereby reduced appellants' remainder interest and they had no right in the benefits which subsequently accrued to appellee by virtue of this lease. (Those benefits consisted of profits accruing from a sublease of the property.)

Our problem is whether a fiduciary relationship exists between *coremaindermen* similar to that existing between *cotenants*. We think it does. Though there is lacking a unity of possession, there is a unity of title created by a single deed vesting equal remainder interests in appellants and appellee. As in the case of joint tenants or tenants in common, public policy dictates that a remainderman shall not impair the title or interests of his coremaindermen. As said in Thompson on Real Property (1961), Vol. 4A, section 2001 (page 525):

"Most cases hold that coremaindermen like cotenants of possessory estates have a fiduciary relationship so that if one acquires an outstanding interest he acquires it for all."

Cases supporting that statement are Clark v. Lindsey, 47 Ohio St. 437, 25 N.E. 422, 9 L.R.A. 740; Harrison v. Harrison, 56 Miss. 174; Wilson v. Linder, 21 Idaho 576, 123 P. 487, 42 L.R.A.,N.S. 242.

There are cases which apparently take a contrary view. Jinkiaway v. Ford, 93 Kan. 797, 145 P. 885, L.R.A.1915E, 343; Crawford v. Meis, 123 Iowa 610, 99 N.W. 186, 66 L.R.A. 154.

This case points up the necessity for recognizing a fiduciary relationship between coremaindermen. Here appellee acquired from the life tenant, nine days before her death, a long term lease which affected the remainder interests of appellants and from which appellee has and will realize substantial benefits. The unity of title as remaindermen and the family relationship make it inequitable for appellee to obtain this advantage, against those who are now his cotenants, by so dealing with the property in which they had, since the execution of the original deed, a common interest. We hold that the benefits of this lease inure to the benefit of appellants as well as to appellee. Of course appellee is entitled to contribution for their rateable share of appellee's expenditures, if any, in the acquisition and exploitation of this lease. 48 C.J.S. Joint Tenancy § 11, p. 933; 98 A.L.R. 865.

The judgment is affirmed in part and reversed in part, with directions to modify the judgment consistent with this opinion.

Problem

In what instance can a cotenant acquire a title superior to that of the cotenancy without being under a duty to hold it for the benefit of his cotenants?

Suppose, for example, the property is subject to a mortgage and that at the sale resulting from foreclosure one of the tenants purchases the entire property? Does he now hold the property for the benefit of his cotenants and if so should he be entitled to contribution from them? See 2 A.L.P. § 6.16, page 67; Annotation, 54 A.L.R. 874 (1928).

GILES v. SHERIDAN

Supreme Court of Nebraska, 1965.
179 Neb. 257, 137 N.W.2d 828.

SPENCER, Justice. This is an equitable action to determine and establish the interests of the parties in Lot 3, Randolph Terrace Third Addition to Lincoln, Lancaster County, Nebraska, on which a duplex is located, and for partition.

The plaintiff is Minnie Giles, who at the time of the acquisition of said property was 83 years of age. The initial defendants were John V. Sheridan and Helen M. Sheridan, husband and wife, who will hereafter be referred to as defendant and Helen. Helen was a niece of plaintiff. The petition was filed May 27, 1963. Helen died February 23, 1964 and was survived by defendant and their three children, Barbara Littlejohn, Sally Sheridan, and James Sheridan, the last two being minors. The deed to the property in question is dated October 31, 1962, and describes as grantees Minnie Giles, a single person, and John V. Sheridan and Helen M. Sheridan, husband and wife, as joint tenants and not as tenants in common. Subsequent to the filing of the action, by a warranty deed dated November 9, 1963, plaintiff conveyed an undivided ¹/₂₀ of her interest in said property, subject to a life estate, to a nephew, Harley Giles.

The case went to trial on the third amended petition, which was filed April 28, 1964, and the cross-petition of the defendant, filed June 4, 1964. Service had been perfected on the minor children of Sheridan, Barbara's spouse and Harley Giles and his spouse, and a guardian ad litem was appointed for the minor defendants. Trial was held July 21, 1964, and a decree was entered March 5, 1965, confirming the shares of the parties and appointing a referee. Defendant has perfected an appeal to this court.

The petition of the plaintiff seeks to establish the interests of the parties on the basis of the contribution made to the purchase price of the property. Plaintiff attempted to prove that Helen came to her home in Hastings in 1961 to induce plaintiff to buy an apartment in Lincoln for joint occupancy and agreed to pay one-half of the costs thereof, and that pursuant to that agreement Helen found the duplex and the plaintiff signed an offer to purchase after looking it over with the Sheridans. This testimony was excluded as a transaction with a deceased, within the provisions of section 25–1202, R.R.S.1943, the dead man's statute.

It is undisputed that the offer to purchase, dated August 25, 1962, which was signed only by the plaintiff, was prepared by the defendant. The purchase price was $33,325. Plaintiff deposited $1,000 with the offer, which was accepted, and agreed to assume a mortgage to the First Federal Savings and Loan Association of Lincoln in the approximate sum of $20,500, and to pay the balance on or before November 1, 1962. The sale was consummated October 31, 1962. Plaintiff paid $12,121.04 at that time to the grantors, and the deed described above was delivered. Plaintiff offered to prove the deed was executed in this manner because Helen demanded that she and her husband be included in the title, but the testimony was excluded. In this connection it is of interest that on examination by his own attorney, defendant testified as follows: "Q Mr. Sheridan, did you ever ask that your name be placed on this deed? A My wife did. Q Did you? A I doubt if I did; I think it was my wife that did." The deed was drawn by a representative of the First Federal Savings and Loan Association of Lincoln, and the evidence is that the defendant told him how it was to be drawn.

The mortgage was paid December 28, 1962. On that date plaintiff gave a check to the First Federal Savings and Loan Association in the amount of $19,003.96, and Helen gave a check in the amount of $686.49. Plaintiff had previously paid $205.50 on the mortgage. On the same day, Helen issued a check to the county treasurer for taxes in the amount of $257.95.

It is defendant's contention that the Sheridans were to pay only $1,000 on the purchase price, and that the plaintiff was to pay the balance. It is his contention that the two items enumerated above constitute a part of the $1,000 they were to pay. There is no other testimony in this record to prove that the Sheridans actually paid $1,000 on the purchase price. Defendant's testimony is contradicted by plaintiff, who insists she always demanded one-half of the purchase price.

The trial court found as follows: "IT IS, THEREFORE ORDERED, CONSIDERED AND ADJUDGED, BY THE COURT, that said shares of each of the parties and their respective interests in said real estate are: 1. Minnie Giles, Plaintiff, Nineteen-twentieths ($^{19}/_{20}$) of a One-third ($^{1}/_{3}$) interest in said property, plus and in addition thereto the sum of $13,135.50 from her co-tenants and the survivor to reimburse said Minnie Giles for her payment of the mortgage on said premises, and said sum shall be and constitute a lien on said cotenants (sic) share; and a life tenancy in the undivided one-sixtieth ($^{1}/_{60}$) interest of Harley Giles therein. 2. Harley Giles, an undivided one-sixtieth ($^{1}/_{60}$) interest therein, subject to the life estate of the plaintiff, Minnie Giles, who on November 9, 1963, was 85 years of age. 3. John V. Sheridan (his own interests and as surviving joint tenant of Helen M. Sheridan) two-thirds ($^{2}/_{3}$) interest in said property, subject to and charged with the payment and reimbursement of the said sum of $13,135.50 to Minnie Giles, advanced and contributed in payment and release of the mortgage lien thereon."

The plaintiff did not file a motion for a new trial or a cross-appeal on the finding of the interests of the parties in said property, so we limit our discussion of that phase except as it is necessary to an understanding of the other questions involved.

Defendant urges that plaintiff's petition is defective because plaintiff did not allege that she was a joint tenant or a tenant in common, or specify the nature of the interests and estates of the defendant. Section 25–2170, R.R.S.1943, provides in part: "The petition must describe the property, and the several interests and estates of the several joint owners, or lessees thereof, if known." There is no merit to the defendant's contention.

The plaintiff pleaded the facts in detail, decribed the monetary interests of the parties therein, alleged in effect a cotenancy by virtue of said facts, set out the fractional interests by a monetary proportion, prayed for a determination that the parties were owners as tenants in common, for a determination of their exact interest, and for a partition.

The nature of the interest and the estate is what the plaintiff sought to have determined in the action as well as for a partition after the determination was made. Where plaintiff pleads the facts which show the interest, she is not required to define the nature of the interest where there may be a question because of contribution, mistake, or otherwise.

Plaintiff had the burden of the proof to establish that the estate described in the deed was other than it purported to be. If the plaintiff had not been prevented by the dead man's statute, the indication is that she would have attempted to prove a joint tenancy between the plaintiff and Helen, with each being required to make an equal contribution. This she could not do because of the statute. Reading the deed in the light of its expressed intent and in the absence of proof to indicate otherwise, we must conclude that the deed created a joint tenancy with the three grantees as joint tenants. As such they were seized of the entire estate for the purpose of tenure and survivorship, but only of an undivided interest for the purpose of conveyance.

In Hoover v. Haller, 146 Neb. 697, 21 N.W.2d 450, we held: "Where a conveyance of property is made to two or more persons, and the instrument is silent as to the interest which each is to take, the rebuttable presumption is that their interests are equal."

When plaintiff on November 9, 1963, conveyed a portion of her intertest to Harley Giles, she terminated the joint tenancy as to her, and converted her interest and that of her grantee to a tenancy in common.

In DeForge v. Patrick, 162 Neb. 568, 76 N.W.2d 733, we said: "An estate in joint tenancy can be destroyed by an act of one joint tenant which is inconsistent with joint tenancy and such act has the effect of destroying the right of survivorship incidental to it.

"Any act of a joint tenant which destroys one or more of its necessarily coexistent unities operates as a severance of the joint tenancy and extinguishes the right of survivorship."

This, however, raises a question as to the nature of the interest of the other two joint tenants, Helen and defendant. If one of two joint tenants disposes of his interest by conveyance inter vivos, the other joint tenant and the grantee become tenants in common, while, if one of three or more joint tenants conveys his interest to a third person, the latter then becomes a tenant in common, instead of a joint tenant, with the others, though such others remain joint tenants as between themselves. 2 Tiffany, Real Property (3d ed.), s. 425, p. 209, note 67, and cases cited therein. See, also, 4 Thompson on Real Property (Perm.Ed.), Joint Tenancy, s. 1780, p. 317; 20 Am.Jur.2d, Cotenancy and Joint Ownership, s. 16, p. 109.

With relation to the payment of the encumbrance on the property, a different question arises. The evidence is undisputed that plaintiff paid off the mortgage with a slight assist from Helen which defendant contends was to be applied on the $1,000 they were to pay on the purchase price. We note that the deed under which the defendant is claiming has the following provision: " * * * subject to the unpaid balance of an existing mortgage to FIRST FEDERAL SAVINGS AND LOAN ASSOCIATION OF LINCOLN, which the grantees assume and agree to pay." The deed would indicate, therefore, that the mortgage is a joint obligation of all of the grantees and if defendant seeks to avoid the effect of this language he of course would have the burden to prove an agreement otherwise.

In Carson v. Broady, 56 Neb. 648, 77 N.W. 80, 71 Am.St.Rep. 691, we said: "In the case of Brown v. Homan, 1 Neb. 448, it was held that the purchase by a tenant in common of an outstanding title to, or incumbrance on, the joint estate, would inure to the common benefit, and entitle the purchaser to contribution. And this is believed to be the universal rule."

In Oliver v. Lansing, 57 Neb. 352, 77 N.W. 802, we held: "As between themselves, co-tenants are liable for the payment of liens and incumbrances existing against the common estate, in proportion to their respective interests therein, each being surety for the others."

In Exchange Elevator Co. v. Marshall, 147 Neb. 48, 22 N.W.2d 403, we held: "A joint or joint and several debtor who has been compelled to pay more than his share of the common debt has the right of contribution from each of his codebtors."

The deed which created the joint tenancy specifically provided that the grantees assumed and agree to pay the mortgage. By its terms, therefore the parties were equally liable for the discharge of the obligation. Defendant has not met his burden to prove that the mortgage was otherwise than the joint obligation of the parties. We hold that a joint tenant who pays off an encumbrance on the property, under such circumstances, does so for the common benefit of the joint tenants and is entitled to contribution.

For the reasons given, we hold that the judgment of the trial court was correct and should be and is affirmed.

Affirmed.

SEBOLD v. SEBOLD [4]

United States Court of Appeals, 1971.
143 U.S.App.D.C. 406, 444 F.2d 864.

MacKINNON, Circuit Judge. The issues here revolve around the effect of a divorce in Maryland upon the title to District of Columbia real estate held by the parties during their marriage as tenants by the entirety. We remand the case for additional hearing and disposition in accordance with the principles hereafter set forth.

I

For a year and one half prior to her marriage, appellant worked as a waitress and turned over her earnings to her husband (appellee) and she continued to do so after their marriage in 1938 until 1943 when she became pregnant with her second child and ceased working. Thereafter, until about 1947, they usually kept a roomer in the house. During the early years of their marriage the couple purchased a residence in the District of Columbia which they sold in 1950 to move to a newly purchased home in Maryland. The purchase price of the Maryland property was partially financed out of the proceeds of the sale of their prior home and the title was placed in the names of the husband and wife as tenants by the entirety. In connection with the sale of the District property the parties took back a second deed of trust and appellant endorsed the note over to appellee, who deposited it in the bank for collection to the credit of his account.

From 1950 through 1960, the parties acquired four other pieces of property in the District of Columbia (the District properties) as follows:

May 16, 1950	425 New Jersey Avenue, S.E.
March 23, 1955	114–11th Street, S.E.
May 13, 1960	431–7th Street, S.E.
March 6, 1961	1208 C Street, N.E.

The title of each of these District properties was placed in the names of the parties hereto, as tenants by the entirety, and they were used primarily for income-producing purposes. A fifth District property acquired by appellee in 1955 at 910–12th Street, S.E. for $2,150 was placed in his name alone.

In 1964, the parties separated and in 1965 a consent order was entered in the Circuit Court for Montgomery County, Maryland, providing that appellee would pay appellant $300 per month separate maintenance, would make "house payments" (of principal and interest) on the Maryland property as they became due, would pay for the taxes, insurance, heat, gas, water and electricity on that property and would provide certain other benefits for appellant. The District properties were not referred to in the order of the Maryland court.

---

4. Most footnotes of the court have been omitted. Those retained have been renumbered. Ed.

In 1967 appellee filed a Bill of Complaint in Maryland for an absolute divorce and appellant responded with a Cross Bill. On September 13, 1967 the Maryland court dismissed appellee's complaint and awarded appellant a divorce *a vinculo matrimoni* on her Cross Bill on the grounds of constructive desertion. The decree of divorce incorporated that part of the consent order mentioned above with reference to alimony and other benefits but, again, the District properties were not mentioned.

In March of 1968, appellee commenced the instant action in the United States District Court for the District of Columbia seeking to have title to the four District properties placed in his name. Appellant counterclaimed for an accounting of the monies which appellee had received from the rental of the District properties from and after the date of the entry of the Maryland divorce decree.

The District Court after trial without a jury, awarded appellee title to all of the District properties save the one located at 425 New Jersey Avenue, S.E. In its findings of fact and conclusions of law, which were announced orally in court, it was found that appellant had contributed her earnings to appellee during the early years of their marriage and that, during the period in which they had rented rooms in their initial house, the income so received was placed in a joint fund. The court also found that the appellant made various non-monetary contributions to the household, chiefly through her efforts in maintaining the home and bringing up the children. Dealing with the case on "the theory that the parties own five properties altogether" (the Maryland house and the four income properties in the District) and holding that the appellant should be entitled to "more than just one of the five pieces of property," the court awarded appellee title in fee simple absolute to all the District properties except that on New Jersey Avenue, title to which it left without any declaration as to its status. On appellant's counterclaim, the court awarded her an accounting of the rents received from the District properties since the date of the entry of the decree of absolute divorce, but allowed appellee an offset for the payments he had made on their Maryland home pursuant to the divorce decree.

From this decision and order appellant appeals and raises nine issues which we consolidate into three principal questions:

(1) Did the District Court have jurisdiction to make the award that it did?

(2) What was the effect of the entry of the decree of divorce in Maryland on the title to the District properties?

(3) Was it proper for the District Court to divide the District properties without first determining the shares to which the parties were entitled or, in any event, to award appellant less than one-half of those properties?

[Appellant's jurisdictional challenge was rejected.]

*   *   *

IV

We next come to consider the effect on the title to the District properties of the divorce in Maryland. These properties were held by the parties while married as tenants by the entirety and the entry of the divorce decree could have affected the state of the title to those properties in one of two ways: It could be held that (1) the tenancy by the entirety was simply dissolved and final disposition of title had to await further action by a court, or that (2) the tenancy by the entirety was dissolved and the parties immediately became tenants in common.[5]

Dissolution of the tenancy by the entirety in either case was accomplished through the operation of D.C.Code § 16–910 (1967).[6] That section, as construed by this court, has two parts, the first of which is the only one of importance in the instant case. In Scholl v. Scholl, 80 U.S. App.D.C. 292, 152 F.2d 672 (1945), we said that the first part of § 16–910, which provides for the dissolution of a tenancy by the entirety upon the entry of a final decree of absolute divorce, was substantive law regarding the effect of a divorce on a tenancy by the entirety. In Heath v. Heath, 89 U.S.App.D.C. 68, 189 F.2d 697 (1951), we held that a property settlement agreement which related to real property in the District of Columbia would be effective under § 16–910 even though it was a foreign decree of divorce that was involved. And logic dictates that the section be held to be triggered by foreign divorces when no settlement agreement is in effect covering property in the District, a situation such as the one at hand.

Although § 16–910, as so construed, dictates that a tenancy by the entirety is dissolved upon entry of a divorce decree, it does not expressly state what happens next. There is some indication in the cases that title is simply dissolved and hangs in limbo until a court decides what shall then happen to it.[7] If possible, such result should be avoided for it necessarily would have an undesirable effect on the stability and certainty with which title to real property should be clothed.

---

5. Counsel for the parties here agree that upon entry of the divorce decree in Maryland, appellant and appellee become tenants in common of the District properties. Tr. 18, 179. Since this is a question of law, however, the agreement of counsel is not binding on this court. Case v. Los Angeles Lumber Products Co., 308 U.S. 106, 114, 60 S.Ct. 1, 84 L.Ed. 110 (1939); Gunn v. United States, 283 F.2d 358, 364 (8th Cir.1960).

6. Upon the entry of a final decree of annulment or absolute divorce, in the absence of a valid antenuptial or postnuptial agreement in relation thereto, all property rights of the parties in joint tenancy or tenancy by the entirety shall stand dissolved and, in the same proceeding in which the decree is entered, the court may award the property to the one lawfully entitled thereto or apportion it in such man-

ner as seems equitable, just, and reasonable.

D.C.Code § 16–910 (1967).

7. E.g., Heath v. Heath, 89 U.S.App. D.C. 68, 69, 189 F.2d 697, 698 (1951) (emphasis added):

The first part of the statute was found to be subtantive; a final divorce terminated the estate by the entireties unless an agreement had been formulated to the contrary. The second provision of [§ 16–910] * * * allows the court when the parties are in that situation to award or apportion the property *left without defined ownership by the first part of the statute.*

In the instant case, such an interpretation would leave unresolved the status of the title of the New Jersey Avenue property since the District Court simply left it "undisturbed." * * *

There is no hint in the debates which accompanied the passage of § 16–910 that such was the result Congress "intended" but the legislative record is neutral on the point and would not seem to prohibit such result. The better rule, however, would seem to be that upon dissolution of the tenancy by the entirety, the parties became tenants in common. Such a result has been reached by various judges of the District Court. Scholl v. Scholl, 72 F.Supp. 823 (D.D.C.1947); Bowles v. Wray, 72 F.Supp. 822 (D.D.C.1942); see Brown v. Brown, 97 F.Supp. 237, 238 (D.D.C.1950), and accords with the majority view in other jurisdictions. * * * Thus, we hold that at the commencement of this suit, the parties held the District properties as tenants in common [8] and the remedy sought by appellee can be considered as being partition of real property between such tenants.

The fact that the parties were tenants in common, however, does not mean that they each had to receive one-half of the property, for the rule is that, in a suit for partition, the court must first determine the respective shares which the parties hold in the property, before the property can be divided. * * * See generally Annot., 156 A.L.R. 508 (1945). Since the tenancy in common held by the parties to this litigation evolved from a tenancy by the entirety, the normal presumption is that they held equal shares in the tenancy in common. As the Supreme Court of Wisconsin has stated:

> The rule is, therefore, that the interests of joint tenants being equal during their lives, a presumption arises that upon dissolution of the joint tenancy during the lives of the cotenants, each is entitled to an equal share of the proceeds. This presumption is subject to rebuttal, however, and does not prevent proof from being introduced that the respective holdings and interests of the parties are unequal. This presumption may be rebutted by evidence showing the source

---

8. Another possibility, that upon dissolution of the tenancy by the entirety the parties became joint tenants, does not appear to have merit. In the first place, § 16–910 manifests an "intent" that both joint tenancies and tenancies by the entirety be dissolved by divorce. While resolution of a tenancy by the entirety into a joint tenancy would not violate the letter of that section, it would seem to violate its spirit. In the second place, while a tenancy by the entirety resembles a joint tenancy in that both have the unities of time, title, interest and possession, with the unity of person added to the former, a tenancy by the entirety is not simply a joint tenancy with the added unity of person. In a joint tenancy, each person holds "an undivided moiety of the whole." 4 G. Thompson, Commentaries on the Modern Law of Real Property § 1776 (Grimes ed. 1961). The estate can be partitioned. D.C.Code § 16–2901 (1967). In a tenancy by the entirety, there are no moieties. Each party holds the entire estate. 4 G. Thompson, supra, at § 1784; Fairclaw v. Forrest, 76 U.S.App.D.C. 197, 201, 130 F.2d 829, 933

(1942). The estate cannot be partitioned. See D.C.Code § 16–2901 (1967). There is no reason, therefore, why, upon dissolution, a tenancy by the entirety should resolve itself into anything other than what might be called the least common denominator of concurrent ownership. See 4 G. Thompson, supra, § 1793. Finally, as was said in the case of Stelz v. Shreck, 128 N.Y. 263, 28 N.E. 510, 511 (1891):

[O]ur statute provides that every estate granted or devised to two or more persons in their own right shall be a tenancy in common, unless expressly declared to be a joint tenancy. * * * The conveyance did not expressly declare that the tenancy was to be a joint tenancy, and therefore, when the original character of the tenancy by the entirety is changed, it cannot be transformed into that of a joint tenancy without a clear violation of our statute.

The District of Columbia has a statute similar to the one under discussion in Stelz, D.C.Code § 45–816 (1967), and the same reasoning applies.

of the actual cash outlay at the time of acquisition, *the intent of the cotenant creating the joint tenancy to make a gift of the half-interest to the other cotenant,* unequal contribution by way of money or services, unequal expenditures in improving the property or freeing it from encumbrances and clouds, or other evidence raising inferences contrary to the idea of equal interest in the joint estate.

Jezo v. Jezo, 23 Wis.2d 399, 127 N.W.2d 246, 250 (1964) (emphasis added).

During the trial, conflicting evidence was introduced concerning the contributions, both monetary and otherwise, made by each of the parties to the District properties. The court found that appellant had made some contributions. But such finding is not controlling here on the disposition of these properties because in the District of Columbia there is another doctrine to the effect that even if real property is purchased entirely by one spouse, and title is taken in the names of both as tenants by the entirety or joint tenants, the consideration to be implied for the share of the non-purchasing spouse is the faithful performance of his or her marriage vows. * * * Thus even if appellant had not contributed any money to the purchase or upkeep of the District properties, since she held title thereto as a tenant by the entirety, she was entitled to a share of them subject to the condition that she faithfully performed her marriage vows.[9]

Because a tenancy by the entirety has all the unities found in a joint tenancy, plus the unity of marriage, the parties to a tenancy by the entirety must enjoy a unity of interest in the property. See Fairclaw v. Forrest, 76 U.S.App.D.C. 197, 200, 130 F.2d 829, 832 (1942). In turn, "[u]nity of interest requires that the shares of the joint trenants, whatever their number, shall be equal." 4 G. Thompson, Commentaries on the Modern Law of Real Property § 1776, at 16 (Grimes ed. 1961). See also 2 H. Tiffany, The Law of Real Property § 419, at 198 (Jones ed. 1939). Thus the non-purchasing spouse, in this case the appellant, took an equal share in the property held in the tenancy by the entirety in consideration of faithful performance of her marriage vows.

The decree of divorce awarded to the wife is conclusive of the fact that she faithfully performed her marriage vows since the husband's suit for divorce was dismissed and Maryland recognizes the doctrine of recrimination. Abare v. Abare, 221 Md. 445, 157 A.2d 427 (1960); Courson v. Courson, 208 Md. 171, 117 A.2d 850 (1955). She therefore fully performed the consideration the law implies for an equal share of the property and she should receive an equal share upon its division.[10]

---

9. In none of the District of Columbia cases does the court appear to have been concerned with the intention of the parties. The implied "consideration" appears to be implied by law rather than by fact. See Richardson v. Richardson, 72 App.D.C. 67, 69, 112 F.2d 19, 21 (1940):

When property is conveyed to one spouse under the circumstances of this case without financial consideration, we have said the consideration or condition underlying the conveyance is the faithful performance of the marriage vows.

Thus, although phrased in contractual terms, the rule is one of quasi-contract and presents no problem for the preexisting duty rule. See generally 1 S. Williston, A Treatise on the Law of Contracts §§ 3A, 32A (Jaeger ed. 1957).

10. We have considered Slaughter v. Slaughter, 83 U.S.App.D.C. 301, 171 F.2d 129 (1948); Hipp v. Hipp, 191 F.Supp. 299

In dividing the property equally, we consider it error to take into account that five properties are "involved." By operation of law, the appellant and the appellee are tenants in common with equal shares in the Maryland property. McCally v. McCally, 250 Md. 541, 243 A.2d 538 (1968). They have reached an agreement concerning how that tenancy in common will be shared and the courts of the District of Columbia have no jurisdiction over Maryland property. Had they desired that arrangement to be contingent upon a certain disposition of the District properties they could have so agreed in connection with the divorce. That there was no agreement to do so should simply remove the status of the Maryland property from consideration in the proceeding which is before us, leaving the District properties for distribution as a separate group.

V

Finally, we hold that appellant is entitled to an accounting of the rents and profits from the District properties and of any investments made from such income, at least from the date on which the parties became tenants in common, i.e., the date on which the decree of divorce was entered. See Schultze v. Schultze, 112 U.S.App.D.C. 162, 164, 300 F.2d 917, 919 (1962); 2 H. Tiffany, The Law of Real Property § 450 (Jones ed. 1939); 4 G. Thompson, Commentaries on the Modern Law of Real Property § 1804 (Grimes ed. 1961). For reasons discussed above, we might question whether it is proper to give the appellee a credit for the "house payments" he is making pursuant to the agreement incorporated in the Maryland decree, but since neither party is contesting that part of the District Court's order which provided for the accounting, we therefore conclude there is no need for this court to consider the propriety of such credits or whether appellant is entitled to an accounting for any period of time prior to the divorce. See Minnesota Mining & Mfg. Co. v. Coe, 73 App.D.C. 146, 148, 118 F.2d 593, 595 (1941).

In light of the foregoing, and particularly the fact that it is impossible from the record here to ascertain the value of the share of the District properties awarded to appellant, we reserve the decision and re-

(D.D.C.1960), aff'd 111 U.S.App.D.C. 307, 296 F.2d 429 (1961) and Lundregan v. Lundregan, 176 A.2d 790 (D.C.App.1962) relied upon by appellee, but find them distinguishable. In *Slaughter*, the husband had supplied all but $100 of the money used to purchase the property and was awarded the divorce on grounds of the wife's desertion. *Lundregan* was a combined divorce and property settlement proceeding in which the parties had made no voluntary agreement concerning the division of any of their property. *Hipp* was, in effect, the same kind of proceeding. In the instant case, we are faced simply with a suit for partition of property owned concurrently by two parties each of whom has given full consideration for an equal share. That equal shares are here required, however, does not mean that they are always required. Special equities may sometimes vary the share to be received by a party when a tenancy in common derived from a tenancy by the entirety is partitioned. See Jezo v. Jezo, 23 Wis.2d 399, 127 N.W.2d 246, 250 (1964). Compare Kollar v. Kollar, 155 Fla. 705, 21 So.2d 356 (1945); Jones v. Jones, 121 So.2d 811 (Fla.App.1960); Latta v. Latta, 121 So.2d 42 (Fla.App.1960) with Wood v. Wood, 104 So.2d 879 (Fla.App. 1958).

mand it to the trial court for determination of the value of the District properties and for their division into equal shares.[11]

Reversed and remanded.

B. COMMUNITY PROPERTY

Dower, curtesy, and estates by the entirety all reflected a common law recognition of special property rights in husband and wife. In the discussion of marital property, supra, we have seen statutory provisions which have gone further in seeking an appropriate adjustment of those rights. In eight states (Arizona, California, Idaho, Louisiana, Nevada, New Mexico, Texas and Washington) a different system of marital property called Community Property is established. It represents a more extensive and elaborate effort to establish a firm and fair property base for the institution of marriage. It was a creature of the civil-law systems and was imported relatively late in United States history. In some respects, the statutory developments in common law states bring them closer to the results of the Community Property system, but there are significant differences. The "equitable distribution" provisions of a divorce statute, as we have seen, produce a species of interest, but it is uncertain when it vests, and uncertain as to the share which may reach a spouse. The Community Property system, however, starts with a theory that property acquired during the marriage results from the joint efforts of husband and wife which entitles each to *equal* ownership, and that such *equal* ownership is to be recognized immediately when the property comes into the marriage. Rules governing management, alienability, and devolution on death apply to property acquired during marriage by either husband or wife or both as a result of labor, industry or skill.[12]

11. Under D.C.Code § 16–2901, if the property cannot be divided in kind equally, the court may order a sale and division of proceeds. * * *

12. The following sections of the California Civil Code indicate the nature of the basic legislation:

"A husband and wife may hold property as joint tenants, tenants in common, or as community property." (§ 5104).

"The respective interests of the husband and wife in community property during continuance of the marriage relation are present, existing and equal interests. This section shall be construed as defining the respective interests and rights of husband and wife in community property." (§ 5105).

"All property of the wife, owned by her before marriage, and that acquired afterwards by gift, bequest, devise, or descent, with the rents, issues, and profits thereof, is her separate property. The wife may, without the consent of her husband, convey her separate property." (§ 5107).

"All property owned by the husband before marriage, and that acquired afterwards by gift, bequest, devise, or descent with the rents, issues, and profits thereof, is his separate property. The husband may, without the consent of his wife, convey his separate property." (§ 5108).

"Except as provided in sections 5107, 5108, and 5109, all real property situated in this state and all personal property wherever situated acquired during the marriage by a married person while domiciled in this state, and property held in trust pursuant to Section 5113.5, is community property; but whenever any real or personal property, or any interest therein or encumbrance thereon, is acquired prior to January 1, 1975, by a married woman by an instrument in writing, the presumption is that the same is her separate property, and if so acquired by such married woman and any other person the presumption is that she takes the part acquired by her, as tenant in common, unless a different intention is expressed in the instrument; except, that when any of such prop-

The most difficult question in the administration of a community property system is in distinguishing between community and separate

erty is acquired by husband and wife by an instrument in which they are described as husband and wife, unless a different intention is expressed in the instrument, the presumption is that such property is the community property of said husband and wife. When a single-family residence of a husband and wife is acquired by them during marriage as joint tenants, for the purpose of the division of such property upon dissolution of marriage or legal separation only, the presumption is that such single-family residence is the community property of said husband and wife. The presumptions in this section mentioned are conclusive in favor of any person dealing in good faith and for a valuable consideration with such married woman or her legal representatives or successors in interest, and regardless of any change in her marital status after acquisition of said property.

"In cases where a married woman has conveyed, or shall hereafter convey, real property which she acquired prior to May 19, 1889, the husband, or his heirs or assigns, of such married woman, shall be barred from commencing or maintaining any action to show that the real property was community property, or to recover the real property from and after one year from the filing for record in the recorder's office of such conveyances, respectively.

"As used in this section, personal property does not include and real property does include lease interests in real property." (§ 5110.)

"(a) Except as provided in subdivisions (b), (c), and (d) and Sections 5113.5 and 5128, either spouse has the management and control of the community personal property, whether acquired prior to or on or after January 1, 1975, with like absolute power of disposition, other than testamentary, as the spouse has of the separate estate of the spouse.

"(b) A spouse may not make a gift of community personal property, or dispose of community personal property without a valuable consideration, without the written consent of the other spouse.

"(c) A spouse may not sell, convey, or encumber the furniture, furnishings, or fittings of the home, or the clothing or wearing apparel of the other spouse or minor children which is community personal property, without the written consent of the other spouse.

"(d) A spouse who is operating or managing a business or an interest in a business which is community personal proper-

ty has the sole management and control of the business or interest.

"(e) Each spouse shall act in good faith with respect to the other spouse in the management and control of the community property." (§ 5125.)

"Except as provided in Sections 5113.5 and 5128, either spouse has the management and control of the community real property, whether acquired prior to or on or after January 1, 1975, but both spouses either personally or by duly authorized agent, must join in executing any instrument by which such community real property or any interest therein is leased for a longer period than one year, or is sold, conveyed, or encumbered; provided, however, that nothing herein contained shall be construed to apply to a lease, mortgage, conveyance, or transfer of real property or of any interest in real property between husband and wife; provided, also, however, that the sole lease, contract, mortgage or deed of the husband, holding the record title to community real property, to a lessee, purchaser, or encumbrancer, in good faith without knowledge of the marriage relation, shall be presumed to be valid is executed prior to January 1, 1975, and that the sole lease, contract, mortgage, or deed of either spouse, holding the record title to community real property to a lessee, purchaser, or encumbrancer, in good faith without knowledge of the marriage relation, shall be presumed to be valid if executed on or after January 1, 1975. No action to avoid any instrument mentioned in this section, affecting any property standing of record in the name of either spouse alone, executed by the spouse alone, shall be commenced after the expiration of one year from the filing for record of such instrument in the recorder's office in the county in which the land is situate, and no action to avoid any instrument mentioned in this section, affecting any property standing of record in the name of the husband alone, which was executed by the husband alone and filed for record prior to the time this act takes effect, in the recorder's office in the county in which the land is situate, shall be commenced after the expiration of one year from the date on which this act takes effect." (§ 5127.)

"Notwithstanding the provisions of Section 5125 or 5127 granting the husband the management and control of the community property, to the extent necessary to fulfill a duty of a wife to support her children, the wife is entitled to the management and control of her share of the community property.

property. For example, property acquired before marriage is not part of the community. Suppose one spouse before marriage enters into a contract for the purchase of a tract of land and makes partial payment of the purchase price. After the marriage the transaction is completed by the payment of the balance of the purchase price and a delivery of a deed naming the contracting spouse as grantee. Arguably ownership of the land in question was "acquired" before marriage in the sense that the contracting spouse had equitable ownership as a result of his specifically enforceable agreement to purchase, even though acquisition of the legal title was dependent on payment of the balance of the purchase price. Perhaps the most reasonable solution, and one for which there is some authority, is to apportion the property so acquired between community and separate property in accordance with the source of funds used for the acquisition. Alternatively, a number of courts follow a so-called inception-of-right theory. This causes the status of the property to be determined by the status of the acquiring spouse at the inception of that right which later resulted in complete ownership. Under this theory the community is entitled to reimbursement for any community funds used to complete the acquisition.

Each spouse has equal undivided ownership of community property. Management and control during their joint lives was, until recently, largely in the hands of the husband, who was required, however, to act more like a fiduciary than as sole owner. Recently there has been considerable statutory modification of this principle, the result of which is to grant power of equal control and curtail the power of the husband to deal with the property without his wife's consent. Most jurisdictions forbid the transfer or encumbrance of land held as community property without the joinder of both spouses.

At the death of one spouse, one-half of the community property, subject to various tax liabilities and certain creditors' claims, passes to the surviving spouse. With some variations among the states, each spouse is given the right of testamentary disposition over his or her share of the community property. Intestate succession laws vary as to the respective shares of the surviving spouse and the descendants of the decedent. Generally a decedent's share of the community property passes to the surviving spouse in the absence of descendants.

Since the income of a spouse is usually community property, for income tax purposes half of such income is reported by each spouse. For

"The wife's interest in the community property, including the earnings of her husband, is liable for the support of her children to whom the duty to support is owed, provided that for the purposes of this section, prior support liability of her husband plus three hundred dollars ($300) gross monthly income shall first be excluded in determining the wife's interest in the community property earnings of her husband.

"The wife may bring an action in the superior court to enforce such right provided that such action is not brought under influ-

ence of fraud or duress by any individual, corporation or governmental agency.

"A natural father is not relieved of any legal obligation to support his children by the liability for their support imposed by this section and such contribution shall reduce the liability to which the interest of the wife in the community property is subject." (§ 5127.5)

Extensive treatment of the major aspects of community property law can be found in Reppy and Samuel, Community Property in the United States, 2d ed. (1982).

many years this gave a tax advantage to spouses under a community property system. This fact induced several states without community property systems to enact community property laws. Such statutes appeared in Michigan, Nebraska, Oklahoma, Oregon, Pennsylvania,[13] and Hawaii. In 1948 the federal Internal Revenue Code was amended to permit husband and wife to split their income for income tax purposes, thus placing married taxpayers in all states on the same basis. Soon thereafter the late-coming community property statutes were repealed. These shifts have left problems which may trouble lawyers for many years.[14]

The existence of two diverse systems of marital property necessarily produces problems. For example, suppose the death of a resident of Texas (a community property state) who owns (in his own name) some land and some personal property in Missouri (a common law state). How do we decide questions of title, of testate or intestate succession, of probate procedure or questions in any other area of the law? See In re Estate of Perry, 480 S.W.2d 893 (Mo.1972) for a relatively simple case which illustrates a very complex area of law known as conflict of laws. Certain principles have been developed to be generally applied in all states, so that legal results do not depend entirely upon the particular forum in which the matter is being adjudicated. It may be recognized, for example, that questions relating to title to real property are governed by the law of the state in which the land is located. The growing migratory nature of our population has increased the incidence and complexity of conflicts problems, especially in respect to the property of spouses who move to or from community-property states. Consider, for example, the difficulties involved in dealing with the interests of spouses who sell community land in a community property state and use or invest the proceeds in a non-community property state—or vice versa. Here we mean only to suggest the dimensions of the problem. See Cantwell, Estate and Tax Planning, Effects of State Lines on Estate Planning, 99 Trusts & Est. 922 (1960).

13. The Pennsylvania statute was declared unconstitutional in Willcox v. Penn Mutual Life Ins. Co., 357 Pa. 581, 55 A.2d 521, 174 A.L.R. 220 (1947). See 46 Mich.L. Rev. 422 (1947); 9 U. of Pitts.L.Rev. 105 (1947).

14. Since the Pennsylvania statute was declared unconstitutional, these problems were avoided.

Chapter 4

LANDLORD AND TENANT

The history of the law of Landlord and Tenant reveals more striking shifts in conceptual analysis and its consequences than perhaps any other of our property institutions. In the late medieval period in England leases were first used primarily as a money lender's device by which the ecclesiastical rules against usury were circumvented. Usury in those days meant lending money at any interest. The holder of land in fee simple would borrow money, and repayment would be made by transferring to the lender the right to possess land for a fixed term, the value of which exceeded the amount of the debt.

To begin with a lessee had no specific remedy to protect his possession, but only an action of covenant against the lessor. Lacking seisin, he was denied the established real actions, including the writ of novel disseisin, by which a disseised feeholder could proceed against a disseisor. By the 16th century, however, the courts had developed the action of ejectment, which, as we have seen, ultimately became the principal action by a landowner to assert his title and recover possession. In its beginnings, however, ejectment was limited to the recovery of possession by a tenant from his lessor or a third party, in the event of the tenant's wrongful dispossession.

This marked the beginning of the notion that a tenant of land under a lease had a protectable property interest, an estate, in the land, the creation of which established the relation of landlord and tenant. This relationship assumed characteristics that were analogous to feudal tenure, that is, it was a "tenure" relationship, by which a tenant held land "under" his landlord, and rules were evolved to regulate the relationship. In fact the modern practice of including in a lease a covenant or promise to pay rent, as well as other covenants, was not common. Rather a landowner by his lease would "reserve" a certain rent, often in the form of produce from the land, and rent so reserved was itself thought to constitute an interest in the land. In those days there was little reason to include the elaborate provisions relating to the respective rights of the parties that in modern times appear as contractual terms of a lease. Hence a lease was a conveyance, with property consequences. But this sort of property arrangement bore the marks of its origin, so that a tenant's estate was nonfreehold, and was treated as personal property, that is, a chattel real, which, if it did not expire at a lessee's death, was administered as part of his chattels and other personal property and did not descend to his heirs.

The usual contractual provisions found in modern leases, however, are not new. The gradual growth in the resort to such terms long ago reached the point where they constituted the major part of most leases. As a consequence, certain contractual terms became common and standard, and came to supersede the otherwise applicable rules that would govern the landlord-tenant relation in their absence. This has reached a sometimes ambiguous equilibrium that at least requires us to say that the usual lease serves a dual function. It is both a *conveyance* and a *contract*, with varying emphasis upon the two functions, depending on the terms of the lease and upon the kind of issue that arises between the parties.

A recent development must now be noted, which may cause one to reflect that the wheel has come full circle. As you will discover in some of the materials which follow, certain problems have arisen which have caused courts to minimize the conveyancing consequences of residential leases and to lay predominant emphasis upon them as contracts. Such a shift in emphasis, of course, has not eliminated the conveyancing feature of leases, which for some purposes remains as important as it ever was.

In fact, as we shall see, the limits that courts have recently put upon a landlord's ability to dictate the contractual terms of residential leases, indicate that the emphasis has really shifted more widely than we have suggested, not only from property to contract, but from contract to something that is neither of these. What that is remains for us to discover as we proceed.*

SECTION 1.　LEASEHOLD ESTATES—CREATION, DURATION, TERMINATION

The leasehold estates, which we sometimes call tenancies, differ from one another and from other estates not only in respect to their duration, but also in respect to the methods of creating them. Some of them can be created orally. Not all leasehold estates are expressly limited in duration to definite periods of time. Some continue until properly terminated either by the lessor or the lessee. In such cases duration is more properly a matter of terminability.

Leasehold estates are identified and classified on the basis of (1) the expressed intention of the parties respecting the identity of the tenancy or its duration or terminability; (2) the agreement of the parties concerning the periodic payments of rent; or (3) the acts of the parties, such as by a tenant's merely taking possession of land with consent of the owner.

A tenant's obligation to pay rent is usually expressed, both in respect to its duration and the method and times of payment; but if it is not expressed, it will be implied from the fact of the creation of a tenancy, and in an amount that is usually determined by the rental value of the land. Normally the duration of a tenant's obligation to pay rent is

---

* A good detailed treatment of the law of Landlord and Tenant may be found in 1 A.L.P., part 3. For a less detailed but still comprehensive treatment, see Cunningham, ch. 6.

governed by the duration or the continuance of the tenancy, but this is not always true, as we shall see.

One further preliminary matter. Unlike the creation of other estates, it has been a traditional rule that a leasehold estate does not arise upon the proper execution of a lease, but only when the lessee takes possession under his lease. Until then his interest is called an *interesse termini*. The origin and consequences of this concept are not entirely clear. It is clear that a lessee out of possession but entitled to possession can recover possession from his lessor or a third person. Indeed the continued observance of this distinction would seem to be in doubt, and it has been argued that it is a barren and useless relic. 1 A.L.P. § 3.22.

The distinction last mentioned is one of several reasons why we have two sets of labels designating the parties involved in the creation or continuance of leasehold estates. A *tenant* is one who has a leasehold estate in the land of another, who is his *landlord*. *Lessor* and *lessee* are of course the parties to a lease. Technically, where either a lessor or a lessee has assigned or conveyed his interest to a third person, the lessor is no longer landlord, or, as the case may be, the lessee is no longer tenant. In common usage for many purposes, however, we use the two sets of labels interchangeably.

Here in summary terms are the several tenancies, together with their methods of creation, and some methods of termination.

A. THE SEVERAL TENANCIES

(1) The Term for Years

a. Duration—For a fixed time in units of one year or multiples or divisions thereof, e.g., a lease for one year, for five years, for one month, for six months. The term may be subject to a possibility of reverter, a right of entry, or an executory limitation.

b. Creation—By agreement, i.e., a lease, oral or written, subject to the requirements of the applicable statute of frauds, mentioned below. The landlord's ownership is subject to the outstanding term for years and is described as a reversion. As security for the payment of rent and the performance of other tenant's obligations, it is common for the landlord to retain a right of entry, i.e., a power of termination. The right to exclusive possession as of the date on which the term begins is in the tenant, for example, L to T "for a term of five years commencing January 1, 1973, but on the condition that if default be made in the payment of rent or in any of the covenants herein contained to be kept by the lessee, lessor may declare said term ended and re-enter." The interest of T is a term for years. The interest of L is a reversion coupled with a right of entry to secure the payment of rent and other commitments of T.

c. Termination—By expiration of the stated period of time, by happening of a stated limitation or contingency if such occurs within the specified term, by *surrender* of the unexpired portion of the term, i.e., a conveyance by tenant to landlord of the tenant's interest, by *release*, i.e., a conveyance by landlord to tenant of the landlord's interest, by *condemnation*, by expiration of the landlord's estate, or by certain other circumstances to be noted later.

If the tenancy is on a contingency with the lessor retaining a right of entry rather than a possibility of reverter, the lessor must affirmatively exercise his right of entry to effect a termination of the leasehold interest.

(2) The Periodic Tenancies

a. Duration—For successive like periods until terminated by appropriate notice given by either landlord or tenant. The controlling period may be a day, a week, a month, a year, or multiples or divisions of any one of these, e.g., a lease from month to month, or year to year. It is possible but uncommon for a periodic tenancy to be subject to a possibility of reverter, right of entry, or executory limitation.

b. Creation—By agreement, i.e., the express terms of an oral or written lease, by the landlord giving possession to the tenant for an indefinite or unspecified period of time with an agreement that rent will be paid periodically, by a tenant's remaining in possession with consent of the landlord subsequent to termination of a prior tenancy (the holdover situation hereafter considered), by a tenant's taking possession under a void lease, but making periodic rental payments.

c. Termination—At common law, by notice given by landlord or tenant six months prior to the end of the current period if the tenancy is from year to year. For periodic tenancies in which the period is less than one year, the notice required is a full period prior to the end of the current period. In most states the notice period has been modified by statute. The prior notice required to terminate a year-to-year tenancy varies from thirty days to two, three or six months. Thirty days prior notice is usually sufficient to terminate a month-to-month tenancy. The basic distinction in duration between the term for years and the periodic tenancy is that the former terminates upon the expiration of the term provided, while the latter continues until terminated by appropriate notice. Except for this difference, the discussion above under "Term for Years—Termination" is equally applicable here.

Under this tenancy, as under the Term for Years, the landlord's interest is called a reversion or ownership subject to an outstanding periodic tenancy.

(3) The Tenancy at Will

a. Duration—As the name implies, it continues only so long as both landlord and tenant refrain from taking any action inconsistent with its continuation. There is neither a fixed term nor successive periods during which the tenant's right to possession will continue. Taking possession with the consent of the owner in fee, there being no agreement as to term or rent, and no pattern of rental payments, creates a tenancy terminable at the will of either party. The landlord's interest is a reversionary interest or ownership subject to the terminable possessory right of the tenant.

b. Creation—By agreement of the parties, by the taking of possession with the consent of the owner without more, by entry into possession under a void lease prior to making periodic rental payments.

c. Termination—At common law, by either party without formal notice of termination. A landlord's demand for possession is sufficient to end the tenant's right to possession, but in such a case the tenant does have a reasonable time within which to vacate. Because the tenant's right to possession is dependent on the continuing will of the landlord and the tenant's obligations are limited by his own continuing will, a conveyance of the fee by the landlord, an attempted assignment of his interest by the tenant, or the death of either landlord or tenant, effects a termination.

(4) Tenancy at Sufferance

a. Duration—Until demand for possession by landlord or until landlord elects to treat tenant as other than a tenant at sufferance.

b. Creation—By one entering into possession rightfully and retaining possession wrongfully. This "tenancy", really no tenancy at all, describes the relationship between the owner in fee and one who was originally in possession rightfully, but who continues in possession beyond the expiration of his right. It distinguishes the holdover tenant from one whose intrusion has no basis in right. A tenant in possession under a tenancy for years who remains in possession following the expiration of the term without the consent of the owner in fee becomes a tenant at sufferance.

c. Termination—In a technical sense, there being no formal landlord-tenant relationship, there is no tenancy to terminate. The wrongdoer has possession, which cannot be defended against any reasonable action of the owner in fee.

In most jurisdictions when a tenant fails timely to surrender possession upon expiration of his tenancy, the landlord is given a reasonable time to make an election between two alternatives. He may consider the tenant as holding under a new tenancy for an additional period of time, or as a wrongdoer from whom possession can be recovered immediately. We will consider later some of the complications of this problem.

B. STATUTORY MODIFICATIONS

(1) The Statute of Frauds

The effect of the Statute of Frauds of 1677 was to require the transfer of all interests in land other than those by act and operation of law to be in writing except leases "not exceeding the term of three years from the making thereof." Most American statutes, being based upon the English Statute, contain a like short-term exception. A modern statute may, however, limit the permissible parol lease to one rather than three years. Where the lessor seeks to create a tenancy by parol for a term longer than permitted by the appropriate statute, the agreement *as to the duration* of the lease is void. Other terms of the tenancy are held enforceable. Since the entry under such oral lease is rightful, and the tenant continues in possession with the consent of the landlord, the tenancy resulting is a tenancy at will. In most states, this tenancy will become a periodic tenancy upon payment of rent, the period being determined by the manner agreed upon for the payment of rent.

(2) *Statutory Definitions of the Tenancy at Will and the Tenancy at Sufferance*

It is important to keep in mind that statutes in many states provide a different scheme of classification of some of the lesser tenancies than that which was developed in the common law. A survey of these changes would produce a confusing array of variations. Most of these statutes supply new definitions of common-law labels. The result is often less change in substance than the changes in terminology seem to suggest. Often the basic statute is a provision of a statute of frauds, which prescribes the consequences of attempting to create an estate in land without an instrument in writing.

Massachusetts provides that any attempt to create an estate in land otherwise than by an instrument in writing shall create a tenancy at will. Three-months notice is required for termination, unless the rent is payable at shorter intervals, which correspondingly shortens the notice requirement.

The Maine statutes are similar, except that a 30-day notice of termination is prescribed.

The District of Columbia Code provides for the express creation of periodic estates and estates at will, but an attempt to create an estate for a greater term than one year, without a writing, results in an estate at sufferance. It is further provided that all letting of premises without agreement as to the term, that is, where rent is payable or paid on a periodic basis, or where a tenant holds over and pays rent, creates a tenancy at sufferance. Thirty-days notice is required to terminate a tenancy at sufferance. Apparently, however, if a tenant holds over wrongfully, and the landlord acts promptly to evict him, the 30-day notice is not required.

Florida defines tenancies at will so as to embrace periodic tenancies, that is, periodic tenancies are variations of the "tenancy at will." It is also provided that if a tenant holds over wrongfully at the end of his tenancy he is a tenant at sufferance, and this status is not changed by the payment and acceptance of rent, and so he remains liable to be evicted without notice.

One should consult the statutes of any state in which he is particularly interested.

(3) The Uniform Residential Landlord and Tenant Act

In 1972 the Commissioners on Uniform State Laws promulgated the Uniform Residential Landlord and Tenant Act (hereafter, URLTA),[1] based on the American Bar Foundation's 1969 Tentative Draft of a Model Residential Landlord-Tenant Code.   At least seventeen states have now adopted comprehensive new landlord-tenant legislation based on the URLTA,[2] and two other states have adopted similar legislation based on the Model Code.[3] The URLTA applies to most residential leasing arrangements, with specified exceptions.[4] In some of the statutes modelled on the URLTA, additional exceptions have been made.[5] URLTA § 401(d) provides: "Unless the rental agreement fixes a definite term, the tenancy is week-to-week in case of a roomer who pays weekly rent and in all other cases month-to-month."[6]

1. For the full text of the URLTA with the Commissioners' Official Comments, see 7A Uniform Laws Annotated 503–559 (1978).

2. Alaska Stat. §§ 34.03.010 to 34.03.380 (1977 and Supp.1982); Ariz.Rev. Stat.Ann. §§ 33–1301 to 33–1381 (1974 and Supp.1982–83);   Conn.Gen.Stat.Ann. §§ 47a–1 to 47a–20 (1978 and Supp.1982); Fla.Stat.Ann. §§ 83.40 to 83.63 (West. Supp.1982); Iowa Code Ann. §§ 562A.1 through 562A.37 (1976 and Supp.1982–83); Kan.Stat.Ann. §§ 58–2540 through 58–2573 (1976 and Supp.1981); Ky.Rev. Stat.Ann. §§ 383.505 to 383.715 (Supp. 1982); Mont.Code Ann. §§ 70–24–101 to 70–24–442 (1981);   Neb.Rev.Stat. §§ 76–1401 to 76–1449 (1981); Nev.Rev. Stat. §§ 118A.010 to 118A.530 (1979); N.M.Stat.Ann. §§ 47–8–1 to 47–8–51 (1982); Ohio Rev.Code Ann. §§ 5321.01 to 5321.19 (Page 1981); Okla.Stat.Ann. tit. 41, §§ 101 to 135 (Supp.1981–82); Or.Rev.Stat. §§ 91–700 to 91–865 (1979); Tenn.Code Ann. §§ 66.28.101 to 66.28.516 (1982); Va. Code §§ 55.248.2 to 55.248.40 (1981 and Supp.1982); Wash.Rev.Code Ann. §§ 59.-18.010 to 59.18.900 (Supp.1982).

3. Del.Code Ann. tit. 25, §§ 5501–5517 (1975 and Supp.1982); Hawaii Rev.Stat. §§ 521–1 through 521–77 (1976 and Supp. 1982).

4. URLTA § 1.202 provides as follows:

Unless created to avoid the application of this Act, the following arrangements are not governed by this Act:

(1) residence at an institution, public or private, if incidental to detention or the provision of medical, geriatric, educational, counseling, religious, or similar service;

(2) occupancy under a contract of sale of a dwelling unit or the property of which it is a part, if the occupant is the purchaser or a person who succeeds to his interest;

(3) occupancy by a member of a fraternal or social organization in the portion of a structure operated for the benefit of the organization;

(4) transient occupancy in a hotel, or motel [or lodgings [subject to cite state transient lodgings or room occupancy excise tax act]];

(5) occupancy by an employee of a landlord whose right to occupancy is conditional upon employment in and about the premises;

(6) occupancy by an owner of a condominium unit or a holder of a proprietary lease in a cooperative;

(7) occupancy under a rental agreement covering premises used by the occupant primarily for agricultural purposes.

5. E.g., Ariz.Rev.Stat.Ann. § 33–1308(7) and Wash.Rev.Code Ann. § 59.18.040(7) exclude public housing; Hawaii Rev.Stat. § 521–7(7) excludes leases for 15 years or more, and Neb.Rev.Stat. § 76.1408(8) excludes leases for 5 years or more; and Va.Code Ann. § 55–248.5(10) excludes any single-family dwelling whose landlord owns ten or more dwellings.

6. URLTA defines "rental agreement" to mean "all agreements, written or oral, and valid rules and regulations adopted under Section 3.102 embodying the terms and conditions concerning the use and occupancy of a dwelling unit and premises," and defines "roomer" to mean "a person occupying a dwelling unit that does not include a toilet and either a bathtub or a shower and a refrigerator, stove, and kitchen sink, all provided by the landlord, and where one or more of these facilities are used in common by occupants in the structure." URLTA § 1.301(11) and (12).

(4) A New Kind of Tenancy in New Jersey

A statute enacted in New Jersey in 1974, and since amended, forbids the removal of a tenant from premises leased for residential purposes except for good cause. N.J.Stat.Ann. § 2A:18–61.1 et seq. The act is not applicable to owner-occupied premises with not more than two rental units. An elaborate array of thirteen causes for removal are specified. In substance these include: failure to pay rent due, disorderly conduct, wilful or grossly negligent injury to the premises, failure to observe the landlord's rules and regulations governing the premises, breach of covenant in the lease where a right of entry is reserved, the case where an owner seeks to retire a residential building permanently from residential use, where a landlord seeks, at the termination of a lease, reasonable changes in the terms of the lease which the tenant after written notice fails to accept, or where the owner of a building of no more than three residential units seeks personally to occupy a unit. Any provision in a lease whereby a tenant waives any rights under the act is unenforceable.

In Sabato v. Sabato, 135 N.J.Super. 158, 342 A.2d 886 (1975), the general validity of the statute was not challenged, but the court said that generally it was a valid exercise of the state's police power. The act was challenged on the ground that at that time it prohibited an owner from evicting a tenant where the owner in good faith sought to occupy a dwelling unit for himself. The court held that such a limitation amounted to an unconstitutional taking of property without due process. But in Stamboulos v. McKee, 134 N.J.Super. 567, 342 A.2d 529 (1975), the court held that such a restriction on a landlord's recovery of possession was not an unlawful impairment of contract rights. In the same year the act was amended to permit eviction for such a purpose in limited circumstances, as indicated above.

ARBENZ v. EXLEY, WATKINS & CO.

Supreme Court of Appeals of West Virginia, 1905.
57 W.Va. 580, 50 S.E. 813.

BRANNON, P. John Arbenz, Sr., made a written lease, but not under seal, to Exley, Watkins & Co., leasing for a term of five years and three months a brick building, including the vacant parts of certain lots, in the City of Wheeling, the term commencing January 1, 1896, and ending March 31, 1902, for the annual rent of $700.00, commencing April 1, 1896, payable in monthly instalments. The lessees took possession on the first week of January, and occupied the premises, paying rent monthly. On September 15, 1898, a fire totally destroyed said building. The lessees paid rent for that September and also for October, but with the rent of October sent a letter, October 31, 1898, to Arbenz, informing him that they "hereby" vacate the premises and surrender them to him.

In November, 1898, [sic–1899?] Arbenz sued out a distress warrant against said lessees for rent from November 1, 1898, to October 31, 1899, and the same having been levied, a forthcoming bond was given, and in the proceedings upon it in the circuit court of Ohio county a verdict was rendered for the plaintiff for $502.54, after deducting for failure to repair an engine, and judgment given thereon, and the defendants took a writ of error. The defendants filed a plea denying grounds of attachment, and denying all liability for the rent claimed.

The judgment below was affirmed by this Court. Those matters will appear in 52 W.Va. 476, 44 S.E. 149, 61 L.R.A. 957. On August 1, 1903, Arbenz brought assumpsit against Exley, Watkins & Co. to recover rent accruing later than that recovered in the proceeding above mentioned—to recover rent for the period beginning November 1, 1899, and ending December 31, 1902, a period of 38 months, at $700.00 per year, and the suit resulted in a verdict for only $148.15, that is, for the two months of November and December, 1899, the court holding that no recovery could be had after the current year ending that date, on the theory that the tenancy from year to year then closed. The theory against the right to recover is, that a few days after the fire the defendants wrote Arbenz the following letter: "Oct. 31st, 1898. Mr. John Arbenz, City—Dear Sir: We beg to advise that we have vacated, the premises known as west building on 20th street, destroyed by fire Sept. 15th, last, and hereby surrender possession of same. Yours truly, Exley, Watkins & Co."

On the former writ of error we held that for want of a seal to the lease the term of years named in it was not created,* but that it created an estate from year to year, and that said letter did not operate as a notice to quit, to end the tenancy so as to preclude recovery of rent up to November 1, 1899, the rent in litigation in the former proceeding. We did not go further, as no later rent was involved in that case. The question presented in the second suit is, Did the tenancy end 31st December, 1899? Did that letter close the tenancy and stop the rent at that date, the close of the current year 1899? For the defendants the contention is, that the letter, accompanied by actual vacation of the premises, and coupled with the fact that in the circuit court in April, 1899, Exley, Watkins & Co. made defense in the former proceeding denying liability for rent, operated as a notice to quit and closed the tenancy 31st December, 1899.

Take the letter. The question rests mainly on it. It states the facts that the lessees had vacated, and then surrendered possession. It does not notify that at the end of a current year in future the tenant would quit, but states present acts or past, vacation and surrender. The common law, for centuries, has required, in order that lessor and lessee, under a tenancy from year to year, may close the tenancy of his own motion, that a notice to quit should be given six months before the end of the current year. That period or time of notice must be prior to the close of the year. The Code 1899, chapter 93, section 5, provides that "a tenancy from year to year may be terminated by either party giving notice in writing to the other, prior to the end of any year, for three

* The demise of the significance of the seal in most jurisdictions would make it highly unlikely today that a court would conclude that for want of a seal this lease is no better than if it had been wholly in parol.

months, of his intention to terminate the same." That provision recognizes as still continuing the common law estate of tenancy from year to year and the process of terminating it by notice to quit, and changed it only in requiring written notice and fixing a shorter time of notice. Hence it seems that we must appeal to the common law and its mode of notice to test the efficiency of the letter as notice to quit. It does not notify of a future act of quitting, but relies on past vacation and present surrender of possession for the effect of the letter. It does not name a day or time in future when the tenancy is to end. The profession has always regarded this as a requisite in a notice to quit, I think, 2 Taylor, Landlord & Ten. § 476, says: "Form of.—The notice may be given to quit on a particular day; or, in general terms, at the end of the current year of the tenancy, which will expire next after the service of the notice; or, in one month after the next rent-day. The latter form of expression is generally used where the landlord is ignorant of the period when the tenancy commenced; and it is preferable even when the commencement of the tenancy is known, as it provides against any misapprehension of the exact day when the tenant entered." 1 Washburn Real Prop. § 810 says: "Notice. The Time—Whether a longer or shorter time of notice is required, it must, in order to be binding, clearly indicate the time when the tenancy is to expire, and, of course, must be given a sufficient number of days before the time so indicated."

The particular question before us is, whether that letter is bad as a notice to quit because (1) it is a quitting at its date, not notice of a future quitting at the end of a year, and (2) because it fails to state a time for quitting. Under the above and many other authorities we are driven to say that it did not end the tenancy at any time. * * * The textbook writers seem to so regard the law. * * *

Of course, much force is to be given to the harmonious construction of the many cases by the text writers. Still, I have had a question whether the cases mean only that period of time before the termination must expire on the day of the close of the year, or that the notice must designate the time when the tenant intends to quit. Such seems to be the law. The only question is, Does it fit this case? It does seem of great force to say that the only object of notice is to manifest an intent of one party to end the tenancy, and to inform the other party of that intent, and that the letter in this case did that. Arbenz surely knew that his tenants designed to end the tenancy, because he knew that they had quit the premises and surrendered possession. What more could formal notice do? True, it could not go to end the tenancy 31st December, 1898, because from the letter to that date was not three months. But could it not end the tenancy at close of 1899? Now, if the tenants had on the date of the letter given notice that they would quit 31st December, 1899, who would say that it would not be sufficient? Did not that letter disclose intent to quit? By law it could not operate to close the tenancy 31st December, 1898, because the time would be too short. Would it not operate then as soon as the law would let it, just as a formal notice at the date of the letter would have done, that is, December 31, 1899? Arbenz had notice of his tenants' intention to quit. Why could not that notice operate at the earliest date the law would allow it to operate? In addition, if anything more could in reason be demanded to disclose the intention of the tenants to stop the tenancy and to inform Arbenz of such intention, we add that the tenants in April, 1899, in court defended the claim of Arbenz to rent prior to November, 1899. Their defense was that the building was destroyed and they had sent that letter and abandoned possession. But here comes in the answer that the statute, reiterating common law prevalent for centuries, tells how the tenant must end his tenancy, that is, by written notice. It is dangerous for us to insert an exception by saying that if the landlord had knowledge of the tenant's intention, it stands for notice. It may not be improper to say that I have given labored investigation of this case, as other members of the Court have, and I have been impressed with the weight of the line of defense just stated, and have struggled to find a justification for adopting it, as the payment of the whole rent by the defendants, without any return, works a hardship, which all the members of the Court appreciate; but I am compelled to say that to decide against the plaintiffs would be to fly in the face of practically a unanimity of authorities through several hundred years in all quarters where the common law rules. As applied generally the rule is right; as applied in this case, it works hardship; but we cannot bend a fixed rule to suit a hard case.

Counsel says that the statute only requires three months notice before end of year, and that the written notice need not specify time of quitting, and that to say so is to read such a requirement into the statute. We answer that the statute only recognizes as the law already the requirement of notice to terminate a tenancy from year to year, and it has not changed the common law requisites of the notice.   *   *   *

We do not go on the theory that the former decision is res judicata to fix right to recover the rent involved in the present case. That case was for rent for a certain period of time—this for another. That case is res judicata to establish that it was a tenancy from year to year, but did not say how long. A case may settle principle, but not be res judicata as to matters not immediately involved.

We are compelled to reverse the judgment and render judgment for the plaintiff for his demand. Reversed.

Notes

1.   In Worthington v. Moreland Motor Truck Co., 140 Wash. 528, 250 P. 30 (1926), a month-to-month tenant vacated the leased premises and sent the landlord the keys and a letter stating that the landlord could take possession on "this date." The court held that the notice was insufficient to terminate at the end of the current month, but was sufficient to terminate at the end of the succeeding month. The court indicated that a notice which does not fix a time of termination might not be sufficient if given by a landlord to a tenant.

In T.W.I.W., Inc. v. Rhudy, 96 N.M. 753, 630 P.2d 753 (1981), a notice to vacate immediately was held sufficient to terminte at the earliest possible date under the applicable statute.

As to the requisites of an effective notice of termination, see Annot., 86 A.L.R. 1346 (1933).

2. In Lonergan v. Connecticut Food Store, 168 Conn. 122, 357 A.2d 910 (1975), a lease contained the following clause: "Upon the expiration of the term of this lease, the same, including this clause, shall automatically be extended for a period of one year and thence from year to year, unless the Lessee shall give notice to the Lessor of termination at least 60 days before the end of the original term or any extension thereof." What kind of tenancy is this? The court held that the clause did not constitute an option for perpetual renewal, for such are not favored. The court held that after the first extension the tenancy became one from year to year. The court was influenced in its construction by the absence of any provision for increased rent and by a provision in the lease requiring that the lessor repair the buildings.

3. Why did not the total destruction of the building on the leased premises terminate the tenancy and release the tenant from further rent liability? The answer lies in the common law concept of a leasehold tenancy—even a mere periodic tenancy—as an estate in the land, which carried with it the usual risks of ownership, including the risk of loss from fire or other casualty. Since the tenant in a case like *Arbenz* still had his estate in the land, there was no failure of consideration when the building on the leased premises was destroyed. Unless the lease or rental agreement expressly provided for termination of the tenancy upon destruction of buildings on the leased premises, the tenant's liability for the agreed rent would continue until the tenancy was terminated in some other fashion. (Cf. Siegel, Is the Modern Lease a Contract or a Conveyance—A Historical Inquiry, 52 J. Urban L. 649, 656 (1975), arguing that the common law rule as to risk of loss is essentially contractual, and that the risk of loss is placed on the tenant because he could have foreseen the possibility of loss but failed to provide for termination of the tenancy and of his liability for rent if a leased building should be destroyed or severely damaged by fire or other casualty.)

4. Most courts have modified the common law rule as to risk of loss so that it is not applicable where the leased premises consist of an apartment or other unit in a larger building which has been destroyed by fire or other casualty. This modification has been explained on the ground that in such cases the subject matter of the tenancy has been destroyed and there is no longer any basis for enforcement of the agreement to pay rent. The modified rule is certainly in accord with normal expectations of the parties.

As we shall see, the common law rule as to risk of loss applied in the *Arbenz* case has been changed by statute in many states.

SECTION 2. THE HOLD–OVER PROBLEM

A. THE STATUS OF THE HOLD–OVER TENANT

CRECHALE & POLLES, INC. v. SMITH

Supreme Court of Mississippi, 1974.
295 So.2d 275.

RODGERS, Presiding Justice. This action originated in the Chancery Court of the First Judicial District of Hinds County, Mississippi, pursuant to a bill for specific performance of a lease contract filed by Crechale and Polles, Inc., appellant herein. The court awarded the complainants one thousand seven hundred and fifty dollars ($1,750.00) in back rent payment, and seven hundred sixty dollars ($760.00) for damages to the leasehold premises, as well as costs incurred in the proceeding. From this judgment appellant files this appeal and appellees cross-appeal.

The testimony shows that on February 5, 1964, the appellant, Crechale and Polles, Inc., a Mississippi corporation, entered into a lease agreement with appellees, John D. Smith, Jr. and Mrs. Gloria Smith, with appellant as lessor and appellees as lessees. The lease was for a term of five (5) years commencing February 7, 1964, and expiring February 6, 1969, with rental in the amount of one thousand two hundred fifty dollars ($1,250.00) per month.

Smith was informed near the end of his lease that the new building which he planned to occupy would not be complete until a month or two after his present lease expired. With this in mind, he arranged a meeting with his landlord, Crechale, in late December, 1968, or early January, 1969, for the purpose of negotiating an extension of the lease on a month-to-month basis. The outcome of this meeting is one of the focal points of this appeal and the parties' stories sharply conflict. Crechale maintains that he told Smith that since he was trying to sell the property, he did not want to get involved in any month-to-month rental. Smith asserts that Crechale informed him that he was trying to sell the building, but that he could stay in it until it was sold or Smith's new building was ready. Smith's attorney drafted a thirty (30) day extension, but Crechale refused to sign it, saying, "Oh, go ahead. It's all right." Crechale denies that he was ever given the document to sign.

The following is a chronological explanation of the events which led to the subsequent litigation:

February 4, 1969—Smith sent a letter to Crechale confirming their oral agreement to extend the lease on a monthly basis.

February 6, 1969—Crechale wrote Smith denying the existence of any oral agreement concerning extension of the lease and requesting that Smith quit and vacate the premises upon expiration of the term at midnight, February 6, 1969. The letter also advised Smith that he was subject to payment of double rent for any holdover.

March 3, 1969—Smith paid rent for the period of February to March. The check was accepted and cashed by Crechale.

April 6, 1969—Smith paid rent for the period of March to April, but the check was not accepted by Crechale, because it was for "final payment".

April 7, 1969—Smith sent a telegram to Crechale stating that he was tendering the premises for purposes of lessor's inventory. The telegram confirmed a telephone conversation earlier that day in which Crechale refused to inventory the building.

April 19, 1969—Approximately three and one-half (3½) months after the expiration of the lease, Crechale's attorney wrote Smith stating that since the lessee had held over beyond the normal term, the lessor was treating this as a renewal of the lease for a new term expiring February 6, 1974.

April 24, 1969—Smith again tendered the check for the final month's occupancy and it was rejected by Crechale.

April 29, 1969—Crechale's attorney wrote Smith again stating the lessor's intention to consider the lessees' holdover as a renewal of the terms of the lease.

There was no further communication between the parties until a letter dated May 15, 1970, from Crechale to Smith requesting that Smith pay the past-due rent or vacate the premises.

May 27, 1970—Smith's attorney tendered the keys to the premises to Crechale.

Subsequently, this lawsuit was filed by Crechale to recover back rent and damages beyond ordinary wear and tear to the leasehold premises. From the chancellor's decision, appellant files the following assignments of error:

(1) The lower court erred in holding that the appellees were not liable as hold-over tenants for an additional term of one (1) year.

(2) The lower court's award of damages to the appellant was so inadequate in its amount as to be contrary to the overwhelming evidence.

The cross-appellants, John D. Smith, Jr. and Mrs. Gloria Smith, assign the following as error:

(1) That the chancellor erred in overruling cross-appellants' general demurrer to the original bill for specific performance.

(2) That the lower court erred in assessing damages against the cross-appellants.

The appellant, Crechale and Polles, Inc., contends that the appellees became hold-over tenants for a new term under the contract at the election of the landlord appellant, and that appellees owe appellant the rent due each month up to the filing of suit, less the rent paid; and, in addition thereto, it is entitled to specific performance of the holdover contract. This argument is based upon the general rule expressed in 3 Thompson on Real Property § 1024, at 65–66 (1959), wherein it is said:

"As a general rule, a tenancy from year to year is created by the tenant's holding over after the expiration of a term for years and the continued payment of the yearly rent reserved. * * * By remaining in possession of leased premises after the expiration of his lease, a tenant gives the landlord the option of treating him as a trespasser or as a tenant for another year, * * *."

In support of this rule the appellant cites Tonkel, et al. v. Riteman, 163 Miss. 216, 141 So. 344 (1932) wherein it is said:

"It is firmly established that where, without a new contract, a tenant continues to occupy the property which he has held under an annual lease, he becomes liable as tenant for another year at the same rate and under the same terms. Love v. Law, 57 Miss. 596; Usher v. Moss, 50 Miss. 208. It is the duty of a tenant when his period of tenancy has expired to surrender the premises to his landlord or else to have procured a new contract, and, if he fails to do either, the landlord may treat him as a trespasser or as a tenant under the previous terms, according to the option of the landlord." 163 Miss. at 219, 141 So. at 344.

An examination of the testimony in this case has convinced us that the appellant is not entitled to specific performance so as to require the appellees to pay rent for a new term of the rental contract as a hold-over tenant for the following reasons.

After receiving a letter from one of the appellees in which appellee Smith confirmed an alleged agreement to extend the lease on a month-to-month basis, Crechale immediately wrote Smith and denied that there was such an agreement, and demanded that Smith quit and vacate the premises at the end of the lease.

In addition to the rule expressed in 3 Thompson on Real Property § 1024, above cited, another rule is tersely expressed in American Law of Property § 3.33, at 237 (1952) as follows: "When a tenant continues in possession after the termination of his lease, the landlord has an election either to evict him, treat him as a trespasser it is said, or to hold him as a tenant."

The letter from the appellant dated February 6, 1969, was an effective election on the part of appellant to terminate the lease and to treat the appellees as trespassers.

After having elected not to accept the appellees as tenants, the appellant could not at a later date, after failing to pursue his remedy to evict the tenants, change the election so as to hold the appellees as tenants for a new term.

It is pointed out by the text writer in 49 Am.Jur.2d under the title of Landlord and Tenant that:

"After the landlord has once exercised his election not to hold the tenant for another term, his right to hold him is lost. On the other hand, if he has signified his election to hold the tenant for another term he cannot thereafter rescind such election and treat the tenant as a trespasser, *since his election when once exercised is binding upon the landlord as well as the tenant.*" (Emphasis added) 49 Am.Jur.2d Landlord and Tenant § 1116, at 1070 (1970).

Although the landlord, appellant, expressly refused to extend the lease on a month-to-month basis, nevertheless, the appellant accepted and cashed the rent check for the month of February. The normal effect of such action by the landlord is tantamount to extension of the lease for the period of time for which the check was accepted, unless, of course, the landlord had elected to treat the tenant as a hold-over tenant.

The following excerpt from Annot., 45 A.L.R.2d 827, 831 (1956) points out this rule: "It is the rule that, absent evidence to show a contrary intent on the part of the landlord, a landlord who accepts rent from his holding-over tenant will be held to have consented to a renewal or extension of the leasing."

Although there is authority to the contrary [*see* Annot., 45 A.L.R.2d at 842] the overwhelming weight of authority has adopted the rule above expressed.

On April 6, 1969, the tenants mailed a check for rent for the month of March accompanied by a letter stating that the enclosed check represented the final payment of rent. The next day the tenants tendered the lease premises to the landlord and requested an inventory of certain personal property described in the lease. The landlord refused to accept the tender and rejected the check as a final payment. On April 19, 1969 [three and one-half (3½) months after the expiration of the lease] the landlord attempted to change its position. It then notified the tenants that it had elected to treat them as holdover tenants so as to extend the lease for another term.

We are of the opinion that once a landlord elects to treat a tenant as a trespasser and refuses to extend the lease on a month-to-month basis, but fails to pursue his remedy of ejecting the tenant, and accepts monthly checks for rent due, he in effect agrees to an extension of the lease on a month-to-month basis. *See* Lally v. The New Voice, 128 Ill. App. 455 (1906); Stillo v. Pellettieri, 173 Ill.App. 104 (1912).

There is authority to the contrary, but we believe this rule to be based on the best reasoned authority.

The appellant contends that the decree of the trial court awarded inadequate damages to the appellant. The appellant fails, however, to point out any fact which would indicate to this Court wherein the decree of the trial court is manifestly wrong. We think that this issue of damages was a question of fact for the chancellor, and from an examination of the record we cannot say that the chancellor was manifestly wrong.

*   *   *

The cross-appellants, the Smiths, contend that the trial court erred in overruling their demurrer upon the ground that the landlord had an adequate remedy at law. They cite Roberts v. Spence, 209 So.2d 623, 626 (Miss.1968) wherein this Court said: [O]rdinarily a court of equity will not attempt to enforce a contract by specific performance where the parties have an adequate remedy at law to recover damages growing out of the failure of a contracting party to carry out the terms of the contract."

The landlord does have a remedy at law to evict a tenant [Mississippi Code Annotated § 89–7–27 (1972)]; nevertheless, a landlord may also proceed in chancery to enforce specific performance of a renewed contract, and the mere fact that the chancellor held that specific performance would not be allowed does not retroactively deprive the chancery court of jurisdiction. This Court said in Roberts v. Spence, supra: "The application for specific performance is addressed to the sound discretion of the chancery court." [209 So.2d at 625]. The chancellor was correct in overruling the demurrer.

We cannot agree with the cross-appellants' contention that the chancellor was manifestly wrong in awarding the amount of damages for the items set out in the decree of the chancery court. We have carefully examined each item in the light of the briefs, and we find no reversible error in the ruling of the trial court.

We hold, therefore, that the decree of the trial court should be and is hereby affirmed.

Affirmed.

Notes

1. If a tenant who holds over without consent of the landlord is a tenant at sufferance, this label alone does not indicate his status, for, as stated in *Crechale*, it merely raises a right of election in the landlord. If the landlord treats the tenant as a trespasser, his remedies are recovery of possession as well as the value of the tenant's use and occupancy of the premises during the hold-over period. If the landlord elects to treat the tenant as continuing under a new tenancy, there is some variation in the decisions on the nature and duration of the new tenancy.

If the rent under the original lease was payable annually (or on an annual basis, payable monthly), some courts hold that the new tenancy is either for one year or from year to year; if the rent was payable monthly, the new tenancy is either for one month or from month to month. Other courts hold that the nature of the new tenancy depends on the term of the original lease; that is, if the term was for a year or more, the new tenancy is either for one year or from year to year; otherwise it depends on how the rent was payable under the original lease. Some of these variations, and others, are dictated by statute.

Whatever the nature of the new tenancy, the terms of the old lease continue unless changed by express or implied agreement of the parties.

No formalities are required for the landlord's election; it may be expressed by words or conduct, the most common example being the acceptance of rent. But having made his election, he will be held to it. What if a landlord delays making his election? There is some conflict upon whether such a delay, if unreasonable, amounts to a consent to the hold-over.

See 1 A.L.P. §§ 3.33, 3.35.

2. Do you see any conflict in *Crechale* between the court's conclusion that the tenant became a trespasser at the landlord's election and the further ruling that a tenancy from month-to-month was created?

What reason or justification was there for the judgment allowing recovery of rent from the tenant of only $1750? Does the result mean that the tenant enjoyed possession of the premises for over a year rent-free?

3. In Union Minerals & Alloys Corp. v. Port Realty & Warehousing Corp., 129 N.J.Super. 41, 322 A.2d 192 (1974), a lessor was given affirmative equitable relief against a prospective holding over by the lessee on account of the removal of extensive machinery and equipment. The lessee was directed to take specific action either to remove the equipment or dispose of it. The court spoke of the lessee's conduct, in failing to take the necessary steps in due time, as constituting an anticipatory breach of the lease agreement.

4. URLTA § 4.301 provides as follows:

URLTA

(c) If the tenant remains in possession without the landlord's consent after the expiration of the term of the rental agreement or its termination, the landlord may bring an action for possession and if the tenant's holdover is willful and not in good faith the landlord may also recover an amount not more than [3] month's periodic rent or [threefold] the actual damages sustained by him, whichever is greater, and reasonable attorney's fees. If the landlord consents to the tenant's continued occupancy, Section 1.401(d) applies [creates a month-to-month tenancy. Ed.]

MAGUIRE v. HADDAD

Supreme Judicial Court of Massachusetts, 1950.
325 Mass. 590, 91 N.E.2d 769.

COUNIHAN, Justice. This is an action of summary process under G.L. (Ter.Ed.) c. 239, § 1, as amended, to recover possession of an apartment occupied by the defendant as a tenant at will of the plaintiffs. * * * The judge denied certain requests of the defendant for rulings and made a finding for the plaintiffs for possession, and the action comes here on a bill of exceptions of the defendant.

The only evidence offered was in the form of an "agreed statement of facts" which we shall treat as an agreement as to evidence and not as a case stated. * * * The evidence may be summarized as follows: From February, 1948, the defendant occupied the apartment as a tenant at will at a monthly rent of $60 payable in advance. * * * On May 14, 1948, the plaintiffs delivered to the defendant the following notice dated May 10, 1948. "This is to notify you to quit and deliver up at the end of that term of your tenancy next beginning after the receipt of this notice the upper or second floor apartment situated at 470 Center Street, Jamaica Plain District of the City of Boston, Massachusetts, unless you are willing after that date to pay the amount of rental of eighty-five dollars monthly * * *." The defendant continued to occupy the premises after July 1, 1948, and sent the plaintiffs on the first day of each month from July 1, 1948, to the date of the trial a check for $60 for each month payable in advance.

Each month the plaintiffs sent the defendant receipts similar in form to the following receipt:

"July 1, 1948

"Dr. F.K. Haddad No. 470 Centre St.J.P.

"Amount $85.00 Due July 1st Month Ending July 31st.

"You are advised that rent as set forth above should be forwarded to this office.

Rec. Payment	$60.00
Bal. Due	25.00

"Very truly yours,
Mrs. Katharine J. Maguire
Received payment:
by _____"

None of the defendant's checks mentioned the purpose for which it was drawn, and the receipts monthly carried forward the balance which the plaintiffs claimed was due them. On September 25, 1948, the defendant was served with a notice to vacate in substance as follows:

"September 25, 1948

"To F.K. Haddad

"Your rent being in arrear, you are hereby notified to quit and deliver up fourteen days from receipt of this notice the premises now held by you as my tenant namely: Upper floor or second floor apartment consisting of eight rooms and bath situated at 470 Center Street, Jamaica Plain District of Boston, Mass. together with all the privileges and appurtenances thereto belonging. * * *

"Amount of Rent $85.00 monthly advance. Amount of rent due $75.00.

"Rental period for which rent is due account of September 1948.

"Cause of Eviction Non-Payment of Rent.

"/s/ Mary J.C. Maguire
Co-Owner."

* * * The defendant's requests for rulings which the judge denied were as follows: "3. The evidence warrants a finding for the defendant. 4. That upon the evidence the defendant is entitled to a finding in his favor."

The plaintiff contends that, because the tenant continued in possession after July 1, 1948, he impliedly assented to the increase in rent requested in the notice dated May 10, 1948, and thus became in arrears of rent on September 25, 1948, when the notice to vacate for nonpayment of rent was given. To support this theory, assent of the tenant express or implied must be found, for it has been established that a new tenancy at will, with terms different from those of a former tenancy, cannot be created except with the mutual consent of the landlord and the tenant. * * * Here there plainly was no assent on the part of the tenant by silence or acquiescence, or by paying the increase, for he steadfastly refused to pay it. The notice to vacate dated May 10, 1948, is clearly equivocal. On the one hand it demands possession and on the other it invites the tenant to remain in possession at an increased rental. When the tenant failed to vacate, the landlords did not treat him as a tenant as sufferance which he was if the notice was good. * * * On the contrary, they recognized him as a tenant at will and proceeded to evict him for nonpayment of rent. * * *

The landlords could not blow hot and blow cold. They had to choose one position and stick to it. If negotiations failed to bring about an adjustment in the rent, the landlords could have terminated the tenancy by an unequivocal notice and instituted proper eviction proceedings under G.L. (Ter.Ed.) c. 239, § 1, as amended.

No Massachusetts decision has been brought to our attention and we have discovered none in which a notice such as this, in the alternative, has been discussed. * * * We conclude that the notice dated May

10, 1948, did not effect an increase in the rent of the tenant, and likewise did not terminate the tenancy at will.

Since no increase in rent of the tenant ever became effective, it follows that, if the tenant continued to pay rent at the old rate, as he did, he was not in arrears in rent on September 25, 1948, when he was served with the notice to vacate for nonpayment of rent. In these circumstances no proceedings under G.L. (Ter.Ed.) c. 186, § 12, as appearing in St.1946, c. 202, could be instituted.   *   *   *

Exceptions sustained. Judgment for the defendant.

Notes

1. Obviously a landlord cannot without the tenant's consent raise the rent specified in a lease for a definite term. Landlords, however, frequently give notice that if a tenant wishes to continue beyond the end of the term, he will be subject to an increased rent. It is generally held that if the tenant holds over without otherwise responding to such a proposal, he will be held to have impliedly consented. E.g. Garrity v. United States, 107 Ct.Cl. 92, 67 F.Supp. 821 (1946); Heckman v. Walker, 167 Neb. 216, 92 N.W.2d 548 (1958). If he holds over after having expressed his rejection of such an increase, the cases are divided on whether the rent increase will take effect. See 109 A.L.R. 197 (1937). But at least one court has held that no contract for an increased rent can be made without the consent of both parties and that the silence of the tenant cannot be construed as consent. Iorio v. Donnelly, 343 Mass. 772, 178 N.E.2d 28 (1961), citing Maguire v. Haddad.

2. Suppose a landlord wishes to raise the rent under a periodic tenancy. As in the case of a lease for a term of years, it would seem that he cannot change the rent agreed upon without the tenant's consent so long as the tenancy continues. But he is not required to continue the tenancy indefinitely. Since he can terminate only by giving a proper notice, how may he also indicate his willingness to create a new tenancy at a higher rent? If he combines an otherwise proper notice of termination with a notice of a rent increase under a successive tenancy, is he really "blowing hot and cold," so that his notice is without any effect? Compare the views of some recent New York lower courts, one of which held the same as the Massachusetts court in Maguire v. Haddad, that is, a notice to terminate coupled with a demand for increased rent if the tenant remains is equivocal and ineffective. (Spencer v. Faulkner, 65 Misc.2d 298, 317 N.Y.S.2d 374 (1971). Two other courts held that if a landlord gives notice of a rent increase without a notice of termination, the notice is ineffective either to increase the rent or to terminate the lease. Aronson v. Markulin, 39 Misc.2d 273, 240 N.Y.S.2d 689 (1963); 62 Spruce St. Realty Co. v. Murray, 62 Misc.2d 973, 310 N.Y.S.2d 625 (1970). Spencer v. Faulkner was followed in T.W.I.W. Inc. v. Rhudy, 96 N.M. 354, 630 P.2d 753 (1981).

A California statute permits a landlord to modify the terms of a month-to-month tenancy by giving notice thereof 30 days prior to the end of any month. A landlord gave notice to terminate as of a certain date, but specified a higher rent if the tenant remained on the premises. The court held that this notice did not comply with the statute because it was a notice to terminate, and so was ineffective to raise the rent. Colyear v. Tolbriner, 7 Cal.2d 735, 62 P.2d 741 (1936).

In several jurisdictions it has been held that under a periodic tenancy a timely notice which expresses a landlord's intention either to terminate or to continue at a higher rent results in the continuation of the tenancy at the higher rent if the tenant holds over beyond the date specified. Welk v. Bidwell, 136 Conn. 603, 73 A.2d 295 (1950); Bhar Realty Corp. v. Becker, 49 N.J.Super. 585, 140 A.2d 756 (1958). The same result has been reached by a few other courts where the notice purported to be merely a notice of a rent increase. Russells Factory Stores, Inc. v. Fielden Furniture Co., 33 Tenn.App. 688, 232 S.W.2d 592 (1950); 109 A.L.R. 197, 212 (1937). But there are other decisions that such a result does not follow if the tenant indicates his rejection of the rent increase. Groner v. Townhouse Realty, Inc., 235 A.2d 324 (D.C.App.1967); cf. Moll v. Main Motor Co., 213 Ark. 28, 210 S.W.2d 321 (1948). What is the status of the tenant if the increase is not effective?

In Stewart v. Melnick, 1 Hawaii App. 87, 613 P.2d 1336 (1980), a timely notice was given of a rent increase in a periodic tenancy. The notice said nothing about the duration or termination of the tenancy. The tenant replied rejecting the increase, but stayed on for three months. During the first of these months the landlord gave due notice to terminate within five days for failure to pay the increased rent. The tenant had tendered the original rent for that month. The court held that the notice to quit was invalid. The statutory five-day notice was available only when a tenant is in default, and here the tenant was not in default.

One court held that a notice of a rent increase which is exorbitant and in the nature of a penalty is ineffective. Di Costanzo v. Tripodi, 137 Conn. 513, 78 A.2d 890 (1951).

Suppose a tenant for a term of years holds over and thereafter the landlord notifies him that if he wishes to stay on he must pay a higher rent. Is this situation governed by any of the above authorities? In Moll v. Main Motor Co., 213 Ark. 28, 210 S.W.2d 321 (1948), the court held that the landlord was entitled only to reasonable compensation for the tenant's use and occupancy of the premises.

3. The dire consequences of the hold-over doctrine have been somewhat countered by a tendency to interpret the facts so as not to amount to a retention of possession beyond the date on which the tenancy came to an end or by recognition of an outright exception.

In a leading case, Herter v. Mullen, 159 N.Y. 28, 53 N.E. 700 (1899), the tenant admittedly was prevented from vacating one room of the premises by reason of the critical illness of a member of the family. The landlord claimed rent for the succeeding year, although the hold-over lasted only 14 days. A defense of impossibility of performance was upheld. The court said:

"It is also well settled that, where a duty or charge is created by law, and the performance is prevented by inequitable accident or the act of God, without fault of the party sought to be charged, he will be excused, but where a person absolutely, and by express contract, binds himself to do a particular thing, which is not at the time impossible or unlawful, he will not be excused, unless through the fault of the other party. The reason given for the latter portion of this rule is that he might have provided by his contract against inevitable accident or the act of God. Harmony v. Bingham, 12 N.Y. 99, 62 Am.Dec. 142; Tompkins v. Dudley, 25 N.Y. 272, 82 Am.Dec. 349; Dexter v. Norton, 47 N.Y. 62, 7 Am.Rep. 415. Thus the most that can be said of the obligation that arises from the relation of landlord and tenant and follows by a general lease is that the tenant is charged with the duty of vacating the premises at the end of his term. If he fails, it is a breach of his duty, and ordinarily the law implies or creates a liability on his part for another year's rent. This being a duty implied or created by law, and not by an express or absolute agreement, it falls within the first part of the foregoing rule, and hence it is obvious that, if the tenant's removal was rendered impossible by inevitable accident or the act of God, he is excused for his omission to surrender the premises, as least so far as it creates a liability for a year's rent which is implied by law. The reason for the distinction between the effect of impossibility of performance, occasioned by inevitable accident or the act of God, upon an obligation created by express contract and upon an obligation which the law implies, has been held to rest 'upon the unwillingness of the law to at once create, impose, and exact the performance of an obligation forbidden or rendered impractible by the interposition of Providence.' School Dist. v. Dauchy, 25 Conn. 530, 68 Am.Dec. 371."

B. RECOVERY OF POSSESSION BY LANDLORDS

(1) Forcible Repossession

PROSSER, THE LAW OF TORTS

Fourth Edition, 1971.

23. FORCIBLE ENTRY ON LAND

The privilege of one entitled to the possession of land to enter and recover it by force has been a source of long standing confusion in the courts. In 1381, under Richard the Second, a statute made such forcible entry a criminal offense. The English courts refused to treat this statute as a basis for any civil action for trespass to the land, on the ground that the plaintiff, having no right to the possession, could sustain no injury when he was deprived of it. But in Newton v. Harland,[*] it was held that the privilege of entry did not extend to the use of force upon the person of the occupant, and that an action for assault and battery would lie in such a case. This decision was overruled in England in 1920, but in the meantime it had received a great deal of acceptance in the United States.

The criminal statute of Richard II has been accepted as part of the common law, or re-enacted, by nearly all of the American states. In addition, many states also provide a specific, and speedy, civil remedy for such forcible entry. The interpretation placed upon such statutes necessarily controls the rule to be adopted, and discussion of them obviously is beyond the scope of this treatise. With due regard to the varying effect of such legislation, it may be said in general that the majority of the states have followed Newton v. Harland, and hold that the occupant may recover for assault and battery, or for trespass to his goods, if any such force is used in the course of the forcible entry. A smaller group adopt the present English rule, that the privilege extends to the use of reasonable force to expel the occupant and his property.

The majority rule seems clearly the desirable one. In virtually all jurisdictions, a summary procedure exists by which the owner may recover possession by legal process, with only a brief delay. Few things are more likely to lead to a brawl than an evicting landlord, throwing out his tenant by main force. Land cannot be sequestered or removed, and the public interest in preserving the peace would seem to justify the temporary inconvenience to the owner.

---

[*] 1840, 1 Man. & G. 644, 133 Eng.Rep. 490. Accord, Beddall v. Maitland, 1881, 17 Ch.Div. 174. [All the other footnotes by the author have been omitted. Ed.]

The same arguments might be advanced, with somewhat less force, against the mere privilege of entry itself. Most states, however, deny any common law remedy for trespass, and permit recovery, if at all, only in the form of an action provided by statute for forcible entry. Even here, a provision in the lease may give the landlord the privilege of entry by force, notwithstanding the statute. In all cases, however, he is liable for the use of any force beyond that reasonably necessary.

The statutes of forcible entry protect only a plaintiff who is himself in peaceable possession of the property. A mere "scrambling" possession is not enough. A trespasser who ousts the owner acquires no such possession as will entitle him to protection against an immediate forcible reentry, even though it may involve assault and battery. What is required is "something like acquiescence in the physical fact of his occupation on the part of the rightful owner." Mere delay in taking effective action, even for a period of months, will not make the entry tortious, where the owner has not discovered his dispossession, or has made persistent efforts to enter; but acquiescence or toleration of the wrongful possession, even for a day, may bring him within the statute.

It is quite generally conceded that the owner may await his opportunity, and if he can regain possession peaceably, may then maintain it, and lawfully resist an attempt to oust him. But what constitutes such "peaceable" entry is very largely a question of the terms of the particular statute; and in some jurisdictions unlocking a door, or breaking it down, is regarded as peaceable, while in others deception, or a mere entry without the consent of the possessor, remains wrongful.

(2) Summary Actions for the Recovery of Possession

By the traditional law of landlord and tenant, a landlord could recover possession of premises from a tenant only when the leasehold had terminated by expiration of the term of a lease, by proper notice when the tenancy was of indefinite duration, or by the exercise of a right of entry (or power of termination) expressly reserved in a lease. In the absence of such a right of entry, breach of a promise by a tenant, including a promise to pay rent, did not confer on a landlord the right of eviction. In property terms, a right of entry is a property interest which can be created only by expressly reserving it in a lease or other conveyance. In recognition of the fact that most leases are also contracts, the traditional interpretation of leases has been that the respective promises of the parties are "independent," so that breach of a promise by either does not excuse performance of a promise by the other.

Statutes exist in most states which extend the remedy of landlords for the recovery of possession of demised premises, although they are framed in general terms so as not to be limited to the landlord-tenant relation. The grounds stated for such a remedy vary, but usually include non-payment of rent due under a lease. The procedure prescribed is more simple and expeditious than the traditional general remedies for establishing title to or recovering possession of land. This of course is the main purpose of such statutes. Hence the term "summary possession statute" is commonly employed as a label. In some states a "Forcible Entry and Detainer" statute will include these features, together with provisions prohibiting forcible entries upon land. Consistently with the objectives of these statutes, they have been construed, if they do not expressly provide, that "affirmative" or "equitable" defenses may not be raised in such actions. This means that a tenant in such an action may not plead breaches by the landlord of any of his obligations under a lease and set them off against the tenant's liability for rent. But it also means more than that. Traditional adherence to the doctrine of the independence of covenants in a lease means that a tenant's promise to pay rent, or any other promise, is not excused by any breach of promise by the landlord. Both of these aspects of the law, that is, the independence of the covenants of landlord and tenant, and the procedural limitations of the summary possession statutes, should be fixed firmly in your minds, for they are the focal point of attack in recent decisions which declare the traditional law inadequate for current needs in the ordering of landlord and tenant relations. We will examine these cases in due course. Provisions of the Iowa statute on summary possession are offered here merely as an example of statutes of this type. The statutes vary considerably in detail.

IOWA CODE ANNOTATED

(as amended, 1973)

Forcible Entry or Detention of Real Property

648.1

A summary remedy for forcible entry or detention of real property is allowable:

1. Where the defendant has by force, intimidation, fraud, or stealth entered upon the prior actual possession of another in real property, and detains the same.

2. Where the lessee holds over after the termination of his lease.

3. Where the lessee holds contrary to the terms of his lease.

4. Where the defendant continues in possession after a sale by foreclosure of a mortgage, or on execution, unless he claims by a title paramount to the lien by virtue of which the sale was made, or by title derived from the purchaser at the sale; in either of which cases such title shall be clearly and concisely set forth in the defendant's pleading.

5. For the nonpayment of rent, when due.

6. When the defendant or defendants remain in possession after the issuance of a valid tax deed.

648.3   Notice to Quit

Before action can be brought in any except the first of the above classes, three days notice to quit must be given to the defendant in writing. [Qualified in case of tenant of a mobile home.]

648.4   Notice Terminating Tenancy

When the tenancy is at will and the action is based on the ground of the nonpayment of rent when due, no notice of the termination of the tenancy other than the three-day notice need be given before beginning the action.

648.5   Jurisdiction

The court within the county shall have jurisdiction of actions for the forcible entry or detention of real property. It shall be tried as an equitable action. Unless commenced as a small claim, a petition shall be presented to a district court judge. The court shall make an order fixing the time and place for hearing upon said petition and shall prescribe that notice of the hearing be personally served upon the defendant or defendants, which service shall be at least five days prior to the date set for hearing.

648.10   Service by Publication

Where it is made to appear by affidavit that personal service of the original notice in such action cannot be made upon the defendant within the state, the same may be made by publication in the same manner and for the same length of time as is required in other cases where such substituted service may be made.

648.16   Priority of Assignment

Such actions shall be accorded reasonable priority for assignment to assure their prompt disposition. No continuance shall be granted for the purpose of taking testimony in writing.

648.17   Remedy Not Exclusive

Nothing contained in sections 648.13 to 648.16, inclusive, shall prevent a party from suing for trespass or from testing the right of property in any other manner.

648.18   Possession—Bar

Thirty days peaceable possession with the knowledge of the plaintiff after the cause of action accrues is a bar to this proceeding.

648.19   No Joinder or Counterclaim

An action of this kind cannot be brought in connection with any other, nor can it be made the subject of counterclaim.

648.20   Order for Removal

The order for removal can be executed only in the daytime.

648.22   Judgment

If the defendant is found guilty, judgment shall be entered that he be removed from the premises, and that the plaintiff be put in possession thereof, and an execution for his removal shall issue accordingly, to which shall be added a clause commanding the officer to collect the costs as in ordinary cases.

648.23   Restitution

The court, on the trial of an appeal, may issue an execution for removal or restitution, as the case may require.

Notes

1. See Annotation, 6 A.L.R.3d 177 (1966).

2. A section of the Illinois Forcible Entry and Detainer statute provides that upon the filing of a complaint by the party entitled to possession stating that such party is entitled to possession and that the defendant unlawfully withholds possession from him, the clerk of the court shall issue a summons. The section further provides,

"The defendant may under a general denial of the allegations of the complaint give in evidence any matter in defense of the action. No matters not germane to the distinctive purpose of the proceeding shall be introduced by joinder, counterclaim or otherwise: Provided, however, that a claim for rent may be joined in the complaint, and judgment obtained for the amount of rent found due."

Illinois Annotated Statutes, ch. 110, ¶ 9–106 (Smith-Hurd, Pamph.1982).

3. The District of Columbia Code provides for an action to recover possession of real property that is of a more summary nature than the action of ejectment. A section of that statute which preserved the right to a jury trial was repealed by Congress in 1970. A landlord sought to recover possession from a tenant for nonpayment of rent. The tenant alleged certain matters by way of defense and requested a jury trial. The request was denied, and the Court of Appeals affirmed. The Supreme Court treated the statutory action as an action at law, rather than a suit in equity, so that a jury trial was required under the Seventh Amendment. Pernell v. Southall Realty Co., 416 U.S. 363, 94 S.Ct. 1723, 40 L.Ed.2d 198 (1974).

SECTION 3.   LANDLORDS' WARRANTIES RESPECTING TITLE AND POSSESSION

HANNAN v. DUSCH

Supreme Court of Appeals of Virginia, 1930.
154 Va. 356, 153 S.E. 824.

PRENTIS, C.J. The declaration filed by the plaintiff, Hannan, against the defendant, Dusch, alleges that Dusch had on August 31, 1927, leased to the plaintiff certain real estate in the city of Norfolk, Va., therein described, for fifteen years, the term to begin January 1, 1928, at a specified rental; that it thereupon became and was the duty of the defendant to see to it that the premises leased by the defendant to the plaintiff should be open for entry by him on January 1, 1928, the beginning of the term, and to put said petitioner in possession of the premises on that date; that the petitioner was willing and ready to enter upon and take possession of the leased property, and so informed the defendant; yet the defendant failed and refused to put the plaintiff in possession or to keep the property open for him at that time or on any subsequent date; and that the defendant suffered to remain on said property a certain tenant or tenants who occupied a portion or portions thereof, and refused to take legal or other action to oust said tenant or tenants or to compel their removal from the property so occupied. Plaintiff alleged damages which he had suffered by reason of this alleged breach of the contract and deed, and sought to recover such damages in the action. There is no express covenant as to the delivery of the premises nor for the quiet possession of the premises by the lessee.

The defendant demurred to the declaration on several grounds, one of which was "that under the lease set out in said declaration the right of possession was vested in said plaintiff and there was no duty as upon the defendant, as alleged in said declaration, to see that the premises were open for entry by said plaintiff."

The single question of law therefore presented in this case is whether a landlord, who without any express covenant as to delivery or possession leases property to a tenant, is required under the law to oust trespassers and wrongdoers so as to have it open for entry by the tenant at the beginning of the term; that is, whether without an express covenant there is nevertheless an implied covenant to deliver possession.

For an intelligent apprehension of the precise question it may be well to observe that some questions somewhat similar are not involved.

It seems to be perfectly well settled that there is an implied covenant in such cases on the part of the landlord to assure to the tenant the legal right of possession; that is, that at the beginning of the term there shall be no legal obstacle to the tenant's right of possession. This is not the question presented. Nor need we discuss in this case the rights of the parties in case a tenant rightfully in possession under the title of his landlord is thereafter disturbed by some wrongdoer. In such case the tenant must protect himself from trespassers, and there is no obligation on the landlord to assure his quiet enjoyment of his term as against wrongdoers or intruders.

Of course, the landlord assures to the tenant quiet possession as against all who rightfully claim through or under the landlord.

The discussion then is limited to the precise legal duty of the landlord in the absence of an express covenant, in case of a former tenant, who wrongfully holds over, illegally refuses to surrender possession to the new tenant. This is a question about which there is a hopeless conflict of the authorities. It is generally claimed that the weight of the authority favors the particular view contended for. There are, however, no scales upon which we can weigh the authorities. In numbers and respectability they may be quite equally balanced.

It is then a question about which no one should be dogmatic, but all should seek for that rule which is supported by the better reason.
* * *

It is conceded by all that the two rules, one called the English rule, which implies a covenant requiring the lessor to put the lessee in possession, and that called the American rule, which recognizes the lessee's legal right to possession, but implies no such duty upon the lessor as against wrongdoers, are irreconcilable.

The English rule is that, in the absence of stipulations to the contrary, there is in every lease an implied covenant on the part of the landlord that the premises shall be open to entry by the tenant at the time fixed by the lease for the beginning of his term. These cases appear to support that rule: *   *   *

It must be borne in mind, however, that the courts which hold that there is such an implied covenant do not extend the period beyond the day when the lessee's term begins. If after that day a stranger trespasses upon the property and wrongfully obtains or withholds possession of it from the lessee, his remedy is against the stranger and not against the lessor.

It is not necessary for either party to involve himself in uncertainty, for by appropriate covenants each may protect himself against any doubt either as against a tenant then in possession who may wrongfully hold over by refusing to deliver the possession at the expiration of his own term, or against any other trespasser.   *   *   *

King v. Reynolds, 67 Ala. 229, 42 Am.Rep. 107, has been said to be the leading case in this country affirming the English rule.   *   *   *

Another case which supports the English rule is Herpolsheimer v. Christopher, 76 Neb. 352, 107 N.W. 382, 111 N.W. 359, 360, 9 L.R.A.,N.S., 1127, 14 Ann.Cas. 399, note. In that case the court gave these as its reasons for following the English rule: "We deem it unnecessary to enter into an extended discussion, since the reasons pro and con are fully given in the opinions of the several courts cited. We think, however, that the English rule is most in consonance with good conscience, sound principle, and fair dealing. Can it be supposed that the plaintiff in this case would have entered into the lease if he had known at the time that he could not obtain possession on the 1st of March, but that he would be compelled to begin a lawsuit, await the law's delays, and follow the case through its devious turnings to an end before he could hope to obtain possession of the land he had leased? Most assuredly not. It is unreasonable to suppose that a man would knowingly contract for a lawsuit, or take the chance of one. Whether or not a tenant in possession intends to hold over or assert a right to a future term may nearly always be known to the landlord, and is certainly much more apt to be within his knowledge than within that of the prospective tenant. Moreover, since in an action to recover possession against a tenant holding over the lessee would be compelled largely to rely upon the lessor's testimony in regard to the facts of the claim to hold over by the wrongdoer, it is more reasonable and proper to place the burden upon the person within whose knowledge the facts are most apt to lie. We are convinced, therefore, that the better reason lies with the courts following the English doctrine, and we therefore adopt it, and hold that ordinarily the lessor impliedly covenants with the lessee that the premises leased shall be open to entry by him at the time fixed in the lease as the beginning of the term." * * *

So let us not lose sight of the fact that under the English rule a covenant which might have been, but was not, made is nevertheless implied by the court, though it is manifest that each of the parties might have provided for that and for every other possible contingency relating to possession by having express covenants which would unquestionably have protected both.

Referring then to the American rule: Under that rule, in such cases, "the landlord is not bound to put the tenant into actual possession, but is bound only to put him into legal possession, so that no obstacle in the form of a superior right of possession will be interposed to prevent the tenant from obtaining actual possession of the demised premises. If the landlord gives the tenant a right of possession he has done all that he is required to do by the terms of an ordinary lease, and the tenant assumes the burden of enforcing such right of possession as against all persons wrongfully in possession, whether they be trespassers or former tenants wrongfully holding over." This quoted language is Mr. Freeman's, and he cites these cases in support thereof: * * *

So that, under the American rule, where the new tenant fails to obtain possession of the premises only because a former tenant wrongfully holds over, his remedy is against such wrongdoer and not against the landlord—this because the landlord has not covenanted against the wrongful acts of another and should not be held responsible for such a tort, unless he has expressly so contracted. This accords with the general rule as to other wrongdoers, whereas the English rule appears to create a specific exception against lessors. It does not occur to us now that there is any other instance in which one clearly without fault is held responsible for the independent tort of another in which he has neither participated nor concurred, and whose misdoings he cannot control. * * *

There are some underlying fundamental considerations. Any written lease, for a specific term, signed by the lessor, and delivered, is like a deed signed, sealed, and delivered by the grantor. This lease for fifteen years is and is required to be by deed. It is a conveyance. During the term the tenant is substantially the owner of the property, having the right of possession, dominion, and control over it. Certainly, as a general rule, the lessee must protect himself against trespassers or other wrongdoers who disturb his possession. It is conceded by those who favor the English rule that, should the possession of the tenant be wrongfully disturbed the second day of the term, or after he has once taken possession, then there is no implied covenant on the part of his landlord to protect him from the torts of others. The English rule seems to have been applied only where the possession is disturbed on the first day, or, perhaps more fairly expressed, where the tenant is prevented from taking possession on the first day of his term; but what is the substantial difference between invading the lessee's right of possession on the first or a later day? To apply the English rule you must imply a covenant on the part of the landlord to protect the tenant from the tort of another, though he has entered into no such convenant. This seems to be a unique exception, an exception which stands alone in implying a contract of insurance on the part of the lessor to save his tenant from all the consequences of the flagrant wrong of another person. Such an obligation is so unusual and the prevention of such a tort so impossible as to make it certain, we think, that it should always rest upon an express contract.

For the reasons which have been so well stated by those who have enforced the American rule, our judgment is that there is no error in the judgment complained of.   *   *   *

We are confirmed in our view by the Virginia statute, providing a summary remedy for unlawful entry or detainer, Code, § 5445 et seq. The adequate, simple, and summary remedy for the correction of such a wrong provided by that statute was clearly available to this plaintiff. It specifically provides that it shall lie for one entitled to possession in any case in which a "tenant shall detain the possession of land after his right has expired, without the consent of him who is entitled to the possession." Section 5445.

Certainly there should be co-operation between the lessor and lessee to impose the resulting loss upon such a trespasser, but whatever the other equities may have arisen, when the plaintiff found that the premises which he had leased were occupied by a wrongdoer who unlawfully refused to surrender possession, it is manifest that he (the lessee, Hannan) had the right to oust the wrongdoer under this statute. His failure to pursue that remedy is not explained.   *   *   *

The plaintiff alleges in his declaration as one of the grounds for his action that the defendant suffered the wrongdoer to remain in possession, but the allegations show that he it was who declined to assert his remedy against the wrongdoer, and so he it was who permitted the wrongdoer to retain the possession. Just why he valued his legal right to the possession so lightly as not to assert it in the effective way open to him does not appear. Whatever ethical duty in good conscience may possibly have rested upon the defendant, the duty to oust the wrongdoer by the summary remedy provided by the unlawful detainer statute clearly rested upon the plaintiff. The law helps those who help themselves, generally aids the vigilant, but rarely the sleeping, and never the acquiescent.

Affirmed.

Notes

1. The measure of damages for breach of an express or implied covenant to give possession is the excess of the rental value of the premises over the agreed rent, plus certain special damages if proved. Although loss of profits may be included as special damages, they seldom are recovered, for lack of adequate proof. Annotation, 88 A.L.R.2d 1024, 1032 (1963).

2. The court in *Hannan* made casual references to two covenants other than the implied covenant to give possession. Either of these may be expressed in a lease, but both will be implied if not expressed, at least where the lessor expressly purports to "demise" or "grant" a leasehold estate.

Power to Demise. By this covenant a lessor warrants that he has such interest in the leased premises as enables him to convey the interest he purports to convey to the lessee. The covenant is broken, if at all, when the lease is made. If the lessee takes possession, only nominal damages can be recovered, unless there is a subsequent eviction. In the latter event, the covenant of quiet enjoyment is also breached, and a suit for damages is usually for breach of that covenant.

Quiet Enjoyment. Most courts hold that this covenant is implied whenever a landlord-tenant relation is created, including the case of an oral lease. The covenant is breached by an eviction of the tenant, actual or constructive, either by the lessor or his successor in interest or by one who asserts a paramount title. In the latter case the covenant of power to demise may also have been breached. The lessor by this covenant does not warrant against invasions by strangers to the title or by assertions of governmental authority in exercise of the power of eminent domain.

For breach of covenant a lessee has a variety of remedies. He may sue to recover possession. He may treat the lease as terminated, including the obligation to pay rent. He may sue for damages, which are measured by the difference between the rental value of the premises for the remainder of a term and the rent prescribed in the lease, plus special damages in certain circumstances. Special rules regarding the requirements and consequences of a "constructive" eviction are considered in several of the cases appearing below.

The cases are divided upon the question whether there can be a breach of a covenant of quiet enjoyment on account of interferences with a tenant's possession short of eviction, that is, whether a tenant who remains in possession can sue for damages for breach of the covenant. Clearly unlawful intrusions by a lessor are tortious, for which of course damages are recoverable. But invasions which do not produce an eviction, actual or constructive, do not permit a tenant to terminate the lease in the absence of express provision otherwise in the lease.

See 1 A.L.P. c. IV.

URLTA

Section 2.103. [Landlord to Deliver Possession of Dwelling Unit]

At the commencement of the term a landlord shall deliver possession of the premises to the tenant in compliance with the rental agreement and Section 2.104. [duties to maintain premises. Ed.] The landlord may bring an action for possession against any person wrongfully in possession and may recover the damages provided in Section 4.301(c). [See notes at page 354 supra: Ed.]

Section 4.102 [Failure to Deliver Possession]

(a) If the landlord fails to deliver possession of the dwelling unit to the tenant as provided in Section 2.103, rent abates until possession is delivered and the tenant may

    (1) terminate the rental agreement upon at least [5] days' written notice to the landlord and upon termination the landlord shall return all prepaid rent and security; or

    (2) demand performance of the rental agreement by the landlord and, if the tenant elects, maintain an action for possession of the dwelling unit against the landlord or any person wrongfully in possession and recover the actual damages sustained by him.

(b) If a person's failure to deliver possession is willful and not in good faith, an aggrieved person may recover from that person an amount not more than [3] months' periodic rent or [threefold] the actual damages sustained, whichever is greater, and reasonable attorney's fees.

Comment

"Aggrieved person" includes a landlord entitled to proceed under Sections 2.103 and 4.301(c) as well as a tenant entitled to possession.

SECTION 4. DUTIES RESPECTING FITNESS AND REPAIR OF LEASED PREMISES

A. THE TRADITIONAL LEGAL DOCTRINE

ANDERSON DRIVE–IN THEATRE v. KIRKPATRICK

Appellate Court of Indiana, In Banc, 1953.
123 Ind.App. 388, 110 N.E.2d 506.

ROYSE, Chief Judge. Appellees brought this action against appellant for rent under the terms of a twenty-five year lease of real estate owned by appellees. The complaint was in the usual form. Appellant answered by a denial of the allegations of each rhetorical paragraph of the complaint. It also filed an amended second paragraph of answer and cross-complaint. Appellees' demurrer to that answer and cross-complaint was sustained. That ruling is the sole question presented by this appeal.

The lease which is the subject of this action provided the real estate was to be used for the construction and operation of a drive-in theatre and for any other lawful purpose not in competition with any business operated by a trailer camp situated immediately east of the leased property. The lease *made no warranty as to the suitability of the land for the purpose which appellant intended to use it.*

The material averments of the second amended paragraph of answer and cross-complaint may be summarized as follows: That appellees were farmers, and for a long time had been engaged in the cultivation of the land leased, and were possessed of full, accurate and complete knowledge of the future use of the land to be made by appellant; that appellees knew that appellant did not have knowledge of the nature and character of the land and depended upon representations of appellees that the said land was suitable for the purpose for which leased; that the land was either boggy or wet or muck ground; that it gave an outward appearance of being ordinary ground; but it would not carry or bear the weight of many tons of buildings and equipment necessary for appellant's purpose; that appellees knew that the surface of the land leased was soft and yielding, and that the weight of the necessary buildings and equipment for such outdoor theatre could not be borne by the land; that appellees, by the lease, warranted, either expressly or impliedly, that said land would be suitable for the purposes intended; that appellees, knowing the land was not fit and suitable for appellant's purposes, failed and neglected to give appellant the true facts as to the condition of said land, but purposely and knowingly either misrepresented the nature of said land or failed to reveal that the land was unsuitable for appellant's purposes; that after the lease was signed, appellant employed skilled and experienced persons to test the said land, and thereby learned that the land was entirely unfit for such purposes, and that appellees had concealed the fact that the land was unfit for appellant's purposes; that appellees knew that appellant did not know of the true character of the land, and that the only information appellant had about the character of the land was as described in the lease executed by both parties; that appellees knew that appellant would not execute the lease if the true facts as to the nature of the land were revealed to it.

The demurrer was on the grounds that the said answer and cross-complaint did not state facts sufficient to constitute an affirmative answer or cross-complaint against appellees.

In the memorandum to their demurrer appellees, in substance, asserted it is the law that because a lease designates the use to which the premises are to be put it does not imply that the premises are suitable or fit for the use intended; that in such matters the rule of caveat emptor applies; that nowhere in the written lease is there any warranty that the land was suitable for appellant's use; that any verbal representation made by appellees could not be claimed to vary the terms of the written agreement; that the cross-complaint avers after the execution of the lease appellant employed skilled and experienced persons to test the land to ascertain whether or not it would bear the weight of the buldings for its special use; that such allegation shows appellant was going to use the premises for a particular and special use with which it was familiar, but of which appellees had no knowledge, and it further shows appellant had the means and opportunity to have examined and tested the land prior to the execution of the lease.

Appellant contends its second paragraph of answer and cross-complaint alleges facts disclosing fraud which would vitiate the lease. In support of this contention it asserts its answer avers facts which show latent defects in the land which it was the duty of the appellees to disclose to it. * * *

The answer and cross-complaint herein do not allege appellees made any statements as to the nature of the land. They do not allege the defects were not reasonably discoverable. On the other hand it avers that after the execution of the lease it caused tests of the land to be made and thereby discovered its unsuitability. There are no averments that appellants did not have an opportunity to inspect the land or to make such tests before executing the lease.

A purchaser of property has no right to rely upon the representations of the vendor of the property as to its quality, where he has a reasonable opportunity of examining the property and judging for himself as to its qualities. Shepard v. Goben, 1895, 142 Ind. 318, 39 N.E. 506.

There is no implied warranty that leased premises are fit for the purposes for which they are let. When an action is based on fraudulent concealment, a duty to disclose the truth must be shown. The rule of caveat emptor applies in the relation of landlord and tenant unless material representations constituting fraud are specifically alleged, or there is a showing of a fiduciary relationship between the parties. * * *

Judgment affirmed.

Note

The doctrine of *caveat emptor* is not the last word to be spoken on a landlord's duties respecting the condition of leased premises at the beginning of the term. Certain exceptions to that doctrine have evolved relating to a landlord's liability in tort for injuries to the person or property of a tenant or certain other persons resulting from the condition of the premises. These problems will be considered below in Section 6, rather than at this point, because a landlord's tort liabilities also include the problem whether and to what extent certain breaches of contract by a landlord can also be treated as tortious. The existence and intepretation of contractual obligations concerning the repair or maintenance of leased premises is our main concern throughout the remainder of this section.

CHAMBERS v. THE NORTH RIVER LINE

Supreme Court of North Carolina, 1920.
179 N.C. 199, 102 S.E. 198.

This is an action to recover damages for failure to rebuild a wharf known as "Shiloh" wharf, and for rent under the lease thereof. The case was submitted upon facts agreed. It appeared therefrom that the defendant lessee covenanted "to maintain the said wharf in its present condition during the continuance of this lease"; that the defendant company went into possession of the premises and paid the rents provided therein up to 31 December, 1917; that on 15 January, 1918, 270 yards of said wharf were totally destroyed, leaving standing and remaining only 100 yards thereof next to the shore, built over shallow water, and about one-half of the pier-head. The freight house at end of said wharf was also completely destroyed.

It was also stated in the facts agreed that "the destruction of said 270 yards of wharf, including the freight house as aforesaid, was due solely to the freezing of Pasquotank River, and the subsequent breaking up of the ice therein, which swept the same away, and the destruction was not due in any part to any fault or negligence on the part of the defendant company. The 100 yards of wharf remaining, as aforesaid, including the one-half of the pier-head also remaining, and all other property rights mentioned in said lease, are absolutely incapable of use for the purpose mentioned in the lease, unless the 270 yards of wharf and the freight house, swept away as aforesaid, be rebuilt."

It was further agreed by the parties that "said freeze began on 31 December 1917, and continued till 24 January 1918, and there had been only three such freezes in that locality in the last forty years." It is admitted that immediately after the destruction of the property aforesaid, the plaintiffs called upon the defendant to replace the same, and the defendant declined to do so, denying any further liability under the lease, and has made no use of the premises since that time. It was agreed, at the time of the refusal of the defendant to rebuild, that the cost of rebuilding the wharf and freight house would be $1,000.

Upon the above admissions the court rendered judgment that under the terms of the lease the plaintiff recover $1,000, the cost of replacing said property, and $420, the rent accrued since 31 December 1917, up to 30 September 1919, and the costs. Appeal by defendants.

CLARK, C.J. The court properly held that by reason of the failure of the defendant to rebuild the 270 yards of wharf and repair the damages to the freight house there was a breach in its covenant "to maintain the said wharf in its present condition during the continuance of this lease." And that the defendant was liable for rent to the trial, notwithstanding the destruction of the wharf, and for the damages, $1,000, which it was agreed by the parties would be the cost of replacing the destroyed wharf and repairing the freight house.

The defendants contended that said covenant did not obligate the defendant to replace the property, which had been destroyed without fault or negligence on its part, and that the destruction of the property also released the defendant from liability for rent. The court rendered judgment against the defendant on these points, and it appealed. The plaintiff contended that the defendant was further liable not only for rent and $1,000 agreed upon as the cost of replacing the wharf, but also for the difference in value of the property before and after the destruction of the wharf, plus the present cash value of the rent for the remainder of the unexpired term. The court held against this contention, and the plaintiff did not appeal.

The covenant "to maintain the premises in their present condition during the continuance of this lease" is equivalent to a general covenant to repair and leave in repair under the common law. It is well settled by the authorities that under a covenant of this kind, "when the property is destroyed by fire, flood, tempest, or other act of God or the public enemy," it is the duty of the contracting party to rebuild, unless relieved therefrom by statute or exceptions specially incorporated in the lease.

The law is thus summed up in 16 R.C.L., title "Landlord and Tenant," sec. 605: "It is the well settled common-law rule that a tenant's general covenant to repair the demised premises binds him under all circumstances, even though the injury proceeds from an act of God, from the elements, or from the act of a stranger, and if he desires to relieve himself from liability to injuries resulting from any of the causes above enumerated, or from any other cause whatever, he must take care to except them from the operation of his covenant. Under this rule, if the tenant enters into an express and unconditional covenant to repair and keep in repair, or to surrender the premises in good repair, he is liable for the destruction of buildings not rebuilt by him, though the destruction may have occurred by a fire or other accident or by the act of enemies, and without fault on his part."

In 18 A. & E. (2 ed.), 249, the rule is thus stated: "A general covenant by the tenant to repair or keep premises in repair includes a covenant to rebuild, and it was settled at an early date that such covenant
imposes upon the tenant the obligation to rebuild in case the premises
were destroyed." It is further said that "the obligation to rebuild in
case of the destruction of the premises imposed by the lessee's covenant
to repair, exists irrespective of whether the destruction was caused by
storm, flood, fire, inevitable accident, or the act of a stranger."

The word "maintain is practically the same thing as repair, which
means to restore to a sound or good state, after decay, injury, dilapida-
tion, or partial destruction." R.R. v. Bryan (Texas), 107 S.W. 576, citing
Verdin v. St. Louis (Missouri), 27 S.W. 447.

In R.R. v. Iron Co., 118 Tenn. 194, 101 S.W. 414, it was held that
where a railroad company agreed to construct and lay a branch track to
the mines of a mining company, and to "maintain and operate the
same," the railroad company was obligated to reconstruct a bridge constructed by the mining company after the bridge was washed away by
an extraordinary freshet, though the bridge under the contract would
become the property of the mining company after completion.

In Pasteur v. Jones, 1 N.C. 393, the Court held: "That where a tenant covenanted to build and leave in repair, and did build, but the houses were destroyed by fire, the Court of Equity would compel him either
to rebuild or pay the value of the buildings."

The defendant is not relieved by Rev., 1935, which provides: "An
agreement in a lease to repair a demised house shall not be construed to
bind the contracting party to rebuild or repair in case the house shall be
destroyed or damaged to more than half of its value by accidental fire
not occurring from the want of ordinary diligence on his part." This
statute was enacted to change the rule, formerly existing, but limits its
application to the destruction of a house by accidental fire, and only
then where it is damaged to more than half its value. It does not apply
to this case where the destruction is not by fire, but by ice and flood.
In 18 A. & E., 307, "the question as to the liability of the tenant, in case
of the accidental destruction of the buildings, has chiefly arisen where
the buildings have been accidentally burned, but applies equally whatever the causes of their destruction. The tenant is not relieved from future rents though the demised building is destroyed by reason of inherent defects existing at the time of the letting."

The same rule is laid down in 24 Cyc., 1089: "According to the common-law rule, which has been followed generally in this country, a covenant on the part of the lessee to repair or keep in good repair imposes
on him an obligation to rebuild the demised premises if they are destroyed during the term by fire or other casualty, even where he is
without fault," citing a large number of cases. It is pointed out, however, that in some States this rule has been modified by statute. In this
State the only modification has been as above stated in the case of a
house destroyed by fire or damaged to more than one-half.

As to rent, this Court has sustained the common-law rule as to the liability of the tenant therefor, notwithstanding the premises have been destroyed by fire. Improvement Co. v. Coley-Bardin, 156 N.C. 257, 72 S.E. 313, where the Court said: "The common law regards such a case as the one in evidence as the grant of an estate for years to which the lessee takes title. The lessee is bound to pay the stipulated rent, notwithstanding injury by flood, fire, or other external causes. It required a statute of the State to relieve the lessee where the property is destroyed by fire."

The liability of the defendant for rent is in no wise affected by Rev., 1992. An inspection of this statute will show that not only is it in terms confined to a demised house or other building, but that it expressly excepts from its provisions those leases in which there is an "agreement respecting repairs." An inspection of the statute will further disclose that by its express terms it requires, as a condition precedent to its application, that a lessee "surrender his estate in the demised premises by a writing to that effect, delivered or tendered to the landlord within ten days from the damage."

It thus appears that the liability for rent upon the part of the defendant is controlled by the rule of the common law, unaffected by any statutory provisions.

Affirmed.

Note on Statutory Modification of Risk of Loss

Although held not to be applicable in the *Chambers* case, the statute mentioned at the very end of the opinion obviously modified the common law rule placing the risk of loss on the tenant and requiring him to continue paying rent after damage to or destruction of buildings on the leased premises. In 1972, at least six states had legislation providing that if the premises are so destroyed or injured as to be untenantable or unfit for occupancy, the tenant may surrender possession and avoid further liability for rent. These states were Arizona, Connecticut, Michigan, Minnesota, Mississippi, and Wisconsin. West Virginia then had a statute providing for " * * * a reasonable reduction of the rent for such time as may elapse until there be placed again upon the premises buildings, or other structures, of as much value to the tenant for his purposes as those destroyed." The Uniform Residential Landlord and Tenant Act (1972), which has been adopted in at least seventeen states, contains the following provision:

Section 4.106. [Fire or Casualty Damage]

(a) If the dwelling unit or premises are damaged or destroyed by fire or casualty to an extent that enjoyment of the dwelling unit is substantially impaired, the tenant may

(1) immediately vacate the premises and notify the landlord in writing within [14] days thereafter of his intention to terminate the rental agreement, in which case the rental agreement terminates as of the date of vacating; or

(2) if continued occupancy is lawful, vacate any part of the dwelling unit rendered unusable by the fire or casualty, in which case the tenant's liability

for rent is reduced in proportion to the diminution in the fair rental value of the dwelling unit.

(b) If the rental agreement is terminated the landlord shall return all security recoverable under Section 2.101 and all prepaid rent. Accounting for rent in the event of termination or apportionment shall be made as of the date of the fire or casualty.

Most written leases, especially leases of premises for commercial use, contain express covenant with respect to the rights of the parties in the event of damage to or destruction of a leased building by fire or other casualty. Consider the adequacy of the following typical lease clauses dealing with this problem.

6. It is further agreed that in the event said premises are damaged by fire or other casualty, Landlord shall promptly repair said premises unless the damage is such as to render the premises untenantable in which event this lease shall terminate as of the date of the fire or other casualty, unless, within ten days from the date of the fire or other casualty, Landlord gives written notice to Tenant that Landlord elects to repair or rebuild, as the case may be. In the event Landlord does elect to repair or rebuild,

(a) Landlord shall complete the necessary repairs or rebuilding within six months from the date of the fire or other casualty.

(b) If the Landlord fails to complete the necessary repairs or rebuilding within the time specified in the preceding subparagraph (a), Tenant shall have the option to terminate this lease as of the date of the fire or other casualty by written notice to Landlord within ten days from the expiration of the time specified in the preceding subparagraph (a).

(c) Tenant shall have no obligation to pay rent for that period during which said premises remain untenantable and until the repair or rebuilding has been completed.

7. Subject to the provisions of paragraph 6 hereof, Tenant shall during the term of the lease, at Tenant's expense, keep the premises in good order, condition and repair.

8. Upon termination of this lease, Tenant shall surrender the premises to Landlord in the same condition as when received except for ordinary wear and tear and loss by fire or other casualty not the fault of Tenant.

Is clause 8 consistent with clauses 6 and 7?

Note on the Duty to Repair

In the light of the traditional doctrine of *caveat emptor*, it is not surprising that, prior to certain recent developments, and in the absence of an express promise in a lease, a landlord owed no duty to repair leased premises. Such a duty in fact was imposed on the tenant. It was implicit in the law of *waste*. In other words, it was inherent in the relation of landlord and tenant that a tenant for years, or under a periodic tenancy, like a life tenant, was bound not to commit either voluntary or permissive waste. In the landlord-tenant relation, problems of permissive waste are much more common than those of voluntary waste. And the obligation not to commit such waste is nothing other than an obligation imposed by law on a tenant to keep the premises in repair. Unfortunately, however, the scope of the duty has never been very precisely defined. It has been said that a tenant must keep the premises "wind and water tight." Or that a tenant must make ordinary or minor repairs. He was not bound to repair or restore premises damaged by fire or other casualty which occurred without his fault. Nor was he bound to repair conditions existing at the beginning of his lease.

As the *Chambers* case demonstrates, covenants by a tenant "to keep the leased premises in repair," or "to maintain the premises in their present condition during the continuance of the lease," or the like may be held to be unconditional and to obligate the tenant to rebuild large structures that have been seriously damaged or destroyed by fire or other casualty.

In Publishers Building Co. v. Miller, 25 Wn.2d 927, 172 P.2d 489 (1946), a lessee of parts of a building which included the basement furnace room, covenanted to keep the premises, including the plumbing, in good repair, and to surrender the premises at the end of the term in good and clean condition, excepting reasonable wear and damage by fire. Several sections of the boiler in the furnace were damaged by lack of water and had to be replaced at a cost of $717. The landlord was allowed to recover this sum from the tenant. The court approved the rule followed in the Chambers case. The "reasonable wear" exception was held not to apply, because that referred to gradual deterioration from use, lapse of time, and to a certain extent the operation of the elements, but not to destruction, in whole or in part, of a structure by some sudden catastrophe.

In Atlantic Discount Corp. v. Mangel's, 2 N.C.App. 472, 163 S.E.2d 295 (1968), the court distinguished the Chambers case. The lessor covenanted to make all repairs and replacements necessary to keep the premises in good order and repair, the leased premises being two retail store areas in a larger building. The building was destroyed by fire. The landlord was held not liable on the covenant. The rule of the Chambers case was held not to be applicable to the lease of a part of a building when the whole building is destroyed by fire.

In Monterey Corp. v. Hart, 216 Va. 843, 224 S.E.2d 142 (1976), an exception to the lessee's promise to keep and deliver up the premises in good order and condition referred to "damages by accidental fire." The court held that the exception covered loss from fire caused by the lessee's own negligence.

In Evco Corp. v. Ross, 528 S.W.2d 20 (Tenn.1975), the lessor promised to be responsible for all major repairs and to carry fire insurance on the leased building. The lessor was held liable to restore fire damage. Cf. Koennecke v. Waxwing Cedar Products, 273 Or. 639, 543 P.2d 669 (1975).

Some courts do not accept the basic rule applied in the *Chambers* case. See, e.g., Brockett v. Carnes, 273 Pa.Super. 34, 416 A.2d 1075 (1979), where the court also held that "maintain" was not equivalent to "repair." Generally, see 1 Am.L.Prop. § 3.79.

GADDIS v. CONSOLIDATED FREIGHTWAYS, INC.

Supreme Court of Oregon, 1965.
239 Or. 553, 398 P.2d 749.

SLOAN, Justice. Plaintiff is the lessor, defendants the lessees of a building in Portland. The lease was entered into in 1958 for a term of 20 years. The rent reserved for the full term was almost one-half million dollars. Defendants were granted an option to purchase the property for a specified sum at any time after the first ten years of the leased term. In 1962, the Oregon State Bureau of Labor, following an inspection of two freight elevators in the building, requested certain repairs * to be made to the elevators. Defendants refused to comply with the plaintiff's demand that they make and pay for the ordered repairs. To avoid possible penalties plaintiff made the repairs. The repairs cost about $7400. He then brought this declaratory judgment proceeding to determine the obligations of the parties as found in the lease. Defendants prevailed in the trial court. Plaintiff appeals.

The pertinent provisions of the lease are:

"8. USE AND OCCUPATION OF THE PREMISES. Lessee has examined the Premises, knows the condition thereof, and accepts the same in its present condition, and hereby affirms that no representations, express or implied, have been made by Lessor or his agents as to the condition of the Premises. The Premises may be used by Lessee, and others lawfully thereon, for any lawful purpose not in violation of any term or covenant of this lease;   *   *   *."

"8.1 COMPLIANCE WITH LAW. Lessee shall conform to and comply with all applicable laws, provided that Lessee may in good faith dispute the validity or applicability of any such law so long as Lessor's title and rights under this Lease are not thereby jeopardized."

       *   *   *

"8.3 MAINTENANCE AND REPAIR BY LESSEE. Lessee, at its own expense, shall maintain the Premises, including exterior walls, roofs, windows, sky lights, and other structural portions thereof, and the adjacent sidewalks, in a safe, sanitary and weather-proof condition, free of ice and snow, and in as good order and repair as when received, reasonable wear and tear excepted,   *   *   *."

"8.4 ALTERATIONS AND CONSTRUCTION. Lessee may, at its sole expense, add any improvements or change or alter any improvement in any manner, provided that all plans and specifications therefor, including demolition of existing improvements or portions thereof shall be first submitted to and approved by Lessor in writing, and provided, further, that Lessee shall not be or become in default of any covenant of this Lease. Lessor shall not unreasonably or arbitrarily withhold its consent in event of any such submission. The provisions of this Section 8.4 shall not apply to the removal of interim partitions and other minor changes or alterations convenient or necessary to adapt the Premises to the uses of lessee or any sublessee hereunder, and Lessor hereby consents to the making of the alterations and changes referred to in this sentence."

It hardly need be repeated that in the absence of an agreement in the lease to the contrary, the lessee bears the obligation to repair. Schenk v. Lamp, 1961, 229 Or. 72, 75, 365 P.2d 1068. This is mentioned to show that if the presently contested repairs to the elevators had been necessitated by use or because of any other failure the burden of repair

---

* We used the word "repairs" because that is the word used by the parties in reference to the work done on the elevators. As it appears later herein we do not know the extent to which the Bureau order required new facilities, replacement, renovation or repair in the usual sense of the word.

[Other footnotes by the court have been omitted. Ed.]

admittably would have been on defendants. It is only because the repairs here were required by a governmental order that gives the lessees-defendants any reason to contest the matter at all. The decisions of the courts are divided as to the extent to which a governmental order may shift the burden of paying for the required changes.

The cases on the subject have been collated in an Annotation at 33 A.L.R. beginning at page 530. Peculiarly, there have been very few cases decided since the date (1924) of that annotation. Comparison of the cases cited and commented on in 3A Thompson, Real Property (1959 Replacement) § 1235, page 184, et seq., with those in the annotation discloses that most of them are the same. The same is true of analysis of the cases found at 1 American Law of Property, 1952, § 3.80, page 353. The last citation provides the most concise review of the cases we have been able to find.

Inasmuch as most of the cases are cited and commented on in the authorities just cited we think it unnecessary to repeat the process here. We agree with the statement in Evans Theatre Corporation v. De Give Investment Co., (1949) 79 Ga.App. 62, 52 S.E.2d 655, 659 and 660, wherein it was said: "* * * An examination in that annotation (33 A.L.R. 530) will reveal that the authorities are divided and it is impossible to lay down a rule applicable to all cases. * * * So it will thus be seen that each case must stand on its particular facts and circumstances." We have found no case which holds categorically that either the lessor or the lessee is bound to make such repairs. The reasons are rather obvious. For a short time lessee to make extensive structural repairs that will shortly revert to the lessor is obviously inequitable. It would be equally inequitable to require a landlord to make repairs when the lease is for a long term and the repairs, or alterations, will be substantially or solely for the benefit of the lessee. In England, it is interesting to note, the regulatory statutes usually provide that any dispute as to an apportionment of the costs of a newly required building change will be referred to a designated court. The court is to apportion costs by a test of what would be equitable and fair. Adaptations in Smoke Control Areas, Who Will Pay—Landlord or Tenant?, 1961, 105 Sol J 539.

We have examined all of the available authority on the subject and conclude, as stated above, that the criterion applied by the courts is briefly but fully stated in 1 American Law of Property, supra, beginning at page 353. Because the statement is concise we copy it in full:

"* * * If the lessee does not expressly covenant to repair, it would seem clear that he generally should be under no duty to make alterations and repairs required by governmental authority in order to conform the premises to health and safety laws. Any changes likely to be ordered for this purpose would be beyond the scope of the tenant's common law duty to repair, and the expenses of compliance are properly regarded either as capital expenditures or as necessary carrying charges to be paid out of the rent.

"Where the lessee covenants to repair, the question of who should bear the cost of compliance depends upon the nature of the alteration or improvement and the reason for requiring it. If the order involves mere repairs which the lessee would normally be required to make under his covenant, he should bear the cost. Likewise, the burden is on the lessee where the alteration is required only because of the particular use which he is making of the premises, although it may be questioned whether even in the case, the courts would place the burden of extensive and lasting improvements on the lessee, except perhaps where the lease is for a long term. At any rate, if the order requires the making of such improvements, so-called 'structural' changes, and they are not required because of the particular use made of the premises by the lessee, the lessor must bear the burden of compliance."

When we apply the tests just mentioned to the facts in this case we conclude that nearly all of the factors to be considered weigh against the tenant. It was acknowledged by the tenant that the repairs required by the Bureau of Labor would have been made at the tenant's expense if they were caused by ordinary wear and tear. We think the same rule would apply for repairs necessitated by the demands of safety to persons and property when no governmental rule was involved. Garrett v. Eugene Medical Center, 1950, 190 Or. 117, 127, 224 P.2d 563. The lease was for a long term, the cost of the repairs were nominal in comparison to the total rental. Melcher v. Sobel, 1923, 120 Misc. 378, 198 N.Y.S. 318. It is doubtful that the benefit of the repairs would have survived the term of the lease and thus revert to the plaintiff. Defendants were not restricted in the use of the building, a consideration mentioned in the cases. Taylor v. Finnigan, 1905, 189 Mass. 568, 78 N.E. 203, 2 L.R.A.,N.S., 973. And, the option to purchase made any reversion only probable. In this respect we note that in a very exhaustive opinion by Mr. Chief Justice Weintraub in Crewe Corp. v. Feiler, 1958, 28 N.J. 316, 146 A.2d 458, 68 A.L.R.2d 1279, an option to purchase was given considerable weight in deciding whether a landlord or tenant should pay an unexpected substantial tax increase caused by the tenant's improvements.

We assume that all of the repairs were required for purposes of safety. The lease required that defendants were to keep the premises in a safe condition. And, the change in the law which created the need for the repairs was not an extraordinary change of policy, nor one that could not have been reasonably anticipated. For a discussion of the latter variable see Deutsch v. Robert Hoe Estate Co., 1916, 174 App.Div. 685, 161 N.Y.S. 968.

In the instant case we are somewhat limited by the facts presented. The case was tried upon a stipulation of facts which provides very little information as to the nature of the repairs required. In many of the cases the courts have recited detailed evidence as to the character of the repairs in reaching a decision. Here, we can only assume that most of the work required was not structural in the same sense that rebuilding a wall, for example, would be. And it is apparent that some of the requirements would be of the housekeeping variety or that they would last no more than a few years at best. Our examination of the cases and the facts presented cause us to hold that the repairs in this instance should have been made by defendants.

Reversed.

Notes

1. For decisions involving a lessee's obligation to comply with government orders and regulations under either (1) a covenant to repair or (2) a covenant to comply with such orders, see Annotation, 22 A.L.R.3d 521 (1968).

2. In Mid-Continent Life Insurance Co. v. Henry's Inc., 214 Kan. 350, 520 P.2d 1319 (1974), the lessee covenanted to maintain the exterior and interior of the premises in first class condition except for damage by casualty. A neighboring building which abutted the wall of the leased building was altered by the removal of the top floor, exposing the leased building. This required repairs to conform to the state building code. The court held that the lessee was not responsible for such repairs, since such unusual, extraordinary, and unexpected conditions were not within the contemplation of the parties. The court also cited *Gaddis* and included the quotation from the A.L.P. that was also quoted in *Gaddis*.

See also Scott v. Prazma, 555 P.2d 571 (Wyo.1976).

3. In Pingree v. Continental Group, 558 P.2d 1317 (Utah 1976), the lessee of premises to be used as a restaurant covenanted to repair. The lessee undertook to use the second floor of the leased building for banquets and special groups. This resulted in an order from local authorities to install a fire escape. The court said that in such circumstances, the lessee must bear the cost of installing a fire escape. In fact, the lessee escaped such a duty by refraining thereafter from the use of the second floor.

4. Some difficulty may be encountered in interpreting the common exception to a covenant to repair, that referring to "reasonable wear and tear." See the definition of the court in Publishers Bldg. Co. v. Miller, note 1 following the Chambers case, supra. Suppose, as in clauses 7 and 8 of the sample lease provisions set out in the introduction to this section, a wear-and-tear exception is included in the covenant to return the premises in good condition, but not included in the covenant relating to repair. See Corbett v. Derman Shoe Co., 338 Mass. 405, 155 N.E.2d 423 (1959). See the same case for the court's treatment of the problem created by the fact that the disrepair may have been caused in part by reasonable wear and tear and in part by conduct of the lessee for which he was not excused. The court also dealt with the question who bears the burden of proof that disrepair was or was not caused by wear and tear.

In Scott v. Prazma, supra note 2, the court said, "An ordinary covenant to keep the premises in good repair does not include the restoration of a part of a building which has become so run-down that it cannot be repaired * * * . Ordinary wear and tear includes any usual deterioration from the use of the premises and by the lapse of time." How does this square with the rule of the *Chambers* case? In fact, the court had previously rejected the rule of the *Chambers* case.

5. "Plaintiffs are the executors of the will of Jacob Borin deceased, and the trustees under the will of Nathan Borin, deceased. The two decedents died possessed of the lessor's interest in a 99-year lease of real estate. Defendant bank is the administrator c. t. a. of the estate of Augusta L. Voigt, deceased, who held the lessee's interest at her death. Involved in this matter are plaintiffs' claims, filed against defendant estate, for rent, taxes, insurance premiums and expenses for repairs to become due and payable in the future under the

lease. The probate court disallowed the claims. On appeal the circuit court allowed them. Defendant appeals. * * *

"The circuit court also allowed as an absolute fifth class claim the sum of $15,000 as the amount necessary to place the building on the leased premises in good condition and repair at the present time, which the court found the lessee had failed but was required to do under the lease. This amount was allowed on the strength of testimony of plaintiffs' witnesses that they estimated that the cost of necessary repairs would come to that total. Plaintiffs have not made these repairs. If they were allowed and paid this sum, there is no assurance that they would make the repairs during defendant's tenancy. If necessary to defendant's use and enjoyment of the premises defendant might be left with the necessity of making these repairs after having paid plaintiffs for them. Clearly plaintiffs are not entitled to payment of the cost of such repairs under such circumstances. No proofs of injury done to the reversion were adduced. In an action begun before termination of the lease, that, not cost of repairs, is the measure of damages. Pennsylvania Cement Co. v. Bradley Contracting Co., 2 Cir., 11 F.2d 687; Glickman v. DeBerry, Tex.Civ.App.1928, 11 S.W.2d 367; Bloom v. Southern Amusement Company, 228 La. 44, 81 So.2d 763. It follows that plaintiffs have made no case for allowance of this item as an absolute claim. * * * *" National Bank of Detroit v. Voigt's Estate, 357 Mich. 657, 99 N.W.2d 504 (1959).

MILLER v. GOLD BEACH PACKING CO.

Supreme Court of Oregon, 1929.
131 Or. 302, 282 P. 764, 66 A.L.R. 858.

This is a suit to establish in favor of the plaintiffs, lessors, an interest in a sum of money, which the defendant National Fire Insurance Company promised to pay in the event of the destruction by fire of a building situated upon the land of the lessors; the policy of insurance was obtained by the other defendant, who is the respondent, and who is the assignee of the lessee; the building was built by the original lessee. The term of the lease extended from May 20, 1916, to April 1, 1931, and contains this provision:

"It is further understood and agreed that all buildings and other permanent improvements erected or placed upon the premises herein-before described shall remain thereon and shall not be removed therefrom and that at the expiration of this lease, any and all such buildings and improvements shall be and become the property of said lessors."

The land, which was vacant at the time of the renting, was upon the shores of the Rogue river, near Gold Beach. Immediately upon the execution of the lease the lessee constructed the building which became the subject-matter of the policy of fire insurance with which this suit is concerned. * * *

The building was destroyed by fire February 20, 1927. When this event occurred the respondent declined to rebuild and denied that the plaintiffs, who are the appellants, had any interest in the insurance money. Thereupon the latter instituted this suit. The insurance company being willing to pay $4,250 to discharge its liability, but uncertain to whom the money belonged, paid that sum into the registry of the circuit court pursuant to a stipulation that its deposit should terminate its liability. While the complaint contains an allegation that the respondent is insolvent, the findings below recite that the plaintiff "has failed to establish" this allegation. The decree of the circuit court was in favor of the respondent.

* * *

ROSSMAN, J. The controlling issues are (1) whether the covenant of the lease quoted in the preceding statement required the tenant to rebuild the structure in event it was destroyed by fire; (2) whether a tenant, who procures a policy of insurance for the full value of the building and who, upon the latter's destruction, collects insurance money in an amount representing the value of the two estates in the building, may retain only such portion of it as represents the value of his estate and must account to the remainderman for the balance. * * *

[The court held that the lease could not be construed so as to impose on the lessee the duty to repair or rebuild the premises destroyed by fire.]

In arguing that the procurement of fire insurance to the full value of the building and its collection upon the destruction of the latter is conclusive evidence that the tenant insured both estates, and that therefore he must account for the portion of the proceeds of the insurance which represents the value of the remainderman's estate, the plaintiffs concede that their contention is opposed by the majority of the adjudications which have passed upon similar sets of facts. This admission upon their part is supported by the authorities: Cooley's Briefs on Insurance, 2d ed. p. 6262, and note in 35 A.L.R. 40. The various considerations, which have moved some courts to adopt the view advocated by the plaintiffs and others to favor that urged by the defendant, are ably reviewed in the majority and the dissenting opinions in the recent case of Clark v. Leverett, 159 Ga. 487, 126 S.E. 258, 37 A.L.R. 180, and in the opinions in the other two recent cases of Thompson v. Gearhart, 137 Va. 427, 117 S.E. 67, 35 A.L.R. 36, and Brownell v. Board of Education, 239 N.Y. 369, 146 N.E. 630, 37 L.R.A. 1319; the note in 35 A.L.R. 40 is exhaustive. Due to the fact that the authorities have thus recently reviewed, analyzed and compared, we find no occasion for setting forth our review of them. The courts, which have reached the conclusion that the remainderman is entitled to no interest in insurance money obtained by a tenant upon a policy of insurance procured by him without any agreement between the two that he should obtain protection for both, premise their holdings upon the following grounds: (1) the tenant as well as the remainderman has an insurable interest; (2) the tenant is under no obligation to insure the property for the benefit of the remainderman; (3) the contract of insurance, which either obtains, is personal to him, and the other has no interest in it; (4) if the tenant obtains from the insurance company more than the value of his estate, the remainderman does not thereby become entitled to the surplus, because the contract of insurance does not undertake to indemnify him; (5) the tenant is neither required to rebuild nor to provide a fund to take the place of the building upon its destruction; (6) the proceeds of the fire insurance contract are not proceeds of the destroyed building; they come to the tenant from a third party as the result of a contract for indemnity; (7) the insurable estates of the tenant and the remainderman are separate and distinct; they are not united or merged under the contract of insurance and hence the latter affords the remainderman no basis for any relief; (8) the amount of the insurance policy obtained by the tenant, and the amount ultimately collected is for the determination of the tenant and the insurer, and it does not affect the remainderman; (9) if a tenant in obtaining a policy of insurance or in obtaining a settlement places an excessive value upon his interest in the property his act does not constitute him the agent of the remainderman so that the latter becomes entitled to any part of the insurance money.

The cases, which represent the minority view, do not adopt reasons which can be as clearly stated as the foregoing, and in some instances the reasons which have persuaded one court apparently do not appeal to all of the others. The following, we believe, is a fair statement of the reasons found in this group of cases: (1) public policy is violated by a policy of insurance which promises to pay to a tenant an amount equal to the value of the remainderman's estate in addition to the value of his own, and, therefore, since the law favors a construction upon contracts which will not impute to the parties bad faith, it will assume that the tenant, who obtained a policy stipulating for the payment of an amount equal to the full value of the building, secured protection not only for himself but also for the remaindermen; (2) the tenant is a quasi-trustee for his remainderman, and, therefore, the insurance contract obtained by him is available to both; (3) the duty owed by a life tenant to exercise ordinary care in preserving the property may include a duty upon his part to insure the property; (4) the insurance money takes the place of the destroyed building, and should be used to restore it; (5) the policy of insurance runs with the land, and, therefore, protects all as their interests may appear; (6) if the amount obtained by the tenant is no more than the amount of his loss he may keep all of it, but if it is greater he must account to the remainderman for the surplus.

In this minority group is South Carolina; it has carried the idea that the life tenant is a quasi-trustee to such a length that it has impressed a trust in favor of the remainderman, upon properties in which the tenant invested the proceeds of the insurance contract: Green v. Green, 50 S.C. 514, 27 S.E. 952, 62 Am.St.Rep. 846. The New York Court of Appeals in Brownell v. Board of Education, 239 N.Y. 369, 146 N.E. 630, 37 A.L.R. 1319, has described some of the reasoning of the minority group thus: "These reasons may savor of layman's ideas of equity, but they are not law." It seems to us that the reasons employed by the minority are not sound. While it is true that public policy is opposed to contracts for over-insurance, this rule of law is misused when invoked for the first time after the insurance money is paid, and when it is sought to divert a portion of it to one who was too indifferent to procure protection for himself. The rule of construction which requires a court to place upon a writing a lawful purpose, rather than one which is opposed to public policy, is available only when such a construction will not do violence to the plain meaning of the words. Here it is clear that the policy was not intended to indemnify the plaintiffs, and since the validity of the contract is not the point at issue the aforementioned rule of public policy has no proper place in this controversy. Next, while it is true that an occasional decision speaks of the relationship of a life tenant to his remainderman as of a quasi-fiduciary nature, we fail to understand how this relationship, even if admitted, can add to the trust property a contract of insurance obtained by the tenant with his personal funds for the protection of his separate estate. The contention that a life tenant's duty may include the procurement of insurance for the protection of the remainderman finds practically no support in the authorities. There can be no occasion for holding that the insurance money shall take the place of the destroyed building and shall be used to restore it, when the tenant was under no obligation to rebuild. The argument that the insurance runs with the land does violence to the contract of the parties; the insurer would never know the name of the insured, and might thus have forced upon it one whom it would not care to insure. Finally, to concede that a tenant, who has received an amount equivalent to the value of his interest, may keep all of it, but contend that another, who has received more, must account to the remainderman for the surplus, discloses the weakness of much of the reasoning employed by the minority group of cases. It is in harmony with the use made by the minority of the agreement concerning public policy, but misfits the rest of the contentions. Should a case develop within the jurisdiction of the minority courts wherein the remainderman was fully protected by insurance, obtained by himself, or had a cause of action against a tortious party, whose act caused the fire, those courts would find it difficult to know what disposition should be made of the tenant's surplus. In such a situation all of their reasons would have to be discarded and yet the facts would remain that the tenant had obtained more than a fair award.

* * *

It seems clear to us that the contract was personal in the present suit; the tenant was not the plaintiffs' agent and was not their trustee. If the plaintiffs [defendants?] obtained more than fair compensation we know of no rule of law which authorizes us to give the surplus to the plaintiffs. The plaintiffs cannot find in this generous award a right whereby they may demand a part of it. They were strangers to the contract of insurance, and must now be content to remain strangers to its fruits.

The appellants also object to the cost bill filed by the defendant; we have given this matter careful consideration but find no merit in the appellants' contentions.

It follows that the conclusion below must be affirmed.

Affirmed.

Notes and Problems

1. A lessee promises in the lease to keep the premises fully insured for the benefit of the lessor. Instead the lessee insures the premises in his own name. In case of loss does the lessor have any right to the proceeds? Houston Can-

ning Co. v. Virginia Can Co., 211 Ala. 232, 100 So. 104 (1924); Eberts v. Fisher, 54 Mich. 294, 20 N.W. 80 (1884); see Alexander v. Security-First Nat. Bank, 7 Cal.2d 718, 724, 62 P.2d 735, 738 (1936). Would the lessor have a direct remedy against the insurance company? Home Insurance Co. of New York v. Gibson, 72 Miss. 58, 17 So. 13 (1894). See generally, 66 A.L.R. 864 (1930). Sears, Roebuck & Co. v. Kelsey Holding Co., 30 N.J.Super. 307, 104 A.2d 708 (1954) is an interesting case in which the lease required that the interest of both parties be protected by insurance, that in case of destruction by fire, etc., the premises were to be rebuilt by the lessor to the extent allowed by the proceeds of the insurance. The insurance policy, however, failed to include the name of the lessee. The premises were destroyed by an explosion. The lessee restored the premises with the encouragement of the lessor. The insurance company paid off the lessor. Then the lessor disclaimed any duty to reimburse the lessee. The lessee sued the lessor for the amount expended in the restoration, and was allowed to recover.

2. Insurance is taken out in the name of both lessor and lessee, "as their interests may appear." Buildings on the premises are destroyed by fire. What are the rights of the parties in the insurance proceeds? Ingold v. Phoenix Assurance Co., 230 N.C. 142, 52 S.E.2d 366, 8 A.L.R.2d 1439 (1949).

It is not likely that insurance companies today would issue a policy solely to a tenant otherwise than by what is called a "tenant's policy." Under such a policy a tenant would be paid only for the loss he has sustained as a tenant. Is a tenant adequately protected by either of the two kinds of policies mentioned in this note, without any provision in the lease respecting the effect of fire or other casualty?

BARASH v. PENNSYLVANIA TERMINAL REAL ESTATE CORP.

Court of Appeals of New York, 1970.
26 N.Y.2d 77, 308 N.Y.S.2d 649, 256 N.E.2d 707.

BREITEL, Judge. Defendant landlord appeals from an affirmed order denying its motion to dismiss tenant's complaint for legal insufficiency (CPLR 3211, subd. [a], par. 7). The allegations for this purpose are accepted as true (Cohn v. Lionel Corp., 21 N.Y.2d 559, 562, 289 N.Y.S.2d 404, 407, 236 N.E.2d 634, 636).

The first cause of action, alleging a partial actual eviction, is to relieve tenant from payment of rent, and, notably, is not a claim for damages. The second is for reformation of the lease to conform to alleged prior oral agreements.

With respect to the first cause of action, the question is whether landlord's allegedly wrongful failure to supply a continuous flow of fresh air on evenings and weekends to offices leased by tenant constitutes a partial actual eviction relieving tenant from the payment of rent or, at most, a constructive eviction requiring the tenant to abandon the premises before he may be relieved of the duty to pay rent. Also at issue is whether grounds for reformation are pleaded by the second cause of action.

Plaintiff, a lawyer, alleges that on September 15, 1967, while the premises known as 2 Pennsylvania Plaza in New York City were being constructed, he entered into a written lease with defendant landlord for rental of office space to be used for the practice of law. Involved is a 29-story glass-enclosed, completely air-conditioned office building. Its windows are sealed and the supply and circulation of air inside the building is under the landlord's exclusive control.

Defendant landlord, through its authorized renting agents, had represented that the building would be open 24 hours a day, 7 days each week, to enable tenants and others to occupy the offices at all times. Prior to signing the lease, plaintiff inquired as to the manner in which air would be circulated "when the air-conditioning system was not in operation." He was informed, fraudulently he alleges, "that the offices in question would be constructed with a duct system, which would always provide a natural and continuous flow of air * * * [making] the offices * * * comfortable and usable at all evening hours and also on weekends, even when the air-conditioning and heating systems were not in operation." The tenant, on the basis of these representations, known by the landlord to be false, signed the lease.

The lease provides, in pertinent part: "As long as Tenant is not in default under any of the covenants of this lease Landlord shall furnish air cooling during the months of June, July, August and September on business days from 9 A.M. to 6 P.M. when in the judgment of the Landlord it may be required for the comfortable occupancy of the demised premises and at other times during business days and similar hours, ventilate the demised premises."

The lease also contains a general merger clause: "Landlord or Landlord's agents have made no representations or promises with respect to said building, the land upon which it is erected or the demised premises except as herein expressly set forth and no rights, easements or licenses are acquired by Tenant by implication or otherwise except as expressly set forth herein. The taking possession of the demised premises by Tenant shall be conclusive evidence, as against Tenant, that Tenant accepts the same, 'as is' and that said premises and the building of which the same form a part were in good and satisfactory condition at the time such possession was so taken."

Plaintiff tenant took possession on May 15, 1968 and that evening at 6:00 P.M. defendant "turned off all air" in the offices. By 7:00 P.M. the offices became "hot, stuffy, and unusable and uninhabitable". Upon protest the landlord refused to provide afterhour ventilation unless paid for by the tenant at a rate of $25 per hour. The tenant refused to pay the reserved rent or the additional charge and brought the instant action. The landlord sought dispossession for the nonpayment. This was denied, but the tenant was directed to pay rent into court pending the outcome of the instant action.

The first cause of action, based on the unreformed lease, alleges a partial actual eviction. Even assuming that the leased premises became "hot, stuffy, and unusable and uninhabitable" so that no one was able to work or remain in the offices after 7:00 P.M., these allegations are insufficient, as a matter of law, to make out an actual eviction.

To be an eviction, constructive or actual, there must be a wrongful act by the landlord which deprives the tenant of the beneficial enjoyment or actual possession of the demised premises (Edgerton v. Page, 20 N.Y. 281; 1 Rasch, Landlord and Tenant, § 849). Of course, the tenant must have been deprived of something to which he was entitled under or by virtue of the lease (52 C.J.S. Landlord & Tenant § 477, p. 292). A right to 24-hour ventilation cannot be established, in the absence of reformation of the lease, by alleging fraudulent representations concerning ventilation when the lease itself expressly limits ventilation rights.

But even if the lease were to be read to include the allegations concerning ventilation (the gravamen of the tenant's second cause of action in reformation), the facts alleged, and accepted as true, would still fall short of, and not constitute, an actual eviction.

An actual eviction occurs only when the landlord wrongfully ousts the tenant from physical possession of the leased premises. There must be a physical expulsion or exclusion (Fifth Ave. Bldg. Co. v. Kernochan, 221 N.Y. 370, 117 N.E. 579; 2 McAdam, Landlord and Tenant [5th ed.], § 329, p. 1391; 1 N.Y. Law of Landlord and Tenant [Edward Thompson Co.], § 250). And where the tenant is ousted from a portion of the demised premises, the eviction is actual, even if only partial (Fifth Ave. Bldg. Co. v. Kernochan, supra; 524 West End Ave. v. Rawak, 125 Misc. 862, 212 N.Y.S. 287).

Thus, for example, where the landlord barred the tenant from entering the premises it has been held a partial actual eviction (Lawrence v. Edwin A. Denham Co., 58 Misc. 543, 109 N.Y.S. 752 [App.Term]; 2 McAdam, op. cit., supra, § 332, p. 1410). Similarly, where the landlord changes the lock, or padlocks the door, there is an actual eviction (see Lester v. Griffin, 57 Misc. 628, 108 N.Y.S. 580 [App.Term]; Morgan v. Short, 13 Misc. 279, 34 N.Y.S. 10).

On the other hand, constructive eviction exists where, although there has been no physical expulsion or exclusion of the tenant, the landlord's wrongful acts substantially and materially deprive the tenant of the beneficial use and enjoyment of the premises (City of New York v. Pike Realty Corp., 247 N.Y. 245, 160 N.E. 359; Ann.—Nonhabitability of Leased Dwellings, 4 A.L.R. 1453, 1461–1463, supp. 29 A.L.R. 52, supp. 34 A.L.R. 711; 1 Rasch, op. cit., supra, §§ 871–875). The tenant, however, must abandon possession in order to claim that there was a constructive eviction (Boreel v. Lawton, 90 N.Y. 293, 297; Two Rector St. Corp. v. Bein, 226 App.Div. 73, 76, 234 N.Y.S. 409, 412; 1 N.Y. Law of Landlord and Tenant [Edward Thompson Co.], supra, § 253).

Thus, where the tenant remains in possession of the demised premises there can be no constructive eviction (Edgerton v. Page, 20 N.Y. 281, 284, supra). It has been said to be inequitable for the tenant to claim substantial interference with the beneficial enjoyment of his property and remain in possession without payment of rent (City of New York v. Pike Realty Corp., supra, 247 N.Y., at p. 247, 160 N.E. 359, 360; Edgerton v. Page, supra).

In the case of actual eviction, even where the tenant is only partially evicted liability for all rent is suspended although the tenant remains in possession of the portion of the premises from which he was not evicted. In the leading case of Fifth Ave. Bldg. Co. v. Kernochan (221 N.Y. 370, 373, 117 N.E. 579, 580, supra), the court stated: "We are dealing now with an eviction which is actual and not constructive. If such an eviction, though partial only, is the act of the landlord, it suspends the entire rent because the landlord is not permitted to apportion his own wrong."

This then presents the nub of the appeal. The tenant, who has not abandoned the premises, asserts that there has been an actual eviction, though partial only, thus permitting him to retain possession of the premises without liability for rent. To support this contention it is claimed that failure to supply fresh air constitutes actual eviction, if only, albeit, during the hours after 6:00 P.M. and on weekends.

There is no previous known reported case involving a like situation in a substantially sealed building. The resolution of this appeal turns therefore on the application of general principles to the novel complex of facts presented.

All that tenant suffered was a substantial diminution in the extent to which he could beneficially enjoy the premises. Although possibly more pronounced, tenant's situation is analogous to cases where there is a persistent offensive odor, harmful to health, arising from a noxious gas (Tallman v. Murphy, 120 N.Y. 345, 24 N.E. 716), an open sewer (Sully v. Schmitt, 147 N.Y. 248, 41 N.E. 514), or defective plumbing (Lathers v. Coates, 18 Misc. 231, 41 N.Y.S. 373 [App.Term]). The possible odor-producing causes are innumerable (see, generally, 1 Rasch, op. cit., supra, § 891). In all such cases there has been held to be only a constructive eviction.

In the Tallman case (supra), which involved coal gas, the court stated: "In such a building as the one under consideration there is very much that remains under the charge and control of the landlord * * * [I]f he persistently neglects them, and by reason of such neglect * * * his apartments are filled with gas or foul odors * * * and the apartments become unfit for occupancy, the tenant is deprived of the beneficial enjoyment thereof * * * and there is a constructive eviction" (id. 120 N.Y. at p. 352, 24 N.E. at p. 718).

Given these well-established rules, proper characterization of the instant failure to ventilate follows easily, assuming there be such duty under the lease as written, or as reformed to conform to the representations. The tenant has neither been expelled nor excluded from the premises, nor has the landlord seized a portion of the premises for his own use or that of another. He has, by his alleged wrongful failure to provide proper ventilation, substantially reduced the beneficial use of the premises.

As long as the tenant remains in possession it matters little whether he can remedy the situation by his independent action. Nor does it matter whether the proposed 24-hour use has become practically impossible.

In City of New York v. Pike Realty Corp. (supra), the land was leased from the city for construction of a parking garage. The city, however, thereafter refused to give tenant a building permit. The court held this refusal "was at most a   *   *   *   constructive eviction" (id. 247 N.Y. at p. 247, 160 N.E. at p. 360).

Tenant's reliance on Schulte Realty Co. v. Pulvino, 179 N.Y.S. 371 [App.Term, per Lehman, J.], which held that a tenant had suffered a partial actual eviction, is misplaced. The landlord, in that case, interfered with tenant's "easement" of light and air by allowing another to cover a large portion of an airshaft upon which tenant's windows opened. The court, relying on Adolphi v. Inglima, 130 N.Y.S. 130 [App. Term], held that the lease included a right to light and air from the shaftway, and that there was, therefore, a partial eviction. It was observed that there could be no constructive eviction because the premises had not been rendered untenantable. In the Adolphi case a landlord had sealed up a window on the tenant's premises, and it was said to justify a finding of a partial eviction. On the other hand, in Solomon v. Fantozzi, 43 Misc. 61, 86 N.Y.S. 754 [App.Term] the court held that blocking the ventilation of a water closet did not constitute a partial constructive eviction, let alone a partial actual eviction. The distinguishing feature of these cases, if indeed they be not anomalies, is that they deal with the destruction of an easement or appurtenance of light and air granted by the landlord (1 Rasch, op. cit., supra, § 895). Here there is no claim to an appurtenant right to air external to the demised premises but rather the failure to provide an essential service within the demised premises, which failure traditionally constitutes a constructive eviction (Tallman v. Murphy, supra).

It would seem moreover, apart from or despite the cases last discussed, that interference with easements or appurtenances of light and air insofar as they diminish the tenant's beneficial enjoyment of the demised premises, constitutes a constructive and not an actual eviction. Thus in Two Rector St. Corp. v. Bein (226 App.Div. 73, 234 N.Y.S. 100, supra) the substantial "diminution of light, air and view" constituted at most a constructive eviction requiring a surrender by the tenant (id. at pp. 75–76, 234 N.Y.S. at p. 411). (See, generally, 52 C.J.S. Landlord & Tenant § 458, p. 312.)

Since the eviction, if any, is constructive and not actual, the tenant's failure to abandon the premises makes the first cause of action insufficient in law (33 N.Y.Jur., Landlord & Tenant, § 170, and cases cited). The first cause of action, therefore, should have been dismissed.
*   *   *

[The court held that the tenant had not properly pleaded his second cause of action for reformation. Ed.]

Although it is necessary to dismiss the complaint because neither cause of action is legally sufficient, plaintiff may wish to move for permission to replead. The record does not reveal that plaintiff sought leave to replead in the event that the motion to dismiss was granted. Consequently, plaintiff may not be granted leave to replead based on the present state of the record (see CPLR 3211, subd. [c]).

Accordingly, the order of the Appellate Division should be reversed, the question certified answered in the negative, with costs to abide the ultimate event, the complaint dismissed, but with leave to plaintiff tenant to apply at Special Term for leave to replead, if so advised.

FULD, Chief Judge (dissenting in part).

Notes

1. In Talbot v. Citizens National Bank, 389 F.2d 207 (7th Cir.1968), the court, in purporting to apply Indiana law, held that in a case of an alleged actual eviction from part of leased premises, the lessee, to sustain his right of rescission, must show that he was evicted from a material part of the leased premises or that the eviction was a material breach of the lessor's implied covenant of quiet enjoyment. On this basis the court held that the lessee had failed to sustain its motion for a summary judgment.

2. In *Barash* suppose the lessee had left the premises, claiming constructive eviction. Could he have sustained his claim? Under what circumstances can a lessor's *failure* to do something constitute a breach of the covenant of quiet enjoyment and a basis for constructive eviction?

In Scott v. Prazma, 555 P.2d 571 (Wyo.1976), a building inspector ordered that the use of leased premises cease unless an extensive list of repairs were made. The lessor refused to make the repairs because of a covenant in the lease imposing on the lessee the duty to make repairs, with the usual exceptions. The lessee left the premises and claimed constructive eviction. The court found that the lessee's covenant did not obligate him to make such repairs, on the same reasoning as in *Gaddis*, supra page 381. What duty did the lessor owe the lessee in this regard?

3. The courts are in conflict on the right of a tenant to sue his landlord for damages for breach of the covenant of quiet enjoyment while remaining in possession. 1 A.L.P. § 3.50. Such a recovery was allowed in Nate v. Galloway, 408 N.E.2d 1317 (Ind.App.1980).

RESTE REALTY CORP. v. COOPER

Supreme Court of New Jersey, 1969.
53 N.J. 444, 251 A.2d 268.

FRANCIS, J. Plaintiff-lessor sued defendant-lessee to recover rent allegedly due under a written lease. The suit was based upon a charge that defendant had unlawfully abandoned the premises two and a quarter years before the termination date of the lease. The trial court, sitting without a jury, sustained tenant's defense of constructive eviction and entered judgment for defendant. The Appellate Division reversed, holding (1) the proof did not support a finding of any wrongful act or omission on the part of the lessor sufficient to constitute a constructive eviction, and (2) if such act or omission could be found, defendant waived it by failing to remove from the premises within a reasonable time thereafter. We granted defendant's petition for certification. 51 N.J. 574, 242 A.2d 378 (1968).

On May 13, 1958 defendant Joy M. Cooper, leased from plaintiff's predecessor in title a portion of the ground or basement floor of a commercial (office) building at 207 Union Street, Hackensack, N.J. The term was five years, but after about a year of occupancy the parties made a new five-year lease dated April 1959 covering the entire floor except the furnace room. The leased premises were to be used as "commercial offices" and "not for any other purpose without the prior written consent of the Landlord." More particularly, the lessee utilized the offices for meetings and training of sales personnel in connection with the business of a jewelry firm of which Mrs. Cooper was branch manager at the time. No merchandise was sold there.

A driveway ran along the north side of the building from front to rear. Its inside edge was at the exterior foundation wall of the ground floor. The driveway was not part of Mrs. Cooper's leasehold. Apparently it was provided for use of all tenants. Whenever it rained during the first year of defendant's occupancy, water ran off the driveway and into the offices and meeting rooms either through or under the exterior or foundation wall. At this time Arthur A. Donigian, a member of the bar of this State, had his office in the building. In addition, he was an officer and resident manager of the then corporate-owner. Whenever water came into the leased floor, defendant would notify him and he would take steps immediately to remove it. Obviously Donigian was fully aware of the recurrent flooding. He had some personal files in the furnace room which he undertook to protect by putting them on 2×4's in order to raise them above the floor surface. When negotiating with defendant for the substitute five-year lease for the larger space, Donigian promised to remedy the water problem by resurfacing the driveway. (It is important to note here that Donigian told Walter T. Wittman, an attorney, who had offices in the buiding and who later became executor of Donigian's estate, that the driveway needed "regrading and some kind of sealing of the area between the driveway which lay to the north of the premises and the wall." He also told Wittman that the grading was improper and was "letting the water into the basement rather than away from it.") The work was done as promised and although the record is not entirely clear, apparently the seepage was somewhat improved for a time. Subsequently it worsened, but Donigian responded immediately to each complaint and removed the water from the floor.

Donigian died on March 30, 1961, approximately two years after commencement of the second lease. Whenever it rained thereafter and water flooded into the leased floor, no one paid any attention to defendant's complaints, so she and her employees did their best to remove it. During this time sales personnel and trainees came to defendant's premises at frequent intervals for meetings and classes. Sometimes as many as 50 persons were in attendance in the morning and an equal number in the afternoon. The flooding greatly inconvenienced the conduct of these meetings. At times after heavy rainstorms there was as much as two inches of water in various places and "every cabinet, desk and chair had to be raised above the floor." On one occasion jewelry kits that had been sitting on the floor, as well as the contents of file cabinets, became "soaked." Mrs. Cooper testified that once when she was conducting a sales training class and it began to rain water came into the room making it necessary to move all the chairs and "gear" into another room on the south side of the building. On some occasions the meetings had to be taken to other quarters for which rent had to be paid; on others the meetings were adjourned to a later date. Complaints to the lessor were ignored. What was described as the "crowning blow" occurred on December 20, 1961. A meeting of sales representatives from four states had been arranged. A rainstorm intervened and the resulting flooding placed five inches of water in the rooms. According to Mrs. Cooper it was impossible to hold the meeting in any place on the ground floor; they took it to a nearby inn. That evening she saw an attorney who advised her to send a notice of vacation. On December 21 she asked that the place be cleaned up. This was not done, and after notifying the lessor of her intention she left the premises on December 30, 1961.

Plaintiff acquired the building and an assignment of defendant's lease January 19, 1962. On November 9, 1964 it instituted this action to recover rent for the unexpired term of defendant's lease, i.e., until March 31, 1964.

At trial of the case defendant's proofs showed the facts outlined above. Plaintiff offered every little in the way of contradiction. It seemed to acknowledge that a water problem existed but as defense counsel told the court in his opening statement, he was "prepared to show that the water receded any number of times, and therefore the damage, if it was caused by an act that can be traced to the landlord, [the condition] was not a permanent interference" with the use and enjoyment of the premises. Plaintiff contended further that the water condition would not justify defendant's abandonment of the premises because in the lease she had stipulated that prior to execution thereof she had "examined the demised premises, and accept[ed] them in their [then] condition * * *, and without any representations on the part of the landlord or its agents as to the present or future condition of the said premises"; moreover she had agreed "to keep the demised premises in good condition" and to "redecorate, paint and renovate the said premises as may be necessary to keep them in good repair and good appearance."

The trial judge found that the "testimony is just undisputed and overwhelming that after every rainstorm water flowed into the leased premises of the defendant" and nothing was done to remedy the condition despite repeated complaints to the lessor. He declared also that the condition was intolerable and so substantially deprived the lessee of the use of the premises as to constitute a constructive eviction and therefore legal justification for vacating them.

On this appeal the plaintiff-landlord claims that under the long-settled law, delivery of the leased premises to defendant-tenant was not accompanied by any implied warranty or covenant of fitness for use for commercial offices or for any other purpose. He asserts also that by express provision of both the first and second leases (which are identical printed forms, except that the second instrument covers the additional portion of basement floor), the tenant acknowledged having examined the "demised premises," having agreed to accept them in their "present condition," and having agreed to keep them in good repair, which acknowledgment, as a matter of law, has the effect of excluding any such implied warranty or covenant.

It is true that as the law of leasing an estate for years developed historically, no implied warranty or covenant of habitability or fitness for the agreed use was imposed on the landlord. Because the interest of the lessee was considered personal property the doctrine of *caveat emptor* was applied, and in the absence of an express agreement otherwise, or misrepresentation by the lessor, the tenant took the premises "as is." * * *

Modern social and economic conditions have produced many variant uses and types of leases, e.g., sale and leaseback transactions, mortgaging of leasehold interests, shopping center leases, long-term leases. Moreover, an awareness by legislatures of the inequality of bargaining power between landlord and tenant in many cases, and the need for tenant protection, has produced remedial tenement house and multiple dwelling statutes. * * *

It has come to be recognized that ordinarily the lessee does not have as much knowledge of the condition of the premises as the lessor. Building code requirements and violations are known or made known to the lessor, not the lessee. He is in a better position to know of latent defects, structural and otherwise, in a building which might go unnoticed by a lessee who rarely has sufficient knowledge or expertise to see or to discover them. A prospective lessee, such as a small businessman, cannot be expected to know if the plumbing or wiring systems are adequate or conform to local codes. Nor should he be expected to hire experts to advise him. Ordinarily all this information should be considered readily available to the lessor who in turn can inform the prospective lessee. These factors have produced persuasive arguments for reevaluation of the *caveat emptor* doctrine and, for imposition of an implied warranty that the premises are suitable for the leased purposes and conform to local codes and zoning laws. Proponents of more liberal treatment of tenants say, among other things, that if a lease is a demise of land and a sale of an interest in land in the commercial sense, more realistic consideration should be given to the contractual nature of the relationship. See Skillern, "Implied Warranties in Leases: The Need for Change," 44 Den.L.J. 387 (1967); 2 Prospectus, "Michigan Landlord—Tenant Law: Course of Statutory Reform," 225, 233 (1968); Schoshinski, "Remedies of the Indigent Tenant: Proposal For Change," 54 Geo.L.J. 519 (1966); Note, 21 Vand.L.Rev. 1117 (1968); 23 Halsbury's Laws of England (3d ed. 1958), Landlord and Tenant § 1250, p. 575; * * * It will not be necessary to deal at any length with the suggested need for reevaluation and revision of the doctrines of *caveat emptor* and implied warranties in leases beyond consideration of matters projected into the case by the various contentions of the landlord. Since the language of the two leases is the same, except that the second one describes the larger portion of the basement taken by the tenant, evaluation of the landlord's contentions will be facilitated by first considering the original lease and the factual setting attending its execution. Although the second or substitutionary lease is the controlling instrument, we take this approach in order to focus more clearly upon the effect of the change in the factual setting when the second lease was executed. This course brings us immediately to the landlord's reliance upon the provisions of the first lease (which also appear in the second) that the tenant inspected the "demised premises," accepted them in their "present condition" and agreed to keep them in good condition. The word "premises," construed most favorably to the tenant, means so much of the ground floor as was leased to Mrs. Cooper for commercial offices. The driveway or its surfacing or the exterior wall or foundation under it cannot be considered included as part of the "premises." In any event there is nothing to show that the inspection by Mrs. Cooper of the driveway or the ground floor exterior wall and foundation under it prior to the execution of the first lease would have given or did give her notice that they were so defective as to permit rainwater to flood into the leased portion of the interior. The condition should have been and probably was known to the lessor. If known, there was a duty to disclose it to the prospective tenant. Certainly as to Mrs. Cooper, it was a latent defect, and it would be a wholly inequitable application of *caveat emptor* to charge her with knowledge of it. The attempted reliance upon the agreement of the tenant in both leases to keep the "demised premises" in repair furnishes no support for the landlord's position. The driveway, exterior ground floor wall and foundation are not part of the demised premises. Latent defects in this context, i.e., those the existence and significance of which are not reasonably apparent to the ordinary prospective tenant, certainly were not assumed by Mrs. Cooper. In fact in our judgment present day demands of fair treatment for tenants with respect to latent defects remediable by the landlord, either within the demised premises or outside the demised premises, require imposition on him of an implied warranty against such defects. See Buckner v. Azulai, 251 Cal.App.2d Supp. 1013, 59 Cal.Rptr. 806 (1967); Charles E. Burt, Inc. v. Seven Grand Corp., 340 Mass. 124, 163 N.E.2d 4, 6, n. 2 (1959); Pines v. Perssion, supra, 111 N.W.2d at 412–413. Such warranty might be described as a limited warranty of habitability. In any event we need not at this point deal with the scope of the warranty, nor with issues of public policy that might be involved in certain types of cases where express exclusion of such warranty is contained in the lease. * * *

In Pines v. Perssion, supra, the Supreme Court of Wisconsin after noting that the frame of reference in which the old common law rule operated has undergone a change, declared:

"Legislation and administrative rules, such as the safeplace statute, building codes and health regulations, all impose certain duties on a property owner with respect to the condition of his premises. Thus, the legislature has made a policy judgment—that it is socially (and politically) desirable to impose these duties on a property owner—which has rendered the old common law rule obsolete. To follow the old rule of no implied warranty of habitability of leases would, in our opinion, be inconsistent with the current legislative policy concerning housing standards. The need and social desirability of adequate housing for people in this era of rapid population increases is too important to be rebuffed by that obnoxious legal cliché, *caveat emptor*." 111 N.W.2d at 412–413.

The letting of a one-family home to college students was involved in the case. Although the young men had gone through the house before renting it, the court pointed out they had no way of knowing that the plumbing, heating and wiring systems were defective. Under the circumstances an implied warranty of habitability was said to exist, and its breach by the landlord relieved the tenants of liability for rent, except for such rent as would be reasonable for the one month of their occupancy. * * * Similarly we believe that at the inception of the original lease in the present case, an implied warranty against latent defects exists.

But the landlord says that whatever the factual and legal situation may have been when the original lease was made, the relationship underwent a change to its advantage when the second was executed. This contention is based upon the undisputed fact that in April 1959, after a year of occupancy, defendant, with knowledge that the premises were subject to recurrent flooding, accepted a new lease containing the same provisions as the first one. This acceptance, the argument runs, eliminates any possible reliance upon a covenant or warranty of fitness because the premises were truly taken then "as is." While it is true that a tenant's knowing acceptance of a defective leasehold would normally preclude reliance upon any implied warranties, the landlord's position here is not sustainable because it is asserted in disregard of certain vital facts—the agent's promise to remedy the condition and the existence of an express covenant of quiet enjoyment in the lease. * * *

This brings us to the crucial question whether the landlord was guilty of a breach of a covenant which justified the tenant's removal from the premises on December 30, 1961. We are satisfied there was such a breach.

The great weight of authority throughout the country is to the effect that ordinarily a covenant of quiet enjoyment is implied in a lease. * * * We need not deal here with problems of current serviceability of that rule because as has been indicated above, the lease in question contains an express covenant of quiet enjoyment for the term fixed. Where there is such a covenant, whether express or implied, and it is breached substantially by the landlord, the courts have applied the doctrine of constructive eviction as a remedy for the tenant. Under this rule any act or omission of the landlord or of anyone who acts under authority or legal right from the landlord, or of someone having superior title to that of the landlord, which renders the premises substantially unsuitable for the purpose for which they are leased, or which seriously interferes with the beneficial enjoyment of the premises, is a breach of the covenant of quiet enjoyment and constitutes a constructive eviction of the tenant. * * *

Examples of constructive eviction having close analogy to the present case are easily found. Failure to supply heat as covenanted in the lease so that the apartment was "unlivable" on cold days amounted to constructive eviction. * * * So too, when the main waste pipe of an apartment building was permitted to become and remain clogged with sewage for a long period of time causing offensive odors and danger to health, the covenant of quiet enjoyment was breached and justified the tenant's abandonment of his premises. * * *

If a landlord lets an apartment in his building to a tenant as a dwelling and knowingly permits another part to be used for lewd purposes which use renders the tenant's premises "unfit for occupancy by a respectable family," his failure to terminate the use when he has the legal power to do so constitutes a constructive eviction. * * *

As noted above, the trial court found sufficient interference with the use and enjoyment of the leased premises to justify the tenant's departure and to relieve her from the obligation to pay further rent. In our view the evidence was sufficient to warrant that conclusion, and the Appellate Division erred in reversing it. Plaintiff argued and the Appellate Division agreed that a constructive eviction cannot arise unless the condition interferes with the use in a permanent sense. It is true that the word "permanent" appears in many of the early cases. * * * But it is equally obvious that permanent does not signify that water in a basement in as case like this one must be an everlasting and unending condition. If its recurrence follows regularly upon rainstorms and is sufficiently serious in extent to amount to a substantial interference with use and enjoyment of the premises for the purpose of the lease, the test for constructive eviction has been met. Additionally in our case, the defective condition of the driveway, exterior and foundation walls which permitted the recurrent flooding was obviously permanent in the sense that it would continue and probably worsen if not remedied. There was no obligation on the tenant to remedy it. * * *

[W]hether the landlord's default in the present case is treated as a substantial breach of the express covenant of quiet enjoyment resulting in a constructive eviction of the tenant or as a material failure of consideration, (i.e., such failure as amounts to a substantial interference with the beneficial enjoyment of the premises) the tenant's vacation was legal. Thus it is apparent from our discussion that a tenant's right to vacate leased premises is the same from a doctrinal standpoint whether treated as stemming from breach of a covenant of quiet enjoyment or from breach of any other dependent covenant. Both breaches constitute failure of consideration. The inference to be drawn from the cases is that the remedy of constructive eviction probable evolved from a desire by the courts to relieve the tenant from the harsh burden imposed by common law rules which applied principles of *caveat emptor* to the letting, rejected an implied warranty of habitability, and ordinarily treated undertakings of the landlord in a lease as independent covenants. To alleviate the tenant's burden, the courts broadened the scope of the long-recognized implied covenant of quiet enjoyment (apparently designed originally to protect the tenant against ouster by a title superior to that of his lessor) to include the right of the tenant to have the beneficial enjoyment and use of the premises for the agreed term. It was but a short step then to the rule that when the landlord or someone acting for him or by virtue of a right acquired through him causes a substantial interference with that enjoyment and use, the tenant may claim a constructive eviction. In our view, therefore, at the present time whenever a tenant's right to vacate leased premises comes into existence because he is deprived of their beneficial enjoyment and use on account of acts chargeable to the landlord, it is immaterial whether the right is expressed in terms of breach of a covenant of quiet enjoyment, or material failure of consideration, or material breach of an implied warranty against latent defects.

Plaintiff's final claim is that assuming the tenant was exposed to a constructive eviction, she waived it by remaining on the premises for an unreasonable period of time thereafter. The general rule is, of course, that a tenant's right to claim a constructive eviction will be lost if he does not vacate the premises within a reasonable time after the right comes into existence.   *   *   *   What constitutes a reasonable time depends upon the circumstances of each case. In considering the problem courts must be sympathetic toward the tenant's plight. Vacation of the premises is a drastic course and must be taken at his peril. If he vacates, and it is held at a later time in a suit for rent for the unexpired term that the landlord's course of action did not reach the dimensions of constructive eviction, a substantial liability may be imposed upon him. That risk and the practical inconvenience and difficulties attendant upon finding and moving to suitable quarters counsel caution.

Here, plaintiff's cooperative building manager died about nine months before the removal. During that period the tenant complained, patiently waited, hoped for relief from the landlord, and tried to take care of the water problem that accompanied the recurring rainstorms. But when relief did not come and the "crowning blow" put five inches of water in the leased offices and meeting rooms on December 20, 1961, the tolerance ended and the vacation came ten days later after notice to the landlord. The trial court found as a fact that under the circumstances such vacation was within a reasonable time, and the delay was not sufficient to establish a waiver of the constructive eviction. We find adequate evidence to support the conclusion and are of the view that the Appellate Division should not have reversed it.   *   *   *

For the reasons expressed above, we hold the view that the trial court was correct in deciding that defendant had been constructively evicted from the premises in question, and therefore was not liable for the rent claimed. Accordingly, the judgment of the Appellate Division is reversed and that of the trial court is reinstated.

Notes and Questions

1. Since the covenant of quiet enjoyment only protects a tenant from "eviction" by the landlord, and since a "constructive eviction" cannot be established—in the absence of an "actual eviction"—without proof of a breach of some independent duty of the landlord which interferes substantially with the

tenant's use and enjoyment of the premises, how did the court find a "constructive eviction" in the principal case?

2. A possible solution of the tenant's problem in deciding whether to vacate the premises and run the risk that a court will later find that he was not justified in vacating is indicated in Charles E. Burt, Inc. v. Seven Grand Corp., 340 Mass. 124, 163 N.E.2d 4 (1959). Plaintiff leased space on the fifth floor of a building owned by the defendant. The lease provided that the lessor would furnish electric power, sufficient heat, and elevator service, except when prevented by unavoidable causes. For failure to provide such services plaintiff suffered damages nearly equal to the rent for a period of six months. Plaintiff sued to enjoin the lessor from collecting rents under the lease, to have the lease "rescinded and declared a nullity," and for damages. The failure to provide these services was found not to be from unavoidable causes, and the trial court decreed that the lease be rescinded as of the date the suit was filed, and ordered payment of the damages claimed in the amount of $2035, which included costs of supplying electric current and loss of profits. This decree was affirmed on appeal. A provision in the lease that no interruption of the services should be deemed a constructive eviction was construed to apply only to excusable failures. The defendant's default was treated as a breach of its covenant of quiet enjoyment, which enabled the lessee to recover damages, and, if he abandoned the premises, provided him with the defense of constructive eviction. The court continued as follows:

"In seeking what it refers to as rescission and that the lease be 'declared a nullity' Burt asked little more (see Corbin, Contracts, § 1223, p. 921) than declaratory relief as to its rights. Its prayer, however, that the lease be rescinded, even if it has not abandoned the premises, can reasonably be construed as an election, if its contentions in fact should be sustained, to abandon because of a constructive eviction.

"At law the tenant's abandonment of the leased premises must take place within a reasonable time   *   *   *   after the acts alleged to constitute constructive eviction   *   *   *, but 'abandonment of the [leased] premises is not essential to seeking equitable relief.'   *   *   *   In the case of material breaches of a lease by a lessor, where the injury is sufficiently serious, equitable relief by way of injunction or specific performance may be granted.   *   *   *   We perceive no reason why equitable relief, in appropriate circumstances, should not be given by way of (1) a declaration under G.L. c. 231A that the wrongful acts of the lessor justify treating those acts as a constructive eviction, (2) appropriate consequential relief, and (3) assessment of damages. Although equitable relief was denied in Barry v. Frankini, 287 Mass. 196, 201, 191 N.E. 651, 93 A.L.R. 1240, there (see 287 Mass. at pages 199–200, 191 N.E. at page 653) the lessor's breach of covenant to pay taxes was 'not of such a material   *   *   * nature as to excuse the party suing from proceeding with the contract.' That case, however, did not decide that equitable relief must be denied where breach of covenant constituting failure of consideration 'goes to the essence' of the contract.   *   *   *   Such relief is more nearly adequate than the incomplete and hazardous remedy at law which requires that the lessee (a) determine at its peril that the circumstances amount to a constructive eviction, and (b) vacate the demised premises, possibly at some expense, while remaining subject to the risk that a court may decide that the lessor's breaches do not go to the essence of the lessor's obligation. The trial judge could properly (1) declare that Seven Grand's material breach of the lease constituted, or would constitute, a constructive eviction upon Burt's abandonment of the premises, and that Burt, upon such abandonment, was or would be excused from further performance of the lease and (2) assess damages.

"The present record does not reveal whether abandonment of the premises has taken place and, if it has, when that occurred. The bill may imply that Burt's possession of the premises continued at least through the date of the bill. In view of the absence of findings about abandonment, the decree of unconditional rescission must be modified, after appropriate findings as to abandonment, to declare either (a) that Burt has been constructively evicted, if abandonment has in fact taken place, or (b) that Burt is entitled to abandon the premises within a reasonable time and to treat Seven Grand's conduct as a constructive eviction.

"No issue of future damage   *   *   *   to Burt by reason of its constructive eviction has been argued. The only damages found are those for Seven Grand's past actions. The appropriate measure of damage thus is the difference between the value of what Burt should have received and the fair value of what it has in fact received.   *   *   *

"The provisions of the lease are established by the pleadings. Upon the lease and the master's subsidiary findings, the trial judge could reasonably conclude (a) that the rent reflected the benefit of what Seven Grand received from Burt during the period of Seven Grand's defaults and also the fair value of what Burt should have received if Seven Grand had performed its obligations fully, and (b) that the value of what Burt in fact received was less than the rent by at least the amount which Burt was obliged to expend for services not furnished by Seven Grand, viz. the aggregate amount ($1,300) spent by Burt for use of diesel engines to produce electric current and for current from other sources. Nothing in the record suggests that incurring these expenses was unreasonable.   *   *   *

"The master could reasonably conclude that the damage to Burt's machinery from cold, the loss of profits during suspension of operations, and the damage resulting from Seven Grand's failure to operate the elevator, reduced the value of what Burt in fact received from Seven Grand.   *   *   *   There is no showing that his ultimate conclusion upon the amount of damage was not justified by his subsidiary findings.

"Because of the absence of findings about the date of abandonment one further uncertainty must be mentioned. If Burt did not abandon the premises within a reasonable time after the date of the bill, when Burt indicated its election to treat Seven Grand's defaults as a constructive eviction, Seven Grand is entitled to a further credit of the fair value, if any, of Burt's occupation of the premises after the date of the bill. If Burt paid any rent after the date of the bill, Burt is entitled to a further recovery of the amount by which that rent exceeded the fair value of its use and occupation during the period after May 22, 1958. Burt must give Seven Grand full credit for the benefits, if any, received by Burt after the date of the bill, for relief of this character should 'be granted [only] upon such equitable conditions as [will] amply protect the rights of the defendant.' "

3. Compare the *Seven Grand* case in Note 2 with Lipkin v. Burnstine, 18 Ill.App.2d 509, 152 N.E.2d 745 (1959); Stevan v. Brown, 54 Md.App. 235, 458 A.2d 466 (1983).

If a lessee seeks injunctive relief against conduct of a lessor which is a violation of the lessee's rights, his principal obstacle is in proving that his legal remedy is inadequate. See Continental & Vogue Health Studios, Inc. v. Abra Corp., 369 Mich. 561, 120 N.W.2d 835 (1963), where equitable relief was denied. In Biscayne Plaza Unit Three Corp. v. G.R. Kinney Co., 113 So.2d 244 (Fla.App. 1959), the court approved an injunction against the maintenance by the lessor of a snack bar in front of the store operated by the lessee, on the ground that the lessee was deprived of full use of the leased premises. See also Blue Cross Association v. 666 Lake Shore Drive Association, 100 Ill.App.3d 647, 56 Ill.Dec. 190, 427 N.E.2d 270 (1981).

Equitable relief in the form of rescission of the lease for breaches by a lessor which amount to constructive eviction faces a more serious obstacle: the traditional rule that constructive eviction requires the lessee to vacate the premises as a condition of any affirmative or defensive remedies. The decision in the *Burt* case may seem like a sensible qualification of the old rule. In the light of prevailing prior law, the decision has major significance as a precedent.

If constructive eviction is a risky defense for a tenant to resort to, which may justify a court in approving the remedy sought by the tenant in the *Burt* case, the rule in that case does require that the tenant surrender the premises on or before obtaining his decree. Can this consequence also constitute such a burden upon a tenant that some remedy should be recognized which allows him to remain in possession? This is the problem which was faced in the cases which follow.

B. THE NEW DUTIES OF RESIDENTIAL LANDLORDS

In the *Reste Realty* case the New Jersey court cited Pines v. Perssion, 14 Wis.2d 409, 111 N.W.2d 409 (1961), for the proposition that every lease of residential premises includes "an implied warranty" against "latent defects remediable by the landlord, either within the demised premises or outside the demised premises." Although Pines v. Perssion is usually considered the first case to recognize such an "implied warranty," the Minnesota Supreme Court had previously held, in Delamater v. Foreman, 184 Minn. 428, 239 N.W. 148 (1931), that there was such an "implied warranty" in the leasing of an apartment unit in a modern apartment building—whether the apartment was furnished or not, and whether the lease was for a long or a short term. But the modern era of judicial activism in expanding tenants' rights really began with the *Pines* case in 1961, where the court seems to have thought that recognition of an "implied warranty of habitability" would provide an effective, though indirect, method of enforcing state and municipal housing codes. In the *Pines* case the court asserted that the traditional *caveat emptor* rule was "inconsistent with the current legislative policy concerning housing standards" as exemplified in "legislative and administrative rules, such as the safeplace statute, building codes and health regulations" all of which "impose certain duties on a property owner with respect to the condition of his premises."

Before looking at more recent cases and statutes in which the concept of an "implied warranty of habitability" is further developed, it is necessary to look briefly at the "housing code" approach to the problem of keeping rental property in habitable condition.

(1) The Housing Code Approach

The direct ancestor of all modern "housing codes" is the New York Tenement House Law of 1867, which applied only to lodging houses and multiple dwellings located in New York City. This statute required that "tenement houses" should have watertight roofs, adequate chimneys, fire escapes, ventilators, refuse containers, and "good and sufficient water closets or privies." That the principal purpose of the statute was to safeguard public health is apparent from the designation of the Metropolitan Board of Health (created the previous year) as the enforcement agency. Massachusetts enacted a statute applicable only to Boston and modelled on the 1867 New York statute in 1868. In New York a new Tenement House Law (applicable to New York City and Buffalo) was enacted in 1901. This statute provided for a system of tenement house registration and occupancy permits. The pioneering New York and Massachusetts statutes provided the basis for the modern "housing code," defined as follows: [1]

"A housing code deals with the owner's and occupant's duty to keep existing housing in decent condition—to see to it that it is not occupied by more persons than are legally permitted for housing accommodations of that size; to keep it in proper repair; to maintain it in a sanitary condition; to see that it remains properly ventilated and lighted; to make sure that it has the required facilities for fire safety; that required machinery—elevators, boilers and heating plants, etc.—are kept in working order; and that required services—heat, hot and cold water—are provided in accordance with minimal requirements of law."

There are broad similarities in the current housing codes of different communities, most of which are based to a considerable extent on one of four or five model codes, which are themselves quite similar. In addition to municipal housing codes, there are several state housing codes. The substantive content of state housing codes is substantially like that of the model codes and their municipal derivatives. Some of the state housing codes apply statewide; others are applicable only to certain cities or to municipalities falling in certain classifications. Some are "mandatory" but allow municipalities to adopt more stringent requirements; others are "optional"—i.e., municipalities may, but need not, adopt them as local ordinances. [2]

A housing code generally provides minimum standards in regard to four different features of the housing it regulates: (1) structural elements such as walls, roofs, ceilings, floors, windows, and staircases; (2) facilities such as toilets, sinks, bathtubs, radiators or other heating fixtures, stoves, electrical outlets, window screens, and door and window locks; (3) services such as heat, hot and cold water, sanitary sewage disposal, electricity, elevator service, central air conditioning, and repair and maintenance services for each dwelling unit; and (4) occupancy standards setting limits on the number of occupants per dwelling or per bedroom. [3]

1. F. Grad, Legal Remedies for Housing Code Violations 2 (Research Report 14, prepared for the National Commission on Urban Problems, 1968). As Grad points out, the term "housing code" really means more than a particular municipal ordinance or state statute. "Realistically, it includes the entire body of state and local law that prescribes housing standards and that may be relied upon to provide the source of power or authority for enforcement sanctions and remedies." Id. at 8.

2. See E. Mood, The Development, Objectives, and Adequacy of Current Housing Code Standards, In Housing Code Standards: Three Critical Studies (prepared for National Comm'n on Urban Problems, Research Rep. No. 19, 1969), surveying the requirements of four model housing codes, nine state housing codes, and sixteen city or county housing codes.

3. Abbott, Housing Policy, Housing Codes and Tenant Remedies: An Integra-

Until very recently, violation of a housing code provision was not considered a breach of any duty owed by the landlord directly to his tenants, and tenants had no direct remedies when code violations occurred. Enforcement of the early tenement house laws was delegated to local administrative agencies charged with a duty to inspect buildings covered by such laws both on a regular periodic basis and in response to tenant complaints, and this has continued to be the normal mode of enforcement of modern housing codes.[4] If the issuance of a violation notice and one or more informal or formal administrative hearings do not lead to correction of the violation, the enforcement agency has traditionally been authorized to obtain an order for vacation of the building, followed by an order for demolition if the owner does not correct the violation within a designated time;[5] and to bring a criminal action against the building owner.[6] In some states additional modes of agency enforcement are authorized; these may include obtaining a mandatory injunction requiring the building owner to bring his building into compliance with the housing code[7] suits to impose a "civil" penalty on the building owner,[8] direct agency action to correct code violations by making repairs and improvements,[9] and suits for appointment of a receiver to take over the building and apply its rents to correction of code violations.[10]

If some or all of the traditional modes of housing code enforcement listed above had proven effective, it is possible that the "revolution" of the 1960's and 1970's in landlord-tenant law would not have occurred. But all observers agree that local governments have been notably unsuccessful in code enforcement.[11] In part the lack of success stems from the institutions charged with enforcement. Most code enforcement agencies are understaffed and underfunded because of the low level of public awareness of code enforcement problems and lukewarm support by local elected officials.[12] Periodic inspections are not carried out on any regular schedule and, since housing inspectors are not very well paid, code enforcement has been hindered by corruption.[13] Even honest housing inspectors may grow discouraged and apathetic because

tion, 56 B.U.L.Rev. 1, 40 (1976). For a more extended discussion of the contents of housing codes, see Grad, Hack and McAvoy, Housing Codes and Their Enforcement 195–216 (Study prepared for HUD, 1966).

4. F. Grad, supra note 1, at 5. When a housing code enforcement officer discovers and reports code violations, the code enforcement agency usually sends a violation notice to the owner of the building with a request that the violations be corrected.

5. F. Grad, supra note 1, at 56–61.

6. Id. at 22–23.

7. Id. at 40–42.

8. Id. at 34–39.

9. Id. at 62–69.

10. Id. at 42–55.

11. The literature is voluminous. See, e.g., M. Teitz and S. Rosenthal, Housing Code Enforcement in New York City (1971); B. Lieberman, Local Administration and Enforcement of Housing Codes: A Survey of 39 Cities (1969); J. Slavet and M. Levin, New Approaches to Housing Code Administration (Research Report 17, for National Commission on Urban Problems, 1969); F. Grad, supra note 1; Abbott, supra note 3, at 49–56.

12. Abbott, supra note 3, at 54–55.

13. See J. Slavet and M. Levin, New Approaches to Housing Code Administration 179 (Research Report 17, prepared for The National Commission on Urban Problems, 1969).

of the ease with which landlords can obtain "variances,"[14] and public prosecutors rarely demonstrate much zeal in code enforcement.[15] Consequently, legislatures have enacted statutes authorizing tenants to withhold rent when their landlords failed to correct serious code violations which rendered their rental units "uninhabitable." Although two states adopted legislation of this type before New York,[16] the New York legislation of 1929 was the first significant rent withholding statute.[17] New York enacted additional rent withholding legislation, with broader coverage, in 1939 and in the 1960's.[18] And in the 1960's a number of other states enacted similar legislation.[19] This legislation generally authorizes withholding of rent while serious code violations exist, and leaves for judicial determination the question whether a particular code violation or combination of violations is, in fact, serious enough to justify the withholding of rent. Most of the statutes also require a tenant to show—in order to justify rent withholding—that an official inspection of his dwelling was made and that the inspecting officer reported one or more code violations to the code enforcement agency.

Some of the rent withholding statutes apply to all kinds of rental housing; some apply only to multifamily dwellings—usually defined as buildings with three or more dwelling units; and some have an even more limited application. Many of the statutes include or are coupled with provisions designed to protect the tenant from retaliatory action by the landlords, and most of them expressly prohibit any waiver of the

---

14. Lieberman reported that most code enforcement personnel believed that variance boards act on the basis of political considerations or emotion. "The results are disrespect for the inspector and his superiors; ineffective systematic code compliance programs; and disrespect for local regulatory measures." B. Lieberman, Local Administration and Enforcement of Housing Codes: A Survey of 39 Cities 23 (1969).

15. " * * * Few housing code enforcement agencies have legal staffs of their own, and even the ones that do must usually bring prosecutions through the municipality's regular legal department; i.e., through the city attorney or corporation counsel, or through the city or county prosecutor. In the usual course, the municipal law officer or his deputies have little experience or knowledge of housing matters and tend to regard housing prosecutions as a very minor, troublesome, and unexciting area for the application of their legal expertise. Even in large cities, where hundreds and thousands of housing cases may be brought each year, they represent a low-prestige area of activity, for a young lawyer in the city's legal department gains neither friends nor glory by successfully prosecuting housing cases." F. Grad, supra note 1, at 25. See also Philadelphia Housing Ass'n, Impediments to Housing Code Compliance iv (1963), cited

by Grad. And see Abbott, supra note 3, at 53–54.

16. See Conn.Gen.Stat.Ann. §§ 19–371, 19–400 (Supp.1982) (originally enacted in 1905, this statute provided that failure to obtain a certificate of compliance with the state housing law should bar any action by the landlord to recover rent or to evict for nonpayment of rent; the statute in its present form, is applicable to all multi-family housing except public housing); Iowa Code § 413–106 (1976) (originally enacted in 1919, the statute was similar to the Connecticut statute). See Cunningham, The New Implied and Statutory Warranties of Habitability in Residential Leases: From Contract to Status, 16 Urban L. Annual 3, 23 (1979).

17. N.Y. Multiple Dwelling Law § 302. The Multiple Dwelling Law was enacted in 1929 to replace the 1901 Tenement House Law; Buffalo, however, remained subject to the latter until 1950, when it was brought under the Multiple Dwelling Law. Section 302 of the latter was similar to the Connecticut and Iowa rent withholding statutes, supra note 16.

18. See discussion of these statutes in Cunningham, supra note 16, at 24, 26–35.

19. See discussion of these statutes in Cunningham, supra note 16, at 35–51, and other discussions of these statutes cited id., at 25 n. 97.

tenant's right to withhold rent because of serious code violations. But the statutes differ substantially with respect to the way in which rent withholding may be initiated and the disposition of withheld rents.

Most of the recently enacted rent withholding statutes require the payment of withheld rents either into court or to some other agency to be held in escrow. These statutes may be broadly divided into two groups: (a) those that require the tenant to bring suit and to obtain a court order authorizing the withholding of rents;[20] and (b) those that do not require the tenant to bring suit, but allow him to set up the landlord's failure to provide him with a habitable dwelling unit as a defense to any action by the landlord to recover unpaid rent or to evict for nonpayment of rent.[21] In addition, these statutes may be classified according to whether or not they provide for application of the withheld rents, under the direction of the court or some other agency, to the correction of the conditions that make the dwelling unit uninhabitable;[22] and whether they provide for rent abatement as well as rent withholding.[23] Some of the rent withholding statutes authorize other remedies, such as damages, injunctive relief, or even the appointment of a receiver to collect the rents and make necessary repairs.[24]

In most of the states where use of escrowed rents to make necessary repairs is authorized by statute, all the unexpended rents must be paid over to the landlord after the repairs are made. In Michigan, however, the local code enforcement agency must return to the landlord any unexpended part of the rent paid into escrow "attributable to the unexpired portion of the rental period, where the occupant terminates his tenancy * * * prior to the undertaking to repair," but the statute is silent as to disposition of any unexpended rents when the tenant remains in possession and the necessary repairs are in fact made. In Pennsylvania, the unexpended rents may be paid over to the landlord only if "the dwelling is certified as fit for human habitation" within six months of the date when it was certified as unfit.

The following Pennsylvania statute, originally enacted in 1966, is less elaborate than many of the rent withholding statutes.

20. E.g., Mass.Laws Ann. c. 111, §§ 127C et seq. (Supp.1977); N.J.Stat.Ann. §§ 2A:42–85 through 2A:42–96 (Supp. 1977); N.Y. Real Property Actions and Proceedings Law, Art. 7–A (Supp.1977).

21. E.g., Mass.Laws Ann. c. 239, § 8A (Supp.1977); N.Y. Multiple Dwelling Law § 302–a (Supp.1977); 35 Pa.Stat.Ann. § 1700–1 (1977); R.I.Gen.Laws § 45–24.2–11 (1970).

22. Application of rents by court order is provided for in Conn.Gen.Stat.Ann. § 19–347n (Supp.1977) (if receiver is appointed); Mass.Laws Ann. c. 111, § 127F (Supp.1977); id. c. 239, § 8A (Supp.1977); N.J.Stat.Ann. § 2A:42–92 (Supp.1977); N.Y. Real Property Actions and Proceedings Law § 7–A (Supp.1977); Mich.Comp. Laws Ann. § 125.534(4) (1976) empowers the code enforcement agency to pay over

escrowed rents "to the landlord or any other party authorized to make repairs, to defray the cost of correcting the violations. 35 Pa.Stat.Ann. § 1700–1 (1977) authorizes use of "funds deposited in escrow, for the purpose of making such dwelling fit for human habitation and for the payment of utility services for which the landlord is obligated," but does not indicate who is empowered to authorize such use of the escrowed rents.

23. Abatement, as well as withholding of rent, is authorized by Mass.Laws Ann. c. 111, § 127F (Supp.1977); id. c. 239, § 8A (Supp.1977); N.Y. Multiple Dwelling Law § 302(1)(b) (1974).

24. E.g., Conn.Gen.Stat.Ann. § 19–347q (Supp.1977); N.J.Stat.Ann. § 2A:-42–93 (Supp.1977); Mich.Comp.Laws Ann. § 125.535 (1976).

PENNSYLVANIA RENT WITHHOLDING ACT

(35 Pa.Stat.Ann. § 1700–1).

Notwithstanding any other provision of law, or of any agreement, whether oral or in writing, whenever the Department of Licenses and Inspections of any city of the first class, or the Department of Public Safety of any city of the second class, second class A, or third class as the case may be, or any Public Health Department of any such city, or of the county in which such city is located, certifies a dwelling as unfit for human habitation, the duty of any tenant of such dwelling to pay, and the right of the landlord to collect rent shall be suspended without affecting any other terms or conditions of the landlord-tenant relationship, until the dwelling is certified as fit for human habitation or until the tenancy is terminated for any reason other than nonpayment of rent. During any period when the duty to pay rent is suspended, and the tenant continues to occupy the dwelling, the rent withheld shall be deposited by the tenant in an escrow account in a bank or trust company approved by the city or county as the case may be and shall be paid to the landlord when the dwelling is certified as fit for human habitation at any time within six months from the date on which the dwelling was certified as unfit for human habitation. If, at the end of six months after the certification of a dwelling as unfit for human habitation, such dwelling has not been certified as fit for human habitation, any moneys deposited in escrow on account of continued occupancy shall be payable to the depositor, except that any funds deposited in escrow may be used, for the purpose of making such dwelling fit for human habitation and for the payment of utility services for which the landlord is obligated but which he refuses or is unable to pay. No tenant shall be evicted for any reason whatsoever while rent is deposited in escrow.

(2) Implied and Statutory Warranties of Habitability

KING v. MOOREHEAD

Missouri Court of Appeals, Kansas City District, 1973.
495 S.W.2d 65.

SHANGLER, Judge. This action was commenced in the magistrate court by a landlord's complaint which alleged that defendant occupied certain premises as a tenant of the plaintiff leased on the 6th day of March, 1969, from month to month at the rate of $85 per month and that the sum of $109 was due plaintiff as rent. The complaint sought judgment for possession and rent in the sum demanded, and the magistrate entered judgment accordingly.

The tenant appealed to the circuit court and filed an answer in which she admitted the lease of the premises for use as a single family dwelling as a month to month tenant of the plaintiff for the agreed rent of $85 per month, that she paid rent through the month ending May 6, 1969, but refused to do so thereafter until plaintiff corrected and abated certain substantial housing code violations, and admitted that she did not vacate the premises until August 1, 1969, when she was finally able to obtain other housing. Defendant then denied indebtedness to plaintiff for any rent for her occupancy from and after May 6, 1969, and as the basis for this denial asserted two affirmative defenses.

The first affirmative defense alleged that the rental agreement was illegal, void and unenforceable because in violation of the Housing Code of Kansas City, Missouri.[25] The defense pleaded as exhibits numerous provisions of the Code, among them, Section 20.16 which renders it unlawful for any person to use or occupy, or for any owner to permit any dwelling unit to be used or occupied, as a place for human habitation unless in compliance with the requirements of the Code, and declaring any building for habitation and which does not conform to the regulations to be a nuisance; and, Section 20.34 which requires the owner of a dwelling to maintain it in good order and repair and fit for human habitation; and, Section 20.10 which renders a violation of the Code a misdemeanor and provides for a fine of not more than $100 for each offense. The defendant also alleged fourteen specific conditions, including rodent and vermin infestation, defective and dangerous electrical wiring, leaking roof, inoperative toilet stool, unsound and unsafe ceilings, which at the time of letting the plaintiff knew or should have known were in violation of the Housing Code and rendered the premises unfit for human habitation.[26] In consequence, the defendant alleged the unenforceability of the rental agreement in the pending action. The second affirmative defense reasserted the allegations of the illegality defense and further alleged that at the time of the letting, plaintiff impliedly covenanted to provide premises in a safe, sanitary and habitable condition, and to so maintain them in compliance with state and local laws, including the provisions of the Housing Code. This defense also alleged that the refusal of the plaintiff to abate the conditions constituting violations of the Housing Code rendered the premises wholly unsuitable for human habitation, was a substantial breach of the implied covenant, and amounted to a failure of consideration on the part of the plaintiff so as to relieve defendant of her obligation to pay rent in whole or in substantial part.[27]

25. The Housing Code, Chapter 20 of the Code of General Ordinances of Kansas City, Missouri, was repealed on October 15, 1971 and a new title adopted. The Property Maintenance Code, as Chapter 20 is now designated, encompasses the substance of the predecessor. Housing Code, and in Section 20.2 asserts with renewed emphasis: "The purpose of this code is to provide minimum requirements for the protection of life, limb, health, property, safety, and welfare of the general public and the owners and occupants of residential and nonresidential buildings." [Footnotes are the court's.]

26. The other violations of the Housing Code alleged were lack of window screening, absence of bathroom venting, loose and insecure front porch column, defective trap under the kitchen sink, broken eaves, improper basement drainage and broken

and defective basement steps. The provisions of the Housing Code violated were alleged to be sections 20.17, 20.19, 20.27, 20.29, 20.33 and 20.34.

27. The defense of illegality, incorporated by reference, also asserted that the defendant had requested, and the plaintiff promised but failed, to abate these conditions; that finally in May of 1969, defendant refused to make further payment of rent until the plaintiff complied, but plaintiff refused to do so throughout the remainder of defendant's occupancy. After inspection of the premises by the Housing Section of the City Health Department, on May 29, 1969, the Director of Health ordered plaintiff to correct these violations and when plaintiff failed to comply, on July 15, 1969, the Director issued first a preliminary order and then a final order re-

The circuit court determined that the defendant's answer admitted occupancy of the premises without payment of the accrued rent for the period alleged in the complaint, and thus failed to state a legal defense to the plaintiff's claim. The court ordered the first and second affirmative defenses stricken and entered judgment for plaintiff for $109 and his costs. The effect of the judgment of the circuit court that the allegations of illegality of lease and breach of an implied warranty of habitability were not sufficient as legal defenses to the plaintiff's claim for rent was to concede the truth of the facts well pleaded by defendant. We test the propriety of the trial court's judgment in the perspective of that concession. Higday v. Nickolaus, 469 S.W.2d 859, 864[10] (Mo.App. 1971).

At early common law, a lease was considered a conveyance of an estate in land and was equivalent to a sale of the premises for the term of the demise. Warner v. Fry, 360 Mo. 496, 228 S.W.2d 729, 730[1] (1950); 2 Powell, The Law of Real Property, § 221(1) at 178. As a purchaser of an estate in land, the tenant was subject to the strict property rule of *caveat emptor*—let the buyer beware. The lessee's eyes were his bargain. He had the duty to inspect the property for defects and took the land as he found it. "[F]raud apart, there (was) no law against letting a tumble-down house." Robbins v. Jones, 15 CBNS 221, 143 Eng.Rep. 768, 776 (1863). There was no implied warranty by the lessor that the leased premises were habitable or fit. The common law traditionally assumed that the landlord and tenant were of equal bargaining power. So, if the tenant wished to protect himself as to the fitness of the premises, he could exact an express covenant from the landlord for that purpose. Burnes v. Fuchs, 28 Mo.App. 279, 281 (1887); Griffin v. Freeborn, 181 Mo.App. 203, 168 S.W. 219, 220[1–5] (1914); See also, Landlord and Tenant—Implied Warranty of Habitability—Demise of the Traditional Doctrine of Caveat Emptor, 20 DePaul L.Rev. 955 (1970–1971).

The law of leasehold originated in an era of agrarian economy which assumed that the land was the most important feature of the conveyance. The tenant was only the conduit for the rent which was conceived to issue from the land itself "without reference to the condition of the buildings or structures on it". Hart v. Windsor, 12 M & W 68, 152 Eng. Rep. 1114, 1119. If the buildings were not habitable, the rent—which was the *quid pro quo* of the tenant's possession—was still due from him.[28] Thus, even where the tenant was successful in exacting a covenant that the lessor make repairs this covenant was considered only incidental to the land and independent of the tenant's covenant to pay rent.[29] Hence a breach by the landlord did not suspend the obligation of rent; the tenant's only remedy was to sue for damages arising from

quiring plaintiff to correct or abate the violations.

28. 2 Pollock & Maitland, The History of English Law 131 (2d ed. 1923); Javins v. First National Realty Corporation, 428 F.2d 1071, 1077 (D.C.App.1970); Quinn & Phillips, The Law of Landlord-Tenant; A Critical Evaluation of the Past With Guide-

lines for the Future, 38 Forham L.Rev. 225, 227–8 (1969).

29. Legal scholarship suggests that the doctrine of independence of covenants in the landlord-tenant law is an historical accident, that it developed before the contract principle of mutually dependent obligations was established. Lesar, Landlord

the breach. For all practical purposes, the obligation to pay rent was absolute.

This rule of law where rigorously applied had harsh results.[30] The severity of the rule has been softened by judicially created exceptions which recognize a lease as a conveyance but, in certain circumstances, treat the landlord-tenant relationship as if governed by principles of contract law. Thus, even the earliest common law lease was understood to be "a contract for title to the estate" and thus to imply a covenant of quiet enjoyment of the demised premises.[31] If the landlord evicts a tenant by physically depriving him of possession, he breaches the implied covenant of quiet enjoyment and the obligation of the tenant to pay rent is suspended. Dolph v. Barry, 165 Mo.App. 659, 148 S.W. 196, 198 (1912). The covenant of quiet enjoyment is not only an exception to *caveat emptor* but also to the doctrine that the covenants of a lease are independent.[32]

Upon this exception was built another exception, the doctrine of constructive eviction. The courts soon came to realize that a tenant's possession and quiet enjoyment could be molested by something less than physical extrusion by the landlord. A constructive eviction arises when the lessor, by wrongful conduct or by the omission of a duty placed upon him in the lease, substantially interferes with the lessee's beneficial enjoyment of the demised premises. Under this doctrine the tenant is allowed to abandon the lease and excuse himself from the obligations of rent because the landlord's conduct, or omission, not only substantially breaches the implied covenant of quiet enjoyment but also "operates to impair the consideration for the lease". Dolph v. Barry, 165 Mo.App. 659, 148 S.W. 196, 198[3] (1912).[33] Thus, the first remedy created by the courts to insure habitability, and to exonerate the tenant's obligation for rent under a lease for lack of it, was "designed to operate as though there were a substantial breach of a material covenant in a bilateral contract". Lemle v. Breeden, 51 Haw. 426, 462 P.2d 470, 475[5] (1969).

*   *   *

Although the early agrarian lease was viewed as a conveyance, the authorities agree that the modern lease is both a conveyance and a contract.[34] With the change from an agricultural to an urban society, the

---

and Tenant Reform, 35 N.Y.U.L.Rev. 1279 (1960); Williston, Contracts, § 890 at 585–8 (3rd ed. W. Jaeger 1962).

30. In O'Neil v. Flanagan, 64 Mo.App. 87 (1895) the tenant was not discharged from his obligation to pay rent although the building was destroyed by fire. In Burnes v. Fuchs, 28 Mo.App. 279 (1887) the obligation to pay rent was not discharged although the premises were in such deplorable condition as to be condemned by municipal authorities.

31. Hart v. Windsor, 12 M & W 68, 152 Eng.Rep. 1114, 1122 (1843); 1 American Law of Property, Secs. 3.47–3.58 at 271–284 (Casner ed. 1952).

32. 1 American Law of Property, Sec. 3.50 at 278 (Casner ed. 1952).

33. See, also, Dyett v. Pendleton, 8 Cow. 727 (N.Y.1827) where the doctrine of constructive eviction was first articulated, l.c. 7.30, on the "universal principle in all cases of contract, that a party who deprives another of the consideration on which his obligation was founded, can never recover damages for its non-fulfillment".

34. Corbin on Contracts, § 686 (1960 ed.); Williston on Contracts, § 890 (3rd ed. Jaeger); Thompson on Real Property, § 1110 (1959 replacement).

function of the lease has also changed. The land itself, once the central reason for the lease, is of no value to an urban dweller. The minds of the parties to a modern lease contemplate more than the mere delivery of possession and the fixing of rent. The urban lessee seeks and expects "a well known package of goods and service—a package which includes not merely walls and ceilings, but also adequate heat, light and ventilation, serviceable plumbing facilities, secure windows and doors, proper sanitation and proper maintenance." Javins v. First National Realty Corporation, 138 U.S.App.D.C. 369, 428 F.2d 1071, 1074[1] (1970). Thus, the importance of a lease to such a tenant today is not to create a tenurial relationship but to arrange for a habitable dwelling. Kline v. Burns, 111 N.H. 87, 276 A.2d 248, 251 (1971).

The recognition that modern housing leases are bilateral contracts as well as conveyances of a property interest has resulted in re-examination of the no-repair rule enjoyed by the landlord under *caveat emptor*. In a context other than, but related to, the circumstances and question presented here, our Supreme Court in Minton v. Hardinger, 438 S.W.2d 3 (1968) approved the American Law of Property text criticism of the common law rule which imposes the duty of repairs upon the tenant, vol. I, p. 347:

> The rule that the tenant must make repairs was probably fair when applied in an agrarian economy where the materials for repairs were simple and at hand, and the tenant capable of making them himself. At least as concerns the actual making of repairs, the rule seems archaic and completely out of harmony with the facts when applied in a complicated society to urban dwellings occupied by persons on salary or weekly wage. Common experience indicates that the tenant in such cases seldom makes or is expected to make repairs even of the minor type covered by the common law duty. * * * It would seem that the lessor is in the better position, from the viewpoint of economic situation and interest, to make repairs, and that the tenant ought to have no duty in the absence of a specific covenant.

In recent years those courts which have considered the question have uniformly rejected the applicability of *caveat emptor* to residential leases and have implied a warranty of habitability and fitness for use of the premises on principles of contract law.[35] The warranty is the implied effect intended by the parties to the lease agreement. Marini v. Ireland, 56 N.J. 130, 265 A.2d 526, 533[15] (1970). "It affirms the fact that a lease is, in essence, a sale as well as a transfer of an estate in land and is, more important, a contractual relationship." Lemle v. Breeden, 51 Haw. 426, 462 P.2d 470, 474[1–3] (1969); Javins v. First Na-

---

35. Pines v. Perssion, 14 Wis.2d 590, 111 N.W.2d 409 (1961); Lemle v. Breeden, 51 Haw. 426, 462 P.2d 470 (1969); Marini v. Ireland, 56 N.J. 130, 265 A. 526 (1970); Javins v. First National Realty Corporation, 138 U.S.App.D.C. 369, 428 F.2d 1071 (1970); Amanuensis, Ltd. v. Brown, 65 Misc.2d 15, 318 N.Y.S.2d 11 (1971); Kline v. Burns, 276 A.2d 248 (N.H.1971); Mease v. Fox, 200 N.W.2d 791 (Iowa 1972); Hinson v. Delis, 26 Cal.App.3d 62, 102 Cal. Rptr. 661 (1972); Jack Spring, Inc. v. Little, 50 Ill.2d 351, 280 N.E.2d 208 (1972). See, also, 40 A.L.R.3d 646, Annotation— Modern Status of Rules as to Existence of Implied Warranty of Habitability or Fitness for Use of Leased Premises.

tional Realty Corporation, 138 U.S.App.D.C. 369, 428 F.2d 1071 (1970); Jack Spring, Inc. v. Little, 50 Ill.2d 351, 280 N.E.2d 208 (1972).

Considerations which justify reappraisal of common law principles of landlord and tenant in favor of an implied warranty of habitability in residential leases include 1) the contemporary housing shortage and resultant inequality in bargaining power between the landlord and tenant (Javins v. First National Realty Corporation, supra, 428 F.2d l.c. 1079; Lemle v. Breeden, supra, 462 P.2d l.c. 474[1–3]; Chapter 99 RSMo 1969); 2) housing codes which impose repair, maintenance and other standards of habitability upon landlords (§ 441.510 et seq., RSMoSupp.1973; § 20, Code of General Ordinances of Kansas City, Missouri; Pines v. Perssion, 14 Wis.2d 590, 111 N.W.2d 409, 412 (1961); Jack Spring, Inc. v. Little, 50 Ill.2d 351; 280 N.E.2d 208, 217[10, 11] (1972)); 3) the common experience that the landlord has superior knowledge of the condition of the premises, including any latent defects, and that the housing requirements and violations are usually known or made known to the landlord (Kline v. Burns, 276 A.2d 248, 251 (N.H.1971)); 4) a residential lessee is a purchaser of "a well known package of services" who must rely on the skill and honesty of the supplier to assure the quality of such services, and thus a residential tenant is entitled to the benefit of consumer protection law (Javins v. First National Realty Corporation, supra, 428 F.2d l.c. 1075; Lemle v. Breeden, supra, 462 P.2d l.c. 474).

The Supreme Court of Wisconsin in Pines v. Perssion, 14 Wis.2d 590, 111 N.W.2d 409 (1961), found an implied covenant of habitability necessary in order for the lease to be consistent with the housing laws. A single family dwelling was leased to a group of college students. When the students moved in, they found the premises uninhabitable, and after an unsuccessful attempt to repair the premises themselves, they moved out and brought suit to recover their deposit. Although the students had inspected the house before renting it, the court pointed out that they had no way of knowing that the plumbing, heating and wiring were defective, l.c. 412–413:

> Legislation and administrative rules   *   *   *   building codes and health regulations, all impose certain duties on a property owner with respect to the condition of his premises. Thus, the legislature has made a policy judgment—that it is socially (and politically) desirable to impose these duties on a property owner—   *   *   *   To follow the old rule of no implied warranty of habitability in leases would, in our opinion, be inconsistent with the current legislative policy concerning housing standards.

      *   *   *

In Javins v. First National Realty Corporation, 138 U.S.App.D.C. 369, 428 F.2d 1071 (1970), the landlord sought to evict a tenant for nonpayment of rent. The tenant asserted the defense that numerous housing code violations had arisen on his premises after the commencement of a tenancy. The court sustained the defense and held that, l.c. 1072, 1074, 1075, 1076, 1077, 1080:

[A] warranty of habitability, measured by the standards set out in the Housing Regulations for the District of Columbia, is implied by operation of law into leases of urban dwelling units covered by these Regulations and that breach of this warranty gives rise to the usual remedies for breach of contract.

*   *   *

Modern contract law has recognized that the buyer of goods and services in an industrialized society must rely upon the skill and honesty of the supplier to assure that goods and services purchased are of adequate quality. In interpreting most contracts, courts have sought to protect the legitimate expectations of the buyer and have steadily widened the seller's responsibility for the quality of goods and services through implied warranties of fitness and merchantability.

*   *   *

Implied warranties of quality have not been limited to cases involving sales. *   *   * Courts have begun to hold sellers and developers of real property responsible for the quality of their product. For example, builders of new homes have recently been held liable to purchasers for improper construction on the ground that the builders had breached an implied warranty of fitness. *   *   * (W)e believe that the consumer protection cases discussed above require that the old rule be abandoned in order to bring residential landlord-tenant law into harmony with the principles on which those cases rest.

*   *   *

Our approach to the common law of landlord and tenant ought to be aided by principles derived from the consumer protection cases *   *   * In a lease contract, a tenant seeks to purchase from his landlord shelter for a specified period of time. The landlord sells housing as a commercial business man and has much greater opportunity, incentive and capacity to inspect and maintain the condition of his building. Moreover, the tenant must rely upon the skill and *bona fides* of his landlord at least as much as a car buyer must rely upon the car manufacturer.

The social realities, legislative policies and judicial disposition to reexamine an outworn common law doctrine which have prompted these courts to imply a warranty of habitability in residential leases obtain also in Missouri. The Missouri Legislature in 1939 enacted the Housing Authorities Law, Chapter 99 RSMo 1969, which authorized the improvement and construction of dwelling units to relieve the "shortage of safe or sanitary dwelling accommodations available at rents which persons of low income can afford". Thereafter, the apparent legislative recognition of the fact, commonly known, that even with such governmental assistance, new construction was not keeping pace with the obsolescence and deterioration of the existing housing inventory in the cities, resulted in the enactment in 1969 of the Enforcement of Minimum Housing Code Standards Act, §§ 441.500–441.640, RSMo Supp.1973.

This statute has as its purpose the coercive repair, by the landlord or from his property [*sic*], of conditions harmful to the life, health and safety of occupants of a dwelling unit resulting from violations of the housing code. If within a reasonable time after notice the landlord fails to repair such a deficiency, a receiver, appointed upon the petition of the code enforcement agency of a municipality or the requisite number of tenants, is authorized to collect rent and encumber the property to meet the cost of abatement of the housing code violations. Such statutes have been effective in extending the life of residential housing accommodations which otherwise would have lapsed into blight.[36]

The Enforcement of Minimum Code Standards statute effectively 1) recognizes the minimum standards for occupancy of municipal housing codes as standards for the habitability of residential dwellings, 2) alters the common law no-repair rule by coercing repairs by the landlord or from his property to restore the tenant's occupancy to the minimum housing code standards for life, health and safety and 3) reads into every residential lease the minimum standards for occupancy of the applicable municipal housing code.

The earliest housing codes, adopted at the turn of the century were exercises in paternalism. They were aimed not at habitability but at preventing tenements from becoming sources of communicable disease. The sanction for non-compliance was a benign vacate order. If a building became so dilapidated as to be unfit for occupancy, the code enforcement agency condemned the building and forced the tenants to move. This procedure was followed during the period of favorable "vacancy ratio", when a dispossessed tenant could readily find other accommodations.[37] The serious housing shortage brought about by the influx of population to the cities, spurred by rapid industrial growth, resulted in the elimination of the vacate order. As a consequence, housing codes adopted stricter requirements of habitability and repair with provision for criminal prosecution of violators.[38]

The Housing Code of Kansas City, which adopts the minimum standards for occupancy (Article II), requires repair or other correction of a dwelling unfit for habitation (§ 20.5) and places the onus of compliance on the landlord (§ 20.34)—a duty unknown at common law—under threat of fine (§ 20.10), evinces a purpose to maintain the habitability of dwellings throughout the period of occupancy, and thus to preserve

36. Gribetz and Grad, Housing Code Enforcement: Sanctions and Remedies, 66 Colum.L.Rev. 1254 at 1272–74 (1966).

37. E.g., Articles II, IV & V, Revised Ordinances of Kansas City (1898) and Article III, § 727, Revised Ordinances of St. Louis (1887). Such ordinances were construed to impose upon a landlord an obligation to the public authorities only. Thus, it was held in Burnes v. Fuchs, 28 Mo.App. 279 (1887), that the breach of a municipal ordinance which charged the owners of a dangerous building with the duty of repair was not available to a tenant as a defense to an action for rent. The court's holding,

although only dictum, has been influential, l.c. 282:

We may add that the ordinance of the city of St. Louis, which charges the owners of dangerous buildings with the obligation to repair, can have no influence in the decision of this question. As between the owner and the city, the obligation under such a police regulation may well rest upon the owner; and yet, as between the owner and his tenant, the rule of the common law will prevail, which casts the obligation upon the landlord.

38. Gribetz & Grad, supra, note 36 at 1260–62.

them for the housing market. It is a purpose consonant with the design of the Housing Authorities Law, §§ 99.010 to 99.230, RSMo 1969 [39], to provide habitable dwellings for persons of low incomes, and of the Land Clearance for Development Authority Law, §§ 99.300 to 99.660 RSMo 1969, for the reclamation and rehabilitation of blighted neighborhoods. The Enforcement of Minimum Housing Code Standards Act, §§ 441.500 to 441.640, coerces repairs by landlords to meet minimum standards of habitability and thus alters the common law. The Act expressly adopts the maintenance provisions, and therefore the purposes, of applicable housing codes in furtherance of state legislative policy. By adopting these standards, the Legislature has clearly made a judgment that the landlord does not agree to lease merely space, but habitable space. The insight of Judge Cardozo given in a related context is particularly appropriate, Altz v. Leiberson, 233 N.Y. 16, 134 N.E. 703, l.c. 704 (1922):

> The Legislature must have known that unless repairs in the rooms of the poor were made by the landlord, they would not be made by any one. The duty imposed became commensurate with the need. The right to seek redress is not limited to the city or its officers. The right extends to all whom there was a purpose to protect.

It is consistent with these legislative policies that in every residential lease there be an implied warranty by the landlord that the dwelling is habitable and fit for living at the inception of the term and that it will remain so during the entire term. The warranty of the landlord is that he will provide facilities and services vital to the life, health and safety of the tenant and to the use of the premises for residential purposes. It is an obligation which the landlord fulfills by substantial compliance with the relevant provisions of an applicable housing code. Jack Spring, Inc. v. Little, supra, 280 N.E.2d l.c. 217[10, 11]; Kline v. Burns, supra, 276 A.2d l.c. 251[1]; Marini v. Ireland, supra, 265 A.2d l.c. 534[15–19].

We are drawn to this conclusion also by the compelling analogy of another development in the law. In Missouri the rule of *caveat emptor* has steadily given way to a warranty of fitness for use implied by law, without any agreement, in sales transactions. The history of this demise is given in Smith v. Old Warson Development Co., 479 S.W.2d 795 (Mo. banc 1972). In *Smith*, the court determined that an implied warranty of fitness is read into a contract for the sale of a new home by a vendor-builder. The court adopted the opinion of the (then) St. Louis Court of Appeals, l.c. 799[4] and 801[12–15]:

> Although considered to be a "real estate" transaction because the ownership of land is transferred, the purchase of a residence is in most cases the purchase of a manufactured product—the house. *The land involved is seldom the prime element in such a purchase, certainly not in the urban areas of the state.* (Emphasis added.)

* * *

39. The Housing Code was repealed by the City Council in 1971 and the Property Maintenance Code which has succeeded it is specifically referenced to the provisions of § 99.010 of the Revised Statutes of Missouri.

The ordinary "consumer" can determine little about the soundness of the construction but must rely upon the fact that the vendor-builder *holds the structure out to the public as fit for use as a residence, and being of reasonable quality.* (Emphasis added.)

* * *

Common sense tells us that a purchaser under these circumstances should have at least as much protection as the purchaser of a new car, a gas stove, or a sump pump, or a ladder.

* * *

"The *caveat emptor* rule as applied to new houses is an anachronism patently out of harmony with modern home buying practices."

The reasoning of this decision is also a postulate of those courts which have rejected *caveat emptor* in favor of an implied warranty of habitability in residential leases. Javins v. First National Realty Corporation, supra, 428 F.2d l.c. 1076; Lemle v. Breeden, supra, 462 P.2d l.c. 473; Mease v. Fox, supra, 200 N.W.2d l.c. 795. It is a persuasive augury that, if presented with the question, the Supreme Court of Missouri would determine, as we now do, that a warranty of habitability is implied by operation of law in every residential lease.

We adopt the view that a lease is not only a conveyance but also gives rise to a contractual relationship between the landlord and tenant from which the law implies a warranty of habitability and fitness by the landlord. Under contract principles a tenant's obligation to pay rent is dependent upon the landlord's performance of his obligation to provide a habitable dwelling during the tenancy. Lemle v. Breeden, supra, 462 P.2d l.c. 475[6, 7]; Javins v. First National Realty Corporation, supra, 428 F.2d l.c. 1082[7–10]. A more responsive set of remedies are thus made available to the tenant, the basic remedies for contract law, including damages, reformation and rescission. Kline v. Burns, supra, 276 A.2d l.c. 252[2]; Lemle v. Breeden, supra, 462 P.2d l.c. 475[6, 7].

The materiality of a breach of warranty claimed by a tenant shall be determined by factors, among others, of the nature of the deficiency or defect, its effect on the life, health or safety of the tenant, length of time it has persisted and the age of the structure. Minor housing code violations which do not affect habitability will be considered *de minimis.* Also, the violation must affect the tenant's dwelling unit or the common areas which he uses. The tenant is under an obligation to give the landlord notice of the deficiency or defect not known to the landlord and to allow a reasonable time for its correction. The contract principle that a person may not benefit from his own wrong will exonerate a landlord for a defect or deficiency caused by a tenant's wrongful conduct. Javins v. First National Realty Corporation, supra, 428 F.2d l.c. 1082, note 62[7–10]; Hinson v. Delis, 26 Cal.App.3d 62, 102 Cal.Rptr. 661, 666[3–8]; Mease v. Fox, supra, 200 N.W.2d l.c. 796[5].

In this action, the tenant-appellant sufficiently pleads a residential lease, the warranty of habitability implied from that contractual relationship, substantial violations of the municipal housing code materially affecting her life, health and safety in breach of the implied warranty, reasonable notice of the defects to the landlord, and refusal of the landlord to restore the premises to habitability. At the time the tenant pleaded in the circuit court, she had already relinquished possession. The affirmative defenses of the tenant-appellant do not seek restoration to a habitable dwelling but are in the nature of counterclaims, alternatively pleaded, for exoneration from rent on the theory of illegality of contract or for set-off in damages against the rent for breach of the implied warranty of habitability.

Where there has been a material breach of implied warranty, the tenant's damages are reasonably measured by the difference between the agreed rent and the fair rental value of the premises as they were during occupancy by the tenant in the unhealthful or unsafe condition. Kline v. Burns, supra, 276 A.2d l.c. 252[5]; Pines v. Perssion, supra, 111 N.W.2d l.c. 413. After a tenant vacates, he is unaffected by the condition of the premises "and that factor loses relevance in the damage equation. For the balance of the term, (the) tenant has lost the benefit of his bargain, assuming he had an advantageous lease. He is therefore entitled to recover at that time for the value of the lease for the unexpired term, that is, the then difference between the fair rental value of the premises, if they had been as warranted and the promised rent, computed for that period. 11 Williston on Contracts, § 1404, at p. 562 (3d ed. 1968)." Mease v. Fox, supra, 200 N.W.2d l.c. 797[6, 7].

The implied warranty of habitability remedy developed, in measure, as response to a chronic and prolonged housing shortage, particularly for those of low income. Javins v. First National Realty Corporation, supra, 428 F.2d l.c. 1079. Common law constructive eviction, (based upon a fiction which the implied warranty remedy discards) could be claimed only by a tenant who abandoned the premises within a reasonable time. Abandonment was required to maintain the fiction of an eviction and thus the breach of the dependent covenant of quiet enjoyment. The effect of the abandonment requirement was to prevent a tenant from remaining in possession without paying rent. Dolph v. Barry, supra, 148 S.W. l.c. 198–200[4]. Constructive eviction has proved an insufficient remedy for those most likely to have resort to it, low income tenants. The dilemma it raises for them is that they must continue to pay rent and endure the conditions of untenantability or abandon the premises and hope to find another dwelling which, in these times of severe housing shortage, is likely to be as uninhabitable as the last.

This dilemma is avoided by recognizing that the modern lease is a bilateral contract so that the tenant's obligation for rent is dependent upon the landlord's performance of his responsibilities, among them, his implied warranty of habitability. Breach of this duty justifies retention of possession by the tenant and withholding of rent until habitability has been restored. A tenant who retains possession, however, shall be required to deposit the rent as it becomes due, *in custodia legis* pending the litigation. See and compare Javins v. First National Realty Corporation, supra, 428 F.2d l.c. 1083 note 67[14, 15]; Hinson v. Delis, supra, 102 Cal.Rptr. l.c. 666[9]. This procedure assures the landlord that those rents adjudicated for distribution to him will be available to correct the defects in habitability, and will also encourage the landlord to minimize the tenant's damages by making tenantable repairs at the earliest time. Also, for good cause and in a manner consistent with the ultimate right between the parties, a trial court will have discretion to make partial distribution to the landlord before final adjudication when to deny it would result in irreparable loss to him. We conclude also that this procedure is that most compatible with policy of our Legislature, of the Housing Code of Kansas City and of the implied warranty of habitability remedy itself that there be preserved and maintained an adequate supply of habitable dwellings.

For all these reasons, we determine that the answer of the tenant-appellant sufficiently pleads an implied warranty of habitability and its breach, an issue properly asserted as defense and counterclaim to the landlord-respondent's claim for rent.

The tenant-appellant contends also that the circuit court erred in striking her affirmative defense of illegality of lease. She pleads that the lease agreement upon which the claim for rent rests was made with the landlord's knowledge and intent that the premises be used for human habitation in substantial violation of the Kansas City Housing Code, so that the lease is an agreement void, illegal and unenforceable from which no obligation for rent can arise.

In Missouri, as elsewhere, it is generally recognized that a contract or transaction prohibited by law is void. State ex rel. American Surety Co. of New York v. Haid, 325 Mo. 949, 30 S.W.2d 100, 103[2] (1930). Such contracts are based upon illegal consideration and cannot be enforced either at law or in equity. Twiehaus v. Rosner, 362 Mo. 949, 245 S.W.2d 107, 111[6] (1952). Agreements violating municipal ordinances are illegal to the same extent as agreements violating enactments of the legislature. 17 C.J.S. Contracts § 208. "'All persons who contract with reference to a subject-matter within the limits of a municipality as to which there are police regulations * * * are charged with knowledge of and are presumed to know the provisions of the regulations and to have entered into such contracts with reference thereto * * * and such provisions become an integral part of the contract.'" Lazare v. Hoffman, 444 S.W.2d 446, 450[1] (Mo.1969). A police regulation is one which promotes "order, safety, health, morals and general welfare". Marshall v. Kansas City, 355 S.W.2d 877, 883[10] (Mo. banc 1962). The Kansas City Housing Code which establishes minimum standards for occupancy and habitability is such a police regulation. Thus, the parties to a lease transaction to which such a housing code appertains "'must be conclusively presumed to know the relevant law'". Sachs Steel & Supply Co. v. St. Louis Auto Parts & S. Co., 322 S.W.2d 183, 186[2–5] (Mo.App.1959).

Leases are generally subject to the rule applicable to illegality of contracts. 49 Am.Jur.2d, Landlord and Tenant, § 41.

The Kansas City Housing Code provides, § 20.16:

It shall be unlawful for any person to use or occupy, or for any owner or other person deemed to be the owner, as herein defined, to *permit any dwelling unit to be used or occupied as a place for human habitation unless the same complies with* the rules and regulations of *this article*. (Emphasis supplied.)

and § 20.34:

Every premise, dwelling and every part thereof shall be maintained in good order and repair fit for human habitation by the owner or his agent.

and § 20.10:

Any person violating any of the provisions of this chapter * * * shall be subject to fine.

These provisions expressly prohibit an owner from permitting occupancy of a dwelling unit which is unfit for human habitation because of violations of the housing code. These regulations in terms forbid the lease bargain pleaded by the tenant and fix a penalty to it. The general rule is that any act forbidden by a legislative enactment, if passed for the protection of the public and which provides for a penalty, cannot be the foundation of a valid contract. Longenecker v. Hardin, 130 Ill.App. 2d 468, 264 N.E.2d 878, 880[6] (1970). The housing code obviously intends to render void the act it prohibits.

Other courts, presented with this question, have held such leases to be illegal contracts and unenforceable. In Brown v. Southall Realty Co., 237 A.2d 834 (D.C.App.1968), the landlord knew at the time of the letting of the dwelling that substantial housing code violations existed. When the tenant's rent became delinquent, the landlord sued for rent and possession. In defense the tenant asserted the illegality, and hence unenforceability, of the lease. The court agreed, l.c. 836–837:

It appears that the violations known by * * * (the landlord) to be existing on the leasehold at the time of the signing of the lease agreement were of a nature to make the "habitation" unsafe and unsanitary * * * The lease contract was, therefore, entered into in violation of the Housing Regulations requiring that they be safe and sanitary and that they be properly maintained.

* * *

"[T]he general rule is that an illegal contract, made in violation of the statutory prohibition designed for police or regulatory purposes, is void and confers no right upon the wrongdoer."

* * *

To uphold the validity of this lease agreement, in light of the defects known to be existing on the leasehold prior to the agreement * * * would be to flout the evident purposes for which (the housing regulations) were enacted * * * (and which) do indeed "imply a prohibition" as to render the prohibited act void.

See, also, Shephard v. Lerner, 182 Cal.App.2d 746, 6 Cal.Rptr. 433 (1960); Longenecker v. Hardin, supra, 264 N.E.2d l.c. 880[6]. While the holding in *Brown* spoke in terms of the landlord's knowledge of violations at the time of letting, our law imposes no such requirement. Haggerty v. St. Louis Ice Mfg. & Storage Co., 143 Mo. 238, 44 S.W. 1114, 1116 (1898); Hall v. Bucher, 240 Mo.App. 1239, 227 S.W.2d 96, 98[2] (1950).

The law will leave parties to an illegal agreement in the position in which they put themselves. State v. County of Camden, 394 S.W.2d 71, 78[10, 11] (Mo.App.1965). The affirmative defense of the tenant-appellant, which pleads that the landlord-respondent leased to her premises in a condition of substantial violation of the housing code pleads a sufficient illegality of lease as a defense to the landlord's action for rent.

The tenant-appellant does not seek recoupment of her performance under the illegal lease, nor any other affirmative relief, but only to defeat the landlord's claim for rent due and unpaid under the lease. We need not determine, therefore, whether the tenant was *in pari delicto* and if so whether considerations of public policy or equity require that relief be granted as against the illegal contract. Gardine v. Cottey, 360 Mo. 681, 230 S.W.2d 731, 740[13] (banc 1950); Twiehaus v. Rosner, supra, 245 S.W.2d l.c. 112, 114[10].

While the law denies the landlord who has leased premises in substantial violation of the housing code the consideration of his illegal bargain, sound public policy dictates that such a landlord may recover the reasonable value of the premises in its condition during occupancy. The same public policy which recognizes the implied warranty of habitability as a means of preserving housing for the rental market will deny a tenant the use and occupancy at no cost of a sub-habitable dwelling and thus deprive a landlord of his basic, and perhaps only, resource for restoration of the premises to habitability. The only court which has considered the question has allowed, as we do, recovery to a landlord for the reasonable value of the premises during occupancy by a tenant who entered into possession under a lease void and illegal because the premises were in substantial violation of the housing regulations. William J. Davis, Inc. v. Slade, 271 A.2d 412 (D.C.App.1970). This result proceeded from the "generally accepted view * * * that entry upon a premises under a void and unenforceable lease creates a tenancy at will" (Diamond Housing Corporation v. Robinson, 257 A.2d 492, 495[7, 8] (D.C. App.1969), and since the law has accorded such a status, "[t]his tenancy, unlike the tenancy attempted by the lease, is legal" and the landlord is entitled to its reasonable value. Davis v. Slade, supra, 271 A.2d l.c. 416[6]. The unenforceable lease which gives rise to a tenancy at will under the "generally accepted view", however, is one which is made void by a formal defect—such as noncompliance with the requirements of the Statute of Frauds—and not where the consideration for the lease, the performance itself, is illegal and prohibited. Thompson on Real Property, § 1018; 6 A.L.R.2d 685, Annotation, Tenancy Under Void Lease. We prefer to base our decision openly on the hard reality that if, under existing conditions, landlords were deprived of all rents because of noncompliance with housing codes there would be far fewer low income housing units available—landlords would find it to their economic advantage to abandon their properties rather than spend their separate resources to restore them to habitability. See, Samuelson v. Quinones, 119 N.J.Super. 338, 291 A.2d 580, 583 (1972).

Upon remand, the court will allow the landlord-respondent, if he should choose, to file a reply to the affirmative defense of illegality of contract to allege a claim for the reasonable value of the tenant's occupancy after May 6, 1969. We conclude also that the affirmative defense of illegality of lease is inconsistent with the affirmative defense of breach of the implied warranty of habitability of that lease. The first defense asserts the unenforceability of the contract and the second that a breach of a term of that contract is enforceable and should yield damages. The proof of one defense necessarily disproves the other, so the defenses are inconsistent. Payne v. White, 288 S.W.2d 6, 9[7] (Mo.App. 1956). A litigant may not pursue to judgment defenses which at once approbate and reprobate, affirm and disaffirm, a contract. Berger v. Mercantile Trust Company, 352 S.W.2d 644, 650[6] (Mo.1961). Upon remand, the tenant-appellant will be put to her election between these defenses and will be permitted to follow only one of them to judgment.

The judgment is reversed and remanded for proceedings consistent with our directions.

DIXON, C.J., and SWOFFORD and WASSERSTROM, JJ., concur.

PRITCHARD, J., concurs in result in separate concurring opinion filed.

PRITCHARD, Judge (concurring in result).

I concur in the result of the main opinion. It is sufficient to rely upon the more recent cases extensively cited, quoted and footnoted therein, and the statutes and ordinances cited. Those cases have long ago uniformly abrogated the common law doctrine of *caveat emptor* in the legal relationship between a landlord and his tenant, assuming that such old rule is the basis, which is not clear, that the trial court employed in striking appellant's affirmative defenses.

Note on the Judge-Made "Implied" Warranty of Habitability

As previously noted, the first significant case to hold that a warranty of habitability should be implied in residential leases was Pines v. Perssion.[40] Although Pines v. Perssion was arguably later overruled *sub silentio*,[41] and has in any case been at least partly superseded by subsequent Wisconsin legislation,[42] the highest courts of at least twelve other jurisdictions followed the Wisconsin court's lead in adopting the "implied" warranty of habitability by judicial decision. These jurisdictions are California,[43] the District of Columbia,[44] Ha-

---

40. 14 Wis.2d 590, 111 N.W.2d 409 (1961).

41. See Posnanski v. Hood, 46 Wis.2d 172, 174 N.W.2d 528 (1970).

42. Wis.Stat.Ann. § 704.07 (West Supp. 1982–83).

43. Green v. Superior Court, 10 Cal.3d 616, 111 Cal.Rptr. 704, 517 P.2d 1168 (1974).

44. Javins v. First National Realty Corp., 428 F.2d 1071 (D.C.Cir.1970), cert. denied 400 U.S. 925, 91 S.Ct. 186, 27 L.Ed. 2d 185.

waii,[45] Illinois,[46] Iowa,[47] Kansas,[48] Massachusetts,[49] New Hampshire,[50] New Jersey,[51] Pennsylvania,[52] Texas,[53] Washington,[54] and West Virginia.[55] In addition, lower courts have recognized the "implied" warranty in Indiana,[56] Missouri,[57] New York [58] and Ohio.[59] It should be noted, however, that the judge-made "implied" warranty has been wholly or largely superseded in Hawaii, Iowa, Kansas, and Washington by provisions in new comprehensive residential landlord-tenant statutes imposing upon landlords a duty—set out in considerable detail—to put and keep the leased premises in a habitable condition.[60] Moreover, the new "implied" warranty has been put in statutory form in the District of Columbia, New York, and West Virginia, although these jurisdictions have not enacted comprehensive new residential landlord-tenant legislation.[61]

1. Rental Housing Covered by the "Implied" Warranty.

In jurisdictions where the new tenant's right to a habitable dwelling is based only on judicial decisions recognizing an "implied warranty of habitability, it is not always clear just what rental housing is subject to the "implied" warranty. In *Javins v. First Nat. Realty Corp.*,[62] the court held that the District of Columbia housing code required "implication" of a warranty of habitability in the leasing of all housing covered by the code, and also suggested that, even without reference to the code, a warranty of habitability should "be implied into all contracts for urban dwellings" as a matter of common law.[63] The latter suggestion really had no significance with respect to the District of Columbia, however, since the D.C. housing code applied to "any habitation" in the District [64] and all rental housing in the District is clearly "urban." A later decision by a lower court has interpreted *Javins* as applying only to dwelling units covered by the D.C. housing code.[65]

After *Javins*, the highest courts of California, Illinois, Iowa, Massachusetts, New Jersey, Pennsylvania, Washington, and West Virginia held that the new warranty of habitability should be "implied" in all residential leases; [66] and in

45. Lemle v. Breeden, 51 Hawaii 426, 462 P.2d 470 (1969); Lund v. MacArthur, 51 Hawaii 473, 462 P.2d 482 (1969).

46. Jack Spring, Inc. v. Little, 50 Ill.2d 351, 280 N.E.2d 208 (1972); Pole Realty Co. v. Sorrells, 84 Ill.2d 178, 49 Ill.Dec. 283, 417 N.E.2d 1297 (1981).

47. Mease v. Fox, 200 N.W.2d 791 (Iowa 1972).

48. Steele v. Latimer, 214 Kan. 329, 521 P.2d 304 (1974).

49. Boston Housing Authority v. Hemingway, 363 Mass. 184, 293 N.E.2d 831 (1973).

50. Kline v. Burns, 111 N.H. 87, 276 A.2d 248 (1971).

51. Marini v. Ireland, 56 N.J. 130, 265 A.2d 526 (1970); Berzito v. Gambino, 63 N.J. 460, 308 A.2d 17 (1973).

52. Pugh v. Holmes, 486 Pa. 272, 405 A.2d 897 (1979).

53. Kamarath v. Bennett, 568 S.W.2d 658 (Tex.1978).

54. Foisy v. Wyman, 83 Wn.2d 22, 515 P.2d 160 (1973).

55. Teller v. McCoy, 253 S.E.2d 114 (W.Va.1978).

56. Old Town Development Co. v. Langford, 349 N.E.2d 744 (Ind.App.1976).

57. King v. Moorehead, 495 S.W.2d 65 (Mo.App.1973).

58. Tonetti v. Penati, 48 App.Div.2d 25, 367 N.Y.S.2d 804 (1975).

59. Glyco v. Schultz, 35 Ohio Misc. 25, 289 N.E.2d 919 (Mun.Ct.1972).

60. See post, Uniform Residential Landlord and Tenant Act.

61. D.C. Landlord-Tenant Regulations § 2902.2 (1970); N.Y. Real Prop.L. § 235–b (Supp.1981–82); W.Va.Code Ann. § 37–6–30 (Supp.1982).

62. Supra note 44.

63. 428 F.2d at 1080.

64. District of Columbia, Landlord-Tenant Regulations §§ 2304, 2501 (1970).

65. Winchester Management Corp. v. Staten, 361 A.2d 187, 190 (D.C.App.1976).

66. Green v. Superior Court, supra note 43; Pole Realty Co. v. Sorrells, supra note 46; Mease v. Fox, supra note 48; Marini v. Ireland, supra note 51; Pugh v. Holmes, supra note 52; Kamarath v. Bennett, supra note 53; Foisy v. Wyman, supra note 54; Teller v. McCoy, supra note 55.

Iowa, Washington, and West Virginia, this broad coverage was confirmed by legislation establishing a statutory warranty of habitability. In New Hampshire, on the other hand, the "implied" warranty is limited to multi-family dwelling units; [67] in Kansas, the "implied" warranty was originally limited to "urban residential property," [68] but was later broadened by statute to cover all property leased for residential use.

Where the courts have "implied" a warranty of habitability in residential leases without the aid of legislation, the relationship between the new "implied" warranty and the standards set out in applicable housing codes is not always clear. In general, the cases indicate that proof of housing code violations having a substantial adverse impact on health and/or safety will be sufficient to establish a breach of the "implied" warranty.[69] On the other hand, most of the cases recognize that some housing code violations, standing alone, do not pose any substantial threat to the health or safety of tenants, and hence that a breach of the "implied" warranty is not proved merely by proof of the existence of a code violation (or violations).[70] As the court observed in *Javins*, "one or two minor violations standing alone, which do not affect habitability, are *de minimis*." [71]

Assuming that most courts will not find a breach of the implied warranty of habitability on the basis of housing code violations unless the code violations are serious enough to pose a threat to the health or safety of the tenant, the question remains whether a breach may be found where there is no code violation at all. It is not clear what position the *Javins* court would have taken on this question, but the District of Columbia Court of Appeals subsequently interpreted *Javins* as holding that the implied warranty is measured solely "by the standards set out in the [D.C.] Housing Regulations" and has refused to "stray from or expand upon that holding." [72] In several other jurisdictions, however, the courts have defined the implied warranty of habitability broadly enough to include all cases where the leased premises are unfit for human habitation because of health or safety hazards, whether or not there is a violation of any housing code provision.[73] Thus several courts [74] have stated that whether defects are so substantial as to render the leased premises unsafe or unsanitary, and thus unfit for habitation, is a factual issue to be determined in light of the

---

67. Kline v. Burns, supra note 50.

68. Steele v. Latimer, supra note 48.

69. Javins v. First National Realty Corp., supra note 44; Green v. Superior Court, supra note 43; Jack Spring, Inc. v. Little, supra note 46; Boston Housing Authority v. Hemingway, supra note 49; King v. Moorehead, supra note 57; Kline v. Burns, supra note 50; Berzito v. Gambino, supra note 51; Pugh v. Holmes, supra note 52; Foisy v. Wyman, supra note 54; Teller v. McCoy, supra note 55.

70. Javins v. First National Realty Corp., supra note 44; Green v. Superior Court, supra note 43; Lund v. MacArthur, supra note 45; Boston Housing Authority v. Hemingway, supra note 49; King v. Moorehead, supra note 57; Berzito v. Gambino, supra note 55; Foisy v. Wyman, supra note 54.

71. 428 F.2d at 1082 n. 63.

72. Winchester Management Corp. v. Staten, 361 A.2d 187, 190 (D.C.App.1976).

73. Green v. Superior Court, 10 Cal.3d 616, 111 Cal.Rptr. 704, 517 P.2d 1168 (1974); Lemle v. Breeden, 51 Hawaii 426, 462 P.2d 470 (1969); Mease v. Fox, 200 N.W.2d 791 (Iowa 1972); Old Town Development Co. v. Langford, 349 N.E.2d 744 (Ind.App.1976); Boston Housing Authority v. Hemingway, 363 Mass. 184, 293 N.E.2d 831 (1973); King v. Moorehead, 495 S.W.2d 65 (Mo.App.1973); Kline v. Burns, 111 N.H. 87, 276 A.2d 248 (1971); Marini v. Ireland, 56 N.J. 130, 265 A.2d 526 (1970); Berzito v. Gambino, 63 N.J. 460, 308 A.2d 17 (1973); Tonetti v. Penati, 48 A.D.2d 25, 367 N.Y.S.2d 804 (1975); Pugh v. Holmes, 486 Pa. 262, 405 A.2d 897 (1979).

74. E.g., Mease v. Fox, Boston Housing Authority v. Hemingway, King v. Moorehead, Kline v. Burns, Marini v. Ireland, and Berzito v. Gambino, supra note 73.

circumstances of each case; that ordinarily one such circumstance would be whether the alleged defect violates an applicable housing code; and that other factors to be considered are the nature of the defect, its effect on safety and sanitation, the length of time it has persisted, the age of the structure, and the amount of the rent.

Although most of the court opinions focus on "defects" in the premises serious enough to pose a threat to the health or safety of the tenant, it seems clear that the implied warranty generally requires the provision of "essential" or "vital" services such as hot water, heat, and elevators (in high rise buildings), even if these services are not strictly necessary to protect the tenant's health or safety.[75] Of course, where a housing code is applicable, it will usually require that such services be provided by the landlord.[76]

2. "Patent" and "Latent" Defects; Continuing Duty to Keep Premises "Habitable".

To the extent that the landlord's obligation is to assure that the leased premises are habitable at the beginning of the tenancy, the further question may arise as to whether the obligation covers "patent" as well as "latent" defects. In Pines v. Perssion,[77] many of the defects that made the premises "uninhabitable" were "patent," but some were "latent." The court, however, said nothing to suggest any distinction between "patent" and "latent" with respect to the newly discovered implied warranty. In Lemle v. Breeden [78] and Lund v. MacArthur,[79] all the defects appear to have been "latent," but the court did not indicate that this was significant. In Javins v. First National Realty Corp.,[80] the tenants offered to prove that there were some 1500 violations of the District of Columbia housing code, but they conceded that "this offer of proof reached only violations which have arisen since the term of the lease had commenced." [81] Thus the court had no reason to discuss the question whether the newly discovered implied warranty would cover patent defects existing at the beginning of the lease term. But the *Javins* opinion does include a dictum that the shortage of housing in the District of Columbia compels tenants to accept rental units notwithstanding observable defects; [82] and the court's emphasis on the need to give tenants new remedies to enforce their right to a habitable dwelling that substantially complies with the housing code suggests that the *Javins* court would draw no distinction between "latent" and "patent" defects.

In New Jersey, on the other hand, it has been held that the warranty of habitability implied in a residential letting is "that at the inception of the lease, there are no *latent* defects in facilities vital to the use of the premises for residential purposes because of original faulty construction or deterioration from age or normal usage." [83] This language was later adopted by the New Hamp-

---

75. Winchester Development Corp. v. Staten, supra note 72 (hot water, but not air conditioning, is required by housing code and, thus, by the implied warranty); Marini v. Ireland, supra note 73 ("facilities vital to the use of the premises for residential purposes); Berzito v. Gambino, supra note 73 (same); Academy Spires v. Brown, 111 N.J.Super. 477, 268 A.2d 556 (1970) (garbage disposal, hot water, elevator service); Park Hill Terrace Associates v. Glennon, 146 N.J.Super. 271, 369 A.2d 938 (1977) (air conditioning); Pugh v. Holmes, supra note 38 (hot water); Foisy v. Wyman, 83 Wn.2d 22, 515 P.2d 160 (1969) (same).

76. E.g., Winchester Development Corp. v. Staten, supra note 72.

77. 14 Wis.2d 590, 111 N.W.2d 409 (1961).

78. Supra note 73.

79. Ibid.

80. 428 F.2d 1071 (D.C.Cir.1970).

81. 428 F.2d at 1073.

82. 428 F.2d at 1079 n. 42.

83. Marini v. Ireland, 56 N.J. at 144, 265 A.2d at 534 (emphasis added). The quoted language was repeated with approval in Berzito v. Gambino, 63 N.J. at 466, 308 A.2d at 20. The *Berzito* case in-

shire [84] and Iowa courts.[85] But the significance of the "latent" defect limitation is hard to determine, since the Iowa, New Hampshire, and New Jersey courts have all held that the implied warranty also includes a continuing duty to keep the premises in a habitable condition.[86] It is probable that this continuing duty extends to the repair of "patent" as well as "latent" defects.[87] And in Massachusetts it is clear that the implied warranty of habitability covers both "latent" and "patent" defects existing at the beginning of the tenancy.[88]

The opinion in Pines v. Perssion,[89] proclaiming the existence of an "implied" warranty that residential premises are habitable at the inception of a tenancy, contains no language indicating that there is also a continuing duty of the landlord to maintain the premises in a habitable condition, although the legislative policy embodied in housing codes arguably supports the view that there should be such a continuing duty running directly from landlord to tenant and enforcible by "private" tenant remedies. And neither of the "implied" warranty cases from Hawaii [90] contains any language suggesting that the implied warranty includes any continuing duty of the landlord to maintain the premises in habitable condition. But in Javins v. First National Realty Corp.[91] the sole issue was whether the landlord was subject to such a continuing duty—more precisely, whether he had a duty to correct numerous housing code violations which were assumed to have "arisen since the term of the lease commenced." The *Javins* court's affirmative answer is clearly not based on the supposed analogy to the "consumer protection" cases relied on by Judge Wright,[92] but it does seem to be justified by the policy underlying the District of Columbia housing code. Since *Javins*, although most of the cases have involved defective conditions in existence at the beginning of the tenancy, the courts have consistently said that the new "implied" warranty includes a continuing duty to maintain the dwelling unit in a habitable condition—i.e., to make all repairs necessary to keep the premises habitable, whether the conditions requiring the repairs existed when the tenancy began or only arose later.[93] None of the opin-

volved an express rather than an implied warranty of habitability, and the only real issue was the scope of the remedies for breach of such a warranty, whether express or implied.

84. Kline v. Burns, 111 N.H. 87, 276 A.2d 248 (1971).

85. Mease v. Fox, 200 N.W.2d 791 (Iowa 1972).

86. Mease v. Fox, supra note 85; Kline v. Burns, supra note 84; Marini v. Ireland, 56 N.J. 1, 144, 265 A.2d 526, 534 (1970). In Iowa, the implied warranty of habitability recognized in Mease v. Fox has been superseded by the statutory warranty of habitability established by Iowa Code Ann. § 562A.15, which clearly covers both "latent" and "patent" defects (based on Uniform Residential Landlord and Tenant Act § 2.104(a) (1972)).

87. It should be noted that both Mease v. Fox, supra note 85, and Berzito v. Gambino, supra note 83 (quoting *Mease*) contain statements that the court should consider, in a particular case, "whether the tenant voluntarily, knowingly and intelligently waived the defects." This clearly suggests that merely accepting possession when "patent" defects exist would not sat-

isfy the stated requirement that any waiver should be made "knowingly and intelligently."

88. Boston Housing Authority v. Hemingway, 363 Mass. 184, 199, 293 N.E.2d 831, 843 (1973) (implied warranty that "at the inception of the rental there are *no latent or patent defects* in facilities vital to the use of the premises for residential purposes"). (Emphasis added.)

89. 14 Wis.2d 590, 111 N.W.2d 409 (1961).

90. Lemle v. Breeden, 51 Hawaii 426, 462 P.2d 470 (1969); Lund v. MacArthur, 51 Hawaii 473, 462 P.2d 482 (1969).

91. 428 F.2d 1071 (1970), cert. denied 400 U.S. 925, 91 S.Ct. 186, 27 L.Ed.2d 185 (1970).

92. Id. at 1079.

93. E.g., Green v. Superior Court, 10 Cal.3d 616, 111 Cal.Rptr. 704, 517 P.2d 1168 (1974); Jack Spring, Inc. v. Little, 50 Ill.2d 351, 280 N.E.2d 208 (1972); Boston Housing Authority v. Hemingway, supra note 88; Marini v. Ireland, 56 N.J. 1, 144, 265 A.2d 526, 534 (1970); Berzito v. Gambino, 63 N.J. 460, 308 A.2d 17 (1973); Pugh v. Holmes, 486 Pa. 272, 405 A.2d 897

ions limits the landlord's duty of repair to those "latent" conditions existing at the inception of the tenancy which first become apparent during the course of the tenancy.[94]

Note on the Defense of Illegality

In King v. Moorehead, supra, the court held that the tenant could assert a defense based either on breach of the implied warranty of habitability or on the theory that the lease was an "illegal contract" and therefore "void." The questions whether a lease is invalid, in whole or in part, because it is contrary to law or public policy, and what the consequences of "illegality" should be, are complex and fraught with much analytical confusion. Perhaps because of the conveyancing feature of leases, these problems are even more difficult than such problems in respect to contracts generally. Such problems are the least difficult where the making of a particular kind of lease is contrary to law. They are the most difficult in cases where only a single provision of a lease is illegal, such as the case where the lease calls for a particular use of the premises that is contrary to law. The problem of illegality in such a case may also be accompanied by other difficult questions, such as mistake, risk of loss, and conditional promises. Compare Economy v. S.B. & L. Bldg. Corp., 138 Misc. 296, 245 N.Y.S. 352 (App.Term, 1930), with Warshawsky v. American Automotive Products Co., 12 Ill.App.2d 178, 138 N.E.2d 816 (1956).

In Brown v. Southall Realty Co., 237 A.2d 834 (D.C.App.1968), in an action for possession for nonpayment of rent, the lessee pleaded substantial housing code violations existing at the beginning of the term. In reversing a judgment for the lessor, the court held that the lease was illegal, on the basis of its violation of a code provision that no person shall rent any habitation unless it is in a "clean, safe, and sanitary condition." Robinson v. Diamond Housing Corp., 463 F.2d 853 (D.C.Cir.1972), was the culmination of a series of proceedings that began with a similar sort of case. The lessor was denied recovery on the authority of *Brown*. The lessor then claimed the right to evict the tenant as a trespasser, since the lease was illegal. Such relief was also denied. The court said that the effect of the lessee's possession under an illegal lease was to make him a "tenant at sufferance" under the statutory definition of that term. 257 A.2d 492 (D.C.App.1969). Such a tenancy required a thirty-day notice to quit. Thereafter the lessor gave such notice and then again sued for possession. Again he lost, on the ground that in such circumstances the lessor's effort to evict the tenant was presumed to have been a "retaliatory eviction." For a further summary of the court's opinion on this point see the Note following Dickhut v. Norton, infra at page 441.

If an initial lease is illegal for violation of the code provision mentioned above, why is not a resulting tenancy at sufferance equally illegal? In the *Diamond Housing* proceedings, the court said, "The defense of illegality does not rescind the illegal agreement, but merely prevents a party from using the courts to enforce such an agreement."

LINDSEY v. NORMET

Supreme Court of the United States, 1972.
405 U.S. 56, 92 S.Ct. 862, 31 L.Ed.2d 36.

Appellants were month-to-month tenants of appellee and paid $100 a month for the use of a single-family residence in Portland, Oregon. On

(1979); Foisy v. Wyman, 83 Wn.2d 22, 515   **94.** Ibid.
P.2d 160 (1973).

November 10, 1969, the City Bureau of Buildings declared the dwelling unit unfit for habitation due to substandard conditions on the premises. Appellants requested appellee to make certain repairs which, with one minor exception, appellee refused to do. Appellants, who had paid the November rent, refused to pay the December rent until the requested improvements had been made.   *   *   *   [Appellee threatened eviction, and on January 7, 1970, appellants filed suit in the federal district court seeking a declaratory judgment that the Oregon Forcible Entry and Detainer Statute (FED) was unconstitutional on its face, and an injunction against its continued enforcement. A three-judge court was convened, which issued a temporary restraining order against enforcement of the FED statute, and appellants were ordered to pay rent into an escrow account pending a hearing on the merits. In due course, the court granted appellee's motion to dismiss the complaint, concluding that the FED statute was not unconstitutional under either the due process or the equal protection clause of the Fourteenth Amendment. Appellants appealed to the Supreme Court.]

Mr. Justice White delivered the opinion of the Court.

      *   *   *

I

The Oregon Forcible Entry and Wrongful Detainer Statute establishes a procedure intended to insure that any entry upon real property "shall be made in a peaceable manner without force." § 105.105. A landlord may bring an action for possession whenever the tenant has failed to pay rent within 10 days of its due date, when the tenant is holding contrary to some other covenant in a lease, and whenever the landlord has terminated the rental arrangement by proper notice and the tenant remains in possession after the expiration date specified in the notice. § 105.115. Service of the complaint on the tenant must be not less than two nor more than four days before the trial date, § 105.135; a tenant may obtain a two-day continuance, but grant of a longer continuance is conditioned on a tenant's posting security for the payment of any rent which may accrue, if the plaintiff ultimately prevails, during the period of the continuance. § 105.140. The suit may be tried to either a judge or a jury, and the only issue is whether the allegations of the complaint are true. §§ 105.145, 105.150. The only award which a plaintiff may recover is restitution of possession. § 105.155. A defendant who loses such a suit may appeal only if he obtains two sureties who will provide security for the payment to the plaintiff, if the defendant ultimately loses on appeal, of twice the rental value of the property from the time of commencement of the action to final judgment. § 105.160.

Appellant's principal attacks are leveled at three characteristics of the Oregon FED Statute: the requirement of a trial no later than six days after service of the complaint unless security for accruing rent is provided; the provisions of § 105.145 which, either on their face or as construed, are said to limit the triable issues in an FED suit to the tenant's default and to preclude consideration of defenses based on the

landlord's breach of a duty to maintain the premises; and the requirement of posting bond on appeal from an adverse decision in twice the
amount of the rent expected to accrue pending appellate decision.
These provisions are asserted to violate both the Equal Protection and
Due Process Clauses of the Fourteenth Amendment. Except for the
appeal bond requirement * * * we reject these claims.

II

We are unable to conclude that either the early-trial provision or the
limitation on litigable issues is invalid on its face under the Due Process
Clause of the Fourteenth Amendment. In those recurring cases where
the tenant fails to pay rent or holds over after expiration of his tenancy
and the issue in the ensuing litigation is simply whether he has paid or
held over, we cannot declare that the Oregon statute allows an unduly
short time for trial preparation. * * *

Nor does Oregon deny due process of law by restricting the issues in
FED actions to whether the tenant has paid rent and honored the covenants he has assumed, issues that may be fairly and fully litigated under the Oregon procedure. The tenant is barred from raising claims in
the FED action that the landlord has failed to maintain the premises,
but the landlord is also barred from claiming back rent or asserting other claims against the tenant. The tenant is not foreclosed from institut-
ing his own action against the landlord and litigating his right to damages or other relief in that action.

Due process requires that there be an opportunity to present every
available defense. American Surety Co. v. Baldwin, 287 U.S. 156, 168,
53 S.Ct. 98, 102, 77 L.Ed. 231 (1932). See also Nickey v. Mississippi, 292
U.S. 393, 396, 54 S.Ct. 743, 744, 78 L.Ed. 1323 (1934). Appellants do not
deny, however, that there are available procedures to litigate any claims
against the landlord cognizable in Oregon. Their claim is that they are
denied due process of law because the rental payments are not suspended while the alleged wrongdoings of the landlord are litigated. We see
no constitutional barrier to Oregon's insistence that the tenant provide
for accruing rent pending judicial settlement of his disputes with the
lessor.

The Court has twice held that it is permissible to segregate an action
for possession of property from other actions arising out of the same
factual situation which may assert valid legal or equitable defenses or
counterclaims. In Grant Timber & Mfg. Co. v. Gray, 236 U.S. 133, 35
S.Ct. 279, 59 L.Ed. 501 (1915) (Holmes, J.), the Court upheld against due
process attack a Louisiana procedure which provided that a defendant
sued in a possessory action for real property could not bring an action
to establish title or present equitable claims until after the possessory
suit was brought to a conclusion. In Bianchi v. Morales, 262 U.S. 170,
43 S.Ct. 526, 67 L.Ed. 928 (1923) (Holmes, J.), the Court considered
Puerto Rico's mortgage law which provided for summary foreclosure of
a mortgage without allowing any defense except payment. The Court
concluded that it was permissible under the Due Process Clause to "exclude all claims of ultimate right from possessory actions," id. at 171, 43

S.Ct., at 526, and to allow other equitable defenses to be set up in a separate action to annul the mortgage.

Underlying appellants' claim is the assumption that they are denied due process of law unless Oregon recognizes the failure of the landlord to maintain the premises as an operative defense to the possessory FED action and as an adequate excuse for nonpayment of rent. The Constitution has not federalized the substantive law of landlord-tenant relations, however, and we see nothing to forbid Oregon from treating the undertakings of the tenant and those of the landlord as independent rather than dependent covenants. Likewise, the Constitution does not authorize us to require that the term of an otherwise expired tenancy be extended while the tenant's damage claims against the landlord are litigated. The substantive law of landlord-tenant relations differs widely in the various States. In some jurisdictions, a tenant may argue as a defense to eviction for nonpayment of rent such claims as unrepaired building code violations, breach of an implied warranty of habitability, or the fact that the landlord is evicting him for reporting building code violations or for exercising constitutional rights. Some States have enacted statutes authorizing rent withholding in certain situations. In other jurisdictions, these claims, if cognizable at all, must be litigated in separate tort, contract, or civil rights suits. There is no showing that Oregon excludes any defenses it recognizes as "available" on the three questions (physical possession, forcible withholding, legal right to possession) at issue in an FED suit.

We also cannot agree that the FED Statute is invalid on its face under the Equal Protection Clause. It is true that Oregon FED suits differ substantially from other litigation, where the time between complaint and trial is substantially longer, and where a broader range of issues may be considered. But it does not follow that the Oregon statute invidiously discriminates against defendants in FED actions.

The statute potentially applies to all tenants, rich and poor, commercial and noncommercial; it cannot be faulted for over-exclusiveness or under-exclusiveness. And classifying tenants of real property differently from other tenants for purposes of possessory actions will offend the equal protection safeguard "only if the classification rests on grounds wholly irrelevant to the achievement of the State's objective," McGowan v. Maryland, 366 U.S. 420, 425, 81 S.Ct. 1101, 1105, 6 L.Ed.2d 393 (1961), or if the objective itself is beyond the State's power to achieve, Gomillion v. Lightfoot, 364 U.S. 339, 81 S.Ct. 125, 5 L.Ed.2d 110 (1960); N.A.A.C.P. v. Alabama ex rel. Flowers, 377 U.S. 288, 84 S.Ct. 1302, 12 L.Ed.2d 325 (1964); Douglas v. California, 372 U.S. 353, 83 S.Ct. 814, 9 L.Ed.2d 811 (1963). It is readily apparent that prompt as well as peaceful resolution of disputes over the right to possession of real property is the end sought by the Oregon statute. It is also clear that the provisions for early trial and simplification of issues are closely related to that purpose. The equal protection claim with respect to these provisions thus depends on whether the State may validly single out possessory disputes between landlord and tenant for especially prompt judicial settlement. In making such an inquiry a State is "presumed to have acted within [its] constitutional power despite the fact that, in practice [its] laws result in some inequality." McGowan v. Maryland, supra, at 366 U.S. 425–426, 81 S.Ct., at 1105.

At common law, one with the right to possession could bring an action for ejectment, a "relatively slow, fairly complex and substantially expensive procedure." But as Oregon cases have recognized, the common law also permitted the landlord to "enter and expel the tenant by force, without being liable to an action of tort for damages, either for his entry upon the premises, or for an assault in expelling the tenant, providing he uses no more force than is necessary and do[es] no wanton damage." Smith v. Reeder, 21 Or. 541, 546, 28 P. 890, 891 (1892). The landlord-tenant relationship was one of the few areas where the right to self-help was recognized by the common law of most States, and the implementation of this right has been fraught with "violence and quarrels and bloodshed." Entelman v. Hagood, 95 Ga. 390, 392, 22 S.E. 545 (1895). An alternative legal remedy to prevent such breaches of the peace has appeared to be an overriding necessity to many legislators and judges.

Hence the Oregon statute was enacted in 1866 to alter the common law and obviate resort to self-help and violence. The statute, intended to protect tenants as well as landlords, provided a speedy, judicially supervised proceeding to settle the possessory issue in a peaceful manner.

*   *   *   The objective of achieving rapid and peaceful settlement of possessory disputes between landlord and tenant has ample historical explanation and support. It is not beyond the State's power to implement that purpose by enacting special provisions applicable only to possessory disputes between landlord and tenant.

There are unique factual and legal characteristics of the landlord-tenant relationship that justify special statutory treatment inapplicable to other litigants. The tenant is, by definition, in possession of the property of the landlord; unless a judicially supervised mechanism is provided for what would otherwise be swift repossession by the landlord himself, the tenant would be able to deny the landlord the rights of income incident to ownership by refusing to pay rent and by preventing sale or rental to someone else. Many expenses of the landlord continue to accrue whether a tenant pays his rent or not. Speedy adjudication is desirable to prevent subjecting the landlord to undeserved economic loss and the tenant to unmerited harassment and dispossession when his lease or rental agreement gives him the right to peaceful and undisturbed possession of the property. Holding over by the tenant beyond the term of his agreement or holding without payment of rent has proved a virulent source of friction and dispute. We think Oregon was well within its constitutional powers in providing for rapid and peaceful settlement of these disputes.

Appellants argue, however, that a more stringent standard than mere rationality should be applied both to the challenged classification and its stated purpose. They contend that the "need for decent shelter" and the "right to retain peaceful possession of one's home" are fundamental interests which are particularly important to the poor and which may be trenched upon only after the State demonstrates some superior interest. They invoke those cases holding that certain classifications based on unalterable traits such as race and lineage are inherently suspect and must be justified by some "overriding statutory purpose." They also rely on cases where classifications burdening or infringing constitutionally protected rights were required to be justified as "necessary to promote a compelling governmental interest."

We do not denigrate the importance of decent, safe and sanitary housing. But the Constitution does not provide judicial remedies for every social and economic ill. We are unable to perceive in that document any constitutional guarantee of access to dwellings of a particular quality or any recognition of the right of a tenant to occupy the real property of his landlord beyond the term of his lease, without the payment of rent or otherwise contrary to the terms of the relevant agreement. Absent constitutional mandate, the assurance of adequate housing and the definition of landlord-tenant relationships is a legislative not a judicial function. Nor should we forget that the Constitution expressly protects against confiscation of private property or the income therefrom.

Since the purpose of the Oregon Forcible Entry and Detainer Statute is constitutionally permissible and since the classification under attack is rationally related to that purpose, the statute is not repugnant to the Equal Protection Clause of the Fourteenth Amendment.

IV

*   *   *

[The Court held that the double-bond requirement for appealing the decision in an FED action does violate the equal protection clause, however, because it arbitrarily discriminates against tenants wishing to appeal.]

[Justice Douglas dissented from those parts of the decision which sustained the early-trial provision and the provision restricting litigable issues. He did not agree that the Oregon FED statute satisfies the requirements of due process. He believed that there are defects in the Oregon procedures which go to the essence of a litigant's right of access to the courts. The summary procedure prescribed, he thought, means that actually a tenant has no real opportunity to be heard.]

JACK SPRING, INC. v. LITTLE

Supreme Court of Illinois, 1972.
50 Ill.2d 350, 280 N.E.2d 208.

[These were actions by two landlords to recover possession for nonpayment of rent. The defendants denied the allegations of the complaints and pleaded affirmative defenses. Both defendants alleged as a defense that their landlords had violated express covenants to repair, and defendant Little also alleged a breach by her landlord of an implied warranty of habitability in her "oral lease." The trial court granted plaintiffs' motions to strike the affirmative answers and entered judgment for possession. The cases were consolidated on appeal. The Supreme Court, in a three-four decision, reversed and remanded both cases. In dealing with the affirmative defenses raised by the defendants, the court had to respond to the plaintiffs' contentions that under the Illinois Forcible Entry and Detainer Act the only issue is the right to possession and that no equitable defenses may be set up by a tenant in an action under the Act. An amendment to the Section 5 of the Act provided: "No matters not germane to the distinctive purpose of the proceeding shall be introduced by joinder, counterclaim, or otherwise." A later amendment added this qualification: "Provided, however, that a claim for rent may be joined in the complaint, and judgment obtained for the amount of rent found due." In response to the plaintiffs' contention, the court said:]

At the time of the enactment of the 1935 amendment the sole remedy available under the Act, and therefore the 'distinctive purpose' of any proceeding based thereon, was recovery of the premises. Upon enactment of the 1937 amendment with its provision for recovery of rent, the proceeding, to some extent, lost its distinctive purpose. To hold that a landlord, at his option, may expand the issues in a proceeding brought under the statute and the tenant may not is violative of common sense and accepted rules of statutory interpretation.

Section 2 of the Forcible Entry and Detainer Act provides that one entitled to the possession of lands may be restored thereto under this Act when, *inter alia*, "a peaceable entry is made and the possession unlawfully withheld." In these cases there is no question that when defendants, in one instance under an oral agreement, and in the other under a written lease, entered upon possession of the premises, they were peaceable entries, and unless, as claimed by plaintiffs, rent is due and remains unpaid, possession is not "unlawfully withheld." It is apparent, therefore, that even though the plaintiffs do not seek to recover rent in these actions, the question of whether rent is due and owing is not only germane, but in these cases where the right to possession is asserted solely by reason of non-payment, is the crucial and decisive issue for determination.

We have stated above the respective contentions of the parties. With respect to plaintiffs' first contention that the only issue in a forcible detainer action is the right to possession and no equitable defenses can be recognized, Rosewood Corp. v. Fisher, 46 Ill.2d 249, 263 N.E.2d 833, holds to the contrary.

It is established law that liability for rent continues so long as the tenant is in possession and equally well established that a tenant may bring an action against his landlord for breach of a covenant or may recoup for damages in an action brought to recover rent. Rubens v. Hill, 213 Ill. 523, 534, 72 N.E. 1127; Selz v. Stafford, 284 Ill. 610, 617, 120 N.E. 462.

The salutary trend toward determination of the rights and liabilities of litigants in one, rather than multiple proceedings, is demonstrated by our opinions in Miller v. DeWitt, 37 Ill.2d 273, 226 N.E.2d 630, and Muhlbauer v. Kruzel, 39 Ill.2d 226, 234 N.E.2d 790. It would be paradoxical, indeed, to hold that if these were actions to recover sums owed for rent the defendants would be permitted to prove that damages suffered as the result of the plaintiffs' breach of warranty equalled or exceeded the rent claimed to be due, and therefore, that no rent was owed, and at the same time hold that because the plaintiffs seek possession of the premises, to which admittedly, they are not entitled unless rent is due and unpaid after demand, the defendants are precluded from proving that because of the breach of warranty no rent is in fact owed. The argument that the landlords' claim is for rent and the tenants' for damages should not be permitted to obfuscate the sole and decisive issue, which simply stated is whether the tenants owe the landlords rent which is due and remains unpaid.

Insofar as defendants' affirmative defenses alleged the breach of express covenants to repair, they were germane to the issue of whether the defendants were indebted to plaintiffs for rent and we find no impediment in our earlier opinions to the determination of the issue in one rather than multiple actions. We hold, therefore, that the trial court erred in striking these affirmative defenses.

[The court then considered at some length the question whether the "implied" warranty of habitability should be recognized in Illinois, and, after quoting at length from Javins v. First National Realty Corp., said:]

We find the reasoning in *Javins* persuasive and we hold that included in the contracts, both oral and written, governing the tenancies of the defendants in the multiple unit dwellings occupied by them, is an implied warranty of habitability which is fulfilled by substantial compliance with the pertinent provisions of the Chicago building code. We hold further that the defendants' answers sufficiently plead the existence and breach of the implied warranties. The issues raised were germane to the decisive question of whether the defendants were indebted to plaintiffs for rent and the trial court erred in striking the affirmative defenses alleging breach of the implied warranty.

* * *

[The written lease of defendant Price also contained a provision that no representation as to the condition or repair of the premises not expressed in the lease had been made by the lessor, and that no promise to repair, not contained in the lease, had been made by the lessor. The court said that, insofar as the defendant's affirmative defense raised the issue as to whether this provision precluded implication of a warranty of habitability or proof of alleged express agreement to repair, that issue was also germane to the question whether rent was due, and the trial court erred in striking it.]

Note

It is frequently said that the traditional unwillingness of courts to excuse performance of the tenant's duties when there was a breach of the landlord's duty—i.e., the doctrine of "independent covenants"—is a result of the erroneous tendency of courts to treat a lease as a "conveyance" rather than a "contract." This is complete nonsense if we look at the history of landlord-tenant law. A lease has always, in fact, been treated as *both* a conveyance and (usually) a set of contracts between landlord and tenant. In Humbach, The Common-Law Conception of Leasing: Mitigation, Habitability, and Dependence of Covenants, 60 Wash.U.L.Q. 1213 (1983), the author challenges the currently fashionable pure "contract" analysis of residential leases, asserting that the interests of tenants—including such tenants' interests in the habitability of leased premises—are better protected under the traditional "conveyance" or "conveyance-cum-contract" analysis than under the pure "contract" analysis. The author's thesis is especially helpful in dealing with the conceptually confused problem of the legal consequences of a tenant's abandonment of leased premises, which is considered in the last section of this chapter.

Note on Remedies for Breach of Implied Warranty

In states where the implied warranty of habitability has been established by judicial decision, it is not always clear what the full range of remedies for breach of the implied warranty will be. The cases decided to date, however, strongly suggest that the remedies for breach of the implied warranty will include (1) termination of the tenancy;[95] (2) recovery of damages, whether the tenancy is terminated or not;[96] (3) rent withholding, with an abatement of the rent effected in court proceedings;[97] and, perhaps, (4) allowing the tenant to make repairs at his own expense and deduct the cost from the rent.[98] Lan-

95. E.g., Lemle v. Breeden, 51 Hawaii 426, 462 P.2d 470 (1969); King v. Moorehead, reprinted supra p. 410 as a principal case; Pines v. Perssion, 14 Wis. 2d 590, 111 N.W.2d 409 (1961).

96. E.g., Lund v. MacArthur, 51 Hawaii, 473, 462 P.2d 482 (1969) (tenant had terminated); Mease v. Fox, 200 N.W.2d 791 (Iowa 1972) (same); King v. Moorehead, reprinted supra p. 401 as a principal case (same); Steele v. Latimer, 214 Kan. 329, 521 P.2d 304 (1974) (tenant in possession).

97. E.g., Green v. Superior Court, 10 Cal.3d 616, 111 Cal.Rptr. 704, 517 P.2d 1168 (1974); Javins v. First National Realty Corp., 428 F.2d 1071 (D.C.Cir.1970), cert. denied 400 U.S. 925, 91 S.Ct. 186 (1970); Jack Spring, Inc. v. Little, 50 Ill.2d 351, 280 N.E.2d 208 (1972); Fritz v. Warthen, 298 Minn. 54, 213 N.W.2d 339 (1973) (statutory warranty); Rome v. Walker, 38 Mich.App. 458, 196 N.W.2d 850 (1972) (statutory warranty); Foisy v. Wyman, 83 Wn.2d 22, 515 P.2d 160 (1973).

98. Marini v. Ireland, 56 N.J. 130, 265 A.2d 526 (1970). Although the *Marini* court said that a breach of the "implied" warranty of habitability gives the tenant "only the alternative remedies of making the repairs or removing from the premises," the New Jersey Supreme Court later rejected this "restrictive reading" of *Marini* and held that other contract remedies are available to the tenant. Berzito v. Gambino, 63 N.J. 460, 468–69, 308 A.2d 17, 21–22 (1973). It seems likely that other courts will recognize the "repair-and-de-

duct" remedy for breach of the "implied" warranty of habitability, since this remedy is available to the tenant when the landlord fails to perform an express covenant to keep the leased premises in repair; indeed, where the repairs are of a minor nature, this appears to be the tenant's exclusive remedy. E.g., Tyson v. Weil, 169 Ala. 558, 53 So. 912 (1910); Sieber v. Blanc, 76 Cal. 173, 18 P. 260 (1888).

It should be noted that the "repair-and-deduct" remedy was made available to tenants by several 19th century statutes which expressly required landlords generally (not just lessees of dwelling units) to keep the leased premises in repair. All of these statutes are still in force. See La. Stat.Ann., Civ.Code arts. 2639, 2693 (West 1952); Ga.Code Ann. §§ 61–611 (1966); Cal.Civ.Code Ann. §§ 1941, 1942 (Deering 1972); Mont.Rev.Codes Ann. tit. 42, §§ 201, 202 (1961); Okla.Stat.Ann. tit. 41, §§ 31, 32 (1954); N.D.Cent.Code §§ 47–16–12, 47–16–13 (1960); S.D.Comp. Laws §§ 43–32–8, 43–32–9 (1967). The Louisiana statute is based on the Code Napoleon. The California statute is based on the Field Code; and the Montana, Oklahoma, North Dakota, and South Dakota statutes are based on the California statute. All of these statutes authorize the tenant to terminate the lease as an alternative to making the necessary repairs and deducting the cost of repairs from the rent when the landlord fails to perform his statutory duty to keep the premises in habitable condition.

guage in some of the cases suggests that injunctive relief ("specific performance") is also an available tenant remedy, but so far there is no holding on the point.[99]

Termination of the tenancy because the landlord's breach of the implied warranty of habitability is clearly a remedy available to any tenant who is willing to vacate the leased premises. Even without adopting the new theory that performance of the landlord's warranty obligations and performance of the tenant's obligations under the lease are mutually dependent, the right to terminate would exist under the well-recognized doctrine of "constructive eviction." It seems clear that the right to terminate—or "rescind," as some courts term it—is conditional on the tenant's vacating the leased premises, but it seems probable that the old requirement that the tenant must vacate "within a reasonable time" after the breach will be eliminated, since most courts have held that the tenant may withhold rent because of a breach of the warranty of habitability without vacating the premises at all. The courts may well decide that the tenant, faced with a breach of the warranty, may stay in possession and withhold rent for a very substantial time without forfeiting his right to terminate the lease and vacate the premises at a later time. Cf. Charles E. Burt, Inc. v. Seven Grand Corp., supra at page 394, Note 2.

It is clear that the tenant has a right to damages for any breach of the warranty of habitability, if damages are provable, whether he elects to terminate the tenancy or not. The tenant's right to damages may be asserted in a direct action—more likely to be brought when the tenant has terminated the tenancy [1]—or as a counterclaim in the landlord's action to recover unpaid rent,[2] or as defense in the landlord's summary action to evict the tenant for nonpayment of rent.[3] The tenant's right to assert his right to damages for breach of the warranty of habitability as a defense against eviction for nonpayment of rent—generally termed a right to "abatement" of the rent—is the basis (as previously indicated) of the tenant's right to withhold rent because of the breach of the warranty.

The proper measure of damages for breach of the warranty of habitability is probably the most difficult one arising from the widespread adoption of statutory or implied warranties of habitability. Broadly speaking, the courts have so far enunciated three different damage formulas: *first*, that the damages for breach of the warranty are "the difference between the agreed rent and the fair rental value of the premises as they were during their occupancy by the tenant in the unsafe, unsanitary or unfit condition";[4] *second*, that damages

---

99. In Steele v. Latimer, supra note 96, the tenant sought both damages and specific performance (i.e., an injunction against continued violation of the housing code), but most of the court's opinion dealt with the question whether an "implied" warranty should be recognized; the court said nothing specifically about the claim for specific relief, although it said that "traditional remedies for breach of contract are available to the tenant, including the recovery of damages." In several other cases, there are general statements to the effect that all the usual remedies for breach of contract, including specific performance, are available to the tenant. In cases where the landlord fails to perform an express covenant to repair and the repairs are extensive and costly, there is some authority for permitting the tenant

to obtain specific performance. Jones v. Parker, 163 Mass. 564, 40 N.E. 1044 (1895); see also Darnall v. Day, 240 Iowa 665, 37 N.W.2d 277 (1949) (relief refused because not equitable under the circumstances).

1. Pines v. Perssion, supra note 95; Lemle v. Breeden, supra note 95; Lund v. MacArthur, supra note 96.

2. Mease v. Fox, supra note 96; King v. Moorehead, reprinted supra p. 401 as a principal case; Kline v. Burns, 111 N.H. 87, 276 A.2d 248 (1971).

3. See, e.g., cases in note 97, supra.

4. Kline v. Burns, supra note 2; Glyco v. Schultz, 35 Ohio Misc. 25, 62 Ohio Op.2d 459, 289 N.E.2d 919 (Mun.Ct.1972). See also Pines v. Perssion, supra note 95, where the court said that the tenants were "ab-

should be measured by "the difference between the fair rental value of the premises if they had been as warranted and the fair rental value of the premises as they were during occupancy in the unsafe or unsanity condition"; [5] and *third*, that the agreed rent should be reduced by a percentage equal to the percentage of the tenant's rightful use and enjoyment which has been lost to him because of the breach of warranty.[6]

The *first* damage formula above apparently assumes that the "agreed rent" is the fair value of the leased premises when in compliance with the warranty of habitability. It produces the same result as the formula used in Pines v. Perssion,[7] where the court said that "[s]ince there was a failure of consideration, respondents [tenants] are absolved from any liability for rent under the lease and their only liability is for the reasonable rental value of the premises during the time of actual occupancy." But if, in fact, the "agreed rent" represents the value of the premises subject to defects that make them "uninhabitable"—which is likely to be the case in urban slums where the defects are generally "patent" at the inception of the tenancy—this damage formula will result in a finding that the damages are nil.

The *second* damage formula set out above does not assume that the "agreed rent" is the fair rental value of the premises if they had been as warranted, but it will obviously produce the same result as the first formula if, in fact, this is the case. Like the first formula, the second formula is workable if the dwelling unit is in compliance with the warranty of habitability at the inception of the tenancy and later becomes "uninhabitable." But suppose that "patent" defects rendering the premises "uninhabitable" exist at the inception of the tenancy, in which case the fair rental value of the premises "as they were during occupancy in the unsafe or unsanitary condition" may well be exactly equal to the contract rent. Under the second damage formula, the tenant would be entitled to recover the excess of the fair rental value of the dwelling unit "as warranted" over the contract rent, and the landlord might—in theory—have to pay the tenant for living in the unit if the unit were in bad enough condition.[8]

solved from any liability for rent under the lease and their only liability is for the reasonable rental value of the premises during the time of actual occupancy"—a formula that may be appropriate where the tenants terminate the lease shortly after the beginning of the term because of conditions then existing. The net result is the same as under the *first* formula stated in the text above. In Berzito v. Gambino, supra note 98, the court said the tenant should "be charged only with the rental value of the property in its imperfect condition during his period of occupancy," which is similar to the *Pines* formula.

5. E.g., Green v. Superior Court, supra note 97; Steele v. Latimer, supra note 96; Boston Housing Authority v. Hemingway, 363 Mass. 184, 293 N.E.2d 831 (1973).

6. Academy Spires, Inc. v. Brown, 111 N.J.Super. 477, 268 A.2d 556 (County Dist. Ct.1970) (25% reduction); Morbeth Realty Corp. v. Rosenshine, 67 Misc.2d 325, 323 N.Y.S.2d 363 (N.Y.City Civ.Ct.1971) (20% reduction); Morbeth Realty Co. v. Velez, 73 Misc.2d 996, 343 N.Y.S.2d 406 (N.Y.City Civ.Ct.1973) (50% reduction); Glyco v. Schultz, supra note 4 ($\frac{2}{3}$ reduction). See also

Cooks v. Fowler, 455 F.2d 1281 (D.C.Cir. 1971). The "percentage reduction" formula is apparently derived from the American Bar Foundation's Model Code § 2–207 (Tent.Draft 1969).

7. Supra note 95. See comment on *Pines* supra note 4.

8. Suppose, e.g., that the rental value as warranted is $200 per month; that the value "as is" is $50 per month; and that the contract rent is $100 per month. Using the *second* damage formula, the damages are $150 per month; thus the damages exceed the contract by $50 per month, and the tenant would be entitled to $50 per month from the landlord as long as he remains in possession! It is interesting to note that, in a recent Massachusetts case, the court said that "it is possible, in a given instance, for substantial defects to reduce the fair rental value of the premises to zero"—a proposition that is difficult to accept—but that, "[i]n any event the tenant shall not be awarded damages in excess of the rent actually paid by him during the period of his occupancy of the premises." McKenna v. Begin, 3 Mass.

The *third* damage formula set out above is essentially a practical expedient adopted by some courts because of the difficulty of establishing damages under either of the other formulas. As a perceptive commentator has pointed out, under this formula "the tenant's recovery really amounts to a civil fine levied on the landlord which recaptures some or all of the contract rent depending upon the court's judgment as to the condition of the [dwelling] unit." [9] This formula has been adopted in Pennsylvania.[10] A recent Massachusetts intermediate court case also adopted the third damage formula despite the fact that it had previously insisted that the second damage formula was the proper one.[11]

King v. Moorehead, supra p. 401, introduced a further complication by asserting that different damage formulas should be applied to the periods before and after a tenant vacates because of a breach of the warranty of habitability: the *first* formula discussed above should be applied to the period while the tenant was in possession; for the period after the tenant vacates the premises, however, "he is unaffected by the condition of the premises" and he is therefore entitled to recover "for the value of the lease for the unexpired term, that is, the then difference between the fair rental value of the premises if they had been as warranted and the promised rent, [if any,] computed for that period." In Mease v. Fox,[12] on the other hand, although the court adopted the damage formula suggested in *King* for the period after the tenant vacates, the Iowa court held that the *second* damage formula discussed supra should be applied to the period while the tenant was in possession.

The first case to sanction rent withholding as a remedy for breach of the warranty of habitability was Javins v. First National Realty Corp.,[13] where the court not only recognized an "implied" warranty of habitability in all leases of property covered by the District of Columbia housing code but also held that the landlord's breach of the "implied" warranty could be set up as a defense in a summary action to evict for nonpayment of rent. In an oft-quoted passage, the *Javins* opinion concluded as follows: [14]

"At trial, the finder of fact must make two findings: (1) whether the alleged violations [of the housing code] existed during the period for which past due rent is claimed, and (2) what portion, if any or all, of the tenant's obligation to pay rent was suspended by the landlord's breach. If no part of the tenant's rental obligation is found to have been suspended, then a judgment for possession may issue forthwith. On the other hand, if the jury determines that the entire rental obligation has been extinguished by the landlord's total breach, then the action for possession on the ground of nonpayment must fail.

"The jury may find that part of the tenant's obligation has been suspended but that part of the unpaid back rent is indeed owed to the landlord. In these circumstances, no judgment for possession should issue if the tenant agrees to

App.Ct. 168, 325 N.E.2d 587, at 591, 592 (1975).

9. Abbott, Housing Policy, Housing Codes, and Tenant Remedies: An Integration, 56 B.U.L.Rev. 1, 24 (1976).

10. McKenna v. Begin, 3 Mass.App.Ct. 168, 362 N.E.2d 548, 553 (1977) (second appeal; trial judge directed to "assess the major code violations and determine the percentage by which the use and enjoyment of the apartment has been diminished by the existence of these violations * * * and then assess as damages that percentage of McKenna's weekly rent for

each of the weeks during which the defect remained unrepaired."). The second damage formula discussed in the text above was announced in Boston Housing Authority v. Hemingway, supra note 5—a fact recognized in both the first and second opinions of the intermediate appellate court in McKenna v. Begin.

11. Pugh v. Holmes, 486 Pa. 272, 405 A.2d 897 (1979).

12. Supra note 97.

13. Supra note 97.

14. 428 F.2d at 1082–83.

pay the partial rent found to be due. If the tenant refuses to pay the partial amount, a judgment for possession may then be entered."

The court's reference in *Javins* to "suspension" or "extinguishment" of the tenant's obligation to pay rent is puzzling. Perhaps all the court meant was that the damages for breach of the implied warranty of habitability are to be set off against the rent otherwise due to the landlord, and that the jury may find either that there is still a balance due to the landlord or that the damages are equal to or in excess of the rent claim. If this is all the court meant, however, it is hard to see the relevance of the court's prefatory statement that, "[u]nder contract principles, * * * the tenant's obligation to pay rent is dependent upon the landlord's performance of his obligations, including his warranty to maintain the premises in habitable condition." [15] Certainly adoption of the theory of mutual dependency of lease covenants is not required to justify a set-off of damages for breach of warranty against the rent claimed under the lease; and only a decision that such a set-off is "germane" to the purpose of a summary eviction action is required to justify allowing the tenant to set up the breach of warranty as a defense in such an action.

The *Javins* language as to dependency of lease covenants is drawn from Pines v. Perssion,[16] and it may be that the *Javins* court meant—as the *Pines* opinion stated—that the breach of the warranty of habitability relieved the tenant of his obligation to pay the lease rent and left him with only a quasi-contractual obligation to pay the fair rental value of his use and occupation. But in the *Pines* case the breach of the "implied" warranty occurred at the inception of the tenancy, which enabled the tenants to avoid the lease *ab initio*, whereas in *Javins* the breach was assumed to have occurred after the tenancy began and the tenants did not seek to avoid or terminate the lease; and it is not easy to see how the tenant can retain all the benefits of the lease without remaining subject to the duty to pay the agreed rent—although the tenant may have an off-setting claim for damages. In any case, one wonders why the *Javins* did not—like the *Jack Spring* court—set out the text of the applicable summary eviction statute and explain why the tenant's off-setting claim for breach of the implied warranty of habitability was "germane" to the purpose of the summary action to evict for non-payment of rent.

If the *Javins* court did mean to adopt the *Pines* formula, the results (as previously indicated) should be the same as under the *first* damage formula discussed above. If the facts were as they were assumed to be by the *Javins* court—i.e., if all the housing code violations actually arose after the inception of the tenancy—the tenant should have been able to prove substantial damages and thus obtain a substantial "abatement" of the rent claimed by the landlord under either the *first* or *second* damage formulas discussed above. If, however, the premises were subject to serious code violations at the inception of the tenancy—which is more likely—the *first* formula would produce little or no "abatement" of the rent claimed, while the *second* formula might result in a finding that the obligation to pay rent was completely "extinguished" because the damages for breach of warranty were equal to the agreed rent.

Assuming that the tenant really wants to prevent rather than merely to postpone eviction, rent withholding is a feasible remedy only if proof of a breach of the warranty of habitability resulting in a partial abatement of the rent claimed will enable the tenant to remain in possession by paying what is found to be due. If the tenant must prove that the damages resulting from the breach equal or exceed the rent otherwise due in order to avoid eviction, rent

15. Id. at 1082.
16. Supra note 95.

withholding will be too risky to be a useful remedy except in very unusual circumstances. But most courts have indicated that, when the tenant proves a breach of the warranty which entitles him to a partial rent abatement, the tenant will be given time to pay the balance found to be due and thus avoid eviction. In some states, the summary eviction statute itself provides a specified period of grace for payment of the rent found to be due;[17] in other states, the courts have exercised their equity powers to grant the tenant a reasonable time to pay the amount found to be due.[18]

In King v. Moorehead, supra p. 401, the court held that a tenant who retains possession of leased premises while withholding rent "shall be required to deposit the rent as it becomes due, in *custodia legis* pending the litigation" in order to assure the landlord "that those rents adjudicated for distribution to him will be available to correct the defects in habitability," and to "encourage the landlord to minimize the tenant's damages by making tenantable repairs at the earliest time." Several other courts have indicated that the trial court has discretion to enter a "protective order" requiring the tenant to pay into court the "abated rent," as determined by the court, until the landlord makes the tenant's dwelling unit "habitable."[19]

Where an "implied" warranty of habitability has been superimposed on legislation creating and defining tenants' rights to withhold rent because of serious housing code violations, it will be necessary for the courts to decide how to make the new "common law" rights of residential tenants consistent with their existing statutory rights. In Massachusetts, the courts have dealt with this problem by holding that, although the new "implied" warranty provides the tenant with a variety of new remedies for breach of the warranty, his exercise of the right to withhold rent must be exercised in the manner directed by the statute; and that failure to follow the statutory requirements will leave the tenant subject to eviction for nonpayment of rent.[20]

STATUTORY WARRANTIES OF HABITABILITY IN LEASES

While some states were establishing an "implied" warranty of habitability by judicial decision, a much larger group of states was establishing a warranty of habitability in residential leases by statute. Idaho, Maine, Michigan, Minnesota, New York, Rhode Island, West Virginia, and Wisconsin have recently enacted short statutes which impose on landlords a new duty to provide tenants with a habitable dwelling, often referred to as a "warranty" or "covenant" of habitability.[21] The Maine and New York statutes[22] create a warranty that the premises leased for residential use *are* habitable, without creating any express

---

17. E.g., Mich.Comp.Laws Ann. § 600.5744(6) (Supp.1978–79) ("When the judgment for possession is for nonpayment of money due under a tenancy * * * the writ of restitution shall not issue, if within * * * [10 days after entry of judgment], the amount as stated in the judgment * * * is paid to the plaintiff."). This makes rent withholding "safe" for the tenant in view of Mich. Comp.Laws Ann. § 600.5741 (Supp. 1978–79) ("the jury or judge shall deduct any portion of the rent which the jury or judge finds to be excused by the plaintiff's breach of the lease or by his breach of one or more statutory covenants").

18. E.g., Javins v. First National Realty Corp., supra note 97.

19. E.g., Javins v. First National Realty Corp., supra note 97; Bell v. Tsintolas Realty Co., 430 F.2d 474 (D.C.Cir.1970); Green v. Superior Court, supra note 97; Fritz v. Warthen, supra note 97.

20. Boston Housing Authority v. Hemingway, supra note 5.

21. Idaho Code §§ 6–320 through 6–323 (1981); Me.Rev.Stat.Ann. tit. 14, § 6021 (Supp.1982–83); Mich.Comp.Laws Ann. § 554.139 (Supp.1982–83); Minn.Stat.Ann. § 504.18 (West Supp.1982); N.Y. Real Prop.L. § 235–b (Supp.1981–82); R.I.Gen. Laws § 34–18–16 (1970); W.Va.Code Ann. § 37–6–30 (Supp.1982); Wis.Stat.Ann. § 704–07 (West Supp.1982–83).

22. Supra note 21.

duty to *keep* them in a habitable condition; but the Maine statute contains other language making it clear that the landlord has a duty to *keep* the premises
habitable.[23] The Idaho, Michigan, Minnesota, Rhode Island, and West Virginia
statutes expressly require the landlord to *keep* the premises in a habitable condition.[24] The Michigan, Minnesota, and West Virginia statutes also require the
landlord to keep the premises in compliance with applicable housing codes.[25]
The Wisconsin statute expressly imposes a duty on the landlord to keep the
premises in a habitable condition but does not expressly create any "warranty"
or "covenant" that the premises are habitable at the beginning of the tenancy.[26]
Only the Idaho, Maine, and Wisconsin statutes expressly provide for tenant
remedies for breach of the landlord's new statutory duty,[27] but in several states
a breach of the duty has been held to give rise to a variety of "contractual"
remedies on the theory that performance of the landlord's statutory duty is a
condition precedent to the tenant's duty to perform.[28]

Maryland now has new landlord-tenant legislation which contains a very detailed statement of the residential landlord's duty to maintain all dwelling units
(except in farm buildings) in habitable condition and prescribes in detail the
remedies of the tenant in the event of any breach of the landlord's duty.[29] This
statute provides that residential landlords have a duty "to repair and eliminate
conditions and defects which constitute, or if not promptly corrected will constitute, a fire hazard or a serious and substantial threat to the life, health or safety of occupants, including but not limited to: (1) Lack of heat, of light, electricity, or of hot or cold running water, except where the tenant is responsible for
the payment of the utilities and the lack thereof is a direct result of the tenant's
failure to pay the charges; or (2) Lack of adequate sewage disposal facilities; or
(3) Infestation of rodents in two or more dwelling units; or (4) The existence of
paint containing lead pigment on surfaces within the dwelling unit; or (5) The
existence of any structural defect which presents a serious and substantial
threat to the physical safety of the occupants; or (6) The existence of any condition which presents a health or fire hazard to the dwelling unit." The statute
further states that it "does not provide a remedy for the landlord's failure to
repair and eliminate minor defects or, in those locations governed by such
codes, housing code violations of a nondangerous nature." [30]

The largest group of current statutes imposing on residential landlords a
duty to put and keep dwelling units in habitable condition is that based either
on the Model Residential Landlord-Tenant Code or the Uniform Residential
Landlord and Tenant Act (URLTA).[31] Both the Model Code and the URLTA
include a comprehensive listing of the duties of both landlord and tenant, and
have the effect of imposing on the landlord of a residential dwelling unit duties
which comprise, in the aggregate, a covenant or warranty to put and keep that
unit in a habitable condition for the duration of the tenancy. Although the
provisions of the recently enacted statutes based on the Model Act or the
URLTA are generally quite similar with respect to the duties imposed on the
landlord, several states made substantial changes in the scope of that duty,[32]
since it is not possible here to set out the provisions of these statutes relating to

23. Ibid.

24. Ibid.

25. Ibid. W.Va.Code Ann. § 37–6–30
(Supp.1982) is obviously derived from Uniform Residential Landlord and Tenant
Code § 2.104, but West Virginia did not
adopt any of the other URLTA provisions.

26. Supra note 21.

27. Ibid.

28. E.g., Teller v. McCoy, 253 S.E.2d
114 (W.Va.1978).

29. Md.Code Ann., Real Property
§ 8–211 (1981).

30. Ibid.

31. See discussion of the URLTA ante
Section 1.

32. E.g., Wash.Rev.Code Ann. § 59.-
18.060 spells out the landlord's duties in

the landlord's duties or even to summarize their variations from their models, we shall simply set out the URLTA provisions dealing with the landlord's duties and the tenant's remedies for breach of those duties.

UNIFORM RESIDENTIAL LANDLORD AND TENANT ACT

Section 2.104.   [Landlord to Maintain Premises]

(a) A landlord shall

(1) comply with the requirements of applicable building and housing codes materially affecting health and safety;

(2) make all repairs and do whatever is necessary to put and keep the premises in a fit and habitable condition;

(3) keep all common areas of the premises in a clean and safe condition;

(4) maintain in good and safe working order and condition all electrical, plumbing, sanitary, heating, ventilating, air-conditioning, and other facilities and appliances, including elevators, supplied or required to be supplied by him;

(5) provide and maintain appropriate receptacles and conveniences for the removal of ashes, garbage, rubbish, and other waste incidental to the occupancy of the dwelling unit and arrange for their removal; and

(6) supply running water and reasonable amounts of hot water at all times and reasonable heat [between [October 1] and [May 1]] except where the building that includes the dwelling unit is not required by law to be equipped for that purpose, or the dwelling unit is so constructed that heat or hot water is generated by an installation within the exclusive control of the tenant and supplied by a direct public utility connection.

(b) If the duty imposed by paragraph (1) of subsection (a) is greater than any duty imposed by any other paragraph of that subsection, the landlord's duty shall be determined by reference to paragraph (1) of subsection (a).

(c) The landlord and tenant of a single family residence may agree in writing that the tenant perform the landlord's duties specified in paragraphs (5) and (6) of subsection (a) and also specified repairs, maintenance tasks, alterations, and remodeling, but only if the transaction is entered into in good faith and not for the purpose of evading the obligations of the landlord.

(d) The landlord and tenant of any dwelling unit other than a single family residence may agree that the tenant is to perform specified repairs, maintenance tasks, alterations, or remodeling only if

(1) the agreement of the parties is entered into in good faith and not for the purpose of evading the obligations of the landlord and is set forth in a separate writing signed by the parties and supported by adequate consideration;

somewhat more detail than does URLTA
§ 2.104.

(2) the work is not necessary to cure noncompliance with subsection (a)(1) of this section; and

(3) the agreement does not diminish or affect the obligation of the landlord to other tenants in the premises.

(e) The landlord may not treat performance of the separate agreement described in subsection (d) as a condition to any obligation or performance of any rental agreement.

*   *   *

Section 4.101.   [Noncompliance by the Landlord—In General]

(a) Except as provided in this Act, if there is a material noncompliance by the landlord with the rental agreement or a noncompliance with Section 2.104 materially affecting health and safety, the tenant may deliver a written notice to the landlord specifying the acts and omissions constituting the breach and that the rental agreement will terminate upon a date not less than [30] days after receipt of the notice if the breach is not remedied in [14] days, and the rental agreement shall terminate as provided in the notice subject to the following:

(1) If the breach is remediable by repairs, the payment of damages or otherwise and the landlord adequately remedies the breach before the date specified in the notice, the rental agreement shall not terminate by reason of the breach.

(2) If substantially the same act or omission which constituted a prior noncompliance of which notice was given recurs within [6] months, the tenant may terminate the rental agreement upon at least [14 days'] written notice specifying the breach and the date of termination of the rental agreement.

(3) The tenant may not terminate for a condition caused by the deliberate or negligent act or omission of the tenant, a member of his family, or other person on the premises with his consent.

(b) Except as provided in this Act, the tenant may recover actual damages and obtain injunctive relief for any noncompliance by the landlord with the rental agreement or Section 2.104.   If the landlord's noncompliance is willful the tenant may recover reasonable attorney's fees.

(c) The remedy provided in subsection (b) is in addition to any right of the tenant arising under Section 4.101(a).

(d) If the rental agreement is terminated, the landlord shall return all security recoverable by the tenant under Section 2.101 and all prepaid rent.

*   *   *

Section 4.103.   [Self-Help for Minor Defects]

(a) If the landlord fails to comply with the rental agreement or Section 2.104, and the reasonable cost of compliance is less than [$100], or an amount equal to [one-half] the periodic rent, whichever amount is greater, the tenant may recover damages for the breach under Section 4.101(b) or may notify the landlord of his intention to correct the condition at the landlord's expense. If the landlord fails to comply within [14] days after beng notified by the tenant in writing or as promptly as conditions require in case of emergency, the tenant may cause the work to be done in a workmanlike manner and, after submitting to the landlord an itemized statement, deduct from his rent the actual and reasonable cost or the fair and reasonable value of the work, not exceeding the amount specified in this subsection.

(b) A tenant may not repair at the landlord's expense if the condition was caused by the deliberate or negligent act or omission of the tenant, a member of his family, or other person on the premises with his consent.

Section 4.104. [Wrongful Failure to Supply Heat, Water, Hot Water, or Essential Services]

(a) If contrary to the rental agreement or Section 2.104 the landlord willfully or negligently fails to supply heat, running water, hot water, electric, gas, or other essential service, the tenant may give written notice to the landlord specifying the breach and may

(1) procure reasonable amounts of heat, hot water, running water, electric, gas, and other essential service during the period of the landlord's noncompliance and deduct their actual and reasonable cost from the rent; or

(2) recover damages based upon the diminution in the fair rental value of the dwelling unit; or

(3) procure reasonable substitute housing during the period of the landlord's noncompliance, in which case the tenant is excused from paying rent for the period of the landlord's noncompliance.

(b) In addition to the remedy provided in paragraph (3) of subsection (a) the tenant may recover the actual and reasonable cost or fair and reasonable value of the substitute housing not in excess of an amount equal to the periodic rent, and in any case under subsection (a) reasonable attorney's fees.

(c) If the tenant proceeds under this section, he may not proceed under Section 4.101 or Section 4.103 as to that breach.

(d) Rights of the tenant under this section do not arise until he has given notice to the landlord or if the condition was caused by the deliberate or negligent act or omission of the tenant, a member of his family, or other person on the premises with his consent.

Section 4.105. [Landlord's Noncompliance as Defense to Action for Possession or Rent]

(a) In an action for possession based upon nonpayment of the rent or in an action for rent when the tenant is in possession, the tenant may [counterclaim] for any amount he may recover under the rental agreement or this Act. In that event the court from time to time may order the tenant to pay into court all or part of the rent accrued and thereafter accruing, and shall determine the amount due to each party. The party to whom a net amount is owed shall be paid first from the money paid into court, and the balance by the other party. If no rent remains due after application of this section, judgment shall be entered for the tenant in the action for possession. If the defense or counterclaim by the tenant is without merit and is not raised in good faith, the landlord may recover reasonable attorney's fees.

(b) In an action for rent when the tenant is not in possession, he may [counterclaim] as provided in subsection (a) but is not required to pay any rent into court.

Notes and Questions

1. The URLTA is reasonably even-handed in allocating duties with respect to maintenance of dwelling units. Thus, e.g., URLTA § 3.101 provides as follows:

A tenant shall

(1) comply with all obligations primarily imposed upon tenants by applicable provisions of building and housing codes materially affecting health and safety;

(2) keep that part of the premises that he occupies and uses as clean and safe as the condition of the premises permit;

(3) dispose from his dwelling unit all ashes, garbage, rubbish, and other waste in a clean and safe manner;

(4) keep all plumbing fixtures in the dwelling unit or used by the tenant as clean as their condition permits;

(5) use in a reasonable manner all electrical, plumbing, sanitary, heating, ventilating, air-conditioning, and other facilities and appliances including elevators in the premises;

(6) not deliberately or negligently destroy, deface, damage, impair, or remove any part of the premises or knowingly permit any person to do so; and

(7) conduct himself and require other persons on the premises with his consent to conduct themselves in a manner that will not disturb his neighbors' peaceful enjoyment of the premises.

In addition, URLTA § 3.102 gives the landlord a limited power to adopt and enforce rules and regulations, as follows:

(a) A landlord, from time to time, may adopt a rule or regulation, however described, concerning the tenant's use and occupancy of the premises. It is enforceable against the tenant only if

(1) Its purpose is to promote the convenience, safety, or welfare of the tenants in the premises, preserve the landlord's property from abusive use, or make a fair distribution of services and facilities held out for the tenants generally;

(2) it is reasonably related to the purpose of which it is adopted;

(3) it applies to all tenants in the premises in a fair manner;

(4) it is sufficiently explicit in its prohibition, direction, or limitation of the tenant's conduct to fairly inform him of what he must or must not do to comply;

(5) it is not for the purpose of evading the obligations of the landlord; and

(6) the tenant has notice of it at the time he enters into the rental agreement, or when it is adopted.

(b) If a rule or regulation is adopted after the tenant enters into the rental agreement that works a substantial modification of his bargain it is not valid unless the tenant consents to it in writing.

2. In providing remedies for breach of the landlord's obligation to put and keep residential premises in habitable condition—see URLTA § 4.101(b)—why did the draftsman omit any direction as to the appropriate measure of damages? If a tenant seeks "injunctive relief" under Section 4.101(b), *must* courts grant such relief whenever a breach of the landlord's duty under Section 4.104, or may they exercise their traditional discretion to withhold injunctive relief on equitable grounds? If it is available in a particular case, is injunctive relief likely to be more satisfactory from the tenant's viewpoint than other remedies such as termination, damages, or rent withholding which are made available under the URLTA?

3. How useful are the tenant remedies provided by URLTA § 4.104 likely to be? If the landlord "fails to supply heat, running water, hot water, electric, gas, or other essential service," is the tenant of a dwelling unit in a multi-family building likely to be able to "procure" such essential services? If a tenant in such a case elects to "procure reasonable substitute housing during the period of the landlord's noncompliance," why would he wish to keep the lease in force—even though he is "excused from paying rent for the period of the landlord's noncompliance"—instead of simply terminating the lease under Section 4.101(a)?

4. Why did the draftsmen of URLTA § 4.105 authorize a "[counterclaim] for any amount he may recover under the rental agreement or this Act," instead of authorizing the court to "abate" the rent for which the tenant is liable? Suppose the tenant has a valid counterclaim for breach of the landlord's duty to put and keep the leased premises habitable. Can the tenant, under URLTA Section 4.105, safely withhold all the rent otherwise payable? Suppose the court, in a summary action by the landlord to evict the tenant for nonpayment of rent, determines that a net amount less than the landlord claims is due and that the tenant pays this amount and remains in possession. Can the tenant then, under URLTA § 4.105, safely begin withholding the rent again if, in his judgment, the landlord has not properly cured his breach of duty?

5. In states where the courts first established an "implied" warranty of habitability by decision and the legislature later enacted a statute establishing a duty to put and keep leased residential units in habitable condition, does the statute completely supersede the judicially established "implied" warranty? Presumably the answer, in general, is "yes." But in Washington the "implied" warranty established in Foisy v. Wyman, 83 Wn.2d 22, 515 P.2d 160 (1973), remains applicable to residential leases not covered by the Washington URLTA-based statute, the most important of which are leases of houses on farms. And in states where the legislature has merely provided new tenant remedies for violation of applicable housing codes the courts have sometimes recognized an "implied" warranty of habitability as a basis for additional tenant remedies. This is the case in Massachusetts. Compare Mass.Ann.Laws ch. 239, § 8A and ch. 111, §§ 127A–127N (Supp.1983), with Boston Housing Authority v. Hemingway, 363 Mass. 184, 293 N.E.2d 831 (1973). Both of the Massachusetts statutes were originally enacted in 1965. In California, which has for over a century had a statutory warranty of fitness (including a continuing duty to keep the leased premises in repair), the courts have recognized an "implied" warranty of habitability as a basis for allowing remedies for breach of the "implied" war-

ranty to supplement the specifically prescribed remedies provided for breach of the statutory warranty of habitability. Compare Cal.Civ.Code §§ 1941, 1942 (Deering 1972), with Green v. Superior Court, 10 Cal.2d 616, 111 Cal.Rptr. 704, 517 P.2d 1168 (1974).

Note on the Waivability of the Warranty of Habitability

The URLTA provides in § 2.104(c) through (e) for written agreements that shift some of the landlord's statutory duties to the tenant and, to that extent result in a waiver by the tenant of the benefits of the statutory warranty of habitability. It is not clear, however, just what is meant by the qualification— which appears in both subsection (c) and in subsection (d)(1)—allowing the shifting of duties "only if the transaction is entered into in good faith and not for the purpose of evading the obligations of the landlord." Nor is it clear whether the landlord may include in the original lease the written agreement contemplated by § 2.104(c). Note that the agreement authorized by § 2.104(d) must be "set forth in a separate writing." It should be noted that the agreement authorized by § 2.104(d) must be "supported by an adequate consideration," while the agreement authorized by § 2.104(c) need not be "supported by a separate consideration." And note that the landlord's duties under the rental agreement are "independent" of those created by any "separate agreement" entered into pursuant to § 2.104(d).

Some of the statutes creating a warranty of habitability—other than the URLTA and statutes containing its provisions—contain provisions as to waiver, and some do not. The New York statute forthrightly declares that "[a]ny agreement by a lessee or tenant of a dwelling waiving or modifying his rights * * * shall be void as contrary to public policy." The Michigan statute includes a provision that "[t]he parties to the lease * * * may modify the obligations imposed by this section where the lease * * * has a current term of at least one year." The Michigan legislature presumably intended to bar any modification of the warranty of habitability if the lease term is less than one year, but it is not whether "modification" includes a complete waiver.

Where "implied" warranties of habitability have been judicially recognized, without express statutory authorization, most of the cases have followed Javins v. First National Realty Co. [33] in rejecting the possibility of an effective waiver by the tenant of the protection afforded by the "implied" warranty.[34]

In those states where the courts have not yet decided whether the benefit of the "implied" warranty of habitability can be waived, Section 5.6 of the Landlord and Tenant part of the Second Property Restatement [35] seems likely to influence future judicial decisions on that point. Section 5.6 allows the parties by agreement "to increase or decrease what would otherwise be the obligations of the landlord with respect to the condition of the leased property and * * * to expand or contract what would otherwise be the remedies available to the tenant for the breach of those obligations," provided the agreement is not "un-

---

33. 428 F.2d 1071 (D.C.Cir.1970), cert. denied 400 U.S. 925, 91 S.Ct. 186, 27 L.Ed. 2d 185 (1970).

34. In Javins, supra note 33, the court refused to consider whether the tenant's express covenant to repair constituted a waiver of the "implied" warranty of habitability because "the implied warranty of the landlord could not be excluded" and any private agreement to shift the burden of compliance with the housing code to the

tenant would be "illegal and unenforceable." Most of the other cases have followed Javins in holding or stating that the "implied" warranty of habitability cannot be waived. See, e.g., Green v. Superior Court, 10 Cal.3d 616, 111 Cal.Rptr. 704, 517 P.2d 1168 (1974); Boston Housing Authority v. Hemingway, 363 Mass. 184, 293 N.E.2d 831 (1973); Foisy v. Wyman, 83 Wn.2d 22, 515 P.2d 160 (1973).

35. Rest.2d (L & T) § 5.6 (1977).

conscionable or significantly against public policy." A wide variety of factors "which may be considered in determining whether an agreement in a lease is in whole or in part unenforceable because unconscionable or against public policy" is listed in a Comment.[36]

The Second Property Restatement unequivocally states in another Comment that "[t]he tenant as a matter of law is unable to waive any remedies [for breach of the landlord's duty] available to him at the time of entry, if at the time of entry it would be unsafe or unhealthy to use the leased premises in the manner contemplated by the parties,"[37] and further states in a Reporter's Note that "[t]he rule of this section does not allow waiver of housing code violations" because of "public policy considerations."[38] The latter statement clearly goes beyond a mere refusal to allow waiver when there are conditions on the leased premises hazardous to health or safety, since it is obvious that not all housing code violations endanger health or safety and that many violations are quite trivial in character.[39]

To the extent that the legislatures and the courts refuse to give effect to provisions waiving the tenant's right to enforce statutory or "implied" warranties of habitability, it becomes possible to assert—as a recent article does—that the last two decades have witnessed "the transition of residential leases from the private law fields of property and contract to an area in which public regulatory law predominates."[40]

C. THE RETALIATORY EVICTION DOCTRINE

DICKHUT v. NORTON

Supreme Court of Wisconsin, 1970.
45 Wis.2d 389, 173 N.W.2d 297.

[Defendant was a tenant under an oral month-to-month lease. Timely notice of termination was given him, and the plaintiff-landlord sued for possession. Defendant answered that the reason for the suit was defendant's complaint to housing officials of the unsanitary condition of the premises. Judgment on the pleadings was entered for the plaintiff, after the defendant's plea of retaliatory eviction was stricken as immaterial. Defendant appealed.]

BEILFUSS, Justice. The issue is whether a tenant, in an unlawful detainer action, can assert as a valid defense an allegation that the landlord's attempt to terminate the tenancy and evict the tenant was motivated as retaliation for the tenant's complaint to the health authorities of a housing code sanitary violation.

36. Id. § 5.6, Comment e (emphasis added).

37. Id. § 5.3, Comment c.

38. Id. § 5.3, Reporter's Note 35.

39. Although § 5.1 creates an "implied" warranty of suitability for residential use that would not be broken by unsubstantial housing code violations—see Comment e following the § 5.1 blackletter—§ 5.5 creates (*inter alia*) a continuing duty of the landlord "to keep the leased property in a condition that meets the requirements of governing health, safety, and housing codes" not qualified by any language indicating that the duty is only to keep the property free from substantial code violations that affect health or safety. It thus appears that the draftsman's intent was not to allow effective waiver of the tenant's right to have full compliance with all housing code requirements, however unsubstantial, or even trivial, in nature.

40. Glendon, The Transformation of American Landlord-Tenant Law, 23 B.C.L. Rev. 503, 552 (1982).

The defendant contends that he has a federally guaranteed constitutional right to make such complaints and that for a state to permit such retaliation violates or abridges his constitutional rights. He further contends that public policy of this state as expressed or derived from housing laws, health laws, and local ordinances would be frustrated if he is not permitted to assert this defense. * * *

[The court set out statutory provisions relating to proceedings to recover possession from a tenant who holds over after the expiration or proper termination of a tenancy, without permission of the landlord.]

The argument of the defendant upon constitutional grounds is that the first amendment of the United States constitution guarantees to him the right to petition his government for redress of grievances as well as what he labels the inherent right to report violations of the law (housing code violations) to appropriate authorities.

The first amendment provides, in part: "Congress shall make no law * * * abridging * * * the right of the people * * * to petition the Government for a redress of grievances." And the fourteenth amendment provides, in part: "* * * No State shall make or enforce any law which shall abridge the privileges or immunities of citizens of the United States; nor shall any State deprive any person of life, liberty, or property, without due process of law; nor deny to any person within its jurisdiction the equal protection of the laws."

The right protected by the first and fourteenth amendments is that the government shall not make laws to abridge these rights. Here, it is the action of one private party as against another that is complained of. Neither the legislature by statute, nor the city council by ordinance, have in any way prohibited the defendant from complaining of housing code violations. The argument, supported to some extent by the cases cited by the defendant, is that the state, by legislatively and judicially affording a means to the plaintiff to evict him because of the exercise of his first amendment rights, is acting in violation of the federal constitution.

While we express our reservations as to whether the facts and factors of this action bring it within the concept proposed by the defendant, we find it unnecessary to reach the constitutional question because of our opinion that the legislative public policy of this state permits the defense to be raised.

There can be no doubt that the legislature and the common council of the city of Milwaukee have both recognized that blighted, substandard and insanitary housing conditions do exist and that they are detrimental to the public interest.

Sec. 66.435, Stats., known as the Urban Renewal Act, provides:

"(2) *Findings.* It is hereby found and declared that there exists in municipalities of the state slum, blighted and deteriorated areas which constitute a serious and growing menace injurious to the public health, safety, morals and welfare of the residents of the state, and the findings and declarations made before August 3, 1955 in s. 66.43(2) are in all respects affirmed and restated; that while certain slum, blighted or deteriorated areas, or portions thereof, may require acquisition and clearance, as provided in s. 66.43, since the prevailing condition of decay may make impracticable the reclamation of the area by conservation or rehabilitation in such a manner that the conditions and evils hereinbefore enumerated may be eliminated, remedied or prevented, and to the extent feasible salvable slum and blighted areas should be conserved and rehabilitated through voluntary action and the regulatory process; and all acts and purposes provided for by this section are for and constitute public uses and are for and constitute public purposes, and that moneys expended in connection with such powers are declared to be for public purposes and to preserve the public interest, safety, health, morals and welfare. Any municipality in carrying out the provisions of this section shall afford maximum opportunity consistent with the sound needs of the municipality as a whole to the rehabilitation or redevelopment of areas by private enterprise."

The city of Milwaukee, in almost identical language, found such conditions to exist in its housing ordinance   *   *   *.

This court, heretofore, has taken cognizance of the legislative policy in the area of urban blight and housing code regulations. In Pines v. Perssion (1961), 14 Wis.2d 590, 595, 596, 111 N.W.2d 409, 412, the court stated:

"Legislation and administrative rules, such as the safe-place statute, building codes and health regulations, all impose certain duties on a property owner with respect to the condition of his premises. Thus, the legislature has made a policy judgment—that it is socially (and politically) desirable to impose these duties on a property owner—which has rendered the old common-law rule obsolete. To follow the old rule of no implied warranty of habitability in leases would, in our opinion, be inconsistent with the current legislative policy concerning housing standards. The need and social desirability of adequate housing for people in this era of rapid population increases is too important to be rebuffed by that obnoxious legal cliché *caveat emptor*. Permitting landlords to rent 'tumble-down' houses is at least a contributing cause of such problems as urban blight, juvenile delinquency and high property taxes for conscientious landowners."

It is our opinion that public policy as espoused in ch. 66, Stats., clearly indicates that the legislature intended that housing code violations should be reported. If a landlord could terminate a tenancy solely because his tenant had reported a violation the intention of the legislature would be frustrated.

In a case decided by the United States Court of Appeals, District of Columbia, Edwards v. Habib (1968), 130 U.S.App.D.C. 126, 397 F.2d 687, 701, 702, involving almost the identical problem, the court stated:

"In trying to effect the will of Congress and as a court of equity we have the responsibility to consider the social context in which our decisions will have operational effect. In light of the appalling condition and shortage of housing in Washington, the expense of moving, the inequality of bargaining power between tenant and landlord, and the social and economic importance of assuring at least minimum standards in housing conditions, we do not hesitate to declare that retaliatory eviction cannot be tolerated. There can be no doubt that the slum dweller, even though his home be marred by housing code violations, will pause long before he complains of them if he fears eviction as a consequence. Hence an eviction under the circumstances of this case would not only punish appellant for making a complaint which she had a constitutional right to make, a result which we would not impute to the will of Congress simply on the basis of an essentially procedural enactment, but also would stand as a warning to others that they dare not be so bold, a result which, from the authorization of the housing code, we think Congress affirmatively sought to avoid.

"The notion that the effectiveness of remedial legislation will be inhibited if those reporting violations of it can legally be intimidated is so fundamental that a presumption against the legality of such intimidation can be inferred as inherent in the legislation even if it is not expressed in the statute itself."

In addition it was said in Edwards v. Habib, supra, pp. 699, 700, 701:

"* * * while the landlord may evict for any legal reason or for no reason at all, he is not, we hold, free to evict in retaliation for his tenant's report of housing code violations to the authorities. As a matter of statutory construction and for reasons of public policy, such an eviction cannot be permitted.

"* * * the codes obviously depend in part on private initiative in the reporting of violations. * * * To permit retaliatory evictions, then, would clearly frustrate the effectiveness of the housing code as a means of upgrading the quality of housing * * *."

We likewise conclude that a landlord may terminate a tenancy at will or from month-to-month (or lesser periods) for any legitimate reason or no reason at all, but he cannot terminate such tenancy simply because his tenant has reported an actual housing code violation as a means of retaliation.

We therefore hold that the defendant can raise the defense of retaliatory eviction. To be successful in this defense, however, he must prove by evidence that is clear and convincing that a condition existed which in fact did violate the housing code, that the plaintiff-landlord knew the tenant reported the condition to the enforcement authorities, and that the landlord, for the sole purpose of retaliation, sought to terminate the tenancy.

A question was raised at oral argument regarding the repercussions in landlord-tenant law of the creation of a defense of retaliatory eviction. It was observed that the logical extension of such a rule would be to create a permanent tenancy as long as a jury could be convinced of the landlord's evil motive. The analysis of the District of Columbia Court of Appeals in Edwards v. Habib, supra, pp. 702, 703, tends to shed some light on this problem:

"This is not, of course, to say that even if the tenant can prove a retaliatory purpose she is entitled to remain in possession in perpetuity.

If this illegal purpose is dissipated, the landlord can, in the absence of legislation or a binding contract, evict his tenants or raise their rents for economic or other legitimate reasons, or even for no reason at all. The question of permissible or impermissible purpose is one of fact for the court or jury, and while such a determination is not easy, it is not significantly different from problems with which the courts must deal in a host of other contexts, such as when they must decide whether the employer who discharges a worker has committed an unfair labor practice because he has done so on account of the employee's union activities. As Judge Greene said, 'There is no reason why similar factual judgments cannot be made by courts and juries in the context of economic retaliation [against tenants by landlords] for providing information to the government.' "

Judgment reversed and a new trial ordered consistent with this opinion. No costs to be awarded because of failure to comply with the rule set forth in sec. 251.38(1), Stats.

[HANSEN and HANLEY, JJ., dissented.]

Note

Reference is made to the "saga" of Diamond Housing Corp. v. Robinson, supra page 420. In Robinson v. Diamond Housing Corp., 463 F.2d 853 (D.C.Cir. 1972), the United States Court of Appeals reversed the judgment of the District of Columbia Court of Appeals, which had affirmed a judgment awarding possession to the landlord. The court refused to concede that the rule of Edwards v. Habib was inapplicable, saying that an attempt to evict a tenant as a punishment for withholding rent is as much prohibited as an eviction for reporting housing code violations. The landlord's affidavit that it was not willing to rent the premises does not resolve the issue of retaliatory eviction. The court declared that an unexplained eviction following a successful assertion of a Javins or a Southall Realty defense gives rise to a presumption of retaliatory eviction. An expressed desire to take the property off the market does not rebut the presumption, because it raises the further question why the landlord wishes to do so. An unwillingness to repair the premises is insufficient. An asserted inability to make such repairs is not sufficient unless the jury finds that the landlord in fact is unable to do so. And even such a finding may not be sufficient to justify a judgment for the landlord, for the existence of a legitimate reason for the landlord's actions will not help him if the jury finds that in fact he was motivated by an illegitimate reason. The court conceded that a jury is not authorized to inspect a landlord's motives if he chooses to go out of business altogether.

As to the code provision prohibiting the occupancy of any habitation which is in violation of the code, the court said that, since the code places primary responsibility for repair of housing violations on the landlord, and makes retaliatory eviction unlawful, estoppel principles prevent his relying on his own neglect of duty as a ground for evicting his tenant. In response to the contention that the court's ruling will lead to many families living indefinitely in substandard housing without paying rent, the court responded that if the landlord is unable to repair premises, he may take them off the market, but if he is able but unwilling to repair, the tenant is entitled to remedies which will enforce the landlord's duty to make the premises habitable.

In respect to the fact that the tenant in this case had left the premises during the litigation, the court ruled that this fact would make the controversy moot only if she left voluntarily or because her own conduct had rendered the premises uninhabitable, but not if the landlord's code violations had caused her departure.

Judge Robb dissented, saying in part, "The theory of the majority seems to be that if not an outlaw a landlord is at least a public utility, subject to regulation by the court in conformity with its concept of public convenience and necessity. I reject that notion, which in practical application will commit to the discretion of a jury the management of the landlord's business and property."

UNIFORM RESIDENTIAL LANDLORD AND TENANT ACT

Section 5.101. [Retaliatory Conduct Prohibited]

(a) Except as provided in this section, a landlord may not retaliate by increasing rent or decreasing services or by bringing or threatening to bring an action for possession after:

> (1) the tenant has complained to a governmental agency charged with responsibility for enforcement of a building or housing code of a violation applicable to the premises materially affecting health and safety; or

> (2) the tenant has complained to the landlord of a violation under Section 2.104; or

> (3) the tenant has organized or become a member of a tenant's union or similar organization.

(b) If the landlord acts in violation of subsection (a), the tenant is entitled to the remedies provided in Section 4.107 and has a defense in any retaliatory action against him for possession. In an action by or against the tenant, evidence of a complaint within [1] year before the alleged act of retaliation creates a presumption that the landlord's conduct was in retaliation. The presumption does not arise if the tenant made the complaint after notice of a proposed rent increase or diminution of services. "Presumption" means that the trier of fact must find the existence of the fact presumed unless and until evidence is introduced which would support a finding of its nonexistence.

(c) Notwithstanding subsections (a) and (b), a landlord may bring an action for possession if:

> (1) the violation of the applicable building or housing code was caused primarily by lack of reasonable care by the tenant, a member of his family, or other person on the premises with his consent; or

> (2) the tenant is in default in rent; or

> (3) compliance with the applicable building or housing code requires alteration, remodeling, or demolition which would effectively deprive the tenant of use of the dwelling unit.

(d) The maintenance of an action under subsection (c) does not release the landlord from liability under Section 4.101(b).

Comment

*   *   *

A number of states by statute have recognized the defense: Cal.C.C. Sec. 1942.5; Conn.Gen.St.Ann., Sec. 42–540a [Supp.1969]; Del.Ch. 25 Sec. 5917 [Supp.1971]; Ha.Ch. 666 Sec. 43 [Supp.1971]; Ill.Rev.St. Ch. 80, Sec. 71 [Supp.1971]; Me.Rev.St. Tit. 14 Sec. 6001, 6002; Md.Laws Ch. 687 Sec. 9–10 [Supp.1971]; Mass.Comp.Laws Ann., Ch. 186 Sec. 18 [Supp.1970]; Mich.Comp.Laws Ann., Ch. 600, Sec. 5646 [Am'd P.S.1969]; Minn.Stat. Ch. 240 Sec. 566.03 [Supp.1971]; N.J.Stat.Ann. 2A Sec. 42–10.10; N.Y.Uncont'd Laws, Tit. 23 Sec. 8590, 8609 [Supp.1971]; Pa. St.Ann. Ch. 35, Sec. 1700–1 [Supp.1971]; R.I.Gen.Laws Ann. Sec. 34–20–10 [1968]. The legislatures of Maine, Massachusetts, New Jersey, Michigan, and Rhode Island also protect tenants from eviction if they have organized or become a member of a tenants' union or similar organization.   *   *   *

Notes and Questions

1. The statutes listed in the official Comment to URLTA § 5.101, supra, were all adopted before the URLTA was promulgated by the Commissioners on Uniform State Laws. However, the Hawaii and Delaware statutory provisions are parts of comprehensive landlord-tenant legislation based on the American Bar Foundation's Model Code. None of the other states represented in the Comment subsequently enacted the URLTA.

2. What is the purpose and effect of the exception in URLTA § 5.101(c)(2)? Will it preclude the tenant's reliance on the defense of "retaliatory eviction" in a case where he is withholding rent pursuant to URLTA § 4.105 because of a breach of the landlord's duty to put and keep the premises in habitable condition? In such a case, can the tenant successfully argue that he is not "in default in rent" because, under URLTA § 4.105(a), "the court may from time to time order the tenant to pay into court all or part of the rent accrued and thereafter accruing"?

3. Suppose a tenant has done one of the acts specified in URLTA § 5.101(a), and that the term of his lease expires shortly thereafter. If the tenant refuses to vacate and the landlord brings an action for possession, can the tenant rely on the defense of "retaliatory eviction"? Arguably the tenant can do so, since Section 5.101 is not limited to cases where the landlord purports to terminate a periodic tenancy and recover possession after the tenant does one of the acts specified in Section 5.101(a). But if the "retaliatory eviction" defense is allowed, the result may be that a tenancy for a definite term will be extended for an indefinite period. Is it likely that the draftsmen of Section 5.101 really intended that result?

Bibliographical Note

For extensive general discussions of the development of the new rules requiring residential landlords to put and maintain leased units in habitable condition and prohibiting "retaliatory" conduct by such landlords, see Cunningham, The New Implied and Statutory Warranties of Habitability in Residential Leases: From Contract to Status, 16 Urban L.Ann. 3 (1979); Glendon, The Transformation of American Landlord-Tenant Law, 23 B.C.L.Rev. 503 (1982).

See also Am.L.Inst., Restatement, Property (Second) §§ 5.1–5.6 (1977) (especially the commentary).

For discussion of the effect of the widespread adoption of statutory or implied warranties of habitability on the real life behavior of landlords and tenants, see Abbott, Housing Policy, Housing Codes and Tenant Remedies: An Integration, 56 B.U.L.Rev. 1, 62–64, 139–146 (1976) (based on a study of Boston Housing Court records); Note, The Great *Green* Hope: The Implied Warranty of Habitability in Practice, 28 Stan.L.Rev. 729 (1976); Heskin, The Warranty of Habitability Debate: A California Case Study, 66 Calif.L.Rev. 37 (1978); Mosier & Soble, Modern Legislation, Metropolitan Court, Miniscule Results: A Study of Detroit's Landlord-Tenant Court, 7 U.M.J. of Law Reform 8 (1973); Rose & Scott, "Street Talk" Summonses in Detroit's Landlord-Tenant Court: A Small Step Forward for Urban Tenants, 52 J. of Urban Law 967 (1975); Krumholz, Rent Withholding as an Aid to Housing Code Enforcement, 25 J. of Housing 242 (1969); Comment, The Pennsylvania Project—A Practical Analysis of the Pennsylvania Rent Withholding Act, 17 Vill.L.Rev. 821, 860–85 (1972).

For theoretical discussion of the long-term effects of the widespread adoption of statutory or implied warranties of habitability on the "low-income" housing supply, see Ackerman, Regulating Slum Housing Markets on Behalf of the Poor: Of Housing Codes, Housing Subsidies, and Income Redistribution Policy, 80 Yale L.J. 1093 (1971); Komesar, Return to Slumville: A Critique of the Ackerman Analysis of Housing Code Enforcement and the Poor, 82 Yale L.J. 1175 (1973); R. Posner, Economic Analysis of Law 259–63 (1972); Meyers, The Covenant of Habitability and the American Law Institute, 27 Stan.L.Rev. 879, 563, 889–93 (1975); Abbott, supra, at 66–86. For an empirical study of the effect of the warranty of habitability on rents, see Hirsch, Hirsch & Margolis, Regression Analysis of the Effects of Habitability Laws Upon Rent: An Empirical Observation on the Ackerman-Komesar Debate, 63 Calif.L.Rev. 1098, 1116–36 (1975).

D. REGULATION OF SECURITY DEPOSITS

Disputes over the amount and disposition of the security deposits required by most landlords of their tenants have given rise to much litigation and, in recent years, to a good deal of new legislation. The URLTA includes the following provision:

Section 2.101. [Security Deposits; Prepaid Rent]

(a) A landlord may not demand or receive security, however denominated, in an amount or value in excess of [1] month[s] periodic rent.

(b) Upon termination of the tenancy property or money held by the landlord as security may be applied to the payment of accrued rent and the amount of damages which the landlord has suffered by reason of the tenant's noncompliance with Section 3.101 all as itemized by the landlord in a written notice delivered to the tenant together with the amount due [14] days after termination of the tenancy and delivery of possession and demand by the tenant.

(c) If the landlord fails to comply with subsection (b) or if he fails to return any prepaid rent required to be paid to the tenants under this Act the tenant may recover the property and money due him together with damages in an amount equal to [twice] the amount wrongfully withheld and reasonable attorney's fees.

(d) This section does not preclude the landlord or tenant from recovering other damgaes to which he may be entitled under this Act.

(e) The holder of the landlord's interest in the premises at the time of the termination of the tenancy is bound by this section.

Comment

Widely varying legislation has been enacted affecting security deposits:

California. Chapter 1317, Acts of 1970, West.Cal.Civ.Code, Sec. 1951.

Colorado. H.B. No. 1230, Acts of 1971, Colo.Rev.Stat.Ann., Ch. 58 (Forcible Entry and Detainer), Sec. 1–26–28.

Delaware. H.B. 433, Acts of 1971, Del.Code Ann. (Landlord-Tenant), Title 25, Ch. 51, Sec. 5912.

Florida. Chapter 70–360, Acts of 1970, Fla.Stat.Ann.Civil Practice and Procedure, Ch. 83 (Landlord and Tenant), Sec. 83.261.

Illinois. P.A. 77–705, Sec. 3, Acts of 1971, Ill.Stat.Ann. Ch. 74 (Interest), Sec. 91–93.

Maryland. Chapter 633, Sec. 1 of Acts of 1969, as amended by Chapter 291 of Acts of 1971, Md.Ann.Code, Art. 53 (Landlord and Tenant), Sec. 41–43.

Massachusetts. Chapter 244, Sec. 1 of Acts of 1969, as amended by Chapter 666, Sec. 1 of Acts of 1970, Mass.Gen.Laws Ann., Ch. 186 (Title to Real Property), Sec. 15B.

Minnesota. Chapter 784 of Acts of 1971, Minn.Stat. Ch. 504 (Landlord and Tenant), Sec. 504.19.

New Jersey. S.B. 904, Acts of 1970, N.J.Rev.Stat., Sec. 2A:46–8.

New York. Chapter 680, Sec. 70 of Acts of 1967, as amended, N.Y. Gen.Obligation Laws, Sec. 7–103 and 7–105.

Pennsylvania. Pa.Stat.Ann., Title 68 (Real and Personal Property), Sec. 250.512.

These statutes generally require a landlord to return security deposits to tenants within a specified time period, account for his claim to any part of the security deposit and provide for penalty in the event landlord fails to comply.

Difficulties in administration and accounting of security deposits have led some authorities to advocate their abolition (see Interim Report Landlord and Tenant Law Applicable to Residential Tenancies, Ontario Law Reform Commission [1968] pgs. 21 and 28). The Uniform Act preserves the security deposit but limits the amount and prescribes penalties for its misuse.

Subsection (e) of this section resolves a split of authority among the states. See 1 A.L.P. Section 3.73, nn. 9–15. Note that under Section 2.105(a) of the Act the original landlord is bound.

Note on Tenants' Rights in Public Housing

The maze of extensive and intricate congressional legislation concerning housing would require a separate course even to give a perspective of its dimensions and ingredients. For our purposes brief mention may be made of several federal programs. One of the earliest and most significant programs was launched as part of the New Deal legislation in the 1930's to provide mortgage insurance for middle and upper income housing and government ownership of low income housing. Under the latter, the federal government did not itself enter the housing market, but provided loans and grants to local housing authorities established under state enabling acts. See United States Housing Act, as amended, 42 U.S.C.A. §§ 1401–1436. The program was designed to leave considerable authority and discretion in the local agencies, but was subject, nevertheless, to extensive federal administrative rules and regulations. Such regulation related not only to the acquisition and construction of housing facilities, but also to the on-going administration of such facilities for low income tenants. In this manner, government took on the mantle of landlord of private tenants.

In order to preserve the basic purpose of the program, administrative regulations at the federal level covered such matters as allowable rents and eligibility requirements. A principal feature of the latter related to the permissible income level of public housing tenants. In order to protect against tenant abuses and to preserve the integrity of a local housing project, many local housing agencies imposed "desirability" requirements, which have been the source of much controversy between local authorities and tenants.

Later Congress undertook to bring private capital into the low and middle income housing market. Several programs were established to insure mortgages and to provide interest subsidies for private nonprofit corporations or associations or limited dividend corporations. See 12 U.S.C.A. §§ 1715*l*, 1715*z*–1. Congress also authorized loans to similar organizations to provide housing for elderly or handicapped persons. 12 U.S.C.A. § 1701*q*. In addition, a rent supplement program was enacted to provide funds in the nature of rent supplements to housing owners on behalf of qualified low income tenants. 12 U.S.C.A. § 1701*s*. Mortgagors of insured mortgages were made subject to regulations issued by the Federal Housing Administration relating to rents and methods of operation which are similar to those prescribed for local housing authorities. Such regulations are usually imposed by an initial regulatory agreement between the mortgagor and the Federal Housing Administration.

The host of problems, political and economic, encountered in creating public housing, and the problems which have arisen in administering it where it has been established, cannot be surveyed here. Many of the problems of administration arise in the form of grievances asserted by prospective or existing tenants concerning their admission to or continuance in public housing. Such problems, of course, raise the question as to what rights, if any, such persons have as existing or prospective tenants. One such problem has particular relevance to our limited purposes. It can be baldly put as involving the eviction of tenants from public housing. Do tenants in public or government supported housing have rights which limit their eviction other than such rights as are created in their lease agreements? It will be readily seen that such a question goes to the nature of a tenancy in public housing.

Our experience with the private law of landlord and tenant would prepare us to say that the termination of any tenancy depends on the terms of the transaction creating the tenancy. Most tenancies in public housing in fact are periodic tenancies of the month-to-month variety, terminable by either party on one month's notice. But it is also clear that few tenancies in public housing are terminated by housing authorities except for reasons which relate to the qualifications or the conduct of the tenants. Effective maintenance of public housing obviously requires an orderly regime of administration and the ability to rid such property of irresponsible tenants. It is also obvious that such administration can produce abusive treatment of tenants, which is aggravated by the fact that the loss of a tenancy in public housing can produce greater hardship than the termination of a leasehold estate in the private market. This has been the focal point of alleged grievances of tenants respecting eviction practices.

The regulations of HUD (Department of Housing and Urban Development) currently include extensive provisions concerning lease and grievance procedures. 24 C.F.R. §§ 866.1–866.6, 866.50–866.59 (1982).

In respect to the rights and duties of the parties to leases of property owned by public housing agencies (PHAs) or leased to them and subleased to tenants, the regulations do not purport to declare such duties directly; but rather elaborately prescribe the terms of leases entered into with tenants. Many of the provisions prescribed bear a striking resemblance to the URLTA. For example, a lease shall prescribe the PHA's obligations, which include the obligation to maintain the premises in decent, safe and sanitary condition, to comply with building and housing codes and HUD regulations materially affecting health and safety, and to make necessary repairs. Tenant obligations are specified and may include a provision for maintenance tasks, if included in good faith and not for the purpose of evading the PHA's obligations. A lease shall provide that the PHA shall not terminate or refuse to renew the lease other than for serious or repeated violations of the terms of the lease, or for other good cause. Notice requirements for termination are specified.

The regulation forbids the use of exculpatory clauses and certain other oppressive procedural obstacles to tenants' remedies.

The regulation concerning grievance procedures defines a "grievance as a dispute which a tenant may have with respect to a PHA action or failure to act in accordance with a lease or PHA regulations which adversely affect an individual tenant's rights, duties or status. Informal, oral or written, presentation of grievances is first prescribed, with a written summary of discussion without a hearing. A complainant may submit a written request for a hearing within a reasonable time of receipt of the summary. Grievances are to be heard by a hearing officer or a hearing panel. In case of a hearing of a grievance involving the amount of rent, the complainant will deposit rent due under the lease in an account until a decision is reached. At a hearing, a complainant is given the opportunity to examine relevant documents and records, to be represented by counsel, to present evidence and controvert evidence, to cross-examine witnesses, and a right to a private hearing unless the complainant requests a public hearing. A written decision is required within a reasonable time after the hearing, a copy of which is to be sent to the complainant. If the hearing officer or panel upholds a PHA's action to terminate a tenancy, the PHA shall not begin an action in court to evict the tenant until it has served a notice to the tenant to vacate within the applicable statutory period.

Under a lease complying with the HUD regulations, what is the estate held by a tenant in public housing? Compare the New Jersey statute, page 341 supra.

What about the similar claims of tenants in privately owned but federally subsidized housing? In Joy v. Daniels, 479 F.2d 1236 (4th Cir.1973), the plaintiff was a tenant in quasi-public, federally subsidized housing, i.e., the defendant landlord received mortgage benefits, as well as rent supplements, from the FHA. Plaintiff's lease was for one year with automatic renewal from month to month, but terminable by either party on 30 days' notice. Plaintiff was given such notice, which did not specify any cause for eviction, and she sued for declaratory and injunctive relief, raising constitutional objections. The court held that defendant's action in seeking eviction was "state action" under the due process clause of the 14th Amendment. The court specified the federal benefits received by the defendant, which were conditioned upon state approval, and the utilization of state eviction procedure. The court said that in view of congressional policies of providing a decent home for every American family and of prohibiting arbitrary and discriminatory action, the scheme of federal housing legislation produces "a property right or entitlement to continue occupancy until there exists a cause to evict other than the mere expiration of the lease." The court cited Perry v. Sinderman, 408 U.S. 593, 92 S.Ct. 2694 (1972) (discussed in Note, supra, at page 19). In respect to the question of the requirements of procedural due process where sufficient cause for eviction is alleged, the court found that the particular state eviction procedures were adequate, since a jury trial was required, a landlord must prove his allegations, and public housing tenants are not evicted until basic due process requisites are satisfied. The court noted that in states having summary eviction procedures full administrative hearings must be afforded. See Comment, Joy v. Daniels: Due Process and Quasi-Public Housing, 23 Cath.U.L.Rev. 375 (1973).

In Lopez v. Henry Phipps Plaza South, 498 F.2d 937 (2d Cir.1974), eviction of a tenant in federally supported housing was sought on the ground of a number of acts of misconduct by the tenant and members of his family. Notice of the lessor's intention not to renew the tenant's one-year lease was given and a hearing was provided by a hearing officer, at which the opportunity was afforded to be represented by counsel and present witnesses. The hearing officer was the manager of a similar housing project of a non-profit corporation whose stock was owned by the same parent corporation that owned the stock of the defendant. The court asserted the same constitutional basis for procedural due process as declared in Joy v. Daniels. But the court found here that those due process requirements were satisfied.

See also Anderson v. Denny, 365 F.Supp. 1254 (W.D.Va.1973); Short v. Fulton Redevelopment Co., 390 F.Supp. 517, 398 F.Supp. 1235 (S.D.N.Y.1975); and Green v. Copperstone, Ltd. Partnership, 28 Md.App. 498, 346 A.2d 686 (1975). In Anderson eviction was sought for alleged misconduct of the tenant; but in the other two cases, the landlords relied merely on notices to terminate according to the terms of the leases. All three courts found constitutionally protected property interests, as in Joy v. Daniels. In Anderson and Green, the courts not only found state action sufficient to invoke the 14th Amendment, but also sufficient federal involvement to invoke the due process clause of the 5th Amendment. In all three cases the courts considered the kind of hearing necessary to satisfy due process requirements. In Green the court simply said that the Maryland summary eviction procedures were sufficient if proper notice is given and good cause for eviction is shown at the hearing. In reaching much the same conclusion, the court in Short noted that proceedings in state courts have the advantages of being least costly to implement and of assuring neutral decision makers who can capitalize on their experience in the landlord-tenant field. In Anderson the court supported the resort to state court procedures on the ground that such courts were bound, under the supremacy clause (Article VI) of the United States Constitution, to apply the federal law concerning the termination of tenancies as declared in this case.

Apart from the refinements of constitutional doctrine involved in these cases, which are beyond our present competence to pursue fully here, look back over what appears to be the legislative-administrative law applicable to public housing, and the constitutionally imposed requirements respecting quasi-public housing, and consider what all this does to the substantive law of landlord and tenant concerning the nature and duration of leasehold estates. If the law remains as it now appears to be, what is the nature of the estate of a tenant in public or quasi-public housing? Compare the New Jersey statute described supra at page 341.

In view of matters previously considered concerning landlords' duties respecting the condition of leased premises, it may occur to you to inquire whether such duties exist in favor of tenants in public housing. The question involves a number of issues, some of which we are not at this point prepared to explore. For example: (1) is any question of "sovereign immunity" involved; (2) do the federal statutes impliedly prescribe an answer, either on a statutory or constitutional basis; (3) are state housing codes intended to be applicable, or an implied warranty of habitability; (4) under federal statutes or regulations or under state law, is it intended that the administration of public housing projects be subject to judicial review; and (5) assuming that public landlords owe duties of this sort to their tenants, what kind of remedies are applicable or practicable? Cf. Knox Hill Tenant Council v. Washington, 448 F.2d 1045 (D.C.Cir.1971).

Alexander v. United States Dept. of HUD, 555 F.2d 166 (7th Cir.1977), is the only case so far giving a clear answer to the question. That case involved a federally assisted housing project that HUD acquired upon a mortgage foreclosure. Recognizing that the premises were plagued by unsafe conditions, nonpayment of rents, and excessive costs in bringing the property into good condition, HUD issued notices to quit to all tenants, intending to terminate the project. A group of tenants sued to recover deposits withheld because they were in default on their rent, alleging that they were excused from rental payments because of breach of an implied warranty of habitability. The decision of the trial court dismissing the complaint was affirmed. Recognizing that the rule of decision governing the case must be federal, the court declared that such warranties should not be implied in leases of units constructed and operated as public housing projects. In explanation the court said, "As such, the implication of a warranty of habitability in leases pertaining to public housing units is a warranty that the stated objectives of national policy have been and are being met. We feel that the establishment of any such warranty that national policy goals have been attained or that those goals are being maintained is best left to that branch of government which established the objectives." See Note, 19 B.C.L.Rev. 343 (1978).

It does not clearly appear from the opinion what the result would have been if the property were still owned and managed by a private landlord with federal financial support.

Note on Fair Housing Laws

Numerous state statutes and local ordinances prohibit discrimination in the sale or rental of housing on the basis of race, color, religion, sex, or national origin. The most important legislation dealing with discrimination is, however, the federal Fair Housing Act of 1968, which constitutes Title VIII of the Civil Rights Act of 1968, 42 U.S.C.A. §§ 3601 et seq. The Act as amended makes it unlawful for any person, on account of race, color, religion, sex, or national origin, to refuse to sell or rent to any person, to discriminate in the terms and conditions of the sale or rental of a dwelling or in the provision of services or facilities in connection therewith, to publish any statement that indicates any discrimination in the sale or rental of a dwelling, to represent to any person that any dwelling is not available for sale or rental when it is in fact so available, or, for profit, to induce any person to sell or rent any dwelling by representations regarding the entry into a neighborhood of persons of a particular race, etc. An exception is provided for the sale or rental of a single-family house sold or rented by an owner under certain circumstances.

The Act also prohibits certain discriminatory acts by institutions in respect to provisions for the financing of housing, and certain discriminatory acts in provisions for brokerage services.

Although the Fair Housing Act of 1968 applies to both sale and rental housing, its principal application appears to have been in connection with new single-family housing offered for sale by land developers. For a more detailed discussion of the Fair Housing Act, see the extended Note, post Chapter 12, Section 1.

SECTION 5. FITNESS OF LEASED PREMISES— LANDLORDS' TORT LIABILITY

BORDERS v. ROSEBERRY

Supreme Court of Kansas, 1975.
216 Kan. 486, 532 P.2d 1366.

PRAGER, Justice. This case involves the liability of a landlord for personal injuries suffered by the social guest of the tenant as the result of a slip and fall on the leased premises. The facts in this case are undisputed and are as follows: The defendant-appellee, Agnes Roseberry, is the owner of a single-family, one-story residence located at 827 Brown Avenue, Osawatomie, Kansas. Several months prior to January 9, 1971, the defendant leased the property on a month to month basis to a tenant, Rienecker. Just prior to the time the tenant took occupancy of the house the defendant landlord had work performed on the house. The remodeling of the house included a new roof. In repairing the house the repairmen removed the roof guttering from the front of the house but failed to reinstall it. The landlord knew the guttering had been removed by the workmen, intended to have it reinstalled, and knew that it had not been reinstalled. The roof line on the house was such that without the guttering the rain drained off the entire north side of the house onto the front porch steps. In freezing weather water from the roof would accumulate and freeze on the steps. The landlord as well as the tenant knew that the guttering had not been reinstalled and knew that without the guttering, water from the roof would drain onto the front porch steps and in freezing weather would accumulate and freeze. The tenant had complained to the landlord about the absence of guttering and the resulting icy steps.

On January 9, 1971, there was ice and snow on the street and ice on the front steps. During the afternoon the tenant worked on the front steps, removing the ice accumulation with a hammer. The plaintiff-appellant, Gary D. Borders, arrived on the premises at approximately 4:00 p.m. in response to an invitation of the tenant for dinner. It is agreed that plaintiff's status was that of a social guest of the tenant. There was ice on the street and snow on the front steps when plaintiff arrived. At 9:00 p.m., as plaintiff Borders was leaving the house he slipped and fell on an accumulation of ice on the steps and received personal injuries. There is no contention that the plaintiff Borders was negligent in a way which contributed to cause his injuries. After a pretrial conference the case was tried to the court without a jury. Following submission of the case the trial court entered judgment for the defendant, making findings of fact which are essentially those set forth above. The trial court based its judgment upon a conclusion of law which stated that a landlord of a single-family house is under no obligation or duty to a social guest, a licensee of his tenant, to repair or remedy a known condition whereby water dripped onto the front steps of a house fronting north, froze and caused plaintiff to slip and fall. The plaintiff has appealed to this court.

The sole point raised on this appeal by the plaintiff, Gary D. Borders, is that the trial court committed reversible error in concluding as a matter of law that a landlord of a single-family house is under no obligation or duty to a social guest of his tenant to repair or remedy a known condition whereby water dripped from the roof onto the front steps of a house fronting north, froze and caused the social guest to slip and fall.

At the outset it should be emphasized that we do not have involved here an action brought by a social guest to recover damages for personal injuries from his host, a possessor of real property. The issue raised involves the liability of a lessor who has leased his property to a tenant for a period of time. Furthermore, it should be pointed out that the plaintiff, a social guest of the tenant, has based his claim of liability against the landlord upon the existence of a defective condition which existed on the leased property *at the time the tenant took possession.*

Traditionally the law in this country has placed upon the lessee as the person in possession of the land the burden of maintaining the premises in a reasonably safe condition to protect persons who come upon the land. It is the tenant as possessor who, at least initially, has the burden of maintaining the premises in good repair. (Bailey v. Kelly, 93 Kan. 723, 145 P. 556, overruling a prior decision in the same case, Bailey v. Kelly, 86 Kan. 911, 122 P. 1027.) The relationship of landlord and tenant is not in itself sufficient to make the landlord liable for the tortious acts of the tenant. (Greiving v. La Plante, 156 Kan. 196, 131 P.2d 898; Campbell v. Weathers, 153 Kan. 316, 111 P.2d 72.) When land is leased to a tenant, the law of property regards the lease as equivalent to a sale of the premises for the term. The lessee acquires an estate in the land, and becomes for the time being the owner and occupier, subject to all of the responsibilities of one in possession, both to those who enter onto the land and to those outside of its boundaries. Professor William L. Prosser in his Law of Torts, 4th Ed. § 63, points out that in the absence of agreement to the contrary, the lessor surrenders both possession and control of the land to the lessee, retaining only a reversionary interest; and he had no right even to enter without the permission of the lessee. There is therefore, as a general rule, no liability upon the landlord either to the tenant or to others entering the land, for defective conditions existing at the time of the lease.

The general rule of non-liability has been modified, however, by a number of exceptions which have been created as a matter of social policy. Modern case law on the subject today usually limits the liability of a landlord for injuries arising from a defective condition existing at the time of the lease to six recognized exceptions. These exceptions are as follows:

1. Undisclosed dangerous conditions known to lessor and unknown to the lessee.

This exception is stated in Restatement, Second, Torts § 358 as follows:

"§ 358. Undisclosed Dangerous Conditions Known to Lessor

"(1) A lessor of land who conceals or fails to disclose to his lessee any condition, whether natural or artificial, which involves unreasonable risk of physical harm to persons on the land, is subject to liability to the lessee and others upon the land with the consent of the lessee or his sublessee for physical harm caused by the condition after the lessee has taken possession, if

"(a) the lessee does not know or have reason to know of the condition or the risk involved, and

"(b) the lessor knows or has reason to know of the condition, and realizes or should realize the risk involved, and has reason to expect that the lessee will not discover the condition or realize the risk.

"(2) If the less[or] actively conceals the condition, the liability stated in Subsection (1) continues until the lessee discovers it and has reasonable opportunity to take effective precautions against it. Otherwise the liability continues only until the vendee has had reasonable opportunity to discover the condition and to take such precautions."

In Kansas we have recognized and applied this exception to impose liability upon the landlord * * * [citations omitted]. It should be pointed out that this exception applies only to latent conditions and not to conditions which are patent or reasonably discernible to the tenant. (Branstetter v. Robbins, supra.)

2. Conditions dangerous to persons outside of the premises.

This exception is stated in Restatement, Second, Torts § 379 as follows:

"§ 379. Dangerous Conditions Existing When Lessor Transfers
          Possession

"A lessor of land who transfers its possession in a condition which he realizes or should realize will involve unreasonable risk of physical harm to others outside of the land, is subject to the same liability for physical harm subsequently caused to them by the condition as though he had remained in possession".

The theory of liability under such circumstances is that where a nuisance dangerous to persons outside the leased premises (such as the traveling public or persons on adjoining property) exists on the premises at the time of the lease, the lessor should not be permitted to escape liability by leasing the premises to another. The liability of the landlord for structural defects on leased property which causes injuries to persons outside of the premises was recognized and made the basis of a judgment against the landlord in Mitchell v. Foran, 143 Kan. 191, 53 P.2d 490. *Mitchell* involved an awning hook which was fastened to the leased building and projected onto the public sidewalk and caused injury to a nine-year-old pedestrian.

3. Premises leased for admission of the public.

The third exception arises where land is leased for a purpose involving the admission of the public. The cases usually agree that in that situation the lessor is under an affirmative duty to exercise reasonable care to inspect and repair the premises before possession is transferred, to prevent any unreasonable risk or harm to the public who may enter. This exception is stated in § 359 of Restatement, Second, Torts as follows:

"§ 359. Land Leased for Purpose Involving Admission of Public

"A lessor who leases land for a purpose which involves the admission of the public is subject to liability for physical harm caused to persons who enter the land for that purpose by a condition of the land existing when the lessee takes possession, if the lessor

"(a) knows or by the exercise of reasonable care could discover that the condition involves an unreasonable risk of harm to such persons, and

"(b) has reason to expect that the lessee will admit them before the land is put in safe condition for their reception, and

"(c) fails to exercise reasonable care to discover or to remedy the condition, or otherwise to protect such persons against it."

This exception has been recognized in Kansas * * * [citations omitted]. In Mathes v. Robinson, 205 Kan. 402, 469 P.2d 259, we held that the owner of a rooming house was liable to a guest of his tenant who was asphyxiated as the result of an unvented gas heater of which the defendant had knowledge. Liability in the case was predicated upon *wanton misconduct* on the part of the landlord of the building. No attempt was made by the court to base liability upon one of the recognized exceptions. Liability for simple negligence was not claimed in the case and the plaintiff relied solely upon wantonness. Under similar factual circumstances in other jurisdictions liability of the landlord has been predicated on the theory that a rooming house, along with a hotel and motel, falls within the exception of property leased for public use and therefore the owner as lessor should be held liable for a dangerous condition existing at the time of the lease and of which the lessor had knowledge. (See the cases cited in the annotation in 17 A.L.R.3d 873.)

4. Parts of land retained in lessor's control which lessee is entitled to use.

When different parts of a building, such as an office building or an apartment house, are leased to several tenants, the approaches and common passageways normally do not pass to the tenant, but remain in the possession and control of the landlord. Hence the lessor is under an affirmative obligation to exercise reasonable care to inspect and repair those parts of the premises for the protection of the lessee, members of his family, his employees, invitees, guests, and others on the land in the right of the tenant. This exception is covered in Restatement, Second, Torts §§ 360 and 361 which provide as follows:

"§ 360.   Parts of Land Retained in Lessor's Control Which Lessee is Entitled to Use

"A possessor of land who leases a part thereof and retains in his own control any other part which the lessee is entitled to use as appurtenant to the part leased to him, is subject to liability to his lessee and others lawfully upon the land with the consent of the lessee or a sublessee for physical harm caused by a dangerous condition upon that part of the land retained in the lessor's control, if the lessor by the exercise of reasonable care could have discovered the condition and the unreasonable risk involved therein and could have made the condition safe."

"§ 361.   Parts of Land Retained in Lessor's Control but Necessary to Safe Use of Part Leased

"A possessor of land who leases a part thereof and retains in his own control any other part which is necessary to the safe use of the leased part, is subject to liability to his lessee and others lawfully upon the land with the consent of the lessee or a sublessee for physical harm caused by a dangerous condition upon that part of the land retained in the lessor's control, if the lessor by the exercise of reasonable care

"(a) could have discovered the condition and the risk involved, and

"(b) could have made the condition safe."

In Kansas this exception has been recognized   *   *   *   [citations omitted].

5.   Where lessor contracts to repair.

At one time the law in most jurisdictions and in Kansas was that if a landlord breached his contract to keep the premises in good repair, the only remedy of the tenant was an action in contract in which damages were limited to the cost of repair or loss of rental value of the property. Neither the tenant nor members of his family nor his guests were permitted to recover for personal injuries suffered as a result of the breach of the agreement. (Murrell v. Crawford, 102 Kan. 118, 169 P. 561.) In most jurisdictions this rule has been modified and a cause of action given in tort to the injured person to enable him recovery for his personal injuries. *Murrell* was expressly overruled in Williams v. Davis, 188

Kan. 385, 362 P.2d 641. This exception is found in Restatement, Second, Torts § 357 which states as follows:

"§ 357. Where Lessor Contracts to Repair

"A lessor of land is subject to liability for physical harm caused to his lessee and others upon the land with the consent of the lessee or his sublessee by a condition of disrepair existing before or arising after the lessee has taken possession if

"(a) the lessor, as such, has contracted by a covenant in the lease or otherwise to keep the land in repair, and

"(b) the disrepair creates an unreasonable risk to persons upon the land which the performance of the lessor's agreement would have prevented, and

"(c) the lessor fails to exercise reasonable care to perform his contract."

In Kansas this exception has been followed   *   *   *   [citations omitted]. In Vieyra v. Engineering Investment Co., Inc., 205 Kan. 775, 473 P.2d 44, we held that although the landlord has a duty to keep the premises in repair by virtue of a covenant to repair in the lease, if the lease does not require the lessor to inspect the premises, the lessor is not liable until the lessee has given him notice of the need for repairs and the lessor thereafter fails to exercise reasonable care and diligence in making the repairs. In Steele v. Latimer, 214 Kan. 329, 521 P.2d 304, we held that the provisions of a municipal housing code prescribing minimum housing standards are deemed by implication to become a part of a lease of urban residential property, giving rise to an implied warranty on the part of the lessor that the premises are habitable and safe for human occupancy in compliance with the pertinent code provisions and will remain so for the duration of the tenancy. Such an implied warranty creates a contractual obligation on the lessor to repair the premises to keep them in compliance with the municipal housing standards as set forth in a municipal housing code.

6. Negligence by lessor in making repairs.

When the lessor does in fact attempt to make repairs, whether he is bound by a covenant to do so or not, and fails to exercise reasonable care, he is held liable for injuries to the tenant or others on the premises in his right, if the tenant neither knows nor should know that the repairs have been negligently made. This exception is stated in Restatement, Second, Torts § 362:

"§ 362. Negligent Repairs by Lessor

"A lessor of land who, by purporting to make repairs on the land while it is in the possession of his lessee, or by the negligent manner in which he makes such repairs has, as the lessee neither knows nor should know, made the land more dangerous for use or given it a deceptive appearance of safety, is subject to liability for physical harm caused by the condition to the lessee or to others upon the land with the consent of the lessee or sublessee."

§ d of Section 362 declares that the lessor is subject to liability if, but only if, the lessee neither knows nor should know that the purported repairs have not been made or have been negligently made and so, relying upon the deceptive appearance of safety, subjects himself to the dangers or invites or permits his licensees to encounter them. Conversely it would follow that if the lessee knows or should know that the purported repairs have not been made or have been negligently made, then the lessor is not liable under this exception. This exception has been recognized in Kansas * * * [citations omitted].

With the general rule and its exceptions in mind we shall now examine the undisputed facts in this case to determine whether or not the landlord can be held liable to the plaintiff here. It is clear that the exceptions pertaining to undisclosed dangerous conditions known to the lessor (exception 1), conditions dangerous to persons outside of the premises (exception 2), premises leased for admission of the public (exception 3), and parts of land retained in the lessor's control (exception 4) have no application in this case. Nor do we believe that exception 5, which comes into play when the lessor has contracted to repair, has been established by the court's findings of fact. It does not appear that the plaintiff takes the position that the lessor contracted to keep the premises in repair; nor has any consideration for such an agreement been shown. As to exception 6, although it is obvious that the repairs to the roof were not completed by installation of the guttering and although the landlord expressed his intention to replace the guttering, we do not believe that the factual circumstances bring the plaintiff within the application of exception 6 where the lessor has been negligent in making repairs. As pointed out above, that exception comes into play only when the lessee lacks knowledge that the purported repairs have not been made or have been negligently made. Here it is undisputed that the tenant had full knowledge of the icy condition on the steps created by the absence of guttering. It seems to us that the landlord could reasonably assume that the tenant would inform his guest about the icy condition on the front steps. We have concluded that the factual circumstances do not establish liability on the landlord on the basis of negligent repairs made by him.

In his brief counsel for the plaintiff vigorously argues that the law should be changed to make the landlord liable for injuries resulting from a defective condition on the leased premises where the landlord has knowledge of that condition. He has not cited any authority in support of his position, nor does he state with particularity how the existing law pertaining to a landlord's liability should be modified. We do not believe that the facts and circumstances of this case justify a departure from the established rules of law discussed above.

The judgment of the district court is affirmed.

Notes

1. **The "Furnished House" Exception.** In addition to the exceptions mentioned by the court in *Borders* to the traditional rule of nonliability of landlords in tort, it has been held in some jurisdictions that in a lease of a furnished

house for a short term for immediate occupancy there is an implied warranty by the lessor that the premises are fit for human occupancy. The basis for the implication is that in such circumstances the lessee cannot be expected to make an adequate inspection of the premises before entering the lease. The restrictive qualifications placed on this rule are not easy to administer, and create pressures on a court to ignore them, but for the most part the courts have not done so. Recoveries of damages for injuries received on defective premises have been allowed. 1 A.L.P. § 3.45.

2. **Violations of Statutes or Administrative Regulations.** The answer to the problem of tort liability for violations of this kind has produced the most significant exception to the traditional rule of *caveat emptor* as applied to landlords. Yet it is never mentioned by courts or commentators as such. Probably the reason is that it is not a rule specifically designed for landlord-tenant relations, but is a general rule of tort law. Such violations normally have penal or administrative consequences. The problem of translating penal liability into tort liability is analogous to translating contract liability into tort liability. In either situation, there is no necessary connection between the two. One question involved in the violation of statutes is who, as between landlord and tenant, is responsible for compliance. See Gaddis v. Consolidated Freightways, Inc., supra page 372. If it is decided that the onus falls on the landlord, courts have insisted that the statute or regulation must be designed to protect identifiable classes of persons, and the plaintiff must be within such a class. Then is it enough that a landlord has violated a statute, usually by failing to take action to repair defective premises? Some courts say that such a violation is negligence *per se*. Others that such a violation is only evidence of negligence. The Restatement (Second) of Torts § 288B says that a violation is "negligence in itself," provided the defendant cannot bring himself within a list of "excused violations," which are as follows:

    (a) the violation is reasonable because of the actor's incapacity;

    (b) he neither knows nor should know of the occasion for compliance;

    (c) he is unable after diligence or care to comply;

    (d) he is confronted by an emergency not due to his own misconduct; or

    (e) compliance would involve a greater risk of harm to the actor or to others.

The excused violations seem to reduce "negligence in itself" to something approaching simple negligence. In contrast, the new Restatement (Second) of Property (Landlord and Tenant) § 17.6 states a simple rule which is indeed a rule of ordinary negligence. This section is set out in the opinion in Rivera v. Selfon Home Repairs & Improvement Co., infra page 464.

A reason why statutory violations have assumed central importance in respect to the tort liability of landlords is the recent widespread enactment of building and housing codes, at state or local levels. Of even greater importance are all the recent statutes which, like the URLTA, have enlarged the duty of landlords respecting the condition of leased premises to a degree approximating the judicially created implied warranty of habitability.

We are left to face the question, in all but a few American jurisdictions: what are the tort consequences of a violation by a landlord of an implied warranty of habitability or a statutory duty of similar dimensions? The several abridged cases which follow represent courts' responses to this problem.

DAPKUNAS v. CAGLE, 42 Ill.App.3d 644, 1 Ill.Dec. 387, 356 N.E.2d 575 (1976). The plaintiff was a month-to-month tenant under an oral lease of a house and lot. She was injured by falling on steps at the rear entrance of the house, which consisted of loosely laid bricks and concrete blocks. The plaintiff sued for damages for negligence and breach of warranty of habitability. Dismissal of the complaint was affirmed.

The court said that the plaintiff's case did not come within any of the exceptions to the traditional rule regarding a lessor's tort liability. In respect to the allegation of breach of warranty the court distinguished Jack Spring, Inc. v. Little, supra, page 425 on the grounds: (1) Jack Spring involved multiple unit dwellings, and (2) Jack Spring involved violations of a building code. The court added:

"We also note that *Jack Spring* involved a forcible entry and detainer action brought by the landlord against certain tenants for the failure of the tenants to pay rent. The implied warranty of habitability was asserted by the tenants merely as a defense, and was found to be 'germane to the decisive question of whether the defendants were indebted to plaintiffs for rent.' 280 N.E.2d at 217. Nowhere in *Jack Spring* do we find an indication that the Supreme Court, by applying an implied warranty of habitability in multiple unit dwelling rentals intended to change the established law in Illinois governing personal injury suits by tenants against landlords. Such a change would have far reaching and serious consequences. For this court to find that the Supreme Court contemplated such a serious change in the law, when it made no discussion on the subject, would be entirely inappropriate. We are, therefore, unwilling to adopt plaintiff's argument with respect to the applicability of *Jack Spring* to the instant case. * * *

"Because of the express limitations placed upon the ruling in *Jack Spring*, as discussed above, it cannot be said that *Jack Spring* like Kline v. Burns [111 N.H. 87, 276 A.2d 248 (1971)] has completely discarded the rule of *caveat emptor*. *Caveat emptor* still remains a part of landlord-tenant law in this state, although perhaps not to the same extent that it was at one time. Moreover, we are not convinced that landlord-tenant law would be 'modernized' by totally discarding the rule. * * *"

KAPLAN v. COULSTON, 85 Misc.2d 745, 381 N.Y.S.2d 634 (Civ.Ct. 1976). Plaintiffs, tenants of an apartment, were injured when a kitchen cabinet fell. They originally sued for damages, alleging the negligence of the landlord. Later they sought to amend their complaint to assert a cause of action for damages for breach of an implied warranty of habitability, on the assumption that such a breach would result in strict liability, without proof of any notice to the landlord of any defect in the leased premises. The court granted the motion to amend. The court stated the arguments both for and against strict liability as follows:

"Militating against strict liability are several persuasive arguments. First, a lease is not a sale of a product. Second, an apartment may be new or, more likely, many years old. Should a landlord of a 40–50 year old apartment be held strictly liable? Third, some defective conditions may exist at the time of the letting, while others may occur weeks, months or years after the letting. Is the warranty to be a continuing one and, if so, for how long? Fourth, the landlord may have constructed the building or purchased it when it was 30, 40 or 50 years old. In the case of a new building he may still have recourse against his suppliers and contractors, but in an old building he probably would not have such recourse and may not even know who created the defective condition. Fifth, isn't the notice requirement based upon the idea that the tenant and not the landlord has possession and control of the apartment, and therefore, the tenant should be required to notify the landlord so that the landlord may take corrective action? If neither party had notice why should the landlord be liable? * * *

"Arrayed against these arguments are the policy considerations behind strict liability as to products and the policy trend in tort and landlord and tenant law. * * *

"One reason for imposing strict liability upon a seller of a product is that the seller has superior knowledge and is in a better position to prevent defects, while the consumer is encouraged to rely on his skill, reputation and implied warranty of safety. Nevertheless, no matter how many tests and inspections a manufacturer performs and whether or not he is aware of the defect, if the defect exists and is the proximate cause of the injury, he is held strictly liable in products liability cases. Certainly, a landlord is in a similar position to a seller, in that he has superior knowledge and is in a better position to prevent defects and a tenant is in a similar position to a purchaser in that he relies on the skill and implied warranty.

"Secondly, products liability was partly based upon the idea that the seller was in a better position to bear and distribute the loss. This is also true of a landlord who can purchase liability insurance and (except possibly for rent controlled apartments) pass the costs on to all of the tenants.

"A final reason for imposing strict liability on the sale of products was to eliminate the difficulty of having to prove negligence. Of course, the plaintiff still has to prove a defective condition. The defect may have been created by an affirmative act of the landlord, or a third person, or by the failure of the landlord to discover or repair a defective condition. In any of these cases the lessee is in the same position as a purchaser and it may be impossible to prove that the landlord knew or should have known of the defective condition.

"In summary, like the typical consumer, the tenant relies upon the landlord's skill, reputation and implied representation of safety. Builder-vendees of real property, sellers of used property and lessors of personal property have all been held strictly liable.

"In Louisiana the landlord is liable for defects existing at the time the lease was made, and even if they have arisen since. L.S.A.–C.C., Art. 2695.

'Thus plaintiff's right to recover from his lessor and the lessor's insurer does not depend solely upon fault or negligence * * * This article provides for liability without fault * * * A lessee needs only to show injury from an accident caused by a defect on the premises.' Joyner v. Aetna Casualty & Surety Co., La.App., 240 So. 2d 545 (Ct.App.La., 2nd Cir., 1970).

"Taking all of the foregoing arguments into account it seems to this court that the imposition of strict liability on the part of a landlord for injuries caused by a defect in the premises would best serve the interests of justice. He is in a better position to inspect and examine. He is in a better position to know when to repair or replace items. He does make the profit from the venture. He is in a better position to spread the loss. As between landlord, collecting rent, and an innocent tenant, the landlord should bear the loss. The development of the tort and lease aspects of our law seem to lead to this conclusion."

Note

The New York lower courts are divided on the rule of *Kaplan*. *Kaplan* was approved in McGuinness v. Jakubiak, 106 Misc.2d 317, 431 N.Y.S.2d 755 (Sup.Ct.1980), and in McBride v. 218 E. 70th St. Associates, 102 Misc.2d 279, 425 N.Y.S.2d 910 (App.Term 1979). But in Mahlmann v. Yelverton, 109 Misc.2d 127, 439 N.Y.S.2d 568 (Civ.Ct.1980), the court construed Section 235–b of the New York Real Property Law, which essentially codifies for residential leases the warranty of habitability. The court, although not deciding the question, expressed its opinion that the section was not intended to impose strict liability on landlords. See also Hamel v. Schmidt, 106 Misc.2d 315, 431 N.Y.S.2d 770 (Sup.Ct.1980). See also Note, New York's Search for an Effective Implied Warranty of Habitability in Residential Leases, 43 Alb.L.Rev. 661 (1979) (criticizing *Kaplan*).

No court of last resort has yet declared strict liability for landlords. Massachusetts has come the closest, but the court's position remains in doubt. See Crowell v. McCaffrey, 377 Mass. 443, 386 N.E.2d 1256 (1979). Cf. Shroades v. Rental Homes, Inc., 68 Ohio St.2d 20, 427 N.E.2d 774 (1981).

See generally Browder, The Taming of a Duty—The Tort Liability of Landlords, 81 Mich.L.Rev. 99 (1982).

RIVERA v. SELFON HOME REPAIRS & IMPROVEMENT CO., 294 Pa.Super. 41, 439 A.2d 739 (1982). Plaintiff was injured when she fell through a landing at the top of a wooden stairway that provided access to her apartment. Plaintiff sued for damages, alleging negligence of the landlord. The entry of a nonsuit below was reversed on appeal. Following is part of the court's opinion:

"In Pugh v. Holmes, 486 Pa. 272, 405 A.2d 897 (1979), decided more than a year before the decision of the lower court *en banc* denying plaintiff's motion to take off the nonsuit and motion for reconsideration of the motion to amend plaintiff's complaint, our supreme court adopted an implied warranty of habitability in residential leases. The court said:

'The implied warranty is designed to insure that a landlord will provide facilities and services vital to the life, health, and safety of the tenant and to the use of the premises for residential purposes. King v. Moorehead, at 495 S.W.2d 75.' Pugh v. Holmes, [253 Pa. Super. 87], 384 A.2d at 1240. This warranty is applicable both at the beginning of the lease and throughout its duration. Id. citing Old

Town Development Co. v. Langford, 349 N.E.2d 744, 764 (Ind.App. 1976) and Mease v. Fox, 200 N.W.2d 791, 796 (Iowa 1972).

*   *   *

'Additionally, we agree with the Superior Court that, to assert a breach of the implied warranty of habitability, a tenant must prove he or she gave notice to the landlord of the defect or condition, that he (the landlord) had a reasonable opportunity to make the necessary repairs, and that he failed to do so. [253 Pa.Super. 88], 384 A.2d at 1241.'

Id. 486 Pa. at 289, 290, 405 A.2d at 905, 906.

"Instantly, the evidence would support a factual finding by the trier of fact that a dangerous condition existed with respect to the premises to be leased, that the landlord was aware of the dangerous condition and failed to exercise reasonable care to repair the condition and finally that the existence of the condition is a violation of an implied warranty of habitability. This is precisely the subject of the Restatement, Second, Property (Landlord and Tenant) § 17.6, Comment a, b, c (1977), representing the modern weight of authority in this area of the law:

"Landlord Under Legal Duty to Repair Dangerous Condition

"A landlord is subject to liability for physical harm caused to the tenant and others upon the leased property with the consent of the tenant or his subtenant by a dangerous condition existing before or arising after the tenant has taken possession, if he has failed to exercise reasonable care to repair the condition and the existence of the condition is in violation of:

(1) an implied warranty of habitability; or

(2) a duty created by statute or administrative regulation.

Cf. Ford v. Ja-Sin., Del.Super., 420 A.2d 184, 187 n. 4 (1980). (The court held that a tenant's guest could recover for her personal injuries against the landlord upon a showing of simple negligence under the Delaware Landlord-Tenant Code, 25 Del.C. § 5101 et seq., 58 Del.Laws, c. 472, effective September 27, 1972, which is entirely consistent with Restatement, Second, Property (Landlord and Tenant) § 17.6 (1977)).

"We hold that under the authority of *Pugh* and the Restatement, Second, Property (Landlord and Tenant) § 17.6 (1977), and under the specific and particular facts of the instant case, it was a matter for the fact finder to determine whether or not the landlord was subject to liability for physical harm caused to the plaintiff, Delia Rivera, based upon an alleged dangerous condition existing before the tenant had taken possession; further a question for the fact finder as to whether or not the landlord failed to exercise reasonable care to repair the condition and whether or not the existence of the condition was in violation of an implied warranty of habitability.

"As we have seen, in the modern view expressed in *Pugh* and the Restatement, Second, Property (Landlord and Tenant) § 17.6 (1977), plaintiff had a valid cause of action for submission to the fact finder as *pleaded in her original complaint*; specifically, that the defendant

Selfon negligently had failed to properly maintain the residence at 529 Terrace Road; negligently failed to satisfactorily provide a means of ingress and egress to the apartment; negligently permitted the wooden structure of the stairway and landing to become decayed, rotten and otherwise unstable, and negligently failed to provide a workman to repair this condition despite previous requests to do so.

"Order of the lower court *en banc* is reversed and the case is remanded for trial consistent with this opinion."

Note

In Henderson v. W.C. Haas Realty Management, 561 S.W.2d 382 (Mo.App. 1978), the court said,

"Under the facts of this case, and the status of the law at this time, there seems to be no legitimate basis for imposing liability upon respondents just by reason of their existent implied warranty of habitability of the leased premises. No case has been cited, nor has one been found, imposing strict liability upon the non-builder landlord for latent defects, rendering the premises unsafe or dangerous, absent some actual or constructive notice or knowledge of the defects. This notice requirement would seem to reduce the concept of implied warranty of habitability to one of negligence. * * * Nevertheless, the concept of implied warranty of habitability by prevailing authority * * * includes the requirement of some type of notice of defects. There is no evidence in this case of any notice of any kind of the defective condition of the wiring in the basement common area, hence the trial court did not err in sustaining respondents' after-trial motion and entering judgment for them in accordance with their motion for directed verdict made at the close of the whole case."

SARGENT v. ROSS, 113 N.H. 388, 308 A.2d 528 (1973). Portions of the court's opinion are as follows:

"KENISON, Chief Justice.

"The question in this case is whether the defendant landlord is liable to the plaintiff in tort for the death of plaintiff's four-year-old daughter who fell to her death from an outdoor stairway at a residential building owned by the defendant in Nashua. The defendant resided in a ground floor apartment in the building, and her son and daughter-in-law occupied a second story apartment serviced by the stairway from which the child fell. At the time of the accident the child was under the care of the defendant's daughter-in-law who was plaintiff's regular baby-sitter.

"Plaintiff brought suit against the daughter-in-law for negligent supervision and against the defendant for negligent construction and maintenance of the stairway which was added to the building by the defendant about eight years before the accident. There was no apparent cause for the fall except for evidence that the stairs were dangerously steep, and that the railing was insufficient to prevent the child from falling over the side. The jury returned a verdict for the daughter-in-law but found in favor of the plaintiff in her action against the defendant landlord. The defendant seasonably excepted to the denial of her motions for a nonsuit, directed verdict, judgment n.o.v., and to have the verdict set aside, and all questions of law where reserved and transferred to this court by *Dunfey*, J. * * *

"The anomaly of the general rule of landlord tort immunity and the inflexibility of the standard exceptions, such as the control exception, is pointedly demonstrated by this case. A child is killed by a dangerous condition of the premises. Both husband and wife tenants testify that they could do nothing to remedy the defect because they did not own the house nor have authority to alter the defect. But the landlord claims that she should not be liable because the stairs were not under her control. Both of these contentions are premised on the theory that the other party should be responsible. So the orthodox analysis would leave us with neither landlord nor tenant responsible for dangerous conditions on the premises. This would be both illogical and intolerable, particularly since neither party then would have any legal reason to remedy or take precautionary measures with respect to dangerous conditions. In fact, the traditional "control" rule actually discourages a landlord from remedying a dangerous condition since his repairs may be evidence of his control. Hunkins v. Amoskeag Mfg. Co., 86 N.H. 356, 169 A. 3 (1933); see Flanders v. New Hampshire Sav. Bank, 90 N.H. 285, 7 A.2d 233 (1939). Nor can there be serious doubt that ordinarily the landlord is best able to remedy dangerous conditions, particularly where a substantial alteration is required. See Kline v. Burns, 111 N.H. 87, 276 A.2d 248 (1971); Note, 62 Harv.L.Rev. 669 (1949). * * *

"We think that now is the time for the landlord's limited tort immunity to be relegated to the history books where it more properly belongs.

"This conclusion springs naturally and inexorably from our recent decision in Kline v. Burns, 111 N.H. 87, 276 A.2d 248 (1971). *Kline* was an apartment rental claim suit in which the tenant claimed that the premises were uninhabitable. Following a small vanguard of other jurisdictions, we modernized the landlord-tenant contractual relationship by holding that there is an implied warranty of habitability in an apartment lease transaction. As a necessary predicate to our decision, we discarded from landlord-tenant law 'that obnoxious legal cliché, *caveat emptor*'. Pines v. Perssion, 14 Wis.2d 590, 596, 111 N.W.2d 409, 413 (1961). In so doing, we discarded the very legal foundation and justification for the landlord's immunity in tort for injuries to the tenant or third persons. 'Judicial discarding of the sale concept [and, hence, of *caveat emptor*] would leave the courts with an easy recourse to established principles of law; the lessor would fall within the general proposition underlying many areas of tort law that he who owns or is in a position to control or is responsible for things or persons has the duty to prevent their harming others. And the large body of negligence principles which have developed in other fields would bound this duty.' Note, 62 Harv.L.Rev. 669, 678–79 (1949).

"To the extent that Kline v. Burns did not do so, we today discard the rule of 'caveat lessee' and the doctrine of landlord nonliability in tort to which it gave birth. We thus bring up to date the other half of landlord-tenant law. Hence forth, landlords as other persons must exercise reasonable care not to subject others to an unreasonable risk of harm. A landlord must act as a reasonable person under all of the circum-

stances including the likelihood of injury to others, the probable seriousness of such injuries, and the burden of reducing or avoiding the risk.
See generally Note, 121 U.Pa.L.Rev. 378 (1972). We think this basic
principle of responsibility for landlords as for others 'best expresses the
principles of justice and reasonableness upon which our law of torts is
founded.' Dowd v. Portsmouth Hosp., 105 N.H. 53, 59, 193 A.2d 788,
792 (1963) (on rehearing). The questions of control, hidden defects and
common or public use, which formerly had to be established as a prerequisite to even considering the negligence of a landlord, will now be relevant only inasmuch as they bear on the basic tort issues such as the
foreseeability and unreasonableness of the particular risk of harm. Cf.
Clarke v. O'Connor, 140 U.S.App.D.C. 300, 435 F.2d 104, 111–113 (1970).
* * *

"Our decision will shift the primary focus of inquiry for judge and
jury from the traditional question of 'who had control?' to a determination of whether the landlord, and the injured party, exercised due care
under all the circumstances. Perhaps even more significantly, the ordinary negligence standard should help insure that a landlord will take
whatever precautions are reasonably necessary under the circumstances
to reduce the likelihood of injuries from defects in his property. 'It is
appropriate that the landlord who will retain ownership of the premises
and any permanent improvements should bear the cost of repairs necessary to make the premises safe * * *.' Kline v. Burns, 111 N.H. 87,
92, 276 A.2d 248, 251 (1971).

"Although the trial court's instructions to the jury in the instant
case were cast according to the traditional exceptions of control and hidden danger, the charge clearly set forth the elements of ordinary negligence which were presented by the court as a prerequisite to a finding
of liability on either issue. Thus, the jury could find that the defendant
was negligent in the design or construction of the steep stairway or in
failing to take adequate precautionary measures to reduce the risk of
injury. We have carefully reviewed the record and conclude that there
is sufficient evidence, on the basis of the principles set forth above, to
support the verdict of the jury which had the benefit of a view. Both
plaintiff and the wife tenant testified that the stairs were too steep, and
the husband tenant testified that his wife complained to him of this fact.
While the defendant landlord did not testify, the jury could find that she
knew that this steep stairway was frequently used by the young children for whom her daughter-in-law was the regular, daily babysitter.
In any event, the use of these steps by young children should have been
anticipated by the defendant. Saad v. Papageorge, 82 N.H. 294, 133 A.
24 (1926); see Manning v. Freeman, 105 N.H. 272, 198 A.2d 14 (1964).

"The verdict of the jury is sustained, and the order is

"Exceptions overruled; judgment on the verdict."

Note on Exculpatory Contracts

Leases may contain provisions designed to relieve a landlord or his agents or
employees from liability for personal injuries or property damage resulting
from the condition of leased premises or the conduct of the landlord's employ-

ees, or to save the landlord harmless from any claim for damages. Traditionally such provisions were upheld in vindication of freedom of contract.

Recently the trend is to find grounds for declaring such provisions void as in violation of public policy. The public policy may be limited to findings of unequal bargaining power or other bases for a finding of unconscionability. Several courts have distinguished between active and passive negligence, finding an exculpatory clause illegal only when it purports to excuse a landlord from active negligence. In application, however, such a distinction tends to break down in the direction of finding active negligence. It may be surprising that the Mississippi court is the only one found, apart from statute, to declare the illegality of exculpatory clauses without reference to specific proof or circumstances. See Cappaert v. Junker, 413 So.2d 378 (Miss.1982).

The reason why more courts have not taken the same step may be the appearance of numerous relevant statutes. Several of these have expressly prohibited exculpatory clauses. The URLTA so provides (Section 1.403), as do a number of states that have enacted the URLTA in whole or in part. Account must be taken, however, of the provisions in the URLTA (Section 2–104) which, in respect to multi-unit residences, permit the shifting of the burden of specified repairs from landlords to tenants by means of a separate writing, supported by adequate consideration, entered in good faith and not for the purpose of evading duties imposed on landlords by the statute. A number of recently enacted statutes include such a provision. A number of others are more liberal, authorizing such a shift in burdens if done in good faith and not to evade landlords' duties. Several permit such a shift in burdens in leases whose terms exceed a specified duration.

See Browder, The Taming of a Duty—The Tort Liability of Landlords, 81 Mich.L.Rev. 99, 141 (1982).

KLINE v. 1500 MASSACHUSETTS AVE. CORP.*

United States Court of Appeals, District of Columbia Circuit, 1970.
141 U.S.App.D.C. 370, 439 F.2d 477.

WILKEY, Circuit Judge. The appellee apartment corporation states that there is "only one issue presented for review * * * whether a duty should be placed on a landlord to take steps to protect tenants from foreseeable criminal acts committed by third parties". The District Court as a matter of law held that there is no such duty. We find that there is, and that in the circumstances here the applicable standard of care was breached. We therefore reverse and remand to the District Court for the determination of damages for the appellant.

I

The appellant, Sarah B. Kline, sustained serious injuries when she was criminally assaulted and robbed at approximately 10:15 in the evening by an intruder in the common hallway of an apartment house at 1500 Massachusetts Avenue. This facility, into which the appellant Kline moved in October 1959, is a large apartment building with approximately 585 individual apartment units. It has a main entrance on Mas-

---

* Certain footnotes of the court have been omitted. Footnotes retained have been renumbered. Ed.

sachusetts Avenue, with side entrances on both 15th and 16th Streets. At the time the appellant first signed a lease a doorman was on duty at the main entrance twenty-four hours a day, and at least one employee at all times manned a desk in the lobby from which all persons using the elevators could be observed. The 15th Street door adjoined the entrance to a parking garage used by both the tenants and the public. Two garage attendants were stationed at this dual entranceway; the duties of each being arranged so that one of them always was in position to observe those entering either the apartment building or the garage. The 16th Street entrance was unattended during the day but was locked after 9:00 P.M.

By mid-1966, however, the main entrance had no doorman, the desk in the lobby was left unattended much of the time, the 15th Street entrance was generally unguarded due to a decrease in garage personnel, and the 16th Street entrance was often left unlocked all night. The entrances were allowed to be thus unguarded in the face of an increasing number of assaults, larcenies, and robberies being perpetrated against the tenants in and from the common hallways of the apartment building. These facts were undisputed, and were supported by a detailed chronological listing of offenses admitted into evidence. The landlord had notice of these crimes and had in fact been urged by appellant Kline herself prior to the events leading to the instant appeal to take steps to secure the building.

Shortly after 10:00 P.M. on November 17, 1966, Miss Kline was assaulted and robbed just outside her apartment on the first floor above the street level of this 585 unit apartment building. This occurred only two months after Leona Sullivan, another female tenant, had been similarly attacked in the same commonway.

II

At the outset we note that of the crimes of violence, robbery, and assault which had been occurring with mounting frequency on the premises at 1500 Massachusetts Avenue, the assaults on Miss Kline and Miss Sullivan took place in the hallways of the building, which were under the exclusive control of the appellee landlord. Even in those crimes of robbery or assault committed in individual apartments, the intruders of necessity had to gain entrance through the common entry and passageways. These premises fronted on three heavily traveled streets, and had multiple entrances. The risk to be guarded against therefore was the risk of unauthorized entrance into the apartment house by intruders bent upon some crime of violence or theft.

While the apartment lessees themselves could take some steps to guard against this risk by installing extra heavy locks and other security devices on the doors and windows of their respective apartments, yet this risk in the greater part could only be guarded against by the landlord. No individual tenant had it within his power to take measures to guard the garage entranceways, to provide scrutiny at the main entrance of the building, to patrol the common hallways and elevators, to set up any kind of a security alarm system in the building, to provide additional locking devices on the main doors, to provide a system of announcement for authorized visitors only, to close the garage doors at appropriate hours, and to see that the entrance was manned at all times.

The risk of criminal assault and robbery on a tenant in the common hallways of the building was thus entirely predictable; that same risk had been occurring with increasing frequency over a period of several months immediately prior to the incident giving rise to this case; it was a risk whose prevention or minimization was almost entirely within the power of the landlord; and the risk materialized in the assault and robbery of appellant on November 17, 1966.

III

In this jurisdiction, certain duties have been assigned to the landlord becuse of his *control* of common hallways, lobbies, stairwells, etc., used by all tenants in multiple dwelling units. This Court in Levine v. Katz, 132 U.S.App.D.C. 173, 174, 407 F.2d 303, 304 (1968), pointed out that:

> It has long been well settled in this jurisdiction that, where a landlord leases separate portions of property and reserves under his own control the halls, stairs, or other parts of the property for use in common by all tenants, he has a duty to all those on the premises of legal right to use ordinary care and diligence to maintain the retained parts in a reasonably safe condition.

While Levine v. Katz dealt with a physical defect in the building leading to plaintiff's injury, the rationale as applied to predictable criminal acts by third parties is the same. The duty is the landlord's because by his control of the areas of common use and common danger he is the only party who has the *power* to make the necessary repairs or to provide the necessary protection.

As a general rule, a private person does not have a duty to protect another from a criminal attack by a third person. We recognize that this rule has sometimes in the past been applied in landlord-tenant law, even by this court. Among the reasons for the application of this rule to landlords are: judicial reluctance to tamper with the traditional common law concept of the landlord-tenant relationship; the notion that the act of a third person in committing an intentional tort or crime is a superseding cause of the harm to another resulting therefrom; the oftentimes difficult problem of determining foreseeability of criminal acts; the vagueness of the standard which the landlord must meet; the economic consequences of the imposition of the duty; and conflict with the public policy allocating the duty of protecting citizens from criminal acts to the government rather than the private sector.

But the rationale of this very broad general rule falters when it is applied to the conditions of modern day urban apartment living, particularly in the circumstances of this case. The rationale of the general rule exonerating a third party from any duty to protect another from a criminal attack has no applicability to the landlord-tenant relationship in multiple dwelling houses. The landlord is no insurer of his tenants' safety, but he certainly is no bystander. And where, as here, the landlord has notice of repeated criminal assaults and robberies, has notice that these crimes occurred in the portion of the premises exclusively within his control, has every reason to expect like crimes to happen again, and has the exclusive power to take preventive action, it does not seem unfair to place upon the landlord a duty to take those steps which are within his power to minimize the predictable risk to his tenants.

This court has recently had occasion to review landlord-tenant law as applied to multiple family urban dwellings. In Javins v. First National Realty Corporation,[1] the traditional analysis of a lease as being a conveyance of an interest in land—with all the medieval connotations this often brings—was reappraised, and found lacking in several respects. This court noted that the value of the lease to the modern apartment dweller is that it gives him "a well known package of goods and services—a package which includes not merely walls and ceilings, but also adequate heat, light and ventilation, serviceable plumbing facilities, *secure windows and doors*, proper sanitation, and proper maintenance." It does not give him the land itself, and to the tenant as a practical matter this is supremely unimportant. Speaking for the court, Judge Wright then went on to state, "In our judgment the trend toward treating leases as contracts is wise and well considered. Our holding in this case reflects a belief that leases of urban dwelling units should be interpreted and construed like any other contract."

Treating the modern day urban lease as a contract, this court in *Javins*, supra, recognized, among other things, that repair of the leased premises in a multiple dwelling unit may require access to equipment in areas in the control of the landlord, and skills which no urban tenant possesses. Accordingly, this court delineated the landlord's duty to repair as including continued maintenance of the rented apartment throughout the term of the lease, rightfully placing the duty to maintain the premises upon the party to the lease contract having the capacity to do so, based upon an implied warranty of habitability.[2]

In the case at bar we place the duty of taking protective measures guarding the entire premises and the areas peculiarly under the landlord's control against the perpetration of criminal acts upon the landlord, the party to the lease contract who has the effective capacity to perform these necessary acts.

As a footnote to *Javins*, supra, Judge Wright, in clearing away some of the legal underbrush from medieval common law obscuring the modern landlord-tenant relationship, referred to an innkeeper's liability in comparison with that of the landlord to his tenant. "Even the old common law courts responded with a different rule for a landlord-tenant relationship which did not conform to the model of the usual agrarian

1. 138 U.S.App.D.C. 369, 428 F.2d 1071 (1970).

2. The landlord's duty to repair was held to include the leased premises in Whetzel v. Jess Fisher Management Co., 108 U.S.App.D.C. 385, 282 F.2d 943 (1960). In that case, we held that the Housing Regulations altered the old common law rule, and further, that the injured tenant had a cause of action in *tort* against the landlord for his failure to discharge his duty to repair the premises. Our recent decision in Kanelos v. Kettler, 132 U.S.App. D.C. 133, 406 F.2d 951 (1968), reaffirms the position taken in Whetzel.

lease. Much more substantial obligations were placed upon the keepers of inns (the only multiple dwelling houses known to the common law)."

Specifically, innkeepers have been held liable for assaults which have been committed upon their guests by third parties, if they have breached a duty which is imposed by reason of the innkeeper-guest relationship. By this duty, the innkeeper is generally bound to exercise reasonable care to protect the guest from abuse or molestation from third parties, be they innkeeper's employees, fellow guests, or intruders, if the attack could, or in the exercise of reasonable care, should have been anticipated.[3]

Liability in the innkeeper-guest relationship is based as a matter of law either upon the innkeeper's supervision, care, or control of the premises, or by reason of a contract which some courts have implied from the entrustment by the guest of his personal comfort and safety to the innkeeper. In the latter analysis, the contract is held to give the guest the right to expect a standard of treatment at the hands of the innkeeper which includes an obligation on the part of the latter to exercise reasonable care in protecting the guest.

Other relationships in which similar duties have been imposed include landowner-invitee, businessman-patron, employer-employee, school district-pupil, hospital-patient, and carrier-passenger. In all, the theory of liability is essentially the same: that since the ability of one of the parties to provide for his own protection has been limited in some way by his submission to the control of the other, a duty should be imposed upon the one possessing control (and thus the power to act) to take reasonable precautions to protect the other one from assaults by third parties which, at least, could reasonably have been anticipated. However, there is no liability normally imposed upon the one having the power to act if the violence is sudden and unexpected provided that the source of the violence is not an employee of the one in control.

We are aware of various cases in other jurisdictions following a different line of reasoning, conceiving of the landlord and tenant relationship along more traditional common law lines, and on varying fact situations reaching a different result from that we reach here. Typical of these is a much cited (although only a 4–3) decision of the Supreme Court of New Jersey, Goldberg v. Housing Authority of Newark, supra relied on by appellee landlord here. There the court said:

> Everyone can foresee the commission of crime virtually anywhere and at any time. If foreseeability itself gave rise to a duty to provide "police" protection for others, every residential curtilage, every shop, every store, every manufacturing plant would have to be patrolled by the private arm of the owner. And since hijacking and attack upon occupants of motor vehicles are also foreseeable, it would be the duty of every motorist to provide armed protection for his passengers and the property of others. Of course, none of this is at all palatable.

3. An excellent discussion of the innkeeper's duty to his guest, including citations to relevant case material, is found in: Annot., 70 A.L.R.2d 621 (1960).

This language seems to indicate that the court was using the word *foreseeable* interchangeably with the word *possible*. In that context, the statement is quite correct. It would be folly to impose liability for mere possibilities. But we must reach the question of liability for attacks which are foreseeable in the sense that they are *probable* and *predictable*. Thus, the United States Supreme Court, in Lillie v. Thompson encountered no difficulty in finding that the defendant-employer was liable to the employee because it "was aware of conditions which created a likelihood" of criminal attack.

In the instant case, the landlord had notice, both actual and constructive, that the tenants were being subjected to crimes against their persons and their property in and from the common hallways. For the period just prior to the time of the assault upon appellant Kline the record contains unrefuted evidence that the apartment building was undergoing a rising wave of crime. Under these conditions, we can only conclude that the landlord here "was aware of conditions which created a likelihood" (actually, almost a certainty) that further criminal attacks upon tenants would occur.

Upon consideration of all pertinent factors, we find that there is a duty of protection owed by the landlord to the tenant in an urban multiple unit apartment dwelling.

Summarizing our analysis, we find that this duty of protection arises, first of all, from the logic of the situation itself. If we were answering without the benefit of any prior precedent the issue as posed by the appellee landlord here, "whether a duty should be placed on a landlord to take steps to protect tenants from foreseeable criminal acts committed by third parties," we should have no hesitancy in answering it affirmatively, at least on the basis of the facts of this case.

As between tenant and landlord, the landlord is the only one in the position to take the necessary acts of protection required. He is not an insurer, but he is obligated to minimize the risk to his tenants. Not only as between landlord and tenant is the landlord best equipped to guard against the predictable risk of intruders, but even as between landlord and the police power of government, the landlord is in the best position to take the necessary protective measures. Municipal police cannot patrol the entryways and the hallways, the garages and the basements of private multiple unit apartment dwellings. They are neither equipped, manned, nor empowered to do so. In the area of the predictable risk which materialized in this case, only the landlord could have taken measures which might have prevented the injuries suffered by appellant.

We note that in the fight against crime the police are not expected to do it all; every segment of society has obligations to aid in law enforcement and to minimize the opportunities for crime. The average citizen is ceaselessly warned to remove keys from automobiles and, in this jurisdiction, may be liable in tort for any injury caused in the operation of his car by a thief if he fails to do so, notwithstanding the intervening criminal act of the thief, a third party. Gaither v. Myers, 131 U.S.App. D.C. 216, 404 F.2d 216 (1968). In addition, auto manufacturers are per-

suaded to install special locking devices and buzzer alarms, and real estate developers, residential communities, and industrial areas are asked
to install especially bright lights to deter the criminally inclined. It is
only just that the obligations of landlords in their sphere be acknowledged and enforced.

Secondly, on the rationale of this court in Levine v. Katz, Kendall v.
Gore Properties, and Javins v. First National Realty Corporation, supra,
there is implied in the contract between landlord and tenant an obligation on the landlord to provide those protective measures which are
within his reasonable capacity. Here the protective measures which
were in effect in October 1959 when appellant first signed a lease were
drastically reduced. She continued after the expiration of the first term
of the lease on a month to month tenancy. As this court pointed out in
Javins, supra, "Since the lessees continue to pay the same rent, they
were entitled to expect that the landlord would continue to keep the
premises in their beginning condition during the lease term. It is precisely such expectations that the law now recognizes as deserving of
formal, legal protection."

Thirdly, if we reach back to seek the precedents of common law, on
the question of whether there exists or does not exist a duty on the
owner of the premises to provide protection against criminal acts by
third parties, the most analogous relationship to that of the modern day
urban apartment house dweller is not that of a landlord and tenant, but
that of innkeeper and guest. We can also consider other relationships,
cited above, in which an analogous duty has been found to exist.

IV

We now turn to the standard of care which should be applied in judging if the landlord has fulfilled his duty of protection to the tenant. Although in many cases the language speaks as if the standard of care
itself varies, in the last analysis the standard of care is the same—reasonable care in all the circumstances. The specific measures to achieve
this standard vary with the individual circumstances. It may be impossible to describe in detail for all situations of landlord-tenant relationships, and evidence of custom amongst landlords of the same class of
building may play a significant role in determining if the standard has
been met.

In the case at bar, appellant's repeated efforts to introduce evidence
as to the standard of protection commonly provided in apartment buildings of the same character and class as 1500 Massachusetts Avenue at
the time of the assault upon Miss Kline were invariably frustrated by
the objections of opposing counsel and the impatience of the trial judge.
At one point during appellant's futile attempts the judge commented
with respect to the degree of proof required to show a custom: "I think
the old proverb that one swallow does not make a summer applies. If
you can get 100 swallows, you say this must be summertime."

Later, but still during appellant's efforts on this point, the judge commented to opposing counsel,

[M]ay I remind you that it is very dangerous to win a case by excluding the other side's testimony because the Court of Appeals might say that testimony should have been admitted even though you might have won the case with the testimony in.

Appellant then attempted to offer evidence of individual apartment houses with which she was familiar. The trial judge became impatient with the swallow by swallow approach, and needled by opposing counsel's objections, disregarded his own admonition and cut short appellant's efforts in this direction. The record as to custom is thus unsatisfactory but its deficiencies are directly chargeable to defendant's counsel and the trial judge, not appellant.

We therefore hold in this case that the applicable standard of care in providing protection for the tenant is that standard which this landlord himself was employing in October 1959 when the appellant became a resident on the premises at 1500 Massachusetts Avenue. The tenant was led to expect that she could rely upon this degree of protection. While we do not say that the precise measures for security which were then in vogue should have been kept up (e.g., the number of people at the main entrances might have been reduced if a tenant-controlled intercom-automatic latch system had been installed in the common entryways), we do hold that the same relative degree of security should have been maintained.

The appellant tenant was entitled to performance by the landlord measured by this standard of protection whether the landlord's obligation be viewed as grounded in contract or in tort. As we have pointed out, this standard of protection was implied as an obligation of the lease contract from the beginning. Likewise on a tort basis, this standard of protection may be taken as that commonly provided in apartments of this character and type in this community, and this is a reasonable standard of care on which to judge the conduct of the landlord here.

V

Given this duty of protection, and the standard of care as defined, it is clear that the appellee landlord breached its duty toward the appellant tenant here. The risk of criminal assault and robbery on any tenant was clearly predictable, a risk of which the appellee landlord had specific notice, a risk which became reality with increasing frequency, and this risk materialized on the very premises peculiarly under the control, and therefore the protection, of the landlord to the injury of the appellant tenant. The question then for the District Court becomes one of damages only. To us the liability is clear.

Having said this, it would be well to state what is *not* said by this decision. We do not hold that the landlord is by any means an insurer of the safety of his tenants. His duty is to take those measures of protection which are within his power and capacity to take, and which can reasonably be expected to mitigate the risk of intruders assaulting and robbing tenants. The landlord is not expected to provide protection commonly owed by a municipal police department; but as illustrated in this case, he is obligated to protect those parts of his premises which are not usually subject to periodic patrol and inspection by the municipal police. We do not say that every multiple unit apartment house in the District of Columbia should have those same measures of protection which 1500 Massachusetts Avenue enjoyed in 1959, nor do we say that 1500 Massachusetts Avenue should have precisely those same measures in effect at the present time. Alternative and more up-to-date methods may be equally or even more effective.

Granted, the discharge of this duty of protection by landlords will cause, in many instances, the expenditure of large sums for additional equipment and services, and granted, the cost will be ultimately passed on to the tenant in the form of increased rents. This prospect, in itself, however, is no deterrent to our acknowledging and giving force to the duty, since without protection the tenant already pays in losses from theft, physical assault and increased insurance premiums.

The landlord is entirely justified in passing on the cost of increased protective measures to his tenants, but the rationale of compelling the landlord to do it in the first place is that he is the only one who is in a position to take the necessary protective measures for overall protection of the premises, which he owns in whole and rents in part to individual tenants.

Reversed and remanded to the District Court for the determination of damages.

MacKINNON, Circuit Judge (dissenting):

I respectfully dissent from the panel decision that the plaintiff has proved liability as a matter of law. My inability to join in that disposition of the case is based primarily in my disagreement as to what facts were proved at the trial of that issue by the court without a jury. In my view the panel opinion errs by overstating the facts which might be construed as being favorable to appellant and by failing to recognize gross deficiencies in appellant's proof, thereby applying a more strict standard of responsibility to the landlord than the opinion actually states to be the law. * * *

Notes

1. In Sherman v. Concourse Realty Corp., 47 A.D.2d 134, 365 N.Y.S.2d 239 (1975), the lessor of a multiple dwelling building failed to repair a defective lobby door lock. The plaintiff tenant was assaulted in the lobby by an intruder. The trial court denied recovery of damages on the ground that the lessor's negligence was not the proximate cause of the injury. This judgment was reversed. The court referred to the fact that the lessor had agreed, in consideration of increased rents, to install a protective buzzer system, and also referred to evidence of prior crimes in the building. Foreseeability of the injury was stressed. The court said that probable cause is a policy decision determining how far removed an effect may be from its cause for the actor nevertheless to be liable. *Kline* was cited with approval, although the court said it was not reaching the issue decided in that case. What was the issue in *Kline*?

See also Johnston v. Harris, 387 Mich. 569, 198 N.W.2d 409 (1972).

2.   In Scott v. Watson, 278 Md. 160, 359 A.2d 548 (1976), the court responded to three certified questions. (1) Does Maryland law impose on a lessor of an
urban apartment complex a duty to protect tenants from criminal acts of third
parties in common areas? The answer was "No." (2) If there is not such duty
generally, would such a duty be imposed if the lessor has knowledge of increasing criminal activity in the premises or in the immediate neighborhood? The
answer was that if a lessor knows or should know of criminal activity in common areas, he has a duty to take reasonable measures to eliminate conditions
contributing to criminal activity. Such a duty does not arise from knowledge of
criminal activity in the neighborhood. (3) In response to a third question, the
court declared that probable cause was vital, but relied on cases from other
jurisdictions for a notion of "enhancement of risk" by the lessor's conduct. In
other words, a breach of duty results in liability only if the breach enhanced the
likelihood that this particular criminal activity would occur. Restatement,
Torts, Second § 448 was accepted.

3.   In Samson v. Saginaw Professional Building, 393 Mich. 393, 224 N.W.2d
843 (1975), the owner of an office building was found liable for negligence in
renting premises to a mental clinic without making a reasonable effort to protect other tenants and their employees from foreseeable criminal acts by the
client's patients. See also Note, The Duty of a Landlord to Exercise Reasonable Care in the Selection and Retention of Tenants, 30 Stan.L.Rev. 725 (1978),
where the author proposes a broader standard of liability for landlords than
that declared in the *Samson* case.

4.   Of the courts in which the problem has arisen since *Kline*, only Illinois
has refused to extend traditional tort liability to impose a duty on landlords
respecting criminal intrusions on leased premises. See Phillips v. Chicago
Housing Authority, 91 Ill.App.3d 544, 47 Ill.Dec. 17, 414 N.E.2d 1133 (1981);
Pippin v. Chicago Housing Authority, 78 Ill.2d 204, 35 Ill.Dec. 530, 399 N.E.2d
596 (1979); Cross v. Wells Fargo Alarm Services, 82 Ill.2d 313, 45 Ill.Dec. 121,
412 N.E.2d 472 (1980). Liability has been imposed where a landlord undertakes
to provide security but does so negligently. There are possibly other unidenti-
fied exceptions. See Stribling v. Chicago Housing Authority, 34 Ill.App.3d 551,
340 N.E.2d 47 (1975).

The California appellate courts seem to be moving from resistance to the
notion that a special relationship exists between landlord and tenant like the
innkeeper-guest relation to an acceptance of the idea as the basis for a duty to
act. Compare Totten v. More Oakland Residential Housing, Inc., 63 Cal.App.3d
538, 134 Cal.Rptr. 29 (1977), with Kwaitkowsky v. Superior Trading Co., 123
Cal.App.3d 324, 176 Cal.Rptr. 494 (1981).

At the other extreme from the Illinois position, the New Jersey court has
declared a duty on landlords to provide reasonable security from the risk of
criminal activities, which is defined not to require any proof of knowledge by a
landlord of any risks, nor that a plaintiff shall have given notice of any unsafe
condition. Trentacost v. Brussel, 82 N.J. 214, 412 A.2d 436 (1980). This startling position, which approaches strict liability for injuries caused by criminal
intrusions, has not appeared elsewhere, except perhaps in a federal court in
Kansas. Flood v. Wisconsin Real Estate Investment Trust, 503 F.Supp. 1157
(D.Kan.1980). Such a view is founded on the assumption that if an implied
warranty of habitability is declared in leases, a breach of warranty, for tort
purposes, requires no proof of negligence. As we have seen, and as explicitly
provided in the Restatement (Second) of Property (Landlord and Tenant) § 17.6,
such an assumption is not necessary and perhaps not desirable. Compare Feld

v. Merriam, ___ Pa.Super. ___, 461 A.2d 225, 232 (1983), where the court in stating a requirement of reasonable care, also said, "a plaintiff must present evidence showing that the landlord had notice of criminal activity which posed risk of harm to his tenants, that he had the means to take precautions to protect the tenant against this risk of harm, and that his failure to do so was the proximate cause of the tenant's injuries." The court also dealt at length with standards for imposing both compensatory and punitive damages, and affirmed the imposition of both in this case, which totaled $3,500,000 in favor of one of the plaintiffs.

SECTION 6. PROTECTION OF TENANTS' ECONOMIC BENEFITS

KULAWITZ v. PACIFIC WOODENWARE & PAPER CO.

Supreme Court of California, 1945.
25 Cal.2d 664, 155 P.2d 24.

SHENK, Justice. This is an appeal by the defendant from a judgment in its favor on a cross-complaint in an action in which the plaintiff sought the rescission of a lease.

The defendant leased store premises in a building owned by it in Oakland, to the plaintiff for a term of four years from July 1, 1938, at a minimum monthly rental of $350. The lease provided that the premises were to be used for the conduct of a general furniture business exclusively, and the lessee agreed not to allow any sale of property by auction on the premises except upon retiring from business. The defendant as lessor covenanted that during the term of the lease it would not let or permit occupation of any other space or storeroom in the same building "for the purpose of conducting therein a furniture store." The lease also provided that should the lessee abandon or vacate the premises during the term of the lease the lessor might at his option without notice to the lessee relet the premises, and the lessee should satisfy any deficiency between the amount realized from the reletting and the amount of the rents reserved.

The lessee took possession and conducted a general furniture business until January, 1941, when, because of illness, he became unable to give his personal attention to the business. He held an auction sale and retired from the conduct of the furniture business on the leased premises. He turned over the keys to the defendant's renting agent with instructions to find a tenant and if necessary at a rental of as much as $100 per month less than that provided in the lease. A tenant was not found. The plaintiff did not pay the rent for February, March or April, but prior to April 18, 1941, commenced to clean and restock the store in preparation for a reopening for business. While making these preparations he observed a sign on an adjoining store in the same building that it would open on May 1st for the sale of carpets, rugs and linoleum. On April 2d the defendant had let the adjoining store to one Smith on a month to month basis commencing May 1, 1941, for the specified purpose of conducting therein the "sale of linoleum and kindred products." On April 21st the plaintiff gave the lessor a telephonic notice of the claimed breach of the restrictive covenant in the lease, and on April 24th he served written notice that competition in the same building in the important items of "carpets, rugs and linoleum" would constitute a difference between a net profit and a definite loss in his conduct of the furniture business in the same building; that the breach of the covenant went to the essence of the lease agreement; that he would no longer be bound by the provisions of the lease; and that since the telephonic communication of April 21st, he had removed his stock of furniture from and had given up the possession of the premises. On April 29th the lessor replied by letter stating that it denied any breach of the restrictive covenant; that the lessee had "retired" from the furniture business; that the claimed breach was a mere pretext, and that it would continue to hold the lessee to the performance of the lease provisions. The Smith tenancy for the sale of linoleum and kindred products continued and was in existence at the time of trial.

In October, 1941, the plaintiff filed his complaint for rescission. Various amended and supplemental cross-complaints were filed by the defendant by which it sought recovery of unpaid rentals for the full unexpired term. They will be referred to as the cross-complaint. By his answer to the cross-complaint the plaintiff admitted that rental was due to May 1, 1941, offered to pay the same, and alleged defensive matter to prevent the recovery of rentals for the remainder of the term by reason of his eviction from the leased premises by the defendant.

The trial court found the facts as above stated, and denied to the plaintiff any relief on his complaint. As to the issues raised by the cross-complaint and the plaintiff's answer thereto, the court concluded that the defendant had violated the restrictive covenant in a substantial respect, that the lease had terminated as of May 1, 1941, and that the defendant was entitled to recover only the unpaid rentals due to that date. The defendant had judgment accordingly.

On the appeal the defendant contends that the plaintiff was not entitled to a declaration that the lease had terminated and be relieved of his obligation to pay rentals for the full term when he was himself in default in the payment of prior rental under the lease; that the plaintiff's "retirement" from the conduct of the furniture business on the leased premises in January, 1941, rendered the lessor's restrictive covenant inoperative; that before the defendant could be placed in default of the restrictive covenant it was entitled to reasonable notice to afford an opportunity to remove the source of the objection; and that the evidence does not support the finding of a substantial breach of the restrictive covenant.

The plaintiff, being in default under the lease, was not entitled to rescind without curing his default by tendering the amount due to the time of the claimed breach by the lessor. Breach of the restrictive covenant would not entitle the plaintiff to escape his obligation to pay that portion of the rentals which had accrued to the date of the alleged breach and which he was bound to pay. His notice was not accompanied by payment of that portion of the obligation which was incontrovertibly due. He therefore had not effected rescission of the lease and the trial court correctly concluded that he was not entitled to prevail on his complaint. Civ.Code, § 1691. * * * The question of the correctness of the trial court's findings and conclusions is therefore resolved by a consideration of the issues raised by the defendant's cross-complaint and the plaintiff's answer thereto.

A covenant not to let other premises in the lessor's property or permit their use for certain purposes during the existence of the lease with the covenantee is binding and a breach thereof entitles the lessee to terminate the lease. Medico-Dental Bldg. Co. v. Horton & Converse, 21 Cal.2d 411, 132 P.2d 457; University Club v. Deakin, 265 Ill. 257, 106 N.E. 790, L.R.A.1915C, 804; Hiatt Inv. Co. v. Buehler, 225 Mo.App. 151, 16 S.W.2d 219. The result in such cases is based on the rule that the condition broken by the covenantor excuses performance by the covenantee. That rule applies ordinarily without the express intention of the parties, in cases of agreed exchange, such as Cameron v. Burnham, 146 Cal. 580, 80 P. 929, and Rathbun v. Security Mfg. Co., 82 Cal.App. 793, 256 P. 296. See Rest., Contracts, §§ 266, 397; Cal.Ann., pp. 143, 226. For historical or other reasons it was not made applicable to leases, unless by the intention of the parties, expressed or necessarily implied, performance by one was conditioned upon performance by the other. (See Rest., Contracts, § 290; Cal.Ann., pp. 155–156.) Therefore breach or failure to perform by a party to a lease is not a defense unless the covenant broken was a condition precedent to performance by the party defending. Alderson v. Houston, 154 Cal. 1, 96 P. 884; Civ. Code, § 1439; 6 Cal.Jur. 489.

In this case performance of the restrictive covenant by the lessor was essential to the beneficial enjoyment of the property by the lessee for the purposes intended. It was therefore a condition precedent to the lessee's performance, and breach thereof may be said to amount to a constructive eviction of the lessee and was found to be such by the trial court. Any interference by the landlord by which the tenant is deprived of the beneficial enjoyment of the premises amounts to a constructive eviction if the tenant so elects and surrenders possession, and the tenant will not be liable for rentals for the portion of the term following his eviction. * * *

Default by the lessee in the payment of rentals does not waive the lessor's performance of the restrictive covenant unless the lease provides expressly or by necessary implication that performance thereof depends upon the payment of rentals. No such provision or intention appears from the agreement here involved. Under this lease the result flowing from the nonpayment of the rent gave to the lessor only the right to the rent or at his option to a termination of the lease. If he did not exercise the option the lease continued in existence. So long as the lease continued in existence the lessor was bound not to interfere with the beneficial enjoyment of the premises by the lessee for the purposes intended. Therefore upon the lessee's default in the payment of rent the lessor could at its option have terminated the lease; but as it elected to consider the lease in force it was bound to an observance of its covenant. Standard Livestock Co. v. Pentz, 204 Cal. 618, 269 P. 645, 62 A.L.R. 1239.

The lessee's "retirement" sale in January, 1941, did not release the lessor from that covenant. The lease term was an estate in lands vested in the lessee. His "retirement" sale did not constitute a surrender nor an offer to surrender the leasehold. In fact the conduct of the parties indisputably showed their intention to consider the lease as continuing. The lessee sought to sublet the premises through the lessor's agent and to discharge his obligation for any deficiency in rentals. The lessor at all times unmistakably indicated its intention to treat the lease as in existence until the expiration of the stipulated term. There is no evidence of abandonment by the lessee by virtue of the "retirement" sale nor of acceptance of any such abandonment by the lessor. The lessee's title continued and he had a right to resume possession at any time until the expiration of the term, and the lessor had no right to interfere with his dominion and control. Welcome v. Hess, 90 Cal. 507, 27 P. 369, 25 Am.St.Rep. 145. The foregoing considerations render inapplicable cases such as M.M. Ullman & Co. v. Levy, 172 La. 79, 133 So. 369, where, on the lessor's sale of the goodwill of a business, his agreement not to engage in the same business in the vicinity for a specfied number of years was held ineffective after the termination of the lease period and the tenant's retirement from business prior to the expiration of the agreed term of restraint.

The evidence in the present case is that the lessee surrendered possession of the premises when he gave to the lessor the notice dated April 24, 1941. Upon surrender of possession by the lessee before the expiration of the lease term, the lessor had three remedies: (1) To consider the lease as still in existence and sue for the unpaid rent as it became due for the unexpired portion of the term; (2) to treat the lease as terminated and retake possession for its own account; or (3) to retake possession for the lessee's account and relet the premises, holding the lessee for the difference between the lease rentals and what it was able in good faith to procure by reletting. * * * The defendant followed the first course. It filed a cross-complaint by which it sought to recover rentals unpaid to the expiration of the lease term. It successfully resisted the plaintiff's claim of rescission inasmuch as the defendant's breach did not excuse the plaintiff's liability for rentals due prior thereto (Civ.Code, § 1511, subd. 3), and the plaintiff had failed to discharge his liability. But the defendant's breach placed it in a position of being unable to resist successfully defensive matter interposed to its own action. It could not compel a performance which depended upon performance of its own broken covenant. When, upon the constructive eviction by the lessor, the lessee exercised his right to terminate the lease and surrender possession of the premises, the result was a constructive reentry by the landlord. All issues between the parties were thus set at rest with the exception of the single issue of the liability of the lessee for unpaid rentals to the date of reentry. * * *

But, complains the defendant, the plaintiff has in effect received the relief sought by his complaint. This as a legal proposition is not so. In such a case the lessee has a choice of several remedies: he may rescind and become absolved from further payment of rentals; he may continue under the lease and sue for loss of profits; or he may treat the violation as putting an end to the lease for the purposes of performance and sue for damages. Medico-Dental Bldg. Co. v. Horton & Converse, supra, 21 Cal.2d at page 434, 132 P.2d 457; Hiatt Inv. Co. v. Buehler, supra, 16 S.W.2d at page 226. Here the plaintiff ineffectually sought the first named remedy. The fact that he failed to establish his right to rescission did not preclude him from any other relief that might be open to him. The rule that a party is not to be denied relief because he has mistaken his remedy is applicable in such a case. Agar v. Winslow, supra, 123 Cal. at page 591, 56 P.2d 422, 69 Am.St.Rep. 84. The plaintiff may not be denied a lawful defense against an unjust claim for rentals because he misconceived his right to rescission. Here the court has merely given effect to the plaintiff's treatment of the lessor's violation of the restrictive covenant as putting an end to the lease for purposes of performance. * * *

In its answer to the plaintiff's complaint the defendant affirmatively admitted that its covenant not to let any space in the same building for use as a furniture store was a material and essential part of the agreement and of the inducement and consideration therefore, without which the plaintiff would not have entered into the lease. Its contention, however, that the breach of the covenant was in an immaterial respect and that the plaintiff was not entitled to abandon the lease for such a trivial cause is not supported by the record. A breach of a covenant not to permit a similar sales business to be conducted occurs if but one of several classes of articles is permitted to be sold by the competitor. * * * The trial court found on sufficient evidence that linoleum and kindred products constituted a big item in the furniture business; that such products were sold at the plaintiff's furniture store, and that competition in that respect would result in serious losses to him.

This court said in Medico-Dental Bldg. Co. v. Horton & Converse, supra, 21 Cal.2d at page 428, 132 P.2d 457, that in measuring the breach of such a covenant in a case where the objectionable competition is in connection with a business different from that of the lessee who is entitled to protection from the lessor, technical subterfuges would be disregarded and the substance of the situation would determine the issue. Even considering the businesses here involved to be of such different character, the defendant's claim of pretext is not supported, in view of the trial court's findings on sufficient evidence that the sale of linoleum and kindred products constituted an important item in the furniture business and that the plaintiff was preparing to reopen his furniture store on the leased premises at the time of the defendant's breach. Here, as in the Horton & Converse case, the covenant was of such character that its contemplated breach would defeat the entire object of the lease, render further occupancy a matter of continued financial loss, and therefore in effect destroy the consideration for the lease. The sufficiency of the evidence in these respects, the surrender of the premises by the plaintiff following his notice to the defendant, the latter's immediate denial of the breach in response thereto and its refusal to take any action thereon except to hold the plaintiff to his lease and at the same time collect the rents from Smith, were justification under the law for the trial court's conclusion that the lease had been terminated. As we said in University Club v. Deakin, supra, 106 N.E. at page 792, if the lessor chose to ignore the provision of the contract it did so at the risk of the lessee's exercising his right to terminate the lease and surrender possession of the premises.

Other contentions of the parties need not be discussed.

The judgment is affirmed.

SCHAUER, Justice (dissenting). I dissent. The majority opinion, in my view, transgresses fundamental rules of both law and equity. It sets a precedent which certainly is potentially inimical to the interest of every owner of income property in California of a class similar to that here involved and, by reason of the character of the rules which are breached, may well affect other types of income property. Briefly, the majority opinion grants equitable relief—full release from the executory obligation to pay rent, evidenced by a written lease—to a defaulting tenant who had abandoned the leased premises had failed to pay the rent, and had unconditionally renounced his obligations under the lease while the lessor was in no way in default.

The grounds upon which the majority place their conclusion are: (1) that the lessor breached a restrictive covenant to protect the lessee against competition in the same building by renting an adjoining store in that building for a somewhat similar business *after the lessee had retired from his business, had ceased paying rent, and had abandoned the premises*, and (2) that by so renting the adjoining store the lessor either constructively evicted the tenant or accepted his abandonment of the lease and released him from his obligations thereunder.
* * *

As to the suggestion that the lessor constructively evicted the tenant after the tenant had previously abandoned the premises and unconditionally renounced his obligations under the lease, it seems to me that the very statement of the proposition sufficiently exposes its infirmity. How can a tenant be evicted from that which he has already abandoned? And the contention that defendant accepted the tenant's abandonment of the premises and released him from his obligations under the lease by renting an adjoining store for a somewhat similar business *after the tenant had ceased doing business and had abandoned the premises and renounced his obligations*, seems likewise devoid of merit in law and justice, * * *.

[The concurring opinion of Carter, J., has been omitted. Justice Carter concurred in the result on the ground that the conduct of the parties constituted a surrender by operation of law.]

Notes

1. Cal.Civ.Code (West's Anno.) § 1691, on which the court relied to deny the plaintiff the right to rescind the lease, provides that a party entitled to re-

scind a contract must give notice of rescission to the party as to whom he rescinds and restore to him everything of value which has been received from him under the contract or offer to restore on condition that the other party do likewise.

The word "rescission," as used in respect to leases, is often misleading. In contracts law generally, rescission may mean a mutual agreement by the parties which discharges or terminates all rights and duties. In such cases questions may be left about the scope of the rescission; for example, about the effect of rescission after part performance. Rescission is also used to refer to a remedy in one party to a contract as a result of a breach of contract by the other party. Assuming that the breach is one which justifies rescission, the term implies not merely a discharge of all unperformed duties, but an undoing of what the parties may have done under the contract, so as to place them in status quo. For obvious equitable reasons, such rescission is associated with principles of restitution. In the case of a sale of goods, for example, upon breach of an express or implied warranty by the seller, a buyer may in certain circumstances rescind, with the purpose (and the duty) of returning the goods to the seller. He may correspondingly have the right to the return of the purchase price already paid by him. It is conceivable, although not likely, that a lessee would resort to such a remedy; that is, he would assert his remedy in proper circumstances by demanding the return of all rent paid by him, but thereby subjecting himself to liability to the lessor for the reasonable value of his actual possession of the premises.

In Kulawitz, when the lessee brought his suit for rescission, the court must have treated his suit as proceeding on this basis. Among the three remedies available to the lessee in the circumstances, the court mentioned rescission as an alternative to treating "the violation as putting an end to the lease for the purposes of performance." The court also invoked the terms of a section of the California Civil Code on the rescission of contracts, cited above, which requires that the rescinding party restore or offer to restore everything of value which he has received under the contract. Since the lessee was in default in the payment of rent, the court held that he could not maintain his suit for rescission.

This is not the meaning of rescission as it is commonly used by courts in lease cases. Under other principles of general contract law, certain promises by one party to a contract may be treated as dependent or conditional upon performance of one or more promises by the other party. Breach of a promise by one party excuses performance of a dependent or conditional promise by the other party. In many contracts consisting of an exchange of single promises on each side, this explanation is sufficient. But what about contracts which have a variety of promises on each side? What about leases, which may have not only several promises on each side, but in which the lessee receives, in partial consideration for his promise, a conveyance of an estate in the land? It is hardly conceivable that every promise on one side is dependent on every promise on the other side. Is it even permissible to say that a lessee's promise to pay rent is dependent on certain promises by the lessor, if this means that a breach by the lessor excuses the duty to pay rent without affecting any other promise or the continuance of the lessee's estate in the land? These complications are at least a partial explanation for the traditional landlord-tenant doctrine that covenants in leases are independent. Courts which casually talk about abandoning the old rule and adopting the contracts doctrine on dependency of covenants for leases have not sufficiently taken account of the complexities of the problem.

Such difficulties are avoided if, upon breach of a dependent promise in the lease, or one which is vital to the bargain, the injured party is permitted to treat all unperformed duties as terminated or discharged, and the lessee's estate revested in the lessor. The traditional law on constructive eviction can be explained in these terms without resort to the notion of eviction, provided the lessee subjects himself to the consequences of termination, that is, by leaving the premises. In fact where the lessor's breach produces economic rather than physical injuries, as in Kulawitz, it seems peculiarly inappropriate to speak in terms of eviction. This sort of result appears to be what the court in Kulawitz meant by saying that the lessee could treat the lessor's violation "as putting an end to the lease for the purposes of performance." In treating this defense as distinct from a strict rescission, the defense remained available, although rescission was barred. This sort of remedy is what other courts usually have in mind when they speak of the rescission of leases. Compare Charles E. Burt, Inc. v. Seven Grand Corporation, supra p. 398.

Note, however, that Kulawitz stands for the proposition that a defense of constructive eviction or the equivalent is available to a lessee who was himself in default in the payment of rent at the time when the lessor's breach occurred. We have found surprisingly little other authority on that point. See Leider v. 80 William St. Co., 22 App.Div. 952, 255 N.Y.S.2d 999, 1001 (1964); cf. Herstein Co. v. Columbia Pictures Corp., 4 N.Y.2d 117, 172 N.Y.S.2d 808, 149 N.E.2d 328 (1958).

You may wish to re-examine the position taken by Justice Carter in his concurring opinion after you have considered the cases below on the surrender of leases.

2. In Hindquarter Corp. v. Property Development Corp., 95 Wn.2d 809, 631 P.2d 923 (1981), a tenant under a commercial lease sought to exercise an option to renew the term when it was in default in the payment of rent. The tenant was denied a declaratory judgment establishing its right to exercise the option. Although the lease was not explicit on the point, the court found that certain provisions of the lease supported the proposition that the right to exercise the option was impliedly conditioned on the tenant's promise to pay rent. This conclusion was not precluded by the usual explicit provision giving the landlord the right, upon notice, to terminate the lease for a default by the tenant. Although perhaps not necessary to the decision, the court went so far as to say that reciprocal promises generally in leases are inherently dependent, reflecting similar remarks made by courts in regard to increased landlord duties under residential leases. This line of reasoning starts with the proposition that leases are no longer conveyances, but contracts. Then it appears to be assumed that contract law dictates that all covenants on one side are dependent on all the covenants on the other side. Assuming that contract law governs leases, contract law does not dictate any such result.

3. In Teodori v. Werner, 490 Pa. 58, 415 A.2d 31 (1980), a landlord under a commercial lease in a shopping center obtained a confessed judgment against the tenant for default on the payment both of the fixed rent and the specified percentage of gross sales proceeds. The tenant petitioned to open the judgment, arguing violation by the landlord of a "non-competition" clause respecting the use of space in the shopping center for a jewelry or gift shop. The trial court dismissed the tenant's petition. In reversing, the Supreme Court gave three grounds:

(1) An early decision that among a tenant's remedies for a landlord's default on a covenant to provide heat was the retention of possession and deducting from the rent the difference between the rental value of the premises with and

without compliance with the covenant. McDanel v. Mack Realty Co., 315 Pa. 174, 172 A. 97 (1934). The court thought that decision was inconsistent with any independence of covenants doctrine.

(2) Independence of covenants is to be rejected where the landlord's promise to perform "is a significant inducement to the making of the lease by the tenant."

(3) The old law on independence of covenants turned on reliance on property rather than contract law and has no place in modern jurisprudence.

CARTER v. ADLER

California District Court of Appeal, Second District, Division 2, 1956.
138 Cal.App.2d 63, 291 P.2d 111.

MOORE, Presiding Justice. From a judgment declaring that the lease to defendants does prevent plaintiffs (landlords of defendants) from conducting a supermarket on an adjoining parcel for the sale of merchandise specified in the lease to be sold exclusively by defendants, plaintiffs appeal.

Respondents' original lease was in writing, executed by Williams and Keeler under date of August 20, 1951, and the land will be referred to herein as parcel 1. The premises demised to respondents and designated as units 4, 5, 6, 7, 8, 9, 20, 21, 22 and 23 of a larger parcel of realty were owned by Williams and Keeler and are commonly known as "Valley Market Town" located at 6127 Sepulveda Boulevard, Van Nuys, Los Angeles County. Pertinent passages of the lease are as follows:

"2. Use of Premises. The demised premises shall be used for the purpose of conducting therein: Grocery, Delicatessen, Meats, Produce, Fish and Poultry, and for no other purpose without the written consent of Lessors.

"It is understood that Lessees have the exclusive rights on Grocery, Delicatessen, Meats, Produce, Fish and Poultry in Valley Market Town, located at 6127 Sepulveda Boulevard, Van Nuys, City of Los Angeles, County of Los Angeles, State of California. It is understood that the exclusive rights given herein does not forbid any operator in another category of business from handling any product customarily handled in a similar business operated outside of Valley Market Town.   *   *   *

"3. Rental: Lessees agree to pay Lessors One Thousand ($1,000.00) Dollars per month in advance each month during the term hereof.

"Then, when the gross volume of sales in all departments have reached Fifty Thousand ($50,000.00) Dollars in any month, then the rental shall be one and one-fourth (1¼%) per cent only on the gross sales volume of all departments between the amount of Fifty Thousand ($50,000.00) Dollars and One Hundred Thousand ($100,000.00) Dollars in said month.

"Then when the gross sales of all departments combined shall have reached One Hundred Thousand ($100,000.00) Dollars in any month there shall be paid a rental of only one (1%) per cent of the combined total gross sales over One Hundred Thousand ($100,000.00) Dollars until a maximum rental of Twenty-Five Hundred ($2,500.00) Dollars per month shall have been reached. *   *   *

"The term 'gross sales' as used in this lease shall mean the total amount of actual gross charges made by Lessees for all merchandise sold and services performed in or from demised premises, whether for cash or other considerations, or on credit, and regardless of collection in payment of such charges. There shall be deducted however, in computing gross sales for each period, the amount of all sales and excise taxes collected from customers during such period and the amounts of any credits or refunds given for merchandise sold on the premises and returned by customers for credit. *   *   *

"It is hereby agreed by both Lessors and Lessees that if the combined gross volume of sales of the Grocery, Delicatessen, Meats, Produce, Fish and Poultry departments, and any other department covered by this lease and operated by Lessees, falls below the sum of Fifty Thousand ($50,000.00) Dollars gross sales for a period of two (2) months, then, and at that time, *Lessors* shall have the right upon giving a thirty (30) day notice in writing to Lessees to cancel and void this lease and cause to be vacated all property covered by this lease. *   *   *

"6.   A plot plan of what is legally considered Valley Market Town, 6127 Sepulveda Boulevard, Van Nuys, City of Los Angeles, County of Los Angeles, State of California, including the parking area, shall be made a part of this lease. *   *   * ''

The document was prepared entirely by Williams and Keeler.

In November, 1953, appellants entered the scene. They purchased the entire parcel of ground of which the demised premises are a part. At the same time they acquired all the interest of Williams and Keeler under their lease to respondents. Appellants' plans became ambitious. At the same time of their acquisition of parcel 1 and the interest of Williams and Keeler in the lease to respondents, appellants acquired a long-term lease on a large unimproved parcel of realty from Owen Michel and his wife Louise. It is herein referred to as parcel 2. It lies immediately to the north of, and is adjacent to parcel 1. The two parcels adjoin on the west side of Sepulveda Boulevard with a combined frontage of about 842.5 feet and they comprise a total area of 23 acres. Appellant's purpose in acquiring such leasehold was to increase the area of Valley Market Town by the inclusion of both parcels 1 and 2 and to make the entire area known as 6127 Sepulveda Boulevard, Van Nuys, and to operate the total area under the name of "Valley Market Town" or "Mr. Carter's Market Place."

Pursuant to such purpose, during the latter part of 1953 and continuing through March 1954, appellants published and circulated advertising matter announcing their new acquisitions and their plans to develop their combined area into one supermarket under a single name to be selected by the public. Also, they engaged respondents in conferences relating to their master plan and displayed their maps and drawings to demonstrate their new scheme for an integrated market center on parcels 1 and 2. In the course of their conversations, appellants demanded that respondents yield their exclusive rights under the Williams-Keeler lease, in return for which appellants offered to build for respondents a new market building and would promote increased trade by means of competition within Valley Market Town. The negotiations initiated by such conferences continued for a time. At all times, respondents stood firm for some consideration for the waiver of their exclusive rights to sell the merchandise named in their lease within Valley Market Town.

Notwithstanding respondents' refusal to surrender their contractual rights vouchsafed by the original lease, appellants continued to urge their demands while they went forward with the development of their plans for a single integrated market by including both parcels 1 and 2. Not until after appellants' drive for respondents to give up their exclusive rights had failed did appellants suggest the plan of constructing and operating a market on parcel 2 and of "breaking" respondents. Promptly following the latter's refusal to grant the concessions demanded, appellants filed the instant action for declaratory relief. * * *

It requires no Newton to compute that a supermarket operated on parcel 2 adjacent to respondents' premises, selling the entire line of produce, meat, poultry, fish and other items sold by respondents in their Valley Market Town, would be in competition with respondents and would reduce the quantum of the latter's sales. Such fact is common knowledge of which judicial notice is taken. * * * Of course, it could not be questioned that for appellants to set up a commercial establishment in direct competition with their tenants would be a violation of the good faith pledged when Williams and Keeler granted respondents the exclusive right to sell the specified merchandise in Valley Market Town. The mutual covenants of the lease abhor the very suggestion of such conduct as that proposed by appellants. * * *

A restrictive covenant, such as the grant of the exclusive mercantile rights to respondents, is not merely ornamental words inserted to please the eye. It is a living expression of the grantor incorporated in a lease as a consideration for the lessee's faithful performance. Concomitant with such a covenant is the implied obligation of the lessor not to cancel the covenant or derogate from its force by so using his adjoining property as substantially to impair the lessee's enjoyment of the leased premises. * * *

It is generally held that a lease of a portion of a building for specified uses is violated where the lessor subsequently leases to a competitor outside rooms of the same premises, Schmidt v. Hershey, 154 Md. 302, 305, 140 A. 363, 364; where the space named in the subsequent lease had been previously excluded from the lease, Strates v. Keniry, 231 Mass. 426, 429, 121 N.E. 151; where the hotel built an addition to its building, with a door leading through a common wall, and used the new addition for the sale of liquor and cigars, the exclusive right to which had been granted to another by a prior lease, it was held that the building of the addition "was a mere subterfuge to avoid the consequences of the restrictions in the leases. The annex became and is a

component part of the hotel building. * * * When the added structure became an integral part of the block, so constructed and designed
to be such, the covenant, being continuing, should be construed to cover
the block in its entirety, in whatever shape it may be, during the life of
the lease." Shaft v. Carey, 107 Wis. 273, 278, 83 N.W. 288, 290. In a
New York case, after the landlord had leased to one Topol certain premises with a covenant that Topol should have the exclusive right there to
handle specific lines of business, he leased a store to the corporate defendant, one block away from Topol's location in which the corporation
was to conduct a business in competition with Topol. The corporation
had knowledge of the restrictive covenant in Topol's lease. The court
held that the restrictive covenant in the lease should be broadly construed to effectuate the clear intent of the parties to the lease and
would prohibit the lessor from leasing any other store of the lessor in
the entire city block. Topol v. Smoleroff Development Corporation, 264
App.Div. 164, 34 N.Y.S.2d 653, 656.

In addition to the support of the cited decisions, it will be recalled
that the lease at bar was prepared entirely by the original lessors. Under the rule that any uncertainties in the construction of a lease will be
resolved strictly against the lessor who prepared the document, Bell v.
Minor, 88 Cal.App.2d 879, 881, 199 P.2d 718; Lori, Ltd., v. Wolfe, 85 Cal.
App.2d 54, 65, 192 P.2d 112, the only reasonable explanation of the presence in the lease of the grant of exclusive rights is that such covenant
was bargained for by respondents as a necessary part of their transaction. It is easy to see that if the chancellor had not given a broad construction to the lease by reducing the chances for appellants to cancel
the lease on account of the dwindling of respondents' monthly gross
sales below $50,000 for two months in succession, a great injustice
might easily have befallen respondents. The court properly construed
respondents' exclusive rights to sell the specified products in connection
with the clause relating to the cancellation. Civ.Code, § 1641.

The contention that competition is not an issue is to disregard the
presence of the lease as an exhibit. In view of its provision that either
party may terminate the lease in the event that the gross amount of
sales should be less than $50,000 per month for two consecutive months
it cannot be seriously asserted that competition is not an issue. After
finding that parcel 2 would be the situs of appellants' proposed supermarket and that it adjoins parcel 1, occupied by respondents under lease
of August 20, 1951, the court had judicial knowledge that a supermarket on parcel 2 would be a competitor with respondents' market on parcel 1. In addition, evidence was received to the effect appellants had
first declared that if respondents did not give up their exclusive right to
sell the products and groceries granted by their lease, appellants
"would be forced to build another market in competition" with respondents that Mr. Carter had said "he knew of somebody that would go
into that particular market in competition" with respondents.

It was a reasonable inference from the declarations of appellants
that they had a fixed purpose to take over Market Town; to oust respondents by reducing their sales or by some unfair means to deprive

respondents of their exclusive rights to sell the food products granted by their lease and that appellants would undertake the erection of a supermarket on parcel 2 to compete with respondents and to accomplish their purpose.

It is the law that when a tenant occupies a store under a lease which fixes the rental at a minimum rental or a definite percentage of the gross receipts from sales, he cannot avoid liability by diverting his business to another store he operates in the same vicinity, when such diversion is effected for the sole purpose of reducing the amount of the gross sales below a specified sum whereby to lay the basis for a cancellation of the lease. "Such conduct would be in direct violation of the covenant of good faith and fair dealing which exists in every contract." Goldberg 168–05 Corporation v. Levy, 170 Misc. 292, 9 N.Y.S.2d 304, 305, 306. A landlord is governed by the same rule. He cannot by any circumlocution or tergiversation avoid the covenant of good faith which attends him in the performance of his obligations to his lessee. Neither lessee nor lessor can avoid liability for damages where they are operating under a percentage rental lease and either conducts a competing business on adjacent premises, causing a reduction of the gross receipts on the demised premises. Cissna Loan Co. v. Baron, 149 Wash. 386, 390, 270 P. 1022. In an Illinois case, the lessee occupied the premises to operate a gasoline filling station at a rental of $1\frac{1}{4}$ cents for every gallon sold. Although the lease made no provision for a minimum rental and made no covenant not to operate a competing station elsewhere, yet after he had acquired the adjoining lot, and by his operations thereon caused his sales on the leased premises to fall only a few gallons per month, the court scorned his behavior and opined that "the law will not stand by and allow such an evident wrong to be committed without finding some remedy." Seggebruch v. Stosor, 309 Ill.App. 385, 389, 33 N.E.2d 159, 160.

To be justifiable, competition can be only that which is carried on in good faith, not that by which the wrongful party is seeking to gratify his feeling of chagrin, disappointment or hatred for another. Prosser's Law of Torts, p. 751, 2d Edition. Such competition has no rightful place in the commerce of the modern world: the man on the street abhors it, the publicist stands aghast at it and the courts condemn it. Where lessees have undertaken to conduct an honorable, profitable business on the lands of their lessor, the latter will not be permitted to frustrate the mutual purposes of the parties or drive the lessees from the business world. He will not be applauded for either taking advantage of the lessee while operating fairly on the demised premises or for subsequently acquiring adjacent land and operating a cut-throat competition with his lessee.

The authorities urged by appellants: Cousins Investment Co. v. Hastings Clothing Co., 45 Cal.App.2d 141, 113 P.2d 878; Masciotra v. Harlow, 105 Cal.App.2d 376, 233 P.2d 586; Palm v. Mortgage Inv. Co., Tex.Civ.App., 229 S.W.2d 869; Freeport Sulphur Co. v. American Sulphur Royalty Co., 117 Tex. 439, 6 S.W.2d 1039, 60 A.L.R. 890; Hicks v. Whelan Drug Co., 131 Cal.App.2d 110, 280 P.2d 104—are not helpful.

They have to do with the interpretation of percentage rental leases which provided for absolute payment of substantial minimum rentals, where the right of cancellation of the lease was not in issue and where the wrongful conduct of either party in attempting to destroy the lessee's business would fail to effect complete frustration of the original purposes of the parties.

Judgment affirmed.

FOX, J., and ASHBURN, J. pro tem., concur.

Hearing denied; McCOMB, J., not participating.

Notes

1. The reference in Carter v. Adler to the authority of Prosser on Torts is to that author's analysis of tort liability for interference with a prospective economic advantage. This includes certain kinds of competition, such as competition which is malicious in the sense of being intended to injure another, rather than to gain an advantage. Also included is a variety of competitive conduct which is regarded as unfair.

2. In Tabet v. Sprouse-Reitz Co., 75 N.M. 645, 409 P.2d 497 (1966), defendant leased a store building for a rental variety business for a monthly rental of $83 plus 5% of the net retail sales in excess of $20,000 a year. During the term of the lease, plaintiff-lessor built a shopping center in the immediate area and leased a portion of it to another lessee for a type of business identical to defendant's. Thereupon defendant ceased using the leased premises for its business and used them only for storage. Plaintiff sued for damages for defendant's failure to use the premises for its retail business. The trial court directed a verdict for the defendant. This was affirmed on appeal. The court found an implied covenant against plaintiff's leasing of its property for a business which competed with defendant's business, based on the percentage feature of defendant's lease. The court spoke of the existence of a mutual covenant by the parties of extreme good faith in the interpretation and performance of the lease agreement, and relied on Carter v. Adler.

3. In Crest Commercial, Inc. v. Union-Hall, Inc., 104 Ill.App.2d 110, 243 N.E.2d 652 (1968), defendant leased a portion of a shopping center owned by plaintiff. The case does not indicate what rent defendant agreed to pay. The lease prohibited plaintiff from leasing "any of the shopping center area to a business that substantially competes with" defendant's business. The lease defined the shopping center for the purposes of the lease as consisting of certain parcels of land designated as Parcel A, Parcel B, and Parcel C. A year after the lease was made, plaintiff acquired Parcel D, which was adjacent to Parcel B. Plaintiff developed this parcel and proposed to lease it for a purpose which would compete with defendant's business. When the parties to the lease in question were unable to agree that no violation would occur, plaintiff sued for a declaratory judgment authorizing the proposed second lease. The court affirmed a judgment of the trial court that the restrictive covenant in defendant's lease did not apply to the proposed lease. The court relied on the principle that restrictive covenants are to be strictly construed. Carter v. Adler and other cases were distinguished. The court said, "Many of these cases turn on the good faith of the parties. A tenant is deluded into believing himself protected and then the center is expanded to evade the restriction. We cannot presume bad faith and there is nothing in the record before us from which such a conclusion can be drawn." Recognizing that this was a special problem in respect to

shopping centers, the court said further, "We recognize the problem presented but the defendant could have avoided any difficulty by simply drawing the lease to cover the shopping center as it then existed and as it might exist at any time in the future. The parties clearly expressed themselves in the lease. This court has no right to re-make their agreement."

4. Suppose in similar circumstances a lease provides: "It is * * * understood and agreed between the Lessors and Lessee * * * that no other supermarket, grocery, meat or vegetable market will be permitted to occupy space on the adjacent property owned by the Lessors during the term of this lease or the renewals herein granted." The lessee's supermarket was the sole mercantile establishment in the development when the lease was made. Thereafter lessors further developed the center on land owned by them when the lease was made. Still later lessors extended the center to other land acquired by them thereafter. Lessors leased a portion of this land for a business which was in competition with the original lessee's business. Lessee sued to enjoin the use of this land for other food markets. What should be the result? See Great Atlantic & Pacific Tea Co. v. Bailey, 421 Pa. 540, 220 A.2d 1 (1966).

5. **Implied Covenant of Continued Operation.** The wide use of percentage leases, that is, leases providing for rent in the form of a percentage of sales, income, etc., has created the problem of a tenant who ceases or reduces his business operations on leased premises without surrendering possession or seeking termination of the lease. In the absence of inconsistent language in a lease, an implied covenant of continued business operation came to be recognized by the courts. Usually a percentage lease will contain a minimum fixed rental. The question then arose whether the presence of the duty to pay at least a fixed rent precluded the implication of a covenant of continued operation. No single or simple answer can be given. It seems to depend largely on the adequacy of the fixed rent, that is, the extent to which the fixed rent departs from the fair rental value of the premises. Several recent decisions may be noted.

In The Kroger Co. v. The Bonny Corp., 134 Ga.App. 834, 216 S.E.2d 341 (1975), the implication of a covenant was denied where it appeared that such a covenant had been expressly included in another lease by the same lessor in the same shopping center. In Continental Oil Co. v. Bradley, 198 Colo. 331, 602 P.2d 1 (1979), the Colorado court, in addressing the question for the first time, found an implied covenant. The percentage lease merely stated that the percentage rental should not fall below a fixed sum. Without mentioning the adequacy of that sum, the court said that the stated provision was intended to set a floor, not to provide an alternative basis for computing rent. In Walgreen Arizona Drug Co. v. Plaza Center Corp., 132 Ariz. 512, 647 P.2d 643 (App.1982), the lessor sought an implied covenant in a lease that included no percentage rental. Apparently the rent had been fixed low because the lease represented an effort to make the lessee's store a "magnet store" to attract customers into the area. The court said that the inadequacy of a fixed rent, where there is no percentage provision, cannot be the basis for any implied covenant.

In Bastian v. Albertson's, Inc., 102 Idaho 909, 643 P.2d 1079 (App.1982), a percentage lease provided for a fixed minimum rent that was found to be inadequate; but the court found that the rights granted to the tenant to assign the lease and to remove fixtures were inconsistent with the implication of a covenant of continued operation. The court held instead, however, that there was an implied covenant to pay "a reasonable and adequate rental." This was to be determined by the fair rental value of the premises from the time of the breach, that is, the time when the tenant ceased business operations.

SECTION 7. ASSIGNMENT OF LEASES

PEOPLE v. KLOPSTOCK

Supreme Court of California, 1944.
24 Cal.2d 897, 151 P.2d 641.

CURTIS, Justice. This is an action to condemn a right-of-way in fee for state highway purposes. The only point in controversy is the matter of participation in the compensation award incident to the state's exercise of its right of eminent domain. The trial court adjudged the entire damage recovery in favor of the defendants Northwestern Pacific Railroad Company and City Bank Farmers Trust Company, and decreed the interest in the condemned property asserted by the defendant Elerding to be noncompensable. From the judgment accordingly entered in rejection of his damage claim, the defendant Elerding prosecutes this appeal.

The material facts affecting the disposition of this litigation are not in dispute: The defendant Elerding's position herein rests upon his claim as assignee, through a succession of assignments, of a lease executed in 1924 by the defendant Northwestern Pacific Railroad Company, as lessor, and Pacific States Construction Company, as lessee. That lease covered a portion of the premises here involved and was for a period of one year at a monthly rental of $10. It provided that in case the lessee should hold over, such holding should be deemed a tenancy from month to month. The lease also contained a provision against assignment without the written consent of the lessor and a stipulation that the lessee, if not in default as to its covenants, was entitled, within thirty days after demand for surrender of possession, to remove any buildings or structures it had placed on the leased premises. The lessee went into possession and erected on the property an asphalt plant and appurtenant facilities. It remained in possession under the lease until March 20, 1940, at which time Consumers Rock & Cement Company went into possession under an assignment of the lease and a bill of sale covering the plant and its appurtenances. The lessor did not give its written consent to the assignment and it declined the assignee's tender of the monthly rental provided in the lease. The lessor wrote three letters to the assignee—dated March 27, April 8 and May 13, 1940—stating that it refused to recognize the validity of the assignment and requesting the removal of any property owned by the assignee on the premises, but it served no notice terminating or declaring a forfeiture of the lease. Thereafter the lessor commenced an action in unlawful detainer against Consumers Rock & Cement Company. In that action the trial court denied judgment for restitution of the premises upon finding that no notice had been served terminating or forfeiting the lease, but it entered its judgment in favor of the lessor for the claimed rental value of the premises which was in excess of the rental provided in the lease. Upon the appeal in that action the portion of the judgment awarding rental in excess of that provided in the lease was reversed. Northwestern Pacific Railroad Co. v. Consumers Rock & Cement Co., 50 Cal.App. 2d 721, 123 P.2d 872.

On February 23, 1940, the present proceeding in eminent domain was commenced. Under the provisions of section 14, article I of the Constitution of California, the trial court on said date made its order to the effect that plaintiff could immediately enter upon possession of the real property sought to be condemned as a right-of-way, immediately remove all obstacles from the land and construct the desired highway thereon. At the same time the plaintiff was ordered to, and it did, deposit in court certain moneys in favor of the defendants Northwestern Pacific Railroad Company and City Bank Farmers Trust Company, the owner in fee and mortgagee, respectively, of the parcels of property involved, to secure payment of just compensation to be thereafter determined in this action. Thereafter the plaintiff took possession of said real property and on July 23, 1940, completely wrecked and destroyed the above-mentioned asphalt plant and appurtenances, which stood in the path of the proposed highway project. As appears from his answer herein, the defendant Elerding's interest stems from mesne assignments transferring to him under date of May 28, 1941, all of the rights of the lessee under the aforementioned lease—and, in particular, "all claims and demands of every kind and character against * * * all persons, including the State of California, for damage to and the destruction, dismantling and removal of said plant and its appurtenances and the value thereof." No written consent from the lessor was ever obtained for the various assignments of the lease. The successive transfers of property interest on the leased premises—through assignment and bill of sale—were duly recorded. The trial court found that the various assignments under which the defendant Elerding claimed "were ineffective to vest any right, title or interest in the defendant Bert Elerding, and that said defendant Bert Elerding has no interest in the parcels sought to be condemned and is not entitled to participate in the award or receive any compensation for his alleged interest therein."

The trial court's rejection of the defendant Elerding's damage claim cannot be sustained as a matter of law. The identical legal principle determinative of the point in issue in the unlawful detainer action brought with regard to this same lease and the breach of the covenant thereunder as to the condition of assignment (Northwestern Pacific Railroad Co. v. Consumers Rock & Cement Co., supra) is likewise applicable in this condemnation proceeding in establishing the rights of participation in the compensation award incident thereto. As is there stated at page 723 of 50 Cal.App.2d, at page 872 of 123 P.2d: "The assignment of the lease without the consent of the lessor did not of itself terminate the lease or render the assignment void but the making of such assignment merely gave to the lessor certain rights to be exercised in the manner provided by law. * * * If the lessor desired to stand upon the covenant against assignment, he could have given notice of his election to declare a forfeiture of the lease and could have sued for breach of the covenant. He could also have had his remedy in unlawful detainer if possession had been thereafter withheld following proper notice. But we find no authority indicating that the lessor had the option of merely giving notice of the invalidity of the assignment without declaring a forfeiture * * *."

The restriction as to the condition of assignment is a personal covenant for the benefit of the lessor and until he elects to take advantage of the breach as authorized by law, the assignment remains a valid and binding conveyance of the leasehold interest as to all other parties. * * * Upon this premise the successive assignments, including that to the defendant Elerding, though made without the written consent of the lessor, were merely voidable, not void; there was no ipso facto termination of the lease by reason of the lessee's failure to obtain the lessor's written consent to assignment. Since the lessor did not elect to exercise its option to avoid the original assignment in the manner prescribed by law, its notice in its above mentioned letters to the first assignee, Consumers Rock & Cement Company, that it did not recognize the validity of the assignment gave no legal force to its demand therein that such assignee remove all property owned by it from the leased premises within a stated period of time. There was yet *no effective demand by the lessor for surrender of possession* as contemplated under the provisions of the lease to be the base starting point for the limitation of time allowed the lessee (or its assignee) to protect its right to remove its property from the premises. By such action the lessor was not following the procedure required for the enforcement of the terms of the lease, and therefore the original assignee of the lessee was in lawful possession of the premises. Northwestern Pacific Railroad Co. v. Consumers Rock & Cement Co., supra. While the course of action pursued by the lessor—notice to the assignee of the "invalidity of the assignment" coupled with the demand that it remove its property from the premises and the refusal to accept the tender of rent—unquestionably was sufficient to apprise the assignee that it *might be* dispossessed because of the lessee's violation of the covenant in question, under the authorities above cited the lessor's option to *void* the objectionable transfer depended upon its *declaration of a forfeiture upon proper notice* as provided by law. But the lessor did not take advantage of the exclusive remedy available to it for termination of the lease and accordingly the defendant Elerding, through mesne assignments, succeeded to all the rights of the lessee.

The state Constitution, art. I, § 14, provides that compensation for the taking of private property shall be paid to the owner. In fixing awards in condemnation cases compensation must be paid to the owners as their respective interests shall appear at the time when the taking of property for a public use is deemed to occur—at the date of the issuance of summons. * * *

At the time of the constructive taking here—February 23, 1940—the lessee indisputably was the owner of the asphalt plant and appurtenances it had theretofore erected on the leased premises, and it had the right to remove them therefrom according to the terms of the lease. Subsequently the defendant Elerding succeeded—through assignment and bill of sale—to the right to compensation for the state's destruction of this original property interest of the lessee. Upon such basis there can be no question as to the propriety of his claim to participate in the condemnation award. * * *

Under these legal principles the defendant Elerding properly claims compensation for the state's invasion of his property rights through destruction of the asphalt plant and appurtenant facilities on the condemned premises. The judgment is therefore reversed with directions to the trial court to amend its findings in accordance with the views herein expressed and to include in its compensation award such damages in favor of the defendant Elerding as it shall determine from the record herein to be properly representative of the value of his loss.

Notes

1. In First American Nat. Bank v. Chicken System of America, 510 S.W.2d 906 (Tenn.1974), it was held that an assignee of a lessee was bound by covenants made by the lessee and it was no defense that the assignment had been made in violation of a covenant by the lessee not to assign without consent of the lessor. *Klopstock* was cited with approval.

2. Restraints upon the alienation of terms of years or lesser leasehold interests, whether in the form of a covenant not to assign or a condition of forfeiture on breach, are valid, without regard to the length of the term. 6 A.L.P. § 26.5. The justification offered for the rule is the protection of the interests of the lessor.

Most common is the covenant against assignment without consent of the lessor. The question here is not so much the validity of the restriction as whether the lessor can withhold consent arbitrarily. It is generally held that he can. For a recent case so holding see B & R Oil Co. v. Ray's Mobile Homes, 139 Vt. 122, 422 A.2d 1267 (1980), rejecting the rule of Restatement (Second) § 15.2. But see contra, Boss Barbara, Inc. v. Newbill, 97 N.M. 239, 638 P.2d 1084 (1982), emphasizing that a lease is a contract, governed by general contractual principles of good faith and commercial reasonableness. Even where the lease provides that the lessor shall not withhold consent unreasonably, some courts have construed this provision not to impose any duty on the lessor so as to make him liable in damages for breach, but merely to be a modification of the lessee's covenant. 31 A.L.R.2d 831 (1953). But in Passaic Distributors v. The Sherman Co., 386 F.Supp. 647 (S.D.N.Y.1974), the court held that such a covenant constituted an affirmative obligation for breach of which the lessor could be liable for damages. See also Jack Frost Sales v. Harris Trust & Savings Bank, 104 Ill.App.3d 933, 60 Ill.Dec. 703, 433 N.E.2d 941 (1982).

The court in B & R Oil Co. v. Ray's Mobile Homes, supra, contra to *Klopstock*, held that an assignment in violation of a covenant was void.

SECTION 8. ABANDONMENT AND SURRENDER

THE LIBERTY PLAN CO. v. ADWAN

Supreme Court of Oklahoma, 1962. 370 P.2d 928.

PER CURIAM.* Theo Adwan, hereinafter called plaintiff, commenced this action against The Liberty Plan Company, hereinafter

* Footnotes of the court have been omitted. Ed.

called defendant, to recover $7,125 for rents due from August 1, 1953, to August 1, 1958. The judgment was for the plaintiff for the full amount of the prayer, after a verdict of the jury, and defendant appealed.

The evidence discloses that plaintiff and defendant executed a lease under date of February 14, 1950, covering the north room of a building at 3002 Paseo, Oklahoma City, Oklahoma. This lease was for a provisional maximum of ten years, renewable by options at certain periods during the ten years. The last option to renew was exercised under the terms of the lease in 1952, and the expiration date of the lease under the option was March 1, 1960. On the 30th day of July, 1953, defendant wrote the following letter:

"Dear Mr. Adwan:

"We have vacated property at 3002 Paseo Street, Oklahoma City and desire to relinquish our lease on the property as of now.

"Air Conditioner, Electric Light Fixtures, Second Rest Room equipment, etc. which we did not remove may now be considered your property. They should help some in assisting you in finding a new tenant.

"Yours very truly,
THE LIBERTY PLAN
COMPANY
BY: /s/ Earnest H. Gill
President.

EHG:av
PS: Key to property is
enclosed herewith."

On August 7, 1953, plaintiff wrote the following letter to defendant:

"The Liberty Plan Company
107 North Broadway
Oklahoma City, Oklahoma.

"Attention Mr. Earnest Gill

"Gentlemen:

"We have been employed by Mr. Theodore B. Adwan. We represent him in connection with the lease on the property at 3002 Paseo. We are unable to understand your position in this matter, and this letter is to notify you that acceptance of the keys to the property by Mr. Adwan does not in any manner constitute a waiver on his part, or evince an intention on his part to relieve you of your obligation under this lease.

"Mr. Adwan will immediately take steps to advertise the property and make every effort to mitigate your damages, but will definitely hold you liable for all costs of advertising, loss of rent and damage to the property sustained while you were in possession.

> "Very truly yours,
> PRIEST, BELISLE &
> FAUSS
> By: /s/ Edward J. Fauss

EJF:mh"

The property remained vacant for several months. It was then rented and it was stated by the defendant at the trial that the $7,125 is the correct balance due under the lease which it was obligated to pay unless the issues raised in the answer and cross-petition filed by the defendant prevailed.

Defendant first argues that the plaintiff accepted the property set out in the letter of July 30, 1953, took possession of the premises, altered them to suit a new tenant and therefore the obligation under the lease is ended.

In Conner v. Warner, 52 Okl. 630, 152 P. 1116, it is stated:

"If a tenant wrongfully abandons leased premises before the expiration of the terms, the landlord may, at his election: (a) At once enter and terminate the contract and recover the rent due up to the time of abandonment; or (b) he may suffer the premises to remain vacant and sue on the contract for the entire rent; or (c) he may give notice to the tenant of his refusal to accept a surrender, when such notice can be given, and sublet the premises for the unexpired term for the benefit of the lessee to reduce his damages—but if the landlord forcibly takes possession of the premises, without the consent of the tenant, and retains the same, he cannot recover to exceed the amount of rent due up to the time he took possession."

In Higgins v. Street, 19 Okl. 45, 92 P. 153, 13 L.R.A.,N.S., 398, it is stated:

" * * * In order to constitute a surrender there must be shown a mutual agreement between the lessor and lessee. A lease in writing constitutes a written contract, and the lessee cannot surrender it or be released from its terms without the consent of the lessor, and it is absolutely essential to the termination of the term that both the lessor and lessee agreed to the surrender; and, when this is shown, the tenant is no longer liable. * * * "

Defendant cites Hargrove v. Bourne, 47 Okl. 484, 150 P. 121, and Rucker v. Mason, 61 Okl. 270, 161 P. 195, and states that the plaintiff waived any right to claim under the lease by failing to notify the defendant that he was reletting the premises in its behalf. These cases are not applicable. In the Hargrove case the landlord personally took possession of the leased hotel and operated the same and such acts were found to be so incompatible with restricted entry as to amount to an acceptance of the tenant's surrender and termination of the lease. In the Rucker case the later leases, after surrender by the original tenant, stated the leasing was to mitigate the damages chargeable to the original defaulting tenant. This was cited as evidence of the landlord's intention not to accept a surrender of the premises, or release the defendant from the terms of the lease. In the present case the plaintiff gave notice of refusal to release defendant and intent to mitigate defendant's liability by renting the premises. The acts of plaintiff were in accord with the above stated law.

In Hoke v. Williamson, 98 Kan. 580, 158 P. 1115, it is stated:

"Consent of the landlord is not implied from the mere fact of a reletting, or from failure to notify the tenant of a reletting, and notice to the tenant of a reletting is not essential in order to prevent surrender by operation of law."

The items left in the building were fixtures and the acceptance of the building under the circumstances did not bind the plaintiff or prevent his recovery under the lease.

* * *

Judgment affirmed.

Notes

A *surrender* of a leasehold interest from a tenant to his landlord, like a *release* of a landlord's interest to his tenant, is a conveyance, requiring compliance with the Statute of Frauds. Surrenders by operation of law, that is, a surrender based on the conduct of a landlord after a tenant abandons the premises, are usually held expressly or impliedly to be exempt from the statute. Surrenders by operation of law are still often spoken of as based on the intention of the parties, that is, the tenant by abandoning offers to surrender, and the landlord by his conduct has accepted the offer. But usually in the case of a reletting of the premises by the landlord, he really has no intention to accept the tenant's offer. In reality, if a reletting is held to constitute an acceptance of the offer to surrender, the result is better founded on the difficulty in concluding that there can be two tenants of the same property at the same time. This logical impasse has been avoided by treating the reletting as merely an assignment by the landlord of the tenant's term. The difficulty with this, of course, is in finding authority in the landlord to act for the tenant if the tenant has not in fact agreed to the reletting. The view that notice to the tenant of an intention to relet is sufficient is not an entirely satisfactory solution to the problem, at least on a theoretical basis, although it may seem perfectly reasonable as a practical matter.

Perhaps a better way to avoid these difficulties was adopted in Novak v. Fontaine Furniture Co., 84 N.H. 93, 146 A. 525 (1929). There the tenant abandoned and the landlord relet to a tenant who stayed for only three months, after which the premises remained vacant until the time of the suit. The landlord sued for damages and the tenant defended on the ground that the reletting constituted a surrender. The court conceded that the reletting may have constituted a surrender, but that such surrender of the tenant's estate did not terminate his liability for breach of contract, and that for such breach the landlord could recover such damages for the entire period of the lease as were "the natural probable result of the defendant's failure to perform its part of the contract." Here the amount of such damages was stipulated by the parties.

SOMMER v. KRIDEL

Supreme Court of New Jersey, 1977.
74 N.J. 446, 378 A.2d 767.

PASHMAN, J. We granted certification in these cases to consider whether a landlord seeking damages from a defaulting tenant is under a duty to mitigate damages by making reasonable efforts to relet an apartment wrongfully vacated by the tenant. Separate parts of the Appellate Division held that, in accordance with their respective leases, the landlords in both cases could recover rents due under the leases regardless of whether they had attempted to re-let the vacated apartments. Although they were of different minds as to the fairness of this result, both parties agreed that it was dictated by Joyce v. Bauman, 113 N.J.L. 438, 174 A. 693 (E. & A.1934), a decision by the former Court of Errors and Appeals. We now reverse and hold that a landlord does have an obligation to make a reasonable effort to mitigate damages in such a situation. We therefore overrule Joyce v. Bauman to the extent that it is inconsistent with our decision today.

I

A. SOMMER v. KRIDEL

This case was tried on stipulated facts. On March 10, 1972 the defendant, James Kridel, entered into a lease with the plaintiff, Abraham Sommer, owner of the "Pierre Apartments" in Hackensack, to rent apartment 6–L in that building.[1] The term of the lease was from May 1, 1972 until April 30, 1974, with a rent concession for the first six weeks, so that the first month's rent was not due until June 15, 1972.

One week after signing the agreement, Kridel paid Sommer $690. Half of that sum was used to satisfy the first month's rent. The remainder was paid under the lease provision requiring a security deposit of $345. Although defendant had expected to begin occupancy around May 1, his plans were changed. He wrote to Sommer on May 19, 1972, explaining

> I was to be married on June 3, 1972. Unhappily the engagement was broken and the wedding plans cancelled. Both parents were to assume responsibility for the rent after our marriage. I was discharged from the U.S. Army in October 1971 and am now a student. I have no funds of my own, and am supported by my stepfather.

> In view of the above, I cannot take possession of the apartment and am surrendering all rights to it. Never having received a key, I cannot return same to you.

---

1. Among other provisions, the lease prohibited the tenant from assigning or transferring the lease without the consent of the landlord. If the tenant defaulted, the lease gave the landlord the option of re-entering or re-letting, but stipulated that failure to re-let or to recover the full rental would not discharge the tenant's liability for rent. [Footnotes are the court's.]

I beg your understanding and compassion in releasing me from the lease, and will of course, in consideration thereof, forfeit the 2 month's rent already paid.

Please notify me at your earliest convenience.

Plaintiff did not answer the letter.

Subsequently, a third party went to the apartment house and inquired about renting apartment 6–L. Although the parties agreed that she was ready, willing and able to rent the apartment, the person in charge told her that the apartment was not being shown since it was already rented to Kridel. In fact, the landlord did not re-enter the apartment or exhibit it to anyone until August 1, 1973. At that time it was rented to a new tenant for a term beginning on September 1, 1973. The new rental was for $345 per month with a six week concession similar to that granted Kridel.

Prior to re-letting the new premises, plaintiff sued Kridel in August 1972, demanding $7,590, the total amount due for the full two-year term of the lease. Following a mistrial, plaintiff filed an amended complaint asking for $5,865, the amount due between May 1, 1972 and September 1, 1973. The amended complaint included no reduction in the claim to reflect the six week concession provided for in the lease or the $690 payment made to plaintiff after signing the agreement. Defendant filed an amended answer to the complaint, alleging that plaintiff breached the contract, failed to mitigate damages and accepted defendant's surrender of the premises. He also counterclaimed to demand repayment of the $345 paid as a security deposit.

The trial judge ruled in favor of defendant. Despite his conclusion that the lease had been drawn to reflect "the 'settled law' of this state," he found that "justice and fair dealing" imposed upon the landlord the duty to attempt do re-let the premises and thereby mitigate damages. He also held that plaintiff's failure to make any response to defendant's unequivocal offer of surrender was tantamount to an acceptance, thereby terminating the tenancy and any obligation to pay rent. As a result, he dismissed both the complaint and the counterclaim. The Appellate Division reversed in a *per curiam* opinion, 153 N.J.Super. 1 (1976), and we granted certification. 69 N.J. 395, 354 A.2d 323 (1976).

B.   RIVERVIEW REALTY CO. v. PEROSIO

This controversy arose in a similar manner. On December 27, 1972, Carlos Perosio entered into a written lease with plaintiff Riverview Realty Co. The agreement covered the rental of apartment 5–G in a building owned by the realty company at 2175 Hudson Terrace in Fort Lee. As in the companion case, the lease prohibited the tenant from subletting or assigning the apartment without the consent of the landlord. It was to run for a two-year term, from February 1, 1973 until January 31, 1975, and provided for a monthly rental of $450. The defendant took possession of the apartment and occupied it until February 1974. At that time he vacated the premises, after having paid the rent through January 31, 1974.

The landlord filed a complaint on October 31, 1974, demanding $4,500 in payment for the monthly rental from February 1, 1974 through October 31, 1974. Defendant answered the complaint by alleging that there had been a valid surrender of the premises and that plaintiff failed to mitigate damages. The trial court granted the landlord's motion for summary judgment against the defendant, fixing the damages at $4,050 plus $182.25 interest.[2]

The Appellate Division affirmed the trial court, holding that it was bound by prior precedents, including Joyce v. Bauman, supra, 138 N.J. Super. 270, 350 A.2d 517 (App.Div.1976). Nevertheless, it freely criticized the rule which it found itself obliged to follow:

> There appears to be no reason in equity or justice to perpetuate such an unrealistic and uneconomic rule of law which encourages an owner to let valuable rented space lie fallow because he is assured of full recovery from a defaulting tenant. Since courts in New Jersey and elsewhere have abandoned ancient real property concepts and applied ordinary contract principles in other conflicts between landlord and tenant there is no sound reason for a continuation of a special real property rule to the issue of mitigation. * * * [138 N.J. Super. at 273-74, 350 A.2d at 519; citations omitted]

We granted certification. 70 N.J. 145, 358 A.2d 191 (1976).

II

As the lower courts in both appeals found, the weight of authority in this State supports the rule that a landlord is under no duty to mitigate damages caused by a defaulting tenant. * * *. [Citations omitted.] This rule has been followed in a majority of states. Annot. 21 A.L.R.3d 534, § 2[a] at 541 (1968), and has been tentatively adopted in the American Law Institute's Restatement of Property. Restatement (Second) of Property, § 11.1(3) (Tent.Draft No. 3, 1975).

Nevertheless, while there is still a split of authority over this question, the trend among recent cases appears to be in favor of a mitigation requirement. Compare Dushoff v. Phoenix Co., 23 Ariz.App. 238, 532 P.2d 180 (App.1975); Hirsch v. Merchants National Bank & Trust Co., 336 N.E.2d 833 (Ind.App.1975); Wilson v. Ruhl, 277 Md. 607, 356 A.2d 544 (1976) (by statute); Bernstein v. Seglin, 184 Neb. 673, 171 N.W.2d 247 (1969); Lefrak v. Lambert, 89 Misc.2d 197, 390 N.Y.S.2d 959 (N.Y. Cty.Ct.1976); Howard Stores Corp. v. Rayon Co., Inc., 36 A.D.2d 911, 320 N.Y.S.2d 861 (App.Div.1971); Ross v. Smigelski, 42 Wis.2d 185, 166 N.W.2d 243 (1969); with Chandler Leas. Div. v. Florida-Vanderbilt Dev. Corp., 464 F.2d 267 (5 Cir.1972) cert. den. 409 U.S. 1041, 93 S.Ct. 527, 34 L.Ed.2d 491 (1972) (applying Florida law to the rental of a yacht); Winshall v. Ampco Auto Parks, Inc., 417 F.Supp. 334 (E.D.Mich.1976) (finding that under Michigan law a landlord has a duty to mitigate damages where he is suing for a breach of contract, but not where it is solely a

---

2. The trial court noted that damages had been erroneously calculated in the complaint to reflect ten months rent. As to the interest awarded to plaintiff, the parties have not raised this issue before this Court. Since we hold that the landlord had a duty to attempt to mitigate damages, we need not reach this question.

suit to recover rent); Ryals v. Laney, 338 So.2d 413 (Ala.Civ.App.1976); B.K.K. Co. v. Schultz, 7 Cal.App.3d 786, 86 Cal.Rptr. 760 (App.1970) (dictum); Carpenter v. Riddle, 527 P.2d 592 (Okl.Sup.Ct.1974); Hurwitz v. Kohm, 516 S.W.2d 33 (Mo.App.1974).

The majority rule is based on principles of property law which equate a lease with a transfer of a property interest in the owner's estate. Under this rationale the lease conveys to a tenant an interest in the property which forecloses any control by the landlord; thus, it would be anomalous to require the landlord to concern himself with the tenant's abandonment of his own property. Wright v. Baumann, 239 Or. 410, 398 P.2d 119, 120–21, 21 A.L.R.3d 527 (1965).

For instance, in Muller v. Beck, supra, where essentially the same issue was posed, the court clearly treated the lease as governed by property, as opposed to contract, precepts.[3] The court there observed that the "tenant had an estate for years, but it was an estate qualified by this right of the landlord to prevent its transfer," 94 N.J.L. at 313, 110 A. at 832, and that "the tenant has an estate with which the landlord may not interfere." Id. at 314, 110 A. at 832. Similarly, in Heckel v. Griese, supra, the court noted the absolute nature of the tenant's interest in the property while the lease was in effect, stating that "when the tenant vacated, * * * no one, in the circumstances, had any right to interfere with the defendant's possession of the premises." 12 N.J.Misc. at 213, 171 A. 148, 149. Other cases simply cite the rule announced in Muller v. Beck, supra, without discussing the underlying rationale. See Joyce v. Bauman, supra, 113 N.J.L. at 440, 174 A. 693; Weiss v. I. Zapinski, Inc., supra, 65 N.J.Super. at 359, 167 A.2d 802; Heyman v. Linwood Park, supra, 41 N.J.Super. at 411, 125 A.2d 345; Zucker v. Dehm, supra, 128 N.J.L. at 436, 26 A.2d 564; Tanella v. Rettagliata, supra, 120 N.J.Super. at 407, 294 A.2d 431.

Yet the distinction between a lease for ordinary residential purposes and an ordinary contract can no longer be considered viable. As Professor Powell observed, evolving "social factors have exerted increasing influence on the law of estates for years." 2 Powell on Real Property (1977 ed.), § 221[1] at 180–81. The result has been that

[t]he complexities of city life, and the proliferated problems of modern society in general, have created new problems for lessors and lessees and these have been commonly handled by specific clauses in leases. This growth in the number and detail of specific lease covenants has reintroduced into the law of estates for years a predominantly contractual ingredient. [Id. at 181]

Thus in 6 Williston on Contracts (3 ed. 1962), § 890A at 592, it is stated:

There is a clearly discernible tendency on the part of courts to cast aside technicalities in the interpretation of leases and to concen-

---

3. It is well settled that a party claiming damages for a breach of contract has a duty to mitigate his loss. See Frank Stamato & Co. v. Borough of Lodi, 4 N.J. 14, 71 A.2d 336 (1950); Sandler v. Lawn-A-Mat Chem. & Equip. Corp., 141 N.J.Super. 437, 455, 358 A.2d 805 (App.Div.1976); Wolf v. Marlton Corp., 57 N.J.Super. 278, 154 A.2d 625 (App.Div.1956); 5 Corbin on Contracts (1964 ed.), § 1039 at 241 et seq.; McCormick, Damages, § 33 at 127 (1935). See also N.J.S.A. 12A:2–708.

trate their attention, as in the case of other contracts, on the intention of the parties, * * *.

This Court has taken the lead in requiring that landlords provide housing services to tenants in accordance with implied duties which are hardly consistent with the property notions expressed in Muller v. Beck, supra, and Heckel v. Griese, supra. See Braitman v. Overlook Terrace Corp., 68 N.J. 368, 346 A.2d 76 (1975) (liability for failure to repair defective apartment door lock); Berzito v. Gambino, 63 N.J. 460, 308 A.2d 17 (1973) (construing implied warranty of habitability and covenant to pay rent as mutually dependent); Marini v. Ireland, 56 N.J. 130, 265 A.2d 526 (1970) (implied covenant to repair); Reste Realty Corp. v. Cooper, 53 N.J. 444, 251 A.2d 268 (1969) (implied warranty of fitness of premises for leased purpose). In fact, in Reste Realty Corp. v. Cooper, supra, we specifically noted that the rule which we announced there did not comport with the historical notion of a lease as an estate for years. 53 N.J. at 451–52, 251 A.2d 268. And in Marini v. Ireland, supra, we found that the "guidelines employed to construe contracts have been modernly applied to the construction of leases." 56 N.J. at 141, 265 A.2d at 532.

Application of the contract rule requiring mitigation of damages to a residential lease may be justified as a matter of basic fairness.[4] Professor McCormick first commented upon the inequity under the majority rule when he predicted in 1925 that eventually

> the logic, inescapable according to the standards of a 'jurisprudence of conceptions' which permits the landlord to stand idly by the vacant, abandoned premises and treat them as the property of the tenant and recover full rent, will yield to the more realistic notions of social advantage which in other fields of the law have forbidden a recovery for damages which the plaintiff by reasonable efforts could have avoided. [McCormick, "The Rights of the Landlord Upon Abandonment of the Premises by the Tenant," 23 Mich.L.Rev. 211, 221–22 (1925)]

Various courts have adopted this position. See Annot., supra, § 7(a) at 565, and ante at 770–771.

The pre-existing rule cannot be predicated upon the possibility that a landlord may lose the opportunity to rent another empty apartment because he must first rent the apartment vacated by the defaulting tenant. Even where the breach occurs in a multi-dwelling building, each apartment may have unique qualities which make it attractive to certain individuals. Significantly, in Sommer v. Kridel, there was a specific request to rent the apartment vacated by the defendant; there is no reason to believe that absent this vacancy the landlord could have succeeded in renting a different apartment to this individual.

---

4. We see no distinction between the leases involved in the instant appeals and those which might arise in other types of residential housing. However, we reserve for another day the question of whether a landlord must mitigate damages in a commercial setting. Cf. Kruvant v. Sunrise Market, Inc., 58 N.J. 452, 456, 279 A.2d 104 (1971), modified on other grounds, 59 N.J. 330, 282 A.2d 746 (1971).

We therefore hold that antiquated real property concepts which served as the basis for the pre-existing rule, shall no longer be controlling where there is a claim for damages under a residential lease. Such claims must be governed by more modern notions of fairness and equity. A landlord has a duty to mitigate damages where he seeks to recover rents due from a defaulting tenant.

If the landlord has other vacant apartments besides the one which the tenant has abandoned, the landlord's duty to mitigate consists of making reasonable efforts to re-let the apartment. In such cases he must treat the apartment in question as if it was one of his vacant stock.

As part of his cause of action, the landlord shall be required to carry the burden of proving that he used reasonable diligence in attempting to re-let the premises. We note that there has been a divergence of opinion concerning the allocation of the burden of proof on this issue. See Annot., supra, § 12 at 577. While generally in contract actions the breaching party has the burden of proving that damages are capable of mitigation, see Sandler v. Lawn-A-Mat Chem. & Equip. Corp., 141 N.J. Super. 437, 455, 358 A.2d 805 (App.Div.1976); McCormick, Damages, § 33 at 130 (1935), here the landlord will be in a better position to demonstrate whether he exercised reasonable diligence in attempting to re-let the premises. Cf. Kulm v. Coast to Coast Stores Central Org., 248 Or. 436, 432 P.2d 1006 (1967) (burden on lessor in contract to renew a lease).

III

The Sommer v. Kridel case presents a classic example of the unfairness which occurs when a landlord has no responsibility to minimize damages. Sommer waited 15 months and allowed $4658.50 in damages to accrue before attempting to re-let the apartment. Despite the availability of a tenant who was ready, willing and able to rent the apartment, the landlord needlessly increased the damages by turning her away. While a tenant will not necessarily be excused from his obligations under a lease simply by finding another person who is willing to rent the vacated premises, see, e.g., Reget v. Dempsey-Tegler & Co., 70 Ill.App. 2d 32, 216 N.E.2d 500 (Ill.App.1966) (new tenant insisted on leasing the premises under different terms); Edmands v. Rust & Richardson Drug Co., 191 Mass. 123, 77 N.E. 713 (1906) (landlord need not accept insolvent tenant), here there has been no showing that the new tenant would not have been suitable. We therefore find that plaintiff could have avoided the damages which eventually accrued, and that the defendant was relieved of his duty to continue paying rent. Ordinarily we would require the tenant to bear the cost of any reasonable expenses incurred by a landlord in attempting to re-let the premises, see Ross v. Smigelski, supra, 166 N.W.2d at 248–49; 22 Am.Jur.2d, Damages, § 169 at 238, but no such expenses were incurred in this case.[5]

5. As to defendant's counterclaim for $345, representing the amount deposited with the landlord as a security deposit, we note that this issue has not been briefed or argued before this Court, and apparently has been abandoned. Because we hold

In Riverview Realty Co. v. Perosio, no factual determination was made regarding the landlord's efforts to mitigate damages, and defendant contends that plaintiff never answered his interrogatories. Consequently, the judgment is reversed and the case remanded for a new trial. Upon remand and after discovery has been completed, R. 4:17 et seq., the trial court shall determine whether plaintiff attempted to mitigate damages with reasonable diligence, see Wilson v. Ruhl, supra, 356 A.2d at 546, and if so, the extent of damages remaining and assessable to the tenant. As we have held above, the burden of proving that reasonable diligence was used to re-let the premises shall be upon the plaintiff. See Annot., supra, § 11 at 575.

In assessing whether the landlord has satisfactorily carried his burden, the trial court shall consider, among other factors, whether the landlord, either personally or through an agency, offered or showed the apartment to any prospective tenants, or advertised it in local newspapers. Additionally, the tenant may attempt to rebut such evidence by showing that he proffered suitable tenants who were rejected. However, there is no standard formula for measuring whether the landlord has utilized satisfactory efforts in attempting to mitigate damages, and each case must be judged upon its own facts. Compare Hershorin v. La Vista, Inc., 110 Ga.App. 435, 138 S.E.2d 703 (App.1964) ("reasonable effort" of landlord by showing the apartment to all prospective tenants); Carpenter v. Wisniewski, 139 Ind.App. 325, 215 N.E.2d 882 (App.1966) (duty satisfied where landlord advertised the premises through a newspaper, placed a sign in the window, and employed a realtor); Re Garment Center Capitol, Inc., 93 F.2d 667, 115 A.L.R. 202 (2 Cir.1938) (landlord's duty not breached where higher rental was asked since it was known that this was merely a basis for negotiations); Foggia v. Dix, 265 Or. 315, 509 P.2d 412, 414 (1973) (in mitigating damages, landlord need not accept less than fair market value or "substantially alter his obligations as established in the pre-existing lease"); with Anderson v. Andy Darling Pontiac, Inc., 257 Wis. 371, 43 N.W.2d 362 (1950) (reasonable diligence not established where newspaper advertisement placed in one issue of local paper by a broker); Scheinfeld v. Muntz T.V., Inc., 67 Ill.App.2d 8, 214 N.E.2d 506 (Ill.App.1966) (duty breached where landlord refused to accept suitable subtenant); Consolidated Sun Ray, Inc. v. Oppenstein, 335 F.2d 801, 811 (8 Cir.1964) (dictum) (demand for rent which is "far greater than the provisions of the lease called for" negates landlord's assertion that he acted in good faith in seeking a new tenant).

IV

The judgment in Sommer v. Kridel is reversed. In Riverview Realty Co. v. Perosio, the judgment is reversed and the case is remanded to the trial court for proceedings in accordance with this opinion.

---

that plaintiff breached his duty to attempt to mitigate damages, we do not address defendant's argument that the landlord accepted a surrender of the premises.

Notes

1. Was the landlord in *Sommer* suing for damages? If not, why did the court decide the case on the basis of a requirement that he mitigate damages? Compare Winshall v. Ampco Auto Parks, Inc., 417 F.Supp. 334 (E.D.Mich.1976), cited in *Sommer*, where the court said that mitigation was applicable only in suits for damages, not in suits for the recovery of unpaid rent.

In Mar-Son, Inc. v. Terwaho Enterprises, Inc., 259 N.W.2d 289 (N.D.1977), the court, in applying the rule of Sommer v. Kridel, held that the lessor, in offering its property for a rent $12,600 a year more than the $21,000 minimum annual rent in the original lease, had not made a good faith effort to mitigate damages.

Rest.2d (L & T) § 12.1(3) states that a landlord is under no duty to attempt to relet abandoned premises or mitigate the tenant's responsibility under the lease. The reason given is that abandonment invites vandalism, and the law should not encourage such conduct by putting a duty of mitigation on the landlord. The URLTA § 4.203(c) provides that if a tenant abandons, the landlord shall make reasonable efforts to rent the premises at a fair rental value, and that if a landlord fails to use reasonable efforts so to rent, the rental agreement is deemed terminated by the landlord as of the date the landlord has notice of the abandonment.

2. "Appellant finally insists that an action to recover rentals for the full term cannot be maintained until the expiration of the term of the lease. Appellee relies upon the doctrine of anticipatory breach as justifying the maintenance of the action to recover future rentals. We recognize that under that rule an unequivocal repudiation or renunciation of an executory contract in advance of the time of performance may, at the election of the injured party, be regarded as an anticipatory breach and support an immediate action for damages without waiting for the time of performance. Although not recognized in all jurisdictions, the doctrine of anticipatory breach is recognized in Kentucky. * * * The doctrine may be applied to rental as well as other contracts. * * * However, we do not regard the rule as justifying the acceleration of payments under a contract where the due dates of such payments are definitely fixed by the contract. If the doctrine could accelerate future rental payments, it might reasonably follow that it could precipitate the due date of a note if the maker should renounce the note in advance of its maturity. Such an application of the rule was never intended. * * * We do not regard this action as one to recover damages. Should we so regard it, the general rule as to minimizing damages would apply." Jordan v. Nickell, 253 S.W.2d 237, 239 (Ky.App.1952).

3. "Some mention should also be made of the lessee's liability in damages to the lessor under the circumstances which we are here discussing. Of course, the parties may mutually agree to a surrender and acceptance of the leasehold estate without further liability on the part of the lessee, in which event there can be no recovery by the lessor of damages for the loss of future rents nor for any damages other than those existing at the time of the termination of the lease agreement. And, as heretofore noted, the lessor may accept the surrender of the premises and thereafter re-enter and relet on the account of the lessee, either by virtue of a stipulation to that effect in the lease or on the basis of such a qualification or condition expressly or impliedly attached to the lessor's acceptance of the lessee's surrender of the premises. It has been held that in these circumstances, there has been no determination of the leasehold estate, that the lease term is still in existence, and that the claim by the lessor for the difference between the amount received on a reletting and the amount stipulat-

ed in the lease is a claim for rent rather than for damages. See Kottler v. New York Bargain House, 242 N.Y. 28, 150 N.E. 591; Dorcich v. Time Oil Co., 103 Cal.App.2d 677, 230 P.2d 10; Wukasch v. Hoover, Tex.Civ.App., 247 S.W.2d 593. Other decisions seem to be based on the fact that a reletting in such circumstances is merely in mitigation of damages—that the leasehold estate is ended and that the contract remains alive only for the purpose of measuring the damages, and that the lessor's claim for the difference between the amount received on the reletting and the amount stipulated in the contract is one for damages rather than for rent. See Crow v. Kaupp, Mo.Sup., 50 S.W.2d 995; Shea v. Leonis, 29 Cal.App.2d 184, 84 P.2d 277; Brill v. Haifetz, supra; Weinsklar Realty Co. v. Dooley, 200 Wis. 412, 228 N.W. 515, 67 A.L.R. 875; Marathon Oil Co. v. Edwards, Tex.Civ.App., 96 S.W.2d 551; Stewart v. Kuskin & Rotberg, Inc., Tex.Civ.App., 106 S.W.2d 1074; Lips v. Opp, 150 Kan. 745, 96 P.2d 865; Carey v. Hejke, 119 N.J.L. 594, 197 A. 652; Friedman v. Colonial Oil Co., 236 Iowa 140, 18 N.W.2d 196. See also Williams v. Aeroland Oil Company, 155 Fla. 114, 20 So.2d 346, 348, where this court stated that the claim would be for 'general damages for the difference between the rentals stipulated to be paid and what, in good faith, the landlord is able to recover from a reletting'. In those jurisdictions where it is held that the claim is for damages, not for rent, the lessee 'is not in position, after having violated his lease by abandoning the premises, to turn that breach into gain for himself by asserting a claim to the excess of the rental obtained on the reletting above that provided in his lease.' 32 Am.Jur., Landlord and Tenant, § 520, page 427.

"But we do not conceive that, upon a 'relinquishment' or abandonment of the leasehold premises by the lessee under such circumstances as to amount to a repudiation of the lease agreement, the lessor is required to relet the premises for the account of the lessee in order to preserve his right to general damages for the loss of future rents. As indicated in Williams v. Aeroland Oil Co., supra, there is authority for the proposition that when a lessee repudiates his contract, a cause of action immediately arises in favor of the lessor for full damages, present and prospective, which were the necessary and direct result of the breach, the measure of which is the difference (reduced to present worth) between the rent fixed in the lease and the present fair rental value of the premises for the remainder of the term, together with such special damages as may have resulted from the breach. This is simply an application to lease contracts of the doctrine of 'anticipatory breach' in general contract law, the reason for which is fully explained in Hawkinson v. Johnston, 8 Cir., 122 F.2d 724, 137 A.L.R. 420. See also Hyman v. Cohen, Fla., 73 So.2d 393, and cases cited therein; 51 C.J.S. Landlord and Tenant, § 250, page 883; Wukasch v. Hoover, Tex.Civ.App., 247 S.W.2d 593.

"And where, as here, a lease agreement contains mutually dependent executory covenants to be performed on either side, there would appear to be no valid reason for refusing to apply the doctrine of anticipatory breach to a repudiation of the contract by the lessee. In such event, the lessor has a right to consider the contract ended insofar as further performance by the lessee of its terms is concerned and may resume possession of the leasehold *premises;* but he may refuse to accept the surrender of the leasehold *estate* insofar as his right to recover damages for the breach is concerned. Where such right is preserved, the lessor's intention in resuming possession of the premises (whether on his own account or for the account of the lessee) is important only to a determination of the time at which he intends to collect for his damages for the total breach of the contract. He may resume possession on his own account and sue immediately for his damages, the measure of which is as noted above; or he may resume possession of the premises and relet for the account of the lessee and, at the end of the term, collect the difference between the amount received on the reletting and the amount stipulated in the lease agreement for the remainder of the term. In either case, the lessor is entitled to recover for any special damages chargeable against the lessee and, in the latter case, for the expenses reasonably necessary in order to obtain a tenant and mitigate damages under the lease. C.D. Stimson Co. v. Porter, 195 F.2d 410 (10th Cir. 1952). For the measure of damages for the breach of a long-term lease, see Hawkinson v. Johnston, supra, and the annotation in 85 L.Ed. at page 352." Kanter v. Safran, 68 So.2d 553, 557 (Fla.1953).

In White v. Watkins, 385 S.W.2d 267 (Tex.Civ.App.1964), the court said that when a tenant abandons and the lessor has relet the premises for only a portion of the unexpired term, the measure of damages for that period is the difference between the rental reserved and the amount realized by the reletting; and as for the period not covered by the reletting the measure is the difference between the present value of the rentals contracted for in the lease and the reasonable cash market value of the lease for that period.

4. See Humbach, The Common-Law Conception of Leasing: Mitigation, Habitability and Dependence of Covenants, 60 Wash.U.L.Quart. 1213 (1983).

Note on Tenants' Fixtures

Few conveyances of land are of vacant land; and few conveyances of improved land specify the improvements. Most parties to conveyances rely on the law of fixtures. That law provides answers to the question: what things which were once chattels have become part of the land so as to pass by a conveyance without being mentioned? The answer is usually easy with respect to houses or other buildings situated on the land. In some circumstances the answer is not easy. The leading case, Teaff v. Hewitt, 1 Ohio St. 511 (1853), stated certain criteria for deciding whether a chattel had become a fixture. These were:

"1st. Actual annexation to the realty, or something appurtenant thereto.

"2d. Appropriation to the use or purpose of that part of the realty with which it is connected.

"3d. The intention of the party making the annexation to make the article a permanent accession to the freehold—this intention being inferred from the *nature* of the article affixed, the *relation* and *situation of the party* making the annexation, the structure and mode of annexation, and the purpose or use of which the annexation has been made."

These criteria suggest the difficulty of the problem. Normally physical annexation to the land is required; but in certain cases a close physical relation between land and chattel will do without fixing the one to the other, as in the case of heavy machinery situated in a building. On the other hand, a chattel may retain its chattel nature despite some connection to the land. Customary practices may be controlling in the case of certain commonly used facilities or appliances. It is often said that the intention of the original owner of both land and chattel is the ultimate test; but such intention is determined by what he does and the circumstances of his doing it, rather than by what he thinks and what he says he thought. Most of the fixture cases today arise in more complicated circumstances. For example, an owner of land may mortgage the land, the mortgage by its terms covering property after-acquired by the mortgagor. The mortgagor later buys a chattel under a conditional-sale contract which reserves title in the seller until full payment of the purchase price. The chattel is then attached to the land or so used that it would be treated as a fixture if the mortgagor had owned the chattel and sold the land. The contest becomes one between the mortgagee of the land and the seller of the chattel. These problems are treated in the Uniform Commercial Code and are dealt with in courses on Commercial Transactions.

Where land is leased, a fixture problem may arise which is similar to the case of a sale of land. The main fixture problem in landlord-tenant relations, however, has to do with chattels originally owned by the tenant and affixed or otherwise used by him in his use of the land. Apart from landlord-tenant relations, if one attaches chattels to the land of another in such a way that they would be fixtures if he owned the land and sold it, the chattels do not become the property of the landowner if they were affixed with the permission of the landowner. If the affixing is done by a trespasser, it has been held that the chattels become the property of the landowner. The harshness of this result in cases where the chattel-owner did not know he was trespassing has led to statutes and decisions to the contrary.

The fixture problem in landlord-tenant relations usually arises with the assumption that the tenant's chattel became a fixture, but involves the question whether the tenant can nevertheless remove it. It was early held that a tenant could remove his "trade fixtures" prior to the expiration of his tenancy. These were fixtures used by a tenant in his trade or business on the premises. Early cases refused to extend this rule to the agricultural fixtures of a tenant farmer; but such a distinction has been rejected in later cases. It has also been held that a tenant can remove "domestic fixtures." The term suggests improvements made for personal comfort or enjoyment. One should be wary of relying on such a label, for fixtures which serve such a purpose may in fact be held to be of such a nature, or to have been acquired in such circumstances, that they are held to be permanent additions to the land. The question whether the above categories leave out any kind of tenant's fixtures has been answered by some courts which have declared that the rule relating to removal extends to any kind of fixture which furthers the use of the premises contemplated by the lease.

There remains, however, a limitation on a tenant's right to remove fixtures. This has been put in various terms, with some variances of substance, but it generally prevents removal of a fixture where such removal would do substantial damage to the leased premises. Obviously this means damage other than the loss of the fixture itself. Most of the litigation on fixtures as between landlord and tenant involve the application of this principle in a variety of circumstances. It can be argued that a tenant should be permitted to remove any fixture, provided he repairs the damage or restores the premises to their original condition. Procedural difficulties may stand in the way of such a result. In any event, such a rule has not been accepted. But some courts, in applying the limitation, have been very liberal in the tenant's favor. The ultimate question concerning removal is really only a variation of the basic fixture question: do all the relevant circumstances justify the conclusion that the tenant must be treated as if he had intended that the chattel in question was to become a permanent part of the land.

Except where the parties otherwise agree, a tenant's right to remove fixtures must be exercised before his tenancy ends (or in certain circumstances within a reasonable time thereafter); otherwise the right of removal is lost.

Where the removal problem is or should be anticipated, it should be explicitly covered by the terms of the lease.

See generally Brown, Personal Property, c. XVI (3d ed. 1975).

Chapter 5

EASEMENTS

SECTION 1. NATURE AND TYPES

"Easements are sometimes divided into affirmative and negative. An affirmative easement is one which authorizes the doing of acts which, if no easement existed would give rise to a right of action, while a negative easement is one the effect of which is not to authorize the doing of an act by the person entitled to the easement, but merely to preclude the owner of the land subject to the easement from the doing of an act which, if no easement existed, he would be entitled to do. In other words, an affirmative easement involves the creation of a privilege, while a negative easement involves the withdrawal of a privilege." 3 Tiffany, Real Property § 756, p. 201 (3d ed. 1939).*

Restatement Property (1936)†

§ 9. Estate

The word "estate," as it is used in this Restatement, means an interest in land which

(a) is or may become possessory; and

(b) is ownership measured in terms of duration.

§ 450. Easement

An easement is an interest in land in the possession of another which

(a) entitles the owner of such interest to a limited use or enjoyment of the land in which the interest exists;

(b) entitles him to protection as against third persons from interference in such use of enjoyment;

(c) is not subject to the will of the possessor of the land;

(d) is not a normal incident of the possession of any land possessed by the owner of the interest, and

(e) is capable of creation by conveyance.

* Reprinted with permission of Callaghan & Co., 3201 Old Glenview Road, Wilmette, Illinois 60091. For a detailed treatment of the law of Easements, see 2 A.L.P. §§ 8.1–8.108. For a more concise treatment, see Cunningham §§ 8.1–8.12.

† Copyright, 1936 by the American Law Institute. Reprinted with permission of the American Law Institute.

DETERDING v. UNITED STATES

United States Court of Claims, 1953.
69 F.Supp. 214.

MADDEN, Judge. The United States has demurred to the plaintiff's petition. The allegations of the petition are in substance as follows: The plaintiff's predecessor in title, Margaret C. Hamilton, made a deed to Anderson in 1909, and Anderson thereafter conveyed his interest to the United States. The deed described the land, the interests in which are involved in this suit, which lay adjacent to the Sacramento River in California. The deed contained the following language:

"To have and to hold all and singular the said premises, together with the appurtenances, unto the said party of the second part and to his heirs and assigns forever.

"The said land hereby conveyed is to be used for the purpose of widening and straightening the Sacramento River from Rio Vista to Collinsville or for works or purposes incidental thereto and in connection therewith; and it is understood that the grantors or their assigns shall have at all times the right to make such use of the lands hereby conveyed as may in the judgment of the grantee or his assigns hereunder be made without interfering in any manner with the said works or purposes for which this deed is made.

"And it is further understood that the grantors and their assigns, owners of the land adjacent on the northwest to the land hereby conveyed, shall have and do hereby reserve the right of access across the land hereby conveyed to and from the bank of the river as now or hereafter located, for the purpose of shipping and receiving freight upon or from boats or vessels plying in the river, provided that such right of way shall be used in such manner, and provided that such right of way can be used in such manner, as not to interfere in any way with the works or purposes for which this deed is made."

The plaintiff succeeded to all the interests of Hamilton in the lands mentioned in the deed. Prior to July 1, 1942 the plaintiff leased the lands here involved to the Amerada Oil Company and the American Petroleum Corporation for the production of oil and gas. On July 1, 1942 the United States entered into a compensatory royalty agreement with the Amerada Oil Company which had gas leases on other lands in the neighborhood of the land here involved, under the terms of which the United States agreed not to drill or permit the drilling of gas wells on the land here involved, and the Amerada Company agreed to pay to the United States as a compensatory royalty a share, proportionate to the acreage of the land here involved in relation to the whole area from which gas was to be taken, of the sale price which Amerada should receive from the sale of gas taken from wells in the area. The United States agreed to make a contribution of $25,000, which was one-half the cost of a well, and $100 per month for upkeep and current expense. The agreement contained the following language in its introductory part:

" *   *   * Whereas, the Secretary of the Interior represents that he has the power and authority under the provisions of said Executive Order, and his general administrative authority, including powers vested in him by the Act of February 25, 1920 (41 U.S.Stats. 437), as amended by the Act of August 21, 1935 [49 Stat. 674] (46 U.S.Stats. 1523), and other applicable acts of Congress, rules, regulations and orders, to enter into this agreement; *   *   *."

and also the following final paragraph

"9.   Government does not warrant title to said parcels but if at any time it shall be finally determined by a final judgment or decree of a Court of competent jurisdiction, or otherwise, that the United States has no title to the mineral rights underlying said parcels or any portion or portions thereof, no further payment shall be required by Amerada hereunder with respect to any such parcel or any portion or portions thereof. *   *   *."

After having made this agreement with the United States, the Amerada Company did not continue its oil and gas lease from the plaintiff, which expired on September 17, 1942.   It has paid the United States some $80,000 under the agreement described above.   The plaintiff seeks, in this suit, to recover the amount which the United States has so received.   She seeks, in the alternative, to recover the entire present value of the gas interests in the land, on the theory that the United States has taken those interests.

The plaintiff claims that after the deed from Hamilton to Anderson, Hamilton, and now the plaintiff as her successor, continued to be the owner of the gas in the land described in the deed, or of the sole right to produce and recover the gas.   She says that the deed conveyed to Anderson only an easement to do upon the land whatever was necessary for widening and straightening the river, leaving in the grantor all other uses and interests in the land.   She further says that if Anderson received more than an easement, and became the owner of corporeal interests in the land, still the language of the deed made it plain that the grantor was to retain many interests in the land, and that those interests, whether they be easements, profits a prendre, or rights under running covenants, include the right here in question, the sole right to take gas from the land.

We think that the plaintiff owns the exclusive right to take gas from the land.   We think that the deed to Anderson, when properly analyzed, may more properly be said to have granted an easement than a corporeal interest.   From a reading of the whole deed it is plain that the words of purpose contained in it were not insignificant surplusage, as words of purpose, without more, are frequently held to be.   That the grantee was to have the land only for the stated purpose is made plain by the succeeding language which provides in substance that the grantor is to have the right to make all other uses of the land not inconsistent with the stated purpose.   Since the purpose of entering on the land to change the course of the stream is much more in the nature of a jus in re aliena than the right, for example, which the grantor was clearly intended to have, to occupy and cultivate the land, we think the conventional pattern of legal interests is better followed by treating the grantee's particular interest as the easement, and the grantor's retained interest as the corporeal and residuary interest in the land.

We agree, however, with the plaintiff, that the application of particular names to the interests involved is not decisive of the ownership of the interests. The right to take gas from the land of another is a conventional subject matter of a profit a prendre, hence if the parties intended, or if the law of the State of California requires, and we are not suggesting that it does, that the deed given to Anderson granted corporeal interests to him, the right of the grantor to take gas from the granted land was nevertheless a lawful and conventional interest.

The provisions of the California Civil Code reenforce our views. Sections 1641 and 1066, which require that the whole document be read before a decision is reached as to the effect of any part of it, and Section 1069, which says that reservations in deeds should be construed in favor of the grantor, are applicable. The spirit of the latter section is surely applicable to a provision, other than a technical reservation, which expresses an intent that, in spite of the deed, the grantor is still to have interests in the land as, for example, by way of an exception or of a covenant running with the land.

We have concluded, then, that the plaintiff is the sole owner, of the right to take gas from the land in question. The United States has, under its agreement with the Amerada Company, received money for its agreement to refrain from doing what it had no right to do. The plaintiff sues for the money so received. The United States urges that this court has no jurisdiction to grant the relief demanded. The question is difficult, indeed. The basis of our jurisdiction, if it exists, is that the plaintiff has rights arising out of a contract which the United States has breached. We think that the relation between the plaintiff and the United States, in relation to their respective rights in the land in question, is a conventional or contractual relation, within the meaning of our jurisdictional statute, 28 U.S.C.A. § 41 et seq. See Fletcher v. Peck, 6 Cranch 87, 136, 3 L.Ed. 162. The deed from the plaintiff's predecessor to the predecessor of the United States was a determination and statement of what rights the parties and their successors were to have in this land. When the United States took the Anderson title, it took it, not by acquisition in some overriding capacity as sovereign, but as successor to Anderson, and subject to his obligations, as they were stated in the deed. His obligations became those of the United States, because it was the intent of the parties, and is the rule of law, that successors shall be bound.

The question remains, Was it a breach of contract for the United States to enter into the compensatory royalty agreement with Amerada, and receive the payments provided in that agreement? The only rational basis for the agreement was that the United States was asserting ownership of the right to the gas, though it refused to warrant its title to it, and the Amerada Company was buying protection from a possible competing well located on the land in question. We think that the provision in the deed to Anderson, that the grantor and its successors should have the use of the land for all purposes except the stated purpose for which the grantee might use it, constituted an agreement that the grantee and its successors would not claim rights inconsistent with that provision, and thereby cast doubts upon the grantor's title to the rights promised her. And we conclude that when the United States, solely on the basis of the documents here involved, asserted title to and sold for money an interest which belonged to the plaintiff, and which, as we have construed the transaction, it had agreed that it would not assert, it breached the contract contained in the deed to Anderson. In these circumstances we think that the net amount of the money received by the United States belongs to the plaintiff, as a fair measure of the damage caused her and as a restitution to her of what the United States has gained by its breach of its contract.

The defendant's demurrer is overruled.

It is so ordered.

WHITAKER and LITTLETON, Judges, and WHALEY, Chief Justice, concur.

JONES, Judge (dissenting). It is my view that the term "use" as set out in the reservation is not sufficient to cover the right on the part of plaintiff to remove and dispose of the oil and gas.

Oil and gas while in the ground are a part of the corpus of the property. Taking them out and disposing of them is not merely a use of the property, but is a removal and sale of a part of the body of the property. The reservation of the right to use the property does not so limit a deed that is otherwise complete as to permit the grantor to sell the property or any part thereof.

While this viewpoint is somewhat weakened by the stated purpose of the transfer, to wit, "widening and straightening the Sacramento River," yet when the whole instrument is considered, it seems to me that the stated purpose is the reason for making the deed rather than a limitation that would make the transfer a mere easement.

In my judgment this reservation is insufficient to support plaintiff's claim.

Note

The court in the Deterding case said that the amount received by the United States under the compensatory royalty agreement "is a fair measure of the damage caused her [the plaintiff] and as a restitution to her of what the United States gained by breach of its contract." This remark indicates a basic problem in deciding what restitutionary remedies are available for breach of contract and the difficulty that may be encountered in deciding whether a money judgment indicates a recovery of damages or restitution for unjust enrichment. These questions cannot be pursued here. One may question the court's assertion that the specification of the rights reserved by the plaintiff's predecessor in his deed to Anderson constituted a contract that the grantee and his successors would not claim rights inconsistent with that provision. Courts normally have no occasion so to construe language in a deed describing the interest conveyed or the interest reserved. Such a contract, if implied, might be better regarded as implied by law for equitable or policy reasons rather than as implied in fact on the basis of the intention of the parties. If the implication of such a contract permits the court in the Deterding case to treat the recovery as one for damages, it does not change the fact that the basic problem remains whether the plaintiff was wrongfully injured or the defendant wrongfully benefitted by the defendant's conduct. If one looks at the problem as essentially one of unjust enrichment, is there some general duty, apart from any prior transaction between the parties, which prevents one person from taking a benefit from a third party by means of an assertion of title to another person's land?

The case might be more easily analyzed if the United States had entered into a typical oil and gas lease with Amerada and gained the usual royalty from some ensuing oil or gas production on the land in question. The main source of difficulty in this case is the peculiar nature of a compensatory royalty agreement. On the surface at least, one might wonder what concern it was of the plaintiff's that Amerada paid the United States for not doing something which it had no right to do. On the other hand the analytical difficulties of this case may not prevent one from a sense that somehow the United States has been inequitably enriched at the plaintiff's expense. But a further problem involved in so declaring is whether Amerada might, upon showing the plaintiff's true title, have recovered the sum it paid. At any rate, so far as we know, the Deterding case is without precedent in respect to the remedy allowed.

Compare the situation discussed in Note 5, page 148 supra. See Palmer, Restitution §§ 4.9, 21.4 (1978).

Problem

Hilgarten Marble Co. conveyed land to the Los Angeles Gas and Electric Corp., retaining land of which the granted land was previously a part. After the granting clause and description of the property, this further clause followed:

"This transfer is made subject to reservations and conditions as follows: The grantor hereby reserves for itself, its successors and assigns the right to lay and maintain pipes * * * under and across the land hereby conveyed * * *; and also the right to use the surface of said land for any lawful purpose, except that no building or other structure shall be erected thereon and no use of said land made by the grantor which shall interfere or be inconsistent with the use by the grantee: it being a further condition of this transfer * * * that no poles or towers or other structures or buildings * * * shall ever be constructed * * * by the grantee upon the land hereby conveyed, the use of said land by the grantee to be limited to the carrying of elevated wires and cables over said land at the usual height above the surface, * * * or carrying such wires or cables under said land. * * * "

Plaintiffs are successors to all rights conveyed to the grantee; defendants are successors of all rights reserved by the grantor. Defendants built fences around three sides of the property, and used the property for the parking and storage of certain automotive equipment. This led to a dispute and to a suit by the plaintiffs for a declaration of the rights and duties of the parties and for certain other relief. The court held that the plaintiffs were owners in fee in trust for the limited purpose of carrying elevated wires and cables as specified in the deed; that the defendants were owners of an easement over and upon the property; and that the defendants were to be enjoined in respect only to maintaining their fences at a certain height with provision for an unlocked gate. This judgment was affirmed on appeal. City of Los Angeles v. Savage, 165 Cal.App.2d 1, 331 P.2d 211 (1958). Do you agree with this analysis? If this property had proven valuable for oil and gas purposes, which of these parties would have been entitled to take the minerals?

TEXAS CO. v. O'MEARA, 377 Ill. 144, 36 N.E.2d 256 (1941). The following paragraph is taken from the opinion of the court:

"A greater portion of appellants' brief is devoted to citations and argument intended to show that the conveyance in question was 'in fee' and the arguments pro and con as to this point are urged by them as determinative of the result. We do not believe this to be true. In Oswald v. Wolf, 126 Ill. 542, 19 N.E. 28, we were, as here, considering a title to a right-of-way. We there pointed out on authority of Blackstone that the word 'fee,' as meaning an estate of inheritance, is applicable to and may be had in any kind of hereditament, either corporeal or incorporeal. We held that an easement of way is an incorporal hereditament, not subject to livery of seisin, but subject only to grant; that rights-of-way have attached to them the same idea of duration or quantity of estate as is applied to corporeal hereditaments; that the duration of the estate, or the time for which the enjoyment is to continue forms the quantity of the estate, and hence, if the grant be an estate of inheritance either in the hereditaments corporeal or incorporeal, a fee is taken, while if for life only, a life estate would be granted."

STANTON v. T. L. HERBERT & SONS

Supreme Court of Tennessee, 1919.
141 Tenn. 440, 211 S.W. 353.

GREEN, J. The bill in this case was filed by the complainants to enjoin the defendants from removing sand and gravel from Hill's Island in the Cumberland river, about 20 miles above Nashville, and to recover damages. This island is the property of the complainants, and the defendants are building contractors at Nashville and were removing sand and gravel from said island and the water adjacent thereto for use in contracts which they had for the erection of buildings at the powder plant.

A demurrer coupled with an answer was filed by the defendants. The Chancellor sustained the demurrer and dismissed the bill, and the complainants have appealed to this court.

Hill's Island was formerly the property of Mrs. Mary Nolan and William E. Jordon. On June 12, 1911, they conveyed to complainants, Mrs. Elizabeth Stanton and Rush Hawes. Said deed described the property and was in the usual form of a warranty deed, except that in the habendum clause there were these words:

"Subject, however, to an easement, right, or privilege, to remove sand from said property for a period of ten years from the date of this conveyance, and such rights, privileges, and easements as may be necessary and proper for such use which easements, privileges, and rights are hereby retained by the grantors herein."

It was averred in the bill that the grantors had attempted to assign their right to remove sand from said island to their codefendants, W.T. Hardison & Son, T.L. Herbert & Sons, and the Nashville Builders' Supply Company, and that the said codefendants, along with Jordan, were removing tremendous quantities of sand and gravel from said island and the water adjacent thereto, for use in their powder plant contracts as aforesaid, and that they were very seriously damaging the complainant's property. It was alleged that these codefendants were acting illegally in the premises, since the complainants were advised that the reservation or exception of the right to remove sand contained in said deed was void for uncertainty, and for that it was contradictory to and destructive of the grant, and that, at any rate, the right of the original grantor to remove sand was personal and not assignable nor divisible.

All these propositions of law were challenged by the demurrer, and the allegations of fact contained in the bill were rather generally denied by the answer.

As is apparent from the foregoing statement, numerous questions are raised in this case, and they have been debated with much learning and ability. It will not be necessary to consider them all. A determination of the nature of the right or interest reserved in this property by the original grantor simplifies the solution of the case.   *   *   *

We think the right to remove sand reserved to the grantors under this deed was not exclusive. There is nothing in the language used in the deed to indicate that such right was intended to be exclusive. The right was described "as an easement, right, or privilege." The indefinite article "an" was used, not "the." In addition to the right to remove sand, only such other rights and privileges were reserved as were necessary to effectuate the principal right. There is nothing to show an intention to deprive Stanton and Hawes of the right to remove sand themselves. Under the authorities, the presumption is against an exclusive grant or reservation of this nature.

The first case dealing with the question involved here was that of Earl of Huntington v. Lord Mountjoy, 4 Leo. 147; 1 And. 307; and Godb. 18.

This case has been variously reported, and not always to the same effect; but the case has always been understood to have declared that a mere grant of liberty to dig coals did not confer on the grantees an exclusive right to dig them.

In Chetham v. Williams, 4 East. 469, Lord Ellenborough said:

"No case can be named where one who has only a liberty of digging for coals in another's soil has an exclusive right to the coals, so as to enable him to maintain trover against the owner of the estate for coal raised by him."   *   *   *

In Duke of Sutherland v. Heathcote (1892) 1 Ch. 475, there was a reservation of a right to dig and carry away coal quite similar to the reservation of the right to dig sand, in the deed before us. Lord Lindley said of the grantors:

"They reserved a profit à prendre, an incorporeal hereditament, not a mere personal license.   *   *   * A profit à prendre is a right to take something of another person's land; such a right does not prevent the owner from taking the same sort of thing from off his own land; the first right may limit, but does not exclude the second. An exclusive right to all the profit of a particular kind can no doubt be granted; but such a right cannot be inferred from the language when it is not clear and explicit."

In Gloninger v. Franklin Coal Co., 55 Pa. 9, 93 Am.Dec. 720, there was a deed granting "the free right to dig coal at the coal bed under the foot of the mountain on my lot. No. 22, in third division of lands in Wilkes-Barre, with the privilege freely to carry the coal * * * to and from said coal bed through my land at all times hereafter, doing as little damage as may be, in the uses aforesaid." It was held that the language used created an incorporeal hereditament and not an exclusive right to all the coal. * * *

It is obvious from these authorities that a mere grant of the right or privilege of removing minerals from the land of another does not in itself create an exclusive right or privilege in the grantees. Such cases are to be distinguished from those in which there is a grant of all the minerals in certain property or a grant of an exclusive right to remove the minerals.

The latter class of cases is illustrated by Caldwell v. Fulton, 31 Pa. 475, 72 Am.Dec. 760. The language used in the grant there considered was construed to mean that the grantee was entitled to take all the coal in the land. The deed was held to be a conveyance of the coal itself. It was said that coal and minerals in place are land, and that it was no longer to be doubted that they were subject to conveyance as land. The deed, therefore, was held to pass an interest in the land—a corporeal interest.

Likewise in the case of Massot v. Moses, 3 S.C. 168, 16 Am.Rep. 697, there was a conveyance held to pass all the phosphates on a particular tract of land, and it was declared that this created an exclusive interest in such minerals in the grantee. A part of the land itself was conveyed. This case of Massot v. Moses is a learned review of the authorities on this subject and a very clear statement of the established rules of law, although not so easy to follow in its application of the principles stated to the facts of the particular case.

The distinction between a conveyance of all the minerals in a particular tract of land, or an exclusive right to the minerals, and a deed granting a right to remove minerals from land by the grantee to be enjoyed in common with the grantor, appears in numerous cases collected in notes in 26 L.R.A., N.S., 614, and 18 L.R.A. 491. In many cases the land itself is demised, which, of course, confers an exclusive right to the minerals.

The effect of this distinction is this: If all the minerals are conveyed, or an exclusive right thereto, an interest in the land passes. This is a corporeal interest, which may be assigned, divided, or dealt with as any other interest in land. If, under the grant, there passes only a right to remove minerals in common with the grantor, an incorporeal hereditament results.

Such an incorporeal hereditament is referred to in some of the cases as a license, and in some of them as an easement in gross. It is not, however, a revocable license, and it is not an easement that is personal to the grantee. It is a profit à prendre, and under the weight of authority a profit à prendre is both inheritable and assignable. Post v. Pearsall, 22 Wend. (N.Y.) 425; Boatman v. Lasley, 23 Ohio St. 614; Tinicum Fishing Co. v. Carter, 61 Pa. 21, 100 Am.Dec. 597.

While a profit à prendre is assignable, it is not divisible. This rule is applicable to mining cases and is recognized in Caldwell v. Fulton, supra, and in Massot v. Moses, supra, and was applied in Lord Mountjoy's Case.

Such an incorporeal hereditament is similar in legal contemplation to commons of estovers or fishery. These were held to be indivisible, and, if an attempt to divide or apportion them was made, a destruction of the right resulted.

In the case before us, it appears that the grantors undertook to assign rights to remove sand from Hill's Island to W.T. Hardison & Son, T.L. Herbert & Sons, and Nashville Builders' Supply Co. In the answer filed by these defendants, they justify their removal of sand from the island on the ground that they are assignees of the reserved rights of the grantors in the deed to these complainants. It is not a fair construction of the pleadings to conclude that these defendants were users of a "common stock," as said in Lord Mountjoy's Case, or were engaged in any joint enterprise. They were separate contractors, and each had contracts with reference to the building of the powder plant. They claim as "assignees" of the grantors, not as "assignee."

In Van Rensselaer v. Radcliff, 10 Wend. (N.Y.) 639, 25 Am.Dec. 582, it was held that a common of estovers was not apportionable, and, if the tract to which the common was appurtenant was conveyed to different persons, the common was extinguished. * * *

From the authorities discussed it is manifest that the grantors by the reservation contained in their deed only obtained a right in common with their grantees to remove sand from this island. Such a right was a mere incorporeal hereditament, and could not be divided as here undertaken. The attempted division has destroyed the reservation. The assignees of the grantors, therefore, were not entitled to this sand.

We cannot undertake a further review of the authorities cited by counsel. We are content to follow the courts of England and of Pennsylvania. These courts have largely developed the law relating to mines and mineral rights, in so far as the subject is not controlled by statute, and their decisions on this subject are entitled to the greatest consideration owing to the magnitude of such interests in these jurisdictions, to say nothing of the ability of the judges.

Indeed, there is little conflict of authority. Cases relied on by the defendants are, almost without exception, cases in which there was an exclusive right considered, and, as heretofore seen, such a right is both assignable and divisible. It is an interest in the land.

The case of Chandler v. Hart, 161 Cal. 405, 119 P. 516, Ann.Cas. 1913B, 1094, is not in point. It was there held that a lease of oil rights might be divided, but there was a demise of the land itself with the exclusive right to take the oil. The court distinguishes the case from Lord Mountjoy's Case, and those following the earlier authority, on the ground that the grantee in the California case had the exclusive right to remove oil, and on the other ground that the development of oil lands differs in character from the development of mines. Chandler v. Hart was properly decided on these facts, and we see nothing in the reasoning of the court that conflicts with what has been heretofore said. We do not understand this case as disapproving Lord Mountjoy's Case.

The justice of the rule against the apportionment or division of an incorporeal hereditament, such as this, is strikingly illustrated in the case before us. The complainants here might very well have agreed that their immediate grantors, one of whom was a contractor, should reserve enough sand for use in their own business. The grantors, however, undertook to assign this right to three of the largest contractors in Nashville, who were engaged in the building of the largest plant in the United States—a plant demanded by the exigencies of the great war, and designed by the government to manufacture enough powder to supply the needs of the United States and all its Allies. To permit the grantor to apportion his right to sand among three such contractors engaged in such an enterprise would have required quantities of sand never dreamed of by the parties at the time this deed was made. It would, indeed, have been a surcharge of the land.

It follows that the Chancellor was in error in holding that complainants were not entitled to injunctive relief. * * *

The case will be remanded for further proceedings, not inconsistent with this opinion, with leave to complainants to set up and recover all damages to which they may be entitled under the proof and the law.

Defendants will pay the costs of this court. The costs below will be adjudged by the Chancellor.

MARTIN v. MUSIC

Court of Appeals of Kentucky, 1953.
254 S.W.2d 701.

CULLEN, Commissioner. This action involves the construction of the following agreement:

"This mutual agreement, made and entered into by and between Martin Music, of Prestonsburg, Kentucky, party of the first part, and Fred Martin, of Prestonsburg, Kentucky, party of the second part.

"Witnesseth: That for and in consideration of the sum of One ($1.00) Dollar, and other considerations hereinafter set out, parties of the first and second part mutually agree:

"Party of the first part gives and grants to second party the right to construct and maintain a sewer line under and through his property located in the Layne Heirs addition to the City of Prestonsburg,

Kentucky, in the Garfield Bottom, and being lots Nos. 17 through 24 inc. of said addition.

"In consideration of said right, second party agrees to lay said sewer line at sufficient depth to not interfere with first party's use and enjoyment of said property; and to place an intake connection in said line for use of said party at a point to be designated by him; and further agrees to pay to first party any damage which may result to his property by reason of the laying, maintaining, repairing and operation of said sewer line.

"Given under our hands, this December 3, 1949."

At the time the agreement was executed, the eight lots owned by Music were unoccupied, except for a garage building used by Music for the vehicles operated by him in his business as a bulk distributer of oil and gasoline. Martin constructed his sewer across the lots, and thereafter Music sold six of the lots to one Moore, who in turn sold three each to the appellees Wells and Allen. Wells and Allen each commenced the construction of a dwelling house on his lots, and prepared to connect with Martin's sewer. Martin then brought this action for a declaration of rights, maintaining that the right to connect with the sewer was personal to Music alone, for the purpose of serving a dwelling house which Music had planned to build, and that the right did not accrue to Wells and Allen. The court adjudged that Music, Wells and Allen each had the right to connect with the sewer, provided that the connection was made through the one intake connection provided for in the written contract. Martin appeals.

Considerable evidence was introduced concerning the circumstances surrounding the execution of the agreement, and the situation that existed at the time the agreement was made. It appears that the lots owned by Music had a depth of 120 feet, from east to west, and a width of 25 feet each, fronting on a street on the west and an alley on the east. Across the alley to the east, Martin owned six lots on which he had his private residence and a motel. Martin's northernmost lot was opposite Music's southernmost lot. The Big Sandy River lies some 600 feet west of Martin's property, and he desired to run the sewer line from his property to the river.

Martin's evidence was that he first proposed to construct his sewer down the alley between his lots and those of Music, but that Music, upon learning of this plan, offered to let the sewer cross his lots, in return for an intake connection privilege. Martin testified that the understanding was that Music was to build a home on his lots, and that the sewer connection was for that purpose.

Music's evidence was that Martin did not want to run his sewer down the alley, for fear that it then would be classified as a public sewer, to which anyone could connect; that Music offered to let the sewer go across his lots in return for a connection privilege; that there was no understanding that the intake was to be limited to one dwelling to be erected by Music, but on the contrary it was clearly understood that the intake was to be available for each of the eight lots.

Martin's sewer is a six-inch main, which the appellees' evidence tends to show is capable of handling the sewage from their buildings, in addition to that from Martin's properties, with no difficulty. On the other hand, Martin testified that the sewer line had a low grade of descent, and that in times of heavy rains, when the river was high, there would be danger of the sewer backing up into his basement. He complains particularly of the proposal of the appellees to connect their eaves and downspouts to the sewer, which he claims will create too great a flow of water for the sewer line to accommodate.

Martin maintains that the agreement provides for an easement in gross, rather than one running with the land. He relies upon Mannin v. Adkins, 199 Ky. 241, 250 S.W. 974, which we do not consider to be in point. In that case, the grantor of a piece of property reserved the right to " 'have, use, and get coal off the lands hereby conveyed for fuel for his own purposes or home consumption as fuel' ". The court held that the reservation was personal to the grantor, and did not run with the adjoining land which he occupied as his home place at the time of the conveyance. There, the reserved privilege was not related to a particular piece of property as a dominant estate, and it necessarily was personal. Here, the sewer connection privilege necessarily is limited to the parcel of land over which the sewer line runs.

If an easement is to be exercised in connection with the occupancy of particular land, then ordinarily it is classified as an easement appurtenant. 28 C.J.S., Easements, § 4(b), p. 635. We think it is clear that the right to connect to Martin's sewer line was to be exercised only in connection with the occupancy of the land through which it ran, and that Music was not granted the right to run a sewer line to the intake point from some parcel of land he might own or acquire in another block. Therefore, the easement must be considered to be an easement appurtenant.

It is the general rule that easements in gross are not favored, and that an easement will never be presumed to be a mere personal right when it can fairly be construed to be appurtenant to some other estate. 28 C.J.S., Easements, § 4(c), p. 638. This rule prevails in Kentucky. Buck Creek R. Co. v. Haws, 253 Ky. 203, 69 S.W.2d 333.

We think the controlling question is whether the use of the sewer by Wells and Allen, as well as by Music, will unduly burden the servient tenement (in this case, the sewer line). It appears to be the general rule that the dominant estate may be divided or partitioned, and the owner of each part may claim the right to enjoy the easement, if no additional burden is placed upon the servient estate. 17 Am.Jur., Easements, § 126, p. 1014.

Here, it cannot be ascertained from the written agreement, nor can it be ascertained with certainty from the evidence of the circumstances and conditions surrounding the execution of the agreement, just what burden it was contemplated might be imposed by way of connection with the sewer line. As far as the face of the agreement is concerned, Music could have built an apartment house, a hotel, or even a factory, upon his lots, and connected them with the sewer. Either of these would have required only one intake connection. The agreement does not limit the kind of use that Music was to make of the sewer. Since, under the words of the agreement, Music could have placed a much greater burden upon Martin's sewer we do not believe that two or three dwellings will increase the burden contemplated by the parties as expressed in their agreement.

If we go beyond the words of the agreement, and accept all of the evidence as to what the parties intended, then we find a conflict of evidence, upon which we could not say that the chancellor erred.

The judgment is affirmed.

Problem

Compare the profit in gross involved in Stanton v. Herbert, supra, with the case of a profit appurtenant. Such cases are not common. But suppose A grants to B:

(a) the right to take gravel and seaweed from the beach on A's land for use on B's land; or

(b) the right to cut timber on A's land to build fences on B's land. In either case what would be the effect on the right granted if B should convey a portion of his land to C, or if B should divide his land by conveyances to C and D. See Hall v. Lawrence, 2 R.I. 218, 57 Am.Dec. 272 (1852); Clark, Covenants and Interests Running With the Land 66 (2d ed. 1947).

LOCH SHELDRAKE ASSOCIATES v. EVANS

Court of Appeals of New York, 1954.
306 N.Y. 297, 118 N.E.2d 444.

DESMOND, Judge. Our question is as to the meaning and effect of a reservation of water rights appertaining to a natural lake or pond known as Loch Sheldrake, in Sullivan County. Into a deed, which was given in 1919 to Greenspan and others (predecessors of plaintiff) by persons named Divine, and which conveyed to plaintiff's predecessors the whole of Loch Sheldrake and all its shores, there was written this language: "The parties of the first part hereby expressly except and reserve from this conveyance the right and privilege of damming the Sheldrake Lake or Pond and the outlet thereof, and of impounding the waters of said Lake or Pond and raising and drawing the same, together with the right of ingress and egress for the purpose of construction, repairing and maintaining the said dam, or any part or portion thereof, and any and all conduits, raceways or pipes connected therewith or leading therefrom, which now exist or may hereafter be constructed. Such waters, however, shall not be drawn lower than the natural low water mark of the said Lake or Pond, and they shall not be raised higher than the normal or natural high water mark of said Pond, except that in case of unusual or extraordinary flood the same may be impounded for not to exceed forty-eight (48) hours at any one time."

All the rights thus reserved were, in 1927, conveyed, together with a so-called "mill lot" some distance south of Loch Sheldrake, by the Divines, to Isidore Evans, defendant's husband and predecessor in title.

Beginning about 1915, and continuously since then, Mr. and Mrs. Evans have operated a large summer hotel on other lands owned by them, not acquired from the Divines, south of the mill lot, and about a half mile south of Loch Sheldrake. Many years before any of the deeds herein referred to were given, a dam had been built, in an outlet of Loch Sheldrake, by the Divines, and from it, through a pipe, water was carried by gravity to and for a mill formerly operated by the Divines on the "mill lot", the water flowing, after such use, out of the mill's tailrace into a brook. Undoubtedly, the Divines made the 1919 reservation of the Loch Sheldrake water rights, because of their then ownership and operation of the mill, but the reservation itself not only did not limit the water diversion to mill uses (it does not mention either the mill lot or the mill), but, on the contrary, the reservation, (supra) embodied its own sole limitation, that is, that the dam be so used that the waters of the lake will be not drawn below low-water mark, or flooded above high-water mark. Before and after the giving by the Divines of the 1919 deed first above mentioned, in which the water rights were reserved, the Divines at times sold, to Mr. and Mrs. Evans, for use at their hotel, water which had been carried by the outlet pipe to the mill lot. After the hotel owners had acquired the mill lot, the mill operations were (in about 1935) discontinued and, ever since, large quantities of water, drawn from the lake through the pipe to the old mill lot, have been piped further on into the hotel grounds for use at the hotel by defendant.

This suit was brought to obtain, for plaintiff, present owner of the lake and its shores, a declaratory judgment that defendant, by the water right reservation (supra), obtained no more than an easement which was appurtenant to the mill lot and which, as plaintiff asserts, permitted the use of the water for the now discontinued mill uses only. Plaintiff demanded an injunction and money damages, also. Defendant's opposing position, with which we will agree herein, is, as expressed in her answer, that by her succession to the water rights reserved in the 1919 deed, she "is entitled to the sole, absolute and free use of the waters of Loch Sheldrake between the low and high water marks for the benefit of her business and business properties."

The trial court came to the conclusion "that the reservation of the right and privilege to the use of the waters of Loch Sheldrake was a reservation in connection with and appurtenant to the mill lot and for which property only the privilege reserved was intended", that defendant, succeeding to the rights of the Divines under that reservation, has no right to draw or use the lake waters except for mill or manufacturing uses on the mill lot, and that such rights as defendant has are not exclusive and do not exclude plaintiff from drawing and using the lake waters. The judgment, entered after trial, perpetually restrained defendant from drawing water other than for mill purposes.

On defendant's appeal to the Appellate Division, that court took a view of the case much more favorable to her. It concluded that the 1919 reservation was not limited, expressly or by implication, to use of the water for mill purposes, and that, while defendant's assertion of an exclusive right to use the water for any purpose whatsoever is perhaps too broad, "she has the right", said the Appellate Division, "to use the water for the purposes the Divine family used the same for at the time they conveyed the lake to Greenspan and others," 280 App.Div. 51, 58, 111 N.Y.S.2d 371, that is, at the time of the giving of the 1919 Divine-Greenspan deed containing the reservation.

Plaintiff alone appealed to this court, so we are powerless to modify the judgment, in defendant's favor. Despite holdings or seeming holdings by both courts below, and concessions or seeming concessions made at one time or another by both parties, that the reservation quoted in the first paragraph hereof from the 1919 deed, created an "easement appurtenant" to the mill lot only, we do not think that such was the result. We think that what the grantors Divine reserved, and what defendant's husband, and defendant, as his successor, got by subsequent grant from the Divines was not, in strictest terms, an easement at all, but an interest in the Loch Sheldrake lands, in the nature of a right to take a "profit" from those lands. See Huntington v. Asher, 96 N.Y. 604, 609; De Witt v. Harvey, 4 Gray 486, 488, 489, 70 Mass. 486, 488, 489; Goodrich v. Burbank, 12 Allen 459, 461, 94 Mass. 459, 461; French v. Morris, 101 Mass. 68, 71. Such a right, not appurtenant to any other lands, may be used by its owner at any place or in any manner. As the Supreme Judicial Court of Massachusetts pointed out in Goodrich v. Burbank, supra, 12 Allen at page 462: "Rights of water duly granted by deed, not appurtenant to any particular parcel of land, may be used by the owner at any place or in any manner, so long as he does not interfere with or impair the rights of others". In that same decision, the Massachusetts court recognized "the right to take a certain quantity of water from a mill pond as a distinct and substantive subject of grant, without restriction as to its use at any designated place". 12 Allen at page 462. The New York cases above cited are in agreement with those statements of law.

The briefs here join in debate as to whether the Divine-Greenspan 1919 deed reservation created an "easement appurtenant" or an "easement in gross". If we are to speak with strictest accuracy, there is no such thing as an "easement in gross" (although the phrase enjoys respectable usage, as in Wilson v. Ford, 209 N.Y. 186, 196, 102 N.E. 614, 617, and other New York opinions), since an easement presupposes two distinct tenements, one dominant, the other servient. Rangeley v. Midland Ry. Co., L.R. 3 Ch. 306, 309, Eng.; Pierce v. Keator, 70 N.Y. 419, 421. Obviously, the reservation we are construing was not the sort of mere personal, nonassignable, noninheritable privilege or license sometimes loosely described as an "easement in gross". See Saratoga State Waters Corp. v. Pratt, 227 N.Y. 429, 443, 125 N.E. 834, 839. What the Divines reserved in their deed to Greenspan and his associates was an absolute right to take profit or produce from the land conveyed, a right which was capable of being conveyed in gross and was so transferred by deed to defendant, and is now held, by defendant, without reference to use on any particular lands. Huntington v. Asher, supra, and see Saratoga State Waters Corp. v. Pratt, supra, 227 N.Y. at pages 443–445, 125 N.E. at pages 838–839. Of course, such a right to take water from a distant source might, by other and appropriate kinds of verbiage, be so granted as to be appurtenant to specific lands separated from the source of supply. Cady v. Springfield Water Works Co., 134 N.Y. 118, 121, 31 N.E. 245, 246. But a reservation or grant in a deed, like every other contract "must be construed according to the intent of the parties, so far as such intent can be gathered from the whole instrument, and is consistent with the rules of law." Real Property Law, § 240, subd. 3, McK.Consol.Laws, c. 50. It is only when language used in a conveyance "is susceptible of more than one interpretation" that the courts will look into surrounding circumstances, the situation of the parties, etc. French v. Carhart, 1 N.Y. 96, 102; Clark v. Devoe, 124 N.Y. 120, 124, 26 N.E. 275, 276; Wilson v. Ford, supra, 209 N.Y. at page 196, 102 N.E. at page 617, and authorities there cited. The settled rule for the construction of such instruments is that all evidence must be excluded which is offered "to vary, explain, or contradict a written instrument that was complete in itself, and without ambiguity in its terms" since, when words in a deed "have a definite and precise meaning, it is not permissible to go elsewhere in search of conjecture in order to restrict or extend the meaning." Uihlein v. Matthews, 172 N.Y. 154, 159, 64 N.E. 792, 794, and cases cited. That is the first rule of construction, and in this case we need no other. The reservation in the 1919 Divine-Greenspan deed, in plain words of common use reserved from the conveyance, the "right and privilege" of damming the lake and its outlet, of impounding its waters "and raising and drawing the same", subject to two conditions only, that is, that the waters should not be drawn lower than the lake's natural low-water mark or raised higher than its natural high-water mark. In that reservation there was no ambiguity whatever, and so it was not necessary or permissible in this lawsuit to look beyond the deed itself for evidence which might suggest a lesser meaning. Obviously, no outside evidence could properly be taken as to the parties' intent concerning the amount of water to be drawn off, since the reservation itself, in its references to low- and high-water marks, states its own precise quantitative limitations.

Plaintiff's contention that the reservation resulted in the creation not of any absolute right but of an easement appurtenant to the mill lot only, is not based on anything in the Divine-Greenspan deed itself, but on the terms of an entirely different deed made by the Divines in 1918 to one Le Roy. That conveyance passed title, from the Divines to Le Roy, to a piece of land lying south of the lake property and between it and the mill lot, and not including any part of either of those two parcels. The grantors Divine, then still owning the lake and its shores to the north of the lands deeded to Le Roy, and the mill lot to the south of Le Roy's parcel, excepted from the Le Roy grant the right to divert the outlet waters which ran from the lake and across the premises deeded to Le Roy, "for the use and operation of the mill and turning shop and other manufacturing purposes" on the mill lot adjoining the Le Roy piece to the south, and the right to carry the diverted waters through Le Roy's land in pipes or conduits, etc. In other words, the Divines originally owned the lake and its shores (northerly piece), the mill lot (southerly piece) and a middle piece between those two, which middle piece they sold to Le Roy before they sold the lake to Greenspan and the mill lot to Evans. In the Le Roy deed, unlike the later Greenspan deed, the Divines reserved a true easement, expressly stated as being appurtenant to the mill lot, to run a pipe through the Le Roy lands to carry the waters from the Divines' lake to the Divines' mill lot. Clearly, that Divine-Le Roy exception or reservation set up a true easement appurtenant, but that deed is not in the chain of title (to the lake lands) which we are examining and is not mentioned or referred to in the later (1919) Divine-Greenspan reservation. As the Presiding Justice put it in his opinion for the Appellate Division, 280 App.Div. at page 57, 111 N.Y.S.2d at page 370: "The Divines were not bound by the language of a separate easement, created by a different deed, and for a different purpose, at a time when they could have used all the water in the lake if they so desired." It would be fatuous to deny that the Divines in their 1919 reservation of water rights, were thinking of the easement they had already carved out of their grant to Le Roy, to carry waters over Le Roy's lands and for the Divine mill to the south. But, in the later Divine-Greenspan reservation, the reservees fettered themselves with no such limitations as are found in the Le Roy easement. In the Greenspan deed the Divines retained, and surely they had the right to reserve, an absolute, total and unlimited right to draw off, not for any particular purpose or for use at any particular place, the lake waters down to low-water mark. The Divine-Le Roy deed displays a background, and supplies a reason, for the Greenspan reservation, but, by settled rules, it cannot vary it. Even if we were to read the Divine-Greenspan deed as stating (and it does not state) the purpose or reason for the reservation, such a statement alone would not limit the otherwise absolute character of the reservation. See Borst v. Empie, 5 N.Y. 33, 40; Lindenmuth v. Safe Harbor Water Power Corp., 309 Pa. 58, 163 A. 159, 89 A.L.R. 1180.

Since we hold that the Divine-Greenspan reservation is nonambiguous, it is unnecessary for us to discuss the question, as to which the courts below differed, of the admissibility of certain testimony tending to fix the time when water was first sold by the Divines for use at defendant's hotel.

The views stated herein would, logically, lead to a conclusion, more favorable to defendant than the judgment appealed from, since our views would produce a holding that the right to draw off water in the lake is in defendant to the exclusion of plaintiff, and that there is no applicable limitation at all as to the purpose of such use. However, the appeal is by plaintiff alone, so we affirm.

The order should be affirmed, with costs. Of the question certified to us by the Appellate Division, the first should be answered in the negative, the second not answered.

Problems

1. "The Grantee and his immediate family only, shall enjoy the free use of the swimming pool." The language was held to create an easement appurtenant to the lot conveyed to the grantee. Maranatha Settlement Association v.

Evans, 385 Pa. 208, 122 A.2d 679 (1956). What is the nature of the interest of the members of the grantee's family, if any?

2. A grants to B a certain tract of land together with a right of way from the land conveyed across the land retained by A for "so long as B shall live." How would you classify this easement? Is it "personal"? Is it in gross?

MILLER v. LUTHERAN CONFERENCE & CAMP ASSOCIATION

Supreme Court of Pennsylvania, 1938.
331 Pa. 241, 200 A. 646, 130 A.L.R. 1245.

STERN, Justice. This litigation is concerned with interesting and somewhat novel legal questions regarding rights of boating, bathing, and fishing in an artificial lake.

Frank C. Miller, his brother Rufus W. Miller, and others, who owned lands on Tunkhannock Creek in Tobyhanna Township, Monroe County, organized a corporation known as the Pocono Spring Water Ice Company, to which, in September 1895, they made a lease for a term of ninety-nine years of so much of their lands as would be covered by the backing up of the water as a result of the construction of a 14-foot dam which they proposed to erect across the creek. The company was to have "the exclusive use of the water and its privileges." It was chartered for the purpose of "erecting a dam   *   *   *, for pleasure, boating, skating, fishing and the cutting, storing and selling of ice." The dam was built, forming "Lake Naomi," somewhat more than a mile long and about one-third of a mile wide.

By deed dated March 20, 1899, the Pocono Spring Water Ice Company granted to "Frank C. Miller, his heirs and assigns forever, the exclusive right to fish and boat in all the waters of the said corporation at Naomi Pines, Pa." On February 17, 1900, Frank C. Miller (his wife Katherine D. Miller not joining), granted to Rufus W. Miller, his heirs and assigns forever, "all the one-fourth interest in and to the fishing, boating, and bathing rights and privileges at, in, upon and about Lake Naomi   *   *   *; which said rights and privileges were granted and conveyed to me by the Pocono Spring Water Ice Company by their indenture of the 20th day of March, A.D.1899." On the same day Frank C. Miller and Rufus W. Miller executed an agreement of business partnership, the purpose of which was the erection and operation of boat and bath houses on Naomi Lake and the purchase and maintenance of boats for use on the lake, the houses and boats to be rented for hire and the net proceeds to be divided between the parties in proportion to their respective interests in the bathing, boating and fishing privileges, namely, three-fourths to Frank C. Miller and one-fourth to Rufus W. Miller, the capital to be contributed and the losses to be borne in the same proportion. In pursuance of this agreement the brothers erected and maintained boat and bath houses at different points on the lake, purchased and rented out boats, and conducted the business generally, from the spring of 1900 until the death of Rufus W. Miller on October 11, 1925, exercising their control and use of the privileges in an exclusive, uninterrupted and open manner and without challenge on the part of anyone.

Discord began with the death of Rufus W. Miller, which terminated the partnership. Thereafter Frank C. Miller, and the executors and heirs of Rufus W. Miller, went their respective ways, each granting licenses without reference to the other. Under date of July 13, 1929, the executors of the Rufus W. Miller estate granted a license for the year 1929 to defendant, Lutheran Conference and Camp Association, which was the owner of a tract of ground abutting on the lake for a distance of about 100 feet, purporting to grant to defendant, its members, guests and campers, permission to boat, bathe and fish in the lake, a certain percentage of the receipts therefrom to be paid to the estate. Thereupon Frank C. Miller and his wife, Katherine D. Miller, filed the present bill in equity, complaining that defendant was placing diving boats on the lake and "encouraging and instigating visitors and boarders" to bathe in the lake, and was threatening to hire out boats and canoes and in general to license its guests and others to boat, bathe and fish in the lake. The bill prayed for an injunction to prevent defendant from trespassing on the lands covered by the waters of the lake, from erecting or maintaining any structures or other encroachments thereon, and from granting any bathing licenses. The court issued the injunction.

It is the contention of plaintiffs that, while the privileges of boating and fishing were granted in the deed from the Pocono Spring Water Ice Company to Frank C. Miller, no bathing rights were conveyed by that instrument. [The court affirmed this contention but held that Frank C. Miller and Rufus W. Miller had acquired title to the bathing rights by prescription.]

We are thus brought to a consideration of the next question, which is whether the boating, bathing and fishing privileges were assignable by Frank C. Miller to Rufus W. Miller. What is the nature of such rights? In England it has been said that easements in gross do not exist at all, although rights of that kind have been there recognized. In this country such privileges have sometimes been spoken of as licenses, or as contractual in their nature, rather than as easements in gross. These are differences of terminology rather than of substance. We may assume, therefore, that these privileges are easements in gross, and we see no reason to consider them otherwise. It has uniformly been held that a profit in gross—for example, a right of mining or fishing—may be made assignable.

In regard to easements in gross generally, there has been much controversy in the courts and by textbook writers and law students as to whether they have the attribute of assignability. There are dicta in Pennsylvania that they are non-assignable. Tinicum Fishing Co. v. Carter, supra [61 Pa.] pages 38, 39 [100 Am.Dec. 597]; Lindenmuth v. Safe Harbor Water Power Corporation, 309 Pa. 58, 63, 64, 163 A. 159, 89 A.L.R. 1180; Commonwealth v. Zimmerman, 56 Pa.Super. 311, 315, 316. But there is forcible expression and even definite authority to the contrary. Tide Water Pipe Co. v. Bell, 280 Pa. 104, 112, 113, 124 A. 351, 40 A.L.R. 1516; Dalton Street Railway Co. v. Scranton, 326 Pa. 6, 12,

191 A. 133. Learned articles upon the subject are to be found in 32 Yale Law Journal 813 [by Vance]; 38 Yale Law Journal 139 [by Clark]; 22 Michigan Law Review 521 [by Simes]; 40 Dickinson Law Review 46 [by Lewis]. There does not seem to be any reason why the law should prohibit the assignment of an easement in gross if the parties to its creation evidence their intention to make it assignable. Here, as in Tide Water Pipe Company v. Bell, supra, the rights of fishing and boating were conveyed to the grantee—in this case Frank C. Miller—"his heirs and assigns," thus showing that the grantor, the Pocono Spring Water Ice Company, intended to attach the attribute of assignability to the privileges granted. Moreover, as a practical matter, there is an obvious difference in this respect between easements for personal enjoyment and those designed for commercial exploitation; while there may be little justification for permitting assignments in the former case, there is every reason for upholding them in the latter.

The question of assignability of the easements in gross in the present case is not as important as that of their divisibility. It is argued by plaintiffs that even if held to be assignable such easements are not divisible, because this might involve an excessive user or "surcharge of the easement" subjecting the servient tenement to a greater burden than originally contemplated. The law does not take that extreme position. It does require, however, that if there be a division, the easements must be used or exercised as an entirety. This rule had its earliest expression in Mountjoy's Case, which is reported in Co.Litt. 164b, 165a. It was there said, in regard to the grant of a right to dig for ore, that the grantee, Lord Mountjoy, "might assign his whole interest to one, two, or more; but then, if there be two or more, they could make no division of it, but work together with one stock."

In Caldwell v. Fulton, 31 Pa. 475, 477, 478, 72 Am.Dec. 760, and in Funk v. Haldeman, 53 Pa. 229, that case was followed, and it was held that the right of a grantee to mine coal or to prospect for oil might be assigned, but if to more than one they must hold, enjoy and convey the right as an entirety, and not divide it in severalty. There are cases in other jurisdictions which also approve the doctrine of Mountjoy's Case, and hold that a mining right in gross is essentially integral and not susceptible of apportionment; an assignment of it is valid, but it cannot be aliened in such a way that it may be utilized by grantor and grantee, or by several grantees, separately; there must be a joint user, nor can one of the tenants alone convey a share in the common right: Grubb v. Baird, Federal Case No. 5,849 (C.Ct.E.D.Pa.); Harlow v. Lake Superior Iron Co., 36 Mich. 105, 121; Stanton v. T.L. Herbert & Sons, 141 Tenn. 440, 211 S.W. 353.

These authorities furnish an illuminating guide to the solution of the problem of divisibility of profits or easements in gross. They indicate that much depends upon the nature of the right and the terms of its creation, that "surcharge of the easement" is prevented if assignees exercise the right as "one stock," and that a proper method of enjoyment of the easement by two or more owners of it may usually be worked out in any given instance without insuperable difficulty.

In the present case it seems reasonably clear that in the conveyance of February 17, 1900, it was not the intention of Frank C. Miller to grant, and of Rufus W. Miller to receive, a separate right to subdivide and sub-license the boating, fishing and bathing privileges on and in Lake Naomi, but only that they should together use such rights for commercial purposes, Rufus W. Miller to be entitled to one-fourth and Frank C. Miller to three-fourths of the proceeds resulting from their combined exploitation of the privileges. They were to hold the rights, in the quaint phraseology of Mountjoy's Case, as "one stock." Nor do the technical rules that would be applicable to a tenancy in common of a corporeal hereditament apply to the control of these easements in gross. Defendant contends that, as a tenant in common of the privileges, Rufus W. Miller individually was entitled to their use, benefit and possession and to exercise rights of ownership in regard thereto, including the right to license third persons to use them, subject only to the limitation that he must not thereby interfere with the similar rights of his cotenant. But the very nature of these easements prevents their being so exercised, inasmuch as it is necessary because of the legal limitations upon their divisibility, that they should be utilized in common and not by two owners severally, and, as stated, this was evidently the intention of the brothers.

Summarizing our conclusions, we are of opinion (1) that Frank C. Miller acquired title to the boating and fishing privileges by grant and he and Rufus W. Miller to the bathing rights by prescription; (2) that he made a valid assignment of a one-fourth interest in them to Rufus W. Miller; but (3) that they cannot be commercially used and licenses thereunder granted without the common consent and joinder of the present owners, who with regard to them must act as "one stock." It follows that the executors of the estate of Rufus W. Miller did not have the right, in and by themselves, to grant a license to defendant.

The decree is affirmed; costs to be paid by defendant.

Note

Fry granted to Witmer, his heirs and assigns, "the right * * * to cause by the erection of dams and other works the water of the Susquehanna River to flow back upon or be withdrawn from Fry's land, together with all the rights, easements, privileges and appurtenances in and to said lands which will be required or needed for the full enjoyment of the right of backing and flowage." The plaintiff was the successor in title to Fry, the defendant the assignee by a series of express assignments of the rights of Witmer. Twenty-four years after the above grant, the defendant built a dam six miles below the plaintiff's property. There is nothing in the report of the case to indicate who owned the land on which the dam was built at the time of the above grant. In preparation for the resulting flooding of the plaintiff's land, the defendant began clearing the land of large trees. This suit for an injunction followed. The bill was dismissed, and this decree was affirmed on appeal. The court said,

"The easement granted to Witmer and his assigns was clearly not an easement so personal to Witmer as to constitute an easement in gross, which is a right of only slightly higher degree than a mere license, but as abundantly appears from the deed of grant and from all of the matters aliunde, it was an easement appurtenant to the land on which Witmer or his assigns were to build the dam and to the dam itself when it came into substantial being. It was therefore assignable in law." Lindenmuth v. Safe Harbor Water Power Corp., 309 Pa. 58, 163 A. 159, 89 A.L.R. 1180 (1932). See Restatement, Property § 543, comment *a*.

JOHNSTON v. MICHIGAN CONSOLIDATED GAS CO., 337 Mich. 572, 60 N.W.2d 464 (1953). A part of the court's opinion is as follows:

"In their brief, plaintiffs contend that the way in question is an easement in gross and, therefore, unassignable; that it was terminated by the attempted assignment from Austin Field Pipe Line Company to defendant. The question was not set forth in the reasons and grounds for appeal and is raised for the first time in this court. We would not consider it, Michigan Court Rule No. 67 (1945); Poelman v. Payne, 332 Mich. 597, 52 N.W.2d 229, were it not for the fact the instant case is one of a series of cases now pending in the circuit courts and the question is briefed and stressed by plaintiffs. In Stockdale v. Yerden, 220 Mich. 444, 190 N.W. 225, we adopted the reasoning of the leading case of Boatman v. Lasley, 23 Ohio St. 614, in holding that easements in gross are unassignable. However, the easement there in question was only the right to pass over the lands of another. The easement in the instant case is of a very different nature, for here the right is to bury and install pipe lines which when installed use up a part of the land itself. While we are not directed to any cases involving the latter type of easements among our own decisions, we have carefully examined those of our sister States and find that according to the weight of authority easements for pipe lines, telephone and telegraph lines and railroads are generally held to be assignable even though in gross. McClung v. Sewell Valley R. Co., 97 W.Va. 685, 127 S.E. 53; Columbus, Hope & Greensburg Ry. Co. v. Braden, 110 Ind. 558, 11 N.E. 357; Morgan v. Des Moines Union Ry. Co., 113 Iowa 561, 85 N.W. 902; Junction R. Co. v. Ruggles, 7 Ohio St. 1; Garlick v. Pittsburgh & West Ry. Co., 67 Ohio St. 233, 65 N.E. 896. In the leading case of Standard Oil Co. v. Buchi, 72 N.J.Eq. 492, 66 A. 427, 432, it was held that the interest gained by a deed of a right of way to lay pipe lines for the transportation of oil is assignable. The court said:

" 'I think the present grant is something more than an easement, although undoubtedly it includes easements, and I think that it is a great deal more than a license, in that it gives an irrevocable interest in the land and creates, by apt words, an estate, is expressed to be upon a consideration, and is sealed by the seal of the grantor.'

"To the same effect see Geffine v. Thompson, 76 Ohio App. 64, 62 N.E. 2d 590.

"Although the rationale and reasoning varies in the different cases, they are quite uniform in their result. A multitude of them may be found in Vance, Assignability of Easements in Gross, 32 Yale L.J. 813; Simes, The Assignability of Easements in Gross in American Law, 22 Mich.L.Rev. 521; and Kloek, Assignability and Divisibility of Easements in Gross, 22 Chicago-Kent L.Rev. 239.

"In the early case of Hall v. City of Ionia, 38 Mich. 493, we held that the right in gross to take water from a stream was assignable, and the reasoning and language we used there seems equally applicable here:

" 'Upon a careful inspection of the record, we think there is very little room for controversy. It is manifest from the conveyance of Samuel Dexter, that if it is legally possible for him to secure and retain for himself the right to the water and the right to divert it into an artificial channel, he has done so. It is not at all important to find any technical name for his method, or to spend time in the legal etymology of exceptions and reservations, which terms have been used with some carelessness and confusion. The general and as we think the correct method of construing such provisions as those in question, is to give them the force which the deeds evidently intended they should have; and we can have no doubt what intention is manifested by the terms of these instruments.' * * *

"There is no persuasive reason for holding the easement in question unassignable and we, therefore, refuse to so hold. Further support for this result is found in American Law Institute's Restatement of the Law of Property, § 489:

" 'Easements in gross, if of a commercial character, are alienable property interests.'

"Judgment for plaintiffs is affirmed, with costs to defendant."

Problem

What do you think is the legal effect of language such as the following:

"Reserving, however, unto the first party, her successors and assigns, as and for an appurtenance to the real property hereinafter particularly described and designated as 'Parcel A' and any part thereof, a perpetual easement of right to receive light, air and unobstructed view over that portion of the real property hereinabove described, to the extent that said light, air and view will be received and enjoyed by limiting any structure, fence, trees or shrubs upon said property above a horizontal plane 28 feet above the level of the sidewalk of Franklin Street as the sidewalk level now exists at the junction of the southern and western boundary lines of the property hereinabove described. * * * "

See Petersen v. Friedman, 162 Cal.App.2d 245, 328 P.2d 264 (1958).

Note

A negative easement of prospect or view seems to have been recognized by the civil law of Europe. But in England it was held at an early date that, "although there can be an easement of light where a defined window receives a defined amount of light, there can be no easement of prospect (i.e., the right to a view)." As the English court rather quaintly declared, "for prospect, which is a matter only of delight, and not of necessity, no action lies for stopping thereof * * * [for] the law does not give an action for such things as delight." See William Aldred's Case, 9 Co.Rep. 57b (1610). In the United States, however, there is substantial case law recognizing a common-law negative easement of prospect or view. Although there are dicta in Michigan and South Carolina cases to the effect that such easements are not recognized in those States, the dicta in both cases are based on earlier cases that are clearly not in point. The Michigan court, moreover, suggested in another case that there is such a thing as a "common-law negative easement of air, light, and view." Common-law negative easements of prospect or view have been recognized in California, Massachusetts, and Rhode Island, at least, and apparently also in New York, Vermont, and Wisconsin.

In recent years so-called "scenic" and "conservation" easements have come into common use. It is not clear whether "scenic easements" should be regarded as common-law negative easements of prospect or view or as "equitable servitudes." The Appraisal and Terminology Handbook of the American Institute of Real Estate Appraisers defines a "scenic easement" as "a restriction imposed upon the use of the property of the grantor for the purpose of preserving the natural state of scenic and historical attractiveness of adjacent lands of the grantee, usually the city, county, state or federal government." "Scenic easement" forms in common use usually include the following:

1. A restriction of new buildings and structures (or major alterations) to farm and residential buildings and structures only, plus a specific prohibition of further nonresidential buildings—with a saving clause permitting the continuance of existing nonconforming uses.

2. An authorization for necessary public utility lines and roads.

3. A prohibition against cutting "mature trees and shrubs," but with a provision authorizing normal maintenance.

4. A prohibition against dumping.

5. A prohibition against outdoor advertising, except for activities located on the premises.

In addition to the above restrictions or "negative rights," a "scenic easement" may, of course, also include one or more affirmative privileges,—e.g., a public right of entry to a limited area for a scenic overlook along a highway, or a public (i.e., highway department) right of entry to remove structures or plantings which are in violation of the restrictions, or to repair damage done to plantings or other vegetation in violation of the restrictions.

The term "conservation easement" is now in common use, and is often used in conjunction with the term "scenic easement." Although the two are not synonymous, there is clearly a good deal of overlap between the "scenic easement" and the "conservation easement." A proposed Pennsylvania statute defined "conservation easements" as follows:

"An aggregation of easements in perpetuity designed to preserve in their natural state lands of cultural, scenic, historic, or other public significance. Such easements could include restrictions against erecting buildings or other structures; constructing or altering private roads or drives; removal or destruction of trees, shrubs or other greenery; changing existing uses; altering public utility facilities; displaying any form of outdoor advertising; dumping of trash, wastes, or unsightly or offensive materials; changing any features of the natural landscape; and any changes detrimental to existing drainage, flood control, erosion control, or soil conservation; any other activities inconsistent with the conservation of open spaces in the public interest. Conservation easements will permit all present normal and reasonable uses, not conflicting with the purposes indicated above, to be engaged in by the landowners, their heirs, successors and assigns."

Although the proposed statute from which the above definition is taken was not enacted, Pennsylvania did enact, in 1964, a statute authorizing "the [public] acquisition of lands for recreation, conservation and historical purposes before such lands are lost forever to urban development or become prohibitively expensive." The statute expressly authorizes public acquisition of "easements" as well as other interests in real property for such purposes, and defines "conservation purposes" to include "any use of land for water supply, flood control, water quality control development, soil erosion control, reforestation, wild life reserves or any other uses that will maintain, improve or develop the natural environment of soil, water, air, minerals or wild life * * * so as to assure their optimum use."

New Jersey enacted a somewhat similar statute, the "New Jersey green acres land acquisition act of 1961," which authorizes public acquisition of "lands for public recreation and the conservation of natural resources" and defines "recreation and conservation purposes" to mean "use of lands for parks, natural areas, forests, camping, fishing, water reserves, wildlife, reservoirs, hunting, boating, winter sports and similar uses for public outdoor recreation and *conservation of natural resources.*" The definition of "land" or "lands" in the New Jersey statute is substantially identical with the definition in the Pennsylvania act, and in addition the New Jersey act expressly states that it authorizes public acquisition of "an interest or right consisting, in whole or in part, of a restriction on the use of land by others including owners of other interests therein; such interest or right sometimes known as a *'conservation easement.'* " (Emphasis added.)

It would thus appear that the objectives of "conservation easements" are somewhat broader than those of "scenic easements," in that the "conservation easement" may be designed to conserve all kinds of natural resources such as agricultural land, water, forests, and wildlife, as well as scenic landscape values. Moreover, "conservation easements" may often be coupled with affirmative easements designed to promote public recreational use of private land,— e.g., hunting, fishing, boating, and camping easements. And it would seem that "conservation easements" are less likely than "scenic easements" to be created under circumstances that will make them appurtenant to a highway or other dominant tenement.

Although all the legislation referred to in this Note provides for acquisition of "scenic" or "conservation" easements by public authorities, it is obvious that such interests may also be acquired by private persons, either individuals or corporations. Indeed, the acquisition of such easements has been an important aspect of the activities of private organizations engaged in preserving open space. But the most extensive "scenic easement" acquisition programs have been carried out by the states bordering the Mississippi River in connection with the Great River Road (formerly the Mississippi River Parkway) and, more recently, by a number of other states in connection with highway beautification efforts stimulated by enactment of the Highway Beautification Act of 1965.

In Hardesty v. State Roads Commission, 276 Md. 25, 343 A.2d 884 (1975), the Commission filed a condemnation petition for a perpetual scenic easement which apparently would have prevented the property owner from removing certain trees. The Commission deposited with the court a sum of money estimated to be the fair value of the property to be acquired. The parties were unable to agree on the value of the property, and seven months after the petition was filed, the Commission sought to abandon the proceedings and recover the sum deposited. A statute forbade such an abandonment after a taking had occurred, and provided that property is deemed taken when the "plaintiff has taken possession of the property and actually and lawfully appropriated it to the public purposes of the plaintiff." The Commission argued that there had been no taking because no physical entry on the land had occurred. The court, however, held that in view of the nature of the property interest involved, the "immediate entry procedure" employed by the Commission, the fact that the public enjoyment of the scenic beauty of the property was immediate, the legal restriction placed on the property pending the proceedings, and the length of time involved before the Commission sought to abandon the proceedings, a taking of property for some period had occurred, for which compensation must be paid, whatever ultimate disposition of the case might be made after an amendment by the Commission of its claim.

In United States v. Albrecht, 496 F.2d 906 (8th Cir.1974), the authority of the Department of the Interior to acquire a conservation easement preventing the draining or filling of certain land was found to have been granted by Congress in The Hunting Stamp Act, 16 U.S.C.A. § 718 et seq. Such authority was held to prevail over a contention that under the law of the state such an easement was not recognized.

SECTION 2.   METHODS OF CREATION

A. GRANT AND THE EFFECT OF INFORMAL GRANT OR LICENSE

Most easements are created expressly by an instrument in writing. In the old law this process was called a *grant*. A grant implied a written instrument under seal, which was called a deed. Many modern statutes dispense with the requirement of a seal. Even in the absence of such a statute, the requirement has been dispensed with by treating an unsealed written instrument as effective to create an easement "in equity". The requirement of a written instrument, however, remains. If this were not a continuing requirement of the common law, it would be established by the modern statutes of frauds. With some variations of detail, these statutes require a written instrument for (1) the creation of an interest in land (except short-term leasehold interests, usually for terms of one year or less), and also for (2) the creation of a contract to convey any interest in land (with similar exceptions).

An easement can be created by a deed which simply grants an easement in the land of the grantor. More often an easement is granted by a deed which also operates to convey certain land to which the easement is appurtenant, or is reserved by a grantor in a deed which conveys land intended as the servient estate. Examples of each of these methods of creating an easement by express language in a deed appear in the preceding materials in this chapter.

Some serious legal problems can be created when land owners orally or informally undertake to confer upon other persons the privilege of making certain uses of their land.

RICENBAW v. KRAUS

Supreme Court of Nebraska, 1953.
157 Neb. 723, 61 N.W.2d 350.

WENKE, Justice. This is an appeal from the district court for Seward County. It involves the appellee's, Norman A. Ricenbaw, right to maintain a dual system of drainage across appellants', Emil E. Kraus and Josephine H. Kraus, husband and wife, land.

Appellee is the owner of the northwest quarter and appellants are the owners of the northeast quarter of Section 23, Township 9, Range 1 East of the 6th P.M., in Seward County. The natural drainage of the moisture falling on the east side of appellee's land and on appellants' land is toward the east, although it is slightly toward the northeast as it crosses appellants' land. It ultimately flows into the Blue River. Since 1901 the natural surface drain of a small area or pocket on appellee's land, consisting of about 2 acres, has been supplemented by a tile drain. This pocket is just west of the parties' line fence and about 60 rods north of appellee's south line. It collects surface water from about 50 to 60 acres of appellee's land and when it fills with water from rain or melting snows it overflows through a small swale at the parties' line fence.

In regard to the tile drain the trial court decreed: "It is therefore, Ordered, Adjudged and Decreed that the plaintiff has an easement over the defendants' land, * * * which is an appurtenance of the plaintiff's land, * * * where the tile drain is located, with the right to maintain said tile drain, including the right to go upon the defendants' land, solely, however, as may be necessary, for the purpose of opening and restoring said tile drain to a functioning condition, and to maintain the same in a functioning condition, with the obligation on the plaintiff and his successors in title, after any work on said tile drain, to restore the surface of defendants' land to substantially the same condition as before performance of said work.

"It is further, Ordered, Adjudged and Decreed that the defendants are hereby enjoined from interfering with or molesting said tile drain and from interfering with the plaintiff in the restoration and maintenance of the same in a functioning condition; * * *."

In considering this appeal we apply the following principle: "It is the duty of this court in an equity case to try the issues de novo and to reach an independent decision without being influenced by the findings of the trial court except if the evidence is in irreconcilable conflict this court may consider that the trial court saw the witnesses, observed their manner of testifying, and accepted one version of the facts rather than the opposite." Keim v. Downing, 157 Neb. 481, 59 N.W.2d 602, 603.

The evidence shows that in 1900 Oscar Knutson was the owner of the northeast quarter. That fall A.L. Hannah bought the northwest quarter. After buying the northwest quarter Hannah obtained oral permission from Knutson to put a tile across Knutson's land in order to drain this small pocket which then existed on the land Hannah had purchased. This permission was given with the understanding that the tiling was to be done in such a manner that it would not bother Knutson in the farming of his land, that is, Hannah was to level off the ground after laying the tile and thereafter take care of it.

Hannah, who was from Illinois, moved to Nebraska in the spring of 1901. He brought with him 400 four-inch tile. These he used to drain this pocket. He started laying the tile at the low point of the pocket, which was some 100 to 110 feet west of the line fence. In laying the tile Hannah followed the natural drain, as evidenced by a small swale, onto and across Knutson's land for a distance somewhere between 160 and 250 feet. The tile were laid to where the swale ended, thus emptying the water flowing therefrom into a draw. The tile successfully drained this pocket until the spring of 1952 when appellant Emil Kraus, because of other difficulties with appellee, either plugged, or caused to be plugged, the outlet thereof which is located on his land.

As stated in Walsh v. Walsh, 156 Neb. 867, 58 N.W.2d 337, 340, by quoting from Atchison, T. & S.F. Ry. Co. v. Conlon, 62 Kan. 416, 63 P. 432, 53 L.R.A. 781: " 'Mere use under a naked license, however long continued, cannot ripen into a prescriptive right.' "

And as stated in Bone v. James, 82 Neb. 442, 118 N.W. 83, 84: " * * * if the use of this way was commenced and continued by license or permission had from the plaintiff, then no right by prescription could be acquired, however, long such use was continued."

But here, after obtaining from Knutson the oral license or permit to use his land to drain this pocket, Hannah went to the trouble and expense of actually putting in the tile. As stated in Fitzsimmons v. Gilmore, 134 Neb. 200, 278 N.W. 262, 266: " 'It is an ancient and well-settled doctrine of the common law that a mere license, whether by deed or by parol, is revocable at pleasure.' 17 R.C.L. 576, § 89. But, to this rule there always has been two recognized exceptions, viz.: Where the license is executed, and where by reason of the expenditures by the licensee on the strength of the license, it would otherwise be inequitable to permit the licensor to effect a revocation. 17 R.C.L. 577, § 89." See, also, Arterburn v. Beard, 86 Neb. 733, 126 N.W. 379; Magnuson v. Coburn, 154 Neb. 24, 46 N.W.2d 775, 778.

As said in Magnuson v. Coburn, supra, quoting from 3 Tiffany, Real Property, 3d Ed., c. 15, § 834, p. 416: " 'Accordingly, the decisions that a license cannot be revoked after the making of improvements on the faith thereof appear properly to involve merely the assertion of a rule of construction, that an oral permission to make a particular use of land, which use is such that it will be necessary or desirable to make expenditures in order to avail oneself of the permission, is to be construed as an attempt orally to grant an easement in the land, which is absolutely invalid as a grant, but operates by way of equitable estoppel in favor of the intended grantee if he subsequently makes expenditures on the assumption that he acquired an easement thereby, although, as a matter of fact, he originally acquired, by reason of the invalidity of the grant, merely a license.' "

We find, under the circumstances here shown, that Hannah, by reason of putting in the tile drain, obtained an irrevocable easement appurtenant to the northwest quarter. * * *

Notes

1. The most simple and common kind of license results from words or conduct by a landowner which indicate his intention that one or more persons may enter his land for business or social purposes. The privilege thus conferred is implicitly of limited duration and for a limited purpose. The only significant

legal attribute of such a privilege is to relieve the licensee of any charge of trespass. A license in any event is revocable at will and unassignable, and is ended by the death of either party. But the legal category of licenses also embraces at the other extreme cases where a landowner has undertaken to grant an easement by a writing which is ineffective for this purpose because of some formal defect in the transaction. In between these two extremes are cases where the intention of the licensor is not clear. In either of the latter two situations the question presented is whether there are grounds in policy or equity for suspending the requirements of the statutes of frauds, and treating the licensee as having something more than a bare license.

2. Did the court in the Ricenbaw case hold that the plaintiff had acquired an easement or merely that the defendant was estopped to deny that an easement had been created? Restatement, Property § 519, comment *e*, states merely that in such circumstances the licensor is estopped to revoke the license. Does it make any real difference which explanation is accepted? In Phillips v. Cutler, 89 Vt. 233, 235, 95 A. 487 (1915), in holding that a license to lay tile for the procurement of water from a spring on the licensor's land had become irrevocable, the court said, "Under the rule established in this State, the right to the water will pass as appurtenant to the property benefitted, and neither the death of the owner of the spring nor his conveyance of the land will operate as a revocation."

3. Another theoretical explanation for a result such as that reached in the Ricenbaw case is that the circumstances result in the creation of a contract to grant an easement, the making of expenditures serving both (1) to provide consideration for the implied promise to grant an easement, and also (2) to provide part performance of such contract sufficient to escape the sanction of the statute of frauds. The contract then is regarded as specifically enforceable, and in fact as if it had already been performed, so that the licensee may recover damages for interference with his interest. See Rerick v. Kern, 14 Serg. & R. 267 (Pa.1826).

4. Are we to infer from these cases that every substantial expenditure in reliance upon an otherwise unenforceable license will result in the creation of an irrevocable interest? Does the declaration of an "estoppel" by the court in the Ricenbaw case suggest the limits of this doctrine? Suppose that in offering the privilege the landowner expressly reserves the right to withdraw it any time?

5. In fact some courts have refused to follow the lead of the above courts by an argument which goes something like this: the licensee must be held to know that he received only a license which was revocable at will; so what equitable basis is there for allowing him to claim some greater interest? See Nelson v. American Telephone & Telegraph Co., 270 Mass. 471, 170 N.E. 416 (1930). One distinguished writer described the situation in this way, "Instead of the picture of a licensor prevented by the courts from taking advantage of his own fraud, it is suggested that a truer picture is that of the kind, neighborly individual who finds himself outwitted, under this rule of law, by a clever landgrabber." Clark, Covenants and Interests Running with the Land 61 (2d ed. 1947).

In Keck v. Scharf, 80 Ill.App.3d 832, 36 Ill.Dec. 83, 400 N.E.2d 503 (1980), an easement by estoppel was denied because of insufficient expenditures by the plaintiff. The court felt it was not impossible or impractical to restore the plaintiff to his original position, also taking into account that the circumstances leading to the claim constituted a neighborly arrangement.

6. Some courts which refuse to declare irrevocable interests in these circumstances hold that the equity of the licensee may be satisfied by reimbursement for his expenditures by the licensor, as a condition of his revocation. See Annotation, 120 A.L.R. 549 (1939).

7. Where an easement results from circumstances of this sort, should there be any limitation on the duration of the easement? Is it in fee? Restatement, Property § 519(4) (1944) states that the licensee is privileged to continue the use permitted by the license to the extent reasonably necessary to realize upon his expenditures. See also Phillips v. Cutler, supra.

8. Defendant's land lay between the plaintiff's land and a highway. A circular road ran from one point on the highway across the defendant's land to within 600 feet of the plaintiff's land, and then returned to the highway. Defendant, by a proper writing granted plaintiff a right of way from the parties' boundary line to the road. This was the only access plaintiff had to his land. In reliance thereon, plaintiff improved his property. Later defendant removed a bridge on the road, plowed part of the road, and did other acts of alleged "harassment." Plaintiff sued for restoration of the road and for damages. The court held that the plaintiff had acquired an easement by estoppel in the road and declared that the expenditures necessary to raise such an estoppel need not have been made on the servient estate, but could be made on the dominant estate. See Exxon Corp. v. Schutzmaier, 537 S.W.2d 282 (Tex.Civ.App. 1976). Does it appear that the plaintiff may have had another ground for his claim?

9. See generally Conard, Unwritten Agreements for the Use of Land, 14 Rocky Mt.L.Rev. 153 (1942); 3 Powell, Real Property ¶ 429 (1952).

10. Suppose a person buys a ticket to enter a theater to see some sort of performance (and perhaps to sit in a designated seat). He enters the theater at the proper time and takes his seat. Some disturbance ensues which he may or may not have been involved in. The theater manager appears and asks him to leave. Upon refusing, he is escorted out of the theater by one or more insistent attendants who have the physical capacity to enforce their demands. What claims should this patron have against the proprietor? What rights did he acquire by buying his ticket? Assume he had not engaged in any misconduct. What objections do you see to a claim by him that he acquired an easement? If he acquired an easement, what remedy should he have in the circumstances? If he did not acquire an easement, what remedy should he have, if any? See Marrone v. Washington Jockey Club, 227 U.S. 633, 33 S.Ct. 401, 57 L.Ed. 679 (1913); Hurst v. Picture Theatres [1915] 1 K.B. 1; 3 Powell ¶ 428 (1952); Conard, The Privilege of Forcibly Ejecting an Amusement Patron, 90 U.Pa.L.Rev. 809 (1942).

B. IMPLICATION

This term suggests that easements may be created as a consequence of a written instrument of conveyance without express language to that effect. The instrument will normally be one which conveys a fee simple estate in land. The implication from such an instrument which results also in the creation of an easement depends so much more upon the extrinsic conduct of the parties than upon the terms of the instrument itself that it seems preferable to deal here with problems of this sort than to relegate them to a heading under Conveyancing.

ROMANCHUK v. PLOTKIN

Supreme Court of Minnesota, 1943.
215 Minn. 156, 9 N.W.2d 421.

PETERSON, Justice. In 1915 defendants acquired the real property at the northeast corner of Twelfth avenue north and Humboldt avenue north in Minneapolis, on which there was a duplex dwelling near the corner facing Twelfth avenue, known as 1312 Twelfth avenue north, and a small dwelling toward the rear facing Humboldt, known as 1206 Humboldt avenue north. Both houses were equipped with plumbing serviced by a common sewer drain which connected with the public sewer in Humboldt avenue.

On February 23, 1921, defendants acquired the real property now owned by plaintiffs, located immediately east of the duplex and known as 1310 Twelfth avenue north. At that time this property was without plumbing and sewer connection. There has not been, nor is there now, a public sewer in Twelfth avenue north. In 1922 defendants installed plumbing in the house at 1310 Twelfth avenue, which they connected with a sewer drain they laid below the basement floor and underground extending from the rear of the house across the properties of the parties into the basement of the duplex, where it was connected with the sewer drain from the duplex to the street. After this connection was made the one sewer drain connecting with the public sewer in Humboldt avenue serviced the three houses on defendants' property.

All the sewer drainpipes are four inches in diameter. The pipes became obstructed and clogged on numerous occasions, causing sewage to back up and thus creating an unsanitary and unhealthful condition. This condition is likely to recur periodically. A separate sewer drain connecting the property now owned by plaintiffs with the public sewer in Humboldt avenue could be installed at a cost of $175. This would have to be laid in Twelfth avenue north. A permit to use the street for that purpose is necessary. It was not shown that a permit could be obtained.

On February 25, 1921, two days after defendants became the owners of 1310 Twelfth avenue north and about one year before they installed the plumbing and made the sewer connection there, they executed a mortgage of the property, with the appurtenances thereto belonging, to one Margaret Roggeman. The mortgage contained the usual covenants of a warranty deed. In July, 1936, Margaret Roggeman acquired title through foreclosure of the mortgage. She did not inspect the property either when she took the mortgage or when she foreclosed it. She dealt through an agent, who afterwards looked after the renting and who, out of rents collected, paid defendant Plotkin for cleaning and repairing the sewer.

On August 8, 1938, plaintiffs purchased the property from Roggeman. They dealt through Roggeman's agent. Plaintiff Nicholas Romanchuk testified that he observed the drainpipes in an unfinished and unused part of the basement. Over objection, he also testified that the agent told him that the sewer drain connected with the public sewer in the street.

Neither the mortgage to Roggeman nor the deed to plaintiffs mentions any easement in the sewer across defendants' land.

In 1941 the common drain connecting these properties with the city sewer became clogged, necessitating repairs. Plaintiffs' proportionate share of the repairs was $25, of which they paid five dollars prior to trial and the balance during the trial.

In 1915, when defendants acquired the property with the duplex on it, and ever since, there has been a fence between their and plaintiffs' properties. The fence encroached on plaintiffs' property one foot and five inches according to the description thereof in the mortgage and deed. In 1941 defendants gave their consent to plaintiffs' entry on their land for the purpose of putting some asbestos siding on their house.

On October 22, 1941, defendant Samuel Plotkin notified plaintiffs that on November 5, 1941, the connection of the sewer drain serving their property with the drain to the sewer in the street would be severed. Plaintiffs then brought this action to enjoin defendants from disconnecting their sewer connection and to compel them to remove the fence.

The court below found that plaintiffs had an easement for the use and maintenance of the sewer drain across defendants' property connecting with the sewer in Humboldt avenue north, subject to the requirement that they pay their proportionate share of the cost of repairing and maintaining the same, and that the fence encroached one foot and five inches on plaintiffs' land. As conclusions it ordered judgment enjoining defendants to refrain from interfering with plaintiffs' use of the sewer drain and from severing the connection of their sewer drain with the sewer leading to the street, and to remove the fence so as not to obstruct the one foot and five inches of plaintiffs' property mentioned. * * *

1. The doctrine of implied grant of easement is based upon the principle that where, during unity of title, the owner imposes an apparently permanent and obvious servitude on one tenement in favor of another, which at the time of severance of title, is in use and is reasonably necessary for the fair enjoyment of the tenement to which such use is beneficial, then, upon a severance of ownership, a grant of the dominant tenement includes by implication the right to continue such use. That right is an easement appurtenant to the estate granted to use the servient estate retained by the owner. Under the rule that a grant is to be construed most strongly against the grantor, all privileges and appurtenances that are obviously incident and necessary to the fair enjoyment of the property granted substantially in the condition in which it is enjoyed by the grantor are included in the grant. * * * Prior to the severance and while there is unity of title, the use is generally spoken of as a quasi-easement appurtenant to the dominant tenement. Wiesel v. Smira, 49 R.I. 246, 142 A. 148, 58 A.L.R. 818.

It is commonly said that three things are essential to create an easement by implication upon severance of unity of ownership, viz.: (1) a separation of title; (2) the use which gives rise to the easement shall have been so long continued and apparent as to show that it was intended to be permanent; and (3) that the easement is necessary to the beneficial enjoyment of the land granted. Read v. Webster, 95 Vt. 239, 113 A. 814, 16 A.L.R. 1068; Berlin v. Robbins, 180 Wash. 176, 38 P.2d 1047.

Defendants contend that the sewer was not an apparent quasi-easement at the time of severance of ownership, upon the theory that the severance took place when the mortgage was given, which was approximately one year before the sewer drain was installed on plaintiffs' property, citing Mt. Holyoke Realty Corp. v. Holyoke Realty Corp., 284 Mass. 100, 187 N.E. 227. In Massachusetts and some other states a mortgage of real property conveys the title subject to defeasance upon payment of the mortgage debt or upon fulfillment of the conditions of the mortgage. We do not follow that rule. Under Minn.St.1941, § 559.17 (Mason St.1927, § 9572), the rule that a mortgage of real estate conveyed the legal title was abrogated and the rule adopted that a mortgage creates a lien in favor of the mortgagee as security for his debt with right of ownership and possession in the mortgagor until foreclosure and expiration of the period of redemption. * * * Where a mortgage on real estate creates a lien, the execution of the mortgage does not affect a severance of title, but the foreclosure of the mortgage does. Naccash v. Hildansid Realty Corp., 140 Misc. 730, 252 N.Y.S. 383, reversed on other grounds 236 App.Div. 686, 257 N.Y.S. 750, second case, motion denied 236 App.Div. 758, 258 N.Y.S. 1040; Amalgamated Properties, Inc., v. Oakwood Gardens, Inc., 148 Misc. 426, 266 N.Y.S. 381, affirmed 238 App.Div. 867, 263 N.Y.S. 927; Berlin v. Robbins, 180 Wash. 176, 38 P.2d 1047, supra. Under the title theory, a use created after the giving of a mortgage does not give rise to an easement in favor of the mortgagee, Mt. Holyoke Realty Corp. v. Holyoke Realty Corp., 284 Mass. 100, 187 N.E. 227, supra; but, under the lien theory, it does and passes to the purchaser at the foreclosure sale, Farina v. Lucisano, 246 App.Div. 553, 282 N.Y.S. 832. In Cannon v. Boyd, 73 Pa. 179, the court held, without any particular discussion of the distinction in question, that an implied easement passed to the purchaser under mortgage foreclosure sale where the use on which it was based came into existence after the execution of the mortgage, but prior to the foreclosure sale.

It cannot be seriously contended that the sewer in question was not continuous and permanent. It is urged, however, that, since the sewer, both in plaintiffs' house and outside in plaintiffs' and defendants' yards, was underground, it was not apparent. "Apparent" does not necessarily mean "visible." The weight of authority sustains the rule that "apparent" means that indicia of the easement, a careful inspection of which by a person ordinarily conversant with the subject would have disclosed the use, must be plainly visible. An underground drainpipe, even though it is buried and invisible, connected with and forming the only means of draining waste from plumbing fixtures and appliances of a dwelling house, is apparent, because a plumber could see the fixtures and appliances and readily determine the location and course of the sewer drain. Wiesel v. Smira, 49 R.I. 246, 142 A. 148, 58 A.L.R. 818, supra, annotation, 58 A.L.R. 832. In 17 Am.Jur., Easements, p. 985, § 80, the text reads:

"As a general rule, implied easements are restricted to servitudes which are apparent. Although there is some conflict of authority as to whether existing drains, pipes, and sewers may be properly characterized as apparent, within such rule most courts take the view that appearance and visibility are not synonymous and that the fact that a pipe, sewer, or drain may be hidden underground does not negative its character as an apparent condition, at least, *where the appliances connected with, and leading to, it are obvious.*" (Italics supplied.)

In Larsen v. Peterson, 53 N.J.Eq. 88, 93, 94, 30 A. 1094, 1097, is an elaborate discussion of the principle as applied to underground water pipes leading from a well to a pump inside a house, where the pump was visible but the pipes were not. The court said:

"In the case in hand the controlling fact is that the pump was there visible and in use, and by its connection with the invisible pipe leading to *some* fountain the house conveyed to complainant was supplied with water. *   *   *

"*   *   *   In short, in my opinion all that is meant by 'apparent,' in that connection, is that the parties should have either actual knowledge of the *quasi*-easement or knowledge of such facts as to put them upon inquiry."

In the instant case the plumbing fixtures and their connection with the sewer pipes were plainly visible. The pipes extended from the rear of plaintiffs' house toward defendants' duplex. A plumber easily could have ascertained that the pipes, although underground and invisible, extended under the duplex, where they connected with the drain leading from the duplex to the sewer in the street.

The authorities are in conflict as to what is meant by "necessary" in this connection. Some hold that "necessary" means substantially the same as indispensable. Others hold that it means reasonably necessary or convenient to the beneficial enjoyment of the property. Vice-Chancellor Pitney in Toothe v. Bryce, 50 N.J.Eq. 589, 595, 603, 25 A. 182, 184, points out that this requirement was adopted from a statement by Gale in his work on Easements. His conclusion was that "the so-called 'necessity' upon which the judges relied was, in fact, no necessity at all, but a mere beneficial and valuable convenience." Jones, Easements, pp. 127, 128, §§ 154, 155, adopts that view. The weight of authority supports the view that "necessary" does not mean indispensable, but reasonably necessary or convenient to the beneficial use of the property. Wiesel v. Smira, 49 R.I. 246, 142 A. 148, 58 A.L.R. 818, supra, and annotation at page 829. *   *   *

In the instant case the use of the drain was highly beneficial and convenient to the use of plaintiffs' property. The reasonable construction of the mortgage under which plaintiffs claim title in the light of the surrounding circumstances is that the use of the sewer drain was an appurtenance to plaintiffs' property which passed under the mortgage.

Further, it appears that the parties placed a practical construction on their rights by which they in effect recognized plaintiffs' right to the easement. Plaintiffs were permitted to continue to use the sewer. Defendants charged them for repairs and maintenance, and plaintiffs paid the charges. A practical interpretation by the parties that an easement exists supports an inference that the easement is one of legal right. Winston v. Johnson, 42 Minn. 398, 45 N.W. 958.

As a word of caution, we do not hold that in all cases the existence of the three characteristics mentioned are necessary to create an easement by implication. Rules of construction are mere aids in ascertaining the meaning of writings, whether they are statutes, contracts, deeds, or mortgages. Being such, they are neither ironclad nor inflexible and yield to manifestation of contrary intention. Lawton v. Joesting, 96 Minn. 163, 104 N.W. 830; Bull v. King, 205 Minn. 427, 286 N.W. 311. As said in Long v. Fewer, 53 Minn. 156, 159, 54 N.W. 1071: "the day is past for adhering to technical or literal meaning of particular words in a deed or other contract against the plain intention of the parties as gathered from the entire instrument." In Wiesel v. Smira, 49 R.I. 246, 142 A. 148, 58 A.L.R. 818, supra, the court said that the presence or absence of any or all of the characteristics should not be deemed conclusive. In 3 Tiffany, Real Property, 3 Ed., p. 254, § 780, the author says:

"The rules declared by the courts as to the creation of easements corresponding to preexisting quasi easements, and of easements of necessity, constitute in reality merely rules of construction for the purpose of determining the scope of the conveyance. And the grant of the easement is implied only in the sense that the easement passes by the conveyance although not expressly mentioned, just as an easement previously created passes upon a conveyance of the land to which it is appurtenant without any express mention of the easement. It is immaterial, from a legal point of view, whether the easement passes because the instrument expressly says that it shall pass, or because the circumstances are such as to call for a construction of the language used as so saying."

We leave open the scope and effect of the characteristics mentioned in the process of construction. For present purposes, it is sufficient to hold that, tested by all three characteristics, an implied easement to the use of the sewer across defendants' land passed under the mortgage and the foreclosure thereof and that plaintiffs became the owners of the easement as grantees of the purchaser at the mortgage foreclosure sale. * * *

Affirmed.

Notes

1. In Frantz v. Collins, 21 Ill.2d 446, 173 N.E.2d 437 (1961), the court reached a result similar to that in Romanchuk v. Plotkin. In its opinion the court said,

"It is generally held where the owner of a single tract has arranged or adapted it so that one portion thereof derives a benefit from the other of an apparent and continuous character, and then sells one of such parts without mention being made of these incidental uses, the grantee takes his property with all the rights and obligations which formerly existed. * * * It is not required that the alleged easement be essential to the enjoyment of the claimants' property but it is sufficient if it would be highly convenient and beneficial thereto."

In what respects, if any, are the standards for the implication of easements stated here different from those declared by the court in Romanchuck v. Plotkin?

Among the courts stating that a pre-existing quasi-easement must be "continuous," several took a restricted view of the requirement. In Morgan v. Meuth, 60 Mich. 238, 27 N.W. 509 (1886), an easement appurtenant had been expressly granted for the use of an alley as a way, followed by a merger of the dominant and servient estates. In denying that a similar easement arose upon a later conveyance of the original dominant estate, the court said,

"The dominant and servient tenements were unified; and the question arises whether, by the conveyance to complainant and consequent severance of the ownership of the dominant tenement, this alley, or right of way, passed by the words, 'together with the hereditaments and appurtenances thereunto belonging, or in anywise appurtaining.' This depends upon the nature of the easement. This alley was created for a passageway, and nothing else. The only benefit or advantage claimed for it is that of a right of way. It is therefore a discontinuous easement,—one the use of which can only be had by the interference of man. It is not like a drain or sewer, which are used continually without the intervention of man. Continuous easements pass, on the severance of the two tenements, as appurtenances, but a right of way does not, unless the grantor in the conveyance uses language sufficient to create the easement *de novo*, or because its use is absolutely necessary to the enjoyment of the premises conveyed."

This peculiar interpretation of the meaning of the requirement that a preexisting quasi-easement be continuous before it can ripen into an actual easement by implication upon severance of the land benefitted by it was adopted by the courts in several other states in early cases. Michigan was a stronghold for such a view, for Morgan v. Meuth was followed in a number of later cases. The extent of recognition generally has never been quite clear, for it appears only vaguely as a factor in some early cases which held that an easement of way cannot be implied, either by grant or reservation, unless it qualifies as a way of necessity. Annotations, 34 A.L.R. 233 (1925); 100 A.L.R. 1321 (1936). This rule has been rejected by a number of courts. 3 Powell, Real Property 411 (1952). It has simply been ignored by other courts some of whom had previously accepted it, as in the manner of the Michigan court in Harrison v. Heald, supra, in which the earlier line of authority was not even mentioned. You will note below that the Restatement does not even include continuity as one of the requirements for the implication of easements.

2. "The importance of an allegation concerning unity of title is basic. An implied easement cannot exist where neither the party claiming it, nor the owner of the land over which it is claimed, nor anyone under whom they or either of them claim, was ever seised of both tracts of land. Such easements are created only when land is broken up, and failure to allege that both estates were formerly one is a fatal omission." Shannon, J., in Dinkins v. Julian, 122 So.2d 620 (Fla.App.1960).

3. "The record discloses that prior to April 28, 1953, the Chicago Title and Trust Company, as trustee, owned certain real estate, * * * upon which it had constructed six 2-story and basement townhouses for sale to the public. The houses constituted one single unbroken structure, divided by party walls into the six houses, each of which has a separate entrance in the front and rear. The structure is situated along the west side of North Winchester Avenue, a north and south thoroughfare, and the first intersecting street from the west is about 165 feet north of the northernmost townhouse. A cement service walk was laid along the rear of the townhouses for the entire length of the structure from north to south, and thence east along the northern wall thereof to the sidewalk running in front of the townhouses. This latter portion, extending from the front sidewalk west to the service walk in the rear, is the subject of dispute in this case." Over a period of several months the houses were sold to different purchasers. Obviously, prior to being offered for sale, no use was made of the walk in question. Nothing was said about the use of the walks in any of the deeds to the separate parcels. Is there a proper basis here for the implication of easements for the use of the walk in question? See Gilbert v. Chicago Title & Trust Co., 7 Ill.2d 496, 131 N.E.2d 1 (1955).

4. Ways of Necessity. "If one conveys a part of his property entirely surrounded by other lands of the grantor and without any way to the property conveyed, the law, acting upon the assumption that grantor intended for his grantee to enjoy the thing granted, will imply an easement to provide access for a public way." Smith v. Moore, 254 N.C. 186, 118 S.E.2d 436 (1961). The so-called "way of necessity," as described above, was one of the earliest kinds of implied easements. It could be established by proof of necessity alone and without proof of any pre-existing use or quasi-easement. It would be implied as readily by reservation in favor of a landlocked grantor as in favor of a grantee.

In Leonard v. Bailwitz, 148 Conn. 8, 166 A.2d 451 (1960), a way of necessity was claimed. The land over which the way was claimed had been mortgaged, and at the time of the mortgage, the mortgagor had access to unmortgaged land retained by him. He later conveyed a portion of the land retained, which left him with land which was without access to any public way, except over the mortgaged land. The mortgage was foreclosed and the mortgaged land was sold. A way of access was then claimed against the purchaser. The claim was denied. Contrary to the position taken in Romanchuck v. Plotkin, supra, the court in applying the "title theory" of mortgage law, said that the severance of the mortgaged land took place at the time the mortgage was given, rather than at the time of foreclosure, and that at that time there was no necessity for a way of access.

In Hellberg v. Coffin Sheep Co., 66 Wn.2d 664, 404 P.2d 770 (1965), a way of necessity was held to have been created in favor of a lessee under a ten-year lease. The lease also provided for the sale of the dominant land to the lessee at the end of the term. The lessor was enjoined from interfering with the lessee's ingress and egress "at least so long as the landlord-tenant relationship continues."

OTERO v. PACHECO, 94 N.M. 524, 612 P.2d 1335 (App.1980). Defendants owned lots 4 and 5 in a certain city block. Lot 5 fronted Conchiti Street and lot 4 sided on Taos Street. Defendants' home was built on lot 5 and partly on lot 4, and was served by a septic tank located on lot 4. City officials ordered the discontinuance of the use of the septic tank, and defendants built a sewer line from their home across lot 4 to the Taos Street sewer. There was no sewer in Conchiti Street. Later defendants built another house on lot 4 and connected it to the same sewer line. Defendants sold the latter house and that part of lot 4 on which it stood to a predecessor of the plaintiffs. Plaintiffs sued for damages caused by the back-up of the sewer line on several occasions. Defendants counter-claimed alleging that they had an easement across plaintiffs' property. One of the plaintiffs testified that he did not know about the existence of the sewer line until nine years after the plaintiffs' land had been sold to plaintiffs' predecessor. The trial court entered judgment for the defendants. This judgment was affirmed. Part of the court's opinion follows.

"Although the trial court did not characterize the type of easement, it is readily apparent from the findings that the court was speaking of an easement by implied reservation. Whether such an easement is recognized by the appellate courts of this State is a matter of first impression. However, the converse, i.e., an easement by implied grant, was recognized by our Supreme Court in Venegas v. Luby, 49 N.M. 381, 164 P.2d 584 (1945):

'It seems well settled * * * that if the owner of land subjects one part of it to a visible servitude in favor of another and then conveys away the dominant portion while it is enjoying the servitude of the portion retained, and the use is reasonably necessary for the full enjoyment of the part granted, an implied easement arises in favor of the premises conveyed and passes by the conveyance without mention.'

The nature of and rationale for these two types of easements was very ably set forth by the Supreme Court of Texas in *Mitchell v. Castellaw*, 151 Tex. 56, 246 S.W.2d 163 (1952):

"It is universally recognized that where the owner of a single area of land conveys away part of it, the circumstances attending the conveyance may themselves, without aid of language in the deed, and indeed sometimes in spite of such language, cause an easement to arise as between the two parcels thus created—not only in favor of the parcel granted ("implied grant") but also in favor of the one remaining in the ownership of the grantor ("implied reservation"). The basis of the doctrine is that the law reads into the instrument that which the circumstances show both grantor and grantee must have intended, had they given the obvious facts of the transaction proper consideration. And in the case of an implied reservation it is not necessarily a bar to its creation that the grantor's deed, into which the law reads it, actually warrants the servient tract thereby conveyed to be free of incumbrance."

There is a split in authority over the question of the degree of necessity that is required to imply the retention of an easement. According to one view, an easement is implied by reservation only where there is strict necessity. Winthrop v. Wadsworth, 42 So.2d 541 (S.Ct.Fla., 1949).

The other view was set forth by the Supreme Court of Oregon in Jack v. Hunt, 200 Or. 263, 264 P.2d 461 (1953):

> 'The majority rule makes no distinction between the degree of necessity in the granting or the retaining of an implied easement. In either circumstances the degree of necessity is answered "if necessary to the reasonable enjoyment of the property'".

The trial court thought that reasonable necessity was the better view, and so do we. This view is more in harmony with Venegas v. Luby, supra, than is strict necessity. However, in Venegas, it is clearly indicated that reasonable necessity is not synonymous with mere convenience.

"Applying the foregoing to the facts of this case, the trial court was correct in deciding that the defendants had an easement by implied reservation as the result of a reasonable necessity which continues to exist.

"The plaintiffs' third point of error is that they were allegedly bona fide purchasers for value of lot 4, and that they took free and clear of any easement of which they had no notice. The general rule is that a bona fide purchaser does not take subject to an easement unless he has actual or constructive knowledge of its existence. Southern Union Gas Co. v. Cantrell, 56 N.M. 184, 241 P.2d 1209 (1952). However, the law charges a person with notice of facts which inquiry would have disclosed where the circumstances are such that a reasonably prudent person would have inquired. Sanchez v. Dale Bellamah Homes of New Mexico, Inc., 76 N.M. 526, 417 P.2d 25 (1966).

> 'While there is some conflict of authority as to whether existing drains, pipes, and sewers may be properly characterized as apparent, within the rule as to apparent or visible easements the majority of the cases which have considered the question have taken the view that appearance and visibility are not synonymous, and that the fact that the pipe, sewer, or drain may be hidden underground does not negative its character as an apparent condition; at least, where the appliances connected with and leading to it are obvious. 58 A.L.R. 832; Helle v. Markotan, 137 N.E.2d 715 (Ohio Com.Pl.1955); Frantz v. Collins, 21 Ill.2d 446, 173 N.E.2d 437 (1961).'

The circumstances in this situation were such that a reasonably prudent person would have inquired.

"We need not consider plaintiffs' fourth point of error because, even if we were to decide that it had merit, it would not alter the outcome of this case.

"The judgment is affirmed.

"IT IS SO ORDERED.

"ANDREWS, Judge (dissenting).

"I dissent.

"I cannot agree with the majority that the circumstances were such as to put the Oteros on constructive notice of the existence of the sewer line.

'* * * the purchaser of property may assume that no easements are attached to the property purchased which are not of record except those which are open and visible, and he cannot otherwise be bound with notice. There should be such a connection between the use and the thing as to suggest to the purchaser that the one estate is servient to the other.'

Southern Union Gas Co. v. Cantrell, 56 N.M. 184 at 190, 241 P.2d 1209 at 1213 (1952).

"The facts in this case do not support the inference that the Oteros had constructive notice of the existence of the sewer line. While the appearance of the adjoining Pacheco property was such as to suggest that it was connected to a sewer line, there is nothing in the record to indicate that it was in any way apparent that it, *at one time*, had been necessary to lay such a line under the Oteros' land. The history of the development of the sewer system in the area is not apparent to the average purchaser, and the Oteros were justified in assuming that the Pachecos' sewer connections did not impinge on the property rights of the surrounding landholders.

"I would reverse."

Note

The startling notion, announced in *Romanchuck* and repeated in *Otero*, about why an underground drain can be regarded as "apparent," may justify contrasting reactions, depending on whether the easement is claimed by grant or by reservation. When a drainage or similar easement is asserted against a grantor as an implied grant, one may be inclined to deal lightly with the "apparent" requirement. Indeed one may wonder what useful purpose the requirement serves, in view of the fact that the grantor surely knows about the drain and usually in fact is the one who installed it.

But when such an easement is asserted against a grantee of land as an implied reservation, if the grantee knows nothing about the drain, one may shrink from so broad a view of the notice ingredient. Note that the question can be raised by two different contentions. It can be argued that no easement was ever created, for want of an apparent quasi-easement. Or it can be contended by a subsequent purchaser from an original grantee of the quasi-servient estate that he is a subsequent purchaser for value without notice of the easement, and so should not be burdened by it. It is implicit in the opinion in *Otero* that both arguments are rejected. Is there room to argue that, however one defines an "apparent" quasi-easement, a proper doctrine of bona fide purchase is distorted by such an interpretation. Even if one were to challenge the decision at the level of defining "apparent," does it not seem odd to say that because a house has modern plumbing, one is bound to inquire where the plumbing goes? Does the view suggest a time long in the past when a house equipped with modern plumbing was a curiosity, moving people to make inquiries about how it worked? How rational is the view that anyone buying a house should inquire whether and where one's household equipment is connected to a sewer?

Restatement, Property (1944) *

§ 476. Factors Determining Implication of Easements.

In determining whether the circumstances under which a conveyance of land is made imply an easement, the following factors are important

(a) whether the claimant is the conveyor or the conveyee,

(b) the terms of the conveyance,

(c) the consideration given for it,

(d) whether the claim is made against a simultaneous conveyee,

(e) the extent of necessity of the easement to the claimant,

(f) whether reciprocal benefits result to the conveyor and the conveyee,

(g) the manner in which the land was used prior to its conveyance, and

(h) the extent to which the manner of prior use was or might have been known to the parties.

Note

You should observe that the approach to the implication of easements declared by the Restatement is significantly different from that stated in the cases referred to above, and in ways other than the inclusion of more and somewhat different specific criteria. It appears that some courts approach the problem in the traditional manner and then simply cited the Restatement, as though the Restatement did no more than codify the traditional requirements. For a consideration of the influence of the Restatement upon the courts see Comment, 57 Mich.L.Rev. 724 (1959). But compare Thomas v. Deliere, 241 Pa. Super. 1, 359 A.2d 398 (1976), where the court weighed all applicable relevant factors stated in the Restatement to conclude that no easement was implied. The court said that no single factor is dispositive nor is any purely mathematical weighing of factors authorized.

KRZEWINSKI v. EATON HOMES, INC.

Court of Appeals of Ohio, 1958.
108 Ohio App. 175, 161 N.E.2d 88.†

HUNSICKER, Presiding Judge. David R. Krzewinski and his wife, Guinevere L. Krzewinski, filed an action in the Common Pleas Court of Lorain County, in behalf of themselves and all others similarly situated, to compel Eaton Homes, Inc., the appellant herein, "to specifically perform its agreement with plaintiffs and all others similarly situated, by ordering said defendant [Eaton Homes, Inc.] to install or to provide for the installation of Alton Drive as a through and uninterrupted street * * *."

Eaton Homes, Inc., laid out a subdivision in Eaton Township, Lorain County, Ohio bordering Island Road and the Elyria-Twinsburg Road

---

† Appeal dismissed, 169 Ohio St. 86, 157 N.E.2d 339 (1959).

(Route 82). The plat of this subdivision, dated February 1, 1955, was approved by all of the necessary parties, and thereafter recorded on April 8, 1955, in volume 17, page 38, of the records of plats of Lorain County, Ohio. This plat, among other things, shows a street, designated as "Alton Drive," running from Eaton Boulevard to Elm Road, and paralleling Island Road, a previously-existing highway. The plat shows that there are three streets which intersect Alton Drive and run into Island Road. They are, from south to north, Elm Road, Mencl Road and East Road.

Eaton Homes, Inc., built two houses on Island Road for display purposes before any work was done in laying out and grading the streets, lots, or other areas, of the subdivision.

On August 2, 1955, Mr. and Mrs. Krzewinski signed an offer, to buy a house and lot, which reads in part as follows:

"The undersigned hereby agrees to purchase the parcel of real estate improved with a 3-bedroom dwelling, known as the National Homes 'B Pacemaker' model, to be located on Sublot No. 90, Alton Road [sic], in the Township of Eaton, County of Lorain, Ohio, together with all appurtenances belonging thereunto."

This offer was accepted by Eaton Homes, Inc., which later delivered a deed to Mr. and Mrs. Krzewinski, wherein the land was described as follows:

" * * * situated in Township of Eaton, County of Lorain, and state of Ohio, and known as being Sublot 90 in the Eaton Homes Subdivision of part of Lot 36, as shown by the recorded plat of Volume 17 of Maps, Page 38, of Lorain County Records."

The sale of the lot in this subdivision to these plaintiffs, as well as sales to other persons living on Alton Drive, was made by reference to the plat only, since the streets were not laid out, and hence the exact location of a lot could not be determined by an inspection of the premises.

An easement across the subdivision lands existed, prior to the preparation of the plat, in favor of the Buckeye Pipe Line Company. An agreement was entered into between Eaton Homes, Inc., and the Buckeye Pipe Line Company, whereby the latter company consented to a restriction of their easement to a strip 60 feet wide, running east and west through the subdivision along the path designated on the recorded plat as Mencl Road. As a consequence, Alton Drive was barricaded at its intersection with Mencl Road.

In order for Alton Road [sic] to be made a through highway across Mencl Road, it will be necessary to encase the pipeline, and do other work to protect the easement of the Buckeye Pipe Line Company.

The Buckeye Pipe Line Company was made a party defendant in the original action, and is an appellee in this court. They have, by answer and cross-petition, asked that their rights be protected, and their title be quieted. They do, however, say, by memorandum filed in this court, and by oral statement of their counsel, that, in the event the issues are decided in favor of Mr. and Mrs. Krzewinski, then Eaton Homes, Inc., has agreed to protect the pipeline.

The trial court decided the issue in favor of Mr. and Mrs. Krzewinski, and, when a journal entry was prepared and placed on record by a deputy clerk of courts, the trial court vacated and set aside such entry, and thereafter prepared a new entry properly signed by the judge. All of this was done within the same term of court.

We do not believe the trial court committed an error in thus correcting his record. A motion was filed herein by the plaintiffs-appellees to dismiss this appeal. We conclude that such motion must be overruled.

The action is before us as an appeal on questions of law and fact.

This case concerns the rights of grantees of lands, purchased with reference only to a recorded plat, to the road abutting such lands, which road, as shown on the recorded plat, is a through highway.

The general rule, with respect to the sale of property by lot number from a recorded plat, as stated in III American Law of Property, Section 12.103 (p. 406), to be as follows:

"When land is conveyed as a unit, or as part of a unit, of a recorded plat, the plat becomes as much a part of the description as would be the case if copied into the instrument or if the data furnished by it were set out in full."

Statements to the same effect may be found in 11 C.J.S. Boundaries § 24, and 26 C.J.S. Deeds § 101b. See also: 2 Tiffany on Real Property (2 Ed.) Section 366(b) (p. 1319).

The authorities cited in these texts support the statement as set out above.

In the case of Finlaw v. Hunter, 87 Ohio App. 543, 96 N.E.2d 319, 320 the court said, with reference to an undedicated plat, that:

"3. Where a deed describes the lot conveyed by number and reference to an undedicated plat upon which the lot is shown to front upon a street, the grantor is estopped to deny the right of the grantee to use the land for street purposes, and the easement which the grantee acquires is not limited to that part of the described street in front of his lot but it extends to the whole street shown so far as it was owned by the grantor when the deed was executed."

That case arose in Cincinnati, Hamilton County, Ohio, and it did not follow the rule laid down in an earlier case arising out of the district court for Hamilton County, where the rule was stated, in the case of Huelsman v. Mills & Kline, 12 Am.Law Rec. 301, 6 Dec.Rep. 1192, to be as follows:

"The purchaser of a lot bounded on an unopened street is 'entitled to a right of way over it if it is of the lands of his vendor, to its full extent and dimensions only, until it reaches some other street or public way. To this extent will the vendor be held by the implied covenant of his deed, and no further.' "

See also: Scott v. Snyder, 73 Ohio App. 424, 54 N.E.2d 157.

An examination of the authorities in other jurisdictions discloses three views with reference to the problem herein. These views are clearly set forth in a note on the subject in 19 University of Cincinnati Law Review, at page 267 et seq.

An extensive annotation on the question of whether such a conveyance as we have herein creates in the purchaser a right to use and enjoy such streets, alleys, parks, or other similar areas, which do not abut the property conveyed, may be found in 7 A.L.R.2d at page 607 et seq. The text writers designate these rules as: (1) The "broad" or "unity" rule; (2) the "intermediate," "beneficial" or "full enjoyment" rule; and (3) the "narrow" or "necessary" rule.

We have examined many of the cases cited in the annotation in 7 A.L.R.2d, supra, some of which bear directly on the problem presented in this appeal. We find that some states, such as New York, West Virginia, and Wisconsin, have a conflict in certain of their reported cases.

The fact that the plat of this subdivision was approved by the county commissioners and township trustees does not make the roads delineated thereon county or township roads. See: Section 711.041, Revised Code.

We do not need to consider the question of a dedication to public use of Alton Drive, because the plaintiffs-appellees, Krzewinski, purchased the land and now live in a house abutting on Alton Drive.

We do not consider herein the right of Mr. and Mrs. Krzewinski in nonabutting streets or recreation areas. We are concerned only with their right to have Alton Drive extended across Mencl Road.

We believe that, when Eaton Homes, Inc., displayed to Mr. and Mrs. Krzewinski a plat showing Alton Drive as a through highway across Mencl Road, they impliedly promised to the purchasers that such roadway would be completed as shown on the plat. This promise became a part of the transaction as though written into the offer of purchase and the deed of conveyance. Mr. and Mrs. Krzewinski, upon the purchase of the land, obtained an easement to use Alton Drive for the full length shown on the plat. The better-reasoned authorities support the view above expressed. See: 17A American Jurisprudence, Easements, Section 39, and 18 Ohio Jurisprudence (2d), Easements, Section 28, and authorities cited in both texts.

One of the early cases on this general subject is Cook v. Totten, 49 W.Va. 177, 38 S.E. 491, 87 Am.St.Rep. 792, where the court said:

"2. When lands are laid off into lots, streets, and alleys, and a map plat thereof is made, all lots sold and conveyed by reference thereto, without reservation, carry with them, as appurtenant thereto, the right to the use of the easement in such streets and alleys necessary to the enjoyment and value of such lots.

"3. When such land owner refuses to such lot owner the use of such streets and alleys, a court of equity will compel him to specifically perform his contract, and require him to open such streets and alleys for the benefit of such lot owners, although the dedication to public use of such streets and alleys has not been accepted by the public authorities."

This case has been quoted with approval in Lindsay v. James, 188 Va. 646, 51 S.E.2d 326, 7 A.L.R.2d 597; Cason v. Gibson, 217 S.C. 500, 61 S.E.2d 58; and Merino v. George F. Fish, Inc., 112 Conn. 557, 153 A. 301.

In those cases where the street sought to be opened as a through highway abuts the property of one who purchased the land from a plat, as in this case, the majority rule is that such street must be open, so as to be used for travel by the abutting land owner-purchaser, for its full length.

Thus, in the case of Westbrook v. Comer, 197 Ga. 433, 29 S.E.2d 574, 575, the Supreme Court of Georgia said:

"2. Where a deed or grant refers to a plat as furnishing the description of the land conveyed, the plat itself and the words and marks on it are as much a part of the grant or deed, and control, so far as limits are concerned, as if such descriptive features were written out on the face of the deed or grant itself."

To the same effect are the following authorities: Lagorio v. Lewenberg, 226 Mass. 464, 115 N.E. 979; Vinso v. Mingo, 162 Pa.Super. 285, 57 A.2d 583; Kerrigan v. Backus, 69 App.Div. 329, 74 N.Y.S. 906; Fiebelkorn v. Rogacki, 280 App.Div. 20, 111 N.Y.S.2d 898; Gerald Park Improvement Ass'n, Inc. v. Bini, 138 Conn. 232, 83 A.2d 195; Rudd v. Kittinger, 309 Ky. 315, 217 S.W.2d 651.

In the instant case the action, as brought by the Krzewinskis, is for specific performance of the contract to open Alton Drive across Mencl Road, by removing the barricades now closing that portion of the highway.

Our examination of the cases shows that the action usually instituted to secure a redress of the alleged grievance is a mandatory injunction to remove obstructions placed in the highway. We do not believe that mandatory injunction is an exclusive remedy. We have herein indicated that the plat of the premises becomes a part of the contract and a part of the deed of conveyance, and that there was an implied promise by the vendor that it would keep Alton Drive open as a through highway if Mr. and Mrs. Krzewinski would buy a lot abutting upon such road. Since we adopt this view, we conclude that specific performance is a proper method to enforce this agreement.

We therefore determine herein, that, when Mr. and Mrs. Krzewinski bought the lot on Alton Drive from a plat prepared and recorded by Eaton Homes, Inc., which lot was designated in the contract of sale and the deed of conveyance by reference to such recorded plat, such plat, with Alton Drive delineated thereon as a highway crossing Mencl Road, became a part of the contract of sale and the deed of conveyance, as though fully written therein; and that there then arose a contract implied from such facts that Eaton Homes, Inc., would have Alton Drive opened across Mencl Road, so that these abutting property owners could travel over Alton Drive, as shown on the plat of the subdivision.

We further determine that Mr. and Mrs. Krzewinski, and all others similarly situated, are entitled to have this contract, set out above, specifically performed by Eaton Homes, Inc., the barricades removed, and Alton Drive opened for travel.

A decree for Mr. and Mrs. Krzewinski, in behalf of themselves and all others similarly situated, directing the performance of the acts hereinbefore set forth, may be prepared, at the costs of Eaton Homes, Inc.

Decree for appellees.

Notes

1. The three rules referred to by the court in the principal case, as listed in the annotation in 7 A.L.R.2d 608 (1949), are as follows:

(1) The "broad" or "unity" view, under which the easement is created in all of the streets and alleys delineated on the map or plat.

(2) The "intermediate" or "beneficial" view, under which the easement is created in such of the streets and alleys shown on the map or plat as are reasonably or materially beneficial to the grantee and where a deprivation of such an interest would reduce the value of the grantee's lot.

(3) The "narrow" or "necessary" view, under which the easement exists only in such streets as abut the grantee's lot and such others as are necessary to give the grantee access to a public way.

The process whereby an owner of land can dedicate streets or alleys or to other public uses is dealt with in a later chapter. Where a proper dedication to public use is consummated and streets and alleys are improved and opened to public use, no special problem about the right of abutting owners to the use of such ways will arise. Such a problem, however, may arise prior to the opening of such ways to the public or if in fact no public way is ever opened. It can also arise where, upon appropriate action by local governmental authority, such a way is vacated as a public way.

Suppose a subdivider of land frames his plat so as to make reference thereon only to ways which at the time are duly established public ways. If such a way should be vacated, do you see any basis for denying to grantees of lots covered by the plat the right to assert the existence of private ways? See Highway Holding Co. v. Yara Engineering Corp., 22 N.J. 119, 123 A.2d 511 (1956).

2. Lots in a subdivision were sold according to a recorded plat. The plat showed not only streets, but a lake designated as Tommy Walker Memorial Park. The lots apparently did not abut on the lake. The lot owners sued to restrain the developer from building a club and condominiums around the lake. The court affirmed a judgment for the plaintiffs on the ground that they had acquired an easement in the lake. Walker v. Duncan, 236 Ga. 331, 223 S.E.2d 675 (1976).

C. PRESCRIPTION

HESTER v. SAWYERS

Supreme Court of New Mexico, 1937.
41 N.M. 497, 71 P.2d 646.

BRICE, Justice. It will be unnecessary to refer to the pleadings. The question is whether the district court erred in holding that appellee has title by prescription to a right of way over appellant's land.

If there is substantial evidence to support the findings and judgment of the court, it will not be disturbed by us. The evidentiary facts are practically undisputed and are as follows:

The parties are adjoining landowners. At the time and before appellee bought his property in 1920, appellant was the owner of the land over which the easement is claimed. Persons owning land on three sides had theretofore built fences around their own land, thus in effect placing fences on three sides of appellant's land; but the east side was open and all persons desiring so do to, could pass across it.

The two tracts of land are separated by a fence belonging to appellee, which is appellant's west boundary. The original way had its beginning at appellee's house, passed an opening in the fence, and ran easterly across appellant's land to a road along her boundary, which at that time was unfenced.

In 1922 a golf club secured the consent of appellant to place a fence along the east boundary, thus inclosing the land; after which it was used in part as a golf course. Appellee claimed a right to pass over the land at that time, though he did not know who owned it. The golf club secured his consent to the building of the fence. He had no deed to the road, paid no taxes on it, and based his claim of right on the fact that "it was the only way to get in and out and had been used for years."

At the time the east fence was built the road was materially changed. From the west boundary it followed the old road a very short distance, then turned away to the south of it some distance, thereafter paralleling it for the greater distance across appellant's land, and terminated on the road at the east side in a lane south of "the old road." A map was introduced in evidence showing the "old road," and the "present road," from which it appears that they are not substantially at the same location, though practically parallel.

Since the east fence was built, appellee, his tenants, visitors, and those having business with him (and no other persons), have used the road daily and openly, without interruption or objection from any one until just prior to the filing of this suit in the district court. Appellee did not have the affirmative consent or authority of appellant, or any person, to use the road. When he gave his consent to the golf club to build the fence, he stated to its representative: "I don't lose my right to come down and out of this canyon." He sells lumber at his house and has no other way out. He did not buy his land from appellant. He testified: "My business is selling lumber at my claim up above my house, with no other way than this road to get to and from my place. I have rent houses and this road is the only way my tenants have to go back and forth. If the road is closed I will have to discontinue my business and move out of there. I claim this road as my right of way."

Since the east fence was built, more than ten years prior to the filing of this suit, appellee has continuously graded and kept the road in condition for travel for his own use.

Just prior to the filing of this suit the appellant saw the appellee and insisted that he change the road to run further north so that it would interfere less with her property. Appellee agreed to do this, and to that end began the grading of a new road. This appellant claimed did not comply with her directions, so she closed appellee out with a fence, which was torn down by him. This suit followed.

There is no specific statute in this state under which title to an easement or other incorporeal hereditament can be obtained by prescription, but appellant claims that section 83–122, Comp.St.1929, applies to corporeal and incorporeal hereditaments. It reads in part as follows: "No person or persons, nor their children or heirs, shall have, sue or maintain any action or suit, either in law or equity, for any lands, tenements or hereditaments, against any one having adverse possession of the same continuously in good faith, under color of title, but within ten years next after his, her or their right to commence, have or maintain such suit shall have come, fallen or accrued, and all suits, either in law or equity, for the recovery of any lands, tenements or hereditaments so held, shall be commenced within ten years, next after the cause of action therefor has accrued: * * * 'Adverse possession' is defined to be an actual and visible appropriation of land, commenced and continued under a color of title and claim of right inconsistent with and hostile to the claim of another."

If this statute applies to easements, then appellee has no title for he does not claim, nor did he prove, color of title.

It was the ancient rule of law that the words "lands, tenements or hereditaments" comprehended only freehold estates and did not apply to easements or other incorporeal hereditaments, Hutchinson v. Bramhall, 42 N.J.Eq. 372, 7 A. 873; likewise statutes of limitation like that to which we have referred, which bar actions to recover lands held adversely under color of title for a period of years, are generally, held to apply to corporeal hereditaments only.

"Prescription may be defined to be a mode of acquiring title to incorporeal hereditaments by continued user, possession or enjoyment had during the time and in the manner fixed by law. The term properly applies only to incorporeal rights. An interest in the land of another greater than an incorporeal hereditament, such as the possession and use of a building thereon, cannot be established by prescription. Prescription is distinguished from custom in that the former is a personal usage or enjoyment confined to the claimant and his ancestors or those whose estate he has acquired, while the latter is a mere local usage, not connected to any particular person, but belonging to the community rather than to its individuals. Adverse possession is distinguished from prescription in that it is, properly speaking, a means of acquiring title to corporeal hereditaments only, and is usually the direct result of the statute of limitations; while prescription is the outgrowth of common-law principles, with but little aid from the legislature, and has to do with the acquisition of no kind of property except incorporeal hereditaments." 1 Thompson on Real Property, § 372.

Appellant does not seriously contend that the statute of limitation applies to easements, but insists that if it does not, then the right is one at common law and that twenty years use is necessary to acquire title by prescription.

The courts of England and, with few exceptions, of the United States, have adopted the rule that the period of use for acquiring such title by prescription corresponds to the local statute of limitation for acquiring title to land by adverse possession.

"The period for acquiring an easement in land corresponds to the local statute of limitation as to land. It would be irrational to hold that an easement may not be acquired by the same lapse of time required to confer title to the land by adverse possession. The period of limitation for the bringing of actions to recover the possession of land is generally adopted as the period for perfecting easements by prescription. This rule is based upon the assumption that if there had been no grant, the owner would have put an end to the wrongful occupation before the full period of limitation had expired. And while it is often said that from such user a grant will be presumed, the presumption in effect amounts to a positive rule of law, and evidence that no grant was made would not be material. * * *" 1 Thompson on Real Property, § 374.
* * *

Appellant, anticipating this holding, insists that if, following the general rule, we adopt the period of time provided by statute under which adverse possession will bar an action to recover possession of real property, then we should hold that appellee must establish color of title and that he had paid taxes as required by the statute of limitation in question, and cites Harkness et al. v. Woodmansee et al., 7 Utah, 227, 26 P. 291; North Point Consolidated Irrigation Co. v. Utah, Etc., Canal Co., 16 Utah, 246, 52 P. 168, 40 L.R.A. 851, 67 Am.St.Rep. 607; Funk v. Anderson, 16 Utah, 246, 61 P. 106; Coleman v. Hines, 24 Utah, 360, 67 P. 1122; Quanah, A. & P. R. Co. v. Wiseman (Tex.Civ.App.) 247 S.W. 695; Smith v. Jensen, 156 Ga. 814, 120 S.E. 417; Louisville & Nashville R. Co. v. Hays, 11 Lea (Tenn.) 382, 47 Am.Rep. 291. These cases in the main sustain the position of appellant, but we think are against the weight of authority. Also see Humphreys v. Blasingame, 104 Cal. 40, 37 P. 804, 805.

That an easement may be created by prescription, appellant agrees. If we should hold that one claiming an easement because of use for ten years is burdened further with proving he had color of title to such easement, and had paid taxes thereon if levied, then we would be applying the statute of limitation and not the law of prescription to easements, though we have just held the statute of limitation did not apply.

Adverse possession of land could not apply to easements, for the use necessary to acquire them is not necessarily constant or exclusive. Cooper v. Smith, 9 Serg. & R. (Pa.) 26, 11 Am.Dec. 658. A prescriptive right is obtained by use alone and does not depend upon any statute. It is founded upon the presumption of a grant, though there may never have been one. The reason for the adoption by the courts of England and generally by those of the United States, of a time of use analogous to that required by statutes of limitation regarding adverse possession of land, is because the common law fixed no definite time. It was, "For a time whereof the memory of man runneth not to the contrary." The courts, through gradual change, ultimately adopted by analogy the time as that for the running of the statute of limitation in cases of lands held by adverse possession as the period of use necessary for a conclusive presumption of a grant. Statutes of limitation are not otherwise involved or material.

We hold that the period of use necessary to create an easement by prescription is ten years, following our statute of limitation with reference to adverse possession of lands. 19 C.C. title Easements, §§ 17 and 18; 9 R.C.L. title Easements, § 32; 1 Thompson on Real Property, § 374. We cite these texts only because the cases are numerous and are cited supporting the textbooks and encyclopedias. * * *

The use necessary to acquire title by prescription must be open, uninterrupted, peaceable, notorious, adverse, under a claim of right, and continue for a period of ten years with the knowledge or imputed knowledge of the owner. 19 C.J. title Easements, § 32.

Having disposed of these questions of law, we come to apply the facts, about which there is little dispute. The evidence and findings establish appellee's user was continuous, open, uninterrupted, peaceable, notorious, and continued for a period of more than ten years; but it is contended by appellant that it was neither proven to be adverse under a claim of right, nor that it was with the knowledge, or imputed knowledge, of the owner.

If the user was open, adverse, notorious, peaceable, and uninterrupted, the owner is charged with knowledge of such user, and acquiescence in it is implied. 1 Thompson on Real Property, § 462. The real question in the case is whether the user was adverse under a claim of right or only permissive.

A prescriptive right cannot grow out of a strictly permissive use, no matter how long the use. 1 Thompson on Real Property § 471.

A road existed across appellant's uninclosed land before the appellee bought his land; and after he acquired it he continuously used this road that others had used before his time, until the east boundary fence was built. But there was no substantial evidence of an adverse user under claim of right.

Appellant quotes Boullioun v. Constantine et al., 186 Ark. 625, 54 S.W.(2d) 986, 987, as follows: "While not universally recognized, the prevailing rule seems to be that, where the claimant has openly made continuous use of the way over occupied lands unmolested by the owner for a time sufficient to acquire title by adverse possession, the use will be presumed to be under a claim of right; but, where the easement enjoyed is across property that is unenclosed, it will be deemed to be by permission of the owner and not to be adverse to his title." In the Boullioun Case it is also stated: "Cases might and do arise where those using a private way over unenclosed lands may, by their conduct, openly and notoriously pursued, apprise the owner that they are claiming the way as of right and thus make their possession adverse."

In this state, where large bodies of privately owned land are open and uninclosed, it is a matter of common knowledge that the owners do not object to persons passing over them for their accommodation and convenience, and many such roads are made and used by neighbors and others. Under these circumstances it would be against reason and justice to hold that a person so using a way over lands could acquire any permanent right, unless his intention to do so was known to the owner, or so plainly apparent from acts that knowledge should be imputed to him. Waller v. Hidlebrecht, 295 Ill. 116, 128 N.E. 807; Evans v. Bullock, 260 Ky. 214, 84 S.W.(2d) 26; Shroer v. Brooks, 204 Mo.App. 567, 224 S.W. 53; Bridwell v. Arkansas Power & Light Co., 191 Ark. 227, 85 S.W.(2d) 712; 1 Thompson on Real Property, § 478.

So far as the record shows there was no claim of right to the use of the road communicated to appellant, or evidenced by any acts that indicated a claim of right, prior to the inclosure of the lands by the building of the fence on the east side by the golf club in 1922. The substance of the evidence is that the road was there when appellee bought his place and he used it not knowing to whom it belonged. It is presumed that the original use of the road by appellee and others was permissive.

A prescriptive right may be acquired, although the use was originally permissive, if in fact it became adverse. But the adverse user must be for the full ten years, which excludes the time under which the user was permissive. 1 Thompson on Real Property, § 472. If there was an adverse user by appellee it must have begun at the time the east fence was placed around the property by Hahn in 1922.

If a use has its inception in permission, express or implied, it is stamped with such permissive character and will continue as such until a distinct and positive assertion of a right hostile to the owner is brought home to him by words or acts. * * *

"A use acquired merely by consent, permission, or indulgence of the owner of the servient estate can never ripen into a prescriptive right, unless the user of the dominant estate expressly abandons and denies his right under license or permission, and openly declares his right to be adverse to the owner of the servient estate." Howard v. Wright, 38 Nev. 25, 143 P. 1184, 1186.

If the only evidence of an assertion by appellee of a hostile right to the use of a way across appellant's land after the fence was built was the fact that "he continually worked and graded" the road, it may be doubted (though we do not decide) whether this was sufficient to change a friendly and permissive use to a hostile and adverse one, according to the authorities we have cited. But after the fence was built a new road was established. A map introduced in evidence shows "the old road" used prior to the building of the fence and "the present road" made and used after the fence was built. The parties do not contend they are the same and all the evidence shows they are different. The two roads converge a short distance from appellee's land and pass through the same opening, otherwise they are entirely different roads. If appellee had used the present road for only eight years, he could not have tacked the use of the old road on it to give him a prescriptive right.

* * *

The permissive right was to use the old road, not the new one. When appellee abandoned the old road, he established a new road over inclosed lands. He kept the road graded and in repair, exercising control over the strip of land as though his own, for more than ten years. In the absence of proof that this use was permissive (and there is no such proof), it is presumed, after ten years use, to have been hostile, adverse, and acquiesced in by appellant. Carmody v. Mulrooney, 87 Wis. 552, 58 N.W. 1109.

There is substantial evidence to support the judgment of the district court, and it is accordingly affirmed.

It is so ordered.

SHANKS v. FLOOM

Supreme Court of Ohio, 1955.
162 Ohio St. 479, 124 N.E.2d 416.

The appellants, hereinafter referred to as plaintiffs, are the successors in title to a property on the south side of West Maple Street in North Canton, Ohio, formerly owned by Austin Schiltz. Schiltz purchased this property in 1910 and erected a house on it in 1911. At the same time, he constructed a driveway from West Maple Street to the rear of his lot. A few years later, William Floom purchased the vacant lot adjacent to the Schiltz property on the west and built a house on it. For four or five years thereafter, both Floom and his family and Schiltz used this unimproved driveway on the Schiltz property.

About 1924 or 1925, Schiltz and Floom, pursuant to an oral agreement, constructed a cement driveway, seven feet wide and 110 feet long, between and on their two properties, each owner bearing one-half the cost thereof. Cement aprons from the common driveway to the respective garages were constructed at the same time. Each owner continued to use the common driveway until the year 1948 when Schiltz sold his property to the plaintiffs, and the appellees, hereinafter referred to as defendants, inherited their property from William Floom, who died in that year.

Shortly after the acquisition of their respective properties, difficulties arose between the present owners. On July 26, 1951, plaintiffs commenced an action in the Court of Common Pleas of Stark County, seeking to enjoin the defendants' use of the common driveway and to quiet the title of the plaintiffs against any claims of the defendants.

The Common Pleas Court denied the injunction, holding that nothing had occurred to alter the obligation of each party to recognize the right of the other to use the driveway.

On appeal to the Court of Appeals on questions of law and fact, that court quieted the title of the plaintiffs as to the west line of their property, and held that both properties are subject to an easement for driveway purposes, where the cement drive is now located, by reason of more than 21 years of adverse use.

The cause is now before this court pursuant to allowance of a motion to certify the record.   *   *   *

BELL, Judge.   The agreement which resulted in the construction of the driveway came about, according to the testimony of Austin Schiltz, as follows:

"A.   One evening Mr. Floom said, 'Aust, how about making this drive in the center; you pay half and I'll pay half' and I said, 'O.K.' and it was done and I paid my share and he paid his."

It is conceded by defendants that if their use of the driveway, and that of their predecessors in title, pursuant to this agreement, was permissive only such use under the law of Ohio could not ripen into an easement.   Pavey v. Vance, 56 Ohio St. 162, 46 N.E. 898; Railroad Co. v. Village of Roseville, 76 Ohio St. 108, 81 N.E. 178; Pennsylvania R. Co. v. Donovan, 111 Ohio St. 341, 145 N.E. 479.   Defendants' contention is that there was an adverse use under a claim of right which ripened into an easement after 21 years.

This precise question is before this court for the first time.   However, the case of Rubinstein v. Turk, 29 Ohio Law Abst. 653, decided by the Court of Appeals for the Eighth Appellate District, presented the identical problem.   In that case, the parties' predecessors in title acquired adjoining sublots in 1909.   Both sublots were improved with dwellings.   Shortly afterwards, the owners of the two lots agreed to construct a driveway for their joint use, substantially one-half of which was to be on each lot.   The agreement was not in writing.   Pursuant to the agreement, the driveway was constructed and the owner of each lot paid one-half of the cost of construction.   More than 21 years later, differences arose between the owners and defendant attempted to construct a fence across the driveway.   In granting an injunction to the plaintiff, the majority of the Court of Appeals held:

"When   *   *   *   the owners   *   *   *   constructed a joint driveway by agreement between themselves, each owner thereafter claimed the right of an easement in the part of the driveway on his neighbor's lot, in consideration of having given his neighbor a similar easement on his own lot.   Thereafter   *   *   *   the 'possession and use' of each owner was under a 'claim of right' and therefore adverse.   This adverse possession continued for more than 21 years and therefore ripened into a prescriptive right."

The reasoning of the Court of Appeals was based largely on the definition of "hostile use" set out as follows by this court in Kimball v. Anderson, 125 Ohio St. 241, 244, 181 N.E. 17, 18:

"To establish hostility it is not necessary to show that there was a heated controversy, or a manifestation of ill will, or that the claimant was in any sense an enemy of the owner of the servient estate; the facts which prove hostility might greatly differ in different cases, and it has been held in many cases that it is sufficient if the use is inconsistent with the rights of the title owner and not subordinate or subservient thereto. Hostile use is sometimes described as possession and use under a claim of right."

The Kimball case also involved a driveway between two lots. It differs from the present case, however, in that the driveway there was constructed by a single owner of the two lots, followed by a sale of one lot by warranty deed without a reservation of that part used for the driveway. This court held that the warranty deed did not prevent the grantor's subsequent use of the driveway from being adverse.

The acquisition of a prescriptive right in a common driveway has been decided by courts of last resort in several jurisdictions outside Ohio. The cases are collected in an annotation in 98 A.L.R. 1098, following the report of Johnson v. Whelan, 171 Okl. 243, 42 P.2d 882, 98 A.L.R. 1096.

The facts set out as follows in the Johnson case appear to be almost identical with those of the present case:

"Plaintiff and defendant own adjacent lots in Oklahoma City. Plaintiffs own the west lot and defendant the east lot. Both lots face the north, and in 1908 were improved with substantial residential buildings on the northerly portion and smaller buildings to rear on the south. In 1908 one Binns owned the west lot and one Collet the east lot. These owners jointly constructed a concrete paved driveway on their medial line, from the street on the north to small buildings on rear, each furnishing half of the expense. Apparently each intended to furnish half the ground for the seven-foot driveway. However, a survey in 1931 showed some six or nine inches more on the east than on the west lot. No writing was executed by either owner, nor by subsequent owners, granting to the other any rights or privileges in the lot of the other.

" * * * At all times the driveway has been used jointly by the occupants of the two lots. In 1931 defendant built an additional strip of pavement on her side, and threatened to construct a wall or fence along the lot line, which would have left insufficient room for a driveway between the house of the plaintiffs and the property line. Plaintiffs brought this suit to enjoin the defendant from interfering with their use of the driveway."

The Supreme Court of Oklahoma, in granting the injunction, held:

"While the mere permissive use of a way over the land of another will not ripen into an easement, yet one who joins his adjacent landowner in the construction of a paved private way over and along the medial line has given such adjacent owner more than a mere license. Each owner, by use of the driveway, is continuously asserting an adverse right in the portion of the way on the other's lot. And from such use for 15 years the law raises a presumption of the grant of an easement."

Similar conclusions have been reached in cases in Arkansas, Georgia, Iowa, Kentucky, Maryland, Massachusetts, Minnesota, Nebraska, New Jersey, New York and South Carolina. See 98 A.L.R. 1098, and Plaza v. Flak, 7 N.J. 215, 81 A.2d 137, 27 A.L.R.2d 332.

We are not unaware of contrary holdings in Michigan and Illinois in the cases of Wilkinson v. Hutzel, 142 Mich. 674, 106 N.W. 207; Banach v. Lawera, 330 Mich. 436, 47 N.W.2d 679; and Lang v. Dupuis, 382 Ill. 101, 46 N.E.2d 21. But we believe the rule of Johnson v. Whelan, supra, and Rubinstein v. Turk, supra, represents the majority view in this country and the better-reasoned rule.

We believe it is unreasonable to assume that the owners of these properties, at the time this driveway was constructed and the use thereof began, each felt that he was using his half as a matter of right and the other's half merely by permission. On the contrary, the nature and permanence of the improvement, that it was constructed of concrete, and that it was constructed on what the owners considered to be the boundary line between their properties are more consistent with a claim of right on the part of each than with a day-to-day permissive use. We hold, therefore, that the use in this case was under a claim of right and as such was adverse and not permissive. Such use being for more than 21 years, it follows that an easement for the common use of this driveway has been acquired by both parties.

In the case of Yeager v. Tuning, 79 Ohio St. 121, 86 N.E. 657, paragraph two of the syllabus, 19 L.R.A., N.S., 700, 128 Am.St.Rep. 679, cited by plaintiffs, this court recognized that an easement can be created by prescription. But there had been a use in that case for only three years and the court was not called upon to decide whether the use was sufficient to create a prescriptive easement.

Similarly, the case of Pennsylvania R. Co. v. Donovan, supra, is distinguishable on the facts from the present case. In that case the use was purely permissive, there being no mutual dedication of land for a common use.

The judgment of the Court of Appeals is hereby affirmed.

Judgment affirmed.

ZIMMERMAN, Judge (dissenting). As is pointed out in the majority opinion, this is the first time the precise question here involved has been before this court. A situation is presented where two friendly neighbors owned adjoining residence properties. At the suggestion of one of them and by mutual oral agreement each contributed a part of his land to form a common driveway and each contributed to the cost of constructing it. There was nothing hostile or adverse in the creation of the driveway or in its subsequent use by such adjoining-property owners, nor was there any claim of absolute right by either in the other's property.

In a situation of this kind the writer is of the opinion that no adverse use occurs but merely a revocable parol license and that, therefore, no easement by prescription can arise.

It is elementary that a permissive use of a right of way over another's land will not ripen into an easement by prescription no matter how long continued. Pennsylvania R. Co. v. Donovan, 111 Ohio St. 341, 145 N.E. 479; 28 C.J.S. Easements, § 18d, p. 666; 17 American Jurisprudence, 978, Section 67.

Upon such basis, the writer entertains the view that the sounder and more cogent reasoning is found in those cases which hold that a parol agreement by the owners of adjoining lots establishing a driveway for their mutual convenience, a part of such driveway being on each lot, constitutes no more than a license revocable by either party, and the mere acquiescence for a long term of years in such joint use does not create title by prescription in and to the land of the other in either party.

Attention is directed to the Michigan and Illinois cases cited in the majority opinion and to the cases not inconsiderable in number, found in the annotations in 98 A.L.R. 1098, 1103, and 27 A.L.R.2d 332, 351, 359.

Moreover, the conclusion reached herein is in harmony with expressions by this court in Yeager v. Tuning, 79 Ohio St. 121, 86 N.E. 679, and Fowler v. Delaplain, 79 Ohio St. 279, 87 N.E. 260, 21 L.R.A., N.S., 100.

STEWART, J., concurs in the foregoing dissenting opinion.

Notes

1. The cases are divided on the common driveway problem. For a case contra to Shanks v. Floom, see Banach v. Lawera, 330 Mich. 436, 47 N.W.2d 679 (1951), noted in 50 Mich.L.Rev. 776 (1952). See Annotations, 98 A.L.R. 1098 (1935); 27 A.L.R.2d 332 (1953).

2. Reineke v. Schlinger, 240 Minn. 478, 61 N.W.2d 505 (1953), was another common driveway case. The evidence did not show when or under what circumstances the driveway had been built. The defendant testified as follows on a conversation he had with the plaintiff's predecessor during the prescriptive period,

"Well, I says to Lou, I says, you are driving over some on mine, and I would have the car shed correct. Well, he says, let it go. I won't claim any of yours and you don't I suppose claim any of mine. I says, fine and dandy. And that is the way it was left."

What effect should this testimony have on the outcome of the case?

3. Do you see a ground in support of the defendants' claim in Shanks v. Floom other than an acquisition of an easement by prescription? See Oliver v. Wilhite, 227 Mo.App. 538, 55 S.W.2d 491 (1932).

4. Among the ingredients required for a prescriptive use some courts have declared that such use must have been with the "acquiescence" of the owner of the land. This reflects the initial theory of prescription as having been founded on the presumption of a lost grant. The fact that an owner acquiesces in a use of his land is an indication that the use began under some express grant. As the courts came to believe that the true basis for prescription is by way of analogy to adverse possession, they first declared that the presumption of a lost grant became conclusive upon showing of an open, continuous, adverse use. In time most courts ceased speaking of any lost grant, but some of them contin-

ued to include the acquiescence ingredient, without appreciating that such an ingredient is hardly relevant to proof of adverse use. In fact one court made a point of questioning how an adverse use could be with the acquiescence of the owner without being permissive. Zollinger v. Frank, 110 Utah 514, 175 P.2d 714 (1946). Similarly the same court questioned whether a use could be both "peaceable" and "hostile." One can, of course, make proper distinctions in both instances. But the main point is that the words "acquiescence" and "peaceable" should be dropped from the requirements for an adverse use if one follows modern prescription theory. Suppose the owner of land which is being adversely used by another verbally or in writing protests against such use. Should such protests have any effect on the acquisition of a prescriptive easement? A few courts which have not yet entirely detached themselves from the lost-grant theory have held that such protests show a lack of acquiescence which defeats the prescription. If the emphasis is properly upon the adverseness of the claimant's use, such protests, so far from vitiating the prescription, would seem to strengthen it. This is now the prevailing view. See, for example, Lehigh Valley Railroad v. McFarlan, 43 N.J.L. 605 (Ct.Err. & App.1881). Suppose now that a landowner, instead of protesting an unlawful use by another, decides that the best way of dealing with the situation is openly to express his permission to the continuance of such a use. Should this affect the nature of the prescriptive use? See Huff v. Northern Pacific Railway, 38 Wn.2d 103, 228 P.2d 121 (1951).

5. Considerable controversy has recently appeared over the question whether the use of a way by the servient owner affects the adverse nature of the similar use made by one claiming an easement. Some courts have found the claimant's use to be not adverse on one of two grounds: (a) the claimant's use is not "exclusive," and (b) such use by the claimant is presumed to be permissive. Decision supporting (a): Brooks v. Jones, 578 S.W.2d 669 (Tex.1979); decision supporting (b): Gibson v. Buice, 394 So.2d 451 (Fla.App.1981).

On the other hand, two courts have properly held that the requirement of "exclusive" possession for adverse possession has no counterpart for prescriptive easements, and so the use of a way can be adverse, even though such use is shared with the servient owner. Gilman v. McCary, 97 N.M. 376, 640 P.2d 482 (1982); Patch v. Baird, 140 Vt. 60, 435 A.2d 690 (1981). It has been suggested that the "exclusive" requirement has a proper place in prescriptive easements, so as to preclude adverse use to one whose use is shared by the public generally. Zehner v. Fink, 19 Md.App. 338, 311 A.2d 477 (1973).

The prevailing rule that the use of a way is presumed to be adverse was recently followed. Matsu v. Chavez, 96 N.M. 775, 635 P.2d 584 (1981). The minority rule that such use is presumed to be permissive was also recently asserted, but the court found that the presumption had been overcome. Potts v. Burnette, 301 N.C. 663, 273 S.E.2d 285 (1981).

SECTION 3. SCOPE

KANEFSKY v. DRATCH CONSTRUCTION CO.

Supreme Court of Pennsylvania, 1954.
376 Pa. 188, 101 A.2d 923.

HORACE STERN, Chief Justice. This controversy is over defendants' right to use a driveway which is located in the rear of plaintiffs' houses.

Dratch Construction Company, one of the defendants, owned a plot of ground in the City of Philadelphia constituting the easterly half of a square city block bounded by Rugby Street on the east, Phil-Ellena Street on the south, Woolston Avenue on the west, and Vernon Road on the north. Its property ran for a distance of about 729 feet along Rugby Street and extended in depth toward Woolston Avenue for a distance of approximately 115 feet. In 1948 it constructed on its land a 15 foot driveway extending between Phil-Ellena Street and Vernon Road and paralleling, at a distance therefrom of three feet, the boundary line between the Dratch property and the Woolston Avenue property to the rear. It then constructed 39 houses along the Rugby Street frontage and sold them to various home buyers, among whom were the present plaintiffs. The deed to each of the purchasers included the area of the driveway in the rear of the property conveyed but not the three feet beyond the driveway.[1] Every deed granted the use of the driveway and also contained the following reservation in the habendum clause: "And also reserving unto the said grantor, its successors and assigns, the right and privilege of granting the use of the aforesaid driveway to any person or persons, corporation or corporations to whom all or any part of the remaining ground owned by it may at any time hereafter be sold and conveyed."

The parties do not agree as to the reason for the retention by Dratch Construction Company of the three foot strip. Plaintiffs claim that Dratch told them it was for their protection so that the occupants of the Woolston Avenue properties in the rear would not be able to use the driveway but would have to build a separate one for themselves. How plaintiffs would be better protected in that regard by having Dratch Construction Company retain title to the strip instead of deeding it to plaintiffs is not apparent. Dratch denies having made any such statement. In 1950 Dratch Construction Company sold and conveyed the three foot strip to Cora E. Milligan, who then owned the remaining half of the block, by a deed which contained the following grant: "Together with the free and common use, right, liberty and privilege of said fifteen feet wide driveway as and for a passageway, driveway and watercourse at all times hereafter forever, for any buildings hereafter built by the purchaser or nominee, his or her heirs and assigns on Woolston Avenue between Vernon Road and Phil-Ellena Street or on the Northwest side of Phil-Ellena Street between Woolston Avenue and said fifteen feet wide driveway, this use to be for its entire distance from Phil-Ellena Street to Vernon Road. * * *" In 1951 Cora E. Milligan conveyed the three foot strip together with all the rest of her ground to defendant Parkman Homes, Inc., by a deed which contained this same grant of the right to use the driveway. Parkman Homes, Inc., and defendant Fishman and Park, builders, began constructing houses along Woolston Avenue and, in connection with that operation, started using the driveway to bring in the necessary building materials. Thereupon

1. Dratch Construction Company retained title to the three foot strip only for a distance of approximately 631 feet northerly from Phil-Ellena Street. Beyond that point to Vernon Road its deeds to purchasers conveyed title all the way to the boundary line of the property to the rear. [Footnotes are the court's. Ed.]

plaintiffs filed a complaint in equity seeking an injunction to restrain those defendants from using or trespassing on the driveway and praying also that plaintiffs' deeds be reformed by deleting therefrom the right reserved by Dratch Construction Company to grant the use of the driveway to any persons to whom it might thereafter convey all or any part of the remaining ground owned by it.[2] The court entered a decree granting their prayer to reform the deeds and issuing the injunction requested. Dratch Construction Company, Parkman Homes, Inc., and Fishman and Park appeal from that decree.

Much argument pro and con is devoted by the parties to the question whether Dratch Construction Company was guilty of deception and fraud in its dealings with plaintiffs by concealing from them its allegedly real intention to enable, in some way, subsequent purchasers of lots on the Woolston Avenue front to make use of the driveway in common with the property owners on Rugby Street. In view of what we conceive to be the controlling issue in the case it is not necessary for us to discuss the question thus argued, nor whether, even if any such fraud was perpetrated, it can properly be imputed to the other defendants on the ground of constructive notice.

The real and determinative question is in regard to the interpretation of the reservation in the deed from Dratch Construction Company to plaintiffs of the right of the grantor to grant the use of the driveway to any persons to whom all or any part of the remaining ground owned by it might at any time thereafter be sold and conveyed. This language is not ambiguous, and it must therefore be construed according to its clear and literal terms and not as colored or amended by any oral conversations between Dratch and the plaintiffs or by any alleged intention of Dratch, secret or revealed. As was stated in Nallin-Jennings Park Co. v. Sterling, 364 Pa. 611, 615, 73 A.2d 390, 392, 20 A.L.R.2d 793, quoting from Witman v. Stichter, 299 Pa. 484, 488, 149 A. 725, 726: " ' "In construing the grant or other instrument whereby the easement is created, the document itself, and that only, can, in the first instance, be looked at to discover the extent and nature of the agreement and the terms of the grant. If on the face of the document no doubt arises that the words are used in their primary sense, and if, read in that sense, they are plain and unambiguous, the matter is concluded." Gale on Easements, page 80. * * * The terms of the grant, as they can be learned either by words clearly expressed, or by just and sound construction, will regulate and measure the rights of the grantee. * * * ' " And in Liquid Carbonic Co. v. Wallace, 219 Pa. 457, 460, 68 A. 1021, 26 L.R.A., N.S., 327, it was said, quoting from Hopewell Mills v. Taunton Savings Bank, 150 Mass. 519, 23 N.E. 327, 6 L.R.A. 249: "The intention to be sought is not the undisclosed purpose of the actor, but the intention implied and manifested by his act. It is an intention which settles, not merely his own rights, but the rights of others who have or may acquire interests in the property. They cannot know his secret purpose, and their rights

2. Subsequently the 35 remaining owners and occupants of the houses in the Rugby Street row were allowed to intervene as party plaintiffs and 4 purchasers of the houses on Woolston Avenue as parties defendants.

depend, not upon that, but upon the inferences to be drawn from what is external and visible."

It is first to be noted that, as all the parties agree, the reservation of the right to grant the use of the driveway to persons becoming the purchasers of other ground owned by the grantor was not the reservation of a right to grant an easement in gross but only an easement as an appurtenance to such other ground. Ulrich v. Grimes, 94 Pa.Super.Ct. 313, 316.

What was the "remaining ground" then owned by the Dratch Construction Company? It owned the Rugby Street half of the block, and it is obvious that, as it sold off lots from out of this area to home buyers and gave to each of them an easement for the use of the 15 foot driveway over the properties of the other purchasers, it was naturally obliged to reserve in each deed the right to grant to such other purchasers the use of the driveway over the lot of the grantee in that particular deed. In addition to the Rugby Street ground remaining in its ownership Dratch Construction Company, having retained title thereto, owned the three foot strip to the rear of the driveway; therefore the use of the driveway—for what such easement might be worth—became appurtenant to that strip also. No other ground was owned then, or indeed at any later time, by Dratch Construction Company, and therefore to no other ground than as thus stated did the reservation of the right to grant the use of the driveway apply.

Did the acquisition by Cora E. Milligan of the title to the three foot strip, thereby adding it to her ownership of the half of the block fronting on Woolston Avenue, entitle her to the use of the driveway as an appurtenance not only to that strip but to all such other ground? In the deed to her from Dratch Construction Company it undertook to grant the use of the driveway "for any buildings hereafter built by the purchaser or nominee, his or her heirs and assigns on Woolston Avenue * * *." But did it have the right to make such a grant and did Cora E. Milligan have the right in turn to convey it to defendants? Clearly, the answer to that question must be in the negative. It is elementary law that an easement cannot be extended by the owner of the dominant tenement to other land owned by him adjacent to or beyond the land to which it is appurtenant,[3] for such an extension would constitute an unreasonable increase of the burden of the servient tenement. It is clear, therefore, that these defendants had no right to use the driveway for the purpose of their operations in connection with the building of houses on Woolston Avenue, nor do the purchasers of the lots on Woolston Avenue have any such right by virtue of their ownership and occupancy of those lots and the buildings thereon.

3. Watson v. Bioren, 1 Serg. & R. 227, 230; Kirkham v. Sharp, 1 Whart. 323, 334; Lewis v. Carstairs, 6 Whart. 193, 207; Shroder v. Brenneman, 23 Pa. 348; Coleman's Appeal, 62 Pa. 252, 275; Schmoele v. Betz, 212 Pa. 32, 36–38, 61 A. 525, 526, 527; Percy A. Brown & Co. v. Raub, 357 Pa. 271, 284, 285, 293, 54 A.2d 35, 42, 46; Hollenback v. Tiffany, 50 Pa.Super. 297; Shawnee Lake Association v. Uhler, 131 Pa.Super. 146, 156, 198 A. 910, 914, 915; Walker v. Walker, 153 Pa.Super. 20, 27, 28, 33 A.2d 455, 459; Davis v. Winsor, 165 Pa. Super. 212, 214, 215, 67 A.2d 569, 570, 571; Myers, Trustee, v. Birkey, 5 Phila. 167, 170; Walker v. Gerhard, 9 Phila. 116.

The Parkman defendants contend that the court should not have granted the injunction because they have been constructing houses on Woolston Avenue at a cost of over $400,000 and because it will be a great hardship on the purchasers of those houses to be obliged to construct a driveway of their own on the rear of their properties, whereas the benefit that the plaintiffs will derive from the injunction is comparatively slight. Since, however, plaintiffs have a right of property it makes no difference that the right may be insignificant in value to them as compared with the advantages that would accrue to defendants from its violation. Even though greater injury may result from granting than refusing an injunction, a plaintiff is entitled thereto if the defendant's act is tortious. Sullivan v. Jones & Laughlin Steel Co., 208 Pa. 540, 554, 555, 57 A. 1065, 1071, 66 L.R.A. 712; Stuart v. Gimbel Bros. Inc., 285 Pa. 102, 106–108, 131 A. 728, 729; Weiss & Maen v. Greenberg, 101 Pa.Super. 24, 30. Defendants also invoke the doctrine of laches, but they did not begin to construct the houses on Woolston Avenue and to use the driveway until the end of February, 1952, and plaintiffs filed the present complaint in equity only six weeks later, so there is no ground for an accusation against them of undue delay.

Whether or not there was, as alleged, any fraud on the part of Dratch Construction Company, the court should not have deleted from plaintiffs' deeds the clause reserving to the grantor the right to grant the use of the driveway to persons who might thereafter purchase all or any part of the remaining ground owned by it, since that reservation was, and is necessary, as previously pointed out, to assure to each of the purchasers of the houses on Rugby Street the right to use the driveway over the properties of the other purchasers.

As thus modified the decree is affirmed, at the cost of appellants.

BELL, Justice (dissenting). Plaintiffs, grantees of Dratch Construction Company, prayed (1) for an injunction, and (2) for a reformation of their respective deeds by deleting therefrom Dratch's right to grant the use of the present 15 foot driveway.

Dratch Construction Company, owners and developers of a large piece of ground fronting on Rugby Street, conveyed parcels of said ground to plaintiffs "reserving unto the said Grantor, its Successors and Assigns, the right and privilege of granting the use of the aforesaid driveway to any person or persons, * * * to whom all or *any part of the remaining ground owned by it may at any time hereafter be sold and conveyed.*" Could any reservation be clearer or more explicit?

The question involved is: Did Dratch Construction Company have a legal right to grant to these defendants the use of the present 15 foot driveway?

It is important to note at the outset that the majority opinion does not assert any fraud on the part of Dratch or any party in this case; and that those defendants who claim title from the owner and common grantor, Dratch, are innocent purchasers for value—without notice of any claim by plaintiffs or by anyone questioning or seeking to limit or invalidate the clear and explicit reservation—and that all the deeds containing the aforesaid reservation of the right to grant the use of the driveway were *recorded*. Nevertheless, plaintiffs contend that Dratch, the common grantor, instead of deeding to them the 3 foot strip of ground bordering their land, *retained title thereto for the purpose of better protecting them*. Such a contention is absurd. Dratch, as the owner and common grantor, could have reserved, as has been done thousands of times before, the right to grant the use of this driveway to others in each deed it made to the purchaser of each of its lots fronting on Rugby Street, without the necessity of reserving to itself the title to a 3 foot strip of land or any land whatsoever. The majority opinion points out that plaintiffs' contention is unreasonable and absurd; yet strangely decides that that is what the reservation in effect meant. The majority hold that the developer (grantor) who owned the 3 foot strip, even if it bought the property adjoining the 3 foot strip, could not allow subsequent purchasers of that property to use the driveway. The effect of the majority's opinion is to make the ownership and reservation of the 3 foot strip—with its right to grant to a subsequent purchaser the use of the 15 foot driveway—absolutely useless, meaningless and absurd, for it is obvious and indisputable (1) that no building of any kind could be erected on a 3 foot strip of land; and (2) that the grantor, *by virtue of owning the remaining ground with Rugby Street frontage*, could grant such easement to all subsequent purchasers of that land without reserving to itself the ownership of this 3 foot strip of land. What possible use was there, therefore, for this 3 foot strip of land except the use contended for by Dratch and the other defendants herein? What possible good could that 3 foot strip of land be to Dratch if it did not intend either (a) to purchase the ground on the other side of the 3 foot strip which fronted on Woolston Avenue, divide it into lots and allow the purchasers thereof to use this driveway, or (b) to sell the 3 foot strip to the owner or owners of the adjoining contiguous land, granting him or them in turn the right to use the driveway. Any other construction is so unreasonable as to be unbelievable. This reservation is explicit and clear as crystal. Where a contract is clear, its meaning must be ascertained by the Court from its language; it must receive a reasonable interpretation; and if it is susceptible of two interpretations a construction will not be adopted which is unreasonable or absurd or which will produce a result that is unreasonable or absurd. Cf. Brown & Co. v. Raub, 357 Pa. 271, 54 A.2d 35; Mowry v. McWherter, 365 Pa. 232, 238, 74 A.2d 154; Com. v. Hallberg, 374 Pa. 554, 97 A.2d 849; Statutory Construction Act of May 28, 1937, § 52, P.L. 1019, 46 P.S. § 552.

That our construction accurately evidences the intention of the parties is further confirmed by the fact that a little more than a year thereafter Dratch Construction Company, unable to purchase the adjoining ground, sold and conveyed the 3 foot strip to the owner of this adjoining contiguous remaining half of the block by a deed which contained the following grant: "Together with the free and common use, right, liberty and privilege of said Fifteen feet wide driveway as and for a passageway, driveway and watercourse at all times hereafter forever, for any buildings hereafter built by the purchaser, or nominee, his or her heirs and assigns, on Woolston Avenue between Vernon Road and Phil-Ellena

Street or on the Northwesterly side of Phil-Ellena Street between Woolston Avenue and said Fifteen feet wide driveway, this use to be for its entire distance from Phil-Ellena Street to Vernon Road, * * *."

The authorities cited by the majority that "an easement cannot be extended by the owner of the dominant tenement to other land owned by him adjacent to or beyond the land to which it is appurtenant, [where] such an extension would constitute an unreasonable increase of the burden of the servient tenement", are, *on their facts*, clearly distinguishable. Furthermore, the fallacy of applying such a principle to the facts in the instant case is, on analysis, clear, because the burden is not *increased* by this extension, *for* (according to the majority) *no burden can exist at all* by virtue of the 3 foot strip ownership. Moreover, when an easement is granted or reserved, the fact that the burden of the servient tenement will be increased by future use is immaterial if the language of the grant or reservation is broad enough to permit, as here, such use.

I would reverse the decree of the Court below and dismiss plaintiffs' Bill of Complaint.

Questions

1. A owns a tract of land which is bounded on the west by a public road. A conveys the west half of his land to B, his deed including the following provision: "reserving, however, to said grantor a right of way for road purposes across the above described premises." Thereafter A begins using an unimproved strip running from the northwest corner of his land along but inside the northern boundary of B's land. Later A sells the south half of the land he retained to C, no mention being made in his deed of the right of way. What rights, if any, does C have to a way across B's land? See Wood v. Ashby, 122 Utah 580, 253 P.2d 351 (1952).

2. A owns a tract of land which is bounded on the west by a public street. A conveys the east half of this tract to B, together with a 16-foot right of way across the land retained by A for ingress and egress. Later B acquires a further tract of land lying adjacent to his land on the east. He then builds a building for use as a bowling alley, which is located partially on the land he acquired from A and partially on the later-acquired tract. Now B and his customers use the way across A's land for ingress and egress to and from the bowling alley. A brings suit to enjoin the use of the way for any purpose. What are the rights of the parties? See McCullough v. Broad Exchange Co., 101 App.Div. 566, 92 N.Y.S. 533 (1902); Penn Bowling Recreation Center v. Hot Shoppes, 86 U.S.App.D.C. 58, 179 F.2d 64 (1949).

3. Could Dratch have reserved the power to make the easement appurtenant to land in the west half of the block? See Restatement § 453, Comment a.

CAMERON v. BARTON

Court of Appeals of Kentucky, 1954.
272 S.W.2d 40.

CLAY, Commissioner. In this suit appellant sought to enjoin the State Highway Department from using a passway over her property for the movement of vehicles, trucks and equipment. The Chancellor dismissed the petition.

In 1931 appellant purchased a lot facing on North Street in the City of Carlisle. In 1950 the State Highway Department purchased a two acre tract behind this lot for the purpose of building a highway garage. In carrying on its operations the Highway Department used a passway over appellant's property.

A passway right, for the benefit of the Highway Department's lot, was created by a conveyance of the original owner of both pieces of property in 1876. This deed apparently was lost and it was not recorded; consequently, the precise nature of the granted easement is not known. However, all subsequent deeds in appellant's chain of title recite that the "same right of passway" originally created was reserved for the benefit of the property owned by the Highway Department. This tract was known as the Slaughter House Lot.

In appellant's deed is the following provision: "The right of passway leading from the Slaughter House Lot to North Street is included in this conveyance."

The facts show that a slaughter house once occupied the premises owned by the Highway Department and for many years the passway over appellant's lot was used for the purpose of bringing in animals and taking out the products of the slaughter house. About 35 or 40 years ago the slaughter house burned and thereafter the property was occupied for farming purposes. The passway was thereafter used for taking in and out farm machinery and for the removal of crops.

In substance it is appellant's contention that since the terms of the original grant are not known, the use of this passway must be restricted to that for which it has heretofore been used, and the Highway Department's grantor had no right to grant it a right of way over appellant's property to move its vehicles and equipment. The principal question before us is whether the right to use this passway is a restricted or a general one.

Appellant's position perhaps would have merit if we were considering an easement by prescription, but this one was created by deed. As far as the record shows there were no restrictions imposed on the use of the passway. The history of its use shows that it changed with the changing type of occupancy of the dominant estate. Since this was permitted without objection, prior to this suit, by subsequent owners of the servient estate, we must conclude that the owners of the servient estate interpreted the original grant as being one for general passway purposes.

The following quotation from Restatement, Property Servitudes, Section 484, which is quoted in Cincinnati, New Orleans & Texas Pacific Ry. Co. v. Barker, Ky.1951, 247 S.W.2d 943, 946, is applicable here:

" 'In ascertaining, in the case of an easement appurtenant created by conveyance, whether additional or different uses of the servient tenement required by changes in the character of the use of the dominant tenement are permitted, the interpreter is warranted in assuming that the parties to the conveyance contemplated a normal development of the use of the dominant tenement.' "

Considering the numerous deed references in appellant's chain of title, which simply refer to the "right of passway" without fixing any limitations, and considering the permitted use of the passway for a great many years for a purpose different from that for which it was used following the original grant, we must presume that the original grant was a general one. Such is the practical interpretation of the scope of the easement. See Cincinnati, New Orleans & Texas Pacific Ry. Co. v. Barker, Ky.1951, 247 S.W.2d 943, just above cited. This being so, the passway may be used in such a manner as is necessary in the proper and reasonable occupation and enjoyment of the dominant estate. See Newberry v. Hardin, Ky.1952, 248 S.W.2d 427. As the passage of time creates new needs and the uses of property change, a normal change in the manner of using a passway does not constitute a deviation from the original grant, and modern transportation uses are not restricted to the ancient modes of travel. See Hodgkins v. Bianchini, 323 Mass. 169, 80 N.E.2d 464.

Appellant argues that the Highway Department's grantor had no right to grant an easement 12 feet wide across her property, which he attempted to do in his deed. This question is not before us as the Chancellor did not undertake to define the physical limits of the passway. However, we may point out that in Newberry v. Hardin, Ky.1952, 248 S.W.2d 427, above cited, we recognized that a 12-foot passway of this nature was a reasonable one.

Appellant finally contends that the easement in controversy was extinguished by merger when a former owner of the dominant estate bought an adjoining lot which offered a means of ingress and egress to and from the Highway Department's property. The answer to this contention is that the doctrine of merger could not apply because the former owner of the dominant estate did not acquire the servient estate.

The Chancellor carefully analyzed all of the material issues in an excellent opinion, and we are in accord with each of the conclusions reached.

The judgment is affirmed.

FRISTOE v. DRAPEAU, 35 Cal.2d 5, 215 P.2d 729 (1950). An easement for the use of a roadway was created by implication upon the division of land owned by a common grantor. At the time of this severance, the dominant estate was used for access to and the servicing of lemon and avocado groves. The dominant owner later undertook to build a place of residence on her land. She sued to enjoin interference with the use of the roadway for residence purposes. Judgment for the plaintiff was affirmed. A part of the court's opinion follows:

"The Restatement sets forth the rule as follows: 'The extent of an easement created by implication is to be inferred from the circumstances which exist at the time of the conveyance and give rise to the implication. Among these circumstances is the use which is being made of the dominant tenement at that time. Yet it does not follow that the use authorized is to be limited to such use as was required by the dominant tenement at that time. It is to be measured rather by such uses as the parties might reasonably have expected from the future uses of the dominant tenement. What the parties might reasonably have expected is to be ascertained from the circumstances existing at the time of the conveyance. It is to be assumed that they anticipated such uses as might reasonably be required by a normal development of the dominant tenement. It is not to be assumed, however, that they anticipated an abnormal development. Hence, the scope of an easement created by implication does not extend to uses required by such development.' Rest., Property, § 484, comment *b*.

"Accordingly, in determining the intent of the parties as to the extent of the grantee's rights, we are of the opinion that consideration must be given not only to the actual uses being made at the time of the severance, but also to such uses as the facts and circumstances show were within the reasonable contemplation of the parties at the time of the conveyance. Under all of the circumstances existing at the time of severance in the present case, we cannot say as a matter of law that the use of the road for purposes connected with a private residence was not within the contemplation of the parties or that the trial court erred in failing to limit plaintiff's rights in the roadway to use thereof for agricultural purposes. If at some future date there is an improper extension of the burden on defendants' parcel, they may at that time seek appropriate relief. The courts, however, are not required to anticipate an improper extension of such an easement and are not called upon to prohibit acts which do not appear to be threatened or likely to occur. See De Haviland v. Warner Bros. Pictures, 67 Cal.App.2d 225, 238, 153 P.2d 983; Fairbanks v. Macready, 92 Cal.App. 156, 159, 267 P. 716, 268 P. 947."

GLENN v. POOLE

Appeals Court of Massachusetts, 1981.
12 Mass.App.Ct. 292, 423 N.E.2d 1030.

KASS, Justice. As is often the case with easements, the governing principles are easier to state than to apply. So, for example, it is familiar law that a right of way may be acquired by prescription through twenty years of uninterrupted, open, notorious and adverse use. Nocera v. DeFeo, 340 Mass. 783, 164 N.E.2d 136 (1959). Ryan v. Stavros, 348 Mass. 251, 263, 203 N.E.2d 85 (1964). G.L. c. 187, § 2. And the extent of an easement so obtained is fixed by the use through which it was created. Baldwin v. Boston & Me. R.R., 181 Mass. 166, 168, 63 N.E. 428 (1902). Lawless v. Trumbull, 343 Mass. 561, 562–563, 180 N.E.2d 80 (1962). Restatement of Property § 477 (1944). See Dunham v. Dodge, 235 Mass. 367, 372, 126 N.E. 663 (1920). Yet, the use made during the prescriptive period does not fix the scope of the easement eternally. See Lawless v. Trumbull, supra 343 Mass. at 563, 180 N.E.2d 80. It may change over time, Restatement of Property § 479, comment *a* (1944), and uses satisfying the new needs are permissible, id., "[b]ut the variations in use cannot be substantial; they must be consistent with the general pattern formed by the adverse use." Lawless v. Trumbull, supra at 563, 180 N.E.2d 80. See also Hodgkins v. Bianchini, 323 Mass. 169, 173, 80 N.E.2d 464 (1948), which holds that once an easement is created, every right necessary for its enjoyment is included by implication.

With these principles in mind we turn to the facts found by the Land Court judge. The proceeding was one to register and confirm title under G.L. c. 185, § 1, in which the petitioner, Glenn, sought to eliminate entirely roads shown on the plan filed with the registration petition and, in the alternative, to establish that the use being made by the Poole family of the road called the "Gravel Road" constituted an overload of that easement. Facts found by a Land Court judge in registration proceedings shall not be disturbed by us if warranted on any view of the evidence and all reasonable inferences therefrom. Lyon v. Parkinson, 330 Mass. 374, 375, 113 N.E.2d 861 (1953). Otis Power Co. v. Wolin, 340 Mass. 391, 395–396, 164 N.E.2d 306 (1960). Norton v. West, 8 Mass. App. 348, 394 N.E.2d 1125 (1979). Daley v. Swampscott, ___ Mass.App. ___, ___, ___, 421 N.E.2d 78 (1981).

Glenn's land is a triangular parcel of 22.681 acres, "more or less", in Rockport. The base of the triangle bounds along the northerly sideline of Thatcher Road, a well travelled public street. Two right of way easements were originally in dispute: the "Gravel Road," which runs fairly directly from Thatcher Road in a northeasterly direction to the Poole property; and the "Wood Road," which, as shown on the filed plan, runs in a more meandering fashion from the easterly corner of Glenn's property at a point on Thatcher Road and eventually links up with the Gravel Road. As to the Wood Road, the judge determined that no prescriptive easement had developed, and only the status of the Gravel Road is the subject of contention on appeal. Three generations of Pooles, the Land Court judge found, had used the Gravel Road from early in this century in travelling back and forth from their property, particularly to haul out wood. Those hauling operations were first conducted by horse-drawn wagon and, beginning in 1920, by truck. For a period of time the Pooles also operated a gravel pit and moved gravel to purchasers over the Gravel Road.

In the 1930's the Pooles got into the construction and snow plowing business and ran their equipment over the Gravel Road to their land, on which they stored their trucks, tractors and accessory gear. The fire chief of Rockport used heavy vehicles on the Gravel Road to fight fires, and other citizens of the town had used the road to gain access to a thickly forested area north of the locus. Over the years, the path of the Gravel Road did not change. Its surface, however, was gradually improved by the Pooles with gravel from their land and by the installation of a drainage pipe at a point about fifty feet in from Thatcher Road. As to the degree of improvement, i.e., as to width, clearing of brush and packing down of gravel, the evidence was conflicting. The judge found the surface to be "greatly improved" by the Pooles in 1972. As to use of the Gravel Road, the judge found that it had markedly increased since 1972. In May of that year the Pooles had obtained a zoning variance to use their back land for a garage and repair shop.[4] All in all, however, the judge found the variation in the Pooles' use of the Gravel Road was "moderate" and "consistent with the general pattern formed by the adverse use." Glenn appeals from so much of the Land Court decision as preserved a right of way over the Gravel Road in favor of the Pooles.

1. Acquisition of easement by prescription.

In view of the abundant evidence of seven decades of open, uninterrupted and notorious use of the Gravel Road, a presumption arises that the use is adverse. Flynn v. Korsack, 343 Mass. 15, 18–19, 175 N.E.2d 397 (1961). Ivons-Nispel, Inc. v. Lowe, 347 Mass. 760, 763, 200 N.E.2d 282 (1964). Bills v. Nunno, 4 Mass.App. 279, 280–281, 346 N.E.2d 718 (1976). Cf. Uliasz v. Gillette, 357 Mass. 96, 101–102, 256 N.E.2d 290 (1970). Indeed, Glenn, who has owned a portion of the property over which the Gravel Road runs since 1951, said he never gave the Pooles permission to use it. Glenn does not so much contest that the Pooles have some prescriptive rights in the Gravel Road as he contests the extent of those rights.

2. Extent of the easement.

We turn then to the question whether the Pooles have overburdened the easement. The easement established during the prescriptive period was for vehicular access and for hauling. In this essential character it has not changed over the years. Compare Socony Mobil Oil Co. v. Cottle, 336 Mass. 192, 194, 197, 143 N.E.2d 265 (1957), in which it was held that an easement to certain premises, so long as a garage was maintained on them terminated when the garage no longer housed automobiles but a car upholstery repair business. In the law of easements, a mutation is not within the scope of normal development. The progression from horse or ox teams to tractors and trucks is a normal development of the sort which, in the language of the Restatement of Property § 479, comment *b* (1944), "accords with common experience." See Swensen v. Marino, 306 Mass. 582, 587, 29 N.E.2d 15 (1940), in which the court said, "We should be very slow to hold that even ancient rights of way, not expressly restricted as to the type of vehicle * * * could not be employed at all for the means of transportation in common use by a succeeding generation."[5] See also Hodgkins v. Bianchini, 323 Mass. at 172–173, 80 N.E.2d 464; Restatement of Property § 484 (1944). Moreover, the Pooles had been running heavy motorized equipment (e.g., a ten-wheel truck and a tractor) over the Gravel Road for suffi-

---

4. Before the variance, the Pooles maintained their storage and repair facility on Thatcher Road. It must have been something less than a tourist attraction for Rockport. One of several conditions attached to the variance required that the Pooles move their "shop" off Thatcher Street and the Land Court judge, after viewing the interior facility, observed: "The Court can well imagine the relief of the Zoning Board of Appeals to get these [carcasses of assorted vehicles] off the main street and into the woods, as it resembles a car wrecking yard with some animals wandering about." [The court's footnotes have been renumbered. Some have been omitted.]

5. It was not known in the *Swensen* case whether the easement arose through prescription or through grant.

cient years before Glenn began to assemble his property so as to have attained that right by prescription.

The improvements to the Gravel Road did not in and of themselves constitute an overburdening of the easement. Some of them, clearing of brush and laying down gravel and clinkers, had occurred during the prescriptive period. It is permissible for the owner of the dominant estate to make necessary repairs to the easement. Guillet v. Livernois, 297 Mass. 337, 340, 8 N.E.2d 921 (1937). Mt. Holyoke Realty Corp. v. Holyoke Realty Corp., 298 Mass. 513, 514, 11 N.E.2d 429 (1937). Restatement of Property § 480, comment *a* (1944). Clearing limbs from a roadway, smoothing the surface of a way, placing gravel on a road, or even paving a road have been condoned as reasonable repairs, if necessary to enjoyment of the easement. See Appleton v. Fullerton, 1 Gray 186, 193 (1854); Sargent v. Hubbard, 102 Mass. 380, 383 (1869); Hodgkins v. Bianchini, 323 Mass. at 173, 80 N.E.2d 464. The most pronounced improvement which the Pooles made in the Gravel Road was to flare the corners of the entrance onto the Gravel Road from the public way (Thatcher Road), so that access can be less abrupt and so that the field of vision of drivers turning off and into Thatcher Road is enlarged. We do not think an improvement so consistent with safety goes beyond the principles we have discussed. The hazard of blind entry into Thatcher Road is not one which the owner of the easement must endure indefinitely, so long as the improvement does not "unreasonably increase the burden on the servient tenement." Restatement of Property § 480, comment *a* (1944).

There is left to discuss the matter of the intensity of use. It is no coincidence that the Pooles' use of the Gravel Road "markedly increased," as the judge found, after the variance granted in 1972. With more of their business now located on their back land, the frequency of the Pooles' travel along the easement obviously grew. Some change in extent of use has been accepted under our cases. So where a prescriptive easement served a manufactory it could when the original building burned down, serve a manufactory and storehouse, the change being only in degree. Parks v. Bishop, 120 Mass. 340, 342 (1876). In Baldwin v. Boston & Me. R.R., 181 Mass. at 167, 169–170, 63 N.E. 428, an easement which originally served one dwelling was permitted to serve several dwellings. Closer to the facts in the instant case, in Hodgkins v. Bianchini, 323 Mass. at 172–173, 80 N.E.2d 464, an easement originally confined by grant to the "privilege of a cart road to pass to and from the main street to the said premises" did not preclude travel by gravel trucks carrying as much as fifteen to twenty loads per day. Contrast Swensen v. Marino, 306 Mass. at 586–587, 29 N.E.2d 15, where the hauling of sand and gravel was so intense as to impermissibly disturb occupants of the plaintiff's land and the easement was held to be overloaded. See also Lawless v. Trumbull, 343 Mass. at 564, 180 N.E. 80 in which the court held that a general right to travel by vehicles would overload an easement in circumstances where the prior use of the way was relatively infrequent. As to increase in intensity of use, the Land Court judge concluded that "[t]he variation in use is moderate and is consis-

tent with the general pattern formed by the adverse use   *   *   *
While respondents' recent use of the easement has doubtless caused the
petitioner some annoyance it does not appear to be so substantial as to
be unreasonable."

Upon a review of the record, we cannot say these findings are insup-
portable. There was no evidence of constant traffic or of debris or dust
being cast on Glenn's land. If not exceeded, however, the limits of the
Pooles' easement have been "closely approached, if not reached."
Hodgkins v. Bianchini, 323 Mass. at 173, 80 N.E.2d 464. Additional expansion of the uses and width of the easement would probably be over
those limits. As to the rights of the owner of the servient estate, see
Western Massachusetts Elec. Co. v. Sambo's of Massachusetts, Inc., 8
Mass.App. 815, 398 N.E.2d 729 (1979).

Decision affirmed.

Note and Question

In O'Brien v. Hamilton, 15 Mass.App. 960, 446 N.E.2d 730 (1983), the court,
in following Glenn v. Poole, held that a prescriptive easement for a roadway,
acquired by using six-wheel dump trucks making six or seven trips a day did
not embrace the use of noisy ten-wheel and 18-wheel trucks making as much as
50 trips a day. The increase in the burden was found to be undue as to type of
vehicle, volume carried, and number of loads. Referring to Restatement § 477,
the court said that if such a change in use had occurred during the prescriptive
period, it would have induced action by the servient owners.

Who should have the right or duty to keep the servient land in such a state
of repair that an easement can be fully exercised? Suppose in the case of a
prescriptive easement no acts of repair were performed by anyone during the
prescriptive period. 2 A.L.P. § 8.70; Tiffany § 810. Suppose that B has an
easement to use a roadway over A's land. Should B be allowed to black-top the
road surface? See Hyland v. Fonda, 44 N.J.Super. 180, 129 A.2d 899 (1957).

On the scope of easements by prescription, see Restatement §§ 477–481.

PASADENA v. CALIFORNIA–MICHIGAN
LAND & WATER CO.

Supreme Court of California, 1941.
17 Cal.2d 576, 110 P.2d 983, 133 A.L.R. 1186.

GIBSON, Chief Justice. This is an action for injunction and damages based on the defendant's alleged past and threatened future invasion of certain easements owned by the plaintiff. The case was tried by
the court sitting without a jury, and from a judgment entered for the
defendant the plaintiff prosecutes this appeal.

The parties are competing vendors of water sevice in an incorporated
area situated between the cities of Arcadia and Pasadena. The defendant, under claim of right and with the admitted permission of the servient owners, installed water mains and service connections in certain
five-foot easements theretofore granted to the plaintiff and partly occupied by its water mains and connections. This action was commenced
by the plaintiff on the theory that the owners of the servient tenements
had no power to grant easements similar to plaintiff's in the same five-

foot strip of land to the defendant company, a competing distributor of water service. Plaintiff's contention was that it had a right to occupy the five-foot strip completely if the necessity arose, and that the defendant's installation substantially interfered both with plaintiff's present partial occupation of the land and with its possible future use of the land for its pipes and connections. The trial court found against the plaintiff and for the defendant upon conflicting evidence. In this appeal plaintiff contends primarily that the easement granted to the defendant was an unreasonable interference with its prior easement as a matter of law. It is asserted that there was no need to resort to evidence of the surrounding facts and circumstances, and that the court should have found for the plaintiff upon the ground that the defendant's mains interfere in law with the easement previously granted to the city, entirely apart from the question of physical interference upon which the trial court found against plaintiff. There is also a contention that the findings of the trial court are not supported by the evidence. We find ample evidence, however, to sustain the findings. We shall confine our opinion, therefore, to a consideration of the appellant's primary contention, that the easements granted to the defendant interfered with its prior easements as a matter of law.

The easements involved in the present case are described as follows in the instrument creating them: "Easements for the purpose of installing and maintaining water mains and connections thereto * * * all of said easements being five feet in width, to-wit: a. In lots 1 to 12, both inclusive, along the south line thereof. * * *". This language eliminates at once the suggestion that appellant's easement was a so-called "exclusive easement". Under section 806 of the Civil Code "the extent of a servitude is determined by the terms of the grant * * *", and there is no language in this grant which indicates any intention to make the easement held by the City of Pasadena an exclusive one. Indeed, appellant does not make a serious claim that there was an intention to make this an exclusive easement; and any such intention would seem clearly contrary to the admitted facts, since prior easements in the same land were in effect at the time when appellant's easements were granted. Furthermore, an "exclusive easement" is an unusual interest in land; it has been said to amount almost to a conveyance of the fee. 2 Thompson, Real Property, 1939, § 578; Jones, Easements, § 378, p. 302. No intention to convey such a complete interest can be imputed to the owner of the servient tenement in the absence of a clear indication of such an intention. See Reiver v. Voshell, 18 Del.Ch. 260, 264, 158 A. 366; Jones, supra, § 379, p. 303.

The determination of this appeal turns upon the rights which the owner of the servient tenement retains in the land over which he has granted an easement for the laying of water pipes. It is established that the right to lay underground pipes over the land of another is an easement and is governed generally by the rules of law which govern ordinary easements of way. * * * Where the easement is founded upon a grant, as here, only those interests expressed in the grant and those necessarily incident thereto pass from the owner of the fee. The general rule is clearly established that, despite the granting of an easement, the owner of the servient tenement may make any use of the land that does not interfere unreasonably with the easement. Hoyt v. Hart, 149 Cal. 722, 87 P. 569; Durfee v. Garvey, 78 Cal. 546, 21 P. 302; Dierssen v. McCormack, 28 Cal.App.2d 164, 82 P.2d 212; Perley v. Cambridge, 220 Mass. 507, 513, 108 N.E. 494, L.R.A.1915E, 432; 3 Tiffany, Real Property, 3d Ed., 1939, § 811. It is not necessary for him to make any reservation to protect his interests in the land, for what he does not convey, he still retains. Jones, Easements, § 391 et seq., p. 313. Furthermore, since he retains the right to use the land reasonably himself, he retains also the power to transfer these rights to third persons. Galletly v. Bockius, 1 Cal.App. 724, 727, 82 P. 1109; Hoyt v. Hart, supra, 149 Cal. page 728, 87 P. 569; 3 Tiffany, supra, § 811; 17 Am.Jur. 994, 995. Thus, in the instant case, the right of the defendant to use the particular land in controversy is derived from the owner of the servient tenements, and whether it is a permissible use is to be determined by whether the owner of the servient tenements could have used the land in that manner.

Whether a particular use of the land by the servient owner, or by someone acting with his authorization, is an unreasonable interference is a question of fact for the jury. * * * In the present case, the trial court found that there was no such unreasonable interference, and this finding based upon conflicting evidence would ordinarily be conclusive.

Appellant urges the application of a different rule to the instant case upon the following grounds: That these easements are created by grant, and the language of the grant is so clear and definite that a court as a matter of law can define the relative rights of the parties from the instrument alone, without resorting to an examination of the surrounding facts and circumstances. This is said to be so because this is an easement of defined width and location, the theory being that where the easement has a defined width, the easement holder has the right to occupy it to the full width if it ever desires to do so. Therefore, it is asserted, any use of the strip of land for laying other water pipes should be held to be unreasonable interference as a matter of law.

Appellant relies upon cases which hold that a surface right of way of defined width gives the easement holder the absolute right to occupy the surface to that width whenever he chooses. These cases depend upon the theory that the easement granted is completely and clearly defined because the width and location of the right of way is specified in the grant. See, for example, Ballard v. Titus, 157 Cal. 673, 110 P. 118; Herman v. Roberts, 119 N.Y. 37, 23 N.E. 442, 7 L.R.A. 226, 16 Am.St. Rep. 800. They do not necessarily require a similar conclusion where the easement is for the limited purpose of laying underground water pipes to serve the surrounding property with water for domestic purposes. There is a clear distinction in purpose between a right of way over the surface of the land to be used by moving vehicles and an easement for the laying of water mains in a relatively fixed and permanent position. In the case of an easement for laying underground water pipes there are important factors to be considered in addition to the width and location of the easement. These include, for example, the number and size of the pipes, the right to shift the pipes around at will, and the depth at which the pipes are to be laid. To state the point more generally, with such an easement the extent of the burden which the parties intend to impose upon the servient tenement is not definitely fixed merely by a specification of width and location. Indeed, even with surface rights of way, a specification of width and location does not always determine the extent of the burden imposed upon the servient land. See Johnson v. Kinnicutt, 2 Cush. 153, 56 Mass. 153, 157; Smith & Sons Carpet Co. v. Ball, 143 App.Div. 83, 127 N.Y.S. 974.

Appellant's position does not take into consideration the difference between the burden which the easement imposes upon the servient land and the location at which the burden is to be imposed. In Winslow v. Vallejo, supra, a case which is strongly relied upon by appellant, the court holds that where the grant is indefinite the court may consider additional factors in determining the extent of the burden intended to be imposed upon the land. At page 725 of 148 Cal., at page 192 of 84 P., 5 L.R.A., N.S., 851, 113 Am.St.Rep. 349, 7 Ann.Cas. 851, the court says: "But the conveyance is general in its terms and affords no basis for determining the number of pipes, their size, or their exact location." It is here recognized that there are factors other than mere location to be considered, and that the extent of the burden is not determined merely by fixing the location of such an easement. It is, of course, possible to draft an instrument which would fully define both the location and the burden of the easement, or which would make the easement exclusive. But the very general language used in the instrument under consideration here cannot be given any such effect. Considering the fact that these easements were granted for the limited purpose of securing domestic water service for the individual owners in this real estate subdivision and that no indication appears that the parties intended to protect the city against competition, we are unable to find any intent, either expressed or implied, that the owners were never to grant similar easements to anyone else. Hence, the mere granting of the second easement to the defendant did not interfere with appellant's prior easement as a matter of law. Whether the particular use under a second easement amounts to an unreasonable interference is, as we have heretofore pointed out, a question of fact, and the finding, made upon conflicting evidence, that defendant's use of its easement was not such an unreasonable interference is conclusive upon the question so far as this appeal is concerned.

We do not wish to be understood, however, as limiting the rights granted to the City of Pasadena under its easements which were properly found to be prior and paramount to those of the defendant. The rule is established that the grant of an unrestricted easement, not specifically defined as to the burden imposed upon the servient land, entitles the easement holder to a use limited only by the requirement that it be reasonably necessary and consistent with the purposes for which the easement was granted. Murphy Chair Co. v. Radiator Co., 172 Mich. 14, 28, 137 N.W. 791; Chapman v. Newmarket Mfg. Co., 74 N.H. 424, 425, 68

A. 868; Dalton v. Levy, 258 N.Y. 161, 167, 179 N.E. 371; Fendall v. Miller, 99 Or. 610, 615, 196 P. 381; see 15 L.R.A., N.S., 292; 2 Thompson, supra, § 572, p. 175; 3 Tiffany, supra, § 803, p. 323; 17 Am.Jur. 994, 996. The language of the easements here involved does not sufficiently define the burden intended to be imposed so that defendant's easement can be termed an unreasonable interference as a matter of law, but neither does it restrict the right granted to the City of Pasadena to make the fullest necessary use of the five-foot strip.

It is possible that the city may, at some future time, be faced with the necessity of expanding or changing its present system, and on its behalf it is asserted that the presence of defendant's pipes may seriously hamper the reasonable use of the city's prior easement under such circumstances. But if, in the reasonable use of its prior easement, the city requires the space occupied by the pipes of the defendant, its paramount right must prevail. In Colegrove Water Co. v. Hollywood, 151 Cal. 425, 90 P. 1053, 13 L.R.A.,N.S., 904, plaintiff sought to make use of the servient tenement for laying water pipes despite the fact that an easement for highway purposes had already been granted to the defendant municipality. The court permitted this after a finding that the water pipes would not interfere with the use then being made of the highway easement by the city and added (151 Cal. page 429, 90 P. page 1055, 13 L.R.A.,N.S., 904): " * * * but the municipality may, and frequently does, occupy the soil beneath the surface for the accommodation of sewers, gas and water pipes, electric wires, and conduits for railroads. Where the city undertakes to occupy the space above or below the surface of the street for any purpose within the scope of the public uses to which highways may be put, the use by the owner of the fee must yield to the public use." Until a point of unreconcilable conflict is reached, however, such a concurrent use of the land for similar purposes as is illustrated here should be governed by principles permitting an equitable adjustment of the conflicting interests. The respective rights of the two parties are not absolute, but must be construed to permit a due and reasonable enjoyment of both interests so long as that is possible. Murphy Chair Co. v. Radiator Co., supra; Bakeman v. Talbot, 31 N.Y. 366, 369, 88 Am.Dec. 275; Pomeroy v. Salt Co., 37 Ohio St. 520, 524; Minto v. Salem Water, etc., Co., 120 Or. 202, 212, 250 P. 722; 3 Tiffany, supra, § 811, p. 355; 17 Am.Jur. 993.

In Murphy Chair Co. v. Radiator Co., supra, successive rights of way in the same land were involved and the court held that both easements could be used simultaneously under the existing facts, but indicated that the subsequent grant must be considered subordinate if it should ever interfere with the reasonable use of the prior easement. In Pomeroy v. Salt Co., supra, 37 Ohio St. page 524, the court held that the holder of an underground easement for the purpose of mining coal could not object to the placing of a second tunnel which would intersect his and would cross it at the same level. The court was clearly of the opinion that the prior easement was paramount but said that the second tunnel would not interfere substantially with the first easement under the existing facts. The proper rule is indicated by the language of the court in Bakeman v. Talbot, supra, 31 N.Y. page 369, 88 Am.Dec. 275, in which a conflict arose between the use by the holder of the easement and the use by the landowner. The court said: "The defendant [landowner] certainly has no right to preclude the plaintiff [easement holder] from availing himself of the right of passage, or to render the exercise of that right unusually or unreasonably difficult or burthensome. I think he is not shown to have done so. * * * There is nothing inconsistent in holding, that the present arrangements are suitable and sufficient under existing circumstances; and after these circumstances have changed, and the question shall arise as to what shall then be proper, to determine that a passage perpetually open or a system of gates better adapted to such increased use * * * shall be required of the defendant. It would not be right at this time * * * to furnish facilities for a state of affairs which may never arise, or which may not arise until some remote period."

Under the present facts no basis is shown for the relief sought. Whether a different conclusion may be required by changed circumstances in the future cannot now be determined with certainty, and need not therefore be decided.

The judgment is affirmed.

[The dissenting opinion of SHENK, J., is omitted.]

SAKANSKY v. WEIN

Supreme Court of New Hampshire, 1933.
86 N.H. 337, 169 A. 1.

Petition for injunction. The facts were found by a master.

At the time of the filing of the petition, the plaintiff Sakansky was the owner of a certain parcel of land with the buildings thereon, situated on the westerly side of Main Street in Laconia. The deed by means of which he took title also conveyed to him a right of way, eighteen feet in width, over land which for the purposes of this case may be regarded as belonging to the defendants. Before trial Sakansky conveyed this property, together with the right of way, to the plaintiff, J.J. Newberry Company, and took back a mortgage thereon. This right of way, with no expressed limitation as to mode of use, originated in a deed to the plaintiff's ancestor in title in 1849. This deed gave the right of way definite location upon the ground.

The defendants wish to develop their servient estate by erecting a building over the land subjected to the plaintiff's easement. They proposed to leave an opening in their new building at the place where it crosses the way; this opening to allow headroom of eight feet for the way where it passes under the defendant's building. They also propose to lay out a new way over level ground around the westerly end of the new building, which new way will give access to the same point on the dominant estate as the old way. This new way is free from obstruction and affords an easy means of access for vehicles whose height would prevent them from continuing to use the old way. The plaintiff objected and excepted to the introduction of evidence concerning the proposed new way.

The master ruled that neither party had any absolute or unlimited rights in the old right of way, but that the rights of each were to be determined by the rule of reasonableness. He further ruled that what was reasonable was a question of fact, to be determined by considering all the circumstances of all of the property, including the advantages accruing to the defendants and the disadvantages to be suffered by the plaintiff.

Applying the above principles he found that, considering the proposed additional right of way, the defendants' proposed reduction in height of the old right of way was not an unreasonable interference with the plaintiff's rights. But he found further that if it was not proper for him to take into consideration the proposed new way, then a reduction in height of the old way, as proposed, would be an unreasonable interference with the plaintiff's rights. On the basis of the above rulings of law and findings of fact, and giving consideration to the proposed new way, he recommended a decree permitting the defendants to build over the old way upon condition that they provide the plaintiff with the new way as proposed by them.

The plaintiff's exception to the admission of evidence concerning the new right of way, and the question of whether the plaintiff is entitled to an injunction, were transferred without ruling by Burque, J.

WOODBURY, Justice. In this state the respective rights of dominant and servient owners are not determined by reference to some technical and more or less arbitrary rule of property law as expressed in some ancient maxim * * * but are determined by reference to the rule of reason. The application of this rule raises a question of fact to be determined by consideration of all the surrounding circumstances, including the location and uses of both dominant and servient estates, and taking into consideration the advantage to be derived by one and the disadvantage to be suffered by the other owner. * * * The same rule has been applied to easements other than rights of way; for example, to aqueduct rights (Stevenson v. Wiggin, 56 N.H. 308; Olcott v. Thompson, 59 N.H. 154, 47 Am.Rep. 184); to rights of flowage, both as to surface water (Franklin v. Durgee [71 N.H. 186, 51 A. 911, 58 L.R.A. 112]); and as to water in a stream (Chapman v. Newmarket Mfg. Co., 74 N.H. 424, 68 A. 868, 15 L.R.A.,N.S., 292). In the somewhat analogous cases involving the reciprocal rights of adjoining owners the same principle has been applied. Horan v. Byrnes [72 N.H. 93, 54 A. 945, 62 L.R.A. 602, 101 Am.St.Rep. 670]; True v. McAlpine, 81 N.H. 314, 125 A. 680. The master's general rulings of law are in accordance with the foregoing and are therefore correct.

The error arises in the application of the above principle to the situation presented in the case at bar.

Implicit in the master's findings of fact is the finding that it is reasonable for the plaintiff to have access to the rear of its premises for vehicles over eight feet high. The master has applied the rule of reason to deflect this reasonable use over the new way which the defendants propose to create. This may not be done under the circumstances of this case.

The rule of reason is a rule of interpretation. Its office is either to give a meaning to words which the parties or their ancestors in title have actually used, as was done in Farmington, etc., Ass'n v. Trafton, 84 N.H. 29, 146 A. 169, in which the word "necessary" was held to mean "reasonably necessary," or else to give a detailed definition to rights created by general words either actually used, or whose existence is implied by law. * * * This rule of reason does not prevent the parties from making any contract regarding their respective rights which they may wish, regardless of the reasonableness of their wishes on the subject. The rule merely refuses to give unreasonable rights, or to impose unreasonable burdens, when the parties, either actually or by legal implication, have spoken generally.

In the case at bar the parties are bound by a contract which not only gave the dominant owner a way across the servient estate for the purpose of access to the rear of its premises, but also gave that way definite location upon the ground. The use which the plaintiff may make of the way is limited by the bounds of reason, but within those bounds it has the unlimited right to travel over the land set apart for a way. It has no right to insist upon the use of any other land of the defendants for a way, regardless of how necessary such other land may be to it, and regardless of how little damage or inconvenience such use of the defendants' land might occasion to them. No more may the defendants compel the plaintiff to detour over other land of theirs.

The rule of reason is to be applied to determine whether or not the plaintiff has the right to approach the rear of its building with vehicles over eight feet high. This question having been answered in the affirmative, the plaintiff, by virtue of the grant, has the right to use that land, and only that land, which was set apart for the purpose of a way, and it may insist upon that right regardless of whether such insistence on its part be reasonable or not.

This does not mean that the defendants may not build over the old way at all. The plaintiff has no absolute right to have the way remain open to the sky. What, if any, structure, the defendants may build over the way depends upon what is reasonable. Tiffany on Real Property, 2d Ed., vol. 2, § 371; 19 C.J. § 239. See, also, Garland v. Furber [47 N.H. 301]. The master has already found that a height of only eight feet for the old way is not reasonable. The defendants must provide more headroom. How much more is a question of fact, which may be determined later in further proceedings before the master if the defendants wish for a definition of the extent of this right.

In view of the fact that the rule of reason may not be invoked to deflect the plaintiff's reasonable travel over the new way, evidence concerning that way becomes immaterial and irrelevant, and hence it was error for the master to have admitted it. * * *

The argument advanced that what is reasonable must be considered in the light of the situation as it was at the time the way was granted in 1849 is without merit. What is or is not a reasonable use of the way does not become crystallized at any particular moment of time. Changing needs of either owner may operate to make unreasonable a use of the way previously reasonable, or to make reasonable a use previously unreasonable. There is an element of time as well as of space in this question of reasonableness. In the absence of contract on the subject, the owner of the dominant estate is not limited in his use of the way to such vehicles only as were known at the time the way was created, but he may use the way for any vehicle which his reasonable needs may require in the development of his estate. * * * In this respect the use of the way is analogous to the use of a highway. * * *

Case discharged.

All concurred.

Problem

A owned land over which B had been expressly granted the right to use a roadway 10 feet wide. A objected to alleged excessive speed and other uses of the roadway by B. Having been unsuccessful in his effort to negotiate a surrender of at least a part of the right of way, A installed asphalt mounds five inches high across the roadway, designed as "speed breakers." He also built a woven wire fence along his boundary, with a 10 foot opening where the roadway crossed his boundary and steel posts at the terminal points of the fence on each side of the roadway. He also erected field stones and steel posts along the boundary of the roadway. B sued to enjoin A from obstructing his use of the roadway in this manner. The trial court held that the objects erected by A were an unreasonable interference with the use of the right of way and ordered A to remove the mounds and also to relocate the stones and posts to points no closer than two feet from the boundary of the roadway.

A did not appeal the ruling about removing the mounds, but he objected otherwise to the decision on the ground that the alleged obstructions would not be an invasion of B's rights so long as they were located on land not subject to the easement. What ruling on appeal? See Hunter v. McDonald, 78 Wis.2d 338, 254 N.W.2d 282 (1977).

SECTION 4.   EXTINGUISHMENT

Where an easement is limited in its creation so that it is less than an easement in fee, that is, where it is limited for a period of years or for life or during the continuance of certain circumstances, the easement will end by the lapse of the specified time or upon the happening of a stated event. Easements have this feature in common with estates. This is not what we mean by extinguishment.

It is a postulate of our land law that an estate in land may not be extinguished. Estates may only be transferred. Estates less than a fee simple absolute may be terminated by the merger of the possessory estate with the future estate which is limited after it. But this of course is the result of a conveyance of the possessory estate to the holder of the future estate, or a conveyance by both of these parties to a third party. Since theoretically easements are not segments of, but are rather burdens upon, title or ownership, it is possible to extinguish easements in ways other than by conveyance.

If extinguished by conveyance from the dominant to the servient owner, the instrument is known as a *release.* Conveyances other than releases may operate to extinguish easements.

Problems

1. A granted to B, a contractor, the privilege of taking sand and gravel from A's land. B transferred this interest to C. Later A conveyed his land to C. C later conveyed the land to D. Does C still have the right to take sand and gravel from the land. Restatement, Property § 499 (1944).

2. A has an easement of way across B's land, appurtenant to land owned by A. A conveys his land to C. B later conveys his land to C. C later conveys to D the land acquired from B. Does C have an easement in D's land? Restatement, Property § 497 (1944).

3. A has an easement of way across B's land, appurtenant to land owned by A. B dies, devising his land to C for life, remainder to D. A conveys his land to C. C dies devising the original dominant estate to E. Does E have an easement in D's land? Restatement, Property § 497, comment *d* (1944); cf. Rogers v. Flick, 144 Ky. 844, 139 S.W. 1098 (1911).

LINDSEY v. CLARK

Supreme Court of Appeals of Virginia, 1952.
193 Va. 522, 69 S.E.2d 342.

BUCHANAN, Justice. This suit was instituted by the Lindseys to enjoin the Clarks from using a driveway along the north side of the Lindsey lots and to have themselves adjudged the fee simple owners of the two lots claimed by them. The trial court held that the Clarks owned a right of way on the south side of the Lindsey lots and, in effect, put the Lindseys on terms to make it available to them or else allow the Clarks to continue using the one on the north side.

There is no controversy about the controlling facts.

In 1937 the Clarks were the owners of four adjoining lots, Nos. 31, 32, 33 and 34, each fronting 25 feet on the east side of Magnolia avenue in West Waynesboro, and running back 150 feet to a 20-foot alley. The Clark residence was on Nos. 31 and 32.

By deed dated July 24, 1937, the Clarks conveyed to C.W. Six and Mabel G. Six, his wife, the latter being a daughter of the Clarks, the front two-thirds of Lots 33 and 34, being a frontage of 50 feet and extending back 100 feet. On the rear one-third of these two lots Clark erected a dwelling and garage for rental purposes. After this conveyance the Sixes built a house on their property, approximately 15 feet from the Clark line on the north and about 8 feet from their own line on the south. The Clark deed to the Sixes contained this reservation: "There is reserved, however, a right-of-way ten (10) feet in width, along the South side of the two lots herein conveyed, for the benefit of the property in the rear."

By deed of January 16, 1939, the Sixes conveyed the property to William H. McGhee and wife, with the same reservation; and by deed of March 16, 1944, the McGhees conveyed the property to the Lindseys, without any reservation.

These three deeds were all made with general warranty and both the deed to the Sixes and the deed to the McGhees were duly recorded prior to the date of the deed to the Lindseys.

Notwithstanding that the 10-foot right of way was reserved by Clark along the south side of the property conveyed to the Sixes, now owned by the Lindseys, Clark proceeded to use it along the north side of the Six property, and has so used it ever since, without objection by the Sixes, or by the McGhees, or by the Lindseys until a few months before this suit was brought. There is no explanation of this change of location. Six, a witness for the Lindseys, testified that Clark stood in the driveway on the north and said, "I am reserving this driveway to get to my back property." The time of that statement is not shown, but the words suggest it was at or before the time of the conveyance to the Sixes. When the McGhees bought the property in 1939, Six pointed out to them the driveway on the north, but the reservation in the deed he made to the McGhees was, as stated, on the south.

In 1946 the Lindseys had their attorney write to Clark, referring to the right of way in the deed to the McGhees, their grantors, and complaining, not of its location, but of its being used for parking purposes. Again, on November 7, 1949, they had their attorney write Clark, calling attention to the fact that the reservation was along the south side of their property and complaining about the use of a water line on their property which had not been reserved. The Lindseys, the letter stated, wanted to erect a line fence and suggested a discussion of the matter before this was done.

The Lindseys contend that the Clarks now have no right of way across their property because none was reserved along the north side and the one reserved on the south side has been abandoned and thereby extinguished. The trial court held it had not been abandoned and that holding was clearly right.

Abandonment is a question of intention. A person entitled to a right of way or other easement in land may abandon and extinguish such right by acts *in pais;* and a cessation of use coupled with acts or circumstances clearly showing an intention to abandon the right will be as effective as an express release of the right. Scott v. Moore, 98 Va. 668, 687, 37 S.E. 342, 348; Daniel v. Doughty, 120 Va. 853, 858, 92 S.E. 848, 850; Magee v. Omansky, 187 Va. 422, 430, 46 S.E.2d 443, 448.

But mere non-user of an easement created by deed, for a period however long, will not amount to abandonment. In addition to the non-user there must be acts or circumstances clearly manifesting an intention to abandon; or an adverse user by the owner of the servient estate, acquiesced in by the owner of the dominant estate, for a period sufficient to create a prescriptive right. Watts v. C.F. Johnson &c. Corp., 105 Va. 519, 525, 54 S.E. 317, 319, 28 C.J.S., Easements, § 60, p. 724. Nor is a right of way extinguished by the habitual use by its owner of another equally convenient way unless there is an intentional abandonment of the former way. Scott v. Moore, supra, 98 Va. at page 686, 37 S.E. at page 348. 17 Am.Jur., Easements, § 144, p. 1029.

The burden of proof to show the abandonment of an easement is upon the party claiming such abandonment, and it must be established by clear and unequivocal evidence. Daniel v. Doughty, supra, 120 Va. at page 858, 92 S.E. at page 850; Blanford v. Trust Co., 142 Va. 73, 82, 128 S.E. 640, 643.

Clark specifically reserved a right of way over the lots now owned by the Lindseys. Very clearly he had no intention of abandoning that right of way. He was evidently mistaken as to where it was located; but his grantees, the Sixes, were likewise mistaken, as were also their grantees, the McGhees. Clark's use on the wrong location of the right of way reserved by him did not establish an intention on his part to abandon his right of way on the right location. He could not have intended to abandon his easement on the south of the Lindsey lots when he did not know that that was where his easement was.

The residence built by the Sixes, and now occupied by the Lindseys, encroaches by about two feet on the 10-foot alley when located on the south side, and the Lindsey property on that side within the 10-foot space is terraced and planted with shrubbery and a tree. The Lindseys argue that the Clarks are estopped from claiming a right of way on that side because Clark knew where the Sixes were building the house. The only testimony about that is from Six, who said that Clark was away at work when the house was being built but came and went every day to and from his home on the adjoining property, saw where the house was located and made no objection; but Six also said that Clark had nothing to do with locating the house. There is no evidence that Clark knew, any more than Six knew, that the house was encroaching on the right of way. Clark did not think the right of way was on that side. Even if he had known it was there, he would not likely have known that Six was building on it. The location of the house was not influenced by anything Clark did or said. Clark knew nothing about the matter that Six did not know.

"It is essential to the application of the principles of equitable estoppel, or estoppel *in pais*, that the party claiming to have been influenced by the conduct or declarations of another to his injury, was not only ignorant of the true state of facts, but had no convenient and available means of acquiring such information, and where the facts are known to both parties, and both had the same means of ascertaining the truth, there can be no estoppel." Lindsay v. James, 188 Va. 646, 659, 51 S.E.2d 326, 332, 7 A.L.R.2d 597.

The Lindseys had both actual and constructive knowledge of the situation. The driveway was there on the north side when they bought the property and Lindsey testified he could see where cars had been using it. They negligently failed to have their title examined but they are, of course, chargeable with the information contained in the recorded deeds. Pillow v. Southwest, &c. Imp. Co., 92 Va. 144, 152, 23 S.E. 32,

34; Florance v. Morien, 98 Va. 26, 33, 34 S.E. 890, 891; 15 M.J., Recording Acts, § 15, p. 561.

The suit therefore developed this situation: The Clarks were entitled to a 10-foot right of way along the south side of the Lindsey property. That right of way was partially blocked by the Lindsey house with its terraces and shrubbery. To require their removal would be very expensive to the Lindseys and damaging to their property. The Clarks were willing to let their right of way continue to be located on the north side.

The court was well warranted in resolving the matter by applying the maxim "He who seeks equity must do equity." That means that "he who seeks the aid of an equity court subjects himself to the imposition of such terms as the settled principles of equity require, and that whatever be the nature of the controversy between the parties and whatever be the nature of the remedy demanded, the court will not confer its equitable relief on the party seeking its interposition and aid, unless he has acknowledged and conceded, or will admit and provide for, all the equitable rights, claims, and demands justly belonging to the adversary party, and growing out of, or necessarily involved in, the subject matter of the controversy." 30 C.J.S., Equity, § 91, p. 461. 2 Pom. Eq.Jur., 5th ed., § 385, pp. 51–2.

A court of equity may in a case in which the principles and rules of equity demand it, condition its granting of the relief sought by the complainant upon the enforcement of a claim or equity held by the defendant which the latter could not enforce in any other way. United Cigarette Mach. Co. v. Brown, 119 Va. 813, 825, 89 S.E. 850, 855, L.R.A.1917F, 1100; 2 Pom.Eq.Jur., supra, § 386a, p. 57; 19 Am.Jur., Equity, § 463, p. 319.

The decree of the trial court provided: "The Court will not require the expensive removal of the obstruction, so long as the right-of-way along the north side of the property is made available. However, it is ordered that the defendants desist from the use of the right-of-way for any purpose other than the use of the rear one-third portion of Lots 33 and 34, and only for the right of passage over and across the said right-of-way to and from the property in the rear." And, further, "Should the complainants make an election under this order, a further order will be entered fixing the rights of the respective parties."

The decree appealed from is affirmed and the cause is remanded for further decree as indicated.

Affirmed and remanded.

CARR v. BARTELL

Supreme Court of Michigan, 1943.
305 Mich. 317, 9 N.W.2d 556.

STARR, Justice. This case involves a dispute over a joint driveway between residence properties in the city of Lansing.

In 1908 Charles Foster and wife, who owned lot four, block 186, of the city of Lansing, conveyed the north ½ of such lot to a predecessor in plaintiffs' chain of title, the deed of conveyance providing: "Reserving a strip of land four (4) feet in width off the south side of said above-described land which with a strip of land four (4) feet in width off the north side of the next adjoining same on the south is to be used as a joint driveway."

In 1910 the Fosters conveyed the south ½ of said lot four to a predecessor in defendants' chain of title, the deed of conveyance providing: "Except four (4) feet off the north side which with four (4) feet off the south side of land adjoining the above on the north is to be used as a driveway for occupants of lot four (4)."

The record indicates that subsequent conveyances of these two parcels of land contained substantially the same reservations and provisions regarding the use of four feet off each parcel for joint driveway purposes. In April, 1911, defendants purchased the south ½ of such lot, and since then have used and occupied the same for residential purposes. In April, 1934, plaintiffs purchased the north ½ of such lot on a land contract which contained substantially the same joint driveway reservations. Since their purchase they have occupied and used such land for residential purposes.

In July, 1940, plaintiffs filed bill of complaint, alleging in substance that both parcels of land were subject to the abovementioned driveway reservations and rights; that defendants had encroached upon and interfered with their use of the driveway by erecting and maintaining a wire fence which extended along the center line of the west (rear) 80 feet of the driveway; and that defendants had placed stones, nails, and other obstructions on the driveway. Defendants answered admitting the mutual driveway reservations, but alleging that they had acquired the right to maintain the fence on the driveway by adverse possession and use. In their answer they denied having placed stones, nails, and other obstructions on the driveway and denied plaintiffs' right to the relief sought.

The trial court's opinion determined that the fence in question had been constructed by defendants "under a permissive arrangement" with a former owner of plaintiffs' adjoining property and that their claim of adverse possession could not be predicated on such permissive use. The court also found that about 1914 a predecessor in plaintiffs' chain of title had erected a barn on the rear of his land, which encroached in part on the driveway and which was maintained for about 20 years until removed by plaintiffs. The court determined that the permanent character of the barn and its maintenance for such period of time extinguished the easement in the west portion of the driveway. The court also found that defendants had placed stones, and ashes containing nails on the east part of the driveway. A decree was entered May 19, 1941, terminating the easement as to the west 51.4 feet of the driveway but ordering defendants to remove the east 38 feet of the fence in question. The decree also ordered them to remove all stones, nails, and other obstructions in the balance of the driveway.

The record indicates that the driveway as created extended the entire length of lot four, i.e., 165 feet. The trial court's decree, in effect, confirmed the joint driveway rights of the parties in and to the east 113.6 feet and extinguished their joint driveway rights in and to the west 51.4 feet. Defendants appeal. This being a chancery case, we consider the same de novo.

As land contract purchasers plaintiffs were entitled to maintain the present action. The fence in question, which was about 80 feet long and constructed of cedar posts with meshed wire attached, was built by defendants about 1913 and, with some repairs, had been maintained ever since. The record clearly indicates that the fence was built by defendants in pursuance of permission or license from one Theodore Morton, a former owner of plaintiffs' property. Defendant Joseph Bartell testified in part:

"Mr. Morton and I had a talk about putting up the fence before I put it up. * * *

"I said we should have a fence because always people before chased around on his property and my property. * * *

"Mr. Morton said it was O.K. with him. He said go ahead and make one, it is good for both sides. * * * Mr. Morton did not assist me in any way. * * *

"Mr. Morton did not pay any part of the costs of the fence and posts. I did not have any talk with him about that. * * * He (Morton) allowed me to build the fence."

Theodore Morton testified in part:

"I recall that Mr. Bartell (defendant) moved next door in April, 1911. * * * Mr. Bartell came and asked me to put a fence through there. I gave him permission. * * *

Mr. Bartell asked permission to put the fence up and I told him to go ahead and put it up. * * *

"I built the barn. The barn was within two or three feet of the fence I should judge. The fence came up past the barn."

The trial court properly determined that, as defendants had built and maintained the fence in pursuance of permission or license from the former owner of plaintiffs' property, they could not defeat plaintiffs' driveway easement under a claim of adverse possession and use. Bankers Trust Co. v. Robinson, 280 Mich. 458, 273 N.W. 768; Martin v. Allen, 258 Mich. 504, 243 N.W. 42; King v. Battle Creek Box Co., 235 Mich. 24, 209 N.W. 133; Berkey & Gay Furniture Co. v. Valley City Milling Co., 194 Mich. 234, 160 N.W. 648.

We agree with the trial court that the building and maintenance of the barn as a permanent structure on a part of the driveway, evidenced an intention to abandon that part of the driveway west of the front of the barn, and extinguished and terminated the joint easements in the west 51.4 feet. Lathrop v. Elsner, 93 Mich. 599, 53 N.W. 791; 28 C.J.S., Easements §§ 58, 59, pp. 722, 723; 17 Am.Jur. § 143, p. 1028. Furthermore, in their brief plaintiffs admit that the building and maintenance of the barn operated to extinguish the driveway easements as to the west 51.4 feet of the driveway.

The trial court's decree properly ordered defendants to remove stones, ashes containing nails, and other obstructions which the testimony shows they had placed on the east portion of the driveway.

The decree of the trial court is affirmed. Plaintiffs shall recover costs.

Questions

Might not the defendant in Carr v. Bartell have based his claim of the extinguishment of the easement by virtue of the fence on a ground other than adverse use?

In Kitzinger v. Gulf Power Co., 432 So.2d 188 (Fla.App.1983), the court, citing Powell, said that a clearer showing of adversity is necessary to extinguish an easement than to create one by prescription. Why, do you suppose?

Problem

Young by deed granted to Witmer "the right at any and at all times hereafter, to cause the water of the Susquehanna River to flow back upon, and overflow, or be withdrawn from the land" of the grantor, which was described in the deed. Four years later Young conveyed the land described in the above deed to Lindemuth. Lindemuth engaged in farming operations on this land, making use in the same connection of the buildings which were on the land. This activity was continued for 25 years by successors in interest, including the plaintiff, who now sues in trespass for the flooding of his land by the erection of a dam by the defendant, successor in interest to Witmer. Plaintiff contends that the flooding right was extinguished by adverse use. What do you think of this argument? See Graham v. Safe Harbor Water Power Corp., 315 Pa. 572, 173 A. 311 (1934).

On extinguishment by adverse use and abandonment see Annotation, 25 A.L.R.2d 1265 (1952).

Note

When servient land is taken under the power of eminent domain for a purpose which is inconsistent with the continued exercise of the easement, the easement will be extinguished. A troublesome problem is presented in such cases in the valuation of the interest thereby taken from the owner of the easement. A difference of opinion exists on this point. One view is that the total condemnation award should not exceed the value of an estate in fee simple in the servient land, so that the value of the easement is the difference between the value of the servient land free of the easement and the value subject to the easement. The other view is that just compensation to the dominant owner of an easement appurtenant should embrace the diminution in value of the dominant estate by virtue of the taking. Where the easement is in gross, the effect of the taking on the value of the servient land is probably the only practicable way of determining the value of the easement. See Restatement, Property §§ 507, 508; 3 Powell ¶ 426.

Other methods by which easements may be extinguished include (1) execution of a license to obstruct, (2) destruction of the dominant or servient tenement (usually when they are buildings and do not include the underlying land), and (3) sale of the servient tenement for nonpayment of taxes.

Chapter 6

PROMISES RESPECTING THE USE AND ENJOYMENT OF LAND

We have seen how, in order to meet the great variety of human needs and desires respecting the use and enjoyment of land, our legal structure of ownership must not only provide a variety of possible fragments of ownership in the form of present and future estates, but must also allow the creation of a variety of lesser rights or interests, which we describe by such terms of easements, profits, and licenses. All this intricate panoply of devices still does not exhaust the kinds of legal relations which must be recognized in order to meet recurrent needs respecting the use of land. Persons who have interests in land of one kind or another often find it necessary to enter into contractual relations with others concerning their use of the land. For the most part, the generally applicable contract law is adequate for this purpose. In certain types of cases, however, it is not. These are cases in which the question is raised whether persons to whom property interests have been transferred gain the benefit of or are bound by contracts which have been entered into by their predecessors.

It is a natural assumption that only the parties to a contract can enforce or be bound by that contract. Exceptions which contract law recognizes are to be found in the law on the assignment of contract rights and third-party beneficiary contracts. Apart from these doctrines, which are relatively recent developments in contract law, it was very early recognized that persons could indeed have the benefit of or be bound by contracts relating to interests in land, although they were not parties to such contracts. A moment's thought will indicate the reason why this is so. In certain contracts relating to land, such as a contract by a tenant with his landlord to repair the leased premises, it should be evident that if the tenant transfers his term, it would be very awkward if the assignee were not bound by the tenant's promise to repair. There is a comparable basis for saying that, if a tenant promises his landlord to pay rent, one to whom the landlord conveys the land subject to the lease ought to be able to enforce this obligation. The average layman is not at all astonished by such a proposition. The difficulties which the courts have encountered in vindicating such a sensible idea have in part been caused by the need to define its proper limits. The mere fact that parties to a contract are owners of interests in land does not mean that every agreement between them should affect their respective successors in interest. To have this effect, their contract must so relate to one or the other or both of their interests in the land as to justify us in saying that it is not the identity of the parties as persons but their status as owners of interests in the land which is the gist of the contract's enforceability. It is not always easy to draw this line. In addition, when a contractual obligation follows the ownership of the land, so to speak, a problem is encountered about whether the title is thereby burdened in a way which affronts the policy against undue fetters on the alienability of land.

In any event, whenever one who is not the promisee is allowed to enforce a contract respecting land, or one who is not the promisor is bound by it, we traditionally use the quaint expression that it is a "covenant running with the land." Originally, a covenant was a promise under seal. With the gradual elimination of the efficacy of the seal, the "running" question now usually relates to promises not under seal, which does not affect the essence of the question, and so the old expression continues in common usage. A covenant which runs is often called a "real" covenant, as distinguished from a "personal" covenant, which does not run.

It seems convenient to deal with this problem in two categories. First, we look at the problem as it relates to contracts between landlord and tenant. Then we will deal with cases involving contracts between owners of land in fee. Although the problem is basically the same in both categories, there are differences between them which justify separate treatment.

Generally, see 2 A.L.P., part 9, chs. I, II; Cunningham §§ 8.13–8.33; Berger, Promises Respecting the Use of Land, 55 Minn.L.Rev. 167 (1970).

SECTION 1. CONTRACTS BETWEEN LANDLORD AND TENANT

The running of covenants made by landlord or tenant was recognized at an early date in English law. In respect to the rights or duties of tenants, it goes back beyond the Tudor period. It took a statute in the reign of Henry VIII, however, to extend the doctrine so as to benefit or burden the assignee of a landlord's reversionary interest.

In Spencer's Case, 5 Coke 16a, 77 Eng.Rep. 72 (1583), a tenant covenanted in his lease, for himself, his executors and administrators, to build a brick wall on part of the demised premises. He then assigned his term to another, who in turn assigned to the defendant. The landlord sued for breach of this covenant. The judgment in this case is revealed in a series of resolutions laid down by the King's Bench, the first two of which have reverberated in the courts down through the centuries. The first resolution declared that when a covenant extends to a thing *in esse*, it shall go with the land and bind the assignee, although he be not bound by express words. Such would be a covenant to repair a house demised. But if the covenant concerns a thing not *in esse* at the time of the demise, but to be newly built thereafter, it will not bind the assignee unless the covenant purports to bind assigns. The second resolution states the same proposition in different terms. If the lessee covenants for himself and his assigns to make a new wall on the demised land, it will bind the assignee for it is to be made on the thing demised, and the assignee is to take the benefit of it.

This strange distinction between covenants relating to things *in esse and* those not *in esse*, and between language binding assigns and that which does not, may have made some sense in its setting or time which now escapes us. It may be surprising to you that this dictum has made itself felt even in our time. If the test is basically one of intention of the parties that the covenant shall run, some courts have been able to find that intention in other ways. In fact the technicalities of Spencer's Case have now largely disappeared into a test of intention which may be satisfied by other language than a reference to "assigns", or which is often referred or taken for granted if the covenant in fact is one which concerns the land in a substantial way. This brings us to what is by far the most significant language in Spencer's Case, and which appears unobtrusively in the statement of the second resolution, as if in contrast to its main point: "But although the covenant be for him and his assigns, yet if the thing to be done be merely collateral to the land and doth not touch or concern the thing demised in any sort, there the assignee shall not be charged." This comes to the real heart of the matter. This is the traditional "touch and concern" requirement. It may sound quaint as put by the court in Spencer's Case, but it is nothing more than the distinction noted in the introduction to this chapter, which is such an essential part of the problem that it is virtually impossible to state the meaning of the running of covenants except in terms of the distinction. But applying it is another matter.

Fortunately most of the promises which ordinarily appear in leases satisfy the touching and concerning requirement. The following promises by lessor or lessee have been held to run with the term or the reversion or both, as the case may be:

1. By the lessee to pay rent.

2. By the lessee to pay taxes on the leased premises.

3. By the lessor or the lessee to repair the premises, or do, or refrain from doing, some other act affecting the physical condition of the premises.

4. By the lessor to provide services, such as heat, water, etc., to the premises.

5. By the lessee not to assign or sublet, or not to do so without consent of the lessor.

6. By the lessor to renew the lease or convey the reversion to the lessee.

See 2 A.L.P. § 9.4.

ABBOTT v. BOB'S U–DRIVE

Supreme Court of Oregon, 1960.
222 Or. 147, 352 P.2d 598, 81 A.L.R.2d 793.

O'CONNELL, Justice. This is an appeal from a judgment based upon an arbitration award in favor of the plaintiff and against the defendants, jointly and severally.

The facts are as follows. In April, 1952, plaintiff leased certain premises to Robert E. Thompson under the terms of which the lessee agreed to operate an automobile "U-Drive" business and an automobile leasing business. The lease contained a provision requiring the parties to submit to arbitration any controversy arising out of the lease. In February, 1953, Thompson caused to be incorporated the defendant Bob's U-Drive, and in October, 1953, he caused to be incorporated the defendant Continental Leasing Company. Bob's U-Drive engaged in the business of making short-term rentals of automobiles, and Continental Leasing Company leased automobiles for twelve months or longer. Thompson was president and manager of both corporations and owned fifty percent of the stock of each corporation. The automobile rental and leasing business which Thompson conducted on the leasehold premises as an individual was continued by the defendant corporations after their formation.

In August, 1954, Thompson assigned all of his interest in the lease to the defendant Bob's U-Drive. The assignment was in writing. No assignment was made to defendant Continental Leasing Company, although it continued to carry on its business from the leasehold premises as before.

The operations of the two corporations were not strictly segregated. All the business was conducted from one office. There was some evidence that in the operation of the business the records did not always clearly reflect which corporation was acting in the particular instance. However, each corporation kept separate business records, separate bank accounts, separate telephones and separate stationery.

A controversy arose between the parties as to the performance of the terms of the lease by the defendants and on April 22, 1957, plaintiff, purporting to act pursuant to ORS 33.210 et seq., filed a petition for the purpose of securing an order directing the defendants to proceed to arbitration. An amended petition was filed in July, 1957. The defendant Continental Leasing Company filed its answer. The defendant Bob's U-Drive prepared an answer which was never filed. At the hearing in the circuit court for Multnomah county on the petition to order arbitration the attorney for defendant Bob's U-Drive, who was also the attorney for Continental Leasing Company, indicated that Bob's U-Drive was willing to arbitrate, whereupon Bob's U-Drive ceased to participate in the proceedings and the hearing continued as to defendant Continental Leasing Company alone.

The defendant Continental Leasing Company prayed for a dismissal of the petition on the ground that there was no assignment of the lease to it and no written arbitration agreement as required by ORS 33.230. An order was entered by the circuit court for Multnomah county requiring the defendant Continental Leasing Company to proceed forthwith to arbitrate the controversy. No order was entered directing the defendant Bob's U-Drive to arbitrate. A hearing was then held before a board of arbitrators, which culminated in an award of $2,938.88 for the plaintiff. Both defendants filed objections to the judgment setting forth various grounds. An order was entered overruling the objections and finally on July 8, 1958, a joint and several judgment was entered against the defendants in accordance with the award. * * *

A more serious question is presented by the second assignment of error. It is urged that the defendant Continental Leasing Company could not be required to submit to arbitration under ORS 33.210 et seq. because it had not been a party to a written contract containing an agreement to submit to arbitration which is required by ORS 33.220.

It is conceded that no written assignment of the lease was ever made to Continental Leasing Company. The assignment ran to Bob's U-Drive only. There is no satisfactory explanation given for limiting the assignment to the one corporation. At the time of the assignment both corporations were occupying portions of the leasehold premises and had been paying rent. Until the assignment was made Thompson continued to be the lessee but he managed both corporations and apparently treated each corporation as having an equal right to the occupancy of the leasehold premises. Although the long-term leasing business of Continental Leasing Company was not developed until after the short-term rental business had been in operation by Bob's U-Drive for some time, there is no evidence that Continental Leasing Company was a sublessee under Bob's U-Drive. Both corporations had an equal status as tenants of Thompson. The looseness of the arrangement was satisfactory as long as Thompson was the common manager. It was only after Thompson decided to sell his interest in the businesses that an assignment of the lease assumed importance.

The plaintiff maintains that Continental became a party to the written lease by virtue of ratifying an act of its promoter, by adoption of a contract of its officers and by accepting the benefits under the lease.

We are of the opinion that Continental became a co-assignee of the lease together with Bob's U-Drive prior to the written assignment of lease. When a person other than the lessee is in possession of leased premises paying rent to the lessor, there is a presumption that the lease has been assigned to the person in possession. * * *

In a majority of the modern cases applying this rule the implied assignment arising out of possession is regarded as effective to form the basis for the running of covenants in the lease so as to burden or benefit the assignee. * * * It is said in Leadbetter v. Pewtherer, 1912, 61 Or. 168, 171, 121 P. 799, 800, Ann.Cas.1914B, 464, that "This cannot amount to or be shown to establish a formal assignment, for the purpose of binding defendant by the covenants of the lease; but it is an oral assignment, and when he enters and is recognized thereunder by the lessor he becomes liable for the rental specified therein." * * *

The court, in the Leadbetter case, held that the possessor was liable for the rent covenanted to be paid in the written lease. Apparently the recovery was deemed to be for use and occupation rather than for the breach of a covenant running with the land. We believe, however, that the cases holding that the implied assignment carries with it liability on the covenants which run with the land state the better rule and we adopt it. But cf., Tiffany, Landlord and Tenant, § 158, p. 973. If the possessor's interest is regarded as arising out of an implied assignment, it seems only consistent to treat him as standing in the same position as an assignee who occupies the premises under a written assignment. The occupation of the premises and the payment of rent should be sufficient to take the case out of the statute of frauds. * * * This is sometimes expressed in terms of estoppel as in Mann v. Ferdinand Munch Brewery, 225 N.Y. 189, 121 N.E. 746, 747, where it was said:

"* * * A person in possession who holds himself out to the landlord as assignee is estopped from denying the assignment or objecting that the assignment was not in writing. Carter v. Hammett, 18 Barb., 608."

If the policy of the statute of frauds is satisfied and if it is assumed that the privilege of occupancy arises out of an assignment of the term, there would be no reason for limiting the operative effect of the assignment as suggested in the Leadbetter and Culver cases, supra. In the instant case the opportunity for fraud was minimal. The gap in written proof to establish liability under the lease was in the transaction between Thompson as lessee and Thompson as manager of Continental. Under these circumstances there is little danger that the policy of the statute of frauds would be violated by recognizing the oral transactions as an assignment of the lease.

We have assumed that the covenant to submit to arbitration controversies arising out of the lease is such that it will be binding upon the assignees of the leasehold. It may be noted that the defendant Bob's U-Drive admitted that the covenant to arbitrate was binding on it. If the covenant is binding on an assignee it should make no difference whether the assignment is express or implied. We are of the opinion that the covenant to submit to arbitration ran with the assignment of the lease.

To bind the assignee of a leasehold the covenant must "touch and concern" the leasehold estate. There is considerable confusion and uncertainty as to the meaning of this requirement, not only in the adjudicated cases but among the scholars as well. The various tests and the cases on the subject of "touching and concerning" are thoroughly examined in Clark on Covenants. Probably the most definitive test is that suggested in Bigelow, The Content of Covenants in Leases, 12 Mich.L. Rev. 639 (1914). The Bigelow test is summarized by Judge Clark in his book "Covenants and Interests Running with Land (2nd ed.)" as follows:

"* * * The method he states is to ascertain the exact effect of the covenant upon the legal relations of the parties. In effect it is a measuring of the legal relations of the parties with and without the covenant. If the promisor's legal relations in respect to the land in question are lessened—his legal interest as owner rendered less valuable by the promise—the burden of the covenant touchs or concerns that land; if the promisee's legal relations in respect to that land are increased—his legal interest as owner rendered more valuable by the promise—the benefit of the covenant touches or concerns that land. It is necessary that this effect should be had upon the legal relations of the parties as owners of the land in question, and not merely as members of the community in general, such as taxpayers, or owners of other land, in order that the covenant may run." Pages 97, 98.

Although this analysis is frequently helpful in testing covenants for their character as "real" or "personal" covenants, it still leaves open to judicial inquiry in each case the question of whether the interests of the parties affected by the covenant are those which they have "as owners of the land in question" or separate and apart from such ownership. To this extent, then, the test begs the original question.

In the case at bar the covenant to arbitrate is invoked to require the lessee to submit to arbitration a matter relating to rental payments under the lease. A covenant to pay rent clearly "touches and concerns" the land. It would seem to follow that a covenant to arbitrate a question with respect to rental payments should also be regarded as relating to the property interests of the original covenanting parties as lessor and lessee. As stated in Clark, op.cit. supra, page 99, "there would seem to be no reason for applying the rule of touching and concerning in an overtechnical manner, which is unreal from the standpoint of the parties themselves." Clark suggests the following as a practical test:

"* * * Where the parties, as laymen and not as lawyers, would naturally regard the covenant as intimately bound up with the land, aiding the promisee as landowner or hampering the promisor in similar capacity, the requirement should be held fulfilled."

In applying this test we believe that it is important not only to consider how the original parties as laymen would naturally regard the covenant, but how one taking a lease as assignee would regard it. Assuming this to be a test to be judicially applied, we believe that the average person accepting the assignment of a lease containing a covenant to arbitrate questions relating to the terms of the lease would normally assume that he was bound by the covenant. In this connection it may be noted again that Bob's U-Drive (represented by legal counsel, to be sure) assumed that it was bound by the covenant to arbitrate. The case law on the specific question before us is sparse. Young v. Wrightson, 11 Ohio Dec.Repr. 104; 24 Cinc.L.Bull. 457 (1890) supports the view we take. In that case the lease contained a covenant that at the end of stated periods the leasehold would be reappraised and the rent computed on the new appraised value. The court held that "It is too plain to admit of argument that the covenant in question is one which is capable of running with the land." In Worthington v. Hewes & McCann, 1869, 19 Ohio St. 66 a stipulation in a lease as to appraisement of the leasehold was held to run with the land. The court said, at pages 73, 74:

"We think the covenant regarding the mode of revaluing the premises, equally with the covenants for revaluation, and for payment of a rent based upon the valuation, runs with the land. The three are inseparably connected, and reflect upon each other."

* * *

We hold, therefore, that the possession of Continental and Bob's U-Drive made them co-assignees of the lease and that the implied assignment to Continental was sufficient to carry with it the covenant to arbitrate contained in the written lease. Were we to hold that Continental's possession was not under the lease we would, in effect, endorse a practice by which a lessee, through the formation of a corporation, could enjoy the benefits of the lease and at the same time insulate himself from liability on the covenants contained in it.

The opportunity for fraud through such a device is illustrated in the present case. The lease called for the payment of a minimum rent of $75 per month and an additional rental of $10 per month for each car over eight "owned by Thompson's U-Drive Company." Plaintiff testified that most of the cars were registered in the name of Continental Leasing Company and that a part of the cars so registered were used in the short-term rental business carried on by Bob's U-Drive. When plaintiff's accountant asked to examine the books of both companies he was denied access to Continental's books.

This confusion of affairs of the two corporations could afford yet another basis for regarding Continental as an assignee of the lease. It is well established that where corporate affairs are confused with those of the stockholders, a subsidiary or an affiliate corporation the corporate veil may be lifted to protect persons whose rights have been jeopardized by the corporate device. * * * We would be justified on the basis of the evidence in this case to treat the two affiliate corporations as one and regard the assignment of the lease to Bob's U-Drive as inuring to Continental as well. However, we are satisfied to rest the decision upon the ground previously stated. * * *

The judgment of the lower court is affirmed.

DUNCAN, Justice pro tem. (dissenting in part).

Defendant Continental Leasing Co. raised timely objection to the petition seeking to require it to arbitrate under the lease between plaintiff, as lessor, and Robert E. Thompson, as lessee. Defendant also objected to the entry of judgment against it by the circuit court based on the award of the arbitrators.

Defendant Continental was not a party to the lease; the lease contained no provision binding assignees or sublessees to the covenants thereof; nor did defendant expressly assume any of the obligations of the lease.

When a party other than the lessee is shown to be in possession and occupancy of leased premises, the law will presume that the lease has been assigned to such party, and the party may be held liable for the payment of the rent unless able to overcome the presumption by proof that some other relationship exists between that party and the original lessee. * * *

However, in the absence of an express agreement by the assignee to be bound by the lease covenants, the assignee is bound only by those covenants which run with the land. No privity of contract arises from the naked assignment, but only privity of estate. * * * Only real covenants run with the land. It is an essential quality of a real covenant that it relates to the realty, having for its object something annexed to or inherent in or connected with the land or other real property. * * *

Under authority of that case, a covenant to pay rent runs with the land. It is deemed, however, that a covenant to arbitrate is personal and does not run with the land. Accordingly, defendant was entitled to have its alleged obligation to pay rent tried out in an appropriate law action.

It is unnecessary to impose a contractual relationship on defendant where none was entered into by it. If fraud existed, plaintiff had a remedy. Also, plaintiff could have fully protected himself, if desired, by a clause in the lease prohibiting an assignment or subletting or by a clause expressly binding assignees and sublessees to all obligations of the lease.

The trial court was without jurisdiction to compel defendant Continental Leasing Co. to arbitrate and the judgment against that defendant based on the arbitration award should be reversed.

Notes

1. In First National Bank v. Hazelwood Co., 85 Or. 403, 166 P. 955 (1917), cited by the dissenting justice in Abbott v. Bob's U-Drive, the plaintiff leased premises which included a creamery plant and certain personal property in the creamery to the Klock Produce Co. The term of the lease was three years. In the lease the lessee agreed "that he will, during the term of this lease, operate said creamery plant as an independent creamery"; and further "that the cream routes now serving said creamery, shall be considered a part of said demised premises, as far as may be, and that both parties will do their utmost to retain said routes for the benefit of said creamery." The lessee assigned the lease to the defendant. The plaintiff sued for damages for breach of both covenants, and had judgment on both counts. On appeal the judgment was affirmed on the first count but reversed on the second. As to the latter judgment the court said that real covenants are those which have for their object something annexed to, or inherent in, or connected with land. Admitting that the cream routes were intimately connected with the business operated on the demised premises and that the leased property had little value in the absence of the creamery business and that such business could not be conducted without the cream routes. "The cream routes, nevertheless, are not attached to real property. The covenants with reference to them are collateral to the real covenants contained in the lease. They are to be distinguished from those covenants whereby an owner of land charges it with a servitude in favor of demised premises in the hands of his lessee. Norman v. Wells, 17 Wend. (N.Y.) 136. Plaintiff had no property right in these cream routes; they were not incorporeal hereditaments. The covenants with reference to them were not real, but personal covenants binding only upon the parties to the lease."

Considering the test of the running of covenants by Clark, quoted in the opinion in the *Abbott* case, would you agree with the court's decision? Do you think that decision is consistent with the later decision of the same court in the *Abbott* case?

2. Covenants by a lessee which most obviously meet the test of running are those which prescribe what may be done on or to the leased premises. Included are those which relate to how a business is to be conducted on the leased premises. 2 A.L.P. § 9.4, n. 16; e.g. Lewin v. American and Colonial Distributors, Ltd., [1945] 1 Ch. 225, where the covenant was to the effect that a certain named person was not to have any interest in the lease or in the conduct of the business to be conducted on the premises.

Suppose, on the other side, a lessor promises not to engage in any business within a stated area which would compete with the business to be conducted by the lessee on the leased premises. In Thomas v. Hayward, L.R. 4 Exch. 311 (1869), it was held that the benefit of this covenant would not run to an assignee of the lessee. The court said that the covenant relates only to the mode of occupying the land, not to the land itself. But in Norman v. Wells, 17 Wend. (N.Y.) 136 (1837), referred to by the court in the Hazelwood case, supra note 1, on similar facts, the court held for the plaintiff assignee. The court said, "The covenant respected the premises; it regulated their value, it fixed the amount of the rent, it was co-extensive with the estate, it benefitted the owner of the demised premises, and nobody but the owner."

Promises relating to competition are most likely to appear today in shopping-center leases. If a lessor promises not to compete with his lessee in the shopping center or on other neighboring land, the right of an assignee of the lessee to enforce such a promise is the problem involved in the cases mentioned above. A related problem is whether the burden of such a promise will run with land to which it relates and which the lessor has conveyed to a third person. Since the interest conveyed is not the reversionary interest of the lessor in the leased premises, the problem, strictly speaking, is not a problem involving the running of promises with the interests of the parties to a lease. Rather the problem involves the running of promises with land held and transferred in fee simple. This is the subject-matter of the succeeding section of this chapter. Although these two kinds of problems relating to the running of promises not to compete are analogous, the fee cases present special problems not encountered in the landlord-tenant cases. See Note 2 infra page 663.

For a shopping center case in accord with Norman v. Wells, see Neiman-Marcus Co. v. Hexter, 412 S.W.2d 915 (Tex.1967).

3. In most states, statutes require assignments of leasehold interests to be in writing, at least when the lease term is more than 1 year. See Rest.2d (Landlord & Tenant) § 15.1, Stat. Note 7.

THRUSTON v. MINKE

Court of Appeals of Maryland, 1870.
32 Md. 487.

BARTOL, C.J., delivered the opinion of the Court.

It appears from the record, that before the 24th day of October, 1867, the appellant and Frederick Minke, (the appellee,) were seized in fee as tenants in common, of a lot of ground in the town of Cumberland, on the north-west corner of Baltimore and George streets; the appellant owning one-fourth, and Minke three-fourths thereof. The lot was improved by a three story building known and occupied as "St. Nicholas Hotel." The building was situated on the corner of the streets mentioned, leaving on the west thereof a part of the lot fronting on Baltimore street vacant or unimproved.

On the 24th day of October, 1867, the appellant leased to Minke, for the term of ninety-nine years, renewable forever, his undivided fourth part of a portion of the vacant or unimproved part of the lot; commencing at the westerly wall of the hotel and binding thereon *   *   *.

After describing the parcel demised, the lease contains, among others, the following provisions:

"*   *   * Provided, however, and this lease is on this condition, that said lessee and his assigns shall not at any time hereafter erect, build or construct, on the part of the lot hereby demised, which fronts eleven feet on Baltimore street next to said hotel building, and runs back ___ feet in depth, any building or tenement, any portion or part of which shall be higher than the present level of said third story floor of said hotel building *   *   *."

The bill of complaint filed by the appellant states that the above conditions were put in the lease "for the express purpose of preventing Minke, or his assigns, from shutting up, or excluding the light from the west window in the third story hall of the main hotel building, and other windows on the west side of said hotel building, in the third story, and also to prevent Minke from building any tenement or house higher than the third story floor of said hotel building, for the space of eleven feet westerly therefrom."

And the bill charges "that Minke has directly violated and broken said condition."

That "said Minke, without any agreement on the part of the complainant, or waiver or release of said condition, and in opposition to the repeated remonstrances of the complainant, is now proceeding to erect and construct a building, and is actually constructing the same of brick, to a height several feet above the roof of the main hotel building, and shutting up the whole space of eleven feet in width on Baltimore street, for the whole depth of thirty-two and a quarter feet, by occupying the whole thereof with such building."

The bill further charges that Minke is proceeding to construct a large wooden cornice on and against the westerly wall of the hotel building, at and near the front thereof, on Baltimore street, and putting the same far over and above the roof of the main hotel building, thereby, as alleged, increasing the danger to the same in case of fire. And the effect of such violation of the conditions of the lease is alleged to be to shut out and obstruct the light and ventilation from the hall of the third story of the hotel, and greatly to injure and impair the value of the same and of the complainant's interest therein.

An injunction was issued to prevent and restrain Minke from proceeding with the construction of the proposed building, contrary to, and in violation of the covenant and conditions contained in the lease.

In the progress of the case in the Court below, the fact was disclosed that the appellant, Thruston, after making the lease, on the 30th day of October, 1867, conveyed to John B.H. Campbell all his reversionary interest and estate in the property demised, and assigned the covenants therein, and the respondent contended that the effect of such conveyance and assignment was to confer upon Campbell the exclusive right to enforce the particular covenant or condition under consideration, and to divest the complainant of the right to maintain any action at law or in equity for the breach or violation thereof. This defence was ruled good by the Circuit Court, and its decree dissolving the injunction appears to have rested mainly on that ground.

In this view we do not concur. It is plain, from the nature of the condition, that it was inserted, as alleged in the bill, only for the benefit and protection of the hotel property, in which the lessor retained his estate, and that it was not in any respect intended for the benefit of the lessor as owner of the reversion in the property leased. It was, in its nature, an independent covenant or condition, made with Thruston, as owner of the contiguous property, for the benefit and protection of which it was intended; it was not a covenant running with the land demised, and did not pass to the assignee of the reversion.

The effect of the condition was to create a right or interest in the nature of an incorporeal hereditament or easement appurtenant to the contiguous hotel property, and arising out of the parcel of land demised by the lease. The principle is correctly stated by the Court in Whitney v. Union R. Co., 11 Gray, Mass., 359, 71 Am.Dec. 715, as follows:

"When it appears, by a fair interpretation of the words of the grant, that it was the intent of the parties to create or reserve a right in the nature of a servitude or easement in the property granted, for the benefit of the other land owned by the grantor, and originally forming, with the land conveyed, one parcel, such right shall be deemed appurtenant to the land of the grantor, and binding on that conveyed to the grantee, and the right and burden thus created will respectively pass to and be binding on all subsequent grantees of the respective parcels of land." * * *

[T]he appellant, as partner of the hotel property, is entitled to the benefit of the condition in the lease, and * * * it did not pass to Campbell by the assignment of the reversion. Is he entitled to relief by a writ of injunction to prevent its violation? * * *

In 2 Story's Eq.Jur. § 927, it is said: "Where easements or servitudes are annexed, by grant or covenant or otherwise to private estates * * * the due enjoyment of them will be protected against encroachments, by injunction."

That is the nature of the right that has been encroached upon here. In this case the covenant or condition in the lease is express and positive, and, as we have before said, the appellant, as part owner of the hotel property, for the protection or benefit of which it was made, has a right to insist on its observance by the lessee.

The consequence of its violation in the manner charged in the bill, as shown by the evidence, is, to shut out, or materially obstruct the light and ventilation of the third story of the hotel.

For such damage and injury, an action at law would not, in our opinion, afford an adequate and complete remedy, and therefore, the appellant is entitled to relief by injunction.

For the reasons stated, the order of the Circuit Court dissolving the injunction will be reversed, with costs to the appellant, and the cause will be remanded.

Reversed and remanded.

Notes and Questions

1. The restriction in the lease in Thruston v. Minke was stated in the form of a condition. If in fact the lessee's interest in the land was subject to a condition, it would seem that the lessor had reserved a right of entry or power of termination, which upon breach of condition, would be enforced by the lessor so as to forfeit the lessee's estate. The court, however, speaks of the restriction as a "covenant or condition," and says that "the effect of the condition was to create a right or interest in the nature of an * * * easement appurtenant to the contiguous hotel property." This must mean that the court is treating the restriction as a covenant which touched and concerned the hotel property so as to run with that property in a manner that is analogous to a negative easement appurtenant. In fact the difference between a negative easement and a restrictive covenant which runs with land is not substantial. Normally the latter is created by words of promise, the former by words of grant. Technically an easement creates a property interest, an interest in rem, in the one to whom it has been granted, while a covenant creates only a contractual right, in personam, in the covenantee. The consequences of this distinction are only rarely significant. In fact the distinction itself may be open to question in respect to certain types of restrictive covenants, considered below, which are enforceable only in equity. A covenant can be enforced by a suit for damages for breach of contract, while a negative easement presumably can be enforced against the servient owner by a tort action for damages. More often both are enforced by injunction, in which case the label applied is of no consequence. See 2 A.L.P. § 9.12.

It should also be noted that while the difference in enforceability noted above between a condition and a covenant is significant, courts do not always follow the form of the language used in a particular case, but in ascertaining the intent of the parties to an instrument, may find that words of condition were really intended to operate as a covenant. See e.g. Post v. Weil, 115 N.Y. 361, 22 N.E. 145 (1889).

2. Thruston v. Minke is important for our purposes because it forces us to consider two basic problems in respect to the touching and concerning requirement. *First*, certain promises are to do upon premises other than the leased premises certain acts which if they were to be done on the leased premises would clearly run with the land; or, as in Thruston v. Minke, to engage in conduct or refrain from conduct on the leased premises which affects some interest of the promisee other than his interest in the leased premises. *Second*, as a consequence of these possibilities, it becomes necessary that the running of the burdens and the benefits of covenants should be considered separately. Every promise between two persons, at least every kind of promise we are here concerned with, confers what we may call a benefit on the promisee and places

what we may call a burden on the promisor. This obvious fact has no special significance for contract law generally. But it is of considerable importance to the property side of contract law, that is, to the running of promises with the property interests of the parties. In fact, it is misleading even to talk of a covenant or promise running with the land. We must ask, with what land? Obviously either the term of the tenant or the reversion of the landlord. But which? If the lessee makes a promise to the lessor and then assigns his term, the question will be whether the obligation or burden of his promise will run with the term. There is no problem about the running of the benefit, the right to sue the lessee or his assignee, for the reversion has not been assigned. If, on the other hand, the lessee does not assign his term, but the lessor conveys his reversion, the question relates to the running of the benefit only, the right of the assignee to sue on the promise. If both parties have assigned their interests, and if the assignee of the reversion wants to sue the assignee of the term, the question will be whether both benefit and burden will run. Where the promise has been made by the lessor to the lessee, the same sort of questions can be put, except that here the burden and benefit are reversed. The reason why we go through this routine is brought out in Thruston v. Minke: it is possible that the benefit of a particular covenant touches the land in question but the burden does not, or vice versa. But we are left in considerable doubt in some cases because the courts have failed to go through this routine for our benefit, but have talked about "the covenant" running or not running, without telling us whether they were referring to the burden or the benefit or both.

"It would seem, therefore, that where a land owner's legal relations as such owner are increased and made more valuable by a covenant, the benefit of such covenant is of such a nature as may pass to his assigns; that where his legal relations as such owner are lessened and made of less value by a covenant, the burden of such covenant is of such a nature as may pass to his assigns; and that the running of benefit and the running of burden should be considered as separate and distinct questions." Clark, Covenants and Interests Running with the Land 111 (2d ed. 1947).

Keeping all these points in mind, consider now these cases:

(1) L leases premises to T for use as a gasoline service station and T promises to buy all petroleum products from L.

(2) L leases to T and T promises that he will not conduct on the leased premises any business which will compete with the business which L is conducting on other land.

(3) L leases to T and L promises that he will not conduct on other nearby premises any business which will compete with the business which T is to conduct on the leased premises.

Should the burden or the benefit of these covenants, or both, run with the respective interests of L and T in the leased land?

See 2 A.L.P. § 9.4; Cunningham § 8.15.

BURTON v. CHESAPEAKE BOX & LUMBER CORPORATION

Supreme Court of Appeals of Virginia, 1950.
190 Va. 755, 57 S.E.2d 904.

SPRATLEY, Justice. This case presents for our consideration the proper construction of the terms of a lease of land. The facts are without substantial conflict, and the decision depends solely upon questions of law.

On September 15, 1943, George H. Burton, by written lease, demised unto C.L. Burroughs and R.T. Blanchard, trading as Blanchard Box & Crate Company, his building and certain furniture and fixtures therein, located on Wilson Road in South Norfolk, Virginia, for one year, beginning October 1, 1943. The lease provided that in the absence of a written notice from one of the parties of a desire to terminate it, given sixty days prior to the end of a rental year, the lease would continue from year to year.

The lease contained the following covenants and agreements:

"The parties of the second part agree to pay as rental for the above mentioned property and equipment, the sum of $112.50 per month, payable on the first day of each and every month, in advance, to the party of the first part, or to his duly appointed representative, $112.50 is to be paid upon signing of this lease, receipt of which is hereby acknowledged, and said sum is to cover the rent for the month of October, 1943.

"It is further agreed by the parties hereto, that in event that the parties of the second part shall be in default ten days in their rent, as above set forth, that the party of the first part shall at his option have the right to forthwith reenter upon the said property and declare this lease null and void, and take possession of said property as for breach of contract, either with or without process of law.

"It is further agreed that the parties of the second part shall have issued at their expense, and maintain during the tenure of this lease a fire insurance policy in amount of $5,000.00 to indemnify the party of the first part against any and all loss sustained by fire during the tenure of lease, $4,500.00 of which shall be to cover loss on the building, and $500.00 on the office furniture and fixtures, and in event of loss, this amount shall be paid to the party of the first part.

"It is further agreed, that the parties of the second part shall have the right to alter, change, build and or repair the building and fences, that they will maintain and keep the premises in the same good condition that it was in upon their entry into, and that in the event of their terminating this lease, they will leave the premises in the same good condition that it was in when this lease was signed, that the foundation walls, and roof shall in no way be weakened or damaged."

By agreement dated April 6, 1944, Burroughs and Blanchard in consideration of $250 cash, contracted to sell and convey to Forest Land and Development Corporation its rights in the above lease, together with certain office furniture and fixtures, for the sum of $2,018.50. The fourth paragraph of that contract reads as follows:

"All of the right, title and interest of Vendors in and to a certain lease from George H. Burton, demising the above premises to them for a term of one year from October 1, 1943, at a monthly rental of One Hundred Twelve Dollars and Fifty Cents ($112.50) plus an amount equal to the premiums on the fire insurance on said property, which said lease is to be properly assigned to Vendee, and Vendors agree that they will pay all rental accruing thereunder prior to May 1, 1944."

On April 24, 1944, Burroughs and Blanchard, in consideration of the sum of $2,018.50, executed a deed to the Forest Land and Development Corporation for the rights and property described in its contract above. The deed described the rights in the lease thereby assigned as follows:

"All of the right, title and interest of Vendors in, to and under that certain lease from Geo. H. Burton, as lessor, to Vendors, as lessees, bearing date on the 15th day of September 1943, demising to Vendors for a term of one year, beginning on the 1st day of October, 1943, and ending on the 30th day of September, 1944, the premises above referred to, situated at Wilson Road and the Norfolk Southern Railroad right of way, in the City of South Norfolk, Virginia, together with certain office furniture, fixtures and equipment described in the said lease, a copy of which said lease is hereto attached and hereby expressly made a part hereof."

Neither the contract nor the deed was signed by either of the defendants. The lease was not attached to the deed, and other than the recital therein was no evidence that it had been actually attached thereto. In neither instrument did the Forest Land and Development Corporation assume the obligations of the lease.

Forest Land and Development Corporation took possession of the property and conducted business under its own name and sometimes as Chesapeake Box and Lumber Company. It was recognized by plaintiff as his tenant, and as such paid plaintiff a monthly rental of $112.50 up to September 30, 1947, the date of the termination of the lease. However, while in possession of Forest Land and Development Corporation, the demised building and some of its chattels were seriously damaged by a fire on May 2, 1945. There was then no fire insurance on the property.

Chesapeake Box and Lumber Corporation, one of the defendants, as distinguished from Chesapeake Box and Lumber Company, was not chartered until 1946, and consequently it was not in possession of the premises at the time of the fire.

Burton instituted this action in assumpsit against the Chesapeake Box and Lumber Corporation and Forest Land and Development Corporation on March 23, 1948, to recover damages in the sum of $5,000 for loss occasioned by the fire. He alleged that his loss was caused by the failure of the defendants to procure fire insurance as agreed and to return the leased premises at the termination of the lease in the same condition they were in upon their entry thereon.

A jury was waived and all matters of law and fact were submitted to the court. The court, upon consideration of the law and the evidence, dismissed the action as to the Chesapeake Box and Lumber Corporation. To this ruling there is no assignment of error.

The court being further of opinion that the Forest Land and Development Corporation did not assume the obligation of the lease and that the covenant to insure the premises was a mere personal covenant of the original lessees, and not a covenant running with the land, held that the Forest Land and Development Corporation was not liable for the damage, and entered judgment accordingly.

The sole assignment of error is that the judgment of the court is contrary to the law and the evidence and plainly wrong. Four grounds are asserted in support of this assignment. The first ground is that the agreement in the lease to insure the property was a covenant running with the land. The second and third grounds are that the covenants to maintain and keep the premises in good condition, and to leave them in the same condition that they were in when the lease was signed, imposed upon the defendants the duty to repair the fire damage. Under the fourth ground, it is claimed that Forest Land and Development Corporation having accepted an assignment of the lease, the plaintiff had the right under Virginia Code 1942 (Michie), section 5143, Code of Virginia, 1950, section 55–22, to hold it liable in the event of failure of the performance of its provisions.

* * *

After the fire, the defendant insured the building in its name. It did not deliver the policy of insurance to the plaintiff. This fact does not aid us in determining whether or not the covenant to insure in the lease ran with the land.

A considerable portion of the evidence was devoted to the question of the amount of damages. In view of the judgment of the court, there is no necessity for its consideration by us.

The language of the contract "a monthly rental of One Hundred Twelve Dollars and Fifty Cents ($112.50) plus an amount equal to the premiums on the fire insurance on said property," was merely a description of the amount of the rental due from lessees. The covenants for rent and for insurance are separate and independent of each other. If the insurance premium constituted a part of the rent payable by defendant, it was liable only for its failure to pay the amount of the premium, a sum which has not been disclosed. An obligation to pay rent did not make the defendant liable for the fire damage.

The first question of law is whether the covenant to insure ran with the land. The development of the law with respect to such covenants is most interesting. In Minor on Real Property, II Edition, Ribble, Vol. I, page 541, it is said:

"Covenants contained in a lease or conveyance of land are said to run with the land when they are of such character that the benefits and burdens thereof *pass with the land* to the *assignee*, into whosesoever hands the land may come." 2 Minor's Institutes, 775.

The authorities make a clear distinction between a bare covenant to insure and a covenant to insure coupled with a covenant to rebuild. In a bare covenant to insure without a reciprocal obligation from the lessor to restore the premises in the event of fire, the assignee receives no benefit from the covenant, unless the proceeds of insurance are used to restore the property, and he is thereby enabled to enjoy its occupancy. On the other hand, if the covenant is so related to the land that the performance thereof would be of benefit to an assignee in his occupancy of the land, it is said to run with the land.

In 1 Taylor's Landlord & Tenant, sec. 400, the distinction is stated as follows:

"The bare covenant to insure is personal, extending only to the covenantor and his personal representatives, without binding the assignee of the term, and, in general, gives the landlord no right to receive the insurance-money; but when it contains a clause for reinstating the premises with the insurance-money, he may not only require it to be so applied, but it becomes a covenant, running with the land and enabling the assignee of the reversion to maintain an action for its breach."

In Sutherland on Damages, 4th Ed., page 3175, we find:

"The bare covenant to insure is personal, extending only to the covenantor. * * * but when it contains a clause for reinstating the premises with such money, he may not only require it to be so applied but it becomes also a covenant running with the land."

In Masury v. Southworth, 9 Ohio St. 340, 341, 348, this is said:

" * * * from the earliest times, the distinction between such covenants as may run with the land, and such as are collateral and cannot, has been taken and maintained. It has been a matter of some dispute, whether a covenant to insure might run with the land. A covenant to run with the land, must have for its subject matter something which sustains the estate and the enjoyment of it, and *is therefore beneficial both to lessor and lessee*. A covenant to insure, which had for its object the benefit of the lessor only, as where the money paid in the event of a loss would go to him, has been regarded as collateral; but if the money is to be applied to repair or rebuild, then it is in its character like a covenant to repair, which may run with the land." (Italics added.)

      *   *   *

It will be noted that the lease under review contained no provision requiring the lessor to restore the premises in event of fire. It required the original lessee to insure the property merely to indemnify the lessor against loss. If the property had been insured and its proceeds paid to the lessor, there was no obligation upon him to rebuild so that the assignee could retain its occupancy.

It is true that some textbook writers have made the general statement that a covenant to insure runs with the land, but an examination of the cases relied upon by them shows that they principally involve instances where it was assumed that the proceeds of the insurance were required to be used to restore the damage. We have been cited no case to the contrary.

The next question is whether the covenant to maintain, keep, and leave the premises in good repair imposed a liability upon the assignee for the fire damage. It is expressly provided in Virginia Code 1942 (Michie), section 5180, Code of Virginia, 1950, section 55–226, that such covenant shall not have the effect of obligating a tenant to repair fire damage "unless there be other words showing it to be the intent of the parties that he should be so bound."

The covenant to repair relates to the right of the lessees to make alterations and changes in the leased property, and to their duty to make needed repairs because of alterations, wear, tear and usage. It contains no language showing the intent of the parties that the tenant should be personally bound for fire damage. It is separate from and independent of the covenant to insure, which, as we have seen, is a bare, personal covenant extending only to the covenantors, the lessees, Blanchard and Burroughs.

*   *   *

We find no error in the judgment complained of, and it will be accordingly affirmed.

Affirmed.

Notes and Questions

In First American National Bank v. Chicken System of America, Inc., 510 S.W.2d 906 (Tenn.1974), the trial court held that the assignee of a lessee was liable for "unpaid rent, taxes, and insurance." This judgment was affirmed without discussion of what covenants ran with the land, the principal issue on appeal being the effect of an assignment without consent of the lessor.

Covenants to pay money present a special problem. Obviously such a covenant does not touch and concern the land in the same direct way as a covenant to do some physical act on or to the leased premises. This of itself is no bar to the running of the covenant, for as we have seen covenants to pay rent or to pay taxes on the demised premises have easily cleared the hurdle.

1. In the light of the distinction which the court made in the Burton case, suppose a lessee promises to leave the demised premises in good condition at the end of the term. Would the fact that the lessee may derive no benefit from this covenant prevent its binding his assignee? Suppose the lessee promises to pay the lessor the cost of putting the premises in good repair, on account either of deterioration caused by the lessee's use or some casualty. Would the promise run, even though the lessor were not bound to use the money to repair or restore the premises?

2. A lessor promises his lessee to reimburse him at the end of the term for the cost of improvements of the leased premises. Where the lessee has neither obligated himself to make improvements, nor reserved the right to remove the improvement if not paid for by the lessor, does such a promise touch and concern the land? Suppose the lessee has reserved the right of removal?

3. A lessor exacts from his lessee a sum of money as security for the lessee's performance of his obligations under the lease. The lessor promises in the lease to refund this deposit at the end of the term if the lessee's obligations have been fully performed. Should an assignee of the lessor be bound by this promise? In Moskin v. Goldstein, 225 Mich. 389, 196 N.W. 415 (1923), an assignee of the reversion was held bound even though he did not receive the deposit money. Contra: McDonald's Corp. v. Blotnik, 28 Ill.App.3d 732, 328 N.E.2d 897 (1975). See Note, 24 Colum.L.Rev. 432 (1924).

4. A lessee by the terms of his lease promised to pay the taxes assessed against the leased premises and also to pay the taxes on adjacent premises owned by the lessor but not included in the lease. In Gower v. Postmaster

General, 57 Law Times, N.S. 527 (Ch.Div.1887), it was held that the lessor could not recover from an assignee of the lessee for the taxes payable on the adjoining premises. But this language of the court appears in the opinion, "If it were meant to make that sum payable by whomsoever this lease may be assigned to, the matter would have been easy. It might have been reserved as rent, and then of course anybody to whom the lease was assigned would have to pay it."

5. Suppose a lease provided that the lessee was to insure the leased premises and that the cost of insurance was to be treated as part of the rent. Would an assignee of the lessee be bound to pay the insurance costs as rent? Suppose the lease provided that if conduct of the lessee should result in increased insurance premiums on the building of which the leased premises were a part or on the stock of the lessor in the store in such building, the lessee would pay the increase, or if not, the lessor could pay it and add it to the rent. In St. Regis Restaurant v. Powers, 219 App.Div. 321, 219 N.Y.S. 684 (1927), the court held that the lessor could not recover from an assignee of the lessee on the covenant to pay increased insurance costs, but insofar as the covenant was one to pay additional rent, it would run with the land. The court said, "We think that what the lessor had in mind was to assure to itself the net rental reserved in the lease."

6. A lessee promised, in "part payment of the rent," to pay a promissory note given by his lessor to a third party. The note was assigned to the plaintiff, and the lease was assigned to the defendant. In Dolph v. White, 12 N.Y. 296 (1855), the plaintiff was denied recovery on the note. One of the judges quoted this statement from an earlier English case, "By the terms, collateral covenants which do not pass to the assignee, are meant such as are beneficial to the lessor without regard to his continuing the owner of the estate." The judge then added, "In the present case White, the lessor, made provision for the payment of the note, and its payment would be beneficial to him without regard to his continuing the owner of the estate. The law touching lessor and lessee, and their grantees or assignees, has no application whatever to the case."

See generally 2 A.L.P. § 9.4; Cunningham § 8.15.

GERBER v. PECHT

Supreme Court of New Jersey, 1954.
15 N.J. 29, 104 A.2d 41.

JACOBS, J. The Appellate Division affirmed a judgment for the plaintiff, entered in the Superior Court, Law Division. We granted certification under R.R. 1:10–2, 14 N.J. 13, 101 A.2d 116.

The plaintiff's predecessor, as lessor, and the defendant Pecht, as lessee, executed a five-year lease for store premises located in Irvington, New Jersey. The fifth paragraph of the printed terms of the lease prohibited any assignment thereof but a typewritten addition stipulated that "The tenant may assign his lease, provided he gets a written consent from the landlord." On November 9, 1948 the defendant Pecht assigned the lease to Moskowitz; the assignment was made with the plaintiff's written consent and upon condition that the assignor and the assignee were to remain liable on the lease for the balance of its term. On February 14, 1950 Moskowitz assigned the lease to Maria and Wilfred Christensen who agreed to comply with all of its provisions; this assignment was made with the plaintiff's written consent but without the defendant Pecht's consent. After the Christensens had defaulted and had vacated the premises the plaintiff instituted her action against the defendant Pecht and the assignees claiming rent and water charges due under covenants in the lease and damages for breach of a covenant to keep the premises in repair. Summary judgment for rent in the sum of $1,172.50 and water charges in the sum of $45 was entered in the Law Division and the defendant Pecht appealed, contending that upon the first assignment of the lease he became a surety and that upon the second assignment without his consent he was discharged from further liability on the lease.   *   *   *

The assignment of a lease does not relieve the lessee of his contractual undertakings in the lease even though the lessor has consented to the assignment and has accepted rental payments from the assignee. *   *   *   The lessor may, of course, expressly release the lessee from further liability or may engage in conduct which has the same legal effect.   *   *   *   Thus the lessor may enter into a direct leasing arrangement with the assignee which effectively establishes a new tenancy relationship while terminating the old.   *   *   *   Or the lessor and assignee may, by agreement, materially vary the terms of the original lease with like consequences. See Walker v. Rednalloh Co., 299 Mass. 591, 13 N.E.2d 394, 397 (Sup.Ct.Jud.1938); 2 Walsh Commentaries, Law of Real Property, 281, n. 4 (1947).

After the defendant Pecht assigned the lease to Moskowitz their relationship *inter se* was comparable to that of principal and surety; they both were liable to the lessor but as between themselves Moskowitz was primarily and Pecht was secondarily liable. Conflicting expressions may be found in the cases as to whether the relationship included the lessor. In Carrano v. Shoor, [118 Conn. 86, 171 A. 17 (1934),] Chief Justice Maltbie adopted the views stated in Baynton v. Morgan, 22 Q.B.D. 74 (1888), that the relationship did not include the lessor and that, as regards him, the original lessee "still remained a principal debtor by reason of his covenant to pay rent." [118 Conn. 86, 171 A. 21.]   *   *   * On the other hand, in Gholson v. Savin, 137 Ohio St. 551, 31 N.E.2d 858, 862, 139 A.L.R. 75 (Sup.Ct.1941), Judge Hart expressed the rule to be that "when a lease is assigned by the lessee, the assignee becomes the principal obligor for the payment of the rent thereafter accruing and the future performance of the covenants, and the lessee assumes the position of surety toward the lessor." See 1 American Law of Property, 311 (1952). While the latter approach has been questioned we need not pursue the matter of labels or nomenclature (Busch v. Plews, 12 N.J. 352, 358, 96 A.2d 761 (1953)) since we are satisfied that Pecht's claim for discharge of liability must, in any event, rest upon a showing that the second assignment constituted a material and prejudicial variation in the terms of the lease. See Walker v. Rednalloh Co., supra [299 Mass. 591, 13 N.E.2d 397], where Justice Dolan set forth the principles which we consider to be generally applicable:

"Regardless of the precise analysis of the theories by which the lessee may be relieved of liability by an assignment, the principle is clear that an agreement between the lessor and the assignee materially varying the terms of the original lease will on one theory or another result in the termination of the lessee's covenant to pay rent. Fifty Associates v. Grace, 125 Mass. 161, 163, 28 Am.Rep. 218; T.A.D. Jones Co. v. Winchester Repeating Arms Co., D.C., 55 F.2d 944, at page 948; Kaskel v. Hollander, 1 Cir., 68 F.2d 265, 267; Fairchild v. Cahn, 120 Cal.App. 418, 420, 7 P.2d 1051; Keeley v. Beenblossom, 183 Iowa 861, 863, 864, 167 N.W. 638; Seeburger v. Cohen, 215 Iowa, 1088, 1092, 247 N.W. 292, 89 A.L.R. 427. Compare Essex Lunch, Inc. v. Boston Lunch Co., 229 Mass. 557, 559, 560, 118 N.E. 899. The lessee is not discharged, however, by variations which inure to his benefit. Eastman v. Nelson, 8 Alaska 548, 555, 556; Gates v. Kehlet, 43 Cal.App. 738, 741, 185 P. 983; Wade v. March, 39 Ohio App. 111, 116, 176 N.E. 687. Compare In re United Cigar Stores Co., 2 Cir., 85 F.2d 134. Nor is the lessee discharged by agreements between lessor and assignee which may increase the liability of the lessee, but which are permitted by the terms of the original lease, to the benefits of which the assignee is entitled. Wall v. Hinds, 4 Gray [Mass.] 256, 266, 267, 64 Am.Dec. 64."

Unlike the situation presented in Silver v. Friedman, [18 N.J.Super. 367, 87 A.2d 336 (App.Div.1952),] the lease in the instant matter embodied an express provision which authorized the tenant to assign the lease with the landlord's consent. When the defendant Pecht executed his assignment to Moskowitz he did not impose limitations (as he might have) but unconditionally transferred the lease with all of its privileges; included was the provision permitting an assignment. When Moskowitz assigned the lease he complied strictly with its terms; at no time was there any waiver or alteration of its provisions or enlargement of its burdens. Under the circumstances the defendant Pecht may not justly complain about the conduct of the lessor or Moskowitz and is in no position to assert that his consent was a condition precedent to the second assignment. See Portnoff v. Medinkowitz, [27 N.J.Super. 301, 99 A.2d 364 (App.Div.1953),] * * * where it was held that a lessee who, with his landlord's consent, unconditionally assigned his lease as permitted by the express terms thereof, was not discharged by a subsequent assignment consented to by the landlord.

We find no merit whatever in the appellant's point that the summary judgment should not have included the item for water charges. Under the terms of the lease the defendant Pecht was liable not only for rent but also for water charges and under the pretrial order the plaintiff was entitled, in the event of recovery, to the amounts stipulated on both claims. The judgment entered in the Law Division was entirely proper and is:

Affirmed.

Notes

1. DeWolf leased premises for a 99-year term to Slosson. Ten years later Slosson executed an assignment of his interest to Springer "in consideration of the assumption by the said Warren Springer of all the obligations and liabilities of the lessee arising under said lease." Springer went into possession and eight years later assigned his interest to McGinniss. Shortly thereafter McGinniss assigned to Miller. The lessor sued to recover rent in the amount of

$12,876, joining as parties defendant Slosson, McGinniss, and Miller. $9,293 of this sum was for rent accruing after the assignment to Miller, the balance apparently having accrued during Springer's tenure. Which of these parties should be liable, and to what extent? Springer v. DeWolf, 194 Ill. 218, 62 N.E. 542 (1902). In its opinion the court said, "* * * we must consider whether there was privity of contract as well as of estate between the appellant and the appellee. As between the lessor and the lessee both exist, but the privity of estate may be terminated by an assignment of the lease by the lessee. Not so as to the privity of contract. The lessee cannot shake off his contractual liability by making such an assignment. When there is no assumption by the assignee of the obligations of the lease, then, as between the lessor and the assignee, there is privity of estate only, and the assignee is liable for the rent while such privity of estate exists, and no longer. But the assignee may terminate such liability by assigning the lease and going out of possession." See also Cork-Oswalt, Inc. v. Hickory Hotel Co., Inc., 20 Ill.App.2d 406, 156 N.E.2d 259 (1959).

2. Call leased to Oliver. Oliver assigned to Catalina Groves, Inc., the instrument of assignment containing the following language, "We hereby assume all responsibilities and obligations of the Lessee as set forth in the above described lease." Catalina Groves later assigned to Levin. Levin defaulted in his rent. Call sued all parties, but service of process was had only upon Oliver and Catalina Groves. Oliver cross-claimed against Catalina, asking that if he be held liable to Call, that Catalina be held liable over to him for any such amount. Call had judgment in his favor, which Oliver paid. Oliver had judgment against Catalina. Catalina appealed. Held, affirmed. Catalina Groves, Inc. v. Oliver, 73 Ariz. 38, 236 P.2d 1022 (1951).

3. Suppose a lease contains a covenant against assignment without consent of the lessor, in addition to a covenant to pay rent. The lessee, T, assigns to A with consent of the lessor. Then A assigns to B without consent. Then B defaults in payment of the rent. Assuming that the covenant against assignment was binding on A, can A be held liable for the rent accruing after the assignment to B? See People v. Klopstock, 24 Cal.2d 897, 151 P.2d 641 (1949); 2 A.L.P. § 9.5; Cunningham § 6.67.

JABER v. MILLER

Supreme Court of Arkansas, 1951.
219 Ark. 59, 239 S.W.2d 760.

GEORGE ROSE SMITH, Justice. This is a suit brought by Miller to obtain cancellation of fourteen promissory notes, each in the sum of $175, held by the appellant, Jaber. The plaintiff's theory is that these notes represent monthly rent upon a certain business building in Fort Smith for the period beginning January 1, 1950, and ending March 1, 1951. The building was destroyed by fire on December 3, 1949, and the plaintiff contends that his obligation to pay rent then terminated. The defendant contends that the notes were given not for rent but as deferred payments for the assignment of a lease formerly held by Jaber. The chancellor, in an opinion reflecting a careful study of the matter, concluded that the notes were intended to be rental payments and therefore should be canceled.

In 1945 Jaber rented the building from its owner for a five-year term beginning March 1, 1946, and ending March 1, 1951. The lease reserved a monthly rent of $200 and provided that the lease would terminate if the premises were destroyed by fire. Jaber conducted a rug shop in the building until 1949, when he sold his stock of merchandise at public auction and transferred the lease to Norber & Son. Whether this instrument of transfer is an assignment or a sublease is the pivotal issue in this case.

In form the document is an assignment rather than a sublease. It is entitled "Contract and Assignment." After reciting the existence of the five-year lease the instrument provides that Jaber "hereby transfers and assigns" to Norber & Son "the aforesaid lease contract * * * for the remainder of the term of said lease." It also provides that "in consideration of the sale and assignment of said lease contract" Norber & Son have paid Jaber $700 in cash and have executed five promissory notes for $700 each, due serially at specified four-month intervals. Norber & Son agree to pay to the owner of the property the stipulated rental of $200 a month, and Jaber reserves the right to retake possession if Norber & Son fail to pay the rent or the notes. The instrument contains no provision governing the rights of the parties in case the building is destroyed by fire.

Later on the plaintiff, Miller, obtained a transfer of the lease from Norber & Son. Miller, being unable to pay the $700 notes as they came due, arranged with Jaber to divide the payments into monthly installments of $175 each. He and the Norbers accordingly executed the notes now in controversy, which Jaber accepted in substitution for those of the original notes that were still unpaid. When the premises burned Miller contended that Jaber's transfer to Norber & Son had been a sublease rather than an assignment and that the notes therefore represented rent. Miller now argues that, under the rule that a sublease terminates when the primary lease terminates, his sublease ended when the fire had the effect of terminating the original lease.

In most jurisdictions the question of whether an instrument is an assignment or a sublease is determined by principles applicable to feudal tenures. In a line of cases beginning in the year 1371 the English courts worked out the rules for distinguishing between an assignment and a sublease. See Ferrier, "Can There be a Sublease for the Entire Term?", 18 Calif.L.Rev. 1. The doctrine established in England is quite simple: If the instrument purports to transfer the lessee's estate for the entire remainder of the term it is an assignment, regardless of its form or of the parties' intention. Conversely, if the instrument purports to transfer the lessee's estate for less than the entire term—even for a day less—it is a sublease, regardless of its form or of the parties' intention.

The arbitrary distinction drawn at common law is manifestly at variance with the usual conception of assignments and subleases. We think of an assignment as the outright transfer of all or part of an existing lease, the assignee stepping into the shoes of the assignor. A sublease, on the other hand, involves the creation of a new tenancy between the sublessor and the sublessee, so that the sublessor is both a tenant and a landlord. The common law distinction is logical only in the light of feudal property law.

In feudal times every one except the king held land by tenure from some one higher in the hierarchy of feudal ownership. "The king himself holds land which is in every sense his own; no one else has any proprietary right in it; but if we leave out of account this royal demesne, then every acre of land is 'held of' the king. The person whom we may call its owner, the person who has the right to use and abuse the land, to cultivate it or leave it uncultivated, to keep all others off it, holds the land of the king either immediately or mediately. In the simplest case he holds it immediately of the king; only the king and he have rights in it. But it well may happen that between him and the king there stand other persons; Z holds immediately of Y, who holds of X, who holds of V, who holds * * * of A, who holds of the king." Pollock and Maitland, History of English Law (2d Ed.), vol. I, p. 232. In feudal law each person owed duties, such as that of military service or the payment of rent, to his overlord. To enforce these duties the overlord had the remedy of distress, being the seizure of chattels found on the land.

It is evident that in feudal theory a person must himself have an estate in the land in order to maintain his place in the structure of ownership. Hence if a tenant transferred his entire term he parted with his interest in the property. The English courts therefore held that the transferee of the entire term held of the original lessor, that such a transferee was bound by the covenants in the original lease, and that he was entitled to enforce whatever duties that lease imposed upon the landlord. The intention of the parties had nothing to do with the matter; the sole question was whether the first lessee retained a reversion that enabled him to hold his place in the chain of ownership.

The injustice of these inflexible rules has often been pointed out. Suppose that A makes a lease to B for a certain rental. B then executes to C what both parties intend to be a sublease as that term is generally understood, but the sublease is for the entire term. If C in good faith pays his rent to B, as the contract requires, he does so at his peril. For the courts say that the contract is really an assignment, and therefore C's primary obligation is to A if the latter elects to accept C as his tenant. Consequently A can collect the rent from the subtenant even though the sublessor has already been paid. For a fuller discussion of this possibility of double liability on the part of the subtenant see Darling, "Is a Sublease for the Residue of a Lessee's Term in Effect an Assignment?", 16 Amer.L.Rev. 16, 21.

Not only may the common law rule operate with injustice to the subtenant; it can be equally harsh upon the sublessor. Again suppose that A makes a lease to B for a certain rental. B then makes to C what B considers a profitable sublease for twice the original rent. But B makes the mistake of attempting to sublet for the entire term instead of retaining a reversion of a day. The instrument is therefore an assignment, and if the original landlord acquires the subtenant's rights there is a merger which prevents B from being able to collect the increased rent. That was the situation in Webb v. Russell, 3 T.R. 393, 100 Eng. Reprint 639. The court felt compelled to recognize the merger, but in doing so Lord Kenyon said: "It seems to me, with all the inclination which we have to support the action (and we have hitherto delayed giving judgment in the hopes of being able to find some ground on which the plaintiff's demand might be sustained), that it cannot be supported. The defence which is made is made of a most unrighteous and unconscious nature; but unfortunately for the plaintiff the mode which she has taken to enforce her demand cannot be supported." Kent, in his Commentaries (14th Ed.), p. 105, refers to this case as reaching an "inequitable result"; Williams and Eastwood, in their work on Real Property, p. 206, call it an "unpleasant result." Yet when the identical question arose in California the court felt bound to hold that the same distasteful merger had taken place. Smiley v. Van Winkle, 6 Cal. 605.

A decided majority of the American courts have adopted the English doctrine in its entirety. Tiffany, Landlord & Tenant, § 151. A minority of our courts have made timid but praiseworthy attempts to soften the harshness of the common law rule. In several jurisdictions the courts follow the intention of the parties in controversies between the sublessor and the sublessee, thus preserving the inequities of feudal times only when the original landlord is concerned. * * *

In other jurisdictions the courts have gone as far as possible to find something that might be said to constitute a reversion in what the parties intended to be a sublease. In some States, notably Massachusetts, it has been held that if the sublessor reserves a right of reentry for nonpayment of rent this is a sufficient reversionary estate to make the instrument a sublease. * * * But even these decisions have been criticized on the ground that at common law a right of re-entry was a mere chose in action instead of a reversionary estate. See, for example, Tiffany, supra, § 151.

The appellee urges us to follow the Massachusetts rule and to hold that since Jaber reserved rights of re-entry his transfer to Norber & Son was a sublease. We are not in sympathy with this view. It may be true that a right of re-entry for condition broken has now attained the status of an estate in Arkansas. See Moore v. Sharpe, 91 Ark. 407, 121 S.W. 341, 23 L.R.A., N.S., 937; Core, "Transmissibility of Certain Contingent Future Interests," 5 Ark.L.Rev. 111. Even so, the Massachusetts rule was adopted to carry out the intention of parties who thought they were making a sublease rather than an assignment. Here the instrument is in form an assignment, and it would be an obvious perversion of the rule to apply it as a means of defeating intention.

In Arkansas the distinction between a sublease and an assignment has been considered in only one case, and then in such circumstances that the litigants were in agreement as to the law. In Pennsylvania Min. Co. v. Bailey, 110 Ark. 287, 161 S.W. 200, the transcript in this court at first contained an instrument purporting to transfer possession for only ten years out of a term of about eighteen years. The appellant accordingly argued that the instrument was a sublease under the orthodox common law rule. The appellee then had the transcript amended to show that the original lessee had later executed an instrument purporting to transfer the entire remaining term. In view of this amendment to the transcript the appellee merely adopted the appellant's argument as to the distinction between an assignment and a sublease. It was therefore to be expected that the court would announce the traditional view, since both parties were urging that position. In one other case, Crump v. Tolbert, 210 Ark. 920, 198 S.W.2d 518, we adverted by dictum to the customary distinction between the two instruments.

In this state of the law we do not feel compelled to adhere to an unjust rule which was logical only in the days of feudalism. The execution of leases is a very practical matter that occurs a hundred times a day without legal assistance. The layman appreciates the common sense distinction between a sublease and an assignment, but he would not even suspect the existence of the common law distinction. As *Darling*, supra, puts it: "Every one knows that a tenant may in turn let to others, and the latter thereby assumes no obligations to the owner of the property; but who would guess that this could only be done for a time falling short by something—a day or an hour is sufficient—of the whole term? And who, not familiar with the subject of feudal tenures, could give a reason why it is held to be so?" It was of such a situation that Holmes was thinking when he said: "It is revolting to have no better reason for a rule than that so it was laid down in the time of Henry IV. It is still more revolting if the grounds upon which it was laid down have vanished long since, and the rule simply persists from blind imitation of the past." The Path of the Law, 10 Harv.L.Rev. 457, 469. The rule now in question was laid down some years before the reign of Henry IV.

The English distinction between an assignment and a sublease is not a rule of property in the sense that titles or property rights depend upon its continued existence. A lawyer trained in common law technicalities can prepare either instrument without fear that it will be construed to be the other. But for the less skilled lawyer or for the layman the common law rule is simply a trap that leads to hardship and injustice by refusing to permit the parties to accomplish the result they seek.

For these reasons we adopt as the rule in this State the principle that the intention of the parties is to govern in determining whether an instrument is an assignment or a sublease. If, for example, a tenant has leased an apartment for a year and is compelled to move to another city, we know of no reason why he should not be able to sublease it for a higher rent without needlessly retaining a reversion for the last day of the term. The duration of the primary term, as compared to the length of the sublease, may in some instances be a factor in arriving at the parties' intention, but we do not think it should be the sole consideration. The Bailey case, to the extent that it is contrary to this opinion, is overruled.

In the case at bar it cannot be doubted that the parties intended an assignment and not a sublease. The document is so entitled. All its language is that of an assignment rather than that of a sublease. The consideration is stated to be in payment for the lease and not in satisfaction of a tenant's debt to his landlord. The deferred payments are evidenced by promissory notes, which are not ordinarily given by one making a lease. From the appellee's point of view it is unfortunate that the assignment makes no provision for the contingency of a fire, but the appellant's position is certainly not without equity. Jaber sold his merchandise at public auction, and doubtless at reduced prices, in order to vacate the premises for his assignees. Whether he would have taken the same course had the contract provided for a cancellation of the deferred payments in case of a fire we have no way of knowing. A decision either way works a hardship on the losing party. In this situation we do not feel called upon to supply a provision in the assignment which might have been, but was not, demanded by the assignees.

Reversed.

HOLT, J., not participating.

Notes

1. It is the traditional view that a sublease creates a landlord-tenant relationship between the sublessor (T) and sublessee (S), but that there is no "privity of estate", no landlord-tenant relation, between the main lessor (L) and the sublessee. It follows that neither L nor S can sue the other in actions at law for breach of the covenants of the main lease.

It does not follow that neither has any remedies against the other. It has been held that L has equitable remedies against S for breach of those covenants of which he has notice, upon the principles considered in the next section relating to the running of covenants in equity, since the requirement of privity of estate is avoided in equity. L also may assert a statutory lien or levy distress upon S's goods for non-payment of rent, where such remedies have been made available. Where the main lessee is insolvent, L may proceed directly against S for rent in an equitable proceeding. Where by statute or the terms of a lease L has the power to terminate the main lease, such termination also terminates S's interest. And if S has promised either L or T to perform the covenants of the main lease, no privity of estate is required to enable L to enforce such a promise.

The sublessee's rights against the lessor include his right to sue L for trespass if L wrongfully invades his possessory interests. Upon further tort principles, S has remedies against L for injuries received on those parts of premises remaining in L's control, or under the rule relating to "hidden defects."

By statute in a few states, a sublessee has the same rights against the lessor as he has against his sublessor.

See generally 1 A.L.P. §§ 3.57, 3.62; Cunningham §§ 6.66, 6.68; Note, 40 Colum.L.Rev. 1049 (1940).

2. Where a lessee transfers his entire interest without variations to a physical part of the demised premises, it is usually held that there has been an assignment pro tanto, although there is authority contra. 1 A.L.P. § 3.57; 2 A.L.P. § 9.6; Cunningham § 6.66.

3. In addition to those courts which, like the Massachusetts court, have held that the reservation by T in his transfer to S of a right of entry renders the transfer a sublease, some courts have held that the same result is produced by the exaction from S of covenants not found in the main lease. Id. In the latter case, even more than in the former, a strain is put upon the technical requirements of privity of estate. In both instances these qualifications seem to reflect dissatisfaction with the rigidities of the traditional distinction.

4. It is easier to find faults in the traditional distinction between an assignment and a sublease than to fashion a better substitute. Apparently under the rule announced in Jaber v. Miller, the traditional distinction may survive to the limited extent of being one factor in arriving at the parties' intention. Do you understand the meaning of the intention test? Suppose this question is put to a proper party: did you intend to execute an assignment or a sublease? One must first establish what we mean by either label if the traditional standard is gone. If laymen may be misled by the traditional distinction, may they not also be misled by the substitute? Will the two parties to a transaction have the same notion? Will intention be determined by the label the parties attach to their transaction? If one recoils from any conclusive presumption from a label, it can certainly be expected that the label would at least raise a rebuttable presumption. Suppose no label is used. What sort of evidence should one expect to find concerning the parties' intention? Consider that under any test for making the distinction, the parties to an assignment or sublease can by contract exercise considerable freedom in fashioning their respective rights and duties. Or if a landlord believes he needs to retain control over the way in which his tenant deals with his leasehold interest, it is easy enough to do so by some variant of the common covenant by a lessee not to assign or sublet without the written consent of the lessor. Does this suggest that we need no labels at all, and that we could ignore or abolish the distinction between an assignment and a sublease? With what effect?

Is the traditional distinction purely a technical, historical quirk? Do not laymen understand the import of the difference between two situations: (1) a merchant-lessee goes out of business and leaves town after transferring to B all his interest under his lease, and (2) a student under a lease for one year or more agrees to let C have his interest for one or more months in the summer?

See 1 A.L.P. § 3.57; Cunningham § 6.66; Wallace, Assignment and Sublease, 8 Ind.L.J. 359 (1933); Ferrier, Can There Be a Sublease for the Entire Unexpired Portion of a Term, 18 Calif.L.Rev. 1 (1929).

5. For recent cases which accepted the traditional distinction between assignments and subleases in rather complicated circumstances, see Urban Investment & Development Co. v. Maurice L. Rothschild & Co., 25 Ill.App.3d 546, 323 N.E.2d 588 (1975); Jensen v. O.K. Investment Corp., 29 Utah 2d 231, 507 P.2d 713 (1973). In Walgreen Arizona Drug Co. v. Plaza Center Corp., 132 Ariz. 512, 647 P.2d 643 (App.1982), the court re-asserted the traditional view in the face of an argument that it was based on "archaic formalism."

SECTION 2. CONTRACTS BETWEEN OWNERS IN FEE

A. THE ENGLISH LAW

KEPPELL v. BAILEY

Court of Chancery, 1834.
2 My. & K. 517, 39 Eng.Rep. 1042.

[Edward Kendall and Jonathan Kendall were the lessees of premises called the Beaufort Ironworks. These persons, together with the proprietors of certain other iron works, and a number of other persons, formed a joint stock company for the construction of a railroad called the Trevil Railroad. By a written instrument the above parties established a body of rules and regulations for the management of the shareholders. Included in the instrument was a provision by which the Kendalls, in consideration of the other provisions thereof, did agree for themselves, their heirs, executors, administrators, and assigns, to procure all limestone for use by them in their iron works from a certain lime quarry, and to cause such limestone to be carried from the quarry to their iron works by means of the Trevil Railroad, and to pay a stated toll for such transportation. Upon the death of the Kendalls the ownership of their iron works came into the hands of several persons, who in turn entered into a contract to sell their interest in the Beaufort Ironworks to two men named Bailey, giving the latter full notice of their obligations under the above agreement. The Baileys paid part of the purchase money and entered into possession of the iron works. Shortly thereafter they commenced the formation of a new railroad from the Beaufort Ironworks to certain other lime quarries. The shareholders of the Trevil Railroad filed a bill to restrain the Baileys from using any railroad except the Trevil Railroad for this purpose.]

The Lord Chancellor [Brougham] * * * [U]pon the best consideration which I can give to the nature of the covenant, it appears to me very clearly that the covenant does not run with the land, and therefore is not binding upon the assignees of the * * * [covenantors]. This is the opinion which I have entertained from the moment I saw it, and which further reflection has served only to confirm.

Between the estates of the occupiers of the three ironworks, and the estates or the persons of their associates in the railway speculation with whom they covenant, there is no privity, no connection whatever of which the law can take notice. There is no relation at all in point of fact, any more than in point of law. The Kendalls, for instance, upon whose covenant the present Plaintiffs rely, contending that it binds the Defendants as purchasers of the Beaufort Ironworks, did not stand in any such relation to the other shareholders, as from its nature could enure to affect the property sold by them. There was no unity of title in the estates of the contracting parties; the ironworks and the lime-pits or railway did not come to them severally from the same owner; they were not held by them severally under the same landlord; but what is of more importance, inasmuch as it is by no means clear that even the kinds of privity I have mentioned would suffice, the parties did not stand in the relation of lessor and lessee towards each other; and there is, therefore, no reversionary interest now in the covenantees to which the right claimed against the assignees of the covenantors may be annexed; and those assignees are called upon to perform the covenant solely in respect of the estate which they have purchased, and, in respect of persons who, except under that covenant, have no connection whatever with the estate. It is the case of mere strangers; it is a covenant by the owner of a messuage and land with the owner of a neighbouring limework and railroad, that he and his executors and assigns will always use that limework and railroad, for making iron at, and carrying it from, such messuage.

Whether the word "assigns" in this covenant, used as it is in a very peculiar manner several times in the deed, means assigns of the works, or only of the railway shares, has been made a question; and if it were necessary to decide it I incline much to the latter construction which, if adopted, would render it unnecessary to pursue the argument further. But I think this admits of sufficient doubt to make it more advisable that the decision should not turn upon it.

Assuming then for the present that the Kendalls covenanted for their assigns of the Beaufort Works, could they, by such a covenant with parties who had no relation whatever to those works except that of having a lime quarry, and a railway in the neighbourhood, bind all persons who should become owners of those works, either by purchase or descent, at all times to buy their lime at the quarry and carry their iron on the railway? Or could they do more, if the covenant should not be kept, then give the covenantees a right of action against themselves and recourse against their heirs and executors as far as these received assets?

Consider the question first upon principle. There are certain known incidents to property and its enjoyment; among others, certain burthens wherewith it may be affected, or rights which may be created and enjoyed over it by parties other than the owner; all which incidents are recognised by the law. In respect of possession, the property may be in one, while the reversion is in another; in respect of interest, the life estate in one, the remainder in tail in a second, and the fee in reversion in a third. So in respect of enjoyment; one may have the possession and the fee-simple, and another may have a rent issuing out of it, or the tithes of its produce, or an easement, as a right of way upon it, or of common over it. And such last incorporeal hereditament may be annexed to an estate which is wholly unconnected with the estate affected by the easement, although both estates were originally united in the same owner, and one of them was afterwards granted by him with the benefit, while the other was left subject to the burthen. All these kinds of property, however, all these holdings, are well known to the law and familiarly dealt with by its principles. But it must not therefore be supposed that incidents of a novel kind can be devised and attached to property at the fancy or caprice of any owner. It is clearly inconvenient both to the science of the law and to the public weal that such a latitude should be given. There can be no harm in allowing the fullest latitude to men in binding themselves and their representatives, that is, their assets real and personal, to answer in damages for breach of their obligations. This tends to no mischief, and is a reasonable liberty to bestow; but great detriment would arise and much confusion of rights if parties were allowed to invent new modes of holding and enjoying real property, and to impress upon their lands and tenements a peculiar character, which should follow them into all hands, however remote. Every close, every messuage, might thus be held in a several fashion; and it would hardly be possible to know what rights the acquisition of any parcel conferred, or what obligations it imposed. The right of way or of common is of a public as well as of a simple nature, and no one who sees the premises can be ignorant of what all the vicinage knows. But if one man may bind his messuage and land to take lime from a particular kiln, another may bind his to take coals from a certain pit, while a third may load his property with further obligations to employ one blacksmith's forge, or the members of one corporate body, in various operations upon the premises, besides many other restraints as infinite in variety as the imagination can conceive; for there can be no reason whatever in support of the covenant in question, which would not extend to every covenant that can be devised.

The difference is obviously very great between such a case as this and the case of covenants in a lease, whereby the demised premises are affected with certain rights in favour of the lessor. The lessor or his assignees continue in the reversion while the term lasts. The estate is not out of them, although the possession is in the lessee or his assigns. It is not at all inconsistent with the nature of property that certain things should be reserved to the reversioners all the while the term continues; it is only something taken out of the demise, some exception to the temporary surrender of the enjoyment; it is only that they retain, more or less partially, the use of what was wholly used by them before the demise, and what will again be wholly used by them when that demise is at an end. Yet even in this case, the law does not leave the reversioner the absolute licence to invent covenants which shall affect the lands in the hands of those who take by assignment of the term. The covenant must be of such a nature as to "inhere in the land," to use the language of some of the cases; or "it must concern the demised premises and the mode of occupying them," as it is down in others; "it must be *quodammodo* annexed and appurtenant to them," as one authority has it; or, as another says, "it must both concern the thing demised, and tend to support it and support the reversioner's estate." Within such limits restraints upon the land demised may be imposed, which shall follow into the hands of persons who are strangers to the contract of lease, and who only become privy to the lessor through the estate which they take by assignment in the demised premises. But this is no more than saying that, within such limits, the owner of the land may retain to himself and his assignees of the reversion a certain controul over, or use of, the property which remains in himself, or which he has conveyed to those assignees; and that he may so retain it, into whose hands soever, as lessee, the temporary possession may have come. Even he, the continuing owner, is confined within certain limits by the view which the law takes of the nature of property; and if beyond those limits he were to imagine a stipulation, the covenant in which he should embody it would not run with the land, but only bind the lessee personally and his representatives. * * *

If such would be its construction at law, does the notice which the purchaser had of its existence alter the case in this Court, upon an application for an injunction? or would it, upon the application of a co-relative and co-extensive nature, for a specific performance? Certainly not. The knowledge by an assignee of an estate, that his assignor had assumed to bind others than the law authorises him to affect by his contracts—had attempted to create a real burthen upon property, which is inconsistent with the nature of that property, and unknown to the principles of the law, cannot bind such assignee by affecting his conscience. If it did, then the illegality would be of no consequence; and however wild the attempt might be to create new kinds of holding and new species of estate, and however repugnant such devices might be to the rules of law, they would prove perfectly successful in the result, because equity would enable their authors to prevail; nay, not only to compass their object, but to obtain a great deal more than they could at law, were their contrivances ever so accordant with strict legal principle. This Court would be occupied in compelling persons by way of injunction and decree to perform covenants which the law repudiated, and for the breach of which no damages could ever be recovered. * * *

The injunction must, therefore, be dissolved. * * *

Note

The idea that the absence of privity of estate (meaning a landlord-tenant relation) between covenantor and covenantee is a basis for invoking a doctrine against creating "novel incidents" of ownership naturally makes one wonder about the meaning and purpose of such a policy. It is most obviously vindicated in respect to the doctrine of estates, where it seems to be conceded and has on occasion been held that one is not free to fashion some new kind of estate to suit his dispositive fancy. Since we know that new kinds of estates were in history fashioned by the courts to meet the needs of the time, the policy is to be understood not as one against change in law, but rather that the forms of ownership are not open to individual determination.

The same policy encountered more difficulty in respect to easements, which may seem by their nature to contemplate such specific uses of land as suit the needs of interested parties. But in England the policy was served by the notion that only certain established kinds of easements were to be recognized. The fact that the courts came to recognize enough kinds of easements to serve most of the needs does not wholly subvert the policy. In this country the policy has had little recognition except as it may clothe decisions reached on other grounds. See Conard, Easement Novelties, 30 Calif.L.Rev. 125 (1942).

In respect to covenants, the policy is submerged in England in the announced rule that the burdens of covenants will not run with ownership in fee. If anyone is still concerned about the true ground for such a rule, it is pertinent to ask what more ultimate policy lies behind the policy against novel incidents. Does the opinion in Keppell v. Bailey indicate the answer? Do you have any reason to doubt whether such a policy is relevant to current American systems of ownership and conveyancing?

TULK v. MOXHAY

Court of Chancery, 1848.
2 Phil. 774, 41 Eng. Reprint 1143.

In the year 1808 the plaintiff, being then the owner in fee of the vacant piece of ground in Leicester Square, as well as of several of the houses forming the square, sold the piece of ground by the description of "Leicester Square Garden or Pleasure Ground, with the equestrian statue then standing in the centre thereof, and the iron railing and stone work round the same," to one Elms in fee: and the deed of conveyance contained a covenant by Elms, for himself, his heirs, and assigns, with the plaintiff, his heirs, executors, and administrators:

"That Elms, his heirs, and assigns, should, and would from time to time, and at all times thereafter at his and their own costs and charges, keep and maintain the said piece of ground and Square Garden, and the iron railing round the same in its then form, and in sufficient and proper repair as a Square Garden and Pleasure Ground, in an open state, uncovered with any buildings, in neat and ornamental order; and that it should be lawful for the inhabitants of Leicester Square, tenants of the plaintiff, on payment of a reasonable rent for the same, to have keys at their own expense and the privilege of admission therewith at any time or times into the said Square Garden and Pleasure Ground."

The piece of land so conveyed passed by divers mesne conveyances into the hands of the defendant, whose purchase deed contained no similar covenant with the vendor: but he admitted that he had purchased with notice of the covenant in the deed of 1808.

The defendant having manifested an intention to alter the character of the Square Garden, and asserted a right, if he thought fit, to build upon it, the plaintiff, who still remained owner of several houses in the Square, filed this bill for an injunction; and an injunction was granted by the Master of the Rolls, to restrain the defendant from converting or using the piece of ground and Square Garden, and the iron railing round the same, to or for any other purpose than as a Square Garden and Pleasure Ground in an open state, and uncovered with buildings.

On a motion, now made, to discharge that order.

THE LORD CHANCELLOR. * * * That this court has jurisdiction to enforce a contract between the owner of land and his neighbour purchasing a part of it, that the latter shall either use or abstain from using the land purchased in a particular way, is what I never knew disputed. Here there is no question about the contract; the owner of certain houses in the Square sells the land adjoining, with a covenant from the purchaser not to use it for any other purpose than as a Square Garden. And it is now contended, not that the vendee could violate that contract, but that he might sell the piece of land, and that the purchaser from him may violate it without this court having any power to interfere. If that were so, it would be impossible for an owner of land to sell part of it without incurring the risk of rendering what he retains worthless. It is said that, the covenant being one which does not run with the land, this court cannot enforce it; but the question is, not whether the covenant runs with the land, but whether a party shall be permitted to use the land in the manner inconsistent with the contract entered into by his vendor, and with notice of which he purchased. Of course, the price would be affected by the covenant, and nothing could be more inequitable than that the original purchaser should be able to sell the property the next day for a greater price, in consideration of the assignee being allowed to escape from the liability which he had himself undertaken.

That the question does not depend upon whether the covenant runs with the land, is evident from this, that if there was a mere agreement and no covenant, this court would enforce it against a party purchasing with notice of it; for if an equity is attached to the property by the owner, no one purchasing with notice of that equity can stand in a different situation from the party from whom he purchased. There are not only cases before the Vice-Chancellor of England, in which he considered that doctrine as not in dispute; but looking at the ground on which Lord Eldon disposed of the case of the Duke of Bedford v. The Trustees of the British Museum, 2 My. & K. 552, it is impossible to suppose that he entertained any doubt of it.   *   *   *

With respect to the observations of Lord Brougham in Keppell v. Bailey [2 M. & K. 547] he never could have meant to lay down, that this court would not enforce an equity attached to land by the owner, unless under such circumstances as would maintain an action at law. If that be the result of his observations, I can only say that I cannot coincide with it.

I think the cases cited before the Vice-Chancellor and this decision of the Master of the Rolls perfectly right, and, therefore, that the motion to discharge this injunction must be refused with costs.

Notes

1. "The doctrine of that Case [Tulk v. Moxhay], rightly considered appears to me to be either an extension in equity of the doctrine of Spencer's Case to another line of cases, or else an extension in equity of the doctrine of negative easements; such, for instance, as a right to the access of light which prevents the owner of the servient tenement from building so as to obstruct the light. * * * Where there is a negative covenant expressed or implied, as, for instance, not be build so as to obstruct a view, or not to use a piece of land otherwise than as a garden, the Court interferes on one or other of the above grounds. This is an equitable doctrine, establishing an exception to the rules of Common Law which did not treat such a covenant as running with the land, and it does not matter whether it proceeds on analogy to a covenant running with the land or on analogy to an easement. The purchaser took the estate subject to the equitable burden, with the qualification that if he acquired the legal estate for value without notice he was freed from the burden. The qualification, however, did not affect the nature of the burden; the notice was required merely to avoid the effect of the legal estate, and did not create the right, and if the purchaser took only an equitable estate he took subject to the burden, whether he had notice or not." Jessel, M.R., in London and South Western Railway Co. v. Gomm, 20 Ch.Div. 562 (1882).

2. Tulk v. Moxhay followed Keppell v. Bailey by a lapse of only fourteen years. Note how easily the court was able to turn around on its willingness to do in equity what could not be done at law.

3. *Affirmative Burdens.* The language of the promise in Tulk v. Moxhay was put in affirmative terms, but the promise was enforced by way of injunction against a use contrary to that promised. In any event Tulk v. Moxhay is regarded as authority for the enforcement in equity of restrictive covenants between landowners. What about affirmative covenants which cannot be enforced by a restrictive decree? Clearly they cannot be enforced in England by any action at law. Doubt remained for a time about enforcement by specific

performance or mandatory injunction, but the matter was finally settled that such equitable remedies would be denied. Haywood v. Brunswick Bldg. Soc., 8 Q.B.D. 403 (1881). The reason for this rule has not been made clear. It has been suggested that it lies in the administrative difficulty in supervising the performance of such promises.

4. Will the burden of a covenant run, at law or in equity, where the benefit is in gross? In London County Council v. Allen, L.R. [1914] 3 K.B. 642, the council conveyed to Allen, who covenanted not to build upon certain designated portions of the land conveyed, which were to be reserved for the making of roads. Allen conveyed to Mrs. Allen, who built three houses on the restricted area. The council sued for a mandatory injunction for the removal of the houses. It was agreed that the burden of the covenant would not run at law so as to bind assigns. The court held that it also would not run in equity under the doctrine of Tulk v. Moxhay, because the council owned no land for the benefit of which the covenant was created. Since the English courts refuse to recognize easements in gross, the result in this case is not surprising.

5. *Running of Benefits.* The objections to the running of burdens have not been raised against the running of the benefit of covenants, and such covenants will run with the land of the promisee provided they touch and concern that land. Megarry & Wade, The Law of Real Property 720 (2d ed. 1959).

6. The delimitations noted above mark out with some degree of clarity the dimensions of the English law on the running of covenants between owners in fee. Do we conclude that the burden of covenants will not run at law, but that the burden of restrictive covenants will run in equity? Should the main emphasis be on the difference in result at law and in equity, or on the difference between restrictive and affirmative burdens? It may be relevant to that question to ask: how important is it that the burden of a restrictive covenant will not run at law if it can be specifically enforced in equity? Maybe the most important feature of the English law is that affirmative burdens will not run either at law or in equity.

Our next inquiry is into the status of the American law on this matter.

B. THE AMERICAN LAW

WHEELER v. SCHAD

Supreme Court of Nevada, 1872.
7 Nev. 213.

By the Court, LEWIS, C.J. On the fifth day of June, A.D. 1862, M.S. Hurd, Ferdinand Dunker and Peter Bossell, being the owners and in possession of a certain mill-site and water privilege, regularly conveyed to Charles Doscher, Charles Itgen, Charles D. McWilliams and William C. Duval a portion thereof, together with the water privilege connected therewith. The grantees entered into possession and erected a quartz mill on the premises thus conveyed. The stream was first conducted to the mill of Hurd and associates, and thence to that of their grantees. On the eleventh day of the same month, the respective parties entered into an agreement which, after reciting the necessity of constructing a dam across the river and a flume to conduct the water to their several mills, provided that the dam and flume should be constructed at their joint expense, Hurd and his associates, however, agreeing to pay five hundred dollars more than one-half the cost, and the other parties the balance; the dam and flume, when completed, to be owned and enjoyed jointly in equal shares. It was also agreed that they should be kept in good order and repair at the joint and equal expense of the respective parties. Some time after the construction of these works, Wheeler succeeded to the interest of Bossell, and he, together with Hurd and Dunker, continued in the ownership and remained in possession of the first mill, known as the Eureka.

Doscher and his associates having mortgaged their mill some time between January and March, 1868, put the assignee of the mortgage (defendant) in possession, who continued to hold the property under the mortgage until he obtained the absolute title by virtue of foreclosure and sale under his mortgage, which occurred in October, A.D. 1868. Early in the year 1868, while the defendant was in possession under the mortgage, the dam and flume were damaged to such an extent that it became necessary to make extensive repairs upon them. Before proceeding with the work, the plaintiffs notified the defendant of their damaged condition, and requested him to unite with them in making the proper repairs. The defendant agreed that the work should proceed, and requested the plaintiff Wheeler to superintend it and "take charge of the workmen." The repairs were made in due time, at an expense of three thousand five hundred dollars, one-half of which is now sought to be recovered. Judgment for defendant; plaintiffs appeal; and it is argued on their behalf: first, that the defendant is liable on the agreement entered into between the defendant's grantors and the plaintiffs; and secondly, if not, that he is so upon his own agreement with the plaintiffs, authorizing the work to be done.

To maintain the first point, it is contended that the deed of conveyance of the mill-site to the grantors of the defendant and the agreement referred to, should be held to be one instrument; that the stipulations of the latter should be engrafted upon the deed and held to be covenants running with the land. But nothing is clearer than that the two instruments are utterly disconnected, as completely independent of each other as they possibly could be. The deed was executed on the fifth day of June, at which time it does not appear that there was any thought of an agreement to construct or keep in repair any dam or flume. There is no evidence that such a project was in contemplation even by any of the parties, much less that any agreement of this character was in view. It was not, in fact, executed until six days afterwards, and there can be no presumption other than that it was not contemplated until such time. Had it entered into the transaction; had it been understood between the parties at the time of the conveyance that such contract should be executed, there might be some ground for the claim that the agreement and deed constituted but one transaction, and therefore should be construed as one instrument; but unfortunately for the appellants, there is no such showing in the case. If, in fact, the agreement did not enter into the conveyance, or was not contemplated at the time, it is of no consequence how soon afterwards it may have been executed; a day or an hour would as completely separate the instruments and make them independent of each other, as a year. It is impossible, under the evidence in this case, to merge the deed and agreement into one instrument, and construe them as if executed simultaneously.

Unless they constituted one instrument or transaction, it cannot be claimed that the covenants of the agreement run with the land so as to charge the grantee of the covenantor. To make a covenant run with the land, it is necessary, first, that it should relate to and concern the land; and secondly, a covenant imposing a burden on the land can only be created where there is privity of estate between the covenantor and covenantee. Whether a covenant for the benefit of land can be created where there is no privity is still questioned by some authorities; but it was held in Packenham's case, determined as early as the time of Edward III, that a stranger might covenant with the owner in such manner as to attach the benefit of a covenant to the land and have it run in favor of the assignees of the covenantee; and the rule there established has since been frequently recognized as law, although questioned by text writers, and the broad doctrine sought to be maintained that privity of estate is absolutely essential in all cases, to give one man a right of action against another upon a covenant, when there is no privity of contract.

Whether the rule announced in Packenham's case be law or not, is not necessary to determine here, for all the courts hold that the *burden* of a covenant can only be imposed upon land so as to run with it when there is privity of estate between the covenantor and covenantee. It was said by Lord Kenyon, in Webb v. Russell, 3 Term, 393, that "it is not sufficient that a covenant is concerning the land, but in order to make it run with the land there must be a privity of estate between the covenanting parties." That was the law long prior to the time of Kenyon, and has never been doubted, although perhaps cases may be found where an erroneous application of the rule has been made. To render a covenant binding on the assignee of the covenantor, it must therefore not only be meant to bind his estate as well as his person, but the relation between the parties must be such as to render the intention effectual—that is, there must be privity of estate between the covenanting parties. To constitute such relation, they must both have an interest in the land sought to be charged by the covenant. It is said their position must be such as would formerly have given rise to the relation of tenure. A covenant real is, and can only be, an incident to land. It cannot pass independent of it. It adheres to the land, is maintained by it, is in fact a legal parasite, created out of and deriving life from the land to which it adheres. It follows, that the person in whose favor a covenant is made must have an interest in the land charged with it; for he can only get the covenant through, and as an incident to, the land to which it is attached. * * *

Did the plaintiffs in this case have any estate in the land owned by the defendant at the time this agreement was entered into? It is not even claimed they had. Nor did the agreement itself create any such interest. There is no attempt in it to convey any estate to them, nor a word of grant in the whole instrument. It is a mere contract for the erection of a dam, which does not appear to be on the premises either of the plaintiffs or defendant, and a flume to conduct water to their respective mills, and to maintain them in good order. Suppose the grantors of the defendant had entered into an agreement binding themselves to build the dam and flume for the benefit of the plaintiffs, for a stipulated sum of money; will it be claimed that such an agreement could be held a covenant running with land owned by such grantors, and which was entirely distinct from that upon which the work was to be performed? We apprehend not. Where the distinction, as to its capacity to run with the land, between such a covenant and that entered into here, where instead of compensation in money the defendant's grantors were to receive a benefit from the improvement itself?

As the grantors had no estate in the land owned by the defendant when the agreement was entered into, but were mere strangers to it, the case comes directly within the rule announced by Lord Coke, and very uniformly followed both by the English and American courts since his time. Webb v. Russell, 3 Term, and Stokes v. Russell, Id.; Hurd v. Curtis, 19 Pick. 459; Plymouth v. Carver, 16 Pick. 183. See also an elaborate review of the question in 1 Smith's Leading Cases, note to Spencer's Case; 2 Washburn on Real Property, 16 Pick. 183. *   *   *

There being no privity of estate, or of contract between the parties, it only remains to determine whether the defendant is holden on his own promise made to the plaintiffs. First, the action is not based on any such promise or contract. The complaint is framed with reference exclusively to the written agreement, and upon that alone relief is sought. Nothing is charged in the complaint tending to charge the defendant with any personal obligation, except that the repairs were made with his knowledge. As the complaint does not allege any personal promise or contract on the part of the defendant, it would hardly be conformable to the rules of law to award relief upon the assumption of its existence. No personal promise or agreement by the defendant could properly be proven under the complaint; for proof is only admissible to establish the case made by the allegations of the pleading.

But again, if any such promise was made, it is undoubtedly barred by the statute of limitations, not being evidenced by writing. It cannot be said that the defendant adopted the written agreement as his own, and thereby bound himself to it, for it is not shown that he knew of its existence. But even if he knew of it, the only evidence of his obligation upon it was in parol, and therefore it cannot with any degree of reason be said that if he had directly adopted the contract by a parol promise, his obligation would not be barred by the limitation prescribed for parol contracts.

The judgment below must be affirmed.

CARLSON v. LIBBY

Supreme Court of Errors of Connecticut, 1950.
137 Conn. 362, 77 A.2d 332.

INGLIS, Judge. The parties in this case are in dispute as to what right, if any, the plaintiff has to the use of a railroad siding which is owned by the defendant and extends in part over the plaintiff's land. The finding, in which no changes may be made, discloses that the controversy arises out of a deed given by Cheney Brothers to Valvoline Oil Company on April 16, 1921. At that time Valvoline Oil Company owned property in Manchester which abutted property of Cheney Brothers on the east. The land of both was bounded on the south by the right of way of the New York, New Haven and Hartford Railroad Company. The deed in question conveyed to Valvoline Oil Company and its successors and assigns "all such rights as are necessary and convenient for it to have for the proper construction and maintenance of a railroad siding for trackage purposes over" a described triangular tract of the grantor's land adjacent to the railroad property. From the description, it is apparent that the purpose of the parties was to permit Valvoline Oil Company to construct and maintain a siding extending westerly from its property over the strip described and then over the property of the railroad company to connect with the main tracks of the railroad.

Following the description, the deed contains these provisions: "It is understood and agreed that the above grant is hereby made and accepted subject to the following conditions: 1. That the right granted aforesaid shall continue only so long as the said trackage is used for car service facilities in connection with the use of the property [contiguous] on the East to the above described [triangular] tract belonging to the Grantee, its successors and assigns, and if at any time, the said trackage is removed, abandoned, or the use thereof discontinued by the owner of said contiguous property on the East as aforesaid, then and thereupon the above grant is to become null, void and of no effect. 2. That the owners, whomsoever they may be, of the land contiguous on the North to the above described [triangular] tract shall be given at all times without charge therefor the use of said siding or [tract] for the loading or unloading opposite their respective properties such Railroad cars as may be necessary and convenient for them."

The plaintiff is now the owner of the triangular tract described in that deed and of the land contiguous on the north. He acquired title from Cheney Brothers by two deeds dated December 5, 1938 and February 5, 1947, respectively. In each of these conveyances it is stated that the land conveyed is "subject to an easement for and in connection with the construction, maintenance and repair" of the railroad siding described in the deed to Valvoline Oil Company. Neither deed makes any specific reference to the right of Cheney Brothers to use the siding, but the land was conveyed together with its appurtenances.

On August 28, 1942, Valvoline Oil Company conveyed to the defendant its property "Together with all such rights, title and interest which the grantor * * * may have, or claim to have, or are, or as may be appurtenant to the above described pieces or parcels of land see *   *   * deed of Cheney Brothers to the Valvoline Oil Company *   *   * dated April 16th., 1921. *   *   *" The record is devoid of any finding as to when the siding was built, but it was built by Valvoline Oil Company as contemplated in the deed of April 16, 1921. It extends from the defendant's land westerly across the land of the plaintiff about seventy feet and continues for several hundred feet on the land of the railroad company until it connects with the main tracks of the latter. The defendant now owns, maintains, repairs and uses it. There is still in effect a contract dated October 28, 1942, between the defendant and the railroad company whereby the latter agreed to continue to treat the siding in question as a sidetrack and to switch to and from it carload freight consigned to and from the defendant. This contract provides that the defendant shall maintain the siding in proper condition, that he shall not assign or lease or otherwise convey any right to its use except with the written consent of the railroad company and that the contract is terminable on thirty days' notice by either party.

The plaintiff is engaged in the trucking business, and it is necessary and convenient for him to use the siding for loading and unloading railroad cars on the premises which he acquired from Cheney Brothers. The railroad company is willing to "spot" cars on the siding for him, but only with the permission of the defendant. The defendant refuses to grant that permission unless the plaintiff will pay him a consideration for the privilege.

The essence of the deed of April 16, 1921, was that Cheney Brothers conveyed to Valvoline Oil Company, its successors and assigns, a conditional easement to construct and maintain the siding and that the grantee covenanted with the grantor that the owners, whoever they might be, of the land then owned by the grantor to the north of the strip which was made subject to the easement might use the siding without charge. It is upon this covenant that the plaintiff predicates his case. That it was the intent of the parties that the provision was to be construed as a covenant rather than a condition is apparent from all of the attendant circumstances. The principal question in the case, therefore, is whether this covenant was a covenant real. An affirmative answer depends on the existence of two factors: first, that the benefit of the covenant runs with the land now owned by the plaintiff, and, second, that its burden runs with the easement now enjoyed by the defendant.

Whether a promise with respect to the use of land is a covenant real as distinguished from a personal covenant depends upon the intent of the parties to the promise, to be determined in the light of the attendant circumstances. If it touches the land involved to the extent that it materially affects the value of that land, it is generally to be interpreted as a covenant which runs with the land. *   *   *

So far as the benefit of the covenant in question is concerned, it is to be noted that it provides in terms that those who are given the right to use the siding are "the owners, whomsoever they may be, of the land contiguous on the North." On its face, the benefit of the covenant is not limited to Cheney Brothers. It is extended to any person who might in the future own the land then owned by Cheney Brothers. Moreover, the right to use the siding covenanted for was one which clearly enhanced the value of the covenantee's land. It was, therefore, a covenant which ran with the land and came to the plaintiff as an appurtenance when he took title to the land. * * * There are two cases in other jurisdictions which are closely analogous to the present case in that each of them involved a covenant, on the part of a railroad company, to run a sidetrack to serve land of the covenantee. They are Lydick v. Baltimore & O.R. Co., 17 W.Va. 427, and Whalen v. Baltimore & O.R. Co., 108 Md. 11, 69 A. 390, 17 L.R.A.,N.S., 130. In both cases it was held that the covenant ran with the land. Clearly, the plaintiff in the instant case as the grantee of Cheney Brothers is entitled to enforce the covenant.

On the question whether the burden of the covenant has fallen upon the defendant, it should be noted in the first place that, by the fact that Valvoline Oil Company accepted the deed in which it was stated that it agreed that Cheney Brothers should have the right to use the siding, the oil company bound itself to that covenant even though it did not sign the document. Hubbard v. Ensign, 46 Conn. 576, 582; Restatement, 5 Property § 532, comment c. The oil company having bound itself to the promise, it was not essential, for the covenant to be binding on its successors and assigns, that the oil company should so agree in express terms. 7 Thompson, Real Property (Perm.Ed.) § 3625.

In approaching the question whether the covenant with which we are concerned in so far as it is a burden is a covenant real, it must first be determined what the land was with which it was to run. The promise was made not in connection with the transfer of the fee of any land. It was made in connection with the grant of an easement. The burden of a covenant will run with land only when the transaction of which the covenant is a part includes a transfer of an interest in land which is either benefited or burdened thereby, or the covenant is made in the adjustment of the mutual relationships arising out of the existence of an easement held by one of the parties in the land of the other. Restatement, 5 Property § 534. If it is made in connection with a transfer of property, as was the situation in this case, it is not essential that the transfer be of the fee to the land. It is adequate if it is the grant of an easement. Restatement, 5 Property § 534, comment e; * * *. Accordingly, the fact that the covenant made by Valvoline Oil Company was made in connection with a grant to it of an easement rather than a conveyance of land does not preclude the covenant from being real rather than personal. If the burden of it runs with anything, it runs with the easement of the right to construct and maintain the siding.

To determine whether the covenant does run with the easement we seek the intent of the parties. * * * The covenant is not in express terms made binding on the successors and assigns of Valvoline Oil Company. It is apparent, however, that it touched the easement in the sense that the right to use the siding promised to Cheney Brothers and its successors in ownership diminished the value of Valvoline Oil Company's easement itself. It was the design of the parties to the deed of

April 16, 1921, that the siding should be used by them mutually. It could hardly have been their intent that the right of Cheney Brothers and its successors to use the siding should be cut off by the conveying of the easement by the Valvoline Oil Company and yet the right of the oil company's grantees to use it should continue. Clearly, the intent of the parties was that the burden of the covenant should run with the easement, and we therefore conclude that it did so run. * * *

From the foregoing it is apparent that the benefit of the covenant runs with the land owned by the plaintiff and the burden of it runs with the easement now enjoyed by the defendant. Accordingly, the covenant is a covenant real.

We come to the question of the proper construction of the language of the covenant. The defendant contends that, inasmuch as the easement granted was the right to construct and maintain the siding on the land of Cheney Brothers only, when the covenant provided that Cheney Brothers should have the use "of said siding" it referred solely to so much of the siding as was on Cheney Brothers' land. This contention overlooks the fact that earlier in the deed the grant of the easement was stated to be for the purpose of "the proper construction and maintenance of a railroad siding." A siding, at least a proper siding, is a spur track making a connection with some railroad affording communication with a market. * * * An isolated piece of track not connected with a railroad could hardly be referred to as a siding. It is clear, therefore, that when the covenant speaks of a siding it refers to an entire track connected with the main tracks of the railroad.

The defendant makes the further contention that no declaratory judgment should have been entered in the case concerning that portion of the track which is on the railroad company's land because that company is not a party. The declaratory judgment entered adjudges that the plaintiff has the right to use without charge the siding located on his property for loading and unloading cars and also the right to use without charge, in order to accomplish that purpose, the siding or track owned by the defendant on land of the railroad company. That is, it adjudges only the obligations of the defendant under the covenant. It does not purport to adjudicate any obligations of the railroad company.

The judgment enjoins the defendant from interfering with the plaintiff's right to use the siding and orders him to grant such permission as is necessary for the plaintiff to make use of that right. Here again no obligations of the railroad company are adjudicated. Specifically, it does not require the railroad company to waive the provisions of its contract with the defendant that he may not assign his right to use the siding without the railroad company's written permission or that the contract may be terminated by the railroad company on thirty days' notice. The relief granted is suitable in equity to compel the performance by the defendant of his obligation under the covenant.

There is no error.

In this opinion the other Judges concurred.

Notes and Questions

1. In Carlson v. Libby why did not the language which the court said created a covenant (rather than a condition) really create an easement appurtenant to the land "on the North"? Compare Martin v. Music, supra page 522.

2. Why was a covenant necessary to allow Cheney Brothers to make the stated use of their own land?

3. Cook conveyed land to Hull, together with the privilege of using and improving a mill pond on land retained by Cook, and together with access to any part of the land on which the pond was located to dig and carry away any part of the soil. Hull conveyed the same premises to the plaintiff. Later Cook covenanted with the plaintiff, his heirs and assigns, that he would draw off his pond in the months of August and September to give the plaintiff an opportunity of digging and carrying out mud from the pond. The plaintiff sued for breach of this agreement by the defendant, successor in interest of Cook. Held, for the plaintiff. Morse v. Aldrich, 19 Pick. (Mass.) 449 (1837).

Do you see any basis for distinguishing this case from Wheeler v. Schad, supra?

4. On the requirement of privity between the contracting parties see: Clark, Covenants and Interests Running with the Land 116–137 and App. III (2d ed. 1947); 2 A.L.P. § 9.11; 5 Powell ¶ 674; Restatement, §§ 534, 548; Cunningham § 8.18.

5. *Running of Benefits.* It has been noted that the English courts permit the running of the benefit of a covenant between owners of land in fee so that a successor of the covenantee can enforce the covenant either at law or in equity. See Note 5 page 633, supra. Since a number of American courts have permitted the running of the burden of such a covenant only if "privity of estate" between the contracting parties is present, one might infer, in the light of the English experience, that such a requirement is not imposed for the running of the benefit. Any policy which has ever been declared in support of the privity requirement relates to the effect of the burden of a covenant as an encumbrance on land. No policy is perceived for restricting the running of the benefit of covenants which are intended to run and which touch and concern the land. There is authority for such a proposition, that is, that privity of estate between the contracting parties is not required for the running of benefits. This is the position taken in Section 548 of the Restatement. A recent case so holding is City of Reno v. Matley, 79 Nev. 49, 378 P.2d 256 (1963). See also the dictum in Wheeler v. Schad, supra, page 635. But there is authority to the contrary. In fact the courts seldom analyze the problem in terms of a separate consideration of the running of benefits and burdens. 2 A.L.P. § 9.11; Cunningham § 8.19.

6. *Vertical Privity.* Whatever view a court may follow concerning the existence or nature of a requirement of privity of estate between a promisor and promisee, it is generally conceded that, in order for the burden of a covenant to bind a successor to the promisor, not only must the burden touch and concern land of the promisor, but the successor must succeed to the promisor's estate in that land. Strictly speaking, the covenant runs not with the land, but with the promisor's estate in the land. Most often this rule has been applied in the lessor-lessee relation in application of the traditional distinction between an assignment and a sublease. The requisite privity exists where the promisor's estate passes to his heirs, his devisees, as well as to purchasers under a sale, including a judicial sale. See 2 A.L.P. § 9.15. In Old Dominion Iron & Steel Corp. v.

Virginia Electric & Power Co., 215 Va. 658, 212 S.E.2d 715 (1975), it was held that a vendee under a contract to purchase burdened land was not bound by a promise respecting such land.

Where only a geographical portion of the promisor's land passes to a successor, the assignee will be proportionately liable so long as he succeeds to a portion of the land which the covenant touches and concerns. Sometimes difficulties are encountered in making such an apportionment. 2 A.L.P. § 9.15.

When a promisor transfers his estate, it is arguable that he still remains in privity of contract with the promisee. As you have already learned, a lessor remains liable on his promise after a transfer of his estate. But courts have departed from this principle in respect to promises between owners in fee, finding an implied release of the promisor by way of construing the terms of the promise to continue only so long as the promisor retains his estate in the land. Id. § 9.18.

In respect to the running of the benefit of covenants, some courts have been more liberal in imposing privity requirements than in cases involving the running of burdens, and have allowed a life tenant or a lessee to enforce the benefit, on the theory that the benefit of a covenant is attached to the possession of the promisee's estate, so that any assignment which carries a possessory interest will suffice. See Old Dominion Iron & Steel Corp. v. Virginia Elec. & Power Co., supra. But one who acquires a benefitted estate by adverse possession is not in privity with the promisee and gains no benefit of the covenant. 2 A.L.P. § 9.20; Cunningham § 8.17.

Upon assignment of his estate by a promisee, he is treated as having also impliedly assigned his contract rights in respect to future performance and can no longer enforce the promisee. Id. § 9.19.

TRUSTEES OF COLUMBIA COLLEGE v. LYNCH, 70 N.Y. 440 (1877). An agreement was entered into between adjacent landowners whereby one of them, Beers, in consideration of similar reciprocal covenants, agreed for himself, his heirs, assigns and tenants, not to use or permit the use of his land for any business purpose. Lynch acquired title to Beers' land and erected a building thereon. Other defendants, tenants of Lynch, used portions of his building for business offices. Plaintiffs, parties to the agreement, sued to restrain the business operations. Judgment for defendants below was reversed on appeal. Part of the court's opinion follows:

"The purpose and intent of the parties to the agreement is apparent from its terms preceded by the recital. The agreement recites the ownership by the respective parties of adjacent premises particularly described, and these constitute the subject-matter of the mutual covenants. There was no privity of estate, or community of interest between the parties, but each could, by grant, create an easement in his own lands for the benefit of the lands owned by the other, and the purpose of the agreement was to create mutual easements, negative in their character, for the benefit of the lands of each. It was the design to impose mutual and corresponding restrictions upon the premises belonging to each and thus to secure a uniformity in the structure and position of buildings upon the entire premises, and to reserve the lots for, and confine their use to, first-class dwellings, to the exclusion of trades and all business, and all structures which would derogate from their value for private residences. The purpose clearly disclosed was, by the restrictions mutually imposed by the owners respectively upon the use of their several properties, to make the lots more available and desirable as sites for residences, and the agreement professes to, and does in terms, impose, for the common benefit, the restrictions in perpetuity, and to bind the heirs and assigns of the respective covenantors. This should be construed as a grant by each to the other in fee of a negative easement in the lands owned by the covenantors. An easement in favor of, and for the benefit of lands owned by third persons, can be created by grant, and a covenant by the owner, upon a good consideration, to use, or to refrain from using, his premises in a particular manner, for the benefit of premises owned by the covenantor, is, in effect, the grant of an easement, and the right to the enjoyment of it will pass as appurtenant to the premises in respect of which it was created. * * * The right sought to be enforced here is an easement, or, as it is sometimes called, an amenity, and consists in restraining the owner from doing that with, and upon, his property which, but for the grant or covenant, he might lawfully have done, and hence is called a negative easement, as distinguished from that class of easements which compels the owner to suffer something to be done upon his property by another. (Wash. on Easements, 5.) Easements of all kinds may be created and exist in favor of any third person, irrespective of any privity of estate or community of interest between the parties; and, in this respect, there is no distinction between negative easements and those rights that are more generally known as easements as a way, etc. * * *

"It is strenuously urged, in behalf of the defendants and respondents, that there was no privity of estate between the mutual covenantors and covenantees, in respect of the premises owned by them respectively, and which were the subjects of the covenants and agreements, and that the covenants did not therefore run with the lands, binding the grantees, and subjecting them to a personal liability thereon. This may be conceded for all the purposes of this action. It is of no importance whether an action at law could be maintained against the grantees of Beers, as upon a covenant running with the land and binding them. Whether it was a covenant running with the land or a collateral covenant, or a covenant in gross, or whether an action at law could be sustained upon it, is not material as affecting the jurisdiction of a court of equity, or the right of the owners of the dominant tenement to relief upon a disturbance of the easements. * * *

"Here each successive grantee, from Beers, the covenantor, down to and including the defendant Lynch, the present owner, not only had notice of the covenant, and all equities growing out of the same, but took their title in terms subject to it, and impliedly agreeing to observe it. It would be unreasonable and unconscientious to hold the grantees absolved from the covenant in equity for the technical reason assigned, that it did not run with the land, so as to give an action at law. A distinguished judge answered a like objection in a similar case by saying, in substance, that, if an action at law could not be maintained, that was an additional reason for entertaining jurisdiction in equity and preventing injustice. The action can be maintained for the establishment and enforcement of a negative easement created by the deed of the original proprietor, affecting the use of the premises now owned and occupied by the defendants, of which they had notice, and subject to which they took title. There is no equity or reason for making a servitude of the character of that claimed by the plaintiffs in the lands of the defendant, an exception to the general rule which charges lands in the hands of a purchaser with notice with all existing equities, easements, and servitudes. The rule and its application does not depend upon the character or classification of the equities claimed, but upon the position and equitable obligation of the purchaser. The language of courts and of judges has been very uniform and very decided upon this subject, and all agree that whoever purchases lands upon which the owner has imposed an easement of any kind, or created a charge which would be enforced in equity against him, takes the title subject to all easements, equities and charges however created, of which he has notice." * * *

Note

Compare the English court's analysis of the running of burdens in equity in London & S.W. Ry. v. Gomm, 20 Ch.Div. 562 (1882), Note 1 page 632 supra.

Not all American courts have explained the running of burdens in equity in the same terms as those offered in Trustees of Columbia College v. Lynch. Their analysis seems to be purely contractual, that is, that a court is merely granting a specific performance of a contract concerning land. Usually it makes no difference which theory is adopted. But if a covenant is treated as creating a property interest in the nature of an easement, which is the view more widely expressed, then there is a special significance in the requirement that a successor to a covenantor must have had notice of the covenant. If the promisee of a covenant has a property interest, must the promise not only be in writing to satisfy the Statute of Frauds (See 2 A.L.P. § 9.25), but is the instrument containing the promise subject to the requirements of the American recording laws, so that if the instrument is recorded, a subsequent purchaser of the burdened land will take with constructive notice of it, or if it is not recorded, he will not be bound without actual notice of the covenant? Without pursuing here the intricacies of the recording laws in this regard, which are reserved for a later chapter, most courts proceed on the assumption that covenants enforceable in equity are for these purposes to be treated as property interests. See 2 A.L.P. § 9.24; Restatement § 539; Cunningham § 8.22.

Consider also how the nature of such interests is involved where the question is presented as to who is entitled to compensation when land burdened by a covenant is taken in an eminent domain proceeding. See note page 686 infra.

To the extent that covenants are treated as creating equitable burdens or servitudes upon land, the emphasis given in Tulk v. Moxhay upon the requirement of notice to a subsequent purchaser falls into better perspective. It is really not accurate to say that a promise runs in equity because a transferee of the promisor had notice of it. The promise runs for other reasons, but one who has no notice of it has a defense to its enforcement against him. See London & S.W. Ry. v. Gomm, Note 1 page 632 supra.

FITZSTEPHENS v. WATSON, 218 Or. 185, 344 P.2d 221 (1959). Davies and wife owned a ranch on which springs fed a small stream. Davies installed a water system by placing a pipe in the creek bed, from which water flowed into a storage tank. Another pipe conveyed water from the tank for use on the ranch. Davies and wife conveyed a portion of the ranch to Mairs and wife. Thereafter Davies and wife executed and delivered to the Mairs another instrument which provided:

"Now this Indenture Witnesseth that the grantors hereby covenant that they, their heirs and assigns will maintain a reservoir on the property now known as the Davies Ranch and a pipeline leading from the said premises to the above described premises owned by the grantees and will furnish to the grantees, their heirs or assigns, water equal to three-eighths of the volume now flowing through the pipeline presently carrying water from the Davies Ranch premises to the above described premises owned by the grantees."

Later the Mairs conveyed to the plaintiff two-thirds of the tract acquired from the Davies, no mention being made in the deed to the water right. Davies and wife conveyed the servient tract to the defendants. The defendants shut off the flow of water to the plaintiff's land. The plaintiff sued to enjoin such interference, and had a decree in the court below.

The defendants alleged that they had obtained an official certification of water under the state's prior appropriation statute and that they have a prior right to the use of the water as against the plaintiff who had no official water permit. The court considered the effect of the statutory system of appropriation upon the pre-existing doctrines of riparian rights, and concluded that riparian rights survived the statute except where inconsistent therewith. When Davies and wife were owners of the land, part of their ownership was the riparian right to use the waters of the stream. The court said that this interest was transferable to the Mairs. Whether or not such a grant to a nonriparian owner is effective against other riparian owners, it is at least binding on the grantor. The defendants, therefore, took their land encumbered by an easement appurtenant to the Mairs' land, a part of which is now owned by the plaintiff.

Since the instrument creating the right was in terms of a covenant rather than the grant of an easement, the court then addressed itself to the question whether a different result would follow if the instrument were treated as giving rise to a covenant only. A part of the court's opinion follows:

"The conclusion that an easement was created dispenses with the defendants' argument that the agreement did not bind the defendants because there was no privity of estate between the parties to the instrument. Privity is not necessary in the creation of an easement (although it may in fact arise through a succession of interests from grantor to grantee). Even though the 'Easement Deed' were regarded as creating only a covenant to furnish water and no privity of estate existed between the covenanting parties, the burden and benefit of the covenant would pass with the land to the successors of the covenantors and the covenantees, respectively, in equity. Although the prevailing view is that privity of estate between the covenantor and covenantee is necessary for a covenant to run at law, such privity is not necessary to create an enforceable equitable servitude against a subsequent purchaser of the servient estate if he has notice of the covenant. 2 American Law of Property, § 9.26; 5 Powell on Real Property, pp. 161–2, 188; 5 Restatement, Property, Servitudes, § 539, Comment i; but see Hall v. Risley, 1950, 188 Or. 69, 213 P.2d 818.

"If the instrument in the present case is regarded as giving rise to a covenant only, it imposed upon the covenantor an obligation of the type which creates in the land a servitude enforceable in equity.   *   *   *   The obligation may be regarded as imbedding itself in the soil of the covenantor imposing its burden upon successive possessors of the land if they have actual or constructive notice of the covenant. See 5 Restatement, Property, Servitudes, § 539.

"Although there is authority for the proposition that affirmative covenants will not run with the land,   *   *   *   the prevailing view is to the contrary.   *   *   *   We accept the latter view.   *   *   *

"The 'Easement Deed' having been recorded gave notice of plaintiff's interest to subsequent purchasers of the servient estate, including the defendants. In fact, the deed to the defendants Watson expressly excepted the interest created by the 'Easement Deed.' Even though the instrument had not been recorded the defendants would have had notice of plaintiff's interest from the presence of the pipeline running from the water source on defendants' land to the land of the plaintiff.   *   *   *   Having purchased the servient land subject to the easement and covenant the defendants could not vitiate those interests by obtaining a water permit from the State Engineer. Duckworth v. Watsonville Water & Light Co., 1910, 158 Cal. 206, 110 P. 927."

Note

The statement by the court in the Fitzstephens case about the running of affirmative covenants and the accompanying citations of authority do not reflect any concern like that of the English courts about enforcing affirmative burdens in equity. The facts of the Fitzstephens case were not such as to give a proper focus on that question. Although the covenant was to furnish water, the plaintiffs sued to enjoin interference with the flow of water. In this regard, what essential factual difference exists between Fitzstephens and Tulk v. Moxhay, which has always been thought to stand for the enforcement against successors of restrictive covenants in equity? There has been some confusion in dicta and commentary on this point. Many of the cases cited for the running of affirmative burdens in equity are cases in which nominally affirmative burdens were enforced by restrictive decrees. In fact there is some dicta in American cases approving the English opposition to the running of affirmative burdens in equity.

See 2 A.L.P. § 9.36; Note 3 page 632, supra; Clark, Covenants and Interests Running with Land 179 (2d ed. 1947). See also Pratte v. Balatsos, 99 N.H. 430, 113 A.2d 492 (1955).

If the force of American precedents for the enforcement of affirmative burdens in equity must be qualified by the fact that some of them really involved restrictive burdens in disguise, Petersen v. Beekmere, Inc., which follows, is particularly significant.

PETERSEN v. BEEKMERE, INC.

Superior Court of New Jersey, 1971.
117 N.J.Super. 155, 283 A.2d 911.

LORA, J.S.C. This is a class action to construe a covenant compelling purchasers of property in a subdivision, known as Allison Acres, to purchase a share of stock in a community association Beekmere, Inc. Said action has been consolidated with a county district court suit instituted by Beekmere against each of the plaintiffs herein for $100 for a required stock subscription, and for $75 representing the 1969 annual assessment as against each of them.

The pertinent facts reveal that the original tract surrounding a small lake was owned by Glendale Investments Corp., which subdivided said tract into five sections, the fifth and final subdivision being filed March 18, 1968. The principal stockholders of Glendale, Charles and Elizabeth Decker, formed Beekmere, Inc., a corporation for profit under Title 14 of the Revised Statutes (now N.J.S.A. 14A), said corporation's ostensible purpose, as gleaned from its certificate of incorporation, being the development of land for recreational pursuits, the sale of merchandise incidental thereto, the operation of a private club for the limited membership of lot owners in various real estate developments, and to deal in lands generally.

On January 31, 1961 Glendale conveyed to Beekmere the lake and a certain access lot to the lake in Section Two of the subdivision. A set of covenants, one of which is at issue herein, was not annexed to the deed. On June 29, 1962 Beekmere conveyed back to Glendale; no restrictions were involved. Thereafter, on October 16, 1967 Glendale reconveyed to Beekmere the lake and access lot together with an easement retained by the grantor over two lots with access to the lake in Section Five of the subdivision; no covenants were annexed to the deed.

Individual lots were conveyed by Glendale to purchasers who were predecessors in title of the within plaintiffs, and a copy of the covenants were annexed to all deeds in these original conveyances. In subsequent conveyances by these individual lot owners to plaintiffs, the covenants were not annexed to some of the deeds. The covenant in dispute, set forth in a document annexed to such deeds and entitled "Covenants for Insertion in Deeds 'Allison Acres,' Sections * * *," recited:

> Whereas, the Purchaser (hereinafter designated as the Owner), agrees to apply for membership in Beekmere, Incorporated (hereinafter designated as Beekmere), and member to purchase one share of the common stock of said Beekmere, for a sum not in excess of $100.00 and to comply with and conform to the Constitution and By-Laws of said Beekmere * * *.

The threshold question for the court is whether this covenant, being affirmative in nature, can be enforced at law through the medium of the county district court action, or in equity, by plaintiffs' action to construe the covenant. Plaintiffs argue that under the law of this State affirmative covenants cannot be enforced, relying on Furness v. Sinquett, 60

N.J.Super. 410, 159 A.2d 455 (Ch.Div.1960), which involved an action against subsequent grantees for the enforcement by mandatory injunction of a covenant to construct sidewalks in front of their homes and to remove certain obstructions in street areas.

It appears from the opinion that each original conveyance from the common developer contained the covenant. Testimony was adduced that practically all the lots upon which residences were constructed were made subject to the covenant, the respective parties involved having obtained possession by mesne conveyances, and defendants did not deny that a similar covenant was contained in their chain of title. The court noted that plaintiff had proved a "neighborhood scheme" by showing that the grantor had inserted in each deed, like restrictions concerning the use of the lands from the original owner, but stated that the fact that such a "neighborhood scheme" had been shown did not alter the fact that the covenant sought to be enforced was affirmative rather than negative in nature.

The court in *Furness* stated that beginning with the English case of Spencer's Case, 1 Smith's Lead.Cas. 145, 5 Coke 16a, and followed in New Jersey by Brewer v. Marshall and Cheeseman, 19 N.J.Eq. 537, 546 (E. & A.1868) our courts have refused enforcement of affirmative covenants, quoting dictum from De Gray v. Monmouth Beach Club House Co., 50 N.J.Eq. 329, 332–333, 24 A. 388 (Ch.1892), aff'd p.c., 67 N.J.Eq. 731, 63 A. 1118 (E. & A.1894):

> It is settled that a court of equity will restrain the violation of a covenant, entered into by a grantee, restrictive of the use of lands conveyed, not only against the covenantor, but against all subsequent purchasers of the lands with notice of the covenant, irrespective of the questions whether the covenant is of a nature to run with the land, or whether it creates an easement; provided, however, that its enforcement is not against public policy. [Citations omitted]
> * * *
>
> This rule of equity being an encroachment on the general doctrine of the common law, that the burden of a covenant does not run with the land [citations omitted], its application is not to be extended beyond the class of cases in which it has been heretofore enforced [citation omitted], and is to be confined to negative covenants.

However, whether affirmative covenants are enforceable at law or in equity does not appear to be settled in this State. The De Gray case, upon which the court relied in Furness v. Sinquett, supra, involved a negative rather than an affirmative covenant, and thus the Court of Errors and Appeals did not pass on the question. Javna v. D.J. Fredricks, Inc., 41 N.J.Super. 353, 360, 125 A.2d 227 (App.Div.1956), noted but likewise did not rule thereon. In addition to De Gray v. Monmouth Beach Club House Co., supra, the cases of Brewer v. Marshall and Cheeseman, 18 N.J.Eq. 337 (Ch.1867), aff'd 19 N.J.Eq. 537 (E. & A.1868), and Costigan v. Pennsylvania R.R. Co., 54 N.J.L. 233, 242, 23 A. 810 (Sup.Ct. 1892), contained some very early statements that the burdens of covenants, affirmative or otherwise, do not run at law except as between landlord and tenant.

The court in Conover v. Smith, 17 N.J.Eq. 51, 55 (Ch.1864), while it did not have the question of affirmative covenants directly before it, stated by way of dictum that if a lessee covenanted for himself and his assigns to make a new wall upon the demised premises, the assignee was bound; and Child v. C.H. Winans Co., 119 N.J.Eq. 556, 183 A. 300 (E. & A.1936), which involved a covenant by the grantee to pay taxes and assessments on land retained by the grantor, although held not to be a covenant running with the land, allowed enforcement against a subsequent purchaser under a theory of an equitable lien.

A view of other jurisdictions indicates that the weight of authority permits the enforcement of affirmative covenants, although courts have not distinguished between the rubrics under which such enforcement is effected, whether it be by covenant running with the land at law, or as an equitable servitude enforceable against a subsequent purchaser with notice. Adaman Mutual Water Co. v. United States, 278 F.2d 842 (9 Cir. 1960); Note, "Affirmative Duties Running with the Land," 35 N.Y.U.L. Rev. 1344 (1960), and appendix at 1365–1369; 7 Thompson, Real Property § 3153 at 78 (1962); 2 American Law of Property (Casner ed. 1952), § 9.36 at 438–439; 20 Am.Jur.2d Covenants, Conditions and Restrictions, § 37 at 607, where it was stated that courts make no distinction between affirmative and negative covenants regarding their running with the land, the chief consideration in running being whether the covenant relates to the land so as to enhance its value and confer benefit, rather than whether it is affirmative or negative in nature. See also, Annotation, "Affirmative Covenants as Running with the Land," 68 A.L.R.2d 1022, § 4 at 1026 (1959), and cases in earlier annotations at 41 A.L.R. 1363 (1926), 51 A.L.R. 1326 (1927), 102 A.L.R. 781 (1936) and 118 A.L.R. 982 (1939).

In New York the courts adhered to the old English rule that affirmative covenants did not run with the land so as to charge the burden of performance upon a subsequent grantee. Miller v. Clary, 210 N.Y. 127, 103 N.E. 1114 (Ct.App.1913). However, such position has been eroded in that state due to recognized exceptions, and in subsequent cases that in all but letter appear to overrule Miller v. Clary. In accord with the view that New York has thus changed its position, see 7 Thompson, Real Property, § 3153 at 78, note 7 (1962); 2 American Law of Property (Casner ed. 1952), § 9.36 at 438; 20 Am.Jur.2d Covenants, Conditions and Restrictions, § 37, p. 607, 5 Powell, Real Property, § 677 at 195 (1970). Cf. Tarantelli v. Tripp Lake Estates, Inc., 63 Misc.2d 913, 314 N.Y.S.2d 21 (Sup.Ct.1970), for an apparent statement that an affirmative covenant will not run. In Nicholson v. 300 Broadway Realty Corp., 7 N.Y.2d 240, 196 N.Y.S.2d 945, 949–950, 164 N.E.2d 832, 835 (1959), which involved a covenant to furnish heat, the Appellate Division stated:

The burden of affirmative covenants may be enforced against subsequent holders of the originally burdened land whenever it appears that (1) the original covenantor and covenantee intended such a result; (2) there has been a continuous succession of conveyances between the original covenantor and the party now sought to be burdened; and (3) the covenant touches or concerns the land to a substantial degree.

The Appellate Division relied on a case very similar on its facts to the present one: Neponsit Property Owners' Ass'n v. Emigrant Industrial Sav. Bank, 278 N.Y. 248, 15 N.E.2d 793 (Ct.App.1938). In that case an action was brought by an association of property owners, as assignee of the original covenantee, to foreclose a lien upon defendant's land, the lien arising from a covenant contained in a deed from the original owner-developer to defendant's predecessor in title. The covenant required payment of an annual charge to be devoted to maintenance purposes of roads, parks, beach and such. Noting that this was an affirmative covenant to pay money for use in connection with, but not upon, the land, the court in a well reasoned opinion stated:

> It has been often said that a covenant to pay a sum of money is a personal affirmative covenant which usually does not concern or touch the land. Such statements are based upon English decisions which hold in effect that only covenants, which compel the covenanter to submit to some *restriction on the use* of his property, touch or concern the land, and that the burden of a covenant which requires the covenanter to do an affirmative act, even on his own land, for the benefit of the owner of a 'dominant' estate, does not run with his land. * * * [t]here were some exceptions or limitations in the application of the general rule. Some promises to pay money have been enforced, as covenants running with the land, against subsequent holders of the land who took with notice of the covenant. [Citations omitted.] It may be difficult to classify these exceptions or to formulate a test of whether a particular covenant to pay money or to perform some other act falls within the general rule that ordinarily an affirmative covenant is a personal and not a real covenant, or falls outside the limitations placed upon the general rule. At least it must 'touch' or 'concern' the land in a substantial degree, and though it may be inexpedient and perhaps impossible to formulate a rigid test or definition which will be entirely satisfactory or which can be applied mechanically in all cases, we should at least be able to state the problem and find a reasonable method of approach to it. It has been suggested that a covenant which runs with the land must affect the legal relations—the advantages and the burdens—of the parties to the covenant, as owners of particular parcels of land and not merely as members of the community in general, such as taxpayers or owners of other land. [Citations omitted]. That method of approach has the merit of realism. The test is based on the effect of the covenant rather than on technical distinctions. Does the covenant impose, on the one hand, a burden upon an interest in land, which on the other hand increases the value of a different interest in the same or related land?

Even though we accept that approach and test, it still remains true that whether a particular covenant is sufficiently connected with the use of land to run with the land, must be in many cases a question of degree. A promise to pay for something to be done in connection with the promisor's land does not differ essentially from a promise by the promisor to do the thing himself, and both promises constitute, in a substantial sense, a restriction upon the owner's right to use the land, and a burden upon the legal interest of the owner. On the other hand, a covenant to perform or pay for the performance of an affirmative act disconnected with the use of the land cannot ordinarily touch or concern the land in any substantial degree. Thus, unless we exalt technical form over substance, the distinction between covenants which run with land and covenants which are personal, must depend upon the effect of the covenant on the legal rights which otherwise would flow from ownership of land and which are connected with the land. The problem then is: Does the covenant in purpose and effect substantially alter these rights? [278 N.Y. at 256–258, 15 N.E.2d at 795–796].

It would thus appear, by the weight of authority and logic, that the distinction between "affirmative" and "negative" covenants is an anachronism which all too often precludes an analysis of the covenant itself in order to determine whether it should be enforced, whether at law as a covenant running with the land or in equity as an equitable servitude enforceable against the original grantee and all successors having notice. See Caullett v. Stanley Stilwell & Sons, Inc., 67 N.J.Super. 111, 116, 170 A.2d 52 (App.Div.1961), where the court used the law and equity analysis in its review of a restrictive covenant. For the position of treating affirmative and negative covenants similarly, see, in addition to authorities heretofore cited, Berger, "A Policy Analysis of Promises Respecting the Use of Land," 55 Minn.L.Rev. 167, 190–193 (1970). See, also, a critical analysis of the Furness v. Sinquett, supra, decision at 15 Rutgers L.Rev. 290 (1961).

The Appellate Division in *Caullett*, supra, set forth the requirements of a covenant directly restrictive of title to land. Of the primary requirement that it "touch and concern" the subject property, the court stated:

> To constitute a real rather than a personal covenant, the promise must exercise direct influence on the occupation, use or enjoyment of the premises. It must be a promise "respecting the use of the land," that is, "a use of identified land which is not merely casual and which is not merely an incident in the performance of the promise." 5 Restatement, Property, Scope Note to Part III, pp. 3147–3148 (1944) [67 N.J.Super. at 116, 170 A.2d at 54]

The meaning of the "touch and concern" requirement is unclear, especially with respect to affirmative covenants, in New Jersey. Although Caullett v. Stanley Stilwell & Sons, Inc., supra, and Brewer v. Marshall and Cheeseman, supra, 19 N.J.Eq. 537 (E. & A.), spoke in terms of the physical use of the land, both cases involved negative covenants (that the grantor reserved the right to build the original building on the premises, and a covenant not to sell marl). In addition, New Jersey seems to distinguish between burden and benefit as they relate to the "touch and concern" requirement. Compare *Brewer*, supra, and

National Union Bank at Dover v. Segur, 39 N.J.L. 173, 186 (Sup.Ct. 1877); and see 5 Powell, Real Property § 678 at 197–199 (1970).

The covenant here under consideration requires individual lot owners to purchase stock in a property owners' association, and make payment of assessments, which ostensibly will be put to use for the development and maintenance of the lake area. Under such a scheme both the burden and benefit of the covenant would be linked to each parcel found subject to the covenant.

As was stated in Neponsit Property Owners' Ass'n v. Emigrant Industrial Sav. Bank, supra:

> In order that the burden of maintaining public improvements should rest upon the land benefited by the improvements, the grantor exacted from the grantee of the land with its appurtenant easement or right of enjoyment a covenant that the burden of paying the cost should be inseparably attached to the land which enjoys the benefit. It is plain that any distinction or definition which would exclude such a covenant from the classification of covenants which "touch" or "concern" the land would be based on form and not on substance. [278 N.Y. at 260, 15 N.E.2d at 797]

For other cases enforcing similar covenants, see Harrison-Rye Realty Corp. v. New Rochelle Trust Co., 177 Misc. 776, 31 N.Y.S.2d 1005 (Sup. Ct.1941); Lawrence Park Realty Co. v. Crichton, 218 App.Div. 374, 218 N.Y.S. 278 (App.Div.1926); Kennilwood Owners Ass'n v. Jaybro R. & D. Co., 156 Misc. 604, 281 N.Y.S. 541 (Sup.Ct.1935); Rodruck v. Sand Point Maintenance Comm'n, 48 Wash.2d 565, 295 P.2d 714 (Sup.Ct.1956) (where the amounts of the individual assessments were governed by a set standard, "according as the area of such tract bears to the entire area of the tracts assessed, that is, on the square footage basis, and without reference to the value of the front footage thereof; * * * *"); Maher v. Cleveland Union Stockyards Co., 55 Ohio App. 412, 9 N.E.2d 995 (Ct.App.1936).

Examining the covenant therein under consideration, the court in Caullett v. Stanley Stilwell & Sons, Inc., supra, 67 N.J.Super. at 118, 170 A.2d 52, stated that prerequisite to a conclusion that a covenant runs with the land at law is a finding that both burdened and benefited properties exist and were intended to be so affected by the contracting parties. That the properties were intended to be so affected in the present case appears evident by the incorporation of Beekmere with its ostensible purpose of subdivision development, together with the pattern of original conveyances by the grantor annexing the restrictions to all deeds. As to the existence of burdened and benefited properties, it would seem that both are merged into the individual lots of Allison Acres subject to the covenant, since they reap the benefits of lake area development and provide the source for necessary funds.

Although not discussed in Caullett v. Stanley Stilwell & Sons, Inc., supra, there perhaps is an additional requirement in order for a covenant to run at law, namely, privity of estate. Early cases in this State seem to require a tenurial relationship in order to constitute privity.

See Costigan v. Pennsylvania R.R., Co., 54 N.J.L. 233, 23 A. 810 (Sup.Ct. 1892) (negative duty held unenforceable in the absence of a landlord-tenant relationship); The Inhabitants of City of Bordentown v. Anderson, 81 N.J.L. 434, 79 A. 281 (E. & A.1910), writ of error dism. 223 U.S. 714, 32 S.Ct. 521, 56 L.Ed. 626 (1911) (burden of a covenant will not run with the land in the absence of lessor-lessee relationship). For a contrary view, see Clark, Real Covenants and Other Interests Which "Run With the Land" (2d ed. 1947), 111–137, which takes the position that logically and historically the only privity requirement is that between the promisor and the assignee which is satisfied by a succession to the estate of the promisor. While the covenant herein under consideration might perhaps fail at least as to the privity requirement, such is not a problem when the covenant is sought to be enforced in equity under a theory of equitable servitude.

> The English doctrine of equitable servitudes was based on notice. In that country (which had no recording system) notice had to mean principally actual notice. In this country which has had a well-developed recording system since its beginning, the record was deemed to be notice to the subsequent purchaser, and thus so long as the agreement was recorded, it was a stable and sure way to bind subsequent parties to private use arrangements. [Berger, A Policy Analysis of Promises Respecting the Use of Land, supra, 55 Minn.L.Rev. at 186 (1970)]

As to the privity requirement it has been stated that "Problems as to the existence of 'privity' have no significance when * * * [t]he controversy is in equity for the enforcement against a successor of the promisor of a promise with notice of which the ownership has been acquired * * *." 5 Powell, Real Property, § 674 at 171, citing Restatement, Property, § 539, comment (a) (1944). Likewise, our courts have "consistently enforced the covenantal rights of an owner of benefited property against a successor, with notice, to the burdened land, even though the covenant did not run with the land at law." Caullett v. Stanley Stilwell & Sons, Inc., supra, 67 N.J.Super. at 118, 170 A.2d 52; Cotton v. Cresse, 80 N.J.Eq. 540, 85 A. 600 (E. & A.1912).

Thus, although the question whether an affirmative covenant is enforceable at law as a covenant running with the land is here expressly left open, it is the conclusion of this court that such a covenant is, in equity, enforceable as an equitable servitude against a subsequent grantee who takes with notice. That the covenant was not annexed to all of plaintiffs' deeds is of no consequence since they acquired title with notice of the covenant, its presence in their chain of title charging them with such notice. Olson v. Jantausch, 44 N.J.Super. 380, 388, 130 A.2d 650 (App.Div.1957).

[Contrary to what might have been expected from the tenor of the opinion reported above, the court held that the covenants in question would not run with the land. The reason was not related to their being affirmative covenants, nor that they did not touch and concern the land, but rather because of their "vagueness of terms and consequent restraints on alienation." See Kell v. Bella Vista Property Owners Association, reported infra page 675.]

Notes

1. Three phases in the development of the English doctrine on running covenants should be recalled. First was the confinement of the running of burdens to landlord-tenant cases under the announced requirement of privity of estate between the contracting parties. Second was the opening of the door to the enforcement of restrictive burdens in equity under Tulk v. Moxhay. Third was the refusal to extend the equitable doctrine to affirmative burdens. Since it makes little difference whether one can enforce a restrictive promise at law if one can get injunctive relief, it seems obvious that the policy of the English law is really against the enforcement of affirmative burdens between owners in fee.

When the American courts began to liberalize the English privity requirement, so that in most circumstances that requirement is met, it is obvious that the American doctrine could not be regarded as primarily against the enforcement of affirmative burdens, for the privity requirement is as often satisfied where the burden is affirmative as where it is negative. It might seem to follow, therefore, that when the doctrine of Tulk v. Moxhay was accepted and was applicable in the absence of privity, it should also be applicable equally to affirmative and negative burdens, unless there is some objection to affirmative burdens other than that implicit in the English doctrine. The notion that affirmative burdens could not be enforced in equity because of an aversion to mandatory injunctions was rejected as the reason for the English rule. Kaywood v. The Brunswick Perm. Ben. Bldg. Soc., 8 Q.B. 403 (1881). That notion has not been discovered in the American cases.

For a conclusive answer to the question one would seek American cases in which an affirmative burden was enforced in equity in the absence of privity. Such cases seldom arise. A few early cases are inconclusive on the point. There is a little early authority that seems simply to follow the English precedents. In Smith v. Kelly, 56 Me. 64 (1868), the court refused specific performance of an affirmative burden for want of privity, but no mention was made of any equitable doctrine under Tulk v. Moxhay. And in Kettle River Railroad v. Eastern Railway, 41 Minn. 461, 43 N.W. 469 (1889), the court refused to enforce an affirmative burden in equity, under the authority of Keppel v. Bailey. But in Town of Middletown v. Newport Hospital, 16 R.I. 319, 15 A. 800 (1888), after saying that an affirmative burden would not run at law under the authority of the English cases on privity, the court held the defendant bound in equity, since he took with notice. The authority of Keppel v. Bailey was specifically rejected. See also Stevens v. Annex Realty Co., 173 Mo. 511, 73 S.W. 505 (1903); Pittsburgh, Cincinnati & Saint Louis Railway v. Bosworth, 46 Ohio St. 81, 18 N.E. 533 (1888).

Among the more recent cases, if the authority and language of *Fitzstephens* extends beyond the restrictive enforcement of affirmative burdens to true affirmative covenants, that case would stand as authority for the obliteration of any impediment to the enforcement of affirmative burdens in equity. See also Anthony v. Brea Glenbrook Club, 58 Cal.App.3d 506, 130 Cal.Rptr. 32 (1976), where in a case similar to *Beekmere*, the court, after finding that the covenant would run with the land, added that it could be enforced in equity even if it did not fulfill the technical requirements for a covenant running with the land. Compare Clear Lake Apartments, Inc. v. Clear Lake Utilities, 549 S.W.2d 385 (Tex.1977), where a contract to furnish water and sewer service to certain land was held not enforceable against a subsequent purchaser of the land. The court said the promise was not enforceable in equity, not because it was affirmative, but rather because it was really a restriction on competition which touched the land only collaterally.

In a number of other states, cases have been appearing in which affirmative burdens have been enforced in equity without any consideration of the question whether the covenant would run at law. As one might expect, it does appear in these cases that if the privity requirement had been invoked by an effort to enforce the burden at law, that requirement would have been satisfied. See e.g. Mobil Oil Corp. v. Brennan, 385 F.2d 951 (5th Cir.1967); Hunt v. DelCollo, 317 A.2d 545 (Del.Ch.1974); Frumkes v. Boyer, 101 So.2d 387 (Fla.App.1958); Greenspan v. Rehberg, 56 Mich.App. 310, 224 N.W.2d 67 (1974); see also Annotation, 68 A.L.R.2d 1022 (1959). Enforcement has been had by way of the declaration and enforcement of a lien to secure a promised payment of the costs of a certain improvement of land, even where the promise itself conferred no lien. Mendrop v. Harrell, 233 Miss. 679, 103 So.2d 418 (1958).

The recognition in *Beekmere* that affirmative burdens would run in equity, even though they would not run at law, is the strongest indication so far that there is no general objection to the running of affirmative burdens in equity. That conclusion would seem to apply a fortiori in other jurisdictions in which covenants like that in *Beekmere* have been found enforceable at law. Generally, see 2 A.L.P. § 9.36; Cunningham § 8.24.

If in fact both affirmative and negative covenants will generally be enforceable in equity, it should be obvious that the American law on privity has become virtually a dead letter. It would remain only as the capricious proposition that in those infrequent cases where the privity requirement is not met, a plaintiff can compel performance of a promise, but cannot get damages for failure to perform it.

2. As stated in *Beekmere*, the history of affirmative covenants in New York and New Jersey was quite different. Miller v. Clary (cited in *Beekmere*) recognized that the true nature of the English doctrine was to be understood as essentially a rule against the running of affirmative burdens. But a number of exceptions were declared that may have signified the recognition that the English rule was not altogether suited to American conditions or attitudes. This led to commentary that the court was moving toward an abandonment of its rule about affirmative burdens. In fact, one may refer to the discussion in *Beekmere* of the leading New York case, Neponsit Property Owners' Association v. Emigrant Industrial Savings Bank where the court appeared to reduce the problem to one involving merely a proper application of the touching and concerning requirement. In Nicholson v. 300 Broadway Realty Corp. (also cited in *Beekmere*) the court again had the opportunity to clarify its law on affirmative burdens. There a landowner promised another landowner to furnish steam heat to the latter's building and to maintain the necessary steam pipes for that purpose, in consideration for a promise by the latter to pay $50 a year. The defendant, purchaser of the promisor's property, was held liable for damages for breach of this promise. The court purported to follow Neponsit, and did not overrule any prior cases, nor did it concede that the rule against the running of affirmative burdens had been wholly abrogated. The only language that gave any indication that the old rule still had some room to operate was the following, "The fear expressed that the covenant imposes an undue restriction on alienation or an onerous burden in perpetuity is dispelled by the fact that by its terms it may run with the land only so long as both buildings are standing and in use."

It appears that New Jersey also at one time may have taken a position against the enforcement of affirmative burdens. It is not clear what, if any, exceptions like those in New York would be recognized. If *Beekmere* is followed in New Jersey, however, it will not matter much whether such exceptions are recognized at law. Whether New Jersey, like New York, will still leave room to find certain kinds of affirmative covenants objectionable is a question we may keep in mind when we consider Kell v. Bello Vista Property Owners Ass'n, page 675 infra.

3. One should recognize that the doctrine of restrictive equitable servitudes, as indicated in Trustees of Columbia College v. Lynch, supra, is hardly distinguishable from, if it is not a part of, the law relating to negative easements. On the other hand, an affirmative promise is quite different from an affirmative easement. An affirmative easement gives one who owns it a right to make some limited use of the servient owner's land; but an affirmative promise requires the promisor to do something to or for the benefit of the promisee's land. If affirmative promises are recognized in equity as binding and running with land, a new kind of property interest has been created. This may be of little concern to most of us, but it was the reason given in England for refusing to enforce affirmative burdens in equity in the first place. If new kinds of interests are not to be rejected merely because of their novelty, it may still remain for us to consider whether there remains at least a remnant of the English objection to affirmative burdens. If burdens are not prevented from running merely because they are affirmative, is it fair to suggest that at least some kinds of affirmative burdens are so peculiarly burdensome that they constitute unreasonable restraints upon alienation?

EAGLE ENTERPRISES, INC. v. GROSS

Court of Appeals of New York, 1976.
39 N.Y.2d 505, 384 N.Y.S.2d 717, 349 N.E.2d 816.

GABRIELLI, Justice. In 1951, Orchard Hill Realties, Inc., a subdivider and developer, conveyed certain property in the subdivision of Orchard Hill in Orange County to William and Pauline Baum. The deed to the Baums contained the following provision:

"The party of the first part shall supply to the party of the second part, seasonally from May 1st to October 1st, of each year, water for domestic use only, from the well located on other property of the party of the first part, and the party of the second part agrees to take said water and to pay the party of the first part, a fee of Thirty-five ($35.00) dollars per year, for said water so supplied."

In addition, the deed also contained the following:

"It is expressly provided that the covenants herein contained shall run with the land * * * and shall bind and shall enure to the benefit of the heirs, distributees, successors, legal representatives and assigns of the respective parties hereto".

Appellant is the successor in interest of Orchard Hill Realties, Inc., and respondent, after a series of intervening conveyances, is the successor in interest of the Baums. The deed conveying title to respondent does not contain the aforementioned covenant to purchase water and, in fact, none of the deeds following the original deed to the Baums contained the mutual promises regarding water supply. While some of the deeds in the chain of title from Baum contained a provision that they were made subject to the restrictions in the deed from Orchard Hill Realties to Baum, the deed to respondents contained no such covenants, restrictions or "subject to" clause.

According to the stipulated facts, respondent has refused to accept and pay for water offered by appellant since he has constructed his own well to service what is now a year-round dwelling. Appellant, therefore, instituted this action to collect the fee specified in the covenant (contained only in the original deed to Baum) for the supply of water which, appellant contends, respondent is bound to accept. The action was styled as one "for goods sold and delivered" even though respondent did not utilize any of appellant's water. Two of the lower courts found that the covenant "ran" with the land and, hence, was binding upon respondent as successor to the Baums, but the Appellate Division reversed and held that the covenant could not be enforced against respondent. We must now decide whether the promise of the original grantees to accept and make payment for a seasonal water supply from the well of their grantor is enforceable against subsequent grantees and may be said to "run with the land." We agree with the determination of the Appellate Division and affirm its order.

* * *

Even though the parties to the original deed expressly state in the instrument that the covenant will run with the land, such a recital is insufficient to render the covenant enforceable against subsequent grantees if the other requirements for the running of an affirmative covenant are not met. The rule is settled that "[r]egardless of the intention of the parties, a covenant will run with the land and will be enforceable against a subsequent purchaser of the land at the suit of one who claims the benefit of the covenant, only if the covenant complies with certain legal requirements" (*Neponsit*, supra, 278 N.Y. p. 254, 15 N.E.2d p. 795; see, also Morgan Lake Co. v. New York, New Haven & Hartford R.R. Co., supra, 262 N.Y. p. 238, 186 N.E. p. 686). Thus, although the intention of the original parties here is clear and privity of estate exists, the covenant must still satisfy the requirement that it "touch and concern" the land.

It is this third prong of the tripartite rule which presents the obstacle to appellant's position and which was the focus of our decisions in Neponsit and Nicholson v. 300 Broadway Realty Corp. (7 N.Y.2d 240, 244, 196 N.Y.S.2d 945, 948, 164 N.E.2d 832, 834, supra). *Neponsit* first sought to breathe substance and meaning into the ritualistic rubric that an affirmative covenant must "touch and concern" the land in order to be enforceable against subsequent grantees. Observing that it would be difficult to devise a rule which would operate mechanically to resolve all situations which might arise, Judge Lehman observed that "the distinction between covenants which run with land and covenants which are personal, must depend upon the effect of the covenant on the legal rights which otherwise would flow from the ownership of land and which are connected with the land" (*Neponsit*, supra, 278 N.Y. p. 258, 15 N.E.2d p. 796). Thus, he posed as the key question whether "the covenant in purpose and effect substantially alter[s] these rights" (p. 258, 15 N.E.2d p. 796). In *Nicholson,* this court reaffirmed the soundness of the reasoning in *Neponsit* as "a more realistic and pragmatic approach" (supra, 7 N.Y.2d p. 245, 196 N.Y.S.2d p. 949, 164 N.E.2d p. 835).

The covenants in issue in *Neponsit* required the owners of property in a development to pay an annual charge for the maintenance of roads, paths, parks, beaches, sewers and other public improvements. The court concluded that the covenant substantially affected the promisor's legal interest in his property since the latter received an easement in common and a right of enjoyment in the public improvements for which contribution was received by all the landowners in the subdivision (supra, 278 N.Y. pp. 259–260, 15 N.E.2d p. 797).

A close examination of the covenant in the case before us leads to the conclusion that it does not substantially affect the ownership interest of landowners in the Orchard Hill subdivision. The covenant provides for the supplying of water for only six months of the year; no claim has been advanced by appellant that the lands in the subdivision would be waterless without the water it supplies. Indeed, the facts here point to the converse conclusion since respondent has obtained his own source of water. The record, based on and consisting of an agreed stipulation of facts, does not demonstrate that other property owners in the subdivision would be deprived of water from appellant or that the price of water would become prohibitive for other property owners if respondent terminated appellant's service. Thus, the agreement for the seasonal supply of water does not seem to us to relate in any significant degree to the ownership rights of respondent and the other property owners in the subdivision of Orchard Hill. The landowners in *Neponsit* received an easement in common to utilize public areas in the subdivision; this interest was in the nature of a property right attached to their respective properties. The obligation to receive water from appellant resembles a personal, contractual promise to purchase water rather than a significant interest attaching to respondent's property. It should be emphasized that the question whether a covenant is so closely related to the use of the land that it should be deemd to "run" with the land is one of degree, dependent on the particular circumstances of a case (*Neponsit,* supra, 278 N.Y. p. 258, 15 N.E.2d p. 796). Here, the meager record before us is lacking and woefully insufficient to establish that the covenant "touches and concerns" the land, as we have interpreted that requirement.

There is an additional reason why we are reluctant to enforce this covenant for the seasonable supply of water. The affirmative covenant is disfavored in the law because of the fear that this type of obligation imposes an "undue restriction on alienation or an onerous burden in perpetuity" (Nicholson v. 300 Broadway Realty Corp., 7 N.Y.2d 240, 246, 196 N.Y.S.2d 945, 950, 164 N.E.2d 832, 835, supra). In *Nicholson,* the covenant to supply heat was not interdicted by this concern because it was conditioned upon the continued existence of the buildings on both the promisor's and the promisee's properties. Similarly, in *Neponsit,* the original 1917 deed containing the covenant to pay an annual charge for the maintenance of public areas expressly provided for its own lapse in 1940. Here, no outside limitation has been placed on the obligation to purchase water from appellant. Thus, the covenant falls prey to the criticism that it creates a burden in perpetuity, and purports to bind all future owners, regardless of the use to which the land is put. Such a result militates strongly against its enforcement. On this ground also, we are of the opinion that the covenant should not be enforced as an exception to the general rule prohibiting the "running" of affirmative covenants.

Accordingly, the order of the Appellate Division should be affirmed, with costs.

Note

Apparently some courts that do not follow the New York view about affirmative covenants are concerned about the effect of certain running covenants as fetters on alienability. On the one hand the Georgia court was willing to dismiss the problem when it asserted the obvious proposition that a covenant to pay an annual stated assessment for membership in a beach club did not violate the Rule Against Perpetuities. Lowry v. Norris Lake Shore Development Corp., 231 Ga. 549, 203 S.E.2d 171 (1974). In Henthorn v. Tri Par Land Development Corp., 221 So.2d 465 (Fla.App.1969), however, such an assessment for maintenance of common areas, effective until January 1, 2000 and renewable thereafter for ten-year periods unless changed by a majority vote of the lot owners, was held to be valid for the initial period, but invalid thereafter "for the same policy reasons which invalidate the remote vesting of property interests." The court relied on Collins v. Pic-Town Water Works, 166 So.2d 760 (Fla. App.1964), where in respect to a promise of a mobile home lot owner to pay a fee for maintenance, lights, and water, the court held that such a contract, if for an indefinite time or perpetual, is terminable at the will of either party, for to enforce a perpetual contract would place an endless duty on the court, which is "inappropriate to its functions."

The language in *Eagle Enterprises* may suggest that the trouble does not lie merely in the duration of a covenant, but in the fact that the covenant would continue "regardless of the use to which the land is put." What concern can there be about duration so long as the conditions which prompted the covenant continue? It may seem that an affirmative covenant becomes an objectionable or unreasonable restraint on alienation only when, because of changed conditions, it does not serve its initial purpose, or the burden imposed greatly outweighs its value to the promisee. This seems to mean that an affirmative covenant should not be found void merely because no limit has been set upon its duration or because it might at some future time become an unreasonable burden.

Where do restrictive covenants stand on this matter? Unless affirmative covenants are inherently more oppressive than restrictive covenants, one might expect that restrictive covenants are also subject to the charge of being unreasonable restraints on alienation. If affirmative covenants are in fact thought to be, on the whole, more burdensome than restrictive covenants, there is little reason to conclude that restrictive covenants should be immune from the charge of being unreasonable restraints on alienation. In fact, as we will see in the next case, the problem of the duration of restrictive covenants is largely absorbed in the doctrine of changed conditions as a defense to the enforcement of a covenant. Courts applying that doctrine have not explained its essence beyond saying that changed conditions may render enforcement of a covenant inequitable. It will be inequitable, at least in part, because it has become an unreasonable restraint on alienation. In due course we might expect that the doctrine of changed conditions will be extended to affirmative covenants (Brendonwood Common v. Franklin, 403 N.E.2d 1136 (Ind.App.1980)). On the other hand, several courts have examined certain restrictive covenants in terms of whether the burdens were reasonable in the circumstances but not necessarily reasonable for all time. Doo v. Packwood, 265 Cal.App.2d 752, 71 Cal.Rptr. 477 (1968); Hall v. American Oil Co., 504 S.W.2d 313 (Mo.App.1973); Moore v. Smith, 443 S.W.2d 552 (Tex.1969).

See Browder, Running Covenants and Public Policy, 77 Mich.L.Rev. 12 (1978).

OLIVER v. HEWITT

Supreme Court of Appeals of Virginia, 1950.
191 Va. 163, 60 S.E.2d 1.

MILLER, Justice. Prior to January 28, 1946, and until the present date, appellant, S.J. Oliver, has owned and operated a store on Lincoln Street in the city of Portsmouth, wherein groceries and soft drinks are sold. It is located a short distance from two other lots of land that he owned which adjoin each other and are described as Lots Nos. 1 and 2, Block 30, Prentis Park Plat.

On January 28, 1946, appellant and wife sold and conveyed to J. Preston Hewitt and Helen H. Alexander the two lots in Prentis Park. The deed conveying these lots was recorded on January 30, 1946, and contained the following covenant:

"The above conveyance is made upon the condition that said parties of the second part, nor their assigns, shall sell in any building to be erected upon said lots, any groceries or bottled drinks, except that bottled High Rock may be sold on said premises, on any day after six o'clock P.M."

On July 7, 1947, Helen H. Alexander and husband, and J. Preston Hewitt deeded the two lots to Pauline H. Hewitt. This deed did not contain the covenant or make any reference thereto. However, the grantee, who is the wife of J. Preston Hewitt, had actual and constructive notice of the existence of the covenant. She leased the premises to W.H. Boyd, who is using the building thereon for the sale of groceries and soft drinks of any character. Though due to the recordation of the deed of January 28, 1946, he had constructive notice of the covenant, it does not appear from the record that he had actual notice of its existence when he leased the property.

S.J. Oliver claims that these facts prove that there has been a violation of the covenant by Pauline H. Hewitt and her lessee, W.H. Boyd, and that he is entitled to an injunction restraining such continued infraction of its terms. From a final decree which decided that the covenant was personal; that it did not run with the land; that it was not binding upon either Pauline H. Hewitt or her lessee, and denying the relief prayed for, appellant appealed.

It is apparent from the pleadings and evidence, and not denied, that the covenant was for the protection of appellant's business, and that the unrestricted use of the lots in question for the sale thereon of groceries and all kinds of soft drinks is in competition with and detrimental to appellant's interests.

We are therefore called upon to decide (1) whether or not the covenant is enforceable in equity against Pauline H. Hewitt who had constructive and actual notice of its existence when she purchased the land, and (2) whether or not it is enforceable in equity against W.H. Boyd who had constructive notice of its existence when he leased the property.

We have no difficulty in concluding that the restriction imposed upon the use of the land is a personal covenant for appellant's sole benefit as distinguished from a covenant that runs with the land. Allison v. Greear, 188 Va. 64, 49 S.E. 279, and 14 Am.Jur., "Covenants", sec. 27, p. 503. It is not for the natural use and enjoyment of the land retained by the grantor but is merely a restriction imposed upon the use of the land conveyed which is simply for the purpose of protecting from injurious competition the business operated by the grantor. It is therefore a mere personal covenant that does not run with the land in equity.

This personal covenant is, however, binding between the original parties, both at law and in equity. More specifically stated, it falls within that class of covenants which at law bind only the original parties as it does not run with the land; but, in equity, one is bound by such a personal restrictive covenant even though it does not run with the land if he takes title with knowledge of its existence, even though the deed to him did not recite the restriction.

This principle is clearly announced in 26 C.J.S., Deeds, § 167, p. 547, where it is stated: " * * * So, regardless of whether a covenant not to use the land for certain purposes runs with the land, a court of equity will, nevertheless, enforce it against a grantee taking title through a deed reciting the covenant and subject thereto, or against a grantee taking title with full knowledge of its existence, although it be omitted from his deed * * *."

The following authorities recognize and adhere to the above principle: Tulk v. Moxhay, 2 Phillips 774; Cheatham v. Taylor, 148 Va. 26, 138 S.E. 545; Whitney v. Union Railway Co., 11 Gray 359, 11 Mass. 359, 71 Am.Dec. 715; Pomeroy on Equity Jurisprudence, 4th Ed., Vol. 4, secs. 1694, 1695; Northrup on Law of Real Property, p. 377, and 24 Harvard Law Review 574.

It is provided by section 3393, Code 1942, sec. 17–60, Code 1950, that "All deeds * * * and all contracts in reference to real estate, which have been acknowledged as required by law, * * * and all other writings relating to or affecting real estate, which are authorized to be recorded, shall, unless otherwise provided, be recorded in a book to be known as the deed book."

This section, as well as section 5194, Code 1942, sec. 55–96, Code 1950, having to do with the recordation of deeds, was complied with when the deed of July 28, 1946, which imposed the restriction was admitted to record. Though it is not shown that W.H. Boyd, lessee of the premises had actual knowledge of the covenant, it does appear that through recordation of this deed, he had constructive notice. It was constructive notice to the subsequent grantee, Pauline H. Hewitt, and her lessee, W.H. Boyd. Cheatham v. Taylor, supra, and Saffell v. Orr, 109 Va. 768, 64 S.E. 1057. Under these facts, in equity the restrictive personal covenant limits the use to which either or both may put the lots in question. 51 C.J.S., Landlord and Tenant, § 238, p. 866.

Nor do we deem the covenant illegal for its terms afford only fair protection to the interests of appellant and are not so broad as to interfere with the public interest. * * *

Whitney v. Union Railway Co., supra, is considered a leading case on the question presented. There Mrs. Whitney was the owner of a tract of land, which she subdivided into lots and conveyed one of them to White by a deed containing restrictions as to use. She continued to be the owner of a part of the original tract and occupied a dwelling house thereon.

In holding that equity would restrain the violation of the covenant in the suit of Mrs. Whitney against White's successors in title, the court said:

" * * * Every owner of real property has the right so to deal with it as to restrain its use by his grantees within such limits as to prevent its appropriation to purposes which will impair the value or diminish the pleasure of the enjoyment of the land which he retains. The only restriction on this right is, that it shall be exercised reasonably, with a due regard to public policy, and without creating any unlawful restraint of trade. * * * " 11 Gray 359, 11 Mass. 359, 71 Am.Dec. 716–17.

"In this view, the precise form or nature of the covenant or agreement is quite immaterial. It is not essential that it should run with the land. A personal covenant or agreement will be held valid and binding in equity on a purchaser taking the estate with notice. It is not binding on him merely because he stands as an assignee of the party who made the agreement, but because he has taken the estate with notice of a valid agreement concerning it, which he cannot equitably refuse to perform: * * * ". Id., 11 Gray 359, 11 Mass. 359, 71 Am.Dec. at page 718. * * *

We conclude that appellant is, so long as he conducts his store for the sale of groceries and soft drinks (14 Am.Jur., "Courts", sec. 205, p. 616), entitled to an injunction restraining Pauline H. Hewitt, the owner of the lots, and her lessee, W.H. Boyd, from operating the store wherein groceries and soft drinks are sold and dispensed (excepting High Rock after 6:00 o'clock p.m.).

The decree is reversed and the cause remanded to the trial court for the entry of an injunction in conformity with this opinion.

Reversed and remanded.

Notes

1.　Kibbe conveyed a quarry to Flynt and covenanted, with language which purported to bind or benefit the heirs and assigns of both parties, not to open or work any quarry on other designated land owned by him.　Plaintiff, successor to Flynt, sued the successor to Kibbe's other land to enjoin him from quarrying stone thereon.　The bill was dismissed.　Norcross v. James, 140 Mass. 188, 2 N.E. 946 (1885).　Holmes, J., in the opinion of the court said:

"The principle of policy applied to affirmative covenants, applies also to negative ones.　They must 'touch and concern' or 'extend to the support of the thing' conveyed.　5 Coke, 16a; Id. 24b.　They must be 'for the benefit of the estate.'　Cockson v. Cock, Cro.Jac. 125.　Or, as it is said more broadly, new and unusual incidents cannot be attached to land by way either of benefit or of burden.　Keppell v. Bailey, 2 Mylne & K. 517, 535; Ackroyd v. Smith, 10 C.B. 164; Hill v. Tupper, 2 Hurl. & C. 121.

"The covenant under consideration, as it stands on the report, falls outside the limits of this rule, even in the narrower form.　In what way does it extend to the support of the plaintiff's quarry?　It does not make the use or occupation of it more convenient.　It does not in any way affect the use or occupation; it simply tends indirectly to increase its value, by excluding a competitor from the market for its products.　If it be asked what is the difference in principle between an easement to have land unbuilt upon, such as was recognized in Brooks v. Reynolds, 106 Mass. 31, and an easement to have a quarry left unopened, the answer is that, whether a difference of degree or of kind, the distinction is plain between a grant or covenant that looks to direct physical advantage in the occupation of the dominant estate, such as light and air, and one which only concerns it in the indirect way which we have mentioned.　The scope of the covenant and the circumstances show that it is not directed to the quiet enjoyment of the dominant land."

2.　*Covenants Relating to Competition.*　The restricted view of the touching and concerning requirement announced in Norcross v. James and recognized in Oliver v. Hewitt was adopted in Section 537 of the Restatement.　But the Restatement indicates that the burden of a promise not to compete with the promisee may bind successors in equity.　Restatement § 539, comment *k*. Such a distinction is declared in Oliver v. Hewitt, although you will note that Norcross v. James also involved a suit in equity.　Do you discover any justification for such a distinction?　Is the court in Oliver v. Hewitt really saying that under the rule of Tulk v. Moxhay a court need not be concerned with any touching and concerning requirement?

Unless limited in scope, covenants relating to competition may be regarded as offensive as being in restraint of trade and tending to produce a monopoly of trade or business.　A covenant which is unreasonably restrictive in this regard may be declared illegal and therefore not enforceable even between the original parties.　If such a covenant is not found illegal, it may be that some courts in refusing to permit such a covenant to run with the land are moved at least in part by such policy considerations.　If so, it should not matter whether enforcement against a successor is sought by a legal or an equitable remedy.

The Massachusetts court reaffirmed the rule of Norcross v. James in Shell Oil Co. v. Henry Ouellette & Sons Co., 352 Mass. 725, 227 N.E.2d 509 (1967). The court recognized the criticism that has been directed against Norcross v. James and the present demand for covenants of this kind "particularly for shopping centers and service stations."　But the court stressed past reliance by the bar of the state on the rule of Norcross v. James as justification for its refusal to overturn that rule. See also Bill Wolf Petroleum Corp. v. Chock Full of Power Gasoline Corp., 41 A.D.2d 950, 344 N.Y.S.2d 30 (1973). Compare Gulf Corp. Finally, in Whitinsville Plaza v. Kotseas, 378 Mass. 85, 390 N.E.2d 243 (1979), the Massachusetts court overruled Norcross v. James in respect to competition covenants entered into after the *Ouellette* case. Such covenants will run if consistent with a reasonable over-all purpose to develop real estate for commercial use and if "the ordinary requirements for creation and enforcement of real covenants" are met.

In other jurisdictions the cases are in conflict, but with more cases favoring enforcement, and there appears to be little recognition of any distinction in this respect between actions at law and suits in equity. See A.L.P. § 9.13a. Among the recent cases compare Gillen-Crow Pharmacies, Inc. v. Mandzak, 5 Ohio St.2d 201, 34 O.O. 217, 215 N.E.2d 377 (1966) with Savings, Inc. v. City of Blytheville, 240 Ark. 588, 401 S.W.2d 26 (1966). In the latter case a covenant by a lessor not to compete with his lessee was held to be personal to the lessor. The court relied in part on the rationale of Norcross v. James and in part on an interpretation of the covenant as not intended to bind successors. In Doo v. Packwood, 265 Cal.App.2d 752, 71 Cal.Rptr. 477 (1968), a covenant by a grantee not to use the premises for a grocery store was enforced against his lessee, who took with notice. The court relied in part on Oliver v. Hewitt. And in Alexander's Department Stores v. Arnold Constable Corp., 105 N.J.Super. 14, 250 A.2d 792 (1969), a covenant in a deed that the grantee would not use the granted land for a shopping center or a store, which was expressly made for the benefit of designated land of the grantor, was held enforceable by a lessee of the grantor against a successor of the grantee, despite the fact that the grantor, after the lease, had purported to release the restriction. See also Hall v. American Oil Co., 504 S.W.2d 313 (Mo.App.1973), and Quadro Stations, Inc. v. Gilley, 7 N.C.App. 227, 172 S.E.2d 237 (1970), involving promises not to operate gasoline service stations. But in Clear Lake Apartments, Inc. v. Clear Lake Utilities Co., 549 S.W.2d 385 (Tex.1977), a covenant, not connected with any conveyance, granting the utilities company the exclusive right to furnish water and sewer services to the land owned by the covenantor, was held not binding on its successor. The court said that the covenant was not enforceable in equity because, since it did not obligate the covenantor to use its land in any particular manner, it was personal only.

Does the same problem exist with respect to the running of the benefit of a competition covenant? According to the Restatement the benefit of such a covenant does meet the touching and concerning requirement. Restatement § 543(2)(b). Language in the opinion in Norcross v. James appears to be to the contrary. A number of other cases support the Restatement view. 2 A.L.P. §§ 9.13a, 9.28. One trouble in assessing the cases lies in the fact that, as in Norcross v. James, it is sometimes not clear whether the decision relates to the running of the benefit or of the burden or both. It can be argued at least that the policy factors which complicate the problem of the running of the burden are not applicable to the running of the benefit.

3. *Benefit in Gross?* Reference is made to the view of the English courts that the burden of a restrictive covenant will not bind successors if the benefit is in gross. See Note 4 page 633 supra. Such a view is consistent with the English refusal to recognize easements in gross. Since a more liberal view exists in this country regarding easements in gross, it might be expected that the courts would not object to the running of burdens when the benefit is in gross. But the few American cases in point are in conflict, with substantial authority favoring the English rule. See 2 A.L.P. § 9.32.

In Bill Wolf Petroleum Corp. v. Chock Full of Power Gasoline Corp., 41 A.D.2d 950, 344 N.Y.S.2d 30 (1973), an agreement made after a conveyance of land that the grantee would purchase all its requirements for gasoline to operate a service station from the plaintiff was not enforceable against the covenantor's successor. The court said that the burden did not touch and concern the land, which seems to mean that it must affect the land in a physical sense. The court also followed the rule that a burden will not run in equity where the benefit is in gross and offered in support of the rule the policy that favors free alienability and maximum utility of land. See also Brown v. Fuller, 347 A.2d 127 (Me.1975).

For an interesting case in which the burden of such a covenant was held to run see Pratte v. Balatsos, 99 N.H. 430, 113 A.2d 492 (1955), 101 N.H. 48, 132 A.2d 142 (1957). The case involved a promise to permit the installation of a jukebox in the promisor's place of business for a term of 14 years, to pay the promisee a percentage of income it produced, and not to permit the installation of any similar equipment by anyone else. A successor to the promisor sought the removal of the machine, but was enjoined from breaching the agreement. The court conceded that the benefit was in gross, but that this was no bar to the running of the burden in equity. The court said that the rule extended to affirmative covenants. Note, however, the enforcement by injunction.

4. *Vertical Privity in Equity.* The requirement of privity of estate between each of the parties to a covenant and his successors in interest has been previously mentioned. See Note 6 page 641 supra. A significant element in the doctrine of equitable servitudes which has developed from the rule of Tulk v. Moxhay is the elimination of this requirement, as well as the requirement of privity of estate between the contracting parties. One who takes any possessory interest in land burdened by a promise which is otherwise enforceable against successors in equity will be subject to the burden of the promise. A purchaser with notice from the promisor is bound in theory, not upon a contractual obligation, but because the land is burdened by an incorporeal property interest for the benefit of another. There is authority that this principle extends to one who acquires title to burdened land by adverse possession, unless the possession was also adverse to the requirements of the promise. Restatement § 539, comment i; 2 A.L.P. § 9.31.

The same principle applies to the running of the benefit of an equitable servitude, except that no authority has been found which permits one who gains title to benefitted land by adverse possession to enforce the covenant. But see Holmes, J., in Norcross v. James, 140 Mass. 188, 2 N.E. 946, 947 (1885).

It has been held that when a promisee transfers all his interest in land benefitted by the promise of another, he deprives himself of any further right of enforcement. 2 A.L.P. § 9.27.

RODGERS v. REIMANN

Supreme Court of Oregon, 1961.
227 Or. 62, 361 P.2d 101.

O'CONNELL, Justice. This is a suit in equity to enforce a building restriction contained in a land sale contract under which defendants were purchasers of a lot in the city of Salem, Oregon.

Defendants own the restricted lot, hereafter referred to as Lot 11, which abuts Kingwood drive on the east. The lot owned by plaintiffs abuts Kingwood drive on the west, directly across the street from Lot

11. Plaintiffs purchased their lot from Dr. and Mrs. Lebold on January 31, 1957. We shall refer to plaintiffs' parcel as the Lebold lot. At the time plaintiffs purchased the Lebold lot, Mr. and Mrs. Willett owned the lot adjoining the Lebold lot on the north. At that time also, the Lebolds and the Willetts owned Lot 11. On December 15, 1959 the Lebolds and the Willetts joined together to convey Lot 11 under a land sale contract to the defendants. The contract contained the following covenant:

"That no dwelling house shall be constructed on said real premises the floor level of which shall be more than one foot higher than the street curb of Kingwood Drive adjacent to said real premises."

Soon after defendants entered into the contract for the purchase of Lot 11 they commenced construction of a dwelling house on the lot. Plaintiffs brought this suit to enjoin the construction of the dwelling house allegedly in violation of the covenant. The trial court entered a decree dismissing plaintiffs' complaint, from which decree plaintiffs appeal.

To be entitled to enforce the covenant plaintiffs must show that the building restrictions imposed upon Lot 11 were intended to benefit them as the owners of the Lebold lot and that defendants entered into the covenant with notice that the covenant was to have this effect. * * *

However, the intention to benefit a particular parcel of land through the imposition of the restrictions on the land conveyed need not be expressly recited in the contract or deed. * * *

It is not reasonable to presume that building restrictions such as we are concerned with here are intended simply for the personal benefit of the vendors. * * * Rather it is reasonable to presume that the covenant in the case at bar was intended to benefit at least the land which was retained by the Willetts at the time they joined with the Lebolds in conveying Lot 11.

It is somewhat more difficult to assume that such a covenant is intended to benefit a prior grantee of the vendor, or, as in this case, the prior grantee of one of the two co-grantors. Where the restrictions are a part of a general building plan the courts generally recognize that a prior purchaser from the covenantee can enforce the covenants subsequently entered into between his grantor and subsequent grantees. 2 American Law of Property (1952) § 9.30; 5 Restatement, Property, Servitudes (1944) Intr. Note, Ch. 46, p. 3244, and § 541, comment f. If the covenants touch and concern the land previously conveyed out of an area subdivided pursuant to a general building plan, it is ordinarily held that in the absence of evidence of a contrary intent it will be assumed that the parties intended to benefit such land. * * *

However, where, as here, there is no general building plan, the inference that the covenant is intended to benefit land previously conveyed by the common grantor is ordinarily more difficult to draw. Some courts take the view that in the absence of a general building scheme a covenant cannot inure to the prior grantee even though the covenantor and covenantee intended to benefit the land previously conveyed. Snow v. Van Dam, 1935, 291 Mass. 477, 197 N.E. 224, 228; Hazen v. Mathews,

1903, 184 Mass. 388, 68 N.E. 838, 839; Roberts v. Scull, 1899, 58 N.J.Eq. 396, 402, 43 A. 583. But, as pointed out by the Restatement of Property, the prevailing view is to the contrary: "It has, however, come to be the prevailing view that beneficiaries of a promise other than the promisee can enforce the promise (see Restatement of Contracts, Chapter 6) even though the promise is not part of a general plan. To the extent to which this is true, the fact that a promise respecting the use of land is not made pursuant to a general plan of land development is not a barrier to the enforcement of the promise by third parties who are beneficiaries of the promise." 5 Restatement, Property, Servitudes, 1944, Intr. Note, Ch. 46, p. 3244. We adopt the prevailing view.

We find no difficulty in recognizing the principle that a prior grantee may sue upon a covenant subsequently made by his grantor, if all of the elements essential to the enforcement of the covenant are present. Some courts have regarded the prior grantee as a third-party beneficiary of a contract entered into between his grantor and the covenantor. * * * The Restatement adopts this view. 5 Restatement, Property, Servitudes, 1944, § 541, Comments c and f. A second theory, recognized by some courts, recognizes the creation of an implied reciprocal servitude. This theory is explained in 2 American Law of Property, 1952, § 9.30, p. 426, as follows:

"* * * when the prior purchaser acquires his land in expectation that he will be entitled to the benefit of subsequently created servitudes, there immediately arises an implied reciprocal servitude against the common grantor's remaining land. If so, then he is enforcing, not the express agreement made by the common grantor when he subsequently sells his remaining land, but this implied reciprocal servitude created by implication at the time of the conveyance to the prior purchaser."

We feel free to employ either of these theories, as the case may demand, in determining whether a prior grantee should be entitled to enforce a covenant inserted in a subsequent deed. Cf., Bristol v. Woodward, 1929, 251 N.Y. 275, 167 N.E. 441, 445–446; 2 American Law of Property, 1952, § 9.30, pp. 426–427.

To establish a reciprocal servitude it is necessary to find that the prior grantee purchased his land in reliance upon his grantor's promise to impose restrictions upon the retained parcels when conveyed by the common grantor to subsequent purchasers. The evidence in the case at bar is not sufficient to establish such reliance by the plaintiffs. Dr. Lebold testified that he was not certain whether he discussed with plaintiffs the imposition of restrictions on Lot 11 before or after the conveyance to plaintiffs. Mr. Rodgers testified that he believed "quite strongly" that he discussed the matter with Dr. Lebold prior to purchasing his lot, but that he was not certain. This is not sufficient evidence to create a servitude upon Lot 11 in favor of the Lebold lot.

We are willing to recognize, as many courts do, that the Statute of Frauds, ORS 41.580, is not an impediment in the creation of such a servitude. * * * But this relaxation of the requirement that the creation of interests in land must be in writing should be attended with the safeguard furnished by satisfactory evidence of a clear and unequivocal agreement between the prior grantee and his grantor, as well as a satisfactory showing that the subsequent grantee had notice of the agreement. In the present case Lebold and Rodgers did not clearly and unequivocally agree, as a part of their bargain in the sale of the Lebold lot, that Lebold would restrict Lot 11 for the benefit of the Lebold lot.

Will the evidence sustain the theory that a third-party beneficiary contract was created? The scope of a third-party beneficiary's rights and remedies in Oregon is not clearly defined. See, Howard, The Restatement of the Law of Contracts with Oregon Notes (Sections 133–147, Chapter 6), 1933, 12 Or.L.Rev. 263; Note, Contracts—Third Party Beneficiaries—Donee's Rights in Oregon, 1943, 22 Or.L.Rev. 297. However, we shall not at this time attempt to reappraise our cases touching upon this part of the law. For purposes of this case it is enough to recognize that under accepted principles relating to the enforcement of restrictive covenants by third persons, plaintiffs do not make out a sufficient case to qualify as either creditor or donee beneficiaries. 5 Restatement, Property, Servitudes, 1944, § 541, Comment e, p. 3248, states the following principle:

"In order to make a third person the beneficiary of a promise it must be shown that the promise was sufficiently comprehensive to include the benefit of the third person within its intended operation. In the case of promises respecting the use of land, it is often true that others besides the promisee would be equally benefited by the performance of the promise. Such others are not entitled to enforce the performance of the promise merely because of that fact (see Illustration 1). It must be shown that benefit to them was one of the things bargained for between the promisee and the promisor."

And see Hall v. Risley and Heikkila, 1950, 188 Or. 69, 213 P.2d 818. In the case at bar it was not shown that the benefit to plaintiffs was one of the things bargained for between the promisee and the promisor. The requirement that benefit to plaintiffs' lot must be shown to be one of the things bargained for between the common grantor and the subsequent grantee may also be regarded as an application of the rule that a purchaser of land will not be bound by a restriction unless he has notice of it. The purchaser must not only have notice that there is a restriction imposed upon the land he is purchasing but he must have notice of its scope, i.e., the extent to which others may enforce it. We recognize that such proof need not be direct and that it may rest upon "reasonable inferences from the circumstances under which the promise was made." 5 Restatement, Property, Servitudes, 1944, § 541, Comment e. But the inferences are not strong enough in the present case. The evidence tending to prove that the bargain between defendants and their grantors had for one of its purposes the benefiting of plaintiffs' land was equivocal.

The evidence may be regarded as establishing that both the Lebolds and the Willetts intended the restriction on Lot 11 to benefit plaintiffs' lot. They purchased Lot 11 to protect their view. Dr. Lebold testified that they even contemplated building a dwelling house, of such size and location so as not to interfere with their view, on Lot 11 to assure themselves of an unobstructed view. Dr. Lebold further testified that the restriction was placed in the contract of sale with the intention of protecting the view from plaintiffs' lot, although he admitted that he did not directly participate in the drafting of the contract. Mr. Willett was in charge of closing the sale of Lot 11, but Dr. Lebold testified that "I felt that he [Willett] had the interest of both pieces of property in mind when we talked about selling that [Lot 11.]" But, although the evidence is reasonably clear that at least the Lebolds intended the restrictions to benefit plaintiffs' lot, the evidence that defendants had either actual or constructive notice of this purpose was insufficient to meet plaintiffs' burden of proof.

Defendants could not have learned of the purpose of the restrictions from the Willetts or Lebolds because the sellers' negotiations for the sale of Lot 11 were handled exclusively by Mr. Hutchison, the real estate agent who showed Lot 11 to defendants. At no time prior to the purchase of Lot 11 did defendants discuss with the Lebolds or the Willetts the purpose of the restrictions. Mr. Hutchison testified that he informed the defendants that the Lebolds and the Willetts would insist upon building restrictions as a condition to the sale of the lot. He also testified that he informed defendants of the purpose of the restrictions. But there was no evidence to show precisely what Mr. Hutchison understood this purpose to be, nor was it shown what he communicated to defendants. He simply testified that the sellers, i.e. the Lebolds and the Willetts, told him why the restriction would be imposed upon Lot 11 and that he communicated this purpose to Mr. Reimann. In order to conclude that Hutchison informed Reimann that the restrictions were to benefit plaintiffs' lot, we would have to infer that Hutchison was informed by the Lebolds (or by their representatives, the Willetts) that they wanted to benefit the lot they had previously conveyed to plaintiffs. We do not feel that we can supply this inference.

To be weighed against any inference which might be drawn that the parties intended the restriction to benefit the Lebold lot is the testimony of Mr. Reimann. He testified as follows:

"A. He told me that there will be restrictions. He told me about the Willett property. He never mentioned Mr. Rodgers and I never knew the man until this suit came up but only that—but the real estate man told me that Mr. Lebold has sold the house and he didn't have anything to do with it any more.

     *   *   *

"Q. Now, did Mr. Hutchison ever tell you about any restrictions that would be on the property? A. He said there would be restrictions on the property of one foot above the curb line.

"Q. And did he tell you who that was to benefit? A. Yes, he told me it was to benefit Mr. Willett. He hadn't sold it yet.

"Q. Did he tell you what the purpose of the restriction was?

     *   *   *

"A. Yes.

"Q. He did. What did he tell you the restrictions were for? A. It was to help Mr. Willett sell his property.

"Q. Did he ever tell you the purpose of those restrictions was to protect the view from either the Willett or the Lebold lot? A. The Lebold property was never mentioned nor were the Rodgers either.

"Q. What about the Willett property? A. That was mentioned.

"Q. What about the view? A. That was, I think, mentioned, too, but the way I understand Willett it was absolutely all right with his view property.

"Q. Didn't he tell you that the restrictions would be on there to protect the view? A. Well, I don't know exactly what he said at that minute, I don't know.

"Q. But you think something was mentioned about the view? A. Well, I bought the property just for the view of it. Now, there is also a time that view was mentioned—what he exactly said I don't know, I couldn't remember if I wanted to.

     * * *

"Q. Now, you heard Mr. Hutchison testify here this morning, did you not, Mr. Reimann? A. Yes.

"Q. Can you remember what he did testify—I'm not going to ask you to repeat it—but do you remember what he did testify to substantially? A. Well, I don't know what you mean by that. You better give me a certain point and I can say yes or no.

"Q. As I recall it, Mr. Hutchison testified that he told you what the reason for the restrictions were; he didn't testify what that reason was, but he testified that he did tell you what the reason for the restrictions were, do you remember that? A. If the stenographer knows, I don't know. I don't remember those things.

"Q. Well, are you denying that he did tell what the reason for the restrictions were? A. I don't deny anything.

"Mr. Banks: No further questions."

Plaintiffs argue that the intention to benefit plaintiffs' lot can be inferred from the juxtaposition of plaintiffs' and defendants' lots. As we have already stated, the purpose of a restriction may be arrived at by drawing reasonable inferences from the circumstances under which the restriction was created. One of these circumstances is the location of the burdened property in relation to the land of the person claiming the benefit of the restriction. In the usual case the inference is drawn from the fact that the claimants' and defendants' land are a part of a general plan of development. * * * And in some cases notice of restrictions has been imputed to the purchaser from the physical appearance of the neighboring land in the subdivision. * * * However, the inference that the restriction was intended to benefit the complainants' property may also be drawn where a general plan of development does not exist. * * *

In the present case we would be willing to find that defendants had notice that the restrictions on Lot 11 were intended to benefit plaintiffs' lot if the circumstances strongly supported that inference. But as we read the record the inference is not strong. A dwelling house could be constructed on Lot 11 in such a way as to interfere with the view from the Willetts' lot. It is, therefore, possible and not unreasonable to construe the restriction to have been inserted in the contract of sale for the purpose of benefiting Willetts' lot only. And that, according to Mr. Reimann's testimony, was precisely his understanding of the purpose of the restriction. To accept plaintiffs' position we would have to disbelieve Reimann and, in addition, draw an inference from a highly equivocal circumstance. A burden on land, created by covenant, should rest upon a more substantial foundation of proof.

The decree of the trial court is affirmed. Neither party to recover costs.

SLOAN, J., dissents.

SANBORN v. McLEAN

Supreme Court of Michigan, 1925.
233 Mich. 227, 206 N.W. 496.

WIEST, J. Defendant Christina McLean owns the west 35 feet of lot 86 of Green Lawn subdivision, at the northeast corner of Collingwood avenue and Second boulevard, in the city of Detroit, upon which there is a dwelling house, occupied by herself and her husband, defendant John A. McLean. The house fronts Collingwood avenue. At the rear of the lot is an alley. Mrs. McLean derived title from her husband, and, in the course of the opinion, we will speak of both as defendants. Mr. and Mrs. McLean started to erect a gasoline filling station at the rear end of their lot, and they and their contractor, William S. Weir, were enjoined by decree from doing so and bring the issues before us by appeal. Mr. Weir will not be further mentioned in the opinion.

Collingwood avenue is a high grade residence street between Woodward avenue and Hamilton boulevard, with single, double, and apartment houses, and plaintiffs, who are owners of land adjoining and in the vicinity of defendants' land, and who trace title, as do defendants, to the proprietors of the subdivision, claim that the proposed gasoline station will be a nuisance per se, is in violation of the general plan fixed for use of all lots on the street for residence purposes only, as evidenced by restrictions upon 53 of the 91 lots fronting on Collingwood avenue, and that defendants' lot is subject to a reciprocal negative easement barring a use so detrimental to the enjoyment and value of its neighbors. Defendants insist that no restrictions appear in their chain of title and they purchased without notice of any reciprocal negative easement, and deny that a gasoline station is a nuisance per se. We find no occasion to pass upon the question of nuisance, as the case can be decided under the rule of reciprocal negative easement.

This subdivision was planned strictly for residence purposes, except lots fronting Woodward avenue and Hamilton boulevard. The 91 lots on Collingwood avenue were platted in 1891, designed for and each one sold solely for residence purposes, and residences have been erected upon all of the lots. Is defendants' lot subject to a reciprocal negative easement? If the owner of two or more lots, so situated as to bear the relation, sells one with restrictions of benefit to the land retained, the servitude becomes mutual, and, during the period of restraint, the owner of the lot or lots retained can do nothing forbidden to the owner of the lot sold. For want of a better descriptive term this is styled a reciprocal negative easement. It runs with the land sold by virtue of express fastening and abides with the land retained until loosened by expiration of its period of service or by events working its destruction. It is not personal to owners, but operative upon use of the land by any owner having actual or constructive notice thereof. It is an easement passing its benefits and carrying its obligations to all purchasers of land, subject to its affirmative or negative mandates. It originates for mutual benefit and exists with vigor sufficient to work its ends. It must start with a common owner. Reciprocal negative easements are never retroactive; the very nature of their origin forbids. They arise, if at all, out of a benefit accorded land retained, by restrictions upon neighboring land sold by a common owner. Such a scheme of restriction must start with a common owner; it cannot arise and fasten upon one lot by reason of other lot owners conforming to a general plan. If a reciprocal negative easement attached to defendants' lot, it was fastened thereto while in the hands of the common owner of it and neighboring lots by way of sale of other lots with restrictions beneficial at that time to it. This leads to inquiry as to what lots, if any, were sold with restrictions by the common owner before the sale of defendants' lot. While the proofs cover another avenue, we need consider sales only on Collingwood.

December 28, 1892, Robert J. and Joseph R. McLaughlin, who were then evidently owners of the lots on Collingwood avenue, deeded lots 37 to 41 and 58 to 62, inclusive, with the following restrictions:

"No residence shall be erected upon said premises which shall cost less than $2,500, and nothing but residences shall be erected upon said premises. Said residences shall front on Helene (now Collingwood) avenue and be placed no nearer than 20 feet from the front street line."

July 24, 1893, the McLaughlins conveyed lots 17 to 21 and 78 to 82, both inclusive, and lot 98 with the same restrictions. Such restrictions were imposed for the benefit of the lands held by the grantors to carry out the scheme of a residential district, and a restrictive negative easement attached to the lots retained, and title to lot 86 was then in the McLaughlins. Defendants' title, through mesne conveyances, runs back to a deed by the McLaughlins dated September 7, 1893, without restrictions mentioned therein. Subsequent deeds to other lots were executed by the McLaughlins, some with restrictions and some without. Previous to September 7, 1893, a reciprocal negative easement had attached to lot 86 by acts of the owners, as before mentioned, and such easement is still attached and may now be enforced by plaintiffs, provided defendants, at the time of their purchase, had knowledge, actual or constructive, thereof. The plaintiffs run back with their title, as do defendants, to a common owner. This common owner, as before stated, by restrictions upon lots sold, had burdened all the lots retained with reciprocal restrictions. Defendants' lot and plaintiff Sanborn's lot, next thereto, were held by such common owner, burdened with a reciprocal negative easement, and, when later sold to separate parties, remained burdened therewith, and right to demand observance thereof passed to each purchaser with notice of the easement. The restrictions were upon defendants' lot while it was in the hands of the common owners, and abstract of title to defendants' lot showed the common owners, and the record showed deeds of lots in the plat restricted to perfect and carry out the general plan and resulting in a reciprocal negative easement upon defendants' lot and all lots within its scope, and defendants and their predecessors in title were bound by constructive notice under our recording acts. The original plan was repeatedly declared in subsequent sales of lots by restrictions in the deeds, and, while some lots sold were not so restricted, the purchasers thereof, in every instance, observed the general plan and purpose of the restrictions in building residences. For upward of 30 years the united efforts of all persons interested have carried out the common purpose of making and keeping all the lots strictly for residences, and defendants are the first to depart therefrom.

When Mr. McLean purchased on contract in 1910 or 1911, there was a partly built dwelling house on lot 86, which he completed and now occupies. He had an abstract of title which he examined and claims he was told by the grantor that the lot was unrestricted. Considering the character of use made of all the lots open to a view of Mr. McLean when he purchased, we think, he was put thereby to inquiry, beyond asking his grantor, whether there were restrictions. He had an abstract showing the subdivision and that lot 86 had 97 companions. He could not avoid noticing the strictly uniform residence character given the lots by the expensive dwellings thereon, and the least inquiry would have quickly developed the fact that lot 86 was subjected to a reciprocal negative easement, and he could finish his house, and, like the others, enjoy the benefits of the easement. We do not say Mr. McLean should have asked his neighbors about restrictions, but we do say that with the notice he had from a view of the premises on the street, clearly indicating the residences were built and the lots occupied in strict accordance with a general plan, he was put to inquiry, and, had he inquired, he would have found of record the reason for such general conformation, and the benefits thereof serving the owners of lot 86 and the obligations running with such service and available to adjacent lot owners to prevent a departure from the general plan by an owner of lot 86.

While no case appears to be on all fours with the one at bar, the principles we have stated, and the conclusions announced, are supported by Allen v. City of Detroit, 167 Mich. 464, 133 N.W. 317, 36 L.R.A.,N.S., 890; McQuade v. Wilcox, 215 Mich. 302, 183 N.W. 771, 16 A.L.R. 997; French v. White Star Refining Co., 229 Mich. 474, 201 N.W. 444; Silberman v. Uhrlaub, 116 App.Div. 869, 102 N.Y.S. 299; Boyden v. Roberts, 131 Wis. 659, 111 N.W. 701; Howland v. Andrus, 80 N.J.Eq. 276, 83 A. 982.

We notice the decree in the circuit directed that the work done on the building be torn down. If the portion of the building constructed can be utilized for any purpose within the restrictions, it need not be destroyed.

With this modification, the decree in the circuit is affirmed, with costs to plaintiffs.

Notes

1. A finding of "reciprocal negative easements" in lots in a subdivision implies the resolution of at least two basic problems in allowing each lot owner to enforce restrictions against other lot owners. One question relates to the running of the burden of such a restriction against one whose own deed may not have contained the restriction. The other relates to the running of the benefit, that is, the necessary proof that the benefit of a covenant in any particular deed was intended to benefit other owners in the subdivision. The lack of such proof was the difficulty the court faced in Rodgers v. Reimann, supra. The necessary proof was supplied in Sanborn v. McLean in the form of proof of a "general plan" of restriction within the subdivision. This raises the question how such general plan can be proved.

The most conclusive sort of proof is to enter restrictions on or as part of a plat of the subdivision which is filed for record, reference to which is then made in each conveyance of the separate lots. There is some authority that the intention that restrictive covenants are for the benefit of certain land, including restricted land under a common plan, must appear in some form in the deed to any party against whom enforcement is sought. See Werner v. Graham, 181 Cal. 174, 183 P. 945 (1919). Generally, however, it is held that such proof may be extrinsic. Evidence that the common grantor publicized in advance of any sales of lots the restricted nature of the subdivision, or that he exhibited a map or plat of the entire tract at the time of the sale of one of the lots involved, or that the grantor at the time of the sale of a restricted lot represented that similar restrictions would be imposed on other lots, have been held to be evidence of a general plan of restriction. So also even with proof of a substantial uniformity in the restrictions imposed in the several deeds, although it has been held that that factor alone may be insufficient proof, depending perhaps on the time when a lot in question was sold in relation to the time of the sale of other lots. Note what the court accepted as sufficient proof of a general plan in Sanborn v. McLean.

2. A more serious problem exists in respect to the imposition of reciprocal negative easements against lot owners who take deeds without express restrictions. Sanborn v. McLean held that such reciprocal servitudes will be implied where proof of a general plan is adequate. See Mid State Equipment Co. v. Bell, 217 Va. 133, 225 S.E.2d 877 (1976), for a recent case in accord with Sanborn v. McLean in respect to the sort of notice of such reciprocal servitudes that will be held sufficient. On the other hand some courts have refused to imply such a servitude on extrinsic proof alone, and, under the authority of the Statute of Frauds, require that a grantor's obligation, after conveying lots with restrictions, to convey the remaining lots with the same restrictions, must be evidenced by a writing. See Houghton v. Rizzo, 361 Mass. 635, 281 N.E.2d 577 (1972), for a recent case reasserting the Massachusetts rule to this effect.

3. For an unusual and limited definition of the meaning of a general plan, see Vickery v. Powell, 267 S.C. 23, 225 S.E.2d 856 (1976).

See generally 2 A.L.P. §§ 9.29, 9.30; 5 Powell ¶ 679; Cunningham §§ 8.32, 8.33.

Problems

1. Bishop, owner of a tract of land, conveyed two lots out of the larger whole, which were described by metes and bounds. These lots were sold without restrictions upon their use. Later three more lots were sold, each containing simple restrictions against use of the premises for commercial purposes and keeping livestock thereon. Two Bishop brothers succeeded as heirs to title to the balance of the original tract. This tract was subdivided into eight lots, all of which were sold with a list of ten restrictions that were much more elaborate than those in the earlier deed. One of these lots was conveyed to the complainants in 1950. Another was conveyed to the respondents in 1951. Neither deed contained any covenant by the grantors that they would convey the remaining portion of the tract subject to the restrictions. Complainants sue to enjoin the respondents from violating certain of the restrictions contained in their deed. The lower court granted the relief prayed for, and the respondents appealed. What result? Bessette v. Guarino, 85 R.I. 188, 128 A.2d 839 (1957).

2. Suppose A acquires a lot in a subdivision and his deed contains a restrictive covenant inserted as part of a general plan. Later A subdivides his lot into two parts and conveys these two parcels to B and C, neither deed containing any covenants. Assuming that B and C both have notice of the restrictions in A's deed, what are the rights and duties of B and C respecting the restrictions? See Restatement § 527, comment c; cf. Erwin v. Bayless, 272 Or. 324, 536 P.2d 1242 (1975).

KELL v. BELLA VISTA VILLAGE PROPERTY OWNERS ASSOCIATION

Supreme Court of Arkansas, 1975.
258 Ark. 757, 528 S.W.2d 651.

BYRD, Justice. This litigation arises out of the covenant assessments contained in the bill of assurance of a planned community development for the maintenance and operation of specified common properties developed for the use and benefit of all property owners in the platted area. The litigants are the appellants, George C. Kell, Jr. and Sharon A. Kell, his wife, property owners, and the appellee, Bella Vista Village Property Owners Association, a non profit corporation organized to act as trustee for the property owners. The matter was submitted to the trial court upon the pleadings and the testimony of John A. Cooper, Jr. and James A. Hatcher. The trial court held the assessments valid and secured by a continuing lien upon the land. Based upon that holding the trial court entered a judgment foreclosing the delinquent and unpaid assessments in favor of appellee. For reversal, the appellants raise the issues hereinafter discussed.

POINT 1. Appellants here contend that since the property constituted their homestead under Article 9, § 3 of the Constitution of Arkansas, their property is not subject to the lien of the assessments. The particular section of the declaration in the bill of assurance, which is challenged, provides:

".   .   . The annual and special assessments, together with such interest thereon and costs of collection thereof as hereinafter provided, shall be a charge on the land and shall be a continuing lien upon the property against which each such assessment is made."

The foregoing language is equally as strong and specific as a mortgage provision extending the lien thereof to future advances, and we can see no reason why the language employed should not be considered as creating a continuing lien on the property for future assessments.

POINT 2. The appellants here argue that they are not bound to pay the annual assessments because the covenant does not run with the land. We find no merit in this contention. See Neponsit Property Owners' Ass'n v. Emigrant Industrial Sav. Bank, 278 N.Y. 248, 15 N.E.2d 793, 118 A.L.R. 973 (1938). Furthermore, the proof here shows that the common properties to be maintained add a value to each lot or living unit subject to the covenants.

POINT 3. Even though the record shows that the lien created by the bill of assurance was recorded, the appellants argue that they are not bound by the lien created thereby because they were not orally advised that such a lien existed. We find no merit to this contention. See Ark.Stat.Ann. § 16–114 (Repl.1968), which makes the recording of such instruments constructive notice to all persons.

POINT 4. Appellants contend that the covenant constitutes a perpetuity contrary to Article 2, § 19 of the Constitution of Arkansas. The bill of assurance provides that the assessment covenant will remain outstanding for a term of 26 years and for successive ten year periods thereafter, until an instrument is signed and recorded by the then owners of two-thirds of the lots or living units. We find no merit to this contention. See Lowry v. Norris Lake Shores Development Corporation, 231 Ga. 549, 203 S.E.2d 171 (1974). There is nothing here which keeps the property from vesting.

POINT 5. Under Article III, Section 2 of the declaration in the bill of assurance, the developer is classified as the only Class "B" member of the property owners association, and as such, it is entitled to ten votes for each lot or living unit of which it is the record owner. However, in so far as any action to increase the annual assessments is concerned, the Class "B" member only has a veto over such assessments, and its votes are not counted against the Class "A" members, such as appellants. Such class distinctions are ordinarily upheld among corporate shareholders, and in the absence of authority to the contrary, we can see no reason why such a veto power over increased assessments should be prohibited in matters involving private contract rights.

POINT 6. The allegation that the assessments amount to an unlawful delegation to tax in violation of Article 2, § 23 of the Constitution of Arkansas overlooks the fact that the assessments here arise out of contract and that they constitute a benefit to the property owner. Other courts recognize that such assessments are not an unlawful delegation of the State's taxing power, Henlopen Acres v. Potter, 36 Del.Ch. 141, 127 A.2d 476 (1956).

POINT 7. Appellants contend that the purposes for which the assessments are made are so vague and indefinite that they amount to a restraint on alienation. The "Covenant for Maintenance Assessments" in so far as here applicable provides:

"ARTICLE X

Covenant For Maintenance Assessments

"Section 1. Creation of Lien. The Developer for each Lot and Living Unit owned by it within The Properties hereby covenants and each Owner of any Lot or Living Unit by acceptance of a deed therefor, or by entering into a contract of purchase with the Developer, whether or not it shall be so expressed in any such deed, contract of purchase, or other conveyance, shall be deemed to covenant and agree to pay to the Club: (1) annual assessments of charges; (2) special assessments for capital improvements, such assessments to be fixed, established and collected from time to time as hereinafter provided. The annual and special assessments, together with such interest thereon and costs of collection thereof as hereinafter provided, shall be a charge on the land and shall be a continuing lien upon the property against which each such assessment is made.

"Section 2. Purpose of Assessments. The assessments levied hereunder by the Club shall be used exclusively for the purpose of promoting the recreation, health, safety, and welfare of the residents in The Properties and in particular for the improvement and maintenance of properties, services and facilities devoted to this purpose and related to the use and enjoyment of the Common Properties and the improvements situated upon The Properties, including, but not limited to, the payment of taxes and insurance thereon, and repair, replacement, and additions thereto, and for the cost of labor, equipment, materials, management and supervision thereof. The limitation aforesaid shall not preclude the use of assessments levied hereunder for maintenance of roads and streets within The Properties, even though same have been dedicated to the public.

"Section 3. Basis and Maximum of Annual Assessments. Until the year beginning January, 1970, the annual assessment shall be $60.00 per Lot or Living Unit. From and after January 1, 1970, the annual assessment may be increased by vote of the members, as hereinafter provided, for the next succeeding three years and at the end of each such period of three years for each succeeding period of three years. Unless the annual assessment shall be increased as aforesaid, it shall remain at $60.00 per Lot or Living Unit.

"The Board of Directors of the Club may, after consideration of current maintenance costs and future needs of the Club, fix the actual assessment for any year at a lesser amount. Likewise, the Board of Directors of the Club may, after consideration of the lack of improvements as to lots in a certain area, fix the actual assessment for any year as to these particular lots at a lesser amount.

"Section 4. Special Assessments for Capital Improvements. In addition to the annual assessments authorized by Section 3 hereof, the Club may levy in any assessment year a special assessment, applicable

to that year only, for the purpose of defraying, in whole or in part, the cost of any construction or reconstruction, unexpected repair or replacement of the roads and streets within The Properties, even though same may have been dedicated to the public, and also a described capital improvement upon the Common Properties, including the necessary fixtures and personal property related thereto, provided that any such assessment shall have the assent of 51% of the votes of each class of members who are voting in person or by proxy at a meeting duly called for this purpose, written notice of which shall be sent to all Members at least 30 days in advance and shall set forth the purpose of the meeting. The Board of Directors of the Club may, after consideration of lack of improvements as to lots in a certain area, fix the asssessment for any year as to these particular lots at a lesser amount.

"Section 5. Change in Basis of Maximum of Annual Assessments. Subject to the limitations of Section 3 hereof, and for the purpose therein specified, the Club may change the maximum and basis of the assessments fixed by Section 3 hereof prospectively for any such period provided that any such change shall have the assent of 51% of the votes of each Class of Members who are voting in person or by proxy, at a meeting duly called for this purpose, written notice of which shall be sent to all Members at least 30 days in advance and shall set forth the purpose of the meeting."

As we read the foregoing provisions, the annual assessments are levied for the purposes of improvement and maintenance of the properties held for the joint use of the properties which include, "the payment of taxes and insurance thereon, and repair, replacement, and additions thereto, and for the cost of labor, equipment, materials, management and supervision thereof." Of course, for these purposes the appellee acts as a trustee for the use and benefit of the property owners. In such capacity it has some discretion as to expenditures, but under those circumstances, a property owner would have recourse in a court of equity to prevent any arbitrary or capricious action on the part of appellee. By virtue of this recourse in equity for relief, the covenants contain a formula from which assessments can be determined, and for these purposes, the assessments are not vague and indefinite and do not constitute a restraint on alienation.

The courts that have considered such assessments have upheld them where the purpose of the assessments has been stated so that a formula for the calculation of the amount thereof can be determined. See Rodruck v. Sand Point Maintenance Commission, 48 Wash.2d 565, 295 P.2d 714 (1956). Likewise, such assessments have been struck down as a restraint upon alienation where the covenants do not contain a formula for the calculation of the amount of the assessment. See Peterson v. Beekmere, Incorporated, 117 N.J.Super. 155, 283 A.2d 911 (1971), and the cases from other jurisdictions cited therein. The courts that have considered the matter of assessment covenants have also refused to enforce such covenants when they do not apply alike to all units in the same subdivision enjoying the benefits to the common properties, Peterson v. Beekmere, Incorporated, supra. The reason is that the property bound by such covenants would be forced to tender larger proportionate amounts through assessments although such non-contributing neighbors would enjoy the same benefits.

When we consider the foregoing authorities, the term "a described capital improvement" in Article X, § 4 requires some discussion. If it is construed to mean the erection of any future improvement that the majority desire (such as an astrodome), then it clearly would amount to a restraint on alienation and would be void. However, the term "a described capital improvement" can be construed to mean those improvements described by the covenants and necessarily contemplated in the use or enjoyment thereof, such as an additional water tower to supply sufficient water pressure for domestic use and fire protection for some or all of the property owners. Applying the latter usage, the term "a described capital improvement" would furnish a sufficient formula for the calculation of the amount of the special assessment and would not constitute a restraint on alienation. Since, in the interpretation of contracts, we are to give a written contract, susceptible to more than one interpretation, a construction that will make it valid, it follows that when the term "a described capital improvement" is given the latter interpretation, we must uphold this Article X, § 4 provision as being valid and binding.

The provisions in Sections 3 and 4 of Article X, supra, providing that appellee ". . . may, after consideration of the lack of improvements as to lots in a certain area, fix the actual assessment for any year as to these particular lots at a lesser amount" appears to be invalid since the owners thereof have the same privilege of using the common facilities as do any of the residents of improved lots.

The foregoing invalid provisions can easily be separated from the valid provisions. Since the bill of assurance contains a severability clause and since the assessments here are not affected by the invalid provision, we find that it does not impair or otherwise invalidate the annual assessments for maintenance and repair.

POINT 8. The contention of appellants that the property owners' association has no standing to enforce the covenant to pay annual assessments is without merit. See Neponsit Property Owners' Ass'n v. Emigrant Industrial Sav. Bank, supra.

Affirmed as modified.

Notes

1. In Japanese Gardens Mobile Estates, Inc. v. Hunt, 261 So.2d 193 (Fla. App.1972), the court, in approving a plan for increasing assessments similar to that in the principal case, remanded the case for a determination whether the assessment was reasonably related to the reasonable expenses of maintenance. In Anthony v. Brea Glenbrook Club, 58 Cal.App.3d 506, 130 Cal.Rptr. 32 (1976), obligatory membership in a home owners' association was enforced without any inquiry into the existence of any limitations on the use by the association of membership fees.

2. In Petersen v. Beekmere, Inc., 117 N.J.Super. 155, 283 A.2d 911 (1971), distinguished by the court in *Kell*, an original "neighborhood scheme" was

found to have been abandoned because the original developer had sold some lots without the generally imposed covenant concerning lot assessments. The court said that it would be inequitable to enforce the burden of the covenant only against those lot owners whose lots were originally sold subject to the covenant, that such lot owners would be bearing a disproportionate burden in relation to the benefits that all lot owners enjoyed to some degree. Although no point was made of it, such a conclusion might seem to depend on the reasonable expectations of original purchasers in that regard, that is, whether they purchased with notice of a reserved power in the grantor to waive the covenant in some cases. In Nelle v. Loch Haven Homeowners' Association, 413 So.2d 28 (Fla.1982), the developer reserved the right to approve exceptions or variations respecting the covenants without notice to other lot owners. The court rejected the contention that such a reservation defeated the general plan. It could be regarded as only one relevant factor. The court also said that other courts have by construction limited reserved powers to reasonable exercise so as not to vitiate a general plan. In Wright v. Cypress Shores Development Co., 413 So.2d 1115 (Ala.1982), the power to waive restrictions was reserved to an architectural committee composed of persons affiliated with the developer. The court held that such a power must be exercised reasonably and not inconsistently with the general plan. On that basis, the waiver involved in this case was held void.

3. *Discretionary Servitudes.* It may be assumed that a general scheme of building or use restrictions may prove inadequate over long periods of time because of its inflexibility. In any case, it has become common in subdivision developments to impose restrictions that prevent the erection of any buildings, or certain kinds of buildings, or that otherwise restrict the use of land, without the approval of the developer-grantor, his heirs and assigns, a committee appointed by the developer, or a majority of the lot owners. It is now generally held that such restrictions are valid and enforceable according to their terms, and burden the affected lots as servitudes running with the land. Often such restrictions specify standards to be applied in their enforcement. It has been held, however, that the absence of such standards does not invalidate the restrictions. On the other hand, it is generally held that the discretionary powers must be exercised reasonably and in good faith. It is not yet entirely clear what such a standard means. It seems at least that the burdens must be enforced for the benefit of the lot owners and not to serve the personal whims of the developer or others, and that they must serve the purposes of the general plan. See e.g. Friedberg v. Riverpoint Building Committee, 218 Va. 659, 239 S.E.2d 106 (1977). Reichman, Residential Private Governments: An Introductory Survey, 43 U.Chi.L.Rev. 253, 291 (1976); Annotation, 40 A.L.R.3d 864 (1971). Occasionally one finds a decision that such covenants are personal to the developer and cannot be enforced by any one else after he has disposed of all his interest in the subdivision. Compare Pulver v. Mascolo, 155 Conn. 644, 237 A.2d 97 (1967), with Johnson v. Linton, 491 S.W.2d 189 (Tex.Civ.App.1973).

Note on Cooperative Apartments, Condominiums, and Time-Sharing Arrangements

There are several different legal devices which land developers and landowners may use in creating living arrangements in which each participant exercises some control over his neighbors and is in turn controlled by them. Any detailed study of these arrangements is beyond the scope of this book, but we may note the principal forms of such arrangements.

The Cooperative Apartment. As previously indicated in the Landlord and Tenant chapter, the traditional housing "co-op" involves the creation of a corporation which acquires title to a multi-unit apartment building and leases the individual units to tenants. The tenants' rights to possession of their units are secured by "proprietary leases," and each tenant is also a shareholder in the corporation which owns the apartment building.

The Condominium. More recently, the condominium form of cooperative housing has come into vogue. From the occupant's viewpoint, the principal advantage of the condominium form is that, in addition to preserving the cooperative features of the traditional arrangement, the condominium permits the acquisition of the separate living units in fee simple and the financing of unit acquisition by a separate mortgage on each unit. Unit owners generally own the so-called common elements of the condominium development concurrently, as tenants in common and, in addition, have interests in the nature of easements in the walls, floors, and roofs of buildings in the development.

From the viewpoint of the owner of an apartment building, the condominium arrangement is often very attractive from an economic standpoint. Indeed, it has become so attractive that there has been widespread conversion of rental apartment buildings to condominium status. The result, in many areas has been an acute shortage of rental housing. Regulations which forbid or control conversion have resulted. See Comment, The Condominium Conversion Problem: Causes and Solutions, 1980 Duke L.J. 306 (Apr.1980); Note, Regulatory Responses to the Condominium Conversion Crisis, 59 Wash.U.L.Q. 513 (1981); Note, The Validity of Ordinances Limiting Condominium Conversions, 78 Mich. L.Rev. 124 (1979).

Whether a condominium development is created by new construction or by conversion of an existing rental apartment, the basic instrument for creating the condominium is a document, usually designated by statute as the "Declaration" or the "Master Deed," which must be filed for public record. The enabling statutes generally prescribe the creation of a unit-owners' association, which may or may not be incorporated, as well as machinery for the making of assessments against the individual units to cover the costs of maintaining the common elements—which may include recreational areas, parking lots, and the like—and other administrative expenses. Provision is usually made for constituting such assessments, when properly made, liens upon the individual units.

All of these arrangements require fairly elaborate statutory provisions if they are to work well. There is now available a Common Interest Ownership Act, promulgated by the Conference of Commissioners on Uniform State Laws, which permits a state to achieve, in adopting one act, the same statutory result as would be achieved if the state were to adopt simultaneously the Uniform Condominium Act, the Uniform Planned Community Act, and the Model Real Estate Cooperative Act. There has been some commentary on earlier acts. See Rohan, The Model Condominium Code—A Blueprint for Modernizing Condominium Legislation, 78 Columbia L.Rev. 587 (1978); Jackson and Colgan, The Uniform Condominium Act From a Local Government Perspective, 10 The Urban Lawyer, 429 (1978); Comment, Areas of Dispute in Condominium Law, 12 Wake Forest L.Rev. 979 (1976).

Condominium projects, when duly established, escape the necessity for resort to the law on the running of covenants or equitable servitudes for the enforcement of the obligations of the unit owners, for such obligations are imposed, by statute or by authority conferred by statute, upon all the unit owners without regard to the time when or the persons from whom they may have acquired their units. This is not to say, however, that there are no problems arising with respect to condominium rules and regulations. May families with children under 12 be excluded? May leasing be restrained? May the association assert a "first refusal" upon sale or transfer? How are the restrictions to be enforced? See Note, Condominium Rule Making—Presumptions, Burdens and Abuses: A Call for Substantive Judicial Review in Florida, 34 U.Fla.L.Rev. 219 (1982); Poliakoff, Conflicting Rights in Condominium Living, 54 Fla.B.J. 756 (1980); Comment, The Enforceability of Age Restrictive Covenants in Condominium Developments, 54 So.Calif.L.Rev. 1397 (1981). And see Franklin v. White Egret Condominium, Inc., 358 So.2d 1084 (Fla.App.1978).

It is obvious from the *Kell* case and others like it that some of the features of cooperative housing are now sought for subdivisions in which lots or houses and lots are sold for single-family use. It is now common for a developer of a subdivision to provide places and facilities for recreational or other benefits for all the lot owners. It is not clear from the terms of the condominium statutes what physical variations from the standard multi-unit structures are authorized, that is, whether or when a subdivision developer could if he wished bring his project under the provisions of the condominium law. In any case, the practice prevails of providing for some of the incidents or embellishments of modern subdivisions by the use of contractual arrangements which invoke the rules relating to running covenants and equitable servitudes. It is also evident that some form of organization of the several unit owners, or one which serves their needs, is necessary or desirable for the administration and enforcement of some of these obligations. The inescapable intricacies of the condominium structure suggest the dimensions of the problems involved in attaining the objectives sought by the developers in the *Kell* case. Does the result in the *Kell* case indicate the inadequacy of the applicable law for obtaining some of these objectives, or does it merely show a lack of proper care in implementing those objectives?

Time-Sharing Arrangements. An arrangement called "time-sharing" is perhaps the most rapidly developing new concept in real estate law, as people seek variety in vacation housing arrangements. "Time-sharing" arrangements, which are not always uniform, have been generally described as follows:

"Under a timesharing plan, a person may acquire an interest in property for a segment of time, normally one or two weeks each year. Virtually any piece of property—a house, a condominium, a hotel, even a yacht—can be timeshared. * * *

"A timesharing interest may take a variety of forms. The buyer may obtain a proprietary interest in the property in the form of a fee interest, a life estate, or a term of years. Or, the purchaser may receive a non-proprietary interest in the unit, whereby the seller retains title to the property and the buyer receives an interest analogous to a lease. These interests are generally termed vacation licenses or club memberships and permit the buyer to use the unit for a period of time over a fixed term of years. The non-proprietary interests may be either 'fixed' or 'floating.' Under a fixed program the buyer occupies the same unit for the same period of time each year. With the floating programs, however, the buyer is guaranteed only an unslotted, finite segment of time, which he must reserve in advance each year. The buyer, under the floating arrangement, normally does not receive the right to occupy a particular unit; instead, the units are assigned at the discretion of the entity which manages the program." Comment, Regulating Vacation Timesharing: A More Effective Approach, 29 U.C.L.A.L.Rev. 907 (1982). (Footnotes omitted.) This comment provides a bibliography and an excellent summary of statutory developments, including comment on the Uniform Real Estate Time Share Act. See also, Eastman, Time Share Ownership: A Primer, 57 N.D.L.Rev. 151 (1981).

OSBORNE v. HEWITT

Court of Appeals of Kentucky, 1960.
335 S.W.2d 922.

CULLEN, Commissioner. The question presented is whether there has been such a change in the character of the neighborhood of a particular tract of land platted as a residential subdivision as to warrant nullification of restrictive covenants against commercial use. The lower court answered the question in the negative.

The appellants, L.L. Osborne and wife, own five vacant lots in Block A of the Fairview Heights Subdivision, near the city of Bowling Green. In this block there are two sets of thirteen 50-foot lots running from north to south, one set facing Grider Street on the west and the other facing Riverwood Drive on the east. At the south end of the block there are four large lots facing Fairview Avenue which runs east and west. The original owner who laid out the subdivision in 1945 placed restrictions in the deeds to all of the lots, limiting them to residential use. In 1949 the U.S. 31–W By-Pass was constructed around Bowling Green, to divert major traffic around the city. A section of the by-pass crossed through property immediately to the west of Grider Street, leaving a triangular shaped tract between Grider Street and the by-pass. The base of this triangle, facing Fairview Avenue on the south, is some 400 feet wide, and the triangle gradually narrows going north-ward, coming to its apex at the intersection of Grider Street with the by-pass, immediately above the north line of Block A of the Fairview Heights Subdivision. The triangular tract has come to be occupied exclusively by commercial enterprises, with their main entrances on the by-pass but with back entrances on Grider Street. Also, by reason of the fact that Fairview Avenue extended to the southeast is a county highway, persons living along that highway have made Grider Street a thoroughfare for travel between their homes and the by-pass to Bowling Green.

The vacant lots owned by the appellants are the five southern-most facing on Grider Street. The appellants own also the large lot facing Fairview Avenue at the intersection of that avenue and Grider Street, and on this lot they maintain their residence. With the exception of the appellants' five lots and two other vacant lots facing on Grider Street, all of Block A is occupied by residences.

Before the instant action was brought the appellants succeeded in obtaining a written waiver of the restrictions from most of the owners of lots in Block A. However, a few owners, including Aubrey Hewitt and wife whose home is on the large lot immediately south of the appellants' home, declined to sign a waiver. Thereupon the appellants brought this action seeking a declaratory judgment, against the Hewitts individually and as representatives of other property owners similarly situated.

The Hewitts did not file answer or enter their appearance in the action (although they were present at the taking of the appellants' depositions and asked some questions). The case was submitted on the complaint and appellants' depositions. The trial court concluded that the change in the character of the neighborhood was not such as to authorize a cancellation of the restrictions, and entered judgment dismissing the complaint.

The appellants maintain that under CR 8.04 the averments in their complaint were required to be taken as admitted, because no responsive pleading was filed. However, we think no responsive pleading was required, because in stating the nature of the controversy upon which a declaratory judgment was sought the complaint alleged not only the contentions of the plaintiffs but also those of the defendants.

Upon the merits of the case the appellants point out that the construction of the by-pass was not contemplated when the subdivision was laid out; the triangular tract immediately across Grider Street from the subdivision has acquired a completely commercial character; the traffic on Grider Street has become heavy; there is practically no market as residential property for the vacant lots facing Grider Street; and the area has been rezoned for commercial uses.

These points may be answered as follows: (1) The by-pass does not touch the block in question. (2) There has been no commercial development within the restricted area itself, see Cochran v. Long, Ky., 294 S.W.2d 503, and the mere fact that there has been commercial development across the street from the restricted property is not enough to warrant relief from the restrictions. Hardesty v. Silver, Ky., 302 S.W.2d 578; Franklin v. Moats, Ky., 273 S.W.2d 812. (3) Heavy traffic on the abutting street does not furnish justification for removing the restrictions. Smith v. Tygrett, Ky., 302 S.W.2d 604. (4) There was evidence that although the lots in question would be much more valuable if freed for commercial uses, they still have some value with the restrictions on them, perhaps as much as $500 each. (5) The action of the planning and zoning authorities in rezoning the area could not operate to relieve the land from the restrictions. Parrish v. Newbury, Ky., 279 S.W.2d 229.

It is our opinion that this case cannot be distinguished from Cochran v. Long, Ky., 294 S.W.2d 503. Applying the test stated in that case, the trial judge was warranted in finding that the change in character of the neighborhood was not such as to make it impossible longer to secure in a substantial degree the benefits sought to be realized through the performance of the restrictive covenants.

The judgment is affirmed.

Notes

1. In Cochran v. Long, which the court in Osborne v. Hewitt relied on and found to be indistinguishable, a 60-foot highway was built across one end of several of the restricted lots, and the evidence showed that from 400 to 500 vehicles passed over this roadway every hour. It was a further fact in that case, however, that only two business places had been built in the area since the highway was built, although other places of business had been built a block away. Cf. Trustees of Columbia College v. Thacher, 87 N.Y. 311 (1882).

The equitable defense of "changed conditions" is generally recognized. The major difficulty in applying it is in determining where the changes must occur, that is, whether changed conditions outside the restricted area are enough. As in the principal case, it is usually stated that they are not. But there is authority contra. See e.g., Downs v. Kroeger, 200 Cal. 743, 254 P. 1101 (1927). The economic pressure where border lots abut on land which has become predominantly commercial should be evident. You should also perceive the argument against yielding to such pressure. Occasionally these pressures become so great that a court has yielded to them, while maintaining in other cases its determination not to do so. It would be foolish to rely on the proposition that outside changed conditions cannot in any circumstances affect the outcome. Perhaps a better standard is that stated by the court in the principal case in the last sentence of its opinion: whether the changes are such as "to make it impossible longer to secure in a substantial degree the benefits sought to be realized through the performance of the restrictive covenants." This is the standard stated in Section 564 of the Restatement of Property. This standard will also prove unsatisfactory unless it is understood to be applicable to the restricted area as a whole and not piecemeal. The comments and illustration in the Restatement indicate that the former is intended. A comparable problem arises if a court denies enforcement of restrictions against a border lot because of the effect of adjacent areas. What is the effect of such a decree upon the status of interior lots? See 5 Powell, § 684.

See generally on the effect of changed conditions: 2 A.L.P. § 9.39; 5 Powell § 684; Cunningham §§ 8.20, 8.30; Annotation, 4 A.L.R.2d 1111 (1949), and prior annotations referred to therein.

2. The holding of the court in the principal case that a change in the applicable zoning law could not effect the restrictions is generally followed. 2 A.L.P. § 9.40. Is it clear why this should be so? Should it always be so? Park Ridge Home Owners v. Pena, 88 N.M. 563, 544 P.2d 278 (1975), is a recent assertion of the traditional rule that a zoning law less restrictive than applicable restrictive covenants does not affect the covenants. It is not often that there is a real conflict between a zoning ordinance and a restrictive covenant, that is, where the use required by the covenant is forbidden by the ordinance. It may be assumed in such a case that the ordinance prevails unless there is a constitutional obstacle. In Rofe v. Robinson, 93 Mich.App. 749, 286 N.W.2d 914 (1980), it was so held without mention of any constitutional issue.

In House v. James, 232 Ga. 443, 207 S.E.2d 201 (1974), a statute providing that restrictive covenants that have run for more than 20 years in a city having zoning laws are unenforceable was held not to be an unconstitutional impairment of the obligation of contracts when applied to covenants in effect before the effective date of the statute.

3. There are defenses to the enforcement of equitable servitudes other than changed conditions. (1) The equitable *clean-hands* doctrine may be applied against a plaintiff who has himself violated similar restrictions. (2) The defense of *acquiescence* may be applied against a plaintiff who has failed to take action against similar violations by third parties. (3) The doctrine of *laches* may be invoked against a plaintiff who has delayed unreasonably in taking action against a defendant after knowledge of the breach. See 2 A.L.P. § 9.38; Cunningham § 8.30.

In Pool v. Denbeck, 196 Neb. 27, 241 N.W.2d 503 (1976), a defense of acquiescence was not allowed where prior violations occurred at considerable distance from the plaintiff's property, which was not much affected by them.

Note on Effect of Condemnation

A problem similar to that noted in respect to easements exists when land burdened by an equitable servitude is condemned by public authority. It is clear that if land is condemned for a use that is inconsistent with the terms of the servitude, the servitude is extinguished. Does this entitle those who could otherwise have enforced it to share in the compensation paid for the taking? To the extent that the benefits of such restrictions are regarded as property interests, it would seem that those who had such interests are entitled to be paid for their loss. But the cases are in conflict. A variety of arguments have been offered for denying compensation. In Arkansas State Highway Comm. v. McNeill, 238 Ark. 244, 381 S.W.2d 425 (1964), the following argument appears:

"Another illustration to demonstrate the fallacy in the decisions allowing compensation: Assume the existence of a purely residential area that is in part restricted and in part unrestricted. If a highway should be constructed just within the restricted section the landowners on that side of the highway would receive compensation while those on the other side, although suffering identical damage, would be without a remedy. Under such a rule it is evident that whenever the owners of property in an unrestricted neighborhood learn that a throughway is coming in their direction it is to their advantage to enter into an agreement imposing restrictions. In that way, by merely signing a piece of paper which they may destroy at will they are able to pluck valuable causes of action from the thin air."

If compensation must be paid for the extinguishment of equitable servitudes, a further question arises, like that in the case of land burdened by an easement, as to the proper measure of compensation. Is the compensation to be a sum fixed by ascertaining the value of the land taken as though it were not encumbered by the servitudes, which is then divided among all those who have interests in the land in proportion to the value of their respective interests? Or are the owners of the several interests to be separately compensated for the loss of depreciation suffered by each? There is authority for each of these standards. Assuming that the two standards will in many cases produce different results, which is to be preferred?

See 2 A.L.P. § 9.40; Restatement § 566.

Reference is made to the comparable problems in the easement cases, Note, page 597, supra.

Part Two

THE TRANSFER OF OWNER-SHIP–CONVEYANCING

Chapter 7

DEVOLUTION OF PROPERTY UPON THE OWNER'S DEATH

SECTION 1. INTESTATE SUCCESSION

Our modern law of intestate succession is based upon two sources: (1) The English feudal law which grew up in the Middle Ages to govern succession to the ownership of land; and (2) The English ecclesiastical law, itself based ultimately upon the Roman law, which grew up in the Middle Ages to govern succession to the ownership of tangible personal property.

A. DESCENT OF LAND IN ENGLAND

The principal characteristics of the English law of descent were the following:

(a) The rule of primogeniture: among males and females equally closely related to the decedent, the eldest male inherited to the exclusion of the others. The rule prevailed throughout England until 1925, except in Kent, where by local custom recognized in the courts all sons inherited equally, and in certain boroughs where, by local custom, all the land descended to the youngest son. (This custom was called "Borough English" because, at Nottingham, it was the custom of the English, as distinguished from the French borough. But it was not confined to Nottingham.)

(b) The rule that where there were no sons, daughters took equal shares as co-owners (called "coparceners," and regarded collectively as a single heir).

(c) The exclusion of inheritance by ancestors (but not by collateral relations). Exclusion of inheritance by spouse.

(d) The doctrine of ancestral property: in descent to collaterals, only those persons would inherit who were "of the blood of the first purchaser"—i.e., the person who first brought ownership of the land into the family. E.g., if John bought Blackacre and it descended to his son James, and James died intestate without issue, brothers or sisters, the land could descend only to paternal cousins, not to maternal cousins.

B. DISTRIBUTION OF PERSONALTY IN ENGLAND

At the time of Magna Carta, intestate personalty was taken by the ordinary (i.e., the ecclesiastical official having judicial authority, usually the bishop) and administered by him for the good of the soul of the deceased. He was not bound to pay the debts of the intestate or make any distribution to his family. There seem to have been grave abuses, and in 1285 a statute was enacted requiring the ordinary to pay debts; and in 1357 another statute required the ordinary to appoint as administrator someone "from the next and most lawful friends" of the deceased. Although the administrator had to give bond to the ordinary to guarantee the faithful performance of his duties, there were many difficulties in the path of a member of the family who wished to force the administrator to distribute what was left of the personalty after debts were paid, and these difficulties were accentuated by jurisdictional squabbles between the ecclesiastical courts and the royal (secular) courts. Finally, in 1670, Parliament passed the Statute of Distribution, which is the basis of practically all the American statutes dealing with descent and distribution. The chief features of the Statute of Distribution were as follows:

(a) Rights of the surviving spouse: If there were children, the surviving spouse took $\frac{1}{3}$; if there were no children, the surviving spouse took $\frac{1}{2}$.

(b) Rights of children: If there was a surviving spouse, the children (and issue of deceased children) took $\frac{2}{3}$; if there was no surviving spouse, the children took the entire estate.

(c) Issue of a deceased child took the share that child would have taken had he or she survived the decedent, i.e., the issue took by "right of representation."

(d) Rights of the next of kin (nearest relatives other than a spouse or issue of the decedent): They took nothing if there were any issue of the decedent; $\frac{1}{2}$ if there was a surviving spouse but no issue; the entire estate if neither spouse nor issue survived the decedent. The relatives in closest degree of kinship, in general, took all to the exclusion of more distant kindred. Kinship between A and B was computed by counting up from A to the nearest common ancestor and then down to B. Thus parents were 1st degree; brothers and sisters, and grandparents were 2nd degree; aunts and uncles, and nieces and nephews were in the 3rd degree. Logically, therefore, grandparents would have equal rights with brothers and sisters when neither parent survived the decedent. But it was decided that brothers and sisters took the entire estate in preference to a grandparent, a result which can be explained on the theory that brothers and sisters really took their parents' share by "right of representation." When there were brothers and sisters and also children of deceased brothers and sisters, the latter were permitted to take by "right of representation"; but when the next of kin were all nieces and nephews, they would take "per capita." And if there were aunts and uncles as well as nieces and nephews, the former would take "per capita," along with the latter, all being related in the third degree although the aunts and uncles were in a more remote line. In theory this rule is inconsistent with the one preferring brothers and sisters to grandparents.

(e) Miscellaneous rules: Collaterals of the half blood shared equally with those of the whole blood. Relatives by marriage, other than the surviving spouse, had no rights. Doctrine of ancestral property had no application. An illegitimate child could inherit from his spouse or his descendants, but not from any ancester or collateral.

It will be noted that, although the surviving spouse was entitled to a share under the Statute of Distribution, he or she was not an heir with respect to land. However, the surviving spouse was protected by the institutions of "dower" and "curtesy." See Chapter 3 supra, pages 286, 287 et seq.

Both dower and curtesy were exempt from claims of the decedent's creditors; both became important parts of the American land law, and continue to exist except so far as they have been abolished or modified by statute.

C. DESCENT AND DISTRIBUTION OF REAL AND PERSONAL PROPERTY IN THE UNITED STATES

The Statute of Distribution (1670) established a pattern which has been widely followed in American statutes of descent and distribution. In more than half the states the statutes apply to both real and personal property. In the other states widely varying differences are established in the treatment of real and personal property. Most of these relate to provisions for a surviving spouse. In a few states a spouse is entirely excluded from the descent of land, which, however, is subject to dower or curtesy or statutory substitutes therefor. In other states the share of a surviving spouse in land differs in some degree from the spouse's share of personal property. These differences of course affect the shares taken by other persons. Descendants, no matter how remote, exclude all ancestors and collaterals. While a living person always excludes his children, the issue of a predeceased child represent the latter and take the share which would otherwise have gone to the predeceased child. Usually it is provided that brothers and sisters or their issue inherit only in the absence of parents, although in a few states they share equally with parents of the decedent. Some statutes then mention grandparents, or uncles and aunts and their issue as being the next in line. Most intestate laws provide that, failing takers in any of the prior designated classes, the property goes to the "next of kin." Under many of the statutes, failing all persons in the designated categories, the property "escheats" to the state.

The following is a fairly typical intestate statute:

OHIO REVISED CODE ANNOTATED (Page, 1968)

Descent and distribution [§ 2105.06]—When a person dies intestate having title or right to any personal property or to any real estate or inheritance in this state, such personal property shall be distributed and such real estate or inheritance shall descend and pass in parcenary, except as otherwise provided by law, in the following course:

(A) If there is no surviving spouse, to the children of such intestate or their lineal descendants, per stirpes;

(B) If there is a spouse and one child or its lineal descendants surviving, one half to the spouse and one half to such child or its lineal descendants, per stirpes; *

(C) If there is a spouse and more than one child or their lineal descendants surviving, one third to the spouse and the remainder to the children equally, or to the lineal descendants of any deceased child, per stirpes; *

(D) If there are no children or their lineal descendants, three fourths to the surviving spouse and one fourth to the parents of the intestate equally, or to the surviving parent; if there are no parents, then the whole to the surviving spouse; *

(E) If there is no spouse and no children or their lineal descendants, to the parents of such intestate equally, or to the surviving parent;

(F) If there is no spouse, no children or their lineal descendants, and no parent surviving, to the brothers and sisters, whether of the whole or of the half blood of the intestate, or their lineal descendants, per stirpes;

(G) If there are no brothers or sisters or their lineal descendants, one half to the paternal grandparents of the intestate equally, or to the survivor of them, and one half to the maternal grandparents of the intestate equally, or to the survivor of them;

(H) If there is no paternal grandparent or no maternal grandparent, one half to the lineal descendants of such deceased grandparents, per stirpes; if there are no such lineal descendants, then to the surviving grandparents or their lineal descendants, per stirpes; if there are no surviving grandparents or their lineal descendants, then to the next of kin of the intestate, provided there shall be no representation among such next of kin;

(I) If there are no next of kin, to stepchildren or their lineal descendants, per stirpes;

(J) If there are no stepchildren or their lineal descendants, escheat to the state.

---

* Although this statute as reproduced above is still a typical intestate statute, it was in fact amended in 1975 to increase the share of a surviving spouse as follows:

"(B) If there is a spouse and one child or his lineal descendants surviving, the first thirty thousand dollars if the spouse is the natural or adoptive parent of the child, or the first ten thousand dollars if the spouse is not the natural or adoptive parent of the child, plus one-half of the balance of the intestate estate to the spouse and the remainder to the child or his lineal descendants per stirpes;

"(C) [Same except that it applies where there is a spouse and more than one child and gives one-third of the balance rather than one-half to the spouse.]

"(D) If there are no children or their lineal descendants, then the whole to the surviving spouse;"

These amendments are similar to those proposed by Section 2–102 of the Uniform Probate Code.

Equality among children [§ 2105.11]—When a person dies intestate leaving children and none of the children of such intestate have died leaving children or their lineal descendants, such estate shall descend to the children of such intestate, living at the time of his death, in equal proportions.

Descendants of equal degree [§ 2105.12]—When all the descendants of an intestate, in a direct line of descent, are on an equal degree of consanguinity to the intestate, the estate shall pass to such persons in equal parts, however remote from the intestate such equal and common degree of consanguinity may be.

Descendants of unequal degree [§ 2105.13]—If some of the children of an intestate are living and others are dead, the estate shall descend to the children who are living and to the lineal descendants of such children as are dead, so that each child who is living will inherit the share to which he would have been entitled if all the children of the intestate were living, and the lineal descendants of the deceased child will inherit equal parts of that portion of the estate to which such deceased child would be entitled if he were living.

SECTION 2. TESTAMENTARY DISPOSITION

A will is a person's declaration of what is to be done with his property after his death, which declaration is (1) revocable during his lifetime, and (2) applicable to the situation which exists at his death.

A. THE ENGLISH LAW OF WILLS

Under the feudal law in England, land could not be "devised"—i.e., disposed of by will—except by local custom, as in Kent and a few other localities. But the Statute of Wills in 1540 permitted the devise of land by will with certain exceptions which have long since been removed. The only requirement was that the will be in writing. A century and a quarter later the Statute of Frauds (1677) required that a devise of land "shall be in writing, and signed by the party so devising the same, or by some other person in his presence and by his express direction, and shall be attested and subscribed in the presence of the said devisor by three or four credible witnesses."

There never was any legal objection to wills (or "testaments" as they were technically called) of personalty. At an early period it seems to have been customary for the priest to receive the testament orally as part of the last confession; but as time went on written testaments became more usual. The Statute of Frauds (1677) imposed the first formal requirements, providing that no "nuncupative" (i.e., oral) testament of personalty in excess of £ 30 should be valid unless (a) it was proved by the oath of three witnesses present when it was made, and (b) the testator bade the persons present to bear witness to his will, and (c) the will was made in the last sickness of the testator, and (d) the testimony of the witnesses was given within 6 months or committed to writing within 6 days after the oral testament was made. Although oral testaments of personalty were still permitted by the Statute of Frauds, and a written testament did not have to be attested, it became customary thereafter to make a written "last will and testament" to dispose of both realty and personalty.

The Wills Act of 1837, for the first time in England, imposed identical formal requirements upon wills of both realty and personalty. It provided that a will "shall be in writing, shall be signed at the foot or end thereof by the testator, or by some other person in his presence and by his direction; and such signature shall be made or acknowledged by the testator in the presence of two or more witnesses present at the same time, and such witnesses shall attest and shall subscribe the will in the presence of the testator."

B. THE AMERICAN LAW OF WILLS

Most American statutes relating to wills are based either upon the English Statute of Frauds (1677) or Wills Act (1837). For example, Massachusetts General Laws, Annotated c. 191 § 1, is in substance a reenactment of the Statute of Frauds, c. 3, sec. 5. It provides: "Every person of full age and sound mind may by his last will in writing, signed by him or by a person in his presence and by his express direction, and attested and subscribed in his presence by three or more competent witnesses, dispose of his property, real and personal * * *." The New Jersey statute, on the other hand, is based on the Wills Act (1847). N.J. S.A. 3A:3—2 provides: " * * * a will to be valid shall be in writing and signed by the testator, which signature shall be made by the testator, or the making thereof acknowledged by him and such writing declared to be his last will in the presence of 2 witnesses present at the same time, who shall subscribe their names thereto, as witnesses, in the presence of the testator."

Note that the requirement that the testator declare the instrument to be his will is a new one, not found in either the English Statute of Frauds or the Wills Act (1837), but included in the New Jersey statute. Note also that the requirement of the Wills Act that the witnesses be present at the same time and subscribe their names in the presence of the testator is retained in the New Jersey statute.

Most states today require only two witnesses to a will—a provision taken from the English Wills Act (1837)—but the New England states (except Rhode Island) and Georgia and South Carolina still insist upon the three witnesses originally prescribed in the Statute of Frauds.

The prescribed statutory formalities must be literally complied with. Under the New Jersey statute, supra, the testator must actually sign the will, although his hand may be guided or steadied by another; it is not sufficient that the signature is made by another in the testator's presence and at his direction—although this would be sufficient under the Massachusetts statute, supra. Moreover, the provision requiring the witnesses to sign in the presence of the testator—found in the Massachusetts and New Jersey statutes—is not complied with where the witnesses sign the will in an adjoining room out of the testator's sight, although the door between the rooms is open. (Many other examples could be given.)

Is it sufficient for an attorney to make sure that his client executes his will in accordance with the requirements of the state in which the client resides? Clearly not, for the law of the place in which the client resides may govern the validity of the will at the testator's death with reference to little or none of his property. The law of the state where real property is located will govern the validity of a will insofar as it disposes of realty, while the law of the domicil of the testator *at the time of his death* will be controlling with regard to the validity of the will insofar as it disposes of personalty. Thus a lawyer supervising the execution of a will must make sure that the will is executed in such a manner as to be valid according to the law of any state in which it may be offered for probate; in short, he must be sure that the will is executed in accordance with the *maximum* formalities required in *any* jurisdiction in the United States. For example, there should always be at least three witnesses.

C. REVOCATION OF WILLS

"Prior to the Statute of Frauds a will could be revoked by oral declarations. This obvious opportunity for fraud was precluded by provisions of that statute, to the effect that no written will of personalty could be repealed or altered by oral words, and that no devise of realty should be revoked except by instrument executed with the formalities of the will or by burning, cancelling, tearing, or obliterating. By the Wills Act, 1837, the language of the earlier provision as to revocation of wills of realty was altered but its substance retained and applied to wills of personalty as well. While the terms of the Statute of Frauds seemed to imply that no other manner of revocation is possible, the courts recognized revocation by operation of law in certain cases, such as the marriage and birth of issue to a male testator, or the marriage of a testatrix, but the Wills Act, 1837 made express exclusive provisions for revocation by operation of law.

"In the United States the statutes universally recognize revocation by subsequent instrument, and except in one state there is provision for revocation by physical act. In addition, there is frequently specific provision for revocation by operation of law, and elsewhere that common-law doctrine is usually recognized." Atkinson, Wills 420 (2d ed. 1953).

The mere fact that an instrument is called "Last Will and Testament" does not, *ipso facto*, cause it to revoke a prior will, though the prior will is of course superseded to the extent that the subsequent will makes inconsistent dispositions of the testator's property. In most jurisdictions, a will may be revoked by a subsequent instrument executed with the formalities required for a will, though it does not itself make any disposition of the testator's property. And, of course, a will may be partly revoked by a duly executed "codicil" which makes a different disposition of part of the testator's property. Whenever a testator executes a new will, there should be an express clause revoking all prior wills and codicils if that is the intent of the testator; or, if the intent is otherwise, an express clause stating what other testamentary instruments exist and how far they are to be considered as still in force.

Most American wills statutes permit revocation by the physical acts specified either in the Statute of Frauds,—"burning, canceling, tearing or obliterating," or the English Wills Act of 1837,—"burning, tearing, or otherwise destroying." But no competent attorney would advise a testator to rely upon such methods of revocation, except perhaps in a case of extreme emergency.

Wills may also be revoked by operation of law in certain circumstances, with considerable variations among the states. Marriage or divorce of a testator are the two basic changes in circumstances that may revoke his will. In some states marriage must also be followed by the birth of issue, at least in the case of male testators. And in a number of states divorce must be accompanied by a property settlement. Section 2–508 of the Uniform Probate Code provides that divorce will revoke any provision a testator has made for his former spouse, but no other change of circumstances will revoke a will.

Note on Certain Will Substitutes

As you learned in the study of Estates in Chapter 3, most divisions of ownership into present and future estates occur by way of testamentary or inter vivos dispositions in trust, which of course also separate the "legal" ownership of a trustee from the "equitable" interests of trust beneficiaries (also called cestuis que trust). In other words, it is the beneficial interests which are divided into present and future estates. Typically, the trust property is income-producing,—whether it be land, corporate stocks, bonds, or some other form of intangible personal property,—and the trustee is charged with the duty of managing the trust property for the benefit of one or more beneficiaries. The trustee is directed to pay income to one or more beneficiaries, concurrently or successively, and at a stated time, to pay over the principal of the trust estate to one or more beneficiaries. A common arrangement is for the owner of income-producing property to transfer legal ownership to a trustee, with the transferor or "settlor" as beneficiary for his own life, and other persons as remaindermen. The "settlor" may direct that the trustee continue to hold the property in trust after the death of the "settlor," paying over the income periodically to designated persons, or that the legal ownership of the trust property be transferred to the remaindermen after the death of the "settlor." In either case, the "settlor" may retain the power to revoke the trust and take back the legal ownership of the trust property at any time during his own lifetime. Thus the trust with a reserved equitable life estate and power of revocation is in some ways very much like a will, which is also revocable during the testator's lifetime and which leaves the testator in complete control of his property right down to the time of his death.

The analogy between a trust with a reserved equitable life estate and power of revocation, on the one hand, and a will, on the other, is even more striking when the settlor declares himself trustee of property owned by him, and perhaps includes himself as one of the beneficiaries, and reserves to himself the power to amend or revoke the trust. In such a case the settlor, for practical purposes, continues to have full control of his property until the time of his death, as he would after making a will disposing of the property in question. Yet the trust is regarded as an "inter vivos" rather than "testamentary" disposition, and thus is not subject to the requirements of the statutes of wills as to execution. A transfer of property in trust by will, of course, must meet the formal requirements for the making of wills. An inter vivos conveyance of property in trust must also pass the legal title to the trustee, and so it must meet the same formal requirements as a conveyance not in trust. A conveyance of land in trust must meet the requirements of the Statute of Frauds, and so must be in writing and signed by the transferor (settlor). A transfer of personal property in trust must meet the requirements applicable to gifts of personal property, that is, as we shall see, it must meet the requirement of delivery. As indicated above, a donor may create a trust without any transfer of the legal title to property, that is, by declaring himself trustee. This is the so-called "self-declared trust." Such a declaration of trust of land must be in writing and signed by the settlor. But in most states a self-declared trust of personal property need meet no formal requirements, that is, it can be oral. This contrast with a gift of property by will, or even an inter vivos gift of personal property outright, is striking. This distinction is relevant to some of the problems encountered in the following chapter on gifts of personal property.

Chapter 8

GIFTS OF PERSONAL PROPERTY

SECTION 1. GIFTS IN GENERAL

It is possible to make a gratuitous transfer of ownership of land, provided appropriate acts are performed, and the transaction would properly be called a gift. It has occasionally been asserted that one can make an effective oral gift of land but, as will be observed later, the Statute of Frauds, as well as other statutes relating to the manner in which interests in land may be conveyed, normally require the execution of an appropriate written instrument for such purpose. In any event, the materials here are confined to transactions involving gratuitous transfers of personal property.

The desire of an owner of chattels to transfer ownership to another person may take many forms. It is not uncommon to encounter a donor who desires one of the following diverse arrangements:

1. An immediate and irrevocable transfer.

2. An arrangement whereby the donee will get the property only after the donor's death, and in the meantime the donor wants to retain complete ownership and complete freedom to change his mind.

3. An arrangement whereby the donee gets the actual enjoyment of the property only after the donor's death, but which, in the meantime, shall be irrevocable and binding on the donor.

4. An arrangement whereby the donor keeps the legal ownership in himself but creates an equitable interest (i.e., the right to the benefits) in the donee.

5. An arrangement whereby the donee gets joint enjoyment with the donor during the latter's life and thereafter sole enjoyment of the property that remains.

6. An arrangement by which the donee gets the property only upon certain contingencies.

The material that follows will indicate the nature of the legal difficulties which may be encountered in attempting to effectuate those desires, and the methods that are available.

The first case in the section indicates the two fundamental methods by which gifts of legal ownership may be made: (a) by deed; (b) by delivery of the subject matter of the gift to the donee. One must compare, however, the requirements for creating the trust relationship in which no legal ownership is transferred but only an equitable interest, and the requirements for creating joint interests.

On this whole subject, see Mechem, The Requirement of Delivery in Gifts of Chattels and of Choses in Action Evidenced by Commercial Instruments, 21 Ill.L.Rev. 341, 457, 568 (1926–1927); Roberts, The Necessity of Delivery in Making Gifts, 32 W.Va.L.Q. 313 (1926).

See also, Restatement, Contracts, 1932, § 158; Bruton, The Requirement of Delivery as Applied to Gifts of Choses in Action, 39 Yale L.J. 837 (1930); Williston, Gifts of Rights Under Contracts in Writing by Delivery of the Writing, 40 Yale L.J. 1 (1930).

COCHRANE v. MOORE

Court of Appeal, 1890.
25 Q.B.Div. 57.

[One Benzon owned a race horse, the horse being in the stables of one Yates. Benzon made a verbal gift to Moore of a one-fourth interest in the horse, and a few days later notified Yates of this gift. Subsequently Benzon executed a bill of sale of the horse to Cochrane to pay for advances made by the latter. Moore's interest was mentioned at the time and Cochrane undertook that it should be "all right." The horse was subsequently sold and an interpleader was filed to settle the right to one-fourth of the proceeds. Appeal from the judgement of Lopes, L.J.]

FRY, L.J. * * * On these facts it was argued that there was no delivery and receipt of the one-fourth of the horse, and consequently, that no property in it passed by the gift. The learned judge has, however, held that delivery is not indispensable to the validity of the gift.

The proposition on which the Lord Justice proceeded may perhaps be stated thus: that where a gift of a chattel capable of delivery is made per verba de praesenti by a donor to a donee, and is assented to by the donee, and that assent is communicated to the donor by the donee, there is a perfect gift, which passes the property without delivery of the chattel itself. This proposition is one of much importance, and has recently been the subject of some diversity of opinion. We therefore feel it incumbent upon us to examine it, even though it might be possible in the present case to avoid that examination.

The proposition adopted by the Lord Justice is in direct contradiction to the decision of the Court of King's Bench in the year 1819 in Irons v. Smallpiece, 2 B. & A. 551. That case did not proceed upon the character of the words used, or upon the difference between verba de praesenti and verba de futuro, but upon the necessity of delivery to a gift otherwise sufficient. The case is a very strong one, because a Court consisting of Lord Tenterden, C.J., and Best and Holroyd, JJ., refused a rule nisi, and all held delivery to be necessary. The Chief Justice said: "I am of opinion that, by the law of England, in order to transfer property by gift there must either be a deed or instrument of gift, or there must be an actual delivery of the thing to the donee," and he went on to refer to the case of Bunn v. Markham, 2 Marsh. 532, as a strong authority.

These observations of the Chief Justice have created some difficulty. What did he mean by an instrument as contrasted with a deed? If he meant that an instrument in writing not under seal was different from parol in respect of a gift inter vivos, he was probably in error; but if in speaking of the transfer of property by gift, he included gifts by will as well as gifts inter vivos, then by instrument he meant testamentary instrument, and his language was correct.

Holroyd, J., was equally clear on the principal point: "In order to change the property by gift of this description" (by which we understand him to mean, a gift inter vivos) "there must be a change of possession."

The correctness of the proposition thus laid down has been asserted in many subsequent cases of high authority. * * *

The first note of dissent was sounded in the year 1841, or twenty-two years after the decision of the case of Irons v. Smallpiece, 2 B. & A. 551, by Serjeant Manning in a note on the case of the London and Brighton Ry. Co. v. Fairclough, 2 Man. & G. 674, at p. 691, in which he impugned the accuracy of Irons v. Smallpiece, and asserted that after the acceptance of a gift by parol the estate is in the donee without any actual delivery of the chattel. The authority cited in that note we shall hereafter consider. * * *

There is thus some difference of judicial opinion as to the rule stated in Irons v. Smallpiece. We cannot think that the few recent decisions to which we have referred are enough to overrule the authority of that decision, and the cases which have followed it, but they make it desirable to inquire whether the law as declared before 1819 was in accordance with that decision, or with the judgment of Pollock, B., in Danby v. Tucker, 31 W.R. 578. * * *

This inquiry into the old law on the point is one of some difficulty, for it leads into rarely-trodden paths, where (as is very natural) we have not had the assistance of counsel, and where the materials for knowledge are for the most part undigested.

The law enunciated by Bracton in his book "de acquirendo rerum dominio," seems clear to the effect that no gift was complete without tradition of the subject of the gift. * * *

In Bracton's day, seisin was a most important element of the law of property in general; and, however strange it may sound to jurists of our day and country, the lawyers of that day applied the term as freely to a pig's ham (Select Pleas in Manorial Courts, p. 142; see also Professor Maitland's papers on the Seisin of Chattels, the Beatitude of Seisin, and the Mystery of Seisin, Law Quarterly Rev. i, 324; ii, 484; iv, 24, 286) as to a manor or a field. At that time the distinction between real and personal property had not yet grown up: the distinction then recognized was between things corporeal, and things incorporeal: no action could then be maintained on a contract for the sale of goods, even for valuable consideration, unless under seal: the distinction so familiar to us now between contracts and gifts had not fully developed itself. The law recognized seisin as the common incident of all property in corporeal things, and tradition or the delivery of that seisin from one man to another as essential to the transfer of the property in that thing, whether it were land or a horse, and whether by way of sale or of gift, and whether by word of mouth or by deed under seal. This necessity for delivery of seisin has disappeared from a large part of the transactions known to our law; but it has survived in the case of feoffments. Has it also survived in the case of gifts?

It has been suggested that Bracton, whilst purporting to enunciate the law of England, is really copying the law of Rome. But by the law of Rome, at least since the time of Justinian, gift had been a purely consensual transaction, and did not require delivery to make it perfect (Inst. ii, vii).

Coming next to the great law-writers of the reign of Edward I, they hold language substantially the same as that of Bracton, except indeed that the difference between transactions purely voluntary, or for pecuniary consideration, appears to be growing somewhat more important. * * *

In the reign of Edward IV a step seems to have been taken in the law relative to gifts which resulted in this modification: that whereas under the old law a gift of chattels by deed was not good without the delivery of the chattel given, it was now held that the gift by deed was good and operative until dissented from by the donee.

Thus in Michaelmas Term, 7 Edw. 4, pl. 21, fol. 20, it was held by Choke and other justices that if a man executes a deed of gift of his goods to me that this is good and effectual without livery made to me, until I disagree to the gift, and this ought to be in a Court of Record.

In Hilary Term, 7 Edw. 4, pl. 14, fol. 29, it was alleged by counsel (Catesby and Pigot), that if a man give to me all his goods by a deed, although the deed was not delivered to the donee, nevertheless the gift is good, and if he chooses to take the goods he can justify this by the gift, although notice has not been given to him of the gift; and further, that if the donee commit felony before notice, &c., still the king will have the goods, and although notice may be material, nevertheless when he has notice, this would have relation to the time of the gift, &c. But the Court said that such a gift is not good without notice, for a man cannot give his goods to me against my will. * * *

It was in the reigns of the early Tudors that the action on the case on indebitatus assumpsit obtained a firm foothold in our law; and the effect of it seems to have been to give a greatly increased importance to merely consensual contracts. It was probably a natural result of this that, in time, the question whether and when property passed by the contract came to depend, in cases in which there was a value consideration, upon the mind and consent of the parties, and that it was thus gradually established that in the case of bargain and sale of personal chattels, the property passed according to that mind and attention, and a new exception was thus made to the necessity of delivery.

This doctrine that property may pass by contract before delivery appears to be comparatively modern. It may, as has been suggested, owe its origin to a doctrine of the civil law that the property was at the risk of the purchaser before it passed from the vendor; but at any rate the point was thought open to argument as late as Elizabeth's reign (see Plowd. 11 b, and see a learned note, 2 Man. & Ry. 566).

Flower's Case, Noy, 67 (which seems to have been decided in 39 Elizabeth, see p. 59), appears to shew that the necessity of delivery was then upheld by the Court. The case is thus stated by Noy (p. 67):

"A. borrowed one hundred pound of B. and at the day brought it in a bagg and cast it upon the table before B. and B. said to A. being his nephew, I will not have it, take it you and carry it home again with you. And by the Court, that is a good gift by paroll, being cast upon the table. For then it was in the possession of B. and A. might well wage his law. By the Court, otherwise it had been, if A. had only offer'd it to B. for then it was chose in action only, and could not be given without a writing."

The Court seems to have held that delivery was necessary, but that by the casting of the money on the table it came into the possession of the uncle, and that the nephew taking the money in his uncle's presence and by his direction, there was an actual delivery by the uncle to the nephew—so that the nephew might wage his law, i.e., might conscientiously swear that he was not indebted to his uncle (see the case discussed in Douglas v. Douglas, L.T., N.S., 127). * * *

Blackstone's discussion of the subject of gifts of chattels is perhaps not so precise as might be desired; but his language does not seem to us essentially to differ from the earlier authorities: "A true and proper gift or grant is," he says, "always accompanied with delivery of possession and takes effect immediately." "But if the gift does not take effect by delivery of immediate possession, it is then not properly a gift, but a contract: and this a man cannot be compelled to perform" (Book 2, c. 30).

This review of the authorities leads us to conclude that according to the old law no gift or grant of a chattel was effectual to pass it whether by parol or by deed, and whether with or without consideration unless accompanied by delivery: that on that law two exceptions have been grafted, one in the case of deeds, and the other in that of contracts of sale where the intention of the parties is that the property shall pass before delivery: but that as regards gifts by parol, the old law was in force when Irons v. Smallpiece, 2 B. & A. 551, was decided: that that case therefore correctly declared the existing law: and that it has not been overruled by the decision of Pollock, B., in 1883, or the subsequent case before Cave, J.

We are therefore unable in the present case to accept the law on this point as enunciated by Lopes, L.J., in deference to the two latest decisions.

But assuming delivery to be necessary in the case of the gift of an ordinary chattel, two questions would remain for consideration in the present case—the first, whether the undivided fourth part of the horse admits delivery, or whether on the other hand it is to be regarded as incorporeal and incapable of tradition; the other, whether the letter written by Benzon to Yates was either a constructive delivery of this undivided fourth part of the horse, or an act perfecting the gift of this incorporeal part as far as the nature of the subject-matter of the gift admits. On these points we do not think it needful to express any decided opinion, because in our judgment what took place between Benzon and Cochrane before Benzon executed the bill of sale to Cochrane, constituted the latter a trustee for Moore of one-fourth of the horse Kilworth.

Notes

1. The requirement of delivery may give rise to complications because of the nature of the subject matter (how does one deliver a herd of cattle? a mere intangible chose in action?), because the intended donee is already in possession, or because the subject of the gift is not readily available. Cases in which delivery of the means of access has been held adequate give rise to the question of how much validity there is today in continuing the requirement. Professor Mechem has suggested the following reasons for continuing the requirement today: (1) It protects the donor because the act of delivery impresses him with the finality of the transaction; (2) it furnishes *objective* evidence of the donative intent of the donor; and (3) it furnishes the donee with concrete evidence to substantiate his claim. Mechem, The Requirement of Delivery in Gifts of Chattels and of Choses in Action Evidenced by Commercial Instruments, 21 Ill.L. Rev. 341, 457, 586 (1926).

Another problem of delivery—one which emphasizes the agency aspect, is involved where the chattel is given to a third person for ultimate delivery to the donee. Factual inquiries to determine for whom the intermediary is acting, who controls his conduct, when ultimate delivery is intended, are of importance, particularly in gifts causa mortis.

The normal method of accomplishing the second desire listed in the introductory note is the making of a will. A will is usually ambulatory until the testator dies, revocable at any time and yet donations expressed therein will be enforced after the testator's death. Because fraudulent claims can easily be made after an owner is dead and unable to refute the claims, some rather rigid formalities are required to make an effective will. Those matters are extensively considered elsewhere in the curriculum, but the underlying policies which have led to the formal requirements are worth considering in connection with certain of the cases in this chapter.

See Jones, Corroborating Evidence as a Substitute for Delivery in Gifts of Chattels, 12 Suff.U.L.Rev. 16 (1978).

2. In Hengst v. Hengst, 491 Pa. 120, 420 A.2d 370 (1980), United States savings bonds were issued to an employee under a thrift plan involving salary deductions and employer contributions. These were issued in the employee's name. In a suit for partition of assets brought by the employee's wife, both she and her husband testified that they regarded this property as jointly owned. The court held that a valid gift of a half interest in the bonds had been made by the husband to his wife. The court said that lack of delivery cannot defeat a gift where the donor in open court testifies as to his intent; that is, the court found the reason for the delivery rule absent in this case.

See Jones, Corroborating Evidence as a Substitute for Delivery in Gifts of Chattels, 12 Suff.U.L.Rev. 16 (1978).

3. While it is true that an owner of chattels may effectively create a trust of the property by declaring himself trustee thereof, and that so far as personal property is concerned, that declaration need not be in writing, one must not conclude that every gift which fails for want of effective delivery can be sustained as an oral trust. The express trust arises only as a result of a manifestation that such was the intention of the donor. It does not require particularly acute perception to note the vast difference between an intention to transfer full and complete legal ownership (a gift) and an intention to transfer only the beneficial interest in the property meanwhile retaining the control, management and legal ownership thereof (a declaration of trust). The Pennsylvania court has thus expressed itself:

"What is clearly intended as a voluntary assignment or a gift, but is imperfect as such, cannot be treated as a declaration of trust. If this were not so, an expression of present gift would in all cases amount to a declaration of trust, and any imperfect gift might be made effectual simply by converting it into a trust. There is no principle of equity which will perfect an imperfect gift, and a court of equity will not impute a trust where a trust was not in contemplation." Smith's Estate, 144 Pa. 428, 22 A. 916, 27 Am.St.Rep. 641 (1891). An excellent discrimination between the two ideas is found in Farmers Loan & Trust Co. v. Winthrop, 207 App.Div. 356, 202 N.Y.S. 456 (1923), noted in 24 Col.L.Rev. 545 (1924), 238 N.Y. 477, 144 N.E. 686 (1924), opinion by Cardozo, J.

Is Cochrane v. Moore consistent with the above-quoted statement?

MATTER OF COHN

Supreme Court of New York, 1919.
187 App.Div. 392, 176 N.Y.S. 225.

SHEARN, J. This appeal involves the validity of a gift of certificates of stock, effected by the execution and delivery of an instrument of gift, unaccompanied by actual delivery of the certificates.

On September 20, 1911, the decedent, Leopold Cohn, a resident of the city of New York but then temporarily residing with his family at West End, N.J., wrote out and delivered to his wife, in the presence of his entire family, on his wife's birthday, the following paper:

"West End, N.J., Sept. 20, 1911.

"I give this day to my wife, Sara K. Cohn, as a present for her (46) forty-sixth birthday (500) five hundred shares of American Sumatra Tobacco Company common stock.

"Leopold Cohn."

The donor died six days after the delivery of this instrument. At the time of the gift the donor was the owner of 7,213 shares of the common stock of the American Sumatra Tobacco Company, but the stock was in the name and possession of his firm of A. Cohn & Co. and deposited in a safe deposit box in the city of New York, which was in the name of and belonged to the firm. This firm consisted of the donor, his brother Abraham, and his nephew Leonard A. Cohn, and was dissolved by the death of Abraham Cohn on August 30, 1911. Prior to that time the firm had 18,033 shares of the Sumatra stock in certificates of 100 shares each, standing in the firm name, but there had never been an actual delivery of the certificates by the firm to the donor in his lifetime. Just prior to his death the donor had agreed to enter into a new partnership and he was to contribute some of the shares to a new firm as an asset. On September 22, 1911, two days after the delivery of the instrument of gift, the donor directed his counsel to hurry the new partnership agreement, because he wished to get the Sumatra stock belonging to him, which was to be delivered when the new partnership agreement was signed, which matter was to be closed on September 26, 1911, the day the donor died. The execution and delivery of the instrument of gift was established by the testimony of the two daughters of the donor, who were present at the time of its delivery, and their testimony is to the effect that their father handed the paper to the mother, in the presence of the whole family and said he gave it to her as a brithday present, that he had not possession of the stock, but as soon as he got it he would give it to her. Some stress is laid by the appellants upon the testimony that the donor "said that he could not give her the stock because it was in the company, but as soon as he could get it he would give it to her," which it is claimed evidences an intent to make a gift in the future instead of a present gift. This contention is completely overborne by the wording of the instrument itself, which reads: "I give this day;" also by the plain intention of the donor to make a birthday gift to his wife, the birthday being the day on which the instrument of gift was executed and delivered. When the donor explained that he could not "give" her the stock that day "because it was in the company" and said that "as soon as he could get it he would give it to her," it is quite obvious that he meant that he could not deliver the stock that day but would as soon as he could get it.

There being no rights of creditors involved, no suggestion of fraud, the intention to make the birthday gift being conclusively established, the gift being evidenced by an instrument of gift executed and delivered to the donee on her birthday, and ever since retained by her, and the circumstances surrounding the making of the gift affording a reasonable and satisfactory excuse for not making actual delivery of the certificates at the time the gift was made, there was in my opinion a valid and effectual gift of the certificates mentioned in the instrument of gift.

There is no doubt that it has been held in a long line of cases in this State that delivery of the thing given is, as a general rule, one of the essential elements to constitute a valid gift. * * * But it is equally true that the rule requiring actual delivery is not inflexible. * * *

As the rule requiring delivery is clearly subject to exceptions, in order to apply it correctly in varying circumstances resort should be had to the reason for the rule. Under the civil law delivery was not requisite to a valid gift, but it was made a requisite by the common law as a matter of public policy, to prevent mistake and imposition. Noble v. Smith, 2 Johns. 52, 56, 3 Am.Dec. 399; Brinckerhoff v. Lawrence, 2 Sandf.Ch. 400, 406. The necessity of delivery where gifts resting in parol are asserted against the estates of decedents is obvious; but it is equally plain that there is no such impelling necessity when the gift is established by the execution and delivery of an instrument of gift. An examination of a large number of cases in this State discloses the significant facts that (1) in every case where the gift was not sustained, the gift rested upon parol evidence; and (2) in every case of a gift evidenced by the delivery of an instrument of gift, the gift has been sustained. * * * It is interesting to note that in Matson v. Abbey, 70 Hun 475, 24 N.Y.S. 284, 53 N.Y.St.Rep. 794; affd., as to the gift, 141 N.Y. 179, 36 N.E. 11, sustaining a gift evidenced by an instrument of assignment without delivery of the property assigned, the court quotes with approval the statement of the English law in Irons v. Smallpiece, 2 Barn. & Ald. 551, 552, made by Abbott, C.J.: "I am of opinion that by the law of England, in order to transfer property by gift, there must either be a deed or instrument of gift, or there must be an actual delivery of the thing to the donee." Based upon decisions in numerous other jurisdictions, it is stated in 20 Cyc. 1197 that: "The general rule is that a gift of property evidenced by a written instrument executed by the donor is valid without a manual delivery of the property." I am inclined to think that this is a broader statement than the New York cases would justify, especially in view of Matter of Van Alstyne (supra), for it does not assume a delivery of the instrument of gift. But in view of the decision of this court in McGavic v. Cossum (supra) it seems to me beyond serious question that the delivery of the instrument of gift in the instant case constituted a good symbolical delivery. In the McGavic case a woman owning bonds which had been deposited by her in a bank for safekeeping during an illness from which she died three weeks later gave to her niece the original memorandum of the purchase of the bonds indorsed with the following statement:

"Poughkeepsie, November 23, 1901.

"I have this day given my niece, Fannie H. McGavic, bond 2000 Reg. 4 per cent.

"Delia C. Robinson."

Mr. Justice McLaughlin said: "We are of the opinion that the plaintiff was entitled to the bonds; that what was done constituted a good gift inter vivos. Actual delivery, by reason of the illness of the owner of the bonds, and their possession at that time by the bank, was physically impossible, but there was present, as evidenced by the writing of the deceased, not only the intention to *then* give, but also the intention to *then* deliver the thing given. The owner did all she could do in this respect. It was a good constructive or symbolical delivery, and this, under the circumstances, was sufficient to vest good title in the plaintiff. 14 Am. & Eng.Ency. of Law, 2d Ed., 1021, and cases cited." In the instant case, on the day the gift was made at West End, N.J., the certificates of stock were in a safe deposit box in New York City. Furthermore, there were the complications above referred to in the partnership relations and in the fact that the certificates were in the partnership strong box, made out in the name of the firm. These were circumstances and surroundings tending to excuse manual delivery and to make a symbolical delivery effective. In addition, as was said by Mr. Justice McLaughlin in the McGavic case, "there was present, as evidenced by the writing of the deceased, not only the intention to *then* give, but also the intention to *then* deliver the thing given. * * * It was a good constructive or symbolical delivery." The instrument of gift was a symbol which represented the donee's right of possession. * * *

Therefore, applying the rule of delivery in the light of the reason which gave birth to it, and finding here no possibility of fraud or imposition, and no doubt whatever concerning the intention of the donor, and finding full support in the precedent of McGavic v. Cossum, (supra), it is my opinion that there was a good constructive or symbolical delivery, consisting of the delivery of the instrument of gift, and that the gift should be sustained. * * *

The decree of the surrogate should be affirmed, with costs and disbursements to the respondents executrix and trustees, and disbursements of the special guardian, respondent.

CLARKE, P.J., and SMITH, J., concurred; DOWLING and PAGE, JJ., dissented.

PAGE, J., dissenting. In my opinion there was not a valid gift inter vivos of the 500 shares of stock of the American Sumatra Tobacco Company by the testator to Sara K. Cohn. * * *

Any one of the partners, * * * at any time, could have taken his proportion of the stock which was in certificates of $100 each and caused the same to be transferred to himself, individually, but by reason of the desire to control the election of directors from which they obtained a business advantage, they allowed the stock to remain in the firm name. Abraham Cohn died in August, 1911, and the two surviving partners began liquidation of the firm's business. Negotiations were opened for the organization of a copartnership, consisting of the testator, Leonard A. Cohn and one Lichtenstein. The testator agreed to contribute some of this stock as an asset to the new copartnership and as it required 7,000 shares to secure the election of a director, the testator's holdings were to be kept intact, so that the new copartnership should have the benefit thereof. * * *

In the present case the writing, taken alone, would seem to show the intention of the donor to make an actual present gift, for he says, "I give this day to my wife," yet the delivery of the writing was accompanied by the statement "that he could not give her the stock because it was in the company, but as soon as he could get it he would give it to her." There is, therefore, a clearly expressed intention to give at a future day, and the acts of the testator showed an intention to retain the dominion and control of the stock, meanwhile, in himself. * * *

The respondents claim, however, that the delivery of this paper writing was a constructive delivery of the stock, and argues that the above rules only apply to gifts inter vivos where the evidence of the gift rests in parol, and that where there is a writing which evidences the donor's intention, the courts will give effect to the delivery of the writing as a constructive delivery of the subject of the gift. This, however, in my opinion, is not the law. The writing must be such as to transfer the right of possession. There may be a symbolic delivery, or there may be a constructive delivery, but whether it be symbolic or constructive, it must be such a delivery as divests the donor with title, dominion and right of possession, and it must be the best delivery that can be made under the circumstances of the case, having due regard to the character of the property. *　*　*

In the instant case there was no physical or other impossibility to the actual delivery of the stock; it stood in the name of the company; but the stock to the extent of 7,213 shares was the property of the testator and it had been so held merely as a matter of business convenience of the old copartnership and at the time was so held, pending the formation of a new copartnership, when it might be desirable to hold all the certificates of the stock in solido for the same business advantages. This latter consideration, in my opinion, was the controlling cause of the failure to make an immediate delivery of the stock, and the reason why the testator retained possession, dominion and control of the certificates. In Matter of Mills (supra) the testator was in California, the stock was in the possession of his son in New York, and this court said the stock which was the subject of the gift was "in possession of one of the donees, and no further act of Mr. Mills could make his possession more complete." And as to the daughter, we held that the delivery of the stock to the son for and on behalf of the daughter was a good delivery.

I have been unable to find that the courts in this jurisdiction have held, heretofore, that it is only where a parol gift is sought to be established that delivery is essential, and that where the intention to give is evidenced by a writing delivery is not necessary. Among the cases cited in the prevailing opinion as tending to sustain the proposition that the requirement for delivery of the thing given is limited to oral gifts, will be found cases where gifts evidenced by a writing have been declared invalid. It will also be found that many of those cases relate to gifts causa mortis and not to gifts inter vivos. So far as this State is concerned, it is in my opinion settled: "Delivery by the donor, either actual or constructive, operating to divest the donor of possession of and dominion over the thing, is a constant and essential factor in every transaction which takes effect as a completed gift. Anything short of this strips it of the quality of completeness which distinguishes an intention to give, which alone amounts to nothing, from the consummated act, which changes the title. The intention to give is often established by most satisfactory evidence although the gift fails. Instruments may be ever so formally executed by the donor, purporting to transfer title to the donee, or there may be the most explicit declaration of an intention to give, or of an actual present gift, yet unless there is delivery the intention is defeated." Beaver v. Beaver, supra.

The writing given to Mrs. Cohn did not purport to assign, transfer or set over to her the stock. It was not a deed or instrument of gift that divested the testator of possession over and dominion of the stock. That it was not intended that it should do so is clearly shown by the subsequent acts of the testator.

In my opinion the decree should be modified by declaring the attempted gift void and sustaining the objections to the account to that extent and the executors and trustees be surcharged with the proceeds of the said 500 shares of stock, and that the same forms a part of the principal of the trust estate.

DOWLING, J., concurred. Decree affirmed, with costs and disbursements to respondents executrix and trustees, and disbursements of special guardian, respondent.

Notes

1. See Note on Gifts of Shares of Stock, infra page 754.

2. The court in the Cohn case said that the delivery of the instrument of gift constituted "a good symbolical delivery." But the reference to the "instrument" of gift raises a question about whether the gift in that case was really made by "deed." The court in Cochrane v. Moore supra recognized the early English rule that a gift could be made by deed without delivery of the chattel itself. This implied that the deed itself must be delivered. At the time this rule arose a deed was a written instrument under seal. The affixing of a seal was a formality which gave some special assurance of the authenticity of the transaction. By statute today in most states the efficacy of a seal has been abolished, and in many states an unsealed instrument conveying land is valid, although such instruments are still called deeds. By the same token, can an unsealed instrument now serve as a deed of gift of a chattel? If so, you can see a source of confusion about whether delivery of an instrument of gift is a gift by deed or a symbolical delivery of the chattel which is the subject matter of the writing.

What difference does it make? It is generally held, since a symbolical delivery is a substitute for delivery of the chattel itself, that it can be resorted to only where delivery of the chattel itself is impossible or so inconvenient as to constitute an unreasonable burden. Note that the dissenting opinion in the Cohn case stressed that there was no physical impossibility of actual delivery of the stock in question. Such a requirement has been criticized by Professor Mechem, who asserted a general non-possessory test of delivery. In other words, it can be argued that an insistence upon delivery as a change of possession invokes all the uncertainties inherent in the concept of possession, and is not necessary to preserve the objectives of the delivery requirement. It is arguable that the proper role of delivery is or should be ceremonial in the sense of providing a reliable and objective manifestation of the intent to give. See Mechem, The Requirement of Delivery in Gifts of Chattels and Choses in Action Evidenced by Commercial Instruments, 21 Ill.L.Rev. 341, 354, 474 (1926, 1927).

In any event, there is much confusion in the cases about what sort of a writing will serve as a vehicle for a gift, and in what circumstances. There should be no trouble about instruments which are actually under seal. There ought to be no trouble about instruments which are formal in every sense other than bearing a seal in states where the efficacy of seals has been abolished. The most trouble comes from writings of varying degrees of informality, such as ordinary correspondence. The cases here are in conflict. For two recent examples of this conflict compare Lewis v. Burke, 214 N.E.2d 186 (Ind.App. 1966) with In re Dodge, 90 N.J.Super. 198, 216 A.2d 757 (1966). See also Brown, Personal Property § 7.10 (3d ed. 1975) Annotations, 63 A.L.R. 537 (1929); 48 A.L.R.2d 1405 (1956). Where gifts by way of informal expressions in writing of the intent to give are held insufficient, the reasons given may be that delivery of chattel itself might have been made, or that the terms of the writing were not sufficient to indicate a present intent to give, or that the donor had not parted with all dominion and control over the chattel. The last of these is a commonly expressed cliche which, if strictly adhered to, would prevent any sort of substitute for manual delivery.

In Carey v. Jackson, 603 P.2d 868 (Wyo.1979), a mother and daughter lived together in a house owned by them as joint tenants. Certain articles of personal property, owned by the mother, were in the house. She and her daughter executed a formal agreement purporting to give these articles to the daughter. This was upheld as a good gift. The court said that the execution and delivery of a written instrument is sufficient delivery. Compare Garrison v. Grayson, 284 Ala. 247, 224 So.2d 606 (1969), where informal letters expressing the intent to give certain bonds were held to be insufficient delivery because the bonds were available for manual delivery.

In Foster v. Reiss, 18 N.J. 41, 112 A.2d 553 (1955), decedent, about to enter a hospital, wrote a note to her husband telling him where to find some money, a bank passbook, and a building and loan stock book, and telling him they were his. The husband received the note and while his wife still lived, took actual possession of the named items. The wife died after the operation. Held: The gift fails for want of delivery, and the informal writing is not sufficient by itself. Three judges dissented, and the case is critically noted in 54 Mich.L.Rev. 572 (1956); 59 Dick.L.Rev. 272 (1955); 17 U.Pittsburgh L.Rev. 105 (1955); and 10 Rutgers U.L.Rev. 457 (1955).

3. Suppose a donor who owns a herd of cattle adopts and records in a public registry in the name of his daughter a distinctive brand, with which he brands certain of his cattle which he intends to give to his daughter. Thereafter such cattle remain mingled with the donor's herd until his death. Can the daughter claim the branded cattle by way of gift? See Barber v. Barber, 128 Fla. 645, 175 So. 713 (1937); cf. Love v. Hudson, 24 Tex.Civ.App. 377, 59 S.W. 1127 (1900).

4. **Constructive Delivery.** The terms "constructive" and "symbolical" delivery are sometimes used by the courts as if they were synonymous. Strictly speaking they are not. Symbolical delivery refers to the delivery of some thing in lieu of the thing which is the subject-matter of the gift, the one being intended to represent or signify the other. Constructive delivery means the delivery of the means of obtaining possession or control of the thing given. Delivery of a key is the most common example. Virtually all courts recognize some forms of constructive delivery. But here, as well as with symbolical delivery, the courts with varying degrees of liberality, invoke the requirement that constructive delivery is possible only where manual delivery is impossible or impracticable.

NEWMAN v. BOST

Supreme Court of North Carolina, 1898.
122 N.C. 524, 29 S.E. 848.

Civil action tried before COBLE, J., and a jury at Fall Term, 1897, of Iredell Superior Court. * * *

On the trial it appeared that the intestate's wife died about 10 years before he died and without issue; that the intestate lived in his dwelling after his wife's death in Statesville until his death and died without issue; that about the last day of March, 1896, he was stricken with paralysis and was confined to his bed in his house and was never able to be out again till he died on the 12th day of April, 1896; that shortly after he was stricken he sent for Enos Houston to nurse him in his last illness; that while helpless in his bed soon after his confinement and in extremis he told Houston to call plaintiff into his room; he then asked the plaintiff to hand him his private keys, which plaintiff did, she having gotten them from a place over the mantel in intestate's bedroom in his presence and by his direction; he then handed plaintiff the bunch of keys and told her to take them and keep them, that he desired her to have them and everything in the house; he then pointed out the bureau, the clock, and other articles of furniture in the house and asked his chamber door to be opened and pointed in the direction of the hall and other rooms and repeated that everything in the house was hers—he failed soon after the delivery of the keys and these declarations, so that he could never talk again to be understood except to indicate yes and no, and this generally by a motion of the head; the bunch of keys delivered to the plaintiff, amongst others, included one which unlocked the bureau pointed out to plaintiff as hers (and other furniture in the room), and the bureau drawer, which this key unlocked, contained in it a life insurance policy payable to intestate's estate and a few small notes, a large number of papers, receipts, etc., and there was no other key that unlocked this bureau drawer, this bureau drawer was the place where intestate kept all his valuable papers; plaintiff kept the keys as directed from time given her and still has them; at the death of intestate's wife he employed plaintiff, then an orphan about eighteen years old, to become his housekeeper, and she remained in his service for ten years and till his death, and occupied rooms assigned her in intestate's residence; in 1895 the intestate declared his purpose to marry plaintiff within twelve months; nobody resided in the house with them. * * * Other facts in relation to the plaintiff's claim appear in the opinion. There was a verdict, followed by judgment for the plaintiff, and defendant appealed.

FURCHES, J. The plaintiff, in her complaint, demands $3,000, collected by defendant, as the administrator of J.F. Van Pelt, on a life insurance policy, and now in his hands; $300, the value of a piano upon which said Van Pelt collected that amount of insurance money; $200.94, the value of the household property sold by defendant as belonging to the estate of his intestate; and $45, the value of property in the plaintiff's bedroom, and sold by the defendant as a part of the property belonging to the intestate's estate. The $3,000, money collected on the life insurance policy, and the $200.94, the price for which the household property sold, plaintiff claims belonged to her by reason of a donatio causa mortis from said Van Pelt. The $45, the price for which her bedroom property sold, and the $300, insurance money on the piano, belonged to her also, by reason of gifts inter vivos. The rules of law governing all of these claims of the plaintiff are in many respects the same, and the discussion of one will be to a considerable extent a discussion of all.

To constitute a donatio causa mortis, two things are indispensably necessary,—an intention to make the gift, and a delivery of the thing given. Without both of these requisites, there can be no gift causa mortis; and both these are matters of fact to be determined by the jury, where there is evidence tending to prove them. * * *

As to what constitutes or may constitute delivery has been the subject of discussion and adjudication in most or all the courts of the Union and of England, and they have by no means been uniform; some of them holding that a symbolical delivery—that is, some other article delivered in the name and stead of the thing intended to be given—is sufficient; others holding that a symbolical delivery is not sufficient, but that a constructive delivery is,—that is, the delivery of a key to a locked house, trunk, or other receptacle is sufficient. They distinguish this from a symbolical delivery, and say that this is in substance a delivery of the thing, as it is the means of using and enjoying the thing given; while others hold that there must be an actual manual delivery to perfect a gift causa mortis. * * *

It [the doctrine of gifts causa mortis] is a doctrine, in our opinion, not to be extended but to be strictly construed and confined within the bounds of our adjudged cases. We were at first disposed to confine it to cases of actual manual delivery, and are only prevented from doing so by our loyalty to our own adjudications. But it is apparent from the adjudications that our predecessors felt the restrictions of former adjudications, and that they were not disposed to extend the doctrine. * * *

The case of Thomas v. Lewis, 89 Va. 1, 15 S.E. 389, 37 Am.St.Rep. 878, was probably more relied on by the plaintiff than any other case cited, and for that reason we mention it by name. This case, in its essential facts, is distinguishable from the case under consideration. There the articles present were taken out of the bureau drawer, handed to the donor, and then delivered by him to the donee. According to all the authorities, this was a good gift causa mortis. The box and safe, the key to which the donor delivered to the donee, were not present, but were deposited in the vault of the bank; and, so far as shown by the case, it will be presumed, from the place where they were, and the purpose for which things are usually deposited in a bank vault, that they were only valuable as a depository for such purposes, as holding and preserving money and valuable papers, bonds, stocks, and the like. This box and safe would have been of little value to the donee for any other purpose. But, more than this, the donor expressly stated that "all you find in this box and this safe is yours." There is no mistake that it was the intention of the donor to give what was contained in the box and in the safe. As my Lord Coke would say, "Note the diversity" between that case and the case at bar. There the evidences of debt contained in the bureau, which was present, were taken out, given to the donor, and by him delivered to the donee. This was an actual manual delivery, good under all the authorities. But no such thing was done in this case as to the life insurance policy. It was neither taken out of the drawer, nor mentioned by the donor, unless it is included in the testimony of Enos Houston, who at one time, in giving in his testimony, says that Van Pelt gave her the keys, saying, "What is in this house is yours;" and at another time, on cross-examination, he said to Julia, "I intend to give you this furniture in this house;" and at another time, "What property is in this house is yours." The bureau in which was found the life insurance policy, after the death of Van Pelt, was present in the room where the keys were handed to Julia; and the life insurance policy could easily have been taken out and handed to Van Pelt, and by him delivered to Julia, as was done in the case of Thomas v. Lewis, supra. But this was not done. The safe and box, in Thomas v. Lewis, were not present, so that the contents could not have been taken out and delivered to the donee by the donor. The ordinary use of a stand of bureaus is not for the purpose of holding and securing such things as a life insurance policy, though they may often be used for that purpose, while a safe and a box deposited in the vault of a bank are. A bureau is an article of household furniture, used for domestic purposes, and generally belongs to the ladies' department of the household government, while the safe and box, in Thomas v. Lewis, are not. The bureau itself, mentioned in this case, was such property as would be valuable to the plaintiff. * * *

It is held that the law of delivery in this State is the same in gifts inter vivos and causa mortis. * * *

We feel bound to give effect to constructive delivery, where it plainly appears that it was the intention of the donor to make the gift, and where the things intended to be given are not present, or, where present, are incapable of manual delivery from their size or weight; but where the articles are present, and are capable of manual delivery, this must be had. This is as far as we can go. It may be thought by some that this is a hard rule,—that a dying man cannot dispose of his own. But we are satisfied, when properly considered, it will be found to be a just rule. But it is not a hard rule. The law provides how a man can dispose of all his property, both real and personal. To do this, it is only necessary for him to observe and conform to the requirement of these laws. It may be thought by some persons to be a hard rule that does not allow a man to dispose of his land by gift causa mortis, but such is the law. The law provides that every man may dispose of all of his property by will, when made in writing. And it is most singular how guarded the law is to protect the testator against fraud and imposition by requiring that every word of the will must be written and signed by the testator, or, if written by someone else, it must be attested by at least two subscribing witnesses, who shall sign the same in his presence and at his request, or the will is void. This is as to written wills. But the law provides for another kind of will, not written before the testator's death, called "nuncupative wills." This kind only applies to personal property, and until recently was limited to small amounts. See how much more guarded they are than gifts causa mortis. Such wills as these must be witnessed by at least two witnesses called by the testator specially for that purpose, and they must be reduced to writing within ten days, and proved and recorded within six months.

*   *   *

The statute of wills is a statute against fraud, considered in England and in this state to be demanded by public policy. And yet, if symbolical deliveries of gifts causa mortis are to be allowed, or if constructive deliveries be allowed to the extent claimed by the plaintiff, the statute of wills may prove to be of little value. For such considerations, we see every reason for restricting, and none for extending, the rules heretofore established, as applicable to gifts causa mortis.

It being claimed and admitted that the life insurance policy was present in the bureau drawer in the room where it is claimed the gift was made, and being capable of actual manual delivery, we are of the opinion that the title to the insurance policy did not pass to the plaintiff, but remained the property of the intestate of the defendant. But we are of the opinion that the bureau and any other article of furniture, locked and unlocked by any of the keys given to the plaintiff, did pass, and she became the owner thereof. This is upon the ground that while these articles were present, from their size and weight, they were incapable of actual manual delivery; and that the delivery of the keys was a constructive delivery of these articles, equivalent to an actual delivery if the articles had been capable of manual delivery. Still following Ward v. Turner, Dick. 170, 21 Eng. Reprint 234, s. c. 2 Ves.Sr. 431, 28 Eng. Reprint 275, 1752, we are of the opinion that the other articles of household furniture (except those in the plaintiff's private bedchamber) did not pass to the plaintiff, but remained the property of the defendant's estate.

We do not think the articles in the plaintiff's bedchamber passed by the donatio causa mortis, for the same reason that the other articles of household furniture did not pass,—want of delivery, either constructive or manual. But, as to the furniture in the plaintiff's bedroom ($45), it seems to us that there was sufficient evidence of both gift and delivery to support the finding of the jury, as a gift inter vivos. The intention to give this property is shown by a number of witnesses, and contradicted by none. The only debatable ground is as to the sufficiency of the delivery. But, when we recall the express terms in which he repeatedly declared that it was hers; that he had bought it for her, and had given it to her; that it was placed in her private chamber, her bedroom, where we must suppose that she had the entire use and control of the same,— it would seem that this was sufficient to constitute a delivery. *   *   *

As to the piano there was much evidence tending to show the intention of Van Pelt to give it to the plaintiff, and that he had given it to her, and we remember no evidence to the contrary. And as to this, like the bedroom furniture, the debatable ground, if there is any debatable ground, is the question of delivery. It was placed in the intestate's parlor where it remained until it was burned. The intestate insured it as his property, collected and used the insurance money as his own, often saying that he intended to buy the plaintiff another piano, which he never did. It must be presumed that the parlor was under the dominion of the intestate, and not of his cook, housekeeper, and hired servant. And unless there is something more shown than the fact that the piano was bought by the intestate, placed in his parlor, and called by him "Miss Julia's piano," we cannot think this constituted a delivery. * * * We see no ground upon which the plaintiff can recover the insurance money, if the piano was not hers. * * *

New trial.

Problems

1. A on his death bed gives B the key to his safety deposit box and tells her the contents are hers. Braun v. Brown, 14 Cal.2d 346, 94 P.2d 348, 127 A.L.R. 773 (1939).

2. A does the same thing but the rules of the safety deposit company provide that no person shall have access except "the renter, a deputy authorized in writing as his personal representative." Is the gift valid? Compare Harrison v. Foley, 206 F. 57 (8th Cir.1913), with In re Estate of Evans, 467 Pa. 336, 356 A.2d 778 (1976).

3. A says to B that all his property is to go to her and hands her a bunch of keys one of which opens his safety deposit box in which there is $21,000 and another of which opens his office in which there is a locked desk containing $63,000. No key unlocks the desk. Is any part of the intended gift valid? In re Elliott's Estate, 312 Pa. 493, 167 A. 289, 90 A.L.R. 360 (1933).

4. Suppose a donor wishes to make a gift of a chattel which is in the possession of the intended donee who is holding it as a bailee. How is such a chattel to be delivered? The courts have held that the delivery requirement may be disregarded in such cases. It is often said that to require the donee to return the chattel to the donor so that it could then be delivered back to him would be a senseless formality. See Matter of Mills' Estate, 172 App.Div. 530, 158 N.Y.S. 1100 (1916); Brown, Personal Property § 7.7 (3d ed. 1975). Is there any other alternative?

5. A similar problem appears in Newman v. Bost. It might be argued that the furniture in plaintiff's bedroom was in the joint possession of donor and donee. Are you satisfied with the way the court disposed of this gift? Did the court in effect dispense with the delivery requirement? See Brown, Personal Property § 7.6 (3d ed. 1975).

BRIND v. INTERNATIONAL TRUST CO.

Supreme Court of Colorado, 1919.
66 Colo. 60, 179 P. 148.

BURKE, J. This is an action in replevin by J. Fitz. Brind, administrator with the will annexed of the estate of Maria E. Brind, deceased, plaintiff, against the International Trust Company, defendant, to recover of the defendant certain jewelry, deposited with it by the decedent for delivery, under certain conditions, to Mrs. U.S. Hollister et al., interveners, who now claim the property.

Demurrers to the answer of the defendant and the petitions of intervention were overruled. Answers and replications were filed, and the cause was tried to a jury. Plaintiff moved the court to direct a verdict in his favor, which motion was denied. The jury found for the interveners. Motion for new trial was overruled, judgment was entered in favor of the interveners for possession of the property, and the cause comes here for review on error.

It appears that on August 18, 1914, Maria E. Brind, then the wife of the plaintiff, addressed to defendant the following communication:

"Gentlemen: In view of the fact that I am about to undergo a very serious surgical operation for the removal of a tumor, and in anticipation of the fact that said operation may result in my death, I hereby deliver into your hands the following mentioned articles of personal jewelry, inclosed separately, one each in box, each article as a gift causa mortis to the person for whom it is mentioned, viz., to wit: [Here follows a description of each article and the name of the person to whom it is to be delivered.] The same to be delivered by you to each of said persons in the event of my death as a result of said surgical operation. In the event I do not die from said operation, then each and all of said articles of jewelry to be returned to me on demand.

> "[Signed] Marie Evaline
> Brind."

This document, with the jewelry, was delivered to the defendant, which receipted therefor and agreed to act thereunder. It was drawn by decedent's attorney, and executed after consulting with him and upon his advice. At the time of the death of said Maria E. Brind, November 8th, the property was still in the possession of the defendant. It is contended by the plaintiff that his wife did not die as a result of the contemplated operation; hence the gift is invalid, and the property must be returned to him, as administrator. Defendant and interveners assert that she did die as a result of said operation, or as a result of said operation and the malady for which it was to be performed; further, that prior to her death she reaffirmed the gifts made by the instrument and never demanded the return of the property. There is no serious conflict in the evidence. It appears therefrom that on the date of the execution of the instrument in question decedent went to a hospital in Denver for the purpose of the operation therein contemplated; that on the following day an incision was made by the surgeon in charge of the case, and such a condition discovered as convinced him that the contemplated operation could only result in Mrs. Brind's death, whereupon the wound made by the incision was sewed up. The incision made was not a serious operation and had perfectly healed, and from it she fully recovered. About September 8th, following, she was sufficiently recovered to leave the hospital and return to her home. The direct cause of her death was the original ailment for which the operation was contemplated. She was fully informed by the surgeon that the contemplated operation had not been performed, and understood the reasons why. She visited the office of the defendant after leaving the hospital, and in the latter part of October, made visits downtown to take X-ray treatments. There is testimony that she said, after leaving the hospital, "I think this is fatal, and I will never get over it"; that she said to one of the witnesses, "In case of my passing away, I should like those things to go, as listed, to my friends"; that the disposition which she had made was the most satisfactory to her; that the jewelry was in the vault of the trust company, and was disposed of by her, and was no longer her property; that she wanted something done in order to insure that the articles would go to the particular individuals mentioned.

H.V. Johnson, attorney for decedent, who drew the instrument in question, testified that he advised her concerning her right to make what the law called a gift causa mortis, which might be made by a person in imminent danger of death; that if the death took place the gift would stand; that if the death did not occur she could get possession of the things she had given them; that about November 3d, when Mrs. Brind was quite ill, he visited her at her home. She spoke of her husband and of a will, and said, "I hardly know what to do about it, but I am particularly anxious about those matters with the International Trust Company." She said she was feeling very badly. It seems she had executed a will, which her attorney told her she had a right to change, and advised her not to wait too long; also that, if she wished to make any change in the document deposited with the defendant he was at her service. She then said, "Well, I will think about it, and if I determine to do anything I will call on you." He reminded her that the instrument which she executed, and under which she had delivered the articles to the trust company, states that whereas, she was about to undergo a dangerous operation for a tumor, and that she might die therefrom, and, as a certain operation had been performed in August, "as I was informed by her, and she had not died immediately after the operation, and was still living, that there might possibly be some question about the validity of the gift." Later, about November 5th, he communicated by telephone with Mrs. Brind, through a third person, and was advised, that if Mrs. Brind wanted him for any purpose later, she would call. This she never did.

The verdict of the jury and the judgment of the court upheld this transaction as a valid gift causa mortis. If such determination was erroneous, plaintiff's motion for a directed verdict should have been sustained, and the judgment entered by the trial court cannot stand.

"A gift causa mortis is subject to the conditions: (1) It must be made in contemplation, fear or peril of death; (2) the donor must die of the illness or peril which he then fears or contemplates; and (3) the delivery must be made with the intent that the title shall vest only in case of death." O'Neil v. O'Neil, 43 Mont. 505–511, 117 P. 889, 890, Ann.Cas. 1912C, 268.

That decedent executed the instrument, and made the delivery of the property (if delivery was made) in fear of death, is established by her signed statement, and is not disputed.

We think it clearly appears from the evidence that there was a delivery of the property in question. The articles passed into the possession of the defendant, which receipted for them and agreed to execute the gift. The evidence shows that the box was set apart by the trust company and the keys retained by the company. Such a delivery to another for the use of a donee is a sufficient delivery to uphold a gift causa mortis. * * *

The first and third essentials of a gift causa mortis, as laid down in O'Neil v. O'Neil, supra, being thus established, there remains for consideration the second: Did Mrs. Brind die of the illness or peril which she feared or contemplated at the time of the execution of the instrument in question? (Not as erroneously and indefinitely stated in the brief of counsel for defendant and interveners, Did she die "of an ailment or peril?")

There can be no better guide for determining just what was the illness or peril which Mrs. Brind feared or contemplated than reference to the instrument which she herself signed and upon which the gift was based. In that instrument she refers only incidentally to the illness or malady for which an operation was to be performed. From a perusal of the writing it is very evident that the cause of her immediate dread, the peril in view of which she made the gift, was the operation itself. She says, "In anticipation of the fact that said operation may result in death." Further, she directed that these gifts were to be delivered "in the event of my death as a result of said surgical operation. In the event I do not die from said operation, then each of said articles of jewelry to be returned to me on demand." It seems to us impossible to read this document and come to the conclusion that at the time of its execution the mind of Mrs. Brind was running ahead or beyond the result of the operation itself, or was taking into consideration any possibility of death from her original malady. That she did not, in fact, die as a result of the said surgical operation, seems to us, from the evidence, beyond question. The slight operation or incision which was, in fact, performed had nothing to do with her death; she unquestionably died as a result of her original malady; her death was in no way connected with the operation she then contemplated, or with any operation.

The contention that the fact that Mrs. Brind died of the contemplated peril was settled by the verdict of the jury cannot be upheld. There is no evidence to support it, and the jury was not limited to that question by the instructions, but permitted to consider whether she died of her original disease and the operation.

The principal case relied upon to sustain the existence of this second essential to a gift causa mortis is Ridden v. Thrall, 125 N.Y. 572, 26 N.E. 627, 11 L.R.A. 684, 21 Am.St.Rep. 758. By its very language it is inapplicable. That court says:

"We therefore confine our decision to the precise facts of this case, and we go no further than to hold that when a gift is made in the apprehension of death from some disease from which the donor did not recover, and the apparent immediate cause of death was some other disease with which he was afflicted at the same time, the gift becomes effectual."

This authority would be applicable only in case Mrs. Brind had not recovered from the operation at the time she died from the tumor. Shall we stretch this rule to cover the instant case where there was a recovery from the operation? Counsel's own authority, just quoted, answers the question thus:

"Sound policy requires that the laws regulating gifts causa mortis should not be extended, and that the range of such gifts should not be enlarged."

On the question of Mrs. Brind's reaffirmation of the gifts after her recovery from the operation, it is sufficient to point out that this contention is fully answered by the testimony of her attorney, Johnson. From him she learned of the probable invalidity of the gifts by reason of her recovery from the operation, of the importance of further action in case of her conclusion to reaffirm them, and of the availability of his services to that end, and from him we learn her decision: "Well, I will think about it, and if I determine to do anything I will call on you." In view of this undisputed testimony, it must be held that her statements of an intention that, notwithstanding her recovery from the operation, these gifts should go to interveners, were nothing more than statements of what she then contemplated she would do, but what she herself well knew she had not done.

We therefore conclude that the second essential element of a valid gift causa mortis, as laid down in O'Neil v. O'Neil, supra—i.e., that the donor must die of the illness or peril which he then fears or contemplates—was absent in this case; that Mrs. Brind's recovery from the operation revoked the gifts; that there was no reaffirmance by her; that plaintiff's motion for a directed verdict should therefore have been sustained.

The judgment of the trial court is reversed, with directions to enter judgment herein in favor of the plaintiff.

Note

Compare with the statement of the requirements for a gift causa mortis in the Brind case the following:

"These elements are: (1) the gift must be made in view of approaching death from some existing sickness or peril; (2) the donor must die from such sickness or peril without having revoked the gift; (3) there must be a delivery, either actual, constructive, or symbolical, of the subject of the gift to the donee or to some one for him, with the intention of passing title thereto, subject, however, to revocation in the event of recovery from the pending sickness."

In re McDonald's Estate, 60 Wn.2d 452, 374 P.2d 365, 366 (1962).

A gift causa mortis is a gift made in contemplation of death. This does not mean the realization of mortality that all people have and which may be the inducement to the making of a will. On the other hand, it does not require that the donor be *in extremis* or on his death bed. Rather it means that the motivation for the gift must be a fear of approaching death on account of some existing ailment. It is possible, therefore, for a mortally sick person to make a good gift inter vivos. It has been held that gifts made in fear of death in military combat cannot be sustained as gifts causa mortis. It is not clear whether fear of death from any external cause is disqualified, although this proposition has been asserted. Gifts made in contemplation of suicide have been held void, usually on the ground of public policy, although there is authority contra.

Robert and Catherine lived together for some 15 years. Following severe injury, a car accident, Catherine was very depressed. On the day of her death, she had received a check for $17,400 from her lawyer, in settlement of her claim. She died by jumping from the apartment building in which she resided. The check was found on the kitchen table, along with two notes, one of which "bequeathed" to Robert all her property, including "the check for $17,400." The check was endorsed in blank.

Is this a valid gift causa mortis? Is any policy involved in determining whether the gift is made in contemplation of death? See Scherer v. Hyland, 75 N.J. 127, 380 A.2d 698 (1977).

Gifts causa mortis are inherently conditional, that is, revocable. As stated in Brind v. International Trust Co., recovery from the illness which motivated the gift is said automatically to revoke the gift. Some nice questions of degree can be posed in this regard, such as the length of time which can elapse between the making of the gift and the death of the donor, or the exact cause of the death which does ensue. See Fendley v. Laster, 260 Ark. 370, 538 S.W.2d 555 (1976). A gift causa mortis is also revocable by the donor at will during his lifetime, and without regard to whether he later dies of the ailment which caused him to make the gift. It has been held that the making of a later will does not revoke a prior gift causa mortis. This is an obvious result where the will does not reveal an intention that it was to have that effect. This result has, however, been justified on the technical ground that a will takes effect only upon the death of the testator.

In general the delivery requirement is the same for gifts causa mortis and gifts inter vivos, except that in certain types of cases some courts may apply the requirement more strictly to gifts causa mortis.

See Brown, Personal Property, §§ 7.15 et seq. (3d ed. 1975).

IN RE NOLS' ESTATE

Supreme Court of Wisconsin, 1947.
251 Wis. 90, 28 N.W.2d 360.

The appeal is from a judgment ordering the defendant administrator Fred Will to strike from the inventory in the estate of Frank Nols items of personal property consisting of cash and a check, postal savings certificates and corporate stock certificates payable to the deceased but not endorsed or assigned. It was adjudged that these items be delivered to the plaintiff George Vander Zanden as the donee of a gift causa mortis. The administrator appeals.

RECTOR, Justice. * * * Upon the question as to whether there was a valid gift, the trial court found that the deceased delivered the items of personal property involved to Vander Zanden by walking into Vander Zanden's store, placing a parcel containing the property on a showcase and saying, "Here is a parcel and you keep it, and if I don't come back, you can have it." It found that at the time of the delivery of the parcel the decedent was seriously ill with a disease which caused his hospitalization the next day and which shortly thereafter was responsible for his death, and that at the time of the delivery he realized the seriousness of his condition. It also found that the deceased delivered the parcel intending a gift to Vander Zanden and that he died without revoking it. In a memorandum decision accompanying the findings it said that at the time the gift was made the deceased realized his death was not far off and that the language "if I don't come back" had reference to that contingency.

We cannot say that these findings are contrary to the great weight and clear preponderance of the evidence, and we are accordingly bound by them. State v. M. Supple & Sons Co., 1940, 234 Wis. 255, 290 N.W. 139. It would serve no useful purpose to review evidence which would warrant other findings.

The most difficult question presented is whether the findings support the judgment. The appellant, relying upon Basket v. Hassell, 1882, 107 U.S. 602, 2 S.Ct. 415, 27 L.Ed. 500, and Schultz v. Becker, 1907, 131 Wis. 235, 110 N.W. 214, contends that they do not. The contention is based upon the argument that a gift made to take effect upon death is a testamentary disposition and invalid unless there is compliance with the statute of wills.

Basket v. Hassell is authority for the appellant's position. It clearly held that a gift causa mortis conditioned upon the donor's death is invalid as a testamentary disposition and that in order to be valid such a gift must pass title in praesenti upon the conditions subsequent of revocation and the other happenings which have been held to defeat it.

Basket v. Hassell was approved by this court in Schultz v. Becker. In Hoks v. Wollenberg, 1932, 209 Wis. 276, 243 N.W. 219, 245 N.W. 128, we upheld a gift made in terms of death as a condition precedent and arrived at a result diametrically at variance with Basket v. Hassell and Schultz v. Becker. The question we have to decide is whether we will adhere to Hoks v. Wollenburg or return to Schultz v. Becker.

We hold to the rule of Hoks v. Wollenberg. We do not believe there is any basis for a distinction between conditions precedent and subsequent in such a case. As a practical matter it should be obvious that out of a thousand would-be donors there would probably not be one who would normally make a gift in the form of conditions subsequent. He would normally make it in terms of "This is yours if I die"—a condition precedent. Therefore, if we were to adhere to a rule of law requiring that such gifts be made upon conditions subsequent, we would in effect invalidate practically all such gifts that are not made under advice of counsel; and such advise is infrequent by reason of the very nature of the gifts and the circumstances under which they are made.

A great deal has been written by courts and textbook writers upon the subject of gifts causa mortis. It is generally agreed that during the lifetime of the donor the donee holds an inchoate title which ripens into absolute title at the donor's death from the illness or peril which he apprehended in making the gift. This court has so stated. "A donatio causa mortis is a gift absolute in form, made by the donor in anticipation of his speedy death, and intended to take effect and operate as a transfer of title only upon the happening of the donor's death." Crook v. The First National Bank of Baraboo, 1892, 83 Wis. 31, 52 N.W. 1131, 1132, 35 Am.St.Rep. 17.

If an absolute title is intended to vest only upon the donor's death, it is immaterial whether it was intended to vest by fulfillment of a condition precedent or removal of conditions subsequent. In either case, death being the contemplated event upon which absolute title is to pass, the disposition is in a broad sense testamentary. For that matter, gifts causa mortis have long been recognized as testamentary in character. In the quaint style of his time an eminent British author described such a gift as: "* * * when any being in perill of death, doth give something, but not so, that it shall presently be his that received it, but in case the giver do dye. This * * * kinde of gift is that which is compared to a legacy * * *." Swinburne, Wills (1640 ed.) 27, sec. 7.

In Jones v. Brown, 1857, 34 N.H. 439, it is said: "* * * a donatio causa mortis is of the nature of a legacy. It becomes a valid gift only upon the decease of the donor."

There have been many other statements to the same effect.

With due deference to the attempts that have been made to in some way account for the transfer of title during life, it seems to us that such considerations are not important. It might be important in relation to collateral matters to determine whether title passes during life or at death, but for purposes of determining whether such gifts are valid, it is not. They have been held valid with practical unanimity for many years in the face of deliveries upon condition that they shall take effect at death. Actually, the doctrine of gifts causa mortis appears to be an exception to the rule against testamentary disposition except by will. It has probably been established and recognized upon the basis of an unspoken acceptance that delivery of the subject of the gift during life is an adequate safeguard against abuses at which the statute of wills is aimed.

The requirements of a valid gift causa mortis are that there be an intention to make a gift effective at death; it must be made with a view to the donor's death from present illness or from an external and apprehended peril; the donor must die of that ailment or peril; there must be a delivery. Hoks v. Wollenberg, supra. The only question raised here as to the sufficiency of the findings in support of these requirements is in reference to delivery. That requirement was clearly met so far as physical delivery was concerned. The condition precedent, upon which the delivery was made, did not affect its validity because it expressed only that which the law implies.

Judgment affirmed.

Note

"It is insisted that the language of the donor, 'if I die, or anything happen to me,' which accompanied the delivery of the money, was a condition attached to the gift that it was not to take effect until the donor's death, and shows that a testamentary disposition was intended, and not a gift *causa mortis*. The language used by the donor is but the expression of the condition attached by implication of law to every gift *causa mortis*—that it does not take effect absolutely and irrevocably except in case of the death of the donor. It is not necessary that the donor should express the condition, but, if he does so, it tends to make plain the character of the gift, rather than to cast doubt upon it. So far as we have had access to the authorities, they are practically unanimous in holding that the language 'if I die,' when used by the donor in making the gift, is but an inference of law from the circumstances, and does not impair the gift." Johnson v. Colley, 101 Va. 414, 418, 44 S.E. 721, 722 (1903).

Contra: Adams v. Fleck, 171 Ohio St. 451, 172 N.E.2d 126 (1961), in which the court approved the rule of Basket v. Hassell, which was discussed and rejected in the Nols case, that a gift causa mortis is invalid if the death of the donor is a condition precedent to the vesting of title in the donee. Emphasis was placed on the belief that gifts causa mortis are in the nature of legacies and are therefore not favored by the law so long as there is provision by the statute of wills and the law of descent for the transmission of all property rights.

BICKFORD v. MATTOCKS

Supreme Judicial Court of Maine, 1901.
95 Me. 547, 50 A. 894.

SAVAGE, J. The defendant's intestate, Thomas R. Heath, loaned $500 to one Sturgis. The latter, by direction of Heath, gave his note for the same, payable to the plaintiff. The note was secured by a mortgage running to the plaintiff. The plaintiff was not present, and knew nothing of the transaction at the time. After the note and mortgage were executed, Heath asked the attorney who was the scrivener to get the mortgage recorded, and, when the mortgage was received from the registry of deeds, to mail it, with the note, to the plaintiff. The attorney filed the mortgage in the registry, and took possession of the note. He did not take the mortgage from the registry. He forgot it, or, to use his own expression, "it left his mind." He kept the note for about a year, and then delivered it to Heath. In the meantime the maker of the note had made certain payments on it to the attorney, who paid the money to Heath. Afterwards the balance due was paid to Heath, and he surrendered the note to the maker. Neither the note nor the mortgage was ever delivered to the plaintiff by Heath or the attorney; nor were any of moneys collected by Heath paid or delivered to her. Some months after the note and mortgage were executed, she executed, at the request of Heath, a release of a portion of the mortgaged premises, and when the note was paid she discharged the mortgage, likewise at the request of Heath.

The plaintiff claims that the transaction constituted a gift of the note to her, and has brought this suit to recover the amount of the proceeds of the note which were paid to the defendant's intestate. The defendant claims that no gift was intended, and that Heath adopted the plan of making the note payable to the plaintiff, who was his niece, in order that he might more easily escape taxation upon the loan; and, further, that, if a gift was intended, that it never became complete and effective for want of delivery.

We think the evidence preponderates in favor of the theory that Heath intended to give the note to the plaintiff. He so declared his intention on the occasion when the note was made, and even before then; and it may be that he thought he had accomplished his purpose, for shortly after the note was made he told the plaintiff and others that he had given her $500; and about the time the note was paid in full, speaking with reference to that fact, he asked her what he should do with the money, to which she replied, "Keep it for me, and invest it again."

To constitute a valid gift inter vivos it must be made with intent that it shall take effect immediately and irrevocably, and it must be fully executed by a complete and unconditional delivery. These principles are elementary. Delivery is essential. * * * Mere intention cannot take the place of it, nor can words, nor can actions. * * * It is the act which completes the gift. It is the test which shows whether the gift was actually consummated, as well as intended. Since many of the cases cited by counsel on both sides in this case involved only gifts causa mortis, it is proper to observe that, while delivery is essential to the validity of each of these classes of gifts, and while there is in this respect no difference in the requisites of good delivery, the effect is widely different. Thornt. Gifts, 105. In gifts causa mortis the delivery is made in expectation of death, but so long as the donor lives the gift is ambulatory, revocable. Only death completes the gift. Before death it is subject to the will of the donor; while in gifts inter vivos it is the delivery itself which completes the gift and makes it irrevocable. The delivery must be absolute. * * *

Now, in the case at bar, it is not claimed that there was any delivery whatever to the plaintiff personally of the note or its proceeds. But delivery may be made to the donee; or, as is commonly, but somewhat loosely, said, it may be made to a third person for the donee, or for the use of the donee. * * *

Not every delivery to a third person is a delivery for the donee, or for the use of the donee, in the sense in which these phrases are used in the cases cited. There may be a delivery to a third person which constitutes him the agent of the donor, and there may be a delivery which constitutes him a trustee for the donee, and the distinction lies in the intention with which the delivery is made. If the donor deliver the property to the third person simply for the purpose of his delivering it to the donee as the agent of the donor, the gift is not complete until the property has actually been delivered to the donee. Such a delivery is not absolute, for the ordinary principle of agency applies, by which the donor can revoke the authority of the agent, and resume possession of the property, at any time before the authority is executed. On the other hand, if the donor delivers the property to the third person with the intent that the gift shall take effect immediately, and thus parts with all present and future dominion over it, the third person holds as trustee for the donee, and the gift is in that respect complete. * * *

Now let us apply these rules of law to the facts in this case. Did the donor here, by leaving the note in the hands of the attorney with directions to mail it to the donee, intend to vest the title to the note then and there in the donee, or did he merely intend that the attorney, as his agent, should deliver the note by mailing it to the donee? We are constrained to think the latter. The attorney was the donor's attorney, not the donee's. He was employed to draft the note and mortgage by the donor, not by the donee. He was paid by the donor, not by the donee.

The mailing of the note was only an extension of his service to his client, only the completion of the transaction in which he was engaged. The donor's direction to the attorney was to mail the note. He had no other duty respecting it. He was not to hold it or keep it; he was to send it. It was left with him solely for that purpose. Had he been directed to send it by the next mail, we think no one would have attached the idea of a trust to his service. If he had done so, no one would have regarded him as the agent of the donee in mailing the note to her, but rather the agent of the donor. If the note had then been lost in the mail, we think no one would have claimed that there had been a good delivery. But the length of time which was expected to elapse before the note was mailed is only a circumstance bearing on the question of intent, and of little importance, unless the delay was due to the performance of some duty in connection with the note itself. That the attorney was not expected to mail the note immediately was not due to anything connected with the note, but to the fact that it would take time to get the mortgage recorded, and it would be convenient to mail both together. Except for convenience, the note might as well have been mailed the day it was signed. We think the donor, in giving directions for mailing, had no other thought than that he was using the attorney as his own hand to make delivery,—that the attorney was his agent. This view is strengthened by the subsequent history of the note. If the note was delivered to the donee, or to the attorney in trust for the donee, the donor had no further dominion over it or interest in it. He could not collect it. He had no right to touch it. But if it was in the hands of the attorney as agent for the mere purpose of making delivery, the donor had a right to revoke the authority, to recall the note and collect it himself. And that is what he did do. Although he probably intended that his agent should make delivery, he undoubtedly learned afterwards that the note was still in the agent's hands undelivered. He then, in effect, revoked the authority of the agent, and in this way: As we have already stated, payments on the note were received by the attorney. They were paid over by him to the donor. Then the note itself was taken back from the attorney; and finally the donor received payment in full, and surrendered the note to the maker. He was still exercising dominion over the note, and none of the money was paid over to the donee. All this tends to show that Heath regarded the attorney as his agent, and did not regard his delivery of the note to the attorney as completing an irrevocable gift to the plaintiff. It may be that Heath still intended that the plaintiff should have the money at some time. It may be that he intended to keep it, and invest it for her. But that was not sufficient. He had not delivered to her either the note or the money, and for that reason the attempted gift was invalid.

Judgment for defendant.

Note

In the preceding case there was some evidence other than the fact that the subject matter of the gift had been handed to a third person from which a court might draw an inference as to whether that third person was holding on behalf of the donor or on behalf of the donee. Where there is no such other evidence, should there be any presumption? Compare the following extracts from cases which involved such a situation:

"It has often been held that the law will presume, unless the contrary appears, that the person to whom the delivery is made takes as trustee of the donee." In re Estate of, White, 129 Wash. 544, 548, 225 P. 415, 1924.

"There is no proof that she (donor) constituted them (the third parties) the agents of the defendants (donees), and in the absence of such proof they must be presumed to have acted as her agents; * * * " Clapper v. Frederick, 199 Pa. 609, 612, 49 A. 218, 1901.

What inference as to intention would you draw from the following facts: A gave $10,000 to B, his brother-in-law, a minister, with directions to take care of it. In 1940, he told B that he wanted B to hold the money "for my brothers and sisters. I want you to take it out of the bank and put it in a lock box and hold it and deliver it to them at my death." In 1943, A asked B to borrow $1,000 and received that amount, promising to repay it. Later in 1943, he asked for $5,000 which was placed in his own account. A died in 1944. See Baugh v. Howze, 211 Ark. 222, 199 S.W.2d 940, 1947.

What inference would you draw from these facts: A made a will devising land to her five sisters. Shortly before her death she sold the land and put the proceeds in a bank, taking certificates of deposit. She handed these certificates to her father, requesting him to deliver them to her sisters. He left the papers with a bank for safekeeping, endorsing on the envelope "Certificates of deposit of A." A died about a month later, with the certificates still with the bank. See Nelson v. Olson, 108 Minn. 109, 121 N.W. 609, 1909.

INNES v. POTTER

Supreme Court of Minnesota, 1915.
130 Minn. 320, 153 N.W. 604, 3 A.L.R. 896.

HALLAM, J. 1. Warren Potter was the owner of 1,370 shares of stock, of the par value of $100 a share, in the Potter-Casey Company, a business corporation of Aitkin county. In 1910 he was a man advanced in years. He had made a will some years before. In the meantime his business associate, Mr. Casey, had died and his estate had been probated. There was "considerable noise" about the amount of his property, and a substantial inheritance tax had been paid. On December 27, 1910, after some talk with J.A. Casey, son of his former associate, in which deceased stated that he wanted to leave a certain amount of property to his daughter, he took a certificate of 1,000 shares of stock of the Potter-Casey Company, indorsed upon it an absolute assignment to the defendant, and wrote a letter addressed to her in which he stated that he had transferred this stock to her, and making certain requests. The certificate, with the indorsement upon it, and this letter he inclosed in an envelope, securely sealed it, and indorsed thereon the following:

"The Certificate No. 1 for 1,000 m shares to be sent by Registered letter to H. Marcia Potter if not Present or Handed to her, taking her Receipt for the same, _____. These certificates to be held by J.A. Casey and delivered to the above parties only in case of the death of

"Warren Potter."

This he then delivered to J.A. Casey, and Casey held it until Mr. Potter's death. Deceased never mentioned the matter to Casey again, and never exercised nor attempted to exercise any control over the stock. Warren Potter died in February, 1914. After his death, J.A. Casey delivered the envelope and its contents to the defendant. She opened the envelope and took therefrom the letter and the certificate. Potter's will was admitted to probate, and plaintiff was appointed administrator with the will annexed. He commenced this action to recover possession of the certificate of stock or its value. The trial court found that defendant owned the stock, that deceased intended to and did relinquish all control over the stock and all rights in it, that he intended to and did give the stock to defendant, and intended that the gift take effect at once on the delivery to Casey, but that the right of defendant to the beneficial enjoyment thereof was postponed until the death of deceased.

2. The first question is this: Is it competent for a person to make a gift of personal property by delivery of the subject of the gift to a trustee where delivery by the trustee to the donee and beneficial enjoyment by the donee are postponed until the death of the donor?

As to deeds of real estate the law in this state is well settled. Where a grantor executes a deed and deposits it with a third person, to be delivered by him to the grantee after the death of the grantor, and reserves to himself no right to control or recall the instrument, the transaction is a valid one and full and complete title is vested in the grantee after death of the grantor. * * * This is true even though the enjoyment of the estate granted is postponed until the death of the grantor, and even though the deed thereof expressly reserves a life estate in the grantor * * *, and even though the grant is subject to the contingency that the grantee survive the grantor, or to any contingency, as long as it is one over which the grantor has no control. * * *

3. Anciently there was no such thing recognized in law as an expectant estate in personal property. This was because of the perishable nature of such property, its movable characteristics, and its insignificance. An exception was early made in favor of chattels real. Manning's Case, 8 Co. (Eng.) 94b; Lampet's Case, 10 Co. (Eng.) 46b. But in that case only as to interests created by will, and when merely the *use* of the chattel was given to the first legatee. 2 Bl.Com. 398. The exception was later extended from chattels real to chattels personal under like restrictions. 2 Bl.Com. 398; 1 Eq.Cas.Abr. (Eng.) 360. These limitations one by one dropped away. In chancery before the close of the seventeenth century it was settled that a bequest of an expectant estate in goods to another was good, whether the goods or the use of the goods were given to the first legatee. Hyde v. Parrat, 1 P.Wms. (Eng.) 1. And in recent times it has not been necessary in England that limitations of this sort be made by will. They are equally good when made by deed of trust. * * *

The doctrine that personal property may be limited by way of remainder after a life interest created at the same time was early recognized in the United States. 2 Kent, Com. (13th Ed.)* 352, 353, and notes; Executors of Moffat v. Strong, 10 Johns. (N.Y.) 12; Langworthy

v. Chadwick, 13 Conn. 42. The disposition of the later cases has been to dispense with all fictitious distinctions between transfers of real and personal property and to apply the same rules to both, except where distinctions are founded upon some substantial principle of law or are required by some statutory enactment. In this state expectant interests in personal property are recognized. State ex rel. Tozer v. Probate Court, 102 Minn. 268, 291, 113 N.W. 888. Since it is competent for a person to create an expectant interest in personal property, we see no ground for saying that he may not do so either by will, by sale, or by gift. Nor do we see any reason why the rules as to delivery to a third person, with direction to deliver to the donee on the death of the donor, should not apply to personal as well as to real property. Delivery is of course necessary to give effect to a gift, but so it is to give effect to a deed. If valid delivery may be made to a trustee in case of a gift of a deed of real property, why not in case of a gift of personal property? Not only do we think there should be no distinction between the two classes of property in this respect, but we are equally convinced that it is the settled law in most of the states of the Union that no such distinction does exist. * * *

We accordingly hold that the owner of personal property may make a valid gift thereof with the right of enjoyment in the donee postponed until the death of the donor, if the subject of the gift be delivered to a third person with instruction to deliver it to the donee upon the donor's death, and if the donor parts with all control over it, reserves no right to recall, and intends thereby a final disposition of the property given.

4. The next question is, Did this transaction constitute such a gift? Plaintiff's contention is that the transaction was not a gift at all, but that it is testamentary in character and void. The gift, if sustainable at all, must be sustained as a gift inter vivos. It was in no sense a gift causa mortis. Effect should be given to the transaction if possible. Thomas v. Williams, 105 Minn. 88. If, as plaintiff claims, the documents were testamentary in character the transaction was void, for the formalities required for the execution of a will were not followed. It is only by construing the transaction as an executed gift that effect can be given to it at all. It is not always easy to determine whether or not an instrument is testamentary in character. It depends upon the intention of the maker. The fact that the instrument postpones the enjoyment of the subject-matter until after the death of the grantor is not decisive that the instrument is testamentary in character. The test is whether the maker intended the instrument to have no effect until after the maker's death, or whether he intended it to transfer some present interest. If some interest vests at once in right, though the enjoyment of it be postponed, the instrument is not a will, and it is irrevocable. Thomas v. Williams, 105 Minn. 88, 117 N.W. 155. We think the evidence sustains the finding of the trial court that the transaction constituted an absolute and irrevocable gift from deceased to defendant.

5. Plaintiff contends that the direction to deliver "only in case of death" of the donor signifies a condition attached to the delivery and an intent that the gift shall become operative only in the event that the

donee survived the donor. There is some authority sustaining plaintiff's contention. Sterling v. Wilkinson, 83 Va. 791, 3 S.E. 533. We do not, however, agree as to this effect of the words "in case of death." If the donor were at the time suffering with some illness, as in the case of Basket v. Hassell, 107 U.S. 602, 2 S.Ct. 415, 27 L.Ed. 500, such language might well be construed to imply a condition that the gift should be operative only in the event of death from such illness, and the survival of the donee. But Warren Potter was not ill, nor was there anything that suggested impending death. Under the circumstances, we think the language "in case of death," which was certain sooner or later to occur, meant nothing more or less than that delivery should be made upon the death of the donor. And this is sustained by authority. Small v. Marburg, 77 Md. 11, 19, 25 A. 920; Goodell v. Pierce, 2 Hill (N.Y.) 659; Ewing v. Winters, 34 W.Va. 23, 11 S.E. 718.

Plaintiff lays much stress upon the fact that J.A. Casey testified that if Potter had in his lifetime demanded a return of the envelope and its contents he would have returned it to him. It is not certain that this expressed anything more than Casey's mistaken view of the law applicable to such a case or his submission to Potter's judgment. But in any event the evidence is not decisive. The intention of Potter, not of Casey, controls.

Nor do we attach great importance to the statement of Casey that Potter said that he wanted to "leave" a certain amount of property to his daughter Marcia. The word "leave" is often used in reference to property left by will, but the word is often loosely used and its use should not be given controlling importance.

Plaintiff also urges strongly that deceased was endeavoring by this transaction to evade the payment of the inheritance tax. We are not sure that he did not have such a purpose. But we cannot see that it is important whether he did or not. It seems to be conceded that he did not succeed and that his property is subject to tax whether this be construed as a gift or not. If the construction of this as a gift would result in a fraud upon the state, that circumstance might be a reason for not adopting that construction, but this is not such a case.

Judgment affirmed.

Notes

1. In Beals v. Lord, 86 R.I. 241, 134 A.2d 127 (1957), a gift of a bond payable to bearer by handing over the bond to the donee was upheld, although the bond was immediately returned to the donor for safekeeping, and although the donor reserved the right to take the interest from the bond for the rest of his life.

2. In Bothe v. Dennie, 324 A.2d 784 (Del.Sup.1974), A added B's name to his safety deposit box, but kept the key. An informal writing referred to certain bonds in the box and directed B to distribute them as directed therein. This instrument was enclosed in an envelope on which was a direction that it be opened immediately after A's death. The envelope and enclosure were delivered to B. On A's death, B sued A's executrix to recover the bonds. It was held that there was no valid conveyance of the bonds in trust for want of delivery.

3.   A executed a power of attorney in writing authorizing B to take possession of certain assets, including bank accounts, and to draw checks thereon for the benefit of A.   Later A told his attorney and another person that he wanted B to have the balance in the accounts at his death.   It was held that, since B was only an agent of A, he was not entitled to the balance.   In re Estate of Simms, 423 S.W.2d 758 (Mo.1968).

ACCEPTANCE

Cases sometimes arise which present the question as to whether acceptance by the donee is necessary to effectuate a change in ownership. For example, A, intending to make a gift to C, delivers the subject matter to B to hold for the benefit of C.   A dies before C ever learns about the transaction.   Can C prevail against A's administrator?   Against A's creditors?   Or, suppose A leaves a will in which he gives "all the personal property which I own at my death" to X.   Can C prevail against X?

Conceptualists would phrase the question thus: Is a gift a "unilateral" or a "bilateral" transaction?   More specifically, consider the following possible views:

1.   A gift needs the assent of the donee to make it complete.   2. But since assent may be evidenced by what a person does as well as by what he says the conduct of the donee normally will sufficiently indicate his acceptance.   3. Since a gift is normally beneficial and would be accepted if the donee knew of it, in cases where he does not it is reasonable to presume an acceptance and treat him as though he had accepted.   4. This position is practically equivalent to saying that no assent is necessary, and it is more honest to be direct and say that the gift is completed when the donor has done all that he has to do.   Consider for example a gift to an insane person.   5. Is this position that donee is "presumed to accept" to be applied in all instances or only where a de facto acceptance is impossible?   6. In any event it must be admitted that a gift cannot be thrust on a person against his will and if he manifests an intent not to accept the gift, the gift fails.   Query, is it never a valid gift or is it invalid only from the rejection?   Does the answer to this depend on what has happened in the meanwhile? *

SECTION 2.   SPECIAL PROBLEMS RELATING TO BANK ACCOUNTS

Note

See, generally, Kepner, The Joint and Survivorship Bank Account—A Concept Without a Name, 41 Cal.L.Rev. 596 (1953);   Kepner, Five More Years of the Joint Bank Account Muddle, 26 U.Chi.L.Rev. 376 (1959);   Wellman, The

---

* Compare the following cases: Miller v. Hertzfeld, C.C.A.N.J., 4 F.2d 355, 1925, noted in 3 Wis.L.R. 492, 1926; Gottstein v. Hedges, 210 Iowa 272, 228 N.W. 93, 67 A.L.R. 1218, 1929; Mahoney v. Martin, 72 Kan. 406, 83 P. 982, 1905; Malone's Committee v. Lebus, 116 Ky. 975, 77 S.W. 180, 25 Ky.Law Rep. 1146, 1903; Cincinnati Finance Co. v. Atkinson's Adm'r, 235 Ky. 582, 31 S.W.2d 890, 1930, noted in 28 Mich. L.Rev. 936, 1931; 15 Minn.L.Rev. 484, 1931; 9 Tenn.L.Rev. 113, 1931; Scott v. Berkshire Co. Sav. Bank, 140 Mass. 157, 165, 2 N.E. 925, 1885.

Joint and Survivor Account in Michigan—Progress Through Confusion, 63 Mich.L.Rev. 629 (1965); Townsend, Creation of Joint Rights Between Husband and Wife in Personal Property, 52 Mich.L.Rev. 779, 957 (1954); Miller, Joint Tenancy in Wisconsin, Especially as Regards Personal Property, 1955 Wis.L. Rev. 154; Comment, The Law of Joint Bank Accounts in Texas, 11 Southwestern L.J. 483 (1957); Note, The Right of the Individual Creditor Against the Joint and Survivorship Bank Account, 42 Ia.L.Rev. 551 (1957); Note, Concurrent Bank Interests—Contracts or Gifts, 16 U.Pittsburgh L.Rev. 262 (1955); Jones, The Use of Joint Bank Accounts as a Substitute for Testamentary Disposition of Property, 17 U.Pittsburgh L.Rev. 42 (1955); Note, Personal Property: Co-ownership: Bank Accounts and Stock Certificates, 6 Okl.L.Rev. 107 (1953); Farnham, Joint Tenancy and Joint Bank Accounts—Danger, Handle With Care, 17 Idaho L.Rev. 101 (1980).

DYSTE v. FARMERS' & MECHANICS' SAVINGS BANK OF MINNEAPOLIS

Supreme Court of Minnesota, 1930.
179 Minn. 430, 229 N.W. 865.

TAYLOR, C. Louis B. Knudsen died in the city of Minneapolis, November 23, 1927. The plaintiff, as administratrix under his will, brought three actions—the first against the Farmers' & Mechanics' Savings Bank of Minneapolis and Olina Langmo; the second against the Minneapolis Savings & Loan Association and Olina Langmo; and the third against the Hennepin Savings & Loan Association and Esther C. Langmo. In each of the cases it was conceded that the corporation defendant therein was a mere stakeholder ready and willing to pay the money in controversy to the one entitled thereto, and it took no part in the trial. Defendant Olina Langmo is a daughter of the decedent born out of wedlock, and defendant Esther C. Langmo is a daughter of Olina Langmo and a granddaughter of the decedent.

Section 7711, G.S.1923, provides:

"Whenever any deposit shall be made by any person in trust for another and no other written notice of the existence and terms of any legal and valid trust shall have been given to the bank, in case of the death of such trustee the same or any part thereof, and the dividends or interest thereon, may be paid to the person for whom the deposit was made. And whenever any deposit shall be made by or in the names of two or more persons upon joint and several account, the same or any part thereof and the dividends or interest thereon may be paid to either of such persons or to a survivor of them or to a personal representative of such survivor."

In July, 1924, Louis Knudsen made a written application to the Farmers' & Mechanics' Savings Bank to open a trust account in his name as trustee in trust for his daughter Olina Langmo. At the same time he deposited in the bank the sum of $2,000 and received a pass book which contained the provision of the statute above quoted, and in which the deposit was entered in the name of "Louis Knudsen in trust for Olina Langmo." The first action was brought to determine whether the money in this trust fund belongs to the estate of Louis Knudsen or to Olina Langmo as the cestui que trust.

In July, 1924, Louis Knudsen, under the name of Lars Knudsen, opened an account with the Minneapolis Savings & Loan Association in the name of "Lars Knudsen or Olina Langmo or survivor." The signature card as well as the pass book were in this form, and the signature card was signed by both Louis Knudsen and Olina Langmo. The deposits in this account aggregated $2,700. The second action was brought to determine whether this money belongs to the estate or to Olina Langmo.

In March, 1925, Louis Knudsen opened an account with the Hennepin Savings & Loan Association in the name of "Louis B. Knudsen or Esther C. Langmo," as shown by the pass book. He took Miss Langmo to the bank where a signature card was prepared containing this statement, "You are hereby authorized to recognize either signature below in the payment of funds or the transaction of any other business for my account," and was signed by both. The deposits in this account aggregated the sum of $1,600. The third action was brought to determine whether this money belongs to the estate or to Esther C. Langmo.

Louis Knudsen kept the pass books in a drawer in a desk or table at his home. He gave Olina Langmo a key to the drawer. He made all the deposits in all three of the accounts. He withdrew a few small amounts from each account, but the full amount of the principal still remained therein at his death. Both Olina Langmo and Esther Langmo say that they understood that he had the right to make withdrawals, but that whatever remained in the respective accounts would belong to them respectively at his death.

The plaintiff contended in each case that the action taken by Louis Knudsen was an attempt on his part to make a testamentary disposition of the fund, and that the failure to comply with the statute regulating the execution of wills rendered such action of no effect. The court so held, and directed judgment for plaintiff in each case. Motions for amended findings or for a new trial were denied in each case, and defendants appeal from the several orders.

The record shows beyond question that Louis Knudsen intended that the money placed in the Farmers' & Mechanics' Savings Bank and the money placed in the Minneapolis Savings & Loan Association should go to his daughter Olina Langmo, and that the money placed in the Hennepin Savings & Loan Association should go to his granddaughter Esther C. Langmo. The question presented is whether the steps which he took to carry his intention into effect were sufficient under the law to accomplish his purpose. The record shows that he had been told by the bankers that money deposited in trust as in the first case would go to the cestui que trust at his death, and that money deposited as in the second and third cases would go to the surviving depositor at the death of the other; and that he created these accounts and made the deposits therein in reliance upon such information and in the belief that the fund in each account would go to the beneficiary named therein.

The deposit in trust involved in the first case is similar to the deposit in trust in this same bank considered in Walso v. Latterner, 140 Minn. 455, 168 N.W. 353; and in Walso v. Latterner, 143 Minn. 364, 173 N.W. 711. In those cases it was held that the statute of trusts permitted the creation of such a trust. It was also held in accordance with the great weight of authority that, where a depositor deposits his own money in his own name in trust for another, he thereby creates a valid trust if it appears that he in fact intended the money to go to the other. It was further held that, where he makes such a deposit and dies before the beneficiary without having taken any action to disaffirm the trust, the presumption is that an absolute trust was created as to the balance remaining on deposit at his death. In the present case the fact that Mr. Knudsen intended the money to go to Olina Langmo is fully established, and therefore at his death the trust became absolute. It follows that she is entitled to the money held by the bank, and that it did not become a part of the estate.

The cases involving the deposit accounts present a somewhat different question. Several courts hold that, where the donor makes a deposit payable to himself or the donee or the survivor, to which the donee assents by signing the signature card or the pass book or in some other manner, it creates a contract between the bank and the donor and donee; and that the contract gives the right to either donor or donee to make withdrawals while both are living, and gives to the survivor absolutely the residue remaining at the death of the other. *   *   *

This court, in common with the majority of courts, considers such deposits as in the nature of gifts and governed by the rules applicable to gifts. McLeod v. Hennepin County Savings Bank, 145 Minn. 299, 176 N.W. 987. The courts which adopt the gift theory agree that the decisive question is whether the depositor made the deposit with the intention of making a gift, or made it for convenience or to serve some purpose of his own. They differ as to the circumstances from which an intention to make a gift may be inferred; but are nearly unanimous in holding that, where a depositor in fact intends to make a gift, and makes a deposit payable to himself or the donee for the purpose of giving effect to that intention, it vests in the donee a present interest in the fund which will sustain the gift as valid. *   *   *

The particular form of the deposit is not important if it shows that the donee has the right to make withdrawals therefrom and therefore has a present interest therein. *   *   * And where both donor and donee have the right to make withdrawals it is immaterial whether one or the other has possession of the pass book.

The statute relating to such deposits, previously quoted, provides that, where a deposit is made in the names of two or more, the deposit or any part of it may be paid to either of them or to the survivor or to the personal representative of such survivor. This statute protects the bank in making such payments. It also recognizes that making a deposit in that manner gives to each of the persons named the right to make withdrawals therefrom, and gives to the survivor the right to withdraw the residue.

From the fact that the statute authorizes the payment of the residue to the survivor or to the personal representative of such survivor, a presumption arises that such residue is the absolute property of the survivor, and casts upon those who claim otherwise the burden of proving that such was not the intention of the donor. But here, in addition to the presumption, it affirmatively appears that the donor intended that the deposits in question should become the absolute property of the donees.

As Louis Knudsen intended to make a gift to his daughter and another to his granddaughter, and, for the express purpose of carrying that intention into effect, put the deposits in a form which gave the donee a present right to make withdrawals therefrom, it gave her a present interest in the fund which is sufficient to sustain the validity of the gift.

The several orders appealed from are reversed.

Notes

1. A trustee of property under a duly created trust for the benefit of one or more beneficiaries may deposit trust funds in a bank as trustee. Few problems arise in such cases about the beneficiaries' rights in such funds, for their rights are fixed by the terms of the trust instrument. Since one can create a trust by declaring himself trustee of his own property for the benefit of others, it would seem that he might do so by depositing money in a bank in his own name as trustee for one or more persons. Where nothing other than the deposit appears as evidence of his intention, a question arises as to the validity or the terms of the trust.

Without exploring here the ramifications of this problem, we may take note of a special rule developed by the New York courts and followed by the courts in a number of other states. Such a deposit at least prima facie creates what has come to be called a "Totten trust," the term being taken from the case in which the New York rule was first announced. Matter of Totten, 179 N.Y. 112, 71 N.E. 748 (1904). In brief, since any trust can be made revocable by the settlor, the court held that in these limited circumstances a power of revocation is implied. This permits the depositor-trustee to withdraw funds in his sole discretion without accountability to the designated beneficiary. The trust designation is vindicated by holding that any funds remaining in the account at the depositor's death belong to the beneficiary. The terse statutory authorization of trust deposits referred to in the Dyste case appears to codify this principle, at least on facts such as those in the Dyste case. It is evident that this device permits a depositor to achieve what is essentially a testamentary objective. It has in fact sometimes been called a "poor man's will." But by a liberal interpretation of the requirements for an inter vivos trust, this donative device is held to escape the formal requirements of the applicable statute of wills.

2. When a person opens a so-called joint account, that is, when he deposits money in a bank, and the account designates him "or" another, or where such designation has the added words "or the survivor," the depositor may in fact have one of three different objectives:

(a) He may intend to create in a donee rights equal to his own in all respects. Such was the intention found in the case of two of the deposits in the Dyste case. This means that both parties in whose names the account is created have equal rights to draw upon the account during their joint lives, and that on the death of either, the other is entitled to the balance remaining in the account. Courts often explain the survivorship feature by saying that the deposit in this form creates a joint tenancy between the depositors, and some statutes so designate a deposit of this kind. Some caution is required in applying such a label, for, as we will discover, there are features of a joint account which may not be entirely consistent with a true joint tenancy.

(b) The depositor may intend to create no interest whatever in the person designated as co-depositor, other than the power to make withdrawals on the depositor's behalf; that is, he adopts this kind of account solely for his own convenience in respect to withdrawals. Persons who are ill or otherwise incapacitated, or who expect that they may become so, do resort to the joint account for such a purpose.

(c) As a variation of (b), a depositor may intend to retain sole control over the account during his lifetime, but intend that any balance left on his death will belong to his co-depositor.

It may occur to you to ask why a deposit in the so-called joint form does not necessarily produce the result indicated under (a) above. On what basis can parol evidence be received of an intent like that in (b) or (c) above? Or if the intent as in (c) can be proven, is there any reason why such an intent cannot be given effect? These questions are considered further in the case which follows.

3.   There are a few early cases in which a gift by way of a joint savings bank account was held ineffective for want of delivery because the donor-depositor retained the passbook. Generally today, however, the usual formalities for opening such an account are regarded as sufficient to meet the delivery requirement. See Brown on Personal Property 183 (3d ed. 1975).

A depositor of a joint account with his son handed the passbook to his son expressing his intention to give the son the entire interest. Acting under a power of attorney, the son also attempted to change the account designation on the bank records, but failed because of a misunderstanding by the bank. On the donor's death, inheritance tax liability was asserted against the son on the basis of his original right of survivorship. This was sustained on the ground that delivery of the donor's interest was incomplete. In re Estate of Tippins, 487 Pa. 99, 408 A.2d 1377 (1979). The court held differently in respect to trust accounts in which the son was designated beneficiary. The acts and statements of the donor when the passbooks were handed over were held to render the trust no longer tentative but irrevocable. How would you explain the difference in result?

4.   A third type of account may be encountered in which the deposit is made in the name of the depositor alone, "payable on death" to a named survivor. Such P.O.D. accounts are sometimes challenged as being "testamentary," a will substitute which fails to create any rights in the donee for failure to comply with the formalities prescribed in the statute of wills.

What legal relations are created when a person deposits money in a bank in his own name? If a person varies the usual terms of a deposit so as to add a P.O.D. ingredient for the benefit of a third person, does this change the nature of the transaction? Should such a transaction become subject to the formalities of the statute of wills because the purpose of the depositor in part was to accomplish the same result as he might have accomplished by will? If a court accepts the "contract" theory, so that it avoids arguments that the transaction is testamentary, does such holding affect the rights of the parties while both still live? Can the depositor change the name of the designated survivor? Can he do so in his will?

For an example of a modern statute which authorizes P.O.D. accounts, answers questions of inter vivos rights, and exempts the transaction from compliance with the statute of wills, see Ohio Rev.Code, § 2131.10.

In re ESTATE OF THOMPSON

Supreme Court of Ohio, 1981.
66 Ohio St.2d 433, 423 N.E.2d 90.

In 1954, Richard L. Thompson, appellee herein, opened two joint and survivorship savings accounts, one with Banc-Ohio (then Ohio National Bank), and the second with Hub Federal Savings & Loan Association. Thompson's wife, Carma Lee, was the other party to the accounts.

By June of 1978, the Thompsons were having marital problems, although neither party had taken legal action prior to that month. On June 8, 1978, Richard Thompson closed both accounts and transferred the funds into two new accounts in his name only.

On June 9, 1978, Richard Thompson was served with a complaint that his wife had filed on June 2, 1978, seeking a divorce, separate maintenance and alimony. The complaint was coupled with a motion seeking a restraining order prohibiting, *inter alia*, withdrawal of any funds in the original two joint and survivorship savings accounts.

On July 19, 1978, Carma Lee Thompson became comatose and on September 26, 1978, she succumbed.

Carma Lee Thompson's daughter, Pamela Lee Botts, appellant herein, was appointed executrix of her estate by the Probate Division of the Court of Common Pleas of Franklin County on October 25, 1978. She filed an inventory which included two unliquidated claims against Richard Thompson as constructive trustee for one-half of the amounts which had been in the joint and survivorship accounts.

Richard Thompson filed exceptions to the inventory, including among the items excepted to the above two unliquidated claims. A hearing was held before a referee.

At the hearing it was established that Thompson had transferred the money, which consisted largely of his contributions from the joint and survivorship accounts, after talking with an attorney regarding his marital problems. On cross-examination, Thompson testified that the accounts had been intended as "safekeeping," to be used by his wife in the event of his death or illness. According to Thompson, approximately ten years before his wife's death, when his wife had taken one or two hundred dollars out of one of the accounts, he had advised her that in the event she persisted in such conduct, he would remove her name from the account. Thompson admitted that in his opinion the accounts belonged to both of them, although he maintained possession and control over the passbooks throughout their existence.

The referee's report, approved by the Probate Judge, found that one-half of the balance in the accounts was properly included in the inventory, and that Richard Thompson had improperly withdrawn the funds from the joint and survivorship accounts, breaching a fiduciary relationship he had with his wife who was determined to be co-owner of the funds.

The Court of Appeals reversed, finding that the survivorship aspect of the accounts continued in effect after the transfer because the transfer was a good faith effort to preserve the funds for the mutual benefit of both Richard and Carma Lee Thompson.

The cause is now before this court upon the allowance of a motion to certify the record.

John C. Wheatley and Edward W. Erfurt, Jr., Columbus, for appellee.

Kemp, Schaeffer & Rowe Co., L.P.A., and Stephen D. Rowe, Columbus, for appellant.

CELEBREZZE, Chief Justice.

This court has traditionally utilized contract law concepts to enforce the survivorship rights of the parties to accounts on deposit in financial institutions which are designated as joint and survivorship accounts. In Berberick v. Courtade (1940), 137 Ohio St. 297, 28 N.E.2d 636, this court stated, at page 301, 28 N.E.2d 636, quoting from paragraph two of the syllabus of In re Estate of Hutchison (1929), 120 Ohio St. 542, 166 N.E. 687:

" 'While joint tenancy with the incidental right of survivorship does not exist in Ohio parties may nevertheless contract for a joint ownership with the right of survivorship and at the death of one of the joint owners the survivor succeeds to the title to the entire interest, not upon the principle of survivorship as an incident to the joint tenancy but by the operative provisions of the contract.' "

In Union Properties v. Cleveland Trust Co. (1949), 152 Ohio St. 430, 89 N.E.2d 638, this court stated, at page 433, 89 N.E.2d 638:

"In the case of Cleveland Trust Co. v. Scobie, Admr., 114 Ohio St. 241, 151 N.E. 373, 48 A.L.R. 182, this court laid down the rule, since adhered to in principle, that where one opens a savings account in a bank to the joint credit of himself and another, payable to either or the survivor, and it is apparent that the depositor intended to transfer to the person, to whom he made the account jointly payable, a present joint interest therein equal to his own, the person to whom the acocunt is made jointly payable is entitled to the balance of the money in the account upon the death of the depositor as against the claim thereto of the depositor's personal representative."

Because both a survivorship interest and a present joint interest are created by contract, we have held that the property can be transferred at one of the party's death even though the formal requisites of a will are not present.

Joint and survivorship accounts, however, are frequently utilized without their legal ramifications being fully understood by their creators. As a result, this court has held that the creation of such accounts raises a rebuttable presumption that the parties to the account share equally in the ownership of the funds on deposit, allowing the presumption to be rebutted by a showing of the "realities of ownership." Vetter v. Hampton (1978), 54 Ohio St.2d 227, 375 N.E.2d 804; Steinhauser v. Repko (1972), 30 Ohio St.2d 262, 285 N.E.2d 55; Union Properties, Inc. v. Cleveland Trust Co., supra.

The case at bar illustrates a common problem with this approach. The primary and foremost contributions made to the accounts were by Richard Thompson. When he created the accounts, he intended to maintain control over them during his lifetime; however, he also intended to create a survivorship interest in them. Under a strict contractual analysis, he could not do both.

R.C. 1107.08(A) states:

"When a deposit is made in the name of two or more persons, payable to either, or the survivor, such deposit or any part thereof, or any interest thereon, may be paid to either of said persons, or the guardian of his estate, whether the other is living or not, and the receipt or acquittance of the person paid is a sufficient release and discharge of the bank for any payments so made."

R.C. 1151.19(A) states in part:

"A building and loan association may receive money on deposit or stock deposits from any persons, firms, corporations, and courts, or their agents, officers, and appointees and may pay interest thereon. When such deposits are made to the joint account of two or more persons, whether adults or minors, with a joint order to the association that such deposits or any part thereof are to be payable on the order of any of such joint depositors, and to continue to be so payable notwithstanding the death or incapacity of one or more of the persons making them, such account shall be payable to any of such survivors or order notwithstanding such death or incapacity. No recovery shall be had against such association for amounts so paid and charged to such account."

In the past this court has held that these sections and their predecessors were enacted solely for the benefit and protection of financial institutions and did not affect the relationships of the parties to joint and survivorship accounts nor authorize use of such accounts to transfer property. Fecteau v. Cleveland Trust Co. (1960), 171 Ohio St. 121, 167 N.E.2d 890; Union Properties v. Cleveland Trust Co., supra.

These sections authorizing financial institutions to create and make payments on joint and survivorship accounts implicitly permits use of such accounts to transfer property at death even though such transfers are not pursuant to a testamentary disposition. Because these statutes authorize the use of such accounts, it is not necessary to utilize the rigid contractual analysis of our earlier cases. Instead, our goal should be to effectuate the intent of the party or parties creating such accounts.

In order to do so, we must first realize that such accounts are not necessarily the most desirable means of effectuating intent. Justice Locher recognized this in his concurrence in Vetter v. Hampton, supra, when he stated, 54 Ohio St.2d at pages 233, 234, 375 N.E.2d 804:

"This writer is cognizant that R.C. 1107.08 and 1151.19 make provision for joint and survivorship accounts. My personal observation is that these accounts are frequently litigated. It is thus apparent that there exists an abysmal flaw in their creation. All too frequently, the parties entering into this type of contractual agreement with banks or savings and loan associations are not *really* apprised of all the ramifications that exist when such a contract is consummated. Often depositors are advised that these accounts are the best way to 'avoid probate.' Seldom, if ever, are the clerks in banks and savings and loan associations attorneys or well versed in the legal aspects of this contract. Thus, the end result, in numerous instances, is a defective estate plan that successfully avoids probate at the cost of litigation, great expense, disruption of the deceased's intention and hardship to his family. [Emphasis *sic.*]

"The defect is obvious. Being a modern-day creation of legislation, the joint and survivorship account is, in essence, a substitute testamentary disposition stripped of all its normal safeguards. * * *"

Use of a rebuttable presumption offers a means by which the relationships of the parties to joint and survivorship accounts can be stabilized. To a certain extent, our earlier case law has done this, but because the presumption used failed to distinguish between the treatment of such accounts during the parties' lifetimes and the treatment of such accounts after the death of a party, the effort to effectuate intent was not entirely successful.

Any presumption made must reflect the intent of the average creator of joint and survivorship accounts. As stated, at page 59, 135 N.E.2d 775, in Abdoney v. Bd. of Liquor Control (1955), 101 Ohio App. 57, 135 N.E.2d 775:

"Presumptions conform to the commonly accepted experiences of mankind and the inferences which reasonable men would draw from such experiences."

Section 6–103(a) of the Uniform Probate Code states:

"A joint account belongs during the lifetime of all parties, to the parties in proportion to the net contributions by each to the sums on deposit, unless there is clear and convincing evidence of a different intent."

Section 6–104(a) of that Code states:

"Sums remaining on deposit at the death of a party to a joint account belong to the surviving party or parties as against the estate of the decedent unless there is clear and convincing evidence of a different intention at the time the account is created. If there are two or more surviving parties, their respective ownerships during lifetime shall be in proportion to their previous ownership interests under Section 6–103 augmented by an equal share for each survivor of any interest the decedent may have owned in the account immediately before his death; and the right of survivorship continues between the surviving parties."

We hold that the presumptions created in these two sections accurately reflect the common experiences of mankind in regard to joint and survivorship accounts. As a result, we adopt these specific sections as the law of this state.[1]

Use of these rules does not significantly alter our earlier case law; it merely amends our earlier analytic framework so that the intent of the parties to create joint and survivorship accounts can be better effectuated.

In our earlier cases we ordinarily dealt with the right of survivorship to such accounts, not the right to control the funds on deposit during the lifetimes of the parties to the accounts. The presumption in favor of holding that such an interest exists has been essentially in accord with creator intent and the Uniform Probate Code even though we have required an intent to transfer a present interest, as well as a survivorship interest.

For example, in In re Estate of Svab (1967), 11 Ohio St.2d 182, 228 N.E.2d 609, this court held that a survivorship interest was not created because it was shown that the creator of the account had placed the other party's name on the account solely to allow that other person to assist her in conducting her business affairs. Such evidence of the "realities of ownership" can be used to rebut the presumption of survivorship which we have adopted from Section 6–104(a) of the Uniform Probate Code and of course would buttress the presumption adopted from Section 6–103(a).[2] Similarly, in a case dealing with ownership during the lives of the parties, *Union Properties*, supra, the court affirmed a determination that the sole depositor to the account had sole ownership of the funds on deposit after it was shown that the other party's name was placed on the account because an injury prevented the depositor from going to the bank. The presumption adopted from Section 6–103(a) leads to the same result.

In the case at bar, appellee, in forbidding his wife from making withdrawals, in maintaining possession of the passbooks for the accounts, and in stating that the money was being held for use in the event of his death or illness, exhibited an intent to maintain control of his contributions to the account. In this context, his statement that he considered the accounts to belong to him and his wife reflected his intention to create a survivorship interest and to authorize use at some future time should he become disabled. Certainly he did not exhibit an intent to make his wife a co-owner of the accounts.

As a consequence, on June 8, 1978, appellee was entitled to withdraw from the accounts that amount which was proportionally attributable to his contributions to those accounts. That proportion of the accounts clearly belonged to him. A constructive trust can be imposed over any amounts withdrawn which exceeded those amounts attributable to his contributions. His withdrawal of any such amounts would be a breach

1. In so holding, we do not, at this time, adopt any other sections of the code, nor do we adopt them for use on accounts other than joint and survivorship accounts.

2. On the other hand, it appears that treatment of the accounts as available for the use and benefit of all parties could be used to show that co-ownership of the accounts was intended.

of his fiduciary duty to his wife. Any survivorship rights appellee had in such sums was forfeited.

We modify the judgment of the Court of Appeals and remand the cause to the Probate Division so that it may determine what proportion of the net contributions to the savings accounts is attributable to appellee and so that it may order any amount remaining be included in the inventory.

Judgment accordingly.

WILLIAM B. BROWN, SWEENEY, LOCHER, HOLMES and CLIFFORD F. BROWN, JJ., concur.

PAUL W. BROWN, Justice, dissenting.

The lower courts found, and the parties agreed, that the funds in the joint and survivorship accounts were owned equally by Mr. and Mrs. Thompson. Had the funds not been removed, Mr. Thompson would have been entitled to all the funds on Mrs. Thompson's death pursuant to the survivorship provision of the accounts.

When Mr. Thompson closed out the joint and survivorship accounts, he terminated the contract, including the contractual right to survivorship. He has practically admitted that half the funds were his wife's. If he was afraid that she would dissipate the accounts, he should have withdrawn his one-half of the funds and left her's alone. Mr. Thompson should not be permitted to withdraw all the funds from the joint and survivorship accounts and to transfer them to an account to which only he has access, and then argue that the right to survivorship survived so that he can legally keep everything he took. This is especially true because this is a marital situation in which assets acquired by joint effort are usually considered by the contracting parties to be the property of both, absent agreements or circumstances demonstrating a contrary purpose. Here the joint account is some further acknowledgment that the funds were the property of both. The husband's threat to take his wife's name off the account made at an earlier date is not a claim of exclusive ownership, it is merely the act of a spouse who considers himself the dominant financial party with a veto power over expenditures and has no real legal significance. I consider this a poor case in which to generalize about joint and survivorship accounts. I would reverse the Court of Appeals and reinstate the Probate Judge's order.

Notes

1. The decision has been criticized because the court "saw fit to usurp the legislature and adopt applicable provisions (of the Uniform Probate Code) by judicial fiat." Note, 50 U.Cinn.L.Rev. 852 (1981). It has been reaffirmed in Gillota, Executrix v. Gillota, 4 Ohio St.3d 222, 448 N.E.2d 802 (1983).

2. As the principal case indicates, Ohio was generally committed to a "contract" theory for handling joint bank account cases, generally sustaining rights of survivors as against claims of the depositor's estate. A similar theory is found in Lowry v. Lowry, 541 S.W.2d 128 (Tenn.1976), noted in 7 Memphis St. U.L.Rev. 332 (1977). But, as the case also indicates, the analysis proved unsatisfactory when applied to rights of the parties while both lived, and Ohio deci-

sions which recognized "the realities of ownership" had denied creditors of the non-contributing party any right to the funds. This result is, of course, quite similar to that reached by courts under the conventional analysis of the so-called joint bank account where the only applicable statute is one referred to as a "bank-protection statute", like the one in the Dyste case. In such case, the statute is regarded as intended primarily to protect a bank in making payments in accordance with the terms of the account, and only incidentally creating a presumption respecting the rights of the depositor and his donee *inter se*. These rights were generally determined by applying the law on gifts of personal property. The delivery requirement has proved to be no obstacle, either because it is seldom raised, or because the formalities of a deposit are regarded as sufficient to satisfy that requirement. Under that analysis, where, under the usual bank-protection statute it was proved that a depositor intended to retain full control of the account during his lifetime, the presumption of an intention to make a gift was rebutted and the survivorship feature was defeated on the ground that, since no interest ripened in the donee until the depositor's death, no gift was effected, and the transaction became testamentary.

The courts have not been troubled in the least about varying by parol evidence the written record or evidence of a deposit. This result is at least understandable in the light of the common purpose to resort to a joint account merely for the convenience of the depositor, that is, to enable a third party to draw on the account for the benefit of the depositor. If a statute authorizes a P.O.D. account, is there any similar reason for permitting parol evidence to vary the terms of the account?

3. Statutory solutions to the problems raised by the several kinds of multi-party bank accounts are quite common. Some statutes purport to create a *conclusive* presumption that a gift was intended if a deposit is made in a "joint and survivor" form. They do not always serve to avoid litigation. Typical of the difficulties are those found in Bauer v. Crummy, 56 N.J. 400, 267 A.2d 16 (1970), where the court traces the judicial and statutory history in New Jersey which had produced a statute creating a "conclusive presumption" concerning the rights of a surviving joint tenant. Despite the statutory language, the court found "interpretive" means to avoid rewarding a surviving joint tenant whose conduct was hardly exemplary.

4. The current Michigan statute declares a different presumption, similar examples of which appear in several other states. That statute includes the following provision:

> "The making of the deposit in such form shall, in the absence of fraud or undue influence, be prima facie evidence, in any action or proceeding, to which either any banking institution or surviving depositor or depositors is a party, of the intention of such depositors to vest title to such deposit and the additions thereto in such survivor or survivors." Mich.Comp.Laws Ann. § 487.703.

Under such a statute, what is the effect of evidence that the depositor intended to confer upon his donee co-owner only a right of survivorship, that is, that the account was only for the convenience of the depositor during his lifetime? Does such evidence also defeat the right of survivorship because the donee was intended to have no other rights? Such evidence would render the transaction testamentary where the only statute was a bank-protection statute. It appears that such is not the result in Michigan, that is, the presumption of a right of survivorship is not rebutted by such proof alone. See Wellman, The Joint and Survivor Account in Michigan—Progress Through Confusion, 63 Mich.L.Rev. 629, 636 (1965).

5. The Ohio court specifically limits its "adoption" of the Uniform Probate Code to those sections it found helpful in the case before it. The total coverage in the UPC, §§ 6–101 to 6–112 is discussed infra, p. 777.

BLANCHETTE v. BLANCHETTE *

Supreme Judicial Court of Massachusetts, 1972.
362 Mass. 518, 287 N.E.2d 459.

BRAUCHER, Justice. This is a petition brought in connection with the divorce of the parties by the petitioner Marie to determine her interest in certain property including 168 shares (the stock) of the American Telephone & Telegraph Company (the company). The petition was referred to a master who heard the parties, filed a report, and made general findings, among others, that the respondent Robert was the sole owner of the stock and that there was no gift or attempted gift of the stock to Marie.

Marie objected to that part of the report which related to the stock. After a hearing, the judge issued a decree overruling Marie's exceptions, confirming the report, declaring the stock to be the sole property of Robert and ordering Marie to execute any documents necessary to give effect to the ownership of the stock, as determined by the decree, upon the records of the company. Marie appeals from the decree, contending that the subsidiary facts reported by the master do not support his general findings with respect to the ownership of the stock.

The master's report having been confirmed, his findings establish the facts in the case. Foot v. Bauman, 333 Mass. 214, 219, 129 N.E.2d 916; Flynn v. Town of Seekonk, 352 Mass. 71, 72, 223 N.E.2d 690. We summarize them. The parties were married on November 17, 1945. While married they both worked, with a few interruptions, at steady jobs. In 1955 Robert was working for the company, and under a company plan began to buy shares of stock in the company at eighty-five per cent of market value through a weekly deduction from his pay.

Robert wanted to avoid the expense of probate and legal proceedings if he should die. When he expressed this desire in connection with the stock purchase plan to the people where he worked, he was told that the only way to achieve it was to have the stock issued to himself and Marie as joint tenants. The stock could have been issued to the parties as tenants in common, but Robert purposely avoided that option.

When he started to acquire the stock, he told Marie he put them in both their names as joint tenants "in case something happened" to him and that they would then be hers "without probate or lawyer." The certificates were issued at his request to "Robert L. Blanchette & Mrs. Marie A. Blanchette, Joint Tenants." He executed assignments to himself and Marie "as Joint Tenants with rights of survivorship and not as Tenants in Common," and she also signed some of the documents in this form. The last certificate was issued on June 30, 1964.

* The court's footnotes have been omitted.

Marie took no part in the purchase of the stock and did not know when the stock certificates were issued or how many shares were acquired. Her impression was that they would be hers only after Robert's death, and she did not think she had the right to sell any interest in them or to do anything with them without his signature. She signed dividend checks; on many occasions Robert signed her name to the checks. Robert never told her that she owned half of the stock. The certificates were kept in a wardrobe in their bedroom when they separated on February 7, 1965, and at that time Marie did demand one of two bankbooks usually kept in the same place, but she did not ask for any of the stock. She was content with the bankbook. There is no finding that she made any claim to the stock before the parties' divorce on May 14, 1969.

The master's general findings included the following: Robert "never at any time indicated by conduct or words that he intended to transfer any present interest in these stocks to his wife." The words "Joint Tenants" were used "only because this form of issuance was the only one authorized by Robert's employer which approximated his desire to make his wife 'his beneficiary' if he died. Robert did not in any way attempt to make a gift of these stocks to his wife and no gift of these stocks was in fact made."

1. The master's findings must stand unless they are inconsistent, contradictory or plainly wrong. * * * We have applied to share certificates in joint names the same principles we have applied to joint bank accounts. * * * In disputes arising while both parties to a joint bank account are still alive we have frequently upheld allegations or findings that there was no donative intent. * * * A finding as to the respective interests of the parties in joint deposits during their lives is a pure question of fact. * * *

Share certificates are less likely than bank accounts to be put in joint names merely for convenience, and in two cases we have disapproved findings that share certificates were placed in joint names without donative intent. MacLennan v. MacLennan, 316 Mass. 593, 597, 55 N.E.2d 928; Zambunos v. Zambunos, 324 Mass. 220, 223, 85 N.E.2d 328. Compare McPherson v. McPherson, 337 Mass. 611, 614, 150 N.E.2d 727 (real estate); Goldman v. Finkel, 341 Mass. 492, 494, 170 N.E.2d 474 (real estate). In both of those cases, as in this one, the intention was clear that the husband was to have sole control during his life and that whatever should remain at his death, if the wife survived, should ripen into full ownership by her. The finding that no present gift was intended would logically have the effect of frustrating the intention of the parties by rendering their arrangement testamentary and void. We avoided that result by substituting a finding of an intention to make a present gift of a joint interest, with the effect intended by the parties. In effect, there was a present gift of a future interest, subject to a reserved life estate in the husband and to his power to revoke his wife's interest. The result was based on our duty to draw proper inferences from the subsidiary findings unaffected by the conclusions of the trier of fact. We have the same duty in reviewing the subsidiary findings and conclusions of a master. * * *

We think, however, that it is not necessary to modify the decree here, as was done in the MacLennan and Zambunos cases, to declare that the certificates are held in joint account, subject to the right of control reserved by the respondent. By contesting this suit the respondent has fully manifested his intention to exercise his right of control, and he has been prevented from doing so by the pendency of the suit. The decree does substantial justice, and a modification would be purely formal except so far as it might permit intervening events to affect unjustly the rights of the parties. Compare White v. White, 346 Mass. 76, 79–80, 190 N.E.2d 102. To the extent that the MacLennan and Zambunos cases would require modification, therefore, we overrule those cases. The decree is to be affirmed without modification.

2. To avoid misunderstanding, we emphasize that nothing we say here is intended to impair the right of the survivor to joint bank accounts or to share certificates in joint names, where the donor has died without manifesting an intention to defeat the gift. If the owner of funds, with the assent of another, deposits the funds in an account in both their names, payable to either or the survivor, the deposit if so intended may take effect as a novation, creating contract rights against the bank in both parties in accordance with the deposit agreement. The statute of wills is not involved. As between the bank and the named depositors, the deposit agreement is binding. G.L. c. 167, § 14. Sawyer v. National Shawmut Bank, 306 Mass. 313, 316, 28 N.E.2d 455.

The effect of such a deposit is a present and complete gift of the contract right intended, and it is not fatal that the original owner of the funds retains possession of the bankbook and a right to withdraw funds from the account and thus to defeat the gift. In numerous cases where the original owner had died, we have upheld the right of the survivor to the balance in the account. We have not regarded the form of the account as conclusive between the parties, but have allowed the representative of the estate of the decedent to show by attendant facts and circumstances that the decedent did not intend to make a present completed gift of a joint interest in the account. Thus we have upheld findings of undue influence. * * * It may be shown that the transaction is a fraud on creditors. * * * The donee may take subject to a trust. * * * Or the account may have been established merely for convenience in paying medical bills or the like. * * * In cases of conflicting evidence we have required that the question of donative intent be submitted to the trier of fact. * * * The burden of proof is on the person seeking to show that the transaction is not to be taken at face value. * * * Whereas in the present case the intention has been clear that the donee's interest was to ripen into full ownership on the donor's death, we have overturned findings that there was no donative intent. * * *

3. We recognize that under the cases cited the arrangement of the parties provides a substitute for a will. But we see no harm in that. "If an owner of property can find a means of disposing of it inter vivos

that will render a will unnecessary for the accomplishment of his practical purposes, he has a right to employ it. The fact that the motive of a transfer is to obtain the practical advantages of a will without making one is immaterial." National Shawmut Bank of Boston v. Joy, 315 Mass. 457, 471–472, 53 N.E.2d 113, 122, and cases cited. * * * An unattested testamentary document is ineffective. * * * But a trust is not rendered invalid by a testatmentary motive. "The underlying purpose of the statute of wills against frauds is secured in the formalities attendant upon the execution of trusts and the solemnity of the actual transfer of property to trustees." Second Bank-State St. Trust Co. v. Pinion, 341 Mass. 366, 371, 170 N.E.2d 350, 353. In cases of informal declarations of trust we have sought substitute safeguards in notice to and informal acceptance by the beneficiary. * * * Contractual arrangements vary in their formality. See Krell v. Codman, 154 Mass. 454, 457–458, 28 N.E. 578 (voluntary covenant to pay money after death); Hale v. Wilmarth, 274 Mass. 186, 189–190, 174 N.E. 232 (partnership agreement under seal); Legro v. Kelley, 311 Mass. 674, 676–677, 42 N.E.2d 836 (contract to transfer stock on death); Massachusetts Linotyping Corp. v. Fielding, 312 Mass. 147, 149–150, 43 N.E.2d 521 (contract not to change beneficiary of life insurance); Bettencourt v. Bettencourt, Mass., 284 N.E.2d 238 (mutual wills reciting agreement). In the present case, as in many cases of joint bank accounts, the parties were designated as joint tenants in formal documents embodying the rights in dispute, and there was notice to an implied acceptance by the donee.

Our law in this situation is in harmony with that in many other States. "The formal requisites of wills serve two main purposes: to insure that dispositions are carefully and seriously made, and to provide reliable evidence of the dispositions. Those purposes are adequately served by the institutional setting and the signed writing normally involved in taking out insurance, opening a bank account, buying United States Savings Bonds, or entering a government pension system." 1951 Rep.N.Y.Law Rev.Commn. 587, 597. In a very large number of cases joint bank accounts have been given effect as a "poor man's will." * * * Similar principles have been applied to share certificates in joint form. * * * "The revocable living trust and the multiple-party bank accounts, as well as the experience with United States government bonds payable on death to named beneficiaries, have demonstrated that the evils envisioned if the statute of wills is not rigidly enforced simply do not materialize." Comment, Uniform Probate Code, § 6–201, promulgated in August, 1969. See also §§ 6–103(a), 6–104(a).

Decree affirmed.

Notes

1. In Desrosiers v. Germain, 12 Mass.App.Ct. 852, 429 N.E.2d 385 (1982), the court held that on the evidence a joint bank account was not intended by the donor as a gift, but only for convenience. The court faced the question of the admissibility as evidence of intention of statements made by the depositor after the account was created. Conceding a conflict on the point generally, the court asserted that the creation of an account and the expression of an intent to make

a gift need not occur simultaneously; that is, an account not constituting a gift may become one by a later expression of donative intent. Statements by the depositor after the account was created are admissible for that purpose.

2. In re Estate of Fanning, 263 Ind. 414, 333 N.E.2d 80 (1974), involved the purchase of bank certificates of deposit in the names of the depositor and her daughter with right of survivorship. The daughter did not participate in or know of the deposit until the death of her mother, when the certificates came into the daughter's hands. Administrators of the estate of the depositor sought to recover the certificates. A judgment in their favor was reversed. The court rejected the "gift theory" of joint bank deposits and asserted the law on third-party beneficiary contracts. The court added that under the law of that state the donor could have extinguished the "contingent contractual right" of the beneficiary by requesting the bank to change the beneficiary or by expressing a contrary intent, until the right was accepted or acted upon by the beneficiary. The court added that the form of the account created a rebuttable presumption that the usual rights incident to jointly owned property with right of survivorship was intended. In Robison v. Fickle, 167 Ind.App. 651, 340 N.E.2d 824 (1976), the court in a similar case felt that the ruling in *Fanning* required further explanation. The shift to a contractual theory was said not to dispense with the requirement of proving donative intent, but the implications of *Fanning* concerning the admissibility of extrinsic evidence of intent was declared not to be the basis of any "parol evidence exception" in this case, or in any case where the words of the contract are clear and unambiguous. This analysis was accompanied by a philosophical inquiry into the difference between "meaning" and "intention," as it related to proof of donative intent. Since no objection to extrinsic evidence was made at the trial, the court held that the only relevant extrinsic circumstances were those at the time of the contract, but not thereafter; that the retention of control of the account by the donor, or his retention of dividends and interest, or the donee's lack of knowledge of the certificates of deposit, do not defeat the joint tenancy created; and that such a joint tenancy can be created in personal property without the traditional common-law unities, and is also not defeated by any charge that the transaction was testamentary.

3. Suppose that the intent is established to vest a present interest in a joint account in the donee, either by proof to that effect or the absence of proof to rebut the presumption arising from the form of the account. If either party can draw upon such an account, this leaves a difficult question, which surprisingly has not often arisen, concerning the extent of a party's right of withdrawal. This is the problem involved in the two cases which follow.

PARK ENTERPRISES, INC. v. TRACH

Supreme Court of Minnesota, 1951.
233 Minn. 467, 47 N.W.2d 194.

LORING, Chief Justice. In this case plaintiff, Park Enterprises, Inc., sued defendant Benedict B. Trach, in the municipal court of Minneapolis to enforce payment of rent under an oral lease between the parties. In proceedings ancillary to this action, plaintiff garnisheed a joint bank account standing in the name of defendant and his wife, Dorothy Trach. Mrs. Trach was permitted to intervene in the garnishment proceedings. The Northwestern National Bank of Minneapolis is the garnishee.

Plaintiff obtained a default judgment for $143.45 against defendant in the main action. In the garnishment proceeding, the facts of the case were stipulated, and the parties requested that the court make and enter findings of fact, conclusions of law, and order for judgment on the basis of the facts stipulated.

The facts as stipulated are as follows: At the time the garnishment summons was served, defendant and intervener had a "joint bank account" with the garnishee in which the deposit credit was $327.38. This account was opened and maintained subject to the following terms and conditions, which are printed on the reverse side of a joint account signature card: "The account listed on the reversed side hereof is a joint and several account. All funds now or hereafter deposited in said account by either or any of the depositors shall be the property of the depositors, jointly with the right of survivorship. Each depositor shall have complete and absolute authority over said account during the joint lives of the depositors and may withdraw all or any part of such funds on checks or other withdrawal orders signed by either or any of the depositors and by the survivor or survivors in case of death of any thereof."

Defendant and intervener had independent incomes. Each of them, from time to time, has deposited portions of his or her individual funds to the credit of this joint account and from time to time has withdrawn funds from the account for family or individual purposes. It is impossible to determine on an evidentiary basis the exact amount of funds each of them has contributed to the joint account.

The trial court made findings in conformity with the facts stipulated, and, having concluded that defendant and intervener should be presumed equal owners of the garnisheed account in the absence of proof establishing the amount each has contributed to it, ordered judgment against the garnishee for $143.45, together with interest and costs, the entire judgment not to exceed $163.69, that being one-half the joint account. Judgment was entered accordingly.

Intervener's sole allegation and claim in the garnishment proceeding is that she and defendant are joint owners of the garnisheed bank account, and therefore that the account is not garnishable for defendant's individual debt to plaintiff. Defendant's contentions are the same as those of intervener. These contentions having been rejected by the trial court, defendant and intervener have appealed from the judgment against the garnishee.

This type of account is difficult, if not impossible, to classify under traditional categories of legal ownership. The account is distinguished from a joint tenancy because of the fact that it is joint and several, whereas in a joint tenancy there is joint ownership only. The survivorship feature of the account readily distinguishes it from a tenancy in common, and yet is not sufficient alone to make it a joint tenancy. "Joint and several," when used to designate a type of ownership, is somewhat of a legal anomaly notwithstanding the fact that the term appears in M.S.A. § 48.30. By definition, several ownership is a denial of joint ownership. Since the type of ownership which the bank and its depositors have created by their contract defies classification under traditional concepts of property ownership, we are forced to treat this case as presenting a contract question and must decide what the incidents of this type of ownership are primarily by reference to the terms of the contract creating it.

By the deposit agreement here involved, each depositor has given the other depositor in the account complete and absolute authority over it and unconditional power to withdraw all or any part of the account. By the terms of the agreement, the bank is likewise obliged to pay any part or all of the account to either depositor upon demand.

Since in purpose and legal effect a garnishment proceeding is virtually an action brought by defendant in plaintiff's name against the garnishee, resulting in the subrogation of the plaintiff to the right of the defendant against the garnishee, we have concluded that plaintiff here may not only garnishee this joint account, but also that it would be entitled to recover judgment against the garnishee for the entire amount of the account if its judgment against defendant were sufficient to exhaust it. Defendant is entitled to withdraw any part or all of the account, and plaintiff, in effect, is subrogated to that right.

A case similar to the one at bar arose in Canada, Empire Fertilizers, Ltd. v. Cioci [1934] 4 D.L.R. 804, 805, where the court stated: "If the judgment debtor, B.N. Cioci, had given to the judgment creditor a cheque signed by B.N. Cioci alone on the Royal Bank, Jane and Annette Branch, Toronto, for the amount owing by Cioci on the judgment, the bank, on presentment of such cheque for payment, would have had to pay it, on the penalty of an action for damages by B.N. Cioci, against the bank if such cheque had been dishonoured. I see no reason why this judgment creditor of B.N. Cioci should not have recourse to these proceedings to compel such appropriation of these funds as was within the power of Cioci himself at the time of the issue and service of the garnishee summons on the bank * * *."

We find ourselves entirely in agreement with the reasoning of the Canadian case cited above. Intervener, having agreed to allow defendant to treat the funds in their joint account as his individual property, is in no position to assert that creditors, subrogated to his rights, may not treat them as if they were his individual property. Intervener assumed the risk that defendant would pay these creditors voluntarily, and we fail to see why an involuntary payment stands upon a different footing. If intervener assumed the risk that her husband would voluntarily honor his debts out of this account, we see no meritorious reason why she should be legally entitled to eschew the risk that he will be compelled to do so. The law should not hedge intervener's risk at the exact instant when the degree of her risk rests upon a point of honor. We shall not assume that intervener took the risk that her husband would honor his debts out of this account merely because she thought he could not be compelled to do so.

The peculiar features of a joint bank account, such as this case presents, make it difficult, if not impossible, in most cases, to determine what portion of the account belongs to each depositor. A long series of deposits which cannot be traced to their source, and a similar series of withdrawals which cannot be traced to their destination, are normally involved. This defect is inherent in the severalty feature of such bank accounts wherein each depositor is allowed to treat joint property as if it were entirely his own. Like any loose system of dealing with money, joint bank accounts sacrifice precision to convenience and becloud the respective rights of the depositors. The courts should not encourage parties to do their bookkeeping in court when, by their private contract, they have virtually declared that they do not wish to be inconvenienced by any strict accountability as between themselves. A joint bank account of this kind is a creature of contract between parties avowedly indifferent to the exact percentage of ownership between themselves. The law should take them at their word and give effect to their contract without making detailed and belated evidentiary inquiries to establish factual ownership. Any presumption, whether conclusive or rebuttable, that part or all of these joint accounts are immune from garnishment has the effect of either creating or tending to create a nonstatutory exemption for the parties using them, and any attempt to base the extent of garnishment upon the respective amounts of the account owned by each depositor will compel courts and juries to grope with problems which the depositors themselves have declared to be of no consequence. Let them abide the results which flow from their own declared purposes.

Although the trial court's order limiting judgment against the garnishee is erroneous so far as it limits judgment against the garnishee to one-half the account, plaintiff has not complained of the error in this proceeding, and we accordingly affirm the judgment entered pursuant to the trial court's order.

Affirmed.

BRICKER v. KRIMER

Court of Appeals of New York, 1963.
13 N.Y.2d 22, 241 N.Y.S.2d 413, 191 N.E.2d 795.

DYE, Judge. In this discovery proceeding, pursuant to section 1377–b of the Civil Practice Act, the committee for an incompetent seeks to recover moneys representing the proceeds of two bank accounts which, allegedly, are being wrongfully withheld by the respondent herein.

It is undisputed that on June 27, 1957 the incompetent's husband, Ilija Krimer, used his personal funds to open two accounts in the Harlem Savings Bank, one in the name of "Anna Krimer or Ilija Krimer, payable to either or the survivor" with a deposit of $20,000. In this connection both husband and wife executed signature cards and a joint account agreement on a bank form. At the same time another account was opened by the husband with a deposit of $5,000 viz.: "Ilija Krimer in trust for Anna Krimer". No withdrawals or further deposits were ever made in either account except for periodic crediting of interest until March 4, 1959, when the husband appeared at the bank accompanied by the respondent William Krimer, and executed a withdrawal slip closing the joint survivorship account, and with the proceeds amounting to $21,002.04 opened a new account in the same bank viz.: "Ilija Krimer or William D. Krimer, payable to either or the survivor". On May 4, 1959 the husband again appeared at the savings bank accompanied by his son, William, and closed the account standing in his name as trustee for Anna. The bank issued its check to his order in the amount of $5,293.10, being the whole of the original deposit plus accumulated interest, which check the husband indorsed in blank and handed to William, who concededly received the proceeds. The husband died December 16, 1959 leaving a last will and testament made February 20, 1959.[1] Six months after his death and on July 1, 1960, which was during the pendency of the will contest, the respondent herein proceeded to close the joint account opened in his and his father's name by withdrawing the whole balance in the sum of $22,113.74.

In this proceeding the committee-petitioner contends that upon the husband's death her ward, the incompetent Anna, became the sole and exclusive owner of all moneys in the two accounts opened in 1957, upon the theory that at the time of the changeover to respondent son, the latter was acting as decedent's confidential agent and trustee and that he may not be permitted to retain the funds he thus received, unless he established that the transfers to him were intended by the decedent, were completely free from fraud and were bona fide in every way; in other words, whether at the time of the transfer in 1959 to respondent son the decedent knowingly and consciously understood that he was closing out the accounts opened in 1957 in favor of his wife and himself and was transferring the proceeds. In Matter of Creekmore's Estate, 1 N.Y.2d 284, 152 N.Y.S.2d 449, 135 N.E.2d 193, a Surrogate's Court proceeding, we ruled that section 239 of the Banking Law, Consol.Laws, c. 2, is not necessarily conclusive of a depositor's intention to vest in the survivor title to a deposit made in the form of a joint account where the circumstances are such that the depositor may not have understood what she was doing. In that case there was proof that the decedent, then suffering a terminal illness, had requested her attorney to prepare papers appointing the respondent her attorney in fact so as to permit withdrawal of funds from her bank account to pay expenses incident to her care and maintenance. For reasons urged by the bank she was persuaded not to execute a power of attorney but to change her account to a joint form payable to either or survivor. The decedent had theretofore made a will bequeathing her estate in equal parts to her two

1. The probate of the decedent's last will and testament was contested by his daughter Maria and the special guardian of the incompetent widow, Anna, for alleged lack of testamentary capacity, and that its execution had been procured by fraud and undue influence allegedly practiced by the son, William Krimer, and the additional reason that the testator did not understand the will and its import. Following a trial, on framed issues, the Surrogate directed the jury to enter a verdict admitting the will to probate and dismissed the objections. Upon appeal the Appellate Division, Second Department, affirmed (16 A.D.2d 665 [16]). Upon appeal to this court we reversed the order of the Appellate Division and granted a new trial, in a decision handed down herewith (13 N.Y.2d 739, 241 N.Y.S.2d 866, 191 N.E.2d 917), on the general ground that, upon the evidence adduced, issues of fact were presented that should have been submitted to the jury for determination.

daughters. Her bank account represented the bulk of her estate. We deemed that under such circumstances the survivor was obliged to demonstrate that the decedent knew the crucial difference between giving a power of attorney to respondent for the limited purpose of drawing expense checks against her account and establishing her accounts in joint form payable to either or survivor.

Here we are also dealing with a joint account payable to either or survivor, and created under circumstances open to doubt. Even though the court below has found against the petitioner as to the husband's lack of capacity to make the transfer, there must, nevertheless, be a new trial. Regardless of whether the husband's act of transfer to his son was voluntarily and understandingly made, the wife may, nevertheless, have continued to retain an interest in the account. Thus, had the joint account which the husband established in 1957 with his wife, payable to either or survivor, remained intact to the date of his death, the wife, as survivor, would have been entitled to the whole thereof (Banking Law, § 239, subd. 3; Domestic Relations Law, Consol.Laws, c. 14, § 56–a, eff. April 20, 1959; Matter of Porianda's Estate, 256 N.Y. 423, 176 N.E. 826). The presumption that a joint account was intended, however, is merely a rebuttable presumption as to funds withdrawn prior to the death of the depositor (Matter of Porianda's Estate, supra). As to any moneys withdrawn from such an account during the joint lives of the two named persons, there is still, after the death of either of them, the presumption that the moneys so withdrawn by one had in fact belonged to both (Moskowitz v. Marrow, 251 N.Y. 380, 397, 167 N.E. 506, 511–512, 66 A.L.R. 870; Marrow v. Moskowitz, 255 N.Y. 219, 174 N.E. 460) and this is so whether an account payable to either or the survivor is opened by the depositor in his name and that of his wife, or someone other than his wife (Moskowitz v. Marrow, 251 N.Y. 380, 397, 167 N.E. 506, 511–512, 66 A.L.R. 870, supra; Russo v. Russo, 17 A.D.2d 129, 232 N.Y.S.2d 577; see, also, 1959 Report of N.Y.Law Rev.Comm. [N.Y. Legis.Doc., 1959, No. 65(J)]; cf. Matter of Polizzo, 308 N.Y. 517, 127 N.E.2d 316, and cases there cited involving personal property other than bank accounts in statutory form). In other words, the withdrawal of moneys from the joint account does not destroy the joint tenancy, if one was created. It merely opens the door to competent evidence, if available, that no joint tenancy was intended to be created (Matter of Porianda's Estate, supra). When a joint tenancy is created, each joint tenant has the right as a joint owner of the bank account to withdraw a moiety (half) or less than a moiety for his own use and thus destroy the joint tenancy as to such withdrawals (Matter of Suter's Estate, 258 N.Y. 104, 179 N.E. 310). A joint tenant who withdraws a sum in excess of his moiety is liable to the other joint tenant for the excess so withdrawn (Matter of Juedel's Will, 280 N.Y. 37, 19 N.E.2d 671; Walsh v. Kennan, 293 N.Y. 573, 59 N.E.2d 409; cf. Russo v. Russo, 17 A.D.2d 129, 232 N.Y.S.2d 577, supra).

In the case before us no consideration was given to the question whether or not the husband intended to and did in fact establish a joint tenancy by opening the savings account in 1957 with his wife Anna.

Upon a new trial the wife will be aided by the presumption that the husband intended a joint tenancy with his wife when he opened the 1957 account (Matter of Porianda's Estate, supra). If the presumption is not overcome, the husband's withdrawal in 1959 of all the funds in that account was in derogation of his wife's right and interest in those funds. In such event the wife, or in this case, her committee, would be entitled to at least her moiety (one half) of the account withdrawn without her consent during her lifetime, or, as survivor of her husband, to the whole thereof, if on a new trial the proof fails to establish that the closing out of the 1957 account by the decedent and the subsequent transfer to the son were voluntarily and understandingly made.

Since there is to be a new trial upon which issues of mental capacity, fraud and undue influence must be explored in connection with the transfer of the alleged joint account, we deem it essential that those issues also be explored upon the new trial with respect to the closing out by the husband of the account opened in trust for his wife and the turning over of the proceeds to the respondent without consideration.

The order appealed from should be reversed and a new trial granted, with costs to abide the event.

Notes

1. Two joint savings accounts were in the name of a father and his son. The son, shortly before his death, being gravely ill and in a hospital, directed his attorney to take the passbooks and withdraw all funds from both accounts and re-deposit them in the son's sole name. These directions were carried out. The son died shortly thereafter. Three years later the father died, and the court held that the funds in question were part of his estate. The withdrawals were unlawful, and the father gained sole right to the funds by right of survivorship. State v. Gralewski's Estate, 176 Or. 448, 159 P.2d 211 (1945). The court said,

> "[I]n our opinion the withdrawal by one depositor, without the other's consent, of the entire deposit, and for the manifest purpose of defeating his codepositor's survivorship right, is a violation of the understanding between the parties, as evidenced by the deposit agreement, and an attempted invasion of such co-depositor's title. It does not effect a severance of the joint tenancy, but, as the authorities upon which we rely hold, results only in a change in the form of the deposit, while its joint character and the rights therein of the respective parties remain unaltered."

2. In Vento v. Vento, 256 Pa.Super. 91, 389 A.2d 615 (1978), the court said that where a joint account is in the names of a husband and wife, the power to withdraw "must be exercised in good faith for the mutual benefit of both, and cannot be rightly exercised by the fraudulent withdrawal of the corpus * * * for the exclusive use of one for the purpose of depriving the other of any use thereof or title thereto." The court in following prior cases so holding said that this rule also applies to joint tenants who are not husband and wife.

3. In First National Bank v. Munns, 602 S.W.2d 910 (Mo.App.1980), a mother created a joint account with right of survivorship, with herself, her son, and her daughter as designated owners. The son withdrew all the money, and deposited it in his own name "in trust for" his mother and sister. The same day he pledged the trust account for a personal debt. After default, the creditor was awarded the money over the objection of mother and sister, although they

were given a money judgment against the son for his "conversion" of the funds. The case is noted in 46 Mo.L.Rev. 666 (1981).

4. The Uniform Probate Code, as adopted by the Commissioners on Uniform State Laws, contains provisions relating to P.O.D., trust, and joint accounts. A P.O.D. account belongs to the original payee during his lifetime. A trust account belongs to the trustee (usually the depositor) during his lifetime unless the contrary is manifested by the terms of the account or unless there is other clear and convincing evidence of an irrevocable trust. A joint account, during the lifetime of all parties, belongs to the parties in proportion to the net contributions of each, unless there is clear and convincing evidence of a different intent.

On the death of the original payee of a P.O.D. account, any sums remaining belong to the surviving P.O.D. payee or payees, with no further right of survivorship among them, if more than one. On the death of the trustee of a trust account, any sums remaining belong to the surviving beneficiary or beneficiaries, with no further right of survivorship, if more than one, unless there is clear and convincing evidence of a contrary intent. On the death of one party to a joint account, any sums remaining belong to the surviving party or parties, unless there is clear and convincing evidence of a contrary intent. If there are more than one surviving party, their respective ownership is in proportion to their previous ownership plus an equal share in the interest of the decedent, and the right of survivorship continues between them. The right of survivorship under each of these types of account cannot be changed by will.

See Uniform Probate Code §§ 6–101 through 6–113.

See Note, Multi-Party Accounts: Does Virginia's New Law Correspond With the Expectation of the Average Depositor, 144 Richmond L.Rev. 851 (1980).

5. Michigan has recently adopted a "statutory joint account act." A new kind of joint account can be created by contract between one or more persons and a financial institution that is agreeable to such a contract. The consequences of such a contract are fixed by responses to a series of questions contained in a prescribed form: (1) which of the contracting persons may withdraw funds during their lifetime; (2) which of them may revoke the contract in a specified manner; (3) which of them owns the funds during their lifetime; (4) which of them owns and has the right to withdraw the funds if one of them dies first; and (5) which of the above controls if both or all of them die simultaneously without proof of who survived. Financial institutions are protected in honoring withdrawals in accordance with the terms of a contract. The rights of creditors of the designated parties are determined by the designation of ownership, and the estate of a deceased owner may recover the amount owned by a decedent, where the estate is insolvent, to the extent required to satisfy claims against the estate, or to satisfy a widow's allowance, an allowance for dependent children, or a widow's right of election if the assets of the estate are insufficient for the payment of the widow's share and the deposits were included as part of the estate. A statutory joint account is not affected by the requirements for testamentary dispositions. This statute does not affect non-statutory joint accounts. Mich.Comp.L.Ann. §§ 487.711–487.719 (1978).

Note on Rental of Joint Safe Deposit Boxes

A situation related to the joint bank deposit cases arises when two or more persons enter into an agreement to rent a safe deposit box. They sometimes sign an agreement reading in substance: "It is hereby declared that all property of every kind, at any time heretofore or hereafter placed in said box is the property of said lessees as joint tenants and upon the death of any of them passes to the survivor." Several cases have held that a good joint tenancy with right of survivorship results from the execution of such agreement, and that the survivor is entitled to the contents free from claims of the decedent's estate. See Hausfelder v. Security-First National Bank, 77 Cal.App.2d 478, 176 P.2d 84 (1946); Brown v. Navarre, 64 Ariz. 262, 169 P.2d 85 (1946). The authorities are not unanimous, however, for in Clevidence v. Mercantile Home Bank & Trust Co., 355 Mo. 904, 199 S.W.2d 1 (1947), the court allowed parol evidence to vary the effect of the writing with the result that the survivor did not take all the contents, and in Chadrow v. Kellman, 378 Pa. 237, 106 A.2d 594 (1954), the court denied the survivor any rights to the contents upon a showing that the decedent had retained both keys to the box and there had never been joint access. The last named case is noted in 30 N.Y.U.L.Rev. 506 (1955), where the theoretical difficulties in sustaining such an agreement are pointed out. It is also noted in 6 Syracuse L.Rev. 198 (1954). See also, note, "The Unintentional Creation of a Joint Tenancy in the Contents of a Safe Deposit Box," 32 Cal.L. Rev. 301 (1944).

Note on Gifts of Shares of Stock

A share of corporate stock is one of the many forms of intangible property. It is moreover one of the forms of intangible property which is evidenced by a written instrument. The use of stock certificates as evidence or symbols of the underlying interest is so much taken for granted that we commonly speak of shares of stock as though they were the certificates rather than the interest which the certificates represent. It would be only normal, therefore, to assume that one makes a gift of corporate stock by delivering the certificate with the proper donative intent. This manner of making a gift of stock is approved by most courts.

Corporate regulations usually provided that the transfer of shares can only be effected by complying with prescribed procedures for recording the transfer on the books of the corporation. One may note that this procedure is analogous to those usually prescribed by law for the transfer of title to automobiles. So far as the relation between the stockholders and the corporation is concerned, it is clear that the corporation is protected if it treats as stockholders only those persons whose ownership of shares has been established in this manner. But, nevertheless, the courts continue to recognize as valid between the parties gifts of shares by means of the delivery of the appropriate certificates.

Suppose on the other hand, a donor attempts to make a gift by following the procedure for transfer prescribed by the corporation, which results in the issuance of new certificates in the name of the donee, and the donor receives and retains the new certificates, which he fails to deliver to the donee. There is authority that in such cases the transfer is valid and complete.

The Uniform Stock Transfer Act requires the endorsement of a certificate of stock plus delivery of the endorsed certificate to the transferee. More courts than not have held, however, that this statute also merely regulates the relations between stockholders and the corporation and does not prevent a valid gift as between the parties by means merely of delivery of an unendorsed certificate. See Rogers v. Rogers, 271 Md. 603, 319 A.2d 119 (1974), relying in part on §§ 8–301(1), 8–307, and 8–313(1)(a) of the Uniform Commercial Code.

See Brown, Personal Property § 8.3 (3d ed. 1975).

MILLER v. RIEGLER

Supreme Court of Arkansas, 1967.
243 Ark. 251, 419 S.W.2d 599.

See report of this case at page 307, supra.

Note on Gifts of United States Savings Bonds

United States Savings Bonds are issued subject to regulations which include the following (C.F.R., Title 31, as amended May 28, 1966):

"315.5 *General.* Savings Bonds are issued only in registered form. The registration used on issue or reissue must express the actual ownership of and interest in the bond and,   *   *   *   will be considered as conclusive of such ownership and interest.   *   *   *

"315.7 *Authorized forms of registration.* Subject to any limitations or restrictions contained in these regulations on the right of any person to be named as owner, coowner, or beneficiary, bonds may be registered in the following forms:

"(a) *Natural persons.* In the names of natural persons in their own right.

"(1) *Single owner.* Example: John A. Jones.

"(2) *Coownership form—two persons (only).* In the alternative as coowners.

Examples:

John A. Jones or Mrs. Ella S. Jones.

Mrs. Ella S. Jones or John A. Jones.

"No other form of registration establishing coownership is authorized.

"(3) *Beneficiary form—two persons (only).*

Examples:

John A. Jones payable on death to Mrs. Ella S. Jones.

John A. Jones P.O.D. Mrs. Ella S. Jones.   *   *   *

"315.15 *Limitation on transfer or pledge.* Savings bonds are not transferable and are payable only to the owners named thereon, except as specifically provided in these regulations, and then only in the manner and to the extent so provided   *   *   *.

"315.22 *Payment or reissue pursuant to judgment.*   *   *   *

"(b) *Gifts causa mortis.* A bond belonging solely to one person will be paid or reissued on the request of the person found by a court to be entitled thereto by reason of a gift causa mortis by the sole owner."

These regulations have been modified from time to time, and cases under earlier regulations are not necessarily controlling. For example, Section 315.22 quoted above was added only after some courts had held attempted gifts causa mortis invalid under the earlier regulations. See Fidelity Union Trust Co. v. Tezyk, 140 N.J.Eq. 474, 55 A.2d 26, 173 A.L.R. 546 (1947), noted in 61 Harv.L. Rev. 542 (1948). Moreover, you should know that in some cases, despite the provisions of Section 315.15, inter vivos gifts have been held valid. See Marshall v. Felker, 156 Fla. 476, 23 So.2d 555 (1945). The prohibition on transfer has also been upheld. Connell v. Bauer, 240 Minn. 280, 61 N.W.2d 177 (1953), noted in 3 Kan.L.Rev. 72 (1954).

The regulations raise some questions:

1. Is there any reason why a bank deposit "P.O.D." should be held testamentary while a bond made "P.O.D." to a named beneficiary will be paid to such beneficiary?

2. Is there any reason to distinguish in the regulations between gifts inter vivos and gifts causa mortis?

3. If the Uniform Stock Transfer Act can be held to be only for the protection of the corporation, can these regulations be construed as being only for the protection of the United States government?

4. Conversely, does the fact that the regulations authorize coownership mean that the person designated as coowner is entitled to the proceeds of the bonds even though the one purchasing them furnishes all the money, retains exclusive possession, and never notifies the coowner of his designation?

Chapter 9

CONVEYANCES OF LAND

SECTION 1. THE MODERN DEED OF CONVEYANCE: HISTORICAL DEVELOPMENT AND MODERN FORMS

PATTON, LAND TITLES
Vol. 1, pp. 3–8 (2d ed. 1957).

History of English System of Conveyancing

We do not know the origin of the practice of transferring title to real estate by a written instrument. It may have been in existence and quite highly developed at the very dawn of written history. It appears to have passed from one predominating civilization to the next till it reached the Roman era, and from the latter into the legal systems of continental Europe. But Roman law did not, directly at least, exercise any appreciable influence on English land law. Instead, therefore, of finding transfers of title in England made from the time of the Roman occupation by the execution and delivery of a deed, we find that at no very remote date, possession was the only evidence of title and that proof of a transfer of title existed solely in the memory of witnesses present at the time when the change of possession occurred. As to estates for years, a transfer of title was effected by a mere entry of the new owner, but in the case of freehold estates the change had to be in the form of a symbolic ceremony known as livery of seisin. This was a ceremony consisting of a symbolical delivery of the corporeal possession of land by the grantor, or "feoffor," as he was called, to the grantee, or "feoffee." The parties, with their witnesses, went upon the land, and the feoffor gave to the feoffee a stick, twig, piece of turf, or a handful of earth taken from the land. Sometimes a ring, a cross, or a knife was handed over, anything, in fact as a token of the delivery. As a further part of the ceremony, the feoffor used proper, and technical, words which were to show that he intended to transfer the land to the feoffee, and which also marked out, or limited, the estate, or the interest, in the land which the feoffor intended the feoffee to have. The words "I give" (Latin, "do") were the proper words to use for the conveyance, while the words "to him" (i.e., the feoffee) "and his heirs," or "to him and the heirs of his body," (designating the limitation, either as a fee simple or a fee tail). A distinction was made between livery in deed and livery in law. The former arose when the livery of seisin took place on the land itself; the latter, when the parties were not actually on the land—as when the transfer was made in sight of the premises, but without an actual entry on them. In the latter case, the feoffor, pointing out the land, bade the feofee enter and take possession of it. Should the feoffee do so within the lifetime of the parties, the feoffment was valid in law. Livery of seisin also required an abjuration of the land by the donor, or feoffor; that is, he had to leave, or vacate, the land, leaving the feoffee in possession. No writing was necessary to give evidence to livery of seisin, although writings became customary in very early times. In later times, however, livery of seisin was usually accompanied by a written deed, especially when the limitations of the estate granted were numerous. Such a deed was, however, only an evidence of title, and not a conveyance itself. * * *

* * * But the use of a writing remained optional with the parties till the passage in 1677 of the Statute of Frauds.[1] It was only incorporeal interests and future estates, which were not capable of livery of seisin because of an absence of the element of possession, as to which a transfer of title could be made by a deed alone. The latter was called a deed of grant and was responsible for the common law distinction between things which "lie in livery" and those which "lie in grant." In the case of freehold estates in corporeal real property, the deed required by the Statute of Frauds did not operate to transfer the title, and livery of seisin remained essential in England, theoretically at least, till dispensed with by the Real Property Act 1845, § 3. But the enactment of the Statute of Uses[2] in 1535 had practically that effect in that it brought into almost universal use modes of alienation which did not require the symbolic ceremony. Aside from a more common form of conveyance which indirectly resulted from the statute, as set forth in the next paragraph those directly resulting from the statute were, (1) a contract in the form of a covenant to stand seized of property for the benefit of a beneficiary related to the covenantor by blood or marriage, and (2) a contract, or deed, of bargain and sale of lands "whereby the bargainor for some pecuniary consideration bargains and sells, that is, contracts to convey, the land to the bargainee; and becomes by such bargain, a trustee for or seised to the use of the bargainee."[3] The statute executed the contract in both cases, and thus the purchaser acquired the seisin and possession of the same as though there had been a livery of seisin.

But since the statute enabled a landowner by a mere contract of sale to vest the title in another without livery of seisin or other publicity, the same parliament passed a companion act for the express purpose of preventing clandestine conveyances. This was the Statute of Enrollments.[4] It made a deed of bargain and sale of a freehold interest void unless within six months it was enrolled in a court of record at Westminster, or in certain other public offices. These two statutes were merely part of

1. 29 Charles II, c. 3, § 1. [Footnotes are the editors'. Ed.]

2. 27 Hen. VIII, c. 10.

3. 2 Blackstone, Comm. 339. See also Holdsworth, Historical Introduction to Land Law 292 (1927).

4. 27 Hen. VIII, c. 16.

a plan to provide a general scheme for the transfer of title by deed, and for the recording or registry of land conveyances.[5] But because of a general disposition of the landholding aristocracy to withdraw the details of their family settlements and domestic arrangements from the curiosity of the public their conveyances welcomed the first part of the plan and set themselves to work to frustrate the second. A common-law deed of "lease and release" had previously been somewhat used to effect a transfer of title without the formal livery of seisin; it was now brought into general use to effect a conveyance which would not be within the terms of the Statute of Enrollments. This was possible by reason of the fact that the statute related to freeholds only, and that such an estate could be so divided that none of its component parts amounted to a freehold. All that the conveyancer had to do was to have the owner execute a lease (usually in the form of a bargain and sale deed of an estate for one year), followed at once by a release of the reversion to the lessee.[6] This cumbersome use of two instruments for every transfer continued in England till the necessity for the fictitious lease was abolished in 1841. Four years later the Real Property Act was passed, making a simple deed of grant sufficient to convey all estates.[7]

Conveyancing in the United States

Though livery of seisin was necessarily recognized as effective to transfer title in the few instances in which it was employed in the early days of this country, and though the statute of uses has been frequently relied upon to give effect to an instrument which might otherwise be ineffective to operate as a conveyance,[8] most of the states early adopted statutes authorizing the transfer of title by simple forms of deeds of conveyance without livery of seisin or other ceremony. Many of these follow substantially the wording of the deeds of bargain and sale which came into use with the statute of uses, others resemble common-law deeds of grant (though no longer confined to incorporeal things or future estates), with or without the addition of covenants of warranty, and some are patterned after the early common-law release. In Louisiana, conveyance has always been by deed but by forms derived from those of France rather than of England.[9]

---

5. See Holdsworth, Causes Which Shaped the Statute of Uses, 26 Harv.L. Rev. 108, 115 (1912); Holdsworth, Historical Introduction to Land Law 153, 155 (1927).

6. Holdsworth, Historical Introduction to Land Law 293 (1927); Reeves, Real Property § 1054.

7. 8 & 9 Vict. c. 106, § 2.

8. See, e.g., Bryan v. Bradley, 16 Conn. 474 (1844); Murray v. Kerney, 115 Md. 514, 81 A. 6, 38 L.R.A., N.S., 937 (1911); French v. French, 3 N.H. 234 (1825); Wilson v. Kilcannon, 5 Tenn. (4 Hayw.) 182 (1817); Waldron v. Pigeon Coal Co., 61 W.Va. 280, 56 S.E. 492 (1907). However, the courts have expressly held that the Staute of Uses is not in force in Nebraska, Ohio, and Vermont; and in New York, Michigan, Minnesota, North Dakota, and Wisconsin the legislatures have abolished all uses and trusts except those expressly provided for by state statute. New Jersey, on the other hand, reenacted a rather peculiar version of the Statute of Uses at an early date; see N.J.S.A. 46:3–9.

9. Both the conveyances and mortgages in most common use are in the form of an "act" or certificate of the notary rather than of the grantors, although the latter also join the notary in signing the instruments. They are known as "notarial

The minimum requirements for an effective conveyance of land (or any interest therein) include the following:

(a) An instrument in writing. As indicated above in the excerpt from Patton, Land Titles, this requirement was made practically universal by the English Statute of Frauds in 1677, which declared that all estates "made or created by livery and seisin only, or by parol, and not put in writing, and signed by the parties so making or creating the same, or by their agents thereunto lawfully authorized by writing, shall have the force and effect of leases or estates at will only." [10]

(b) The instrument must be effectively executed; [11]

(c) The instrument must contain language showing the conveying intent;

(d) Not only must there be a grantor but also a grantee,[12] identifiable by the language of the instrument;

(e) The subject matter of the conveyance must be identifiable by resort to the language of the instrument; [13]

(f) The instrument should contain not only the means of identifying the subject matter, physically speaking, but also the extent of the the interest or estate in the subject matter conferred upon the conveyee.

Throughout the country will be found a great many forms of conveying documents. Conveyancers use them, but they should always be used with intelligence and understanding. One without sufficient training should not even pick out a form for use to say nothing about filling it up. It is no impropriety for a competent person to utilize a form, but no one should ever attempt to complete a form unless he is able to prepare an effective instrument of conveyance with no form in front of him. He, of course, needs (a) to understand the facts and the objectives of the parties; (b) to be able to use the English language so that a read-

---

acts" or "authentic acts." In less common use are instruments "under private signature," duly acknowledged before a notary or other officer authorized to take acknowledgments.

10. That an effective gift of land may be made "by parol," on principles analogous to "part performance" of contracts, see Lynch v. Lynch, 239 Iowa 1245, 34 N.W.2d 485 (1948); Hayes v. Hayes, 126 Minn. 389, 148 N.W. 125 (1914); Re Schnoor's Estate, 31 Wash.2d 565, 198 P.2d 184 (1948).

11. "Execution" may include signing, sealing, attestation, acknowledgment and delivery. Signing and delivery are universally required; attestation or acknowledgment are usually necessary only as prerequisites to recordation of the deed. In most states, sealing is no longer necessary for any purpose. It can be argued that there is an additional element in "execution," i.e., "acceptance"; but "acceptance" may also be viewed as the final step in "deliv-

ery" and, in any case, is usually presumed when the conveyance is beneficial to the grantee. "Delivery" will be treated in some detail in Section 4.

12. When there is no identifiable grantee a dedication may possibly be found. See Cincinnati v. White, 6 Pet. (U.S.) 431, 8 L.Ed. 452 (1832). Moreover, it is generally held that when a deed with the name of the grantee in blank is delivered by the grantor with the intention that the title shall pass to the person to whom the deed is delivered, the latter obtains an equitable title to the land and has the implied authority to insert his name in the blank space; and when he does so, he is deemed to have obtained the legal title as of the date of delivery. 2 Patton, Land Titles, § 336 n. 44 (2d ed. 1957) and cases there cited. See also, to the same effect, Womack v. Stegner, 293 S.W.2d 124 (Tex.Civ.App.1956), and cases cited.

13. This is dealt with in Section 3, infra.

er—possibly a later lawyer or judge—may understand it; and (c) to know the applicable law.

There are three basic types of conveyances in use in the United States today:

(1) deeds with covenants for title, usually called "warranty deeds"; (2) deeds without covenants for title, often called "bargain and sale" or "grant deeds"; and (3) "quitclaim deeds."

The *warranty deed* contains at least a covenant by the grantor to warrant and defend the title and possession of the grantee, and usually contains one or more of the other "usual covenants for title": the covenants of seisin, of good right to convey, against encumbrances, and for quiet possession. Sometimes a covenant for further assurances—one of the "usual covenants" in England—is also included. A covenant to warrant and defend against "all lawful claims whatsoever" is a general warranty, and a deed containing such a covenant is a "general warranty deed." A "special warranty deed," in contrast, contains only a covenant to warrant and defend "against the claims and demands of the grantor and all persons claiming or to claim by, through, or under him." [14]

A *deed without covenants* contains no covenants with respect to the title conveyed; it merely purports to convey a fee simple or a designated lesser estate. The operative words of such a deed ordinarily include "grant," "bargain," "sell," "convey," "alien," or words of like import.

A *quitclaim deed* contains no covenants for title and is derived from the old common law deed of release. In such a deed, the grantor usually purports merely to "remise, release and forever quitclaim" to the grantee "all his right, title and interest" in the land described therein; the grantor does not represent that he has any particular interest in the land and the deed will not be effective to transfer an after-acquired interest to the grantee.

The student should acquaint himself with the forms of conveyances in general use in the area where he expects to practice.

The following is a form of general warranty deed in common use in the State of Michigan:

This Indenture, made this _____ day of _____, in the year of our Lord one thousand nine hundred and _____, between _____, part__ of the first part, and _____, part__ of the second part,

Witnesseth, that the said part__ of the first part, for and in consideration of the sum of _____ dollars, to _____ in hand paid by the said part__ of the second part, the receipt whereof is hereby confessed and acknowledged, do__ by these presents grant, bargain, sell, remise, release, alien and confirm unto the said part__ of the second part, and _____ heirs and assigns forever, all _____ certain piece__ or par-

---

14. In addition, the "special warranty deed" may also contain a covenant by the grantor "that he has done no act to encumber the said lands." See N.J.S.A. 46:4–6 for a full explanation of the scope of this "special" or limited covenant against encumbrances.

cel__ of land situate and being in the _____ of _____, County of _____, and State of Michigan, and described as follows, to-wit:

_____

_____

Together with all and singular the hereditaments and appurtenances thereunto belonging or in anywise appertaining: [15] To have and to hold the said premises, as herein described, with the appurtenances, unto the said part__ of the second part, and to _____ heirs and assigns forever.[16] And the said _____, part__ of the first part, for __sel__, __h__ heirs, executors and administrators, do__ covenant, grant, bargain and agree to and with the said part__ of the second part_____ heirs and assigns, that at the time of the ensealing and delivery of these presents _____ well seized of the above-granted premises in fee simple; that they are free from all incumbrances whatever _____ and that _____ will, and _____ heirs, executors, _____ administrators _____ shall, warrant and defend the same against all lawful claims whatsoever _____.[17]

In witness whereof, the said part__ of the first ha__ hereunto set _____ hand__ and seal__ the day and year first above written.[18]

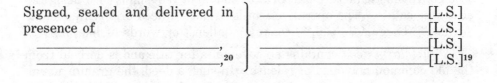

Signed, sealed and delivered in presence of

_____,

_____, 20

_____[L.S.]
_____[L.S.]
_____[L.S.]
_____[L.S.][19]

State of Michigan,
County of _____ } ss.

On this __ day of _____ in the year one thousand nine hundred and __, before me, _____, _____ in and for said county, personally appeared _____, to me known to be the same person__ described in

15. Everything down to this point, including the description (which must be inserted in the blank space provided), is technically known as the "premises." If the deed is to include any reservations, exceptions, restrictions, or special recitals, they will usually be placed immediately after the description. When a printed form is used, that is generally the only place where sufficient blank space can be found for them.

16. This part of the deed is technically called the "habendum and tenendum" clause. If the grantor is conveying a qualified fee simple estate rather than a fee simple absolute, the special limitation, condition subsequent, or executory limitation is ordinarily included in the "habendum

and tenendum" clause. If the estate granted is only a life estate, that fact is ordinarily stated in the "premises" and restated in the "habendum and tenendum" clause.

17. This part of the deed consists of personal covenants with respect to the estate conveyed; but, as we shall later discover, the benefit of some of these covenants "runs with the land conveyed." See Chapter 11, Section 1, infra.

18. This is the "testimonium" clause.

19. The grantor or grantors will sign here.

20. The attesting witnesses (if any) will sign here.

and who executed the within instrument, who _____ acknowledged the same to be _____ free act and deed.

_____,

Notary Public, _____
_____ County, Michigan.

My commission expires _____, 19__.[21]

Does the above Michigan warranty deed form contain all of the "usual covenants" for title mentioned above? Compare the New Jersey statutory warranty deed form, which contains the following covenants by the grantor: "that he is lawfully seized of the said land; that he has the right to convey the said land to the said grantee; that the grantee shall have quiet possession of the said land free from all encumbrances; that the grantor will execute such further assurances of the said land as may be requisite; that he will warrant generally the property hereby conveyed." As to the full meaning of these covenants, see N.J.Stat. Ann. 46:4–2 through 46:4–5, 46:4–7, and 46:4–10.

The Michigan warranty deed form would become a deed without covenants if the sentence preceding the testimonium clause ("In witness whereof," etc.) were eliminated. The warranty deed could be transformed further into a quitclaim deed by striking out the words, "grant, bargain, sell, remise, release, alien and confirm" and substituting therefor the following language: "remise, release and forever quitclaim all his right, title and interest."

Not uncommonly one finds stautory provisions stating terms, simple indeed, that will suffice as a conveyance if properly executed. For example, Cal.Civ.Code § 1092 declares that "A grant of an estate in real property may be made in substance as follows:

"I, AB, grant to CD all that real property situated in (insert name of county) county, state of California, bounded (or described) as follows: (here insert description, or if the land sought to be conveyed has a descriptive name, it may be described by the name, as for instance, 'The Norris Ranch.')

"Witness by hand this (insert day) _____ day of (insert month), _____."

"AB."

This, of course, does not mean that no other combination of words will do.[22]

21. This concludes the certificate of acknowledgment. Officials other than notaries public are often authorized by statute to take and certify the acknowledgment of the grantor of a deed.

22. For an instance of extreme informality, see Metzger v. Miller, 291 F. 780 (U.S.Dist.Ct.1923), where a series of letters was held operative as a conveyance of land.

Other interesting instances of informal documents held effective as conveyances are Brusseau v. Hill, 201 Cal. 225, 256 P. 419, 55 A.L.R. 157 (1927); Barnes v. Banks, 223 Ill. 352, 79 N.E. 117, 8 L.R.A.,N.S., 1037, 114 Am.St.Rep. 331 (1906), in equity. In McGurl v. Burns, 81 N.Y.S.2d 51 (1948), these words were included in the language of a promissory note: "We resign any further claim to property at 9009 Ft. H. Pway, Brooklyn".

Many states provide that use of certain words or certain statutory forms shall have the effects, such as inclusion of covenants for title stated in the statute. Thus in California use of the word "grant" causes the deed to include covenants by the grantor (1) that he has not conveyed any interest in the land to another by a prior deed, and (2) that the land is free of any encumbrance created or suffered by the grantor or anyone claiming under him. Cal.Civ.Code § 1113. And Ill.Rev.Stat. Ann. (Smith-Hurd) c. 30, § 8, incorporates general covenants of seisin and good right to convey, against encumbrances, and of warranty and quiet enjoyment in the following short-form deed:

"The grantor [here insert name or names and place of residence], for and in consideration of [here insert consideration] in hand paid, conveys and warrants to [here insert the grantee's name or names] the following described real estate [here insert description], situated in the county of _____ in the state of Illinois.

"Dated this _____ day of _____, A.D. 18__.

"A.B. [L.S.]"

The two succeeding sections of the Illinois statutes give forms for quit claim deeds and mortgages, with statements of the effects thereof.

At the end of Chapter 183 of the Mass.Gen.Laws Ann. are found a considerable number of forms of instruments relating to real estate. Section 8 of Chapter 183 states that:

"The forms set forth in the appendix to this chapter may be used and shall be sufficient for their respective purposes. They shall be known as 'Statutory Forms' and may be referred to as such. They may be altered as circumstances require, and the authorization of such forms shall not prevent the use of other forms. Wherever the phrase 'Incorporation by reference' is used in the following sections, the method of incorporation as indicated in said forms shall be sufficient, but shall not preclude other methods."

See also Ariz.Rev.Stats. § 33–402; N.J.Stat.Ann. 46:4–1 through 46:4–11 and 46:5–1 through 46:5–9; Wis.Stats.Ann. 235.04 through 235.16 and the "State of Wisconsin" forms authorized by 235.16.

Obviously the student, at this point, should consult the statutes of the state which interests him most.

Note

For a more detailed treatment of "deeds", see 3 A.L.P. §§ 12.1–12.14, 12.35–12.55. See also the briefer treatment in Cunningham §11.1.

Strictly speaking, a "deed", of course, is an instrument under seal. It will be noted from the succeeding material that seals are commonly no longer neces-

In Rosenwald v. Commissioner of Internal Revenue, 33 F.2d 423 (C.C.A.Ill., 1929), the Barnes case is said to depend upon the donee being in possession when the letter of gift was written. See, further, Rood in 4 Mich.L.Rev. 109, 112–116, and cases cited therein. Cf. Eriksen v. Lucas, 284 Mich. 372, 279 N.W. 866 (1938), in which it was held that a letter by a land owner referring to a deed supposedly made out by him in favor of the addressee and stating that he would keep the deed "So all you need do is to have the deed recorded," etc., did not amount to a conveyance. Nor did it constitute delivery of the supposed deed.

sary to effectuate transfers of ownership in land, yet instruments of conveyances are still commonly called "deeds."

Estoppel by Deed and Transfer of After-Aquired Titles

One of the basic rules of the common law is expressed in the famous maxim "Nemo plus juris transferre potest quam ipse habet"—"No one can transfer a better title than he himself has." But suppose a grantor of land has no title to the land which he purportedly conveys and later does acquire the title thereto. Is there any theory on which this after-acquired title may be deemed to pass to the grantee by virtue of the prior conveyance? Consider the following excerpts from 1 Patton, Land Titles (2d ed. 1957):

"§ 215. Conveyance by Nonowner—After-Acquired Title

" * * * a deed made when the grantor has no title, or has title to a lesser estate than he purports to convey, may operate as an agreement to convey which may be enforced in equity in case of a subsequent acquisition of title by the grantor. However, in most states there is no necessity for action by the grantee, in that the courts hold that an after-acquired or a perfected title inures to the grantee, his heirs or assigns, by way of estoppel of the grantor to assert any claim in opposition to his own conveyance, and that such a title vests in the grantee by operation of law as soon as it is acquired by the grantor. The doctrine applies, irrespective of how the subsequent title is acquired, and regardless of whether the grantor, who assumed to convey what he did not have, acted under an honest mistake or committed a fraud. The right of inurement operates in favor of the original grantee, and any person, no matter how remote, holding title under him, and binds, not only the grantor, his heirs, and representatives, but also all parties having notice of the conveyance which gives rise to the right.

"§ 216. Conveyance by Nonowner—Conveyances to Which Doctrine Applies

"In order that the estoppel shall become operative, the instrument upon which it is founded must have been an actual and valid conveyance, and not merely a contract to convey. But its effect is not limited to conveyances which create or transfer an estate; if one mortgages land which he does not own, and thereafter acquires title to it, the mortgage at once becomes a lien thereon; and if in conveying land, he gives an express or implied easement in adjoining land which he does not own, any title which he may thereafter acquire to the adjoining land, either in his hands or in the hands of one charged with notice, will be subject to the easement. At common law the doctrine applied only to conveyances which contained a covenant of warranty. Now, however, any of the title covenants may produce the necessary estoppel. In fact, it is now generally held that if a deed, either expressly or by necessary implication, shows that the grantor intended to convey, and that the grantee expected to acquire an estate of a particular kind, the deed is a foundation for the doctrine, even if it contain no technical covenants whatever. Several legislatures have made a statutory statement of the doctrine in still broader terms to the effect that, whenever a deed purports to convey a greater estate than the grantor then owns, any after-acquired interest of such grantor, to the extent of that which the deed purports to convey, inures to the benefit of the grantee. The effect of such statutes, so far as after-acquired title is concerned, is to read into all deeds, purporting to convey a fee title, full covenants of warranty. Usually, therefore, they bring conveyances by quitclaim deed within the operation of the rule, though this is not always the case. In the absence of statute, it is the general rule in nearly all jurisdictions that a deed which is strictly a quitclaim, and which contains neither covenants nor recitals showing, expressly or by implication, the existence of any estate or interest in the grantor, does not affect an after-acquired title, nor estop the grantor from asserting it. But the rule does apply if the deed bears upon its face evidence that the grantor intended to convey, and the grantee expected to receive, an estate of a particular character—under such circumstances, the grantor and those claiming under him will be as effectively estopped to assert an after-acquired title to the extent of the estate embraced in the conveyance as would be the case if a formal covenant to that effect had been inserted.

"Because of the lack of representations which would raise an estoppel, the doctrine does not apply to official conveyances. For the same reason, there is no estoppel when a deed, even with the strongest of covenants, purports to convey and warrant merely the present interest of the grantor. In fact, many courts hold that unless there is a definite showing, by covenant or recital, of an intention to convey an after-acquired title, it will be construed to relate to the grantor's present title and interest only." *

SECTION 2. PREPARATION OF THE DEED FOR DELIVERY

In preparing a "deed" for delivery, some or all of the following formalities must be observed: signing, sealing, attestation, and acknowledgment. These formalities will now be considered in brief detail.[1]

Signing

At common law, signing was not essential to a "deed." Blackstone seems to have been of the opinion that the Statute of Frauds made signing necessary. The more generally accepted view, however, is that the Statute of Frauds did not, in its requirement of a signature, include instruments under seal. However, that may be, the statutes of the several states in this country quite uniformly require that a "deed" shall be signed by the grantor or his agent in order to be effective as a conveyance. Some statutes—e.g. West's Ann.Cal.Civ.Code § 1091,—require

---

* For a detailed treatment of "estoppel by deed", see 3 A.L.P. §§ 15.17–15.25. For a briefer treatment, see Cunningham § 11.5.

such formalities as a prerequisite to recording. Generally, see 3 A.L.P. §§ 12.57–12.63.

1. The Uniform Simplification of Land Transfers Act (1977) eliminates nearly all

that the instrument be "subscribed." The state statutes should be consulted.

Sealing

The common law "grant," required for conveyance of incorporeal interests in land, was a "deed" and necessarily had to be under seal. Conveyances of corporeal interests in land, such as feoffments and leases operating under the common law, did not even have to be in writing until required to be so by the Statute of Frauds; but the charters of feoffment and the written leases in common use were usually under seal. The Statute of Frauds, itself, did not require that any conveyance be under seal. Of the conveyances operating by force of the Statute of Uses, the covenant to stand seised clearly had to be a "deed" under seal. Moreover, a bargain and sale of a freehold estate was required by the Statute of Enrollments to be in writing and under seal. But since the Statute of Enrollments was never in force in the United States, it is arguable that a bargain and sale would be effective in the United States if in writing and signed by the grantor, though not under seal. In a number of states, however, it was held at an early date that all conveyances must be under seal in order to pass a freehold estate. See, e.g., Jackson ex dem. Gouch v. Wood, 12 Johns. 73 (N.Y.1815), where the court said:

"We have the authority of that learned commentator, unequivocally in favor of the opinion, that a seal is indispensable, in order to convey an estate in fee simple, fee tail, or for life. 2 Black.Com. 297, 312.

"Such seems to have been the practical construction, ever since the statute of Car. II in England, and under our statute of frauds in this state; and to decide now, that a seal is unnecessary to pass a fee, would be to introduce a new rule of conveyancing, contrary to the received opinion, and almost universal practice in our community, and dangerous in its retrospective operation. Construing this statute with reference to the pre-existing common law, and the particular evil intended to be remedied, I think the legislature did not intend to dispense with a seal, where it was before required, as in a conveyance of a freehold estate; but the object was to require such deeds to be signed also, which the Courts had decided to be unnecessary."

Some relatively early statutes in the United States specifically required that conveyances be made by sealed instruments. But other statutes diluted the requirement in various ways. See, e.g., N.J.Stat. Ann. 46:13–3, which provides: "No deed or other instrument [entitled to record], heretofore or hereafter made, excepting deeds or instruments made by a corporation, shall be void for lack of a seal, if the attestation or testimonium clause, or the acknowledgment or proof, shall recite that the same was signed and sealed by the makers thereof; and the record of every such deed shall be admissible in evidence as fully and completely for all purposes as if such deed or instrument had been duly sealed." Other states have followed the more direct approach of providing by statute that a seal is not essential for the effectiveness of a conveyance. It would appear that the necessity for a seal on a "deed" is now completely abolished in at least 34 states. See comment in 3 Utah L.Rev. 83 (1952). Even in states which still purport to require a seal, a modern court may be very lenient in allowing any mark to serve as a "seal", and may be willing to find that a printed parenthetical reference is the equivalent of a seal. See Garrison v. Blakeney, 37 N.C.App. 73, 246 S.E.2d 144 (1978), cert. denied 295 N.C. 646, 248 S.E.2d 251.

Attestation

At common law attestation by witnesses was not necessary for any purpose in connection with deeds. In the United States not uncommonly the statutes require attestation for some purpose. In Ohio and Connecticut attestation by two witnesses is necessary to make the deed valid as a conveyance, even as between the parties. Langmede v. Weaver, 65 Ohio St. 17, 60 N.E. 992; Winsted Sav. Bank & Bldg. Ass'n v. Spencer, 26 Conn. 195.[2] Generally, however, where attestation is called for by the statute it is considered necessary only as a prerequisite to effective recording. In examining a title it is important for the examiner to remember that the law may not always have been the same, and the effectiveness of conveyances must be determined by the law as it was at the time the conveyance was executed.

Acknowledgment

This, too, is wholly a requirement of statute, and generally speaking, as in the case of attestation, is not essential to the validity of the conveyance. Ohio and Arizona are examples, however, of states in which it seems essential to the validity of the conveyance. Hout v. Hout, 20 Ohio St. 119; Lewis v. Herrera, 10 Ariz. 74, 85 P. 245, affirmed 208 U.S. 309, 28 S.Ct. 412, 52 L.Ed. 506. Quite commonly acknowledgment is made necessary to the validity of conveyances of certain special interests, as homesteads, or conveyances by certain persons, as married women. Aside from these, the requirement goes only to the effectiveness of the recording or to the proof required to make the instrument admissible in evidence in litigation. But these are matters of the utmost importance.

In general, *either* attestation *or* acknowledgment, but not both, is a condition precedent to effective recordation of an instrument and to its admission in evidence as a "self-proving" document—i.e., without the necessity for affirmative proof of due execution and delivery by the grantor. As a general rule, acknowledgment rather than attestation is

---

2. The *Winsted* case, on this point, rests on dubious grounds. See Watson v. Wells, 5 Conn. 468 (1825), relied upon in Winsted.

Compare French v. French, 3 N.H. 234 (1825), where a deed subscribed by only one witness was sustained as a covenant to stand seized under the Statute of Uses, although it purported to be a deed of lease and release. A statute provided that a conveyance of land "signed and sealed by the party granting the same, * * * and signed by two or more witnesses, and acknowledged by such grantor * * * and recorded at length * * * shall be valid to pass the same, without any other act, or ceremony in law whatever." The court held that the statutory form of conveyance was not exclusive, and that the legislature intended to allow the continued use of conveyances operating under the Statute of Uses—which, in effect, meant that the requirement as to two witnesses was a nullity.

utilized in order to meet the statutory prerequisites. But the state statutes should be consulted with respect to both attestation and acknowledgment.

Recital of Consideration in the Deed

It will be noted that the Michigan warranty deed form set out above contains a recital of the payment and receipt of consideration for the conveyance. Since a conveyance is not a contract—although it is the result of an agreement—it is never necessary to prove the payment of a consideration in order to establish the validity of the conveyance as between grantor and grantee. The owner of land has the same right to give it away as he has to sell it, provided he is not insolvent and will not be rendered insolvent by making the gift—in which case only his creditors can complain. A recent Florida decision, which seemingly holds that want of consideration rendered two deeds invalid, even though one had been recorded, is probably explainable on other grounds. Florida National Bank & Trust Co. v. Havris, 366 So.2d 491 (Fla.App.1979). But most deeds of conveyance expressly acknowledge the payment and receipt of a consideration—frequently nominal ("one dollar and other valuable consideration")—in order to rebut any implication of a resulting trust or use in favor of the grantor and to furnish support for the conveyance as a deed of bargain and sale under the Statute of Uses. Such acknowledgment while not conclusive as to the amount of the consideration actually paid (if any), is conclusive upon the parties for the purpose (if it should become important) of supporting the conveyance as a bargain and sale and vesting a beneficial interest in the grantee. Moreover, the presence of such a recital may give the grantee the benefit of a presumption that he is a purchaser for value under the recording statutes. The absence of such a recital, however, does not affect the grantee's right to show actual payment of a consideration for the conveyance, if it becomes important for him to do so.

Revenue Stamps

"Federal laws have at different periods required that revenue stamps be affixed to conveyances. An examiner [of title] need not, however, examine as to these, for the reason that their presence or absence, without a state statute on the subject, cannot affect the validity of the instrument, or the sufficiency of the record. Congress may prescribe proper penalties for failure to attach and cancel such stamps, but has no power, under the guise of penalties, to prescribe rules of evidence for states nor to limit methods or means by which property within their borders may be transferred." 2 Patton, Land Titles § 365 (2d ed. 1957).

Since January 1, 1968, federal revenue stamps have not been required on deeds of conveyance. See Int.Rev.Code § 4361 (1972). It may, nevertheless, be helpful to a title examiner to check the revenue stamps on deeds recorded prior to January 1, 1968, in order to discover what the true consideration for a conveyance was where the deed recites payment of only a nominal consideration.

State documentary stamps are required on deeds of conveyance in some jurisdictions.

SECTION 3. DESCRIPTION AND BOUNDARIES

If a written expression of intention is to be effectuated as a conveyance it must identify a subject of ownership which is being conveyed. Consideration has already been given to the idea that estates in land are the subject of conveyances but it is obvious that estates refer to the time and duration of ownership of particular places. Our inquiry here concerns the methods by which the particular places intended may be described.

Parties to a conveyance typically have a precise idea in mind and their writing undertakes to describe it. If the usual land transfer involved a settled establishment with clearly marked boundaries like the English manors of old, one would expect little difficulty in the process of selecting words which refer with fair precision to the area intended. Modern society is relatively fluid, however, and there is considerable pressure for new sizes and shapes of land ownership. As a consequence, reliance frequently must be placed on measurements of the surface of the earth which rarely admit of complete exactness.

You might say: "So what? Grant that the exact area described by a particular deed may be difficult to locate still, once the deed is recorded the area owned is identified and uncertainties are settled." This kind of statement assumes that recording involves an administrative procedure which serves to identify and register private ownerships of particular areas of land. If there were such a procedure, it might settle questions of who owned what by cataloguing all ownerships in the area. One might assume that particular ownerships, *as officially marked on the earth's surface,* could be evidenced by certificates of title which could be endorsed and passed on to new owners upon any sale or gift.

In point of fact, the usual system for evidencing land ownership in public records does not include these features. The usual system operates only to give certain persons notice of the content of private documents which purport to affect land titles. Deeds and other instruments of title are effective to do what a court holds they do in litigation between persons with conflicting claims and contentions. There is no administrative procedure which screens and interprets deeds and registers the determination of who owns what. It is true that all land in a particular political subdivision (usually counties) is mapped and catalogued for real property tax purposes, but while an effort is made to make sure that the tax listings are kept current with ownership as it is affected by recorded instruments, there is no necessary correlation between ownership for tax purposes and ownership between disputing claimants as determined by relevant title documents.

"But," you might ask, "if the difficulty lies in selecting words which admit of exact translation to lines on the ground, why can't we let the lines as actually drawn by surveyors and possessors control the matter?" The rub is the statute of frauds which prohibits transfers of ownership by the simple device of transferring possession, and the logic that the fringe areas of a parcel are as much the subject of land ownership as any other part thereof. With exceptions soon to be noted, words of description in private conveyances control boundary questions irrespective of the actual location of possessions and boundaries and irrespective of the suggestions concerning boundaries which may be found in public records which do not constitute part of the sense of deeds of conveyance.

"Still," you might continue, "is there any real problem? Modern methods of surveying eliminate most of the chances for error and surely parties to a land transaction do all that they can to see to it that the critical language of transfer coincides exactly with the area they intend."

But what happens? When an owner contracts to sell his land he must refer to the particular parcel he is selling with words. He might refer to it by street address but would such a reference, pin down the boundaries of the area he means? Such a description might be read to refer to the area commonly considered to be the lot on which the house bearing the address used is located. But, does the seller own exactly to the apparent line as marked by fences, shrubs and the like? If he does not, he may be unable to perform his contract. If he owns more, he'll be left with ownership he did not intend to keep. These considerations tend to compel a seller to use the words of description which appeared in the instrument by which he received title. Moreover, the seller is obliged to tender a "marketable title" to whatever he has contracted to sell. One test of marketability is the relative ease with which it can be demonstrated from previously recorded instruments of title that the deed tendered by the seller will invest the buyer with a title to the same land which the seller received from a prior owner. There is pressure from this circumstance to repeat the historic description of the parcel in question even though the parties may not know exactly what it embraces.

Will the buyer insist upon a re-survey of what he is getting? He might but the odds are that he will not. A survey entails expense and delay and if the seller has had no boundary difficulty, he is likely to assure the buyer that there is no problem. Moreover, what will a survey accomplish? A surveyor will use reasonable skill and judgment in locating a boundary in accordance with words which constitute the evidence of ownership. If the description he is following is an old one which refers to markings on the earth's surface which are no longer discernible, or contains contradictory or vague references, he can only give an opinion about the proper location of the boundary and there is no assurance that a court would agree with him if it were presented with a boundary dispute. The only surveys which settle matters beyond question are those which are adjudicated to mark a boundary in litigation in which a court has jurisdiction of the subject matter and all persons whose claims may be affected. Well advised purchasers frequently will have a survey made so that they will have an expert's appraisal of the risks involved in one assumption or another concerning the true location of their boundaries. A survey can be very valuable, but be sure that you understand its legal import.

With this background, you will be in better position to understand some of the twists and turns which the law concerning descriptions and boundaries involves, for this is law forged of attempts by courts to resolve boundary disputes in ways consistent with the underlying theory that land ownership cannot be altered without written instruments of conveyance. Perhaps when you have thought through the problems you can see some ways for improving the present system. It's far from clear that we can continue to indulge in the luxury of not worrying about some of its deficiencies.

The story of descriptions and boundaries starts with a look at some of the ways by which land is described by words, and the ways in which courts have resolved contradictions in descriptions. Then we'll look at some of the approaches to problems which arise when a description fits an area different from that to which the parties or their successors have adjusted their possessions.*

A. METHODS OF LAND DESCRIPTION

How does one describe places with written words? There is no single system or method and any arrangement of language which will enable a reader to locate the particular place intended (or possibly intended) is sufficient. Written words as distinguished from other means of communicating intention are required by the Statute of Frauds. The words manifestly cannot do more than to tell a person how to locate the place intended; it is impossible for the words to be the place itself. Therefore, it is frequently impossible to determine whether words of a description are indefinite until an attempt is made to apply them to the area to which they refer. Obviously one should have an area in mind before attempting to select words to describe it.

The common techniques of description involve references to objects located on the surface of the earth from which measurement is possible. A survey involves the location and measurement of one or more parcels of land by reference to existing monuments or monuments placed for the purpose by the surveyor where he is platting new areas or sizes. Vast portions of the United States located outside of the ultimately settled boundaries of the original thirteen states were surveyed pursuant to the statutes and regulations of the Federal government which authorized and directed surveys of the public land. Though there have been many important changes in the system through the years, the basic patterns may be seen by reference to the legislation of the Continental Congress in 1785 which provided for the survey of "the Western Territory." That legislation directed that the territory was to be divided into "townships of six miles square, by lines running due north and south, and others crossing them at right angles." Pursuant to the legislation applicable to a particular area and regulations of the govern-

---

* For a comprehensive discussion of "descriptions and boundaries," see 3 A.L.P. ch. V. See also Cunningham §§ 11.2, 11.8.

CORRECTION LINES AND GUIDE MERIDIANS *

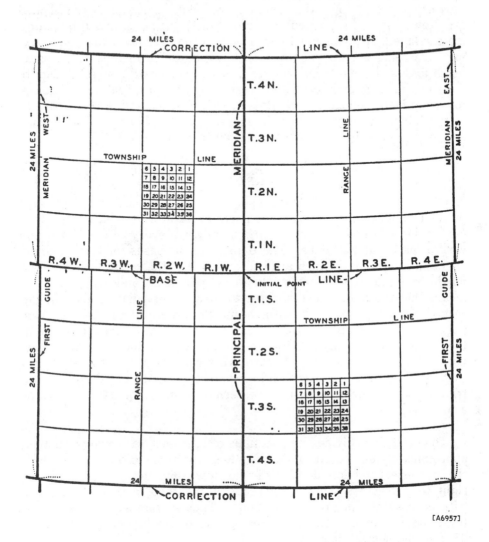

[A6957]

ment land office, an east-west "base-line" is established by astronomic measurement and marked with monuments. A principal meridian, a true north-south line, intersecting the base-line at a given point is marked. Thereafter all areas in the territory are located by reference to the intersection of the base-line and the principal meridian by a method which will be apparent directly. By 1959, thirty-two base-lines and thirty-five principal meridians had been established pursuant to federal legislation.

After a base-line and a principal meridian are located and surveyed monuments are located at six-mile intervals on the base-line and principal meridian, and true north-south lines and east-west lines at right an-

---

* Reprinted by permission of the Chicago Title & Trust Co. from their pamphlet, Legal Descriptions of Land, by Maley and Thuma.

gles thereto are run and their points of intersection marked. The north-south lines are called "range lines" and the east-west lines are called "township lines." The thirty-six-square-mile squares thus established are "townships." A particular tier of townships is described by counting the layers of townships between it and the base-line and by identifying it as being north or south of the base-line. Townships in the same north and south line form "ranges", and a particular "range" is identified by counting to it east and west from the principal meridian. A township identified as T–6–N, R–3–E, would be located in the sixth tier of townships north of the base-line and in the third range of townships east of the principal meridian in the territory described.

Because north-south lines were run on compass lines rather than in parallel, there is a convergence as one proceeds in the direction of the North Pole, which is offset by using "correction lines" (or "standard parallels"), located every 24 miles north and south of a base-line. Correspondingly "guide meridians" are usually run every 24 miles east and west of principal meridians. These lines are the bases for further township and range lines, which are laid out so that the range lines running north from the correction line begin at points six miles apart. This means that the south corners of the townships immediately above a correction line do not coincide with the north corners of the tier of townships lying immediately to the south. Also, because of the curvature of the earth, townships cannot form a perfect square, and all sections cannot contain 640 acres. For this and other reasons, it is provided by law that all deficiencies or excesses in area are to be deducted from or attributed to the northernmost or westernmost line of quarter sections in a township.

Townships are divided into sections of land each of which consists of approximately one square mile. Sections are numbered beginning with the north-east section in a particular township and proceeding from right to left across the top six sections and then in reverse direction with each succeeding row of sections. Thus section 31 of a particular township is located in the southwest corner of the township and section 36 is in the southeast corner.

Each section contains approximately 640 acres of land and quarter sections are thus composed of the familiar 160 acres typical of the size of many farms in the middle west. The dimensions of some of the commonly encountered areas produced by subdivisions formed by reference to the rectangular survey of the public lands and a convenient table of surveyor's measurements may be seen by the illustration on p. 775.

Surveys commonly encountered in today's practice involve *subdivisions* of areas located by the governmental survey, or, in cases where the land was never part of the public domain, of an area as defined by an ancient conveyance from one who owned the whole of that of which the area is a part. In subdivision work, the surveyor's job is to locate the outer limits of the area available for subdivision and to measure and divide it according to the wishes of the owner. Monuments defining the

SECTION OF LAND SHOWING ACREAGE
AND DISTANCES *

1 chain—4 rods or 66 feet

1 mile—320 rods or 5,280 feet

1 section—1 square mile or 640 acres

1 acre—160 square rods or 43,560 square feet

[A69956]

lines of streets and blocks may be planted and, ideally, monuments marking the line of each lot will also be located. The surveyor prepares a plat showing his work, certifies the accuracy of the plat and provides it to the owner. The owner then will seek to make the plat a part of the public land records so that his conveyances of areas defined by reference to the plat will provide purchasers with evidence available in the public land records of the proper location of their ownership. A conveyance of a lot described by reference to an unrecorded plat is possible, but the typical contract of sale of real estate requires the seller to tender a title the marketability of which appears from duly recorded documents and instruments. A full description might appear as follows: "Land located in Washtenaw County, State of Michigan, and more par-

---

* Reprinted by permission of the Chicago Title & Trust Co. from their pamphlet, Legal Descriptions of Land, by Maley and Thuma.

ticularly described as follows: Lots 1 and 2 of Pine Tree Acres Subdivision, part of the southwest $\frac{1}{4}$ of section 32, Township 2 South, Range 6 East, Harrison Townships, according to the plat thereof as recorded in Liber 11 of Plats, page 4, Washtenaw County Records."

The point was made earlier that a survey does not establish boundaries unless it is adjudicated to do so. The governmental survey of public lands has been held to establish boundaries, however. A conveyance of land described "according to the governmental survey thereof" is a conveyance of the area as determined by the monuments as actually located by the official surveyor, irrespective of whether the monuments were located where the discipline of the system indicates they should have been located and irrespective of where plats, maps and field notes of the surveyor might suggest they were located. The actual location of monuments located in a private survey which is later referred to in a conveyance may be determinative also, but the question to be faced here is where the words of description refer to the located monuments. If the reference is to a plat or map, the lines pictured thereon located and measured as suggested in the plat may be determinative even though the plat fails to describe the physical survey it was supposed to follow. Of course, if the plat shows or refers to physical monuments as well as to measurements as means by which lines are to be located and the calls are inconsistent, we face a problem of deciding which of two conflicting meanings is the true one.

Sometimes persons convey land without reference to a survey. One way is by reference to ownership as, for example, in a deed to "all of the lands owned by the grantor herein in Miller township as of the date hereof." This kind of description has been aptly described as a "Mother Hubbard description." If the "cupboard is bare," the deed describes nothing. Sometimes land is described by reference to abutting owners. Obviously these kinds of references send readers to other records and serious ambiguities concerning the time and manner of proof of the ownership referred to may be involved.

A description by "metes and bounds" is a description constituted of words describing the measure and location of sidelines. The boundary lines may be identified by their coincidence with a physical characteristic (a form of monument) as, for example, "bounded on the west by the east line of Plum Alley," or by directions to go from a particular place in a particular direction and for a distance stipulated. An example of the latter would be "beginning at a point south 10° 15 minutes west, 81.5 ft. from a post located at the intersection of the south line of Elm Street and the east line of Main Street; thence south 2° east 150 ft. to a point; thence east 2° north 100 ft. to a point; thence north 2° west 150 ft. to a point; thence west 2° south to the point of beginning." Obviously the description is incomplete unless it includes reference to the political subdivision in which Elm and Main Streets intersect.

It should also be obvious that great care must be taken in a metes-and-bounds description so that the "calls" for the several component lines, when followed in proper sequence, will bring you back to the point of beginning. In other words, the description must "close." If on the face of a deed, or when applied to the ground, the description does not close, a court faces a serious problem, which at times it can resolve by proper construction of one or more of the several calls, or if not, may result in a decision that the conveyance is void.

Problems

1. What is the size, shape and location of land described as follows: Situated in Livingston County, State of Michigan and being the south ½ of the southwest ¼ of the southeast ¼ of the southwest ¼ of Section 36, T–2–N, R–5–E? Also, the northeast ¼ of the northwest ¼ of Section 1, T–1–N, R–5–E?

2. Suppose the owner of a 40-acre parcel bounded on the east and north by land of A and on the south and west by land of B executes a deed describing the following: "A certain piece or tract of land, grist mill and all fixtures thereunto, and one store-house, 28 by 100 feet long, lying and being in Brassfield township, Granville County, N.C., and adjoining the lands of A and B, said lot to contain three acres." Does this language describe any particular tract or direct how a particular tract is to be located? See Harris v. Woodard, 130 N.C. 580, 41 S.E. 790 (1902).

B. DESCRIPTIONS IN ACTION

HOBAN v. CABLE

Supreme Court of Michigan, 1894.
102 Mich. 206, 60 N.W. 466.

MONTGOMERY, J. This is an action of ejectment. The trial was had before a jury, and a verdict rendered for the plaintiff. The defendant brings error. The assignments of error are numerous, but have been carefully grouped by the appellant's counsel, so that the questions may be dealt with under a few heads. The diagram on the following page will furnish an aid to an understanding of the points involved.

The record contains the substance of all the testimony, from which it appears that plaintiff derived title from the heirs of Laurie McLeod, to whom a conveyance was made by Eliza R. McLeod, in 1862, Eliza R. McLeod being then in possession, and the apparent owner. The defendant claims title by adverse possession, and also claims that by a subsequent conveyance to him by Eliza R. McLeod of lot No. 293 the title passed to him, and in this connection contends that the deed to Laurie McLeod contained no sufficient description of any property, and that the record of the deed was, therefore, no notice to him of any right in Laurie McLeod. * * *

As the deed to Laurie McLeod was first recorded, and as defendant claims it in fact read when executed, the description of the land was as follows:

"Beginning on Market street, between the lot hereby intended to be conveyed and a lot confirmed by the government of the United States to Ambrose R. Davenport; thence north, 62 degrees 15 minutes west, 158.96 feet; thence south, 31 degrees west, 60 feet; thence south, 62 degrees 15 minutes west, 158.96 feet, to Market street; thence along said street north, 27 degrees 55 minutes east, to the place of beginning."

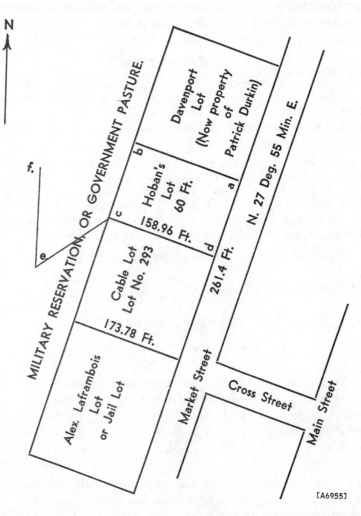

[A6955]

Was this a sufficient description, or must the deed be treated as a nullity? The starting point is definite. The first line, to point "b," is also certain, as is the line between points "b" and "c." But, if the direction of the next line is followed as given in the instrument, the terminus is at "e," and the line named in the succeeding portion of the description would end at "f." But the course given after reaching point "c" is not the only means of identification adopted. That line is described as terminating at Market street. If we exclude the words indicative of the direction of the line, and carry the line in the most direct course to Market street, we have not only a line answering to the other terms of the deed, but one which, with its extension, incloses something, which is, by the terms of the deed, "a lot intended to be conveyed," and which, to answer the terms of the portion of the description relating to the starting point, must lie next to "a lot confirmed by the government of the United States to Ambrose R. Davenport." To make this clearer, the deed contains the statement that from the terminus of the third line named in the description the boundary shall extend along Market street to the place of beginning. We think the intent of the grantor is clear, and that the deed is not a nullity for want of a sufficient description. See Anderson v. Baughman, 7 Mich. 69, 74 Am.Dec. 699; Cooper v. Bigly, 13 Mich. 463; Dwight v. Tyler, 49 Mich. 614, 14 N.W. 567.

A number of defendant's points depend upon this, and it becomes unnecessary to treat in detail some of his assignments of error. The deed being valid to convey the land, the record was notice to subsequent purchasers.

One of the conveyances under which plaintiff claims contained a description as follows:

"A lot 60 feet wide on Market street and 128.90 feet deep, being the north end of lot 293 in the village of Mackinac."

This is claimed to be insufficient, but we think there is no mistaking the land intended to be conveyed. * * *

We think no error to the prejudice of defendant was committed.

The judgment will be affirmed, with costs, and the case remanded.

HALL v. EATON

Supreme Judicial Court of Massachusetts, 1885.
139 Mass. 217, 29 N.E. 660.

Writ of entry to recover a lot of land in the city of Worcester. Plea, nul disseisin. Trial in the Superior Court, without a jury, before Blodgett, J., who allowed a bill of exceptions, in substance as follows:

The land in dispute was a triangular tract on the northerly side of Dix Street, marked on a plan used at the trial, a copy of which is printed in the margin, as "Demanded Premises." It appeared that all the land lying next northerly of Dix Street and between Wachusett Street on the east and Goulding Street on the west was formerly owned by Henry Goulding, and was divided into lots and sold by his executors. The tenants' lot was at the corner of Dix Street and Wachusett Street, and the demandant's lot was part of the lot next westerly, and the question was as to the westerly boundary of the tenants' lot and the easterly boundary of the demandant's lot, under the following deeds:

On February 20, 1869, Goulding's executors conveyed the corner lot to Blackmer and Kelley, (under whom the tenants derive their title,) by the following description: "A certain lot of land situated in the city of Worcester, on the westerly side of Wachusett Street and northerly side of Dix Street, bounded and described as follows, to wit: beginning at the southeasterly corner of the lot conveyed, and at the intersection of said streets; thence running northerly by Wachusett Street one hundred and thirty-four feet, to land of the heirs of Henry Goulding; thence running westerly by land of the heirs of said Goulding, sixty feet; then running southerly by land of said heirs at right angles to said Dix Street one hundred and twenty-five feet to Dix Street; then running easterly by Dix Street sixty-one feet more or less to the first-mentioned bound, containing 7770 feet more or less."

On October 8, 1869, said executors conveyed the residue of the land between the tenants' lot and Goulding Street to one King, by a deed which contained the following description: "Lot of land on the northerly side of Dix Street, bounded as follows: beginning at the southeasterly corner of the lot at a corner of land of Kelley and Blackmer and running westerly on Dix Street one hundred and eighty feet to a new street about to be made; thence turning and running northerly on said new street one hundred and twelve and a half feet, to land belonging to the estate of the late Henry Goulding; thence turning and running easterly on said Goulding estate one hundred and eighty feet, to land of Kelley and Blackmer; thence turning and running southerly on land of said Kelley and Blackmer one hundred and twenty-five feet, to the place of beginning on said Dix Street."

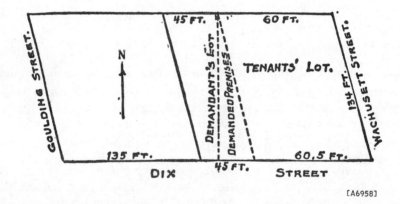

[A6958]

It was agreed that the new street referred to was Goulding Street, and the corner of Goulding Street and Dix Street was a known and fixed bound.

On May 8, 1871, King conveyed to the demandant a part of said lot, forty-five feet wide on Dix Street, bounded as follows: "beginning at the southeasterly corner thereof at corner of land of Kelley and Black-mer, and at a point one hundred and eighty feet distant from the easter-ly line of Goulding Street, thence northerly on land of Kelley and Black-mer one hundred and twenty-five feet, to land of the estate of Henry Goulding; thence westerly on said land of Goulding forty-five feet; thence southerly and parallel with the first-described line one hundred and twenty-five more or less, to said Dix Street; thence easterly on Dix Street forty-five feet, to the place of beginning."

The corner of Dix Street and Wachusett Street was a known and fixed bound, and the northerly line of Dix Street was a known and fixed line.

If the third line described in the deed of the executors to Blackmer and Kelley is drawn at right angles to Dix Street, it strikes a point on Dix Street eighty feet and fifty-two one-hundredths of a foot from Wa-chusett Street, and one hundred and sixty-one feet and ninety-four one-hundredths of a foot from Goulding Street. In such case, the tenants' line on Dix Street is eighty feet and fifty-two one-hundredths of a foot in length, and is shown by the westerly dotted line, and their lot contains 9101 square feet.

If the third line described in said deed to Blackmer and Kelley is drawn so as to strike Dix Street one hundred and eighty feet easterly from Goulding Street, the tenants' line on Dix Street is sixty feet and a half in length, and their lot contains exactly 7770 square feet.

The demandant offered evidence tending to show that, before the several lots were sold by the executors of Henry Goulding, they prepared a plan of them, which was produced at the trial; and it was testified by one of the executors, that the lots were sold by said plan, but there were no monuments at the corners of the lots when the deeds were given, and there was no evidence that Blackmer and Kelley saw the plan before they took their deed. Said plan showed the tenants' lot to have a line of only sixty feet and a half on Dix Street, and showed that the westerly line did not make a right angle with Dix Street.

The demandant also offered evidence tending to show that, in the year 1876, he erected a fence between his said lot and the tenants' lot (Kelley, who had bought Blackmer's interest, then being the owner of the tenants' lot), and by Kelley's consent it was placed on the line as claimed by the demandant, and remained there several years, and until removed by the tenants a short time before this suit was brought.

The demandant asked the judge to rule that it was a question of fact, on all the evidence, whether the tenants' westerly line was to be drawn at right angles to Dix Street, and asked a finding in fact that it was to be drawn at an angle to said Dix Street, so as to strike said street sixty and a half feet from Wachusett Street. The judge ruled, as matter of law, that the said line was to be drawn at a right angle to Dix Street, without regard to the evidence outside of the deeds; and found for the tenants. The demandant alleged exceptions.

W. ALLEN, J. The courses of the lines on Wachusett Street and Dix Street are fixed on the land, and fix the angle contained by them. There is nothing on the land to fix the course of the second or of the third line, for it does not appear that the line of the land of the heirs of Henry Goulding mentioned is fixed. The description in the deed gives the length of the first, second, and third lines, which there is nothing to control, and the angle contained by the third and fourth lines. There is no difficulty in locating this description upon the land, and it makes the length of the fourth line eighty feet and fifty-two one-hundredths of a foot, and the contents of the lot 9101 square feet. The description in the deed gives the length of the fourth line as "sixty-one feet more or less," and the contents of the lot as "7770 feet more or less." This discrepancy of one third in the length of the front line of the lot, and one fifth in its contents, could not have been intended, although the length and dimensions are only approximately given, and it is obvious that there is a mistake, either in the angle given, or in the length of the fourth line.

We do not regard the statement of the quantity of the land as very material. It is the computation of the contents of the figure described in the deed, but which cannot be produced on the land. The fact that to give exactly the quantity of land mentioned when the other particulars of the description are applied to the land, the third line must intersect the fourth at an obtuse angle, and the fourth line must be sixty feet and a half in length, goes to show, what is otherwise sufficiently apparent, that no such discrepancy in the length was intended. There was a mistake either in the angle given or in the length of the fourth line; they cannot both be applied to the land, though either of them may be, and the question is which must be rejected.

The question to be determined is the intention shown in the language of the deed, in the light of the situation of the land and the circumstances of the transaction, and sometimes with the aid of declarations and conduct of the parties in relation to the subject-matter. The rule that monuments, in a description in a deed, control courses and distances, is founded on the consideration that that construction is more likely to express the intention of the parties. The intention to run a line to a fixed object is more obvious, and the parties are less likely to be mistaken in regard to it than in running a given distance or by a given course. But, where the circumstances show that the controlling intention was otherwise, the rule is not applied. * * * So far as the question is as to the relative effect to be given to a course and a distance, neither has in itself any advantage over the other as showing a governing intent. Whether the one in a given case shall outweigh the other, as showing the intention of the parties, must depend upon the circumstances existing at the time.

The angle formed by Dix Street and Wachusett Street is an acute angle; the lot was a corner lot, the front on Dix Street. In laying it out, it would be natural either to have the third line in the description parallel to Wachusett Street, or at a right angle with Dix Street. The latter is for the advantage of the purchasers. The deed shows that the parties had that, and not the other, in mind. Not only is the third line not said to be parallel with Wachusett Street, but it appears that it was not intended to be. The parties understood that the angle at the corner of the streets was an acute angle, and that making the other angle on Dix Street a right angle, would require the line on that street to be longer than the rear line, and they said that the angle should be a right angle, and therefore that the line should be longer. It was not merely giving a course to the third line, but it was expressly fixing the shape of the lot. The length of the fourth line was left indefinite, and to be determined by the angle which was fixed. It is true that the given angle requires a longer line than was supposed; but the angle and the shape of the lot, and not the length of the line, appear to have been the controlling considerations. See Noble v. Googins, 99 Mass. 231.

It is contended by the plaintiff, that it is a case of latent ambiguity, which may be explained by parol evidence. If the difference were between a given course of the third line and measurement of the fourth, it might present such a case, but neither is given. The course of the third line was not run, but it was to intersect Dix Street at a right angle; the fourth line was not measured, but its length was estimated, and apparently estimated as the distance between the point where the third line must meet Dix Street to form a right angle with it and the first corner. A mistake was made in the estimate of the distance. It would seem that the angle was so material a particular in the description of the lot, that the expressed intention in regard to it could not be made doubtful by a mistake in the estimate of the length of the fourth line, which was determined by it; but it is not necessary to decide this. As the case stood at the trial, and upon the evidence offered, the court properly ruled that, as matter of law, the third line was to be at a right angle with Dix Street, without regard to the evidence outside the deed.

The plaintiff relied upon evidence that the executors of Goulding, before the lot was sold, made a plan of this and other lots, by which it appeared that the fourth line was sixty feet and a half in length, and that the angle formed by the third line and Dix Street was an obtuse angle. This plan is not referred to in the deed, and was not seen by the purchasers. The only effect of this evidence would be to show that the grantors knew that the lot described in the deed did not correspond with the one on the plan, and did not inform the grantees.

Eight months after the conveyance to Blackmer and Kelley, the executors conveyed to one King the adjoining lot on Dix Street, extending westerly to a way to be laid out, called Goulding Street, bounding easterly on the land of Blackmer and Kelley and the line on Dix Street, and the rear lines being each one hundred and eighty feet in length. This evidence may tend to show that the executors intended that the third line of the Blackmer and Kelley lot should be parallel with Goulding Street, but such intention was not known to Blackmer and Kelley, and was not expressed or indicated in the deed to them. The demandant also relied upon evidence that King afterwards conveyed to the demandant a lot adjoining Blackmer and Kelley, described as beginning at a corner of their land on Dix Street one hundred and eighty feet from Goulding Street, and that several years after, and seven years after the conveyance to Blackmer and Kelley, and after Kelley had acquired Blackmer's interest, the demandant put up a fence between his lot and Kelley's and, with Kelley's consent, put it on the line now claimed by the demandant, where it remained for several years.

We do not see that any of this evidence is competent to control the construction indicated by the deed itself. It is not sufficient to show a practical construction of the deed by the parties to it, nor an admission by the tenants' grantor which can bind the tenants, nor a mutual agreement as to the boundary, and occupation accordingly. * * * Whether evidence of the construction of the deed by the acts of the parties by locating the third line on the land, or fixing the point of its intersection with Dix Street by a monument or otherwise, would present a question for the jury, we need not consider, because the evidence offered was not sufficient to show such acts, and the question presented was one of law upon the construction of the deed.

A majority of the court are of opinion that the ruling excepted to was correct.

Exceptions overruled.

Problem

An area bounded on the east and west by rows of marked trees and ultimately found to be 180' wide, was severed by a conveyance which described: "the westerly portion (of the area in question) measuring $7\frac{1}{2}$ rods on the road (on which the parcel fronted), the property conveyed being one-half of the piece of property formerly owned by X (a reference to the tree bounded area)." Does the grantee receive an area with $7\frac{1}{2}$ rods (113.75') of frontage or one with a 90' frontage? See Morse v. Kelley, 305 Mass. 504, 26 N.E.2d 326 (1940).

C. WAY AND WATER BOUNDARIES

(1) In General

It is a general rule of construction that a reference to a public way as a boundary is a reference to the center line of the way when the grantor owns so far. That he may own so far assumes that the public way is an easement only and that private ownership subject to the easement remains. Such private ownership is of virtually no significance unless and until the way is abandoned by the public. However, abandonment occurs with surprising frequency and unless the rule of construction described were followed, a grantor who described his land as he knew it, e.g., as being bounded by the highway, would be left with a strip of ownership of virtually no meaning to him and which he probably would not realize that he had retained.

Where the road is mentioned, as in the case supposed, the rule coincides with a more general rule relating to references to monuments having some area but not enough to lead to the conclusion that the area was important to the grantor. Reference to a post, for example, is construed as reference to the center of the post. However, where a line is described by metes and bounds and, when located, is exactly coincident with sideline of a highway, there is more room for doubt as to whether the written description admits of construction that it refers to the center of the way. Nonetheless, the pressure to avoid the conclusion that the grantor retained an isolated strip of ownership of little significance to him has been great enough to lead courts to conclude that such a description carries the grantor's ownership to the center of the way if he owned so far.

Starting with the basic assumption that reference to a public highway is to be construed as a reference to the center of the highway, the courts have looked at language before them to determine if it reveals the grantor's intention to reserve to himself ownership underlying the highway. Though this approach suggests no particular difficulty, trouble is caused by the view, supposedly consistent with the basic analysis suggested above, that a description which refers to the *side* of a highway is to be distinguished from one which simply refers to the highway itself. Thus if the call of a deed suggests a line commencing at the side line of a highway and running along the side line of a highway to another point, the conclusion has been reached that this call carries the grantor's ownership only to the side of the highway and leaves him with the ownership of the area covered by the highway. One does not get to the question of whether the grantor clearly manifested the intent to keep the land covered by the highway, for, under this theory, he has not used language which admits of the construction of extending the subject of his conveyance to the center of the highway. Happily, there are decisions which have rejected the logic of distinguishing between a reference to a road and a reference to the side of a road in favor of reaching a conclusion that the grantor who conveys land abutting an existing, public way has passed ownership to the center of the road if he owned so far unless he has explicitly excluded such ownership.

When the words of a conveyance describe a boundary adjacent to a private road or alley or to an unopened or abandoned public way, problems of considerable difficulty arise. Arguably, the grantor has a greater interest in land on which such a road or alley is located than he would have in land subject to an easement of way then being exercised by the public. Arguably less reason exists for construing his references to the road or alley as references to the center thereof and there are decisions in some of the states to the effect that the rules applicable to highway descriptions have no application to descriptions of land bounded by ways of the sort mentioned. There is substantial authority to the contrary, however.

A second point needs to be made. A public or private way may be established along the boundary of a parcel so that more than one half of the way is situated thereon but with the unencumbered portion of the parcel located wholly on one side of the way. If, in such a case, the owner of the parcel conveys the area adjacent to the street or alley so established without reserving the part of his ownership which is subject to the easement, does his ownership to the center of the way pass or does the conveyance carry all of his ownership beneath the way? It should be obvious that the reasons for saying that the deed carries his ownership to the center here apply to carry his ownership so far as it extends beneath the road and the cases have so concluded.

The interpretation of words describing the boundaries of land adjacent to streams or bodies of water present similar problems. At the core of the matter is the assumption that private ownership exists in submerged lands, an assumption which is clearly applicable if the water in question is non-tidal and non-navigable. If the water in question is tidal, the American decisions, generally speaking, recognize that private ownerships stop at the high water mark. If the water in question is non-tidal but navigable some jurisdictions recognize private ownership as extending beneath the navigable water while others conclude that the public owns the fee of the land beneath the water. Where private ownership exists beneath the lake or stream in question, it is burdened by the fact that other owners whose lands give them access to the water have rights in common in the use of the water. As a result, ownership of the land underneath the water has relatively little significance and is not likely to be the subject of an intended reservation or exception where the owner sells his land abutting the water source. Accordingly, a description of land as being bounded by a stream or lake is interpreted to include all of grantor's ownership to contiguous sub-merged land to the extent that such land is allocated to the area transferred. Again, however, a difficulty has arisen from descriptions carrying a boundary "by the shore" of a body of water and decisions can be found where such descriptions have been held not to carry the grantor's title beneath the water of the stream or lake in question.

See 3 A.L.P. §§ 12.112, 12.113.

(2) Accretion

Accretion is the increase of land "by the addition of portions of soil, by gradual deposition through the operation of natural causes, to that already in the possession of the owner." The deposit itself is generally referred to as "alluvion." The implication is that the land thus created belongs to the owner of the land to which it attached. The title by which such ownership is acquired is, therefore, "original" rather than "derivative," and in that sense may be classified with adverse possession. Since, however, the problem that usually arises out of accretions is one of boundaries, the subject is briefly noted here.

If the space now occupied by the new land was owned by the owner of the land to which it was added, the conclusion of ownership, as above stated, needs no justification. If, however, that space was not so owned, the conclusion is not quite so obvious.

The leading case is Gifford v. Yarborough, 5 Bing. 163, 130 Eng.Rep. 1023 (H. of L.1828). The court there decided that the ownership of the land which touched the sea carried with it the ownership of new land resulting from the accretion process, though the new land occupied space that had been within the territorial rights of the King as "lord of the sea * * *, and also owner of all land to which no individual has acquired a right," etc. The conclusion was based upon a combination of several considerations: (a) public policy, in that the new land, even though small in quantity, would thereby be made immediately productive; (b) fairness to the owner of the upland in that the chance of gain offsets his risk of loss if the water's action instead of adding to his land, were to wear it away; (c) preservation of the owner's valuable privileges, as a littoral or riparian owner, to the uses of the water.

When the water gradually subsides, thus adding usable land to the upland, a process known as "reliction," the same principle applies.

There is little, if any, dissent from the view that, when a boundary line is the center, the low-water mark, the high-water mark, or any other water line, any shifting of that line by gradual and imperceptible change, whether it be by the gradual recession of the water—reliction, or by the gradual extension of the land by the deposit of alluvial soil—accretion, results in a corresponding shift in the boundary line.

The situation is markedly different if the boundary of the claimant's land was fixed at a definite line without regard to the water line.

Not infrequently it is stressed that the accretion or reliction must be a result of natural causes. The fact that action by some one other than the claimant of the benefit of the accretion caused or contributed to the formation should not, however, prejudice his claims.

In cases of sudden and violent changes in the water line ("avulsion"), the boundary is left unaffected. A new channel across a neck of land formed by a bend in the Mississippi river gradually deepened and widened until finally it became the main channel. This was treated as an avulsion so far as any effect upon boundaries was concerned, though the process had been prolonged.

In Valder v. Wallis, 196 Neb. 222, 242 N.W.2d 112 (1976), the Missouri River moved westward creating an island and leaving a "chute" between the island and the Iowa mainland. This was found to be avulsion which changed no boundaries. Later accretion developed eastward from the island and westward from the Iowa mainland. It was held that the accretion to the island belonged to the owner of the island until it met accretion from the mainland, leaving the thread of the chute as a boundary.

A stream, some line of which is a boundary between landowners, may move gradually so far that one owner may lose his ownership completely. An interesting question may arise thereafter if by some chance of nature the side movement of the stream is reversed. Or land owned by X which borders on the sea may be gradually washed away, leaving O's land, which was in the rear, now bordered by the water. Later accretions to O's land may be held to belong to O, though they extend his land into space once owned and occupied by X. See Winkle v. Mitera, 195 Neb. 821, 241 N.W.2d 329 (1976).

See generally 3 A.L.P. § 15.26 et seq.; Annotation, 78 A.L.R.3d 604 (1977).

D. LOCATION OF BOUNDARIES WHERE DESCRIPTION IS INCONSISTENT WITH THE PURPOSES OR ACTS OF THE PARTIES

(1) Reformation for Mistake

It is generally conceded that a deed may be reformed in equity when its terms are the result of a mutual mistake. The parol evidence rule is not thought to bar evidence tending to show mistake or fraud, and the Statute of Frauds frequently has been held inapplicable to enforcement of the real understanding between parties as established in an action for reformation. It is usually said that clear and convincing evidence is necessary to prove mistake and the equitable defenses of laches, bona fide purchase, and the like are available if suggested by the proofs. The problem of when a deed must be reformed in order that the boundary lines intended by the parties may be made the true boundary lines is a complicated one. Its proper answer in any given case involves a determination of whether parol evidence might not be admissible in an action involving construction, or whether the boundary has not been determined by acts of the parties under one of the several theories discussed herein. Nor is it always easy to determine whether the standards and defenses applicable to an action for reformation or the standards and defenses available to an action for construction are being applied in a given case. Boundary questions frequently come up in equitable proceedings to quiet title or to secure a partition of land and unless litigants state the applicable theories succinctly a confusing blend of reformation and construction may be the result. If the defense of bona fide purchase is injected into litigation the choice between reformation and construction would seem to be forced upon the court. As was observed in Cities Service Oil Company v. Dunlap, 115 F.2d 720 (1941): "An innocent purchaser is protected from reformation in equity, but not from construction at law of deeds as written. If the muniments of title he holds are beset with ambiguity, a court of law will resolve that ambiguity according to its own methods." The other side of this proposition is that, even in equity, an innocent purchaser takes subject to ambiguities and doubts of description if the process by which the meaning of the parties is ascertained is viewed as construction rather than reformation.

(2) Adverse Possession

The subject of acquisition of ownership of land by adverse possession is considered elsewhere in the course. It involves the idea that a wrongful possession of another's land which continues until the expiration of the period during which the rightful owner may sue to recover possession, may ripen into ownership for the possessor. When a party to a conveyance physically possesses to boundaries which are located so as to include more land than the language of description entitles him to, he may be an adverse possessor. As such, in time he will become the owner of the excess, and his lawful boundaries will coincide with what he conceives to be his. The principal impediments to moving to a conclusion of title by adverse possession from long continued possession in excess of that indicated by title documents are the following: (1) the question of whether the claimant has possessed the excess area in question. The supposed, but mistaken, boundary may have been marked by a fence enclosing an area of obvious possession, but it may as well have been a tree or trees, a stream, a road, or as marked by stakes or posts placed to show the supposed boundary but hardly constituting the limits of a possession in fact; (2) questions of privity between successive claimants of the excess area. Commonly, the possessions of two or more persons who have succeeded each other as claimants of the area in question need to be tacked together to make one continuous possession extending for the required statutory period. More than likely, the deeds exchanged between such successive holders will repeat the description which the first possessor exceeded by taking possession of the area in question. Hence, these deeds will not show the requisite succession of adverse possession and there may be difficulty in showing privity between the successive possessors with reference to the area in question; (3) the question of whether possession taken under the mistaken assumption that the possessor owned the area involved is adverse.

(3) The Practical Location of Boundaries

LOVERKAMP v. LOVERKAMP

Supreme Court of Illinois, 1943.
381 Ill. 467, 45 N.E.2d 871.

MURPHY, Justice. This is an appeal from a judgment entered in an ejectment suit in the circuit court of Massac county. The chain of title, under which the respective parties claim, runs to a common source in Charles Redmeier, Jr. On and prior to December 5, 1916, Redmeier owned other lands and the north half of the northeast quarter of section twenty-four, township fifteen in said county. On that date, he and his wife conveyed by warranty deed the northwest quarter of the northeast quarter of said section twenty-four to his son Henry. Plaintiff's chain of title is as follows: Charles Redmeier, Jr., to Henry Redmeier, he to Charles Loverkamp, and Charles Loverkamp to plaintiff. Defendant's chain of title is Charles Redmeier, Jr., by descent to Emma Redmeier, his widow, Henry Redmeier, a son, and Lena Dummeier, a daughter, and they to defendant, Lester Loverkamp. All of the conveyances in plaintiff's chain of title described the tract conveyed as the northwest quarter of the northeast quarter and all the deeds in defendant's chain of title described the land conveyed as the northeast quarter of the northeast quarter.

A public highway enters the northeast quarter on the north line at or near the dividing line between the northwest quarter and the northeast quarter of said quarter section and extends due south six chains and then in a southwesterly direction intersecting the south line of the north half of the northeast quarter and then on south. The divergence of the road from a north and south line creates a triangular-shaped tract containing three and one-half acres, which is the tract involved in this litigation. The cause was tried before the court without a jury and resulted in a finding and judgment in favor of defendant.

The complaint contained two counts, the first of which alleged defendant unlawfully withheld from the plaintiff possession of the northwest quarter of the northeast quarter, etc. Count 2 alleged defendant unlawfully withheld from the plaintiff a certain parcel of land described, to-wit:

"All that portion of the Northwest one-fourth ($\frac{1}{4}$) of the Northeast Quarter ($\frac{1}{4}$) of Section No. Twenty-four (24) Township Fifteen (15) South, Range Five (5) East of the Third Principal Meridian, in Massac County, Illinois, which lies East, Southeasterly and South of the public road that runs through said forty acre tract, as the same now exists, containing Three and One Half (3.5) acres, more or less; said parcel of ground being more particularly described; A parcel of ground described as follows:

"Beginning Six (6) chains South of the Northeast corner of the Northwest one-fourth ($\frac{1}{4}$) of the Northeast Quarter ($\frac{1}{4}$) of Section Twenty-four (24), in Township Fifteen (15) South, Range Five (5) East of the Third Principal Meridian, on the East side of the public highway;

thence South 86° 30′ East to the southeast corner of the Northwest one-fourth ($\frac{1}{4}$) of the Northeast one-fourth ($\frac{1}{4}$) of the aforesaid section, Township and Range; thence West 87° East to the public road; thence in a Northeasterly direction, along the public road to the place of beginning, being 3.5 acres, more or less."

Defendant's answer traversed the allegations of unlawful withholding in both counts. Defendant's special defense No. 1 alleged he was possessed of and claimed to be the owner of all of the north one-half of the northeast quarter lying east of the public road, and pleaded the twenty-year statute of limitations of adverse possession. Ill.Rev.Stat. 1941, c. 83, §§ 1–3. Defendant's special defense No. 2, filed after the evidence was heard and the cause argued orally, alleged the defendant claimed to own all of the north one-half of the northeast quarter lying east of the public road and alleged that the dividing line between the northwest quarter of the northeast quarter and the northeast quarter of the northeast quarter was fixed by agreement of Charles Redmeier and Henry Redmeier, which agreement was made when Charles Redmeier sold the land to Henry in 1916, and that by said agreement the public road marked the dividing line between the two tracts. Defendant claimed he was the owner of all of the north one-half located east of the roadway by virtue of said agreement and twenty years' adverse possession by him and his predecessors in title. Plaintiff traversed the material facts in both of defendant's special defenses.

Defendant introduced the evidence of Emma Redmeier, the widow of Charles Redmeier, Jr., Henry Redmeier, a son, and Nora Redmeier, Henry's wife. The evidence of these witnesses tended to prove that a few days prior to the execution of the deed from Charles Redmeier and wife to Henry Redmeier, December 5, 1916, Henry Redmeier and Charles Redmeier, Jr., agreed that the road right-of-way should be the dividing line between the northwest quarter of the northeast quarter and the northeast quarter of the northeast quarter. Plaintiff objected to the introduction of such evidence and now urges its admission and consideration as grounds for reversal. Defendant offered the evidence on the theory that whenever a boundary line between adjoining owners of land is unascertained or in dispute, the parties may establish it by parol agreement and possession in pursuance of that agreement, and contends that when a line is so established it will be binding on the parties and their privies.

It is well established that the rule sought to be invoked by defendant cannot be applied unless at least one of two conditions exists, namely: there must be a dispute between the adjoining owners as to the location of the line, or that the line has not been ascertained. * * * The application of the rule is limited to the establishment of a disputed line or the locating of an unascertained line.

The line between the northwest quarter of the northeast quarter and the northeast quarter of the northeast quarter was not marked by government survey but that survey showed witness marks and monuments by which the location of boundary lines of the whole northeast quarter could be readily located. The boundary line of the northeast quarter being thus determined, it was a simple matter to determine the location of the lines between the quarters of the northeast quarter. For many years prior to December 5, 1916, Charles Redmeier, Jr., owned the whole of the north half of the quarter and he did not establish the line between the two forties. He constructed fences on either side of the road disregarding the location of any of the quarter-quarter lines. Consequently, when he and Henry had their conversation a few days prior to the execution of the deed relative to the location of the line, no dispute had then arisen as to its location.

The elements of the second condition under which the rule can be applied were not present. Appellee contends the evidence of the surveyor and others leaves a doubt as to whether the road right-of-way was on the quarter-quarter line for the first six chains south from the north line of the quarter. The evidence as to the location of the public road on the quarter section to the north and the evidence of the surveyor is convincing that the roadway is on the quarter-quarter line for that distance. Although the line between the two quarter quarters had not been definitely located by measurement or survey, yet the parties knew it would be equidistant from the east and west boundary line of the quarter. When located it would necessarily be a straight line, but all the witnesses who were interrogated as to that matter testified that after the first six chains from the north line of the quarter, the road veered to the west and continued in a southwesterly course to the south line. There is no evidence that any part of the three and one-half acres is on the northeast quarter of the northeast quarter. To give effect to the oral agreement between Charles and Henry Redmeier as testified to by the three witnesses would be to hold that the terms of the oral agreement should overcome the provisions in the deed to convey the northwest quarter of the northeast quarter. The oral agreement would take three and one-half acres from the land deeded from Charles Redmeier to Henry Redmeier. It is clear oral agreements can not be introduced in evidence and given such effect in ejectment suits.

The case of Kesl v. Cobine, 313 Ill. 438, 145 N.E. 148, was an ejectment action where the deed of one of the parties included the disputed strip. Evidence was offered by the other party to prove that the common grantor stated before the conveyances were made that the property line between the two tracts would be a certain designated place, which would indicate the strip in dispute as the property of the one offering the evidence. The trial court rejected the introduction of such evidence. In affirming the ruling this court said: "Appellant's deed did not convey to him the land in question, but appellees' deed from the same grantor did convey to them the disputed land. If it was intended to convey the strip to appellant and not to appellees, that fact could not be shown in defense of an ejectment suit; nor was it competent to prove the grantor of appellant told him, before he purchased, that the line of his land would be 25 feet east of the residence, which would give him the disputed tract." The evidence of the three Redmeier witnesses in reference to the agreement between Charles Redmeier and Henry Redmeier was not admissible in this action.

To overcome plaintiff's record title to the disputed tract, defendant claims benefit of the twenty-year statute of limitations. During Charles Redmeier, Jr.'s, ownership of the north half of the quarter there was a house and other farm buildings on the northwest quarter of the northeast quarter just west of that part of the highway that is located on the quarter-quarter section line. He occupied this as a home. In 1917, subsequent to the making of the conveyance to his son, he erected a house and other farm buildings across the road on the northeast quarter of the northeast quarter and occupied it as a residence until his death July 12, 1933. Thereafter, the widow, Emma Redmeier, occupied it as a home until she conveyed the northeast quarter of the northeast quarter to the defendant in 1937. None of the buildings was located on the tract in dispute and it does not appear that it was ever separately enclosed by a fence. During the lifetime of Charles Redmeier, Jr., Henry Redmeier farmed his father's land located in the northeast quarter of the northeast quarter and the disputed area was included in this farming arrangement. After the death of his father, he continued as a tenant of Emma Redmeier.

From the facts related it is obvious that Charles Redmeier's possession of the disputed strip was not hostile in its inception but was a permissive use, granted by the son to the father. Adverse possession cannot be made out by inference or by implication. The proof to be established must be clear, positive and unequivocal. All presumptions are in favor of the true owner. To entitle the person urging the statute of limitations as a defense the evidence must show that the possession was hostile, actual, visible, notorious and exclusive, and that it has been continuous for twenty years or more under claim of ownership and without any recognition of the title of the true owner.   *   *   *

It should also be noted that during the lifetime of Charles Redmeier, Jr., Henry Redmeier at various dates executed three mortgages creating a lien on the land described as the northwest quarter of the northeast quarter. The last mortgage was foreclosed, and the complaint, decree and master's deed, which was executed November 15, 1938, described the whole of the northwest quarter of the northeast quarter. Near the close of the period of redemption, Henry Redmeier executed a quitclaim deed to the mortgagee, Charles Loverkamp, in which he described the whole of the northwest quarter of the northeast quarter. It is also significant that when the children of Charles Redmeier conveyed to the widow August 12, 1933, they gave a warranty deed describing the land conveyed as the northeast quarter of the northeast quarter. From these facts and others of record, it is evident that the defendant has not shown a right to claim the title to the disputed tract by reason of adverse possession under the twenty-year statute of limitations.

For the reasons assigned the judgment of the circuit court is reversed and the cause remanded with directions to proceed in accordance with the views expressed.

Reversed and remanded, with directions.

Note

In view of the difficulties involved in describing land with such accuracy as to admit of no doubt or conflict over the exact location of particular boundaries, it was only natural that neighboring landowners would undertake to resolve questions about their common boundaries by means short of a lawsuit. Normally they do this informally and often without adequate thought about the ultimate consequences. At best they may expressly agree upon a boundary and then adjust their subsequent use of their respective parcels accordingly. Or without express agreement, one or both of two abutting landowners may erect a barrier, such as a fence or hedge, and they both may act as though such barrier were the boundary. Despite the obvious dangers in encouraging such practices, the courts have been impressed by the public policy to be served by sanctioning such amicable efforts to resolve doubts and differences which can lead to rancorous controversies.

A considerable body of law has therefore developed which provides legal sanction to the efforts of adjacent landowners to provide a "practical location" of their common boundaries. It should be obvious that unless any doctrine of practical location is carefully circumscribed, it can become a means of allowing parties to convey land informally and in violation of the Statutes of Frauds. This was the problem which bothered the court in the Loverkamp case supra. Several theories have been evolved, however, which permit the informal establishment of boundaries so as to bind the parties involved and their successors and preclude contradiction by the later assertion of the terms of a conveyance under which one of the parties is claiming title. See Browder, The Practical Location of Boundaries, 56 Mich.L.Rev. 487 (1958).

(1) **Parol Agreement.** It is recognized by many courts that a boundary line can be conclusively determined by a parol agreement between the affected parties. But in order to safeguard the requirements of the Statute of Frauds, certain conditions must exist prior to such an agreement, and certain further conduct must follow the agreement in order to perfect it. Some courts have said that the agreement must be entered into for the purpose of settling a dispute about the boundary. But most of the courts which recognize parol agreements merely require that the true boundary was uncertain or unascertained or unsettled or doubtful, as it is variously put. Such a vague requirement can cause trouble, as you may note in the Loverkamp case supra. It is not clear whether it is enough that the parties were in doubt in their own minds, or whether such doubt was justified by the facts; in other words, whether they must have made some effort to locate the true boundary.

A more serious complication has been introduced by some, but fortunately not by all, courts. They have said that the agreement is vitiated by proof that it was founded on a mistaken belief of the parties that they had found the true line. This sounds rather like the so-called "mistake" rule in adverse possession. It is doubtful what mistake means in this context, but apparently it introduces a very subtle distinction. If the parties have a survey run and conclude to accept its results on the basis that the surveyor discovered the true line, they are not bound by the agreement upon a later discovery of an error in the survey. In other words, the parties cannot be held to have fixed a boundary when their only purpose was to find it. On the other hand, if at the time of their agreement the parties are still in doubt about the true boundary, and therefore by their agreement undertake to settle the matter, their agreement will be binding. This distinction is unfortunate because it may vitiate a practical location in that type of case which seems most deserving of judicial protection, that is, where the parties have done as much as they could do, short of a lawsuit, to apply their titles to the ground. It also means that the parties are forced to walk a tight rope in this regard, for if they procure a survey and simply ignore it and agree upon a different line, they may be subject to the charge that their agreement was not made to resolve their doubt or uncertainty, but simply amounted to an effort to transfer land without a writing.

It is also clear that if the parties consent to some fence or other barrier for any reason short of fixing their boundary permanently, they will not be bound. It should be obvious why predictability of decision in these cases is very low.

Assuming that the above requirements are met, it is not enough that the parties simply agree upon a line. They must thereafter "acquiesce" in it or possess according to it. This normally means that the line must be visibly designated on the ground, although this usually is not stated as a requirement. It is usually held, however, that no special period of acquiescence is required, and a period short of that required for adverse possession may suffice. A few courts require acquiescence for the statutory period, but on the other hand, a few courts require no period of acquiescence at all, but only that the parties shall have "executed" their agreement by their acts or have changed their position in reliance on it.

The special sense of the word "agreement" in this context must be understood. These so-called agreements are not essentially promissory. They imply merely an express and mutual assent to a line on the ground as a boundary.

(2) **Acquiescence.** An even larger number of courts hold that a boundary can be established simply by acquiescence in a line on the ground as a boundary. Some courts say that the period of acquiescence is the period required for adverse possession. Others have referred merely to "long acquiescence," which usually has been at least as long as the statutory period.

The courts are not agreed, however, upon the theory which would justify the determination of a boundary on this basis. Some courts say that such acquiescence is merely to be regarded as sufficient evidence to prove a boundary agreement; that is, that an agreement is to be implied from their conduct. Usually this also means that the requirements for boundary agreements, such as pre-existing dispute or uncertainty respecting the boundary, are also implied and need not be proven. Generally, however, the courts have not carried over to these cases the so-called "mistake" rule, referred to in connection with express boundary agreements.

But this relatively simple rule does leave plenty of room for argument over what is meant by acquiescence. Is there a difference, for example, between the acquiescence required to support an express agreement and that involved when acquiescence alone is relied on? The term carries a passive connotation. But it also connotes that something significant has been done which the parties have acquiesced in. Perhaps the best way of putting the requirement in brief is that it means a mutual recognition, by words or conduct or both, over a period of time, of a line on the ground as a boundary. So obviously the distinction between express and implied boundary agreements often is not easy to draw. Emphasis surely must be put on the need for mutuality of acquiescence. It is also implicit here too that the acceptance of a line which restricts one's possession does not necessarily mean acceptance of the line as a permanent boundary or as defining the right to possession. And parties' acts are likely to be equivocal in this regard, which leaves considerable room for maneuver by a court, which in turn affects the predictability of result in these cases.

Other courts have imposed the same requirements, but justified them by an entirely different theory. They have resorted to the analogy of adverse possession and treated acquiescence as basically prescriptive, that is, as invoking a "rule of repose." It is sometimes said that long acquiescence is evidence of the true line which is so strong that the parties are precluded from offering evidence to the contrary. Others have dealt with the question in such a way as to leave some doubt whether they regarded acquiescence as distinguishable from adverse possession. Still others have treated the two doctrines as related but distinct, which means that the acquiescence doctrine can sometimes be relied on where one or more of the requirements for adverse possession are absent.

Under any of these variants of the prescriptive theory the courts are also relieved of any need to discover a boundary agreement, express or implied. But the differences in theory do not seem appreciably to affect the nature of the proof required for acquiescence.

(3) **Estoppel.** Courts on occasion have resolved boundary disputes by invoking the term "estoppel" against the party who tries to prove the true line. Among the various meanings of this term, the equitable doctrine of "estoppel in pais" is the closest analogy. That doctrine requires a representation of a material fact by one person to another, who does not know the true facts, and a substantial change in position by the latter in reliance thereon. This doctrine is referred to only as an analogy because often in the boundary cases there is not a full compliance with the stated requirements. Rather the courts have placed major emphasis on the change in position by one party in reliance on a line as a boundary, where the party estopped has by words or conduct or even silence indicated that he too regarded the line as a boundary. In fact, some courts have announced the doctrine where the facts would be sufficient for a practical location by agreement or acquiescence, but also show a change in position by one party in reliance thereon, such as by the erection of valuable improvements or even merely by purchasing land affected thereby.

Effect on Subsequent Purchasers. Under any of the above three types of practical location, the question arises as to the effect thereof upon the titles of successors in interest of the original parties thereto. The answer seems to be clear, although more often than not it is taken for granted rather than expressly decided. Successors in interest are bound and do benefit by the practical location made by their predecessors. Among the relatively small number of cases in which the question has been expressly raised, some courts even hold to this result without regard to the question of notice of the practical location. Others hold a successor bound only if he had notice of the line, but constructive or inquiry notice may be sufficient by virtue merely of the visibility of the line on the ground.

A related but different and more serious question is the possible effect of a practical location, not upon the direct successors of the parties thereto, but upon other boundaries which were not specifically the subject of the practical location, but which, for one reason or another may be dependent upon the boundary which has been located. See Daley v. Gruber, 361 Mich. 358, 104 N.W.2d 807 (1960).

(4) *Plat v. Survey*

ARNOLD v. HANSON

District Court of Appeal, Third District, California, 1949.
91 Cal.App.2d 15, 204 P.2d 97.

ADAMS, Presiding Justice. This is an appeal by defendants from a judgment quieting plaintiffs' title to lots 19 and 20, Block 1, of Clear

Lake Highlands Club House addition in Lake County, which judgment also ordered defendants to restore to its original position the line fence between lots 20 and 21, which fence had been constructed by plaintiffs and moved by defendants; and further awarded plaintiffs damages in the sum of $200 caused by the acts of defendants in cutting down plaintiffs' berry bushes and a tree, and moving the fence.

The controversy involves the location of the boundary line between lots 20 and 21. In April, 1924 Clear Lake Highlands, Inc., owned a large tract of land on or near the shore of Clear Lake which it surveyed and subdivided into numerous lots and blocks. The survey was made by D.R. Morgan, a licensed surveyor, assisted by Carol Hale as transit man; and thereafter a plat of the survey showing lots, blocks and streets, which plat had been made by surveyor Morgan, was approved by the board of supervisors and filed for record July 25, 1924. The lots in question, namely, lots 19, 20 and 21, face Hambaugh Avenue, sometimes called Lake Shore Drive, on the east, while the west ends of the lots are covered by the water of Clear Lake. As shown on the plat, lots 4 to 26, inclusive, are 50 feet in width and rectangular in shape.

When the tract was surveyed into lots in April, 1924, wooden stakes were driven into the ground to mark their corners and side lines. In 1931 Carol Hale, with John T. LaBree who was or had been vice president of Clear Lake Highlands, Inc., subdivider of the tract, and was then owner of lots 19 and 20, located the original wooden stakes, most of which were still in place, and beside them drove into the ground three-quarter inch iron pipe stakes about thirty inches long.

In 1937 Mr. LaBree and his wife contracted with plaintiffs for the purchase of lots 19 and 20, and when the parties were negotiating for such sale Mr. LaBree showed the iron stakes to Mr. Arnold who accepted such stakes as marking the boundaries of the lots. They went into possession in 1937, built a house upon lot 20, erected a fence along the south line for a distance of approximately 81 feet from Hambaugh Avenue, planted berry bushes and a tree near the fence, and later placed a stone wall along the remaining portion of the south boundary of the lot extending toward the lake. Plaintiffs completed the purchase and obtained a deed of conveyance in 1943.

In the spring of 1945 defendants acquired lot 21, a 50 foot lot facing on Hambaugh Avenue and paralleling lot 20 on the south. In the same year they engaged a licensed surveyor, Hamlin A. Witham, to survey lot 21. Mr. Witham concluded that the official plat (plaintiffs' Exhibit 1 in evidence) did not correctly match with monuments on the land, to wit, the iron pipes of which there is one at practically each corner, every 50 feet. He concluded that the bearing on the original plat was off, that the survey had been carelessly made, and that while the lots were staked as approximately shown by the original iron pipes on the front of the lots, the bearings on the original plat were erroneous. He admitted at the trial that his survey would disturb the side lines of lots in the tract numbered from 11 to 21, inclusive, and would have the effect of throwing the line between lots 20 and 21 over onto lot 20, and taking therefrom a triangular section 10.30 feet wide at a point 147 feet from Hambaugh Avenue and 18.24 feet at the rear of the lot.

On receiving the report of surveyor Witham, defendants, without consultation with plaintiffs, took down plaintiffs' fence, removed the berry bushes and tree, and began the construction of a garage extending over into plaintiffs' lot 20.

This action was thereupon brought by plaintiffs, and after trial by the court, without a jury, findings in favor of plaintiffs were filed and the judgment from which this appeal has been taken was entered.

We think that the judgment must be affirmed.

In Kaiser v. Dalto, 140 Cal. 167, 172, 73 P. 828, the court said that the survey as made in the field, and the lines as actually run on the surface of the earth at the time the blocks were surveyed and the plats filed must control; that the parties who own the property have a right to rely upon such lines and monuments, and that, when established they control courses and distances. And in Burke v. McCowen, 115 Cal. 481, 486, 47 P. 367, it was held that where a survey as made and marked upon the ground conflicts with the plat, the survey must prevail. There Whiting v. Gardner, 80 Cal. 78, 22 P. 71, was cited, in which latter case it was said that in the absence of evidence to the contrary it will be presumed that the map correctly represents the survey, and the latter need not be looked to; but that if it be shown that a discrepancy exists between the map and the survey upon which it is based, the survey must prevail. A comparable case from Iowa is Tomlinson v. Golden, 157 Iowa 237, 138 N.W. 448, where it was held that where stakes were set in the ground to indicate boundaries of the lots, and a purchaser found the stakes and relied thereon as monuments fixing the boundaries, as did others, such stakes must control though in a later survey the same surveyor found a discrepancy between the stakes and his field notes—that the field notes and paper plat must give way thereto. In support of its ruling that court cited, among other cases, Burke v. McCowen, supra, and O'Farrel v. Harney, 51 Cal. 125.

In accord are Brauss v. Fayette County, 164 Iowa 606, 146 N.W. 6, and Langle v. Brauch, 193 Iowa 140, 185 N.W. 28, 29. In the latter case the court said: "It is well established that the lines as actually run by the original government surveyor become the true boundary lines. If these lines can be ascertained and determined by reason of monuments erected by the government surveyor, they will control, and courses, distances, measurements, plats, and field notes must all yield to such established monuments."

Appellants' surveyor testified that the official plat does not match the monuments on the land, that is, the iron stakes set in the ground. Under the foregoing authorities the monuments must prevail. This surveyor admitted that his survey would disturb the lines of all of the lots from 11 to 21, inclusive, many of which lots had already been sold. All of those lots are admittedly of the same width, and their side lines are parallel.

Furthermore, we are of the opinion that the trial court was not compelled to accept the testimony of appellants' surveyor as controlling on questions of fact which were involved, but was justified in accepting the monuments set by the original survey as correct. Lohman v. Lohman, 29 Cal.2d 144, 149, 173 P.2d 657.

The only other question raised by appellants is that the judgment is so vague as to be unintelligible because it does not describe plaintiffs' lots by metes and bounds so as to fix the division line between lots 20 and 21—that it does not describe that line so that appellants will know where to replace the fence which it removed. The language used by this court in Morris v. George, 57 Cal.App.2d 665, 677, 135 P.2d 195, 201, is applicable, to wit: that "if appellants desired to have what they were required to do described with such meticulous particularity as their brief would indicate, they should have had a detailed survey and description of said ditch made before they destroyed it." Furthermore, the findings (Finding IV) recite that defendants pulled up the iron pipe on the south line of lot 20, about 91 feet west of the street, and moved the fence over 5 feet 8 inches north from where the iron pipe was driven in the ground on the south line, 91 feet from the street. Also all of the lots numbered 11 to 21, inclusive, are 50 feet wide, and rectangular in shape, so appellants should have no difficulty in finding the original location of the fence and restoring it, as the judgment directs, "to its original position."

The judgment is affirmed.

Questions

1. If the description in the deed to the plaintiffs in Arnold v. Hanson was by reference to the numbers of the lots which they purchased, and as is customary, concluded with the reference "as shown on recorded plat thereof" or the equivalent, what objection could be taken to allowing the location of the stakes on the ground to control the boundaries as shown on the plat? Note the quotation by the court from the opinion in the Iowa case, Langle v. Brauch. Does a case involving government survey lines rest on all fours with a case such as Arnold v. Hanson? It appears in Arnold v. Hanson that the plaintiffs were shown the boundary stakes before they purchased. Do you regard this as an important fact? See Browder, Boundaries: Description v. Survey, 53 Mich.L. Rev. 647 (1955).

2. Do you see any other ground for the court's decision in Arnold v. Hanson than the one offered by the court?

SECTION 4. DELIVERY, CONDITIONAL DEEDS, AND ESCROWS *

A. NONCOMMERCIAL TRANSACTIONS

McMAHON v. DORSEY

Supreme Court of Michigan, 1958.
353 Mich. 623, 91 N.W.2d 893.

SMITH, Justice. This case turns upon the delivery of a deed to certain real property. The deed was found in a safety-deposit box leased in the name of William J. McMahon, the deceased grantor, and Patrick

* See 3 A.L.P. §§ 12.64–12.71; Cunningham § 11.3.

Dorsey, who, with his wife Hazel, as tenants by the entireties, were the grantees. The plaintiffs are Mr. McMahon's sole heirs.

Some 30 years ago, Mr. McMahon took into his home defendant Patrick Dorsey and Patrick's sister Bernice, then about 10 and 11½ years of age, respectively. Here they lived during the years of their youth. Approximately 4 years after graduation from high school Bernice married and left the home. Patrick, however, never left the farm. He had worked it since he was a child, along with Mr. McMahon, and even after his marriage continued to reside on the place, Mr. McMahon having deeded him an acre out of the home farm, on which Patrick built his own home. As Mr. McMahon grew older he was able to do only the lighter work, Patrick doing the rest, in addition to factory work. The trial court found that the farming proceeds were split in no regularized manner, "the farm being worked on a father-and-son arrangement."

On September 18, 1954, two years before his death, Mr. McMahon tidied up his affairs. On this date he executed the deed before us, conveying to Patrick and his wife the farm (120 acres less the one acre previously given Patrick). On this date, also, Patrick and Hazel signed a note promising to pay to each of William's sisters the sum of $500, "to be paid within 90 days following the death of William McMahon; if any of the above named individuals predecease William McMahon, then there shall be no obligation to pay the sum herein specified to the party who is deceased, but only to those remaining." These sums have in fact been paid.

As we have noted, the deed in controversy was found in the joint McMahon-Dorsey safety-deposit box after William McMahon's death and it was thereafter recorded by defendant Patrick Dorsey. Mr. McMahon's will, duly admitted to probate in the probate court for the county of St. Clair, gave the farm property to his wife for life (she, however, had predeceased him), remainder to his "living brothers and sisters, share and share alike." The plaintiffs herein, who are, as we noted, William's sole heirs at law, filed a bill of complaint seeking to have the deed set aside and for other ancillary equitable relief. The trial chancellor having found for defendants, plaintiffs are before us on a general appeal. They here assert that there was never a valid delivery of the deed by William McMahon to Patrick, that such has not been established by a preponderance of the evidence, and that there is no evidence to show that William McMahon ever relinquished control of the purported deed.

The formalism with which the courts anciently treated questions of delivery has been largely abandoned. The modern inquiry places but little emphasis upon manual tradition. It has come to be recognized that, as in other situations involving the concept of "delivery" (e.g., the making of gifts), the significance of delivery is its manifestation of the grantor's intent that the instrument be "a completed legal act." See Aigler's comment in 18 Mich.L.Rev. 314. The Illinois court phrased the problem with accuracy in Berigan v. Berrigan, 413 Ill. 204, 215, 108 N.E.2d 438, 444, when it held:

"Delivery, in its legal and technical connotation, is a vital part of the execution of a deed and is essential to the operation and validity of the conveyance. We have stated many times that delivery of a deed is strictly a matter of the intention of the grantor as manifested and evidenced by the words, acts and circumstances surrounding the transaction. * * * Manual transfer of the deed is not indispensable to delivery but is evidence of delivery. The controlling factor in determining the question of delivery in all cases is the intention of the grantor, and this is particularly the case where the grantor makes a voluntary conveyance to grantees who are very naturally the subject of his bounty. In such cases, courts of equity are strongly inclined to carry out this intention unless to do so would run contrary to very convincing evidence or well-established legal principles."

* * *

Likewise, we have held repeatedly that "the whole object of delivery is to indicate an intent by the grantor to give effect to the instrument." Reed v. Mack, 344 Mich. 391, 73 N.W.2d 917, 920; Gibson v. Dymon, 281 Mich. 137, 274 N.W. 739.

In the case before us, however, we are not forced to the determination of intent from ambiguous circumstances. We have the unequivocal statement of the grantor himself as to his intention. The witness was Mr. Clifford Halsey, an adjoining neighbor, and justice of the peace, who had known Mr. McMahon for some 50 years, and with whom the latter had often discussed his business matters. We will proceed in the words of the record:

"Q. Mr. Halsey, you did have a conversation, you say, with Mr. McMahon then concerning his disposition of this farm, did you? A. Yes.

"Q. And what did he tell you? A. He told me that he had deeded the farm to Pat; he also had his name on the bonds.

"Q. And the reason for that would be why, did he tell you? A. Because he felt that he owed it to him. He said if Pat had not stayed there with him he would have been up against it for help."

The trial chancellor, upon consideration of this and other testimony and exhibits, concluded that "The intention and the desires of William J. McMahon are most obvious," and determined as a matter of fact "that the deed was delivered by William J. McMahon to Patrick Dorsey in William J. McMahon's lifetime." We cannot say that he was in error.

Decree affirmed. Costs to appellees.

Note

Compare Manhattan Life Insurance Co. v. Continental Insurance Co., 33 N.Y.2d 370, 353 N.Y.S.2d 161, 308 N.E.2d 682 (1974), where it was held that giving a deed to the grantor's attorney "to be held by him" was not a good delivery, despite the fact that the deed was also recorded.

In Driskill v. Forbes, 566 S.W.2d 90 (Tex.Civ.App.1978), where a grantor recorded a deed and then retained it in his possession, the court noted decisions where recording was held to be sufficient delivery, but said that where a grantor retains possession of a deed after recording, there must be further inquiry into the intent with which the acts relied on were performed, and that evidence may show that the grantor did not intend the deed to be operative when filed for record. Compare Hanifin v. Marsden, 297 N.W.2d 172 (S.D.1981), where a father contracted to sell a ranch to his son and the son's wife. On the same date the grantor and his wife executed a quitclaim deed of the land to the son and his wife. Later the grantor, after a period during which the son managed the ranch under a lease from his father, the latter decided to give the land to his son. His attorney told him that a deed would be required. Several months later, the grantor filed the quitclaim deed for record. Thereafter until his death three years later the grantor received payments under the contract from his son. Upon the grantor's death, his daughter sued the son to recover half of the balance due under the contract. The judgment of the trial court for the defendant was affirmed, on the basis that the deed had been delivered when it was filed for record. Asserting that execution, acknowledgment, and recording of a deed are prima facie evidence of delivery, the acceptance of contract payments thereafter was found not sufficient rebutting evidence. Evidence showed gifts totalling $24,500 by the grantor over the years to his daughter, leading the court to concede the possible inference that the grantor in making such gifts and in accepting contract payments from his son was trying to equalize the benefits going to his two children.

ERBACH et al. v. BRAUER

Supreme Court of Wisconsin, 1925.
188 Wis. 312, 206 N.W. 62.

The action is one brought by the plaintiffs, the heirs at law of Henry Erbach, deceased, against the defendant, Roman Brauer, to cancel, annul, and set aside a certain deed. The evidence in the case is practically undisputed, and it appears therefrom that Henry Erbach, on the 13th day of September, 1915, was the owner of certain real estate in the Thirteenth ward of the city of Milwaukee, of the value of about $5,000; that at the time of his death, and for some period prior thereto, he occupied a part of said premises, and sublet the balance thereof to the parents of the defendant. Some time prior to the death of the deceased his health was impaired, and from that time until his death the mother of the defendant extended her aid and assistance to the deceased, both in and about the portion of the house occupied by him, and in furnishing him with meals, and during that time the defendant's parents paid no rent for that portion of the premises occupied by them. The defendant, who at the time of the execution of the deed was a minor of the age of about two years, was a special favorite of the deceased.

The deed was signed and sealed by the grantor, was properly witnessed and acknowledged, and inclosed in a sealed envelope, and was then deposited by the grantor in his lock box in the Home Savings Bank of Milwaukee, on which envelope there appeared the following in the handwriting of the deceased:

"Sept. 13, 1915.

"This belong to Mrs. John Brauer and Roman Brauer.

"Henry Erbach.

"She must open it."

The envelope which contained the deed also had inclosed the following letter, written in the handwriting of the deceased:

"Mil. Sept. 15, 1915.

"Dear Mrs. Clara Brauer: Take this deed to the Court House and have it recorded for My Friend Roman and you take care of your Home for Him it is My Wish.

"Your Friend   Henry Erbach.

"Denket an Mich."

The three last words under the signature are in the German language, and the translation is as follows: "Think of me." The deceased alone had access to this lock box, and it could be opened only by means of his key and that of the master key in the possession of the bank. No one but the witnesses, up to the time of the deceased's death, had any knowledge of the execution of the deed. Shortly after the death of the deceased the lock box was opened in the presence of Phillip Erbach, one of the plaintiffs, Mr. Wells, the president of the bank, and Clara Brauer, the mother of the defendant, and the deed contained in the envelope was taken by Mrs. Brauer and recorded.

The trial court found, among other things:

"That the quitclaim deed from Henry Erbach to Roman Brauer on the 13th day of September, 1915, conveying the premises described in the complaint, is null and void for want of delivery thereof, and that no title to said premises passed to the defendant by reason of said deed."

Judgment was therefore entered as above indicated, and from such judgment the defendant has prosecuted this appeal.

DOERFLER, J. (after stating the facts as above). The sole issue involved herein consists of whether or not there was a delivery of this deed. Defendant's counsel take the position that the writings on the envelope and in the letter clearly establish an intention on the part of the deceased of a delivery of the deed at the time of its execution. Plaintiffs' counsel, however, argue that these writings do not manifest an intention as to delivery as of the date of the execution of the instrument, but that they become operative, and speak as of the time of the death of the deceased, and are therefore in the nature of a testamentary disposition. The authorities seem to hold that whether or not there was a delivery is clearly a question of intention, so that, if these writings can be construed as a present intention of delivery as of the date of the deed, a delivery has resulted, even though no manual delivery was effected, and the deed itself at all times up to the death of the deceased remained in the actual possession of the grantor. * * *

This court, in Bogie v. Bogie, 35 Wis. 659, in an opinion rendered by Chief Justice Ryan, quotes with approval the following from 1 Coke, Litt. 36A:

"As a deed may be delivered to the party without words, so may a deed be delivered by words without any act of delivery."

In the case of Cooper et al. v. Jackson et al., 4 Wis. 550, cited in the brief of counsel for the defendant, this court cites with approval the following language, used in the opinion in the case of Doe ex dem. Garnons v. Knight, 5 Barn. & Cress. 671:

"That when a party to any instrument seals it, and declares in the presence of a witness that he delivers it as his deed, but keeps it in his possession, and there is nothing to qualify that, or to show that the executing party did not intend it to operate immediately, except the keeping the deed in his hands, it is a valid and effectual delivery; and delivery to the party who is to take the deed, or to any person for his use, is not essential. * * *"

Bearing in mind the law as it appears from the foregoing citations of authority and opinions, we will now endeavor to determine whether under the facts and circumstances of this case a delivery has resulted. The deed was executed in the presence of a notary, who acted as a witness, and the other subscribing witness. No one but the subscribing witnesses ever knew or heard of either the execution or the existence of the deed. The deed itself contains no language expressive of a delivery or of an intention of delivery.* There is no evidence in the record that at the time of the execution of the deed any oral statement was made by the grantor from which a delivery or an intention of delivery could be presumed. Neither the grantee named in the deed, nor his parents, had any information prior to the grantor's death of this deed. The first intimation that they received of the existence of the deed came to them when the lock box was opened after the grantor's death. Furthermore, the deed remained in the sole possession of the grantor from the time of its execution to the time of his death, in his lock box, to which no one had access but himself. With these facts in mind, there appears not the slightest evidence from which it can be inferred or said that an intention of delivery was shown as of the date of the execution of the instrument. On the contrary, it appears quite conclusive to us that there was no delivery.

While the writing on the outside of the envelope was dated September 13, 1915, does it speak of that date, or of the date when it shall be found in his lock box after his death? This writing, in the light of all the evidence, and particularly in view of the grantor's continued possession, not only of the deed, but of the property, and his failure to orally or in writing express an intention of delivery as of the date of the execution of the deed, and his failure to notify or inform any one but the witnesses that the deed had been executed, is not only persuasive to our minds, but conclusive as a matter of law, that the grantor intended the deed to become effective only after his death.

This case is not ruled by the Cooper case, supra, for there was no declaration in the presence of a witness or witnesses that he delivered the deed as his deed. * * * The language on the envelope must be

---

* This language is criticized in 1940 Wis. L.Rev. 288, because of the implication therein that a delivery might be found on the basis of an intent expressed in the deed itself. This article discusses the general problem of evidence in establishing delivery.

construed as meaning that the deed shall belong to the parties therein indicated at the time when the deed shall be found in the lock box, after the grantor's death. To our minds, the letter, instead of evidencing an intention of a present delivery as of its date, shows a contrary intention, for in it he directs the mother of the defendant to take the deed and have it recorded, and also directs her to take care of the home for the defendant. Here also must be borne in mind all of the evidence referred to in that part of this opinion where we construe the writing on the envelope. It was after the death of the deceased that the grantor intended that a constructive delivery should take place, and at such time and no other was the mother directed to take care of the home for the defendant.

While the continued possession of the deed by the grantor is not conclusive of a nonintention of delivery, it is nevertheless of strong and persuasive evidentiary value in many instances. From the time of the execution of the deed, up to the time of the grantor's death, he occupied the property and had the use thereof. During all this time he could have destroyed the deed, which, however, had there been a delivery, would not have affected the title. It must also be conceded that, if there had been words used evidencing a present delivery, even though the grantee or his parents had no knowledge thereof, the destruction of the deed would not have affected the title, and such destruction would constitute both a legal and a moral wrong against the grantee.

It is claimed by the learned counsel for the defendant that the presumption of delivery, where an infant is a grantee, is much stronger than where a deed is executed to an adult. This undoubtedly is the law. He cites 8 R.C.L. § 70, pp. 1010, 1011. A quotation from this last authority is set forth in defendant's brief, and in it will be found the following:

"The current of decisions has gone far to enable the courts to carry out the intention of the donor and to protect the rights of the donee, but they have never presumed delivery without some evidence that it was the intention of the donor, and probably no case can be found warranting the conclusion that a delivery has been made merely because the grantor has signed and sealed the instrument, without any further circumstances indicative of his intention."

In our opinion the case before us is much stronger for the plaintiffs than a case where a deed is executed to an infant, and where the deed is retained in the possession of the grantor until the time of his death, and where there is nothing to indicate an intention to pass present title, for, as we construe the evidence in this case, an intention of present delivery was not only not expressed, but, on the contrary, an intention in the nature of a testamentary disposition to the effect that the title was not to pass until after the death of the deceased was expressed.

It would be useless to review all of the cases decided by this court, or a considerable number of them, where the question of delivery was raised, for each case must stand or fall upon its own facts.

The judgment of the lower court is affirmed.

Questions

1. Suppose in McMahon v. Dorsey, supra, the grantor had placed his deed in a safe-deposit box in his own name and to which he alone had access. Do you think the same result could have been reached?

2. If delivery does not necessarily require a transfer of possession of the deed from grantor to grantee, but depends upon the intention of the grantor, what sort of intention must we seek? How does delivery of deeds differ from the requirement of delivery in gifts of chattels?

THOMAS v. WILLIAMS

Supreme Court of Minnesota, 1908.
105 Minn. 88, 117 N.W. 155.

START, C.J. This is an appeal from an order of the district court of the county of Blue Earth denying the defendant Williams' motion for a new trial in an action to recover the rent stipulated in a lease of certain real estate situate in the city of Mankato. The trial court upon the facts found, which are not here controverted, directed judgment for the plaintiff for the amount claimed. The sole question presented by the record is whether the plaintiff's intestate, John J. Lewis, died seised of the demised premises. If he did, the order appealed from was right; otherwise, erroneous.

On November 1, 1905, John J. Lewis, then being the owner of the premises, executed and delivered a quitclaim deed to the defendant Williams, which was duly recorded the next day. The here material provisions of the deed are the following: "The said party of the first part [Lewis], in consideration of the sum of one dollar and other valuable consideration to him in hand paid by the said party of the second part [Williams] the receipt whereof is hereby acknowledged, does hereby grant, bargain, sell, remise, release, quitclaim, and convey unto the said party of the second part, his heirs and assigns, forever, all the right of survivorship in and to the following tract or parcel of land: [Here followed a description of the demised premises.] To have and to hold the above quitclaimed premises, together with all the hereditaments and appurtenances thereunto belonging or in any wise appertaining, unto the said party of the second part, his heirs and assigns, forever, in case he survives said John J. Lewis. The intent of this deed being to convey to said second party all of said land in case he survives said first party; otherwise, said land to be vested in first party in case he survives said second party." At the time this deed was made and delivered, and as a part of the same transaction, the defendant Williams made and delivered to John J. Lewis a quitclaim deed containing the same provisions which we have quoted from the first deed, except that the land described therein was a lot in Mankato other than the demised premises.

The contention of the plaintiff is that the deed from Lewis to Williams was testamentary in character, and therefore void. If this claim is correct, then the plaintiff's intestate, Lewis, died seised of the demised premises; but, if it is not, then the defendant Williams is the owner thereof. It is elementary law that a written instrument, no matter what its form may be, which is of a testamentary character only, is a will, and, if not executed as required by the statute relating to wills, is void. *   *   * All courts and text-writers are agreed upon this proposition, but there is much apparent conflict of judicial authority as to the application of the rule to particular instruments. No general and invariable rules for determining whether a given instrument is a deed or a will can be laid down, for in nearly every case the language of the instrument is different. The true test whether an instrument is a deed or a will is the intention of the maker, which is primarily to be determined from its language. If in doubtful cases the instrument cannot be given effect as a will, but may be as a deed, especially if such be its form, it will be construed as such. The fact that an instrument, in form a deed, postpones the enjoyment of the subject-matter of the grant until after the death of the grantor, and is contingent upon the grantee surviving him, is not necessarily conclusive that the deed is testamentary in character. The test in such a case is whether the grantor intended the instrument to be ambulatory, serving no purpose and having no effect until after his death, and therefore revocable, or whether he intended to convey thereby some present right or interest, absolute or contingent, in the subject-matter of the grant, with the enjoyment thereof postponed until after his death. If, by the terms of the instrument, the right or interest passes at once, subject to a contingency over which the grantor has no control, it is a deed, and irrevocable, even though the enjoyment of the thing granted is postponed until his death. *   *   *

Now, if the language of the instrument here in question be read in the light of the general rules we have stated, the intention of the grantor is reasonably clear, although the words used to express it are not aptly chosen. The grant was based upon a valuable consideration moving from the grantee, and the instrument was duly executed, delivered, and recorded as a deed. It expressly states that the grantor "does hereby sell *   *   * and convey" to the grantee and his assigns, forever, all the right of survivorship in and to the land (describing it), which he and his assigns are to hold forever in case the grantee survives the grantor. Again, the deed expressly declares what the intention of the parties and the purpose of the deed are in these words: "The intent of this deed being to convey to said party of the second part all of said land in case he survives said party of the first part; otherwise, said land to be vested in the first party in case he survives said second party"—that is, the intention is to convey at once the land to the grantee upon the contingency of his surviving the grantor, but, if he does not, then the "land [is] to be vested in first party in case he survives said second party." It seems quite obvious that the only reasonable construction that can be given to the language used by the parties to this deed, which will give effect to the whole thereof, is to hold that the grantor intended thereby to convey, and did convey, to the grantee a present contingent right in the land in the nature of a contingent fee, and that, while the enjoyment of such right was, by necessary implication, postponed until the happening of the contingency, yet it vested upon the delivery of the deed. Therefore the right could not be revoked by the grantor, and the deed is not of testamentary character. If, after the defendant's deed had been recorded, the grantor had deeded the premises to a third party, would he have acquired a perfect title thereto?   *   *   *

But, even if this construction may be fairly regarded as doubtful, yet any construction which would render the deed void, because testamentary in character, would be much more doubtful, and it cannot be accepted, for the instrument cannot possibly be given effect as a will, but it may fairly be as a deed. We accordingly hold that the deed is not void, and that upon the death of the grantor the defendant Williams became the owner of the demised premises, and entitled to the rent therefor.

It follows that the order appealed from must be reversed, and the cause remanded to the district court, with direction to change its conclusion of law, so as to direct judgment to be entered for the defendant Williams. So ordered.

Notes

1. It has been held that if a deed has been duly delivered, a statement in the deed that it is not to be effective until the death of the grantor will be upheld as the reservation of a life estate by the grantor. 3 A.L.P. § 12.65 (1952).

2. The question in Thomas v. Williams was the distinction between a deed and a will, between an inter vivos and a testamentary disposition of property. An important reason for making the distinction is that the requirements for making the two types of dispositions are different. In most jurisdictions a deed requires only proper execution by the grantor and delivery. But a will must be attested by two or more witnesses in a designated manner. It should also be evident that the nature of an instrument disposing of property cannot be determined by its form or the label which has been attached to it. We are therefore driven to the question, what is the substantive essence of the distinction between an inter vivos and a testamentary disposition? This question emerges at several points in the materials which follow.

Frequently the word "ambulatory" is offered to indicate the essence of a will. This may be thought to suggest that a will is revocable by the testator. This of course is an essential feature of a will. But we may hesitate to say that this is the essence of the difference between a deed and a will, for, as we will see, there is authority that an inter vivos disposition can also be made revocable, although it will not be so unless the power of revocation is expressly reserved.

"Ambulatory," when applied to a will, properly means that the instrument speaks as a conveyance only upon the death of the testator, that is, it can have no effect upon the title of the testator until that time, and takers under a will can take no interest of any kind until that time. If then an instrument which appears to be a deed, and which purports to convey an interest in property, is attacked as being testamentary, this challenge must mean that the deed, for one reason or another, is not effective as a conveyance at the moment of delivery, but was intended to be so effective only upon the death of the grantor. As we saw in Thomas v. Williams, such a question can be raised by the language of the deed; or, as in some of the cases which follow, because the delivery process was not completed prior to the death of the grantor.

In either case, a discriminating perception of the problem will require a court to sustain any deed, otherwise valid, which can be found to pass any kind of estate or interest, large or small, at the moment of delivery.

See Browder, Giving or Leaving—What is a Will, 75 Mich.L.Rev. 845 (1977).

3. Accord with Thomas v. Williams: Abbott v. Holway, 72 Me. 298 (1881); Pure Oil Co. v. Bayler, 388 Ill. 331, 58 N.E.2d 26 (1944); but cf. Aldridge v. Aldridge, 202 Mo. 565, 101 S.W. 42 (1907). The language construed in Abbott v. Holway was as follows: "This deed is not to take effect and operate as a conveyance until my decease, and in case I shall survive my said wife, this deed is not to be operative as a conveyance, it being the sole purpose and object of this deed to make provision for the support of my said wife if she shall survive me, and if she shall survive me then and in that event only this deed shall be operative to convey to my said wife said premises in fee simple."

ST. LOUIS COUNTY NATIONAL BANK v. FIELDER

Supreme Court of Missouri, 1953.
364 Mo. 207, 260 S.W.2d 483.

HYDE, Judge. Action to determine title to real estate. Plaintiff claims title as testamentary trustee under the will of Paul A. Kessler, deceased, executed September 17, 1947. Defendant claims under a quit-claim deed, executed by Kessler, June 2, 1949, and recorded on that date. Kessler died July 24, 1950. The question for decision is whether the deed is void as an invalid testamentary disposition as contended by plaintiff. The trial court found the deed void, adjudged title in plaintiff and defendant has appealed.

The case was tried on an agreed statement of facts. Kessler's will left all his estate, real and personal, to plaintiff as trustee for his daughter and three grandchildren, the corpus to go to the grandchildren at the daughter's death. The deed conveyed Kessler's residence to defendant. It was in regular form but contained the following reservation: "The said party of the first part hereby reserves a Life Estate in and to said property, with power to sell, rent, lease, mortgage or otherwise dispose of said property during his natural lifetime." Kessler continued to reside in the property until his death, and at no time did he sell, rent, lease, mortgage or otherwise dispose of said property during his natural lifetime or attempt to do so.

Plaintiff contends that "a deed, in order to convey, must vest in the grantee a present irrevocable interest"; that "retention of power to sell, mortgage or otherwise dispose of property during lifetime, by grantor, in deed purporting to convey an estate to commence in the future prevents an immediate and irrevocable interest from being vested in grantee because the retention of such powers is equivalent to the power to revoke the deed"; that the reservation of the power to revoke shows grantor's intention to be that no estate is to pass to grantee until the death of the grantor; and that this reservation makes the deed testamentary in character. Plaintiff relies mainly on Goins v. Melton, 343 Mo. 413, 121 S.W.2d 821, 823 and cases cited therein.

However, the reservation in the deed herein involved says nothing about postponing the passing or vesting of title until the death of the grantor, as is true in every Missouri case we have found holding a deed to be testamentary. See cases cited in article on Testamentary Character of Deeds in Missouri, Ottman, 5 Mo.Law Rev. 350; see also Deed or

Will, Eckhardt, 15 Mo.Law Rev. 383. Instead, this deed unconditionally conveys the title immediately, stating "neither the said party of the first part, nor his heirs * * *. will hereafter claim or demand any right or title to the aforesaid premises." It makes a clear and proper reservation of a life estate and does also reserve the right to sell, mortgage or otherwise dispose of the property during the grantor's lifetime, which plaintiff correctly says is in effect a reservation of the power to revoke to be exercised in a particular manner. See 3 Tiffany, Real Property 14, Sec. 681. Of course, the right to rent or lease is not inconsistent with the life estate; and none of these provisions prevent the immediate vesting of title in the grantee of the remainder in fee. While the grantee's estate might later be defeated by exercise of the power that would only make it a defeasible fee but nevertheless a vested estate. See 31 C.J.S. Estates, § 5, p. 15; 133 Am.Jur. 544, Sec. 88. The deed in the Goins case, in addition to the retention of the right to sell during the grantor's lifetime, stated: "*At his death the title* to all, or whatever part thereof remains unsold, *to pass to and vest in the grantee together with all his personal property and belongings.*" Providing for personal property to thus vest in the grantee at the same time as the title to the land (at the grantor's death) was an added indication of the grantor's intention to make a testamentary disposition not found in many of the cases. This intention, as therein stated, was to be "gathered from the four corners of the instrument". For criticism of the Goins case see Work of Missouri Supreme Court—1938, Property, Eckhardt, 4 Mo.Law Rev. 419. There is nothing like the above quoted provision of the Goins case deed in this case. Indeed the grantor had already made his testamentary disposition by his previously executed will. (For a deed more like the Goins case deed see Wren v. Coffey, Tex.Civ.App., 26 S.W. 142, 143, where the language was "all our right, title, and interest in and to our homestead * * * should we not sell or dispose of the same before death." While this did not prohibit the vesting of title as specifically as did the Goins case deed, the Court held it testamentary, saying it was "a declaration of intention that the conveyance should not have the effect to divest title out of the makers, and invest it in the son, during the lifetime of such makers".) In this case, there is only the reservation of a life estate and a power to revoke during the grantor's lifetime. There is no language indicating an intention to postpone the vesting of the remainder in fee; but instead this deed affirmatively provides for the immediate vesting of title.

For the reasons hereinafter stated, we are convinced that a grantor has the right to reserve the power to revoke and that such a reservation alone does not make a deed testamentary. Insofar as Goins v. Melton indicates this reservation alone to be a reason for declaring a deed testamentary, it should be no longer followed. In fact, it would be more logical to hold the reservation void as repugnant to the grant (see 6 Thompson on Real Property 698, Sec. 3471) and thus leave the conveyance absolute, than it would be to hold that such a reservation makes the deed testamentary. That was the result reached by the Supreme Court of Kansas in Newell v. McMillan, 139 Kan. 94, 30 P.2d 126, 127 where a deed, reserving a life estate to the grantors, provided "The right to mortgage, sell or * * * dispose of the within described real estate is hereby reserved by the grantors, until said grantee shall have attained the age of forty years." The Court held this reservation was a nullity and did not defeat the conveyance of the fee to the grantee.

Apparently that was what the early common law did before the Statute of Uses (see Farwell on Powers, p. 2) for reasons stated by the Supreme Court of California, in Tennant v. John Tennant Memorial Home, 167 Cal. 570, 140 P. 242, loc. cit. 244, as follows: "Under the ancient common law, there was a rule to the effect that, where a transfer was made by feoffment and livery of seisin, any power of revocation reserved in the feoffment itself was void, on the ground that it was repugnant to the grant. The rule arose from the peculiar nature and purpose of the ceremony of livery of seisin, which was a necessary part of an alienation by feoffment. It consisted of a formal delivery of possession on the premises, symbolized by the manual delivery of a clod or piece of turf from the land, all of which was done in the presence of witnesses from the vicinage. The publicity was required because in those times there were no public records of conveyances and it was necessary in some way to preserve evidence of the transfer. For this reason the ceremony was required and the presence of witnesses was necessary. 4 Kent's Comm. 480. As this purpose would be defeated if the accompanying deed contained a reservation of power to revoke it, so that thereby the transfer could be absolutely defeated and a retransfer effected without such public ceremony or witnesses, the courts were forced to hold that such reservation in a feoffment was void. 1 Sugden on Powers, 2." While the Court, in the Tennant case, put the validity of the reservation of the right to revoke on statutory grounds, it also said: "Aside from the implied permission in the above section, * * * the reasonable conclusion would be that it was one of the inherent rights of every landowner to include such a reservation in a grant of his land." * * *

Obviously, therefore, whether the reserved power to revoke was valid or invalid, defendant would have title to the land herein involved. That is, if the grantor had a valid right to revoke, since he did not do so, defendant's title in fee is now absolute. On the other hand, if such a provision was invalid, because the grantor could not reserve such a power, then it was a nullity and his conveyance in fee was absolute. Likewise, it seems clear that neither the existence of a power to revoke nor its validity or invalidity has any bearing whatever on the question of testamentary character of a conveyance. Thus it requires something more than the reservation of a power to revoke alone to show an intention to make a testamentary disposition and there is nothing more in this case.

However, we think we should put our decision on the ground that the reservation of a power to revoke is valid because that is the modern trend. As pointed out in the Tennant case, 140 P. loc. cit. 244, modern statutes for the transfer of lands by deed and the recording thereof have removed all the reasons on which the rule of the common law (holding void the reservation of such a power) was founded. See provisions of Chap. 59 and Chap. 442, RSMo 1949, V.A.M.S. The modern conception of the right to acquire, possess and dispose of property, 140 P. loc. cit. 245, "includes the right to dispose of it, or any part of it, and for that purpose to divide it in any possible manner, either by separating it into estates for successive periods or otherwise, and disposing of one or more of such estates. It also includes the right to impose upon the grant of such estates any reservations or conditions which the grantor may see fit to place in the grant. The only limitation upon these rights is that they must be exercised in a way not forbidden by law." The Kentucky case, Ricketts v. Louisville, St. L. & T. Ry. Co., 15 S.W. 182, answered the contention that the reservation of a power to revoke was against public policy, because it would enable the parties to defeat creditors, by saying: "The deed is notice to the creditors of the reserved power. If they trust the grantee upon the credit of the estate thus granted, they do so knowing the risk, because the deed gives them notice of it."

There is both good reason and authority for holding valid the reservation of a power to revoke. In 3 Tiffany, 3rd Ed. 12, Sec. 681, it is said: "A power of revocation in favor of the grantor himself is, even by the English authorities, perfectly valid in a conveyance by way either of bargain and sale or covenant to stand seised, though it would not have been valid at common law. In this country, as in England, a power of revocation is frequently inserted in a voluntary deed of trust and that there is no such power in a deed of that character has been regarded as an indication that the deed was obtained by undue influence. But such a power is valid in conveyances other than deeds of trust, and the reservation of such a power involves no inconsistency with the conveyance. It merely involves, as before remarked, the creation of an executory limitation in favor of the grantor himself." * * * We therefore, hold that the deed to defendant herein created a defeasible fee subject to a life estate and, since the life estate has terminated and the power to revoke was not exercised, defendant is now the absolute owner.

The judgment is reversed and remanded with directions to enter judgment for defendant.

All concur.

Note

Are you satisfied with a purely technical argument in support of a revocable deed, that is, that the conveyance is effective to transfer a defeasible estate and so is as effective as any other conveyance upon a condition or limitation of defeasance? If one is concerned about the nature of the condition of defeasance in this case, that is, it leaves the grantor only one step removed from complete control over the property, does it follow that his position is substantially the same as if he had made a will?

There are decisions which do not sustain revocable deeds. Some of these have declared the conveyance good, but the power of revocation void, on the ground that the power is "repugnant" to the estate conveyed. What does that mean? Others hold the conveyance void on the ground that it is testamentary. But there is substantial authority in accord with the Fielder case. See Garvey, Revocable Gifts of Legal Interests in Land, 54 Ky.L.J. 19 (1965).

If such a deed is valid as between the parties, do you see any reason why the creditors of the grantor should be able to enforce their claims out of the property conveyed? Apart from the many ramifications of the law on fraudulent conveyances, there is little authority apart from statute on the question whether the rights of creditors are preserved where the only evidence is a deed reserving a power to revoke. What authority there is denies the rights of creditors. But there are statutes in a number of states, based on an early New York statute, which provide that where a grantor reserves an absolute power of revocation, he is still deemed to be absolute owner of the estate conveyed, so far as the rights of "creditors and purchasers" are concerned. Id. at 44. For a recent amendment to such a statute see Michigan Compiled Laws Annotated § 556.128.

SMITH v. FAY

Supreme Court of Iowa, 1940.
228 Iowa 868, 293 N.W. 497.

STIGER, Justice. On December 10, 1918, C.O. White executed a deed conveying his real estate to his brother, George E. White. The deed was drawn and acknowledged by E.M. Hertert at the office of Hertert and Hertert in Harlan, Iowa, and delivered to Mr. Hertert under the circumstances hereinafter set out.

On December 11, 1918, C.O. White made a will leaving all of his personal property to George E. White. George E. White outlived C.O. White, and at the time of the trial the grantor and grantee in the deed and both members of the firm of Hertert & Hertert were deceased.

Plaintiffs, who are collateral heirs of C.O. White, allege they are the owners of the real estate described in the deed because it was never delivered to the grantee.

Defendants, beneficiaries under the will of George E. White, claim the deed operated as an escrow being deposited by the grantor with E.M. Hertert and to be delivered by him to the grantee on the death of the grantor.

The grantor died on November 11, 1936. On November 12, 1936, the grantee secured possession of and recorded the duly acknowledged deed. Under the circumstances the burden of proving nondelivery was on plaintiffs. Heavner v. Kading, 209 Iowa 1275, 228 N.W. 313.

The only witness produced at the trial who had knowledge of the transaction between the grantor and Mr. Hertert was defendants' witness, Peter Heintz, an employee of Hertert and Hertert from 1908 to 1925. Mr. Heintz was the bookkeeper, wrote insurance policies, made real estate sales, took loan applications, and, in general, participated in the business of the firm with the exception of the law business. We will first set out the material portions of his testimony.

About noon on December 10, 1918, the grantor, C.O. White, came to the office of Hertert and Hertert and talked with E.M. Hertert about the execution of a deed to his real estate. Hertert told him to return to the office after lunch and he would have the deed prepared. When the grantor returned to the office he brought with him a small box labeled "C.O. White" identified in the record as Exhibit 2. After further conversation between White and Hertert, Mr. White signed the deed. The grantor then said, "I am going to put the deed in this box and leave it with you." Hertert told him that it would not be legal, that the deed would not be good, and that it would be necessary to deliver the deed to some third party. White replied, "Will you keep it here?" Hertert stated, "We will keep them for you if you want us to." Hertert then placed the deed in an envelope in the presence of White and the witness and wrote the following statement on the envelope: "C.O. White. Papers in this envelope to be delivered to George E. White, after my death." Hertert then gave the sealed envelope to Heintz, who placed it in the "will box" in the vault which was the box in which were placed papers that were to be delivered to third parties. The sealed envelope was in the will box when the witness left the firm of Hertert and Hertert in 1925. The will was placed in another envelope.

On cross-examination Mr. Heintz testified:

"Q. The purpose of putting the real estate in the deed was to save the additional probate expense? A. Yes, to save it from someone else, that is what Charlie told me specially.

"Q. He told you then that he was fixing so that after he was gone George would be sure and get the property? A. Yes, if he should die first for his protection so if Charlie died first, George would be sure to get the property. There was nothing said there about what would happen if George died first that I know of. I never heard Mr. Hertert say that he could come and get his deed back if George died first."

Defendants introduced in evidence the sealed envelope, Exhibit 10, and identified the writing on the envelope as the handwriting of Mr. Hertert. The testimony of Heintz effectively supported the contention of defendants that White delivered the deed to Hertert without any reservation of a right to recall it and with instructions to deliver it to the grantee on the death of the grantor.

Plaintiffs failed to sustain their burden of proving nondelivery which they attempted to establish through attorney Russell F. Swift who testified substantially as follows: The witness was attorney for the administrator of the estate of John Hertert, who died in August, 1936. After his death his daughter remained in the office and looked after the insurance business and the witness looked after the law business. E.M. Hertert predeceased John Hertert. After the death of Charles White in November, 1936, the grantee in the deed, George E. White, asked the witness to go with him to Hertert's office, stating he wanted to get Charlie White's box. The key to the box was in the vault. The witness unlocked the private box of Charles White, Exhibit 2, and stated that he found the deed, will and other papers in that box. He gave the deed to George E. White. With the consent of George White the witness took possession of the will for the purpose of commencing probate proceedings. There was a box in the vault containing wills but there were no deeds in it. The envelope, Exhibit 10, was not in Exhibit 2 or in the will box. The witness published a notice in a newspaper for owners to get their boxes and papers at the office of Hertert and Hertert.

However, evidence introduced by defendants tended to show that Mr. Swift was mistaken in stating that he found the deed in Exhibit 2 in the vault of the office the day after the grantor died.

Hans Hansen, a resident of Harlan for 30 years, testified that he was acquainted with Charles and George White and Hertert and Hertert. After John Hertert's death he helped Catherine Hertert, the daughter of Mr. Hertert, in the office. Catherine and her mother gave the witness the box, Exhibit 2, and told him to take it to Charlie White, who was ill at the Iowa Hotel. The witness delivered the box to George E. White at the hotel, asking him to deliver the box to his brother Charles. George replied that he would do so and the witness saw him go upstairs with the box.

Mrs. Nelson, a nurse who cared for Mr. White three weeks prior to his death, identified Exhibit 2 and stated it was in Mr. White's room when she came to the hotel as his nurse and remained in the room on the dresser until after his death.

The delivery of Exhibit 2 to C.O. White was in accord with the published request of Mr. Swift to owners of boxes to remove them from the office.

Mr. Heintz testified he placed the deed in the will box in the vault in Hertert's office pursuant to the direction of Mr. Hertert the day the deed was executed and that it was in the box when he left in 1925. There is no evidence that the deed was removed from the will box. The presumption is that the situation remained unchanged and that Messrs. Hertert and Hertert maintained the deed in the will box for the purpose of performing their duties under the escrow agreement. Mr. Swift testified that the envelope, Exhibit 10, was not in the will box or Exhibit 2 after the death of the grantor and that he never saw Exhibit 10 until the trial. However, defendants produced the envelope at the trial and it is a reasonable assumption that it was in one of the boxes and with the deed.

We are of the opinion that Exhibit 2 was not in the vault of the office of Hertert and Hertert the day after the death of Charles White and that Mr. Swift obtained the deed from the will box and delivered it to the grantee.

It is obvious that Mr. White intended to give all of his property, real and personal, to his brother. We conclude that when the grantor delivered the deed to Mr. Hertert with instructions to deliver it to grantee on the death of grantor, he parted with all control over the deed with the intention that title pass immediately to the grantee subject to his reserved life estate. It follows that there was a sufficient delivery. In Bohle v. Brooks, 225 Iowa 980, 282 N.W. 351, 354, the court said:

"The effect of thus placing the instrument in the hands of a third person with instructions to deliver after the death of the grantor is to reserve a life estate in the grantor, with the title immediately passing to the grantee, but with his right to possession and enjoyment postponed until the grantor's death." See Goodman v. Andrews, 203 Iowa 979, 213 N.W. 605.

As bearing on the question of intent of the grantor, plaintiffs introduced evidence that subsequent to the delivery of the deed to Hertert the grantor sold and mortgaged some of the property described in the deed. The grantor having parted with dominion over the instrument with the intention of passing title, a sufficient delivery was accomplished and a different or changed intention manifested by the exercise of subsequent acts of ownership must yield to the intention of the grantor at the time of the escrow delivery.

Appellants contend the statement of Mr. Heintz that the grantor told him he was fixing it so if he died first "George would be sure to get the property" establishes an intention of the grantor to make a testamentary disposition rather than a conveyance of a present interest in the real estate. We do not so construe this testimony. The witness testified to statements the grantor made to him at the office of Hertert and Hertert. This witness had stated on cross-examination that he was not present in the room where the grantor talked with Mr. Hertert about his purpose in executing the deed. The purport of the transaction between the grantor and Hertert is revealed by the notation on the envelope and the deposit of the deed in the will box. The most plaintiff can claim from the statement "if Charlie died first, George would be sure and get the property" is that the deed was to be delivered to the grantee on the contingency that he survive the grantor. The question here is not whether the grantee obtained a vested or contingent remainder, the question is whether or not there was an absolute delivery of the deed. The quoted testimony of the witness affects only the nature of the estate granted and does not bear on the question of the delivery of the deed.

Appellants further contend the evidence shows that the grantor reserved the right of recall and therefore, though the right was not exercised, there was no valid delivery, citing the recent case of Orris v. Whipple, 224 Iowa 1157, 280 N.W. 617, which holds that the deposit of a deed in the grantor's safety box where it remained under the control of the grantor until his death was not a sufficient delivery. The decision rests on the proposition that a retention of possession and control of the deed by the grantor is inconsistent with the delivery and an intention to convey a present interest in the property to the grantee. The case of Davis v. Brown College, 208 Iowa 480, 222 N.W. 858, recognized the rule that a delivery of a deed to a third person, with no reservation of the right to recall the deed, to be delivered to the grantee upon the death of the grantor, constituted a good delivery, but further held that an unexercised right to recall would not defeat delivery. This decision had the support of some of our prior cases.

While the case of Orris v. Whipple, supra, pointed out that there was an escrow delivery in the Brown College case and overruled the latter case only in so far as it was in conflict with the opinion, the discussion and pronouncements of the court on the question of delivery in the Orris case are irreconcilable with the decision in the Brown College case. As there is no difference in principle between actual possession and control (safety box cases) and the right of possession and control under a reservation of the right to recall the deed in an escrow delivery, the decision in the Orris case is in conflict with the decision in the Brown College case and the ruling in the Brown College case that an unexercised right of recall of a deed operating as an escrow does not defeat delivery was, in effect, repudiated by the case of Orris v. Whipple, supra. However, appellants' contention cannot prevail because in the instant case we find the grantor parted with all dominion and control over the deed.

We concur in the trial court's view of the law and evidence and the case is affirmed.

Affirmed.*

ATCHISON v. ATCHISON

Supreme Court of Oklahoma, 1946.
198 Okl. 98, 175 P.2d 309.

HURST, Vice Chief Justice. This is an ejectment action commenced by Kate Atchison against Bess A. Atchison to recover the south 80 acres and an undivided ³/₄ interest in the north 80 acres of a certain quarter section of land in Okfuskee County. From a judgment in favor of the plaintiff, the defendant appeals.

The plaintiff is the mother of A.L. Atchison and claims title to the land under a warranty deed executed by him on October 15, 1914, and filed for record on December 1, 1943. The defendant is the widow of A.L. Atchison, who died testate in 1939, and by his will he devised all of his real estate to the defendant. The question for decision is whether the deed above referred to was effective to pass title to the plaintiff.

The record discloses that at and prior to the time of the execution of said deed, Atchison was indebted to his mother. There was introduced in evidence a letter from him to his mother dated November 9, 1913, stating that he was inclosing a quit claim deed to a certain farm to be held as collateral until he could make other arrangements. This quit claim deed was neither produced nor accounted for. With the letter was a statement showing that Atchison owed his mother the sum of $2,450.

The only witness testifying as to the delivery of the warranty deed was a brother of A.L. Atchison, who testified that in 1924 or 1925 A.L. Atchison, who was then about to undergo an operation, handed the deed to him to be delivered to his mother in the event he predeceased her. He testified as follows:

"Q. And the deed was to be delivered in case he died before she did? A. That is right.

"Q. Otherwise not? A. That is right. He said after his death he wanted to see my mother got the deed, and asked me to deliver it to her."

---

* Accord: Ritchie v. Davis, 26 Wis.2d 636, 133 N.W.2d 312 (1965).

The defendant, appellant here, argues that this constituted a conditional delivery to take effect only upon the death of A.L. Atchison if he predeceased his mother, and that consequently it was testamentary in character, and since the deed was not executed in the manner prescribed by law for the execution of wills it is without legal effect. The plaintiff argues that the delivery was absolute and had the effect of vesting in the grantee a present title with the right of possession postponed until the grantor's death. He relies upon Shaffer v. Smith, 53 Okl. 352, 156 P. 1188; Kay v. Walling, 98 Okl. 258, 225 P. 384; Maynard v. Hustead, 185 Okl. 20, 90 P.2d 30; and McCaw v. Hartman, 190 Okl. 264, 122 P.2d 999.

After the deed was delivered in 1924 or 1925, Atchison continued to treat the land as his own, by terracing it in connection with an adjoining tract of land and farming the two tracts as one and by executing right of way grants and leases. These acts were consistent with his continued ownership of the land, and inconsistent with the testimony of his brother, above quoted.

We are of the opinion, and hold, that no estate vested in grantor's mother at the time the deed was delivered to his brother. The delivery by the brother to the mother was contingent upon the grantor predeceasing his mother. If she had predeceased him, then it would have been the duty of the brother to re-deliver the deed to grantor. The delivery to the grantee was subject to a contingency that was not certain to occur—death of the grantor before the death of the grantee. 18 C.J. 206; 26 C.J.S. Deeds, § 43, p. 244. Thus, the grantor did not relinquish full and absolute control of the deed when he delivered it to his brother as escrow holder. The deed was to be effective as a deed only upon the death of the grantor. It was, therefore, testamentary in character and was ineffective as a will because not executed with the formalities required for the execution of a will. See Green v. Comer, 193 Okl. 133, 141 P.2d 258, and Maynard v. Hustead, 185 Okl. 20, 90 P.2d 30, and the authorities therein cited; 8 R.C.L. 930, 932; 16 Am.Jur. 516; Snodgrass v. Snodgrass, 107 Okl. 140, 231 P. 237, 52 A.L.R. 1222, annotation. The authorities relied upon by the plaintiff are distinguishable on their facts.

Reversed with instructions to enter judgment for the defendant.

RILEY, Justice (dissenting).

A warranty deed was executed October 15, 1914. The grantor conveyed land to his mother. He was at the time indebted to her in a substantial amount. Grantor placed the instrument in the hands of a third person. It was to be delivered to grantee by the depositary upon condition that grantor predecease his mother. That condition was fulfilled. In my opinion, the deed effectively conveyed right of possession and title to the land. Shaffer v. Smith, 53 Okl. 352, 156 P. 1188; Kay v. Walling, 98 Okl. 258, 225 P. 384; McCaw v. Hartman, 190 Okl. 264, 122 P.2d 999.

The mere fact that grantor, subsequent to time of the escrow, by which on fulfillment of the condition, parted with title, continued throughout his lifetime to exercise dominion over the land, did not defeat the effectiveness of the grant.

"A future estate may be limited by the act of the party to commence in possession at a future day, either without the intervention of a precedent estate, or on [its] termination, by lapse of time, or otherwise * * *." 60 O.S.1941 § 28.

"* * * a freehold estate * * * may be created to commence at a future day * * *. A fee may be limited * * * upon a contingency * * *." 60 O.S.1941 § 35.

"Where the owner of realty executes a deed thereto and places it beyond recall in the hands of a third person to be delivered to the grantees, on the grantor's death, there is a 'conveyance' passing title to the realty in praesenti with right to possession postponed until grantor's death". Maynard v. Hustead (Hurst, J.), 185 Okl. 20, 90 P.2d 30; 26 C.J.S., Deeds, §§ 45, 46, pp. 246, 247.

The grantor's act in placing his deed beyond his power to recall so long as grantor and grantee were alive, yet limiting delivery of the deed upon the contingency of grantor's death prior to that of grantee, with conditions fulfilled, constituted a conveyance. Anno. 52 A.L.R. 1222.

Seisin in real property once was accomplished by a manual delivery of a token, such as a twig from a tree upon the land, or a clod of its dirt. There can be no doubt that a grantor may, as in the case at bar, by deed limit a grant upon the happening of a future event such as payment of the consideration or any other condition. That which might be accomplished by deed, by act may be done. The judgment should be affirmed.

Notes and Questions

1. **Escrows.** The term "escrow" refers to the use of a third party in the delivery process, to whom the deed is physically transferred. We say in such cases that the deed is delivered in escrow. There is some danger in the latter expression, for a major problem in cases involving escrows is the legal effect of such a transfer. Two deliveries are contemplated. Which one is the legal delivery? Escrow cases are generally of two types:

(a) Gratuitous, family transactions, where the third party is to deliver on an event relating to the death of the grantor. Smith v. Fay and Atchison v. Atchison, supra, are cases of this type.

(b) Commercial transactions, where the third party is to deliver upon the performance of some act or acts by the grantee, such as payment of the purchase price. First National Bank & Trust Co. v. Scott, infra, is a case of this type.

2. The result and its explanation in Smith v. Fay, has considerable support. 3 A.L.P. § 12.67 (1952). The effect is to blend the ingredients of delivery with the divisibility of ownership allowed by the law of estates. If the question were open, you could no doubt state reasons why this sort of thing should not be allowed. But if it is allowed in a case like Smith v. Fay, it may be difficult to understand why the same analysis is not permissible in a case like Atchison v. Atchison. If the only obstacle is the policy of the statutes of wills, and if a deed can escape the charge of being testamentary by a finding that some interest passed at the time of the delivery in escrow, and if an interest passes upon

such delivery in a case like Smith v. Fay, then why does not an interest also pass in the same manner in Atchison v. Atchison? If the only difference is in the nature of the interest which passes in each case, why should this spell the difference between validity and invalidity?

3. John and Joseph Masquart, unmarried brothers, were tenants in common of certain lands. On January 14, 1943 John signed and acknowledged a deed of his one-half interest to Joseph, and on the same day Joseph likewise signed and acknowledged a similar deed in favor of John. These deeds were left with a lawyer, Dick, who prepared them, with instructions to keep both deeds until one of the brothers died, at which time he was to deliver the deed signed by the deceased to the survivor. Neither deed was to be recalled during the lifetime of the brothers without their mutual consent. On the death of John in 1950, the deed signed by him was taken by Mr. Dick from the safe in which both deeds had been kept; it was recorded and handed to Joseph. The other deed was then destroyed by Mr. Dick.

Joseph died in 1953, but shortly after the death of his brother he had executed a will devising all his property to the Shriners' Hospital. Thereafter a partition action was instituted by the heirs at law of John. The defendants were the executor of Joseph's estate and the Hospital. The decree was for the plaintiffs, and the defendants appealed. Held, affirmed. Masquart v. Dick, 210 Or. 459, 310 P.2d 742 (1957).

4. John Noble executed a warranty deed to his son Thomas of certain land. The deed was acknowledged, attested by two witnesses, an delivered in escrow with directions to deliver it to the grantee on the grantor's death, but to remain in the meantime subject to his order. On his death, John Noble left a will by which he gave all of his estate except the land deeded to his son Thomas to his three sons equally. This will was admitted to probate. Two of Noble's daughters filed a bill in partition against the other children, alleging that the deed was void as a conveyance because not delivered in the lifetime of their father. The court held the deed void for want of delivery, and this was affirmed on appeal, but the case was remanded upon other grounds. In the course of further proceedings an effort was made to probate the deed as a will, but probate was denied. On appeal, held, affirmed. The court said, "The inherent difficulty with the instrument involved in this case is, that there is nothing in the writing itself which imparts to it a testamentary character. To give it this character a resort must be had to extrinsic facts depending on parol evidence." The court said that an unambiguous deed cannot be converted into a will by proving testamentary intent in the maker by parol evidence. The court concluded by saying, "It would be a strange result if the same evidence which destroyed the instrument as a deed should bring it to life as a will?" Why would it be strange? Noble v. Fickes, 230 Ill. 594, 82 N.E. 950 (1907).

BALLENTINE, When Are Deeds Testamentary,* 18 Mich.L.Rev. 470, 478, 479 (1920): * * * In O'Brien v. O'Brien,[1] it is said: "To constitute delivery it must clearly appear that it was the grantor's intention to pass title at the time and that he should lose control over the same."[2] It is submitted that the *passing of title at the time* of execution of the deed is not an element of delivery. The question is whether the instru-

* Copyright, 1919–1920, Michigan Law Review Association.

1. 285 Ill. 575, 121 N.E. 243. [Footnotes are the author's. Ed.]

2. So in Pemberton v. Kraper, 289 Ill. 295, 124 N.E. 611; Pollock v. McCarty, 198 Mich. 66, 164 N.W. 391; Felt v. Felt, 155 Mich. 237, 118 N.W. 953; Williams v. Kidd, 170 Cal. 631, 151 P. 1, Ann.Cas.1916E, 703. See also White v. Chellew (1919) 108 Wash. 628, 185 P. 621.

ment is made operative as a consummated or completed legal act.[3] A deed deposited with a third party need not be upheld on the theory that title passes when such deposit is made. An instrument conditionally delivered may be immediately operative to create rights and liabilities, even though it may be an escrow and confer contingent or executory interests, which will vest only upon conditions precedent. A conditional delivery differs from an absolute delivery merely in the fact that the full operation of the deed is subject to a condition; the delivery is in its nature as final and as irrevocable as absolute delivery. The condition that the deed is not to take effect in the event of the grantee dying before the grantor does not show that the grantor did not part with dominion and control over the deed and also over the title. It is an unfounded assumption to say that the grantor retains control over the instrument or its operation.[4] Why does he not lose his right to recall the deed provided the event happens? He has manifested his intention by his acts or words to dispose of his property and to make the deed a valid and effective instrument of conveyance of the estate and interests described therein, subject to a condition precedent that is beyond his control or volition. This constitutes delivery.[5] Delivery is not a question of vesting of title at once, but of making a deed binding or operative at once.

Whether the deed is delivered to take effect upon a certain or upon an uncertain event, it may equally be regarded as beyond the control of the grantor to revoke or defeat its operation. If, however, the *event is sure to happen*, for practical purposes it may be said that the grantee has a *vested estate*, a fixed right of future enjoyment, and that by a kind of subtraction the grantor's estate is reduced to one for life only. Where the event is uncertain absolute title does not pass to the grantee until the event occurs, but nevertheless the deed may be put beyond the control of the grantor.[6] The arbitrary and unreasonable doctrine invalidating delivery to a depositary upon an uncertain condition constitutes a snare and pitfall to honest and innocent grantors and grantees. It has no foundation in intelligent considerations of policy or inconvenience, but is one of those irrational and technical distinctions that spring up in the law, when the courts in "discovering" the law lose sight of its practical ends, and formulate mechanical rules by deduction from unfounded general assumptions. The sole effect of the rule is to defeat the intention of the grantor in seeking to dispose of his property by deed rather than by will. *   *   *

3. Provart v. Harris, 150 Ill. 40, 36 N.E. 958; 17 Mich.L.Rev. 580, 586, 4 Wigmore, Evidence, § 2408.

4. Nolan v. Otney, 75 Kan. 311, 89 P. 690, 9 L.R.A, N.S., 317; Stanton v. Miller, 58 N.Y. 192; Anderson v. Messenger, 158 F. 250; 4 Wigmore, Evidence, Secs. 2405, 2408. See Hall v. Harris, 40 N.C. (5 Ired. Eq.) 303.

5. See Jones v. Schmidt, 290 Ill. 97, 124 N.E. 835.

6. Nolan v. Otney, 75 Kan. 311, 89 P. 690; Hall v. Harris, 40 N.C. 303.

TAKACS v. TAKACS

Supreme Court of Michigan, 1947.
317 Mich. 72, 26 N.W.2d 712.

CARR, Chief Justice. This suit was started in the circuit court to set aside a deed executed by plaintiff to his son and his daughter-in-law, the defendant herein. The material facts leading to the giving of the instrument in question are not in dispute. Plaintiff came to the United States from Hungary in 1922, leaving his wife and son in that country. Approximately 14 years later plaintiff forwarded to his son Stephen Takacs, Jr., money for transportation to Detroit. The young man arrived there in October, 1936. Both plaintiff and the son were employed by the Ford Motor Company.

In March, 1937, Stephen Takacs, Jr., married the defendant in this case. At that time she was 15 years of age. The young couple desired a home and apparently plaintiff was anxious to assist them. As a result a lot was purchased, the conveyance being executed to plaintiff and the son as tenants in common. Thereafter arrangements were made with a contractor to build a house, the construction being financed from the proceeds of a mortgage placed upon the property. Following the completion of the house in June, 1941, plaintiff and the young couple lived therein together until February, 1943, when plaintiff left the premises. During the time that plaintiff remained with his son and daughter-in-law he paid them, at first, $40 per month for his board and room, and thereafter, $45 per month. It appears further that he voluntarily contributed to certain improvements, principally a garage and a fence. Including the amount contributed by him towards the initial price of the lot, plaintiff contributed approximately $1,250 to the home and its improvement.

In February, 1942, while the parties were living together in the home, plaintiff, accompanied by his son and daughter-in-law, went to the office of an attorney, Miss Suzanne Popp, for the purpose of having an instrument drawn and executed that would insure the passing of plaintiff's interest in the property, on his death, to the young couple. The attorney in question, who was a witness on the trial of the case in the circuit court, spoke the Hungarian language, and it appears from the record that she discussed the matter with plaintiff at some length. The preparation of a will was suggested, but plaintiff indicated quite positively that he did not want a will because his son would have to go to court in connection with it and he wished to avoid the necessity for such action. As a result of the conversation and in accordance with plaintiff's desires, a quitclaim deed was prepared conveying plaintiff's interest in the property in question to "Stephen Takacs, Jr., and Mabel R. Takacs, his wife," the instrument being signed by plaintiff and witnessed. The proofs indicate that at that time there was an understanding among the parties that the deed would become effective on the death of plaintiff, and that it was not to be recorded during his lifetime. Following the transaction, and while the parties were still in the attorney's office, the deed was delivered to Stephen Takacs, Jr. It does not appear that thereafter plaintiff had the instrument in his possession at any time, or that he made any attempt to obtain it. No claim is made that he reserved the right, conditional or otherwise, to recall the conveyance.

After plaintiff left the home of his son in February, 1943, defendant caused the deed to be recorded. On December 15, following, Stephen Takacs, Jr., died. Plaintiff claims that thereafter he learned for the first time that the deed had been recorded. He also learned that defendant was trying to sell the property. On July 19, 1944, the bill of complaint was filed, followed by an amended bill of complaint filed September 11, 1944. Plaintiff asked therein that the quitclaim deed above referred to be set aside and declared null and void, that plaintiff be decreed to be the owner of an undivided one-half interest in the property in question, or, in lieu thereof, that defendant be required to pay to plaintiff such sum or sums as might be found due to plaintiff for his equitable interest in the property. Plaintiff also asked for an accounting between the parties, and that defendant be enjoined from selling the property, or encumbering it, during the pendency of the suit. Defendant, by answer, denied plaintiff's right to the relief sought. On the trial the proofs disclosed that the property had actually been sold prior to the service of the papers in plaintiff's suit, and that defendant received the sum of approximately $2,800, the sale being made subject to the outstanding mortgage. It further appears that the payments falling due on the mortgage from time to time had been made by Stephen Takacs, Jr., and the defendant.

The trial court concluded, after listening to the proofs of the parties, that plaintiff was entitled to relief on the ground that there was no legal delivery of the deed to the grantees. A decree was entered in accordance with the court's opinion, requiring defendant to pay plaintiff one-half the amount received by her for the property, together with interest thereon from July 10, 1944. From such decree defendant has appealed. It is her claim, in substance, that the delivery of the conveyance was unconditional, that the terms of the deed cannot be varied by parol evidence, that the attempted oral condition that the deed was not to operate until plaintiff's death was ineffective, and that, in consequence, title vested in her husband and herself. On behalf of appellee it is insisted that the oral stipulation as to when the conveyance should go into effect prevented a legal discovery [sic], that, in consequence, no title passed to the grantees, that defendant was guilty of fraud in causing the instrument to be recorded, and further that plaintiff is entitled to a cancellation of the deed because it was executed without consideration.

It is clearly apparent from the evidence in the case that plaintiff did not wish to execute a will. It was his desire that on his death his son and daughter-in-law should take his interest in the property, without the necessity of any court procedure. He might have delivered the instrument, following its execution, to a third person with directions to deliver it to the grantees following plaintiff's death. * * * Instead of following this course plaintiff turned the instrument over to the grantees without any reservation as to its recall. It remained thereafter in the possession of the grantees. When plaintiff left the home in February, 1943, he asserted no right to recall the deed. Neither does it appear that he at that time asserted any interest whatsoever in the property. The fact that he paid for his board and room is rather significant, especially in view of the further fact that the grantees made the payments on the mortgage. Plaintiff made no claim of any kind until after the death of his son.

This court has in several prior decisions passed on the sufficiency of a manual delivery of an instrument of conveyance made under circumstances analogous to those involved in the case at bar. In Dyer v. Skadan, 128 Mich. 348, 87 N.W. 277, 279, 92 Am.St.Rep. 461, cited and relied on by appellant, the question at issue was whether a deed, executed by the plaintiff's wife to him, had been delivered. In discussing the situation, it was said: "There is nothing in the testimony indicating the parties to the deed expected that Mrs. Dyer might control the deed during the lifetime of her husband, or that she could recall it. The most favorable view for the defendants that can be taken of the testimony is that Mr. and Mrs. Dyer both supposed that, if the deed was not recorded by Mr. Dyer, in the event of his death all it was necessary to do to reinvest the title in Mrs. Dyer was to destroy the deed. Whether it is said there was an unconditional delivery of the deed to the grantee, expecting it would take immediate effect as claimed by Mr. Dyer, or whether it was expected the deed would not take effect until the death of the grantor, cannot, we think, under the authorities, make any difference with the result. The testimony shows the deed was delivered to the grantee, the grantor not reserving any right of control over it. In the one case the title would pass at once. In the other case the grantee would not be in a less favorable position than he would have been had the deed been delivered to a third party with directions to deliver it upon the death of the grantor. We have already seen that in the last-mentioned case the title would take effect when the deed was delivered by the third party, and, except as to intermediate rights, when thus delivered, it would take effect by relation from the first delivery."

The court also cited, with approval, the earlier decision of Dawson, Adm'r, v. Hall et al., 2 Mich. 390, where it was said: " 'It is a well-settled rule of law that, if the grantor does not intend that his deed shall take effect until some condition is performed, or the happening of some future event, he should either keep it himself, or leave it with some other person as an escrow to be delivered at the proper time. That it should operate as an escrow, it is necessary that the delivery should be made to a stranger, and not to the party; for, if one makes a deed and delivers it to the party to whom it is made, as an escrow upon certain conditions, in such case, let the form of the words be whatever it may, the delivery is absolute, and the deed shall take effect presently as his deed, and the party to whom it is delivered is not bound to perform the condition.' "

In Wipfler v. Wipfler, 153 Mich. 18, 116 N.W. 544, 16 L.R.A., N.S., 941, the plaintiff sought to set aside a deed given by him to his wife the defendant, on the ground of insufficient delivery. The grantor, after executing the instrument, kept it in his possession for several years. When departing on a journey that he deemed hazardous he handed the instrument to the grantee with directions that if anything of a fatal nature should happen to him she should cause the instrument to be recorded. Plaintiff returned safely from the trip, but before his return the grantee placed the deed on record. It was held that, assuming plaintiff's claims as to the facts to be correct, the transaction constituted a delivery of the deed to grantee without express reservation of the right of recall, and with the intent that, under a certain contingency, the instrument should be effective without any further act on plaintiff's part. * * *

The Wipfler case is reported in 16 L.R.A., N.S., p. 941, followed by an annotation relating to the question at issue. In said annotation it is said:

"It may be said to be a well-settled rule of law that, where a grantor delivers his deed to the grantee, without any express reservation of the right to recall it, and with intent that in a certain contingency it shall be effective without any further act on the part of the grantor, such delivery is effectual to pass title presently. There are two different grounds upon which the courts arrive at such conclusion: First, upon the well-known rule of evidence that parol testimony is inadmissible to vary the terms of a written instrument; second, that such delivery is an attempt to deliver the deed in escrow to the grantee, which cannot be done, for delivery to a stranger is essential to an escrow.

"In the first class of cases, the authorities will be found to be almost unanimously agreed upon the proposition that, where the grantor has delivered his absolute deed to the grantee, with the intent to relinquish all control over the same, he, or those claiming under him, will not afterwards be permitted to show that such delivery was conditional. * * *

"The great majority of the cases have looked upon a conditional delivery to the grantee, of a deed absolute on its face, as an attempt to deliver the same in escrow, and, as an esrow must necessarily be delivered to a stranger to the deed, to be held until the performance of a condition by the grantee, or until the happening of a certain contingency, have laid down the rule that no delivery in escrow can be made to the grantee, and that an attempt to do so will vest the title absolutely. Such has been the conclusion of every authority ancient and modern." * * *

The decisions of this court above referred to are controlling on the question as to the effectiveness of the delivery of the deed in the instant case. In accordance therewith we hold that the delivery was sufficient to pass title to the grantees, that the terms of the conveyance may not be altered by parol, and that the attempted verbal stipulation as to when the conveyance should become operative was ineffective. * * *

[On the claim that the deed was not supported by consideration the court held that a deed will be supported by a consideration of natural love and affection, or of a close relationship.]

The claim that defendant acted fraudulently in placing the deed on record does not require extended consideration. Such act on her part was in violation of the verbal agreement between the parties, but under the circumstances presented by the record it did not operate to the injury of the plaintiff. In view of the fact that title to the property passed as the result of the delivery of the deed to the grantees, the right to have such conveyance placed on record may well be regarded as a resulting legal incident, notwithstanding the attempted oral stipulation on plaintiff's part. In any event plaintiff is not in position to seek relief on the theory that he was injured by defendant's act in causing the deed to be recorded.

For the reasons indicated the decree of the trial court is vacated, and a decree will enter in this court in conformity with the foregoing opinion, with costs to appellant.

Note

Ritchie v. Davis, 26 Wis.2d 636, 133 N.W.2d 312 (1965) is in accord. Two special features of this case should be noted:

(1) The person to whom the deed was delivered was one of three grantees named in the deed, and the court held that the same principle applied in such a case as in the case where a so-called delivery in escrow is attempted to a single grantee.

(2) The direction given by the grantor to the grantee to whom he gave the deed was that he did not wish the deed recorded while he (the grantor) was around. This was interpreted as amounting to a direction to record the deed only after the grantor's death. In the first part of its opinion the court treated the case as though the deed had been delivered with these instructions to a third party for the benefit of a single grantee. In such cases, the court said, delivery is effective if no right of recall has been reserved, and that the effect of the deed is to convey the fee estate with enjoyment postponed, that is, with the reservation of a life estate in the grantor. See Smith v. Fay, supra page 812. Is this conclusion consistent with the further holding in this case that a delivery cannot be made in escrow to the grantee, and that where attempted the delivery becomes absolute? The court was not required to reconcile its two grounds for decision because no claim was made by the grantees to any benefit of the property prior to the grantor's death.

CHILLEMI v. CHILLEMI, 197 Md. 257, 78 A.2d 750 (1951). Chillemi executed deeds to his wife in anticipation of a military mission and handed them to his wife on condition that she would not record the deeds until such time as he should have been reported missing, killed, or had failed to return, and that if he returned, the deeds should be returned to him and destroyed. His wife, however, recorded the deeds, and on Chillemi's return refused to return them to him. Chillemi then sued his estranged wife to have the deeds annulled. A decree in his favor was affirmed. The court said:

"But there is actually no logical reason why a deed should not be held in escrow by the grantee as well as by any other person. The ancient rule is not adapted to present-day conditions and is entirely unnecessary for the protection of the rights of litigants. After all, conditional delivery is purely a question of intention, and it is immaterial whether the instrument, pending satisfaction of the condition, is in the hands of the grantor, the grantee, or a third person. After the condition is satisfied, there is an operative conveyance which is considered as having been delivered at the time of the conditional delivery, for the reason that it was then that it was actually delivered, although the ownership does not pass until the satisfaction of the conditions. We, therefore, hold that it is the intention of the grantor of a deed that determines whether the delivery of the deed is absolute or conditional, although the delivery is made by the grantor directly to the grantee."

COLES v. BELFORD, 289 Mo. 97, 232 S.W. 729 (1921). Following is an excerpt from the opinion of the court:

"Bearing upon the question of delivery we find only the statement of defendant George F. Belford that Mrs. Phelps gave the deed to Anna Belford, saying, 'You take this and put it in your box and keep it and whenever anything happens you send it to Springfield, Missouri, and have it recorded.' True, by this delivery it may be said that Mrs. Phelps parted with dominion over the deed. However, when she said 'whenever anything happens you send it to Springfield, Missouri, and have it recorded,' that language indicates that it was her intention that the deed was not to become operative until her death. This interpretation is borne out by the further testimony of the witness George Belford, when, in response to an interrogation by the court, 'She told your sister to take the deed and put it in her box?' he replied, 'Yes, sir, and keep it and whenever anything happened to her, when she died, to send it to Springfield, Missouri, and have it recorded.' Accordingly, upon authority of the adjudicated cases, the instrument was testamentary in character, did not pass a present interest in the property to the grantees, and hence was not good as a deed, notwithstanding the intention of Mrs. Phelps that it should take effect at her death. * * * Under these authorities even a valid delivery within the life time of the grantor is not shown. This evidence fails to show that the handing of the deed to one of the grantees was done with the intent of passing an estate in praesenti, and intent is a material matter on the question of delivery. If the grantor did not give the deed to the grantee with intent of passing title at that time, then there was no delivery within contemplation of law."

BERIGAN v. BERRIGAN, 413 Ill. 204, 108 N.E.2d 438 (1952). A deed dated February 19, 1948 to the grantor's nephew John, was proved to have been executed on that date. Testimony established that the grantor on that date stated to a friend that he had just given John a deed to some property. Other testimony was given of statements by the grantor that he had taken care of John, or that John had nothing to worry about, or that John was to have the property after his death, or that he had left John the property after his death. There was other evidence that John, who lived with the grantor, had possession of the deed after its execution or at least that there was common access to it by John and the grantor. The grantor, however, retained possession of the land and received the rents and profits until his death. In a suit by heirs of the grantor to have the deed declared void, a decree upholding the deed was affirmed. The court said in part,

"We believe that the evidence shows that Patrick Berigan intended to make a present grant of a future estate in fee, a future estate to commence at his death and unsupported by any intermediate estate. Under our law it was possible for him to do this, if he carried out his intent by some proper and provable execution. * * * There is a great deal of testimony supporting the theory that whatever estate was created was presently created on February 19, 1948, by a deed that was intended to be a fully executed and delivered conveyance as of that date. The statement of Patrick Berigan to John Teter on that date, 'I just got through giving John a deed for some property, by Judas,' is most persuasive in this regard. Retention of possession of the property and its fruits by Patrick, and seeking and obtaining reimbursement for expenditures made on the property by John, are perhaps interpretable as inconsistent with a present grant of a present estate, but they are not at all inconsistent with a present grant of a future estate in fee to commence upon the death of the grantor."

B. COMMERCIAL ESCROWS

FIRST NATIONAL BANK & TRUST CO. v. SCOTT

The Court of Chancery of New Jersey, 1931.
109 N.J.Eq. 244, 156 A. 836.

LEAMING, Vice Chancellor. [A part of the court's opinion is omitted]

3. Some time before his death testator owned a number of building lots and sold them to various parties, receiving parts of the purchase money and executing written contracts of sale which provided for the payment of the balances of the purchase prices in installments and the delivery of deeds to the several parties when the full installment payments were completed. Deeds in conformity to these several agreements were then executed and acknowledged by testator and his wife to these various purchasers, and these deeds were then deposited with testator's bank, with instructions to the bank to receive for testator the purchase money as the several installments were paid, and as each contract was paid in full, to deliver to the purchaser the deed for the property called for by that contract. Some of these contracts were paid in full, and deeds delivered by the bank to the purchasers in testator's lifetime. As to these no question is herein raised. Payments to the bank have been made on many of the contracts; these payments were some made in testator's lifetime and some since his death. Some of the contracts were executed by testator and his wife, others by testator alone; but deeds were executed by testator and his wife in all cases, and those not yet delivered are in the possession of the bank. The duty of the executors touching these several transactions is made an inquiry herein, since the wife now asserts a dower interest in the several lots or their proceeds.

As to the deeds delivered in the lifetime of testator, no contention is made in behalf of the widow. As to deeds now held by the bank in cases in which the wife joined with her husband in executing the contracts of sale as well as the deeds, no substantial claim can be made by her, since she has contracted to sell. As to the remaining deeds, it is my determination that those delivered since the decease of testator are free from the widow's claim of dower. As to the deeds still in the possession of the bank, I determine it to be the duty of the executors to cause the remaining installments to be collected and the deeds to be delivered by the bank when the installments are fully paid, and in these transactions I hold that the widow cannot properly assert her claim for dower. In cases in which it is found that the installments cannot be collected and the purchasers are obliged to surrender their contracts, the widow's dower right will remain.

These conclusions flow from the recognized doctrine of relation, applied in cases of this nature for the general purpose of effectuating the intention of the parties and to thus promote justice. The controlling inquiry in cases of this class is whether the deeds were executed and given to the custody of the bank with the intent that they should be delivered to the respective parties when full payment for the lots should be made, and it is held to be immaterial whether the deposit of the deeds was made under a formal escrow agreement or in the manner in which the deeds here in question were left with the bank. * * * When so delivered with that intent and the death of the vendor holding the legal title intervenes before the condition is performed, the subsequent performance of the condition entitles the vendees to the deed, and their titles will be protected as of the date of the deposits, in the absence of intervening equities. This was early held in Perryman's Case, 5 Coke's Rep. 84a (77 Eng.Reprint, p. 181), which case is cited with approval in State Bank v. Evans, 15 N.J.Law, 155, at page 160, 28 Am. Dec. 400. In Coare v. Gilbert, 4 East, 94 (102 Eng.Reprint, p. 762, at page 763), the rule as stated in Perryman's Case is later quoted, approved, and applied. In 21 C.J. p. 890, § 36C, the American cases are collected in support of the various aspects and application of the following text:

"An instrument held by a third person as an escrow usually does not take effect until the performance of the condition or the second or final delivery. There are, however, cases where the second delivery, whether actual or constructive, operates retroactively, and by relation back to the first delivery or deposit, is substituted for it in time and effect. This rule has been applied where either of the parties to the instrument dies after it has been deposited as an escrow and before the condition has been performed and final delivery made, whether the death is that of the grantor, of the grantee, or of both parties. Likewise the delivery will relate back to the deposit if in the meantime one of the parties becomes insane, or, being a femme sole, marries. Any title acquired by the grantor between the deposit and the delivery passes by such delivery to the grantee; and if the latter dies before final delivery, the depositary may make delivery to his heirs and it will be held ordinarily to have taken effect in the ancestor so as to transmute title through him to the heirs by inheritance, where nothing intervenes to prevent. Different reasons for the adoption of this fiction are assigned by the courts. By some it is said to be equitable in its nature and intent and devised to promote justice, and hence will never be applied where injustice would result. By others it is said to be for the general purpose of effectuating the intention of the parties; and in case of deeds in consideration of love and affection, it has been said to be resorted to by some courts for the purpose of holding the transaction as in the nature of a testamentary disposition. It has been maintained that the fiction of relation back to the first delivery may be resorted to in courts of equity to ward off intervening claims or liens of the depositor's creditors; but it seems to be the prevailing rule that, in the interval of time between the first and second delivery, title remains in the grantor subject to the claims of his creditors, and that this doctrine of relation cannot be applied for the purpose of defeating such intervening claims. It has also been held that the fiction of relation will not be applied where it will cause a violation of a contract. It has, however, been resorted to for the purpose of supporting a sale of the land by the grantee after the deposit and before the final delivery, of cutting off dower of the grantor's wife, and of giving grantee priority over an intervening purchaser with full knowledge of all the facts, but not over such a purchaser without such notice.

"Where both parties to a deed in escrow abandoned the transaction, subsequent delivery of the deed by one obtaining equitable title from the grantor was not a delivery in pursuance of escrow instructions, and passage of title did not relate back to the time of delivery in escrow."
*   *   *

Defendants cite Flagg v. Teneick, 29 N.J.Law, 25, in which case, at page 31, the following language is used: "It [the deed] was delivered in escrow; but the condition or event on which it was to be delivered never happened in her lifetime, and the deed died with her." No authority touching the latter expression is cited, and obviously it cannot be understood as meaning more than at the death of the vendor the legal title necessarily vested in her heirs, but, of course, subject to any equitable rights of the vendee. As already pointed out, the same court in State Bank v. Evans, supra, recognized an equitable right of the vendee to take under the deed as of the date of its first delivery to the depository, upon the performance of the condition, notwithstanding the death of the vendor prior to the date of performance.

In the present case it is entirely clear that these deeds were executed by testator and his wife and delivered to the bank with the consummated intent and purpose that the vendees should be privileged to complete the stipulated payments to the bank, and then receive these deeds from the bank to convert their equitable estates into complete legal titles as of the prior dates. In such circumstances, the defined principles of equity in effectuating intent of the parties should recognize any legal estate transmuted to heirs by the death of the vendor, who merely held the naked legal estate, as subject to these rights of the vendees as intended by the parties.

Questions

1. Who should be entitled to the rents and profits of land which accrue between the time when the deed was placed in escrow and the time of its final delivery to the grantee? Who should be responsible for the taxes which accrue on the property during the same period? There is authority that relation-back will be applied in the first case, but not in the second. See Cribbett, Principles of the Law of Property 177 (1962). Do you see any reason for such a distinction? See generally, Mann, Escrows—Their Use and Value, 1949 U.Ill.L.F. 398.

2. The doubt about when relation-back applies and when it does not, and the difficulty in finding a consistent principle for applying the doctrine may tend to suggest the question whether there is not some other analysis of the delivery problem which could more successfully be used to cope with the hiatus between a delivery in escrow and the final delivery to the grantee. Does the analysis of the state of title after delivery in escrow which was offered in Smith v. Fay, supra, suggest itself as adaptable to the use of the escrow device in commercial transactions? Is there a basis for arguing that any delivery in escrow without reservation of a right of recall constitutes a legal delivery at the time when the deed is delivered into the hands of the third party? It may occur to you that the same question can be put in a case like Campbell v. Thomas, infra.

A Further Note on Escrows

In note 1 following Atchison v. Atchison, supra, reference was made to the use of a third party in the delivery process by the device called an "escrow." It should be obvious that if a vendor can resort to this device for his convenience and protection in the conveyancing process, so also can the purchaser do likewise in respect to the purchase price: that is, he can pay it, or its equivalent in a transaction involving an extension of credit, to a third party in escrow, under directions to pay over the purchase money or take other action on certain conditions, such as delivery of a proper deed, after title defects, if any, have been cleared. Where both parties to a land transaction desire to resort to this device, it makes sense for them to designate one person to serve them both. A person who acts under escrow instructions, whether jointly given or not, may be called an escrowee, an escrow agent, or escrow holder. His special status or powers have never been adequately defined in the law. In the joint arrangement mentioned, he would appear to be something like an agent for both parties, but he may be more than that, depending on the legal effect that is given to a delivery in escrow.

In commercial real estate transactions, a typical escrow arrangement might operate in the following manner:

Both the deed of conveyance and the purchase money are delivered in escrow, with written instructions to record the deed and order an examination of the vendor's title, and if the title is found to be good and marketable to pay over the purchase money to the vendor. The escrow instructions will also provide that if the vendor's title appears to be defective and the defects are not cured within a specified time, the purchaser shall be entitled to the return of his money upon executing a reconveyance to the vendor. Sometimes a quitclaim deed from the purchaser back to the vendor is executed in advance and deposited in escrow in order to provide for the necessary reconveyance where the vendor's deed is recorded and his title subsequently is found defective. In cases where the vendor's title has not been examined in the recent past, the escrow procedure is often divided into two parts. First, before the vendor's deed is recorded, the escrow holder is instructed to have the vendor's title examined down to the date of the contract. Then, if the vendor's title is good at the date of the contract, the escrow holder is instructed to record the vendor's deed and bring the examination of title down to the date of recordation.

Since the escrow normally is a means of carrying out the terms of a contract of sale, the draftsman should make sure that there is no conflict between the contract and the escrow agreement which embodies the parties' instructions to the escrow holder. In some of the Western states, however it is the general practice to draft the contract itself in the form of an escrow agreement, with a title company as the escrow holder. The parties sign an agreement containing the terms of sale, much like an ordinary purchase and sale contract, but specifying that the vendor's deed and the purchase money are to be deposited in escrow. The title company examines the vendor's title, notifies the vendor of any title defects so that he may correct them, and when all defects have been cleared up, records the deed and pays over the purchase money to the vendor after deducting its own charges.

Sometimes it develops at the title closing that some title defect exists which cannot be eliminated at once, but the parties want to avoid the necessity of another meeting to complete the sale. In such a case, although no escrow was originally contemplated, the parties may agree to deliver the deed and the purchase money to a third party to hold in escrow, with instructions that when the title defect is removed the deed shall be delivered to the purchaser and the purchase money to the vendor. In the same way, part of the purchase money may be put in escrow, to be paid over to the vendor upon proof that he has satisfied some outstanding lien, the amount of which cannot be accurately estimated at the closing.

In every case, escrow instructions should be in writing, and should cover all matters agreed upon, such as the documents to be deposited by the vendor, deposits to be made by the purchaser (purchase money and purchase money mortgage, if any), when the vendor's deed is to be recorded, title defects to which the purchaser will not object, evidence of title to be furnished by the vendor, time allowed the vendor to clear defects in title, how and when the purchase money is to be disbursed, time when the deed is to be delivered to the purchaser, return of deposits to the parties where title defects cannot be removed, and reconveyance to the vendor if his deed has been recorded immediately on signing of escrow agreement and it appears that the title is subject to defects which cannot be removed.

The major advantage of such an escrow arrangement is that the purchaser is assured of receiving, in return for the purchase price, a title free and clear of all defects except those he agreed to take subject to, including encumbrances that might otherwise attach in the interval between the making of the contract and the recording of the vendor's deed; while the vendor is assured that he will receive the purchase money if his title is found to be good and marketable as required by the contract. Where the escrow arrangement provides for immediate recording of the vendor's deed, he can be protected by a provision for reconveyance by the purchaser if the title proves defective and cannot be cured; in such a case, the purchaser cannot recover the purchase money until he reconveys. Moreover, if the vendor's deed is immediately recorded, the purchaser may safely allow the escrow holder to use part of the purchase money to remove encumbrances such as judgment liens, tax liens, and mechanics' liens; and the purchaser is also protected against the vendor's changing his mind and conveying the property to a bona fide purchaser without notice of the contract to sell.

A long-term escrow may also be used when the vendor extends credit to the purchaser for part of the purchase price and retains title as security under an installment land contract. In such a case, deposit of the vendor's deed in escrow gives the purchaser additional assurance that he will obtain the legal title to the property if and when he completes payment of the purchase price.

CAMPBELL v. THOMAS

Supreme Court of Wisconsin, 1877.
42 Wis. 437, 24 Am.Rep. 427.

Appeal from the Circuit Court for Racine County.

The case, stated most favorably to the plaintiff, is briefly as follows: The plaintiff and Thomas entered into a parol agreement for the sale by the latter to the former of certain land, at a stipulated price, to be secured and paid as hereinafter mentioned. In accordance with such parol agreement, the plaintiff paid Thomas a small sum on account of the purchase money, and the latter signed, sealed and duly acknowledged a deed of the premises to the plaintiff (which was in the usual form of a warranty deed), and delivered the same to Judge Hand, his codefendant, with directions to deliver it to the plaintiff if the latter should, two days later, deposit with Hand his notes for a certain sum (part of the price of the land), and a mortgage executed by him on the same land to secure the payment of such notes, and at the same time pay to Hand, for the use of Thomas, the balance of the agreed price. These proceedings were all in accordance with such verbal agreement. At the appointed time, the plaintiff deposited with Hand the notes, mortgage and money as agreed, and demanded the deed of the land; but, acting in obedience to instructions from Thomas, Hand refused to deliver the deed. At the same time, Thomas tendered to the plaintiff the money which the latter paid him when the verbal agreement was made, and, on the refusal of the plaintiff to receive it, left the same with Judge Hand for the plaintiff.

This action was brought to compel Judge Hand to deliver to the plaintiff the deed thus deposited with him by Thomas. The circuit court gave judgment for the plaintiff, that the defendant Hand deliver such deed to him, and that Thomas pay the costs of the action. From this judgment Thomas appealed.

LYON, J. If the deed deposited by Thomas with Judge Hand was an escrow, we have no doubt the conditions upon which the same was to be delivered to the plaintiff, who was the grantee named therein, might lawfully rest in parol and be proved by parol. Was the instrument an escrow? If Thomas, notwithstanding the deposit, retained control of it, it was not, and he might lawfully reclaim it or prevent a delivery of it to the plaintiff. See Prutsman v. Baker, 30 Wis. 644, and cases cited.

It is very clear that unless there was a valid contract between Thomas and the plaintiff for the sale and purchase of the lands described in the deed deposited with Judge Hand, such deposit was the mere voluntary act of Thomas, which in no manner interfered with or affected his control of the instrument. Fitch v. Bunch, 30 Cal. 208.

Hence the controlling question to be determined is, did Thomas and the plaintiff make a valid contract for the sale and purchase of the land?

[The court then went on to point out that there was no such valid contract. The judgment below was reversed. A petition for rehearing having been granted, the case was reargued and the following opinion by LYON, J., was handed down.]

The controlling question in this case is, whether it is essential to the plaintiff's right of action that there was a valid executory contract between the parties for the purchase and sale of the land described in the deed of the defendant deposited with Judge Hand. If this question be answered in the affirmative, the plaintiff cannot recover; for it is certain that no note or memorandum of the alleged agreement under which the plaintiff claims, expressing the consideration thereof, was reduced to writing and subscribed by the defendant. Rev.St.1858, c. 106, § 8.

The learned counsel for the plaintiff has met this question squarely, and, in his elaborate and most able arguments on the motion for a rehearing and on the rehearing of the cause, has maintained the proposition that "it is not true that a person must be under a previous binding executory contract to convey the lands described in the deed to the grantee, in order to place a deed thereof, delivered to a third person on condition for the grantee, beyond the control of the grantor."

Undoubtedly there is a class of cases in which this proposition is true. These are the cases where the deed has been delivered by the grantor to a third person with instructions to deliver the same to the grantee on the happening of a future certain event—as the death of the grantor or some other person,—and such conditional delivery is assented to by the grantee. In such a case, if the grantor reserves no control over the deed, he cannot after such delivery recall it, but the grantee is entitled to it upon the happening of the event, although there is no valid executory contract to support it. The reason of this is, that the first delivery of the deed passes to the grantee the title to the land, and thus relieves him of the obligation to make title through any contract other than that expressed in the deed itself.

But by all of the authorities a deed so deposited with a third person to be delivered to the grantee on the happening of some event in the future which may or may not happen, does not pass title to the land described in it to the grantee until such event occurs, and then only from that time, or perhaps from the actual delivery of the deed to the grantee after the event has occurred. There may be exceptional cases, as where a man delivers his deed in escrow and dies before the conditions of the deposit are fulfilled. In such cases, it has been said that from necessity after the conditions are fulfilled the deed must take effect by relation as of the time of the first delivery. This, however, is not one of the exceptional cases; and it must be conceded, we think, that the deposit of the deed with Judge Hand by the defendant with the assent of the plaintiff did not transfer title to the plaintiff.

Because such deposit did not divest the plaintiff of his title to the land, there is no executed contract for sale; and hence, it seems almost too plain to be questioned or doubted that, before the plaintiff can obtain the delivery of the deed and the title to the land, after the defendant has recalled the deed and repudiated the whole transaction, he must show that the defendant has made a valid and binding agreement to sell and convey the land. And such an agreement can be evidenced only by a written note or memorandum thereof, expressing the consideration and subscribed by the defendant.

In many of the cases cited, there was no valid executory contract for the sale of the land, but the grantor permitted the deed to be delivered by the depositary to the grantee upon performance of the parol conditions of the deposit. Undoubtedly, the final delivery to the grantee in such cases operated to pass the title; as it would in the present case had the defendant seen fit to allow his void parol agreement to be thus consummated. In other cases cited, there was a compliance with the statute of frauds. Everts v. Agnes, 4 Wis. 343, 65 Am.Dec. 314, is one of them. But we have not discovered a single case in which it has been held that one who has deposited a deed of land with a third person with directions to deliver it to the grantee on the happening of a given event, but who has made no valid executory contract to convey the land, may not revoke the directions to the depositary and recall the deed at any time before the conditions of the deposit have been complied with; provided those conditions are such that the title does not pass at once to the grantee upon delivery of the deed to the depositary.

The cases of Welch v. Sackett, 12 Wis. 243, Brandeis v. Neustadtl, 13 Wis. 142, and Prutsman v. Baker, 30 Wis. 644, 11 Am.Rep. 592, as well as that of Thomas v. Sowards, 25 Wis. 631, contain much doctrine in perfect accord with the views here expressed. The latter of these cases, as was observed in the first opinion filed herein, is direct authority that in this case the plaintiff must show a valid executory agreement for the sale and purchase of the land, or fail in the action. And here it should be observed that the language of the opinion in Thomas v. Sowards which was commented on at some length in the former opinion in this case, was manifestly employed with reference to the facts in that case, without any intention to lay down a general rule of law applicable to other cases. In that view, the language seems unexceptionable. So far as those comments are concerned, I am still inclined to the opinion that the views there advanced are correct. The proposition that the executory contract may be proved by the deed (if it is stated therein) is, however, still open in this court for argument and decision in a proper case.

Our conclusion is, that this case was correctly decided in the first instance. The judgment of the circuit court must therefore be reversed, and the cause remanded with the direction to that court to dismiss the complaint.

Notes

1. Most of the authority is in accord. 3 A.L.P. § 12.67; but cf. Calbreath v. Borchert, 248 Iowa 491, 81 N.W.2d 433 (1957), and Farley v. Palmer, 29 Ohio St. 223 (1870). The rule has been much criticized. See 4 Tiffany § 1052; Ai-

gler, Is a Contract Necessary to Create an Effective Escrow, 16 Mich.L.Rev. 569 (1918); Ballantine, Delivery in Escrow, 29 Yale L.J. 831 (1920).

Should it make any difference in a proper analysis of such a transaction that a grantor withdraws his deed from escrow before the grantee has performed or tendered performance of his obligations under the terms of the escrow?

2. G deposited a deed in escrow, the terms of the escrow requiring the deposit by the grantee, H, of his deed to other land to G. H deposited as required a duly executed deed to G, but did not at that time receive the deed executed by G. Several days later T filed a notice of a mechanics' lien against the property conveyed by G and commenced a suit to foreclose the lien. T had notice of all the above facts. Is T's claim superior to H's? See Holman v. Toten, 34 Cal. App.2d 309, 128 P.2d 808 (1942).

CLEVENGER v. MOORE

Supreme Court of Oklahoma, 1927.
126 Okl. 246, 259 P. 219, 54 A.L.R. 1237.

DIFFENDAFFER, C. This is an action brought by the plaintiff for the possession of lot 15, block 10, in the original town of Bartlesville, and for the cancellation of a deed therefor from plaintiff to defendant J.D. Simmons, and also for cancellation of a deed made by J.D. Simmons to defendant D.F. Moore. * * *

[Plaintiff signed and acknowledged a deed to property owned by her, conveying the property to defendant Simmons. She handed the deed over to one Peay, who was to place it in the safe of one Grant until the plaintiff could inspect property owned by Simmons, with a view to taking that property in exchange for the property covered by her deed, but with the understanding that the deed was to be returned to her if she decided not to take the Simmons property. After inspecting the Simmons property, plaintiff told Peay that she did not want the Simmons property and wanted her deed returned to her. Peay promised to get the deed for her, but a week later offered in exchange for plaintiff's property a ranch owned by Simmons. Plaintiff saw the ranch and agreed to take it, but then it was discovered that Simmons did not own the ranch. Attempts were then made to obtain a deed to the ranch from the owner, but this deal fell through for failure to obtain a federal loan on the ranch. Ten days after plaintiff's deed was executed it was filed for record. Thereafter Simmons executed and delivered a deed to the same land to defendant Moore, who paid value therefor without knowledge of the prior circumstances, and took possession of the property. Plaintiff testified that she did not know how or when Simmons got possession of her property or the deed, that all during the negotiation she thought that the deed remained in escrow, and that she made repeated demands for the return of her deed. At the close of the plaintiff's evidence the court sustained a demurrer thereto and dismissed the action, and from that judgment the plaintiff brings this appeal.]

We think the evidence clearly shows that the deed to plaintiff's property was placed in escrow and was delivered to defendant Simmons without the fulfillment of the conditions, and without any authority whatever from plaintiff, and in violation of the escrow agreement, which is sufficient to make out a clear case in favor of plaintiff as against the defendant Simmons, and that the only question for us to consider in this case is: First, where a deed is placed in escrow and the same is delivered to the grantee without performance of the conditions for delivery, is such a deed absolutely void? And, second, what are the rights of one claiming to be an innocent purchaser for value of the property from such grantee, where such grantee is in possession of the property without the knowledge or consent of the grantor? The first question, we think, is well settled in this state. In Hunter Realty Co. v. Spencer et al., 21 Okl. 155, 95 P. 757, 17 L.R.A., N.S., 622, this court in the second syllabus said:

"No title will pass by a deed which is not delivered by the grantor or some one duly authorized by him."

And in the case of Taylor v. Harkins, 74 Okl. 206, 178 P. 117, it was held that a deed does not operate to convey title until delivered, and that, where the possession of a deed placed in escrow is obtained without the performance of the condition upon which delivery thereof was to be made, no title passes therefor.

We think these cases clearly state the rule in cases of this character where the question is between the grantor and grantee.

In the case of Wood v. French, 39 Okl. 685, 136 P. 734, this court said:

"We are of opinion that where the grantor retains the actual possession of the land, as in the present case, although such possession be not notice of his adverse claim * * * an escrow deed is utterly invalid to transfer any right, in the absence of performance of the condition, so that the wrongful yielding of possession of the deed to the grantee by the person with whom it is deposited transfers no title, even though the claimant thereunder be an innocent purchaser for value."

It will be observed that in that case, the court went so far as to say that where a grantor retains possession of the land, though his possession is not notice of his adverse claim, the escrow deed is utterly invalid to transfer any right, in the absence of performance of the conditions, even though the claimant thereunder be an innocent purchaser for value.

The second proposition of plaintiff's brief is that the deed, being obtained from escrow, without performance of the conditions, is absolutely void, passes no title, and the title remains in the grantor. Therefore the grantee has no title which he can pass to an innocent purchaser, and that there can be no innocent purchaser.

In considering this proposition, it must be borne in mind that this class of cases is to be distinguished from those in which the signature to the deed or consent to its delivery from the escrow holder is obtained by fraud. In the latter class, the rule is everywhere recognized to be that an innocent purchaser from such grantee will be protected, and the distinction seems to be made on the ground that where the instrument is obtained from the escrow in violation of the terms thereof, and without the knowledge or consent of the grantor, it is equivalent to taking the instrument from his possession by theft. While in the other class the grantor consents thereto and has knowledge of such delivery, and where it is a question of whether he or another innocent person must suffer from the fraud, he will be held to suffer the loss rather than the innocent purchaser who takes without knowledge.

It is conceded by defendant that the case of Wood v. French, supra, cited by counsel for plaintiff, at least tends to support plaintiff's claim in this case, but defendant insists that Wood v. French, supra, was based upon the fact that the grantor remained in possession of the land. Defendants' counsel state that, so far as their research has led, in no case has it been held that an innocent purchaser from a record owner of land in possession thereof fails to acquire title thereto, by reason of the fact that his grantor's title came through a deed which had been delivered out of escrow before performance of the conditions of the escrow agreement. The general rule, as stated in 21 Corpus Juris, 885, is:

"A transfer to a subvendee of an instrument, wrongfully delivered to the grantee or obligee, confers no right or title upon him where he has notice of such delivery or is put upon inquiry regarding it. Further, although there is some authority to the contrary, according to the weight of authority the same rule applies even in the case of an innocent subvendee without notice of the conditions or event stipulated in the escrow contract, and is especially applied in cases where the escrow has been obtained or delivered through fraud."

There is some authority to the contrary: Hubbard v. Greely, 84 Me. 340, 24 A. 799, 17 L.R.A. 511, and Blight v. Schenck, 10 Pa. 285, 51 Am. Dec. 478. In support of the majority rule, cases are cited from Colorado, Georgia, Illinois, Indiana, Iowa, Kansas, Nebraska, New Jersey, Oregon, Texas, Vermont, Wisconsin, and also the case of Wood v. French, supra.

We have read all the cases cited, and one of the earliest cases on the subject seems to be the case of Smith v. South Royalton Bank, 32 Vt. 341, 76 Am.Dec. 179, where it is held that a deed delivered in escrow to be delivered to the grantee, after the performance of some other act, will not be valid for any purpose until the condition upon which it is to be delivered to the grantee has been performed, and the fact that the deed has since come into the hands of an innocent purchaser for value will not change the rule in that case. However, it does not appear that the grantor had surrendered possession of the property. In that case, the court, however, after discussing the principle of the rule as applied to commercial paper, says:

"But let the principle be as it may, in regard to commercial papers, no question can be made as to a void deed. The case of Van Amringe v. Morton, 4 Whart. [Pa.] 382, 34 Am.Dec. 517, is ruled expressly on the distinction between a void and a voidable deed, and it was there held that a bona fide purchaser for a valuable consideration, from the person holding a void deed, stands in no better situation than such fraudulent holder. The distinction is fully recognized in Price v. Junkin, 4 Watts [Pa.] 85, 28 Am.Dec. 685, and the case decided upon that distinction. So in Arrison v. Armstead, 2 Pa.St. 191, 195, it was held that a deed having been rendered void by an alteration, a purchaser without notice and for valuable consideration was in no better situation than the original parties. The case in 4 Wharton, as in the case at bar, was one where there had been no valid delivery of the deed. So in the case of Pawling v. United States, 4 Cranch, 219 [2 L.Ed. 601], there had been no delivery of the deed. It hardly need be remarked that if a deed wants delivery, it is void ab initio.

"Where a bona fide purchaser for value holds under a vendee who holds by a voidable deed, though he and the creditors of the vendor have equal equities, yet the purchaser has also the legal title, and shall be preferred. In the case at bar, though the billholders of the bank, represented by the treasurer and the orators, have equal equities, yet as the bond and deed are void, the legal title remains in the orators, and they should be preferred, under the common rule, that where the equities are equal, the one having the legal title prevails."

Another early case on the subject is the case of Everts v. Agnes, 4 Wis. 343, 65 Am.Dec. 314, which case was again before the court on a second appeal in Everts v. Agnes, 6 Wis. 453. * * *

In that case Everts, the plaintiff, was the maker of the deed. Agnes, one of the defendants, was the one to whom the deed had been wrongfully delivered from escrow, and Swift, the other defendant, was the one to whom Agnes had conveyed the property and made his defense upon the ground that he was an innocent purchaser for value without notice, and set up in his answer, as did Moore in the instant case, that at the time he made the purchase he caused the record to be examined, obtained full abstract of Agnes' title, and believed he (Agnes) had a good title, and gave him, Swift, one, except as to the balance due on a mortgage, subject to which Swift made the purchase. Also, that before he made the purchase he visited the premises and found Agnes and Bender in possession, that Agnes had been in undisputed possession there the preceding summer, and assured Swift his title was good, denies all notice, at the time of the purchase and payment of consideration money, as to the manner in which Agnes got the deed from Zettler (the escrow holder), and all notice of the conditions under which the deed was left by Everts with Zettler. He further alleges in his answer, that Everts, before any of these transactions, resided in the neighborhood of the premises, and saw Agnes in possession without objection, that the possession was given Agnes at the date of the contract between Everts and Agnes, and that Agnes held possession until he sold the premises to Swift. It will thus be seen that, in that case, the facts appeared more strongly against the plaintiff than in the instant case, for the reason that the evidence in this case, as the record now stands, is that the plaintiff did not know that Simmons ever was in possession, did not know how he obtained possession, if he was in possession, and that such possession was without her knowledge or consent. The court in the case of Everts v. Agnes, supra, held:

"We have not the slightest doubt that the deed of Everts to Agnes was delivered to Zettler as an escrow, to be delivered only upon the performance of the conditions prescribed. That Agnes fraudulently ob-

tained possession of the deed, and fradulently procured it to be recorded. That no title passed to Agnes, and hence he could convey none to
Swift. The latter has his remedy upon his covenant against Agnes if
any there be. This is the only point necessary to be considered at this
time, and we adhere to the language and the conclusion adopted when
this case was under consideration before, viz.: that the fraudulent procurement of a deed, deposited as an escrow, from the depositary, by the
grantee named in the deed, would not operate to pass the title; and that
a bona fide purchaser from such grantee so fraudulently procuring the
deed, could derive no title from him, and would not be protected."

The case of Everts v. Agnes, supra, has been cited by a great number of the courts in other states as the leading case on this question,
and was followed in the case of Dixon v. Bristol Savings Bank, 102 Ga.
461, 31 S.E. 96, 66 Am.St.Rep. 193, where the court on the question of
possession said:

"The question of possession is not material where there has been an
unauthorized delivery of an escrow, or where it has been obtained
fraudulently, for the reason that the parties claiming under the grantee
named in the escrow cannot be protected, unless it is shown that the
grantor ratified its delivery or that the depositary was the grantee's
[sic] agent to procure delivery."

The rule laid down in the Wisconsin case (Everts v. Agnes, supra)
seems to have been followed in the following cases: Chipman v. Tucker,
38 Wis. 43, 20 Am.Rep. 1, Tyler v. Cate, 29 Or. 515, 45 P. 800, and
Weghorst v. Clark, 66 Colo. 535, 180 P. 742, where it is said:

"The only way, if any, in which a grantee of a grantee of a recorded
undelivered deed can claim anything against the grantor in such deed is
by estoppel in pais through the grantor's neglect to take immediate
measures to recover his land, thus leaving an apparently good title
shown by the record." Harkreader v. Clayton, 56 Miss. 383, 31 Am.
Rep. 369; Spotts v. Whitaker (Tex.Civ.App.) 157 S.W. 422; Houston v.
Adams, 85 Fla. 291, 95 So. 859; Jackson v. Lynn, 94 Iowa 151, 62 N.W.
704, 58 Am.St.Rep. 386.

We have given due consideration to the cases cited by defendant
wherein third persons claiming as innocent purchasers have been protected under circumstances somewhat similar to those in the instant
case, but we think the great weight of authority, as well as better reasoning, is found in those cases holding the other way. The defendant in
his brief says:

"In passing upon a demurrer to the evidence the court does not
weigh the evidence. The demurrer admits every fact which the evidence in the slightest degree tends to prove and all inferences and conclusions that may be reasonably and logically drawn from the same,
and, where there is any conflict in the plaintiff's evidence that would
make any part of it unfavorable to the plaintiff or sustains the defense,
the court in passing upon such demurrer should consider such evidence
withdrawn."

Applying this rule, we think the trial court committed error in sustaining the demurrer to plaintiff's evidence, and that for the reasons stated this cause should be reversed and remanded for a new trial.

Note on Acceptance

In an early leading English case, Thompson v. Leach, 2 Vent. 198, 86 Eng. Rep. 391 (1691), it was held that a conveyance was a contract and consequently acceptance thereof by the grantee was a necessary part of the conveyance. But the court added that in normal circumstances such acceptance is presumed unless and until the grantee negates it by express rejection, in which case the estate that came to him by delivery is revested in the grantor. It is objectionable to say that every conveyance is a contract, although many instruments of conveyance do state the terms of a contract that is incidental to the passage of title. But with the presumption of acceptance, and the fact that the incidence of rejections is very rare, it seems sensible to regard the title as passing subject to being divested upon rejection.

Most of the American cases have followed both the view that acceptance is necessary and that normally acceptance is presumed. But they have not followed the view that title passes subject to later rejection, preferring to treat acceptance as the final step in a conveyance, and where necessary to effectuate the intention of the grantor, holding that title relates back upon acceptance to the time of delivery. This view has permitted courts on occasion to refuse to relate back in favor of an accepting grantee if other interests have intervened between the time of delivery and a later knowledge or acceptance of the deed by the grantee. Such intervening claimants are most often subsequent purchasers or creditors of the grantor. See 3 A.L.P. § 1270.

Note on Dedication of Land for Streets and Other Public Uses

The "dedication" of land is "the permanent devotion of private property to a use that concerns the public in its municipal character." Black v. Central R.R., 85 N.J.L. 197, 89 A. 24 (1913). It would appear that the term "dedication" was used in England almost exclusively with respect to highways. In the United States, however, the scope of "dedication" is much expanded. It is well settled that land may be dedicated for any of the following public uses: bridges, squares, parks and other recreational facilities, schools, markets, wharves and landing-places, public buildings, cemeteries and some "charitable uses."

As a general rule any person or corporation capable of conveying land by deed may dedicate land to public use. There need not be any particular "grantee" in existence at the time of dedication, although a municipal corporation or other governmental agency representing the public is usually in existence and capable of accepting the dedication when it is made. Ordinarily land can be dedicated only by one who has a legal fee simple estate therein, but there is some authority that the holder of an equitable estate may make a dedication which will be effective as soon as he acquires the legal estate.

Dedication of land may be effected, at common law, by any conduct of the dedicator which manifests his intent to devote the land in question to public use. The conduct may consist of either written or oral declarations of intent, or of other conduct from which the intent to devote land to a public use can be inferred. The interest acquired by the public may be either a fee simple estate or an easement, whichever is required to effectuate the dedicator's intent. A gift of land to a municipal corporation or other governmental unit by an effective written conveyance is usually called a "dedication," although in such case it would seem that the estate or easement passes by "conveyance" rather than by "dedication" in the strict sense of the term.

A dedicator may reserve to himself all rights in the land not inconsistent with the purpose for which the land is dedicated, and may impose conditions or restrictions as to the mode of public user which are not inconsistent with the legal character of the dedication and do not impair the police power of the municipality or other governmental unit which holds the dedicated interest in trust for the public at large. But the dedicator apparently cannot dedicate land to public use for a limited period of time—e.g., for his lifetime or for a term of years.

Conduct of a landowner manifesting his intent to devote land to a public use is sometimes referred to as an "offer of dedication," although courts usually refer to it simply as a "dedication." Use of the latter term to describe the dedicator's conduct may cause confusion, since "dedication" is also used to describe the entire transaction by which present public rights of user and duties of maintenance are created with respect to privately owned land, i.e., the legal relations which result from the "offer" and the "acceptance" together. It is clear that "dedication" is not complete until there is an "acceptance". That is to say, "acceptance" is a prerequisite to acquisition of any present right of user by the public and to the imposition of any duty upon the public authorities to maintain the area dedicated to public use. But, although "acceptance" usually results from official action by public authorities empowered to act in behalf of the public at large, "acceptance" has sometimes been held to result from an actual enjoyment by the public of the use for such length of time that the public accommodation would be materially affected by a denial or interruption of enjoyment, or public user for twenty years without proof that the public would be seriously discommoded were the use to be interrupted.

Many states have statutes setting forth a procedure for dedication of land to public use. Usually these statutes require the making of a survey and plat, a recital of dedication on the plat, recordation of the plat, and acceptance of the dedication by the appropriate public authorities. Substantial compliance with the statutory procedure is generally sufficient, although some states require strict compliance. Statutory dedication ordinarily results in the transfer of a fee simple estate to the municipality or other governmental unit in trust for the public at large. The statutory procedure may be, but seldom is, exclusive. Common law dedications are usually still permitted, and an unsuccessful attempt at statutory dedication may result in an effective common law dedication.

The type of common law dedication with which we are principally concerned nowadays is that which results from the recording of a subdivision plat showing streets or other public areas such as parks, followed by the sale of lots with reference thereto. This not only creates private easements in the purchasers of the lots but also constitutes a sufficient offer to dedicate the streets or other public areas shown on the plat to public use, provided the plat does not contain a "reservation" or other notation which prevents the inference of intent on the part of the subdivider to dedicate. In some states, at least, the inference of intent to dedicate will arise even though the plat is not recorded. And in New Jersey it has been held that the "deliberate and successful pursuit of" the formalities necessary for subdivision approval by the public authorities, without more, carries "the manifest implication of an *offer* to dedicate for public use those delineated areas which are definitely designated on the map or plan as streets." New Jersey Highway Authority v. Johnson, 35 N.J.Super. 203, 113 A.2d 831, 836 (App.Div.1955). *Sed quaere*, however, whether the resulting dedication should be viewed as based upon common law or statute, in view of the requirements imposed upon the subdivider by statute and ordinance as a condition precedent to subdivision approval.

As is indicated infra in the section dealing with public control of land subdivision, a municipality or other local unit of government may, and often does, accept a subdivider's offer of dedication of streets or other areas by an appropriate ordinance or resolution of its governing body. But an offer of dedication may also be accepted by other official conduct of public authorities which manifests the intent to treat the land in question as dedicated to public use. Thus, e.g., assumption of control over streets or other areas by grading, paving, otherwise improving, or maintaining them has been held to constitute an acceptance. So also, the bringing of an action for possession of the dedicated land or any action in which the municipality asserts that the land has been dedicated to public use may be deemed an acceptance.

The most common method of extinguishing public rights in dedicated lands is a formal proceeding to "vacate" such rights. The mode of proceeding is usually prescribed by statute, and the statute usually requires publication and mailing of notices to persons affected by the proposed "vacation." Final action by the local governing body in "vacating" public rights in dedicated lands is by ordinance or resolution.* Public rights in dedicated land may also be lost by abandonment, but the burden of proof is upon the person alleging that abandonment has occurred and proof is difficult.

---

* In cases where the municipality owns the street in fee simple by virtue of statutory dedication, the statutes usually provide that, upon "vacation" of public rights in the street, the fee simple shall vest in the abutting landowners, with the midpoint of the former street as the new boundary. In cases where the municipality has only an easement in the street, "vacation" of public rights will give the fee simple owners (whoever they may be) an unencumbered right to possession and use of the former street. Usually, but not always, the abutting landowners will own the fee in the street, with the midpoint as the boundary.

Chapter 10

PRIORITIES AND RECORDING

SECTION 1. PRIORITIES: BASIC COMMON LAW AND EQUITY RULES

A. REAL PROPERTY PRIORITIES

Consider the competing claims of A and B in the following situations apart from the application of any statute, in other words, in accordance with the general rules of the common law and equity:

Assuming O to be the owner in fee simple of Blackacre:

(a) He makes an effective conveyance thereof to A and his heirs. Thereafter he executes another conveyance in favor of B and his heirs, B taking (1) with notice, (2) without notice, of the earlier deed to A. Would it be significant that B gave value?

(b) He creates in favor of A an equitable interest in or charge upon Blackacre. Thereafter he purports to create in favor of B another equity, the assertion of which interferes with the enjoyment by A of his equity. Assume that B took (1) with notice, (2) without notice of A's earlier equity. Again would it be significant that B gave value?

(c) He creates in favor of A an equitable interest in or charge upon Blackacre. Thereafter he executes an effective legal conveyance thereof in favor of B and his heirs, B taking (1) as a bona fide purchaser for value, (2) as a donee or with notice.

(d) He executes an effective legal conveyance to A and his heirs. Thereafter he purports to create in the same land an equity in favor of B, who takes (1) for value without notice, (2) as a donee or with notice.

As between successive transfers of land by the same transferor purporting to create legal interests it was the almost invariable rule of the common law that priority in right was determined by priority in time.[1]

---

1. Apparently the only exception, at least in the case of land, was found in those situations where the earlier transfer was tinctured with fraud. The fraud might be aimed either at creditors of the conveyor or at subsequent purchasers from him. Two celebrated statutes of the time of Elizabeth were designed to cover these situations. The statute of 13 Eliz. c. 5, declared all transfers made with intent to hinder, delay and defraud creditors to be null and void as to such creditors.

The statute of 27 Eliz. c. 4, provided in substance that conveyances with the intent and purpose of defrauding subsequent purchasers of the same lands for valuable consideration should be, as to such subsequent purchasers, null and void. Conveyances made bona fide and for good consideration were expressly excepted from the operation of the statute.

In the nature of things most of the conveyances that have been stricken down un-

This followed naturally from the fact that after O had conveyed to A there was no interest left in O which he could transfer to B; first in time was first in right because there was nothing left for the second transferee.[2] Notice and lack of notice were wholly immaterial.

When the contest was in equity between holders of competing equitable interests, priorities again were determined normally on the basis of time. The familiar maxim "Qui prior est tempore potior est jure," is a reflection of this doctrine. In Willoughby v. Willoughby [3] Lord Hardwicke said: "Wherever the legal estate is standing out, either in a prior encumbrancer, or in such a trustee as against whom the puisne incumbrancer has not the best right to call for the legal estate, the whole title and consideration is in equity, and then the general maxim must take place, qui prior est tempore potior est jure." Here, too, as in the case of competing legal claimants, notice is not the basis for determining priority of right.[4]

When the contest is between claimants of the legal ownership, on the one side, and, on the other, claimants of equitable interests, again the normal basis of preferment is priority of time. Here, however, application of the doctrines of bona fide purchase may reverse the order. If the taker of the legal ownership was a purchaser for value without notice, he will be preferred even as against an older equity.[5] In this type of case, then, notice, or the absence thereof, may be of prime importance. The doctrines of bona fide purchaser never went so far as to

der the Stat. 27 Eliz., as having been made with intent to defraud subsequent purchasers, have been gift transfers, and the English court went so far as to hold a gratuitous conveyance to be conclusively fraudulent as against a subsequent purchaser for value, even though such subsequent purchaser took with notice of the earlier deed.

Under that doctrine the donor might be said to retain a power to divest the donee of his gift by executing a deed to a later purchaser who was willing to give value for a conveyance of the same lands.

The courts in the United States have not generally taken such an extreme stand. Indeed, since American courts commonly hold that recording of deeds gives constructive notice thereof to subsequent purchasers and creditors, and since the normal course is for any grantee promptly to record his deed—and since, in addition, American courts have refused to find any "fraud" when a subsequent purchaser takes with notice of a prior gratuitous conveyance by the same grantor—it is clear that American statutes avoiding conveyances made with intent to defraud subsequent purchasers have little operative effect.

The English rule as to subsequent purchasers was changed by Stat. 56 & 57 Vict., c. 21 (1893).

2. This, of course, is the normal result both as to land and goods. The departures therefrom are few and based upon what are deemed compelling reasons.

3. 1 Term.Rep. 763, 1756.

4. There are, however, some apparent exceptions to the rule that priority in these cases depends always on time, and in these situations the matter of notice may be important. It is obviously not within the scope of this book to examine into these so called exceptions. See Tiffany § 1260.

5. The bona fide purchaser has an equity in the mere fact that he has parted with his money or its equivalent in good faith. As between his equity and the earlier one, it might be expected that the scales would incline towards the earlier one simply because it is earlier; but the holder of the later equity has the legal ownership to add to the weight of his equity as an innocent purchaser. It is important, then, to observe that in order to take free of an equity as a bona fide purchaser the purchase, generally speaking, must be of a legal interest. It will be remembered that in the early development of the use, it was cut off in favor of a later bona fide purchaser of the legal ownership.

cut off legal interests in favor of subsequent equity claimants, even though the latter acquired their equities for value and without notice.

B. PERSONAL PROPERTY PRIORITIES

At common law the maxim "Qui prior est tempore potior est jure" also provided the basic rule of priority with respect to transfers of chattels. The same fundamental idea was, perhaps, more frequently expressed in the maxim "Nemo plus juris transferre potest quam ipse habet,"—"No one can transfer a better title than he himself has." To this general rule there were three principal exceptions: (1) Where a purchaser acquired title to goods by fraud, although his title was said to be "voidable" by the defrauded seller, a further transfer to a bona fide purchaser for value gave the latter a "good title" as against the defrauded seller. (2) A seller in possession of goods already sold had power to transfer a "good title" to a subsequent bona fide purchaser for value. (3) A bailor who entrusted goods to one regularly in the business of selling goods of the same type might, under certain circumstances, be estopped to assert his title to the goods as against a bona fide purchaser from the bailee for a valuable consideration. The first two exceptions were codified in the Uniform Sales Act, §§ 24 and 25. The third exception, which can be regarded as a generalized statement of the principle underlying the second exception, was not expressly codified in the Uniform Sales Act, although § 23 refers to this exception.

At the present time all fifty states have adopted the Uniform Commercial Code. In these states the rules of priority with respect to the sale of goods are now codified as follows:

"Section 2–403. Power to Transfer; Good Faith Purchase of Goods; 'Entrusting'.

"(1) A purchaser of goods acquires all title which his transferor had or had power to transfer except that a purchaser of a limited interest acquires rights only to the extent of the interest purchased. A person with voidable title has power to transfer a good title to a good faith purchaser for value. When goods have been delivered under a transaction of purchase the purchaser has such power even though (a) the transferor was deceived as to the identity of the purchaser, or (b) the delivery was in exchange for a check which is later dishonored, or (c) it was agreed that the transaction was to be a 'cash sale,' or (d) the delivery was procured through fraud punishable as larcenous under the criminal law.

"(2) Any entrusting of possession of goods to a merchant who deals in goods of that kind gives him power to transfer all rights of the entruster to a buyer in ordinary course of business.

"(3) 'Entrusting' includes any delivery and any acquiescence in retention of possession regardless of any condition expressed between the parties to the delivery or acquiescence and regardless of whether the procurement of the entrusting or the possessor's disposition of the goods have been such as to be larcenous under the criminal law.

"(4) The rights of other purchasers of goods and of lien creditors are governed by the Articles on Secured Transactions (Article 9), Bulk Transfers (Article 6) and Documents of Title (Article 7)."

For definitions of "Buyer in ordinary course of business," "Good faith," "Purchase," "Purchaser," and "Value," see Uniform Commercial Code, Sec. 1–201(9, 19, 32, 33 and 44).

Uniform Commercial Code, Sec. 3–305 provides as follows:

"To the extent that a holder is a holder in due course he takes the instrument free from

"(1) all claims to it on the part of any person; and

"(2) all defenses of any party to the instrument with whom the holder has not dealt except (a) infancy, to the extent that it is a defense to a simple contract; and (b) such other incapacity, or duress, or illegality of the transaction, as renders the obligation of the party a nullity; and (c) such misrepresentation as has induced the party to sign the instrument with neither knowledge nor reasonable opportunity to obtain knowledge of its character or its essential terms; and (d) discharge in insolvency proceedings; and (e) any other discharge of which the holder has notice when he takes the instrument."

The term "instrument" means "negotiable instrument," as defined in U.C.C. Sec. 3–104. "Negotiation," "Holder in Due Course," "Taking for Value," and "Notice to Purchaser" are defined in U.C.C. Secs. 3–202, 3–302, 3–303, and 3–304.

SECTION 2. EFFECT OF REAL PROPERTY RECORD-ING ACTS ON PRIORITIES: IN GENERAL *

The rules governing competing claims to land at common law and in equity, together with the continued application of the doctrine of *caveat emptor* to sales of land, make it necessary for a prospective purchaser of land to investigate and appraise the "title" of his vendor before he completes his purchase. For when a purchaser of land accepts a deed of conveyance from his vendor, he assumes the risk of loss by reason of the assertion of outstanding claims against the land except insofar as he may protect himself against such loss by obtaining a deed with title covenants or by obtaining title insurance. And the purchaser also assumes the risk of loss by reason of the "unmarketability" of the title—i.e., the risk that he may find it difficult or impossible to sell or mortgage the land at some future time without undertaking more or less expensive "curative" proceedings—except insofar as he may protect himself against such loss by securing title insurance. But how is a prospective purchaser to investigate his vendor's title? He may demand that the vendor deliver to him all his "muniments of title"—i.e., all the original deeds or other instruments upon which the vendor's title depends—but this will not protect the purchaser against claims based upon instruments executed by the vendor or prior grantors to third parties which

---

* As to the recording statutes and their effect on priorities, see 4 A.L.P. §§ 17.4–17.36; Cunningham §§ 11.9–11.11.

may have priority of right under the rules of common law and equity. What is required, obviously, is a system for registering or recording all conveyances and other instruments affecting the title to land.

When the Statute of Uses was enacted in 1535, Henry VIII tried to induce Parliament to pass a comprehensive bill requiring the registration of all conveyances in county registries. This comprehensive bill failed to pass. As a substitute, Parliament enacted a short Statute of Enrollments, which required all conveyances of freehold estates by bargain and sale to be enrolled within six months of the date of conveyance, either in the courts at Westminster or in county registries. By the end of the seventeenth century, the lease and release (i.e., a bargain and sale of a term of years coupled with a common law release) had completely superseded the simple bargain and sale as a method of conveying freehold estates, and, since the lease and release did not have to be enrolled, the Statute of Enrollments became a dead letter in England. But, although it was not received in the American colonies as part of the common law of England, the Statute of Enrollments was the model for many of the early recording statutes enacted in the American colonies, including the famous act adopted by the Massachusetts Bay colony on October 7, 1640. Because of later widespread adoption of recording statutes modelled either upon the Massachusetts act or directly from its English source, the Statute of Enrollments exerted a lasting influence upon the development of the recording system in the United States.

In 1708 the English Parliament enacted the statute of 7 Anne, c. 20, which declared that a memorial of all deeds and conveyances and of all wills and devises whereby any lands in the county of Middlesex "may be any way affected in law or equity, may be registered," and that every such deed or conveyance should be "adjudged fraudulent and void against any subsequent purchaser or mortgagee for valuable consideration, unless such memorial thereof be registered as by this Act directed, before the registering of the memorial of the deed or conveyance under which such subsequent purchaser or mortgagee shall claim." This Middlesex Registry Act became the model for most of the American colonial recording statutes enacted after 1708, and ultimately became the ancestor of many of the American recording statutes presently in force. New Jersey, New York, and Pennsylvania, for example, after experimenting with other types of recording acts, adopted statutes which in substance were identical with the Middlesex Registry Act of 1708, and the Pennsylvania recording act of 1775 was in turn adopted by the governor and judges of the Northwest Territory in 1795. In 1834 those parts of the Northwest Territory and the Louisiana Purchase which were still too sparsely settled to have been formed into states were combined for governmental purposes. Thus the Pennsylvania recording act of 1775, derived from the Middlesex Registry Act of 1708, became the original recording statute of a large part of the American public domain and of the states formed from it.

Recording acts are now in force in all of the American states. In general, all these recording acts provide that, unless recorded, certain instruments affecting land titles shall be void as against certain persons. Although they arrive at the same general result, however, the recording acts vary quite widely in their terms. The following recording act provisions are illustrative of some of the more common types. In reading these provisions you should try to discover the extent to which differences in statutory phraseology result in different answers to the following questions: (1) What instruments are authorized to be recorded? (2) What persons are protected against claims based on unrecorded instruments? (3) What constitutes an effective record?

MASSACHUSETTS GENERAL LAWS ANNOTATED,

Chapter 183

Section 4. A conveyance of an estate in fee simple, fee tail or for life, or a lease for more than seven years shall not be valid as against any person, except the grantor or lessor, his heirs and devisees and persons having actual notice of it, unless it, or an office copy as provided in section thirteen of chapter thirty-six, or with respect to such a lease, a notice of lease, or a notice of assignment of rents or profits, as hereinafter defined, is recorded in the registry of deeds for the county or district in which the land to which it relates lies. * * *

OHIO REVISED CODE

(1970)

Section 5301.23. All mortgages properly executed shall be recorded in the office of the county recorder of the county in which the mortgaged premises are situated, and take effect from the time they are delivered to such recorder for record. If two or more mortgages are presented for record on the same day, they shall take effect in the order of presentation. The first mortgage presented must be the first recorded, and the first recorded shall have preference.

Section 5301.25. [(A)] All deeds, land contracts referred to in division (B)(2) of section 317.08 of the Revised Code, and instruments of writing properly executed for the conveyance or encumbrance of lands, tenements, or hereditaments, other than as provided in section 5301.23 of the Revised Code, shall be recorded in the office of the county recorder of the county in which the premises are situated, and until so recorded or filed for record, they are fraudulent, so far as relates to a subsequent bona fide purchaser having, at the time of purchase, no knowledge of the existence of such former deed or land contract or instrument.

NEW YORK REAL PROPERTY LAW (McKINNEY)

Section 290. 1. The term "real property," as used in this article, includes lands, tenements and hereditaments and chattels real, except a lease for a term not exceeding three years.

2. The term "purchaser" includes every person to whom any estate or interest in real property is conveyed for a valuable consideration, and every assignee of a mortgage, lease or other conditional estate.

3. The term "conveyance" includes every written instrument, by which any estate or interest in real property is created, transferred, mortgaged or assigned, or by which the title to any real property may be affected, including an instrument in execution of a power, although the power be one of revocation only, and an instrument postponing or subordinating a mortgage lien; except a will, a lease for a term not exceeding three years, an executory contract for the sale or purchase of lands, and an instrument containing a power to convey real property as the agent or attorney for the owner of such property. * * *

Section 291. A conveyance of real property, within the state, on being duly acknowledged by the person executing the same, or proved as required by this chapter, and such acknowledgment or proof duly certified when required by this chapter, may be recorded in the office of the clerk of the county where such real property is situated, and such county clerk shall, upon the request of any party, on tender of the lawful fees therefor, record the same in his said office. Every such conveyance not so recorded is void as against any person who subsequently purchases or acquires by exchange or contracts to purchase or acquire by exchange, the same real property or any portion thereof * * * in good faith and for a valuable consideration, from the same vendor or assignor, his distributees or devisees, and whose conveyance, contract or assignment is first duly recorded, and is void as against the lien upon the same real property or any portion thereof arising from payments made upon the execution of or pursuant to the terms of a contract with the same vendor, his distributees or devisees, if such contract is made in good faith and is first duly recorded.

GENERAL STATUTES OF NORTH CAROLINA

(Michie, 1976)

§ 47–18. (a) No (i) conveyance of land, or (ii) contract to convey, or (iii) option to convey, or (iv) lease of land for more than three years shall be valid to pass any property interest as against lien creditors or purchasers for a valuable consideration from the donor, bargainor or lessor, but from the time of registration thereof * * *.

ANNOTATED CODE OF MARYLAND REAL PROPERTY

(Michie, 1974)

§ 3–101. * * * [N]o estate of inheritance or freehold, declaration or limitation of use, estate above seven years, or deed may pass or take effect unless the deed granting it is executed and recorded.

Notes

1. All American recording acts authorize the recording of "conveyances," which may be given a broad statutory definition as in N.Y. Real Prop.Law § 290 (McKinney), supra. All of the American recording acts also authorize the recording of mortgages, either by express language or by construction of the term "conveyances" to include mortgages. Some recording acts expressly authorize the recording of leases and of executory contracts for the sale of land,

though usually with qualifications. The Massachusetts statute, supra, expressly includes leases for a term of more than seven years, and thus by implication
excludes leases for a shorter term. The New York statute, supra, on the other
hand, expressly excludes leases for a term not exceeding three years, and thus
by clear implication includes leases for a longer term. Recording acts that provide for the recording of "conveyances" without additional language from
which the intent of the legislature may be gathered, may or may not be deemed
to include leases. On the one side, terms of years, normally created by lease,
may be viewed as estates and the instruments creating them as conveyances.
On the other hand, the term may be classified as a chattel interest in which case
"conveyance" might not seem applicable to the instrument creating it.

N.Y. Real Prop.Law § 290 (McKinney), supra, expressly excludes "an executory contract for the sale or purchase of lands" from the definition of "conveyance," but a subsequent section of the statute makes special provision for recording such contracts. See N.Y. Real Prop.Law § 294 (McKinney). Unless
expressly referred to, executory contracts for the sale of land are usually not
deemed to come within the statutory authorization to record "conveyances."
Thus in Churchill v. Little, 23 Ohio St. 301 (1872), the court concluded that an
executory contract for the sale of land was not within the terms of a statute
providing for the recording of instruments by which lands are "conveyed or
otherwise affected or incumbered in law." But an executory contract for the
sale of land was held entitled to record under a statute applying to all instruments in writing "affecting the title to real estate." McBee v. O'Connell, 16
N.M. 469, 120 P. 734 (1911). Under a similar statute an assignment of a swamp
land certificate was held to be recordable although the certificate holder had
only an equitable title. And in North Dakota, where the statute had previously
specifically declared that executory contracts should not be deemed to be "conveyances" and was then amended in 1903 by striking out "contracts for the sale
or purchase of land" from the list of excluded instruments, it was held that "a
contract for a deed is a conveyance under the statutory definition and must be
recorded to be effective as constructive notice." Battersby v. Gillespie, 57 N.D.
426, 222 N.W. 480 (1928).

In Second Nat. Bank v. Dyer, 121 Conn. 263, 184 A. 386, 104 A.L.R. 1295
(1936), it was held that a mortgage assignment was within a recording act requiring the record of "conveyances."

A notice of rescission served upon a grantee by a grantor who claimed to
have executed a deed under the influence of fraud, properly acknowledged, was
deemed entitled to record and a claimant under the grantee was charged with
constructive notice under the California statute. Dreifus v. Marx, 40 Cal.App.
2d 461, 104 P.2d 1080 (1940).

As to powers of attorney to convey land, see Johnson v. Johnson, 184 Ga.
783, 193 S.E. 345, 114 A.L.R. 657 (1937). Mich.Comp.L. §§ 565.202, and 565.451
provide for the recording of affidavits regarding parties to instruments affecting realty.

The requirement of recording being wholly statutory, whether or not a giv-
en type of document is entitled to be recorded is dependent upon the language
of the statute. There is no uniformity of language in the statutes in this respect. The New York statute, supra, is among the most inclusive of the recording acts. Similar to it, and perhaps even more inclusive, is the New Jersey
recording act. N.J.Rev.Stat. 46:16–1 contains a long list of instruments affecting land titles which are authorized to be recorded, and id. 46:16–2, for good
measure, authorizes the recording of "All instruments of every kind in anywise
affecting the title to any real estate situate in this state, or any interest therein,

or containing any agreement in relation thereto, or granting any right or interest therein   *   *   *.''

The Uniform Simplification of Land Transfers Act, promulgated by the National Conference of Commissioners on Uniform State Laws in 1976 (and amended in 1977) provides for the broadest possible scope of the recorder's office, and places great emphasis on the indexing of recorded documents with a view to bringing greater efficiency to the process. Article 2 deals with recording and Article 6 with the maintenance of public land records.

2. "**Classification of Recording Acts.** Acts providing for the recording of deeds and other instruments of conveyance are found in all states. None of these requires recording for the purpose of validity of the instrument. But in each it is provided that a person who fails to record may lose his title as against certain other persons. The statutes have sometimes been classified in three groups, based upon the facts required to give priority to a subsequent conveyance when two successive conveyances of the same property have been made. Mr. R.G. Patton's statement of this classification is as follows: '(1) Those which give priority of right to the purchaser who secures priority of record; (2) those which invalidate or subordinate an unrecorded conveyance as against the rights of a subsequent bona fide purchaser; and (3) those which thus protect a subsequent bona fide purchaser provided his conveyance is the first to be recorded.' These have been popularly described as pure race statutes, notice statutes, and notice-race statutes. That is to say, in the first type, it is a pure question of race to the records; the purchaser who first records wins. In the second type, the subsequent purchaser wins if he purchases without notice of the prior deed and before the prior deed is recorded. In the third type, the subsequent purchaser wins if he purchases without notice of the prior deed, and also records his deed before the prior deed is recorded. Formerly, a number of statutes gave full protection to a recorded deed if it was recorded within a designated period of time after the date of its execution. But now such statutes are rare.

"Today, North Carolina and Louisiana are the only states which apply the pure race-to-the-records rule to instruments of conveyancing generally. In a few other states the rule is in force as to mortgages. The states having the notice type of statute and those having the race-notice type, or having construed their statutes to be of the race-notice type, are rather equally divided." Simes, Handbook for More Efficient Conveyancing 18–19 (1961).*

How would you classify the statutes set out above according to the three types discussed in the above excerpt?

Suppose under the Maryland statute a grantor delivers an unacknowledged deed to the grantee, who is therefore unable to record it. What result if (a) the grantee is in possession of the land and the grantor brings ejectment, or (b) the grantor is still in possession and the grantee brings ejectment?

That recording may be required by statute for an instrument to be effective at all, see Klasen v. Thompson, 189 Minn. 254, 248 N.W. 817 (1933), dealing with a tax sale certificate.

Does the first sentence of Section 5301.23 of the Ohio recording act make delivery of a mortgage to the county recorder the final step in the execution of the instrument, necessary for its effectiveness between mortgagor and mortgagee? Or does it merely require delivery to the recorder in order that a mortgage shall be effective as against a competing mortgagee? What result if a land owner gives successive mortgages to A and B, neither of whom records?

---

* Copyright, 1961, University of Michigan.

3. "Most of the recording acts are phrased in terms of declaring the priorities between two inconsistent conveyances of the same property. Thus it is assumed that the owner, A, first conveyed the property to B and thereafter conveyed it to C. The statute ordinarily declares when C's conveyance takes priority over the conveyance to B. At common law, and in the absence of a recording act, if A had legal title, then B would always win over C, since B's conveyance was first. The recording act, however, gives C a priority when B fails to record, if, in a notice state, C pays value and has no notice of the deed to B, or in a notice-race state, if C pays value without notice of B's deed, and thereafter records before B records. Thus, in a notice state, C must record only to protect himself against subsequent conveyances, but not against the conveyance to B; but in a notice-race state, C must record to protect himself both against B and against subsequent conveyances.

"The theory of the operation of the recording acts may be expressed in two ways, as follows. First, the statute gives to the person appearing by the record to be the owner, a power to pass the title to a bona fide purchaser; and the person holding under an unrecorded instrument is under a corresponding liability to lose his title. If, however, the first grantee complies with the recording act and takes all steps necessary to record, he preserves his common law priority and no such power-liability relation exists. Second, the recording act places the taker under an unrecorded deed practically in the position of a person having only an equitable title. Thus, his interest is subject to extinguishment in the hands of a subsequent bona fide purchaser for value. Recording constitutes notice to all subsequent purchasers and, therefore, prevents them from taking bona fide or from extinguishing the recorded interest.

"Of course, it must be noted that, whatever the theory, the recording of an instrument may, for some purposes, entirely aside from the operation of the recording acts, constitute notice. Thus, if A conveys land to B under an instrument which states that B is to hold in trust for C and spells out the terms of the trust, and B records this instrument, no one can be a bona fide purchaser from B. Therefore, no one can cut off C's equitable interest, because any purchaser would have notice of the terms of the recorded instrument. These two theories of the operation of the recording acts may be designated as the power theory and the notice theory. Although these theories are not necessarily mutually exclusive, it is believed that most modern courts tend toward the second theory. Some statutes are phrased in terms of that theory. Doubtless in most situations it makes little difference which theory is employed." Simes, Handbook for More Efficient Conveyancing 20–21 (1961).

Test your understanding of the foregoing material on the different types of recording acts by addressing yourself to the following problems.

Problems

In each of the following problems, assume that A had a fee simple estate in Blackacre to begin with; that A conveyed Blackacre to B on January 2, and that A conveyed Blackacre to C on January 9; that both B and C paid a substantial price for Blackacre; and that neither B nor C when he received his deed and paid the price had actual notice of the conveyance to the other.

1. Who is the owner of Blackacre if B's deed was recorded on January 8 and C's deed was recorded on January 10? Consider what the result should be under each of the recording acts set out above.

2. Who is the owner of Blackacre if B's deed was recorded on January 10 and C's deed was recorded on January 11? Consider what the result should be under each of the recording acts set out above.

3. Who is the owner of Blackacre if B's deed was recorded on January 11 and C's deed was recorded on January 10? Consider what the result should be under each of the recording acts set out above.

MESSERSMITH v. SMITH

Supreme Court of North Dakota, 1953.
60 N.W.2d 276.

MORRIS, Chief Justice. This is a statutory action to quiet title to three sections of land in Golden Valley County. The records in the office of the register of deeds of that county disclose the following pertinent facts concerning the title: For some time prior to May 7, 1946, the record title owners of this property were Caroline Messersmith and Frederick Messersmith. On that date, Caroline Messersmith executed and delivered to Frederick Messersmith a quitclaim deed to the property which was not recorded until July 9, 1951. Between the date of that deed and the time of its recording the following occurred: On April 23, 1951, Caroline Messersmith as lessor, executed a lease to Herbert B. Smith, Jr., lessee, which was recorded May 14, 1951. On May 7, 1951, Caroline Messersmith, a single woman, conveyed to Herbert B. Smith, Jr., by mineral deed containing a warranty of title, an undivided one-half interest in and to all oil, gas and other minerals in and under or that may be produced upon the land involved in this case. This deed was recorded May 26, 1951. On May 9, 1951, Herbert B. Smith, Jr., executed a mineral deed conveying to E.B. Seale an undivided one-half interest in all of the oil, gas and other minerals in and under or that may be produced upon the land. This deed was also recorded in the office of the Register of Deeds of Golden Valley County, on May 26, 1951. Seale answered plaintiff's complaint by setting up his deed and claiming a one-half interest in the minerals as a purchaser without notice, actual or constructive, of plaintiff's claim. To this answer the plaintiff replied by way of a general denial and further alleged that the mineral deed by which Seale claims title is void; that it was never acknowledged, not entitled to record and was obtained by fraud, deceit and misrepresentation. The defendant Herbert B. Smith, Jr., defaulted.

For some time prior to the transactions herein noted, Caroline Messersmith and her nephew, Frederick S. Messersmith, were each the owner of an undivided one-half interest in this land, having acquired it by inheritance. The land was unimproved except for being fenced. It was never occupied as a homestead. Section 1 was leased to one tenant and Sections 3 and 11 to another. They used the land for grazing. One party had been a tenant for a number of years, paying $150 a year. The amount paid by the other tenant is not disclosed. The plaintiff lived in Chicago. Caroline Messersmith lived alone in the City of Dickinson where she had resided for many years. She looked after the renting of the land, both before and after she conveyed her interest therein to her nephew. She never told her tenants about the conveyance.

On April 23, 1951, the defendant Smith, accompanied by one King and his prospective wife, went to the Messersmith home and negotiated an oil and gas lease with Miss Messersmith covering the three sections of land involved herein. According to Miss Messersmith, all that was discussed that day concerned royalties. According to the testimony of Mr. Smith and Mr. King, the matter of the mineral deed was discussed.

Two or three days later, Smith and King returned. Again the testimony varies as to the subject of conversation. Miss Messersmith said it was about royalties. Smith and King say it was about a mineral deed for the purchase of her mineral rights. No agreement was reached during this conversation. On May 7, 1951, Smith returned alone and again talked with Miss Messersmith. As a result of this visit, Miss Messersmith executed a mineral deed for an undivided one-half interest in the oil, gas and minerals under the three sections of land. Smith says this deed was acknowledged before a notary public at her house. She says no notary public ever appeared there. She also says that Smith never told her she was signing a mineral deed and that she understood she was signing a "royalty transfer." The consideration paid for this deed was $1,400, which is still retained by Miss Messersmith. After leaving the house Smith discovered a slight error in the deed. The term "his heirs" was used for the term "her heirs." He returned to the home of Miss Messersmith the same day, explained the error to her, tore up the first deed, and prepared another in the same form, except that the error was corrected. According to Smith's testimony, he took the second deed to the same notary public to whom Miss Messersmith had acknowledged the execution of the first deed and the notary called Miss Messersmith for her acknowledgment over the telephone and then placed on the deed the usual notarial acknowledgment, including the notary's signature and seal. The notary, who took many acknowledgments about that time, has no independent recollection of either of these acknowledgments. It is the second deed that was recorded on May 26, 1951, and upon which the defendant, E.B. Seale, relied when he purchased from the defendant, Herbert B. Smith, Jr., the undivided one-half interest in the minerals under the land in question. * * *

The trial court found "that such deeds, or either of them, were not procured through fraud or false representation." The evidence does not warrant this court in disturbing that finding.

The determination that the mineral deed from Caroline Messersmith to Herbert B. Smith, Jr., was not fraudulently obtained by the grantee does not mean that the defendant, who in turn received a deed from Smith, is entitled to prevail as against the plaintiff in this action. At the time Miss Messersmith executed the mineral deed she owned no interest in the land, having previously conveyed her interest therein to the plaintiff. Smith in turn had no actual interest to convey to the defendant Seale. If Seale can assert title to any interest in the property in question, he must do so because the plaintiff's deed was not recorded until July 9, 1951, while the deed from Caroline Messersmith to Smith and the deed from Smith to the defendant Seale were recorded May 26, 1951, thus giving him a record title prior in time to that of the plaintiff. Section 47–1907, NDRC 1943, contains this provision:

"An instrument entitled to be recorded must be recorded by the register of deeds of the county in which the real property affected thereby is situated."

Section 47–1908, NDRC 1943, provides:

"An instrument is deemed to be recorded when, being duly acknowledged or proved and certified, it is deposited in the register's office with the proper officer for record."

The defendant Seale asserts that priority of record gives him a title superior to that of the plaintiff by virtue of the following statutory provision, Section 47–1941, NDRC 1943:

"Every conveyance of real estate not recorded as provided in section 47–1907 shall be void as against any subsequent purchaser in good faith, and for a valuable consideration, of the same real estate, or any part or portion thereof, whose conveyance, whether in the form of a warranty deed, or deed of bargain and sale, or deed of quitclaim and release, of the form in common use or otherwise, first is recorded, or as against an attachment levied thereon or any judgment lawfully obtained, at the suit of any party, against the person in whose name the title to such land appears of record, prior to the recording of such conveyance. The fact that such first recorded conveyance of such subsequent purchaser for a valuable consideration is in the form or contains the terms, of a deed of quitclaim and release aforesaid, shall not affect the question of good faith of the subsequent purchaser, or be of itself notice to him of any unrecorded conveyance of the same real estate or any part thereof."

Section 47–1945, NDRC 1943, in part, provides:

"The deposit and recording of an instrument proved and certified according to the provisions of this chapter are constructive notice of the execution of such instrument to all purchasers and encumbrancers subsequent to the recording."

As against the seeming priority of record on the part of Seale's title, the plaintiff contends that the deed from Caroline Messersmith to Smith was never acknowledged and, not having been acknowledged, was not entitled to be recorded, and hence can confer no priority of record upon the grantee or subsequent purchasers from him.

It may be stated as a general rule that the recording of an instrument affecting the title to real estate which does not meet the statutory requirements of the recording laws affords no constructive notice. * * * The applicability of the rule is easily determined where the defect appears on the face of the instrument, but difficulty frequently arises where the defect is latent. Perhaps the most common instance of this nature arises when an instrument is placed of record bearing a certificate of acknowledgment sufficient on its face despite the fact that the statutory procedure for acknowledgment has not been followed. See Annotations 19 A.L.R. 1074; 72 A.L.R. 1039.

The certificate of acknowledgment on the mineral deed to Smith, while it is presumed to state the truth, is not conclusive as to the fact of actual acknowledgment by the grantor. * * *

In Severtson v. Peoples, 28 N.D. 372, 148 N.W. 1054, 1055, this court, in the syllabus said:

"4. A certificate of acknowledgment, regular on its face, is presumed to state the truth, and proof to overthrow such certificate must be very strong and convincing, and the burden of overthrowing the same is upon the party attacking the truth of such certificate.

"5. To constitute an acknowledgment, the grantor must appear before the officer for the purpose of acknowledging the instrument, and such grantor must, in some manner with a view to giving it authenticity, make an admission to the officer of the fact that he had executed such instrument.

"6. Where, in fact, the grantor has never appeared before the officer and acknowledged the execution of the instrument, evidence showing such fact is admissible, even as against an innocent purchaser for value and without notice."

It avails the purchaser nothing to point out that a deed is valid between the parties though not acknowledged by the grantor—see Bumann v. Burleigh County, 73 N.D. 655, 18 N.W.2d 10—for Caroline Messersmith, having previously conveyed to the plaintiff, had no title. The condition of the title is such that Seale must rely wholly upon his position as an innocent purchaser under the recording act.

Before a deed to real property can be recorded its execution must be established in one of the ways prescribed by Section 47–1903, NDRC 1943. No attempt was made to prove the execution of this deed other than "by acknowledgment by the person executing the same." It is the fact of acknowledgment that the statute requires as a condition precedent to recording. Subsequent sections of Chapter 47–19, NDRC 1943, prescribe before whom and how proof of the fact of acknowledgment may be made. A general form of certificate of acknowledgment is set forth in Section 47–1927. The certificate on the mineral deed follows this form and states:

"On this 7th day of May, in the year 1951, before me personally appeared Caroline Messersmith, known to me to be the person described in and who executed the within and foregoing instrument, and acknowledged to me that she executed the same."

But Caroline Messersmith did not appear before the notary and acknowledge that she executed the deed that was recorded. In the absence of the fact of acknowledgment the deed was not entitled to be recorded, regardless of the recital in the certificate. The deed not being entitled to be recorded, the record thereof did not constitute notice of its execution, Section 47–1945, or contents, Section 47–1919. The record appearing in the office of the register of deeds not being notice of the execution or contents of the mineral deed, the purchaser from the grantee therein did not become a "subsequent purchaser in good faith, and for a valuable consideration" within the meaning of Section 47–1941, NDRC 1943.

In this case we have the unusual situation of having two deeds covering the same property from the same grantor, who had no title, to the same grantee. The only difference between the two was a minor defect in the first deed, for which it was destroyed. The evidence is conflicting as to whether or not the first deed was acknowledged. The second deed clearly was not. It is argued that the transaction should be considered as a whole, with the implication that if the first deed was actually acknowledged, the failure to secure an acknowledgment of the second deed would not be fatal to the right to have it recorded and its efficacy as constructive notice. We must again point out that the right which the defendant Seale attempts to assert is dependent exclusively upon compliance with the recording statutes. His claim of title is dependent upon the instrument that was recorded and not the instrument that was destroyed. Assuming that Smith is right in his assertion that the first deed was acknowledged before a notary public, we cannot borrow that unrecorded acknowledgment from the destroyed deed and, in effect, attach it to the unacknowledged deed for purposes of recording and the constructive notice that would ensue.

In Dixon v. Kaufman, 79 N.D. 633, 58 N.W.2d 797, we sustained the title to nonhomestead lands of purchasers for value and without notice whose title rested upon a deed bearing a certificate of acknowledgment regular on its face but which in fact had not been acknowledged by the grantors. In that case the grantors were the actual owners of the property at the time they signed the deed and as to nonhomestead property the delivery of the deed without acknowledgment was sufficient to pass title which the grantees then had. This title was then purchased by defendants who paid the value therefor in good faith and without notice of any claimed defects in the execution of the deed. The deed executed by the plaintiffs which they sought to attack conveyed a title which, at the most, was voidable. In that case plaintiffs sought relief from the consequences of their own acts which would result in loss to innocent parties. The situation here is entirely different. The plaintiff seeks relief from the consequences of the acts of a third party, Caroline Messersmith, who, after deeding to the plaintiff her entire interest in the property, executed the mineral deed to Smith. This deed contained a warranty but it actually conveyed no title. As a conveyance it was good between the parties only in theory, for the grantor had nothing to convey. For the loss which resulted from her acts, the plaintiff in this case is not to blame. His failure to record his deed will not defeat the title which he holds unless there appears against it a record title consisting of instruments executed and recorded in the manner prescribed by our recording statutes. The title asserted by the defendant Seale does not meet these requirements and the trial court erred in rendering judgment in his favor.

The judgment appealed from is reversed.

On Petition for Rehearing.

MORRIS, Chief Justice. The respondent has petitioned for a rehearing and additional briefs have been filed. From the cases cited and statements of counsel, it appears that there may be a misapprehension concerning the scope of our opinion. We would emphasize the fact that at the time Caroline Messersmith signed and delivered the deed to Herbert B. Smith, Jr., she had no title to convey. Smith therefore obtained no title to convey to E. B. Seale who, as grantee of Smith, claims to be an innocent purchaser. The title had already been conveyed to Frederick Messersmith. The deed to Smith had never been acknowledged and was therefore not entitled to be recorded, although it bore a certificate of acknowledgment in regular form. Seale, whose grantor had no title, seeks through the operation of our recording statutes to divest Frederick Messersmith of the true title and establish a statutory title in himself.

We are here dealing with a prior unrecorded valid and effective conveyance that is challenged by a subsequent purchaser to whom no title was conveyed and who claims that the recording laws vest title in him by virtue of a deed that was not acknowledged in fact and therefore not entitled to be placed of record. This situation differs materially from a case where an attack is made by a subsequent purchaser on a prior recorded deed which actually conveyed title to the grantee but was not entitled to be recorded because of a latent defect. The questions presented by the latter situation we leave to be determined when they arise.

The petition for rehearing is denied.

Notes

1. The Messersmith case illustrates two of the many problems that can be encountered in deciding whether there has been a legally effective recording. We must recognize that most recording acts presently provide that a conveyance is not eligible to be recorded unless it is properly witnessed and acknowledged. With those formalities *required*, what result is to follow in cases such as these:

(a) Suppose that despite the absence of witnesses or of an acknowledgment, the register of deeds accepts the instrument, enters it in the records, and indexes it. (The principal case treats the improperly acknowledged deed as if it were unacknowledged.) We might want to concede that an unacknowledged (or defectively acknowledged deed) would not, even though placed on record, be deemed to give constructive notice to subsequent purchasers. But does that mean it is totally "unrecorded"? Does it mean the record, which looks proper, can be ignored?

(b) Suppose the converse situation where an instrument is in fact properly acknowledged, and hence entitled to be recorded, but the recording officer erroneously omits to include the certificate of acknowledgment when he copies the instrument into the records. Is the "recording" effective? It has generally been held not "recorded" in such cases. See, e.g., Pringle v. Dunn, 37 Wis. 449, 19 Am.Rep. 772 (1875) (mortgage was probably subscribed by attesting witnesses when filed for record, as required by statute, but there was a mistake in transcribing the instrument and the names of the witnesses were omitted); Dean v. Gibson, 34 Tex.Civ.App. 508, 79 S.W. 363 (1904) (recorder failed to copy into the record the certificate of acknowledgment); Williams v. Adams, 43 Ga. 407 (1871) (deed apparently regularly attested appeared, as copied into record, not to have been properly attested).

(c) Suppose the recording officer makes a mistake in copying the instrument. For example, a mortgage is shown as $400 rather than $4000. In general, the courts have held that the consequences of a substantive error must fall on the person named as grantee or mortgagee in the recorded instrument rather than upon subsequent purchasers or mortgagees. As the court said in Terrell v. Andrew County, 44 Mo. 309 (1869), "Hard and uncertain would be the fate of subsequent purchasers if they could not rely upon the records, but must be under the necessity, before they act, of tracing up the original deed to see that it is correctly recorded. The statute says that when the deed is certified and recorded it shall impart notice of the contents from the time of filing. Certainly; but this is to be understood in the sense that the deed is rightly recorded, and the contents correctly spread upon the record. It never was intended to impose upon the purchaser the burden of entering into a long and laborious search to find out whether the recorder had faithfully performed his duty. The obligation of giving the notice rests on the party holding the title. If he fails in his duty, he must suffer the consequences. If his duty is but imperfectly performed, he can not claim all the advantages and lay the fault at the door of an innocent purchaser."

There is, however, a minority view which emphasizes that the applicable recording acts require no more of a party claiming under a particular instrument than that he deposit or file the instrument, properly executed and ready for recording, in the recorder's office. Indeed, some courts have allowed the party who files his instrument for record the full benefit of recordation from the date of filing even if the instrument is never transcribed at all, or is transcribed in the wrong record book. For example, in Gregor v. City of Fairbanks, 599 P.2d 743 (Alaska 1979), the court held that an error by the recorder (allegedly he failed to put the deed in the records at all), did not burden the person who had submitted the deed for recording.

See discussion in 4 A.L.P. § 17.31, especially at nn. 28–36.

Photographic reproduction of instruments filed for record will generally eliminate the kind of mistakes referred to in (b) and (c) above.

(d) Suppose the instrument is properly copied in the records, but no entry is made in the index. Can a purchaser be expected to find it?

2. The statutory requirements which specify prerequisites to recordation are in general not very helpful to the conveyancing process. Many states have found it necessary to adopt "curative" acts of various kinds. These acts are described by Simes as those which provide that, "after the expiration of a specified period of time, a failure to comply with certain formal requirements of the law as to the execution or recording of instruments, as to judicial proceedings, or as to similar matters shall cease to be material. In other words, after the termination of the specified time, the formal requirements cease to apply, and the conveyance or transaction is just as valid as if these requirements had been complied with in the first place." Simes, Handbook for More Efficient Conveyancing, ch. 8 (1961).

The Uniform Simplification of Land Transfers Act (1977) eliminates nearly all requirements for eligibility for recording, and specifically provides in § 2–301(b): "No signature, acknowledgment, seal or witness is required for a document to be eligible for recording." It further attacks the problem by creating a number of presumptions of validity for a recorded document (§ 2–305); by providing a comprehensive one-year curative statute (§ 3–401), by providing comprehensive instructions for recordation and indexing (§§ 2–301–304), by giving certified copies of recorded instruments a presumption of correctness which permits their introduction in evidence even if the original is available (§ 2–306), and by allowing facts stated in recorded affidavits to be presumed true as they relate to real estate, its use, or its ownership (§ 2–307). The curative provision is as follows:

Section 3–401. [Minor Defects Cured by One Year Lapse]

(a) If a document purporting to transfer or affect, or to authorize action affecting, title to real estate has been signed by the owner of the real estate, or by a person acting in a representative, fiduciary, or official capacity, and has been recorded for one year, the document and the record thereof are effective, notwithstanding any one or more of the defects or omissions described in subsection (b), for all purposes as though the document or the record thereof had not been subject to the defects or omissions, unless a proceeding is commenced on account of the defects or omissions, and a notice of the pending proceeding is recorded within the one-year period.

(b) This section applies to the following defects and omissions under prior law or this Act:

(1) a failure or omission of. a document to comply with a requirement of law relating to execution, acknowledgment, or recording, including a requirement relating to a corporate or individual seal or to witnesses, attestation, proof of execution, certificate, or recording of acknowledgment, proof of notarial authority, time and dates of execution or acknowledgment, certificate of recording, recitals of consideration, indications of residences or addresses or statements of payment of tax or documentary stamps;

(2) a failure or omission of an instrument signed by an attorney-in-fact, trustee, personal representative, executor, administrator, conservator, guardian, corporate officer, sheriff, official of any governmental unit or public agency, authority, or corporation, or another person acting in a representative, fiduciary, or official capacity to state or indicate that the signature, acknowledgment, or another act is on behalf of the owner or is in the signer's representative, fiduciary, or official capacity;

(3) in the case of a transfer by an executor, personal representative, or administrator of his decedent's real estate, by a trustee of the real estate held in a testamentary trust, or by a conservator or guardian of his ward's real estate, a defect, irregularity, or omission in the probate or other judicial proceedings if the conveyance has been confirmed by order of the court or administrative body having jurisdiction over the estate; and

(4) in the case of a sale of real estate on execution or pursuant to the terms of an order or decree of a court or on foreclosure of a tax lien or after a forfeiture, a defect, irregularity, or omission in the proceedings pertaining thereto if the sale or forfeiture has been confirmed by the court or administrative body having jurisdiction.

3. In view of the obvious problems created by recordation of instruments which are void for lack of delivery, what type of legislative action might be taken to improve the situation? The Uniform Simplification of Land Transfers Act (1977) provides a presumption that a recorded signed document is delivered notwithstanding a lapse of time between dates on the document and the date of recording (§ 2–305(a)(3)), and further provides that after a conveyance has been of record three years, no action or proceeding may be brought to invalidate it for want of delivery. (§ 3–402(c)).

4. Since Seale, in the principal (Messersmith) case, obtained a properly acknowledged deed from Smith on May 9, 1951, "as a purchaser without notice, actual or constructive, of plaintiff's claim" under the latter's unrecorded deed of May 7, 1946, and since Seale recorded his deed on May 26, 1951 while plaintiff did not record until July 9, 1951, why didn't Seale qualify for protection

under the North Dakota "notice-race" recording act? Wasn't Seale a "subsequent purchaser in good faith, and for a valuable consideration, of [part of] the same real estate, * * * whose conveyance * * * first is recorded"? What is the statutory warrant for the court's statement that plaintiff's "failure to record his deed will not defeat the title which he holds unless there appears against it a record title consisting of instruments executed and recorded in the manner prescribed by our recording statutes"?

The North Dakota court is not the only one which has construed the statutory phrase "whose conveyance * * * first is recorded" as referring to the entire "chain of title" rather than simply the final conveyance under which a claim to land is asserted. See Zimmer v. Sundell, 237 Wis. 270, 296 N.W. 589, 133 A.L.R. 882 (1941). The court was faced with the following situation: O conveyed to A who did not record; O later conveyed the same land to B, who also neglected to record; B then conveyed to C, who recorded promptly and before A recorded; then A recorded his deed; and finally, C recorded the deed from O to B. All parties purchased in good faith and for value. *Held*, under the Wisconsin "notice-race" recording statute, that A's title was superior to C's.

Even assuming that a subsequent purchaser must get his entire chain of title properly on record "first" to prevail under a "notice-race" recording act, does it make sense for the court to say (in Messersmith): "The record appearing in the office of the register of deeds not being notice of the execution or contents of the mineral deed [to Smith], the purchaser [Seale] from the grantee therein did not become a 'subsequent purchaser in good faith, and for a valuable consideration' within the meaning of Section 47–1941, NDRC 1943."?

One should compare the facts of the Messersmith case with the situation which arises in a different kind of case: O conveys to A who does not record. O conveys to B who records, but takes with actual notice of A's unrecorded deed. B conveys to C, who takes for value and without notice and records. It is generally held that even though B could not prevail against A's unrecorded deed (because he had notice), his conveyance to C permits C to win against A's unrecorded deed. Observe that in this case, the apparent record will not create any future problems in tracing the chain of title transactions, whereas if the deed to B is unrecorded, then C has left the way open for future problems. In that sense, a decision that a purchaser must record his entire chain of title under a notice-race statute may well be designed to further the reliability of the record and prevent future problems. The Messersmith case, however, is less appealing because the intermediate deed to Smith was in fact on the record and the defect could not be seen. Only the technical decision that an improperly acknowledged deed should be treated as unacknowledged and therefore as unrecorded could lead to the conclusion that Seale should not be protected.

5. "Suppose O is the record owner of a tract of land. A goes into possession claiming the land in fee simple adversely to O, and remains for the period of the statute of limitations, thus acquiring a title by adverse possession. Thereafter, O conveys the same land to B, who pays value and has no knowledge of A's title by adverse possession. Does B take priority over A? Of course, if, as is usually the case, A is still in possession when B takes his conveyance, this possession is notice of A's title, and * * * B will lose. But suppose, after A has acquired title by adverse possession, he leaves the premises and no one is in possession. If B purchases when no one is in possession, will he take priority over A? The authorities are to the effect that he will not. It is true, the title by adverse possession is not on the record. But then there is no practicable way to put it on the record. However, the chief reason why A wins is that the recording acts simply do not cover this situation. They deal

with the priority of conveyances, and the acquiring of title by adverse possession is not a conveyance in any sense of the word. In some respects it is unfortunate that this is the law, since it means that less reliance can be placed on the record. On the other hand, the running of the statute of limitations is much more relied upon by title examiners to cure an imperfect record title than it is to establish a title entirely outside the record. If title by adverse possession could be extinguished by a purchaser from a record title holder, this function of curing record titles might be greatly impaired." Simes, Handbook for More Efficient Conveyancing 28–29 (1961).

Does the same reasoning apply to prescriptive easements? Should the fact that in prescriptive easement cases the courts sometimes indulge in the fiction of a "lost grant" of the easement affect the result?

See Ferrier, The Recording Acts and Titles by Adverse Possession and Prescription, 14 Calif.L.Rev. 287 (1925). Cases are collected in Annotation, Extinguishment of Easement by Implication or Prescription, by Sale of Servient Estate to a Purchaser Without Notice, 174 A.L.R. 1241 (1948); Annotation, Title by Adverse Possession as Affected by Recording Statutes, 9 A.L.R.2d 850 (1950).

6. Are easements arising by implication, including easements by necessity, within the recording acts' penalties for failure to record? It would seem that the answer is necessarily "no," since there is nothing to record that will give notice of an easement arising by implication. It has sometimes been argued that, since such an easement arises by implication from the terms of the conveyance which "severs" the "dominant" and the "servient" tracts, it is within the terms of the recording acts. It has also been argued that the person who fails to stipulate for the express grant or reservation of an easement is guilty of such negligence as to estop him from asserting an easement by implication against a subsequent bona fide purchaser of the "servient" tract. The problem is particularly difficult with respect to easements of necessity, which may not be used for many years so that there is no visible evidence of the easement on the ground.

The cases are about evenly divided on the question whether a subsequent bona fide purchaser of the "servient" tract takes subject to easements by necessity. See, e.g., Wiesel v. Smira, 49 R.I. 246, 142 A. 148, 58 A.L.R. 818 (1928), where the court recognized the possible hardship to the subsequent bona fide purchaser but nevertheless concluded that, since there had been no failure of duty on the part of the easement holder, his easement by necessity was not divested in favor of the subsequent purchaser. Cf. Backhausen v. Mayer, 204 Wis. 286, 234 N.W. 904, 74 A.L.R. 1245 (1931), where the court decided in favor of the subsequent purchaser and expressly repudiated the rule that "the purchaser of the servient estate takes it subject to the easement [by necessity] whether he had notice thereof or not." In explaining its decision, the court said:

"Such a doctrine would be the exercise of an unreasonable solicitude for a negligent grantee who fails to exact an express covenant granting to him the right of way necessary for the beneficial enjoyment of his premises. We conclude, therefore, that the public record afforded Hanke no notice, actual or constructive, of the existence of this way. Neither were there any visible conditions which amounted to notice thereof. The dominant estate was a wood lot. It was covered with timber. It has not yet all been removed. While it does appear that for the last ten years timber has been hauled from the lot, sometimes over plaintiffs' and sometimes over other adjoining premises, it does not appear that any considerable quantity of timber was hauled prior to 1895.

What hauling was done was in the wintertime, when the snow was on the ground. An inspection of the premises in 1895 would have revealed no evidence whatever of the existence of this way. * * *

"The conclusion seems to be inevitable that the way of necessity with which the servient estate was undoubtedly burdened during the time it was owned by Christian Mayer was extinguished when Christian Mayer conveyed to Hanke in 1895."

Where easements are implied not simply on the basis of necessity but on the basis of a prior "apparent" use, it seems generally to be assumed that the easement will not be valid as against a subsequent bona fide purchaser without notice, but "inquiry notice" to subsequent purchasers of the "servient" tract is usually found to result from visible evidence of the easement's use. This is so even where the marks of use are on the "dominant" tract only.

Generally, see 4 A.L.P. § 17.24.

SECTION 3. PERSONS PROTECTED BY THE RECORDING ACTS

A. BONA FIDE PURCHASERS FOR VALUE

In General

" * * * In a large number of states the form of the statute is to the effect that 'subsequent purchasers in good faith and without notice' are protected, or that they are protected if they first duly record. In order to be a subsequent purchaser in good faith, the person in question must take title and part with value before he has notice of the prior conveyance. A legally binding promise is not sufficient to constitute value. In general, value means money or money's worth, but not necessarily the market value of the land." Simes, Handbook for More Efficient Conveyancing 28 (1961).

In Morris v. Wicks, 81 Kan. 790, 106 P. 1048, 26 L.R.A.,N.S., 681, 19 Ann.Cas. 319 (1910), the consideration paid was one dollar. Held: not sufficient to make out a case of bona fide purchase for value. So also, in Tinnin v. Brown, 98 Miss. 378, 53 So. 780, Ann.Cas.1913A, 1081 (1910). But in Ennis v. Tucker, 78 Kan. 55, 96 P. 140, 130 Am.St.Rep. 352 (1908), a consideration of $40, though inadequate, was held sufficient to make out a case of purchase for value.

In Ten Eyck v. Witbeck, 135 N.Y. 40, 31 N.E. 994, 31 Am.St.Rep. 809 (1892), the subsequent conveyance was made to a child of the grantor in consideration of $10 paid and an agreement by the grantee to pay annually to designated persons the receipts from the property. The property was worth twenty thousand dollars. Held, that the child was not a purchaser for valuable consideration under the recording statute so as to be preferred over an earlier unrecorded deed of the same grantor.

Cf. Strong v. Whybark, 204 Mo. 341, 102 S.W. 968, 12 L.R.A.,N.S., 240, 120 Am.St.Rep. 710 (1907), where the court held that a recited consideration of "natural love and affection of five dollars" made the grantee a purchaser for value. The court said that "five dollars or any other stated sum of money in excess of one cent, one dime, or one dollar, which are the technical words used to express nominal considerations, is a valuable consideration within the meaning of the law of conveyancing."

See also, Dunn v. Barnum, 51 F. 355, 2 C.C.A. 265 (C.C.A.Minn.1892), where the consideration for the second conveyance was $100, the property then being worth $30,000, and at time of the suit $1,000,000; Nichols-Steuart v. Crosby, 87 Tex. 443, 29 S.W. 380, 1895, where $5 was paid for land then worth about $8,000.

The reason why "a legally binding promise is not sufficient to constitute value" is explained as follows in Thomas v. Stone & Graham, Walker Ch. 117 (Mich.Ch.1843): "He has paid nothing. It is not enough that the party has secured the purchase money; he must have paid it, or become bound for it in such a way that this Court could not relieve from the payment of it; as, by a promissory note, which had been negotiated, or the like. The bond for $200, if it has been assigned by Stone (of which there is no evidence) would, in the hands of the assignee, be subject to all equities existing against it before it was assigned."

When a subsequent purchaser obtains a deed from his vendor without having paid the full purchase price, should he be considered a purchaser for value, so as to prevail over a prior grantee holding an unrecorded deed? If so, the prior grantee is, of course, entitled to the unpaid balance of the purchase price as of the date when the subsequent purchaser received notice of the prior unrecorded conveyance; and if the subsequent purchaser pays his vendor the balance after receiving notice of the prior unrecorded conveyance he must pay it again to the prior grantee. See Baldwin v. Sager, 70 Ill. 503 (1873); Green v. Green, 41 Kan. 472, 21 P. 586 (1889). But it can be argued that the subsequent purchaser is not yet a purchaser for value if he has not completed payment of the price before receiving notice of the prior unrecorded conveyance, and hence that the grantee holding the unrecorded deed should retain legal title but be required to reimburse the subsequent purchaser for the amount actually paid before receiving notice. See Henry v. Phillips, 163 Cal. 135, 124 P. 837, Ann.Cas.1914A 39 (1912). Or perhaps the courts should adopt a more flexible approach to this problem.

In Durst v. Daugherty, 81 Tex. 650, 17 S.W. 388 (1891), the subsequent purchaser (plaintiff-appellee in the case) paid half the consideration before notice of any claim adverse to him. The lower court gave judgment for the subsequent purchaser for possession of the entire tract. On appeal, the court held that the subsequent purchaser was entitled to prevail *pro tanto* and suggested consideration of the following matters in arriving at an equitable solution:

"Some of the courts adopt that rule that allows the innocent purchaser to retain of the land purchased the proportion paid for; some admit a lien in favor of the innocent purchaser upon the land for the amount of the purchase money paid; other courts give to the innocent purchaser all the land, with a right in the real owner [i.e., prior grantee] to recover from him the purchase money unpaid at the time of notice. * * * In determining which of these rules should be applied in any case it is necessary to ascertain the equities, if any, of the respective parties; for in the application of these rules the adjustment of the equities of each given case is the primary object to be accomplished. The rule that should be applied in one case may be inequitable if applied to another; consequently, it is not proper that a court select one rule, to the exclusion of the others, as a rule that should govern alike in all cases. In ascertaining what the equities of the parties are it is permissible to inquire into the price paid for the land by the innocent purchaser, and if or not he has placed upon the land permanent and valuable improvements; and if or not the land, situated as it is at the time, is in a condition to be partitioned or divided so that it would not affect or destroy its usefulness, and render it of little or no value to either party, or if a partition could be had without injury to the innocent purchaser; and it is further proper to show the conduct of the parties, with reference to their acts of diligence, laches, or negligence, if any, in order to ascertain what party, if any, is in fault, so that the court can determine who is the more entitled to its equitable relief; and if the land by reason of the improvements, if any, placed thereon by the innocent purchaser, has increased in value since its purchase. *   *   * "

What about subsequent purchasers without legal title? Suppose, e.g., that O executes a deed to A, who neglects to record; thereafter O enters into a contract with X for the sale of the same land and X pays part (or all) of the purchase price without notice of A's claim; but X learns of the prior deed to A before he (X) obtains a deed from O. How should X stand with reference to A? Should X be denied any protection because he has not added the "legal title" to his equity arising out of bona fide purchase for value? Or should he be limited to an equitable lien upon the land in A's hands, to secure a right of reimbursement for the purchase money X paid before notice of A's claim? Or should X be treated as purchaser protected *pro tanto* under the recording act as suggested in the Durst case, supra?

See cases cited in 1 Patton, Land Titles § 13 nn. 77–78 (2d ed. 1957), in support of the propositions that, "In many jurisdictions, 'completing the purchase' is marked by an irrevocable payment of the consideration, whether in cash, property, or by execution of an obligation. A number of cases go further and hold that it includes also the procuring of a conveyance."

Pre-existing Debt as "Value"

Is one who takes a mortgage to secure a pre-existing debt a "purchaser for value"? What about one who takes an absolute conveyance of land in satisfaction of a pre-existing debt?

By the very decided weight of authority, one who takes a mortgage to secure a pre-existing debt without at the same time relinquishing any right or claim as a consideration for the mortgage is not a purchaser for value. But if the creditor surrenders other security for the debt or extends the time for payment of the debt by a binding contract, he is regarded as a purchaser for value. See 5 Tiffany, Real Property, 91–92

(3d ed. 1939) and cases cited. With respect to one who takes an absolute conveyance of land in satisfaction of an antecedent debt, the cases are about equally divided on the question whether he is a purchaser for value. See id., 93–94 and cases cited.

Purchasers at Execution Sales

It is well-settled that a purchaser at an execution sale, other than the judgment creditor himself, is a purchaser for value, as is a purchaser at a judicial sale pursuant to a court order. See 1 Patton, Land Titles § 12 n. 55 (2d ed. 1957) or 4 A.L.P. p. 562 n. 22 (1952) for an extensive citation of cases. But the case of a judgment creditor who buys at his own execution sale presents greater difficulty. Since it can be argued that such a judgment creditor is, in substance, merely taking a conveyance of his judgment debtor's land in satisfaction of an antecedent debt, it would seem that such a judgment creditor might not be deemed a purchaser for value in those jurisdictions where the satisfaction of an antecedent debt is not "value." Patton says the weight of authority considers the judgment creditor who buys at his own execution sale to be a purchaser for value, "because the consideration he pays embraces something more than his pre-existing debt, namely the legal expenses of the proceeding." 1 Patton, Land Titles, 92 at nn. 65–66 (2d ed. 1957). But an examination of the cases cited by Patton, as well as those cited in 4 A.L.P. p. 613 n. 9 and n. 11 (1952) and in 5 Tiffany, Real Property, 93 nn. 30–31 (3d ed. 1939), shows the authorities to be about equally divided on the question. Such an examination also reveals that most courts which hold a preexisting debt not to be "value" do not consider the judgment creditor purchasing at his own execution sale to be a purchaser for value. Conversely, a judgment creditor who buys at his own execution sale is generally regarded as a purchaser for value in states where satisfaction of a pre-existing debt is "value." But there are states where a judgment creditor who buys at his own execution sale is deemed a purchaser for value although, as a general rule, satisfaction of a preexisting debt is not "value."

Of course, in jurisdictions where lien creditors are protected under the recording act, this protection dates from the time when the creditor acquires his lien, and he obtains very little additional protection by virtue of his status as a purchaser for value when he buys at his own execution sale. Even in such jurisdictions, however, the creditor may gain some additional protection since his lien may be subject to outstanding equitable interests arising by operation of law, and therefore not within the recording acts at all. If the creditor buys at his own execution sale without notice of any such outstanding equitable interests, and is deemed to be a purchaser for value, he will acquire the legal title free and clear of any such outstanding equitable interests.

The Uniform Simplification of Land Transfers Act (1977) provides in § 1–201:

"(31) A person gives 'value' for rights if he acquires the rights:

"(i) pursuant to a commitment to extend credit or for the extension of credit;

"(ii) as security for, or in total or partial satisfaction of, a pre-existing claim;

"(iii) under a pre-existing contract; or

"(iv) generally, in return for any consideration sufficient to support a simple contract."

This definition of "value" is consistent with those contained in the Uniform Commercial Code, §§ 1–201(44) and 3–303.

B. PROTECTION OF CREDITORS

"Acts which, by express wording or judicial construction, limit their protection to subsequent purchasers, do not protect general creditors, or judgment and attachment creditors. This is because none of these parties are embraced in the term 'purchaser'; or, because of the general rule that, except as provided otherwise by statute, the lien of a judgment attaches to the actual interest only of the debtor rather than to his apparent interest.

"A number of the recording acts expressly include in their protection the record owner's creditors, or his lien creditors. Others embrace creditors by a general term defining the parties protected, such as 'third persons,' 'all parties,' etc.; or, by making an instrument ineffective generally till recorded, or effective as to certain persons only.   *   *   *

"In several states the question as to whether a creditor must be without notice of prior unrecorded rights, in order to be protected, is expressly covered by the statute. Most of these affirm that proposition. Under a few of them notice is immaterial. When the statute is silent on the point but prescribes that a purchaser to be protected must be without notice, there are numerous decisions that by implication this qualification extends to creditors also; and some decisions to the contrary.   *   *   *   But it should be added that whenever lack of notice is essential to a creditor's protection, receipt of it after the lien has attached is immaterial." 1 Patton, Land Titles, 83–91 (2d ed. 1957).

It should also be noted that, in general, acquisition of a lien is essential to protection of a creditor under the recording acts. This is obviously so where the statute expressly makes unrecorded instruments void as against "lien creditors" or "judgment creditors"; it is also essential where the statute protects creditors by a broad, inclusive reference, as in Massachusetts; and it is even essential in most of the states, such as Illinois, where the statute purports to protect "all creditors." Protection is even more limited under statutes which protect "judgment creditors," since creditors who acquire liens other than by judgment are clearly excluded. But a few recording acts expressly protect non-lien creditors.

Assuming that the creditors protected by recording acts, in general, are those who acquire liens without notice of a prior unrecorded instrument executed by the judgment debtor or a predecessor in title, does the protection of the recording acts extend to those who became creditors before the unrecorded instrument was executed, or only to those who became creditors after the unrecorded instrument was executed? What about recording acts like that of Massachusetts, supra page 848, which protects creditors by broad reference without expressly mentioning them? What about recording acts which expressly protect "subsequent lien creditors" or "subsequent judgment creditors"?

C. NOTICE TO PURCHASER AND CREDITORS

A subsequent purchaser or lien creditor may, of course, actually learn of the existence of a prior unrecorded instrument affecting the title to a particular tract of land before he makes his purchase or acquires his lien. In such case, he is said to have "actual notice." But a wide variety of types of "constructive notice" may be accorded the same legal effect as "actual notice" under the recording statutes. We consider several forms of "constructive notice" here.

Notice from Muniments of Title

BAKER v. MATHER

Supreme Court of Michigan, 1872.
25 Mich. 51.

PER CURIAM. The question in these cases is one of priority between two mortgages. The second mortgage was recorded first, and there is no evidence that the mortgagee therein had actual notice of the existence of the prior mortgage when he took his. It appears, however, that the deed, under which the mortgagor held the land, expressly referred to this prior mortgage, and made his title subject to it. The deed was not recorded, but this is an immaterial circumstance. Everybody taking a conveyance of, or a lien upon, land, takes it with constructive notice of whatever appears in the conveyances which constitute his chain of title. Decrees below affirmed.

Note

In Sweet v. Henry, 175 N.Y. 268, 67 N.E. 574 (1903), the court said:

"The plaintiff's chain of title extends back through the foreclosure sale, the mortgage on which it is based and the mesne conveyances leading up to Van Dresser, the lessor and owner of the fee. The fact that Howden omitted from his quitclaim deed to plaintiff any reference to the exception and reservation mentioned in the prior conveyances is of no importance, as under the rule, to which reference has been made, the plaintiff is presumed to have examined the conveyances in his chain of title and to have investigated all facts therein disclosed in any way affecting his rights under the conveyance he was about to accept. If he failed to make such an investigation, but relied on a quitclaim deed, he is chargeable with negligence and is estopped from availing himself of any benefit he might have derived by reason of due inquiry."

Cf. Ebling Brewing Co. v. Gennaro, 189 App.Div. 782, 179 N.Y.S. 384 (1919): O conveyed to G and took back a purchase money mortgage; G conveyed to H, who mortgaged to P; the deeds from O to G and from G to H were not record-ed, but O's mortgage was referred to in the deed from G to H. In an action to foreclose P's mortgage, the lower court held that P had constructive notice of the unrecorded mortgage because of the recital in the unrecorded deed from G to H. The Appellate Division reversed, holding that it was unreasonable to charge a subsequent purchaser with notice from recitals in unrecorded deeds because the English practice of examining the original title deeds does not pre-vail in this country. Two of the five judges dissented.

Generally, see 4 A.L.P. pp. 589–590.

Notice From Title Records

Is it consistent with the spirit and purpose of the recording acts to hold that the recording of an instrument of title gives notice of instru-ments mentioned in recitals therein, although the instruments referred to are not recorded? The consensus of informed persons is well stated in Simes & Taylor, Improvement of Conveyancing by Legislation 101–102 (1960): "That this places an unreasonable burden upon the title searcher can scarcely be denied. Indeed, it is entirely inconsistent with the spirit and purpose of the recording acts in that it compels the title searcher to investigate the existence of unrecorded instruments."

Section 3–207 of the Uniform Simplification of Land Transfers Act (1977) deals with this situation as follows:

"(a) Unless a reference in a document is a reference to another docu-ment by its record location, a person by reason of the reference is not charged with knowledge of the document or an adverse claim founded thereon, and the document is not in the record chain of title by reason of the reference to it.

"(b) Examples of references that are not to a record location and are too indefinite to charge a person with knowledge of an interest or to bring the document within the record chain of title are:

"(1) subject to the terms of a deed dated July 4, 1976, from A to B;

"(2) subject to a mortgage from A to B;

"(3) subject to existing encumbrances;

"(4) subject to easements of record;

"(5) subject to mortgages of record; and

"(6) excepting so much of the described premises as I have here-tofore conveyed.

"(c) This section does not prevent an indefinite reference from con-stituting a waiver, or exception, or from being taken into account in determining the existence of:

"(1) a contractual obligation or condition between the immediate parties to the document in which the reference occurs,

"(2) any negation of a warranty of title.

"(d) This section does not limit the effect of recording a memoran-dum of lease (Section 2–309) or memorandum of any other document the recording of which is permitted by law."

A number of states already have similar provisions, though they may be more restricted in scope. See Bayse, Clearing Land Titles § 138 (2d ed. 1970).

As previously indicated, conveyances are not entitled to record unless they are acknowledged or authenticated in some similar way. Hence, if the recording officer copies into the records an unacknowledged instrument not otherwise authenticated, the instrument is not deemed to be recorded at all. See Messersmith v. Smith, supra page 853. Suppose, however, that a prospective purchaser or his agent does see the copy of the unacknowledged deed on the record. Can he then be considered a purchaser without notice within the protection of the recording statute? There are decisions both ways on this question, some holding that seeing the unauthorized record gives the purchaser at least "inquiry notice," while other decisions hold that actual knowledge of the unauthorized record copy is not actual notice of a valid original instrument corresponding to the copy and does not place the purchaser upon inquiry. The cases are collected in Note, 3 A.L.R.2d 589 (1949). An especially interesting case is Nordman v. Rau, 86 Kan. 19, 119 P. 351, 38 L.R.A.,N.S., 400, Ann.Cas.1913B 1068 (1911). The majority held that actual knowledge of the unauthorized record of the unacknowledged instrument did not charge the purchaser, whose agent had actually seen it, with notice; the grounds for the majority's holding were as follows:

"* * * To charge him with such notice is to require him to assume, without proof and without competent evidence, that a valid conveyance is in existence corresponding to the unauthorized copy. If he is required to give any attention to the matter at all he may with equal or greater reason suppose the parties to have abandoned whatever intention they may have had to execute such a conveyance, from the fact that they failed to have a certificate of acknowledgment attached. To charge him with actual notice of the existence of a conveyance because he has seen a copy of it which, without legal authority, has been written in a book of public records, is essentially to give such copy the force of a valid record. To hold that the record of an unacknowledged conveyance, if known to a prospective buyer, amounts to actual notice of the instrument, is to compel him to give it force as evidence which the court itself would refuse it. * * *"

There is a vigorous dissent in Nordman v. Rau, supra, containing the following language:

"* * * Where a prospective buyer of land sees upon the record what purports to be the copy of an instrument bearing no certificate of acknowledgment (or a defective one, for the rule would necessarily be the same), the inference which he would naturally and almost necessarily draw would be that the record was made at the instance of the grantee, and that the grantee claimed to have an interest in the land under an instrument in the language of the copy. The record would not be competent legal evidence that such an instrument had been executed, but it would suggest that probability so strongly that a prudent person having knowledge of it would be put upon inquiry. It would give him a definite and tangible clue, which, if diligently followed up, would ordinarily bring the truth of the matter to light. In the present case, if an inquiry had been prosecuted with reasonable diligence, the existence of the mortgage would necessarily have been developed. * * *"

For a discussion of "curative acts" as a remedy for records which are unauthorized because of failure to comply with statutory prerequisites to recordation, see pages 859–60, supra.

Possession as Notice

"* * *. It is the universal rule, both in notice jurisdictions and in notice-race jurisdictions, that a subsequent purchaser is not given priority if he has actual notice of a prior conveyance from the same grantor, even though that notice is derived from something entirely outside the record. One of the most common situations in which this is true is the case where inquiry notice arises from the possession of someone having title. Thus, suppose O, the owner of record of a piece of land, conveys it to A, who fails to record his deed. A, however, goes into possession, and is still in possession when O later conveys the same land to B, who pays value and has no knowledge of the conveyance to A. B would not be protected, even though he should record before A, if an inquiry of A would have disclosed the latter's title. On the other hand, if it could be shown that, for some reason, A would have denied having any title even though B had made inquiry of him, then B is not deemed to have notice of A's title, and would obtain priority over A." Simes, Handbook for More Efficient Conveyancing (1961).

Possession of land is not per se notice to those claiming the benefit of the recording statute, of the interest of the possessor. Its effect is to put them upon inquiry. Facts the notice of which is charged to him are those which a reasonably diligent inquiry, prompted by such possession, would disclose. This is well illustrated by Austin v. Southern Home Bldg. & Loan Ass'n, 122 Ga. 439, 50 S.E. 382 (1905). In light of the foregoing, one must not take literally such language as the following, used by the court in Doll v. Walter, 305 Ill.App. 188, 27 N.E.2d 231 (1940): "Possession of property is equivalent to the recording of a deed."

As to "possession" of a vacant lot, see Ballona v. Petex, 234 Mich. 273, 207 N.W. 836 (1926). In Detrick v. Kitchens, 184 Okl. 293, 86 P.2d 998 (1939), the presence of household goods in a locked outhouse was not sufficient to put one on inquiry.

The Massachusetts recording act, in its current form, is set out above at page 848. In Toupin v. Peabody, 162 Mass. 473, 39 N.E. 280 (1895), the court said: "It is well settled that facts sufficient to put a purchaser upon inquiry are not sufficient to affect him with actual notice of an unrecorded instrument within the meaning of the language of the statute." The court therefore held that an unrecorded lease for five years, with a privilege in the lessee to renew on the same terms for another five years, was void as against a subsequent purchaser of the fee simple, without actual notice, insofar as the lease purported to give the lessee a right to a second term of five years, although inquiry would almost certainly have revealed the existence of the lease and the option.

Does it follow, in Massachusetts, that a purchaser of land may safely ignore the possible interest of a possessor who has no title of record? That a purchaser need not even investigate to determine who is in possession of the land?

Compare Toupin v. Peabody, supra, with Brinkman v. Jones, 44 Wis. 498 (1878). In applying a recording statute which made certain unrecorded instruments void as against "the maker * * *, or his heirs or devisees, or persons having actual notice thereof," the court recognized "the obligation to give some effect to the term 'actual notice,' as distinguished from mere 'notice,'" and held that possession inconsistent with record title would not put a subsequent purchaser upon inquiry unless he had actual knowledge of that possession; but the court also held that actual knowledge of possession inconsistent with record title would put the subsequent purchaser upon inquiry as to the basis of the possession. In the Brinkman case, the court went on to deal with the argument of the subsequent purchaser that "the possession of a grantor cannot be considered hostile to the rights of his grantee." On this point, the court said:

"We are of the opinion that the rule as stated in these cases must be qualified by at least two considerations: first, that such occupation is not inconsistent with the rights of the grantee; and second, that the length of time that the occupancy has continued ought to be considered. The first consideration is recognized by the authorities. Butler v. Phelps, 17 Wend. 642; Cramer v. Benton, 4 Lans. 291; Chalfin v. Malone, 9 B. Monroe 496. * * * The cases last above cited decide that a grantor may hold so adversely against his grantee. We have no doubt of the justice of the rule as stated by the counsel for the respondent, when the occupation has continued but a short time after the date of the deed, or when, though continued for a longer time, it is not inconsistent with the title purporting to be conveyed by the deed. We are, however, of the opinion that when the possession has been for a long period, the presumption of a claim of right hostile to the title granted does arise in every case where such possession is inconsistent with the rights of the grantee, and that in such case a court or jury might find the possession adverse from the nature of the possession, without proof of an express declaration on the part of the occupant that he claimed to hold in hostility to his grant."

With respect to possession as "inquiry notice," see 4 A.L.P. § 17.12; with respect to continued possession by grantor in recorded deed, see id. § 17.14.

In general, "where a title under which the occupant holds has been put on record, and his possession is consistent with what thus appears of record, it shall not be a constructive notice of any additional or different title or interest to a purchaser who has relied upon the record, and has had no actual notice beyond what is thereby disclosed." Pomeroy, Eq.Jur. § 616 (5th ed. 1941). But many courts have made an exception to this rule "in the case of leases where the lessee is in open and visible possession of improved property. Prospective purchasers should inquire of the tenant in possession as to whether there have been any modifications of the recorded lease or any other collateral or subsequent agreements affecting it." Hull v. Gafill Oil Co., 263 Mich. 650, 249 N.W. 24 (1933). The reason given in the Hull case is "the great frequency with which collateral or subsequent agreements are entered into in forms that do not meet the requirements of recording laws. Agreements modifying the terms of written leases are extremely common. Frequently, alterations, improvements and repairs have been made by the lessee in consideration of a reduction in the rent, extension of the term, or some other change or modification of the lease. * * * Such concessions have been made orally as well as in writing, and frequently are neither witnessed nor acknowledged."

With respect to the effect of possession consistent with the record title, where the possessor has another or greater interest under an unrecorded instrument, see generally 4 A.L.P. § 17.13. As to the effect, as notice, of possession without human occupancy, see id. § 17.15.

Problems

1. A, a married woman, having purchased certain lands, had a conveyance of them made to B to hold on her behalf. B later conveyed the premises to A, but the deed was never recorded. After the death of B, his heirs executed a deed of these premises to C, who paid value therefor without knowledge of the rights of A. Since the time of the first conveyance mentioned to B, A and her husband have resided upon the premises. Should C be charged with notice of A's rights? See Kirby v. Tallmadge, 160 U.S. 379, 16 S.Ct. 349, 40 L.Ed. 463 (1896).

What would have been the situation if, instead of A and her husband being in possession, a lessee of A had been occupying the premises? See Hunt v. Luch [1902] 1 Ch. 428; Randall v. Lingwall, 43 Or. 383, 73 P. 1 (1903).

2. A prospective mortgagee examined the premises on September 12th and found the expected mortgagor then in possession; the mortgage was executed on September 16th. Should the mortgagee be deemed a taker with notice of the rights of a claimant under an earlier equity who took possession on the 14th? See Mishawaka-St. Joseph L. & T. Co. v. Neu, 209 Ind. 433, 196 N.E. 85, 105 A.L.R. 881 (1935); Fraser v. Fleming, 190 Mich. 238, 157 N.W. 269 (1916).

3. Does an easement permit of such enjoyment of the servient land that a purchaser thereof may be deemed charged with notice of the existence of the easement by reason of the acts of user and other physical evidences? See Dunford v. Dardanelle & Russellville Railroad Co., 171 Ark. 1036, 287 S.W. 170 (1926); Rock Island & Pacific Railway Co. v. Dimick, 144 Ill. 628, 32 N.E. 291, 19 L.R.A. 105 (1892); Johnson v. Chicago, Burlington & Quincy Railroad Co., 202 Iowa 1282, 211 N.W. 842 (1927); McHugh Inc. v. Haley, 61 N.D. 359, 237 N.W. 835 (1930).

4. Plaintiffs, the children of Manuel Strong and his first wife, Nancy, sued Strong, his second wife, Minnie, and Sun Oil Company to establish title to an undivided $^{15}/_{32}$ interest in a 50.5 acre tract of land, and for partition. The land was community property of Manuel Strong and his first wife, acquired and conveyed to him during their marriage, and plaintiffs claimed as heirs of their mother. Manuel Strong and his second wife, Minnie, admitted the allegations in plaintiffs' petition and joined in the prayer for relief therein. Sun Oil Compa-

ny asserted its ownership of the oil and gas in the 50.5 acre tract under an oil and gas lease executed by Manuel Strong and Minnie to one N.M. Wilson and by Wilson assigned to Sun Oil. Several witnesses testified that it was commonly known in the community where the land was situated that plaintiffs had an interest in the land. There was no evidence showing or tending to show that any one representing Sun Oil knew of the existence of such common knowledge or reputation, or that any representative of Sun Oil was so situated that he would or should learn of such common knowledge or reputation. The undisputed evidence was that at the time Sun Oil acquired the lease the territory in which the land as situated was unproved, that Sun Oil had sent no geologist or other employee or agent there, had taken no steps to ascertain whether anyone other than Manuel Strong had an interest in the land, and had no information about the ownership or occupancy of the land except that contained in an affidavit made by Manuel Strong. In the affidavit Manuel Strong stated in substance that he held a deed to the land duly registered, giving its date, the book and page where recorded, and the name of the grantor, that the land was not encumbered, that he was in possession of the land and had been continuously for at least twenty years, paying all taxes, and that no adverse claim had been made. The community property rights of plaintiffs were not a matter of public record. Manuel Strong and his second wife, Minnie, occupied the land as their homestead, seven children living with them—the two plaintiffs, children of Manuel's first wife, and five children of Manuel and his second wife. They lived as one family and all helped cultivate the farm. One of the plaintiffs was of age and unmarried when the oil and gas lease was executed in 1929. Sun Oil Company acquired the lease, together with a number of other leases of land in the same territory, for $350, of which $50 was paid for the Manuel Strong lease.

What result?   See Strong v. Strong, 128 Tex. 470, 98 S.W.2d 346, 109 A.L.R. 739 (1936).

Effect of Recording a Quitclaim Deed

"* * *. The great weight of authority is to the effect that the record of a quitclaim deed in the chain of title is just as effective to pass a title to a bona fide purchaser under the recording acts as a grant deed or a deed with covenants. Against this view, it may be said that a quitclaim deed indicates that the grantor suspected there were defects in the title, and therefore puts a subsequent purchaser on notice that such defects may exist. Or it may be said that the very language of the deed, 'release, remise and forever quitclaim,' conveys only what the grantor actually has, not what he appears by the record to have. However, if quitclaim deeds are not treated as other conveyances, then the presence of a recorded quitclaim deed in the chain of record title would render the record totally ineffective as a means of effective title search. Doubtless, the majority of courts have realized this in deciding as they have on this question." Simes, Handbook for More Efficient Conveyancing 27 (1961).

The Uniform Simplification of Land Transfers Act (1977) specifically provides that a quitclaim deed is to be treated as any other conveyance (§ 3–203(c)).

SECTION 4.   THE PUBLIC LAND RECORDS AND THE RECORD CHAIN OF TITLE

A. THE PUBLIC LAND RECORDS

In most states the geographical unit on which the recording system is based is the county; i.e., instruments affecting the title to land are recorded in the county where the land is situated. Consequently, the title search can be conducted principally in the county court house.

Filing, Recording and Indexing

One wishing to record an instrument in the county recorder's office delivers it to the recorder or one of his assistants. It is immediately stamped with the date, hour, and minute of its delivery. Usually an entry is made in an "original entry book" or "daily entry sheet" showing the nature of the instrument, the names of the parties, the description of the property affected, and the time of the delivery for record. As soon as practicable the instrument is copied and the copy is bound into a permanent volume of records. Originally, instruments were copied by hand; later, by typing; and at the present time photographic copying has come into general use in order to save time, eliminate mistakes in copying, and reproduce signatures. In some states separate books are kept for each class of recordable instruments. Thus there will be one series of books for deeds, another for mortgages, another for land sale contracts, etc. In other states there is no segregation of the records of different classes of instruments.

"No doubt, for some time after a recording act took effect, it was possible for the title examiner to examine all recorded instruments in order to determine whether a given person had good title. But as the number of recorded instruments increased, it became necessary to make use of indices in order to limit the examination to those instruments directly concerned with the piece of real estate, the title to which was involved. At first these were only name indices. There would commonly be a grantee-grantor index, in which deeds were indexed alphabetically in the names of grantees. Similarly there would be a grantor-grantee index, in which deeds were indexed alphabetically in the names of grantors. There would also be a mortgagee-mortgagor index and a mortgagor-mortgagee index of similar character. There might also be other name indices, such as a miscellaneous index. In practically all states are now found name indices. But in a few states are also found so-called tract indices. These index the instruments in accordance with designated tracts or lots, so that all instruments of conveyance involving a particular tract may be found listed under the designation of that tract." *

A typical form of "grantor" index might have headings and initial entries as follows:

* Simes, Handbook for More Efficient
Conveyancing 19 (1961).

Time filed	Grantor	Grantee	Nature of Instrument	Recorded in Book Vol. Page	Description of Property
2:16 P.M. July 9, 1935	Abner, John	Smith, Edward L.	Deed	195 Deeds 44	NE¼, SE¼ S. 9, T. 5 S. R. 2 E.
8:30 A.M. July 21, 1935	Acheson, William	Daniels, Robert	Deed	197 Deeds 429	NW¼, S. 12, T. 6 S. R. 4 E.

[A6966]

In such a "grantor" index a separate page or series of pages is allotted to each letter of the alphabet and instruments are indexed under the first letter of the last name of the grantor. If a title searcher knows who held the title at a given date in the past, he can begin his search in the grantor index at that date and search the index under the first letter of the then owner's name until he finds when that owner conveyed the land—i.e., when he became a grantor. The searcher can then take the grantee's name and repeat the process, continuing in the same way with successive grantees until he has traced the title down to the present owner. This search of the grantor index also enables the title searcher to discover any conveyances, mortgages, or other encumbrances which would prevail over the chain of title he is investigating, and consequently the search must be continued not only to the point where the record title became vested in the person who now appears to be owner but right down to the final entry in the grantor index.

The "grantee" index is identical with the "grantor" index except that columns two and three are reversed in order, so that the grantees' names appear first, and the entries are arranged alphabetically according to the last names of the grantees. This enables the title searcher to start with the name of a prospective vendor or mortgagor and establish his chain of title by searching backward in the grantee index. Thus, knowing that Edward L. Smith, the prospective vendor or mortgagor, received title on July 9, 1935, the title searcher can work backward in the grantee index under "A" until he finds when Abner became a grantee; then take the name of Abner's grantor and work backward in the grantee index until he finds when Abner's grantor became a grantee; and so on back, as far as the title searcher wants to go. In every case, however, it is necessary to search the grantor index under the name of every owner in the chain of title to determine whether any such owner has executed a recorded deed, mortgage, or other instrument which would prevail over the chain of title under investigation.

As previously indicated, "tract" indexes are maintained in some states. A tract index system is feasible wherever an underlying survey has created convenient subdivisions of land that can be designated by number, letter, or some other short formula. A page in the index book is assigned to each such subdivision and on this page (and continuation pages) there is indexed every recorded instrument affecting the title to land in that subdivision, regardless of who the parties to the instrument may be. The index entries usually include the type of instrument, the volume and page where it is recorded, and, if the instrument did not affect the title to the entire tract, a notation as to what part of the tract it affects. A tract index immensely simplifies title searches, although it is somewhat more difficult to maintain because a single instrument may have to be indexed in several tract books if it affects more than one tract of land.

Tract indexes are generally maintained only in states carved out of the United States public domain, where the government survey divided the land into numbered "ranges," "townships," "sections," and "quarter-sections" and thus made it relatively easy to set up tract indexes based on these survey subdivisions. The systematic numbering or lettering of blocks and lots in townsite or other subdivision plats in urban areas has also made it feasible to set up tract indexes covering towns and cities. In some of the larger cities a combination of the tract and alphabetical index systems is in use. In New York City, for example, each city lot is numbered and separate grantor and grantee indexes are maintained for each lot. Thus the grantee index for the lot can conveniently be used to establish the chain of title to a particular lot and the grantor index can be used to check for recorded instruments that might prevail over the chain of title in question.

A typical form of tract index might contain a heading and entries like the following: **

Section 10, Block 7125.

Grantors	Grantees	Date of Recording, 1927	Conveyance		Serial Number	Remarks
			Liber	Page		
Richards, Frank	John T. Smith	Jan. 2	4122	96	148 Deed	Cor. Ave. M & 14th St. 100 × 100
Martin, Joseph A.	Neil Jordan	Jan. 26	4133	248	2176 Assigt. of Lease	S. side Brown Ave. 40 W. Pearl St. 40 × 100
Smith, John T.	Mary R. Abbott	Feb. 10	4144	432	3354 Deed	Lot 10

[A6959]

The Chain of Title

Neither the alphabetical grantor-grantee indexes nor the tract index will always disclose a complete chain of title to a particular parcel of land. Since the county land records generally include only inter vivos transfers, the name of a grantor who acquired title by descent or devise will not appear in the grantee index, and it will be impossible to discover from that index who his predecessor in title was. A tract index will reveal who that predecessor was, but not how the grantor in question

** North & Van Buren, Real Estate, Titles and Conveyancing 131 (Rev. ed. 1940). Reprinted by permission of Prentice-Hall, Inc., Englewood Cliffs, New Jersey.

acquired title from him. However, a reading of the deed from the grantor in question may reveal how he acquired title, for in many parts of the United States it is customary for each deed to recite the grantor's source of title. If a reading of the deed does not disclose the source of his title, a search of the probate records may enable the searcher to obtain the missing information. But the index to probate records is usually an alphabetical index of decedents rather than of heirs and devisees. Hence it is likely to require luck or a shrewd guess to pick out, in the index of decedents, a decedent who, upon careful examination of his probate file, turns out to be the ancestor or devisor of the grantor in question. Even if the title searcher is fortunate enough to find an estate listing the grantor in question as an heir or devisee, it is still necessary to determine whether the land in question passed to that grantor by descent or devise. If the decedent left no will, it may be impossible to determine this from the probate file; and even if there was a will, it is likely to contain a very indefinite description of the land devised, such as "all my real estate, wheresoever situated." If an inventory of the decedent's assets was filed, this may describe the decedent's real estate with sufficient definiteness so that the title searcher can tell whether it includes the land in question. If so, the searcher can then fit the next link into the chain of title by returning to the county recorder's office and searching the grantee index for the period prior to the decedent's death until a deed to him is found which conveys the land in question. If not, the title searcher must have another look at the probate records.

A break in the chain of title as shown by the indexes may also occur because a grantor is a public official, such as a sheriff, referee, or master in chancery conveying pursuant to court order. In such a case the grantee index obviously will not disclose any conveyance to the public official by the prior owner, but a reading of the deed itself may disclose the name of the owner whose land was conveyed by court order. If not, the deed will almost certainly refer to the judicial proceeding giving rise to the court order for conveyance, and by consulting the record of that proceeding the name of the prior owner can be ascertained.

In order to put himself in position to appraise the title to a given tract of land, the title searcher must not only establish the direct "chain of title" but must also discover all liens and other encumbrances which are a matter of public record. Encumbrances such as mortgages and easements created by deed can be located in the county land records. But the title searcher must look elsewhere for other kinds of encumbrances. As Simes points out—

"The title examiner must also ascertain whether real estate taxes have been paid. Again, this will normally be ascertained and reported by the abstractor or by the title insurance company. But, if the information is not furnished to the lawyer in this way, he will normally have to find it in the public office concerned with tax collection.

"Commonly, a money judgment in a court of general jurisdiction constitutes a lien on the real estate of the judgment debtor. Statutes usually make a judgment a lien only if some record of it is filed in the recorder's office. But, if such statutes are defective, or non-existent, then land titles may be affected by records of court proceedings which are entirely outside the recording office. Similarly, the record of titles derived from mortgage foreclosures or judicial sales, will be found in the courts of general jurisdiction. Unless a statute requires an additional filing in the recorder's office, search must be made in the court files." *

It should be noted that all judgments in a federal District Court create liens which continue for the same period as the liens of judgments rendered in courts of the state in which the federal court sits.[1] Most states have passed "conformity acts" under the Act of August 1, 1888,[2] authorizing "the judgments and decrees of the United States courts to be registered, recorded, docketed, indexed, or otherwise conformed to the rules and requirements relating to the judgments and decrees of the courts of the state." In these states judgments of federal courts are on the same basis as judgments of state courts with respect to the time of attachment of their liens and the geographic area over which their liens extend. The Act of August 1, 1888, allows a good deal of latitude in the details of state "conformity acts." In some states the "conformity act" requires that a judgment of either a state or federal court must be docketed in the office of the clerk of the state court, or that an abstract, transcript, or certified copy of the judgment be filed, or filed and recorded, in the office of the county recorder, in order that a lien shall attach to the real property of a judgment debtor in any county, including the county in which rendered.[3] Under such statutes no judgment search is necessary other than in the county office designated by the statute. Other states have "conformity acts" which provide that judgments of both state and federal courts shall be a lien on land of the judgment debtor in the county where the land is located from the time of rendition, or from the time of the docketing thereof in the office of the clerk of the court rendering the judgment; and that judgments shall be a lien on land of the judgment debtor in other counties from the time of filing or docketing a transcript, abstract, or certified copy of the judgment with the clerk of the state court of such other county.[4] In these states a judgment search must be made in the office of the clerk of both the state and federal court in counties where the federal court sits, and in the office of the clerk of the state court only in other counties.

A few states either have not adopted "conformity acts" or have adopted acts as to which there is uncertainty as to whether they establish the equality required in order to restrict the territorial limits of the lien of federal court judgments.[5] In these states the lien of a federal court judgment extends (or must be deemed to extend) to all the land of

---

* Simes, Handbook for More Efficient Conveyancing (1961).

1. See 28 U.S.C.A. § 1962.

2. 25 Stat. pp. 357–58, c. 729. For the current form of the statute, see 28 U.S. C.A. § 1962.

3. See 2 Patton, Land Titles 587 n. 31 (2d ed. 1957).

4. See id. 585 n. 30.

5. See id. 587–88 nn. 34, 36 (incl. Pocket Part) and text therewith.

the judgment debtor located within the federal judicial district, and the federal judgment search must be made accordingly.[6]

It may also be necessary to search for federal income tax liens in the office of the clerk of the federal District Court. Whenever the person liable for the tax fails to pay it after demand, it becomes a lien in favor of the United States from the time the assessment list is received by the collector of internal revenue against all property belonging to such person,[7] but the lien is not valid as against purchasers, mortgagees, or judgment creditors of the delinquent taxpayer until a notice of lien is filed in "the office designated by the law of the State or Territory in which the property subject to the lien is situated" or, if no such office is designated by state law, in the office of the clerk of the United States District Court for the district where the property subject to the lien is located.[8] Legislation has been enacted in some, but not all states, of the character referred to, authorizing "the filing of such notice in the office of the registrar, or recorder of deeds, of the counties of the state." [9]

Unfortunately, however, there is no provision for filing a notice of federal estate tax liens, although, "unless the tax is sooner paid in full, it shall be a lien for ten years on the gross estate of the decedent." [10] Consequently a title searcher must, "as to any title which has passed by descent or devise since September 8, 1916, ascertain whether the circumstances were such as to make it subject to the tax," [11] and if so, that it has been paid.

The above discussion, though by no means exhaustive, will at least serve to indicate some of the difficulties that may beset the title searcher. In concluding this discussion, it should be noted that in states where the county recorder maintains only alphabetical grantor-grantee indexes, abstract companies and title insurance companies almost invariably maintain their own tract indexes; and they frequently do so even where the county recorder maintains tract indexes. Indeed, title insurance companies in some parts of the United States maintain their own

---

6. With respect to execution liens arising from federal court judgments, see 2 Patton, Land Titles §§ 655–56 (2d ed. 1957).

7. This is true of other internal revenue taxes, except the federal estate tax. See 26 U.S.C.A., 1954 Int.Rev.Code, §§ 6321, 6322, 6323(a, d), 6325(a)(1, 2), 6325(b)(1, 2), 6325(c).

8. 26 U.S.C.A., 1954 Int.Rev.Code, 6323(a and d).

9. See 2 Patton, Land Titles 594 n. 71. For general discussion, see Wright, Title Examinations as Affected by Federal Tax Liens, 51 Mich.L.Rev. 183 (1953); Wright, Michigan Title Examinations and the 1954 Revenue Code's New General Lien Provisions, 53 Mich.L.Rev. 393 (1955); Tapp, et al., Titles as Affected by Liens, 28 Tenn.L. Rev. 352 (1961); Shanks, The Tax Lien Tamed, 8 U.C.L.A. L. Rev. 339 (1961); Report of Committee on Federal Liens (Am.

Bar Ass'n 1958); Plumb, Federal Tax Liens: Association-Sponsored Bills Reintroduced, 47 A.B.A.J. 455 (1961). For definitive treatment, see Plumb & Wright, Federal Tax Liens (1961).

10. 26 U.S.C.A., 1954 Int.Rev.Code, § 6324(a)(1).

11. Detroit Bank v. United States, 317 U.S. 329, 63 S.Ct. 297, 87 L.Ed. 304 (1943). The federal estate tax law has been in force since September 8, 1916. Since the lien exists for only 10 years from the death of the decedent, however, it would seem to be unnecessary to check titles passing by descent or devise more than 10 years prior to the date of title search for compliance with the federal estate tax law. The lien of federal gift taxes also ceases at the end of 10 years from the date of the property owner's death. See Wright, Title Examinations as Affected by Gift and Estate Taxes, 51 Mich.L.Rev. 325 (1953).

"title plants" containing a complete set of duplicates of all the records relating to land within the area where the "title plant" is located.

Proposed Improvements in the Public Land Records

The obvious deficiencies of the system of public land records has led to proposed improvements. In 1964 the Section of Real Property, Probate and Trust Law of the American Bar Association published an excellent Report of its Committee on Improvement of Land Records. (1964 Proceedings, p. 94). The use of shorter forms of documents, the value of tract indexes, the improvement of surveys and descriptions, and the use of photographic and microfilm recording are all examined. The report also concludes that even at that time computer equipment and technology made possible a system of recording which would provide a data bank with random access which would enable a lawyer to obtain in a matter of minutes references to all relevant documents recorded after the system is started. A local experiment for improvement is described in Payne, Self-Indexing System in Action: A Preliminary Report, 36 Ala. Lawyer 64 (1975), and Payne, Experiment in Public Land Indexing, 61 A.B.A.Jnl. 735 (June, 1975).

More recently, the National Conference of Commissioners on Uniform State Laws promulgated the Uniform Simplification of Land Transfer Act (1977) (USOLTA). The prefatory note indicates that the Act "deals with conveyancing, recording, priorities, limitations, construction (mechanics') and other liens, and public land records. In each of these areas it provides comprehensive provisions designed to unify and modernize the law. The purposes of the Act include the furtherance of the security and certainty of land titles, the reduction of the costs of land transfers, the balancing of the interests of all parties in the construction lien area, and the creation of a more efficient system of public land records.

* * *

"The high cost of real estate transfers has been seen by many analysts in recent years as being a substantial cause of the pricing of housing out of the reach of a large segment of the American public and of discouraging new investment in construction. This Act embodies a number of reforms designed to limit these costs. The required period of title search has been shortened through the adoption of marketable record title provisions similar to those which have proved successful in over a dozen states. The scope of the search has been further reduced by almost entirely eliminating interests other than those stated on the official record or those of which a purchaser has actual knowledge. Wasteful formalities have been made unnecessary.

"Considerable attention is paid to the mechanics of the recording system and to the division of functions among the various participants in the process. Persons presenting documents for recording are required to give detailed information to enable the recording officer to index the documents correctly. The recording officer is given discretion in the development of systems for modernization and automation of recording operations and is given the responsibility for moving toward a system of at least limited geographic indexing. At the same time, in anticipation of the eventual computerization of the recording system, the recording office is relieved of all responsibility for making conclusions about the legal effects of documents submitted for recording. The office of state recorder is created to allow for coordination and sharing of experience in the modernization of recording practices."

This Act, when taken in conjunction with the Uniform Land Transaction Act (ULTA) promulgated in 1975 by the National Conference of Commissioners on Uniform Laws, provides an excellent statutory base for badly needed changes in this area of the law.

B. RECORD CHAIN OF TITLE PROBLEMS

LOSEY v. SIMPSON

Court of Chancery of New Jersey, 1856.
11 N.J.Eq. 246.

THE CHANCELLOR. The bill is filed upon a mortgage, given by Ferdinand G. Simpson to Pamela Adams, and by her assigned to the complainants. The controversy is in reference to the priority of this mortgage, and a mortgage given by Calvin A. Kanouse to Noah Estell, now held by the defendant, Mary Estell, as the executrix of the last will of Noah Estell, deceased.

Stephen Adams, being indebted to Noah Estell in the sum of twelve hundred dollars for money lent, had given a mortgage to secure the same on several tracts of land, embracing the land which is covered by the mortgages in dispute. By an arrangement between Adams, Estell and Kanouse, Adams conveyed to Kanouse the portion of the mortgaged premises embraced in the disputed mortgages. The money received by the mortgagee was reduced from $1600 to $1310; and to secure this latter sum Kanouse executed a mortgage to Estell, embracing the land conveyed in the deed from Adams. Estell then cancelled his $1600 mortgage, or delivered it up to Adams for that purpose. The deed from Adams to Kanouse was dated the 2d of August, 1847. The mortgage bears the same date. Both were acknowledged on the 12th of August, 1847. The mortgage was recorded on the 2d day of September of the same year. The deed has never been recorded. It is alleged that it was, some time after its delivery, destroyed by Kanouse. Kanouse entered into the possession of the premises under his deed, and continued in possession until after the execution of the mortgage under which the complainants claim their priority.

The complainants had a claim against Pamela Adams and Calvin A. Kanouse for debt, and were prosecuting it at law. Kanouse offered to compromise this claim. He stated to the complainants, through his attorney, that Pamela Adams owned certain premises, which Stephen Adams held in his name in trust for her, and that the premises were sold to one Ferdinand G. Simpson, who was to give to Pamela Adams a mortgage of sixteen hundred dollars for the purchase money. Kanouse offered this mortgage to the complainants, if they would advance, in cash, the balance of the mortgage money, after deducting their claim of

$797.98. The proposition was acceded to; and on the 6th of December, 1849, Stephen Adams, at the procurement of Kanouse, executed a deed to Simpson for the same premises which he, Adams, had, as before stated, conveyed to Kanouse, and Kanouse had mortgaged to Estell. Simpson executed a mortgage to Pamela Adams to secure the purchase money of $1600, and she assigned the mortgage to the complainants, who, in consideration of the assignment, receipted their claim of $797.98, and for the balance gave their promissory notes, at a short date, which were paid at maturity. The deed to Simpson and the mortgage from Simpson to Pamela Adams were duly recorded. The deed from Stephen Adams to Kanouse, through which Mary Estell, who holds the mortgage from Kanouse to Noah Estell, claims title, has never been recorded.

Both parties claim under Stephen Adams. The complainants' mortgage is subsequent, in date and execution, to that of the defendant, Mary Estell; but the complainants claim priority, on the ground that, at the time their mortgage was executed, the deed from Adams to Kanouse was not recorded; and the title on the record being in Stephen Adams, they insist that the recording of the Estell mortgage afforded no notice of its existence.

On behalf of Mary Estell, it is insisted that the mortgage she holds is protected by the very language of the statute; that the statute declares a mortgage void and of no effect against a subsequent bona fide purchaser or mortgagee for a valuable consideration, unless such mortgage shall be recorded at or before the time of recording the said mortgage or conveyance to such subsequent purchaser or mortgagee, and that, in point of fact, the Estell mortgage was recorded before the subsequent mortgage held by the complainants. But, by the very language of the statute, the deed from Adams to Kanouse is void and of no effect against the subsequent deed from Adams to Simpson, because it was not recorded at or before the time of recording the subsequent deed to Simpson. The defendant Mary Estell, then, claims under a grantor whose deed is void, and who, at the time of the conveyance, had no title against the grantor under whom the complainants hold. Now it could be of no advantage to Simpson that his recorded deed should be valid against the unregistered deed of Kanouse, if a grantee under the latter could claim a title superior to that of Simpson's or of his grantee.

The whole object of the registry acts is to protect subsequent purchasers and encumbrancers against previous conveyances which are not recorded, and to deprive the holder of the previous unregistered conveyance, &c., of the right, which his priority in execution would have given him at the common law. But if the construction contended for be adopted, this object is totally defeated; the registry will afford no protection to an innocent purchaser. When one link in the chain of title is wanting, there is no clue to guide the purchaser in his search to the next succeeding link by which the chain is continued. The title upon the record is the purchaser's protection, and when he has traced the title down to an individual, out of whom the record does not carry it, the registry acts make that title the purchaser's protection. The registry of a deed is notice only to those who claim through or under the grantor by whom the deed was executed. * * * Nor will a purchaser be bound to take notice of the record of a deed executed by a prior grantee whose own deed has not been recorded. * * * And where the deed of a vendor is not recorded, the record of a mortgage given by the vendee for the purchase money will not be notice to a subsequent purchaser. * * * For in any such case the purchaser is without a clue to guide him in searching the record. * * *

The mortgage to Estell is void against the complainants' mortgage, if Simpson, under whom the complainants hold, was a bona fide purchaser for a valuable consideration without notice of the Estell mortgage. * * *

[The court concluded that Simpson was a bona fide purchaser for value.]

But of what was Kanouse's possession notice? It was notice only of the legal or equitable interest which he assumed or claimed in the land, and the greatest extent to which it can be carried is to visit the purchaser with notice of every fact and circumstance which he might have learned by making inquiry of the possessor. The purchaser can be affected only to the extent of the claim which the possessor asserted. In this case every inquiry was made of Kanouse. He denied having any title to the land, and it is now sought to affect an innocent purchaser by a title which he concealed for the very purpose of committing a fraud upon an innocent man. It was contended that this possession imposed the duty of searching the record, not only to ascertain what title Kanouse had, but what title he had parted with. The possession of Kanouse imposed upon the complainants no other duty than that of inquiring of him of what his right of possession consisted, and his response to such inquiry was binding in law and equity upon him, and upon every person claiming under him.

The Estell mortgage must be postponed in payment to the complainant's mortgage.

Notes

1. On the main issue in the principal case, see 4 A.L.P. § 17.17. If conveyances were indexed by tracts rather than alphabetically by the names of the parties, might the result in the principal case be different? See 4 A.L.P. p. 605 at nn. 12–14.

Consider the following extract from Simes, Handbook for More Efficient Conveyancing, 93–94 (1961):

"It has been claimed that legislation providing for official tract indices would be an important reform. In favor of such indices, the following arguments should be noted. The title searcher will more easily find recorded instruments which are out of the "chain of title." In Metropolitan areas, where the volume of recording is very great, the number of instruments to be checked will be materially reduced. For it is probable that there will be more instruments listed in a given segment of the alphabet under the names of the parties than will be listed under a given tract.

"Among disadvantages of a tract index are the following. The use of such an index may mean that the scope of notice of recorded instruments has been unduly extended, so that real estate may be less readily marketable. Thus a purchaser would have notice of a "wild deed" outside the chain of title. Furthermore, official tract indices may duplicate what is already provided unofficially by abstract and title insurance companies, without any added advantage.

"Whether legislation adopting an official tract index is desirable depends upon local conditions. If satisfactory unofficial indices are available, and if the purchaser has the benefit of them, it would seem that there is no point in duplicating indices already existing. Moreover, if conditions do indicate the desirability of a public tract index, it still may be desirable to limit the scope of notice by imposing the 'chain of title' doctrine, or limiting notice by recorded instruments in some other way."

Could the "chain of title" problem in the principal case be solved by requiring anyone who seeks to record an instrument to demonstrate to the recording officer that his grantor, mortgagor, or lessor, is the grantee in a recorded deed?

2. The vast number of recorded instruments in almost every county in the United States makes accurate indexing of the land records absolutely essential. Unless a recorded instrument is properly indexed, it "might as well be buried in the earth as in a mass of records without a clue to its whereabouts," as the court said in Barney v. McCarty, 15 Iowa 510, 83 Am.Dec. 427 (1863). Thus it is quite astonishing to find that, in a majority of the states where the issue has been raised, it has been held that, although provided for by statute, an index is not an essential part of the land records. Under this view, recordation is effective, and subsequent purchasers are charged with notice of the contents of the recorded instrument, even though there is no index entry which will direct him to the record. In a few states (Alaska, Iowa, North Carolina, Pennsylvania, Washington, Wisconsin) the recording acts by express language or by judicial construction make the index an essential part of the land records, so that an instrument is not effectively recorded unless and until it is properly indexed. The failure of legislatures to amend the recording acts in other states so as to make the index an essential part of the land records is hard to explain except on the theory that title searches are now rarely made with the aid of the official indexes, but instead are made with the aid of private tract indexes maintained by the abstract and title insurance companies.

Why should courts be concerned about the "chain of title" in states where the index is not deemed to be an essential part of the land records?

GLORIEUX v. LIGHTHIPE

Court of Errors and Appeals of New Jersey, 1915.
88 N.J.L. 199, 96 A. 94, Ann.Cas.1917E, 484.

SWAYZE, J. This is an action on covenants for title contained in a deed from the defendants, heirs of Charles A. Lighthipe, to William L. Glorieux. The breach alleged is the existence of an incumbrance in the form of building restrictions. This is said to have been created by a covenant in a deed for adjoining land made by Charles A. Lighthipe, the ancestor, to one Marsh, in which Lighthipe covenanted that he would not convey the land subsequently conveyed by his heirs to Glorieux, unless the grantee should enter into a covenant of the same nature, purport, and effect as that made by Marsh, which should be inserted in the deed. Lighthipe's heirs conveyed to Glorieux without inserting the covenant. Glorieux himself testified that he had no actual knowledge of any restrictions upon the land conveyed to him, and his counsel in argument makes the same concession. Since the very foundation of an equitable servitude is notice to the purchaser of the servient tenement, the plaintiff's case fails unless the record of the deed to Marsh constitutes statutory notice. If the Marsh deed were in the plaintiff's chain of title, the case would present no difficulty. It is not, and we are confronted with the question of the effect as notice of a prior recorded deed by the same grantor, but for other lands. Prior to the act of 1883, P.L. p. 215; G.S. p. 882, pl. 143–145, the effect of the record as notice was determined by principles of equity, and was limited to deeds in the chain of title of the person sought to be charged. * * * Such also was the rule in other jurisdictions. * * * And the rule was so stated in this court in Mitchell v. D'Olier, 68 N.J.L. 375, 384, 53 A. 467, 59 L.R.A. 949, although the present question was not necessarily involved in the decision. The reason for imputing notice as stated by Chief Justice Beasley speaking for this court in Brewer v. Marshall, 19 N.J.Eq. 537, 541, 97 Am.Dec. 679, excludes that imputation where the deed relied on is not in the chain of title of the party to be charged. The court said:

"The law conclusively charges him with such information, because the deed which contains this restrictive agreement constitutes one of the muniments of his own title."

The rule is recognized by the text-writers. * * *

The act of 1883 provided that the record should become and be forthwith notice to all persons of the execution thereof. This act was repealed in 1898, P.L. p. 713, and cannot affect the present case since Glorieux did not take title until 1910. The case turns upon the construction of the act respecting conveyances of 1898, P.L. p. 670, and the supplement of 1903, P.L. p. 489; G.S. p. 1552, pl. 53; Id. page 1556, pl. 57a–57c, N.J.S.A. 46:16–2, 46:21–1. The act of 1903 adds nothing material to the present case. It seems to have been intended to permit the record of certain instruments not mentioned in the twenty-first section of the act respecting conveyances, and may have been suggested by the difficulty that arose in Lembeck & Detz Eagle Brewing Co. v. Kelly, 63 N.J.Eq. 401, 51 A. 794. The act of 1903 was not necessary to authorize the record of the deed from Lighthipe to Marsh since that was clearly authorized by section 21. The act added nothing to the effect of the record as notice, since by virtue of section 53 the record was notice, not only of the execution of the deed, but of the contents thereof. The only effect of the act of 1903 was to extend the provisions of section 53 to other instruments. The case turns, therefore, upon the construction of section 53. The language of that section is narrower and more limited than that in the act of 1883. Where the earlier act made the record notice to all persons, the act of 1898 made it notice only to subsequent judgment creditors, purchasers, and mortgagees. The words material to the present case are "subsequent purchasers." Unless Glorieux was a "subsequent purchaser," the statute did not make the record notice as to him. The question otherwise stated is whether "subsequent purchaser" means subsequent purchaser from the same grantor, or subsequent purchaser of the same land. The more natural meaning is subsequent purchaser of the same land. In most cases it is probable that the grantor owns no other land. Even where he holds other tracts, we must logically hold either that the statutory notice applies only to the particular land described in the deed or affects all other land owned by the grantor at least in the same county, whether in the same or different municipalities, whether on the same street or different streets. The limitation to adjoining land suggested by the learned Vice Chancellor in Howland v. Andrus, 80 N.J.Eq. 276, at page 282, 83 A. 982, is not suggested by any language in the statute and would lead to an anomalous situation. It would charge with notice the purchaser of an adjoining lot, but not the purchaser of the next lot but one, on the same large tract.

The construction we adopt is in line with the history and purpose of the registry acts and the doctrine of constructive or statutory notice founded thereon. The purpose was to protect purchasers of land which had already been conveyed by an unrecorded deed by making that deed void as to them. This purpose did not require that the failure to record should make the deed void as to subsequent purchasers of other land. The words "subsequent purchaser" occur in section 54 as well as in section 53, N.J.S.A. 46:22–1, 46:21–1; in fact, their use in connection with the other language of section 54 antedates as matter of legislative history their use in section 53. The former use goes back to the act of 1799, Paterson's Laws, p. 399: the latter to 1898 only. The words ought to have the same construction in both sections. To attribute to them in section 54 the meaning of subsequent purchasers from the same grantor would lead to an absurdity. Section 54 provides that an unrecorded deed shall be void as to a subsequent purchaser in good faith for value, and if subsequent purchaser means a purchaser from the same grantor but of different land, then the owner of land by an unrecorded deed would be unable to sue for a trespass if the trespasser happened to be a subsequent purchaser from the same grantor. This is obviously absurd, and it is absurd because it extends the meaning of the words beyond the necessity of the mischief to be cured. Yet we must go to that extent unless we hold that subsequent purchaser in section 54 means only subsequent purchaser of the land. If we give the words that meaning in section 54, we must give them the same meaning in section 53. This is demonstrated by a consideration of the American doctrine of notice by the record. That doctrine arose by implication from the statutory provision (now found in section 54) making an unrecorded deed void as to subsequent purchasers. The fact that a deed was void as to a subsequent purchaser made it necessary for a careful purchaser to see that all deeds in his chain of title were recorded. The courts would not impute to him a failure to do what he ought to do, but assumed that he had done his duty. If he had, he must have found all the recorded deeds in his chain of title, and might properly be charged with notice thereof and of their contents. Pomeroy, § 649; Losey v. Simpson, 11 N.J.Eq. 246. There was no express statutory provision making the record notice until 1883, and, if that act did in fact broaden the scope of the notice (as to which we express no opinion), it was repealed in 1898. In that year the Legislature, in enacting section 53, limited the notice to the same class of persons to whom it had been limited by construction prior to 1883.

The reason of the legislation and the argument ab inconvenienti point to the same result. The record is held to be constructive notice because a man is bound to examine his own title or take the risk of not doing so. A purchaser may well be held bound to examine or neglect at his peril, the record of the conveyances under which he claims; but it would impose an intolerable burden to compel him to examine all conveyances made by every one in his chain of title. The case differs from the conveyance of an easement or any interest that lies in grant. A grant takes effect regardless of notice; an equitable servitude is the creature of equity alone and depends entirely on the existence of notice. Confessedly, Lighthipe's covenant to insert restrictions in subsequent deeds, was not enforceable at law against Glorieux. It clearly was not a grant.

The result is that the plaintiff failed to prove that the land conveyed to Glorieux was burdened with the restrictions contained in the deed from Lighthipe to Marsh, and the nonsuit should have been granted for that reason.

The judgment must be reversed, to the end that a venire de novo may be awarded.

Notes

1. For a contrary view, see Finley v. Glenn, 303 Pa. 131, 154 A. 299 (1931), where the court reached the opposite result on very similar facts. The rationale of the decision in Finley is to be found in the following excerpt from the opinion:

"The controlling factor in the decision of the case is that the immediate grantors of both plaintiff and defendants were the same. When the latter came to examine the title which was tendered to them, it was of primary consequence that they should know whether their grantors held title to the land which they were to convey. They could determine that question only by searching the records for grants from them. 'The rule has always been that the grantee * * * must search for conveyances * * * made by any one who has held the title.' Pyles v. Brown, 189 Pa. 164, 168, 42 A. 11, 12, 69 Am.St. Rep. 794. 'The weight of authority is to the effect that if a deed or a contract for the conveyance of one parcel of land, with a covenant or easement affecting another parcel of land owned by the same grantor, is duly recorded, the record is constructive notice to a subsequent purchaser of the latter parcel. The rule is based generally upon the principle that a grantee is chargeable with notice of everything affecting his title which could be discovered by an examination of the records of the deeds or other muniments of title of his grantor.' Note, 16 A.L.R. 1013, and cases cited; 2 Tiffany's Real Property, 1920 Ed., p. 2188. So doing, defendants would find the deed from Rosekrans and his wife to plaintiff which had been recorded. Coming upon this conveyance, it was their duty to read it, not, as argued by appellant and decided by the chancellor who heard the case, to read only the description of the property to see what was conveyed, but to read the deed in its entirety, to note anything else which might be set forth in it. The deed was notice to them of all it contained; otherwise the purpose of the recording acts would be frustrated. If they had read all of it, they would have discovered that the lots which their vendors were about to convey to them had been subjected to the buildings restriction which the deed disclosed. It boots nothing, so far as notice is concerned, that they did not acquaint themselves with the entire contents of the deed. It affected them to the same extent as though they had read it all. This is the rule of all our cases and the express declaration of the recording act. Were it otherwise, in the familiar instance where a grantor creates an easement on other property owned by him in favor of his grantee, the easement would not be effective against subsequent purchasers of the retained property."

See also McQuade v. Wilcox, 215 Mich. 302, 183 N.W. 771 (1921). O, owner of a considerable tract of land, subdivided into lots, conveyed various lots with restrictions against uses other than residence, etc. The deeds contained the following: "These conditions are for the benefit of all present and future owners of property in this subdivision," etc. D, to whom O had contracted to sell another lot in the tract, had no knowledge of any restrictions and planned to operate a restaurant on his lot. In a suit by owners of lots subject to the restriction, it was held that D had constructive notice of the restriction upon his lot by reason of the recording of the deeds to other grantees, such deeds containing the restrictive language. The McQuade case is discussed in 20 Mich.L. Rev. 344 (1922), where it is pointed out that since the plaintiff's interest in the restriction was an equity and D's interest, he being merely a contract vendee, was also merely equitable, it was unnecessary to find that the record operated as notice to D.

2. The authorities seem to be about evenly divided on the issue presented in Glorieux and Finley. See 4 A.L.P. § 17.24. The author, R.G. Patton, favors the view adopted in Finley, and says, with respect to cases like Glorieux: "* * * is not the error in [that] line of cases in their holding that the record of the deed conveying Blackacre is outside the chain of title to Whiteacre? It appears to have had a double effect and that it should be so indexed: as having transferred the title to Blackacre and as having created an encumbrance upon Whiteacre. This is clearly recognized when the two results are accomplished by separate instruments." (Id. 602.) But how can the grantee of Blackacre make sure that the deed is indexed "as having created an encumbrance upon Whiteacre"? Must he instruct the recording officer to index the deed in that way and then check to see that he has done so? Suppose the recording officer refuses to index the deed "as having created an encumbrance upon Whiteacre" on the ground that no statute authorizes or requires him to do so?

3. In Sanborn v. McLean, 233 Mich. 227, 206 N.W. 496, 60 A.L.R. 1212 (1925), reprinted supra page 671, the court carried the doctrine of restrictions even further. In the McQuade case, supra, the deeds expressly provided that the "conditions" were "for the benefit of all present and future owners of property in this subdivision." In the Sanborn case, however, no deed in the defendant's direct chain of title from the original subdivider contained any restrictions. But the court held that a reciprocal restriction upon defendant's lot would be implied from the restrictions in the original deeds to other lots in the subdivision, saying, "If the owner of two or more lots, so situated as to bear the relation, sells one with restrictions of benefit to the land retained, the servitude becomes mutual, and, during the period of restraint, the owner of the lot or lots retained can do nothing forbidden to the owner of the lot sold." The reciprocal servitude was held enforceable against the defendant because he and his predecessors in title "were bound by constructive notice under our recording acts." This seems to mean that a purchaser must not only read the entire deed from the common grantor on record but he may have to examine the fact situation in the neighborhood to see whether the restriction he has read implies a similar restriction upon the lot he is buying. See also Denhardt v. De Roo, 295 Mich. 223, 294 N.W. 163 (1940). But see Buckley v. Mooney, 339 Mich. 398, 63 N.W.2d 655 (1954).

It should be noted that, in most states, whether they follow the rule in the Glorieux case or the rule in the Finley case, imposition of restrictions upon lots conveyed does not, in the absence of express provision, impose them by implication on all lots retained by the grantor "so situated as to bear the relation." See Wing v. Forest Lawn Cemetery Ass'n, 15 Cal.2d 472, 101 P.2d 1099, 130 A.L.R. 120 (1940), and Comment in 14 So.Cal.L.Rev. 191 (1940).

4.   It is generally held in the United States that a properly recorded instrument "in the chain of title" gives "record notice" to any subsequent taker whether the instrument creates a "legal" or an "equitable" interest.   It is worth noticing, as a contrast with the generally accepted view in the United States, that the English courts have held, under the Middlesex Registry Act, that registration has no effect beyond preservation of the position one would have by force of the common law; it preserves prior legal interests as against a subsequent conveyance or mortgage for value if the instrument upon which the prior interest depends is duly registered.   But registration does not give constructive notice of an equitable interest created by the registered instrument, and consequently registration will not preserve an equitable interest as against a subsequent purchaser of a legal interest in the same land for value and without notice.

Question

What did the court mean in the Glorieux case when it said: "The case differs from the conveyance of an easement or any interest that lies in grant.   A grant takes effect regardless of notice; an equitable servitude is the creature of equity alone and depends entirely on the existence of notice"?   Would the New Jersey court reach a contrary result if Lighthipe had granted Marsh an easement over the land he retained, instead of covenanting that he would not convey the retained land "unless the grantee should enter into a covenant of the same nature, purport, and effect as that made by Marsh"?

Note: Some Additional Chain of Title Problems

Additional "chain of title" problems which have been the subject of much judicial and scholarly comment are summarized as follows in Simes, A Handbook for More Efficient Conveyancing 24–25 (1961):

" *   *   * Suppose O conveys to A on January 1.   On January 10, O conveys the same land to B, who has actual notice of the deed to A.   B records on the same day on which the deed was delivered to him.   On February 1, the deed from O to A is recorded.   On March 1, B conveys to C, who pays value, has no notice of the deed to A, and records the same day.   While the authorities are divided, it would seem that C should have priority over A.   It is true, A recorded before C, and in a notice-race jurisdiction, it may be said that this fact prevents C from taking.   But, on the other hand, it may be said that, after the date of the record of the deed from O to B, any further conveyances from O would be outside the chain of record title.   Thus, if C, in searching the record, should find the recorded conveyance from O to B, he should not be expected to search further for recorded conveyances from O, but would look for recorded conveyances from B.   Therefore, it may be said that the deed from O to A, while recorded first, is not recorded in the chain of title.   Or if a notice jurisdiction is involved, it may be said that the recording of the deed from O to A was outside the chain of title, and C had no notice of it.

" *   *   * A problem may also arise in connection with a situation where there is a recorded conveyance by a person who was not in the chain of title at the date of the record, but who later did become a grantee in the chain of title. Assume that, on January 1, O is the record owner of a piece of land. On that day, A conveys the land by warranty deed to B, who records the same day. On February 1, O, who is still the owner of record, conveys to A, who records the same day. On February 10, A conveys the same land to C, who pays value and has no actual notice of A's deed to B. C records the same day. The weight of authority is to the effect that C is preferred over B. This is because C, in examining the record, should not be expected to search for recorded conveyances from A before the date when A acquired title. If C does have to make such a search, then he must examine the name index for conveyances to every person whose name appears in the chain of title, for an indefinite period prior to the time when such person acquired title. To do this would be to impose an unreasonable burden upon him. Although the deed from A to B was recorded when the conveyance to C was made and when it was recorded, it was not in the chain of title, and, therefore, C should not be regarded as having notice of it. Or in a notice-race jurisdiction, it may be said that when the deed from A to B was recorded, it was merely a "wild deed," and therefore the requirement of prior recording was not met by the recording of such a deed. It may also be said that where, as in this situation, the doctrine of estoppel by deed conflicts with the policy of the recording acts, the latter should prevail."

However, in the situation discussed in the last preceding paragraph, there is substantial authority preferring B over C, especially in those states where the doctrine of "estoppel by deed" has been made statutory. See, e.g. Bernardy v. Colonial & United States Mortgage Co., 17 S.D. 637, 98 N.W. 166, 106 Am.St. Rep. 791 (1904). Even where a statute provides that after-acquired titles shall pass to the "estoppel grantee" by operation of law, however, there is some authority that a subsequent bona fide purchaser for value from the estopped grantor is entitled to priority. See Ford v. Unity Church, 120 Mo. 498, 25 S.W. 394, 23 L.R.A. 561, 41 Am.St.Rep. 711 (1893).

But suppose the estoppel problem arises in a state which requires maintenance of tract indexes? See Balch v. Arnold, 9 Wyo. 17, 59 P. 434 (1899), holding that a subsequent purchaser for value was charged with notice of an "estoppel deed" executed by a grantor before he took title because under the Wyoming recording act the recorder was required to keep "abstract books" with abstracts of each recorded instrument under "head lines" describing the legal subdivisions of land according to the U.S. government survey, "so that one interested in any tract of land may turn to the proper page of the abstract and find almost at a glance, a description of every instrument in which it is referred to, whether anterior or subsequent to the vesting of the legal title in his grantor. * * * The failure, under such circumstances, to search further than the vesting of title in the purchaser's grantor, would be such inexcusable negligence as to amount to a wilful refusal to receive any information as to the rights or interests of other claimants."

How would this argument apply to a situation arising under the Block Index system in New York City, which is now developed to the point that the index gives all instruments affecting title to each lot?

Where the only official indexes are alphabetical grantor-grantee indexes, is it significant to a solution of the "chain of title problem" that all title examinations are based on abstracts prepared by abstract companies which maintain their own private tract indexes?

The best detailed discussion of the "chain of title" problem is to be found in Cross, The Record "Chain of Title" Hypocrisy, 57 Col.L.Rev. 787 (1957).

Chapter 11

LAND TITLE ASSURANCE

SECTION 1. COVENANTS FOR TITLE *

INTRODUCTORY NOTE

Unlike a sale of chattels which normally imports a warranty of title, a conveyance of land implies no warranties as to the grantor's title. In the absence of fraud or mistake the purchaser accepts a deed of the premises at his own risk. He cannot resist an action for the recovery of the unpaid part of the purchase price, nor can he maintain an action to recover back payments already made, even though it develops that the deed has not given him the bargained-for title to the land. And when relief is sought on the basis of mistake, it must appear that the parties were mistaken as to the contents of the deed delivered, not merely mistaken as to the status of the grantor's title.

Covenants for title are frequently included in the deed of conveyance in order to protect the purchaser from loss as a result of defects in the vendor's title. While playing no direct part in the operation of the deed as a conveyance, such personal covenants are of considerable importance in affording grantees—and perhaps their successors in the chain of title—some redress in case it turns out that the deed, by reason of defects in or encumbrances upon the grantor's title, did not transfer the interest it purported to convey.

Although covenants for title are not implied in conveyances of land, it is not uncommon for statutes to provide that deeds in certain forms or using certain words shall be deemed to contain certain enumerated covenants for title. The covenants thus imported into such deeds are not implied; they are incorporated by reference by the use of particular words declared by the statute to bear such meaning.

The vendor's obligation with respect to inclusion of particular covenants for title in his deed of conveyance when the contract calls for a "warranty deed" or a "deed with the usual full covenants and warranty of title" or simply a "good and sufficient deed" will be discussed in the next chapter. It is there pointed out that there is much variation in judicial views as to the covenants for title which must be included in the deed when the contract is silent with respect to type of deed or inclusion

---

* See 3 A.L.P. §§ 12.124–12.131 for a fuller treatment. Also see Cunningham § 11.13.

of covenants. In such a case, no covenants for title need be included in some states; in other states, a general warranty may be required; in others, only a special warranty; and in some states all the "usual covenants" must be included.

As previously indicated, the "usual covenants" for title are (1) the covenant of seisin; (2) the covenant of good right to convey; (3) the covenant against encumbrances; (4) the covenant for quiet enjoyment; and (5) the covenant of warranty. In a few states, the covenant for further assurances may also be one of the "usual covenants"—or at least may be required if the contract calls for a deed with "full covenants." And since an analysis of the various covenants for title will show that those of seisin, against encumbrances, and of warranty are generally adequate to meet most contingencies, it is possible that these three alone would be held sufficient to satisfy a contract calling for "usual" or "full" covenants.

See deed form page 761 supra.

A. COVENANTS OF SEISIN AND GOOD RIGHT TO CONVEY

(1) In General

The covenant of seisin may vary in its scope according to the way it is worded and the meaning attached to the word "seised." At any early date "seisin" was interchangeable with "possession" and was applicable to chattels as well as land. Later, usage confined "seisin" to land, and meant possession thereof under claim of a freehold estate therein. "Seisin" could thus refer to either wrongful or rightful possession of land. Consequently, in a few states a covenant that the grantor is "seised," or even that he is "lawfully seised," is satisfied by actual possession under a claim of ownership. The grantor is considered as covenanting merely that he is in possession claiming such title as his deed purports to convey, and there is no breach of the covenant if the grantor is in possession when he conveys, although he does not have the title he purports to convey—or any interest in the land at all! In most states, however, the covenant of seisin is construed as a covenant that the grantor has the title which he purports to convey, and there is a breach of the covenant if the grantor does not in fact have an indefeasible estate in, as well as possession of, the land. Where the more limited construction of the covenant of seisin prevails, the draftsman may, of course, enlarge the scope of the covenant by providing that the grantor covenants he is "lawfully seised of an indefeasible estate in fee simple" (or any other estate which the grantor may have contracted to convey).

Where the covenant of seisin, by construction or by express wording, guarantees that the grantor has an indefeasible title, the scope of the covenant of good right to convey is almost coterminous with the covenant of seisin. If the covenant of seisin is not broken, it follows that the covenant of good right to convey cannot be broken. One with good right to convey, however, may not be in a position to warrant that he is lawfully seized of the estate which he purports to convey. This would be true, for example, where the grantor is a life tenant with a power to convey the fee simple, or where he is owner in fee simple but does not have "seisin" because another person is in adverse possession of the land.

The covenants of seisin and good right to convey are "present" covenants which are either broken when the deed is delivered or not at all. If they are broken, the traditional (and still the majority) rule is that the cause of action for breach does not "run with the land" or pass by implied assignment to a grantee of the original covenantee. But a minority of the courts have held that the cause of action passes by implied assignment to the grantees of the covenantee. Under the minority rule, which has been adopted by statute in some states, the cause of action in effect "runs with the land" and can be asserted by a remote grantee when he learns of the breach. Since the breach of covenant starts the applicable statute of limitations running against the covenantee whether he is aware of the breach or not, the cause of action may be barred before the covenantee (or one of his grantees, where the cause of action is held to "run" or to pass by implied assignment) discovers the title defect which creates the breach.

The covenants of seisin and good right to convey are broken whenever the grantor has no title to some or all of the land he purports to convey, or when he has an estate of lesser quantity than he purports to convey—e.g., he has only a life estate rather than a fee simple. At least where the covenant of seisin, by express wording or by construction, is a covenant that the grantor has an indefeasible estate in fee simple, there would clearly be a breach if the grantor has only a defeasible estate in fee simple such as a fee simple determinable, fee simple on a condition subsequent, or fee simple subject to an executory limitation.

(2) Damages for Breach

For a total breach—complete absence of any title to any part of the land—the measure of damages is usually the purchase price of the land, plus interest thereon from the date of breach. For a partial breach— where the covenantor has no title to part of the land, or has an estate smaller in quantity than what he purported to convey—the measure of damages is usually a proportionate part of the purchase price, plus interest from the date of breach. But if the covenantee buys in the outstanding title or interest, the measure of damages is the amount paid for this purpose (if reasonable), not exceeding the purchase price or the appropriate proportion thereof. If the covenantor buys in the outstanding title or interest, some courts hold that the after-acquired title or interest inures to the benefit of the covenantee by operation of law, thus curing the breach and limiting the covenantee to nominal damages. But other courts hold that the covenantee has the option to refuse the after-acquired title and recover full damages from the covenantor.

Since an eviction is not necessary to establish a breach of the covenants of seisin and good right to convey, the covenantee may recover damages based on the purchase price even though he is still in possession of the land (unless the covenantor had possession when he conveyed and the court adopts the narrow construction of the covenant of seisin). But if the covenantee recovers what he paid for the land he should not be allowed to remain in possession of the land, enjoying the rents and profits and perhaps eventually acquiring a good title by adverse possession. Some courts have therefore required the tender of a reconveyance as a condition precedent to a judgment for the purchase price. Other courts have simply held that the judgment itself revests the right to possession in the covenantor. And it has been suggested that, in any case, the court should require a reconveyance to the covenantor as a condition precedent to issuance of execution on the judgment for the purchase price. In substance, the basis of the action is failure of consideration (total or partial), and if the covenantee is given judgment for the entire purchase price he should be required to restore what he received by virtue of the conveyance to him—the right to possession as against the grantor.

The covenants of seisin and of good right to convey may be very useful to the covenantee because they afford protection in situations not covered by the covenants against encumbrances, for quiet enjoyment, or of warranty. Generally speaking, the two latter covenants are broken only by an "eviction." Since the covenants of seisin and of good right to convey will generally support a claim for damages by the mere fact that title is outstanding in another, the covenantee need not wait for an actual eviction, or even for the holder of the outstanding title to bring suit against him, before starting an action for breach of these covenants. In substance, the covenants of seisin and good right to convey give the covenantee, when a breach is discovered, the option to rescind and recover the consideration paid.

B. COVENANT AGAINST ENCUMBRANCES

(1) In General

The covenant against encumbrances is usually so worded that it is broken if, at the time the conveyance takes effect, there is any outstanding mortgage, lien, dower right, easement, or equitable servitude to which the land conveyed is subject. An outstanding estate less than a fee simple may constitute both a breach of the covenant of seisin and a breach of the covenant against encumbrances because such an estate falls within the usual definition of an "encumbrance"—"Every right to, or interest in, the land which may subsist in third persons to the diminution of the value of the land, but consistent with the passing of the fee in it by deed." Like the covenants of seisin and good right to convey, the covenant against encumbrances is a "present" covenant which does not "run with the land" or pass by implied assignment after breach to a grantee of the original covenantee. Many cases hold the covenantor liable for breach of the covenant against encumbrances even though the covenantee knows of the existence of the encumbrance when the deed is delivered. Other cases are contra, at least, where the encumbrance is "an easement obviously and notoriously affecting the physical condition of the land at the time of its sale." For a decision rejecting the view that there is an implied exception with respect to such an "obvious" easement, see Huyck v. Andrews, 113 N.Y. 81, 20 N.E. 581, 3 L.R.A.

789 (1889). See also Memmert v. McKeen, 112 Pa.St. 315, 4 A. 542 (1886); Lavey v. Graessle, 245 Mich. 681, 224 N.W. 436, 64 A.L.R. 1477 (1929). It is difficult to see why the implied exception, if recognized should be limited to cases where the encumbrance is "obvious." If the grantee has actual knowledge of the encumbrance and it is one which cannot be eliminated by a money payment, it seems improbable that the parties intended the grantee to have an immediate cause of action for breach, based on the reduction in land value resulting from the encumbrance. It seems far more likely that the price was adjusted to take account of the "unremovable" encumbrance. Which is a good reason for recognizing an implied exception to the covenant against encumbrances in such cases, is it not?

(2) Damages for Breach

If the covenantee is unable to remove the encumbrance by a money payment, his damages will be the amount by which such encumbrance reduces the value of the land. Otherwise, his damages will be the cost of removing the encumbrances, provided this cost does not exceed the price paid for the land.

C. COVENANTS OF WARRANTY AND FOR QUIET ENJOYMENT

(1) In General

The covenants of warranty and for quiet enjoyment are often run together in expression, and what amounts to a breach of one will almost necessarily be a breach of the other. These covenants are broken only by an "eviction" by one asserting a paramount right to possession or by the covenantor or someone acting under his authority. The covenants do not guarantee the covenantee against eviction or disturbance of his possession by wrongdoers in general. The "paramount title" under which an eviction will cause a breach of the covenants of warranty and for quiet enjoyment may be found in various forms. No enumeration will be attempted here. But it should be pointed out that an exercise of the power of eminent domain is not a breach, although it does result in an eviction.

Assuming that the eviction is under a paramount title or by the covenantor or someone claiming under him, a physical ouster or interference with the normal privileges of a possessor constitutes an actual eviction and therefore a breach of both covenants. But more difficulty is encountered in the field of "constructive" evictions. For there may be a "constructive" eviction although the covenantee is not physically ousted or disturbed in possession. If, for instance, he buys in the outstanding paramount title, he is "constructively" evicted. In such a case, however, he runs a risk, not taken when he yields only to a court's judgment or decree, in that he assumes the burden, in his action for breach of covenant, of establishing the fact that the title to which he yielded was really "paramount." He assumes the same burden when he yields possession without waiting for judicial action. However, if the covenantee has unsuccessfully defended his title against one asserting a "para-

mount title," the judgment establishing the "paramount title" in ejectment is *res judicata* and binds the covenantor provided he was notified
of the ejectment action and was requested to appear and defend it on
behalf of his covenantee. Indeed, some courts consider the ejectment
judgment *res judicata* against the covenantor if he was notified of the
adverse claimant's action, even though he was not requested to appear
and defend.

When the covenantee is unable to get possession of the land because
of an outstanding "paramount title" there is an eviction (whether it be
deemed "actual" or "constructive") and a breach of the covenants of
warranty and for quiet enjoyment. In such a situation, of course, the
covenants of seisin and good right to convey are also broken. And the
covenants of warranty and for quiet enjoyment may ultimately be broken by action taken under, or because of, an outstanding encumbrance
such as a mortgage or judgment lien which constituted an immediate
breach of the covenant against encumbrances. The foreclosure of a
mortgage resulting in an actual or constructive eviction of the covenantee would clearly be such a breach. Moreover, in some cases the exercise of privileges conferred by an outstanding easement or the exercise
of rights under an outstanding equitable servitude may result in a
breach of the covenants of warranty and for quiet enjoyment. An interesting case along this line is Kramer v. Carter, 136 Mass. 504 (1884). D,
the owner of land which had been subjected to building restrictions (equitable servitudes), conveyed it to P by deed with the usual covenants;
P conveyed to A by similar deed; A conveyed to B by similar deed. B,
having suffered damage by reason of the existence of the restrictions,
recovered damages from A for breach of the covenant against encumbrances, and A thereupon sued P and recovered damages for breach of
the same covenant in P's deed to him. P then sought to recover from D
either on the covenant against encumbrances or the covenant of warranty in D's deed to him. The court held recovery on the covenant against
encumbrances barred by the statute of limitations; but recovery on the
covenant of warranty was allowed, the payment of damages to A being
the "constructive" eviction. The cases are in conflict, however, as to
whether public highways and railroad rights of way may constitute or
result in breaches of the covenants of warranty and for quiet enjoyment.

(2) These Covenants "Run With the Land"

Familiar contract principles govern the rights of the covenantee to
recover damages from the covenantor. Not infrequently, however, no
substantial harm has resulted from a breach of a covenant until after
the covenantee has ceased, by reason of death or further conveyance, to
be interested in the performance of the covenant; and a subsequent
grantee—often a remote subsequent grantee—is the person damaged
by the breach. In such a situation the question arises as to whether the
covenant is one that "runs with the land." As we have already seen,
the covenants of seisin and good right to convey are "present" covenants which by the traditional view do not "run with the land"; i.e., only

the covenantee himself has a cause of action for breach, although a subsequent grantee of the land may assert the cause of action if it is expressly assigned to him. The covenant against encumbrances is subject to the same rule. But the covenants of warranty and for quiet enjoyment are "future" covenants which "run with the land" until a breach by eviction occurs. Or, more accurately, these covenants are made with the covenantee in his capacity as owner of an estate or interest in the land so that, when such estate or interest is vested in another person by conveyance, devise, or descent, that other person is looked upon as the covenantee. Instead of the covenant "running with the land," it is really a case of the successor in title moving into the position of his predecessor. As was said by Justice Holmes in Norcross v. James, 140 Mass. 188, 2 N.E. 946 (1885): " *   *   * in order that an assignee should be so far identified in law with the original covenantee, he must have the same estate, that is, the same status or inheritance, and thus the same *persona, quoad* the contract."

Holmes went on to say, however, that "The privity of estate which is thus required [for a covenant to run] is privity of estate with the original covenantee, not with the original covenantor; and this is the only privity of which there is anything said in the ancient books." Yet many courts have concluded that the benefit of the covenants of warranty and for quiet enjoyment cannot pass to a subsequent grantee where the covenantee acquires neither good title nor possession of the land from the covenantor, because in such a case there is no "privity of estate" between the covenantor and the subsequent grantee. Consequently, these courts have denied the subsequent grantee any protection under the covenants of warranty and for quiet enjoyment in precisely the situation where he is most in need of protection. But other courts have held that the benefit of these covenants will pass to a subsequent grantee on one theory or another, despite conceptual difficulties with the "privity of estate" requirement. In Wead v. Larkin, 54 Ill. 489, 5 Am.Rep. 149 (1870), the court said: " *   *   * although the covenant of warranty is attached to the land, *   *   * yet this certainly does not mean that it is attached to the paramount title, nor does it mean that it is attached to an imperfect title, or to possession, and only passes with that, but it means, simply, that it passes by virtue of the privity of estate, created by the successive deeds, each grantor being estopped by his own deed from denying that he has conveyed an estate to which the covenant would attach." For a somewhat more elaborate theory to support the same conclusion, see Solberg v. Robinson, 34 S.D. 55, 147 N.W. 87 (1914), where the court said:

" *   *   * It seems to be generally held that, where the covenantor delivers the possession of the land to his grantee and he, in turn, puts his grantee in possession, this constitutes a privity of estate sufficient to carry the covenant with the land. And it may be taken as true that the reason for the rule originated at a time when physical possession of the land was the chief muniment of title thereto. But this reason no longer exists. A person who has a grant of land from the owner of the fee becomes the absolute owner thereof and is entitled to all the benefits that can be derived therefrom, even though neither of them was ever in actual possession thereof. This being the case, why should it be necessary that actual, as distinguished from constructive, possession should be delivered in order to carry a covenant with the land when the covenantor was without title? * * * In this case, while the Smiths acquired no title to the land by virtue of their deed from the Robinsons, still they had the apparent title even as against Vesey himself [the true owner]. The county records showed that they had a perfect chain of title, and, therefore, the Smiths and their grantees (plaintiffs in this action), as against the defendant [covenantor] should be held to have had constructive possession of the granted premises, and that plaintiffs are entitled to recover against the defendant because of the eviction by Vesey. This, of course, involves the doctrine of estoppel by deed; and we believe this to be a proper case for the application of this doctrine."

Suppose that one or more of the intermediate deeds in the chain of title is a quitclaim deed or other deed without covenants. Will the covenants of warranty and for quiet enjoyment in a prior deed nevertheless "run with the land" so that a remote grantee may sue on them?

(3) Damages for Breach

As a general rule, the measure of damages is the purchase price (or a proportionate part thereof, when the eviction is partial), plus interest from the date of breach. In a few jurisdictions, however, the measure of damages is the value of the land at the time of breach (including "natural appreciation in value"), or the purchase price plus the value added by improvements while the plaintiff was in possession. (In either case, of course, interest from date of breach is added.) In some jurisdictions the recovery of a remote grantee of the covenantee is fixed by the price paid by the covenantee himself, but in other jurisdictions the remote grantee is limited to the price he paid his grantor if that is less than the price paid by the original covenantee. If the plaintiff was forced to buy in an outstanding title or to pay off an encumbrance in order to avoid actual eviction, the amount so paid is the basic measure of damages, if not in excess of the price paid by the covenantee. The courts have generally recognized as an element in damages for breach of the "future" covenants the litigation costs incurred by a grantee who defends unsuccessfully against one claiming paramount title, and a few courts have also allowed attorneys' fees, although most courts do not. Where there is a chain of conveyances by warranty deed, the last grantee may recover on his grantor's warranty, and so on back to the first grantor who warranted his title. But the last grantee may also sue any or all of the prior grantors who warranted the title, and may recover judgments against several of them. These judgments may differ in amount because the land may have been sold for different prices in successive transfers. Even if he obtains two or more judgments, however, the plaintiff is entitled only to one full satisfaction of judgment for breach of warranty.

There is some authority that a grantor who has conveyed with a covenant of warranty and/or quiet enjoyment can be compelled to satisfy a mortgage, judgment lien, or similar encumbrance the enforcement of which would result in the eviction of his grantee or a more remote grantee. It is said that the covenant imposes upon the covenantor a duty to exonerate the covenantee or his grantee.

D. COVENANT FOR FURTHER ASSURANCE

This covenant enables the covenantee or his grantee to compel the covenantor to convey any paramount interest later acquired by the covenantor which is adverse to the estate he previously conveyed to the covenantee. Since the covenant is not broken until the covenantor refuses or neglects to execute the further assurance, it is a "future" covenant and it may be enforced specifically by a remote grantee. The doctrine of after-acquired title or estoppel by deed serves somewhat the same purpose, but enforcement of the covenant for further assurance can help to avoid difficulties which arise with respect to the doctrine of estoppel by deed under the recording statutes. It would seem that the covenant for further assurance should be used more generally in the United States than is now the usual practice.

E. CONCLUDING OBSERVATIONS

The character of the estate to which covenants for title relate must be determined from other parts of the deed, principally from the granting clause. Thus in a deed granting Blackacre "subject to a mortgage" which is identified, covenants for title in general terms will apply only to Blackacre *subject to the mortgage;* the covenants against encumbrances, or warranty, and for quiet enjoyment will not be broken by the existence of such mortgage or by steps taken to enforce it. Generally, however, the covenants are construed individually, so that an exception of a mortgage, for instance, from the covenant against encumbrances will not operate *ipso facto* to withdraw it from the operation of the covenants of warranty and for quiet enjoyment. Indeed, an exception of a particular encumbrance in the covenant against encumbrances without any similar exception in the covenant of warranty or the covenant for quiet enjoyment may well be intentional. Its exception from the covenant against encumbrances is necessary in order to save the covenantor from an immediate breach of that covenant. Since, however, the covenants of warranty and for quiet enjoyment are broken only by an eviction which normally, in the case of a mortgage or other lien, would occur only upon foreclosure, the covenantor who plans to discharge such lien may be quite willing to make a general covenant of warranty and for quiet enjoyment which will protect the covenantee or his grantees in the event of eviction. But is the covenantee well advised to pay the full market value of the land, without a deduction equal to the amount of the outstanding lien, and to rely upon his grantor's covenants of warranty and for quiet enjoyment for protection against loss resulting from enforcement of the lien?

How long does meaningful liability continue against a covenantor who has warranted his title? If the breach occurs during the covenantor's lifetime, his liability continues until the cause of action is barred by the applicable statute of limitations, which is usually a long one. But suppose he dies after the breach and before the statute of limitations has run? Other statutes control actions against heirs and distributees of the assets of a decedent and such statutes would have to be consulted before any satisfactory answer can be given. Generally such statutes bar all claims against the decedent's estate unless they are presented within a specified—usually short—time after the appointment of the executor or administrator. But under such statutes claimants who do not present their claims within the period prescribed by the statute often have a personal action against the heirs or distributees; recovery is usually limited to the value of the assets which the heir has received from the decedent by intestate succession or which the distributee has received under the decedent's will, but the recovery is not dependent upon the retention of such assets by the heir or distributee. If there is no breach of the warranty prior to the covenantor's death, no one is in a position to make any claim against the decedent's estate on account of the warranty; but in the event of a subsequent breach, there may be a personal action against the heirs or distributees of the deceased covenantor, on the basis just described.

SECTION 2. TITLE ASSURANCE BASED ON THE PUBLIC LAND RECORDS

A. IN GENERAL

As we have seen, covenants for title are frequently included in deeds of conveyance in order to afford purchasers, and perhaps their successors in the chain of title, some redress in case it turns out that the conveyance, by reason of defects in or encumbrances upon, the grantor's title, did not transfer to the purchaser the interest it purported to transfer. But, as one writer has recently pointed out,

"As a method of title assurance the warranty deed can never be more than an auxiliary weapon in the conveyancer's arsenal. It is speedily delivered; it can be drafted for a nominal fee; but it secures nothing other than the personal promise of the grantor and is no better than his solvency and availability at some future date when suit may be necessary. Apart from this weakness inherent in all the warranty deeds, the covenants used today are still needlessly technical and hedged about the ancient dogma as to whether they will run with the land, when the breach occurs, the amount of damages due in case of breach, etc., * * * [N]o well-advised purchaser would rely on such a deed as his sole title security." Cribbet, Conveyancing Reform, 35 N.Y.U.L. Rev. 1291, 1300 (1960).*

It is obvious, therefore, that a prudent purchaser or mortgage lender will want some sort of title assurance in addition to the covenants for title, if any, which the vendor includes in his deed of conveyance. The title assurance required by the purchaser or mortgage lender will al-

* Copyright, 1960, Board of New York
University Law Review.

most invariably be based upon a search of the land records and an appraisal of the results of that search. The principal methods of search and title appraisal are summarized as follows in Basye, Clearing Land Titles 13–15 (2d ed. 1970): [**]

"Several different methods of making title searches and appraisals are followed in the United States based upon the recording acts. Throughout New England, in some of the Atlantic and Southern states and in a few Midwest areas the attorney opinion method is commonly followed. A search of title is made of the public land records by an attorney or under his direction, and an abstract is made up from his notes. An opinion is then given based upon this search of the records. In other areas of the East, Midwest and in the West the search is made by an abstractor who compiles an abstract showing all recorded instruments affecting the land in question and certifies that it is a complete and accurate copy of the official record. This abstract is kept up to date with each transfer of ownership and passes to each new owner. The buyer's attorney gives his opinion of the title from his examination of this abstract. A third method is for an abstractor to issue a certificate of title himself based upon his own examination of the record.[1]

"A fourth method of examining and appraising marketability of titles is afforded by the process of issuing title insurance.[2] Most title insurance is not written on a casualty basis but is based upon and issued only after a careful search of the record. Pertinent to the present consideration is the fact that in making their searches and issuing their title policies most title insurance companies maintain their own plant taken from the public records, in which they have converted the grantor-grantee index to a tract index for their own convenience. Only in this way can they make searches of the record with sufficient accuracy and speed to satisfy the demands upon them for service. Thus two sets of indices are maintained at all times—one a public grantor-grantee index and the other a private tract index. The preparation and maintenance of this second private index is, of course, a very great expense to the individual title companies, which could easily be avoided by converting all grantor-grantee indices to tract indices.[3]

[**] Copyright, 1970, West Publishing Company. The footnotes have been renumbered.

1. For a summary of the practices and methods used to assess marketability in the various states in 1953 see Reports of Committee on Acceptable Titles to Real Property, A.B.A.Proc., Section of Real Prop., Prob. and Trust Law 43 (1953); id. 34 (1954). For a fuller description of these methods see Patton, Land Titles § 41 (2d ed. 1957); Russell and Bridewell, Systems of Land Title Examination: An Appraisal, 14 J. of Land & Pub.Util.Econ. 133 (1938); Simes, A Handbook for More Efficient Conveyancing 4 (1961); Flick, Abstract and Title Practice §§ 151–220 (2d ed. 1958); Fiflis, Land Transfer Improvement: The Basic Facts and Two Hypotheses for Reform, 38 Colo.L.Rev. 431 at 438 (1966).

For a discussion of the searcher's potential liability, see Note, Title Searches: The Potential for Liability, 49 Miss.L.J. 689 (1978).

2. Johnstone, Title Insurance, 66 Yale L.J. 492 (1957); Fiflis, Land Transfer Improvement: The Basic Facts and Two Hypotheses for Reform, 38 Colo.L.Rev. 431 (1966).

See also Payne, Title Insurance, The Legislatures and the Constitution, 21 Ala. L.Rev. 25 (1968); Payne, Title Insurance and the Unauthorized Practice of Law Controversy, 53 Minn.L.Rev. 423 (1969).

3. McCormick, Possible Improvements in the Recording Acts, 31 W.Va.L.Q. 79 (1925); Fairchild, Improvement in Recording and Indexing Methods for Real Property Instruments, 28 Georgetown, L.J. 307

"Even when title insurance is issued, the search and opinion on marketability may have been made by the buyer's own attorney who may recommend additional protection of title insurance in the particular case, either because of certain defects in the title or because of the possibility that the record may not disclose everything affecting the title. More likely, however, the search and the opinion on the title will be made by lawyers or laymen in the employ of the title company and without any participation by the attorney for the buyer in the entire process. The title insurance company may even handle the closing of the transaction for both the seller and buyer without the participation of an attorney for either of them. Indeed this is the standard pattern for more and more real estate transactions in the United States today."

In localities where title insurance is in common use, land sale contracts may provide, in the alternative, that the vendor shall furnish the purchaser with a "marketable" abstract of title or a title insurance policy in the usual form insuring the title against all defects and encumbrances except those subject to which the purchaser has agreed to accept the title. In states where Torrens title registration acts are in force, land sale contracts may provide, as a third alternative, that the vendor may furnish a Torrens certificate as evidence of title. See, e.g., paragraph 4 of the Chicago Real Estate Board contract, infra at page 984.

B. ABSTRACTS OF TITLE AND TITLE EXAMINATION

As previously indicated, in many areas of the United States the "title search" in the public land records is made by an "abstractor" who compiles an abstract showing all recorded instruments affecting the land in question and certifies that it is a complete and accurate abstract of the official records. This abstract is examined by the attorney for the prospective purchaser or mortgage lender, or both, and his opinion as to the soundness and marketability of the title is based on this examination.

"The nature and scope of an abstracter's duties may be prescribed and limited by contract; but in the absence of an express contract defining the scope of an abstracter's duties, he impliedly agrees to exercise due and ordinary care in the performance of his task. * * * He is bound to disclose to the person employing him all pertinent information acquired by him in the course of his examination, and to set forth whatever concerns the sources of title and its condition, whether these tend to confirm the title or to impair it. While he is not ordinarily required to go outside the records in his search, he should, if in his search he is put upon notice of anything outside the record which might affect the title, either investigate the same or call attention thereto in the abstract, setting forth the facts so that the person using the abstract may him-

(1939); Simes and Taylor, Improvement of Conveyancing by Legislation 85–89 (1960); Brussack, Reform of American Conveyancing Formality, 32 Hastings L.J. 561 (1981); Report of the Committee on The Improvement and Modernization of Land Records, Real Property Division of the American Bar Association, "Land Information Systems For the Twenty-First Century," 15 Real Property, Probate & Trust J. 890 (1980).

self make the proper investigation relative to the outside facts. He must present a summary of the records of all grants, patents, conveyances, wills, documents and all judicial proceedings which may affect the title in any way; also all mortgages, judgments, taxes, assessments, mechanic's liens, lis pendens, notices, or other liens which may encumber the title in any degree. * * * He must set out every part of an instrument which may have any bearing on the condition of the title, and his employer is entitled to assume that any part not so set out has no bearing on the title. But it is not implied that he should show * * * all the facts and circumstances connected with the conveyances which might affect the title, such as possession, names of legal heirs, and matters of a similar character. It would seem that he is only bound to exercise reasonable care, diligence and skill in preparing the abstract, and that the element of guaranty does not enter into the employment. * * * " Thompson, Abstracts and Titles § 16 (pp. 26–27) (2d ed. 1930).*

The abstract of title is usually delivered to the attorney of the prospective purchaser or mortgage lender, as the case may be, for examination and appraisal. In most localities it is customary for the examining attorney to base his title opinion entirely upon the abstract, without making any independent investigation of the records upon which the abstract is based. The title examiner's function is to determine from the abstract whether the vendor or mortgagor has a "good" title to the land—indefeasible and free of encumbrances—and whether the title is "marketable" as well as "good"—i.e., whether the abstract shows the title to be so clearly "good" that the purchaser or mortgage lender will be free from (a) any reasonable doubt as to its validity and (b) any likelihood of litigation to test its validity. (The topic of "marketability" will be explored in more detail infra in Chapter 12, Section 2.)

The title examiner brings to his employment "only such knowledge, skill and ability as is ordinarily required of members of his profession * * * who engage in work of like character. * * * Aside from his duty to avoid any breach of confidence between himself and his client, the title examiner is not liable except for negligence or want of ordinary skill and legal knowledge. He does not warrant the titles he examines, nor is he a guarantor as to their perfection." Thompson, Abstracts and Titles § 811 (pp. 1037–38).

In some localities it is common practice for abstract companies to issue "certificates of title" to prospective purchasers and mortgage lenders. These certificates are, in legal effect, legal opinions as to the state of the title to the land in question. It seems clear that companies which issue certificates of title are engaging in the practice of law, and that they are subject to the same duty as an attorney engaged to examine the title to land.

The following abstract, taken from Flick, Abstract and Title Practice, Vol. 1, pp. 22–40 (2d ed. 1958),** is complete though too short to be typical.

ABSTRACT OF TITLE

1. CAPTION

Situated in the Township of Audrain, in the County of Dore and in the State of Ohio, and Being the Northwest quarter of the Southeast quarter, and the North half of the Southeast fraction of the Southwest quarter of Section 34, Township one South, of Range five East, containing 83 acres of land, more or less.

1-A-Plat.

Section 34 Tp. 1 South R. 5 East

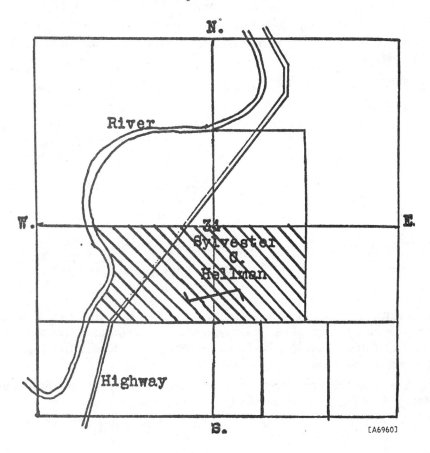

Audrain Township, Dore County, Ohio

2.

STATE DEED

The State of Ohio

TO

John Glander

Date of Instrument? August 5, 1835

Filed: December 16, 1842

Recorded in Volume 12, Page 236 of the Record of Deeds of Dore County, Ohio

Consideration $132.33

Estate conveyed:

What if any defect in instrument? None.

Description: The Southeast fraction of the West half of Section No. 34, Township one South of Range five East within the land and containing 105 acres of land, more or less.

Regularly signed, sealed, witnessed and acknowledged.

3.

WARRANTY DEED

John Glander and Elizabeth Glander, his wife

TO

Henry Joseph Boehmer

Date of Instrument? September 4, 1847

Filed: June 4, 1848

Recorded in Volume 2, Page 315 of the Record of Deeds of Dore County, Ohio

Consideration $390.00

Estate conveyed: Fee simple

What if any defect in instrument? None.

Description: Situated in the County of Dore and State of Ohio and bounded and described as follows, to-wit: The Southeast fraction of the West half of Section No. 34, Township one South, Range five East, containing 105.86 acres, more or less.

Also, the Northeast fraction of Section No. 34, Township one South, Range five East, containing 71.51 acres of land, more or less.

Regularly signed, sealed, witnessed and acknowledged.

4.

<table>
<tr><td>

Henry Joseph Boehmer
and Mary Boehmer,
his wife

TO

Mathias Hellman

</td><td>

WARRANTY DEED

Date of Instrument? January 29,
1848

Filed: November 28, 1848

Recorded in Volume 2, Page 405
of the Record of Deeds of Dore
County, Ohio

Consideration $155.00

Estate conveyed: Fee simple

What if any defect in instrument?
None.

</td></tr>
</table>

Description: Situated in the County of Dore and State of Ohio and bounded and described as follows, to-wit: The Northeast fraction of the Southwest quarter of Section 34, Township one South, Range five East, containing 43.20 acres of land, more or less.

Regularly signed, sealed, witnessed and acknowledged.

5.

<table>
<tr><td>

The State of Ohio

TO

J. C. McCowen

</td><td>

STATE DEED

Date of Instrument? September
16, 1853

Filed: January 7, 1854 at 12:30
P.M.

Recorded in Volume 87, Page 93
of the Record of Deeds of Dore
County, Ohio

Consideration $160.00

Estate conveyed:

What if any defect in instrument?
None.

</td></tr>
</table>

Description: The Southeast quarter of Section No. 34, Township one South, Range five East, containing 160 acres of land.

Regularly signed, sealed, witnessed and acknowledged.

6.

<table>
<tr><td>

John McCowen and Drucilla
McCowen, his wife

TO

Mathias Hellman

</td><td>

WARRANTY DEED

Date of Instrument? August 10,
1854

Filed: November 9, 1854

Recorded in Volume 11, Page 164
of the Record of Deeds of Dore
County, Ohio

Consideration $120.00

Estate conveyed: Fee simple

Defects: None.

</td></tr>
</table>

Description: The West half of the Northwest quarter of the Southeast quarter of Section 34, Twp 1 S of R 5 E, in the County of Dore, Ohio, containing 20 acres of land.

Regularly signed, sealed, witnessed and acknowledged.

7.

WARRANTY DEED

John McCowen and Drucilla
    McCowen, his wife

Date of Instrument? January 14, 1860

Filed: September 12, 1860

TO

Recorded in Volume 14, Page 221 of the Record of Deeds of Dore County, Ohio

Mathias Hellman

Consideration $140

Estate conveyed: Fee simple

What if any defect in instrument? None.

Description: Situated in the County of Dore in the State of Ohio and in _____ and bounded and described as follows: Being the East half of the Northwest quarter of Section 34, Township one South, Range five East, containing 20 acres of land in the County of Dore, Ohio.

Regularly signed, sealed, witnessed and acknowledged.

8.

WARRANTY DEED

Mathias Hellman

Date of Instrument? April 2, 1883

Filed: May 11, 1883

TO

Recorded in Volume 42, Page 426 of the Record of Deeds of Dore County, Ohio

Joseph Hellman

Consideration $3500.00

Estate conveyed: Fee simple

What if any defect in instrument? None.

Description: Situated in the Township of Audrain, in the County of Dore and State of Ohio and being the Northeast fraction of the Southwest fractional quarter, and the Northwest quarter of the Southeast quarter of Section 34, Township one South of Range five East, containing 80 acres of land, more or less.

Regularly signed, sealed, witnessed and acknowledged.

9.

Joseph Hellman and
Bernadina Hellman,
husband and wife

TO

Sylvester C. Hellman

WARRANTY DEED

Date of Instrument? October 17, 1929

Filed: April 28, 1930 at 4:15 P.M.

Recorded in Volume 139, Page 398 of the Record of Deeds of Dore County, Ohio

Consideration $1.00

Estate conveyed: Fee simple

What if any defect in instrument? None.

Description: Situated in the Township of Audrain, County of Dore and State of Ohio, and being the Northeast fraction of the Southwest fractional quarter, and the Northwest quarter of the Southeast quarter of Section 34, Township one South, of Range five East, and containing 80 acres of land, more or less.

Regularly signed, sealed, witnessed and acknowledged.

10.

CERTIFICATE TO RECORDER
REAL ESTATE DEVISED BY WILL

Probate Court, Dore County, Ohio

To the County Recorder of said County:

I the undersigned, Probate Judge of said County, do hereby certify that on the 18th day of March, A.D. 1930, the Last Will and Testament of Joseph Hellmann, late of said County, was duly admitted to probate in this Court, and the same has been duly recorded in Volume P Page 159 of the Records of Wills in this office.

That by the terms of said Will certain real estate was devised to Bernadina Hellmann and Sylvester Hellman.

That the following is a description of said real estate as is contained in the Will to-wit:

Second: I give, devise and bequeath to my beloved wife, Bernadina, the farm on which we now reside together with all chattel property I may have at the time of my decease. She to have full possession of same during her natural life. After the death of my beloved wife, I give to my son, Sylvester, the aforementioned farm located in Section 34, Audrain Township, Dore County, Ohio, containing 83 acres of land, together with all chattels. He, however, must pay all funeral expenses and debts contracted by my said wife. Also to pay my following named children within three years after the death of my said wife as follows:

Witness my signature and the seal of said Court, this 6th day of January, 1931.

W. M. Bunge, *Probate Judge*
By Mary McLeasure,
Deputy Clerk

[*Seal*]
Recorded in Vol. 141, Page 191
Record of Deeds of said County

11.

APPLICATION FOR PROBATE OF WILL

Dore County, Ohio
Probate Court,

In the Matter of
    The Last Will and Testament of   }   Application To Admit
Joseph Hellmann,   To Probate
              Deceased.

To the Probate Court of said County:

Your petitioner respectfully represents that Joseph Hellmann, late a resident of the Township of Audrain in said County, died on or about the 4th day of March, A.D., 1930, leaving an instrument in writing, herewith produced, purporting to be his last Will and Testament;

That the said Joseph Hellmann died leaving Bernadina Hellmann, widow, who resides at Fort Audrain, Ohio, and the following named persons his only next of kin, to-wit:

Name	Degree of Kinship	P.O. Address
Mathias Hellmann	Son	Fort Audrain, Ohio
Otto Hellmann	"	Delton, Ohio
Christina Brinkman	Daughter	Fort Audrain, O.
Bernadina Beining	"	Fort Audrain, "
Mary Hellmann	"	" " "
Sylvester Hellman	Son	" " "

Your petitioner offers said Will for Probate and prays that a time may be fixed for the proving of the same, and that said above named persons resident in this State may be notified according to law of the pendency of said proceedings.

Sylvester Hellmann, *Petitioner*

Properly verified.

12.

LAST WILL AND TESTAMENT

In the Name of the Benevolent Father of All: Amen.

I, Joseph Hellmann, of the Township of Audrain, County of Dore and State of Ohio, being about 70 years of age and of sound and disposing mind and memory, do make, publish and declare this my last will and testament, hereby revoking and annulling any and all will or wills by me made heretofore:

First: My will is that all my just debts and funeral expenses be paid out of my estate as soon after my decease as shall be found convenient.

Second: I give, devise and bequeath to my beloved wife Bernadina the farm on which we now reside together with all chattel property I may have at the time of my decease. She to have full possession of same during her natural life. After the death of my beloved wife I give to my son Sylvester the aforementioned farm located in Section thirty-four, Audrain Township, Dore County, Ohio, containing eighty-three (83) acres of land together with all chattels. He, however, must pay all funeral expenses and debts contracted by my said wife. Also to pay my following named children within three years after the death of my said wife as follows:

Item 3. My son Mathias to get Seven Hundred ($700.00) Dollars, I having paid him Eight Hundred ($800.00) Dollars.

Item 4. My son Otto to get Fifteen Hundred ($1500.00) Dollars.

Item 5. My daughter Christina Brinkman to get Fourteen Hundred ($1400.00) Dollars. She having been paid One Hundred ($100.00) Dollars.

Item 6. My daughter Bernadina Beining to get Fourteen Hundred ($1400.00) Dollars. She having been paid One Hundred ($100.00) Dollars.

Item 7. My daughter Mary to get Eighteen Hundred ($1800.00) Dollars and the privilege of remaining and living on said farm with my son Sylvester, as long as she lives, and to occupy the East upstairs room. However in case Sylvester is forced to sell, then my daughter may so give up the aforesaid privileges.

Item 8. I desire that there be no appraisement of my property and ask that the court omit the same.

Item 9. I hereby revoke any and all wills formerly made by me. In Testimony Whereof, I have set my hand to this my last will and testament at Fort Audrain, Ohio, this 8th day of April in the year of our Lord one thousand nine hundred and twenty-four.

Joseph Hellmann

The foregoing instrument was signed by the said Joseph Hellmann in our presence, and by him published and declared as and for his last will and testament and at his request, and in his presence, and in the presence of each other, we hereunto subscribe our names as attesting witnesses, at Fort Audrain, Ohio, this 8th day of April, A.D., 1924.

Anton J. Berelman   resides at Fort Audrain, Ohio
Rudolph Rasbe   resides at Fort Audrain, Ohio

Filed March 18, 1930

13.

NOTE: The order for hearing, the admission to probate and record, the waiver of notice and consent to probate, the testimony of witnesses to the will, the application for letters, the issuance of letters; the order for bond; and the proof of publication of notice to creditors are all regular and complete and are not set out.

14.

JOURNAL ENTRY

IN PROBATE COURT
Dore County, Ohio
May 13, 1930

In the matter of the Estate of
    Joseph Hellman,[4]   } Estate Not Subject to Tax
        Deceased.

Determination of Inheritance Tax

Sylvester C. Hellman as Administrator of the estate of Joseph Hellman, deceased, having filed an application duly verified, for a finding and order that said estate and the successions therein are exempt from any inheritance tax under the laws of Ohio, the same came on for hearing.

And the Court being fully advised in the premises, finds and determines that the gross value of said estate is $885.86; the debts and costs of administration are $585.00, and the net actual market value thereof is $300.86, (a) Said decedent died leaving three sons and three daughters, and that as a result said estate and the successions therein are exempt from such inheritance tax.

It is ordered that the court costs on this proceeding taxed at $3.00 be certified to the County Auditor to be paid and credited in the manner provided by law.

W.M. Bunge, *Probate Judge*

Filed May 13, 1930.

---

4. The various spellings of the name "Hellmann" are as they appeared in the original documents.

15.

In the Matter of the Estate of	IN PROBATE COURT
Joseph Hellman,	Dore County, Ohio
Deceased.	Saturday May 2, 1931.

The first and final account of Sylvester Hellman, Administrator with will annexed of the estate of Joseph Hellman, deceased, herein filed on the 23rd day of March, A.D., 1931, came in this day for hearing and settlement, due notice thereof having been published according to law. No exceptions having been filed thereto, and no one now appearing to except or object to the same; and the Court having carefully examined said account and the vouchers therewith and all matters pertaining thereto, and being fully advised in the premises, finds the same to be in all respects just and correct and in conformity to law.

It is ordered that the same be and hereby is approved, allowed and confirmed.

The Court further finds said Administrator with will annexed chargeable with the assets of the estate of said Joseph Hellman to the amount of $929.11 and that he is entitled to the credits in the sum of $929.11 and that there is no balance due to said estate.

And the Court further finding that said estate has been duly and fully settled, it is ordered that said Administrator with will annexed be discharged and his bond released from further liability. It is ordered that said account and the proceedings herein be recorded in the records of this office, and that said Administrator with will annexed pay the costs herein taxed at $5.00.

W.M. Bunge, *Probate Judge*

Filed May 2, 1931.

16.

EASEMENT

Sylvester Hellman	Date of Instrument. April 22, 1933
TO	
The General Utilities Co. of Deshler, Ohio	Recorded May 17, 1933 in Volume 143 at Page 596
	No defects in instrument

Grants the right to construct, operate and maintain its lines through and along the following described property: The Northeast 43.1 acres of the Southwest quarter of section 34, Township one South, Range five East.

17.

TAX STATEMENT

The tax duplicates of the Treasurer's Office and the records of the Auditor's Office and Surveyor's Office of Dore County, Ohio, show the following in connection with the taxes levied against caption lands:

Amount of Special Assessments and Terms:
No specials
Description of Land as it Appears on the Duplicates:

Sec. 34 NW ¼ SE ¼	40A
Sec. "N ½ SE fr. SW¼	43.10A
Assessed Value of	
Land	$4390.00
Buildings	$2340.00
Total	$6730.00

Current Taxes:

Paid   Taxes for the first half of the year 1937, due and payable in December 1937 .... $33.65

Unpaid   Taxes for the last half of the year 1937, due and payable in June 1938 .... $33.65

18.

State of Ohio, County of Dore

I hereby certify that the annexed abstract, which is furnished _____, as prospective mortgagee for use in passing on the title to premises covered thereby, is a correct abstract of the title to the land described in the caption thereof, to-wit:

CAPTION LANDS

in the said county and state: that said abstract correctly shows all matters affecting or relating to the said title which are of record or on file in said county, including conveyances, deeds, trust deeds, land and other liens, attachments and foreign or domestic executions in the hands of the sheriff, certificates of authority to pay taxes, suits pending by or against owners of record within the last two years or against Sylvester Hellman, notices of Federal liens, tax sales, tax deeds, probate proceedings, special proceedings, and unsatisfied judgments and transcripts of judgments from United States and State courts against owners of record or against Sylvester Hellman, notices of liens on bail bonds or recognizances filed against said premises, or against owners of record on or since April 1, 1929, or against Sylvester Hellman, under chapter 14, section 13435–5, of laws of Ohio of 1929; that said abstract also shows all bankruptcy proceedings and certified copies of orders of adjudication and orders approving bonds of trustee in bankruptcy proceedings by or against any party who, within three years past, has been an owner of record of said land or against Sylvester Hellman on file or of record in said county; that all taxes and special assessments against said premises are paid in full to and including the first instalment of the taxes for the year 1937 and that there are no outstanding instalments of special assessments to become due in the future.

Dated at _____, Ohio this 2nd day of May, A.D. 19__, at 10:00 o'clock A.M.

C.W. McLain Abstracter

Continued to this date and recertified as above, this _____ day of _____, A.D. 19__, at _____ o'clock __.M.

Problems

1. Is the Caption of the above Abstract consistent with the descriptions included in entries 2, 3, and 4? Are the latter entries consistent?

2. What about entry 7? Is the description correct?

3. What is the significance of the fact, as indicated by entry 9, that the warranty deed dated October 17, 1929, was not filed for record until April 28, 1930, and that in the meantime (as indicated by entries 10–12), the grantor Joseph Hellman died? Does the delay in recording suggest why entries 10–15 were included in the Abstract?

4. What about the discrepancies in names of grantors and grantees in the Abstract? How can the title examiner be sure that "J.C. McCowen" named as grantee in entry 5 is the same person as "John McCowen" named as grantor in entry 6? How can the title examiner be sure that "Joseph Hellman" named as grantee in entry 8 is the same person as "Joseph Hellmann" named as testator in entries 10–12? How can the title examiner be sure that "Sylvester C. Hellman" named as grantee in entry 9 is the same person as "Sylvester Hellmann" named as a "next of kin" and petitioner in entry 11 and as grantor in entry 16? Does it matter: Is it enough that the last names sound alike ("idems sonans")?

5. Do you see any problems that may arise from the vague and general terms in which the easement is granted in entry 16? Suppose the General Utilities Company has already constructed one transmission line across the subject land; would this improve or detract from the marketability of the title?

Note: *"Root of Title" and Period Covered by Search and Abstract of Title*

You will have noticed that the foregoing abstract of title begins, as to each parcel of land involved, with a deed from the State of Ohio. But how did title to the land involved pass from the United States to the State of Ohio? Since Ohio was the first state formed from the old Northwest Territory, wouldn't you expect an abstract of title to Ohio land to begin with a grant or patent from the United States? In those states formed from the old Northwest Territory or from the Louisiana Purchase, an abstract ordinarily does start with a conveyance from the United States either in the form of a special Congressional grant (with or without a patent) or a patent issued pursuant to a general act of Congress; and in parts of the South and the Southwest an abstract ordinarily begins either with a French, Spanish, or Mexican grant, a confirmation of the same by the United States, or a conveyance from the United States. Such patent, grant, or other conveyance is commonly referred to as the "root of title."

In localities where it is feasible to carry the title search all the way back to the inception of private ownership, a contract requiring the vendor to furnish an abstract of title is generally held to require an abstract showing the complete chain of title. In such localities an abstract is generally held insufficient if it begins only with the filing of a plat. In some localities, however, conveyancers regard an abstract as sufficient if it shows the chain of title from the date of platting and also shows the inception of private ownership—the latter being necessary because statutes of limitations do not operate against the sovereign.

In some of the Atlantic seaboard states, where the grants initiating private ownership of the land are very ancient, title searches are normally extended back only far enough to give reasonable assurance that successful attack on the record title is barred by statutes of limitation. In Connecticut the state bar association has adopted a title standard recognizing the sufficiency of a title search extending back 60 years to an instrument of conveyance other than a tax collector's deed, providing the search does not disclose any defect or encumbrance originating prior to the 60 year period. Conn. Title Standard No. 1. In Massachusetts and New Jersey a 50 to 60 year title search is also customary. See Johnson, "Title Examination in Massachusetts," in Casner and Leach, Cases and Text on Property 897 (2d ed. 1969); 13A New Jersey Practice 141 (Abstracts and Titles, by Lieberman, 1966). In Pennsylvania a 50 year search is generally considered sufficient. See Nicholson, Law of Real Estate in Pennsylvania 511 (3rd ed. 1929).

In localities where attorneys are responsible for examining the public records relating to land titles and commercial abstracts prepared by abstract or title companies are not used, each transfer or mortgage of a given parcel of land usually involves a new examination of the records for the full period required to satisfy the requirement of marketability. With his client's consent the attorney employed to search the title sometimes buys a title opinion with respect to the land in question from a reputable attorney who has made a title search in connection with an earlier transaction, and then restricts his examination of the records to the period since the earlier transaction; but this practice does not seem to be general. The waste of time and money resulting from repeated "retracing of the tortuous path of title" is obvious, even when confined to parcels not recently subdivided. Where a large tract has been recently subdivided, the situation with respect to title search often approaches the absurd. For a graphic illustration, see Viele, The Problem of Land Titles, 44 Pol. Sci.Q. 421 at 425 (1929).

In localities where commercial abstracts prepared by abstract or title companies are in general use, many landowners have abstracts of title furnished to them when they acquired their properties. When such a landowner contracts to sell his property, or negotiates for a mortgage, he may satisfy his obligation to furnish a "merchantable abstract" or "abstract of title disclosing a good and merchantable title" by having his "old" abstract "continued" to the date of the current transaction, provided his "old" abstract was compiled by a responsible abstract or title company which is still doing business. This reduces very considerably the necessity for repeated examinations of the same title records for the same period of time with respect to the same parcel of land. However, since the localities in which commercial abstracts of title are in general use are also localities where abstracts customarily show the complete chain of title, all the way back to the inception of private ownership, the period covered by the abstract is constantly increasing and the opportunity for captious objection to ancient defects in the record title is more extensive than it is in localities where the title search is customarily restricted to 50 or 60 years.

The "marketable title" acts adopted in a number of states during the past twenty-five to thirty years are one attempt to deal with the problem of repeated re-examinations of the same title-affecting transactions shown in the earlier parts of the abstract of title. Under these "marketable title" acts, which are discussed in more detail infra, Section 5, the title examiner, having ascertained that the abstract shows a patent or other conveyance from the United States, may substantially limit his examination of the abstract of title to the most recent thirty, forty, or fifty year period. (The period varies in accordance with the particular statute's definition of "marketable record title" as one which is good "of record" for a designated period prior to the date when the determination is made.)

For a comprehensive treatment of "title examination," see 4 A.L.P. §§ 18.1–18.100; R. Patton & C. Patton, Land Titles (2d ed. 1957; 3 vols.).

C. TITLE INSURANCE AND TITLE GUARANTY

(1) Commercial Title Insurance *

Title insurance is the predominant method of assuring real estate titles in the United States today. It was developed more than one hundred years ago, and is an exclusively American invention. It attempts to solve the problems we have discussed in connection with the recording system: the existence of off-record interests, the fact that recorded documents may not be valid, and the limited liability of abstractors and lawyers for title search and examination errors. In substance, a title insurance policy is the insurer's promise that, if the title is not in the condition described by the policy on its effective date, the insurer will indemnify the insured for resulting losses.

There are two kinds of title insurance policies: those insuring the interests of lenders and of owners. The lender's policy is far more significant in economic terms, since it is really lenders and secondary market mortgage investors who have made title insurance the important force in real estate conveyancing that it is today. The secondary market, in which financial institutions (e.g., life insurance companies, savings banks, and certain federally-chartered corporations such as the Federal National Mortgage Association) buy mortgages from local lenders, has been particularly insistent on title insurance. This is a reasonable insistence, since an investor who is acquiring mortgages from many states and localities is understandably reluctant to rely on the opinions and malpractice insurance policies of numerous local lawyers whose qualifications and experience are hard to judge and police. Title insurance provides a standardized, fungible nationwide means of assuring titles, and thus is far more attractive.

Nearly all title insurers obtain title searches and examinations before issuing policies. In some states this is legally mandated, and it is generally considered foolish to do otherwise. The search may be done by a local lawyer who is "approved" by the title company (and who will get his or her fee directly from the client). In this setting, the title

---

* The text of this part, up to the next principal case, is drawn from G. Nelson & D. Whitman, Real Estate Transfer, Finance, and Development 215–221 (2d ed. 1981). Copyright, 1981, West Publishing Company.

company is paid only a "risk premium", since it is not required to perform the search. In other areas or among other companies, the insurer's own employees may perform searches, either in the company's private title plant or in the public records. Under this method, the company generally charges an "all-inclusive" premium to the insured which covers both the search and the risk-assumption aspects. The "approved attorney" approach is predominant in the East and Midwest, especially outside major cities; the "all-inclusive" approach is widely used in the West and in major cities throughout the rest of the nation.

For the reasons mentioned above, many lenders now insist on the issuance of lenders' policies whenever a new mortgage loan is made. It is the nearly universal custom that the borrower must pay the premium for this policy. Owners' policies are not issued quite as frequently. They may be paid for by the buyer of the property (commonly in the East) or by the seller (commonly in the West). As we will see below, there are often significant differences between the coverage of lender's and owner's policies, with the former usually having fewer exceptions and thus absorbing a broader range of risks. In 1970 the American Land Title Association, the trade organization for title insurers, developed a set of forms which are very widely used. At this writing they are the most recent of a long series of standard forms promulgated by ALTA and its predecessor organizations; a new set of "plain language" forms is reported to be in preparation.

AMERICAN LAND TITLE ASSOCIATION OWNERS TITLE INSURANCE POLICY FORM B–1970

[Note: Form A–1970 is similar but does not insure against unmarketability.]

SUBJECT TO THE EXCLUSIONS FROM COVERAGE, THE EXCEPTIONS CONTAINED IN SCHEDULE B AND THE PROVISIONS OF THE CONDITIONS AND STIPULATIONS HEREOF [*name of company*] herein called the Company, insures, as of Date of Policy shown in Schedule A, against loss or damage, not exceeding the amount of insurance stated in Schedule A, and costs, attorneys' fees and expenses which the Company may become obligated to pay hereunder, sustained or incurred by the insured by reason of:

1. Title to the estate or interest described in Schedule A being vested otherwise than as stated therein;

2. Any defect in or lien or encumbrance on such title;

3. Lack of a right of access to and from the land; or

4. Unmarketability of such title.

Schedule of Exclusions from Coverage

The following matters are expressly excluded from the coverage of this policy:

1. Any law, ordinance or governmental regulation (including but not limited to building and zoning ordinances) restricting or regulating or prohibiting the occupancy, use or enjoyment of the land, or regulating the character, dimensions or location of any improvement now or hereafter erected on the land, or prohibiting a separation in ownership or a reduction in the dimensions or area of the land, or the effect of any violation of any such law, ordinance or governmental regulation.

2. Rights of eminent domain or governmental rights of police power unless notice of the exercise of such rights appears in the public records at Date of Policy.

3. Defects, liens, encumbrances, adverse claims, or other matters (a) created, suffered, assumed or agreed to by the insured claimant; (b) not known to the Company and not shown by the public records but known to the insured claimant either at Date of Policy or at the date such claimant acquired an estate or interest insured by this policy and not disclosed in writing by the insured claimant to the Company prior to the date such insured claimant became an insured hereunder; (c) resulting in no loss or damage to the insured claimant; (d) attaching or created subsequent to Date of Policy; or (e) resulting in loss or damage which would not have been sustained if the insured claimant had paid value for the estate or interest insured by this policy.

Conditions and Stipulations

1. Definition of Terms

The following terms when used in this policy mean:

(a) "insured": the insured named in Schedule A, and, subject to any rights or defenses the Company may have had against the named insured, those who succeed to the interest of such insured by operation of law as distinguished from purchase including, but not limited to, heirs, distributees, devisees, survivors, personal representatives, next of kin, or corporate or fiduciary successors.

(b) "insured claimant": an insured claiming loss or damage hereunder.

(c) "knowledge": actual knowledge, not constructive knowledge or notice which may be imputed to an insured by reason of any public records.

(d) "land": the land described, specifically or by reference in Schedule C, and improvements affixed thereto which by law constitute real property; provided, however, the term "land" does not include any property beyond the lines of the area specifically described or referred to in Schedule C, nor any right, title, interest, estate or easement in abutting streets, roads, avenues, alleys, lanes, ways or waterways, but nothing herein shall modify or limit the extent to which a right of access to and from the land is insured by this policy.

(e) "mortgage": mortgage, deed of trust, trust deed, or other security instrument.

(f) "public records": those records which by law impart constructive notice of matters relating to said land.

2. Continuation of Insurance after Conveyance of Title

The coverage of this policy shall continue in force as of Date of Policy in favor of an insured so long as such insured retains an estate or interest in the land, or holds an indebtedness secured by a purchase money mortgage given by a purchaser from such insured, or so long as such insured shall have liability by reason of covenants of warranty made by such insured in any transfer or conveyance of such estate or interest; provided, however, this policy shall not continue in force in favor of any purchaser from such insured of either said estate or interest or the indebtedness secured by a purchase money mortgage given to such insured.

3. Defense and Prosecution of Actions—Notice of Claim to be Given by an Insured Claimant

(a) The Company, at its own cost and without undue delay, shall provide for the defense of an insured in all litigation consisting of actions or proceedings commenced against such insured, or a defense interposed against an insured in an action to enforce a contract for a sale of the estate or interest in said land, to the extent that such litigation is founded upon an alleged defect, lien, encumbrance, or other matter insured against by this policy.

(b) The insured shall notify the Company promptly in writing (i) in case any action or proceeding is begun or defense is interposed as set forth in (a) above, (ii) in case knowledge shall come to an insured hereunder of any claim of title or interest which is adverse to the title to the estate or interest, as insured, and which might cause loss or damage for which the Company may be liable by virtue of this policy, or (iii) if title to the estate or interest, as insured, is rejected as unmarketable. If such prompt notice shall not be given to the Company, then as to such insured all liability of the Company shall cease and terminate in regard to the matter or matters for which such prompt notice is required; provided, however, that failure to notify shall in no case prejudice the rights of any such insured under this policy unless the Company shall be prejudiced by such failure and then only to the extent of such prejudice.

(c) The Company shall have the right at its own cost to institute and without undue delay prosecute any action or proceeding or to do any other act which in its opinion may be necessary or desirable to establish the title to the estate or interest as insured, and the Company may take any appropriate action under the terms of this policy, whether or not it shall be liable thereunder, and shall not thereby concede liability or waive any provision of this policy.

(d) Whenever the Company shall have brought any action or interposed a defense as required or permitted by the provisions of this policy, the Company may pursue any such litigation to final determination by a court of competent jurisdiction and expressly reserves the right, in its sole discretion, to appeal from any adverse judgment or order.

(e) In all cases where this policy permits or requires the Company to prosecute or provide for the defense of any action or proceeding the insured hereunder shall secure to the Company the right to so prosecute or provide defense in such action or proceeding, and all appeals therein, and permit the Company to use, at its option, the name of such insured for such purpose. Whenever requested by the Company, such insured shall give the Company all reasonable aid in any such action or proceeding, in effecting settlement, securing evidence, obtaining witnesses, or prosecuting or defending such action or proceeding, and the Company shall reimburse such insured for any expense so incurred.

4. Notice of Loss—Limitation of Action

In addition to the notices required under paragraph 3(b) of these Conditions and Stipulations, a statement in writing of any loss or damage for which it is claimed the Company is liable under this policy shall be furnished to the Company within 90 days after such loss or damage shall have been determined and no right of action shall accrue to an insured claimant until 30 days after such statement shall have been furnished. Failure to furnish such statement of loss or damage shall terminate any liability of the Company under this policy as to such loss or damage.

5. Options to Pay or Otherwise Settle Claims

The Company shall have the option to pay or otherwise settle for or in the name of an insured claimant any claim insured against or to terminate all liability and obligations of the Company hereunder by paying or tendering payment of the amount of insurance under this policy together with any costs, attorneys' fees and expenses incurred up to the time of such payment or tender of payment, by the insured claimant and authorized by the Company.

6. Determination and Payment of Loss

(a) The liability of the Company under this policy shall in no case exceed the least of:

(i) the actual loss of the insured claimant; or

(ii) the amount of insurance stated in Schedule A.

(b) The Company will pay, in addition to any loss insured against by this policy, all costs imposed upon an insured in litigation carried on by the Company for such insured, and all costs, attorneys' fees and expenses in litigation carried on by such insured with the written authorization of the Company.

(c) When liability has been definitely fixed in accordance with the conditions of this policy, the loss or damage shall be payable within 30 days thereafter.

7. Limitation of Liability

No claim shall arise or be maintainable under this policy (a) if the Company, after having received notice of an alleged defect, lien or encumbrance insured against hereunder, by litigation or otherwise, removes such defect, lien or encumbrance or establishes the title, as insured, within a reasonable time after receipt of such notice; (b) in the event of litigation until there has been a final determination by a court of competent jurisdiction, and disposition of all appeals therefrom, adverse to the title, as insured, as provided in paragraph 3 hereof; or (c) for liability voluntarily assumed by an insured in settling any claim or suit without prior written consent of the Company.

8. Reduction of Liability

All payments under this policy, except payments made for costs, attorneys' fees and expenses, shall reduce the amount of the insurance pro tanto. No payment shall be made without producing this policy for endorsement of such payment unless the policy be lost or destroyed, in which case proof of such loss or destruction shall be furnished to the satisfaction of the Company.

9. Liability Noncumulative

It is expressly understood that the amount of insurance under this policy shall be reduced by any amount the Company may pay under any policy insuring either (a) a mortgage shown or referred to in Schedule B hereof which is a lien on the estate or interest covered by this policy, or (b) a mortgage hereafter executed by an insured which is a charge or lien on the estate or interest described or referred to Schedule A, and the amount so paid shall be deemed a payment under this policy. The Company shall have the option to apply to the payment of any such mortgages any amount that otherwise would be payable hereunder to the insured owner of the estate or interest covered by this policy and the amount so paid shall be deemed a payment under this policy to said insured owner.

10. Apportionment

If the land described in Schedule C consists of two or more parcels which are not used as a single site, and a loss is established affecting one or more of said parcels but not all, the loss shall be computed and settled on a pro rata basis as if the amount of insurance under this policy was divided pro rata as to the value on Date of Policy of each separate parcel to the whole, exclusive of any improvements made subsequent to Date of Policy, unless a liability or value has otherwise been agreed upon as to each such parcel by the Company and the insured at the time of the issuance of this policy and shown by an express statement herein or by an endorsement attached hereto.

11. Subrogation upon Payment or Settlement

Whenever the Company shall have settled a claim under this policy, all right of subrogation shall vest in the Company unaffected by any act of the insured claimant. The Company shall be subrogated to and be entitled to all rights and remedies which such insured claimant would have had against any person or property in respect to such claim had this policy not been issued, and if requested by the Company, such insured claimant shall transfer to the Company all rights and remedies against any person or property necessary in order to perfect such right of subrogation and shall permit the Company to use the name of such insured claimant in any transaction or litigation involving such rights or remedies if the payment does not cover the loss of such insured claimant, the Company shall be subrogated to such rights and remedies in the proportion which said payment bears to the amount of said loss if loss should result from any act of such insured claimant, such act shall not void this policy, but the Company, in that event, shall be required to pay only that part of any losses insured against hereunder which shall exceed the amount, if any, lost to the Company by reason of the impairment of the right of subrogation.

12. Liability Limited to this Policy

This instrument together with all endorsements and other instruments, if any, attached hereto by the Company is the entire policy and contract between the insured and the Company.

Any claim of loss or damage, whether or not based on negligence, and which arises out of the status of the title to the estate or interest covered hereby or any action asserting such claim, shall be restricted to the provisions and conditions and stipulations of this policy.

No amendment of or endorsement to this policy can be made except by writing endorsed hereon or attached hereto signed by either the President, a Vice President, the Secretary, an Assistant Secretary, or validating officer or authorized signatory of the Company.

13. Notices, where Sent

All notices required to be given the Company and any statement in writing required to be furnished the Company shall be addressed to it at the office which issued this policy or to its Home Office. [*insert address*].

14. The Premium Specified in Schedule A is the Entire Charge for Title Search, Title Examination and Title Insurance.

As a part of the ALTA owner's policy, and similarly included as part of most other title insurance policies, there are three schedules containing the following information:

Schedule A: contains basic policy information: the amount of coverage (usually the purchase price for an owner's policy and the loan amount for a lender's policy), the premium amount, the name of the insured, the type of estate being insured (e.g., fee simple, leasehold, etc.), the name of the person in whom the estate is vested (usually the insured in the case of an owner's policy), and in some policies, the legal description of the land.

Schedule B: lists types of claims not covered by the policy and also outstanding interests in the land held by others as disclosed by the title search. Typical of such claims would be existing mortgages (in an owner's policy) or prior mortgages (in a lender's policy), utility easements, the lien of the current year's property taxes if they have not been paid, and so on. In most cases the company will have issued a "preliminary title report" or "binder" prior to the issuance of the policy itself; this report will indicate the matters which the company expects to show on Schedule B of the policy, based on the results of its title search. Sometimes the company can be persuaded that one or more of these matters is so old or so unlikely to be asserted that the company can safely "insure over" it, dropping it from Schedule B. In some areas companies may charge an additional premium (to cover the added risk) when they do so.

Schedule C: In some policies, the legal description of the land is contained here rather than in Schedule A.

The ALTA owner's policy gives owners very broad coverage, and many companies offer an alternative owner's policy, often prepared by a state land title association or copied from one of the earlier (and less comprehensive) ALTA forms, at a lower cost. Such lower-priced policies are purchased much more frequently than ALTA owner's policies in many states, especially in single-family house transactions. ALTA owner's policies, on the other hand, are nearly always purchased where the property is used (or is to be developed) for valuable commercial purposes. In many ALTA policies and nearly all other owners' policies, the matters not covered are shown as general exceptions to coverage on Schedule B, usually being listed just above the individualized exceptions which derive from the results of the company's title search. A typical example is the following language from the Washington Land Title Association's standard owner's policy.

Schedule B, General Exceptions

1. Encroachments or questions of location, boundary and area, which an accurate survey may disclose; public or private easements, streets, roads, alleys or highways, unless disclosed of record by recorded Plat or conveyance, or decree of a Court of record; rights or claims of persons in possession, or claiming to be in possession, not disclosed by the public records; material or labor liens, or liens under the Workmen's Compensation Act not disclosed by the public records; water rights or matters relating thereto; any service, installation or construction charges for sewer, water, electricity, or garbage removal.

2. Exceptions and reservations in United States Patents: right of use, control or regulation by the United States of America in the exercise of powers over navigation; limitation by law or governmental regulation with respect to subdivision, use, enjoyment or occupancy; any prohibition or limitation on the use, occupancy or improvement of the land resulting from the rights of the public or riparian owners to use

any waters which may cover the land; defects, liens, encumbrances, or other matters created or suffered by the insured; rights or claims based upon instruments or upon facts not disclosed by the public records but of which rights, claims, instruments or facts the insured has knowledge.

3. General taxes not now payable; matters relating to special assessments and special levies, if any, preceding the same becoming a lien.

4. "Consumer credit protection," "truth-in-lending," or similar law, or the failure to comply with said law or laws.

————

In addition to these exceptions from coverage, many of the "lower-grade" owners' policies do not cover rights of access and do not insure marketability of title. Several companies in recent years have begun offering upgraded versions of these policies for one-to-four-family home owners; they typically provide coverage for access to a public street and for unrecorded mechanics' liens and tax and assessment liens, and also for interference to the use of the house caused by encroachment of the house on adjoining land or by easements, or by violations of restrictive covenants or zoning ordinances. Such policies thus give coverage which is closer to that of the "full" ALTA owner's policy, although still somewhat deficient. The average owner, of course, has no conception of any of this, and might be quite taken aback to learn that his or her policy did not have "full" coverage.

Another type of improvement made in owners' policies by several companies in recent years is the "inflation protection endorsement", by which the company agrees to increase the dollar coverage of the policy each year by the percentage increase in the Composite Construction Cost Index published by the Department of Commerce, with an upper limit of 150% of the policy's original face amount. This is a valuable change, since without it policy amounts tend to become obsolete very quickly in an inflationary economy.

Lenders' policies differ from owners' policies in several important ways. The insuring language at the beginning of the policy is generally broader; the 1970 ALTA loan policy tracks the 1970 owner's policy reprinted above, but adds the following items after the four in the owner's policy (ending with unmarketability of title):

5. The invalidity or unenforceability of the lien of the insured mortgage upon said estate or interest except to the extent that such invalidity or unenforceability, or claim thereof, arises out of the transaction evidenced by the insured mortgage, and is based upon

a. usury, or

b. any consumer credit protection or truth in lending law;

6. The priority of any lien or encumbrance over the lien of the insured mortgage;

7. Any statutory lien for labor or material which now has gained or hereafter may gain priority over the lien of the insured mortgage, except any such lien arising from an improvement on the

land contracted for and commenced subsequent to Date of Policy not financed in whole or in part by proceeds of the indebtedness secured by the insured mortgage which at Date of Policy the insured has advanced or is obligated to advance.

8. Any assessments for street improvements under construction or completed at Date of Policy which now have gained or hereafter may gain priority over the insured mortgage; or

9. The invalidity or unenforceability of any assignment, shown in Schedule A, of the insured mortgage or the failure of said assignment to vest title to the insured mortgage in the named insured assignee free and clear of all liens.

Lenders' policies, unlike owners' policies, are generally assignable; thus, a secondary market purchaser of the mortgage gets the benefit of the policy. If the mortgagee purchases at a foreclosure sale of the mortgage, the policy's protection continues.

MAYERS v. VAN SCHAICK

Court of Appeals of New York, 1935.
268 N.Y. 320, 197 N.E. 296.

LOUGHRAN, J. On May 8, 1928, the board of trustees of the village of Scarsdale resolved to establish a village park and playground and to assess 70 per cent. of the expense of that improvement against the owners of lands designated upon an assessment map as comprising the district to be benefited thereby. The cost of the project having meantime been determined, the board, on June 12, 1928, apportioned 70 per cent. thereof upon the respective properties so assessed, including premises of Eleanor M. Grieve against which was allotted $960.65 of the localized burden.

The board then further resolved: "That the said assessments become due and payable in forty equal annual installments commencing with the year 1929, with interest on unpaid balances at the rate of four and one-quarter per cent per annum; * * * and * * * that the amount of the said assessments falling due in any year, including interest, shall be included in the annual tax levy of such village for such year and become due concurrently with the general village tax." These proceedings were taken and completed pursuant to section 280 of the Village Law (Consol.Laws, c. 64) and within 15 days thereafter became final and conclusive accordingly.

On May 22, 1933, Lawyers Title & Guaranty Company issued to plaintiff its certificate that title to the premises of Eleanor M. Grieve in the village of Scarsdale was, as of that date, vested in her "clear of all requirements, liens, encumbrances and defects except as in said instrument noted, and agreed to insure plaintiff against the existence of any and all requirements, liens, encumbrances and defects not therein noted." In reliance on this instrument, plaintiff thereupon purchased the title thus insured. The certificate made no reference to the above-mentioned local assessment to be borne by the premises after 1928, as part of the expense of the park and playground improvement laid out in that year by the trustees of the village of Scarsdale. Installments of this assessment had been paid to and including 1932. Under the resolutions of the trustees, further installments were to become due annually thereafter to and including 1968, in the aggregate sum of $863.97.

This is an action to recover that sum as the amount of a liability covered by the certificate of title insurance issued to plaintiff by Lawyers Title & Guaranty Company. No cause of action for negligence in searching the insured title is alleged. The superintendent of insurance, as rehabilitator of Lawyers Title & Guaranty Company, is made defendant. The Special Term granted his motion for judgment on the pleadings and dismissed the complaint. The Appellate Division affirmed. Plaintiff is here by leave of this court.

Title insurance operates to protect a purchaser or a mortgagee against defects in or encumbrances on a title existing at the date of such insurance. It is not prospective in its operation and has no relation to liens or requirements arising thereafter. * * * The full form of the certificate of insurance of plaintiff's title is not before us. We have only so much of the text as has been quoted from his pleading. On that text, the issue is whether the unpaid installments of the assessment in question were on May 22, 1933, an existing requirement of, or a lien or incumbrance on, or a defect in the title then acquired by plaintiff. His contention that such a lien existed at that time is based upon sections 280, 116 and 113 of the Village Law. We find no warrant for his position in these sections.

Section 280 contains the provisions under which the assessment was laid. That section does not provide that any assessment for a local improvement thereby authorized, shall be a lien on property benefited. By subdivision 6 of that section it is provided (and the village trustees here so resolved) that: "If the said assessments are payable in more than one installment, the amount thereof becoming due in any year may be included in the annual tax levy of such year * * * and in case of default in payment said assessments, with interest and penalties, may be collected in the same manner as delinquent village taxes." Section 116 provided: "The annual village tax is a lien * * * on real property on which it is levied from the fifteenth [now the first] day of June of the year in which it is levied. * * * "

All installments of this assessment were paid to and including 1932. No installment unpaid on May 22, 1933 (the date on which the certificate of insurance issued), was then a lien on this title, or could become such a lien before June 15 of that year, by force of anything provided in sections 280 and 116 of the Village Law.

Section 113 of that statute has no application here. It defines the effect of assessments for named purposes which do not include the local improvements authorized by section 280.

The village board of trustees "may declare and provide that the cost of all local improvements or of any other work or benefit to or for abutting property as determined by it, shall be a lien upon the property." Village Law, § 89, subd. 38. The board of trustees of Scarsdale here elected not to follow that course, but rather to adopt the optional alternative method made available by section 280 of the statute. See subdivision 7.

It follows, we think, that Lawyers Title & Guaranty Company no more agreed with plaintiff to protect him against liability for the unpaid assessment in question than it undertook to indemnify him for taxes to be levied against the premises after delivery of its certificate of title insurance.

The judgment should be affirmed, with costs.

FINCH, J. (dissenting). The Lawyers Title & Guaranty Company, by a policy of insurance, agreed to give the plaintiff a clear title, free of all requirements, objections, and defects, except as these were noted in the policy of title insurance. It is not necessary that the objection or requirements should amount to a lien, but what is stated in the policy of title insurance is that any defect is insured against except those noted. Here, by the conceded facts, this plaintiff's property was subjected to a fixed assessment for a local improvement which was to become due and payable yearly in forty equal annual installments, commencing in the year 1929, with interest on the unpaid balance at the rate of $4\frac{1}{4}$ per cent. per annum, the amount of assessment to be added each year to the annual tax.

The certificate upon which the plaintiff relied certified to the plaintiff that title to the premises was vested in Eleanor M. Grieve, clear of all requirements, liens, incumbrances, and defects, except as in said certificate noted, and agreed to insure the plaintiff against the existence of any and all requirements, liens, encumbrances, and defects not therein noted. The complaint is based on the foregoing certificate. The plaintiff alleges in his complaint that this defect amounts also to a lien, but the plaintiff may succeed upon proof that the future installments are an objection to title not noted in the policy although they do not amount to liens. That this assessment for a part constitutes a defect and objection to title admits of no doubt. It is payable in annual installments for 40 years to come, with interest at $4\frac{1}{4}$ per cent. from the time the assessment was completed and could have been paid without interest. Such interest also is to be computed on the entire amount of the assessment, and not on the amount of each installment. The interest is either a penalty for non-payment of the assessment or is a charge for the extension of the time for payment by the exercise of the option to pay in installments. In either case, this evidences the fact that the entire assessment was payable when this amount was determined and lends support to the plaintiff's contention that this objection and defect also amounts to a lien. But, as already noted, this defect in title need not amount to a lien to come within the terms of the certificate, which agrees to protect plaintiff against not only liens but also against all requirements, defects, and objections not noted in the policy by way of exception as not being insured against.

Every year for 40 years this additional amount will be added to plaintiff's ordinary tax bill. In accordance with established practice, the total amount of these unpaid installments of assessments would have been deducted from the purchase price at the time of closing of title, if they had been disclosed to appellant as the title company agreed to do.

The title company urges that although no policy was issued the certificate is to be construed as containing all the terms and conditions contained in the policy ordinarily issued by the company. This contention would not seem justified by the facts, but even assuming that it were so, it does not avail respondent. The agreement of the title company was to note among the exceptions not insured against, the existence of any and all requirements, objections, and defects, and in default thereof to insure against their existence. The fact that the policy of insurance to be issued merely stated that plaintiff was not insured against assessments payable in installments is not material to excuse the failure to comply with the agreement by the title company to bring to the attention of the insured the existence of future installments by way of exception. In any event, the wording of the policy in this regard is ambiguous and in accordance with the usual rule must be taken most strongly against respondent.

The measure of damages of the appellant is at least the difference between the value of the property subject to the assessment and free from it. * * *

Title insurance policies are intended to inform the purchaser of any defects in the title, claims against or burdens or requirements on the property. Unless defects or objections are noted, at least in the exceptions, the policy becomes valueless. An assessment levied against the property, although not a lien nor payable until the future, is clearly a burden on the property concerning which the purchaser seeks information. To hold that although objections to a title are not noted either by way of exception or otherwise, those insuring the title are not liable, is to render useless title insurance.

The judgment dismissing the complaint should be reversed and a trial had for the purpose of determining the damages of plaintiff.

CRANE, C.J., and LEHMAN, O'BRIEN, and CROUCH, JJ., concur with LOUGHRAN, J.

FINCH, J., dissents in opinion in which HUBBS, J., concurs.

Judgment affirmed.

Notes and Problems

1. If no title insurance policy was issued to plaintiff in the principal case, why does the majority refer to "the title thus insured" and discuss the scope of protection under a title insurance policy? Wouldn't the title insurance company's liability (if any) under its "certificate of title" be the same as that of an attorney rendering an opinion on the title? Compare Glyn v. Title Guarantee & Trust Co., 132 App.Div. 859, 117 N.Y.S. 424 (1909), where the court said:

"It will be observed that defendant undertook to act for plaintiff in two capacities—as a conveyancer, who examined the title and undertook to advise her whether it was good and marketable, and as an insurer, who undertook to insure that she had a good and marketable title. In the former capacity, the defendant assumed the same responsibilities and owed to the plaintiff the same duty as if it had been an individual attorney or conveyancer. This involved upon its part the exercise of due care and skill in investigating the title, and the utmost frankness toward the plaintiff in disclosing to her the result of its investigations, and in advising her as to what course she should take in view of the facts which had been discovered respecting the title. It has assumed toward the plaintiff the relation of attorney, and thereby assumed all the obligations of an attorney to his client."

In Metropolitan Life Ins. Co. v. Union Trust Co. of Rochester, 283 N.Y. 33, 27 N.E.2d 225 (1940), where the title company actually issued title insurance policies to plaintiff, the court reached the same conclusion as it did in the principal case (Mayers v. Van Schaick) with respect to the meaning of the terms "encumbrances upon or liens or charges against the title of the mortgagors or grantors," holding that these terms did not include "inchoate" assessments for local improvements.

For a full discussion of the title insurance company's duty to search and to include all defects in title in its title report or certificate, see Comment, Title Insurance: The Duty to Search, 71 Yale L.J. 1161 (1962); Note, Washington Title Insurers' Duty to Search and Disclose, 4 U. Puget Sound L.Rev. 212 (1980).

2. New York Title Guarantee & Trust Co. issued a title insurance policy with the standard exceptions set out to the text preceding the principal (Mayers) case. About a year after the policy was issued, the City of New York undertook to grade the street adjacent to the insured premises. As a result, the street level was raised about seven feet; and the insured was consequently forced to raise his house and fill in his land to conform to the new street grade. When the title insurance was issued there was on file, in the Topographical Bureau of the Borough of Queens, a map of the street system for the area where the insured's property was located, which map indicated that the change in grade of the street adjacent to the insured's property had been proposed. Should Title Guarantee & Trust Co. be liable for the expense incurred by the insured in raising his house and filling in his land to conform to the new street grade? See Sperling v. Title Guarantee & Trust Co., 227 App.Div. 5, 236 N.Y.S. 553 (1929), affirmed 252 N.Y. 613, 170 N.E. 163 (1930).

3. Plaintiff loaned the sum of $10,000 upon a promissory note secured by trust deed of real property, in connection with which transaction the defendant wrote its policy of title insurance, by which it insured plaintiff "as the owner or owners of the indebtedness described in and secured by the mortgage, trust deed or other lien or encumbrance referred to in Schedule A herein, and the successor or successors in interest of said indebtedness (hereinafter called the insured), against all damage or loss of principal, interest or other sums secured by said mortgage, trust deed or other lien or encumbrance, which the said Insured shall sustain by reason of defects in the title of the maker or makers of the said mortgage, trust deed or other lien or encumbrance securing said indebtedness existing at the date of the recording thereof, to the real property described and pledged to the payment of said indebtedness; * * * "

The policy further contained an exception for "estates, interests, defects or objections to title" arising from "rights or claims of parties in possession * * * which rights or claims are not shown by the public records."

Plaintiff sustained losses as a result of the loan and events which followed, by reason of the following facts: The real property belonged to one Katherine Mintener, who at the time of and subsequent to said transaction was, in person and by her tenants, in actual possession of all of the real property. One Tingley, having procured her signature to a document, forged and altered the same into a grant deed of the real property to a fictitious grantee, Larry E. Ketch; he then negotiated a loan of $10,000, with the plaintiff herein and executed in the name of Ketch the note and trust deed. The deed and trust deed were recorded at the same instant, and the policy of insurance was issued simultaneously therewith. Thereafter Katherine Mintener brought an action to quiet title against the plaintiff and defendant herein and others, which action plaintiff called upon defendant to defend, which defendant declined to do. Plaintiff thereupon employed counsel to defend the action, and expended therein the sum of $1,220.47. Katherine Mintener prevailed, and her title was quieted against the lien of the trust deed. In addition to the amount expended in defending the action, plaintiff suffered a loss on account of the money loaned on the trust deed in the amount of $7,847.92, and for these aggregate amounts judgment was given in favor of plaintiff herein.

The defense was that plaintiff's loss was one which was not insured against, and in support thereof reliance is placed upon the exception quoted above from schedule B of the policy. Defendant argued as follows: At the time the policy was issued, Katherine Mintener was in possession of the land; at that identical moment the forged deed was recorded, and thus the rights and claims of Katherine Mintener were not shown on the public records at the time the policy was issued, and therefore were not insured against.

What result? See Coast Mutual Building-Loan Association v. Security Title Insurance & Guarantee Co., 14 Cal.App.2d 225, 57 P.2d 1392 (1936).

4. A mortgagee obtained a policy of title insurance on the mortgaged land in which policy the mortgagee was insured against any loss or damage by reason "of any defect in the title of the insured to the estate or interest described." The mortgage, shortly thereafter, was declared invalid under the Bankruptcy Act as a preference. Such invalidity was not specifically excepted in the policy of title insurance. Does the policy of title insurance protect the mortgagee against such risk? See First National Bank & Trust Company v. New York Title Insurance Co., 171 Misc. 854, 12 N.Y.S.2d 703 (1939).

5. Suppose a title insurance policy contains an exception with respect to claims of "parties in possession" of the premises at the date when the policy was issued. When the insured owners acquired title to the premises and obtained the title policy, they were unaware of a pipeline extending under the land and a recorded easement authorizing such a pipeline. The title insurer apparently missed the recorded easement in its title search and guaranteed that the purchasers of the premises had acquired a good and indefeasible title, subject to the exception for claims of "parties in possession." In an action by the insured owners to recover on the title policy, what result? See Shaver v. National Title & Abstract Co., 361 S.W.2d 867 (Tex.1962).

LAWYERS TITLE INSURANCE CORP. v. McKEE

Texas Court of Civil Appeals, 1962.
354 S.W.2d 401.

MASSEY, Chief Justice. From a judgment in favor of William R. McKee, as plaintiff policyholder, against defendant Lawyers Title Insurance Corporation, the latter appealed.

Judgment reformed and affirmed.

In 1880 a tract of land in Tarrant County, Texas, of rectangular shape but with the eastern boundary a meander line following a ravine, was owned by one Wiggins. The property was known as the Hudgins Homestead. Total acreage of the tract comprised some 72 acres, more or less.

Through a trade with one Nash, his neighbor, Wiggins conveyed approximately 2 acres out of said tract to Nash. By the deed of conveyance the eastern boundary of Wiggins' land became what may be considered as a straight line on the high ground immediately west of the ravine, the ravine passing to Nash, and Wiggins' remaining land comprised some 70 acres. Nash never recorded his deed, but began to run livestock on the 2 acres purchased, as have his heirs since that time.

Subsequently, Wiggins sold the 70 acres remaining to one Wilson. Chain of title thereto from Wilson ultimately passed to the plaintiff in this case. Wilson conveyed the land to one McGinnis, and in the deed the land conveyed was described as though it was the entire original Wiggins tract, the Hudgins Homestead, with the eastern boundary line given in metes and bounds as though it followed the meanders of the ravine, with the following additional language, "except a small tract of one acre conveyed to John W. Nash, by J.S. Wiggins, and wife, *   *   *."

McGinnis conveyed to one Coburn, and in the deed the land was described by metes and bounds identical to the description of the original Wiggins tract, with eastern boundary line the "meanderings of the ravine", and with the further recitation: "It being 78 acres more or less of the Thomas Easter 480 acre survey and known as the W. Hudgins homestead, and being the same land that was conveyed to Jack McGinnis by Jassie E. Wilson by deed dated 8th day of November 1930 and shown of record in Vol. 1102 page 635 Deed records of Tarrant County Texas."

Coburn conveyed to one Tibbits, likewise describing the land by metes and bounds, with the further recitation: "And being the same property described in warranty deed from Jack McGinnis and wife, Corine McGinnis, to R. Lee Coburn and wife, Aline Coburn, dated December 30, 1943, *   *   *."

Tibbits conveyed to plaintiff McKee. The tract conveyed was described as "Being a 73.45 acre tract located about 2 miles Southwest from the Town of Grapevine, Texas, being out of the THOMAS EASTER 480-Acre SURVEY, Patent #792, Volume 9, dated July 10, 1855, known as the W. Hudgins Homestead, described by metes and bounds as follows:" (here followed metes and bounds description in which instead of language as to the eastern boundary as "THENCE North 542 varas with meanderings of the ravine", the calls of the meanderings of such ravine were given according to a survey along same), with the further recitation: "It being the intention of the Grantors herein to convey to Grantee herein the same land described in Deed from R. Lee Coburn and wife, Aline Coburn to Robert Eugene Tibbits and wife, Helen Elizabeth Tibbits, by Deed dated February 12, 1948, filed for record March 16, 1948 *   *   *."

Pursuant to his purchase plaintiff McKee contracted with defendant company, subject to its examination of title, to insure his title to the property. It is not an issue and is undisputed that plaintiff believed he was purchasing land, the eastern boundary of which followed the meanders of the ravine, i.e., that the land included the 2 acres Wiggins had conveyed to Nash. He caused a survey of the land, including the 2 acres, to be prepared and furnished to the company.

The company issued to plaintiff on September 12, 1953, the same date as plaintiff's deed from Tibbits was filed for record, its policy of title insurance. Thereby the company guaranteed to plaintiff, his heirs, executors and administrators that he had good and indefeasible title to the following real property: "Situated in Tarrant County, Texas, being a 73.45 acre tract located about 2 miles Southwest from the Town of Grapevine, Texas, being out of the THOMAS EASTER 480-Acre SURVEY, Patent #792, Volume 9, dated July 10, 1855, known as the W. Hudgins Homestead, described more fully by metes and bounds in Warranty Deed referred to below: * * *." The deed was that to plaintiff from Tibbits, material language from which has been heretofore quoted.

After entering into possession, and using the land extending to the ravine, plaintiff discovered that the heirs of Nash were claiming the 2 acres deeded to Nash by Wiggins. Plaintiff called upon the company to clear his title, but the company did nothing. Plaintiff then filed a trespass to try title suit to settle the title to the 2 acres. Prior to such time plaintiff placed the company on notice that the Nash heirs had declared that they would defend their title in such suit. At all material times the company was kept informed, with continuous demands that it defend plaintiff's title. Even after trial of the suit and after judgment was entered, but in time for steps preparatory for an appeal to be taken therefrom, plaintiff continued to call upon the company to take such measures as it might deem appropriate to defend plaintiff's title. The company chose to do nothing, but to defer any action until judgment in the trespass to try title suit had become final.

The judgment in the trespass to try title case recited that plaintiff was a remote grantee, that he was on constructive notice of the fact of prior conveyance to Nash although the deed was not filed of record, by reason of mention made thereof in deeds in his chain of title, and that the Nash heirs were at all material times in continuous, open and notorious possession of the approximate 2 acres. The judgment divested plaintiff of his claim of title, and was dated November 30, 1959.

Plaintiff then brought his suit under the policy, seeking to recover the sum to which he was thereunder entitled plus attorney's fees and expenses necessary to be expended in the trespass to try title suit. Trial was to a jury. The company did not except to the charge and there were no specially requested issues which appear to have been refused. Upon jury findings made the court entered a judgment in favor of the plaintiff and against the company for the sum of $6,000.00, being the difference in market value of the whole tract, or 72 acres, at $36,725.00, and the tract as reduced by the 2 acres as to which title failed at $30,725.00, as of the date of the trespass to try title judgment,—plus the sum of $2,200.00 as reasonable value of attorney's services in defending plaintiff's title in the trespass to try title suit, plus the sum of $52.10 as the reasonable expenses incurred in the same suit, or a total of $8,252.10.

In resolving points of error presented on appeal we will handle by stating questions, the answers we believe proper, and a discussion.

First Question: Is the company liable to plaintiff under the provisions of the policy because his title failed as to the 2 acres? We have concluded that the company is liable therefor.

Propriety of our answer basically depends upon the determination of whether the property designated by the title insurance policy as that as to which title was guaranteed, included the 2 acres, or whether the company guaranteed the ravine as the eastern boundary.

Were this a suit on a warranty by plaintiff against his grantor, and even had therein been a reference to a prior deed *for all purposes,* the metes and bounds description would control. As notice in and of itself such a reference would have no standing to impair grantee's title where reference to it would not be necessary in the determination of the identity and boundary of the land conveyed. Where conveyance is specific, as by metes and bounds, there can be no mistake and no necessity for invoking the aid of a general description and the specific description would control. * * *."

Such being the case in a suit against a grantor under a warranty, certainly would an insurer of the title, privileged to pass upon and actually designating the description of property it insures by its written contract of insurance, be bound under similar rules of construction, even without reference made to those additional rules of construction applicable to insurance contracts.

A situation or condition to which the protection of the policy was made subject, and as to which coverage was specifically excluded, was any instance where there might be "Any discrepancies, conflicts, or shortages in area or boundary lines, or any encroachments or any overlapping of improvements which a correct survey would show." The company contends that a "correct survey" would have shown that the land received by plaintiff did not include the 2 acres, but that the eastern boundary of the land was west of the ravine. Because thereof, says the company, the 2 acres were excluded as subject of insurance under the policy. No authority is cited by the company in support of the contention.

There is no merit to the contention of the company. As applied to the land intended to be insured by plaintiff and the company, the survey which showed the eastern boundary thereof at the ravine, and including the 2 acres in question, was a "correct survey" within the purport and intent of the policy. * * *

Second Question: If the company is liable under the policy of insurance because of the failure of title in plaintiff to the 2 acres, is the liability of the company controlled by provisions of the policy so that it would be an amount less than the actual difference in the value of the property as and when received (or at time loss should properly be deemed to have been sustained) and as it would have been but for the failure of title as and when the property was received (or at time failure of title should be deemed to have been sustained)? Our holding is that the liability of the company is so controlled. Provisions of the policy under which the amount of liability is limited must be honored in calculation and computation of the amount recoverable in the event of partial failure of title.

The policy contains a provision reading as follows: if " * * * such adverse claim or right shall have been held valid by a court of last resort to which either litigant may apply, and, if such adverse claim or right so established shall be for less than the whole of the property, then the liability of the Company shall be (1) only such part of the whole liability limited above as shall bear the same ratio to the (2) whole liability that the (3) adverse claim or right established may bear to the (4) whole property." (Addition of the numbers and brackets supplied.)

The words following the numbers in the brackets in the above paragraph, which we have added for explanatory purposes, may be clarified when their proper interpretation is recognized. To us (1) means the value of that part of the property as to which title failed; (2) means the amount of the whole or maximum liability of the company if the entire title failed; (3) means the value of the right or property as to which title failed; and (4) means the value of the whole property had there been no failure of title. The whole liability, or maximum liability, would of course be the maximum amount payable under the policy, in this instance the sum of $18,362.50, the amount plaintiff paid for the property at the time of its purchase.

By calculation made from answers returned by the jury the value of the property as to which title failed was $6,000.00 on date the judgment was entered divesting plaintiff of his claim on the title to the 2 acres, and was $3,000.00 on the date the property was deeded to plaintiff. From other answers it is furthermore determinable that the value of the property as it would have been had there been no failure of title was $36,725.00 on date the judgment was entered divesting plaintiff of his title claim, and was $18,362.50 on the date the property was deeded to him. As already mentioned the whole liability under the policy was $18,362.50.

With such information a formula by which the monetary amount of the company's liability may be calculated would be:

(1) : (2) = (3) : (4), or
X   : $18,362.50 = $6,000.00 : $36,725.00, or
X   (company's liability) = $3,000.00.

In other words, the liability under the policy was limited to the sum of $3,000.00, although the actual monetary loss sustained, calculated as of the date of the judgment in the trespass to try title case, was $6,000.00. Texas Standard Form policies for title insurance, issued beginning at a time subsequent to the issuance of the instant policy, prescribe that the values for application to such a formula shall be taken as of the date any particular policy is issued, and were this done in the instant case the amount of the company's liability would be the identical figure, $3,000.00. For our discussion and example we have taken the values as of the date the judgment was entered in the trespass to try title suit; however, it not being necessary to the decision in this case we do not pass upon whether this, or the date the policy was issued, was the proper date for liability calculation purposes.

Third Question: Is the Title Company obliged, in an instance where its insured files a trespass to try title suit to recover the title to real estate which is covered by its policy of title insurance, to furnish at its own cost the expense necessarily incident to the prosecution of the suit as "a defense of the assured on a claim against or right to said land, or a part thereof, adverse to the title guaranteed"? We hold that it is ordinarily so obliged, and was in the instant case.

A provision of the policy in question reads as follows: "Said Company * * * shall, at its own cost, defend said assured in every suit or proceeding on any claim against or right to said land, or any part thereof, adverse to the title hereby guaranteed, provided the party or parties entitled to the defense shall, within a reasonable time after the commencement of such suit or proceeding, and in ample time for defense therein, give said Company written notice of the pendency of the suit or proceeding, and authority to defend, and said Company shall not be liable until such adverse claim or right shall have been held valid by a court of last resort * * *."

The circumstances giving rise to the necessity for plaintiff's filing of the trespass to try title case have been stated. Therefrom it is made plain that plaintiff at all material times attempted to get the company to defend his title. There is no question but that his right to title was cast in issue the moment the defendants in said suit filed their answer and pleaded "not guilty". Plaintiff, being out of possession, stood in peril of losing the title by limitations if he did nothing, and was compelled to prosecute the suit so filed by bringing it to trial and obtaining an adjudication of his title. This was also necessary if plaintiff was to lay a predicate for his suit against the company under the policy, unless he was willing to forget his trespass to try title suit and in suit against the company assume the burden of proving that the Nash heirs' title was superior to his own. Possibly the plaintiff would have incurred attorney's fees and expenses at his peril if the company had come forward and confessed that his title had failed for all purposes of the policy of insurance, and admitted liability (except possibly the monetary extent thereof), etc. This the company did not do, but instead chose to wait watchfully in the apparent hope that plaintiff would prevail in the trespass to try title case.

Coverage of the policy being established in the trial between plaintiff and the company, all the benefits thereof were and are property rights to which plaintiff has shown himself entitled. The company was obligated by the policy to furnish, at its own expense, the legal services and expenses in court costs, witness fees and miscellaneous incidental expenses. In this the company defaulted making it necessary for the

plaintiff to furnish them at his own expense. Those reasonable and necessary fees and expenses supplied the measure of actual damages plaintiff sustained from the company's breach of contract in this particular, and such damages were properly awarded to him by the judgment.
* * *

Fourth Question: In testing the application of statutes of limitation as applied to plaintiff's suit against the company, is the policy provision relative to the time for any suit brought thereunder controlling over the general rules for application of statutes of limitation in suits on contract? Our holding is that the policy provisions control.

The policy contains a provision that the "Company shall not be liable until such adverse claim or right shall have been held valid by a court of last resort". The adverse claim or right referred to, as applied to the instant case, would be the claim of the Nash heirs, litigated in the trespass to try title suit.

From the foregoing policy provision it would appear that plaintiff and the company contracted upon the matter of the date of the accrual of the company's liability thereunder, at least as applied to instances where an adverse claim or right is actually determined by a court of last resort. This is a matter upon which the parties could validly contract.

No appeal was taken from the judgment of the trial court, a Judicial District Court of Texas. That judgment became final. The company was afforded notice and reasonable opportunity to appeal the judgment in the trespass to try title case, which opportunity was declined. Under the construction proper to be given under these circumstances, the District Court was a court of last resort. Under principles of estoppel the company cannot be heard to contend to the contrary. Furthermore, its conduct amounted to a denial of liability under the policy and from and after the time liability was denied the policy clause under consideration was not one upon which the company was entitled to rely.

Since no statutory limitation period could be applicable to the instant case, suit on the policy filed less than one year from the date that judgment in the trespass to try title case became final upon failure of any party thereto to perfect an appeal, there was never raised for determination any issue of limitation and none need have been submitted to the jury. Even had the jury answered the issues thereon which were submitted in favor of the company, which was not the case, the answers could have been disregarded for the matter is resolved as a matter of law. The company's contentions upon the matter of limitation are overruled.

Judgment is reformed so as to award plaintiff William R. McKee judgment for $3,000.00 as the part of his loss recoverable under the policy, rather than the $6,000.00 awarded by the trial court. Judgment in other respects, for attorney's fees and expenses, is not disturbed.

As so reformed, the judgment is affirmed. Costs are adjudged against the company, Lawyers Title Insurance Corporation.

Notes and Problems

1. If we assume that the contract provisions will control the measure of damages for failure of title, does it follow that no other liability may be imposed? For example, is there a possible independent tort action for negligent search, or for wrongful failure to defend, under which damages for emotional distress can be recovered, perhaps in excess of the policy limits? See Jarchow v. Transamerica Title Insurance Co., 48 Cal.App.3d 917, 122 Cal.Rptr. 470 (1975), noted in 1976 Brigham Young U.L.Rev. 895.

2. C.B. Beaullieu brought suit against Atlanta Title & Trust Company for an alleged breach of a contract of title insurance, to the plaintiff's damage. In the petition plaintiff alleged that he bought from B.P. Hancock a certain described parcel of real estate in the County of Fulton, State of Georgia, and contracted to pay therefor $8,000; that the defendant, on March 18, 1937, for a consideration of $60 paid to it, issued to the plaintiff its title guaranty policy by which it insured the plaintiff against all loss or damage, not exceeding $7,000, which the plaintiff should sustain by reason of any defect or defects of title affecting the property which the plaintiff had contracted to purchase; that the plaintiff entered into possession of the land, and, after proceeding to build thereon a house early in the month of March, 1937, he ascertained that Mrs. Hal Padgett had an easement in and over the property; that plaintiff notified the defendant of this fact; that the defendant admitted the validity of the easement and requested the plaintiff to allow it to bring suit in the plaintiff's name against Hancock in order to minimize the damage which the plaintiff had sustained; that the plaintiff agreed to this; that on the date of the issuance of the policy the true market value of the property, if unencumbered by the easement, was $15,000; that on this date the true market value of the property encumbered by the easement was $5,000, and that in order to extinguish the easement, the plaintiff would be obliged to purchase the land to which the easement is appurtenant at a cost of $50,000. The plaintiff alleged that the defendant had, on demand of the plaintiff, failed and refused to pay the loss which the plaintiff sustained by the easement upon the property, to the plaintiff's damage of $7,000.

The defendant filed no general demurrer to the petition, but specially demurred thereto on the ground, among others, that the allegation as to the market value of the property was irrelevant and immaterial, and that the plaintiff in alleging his damage to be the difference between the market value of the property, namely $15,000, without the easement or encroachment thereon, and the value with the easement or encroachment thereon, namely $5,000, alleged the wrong measure of damage by reason of the defendant's breach of its contract of title insurance, and that the correct measure of the plaintiff's damage was the difference between the purchase-money of the property, namely $8,000, and the market vlaue of the property with the easement or encroachment thereon.

What result? See Beaullieu v. Atlanta Title & Trust Co., 60 Ga.App. 400, 4 S.E.2d 78 (1939).

Cf. Overholtzer v. Northern Counties Title Insurance Co., 116 Cal.App.2d 113, 253 P.2d 116 (1953).

3. Some insights into the economics of the title insurance industry may be interesting. For calendar year 1978, the industry's total operating revenues from title activities were about $1,210 million. All losses paid during the same year totalled $36.5 million, and attorney fees and other outside expenses in connection with claims settlements totalled another $11.1 million. The total

amount paid out due to claims was thus $47.6 million, or 3.93 percent of operating revenues. This figure seems extremely low by comparison with property or casualty insurance, but it is typical of the title insurance industry.

One reason for the low "loss ratio" is the fact that in many (although by no means all) cases, title insurance premiums cover both the cost of the title search and the assumption of risk. Where an "all-inclusive" premium is charged, the insured is buying mainly the service of a search and examination of the records. The industry likes to point out that it is mainly in the business of loss prevention through careful searches.

The listing below shows some of the main categories of claims experienced in 1978. They are listed in descending order of numbers of claims; not all categories are shown. The total number of claims made in 1978 was 19,089. Note that some claims tend to give rise to much larger amounts of loss payments than others.

Type of Claim	Number	Amount of Loss Payments
Closing and escrow	6,834	$4.59 million
Property taxes	3,867	$2.07 million
Plant & search error	1,959	$5.50 million
Exam & opinion error	1,789	$3.61 million
Miscellaneous risks	1,242	$2.90 million
Mechanics' liens	1,016	$9.73 million
Forgery	270	$2.47 million

It is interesting that the claims resulting from mechanics' liens tend to average nearly $10,000, the largest average amount of all categories. Many mechanics' lien claims result from cost overruns and developer insolvencies in large commercial or residential construction projects; these, in turn, tend to occur during periods when interest rates are high and construction costs are rising rapidly, as was true during the mid-1970's. Some title companies have simply begun refusing to accept liability for mechanics' liens, inserting exclusionary clauses in their policies on construction loans.

(2) Lawyers' Guaranty Funds

In addition to the insistence of "secondary market" investors in mortgages that their security interests should be protected by title insurance, an important reason for the rapid expansion of title insurance since the Second World War is that title insurance companies can and do vigorously advertise their services and solicit business, whereas their lawyer and Torrens system competitors are inhibited from so doing—lawyers, by their canons of ethics, and Torrens registrars by the traditional reluctance of local government agencies to expend funds for advertisement of their services. However, lawyers tend to resist the expansion of title insurance into small towns and rural areas if it threatens to exclude them from title searches and examinations. And such resistance has generated a movement toward establishment of "lawyers' title guaranty funds" in some states. The genesis and general *modus operandi* of these guaranty funds is described as follows in Basye, Clearing Land Titles 15 (2d ed. 1970):

"An independent movement originated in Florida in 1948 which was designed to provide legal advice to both sellers and purchasers in a land transaction and also furnish title insurance.[5] This was known as the Florida Lawyers' Title Guaranty Fund. Such a plan has now been established in several other states.[6]

"The Lawyers' Title Guaranty Funds are organized either as separate corporations or as trusts. Under this plan a lawyer must become a member of the Fund with payment of a small fee or purchase of a limited amount of stock. Only qualified lawyers who specialize in real estate law are accepted. A lawyer for a purchaser or lender examines the record or abstract in the usual way and writes his opinion on it. At the same time the lawyer is authorized to issue an insurance policy for the Fund on the title which he has examined. A charge is made by the Fund for the policy, which is credited to the lawyer's account and expenses incident to that policy are charged to his account. Likewise losses from any claims due to the lawyer's negligence, oversight or incompetence are charged to his account, but other losses are charged against the Fund as a whole. The Lawyers' Title Guaranty Fund provides title insurance for each title transaction equivalent to an ordinary title insurance policy. Purchasers and lending agencies receive independent legal advice throughout a title transaction, and they also get the benefit of title insurance, which they did not receive under the traditional attorney-opinion method based upon a search of the records or under the attorney-abstract method based upon an examination of an abstract of title."

More detail on the operation of the pioneering Florida Lawyers' Title Guaranty Fund is provided in the following excerpt from Yelen, Lawyers' Title Guarantee Funds: The Florida Experience, 51 A.B.A.J. 1070, 1072–1074 (1965):[7]

" * * * As the pioneering effort in the field, The Florida Bar chose to operate in the form of a Massachusetts trust. This form seems to have been well adapted to the purpose. It has given great flexibility to membership and capital requirements while creating a separate legal entity for the operation of the insurance transactions.

"A declaration of trust was filed with the Secretary of State of Florida in 1947 to establish the Lawyers' Title Guaranty Fund. The declaration states categorically that the fund is to be a perpetual trust and not a partnership. It is specifically declared that only the trust's assets shall be liable to creditors and similarly that the members * * * shall have no interest in the assets except as provided in the declaration it-

5. On Lawyers' Title Insurance organizations generally see Carter, A New Role for Lawyers: The Florida Lawyers' Title Guaranty Fund, 45 A.B.A.J. 803 (1959); Carter, Lawyers' Title Guaranty Fund, 8 U.Fla.L.Rev. 480 (1955); Balbach, Title Assurance: A New Approach to Unauthorized Practice, 41 Notre Dame Lawyer 192 (1965); Rooney, Bar Related Title Insurance: The Positive Perspective, 1980 So.Ill. U.L.J. 263 (1980).

Several other articles too numerous to cite here have appeared in various State Bar Journals.

6. At the present time Funds have been established and are functioning in Arkansas, Colorado, Connecticut, Illinois, Indiana, Kansas, Kentucky, Minnesota, Nebraska, Ohio, Utah and Wisconsin and are being planned in at least six other states. See Fiflis, Land Transfer Improvement: The Basic Facts and Two Hypotheses for Reform, 38 Colo.L.Rev. 431 at 449 (1966).

7. Copyright, 1965, American Bar Association Journal.

self. The members' only right to control or manage the trust estate or activities is the right to elect trustees as provided.

*   *   *

"To become a member of the fund it is necessary to be a member of the Bar with two years' experience in examining titles in individual practice or one year's experience in association with an attorney of five years' practice. A membership committee must pass on all applicants, but it is not intended to reject membership for any but professional reasons. There are provisions for a limited membership for attorneys with less than the required experience.

*   *   *

"Despite the large accumulation of assets and reserves, there is always the danger that a series of large claims might overtax the fund's economic strength. For that reason the fund reinsures certain of its risks. *   *   *

*   *   *

"One of the major features of the fund is that the individual lawyer issues the title guarantee. Each member is authorized to issue the guarantee of the fund up to a principal amount of $100,000. For any commitment over that amount prior review and approval must be secured from the fund. This method fits in ideally with the concept of a title guarantee issued by a lawyer as part of the regular services he performs for his clients.

"The procedure creates a possibility of the fund's being liable for excessive guarantees issued by careless or unscrupulous members. One danger is that a member might deliberately issue a guarantee exceeding $100,000 without prior approval. The policy forms do not state a limit, making it difficult for the fund to deny recovery to an innocent guarantee holder.

*   *   *

"There are some problems which might arise as a result of the fund concept. One is the existence of a possible conflict of interest on the part of an attorney caught between his own client and the fund of which he is a member and an agent.

"One possibility of conflict arises from one of the fund's regulations. Regulation 4(2)(d) refers to the situation in which a member is examining a title previously insured by the fund and finds an unexcepted defect which existed prior to the previously issued guarantee or policy. The regulation requires the member to notify the fund and receive its advice before disclosing his discovery. The fund is then obligated to investigate the defect and attempt to clear the title. This regulation makes the member's duty to the fund superior to the duty to his client—a clear conflict of interest which may work to the detriment of the client and violate the basic tenets of the attorney-client relationship.

"There are a number of situations in which the delay in disclosure to the client would be to his disadvantage. For example, the client may be involved in a number of prospective purchases which would require an immediate decision as to whether to purchase or reject. It is also possible to imagine a seller who refuses other prospective buyers while waiting for a title opinion for his first would-be purchaser. Although there may not be many cases of this nature, the fact remains that there is a possibility of a direct conflict between the attorney's duty to his client and his duty to the fund.

"There is another possible conflict more general in terms. In the event of a claim against the fund, the attorney representing the claimant would be subject to a conflict of interest if he were also a member of the fund. A member of the fund is its cestui que trust, and any recovery against the fund would adversely affect his account. Thus, an attorney representing a claimant would be arguing against his own interest. This could ordinarily be avoided by having claims represented by attorneys who were not members. The very nature of the fund, however, will not permit this easy solution. Since the membership is solely for lawyers, it is quite likely that in any single community the best legal talent will be members; in some communities all attorneys might be members. If this were the case, how could a claimant find counsel? The entire point must rest on the question of where to draw the line to delineate a financial interest sufficient to create a conflict of interest for the attorney. * * * "

The experience of the Florida Lawyers' Title Guaranty Fund does not clearly indicate whether costs to the public are less when insurance is obtained from the Guaranty Fund than when it is obtained from commercial title insurance companies. When the Guaranty Fund first started operating it issued a schedule of rates to be charged to the public which was identical with those of local commercial companies. Subsequently the old rate schedule was revoked and the Guaranty Fund issued a schedule incorporating substantial reductions in charges.

Generally, as to "title insurance," see Cunningham § 11.14.

SECTION 3. IMPROVEMENT OF THE EXISTING SYSTEM OF TITLE ASSURANCE BY LEGISLATION

INTRODUCTORY NOTE

As will more fully appear in the next chapter,[1] purchasers of land are generally under no obligation to complete a contract for the purchase and sale of land unless the vendor's title is "good and marketable." This is true whether the vendor is obligated by the contract to provide an abstract of title for examination by the purchaser's attorney or not; and it is also true even where the vendor has the alternative of supplying a policy of title insurance in lieu of an abstract, unless insurability of the title is expressly substituted for marketability as the criterion of acceptability to the purchaser. In any case, a title insurance company will not insure the marketability of a title unless its own title examiners conclude that the title meets the judicial test of marketability.

---

1. See Chapter 12, Section 2.

The judicial approach to the problem of determining the marketability of land titles, although it has varied a good deal from one state to another and from one period of time to another, can fairly be described as predominantly "negative." Indeed, one writer attributes most of the difficulties connected with the examination of land titles to "the narrow and technical definition of marketable title adopted by the courts." Hendricks, Defects in Titles to Real Estate and the Remedies, 20 Marq. L.Rev. 115 (1936) at 117. Equally important, however, would seem to be the attitude of the attorneys who examine land titles for the purpose of passing upon their marketability. Every title examiner owes a duty to his client to advise him not only whether, in his opinion, the title under examination is good, but whether it is likely to be acceptable to a subsequent title examiner acting for a potential purchaser or mortgage lender. Thus, from the title examiner's point of view, a "marketable" title is not merely one which can be forced upon an unwilling purchaser; it is a title which will be accepted by any other attorney who may be called upon to examine the title at a later time. Although a title examiner may himself be willing to waive a "formal" defect as one not affecting the validity of the title, he must anticipate the possibility that another examiner may subsequently reject the title, or demand that the defect be removed as a condition of completing some later sale or mortgage transaction. If so, the professional reputation of the first examiner will be impaired and his client may suffer substantial financial loss. Since the subsequent examiner of the title may be the most conservative lawyer in the community, the standard of "marketability" tends to become increasingly conservative. As one writer graphically puts it, "unlike water, all conveyancers seek the highest level." Johnson, Mechanics of Title Examination in Massachusetts, in Casner and Leach, Cases and Text on Property 886 (2d ed. 1969), at 887. The result is the practice often referred to as "construing against title," or "fly-specking," which means that the title examiner indulges in a minimum of presumptions of law and fact in favor of the title, demands a full search in every instance, places no reliance upon statutes of limitations, and demands maximum formal proof of title. See Aigler, Clearance of Land Titles—A Statutory Step, 44 Mich.L.Rev. 45 (1945) at 48; Aigler, Clearance of Land Titles—Statutory Steps, 1946 Proceedings of A.B.A. Sec. of Real Prop. Prob. & Trust L. 19, at 21–22; Payne, Increasing Land Marketability Through Uniform Title Standards, 39 Va.L.Rev. 1 (1953) at 9; Payne, The Future of Uniform Title Standards, 1953 Proceedings of A.B.A. Sec. of Real Prop. Prob. & Trust L. 4, at 7; Williams, The Over Meticulous Title Examiner as a Nuisance to the Public and to the Profession, 17 Neb.L.Bull. 98 (Proc.Neb.Bar Assn.1938).

Underlying the uncertainty as to whether a title will be acceptable to another examiner at a later time, which leads to "fly-specking," is the inconclusiveness of the public records as to many matters that may affect the validity of a land title. Among these matters are the following: adverse possession and prescription; forgeries and other frauds; matters of heirship, marriage and divorce; copyists' and recorders' errors; infancy, insanity, and other disabilities; authority of corporate officers; invalidity of acknowledgments; identity of persons; validity of mortgage foreclosures and of judgments and decrees; delivery of instruments; violations of the usury laws; existence of unprobated wills, pretermitted heirs, and posthumous children; falsity of affidavits; revocation of powers of attorney by death or insanity; parol partitions and dedications; inchoate mechanics' liens; extent of restrictive covenants; and facts as to boundaries. McDougal and Brabner-Smith, Land Title Transfer: A Regression, 48 Yale L.J. 1125 (1939) at 1128. Additional matters which cannot be ascertained by searching the public land records are listed by other writers. Because of the inconclusiveness of the public land records, the title examiner must exercise sound legal and practical judgment as to what presumptions of fact and of law he shall rely upon in support of the record title—in what cases he will waive proof of facts necessary to support the record—and, if he decides to insist upon evidence *dehors* the record, as to the nature of the evidence to be required. It is because the lawyer later employed to pass upon the same title may not reach the same conclusions as to presumptions of fact and law and as to proof *dehors* the record, when faced with the same non-conclusive record, that the practice of "fly-specking" has developed. Payne, Increasing Land Marketability Through Uniform Title Standards, 39 Va.L.Rev. 1 (1953) at 2–9; Payne, The Future of Uniform Title Standards, 1953 Proceedings of A.B.A. Sec. of Real Prop. Prob. & Trust L. 4, at 5–7.

The inconclusiveness of the public land records in establishing land titles is paralleled by the inconclusiveness of statutes of limitations designed to cut off ancient interests and encumbrances of record. The major reason for this is that most limitation statutes do not run against owners of future interests, the United States and other governmental units, and "pious or charitable uses," and that the period is extended for persons under disabilities. In addition, the American courts have invented the doctrine of "adverse possession" and have made the operation of limitation statutes relating to land depend upon proof of such adverse possession. As one experienced title examiner has succinctly stated, "the Lord only knoweth when possession is adverse, and all title lawyers will tell you that adverse possession is an exceedingly shaky basis for titles." White, The Title Game, 8 Title News No. 11 (1929) 5, 6. Furthermore, no state requires that titles acquired by adverse possession be made a matter of public record by a proceeding to quiet or register the title; hence there is usually nothing in the public land records to indicate the transfer of title by adverse possession.

The lack of security in land titles based upon inconclusive public records and inconclusive statutes of limitations leads to another basic deficiency in our current system of conveyancing, namely, the requirement of repeated examinations of the same title as successive sale and mortgage transactions occur. Even in localities where the period of search is limited to some period between 40 and 100 years by conveyancing custom, as in New Jersey, it is generally true that each sale or mortgage of a particular tract of land results in a new search and examination of the title over the full period covered by the search. As one writer has pointed out, it is an anomaly that a title passed upon by a competent attorney must thereafter be subjected to another complete scrutiny before a second sale or mortgage can be consummated—an anomaly that constitutes an indictment of the technical skill of searchers and examiners in general; and though it may be argued that there is no assurance that the prior examinations of title were competently performed, such an argument is hardly persuasive when the title has been passed for an institutional mortgage for a large amount and it is certain that the best professional opinion was available. See Payne, The Future of Uniform Title Standards, 1953 Proceedings of A.B.A. Sec. of Real Prop. Prob. & Trust L. 4, at 6. The same writer has also pointed out the paradox of title practice in areas where commercial abstracts are employed, which requires that, on each successive transfer or mortgage, the abstract need merely be "continued" to date, whereas all earlier attorneys' certificates as to the sufficiency of the abstract are ignored and a complete reexamination of the abstract is made. See Payne, The Crisis in Conveyancing, 19 Mo.L.Rev. 214 (1954) at 216, n. 6.

The net result of the defects referred to above has been increasing criticism of our present system of conveyancing as slow, clumsy, wasteful, inefficient, and unduly expensive; as requiring a degree of professional supervision by lawyers incompatible with the use of land as a liquid commercial asset and often disproportionate to the value of the property involved; and as out of keeping with current demands for social institutions of reasonable effectiveness. To this effect, see, in addition to sources already cited herein, Aigler, Title Problems in Land Transfers, 24 Mich.Bar J. 202 (1945) at 213; McDougal, Title Registration and Land Law Reform: A Reply, 8 U. of Chi.L.Rev. 63 (1940) at 65–66; Report on Land Title Law of the State of California (State Land Commission, 1953) 15, 90, 95; Report of Committee on Acceptable Titles to Real Property, 1953 Proceedings of A.B.A. Sec. of Real Prop. Prob. & Trust L. 43, at 43–44; Russell and Bridewell, Land Title Examination: An Appraisal, 14 J.Land & Pub.Util.Econ. 133 (1938); Spies, A Critique of Conveyancing, 38 Va.L.Rev. 245 (1952) at 245–250. Despite the lack of reliable data on the point, it seems clear that the present system is unreasonably expensive. One experienced investigator has estimated that "legal costs"—mainly for title examination—attendant upon the transfer of urban residential property total, on the average between 2 and 3 per cent of the purchase price. Colean, The Impact of Government on Real Estate Finance in the United States (1950) 4, n. 1.

The criticism of the present system has been accompanied by numerous suggestions for improvement. These range from suggested changes in substantive law (e.g., abolishing or modifying the common law estates of dower and curtesy; placing time limits on the duration of possibilities of reverter or powers of termination) to proposed legislation which is specifically designed to bring greater ease in using public land records, greater speed and greater certainty to the conveyancing process. An analysis of defects and possible changes in our present system is found in Whitman, Optimizing Land Title Assurance Systems, 42 George Washington L.Rev. 40 (1973). See also five articles from a Symposium: Computerization of Land Title Records, 43 U. of Cincinnati L.Rev. 465 (1974).

The most important legislative proposals are discussed in the following pages.

A. THE UNIFORM SIMPLIFICATION OF LAND TRANSFERS ACT (1977)

Various portions of the Uniform Simplification of Land Transfers Act (1977) have already been noted in the chapter on priorities and recording. In essence, this Act brings together in a single statute most of the legislative reforms which have been proposed. It specifically limits the duration of a possibility of reverter or power of termination (§ 3–409). It contains a variety of "curative" provisions which are designed to make public land records more conclusive at an earlier date.[2] It establishes a one-year statute of limitations for minor defects in the land records (§ 3–401) and a three-year limitation for proceedings attacking documents which purport to be executed by personal representatives, executors, administrators, guardians, sheriffs and the like on grounds that the records concerning the transactions are incomplete (§ 3–402(a)). A similar limitation is applied to actions alleging a breach of restrictive covenants (§ 3–402(b)). Most importantly, a three-year limitation is established in which to challenge a recorded instrument for lack of delivery (§ 3–402(c)). So far as the general statute of limitations for actions to recover possession of land is concerned, the Uniform Act would establish relatively short periods of five or ten years for most cases (§ 3–404) and markedly reduce the occasions in which the period will be extended by the disability of a claimant (§ 3–407).

The 1981 Southern Illinois University Law Journal, No. 4, contains a series of articles about USOLTA, and includes at page 549, an informative article by Dunham, Reflections of a Statutory Draftsman: The Land Transactions Acts. There are comparisons between the uniform acts and the present Illinois law.

The USOLTA incorporates a "Marketable Record Title" provision, derived from the Model Marketable Act, the operation of which should be noted in more detail.

B. MARKETABLE TITLE LEGISLATION

Marketable title legislation represents one effort at simplifying land transactions. The first statute of this general type was adopted in Iowa in 1919. A later version of this statute was held, in Lane v. Travelers Insurance Co., 230 Iowa 973, 299 N.W. 553 (1941), to be effective to bar contingent remainders. Minnesota adopted a Marketable Title Act in 1943. The Act had serious defects, and was extensively amended in 1945 and again in 1947. A Marketable Title Act somewhat like Minnesota's was adopted in Michigan in 1945. At the present time at least 18 states have Marketable Title Acts. These states are Connecticut, Florida, Illinois, Indiana, Iowa, Kansas, Michigan, Minnesota, Nebraska, North Carolina, North Dakota, Ohio, Oklahoma, South Dakota, Utah,

---

2. The best discussion of "curative" statutes in detail, including a discussion of constitutional limitations, is found in Basye, Clearing Land Titles, Part III (2d ed. 1970).

Vermont, Wisconsin, and Wyoming. A statute of more limited application is found in Indiana—The Dormant Mineral Interests Act, Ind.Code 1971, 32–5–11. The act was recently held to be constitutional in Texaco, Inc. v. Short, 454 U.S. 516, 102 S.Ct. 781, 70 L.Ed.2d 738 (1982). The case is discussed in Pindar, Marketability of Titles—Effect of Texaco, Inc. v. Short, 34 Mercer L.Rev. 1005 (1983).

Set out below, with comments, is that part of the Uniform Simplification of Land Transfers Act which deals with marketable record title, including 1983 amendments.

PART 3. MARKETABLE RECORD TITLE

Introductory Comment

This Part derives from the Model Marketable Title Act, which traces its history to legislation earlier adopted in Michigan, Wisconsin, and Ontario. The Model Act was prepared by Professor Lewis M. Simes and Clarence B. Taylor for the Section of Real Property, Probate and Trust Law of the American Bar Association and for the University of Michigan Law School. It is discussed in L.M. Simes & C.B. Taylor, The Improvement of Conveyancing by Legislation (Ann Arbor: University of Michigan Law School, 1960), pp. 6–16. Legislation based upon the Michigan Act or the Model Act exists in Indiana, South Dakota, Nebraska, North Dakota, Ohio, Oklahoma, Utah, Connecticut, Iowa, Florida, and Vermont. Marketable title legislation on somewhat different patterns is found in a number of other states.

The basic idea of the marketable title act is to codify the venerable New England tradition of conducting title searches back not to the original creation of title, but for a reasonable period only. The Model Act is designed to assure a title searcher who has found a chain of title starting with a document at least 30 years old that he need search no further back in the record.

Provisions for rerecording and for protection of persons using or occupying land are designed to prevent the possibility of fraudulent use of the marketable record title rules to oust true owners of property.

The most controversial issue with respect to marketable title legislation is whether or not an exception should be made for mineral rights. This Act follows the Model Act in making no such exception. Any major exception largely defeats the purpose of marketable title legislation, by forcing the title examiner to search back for an indefinite period for claims falling under the exception.

Section 3–301. [Definitions]

In this Part, unless the context otherwise requires:

(1) "Marketable record title" means a title of record, as indicated in Section 3–302, which operates to extinguish interests and claims, existing before the effective date of the root of title, as stated in Section 3–304.

(2) "Records" includes probate and other official records available in the recording office.

(3) "Person dealing with real estate" includes a purchaser of real estate, the taker of a security interest, a levying or attaching creditor, a real estate contract vendee, or another person seeking to acquire an estate or interest therein, or impose a lien thereon.

(4) "Root of title" means a conveyance or other title transaction, whether or not it is a nullity, in the record chain of title of a person, purporting to create or containing language sufficient to transfer the interest claimed by him, upon which he relies as a basis for the marketability of his title, and which was the most recent to be recorded as of a date 30 years before the time marketability is being determined. The effective date of the "root of title" is the date on which it is recorded.

(5) "Title transaction" means any transaction purporting to affect title to real estate, including title by will or descent, title by tax deed, or by trustee's, referee's, guardian's, executor's, administrator's, master in chancery's, or sheriff's deed, or decree of a court, as well as warranty deed, quitclaim deed, or security interest.

Comment

The definition of root of title has been expanded to make it clear that a quitclaim deed or a forgery can be a root of title.

Section 3–302. [Marketable Record Title]

A person who has an unbroken chain of title of record to real estate for 30 years or more has a marketable record title to the real estate, subject only to the matters stated in Section 3–303. A person has an unbroken chain of title when the official public records disclose a conveyance or other title transaction, of record not less than 30 years at the time the marketability is to be determined, and the conveyance or other title transaction, whether or not it was a nullity, purports to create the interest in or contains language sufficient to transfer the interest to either:

(1) the person claiming the interest, or

(2) some other person from whom, by one or more conveyances or other title transactions of record, the purported interest has become vested in the person claiming the interest; with nothing appearing of record, in either case, purporting to divest the claimant of the purported interest.

Comment

This is the basic section which frees the holder of marketable record title from adverse claims antedating his root of title, even if the root of title is a forgery. See Marshall v. Hollywood, 244 So.2d 743 (Fla.App. 1969), affirmed 236 So.2d 114 (Fla.1970).

Section 3–303. [Matters to Which Marketable Record Title Is Subject]

The marketable record title is subject to:

(1) all interests and defects which are apparent in the root of title or inherent in the other muniments of which the chain of record title is

formed; however, general reference in a muniment to easements, use restrictions, encumbrances or other interests created prior to the root of title is not sufficient to preserve them (Section 3–207) unless a reference by record location is made therein to a recorded title transaction which creates the easement, use, restriction, encumbrance or other interests;

(2) all interests preserved by the recording of proper notice of intent to preserve an interest (Section 3–305);

(3) an interest arising out of a title transaction recorded after the root of title, but recording does not revive an interest previously extinguished (Section 3–304); [and]

(4) the exceptions stated in Section 3–306[; and] [.]

[(5) interests preserved by the [Torrens Title Act.]]

Comment

This section states the types of claims to which a marketable record title is subject. As mentioned in the introductory comment, any extension of this list may defeat the whole purpose of marketable title legislation.

Section 3–304. [Interests Extinguished by Marketable Record Title]

Subject to the matters stated in Section 3–303, the marketable record title is held by its owner and is taken by a person dealing with the real estate free and clear of all interests, claims, or charges whatsoever, the existence of which depends upon an act, transaction, event, or omission that occurred before the effective date of the root of title. All interests, claims, or charges, however denominated, whether legal or equitable, present or future, whether the interests, claims or charges are asserted by a person who is or is not under a disability, whether the person is within or without the state, whether the person is an individual or an organization, or is private or governmental, are null and void.

Comment

This section is designed to make absolutely clear what has already been indicated in Section 3–302, that all interests except those indicated in Section 3–303 are extinguished by marketable record title.

Section 3–305. [Effect Upon Marketable Record Title of Recording Notice of Intent to Preserve an Interest]

A person claiming an interest in real estate may preserve and keep the interest, if any, effective by recording during the 30-year period immediately following the effective date of the root of title of the person who would otherwise obtain marketable record title, a notice of intent to preserve the interest (Section 2–308). No disability or lack of knowledge of any kind on the part of anyone suspends the running of the 30-year period. The notice may be recorded by the claimant or by another person acting on behalf of a claimant who is:

(1) under a disability;

(2) unable to assert a claim on his own behalf; or

(3) one of a class, but whose identity cannot be established or is uncertain at the time of recording the notice of intent to preserve the interest.

Comment

A simple method is provided for persons whose title depends solely upon documents which have been of record for more than 30 years to prevent a later recorded document from cutting off the effect of the documents upon which they rely. Suppose real estate was owned by A in 1930 and that he conveyed to B in 1940, to C in 1950, and to D in 1960. If this Act became effective in 1977, then in 1981 C has a marketable record title free of all claims of A and B and superior to that of D. If C does not record a notice of intent to preserve his interest by 1990, D will obtain a marketable record title and C's interest will be extinguished.

Section 3–306. [Interests Not Barred by Part]

This Part does not bar:

(1) A restriction,* the existence of which is clearly observable by physical evidence of its use;

(2) A use or occupancy inconsistent with the marketable record title, to the extent that the use or occupancy would have been revealed by reasonable inspection or inquiry;

(3) rights of a person in whose name the real estate or an interest therein was carried on the real property tax rolls within 3 years of the time when marketability is to be determined, if the relevant tax rolls are accessible to the public at the time marketability is to be determined;

(4) a claim of the United States not subjected by federal law to the recording requirements of this State and which has not terminated under federal law;

[(5) mineral interests including oil, gas, sulphur, coal, and all other mineral interests of any kind, whether similar or dissimilar to those minerals specifically named.]

Comment

This list of exceptions is designed to be as limited as possible, given the restrictions imposed by federal law and the need to avoid use of marketable record title for fraudulent purposes. The provisions on use or occupancy and on tax assessment should virtually eliminate situations in which more than one person can claim marketable record title to the same property. Paragraph (3) derives from the Florida Marketable Record Title Act, F.S.A. Sec. 712.03(6).

Section 3–307. [Effect of Contractual Liability as to Interests Antedating Root of Title]

This Part does not free a person from contractual liability with respect to an interest antedating his root of title to which he has agreed to

* ["Restriction" is defined in § 1–201(24) to include any "covenant, condition, easement, or other limitation created by agreement, grant or implication affecting the use or enjoyment of real estate."—Ed.]

be subject by reason of the provision of a deed or contract to which he is a party, but a person under contractual liability has power to create a marketable record title in a transferee not otherwise subjected to the interest antedating root of title by the provisions of this Part.

Comment

This section is meant to overcome a possible constitutional problem of impairment of the obligations of contracts. Its application is limited so that it should pose no problem for the title examiner.

Section 3–308. [Limitations of Actions]

This Part shall not be construed to extend the period for the bringing of an action or for the doing of any other required act under a statute of limitations.

Section 3–309. [Abandonment in Fact]

This Part does not preclude a court from determining that a restriction has been abandoned in fact, whether before or after a notice of intent to preserve the restriction has been recorded.

Note

For comment on the Model Marketable Title Act, section-by-section, see Simes & Taylor, Improvement of Conveyancing by Legislation 11–16. For a detailed study of Marketable Title legislation, with an extensive bibliography, see id. 295–361. For a more recent and even more detailed treatment of Marketable Title legislation in the various states where it has been adopted, see Basye, Clearing Land Titles, Ch. 9 (2d ed. 1970).

MARSHALL v. HOLLYWOOD, INC.

District Court of Appeal of Florida, 1969.
224 So.2d 743.

REED, Judge. The appellant in this case, E.E. Marshall, as administrator of the estate of Mathew A. Marshall, deceased, has appealed from a final judgment of the Circuit Court in and for Broward County, Florida, dismissing with prejudice his second amended complaint. Appellant was the plaintiff in the trial court.

E.E. Marshall in his capacity as administrator of the estate of Mathew A. Marshall, deceased, filed his initial complaint in this cause on 13 July 1967. The complaint joined a multitude of defendants and sought relief relating to certain real property in Broward County, Florida, in which the defendants claim to have interests adverse to that of the plaintiff. Ultimately the second amended complaint was filed on 5 April 1968. Upon motion, this complaint was dismissed by a final judgment which dismissed the cause with prejudice. It is from the final judgment of dismissal that the present appeal has been taken.

The following statement of facts is taken from the allegations in the second amended complaint. In 1913 the Atlantic Beach Company, a Florida corporation, acquired title to the real property involved in the suit. Mathew A. Marshall was one of the organizers of that corporation. At the time of his death on 31 December 1923 he owned 334 shares of its capital stock. He was then the president of the corporation and a director. The only other director and officer was Carl P. Weidling, the secretary of the corporation. Mr. Weidling owned the remaining 166 shares of stock in the corporation. No other stock was authorized or outstanding at the time of Mathew A. Marshall's death. Carl P. Weidling died in 1963.

On or about 1 February 1924 Louise L. Marshall, the widow and sole heir of Mathew A. Marshall, deceased, left Florida. At that time she had no knowledge that her deceased husband had owned stock in the Atlantic Beach Company at the time of his death.

Letters of administration were issued by the county judge for Dade County, Florida, to Louise L. Marshall dated 5 February 1924. These were issued pursuant to an application for letters bearing the forged signature of Louise L. Marshall. The application for letters made no reference to the stock in Atlantic Beach Company.

On 13 February 1924 a paper entitled "Minutes Of A Meeting Of The Stockholders Of Atlantic Beach Company" was signed and sworn to by Frank M. Terry. This paper purported to be minutes of a meeting on 5 February 1924 of the stockholders of Atlantic Beach Company at which all of the outstanding shares (500) were represented in person or by proxy. The minutes indicate that Frank M. Terry held a number of the shares individually and a proxy for a majority of the shares. One S. Grover Morrow was indicated as holding a proxy for four shares. Terry signed the minutes falsely pretending to be president of the corporation. These minutes were recorded in Deed Book 28 at page 223, public records of Broward County, Florida, on 13 February 1924. The minutes reflect a resolution of the stockholders authorizing the conveyance of all of the assets of the corporation to the stockholders thereof.

On 6 February 1924 Frank M. Terry executed a deed in the name of Atlantic Beach Company as president. The deed purported to convey all of Atlantic Beach Company's property to Frank M. Terry and the other individuals who purported to be—but were not—owners of all of the stock in the corporation. This deed was recorded on 15 February 1924 in the public records of Broward County, Florida. The deed is alleged to have been "falsely made and forged by Frank M. Terry. * * * "

On 14 February 1924 Frank M. Terry and the other grantees under the deed from Atlantic Beach Company executed a deed to Hollywood Realty Company, a Florida corporation. This deed was recorded in the public records of Broward County, Florida, on 11 April 1924. This deed was alleged to be false, spurious, fraudulent, and forged.

On 6 August 1924 a deed was executed by Hollywood Realty Company to Homeseekers Realty Company, a corporation, and recorded in the public records of Broward County, Florida, on 22 August 1924. This deed was also alleged to be false, spurious and forged.

On 15 February 1924 the Circuit Court for Broward County, Florida, entered a decree dissolving the Atlantic Beach Company. This decree was based on the affidavit purporting to be signed by an attorney representing all stockholders of Atlantic Beach Company and falsely representing that he was authorized to seek the dissolution of the Atlantic Beach Company. The affidavit was false and the name of the attorney was forged thereon.

The foregoing transactions were part of a scheme to perpetrate a fraud on the estate of Mathew A. Marshall.

On 25 April 1929 The Highway Construction Company of Ohio, Inc., obtained a judgment against Homeseekers Realty Company. Following a levy and a sheriff's sale, a sheriff's deed to The Highway Construction Company was recorded on 30 December 1930. The deed purports to convey substantially all of the real property involved in this litigation.

On 21 February 1931 a deed from The Highway Construction Company of Ohio, Inc., to the defendant, Hollywood, Inc., was placed of record in the public records of Broward County, Florida.

Diagrammed, the chain of title to the real property involved in this lawsuit, insofar as it is relevant to the issues here involved, looks like this:

Atlantic Beach Company

↓　　　　warranty deed (claimed
　　　　　to be forged and fraudulent)

Frank M. Terry
recorded 2/15/24

↓　　　　warranty deed

Hollywood Realty Company
recorded 4/11/24

↓　　　　warranty deed

Homeseekers Realty Company
recorded 8/22/24　↘

　　　　　　　　Deeds to defendants
　　　　　　　　other than Hollywood,
　　　　　　　　Inc.

Sheriff's Deed

↓

The Highway Construction Company
of Ohio, Inc., recorded 12/30/30

↓　　　　fee simple deed

Hollywood, Inc.
recorded 2/21/31

[A7000]

There were never any stockholders of the Atlantic Beach Company except Mathew A. Marshall and Carl P. Weidling. The Atlantic Beach Company was never legally dissolved until 14 September 1936 when it was dissolved by a proclamation of the governor for failure to pay capital stock tax.

Defendant Hollywood, Inc. and all other defendants knew the deed to Terry et al., to Hollywood Realty Company, and to Homeseekers Realty Company, was null and void.

The sheriff's deed to The Highway Construction Company of Ohio, Inc., was allegedly void because the judgment debtor (Homeseekers Realty Company) did not own title to the property. The deed is also void because the judgment on which the deed was based was, for various reasons, allegedly void.

The defendants other than Hollywood, Inc., claim interests under recorded instruments purporting to create the same from Homeseekers Realty Company. Hollywood, Inc., of course, claims under the recorded deed from The Highway Construction Company of Ohio, Inc.

Louise L. Marshall died in December 1945 without ever having learned of her husband's interest in the Atlantic Beach Company. The plaintiff, E.E. Marshall, a brother of the deceased, Mathew A. Marshall, did not discover any of the facts alleged in the second amended complaint until 1 November 1966.

The land involved in this litigation is wild, unimproved, and not in the possession of any of the defendants.

The second amended complaint demands a decree establishing the interest of the plaintiff in the aforesaid lands of the Atlantic Beach Company, a confirmation of the ownership of the stock by the plaintiff, as administrator of the estate of Mathew A. Marshall, deceased, and the appointment of a trustee for Atlantic Beach Company to convey the legal title to the real property to the heirs of Mathew A. Marshall.

The order which dismissed the second amended complaint stated that it failed to state a cause of action on the ground that the plaintiff's alleged claim affirmatively appeared to be barred by the Marketable Title Act, Section 712, F.S.1967, F.S.A. The issue which has been presented by the parties to this appeal by briefs and oral argument is whether or not the Marketable Title Act applies to the claim of title asserted by the plaintiff in the second amended complaint and extinguishes the same.

The plaintiff, as administrator of the estate of Mathew A. Marshall, deceased, claims to own two-thirds of the stock of the Atlantic Beach Company in his capacity as administrator. As the owner of two-thirds of the stock in the Atlantic Beach Company, the plaintiff claims equitable title to two-thirds of the real property owned by the corporation at the time it was dissolved and that he and the other heirs of Mathew A. Marshall are entitled to the legal and equitable title to the said real property. See Trueman Fertilizer Co. v. Allison, Fla.1955, 81 So.2d 734.

The plaintiff's theory is that Atlantic Beach Company, at the time it was dissolved, still owned the real property in question because the purported deed executed in the name of that corporation by Terry to himself and others was void as a forgery. While there is some doubt as to whether or not the deed executed by Frank M. Terry pretending to be president of the Atlantic Beach Company may be classified as a forgery under the law of Florida, * * * for the purposes of evaluating the second amended complaint, we will accept the plaintiff's characterization of the deed as a forgery and, as such, void. We think the plaintiff's conclusion that the deed was void under the facts alleged in the complaint is inescapable.

The Florida Marketable Title Act, Section 712.01, F.S.1967, F.S.A., was enacted in 1963 and became effective September 1, 1963. It is undoubtedly the most important piece of legislation dealing with real property titles enacted in the State of Florida in many years. We will attempt to determine the legislative intent based upon the language used, the subject matter of the act and the purpose of the act. * * *

The purpose of the act is to simplify and facilitate land transactions by allowing persons interested therein to rely on a record title. Section 712.10, F.S.1967, F.S.A. The purpose of the act is accomplished basically by the provisions of Sections 712.02 and 712.04, F.S.1967, F.S.A. Section 712.02 reads as follows:

"Any person having the legal capacity to own land in this state, who, alone or together with his predecessors in title, has been vested with any estate in land of record for thirty years or more, shall have a marketable record title to such estate in said land, which shall be free and clear of all claims except the matters set forth as exceptions to marketability in § 712.03. A person shall have a marketable record title when the public records disclosed a title transaction affecting the title to the land which has been of record for not less than thirty years purporting to create such estate either in:

"(1) The person claiming such estate; or

"(2) Some other person from whom, by one or more title transactions, such estate has passed to the person claiming such estate, with nothing appearing of record, in either case, purporting to divest such claimant of the estate claimed."

The word "affecting" as it is used in the second sentence of Section 712.02 in the clause "affecting the title to the land" does not carry the narrow meaning of "changing or altering". The word is used in the broader sense meaning "concerning" or "producing an effect upon". In this broad sense, even a void instrument of record "affects" land titles by casting a cloud or a doubt thereon. * * *

All parts of an act should be read together in an effort to achieve a consistent whole. Ideal Farms Drainage District v. Certain Lands, 1944, 154 Fla. 554, 19 So.2d 234. The interpretation which we give the word "affecting" as used in Section 712.02 attributes to it a meaning consistent with the sense in which the same word is used in Section 712.01(3) in the definition of a "title transaction". "Title transaction" is defined as any recorded instrument or court proceeding which *affects* title to any estate or interest in land. If the word "affects" in the definition of a title transaction is interpreted narrowly to mean a recorded instrument which actually transfers or modifies an estate or interest in land, this would exclude from the definition of a title transaction a recorded instrument which "purported" to transfer or modify an estate or interest in land, but which actually did not do so because of some defect or impediment. Such an interpretation would create an inconsistency within the definition of the term "root of title" because it is defined in Section 712.01(2) in terms of *a title transaction* which *purports* to create or transfer an estate.

The first sentence of Section 712.02 states, "Any person * * * who * * * *has been vested with any estate in land of record* for thirty years or more, shall have a marketable record title to such estate in said land, which shall be free and clear of all claims except the matters set forth as exceptions to marketability in § 712.03." (Emphasis added.) The plaintiff argues that the use of the word "vested" in the first sentence of Section 712.02 indicates a legislative intent to apply the operative provisions of the act only to and in favor of a person who is *in fact* vested with some estate in land as distinguished from one who has an *apparent* estate in land. The plaintiff contends that the defendants never were vested with any estate in land because their predecessors in title had no estate. The defendants, therefore, are not entitled to the benefits of the act, and the act is not operative to bar the claim of the plaintiff.

We disagree with this construction placed upon the first sentence of Section 712.02 by the plaintiff. It ignores the total language of the sentence and particularly the words "of record" used therein. Furthermore, since the purpose of the act is to allow persons to rely on the record title to real property, it would be inconsistent to construe the words "vested * * * of record" in that sentence in such a way as to require an inquiry behind the record. The plaintiff's construction would render the first sentence of Section 712.02 inconsistent with the more explicit definition of "marketable record title" which is contained in the second sentence of Section 712.02. In the second sentence, a marketable record title is defined as a title which is *purportedly* created by recorded instruments or court proceedings without reference to that which might be disclosed by facts outside the record title. We conclude, therefore, that Section 712.02 declares the existence of a marketable record title when a person is shown by the record to have been vested with any estate of land for thirty years or more. In our opinion the application of Section 712.02 is not conditioned upon an actual vesting of some estate or interest in a person claiming the benefit of the act.

Prior to the passage of the Marketable Title Act, the broadest statute purporting to cure titles to real property was sections 1 and 2, Chapter 10171, Laws 1925. These sections were codifed as subsections (1) and (2) of Section 95.23, Florida Statutes, F.S.A. and read as follows:

"(1) After the lapse of twenty years from the record of any deed or the probate of any will purporting to convey lands no person shall assert any claim to said lands as against the claimants under such deed or will, or their successors in title.

"(2) After the lapse of twenty years all such deeds or wills shall be deemed valid and effectual for conveying the lands therein described, as against all persons who have not asserted by competent record title an adverse claim."

In Wright v. Blocker, 1940, 144 Fla. 428, 198 So. 88, Section 95.23, F.S.A., was held not to apply to a deed that was void by reason of a forgery of the grantor's name. In Reed v. Fain, Fla.1961, 145 So.2d 858, the Florida Supreme Court on rehearing held that § 95.23, F.S.A., could not be applied to validate a deed executed in violation of the homestead provisions of Article X of the Florida Constitution of 1885. Based upon these decisions, the plaintiff here argues that the Marketable Title Act does not apply to a void deed to eliminate claims of title depending upon transactions antecedent to the void deed. We appreciate the logic of the plaintiff's argument; however, the Marketable Title Act differs in many respects from Section 95.23 which was before the Florida Supreme Court in Wright v. Blocker and Reed v. Fain, supra. Section 95.23 has no express exceptions. The Marketable Title Act does. The specific enumeration of exceptions to the act in Section 712.03 and the specific provision in Section 712.05 for the protection of valid claims indicates a legislative intent to exclude no other claims from extinction by the operation of Sections 712.02 and 712.04. * * * For this reason, we do not believe that the rationale in Wright v. Blocker and Reed v. Fain, supra is pertinent to the Marketable Title Act and hold that under the circumstances depicted by the second amended complaint, the act may be applied to validate a record title even though it may be based on a void deed. Compare Wilson v. Kelley, Case No. 68–421, decided by the Florida Second District Court of Appeal on 14 May 1969 wherein it held that the Marketable Title Act may be applied to a wild deed.

Section 712.02 correlates with Section 712.04. The first sentence of Section 712.04 states that " * * * such marketable record title shall be free and clear of all estates, interest * * *." The phrase "such marketable record title" refers back to the marketable record title declared and defined in Section 712.02. The second sentence of Section 712.04 amplifies upon the claims which are rendered null and void by the marketable record title.

The allegations in the second amended complaint and the exhibits thereto affirmatively reveal "title transactions" which have been of record for not less than thirty years which purport to create a fee simple estate in the lands involved in this suit in the defendant Hollywood, Inc., and the predecessors in title of the other defendants. One such title transaction is the deed from Hollywood Realty Company to the Homeseekers Realty Company recorded on 22 August 1924. The other title transaction is the deed from The Highway Construction Company of Ohio, Inc., to defendant Hollywood, Inc., recorded 21 February 1931. The complaint affirmatively alleges that all of the defendants other than Hollywood, Inc., claim as successors in title under the deed to Homeseekers Realty Company. That nothing appears of record purporting to divest the defendants of their record title to the property is a necessary implication from the affirmative allegation that the defendants have present claims to the land in question. The defendants, therefore, appear from the allegations of the complaint to have a marketable record title as defined in Section 712.02.

Under Section 712.04 this title is cleared of all estates, interests, claims or charges whatsoever the existence of which depends upon any act, title transaction, event or omission that occurred prior to the effective date of the root of title. The deed from Hollywood Realty Company to Homeseekers Realty Company and the deed from The Highway Construction Company of Ohio, Inc., to Hollywood, Inc., are roots of title within the definition of Section 712.01(2). The plaintiff's claim depends on title transactions which occurred prior to the recording of those deeds. We, therefore, conclude that the allegations in the second amended complaint affirmatively indicate a marketable record title in the defendants as the same is defined by the act. And this marketable record title bars the plaintiff's claim unless the claim is exempt from marketability under either Section 712.03 or Section 712.05. Where the plaintiff has pled facts showing that his claim depends on transactions which occurred prior to the defendants' roots of title and a marketable record title in defendants, the plaintiff, to state a cause of action, was obligated to plead facts showing that his claim of title was not extinguished by the otherwise apparent application of the Marketable Title Act.

The plaintiff argues that the deed of record from the Atlantic Beach Company to Frank M. Terry et al., being a void deed, conveyed nothing. From this premise, the plaintiff proceeds to the conclusion that all subsequent deeds under which the defendants in this case claim title were void and conveyed nothing. Therefore, contends the plaintiff, these deeds contained an "inherent defect" which was not cured or affected by the marketable record title. The plaintiff relies on the language of Section 712.03(1) reading:

"Such marketable record title shall not affect or extinguish the following rights:

"(1) Estates or interests, easements and use restrictions disclosed by and defects inherent in the muniments of title on which said estate is based beginning with the root of title * * *."

The terms "defects inherent in the muniments of title" do not refer to defects or failures in the transmission of title, as the plaintiff's argument suggests, but refer to defects in the makeup or constitution of the deed or other muniments of title on which such transmission depends. To accept the plaintiff's proposition would virtually nullify the act because it would preserve from extinction all claims arising out of defective deeds—no matter how far antecedent to the root of title. We accept as sound the view of Professor Barnett who wrote with respect to the exemption now under consideration:

"This exception apparently protects only those interests or claims disclosed by, or based on defects inherent in, the recorded transactions that form the links in the chain of title of the person claiming a marketable record title. The provision means only those links subsequent to and including the root of title itself, although this is not as obvious in the Model Act as in the Florida and Indiana Acts. *For example, if the root of title is itself a forged deed, the act will not extinguish the interest of the person whose name appears as grantor therein, even though his interest 'depends upon [a] * * * transaction * * * that occurred prior to the effective date of the root of title' and is thus otherwise subject to extinguishment under section 3 of the Model Act. Similarly, the act will not eliminate the problem of forgeries in any link subsequent to the root of title, although it will extinguish the right of owners whose names were forged to links in the chain of title prior to the root. * * *"* (Emphasis added.)

Barnett, Marketable Title Acts—Panacea or Pandemonium, 53 Cornell L.Q. 45, 67 (1967). The factual allegations of the complaint demonstrate no defect in the make up or constitution of the deeds previously identified as roots of title or in the subsequent muniments of title. The exemption, therefore, is inapplicable here.

There are no allegations of fact in the second amended complaint indicting that the plaintiff's claim of title is exempt from the effect of the marketable record title by any other provision of Section 712.03. Also there is no factual allegation which would demonstrate that the claim of the plaintiff to the title was preserved by a notice filed in accordance with Section 712.05. In our opinion these were essential allegations where the facts affirmatively alleged show that, but for such an exemption or filing, the plaintiff's claim would be extinguished by the marketable record title held by the defendants. It does not appear from the pleadings, the record, or the briefs, that the plaintiff by a further amendment to the second amended complaint could show that he made such a filing or that his claim was otherwise exempt; therefore, we conclude that the trial court was correct in dismissing the second amended complaint with prejudice.

Finally, the plaintiff contends that his cause of action is based on fraud. It did not accrue, therefore, until the fraud was discovered on or about 1 November 1966. Under Section 95.11(5)(d), F.S.1967, F.S.A. the plaintiff has three years from the discovery of the fraud within which to commence his action. The plaintiff's contention might be proper if this were an action against Mr. Terry for damages; however, in our opinion Section 95.11, F.S.1967, F.S.A. does not apply to an action for the recovery of real property which is the essential nature of the plaintiff's claim.

Because of the great importance to the general public of the statute with which we are here concerned and the need of the bench and the bar for authoritative precedent dealing with the statute, it is our intention, upon receipt of proper application, to certify the decision under F.A.R. 4.5(c)(6), 32 F.S.A., as one passing upon a question of great public interest.

The judgment appealed is affirmed.

Affirmed.

Note

The decision in the principal case was affirmed by the Florida Supreme Court in 236 So.2d 114 (1970). At the end of its opinion the Supreme Court said:

"In summary, although the Atlantic Beach Company/Terry deed initiating the chain of title here was forged, this deed formed but one link in the chain coming *before* the effective roots of title in this case as defined by the Act, i.e., transactions with either The Highway Construction Company or the Homeseekers Realty Company as grantors. Claims arising out of transactions, whether based upon forgeries or not, predating the effective roots of title are extinguished by operation of the Act unless claimants can come in under any of the specified exceptions to the Act. In this case, petitioner fails to qualify under any of the exceptions to the Act, and therefore, petitioner's claims are barred.

"The certified question involved in this cause was, in effect, whether the Marketable Record Titles to Real Property Act, Ch. 712, F.S. confers marketability to a chain of title arising out of a forged or wild deed, so long as the strict requirements of the Act are met. This question is answered in the affirmative." (236 So.2d at 120.)

Suppose, in the principal case, that Louise L. Marshall, the widow and sole heir of Mathew A. Marshall, had known about her deceased husband's stock ownership in the Atlantic Beach Company; that she assumed that she acquired ownership of the land in question when he died; and that in 1926 she executed a deed conveying the land to X, such deed being promptly recorded. As of the date of the litigation in the principal case, would the Florida Marketable Title Act confer a "marketable record" title on X, or on Hollywood, Inc. and the other respondents?

Suppose, in 1967, that Hollywood, Inc. had contracted to sell its interest in the land in question to Y, and that Y had refused to complete the purchase on the ground that Hollywood, Inc., did not have a "marketable title" to the land. Absent a quiet title judgment like the one in the principal case, could Hollywood, Inc. obtain a judgment for specific performance against Y? See the materials in the next chapter dealing with "marketable title."

In Wilson v. Kelley, 226 So.2d 123 (Fla.App.1969), one set of claimants had a continuous record chain of title back to 1916, except that the deed of that date purported only to quitclaim all the title and interest which the grantors had in an undivided one-half interest in the property. Because the deed did not specify what interest the grantors had in the property, the court held that the Marketable Title Act did not apply; the 1916 deed could not constitute a "root of title" within the statutory definition: "any title transaction purporting to create or transfer the estate claimed by" the person claiming the benefit of the Act. By way of dictum, the court pointed out the methods by which a person claiming ownership of land can prevent an interloping or "wild" deed from cutting off his title under the Act: by being a party to a title transaction within the past thirty years, by filing a notice within the time allowed, by remaining in possession of the land, or by having the land assessed to him on the assessment rolls. Special emphasis was given to the worthy and public purpose which the Act serves in simplifying land title examinations and enhancing the marketability of land titles.

In Whaley v. Wotring, 225 So.2d 177 (Fla.App.1969), the trial court entered judgment quieting title to certain land in the defendant-counter-claimant Wotring, but the District Court of Appeal reversed, holding that Wotring's claim under an 1897 land patent to one Sherman was barred by the Florida Marketable Title Act because a 1908 deed in the plaintiffs' chain of title had been on record more than 30 years. The filing of the patent and of quitclaim deeds to Wotring from the heirs of the patentee in 1966 came too late to preserve the patentee's interest, since the Act gave the heirs only until July 1, 1965 to file the notice which would have protected their claim for another 30 years. The claim of the patentee's heirs was already barred when Wotring obtained the quitclaim deeds from them in 1966. It was immaterial that the plaintiffs' record chain of title began with a "wild deed" in 1863. As the court said:

"The crux of this case is the application of Section 95.23 and Chapter 712, the Marketable Record Title Act. As of December 1, 1897, the sovereign had by means of a patent divested itself of any claim to the subject land. As of said date, the records of Clay County, Florida, reflected that the subject land was owned by Blake & Benedict, as trustees, claiming through predecessors back to 1863. In 1908 Blake and the heirs of Benedict, by an instrument duly recorded in Clay County, Florida, conveyed the subject land * * * to Charles A. Brown, Jr. This constitutes the critical instrument in this cause, for this deed remained of public record for more than thirty years without being assaulted and, thus, constitutes a valid root of title to support the Whaleys' [plaintiffs'] deraignment. Risking redundancy, we emphasize that in 1908 the sovereign had no claims upon the land; the record reflected no claim upon the part of the patentee Sherman, but to the contrary reflected a long-standing chain of title which neither Sherman nor his heirs or their grantees, if any, had ever questioned. But, irrespective of the transactions prior to 1908, the conveyance into Brown, same not being void, constituted a record claim that ripened with the expiration of time into a valid root of title within the meaning of the cited * * * statutes." (225 So.2d at 182.)

What result in Whaley v. Wotring, supra, if the patent to Sherman in 1897 had immediately been recorded? Upon obtaining and recording quitclaim deeds from Sherman's heirs in 1966, could Wotring successfully argue that he was vested with "a marketable record title" under the Marketable Title Act because "the public records disclosed a title transaction [i.e., issuance of the patent] affecting the title to the land which has been of record for not less than thirty years purporting to create" an estate in fee simple in someone [i.e., Sherman] "from whom, by one or more title transactions, such estate has passed to the person claiming such estate [i.e., Wotring], with nothing appearing of record * * * purporting to divest such claimant of the estate claimed"?

The constitutionality of Marketable Title Acts has been affirmed against attacks that they operated retroactively; that they operated to deprive persons of property without due process of law; and that they impair contract rights. See Basye, Clearing Land Titles § 175 (2d ed. 1970); Simes and Taylor, Improvement of Conveyancing by Legislation 271–3; Wichelman v. Messner, 250 Minn. 88, 83 N.W.2d 800, 71 A.L.R.2d 816 (1957). But see, Board of Educ. v. Miles, 15 N.Y.2d 364, 259 N.Y.S.2d 129, 207 N.E.2d 181 (1965).

The best critique of the current marketable title legislation is to be found in Barnett, Marketable Title Acts—Panacea or Pandemonium?, 53 Corn.L.Rev. 45 (1967). Barnett makes the following points:

A. On the Positive Side—

(1) Marketable title acts "completely eliminate the problem of defects in the pre-root chain of the person claiming marketable record title. Such defects, ranging from absence of seals or acknowledgments

to lack of delivery and forgery, are so common that there is hardly a single land title wholly free of them. In most states, curative acts eliminate some of the obvious defects after a stated period of time. The advantage of marketable title acts is that they eliminate all defects, including those that do not appear on the records, against which there is otherwise no protection aside from title insurance." (Id. at 84–85.)

(2) "A marketable title act also eliminates the problem of a gap in the chain prior to the root of title. Such gaps usually result from the failure of a grantee to record his deed, or the failure of an intestate's heirs to have their heirship placed of record. * * * Breaks in the chain of title are cured if the persons appearing subsequently in the chain have been in continuous adverse possession for a period long enough to satisfy the statute of limitations that is effective even against person under disabilities, but 'adverse possession' must ultimately be proved in court. The cure offered by a marketable title act seems preferable, since it requires no litigation." (Id. at 85.)

(3) Marketable title acts cut off many "old recorded interests less than a fee simple, to which the title of the fee simple owner is subject. * * * Easements, equitable servitudes, liens, mineral rights, leases, possibilities of reverter, and powers of termination are typical examples." (Id. at 86.)

(4) Marketable title acts simplify title examination and reduce the amount of curative action needed to make a title good. "Abstracts all the way back to the sovereign will continue to be examined, but title examiners may disregard most matters prior to a root of title at least forty years of record." (Id. at 91.)

B. On the Negative Side—

(1) Marketable title acts, by reversing the priorities that obtained under the recording acts and by favoring the grantee under *any* title transaction that was the *last* to be recorded at least forty years ago, have destroyed the assurance of a grantee by conveyance from the record owner that his interest is indefeasible, provided he has recorded his instrument immediately. This is true even in the case of a fee simple owner who is in possession. "Under a marketable title act, all holders of interests in land, to be safe, must file a notice of claim every forty years after the recording of their instruments of acquisition." (Id. at 84.)

(2) "Under a marketable title act, abstracts become an *essential* part of the conveyancing system in counties where no official tract index is maintained. This may not be obvious at first glance, because the Model Act seems to adopt the chain of title concept. But the exception for 'any interest arising out of a title transaction * * * recorded subsequent to the * * * root of title' is not expressly restricted to interests 'arising out of' the chain of title of the person claiming marketable record title. If it is given a more inclusive meaning, a title examiner can find the excepted interests only by means of a tract index, official or unofficial. Of course, an interest protected from extinguishment by the marketable title act is not necessarily protected from extinguish-

ment by the recording acts. If recorded 'outside the chain of title,' an interest may still be rendered ineffective against a subsequent bona fide purchaser by the recording acts. But this is not the whole story. A wild deed can, under the marketable title acts, form a root of title which may cut off the interest of the record owner. This is a much more serious matter than merely preserving from extinguishment any rights that the parties to a wild deed might otherwise have under the recording acts." (Id. at 84.)

(3) Where one of the links in the record chain of title prior to the root is a forgery, or is missing simply because the grantee in the previous link has never transferred his interest, the interest of the person whose name was forged or who has never conveyed may be cut off automatically by a marketable title act without any notice that there is so much as an adverse claim to his land. "The recording of the subsequent links in the chain can hardly be expected to give him notice, except that, in the case of a forgery, he would probably cease to receive notices for taxes due against the land. Since the persons in the subsequent chain whose title will extinguish his need not be in possession, there is no assurance that the situation of the land will apprise him of an adverse claim. There is not even that minimum effort to notify which litigation requires—notice by publication." (Id. at 85.)

(4) If the objective is to ease the burden of title examination, no really sound argument can be made for cutting off only some of the old recorded interests less than a fee simple disclosed in the pre-root chain. "If the marketable title act makes even one exception for an interest of this type (as do all the statutes considered in this article), then a title examiner must check, at least cursorily, all recorded transactions back to the sovereign, to be sure that no interest of the type so excepted is outstanding of record against the title. And if, for example, he must check pre-root transactions for outstanding easements, his burden would not be greatly increased if he were also required to note any outstanding possibility of reverter. * * * Unfortunately, * * * general statements about the social utility of various types of interests do not stand up under examination. * * * Even if one could validly make general observations on how long a particular type of interest retains its social utility, a marketable title act will not necessarily cause the interest to be extinguished when it has outlived its usefulness. The holder of any interest can preserve it ad infinitum by periodically filing a notice of claim." (Id. at 86–87.)

(5) "Simes and Taylor suggest that the very small number of notices of claim filed under enacted marketable title acts prescribing a forty-year period tends to prove that few of the interests subject to extinguishment are still alive. On the other hand, however, it may prove merely that many holders of outstanding interests are ignorant of the existence and mode of operation of the marketable title acts. * * * The crucial argument made in justification of allowing marketable title acts to extinguish express interests outstanding of record is that, even if live interests of possibly continuing social utility are subject to extinguishment, they can all be preserved by the simple expedient of filing

notices of claim. But how are people going to learn of this saving procedure, or even of the threat of extinguishment? * * * The stock answer to the question is that the recording acts pose a similar threat and offer a like saving procedure: interests based on unrecorded instruments are subject to extinguishment, and all one need do to protect the interest is to record the instrument. The analogy is inappropriate. Since many states adopted recording acts early in their history, the regime imposed by them grew as the states grew. Unlike marketable title acts, they did not revolutionize a mature and full-blown system of private titles. Also, some requirement of affirmative action such as that demanded by the recording acts was essential for the production of subsequent bona fide purchasers; the filing requirement of marketable title acts is not." (Id. at 89–90.)

(6) "Finally, unlike title registration acts, a marketable title act makes no provision for any indemnity fund to recompense persons wrongfully deprived of their interests as a result of the mechanical operation of the act." (Id. at 85.)

Professor Barnett's ultimate conclusion is that the problems intended to be solved by marketable title legislation cannot "be solved completely without resort to some type of official registration of the present state of the title—a sort of official title opinion that is constantly kept up to date. In other words, the need is for some type of Torrens system." (Id. at 92). A brief consideration of systems of official title registration will be found below in Section 6.

For a concise treatment of "curative" and "marketable title" statutes, see Cunningham § 11.13.

C. LAND TITLE REGISTRATION

(1) The Torrens System

The Torrens System mentioned in the Barnett article, supra, is a system under which land titles are registered in somewhat the same way that automobile titles are now registered in most states; it is not simply an improved system for recording title instruments. The Torrens System is far from new. It takes its name from Sir Robert R. Torrens, a native of Ireland, who emigrated to Australia in 1840, later becoming the first premier of South Australia. It is said that it was in 1850, when he was collector of customs at Adelaide, that he first thought of applying to land the method of registering and transferring ownership in ships. In 1858, the first "Torrens Title Act" went into effect in South Australia, largely through the efforts of Sir Robert R. Torrens. Although the system in England and her dependencies and in the United States is known by his name, he was by no means its inventor, so to speak, for similar systems had been in operation in parts of Europe for many years.

In the United States the first difficulty is to draw a statute that will withstand constitutional objections. The first American statute introducing the Torrens System was enacted in Illinois in 1895; the second, in Ohio in 1896. California, Massachusetts, Oregon, Minnesota, Colorado, Washington, and New York followed. The first Torrens Act in Illinois was held unconstitutional. Following that decision, the Illinois Legislature enacted a new statute, which has so far withstood constitutional attacks. The Ohio statute of 1896 also was held invalid. In 1913, the Ohio Legislature, pursuant to provisions of an amendment to the Constitution adopted in 1912, enacted a new statute for registration of land titles.

The statutes are too lengthy to give even in summary. The procedure in bringing land under the system and the manner of dealing therewith afterwards are well stated in the following language used by the Supreme Court of Minnesota in State v. Westfall,[3] in which the court declared the Minnesota Torrens Act constitutional:

"The act provides, among other things, that the owner of any estate or interest in land may have the title thereto registered by making an application in writing, stating certain facts, to the district court of the county wherein the land is situated. Thereupon the court has power to inquire into the state of title, and make all decrees necessary to determine it against all persons, known or unknown. The application must be filed and docketed in the office of the clerk of the court, and a duplicate thereof filed with the register of deeds, who is ex officio registrar of titles. The application is then referred by the court to an examiner of titles, who investigates the titles, and inquires as to the truth of the allegations of the application, particularly whether the land is occupied or not, and makes and files a report of his examination with the clerk. Upon the filing of the report the clerk issues a summons by order of the court, wherein the applicant is named as plaintiff, and the land described, and all other persons known to have any interest in or claim to the land and 'all other persons or parties unknown' claiming any interest in the real estate described in the application are named as defendants. The summons must be directed to such defendants, and require them to appear and answer within twenty days. It must be served in the manner now provided for the service of summons in civil actions, with this exception: That the summons shall be served on nonresident defendants and upon all unknown persons by publishing it in a newspaper printed and published in the county where the application is filed once a week for three consecutive weeks. In addition to such publication the clerk shall, within twenty days after the first publication, mail a copy of the summons to all nonresident defendants whose place or address is known, and the court may order such additional notice of the application as it may direct. Any interested party may appear and answer. If no appearance is made, the court may enter the default, but must take proof of the applicant's right to a decree, and is not bound by the report of the examiner, but may require further proof. If appearance is made, the case shall be set for trial, and heard as other civil actions. If the court finds that the applicant has title proper for registration, a decree confirming the title and ordering registration shall be entered. Every such decree shall bind the lands and quiet title thereto, except as otherwise provided in the act, and shall be forever binding and

3. 85 Minn. 437, 89 N.W. 175 (1902).

conclusive upon all persons, whether mentioned by name or included in the expression 'all other persons or parties unknown,' and such decree shall not open by the reason of absence, infancy, or other disability * * * except as provided in the act. * * * Every person receiving a certificate of title and every subsequent purchaser in good faith takes the same free from all incumbrances, except such as are noted thereon. Upon entering the decree of registration, a certified copy thereof must be filed by the clerk in the office of the registrar of titles, who proceeds to register the title pursuant to the decree. This he does by entering an original certificate in the registry of titles, and delivering a duplicate thereof to the owner, who may thereafter convey his title by the execution of deeds and the surrender of his certificate to the registrar for cancellation, who issues a new certificate to the purchaser."

And such is the only method by which the land, after registration, may be conveyed; the old duplicate certificate must be delivered up and canceled, and a new certificate issued to the new owner. Most of the statutes, as in Minnesota, still preserve the use of the deed, which, however, does not act in itself as a conveyance, even after complete execution.

A feature of the Torrens System that should be mentioned is the assurance or indemnity fund out of which are to be paid the claims of persons wrongfully deprived of land or an interest therein through the registration of the land or through an act or omission of the registrar. This fund is derived from an assessment fixed by the statute, usually a small percentage of the assessed value, payable at the time of registration and, perhaps, at later stages in dealing with the registered tract.

Although occasionally someone in actual occupation of the land is not made a party to the initial registration proceeding, as in Follette v. Pacific Light & Power Corp., 189 Cal. 193, 208 P. 295 (1922), or a person entrusted with the owner's duplicate certificate of title forges a deed and secures the issuance of a new certificate of title in his own name, thus putting himself in position to transfer title to a bona fide purchaser, as in Eliason v. Wilborn, 281 U.S. 457, 50 S.Ct. 382 (1929), such occurrences are very rare. Generally speaking, wherever the Torrens system has been tried, it has produced titles which are both secure and marketable, and has permitted rapid determination of the state of the title to registered land without any need for repeated examinations of voluminous public records. See, e.g., McGill, New York's Land Title Registration Law, 17 A.B.A.J. 689 (1931): "A title that is now registered in this State is one that is indefeasible and stands against anyone in the world. It just simply cannot be upset, nor the owner of the title ousted from his possession." And see the statement of a Massachusetts lawyer to the effect that "the average time expended by a lawyer in ascertaining the state of the title of nonregistered land would be a day and a half, whereas the comparable average required to ascertain the state of a registered title would be not more than one or two hours," quoted in Powell, Registration of Title to Land in the State of New York 192 (1938).

The following is an example of a registered title certificate, drawn from Flick, Abstract and Title Practice, Vol. 1, pp. 199–201 (2d ed. 1958).

Example of Registered Title: Owner's Certificate (Form)

Folio 128208   Volume 10   Page 1205   No. 128208

UNITED STATES
OF AMERICA

STATE OF WASHINGTON
KING COUNTY

Owner's Duplicate Certificate of Ownership

FIRST CERTIFICATE OF TITLE

Pursuant to order of the Superior Court of the State of Washington, in and for King County.

State of Washington,   }   This is to Certify That
County of King City of Seattle   } ss.   Alice S. Potter
State of Washington   }   County of King

is now the owner of the following described land situated in the County of King and State of Washington, to-wit:

Lot Eighteen (18) in Block Eighty-one (81) of a plat of an Addition to the Town (now city) of Seattle as laid off by A.A. Arnheim.

King County   subject to the encumbrances, liens and interests noted
Auditor's Seal   by the memorial underwritten or indorsed thereon sub-
State of   ject to the exceptions and qualifications mentioned in
Washington   the thirtieth section of "An Act Relating to the Regis-
tration and Confirmation of Titles to Land" in the ses-
sion laws of Washington, for the year 1907.

In Witness Whereof, I have hereunto set my hand and affixed the official seal of my office this 17th day of August, A.D., 1958.

James Thurber
Registrar of Titles,
King County, Washington.

MEMORIAL OF ENCUMBRANCES, LIENS AND INTERESTS ON THE LANDS IN THIS CERTIFICATE OF TITLE

File No.	Kind	Running in Favor of	Amount
18732	Mortgage	Equitable Life Assurance Society	$104,000
951097	Tax	General	593.10
83942	Judgment	Brink Co.	2,319.58

By and large, writers in the first half of the 20th century were very favorable to the Torrens system. Among the articles favoring adoption of the system see Beale, Registration of Title to Land, 6 Harv.L.Rev. 369 (1893); Reeves, Progress in Land Title Transfers; The New Registration Law of New York, 8 Col.L.Rev. 438 (1908); Rood, Registration of Land Titles, 12 Mich.L.Rev. 379 (1914); McCall, The Torrens System, After 35 Years, 10 N.C.L.Rev. 329 (1932); Patton, The Torrens System of Land Title Registration, 19 Minn.L.Rev. 519 (1935); Russell and Bridewell, Systems of Land Title Examination: An Appraisal, 14 J. of Land & Pub.Util.Econ. 133 (1938); Fairchild and Springer, A Criticism of Professor Powell's Book Entitled Registration of Title to Land in the State of New York, 24 Corn.L.Q. 557 (1939); McDougal and Brabner-Smith, Land Title Transfer: A Regression, 48 Yale L.J. 1125 (1939); and McDougal, Title Registration and Land Law Reform: A Reply, 8 U. of Chi.L.Rev. 63 (1940). The book by Powell, cited above, contains the only substantial criticism of the Torrens system to be found.

Despite this support, however, use of the system has not progressed. It was adopted in a total of 20 states and territories between 1895 and 1917, but there have been no additional adoptions, and 8 states have since repealed their title registration statutes or have allowed them to expire. At the present time title registration statutes are still in force in only 12 states: Colorado, Georgia, Hawaii, Illinois, Massachusetts, Minnesota, New York, North Carolina, Ohio, Oregon, Virginia and Washington. Only four states have significant current use: Hawaii, Illinois, Massachusetts and Minnesota. Even in these states, however, the use of the Torrens system is still optional, and is confined to certain localities; and even within these localities only a relatively small proportion of the land is registered.

The debate concerning the merits of the system may arise again as a result of two recent studies. Those studies may, however, actually sound the death knell of the idea. One extensive legal and economic study of the operative systems, came to the essentially negative conclusion that "Torrens is not a sound concept for implementation in the United States today." Shick and Plotkin, Torrens in the United States (1978), at p. 10. A second study, conducted as a result of Congressional mandate in Section 13 of the Real Estate Settlement Procedures Act of 1974, is briefly reported in Patterson and Alexander, Land Title Record Modernization: An Update on the RESPA Section 13 Research, 16 Real Property Probate and Trust Journal 630 (1981). With respect to land title registration systems, the report does propose a model which it suggests is workable and affordable. However, it also lists a dozen reforms which would be needed to achieve workability, some of which are unlikely to be widely accepted.[4] Moreover, the report contains other recommendations which are more likely to move forward (e.g., the creation of tract indexes, and the support of the Uniform Simplification of Land Transfers Act, including its marketable record title provisions, and its elimination of formal conveyancing requisites). To the extent that these other proposals are adopted, the present system will be greatly improved, and the perceived need for Torrens greatly reduced.

Without trying to exhaust all factors which account for lack of widespread acceptance of a title registration system, one may note three major reasons: (1) there were structural defects in some of the acts which left numerous interests unaccounted for on the certificate and which produced either procedural problems in filing claims against the assurance fund or the bankruptcy of such fund; (2) the cost of initial registration is too high to attract large numbers of landowners so long as the system remains optional, even though there are potential savings in cost on subsequent transfers of title; and (3) Title insurance companies, abstract companies and title lawyers have, in general, vigorously opposed the Torrens system, fearing that universal adoption of the system would practically remove the need for title insurance, would put abstract companies out of business, and might well require title attorneys to reduce their fees for title examination very substantially.

All of these reasons could be surmounted if there were political desire to do so. A recent Comment, The Torrens System of Title Registration: A New Proposal for Effective Implementation, 29 UCLA L.Rev. 661 (1982) concedes the second and third causes for non-adoption listed above. The author then argues that the advantages of moving to a universal title registration system, which would replace our recordation system, are so great that we must find a way to surmount those deterrents. The proposed plan, derived in part from the English Torrens system, would, (1) replace the grantor-grantee records with official tract indices; (2) require registration of a possessory title to each parcel of land (or interest therein) at the time it is first transferred (but would not require the expensive *in rem* action which is now used in initial registration) and provide a statutory period, after which the initial possessory title would become absolute and conclusive. The article provides an extensive bibliography of the writings concerning title registration.

For a brief discussion of the Torrens System, see Cunningham § 11.15.

(2) Title Registration in England

The substantial rejection of the Torrens system of title registration in the United States should be contrasted with the current acceptance in

---

4. See also U.S. Dept. of Housing & Urban Development, Improving Title Registration (1979).

England of a similar system of title registration. The Land Registration Act of 1925, 15 Geo. 5, ch. 21, introduced the system which is gradually spreading throughout the country. Implementation has been slow, but under the Act, certain areas are designated as "compulsory," and any properties in such areas sold thereafter must be registered. Urban areas are mostly covered now, and additional compulsory areas are being designated. The basic features of the English system are summarized in Fiflis, English Registered Conveyancing: A Study in Effective Land Transfer, 59 N.W.U.L.Rev. 468 (1964). He there points out that the English system has a number of distinctive characteristics, not present in any American title registration act, and suggests we could learn much from the English system in any future effort to institute an effective mode of title registration. In a later article, Security and Economy in Land Transactions: Some Suggestions from Scotland and England, 20 Hastings L.J. 171 (1968), Fiflis concludes that "the real reasons for the extension of compulsory registration were the public pressure for reducing the costs of conveyancing and the solicitors' pressure to reduce the workload resulting from a shortage of manpower in the profession." (Id. at 204.) "One lesson to be learned from this [the English] experience is that even vested interests cannot withstand intense political pressure. It appears that, but for the pressure from without, solicitors might have been content with the status quo. Perhaps if the American public were made sufficiently aware of the unnecessary expense and insecurity of titles caused by retention of the recording system and by title insurance, reform could be brought about in the United States as well." (Id. at 206)

A brief, but enlightening, article by Michael Sturley, in 55 So.Cal.L. Rev. 1417 (1982) describes the system as it functions in conjunction with the Land Charges Act of 1925, 15 Geo. 5, ch. 22, now superseded by Land Charges Act, 1972, ch. 61.

Chapter 12

VENDOR AND PURCHASER

SECTION 1. THE LAND SALE TRANSACTION: IN GENERAL *

A. PARTICIPANTS IN THE LAND SALE TRANSACTION

The purchase and sale of land always involves at least two parties, a vendor and a purchaser. Each of these essential parties may be an individual, a partnership, an unincorporated association, a business corporation, or an eleemosynary corporation. The purchaser may be interested in acquiring realty for residential, agricultural, industrial, commercial, or other use—or merely to hold as an investment. The bulk of the realty available for residential use is "second hand" and both the vendor and the purchaser are likely to be relatively inexperienced in buying and selling realty. Until relatively recently, new housing was not "purchased" like goods, but was "custom built" on the prospective homeowner's land under the supervision of a "general contractor." Since World War II, however, the principal source of new housing has been the builder-developer who lays out entire new residential subdivisions and contracts to sell houses and lots to purchasers on the basis of plans and "model homes" which are open for inspection.

Most land sale transactions involve several participants in addition to the vendor and the purchaser. The most important of these is the mortgage lender—usually an institutional lender such as a savings and loan association, a savings bank, a commercial bank, or a mortgage company—which finances the sale. Occasionally, the purchaser may be able to supply the entire purchase price from his own resources and thus does not need mortgage financing. And sometimes the vendor himself will extend the necessary credit for part of the purchase price, in which case he may either transfer legal title to the purchaser and take back a purchase money mortgage as security for the unpaid balance or retain the legal title under an installment land contract.

In the sale of "second-hand" property, real estate brokers perform a useful function in bringing prospective vendors and purchasers together. The broker is usually employed by the vendor, who "lists" his property for sale with the broker. The broker undertakes to advertise the property for sale, show it to prospective purchasers, and if possible se-

---

* For a detailed treatment of "vendor and purchaser," see 3 A.L.P. §§ 11.3–11.81. See also Cunningham ch. 10.

cure an offer to purchase on the terms specified by the vendor. The vendor ordinarily sets an asking price well above what he is willing to accept, of course, and the purchaser is likely to make an initial offer well below what he is willing to pay. There may be several offers and counter-offers before a sale price is agreed upon. When property is listed with a broker under an "open" listing agreement, the vendor may also list the property for sale with as many other brokers as he wishes; indeed, in some cities the local real estate board (a brokers' organization) maintains a "multiple listing bureau" through which a vendor may list his property with all members of the board under an "open" listing agreement. If the property is listed with more than one broker under an "open" agreement, the broker who first communicates to the vendor an offer to purchase on the terms specified by the vendor, or on different terms accepted by the vendor, is the one entitled to the commission. On the other hand, if the vendor lists his property "exclusively" with a particular broker, the vendor agrees not to list it for sale with any other broker, and usually agrees also that the broker who has received the "exclusive" listing shall be entitled to a commission even if the sale is actually brought about by another broker or by the vendor himself. If the vendor enters into an "exclusive" listing agreement and then sells his property through another broker (not the one with whom the "exclusive" agreement was made), he may be compelled to pay a commission to both brokers unless the brokers have an agreement to split a single commission on the sale. Five, six, or seven per cent of the sale price would be common rates for computing the commission. The percentage may be graduated if the sales price exceeds certain specified amounts. In the absence of an express agreement as to the rate of commission, the broker is usually held entitled to "reasonable" compensation for his services in securing an offer to purchase on the vendor's terms, or on other terms agreed to by the vendor. Local real estate boards usually adopt standard rate schedules for brokers' commissions, based on the sale price, and in the absence of an express agreement as to compensation these standard rates are generally accepted as prima facie reasonable. This practice has been challenged as constituting an illegal price-fixing under the Sherman Act, and the Supreme Court has indicated that despite the local nature of brokerage services, there may be sufficient effect on interstate commerce to confer jurisdiction. McLain v. Real Estate Board of New Orleans, Inc., 444 U.S. 232, 100 S.Ct. 502, 62 L.Ed.2d 441 (1980).

More than thirty states have statutory licensing requirements for real estate brokers, and state licensing boards generally have power to suspend or revoke brokers' licenses for fraud, misrepresentation, or other dishonest or unethical conduct. Moreover, a broker may be found liable to the vendee for negligent misrepresentation. Dugan v. Jones, 615 P.2d 1239 (Utah 1980), noted in 1981 Utah L.Rev. 229. As a practical matter, the broker has a dual responsibility to both vendor and vendee, even though he is normally the agent of the vendor. Expectations of the buyer arise because the broker takes him around to see several possible houses. Some of the problems raised by this dual relationship are discussed in Currier, Finding the Broker's Place in the Typical Residential Real Estate Transaction, 33 U.Fla.L.Rev. 655 (1981).

New housing may be "marketed" by the builder-developer through a local real estate brokerage firm (in which case that firm usually has an "exclusive" listing agreement with the builder), or it may be "marketed" by the builder's own sales organization without the intervention of a broker. Most builder-developers have fixed pricing policies similar to those of retail merchants of goods, and there is little room for haggling over price; the purchaser must either take it or leave it at the price fixed by the vendor. The builder-developer is likely to have obtained a commitment from the FHA, and perhaps also from the VA, to insure loans to purchasers of houses in his "development," and the sale of each house and lot is likely to be a "package deal." That is, the builder-developer handles the details of financing for the purchaser, whether the financing is "FHA," "GI," or "conventional" (not insured either by the FHA or the VA). Mortgage loan arrangements may be made with a local bank or savings and loan association, or with an insurance company which invests in mortgage loans all over the United States.

It should be noted that lawyers may be involved in real estate sales in various ways. The documents used to effect the sale are generally drafted by lawyers, although the parties often use forms that were not specially prepared for the particular transaction. As already noted, the purchaser often employs a lawyer to examine the abstract of title supplied by a title searcher or an abstract company, or, in some states, to make the title search and render an opinion based thereon. The mortgage lender usually employs an attorney to examine titles as well as to draft bonds, notes, and mortgages. Title insurance companies employ lawyers, and frequently some or all of the officers of such companies are lawyers. Moreover, in recent years lawyers in some states have established mutual title insurance organizations to guarantee titles examined and approved by the lawyer-members of the organization. And both the FHA and VA employ a good many lawyers in connection with the loan insurance and guaranty programs mentioned above.

The Federal Government is frequently a party to real estate sales under the loan insurance program administered by the Federal Housing Administration under the National Housing Act of 1934 (as amended)[1] and the loan guaranty program administered by the Veterans' Administration under Public Law 85–857 of 1958 (as amended).[2]

Title II of the National Housing Act of 1934 (as amended)[3] provides for the creation of a mutual insurance fund to insure private mortgage lenders against losses on eligible mortgage loans underwritten by the

---

1. 12 U.S.C.A. § 1701 et seq.

2. 38 U.S.C.A. § 1501 et seq. This is the successor of the Servicemen's Readjustment Act of 1944, the famous "GI Bill of Rights."

3. 12 U.S.C.A. § 1707 et seq. Title II is the part which has most affected the "real estate business," because, under this title, the FHA has established construction standards, subdivision design standards, and mortgage loan terms (including maximum interest rates and amortized payment procedures) for approved loans which have also been extensively adopted or copied in financing the construction and sale of housing outside the FHA mortgage insurance program.

Federal Housing Administration. Chapter 37 of Public Law 85–857 of 1958 [4] provides for Federal Government guaranties of private loans to veterans of World War II and the Korean War to finance the purchase or construction of homes, farms, or business property. A direct Government loan is authorized to any eligible veteran to purchase or construct a home in any rural area or small city or town where "the administrator finds that private capital is not generally available * * * for the financing of loans" for such purposes.[5] During the 1950's a major portion of the new residential construction was financed by FHA and VA insured mortgage loans. At the present time, however, a majority of the mortgage loans for new construction are of the uninsured or "conventional" type.

In addition to its role as an insurer or guarantor of mortgages, the Federal Government has also initiated a number of "secondary mortgage market" agencies—the Federal National Mortgage Association (FNMA), the Government National Mortgage Association (GNMA), and the Federal Home Loan Mortgage Corporation (FHLMC).[6] FNMA is now privately owned by its shareholders, but the President still appoints one-third of its board of directors. GNMA is a government corporation administered by the Department of Housing and Urban Development (HUD). And FHLMC is a government corporation owned by the Federal Home Loan Banks and administered by the Federal Home Loan Bank Board, whose members are appointed by the President. All three of these agencies perform the function of providing a "secondary market"—i.e., a resale market—for mortgage loans "originated" by institutional lenders. FNMA and FHLMC buy both federally insured or guaranteed mortgage loans and "conventional" (not federally-insured) mortgage loans; and both agencies, in effect, "package" pools of mortgage loans for resale to investors. GNMA at one time provided a mechanism for federal subsidization of "below market rate" mortgage loans on "low- and moderate-income" housing projects, but little federal money is now available for "below market rate" subsidy programs. GNMA has, however, found a new and useful function as a guarantor of "packaged" mortgage loans originated by institutional lenders and sold in the secondary market. In most cases, investors are offered participation certificates representing fractional interests in the underlying mortgage "pool" under the FNMA, FHLMC, and GNMA programs. All three of these agencies raise capital funds through issues of bonds and debentures which are sold in the capital markets.

---

4. 38 U.S.C.A. § 1801 et seq.

5. Id. § 1811.

6. For descriptions of these secondary market agencies and their functions, see U.S. Dept. of Housing & Urban Development, Housing in the Seventies 3–39 to 3–48 (1973); Wiggin, Doing Business in the Secondary Mortgage Market, 5 Real Estate Rev. 84 (1975); Ganis, All About the GNMA Mortgage-Backed Securities Market, 4 Real Estate Rev. 55 (1974); GNMA Annual Report, 1979, pp. 2–14; Hendershott & Villani, Secondary Mortgage Markets and the Cost of Mortgage Funds, 8 J.Am.Real Est. & Urban Econ. Ass'n 50 (No. 1, Spring 1980); Note, The GNMA Securities Market: An Analysis of Proposals for a Regulatory Scheme, 9 Ford.Urb.L.Rev. 457 (1980).

Note: "Fair Housing" Laws and Discrimination in the
Sale and Rental of Housing

By 1953 it was settled that restrictive covenants purporting to prohibit occupancy of real property by "any person not of the Caucasian race" could not be enforced in the state courts either by injunction or by an action for damages, because such enforcement would constitute "state action" which would deny to "non-Caucasians" the "equal protection of the laws" guaranteed by the Fourteenth Amendment to the United States Constitution. Shelley v. Kraemer, 334 U.S. 1, 68 S.Ct. 836 (1948); Barrows v. Jackson, 346 U.S. 249, 73 S.Ct. 1031 (1953). The focus of attention then shifted to enactment of legislation against "private" racial discrimination in housing. In 1957, New York City became the first governmental unit to legislate against racial discrimination in housing on a general basis. This was followed in 1958 by a similar ordinance in Pittsburgh, Pennsylvania. In 1959, Colorado, Connecticut, Massachusetts, and Oregon enacted statutes prohibiting racial discrimination in the private housing market. As of June, 1967, at least 19 states and 28 cities had adopted anti-discrimination laws affecting some part of the private housing market. These state and local "fair housing" or "open housing" laws vary widely in their coverage of the private housing market. For a good survey, see Note, Open Housing Meets My Old Kentucky Home: A Study of Open Housing With Special Attention to Implications for Kentucky, 56 Ky.L.J. 140, 187–194 (1967).

The federal government made little use of its power to combat discriminatory practices in housing until the 1960's. In 1962, President Kennedy, fulfilling a campaign promise made two years before, signed an Executive Order (No. 11063) directing federal agencies to take all necessary steps to prevent discrimination in housing programs supported or financially aided by the federal government. This order had a number of limitations, and made no provision for effective enforcement. But in Title VI of the Civil Rights Act of 1964, Congress specifically prohibited discrimination on the basis of race, color, or national origin in most housing programs receiving federal aid. The ultimate sanction under Title VI was refusal to grant the requested financial assistance or the termination of assistance already granted. And in 1968 Congress enacted Title VIII of the Civil Rights Act of 1968, 82 Stat. 73, 42 U.S.C.A. § 3601 et seq., which contained a sweeping prohibition of discrimination in the sale or rental of housing based upon "race, color, religion, or national origir.." An amendment in 1974 prohibits discrimination on the basis of sex. Prior to December 31, 1968, the prohibition applied only to housing owned or operated by the federal government or constructed with federal financial assistance; but since December 31, 1968, the prohibition has applied "to all other dwellings except * * * (1) any single-family house sold or rented by an owner * * * or (2) rooms or units in dwellings containing living quarters occupied or intended to be occupied by no more than four families living independently of each other, if the owner actually maintains and occupies one of such living quarters as his residence." [7]

The enforcement machinery created by Title VIII of the 1968 Civil Rights Act includes efforts by the Secretary of Housing and Urban Development, upon complaint by "any person who claims to have been injured by a discriminatory housing practice or who believes that he will be irrevocably injured by a discriminatory housing practice that is about to occur," to "eliminate or correct the alleged discriminatory housing practice by informal methods of conference,

---

7. The single-family dwelling exception is subject to a series of limiting provisos.

conciliation, and persuasion"; and if the Secretary is unable to obtain voluntary compliance with Title VIII within 30 days after the complaint is filed with him, a "civil action in any appropriate United States district court," by "the person aggrieved * * * against the respondent named in the complaint, to enforce the rights granted or protected by this title, insofar as such rights relate to the subject of the complaint."

The provision for informal attempts by the Secretary to "eliminate or correct the alleged discriminatory housing practice" is subject to a proviso that "wherever a State or local fair housing law provides rights and remedies for alleged discriminatory housing practices which are substantially equivalent to the rights and remedies provided in this title, the Secretary shall notify the appropriate State or local agency of any complaint filed under this title which shall appear to constitute a violation of such State or local fair housing law, and the Secretary shall take no further action with respect to such complaint if the appropriate State or local enforcement official has, within thirty days from the date the alleged offense has been brought to his attention, commenced proceedings in the matter, or, having done so, carries forward such proceedings with reasonable promptness." The right of the "aggrieved person" to bring a civil action in the U.S. district court is also subject to the following proviso: "That no such civil action may be brought in any United States district court if the person aggrieved has a judicial remedy under a State or local fair housing law which provides rights and remedies for alleged discriminatory housing practices which are substantially equivalent to the rights and remedies provided in this title."

In actions brought by an "aggrieved person" to enforce rights under Title VIII of the Civil Rights Act of 1968, the federal or state court is authorized to grant "any permanent or temporary injunction, temporary restraining order, or other order, and may award to the plaintiff actual damages and not more than $1,000 punitive damages, together with court costs and reasonable attorney fees in the case of a prevailing plaintiff," provided the latter "in the opinion of the court is not financially able to assume said attorney's fees." Moreover, the United States Attorney General, whenever he "has reasonable cause to believe that any person or group of persons is engaged in a pattern or practice of resistance to the full enjoyment of any of the rights granted by this title, or that any group of persons has been denied any of the rights granted by this title and this denial raises an issue of general public importance, * * * may bring a civil action in any appropriate United States district court by filing with it a complaint setting forth the facts and requesting such preventive relief, including an application for a permanent or temporary injunction, restraining order, or other order against the person or persons responsible for such pattern or practice or denial of rights, as he deems necessary to insure full enjoyment of the rights granted by this title." [8]

Shortly after passage of the Civil Rights Act of 1968, the Supreme Court held that all racial discrimination, private as well as public, in the sale or rental of property is barred by 42 U.S.C.A. § 1982, and that the statute, thus construed, is a valid exercise of the power of Congress to enforce the Thirteenth Amendment. Jones v. Alfred H. Mayer Co., 392 U.S. 409, 88 S.Ct. 2186, 20 L.Ed.2d 1189 (1968). 42 U.S.C.A. § 1982, which is the current version of part of § 1 of the Civil Rights Act of 1866, provides as follows:

8. See, in general: The Federal Fair Housing Requirements: Title VIII of the 1968 Civil Rights Act, 1969 Duke L.Jnl. 773; Racial Discrimination in the Private Housing Sector: Five Years After, 33 Maryland L.Rev. 289 (1973); The Fair Housing Act of 1968; Its Success and Failure, 9 Suffolk University L.Rev. 1312 (1975).

"All citizens of the United States shall have the same right in every State and Territory, as is enjoyed by white citizens thereof to inherit, purchase, lease, sell, hold, and convey real and personal property."

In discussing the relation between 42 U.S.C.A. § 1982 and Title VIII of the Civil Rights Act of 1968, the Supreme Court said:

" * * * Whatever else it may be, 42 U.S.C.A. § 1982 is not a comprehensive open housing law. In sharp contrast to the Fair Housing Title (Title VIII) of the Civil Rights Act of 1968, * * * the statute in this case deals only with racial discrimination and does not address itself to discrimination on grounds of religion or national origin. It does not deal specifically with discrimination in the provision of services or facilities in connection with the sale or rental of a dwelling. It does not prohibit advertising or other representations that indicate discriminatory preferences. It does not refer explicitly to discrimination in financing arrangements or in the provision of brokerage services. It does not empower a federal administrative agency to assist aggrieved persons. It makes no provision for intervention by the Attorney General. And, although it can be enforced by injunction, it contains no provision expressly authorizing a federal court to order the payment of damages.

"Thus, although § 1982 contains none of the exemptions that Congress included in the Civil Rights Act of 1968, it would be a serious mistake to suppose that § 1982 in any way diminishes the significance of the law recently enacted by Congress. * * * Its enactment had no effect upon § 1982 and no effect upon this litigation, but it underscored the vast differences between, on the one hand, a general statute applicable only to racial discrimination in the rental and sale of property and enforceable only by private parties acting on their own initiative, and, on the other hand, a detailed housing law, applicable to a broad range of discriminatory practices and enforceable by a complete arsenal of federal authority."

The "block-busting" provision of the Act, relating to inducements, for profit, to persons to sell or rent any dwelling by representations regarding the entry into a neighborhood of persons of a particular race, etc., was sustained by one federal court of appeals as within the powers of Congress, under the authority of Jones v. Mayer Company, supra, and not in violation of the First Amendment guaranty of free speech. United States v. Bob Lawrence Realty, Inc., 474 F.2d 115 (5th Cir.1973), certiorari denied 414 U.S. 826, 94 S.Ct. 131 (1973). Another court of appeals held that the provisions of the Act forbidding the publication of discriminatory statements concerning the sale or rental of a dwelling was applicable to a newspaper, and as so applicable, was not a denial of the freedom of the press under the First Amendment or of due process under the 5th Amendment. United States v. Hunter, 459 F.2d 205 (4th Cir.1972), certiorari denied 409 U.S. 934, 93 S.Ct. 235 (1972).

Violations of the Civil Rights Act of 1968 can be established on the basis of discriminatory effect, without the necessity of proving discriminatory intent. See, e.g., Metropolitan Housing Development Corp. v. Village of Arlington Heights, 558 F.2d 1283 (1977); Washington v. Davis, 426 U.S. 229, 96 S.Ct. 2040, 48 L.Ed.2d 597 (1976); United States v. Pelzer Realty Co., Inc., 484 F.2d 438 (5th Cir.1973), cert. denied 416 U.S. 936, 94 S.Ct. 1935, 40 L.Ed.2d 286 (1974).

B. PRINCIPAL DOCUMENTS USED IN REAL ESTATE SALES

(1) The Earnest Money Contract

It should be noted that a real estate sale is normally a two or three-step process characterized by the execution of written documents at each step in the transaction. Contrast this with the usual procedure in the sale of goods at retail, where, except when relatively expensive durable goods are sold under a conditional sale contract, the sale is normally consummated by transfer of the legal title and possession as soon as agreement on the terms of sale is reached. Although the buyer may be given a "bill of sale," this is not essential to the transfer of title. And even when durable goods are conditionally sold (i.e., possession is delivered to the buyer but the seller retains the legal title), the transaction is normally completed simply by payment of the price in full; i.e., the legal title automatically passes to the buyer upon full payment, whether or not a "bill of sale" is then given to the buyer by the seller. But in the analogous real estate sale transaction where the parties enter into a "title retention contract," the legal title to the realty will not pass automatically to the purchaser upon completion of his payments in accordance with the contract; a formal transfer of title by delivery of a deed is still necessary.

Theoretically the vendor could execute a deed of conveyance to the purchaser as soon as the terms of sale are agreed upon, but in practice this almost never happens. Even if the purchaser is in a position to pay the full purchase price in cash without borrowing, he is generally unwilling to pay the price and accept a deed until he has assured himself that the vendor has a "good and marketable title" to the realty he has contracted to sell. Hence the formal transfer of the legal title by deed (often referred to as "the closing of title," or simply "the closing") is almost always delayed until the title has been examined by the purchaser's attorney or by a title company. If the purchaser needs to borrow some or all of the purchase money, additional time is usually required to arrange a mortgage loan; and the mortgage lender will usually wish to have the title examined before giving a commitment to take a mortgage on the property in question.

During the interval between agreement upon the terms of sale and the "closing of title," even when it is contemplated that the "closing" will be delayed only a short time, it is obviously desirable to have the exact terms agreed upon between vendor and purchaser embodied in a written document. In the event of dispute or litigation, the document can be used to prove the existence of the agreement and its terms, and neither party will have to rely upon the memory and the honesty of the other, or upon his own all too fallible memory. Furthermore, even were it not highly desirable to embody the agreement of the parties in a written instrument for the reasons just stated, the local "statute of frauds" will usually make it impossible to enforce an agreement for the sale of realty against an unwilling defendant unless "the agreement upon which such action shall be brought or some memorandum or note thereof, shall be in writing, and signed by the party to be charged therewith."

The more or less formal written instrument used to stabilize the contract for the relatively short period between agreement on the terms of sale and the "closing" is generally called an "earnest money contract" because the purchaser usually makes a deposit of "earnest money" when he signs the instrument. The "earnest money" is applied against the purchase price if the purchaser performs his further obligations at the "closing."

(a) Minimum Requirements: The Written Memorandum

All states have adopted a Statute of Frauds based on the English Statute of Frauds and Perjuries of 1677 (29 Charles II, c. 3). Section 4 of the English Statute provided as follows: "No action shall be brought upon any contract or sale of tenements or hereditaments, or any interest in or concerning them, unless the agreement upon which such action shall be brought, or some memorandum or note thereof, shall be in writing and signed by the party to be charged therewith, or by some person therewith by him lawfully authorized." Most American state Statutes of Frauds contain similar, if not identical, language. It should be noted, however, that the contract provisions of the Statutes of Frauds are applicable only to executory obligations, despite the use of the word "sale." So long as a bilateral contract for the sale of realty remains executory on both sides the reciprocal promises of the vendor to convey and of the purchaser to pay the price are equally "within the statute." If the purchaser pays the price in full, the vendor's promise to convey is still "within the statute." But if the vendor conveys in accordance with his promise, the purchaser's promise to pay the price is a mere promise to pay a sum certain (a "debt" in the technical sense) and is no longer "within the statute."

The Statute of Frauds requires that the contract itself, or "some note or memorandum thereof," shall be in writing. A written memorandum of a contract is not identical with a written contract. A written contract will, of course, satisfy the Statute of Frauds; but a memorandum will also satisfy the Statute of Frauds if it states the terms agreed upon, though not intended or adopted by the vendor and purchaser as a final complete statement of their agreement. No precise formula can be laid down as to the degree of particularity with which the terms of the contract must be stated. There must be "reasonable" certainty as to the identity of the parties, the description of the land, the price, and the terms of payment. Some of the American Statutes of Frauds expressly require that the "consideration" be stated in the written contract or memorandum, but this has generally been construed to mean simply that the agreed price must be stated; and a statement of the price is generally required even though the Statute of the jurisdiction does not refer to "consideration" at all. Only a few cases distinguish the price from the "consideration" for the vendor's promise to convey— which is the purchaser's promise to pay the agreed price. Where the local Statute of Frauds expressly states that the "consideration" need *not* be expressed in the contract or memorandum, as in Illinois, Indiana, Kentucky, Maine, Massachusetts, Michigan, Nebraska, New Jersey, Virginia, and West Virginia, some courts (erroneously) have held that the price need not be stated in the writing, while other courts have held (correctly) that the agreed price is an essential term of the contract which must be expressed in the writing.

A memorandum sufficient to satisfy the Statute of Frauds may consist of several writings, if each writing is signed by the party to be charged and the writings indicate that they relate to the same transaction, or, though only one writing is signed, if the signed writing is physically annexed to the unsigned writings by the party to be charged, or the signed writing refers to the unsigned writings, or it appears from examination of all the writings that the signed writing was signed with reference to the unsigned writings.

Section 4 of the English Statute of Frauds uses the phrase "signed by the party to be charged therewith, or some other person thereunto by him lawfully authorized." The English courts, and most of the American courts when applying statutes containing this phrase, have held that "the person to be charged" is the party to the contract who tries to prevent its enforcement against himself. He is usually the defendant in a judicial proceeding, but sometimes he is the plaintiff, against whose claim the defendant attempts to set up the contract as a defense or as the basis of a counterclaim. By the prevailing view, if either party has signed an otherwise sufficient memorandum of the contract it is enforceable against him as "the party to be charged" even though no memorandum has been signed by the party seeking to enforce or establish the contract. This seems fair enough, since the terms of the contract have been authenticated by the party resisting enforcement of the contract, and the other party cannot enforce it without making it enforceable against himself. That is, the party seeking to enforce or establish the contract necessarily submits himself to the jurisdiction of the court, which may make any decree enforcing the contract conditional upon tender of full performance by the party seeking enforcement. And the court may even require the party seeking enforcement to file in court a signed memorandum for the purpose of assuring the other party an adequate remedy in the event of subsequent breach by the party presently seeking to enforce the contract judicially.

Under the view just stated, it is clear that the written offer signed by one party may be a sufficient memorandum to charge that party, even though the other party has signed no memorandum at all. It is essential, of course, that the other party shall have accepted the offer before it was revoked, but his acceptance can be proved by parol evidence. Conversely, a written offer signed by the purchaser has been held a sufficient memorandum to charge him, although the vendor accepted orally and did not himself sign a written memorandum. First National Bank of St. Johnsbury v. Laperle, 117 Vt. 144, 86 A.2d 635, 30 A.L.R.2d 958 (1952). For a comprehensive annotation, see "Oral Acceptance of Written Offer by Party Sought to be Charged as Satisfying Statute of Frauds," 30 A.L.R.2d 972 (1953).

In some states the phrase "signed by the party to be charged" has been construed to require the signature of the vendor in every case involving a contract for the sale of realty. This seems to be based on the theory that the land contract clause in the Statute of Frauds is solely for the protection of landowners, and not for the protection of purchasers. No such construction has been adopted with respect to other classes of contracts dealt with in the Statute of Frauds. In some states the phrase "signed by the party to be charged" has been omitted from the land contract clause and the phrase "signed by the grantor" or some similar phrase has been substituted. Wherever the signature of the vendor is required, whether by express statutory provision or by construction, the vendor can enforce the contract against the purchaser if he (the vendor) has signed a sufficient memorandum of the contract, even though the purchaser has not signed. But in order to prevent the vendor from taking advantage of the purchaser under this rule the courts have generally held that the memorandum signed by the vendor must have been delivered to the purchaser and assented to by him, before the vendor can hold the purchaser to the contract. That a Statute of Frauds so worded or construed as to require the vendor's signature in every case is less satisfactory than a Statute of Frauds which requires the signature of the party seeking to resist enforcement of the contract seems obvious. And New York recognized this fact in 1944 by amending its Real Property Law § 259, which formerly required the contract or memorandum to be "subscribed by the lessor or grantor," so as to require it to be "subscribed by the party to be charged."

Suppose each party to a contract for the sale of land has signed a different memorandum and that the terms included in the two memorandums differ in one or more respects? See Restatement Contracts § 208(b), Illustration 7.

In the absence of a statutory provision to the contrary, the authority of an agent to make a contract subject to the statute of frauds on his principal's behalf, and to sign a sufficient memorandum thereof, need not be in writing. A number of states, however, have enacted statutes which require that the agent's authority must be in writing and signed by the principal in order for his memorandum to bind the principal to a contract subject to the statute of frauds. See, e.g., N.Y. General Obligations Law § 5–703(2), which requires the "contract, or some note or memorandum thereof," to be in writing, "subscribed by the party to be charged or by his lawful agent thereunto authorized by writing." It should be noted in this connection that an agent may have authority, oral or written, to sign a sufficient memorandum of a contract made by his principal even though he had no authority to make the contract. On the other hand, the authority to execute a written memorandum may be inferred from authority given to make the contract, but this is not a necessary inference. Such an inference certainly should not be drawn merely from an authorization to find a purchaser.

An oral ratification will render sufficient a memorandum signed by one purporting to act as agent but without actual authority if an antecedent oral authorization would have been sufficient; otherwise the ratification must also be in writing, signed by the principal. There is some authority that a statute requiring the authority of an agent to be in writing does not apply to the principal officers of a corporation, on the theory that a corporation can act only through its officers and agents and the action of its principal officers is the action of the corporation itself. There are contrary decisions, however, and the result is likely to turn on the wording of the statute involved.

For a fuller discussion of the Statute of Frauds as it relates to contracts for the sale of land, see 2 Corbin, Contracts, Ch. 17 (1950); for fuller discussion of the memorandum necessary to satisfy the Statute of Frauds, see id. Chaps. 22, 23.

Questions frequently arise with respect to the sufficiency of a written memorandum to satisfy the Statute of Frauds where some term of the contract has not yet been agreed upon when the memorandum is drawn up and signed. Compare Ansorge v. Kane, 244 N.Y. 395, 155 N.E. 683 (1927), and Goldblatt v. Rosenwasser, 275 App.Div. 680, 86 N.Y.S.2d 684 (2d Dept.1949).

The problem in the Ansorge and Goldblatt cases is one that may arise whenever a prospective vendor or purchaser, or both, sign an informal writing that does not include all the terms that would normally be included in a purchase and sale contract. Typically, the real estate broker gets the prospective purchaser to sign a paper, variously called an "offer to purchase," a "binder," or a "receipt," containing an offer to purchase the property in question at the price set by the vendor and a provision that if the vendor accepts the offer by signing the paper a more formal contract will be executed at a later time. Although the broker usually earns his commission simply by obtaining an offer to purchase at the price set by the vendor, he usually acts on the assumption that he is more likely to collect his commission if the prospective vendor and purchaser are contractually bound at the outset; and he attempts to bind the parties by getting the vendor to sign the "offer to purchase" or "binder." Although "offer to purchase" or "binder" forms used by real estate brokers vary in detail, they usually contain the names and designations of the parties (i.e., as vendor and purchaser), a brief description of the property being sold, the price and the terms of payment, a statement that the sale is either free of all encumbrances or subject to stated encumbrances, and some statement as to the date for the "closing of title." The informal writing may or may not state that a more formal contract is to be executed later.

What do you think of a form providing that a "Contract of Sale" will be signed at a specified later time, but also providing that the "binder" is "to remain in force and effect and constitute a valid contract between the parties unless, or until, superseded by further contract between the parties incorporating detailed description and providing for adjustments of taxes, rent, interest, insurance premiums, etc."?

In general, see 1 Corbin, Contracts §§ 95–101 (1950).

(b) Standardized Forms

Most contracts for the purchase and sale of real estate are more formal and detailed than the memoranda necessary to satisfy the Statute of Frauds. Lawyers with a sizeable real estate practice often develop their own contract forms. Attorneys for local real estate boards, land development companies, and title insurance companies also frequently prepare standardized contract forms for the sale of real estate, which may be published and sold for general use or used only in connection with a particular real estate development. The content and phraseology of forms used in different communities tends to vary a good deal, reflecting differing local customs, practices, statutes, and rules of case law; but the forms in use in a given community usually do not differ materially in the wording of particular clauses, although some forms may be more comprehensive than others.

Standardized froms are generally used by real estate brokers in the sale of urban residential real estate. Most of the standard clauses in printed form contracts represent the cumulative experience of brokers and vendors with real estate sales, and they tend to be more favorable to the vendor than to the purchaser. If changes are made in any of the standard clauses, it is likely to be at the purchaser's insistence. But both parties should be aware of the dangers of attempting to handle even "routine" purchase and sale transactions by means of a standardized contract form. And unusual situations clearly call for careful drafting of a contract tailored to fit the particular situation.

Whatever its form, a contract for the purchase and sale of real estate should, of course, contain provisions appropriate to the purposes of the parties, and it should provide so far as possible for all contingencies that can reasonably be anticipated.

The following contract form is in widespread use in Chicago, Illinois.

The Chicago Real Estate Board Sale Contract (Cook County, Ill.) No. 999

_____ agree__ to buy at the price of _____ Dollars which includes the mortgage indebtedness, if any, hereinafter specified, the following described real estate, in Cook County, Illinois,

_____

_____

and _____ agree__ to sell said premises at said price, and to convey or cause to be conveyed to buyer good title thereto by _____ * deed, with release of dower and homestead rights, subject only to: (1) Existing leases expiring _____; (2) Special taxes or assessments for improvements not yet completed; (3) Installments not due at date hereof of any special tax or assessment for improvements heretofore completed; (4) General taxes for the year _____ and subsequent years; (5) Building lines and building and liquor restrictions of record; (6) Zoning and building laws or ordinances; (7) Party wall rights or agreements, if any; (8)

---

* The type of deed is to be specified here.

Roads and highways, if any; (9) Principal indebtedness aggregating $_____ payable _____ bearing interest at the rate of _____% per annum, secured by mortgage—or trust deed—of record; and to

Rents, water taxes, insurance premiums and accrued mortgage interest are to be adjusted pro rata as of date of delivery of deed. Existing leases and insurance policies shall be assigned to buyer. General taxes for the year _____ are to be prorated from January 1, to date of delivery of deed. If the amount of such taxes is not then ascertainable, prorating shall be on the basis of the amount of the most recent ascertainable taxes.

Buyer has paid _____ Dollars earnest money to be applied on purchase price, and agrees to pay, within five days after title is shown good or is accepted by buyer, the further sum of _____ Dollars, provided deed as aforesaid shall be ready for delivery. The balance, $_____ shall be paid as follows:

with interest from date of delivery of deed at the rate of _____% per annum, payable _____ to be evidenced and secured by buyer's notes and trust deed of even date with said deed on said premises in a form ordinarily used by _____.

(If this blank is not filled in, said notes and trust deed shall be in a form ordinarily used by the Chicago Title and Trust Company.)

Within twenty days from date hereof, seller shall deliver to buyer or his agent (which delivery may be made at office of _____) as evidence of title covering date hereof, showing record title in seller (or grantor) one of the following: (1) Merchantable abstract; (2) Owner's Guarantee Policy of Chicago Title and Trust Comany in the amount of the purchase price or its customary preliminary report on title subject to the usual objections contained in such policies, though, if such report be furnished, seller shall deliver such guarantee policy when deed is delivered, but seller, on furnishing such reports shall not be in default for failure to furnish policy until ten days after demand therefor by buyer, such policy or report on title to be conclusive evidence of good title subject only to the exceptions therein stated; (3) Owner's Duplicate Certificate of Title issued by Registrar of Titles, or certified copy thereof, and a Registrar's tax and special assessment search, such Owner's Duplicate to be delivered in any event when deed is delivered.

If abstract be furnished, buyer, within fifteen days after delivery thereof, shall deliver to seller a written statement of his objections to the title, if any, with the abstract, both of which may be delivered at office of _____ otherwise title shown by abstract shall be deemed good.

If evidence of title furnished discloses any defect in title except matters to which this sale is subject by the terms hereof seller shall have sixty days, computed from delivery of objections in case of an abstract, and from delivery of evidence of title in any other case, in which to cure all defects, to which this sale is not subject. Seller, at his election, may cure all objections to title by delivery of guarantee policy covering such objections such as he might have furnished in the first instance. If such defects in title be not cured within such sixty days buyer may terminate this contract or may at his election, take the title as it then is (with right to deduct from purchase price liens of definite or ascertainable amount) on giving seller notice of such election and tendering performance. If no such notice be given or tender made within ten days after notice to buyer of seller's inability to cure such defects, this contract then shall be null and void. If this contract be terminated except for buyer's default earnest money shall be returned.

If buyer defaults hereunder, then, at the option of seller, earnest money shall be forfeited as liquidated damages and his contract then shall be null and void.

If, prior to delivery of deed hereunder, the improvements on said premises shall be destroyed or materially damaged by fire or other casualty, this contract shall, at the option of buyer, become null and void. Payment of purchase price and delivery of deed shall be made at office of _____ but at Registrar's Office if Certificate of Title be furnished.

All notices and demands herein required shall be in writing. The mailing of a notice by registered mail to seller at _____, or to buyer at _____ shall be sufficient service thereof, on date of mailing.

Seller agrees to pay a real estate brokerage commission to _____ computed at the rate acknowledged by the Chicago Real Estate Board to be customary with respect to this sale.

Time is of the essence of this contract. The words "date hereof" mean date of delivery of this contract.

This contract and earnest money shall be held in escrow by _____ for the mutual benefit of parties hereto, and after consummation the canceled contract may be retained by the escrowee. Unless buyer be entitled to a refund of earnest money, it shall be applied first to payment of expenses incurred for seller by said broker, and second to payment of said commission, balance, to be paid to seller.

Dated the _____ day of _____, A.D. 19__.

_____　　　_____

_____　　　_____

Note: Enforcement of Oral Contract—The "Part Performance" Doctrine

Even where no written memorandum sufficient to satisfy the Statute of Frauds has been executed, an oral contract for the purchase and sale of land may become specifically enforcible by virtue of the equitable doctrine of "part performance."

In this connection, consider the following extract from 2 Corbin, Contracts § 420 (1950):

"It is sometimes said that part performance takes a case out of the statute. There is reason for this in the case of a sale of goods, because the statute applicable thereto is expressly limited to cases in which there has been no part payment, nothing given in earnest, and no acceptance and receipt of part of the goods. But the usual statutory provision as to land contains no such limitation; and therefore part performance does not take a case out of that provision. Nevertheless, it is established law that, after certain kinds of part performance by a purchaser, the court will specifically enforce the vendor's promise to convey land, and there are numerous cases giving the same remedy to a vendor on similar grounds. By a course of judicial development, the statute has become inapplicable in these cases, in spite of the fact that they are clearly included within its words. Part performance of a contract for the transfer of land does not take the case out of the statute; but it may be of such a character that it will take the statute out of the case.

"In these cases, the plaintiff is permitted to prove the terms of the agreement by oral testimony; and he has the burden of proof as to what those terms were. It is equally permissible for the defendant to show that the agreement was not as alleged by the plaintiff, that his promise was conditional upon an event that has never occurred, that he promised to convey without warranty, or that he reserved a right of way or other easement.

"Part performance has been held sufficient to compel recognition of an easement in land as well as to compel a conveyance or a payment. Being sufficient to enable the plaintiff to prove all the terms of an oral contract, it is necessarily sufficient to allow the use of oral testimony to supplement an existing memorandum that is deficient in some material respect."

As the foregoing extract indicates, the doctrine of "part performance" is an equitable doctrine generally applicable only in specific performance suits or in cases where the specific enforceability of an oral contract for the sale of an interest in land is asserted by way of defense or counterclaim. Although the law of many states as to "part performance" is doubtful and that of some is extremely confused both in theory and application, American courts seem generally agreed that the "part performance" relied on to "take the statute out of the case" must be (1) in some degree evidential of the existence of a contract relating to the property in question, and (2) pursuant to the alleged contract and prior to notice of repudiation by the other party. But there is no agreement among the courts as to the necessity of showing that "injustice" or "irreparable injury" will result if the court refuses to enforce the contract specifically. The following are the chief kinds of "part performance" which various courts have thought sufficient to justify specific enforcement of an oral contract.

Payment of the Price. Although at an early date it was held in England that payment of all or a substantial portion of the purchase price by the purchaser would entitle the purchaser to have specific performance of an oral contract, this view has been repudiated in England and in most of the United States. The reasons usually given are that payment of money alone is not sufficiently evidential of the existence of a contract relating to the property in question and that the purchaser can be placed in the *status quo ante* by a judgment for restitution in money and thus will suffer no hardship if specific performance is refused. There appear to be only three jurisdictions [9] which still follow the rule that payment of all or part of the purchase price is sufficient "part performance" of an oral contract to render it specifically enforceable.

_____

9. Delaware (decision), Iowa (statute), and Georgia (statute).

Delivery of Possession to the Purchaser. Some fourteen states [10] have indicated that they accept the English view that delivery of possession by the vendor to the purchaser (or his taking possession with the consent of the vendor), standing alone, may be sufficient "part performance" to permit enforcement of an oral contract against the vendor. The English view was based in part, at least, on the theory that since delivery of possession was an important operative fact in the transfer of freehold estates at common law, it could be regarded as a substantial performance of the vendor's promise to convey, although he had not yet executed a written instrument of conveyance. Furthermore, delivery of possession is normally evidential of the existence of some contract between the parties, though it does not furnish any evidence as to the precise terms thereof. In some cases entry by the purchaser into joint occupancy with the vendor has been held sufficient "part performance," but in other cases it has been held insufficient. Continuance of a prior possession by the purchaser has generally been held insufficient, since it bears no resemblance to a livery of seisin and does not evidence the making of a new contract between the parties. In at least sixteen states [11] even the delivery of exclusive possession to the purchaser, standing alone, has been held insufficient "part performance" on the ground that by taking possession the purchaser does not necessarily change his position in such a way as to render it unjust for the court to refuse specific performance of the oral contract. In some seven jurisdictions [12] the decisions and/or dicta are conflicting as to the effect of delivery of possession to the purchaser, standing alone. The question appears to be open in the remaining American jurisdictions.

Delivery of Possession Plus Payment of Purchase Money. In a substantial number of jurisdictions,[13] although delivery of possession to the purchaser, standing alone, is insufficient, such delivery plus payment of all or a substantial part of the purchase price by the purchaser is sufficient "part performance" to permit enforcement of the oral contract against the vendor. There is some authority that even the continuance of a prior possession by the purchaser, coupled with payment, is sufficient "part performance," and the rule is so stated in 1 Restatement, Contracts § 197(b).

Possession Plus the Making of Improvements by the Purchaser. Most of the jurisdictions that recognize the "part performance" doctrine at all will decree specific performance in favor of a purchaser who receives possession of the property in dispute and makes "valuable and permanent improvements" thereon before notice of repudiation by the vendor. The making of such improvements is usually considered as "unequivocally referable" to the alleged contract, and it often creates a situation where it would be difficult to compensate the purchaser fairly by a money judgment for restitution. The courts tend to talk about "virtual" or "equitable" fraud in such cases, either granting the relief asked on the ground that refusal to enforce the oral contract would result in the consummation of such fraud or denying relief because no such fraud would result. It is clear, of course, that no legal fraud can be found in most of these cases. Failure of the vendor to perform his promise to convey does not

---

10. 3 A.L.P. § 11.8 lists Arkansas, California, Connecticut, Delaware, Iowa, Maryland, Minnesota, New Hampshire, New Jersey, North Dakota, Ohio, South Carolina, Washington (dictum), and West Virginia.

11. For various states' application of the doctrine of part performance, see 3 A.L.P. § 11.7 et seq., and 2 Corbin on Contracts § 420 et seq., especially §§ 431–440.

12. Ibid.

13. 8 C.J.S. Specific Performance § 67, n. 24 lists Alabama, Arizona, Arkansas, Florida, Georgia, Massachusetts, Michigan, Nebraska, New Jersey, New Mexico, Wisconsin and Wyoming as accepting this view. See also Corbin on Contracts § 433, p. 488, n. 81 and 3 A.L.P. § 11.11 pp. 39–40. The Alabama decisions are pursuant to Alabama Code § 8–9–2.

constitute legal fraud, even though there has been an expenditure of money and/or labor by the purchaser for which there is no adequate compensatory remedy. Some courts tend to treat the making of "valuable and permanent" improvements as sufficient to justify specific performance without any real consideration of the possible adequacy of restitutionary relief, while other courts at least say that they will not specifically enforce an oral contract unless the purchaser can show that he will suffer "irreparable" injury if the contract is not enforced.[14] Logically, the latter view would require the court to refuse enforcement of an oral contract in any case where restitution is available to the purchaser and would furnish a reasonably adequate remedy. It may be doubted, however, that any court except the Massachusetts court has consistently applied such a rule.

In at least three states, Kentucky, Mississippi, and North Carolina, the doctrine of "part performance" as a basis for the specific enforcement of oral contracts has been wholly repudiated. This seems also to be true in Tennessee, although the exact status of the doctrine in Tennessee is not clear. A recent Tennessee case, Knight v. Knight, 222 Tenn. 367, 436 S.W.2d 289 (1969), denied relief to a purchaser, saying that part performance did not make the contract enforceable, and that in Tennessee this was a rule of property. It also recognized however, that Tennessee courts have sometimes applied a doctrine of equitable estoppel to reach the same result as would be reached under the part performance doctrine. In all of these states, moreover, the terms of the oral contract may be proved by parol evidence as a basis for obtaining restitution of payments made or the value of services rendered to the vendor pursuant to the contract, or the value of improvements made on the land by the purchaser in reliance on the contract. In Kentucky the court has gone so far as to impose a lien upon the land that was the subject-matter of the oral contract as security for the collection of a judgment for restitution in favor of the purchaser. In Kentucky, North Carolina, and Tennessee the courts have also on occasion given judgment to the purchaser for the value of the land itself where the purchaser's performance was such that it could not be accurately valued in money for restitutionary purposes. This is in substance, though not in form, an award of damages for breach of the oral contract, despite the fact that an oral contract within the statute of frauds is normally not enforceable by a common law action for damages.

For a fuller discussion of the "part performance doctrine," see 2 Corbin, Contracts, Ch. 18 (1950). As to the remedy of restitution where defendant pleads the Statute of Frauds, see id. § 321.

(2) Documents Required for Completion of Sale

(a) The Deed of Conveyance

Every sale of real estate is ultimately completed, if the deal does not fall through, by the execution of a deed of conveyance which transfers

---

14. See 3 A.L.P. § 11.10, stating that the rule is well-settled in Massachusetts, and probably also in Pennsylvania, New York, Virginia, and two or three other states; but that even in Massachusetts, "one finds difficulty in reconciling the decisions. Some stress the value of the improvements as the sole criterion for change of position. Others consider extrinsic acts done in reliance upon the promise even where there was possession, partial payment and minor improvements to the land. Usually, even where the facts of possession, payment in part or in whole, exist, the stress is put upon the value of the improvements as the determining factor in whether an award of compensation in money or a decree of specific performance will be made."

the vendor's interest in the land to the purchaser. In Chapter 9, Section 1, of this book we have already considered in some detail the form, contents, and execution of deeds of conveyance.

(b) The Mortgage

As previously indicated, most real estate sale transactions involve borrowing by the purchaser from a third party or the extension of credit to the purchaser by the vendor. The most common method of handling the transaction in such cases is to provide for the transfer of legal title to the real estate to the purchaser by delivery of a deed of conveyance as soon as the title examination has been satisfactorily completed and the loan or extension of credit has been arranged, with a contemporaneous delivery to the third party lender or to the vendor (as the case may be) of an instrument called a mortgage for the purpose of securing repayment of the loan or payment of the balance of the purchase price (as the case may be).

The mortgage is an instrument giving a creditor an interest in real property as security for performance of an obligation. In form, the mortgage usually purports to be a conveyance of legal title in fee simple, with a proviso that if the mortgagor performs his obligations as set out in the instrument such conveyance shall be "void and of no effect." From the standpoint of the purchaser of real estate, the mortgage represents the most usual means of financing his purchase; from the standpoint of the vendor or third party lender, it represents security for his extension of credit or his loan, enforceable against the land which the purchaser acquired in the purchase transaction. When the vendor extends credit for a portion of the purchase price and takes a mortgage to secure payment, the mortgage is called a "purchase money mortgage." When a third party lends the purchaser enough money so that he can pay the entire purchase price in cash and takes a mortgage to secure repayment of the loan, the mortgage is not always called a "purchase money mortgage," but in fact it serves exactly the same purpose and, as regards priority over other types of encumbrances, it is generally treated as a "purchase money mortgage."

The mortgage often takes the form of a deed of trust—i.e., a conveyance of the legal title to a trustee, to hold as security for a debt, in trust to reconvey to the debtor if the debt is paid, and, if it is not paid, to sell the land and pay the creditor out of the proceeds—instead of a conveyance of the legal title to the creditor himself. Technically both the debtor and the creditor are *cestuis que trust*, but the relation between debtor and creditor is basically the same as where the creditor takes a regular mortgage as security. The trust deed mortgage can, of course, be used to secure a purchaser's obligation to pay the unpaid portion of the purchase price to the vendor, and it is accorded the same priority as a regular "purchase money mortgage" in such a case. Although the trust deed mortgage is treated differently in some respects from the regular mortgage, there is a tendency for legislatures and courts to narrow the differences between it and the regular mortgage so far as the substantial rights of the parties are concerned, except where the trust deed mortgage is used to secure an issue of corporate bonds. The trustee under a corporate trust deed mortgage represents all the bondholders *vis a vis* the corporation, and has important duties if there is a default in payment of interest or principal of the bonds necessitating a foreclosure and/or a corporate reorganization.

Prior to the mid-1930s, mortgages generally required repayment of the principal of a mortgage within a relatively short period, and in many cases only interest was payable until the end of the loan term, when the entire principal was payable in a lump sum (a "balloon payment"). As a result of the enactment of Title II of the National Housing Act of 1934, creating a system of federal mortgage insurance and providing that a mortgage would be eligible for such insurance only if it contained "complete amortization provisions satisfactory to the [Federal Housing] Commissioner requiring periodic payments by the mortgagor," it soon became the practice to draft mortgages on residential property so as to require the mortgagor to repay the mortgage loan over a long term (20 to 30 years) in equal monthly installments, each consisting partly of principal and partly of interest. Although a provision for amortization by equal monthly payments was not then mandated by state law, institutional lenders generally adopted the "self-amortizing" mortgage for "conventional" (i.e., not federally insured) loans as well as for federally insured loans; and many states later enacted legislation requiring most residential housing loans to be repaid on a "self-amortizing" basis.

When mortgaged land is sold, the purchaser is likely to "refinance"—i.e., to borrow enough money to pay off the existing mortgage debt in full and to pay the vendor the difference between the mortgage debt and the agreed purchase price, with the purchase money lender taking a new mortgage to secure his loan. But sometimes the vendor is willing to receive only the difference between the existing mortgage debt and the agreed purchase price in cash and to convey the property to the purchaser "subject to the mortgage." The purchaser, in such a case, usually (though not always) "assumes the mortgage" or, more precisely, assumes a personal obligation to pay the balance of the mortgage indebtedness. Sometimes, of course, the vendor is willing to accept a "purchase money mortgage" to secure payment of all or part of the difference between the existing mortgage debt and the agreed purchase price; and sometimes a third party will lend all or part of the difference between the existing mortgage debt and the agreed purchase price, taking a "purchase money mortgage" to secure the loan. In either case, the purchaser usually "assumes" the existing mortgage debt.

Beginning in the late 1960s, as mortgage interest rates continued an escalation that started in the 1950s, institutional mortgage lenders instituted the practice of inserting in mortgages so-called "due-on-sale" clauses empowering them to "accelerate" the maturity of the mortgage indebtedness if and when the mortgaged property is sold. The purpose of such clauses is primarily to enable a mortgage lender to impose upon a prospective purchaser the necessity either to agree to an increase in the interest rate on the mortgage debt, as the price of "assuming" the existing mortgage, or to "refinance" by obtaining a new mortgage loan at the current (usually higher) interest rate to replace the existing mortgage loan. Courts in a few states subsequently held that "due-on-sale" clauses constitute indirect restraints on the alienation of fee simple estates and, therefore, should be enforceable only upon a showing that sale to the prospective purchaser will impair the mortgage holder's security in some way; and a few state legislatures enacted statutes restricting enforcement of "due-on-sale" clauses. In the great majority of states, however, it is now settled that "due-on-sale" causes are "automatically" enforceable at the sole option of the mortgage holder. This is true as to federally-chartered thrift institutions as a result of the Supreme Court's decision in Fidelity Savings & Loan Association v. De La Cuesta,[15] and as to practically all other lending institutions as a result of the enactment of the Garn-St. Germain Depository Institutions Act of 1982.[16]

More or less standardized mortgage forms have come into common use during the past three decades. Federally insured or guaranteed mortgages must utilize forms approved by the Federal Housing Administration or the Veterans' Administration; and mortgage lenders must now use the "uniform instruments" prepared jointly by the Federal National Mortgage Association (FNMA) and the Federal Home Loan Mortgage Corporation (FHLMC) to make their mortgages eligible for purchase by either FNMA or FHLMC in the "secondary market." This is a matter of real significance, since by 1980 the lending institutions that "originate" mortgages were selling almost one-half of their residential mortgages in the secondary market, mainly to FNMA and FHLMC.

(c) The Mortgage Bond or Note

If the purchaser obtains credit from the vendor or borrows from a third party and gives a mortgage to secure his personal obligation to pay the balance of the purchase price or to repay the loan, that obligation is usually embodied in a bond or promissory note (or series of notes). Although mortgage bonds are still used in some states, the more common practice today is to embody the mortgage debtor's obligation in a promissory note, or a series of promissory notes falling due periodically. The note or notes may or may not be negotiable in charac-

---

15. 458 U.S. 141, 102 S.Ct. 3014, 73 L.Ed.2d 664 (1982).

16. Fed.Banking L.Rep. (CCH) ¶ 940 (Special 3) § 341(c)(1). This statute authorized the Federal Home Loan Bank Board to issue regulations pertaining to the new statute's abrogation of state rules restricting the exercise of "due-on-sale" clauses. On May 13, 1983, the FHLBB, in consultation with the Comptroller of the Currency and the National Credit Union Administration Board, issued such regulations. The statute and the regulations allow state law to remain in force in those states where enforcement of "due-on-sale" clauses was restricted by court decisions or statute before adoption of the act, as to mortgage loans originated by non-federal-

ly chartered lenders, national banks, and federally-chartered credit unions for a three-year "window period" beginning October 15, 1982. After October 15, 1985, "due-on-sale" clauses in mortgage loans originated by none-federally chartered lenders will be enforcible as written unless a state legislature acts within the "window period" to restrict enforcement; and mortgage loans originated by national banks and federal credit unions will be enforcible as written unless the COC or the NCUA Board acts within the "window period" to restrict enforcement.

Generally, see Barad & Layden, Due-on-Sale Law as Preempted by the Garn-St. Germain Act, 12 Real Estate L.J. 138 (1983).

ter, but mortgage bonds are almost invariably non-negotiable. For an authoritative definition of a "negotiable instrument," see Uniform Commercial Code §§ 3–104 through 3–114.

(d) The Title Retention Contract

Where a real estate vendor extends credit to the purchaser for part of the purchase price, as an alternative to the deed and purchase money mortgage arrangement, the parties may execute a title retention contract which will serve as a security device for a relatively extended period. The title retention contract usually provides that the purchaser shall pay the price (with interest) in stated periodic installments, and that the vendor shall deliver a deed to the purchaser only when the purchase price has been paid in full, or when the unpaid balance has been reduced to a stated amount. Although the deed and mortgage form of transaction is prevalent in most parts of the country, the "title retention contract" is extensively used in some localities, particularly when satisfactory financing cannot be arranged through a lending institution and the vendor agrees to extend credit to the purchaser.

In cases where a title retention contract is used as a security device, it is likely to be preceded by an informal written memorandum expressing the terms of sale as to which the parties have reached agreement, and in some cases the parties even execute a formal written instrument of the "earnest money" type providing for later execution of a title retention contract of specified character.

It should be noted that the title retention contract, like the conditional sale contract used in the sale of goods, can be used to secure a loan from a third party by the simple expedient of having the vendor immediately assign the contract and transfer his legal title to the third party lender. The Veterans' Administration will guaranty loans secured by title retention contract, and the Federal Housing Administration will insure such loans.

The similarity between the title retention contract used in the purchase and sale of realty and the conditional sale contract used in the purchase and sale of goods is obvious. In both instances the vendor wants to obtain the maximum security and prefers the contract form of security to the mortgage form because he believes that retention of the legal title and the other legal incidents of the contract form of security will assure a swifter and more satisfactory remedy in case the purchaser defaults. Although the similarity between the position of a purchaser-mortgagor and a purchaser in possession under a title retention contract is striking, the rules applied in the event of default are often quite different. In some jurisdictions, for example, the vendor under a title retention contract may, on default by the purchaser, summarily "cancel" the contract, recover possession of the property, and retain all payments made by the purchaser, if the contract so provides. This result, which is completely repugnant to the concept of the mortgagor's "equity of redemption" developed in the English Court of Chancery in the 17th century, came to be permitted during the 19th century when courts were strongly influenced by the concepts of "freedom of contract" and the inviolability of contract obligations.

A modern court may find that where a land contract purchaser has paid a large portion of the agreed price, and then defaulted, it would be "unconscionable" to allow "forfeiture" of the payments and also give the vendor the land. See, e.g., Skendzel v. Marshall, 261 Ind. 226, 301 N.E.2d 641 (1973), certiorari denied 415 U.S. 921, 94 S.Ct. 1421 (1974), where the court refused to enforce the forfeiture provision in the contract, and remitted the vendor to a foreclosure remedy.[17] The Uniform Land Transaction Act, § 3–102, eliminates the difference between the mortgage and the instalment land contract with respect to the rights of the parties on default. It provides that "this Article [Secured Transactions] applies to any transaction, regardless of its form, intended to create a security interest in real estate." Specifically, it applies to "security interests created by contract or conveyance, including a mortgage, deed of trust, trust deed, security deed, contract for deed, land sales contract, lease intended as security, * * * and any other consensual lien or title retention contract intended as security for an obligation."

It is probable that whether land is sold with a title retention contract or by giving the purchaser a deed and taking back a "purchase money" mortgage is heavily influenced by the condition of the real estate market and by the way in which remedial laws to protect land contract purchasers have developed in a given state. See Note, The Changing Status of the Land Contract in Michigan and the Advantages of the Two-Party Mortgage as an Alternative, 28 Wayne L.Rev. 239 (1981).

Title retention contracts are of various types and may be variously referred to as "bonds for title," "contracts for deed," "instalment land contracts," or simply "land contracts." The old-fashioned "bond for title" or "contract for deed" was usually a rather brief instrument. The modern "instalment land contract" is generally a much longer and more detailed instrument. The following form of instalment land contract is in common use in Wisconsin and is similar to forms in common use throughout the Middle West:

---

17. See also H & L Land Co. v. Warner, 258 So.2d 293 (Fla.Ct.App.1972), noted in 26 U.Miami L.Rev. 855 (1972), where a vendee was allowed specific performance even after four years of default.

See an excellent discussion of the problems inherent in the instalment land contract arrangement in Nelson and Whitman, The Instalment Land Contract—A National View, Brigham Young U.L.Rev. 1977: 541.

It has been urged that the instalment land contract, with its speedy remedies, has been a significant factor in providing access to low cost housing by low income families, because the quick and expeditious remedies enable the builder-vendor to live with the high risk conditions of low down payment and minimal credit requirements. Too much tightening by consumer protection holdings could operate to dry up access. See Note, Reforming the Vendor's Remedies for Breach of Installment Land Sale Contracts, 47 So.Cal.L.Rev. 191 (1973).

It has also been urged that the instalment land sale contract should be abolished. Note, Toward Abolishing Instalment Land Sale Contracts, 36 Mont.L.Rev. 110 (1975). See also, Egan, Forfeiture Under Installment Land Contracts in Utah, 1981 Utah L.Rev. 803.

𝕿𝖍𝖎𝖘 𝕬𝖗𝖙𝖎𝖼𝖑𝖊 𝖔𝖋 𝕬𝖌𝖗𝖊𝖊𝖒𝖊𝖓𝖙,

Made and concluded this...day of...A. D., 19........., by and between...

and ....part...........of the first part,

....part..............of the second part.

𝖂𝖎𝖙𝖓𝖊𝖘𝖘𝖊𝖙𝖍: First, That the said part............ of the second part hereby agree......and bind.............................
.................legal representatives, to pay or cause to be paid, to the said part........... of the first part,...................heirs or assigns, the sum of...Dollars, in the manner following:...Dollars, at the ensealing and delivery hereof: ....

....

The said payments to be made to the part........... of the first part, at...
....
and the same being intended to apply, when fully completed as the purchase money for the following tract, piece or parcel of land, situated in the County of...and State of Wisconsin, to-wit:

....

....

The said part ....of the second part further agree...... that.........................will pay, when due and payable, all taxes and assessments which have been assessed or levied on the above described premises since the 1st day of January, A. D., 19..........., and also all such as may be hereafter assessed or levied thereon or upon the interest of said part...........of the first part in said premises; and also all taxes and assessments now or hereafter assessed or levied against any mortgage which may exist against said premises or against the note...... or the indebtedness secured by such mortgage or against the interest in said premises of any party holding a mortgage against said premises during the term of this contract, and promise..... and agree..... that the interest of the part........... of the first part and the interest of the part........... of the second part in said real estate and the interest of any party holding a mortgage against said real estate during the term of this contract, shall be assessed for taxation and taxed together, without separate valuation as unincumbered real estate and shall be paid by the said part........... of the second part and the said part...........of the second part hereby waive..... all rights of offsets or deductions because of the payment of any such taxes and assessments, until the aforesaid purchase money shall be fully paid, in the manner above stated.
The part ....of the second part further agree......that the said part...........of the first part shall insure and keep insured against loss or damage the building......now on said premises and such as may hereafter be erected thereon during the life of this contract in the sum of at least ....Dollars, against loss or damage by fire...

.... , in the name of the part............ of the first part as owner in fee, with clause in said policy that the said part........... of the second part ha...... a land contract interest therein and the loss, if any, under such insurance shall be payable to the said part...........of the first part to the extent of .... interest and the surplus, if any, to the said part........... of the second part, subject, however, to the rights of mortgagees, if any, respecting such insurance: such policy or policies to be held by the said part...........of the first part,......................heirs, legal representatives or assigns, as collateral to this contract; and the said part........... of the second part shall pay the premium on such policy or policies when due, and in case of the failure or neglect of the said part...........of the second part to pay such premiums when due, said part...........of the first part,......................heirs, legal representatives or assigns may pay the same and charge the cost thereof with interest thereon at the legal rate, to the said part...........of the second part, and the same shall be considered and taken to be an additional part of the consideration of this contract.

[A69962]

The part........... of the second part further agree...... to hold the said premises from the date hereof, as the tenant...... by sufferance of the said part...........of the first part, subject to be removed as....................tenant..... .... holding over, by process under the statute in such case made and provided, whenever default shall be made in the payment of any of the installments of purchase money, interest, taxes, assessments or insurance premiums as above specified; and also to keep the building......, fences and improvements on said premises in as good repair and condition as they now are, except ordinary wear and decay, and not to do any act whatsoever. which tends to depreciate the value of said premises.
Second, That the said part........... of the first part hereby agree..... and bind.................................heirs, executors and administrators, that in case the aforesaid sum of ....Dollars, with the interest and other moneys shall be fully paid and all the conditions herein provided shall be fully performed at the times and in the manner above specified,....................will on demand, thereafter cause to be executed and delivered to the said part...........of the second part, or.......................heirs or legal representatives, a good and sufficient Warranty Deed, in fee simple, of the premises above described, free and clear of all legal liens and incumbrances, except the taxes and assessments herein agreed to be paid by the part .... of the second part, and except any liens or incumbrances created by the act or default of the part .... of the second part, ...heirs, legal representatives or assigns ....

....

....

....

Third. It is distinctly agreed and understood by and between the parties hereto, that if the said part............ of the second part shall fail to make any of the payments of purchase money and interest above specified, at the times and in the manner above specified, or fail to pay the taxes and assessments, or fail to insure and keep insured the premises herein as above stipulated. or fail to pay any or all insurance premiums herein specified, or violate any other terms or conditions herein contained, this agreement shall at the option of the said part............ of the first part be henceforth utterly void w'thout any notice whatsoever, and all payments thereon forfeited, subject to be revived and renewed only by the act of the part............of the first part, or the mutual agreement of both parties; and whenever such default or violation shall occur, the part............ of the second part shall have no further right to collect rents from tenants, if any, of the said real estate, or any part thereof, but such rents shall be collected by, and belong to the part............of the first part.

The said part............ of the second part further promise......and agree......that in case of the commencement of an action to foreclose this contract and also in case of the foreclosure thereof,............will pay in addition to the taxable costs and expenses incurred, a reasonable sum of money as attorney's fees.

In Witness Whereof, the said parties have hereunto set their hands and seals this.............................
day of.., A. D., 19............

SIGNED AND SEALED IN PRESENCE OF

.... (SEAL)

.... (SEAL)

.... (SEAL)

.... (SEAL)

State of Wisconsin,
               } ss.
--------------------------------- County.

Personally came before me, this..day of........................A. D., 19............
the above named ....

....

to me known to be the person...... who executed the foregoing instrument and acknowledged the same.

....

Notary Public,..County, Wis.

My commission expires .... A. D., 19..........

[A6963]

(e) The Escrow Agreement

The closing of a real estate sale is frequently handled by means of an "escrow" involving the deposit of all the necessary documents with a third party pending completion of the title examination and determination that the vendor's title is "good and marketable" or that it meets any other standard set out in the sale contract. This matter has already been treated in some detail in Chapter 9, Section 4, under the heading "Delivery, Conditional Deeds, and Escrows." At this point we simply repeat that careful drafting of the escrow agreement is necessary if this form of closing is used. It should also be pointed out that in some of the western states, especially in California, the basic real estate sale contract and the escrow agreement are frequently combined in a single document. When this practice is followed, the "escrow agent" is usually a title insurance company which will conduct the title examination, handle the delivery and recording of the deed, the trust deed or mortgage, and insure the title of the lender and the purchaser. Frequently the title insurance company will be an affiliate or subsidiary of the lending institution which finances the purchase.

(3) The Closing or Settlement *

When the title has been examined, financing arranged, and other necessary conditions satisfied and investigations completed, the buyer and seller will exchange title for purchase price in a process called "closing" or "settlement." The mechanics of title transfer are straightfoward, although somewhat complex. Some "closing agent" will usually handle them. The closing agent's tasks may include the following:

1.   Reviewing the preliminary title report to determine what liens or encumbrances exist on the property, and then inquiring of their holders (e.g., existing lending institutions) what amount will be necessary to pay them off (if title is to be transferred free of them.)

2.   Obtaining executed copies of the deed, the new note and mortgage or other security device if any, and a multitude of other forms and documents, including satisfactions of mortgages or liens being paid off.

3.   Obtaining funds from the buyer and the new lender.

4.   Arranging for completion of some miscellaneous ancillary services, such as surveys, pest inspections, etc.

5.   Computing the necessary adjustments between buyer, seller, and old and new lien holders for such matters as property taxes, insurance, and local assessments.

6.   Seeing that appropriate documents are recorded and mailed to the persons entitled to them.

7.   Disbursing funds to the providers of ancillary services, to taxing authorities if any, and to the seller and prior lienholders who are being paid off.

There is great national variation in the filling of the roles of title examiner and closing agent. Along most of the east coast (with exceptions in New York City and Washington, D.C.) attorneys commonly do both jobs; in fact, they frequently do the actual searches in the public records, although the more sophisticated members of the bar are now beginning to employ lay assistants or independent contractors for this phase of their work. In the mountain west, the west coast, and Texas, the examination of titles is generally done by private title insurance companies, often in their own private "title plants" rather than in the public records. In these areas of the Nation, the closing agent is usually an "escrow agent"—a private corporation (sometimes affiliated with a title company or lending institution) set up to receive and disburse documents and funds in real estate transactions. In the Midwest, title assurance is usually in the form of an "abstract", a book or sheaf of documents which summarize or set forth in full each instrument in the public records. Abstracts are often passed down from one owner to the next, and are updated with each transfer, thus saving a great deal of time and duplication which would be necessary if a complete record

* This part is drawn from G. Nelson & D. Whitman, Real Estate Transfer, Finance, and Development 224–226, 235–239 (2d ed. 1981). Copyright, West Publishing Company, 1981.

search had to be made each time land was sold.   Under the Midwestern practice, the abstract is typically examined by an attorney, who provides his opinion of the title to the new lender and the buyer.   He may also handle the closing function, or the lending institution may do so, perhaps without a separate charge for the service.   The foregoing summary of national practices is sketchy and oversimplified; more detail is found in B. Burke, American Conveyancing Patterns (1978); Payne, Ancillary Costs in the Purchase of Homes, 35 Mo.L.Rev. 455 (1970); U.S. Dept. of Housing and Urban Development & Veterans Administration, Report on Mortgage Settlement Costs (1972).

Throughout the nation procedures for the transfer of single-family homes tend to be routine and mechanical; indeed, you may wonder that attorneys want such work at all, although you may be assured that in many jurisdictions they fight vigorously for their exclusive right to continue doing it.   But whether the closing is handled by an attorney, a title company, an escrow company, or a lending institution, things sometimes go wrong.   The closing agent may have a great deal of other people's money in hand, and the temptation to convert some of it to his own use may be powerful.   In its least innocuous form, this temptation may be manifested by the agent's merely being a bit slow to disburse the funds after the closing is completed; they may rest for a few days or even weeks in his bank account, where (as a so-called "compensating balance") they serve to make his bank more generous with him in other matters.   Sometimes things are worse, with the agent simply accumulating the funds from a number of closings and then skipping town with them.   The usual attitude of the courts in such cases is that the loss falls on the party who was entitled to the funds—the seller and old lender, if the closing has already occurred.   See, e.g., Lawyers Title Ins. Corp. v. Edmar Constr. Co. Inc., 294 A.2d 865 (D.C.App.1972).   Is this a sensible resolution of the conflict, given the unavailability of the crooked closing agent?   In general, is it wise to use institutional closing agents (lenders, large title insurance companies, etc.) to minimize such risks?

During the early 1970's the cost of real estate transfer services became the focus of serious attention by federal officials.   Section 701 of the Emergency Home Finance Act of 1970 instructed the Department of Housing and Urban Development to study the problem, and also authorized HUD and the VA to " *   *   * prescribed standards governing the amount of settlement costs allowable in connection with the financing of *   *   *" FHA and VA homes.   The only tangible result of this mandate was the publication of a Report on Mortgage Settlement Costs in 1971.   HUD and VA did publish a proposed regulation which would have fixed maximum charges for certain settlement services; see 37 Fed.Reg. 13185 (1972).   But opposition from the affected industries was swift, heavy, and effective, for the regulation was never made binding. The process is described in detail in Whitman, Home Transfer Costs: An Economic and Legal Analysis, 62 Geo.L.J. 1311 (1974).   See also Burke, Conveyancing in the National Capital Region: Local Reform with National Implications, 22 Am.U.L.Rev. 527 (1973).

The 1971 Report on Mortgage Settlement Costs provides the results of a nationwide survey of transfer costs in FHA and VA home sales, and thus is helpful in assessing whether title-related closing costs are excessive. The report disclosed an enormously wide variation in average costs, ranging from $56 in North Dakota to $480 in New York. The average of the five lowest cost states was $84, and of the five highest cost states, $418. The geographic distribution of the cost spectrum is instructive. Seven of the ten highest cost states were located in the Middle Atlantic area, while all but one of the 20 lowest cost states were in the Midwest, New England, or the Rocky Mountain states.

* * *

Congressional concern with high costs of settlement services and with allegedly "abusive" practices in the settlement industry resulted in the enactment in 1974 (and substantial amendment in 1975) of the Real Estate Settlement Procedures Act, 12 U.S.C.A. § 2601 et seq., commonly called "RESPA." Its basic thesis is that if consumers are given advance information about settlement services and costs, they will shop more vigorously and will bargain down prices to competitive levels. RESPA § 5 requires lending institutions to give to loan applicants a "special information booklet" prepared by HUD, and a written "good faith estimate" of the settlement costs the borrower is likely to incur, within three days after the loan application is received. It is doubtful, however, that this information has much impact on shopping behavior or prices. It does have the advantage of informing borrowers well in advance of the cash requirements they must meet. Is any form of consumer education or disclosure likely to be much more effective in encouraging shopping? See Stoppello, Federal Regulation of Home Mortgage Settlement Costs: RESPA and its Alternatives, 63 Minn.L.Rev. 367 (1979).[18]

Perhaps the most controversial aspect of RESPA is § 8, which prohibits referral fees and fee-splitting among providers of settlement services, except to the extent that the fee is for the reasonable value of services actually performed. The core language is § 8(a):

> No person shall give and no person shall accept any fee, kickback, or thing of value pursuant to any agreement or understanding, oral or otherwise, that business incident to or a part of a real estate settlement service * * * shall be referred to any person.

Both civil and criminal penalties are provided for violations. Such fees for referrals were very widespread prior to the enactment of RESPA, and there is no doubt that their frequency has declined. Today they are much more likely to take the form of free services, trips, information, food and beverages, etc., rather than cash.

Most of the entities which formerly were heavily involved in paying referral fees, such as title insurers, were pleased with the passage of RESPA § 8. Yet there is by no means universal agreement that it is a good thing, even if effectively enforced. See Owen, Kickbacks, Speciali-

---

18. See also Payne, Conveyancing Practice and the Feds: Some Thoughts About RESPA, 29 Ala.L.Rev. 339 (1978). [Footnote added. Eds.]

zation, Price Fixing, and Efficiency in Residential Real Estate Markets, 29 Stan.L.Rev. 931 (1977), arguing that since real estate brokers are more price-competitive than title insurers, the "monopoly profits" earned by the latter are more likely to filter down to consumers (in the form of lower brokerage commissions) if the title insurers are permitted to pay referral fees to brokers.

Since the passage of § 8, many real estate brokers have attempted to circumvent it by establishing or purchasing title insurance agencies of their own. This practice, known as "controlled business", permits the brokers to refer their customers to their kept title company and to recover the profits in the form of dividends or partnership distributions rather than referral fees. Originally, HUD's interpretation of RESPA appeared to allow this if the dividends were based on a shareholder's capital contributions and not on the relative amount of business which the shareholder referred to the title company. See 24 C.F.R. § 3500.14 and Appendix B, Comment 10. Whether such arrangements should be permitted was a matter of heated debate within HUD, and on July 16, 1980, it issued an interpretive rule which stated that dividends paid to those who also refer business "may" violate § 8 even if the dividends are not based on the amount of business referred. See 45 Fed.Reg. 49360 (July 24, 1980). What would you advise a client under these circumstances?

RESPA § 4 requires that closing agents use a standard form, prescribed by HUD and known as the HUD–1 form, for all home loan closings covered by the Act. The form is designed to make an inherently complex transaction as intelligible as possible to consumers. A copy is reproduced on the next two pages. Following the form is a set of facts and figures on a typical home sale. You are invited to try your hand at completing the form on the basis of these data; you will find it to be a revealing process.

HUD-1 Rev. 5/76

Form Approved
OMB NO. 63-R-1501

A.	B. TYPE OF LOAN
U. S. DEPARTMENT OF HOUSING AND URBAN DEVELOPMENT **SETTLEMENT STATEMENT**	1. ☐ FHA 2. ☐ FmHA 3. ☐ CONV. UNINS. 4. ☐ VA 5. ☐ CONV. INS. 6. File Number: 7. Loan Number: 8. Mortgage Insurance Case Number:

C. NOTE: *This form is furnished to give you a statement of actual settlement costs. Amounts paid to and by the settlement agent are shown. Items marked "(p.o.c.)" were paid outside the closing; they are shown here for informational purposes and are not included in the totals.*

D. NAME OF BORROWER:	E. NAME OF SELLER:	F. NAME OF LENDER:
G. PROPERTY LOCATION:	H. SETTLEMENT AGENT:	I. SETTLEMENT DATE:
	PLACE OF SETTLEMENT:	

J. SUMMARY OF BORROWER'S TRANSACTION		K. SUMMARY OF SELLER'S TRANSACTION	
100. GROSS AMOUNT DUE FROM BORROWER:		**400. GROSS AMOUNT DUE TO SELLER:**	
101. Contract sales price		401. Contract sales price	
102. Personal property		402. Personal property	
103. Settlement charges to borrower (line 1400)		403.	
104.		404.	
105.		405.	
Adjustments for items paid by seller in advance		*Adjustments for items paid by seller in advance*	
106. City/town taxes to		406. City/town taxes to	
107. County taxes to		407. County taxes to	
108. Assessments to		408. Assessments to	
109.		409.	
110.		410.	
111.		411.	
112.		412.	
120. **GROSS AMOUNT DUE FROM BORROWER**		420. **GROSS AMOUNT DUE TO SELLER**	
200. AMOUNTS PAID BY OR IN BEHALF OF BORROWER:		**500. REDUCTIONS IN AMOUNT DUE TO SELLER:**	
201. Deposit or earnest money		501. Excess deposit (see instructions)	
202. Principal amount of new loan(s)		502. Settlement charges to seller (line 1400)	
203. Existing loan(s) taken subject to		503. Existing loan(s) taken subject to	
204.		504. Payoff of first mortgage loan	
205.		505. Payoff of second mortgage loan	
206.		506.	
207.		507.	
208.		508.	
209.		509.	
Adjustments for items unpaid by seller		*Adjustments for items unpaid by seller*	
210. City/town taxes to		510. City/town taxes to	
211. County taxes to		511. County taxes to	
212. Assessments to		512. Assessments to	
213.		513.	
214.		514.	
215.		515.	
216.		516.	
217.		517.	
218.		518.	
219.		519.	
220. **TOTAL PAID BY/FOR BORROWER**		520. **TOTAL REDUCTION AMOUNT DUE SELLER**	
300. CASH AT SETTLEMENT FROM/TO BORROWER		**600. CASH AT SETTLEMENT TO/FROM SELLER**	
301. Gross amount due from borrower (line 120)		601. Gross amount due to seller (line 420)	
302. Less amounts paid by/for borrower (line 220)	( )	602. Less reductions in amount due seller (line 520)	( )
303. CASH (☐ FROM) (☐ TO) BORROWER		**603. CASH (☐ TO) (☐ FROM) SELLER**	

[C3136]

L. SETTLEMENT CHARGES	PAID FROM BORROWER'S FUNDS AT SETTLEMENT	PAID FROM SELLER'S FUNDS AT SETTLEMENT
700. TOTAL SALES/BROKER'S COMMISSION based on price $ @ % =		
Division of Commission (line 700) as follows:		
701. $ to		
702. $ to		
703. Commission paid at Settlement		
704.		
800. ITEMS PAYABLE IN CONNECTION WITH LOAN		
801. Loan Origination Fee %		
802. Loan Discount %		
803. Appraisal Fee to		
804. Credit Report to		
805. Lender's Inspection Fee		
806. Mortgage Insurance Application Fee to		
807. Assumption Fee		
808.		
809.		
810.		
811.		
900. ITEMS REQUIRED BY LENDER TO BE PAID IN ADVANCE		
901. Interest from to @ $ /day		
902. Mortgage Insurance Premium for months to		
903. Hazard Insurance Premium for years to		
904. years to		
905.		
1000. RESERVES DEPOSITED WITH LENDER		
1001. Hazard insurance months @ $ per month		
1002. Mortgage insurance months @ $ per month		
1003. City property taxes months @ $ per month		
1004. County property taxes months @ $ per month		
1005. Annual assessments months @ $ per month		
1006. months @ $ per month		
1007. months @ $ per month		
1008. months @ $ per month		
1100. TITLE CHARGES		
1101. Settlement or closing fee to		
1102. Abstract or title search to		
1103. Title examination to		
1104. Title insurance binder to		
1105. Document preparation to		
1106. Notary fees to		
1107. Attorney's fees to		
(includes above items numbers:)		
1108. Title insurance to		
(includes above items numbers:)		
1109. Lender's coverage $		
1110. Owner's coverage $		
1111.		
1112.		
1113.		
1200. GOVERNMENT RECORDING AND TRANSFER CHARGES		
1201. Recording fees: Deed $; Mortgage $; Releases $		
1202. City/county tax/stamps: Deed $; Mortgage $		
1203. State tax/stamps: Deed $; Mortgage $		
1204.		
1205.		
1300. ADDITIONAL SETTLEMENT CHARGES		
1301. Survey to		
1302. Pest inspection to		
1303.		
1304.		
1305.		
1400. TOTAL SETTLEMENT CHARGES (enter on lines 103, Section J and 502, Section K)		

HUD-1 R [C3141]

NOTE

The following information wil allow you to complete the HUD–1 form.

The transaction is a sale of a newly-constructed house.

Seller: Deluxe Homes, Inc.

Buyers: Frank and Janice Jones

Property location: 1104 Maple Drive, City of Metropole, State of Euphoria.

Legal description: Lot 6, Block B, Outrage Hills addition to the city of Metropole, as recorded in Plat Book 18, page 35, Official Records of Metropole County, State of Euphoria.

Settlement date: February 14, 19__.

Contract sales price: $85,000. Refrigerator to be purchased, $275 extra.

Ad valorem taxes (estimated):

Metropole City = $180

Metropole County = $135

Metropole School District = $755

Taxes are assessed on a calendar year basis and are payable in one annual installment on November 1.

Earnest money deposited with real estate broker (Century Homes, Inc.): $2500.

New mortgage loan: First Federal Savings of Metropole

$68,000, 13% interest, 30 year term

Charges in connection with loan:

Loan origination fee: 2 "points" (%)

Appraisal fee: $150

Credit report: $35

The two latter items were paid at time of loan application.

Lender's reserve requirement: All tax and insurance payments must be paid from reserves, with a two-month "cushion" to be funded at closing of the loan.

Hazard Insurance: County Farm Insurance Co., $190/year paid in advance.

Title and recording charges:

Closing (escrow) fee: $150, split between buyer and seller

Title insurance:

Owner's policy = $205.00, paid by seller

Lender's policy = $85.00, paid by buyer

Recording fees: Deed = $2.00, deed of trust = $4.00

Brokerage commission: 6%, payable entirely to Century Homes, Inc.

Construction loan and other liens on seller's interest:

Balance on construction loan from Second Security Bank = $49,585.

Balance on subordinated deed of trust to former owner of land, Mr. James Link = $8450.

Judgment docketed against Deluxe Homes, Inc. in favor of Capital Credit Corporation = $3480.

Note: on new loan to Mr. & Mrs. Jones, first payment will be due on April 1, and on the first of each month thereafter.

SECTION 2. OBLIGATIONS OF THE VENDOR AS TO TITLE

HEBB v. SEVERSON

Supreme Court of Washington, 1948.
32 Wn.2d 159, 201 P.2d 156.

STEINERT, Justice. Plaintiffs instituted action to compel specific performance of a contract, denominated an earnest money receipt, wherein the defendants promised, subject to specified terms and conditions, to purchase certain real property owned by the plaintiffs. This agreement, setting forth the rights and obligations of the parties thereunder, so far as is material here, reads as follows:

"Earnest Money Receipt

"Seattle, Washington,
"March 31, 1947

"Received from E.H. Severson, Anne M. (His wife) hereinafter called 'purchaser' One Thousand and no/100 ($1000) Dollars as earnest money in part payment of the purchase price of the following described real estate in King County, Washington:

"Lot thirteen (13), Block three (3), Hebb's Avion City addition of the City of Seattle, Washington, commonly known as 5700 East 61st.

"Total purchase price is Twelve Thousand Dollars ($12,000), payable as follows:

"Four Thousand Dollars ($4000) cash, including the amount herein receipted for on closing. Balance to be paid from the proceeds of an F.H.A. loan which the purchaser agrees to apply for through Burwell & Morford, within five (5) days from the date of this receipt. It is understood that purchaser's obligation to purchase is contingent on securing said loan in the amount of Eight Thousand Dollars ($8000).

*   *   *

"Owner shall furnish purchaser, as soon as procurable and within 30 days of date of acceptance of this offer, Puget Sound Title Insurance Company's policy of title insurance or its title report evidencing condition of title.

"If title is not insurable and cannot be made insurable within 60 days from date of title report, earnest money shall be refunded and all rights of purchaser terminated, except that purchaser may waive defects and elect to purchase. But if title is good and purchaser neglects or refuses to complete purchase, the earnest money may, at seller's option, be forfeited as liquidated damages. The agent shall not be responsible for delivery of title.

"The property is to be conveyed by warranty deed, free of encumbrances except: None.

"Rights reserved in federal patents or state deeds, building or use restrictions general to the district, and building or zoning regulations and provisions shall not be deemed encumbrances.

* * *

"Purchaser offers to purchase the property on the terms noted.

"The sale shall be closed within five (5) days after loan is completed and title insurance policy or title insurance company's report is furnished by owner. The purchaser and the seller will, on demand of either, deposit in escrow with the company furnishing the evidence of title all instruments and monies necessary to complete the purchase; the cost of escrow shall be paid one-half each by seller and purchaser."

* * *

Prior to the trial of this action, the parties thereto entered into a written stipulation, setting forth, as agreed upon, the following facts relative to the suit: On March 31, 1947, the appellants, E.H. Severson and Anne M. Severson, executed and delivered to the respondents, Ross P. Hebb and Irene M. Hebb, the earnest money receipt set forth above, wherein the appellants offered to purchase from the respondents a city lot, upon which a house had just been constructed, for the sum of $12,000. At the same time, appellants deposited $1,000 with respondents as earnest money and, on April 7, 1947, the respondents accepted the offer to purchase and signed the earnest money agreement.

It was further stipulated by the parties that, for the purpose of securing funds with which to pay in part the balance of the purchase price owing under the contract, the appellants applied to the mortgage loan firm of Burwell & Morford for a loan in the sum of $8,000. Following the issuance by the Federal housing administration, of its commitment to insure the proposed loan for the full amount, the appellants, on June 9, 1947, made, executed, and delivered to Burwell & Morford, as mortgagee, their promissory note for $8,000, together with a real estate mortgage on the lot above mentioned as security. This mortgage was subsequently recorded, although no part of the loan which it was designed to secure has ever been disbursed by the mortgagee. To insure payment of the remainder of the purchase price, the appellants deposited with the mortgage firm the sum of $3,186.17, but with the instruction to that firm that it should not pay over to the respondents any part of this fund until it was directed by the appellants to do so.

On June 26, 1947, according to the agreed facts, the appellants, through their attorneys, notified respondents that they were rescinding the transaction, and again advised Burwell & Morford not to pay out any of the sum of money deposited with it until further instructed on the matter by the attorneys for appellants.

It was also stipulated that, on August 4, 1947, the respondents furnished to the appellants a title report which showed the title of the property here involved to be subject to (1) an easement for a watermain, but with the notation that the easement had been vacated; (2) the right of the public to make all necessary slopes for cuts or fills upon the lot, in the reasonable original grading of streets, granted in the dedication of the plat; and (3) a declaration of protective restrictions, recorded April 5, 1937. Immediately following this information concerning the declaration of restrictions is a note stating that the title company's inspection of the premises disclosed a breach of one of these restrictions, in that the dwelling house located on the lot involved is less than five feet from the east side line of the premises. The note then continues with the statement:

"The policy to issue will, however, affirmatively insure against loss or damage resulting from such violation and will further affirmatively insure that neither said violation nor any future violation of said restrictions will work a forfeiture or reversion of title to said premises."

Appellants' major assignment of error is that the trial court erred in decreeing that the appellants specifically perform their contract. In support of this assignment, numerous arguments are advanced, but the one to which we shall address our attention and upon which we shall rest our decision is that the title tendered into court by the respondents, though in form a warranty deed covenanting against encumbrances, was in fact subject to the encumbrance, inter alia, of a presently existing violation of a protective restriction; that therefore the title was unmarketable; and that it was not made marketable by a showing of willingness on the part of a title insurance company to insure the appellants against loss incurred by them because of that encumbrance.

A marketable title is one that is free from reasonable doubt and such as reasonably well informed and intelligent purchasers, exercising ordinary business caution, would be willing to accept. * * * Moore v. Elliott, 76 Wash. 520, 136 P. 849; * * * Empey v. Northwestern & Pacific Hypotheekbank, 129 Wash. 392, 225 P. 226; * * *

In discussing the meaning of the term "marketable title," this court said in Moore v. Elliott, supra: * * *

" 'The authorities hold that to render a title marketable it is only necessary that it shall be free from reasonable doubt; in other words, that a purchaser is not entitled to demand a title absolutely free from every possible technical suspicion. He can only demand such title as a reasonably well-informed and intelligent purchaser acting upon business principles would be willing to accept.' Cummings v. Dolan, 52 Wash. 496, 501, 100 P. 989, 991, 132 Am.St.Rep. 986."

In Empey v. Northwestern & Pacific Hypotheekbank, supra, we quoted approvingly the following statement from Dobbs v. Norcross, 24 N.J.Eq. 392, having reference to marketable title (129 Wash. 329, 225 P. 228):

"Every purchaser of land has a right to demand a title which shall put him in all reasonable security and which shall protect him from anxiety, lest annoying, if not successful suits be brought against him, and probably take from him or his representatives, land upon which money was invested. He should have a title which shall enable him not only to hold his land, but to hold it in peace; and if he wishes to sell it, to be reasonably sure that no flaw or doubt will come up to disturb its marketable value."

An "encumbrance" has been defined by this court to be any right to, or interest in, land which may subsist in third persons, to the diminution of the value of the estate of the tenant, but consistent with the passing of the fee; and, also, as a burden upon land depreciative of its value, such as a lien, easement, or servitude, which, though adverse to the interest of the landowner, does not conflict with his conveyance of the land in fee. *   *   *

Keeping these definitions in mind, we have carefully examined the earnest money contract in order to discover what the parties intended, or more specifically, what intention the law imputes to them from the language used in the contract, relative to the quality of title that the appellants bound themselves to accept. The portion of the contract pertinent to our present inquiry is as follows:

"*If title is not insurable* and cannot be made insurable within 60 days from date of title report, earnest money shall be refunded and all rights of purchaser terminated, except that purchaser may waive defects and elect to purchase. *But if title is good* and purchaser neglects or refuses to complete purchase, the earnest money may, at seller's option, be forfeited as liquidated damages. The agent shall not be responsible for delivery of title.

"*The property is to be conveyed by warranty deed, free of encumbrances except: None.*" (Italics ours.)

As we read this part of the contract, three portions thereof stand out as peculiarly significant on the issue of the intent of the parties. First, if the title is not insurable, the appellants may, at their option, terminate the contract; second, if the title is good, the appellants are bound to accept it; and third, the property is to be conveyed by warranty deed, free of encumbrances. It is to be noted that the only expressed intent as to the subject of title insurance is the provision that if title is not insurable, it need not be accepted, and that it is only in the event that title is good that it must be accepted by appellants.

Respondents contend that the intent of the parties, as evidenced by the contract, is that the appellants must accept the title of respondents if it is insurable.

It is without doubt true that a contract for the sale of land may properly contain a provision in effect obligating the vendor to convey only such title as a designated title company will approve and insure, and where such is the case the vendee is of course bound by the agreement and is not justified in refusing a title which conforms thereto merely because it is objectionable on other grounds. *   *   *

We are of the opinion that the contract here under scrutiny contains no such provision. It simply provides that if the title proves non-insurable the appellants need not accept it, and that they need only accept it if it is "good."

The terms "good title," "marketable title," "merchantable title," and "perfect title" are used by the courts to convey the same meaning. 55

Am.Jur. 619, Vendor and Purchaser, § 149; Notes (1928), 57 A.L.R. 1282. * * *

We have no reason to believe that the parties to the earnest money agreement here involved contracted with reference to a different meaning for the term "good title" than the commonly accepted meaning which requires that the title be marketable as hereinbefore defined.

It is to be noted, parenthetically, that even though a title be insurable, it does not follow, necessarily, that the title is also good or marketable. It cannot be gainsaid that any title, no matter how defective, is, from a practical standpoint, insurable, if the premium rate be set high enough, or the list excepting defects which are not insured against be long enough. Therefore, to say that a title is insurable merely means that it is capable of being insured, and not that it is also good or marketable.

A separate and independent reason for holding that the parties herein contracted with reference to marketable title is the fact that their agreement provided that the property was to be conveyed by warranty deed free of encumbrances.

Such a provision in a contract cannot be said to be performed merely by the tender of a warranty deed, but the title must in fact be marketable.

While some of the earlier decisions of other courts have taken the position that a covenant to give a warranty deed is satisfied by furnishing such a deed in form, regardless of the true state of the title, this doctrine has been largely abandoned as being overly technical, and the great majority of the courts, including our own, hold to the better rule that the true intent of the parties, as evidenced by such a provision, is not merely that a deed in the form of a warranty deed must be delivered, but that the actual title of the vendor must in fact conform to the deed, i.e., be marketable, or else the vendee need not accept it. * * *

Even in the absence of any provision in the contract indicating the quality of the title provided for, the law implies an undertaking on the part of the vendor to make and convey a good or marketable title to the purchaser. 55 Am.Jur. 619, Vendor and Purchaser, § 149; Notes (1928), 57 A.L.R. 1256, 1260, wherein Washington cases in support of the rule are collected.

Respondents, however, contend (a) that the appellants had knowledge of the protective restriction at the time they entered into the contract, and that therefore the principles of waiver or estoppel apply, and (b) that the defect is cured by the announced willingness of a title insurance company to insure the appellants against any loss or damage which might be suffered by them as a result of the violation of the protective restriction. A third ground for contention (which, although it is not urged by respondents, we nevertheless mention because it is disclosed by a reading of the contract set forth herein and should therefore receive attention) is (c) that the earnest money contract contains the following provision:

"Rights reserved in federal patents or state deeds, *building or use restrictions general to the district*, and building or zoning regulations and provisions *shall not be deemed encumbrances.*" (Italics ours.)

The first contention, that appellants had knowledge of the protective restrictions prior to the time of their entering into the contract and that they therefore waived the objection or are estopped to deny its existence, is untenable because, even though they may have had knowledge of the restrictions as shown by the declaration of record, there is no evidence that they had any knowledge, at the time the contract was signed or at the time the note and mortgage were executed, that the position of the house on the lot violated these restrictions. On the contrary, the evidence shows that the violation of the protective building restriction was discovered by the appellants at a later time, as the result of a survey made for the purpose of determining the location of a bulkhead which they planned to install on the property, and that they then promptly rescinded the contract, notifying respondents as well as Burwell & Morford to that effect.

The second contention, that the defect of the existing encumbrance is cured by a showing that a certain title company is willing to insure the appellants against loss incurred by them because of the existing violation, is also untenable. The parties cite no cases, nor have we discovered any, passing on the question of whether or not an agreement by an insurance company to indemnify a vendee against loss from an encumbrance on the property cures the defect in the title. We do not venture an opinion on what the law is or should be on this point, because the record herein does not show an agreement on the part of a title company to insure the appellants against *all possible loss* that might be incurred by them as the result of this encumbrance, nor, for that matter, is any agreement of such nature exhibited. If we assume, as the record indicates may well be the case, that a title company is willing to bind itself to defend in court any and all suits that might be brought by the adjoining property owners and to pay all judgments and court costs, and if we discount the inconvenience to the appellants resulting from the necessity of participating in such possible suits, still we cannot say that any title company would be willing to so insure the title in favor of a prospective purchaser of the property from the appellants, or that any loss to appellants because of a refusal to so insure the title would be within the coverage of the policy which the title company's present report indicates will be offered to these appellants.

That the value of a title on resale is an element to be considered in cases such as this is demonstrated by the following language of this court in Flood v. Von Marcard, 102 Wash. 140, 172 P. 884, 886:

"Few titles are good to a mathematical certainty, nor does the law demand that they shall be so, *but the value of a title on a resale is an element to be considered.*

"'A purchaser is entitled to a merchantable title—a marketable title—*such a one as will bring in the market as high a price with, as without the objection.*' Parmly v. Head, 33 Ill.App. 134.

"While the law will not countenance the idle scruples of one interested in withholding the purchase money (Brown v. Witter, 10 Ohio 143) *it will not compel one who seems to be acting in good faith to accept a title if there be reasonable probability of a lawsuit to convince a purchaser on resale, or to quiet the title.* (Moore v. Elliott, supra.)" (Italics ours.)

Finally, the fact that the contract contains a provision that protective restrictions shall not be deemed encumbrances cannot aid the respondents. It is not the existence of the protective restrictions, as shown by the record, that constitutes the encumbrance alleged by the appellants; but, rather, it is the *presently existing violation* of one of these restrictions that constitutes such encumbrance, *in and of itself.* The authorities so hold, on the rationale, to which we subscribe, that to force a vendee to accept property which in its present state violates a building restriction without a showing that the restriction is unenforcible, would in effect compel the vendee to buy a lawsuit. 66 C.J. 911, Vendor and Purchaser, § 590; * * *

For the particular reasons hereinabove given, we are of the opinion that the trial court erred in granting to the respondents specific performance of the contract. In view of this ruling, it becomes unnecessary to pass upon the other matters assigned by appellants as grounds for the same result.

In the proceedings before the trial court the appellants herein requested the affirmative relief of rescission of the contract and asked for the return to them of the earnest money paid to the respondents and all other sums paid by appellants pursuant to the contract. This relief should have been granted. The record shows that the appellants gave timely notice of rescission after learning, through a survey of the property, that the position of the building violated a protective restriction. There is no evidence in the record of any offer by respondents to cure this defect in title; there is only an indication of willingness on the part of a title company to issue, upon certain conditions, its "owners policy of title insurance" in "usual form." Such situation furnishes ground for invoking the rule that where the vendor covenants to convey title by warranty deed free of encumbrances and he is unable to do so, the vendee may rescind the contract and recover the amount of money paid thereunder. 55 Am.Jur. 923, 930, 935, 936, Vendor and Purchaser, §§ 529, 537, 541, 542.

The mortgage firm of Burwell & Morford, which was originally named as a party defendant in the action, was dismissed from the suit on stipulation of the parties and upon agreement by that firm to abide by the decree of the court. The decree to be entered should, therefore, in addition to ordering Burwell & Morford to return to the appellants the sum of money paid over to it under escrow agreement, also command that firm to secure the release of the mortgage of record which appellants as mortgagors executed to Burwell & Morford in contemplation of the final closing of the transaction of sale between the parties here involved.

The decree is reversed with instructions to the trial court to enter in its place a decree rescinding the contract, in accordance with this opinion.

Note: Type of Deed to be Executed by Vendor

The prevailing rule in the United States, in contrast to that in England, is that in the absence of a contract provision to the contrary it is the duty of the vendor to prepare as well as execute the deed of conveyance. The deed must be in proper form to convey the legal title to the property described in the contract, without any conditions, limitations, restrictions, reservations, or exceptions not warranted by the contract, and must also be in proper form to be recorded in the state where the property is situated. If the contract contains an express provision as to the kind of deed to be executed, the vendor's obligation will be determined by the construction given to such provision.

As was previously indicated, there are three basic types of deeds in use in the United States today: (1) warranty deeds; (2) deeds without covenants for title (often called "bargain and sale" or "grant" deeds); and (3) quitclaim deeds. If the contract requires the vendor to convey by a "warranty deed," as in the principal case, it is clear that the deed must at least contain a covenant of warranty. In most states the covenant of warranty must be general in form—i.e., it must obligate the grantor to warrant and defend the grantee's title and possession against "all lawful claims whatsoever"—unless the contract calls for a "special" or "limited" warranty. But in a few states (such as Pennsylvania) an agreement to convey by "warranty deed" is satisfied by a "special" or "limited" warranty deed which warrants the title only as against future claims by the grantor or persons claiming under the grantor. And in some jurisdictions a "warranty deed" must contain some or all of the "usual" covenants for title in addition to the covenant of warranty. For discussion of the "usual" covenants for title and their import, see supra at pages 763 and 892–901.

A contract provision that the vendor shall convey by a "good and sufficient deed" or the like is generally held to require the execution of a "warranty deed" as defined in the particular jurisdiction. A contract to convey by "deed without covenants" or by "quitclaim deed" does not require that any covenants for title be included in the deed. Presumably a contract to convey by "warranty deed" or by "deed with the usual covenants" or the like requires a deed which purports to convey the land itself and not merely the grantor's "right, title, and interest" therein. But an agreement to convey by "quitclaim deed" is satisfied by a deed purporting to convey only the grantor's "right, title, and interest" in the land.

If there is no express provision in the contract as to title covenants or type of deed, there is much variation in judicial views as to the proper rule. In many states, the rule seems to be that a vendor selling for his own benefit must execute the kind of deed customary in the locality when the question first came before the court, with the "usual" covenant or covenants. Thus in some states a deed with a general covenant of warranty is required, and in others a deed with "full covenants" must be tendered. In Pennsylvania, on the other hand, only a special covenant of warranty need be included in the deed; and in a number of states the purchaser is entitled to no covenants for title unless the contract expressly calls for a deed with covenants. In some of the states where the latter rule prevails, a "quitclaim deed" has been held sufficient.

One who conveys property to which he holds title only as a fiduciary cannot be required to execute any covenant except one against his own acts ("the usual trustee covenant") unless the contract expressly obligates him to do so. And no covenants of any kind can be required from an officer of the court selling by court order or mere ministerial grantors, such as sheriffs, tax collectors and others who are made by law the mere media for transfer of title. But the "usual covenants" which could be required of the vendor may ordinarily be required of an agent executing a deed in behalf of his principal, unless the power under which the agent sells expressly provides for a conveyance without covenants or with more limited covenants.

Note: The "Marketable Title" Requirement and Agreements Varying the Requirement

In the early case of Dwight v. Cutler, 3 Mich. 566, 64 Am.Dec. 105 (1855), the court said that, "in every contract for the sale of land, unless the contrary intention is expressed, there is an implied undertaking on the part of the vendor, available at law as well as in equity, while the contract remains executory, to make out a good title clear of all defects and encumbrances." Accord, Hebb v. Severson, supra. This rule seems to have developed as a corollary of the application of *caveat emptor* to the sale of interests in land. With certain exceptions (chiefly by virtue of the recording statutes) a land purchaser cannot acquire any greater interest in the land than his vendor had at the time of conveyance to the purchaser. Once a sale of land is completed and the purchaser accepts a deed of conveyance, he assumes the risk of loss by reason of the assertion of outstanding claims against the land, except insofar as he can effectively protect himself against such loss by obtaining a deed with covenants of title from the vendor or by obtaining title insurance. The extent of protection afforded by covenants of title has already been considered; but it is clear that the effectiveness of such covenants, as a practical matter, depends upon the continued availability and solvency of the vendor. Title insurance may provide a better means of protection for the purchaser, but it is of relatively recent origin and even today is not available in all communities. It is not surprising, therefore, that courts at an early date adopted the rule quoted above, which permits a purchaser to reject the vendor's title and refuse to accept a conveyance if the title is not "good" and "clear of all defects and encumbrances." In the absence of any provision to the contrary in the sale contract, this means not only an unencumbered and indefeasible estate, but such an estate in fee simple, that is, the largest estate that can be had in the premises.

Until early in the 18th century it was the practice of the English Court of Chancery, when a purchaser resisted a suit for specific performance on the ground that the vendor's title was "bad," to decide whether the title was "good"—i.e., indefeasible and unencumbered—or "bad"—i.e., completely lacking, defeasible, encumbered, or otherwise defective—and either compel the purchaser to take the title as "good" or permit him to reject it as "bad." Although the purchaser might cast considerable doubt on the validity of the title, the court would compel him to accept it unless he persuaded the court that the title was "bad." In Marlow v. Smith, 2 P.Will. 198 (1723), however, it was held that the court would not compel a purchaser to accept a title the validity of which was subject to a reasonable doubt, although the court might not be persuaded that it was "bad." Thereafter, "doubtful" titles were classed with titles absolutely "bad." As Lord Eldon said in Stapylton v. Scott, 16 Vesey 272 (Ch.1809), "though in the judgment of the Court the better opinion is, that a title can be made, yet, if there is a considerable, a rational, doubt, the Court has not attached so much credit to its own opinion as to compel a purchaser to take the title; but leaves the parties to Law." Later, the term "marketable" was coined to designate titles which a court of equity would compel a purchaser to take, and the term "unmarketable" to designate those which a purchaser was justified in rejecting. At the present time, the tendency is to use the terms "good" and "marketable," and the terms "bad" and "unmarketable," interchangeably, to designate titles which a court of equity will or will not compel a purchaser to accept.

Real estate sale contracts usually include express provisions as to the title which the vendor is to convey. The Chicago Real Estate Board contract form set out above obligates the vendor "to convey or cause to be conveyed to buyer good title" to the land described, and to deliver within 20 days from the date of the contract "evidence * * * showing record title in seller (or grantor)." Does this change the obligation of the vendor from that which would be imposed by law in the absence of such a provision? Does it set up a single or a double standard for appraising the vendor's title?

"A purchaser may prevent any implied warranty of title from arising by expressly or impliedly assuming the risks of title or agreement for a conveyance of such interest as the vendor has, and under such a contract, if the purchaser receives the interest of the vendor, he cannot complain, in the absence of fraud or concealment, because the title is not good. An agreement to convey the vendor's right, title and interest implies that he has some right, title, or interest; but it does not imply that he has a good title, and the fact that the title is defective is no objection to it, in the absence of fraud or concealment, provided the purchaser gets all the interest the vendor had at the time the contract was entered into." Page, "Vendor and Purchaser," 39 Cyc. 1129 (1912) at 1447–1448. But in Bull v. Weisbrod, 185 Iowa 318, 170 N.W. 536 (1919), it was held that the purchaser was entitled to receive a good title free of encumbrances where the vendor agreed to sell all his "right, title, and interest" in certain lots and to execute and deliver a "warranty deed of said premises." The same result was reached in Henderson v. Beatty, 124 Iowa 163, 99 N.W. 716 (1904), where the vendor agreed to sell his "right, title, and interest" and also to furnish an abstract showing a "good and perfect title" in himself; and in Culley v. Dixon, 199 Iowa 136, 201 N.W 582 (1925), where the vendor agreed to convey his "right, title, and interest" by "warranty deed" and to furnish an abstract showing a "good merchantable title" in himself.

Suppose the contract requires the vendor to convey by "quitclaim deed" and says nothing as to the quality of the title to be conveyed? Can the purchaser resist specific performance and/or recover back his earnest money upon proof that the title is not good and marketable? See Wallach v. Riverside Bank, 206 N.Y. 434, 100 N.E. 50 (1912). The contract was for sale of "all the premises known as Nos. 165 and 167 East 108th Street in the city of New York," and further provided that upon receipt of the price the vendor would execute to the purchaser a "quitclaim deed of said premises." On the closing date the vendor tendered a "quitclaim deed in the usual form of such instruments," but the purchaser refused to take the deed and pay the price because of the existence of an inchoate dower interest in the wife of a former owner of the property. After tender and demand upon the vendor to convey a marketable title, the purchaser sued to recover "the sum paid down and a further sum for the reasonable expense of examining the title." The lower court found for the plaintiff. On appeal, the judgment was affirmed. The court said:

" * * * The covenant was to convey a certain parcel of land, not to convey all the right, title, and interest of the defendant in that land. * * * The plaintiff did not agree to accept a defective title. He agreed to buy 'all the premises' described by clear and unmistakable boundaries, and by implication of law this means in an executory contract a good title to the whole thereof, free and clear from incumbrances. * * * Even if the conveyance is to be made without warranties, still the land itself is to be conveyed, and, as the grantor can convey only that which he has, unless he has title to the land he cannot convey the land. If his title is subject to a right which may take away part of the land, he cannot in the full legal sense convey the land, for there is an outstanding interest which his deed does not touch. If the plaintiff was bound to accept the deed tendered with a partial defect of title, he would have been bound to accept it even if it conveyed nothing whatever, although the consideration named was $22,000.   *   *   *

"The agreement of the plaintiff to accept a quitclaim deed as the means of transfer was not a waiver of the defect. A quitclaim deed is as effective as any other to convey all the title the grantor has, and a deed with all the covenants known cannot strengthen a defective title, but can simply protect from loss on account thereof.   *   *   *

"If the plaintiff knew of the defect when the contract was signed, he had the right to presume from its terms that a good title would be made before the law day. It is a somewhat common practice to agree to sell land without limitation, although both parties know at the time that some outstanding right must be acquired by the vendor in order to enable him to perform his covenant when the law day arrives.

"The defendant insists that the court erred in refusing to find upon its request that the plaintiff knew what a quitclaim deed was and the title it would convey; that before the agreement was executed he had been told by the defendant that the only title it could give was such as it had and no more; and that he knew when he signed the contract that there were existing questions respecting the title.

"Assuming, without holding, that there was sufficient uncontradicted evidence to warrant these findings, the written agreement could not be cut down or limited by such facts. Whatever was said before the instrument was signed being merged therein became wholly immaterial, and it is not an error of law to refuse to find an immaterial fact even upon uncontradicted evidence."

Cf. McManus v. Blackmarr, 47 Minn. 331, 50 N.W. 230 (1891).

How is a court to determine whether the term "quitclaim deed," appearing in the contract, refers only to the form of the conveyance or to the vendor's obligation as to the character of the title to be transferred? What is the effect of an agreement to convey by "special warranty deed"—a deed in which the grantor warrants the title against defects arising from his own acts only?

As to the effect of knowledge by the purchaser of defects in the vendor's title, and parol agreement that the purchaser will accept such title as the vendor has, the weight of authority, seems to be in accord with Wallach v. Riverside Bank, supra. "*   *   * the general rule is that knowledge by the vendee of the vendor's lack of title at the time he entered into the contract is immaterial since he has a right to rely upon the vendor either having a title, or procuring it so as to carry out his agreement. It is no defense for the vendor to show that the vendee knew of the existence of outstanding encumbrances, and that he agreed to take only the title which the vendor then had, where such facts depend upon extrinsic evidence, and are contradictory of the express terms of the contract entered into between the parties." Annotation, 57 A.L.R. 1253, at pp. 1541–2. For an interesting application of this doctrine, see Simpson v. Stallings, 54 N.M. 352, 225 P.2d 139 (1950), where the contract obligated the vendor to convey by "warranty deed *   *   * clear of all liens and encumbrances *   *   *." The court, in holding for the purchaser, said: "The contract is clear and unambiguous *   *   * and leaves no room for claimed prior oral statements to the effect that practically all of the titles in the neighborhood of the land in question were not merchantable under the standards imposed by the * * * lawyers who usually examined the abstracts on such properties, and that defendant * * * would convey only the title he received from his grantor." (225 P.2d at 140.)

The parties may, of course, substitute the test of "insurability" for that of "marketability" with respect to the vendor's title. "One of the important functions of title insurance is to broaden the base for lending transactions and sales of real estate by making it possible for mortgage lenders safely to accept as collateral, or for purchasers to accept without concern, not only perfect titles and marketable titles, but also those titles which are subject to defects which render them technically unmarketable, provided they still are sound, defensible and insurable." Reeve, Guaranteeing Marketability of Titles to Real Estate 31 (1951).

However, if it is the intention of the parties to substitute the test of "insurability" for that of "marketability," this intention should be clearly stated in the contract. Failure of the parties to do so in the contract which came before the court in Hebb v. Severson, supra, resulted in a decision that the title must be "marketable" as well as "insurable." A similar decision was reached in New York Investors, Inc. v. Manhattan Beach Bathing Parks Corp., 229 App.Div. 593, 243 N.Y.S. 548 (2nd Dept.1930). Cf. Haar v. Daly, 232 App.Div. 423, 250 N.Y.S. 59 (1931).

In the absence of a contract provision expressly covering the point, who has the burden of employing a title company when a land sale contract provides that the vendor's title must be such as a title insurance company will approve and insure? See Eastman v. Horne, 205 N.Y. 486, 98 N.E. 758 (1912).

If the contract requires the vendor to tender a title that will be "approved and insured at the usual rates," "guaranteed," or "insurable at the usual rates" by a title insurance or guaranty company, it is clearly not enough for the vendor to tender a title that a court may deem to be "marketable"; the purchaser need not accept the title unless a reputable title insurance or guaranty company (or the designated company, if a particular one is named in the contract) will insure or guarantee the title at the usual rates and without exceptions beyond those specified in the contract.

The contract may, of course, give the vendor an option to satisfy his obligation with respect to title *either* by tendering a marketable title (or abstract of title) *or* by supplying a title insurance policy. (See provision in Chicago Real Estate Board Contract form reprinted, supra.) In that event, the purchaser, in order to recover his earnest money on the ground that the vendor has defaulted on his title obligation, must allege and prove that the vendor has *neither* tendered a marketable title *nor* tendered a satisfactory title insurance policy in accordance with the contract. Continental Southland Savings & Loan Ass'n v. Jones, 142 S.W.2d 401 (Tex.Civ.App.1940).

What is the effect of a provision in the contract requiring that the vendor's title be "satisfactory" to the purchaser? Some courts have held that such a provision is complied with by tendering a good and marketable title because such a title will be "satisfactory" to any reasonable person. Other courts, however, have held that the purchaser is at liberty to reject the title and refuse to buy the property if he is "honestly" dissatisfied with the title. See discussion and authorities cited in Campbell v. Hart, 256 S.W.2d 255 (Tex.Civ.App.1953). Where the contract provides that the title is to be "satisfactory" to a third person such as the purchaser's attorney, the prevailing rule seems to be that such person must actually be satisfied; it is not enough that a reasonable man would be satisfied and that the court regards the title as good and marketable. The third person must act honestly and in good faith in rejecting the title as "unsatisfactory," of course. For an exhaustive collection of cases, see Annotation, "Marketable Title," 57 A.L.R. 1253, 1314–22 (1928).

Mortgage lenders, of course, usually insist upon a title that is "satisfactory," and may refuse to lend money on a title which a court would deem "marketable." A mortgage lender might agree in advance to lend if the title is "marketable," but in practice mortgage lenders rarely if ever commit themselves in this fashion. In any case, the courts have consistently refused to enforce contracts to lend money, whatever the lender's reason for refusing to make the loan.

Note: The Doctrine of Merger

Although there is an implied undertaking, and frequently an express undertaking, that the vendor will tender a good title, free from defects and encumbrances, it should be emphasized that the undertaking lasts only while the contract is executory. The purchaser is given time to satisfy himself as to the "goodness" of the tendered title, and if the transaction is consummated with the purchaser accepting a deed in fulfilment of the contract, the risk of loss from title defects falls upon the purchaser. He must find other ways to protect himself. The contract provision is said to be "merged" in the deed. Thus, in Bennett v. Behring Corp., 466 F.Supp. 689 (1979), the sale contract provided that the seller would deliver deeds "free of all encumbrances." Between the time of the contract and the delivery of the deed, there were some restrictions placed of record which required all owners to rent and help maintain some common recreational facilities. The deed contained a provision that the buyer would comply with the "Declaration of Restrictions" of record. The buyer was held bound by the restrictions since acceptance of the deed merges all preliminary contracts.

The doctrine, however, contains an important exception. Any collateral agreements concerning matters not normally found in deeds, are not "merged" and may continue to be enforced. Thus, in Mallin v. Good, 93 Ill.App.3d 843, 49 Ill.Dec. 168, 417 N.E.2d 858 (1981), the contract required seller to inspect the roof of the house and repair any damage in good and workmanlike manner. The buyer, who had accepted a deed was held entitled to enforce the covenant to repair since it did not relate to the title to the premises. And in Campbell v. Rawls, 381 So.2d 744 (Fla.App.1980), the contract contained a warranty that the "air conditioning and heating systems (will) be in working order at the time of closing. Buyer may inspect 3 days before closing and if discrepancies exist Seller will repair." The court found that buyer was not required to inspect and that merger did not preclude enforcement of antecedent contracts not intended to be incorporated in the deed.

As to the obligation of vendor as to quality of construction and fitness for intended use, see infra, p. 1055.

SIMIS v. McELROY

Court of Appeals of New York, 1899.
160 N.Y. 156, 54 N.E. 674, 73 Am.St.Rep. 673.

O'BRIEN, J. This action was brought by the plaintiffs' testatrix, who died during its pendency, and about five years after it was commenced. The purpose of the action was to recover damages for the breach by the defendant of an executory contract for the sale of certain real estate in the city of New York. It is an admitted fact in the case that both parties made tender of performance on the day specified for that purpose in the contract, and the defense to the action is that at the time of the tender the plaintiff's title was defective and unmarketable, and has so remained ever since. Upon that ground the defendant refused to accept the deed tendered to him, though ready and willing to perform but for the defect in plaintiff's title. At the close of the trial the plaintiff's counsel stated that he asked a verdict for nominal damages only, and the court directed a verdict for the plaintiff for six cents damages, and directed that the defendant's exceptions be heard in the first instance at the general term. On the hearing of the exceptions at the appellate division they were sustained, and the verdict was set aside and a new trial granted. The only question necessary to consider, therefore, is whether the plaintiff made out a case for damages at the trial, or, in other words, whether the facts were of such a conclusive character as to entitle the plaintiff to even nominal damages as matter of law. If the title tendered by the plaintiff was so defective as to be unmarketable, then there was no breach of the contract established, and the plaintiff was not entitled to recover.

It is admitted that, as to a material part of the premises embraced in the contract, the plaintiff had no record title, but she claimed to have good title by adverse possession; and the question presented by this appeal is whether the plaintiff established title in that way so conclusively as to warrant the court in directing a verdict in her favor. It is important to bear in mind that the controversy is not between the party holding or claiming under the record title and the plaintiff claiming by adverse possession, but between the latter and a purchaser by executory contract to recover damages for his refusal to accept a title based entirely on such adverse possession. The holders of the outstanding record title, if any, are not parties to this action, and cannot be bound by the judgment; and hence the defendant, if compelled to accept the deed tendered, might still be obliged to litigate with the true owners the question of title as against them. When the controversy assumes the form of an action of ejectment against the party in possession by one claiming under title by record, the former is in a stronger position to assert his right than when he is litigating with a stranger who refuses to accept his title. In the former case adverse possession is evidence of title in the party asserting it. * * * It might well be held to have the same effect in every case, but for the difficulty, if not impossibility, of establishing the fact as against those who are not parties to the action, or bound by the judgment. In such cases it is frequently very difficult for courts to anticipate what the owner of the outstanding title may be able to prove in a litigation with a party who has taken a title by adverse possession. The former may be able to prove facts tending to show that what appeared to be an adverse possession, in a litigation in which he was not heard, is quite otherwise, and hence this court has frequently refused to compel a purchaser to take a title which he may be called upon to defend by parol proof of adverse possession. * * *

The plaintiff contracted to deliver to the defendant a deed "containing a general warranty, and the usual full covenants for the conveying and assuring to him the fee simple of the said premises free from all incumbrance." The deed tendered did not assure to the defendant the fee simple in the property, since the plaintiff was obliged to prove her title by adverse possession. It was made out in this action by parol proof, which is open to change hereafter in any litigation between the defendant and the parties who have succeeded to the record title. Adverse possession is defined by the Code (sections 369, 373), and, unless the case made by the plaintiff met all the conditions prescribed by these sections, she has failed to establish a breach of the contract on the part of the defendant in refusing to accept the title tendered. The court below, upon a review of the testimony, was of the opinion that she had not. It would require a very clear and a very peculiar case to warrant this court in interfering with the judgment in order to enable the plaintiff to retry a case involving only nominal damages. * * * The plaintiff undoubtedly proved possession of the premises for over 30 years, and, if her right of recovery depended upon that fact alone, it was established. But possession, though a very important element in making out her title, was not the only thing to be considered. In order to prove such an adverse possession as would make her title good, and require the defendant to accept it at the peril of liability in damages for the breach of his contract, she was bound to show that the defendant could not hereafter be called upon to litigate that question with strangers to this action, who might claim title under some former owner. She was bound to show that the title tendered was good, or at least marketable, as against all the world. The proof, we think, fell far short of this requirement, and so we think that the learned court below was right.

The defect in the proof has been very clearly and fully pointed out in the opinions given in the court below, and it is unnecessary to repeat the facts here. In 1856 the premises were conveyed to the plaintiff's remote grantor by a party who, so far as appears, had neither record title or possession. Since that time, by reason of conveyances, the property was repeatedly transferred, until it was deeded to the plaintiff in 1880. Her possession and that of her grantors since 1856 has been clearly shown, but just where the title was prior to that date does not appear. It is quite probable that the plaintiff's title is good, but whether the defendant can be compelled by the courts to accept it is a very different question. It appears that one Kip, who died in the year 1777, was the owner of a considerable tract of land in the city of New York, which included the premises in question. He left a will, which was proved in 1805, devising the land, or some interest in it, to his children. A share which had been devised to a daughter dying before her father was by a codicil devised to her daughter, the testator's grandchild, but for life if she died without issue, with remainder to the surviving children of the testator. It does not appear that the conveyance to the plaintiff's remote grantor in 1856 carried the title of all the Kip heirs, and hence the claim that the plaintiff has title by adverse possession. Adverse possession does not commence to run against heirs taking the title to land by descent or by will until the right of entry has accrued, or while they were under any disability. The remainderman's right of entry does not accrue until the termination of the estate or estates upon which the remainder is limited. Nonresidence, infancy, or other disabilities sometimes operate to prevent the statute of limitations from running. The difficulty with the plaintiff's case is that she has not negatived the possibility of an outstanding claim to this land, or some interest in it, by the heirs of Kip. It may be true that it was impossible to do it, but in such cases the vendor may always describe the title which he has, or intends to convey, in the contract; and, if the vendee agrees to take it, he will be bound. When the contract in terms provides for a deed to vest in the purchaser the title in fee simple, and the vendor's title is open to doubts such as exist in this case, there will be room left for the vendee to resist compulsory performance on his part. This situation arises from the fact that it is impossible in such cases for courts to adjudge with that reasonable certainty which the nature of the case requires that his fears with respect to the title, whether real or assumed, are groundless. In order to make the adverse possession since 1856 good against the heirs of Kip, the proof must be of such a character as to exclude to a moral certainty any right or claim on their part; in other words, it should have been proved that their interest passed to the plaintiff's remote grantor under the deed of that year. Unless it did, they may be able to prove facts which might qualify, if not wholly avoid, the fact of possession in the plaintiff and her predecessors. Whether they are infants, or under some other disability, or nonresidents or remaindermen, does not appear, so that the proof did not warrant the court in directing a verdict. It was thus ruled, as matter of law, that the plaintiff's title was good. The most favorable view that could be taken of the plaintiff's case would not warrant the court in taking the question from the jury, and hence the exception taken by the defendant's counsel to the refusal of the court to submit the question was good. On the whole, we think that the case was well decided below, and that the order must be affirmed, with costs, and judgment absolute be given for the defendant. All concur. Order affirmed, and judgment accordingly.

Questions and Problems

1. Do you agree with the decision in the principal case, assuming that the statute of limitations in force at the time of the litigation barred actions to recover possession of land unless begun within twenty years from the date when the cause of action first accrued? Before expressing an opinion, would you like to know about the provisions of the statute of limitations respecting persons under "disabilities"? How would you decide the principal case if it came up today, under the following New York statutes?

N.Y.R.P.A.P.L. § 511. "Where the occupant or those under whom he claims entered into possession of the premises under claim of title, exclusive of any other right, founding the claim upon a written instrument, as being a conveyance of the premises in question, * * * and there has been a continued occupation and possession of the premises included in the instrument * * * for ten years, under the same claim, the premises so included are deemed to have been held adversely * * *."

N.Y.C.P.L.R. § 208. "If a person entitled to commence an action is under a disability because of infancy or insanity at the time the cause of action accrues, and the time otherwise limited for commencing the action is three years or more and expires no later than three years after the disability ceases, or the person under the disability dies, the time within which the action must be commenced shall be extended to three years after the disability ceases or the person under the disability dies, whichever event first occurs * * * The time within which the action must be commenced shall not be extended by this provision beyond ten years after the cause of action accrues, except, * * * where the person was under a disability due to infancy. * * *."

N.Y.C.P.L.R. § 212. "(a) * * * An action to recover real property or its possession cannot be commenced unless the plaintiff, or his predecessor in interest, was seized or possessed of the premises within ten years before the commencement of the action."

2. How would you decide the principal case if it came up today in a jurisdiction with a Marketable Title Act identical with the USOLTA provisions set out supra at pages 947–951?

3. The following is in the statement of facts in Rehoboth Heights Development Co. v. Marshall, 15 Del.Ch. 314, 137 A. 83 (Ch.1927):

"The contract of sale obligates the vendor to convey a good marketable, fee-simple title clear of all incumbrances. The sole objection to performance of the contract made by the defendant vendee is that the title rendered him is not a good marketable one. The record title in the complainant and its predecessors is conceded to be good as far back as July 7, 1887, when one TreDennick purchased a tract including the blocks in controversy at a judicial sale in execution of a judgment upon foreign attachment obtained by him against Curtis, Hughes and Fallon. The land was seized and sold as the property of these defendants. At the time of the foreign attachment proceedings the last recorded deed shows the title to have been in the Rehoboth Association, a corporation created in 1871. It is admitted that this corporation ceased to function about five years after its creation. How the title got from the association into Curtis, Hughes and Fallon, records in the county of Sussex, where the land is located, fail to show.

"Because of this break in the record chain of title the defendant refuses to complete his contract of purchase. The complainant contends that it and its predecessors have been in open, continuous, notorious and adverse possession of the land ever since 1887 when TreDennick became the purchaser at the judicial sale referred to, and that this possession coupled with the claim of title evidenced by the recorded conveyances since that date gives such a possessory title as will satisfy all the requirements of marketability which the contract demands. * * * It is admitted by the defendant that for thirteen years at least the notorious, continuous and adverse nature of the possession of the complainant and its predecessors in title is clear. But in my opinion the evidence is clear and positive in showing such possession as far back as 1895 (thirty-two years ago) when Charles W. Cullen purchased the lands at an Orphans' Court sale for the payment of debts conducted by the administrator of TreDennick; and is only a little if any less so for the period running back from 1895 to 1887 when TreDennick became the purchaser. This possession was of the whole tract as subdivided.

"Against the force of this evidence the defendant urges that possibly some claimant exists somewhere against whom the possessory title of the complainant would not be good because of the fact that disability of some form would bring such claimant within the saving clause of the applicable statute of limitations so as to permit at this time the successful maintenance of an action to recover possession. * * * Of course if the imaginary claimants were *sui juris*, the twenty year period of limitations has long since barred them. * * * But the statute saves the rights of those under disability. The sections thereof which do so are as follows:

" '4664. Sec. 3. Saving of Rights of Sundry Persons; Limitation Ten Years after Disability Removed:—If at any time when such right of entry upon, or action for any lands or tenements shall first accrue, the person entitled to such entry, or action, shall be an infant or a married woman, insane, or imprisoned, such person, or anyone claiming from, by, or under him, may make the entry, or bring the action, at any time within ten years after such disability shall be removed, notwithstanding the twenty years before limmited in that behalf shall have expired.

" '4665. Sec. 4. Successors in Title to Persons Under Disability; To Have Benefit of Time Limitation:—If the person entitled to an entry, or action, die under any of the disabilities aforesaid, any other person claiming from, by, or under him, shall have the same benefit which the person first entitled would have had, by living until the removal of the disability.'

"There are four classes of disability mentioned in the statute, infancy, coverture, insanity and imprisonment. I suppose our Married Women's Statutes have rendered obsolete the disability of marriage."

How would you decide the case?

Suppose all the events described in the above excerpt occurred 40 years later, and that Delaware had adopted the USOLTA Marketable Title Act in 1960. How would your approach to the problem be changed if the suit for specific performance had been brought in 1967?

DOUGLASS v. RANSOM

Supreme Court of Wisconsin, 1931.
205 Wis. 439, 237 N.W. 260.

Action for specific performance of land contract commenced March 17, 1927; judgment for plaintiff entered October 4, 1930. Defendant appeals.

The parties on January 8, 1927, entered into a contract of sale by defendant to plaintiff of residence property in Waukesha. The contract provided for a $1,000 down payment and payment of the remainder of the purchase price "as soon as merchantable abstract and warranty deed" were furnished by the defendant. The plaintiff delivered defendant his check for the down payment, and the defendant delivered to plaintiff for examination an abstract of title of the premises brought down to January 12, 1927. This abstract did not show as paid the 1926 tax, then a lien on the premises, and did not show as closed the estate of defendant's husband through whom the defendant took title as surviving joint tenant, or show the situation of the said estate other than that there was no income tax payable and that determination of the inheritance tax, if any, was not yet made. The satisfactions of several old mortgages were defective and there were discrepancies in spelling or initials in the names of several parties to the title in instruments to and from them.

This was the situation on January 19th, when, after examination of the abstract by his attorney and getting his opinion to that effect, plaintiff informed defendant that the title was not merchantable and would not be accepted until a marketable title was established. The plaintiff suggested perfecting the title by suit to quiet title. The defendant suggested the filing of affidavits identifying parties to the title where necessary and the procuring of court orders satisfying mortgages the satisfaction of which was not perfect of record. The plaintiff also suggested deducting $150 from the purchase price to cover the expense of a quia timet action and the defendant offered a $75 allowance for that purpose. But no agreement was reached. On February 23d, the defendant returned to plaintiff his $1,000 check with a letter declaring the deal ended. The plaintiff did not return this check to the defendant or reply to her letter and does not know what became of the check. There is no proof that he kept the check good by maintaining a balance in bank to cover it, but he claims that he was at all times willing and able to pay the check and the $6,600 deferred payment of the purchase price. On February 25th the plaintiff filed in the register of deeds office a lis pendens dated February 24th, stating that he had commenced an action to enforce specific performance of the contract. The summons in the action was served, March 17th. The complaint was served August 17th and filed August 18th. The defendant demurred to the complaint, the circuit court overruled the demurrer, and on appeal this court affirmed the order on April 2, 1929. The defendant by her answer claimed that the title shown by the abstract furnished was merchantable and that she had duly tendered a warranty deed which plaintiff had wrongfully refused to accept, and further claimed that the contract was void for fraud perpetrated upon her by the plaintiff. The court found that the contract was free from fraud; that the title shown by the abstract was not merchantable; that the defendant had had the use of the premises pending the suit; that the rental value of the premises was $50 per month, which was (apparently) considered as netting the equivalent of the interest on the purchase price of the premises; that $150 was the reasonable expense of completing the abstract and perfecting the title. The judgment decreed specific performance and gave plaintiff the option of accepting the title as shown by the abstract tendered and deducting $150 from the "balance of the purchase price," and provided that the defendant deliver a warranty deed within sixty days from date of the judgment and perfect the title within that time if plaintiff did not elect to accept the title as shown by the abstract furnished, and that on default of delivery of such deed the judgment stand as a conveyance of the title, and awarded costs to the plaintiff.

FOWLER, J. The appellant's claims may be summarized as that the court erred in finding that: (1) The abstract furnished does not show a merchantable title; (2) the contract is free from fraud; (3) the plaintiff has at all times been able and willing to perform his part of the contract; (4) the reasonable cost of perfecting the title and completing an abstract is $150; (5) in entering judgment as rendered; and (6) in not receiving testimony of witnesses that the title shown by the abstract is merchantable.

As to (2), (3), and (4), we will only say that it appears to us that these findings are amply supported by the evidence and that no good purpose would be served by discussion of them.

(1) The failure to show freedom from tax liens was of itself sufficient to render the title not merchantable. 57 A.L.R. 1403, and cases cited. While it is doubtless true that the abstract would have been extended to show the payment of the 1926 tax had this been asked for and no other objection had been made to the abstract by the plaintiff, the fact remains that the abstract was not so extended. A receipt showing payment of the tax on January 25, 1927, was received in evidence, but the contract provided that a "merchantable abstract" should be furnished and this implies that an abstract should be furnished which showed a merchantable title. * * * The abstract should have further shown such condition of the probate proceedings of the husband's estate as to free the premises from possible lien of an inheritance tax and judgments on claims filed. 57 A.L.R. 1404, 1408, and cases cited. It is not the fact that the grantor has good title, but the appearance of that fact of record, that renders a title merchantable. * * * As the plaintiff was not bound to accept the title until an abstract was furnished showing that no liens existed and that none would arise in progress of the probate proceedings, and was not bound to pay or tender the portion of the purchase price not covered by the check until such an abstract was furnished there was no breach of the contract by the plaintiff when the defendant declared that he had breached it and for that reason declared the deal ended. The retention of the returned check without reply to defendant's letter might perhaps be construed as acquiescence by plaintiff in the defendant's position that the deal was ended but for the filing of the lis pendens on the day following its receipt and the commencement of the action. This negatives such acquiescence and shows intent by plaintiff not to waive his rights under the contract. The defendant could not, by her declaration that the contract was ended and her return of the check when no right to take such action existed impose a duty on the plaintiff to send back the check to her or make other repudiation of her attempt at termination of the contract than commencement of suit to enforce it.

It is contended by appellant that the plaintiff can only assert such defects of title as were covered by his objections first made to the defendant as ground for holding the title not marketable. But the condition of the estate as shown by the abstract was included in the objections presented. And we do not see that any element of estoppel exists to prevent plaintiff from now asserting any valid objection that may exist. Had the defendant, relying on the assumption that no further objections to the title were made by the plaintiff, taken action to remove the defects to which objection was made and tendered an abstract showing their removal and brought action for performance by the plaintiff, she would then be in position to invoke an estoppel or claim a waiver of other defects. * * *

(5) The court concluded in effect that a judgment in a quia timet action to remove clouds from the title was necessary to render the title

merchantable and gave the plaintiff the option to abate $150 from the purchase price to cover the cost of prosecuting such an action and accept the title shown by the abstract or require the defendant to prosecute such an action to judgment. The defects mentioned in (1), while sufficient to render the title unmerchantable, would not require prosecution of such an action to remove them, as their removal would be accomplished merely by bringing the abstract down to date. We must therefore determine whether the other defects claimed render the title unmarketable.

What constitutes a marketable or merchantable (the terms are synonymous) title to real estate has been considered by this court in several cases. The general rule applicable is not difficult of statement, but it is often not easy to determine whether a particular defect falls within the rule. In the opinon of Mr. Justice Pinney in Harrass v. Edwards, 94 Wis. 459, 464, 69 N.W. 69, it is stated that although a title is good, if there is reasonable doubt as to its validity it is not marketable. A material defect is such as will cause a reasonable doubt and just apprehension in the mind of a reasonably prudent and intelligent person acting upon competent legal advice, and prompt him to refuse to accept it. If such doubt exists as to make the title subject to probable attack by legal proceedings, or depends upon facts which can only be established by parol evidence if attack is made upon it in such proceedings, the title is not marketable. In Stack v. Hickey, supra, [151 Wis. 347, 138 N.W. 1011] it is stated that a marketable title is one that can be held in peace and quiet; not subject to litigation to determine its validity; not open to judicial doubt. An exhaustive note on the subject citing a multitude of cases is contained in 57 A.L.R. 1282, without adding much to the statements by this court above given. A marketable title must be salable without abatement of price and salable on the face of the record. * * * The chancery rule in England is that a merchantable title is one "which at all times and under all circumstances, may be forced upon an unwilling purchaser."

Of the clouds considered by the trial court as necessary to be removed by quia timet action, we need mention only two classes to support its conclusion. Mortgages are defectively satisfied of record and discrepancies exist in the names of grantors and titleholders illustrated as where one takes title as John J. Jones and conveys as J. J. Jones. Like discrepancies between the names of the one who should satisfy and the one who executes the satisfaction of mortgages constitutes the defect in most of the satisfactions. The mortgages defectively satisfied are eleven in number, ranging in date of execution from 1840 to 1870. In one of them, dated 1854, there is no similarity between the name of the mortgagee and the one who executed the satisfaction, and no assignment of the mortgage is shown. This leaves the mortgage unsatisfied of record.

It is contended by the appellants that the defects in the mortgage satisfactions are immaterial because the statute of limitations has run against foreclosure. It has been held that an unsatisfied mortgage, although the lapse of time is such as to make it probable that the statute of limitations has run against foreclosure of it, renders a title unmarketable, because the running of the statute may have been tolled by agreement or by payments. * * * This appears to us a reasonable rule and we adopt it.

The discrepancies in names referred to in connection with deeds and mortgages we also consider as resulting in nonmerchantability of title. Counsel for appellant cites 4 Thompson, Real Property, § 2971, to the effect that similarity of names is sufficient evidence of identity of a party in a chain of title in absence of evidence casting doubt upon his identity. This is the rule in cases of ejectment, trespass, and the like where the plaintiff is proving title. The question there is one of good title, actual title, not of merchantable title. Where merchantable title is the issue, the title must be such, on the face of it, as to preclude question of identity. The trial court considered that the discrepancies here involved constituted nonmerchantability, and it has been held by courts whose decisions are entitled to great respect that where the trial court has held a title unmerchantable an appellate court will not force the title upon a purchaser although of opinion that the title is sufficient. * * * It is also to be considered as matter of common knowledge that some examiners of title are more particular and technical than others about passing titles. The examiner for the plaintiff refused to pass the title here involved as merchantable. Acting upon competent legal advice is stated in the Harrass Case, supra, as one element to be considered in determining merchantability. That competent counsel have refused to pass a title as merchantable has been held to render it not merchantable. * * * As we are of opinion that nonmerchantability of title results from the defects mentioned, it is not necessary to discuss other alleged defects in the title.

It is contended that the title might have been sufficiently cleared by permitting satisfaction of the mortgages to be made by court order under section 235.60, Stats.; that this would have been a cheaper method than a quia timet action; and that the court erred in requiring the more expensive procedure. Assuming the statutory method might have been followed as to mortgages, it does not follow that the court erred in requiring the quia timet action. The statutory order satisfying the mortgages would not have affected the defects resulting from discrepancies in the names of the grantors in conveyances other than mortgages.

It is also contended that the court erred in not permitting the clouds on the title resulting from the discrepancies in the names of grantors to be removed by the filing of affidavits of identification. It is sufficient to say upon this point that no such affidavits were offered in evidence. Evidence was received that as to one such case of discrepancy in a mortgage satisfaction an affidavit could be procured, and the witness testified that he believed that affidavits could be procured in all such cases. But this was manifestly not the best evidence of the fact, if it be a fact, and incompetent. Objection to such proof was properly interposed and should have been sustained.

The defendant contends generally that the equities of the case are in favor of the defendant and that specific performance should have been denied because the defendant was willing to correct the title by proceeding under section 235.60 Stats., to procure an order satisfying the mortgages and procuring the recording of affidavits properly identifying the parties to the title. Had the defendant done this and continued the abstract to show the corrections before demanding full payment of the purchase price, we would have an entirely different situation. This might well have resulted in a finding that these defects did not render the title unmerchantable. But merely being willing to do this did not so result. The trial court considered the general equities to be in favor of the plaintiff. Whether specific performance will be decreed under given circumstances "rests in the sound discretion" of the trial court. * * * The court exercised its discretion and we can not say its discretion was unsound. The defendant's hasty attempt to declare the deal at an end smacks more of desire to avoid the contract than to perform it.

It is urged that the judgment is erroneous because it does not fix the date upon which the plaintiff should have made payment and thus fixed the time when interest on the purchase price should begin to accrue. The plaintiff delivered his check for $1,000 and the defendant did not refuse to accept it because it was not cash. This operated as a tender of the down payment and prevented the accrual of interest on that amount. The contract expressly provided that payment of the remaining $6,600 should be made "as soon as merchantable abstract was furnished." As no such abstract has been furnished, the time for payment of the $6,600 has not yet arrived and will not arrive until defendant furnishes such an abstract or the plaintiff under the judgment elects to abate $150 and accept the title shown by the abstract furnished. By fixing the rental value of the premises of which the defendant has retained possession, it would seem that the trial court considered this value the equivalent of all that the defendant was entitled to for nonuse of the purchase price or otherwise, and it does not appear that this view worked injustice to her.

It is urged that time is the essence of the contract and performance should be denied for nonpayment of the purchase price within two weeks, because of the notation at the foot of the contract: "I hereby agree to give possession of this property within two weeks from date, provided the balance of the purchase price, $6,600, is paid on delivery of the deed. If said purchase price is not paid on delivery of the deed, as above provided, this entire contract shall be void and of no effect." This notation obviously contemplates that the "merchantable abstract and warranty deed" provided for in the body of the contract would be furnished within the two weeks period referred to in the note. If a deed was tendered, as defendant claims, a merchantable title was not. The express provision contained in the body of the contract controls the time of payment, and that time has not yet arrived as above shown.

(6) The defendant produced several attorneys in good standing, experienced in the examination of titles who had examined the abstract in evidence, to whom he put the questions (a) whether the title shown by the abstract is merchantable, and (b) whether in such abstracts the plat can be considered as the root of the title and examination be safely

started from that point and prior defects disregarded. Objections to these questions were sustained on the ground that the opinions of the witnesses were incompetent and immaterial.

As to (a) it is plain that the matters stated in (1) rendered the title unmerchantable as matter of law and that no prejudicial error resulted from refusal of the court to permit that question to be answered. It has been squarely held that the question of marketability of a title is one of law and that the opinion of witnesses is not receivable.   *   *   * In Bradway v. Miller, 200 Mich. 648, 167 N.W. 15, the question is held to be one of law, so that an admission of unmarketability by counsel is not binding upon the court although it might naturally affect the court's judgment.

As to (b) we are of opinion that the objection was properly sustained. The question put was not whether the title was marketable notwithstanding defects antecedent to platting, which would be the material point aimed at if the point were material. We are perhaps not called upon to determine whether, if a question to this point had been put, objection to it would have been made and the objection would have been sustained. However, it is not entirely beside the case to say that it may be the custom of examiners of platted lands in some localities not to go back of the plat, and if so titles would doubtless be acceptable locally upon approval of a local examiner. But it would not follow that the title would be acceptable when passed upon by examiners elsewhere, and we consider that to be marketable a title must be marketable generally as distinguished from locally. Marketability is not established by the fact that any particular examiner has passed it. If as stated in (1) a marketable title is one "which at all times and under all circumstances may be forced upon an unwilling purchaser," to constitute marketability the title must be "salable" not only in Waukesha but in Milwaukee and elsewhere in the state.

Some other contentions are made by appellant's counsel, all of which have received attention. So far as these are not covered by what we have said, they are considered as not requiring especial mention.

The judgment is affirmed.

Note: Requirement that Vendor Furnish Abstract of Title and Requirement that Title be Marketable of Record

A vendor of land is under no legal obligation to furnish evidence of his title to the purchaser unless the sale contract expressly requires him to do so. See, e.g., Easton v. Montgomery, 90 Cal. 307, 27 P. 280 (1891). As a general rule, land sale contracts do not expressly require the vendor to furnish evidence of his title in localities where title searches are still performed by lawyers or lawyers employed to examine land titles assume responsibility for having accurate searches made. In these localities, it is customary for the prospective purchaser to employ his own attorney to search the records and render an opinion as to the validity and marketability of the vendor's title, and the purchaser customarily bears the expense of the title examination. But the purchaser does not get an abstract of his title.

In localities where title searches are customarily made by individual abstracters or by abstract companies, land sale contracts usually provide that the vendor shall furnish to the purchaser a "marketable" or "merchantable" abstract of title to the land he has contracted to sell. When a land sale contract contains such a provision, furnishing an abstract of title is just as much a condition precedent to the enforcement of the contract against the purchaser as is the delivery or tender of a deed of conveyance. In the absence of an express contract provision as to the date when the abstract is to be furnished to the purchaser, the vendor must furnish the abstract within a "reasonable" time. Since the vendor usually has the abstract of title which he obtained when he acquired title to the land in question, he ordinarily needs only to have the abstract "continued" to the date specified in the contract or, in the absence of any contract specifying the date, to such date as appears "reasonable" in view of the purpose for which the abstract is furnished. Generally, this means that the abstract must be brought down at least to the date of the contract or shortly thereafter. If the abstract is incomplete, the purchaser is generally held entitled to have it completed at the vendor's expense; and the cost of furnishing the abstract must be borne by the vendor in the absence of a contrary provision in the contract.

A contract for the purchase and sale of realty may require either that the vendor furnish a "merchantable abstract of title" or that the vendor shall convey "a good and clear record and marketable title," or both. The latter requirement, of course, is not met even if the title is "good and marketable" unless it appear so by reference to the public land records. "Even when there is no express provision for a record title, the obligation is frequently created by an agreement that the vendor is to furnish an abstract. Under such a contract, merely a marketable title as defined by the equity courts will not suffice; its character as such must appear from the abstract. And, since in this country an abstract covers only those muniments of title which are of record, such contracts are construed as requiring a marketable title of record." 1 Patton, Land Titles, 172 (2d ed. 1957). Moreover, decisions in some jurisdictions require the vendor's title to be "fairly deducible from the record" to qualify as a marketable title, although the contract neither requires a marketable title "of record" by virtue of express stipulation or by virtue of a provision that the vendor shall furnish an abstract. Some time ago, the Committee on Acceptable Titles to Real Property of the American Bar Association's Section of Real Property, Probate and Trust Law made a study of "the question of adverse possession so far as it tends to create a marketable title." The general conclusion of the study was as follows:

"Of the states studied by the committee it was found that in Massachusetts, New Hampshire, New York, Missouri (if the Missouri contract does not require an abstract showing good title), Arkansas (if the contract does not call for an abstract showing good title), and Wisconsin, a title by adverse possession, clearly established, is regarded as merchantable. In Tennessee, there is doubt whether such title is marketable. In Oklahoma, Colorado, Maine and Texas such title is not regarded as merchantable. In Idaho, Michigan, Ohio and Connecticut such a title is not considered to be marketable until it has been established by a court decree. In New Jersey the status of such a title is regarded as uncertain." 1957 Proceedings of A.B.A. Section of Real Property, Probate and Trust Law 50. See also 1 Patton, Land Titles 166 (2d ed. 1957); Basye, Clearing Land Titles 10 (1953); 3 A.L.P. 128 (1952); Annotation, Marketable Title, 57 A.L.R. 1253, 1324–31 (1928).

It is obvious, of course, that where the vendor is obligated to tender a marketable record title, a title based upon adverse possession will not satisfy the contract unless the title has been "quieted" by a judgment or decree that is binding on all who might otherwise have interests in the land adverse to the vendor. Sometimes persons with possible outstanding interests of record may be persuaded to give quitclaim deeds to the vendor which, when recorded, will give him a marketable title of record. And sometimes special statutory proceedings to remove particular kinds of "clouds on title" may be available to the vendor. In Wisconsin, e.g., as indicated in the principal case, Wis.Stats.Ann. 235.60 provides for an inexpensive proceeding to obtain a court order satisfying ancient mortgages which are either paid or barred by limitations, but which are not properly satisfied of record.

Even in states where a title by adverse possession, "clearly established," is deemed marketable, the cases indicate that it is usually only at the end of a lawsuit that a purchaser will accept such a title. Why this should be so is suggested in Simis v. McElroy, supra.

Note: Common Title Defects, and Objections to Vendor's Title

As Professor Basye has pointed out, "To define marketable title in general terms is relatively easy; to apply the definition to a particular title is often a highly technical and difficult task." Basye, Clearing Land Titles 15 (1953). It is obviously impossible to deal with all the various defects, or apparent defects, which may in particular circumstances be held to render land titles unmarketable. The preceding cases, of course, indicate some title defects which have this effect. It may also be helpful to summarize the results of a study of 71 cases involving the question of marketability of title which reached the appellate courts of Illinois between 1840 and 1950. (Many of these cases involved more than one alleged defect in title.) The title defects alleged in these 71 cases were as follows: Lack of patent or grant from the government, 5; break in the chain of title, 13; defectively executed instruments in the chain of title, 6; variations in names of grantors and grantees in the chain of title, 6; incompetency of grantors in the chain of title, 5; defective descriptions of the land in the chain of title, 2; defective judicial or tax sales in the chain of title, 6; omission of necessary parties to judicial proceedings in the chain of title, 5; outstanding mortgages, 11; outstanding dower interests, 7; outstanding leases, 3; outstanding easements, 2; outstanding land sale contracts, 2; unpaid taxes or special assessments, 3; outstanding judgments, 3; outstanding claims against decedents' estates, 3; restrictions on use of the property, 2; encroachments, 2; lack of possession by the vendor, 2; "wild deed" in the chain of title, 1; title tainted with fraud, 1; and suit pending against vendor, 1. Six cases involved construction of wills, and four cases involved construction of deeds. In nearly 80% of the 71 cases, the title under consideration was held *unmarketable!* Reeve, Guaranteeing Marketability of Titles to Real Estate (1951).

In Easton v. Montgomery, 90 Cal. 307, 27 P. 280 (1891), the court said: "The burden is on the vendee to point out the defects in the title. If the vendor fails within * * * [a reasonable] time to remedy the defects thus pointed out, the purchaser, in any action to recover the purchase money or deposit paid by him, upon the ground that the title is defective, is limited to such defects as were then pointed out." And the court further said that "the acts of payment and conveyance being mutual and dependent, neither party is in default until after tender and demand by the other."

When must the purchaser make his objections to the vendor's title? May he wait until the vendor tenders a deed, or must he make his objections prior to that time? Suppose the vendor furnishes an abstract of title and the purchaser, after submitting it to his attorney for examination, returns it to the vendor without making any objections to the title; may the purchaser still raise objections at the time fixed for the closing of title? Is there any reason for the purchaser either to give notice of title defects or to tender performance if he discovers title defects that are incurable?

See Oppenheimer v. Knepper Realty Co., 50 Misc. 186, 98 N.Y.S. 204 (Sup. Ct.App.Term, 1906). The contract did not require the vendor to furnish any evidence of his title, but obligated him to convey certain property free from all encumbrances (with stated exceptions). On the day fixed for the closing of title, the purchaser raised certain objections to the title and the sale was not consummated. The purchaser then sued to recover his down payment and damages for the vendor's breach of contract. The trial judge apparently found that the southerly wall of the building on the property in question was a party wall, and that two agreements with respect thereto between former owners of the property in question and the owners of the lot adjoining on the south constituted encumbrances upon the property in question. On appeal, the court said:

"It is urged, * * * and the justice apparently considered, that this particular objection was not raised at the time the parties met to conclude the sale, and that it must therefore be deemed to have been waived, and there is much question whether plaintiff's assignor made any effectual tender of performance on his part. The existence of the party wall agreements made it impossible for the defendant to fulfill its contract according to its tenor on the law day. The rule is that tender of performance on the part of the vendee is dispensed with in a case where it appears that the vendor is disabled from performance on the day fixed therefor. In such a case tender of performance on the part of the vendee would be an idle ceremony, and the vendee may, without tender or demand, sue for the money paid on the contract and for damages. * * * This rule, however, does not apply when it appears that the incumbrance constituting an objection to the title is one which is within the power of the vendor to remove. In such a case the vendee may not maintain an action unless he tenders performance and makes his objection at the time fixed for performance; for he will then be deemed to have waived the objection. But, if the incumbrance be one not within the power of the vendor to remove, the vendee, in order to maintain an action, need not make tender or raise the particular objection at the time fixed for closing the title. * * *

"There are certain incumbrances as to which it may be presumed that the vendor, if his attention were called thereto, could and would remove, such as an overdue mortgage or taxes, or a servitude in favor of other property owned by him. Where, however, the incumbrance consists, as in the present case, of a servitude in favor of the property of a stranger, there is no presumption that it lay within the vendor's power to remove or extinguish the incumbrance. In fact, the presumption, if any there be, is quite the other way. Such an incumbrance therefore is not waived, because not raised at the time fixed for performance of the contract, when other objections, untenable in their nature, were raised, and its existence excuses any lack or deficiency there may have been in the vendee's tender and demand of performance. No evidence whatever was offered to show that the vendor could, if the objection had been made at the time, have caused the removal of the incumbrance. In the absence of such evidence, the plaintiff was entitled to recover the money paid on account of the contract and the reasonable damages due to defendant's inability to perform." (98 N.Y.S. at 205–206.)

Should a tender of performance be required of the purchaser even when the title defect is curable, if in fact it has not been cured by the closing date? Suppose the contract makes time "of the essence" and notice of the defect is not

given to the vendor until the closing date? Must the purchaser tender performance even though it is obvious that the vendor cannot cure the defect in time to
convey a good title on the "law day"? Suppose the purchaser gives notice of
the defect prior to the closing date but the vendor does not cure the defect.
Must the purchaser tender performance in such a case, if time is "of the essence"? What should be the consequences of a failure to specify a particular
title defect at or before the closing date, if the defect is curable? Is the purchaser merely precluded from rescinding and recovering his payments under
the contract, or may he be required to accept the title without a reduction in
price because of the defect? Compare the provision in the Chicago Real Estate
Board contract form: "If abstract be furnished, buyer, within fifteen days after
delivery thereof, shall deliver to seller a written statement of his objections to
the title, if any, with the abstract, * * * otherwise title shown by abstract
shall be deemed good."

Note: Improving "Marketability" of Land Titles Through
Adoption of Title Examination Standards

If, as has been stated above, the root cause of "construing against title" or
"fly-specking" is the inability of one title examiner to anticipate the decision of
another examiner on questions involving an exercise of sound practical and legal judgment, it would seem that the most sensible method of eliminating the
practice is by agreements made in advance as to the presumptions which will be
relied on in examining land titles, the period of search, the reliance to be placed
on statutes of limitations, and the effect of specific title records such as notorious receiverships and foreclosures. Such agreements, when adopted by local
bar associations, constitute so-called uniform title standards. The first standards were apparently adopted by the bar association of Livingston County,
Illinois, in 1923. Other bar associations, generally acting without knowledge of
the Illinois standards and without knowledge of each other's activities, adopted
title standards during the next 15 years: in Dodge County, Nebraska, in 1929;
in Gage County, Nebraska, in 1933 or 1934; and in Connecticut, on a state-wide
basis, in 1938. The movement toward adoption of uniform title standards can
fairly be said to have received its major impetus from the Connecticut bar adoption, which was reported to the American Bar Association's Section of Real
Property, Probate and Trust Law in 1939. This aroused widespread interest in
uniform title standards and during the next few years the A.B.A. Section actively promoted adoption of uniform title standards by state and local bar associations. Title standards have now been adopted at the state bar association
level in at least 25 states. These states are Colorado, Connecticut, Florida,
Georgia, Idaho, Illinois, Iowa, Kansas, Maine, Michigan, Minnesota, Missouri,
Montana, Nebraska, New Hampshire, New Mexico, New York, North Dakota,
Ohio, Oklahoma, South Dakota, Utah, Washington, Wisconsin, and Wyoming.[1]

The standards which have been adopted vary so much that generalization
about them is difficult. Nevertheless, there are certain noticeable similarities,
stemming in part from the fact that the Connecticut, Nebraska, Kansas, and
Colorado standards have been widely relied on as models by other bar associations, and in part from the fact that certain problems regularly recur in connection with title examinations in any jurisdiction. Thus, in almost every state
where title standards have been adopted, attention has been given to such problems as identity of parties and the doctrine of *idem sonans;* the effectiveness

1. Adoption in New York, in 1955, was
by the Executive Committee of the State
Bar Association.

of instruments purporting to have been executed by corporations; the effect of unreleased liens and encumbrances; the use of affidavits and recitals; the regularity of probate proceedings and acts of fiduciaries; the effect of recorded instruments executed by persons not in the chain of title; releases and satisfactions of liens; the regularity of judicial and quasi-judicial proceedings; and presumptions as to delivery. Other frequently recurring problems such as the effect of an absence of revenue stamps from a deed; the extent of notice given by the inclusion of the word "trustee" in the name of a party to an instrument; presumptions as to whether a "deed" constitutes a mortgage; and the presumptions attendant upon purported acts of notaries, have received more limited attention. Except as regards problems dependent on peculiar state practice, there is a substantial degree of agreement among the standards on the points listed above, resulting no doubt from the necessity of unanimity which excluded from the scope of the standards all matters as to which there was substantial difference of opinion.

The title standards so far adopted uniformly provide that the prior examiner shall, where possible, be informed of any objection to a title by a later examiner and be given an opportunity to meet such objection. There is diversity, however, with respect to acceptable base titles and period of search, and the standards adopted are sometimes neither entirely clear nor satisfactory. The Connecticut standards make the most drastic and clear-cut limitation of the period of search, generally limiting the period to 60 years. (Connecticut Standard No. 1.) In Utah and Missouri, most defects and encumbrances older than 45 and 50 years, respectively, can be ignored, but apparently it is still necessary to take the chain of title back to the sovereign. (Utah Standard No. 41; Missouri Standard No. 23.) In Idaho and Washington, a recorded patent need not be shown in the abstract if a take-off from the records of the United States Land Office is shown (Idaho Standard No. 12; Washington Standard No. 27); but in North Dakota and Minnesota it is still necessary that a recorded patent be shown except where the title is founded on a Congressional grant which by its terms does not require a patent (North Dakota, Conveyances 1; Minnesota Standard No. 13). Illinois has recognized as acceptable in certain cases an abstract beginning with a plat of subdivided land (Illinois Standard No. 14); and Iowa has adopted the same view (Iowa Standard No. 1.4). In Wisconsin and Nebraska, however, a complete abstract from the inception of private title must still be furnished. (Wisconsin Standard No. 2; Nebraska Standard No. 44.)

In general, the title standards adopt the position that the various statutes creating short periods of limitations, curing ancient irregularities of record, and providing for the termination of the notice of recorded instruments after a certain lapse of time should be given broad curative effect until the courts indicate otherwise. In some cases the standards contained general provisions as to marketability or as to the attitude which should characterize the title examiner. For example, Kansas Standard No. 10 provides in effect that defects in title shall be considered substantial only when they expose the purchaser to the hazard of adverse claims or litigation. In Idaho, the bar association has adopted a separate set of "Standards of Preparation of Abstracts" in addition to the title standards. In Iowa, on the other hand, the title standards themselves prescribe the form of the abstract and the abstracter's certificate. (Iowa Standards Nos. 1.1–1.11; see also Kansas Standards Nos. 3–4.) In Connecticut and Ohio, the certificate of title given by the examining attorney is set out. (Connecticut Standards Nos. 3, 5, 39; Ohio Standard No. 2.3.)

It would seem that the effectiveness of "uniform title standards" could be tremendously increased if land sale contract forms in common use were made to contain a provision that the vendor's title shall conform to the state and/or local title standards. Strangely enough, only two states have standards recommending such a course. (Connecticut Standard No. 67; Oklahoma Standard No. 28. Such a standard has also been proposed in Missouri.)

As the result of a research project sponsored by the University of Michigan Law School and the A.B.A. Section of Real Property, Probate and Trust Law, the University of Michigan Law School published a set of Model Title Standards by Simes and Taylor in 1960. The complete set of title standards adopted by the Georgia bar in 1963 was based on the Model Title Standards and several of the new title standards adopted in other states since 1960 have been based on the Model Title Standards. As Simes and Taylor point out, however,

" * * * there are definite limits to the scope and function of uniform title standards. * * * They cannot change or abolish a rule of law. They cannot do away with the requirement of delivery or of a writing for a valid conveyance; they cannot change the length of the statute of limitations, or abolish provisions for the extension of the period of limitations by disabilities. They cannot make a statute constitutional by declaring it so. In short, so far as rules of law are concerned, they can only resolve ambiguities pending their resolution by the highest court of the jurisdiction. So far as facts are concerned, they can determine what risks it is reasonable to expect a client to assume when a title is approved. Even that question of reasonableness is doubtless subject to review by a court. But if the practice of conveyancers is followed by all, the question is not likely to reach a court, and, even if it does, the court will generally follow the title standard." [2]

In 1947, the Nebraska legislature enacted the Nebraska Title Standards into law. Neb.Rev.Stat. (1943), reissue 1958, §§ 76.601 to 76.644. The enactment brought some regrets (See Morton, Title Standards, 31 Mich.Bar J., May 1952, 7, at 15–17) and in 1973 the act was repealed. Laws 1973, LB 517, § 2. The standards are now promulgated by the Bar Association, and the only statutory provision is § 76–530 which provides that it is not negligence for an attorney to follow the Standards.

Note: Time to Cure Title Defects and Purchaser's Right to Rescind

In Johnson v. Schuchardt, 333 Mo. 781, 63 S.W.2d 17, 89 A.L.R. 914 (1933), the contract expressly provided that the vendors should have a "reasonable time" in which to remedy any defects pointed out by the purchaser, and that the deed should be delivered with the purchaser approved the title. Even if the contract had not expressly given the vendor a "reasonable time," such a provision would undoubtedly have been implied. But suppose the contract had expressly fixed a date for delivery of the deed and payment of the purchase price? In such a case, it has often been said that time is "of the essence" if the question arises "at law." Thus where the vendor is unable to tender the title required by his contract on the "law day" and the purchaser points out the defect

---

2. Simes & Taylor, Model Title Standards 4–5 (1960). With respect to judicial recognition of title standards, Simes & Taylor cite Hughes v. Fairfield Lumber & Supply Co., 143 Conn. 427, 123 A.2d 195 (1956); Siedel v. Snider, 241 Iowa 1227, 44 N.W.2d 687 (1950); In re Baker's Estate, 247 Iowa 1380, 78 N.W.2d 863 (1956); Tesdell v. Hanes, 248 Iowa 742, 82 N.W.2d 119 (1957); B.W. & Leo Harris Co. v. City of Hastings, 240 Minn. 44, 59 N.W.2d 813 (1953); Hartley v. Williams, 287 S.W.2d 129 (Mo.App.1956). Id., 5 n. 5. In Com-

pagna v. Home Owner's Loan Corp., 141 Neb. 429, 3 N.W.2d 750 (1942), the court reversed its earlier decision in the same case, on rehearing, and largely as a result of efforts of the Nebraska Bar Association adopted a rule identical with one set out in the Nebraska Title Standards; but the court made no express reference to the standards. In Grand Lodge v. Fischer, 70 S.D. 562, 21 N.W.2d 213 (1945), the court took judicial notice of an Iowa Title Standard.

and tenders the purchase money, the purchaser will be entitled to recover his earnest money "at law," provided the vendor does not effectively invoke the equity jurisdiction of the court by a counterclaim for specific performance. See Groden v. Jacobson, 129 App.Div. 508, 114 N.Y.S. 183 (2d Dept.1908) (purchaser recovered deposit and cost of title examination; vendor's counterclaim for specific performance denied because he had conveyed the premises to a third party). But "in equity" time is not necessarily "of essence." As the court said in the Johnson case, "Parties to a contract for the sale of real estate may make time of the essence of the contract by express stipulation in the contract to that effect, but, where the contract does not expressly provide that time shall be of its essence, the court will look to the language employed, and to the nature and purpose of the contract and to the circumstances under which it was made in order to determine whether the parties intended that time should be of the essence of the contract." In some localities it is customary to provide expressly in real estate sale contracts that time shall be "of the essence." The Chicago Real Estate Board contract form previously considered contains such provisions.

Even where there is no evidence that the parties originally intended time to be "of the essence" of the contract, "either of the parties * * * may, by a reasonable notice to the other party for that purpose, render the time of performance as of the essence of the contract." Schmidt v. Reed, 132 N.Y. 108, 30 N.E. 373 (1892). The notice is equally binding on both parties, and the party making time "of the essence" cannot later insist upon additional time. If the party receiving the notice acquiesces in the time set for performance, he cannot later question the reasonableness of the period allowed.

Where the time of performance is "of the essence" of the contract, the vendor cannot enforce the contract specifically unless he can show that all valid objections to his title were satisfied on or before the date set for the title closing. But where time is not "of the essence," the courts will usually grant specific performance if the vendor succeeds in clearing his title within a reasonable time after the date set for the closing of title, even though he is "legally" in default. What is a reasonable time to cure title defects depends, of course, on the circumstances of the particular case. Even where the contract expressly states a definite period of time for curing defects, an additional period may be held reasonable, if time is not "of the essence." Where the vendor undertakes to clear his title by judicial proceedings, as in the Johnson case, the necessity for such proceedings and the reasonableness of the time required for their completion is generally a question of law for the court.

The cases generally support the statement in the Johnson case that, "Where * * * time is not of the essence of the contract, a decree for specific performance will be rendered, although the title was not perfected at the time the contract of sale was made, or at the time the suit for specific performance was filed, if it appears that the title is perfected at the time the decree for specific performance is rendered." See Lewis, Specific Performance of Contracts— Perfecting Title After Suit Has Begun, 50 Am.L.Reg. 523 (1902). In Van Riper v. Wickersham, 77 N.J.Eq. 232, 76 A. 1020, 30 L.R.A., N.S., 25 (Err. & App. 1910), it was even held that the vendor was entitled to a reasonable time *after* entry of a conditional decree for specific performance in which to clear his title, where the failure of the purchaser to object to his title until the day of the final hearing of the cause "lulled the complainant into inactivity and a feeling of security as to any objection that might be urged on the score of the title," and where the allowance of such time for perfection of the vendor's title would "not work hardship upon the defendant."

It should be noted, however, that if the vendor has no interest whatever in the land he has contracted to sell, at the date set for conveyance, he generally is not given any additional time in which to acquire title, even though time is not "of the essence" of the contract.

The rule is usually stated to be that a purchaser may not rescind or repudiate a land sale contract before the time for performance because the vendor's title is "bad" or "unmarketable," since the vendor is only obligated to tender a "good" and "marketable" title on the date when the conveyance is to be executed. There are some exceptions to this general rule, however,—exceptions characterized as involving "fraud" on the vendor's part in Easton v. Montgomery, 90 Cal. 307, 27 P. 280 (1891). According to 1 Restatement, Contracts § 283, a land purchaser "need not perform his promise" if the vendor "has not, at the time of contracting, (a) the present ownership of the land * * * or (b) the right to become the owner in time to perform the contract, or (c) a justifiable expectation of becoming the owner in time to perform the contract," and if the purchaser "neither knows nor has reason to know the facts when he enters into the contract, and makes a material change of position after he acquires knowledge of them" and while the facts as to the vendor's lack of ownership continue. A comment to sec. 283 states that the same rule applies to cases where the vendor's interest is encumbered as well as cases where the vendor has no interest in the land. Compare 1 Restatement, Contracts § 284, which states that a land purchaser "need not perform his promise" if the vendor contracts to sell the land to a third person, or subjects the land "to a substantial encumbrance which he apparently cannot remove by the time when his performance is due, * * * unless while the purchaser has not changed his position the seller acquires such ownership as is necessary for the performance of his contract and is free from any duty to sell to a third person." A comment to sec. 284 states that "the action of the seller not only creates a probable inability to perform but is also a manifestation of an intention not to perform."

Suppose a purchaser is in possession under a contract calling for payment of the price in monthly installments over a long period of time. If he discovers that his vendor's title is defective, must he nevertheless continue to make payments under the contract? May he notify the vendor of the defect, tender the entire balance of the contract price, and then maintain a suit to rescind and recover payments already made on the contract?

See 1937 Report of the New York Law Revision Commission, p. 556 (Leg. Doc. 65M, p. 14):

"If the purchaser has defaulted in the payment of intermediate installments, the vendor may sue at law to recover them. Inasmuch as the purchaser's obligation to pay intermediate installments is, in the absence of contrary stipulation in the contract, deemed 'independent' of the vendor's obligation to convey, the vendor need neither tender a valid title before suit nor prove upon the trial that he possesses a marketable title. The fact that the vendor never had title to the premises will be of no avail to the purchaser. He will be compelled to continue his payments unless he can establish either that the title which the vendor does possess is incurably defective, so that there is no probability of a marketable title being tendered on the law day, or that the vendor has, since the execution of the contract, disposed of the property and thus prospectively disabled himself from meeting his obligation to convey."

Cf. Prentice v. Erskine, 164 Cal. 446, 129 P. 585 (1913). The purchaser under an installment contract defaulted and surrendered possession to the vendor, who sued to quiet his title. The purchaser counterclaimed for payments made under the contract and for the cost of improvements, alleging that the vendor was himself in default since he could not convey a good title, the property being encumbered by a perpetual right of way for a public road, by an easement for an irrigation ditch, and by a lien for water charges. *Held:* Judgment for the purchaser for his payments on the contract but not for the cost of the improvements, which was offset by the reasonable value of the use of the property. The court said that although it is the general rule that a defaulting purchaser cannot complain because the vendor was not in a position to convey a good title before the date set for the conveyance, this is a harsh rule and should not be extended. "If the only encumbrance upon the property were the easement for the irrigating ditch and the lien for the water-tax, we might be constrained to hold, under the authorities, that the case would fall within the rule discussed above, but as one of the defects in the vendor's title arose from the existence of a public servitude, we must conclude that plaintiff was himself in default, because that is the sort of cloud which in the nature of things he could not remove by any ordinary method of business negotiation. It would not be like a mortgage, for example, which might be extinguished by payment of the debt thereby secured, or like a lien for unpaid water rent which might be destroyed by settlement of the account. He could not either by adverse possession or by purchase take from the public the right to pass over the land on a dedicated highway. He was as completely helpless and hopeless of conveying a perfect title at any time as if the whole tract had been taken for use as a public park. The vendee might have rescinded the contract at any time even though the time for final payment had not arrived because the vendor, in the nature of things, never could offer a perfect title to him."

See also Reagan v. Daniels, 70 Colo. 373, 201 P. 889 (1921).

SECTION 3. RISK OF LOSS WHILE THE CONTRACT REMAINS EXECUTORY

ANDERSON v. YAWORSKI

Supreme Court of Errors of Connecticut, 1935.
120 Conn. 390, 181 A. 205, 101 A.L.R. 1232.

MALTBIE, C.J. On November 13th, 1933, the plaintiff and the defendant entered into a written agreement by the terms of which the defendant agreed to sell and the plaintiff to buy for $2745 a certain parcel of land with the buildings thereon. The agreement acknowledged the receipt of $100 upon the purchase price and provided that the plaintiff would, on or before April 1st, 1934, pay the defendant the balance of the purchase price, in part in cash and the rest by the assumption of a mortgage already upon the premises and by giving to the defendant a second mortgage for the remaining sum due; and it also provided that if the plaintiff failed to make the payments stated he should forfeit all claims to the premises and all money paid. Upon the execution of the contract the defendant paid a commission of $140 to a real-estate agent for his services in negotiating the sale. The plaintiff intended to occupy the premises as his home. On January 26th, 1934, the dwelling-house on the premises was totally destroyed by accidental fire without the fault of either party. Shortly before April 1st the defendant informed the plaintiff that she would be ready and willing to carry out the contract on March 31st; and she also offered to assign to him all rights under an insurance policy which had been issued to her upon the buildings on the property. This offer the plaintiff refused and, declining to make further payments, he demanded the return of the $100 he had paid. He brought this action to recover that sum, and the defendant filed a counterclaim seeking damages for his failure to perform the contract. The trial court concluded that, as there had been a substantial failure of consideration by the destruction of the dwellinghouse, the plaintiff was relieved of his obligation to fulfil the provisions of the agreement and was entitled to recover the amount he had paid. Judgment entered for the plaintiff upon the complaint and counterclaim and the defendant has appealed.

It is undoubtedly true that the majority of courts have adopted the rule that, where a contract is made to convey real estate upon which a building stands the burden of the loss by the burning of the building without fault of either party falls upon the vendee, no matter how material a part of the substance of the contract it was or whether or not the time for the performance had arrived when it was destroyed. Notes, 22 A.L.R. 575; 41 A.L.R. 1272; 46 A.L.R. 1126. This rule, differing from that applied to contracts for the sale of personal property, is based, as far as legal principles are concerned, upon the nature of the estate of the vendee, which equity regards as arising out of the contract. The legal foundation for the rule does not bear analysis. See Langdell, A Brief Survey of Equity Jurisdiction (2d Ed.) pp. 58 et seq. (1 Harvard Law Review, pp. 373 et seq.); 2 Williston, Contracts, §§ 928 et seq. (9 Harvard Law Review, p. 106). While for many purposes the vendee in equity is recognized as the real owner of the property, it cannot be said with accuracy that the entire beneficial interest has vested in him; for instance, pending the time fixed for the performance of the contract the vendee has not one of the principal incidents of ownership, the right to the enjoyment and profits of the property. 66 C.J. p. 1034, §§ 784 et seq. For this reason, if for no other, the vendor cannot properly be said to be a trustee of the land for the vendee; Brett, L.J., Rayner v. Preston, L.R. 18 Ch.Div. 1, 10; Pound, The Progress of the Law, 33 Harvard Law Review, p. 830; rather their relationship is like that between a mortgagor in possession and the mortgagee, which is more aptly described as one in the nature of a trust than as one of a trust in fact, although, as in similar situations, equity may for certain purposes undoubtedly treat the vendor as a quasi-trustee. Andrews v. New Britain National Bank, 113 Conn. 467, 472, 155 A. 838.

The maxim that equity regards that as done which ought to be done and its outgrowth, the equitable doctrine of conversion, cannot be broadly applied to such a situation as the one before us. The basis of the maxim is the existence of a duty; "unless the equitable *ought* exist, there is no room for the operation of the maxim"; 3 Pomeroy, Equity Jurisprudence (4th Ed.) § 1160; agreements " 'are to be considered as done at the time when, according to the tenor thereof, they ought to have been performed' "; Hall v. Hall, 50 Conn. 104, 111; Manice v. Manice, 43 N.Y. 303, 372; and equity can hardly regard that as presently done which the parties to a contract have agreed shall be done only in the future. The basis of the doctrine of conversion whereby for certain purposes real estate is considered in equity as personal and personal estate as real, is the intent of the party creating a right in the property, or in the case of a contract, the intent of the parties to it; "this, like all other questions of intention, must ultimately depend upon the provisions of the particular instrument." Pomeroy, Op.Cit., § 1162. "The doctrine of equitable conversion is an equitable one, adopted for the purpose of carrying into effect, in spite of legal obstacles, the intent of a testator or settlor. It is not a fixed rule of law, but proceeds upon equitable principles which take into account the result which its application will accomplish. Its application is, therefore, governed by somewhat different considerations, according to the connection in which it is invoked." Emery v. Cooley, 83 Conn. 235, 238, 76 A. 529. In determining the devolution of estates, equity may regard real property as converted into personal or personal into real even though by the terms of a will the actual conversion is postponed to some future time, and may hold that a contract to sell real estate works a conversion in so far as the rights of those interested in the estate of the vendor are concerned, where he dies before the time of performance has arrived. Emery v. Cooley, supra; Bowne v. Ide, 109 Conn. 307, 315, 147 A. 4. But in doing this equity is giving that effect to the transaction which will most nearly work out the rights of those interested in the estate in accordance with the aspect of the property which it may fairly be assumed it had taken in the mind of the deceased. But, as between the parties to the contract, to regard the land as converted into personalty before the time for performance of the contract has come is to do violence to their expressed intent. Under such a contract, the vendor's right to money in lieu of the land and the vendee's right to the land in lieu of the money can arise only when the time agreed upon for performance has arrived.

Nor do the distinctions between the effect of the contract for the sale of real estate and those for the sale of personal property, often adverted to in the opinions, afford sufficient basis for the application of a different rule as to risk of loss. While it is true that in most jurisdictions of this country, by the recording of a contract to sell real estate notice of the rights of the vendee will be imputed to all the world and hence he is protected to a greater extent than is the vendee of personal property, that is only because of the effect of the recording statutes; and a vendee of personal property enjoys a like protection where, as in the case of conditional sales, the statutes provide for the recording of the contract. Liquid Carbonic Co. v. Black, 102 Conn. 390, 394, 128 A. 514; Tire Shop v. Peat, 115 Conn. 187, 189, 161 A. 96. While contracts for the sale of real estate may usually be specifically enforced, but contracts for the sale of personal property can only be so enforced in exceptional circumstances, this distinction is due to the fact that in the case of the latter the disappointed purchaser may ordinarily repair his loss by the purchase of other like property, while each parcel of land has usually its own peculiar characteristics and one parcel cannot often afford a complete and adequate substitute for another in the mind of the purchaser. "Courts of equity decree the specific performance of contracts, not upon any distinction between realty and personalty, but because damages at law may not, in a particular case, afford a complete remedy. Thus a court of equity decrees performance of a contract for land, not because of the real nature of the land, but because damages at law, which must be calculated upon the general money-value of land, may not be a complete remedy to the purchaser, to whom the land may have a peculiar and special value." Adderley v. Dixon, 1 Sim. & St. 607, quoted 5 Pomeroy, Op.Cit., p. 4869. Nor are we impressed with the practical reasons sometimes advanced in support of the majority rule, that as the vendee would have the benefit, upon the performance of the contract, of any excess of value accruing subsequent to its making, it is only just that he should bear any risk of loss due to the destruction of the building upon the property during this time. Whether the one could fairly be set off against the other involves considerations which cannot be definitely ascertained and our own conviction is that to do so does not produce a just result. Moreover, the same considerations are present in sales of personal property, but they have never been considered to justify the abrogation of the rule applied to such sales.

That rule has been stated by us as follows: "Where, from the nature of the contract and the surrounding circumstances, the parties from the beginning must have known that it could not be fulfilled unless, when the time for fulfillment arrived, some particular thing or condition of things continued to exist, so that they must be deemed, when entering into the contract, to have contemplated such continuing existence as the foundation of what was to be done; in the absence of any express or implied warranty that such thing or condition of things shall exist, the contract is to be considered as subject to an implied condition that the parties shall be excused, in case, before breach, performance becomes impossible or the purpose of the contract frustrated from such thing or condition ceasing to exist without default of either of the parties." Straus v. Kazemekas, 100 Conn. 581, 591, 124 A. 234; see Fischer v. Kennedy, 106 Conn. 484, 490, 138 A. 503. We can find no sufficient reason for not applying the same rule to contracts for the sale of real estate. In the latter as much as in those for the sale of personal property, the intention of the parties is that, when the time for performance is reached, the property bargained for shall pass; that intention is just as much frustrated in the one case as in the other by the destruction of the essential value of the property before the day of performance comes; and there is the same reason to imply as a condition of an obligation to perform the contract, that that value should continue to exist. Thompson v. Gould, 37 Mass. (20 Pick.) 134, 139; Gould v. Murch, 70 Me. 288.

In Hough v. City Fire Ins. Co., 29 Conn. 10, we had before us an action upon a fire insurance policy issued to one who had contracted to buy the property insured but had not received a deed of it. The application for the policy requested that it be issued to the insured upon "his frame dwelling-house" and "his barn" and one condition of the policy was that if the interest of the insured in the property was "not absolute" this must be so represented or the policy would be void. The buildings having been destroyed by fire, the insurer contended that the representation of the insured that they were "his" buildings was untrue and that the condition in the policy had not been met. We held that the plaintiff had a vested interest in the property, dependent upon no contingency, and a right to it which he might enforce at his will and of which he could not be deprived without his consent, that he did not misrepresent when he referred to the buildings upon it as "his" and that his interest was not other than "absolute" as that word was used in the condition of the policy. It is true that we did in the opinion state that the risk of loss of property was upon the insured, and other courts, in reaching like conclusions, have sometimes given this as a reason for their decisions. See Petello v. Teutonia Fire Ins. Co., 89 Conn. 175, 93 A. 137; note, 60 A.L.R. 18. That reason is by no means a necessary foundation for such a rule, but it finds adequate basis in the nature of the equitable estate which the vendee acquires under a contract for the sale of land. McCollough v. Home Ins. Co., 155 Cal. 659, 102 P. 814; Johannes v. Standard Fire Office, 70 Wis. 196, 201, 35 N.W. 298; note, 60 A.L.R. 18. Now that we are directly confronted with the question whether, under such a contract the risk of loss is upon the vendee, we are not able to accept as authoritative the statement in the Hough case that it is, at least where possession has not passed, but hold that risk of loss is upon the vendor.

It is true that in the ordinary contract for the sale of real estate, though a building upon it is destroyed by fire, the land remains and the inability of the vendor to perform does not go to the entire subject-matter of the contract; nor should the destruction of a building upon the land or a part of the buildings upon it in all cases discharge the vendee from his obligation to perform. Recognizing this, the Supreme Judicial Court of Massachusetts has stated that the vendee is not released "if the change in the value of the estate is not so great, or if it appears that the buildings did not constitute so material a part of the estate to be conveyed as to result in an annulling of the contract." Hawkes v. Kehoe, 193 Mass. 419, 425, 79 N.E. 766. In dealing with the discharge of contracts for the sale of personal property, the American Law Institute Restatement states that where a "material deterioration" of a specific thing which in the contemplation of both parties is necessary for the performance of a promise in a bargain occurs without the fault of the promisee, the duty to perform the contract, unless a contrary intent appears, is discharged, except that the promisee has a qualified right to demand whatever performance remains possible; Amer.Law Institute Restatement, Contracts, § 460; and in Comment (e) to this section it states that the same rule applies where the subject-matter of the contract is partially destroyed. But in § 281 of the Restatement, though treating of a "prospective inability" to perform due to the destruction of the subject-matter of the bargain, the Restatement gives as a rule applicable to both present and future inability to perform that the promisor is discharged where "substantial performance" has become impossible; and in Comment (b) to this section it states: "Where the means of performance are impaired, but not destroyed, the determination of the question depends upon the degree of impairment."

The phrase "substantial performance" is one made familiar to us in those cases where a contractor is permitted to recover though he has failed, not wilfully, in part to perform his obligation but has substantially performed it; Kelley v. Hance, 108 Conn. 186, 187, 142 A. 683; and we have recognized that whether a contract has been substantially performed is ordinarily a question of fact. Chinigo v. Ehrenberg, 112 Conn. 381, 384, 152 A. 305. The test of substantial performance is more in accord with our legal conceptions and furnishes a sufficient test for the application of the rule we are considering. Whether there has been such performance must depend upon the circumstances of the particular case; the intention of the parties; the use to which the property is capable of being put or to which the vendor knows or should know that the vendee intends to put it, and the extent to which such use will be prevented or interfered with; the relative values of the land and the buildings, if they are wholly destroyed or, if only partially destroyed, of the value of what remains to the value of the whole; and no doubt other considerations. Our conclusion is that, if by reason of the destruction or injury to the buildings upon real estate agreed to be conveyed between the time of the making of the contract and the time fixed for performance, it is no longer possible for the vendor substantially to perform the contract, the vendee may treat it as discharged.

The finding of the trial court that the burning of the dwelling-house upon the property had brought about a substantial failure of consideration is, for all practicable purposes, the equivalent of a finding that after the fire the defendant was no longer able substantially to perform the contract. The plaintiff was therefore entitled to treat it as discharged. The contract being discharged, the provision in it that if the plaintiff failed to make the further payments agreed upon he should forfeit the money paid in pursuance of it falls with the rest of it. He has paid a part of the purchase price but has received no benefit under the contract. He is therefore entitled to recover the sums so paid from the defendant. * * * The trial court was correct in giving judgment for the plaintiff upon both the complaint and the counterclaim.

There is no error.

In this opinion HAINES and AVERY, Js., concurred.

BANKS, J. (dissenting). The ruling of the court presents this question: Where, after the execution of a contract for the sale of land and prior to the delivery of the deed, the buildings thereon are accidentally destroyed, upon whom should fall the burden of the loss, the vendor or the vendee? The plaintiff says that an implied condition of the contract which the parties must have had in mind when it was entered into was the continued existence of the dwelling-house upon the property, that its destruction has made the contract impossible of performance, and relies on the rule that where a specific thing which is essential to the performance of a contract is destroyed the parties are excused from performance. Straus v. Kazemekas, 100 Conn. 581, 592, 124 A. 234; Amer.Law Institute Restatement, Contracts, Vol. 1, § 281. That rule is applicable if, at the time of the destruction of the dwelling, the vendor was its real owner, but not if the contract had been so far executed as to vest the ownership in the vendee. Cases which hold that the buyer is bound to pay in spite of the destruction of the building "are not exceptions to the rule stated in the section [281] since when recovery of the price is allowed, the result is based on the premise that the substantial incidents of ownership had already passed to the buyer before the destruction." Restatement, Contracts, Vol. 1, § 281, Comment c. The authorities all agree that the loss should fall upon the party who is the owner at the time, but differ as to whether the vendor or the purchaser is the owner. 66 C.J. 1052, § 811. The question, therefore, resolves itself into an inquiry as to who was the owner of the house at the time of the fire, and the answer to that inquiry will determine the incidence of the loss.

The legal title, of course, was in the defendant since the deed conveying the property to the plaintiff had not been executed or delivered at the time of the fire. But a binding contract of sale of the property, known with us as a bond for a deed, had been executed, delivered and recorded in the land records. The plaintiff thereby acquired the equitable title to the property. Hough v. City Fire Ins. Co., 29 Conn. 10; Miller Co. v. Grussi, 90 Conn. 555, 557, 98 A. 90; Grippo v. Davis, 92 Conn. 693, 695, 104 A. 165; Rienzo v. Cohen, 112 Conn. 427, 431, 152 A. 394; 27 R.C.L. 464. In Hough v. City Fire Ins. Co., supra, we said (p. 20) that one in possession of real property under a contract of sale had acquired a right of which he could not be deprived against his will, and was the owner of an absolute interest, who must necessarily bear the loss if the property were destroyed, and sustained a charge of the trial court that a perfect legal title was not essential to his recovery upon an insurance policy, and that he might be regarded as the real owner if he had the equitable title. "In some respects, and for some purposes, the contract is executory in equity as well as at law; but so far as the interest or estate in the land of the two parties is concerend, it is regarded as executed, and as operating to transfer the estate from the vendor and to vest it in the vendee. * * * The vendee is looked upon and treated as the owner of the land; an equitable estate has vested in him commensurate with that provided for by the contract, whether in fee, for life, or for years; although the vendor remains owner of the legal estate, he holds it as a trustee for the vendee, to whom all the beneficial interest has passed." I Pomeroy, Equity Jurisprudence (4th Ed.) § 368. Under this doctrine of equity the vendor has the bare legal title to the property; all other incidents of ownership are vested in the vendee who has acquired the full equitable estate. It follows that the latter is entitled to all the benefits accruing from such ownership, and at the same time assumes all the burdens incident thereto. "Equity, from the moment the contract is binding, gives the vendee the entire benefit of the rise in value of the land and all subsequent improvements, and any other advantage that may accrue to the estate. If the vendee is the owner in equity so as to receive all increment, he should be considered owner so as to accept the burden of any loss not due to the vendor's fault." 5 Pomeroy, Equity Jurisprudence (4th Ed.) § 2282.

Accordingly, in the early English case of Paine v. Meller, 6 Ves. 349, it was established as a general rule of equity that, when there was a binding contract capable of specific performance, loss by fire or other accident prior to the transfer of the legal title should fall upon the vendee. This would seem to be a necessary corollary of the accepted rule that the entire equitable interest in the property is then vested in the vendee. The great weight of judicial decisions in this country as well as text-writers upon the subject support this rule. 27 R.C.L. 555, § 293; 66 C.J. 1052, § 811; 22 A.L.R. 575; 41 A.L.R. 1272; 46 A.L.R. 1126. Indeed, an eminent authority has said that it is "a long-settled theory of courts of equity * * * sustained by the overwhelming weight of Anglo-American authority." Pound, The Progress of the Law, 33 Harvard Law Review, 828, note. Our own case of Hough v. City Fire Ins. Co., supra, has been widely cited as an authority in support of the majority rule. Thompson v. Gould, 37 Mass. (20 Pick.) 134, announced the contrary doctrine since adhered to in Massachusetts and followed in a few jurisdictions. In that case there was no enforceable contract, the agreement to purchase being by parol. It was there said that the loss must fall on the owner of the property at the time the loss happened, but the court held that the vendor, being the holder of the legal title, was such owner. The opinion recognized that "a different doctrine has been adopted in equity, founded on the fiction that whatever is agreed to be done shall be considered as actually done," and that under that doctrine the purchaser must bear the loss. In the case of an agreement for the sale of personal property, if the property is destroyed before the sale is completed and title passed the loss must ordinarily be borne by the vendor; and it was said in Thompson v. Gould, supra, that there is no reason why the same rule should not apply in the case of real estate. A contract to sell personal property without the transfer of possession gives only a personal right of action against the vendor for damages in case of a breach of the contract. A contract to sell real estate may be specifically enforced against the vendor and against anyone taking title from him with notice and the recording of the contract charges such taker with constructive notice. The vendee thus acquires the full *jus disponendi*, the substantial equivalent of a legal reversionary interest from the time when performance is due. Williston, 9 Harvard Law Review, 113, 119.

The majority opinion suggests that the vendee has not the entire beneficial interest in the property since, pending the time fixed for the performance of the contract, he has not a right to the possession and enjoyment of the property. Possession is not material with respect to the passing or existence of either legal or equitable title to land, and should not be as to the incidents of equitable title. See Pound, The Progress of the Law, 33 Harvard Law Review, 826, note 68.

The majority opinion apparently assumes that the rule that the vendee must bear the loss depends upon the doctrine of equitable conversion. It is unnecessary to resort to that doctrine to justify the rule; the loss is thrown upon the vendee simply because he is in equity substantially the owner of the property and justice requires that having the benefits he should bear the burden of ownership. Keener, 1 Columbia Law Review, 8.

Since the substantial incidents of ownership have passed to the buyer, equity treats the contract as executed to the extent that the beneficial ownership of the property is vested in him, and the doctrine of impossibility of performance of an executory contract has no application. In my opinion the destruction of the dwelling-house did not relieve either party of the duty to perform on the ground of impossibility of performance of an executory contract, the loss should fall upon the plaintiff as the equitable owner, and he is not entitled to the return of his deposit.

In this opinion HINMAN, J., concurred.

Notes

1. Although the earlier Massachusetts cases of Thompson v. Gould and Hawkes v. Kehoe, cited in the principal case, were actions "at law" and therefore did not really decide that the risk of loss was on the vendor "in equity" under an enforceable contract for the sale of realty, Libman v. Levenson, 236 Mass. 221, 128 N.E. 13, 22 A.L.R. 560 (1920), is clear authority for that proposition. In Libman the property contracted to be sold was substantially damaged by the collapse of a retaining wall prior to the time fixed for conveyance of the legal title. The court dismissed the vendor's bill in equity for specific performance and entered a decree for the purchaser on his cross bill for recovery of an installment paid on the purchase price. It is therefore clear that the rule as to risk of loss in Massachusetts is the same "in equity" as it is "at law." Other jurisdictions which appear to have adopted the Massachusetts rule placing the risk of loss on the vendor pending conveyance of the legal title (in the absence of any contrary provision in the contract) include Connecticut (principal case), Maine, Montana, New Hampshire, Oregon, Rhode Island, and Washington. The doctrinal basis of the rule has been variously stated, but underlying all the statements is the idea that the vendor should not be permitted to enforce the contract unless he is able to render substantial performance himself.

Under the Massachusetts rule it seems to be immaterial whether the vendor or purchaser is in possession when the loss occurs. It should be noted, however, that in the New England states where the rule is most firmly established, the usual form of contract contemplates conveyance of the legal title within a relatively short time and does not provide for transfer of possession until such conveyance is made.

Under the Massachusetts rule, if there is substantial damage to the premises by fire or other casualty, not resulting from the purchaser's negligence or other fault, prior to conveyance of the legal title, the vendor is not entitled to specific performance and the purchaser can recover his deposit and any other payments on the purchase price. If the damage is not substantial, the purchaser will not be permitted to rescind and recover his payments, but he will be entitled to specific performance with an abatement of the price. Presumably the vendor can also enforce the contract with an abatement of the price in such a case or, in the alternative, recover damages for breach of contract if the purchaser does not ask for specific performance. Even where the damage is substantial, there seems to be no good reason why the purchaser should not be given specific performance with abatement of the price if the damage can be fairly assessed; but the cases are divided on this point.

Should it make any difference in allocation of the loss whether the loss occurs before or after the time agreed upon for conveyance of the legal title? Dean Langdell was of the opinion that the risk of loss should be on the vendor until the time agreed upon for conveyance of the legal title, and thereafter on the purchaser unless the vendor is then in such default as to be unable specifically to enforce the contract.[1] But this view has apparently found no support in the cases.

2. Paine v. Meller, 6 Ves.Jr. 349, 31 Eng.Rep. 1088 (Ch.1801), cited in the dissenting opinion in the principal case, has generally been considered to establish the broad doctrine that the making of an enforcible contract to purchase realty vests "equitable ownership" in the purchaser, with the corollary that any loss through accidental damage to or destruction of the realty pending conveyance of the legal title must be borne by the purchaser unless the contract provides otherwise. This means that despite the loss the purchaser must pay the contract price in full (subject to any credit to which he may be entitled because of insurance proceeds received by the vendor) if the vendor seeks specific performance. And despite dicta that the risk of loss remains with the vendor "at law" until the legal title is conveyed, it is clear that if the risk is imposed on the purchaser as "equitable owner" the vendor may recover damages for the purchaser's refusal to perform the contract after the loss occurs; and that the purchaser is not entitled to restitution of any purchase money already paid, provided the vendor is willing and able to convey the legal title in accordance with his contract.

The doctrine of Paine v. Meller is, however, subject to certain well-recognized qualifications. The purchaser as "equitable owner" must bear the loss only if the loss does not arise from the neglect, default, or unwarrantable delay of the vendor in carrying out the contract; and the vendor must bear the loss if, at the time when it occurs, he was not in a position to convey the title which he contracted to convey.[2] In some of the cases so holding, the loss occurred after the time set by contract for conveyance of the legal title, or at the time of the loss the vendor had delayed unreasonably in clearing his title of defects and tendering a deed, no fixed time for conveyance having been stated in the contract. In other cases so holding, the loss occurred either before the time set for conveyance or within a reasonable time after the contract was made, no definite time for conveyance having been fixed. In some of the cases where the vendor's title was defective at the time of the loss, the courts have, for that reason, placed the loss on the vendor even though the purchaser was in possession. And in some cases the loss has been placed on the vendor because the purchaser's duty of performance was subject to a suspensive condition at the time when the loss occurred, or because the vendor then had an option to cancel the contract without liability except for return of the purchaser's payments. In these cases, the purchaser has not been regarded as "equitable owner" by virtue of the contract.

Under the doctrine of Paine v. Meller in its broadest form, it is immaterial whether the vendor or the purchaser is in possession when the loss occurs. However, in some of the cases where the doctrine of "equitable ownership" is stated as the basis of a decision that the risk of loss is on the purchaser, the court has also stressed the fact that the purchaser was in possession under the contract; and in a few such cases the court has indicated that possession may be a necessary element of "equitable ownership." In a few cases, also, the courts have stressed the use of "present" words of sale in the contract as a

---

1. See Langdell, A Brief Survey of Equity Jurisdiction: III, 1 Harv.L.Rev. 355, 374–75 (1888). See also Clark, Some Problems in Specific Performance, 31 Harv.L. Rev. 271, 283–87 (1917).

2. 4 Pomeroy, Equity Jurisprudence 482, 483 (5th ed. 1941).

basis for treating the purchaser as "equitable owner," but this has not generally been deemed essential.

The broad doctrine that the risk of loss is on the purchaser from the time the vendor-purchaser relation arises is approved, with extensive citation of supposedly analogous situations in which the purchaser is regarded as "equitable owner," in Keener, The Burden of Loss as an Incident of the Right to the Specific Performance of a Contract, 1 Col.L.Rev. 1 (1901). Pound also approves the doctrine in this article, Progress of the Law—Equity, 33 Harv.L.Rev. 813 (1920) at 826–828. The doctrine is vigorously disapproved in Langdell, A Brief Survey of Equity Jurisdiction: III, 1 Harv.L.Rev. 355 (1888) at 374–380; Stone, Equitable Conversion by Contract, 13 Col.L.Rev. 368 (1913) at 385–387; Vanneman, Risk of Loss in Equity, 8 Minn.L.Rev. 127 (1924) at 131–137; 7 Williston, Contracts §§ 929–943 (3d ed. 1963). Both Vanneman and Williston (the latter in greater detail) answer Keener's arguments by analogy point by point. For a good brief summary of the arguments pro and con, see 3A Corbin, Contracts § 667 (1960).

3. Professor Williston vigorously championed the view that the risk of loss should remain with the vendor until conveyance of the legal title unless possession of the realty was transferred to the purchaser prior to the conveyance.[3] This view seems to have been adopted by judicial decision in California, South Carolina, and Wisconsin. Moreover, Professor Williston drafted the Uniform Vendor and Purchaser Risk Act, recommended for adoption by the Commissioners on Uniform State Laws in 1935 and subsequently adopted in New York (with substantial additions), South Dakota, Hawaii, Wisconsin, Michigan, California (with minor changes), Oregon, North Carolina (with a minor omission), and Illinois (with an interesting addition to deal with escrows). The text of the Uniform Act, as originally recommended and as adopted in most of the above states, is in part as follows:

"Any contract hereafter made in this State for the purchase and sale of realty shall be interpreted as including an agreement that the parties shall have the following rights and duties, unless the contract expressly provides otherwise:

"(a) If, when neither the legal title nor the possession of the subject matter of the contract has been transferred, all or a material part thereof is destroyed without fault of the purchaser or is taken by eminent domain, the vendor cannot enforce the contract, and the purchaser is entitled to recover any portion of the price that he has paid;

"(b) If, when either the legal title or the possession of the subject matter of the contract has been transferred, all or any part thereof is destroyed without fault of the vendor or is taken by eminent domain, the purchaser is not thereby relieved from a duty to pay the price, nor is he entitled to recover any portion thereof that he has paid."

4. In addition to authorities already cited on the risk of loss problem, see 3 A.L.P. § 11.30 (1952); Simpson, Legislative Changes in the Law of Equitable Conversion by Contract: II, 44 Yale L.J. 754 (1935), at 754–59, 769–77; Hirschler & Fleischer, Risk of Loss in Executory Contracts for the Purchase of Lands, 34 Va.L.Rev. 965 (1948).

5. The doctrine of "equitable conversion" is frequently applied in controversies other than those which involve allocation of the risk of loss. For example, if a vendor dies after the contract of sale is executed, the usual law would mean that his "real property" descends to the heirs, while "personal property"

---

3. 7 Williston, Contracts §§ 938–940 (3d ed. 1963).

goes to the administrator to pay debts, costs of administration, and for distribution to the next of kin (who may not be the same people as the heirs). If the purchaser defaults after the vendor's death, and someone must bring an action to foreclose, should it be the administrator (i.e., is the vendor's interest to be regarded as personalty—the contract right to the unpaid price), or should the heirs bring the action (as owners of the land)? Application of the equitable conversion doctrine would result in having the administrator being the action. Similarly, if a vendor leaves a will devising "real property" to X and "personal property" to Y, the doctrine may be invoked to determine who gets the amount still due on the land contract.

WORLD EXHIBIT CORP. v. CITY BANK FARMERS TRUST CO.

New York Supreme Court, Appellate Division, 2d Dept., 1946.
270 App.Div. 654, 61 N.Y.S.2d 889.

CARSWELL, Justice. On July 25, 1944, defendant's predecessor, pursuant to an option in a lease, sold to its tenant a private amusement park, situated in Coney Island for $275,000. The purchaser made a down payment of $60,000. The vendor was to take back a purchase money mortgage of $125,000, and the balance of $90,000 was to be paid on the closing day, September 15, 1944. On the day the contract was signed, it was assigned by the tenant to Sally L. Draisin, to the knowledge of the vendor. On September 14, 1944, it was assigned by Draisin to the Brooklyn Amusement Corporation. On the same day that corporation also received a similar assignment directly from the tenant, or assignor of Draisin.

On August 12, 1944, a fire destroyed 40% of the improvements on the property. The closing day was adjourned to September 29, 1944, and in the meantime the vendor became entitled to and later received $153,000 of insurance for the property destroyed and damaged. On the closing day the Brooklyn Amusement Corporation, hereinafter called the vendee, demanded title with an abatement of $140,000 which was conceded to be a proper amount, if there were to be an abatement.

The vendor refused to convey on these terms, tendered a deed and demanded the full purchase price. The vendee rejected the vendor's terms, whereupon the vendor made a second tender, i.e., an offer to return the $60,000 down payment and pay $1,000 to cover the cost of title search. The vendee refused this offer and insisted upon a deed with an abatement of $140,000. By mesne assignments the contract and rights thereunder were assigned by the vendee to the plaintiff. It brought this action on May 31, 1945, and obtained a judgment requiring specific performance of the contract with an abatement of $140,000.

The defendant appeals and asserts that the rights of the parties are to be determined by section 240–a, Real Property Law, enacted in 1936, and that its offer complied with that statute. The vendee insists that the contract contains engagements which preclude the statute having any effect herein. The contract provided:

"In the event for any reason the Seller *is unable to cause to be conveyed marketable title* to the premises *or otherwise to comply with* *this agreement,* the only obligation of the Seller hereunder shall be to refund the amounts paid by the Purchaser to the Seller under this agreement and the expenses paid by the Purchaser for a title search * * *.

"The risk of loss or damage to said premises by fire, until the delivery of said deed, is assumed by the Seller." (Italics ours.)

If the contract were silent on the subject of risk of loss in the event of damage to the premises by fire before the law day, under Sewell v. Underhill, 197 N.Y. 168, 170, 90 N.E. 430, 431, 27 L.R.A., N.S., 233, 134 Am.St.Rep. 863, 18 Ann.Cas. 795, in the absence of a statute, such a loss would fall on the vendee and specific performance of the contract could be had. Recognizing the authority of Sewell v. Underhill, supra, effect was given to a similar risk of loss clause in a contract in Polisiuk v. Mayers, 205 App.Div. 573, 200 N.Y.S. 97. There the burden of the loss having been assumed, by specific engagement, by the vendor, specific performance with an abatement was enforced in favor of the vendee. Unless the authority of that case has been impaired by later cases or by the statute, the judgment herein is correct.

The appellant asserts that the Polisiuk case has been overruled, in effect, by Brownell v. Board of Education of Inside Tax District of Saratoga Springs, 239 N.Y. 369, 146 N.E. 630, 37 A.L.R. 1319. But, in Reife v. Osmers, 252 N.Y. 320, 323, 169 N.E. 399, 400, 67 A.L.R. 1101, after noting criticism of the English rule, enforced in Sewell v. Underhill, supra, upon which the decision in Polisiuk v. Mayers was based in part, the court stated: "That doctrine was not weakened in Brownell v. Board of Education, 239 N.Y. 369, 374, 146 N.E. 630 [632], 37 A.L.R. 1319. There the parties by the terms of their contract took themselves out of the rule." The provision referred to was a liquidated damage clause that fixed with precision the rights of the parties in the event that a fire occurred and property damage ensued.

To sustain further its contention, the appellant refers to the citation in the Brownell case of two Massachusetts cases, and points out that the basis of their doctrine was Hawkes v. Kehoe, 193 Mass. 419, 79 N.E. 766, 10 L.R.A.,N.S., 125, 9 Ann.Cas. 1053. Appellant fails to state, however, that the Massachusetts rule is dissimilar to the New York rule, and that the doctrine of the cases cited is distinguished in the Hawkes case from Allyn v. Allyn, 154 Mass. 570, 28 N.E. 779. There a special agreement in respect of who was to bear the risk of loss in the event of the destruction of the property by fire was enforced, and the burden was borne by the vendor. Thus the very cases cited and relied on in Massachusetts recognized that by special covenant the risk of loss can be placed upon the vendor and he can be required to perform the contract just as in Polisiuk v. Mayers, supra. Hence, in the light of the foregoing, the language of the Brownell case, referring to the Massachusetts cases, is to be confined to a situation where the parties have made specific provision on this phase. Moreover, the criticism in Williston on Contracts, in the footnote to section 935, is directed primarily to the English rule upon which the Polisiuk case is founded and has no pertinency to cases in New York, where imperative authority requires effect to be given to that English rule.

Appellant invokes from the above quoted contract a clause which excuses the seller in the event it is unable to convey a marketable title "or otherwise to comply with this agreement." This provision is of no avail to the vendor where it is able to give a marketable title. General language must be confined in its meaning by the specific enumeration which precedes it. If, for instance, title could not be conveyed because the property was taken in whole or part by eminent domain, such an occurrence would come within the phrase "or otherwise to comply," being a form of inability to convey title other than from inability because of a defect rendering the title unmarketable. This interpretation excludes failure to perform by reason of destruction of the property by fire. Any doubt as to the propriety of such a construction vanishes under the impact of the next succeeding language, which specifically provides that in the event of such an occurrence "The risk of loss or damage" is to be borne by the seller. This, of course, means that the seller is subject to the obligations arising from the contract, under the then existing law, which obligations require the seller to respond to the buyer. This specific language relating to the effect of a fire takes precedence over any other general language. As the specific language does not excuse but instead affirmatively imposes obligations on the seller, the preceding general language may not be invoked to excuse the seller. The cases appellant invokes are not to the contrary. They concern contracts with different provisions, and none of them has a provision like "the risk of loss or damage" clause in the instant contract. To be sure, the contract in the Polisiuk case did not have a provision of this character, but that is of no importance as the provision itself does not have the effect for which the appellant contends, which view would make the specific and pertinent risk of loss or damage clause meaningless.

Appellant asserts that the rights of the parties, in respect of risk of loss of property by fire, are to be determined, not by the contract, but by section 240–a of the Real Property Law. It is clear that this statute was enacted primarily to save a vendee from the rigors of the English rule that when property is destroyed before the law day the burden is cast on the vendee. The New York cases in enforcing that rule made no distinction between material and immaterial destruction. The statute, however, does. Except where the destruction is substantial or material, the statute is merely declaratory of the pre-existing New York case Law. The only part of subdivision "a" which makes a change in the law is Clause No. "1" (Williston on Contracts, Rev.Ed., § 943B, f.n. 1). It is the only pertinent statutory provision. It reads:

"Section 240–a. Uniform vendor and purchaser risk act. 1. Any contract hereafter made for the purchase and sale or exchange of realty shall be interpreted, *unless the contract expressly provides otherwise,* as including an agreement that the parties shall have the following rights and duties:

"(a) When neither the legal title nor the possession of the subject matter of the contract has been transferred to the purchaser: (1) *if all or a material part* thereof *is destroyed without fault of the purchaser* or is taken by eminent domain, *the vendor cannot enforce the contract,* and the purchaser is entitled to recover any portion of the price that he has paid; but nothing herein contained shall be deemed to deprive the vendor of any right to recover damages against the purchaser for any breach of contract by the purchaser prior to the destruction or taking; * * *." (Italics ours.)

It provides that the "vendor cannot enforce the contract", and that the purchaser is to be entitled to recover his down payment if the property, or a material part, is destroyed without his fault before the law day. The introductory section provides, inter alia, that a contract for the purchase and sale of realty shall be interpreted to include an agreement that the parties shall have the enumerated rights and duties above stated, "unless the contract expressly provides otherwise." This interpretative directive integrates these provisions into the contract of the parties if the contract is silent on the subject matter of the enumerated rights and duties, because this interpretation is so enjoined "unless the contract expressly provides otherwise." If the vendor and the vendee make a specific engagement in respect of that subject matter, then the statute does not become an integral part of the contract. As was said by Nolan, J., in Auswin Realty Corporation v. Kirschbaum, 270 App.Div. 334, 338, 59 N.Y.S.2d 824, 827, "Effect must be given, if practicable, to all of the language employed, * * * to reach the real intent of the Legislature." Here, the parties have made a contract which "expressly provides otherwise" in precise language which may not be construed to be meaningless.

Accordingly, the statute has not impaired the authority of Polisiuk v. Mayers, supra, or the cases upon which it is founded.

* * *

The judgment for the plaintiff should be affirmed, with costs.

Judgment in favor of plaintiff affirmed, with costs.

* * *

ALDRICH, Justice (dissenting). I dissent and vote to reverse the judgment, in so far as it directs a conveyance, with an abatement of the purchase price, and to dismiss the complaint.

The rights and duties of the parties are controlled by section 240–a of the Real Property Law "unless the contract expressly provides otherwise." Neither the legal title nor the possession of the subject matter of the contract had been transferred to the purchaser by the contract. Therefore, the case comes within subdivision (a) of that section. It clearly appears that the fire destroyed a material part of the buildings without the fault of either party. Therefore subdivision (a) (1) applies. Under that provision, the right of the purchaser was merely to recover any portion of the price that had been paid. The statute does not give the purchaser any right to specific performance with an abatement of the purchase price where a material part of the property is destroyed. This contract nowhere "expressly provides otherwise." The contract provision that "the risk of loss or damage to said premises by fire, until the delivery of said deed, is assumed by the Seller" merely made applicable by express agreement what section 240–a already provided as a statutory matter. The contract also provides as follows:

"In the event for any reason the Seller is unable to cause to be conveyed marketable title to the premises or otherwise to comply with this agreement, the only obligation of the Seller hereunder shall be to refund the amounts paid by the Purchaser to the Seller under this agreement and the expenses paid by the Purchaser for a title search in an amount not exceeding the established net rates of the Title Guarantee and Trust Company." The seller agreed to cause to be conveyed, and the purchaser agreed to purchase, the parcels of land described in the contract, "together with the buildings and improvements erected thereon." When a material portion of the buildings was destroyed by fire, without the fault of either party, the seller became unable to comply with the agreement. To the extent of the buildings destroyed by fire the contract had become impossible of performance. In my opinion, the quoted provision should be construed to cover this situation. Thereunder the only obligation of the seller was to refund the amount paid by the purchaser to the seller, and the expenses paid by the purchaser for a title search. The provision for payment of the expense for the title search was a matter in which "the contract expressly provides otherwise" than the statute provided. The seller, is consequently, liable for the title search.

Notes

1. The decision in the principal case was affirmed without opinion, 296 N.Y. 586, 68 N.E.2d 876 (1949).

2. New York General Obligations Law § 5–1311 (McKinney), formerly Real Property Law § 240–a (construed and applied in the principal case), consists of the Uniform Vendor and Purchaser Risk Act with substantial additions. Paragraph (a) of the Act as adopted in New York is as follows: "When neither the legal title nor the possession of the subject matter of the contract has been transferred to the purchaser: (1) if all or a material part thereof is destroyed without fault of the purchaser or is taken by eminent domain, the vendor cannot enforce the contract, and the purchaser is entitled to recover any portion of the price that he has paid; but nothing herein contained shall be deemed to deprive the vendor of any right to recover damages against the purchaser for any breach of contract by the purchaser prior to the destruction or taking; (2) if an immaterial part thereof is destroyed without fault of the purchaser or is taken by eminent domain, neither the vendor nor the purchaser is thereby deprived of the right to enforce the contract; but there shall be, to the extent of the destruction or taking, an abatement of the purchase price."

Paragraph (b) contains, in addition to the language of the Uniform Act quoted in text note (3), supra, p. 1045, the following proviso: "but nothing herein contained shall be deemed to deprive the purchaser of any right to recover damages against the vendor for any breach of contract by the vendor prior to the destruction or taking."

3. It was customary in New York prior to the principal case to include in contracts for the sale of realty either a provision that "the risk of loss or damage by fire, until delivery of the deed, is assumed by the vendor," or a provision that "the premises are to be delivered in as good condition as they now are,

natural wear excepted." Where loss by fire occurred pending conveyance under a contract that contained the first type of risk of loss provision, the Appellate Division held that the purchaser was entitled to specific performance with an abatement of the price. Polisiuk v. Mayers, 205 App.Div. 573, 200 N.Y.S. 97 (1923), leave to appeal denied 206 App.Div. 765, 200 N.Y.S. 943 (1923). In the principal case, the majority relied on the Polisiuk case, although the vendor contended that it had been overruled by Brownell v. Board of Education, 239 N.Y. 369, 146 N.E. 630, 37 A.L.R. 1319 (1925). The vendor apparently based his contention on the fact that the court did not grant specific performance with an abatement to the purchaser in the Brownell case. In that case, the contract provided that the premises were to be delivered "in as good condition as they now are, natural wear excepted," and that in case either party failed to perform the party so failing should pay to the other the sum of $3,000 as liquidated damages. The purchaser paid $3,000 down, but before the contract was completed the principal building on the premises was destroyed by fire. The vendor collected $28,000 of insurance money, and the purchaser then sued for specific performance with application of the insurance money against the unpaid purchase price of $27,000; or, if this relief should not be granted, for a declaratory judgment stating the rights of the parties. The court held that the purchaser was not entitled to have the insurance money applied on the price, since the vendor's policy was a personal contract of indemnity, and stated that the purchaser's only right was to recover $3,000 (either on the theory of restitution or as liquidated damages under the contract). It seems clear, however, that the purchaser could have secured specific performance if willing to pay the purchase price in full; but the purchaser was precluded from securing an abatement in the full amount of the fire loss because of the liquidated damages clause in the contract. The Brownell case, therefore, could hardly be said to lay down a broad rule denying the purchaser a right to specific performance with abatement where the risk of loss is on the vendor by express contract provision.

4. A contract provision that "the premises shall be conveyed in the same condition as the same now are, reasonable wear and tear excepted," or the equivalent, has generally been held to place the risk of loss from fire or other casualty upon the vendor, although otherwise the risk would be upon the purchaser as "equitable owner." Thus the vendor cannot compel specific performance if substantial loss occurs prior to the time for conveyance, and that in such a case the purchaser may recover any payments made to the vendor. It is also clear that the vendor cannot recover damages for the purchaser's failure to perform. In some states it is clear that the purchaser will be able to obtain specific performance with abatement of the price because of the loss, and where this is so, the purchaser should also be permitted to recover damages for the vendor's breach of contract, as an alternative to compelling specific performance or recovering his payments.

5. If the contract provides that all buildings are to be delivered "in as good condition as they are at the date of this contract, usual wear excepted," or contains equivalent language, it seems clear that the risk of loss will shift to the purchaser if he takes possession under the contract, even though the legal title is still in the vendor, if the risk of loss would otherwise have been thrown upon the purchaser "as equitable owner" as soon as the contract was made. The same result would seem to follow under the Uniform Vendor and Purchaser Risk Act. But suppose the contract provides that the vendor shall *convey* the premises "in as good condition as they are at the date of this contract," and the vendor delivers possession to the purchaser prior to the time for conveyance of

the legal title? Does the risk of loss shift to the purchaser? What result under the Uniform Vendor and Purchaser Risk Act?

6. In the principal case both the majority and the dissenting judge seem to have assumed that the purchaser would not be entitled to specific performance with abatement of the price if the rights of the parties were controlled by Real Property Law § 240–a [now General Obligations Law § 5–1311]. But see Rizzo v. Landmark Realty Corp., 277 App.Div. 1094, 101 N.Y.S.2d 151 (1950), where the statute was apparently held to be controlling. The court reversed a judgment for the vendor on the pleadings in an action by the purchasers for specific performance with abatement, saying: "Section 240–a of the Real Property Law does not deprive a vendee of the right of specific performance with abatement. Said section, * * * renders unenforceable in so far as the vendor is concerned the right to specific performance when the loss is material. It does not, however, destroy any common law right of the vendee to specific performance with abatement." Does this make any sense to you? Since the purchaser was not previously allowed an abatement for loss where the risk of loss was on him, as it was under the New York decisions prior to adoption of the Uniform Vendor and Purchaser Risk Act, what does the court mean by "common law right of the vendee to specific performance with abatement"? And how can the court in the principal (World Exhibit Corp.) case say that, "Except where the destruction is substantial or material, the statute is merely declaratory of the pre-existing New York case law"?

7. For comment on the principal case, see Notes, 21 N.Y.U.L.Q.Rev. 556 (1946) and 21 St. John's L.Rev. 104 (1946); and 1946 Annual Survey of American Law 841. In the latter Professor Simpson reached the following conclusions with respect to the principal case:

> The decision * * * did substantial justice between the parties, in the absence of any general fluctuation in land values. * * * under the doctrine of the case, the purchaser gets an option. He can either enforce with abatement, or resist specific performance and recover his down payment. If the value of the premises has changed independent of the damage, this may give him a choice he was never intended to have. But this is so in all cases of partial performance with compensation at suit of the purchaser only. The matter will probably be taken care of in most future contracts by more specific language.

> As matters now stand, however, it would be a brave lawyer who would give an opinion as to the meaning of the simple clause "the risk of loss is assumed by the vendor" either in New York (until the Court of Appeals sees fit explicitly to discuss the point) or elsewhere, whether or not the Uniform Act is in effect.

8. Does the type of contract provision considered in the principal (World Exhibit Corp.) case adequately protect the purchaser? See Pellegrino v. Guiliani, 118 Misc. 329, 193 N.Y.S. 258 (Sup.Ct.1922), where the purchaser failed to recover his down payment because the damage was due to a windstorm rather than a fire. How should the risk of loss provision be drafted so as to protect the purchaser against loss from any possible type of casualty?

Note: Insurance Protection for Vendor and Purchaser While the Contract Remains Executory

The desirability of insurance protection for both vendor and purchaser pending transfer of the legal title is obvious. Such protection can be provided in various ways. The contract can be drafted so as to impose a duty on one party or the other to maintain insurance in a stated amount. Or each party may simply insure his own interest separately. If the vendor already has adequate insurance coverage on the property the purchaser may, in most jurisdictions, rely on the vendor's existing insurance for his own protection, since in the event of loss the insurance company can be compelled to pay and the vendor will hold the payment in trust for the purchaser. A few American courts, however, have followed the contrary rule established in Rayner v. Preston, 18 Ch.D. 1 (Eng.Ct. App.1881).* The conflicting rules and their rationales are well summarized in Vance, Insurance, § 131 (3d ed. 1951).** Vance concludes as follows:

> It is reasonable to infer that the business public assumes that an executory contract for the sale of insured realty carries the protection of existing insurance policies to the vendee even though it makes no mention of the insurance; that is, that in such cases the insurance runs with the land. If that is the meaning of the transaction in the market place, that should also be its meaning in the courtroom. In any event, such is the meaning which the English Parliament and many of the American courts have given it. Here we have another instance in which business usage substitutes the insurance money for the insured property, despite the general rule that the two are not legally connected; and, as usual, the courts are sluggishly following business.

> There is little evidence, however, of any tendency to extend this doctrine of substituting the insurance money for the insured property, to cases in which the vendee independently procures insurance upon the property sold. Here the contract of insurance is held to be purely a personal arrangement between the vendee and the insurer, and the vendee takes the insurance money free from any liens which the vendor may have against the insured property. The vendor has no equity either in the courtroom or in the market place.

The tentative draft of the Uniform Vendor and Purchaser Risk Act submitted to the Commissioners on Uniform State Laws in 1934 by Professor Williston contained the following provision: "Where a vendor receives compensation from insurance or otherwise for such destruction or taking [of all or a material part of the subject matter of the contract], the purchaser shall be entitled to enforce the contract with an abatement of the price to the extent of such compensation. Where a purchaser receives compensation from insurance or otherwise for such destruction or taking, the vendor shall be entitled either to have such compensation applied to the payment of the price to the extent that is necessary or, at the option of the purchaser, applied to the restoration of the subject matter." This provision, however, was not included in the Uniform Act as finally adopted by the Commissioners and recommended for enactment by the several states.

In recommending the enactment of the Uniform Act in New York, the Law Revision Commission specifically disavowed any purpose to effect a change in existing rules as to rights of vendor and purchaser with respect to insurance, saying: "It has been deemed advisable, in drafting remedial legislation, not to attempt to change the rule as to the insurance. That rule treating the fire insurance policy as a contract of personal indemnity, recognizes the importance of the moral hazard in fire insurance, and should not be disturbed."

In the case of In re Bond & Mortgage Guarantee Co., 63 N.Y.S.2d 120 (Sup. Ct.1946), the court reiterated the rule of Rayner v. Preston in holding that a

---

* The English rule was changed by the Law of Property Act, 1925, 15 Geo. V, c. 20, § 47.

** Copyright, 1951, West Publishing Co.

purchaser who, after loss by fire occurred, expressed a willingness to complete the contract, was not entitled to an assignment of insurance money receivable by the vendor on account of the loss.

Suppose, in New York, that the purchaser pays the premiums on insurance taken out in the vendor's name, the risk of loss being on the purchaser. If the loss insured against occurs, is the purchaser entitled to have the insurance money applied on the purchase price? Does it make any difference whether the contract requires the purchaser to pay the premiums? See Raplee v. Piper, 3 N.Y.2d 179, 143 N.E.2d 919 (1957).

The rights of vendor and purchaser with respect to insurance money are discussed in 3 A.L.P. § 11.31 (1952); 3A Corbin, Contracts § 670 (1960); 7 Williston, Contracts § 942 (3d ed. 1963); Simpson, Legislative Changes in the Law of Equitable Conversion by Contract: II, 44 Yale L.J. 754 (1935) at 763–768; Holland, Risk of Loss and Insurance in Contracts for the Sale of Real Estate, 5 Tex.L.Rev. 249 (1927) at 251–262. The cases are collected and analyzed in detail in the following A.L.R. Annotations: Rights of vendor and purchaser inter se in respect of proceeds of insurance, 37 A.L.R. 1324 (1925), 40 A.L.R. 607 (1926), and 51 A.L.R. 929 (1927); Amount of insurer's liability as affected by insured's executory contract to sell the property, 8 A.L.R.2d 1408 (1949).

Of course, it should be remembered that in the absence of an express contract provision requiring him to do so, the vendor is under no duty either to procure insurance for the purchaser's benefit or to maintain existing insurance for his benefit. Hence it is wise for the purchaser, if his bargaining position permits, to insist upon an express contract provision requiring the vendor to maintain existing insurance for the purchaser's benefit. If the vendor's existing insurance is insufficient in amount, either party may, of course, procure additional insurance in his own name.

The cases adopting the majority rule that the purchaser is entitled to the benefit of the vendor's insurance are based on the view that the vendor's policies insure the whole legal and equitable estate in the property, and not merely the vendor's security interest, i.e., his interest in obtaining payment of the purchase price in full. If the insurance *is* expressly confined to the vendor's security interest, however, it seems clear that the purchaser cannot claim any benefit thereunder. In such a case, if the purchaser paid the price in full the insurer would be relieved of liability; and if the purchaser failed to pay the balance of the price after loss occurred, the insurer could pay the amount of the unpaid balance to the vendor and then enforce the contract against the purchaser under the doctrine of subrogation. In short, the results would be the same as under the rule of Rayner v. Preston. But where the purchaser is not entitled to any benefit from the vendor's insurance (either because the insurance is expressly limited to the vendor's security interest or under the rule of Rayner v. Preston), *quaere* whether the vendor must exhaust his remedies against the purchaser before he can compel the insurer to make payment under the policy.

Installment contracts under which the purchaser goes into possession for a considerable time pending full payment of the contract price and transfer of the legal title usually contain a provision requiring the purchaser to keep the premises insured in a stated amount, in companies satisfactory to the vendor, with loss payable either to the vendor or to the parties "as their respective interests may appear." If a loss covered by such insurance occurs, the vendor is clearly entitled to the insurance money to the extent of any installments of the price then due and unpaid. If the contract expressly provides for application of the insurance money *pro tanto* against the entire unpaid balance of the price, or if it provides that all insurance money over and above the amount necessary to pay installments due and unpaid shall be used to restore the damaged premises, no problem is likely to arise. But in the absence of an express contract provision as to the application of the insurance money after loss, controversy may arise between the parties. In that event, the courts are not in accord as to what should be done with the insurance money.

It is generally held that the vendor is entitled to the insurance money to the full extent of the unpaid balance of the price, including the unmatured installments, and that the vendor need not apply the insurance money to restoration of the premises unless he has agreed to do so. But it has been held by some courts that the purchaser can compel the use of the insurance money for restoration of the premises in the absence of an agreement for such use; and, contrariwise, it has been held that the vendor may rightfully use the insurance money to restore the premises despite the purchaser's demand that it be applied to the unpaid balance of the price.

SECTION 4. OBLIGATIONS OF VENDOR AS TO QUALITY OF CONSTRUCTION AND FITNESS FOR INTENDED USE

HUMBER v. MORTON

Supreme Court of Texas, 1968.
426 S.W.2d 554, 25 A.L.R.3d 372.

NORVELL, Justice. The widow Humber brought suit against Claude Morton, alleging that Morton was in the business of building and selling new houses; that she purchased a house from him which was not suitable for human habitation in that the fireplace and chimney were not properly constructed and because of such defect, the house caught fire and partially burned the first time a fire was lighted in the fireplace. Morton defended upon two grounds: that an independent contractor, Johnny F. Mays, had constructed the fireplace and he, Morton, was not liable for the work done by Mays, and that the doctrine of "caveat emptor" applied to all sales of real estate. Upon the first trial of the case (which was to a jury), Mrs. Humber recovered a judgment which was reversed by the Eastland Court of Civil Appeals and the cause remanded for another trial because of an improper submission of the damage issue. 399 S.W.2d 831 (1966, no writ).[1]

Upon the second trial, defendant Morton filed a motion for summary judgment supported by affidavits, one of which referred to and incorporated therein the statement of the evidence adduced upon the first trial. Plaintiff likewise made a motion for summary judgment. Defendant's motion was granted and that of the plaintiff overruled. Such judgment was affirmed by the Court of Civil Appeals upon the holdings that Mays was an independent contractor and that the doctrine of implied warranty was not applicable to the case. 414 S.W.2d 765. Mrs. Humber, as petitioner, brought the case here, but we shall refer to the parties by their trial court designations.

---

1. The Court of Civil Appeals without discussion overruled a number of points which asserted that Morton was entitled to judgment as a matter of law. [The footnotes are those of the Court, but some have been omitted and renumbered. Ed.]

It conclusively appears that defendant Morton was a "builder-vendor." The summary judgment proofs disclose that he was in the business of building or assembling houses designed for dwelling purposes upon land owned by him. He would then sell the completed houses together with the tracts of land upon which they were situated to members of the house-buying public. There is conflict in the summary judgment proofs as to whether the house sold to Mrs. Humber had been constructed with a dangerously defective fireplace chimney. Construction engineers who testified under oath for Mrs. Humber, as disclosed by the statement of facts upon the first trial which was made a part of the summary judgment record here, stated that the chimney was defective. Mr. Mays, who built the chimney, denied that his work was substandard or deficient in any way.

While there may be other grounds for holding that Mrs. Humber made a case to go to the jury, such as negligence attributable to Morton, failure to inspect and the like, we need not discuss these theories because we are of the opinion that the courts below erred in holding as a matter of law that Morton was not liable to Mrs. Humber because the doctrine of caveat emptor applied to the sale of a new house by a "builder-vendor" and consequently no implied warranty that the house was fit for human habitation arose from the sale. Accordingly, we reverse the judgments of the courts below and remand the cause to the district court for a conventional trial upon the merits.

Mrs. Humber entered into a contract when she bought the house from Mortion in May of 1964 and such house, together with the lot upon which it was situated, was conveyed to her. According to Morton, the only warranty contained in the deed was the warranty of title, i.e. "to warrant and forever defend, all and singular, the said premises unto the said Ernestine Humber, her heirs and assigns, * * *," and that he made no other warranty, written or oral, in connection with the sale. While it is unusual for one to sell a house without saying something good about it, and the statement that no warranty was made smacks of a conclusion, we shall assume that such conversation as may have taken place did not involve anything more than mere sales talk or puffing, and that no express warranties, either oral or written, were involved. However, it is undisputed that Morton built the house and then sold it as a new house. Did he thereby impliedly warrant that such house was constructed in a good workmanlike manner and was suitable for human habitation? We hold that he did. Under such circumstances, the law raises an implied warranty.

* * *

Originally, the two great systems of jurisprudence applied different doctrines to sales of both real and personal property. The rule of the common law—caveat emptor—was fundamentally based upon the premise that the buyer and seller dealt at arm's length, and that the purchaser had means and opportunity to gain information concerning the subject matter of the sale which were equal to those of the seller. On the other hand, the civil law doctrine—caveat venditor—was based upon the premise that a sound price calls for a sound article; that when one sells an article, he implies that it has value. 77 C.J.S. 1159, Sales § 315, Sales 275, Sales, 46 Am.Jur. 275, Sales § 87.

Today, the doctrine of caveat emptor as related to sales of personal property has a severely limited application. Decker & Sons v. Capp, supra; McKisson v. Sales Affiliates, 416 S.W.2d 787 (Tex.Sup.1967); Putman v. Erie City Mfg. Co., supra; O.M. Franklin Serum Co. v. C.A. Hoover & Sons, 418 S.W.2d 482 (Tex.Sup.1967).

In 1884, the Supreme Court of the United States applied the doctrine of implied warranty, the antithesis of caveat emptor, to a real property situation involving false work and pilings driven into the bed of the Maumee River. The case of Kellogg Bridge Company v. Hamilton, 110 U.S. 108, 3 S.Ct. 537, 28 L.Ed. 86, arose in connection with the construction of a bridge. The Supreme Court, (the elder Mr. Justice Harlan writing), said:

"Although the plaintiff in error (Kellogg Bridge Company, defendant in the trial court) is not a manufacturer, in the common acceptation of that word, it made or constructed the false work which it sold to Hamilton. The transaction, if not technically a sale, created between the parties the relation of vendor and vendee. The business of the company was the construction of bridges. By its occupation, apart from its contract with the railroad company, it held itself out as reasonably competent to do work of that character. Having partially executed its contract with the railroad company, it made an arrangement with Hamilton whereby the latter undertook, among other things, to prepare all necessary false work, and, by a day named, and in the best manner, to erect the bridge then being constructed by the bridge company—Hamilton to assume and pay for such work and materials as that company had up to that time done and furnished. Manifestly, it was contemplated by the parties that Hamilton should commence where the company left off. It certainly was not expected that he should incur the expense of removing the false work put up by the company and commence anew. On the contrary, he agreed to assume and pay for, and therefore it was expected by the company that he should use, such false work as it had previously prepared. It is unreasonable to suppose that he would buy that which he did not intend to use, or that the company would require him to assume and pay for that which it did not expect him to use, or which was unfit for use. * * * In the cases of sales by manufacturers of their own articles for particular purposes, communicated to them at the time, the argument was uniformly pressed that, as the buyer could have required an express warranty, none should be implied. But, plainly, such an argument impeaches the whole doctrine of implied warranty, for there can be no case of a sale of personal property in which the buyer may not, if he chooses, insist on an express warranty against latent defects.

"All the facts are present which, upon any view of the adjudged cases, must be held essential in an implied warranty. The transaction was, in effect, a sale of this false work, constructed by a company whose business it was to do such work; to be used in the same way the maker intended to use it, and the latent defects in which, as the maker knew, the buyer could not, by any inspection or examination, at the time discover; the buyer did not, because in the nature of things he could not, rely on his own judgment; and, in view of the circumstances of the case, and the relations of the parties, he must be deemed to have relied on the judgment of the company, which alone of the parties to the contract had or could have knowledge of the manner in which the work had been done. The law, therefore, implies a warranty that this false work was reasonably suitable for such use as was contemplated by both parties. * * *"

In Texas, the doctrine of caveat emptor began its fade-out at an early date. In Wintz v. Morrison, 17 Tex. 369 (1856), involving a sale of personal property, the Texas Supreme Court quoted with approval the following from Story on Sales as to the trend of 19th century decisions:

"[T]he tendency of all the modern cases of warranty is to enlarge the responsibility of the seller, to construe every affirmation by him to be a warranty, and frequently to imply a warranty on his part, from acts and circumstances, wherever they were relied upon by the buyer. The maxim of *caveat emptor* seems gradually to be restricted in its operation and limited in its dominion, and beset with the circumvallations of the modern doctrine of implied warranty, until it can no longer claim the empire over the law of sales, and is but a shadow of itself. * * *"

As to the present personal property rule of implied warranties or strict liability in tort, see, *Decker, Putman, McKisson* and *Franklin*, cited above.

While in numerous common law jurisdictions, the caveat emptor doctrine as applied to the vendor builder—new house situation has overstayed its time, it was said by way of dicta in a Texas Court of Civil Appeals case in 1944 that:

"By offering the (new) house for sale as a new and complete structure appellant impliedly warranted that it was properly constructed and of good material and specifically that it had a good foundation, * * *." Loma Vista Development Co. v. Johnson, Tex.Civ.App., 177 S.W.2d 225, l.c. 227, rev. on other grounds, 142 Tex. 686, 180 S.W.2d 922.

This decision has been described as "a preview of things to come." [2]

The rapid sickening of the caveat emptor doctrine as applied to sales of new houses was exposed by the Miller-Perry-Howe-Weck-Jones-Glisan-Carpenter syndrome.[3] The history of this development is briefly set out in Carpenter v. Donohoe, 154 Colo. 78, 388 P.2d 399 (1964), and in more detail by Professor E.F. Roberts in "The Case of the Unwary Home Buyer: The Housing Merchant Did It," 52 Cornell Law Quarterly

2. 52 Cornell Law Quarterly 835, l.c. 841.

3. Miller v. Cannon Hill Estates, Ltd., [1931] 1 All.E.R. 93 (K.B.); Perry v. Sharon Dev. Co. [1937] 4 All.E.R. 390 (C.A.); Hoye v. Century Builders, Inc., 52 Wash. 2d 830, 329 P.2d 474 (1958); Weck v. A.M. Sunrise Construction Co., 36 Ill.App.2d 383, 184 N.E.2d 728 (1962); Jones v. Gatewood, 381 P.2d 158 (Okl.1963); Glisan v. Smolenske, 153 Colo. 274, 387 P.2d 260 (1963); and Carpenter v. Donohoe, 154 Colo. 78, 388 P.2d 399 (1964).

835 (1967). See also, Williston on Contracts (3rd Ed. Jaeger) § 926A, wherein it is said: "It would be much better if this enlightened approach (implied warranty, Jones v. Gatewood, 381 P.2d 158 [Okl.]) were generally adopted with respect to the sale of new houses for it would tend to discourage much of the sloppy work and jerry-building that has become perceptible over the years." 7 Williston (3rd Ed.) p. 818; 1 Follmer and Friedman, Products Liability, § 5.03[5][b]; Stewart, "Implied Warranties in the Sale of New Houses," Note, 26 U.Pitt.L.Rev. 862 (1965); Haskell, "The Case for an Implied Warranty of Quality in Sales of Real Property," 53 Geo.L.J. 633 (1965); Gibson and Lounsberry, "Implied Warranties—Sales of a Completed House," Comments, 1 Cal.Western L.Rev. 110 (1965); Smith, "Torts, Implied Warranty in Real Estate, Privity Requirement," Comment, 44 N.Car.L.Rev. 236 (1965); Ramunno, "Implied Warranty of Fitness for Habitation in Sale of Residential Dwellings," 43 Denver L.Rev. 379 (1966).

The *Glisan* case (Glisan v. Smolenske), 153 Colo. 274, 387 P.2d 260 (1963), was factually similar to the hypothetical example heretofore set out in this opinion. Smolenske had agreed to purchase a house from Glisan while it was under construction. The court propounded and answered the implied warranty question, thusly:

"Was there an implied warranty that the house, when completed, would be fit for habitation? There is a growing body of law on this question, which, if followed, requires an answer in the affirmative.

"It is the rule that there is an implied warranty where the contract relates to a house which is still in the process of construction, where the vendor's workmen are still on the job, and particularly where completion is not accomplished until the house has arrived at the contemplated condition—namely, finished and fit for habitation. Weck v. A.M. Sunrise Construction Co., supra [36 Ill.App.2d 383, 184 N.E.2d 728]; Jones v. Gatewood, supra [381 P.2d 158]; Hoye v. Century Builders, Inc., 52 Wash.2d 830, 329 P.2d 474; Miller v. Cannon Hill Estates, Ltd., supra [2 K.B. 113]; Perry v. Sharon Development Co., Ltd., supra [4 All.E.L.R.]; Jennings v. Tavenner, 2 All.E.L.R. (1955) 769; Dunham, 'Vendor's Obligation as to Fitness of Land for a Particular Purpose,' 37 Minn.L.Rev. 108 (1953). Contra: Coutraken v. Adams, 39 Ill.App.2d 290, 188 N.E.2d 780."

In the next year, 1964, the Colorado Supreme Court in Carpenter v. Donohoe, 154 Colo. 78, 388 P.2d 399, extended the implied warranty rule announced by it in *Glisan* to cover sales of a new house by a builder-vendor. The court said:

"That a different rule should apply to the purchaser of a house which is near completion than would apply to one who purchases a new house seems incongruous. To say that the former may rely on an implied warranty and the latter cannot is recognizing a distinction without a reasonable basis for it. This is pointedly argued in an excellent article, 'Caveat Emptor in Sales of Realty—Recent Assaults upon the Rule,' by Bearman, 14 Vanderbilt Law Rev. 541 (1960–61.)

"We hold that the implied warranty doctrine is extended to include agreements between builder-vendors and purchasers for the sale of newly constructed buildings, completed at the time of contracting. There is an implied warranty that builder-vendors have complied with the building code of the area in which the structure is located. Where, as here, a home is the subject of sale, there are implied warranties that the home was built in workmanlike manner and is suitable for habitation."

While it is not necessary for us to pass upon a situation in which the vendor-purchaser relationship is absent, the case of Schipper v. Levitt & Sons, 44 N.J. 70, 207 A.2d 314 (1965), is important as much of the reasoning set forth in the opinion as applicable here. The Supreme Court of New Jersey recognized "the need for imposing on builder-vendors an implied obligation of reasonable workmanship and habitability which survives delivery of the deed." This was a case in which a person other than a purchaser had been injured by a defective water heater which had been installed in a new house by Levitt, the builder-vendor. The opinion cited and quotes from Carpenter v. Donohoe but proceeded upon the theory of strict liability in tort.[4] The court placed emphasis upon the close analogy between a defect in a new house and a manufactured chattel. The opinion states:

"The law should be based on current concepts of what is right and just and the judiciary should be alert to the never-ending need for keeping its common law principles abreast of the times. Ancient distinctions which make no sense in today's society and tend to discredit the law should be readily rejected as they were step by step in Henningsen [Henningsen v. Bloomfield Motors, 32 N.J. 358, 161 A.2d 69, 75 A.L.R.2d 1 (1960)] and Santor [Santor v. A and M Karagheusian, 44 N.J. 52, 207 A.2d 305, 16 A.L.R.3d 670 (1965)]. * * *

"When a vendee buys a development house from an advertised model, as in a Levitt or in a comparable project, he clearly relies on the skill of the developer and on its implied representation that the house will be erected in reasonably workmanlike manner and will be reasonably fit for habitation. He has no architect or other professional adviser of his own, he has no real competency to inspect on his own, his actual examination is, in the nature of things, largely superficial, and his opportunity for obtaining meaningful protective changes in the conveyancing documents prepared by the builder vendor is negligible. If there is improper construction such as a defective heating system or a defective ceiling, stairway and the like, the well-being of the vendee and others is seriously endangered and serious injury is foreseeable. The public interest dictates that if such injury does result from the defective construction, its costs should be borne by the responsible developer who

---

4. It is said in the opinion that, "It is true, as Levitt suggests, that cases such as Carpenter (388 P.2d 399) involved direct actions by original vendees against their builder vendors and that consequently no questions of privity arose. But it seems hardly conceivable that a court recognizing the modern need for a vendee occupant's right to recover on principles of implied warranty or strict liability would revivify the requirement of privity, which is fast disappearing in the comparable products liability field, to preclude a similar right in other occupants likely to be injured by the builder vendor's default. * * *"

created the danger and who is in the better economic position to bear the loss rather than by the injured party who justifiably relied on the developer's skill and implied representation."

In Bethlahmy v. Bechtel, 415 P.2d 698 (Idaho 1966), it appeared that the trial court had rendered judgment in accordance with the 1959 holding of the Supreme Court of Oregon in Steiber v. Palumbo, a much cited case which is relied upon by the defendant here. The specific finding of the trial court was:

"There are no implied warranties in the sale of real property. Steiber v. Palumbo, 219 Oreg 479, 347 P.2d 978 [78 A.L.R.2d 440] (1959); Annot., 78 ALR2d 446. The sale of this home carried with it, absent an express warranty, no promise that the floor would not leak."

The Idaho court was then called upon to deal with the Oregon decision and the later decisions of the Colorado Supreme Court in *Carpenter* and that of the New Jersey Supreme Court in *Schipper*. After a careful review of many decisions, including the Oregon, Colorado and New Jersey cases mentioned, the court said:

"The Schipper decision is important here because: (1) it illustrates the recent chan. ʳᵉ in the attitude of the courts toward the application of the doctrine of caveat emptor in actions between the builder-vendor and purchaser of newly constructed dwellings; (2) it draws analogy between the present case and the long-accepted application of implied warranty of fitness in sales of personal property; and (3) the opinion had the unanimous approval of the participating justices. * * *

"The foregoing decisions all (except the Hoye case) rendered subsequent to the 1959 Oregon decision, relied upon by the trial court, show the trend of judicial opinion as to invoke the doctrine of implied warranty of fitness in cases involving sales of new houses by the builder. The old rule of caveat emptor does not satisfy the demands of justice in such cases. The purchase of a home is not an everyday transaction for the average family, and in many instances is the most important transaction of a lifetime. To apply the rule of caveat emptor to an inexperienced buyer, and in favor of a builder who is daily engaged in the business of building and selling houses, is manifestly a denial of justice. See also, Loma Vista Development Co. v. Johnson (Tex.) 177 S.W.2d 225 (1943); Appendix to Staff v. Lido Dunes, Inc., 47 Misc.2d 322, 262 N.Y.S.2d 544, at 553 (1965)."

See also, Waggoner v. Midwestern Development, Inc., 154 N.W.2d 803 (So.Dak., 1967)

In September of 1967, the Houston Court of Civil Appeals handed down its opinion in Moore v. Werner, 418 S.W.2d 918 (no writ), in which, after citing a number of authorities, the court said:

"Many of the authorities cited involve personalty, but we see no reason for any distinction between the sale of a new house and the sale of personalty, especially in a suit between the original parties to the contract, one of whom constructed the house in question. It was the seller's duty to perform the work in a good and workmanlike manner and to furnish adequate materials, and failing to do so, we believe the rule of implied warranty of fitness applies. Hoye v. Century Builders, 52 Wash.2d 830, 329 P.2d 474, 476; Mann v. Clowser, 190 Va. 887, 59 S.E.2d 78, 84; 13 Am.Jur.2d, p. 29, Sec. 27." * * *

If at one time in Texas the rule of caveat emptor had application to the sale of a new house by a vendor-builder, that time is now past. The decisions and legal writings herein referred to afford numerous examples and situations illustrating the harshness and injustice of the rule when applied to the sale of new houses by a builder-vendor,[5] and we need not repeat them here. Obviously, the ordinary purchaser is not in a position to ascertain when there is a defect in a chimney flue, or vent of a heating apparatus, or whether the plumbing work covered by a concrete slab foundation is faulty. It is also highly irrational to make a distinction between the liability of a vendor-builder who employs servants and one who uses independent contractors. Compare, Conner v. Conejo Valley Development Co., 61 Cal.Rptr. 333 (1967). The common law is not afflicted with the rigidity of the law of the Medes and the Persians "which altereth not," and as stated in Cardozo in "The Nature of the Judicial Process," pp. 150–151 (quoted in 415 P.2d 698):

"That court best serves the law which recognizes that the rules of law which grew up in a remote generation may, in the fullness of experience, be found to serve another generation badly, and which discards the old rule when it finds that another rule of law represents what should be according to the established and settled judgment of society, and no considerable property rights have become vested in reliance upon the old rule. * * *"[6]

The caveat emptor rule as applied to new houses is an anachronism patently out of harmony with modern home buying practices. It does a disservice not only to the ordinary prudent purchaser but to the industry itself by lending encouragement to the unscrupulous, fly-by-night operator and purveyor of shoddy work.

The judgments of the courts below are reversed and the cause remanded for trial in accordance with this opinion.

GRIFFIN, J., notes his dissent.

---

5. In the vendor-builder situation, Professor Roberts seems inclined to agree with Mr. Bumble's estimate of the law and points out that when caveat emptor is retained with regard to the sale of new houses, the law seemingly concerns itself little with a transaction which may and often does involve a purchaser's life savings, yet may afford relief by raising an implied warranty of fitness when one is swindled in the purchase of a two dollar fountain pen. 52 Cornell L.Rev. 835. Similarly, in 111 Solicitors' Journal 22, l. c. 25 (London), it is pointed out that, "the purchaser buying a new house with legal assistance is often less well protected legally than the purchaser buying a chattel without legal assistance." It is further urged that "The legal profession should have made it their business to insure proper protection for the purchaser without waiting for building societies to take the initiative" for their own protection since most builders "try to do a good job (but) the reputation of all may be injuriously affected by the low standards of a few."

6. See also, Holmes, Collected Legal Papers, p. 187, quoted in 16 Baylor L. Rev. 263, 277, viz.:

"It is revolting to have no better reason for a rule of law than that it was laid down in the time of Henry IV. It is still more revolting if the grounds upon which it was laid down have vanished long since, and the rule persists from blind imitation of the past."

Note: Caveat Emptor Gives Way to Rules Imposing on the Builder-Vendor Obligations as to Quality of Construction and Fitness for Use

According to Sir Edward Coke, "by the civil law, every man is bound to warrant the thing that he selleth or conveyeth, albeit there be no express warranty, either in deed or in law; but the common law bindeth him not, for caveat emptor." 2 Coke on Littleton, c. 7 § 145 (1633). But the doctrine of caveat emptor with respect to sales of goods has long since practically disappeared. At the present time, sales of goods are subject in all 50 states to the Uniform Commercial Code §§ 2–314 and 2–315, which provide for implied warranties of "merchantability" and "fitness for particular purpose"; the latter warranty is implied "[w]here the seller at the time of contracting has reason to know any particular purpose for which the goods are required and that the buyer is relying on the seller's skill or judgment to select or furnish suitable goods, * * * unless excluded or modified under" § 2–316. The Uniform Land Transactions Act, promulgated by the Conference of Commissioners on Uniform Laws seeks to impose similar implied warranties in sales of real estate as well as some specific warranties applicable only to real estate transactions. The relationship between the two Uniform Acts is analyzed in a Note, Warranties in the Uniform Land Transactions Act of 1975—Progression or Retrogression in Pennsylvania, 49 Temple L.Q. 162 (1975). There is a body of comment on this development: Note, Caveat Emptor and the Morals of the Housing Market, 20 New York Law Forum 803 (1975); Williams, Developments in Actions for Breach of Implied Warranties of Habitability in the Sale of New Houses, 10 Tulsa L.Jnl. 445 (1973); Note, Caveat Emptor in the Sale of Real Property—Epitaph to an Inequitable Maxim, 4 Memphis St.U.L.Rev. 54 (1973); Implied Warranties in the Sale of Real Estate in Colorado: Rational Boundaries of the Doctrine, 53 U.Colo.L.Rev. 137 (1981); Home Sales: A Crack in the Caveat Emptor Shield, 29 Mercer L.Rev. 323 (1977); Implied Warranties in New House Construction, 46 U.Cinn.L.Rev. 207 (1977); Roeser, Implied Warranty of Habitability in the Sale of New Housing: The Trend in Illinois, 1978 So.Ill.U.J. 178 (1978); Virginia's Reaction to an Implied Warranty in Real Estate Transactions, 13 U. Richmond L.Rev. 381 (1979).

Caveat emptor continued to hold sway until very recent times with respect to the sale of housing. The contractor who builds a house would under ordinary contract law, be under an obligation to construct a livable and safe house according to accepted standards of good workmanship. See 13 Am.Jur.2d § 27 (1964). It was even recognized that if a purchaser bought a house before it was completed, he was entitled to the benefit of an implied warranty of good workmanship. Gliesan v. Smolenske, 153 Colo. 274, 387 P.2d 260 (1963). But until quite recently no such duty was implied on the sale of a completed house and lot together by a speculative builder, even though the builder-vendor might be engaged in the mass production of suburban tract homes. For a good statement of the traditional doctrine of caveat emptor and its application in favor of the builder-vendor of a single-family house, see Steiber v. Palumbo, 219 Or. 479, 347 P.2d 978 (1959). See also, Shores v. Spann, 557 S.W.2d 67 (Tenn.App.1977), noted in 8 Memphis St.U.L.Rev. 902 (1978) for a case refusing to imply a warranty of habitability.

It is clear, however, that since the decision in Carpenter v. Donohoe, 154 Colo. 78, 388 P.2d 399 (1964), a sizeable number of courts have moved to provide some protection to a purchaser who buys from a builder-vendor. A definite trend may be observed, and the emphasis will now turn to the subsidiary questions which must be addressed. These include: (1) What is the scope of the implied warranty? (2) Does the warranty extend only to the immediate vendee or may a remote purchaser recover when defects appear after the initial vendee has sold the property? (3) May the warranty be waived by the purchaser? (4) Is a lender who acquires the property of a builder-vendor through foreclosure subject to the same warranty? (5) Will the warranty extend to sales of "second hand" housing? (6) Is the cause of action founded in the tort of negligence, or in contract, or in some notion of strict liability?

With respect to the scope of the warranty, it seems clear that there is a substantial difference in the formulation of the terms of the warranty by those courts which have held the builder-vendor liable to his vendee. Some of these differences may be purely semantic, but there are at least three different warranties that have been recognized. Both procedural and substantive differences arise from the different formulations. The three are: (1) A warranty that the building was constructed in a workmanlike manner; (2) a warranty that the house is fit for human habitation; and (3) a warranty that the house complies with the local zoning and building codes. It has also been held that when land is sold by a deed which restricts the use of the conveyed property to one specific use, the grantor impliedly warrants that at the time of the conveyance the land is usable for that purpose. Hinson v. Jefferson, 287 N.C. 422, 215 S.E.2d 102 (1975), noted in 54 N.C.L.Rev. 1097 (1976). A recent case has held that a builder-vendor is liable to a vendee for failing to supply a "safe site," and must respond in damages when a neighboring hill slid down with resultant damage to the house. ABC Builders, Inc. v. Phillips, 632 P.2d 925 (Wyo.1981), noted in 17 Land and Water Rev. 467 (1982). The decisions of a particular state must be examined with great care in determining the scope of the warranty.

Cases are not uniform on the question of extending the protection to a remote vendee. The Texas court has extended coverage to a remote owner. Gupta v. Ritter Homes, Inc., 646 S.W.2d 168 (Tex.1983). Courts in Ohio and Mississippi have rejected recovery beyond the initial vendee. Insurance Co. of North America v. Bonnie Built Homes, 64 Ohio St.2d 269, 416 N.E.2d 623 (1980), noted in 43 Ohio St.L.J. 951 (1982); Oliver v. City Builders, Inc., 303 So.2d 466 (Miss.1974), noted in 46 Miss.L.J. 510 (1975).

With respect to waiver, a recent Illinois case involved a purchase from a builder-vendor in which the contract contained a provision that "there are no warranties on either house except those manufacturer warranties that are in effect." The court said that a purchaser could waive his protection (it is not against public policy), but held that the waiver must be precise and specific enough to show that the purchaser knew what he is waiving. The quoted waiver clause was held to be not sufficiently express. Conyers v. Molloy, 50 Ill.App. 3d 17, 7 Ill.Dec. 695, 364 N.E.2d 986 (1977).

Where a lender is forced to foreclose on a building project, new problems of his liability for defects may arise. See Note, 53 Denver L.J. 413 (1976). See also § 2–309(f) of ULTA.

Sales of "second hand" housing from one individual to another are likely to continue to be governed by the doctrine of caveat emptor.

To the extent that the underlying theory is that a builder-vendor of housing may be subject to liability for harm proximately caused by the builder-vendor's negligence in construction, it seems clear that either contributory negligence or assumption of risk on the part of the injured party may bar recovery. By way of analogy, see Nichols v. Nashville Housing Authority, 187 Tenn. 683, 216 S.W.2d 694 (1949), where plaintiffs brought an action based on negligence for the wrongful death of their child against their landlord, which knowingly maintained a hot water system which many times produced steam from the bathroom faucets. Plaintiffs' three-year-old child was scalded to death when she was temporarily left alone in the bathroom by her mother. As the mother returned, the child tried to turn on the cold water faucet, accidentally fell into the tub, and accidentally turned on the hot water faucet as she fell. The court held that the mother was contributorily negligent in leaving the child alone in a place the mother knew to be dangerous; that her negligence was imputed to the father; and that recovery for wrongful death was therefore barred because the sole beneficiaries of the action were guilty of contributory negligence.

Can the plaintiff avoid defenses based on contributory negligence or assumption of risk by framing the action as one to impose strict tort liability or liability for breach of implied warranty? Logically, the answer might seem to be "yes." But see Maiorino v. Weco Products Co., 45 N.J. 570, 574, 214 A.2d 18, 20 (1965), a products liability case where the court said, "we are of the view that where a plaintiff * * * fails to act as a reasonably prudent man in connection with use of a warranted product or one which comes into his hands under circumstances imposing strict liability on the maker or vendor or lessor, and such conduct proximately contributes to his injury, he cannot recover." Cases such as Johnson v. Healy, 176 Conn. 97, 405 A.2d 54 (1978) which leave the theory of recovery in doubt are properly subject to criticism. See note, Breach of Warranty in the Sale of Real Property: Johnson v. Healy, 41 Ohio St. L.J. 727 (1980).

Note: Express Warranties as to Quality of Construction and Fitness for Intended Use

A builder-vendor of housing may, of course, give express warranties as to quality of construction and/or fitness for intended use. Such warranties are construed in accordance with the ordinary rules of construction applicable to contracts generally and to warranties in particular. It has been held, however, that an express warranty (which had expired) does not preclude liability on implied warranty grounds. Gable v. Silver, 258 So.2d 11 (Fla. 4th Dist. 1972), noted in 26 U.Miami L.Rev. 838 (1972).

If the sale of housing is to be financed by means of federally insured mortgages, the vendor must be prepared to give the warranty required by 12 U.S. C.A. § 1701j–1(a), which provides as follows:

"(a) The Secretary of Housing and Urban Development is authorized and directed to require that, in connection with any property upon which there is located a dwelling designed principally for not more than a four-family residence and which is approved for mortgage insurance prior to the beginning of construction, the seller or builder, and such other person as may be required by the said Secretary to become warrantor, shall deliver to the purchaser or owner of such property a warranty that the dwelling is constructed in substantial conformity with the plans and specifications (including any amendments thereof, or changes and variations therein, which have been approved in writing by the Secretary * * *) on which the Secretary * * * based his valuation of the dwelling: *Provided*, That the Secretary * * * shall deliver to the builder, seller, or other warrantor his written approval (which shall be conclusive evidence of such approval) of any amendment of, or change or variation in, such plans and specifications which the Secretary deems to be a substantial amendment thereof, or change or variation therein, and shall file a copy of such written approval with such plans and specifications: Provided further, That such warranty shall apply only with respect to such instances of substantial nonconformity to such approved plans and specifications (including any amendments thereof, or changes or variations therein, which have been approved in writing * * * by the Secretary * * *) as to which the purchaser or homeowner has given written notice to the warrantor within one year from the date of conveyance of title to, or initial occupancy of, the dwelling, whichever first occurs: Provided further, That such warranty shall be in addition to, and not in derogation of, all other rights and privileges which such purchaser or owner may have under any other law or instrument * * *."

Part Three

GOVERNMENT CONTROL OF LAND USE

Chapter 13

THE POLICE POWER AND THE REGULATORY "TAKING" PROBLEM

SECTION 1.   INTRODUCTION

HADACHECK v. SEBASTIAN

Supreme Court of the United States, 1915.
239 U.S. 394, 36 S.Ct. 143, 60 L.Ed. 348.

Mr. Justice McKENNA delivered the opinion of the court.

Habeas corpus prosecuted in the Supreme Court of the State of California for the discharge of plaintiff in error from the custody of defendant in error, Chief of Police of the City of Los Angeles.

Plaintiff in error, to whom we shall refer as petitioner, was convicted of a misdemeanor for the violation of an ordinance of the City of Los Angeles which makes it unlawful for any person to establish or operate a brick yard or brick kiln, or any establishment, factory or place for the manufacture or burning of brick within described limits in the city. Sentence was pronounced against him and he was committed to the custody of defendant in error as Chief of Police of the City of Los Angeles.

Being so in custody he filed a petition in the Supreme Court of the State for a writ of *habeas corpus*.   The writ was issued.   Subsequently defendant in error made a return thereto supported by affidavits, to which petitioner made sworn reply.   The court rendered judgment discharging the writ and remanding petitioner to custody.   The Chief Justice of the court then granted this writ of error.   *   *   *   [Petitioner alleged that he was the owner of land within the limits described in the ordinance on which land there was a very valuable bed of clay worth about $800,000 for brick-making purposes, but worth only about $60,000 for any purpose other than the manufacture of brick; that he had made excavations of considerable depth and extent on his land, so that the land could not be used for residential purposes or any purpose other than extraction of the clay and manufacture of brick; that he purchased the land because of the bed of clay located thereon, at a time when the land was outside the limits of the city and distant from any dwellings; that he had erected expensive machinery for the manufacture of bricks on the land; that if the ordinance should be declared valid he would be compelled entirely to abandon his business and would be deprived of the use of his property because the manufacture of brick must necessarily

1068

be carried on where suitable clay is found and the clay cannot be transported to some other location; that there was no reason for the prohibition of the brick making business because it was so conducted as not to be a nuisance; that the district described in the ordinance included only about three square miles, was sparsely settled and contained large tracts of unsubdivided and unoccupied land; that there were at the time of the adoption of the ordinance in other districts of the city thickly built up with residences brick yards maintained more detrimental to the inhabitants of the city, but permitted to be maintained without prohibition or regulation; that no ordinance had been passed at any time regulating or attempting to regulate brick yards or inquiry made whether they could be maintained without being a nuisance or detrimental to health; and that the ordinance in question was enacted for the sole and specific purpose of prohibiting and suppressing the business of petitioner and that of the other brick yard within the district described in the ordinance.

The City of Los Angeles denied the charge that the ordinance was arbitrarily directed against the business of petitioner and alleged that there was another district in which brick yards were prohibited. There was a denial of the allegations that the brick yard was or could be conducted sanitarily and so as not to be offensive to health, with supporting affidavits alleging that the fumes, gases, smoke, soot, steam and dust arising from petitioner's brick factory had from time to time caused sickness and serious discomfort to those living in the vicinity. There was no specific denial of petitioner's allegations as to the value of his property and his inability to move the brick factory elsewhere, but there was a general denial that enforcement of the ordinance would "entirely deprive petitioner of his property and the use thereof."

The Supreme Court of California considered the petitioner's business one which could be regulated and that regulation was not precluded by the fact "that the value of investments made in the business prior to any legislative action will be greatly diminished" or that petitioner had been engaged in brick making in that locality for a long period. The court said the evidence tended to show that the district had become primarily a residential section and that the residents were seriously incommoded by petitioner's operation of his factory; and that such evidence, "when taken in connection with the presumptions in favor of the propriety of the legislative determination, overcame the contention that the ordinance was a mere arbitrary invasion of private right, not supported by any tenable belief that the continuance of the business was so detrimental to the interests of others as to require suppression." The court thus rejected the contention that the ordinance was not in good faith enacted as police measure and that it was intended to discriminate against petitioner. With respect to the charge of discrimination between localities, the court said that the determination where brick making should be prohibited was for the local legislative body.]

We think the conclusion of the court is justified by the evidence and makes it unnecessary to review the many cases cited by petitioner in which it is decided that the police power of a state cannot be arbitrarily exercised. The principle is familiar, but in any given case it must plainly appear to apply. It is to be remembered that we are dealing with one of the most essential powers of government, one that is the least limitable. It may, indeed, seem harsh in its exercise, usually is on some individual, but the imperative necessity for its existence precludes any limitation upon it when not exerted arbitrarily. A vested interest cannot be asserted against it because of conditions once obtaining. * * * To so hold would preclude development and fix a city forever in its primitive conditions. There must be progress, and if in its march private interests are in the way they must yield to the good of the community. The logical result of petitioner's contention would seem to be that a city could not be formed or enlarged against the resistance of an occupant of the ground and that if it grows at all it can only grow as the environment of the occupations that are usually banished to the purlieus.

The police power and to what extent it may be exerted we have recently illustrated in Reinman v. Little Rock, 237 U.S. 171, 59 L.Ed. 900, 35 Sup.Ct.Rep. 511. The circumstances of the case were very much like those of the case at bar and give reply to the contentions of petitioner, especially that which asserts that a necessary and lawful occupation that is not a nuisance *per se* cannot be made so by legislative declaration. There was a like investment in property, encouraged by the then conditions; a like reduction of value and deprivation of property was asserted against the validity of the ordinance there considered; a like assertion of an arbitrary exercise of the power of prohibition. Against all of these contentions, and causing the rejection of them all, was adduced the police power. There was a prohibition of a business, lawful in itself, there as here. It was a livery stable there; a brick yard here. They differ in particulars, but they are alike in that which cause and justify prohibition in defined localities—that is, the effect upon the health and comfort of the community.

The ordinance passed upon prohibited the conduct of the business within a certain defined area in Little Rock, Arkansas. This court said of it: granting that the business was not a nuisance *per se*, it was clearly within the police power of the State to regulate it, "and to that end to declare that in particular circumstances and in particular localities a livery stable shall be deemed a nuisance in fact and in law." And the only limitation upon the power was stated to be that the power could not be exerted arbitrarily or with unjust discrimination. There was a citation of cases. We think the present case is within the ruling thus declared.

There is a distinction between Reinman v. Little Rock and the case at bar. There a particular business was prohibited which was not affixed to or dependent upon its locality; it could be conducted elsewhere. Here, it is contended, the latter condition does not exist, and it is alleged that the manufacture of brick must necessarily be carried on where suitable clay is found and that the clay on petitioner's property cannot be transported to some other locality. This is not urged as a physical impossibility but only, counsel say, that such transportation and the transportation of the bricks to places where they could be used in construction work would be prohibitive "from a financial standpoint." But upon the evidence the Supreme Court considered the case, as we understand its opinion, from the standpoint of the offensive effects of the operation of a brick yard and not from the deprivation of the deposits of clay, and distinguished Ex parte Kelso, 147 Cal. 609, 2 L.R.A. (N.S.) 796, 109 Am.St.Rep. 178, 82 Pac. 241, wherein the court declared invalid an ordinance absolutely prohibiting the maintenance or operation of a rock or stone quarry within a certain portion of the city and county of San Francisco. The court there said that the effect of the ordinance was "to absolutely deprive the owners of real property within such limits of a valuable right incident to their ownership,—viz., the right to extract therefrom such rock and stone as they might find it to their advantage to dispose of." The court expressed the view that the removal could be regulated but that "an absolute prohibition of such removal under the circumstances," could not be upheld.

In the present case there is no prohibition of the removal of the brick clay; only a prohibition within the designated locality of its manufacture into bricks. And to this feature of the ordinance our opinion is addressed. Whether other questions would arise if the ordinance were broader, and opinion on such questions, we reserve.

Petitioner invokes the equal protection clause of the Constitution and charges that it is violated in that the ordinance (1) "prohibits him from manufacturing brick upon his property while his competitors are permitted, without regulation of any kind, to manufacture brick upon property situated in all respects similarly to that of plaintiff in error"; and (2) that it "prohibits the conduct of his business while it permits the maintenance within the same district of any other kind of business, no matter how objectionable the same may be, either in its nature or in the manner in which it is conducted."

If we should grant that the first specification shows a violation of classification, that is, a distinction between businesses which was not within the legislative power, petitioner's contention encounters the objection that it depends upon an inquiry of fact which the record does not enable us to determine. It is alleged in the return to the petition that brickmaking is prohibited in one other district and an ordinance is referred to regulating business in other districts. To this plaintiff in error replied that the ordinance attempts to prohibit the operation of certain businesses having mechanical power and does not prohibit the maintenance of any business or the operation of any machine that is operated by animal power. In other words, petitioner makes his contention depend upon disputable considerations of classification and upon a comparison of conditions of which there is no means of judicial determination and upon which nevertheless we are expected to reverse legislative action exercised upon matters of which the city has control.

To a certain extent the latter comment may be applied to other contentions, and, besides, there is no allegation or proof of other objectionable businesses being permitted within the district, and a speculation of their establishment or conduct at some future time is too remote.

In his petition and argument something is made of the ordinance as fostering a monopoly and suppressing his competition with other brickmakers. The charge and argument are too illusive. It is part of the charge that the ordinance was directed against him. The charge, we have seen, was rejected by the Supreme Court, and we find nothing to justify it.

It may be that brick yards in other localities within the city where the same conditions exist are not regulated or prohibited, but it does not follow that they will not be. That petitioner's business was first in time to be prohibited does not make its prohibition unlawful. And it may be, as said by the Supreme Court of the State, that the conditions justify a distinction. However, the inquiries thus suggested are outside of our province.

There are other and subsidiary contentions which, we think, do not require discussion. They are disposed of by what we have said. It may be that something else than prohibition would have satisfied the conditions. Of this, however, we have no means of determining, and besides we cannot declare invalid the exertion of a power which the city undoubtedly has because of a charge that it does not exactly accommodate the conditions or that some other exercise would have been better or less harsh. We must accord good faith to the city in the absence of a clear showing to the contrary and an honest exercise of judgment upon the circumstances which induced its action.

We do not notice the contention that the ordinance is not within the city's charter powers nor that it is in violation of the state constitution, such contentions raising only local questions which must be deemed to have been decided adversely to petitioner by the Supreme Court of the State.

Judgment affirmed.

Note on the Police Power and Constitutional Limitations Thereon

The "police power" which was the basis of the Los Angeles ordinance challenged in the *Hadacheck* case is one of the inherent powers of the states and was confirmed in them by the Tenth Amendment to the United States Constitution. The federal government has a similar power to regulate land use in those areas where power has been delegated to it by the United States Constitution. Although definitions of the "police power" tend to vary a bit from one judicial opinion to the next, all courts would probably accept the following definition: the police power is the power of a government to regulate human conduct to protect or promote "public health, safety, or the general welfare." The states may delegate their police power to units of local government such as counties and cities.

The power of the federal government to regulate land use is expressly limited by the "due process" and "taking" clauses of the Fifth Amendment to the United States Constitution. Although the Fourteenth Amendment contains no "taking" clause, it has long been settled that the "due process" clause makes the "taking" clause of the Fifth Amendment applicable to the states. Thus the states (and their political subdivisions) are subject to limitations under the Fourteenth Amendment identical with the limitations imposed on the federal government by the Fifth Amendment, as well as the "equal protection" guarantee expressly included in the Fourteenth Amendment.[1] In addition, the power of state and local governments is expressly limited by "due process" and/or "taking" clauses in the various state constitutions.

State statutes and local ordinances regulating land use are frequently challenged on the ground that they deprive the landowner of property without "substantive due process"—as distinct from "procedural due process"—and/or amount to a *de facto* "taking of private property for public use without just compensation." Unfortunately, it is often unclear whether the challenge is based on the state constitution or on the Fourteenth Amendment, and the courts generally do not distinguish clearly between "substantive due process" and "taking" arguments. Where the challenge is based (at least partly) on the Fourteenth Amendment, this is understandable, since the Fourteenth Amendment (as noted above) contains no "taking" clause and the "taking" challenge is thus always, in a sense, a "substantive due process" challenge; i.e., a land use regulation that amounts to a *de facto* "taking" violates the Fourteenth Amendment *only* because it is deemed, ipso facto, to deprive the landowner of his property "without due process of law."

Further confusion has arisen in land use regulation cases because the United States Supreme Court—which establishes the minimum constitutional limitations on the exercise of state and local police power—has not developed any consistent standard to determine the validity of police power regulations challenged under the Fourteenth Amendment. In Mugler v. Kansas,[2] where the Court upheld a Kansas statute that prohibited the manufacture of intoxicating liquors, the Court applied a substantive due process test but declared that the Fourteenth Amendment's due process clause was not "designed to interfere with the power of the States, sometimes termed police power, to prescribe regulations to promote the health, peace, morals, education and good order of the people, and to legislate so as to increase the industries of the State, develop its resources, and add to its wealth and prosperity."[3] Hence, said the Court, the police power of the States "cannot be burdened with the condition that the State must compensate * * * individual owners of property for pecuniary losses they may sustain, by their not being permitted, by a *noxious* use of their property, to inflict injury on the community."[4] In addition, the Court said that a valid legislative act pursuant to the police power, prohibiting the use of property in a manner declared by a state to be "injurious to the health, safety, morals, or safety of the community is not an appropriation of property for the public benefit in the sense in which a taking of property by the exercise of the State's power of eminent domain is such a taking or appropriation."[5] And the Court adopted a deferential attitude with respect to the legislative determination that the manufacture of liquor was "injurious" to the public.[6]

A few years later, in Lawton v. Steele,[7] the Court, in upholding a New York statute that authorized seizure and destruction of illegal fishing nets without compensating the owners, said that a purported exercise of the police power is valid under the Fourteenth Amendment if it appears "first, that the interests of the public * * * require such interference; second, that the means are reasonably necessary for the accomplishment of the purpose, and not unduly oppressive on individuals."[8] This has long been considered the classic statement

---

1. Chicago, B. & Q. R. v. Chicago, 166 U.S. 226, 17 S.Ct. 581, 41 L.Ed. 979 (1897).

2. 123 U.S. 623, 8 S.Ct. 273, 31 L.Ed. 205 (1887).

3. Id. at 663, 8 S.Ct. at 298.

4. Id. at 669, 8 S.Ct. at 301.

5. Id. at 668, 8 S.Ct. at 301.

6. Id. at 660, 8 S.Ct. at 296.

7. 152 U.S. 133, 14 S.Ct. 499, 38 L.Ed. 385 (1894).

8. Id. at 137, 14 S.Ct. at 501.

of the concept of "substantive due process." But, unfortunately, *Lawton* did not indicate the relative weight to be attached to each of the designated factors, proper governmental purpose, reasonable means to achieve the purpose, and the adverse impact of the regulation on the landowner affected by it.

The decision in *Hadacheck* seems consistent with the "noxious use" test and the deferential attitude toward legislative determinations announced in Mugler v. Kansas. But it can be argued that the *Hadacheck* court did not seriously consider whether the Los Angeles ordinance, in view of its economic effect on Hadacheck, satisfied the third test announced in Lawton v. Steele—i.e., that it not be "unduly oppressive on individuals." Hadacheck certainly alleged that the ordinance was "unduly oppressive" on him because it reduced the value of his bed of clay from about $800,000 to about $60,000. Was it an adequate answer to Hadacheck's claim that the ordinance caused him severe economic hardship to say, as the *Hadacheck* court did, that the ordinance did not prohibit the removal of his clay from the ground, although it may have made removal infeasible "from a financial standpoint"?

PENNSYLVANIA COAL CO. v. MAHON

Supreme Court of the United States, 1922.
260 U.S. 393, 43 S.Ct. 158, 67 L.Ed. 322.

Mr. Justice HOLMES delivered the opinion of the Court.

This is a bill in equity brought by the defendants in error to prevent the Pennsylvania Coal Company from mining under their property in such way as to remove the supports and cause a subsidence of the surface and of their house. The bill sets out a deed executed by the Coal Company in 1878, under which the plaintiffs claim. The deed conveys the surface, but in express terms reserves the right to remove all the coal under the same, and the grantee takes the premises with the risk, and waives all claim for damages that may arise from mining out the coal. But the plaintiffs say that whatever may have been the Coal Company's rights, they were taken away by an Act of Pennsylvania, approved May 27, 1921, P.L. 1198, commonly known there as the Kohler Act. The Court of Common Pleas found that if not restrained the defendant would cause the damage to prevent which the bill was brought, but denied an injunction, holding that the statute if applied to this case would be unconstitutional. On appeal the Supreme Court of the State agreed that the defendant had contract and property rights protected by the Constitution of the United States, but held that the statute was a legitimate exercise of the police power and directed a decree for the plaintiffs. A writ of error was granted bringing the case to this Court.

The statute forbids the mining of anthracite coal in such way as to cause the subsidence of, among other things, any structure used as a human habitation, with certain exceptions, including among them land where the surface is owned by the owner of the underlying coal and is distant more than one hundred and fifty feet from any improved property belonging to any other person. As applied to this case the statute is admitted to destroy previously existing rights of property and contract. The question is whether the police power can be stretched so far.

Government hardly could go on if to some extent values incident to property could not be diminished without paying for every such change in the general law. As long recognized, some values are enjoyed under an implied limitation and must yield to the police power. But obviously the implied limitation must have its limits, or the contract and due process clauses are gone. One fact for consideration in determining such limits is the extent of the diminution. When it reaches a certain magnitude, in most if not in all cases there must be an exercise of eminent domain and compensation to sustain the act. So the question depends upon the particular facts. The greatest weight is given to the judgment of the legislature, but it always is open to interested parties to contend that the legislature has gone beyond its constitutional power.

This is the case of a single private house. No doubt there is a public interest even in this, as there is in every purchase and sale and in all that happens within the commonwealth. Some existing rights may be modified even in such a case.   *   *   *   But usually in ordinary private affairs the public interest does not warrant much of this kind of interference. A source of damage to such a house is not a public nuisance even if similar damage is inflicted on others in different places. The damage is not common or public.   *   *   *   The extent of the public interest is shown by the statute to be limited, since the statute ordinarily does not apply to land when the surface is owned by the owner of the coal. Furthermore, it is not justified as a protection of personal safety. That could be provided for by notice. Indeed the very foundation of this bill is that the defendant gave timely notice of its intent to mine under the house. On the other hand the extent of the taking is great. It purports to abolish what is recognized in Pennsylvania as an estate in land—a very valuable estate—and what is declared by the Court below to be a contract hitherto binding the plaintiffs. If we were called upon to deal with the plaintiffs' position alone, we should think it clear that the statute does not disclose a public interest sufficient to warrant so extensive a destruction of the defendant's constitutionally protected rights.

But the case has been treated as one in which the general validity of the act should be discussed. The Attorney General of the State, the City of Scranton, and the representatives of other extensive interests were allowed to take part in the argument below and have submitted their contentions here. It seems, therefore, to be our duty to go farther in the statement of our opinion, in order that it may be known at once, and that further suits should not be brought in vain.

It is our opinion that the act cannot be sustained as an exercise of the police power, so far as it affects the mining of coal under streets or cities in places where the right to mine such coal has been reserved. As said in a Pennsylvania case, "For practical purposes, the right to coal consists in the right to mine it." Commonwealth v. Clearview Coal Co., 256 Pa. 328, 331, 100 Atl. 820, L.R.A.1917E, 672. What makes the right to mine coal valuable is that it can be exercised with profit. To make it commercially impracticable to mine certain coal has very nearly the same effect for constitutional purposes as appropriating or destroying it. This we think that we are warranted in assuming that the statute does.

It is true that in Plymouth Coal Co. v. Pennsylvania, 232 U.S. 531, 34 Sup.Ct. 359, 58 L.Ed. 713, it was held competent for the legislature to require a pillar of coal to be left along the line of adjoining property, that, with the pillar on the other side of the line, would be a barrier sufficient for the safety of the employees of either mine in case the other should be abandoned and allowed to fill with water. But that was a requirement for the safety of employees invited into the mine, and secured an average reciprocity of advantage that has been recognized as a justification of various laws.

The rights of the public in a street purchased or laid out by eminent domain are those that it has paid for. If in any case its representatives have been so short sighted as to acquire only surface rights without the right of support, we see no more authority for supplying the latter without compensation than there was for taking the right of way in the first place and refusing to pay for it because the public wanted it very much. The protection of private property in the Fifth Amendment presupposes that it is wanted for public use, but provides that it shall not be taken for such use without compensation. A similar assumption is made in the decisions upon the Fourteenth Amendment. * * * When this seemingly absolute protection is found to be qualified by the police power, the natural tendency of human nature is to extend the qualification more and more until at last private property disappears. But that cannot be accomplished in this way under the Constitution of the United States.

The general rule at least is, that while property may be regulated to a certain extent, if regulation goes too far it will be recognized as a taking. It may be doubted how far exceptional cases, like the blowing up of a house to stop a conflagration, go—and if they go beyond the general rule, whether they do not stand as much upon tradition as upon principle. * * * In general it is not plain that a man's misfortunes or necessities will justify his shifting the damages to his neighbor's shoulders. * * * We are in danger of forgetting that a strong public desire to improve the public condition is not enough to warrant achieving the desire by a shorter cut than the constitutional way of paying for the change. As we already have said, this is a question of degree—and therefore cannot be disposed of by general propositions. But we regard this as going beyond any of the cases decided by this Court. The late decisions upon laws dealing with the congestion of Washington and New York, caused by the war, dealt with laws intended to meet a temporary emergency and providing for compensation determined to be reasonable by an impartial board. They went to the verge of the law but fell far short of the present act. Block v. Hirsh, 256 U.S. 135, 41 Sup.Ct. 458, 65 L.Ed. 865, 16 A.L.R. 165; Marcus Brown Holding Co. v. Feldman, 256 U.S. 170, 41 Sup.Ct. 465, 65 L.Ed. 877; Levy Leasing Co. v. Siegel, 258 U.S. 242, 42 Sup.Ct. 289, 66 L.Ed. 595, March 20, 1922.

We assume, of course, that the statute was passed upon the conviction that an exigency existed that would warrant it, and we assume that an exigency exists that would warrant the exercise of eminent domain. But the question at bottom is upon whom the loss of the changes desired should fall. So far as private persons or communities have seen fit to take the risk of acquiring only surface rights, we cannot see that the fact that their risk has become a danger warrants the giving to them greater rights than they bought.

Decree reversed.

Mr. Justice BRANDEIS, dissenting. The Kohler Act prohibits under certain conditions, the mining of anthracite coal within the limits of a city in such a manner or to such an extent "as to cause the . . . subsidence of any dwelling or other structure used as a human habitation, or any factory, store, or other industrial or mercantile establishment in which human labor is employed." Coal in place is land; and the right of the owner to use his land is not absolute. He may not so use it as to create a public nuisance; and uses, once harmless, may, owing to changed conditions, seriously threaten the public welfare. Whenever they do, the legislature has power to prohibit such uses without paying compensation; and the power to prohibit extends alike to the manner, the character and the purpose of the use. Are we justified in declaring that the Legislature of Pennsylvania has, in restricting the right to mine anthracite, exercised this power so arbitrarily as to violate the Fourteenth Amendment?

Every restriction upon the use of property imposed in the exercise of the police power deprives the owner of some right theretofore enjoyed, and is, in that sense, an abridgment of the State of rights in property without making compensation. But restriction imposed to protect the public health, safety or morals from dangers threatened is not a taking. The restriction here in question is merely the prohibition of a noxious use. The property so restricted remains in the possession of its owner. The State does not appropriate it or make any use of it. The state merely prevents the owner from making a use which interferes with paramount rights of the public. Whenever the use prohibited ceases to be noxious—as it may because of further change in local or social conditions—the restriction will have to be removed and the owner will again be free to enjoy his property as heretofore.

The restriction upon the use of this property cannot, of course, be lawfully imposed, unless its purpose is to protect the public. But the purpose of a restriction does not cease to be public, because incidentally some private persons may thereby receive gratuitously valuable special benefits. Thus, owners of low buildings may obtain, through statutory restrictions upon the height of neighboring structures, benefits equivalent to an easement of light and air. Welch v. Swasey, 214 U.S. 91, 29 Sup.Ct. 567, 53 L.Ed. 923. Compare Lindsley v. Natural Carbonic Gas Co., 220 U.S. 61, 31 Sup.Ct. 337, 55 L.Ed. 369, Ann.Cas. 1912C, 160; Walls v. Midland Carbon Co., 254 U.S. 300, 41 Sup.Ct. 118, 65 L.Ed. 276. Furthermore, a restriction, though imposed for a public purpose, will not be lawful, unless the restriction is an appropriate means to the public end. But to keep coal in place is surely an appropriate means of preventing subsidence of the surface; and ordinarily it is the only available means. Restriction upon use does not become inappropriate as a means, merely because it deprives the owner of the only use to which the property can then be profitably put. The liquor and the oleomargine cases settled that. Mugler v. Kansas, 123 U.S. 623, 668, 669, 8 Sup.Ct. 273, 31 L.Ed. 205; Powell v. Pennsylvania, 127 U.S. 678, 682, 8 Sup.Ct. 992, 1257, 32 L.Ed. 253. See also Hadacheck v. Los Angeles, 239 U.S. 394, 36 Sup.Ct. 143, 60 L.Ed. 348, Ann.Cas.1917B, 927; Pierce Oil Corporation v. City of Hope, 248 U.S. 498, 39 Sup.Ct. 172, 63 L.Ed. 381. Nor is a restriction imposed through exercise of the police power inappropriate as a means, merely because the same end might be affected through exercise of the power of eminent domain, or otherwise at public expense. Every restriction upon the height of buildings might be secured through acquiring by eminent domain the right of each owner to build above the limiting height; but it is settled that the state need not resort to that power. Compare Laurel Hill Cemetery v. San Francisco, 216 U.S. 358, 30 Sup.Ct. 301, 54 L.Ed. 515; Missouri Pacific Railway Co. v. Omaha, 235 U.S. 121, 35 Sup.Ct. 82, 59 L.Ed. 157. If by mining anthracite coal the owner would necessarily unloose poisonous gases, I suppose no one would doubt the power of the state to prevent the mining, without buying his coal fields. And why may not the state, likewise, without paying compensation, prohibit one from digging so deep or excavating so near the surface, as to expose the community to like dangers? In the latter case, as in the former, carrying on the business would be a public nuisance.

It is said that one fact for consideration in determining whether the limits of the police power have been exceeded is the extent of the resulting diminution in value, and that here the restriction destroys existing rights of property and contract. But values are relative. If we are to consider the value of the coal kept in place by the restriction, we should compare it with the value of all other parts of the land. That is, with the value not of the coal alone, but with the value of the whole property. The rights of an owner as against the public are not increased by dividing the interests in his property into surface and subsoil. The sum of the rights in the parts can not be greater than the rights in the whole. The estate of an owner in land is grandiloquently described as extending ab orco usque ad coelum. But I suppose no one would contend that by selling his interest about 100 feet from the surface he could prevent the state from limiting, by the police power, the height of structures in a city. And why should a sale of underground rights bar the state's power? For aught that appears the value of the coal kept in place by the restriction may be negligible as compared with the value of the whole property, or even as compared with that part of it which is represented by the coal remaining in place and which may be extracted despite the statute. Ordinarily a police regulation, general in operation, will not be held void as to a particular property, although proof is offered that owing to conditions peculiar to it the restriction could not reasonably be applied. See Powell v. Pennsylvania, 127 U.S. 678, 681, 684, 8 Sup.Ct. 992, 1257, 32 L.Ed. 253; Murphy v. California, 225 U.S. 623, 629, 32 Sup.Ct. 697, 56 L.Ed. 1229, 41 L.R.A. (N.S.) 153. But even if the particular facts are to govern, the statute should, in my opinion be upheld in this case. For the defendant has failed to adduce any evidence from which it appears that to restrict its mining operations was an unreasonable exercise of the police power. Compare Reinman v. Little Rock, 237 U.S. 171, 177, 180, 35 Sup.Ct. 511, 59 L.Ed. 900; Pierce Oil Corporation v. City of Hope, 248 U.S. 498, 500, 39 Sup.Ct. 172, 63 L.Ed. 381. Where the surface and the coal belong to the same person, self-interest would ordinarily prevent mining to such an extent as to cause a subsidence. It was, doubtless, for this reason that the Legislature, estimating the degrees of danger, deemed statutory restriction unnecessary for the public safety under such conditions.

It is said that this is a case of a single dwelling house, that the restriction upon mining abolishes a valuable estate hitherto secured by a contract with the plaintiffs, and that the restriction upon mining cannot be justified as a protection of personal safety, since that could be provided for by notice. The propriety of deferring a good deal to tribunals on the spot has been repeatedly recognized. Welch v. Swasey, 214 U.S. 91, 106, 29 Sup.Ct. 567, 53 L.Ed. 923; Laurel Hill Cemetery v. San Francisco, 216 U.S. 358, 365, 30 Sup.Ct. 301, 54 L.Ed. 515; Patsone v. Pennsylvania, 232 U.S. 138, 144, 34 Sup.Ct. 281, 58 L.Ed. 539. May we say that notice would afford adequate protection of the public safety where the Legislature and the highest court of the state, with greater knowledge of local conditions, have declared, in effect, that it would not? If the public safety is imperiled, surely neither grant, nor contract, can prevail against the exercise of the police power. Fertilizing Co. v. Hyde Park, 97 U.S. 659, 24 L.Ed. 1036; Atlantic Coast Line R.R. Co. v. North Carolina, 232 U.S. 548, 34 Sup.Ct. 364, 58 L.Ed. 721; Union Dry Goods Co. v. Georgia Public Service Corporation, 248 U.S. 372, 39 Sup.Ct. 117, 63 L.Ed. 309, 9 A.L.R. 1420; St. Louis Poster Advertising Co. v. St. Louis, 249 U.S. 269, 39 Sup.Ct. 274, 63 L.Ed. 599. The rule that the state's power to take appropriate measures to guard the safety of all who may be within its jurisdiction may not be bargained away was applied to compel carriers to establish grade crossings at their own expense, despite contracts to the contrary (Chicago, Burlington & Quincy R.R. Co. v. Nebraska, 170 U.S. 57, 18 Sup.Ct. 513, 42 L.Ed. 948); and, likewise, to supersede, by an Employers' Liability Act, the provision of a charter exempting a railroad from liability for death of employees, since the civil liability was deemed a matter of public concern, and not a mere private right. Texas & New Orleans R.R. Co. v. Miller, 221 U.S. 408, 31 Sup.Ct. 534, 55 L.Ed. 789. Compare Boyd v. Alabama, 94 U.S. 645, 24 L.Ed. 302; Stone v. Mississippi, 101 U.S. 814, 25 L.Ed. 1079; Butchers' Union Co. v. Crescent City Co., 111 U.S. 746, 4 Sup.Ct. 652, 28 L.Ed. 585; Douglas v. Kentucky, 168 U.S. 488, 18 Sup.Ct. 199, 42 L.Ed. 553; Pennsylvania Hospital v. Philadelphia, 245 U.S. 20, 23, 38 Sup.Ct. 35, 62 L.Ed. 124. Nor can existing contracts between private individuals preclude exercise of the police power. "One whose rights, such as they are, are subject to state restriction cannot remove them from the power of the state by making a contract about them." Hudson Water Co. v. McCarter, 209 U.S. 349, 357, 28 Sup.Ct. 529, 52 L.Ed. 828, 14 Ann.Cas. 560; Knoxville Water Co. v. Knoxville, 189 U.S. 434, 438, 23 Sup.Ct. 531, 47 L.Ed. 887; Rast v. Van Deman & Lewis Co., 240 U.S. 342, 36 Sup.Ct.

370, 60 L.Ed. 679, L.R.A.1917A, 421, Ann.Cas.1917B, 455. The fact that this suit is brought by a private person is, of course, immaterial. To protect the community through invoking the aid, as litigant, of interested private citizens is not a novelty in our law. That it may be done in Pennsylvania was decided by its Supreme Court in this case. And it is for a state to say how its public policy shall be enforced.

This case involves only mining which causes subsidence of a dwelling house. But the Kohler Act contains provisions in addition to that quoted above; and as to these, also, an opinion is expressed. These provisions deal with mining under cities to such an extent as to cause subsidence of—

(a) Any public building or any structure customarily used by the public as a place of resort, assemblage, or amusement, including, but not limited to, churches, schools, hospitals, theaters, hotels, and railroad stations.

(b) Any street, road, bridge, or other public passageway, dedicated to public use or habitually used by the public.

(c) Any track, roadbed, right of way, pipe, conduit, wire, or other facility, used in the service of the public by any municipal corporation or public service company as defined by the Public Service Law, section 1.

A prohibition of mining which causes subsidence of such structures and facilities is obviously enacted for a public purpose; and it seems, likewise, clear that mere notice of intention to mine would not in this connection secure the public safety. Yet it is said that these provisions of the act cannot be sustained as an exercise of the police power where the right to mine such coal has been reserved. The conclusion seems to rest upon the assumption that in order to justify such exercise of the police power there must be "an average reciprocity of advantage" as between the owner of the property restricted and the rest of the community; and that here such reciprocity is absent. Reciprocity of advantage is an important consideration, and may even be an essential, where the state's power is exercised for the purpose of conferring benefits upon the property of a neighborhood, as in drainage projects (Wurts v. Hoagland, 114 U.S. 606, 5 Sup.Ct. 1086, 29 L.Ed. 229; Fallbrook Irrigation District v. Bradley, 164 U.S. 112, 17 Sup.Ct. 56, 41 L.Ed. 369); or upon adjoining owners, as by party wall provisions (Jackman v. Rosenbaum Co., 260 U.S. 22, 43 Sup.Ct. 9, 67 L.Ed. 107, decided October 23, 1922). But where the police power is exercised, not to confer benefits upon property owners but to protect the public from detriment and danger, there is in my opinion, no room for considering reciprocity of advantage. There was no reciprocal advantage to the owner prohibited from using his oil tanks in 248 U.S. 498, 39 Sup.Ct. 172, 63 L.Ed. 381; his brickyard, in 239 U.S. 394, 36 Sup.Ct. 143, 60 L.Ed. 348, Ann. Cas.1917B, 927; his livery stable, in 237 U.S. 171, 35 Sup.Ct. 511, 59 L.Ed. 900; his billiard hall, in 225 U.S. 623, 32 Sup.Ct. 697, 56 L.Ed. 1229, 41 L.R.A. (N.S.) 153; his oleomargarine factory, in 127 U.S. 678, 8 Sup.Ct. 992, 1257, 32 L.Ed. 253; his brewery, in 123 U.S. 623, 8 Sup.Ct. 273, 31 L.Ed. 205; unless it be the advantage of living and doing business in a civilized community. That reciprocal advantage is given by the act to the coal operators.

Notes and Questions

1. It was quite clear, under Pennsylvania law, that the coal company's reserved "right to remove all the coal" without liability for injury caused by subsidence of the surface was a "property" right, not a mere "contract" right. As counsel for the coal company, John W. Davis, pointed out in the oral argument in *Mahon*, "the courts of Pennsylvania have recognized three distinct estates in mining property: (1) The right to use the surface; (2) the ownership of the subjacent minerals; (3) the right to have the surface supported by the subjacent strata." (260 U.S. at 395.) The coal company's reserved right would appear to be an easement burdening the surface estate. Thus, Holmes might simply have said that, to the extent the Kohler Act destroyed or transferred to the surface estate owner the coal company's easement, it was a "taking" or "deprivation" of the coal company's property without compensation, and therefore "without due process of law." Why do you think Holmes rejected this approach in favor of a holding that, where the severity of the consequences of shifting the economic loss involved in improving "the public condition" from the public to the landowner becomes too great, the governmental objective cannot constitutionally be achieved unless just compensation is paid to the landowner? Was Holmes right in finding a duty to compensate where the exercise of the coal company's property right would clearly cause serious injury to occupied land and might well cause physical harm to its inhabitants? Would not the removal of supporting coal "pillars" constitute a "noxious" use of the coal company's property, tantamount to a nuisance, as Brandeis argued in his dissent? In light of Reinman v. Little Rock and Hadacheck v. Sebastian, was it not clear that the Kohler Act was a legitimate exercise of Pennsylvania's police power for the purpose of protecting the public safety and welfare, rather than a "taking" or "deprivation" of the coal company's property? Surely there is no "property right" in a "nuisance." Or was Holmes invoking the "unduly oppressive on individuals" test from Lawton v. Steele?

2. It has sometimes been said that Holmes' opinion in *Mahon* supports the use by the courts of "a balancing test—a weighing of the public benefits of the regulation against the extent of the loss of property values." Bosselman, Callies, and Banta, The Taking Issue 321 (Council on Environmental Quality, 1973). Do you think this is an accurate statement? How can one "balance" a very great danger to public health, safety, or general welfare against a governmental restriction that leaves a landowner with no "reasonable" use of his land and thus reduces its value almost to zero? Does either the Holmes or the Brandeis approach help you with this problem?

3. Even if we accept the Holmes thesis that, "while property may be regulated to a certain extent, if regulation goes too far it will be recognized as a taking," on what basis did Holmes find that the regulation went "too far" in *Mahon*? Was Brandeis not right in arguing that, "[i]f we are to consider the value of the coal kept in place by the restriction, we should compare it with the value of all other parts of the [coal company's] land"? In ignoring this point, did Holmes implicitly hold that requiring "pillars" of coal to be kept in place to support the surface was *ipso facto* a "taking," without regard to the relative value of the "pillars" and "all other parts of the land"?

4. In *Mahon*, Holmes said that "[t]o make it commercially impracticable to mine certain coal [i.e., the "pillars" required for surface support] has very nearly the same effect for constitutional purposes as appropriating or destroying

it." This statement was based on the fact the cost of providing artificial support in lieu of the "pillars" of coal would exceed the value of the "pillars." (See the coal company's argument, 260 U.S. at 395.) Is Holmes' statement consistent with the court's conclusion in Hadacheck v. Sebastian that there was no "taking" despite the fact that transportation of Hadacheck's brick clay to some other locality for manufacturing would be impractical "from a financial standpoint," since the Los Angeles ordinance only prohibited the manufacture of bricks and not the removal of the clay?

SECTION 2. "ZONING" AND OTHER GOVERNMENT RESTRICTIONS ON LAND USE

VILLAGE OF EUCLID v. AMBLER REALTY CO.

United States Supreme Court, 1926.
272 U.S. 365, 47 S.Ct. 114, 71 L.Ed. 303.

Mr. Justice SUTHERLAND delivered the opinion of the Court.

The Village of Euclid is an Ohio municipal corporation. It adjoins and practically is a suburb of the City of Cleveland. Its estimated population is between 5,000 and 10,000, and its area from twelve to fourteen square miles, the greater part of which if farm lands or unimproved acreage. It lies, roughly, in the form of a parallelogram measuring approximately three and one-half miles each way. East and west it is traversed by three principal highways: Euclid Avenue, through the southerly border, St. Clair Avenue, through the central portion, and Lake Shore Boulevard, through the northerly border in close proximity to the shore of Lake Erie. The Nickel Plate railroad lies from 1,500 to 1,800 feet north of Euclid Avenue, and the Lake Shore railroad 1,600 feet farther to the north. The three highways and the two railroads are substantially parallel.

Appellee is the owner of a tract of land containing 68 acres, situated in the westerly end of the village, abutting on Euclid Avenue to the south and the Nickel Plate railroad to the north. Adjoining this tract, both on the east and on the west, there have been laid out restricted residential plats upon which residences have been erected.

On November 13, 1922, an ordinance was adopted by the Village Council, establishing a comprehensive zoning plan for regulating and restricting the location of trades, industries, apartment houses, two-family houses, single family houses, etc., the lot area to be built upon, the size and height of buildings, etc.

The entire area of the village is divided by the ordinance into six classes of use districts, denominated U–1 to U–6, inclusive; three classes of height districts, denominated H–1 to H–3, inclusive; and four classes of area districts, denominated A–1 to A–4, inclusive. The use districts are classified in respect of the buildings which may be erected within their respective limits, as follows: U–1 is restricted to single family dwellings, public parks, water towers and reservoirs, suburban and interurban electric railway passenger stations and rights of way, and farming, non-commercial greenhouse nurseries and truck gardening; U–2 is extended to include two-family dwellings; U–3 is further extended to include apartment houses, hotels, churches, schools, public libraries, museums, private clubs, community center buildings, hospitals, sanitariums, public playgrounds and recreation buildings, and a city hall and courthouse; U–4 is further extended to include banks, offices, studios, telephone exchanges, fire and police stations, restaurants, theatres and moving picture shows, retail stores and shops, sales offices, sample rooms, wholesale stores for hardware, drugs and groceries, stations for gasoline and oil (not exceeding 1,000 gallons storage) and for ice delivery, skating rinks and dance halls, electric substations, job and newspaper printing, public garages for motor vehicles, stables and wagon sheds (not exceeding five horses, wagons or motor trucks) and distributing stations for central store and commercial enterprises; U–5 is further extended to include billboards and advertising signs (if permitted), warehouses, ice and ice cream manufacturing and cold storage plants, bottling works, milk bottling and central distribution stations, laundries, carpet cleaning, dry cleaning and dyeing establishments, blacksmith, horseshoeing, wagon and motor vehicle repair shops, freight stations, street car barns, stables and wagon sheds (for more than five horses, wagons or motor trucks), and wholesale produce markets and salesrooms; U–6 is further extended to include plants for sewage disposal and for producing gas, garbage and refuse incineration, scrap iron, junk, scrap paper and rag storage, aviation fields, cemeteries, crematories, penal and correctional institutions, insane and feeble minded institutions, storage of oil and gasoline (not to exceed 25,000 gallons), and manufacturing and industrial operations of any kind other than, and any public utility not included in, a class U–1, U–2, U–3, U–4 or U–5 use. There is a seventh class of uses which is prohibited altogether.

Class U–1 is the only district in which buildings are restricted to those enumerated. In the other classes the uses are cumulative; that is to say, uses in class U–2 include those enumerated in the preceding class, U–1; class U–3 includes uses enumerated in the preceding classes, U–2 and U–1; and so on. In addition to the enumerated uses, the ordinance provides for accessory uses, that is, for uses customarily incident to the principal use, such as private garages. Many regulations are provided in respect of such accessory uses.

The height districts are classified as follows: In class H–1, buildings are limited to a height of two and one-half stories or thirty-five feet; in class H–2, to four stories or fifty feet; in class H–3, to eighty feet. To all of these, certain exceptions are made, as in the case of church spires, water tanks, etc.

The classification of area districts is: In A–1 districts, dwellings or apartment houses to accommodate more than one family must have at least 5,000 square feet for interior lots and at least 4,000 square feet for corner lots; in A–2 districts, the area must be at least 2,500 square feet for interior lots, and 2,000 square feet for corner lots; in A–3 districts, the limits are 1,250 and 1,000 square feet, respectively; in A–4 districts, the limits are 900 and 700 square feet, respectively. The ordinance contains, in great variety and detail, provisions in respect of width of lots, front, side and rear yards, and other matters, including restrictions and regulations as to the use of bill boards, sign boards and advertising signs.

A single family dwelling consists of a basement and not less than three rooms and a bathroom. A two-family dwelling consists of a basement and not less than four living rooms and a bathroom for each family; and is further described as a detached dwelling for the occupation of two families, one having its principal living rooms on the first floor and the other on the second floor.

Appellee's tract of land comes under U–2, U–3 and U–6. The first strip of 620 feet immediately north of Euclid Avenue falls in class U–2, the next 130 feet to the north, in U–3, and the remainder in U–6. The uses of the first 620 feet, therefore, do not include apartment houses, hotels, churches, schools, or other public and semi-public buildings, or other uses enumerated in respect of U–3 to U–6, inclusive. The uses of the next 130 feet include all of these, but exclude industries, theatres, banks, shops, and the various other uses set forth in respect of U–4 to U–6, inclusive.*

Annexed to the ordinance, and made a part of it, is a zone map, showing the location and limits of the various use, height and area districts, from which it appears that the three classes overlap one another; that is to say, for example, both U–5 and U–6 use districts are in A–4 area districts, but the former is in H–2 and the latter in H–3 height districts. The plan is a complicated one and can be better understood by an inspection of the map, though it does not seem necessary to reproduce it for present purposes.

The lands lying between the two railroads for the entire length of the village area and extending some distance on either side to the north and south, having an average width of about 1,600 feet, are left open, with slight exceptions, for industrial and all other uses. This includes the larger part of appellee's tract. Approximately one-sixth of the area of the entire village is included in U–5 and U–6 use districts. That part of the village lying south of Euclid Avenue is principally in U–1 districts. The lands lying north of Euclid Avenue and bordering on the long strip just described are included in U–1, U–2, U–3 and U–4 districts, principally in U–2.

The enforcement of the ordinance is entrusted to the inspector of buildings, under rules and regulations of the board of zoning appeals. Meetings of the board are public, and minutes of its proceedings are

---

* The court below seemed to think that the frontage of this property on Euclid Avenue to a depth of 150 feet came under U–1 district and was available only for single family dwellings. An examination of the ordinance and subsequent amendments, and a comparison of their terms with the maps, shows very clearly, however, that this view was incorrect. Appellee's brief correctly interpreted the ordinance: "The northerly 500 feet thereof immediately adjacent to the right of way of the New York, Chicago & St. Louis Railroad Company under the original ordinance was classed as U–6 territory and the rest thereof as U–2 territory. By amendments to the ordinance a strip 630 [620] feet wide north of Euclid Avenue is classed as U–2 territory, a strip 130 feet wide next north as U–3 territory and the rest of the parcel to the Nickel Plate right of way as U–6 territory."

kept. It is authorized to adopt rules and regulations to carry into effect provisions of the ordinance. Decisions of the inspector of buildings may be appealed to the board by any person claiming to be adversely affected by any such decision. The board is given power in specific cases of practical difficulty or unnecessary hardship to interpret the ordinance in harmony with its general purpose and intent, so that the public health, safety and general welfare may be secure and substantial justice done. Penalties are prescribed for violations, and it is provided that the various provisions are to be regarded as independent and the holding of any provision to be unconstitutional, void or ineffective shall not affect any of the others.

The ordinance is assailed on the grounds that it is in derogation of § 1 of the Fourteenth Amendment to the Federal Constitution in that it deprives appellee of liberty and property without due process of law and denies it the equal protection of the law, and that it offends against certain provisions of the Constitution of the State of Ohio. The prayer of the bill is for an injunction restraining the enforcement of the ordinance and all attempts to impose or maintain as to appellee's property any of the restrictions, limitations or conditions. The court below held the ordinance to be unconstitutional and void, and enjoined its enforcement. 297 F. 307.

Before proceeding to a consideration of the case, it is necessary to determine the scope of the inquiry. The bill alleges that the tract of land in question is vacant and has been held for years for the purpose of selling and developing it for industrial uses, for which it is especially adapted, being immediately in the path of progressive industrial development; that for such uses it has a market value of about $10,000 per acre, but if the use be limited to residential purposes the market value is not in excess of $2,500 per acre; that the first 200 feet of the parcel back from Euclid Avenue, if unrestricted in respect of use, has a value of $150 per front foot, but if limited to residential uses, and ordinary mercantile business be excluded therefrom, its value is not in excess of $50 per front foot.

It is specifically averred that the ordinance attempts to restrict and control the lawful uses of appellee's land so as to confiscate and destroy a great part of its value; that it is being enforced in accordance with its terms; that prospective buyers of land for industrial, commercial and residential uses in the metropolitan district of Cleveland are deterred from buying any part of this land because of the existence of the ordinance and the necessity thereby entailed of conducting burdensome and expensive litigation in order to vindicate the right to use the land for lawful and legitimate purposes; that the ordinance constitutes a cloud upon the land, reduces and destroys its value, and has the effect of diverting the normal industrial, commerical and residential development thereof to other and less favorable locations.

The record goes no farther than to show, as the lower court found, that the normal, and reasonably to be expected, use and development of that part of appellee's land adjoining Euclid Avenue is for general trade and commercial purposes, particularly retail stores and like establishments, and that the normal, and reasonably to be expected, use and development of the residue of the land is for industrial and trade purposes. Whatever injury is inflicted by the mere existence and threatened enforcement of the ordinance is due to restrictions in respect of these and similar uses; to which perhaps should be added—if not included in the foregoing—restrictions in respect of apartment houses. Specifically, there is nothing in the record to suggest that any damage results from the presence in the ordinance of those restrictions relating to churches, schools, libraries and other public and semi-public buildings. It is neither alleged nor proved that there is, or may be, a demand for any part of appellee's land for any of the last named uses; and we cannot assume the existence of facts which would justify an injunction upon this record in respect of this class of restrictions. For present purposes the provisions of the ordinance in respect of these uses may, therefore, be put aside as unnecessary to be considered. It is also unnecessary to consider the effect of the restrictions in respect of U–1 districts, since none of appellee's land falls within that class.

We proceed, then, to a consideration of those provisions of the ordinance to which the case as it is made relates, first disposing of a preliminary matter.

A motion was made in the court below to dismiss the bill on the ground that, because complainant [appellee] had made no effort to obtain a building permit or apply to the zoning board of appeals for relief as it might have done under the terms of the ordinance, the suit was premature. The motion was properly overruled. The effect of the allegations of the bill is that the ordinance of its own force operates greatly to reduce the value of appellee's lands and destroy their marketability for industrial, commercial and residential uses; and the attack is directed, not against any specific provision or provisions, but against the ordinance as an entirety. Assuming the premises, the existence and maintenance of the ordinance, in effect, constitutes a present invasion of appellee's property rights and a threat to continue it. Under these circumstances, the equitable jurisdiction is clear. * * *

It is not necessary to set forth the provisions of the Ohio Constitution which are thought to be infringed. The question is the same under both Constitutions, namely, as stated by appellee: Is the ordinance invalid in that it violates the constitutional protection "to the right of property in the appellee by attempted regulations under the guise of the police power, which are unreasonable and confiscatory?"

Building zone laws are of modern origin. They began in this country about twenty-five years ago. Until recent years, urban life was comparatively simple; but with the great increase and concentration of population, problems have developed, and constantly are developing, which require, and will continue to require, additional restrictions in respect of the use and occupation of private lands in urban communities. Regulations, the wisdom, necessity and validity of which, as applied to existing conditions, are so apparent that they are now uniformly sustained, a century ago, or even half a century ago, probably would have been rejected as arbitrary and oppressive. Such regulations are sustained, under the complex conditions of our day, for reasons analogous to those which justify traffic regulations, which, before the advent of automobiles and rapid transit street railways, would have been condemned as fatally arbitrary and unreasonable. And in this there is no inconsistency, for while the meaning of constitutional guaranties never varies, the scope of their application must expand or contract to meet the new and different conditions which are constantly coming within the field of their operation. In a changing world, it is impossible that it should be otherwise. But although a degree of elasticity is thus imparted, not to the *meaning*, but to the *application* of constitutional principles, statutes and ordinances, which, after giving due weight to the new conditions, are found clearly not to conform to the Constitution, of course, must fall.

The ordinance now under review, and all similar laws and regulations, must find their justification in some aspect of the police power, asserted for the public welfare. The line which in this field separates the legitimate from the illegitimate assumption of power is not capable of precise delimitation. It varies with circumstances and conditions. A regulatory zoning ordinance, which would be clearly valid as applied to the great cities, might be clearly invalid as applied to rural communities. In solving doubts, the maxim *sic utere tuo ut alienum non laedas*, which lies at the foundation of so much of the common law of nuisances, ordinarily will furnish a fairly helpful clew. And the law of nuisances, likewise, may be consulted, not for the purpose of controlling, but for the helpful aid of its analogies in the process of ascertaining the scope of, the power. Thus the question whether the power exists to forbid the erection of a building of a particular kind or for a particular use, like the question whether a particular thing is a nuisance, is to be determined, not by an abstract consideration of the building or of the thing considered apart, but by considering it in connection with the circumstances and the locality. Sturgis v. Bridgeman, L.R. 11 Ch. 852, 865. A nuisance may be merely a right thing in the wrong place,—like a pig in the parlor instead of the barnyard. If the validity of the legislative classification for zoning purposes be fairly debatable, the legislative judgment must be allowed to control. Radice v. New York, 264 U.S. 292, 294, 44 S.Ct. 325, 68 L.Ed. 690.

There is no serious difference of opinion in respect of the validity of laws and regulations fixing the height of buildings within reasonable limits, the character of materials and methods of construction, and the adjoining area which must be left open, in order to minimize the danger of fire or collapse, the evils of over-crowding, and the like, and excluding from residential sections offensive trades, industries and structures likely to create nuisances. See Welch v. Swasey, 214 U.S. 91, 29 S.Ct. 567, 53 L.Ed. 923; Hadacheck v. Los Angeles, 239 U.S. 394, 36 S.Ct. 143, 60 L.Ed. 349; Reinman v. Little Rock, 237 U.S. 171, 35 S.Ct. 511, 59 L.Ed. 900; Cusack Co. v. City of Chicago, 242 U.S. 526, 529–530, 37 S.Ct. 190, 61 L.Ed. 472.

Here, however, the exclusion is in general terms of all industrial establishments, and it may thereby happen that not only offensive or dangerous industries will be excluded, but those which are neither offensive nor dangerous will share the same fate. But this is no more than happens in respect of many practice-forbidding laws which this Court has upheld although drawn in general terms so as to include individual cases that may turn out to be innocuous in themselves. Hebe Co. v. Shaw, 248 U.S. 297, 303, 39 S.Ct. 125, 63 L.Ed. 255; Pierce Oil Corp. v. City of Hope, 248 U.S. 498, 500, 39 S.Ct. 172, 63 L.Ed. 381. The inclusion of a reasonable margin to insure effective enforcement, will not put upon a law, otherwise valid, the stamp of invalidity. Such laws may also find their justification in the fact that, in some fields, the bad fades into the good by such insensible degrees that the two are not capable of being readily distinguished and separated in terms of legislation. In the light of these considerations, we are not prepared to say that the end in view was not sufficient to justify the general rule of the ordinance, although some industries of an innocent character might fall within the proscribed class. It can not be said that the ordinance in this respect "passes the bounds of reason and assumes the character of a merely arbitrary fiat." Purity Extract Co. v. Lynch, 226 U.S. 192, 204, 33 S.Ct. 44, 47, 57 L.Ed. 184. Moreover, the restrictive provisions of the ordinance in this particular may be sustained upon the principles applicable to the broader exclusion from residential districts of all business and trade structures, presently to be discussed.

It is said that the Village of Euclid is a mere suburb of the City of Cleveland; that the industrial development of that city has now reached and in some degree extended into the village and, in the obvious course of things, will soon absorb the entire area for industrial enterprises; that the effect of the ordinance is to divert this natural development elsewhere with the consequent loss of increased values to the owners of the lands within the village borders. But the village, though physically a suburb of Cleveland, is politically a separate municipality, with powers of its own and authority to govern itself as it sees fit within the limits of the organic law of its creation and the State and Federal Constitutions. Its governing authorities, presumably representing a majority of its inhabitants and voicing their will, have determined, not that industrial development shall cease at its boundaries, but that the course of such development shall proceed within definitely fixed lines. If it be a proper exercise of the police power to relegate industrial establishments to localities separated from residential sections, it is not easy to find a sufficient reason for denying the power because the effect of its exercise is to divert an industrial flow from the course which it would follow, to the injury of the residential public if left alone, to another course where such injury will be obviated. It is not meant by this, however, to exclude the possibility of cases where the general public interest would so far outweigh the interest of the municipality that the municipality would not be allowed to stand in the way.

We find no difficulty in sustaining restrictions of the kind thus far reviewed. The serious question in the case arises over the provisions of the ordinance excluding from residential districts, apartment houses, business houses, retail stores and shops, and other like establishments.

This question involves the validity of what is really the crux of the more recent zoning legislation, namely, the creation and maintenance of residential districts, from which business and trade of every sort, including hotels and apartment houses, are excluded. Upon that question this Court has not thus far spoken. The decisions of the state courts are numerous and conflicting; but those which broadly sustain the power greatly outnumber those which deny altogether or narrowly limit it; and it is very apparent that there is a constantly increasing tendency in the direction of the broader view. * * *

As evidence of the decided trend toward the broader view, it is significant that in some instances the state courts in later decisions have reversed their former decisions holding the other way. * * *

The decisions enumerated in the first group cited above agree that the exclusion of buildings devoted to business, trade, etc., from residential districts, bears a rational relation to the health and safety of the community. Some of the grounds for this conclusion are—promotion of the health and security from injury of children and others by separating dwelling houses from territory devoted to trade and industry; suppression and prevention of disorder; facilitating the extinguishment of fires, and the enforcement of street traffic regulations and other general welfare ordinances; aiding the health and safety of the community by excluding from residential areas the confusion and danger of fire, contagion and disorder which in greater or less degree attach to the location of stores, shops and factories. Another ground is that the construction and repair of streets may be rendered easier and less expensive by confining the greater part of the heavy traffic to the streets where business is carried on. * * *

The matter of zoning has received much attention at the hands of commissions and experts, and the results of their investigations have been set forth in comprehensive reports. These reports, which bear every evidence of painstaking consideration, concur in the view that the segregation of residential, business, and industrial buildings will make it easier to provide fire apparatus suitable for the character and intensity of the development in each section; that it will increase the safety and security of home life; greatly tend to prevent street accidents, especially to children, by reducing the traffic and resulting confusion in residential sections; decrease noise and other conditions which produce or intensify nervous disorders; preserve a more favorable environment in which to rear children, etc. With particular reference to apartment houses, it is pointed out that the development of detached house sections is greatly retarded by the coming of apartment houses, which has sometimes resulted in destroying the entire section for private house purposes; that in such sections very often the apartment house is a mere parasite, constructed in order to take advantage of the open spaces and attractive surroundings created by the residential character of the district. Moreover, the coming of one apartment house is followed by others, interfering by their height and bulk with the free circulation of air and monopolizing the rays of the sun which otherwise would fall upon the smaller homes, and bringing, as their necessary accompaniments, the disturbing noises incident to increased traffic and business, and the occupation, by means of moving and parked automobiles, of larger portions of the streets, thus detracting from their safety and depriving children of the privilege of quiet and open spaces for play, enjoyed by those in more favorable localities,—until, finally, the residential character of the neighborhood and its desirability as a place of detached residences are utterly destroyed. Under these circumstances, apartment houses, which in a different environment would be not only entirely unobjectionable but highly desirable, come very near to being nuisances.

If these reasons, thus summarized, do not demonstrate the wisdom or sound policy in all respects of those restrictions which we have indicated as pertinent to the inquiry, at least, the reasons are sufficiently cogent to preclude us from saying, as it must be said before the ordinance can be declared unconstitutional, that such provisions are clearly arbitrary and unreasonable, having no substantial relation to the public health, safety, morals, or general welfare. Cusack Co. v. City of Chicago, supra, pp. 530–531; Jacobson v. Massachusetts, 197 U.S. 11, 30–31, 25 S.Ct. 358, 49 L.Ed. 643.

It is true that when, if ever, the provisions set forth in the ordinance in tedious and minute detail, come to be concretely applied to particular premises, including those of the appellee, or to particular conditions, or to be considered in connection with specific complaints, some of them, or even many of them, may be found to be clearly arbitrary and unreasonable. But where the equitable remedy of injunction is sought, as it is here, not upon the ground of a present infringement or denial of a specific right, or of a particular injury in process of actual execution, but upon the broad ground that the mere existence and threatened enforcement of the ordinance, by materially and adversely affecting values and curtailing the opportunities of the market, constitute a present and irreparable injury, the court will not scrutinize its provisions, sentence by sentence, to ascertain by a process of piecemeal dissection whether there may be, here and there, provisions of a minor character, cr relating to matters of administration, or not shown to contribute to the injury complained of, which, if attacked separately, might not withstand the test of constitutionality. In respect of such provisions, of which specific complaint is not made, it cannot be said that the land owner has suffered or is threatened with an injury which entitles him to challenge their constitutionality. * * *

 * * * What would be the effect of a restraint imposed by one or more of the innumerable provisions of the ordinance, considered apart, upon the value or marketability of the lands is neither disclosed by the bill nor by the evidence, and we are afforded no basis, apart from mere speculation, upon which to rest a conclusion that it or they would have any appreciable effect upon those matters. Under these circumstances, therefore, it is enough for us to determine, as we do, that the ordinance in its general scope and dominant features, so far as its provisions are here involved, is a valid exercise of authority, leaving other provisions to be dealt with as cases arise directly involving them.

And this is in accordance with the traditional policy of this Court. In the realm of constitutional law, especially, this Court has perceived the embarrassment which is likely to result from an attempt to formulate rules or decide questions beyond the necessities of the immediate issue. It has preferred to follow the method of a gradual approach to the general by a systematically guarded application and extension of constitutional principles to particular cases as they arise, rather than by out of hand attempts to establish general rules to which future cases must be fitted. This process applies with peculiar force to the solution of questions arising under the due process clause of the Constitution as applied to the exercise of the flexible powers of police, with which we are here concerned.

Decree reversed.

Mr. Justice VAN DEVANTER, Mr. Justice McREYNOLDS and Mr. Justice BUTLER, dissent.

Notes

1. The Euclid "building zone" ordinance sustained against constitutional attack in the principal case was modelled on the New York City Building Zone Resolution of 1916. The latter was adopted by the New York City Board of Estimate after three years of careful investigation and study. It comprised a complete, comprehensive system of land use control for the five boroughs of the city, establishing restrictions on the use of land and buildings, the height of buildings, and the amount or percentage of a lot that might be occupied by a building, within designated districts or zones. The resolution provided for three separate classes of districts, regulating "use," height, and land coverage, each expressed in a separate set of maps. "Use" districts were divided into residence districts, business districts, and unrestricted districts. In residence districts, trade and industry of every kind were prohibited. In business districts, specified trades and industries—mainly nuisance types of industry such as boiler-making, ammonia manufacturing, and paint manufacturing—were prohibited. In unrestricted districts any kind of industrial, business, or residential use was permitted. The provisions of the resolution were prospective rather than retroactive in effect; the resolution was intended to furnish a rational basis for future building development in New York City.

Although ordinances like the New York City Building Zone Resolution of 1916 were often called "districting" ordinances in the period immediately after the New York City resolution was adopted, they subsequently came to be called "zoning" ordinances.

2. "Zoning" spread rapidly after 1916. By 1926 some 420 municipalities with a total population of more than 27,000,000 had adopted zoning ordinances, and hundreds of other municipalities were engaged in preparation of zoning ordinances. But judicial acceptance of zoning was far from unanimous prior to 1926. Decisions favorable to the constitutionality of zoning had been rendered by the highest courts of California, Illinois, Kansas, Louisiana, Massachusetts, Minnesota, New York, Ohio, Oregon, and Wisconsin. Adverse decisions had been rendered by the highest courts of Delaware, Georgia, Maryland, Missouri, and New Jersey. The favorable decision of the United States Supreme Court in the principal case removed doubts as to the validity of zoning—in general, at least—under the United States Constitution. Within a relatively few years, zoning had been held valid in every state, although constitutional amendments

were necessary to validate zoning in states where it had been held invalid under state constitutional provisions.

3.   In deciding the *Euclid* case, why did the court substantially ignore the Ambler Realty Company's contention that the effect of the Euclid zoning ordinance was to reduce the market value of its land by somewhere between two-thirds and three-fourths?   Should not this contention have been considered in deciding whether the ordinance "deprived" the Realty Company of its property "without due process of law" under the test laid down in Lawton v. Steele, or a "taking" of its property under the rule laid down in the *Mahon* case?

4.   Shortly after Euclid, the United States Supreme Court decided two other important "zoning" cases.   In Gorieb v. Fox, 274 U.S. 603, 47 S.Ct. 675, 71 L.Ed. 1228 (1927), the court sustained an ordinance creating a set-back or building line for all lots in "business" and "residential" districts.   In Nectow v. City of Cambridge, 277 U.S. 183, 48 S.Ct. 447, 72 L.Ed. 842 (1928), the court invalidated a "residential" classification as applied to specific property, although the Cambridge zoning ordinance was conceded, in its general scope, to be constitutional under *Euclid.*   In *Gorieb*, the court said:

" *   *   *   [W]e recently have held, Euclid v. Ambler, *   *   *   that comprehensive zoning laws and ordinances prescribing, among other things, the height of buildings to be erected *   *   *   and the extent of the area to be left open for light and air and in aid of fire protection, etc., are, in their general scope, valid under the federal Constitution.   It is hard to see any controlling difference between regulations which require the lot-owner to leave open areas at the sides and rear of his house and limit the extent of his use of the space above his lot and a regulation which requires him to set his building a reasonable distance back from the street.   Each interferes in the same way, if not to the same extent, with the owner's general right of dominion over his property. All rest for their justification upon the same reasons which have arisen in recent times as a result of the great increase and concentration of population in urban communities and the vast changes in the extent and complexities of the problems of modern city life.

In *Nectow*, the court relied heavily on the express finding of the master appointed by the trial court that the health, safety, convenience and general welfare of the inhabitants of the part of the city affected would not be promoted by the "residential" zoning of the locus in question, supported by other findings of fact and confirmed by the trial court.   In reaching its decision, the court said it was also clearly established that the invasion of the plaintiff's property rights was "serious and highly injurious," and "since a necessary basis for the support of that invasion is wanting, the action of the zoning authorities comes within the ban of the Fourteenth Amendment and cannot be sustained."

Nectow seemed to foreshadow a continuing oversight of local zoning by the Supreme Court in cases where it was alleged that zoning regulations, "concretely applied to particular premises" were "clearly arbitrary and unreasonable."   But, in fact, the United States Supreme Court did not review any zoning cases between 1928 and 1974, when it decided Village of Belle Terre v. Boraas, reprinted infra at p. 1101.   For a thorough review of zoning law with emphasis on constitutional issues, see Developments in the Law—Zoning, 91 Harv.L.Rev. 1427–1708 (1978).

5.   Although some municipalities adopted zoning ordinances without waiting for enactment of enabling legislation, it was generally thought—and occasionally held by a court—that specific enabling legislation was necessary. Most of the state zoning enabling acts adopted prior to 1923 were modelled on the New York general city enabling act of 1917, which in turn was based on the

special enabling act of 1914 conferring zoning authority on New York City. In January, 1923, however, the United States Department of Commerce published the first draft of a Standard State Zoning Enabling Act which departed substantially in some respects from the New York models. This Standard Act, revised and republished in 1924 and again in 1926, was the model for most of the zoning enabling legislation adopted between 1923 and World War II. At the present time all of the 50 states have zoning enabling legislation for municipalities and 37 states have zoning enabling legislation for counties. Although current zoning acts often embody substantial changes from the original enabling acts, the majority of current municipal zoning acts still retains the substance of the Standard Act.

The Standard State Zoning Enabling Act is set out below.

A STANDARD STATE ZONING ENABLING ACT *

Section 1. Grant of Power. For the purpose of promoting health, safety, morals, or the general welfare of the community, the legislative body of cities and incorporated villages is hereby empowered to regulate and restrict the height, number of stories, and size of buildings and other structures, the percentage of lot that may be occupied, the size of yards, courts, and other open spaces, the density of population, and the location and use of buildings, structures, and land for trade, industry, residence, or other purposes.

Sec. 2. Districts. For any or all of said purposes the local legislative body may divide the municipality into districts of such number, shape, and area as may be deemed best suited to carry out the purposes of this act; and within such districts it may regulate and restrict the erection, construction, reconstruction, alteration, repair, or use of buildings, structures, or land. All such regulations shall be uniform for each class or kind of buildings throughout each district, but the regulations in one district may differ from those in other districts.

Sec. 3. Purposes in View. Such regulations shall be made in accordance with a comprehensive plan and designed to lessen congestion in the streets; to secure safety from fire, panic, and other dangers; to promote health and the general welfare; to provide adequate light and air; to prevent the overcrowding of land; to avoid undue concentration of population; to facilitate the adequate provision of transportation, water, sewerage, schools, parks, and other public requirements. Such regulations shall be made with reasonable consideration, among other things, to the character of the district and its peculiar suitability for particular uses, and with a view to conserving the value of buildings and encouraging the most appropriate use of land throughout such municipality.

Sec. 4. Method of Procedure. The legislative body of such municipality shall provide for the manner in which such regulations and restrictions and the boundaries of such districts shall be determined, es-

---

* The draftsmen's footnotes have been omitted. The Standard State Zoning Enabling Act is no longer in print in its original form as a publication of the U.S. Department of Commerce, but it is reprinted in full, with the draftsmen's footnotes as Appendix A, in American Law Institute, A Model Land Development Code, Tentative Draft No. 1, at p. 210 (April 24, 1968).

tablished, and enforced, and from time to time amended, supplemented, or changed. However, no such regulation, restriction, or boundary shall become effective until after a public hearing in relation thereto, at which parties in interest and citizens shall have an opportunity to be heard. At least 15 days' notice of the time and place of such hearing shall be published in an official paper, or a paper of general circulation, in such municipality.

Sec. 5. Changes. Such regulations, restrictions, and boundaries may from time to time be amended, supplemented, changed, modified, or repealed. In case, however, of a protest against such change, signed by the owners of 20 per cent or more either of the area of the lots included in such proposed change, or of those immediately adjacent in the rear thereof extending _____ feet therefrom, or of those directly opposite thereto extending _____ feet from the street frontage of such opposite lots, such amendment shall not become effective except by the favorable vote of three-fourths of all the members of the legislative body of such municipality. The provisions of the previous section relative to public hearings and official notice shall apply equally to all changes or amendments.

Sec. 6. Zoning Commission. In order to avail itself of the powers conferred by this act, such legislative body shall appoint a commission, to be known as the zoning commission, to recommend the boundaries of the various original districts and appropriate regulations to be enforced therein. Such commission shall make a preliminary report and hold public hearings thereon before submitting its final report, and such legislative body shall not hold its public hearings or take action until it has received the final report of such commission. Where a city plan commission already exists, it may be appointed as the zoning commission.

Sec. 7. Board of Adjustment. Such local legislative body may provide for the appointment of a board of adjustment, and in the regulations and restrictions adopted pursuant to the authority of this act may provide that the said board of adjustment may, in appropriate cases and subject to appropriate conditions and safeguards, make special exceptions to the terms of the ordinance in harmony with its general purpose and intent and in accordance with general or specific rules therein contained.

The board of adjustment shall consist of five members, each to be appointed for a term of three years and removable for cause by the appointing authority upon written charges and after public hearing. Vacancies shall be filled for the unexpired term of any member whose term becomes vacant.

The board shall adopt rules in accordance with the provisions of any ordinance adopted pursuant to this act. Meetings of the board shall be held at the call of the chairman and at such other times as the board may determine. Such chairman, or in his absence the acting chairman, may administer oaths and compel the attendance of witnesses. All meetings of the board shall be open to the public. The board shall keep minutes of its proceedings, showing the vote of each member upon each question, or, if absent or failing to vote, indicating such fact, and shall keep records of its examinations and other official actions, all of which shall be immediately filed in the office of the board and shall be a public record.

Appeals to the board of adjustment may be taken by any person aggrieved or by any officer, department, board, or bureau of the municipality affected by any decision of the administrative officer. Such appeal shall be taken within a reasonable time, as provided by the rules of the board, by filing with the officer from whom the appeal is taken and with the board of adjustment a notice of appeal specifying the grounds thereof. The officer from whom the appeal is taken shall forthwith transmit to the board all the papers constituting the record upon which the action appealed from was taken.

An appeal stays all proceedings in furtherance of the action appealed from, unless the officer from whom the appeal is taken certifies to the board of adjustment after the notice of appeal shall have been filed with him that by reason of facts stated in the certificate a stay would, in his opinion, cause imminent peril to life or property. In such case proceedings shall not be stayed otherwise than by a restraining order which may be granted by the board of adjustment or by a court of record on application on notice to the officer from whom the appeal is taken and on due cause shown.

The board of adjustment shall fix a reasonable time for the hearing of the appeal, give public notice thereof, as well as due notice to the parties in interest, and decide the same within a reasonable time. Upon the hearing any party may appear in person or by agent or by attorney.

The board of adjustment shall have the following powers:

1. To hear and decide appeals where it is alleged there is error in any order, requirement, decision, or determination made by an administrative official in the enforcement of this act or of any ordinance adopted pursuant thereto.

2. To hear and decide special exceptions to the terms of the ordinance upon which such board is required to pass under such ordinance.

3. To authorize upon appeal in specific cases such variance from the terms of the ordinance as will not be contrary to the public interest, where, owing to special conditions, a literal enforcement of the provisions of the ordinance will result in unnecessary hardship, and so that the spirit of the ordinance shall be observed and substantial justice done.

In exercising the above-mentioned powers such board may, in conformity with the provisions of this act, reverse or affirm, wholly or partly, or may modify the order, requirement, decision, or determination appealed from and may make such order, requirement, decision, or determination as ought to be made, and to that end shall have all the powers of the officer from whom the appeal is taken.

The concurring vote of four members of the board shall be necessary to reverse any order, requirement, decision, or determination of any such administrative official, or to decide in favor of the applicant on any matter upon which it is required to pass under any such ordinance, or to effect any variation in such ordinance.

Any person or persons, jointly or severally, aggrieved by any decision of the board of adjustment, or any taxpayer, or any officer, department, board, or bureau of the municipality, may present to a court of record a petition, duly verified, setting forth that such decision is illegal, in whole or in part, specifying the grounds of the illegality. Such petition shall be presented to the court within 30 days after the filing of the decision in the office of the board.

Upon the presentation of such petition the court may allow a writ of certiorari directed to the board of adjustment to review such decision of the board of adjustment and shall prescribe therein the time within which a return thereto must be made and served upon the relator's attorney, which shall not be less than 10 days and may be extended by the court. The allowance of the writ shall not stay proceedings upon the decision appealed from, but the court may, on application, on notice to the board and on due cause shown, grant a restraining order.

The board of adjustment shall not be required to return the original papers acted upon by it, but it shall be sufficient to return certified or sworn copies thereof or of such portions thereof as may be called for by such writ. The return shall concisely set forth such other facts as may be pertinent and material to show the grounds of the decision appealed from and shall be verified.

If, upon the hearing, it shall appear to the court that testimony is necessary for the proper disposition of the matter, it may take evidence or appoint a referee to take such evidence as it may direct and report the same to the court with his findings of fact and conclusions of law, which shall constitute a part of the proceedings upon which the determination of the court shall be made. The court may reverse or affirm, wholly or partly, or may modify the decision brought up for review.

Costs shall not be allowed against the board unless it shall appear to the court that it acted with gross negligence, or in bad faith, or with malice in making the decision appealed from.

All issues in any proceeding under this section shall have preference over all other civil actions and proceedings.

Sec. 8. Enforcement and Remedies. The local legislative body may provide by ordinance for the enforcement of this act and of any ordinance or regulation made thereunder. A violation of this act or of such ordinance or regulation is hereby declared to be a misdemeanor, and such local legislative body may provide for the punishment thereof by fine or imprisonment or both. It is also empowered to provide civil penalties for such violation.

In case any building or structure is erected, constructed, reconstructed, altered, repaired, converted, or maintained, or any building, structure, or land is used in violation of this act or of any ordinance or other regulation made under authority conferred hereby, the proper local authorities of the municipality, in addition to other remedies, may institute any appropriate action or proceedings to prevent such unlawful erection, construction, reconstruction, alteration, repair, conversion, mainte-nance, or use, to restrain, correct, or abate such violation, to prevent the occupancy of said building, structure, or land, or to prevent any illegal act, conduct, business, or use in or about such premises.

Sec. 9. Conflict with other Laws. Wherever the regulations made under authority of this act require a greater width or size of yards, courts, or other open spaces, or require a lower height of building or less number of stories, or require a greater percentage of lot to be left unoccupied, or impose other higher standards than are required in any other statute or local ordinance or regulation, the provisions of the reg-ulations made under authority of this act shall govern. Wherever the provisions of any other statute or local ordinance or regulation require a greater width or size of yards, courts, or other open spaces, or require a lower height of building or a less number of stories, or require a greater percentage of lot to be left unoccupied, or impose other higher standards than are required by the regulations made under authority of this act, the provisions of such statute or local ordinance or regulation shall govern.

Note on County, Regional, and State Land Use Controls

The power to control land use by "zoning" has been exercised by local gov-ernment units since the inception of zoning in the early years of the twentieth century. The Standard State Zoning Enabling Act, supra, gave the zoning pow-er only to "cities and incorporated villages." A few zoning enabling acts au-thorize municipalities to zone unincorporated areas outside their boundaries, but extra-territorial zoning is not common. The constitutionality of extra-terri-torial zoning is still open to serious question; and, in any case, the power can-not be used in metropolitan areas where all or most of the land is already with-in the corporate limits of one municipality or another.

At least thirty-seven states currently have county zoning enabling legisla-tion. In Maryland, the zoning power is exercised exclusively at the county level except for the City of Baltimore, and county zoning has been extensively uti-lized in California.[1] In general, however, counties have not been able to exer-cise the zoning power effectively in metropolitan areas because (1) they cannot zone areas within municipal corporation boundaries; (2) many metropolitan ar-eas contain two or more counties; and (3) many counties are not well organized administratively to perform urban zoning functions.

1. See, e.g., Cal.Gov.Code § 65850 (West 1965):

Pursuant to the provisions of this chap-ter, the legislative body of any county or city by ordinance may:

(a) Regulate the use of buildings, struc-tures and land as between industry, busi-ness, residents, open space, including agri-culture, recreation, enjoyment of scenic beauty and use of natural resources, and other purposes.

(b) Regulate signs and billboards.

(c) Regulate location, height, bulk, num-ber of stories and size of buildings and structures; the size and use of lots, yards, courts and other open spaces; the percent-age of a lot which may be occupied by a building or structure; the intensity of land use.

(d) Establish requirements for off-street parking and loading.

(e) Establish and maintain building set-back lines.

(f) Create civic districts around civic cen-ters, public parks, public buildings or pub-lic grounds and establish regulations therefor.

A possible solution of the problem of zoning in metropolitan areas would be to establish metropolitan regional governments with comprehensive land use planning and zoning powers. At the present time, however, there are only four such regional governments in the United States,[2] and the prospects for creation of more are not encouraging. Thus, although regional planning agencies have existed in some states for more than half a century, there is in most states no agency with power to implement regional land use plans by adopting appropriate zoning and other land use control regulations. Most of the enabling legislation simply authorizes the creation of regional planning agencies but does not make it mandatory;[3] and in no state are local government units required to conform their zoning regulations to the regional land use plan, even if one has been formulated by the regional planning agency.

In recent years there has been much discussion of the need for state governments to "take back" the zoning power—in part, at least—in order to deal effectively with problems of regional and state-wide concern. The first state to do this is Hawaii. In 1961 state-wide zoning power was given to the State Land

2. All of these "regional" governments involve either the consolidation of a central city and the county in which it is located—as in Indianapolis-Marion County, Indiana, Nashville-Davidson County, Tennessee, and Jacksonville-Duval County, Florida—or a federation of a metropolitan county with its constituent municipalities—as in Dade County, Florida (which includes Miami). For discussion of these "regional" governments, see Sofen, The Miami Metropolitan Experiment (2d ed. 1966); Bollens & Schmandt, The Metropolis: Its People, Politics, and Economic Life 327–35 (2d ed. 1970); Advisory Commission on Intergovernmental Relations, Substate Regionalism and the Federal System, Vol. II (Case Studies, 1973).

3. The Standard City Planning Enabling Act, Title IV (U.S. Department of Commerce, 1928), contained provisions for "regional planning and planning commissions." Section 26 of the Act empowered the governor to establish "a region for planning purposes" and to appoint "a regional planning commission for such region" upon petition from the planning commission of any municipality, the county commissioners of any county, "or any 100 citizens." Although the Standard Act's authorization for regional planning was adopted in a number of jurisdictions, the number of regional planning agencies created over the past fifty years pursuant to such authorization is miniscule.

Since World War II regional planning has been heavily influenced by federal legislation. Section 701 of the federal Housing Act offers assistance for comprehensive regional planning not tied to specific program requirements. Other federal legislation is tied to specific federally funded public improvement projects—e.g., under the federal Water Pollution Control Act water quality planning on an area-wide ba-

sis is required as a condition of obtaining federal aid for construction of wastewater treatment plants. Federal legislation has also influenced the governmental structure under which regional planning is carried out. The structure favored by the federal government is the Council of Governments, a voluntary association of local governments which has increasingly been given regional planning responsibilities by federal legislation. Section 208 of the federal Water Pollution Control Act, e.g., designated the Councils of Government as the appropriate regional planning agencies, and they have also been so designated for transportation planning under the federal-aid Highway Act and the Urban Mass Transportation Act.

Probably the most successful regional planning agency so far established is the Metropolitan Council for the Twin Cities Area in Minnesota. Under the authorizing legislation the members of the Metropolitan Council are appointed by the Governor, so the Metropolitan Council does not technically qualify as a Council of Governments. But the Metropolitan Council has been given planning and implementation powers far greater than those possessed by comparable regional planning agencies elsewhere. For additional discussion of the Twin Cities system, see Reichert, Growth Management in the Twin Cities Metropolitan Area: The Development Framework Planning Process (1976); Advisory Commission on Intergovernmental Relations, Substate Regionalism and the Federal System, Vol. II, ch. IV (Case Studies, 1973); Freilich & Ragsdale, Timing and Sequential Controls—The Essential Basis for Effective Regional Planning: An Analysis of the New Directions for Land Use Control in the Minneapolis-St. Paul Metropolitan Region, 58 Minn.L.Rev. 1009 (1974).

Use Commission by the Hawaii Land Use Law.[4] Pursuant to the 1961 legislation, the Commission has divided the entire state into four districts—urban, rural agricultural, and conservation. But the counties were left with authority to formulate comprehensive land use plans and to enact zoning ordinances, and a kind of two-way veto was created: the Commission could change district boundaries but could not compel the counties to make appropriate planning and zoning ordinance changes; and the counties could show areas for various types of land use on their comprehensive plans (adopted by all four counties) and zoning maps but could not compel the Commission to make appropriate district boundary changes. A great deal of tension developed between the Commission and the counties as a result of pressures for expansion of the original urban district into the agricultural district on Oahu. Recent changes in the 1961 legislation have weakened the power of the Commission as the dominant agency in controlling land development in Hawaii.

The Vermont Environmental Control Law of 1970 [5] was a response to pressures from the "second-home" boom and several major industrial developments during the 1960s. While the Hawaii Land Use Law adopts the conventional districting approach used in most local zoning ordinances, the 1970 Vermont legislation sets up a state permit system for major developments throughout the state. Residential, commercial, and industrial developments on sites of more than ten acres must obtain state permits; and if the municipality having jurisdiction of the site has not adopted permanent zoning and subdivision control regulations, a state permit must be obtained for any development on a site of one acre or more. Applications for state permits are reviewed on the basis of statutory criteria aimed at evaluation of the impact of a particular development at the proposed site. Since local approval is also required, the Vermont legislation can also be said to create a double veto system. The legislation also calls for legislative adoption of a state plan to guide the permit approval process, but political differences have so far prevented adoption of such a plan.

The recently completed American Law Institute Model Land Development Code contains provisions for state land use controls intended to be generally applicable anywhere in the United States.[6] These Model Code provisions are in response to perceived weaknesses in the local land use control system and are not intended as a response to any particular environmental or other problem. There are two major components in the Model Code's state land use control system: (a) the designation of areas of critical state concern and the review of local land use regulations applicable within these areas for consistency with the developmental policies adopted by the state land use control agency for such areas; (b) a review process at the state level for "major development"—development of regional impact or benefit—which is disapproved by a local land use control agency. State review of major development is intended to foreclose the

4. Hawaii Rev.Stat. ch. 205, as amended (1976, Supp.1977). For additional discussion of the Hawaii Land Use Law see Bosselman & Callies, The Quiet Revolution in Land Use Control 5–53 (1971); Mandelker, Environmental and Land Controls Legislation ch. VII (1976); Myers, Zoning Hawaii (Conservation Foundation, 1976).

5. Vt.Stat.Ann. tit. 10, ch. 151, as amended (1973, Supp.1978). For additional discussion of the Vermont legislation, see Heeter, Almost Getting It Together in Vermont, in Mandelker, Environmental and Land Controls Legislation ch. VIII (1976).

6. Am.L.Inst., A Model Land Development Code art. 7 (1976). For an application and critique of the Model Code provisions for state-level land use control see Mandelker, supra n. 4, at 63–110, 123–26. Also see Advisory Commission on Intergovernmental Relations, 5 State Legislative Program: Environment, Land Use and Growth Policy (1975) for a model act based on the ALI Model Code, the Florida state comprehensive planning act, and the Oregon comprehensive planning act. The ACIR model act provides both for a comprehensive state development plan and a state land management plan.

local exclusion of development projects that serve needs of more than local impact. State designation of critical areas is intended to provide protection for areas that have value as a resource for the entire state, although this is not the only purpose of such designation. Examples of areas of critical state concern are wetlands and coastal zones. One idiosyncracy of the Model Code is that it does not relate state land use control powers to a state land use plan, which is in keeping with the Code's general preference for a land use control system not based on the implementation of planning policies.

Of all the Model Code's proposals for reform in land use controls, the critical area and development of regional impact (DRI) concepts have received the most attention from state legislatures. See Rosenbaum, Land Use and the Legislatures 73–75 (1976). Only in Florida, however, has the entire Model Code state land use system been adopted, and in Florida its adoption was a response to a perceived environmental crisis arising from a massive development boom that threatened to imperil water resources and a fragile wetlands-coastal zone ecology. The Florida Environmental Land and Water Management Act of 1972,[7] drafted by Fred Bosselman, the Model Code's Associate Reporter and a leading Chicago land use lawyer, is generally faithful to the Code's critical area proposals, but modifies the Code's provisions for review of development of regional impact.

Oregon has created a state-level system which includes authority for limited state regulation of development projects as well as for state administrative review of local plans and implementing regulations.[8] Planning is mandatory at the local level in Oregon. Unlike state programs elsewhere, the administrative structure of the Oregon program is relatively simple. Major administrative responsibility is placed with a state Land Conservation and Development Commission, which is served by staff in a state Land Conservation and Development Department. Both are subject to advice from a Joint Legislative Committee on Land Use. This centralization of authority has its advantages, but also makes the Commission and the Department the direct target of adverse comments about the administration of the program. The Commission has now adopted a series of goals covering a variety of topics such as protection of environmental resources, provision of public facilities, transportation needs, and urbanization policy, and has also adopted guidelines specifying the manner in which these goals are to be achieved. Statewide goals are to be achieved by cities and counties through the exercise of their planning, zoning, and other land use control powers. The Commission may review any local comprehensive plan or land use control ordinance considered to be inconsistent with statewide goals on petition from a city, county, special district, or state agency. The Oregon legislation also provides for regulation at the state level of activities of statewide significance. These activities may not be initiated without a permit from the Commission. In general concept, these provisions for control of activities of statewide significance parallel the provisions of the Model Land Development Code for "development of regional impact," except that the Code provides for state review of local decisions on these developments but does not provide for a state permit. Like the Code, the Oregon statute further also provides for the designation (by the legislature) of areas of critical state concern, for which the Commission may adopt land use standards and regulations.

7. Fla.Stat.Ann. ch. 380.   8. Or.Rev.Stat. ch. 197.

VILLAGE OF BELLE TERRE v. BORAAS

Supreme Court of the United States, 1974.
416 U.S. 1, 94 S.Ct. 1536.

Mr. Justice DOUGLAS delivered the opinion of the Court.

Belle Terre is a village on Long Island's north shore of about 220 homes inhabited by 700 people. Its total land area is less than one square mile. It has restricted land use to one-family dwellings excluding lodging houses, boarding houses, fraternity houses, or multiple-dwelling houses. The word "family" as used in the ordinance means, "[o]ne or more persons related by blood, adoption, or marriage, living and cooking together as a single housekeeping unit, exclusive of household servants. A number of persons but not exceeding two (2) living and cooking together as a single housekeeping unit though not related by blood, adoption, or marriage shall be deemed to constitute a family."

Appellees, the Dickmans, are owners of a house in the village and leased it in December 1971 for a term of 18 months to Michael Truman. Later Bruce Boraas became a colessee. Then Anne Parish moved into the house along with three others. These six are students at nearby State University at Stony Brook and none is related to the other by blood, adoption, or marriage. When the village served the Dickmans with an "Order to Remedy Violations" of the ordinance,[1] the owners plus three tenants[2] thereupon brought this action under 42 U.S.C.A. § 1983 for an injunction and a judgment declaring the ordinance unconstitutional. The District Court held the ordinance constitutional, 367 F.Supp. 136, and the Court of Appeals reversed, one judge dissenting. 2 Cir., 476 F.2d 806. The case is here by appeal, 28 U.S.C.A. § 1254(2); and we noted probable jurisdiction, 414 U.S. 907, 94 S.Ct. 234, 38 L.Ed. 2d 145.

This case brings to this Court a different phase of local zoning regulations from those we have previously reviewed. Village of Euclid v. Ambler Realty Co., 272 U.S. 365, 47 S.Ct. 114, 71 L.Ed. 303, involved a zoning ordinance classifying land use in a given area into six categories.
* * *

The main thrust of the case in the mind of the Court was in the exclusion of industries and apartments, and as respects that it commented on the desire to keep residential areas free of "disturbing noises"; "increased traffic"; the hazard of "moving and parked automobiles"; the "depriving children of the privilege of quiet and open spaces for play, enjoyed by those in more favored localities." Id., at 394, 47 S.Ct., at 120. The ordinance was sanctioned because the validity of the legis-

---

1. * * * The effect of the "Order to Remedy Violations" was to subject the occupants to liability commencing August 3, 1972. During the litigation the lease expired and it was extended. Anne Parish moved out. Thereafter the other five students left and the owners now hold the home out for sale or rent, including to student groups.

[Some of the court's footnotes have been renumbered; others have been omitted.— Ed.]

2. Truman, Boraas, and Parish became appellees but not the other three.

lative classification was "fairly debatable" and therefore could not be said to be wholly arbitrary. Id., at 388, 47 S.Ct., at 118.

Our decision in Berman v. Parker, 348 U.S. 26, 75 S.Ct. 98, 99 L.Ed. 27, sustained a land use project in the District of Columbia against a landowner's claim that the taking violated the Due Process Clause and the Just Compensation Clause of the Fifth Amendment. The essence of the argument against the law was, while taking property for ridding an area of slums was permissible, taking it "merely to develop a better balanced, more attractive community" was not, id., at 31, 75 S.Ct., at 102. We refused to limit the concept of public welfare that may be enhanced by zoning regulations. We said:

"Miserable and disreputable housing conditions may do more than spread disease and crime and immorality. They may also suffocate the spirit by reducing the people who live there to the status of cattle. They may indeed make living an almost insufferable burden. They may also be an ugly sore, a blight on the community which robs it of charm, which makes it a place from which men turn. The misery of housing may despoil a community as an open sewer may ruin a river.

"We do not sit to determine whether a particular housing project is or is not desirable. The concept of the public welfare is broad and inclusive. * * * The values it represents are spiritual as well as physical, aesthetic as well as monetary. It is within the power of the legislature to determine that the community should be beautiful as well as healthy, spacious as well as clean, well-balanced as well as carefully patrolled." Id., at 32–33, 75 S.Ct., at 102.

If the ordinance segregated one area only for one race, it would immediately be suspect under the reasoning of Buchanan v. Warley, 245 U.S. 60, 38 S.Ct. 16, 62 L.Ed. 149 where the Court invalidated a city ordinance barring a black from acquiring real property in a white residential area by reason of an 1866 Act of Congress, 14 Stat. 27, now 42 U.S.C.A. § 1982, and an 1870 Act, § 17, 16 Stat. 144, now 42 U.S.C.A. § 1981, both enforcing the Fourteenth Amendment. 245 U.S., at 78–82, 38 S.Ct. at 19–21. See Jones v. Alfred H. Mayer Co., 392 U.S. 409, 88 S.Ct. 2186, 20 L.Ed.2d 1189.

* * *

The present ordinance is challenged on several grounds: that it interferes with a person's right to travel; that it interferes with the right to migrate to and settle within a State; that it bars people who are uncongenial to the present residents; that it expresses the social preferences of the residents for groups that will be congenial to them; that social homogeneity is not a legitimate interest of government; that the restriction of those whom the neighbors do not like trenches on the newcomers' right to privacy; that it is of no rightful concern to villagers whether the residents are married or unmarried; that the ordinance is antithetical to the Nation's experience, ideology, and self-perception as an open, egalitarian, and integrated society.

We find none of these reasons in the record before us. It is not aimed at transients. Cf. Shapiro v. Thompson, 394 U.S. 618, 89 S.Ct. 1322, 22 L.Ed.2d 600. It involves no procedural disparity inflicted on some but not on others such as was presented by Griffin v. Illinois, 351 U.S. 12, 76 S.Ct. 585, 100 L.Ed. 891. It involves no "fundamental" right guaranteed by the Constitution, such as voting, Harper v. Virginia State Board, 383 U.S. 663, 86 S.Ct. 1079, 16 L.Ed.2d 169; the right of association, NAACP v. Alabama ex rel. Patterson, 357 U.S. 449, 78 S.Ct. 1163, 2 L.Ed.2d 1488; the right of access to the courts, NAACP v. Button, 371 U.S. 415, 83 S.Ct. 328, 9 L.Ed.2d 405; or any rights of privacy, cf. Griswold v. Connecticut, 381 U.S. 479, 85 S.Ct. 1678, 14 L.Ed.2d 510; Eisenstadt v. Baird, 405 U.S. 438, 453–454, 92 S.Ct. 1029, 1038–1039, 31 L.Ed. 2d 349. We deal with economic and social legislation where legislatures have historically drawn lines which we respect against the charge of violation of the Equal Protection Clause if the law be " 'reasonable, not arbitrary' " (quoting F.S. Royster Guano Co. v. Virginia, 253 U.S. 412, 415, 40 S.Ct. 560, 561, 64 L.Ed. 989) and bears "a rational relationship to a [permissible] state objective." Reed v. Reed, 404 U.S. 71, 76, 92 S.Ct. 251, 254, 30 L.Ed.2d 225.

It is said, however, that if two unmarried people can constitute a "family," there is no reason why three or four may not. But every line drawn by a legislature leaves some out that might well have been included.[3] That exercise of discretion, however, is a legislative, not a judicial, function.

It is said that the Belle Terre ordinance reeks with an animosity to unmarried couples who live together. There is no evidence to support it; and the provision of the ordinance bringing within the definition of a "family" two unmarried people belies the charge.

The ordinance places no ban on other forms of association, for a "family" may, so far as the ordinance is concerned, entertain whomever it likes.

The regimes of boarding houses, fraternity houses, and the like present urban problems. More people occupy a given space; more cars rather continuously pass by; more cars are parked; noise travels with crowds.

A quiet place where yards are wide, people few, and motor vehicles restricted are legitimate guidelines in a land-use project addressed to family needs. This goal is a permissible one within Berman v. Parker, supra. The police power is not confined to elimination of filth, stench, and unhealthy places. It is ample to lay out zones where family values,

---

3. Mr. Justice Holmes made the point a half century ago.

"When a legal distinction is determined, as no one doubts that it may be, between night and day, childhood and maturity, or any other extremes, a point has to be fixed or a line has to be drawn, or gradually picked out by successive decisions, to mark where the change takes place. Looked at by itself without regard to the necessity behind it the line or point seems arbitrary.

It might as well or nearly as well be a little more to one side or the other. But when it is seen that a line or point there might be, and that there is no mathematical or logical way of fixing it precisely, the decision of the legislature must be accepted unless we can say that it is very wide of any reasonable mark." Louisville Gas Co. v. Coleman, 277 U.S. 32, 41, 48 S.Ct. 423, 426, 72 L.Ed. 770 (dissenting opinion).

youth values, and the blessings of quiet seclusion and clean air make the area a sanctuary for people.

The suggestion that the case may be moot need not detain us. A zoning ordinance usually has an impact on the value of the property which it regulates. But in spite of the fact that the precise impact of the ordinance sustained in *Euclid* on a given piece of property was not known, 272 U.S., at 397, 47 S.Ct., at 121, the Court, considering the matter a controversy in the realm of city planning, sustained the ordinance. Here we are a step closer to the impact of the ordinance on the value of the lessor's property. He has not only lost six tenants and acquired only two in their place; it is obvious that the scale of rental values rides on what we decide today. When *Berman* reached us it was not certain whether an entire tract would be taken or only the buildings on it and a scenic easement. 348 U.S., at 36, 75 S.Ct., at 104. But that did not make the case any the less a controversy in the constitutional sense. When Mr. Justice Holmes said for the Court in Block v. Hirsh, 256 U.S. 135, 155, 41 S.Ct. 458, 459, 65 L.Ed. 865, "property rights may be cut down, and to that extent taken, without pay," he stated the issue here. As is true in most zoning cases, the precise impact on value may, at the threshold of litigation over validity, not yet be known.

Reversed.

Mr. Justice BRENNAN, dissenting.

The constitutional challenge to the village ordinance is premised *solely* on alleged infringement of associational and other constitutional rights of *tenants*. But the named tenant appellees have quit the house, thus raising a serious question whether there now exists a cognizable "case or controversy" that satisifes that indispensable requisite of Art. III of the Constitution. Existence of a case or controversy must, of course, appear at every stage of review, * * *.

* * *

* * * If the District Court determines that a cognizable case or controversy no longer exists, the complaint should be dismissed. Golden v. Zwickler, 394 U.S. 103, 89 S.Ct. 956, 22 L.Ed.2d 113 (1969).

* * *

Mr. Justice MARSHALL, dissenting.

This case draws into question the constitutionality of a zoning ordinance of the incorporated village of Belle Terre, New York, which prohibits groups of more than two unrelated persons, as distinguished from groups consisting of any number of persons related by blood, adoption, or marriage, from occupying a residence within the confines of the township. Lessor-appellees, the two owners of a Belle Terre residence, and three unrelated student tenants challenged the ordinance on the ground that it establishes a classification between households of related and unrelated individuals, which deprives them of equal protection of the laws. In my view, the disputed classification burdens the students' fundamental rights of association and privacy guaranteed by the First and Fourteenth Amendments. Because the application of strict equal protection scrutiny is therefore required, I am at odds with my Brethren's conclusion that the ordinance may be sustained on a showing that it bears a rational relationship to the accomplishment of legitimate governmental objectives.

I am in full agreement with the majority that zoning is a complex and important function of the State. It may indeed be the most essential function performed by local government, for it is one of the primary means by which we protect that sometimes difficult to define concept of quality of life. I therefore continue to adhere to the principle of Village of Euclid v. Ambler Realty Co., 272 U.S. 365, 47 S.Ct. 114, 71 L.Ed. 303 (1926), that deference should be given to governmental judgments concerning proper land-use allocation. That deference is a principle which has served this Court well and which is necessary for the continued development of effective zoning and land- use control mechanisms. Had the owners alone brought this suit alleging that the restrictive ordinance deprived them of their propety or was an irrational legislative classification, I would agree that the ordinance would have to be sustained. Our role is not and should not be to sit as a zoning board of appeals.

I would also agree with the majority that local zoning authorities may properly act in furtherance of the objectives asserted to be served by the ordinance at issue here: restricting uncontrolled growth, solving traffic problems, keeping rental costs at a reasonable level, and making the community attractive to families. The police power which provides the justification for zoning is not narrowly confined. See Berman v. Parker, 348 U.S. 26, 75 S.Ct. 98, 99 L.Ed. 27 (1954). And, it is appropriate that we afford zoning authorities considerable latitude in choosing the means by which to implement such purposes. But deference does not mean abdication. This Court has an obligation to ensure that zoning ordinances, even when adopted in furtherance of such legitimate aims, do not infringe upon fundamental constitutional rights.

When separate but equal was still constitutional dogma, this Court struck down a racially restrictive zoning ordinance. Buchanan v. Warley, 245 U.S. 60, 38 S.Ct. 16, 62 L.Ed. 149 (1917). I am sure the Court would not be hesitant to invalidate that ordinance today. The lower federal courts have considered procedural aspects of zoning, and acted to insure that land-use controls are not used as means of confining minorities and the poor to the ghettos of our central cities. These are limited but necessary intrusions on the discretion of zoning authorities. By the same token, I think it clear that the First Amendment provides some limitation on zoning laws. It is inconceivable to me that we would allow the exercise of the zoning power to burden First Amendment freedoms, as by ordinances that restrict occupancy to individuals adhering to particular religious, political, or scientific beliefs. Zoning officials properly concern themselves with the uses of land—with, for example, the number and kind of dwellings to be constructed in a certain neighborhood or the number of persons who can reside in those dwellings. But zoning authorities cannot validly consider who those persons are, what they believe, or how they choose to live, whether they are Negro or white, Catholic or Jew, Republican or Democrat, married or unmarried.

My disagreement with the Court today is based upon my view that the ordinance in this case unnecessarily burdens appellees' First Amendment freedom of association and their constitutionally guaranteed right to privacy. Our decisions establish that the First and Fourteenth Amendments protect the freedom to choose one's associates. NAACP v. Button, 371 U.S. 415, 430, 83 S.Ct. 328, 336, 9 L.Ed.2d 405 (1963). Constitutional protection is extended, not only to modes of association that are political in the usual sense, but also to those that pertain to the social and economic benefit of the members. Id., at 430–431, 83 S.Ct., at 336–337; Brotherhood of Railroad Trainmen v. Virginia ex rel. Virginia State Bar, 377 U.S. 1, 84 S.Ct. 1113, 12 L.Ed.2d 89 (1964). The selection of one's living companions involves similar choices as to the emotional, social, or economic benefits to be derived from alternative living arrangements.

The freedom of association is often inextricably entwined with the constitutionally guaranteed right of privacy. The right to "establish a home" is an essential part of the liberty guaranteed by the Fourteenth Amendment. Meyer v. Nebraska, 262 U.S. 390, 399, 43 S.Ct. 625, 626, 67 L.Ed. 1042 (1923); Griswold v. Connecticut, 381 U.S. 479, 495, 85 S.Ct. 1678, 1687, 14 L.Ed.2d 510 (1965) (Goldberg, J., concurring). And the Constitution secures to an individual a freedom "to satisfy his intellectual and emotional needs in the privacy of his own home." Stanley v. Georgia, 394 U.S. 557, 565, 89 S.Ct. 1243, 1248, 22 L.Ed.2d 542 (1969); see Paris Adult Theatre I v. Slaton, 413 U.S. 49, 66–67, 93 S.Ct. 2628, 2640–2641, 37 L.Ed.2d 446 (1973). Constitutionally protected privacy is, in Mr. Justice Brandeis' words, "as against the Government, the right to be let alone * * * the right most valued by civilized man." Olmstead v. United States, 277 U.S. 438, 478, 48 S.Ct. 564, 572, 72 L.Ed. 944 (1928) (dissenting opinion). The choice of household companions—of whether a person's "intellectual and emotional needs" are best met by living with family, friends, professional associates, or others—involves deeply personal considerations as to the kind and quality of intimate relationships within the home. That decision surely falls within the ambit of the right to privacy protected by the Constitution.

The instant ordinance discriminates on the basis of just such a personal lifestyle choice as to household companions. It permits any number of persons related by blood or marriage, be it two or twenty, to live in a single household, but it limits to two the number of unrelated persons bound by profession, love, friendship, religious or political affiliation, or mere economics who can occupy a single home. Belle Terre imposes upon those who deviate from the community norm in their choice of living companions significantly greater restrictions than are applied to residential groups who are related by blood or marriage, and compose the established order within the community. The village has, in effect, acted to fence out those individuals whose choice of lifestyle differs from that of its current residents.

This is not a case where the Court is being asked to nullify a township's sincere efforts to maintain its residential character by preventing the operation of rooming houses, fraternity houses, or other commercial or high-density residential uses. Unquestionably, a town is free to restrict such uses. Moreover, as a general proposition, I see no constitutional infirmity in a town's limiting the density of use in residential areas by zoning regulations which do not discriminate on the basis of constitutionally suspect criteria. This ordinance, however, limits the density of occupancy of only those homes occupied by unrelated persons. It thus reaches beyond control of the use of land or the density of population, and undertakes to regulate the way people choose to associate with each other within the privacy of their own homes.

It is no answer to say, as does the majority that associational interests are not infringed because Belle Terre residents may entertain whomever they choose. Only last Term Mr. Justice Douglas indicated in concurrence that he saw the right of association protected by the First Amendment as involving far more than the right to entertain visitors. He found that right infringed by a restriction on food stamp assistance, penalizing households of "unrelated persons." As Mr. Justice Douglas there said, freedom of association encompasses the "right to invite the stranger into one's home" not only for "entertainment" but to join the household as well. United States Department of Agriculture v. Moreno, 413 U.S. 528, 538–545, 93 S.Ct. 2821, 2828–2831 (1973) (concurring opinion). I am still persuaded that the choice of those who will form one's household implicates constitutionally protected rights.

Because I believe that this zoning ordinance creates a classification which impinges upon fundamental personal rights, it can withstand constitutional scrutiny only upon a clear showing that the burden imposed is necessary to protect a compelling and substantial governmental interest, Shapiro v. Thompson, 394 U.S. 618, 634, 89 S.Ct. 1322, 1331, 22 L.Ed.2d 600 (1969). And, once it be determined that a burden has been placed upon a constitutional right, the onus of demonstrating that no less intrusive means will adequately protect the compelling state interest and that the challenged statute is sufficiently narrowly drawn, is upon the party seeking to justify the burden.

A variety of justifications have been proffered in support of the village's ordinance. It is claimed that the ordinance controls population density, prevents noise, traffic and parking problems, and preserves the rent structure of the community and its attractiveness to families. As I noted earlier, these are all legitimate and substantial interests of government. But I think it clear that the means chosen to accomplish these purposes are both overinclusive and underinclusive, and that the asserted goals could be as effectively achieved by means of an ordinance that did not discriminate on the basis of constitutionally protected choices of lifestyle. The ordinance imposes no restriction whatsoever on the number of persons who may live in a house, as long as they are related by marital or sanguinary bonds—presumably no matter how distant their relationship. Nor does the ordinance restrict the number of income earners who may contribute to rent in such a household, or the number of automobiles that may be maintained by its occupants. In that sense the ordinance is underinclusive. On the other hand, the statute restricts the number of unrelated persons who may live in a home to no more than two. It would therefore prevent three unrelated people from occupying a dwelling even if among them they had but one income and no vehicles. While an extended family of a dozen or more might live in a small bungalow, three elderly and retired persons could not occupy the large manor house next door. Thus the statute is also grossly overinclusive to accomplish its intended purposes.

There are some 220 residences in Belle Terre occupied by about 700 persons. The density is therefore just above three per household. The village is justifiably concerned with density of population and the related problems of noise, traffic, and the like. It could deal with those problems by limiting each household to a specified number of adults, two or three perhaps, without limitation on the number of dependent children.[4] The burden of such an ordinance would fall equally upon all segments of the community. It would surely be better tailored to the goals asserted by the village than the ordinance before us today, for it would more realistically restrict population density and growth and their attendant environmental costs. Various other statutory mechanisms also suggest themselves as solutions to Belle Terre's problems— rent control, limits on the number of vehicles per household, and so forth, but, of course, such schemes are matters of legislative judgment and not for this Court. Appellants also refer to the necessity of maintaining the family character of the village. There is not a shred of evidence in the record indicating that if Belle Terre permitted a limited number of unrelated persons to live together, the residential, familial character of the community would be fundamentally affected.

By limiting unrelated households to two persons while placing no limitation on households of related individuals, the village has embarked upon its commendable course in a constitutionally faulty vessel. I would find the challenged ordinance unconstitutional. But I would not ask the village to abandon its goal of providing quiet streets, little traffic, and a pleasant and reasonably priced environment in which families might raise their children. Rather, I would commend the village to continue to pursue those purposes but by means of more carefully drawn and even-handed legislation.

I respectfully dissent.

Notes

1. *Belle Terre* was the first zoning case to be reviewed by the United States Supreme Court since the late 1920's despite the tone of the majority opinion, which implies that in *Belle Terre* the court was merely filling a small gap in a long worked-over legal mosaic. Berman v. Parker, although characterized by Justice Douglas in *Belle Terre* as refusing "to limit the concept of pub-

---

4. By providing an exception for dependent children, the township would avoid any doubts that might otherwise be posed by the constitutional protection afforded the choice of whether to bear a child. See Molino v. Mayor & Council of Glassboro, 116 N.J.Super. 195, 281 A.2d 401 (1971); cf. Cleveland Board of Education v. LaFleur, 414 U.S. 632, 94 S.Ct. 791, 39 L.Ed. 2d 52 (1974).

lic welfare that may be enhanced by zoning regulations," actually had nothing to do with zoning; it was an eminent domain case. In *Berman*, the Court sustained a District of Columbia urban redevelopment project against a Fifth Amendment challenge based primarily on the argument that a taking of the plaintiff's commercial property—clearly not "slum housing"—under the power of eminent domain could not be justified as a taking for a "public" use or purpose because the project would be carried out largely by private redevelopers. No issue was raised as to the adequacy of the compensation to be paid to the plaintiff for the property taken by the redevelopment agency.

In *Berman* it is true that Justice Douglas said, "Public safety, public health, morality, peace and quiet, law and order—these are some of the more conspicuous examples of the traditional application of the police power to municipal affairs." This statement has sometimes been criticized on the ground that, in the context of an eminent domain case, it indicates that Justice Douglas did not know the difference between the police power and the eminent domain power. But it would seem rather that Justice Douglas was using the term "police power" in its older, broader meaning, to signify all the inherent powers of a sovereign government—in this case, the federal government acting through Congress—and that he merely intended to assert that the "public" *purposes* which justify the taking of private property for a public purpose upon payment of just compensation are essentially the same as those which justify the "regulation" of private property without payment of any compensation.

2. Although Euclid v. Ambler Realty Co. did not deal with the constitutional validity of "exclusive" single-family use districts, it was generally assumed after *Euclid* that such zoning was a proper exercise of the police power. Even prior to *Euclid* the Massachusetts Supreme Court sustained such zoning in Brett v. Building Commissioner of Brookline, 250 Mass. 73, 145 N.E. 269 (1924). The *Brett* rationale was as follows:

"Restriction of the use of land to buildings each to be occupied as a residence for a single family may be viewed at least in two aspects. It may be regarded as preventive of fire. It seems to us manifest that, other circumstances being the same, there is less danger of a building becoming ignited if occupied by one family than if occupied by two or more families. Any increase in the number of persons or of stoves or lights under a single roof increases the risk of fire. A regulation designed to decrease the number of families in one house may reasonably be thought to diminish that risk. The space between buildings likely to arise from the separation of people into a single family under one roof may rationally be thought also to diminish the hazard of conflagration in a neighborhood. Statutes designed to minimize this hazard by regulations as to mechanical construction, air spaces and similar contrivances are familiar and have been upheld. *Stevens, landowner*, 228 Mass. 368, and cases there collected. We cannot say that it may not be a rational means to the same end to require that no more than one family inhabit one house, where conditions as to population permit.

"It may be a reasonable view that the health and general physical and mental welfare of society would be promoted by each family dwelling in a house by itself. Increase in fresh air, freedom for the play of children and of movement for adults, the opportunity to cultivate a bit of land, and the reduction in the spread of contagious diseases may be thought to be advanced by a general custom that each family live in a house standing by itself with its own curtilage. These features of family life are equally essential or equally advantageous for all inhabitants, whatever may be their social standing or material prosperity. There is nothing on the face of this by-law to indicate that it will not operate indifferently for the general benefit. It is matter of common knowledge that there are in numerous districts plans for real estate development involving modest single-family dwellings within the reach as to price of the thrifty and economical of moderate wage earning capacity."

What do you think of the justifications for separation of single-family dwellings from two-family dwellings stated in *Brett*, and the rationale for separation of one- and two-family dwellings from apartment buildings stated in *Euclid*?

3. Compare the *Euclid* and *Brett* rationales for creation of different kinds of residential districts with the following excerpt from D. Hagman, Urban Planning and Land Development Control Law 473–475 (1971): *

"* * * [U]nder most zoning ordinances, there are several residential districts varying from large lot single family zones to multiple family high-rise building zones. What is the basic reason for such a system? * * * [H]ow is it that the single family zone became known as the 'highest use' zone, rather than the multiple [family] residential zones, which had greater densities of people? If zoning is in the interest of the poor, why is it that apartment buildings are the buffer zone between industrial-commercial zones and single-family residential zones, rather than the single-family zones, with fewer people, being the neighbor of the undesirable commercial and industrial uses? If safety of pedestrial children is a major concern, how is it that the apartments housing the poor are on the major traffic arteries rather than the single family homes? If adequate light and air is provided for residents in multiple family high-rise buildings in the interests of their health, safety and welfare, how is the police power justified in providing more light and air by imposing regulations limiting land use to single family development? The several residential districts exist because most people want economic segregation."

4. Fraternities, sororities, and retirement homes have generally been unsuccessful in the state courts in attacking "single-family" zoning classifications. E.g., City of Schenectady v. Delta Chi Fraternity, 5 A.D.2d 14, 168 N.Y.S.2d 754 (1957); Cassidy v. Triebel, 337 Ill.App. 117, 85 N.E.2d 461 (1948); Pettis v. Alpha Alpha Chapter of Phi Beta Pi, 115 Neb. 525, 213 N.W. 835 (1927); Kellogg v. Joint Council of Women's Auxiliaries Welfare Association, 265 S.W.2d 374 (Mo.1954). State courts have generally been favorable to religious groups living together in a "single-family" district. E.g., Carroll v. Miami Beach, 198 So. 2d 643 (Fla.App.1967) (novices living together under supervision of Mother Superior); Missionaries of Our Lady of La Salette v. Whitefish Bay, 267 Wis. 609, 66 N.W.2d 627 (1954) (up to eight priests and lay brothers); Laporte v. New Rochelle, 2 A.D.2d 710, 152 N.Y.S.2d 916 (1956) (dormitory for sixty students in a Roman Catholic college). In Robertson v. Western Baptist Hospital, 267 S.W.2d 395 (Ky.1954), 20 nurses living together were held to be a "family" under an ordinance defining "family" as "one or more persons living as a single housekeeping unit, as distinguished from a group occupying a hotel, club, fraternity or sorority house."

5. Since *Belle Terre*, at least three state high courts located in populous states have rejected the result and the rationale of the majority opinion in *Belle Terre*. In White Plains v. Ferraioli, 34 N.Y.2d 300, 357 N.Y.S.2d 449, 313 N.E.2d 756 (1974), the court held that a group home for juveniles was held to be permitted in a single-family district; the New York court distinguished *Belle Terre* on the ground that the latter involved "a temporary arrangement" in which "[e]very year or so, different college students would come to take the place of those before them," whereas the "group home" in *Ferraioli* "is a permanent arrangement and akin to a traditional family, which also may be sun-

* Copyright 1971, West Publishing Co.

dered by death, divorce, or emancipation of the young" and "[t]he purpose is to emulate the traditional family and not to introduce a different 'life style'."

In both State v. Baker, 81 N.J. 99, 405 A.2d 368 (1979), and City of Santa Barbara v. Adamson, 27 Cal.3d 123, 164 Cal.Rptr. 539, 610 P.2d 436 (1980), the courts rejected the *Belle Terre* result and rationale in striking down restrictive definitions of "single family" in local zoning ordinances, and in both cases the result was to allow occupancy of houses in single-family districts by large groups of persons who did not constitute nuclear families and who had deliberately adopted an "alternative life style." In *Baker*, a single-family house was occupied by a married couple and their three daughters, an unrelated woman and her three children, and "several other persons" who "apparently resided within the household for indeterminate periods of time." Mr. Baker, an ordained Presbyterian minister, testified that the living arrangement arose out of the religious beliefs of the group members and their resultant desire to live as "brothers and sisters," and that they ate together, shared common areas, and held communal prayer sessions. The local zoning ordinance defined a "family" so as to exclude groups including more than four persons "not related by blood, marriage, or adoption." The New Jersey court held that "zoning regulations which attempt to limit residency based upon the number of unrelated individuals present in a single non-profit housekeeping unit" could not "pass constitutional muster." The court refused to follow *Belle Terre*, and based its decision entirely on Article I, para. I of the New Jersey Constitution, which it interpreted as guaranteeing substantive due process.

In *Adamson*, a single-family house was occupied by "a group of 12 adults * * * not related by blood, marriage, or adoption," who shared expenses, rotated chores, and ate evening meals together, and who alleged that they had become "a close group with social, economic, and psychological commitments to each other" which provided them with "emotional support and stability." The Santa Barbara zoning ordinance, as construed by the court, barred such a group of unrelated persons from residing, as of right, anywhere in the city— not just in "one-family zones." The court held that exclusion of such groups violated a provision of the California state constitution guaranteeing the right of "privacy." The court held that Santa Barbara had failed to show that any "compelling [public] interest" justified the infringement on the "fundamental" right of "privacy" resulting from the restrictive definition of "family" in the zoning ordinance. In so holding, the court rejected the city's arguments that (1) "transiency" results from "lack of any biological or marriage relation among the residents" of a dwelling, and (2) that the restrictive definition of "family" was necessary to maintain a low population density, "the essential characteristics of the [residential] districts," and "a suitable environment for family life where children are members of most families." With respect to the last argument, the court went on to say that the "implied goal" of protecting children from "an immoral environment" by prohibiting residence by large groups of unrelated persons "would not be legitimate." The court's opinion on the latter point is rather surprising, since the police power has traditionally been thought to justify regulations designed to protect "morals."

In Town of Durham v. White Enterprises, Inc., 115 N.H. 645, 348 A.2d 706 (1975), the court followed *Belle Terre* in holding that a town could constitutionally restrict the density of occupation of premises in a "single-family" district by unrelated persons while not similarly restricting occupancy by persons related by blood, marriage, or adoption.

For critical commentary on zoning ordinances excluding group living arrangements, see Note, "Burning the House to Roast the Pig": Unrelated Individuals and Single Family Zoning's Blood Relation Criterion, 58 Cornell L.Rev. 138 (1972).

6.   In Moore v. City of East Cleveland, 431 U.S. 494, 97 S.Ct. 1932, 52 L.Ed. 2d 531 (1977), the Supreme Court struck down a provision of the East Cleveland "housing ordinance" which defined "family" to include (*inter alia*), in addition to unmarried children of the nominal head of the household or of the spouse of the nominal head of the household, the spouse and dependent children of "not more than one dependent married or unmarried child of the nominal head of the household or of the spouse of the nominal head of the household." The effect of this provision was to make it unlawful for the appellant to include in her household two grandchildren who were first cousins rather than brothers. Three of the justices joined Justice Powell in holding that the restrictive definition of "family" violated "substantive due process" because it intruded too far on "choices concerning family living arrangements" and it bore only "a tenuous relation to alleviation of the conditions mentioned by the city"—i.e., "overcrowding," "traffic and parking congestion," and "an undue financial burden on East Cleveland's school system." Justice Brennan, in an opinion in which Justice Marshall joined, concurred in the Powell opinion and also noted (1) that the East Cleveland ordinance had a disproportionately adverse impact on black "extended" families; and (2) that the result was consistent with *Belle Terre*, where "[t]he village took special care in its brief to emphasize that its ordinance did not in any manner inhibit the choice of related individuals to constitute a family, whether in the 'nuclear' or 'extended' form." (Emphasis by the court.) Justice Stevens concurred in the result essentially on the grounds stated in the Powell opinion.

Chief Justice Burger dissented on the ground that the appellant had not exhausted her administrative remedies because no effort had been made to apply for a variance as provided in the East Cleveland housing code. Justice Stewart, dissenting, in an opinion in which Justice Rehnquist joined, said:

> * * * When the Court has found that the Fourteenth Amendment place a substantive limitation on a State's power to regulate, it has been in those rare cases in which the personal interests at issue have been deemed "implicit in the concept of ordered liberty." * * * The interest that the appellant may have in permanently sharing a single kitchen and a suite of contiguous rooms with some of her relatives simply does not rise to that level. To equate this interest with the fundamental decisions to marry and to bear and raise children is to extend the limited substantive contours of the Due Process Clause beyond recognition.

Justice Stewart also found no violation of the Equal Protection Clause. Justice White, also dissenting, reviewed the development of substantive Due Process doctrine in the Supreme Court and noted that the court has moved to a highly deferential view of state and local legislative enactments, especially with respect to "legislation seeking to control or regulate the economic life of the state or Nation." He concluded as follows: If there is power to maintain the character of a single-family neighborhood, as there surely is, some limit must be placed on the reach of the "family." Had it been our task to legislate, we might have approached the problem in a different manner than did the drafters of this ordinance; but I have no trouble in concluding that the normal goals of zoning regulation are present here and that the ordinance serves these goals by limiting, in identifiable circumstances, the number of people who can occupy a single household. The ordinance does not violate the Due Process Clause.

Note on Zoning and "Group Homes"

In recent years, the most controversial question in connection with single-family zoning classifications has been whether "group homes" for juveniles, mentally retarded persons, and drug addicts undergoing rehabilitation may be excluded from single-family districts. In a few cases courts have resolved the conflict by construing the zoning ordinance as permitting group homes in single-family districts despite restrictive definitions of "family" in the ordinance. In White Plains v. Ferraioli, 34 N.Y.2d 300, 357 N.Y.S.2d 449, 313 N.E.2d 756 (1974), the court said that requiring "the relationships [to] be those of blood or adoption * * * might be too restrictive," implying that such a definition would be either *ultra vires* or unconstitutional. But the court did not invalidate the White Plains ordinance's definition of "family," although it did, in fact, require the members of a "family" to be related by blood, marriage or adoption. Instead, the court held that the ordinance provision limiting the principal use of land in an R–2 zone to a "single family dwelling for one housekeeping unit only" would permit a group home for unrelated persons because it comprised "one housekeeping unit," despite the fact that the group home clearly did not fit the definition of "family" in the ordinance.

Almost equally disingenuous was the holding in Hessling v. City of Broomfield, 563 P.2d 12 (Colo.1977), which allowed a married couple and six unrelated children to occupy a house in a single-family residence district as a matter of right, although the city's zoning ordinance defined a "family" as "an individual or two or more persons related by blood or marriage, or an unrelated group of not more than three persons living together." The court said that "adopted children" would necessarily be included by construction, though not related to their adoptive parents by blood or marriage, and that since a group of unrelated children living with "surrogate parents" were not distinguishable from adopted children, they should be included as well. The court noted that such a group of unrelated persons was "consistent with the core concept" that "maintenance of a single housekeeping unit" is the true test of a "family." The decision in *Hessling*, although ostensibly based on a "construction" of the zoning ordinance, was undoubtedly influenced by the fact that the local governing body had, by resolution, specifically authorized the use of the house in question as a "live-in home" for a married couple and not more than six mentally retarded children. It seems clear that the governing body could simply have amended its zoning ordinance to allow such group homes in a single-family residence district either as a matter of right or as a conditional use, although an amendatory ordinance rather than a mere resolution would have been required.

Compare State ex rel. Ellis v. Liddle, 520 S.W.2d 644 (Mo.App.1975), with *Ferraioli* and *Hessling*, supra. In *Liddle*, it was conceded that a group home was within the zoning ordinance definition of "family," which allowed not more than ten unrelated persons per dwelling unit, but it was argued that the purpose of the particular group home involved in the litigation was to provide for "detention" of juvenile delinquents, which was prohibited in an R–2 zone, rather than to provide a "residence" for them. The court held, however, that the group home was a "residence," although it housed some juvenile delinquents as well as abandoned and neglected boys.

Also compare Catholic Family & Children's Services v. City of Bellingham, 605 P.2d 788 (Wash.App.1979), where the court held that a "children's residence home" was permitted in a single-family residence zone as of right because the resident children satisfied the ordinance definition of "family," which included "foster children" as well as persons related by "blood, marriage, or adoption."

The court conceded that the "children's residence home" was also within the ordinance definition of "juvenile home," which was authorized only on the basis of a conditional use permit, but held that the status of the children as "foster children" under the supervision of a resident married couple was controlling. It should be noted that the "children's residence home" in this case had been constructed after its sponsor obtained a "group home license," and only then did the board of adjustment seek to impose the conditional use permit requirement.

In several recent cases, group home residents have been held not to constitute a "family" as defined in the local zoning ordinance. See Lakeside Youth Service v. Zoning Hearing Board, 414 A.2d 1115 (Pa.Commw.Ct.1980); Culp. v. City of Seattle, 590 P.2d 1288 (Wash.App.1979); City of Guntersville v. Shull, 355 So.2d 361 (Ala.1978) ("halfway house" for former patients in mental hospital is not permitted in R–3 residential district which may include "dwellings and apartments for any number of families").

Assuming a court is not prepared to invalidate local zoning restrictions excluding group homes from single-family residence zones and that a court is not able to construe the local zoning restrictions so as to permit group homes in such zones, the court may nevertheless decide that group homes should be allowed in such zones either on the basis of "state governmental immunity" or "overriding state policy."

"State governmental immunity" may provide a basis for judicial authorization of group homes in single-family residence zones from which they are excluded under the local zoning ordinance in cases where a state agency operates a group home, or a group home, whether publicly or privately owned, contracts with a state agency which exercises significant control over its operation, and receives state funds to finance its operations. In some cases, courts have found that the legislative intent to make group home operations immune from local zoning restrictions is clear and unequivocal. E.g., People v. St. Agatha Home for Children, 389 N.E.2d 1098 (N.Y.), cert. denied, 444 U.S. 869 (1979) (nonsecure detention facility for children "in need of supervision" was immune from local zoning restrictions where statute required local governments to provide such facilities "notwithstanding any other provision of law").

Where the legislative intent is less clear, courts have usually adopted a balancing test, under which the court weighs various factors—the nature and scope of the group home for which immunity is sought, the extent of the public interest to be served by locating the group home in a single-family zone, and the impact of such location on the legitimate local interests embodied in the zoning restrictions. See, e.g., Berger v. State, 364 A.2d 998, 999 (N.J.1976) (discussed in State v. Baker, supra); City of Temple Terrace v. Hillsborough Ass'n for Retarded Citizens, Inc., 322 So.2d 571, 574 (Fla.App.1975), aff'd, 322 So.2d 610 (Fla.1976). In applying a balancing test, some courts have required a showing that the state have good faith consideration to local zoning concerns as a prerequisite to granting immunity from local zoning restrictions—see, e.g., Brownfield v. State, 407 N.E.2d 1365 (Ohio 1980)—and have been less willing to grant immunity where the group home is likely to have a substantial adverse impact on the community. Thus, courts have been more sympathetic to claims of immunity for group homes for handicapped children than for correctional facilities for juvenile delinquents. Compare Berger v. State, supra, with Pemberton Township v. State, 408 A.2d 832 (N.J.L.1979). Courts have also been reluctant to grant immunity to group homes operating without state funds and/or without significant state supervision—see, e.g., Township of Washington v. Central Bergen Community Mental Health Center, Inc., 383 A.2d 1194

(N.J.L.1979)—and have required a showing that the group home serves a governmental rather than a purely proprietary purpose—see, e.g., Connors v. New York State Ass'n of Retarded Children, Inc., 370 N.Y.S.2d 474 (N.Y.Sup.Ct. 1975).

A distinct, though related, basis on which courts have allowed group homes to locate in single-family zones from which they would otherwise be excluded is that this result is required because of an overriding or preemptive state policy. A court may apply this doctrine where the state legislature has expressly or impliedly manifested the intent to occupy the field to the exclusion of all other governmental entities, in which case contrary local government regulations would obstruct the effectuation of the state policy. Thus, the New York courts have held, on the basis of state enabling and funding legislation and general state constitutional provisions, that small-scale group homes created to care for neglected and delinquent children cannot be barred from single-family zones by local zoning ordinances. See Abbott House v. Village of Tarrytown, 312 N.Y.S.2d 841 (N.Y.App.Div.1970); Nowack v. Department of Audit & Control, 338 N.Y.S.2d 52 (N.Y.Sup.Ct.1973). But a state policy in favor of the establishment of group homes does not necessarily override reasonable local restrictions. Hence courts have upheld local ordinances that require a group home to conform to reasonable standards but do not entirely prohibit or seriously interfere with their establishment and operation. Ibero-American Action League, Inc. v. Palma, 366 N.Y.S.2d 747 (N.Y.App.Div.1975); People v. Renaissance Project, 324 N.E.2d 355 (N.Y.1975).

In order to avoid the uncertainty inherent in reliance on judicial application doctrines such as "state governmental immunity" and "overriding state policy," state legislatures have increasingly enacted statutes designed to assure and facilitate establishment and acceptance of group homes in local communities. These statutes either curtail or revoke the power of local governments to bar group homes from single-family zones, and generally share the following characteristics: (1) the types of group homes covered by the statute are identified and defined; (2) the maximum number of residents allowed in a particular type of group home is specified; (3) state licensing of group homes is required; and (4) the power of local governments to impose conditions not specified in the statute is expressly granted or denied. In addition, about one half of the statutes require "dispersal" of group homes within a given community. Many of the statutes expressly provide that small group homes with a maximum resident population of six to eight persons, excluding surrogate parents, are permitted as of right without being required to meet local zoning requirements, but that larger group homes are to be treated as conditional uses subject to imposition of certain conditions by local authorities. Some of the statutes declare group homes to be appropriate uses in single-family residence zones, but allow local governments to retain significant control over the location of such homes. Many of the statutes expressly allow group homes for handicapped children, foster children, and religious orders in single-family residence zones; few of the statutes allow drug rehabilitation centers, prison halfway houses, or homes whose residents require psychological observation in single-family residence zones.

Courts have generally sustained statutes of the sort here considered, on the ground that they bear a substantial relation to legitimate governmental purposes and deal with a matter of statewide concern which justifies overriding local land controls. See, e.g., Zubli v. Community Mainstreaming Associates, Inc., 423 N.Y.S.2d 982 (N.Y.Sup.Ct.1979); Adams County Ass'n for Retarded Children, Inc. v. City of Westminster, 580 P.2d 1246 (Colo.1978); Los Angeles v. State Dep't of Health, 133 Cal.Rptr. 771 (Cal.App.1976); State ex rel. Thelen v.

City of Missoula, 543 P.2d 173 (Mont.1975). Contra, Garcia v. Sifrin Residential Ass'n, 407 N.E.2d 1369 (Ohio 1980) (Ohio statute unreasonably limited enforcement of municipal powers authorized by state constitution).

For a list of statutes authorizing group homes in single-family residence zones, see Hopperton, A State Legislative Strategy for Ending Exclusionary Zoning of Community Homes, 19 Urb.L.Ann. 47 (1980). See also 19 Urb.L.Ann. 77 (1980) for the text of the Model Zoning Act provision authorizing a group home of six or fewer residents in all residential zones and, specifically, in single-family zones. This provision was the product of the American Bar Association Commission on the Mentally Disabled. The Model Act further provides that any restrictive covenant precluding the use of residential property for group homes is void as against state policy.

For a general discussion of the problems covered in this Note and in the preceding Comments, see Gailey, Group Homes and Single Family Zoning, 4 Zoning & Plan.L.Rep. 97 (1981), on which this Note is based in large measure. See also D. Mandelker & D. Netsch, State and Local Government in a Federal System 408–18 (1977).

MAYOR & COUNCIL OF NEW CASTLE v. ROLLINS OUTDOOR ADVERTISING, INC.

Court of Chancery of Delaware, 1983.
459 A.2d 541.

BROWN, Chancellor. This is an action brought to enforce a zoning regulation. Defendant has moved to dismiss. The issue presented calls into question the legality of a zoning ordinance which seeks to eliminate certain nonconforming uses through a gradual amortization of the value of the use. The question would appear to be one of first impression in this State.

The zoning ordinance involved was adopted by the plaintiff City of New Castle as a part of a 1968 reenactment of the zoning code of the City. It reads in relevant part as follows:

"6. *Gradual Elimination of Certain Uses*—

"Certain non-conformities shall be terminated in accordance with the following provisions:

* * *

"b. Within not more than three years from the date of adoption or amendment of this ordinance by which a use becomes non-conforming, the right to maintain the following non-conformities shall terminate and such non-conformities shall no longer be operated or maintained:

(1) Any junk yard

(2) A non-conformity, which is not enclosed within a structure

(3) Off-site signs."

This case deals with the third category—off-site signs. Specifically, the defendant Rollins Outdoor Advertising, Inc. presently owns two parcels of real estate within the City of New Castle on which advertising billboards are situated. These properties are classified for residential use under the City zoning code. However, they are used solely for off-site advertising purposes by Rollins. No other business or activity is conducted on the premises.

These billboards were in place on the properties and were being used for off-site advertising purposes by Rollins' predecessor in title at the time that a comprehensive zoning code was first adopted by the City of New Castle. The initial zoning classification of the two properties did not permit such a use. Neither does the 1968 reenactment. Accordingly, since the actual use predated the zoning classification, the continued existence of the billboards has been permitted heretofore under the concept of a nonconforming use. As with all nonconforming uses, the theory is that eventually the proscribed use will be terminated or abandoned with the passage of time, after which the property will then be made to comply with the zoning classification.

As to certain uses, however, the passage of time has not produced the curative effect hoped for by the zoning planners. Junk yards and billboards fall within this category. A junk yard, by its very nature, has a tendency to never go away. To perhaps a lesser degree the same is true of billboards. Thus, in recent years, a new approach has been conceived to hasten their respective departures so as to terminate the objectionable use and bring the property into compliance with the overall zoning scheme. This new concept allegedly involves the principle of amortization. This is said to be the basis and justification for the zoning ordinance in issue here insofar as it applies to the off-site signs of the defendant Rollins.

Stated in its simplest terms, the amortization of a nonconforming use contemplates the compulsory termination of a nonconformity at the expiration of a specified period of time—the time period, in theory, being equal to the useful economic life of the nonconformity. The basic idea is to determine the remaining normal useful life of a pre-existing nonconforming use. The landowner is then allowed to continue his use for this period so as to realize (or perhaps recoup) the value of the use. Presumably, this is measured against his capital investment in the use. At the end of the specified period he must terminate the use and conform his property to its classification under the zoning plan. See, Hoffman v. Kinealy, Mo.Supr., 389 S.W.2d 745, 750 (1965).

The parties concede that there is a distinct split of authority throughout the country on the question of the constitutionality of this amortization approach to the elimination of nonconforming uses. On the one hand, the number of cases holding the amortization method of eliminating nonconforming uses or structures to be constitutional is substantial. National Advertising Company v. County of Monterey, Cal.App., 211 Cal.App.2d 375, 27 Cal.Rptr. 136 (1963); Village of Gurnee v. Miller, Ill.App., 69 Ill.App.2d 248, 315 N.E.2d 829 (1966); John Donnelly & Sons, Inc. v. Outdoor Advertising Bd., Mass.Supr., 369 Mass. 206, 339 N.E.2d 709 (1975); Harris v. Mayor and City Council of Baltimore, Md.Spec.App., 35 Md.App. 572, 371 A.2d 706 (1977); Eutaw Enterprises, Inc. v. City of Baltimore, Md.App., 241 Md. 686, 217 A.2d 348 (1966); Grant v. Mayor and City Council of Baltimore, Md.App., 212 Md. 301, 129 A.2d 363 (1957); Inhabitants, Town of Boothbay v. National

Adv. Co., Me.Supr., 347 A.2d 419 (1975); Naegele Outdoor Adv. Co. v. Village of Minnetonka, Minn.Supr., 281 Minn. 492, 162 N.W.2d 206 (1968); Lachapelle v. Town of Goffstown, N.H.Supr., 107 N.H. 485, 225 A.2d 624 (1967); Suffolk Outdoor Advertising Co. v. Hulse, N.Y.App., 43 N.Y.2d 483, 402 N.Y.S.2d 368, 373 N.E.2d 263 (1977); Harbison v. City of Buffalo, N.Y.App., 4 N.Y.2d 553, 176 N.Y.S.2d 598, 152 N.E.2d 42 (1958); Beals v. County of Douglas, Nev.Supr., 93 Nev. 156, 560 P.2d 1373 (1977); State v. Joyner, N.C.Supr., 286 N.C. 366, 211 S.E.2d 320 (1975); City of Seattle v. Martin, Wash.Supr., 54 Wash.2d 541, 342 P.2d 602 (1959); Art Neon Co. v. City and County of Denver, 488 F.2d 118 (10th Cir.1973); Standard Oil Co. v. City of Tallahassee, 183 F.2d 410 (5th Cir.1950), cert. den'd 340 U.S. 892, 71 S.Ct. 208, 95 L.Ed. 647 (1950). In the main, these decisions stand for the proposition that the forced termination of a nonconforming use over a specified period of time is a reasonable exercise of the police power and does not constitute a taking of property in violation of due process.

On the other side of the matter, Rollins cites City of Fayetteville v. S & H, Inc., Ark.Supr., 261 Ark. 148, 547 S.W.2d 94 (1977); Hoffman v. Kinealy, supra; Concord Township v. Cornogg, Pa.C.P., 9 D. & C.2d 79 (1956); and City of Akron v. Chapman, Ohio Supr., 160 Ohio St. 382, 116 N.E.2d 697 (1953), all of which have held that such an amortization ordinance does amount to an improper taking of private property without just compensation.

As applied to off-site signs the rationale offered by the authorities cited by the City of New Castle is that such an ordinance is a reasonable exercise of the police power in that it is related to the general welfare of the community. It is said to be reasonably designed to gradually remove an unwanted, unsightly and value-depreciating commercial intrusion from an otherwise residential area. It is said that the owner of the property having the nonconforming use is compensated for the eventual termination by virtue of being granted, in effect, a monopoly to continue the nonconforming use in the prohibited area, and to profit by it and thus recoup his investment over the duration of the amortization period established by the ordinance. It is pointed out that the ordinance does not take the realty itself but rather it simply brings it within the residential classification and that, as such, the property still has value to the owner. It is further pointed out that in a case such as this the billboards themselves are not taken and thus the owner is free to remove them to another location where such a use is permitted.

In final analysis, the position of the authorities relied upon by the City of New Castle may be summed up in the following statement from Grant v. Mayor and City Council of Baltimore, supra, at 129 A.2d 369:

> "The distinction between an ordinance that restricts future uses and one that requires existing uses to stop after a reasonable time, is not a difference in kind but one of degree and, in each case, constitutionality depends on overall reasonableness, on the importance of the public gain in relation to the private loss."

In this sense the right of the public to be relieved from the onus of commercial billboards in residential areas over a reasonable period of time is said to predominate over the right of a property owner to rely on the nonconforming use concept so as to maintain an off-site sign in a residentially zoned area indefinitely.

The aforesaid authorities cited by Rollins view the matter differently. Those cases recognize that the value of property lies in the right to use it. They stress the principle that a lawful use of property which predates a zoning ordinance constitutes a vested property right which is guaranteed to the landowner as a nonconforming use until such time as it is voluntarily terminated or abandoned. They view an ordinance which compels the termination of the nonconforming use against the will of the landowner, and without compensation, to constitute an unconstitutional taking of private property. As stated by the Ohio Supreme Court in City of Akron v. Chapman, supra, at 116 N.E.2d 700:

> "The right to continue to use one's property in a lawful business and in a manner which does not constitute a nuisance and which was lawful at the time it was acquired is within the protection of Section 1, Article XIV, Amendments, Constitution of the United States, and Section 16, Article I of the Ohio Constitution, which provide that no person shall be deprived of life, liberty or property without due process of law."

And, in Hoffman v. Kinealy, supra, the situation was summed up as follows at 389 S.W.2d at 753:

> "The amortization provision under review would terminate and take from instant relators the right to continue a lawful nonconforming use of their lots which has been exercised and enjoyed since 1910—a right of the character to which the courts traditionally have referred as a 'vested right.' To our knowledge, no one has, as yet, been so brash as to contend that such a pre-existing lawful nonconforming use properly might be terminated *immediately*. In fact, the contrary is implicit in the amortization technique itself which would validate a taking *presently* unconstitutional by the simple expedient of *postponing* such taking for a 'reasonable' time. All of this leads us to suggest, as did the three dissenting justices in Harbison v. City of Buffalo, supra, 152 N.E.2d at 49, that it would be a strange and novel doctrine indeed which would approve a municipality taking private property for public use without compensation if the property was not too valuable and the taking was not too soon, and prompts us to repeat the caveat of Mr. Justice Holmes in Pennsylvania Coal Co. v. Mahon, 260 U.S. 393, 416, 43 S.Ct. 158, 160, 67 L.Ed. 322, 326, 28 A.L.R. 1321, that '[w]e are in danger of forgetting that a strong public desire to improve the public condition is not enough to warrant achieving the desire by a shorter cut than the constitutional way of paying for the change.' " (Emphasis in the original.)

The choice between the respective positions of the parties thus puts at loggerheads two separate constitutional principles, namely, the proposition that through zoning a person shall not be deprived of property rights without due process of law, see Shellburne, Inc. v. Roberts, Del. Supr., 43 Del.Ch. 276, 224 A.2d 250 (1966), versus the now well-established principle that under the police power of the State the use of private property may be reasonably regulated and restricted through zoning so long as it bears a substantial relation to the health, safety and general welfare of the community. Delaware Constitution of 1897, Article II, § 25; 22 Del.C. § 301; In re Ceresini, Del.Super., 38 Del. 134, 189 A. 443 (1936). As applied to an ordinance which purports to amortize and eliminate an otherwise valid nonconforming use, the parties concede that there is logical justification and valid criticism attached to both sides of the argument. As a result, they suggest that the Court will simply have to pick between the two.

I think, however, that the Court has a duty to approach the dilemma in light of our existing case precedents. On this score, there is not much with which to work. But there is something.

To begin with, our law recognizes that the value of property does not consist solely in holding the title to it. As stated in In re Ceresini, supra, "there can be no conception of property aside from its control, use and enjoyment; and upon its use and enjoyment necessarily depends its value." 189 A. 449. Therefore, obviously, it is the use of property that cannot be unreasonably regulated or restricted through zoning.

In the case of New Castle County v. Harvey, Del.Ch., 315 A.2d 616 (1974), at least certain aspects of which were recently approved by our Supreme Court in Hooper v. Del. Alcoholic Beverage Control Com'n, Del.Supr., 409 A.2d 1046 (1979), the following statement concerning the scope of a nonconforming use appears at 315 A.2d 619:

> "In my opinion, the [nonconforming use] exception must be interpreted so as to guarantee that zoning will not take from an owner property rights which he already legally possessed, because to do otherwise would be confiscatory and thus, in all probability, unconstitutional. 2 Rathkopf, The Law of Zoning And Planning 58–1."

And in Shellburne, Inc. v. Roberts, supra, in which it was held that the mere issuance of a building permit for a particular use did not create a vested right in a particular zoning classification, the Supreme Court, in pointing out nonetheless that a substantial change in position in reliance on the permit could overcome a subsequent zoning change, saw fit to state as follows at 224 A.2d 254:

> "Under certain circumstances, the law recognizes a *vested right* to construct and use under a valid building permit issued prior to a zoning change which would otherwise prohibit such construction and usage. *The basis for the rule is the same* as that underlying 9 *Del. C.* § 2620 and Article XVII, Section 1 of the Zoning Code of New Castle County which prevent zoning changes from being retroactively applied to nonconforming uses and structures." (Emphasis added.)

While apparently no reported Delaware case expressly so holds, I think the fair intendment of these decisions is that the owner of a nonconforming use has a vested right to continue to use his property for that purpose despite the enactment of a zoning ordinance under which the nonconforming use would otherwise be prohibited. Compare also, Minquadale Civic Association v. Kline, Del.Ch., 212 A.2d 811 (1965). As such, I think they can be said to further stand for the proposition that such a vested right in a pre-existing use cannot be eliminated by a subsequent zoning enactment.

Simply stated, if such a vested property right cannot be taken away by the initial zoning enactment, how can it be taken away by a later amendment to that enactment, especially when the true underlying justification for the amendment is that the original zoning ordinance has not succeeded in doing away with the vested property right as quickly as it had been hoped? In such a situation the use, and thus the vested property right, has not changed. It has remained constant throughout. The change that has occurred lies in the patience of the original zoning plan.

Viewed from this perspective I find myself unable to agree with the rationale of the authorities cited by the City of New Castle, namely, that the distinction between an ordinance that restricts a future use of property and one that requires existing lawful uses to cease after a reasonable period of time is merely a difference in degree rather than a difference in kind. I think we are talking about a difference in kind here.

The nonconforming use concept was born of due process considerations. It recognized that zoning, even though in the public interest, should not be permitted to take a vested property right from a citizen. Rather, it permits the right, and thus the use, to run its course and to be terminated by the owner of it, whether through voluntary change, abandonment, or otherwise. Once terminated by conduct attributable to the owner of the use, the zoning restriction as to the future use of the property prevents the nonconformity from being revived or renewed. In this sense, the zoning ordinance does not take from the property owner that which he possessed. It leaves the decision to the property owner based upon conditions as to which he is forewarned under the terms of the zoning ordinance.

The amortization approach of the City of New Castle, however, does not do this. It does not leave the decision to the owner of the use. Rather, it tells him when, in the opinion of the municipality, he has had enough. In this sense it is the ordinance itself which takes from him that which he already had. To say that the difference between the two approaches is merely one of degree is, it seems to me, to emphasize the result, i.e., the eventual termination of the nonconforming use, and to disregard the manner in which it is accomplished. But the difference as I see it, is really one in kind since it pits what, in effect, is a voluntary surrender of a vested property right against one that is involuntary. And to say that one is being made to surrender an existing property right on reasonable terms under the particular circumstances does not make it any less involuntary.

It is for this reason that I am persuaded that the ordinance of the city of New Castle here cannot be enforced against Rollins. To uphold it would be to recognize that the City has the power through its zoning authority to cut off the continuation of an otherwise lawful use of property. While concededly it has the power in a proper case to terminate an existing use through eminent domain, and while it could take action to curtail a use which had reached the proportions of a nuisance, I do not feel that it has the authority to accomplish the same result by means of a zoning ordinance.

The general statute by which all municipalities in this State derive their zoning authority is 22 Del.C. § 301. That statute reads as follows:

> "For the purpose of promoting health, safety, morals or the general welfare of the community, the legislative body of cities and incorporated towns may *regulate and restrict the* height, number of stories and size of buildings and other structures, percentage of lot that may be occupied, the size of yards, courts and other open spaces, the density of population, and the location and *use of* buildings, structures and *land for trade, industry,* residence or other purposes." (Emphasis added.)

The key word in this statute is the word "restrict." The City cites various authorities from other jurisdictions for the proposition that the power to prohibit is necessarily encompassed within the meaning of the word "restrict." Indeed, some cases may be construed to have so held in a zoning context such as this.

In Delaware, however, the word restrict has been defined as meaning "to restrain within bounds; to limit; to confine." State v. Terry, Del.Super., 39 Del. 32, 196 A. 163, 167 (1937). Cases from other jurisdictions adopting this same definition have seen fit to add that the meaning of the term does not include the power to destroy or prohibit. Forest Land Co. v. Black, S.C.Super., 216 S.C. 255, 57 S.E.2d 420 (1950); Dart v. City of Gulfport, Miss.Supr., 147 Miss. 534, 113 So. 441 (1927):

The zoning authority given to municipalities by 22 Del.C. § 301 does not expressly grant the power to prohibit or destroy a lawful property use which predates a zoning enactment. It is arguable at best that the word "restrict" as contained in the enabling statute carries this power with it. In my view, it does not and should not be so construed.

Municipalities have no inherent power to zone property except as the General Assembly may delegate. Boozer v. Johnson, Del.Ch., 33 Del.Ch. 554, 98 A.2d 76 (1953). Such being the case, and the ordinance in issue here having been analyzed as one which is intended to prohibit or destroy an otherwise lawfully vested property right of the defendant Rollins to use its property for the purpose of maintaining off-site signs, it is my conclusion that the City of New Castle has not been granted the power by the General Assembly to enact such an ordinance. Accordingly, it will not be enforced in this proceeding.

I can well appreciate the problem caused by the continuation of off-site signs in residential areas. With respect to billboards there is great temptation to support a reasonable means to bring about their removal, especially after a prolonged period of time. In the scheme of things, billboards do not evoke much sympathy. However, it is the concept that is bothersome. It is a concept that is potentially far-reaching.

If a municipality can terminate a billboard use today and a junk yard tomorrow, how long will it take to go after the outdated shopping center or the cattle farm brought within municipal boundaries through the annexation of an area? Certainly, if the so-called amortization of a conflicting use will justify the elimination of the one, it will justify the elimination of the other. The power has awesome potential, especially if misused in the name of the public good. If municipalities are to be given this power, then I think that it should be made clear by the General Assembly and accomplished by means of a legislative grant which can be properly measured against constitutional safeguards. It is not, in my opinion, a power that should be created by judicial decision under less than compelling circumstances.

Judgment will be entered in favor of the defendant dismissing the complaint.

Notes and Questions

1. The Standard State Zoning Enabling Act omitted any reference to nonconforming uses, and most of the early zoning legislation (including the pioneering New York legislation) was as silent as the Standard Act on this point. The omission of any reference to the problem of nonconforming uses was apparently based largely on political considerations; the draftsmen of the early enabling statutes feared that state legislatures would not enact them if they expressly authorized the elimination of nonconforming uses without payment of compensation. Thus, Bassett states that,

"During the preparatory work for the zoning of Greater New York fears were constantly expressed by property owners that existing nonconforming buildings would be ousted. The demand was general that this should not be done. The Zoning Commission went as far as it could to explain that existing nonconforming uses could continue, that zoning looked to the future, and that if orderliness could be brought about in the future the nonconforming buildings would to a considerable extent be changed by natural causes as time went on. It was also stated by the Commission that the purpose of zoning was to stabilize and protect lawful investments and not to injure assessed valuations or existing uses. This has always been the view in New York. No steps have been taken to oust existing nonconforming uses. Consideration for investments made in accordance with the earlier laws has been one of the strong supports of zoning in that city."

E. Bassett, Zoning 113 (rev. ed. 1940).

When the state's zoning enabling act was silent on the subject of nonconforming uses, the early zoning ordinances almost invariably provided expressly that lawfully established nonconforming uses might continue, although many ordinances contained a wide variety of restrictive regulations which were meant to hasten their disappearance. Such provisions are still a feature of almost all local zoning ordinances. Typically, they prohibit or severely restrict the physical extension of nonconforming uses, impose limitations on the repair, alteration, or reconstruction of nonconforming structures, and prohibit the resumption of nonconforming uses after "abandonment" or "discontinuance."

Quite early in the history of zoning, it was occasionally argued that there was no justification for treating established nonconforming uses differently— and more favorably—than merely planned or potential future uses, and that permitting nonconforming uses to continue was arbitrary and discriminatory.

Most of the early cases sustained such differential treatment. See, e.g., State ex rel. Manheim v. Harrison, 114 So. 159 (La.1927) (reasonable measure to avoid unduly harsh treatment of nonconforming uses).

2. "Nonconforming use" is an imprecise term. It may include (a) various types of open land use, such as junkyards, lumber yards, and storage yards for heavy machinery; (b) small structures of a nonconforming type such as a shed or a billboard; (c) buildings designed for a conforming use, or at least capable of such use, which have in fact been devoted to some nonconforming use—e.g., an office or store on the ground floor of a residential building; (d) buildings designed, and really only usable, for nonconforming purposes—e.g., a factory building; (e) the use of a building of a generally conforming type for a conforming use, but with some nonconformity as to lot size, lot frontage, setbacks, height, or bulk.

3. It is not always easy to determine when a nonconforming use has been lawfully established. Where the actual "use"—whether of open land or of a structure—rather than a structure itself is nonconforming, most courts seem to require a quantitatively substantial devotion of the property to that use prior to the date when the zoning regulation prohibiting the use becomes effective. See, e.g., Township of Fruitport v. Baxter, 6 Mich.App. 283, 148 N.W.2d 888 (1967), holding it insufficient that several truckloads of junked cars were moved onto the tract just before the effective date of the zoning regulation. But see Kubby v. Hammond, 68 Ariz. 17, 198 P.2d 134 (1948) (nonconforming junkyard was established by a show of intent to establish such a use—building a fence and placing a few junked cars on the tract); County of DuPage v. Gary-Wheaton Bank, 42 Ill.App.2d 299, 192 N.E.2d 311 (1963) (nonconforming gravel pit was established by one day's work therein).

Where a developer undertakes a building project which becomes nonconforming under new lot area, frontage, setback, height, bulk, density or building type regulations before construction is completed, a more difficult problem is presented. Up to and through the stage where the developer obtains a building permit, very few courts have found that the developer acquires a vested right to a nonconforming use. Subsequent to the building permit stage, however, the developer normally signs contracts for the construction of the project, does clearance work on the site, and makes other expenditures in reliance on the building permit. Some courts find a vested right to a nonconforming use at this stage, and a vested right is even more often found to have accrued when the developer has started to install the foundations on the site. Most courts would probably find a vested right to a nonconforming use when the foundation work is completed and substantial work has been done above ground level.

Although the most important factor in the court's determination as to accrual of a vested right to a nonconforming use is the stage which the project reached before the zoning ordinance prohibited it, other factors may also be significant. Thus, if the developer rushed to beat the deadline on a proposed zoning regulation which he knew was under consideration, courts tend to be unsympathetic to him, viewing his situation, in effect, as one of self-inflicted hardship. On the other hand, if the local governing body rushes to change the zoning regulations in order to block a particular development, or the local officials have obviously been stalling on the issuance of a building permit while trying to get a zoning amendment passed to stop the project, this tends to favor the developer. And courts are likely to be sympathetic to the developer if the local officials have encouraged the developer to go ahead, although courts are reluctant to find that a municipality is estopped by the acts of its officials.

4. In light of *Hadacheck* and *Pennsylvania Coal Co.*, do you think the United States Supreme Court, back in the 1920's, would have sustained zoning regulations requiring termination of nonconforming uses without payment of compensation? Do you think allowance of an "amortization" period would have been regarded as a significant factor in determining the constitutionality of compulsory termination provisions? Doubts as to constitutionality, coupled with fear that state legislatures would not enact zoning enabling legislation if provision was made for compulsory termination of nonconforming uses without compensation, led the draftsmen of the Standard Act to omit any reference at all to nonconforming uses. See E. Bassett, Zoning 113 (rev. ed. 1940). A few of the early zoning enabling acts expressly provided that nonconforming uses should not be terminated without compensation. See, e.g., Mich.Comp.Laws Ann. § 125.583a (1976).

5. In Harbison v. City of Buffalo, cited in the principal case, the court approved the theory that nonconformances may be terminated after a reasonable time, using the following language:

"With regard to prior nonconforming *structures*, reasonable termination periods based upon the amortized life of the structure are not, in our opinion, unconstitutional. They do not compel the immediate destruction of the improvements, but envision and allow for their normal life without extensive alterations or repairs. Such a regulation is akin to those we have sustained relating to restrictions upon the extension or substantial repair or replacement of prior nonconforming structures.

"As to prior nonconforming *uses*, * * * [i]f * * * a zoning ordinance provides a sufficient period of permitted nonconformity, it may further provide that at the end of such period the use must cease. This rule is analogous to that with respect to nonconforming structures. In ascertaining the reasonable period during which an owner of property must be allowed to continue a nonconforming use, a balance must be found between social harm and private injury. We cannot say that a legislative body may not in any case, after consideration of the factors involved, conclude that termination of a use after a period of time sufficient to allow a property owner to amortize his investment and make other plans is a valid method of solving the problem."

The case was remanded for a determination of the question "whether the resultant injury to petitioners [if they were required to terminate their junkyard business] would be so substantial that the ordinance would be unconstitutional as applied to the particular facts of this case." On remand, the trial court concluded that, if the petitioners were required to move their business, it would cost them approximately $20,000 and that the "amortization" requirement was "unconstitutional as applied to the particular facts of this case." Note, 44 Cornell L.Q. 450, 451 (1959).

6. Judge Van Voorhis, dissenting in *Harbison*, was extremely critical of the "amortization" rationale. He said,

"This theory to justify extinguishing nonconforming uses means less the more one thinks about it. It offers little more promise of ultimate success than the other theories which have been tried and abandoned. In the first place, the periods of time vary so widely in the cases which have been cited from different States where it has been tried, and have so little relation to the useful lives of the structures, that this theory cannot be used to reconcile these discordant decisions. Moreover the term 'amortization', as thus employed, has not the same meaning which it carries in law or accounting. It is not even used by analogy. It is just a catch phrase, and the reasoning is reduced to argument by metaphor. Not only has no effort been made in the reported cases where this theory has been applied to determine what is the useful life of the structure, but almost all were decided under ordinances or statutes which prescribe the same time limit for many different kinds of improvements. This demonstrates that it is not attempted to measure the life of the particular building or type of building, and that the word 'amortization' is used as an empty shibboleth. This comment applies to the ordinance at issue on this appeal. There could be no presumption that all junk yards, all auto wrecking or dismantling establishments, and all improvements assessed for tax purposes at not more than $500 will or have any tendency to depreciate to zero in three years. This shows that the ordinance in suit could not possibly have been based on the amortization theory.

"Moreover this theory, if it were seriously advanced, would imply that the owner should not keep up his property by making necessary replacements to restore against the ravages of time. Such replacements would be money thrown away. The amortization theory would thus encourage owners of nonconforming uses to allow them to decay and become slums."

Subsequently, in Modjeska Sign Studies, Inc. v. Berle, 43 N.Y.2d 468, 402 N.Y.S.2d 359, 373 N.E.2d 255 (1977), the court held that a statute requiring removal of outdoor advertising signs from the Catskill and Adirondack State Parks, without compensation, was not unconstitutional *per se*, and remanded the case for consideration of the question whether the six and one-half year "amortization" period was reasonable. On this question, the court said,

* * * Whether an amortization period is reasonable is a question that must be answered in the light of the facts of each particular case. Certainly, a critical factor is the length of the amortization period in relation to the investment. Similarly, another factor considered significant by some courts is the nature of the nonconforming activity prohibited; generally a shorter period may be provided for a nonconforming use as opposed to a nonconforming structure. The critical question, however, that must be asked is whether the public gain achieved by the exercise of the police power outweighs the private loss suffered by the owners of the nonconforming uses. While an owner need not be given that period of time necessary to recoup his investment entirely, the amortization period should not be so short as to result in a substantial loss. In determining what constitutes a substantial loss, the court should look to, for example, such factors as: initial capital investment, investment realization to date, life expectancy of the investment, and the existence or nonexistence of a lease obligation as well as a contingency clause permitting termination of the lease. Generally, most regulations requiring the removal of nonconforming billboards and providing a reasonable amortization period should pass constitutional muster.

7.   For a detailed tabulation of the types of nonconforming uses and structures eliminated by the amortization technique in cases where the technique was held valid and the amortization periods reasonable, see American Law Institute, Model Land Development Code 170–72 (Proposed Official Draft 1975), listing 28 cases. Nine of these involved advertising signs; 5 involved junkyards or auto wrecking yards; and 3 involved gasoline service stations. In Hatfield v. City of Fayetteville, 278 Ark. 544, 647 S.W.2d 450 (1983), the court sustained an ordinance requiring removal of all free-standing nonconforming signs within seven years, holding that the ordinance was constitutional both on its face and as applied. However, in Ailes v. Decatur County Area Planning Commission, 448 N.E.2d 1057 (Ind.1983), U.S.App. pending, the court laid down the broad rule that "an ordinance prohibiting any continuation of a lawful use within a zoned area regardless of the length of time given to amortize that use is unconstitutional as the taking of property without due process of law and an unrea-

sonable exercise of the police power." Consequently, the three- and five-year "amortization" periods allowed before junkyards were required to be removed from residential areas did not make the termination requirement valid. See also Battaglini v. Town of Red River, 669 P.2d 1082 (N.M.1983).

8.   Back in 1970, the American Society of Planning Officials polled its membership to determine the extent to which amortization was being used to eliminate nonconforming uses. Out of 489 cities and counties responding, 159 reported that they had zoning ordinances providing for amortization, but only 27 municipalities reported use of the amortization technique against nonconforming buildings. The report indicated that amortization has most frequently been used against billboards and other land uses involving a small capital investment. R. Scott, The Effect of Nonconforming-Land-Use Amortization (ASPO Planning Advisory Service Rep. No. 280, May 1972). All of this suggests that both courts and local legislative bodies are most receptive to the amortization of "open land uses," billboards, and other structures involving only a small capital investment. If structures which represent a substantial capital investment are to be amortized over a relatively long period—e.g., 20 years, as in Livingston Rock & Gravel Co. v. Los Angeles County, 43 Cal.2d 121, 272 P.2d 4 (1954), or 25 years, as in Swain v. Board of Adjustment of City of University Park, 433 S.W.2d 727 (Tex.Civ.App.1968), appeal dismissed and cert. denied 396 U.S. 277, 90 S.Ct. 563 (1970), rehearing denied 397 U.S. 977, 90 S.Ct. 1085—the municipality is faced with an onerous task of record-keeping to assure that the use is, in fact, terminated at the end of the amortization period. See Comment, Elimination of Nonconforming Uses: Alternatives and Adjuncts to Amortization, 14 U.C.L.A.L.Rev. 354 (1966).

The ASPO report cited above indicated that most of the zoning administrators who responded were dissatisfied with the amortization technique. The American Law Institute has taken a dim view of the amortization technique and, more broadly, of the whole attempt to get rid of nonconforming uses. See Am.Law Inst., Model Land Development Code 173–177 (Proposed Official Draft, 1975). The literature on nonconforming uses is voluminous. In addition to the materials cited in *Harbison* and the preceding Notes, a sampling of the literature might include the following: 1 Anderson, American Law of Zoning ch. 6 (2d ed. 1976); 4 Williams, American Land Planning Law ch. 109 (1975); Wood, Zoning Ordinances Requiring the Termination of a Nonconforming Use, in 1973 S.W. Legal Foundation Inst. on Planning, Zoning & Eminent Domain 65; Katarincic, Elimination of Nonconforming Uses, Buildings, and Structures by Amortization—Concept v. Law, 2 Duquesne L.Rev. 1 (1962); Anderson, Nonconforming Uses—A Product of Euclidean Zoning, 10 Syracuse L.Rev. 214 (1959); Norton, Elimination of Incompatible Uses and Structures, 20 Law & Contemp. Prob. 305 (1955); Noel, Retroactive Zoning and Nuisances, 41 Col.L.Rev. 457 (1941); Note, 50 Calif.L.Rev. 101 (1962); Comment, 57 Nw.U.L.Rev. 323 (1962); Comment, 30 Ind.L.J. 521 (1955).

ARVERNE BAY CONSTRUCTION CO. v. THATCHER

Court of Appeals of New York, 1938.
287 N.Y. 222, 15 N.E.2d 587.

Appeal from a judgment, entered February 28, 1938, upon an order of the Appellate Division of the Supreme Court in the second judicial department reversing, on the law, a judgment in favor of plaintiff entered upon a decision of the court on trial at Special Term and directing a dismissal of the complaint.

LEHMAN, J. The plaintiff is the owner of a plot of vacant land on the northerly side of Linden boulevard in the borough of Brooklyn. Until 1928 the district in which the property is situated was classified as an "unrestricted" zone, under the Building Zone Resolution of the city of New York (New York Code of Ordinances, Appendix B). Then, by amendment of the ordinance and the "Use District Map," the district was placed in a residence zone. The plaintiff, claiming that its property could not be used properly or profitably for any purpose permitted in a residence zone and that, in consequence, the zoning ordinance imposed unnecessary hardship upon it, applied to the Board of Standards and Appeals, under section 21 of the Building Zone Resolution, for a variance which would permit the use of the premises for a gasoline service station. The application was denied, and, upon review in certiorari proceedings, the courts sustained the determination of the board. (People ex rel. Arverne Bay Construction Co. v. Murdock, 247 App.Div. 889, 286 N.Y.S. 785; aff'd 271 N.Y. 631, 3 N.E.2d 457.)

Defeated in its attempt to obtain permission to put its property to a profitable use, the plaintiff has brought this action to secure an adjudication that the restrictions placed upon the use of its property by the zoning ordinance result in deprivation of its property without due process of law and that, in so far as the ordinance affects its property, the ordinance violates the provisions of the Constitution of the United States and the Constitution of the State of New York. In this action it demands as a right what has been refused to it as a favor. * * *

The amendment to the zoning ordinance, about which complaint is made, changed from an unrestricted zone to a residential district the property abutting on Linden boulevard for a distance of four miles, with the exception of a small section at a railroad crossing. The district is almost undeveloped. There had been no building construction in that area for many years prior to the amendment. The chairman of the building zone commission which drafted the zoning ordinance, testifying as an expert witness for the defendant, described the district as in a "transition state from the farms as I knew them thirty and forty years ago south of this location." There are some old buildings used for nonconforming purposes, left from the days when the district was used for farming. There are only three buildings on Linden boulevard in a distance of about a mile. One of these buildings is a cow stable and a second building is used as an office in connection with the dairy business conducted there. A gasoline station erected on that boulevard would, it is plain, not adversely affect the health, morals, safety or general welfare of the people who now live in that neighborhood. Justification, if any, for the ordinance restricting the use of the property on Linden boulevard to residential purposes must be found in the control over future development which will result from such restrictions.

Without zoning restrictions, the self-interest of the individual property owners will almost inevitably dictate the form of the development of the district. The plaintiff claims, and has conclusively shown at the trial, that at no time since the amendment of the zoning resolution could its property be profitably used for residential purposes. The expert witness for the city, to whose testimony we have already referred and whose qualifications are universally recognized, admits that such a residential improvement would, even now after the lapse of ten years, be "premature." The property, then, must for the present remain unimproved and unproductive, a source of expense to the owner, or must be put to some non-conforming use. In a district otherwise well adapted for residences a gasoline station or other nonconforming use of property may render neighboring property less desirable for use as a private residence. The development of a district for residential purposes might best serve the interests of the city as a whole and, in the end, might perhaps prove the most profitable use of the property within such district. A majority of the property owners might conceivably be content to bear the burden of taxes and other carrying charges upon unimproved land in order to reap profit in the future from the development of the land for residential purposes. They could not safely do so without reasonable assurance that the district will remain adapted for residence use and will not be spoilt for such purpose by the intrusion of structures used for less desirable purposes. The zoning ordinance is calculated to provide such assurance to property owners in the district and to constrain the property owners to develop their land in a manner which in the future will prove of benefit to the city. Such considerations have induced the Appellate Division to hold that the ordinance is valid.

There is little room for disagreement with the general rules and tests set forth in the opinion of the Appellate Division. The difficulty arises in the application of such rules and tests to the particular facts in this case. We are not disposed to define the police power of the State so narrowly that it would exclude reasonable restrictions placed upon the use of property in order to aid the development of new districts in accordance with plans calculated to advance the public welfare of the city in the future. We have said that "the need for vision of the future in the governance of cities has not lessened with the years. The dweller within the gates, even more than the stranger from afar, will pay the price of blindness." (Hesse v. Rath, 249 N.Y. 436, 438, 164 N.E. 342.) We have, indeed, recognized that long-time planning for zoning purposes may be a valid exercise of the police power, but at the same time we have pointed out that the power is not unlimited. "We are not required to say that a merely temporary restraint of beneficial enjoyment is unlawful where the interference is necessary to promote the ultimate good either of the municipality as a whole or of the immediate neighborhood. Such problems will have to be solved when they arise. If we assume that the restraint may be permitted, the interference must be not unreasonable, but on the contrary must be kept within the limits of necessity." (People ex rel. St. Albans-Springfield Corp. v. Connell, 257 N.Y. 73, 83, 177 N.E. 313, 316.) The problem presented upon this appeal is whether or not the zoning ordinance as applied to the plaintiff's property is unreasonable.

Findings of the trial judge, sustained by evidence presented by the plaintiff, establish that, in the vicinity of the plaintiff's premises, the city operates an incinerator which "gives off offensive fumes and odors which permeate plaintiff's premises." About 1,200 or 1,500 feet from the plaintiff's land, "a trunk sewer carrying both storm and sanitary sewage empties into an open creek * * *. The said creek runs to the south of plaintiff's premises and gives off nauseating odors which permeate the said property." The trial judge further found that other conditions exist which, it is plain, render the property entirely unfit, at present, for any conforming use. Though the defendant urges that the conditions are not as bad as the plaintiff's witnesses have pictured, yet as the Appellate Division has said: "It must be conceded, upon the undisputed facts in this case, that this property cannot, presently or in the immediate future, be profitably used for residential purposes." (253 App.Div. 285, 286, 2 N.Y.S.2d 112, 114.)

We may assume that the zoning ordinance is the product of far-sighted planning calculated to promote the general welfare of the city at some future time. If the State or the city, acting by delegation from the State, had plenary power to pass laws calculated to promote the general welfare, then the validity of the ordinance might be sustained; for "we have nothing to do with the question of the wisdom or good policy of municipal ordinances." (Village of Euclid v. Ambler Realty Co., 272 U.S. 365, 393, 47 S.Ct. 114, 120, 71 L.Ed. 303, 54 A.L.R. 1016.) The legislative power of the State is, however, not plenary, but is limited by the Constitution of the United States and by the Constitution of the State. It may not take private property without compensation even for a public purpose and to advance the general welfare. (Matter of Eaton v. Sweeny, 257 N.Y. 176, 177 N.E. 412.) "The protection of private property in the fifth amendment presupposes that it is wanted for public use, but provides that it shall not be taken for such use without compensation. A similar assumption is made in the decisions upon the fourteenth amendment. Hairston v. Danville & Western Ry. Co., 208 U.S. 598, 605, 28 S.Ct. 331, 52 L.Ed. 637. When this seemingly absolute protection is found to be qualified by the police power, the natural tendency of human nature is to extend the qualification more and more until at last private property disappears. But that cannot be accomplished in this way under the constitution of the United States." (Pennsylvania Coal Co. v. Mahon, 260 U.S. 393, 415, 43 S.Ct. 158, 160, 67 L.Ed. 322, 28 A.L.R. 1321.)

In the prevailing opinion in that case, Mr. Justice Holmes pointed out that "the general rule at least is, that while property may be regulated to a certain extent, if regulation goes too far it will be recognized as a taking" (p. 415, 43 S.Ct. page 160). Whether a regulation does go too far is "a question of degree—and therefore cannot be disposed of by general propositions," and here Mr. Justice Holmes gave warning that "we are in danger of forgetting that a strong public desire to improve the public condition is not enough to warrant achieving the desire by a shorter cut than the constitutional way of paying for the change" (p. 416, 43 S.Ct. page 160). The dissent of Mr. Justice Brandeis in that case is not based upon difference of opinion in regard to general principles, but upon different evaluation of the degree of the restrictions there challenged.

The warning of Mr. Justice Holmes should perhaps be directed rather to Legislatures than to courts; for the courts have not hesitated to declare statutes invalid wherever regulation has gone so far that it is clearly unreasonable and must be "recognized as taking;" and unless regulation does clearly go so far the courts may not deny force to the regulation. We have already pointed out that in the case which we are reviewing, the plaintiff's land cannot at present or in the immediate future be profitably or reasonably used without violation of the restriction. An ordinance which *permanently* so restricts the use of property that it cannot be used for any reasonable purpose goes, it is plain, beyond regulation, and must be recognized as a taking of the property. The only substantial difference, in such case, between restriction and actual taking, is that the restriction leaves the owner subject to the burden of payment of taxation, while outright confiscation would relieve him of that burden.

The situation, of course, might be quite different where it appears that within a reasonable time the property can be put to a profitable use. The temporary inconvenience or even hardship of holding unproductive property might then be compensated by ultimate benefit to the owner or, perhaps, even without such compensation, the individual owners might be compelled to bear a temporary burden in order to promote the public good. We do not pass upon such problems now, for here no inference is permissible that within a reasonable time the property can be put to a profitable use or that the present inconvenience or hardship imposed upon the plaintiff is temporary. True, there is evidence that the neighborhood is improving and that some or all of the conditions which now render the district entirely unsuitable for residence purposes will in time be removed. Even so, it is conceded that prognostication that the district will in time become suited for residences rests upon hope and not upon certainty and no estimate can be made of the time which must elapse before the hope becomes fact.

During the nine years from 1928 to 1936, when concededly the property was unsuitable for any conforming use, the property was assessed at $18,000, and taxes amounting to $4,566 were levied upon it, in addition to assessments of several thousand dollars; yet, so far as appears, the district was no better suited for residence purposes at the time of the trial in 1936 than it was when the zoning ordinance was amended in 1928. In such case the ordinance is clearly more than a temporary and reasonable restriction placed upon the land to promote the general welfare. It is in substance a taking of the land prohibited by the Constitution of the United States and by the Constitution of the State.

We repeat here what under similar circumstances the court said in People ex rel. St. Albans-Springfield Corp. v. Connell (supra, p. 83, 177 N.E. page 316): "we are not required to say that a merely temporary restraint of beneficial enjoyment is unlawful where the interference is necessary to promote the ultimate good, either of the municipality as a whole or of the immediate neighborhood." There the court held that

the "ultimate good" could be attained and a "productive use" allowed
by a variation of the zoning ordinance that "will be temporary and provisional and readily terminable." Here the application of the plaintiff
for any variation was properly refused, for the conditions which render
the plaintiff's property unsuitable for residential use are general and
not confined to plaintiff's property. In such case, we have held that the
general hardship should be remedied by revision of the general regulation, not by granting the special privilege of a variation to single owners. (Matter of Levy v. Board of Standards & Appeals, 267 N.Y. 347,
196 N.E. 284.) Perhaps a new ordinance might be evolved by which the
"ultimate good" may be attained without depriving owners of the productive use of their property. That is a problem for the legislative authority, not for the courts. Now we hold only that the present regulation *as applied to plaintiff's property* is not valid.

The judgment of the Appellate Division should be reversed and that
of the Special Term affirmed, with costs in this court and in the Appellate Division.

Judgment accordingly.

Notes and Questions

1. Pennsylvania Coal Co. v. Mahon was not the only United States Supreme
Court decision to which the New York Court of Appeals might have looked for
guidance. Recall Hadacheck v. Sebastian, 239 U.S. 394, 36 S.Ct. 143, 60 L.Ed.
348 (1915) (like *Mahon*, reprinted in Chapter 13), upholding a Los Angeles ordinance which prohibited the operation of petitioner's brick factory and (as alleged by petitioner) reduced the value of the brick clay on his land from about
$800,000 to $60,000. Why do you suppose the New York court in *Arverne Bay*
relied on *Mahon* and ignored *Hadacheck?*

2. When the New York court in *Arverne Bay* said that the residential use
classification went "beyond regulation, and must be recognized as a taking of
the property," did it literally mean what it said? Suppose the plaintiff landowner had sought "just compensation" for the "taking" on an "inverse condemnation" theory, instead of simply seeking to invalidate the residential use classification. Would the court have awarded compensation to the plaintiff?

3. In Consolidated Rock Products Co. v. City of Los Angeles, 57 Cal.2d 515,
20 Cal.Rptr. 638, 370 P.2d 342 (1962), app. dismissed for want of a substantial
federal question, 371 U.S. 36, 83 S.Ct. 145 (1962), the California court upheld
zoning which prohibited sand and gravel mining on a large tract owned by Consolidated, despite the trial court's finding that the tract had great value if used
for sand and gravel mining but "no appreciable economic value" for any other
use and that, in view of the "continuing flood hazard and the nature of the
soil," any suggestion that the tract had economic value for any other use, including those uses for which it was zoned, "is preposterous." There was substantial evidence that, even though operated with all possible safeguards, the
extraction of sand and gravel from the tract would still create appreciable
quantities of dust, which would be carried by the prevailing winds to the residences and sanitariums of nearby Sunland and Tujunga; that this dust would
have a damaging effect on the sufferers from respiratory ailments who largely
populated these neighboring communities; and also that sand and gravel mining would adversely affect property values in these communities as well as the

reputation of Sunland and Tujunga "as a haven for sufferers from respiratory ailments."

4. In *Arverne Bay*, the court concluded that the zoning ordinance restricted the use of plaintiff's property that it could not be used for "any reasonable purpose," which it seems to have equated with inability to put the property "to a profitable use." In New York and in many other states, the courts have consistently held that a land use restriction is not a *de facto* "taking" simply because it prohibits the *most* profitable use of the land in question. In some states, a land use restriction that is otherwise valid—i.e., has a proper public purpose and utilizes a reasonable means of achieving that purpose—will not be held invalid as a *de facto* "taking" unless the restriction prevents use of the land for any reasonable purpose (or any profitable use) whatever. In other states, however, the courts have applied a "balancing" test, probably derived from the classic tripartite substantive due process test laid down in Lawton v. Steele, 152 U.S. 133, 14 S.Ct. 499, 38 L.Ed. 385 (1894). Under the "balancing" test, courts attempt to measure net social gains against the economic loss to individual landowners—basically a utilitarian test. Some critics have questioned the fairness of the "balancing" test. See, e.g., Michelman, Property, Utility, and Fairness: Comments on the Ethical Foundations of "Just Compensation" Law, 80 Harv.L.Rev. 1165 (1967). In any case, it is far from clear that courts are really capable of applying the "balancing" test, since it requires them to make subjective evaluations of the public purposes that may justify imposition of substantial economic losses on individual landowners. Moreover, determination of the "loss" to the landowner may present serious difficulties. Should the entire difference in the value of the land for its most profitable use and for the uses permitted by the land use regulations be considered an economic "loss"? If not, how should the "loss" be measured?

5. In recent years, land use regulations have been attached as *de facto* "takings" principally in three types of cases: (1) where, as in *Arverne Bay*, land has been "down-zoned" to a classification that prohibits the most profitable uses of the land; (2) where, as in Just v. Marinette County and Agins v. City of Tiburon, and San Diego Gas & Electric Co. v. City of San Diego, infra, any substantial land development whatever is prohibited by "environmental" or "open space" regulations; and (3) where, as in Penn Central Transportation Co. v. City of New York, infra, development or redevelopment of improved property is substantially prohibited as a result of designating an existing structure as a "landmark" or including it in an "historic district."

JUST v. MARINETTE COUNTY

Supreme Court of Wisconsin, 1972.
56 Wis.2d 7, 201 N.W.2d 761.

These two cases were consolidated for trial and argued together on appeal. In case number 106, Ronald Just and Kathryn L. Just, his wife (Justs), sought a declaratory judgment stating: (1) The shoreland zoning ordinance of the respondent Marinette County (Marinette) was unconstitutional, (2) their property was not "wetlands" as defined in the ordinance, and (3) the prohibition against the filling of wetlands was unconstitutional. In case number 107, Marinette county sought a mandatory injunction to restrain the Justs from placing fill material on their property without first obtaining a conditional-use permit as required by the ordinance and also a forfeiture for their violation of the ordinance in having placed fill on their lands without a permit. The trial court held the ordinance was valid, the Justs' property was "wet-lands," the Justs had violated the ordinance and they were subject to a forfeiture of $100. From the judgments, the Justs appeal.

On this appeal the state of Wisconsin has intervened as a party-re-spondent pursuant to sec. 274.12(6), Stats., because of the issue of con-stitutionality. The state considers the appeal to be a challenge to the underlying secs. 59.971 and 144.26, Stats., and a challenge to the state's comprehensive program to protect navigable waters through shoreland regulation. * * *

HALLOWS, Chief Justice. Marinette county's Shoreland Zoning Or-dinance Number 24 was adopted September 19, 1967, became effective October 9, 1967, and follows a model ordinance published by the Wiscon-sin Department of Resource Development in July of 1967. See Kusler, Water Quality Protection For Inland Lakes in Wisconsin: A Comprehen-sive Approach to Water Pollution, 1970 Wis.L.Rev. 35, 62–63. The ordi-nance was designed to meet standards and criteria for shoreland regula-tion which the legislature required to be promulgated by the department of natural resources under sec. 144.26, Stats. These stan-dards are found in 6 Wis.Adm.Code, sec. NR 115.03, May, 1971, Regis-ter No. 185. The legislation, secs. 59.971 and 144.26, Stats., authorizing the ordinance was enacted as a part of the Water Quality Act of 1965 by ch. 614, Laws of 1965.

Shorelands for the purpose of ordinances are defined in sec. 59.971(1), Stats., as lands within 1,000 feet of the normal high-water ele-vation of navigable lakes, ponds, or flowages and 300 feet from a navi-gable river or stream or to the landward side of the flood plain, which-ever distance is greater. The state shoreland program is unique. All county shoreland zoning ordinances must be approved by the depart-ment of natural resources prior to their becoming effective. 6 Wis. Adm.Code, sec. NR 115.04, May, 1971, Register No. 185. If a county does not enact a shoreland zoning ordinance which complies with the state's standards, the department of natural resources may enact such an ordinance for the county. Sec. 59.971(6), Stats.

There can be no disagreement over the public purpose sought to be obtained by the ordinance. Its basic purpose is to protect navigable wa-ters and the public rights therein from the degradation and deteriora-tion which results from uncontrolled use and development of shore-lands. In the Navigable Waters Protection Act, sec. 144.26, the purpose of the state's shoreland regulation program is stated as being to "aid in the fulfillment of the state's role as trustee of its navigable waters and to promote public health, safety, convenience and general welfare." In sec. 59.971(1), which grants authority for shoreland zoning to counties, the same purposes are reaffirmed. The Marinette county shoreland zoning ordinance in secs. 1.2 and 1.3 states the uncontrolled use of shorelands and pollution of navigable waters of Marinette county ad-versely affect public health, safety, convenience, and general welfare and impair the tax base.

The shoreland zoning ordinance divides the shorelands of Marinette county into general purpose districts, general recreation districts, and conservancy districts. A "conservancy" district is required by the statutory minimum standards and is defined in sec. 3.4 of the ordinance to include "all shorelands designated as swamps or marshes on the United States Geological Survey maps which have been designated as the Shoreland Zoning Map of Marinette County, Wisconsin or on the detailed Insert Shoreland Zoning Maps." The ordinance provides for permitted uses [1] and conditional uses.[2] One of the conditional uses requiring a permit under sec. 3.42(4) is the filling, drainage or dredging of wetlands according to the provisions of sec. 5 of the ordinance. "Wetlands" are defined in sec. 2.29 as "(a)reas where ground water is at or near the surface much of the year or where any segment of plant cover is deemed an aquatic according to N.C. Fassett's "Manual of Aquatic Plants." Section 5.42(2) of the ordinance requires a conditional-use permit for any filling or grading "Of any area which is within three hundred feet horizontal distance of a navigable water and which has surface drainage toward the water and on which there is: (a) Filling of more than five hundred square feet of any wetland which is contiguous to the water * * * (d) Filling or grading of more than 2,000 square feet on slopes of twelve per cent or less."

In April of 1961, several years prior to the passage of this ordinance, the Justs purchased 36.4 acres of land in the town of Lake along the south shore of Lake Noquebay, a navigable lake in Marinette county. This land had a frontage of 1,266.7 feet on the lake and was purchased partially for personal use and partially for resale. During the years 1964, 1966, and 1967, the Justs made five sales of parcels having frontage and extending back from the lake some 600 feet, leaving the property involved in these suits. This property has a frontage of 366.7 feet and the south one half contains a stand of cedar, pine, various hard woods, birch and red maple. The north one half, closer to the lake, is barren of trees except immediately along the shore. The south three fourths of this north one half is populated with various plant grasses

---

1. "3.41   Permitted Uses

(1) Harvesting of any wild crop such as marsh hay, ferns, moss, wild rice, berries, tree fruits and tree seeds.

(2) Sustained yield forestry subject to the provisions of Section 5.0 relating to removal of shore cover.

(3) Utilities such as, but not restricted to, telephone, telegraph and power transmission lines.

(4) Hunting, fishing, preservation of scenic, historic and scientific areas and wildlife preserves.

(5) Non-resident buildings used solely in conjunction with raising water fowl, minnows, and other similar lowland animals, fowl or fish.

(6) Hiking trails and bridle paths.

(7) Accessory uses.

(8) Signs, subject to the restriction of Section 2.0."

2. "3.42   Conditional Uses. The following uses are permitted upon issuance of a Conditional Use Permit as provided in Section 9.0 and issuance of a Department of Resource Development permit where required by Section 30.11, 30.12, 30.19, 30.195 and 31.05 of the Wisconsin Statutes.

(1) General farming provided farm animals shall be kept one hundred feet from any non-farm residence.

(2) Dams, power plants, flowages and ponds.

(3) Relocation of any water course.

(4) Filling, drainage or dredging of wetlands according to the provisions of Section 5.0 of this ordinance.

(5) Removal of top soil or peat.

(6) Cranberry bogs.

(7) Piers, docks, boathouses."

and vegetation including some plants which N.C. Fassett in his manual of aquatic plants has classified as "aquatic." There are also non-acquatic plants which grow upon the land. Along the shoreline there is a belt of trees. The shoreline is from one foot to 3.2 feet higher than the lake level and there is a narrow belt of higher land along the shore known as a "pressure ridge" or "ice heave," varying in width from one to three feet. South of this point, the natural level of the land ranges one to two feet above lake level. The land slopes generally toward the lake but has a slope less than twelve per cent. No water flows onto the land from the lake, but there is some surface water which collects on land and stands in pools.

The land owned by the Justs is designated as swamps or marshes on the United States Geological Survey Map and is located within 1,000 feet of the normal high-water elevation of the lake. Thus, the property is included in a conservancy district and, by sec. 2.29 of the ordinance, classified as "wetlands." Consequently, in order to place more than 500 square feet of fill on this property, the Justs were required to obtain a conditional-use permit from the zoning administrator of the county and pay a fee of $20 or incur a forfeiture of $10 to $200 for each day of violation.

In February and March of 1968, six months after the ordinance became effective, Ronald Just, without securing a conditional-use permit, hauled 1,040 square yards of sand onto this property and filled an area approximately 20-feet wide commencing at the southwest corner and extending almost 600 feet north to the northwest corner near the shoreline, then easterly along the shoreline almost to the lot line. He stayed back from the pressure ridge about 20 feet. More than 500 square feet of this fill was upon wetlands located contiguous to the water and which had surface drainage toward the lake. The fill within 300 feet of the lake also was more than 2,000 square feet on a slope less than 12 percent. It is not seriously contended that the Justs did not violate the ordinance and the trial court correctly found a violation.

The real issue is whether the conservancy district provisions and the wetlands-filling restrictions are unconstitutional because they amount to a constructive taking of the Justs' land without compensation. Marinette county and the state of Wisconsin argue the restrictions of the conservancy district and wetlands provisions constitute a proper exercise of the police power of the state and do not so severely limit the use or depreciate the value of the land as to constitute a taking without compensation.

To state the issue in more meaningful terms, it is a conflict between the public interest in stopping the despoliation of natural resources, which our citizens until recently have taken as inevitable and for granted, and an owner's asserted right to use his property as he wishes. The protection of public rights may be accomplished by the exercise of the police power unless the damage to the property owner is too great and amounts to a confiscation. The securing or taking of a benefit not presently enjoyed by the public for its use is obtained by the government through its power of eminent domain. The distinction between the exercise of the police power and condemnation has been said to be a matter of degree of damage to the property owner. In the valid exercise of the police power reasonably restricting the use of property, the damage suffered by the owner is said to be incidental. However, where the restriction is so great the landowner ought not to bear such a burden for the public good, the restriction has been held to be a constructive taking even though the actual use or forbidden use has not been transferred to the government so as to be a taking in the traditional sense. Whether a taking has occurred depends upon whether "the restriction practically or substantially renders the land useless for all reasonable purposes." Buhler v. Racine County, supra. The loss caused the individual must be weighed to determine if it is more than he should bear. As this court stated in Stefan [Auto Body v. State Highway Comm. (1963), 21 Wis.2d 363] at pp. 369–370, 124 N.W.2d 319, p. 323, "* * * If the damage is such as to be suffered by many similarly situated and is in the nature of a restriction on the use to which land may be put and ought to be borne by the individual as a member of society for the good of the public safety, health or general welfare, it is said to be a reasonable exercise of the police power, but if the damage is so great to the individual that he ought not to bear it under contemporary standards, then courts are inclined to treat it as a 'taking' of the property or an unreasonable exercise of the police power."

Many years ago, Professor Freund stated in his work on The Police Power, sec. 511, at 546–547, "It may be said that the state takes property by eminent domain because it is useful to the public, and under the police power because it is harmful * * * From this results the difference between the power of eminent domain and the police power, that the former recognises a right to compensation, while the latter on principle does not." Thus the necessity for monetary compensation for loss suffered to an owner by police power restriction arises when restrictions are placed on property in order to create a public benefit rather than to prevent a public harm. Rathkopf, The Law of Zoning and Planning, Vol. 1, ch. 6, pp. 6–7.

This case causes us to reexamine the concepts of public benefit in contrast to public harm and the scope of an owner's right to use of his property. In the instant case we have a restriction on the use of a citizen's property, not to secure a benefit for the public, but to prevent a harm from the change in the natural character of the citizen's property. We start with the premise that lakes and rivers in their natural state are unpolluted and the pollution which now exists is man made. The state of Wisconsin under the trust doctrine has a duty to eradicate the present pollution and to prevent further pollution in its navigable waters. This is not, in a legal sense, a gain or a securing of a benefit by the maintaining of the natural *status quo* of the environment. What makes this case different from most condemnation or police power zoning cases is the interrelationship of the wetlands, the swamps and the natural environment of shorelands to the purity of the water and to such natural resources as navigation, fishing, and scenic beauty. Swamps and wetlands were once considered wasteland, undesirable, and not picturesque. But as the people became more sophisticated, an appreciation was acquired that swamps and wetlands serve a vital role in nature, are part of the balance of nature and are essential to the purity of the water in our lakes and streams. Swamps and wetlands are a necessary part of the ecological creation and now, even to the uninitiated, possess their own beauty in nature.

Is the ownership of a parcel of land so absolute that man can change its nature to suit any of his purposes? The great forests of our state were stripped on the theory man's ownership was unlimited. But in forestry, the land at least was used naturally, only the natural fruit of the land (the trees) were taken. The despoilage was in the failure to look to the future and provide for the reforestation of the land. An owner of land has no absolute and unlimited right to change the essential natural character of his land so as to use it for a purpose for which it was unsuited in its natural state and which injures the rights of others. The exercise of the police power in zoning must be reasonable and we think it is not an unreasonable exercise of that power to prevent harm to public rights by limiting the use of private property to its natural uses.

This is not a case where an owner is prevented from using his land for natural and indigenous uses. The uses consistent with the nature of the land are allowed and other uses recognized and still others permitted by special permit. The shoreland zoning ordinance prevents to some extent the changing of the natural character of the land within 1,000 feet of a navigable lake and 300 feet of a navigable river because of such land's interrelation to the contiguous water. The changing of wetlands and swamps to the damage of the general public by upsetting the natural environment and the natural relationship is not a reasonable use of that land which is protected from police power regulation. Changes and filling to some extent are permitted because the extent of such changes and fillings does not cause harm. We realize no case in Wisconsin has yet dealt with shoreland regulations and there are several cases in other states which seem to hold such regulations unconstitutional; but nothing this court has said or held in prior cases indicate that destroying the natural character of a swamp or a wetland so as to make that location available for human habitation is a reasonable use of that land when the new use, although of a more economical value to the owner, causes a harm to the general public.

Wisconsin has long held that laws and regulations to prevent pollution and to protect the waters of this state from degradation are valid police-power enactments. * * * The active public trust duty of the state of Wisconsin in respect to navigable waters requires the state not only to promote navigation but also to protect and preserve those waters for fishing, recreation, and scenic beauty. * * * To further this duty, the legislature may delegate authority to local units of the government, which the state did by requiring counties to pass shoreland zoning ordinances. * * *

This is not a case of an isolated swamp unrelated to a navigable lake or stream, the change of which would cause no harm to public rights.

Lands adjacent to or near navigable waters exist in a special relationship to the state. They have been held subject to special taxation, Soens v. City of Racine (1860), 10 Wis. 271, and are subject to state public trust powers, Wisconsin P. & L. Co. v. Public Service Comm. (1958), 5 Wis.2d 167, 92 N.W.2d 241; and since the Laws of 1935, ch. 303, counties have been authorized to create special zoning districts along waterways and zone them for restrictive conservancy purposes. The restrictions in the Marinette county ordinance upon wetlands within 1,000 feet of Lake Noquebay which prevent the placing of excess fill upon such land without a permit is not confiscatory or unreasonable.

Cases wherein a confiscation was found cannot be relied upon by the Justs. In State v. Herwig (1962), 17 Wis.2d 442, 117 N.W.2d 335, a "taking" was found where a regulation which prohibited hunting on farmland had the effect of establishing a game refuge and resulted in an unnatural, concentrated foraging of the owner's land by waterfowl. In State v. Becker, supra, the court held void a law which established a wildlife refuge (and prohibited hunting) on private property. In Benka v. Consolidated Water Power Co. (1929) 198 Wis. 472, 224 N.W. 718, the court held if damages to plaintiff's property were in fact caused by flooding from a dam constructed by a public utility, those damages constituted a "taking" within the meaning of the condemnation statutes. In Bino v. Hurley (1955), 273 Wis. 10, 76 N.W.2d 571, the court held unconstitutional as a "taking" without compensation an ordinance which, in attempting to prevent pollution, prohibited the owners of land surrounding a lake from bathing, boating, or swimming in the lake. In Piper v. Ekern (1923), 180 Wis. 586, 593, 194 N.W. 159, 162, the court held a statute which limited the height of buildings surrounding the state capitol to be unnecessary for the public health, safety, or welfare and, thus, to constitute an unreasonable exercise of the police power. In all these cases the unreasonableness of the exercise of the police power lay in excessive restriction of the natural use of the land or rights in relation thereto.

* * *

The Justs rely on several cases from other jurisdictions which have held zoning regulations involving flood plain districts, flood basins and wetlands to be so confiscatory as to amount to a taking because the owners of the land were prevented from improving such property for residential or commercial purposes. While some of these cases may be distinguished on their facts, it is doubtful whether these differences go to the basic rationale which permeates the decision that an owner has a right to use his property in any way and for any purpose he sees fit. In Dooley v. Town Plan & Zon. Com. of Town of Fairfield (1964), 151 Conn. 304, 197 A.2d 770, the court held the restriction on land located in a flood plain district prevented its being used for residential or business purposes and thus the restriction destroyed the economic value to the owner. The court recognized the land was needed for a public purpose as it was part of the area in which the tidal stream overflowed when abnormally high tides existed, but the property was half a mile from the ocean and therefore could not be used for marina or boathouse pur-

poses. In Morris County Land I. Co. v. Parsippany-Troy Hills Tp.
(1963), 40 N.J. 539, 193 A.2d 232, a flood basin zoning ordinance was
involved which required the controversial land to be retained in its natural state. The plaintiff owned 66 acres of a 1,500-acre swamp which
was part of a river basin and acted as a natural detention basin for
flood waters in times of very heavy rainfall. There was an extraneous
issue that the freezing regulations were intended as a stop-gap until
such time as the government would buy the property under a flood-con-
trol project. However, the court took the view the zoning had an effect
of preserving the land as an open space as a water-detention basin and
only the government or the public would be benefited, to the complete
damage of the owner.

In State v. Johnson (1970), Me., 265 A.2d 711, the Wetlands Act restricted the alteration and use of certain wetlands without permission.
The act was a conservation measure enacted under the police power to
protect the ecology of areas bordering the coastal waters. The plaintiff
owned a small tract of a salt-water marsh which was flooded at high
tide. By filling, the land would be adapted for building purposes. The
court held the restrictions against filling constituted a deprivation of a
reasonable use of the owner's property and, thus, an unreasonable exercise of the police power. In MacGibbon v. Board of Appeals of Dux-
bury (1970), 356 Mass. 635, 255 N.E.2d 347, the plaintiff owned seven
acres of land which were under water about twice a month in a shoreland area. He was denied a permit to excavate and fill part of his property. The purpose of the ordinance was to preserve from despoilage
natural features and resources such as salt marshes, wetlands, and
ponds. The court took the view the preservation of privately owned
land in its natural, unspoiled state for the enjoyment and benefit of the
public by preventing the owner from using it for any practical purpose
was not within the limit and scope of the police power and the ordinance
was not saved by the use of special permits.

It seems to us that filling a swamp not otherwise commercially usable is not in and of itself an existing use, which is prevented, but rather
is the preparation for some future use which is not indigenous to a
swamp. Too much stress is laid on the right of an owner to change
commercially valueless land when that change does damage to the
rights of the public. It is observed that a use of special permits is a
means of control and accomplishing the purpose of the zoning ordinance
as distinguished from the old concept of providing for variances. The
special permit technique is now common practice and has met with judicial approval, and we think it is of some significance in considering
whether or not a particular zoning ordinance is reasonable.

A recent case sustaining the validity of a zoning ordinance establishing a flood plain district is Turnpike Realty Company v. Town of Ded-
ham (June, 1972), 72 Mass. 1303, 284 N.E.2d 891. The court held the
validity of the ordinance was supported by valid considerations of public
welfare, the conservation of "natural conditions, wildlife and open
spaces." The ordinance provided that lands which were subject to seasonal or periodic flooding could not be used for residences or other pur-

poses in such a manner as to endanger the health, safety or occupancy thereof and prohibited the erection of structures or buildings which required land to be filled. This case is analogous to the instant facts. The ordinance had a public purpose to preserve the natural condition of the area. No change was allowed which would injure the purposes sought to be preserved and through the special-permit technique, particular land within the zoning district could be excepted from the restrictions.

The Justs argue their property has been severely depreciated in value. But this depreciation of value is not based on the use of the land in its natural state but on what the land would be worth if it could be filled and used for the location of a dwelling. While loss of value is to be considered in determining whether a restriction is a constructive taking, value based upon changing the character of the land at the expense of harm to public rights is not an essential factor or controlling.

We are not unmindful of the warning in Pennsylvania Coal Co. v. Mahon (1922), 260 U.S. 393, 416, 43 S.Ct. 158, 160, 67 L.Ed. 322:

> "*   *   * We are in danger of forgetting that a strong public desire to improve the public condition is not enough to warrant achieving the desire by a shorter cut than the constitutional way of paying for the change."

This observation refers to the improvement of the public condition, the securing of a benefit not presently enjoyed and to which the public is not entitled. The shoreland zoning ordinance preserves nature, the environment, and natural resources as they were created and to which the people have a present right. The ordinance does not create or improve the public condition but only preserves nature from the despoilage and harm resulting from the unrestricted activities of humans.

Notes and Questions

1. Since the landowner-plaintiff did not even apply for a conditional use permit before placing fill along the shore of Lake Noquebay, why did he have standing to raise the constitutional issue in the principal case? Should not the court have required him to "exhaust his administrative remedy" by applying for a permit—and having his application rejected—before entertaining a challenge the Marinette County shoreland zoning ordinance?

2. In Potomac Sand & Gravel Co. v. Governor of Maryland, 266 Md. 358, 293 A.2d 241 (1972), cert. denied 409 U.S. 1040, 93 S.Ct. 525, 34 L.Ed.2d 490, the court upheld the constitutionality of a statute absolutely prohibiting dredging and filling in tidal wetlands in an opinion with strong "nuisance" overtones. The court quoted the following passage from Commonwealth v. Tewkesbury, 11 Metc. 55 (Mass.1846), upholding a statute prohibiting the taking of sand, stones or gravel from beaches:

"All property is acquired and held under the tacit condition that it shall not be so used as to injure the equal rights of others, or to destroy or greatly impair the public rights and interests of the community, under the maxim of the common law, *sic utere tuo ut alienum non laedas* *   *   *. In such cases, we think, it is competent for the legislature to interpose, and by positive enactment to prohibit the use of property which would be injurious to the public, *   *   *."

266 Md. at 368, 293 A.2d at 247.

The Maryland court distinguished State v. Johnson, discussed in *Just*, on the ground that *Johnson* dealt with a statute authorizing a permit procedure, while the Maryland statute imposed an absolute prohibition against dredging and filling. But it seems clear that the Maryland court did not mean to suggest that the administrative permit procedure set up by the Maryland Wetlands Act of 1970 was invalid, for the court expressly stated that "State v. Johnson is not the law in Maryland."

3. In Sibson v. State, 115 N.H. 124, 336 A.2d 239 (1975), after noting that it had been urged to reject the traditional "taking" formula of Pennsylvania Coal Co. v. Mahon, the court in fact adopted the views of Brandeis, J., dissenting in *Pennsylvania Coal Co.* The New Hampshire court said that "[u]nder the proposed rule, if the action of the state is a valid exercise of the police power proscribing activities that could harm the public, then there is no taking under the eminent domain clause. It is only when the state action appropriates property for the public use at the expense of the property owner that compensation is due." (115 N.H. at 127, 336 A.2d at 241.) The court then held that filling the plaintiff's saltmarsh was an activity "that would be harmful to the public and that, therefore, there was no taking under the eminent domain clause." The court cited with approval Mugler v. Kansas, 123 U.S. 623, 8 S.Ct. 273, 31 L.Ed. 205 (1887)—also relied on by Brandeis in his *Pennsylvania Coal Co.* dissent—which sustained an early Kansas prohibition law shutting down the plaintiff's brewery without compensation, and quoted the statement in *Just* that "[a]n owner of land has no absolute and unlimited right to change the essential natural character of his land so as to use it for a purpose for which it was unsuited in its natural state and which injures the rights of others."

4. In Bob Graham v. Estuary Properties, Inc., 399 So.2d 1374 (Fla.1981), the court sustained the denial of a permit for a major residential and commercial development in a coastal wetland area on the ground that the proposed development would destroy a large stand of mangroves, which in turn would have an adverse impact on water quality in the adjacent coastal bay. The court said, "the permit was denied because of the determination that the proposed development would pollute the surrounding bays, i.e., cause a public harm. It is true that the public benefits in that the bay will remain clean, but that is a benefit in the form of maintaining the status quo. Estuary [Properties] is not being required to change its development plan so that public waterways will be improved. That would be the creation of a public benefit beyond the scope of the state's police power." The Florida court cited *Just* with approval in support of its decision.

5. Compare the approach of the Massachusetts court in Commissioner of Natural Resources v. S. Volpe, Inc., 349 Mass. 104, 206 N.E.2d 666 (1965), where the court held that the Massachusetts wetlands protection statute was enacted to promote a proper public purpose—and thus was within the police power—but also held that the refusal of a permit to fill in a saltmarsh in order to permit construction of "houses with water rights for boating" might nevertheless amount to a *de facto* "taking" of the defendant's property. The court said,

"In this conflict between the ecological and the constitutional, it is plain that neither is to be consumed by the other. * * * [W]hether the defendant is the uncompensated victim of a taking invalid without compensation depends upon further findings as to what uses the marshland may still be put and possibly other issues which have not been argued * * *. The case is remanded

*   *   * for the taking of further evidence and for further findings on the following matters:

"1. The portions, if any, of the 49.4 acres (the locus) which the owner desires to improve below the line of mean high water (see Commonwealth v. City of Roxbury, 9 Gray, 451, 483).

"2. The uses which can be made of the locus in its natural state (a) independently of other land of the owner in the area; (b) in conjunction with other land of the owner.

"3. The assessed value of the locus for each of the five years, 1960 to 1964, inclusive.

"4. The cost of the locus to the defendant.

"5. The present fair market value of the locus (a) subject to the limitations imposed by the Commissioner; (b) free of such limitations.

"6. The estimated cost of the improvements proposed by the defendant.

"7. Any relevant rules and regulations prescribed by the Director of Marine Fisheries.

"8. Any relevant by-laws (including zoning provisions) or regulations of the town of Wareham.

"Second, for further hearings to develop any relevant evidence on each of the following issues, none of which has been argued and as to which we express no opinion. Briefs and oral arguments should be directed at least to such issues upon any subsequent appeal to this court.

"A. Would the Commonwealth, by the imposition of the proposed restriction, take property without just compensation, if there is no substantial possible use of the locus while subject to the proposed restriction which will yield to the owner of the locus a fair return (1) upon the amount of his investment in the locus, or (2) upon what would be the fair market value of the locus free of the restriction?

"B. If it is contended that the land, if subject to the proposed restriction, may be profitably used in connection with other land, is this relevant, and, if so, to what extent?

"C. Is it relevant to questions A or B that the locus is not suitable in its present state for residential or commercial use?

"D. Is it relevant to questions A and B that the proposed filling, at least in part, will change coastal marshland, subject at times to tidal flow into upland?"

6. For a more sophisticated, modern version of the Brandeis "noxious use" rationale for noncompensatory police power restrictions that leave the landowner practically no economically valuable use of his property, see Sax, Takings, Private Property and Public Rights, 81 Yale L.J. 149 (1971). Addressing himself primarily to "environmental" problems, Sax says: *

"The view here would recognize diffusely-held claims as public rights, entitled to equal consideration in legislative or judicial resolution of conflicting claims to the common resource base, without regard to the manner in which they are held. *   *   * A pristine example of the inextricability of property interests is marine life that breeds along the shallow wetlands shorelines, depending upon maintenance of the shoreline habitat. The wetlands owner thus does not use only his own tract, but demands, as a condition of developing his property, that the ocean users tolerate a change in their use of the ocean. Simi-

* Reprinted by permission of The Yale Law Journal Company and Fred B. Roth- man & Company from The Yale Law Journal, Vol. 81, pp. 149, 159–160.

larly, the ocean users demand that the wetlands owner restrict his use. Most courts view the prohibition imposed upon the wetlands owner as a taking of property by the public, necessitating public purchase of those lands if they are to be preserved. The question raised here is why, if he wishes to impose a restriction on the use of the oceans to promote his activities on his own land, the wetlands owner ought not be compelled to buy *that* right? Id. at 159–60.

Sax goes on to explain that,

"The purpose of the analysis stated above is not to permit a redistribution of land to achieve the most socially beneficial use, but only to put competing resource-owners in a position of equality when each of them seeks to make a use that involves some imposition (spill-over) on his neighbors, and those demands are in conflict. In such cases, and such cases only, there is a conflict in which neither is a priori entitled to prevail, because neither claimant has any more right to impose on his neighbor than his neighbor does on him. Only in such situations may one use be curtailed by the government without triggering the takings clause. Id. at 161.

Sax argues that when the government simply acts as an arbiter between conflicting claims in such a situation, it may enact noncompensatory regulations under the police power favoring either the wetlands owner or the more diffuse public interest in the ocean. Such regulations will be valid if they meet the normal constitutional tests of minimum rationality and nondiscriminatory treatment of those similarly situated."

7. Recent interest in environmental protection has resulted in the resurrection of and extensive reliance upon §§ 10 and 13 of the Rivers and Harbors Act of 1898, 33 U.S.C.A. §§ 403, 407. § 10 of the Act prohibits "creation of any obstruction not affirmatively authorized by Congress, to the navigable capacity of any of the waters of the United States," and also prohibits the excavation or filling "of any navigable water of the United States, unless the work has been recommended by the Chief of Engineers and authorized by the Secretary of the Army prior to the beginning of the same." Section 13 of the Act prohibits the discharge of "any refuse matter of any kind or description whatever other than that flowing from streets and sewers and passing therefrom in a liquid state, into any navigable water of the United States, or into any tributary of any navigable water from which the same shall float or be washed into such navigable water," except under a permit from the Secretary of the Army issued "whenever in the judgment of the Chief of Engineers anchorage and navigation will not be injured thereby." For an interesting case holding that the Secretary of the Army is "entitled, if not required, to consider ecological factors and, being persuaded by them, to deny" a permit for the filling of tidelands under § 10 of the Act, see Zabel v. Tabb, 430 F.2d 199 (5th Cir.1970), cert. denied, 401 U.S. 910, 91 S.Ct. 873, 27 L.Ed.2d 808 (1971).

The dredge and fill permit program of the U.S. Army Corps of Engineers, historically limited to navigable waters, was extended by judicial interpretation to include wetland areas. See Ablard & O'Neill, Wetland Protection and Section 404 of the Federal Water Pollution Control Act Amendments of 1972: A Corps of Engineers Renaissance, 1 Vt.L.Rev. 51 (1976).

7. The literature on "wetlands" protection is voluminous. Particularly useful are Bosselman & Callies, The Quiet Revolution in Land Use Control 108–35, 205–61; Mandelker, Environmental and Land Controls Legislation 248–54 (1976); Kusler, Water Quality Protection for Inland Lakes in Wisconsin: A Comprehensive Approach to Water Pollution, 1970 Wis.L.Rev. 35; Note, Assimilating Human Activity into the Shoreland Environment: The Michigan Shoreland Protection and Management Act of 1970, 62 Iowa L.Rev. 149 (1976); Note,

State Land Use Regulation—A Survey of Recent Legislative Approaches, 56
Minn.L.Rev. 869, 889–901 (1972).

FRED F. FRENCH INVESTING CO. v. CITY
OF NEW YORK

Court of Appeals of New York, 1976.
39 N.Y.2d 587, 385 N.Y.S.2d 5, 350 N.E.2d 381.

BREITEL, Chief Judge.   Plaintiff Fred F. French Investing Co., purchase money mortgagee of Tudor City, a Manhattan residential complex, brought this action to declare unconstitutional a 1972 amendment
to the New York City Zoning Resolution and seeks compensation as for
"inverse" taking by eminent domain.   The amendment purported to create a "Special Park District", and rezoned two private parks in the
Tudor City complex exclusively as parks open to the public.   It further
provided for the granting to the defendant property owners of transferable development (air) rights usable elsewhere.   It created the transferable rights by severing the above-surface development rights from the
surface development rights, a device of recent invention.

Special Term, in a studied and painstaking opinion, declared the
amendment unconstitutional and restored the former zoning classification, R–10, permitting residential and office building development.   The
Appellate Division, 47 A.D.2d 715, 366 N.Y.S.2d 346 unanimously affirmed, without opinion.   By its appeal, the city seeks review of the declaration of unconstitutionality and the denial of its summary judgment
motion on the issue of damages.   By their cross appeals, plaintiff mortgagee and defendants, owners and mortgage interest guarantor, seek
review of the denial of their summary judgment motions for compensation based on an "inverse" taking.

The issue is whether the rezoning of buildable private parks exclusively as parks open to the public, thereby prohibiting all reasonable
income productive or other private use of the property, constitutes a
deprivation of property rights without due process of law in violation of
constitutional limitations.

There should be an affirmance.   While the police power of the State
to regulate the use of private property by zoning is broad indeed, it is
not unlimited.   The State may not, under the guise of regulation by zoning, deprive the owner of the reasonable income productive or other private use of his property and thus destroy all but a bare residue of its
economic value.   Such an exercise of the police power would be void as
violative of the due process clauses of the State and Federal Constitutions (N.Y. Const., art. I, § 6; U.S. Const., 14th Amdt., § 1).   In the
instant case, the city has, despite the severance of above-surface development rights, by rezoning private parks exclusively as parks open to
the public, deprived the owners of the reasonable income productive or
other private use of their property.   The attempted severance of the
development rights with uncertain and contingent market value did not
adequately preserve those rights.   Hence, the 1972 zoning amendment
is violative of constitutional limitations.

Tudor City is a four-acre residential complex built on an elevated level above East 42nd Street, across First Avenue from the United Nations in mid-town Manhattan. Planned and developed as a residential community, Tudor City consists of 10 large apartment buildings housing approximately 8,000 people, a hotel, four brownstone buildings, and two 15,000 square-foot private parks. The parks, covering about 18½% of the area of the complex, are elevated from grade and located on the north and south sides of East 42nd Street, with a connecting viaduct.

On September 30, 1970, plaintiff sold the Tudor City complex to defendant Ramsgate Properties for $36,000,000. In addition to cash, plaintiff took back eight purchase money mortgages, two of which covered in part the two parks. Payment of the mortgage interest for three years was personally guaranteed by defendant Helmsley. Ramsgate thereafter conveyed, subject to plaintiff's mortgages, properties including the north and south parks to defendants, North Assemblage Co. and South Assemblage Co. Each of the mortgages secured in part by the parks has been in default since December 7, 1972.

Soon after acquiring the Tudor City property, the new owner announced plans to erect a building, said to be a 50-story tower, over East 42nd Street between First and Second Avenues. This plan would have required New York City Planning Commission approval of a shifting of development rights from the parks to the proposed adjoining site and a corresponding zoning change. Alternatively, the owner proposed to erect on each of the Tudor City park sites a building of maximum size permitted by the existing zoning regulations.

There was immediately an adverse public reaction to the owner's proposals, especially from Tudor City residents. After public hearings, the City Planning Commission recommended, over the dissent of one commissioner, and on December 7, 1972 the Board of Estimate approved, an amendment to the zoning resolution establishing Special Park District "P". By contemporaneous amendment to the zoning map, the two Tudor City parks were included within Special Park District "P".

Under the zoning amendment, "only passive recreational uses are permitted" in the Special Park District and improvements are limited to "structures incidental to passive recreational use". When the Special Park District would be mapped, the parks are required to be open daily to the public between 6:00 a.m. and 10:00 p.m.

The zoning amendment permits the transfer of development rights from a privately owned lot zoned as a Special Park District, denominated a "granting lot", to other areas in midtown Manhattan, bounded by 60th Street, Third Avenue, 38th Street and Eighth Avenue, denominated "receiving lots". Lots eligible to be receiving lots are those with a minimum lot size of 30,000 square feet and zoned to permit development at the maximum commercial density. The owner of a granting lot would be permitted to transfer part of his development rights to any eligible receiving lot, thereby increasing its maximum floor area up to 10%. Further increase in the receiving lot's floor area, limited to 20% of the maximum commercial density, is contingent upon a public hearing and approval by the City Planning Commission and the Board of Estimate. Development rights may be transferred by the owner directly to a receiving lot or to an individual or organization for later disposition to a receiving lot. Before development rights may be transferred, however, the Chairman of the City Planning Commission must certify the suitability of a plan for the continuing maintenance, at the owner's expense, of the granting lot as a park open to the public.

It is notable that the private parks become open to the public upon mapping of the Special Park District, and the opening does not depend upon the relocation and effective utilization of the transferrable development rights. Indeed, the mapping occurred on December 7, 1972, and the development rights have never been marketed or used.

Plaintiff contends that the rezoning of the parks constitutes a compensable "taking" within the meaning of constitutional limitations.

The power of the State over private property extends from the regulation of its use under the police power to the actual taking of an easement or all or part of the fee under the eminent domain power. The distinction, although definable, between a compensable taking and a noncompensable regulation is not always susceptible of precise demarcation. Generally, as the court stated in Lutheran Church in Amer. v. City of New York, 35 N.Y.2d 121, 128–129, 359 N.Y.S.2d 7, 14, 316 N.E.2d 305, 310: "[G]overnment interference [with the use of private property] is based on one of two concepts—either the government is acting in its enterprise capacity, where it takes unto itself private resources in use for the common good, or in its arbitral capacity, where it intervenes to straighten out situations in which the citizenry is in conflict over land use or where one person's use of his land is injurious to others. (Sax, Taking and the Police Power, 74 Yale L.J. 36, 62, 63.) Where government acts in its enterprise capacity, as where it takes land to widen a road, there is a compensable taking. Where government acts in its arbitral capacity, as where it legislates zoning or provides the machinery to enjoin noxious use, there is simply noncompensable regulation."

As noted above, when the State "takes", that is appropriates, private property for public use, just compensation must be paid. In contrast, when there is only regulation of the uses of private property, no compensation need be paid. Of course, and this is often the beginning of confusion, a purported "regulation" may impose so onerous a burden on the property regulated that it has, in effect, deprived the owner of the reasonable income productive or other private use of his property and thus has destroyed its economic value. In all but exceptional cases, nevertheless, such a regulation does not constitute a "taking", and is therefore not compensable, but amounts to a deprivation or frustration of property rights without due process of law and is therefore invalid.

* * *

In the present case, while there was a significant diminution in the value of the property, there was no actual appropriation or taking of the parks by title or governmental occupation. The amendment was declared void at Special Term a little over a year after its adoption. There was no physical invasion of the owner's property; nor was there an assumption by the city of the control or management of the parks. Indeed, the parks served the same function as before the amendment, except that they were now also open to the public. Absent factors of governmental displacement of private ownership, occupation or management, there was no "taking" within the meaning of constitutional limitations (see City of Buffalo v. Clement Co., 28 N.Y.2d 241, 255–257, 321 N.Y.S.2d 345, 357–359, 269 N.E.2d 895, 903–905). There was, therefore, no right to compensation as for a taking in eminent domain.

Since there was no taking within the meaning of constitutional limitations, plaintiff's remedy, at this stage of the litigation, would be a declaration of the amendment's invalidity, if that be the case. Thus, it is necessary to determine whether the zoning amendment was a valid exercise of the police power under the due process clauses of the State and Federal Constitutions.

*   *   *

A zoning ordinance is unreasonable, under traditional police power and due process analysis, if it encroaches on the exercise of private property rights without substantial relation to a legitimate governmental purpose. A legitimate governmental purpose is, of course, one which furthers the public health, safety, morals or general welfare. Moreover, a zoning ordinance, on similar police power analysis, is unreasonable if it is arbitrary, that is, if there is no reasonable relation between the end sought to be achieved by the regulation and the means used to achieve that end.

Finally, and it is at this point that the confusion between the police power and the exercise of eminent domain most often occurs, a zoning ordinance is unreasonable if it frustrates the owner in the use of his property, that is, if it renders the property unsuitable for any reasonable income productive or other private use for which it is adapted and thus destroys its economic value, or all but a bare residue of its value.

The ultimate evil of a deprivation of property, or better, a frustration of property rights, under the guise of an exercise of the police power is that it forces the owner to assume the cost of providing a benefit to the public without recoupment. There is no attempt to share the cost of the benefit among those benefited, that is, society at large. Instead, the accident of ownership determines who shall bear the cost initially. Of course, as further consequence, the ultimate economic cost of providing the benefit is hidden from those who in a democratic society are given the power of deciding whether or not they wish to obtain the benefit despite the ultimate economic cost, however initially distributed (Dunham, Legal and Economic Basis for Planning, 58 Col.L.Rev. 650, 665). In other words, the removal from productive use of private property has an ultimate social cost more easily concealed by imposing the cost on the owner alone. When successfully concealed, the public is not likely to have any objection to the "cost-free" benefit.

In this case, the zoning amendment is unreasonable and, therefore, unconstitutional because, without due process of law, it deprives the owner of all his property rights, except the bare title and a dubious future reversion of full use. The amendment renders the park property unsuitable for any reasonable income productive or other private use for which it is adapted and thus destroys its economic value and deprives plaintiff of its security for its mortgages. Indeed, as Rathkopf has characterized it, the case is an "extreme example" of a deprivation (1 Rathkopf, op. cit., at p. 6–55; contra Marcus, Mandatory Development Rights Transfer and the Taking Clause: The Case of Manhattan's Tudor City Parks, 24 Buffalo L.Rev. 77, 93–94, 105).

It is recognized that the "value" of property is not a concrete or tangible attribute but an abstraction derived from the economic uses to which the property may be put. Thus, the development rights are an essential component of the value of the underlying property because they constitute some of the economic uses to which the property may be put. As such, they are a potentially valuable and even a transferable commodity and may not be disregarded in determining whether the ordinance has destroyed the economic value of the underlying property.

Of course, the development rights of the parks were not nullified by the city's action. In an attempt to preserve the rights they were severed from the real property and made transferable to another section of mid-Manhattan in the city, but not to any particular parcel or place. There was thus created floating development rights, utterly unusable until they could be attached to some accommodating real property, available by happenstance of prior ownership, or by grant, purchase, or devise, and subject to the contingent approvals of administrative agencies. In such case, the development rights, disembodied abstractions of man's ingenuity, float in a limbo until restored to reality by reattachment to tangible real property. Put another way, it is a tolerable abstraction to consider development rights apart from the solid land from which as a matter of zoning law they derive. But severed, the development rights are a double abstraction until they are actually attached to a receiving parcel, yet to be identified, acquired, and subject to the contingent future approvals of administrative agencies, events which may never happen because of the exigencies of the market and the contingencies and exigencies of administrative action. The acceptance of this contingency-ridden arrangement, however, was mandatory under the amendment.

The problem with this arrangement, as Mr. Justice Waltemade so wisely observed at Special Term, is that it fails to assure preservation of the very real economic value of the development rights as they existed when still attached to the underlying property (77 Misc.2d 199, 201, 352 N.Y.S.2d 762, 764). By compelling the owner to enter an unpredictable real estate market to find a suitable receiving lot for the rights, or a purchaser who would then share the same interest in using additional development rights, the amendment renders uncertain and thus severely impairs the value of the development rights before they were severed (see Note, The Unconstitutionality of Transferable Development Rights,

84 Yale L.J. 1101, 1110–1111). Hence, when viewed in relation to both the value of the private parks after the amendment, and the value of the development rights detached from the private parks, the amendment destroyed the economic value of the property. It thus constituted a deprivation of property without due process of law.

None of this discussion of the effort to accomplish the highly beneficial purposes of creating additional park land in the teeming city bears any relation to other schemes, variously described as a "development bank" or the "Chicago Plan" (see Costonis, The Chicago Plan: Incentive Zoning and the Preservation of Urban Landmarks, 85 Harv.L.Rev. 574; Costonis, Development Rights Transfer: An Exploratory Essay, 83 Yale L.J. 75, 86–87). For under such schemes or variations of them, the owner of the granting parcel may be allowed just compensation for his development rights, instantly and in money, and the acquired development rights are then placed in a "bank" from which enterprises may for a price purchase development rights to use on land owned by them. Insofar as the owner of the granting parcel is concerned, his development rights are taken by the State, straightforwardly, and he is paid just compensation for them in eminent domain. The appropriating governmental entity recoups its disbursements, when, as, and if it obtains a purchaser for those rights. In contrast, the 1972 zoning amendment short-circuits the double-tracked compensation scheme but to do this leaves the granting parcel's owner's development rights in limbo until the day of salvation, if ever it comes.

With respect to damages caused by the unlawful zoning amendment the issue is not properly before the court. The owner never made such an unequivocal claim and still does not. Instead, it claims compensation for value appropriated as for an "inverse" taking in eminent domain. The mortgagees and personal guarantor make parallel claims. That view of the invalid amendment is not adopted for the reasons discussed at length earlier. The city, on the other hand, seeks a declaration with respect to such damages, but in the absence of allegation or proof that such damages lie, are claimed, or how they have been incurred, there can be no abstract declaration, and therefore there is none.

It would be a misreading of the discussion above to conclude that the court is insensitive to the inescapable need for government to devise methods, other than by outright appropriation of the fee, to meet urgent environmental needs of a densely concentrated urban population. It would be equally simplistic to ignore modern recognition of the principle that no property has value except as the community contributes to that value. The obverse of this principle is, therefore, of first significance: no property is an economic island, free from contributing to the welfare of the whole of which it is but a dependent part. The limits are that unfair or disproportionate burdens may not, constitutionally, be placed on single properties or their owners. The possible solutions undoubtedly lie somewhere in the areas of general taxation, assessments for public benefit (but with an expansion of the traditional views with respect to what are assessable public benefits), horizontal eminent domain illustrated by a true "taking" of development rights with corresponding compensation, development banks, and other devices which will insure rudimentary fairness in the allocation of economic burdens.

Solutions must be reached for the problems of modern zoning, urban and rural conservation, and last but not least landmark preservations, whether by particular buildings or historical districts. Unfortunately, the land planners are now only at the beginning of the path to solution. In the process of traversing that path further, new ideas and new standards of constitutional tolerance must and will evolve. It is enough to say that the loose-ended transferable development rights in this case fall short of achieving a fair allocation of economic burden. Even though the development rights have not been nullified, their severance has rendered their value so uncertain and contingent, as to deprive the property owner of their practical usefulness, except under rare and perhaps coincidental circumstances.

The legislative and administrative efforts to solve the zoning and landmark problem in modern society demonstrate the presence of ingenuity. That ingenuity further pursued will in all likelihood achieve the goals without placing an impossible or unsuitable burden on the individual property owner, the public fisc, or the general taxpayer. These efforts are entitled to and will undoubtedly receive every encouragement. The task is difficult but not beyond management. The end is essential but the means must nevertheless conform to constitutional standards.

Accordingly, the order of the Appellate Division should be affirmed, without costs, and the certified questions answered in the affirmative.

Notes

1. The reasons for the adoption of the 1972 amendment rezoning the Tudor City private parks "exclusively as parks open to the public" was explained as follows by the New York City Planning Commission:

"Midtown Manhattan, lying between the East and Hudson Rivers and 38th and 60th Streets, contains some of the most densely [developed] residential and office districts found anywhere in the world. It is generally recognized that in order to maintain an acceptable level of amenity in this area there should be sufficient open space to provide light, air and a measure of repose for both residents and workers.

"Midtown contains a number of privately owned parks which are invaluable components of the Midtown environment. Among these are the two private parks in Tudor City, which are elevated above 42nd Street. They are separated from street noise and traffic fumes making them excellent locations for people to sit and relax. But, these parks provide much more than a place for escape and relaxation. They permit most of the apartments found in the mammoth Tudor City complex to enjoy greater access to light and air than found in most residential developments in this part of the City.

"Furthermore, the parks are an inherent part of the Tudor City design. They unite the individual buildings into a distinguished development of architectural and planning significance.

"These two parks are an essential amenity which could not be duplicated in this crowded part of Midtown.

"Although the Tudor City and other privately owned parks are desirable amenities, they also are potentially redevelopable as part of office or residential building sites. It became apparent that these privately owned parks could eventually disappear unless the City's land use regulations were modified to preserve them."

In the Matter of * * * Establishment of a Special Park District, New York City Planning Commission, No. 224, Dec. 7, 1972.

2. What do you think of the court's holding that there was no compensable "taking" of plaintiff's property because, "while there was a significant diminution in the value of the property, there was no actual appropriation or taking of the parks by title or governmental occupation," so that plaintiff's only remedy "would be a declaration of the amendment's invalidity, if that be the case"? The court seems to have applied the traditional "appropriation" test in determining whether there was a "taking." This is quite surprising, since the court cited, with apparent approval, Sax, Takings and the Police Power, 74 Yale L.J. 36 (1964), where the "appropriation" test is clearly rejected. On the other hand, the result reached by the court is clearly inconsistent with Professor Sax's suggested "government acts in its enterprise capacity" test (id. at 62, 63), since the rezoning amendment in *French* required that the private parks owned by plaintiff be kept open for public use. It is difficult to see how New York City could be viewed as acting only in "its arbitral capacity" when, in effect, it acquired new public parks by the use of its police power.

Cf. Kaiser-Aetna v. United States, 444 U.S. 164, 100 S.Ct. 383, 62 L.Ed.2d 332 (1979), where the Court held that an attempt by the Corps of Engineers to open a privately-developed marina to public use would amount to a "taking" under the Fifth Amendment. The marina was located on a private "pond" connected with the ocean by a channel two feet deep. Kaiser-Aetna bought and developed a 6,000 acre tract including the pond, dredged and filled parts of the pond, and deepened the channel from two to six feet to provide ingress and egress for the marina. The Court said that, "if the Government wishes to make what was formerly Kuapa Pond into a public aquatic park after petitioners have proceeded as far as they have here [in the improvement of their land], it may not, without invoking its eminent domain power and paying just compensation, require them to allow free access to the dredged pond while petitioners' agreement with their customers calls for an annual $72 regular fee." In reaching its decision, the Court held that the federal government's "navigational servitude" did not immunize it from the Fifth Amendment's requirement that compensation be paid when private property is "taken for public use."

Note on Transferable Development Rights

In the principal case the court rejected the city's contention that its provision for a transfer of the Tudor City development rights to other areas in midtown Manhattan provided adequate compensation for the prohibition of development at the Tudor City site. The basis of the concept of "transferable development rights"—generally known as TDR—is simple: the long-accepted idea that title to real estate is not a unitary right but a "bundle of rights," one of which is the right to develop land for economically profitable uses. Hence a landowner whose right to develop a tract of land is severely restricted can nevertheless be permitted to use that development right on other land owned by him so that it may be developed more intensively than would otherwise be permitted. Alternatively, the landowner may be permitted to sell his development right to someone else who can then develop his land to an intensity beyond what is ordinarily permitted. Separation of some of the components of the "bundle of rights" comprised in land ownership from the others is familiar in the case of mineral resources and "air rights" over railroad yards, city streets, and urban expressways. Separation of development rights from land ownership was accomplished in England by the Town and Country Act of 1947, under which the British government appropriated the development rights of all undeveloped land. The Act provided for payment of compensation to all landowners whose development rights were taken, and also required any owner who wished to develop his land to buy back the right to develop from the government by paying a development charge. But the Act did not work well in practice, and has been extensively amended several times in the last quarter century. In the United States, separation of development rights from the other components of land ownership has most often been accomplished by government acquisition of conservation or scenic easements from private landowners.

Proposals for use of the TDR technique as a component of the public system of land use control have been developed in a number of localities. In New York City, it has been used in connection with the City's program of preserving architectural and historical landmarks. The New York City Landmarks Preservation Law, as applied to Grand Central Terminal, was upheld in Penn Central Transportation Co. v. City of New York, reprinted infra p. 1155. The Chicago plan is also designed to help preserve architectural and historical landmarks, and permits (with some limitations) landmark owners to sell development rights to owners of land in designated districts, subject to the power of the city to acquire those rights by condemnation for deposit in a "development rights bank." See the brief discussion of the "Chicago Plan" in Judge Breitel's opinion in *French*. The New Jersey plan seeks to preserve farmland and open space by transferring the right to develop such land to designated districts, and the rural community of Eden, near Buffalo, New York, has adopted a TDR program based on the New Jersey plan. The Puerto Rico plan was designed to preserve the ecologically fragile Phorescent Bay area. Southhampton New York, has adopted an ordinance using TDRs to encourage construction of low- and moderate-income housing. St. George, Vermont, uses TDRs as a device to regulate community growth. The Maryland, Fairfax County (Virginia), and Sonoma County (California) plans, on the other hand, seek to use TDRs as a primary method of land use regulation.

Contrast the court's pessimistic view of the value of the TDRs in *French* with the New York City Planning Commission's view that "[t]he balance of property rights generated by this parcel of land under the existing zoning are reserved to the owner for use in an adjacent area characterized, if anything, by higher land values than the park sites themselves. In our view, this transfer right could under certain circumstances be considered more valuable than the right to develop the same potential on the park sites themselves." In the Matter of * * * Establishment of a Special Park District, supra note 1.

Judge Breitel subsequently commented on the *French* case as follows:

* * * In the *Fred F. French* case, the owner at one point had been offered a tremendous price for those development rights somewhere else in mid-Manhattan. But by the time the case was decided, mid-Manhattan was terribly overbuilt and the value of the TDRs had dropped. That really isn't an accidental circumstance. This is the nature of our economy.

Breitel, A Judicial View of Transferable Development Rights, 30 Land Use Law & Zoning Digest, No. 2, at 5, 6 (1978).* Addressing more generally the problem of using TDRs as compensation for severe restrictions imposed on land development, Judge Breitel pointed out that the question of transferring TDRs

---

* Copyright 1978. Reprinted with the permission of the American Planning Association (formed by consolidation of former American Association of Planners and former American Association of Planning Officials).

is not easily solved, for the neighboring properties where it would be economically and technically feasible to develop air rights are often so profitable in their present use that additional development rights "would have a value only for the future and, therefore, would have to be markedly discounted." Judge Breitel concluded that, to the extent that TDRs are "necessary to compensate the owner of the original site, they must be either in cash, acceptable in kind, or be sufficiently translatable into cash." Id. at 6.

The *French* case is discussed in Costonis, Fred F. French Investing Co. v. City of New York: Losing a Battle but Winning a War, 28 Land Use Law & Zoning Digest, No. 7, at 6 (1976).

In addition to the articles on TDR cited in the *French* opinion and in this Note, see F. James & D. Gale, Zoning for Sale: A Critical Analysis of Transferable Development Rights Programs (Urban Institute 1977); Emanuel, Rural Eden Uses TDR to Save Agricultural Land, Practicing Planner, March 1977, at 15; Costonis, The Disparity Issue: A Context for the *Grand Central* Decision, 91 Harv.L.Rev. 402 (1977); Berry & Steiker, an Economic Analysis of Transfer of Development Rights, 17 Nat. Resources J. 55 (1977); Gale, The Transfer of Development Rights; Some Equity Considerations, 14 Urban L.Ann. 81 (1977); Field & Conrad, Economic Issues in Programs of Transferable Development Rights, 51 and Econ. 331 (1975); J. Costonis & R. DeVoy, The Puerto Rico Plan; Environmental Protection Through Development Rights Transfer (1975); Note, Development Rights Transfer and Landmarks Preservation—Providing a Sense of Orientation, 9 Urban L.Ann. 131 (1975); J. Costonis, Space Adrift (1974); The Transfer of Development Rights: A New Technique of Land Use Regulation (J. Rose ed. 1975); Rose, The Transfer of Development Rights: A Preview of an Evolving Concept, 3 Real Estate L.J. 330 (1975); Rose, A Proposal for the Separation and Marketability of Development Rights as a Technique to Preserve Open Space, 2 Real Estate L.J. 635 (1974), and 51 J.Urban L. 461 (1974); Note, Development Rights Transfer in New York City, 82 Yale L.J. 338 (1972).

PENN CENTRAL TRANSPORTATION CO v. CITY OF NEW YORK

Supreme Court of the United States, 1978.
438 U.S. 104, 98 S.Ct. 2646, 57 L.Ed.2d 631.

[Under New York City's Landmarks Preservation Law (Landmarks Law), which was enacted to protect historic landmarks and neighborhoods from precipitate decisions to destroy or fundamentally alter their character, the Landmarks Preservation Commission (Commission) may designate a building to be a "landmark" on a particular "landmark site" or may designate an area to be a "historic district." The Board of Estimate may thereafter modify or disapprove the designation, and the owner may seek judicial review of the final designation decision. The owner of the designated landmark must keep the building's exterior "in good repair" and before exterior alterations are made must secure Commission approval. Under two ordinances owners of landmark sites may transfer development rights from a landmark parcel to proximate lots. Under the Landmarks Law, the Grand Central (Terminal), which is owned by the Penn Central Transportation Co. and its affiliates (Penn Central) was designated a "landmark" and the block it occupies a "landmark site." Appellant Penn Central, though opposing the designation before the Commission, did not seek judicial review of the final designation decision.   Thereafter appellant Penn Central entered into a lease with appellant UGP, whereby UGP was to construct a multi-story office building over the Terminal.   After the Commission had rejected appellants' plans for the building as destructive of the Terminal's historic and aesthetic features, with no judicial review thereafter being sought, appellants brought suit in state court claiming that the application of the Landmarks Law had "taken" their property without just compensation in violation of the Fifth and Fourteenth Amendments and arbitrarily deprived them of property without due process of law in violation of the Fourteenth Amendment.   The trial court's grant of relief was reversed on appeal, the New York Court of Appeals ultimately concluding that there was no "taking" since the Preservation Law had not transferred control of the property to the City, but only restricted appellants' exploitation of it;   and that there was no denial of due process because (1) the same use of the Terminal was permitted as before;   (2) the appellants had not shown that they could not earn a reasonable return on their investment in the Terminal itself;   (3) even if the Terminal proper could never operate at a reasonable profit, some of the income from Penn Central's extensive real estate holdings in the area must realistically be imputed to the Terminal;   and (4) the development rights above the Terminal, which were made transferable to numerous sites in the vicinity provided significant compensation for loss of rights above the Terminal itself.   (Statement of facts is from the official Syllabus.— Eds.)]

Mr. Justice BRENNAN delivered the opinion of the Court.

* * *

The issues presented by appellants are (1) whether the restrictions imposed by New York City's law upon appellants' exploitation of the Terminal site effect a "taking" of appellants' property for a public use within the meaning of the Fifth Amendment, which of course is made applicable to the States through the Fourteenth Amendment, see Chicago, B. & Q. R. Co. v. Chicago, 166 U.S. 226, 239, 17 S.Ct. 581, 585, 41 L.Ed. 979 (1897), and, (2), if so, whether the transferable development rights afforded appellants constitute "just compensation" within the meaning of the Fifth Amendment.   We need only address the question whether a "taking" has occurred.[1]

A

Before considering appellants' specific contentions, it will be useful to review the factors that have shaped the jurisprudence of the Fifth Amendment injunction "nor shall private property be taken for public use, without just compensation."   The question of what constitutes a "taking" for purposes of the Fifth Amendment has proved to be a problem of considerable difficulty.   While this Court has recognized that the "Fifth Amendment's guarantee   *   *   *   [is] designed to bar Government from forcing some people alone to bear public burdens which, in

---

1.   As is implicit in our opinion, we do not embrace the proposition that a "taking" can never occur unless government has transferred physical control over a portion of a parcel.

all fairness and justice, should be borne by the public as a whole," Armstrong v. United States, 364 U.S. 40, 49, 80 S.Ct. 1563, 1569, 4 L.Ed.2d 1554 (1960), this Court, quite simply, has been unable to develop any "set formula" for determining when "justice and fairness" require that economic injuries caused by public action be compensated by the government, rather than remain disproportionately concentrated on a few persons. See Goldblatt v. Hempstead, 369 U.S. 590, 594, 82 S.Ct. 987, 990, 8 L.Ed.2d 130 (1962). Indeed, we have frequently observed that whether a particular restriction will be rendered invalid by the government's failure to pay for any losses proximately caused by it depends largely "upon the particular circumstances [in that] case." United States v. Central Eureka Mining Co., 357 U.S. 155, 168, 78 S.Ct. 1097, 1104, 2 L.Ed.2d 1228 (1958); see United States v. Caltex, Inc., 344 U.S. 149, 156, 73 S.Ct. 200, 203, 97 L.Ed. 157 (1952).

In engaging in these essentially ad hoc, factual inquiries, the Court's decisions have identified several factors that have particular significance. The economic impact of the regulation on the claimant and, particularly, the extent to which the regulation has interfered with distinct investment-backed expectations are, of course, relevant considerations. See Goldblatt v. Hempstead, supra, 369 U.S., at 594, 82 S.Ct., at 990. So, too, is the character of the governmental action. A "taking" may more readily be found when the interference with property can be characterized as a physical invasion by government, see, e.g., United States v. Causby, 328 U.S. 256, 66 S.Ct. 1062, 90 L.Ed. 1206 (1946), than when interference arises from some public program adjusting the benefits and burdens of economic life to promote the common good.

"Government hardly could go on if to some extent values incident to property could not be diminished without paying for every such change in the general law," Pennsylvania Coal Co. v. Mahon, 260 U.S. 393, 413, 43 S.Ct. 158, 159, 67 L.Ed. 322 (1922), and this Court has accordingly recognized in a wide variety of contexts, that government may execute laws or programs that adversely affect recognized economic values. Exercises of the taxing power are one obvious example. A second are the decisions in which this Court has dismissed "taking" challenges on the ground that, while the challenged government action caused economic harm, it did not interfere with interests that were sufficiently bound up with the reasonable expectations of the claimant to constitute "property" for Fifth Amendment purposes. See e.g., United States v. Willow River Power Co., 324 U.S. 499, 65 S.Ct. 761, 89 L.Ed. 1101 (1945) (interest in high-water level of river for runoff for tailwaters to maintain power head is not property); United States v. Chandler-Dunbar Water Power Co., 229 U.S. 53, 33 S.Ct. 667, 57 L.Ed. 1063 (1913) (no property interest can exist in navigable waters); see also Demorest v. City Bank Co., 321 U.S. 36, 64 S.Ct. 384, 88 L.Ed. 526 (1944); Muhlker v. Harlem R. Co., 197 U.S. 544, 25 S.Ct. 522, 49 L.Ed. 872 (1905); Sax, Takings and the Police Power, 74 Yale L.J. 36, 61–62 (1964).

More importantly for the present case, in instances in which a state tribunal reasonably concluded that "the health, safety, morals, or general welfare" would be promoted by prohibiting particular contemplated uses of land, this Court has upheld land-use regulations that destroyed or adversely affected recognized real property interests. See Nectow v. Cambridge, 277 U.S. 183, 188, 48 S.Ct. 447, 448, 72 L.Ed. 842 (1928). Zoning laws are, of course, the classic example, see Euclid v. Ambler Realty Co., 272 U.S. 365, 47 S.Ct. 114, 71 L.Ed. 303 (1926) (prohibition of industrial use); Gorieb v. Fox, 274 U.S. 603, 608, 47 S.Ct. 675, 677, 71 L.Ed. 1228 (1927) (requirement that portions of parcels be left unbuilt); Welch v. Swasey, 214 U.S. 91, 29 S.Ct. 567, 53 L.Ed. 923 (1909) (height restriction), which have been viewed as permissible governmental action even when prohibiting the most beneficial use of the property. * * *

Zoning laws generally do not affect existing uses of real property, but "taking" challenges have also been held to be without merit in a wide variety of situations when the challenged governmental actions prohibited a beneficial use to which individual parcels had previously been devoted and thus caused substantial individualized harm. Miller v. Schoene, 276 U.S. 272, 48 S.Ct. 246, 72 L.Ed. 568 (1928), is illustrative. In that case, a state entomologist, acting pursuant to a state statute, ordered the claimants to cut down a large number of ornamental red cedar trees because they produced cedar rust fatal to apple trees cultivated nearby. Although the statute provided for recovery of any expense incurred in removing the cedars, and permitted claimants to use the felled trees, it did not provide compensation for the value of the standing trees or for the resulting decrease in market value of the properties as a whole. A unanimous Court held that this latter omission did not render the statute invalid. The Court held that the State might properly make "a choice between the preservation of one class of property and that of the other" and since the apple industry was important in the State involved, concluded that the State had not exceeded "its constitutional powers by deciding upon the destruction of one class of property [without compensation] in order to save another which, in the judgment of the legislature, is of greater value to the public." Id., at 279, 48 S.Ct., at 247.

Again, Hadacheck v. Sebastian, 239 U.S. 394, 36 S.Ct. 143, 60 L.Ed. 348 (1915), upheld a law prohibiting the claimant from continuing his otherwise lawful business of operating a brickyard in a particular physical community on the ground that the legislature had reasonably concluded that the presence of the brickyard was inconsistent with neighboring uses. See also United States v. Central Eureka Mining Co., supra (Government order closing gold mines so that skilled miners would be available for other mining work held not a taking); Atchison, T. & S.F.R. Co. v. Public Utilities Comm'n, 346 U.S. 346, 74 S.Ct. 92, 98 L.Ed. 51 (1953) (railroad may be required to share cost of constructing railroad grade improvement); Walls v. Midland Carbon Co., 254 U.S. 300, 41 S.Ct. 118, 65 L.Ed. 276 (1920) (law prohibiting manufacture of carbon black upheld); Reinman v. Little Rock, 237 U.S. 171, 35 S.Ct. 511, 59 L.Ed. 900 (1915) (law prohibiting livery stable upheld); Mugler v. Kansas, 123 U.S. 623, 8 S.Ct. 273, 31 L.Ed. 205 (1887) (law prohibiting liquor business upheld).

Goldblatt v. Hempstead, supra, is a recent example. There, a 1958 city safety ordinance banned any excavations below the water table and effectively prohibited the claimant from continuing a sand and gravel mining business that had been operated on the particular parcel since 1927. The Court upheld the ordinance against a "taking" challenge, although the ordinance prohibited the present and presumably most beneficial use of the property and had, like the regulations in *Miller* and *Hadacheck*, severely affected a particular owner. The Court assumed that the ordinance did not prevent the owner's reasonable use of the property since the owner made no showing of an adverse effect on the value of the land. Because the restriction served a substantial public purpose, the Court thus held no taking had occurred. It is, of course, implicit in *Goldblatt* that a use restriction on real property may constitute a "taking" if not reasonably necessary to the effectuation of a substantial public purpose, see Nectow v. Cambridge, supra; cf. Moore v. East Cleveland, 431 U.S. 494, 513–514, 97 S.Ct. 1932, 1943, 52 L.Ed.2d 531 (1977) (STEVENS, J., concurring), or perhaps if it has an unduly harsh impact upon the owner's use of the property.

Pennsylvania Coal Co. v. Mahon, 260 U.S. 393, 43 S.Ct. 158, 67 L.Ed. 322 (1922), is the leading case for the proposition that a state statute that substantially furthers important public policies may so frustrate distinct investment-backed expectations as to amount to a "taking." There the claimant had sold the surface rights to particular parcels of property, but expressly reserved the right to remove the coal thereunder. A Pennsylvania statute, enacted after the transactions, forbade any mining of coal that caused the subsidence of any house, unless the house was the property of the owner of the underlying coal and was more than 150 feet from the improved property of another. Because the statute made it commercially impracticable to mine the coal, id., at 414, 43 S.Ct., at 159, and thus had nearly the same effect as the complete destruction of rights claimant had reserved from the owners of the surface land, see id., at 414–415, 43 S.Ct., at 159–160, the Court held that the statute was invalid as effecting a "taking" without just compensation. See also Armstrong v. United States, 364 U.S. 40, 80 S.Ct. 1563, 4 L.Ed.2d 1554 (1960) (Government's complete destruction of a materialman's lien in certain property held a "taking"); Hudson Water Co. v. McCarter, 209 U.S. 349, 355, 28 S.Ct. 529, 531, 52 L.Ed. 828 (1908) (if height restriction makes property wholly useless "the rights of property * * * prevail over the other public interest" and compensation is required). See generally Michelman, Property, Utility, and Fairness: Comments on the Ethical Foundations of "Just Compensation" Law, 80 Harv.L.Rev. 1165, 1229–1234 (1967).

Finally, government actions that may be characterized as acquisitions of resources to permit or facilitate uniquely public functions have often been held to constitute "takings." United States v. Causby, 328 U.S. 256, 66 S.Ct. 1062, 90 L.Ed. 1206 (1946), is illustrative. In holding that direct overflights above the claimant's land, that destroyed the present use of the land as a chicken farm, constituted a "taking," *Causby* emphasized that Government had not "merely destroyed property [but was] using a part of it for the flight of its planes." Id., 328 U.S., at 262–263, n. 7, 66 S.Ct., at 1066. See also Griggs v. Allegheny County, 369 U.S. 84, 82 S.Ct. 531, 7 L.Ed.2d 585 (1962) (overflights held a taking); Portsmouth Co. v. United States, 260 U.S. 327, 43 S.Ct. 135, 67 L.Ed. 287 (1922) (United States military installations' repeated firing of guns over claimant's land is a taking); United States v. Cress, 243 U.S. 316, 37 S.Ct. 380, 61 L.Ed. 746 (1917) (repeated floodings of land caused by water project is taking); but see YMCA v. United States, 395 U.S. 85, 89 S.Ct. 1511, 23 L.Ed.2d 117 (1969) (damage caused to building when federal officers who were seeking to protect building were attacked by rioters held not a taking). See generally Michelman, supra, at 1226–1229; Sax, Takings and the Police Power, 74 Yale L.J. 36 (1964).

B

In contending that the New York City law has "taken" their property in violation of the Fifth and Fourteenth Amendments, appellants make a series of arguments, which, while tailored to the facts of this case, essentially urge that any substantial restriction imposed pursuant to a landmark law must be accompanied by just compensation if it is to be constitutional. Before considering these, we emphasize what is not in dispute. Because this Court has recognized, in a number of settings, that States and cities may enact land-use restrictions or controls to enhance the quality of life by preserving the character and desirable aesthetic features of a city, see New Orleans v. Dukes, 427 U.S. 297, 96 S.Ct. 2513, 49 L.Ed.2d 511 (1976); Young v. American Mini Theatres, Inc., 427 U.S. 50, 96 S.Ct. 2440, 49 L.Ed.2d 310 (1976); Village of Belle Terre v. Boraas, 416 U.S. 1, 9–10, 94 S.Ct. 1536, 39 L.Ed.2d 797 (1974); Berman v. Parker, 348 U.S. 26, 33, 75 S.Ct. 98, 102, 99 L.Ed. 27 (1954); Welch v. Swasey, 214 U.S., at 108, 29 S.Ct., at 571, appellants do not contest that New York City's objective of preserving structures and areas with special historic, architectural, or cultural significance is an entirely permissible governmental goal. They also do not dispute that the restrictions imposed on its parcel are appropriate means of securing the purposes of the New York City law. Finally, appellants do not challenge any of the specific factual premises of the decision below. They accept for present purposes both that the parcel of land occupied by Grand Central Terminal must, in its present state, be regarded as capable of earning a reasonable return, and that the transferable development rights afforded appellants by virtue of the Terminal's designation as a landmark are valuable, even if not as valuable as the rights to construct above the Terminal. In appellants' view none of these factors derogate from their claim that New York City's law has effected a "taking."

They first observe that the airspace above the Terminal is a valuable property interest, citing United States v. Causby, supra. They urge that the Landmarks Law has deprived them of any gainful use of their "air rights" above the Terminal and that, irrespective of the value of the remainder of their parcel, the city has "taken" their right to this superadjacent airspace, thus entitling them to "just compensation" measured by the fair market value of these air rights.

Apart from our own disagreement with appellants' characterization of the effect of the New York City law, see infra, at 2665, the submission that appellants may establish a "taking" simply by showing that they have been denied the ability to exploit a property interest that they heretofore had believed was available for development is quite simply untenable. Were this the rule, this Court would have erred not only in upholding laws restricting the development of air rights, see Welch v. Swasey, supra, but also in approving those prohibiting both the subjacent, see Goldblatt v. Hempstead, 369 U.S. 590, 82 S.Ct. 987, 8 L.Ed.2d 130 (1962), and the lateral, see Gorieb v. Fox, 274 U.S. 603, 47 S.Ct. 675, 71 L.Ed. 1228 (1927), development of particular parcels.[2] "Taking" jurisprudence does not divide a single parcel into discrete segments and attempt to determine whether rights in a particular segment have been entirely abrogated. In deciding whether a particular governmental action has effected a taking, this Court focuses rather both on the character of the action and on the nature and extent of the interference with rights in the parcel as a whole—here, the city tax block designated as the "landmark site."

Secondly, appellants, focusing on the character and impact of the New York City law, argue that it effects a "taking" because its operation has significantly diminished the value of the Terminal site. Appellants concede that the decisions sustaining other land-use regulations, which, like the New York City law, are reasonably related to the promotion of the general welfare, uniformly reject the proposition that diminution in property value, standing alone, can establish a "taking," see Euclid v. Ambler Realty Co., 272 U.S. 365, 47 S.Ct. 114, 71 L.Ed. 303 (1926) (75% diminution in value caused by zoning law); Hadacheck v. Sebastian, 239 U.S. 394, 36 S.Ct. 143, 60 L.Ed. 348 (1915) ($87\frac{1}{2}$% diminution in value); cf. Eastlake v. Forest City Enterprises, Inc., 426 U.S., at 674 n. 8, 96 S.Ct., at 2362 n. 8, and that the "taking" issue in these contexts is resolved by focusing on the uses the regulations permit. See also Goldblatt v. Hempstead, supra. Appellants, moreover, also do not dispute that a showing of diminution in property value would not establish a taking if the restriction had been imposed as a result of historic-district legislation, see generally Maher v. New Orleans, 516 F.2d 1051 (CA5 1975), but appellants argue that New York City's regulation of individual landmarks is fundamentally different from zoning or from historic-district legislation because the controls imposed by New York City's law apply only to individuals who own selected properties.

Stated baldly, appellants' position appears to be that the only means of ensuring that selected owners are not singled out to endure financial

---

2. These cases dispose of any contention that might be based on Pennsylvania Coal Co. v. Mahon, 260 U.S. 393, 43 S.Ct. 158, 67 L.Ed. 322 (1922), that full use of air rights is so bound up with the investment-backed expectations of appellants that governmental deprivation of these rights invariably—i.e., irrespective of the impact of the restriction on the value of the parcel as a whole—constitutes a "taking." Similarly, *Welch, Goldblatt,* and *Gorieb* illustrate the fallacy of appellants' related contention that a "taking" must be found to have occurred whenever the land-use restriction may be characterized as imposing a "servitude" on the claimant's parcel.

hardship for no reason is to hold that any restriction imposed on individual landmarks pursuant to the New York City scheme is a "taking" requiring the payment of "just compensation." Agreement with this argument would, of course, invalidate not just New York City's law, but all comparable landmark legislation in the Nation. We find no merit in it.

It is true, as appellants emphasize, that both historic-district legislation and zoning laws regulate all properties within given physical communities whereas landmark laws apply only to selected parcels. But, contrary to appellants' suggestions, landmark laws are not like discriminatory, or "reverse spot," zoning: that is, a land-use decision which arbitrarily singles out a particular parcel for different, less favorable treatment than the neighboring ones. See 2 A. Rathkopf, The Law of Zoning and Planning 26–4, and n. 6 (4th ed. 1978). In contrast to discriminatory zoning, which is the antithesis of land-use control as part of some comprehensive plan, the New York City law embodies a comprehensive plan to preserve structures of historic or aesthetic interest wherever they might be found in the city,[3] and as noted, over 400 landmarks and 31 historic districts have been designated pursuant to this plan.

Equally without merit is the related argument that the decision to designate a structure as a landmark "is inevitably arbitrary or at least subjective, because it is basically a matter of taste," Reply Brief for Appellants 22, thus unavoidably singling out individual landowners for disparate and unfair treatment. The argument has a particularly hollow ring in this case. For appellants not only did not seek judicial review of either the designation or of the denials of the certificates of appropriateness and of no exterior effect, but do not even now suggest that the Commission's decisions concerning the Terminal were in any sense arbitrary or unprincipled. But, in any event, a landmark owner has a right to judicial review of any Commission decision, and, quite simply, there is no basis whatsoever for a conclusion that courts will have any greater difficulty identifying arbitrary or discriminatory action in the context of landmark regulation than in the context of classic zoning or indeed in any other context.[4]

Next, appellants observe that New York City's law differs from zoning laws and historic-district ordinances in that the Landmarks Law

---

3. Although the New York Court of Appeals contrasted the New York City Landmarks Law with both zoning and historic-district legislation and stated at one point that landmark laws do not "further a general community plan," 42 N.Y.S.2d 324, 330, 397 N.Y.S.2d 914, 918, 366 N.E.2d 1271, 1274 (1977), it also emphasized that the implementation of the objectives of the Landmarks Law constitutes an "acceptable reason for singling out one particular parcel for different and less favorable treatment." Ibid., 397 N.Y.S.2d, at 918, 366 N.E.2d, at 1275. Therefore, we do not understand the New York Court of Appeals to disagree with our characterization of the law.

4. When a property owner challenges the application of a zoning ordinance to his property, the judicial inquiry focuses upon whether the challenged restriction can reasonably be deemed to promote the objectives of the community land-use plan, and will include consideration of the treatment of similar parcels. See generally Nectow v. Cambridge, 277 U.S. 183, 48 S.Ct. 447, 72 L.Ed. 842 (1928). When a property owner challenges a landmark designation or restriction as arbitrary or discriminatory, a similar inquiry presumably will occur.

does not impose identical or similar restrictions on all structures located in particular physical communities. It follows, they argue, that New York City's law is inherently incapable of producing the fair and equitable distribution of benefits and burdens of governmental action which is characteristic of zoning laws and historic-district legislation and which they maintain is a constitutional requirement if "just compensation" is not to be afforded. It is, of course, true that the Landmarks Law has a more severe impact on some landowners than on others, but that in itself does not mean that the law effects a "taking." Legislation designed to promote the general welfare commonly burdens some more than others. The owners of the brickyard in *Hadacheck,* of the cedar trees in Miller v. Schoene, and of the gravel and sand mine in Goldblatt v. Hempstead, were uniquely burdened by the legislation sustained in those cases.[5] Similarly, zoning laws often affect some property owners more severely than others but have not been held to be invalid on that account. For example, the property owner in *Euclid* who wished to use its property for industrial purposes was affected far more severely by the ordinance than its neighbors who wished to use their land for residences.

In any event, appellants' repeated suggestions that they are solely burdened and unbenefited is factually inaccurate. This contention overlooks the fact that the New York City law applies to vast numbers of structures in the city in addition to the Terminal—all the structures contained in the 31 historic districts and over 400 individual landmarks, many of which are close to the Terminal.[6] Unless we are to reject the judgment of the New York City Council that the preservation of landmarks benefits all New York citizens and all structures, both economically and by improving the quality of life in the city as a whole— which we are unwilling to do—we cannot conclude that the owners of the Terminal have in no sense been benefited by the Landmarks Law. Doubtless appellants believe they are more burdened than benefited by

---

5. Appellants attempt to distinguish these cases on the ground that, in each, government was prohibiting a "noxious" use of land and that in the present case, in contrast, appellants' proposed construction above the Terminal would be beneficial. We observe that the uses in issue in *Hadacheck, Miller,* and *Goldblatt* were perfectly lawful in themselves. They involved no "blameworthiness, * * * moral wrongdoing or conscious act of dangerous risk-taking which induce[d society] to shift the cost to a pa[rt]icular individual." Sax, Takings and the Police Power, 74 Yale L.J. 36, 50 (1964). These cases are better understood as resting not on any supposed "noxious" quality of the prohibited uses but rather on the ground that the restrictions were reasonably related to the implementation of a policy—not unlike historic preservation—expected to produce a widespread public benefit and applicable to all similarly situated property.

Nor, correlatively, can it be asserted that the destruction or fundamental alteration of a historic landmark is not harmful. The suggestion that the beneficial quality of appellants' proposed construction is established by the fact that the construction would have been consistent with applicable zoning laws ignores the development in sensibilities and ideals reflected in landmark legislation like New York City's. Cf. West Bros. Brick Co. v. Alexandria, 169 Va. 271, 282–283, 192 S.E. 881, 885–886, *appeal dismissed for want of a substantial federal question,* 302 U.S. 658, 58 S.Ct. 369, 82 L.Ed. 508 (1937).

6. There are some 53 designated landmarks and 5 historic districts or scenic landmarks in Manhattan between 14th and 59th Streets. See Landmarks Preservation Commission, Landmarks and Historic Districts (1977).

the law, but that must have been true, too, of the property owners in *Miller, Hadacheck, Euclid,* and *Goldblatt.*[7]

Appellants' final broad-based attack would have us treat the law as an instance, like that in United States v. Causby, in which government, acting in an enterprise capacity, has appropriated part of their property for some strictly governmental purpose. Apart from the fact that *Causby* was a case of invasion of airspace that destroyed the use of the farm beneath and this New York City law has in no wise impaired the present use of the Terminal, the Landmarks Law neither exploits appellants' parcel for city purposes nor facilitates nor arises from any entrepreneurial operations of the city. The situation is not remotely like that in *Causby* where the airspace above the property was in the flight pattern for military aircraft. The Landmarks Law's effect is simply to prohibit appellants or anyone else from occupying portions of the airspace above the Terminal, while permitting appellants to use the remainder of the parcel in a gainful fashion. This is no more an appropriation of property by government for its own uses than is a zoning law prohibiting, for "aesthetic" reasons, two or more adult theaters within a specified area, see Young v. American Mini Theatres, Inc., 427 U.S. 50, 96 S.Ct. 2440, 49 L.Ed.2d 310 (1976), or a safety regulation prohibiting excavations below a certain level. See Goldblatt v. Hempstead.

C

Rejection of appellants' broad arguments is not, however, the end of our inquiry, for all we thus far have established is that the New York City law is not rendered invalid by its failure to provide "just compensation" whenever a landmark owner is restricted in the exploitation of property interests, such as air rights, to a greater extent than provided for under applicable zoning laws. We now must consider whether the interference with appellants' property is of such a magnitude that "there must be an exercise of eminent domain and compensation to sustain [it]." Pennsylvania Coal Co. v. Mahon, 260 U.S., at 413, 43 S.Ct., at 159. That inquiry may be narrowed to the question of the severity of the impact of the law on appellants' parcel, and its resolution in turn requires a careful assessment of the impact of the regulation on the Terminal site.

Unlike the governmental acts in *Goldblatt, Miller, Causby, Griggs,* and *Hadacheck,* the New York City law does not interfere in any way with the present uses of the Terminal. Its designation as a landmark not only permits but contemplates that appellants may continue to use the property precisely as it has been used for the past 65 years: as a railroad terminal containing office space and concessions. So the law does not interfere with what must be regarded as Penn Central's primary expectation concerning the use of the parcel. More importantly, on this record, we must regard the New York City law as permitting Penn

---

7. It is, of course, true that the fact the duties imposed by zoning and historic-district legislation apply throughout particular physical communities provides assurances against arbitrariness, but the applicability of the Landmarks Law to a large number of parcels in the city, in our view, provides comparable, if not identical, assurances.

Central not only to profit from the Terminal but also to obtain a "reasonable return" on its investment.

Appellants, moreover, exaggerate the effect of the law on their ability to make use of the air rights above the Terminal in two respects.[8] First, it simply cannot be maintained, on this record, that appellants have been prohibited from occupying *any* portion of the airspace above the Terminal. While the Commission's actions in denying applications to construct an office building in excess of 50 stories above the Terminal may indicate that it will refuse to issue a certificate of appropriateness for any comparably sized structure, nothing the Commission has said or done suggests an intention to prohibit *any* construction above the Terminal. The Commission's report emphasized that whether any construction would be allowed depended upon whether the proposed addition "would harmonize in scale, material and character with [the Terminal]." Record 2251. Since appellants have not sought approval for the construction of a smaller structure, we do not know that appellants will be denied any use of any portion of the airspace above the Terminal.[9]

Second, to the extent appellants have been denied the right to build above the Terminal, it is not literally accurate to say that they have been denied *all* use of even those pre-existing air rights. Their ability to use these rights has not been abrogated; they are made transferable to at least eight parcels in the vicinity of the Terminal, one or two of which have been found suitable for the construction of new office buildings. Although appellants and others have argued that New York City's transferable development-rights program is far from ideal, the New York courts here supportably found that, at least in the case of the Terminal, the rights afforded are valuable. While these rights may well not have constituted "just compensation" if a "taking" had occurred, the rights nevertheless undoubtedly mitigate whatever financial burdens the law has imposed on appellants and, for that reason, are to be taken into account in considering the impact of regulation. Cf. Goldblatt v. Hempstead, 369 U.S., at 594 n. 3, 82 S.Ct., at 990 n. 3.

On this record, we conclude that the application of New York City's Landmarks Law has not effected a "taking" of appellants' property. The restrictions imposed are substantially related to the promotion of the general welfare and not only permit reasonable beneficial use of the landmark site but also afford appellants opportunities further to enhance not only the Terminal site proper but also other properties.[10]

Affirmed.

8. Appellants, of course, argue at length that the transferable development rights, while valuable, do not constitute "just compensation." Brief for Appellants 36–43.

9. Counsel for appellants admitted at oral argument that the Commission has not suggested that it would not, for example, approve a 20-story office tower along the lines of that which was part of the original plan for the Terminal. See Tr. of Oral Arg. 19.

10. We emphasize that our holding today is on the present record, which in turn is based on Penn Central's present ability to use the Terminal for its intended purposes and in a gainful fashion. The city conceded at oral argument that if appellants can demonstrate at some point in the future that circumstances have so changed

Mr. Justice REHNQUIST, with whom THE CHIEF JUSTICE and Mr. Justice STEVENS join, dissenting.

Of the over one million buildings and structures in the city of New York appellees have singled out 400 for designation as official landmarks.[11] The owner of a building might initially be pleased that his property has been chosen by a distinguished committee of architects, historians, and city planners for such a singular distinction. But he may well discover, as appellant Penn Central Transportation Co. did here, that the landmark designation imposes upon him a substantial cost, with little or no offsetting benefit except for the honor of the designation. The question in this case is whether the cost associated with the city of New York's desire to preserve a limited number of "landmarks" within its borders must be borne by all of its taxpayers or whether it can instead be imposed entirely on the owners of the individual properties.

Only in the most superficial sense of the word can this case be said to involve "zoning."[12] Typical zoning restrictions may, it is true, so limit the prospective uses of a piece of property as to diminish the value of that property in the abstract because it may not be used for the forbidden purposes. But any such abstract decrease in value will more than likely be at least partially offset by an increase in value which flows from similar restrictions as to use on neighboring properties. All property owners in a designated area are placed under the same restrictions, not only for the benefit of the municipality as a whole but also for the common benefit of one another. In the words of Mr. Justice

that the Terminal ceases to be "economically viable," appellants may obtain relief. See Tr. of Oral Arg. 42–43.

11. A large percentage of the designated landmarks are public structures (such as the Brooklyn Bridge, City Hall, the Statue of Liberty and the Municipal Asphalt Plant) and thus do not raise Fifth Amendment taking questions. See Landmarks Preservation Commission of the City of New York, Landmarks and Historic Districts (1977 and Jan. 10, 1978, Supplement). Although the Court refers to the New York ordinance as a *comprehensive* program to preserve *historic* landmarks, *ante,* at 2651, the ordinance is not limited to historic buildings and gives little guidance to the Landmarks Preservation Commission in its selection of landmark sites. Section 207–1.0(n) of the Landmarks Preservation Law, as set forth in N.Y.C.Admin.Code, ch. 8–A (1976), requires only that the selected landmark be at least 30 years old and possess "a special character or special historical or aesthetic interest or value as part of the development, heritage or cultural characteristics of the city, state or nation."

12. Even the New York Court of Appeals conceded that "[t]his is not a zoning case. * * * Zoning restrictions operate to advance a comprehensive community plan for the common good. Each property owner in the zone is both benefited and restricted from exploitation, presumably without discrimination, except for permitted continuing nonconforming uses. The restrictions may be designed to maintain the general character of the area, or to assure orderly development, objectives inuring to the benefit of all, which property owners acting individually would find difficult or impossible to achieve * * *.

"Nor does this case involve landmark regulation of a historic district. * * * [In historic districting, as in traditional zoning,] owners although burdened by the restrictions also benefit, to some extent, from the furtherance of a general community plan.

* * *

"Restrictions on alteration of individual landmarks are not designed to further a general community plan. Landmark restrictions are designed to prevent alteration or demolition of a single piece of property. To this extent, such restrictions resemble 'discriminatory' zoning restrictions, properly condemned * * *." 42 N.Y.2d 324, 329–330, 397 N.Y.S.2d 914, 917, 918, 366 N.E.2d 1271, 1274 (1977).

Holmes, speaking for the Court in Pennsylvania Coal Co. v. Mahon, 260 U.S. 393, 415, 43 S.Ct. 158, 160, 67 L.Ed. 322 (1922), there is "an average reciprocity of advantage."

Where a relatively few individual buildings, all separated from one another, are singled out and treated differently from surrounding buildings, no such reciprocity exists. The cost to the property owner which results from the imposition of restrictions applicable only to his property and not that of his neighbors may be substantial—in this case, several million dollars—with no comparable reciprocal benefits. And the cost associated with landmark legislation is likely to be of a completely different order of magnitude than that which results from the imposition of normal zoning restrictions. Unlike the regime affected by the latter, the landowner is not simply prohibited from using his property for certain purposes, while allowed to use it for all other purposes. Under the historic-landmark preservation scheme adopted by New York, the property owner is under an affirmative duty to *preserve* his property *as a landmark* at his own expense. To suggest that because traditional zoning results in some limitation of use of the property zoned, the New York City landmark preservation scheme should likewise be upheld, represents the ultimate in treating as alike things which are different. The rubric of "zoning" has not yet sufficed to avoid the well-established proposition that the Fifth Amendment bars the "Government from forcing some people alone to bear public burdens which, in all fairness and justice, should be borne by the public as a whole." Armstrong v. United States, 364 U.S. 40, 49, 80 S.Ct. 1563, 1569, 4 L.Ed.2d 1554 (1960).

* * *

* * * At the time Grand Central was designated a landmark, Penn Central was in a precarious financial condition. In an effort to increase its sources of revenue, Penn Central had entered into a lease agreement with appellant UGP Properties, Inc., under which UGP would construct and operate a multistory office building cantilevered above the Terminal building. During the period of construction, UGP would pay Penn Central $1 million per year. Upon completion, UGP would rent the building for 50 years, with an option for another 25 years, at a guaranteed *minimum* rental of $3 million per year. The record is clear that the proposed office building was in full compliance with all New York zoning laws and height limitations. Under the Landmarks Preservation Law, however, appellants could not construct the proposed office building unless appellee Landmarks Preservation Commission issued either a "Certificate of No Exterior Effect" or a "Certificate of Appropriateness." Although appellants' architectural plan would have preserved the facade of the Terminal, the Landmarks Preservation Commission has refused to approve the construction.

* * *

Appellees have thus destroyed—in a literal sense, "taken"—substantial property rights of Penn Central. While the term "taken" might have been narrowly interpreted to include only physical seizures of property rights, "the construction of the phrase has not been so narrow. The courts have held that the deprivation of the former owner rather than the accretion of a right or interest to the sovereign constitutes the taking." Id., at 378, 65 S.Ct. at 359. See also United States v. Lynah, 188 U.S. 445, 469, 23 S.Ct. 349, 47 L.Ed. 539 (1903); Dugan v. Rank, 372 U.S. 609, 625, 83 S.Ct. 999, 1009, 10 L.Ed.2d 15 (1963). Because "not every destruction or injury to property by governmental action has been held to be a 'taking' in the constitutional sense," Armstrong v. United States, 364 U.S., at 48, 80 S.Ct., at 1568, however, this does not end our inquiry. But an examination of the two exceptions where the destruction of property does not constitute a taking demonstrates that a compensable taking has occurred here.

1

As early as 1887, the Court recognized that the government can prevent a property owner from using his property to injure others without having to compensate the owner for the value of the forbidden use. * * * [Citing and quoting from Mugler v. Kansas, 123 U.S. 623, 668–669, 8 S.Ct. 273, 301, 31 L.Ed. 205.] Thus, there is no "taking" where a city prohibits the operation of a brickyard within a residential area, see Hadacheck v. Sebastian, 239 U.S. 394, 36 S.Ct. 143, 60 L.Ed. 348 (1915), or forbids excavation for sand and gravel below the water line, see Goldblatt v. Hempstead, 369 U.S. 590, 82 S.Ct. 987, 8 L.Ed.2d 130 (1962). Nor is it relevant, where the government is merely prohibiting a noxious use of property, that the government would seem to be singling out a particular property owner. Hadacheck, supra, at 413, 36 S.Ct., at 146.[13]

The nuisance exception to the taking guarantee is not coterminous with the police power itself. The question is whether the forbidden use is dangerous to the safety, health, or welfare of others. * * *

Appellees are not prohibiting a nuisance. The record is clear that the proposed addition to the Grand Central Terminal would be in full compliance with zoning, height limitations, and other health and safety requirements. Instead, appellees are seeking to preserve what they believe to be an outstanding example of beaux-arts architecture. Penn Central is prevented from further developings its property basically because *too good* a job was done in designing and building it. The city of New York, because of its unadorned admiration for the design, has decided that the owners of the building must preserve it unchanged for the benefit of sightseeing New Yorkers and tourists.

Unlike land-use regulations, appellees' actions do not merely *prohibit* Penn Central from using its property in a narrow set of noxious ways. Instead, appellees have placed an *affirmative* duty on Penn Central to maintain the Terminal in its present state and in "good repair." Appellants are not free to use their property as they see fit within broad outer boundaries but must strictly adhere to their past use except where appellees conclude that alternative uses would not detract from

---

13. Each of the cases cited by the Court for the proposition that legislation which severely affects some landowners but not others does not effect a "taking" involved noxious uses of property. See Hadacheck; Miller v. Schoene, 276 U.S. 272, 48 S.Ct. 246, 72 L.Ed. 568 (1928); Goldblatt. * * *

the landmark. While Penn Central may continue to use the Terminal as it is presently designed, appellees otherwise "exercise complete domin-ion and control over the surface of the land," United States v. Causby, 328 U.S. 256, 262, 66 S.Ct. 1062, 1066, 90 L.Ed. 1206 (1946), and must compensate the owner for his loss. Ibid.   *   *   *

2

Even where the government prohibits a noninjurious use, the Court has ruled that a taking does not take place if the prohibition applies over a broad cross section of land and thereby "secure[s] an average reciprocity of advantage." Pennsylvania Coal Co. v. Mahon, 260 U.S., at 415, 43 S.Ct., at 160.[14] It is for this reason that zoning does not constitute a "taking." While zoning at times reduces *individual* prop-erty values, the burden is shared relatively evenly and it is reasonable to conclude that on the whole an individual who is harmed by one aspect of the zoning will be benefited by another.

Here, however, a multimillion dollar loss has been imposed on appel-lants; it is uniquely felt and is not offset by any benefits flowing from the preservation of some 400 other "landmarks" in New York City. Ap-pellees have imposed a substantial cost on less than one one-tenth of one percent of the buildings in New York City for the general benefit of all its people. It is exactly this imposition of general costs on a few individuals at which the "taking" protection is directed.

      *   *   *

As Mr. Justice Holmes pointed out in Pennsylvania Coal Co. v. Mahon, "the question at bottom" in an eminent domain case "is upon whom the loss of the changes desired should fall." 260 U.S., at 416, 43 S.Ct., at 160. The benefits that appellees believe will flow from presevation of the Grand Central Terminal will accrue to all the citizens of New York City. There is no reason to believe that appellants will enjoy a substantially greater share of these benefits. If the cost of pre-serving Grand Central Terminal were spread evenly across the entire population of the city of New York, the burden per person would be in cents per year—a minor cost appellees would surely concede for the benefit accrued. Instead, however, appellees would impose the entire cost of several million dollars per year on Penn Central. But it is pre-cisely this sort of discrimination that the Fifth Amendment prohibits.[15]

---

14. Appellants concede that the preser-vation of buildings of historical or aesthet-ic importance is a permissible objective of state action. Brief for Appellants 12. Cf. Berman v. Parker, 348 U.S. 26, 75 S.Ct. 98, 99 L.Ed. 27 (1954); United States v. Get-tysburg Electric R. Co., 160 U.S. 668, 16 S.Ct. 427, 40 L.Ed. 576 (1896).

For the reasons noted in the text, histor-ic *zoning,* as has been undertaken by cit-ies, such as New Orleans, may well not re-quire compensation under the Fifth Amendment.

15. The fact that the Landmarks Pres-ervation Commission may have allowed ad-ditions to a relatively few landmarks is of no comfort to appellants. Ante, at 2656 n. 18. Nor is it of any comfort that the Com-mission refuses to allow appellants to con-struct any additional stories because of their belief that such construction would not be aesthetic. Ante, at 2656.

Appellees in response would argue that a taking only occurs where a property owner is denied *all* reasonable value of his property.[16] The Court has frequently held that, even where a destruction of property rights would not *otherwise* constitute a taking, the inability of the owner to make a reasonable return on his property requires compensation under the Fifth Amendment. See, e.g., United States v. Lynah, 188 U.S., at 470, 23 S.Ct., at 357. But the converse is not true. A taking does not become a noncompensable exercise of police power simply because the government in its grace allows the owner to make some "reasonable" use of his property. "[I]t is the character of the invasion, not the amount of damage resulting from it, so long as the damage is substantial, that determines the question whether it is a taking." United States v. Cress, 243 U.S. 316, 328, 37 S.Ct. 380, 385, 61 L.Ed. 746 (1917); United States v. Causby, 328 U.S., at 266, 66 S.Ct., at 1068. See also Goldblatt v. Hempstead, 369 U.S., at 594, 82 S.Ct., at 990.

C

Appellees, apparently recognizing that the constraints imposed on a landmark site constitute a taking for Fifth Amendment purposes, do not leave the property owner empty-handed. As the Court notes, ante, at 2654–2655, the property owner may theoretically "transfer" his previous right to develop the landmark property to adjacent properties if they are under his control. Appellees have coined this system "Transfer Development Rights," or TDR's.

Of all the terms used in the Taking Clause, "just compensation" has the strictest meaning. The Fifth Amendment does not allow simply an approximate compensation but requires "a full and perfect equivalent for the property taken." Monongahela Navigation Co. v. United States, 148 U.S., at 326, 13 S.Ct., at 626.

* * *

Appellees contend that, even if they have "taken" appellants' property, TDR's constitute "just compensation." Appellants, of course, argue that TDR's are highly imperfect compensation. Because the lower courts held that there was no "taking," they did not have to reach the question of whether or not just compensation has already been

---

16. Difficult conceptual and legal problems are posed by a rule that a taking only occurs where the property owner is denied all reasonable return on his property. Not only must the Court define "reasonable return" for a variety of types of property (farmlands, residential properties, commercial and industrial areas), but the Court must define the particular property unit that should be examined. For example, in this case, if appellees are viewed as having restricted Penn Central's use of its "air rights," *all* return has been denied. See Pennsylvania Coal Co. v. Mahon, 260 U.S. 393, 43 S.Ct. 158, 67 L.Ed. 322 (1922). The Court does little to resolve these questions in its opinion. Thus, at one point, the Court implies that the question is whether the restrictions have "an unduly harsh impact upon the owner's use of the property," ante at 2661; at another point, the question is phrased as whether Penn Central can obtain "a 'reasonable return' on its investment," ante, at 2666; and, at yet another point, the question becomes whether the landmark is "economically viable," ante, at 2666 n. 36.

awarded. The New York Court of Appeals' discussion of TDR's gives some support to appellants:

> "The many defects in New York City's program for development rights transfers have been detailed elsewhere * * *. The area to which transfer is permitted is severely limited [and] complex procedures are required to obtain a transfer permit." 42 N.Y.2d 324, 334–335, 397 N.Y.S.2d 914, 920, 366 N.E.2d 1271, 1277 (1977).

And in other cases the Court of Appeals has noted that TDR's have an "uncertain and contingent market value" and do "not adequately preserve" the value lost when a building is declared to be a landmark. French Investing Co. v. City of New York, 39 N.Y.2d 587, 591, 385 N.Y.S.2d 5, 7, 350 N.E.2d 381, 383, appeal dismissed 429 U.S. 990, 97 S.Ct. 515, 50 L.Ed.2d 602 (1976). On the other hand, there is evidence in the record that Penn Central has been offered substantial amounts for its TDR's. Because the record on appeal is relatively slim, I would remand to the Court of Appeals for a determination of whether TDR's constitute a "full and perfect equivalent for the property taken." [17]

Notes and Questions

1. Local programs for preservation of historic areas and sites have become widespread in recent years. Places like the French Quarter in New Orleans and Beacon Hill in Boston have been the object of "historic zoning" which seeks to require the owners of buildings in the designated historic areas to maintain their exterior appearance. Such a use of the police power, without providing compensation for property owners who are denied more profitable uses of their land, raises difficult constitutional issues. In all the "first generation" cases involving famous historic districts like the French Quarter and Beacon Hill, the constitutionality of the historic district legislation was sustained.[1]

When an individual "landmark" is designated for preservation, as in the case of Grand Central Station in New York, the legislative action is not sup-

---

17. The Court suggests, ante, at 2663, that if appellees are held to have "taken" property sights of landmark owners, not only the New York City Landmarks Preservation Law, but "all comparable landmark legislation in the Nation" must fall. This assumes, of course, that TDR's are not "just compensation" for the property rights destroyed. It also ignores the fact that many States and cities in the Nation have chosen to preserve landmarks by purchasing or condemning restrictive easements over the facades of the landmarks and are apparently quite satisfied with the results. See, e.g., Ore.Rev.Stat. §§ 271.710, 271.720 (1977); Md.Ann.Code, Art. 41, § 181A (1978); Va.Code §§ 10–145.1 and 10–138(e) (1978); Richmond, Va., City Code §§ 21–23 et seq. (1975). The British National Trust has effectively used restrictive easements to preserve landmarks since 1937. See National Trust Act, 1937, 1 Edw. 8 and 1 Geo. 6 ch. lvii, §§ 4 and 8. Other States and cities have found that tax incentives are also an effective means of encouraging the private

preservation of landmark sites. See, e.g., Conn.Gen.Stat. § 12–127a (1977); Ill.Rev. Stat., ch. 24, § 11–48.2–6 (1976); Va.Code § 10–139 (1978). The New York City Landmarks Preservation Law departs drastically from these traditional, and constitutional, means of preserving landmarks.

1. The rationale of such decisions was well-stated in a recent case upholding an ordinance making the "Old Town" areas of San Diego an historic district, where the court said:

> * * * Preservation of the image of Old Town as it existed prior to 1871, as reflected in the historical buildings in the area, as a visual story of the beginning of San Diego and as an educational exhibit of the birth place of California, contributes to the general welfare; gives the general public attendant educational and cultural advantages; and by its encouragement of tourism is of general economic value.

Bohannan v. City of San Diego, 30 Cal. App.2d 416, 106 Cal.Rptr. 333 (1973).

ported by imposition of comparable restrictions on surrounding buildings, as is the case when an historic district is created. Hence it is easier for the owner of the "landmark" site to argue that the ordinance is discriminatory, that it denies him "equal protection of the laws," and that it also constitutes a "taking" because the owner enjoys no "average reciprocity of advantage" as in historic districting and conventional zoning cases. For an important recent decision finding a "landmark" designation to be "confiscatory" as applied to a particular site, see Lutheran Church in America v. City of New York, 35 N.Y.2d 121, 359 N.Y.S.2d 7, 316 N.E.2d 305 (1974).

Sometimes objections are raised to historic district ordinance requirements that owners of buildings in the district maintain them to prevent deterioration. (A similar objection was raised in *Penn Central.*) The court dealt with this objection in Maher v. City of New Orleans, 516 F.2d 1051 (5th Cir.1975), as follows:

" * * * Once it has been determined that the purpose of the Vieux Carre legislation is a proper one, upkeep of buildings appears reasonably necessary to the accomplishment of the goals of the ordinance. * * * It may be that, in some set of circumstances, the expense of maintenance under the Ordinance— were the city to exact compliance—would be so unreasonable as to constitute a taking."

Id. at 1066–67. See also Lafayette Park Baptist Church v. Scott, 553 S.W.2d 856 (Mo.App.1977), where the court said that "economic considerations cannot be wholly discounted" and that the ordinance must be construed to "authorize demolition when the condition of the structure is such that the economics of restoration preclude the landowner from making any reasonable use of the property." Id. at 862.

For an application of economic analysis to the landmark preservation problem, see Gold, The Welfare Economics of Historic Preservation, 8 Conn.L.Rev. 348 (1976). For additional discussion of the landmark preservation cases, see Gerstell, Needed: A Landmark Decision, 8 Urban L. 213 (1976); Note, Urban Landmarks: Preserving Our Cities' Aesthetic and Cultural Resources, 39 Albany L.Rev. 521 (1974).

2. In *Penn Central* the United States Supreme Court said in footnote 1, supra p. 1156, that "we do not embrace the proposition that a 'taking' can never occur unless the Government has transferred physical control over a portion of a parcel." (Presumably the court meant "asserted" rather than "transferred.") If *Penn Central* has been decided in the Supreme Court before the *French* case, reprinted supra p. 1145, was decided by the New York Court of Appeals, do you think the result in *French* would have been different? Would the New York court perhaps have awarded compensation to the plaintiff?

Suppose the *Arverne Bay* case, reprinted supra p. 1127, had come before the New York Court of Appeals after *Penn Central* was decided by the United States Supreme Court. Do you think *Arverne Bay* would have been decided differently insofar as the decision was based on the conclusion that the plaintiff's property was "taken" in violation of the Fourteenth Amendment?

3. In *Penn Central* the Supreme Court said: " 'Taking' jurisprudence does not divide a single parcel into discrete segments and attempt to determine whether rights in a particular segment have been entirely abrogated. In deciding whether a particular governmental action has effected a taking, this Court focuses rather both on the character of the action and on the nature and extent of the interference with rights in the parcel as a whole, here, the city tax block designated as the 'landmark site.' " Is this consistent with the majority (Holmes) opinion in Pennsylvania Coal Co. v. Mahon, or with the dissenting

(Brandeis) opinion? Is it consistent with the New York Court of Appeals' approach in the *French* case, reprinted supra p. 1145? Was there any finding in *French* that "the parcel as a whole"—the entire Tudor City complex—was deprived of a "reasonable return" by the city's refusal to allow construction of buildings on the private park sites?

4. Are the *Euclid, Hadacheck*, and *Goldblatt* cases, cited by Justice Brennan in his majority opinion in *Penn Central*, really in point? *Euclid* clearly did not deal with the "taking" issue at all, although the Ambler Realty Co. had tried to raise that issue; *Euclid* only decided that the Euclid zoning ordinance was not unconstitutional "on its face." Similarly, *Hadacheck* did not expressly deal with the "taking" issue; indeed, it seems to have followed Mugler v. Kansas in holding that no police power regulation can amount to a "taking." In *Goldblatt*, it is true, the court clearly recognized that "governmental action in the form of regulation" may "be so onerous as to constitute a taking which constitutionally requires compensation"; but, as Justice Brennan conceded, the landowner in *Goldblatt* failed to introduce any evidence to show that the ordinance in that case reduced the value of his land at all. Hence the *Goldblatt* case only decided that, absent such evidence, the ordinance was not clearly "unreasonable" and hence could not be held to violate substantive due process.

5. How much guidance does the majority opinion in *Penn Central* provide for lower federal courts and for state courts seeking to determine when regulations based on the police power should be held to amount to a *de facto* "taking" in violation of the Fourteenth Amendment? Does *Penn Central* establish the proposition that a regulation which "does not interfere in any way with the present uses" of property cannot amount to a de facto "taking" if the "present uses" permit the owner to obtain a "reasonable return" on its investment? What is the significance of the Court's statement in *Penn Central* that "the extent to which the regulation has interfered with distinct investment backed expectations" is a relevant consideration? In Kaiser-Aetna v. United States, 444 U.S. 164, 100 S.Ct. 383, 62 L.Ed. 332 (1979), the distinct investment backed expectations of the defendant seem to have been an important factor in the court's determination that the attempt by the United States to open a private marina to public use amounted to a *de facto* "taking." In Bob Graham v. Estuary Properties, Inc., 399 So.2d 1374 (Fla.1981), on the other hand, the court based its holding that refusal of a permit to dredge and fill coastal wetlands did not amount to a "taking"—at least in part—on the fact that Estuary Properties "had only its own subjective expectation" that the land could be developed as it wished, and, from the start, "recognized that it could not materially alter the property in a way that would have serious adverse impact on the surrounding area."

6. If the majority had found a *de facto* "taking" in *Penn Central*, would it have awarded to the plaintiffs the monetary compensation they originally sought?

AGINS v. CITY OF TIBURON

Supreme Court of California, 1979.
24 Cal.3d 266, 157 Cal.Rptr. 372, 598 P.2d 25, affirmed 447 U.S. 255,
100 S.Ct. 2138, 65 L.Ed.2d 106 (1980).

RICHARDSON, JUSTICE. We review the availability of inverse condemnation as a landowner's remedy when a public agency has adopted a zoning ordinance which substantially limits use of his property. We will conclude that although a landowner so aggrieved may challenge both the constitutionality of the ordinance and the manner in which it is applied to his property by seeking to establish the invalidity of the ordinance either through the remedy of declaratory relief or mandamus, he may not recover damages on the theory of inverse condemnation.

Plaintiffs own five acres of unimproved land in the City of Tiburon, Marin County. Tiburon has an area of 1,676 acres, a population of approximately 6,000, and because of its proximity to San Francisco, its aquatic facilities, temperate climate, and other geographic advantages, is a very desirable suburban residential area. Plaintiffs' real property is ridgeland, possesses views of San Francisco Bay, and was acquired by plaintiffs for residential development.

Tiburon, like every other city in California, is required by state law to prepare a general plan containing, among other things, "A land use element which designates the proposed general distribution and general location and extent of the uses of the land for housing, business, industry, open space   *   *   *   and other categories of public and private uses of land. The land use element shall include a statement of the standards of population density and building intensity recommended for the various districts and other territory covered by the plan." (Gov. Code, § 65302, subd. (a).)

Routinely, the development of a general plan entails a careful examination of numerous social and economic factors. Many cities, especially those which are too small to maintain a staff of sufficient size and technical expertise to undertake such a project, seek the advice of expert consultants. The recommendations of these consultants are considered when the local governmental entity prepares its general plan.

In January 1972 Tiburon retained [two] private consultants, Williams & Mocine and Dean Witter & Co., Incorporated, to prepare advisory reports. The Williams report, issued in October 1972, focused on possible land use designations and recommended that Tiburon attempt to acquire "a substantial portion of Tiburon ridge" for "open space." Plaintiffs' property was identified in the report as one of those parcels of property which were suitable for acquisition for open space. The Witter report, dated July 1972, recommended that the purchase of open space lands be financed through the issuance of $1.25 million of general obligation bonds. The subsequent resolution of the Tiburon City Council approving sale of these bonds did not specifically authorize acquisition of plaintiffs' property or directly refer to it.

By Ordinance No. 124 N.S., effective June 28, 1973, Tiburon adopted widespread zoning modifications which drew upon but did not mirror the consultants' reports. Under the ordinance, plaintiffs' land was designated "RPD-1," defined by Ordinance No. 123 N.S. as a "Residential Planned Development and Open Space Zone." The authorized uses of land so designated are (1) *one-family dwellings*, (2) open space uses, and (3) accessory buildings and accessory uses. The permissible density of buildings is "not less than .2 nor more than 1 dwelling unit per gross acre" depending on other specified provisions. As applied to plaintiffs' five acres "RPD-1" zoning means a maximum of five dwelling units or a minimum of one. Whether plaintiffs are permitted to build five dwelling units, or fewer, will depend upon the particular architectural design contemplated and the results of the required environmental impact report.

Plaintiffs have never made application to use or improve their property following Tiburon's adoption of Ordinance No. 124 N.S., nor have they either sought or received any definitive statement as to how many dwelling units they could build on their land. On October 15, 1973, plaintiffs filed a claim against the City of Tiburon in the amount of $2 million alleging that the adoption of Ordinance No. 124 N.S. had completely destroyed the value of their property. The city rejected the claim on November 12, 1973.

On December 4, 1973, Tiburon filed a complaint in eminent domain against plaintiffs to acquire their property, but on November 1, 1974, filed a notice of abandonment of the proceedings as then authorized by Code of Civil Procedure section 1255a, subdivision (a). (This section was repealed by Stats.1975, ch. 1275, § 1.) The trial court entered its judgment of dismissal of the action on May 20, 1975. The city paid plaintiffs $4,500 for their necessary expenses incurred during the pendency of the action pursuant to section 1255a, subdivision (c), which then fixed the rights of a condemnee upon abandonment of a condemnation proceeding. The remedy was exclusive and the section did not include, as an element of damages, financial impairment during pendency of the eminent domain action of the owner's right to sell. Accordingly, there was no further cause of action available to plaintiffs by reason of the city's eminent domain proceeding.

On June 16, 1975, plaintiffs filed their complaint in the Marin County Superior Court against the City of Tiburon *   *   * alleging, as a first cause of action, a claim in inverse condemnation for $2 million damages and requesting, in a second cause of action, declaratory relief, asserting, among other things, that Ordinance No. 124 N.S. is unconstitutional in that it "constitutes a taking of [plaintiffs'] property without payment of just compensation."

Defendants' general demurrer to the first cause of action (inverse condemnation) was sustained without leave to amend. Similarly, their demurrer to the second cause of action (declaratory relief) was sustained with 10 days leave to amend. Plaintiffs declined to amend their second cause of action and plaintiffs appeal from the ensuing judgment of dismissal with prejudice.

Plaintiffs contend that the limitations on the use of their land imposed by the ordinance constitute an unconstitutional "taking of [plaintiffs'] property without payment of just compensation" for which an action in inverse condemnation will lie. Inherent in the contention is the argument that a local entity's exercise of its police power which, in a given case, may exceed constitutional limits is equivalent to the lawful taking of property by eminent domain thereby necessitating the payment of compensation. We are unable to accept this argument believing the preferable view to be that, while such governmental action is invalid because of its excess, remedy by way of damages in eminent domain is not thereby made available. This conclusion is supported by a leading authority (1 Nichols, Eminent Domain (3d rev. ed. 1975) Nature and Origin of Power, § 1.42(1), pp. 116–121), who expresses his view in this manner: "Not only is an actual physical appropriation, under an attempted exercise of the police power, in practical effect an exercise of the power of eminent domain, but if regulative legislation is so unreasonable or arbitrary as virtually to deprive a person of the complete use and enjoyment of his property, it comes within the purview of the law of eminent domain. *Such legislation is an invalid exercise of the police power since it is clearly unreasonable and arbitrary. It is invalid as an exercise of the power of eminent domain since no provision is made for compensation.*" (Italics added.)

We have previously pointed to the general nature of the appropriate remedy in such cases. In *State of California v. Superior Court (Veta)* (1974) 12 Cal.3d 237, 115 Cal.Rptr. 497, 524 P.2d 1281, real parties had been granted a permit to develop their coastal lands by a regional commission. They brought suit when a permit was denied following an appeal to the California Coastal Zone Commission. We held that declaratory relief was an appropriate remedy by which to seek a declaration that a statute controlling development of coastal lands was facially unconstitutional. Further, insofar as the challenge was to the constitutionality of the act's *application* to the lands of the complaining parties, we concluded that the proper and sole remedy was administrative mandamus.

Similarly, a landowner alleging that a zoning ordinance has deprived him of substantially all use of his land may attempt through declaratory relief or administrative mandamus to invalidate the ordinance as excessive regulation in violation of the Fifth Amendment to the United States Constitution and article I, section 19, of the California Constitution. He may not, however, elect to sue in inverse condemnation and thereby transmute an excessive use of the police power into a lawful taking for which compensation in eminent domain must be paid. * * * To the extent that Eldridge v. City of Palo Alto (1976) 57 Cal.App.3d 613, 129 Cal.Rptr. 575, is contrary, it is expressly disapproved.

There is a clear, direct and unquestionable constitutional basis for the protection of private property. Amendment V of the United States Constitution provides that "No person shall be * * * deprived of * * * property, without due process of law; nor shall private property be taken for public use, without just compensation." In concert with the foregoing Fifth Amendment language article I, section 19, of the California Constitution mandates that "Private property may be taken or damaged for public use only when just compensation, ascertained by a jury unless waived, has been paid to, or into court for, the owner."

"Property," in a legal sense, has been broadly defined. The United States Supreme Court has said that the term "property" is not used in "[the] vulgar and untechnical sense of the physical thing with respect to which the citizen exercises rights recognized by law. * * * [Instead it] denote[s] the group of rights inhering in the citizen's relation to the physical thing, as the right to possess, use and dispose of it. * * * The constitutional provision is addressed to every sort of interest the citizen may possess." (U.S. v. General Motors Corp. (1945) 323 U.S. 373, 377–378, 65 S.Ct. 357, 359, 89 L.Ed. 311.)

While acknowledging the power of government to preserve and improve the quality of life for its citizens through the regulation of the use of private land, we cannot countenance the service of this legitimate need through the uncompensated destruction of private property rights. Such Fifth Amendment property rights have been equated by the constitutional draftsmen with the cherished personal protections against self-incrimination, double jeopardy, and the guarantee of due process of law. These rights are protected by the same amendment.

In balancing the constitutional rights of the landowner against the legitimate needs of government we do not ignore well established precedent. In Pennsylvania Coal Co. v. Mahon (1922) 260 U.S. 393, 43 S.Ct. 158, 67 L.Ed. 322, an injunction was sought to prevent a coal company from causing subsidence of property due to the company's underground mining activities. This Supreme Court opinion has generated some confusion and has even been cited erroneously for the proposition that inverse condemnation is readily available as a remedy in zoning cases because of Justice Holmes' statement that "The general rule at least is, that while property may be regulated to a certain extent, if regulation goes too far it will be recognized as a taking." (*Mahon*, supra, at p. 415.) It is clear both from context and from the disposition in *Mahon*, however, that the term "taking" was used solely to indicate the limit by which the acknowledged social goal of land control could be achieved by regulation rather than by eminent domain. The high court set aside the injunctive relief which had been granted by the Pennsylvania courts and declared void the exercise of police power which had limited the company's right to mine its land. The court did not attempt, however, to transmute the illegal governmental infringement into an exercise of eminent domain and the possibility of compensation was not even considered.

In HFH, Ltd. v. Superior Court (1975) 15 Cal.3d 508, 125 Cal.Rptr. 365, 542 P.2d 237, we examined directly the problem of available remedies for aggrieved landowners and held that inverse condemnation does not lie in zoning actions in which the complaint alleges the mere reduction of market value, and that a zoning action which merely decreases the market value of property does not violate the constitutional provisions forbidding uncompensated taking or damaging of property. In *HFH, Ltd.* we specifically noted that "This case does not present, and we therefore do not decide, the question of entitlement to compensation in the event a zoning regulation forbade substantially *all* use of the land in question. We leave the question for another day." (p. 518, fn. 16, 125 Cal.Rptr. p. 372, 542 P.2d p. 244, italics in original.) We now reach that issue.

While it is true that the land uses which were regulated in *HFH, Ltd.* were commercial, we find no reason to distinguish it on that basis from similar situations in which the regulation affects land used for residential, recreational, or other purposes, or to extend the additional relief of inverse condemnation to the owners of noncommercial property.

(For a discussion of a contrary analysis which recommends the extension of a damages remedy in a noncommercial context, see Ellickson, Suburban Growth Controls: An Economic and Legal Analysis (1977) 86 Yale L.J. 385, 507–511.)

We are persuaded by various policy considerations to the view that inverse condemnation is an inappropriate and undesirable remedy in cases in which unconstitutional regulation is alleged. The expanding developments of our cities and suburban areas coupled with a growing awareness of the necessity to preserve our natural resources, including the land around us, has resulted in changing attitudes toward the regulation of land use. Recognition of this historic trend is not new. The United States Supreme Court perceptively observed more than 50 years ago that with the passage of time and increased concentration of people "problems have developed, and constantly are developing, which require, and will continue to require, additional restrictions in respect of the use and occupation of private lands in urban communities. Regulations, the wisdom, necessity and validity of which, as applied to existing conditions, are so apparent that they are now uniformly sustained, a century ago, or even half a century ago, probably would have been rejected as arbitrary and oppressive. Such regulations are sustained, under the complex conditions of our day, *   *   *. And in this there is no inconsistency, for while the meaning of constitutional guaranties never varies, the scope of their application must expand or contract to meet the new and different conditions which are constantly coming within the field of their operation. In a changing world, it is impossible that it should be otherwise." (Euclid v. Ambler Co. (1926) 272 U.S. 365, 386–387, 47 S.Ct. 114, 118, 71 L.Ed. 303.)

In the half century since *Euclid* the foregoing abstract principles under the force of experience have coalesced into a specific functional requirement. Community planners must be permitted the flexibility which their work requires. As we ourselves have recently observed, "If a governmental entity and its responsible officials were held subject to a claim for inverse condemnation merely because a parcel of land was designated for potential public use on one of these several authorized plans, the process of community planning would either grind to a halt, or deteriorate to publication of vacuous generalizations regarding the future use of land." (Selby Realty Co. v. City of San Buenaventura (1973) 10 Cal.3d 110, 120, 109 Cal.Rptr. 799, 805, 514 P.2d 111, 117.)

Other commentators have recognized that the utilization of an inverse condemnation remedy would have a chilling effect upon the exercise of police regulatory powers at a local level because the expenditure of public funds would be, to some extent, within the power of the judiciary. "This threat of unanticipated financial liability will intimidate legislative bodies and will discourage the implementation of strict or innovative planning measures in favor of measures which are less stringent, more traditional, and fiscally safe." (Hall, Eldridge v. City of Palo Alto: Aberration or New Direction in Land Use Law? (1977) 28 Hastings L.J. 1569, 1597.)

We envisage that the availability of an inverse condemnation remedy in these situations would pose yet another threat to legislative control over appropriate land-use determinations. It has been noted that "The weighing of costs and benefits is essentially a legislative process. In enacting a zoning ordinance, the legislative body assesses the desirability of a program on the assumption that compensation will not be required to achieve the objectives of that ordinance. Determining that a particular land-use control requires compensation is an appropriate function of the judiciary, whose function includes protection of individuals against excesses of government. But it seems a usurpation of legislative power for a court to force compensation. Invalidation, rather than forced compensation, would seem to be the more expedient means of remedying legislative excesses." (Fulham & Scharf, Inverse Condemnation: Its Availability in Challenging the Validity of a Zoning Ordinance (1974) 26 Stan.L.Rev. 1439, 1450–1451; see also Bowden, Legal Battles on the California Coast: A Review of the Rules (1974) 2 Coastal Zone Management J. 273.)

Other budgetary consequences reveal themselves when the land use control is exercised by means of the initiative. "Legislation in the nature of zoning can be and has been enacted by the people through a direct initiative. Are the voters, through the initiative power, also to have this unwelcome power to *inadvertently* commit funds from the public treasury? The logical extension of requiring compensation for the mere enactment of a harsh zoning measure indicates that the answer would be in the affirmative. The potential for fiscal chaos would be great if this were the result." (28 Hastings L.J., supra, at p. 1598, emphasis in original.)

In combination, the need for preserving a degree of freedom in the land-use planning function, and the inhibiting financial force which inheres in the inverse condemnation remedy, persuade us that on balance administrative mandamus or declaratory relief rather than inverse condemnation is the appropriate relief under the circumstances.

Having clarified the nature of the remedies available to an aggrieved landowner, we now consider whether the property owners before us establish their right to declaratory relief. We conclude that they did not.

An ordinance which on its face results in a mere diminution in the value of the property is not per se improper. In HFH, Ltd. v. Superior Court, supra, 15 Cal.3d 508, 125 Cal.Rptr. 365, 542 P.2d 237, we examined a change in zoning which reduced the value of property from $400,000 to $75,000. We concluded that no remedy was available for a mere decrease in the value of property. By this holding we acknowledged a practical truism which had been expressed by Justice Holmes more than 50 years ago in the *Mahon* cases: "Government hardly could go on if to some extent values incident to property could not be diminished without paying for every such change in the general law. As long recognized, some values are enjoyed under an implied limitation and must yield to the police power." (Pennsylvania Coal Co. v. Mahon, supra, 260 U.S. at p. 413, 43 S.Ct., at p. 159.)

Accepting as we must the general proposition that whether a regulation is excessive in any particular situation involves questions of degree, turning on the individual facts of each case, we hold that a zoning ordinance may be unconstitutional and subject to invalidation only when its effect is to deprive the landowner of substantially all reasonable use of his property. The ordinance before us had no such effect. According to the wording of the ordinance, of which we may take note, the RPD–1 zoning allows plaintiffs to build between one and five residences on their property. This belies plaintiffs' claim that development of their land is forever prevented. Taking cognizance of the use which plaintiffs were entitled to make of their land the trial court was justified in finding that the ordinance did not unconstitutionally interfere with plaintiffs' entire use of the land or impermissibly decrease its value. The trial court acted properly in determining that plaintiffs were not, as a matter of law, entitled to a favorable judgment in declaratory relief.

Plaintiffs also argue that the city's "precondemnation activities," those being the authorization of studies which recommended acquisition of plaintiffs' land for open space and bonds for its purchase, and the filing and subsequent abandonment of an eminent domain proceeding, were so unreasoanble as to provide a separate basis for an action for inverse condemnation. Plaintiffs err and we do not find persuasive their reliance on Klopping v. City of Whittier (1972) 8 Cal.3d 39, 104 Cal. Rptr. 1, 500 P.2d 1345, for support for their contention.

Klopping involved a plaintiff's recovery for the decline in market value as the result of an unreasonable delay in the institution of eminent domain proceedings following announcement of intent to condemn, and other unreasonable conduct prior to condemnation. In the matter before us there was no such delay or conduct. Tiburon instituted eminent domain proceedings less than six months after Ordinance No. 124 N.S. was adpoted. It is manifest that general land use planning discussions and related decision-making by elected officials must be both unhampered and public. Together or singly, neither process constitutes a "taking" of the property under consideration. Any other conclusion would violate sound public policy.

Our appellate courts have recognized the appropriate controlling principles. "*Selby* [supra, 10 Cal.3d 110, 109 Cal.Rptr. 799, 514 P.2d 111] made clear that *Klopping* [supra, 8 Cal.3d 39, 104 Cal.Rptr. 1, 500 P.2d 1345] was no support for a claim that planning designations constitute takings." (Navajo Terminals, Inc. v. San Francisco Bay Conservation etc. Com. (1975) 46 Cal.App.3d 1, 4, 120 Cal.Rptr. 108, 110.) As was noted in City of Walnut Creek v. Leadership Housing Systems (1977) 73 Cal.App.3d 611, 140 Cal.Rptr. 690, " * * * the inclusion of the property for public use in a general plan does not give rise to a cause of action. If calling a bond election and urging passage to secure funds for a public purpose constituted a taking, the agency so acting would be subject to suit whether or not the issue carried. The expression of political preference cannot be so burdened." (Pp. 622–623, 140 Cal.Rptr. p. 696.)

Recognizing the constitutionally protected property interests here involved, we also accept the reasonable latitude which must be afforded public officials in the planning for and implementation of legitimate land use goals. These twin purposes will be served by preserving for the landowner, in appropriate cases, declaratory relief or administrative mandamus remedies. However, the use of inverse condemnation with its imposition of money damages upon the public entity would, in our view, unwisely inhibit the proper and necessary exercise of a valid police power.

The judgment is affirmed.

BIRD, C.J., and TOBRINER, MOSK, MANUEL and NEWMAN, JJ., concur.

CLARK, Justice, dissenting. [Omitted.]

Notes

1. In Eldridge v. City of Palo Alto, "expressly disapproved" in the principal case, plaintiff Eldridge brought suit against the City of Palo Alto "for damages in inverse condemnation" after his 750 acres of undeveloped land was "downzoned" from "single-family residential use on minimum 1-acre sites" to "open space" with "a minimum parcel size of 10 acres." Eldridge, however, "conceded the ordinances' validity." The California intermediate appellate court held that Eldridge had stated a cause of action "for damages in inverse condemnation," relying on most of the cases distinguished by the California Supreme Court in the principal case. And in a companion case decided at the same time, the intermediate court held that the *only* action available to the landowner was on "for damages in inverse condemnation"—invalidation was not available as an alternative remedy!

2. A 515-acre tract located in the same general area as the land involved in *Eldridge* was the locus of the litigation in Arastra Ltd. Partnership v. City of Palo Alto, 401 F.Supp. 962 (N.D.Cal.1975), vacated 417 F.Supp. 1125 (1976). In *Arastra,* the developer acquired its tract after it was rezoned from REA (Residential, 1-acre lot minimum) to P–C (Planned Community District) and after a development plan for the tract was approved by the Palo Alto city council. Sometime in early 1868 Arastra began to formulate a new development plan, and on August 1, 1968, it filed an application for approval of the new plan, which called for 1,776 housing units, a 150,000 square foot commercial site, a 200,000 square foot office-professional complex, an elementary school, and other related public facilities, on a 24-acre site, and approximately 250 acres of open space. (This was the "1776 Plan"). On October 29, 1969, the city's planning consultant delivered the first of a series of reports dealing with development of the Foothills area. On March 16, 1970, the city council passed a resolution deferring action on Arastra's 1776 Plan pending receipt of a final report from its planning consultant.

This report was submitted to the City Council in June, 1970; in part, it recommended: (a) that the "lower Foothills" below Foothills Park, including the Arastra tract, be purchased by the City; (b) that the City deny approval to all development proposals for the "lower Foothills"; (c) that the City be prepared to purchase land in the "lower Foothills," when necessary to prevent development; (d) that all "lower Foothills" land be rezoned so as to prohibit more than one dwelling unit per five acres, in order to prevent development prior to acquisition of the land by the City; and (e) that there be further study of alternative means of acquiring such land. On November 9, 1970, the City Council voted to accept the consultant's recommendations, and its action was publicized in local news media as a decision to purchase "the lower Foothills" area, including the Arastra tract. On November 16, 1970, the City Council unanimously voted to deny approval of Arastra's 1776 Plan, and this action was also publicized in local news media as being in furtherance of the decision of the City to purchase "the lower Foothills" area. Arastra in fact believed that Palo Alto had decided to purchase its property and made no further plans to develop its tract, although it made repeated efforts to induce the City to reverse its decision to prohibit development of the tract.

Between January 13 and July 19, 1971, Palo Alto officials proceeded with planning for acquisition of the entire "lower Foothills" area, and on July 19 the City Council adopted an ordinance establishing a six-month moratorium on development in that area. On August 6, 1971, the City Manager rendered a report to the City Council entitled "Foothills Financing Plan" wherein three alternative financing plans were suggested. On August 23, 1971, the City Council passed an ordinance increasing its budget appropriations for "Foothills Land Acquisition" by $665,900 (from $3,334,100 to $4,000,000). On August 30, however, the Palo Alto City Planning Staff reported to the City Council that the receipt of federal funds to aid in the purchase of "the lower Foothills" area was unlikely. On October 4, the City Council in a closed session decided to make no further effort to obtain federal funds for land acquisition in the "lower Foothills" area. On February 28, 1972, the development moratorium was extended for another six-month period. Shortly thereafter, the Council apparently decided that acquisition of the "lower Foothills" with City funds alone would be too expensive.

On June 5, 1972, the Palo Alto City Council added "O–S" Open Space District Regulations to the Municipal Code, and on August 14, 1972, adopted an ordinance reclassifying the "lower Foothills," including both the Eldridge and Arastra tracts, as "O–S" Open Space. On December 20, 1972, Arastra brought an inverse condemnation action against Palo Alto. The court held as follows:

"When the open space ordinance is examined in * * * context, it compels the conclusion that the City had the purpose, by way of zoning regulation, to accomplish without expense to the taxpayers all of the benefits it could have received from the acquisition [of Arastra's tract]. * * *

"It is somewhat ironic for the defendant to contend that there is an absolute bar to inverse condemnation because there has been no physical invasion of plaintiff's property. Of course, physical invasion of the property is precisely what the City is attempting to prevent. Their whole objective is to have the property remain unused, undisturbed, and in natural state so that the open space and scenic qualities may be preserved. * * * There has clearly been the appropriation of a valuable property right of the plaintiff * * * whether the taking be deemed a scenic easement, an open space easement, or something different.

 * * *

"Considered narrowly, the damages here might be computed solely upon the basis of the easements constructively acquired by the City and the losses resulting. This, however, would leave the parties in intolerable positions. The City would have paid out amounts which well could approach the full value of fee title but would have no title. The plaintiff, on the other hand, would have title but little more.

"Relief in such a matter should be framed as equitably as possible, considering the position of both parties. The original plan of the City was to acquire the fee; it has never abandoned its purpose to do so. Requiring it to carry out that purpose would serve the interest of both parties. The City with fee title could deal with the entire property in any fashion that public purposes required, including its original concept of land banking some portion of the land for future controlled development. Plaintiff on the other hand would be fully compensated for its property without being left with a naked fee that could well be a liability rather than an asset. Accordingly, * * * the measure of plaintiff's damages shall be the fair market value of the fee title on the effective date of the Open Space Ordinance, and it will be further ordered that, concurrently with payment therefor, plaintiff shall convey such fee title to the City.

"The sole remaining question is whether, at the trial to determine fair market value, the Court may decide as a matter of law, the density to which the property might probably have been permitted to be developed, had not the taking intervened, or whether that is a question of fact to be decided by the jury. It would appear that this determination, just as all other facts affecting compensation, must be left to the jury. * * * The Court has, however, already heard what may well be all of the evidence which will bear upon this issue. On the present record, the Court would be constrained to find that there is no evidence which would support a jury finding that development would probably have been permitted to an intensity in excess of 1,250 residential units, plus office and commercial structures, all subject to the then requirements of the P–C (Planned Community) zoning regulations. 401 F.Supp. at 980, 981–82."

Before any judicial determination of Arastra's compensation was made, the parties settled out of court for more than $7,000,000 and the judgment of the district court was vacated. See 417 F.Supp. 1125 (N.D.Cal.1976).

3. When the United States Supreme Court decided to review Agins v. City of Tiburon, persons interested in the "taking" and "compensation" issues thought that the Court would rule on the question whether compensation is constitutionally required when a court finds that a regulatory "taking" has occurred. The Court, however, never reached the "compensation" issue because it agreed with the California Supreme Court that the Tiburon zoning regulations, as applied to the Agins tract, did not result in a "taking" at all. The Court's opinion, by Justice Powell, does little to dispel the prevailing confusion as to when—if ever—regulation amounts to a *de facto* "taking." Justice Powell said that, "[b]ecause the appellants have not submitted a plan for development of their property as the ordinances permit, there is as yet no concrete controversy regarding the application of the specific zoning provisions. * * * Thus, the only question properly before us is whether the mere enactment of the zoning ordinances constitutes a taking." In other words, until the landowner, upon submitting a plan for development, ascertained what the allowable density of development on their tract would be, they could not raise the issue whether a density of less than one single-family dwelling per acre would effect a *de facto* "taking." Assuming that the city authorities might allow the maximum density of one dwelling per acre, the zoning classification was valid because it did not deny appellants the "justice and fairness" guaranteed by the Fifth and Fourteenth Amendments.

Justice Powell's assertion that "application of a general zoning law to particular property effects a taking if the ordinance does not substantially advance legitimate state interests" is, of course, demonstrably incorrect. In such a case, the zoning is invalid because it violates substantive due process, but it does *not* effect a "taking."

The United States Supreme Court's opinion in *Agins* is reported in 447 U.S. 255, 100 S.Ct. 2138, 65 L.Ed.2d 106 (1980). On the same day it filed its *Agins* opinion, the Court tentatively agreed to review another "regulatory taking—compensation" case, San Diego Gas Co. v. City of San Diego.

SAN DIEGO GAS & ELECTRIC CO. v. CITY OF SAN DIEGO

Supreme Court of the United States, 1981.
450 U.S. 621, 101 S.Ct. 1287, 67 L.Ed.2d 551.

Justice BLACKMAN delivered the opinion of the Court.

Appellant San Diego Gas & Electric Company, a California corporation, asks this Court to rule that a State must provide a monetary remedy to a landowner whose property allegedly has been "taken" by a regulatory ordinance claimed to violate the Just Compensation Clause of the Fifth Amendment.[1] This question was left open last Term in Agins v. City of Tiburon, 447 U.S. 255, 263, 100 S.Ct. 2138, 2142, 65 L.Ed.2d 106 (1980). Because we conclude that we lack jurisdiction in this case, we again must leave the issue undecided.

I

Appellant owns a 412-acre parcel of land in Sorrento Valley, an area in the northwest part of the city of San Diego, Cal. It assembled and acquired the acreage in 1966, at a cost of about $1,770,000 as a possible site for a nuclear power plant to be constructed in the 1980's. Approximately 214 acres of the parcel lie within or near an estuary known as the Los Penasquitos Lagoon.[2] These acres are low-lying land which serves as a drainage basin for three river systems. About a third of the land is subject to tidal action from the nearby Pacific Ocean. The 214 acres are unimproved, except for sewer and utility lines.[3]

When appellant acquired the 214 acres, most of the land was zoned either for industrial use or in an agricultural "holding" category.[4] The city's master plan, adopted in 1967, designated nearly all the area for industrial use.

1. "[N]or shall private property be taken for public use, without just compensation."

The Fifth Amendment's prohibition applies against the States through the Fourteenth Amendment. Chicago, B., & Q.R. Co. v. Chicago, 166 U.S. 226, 239, 17 S.Ct. 581, 585, 41 L.Ed. 979 (1897); Webb's Fabulous Pharmacies, Inc. v. Beckwith, 449 U.S. 155, 160, 101 S.Ct. 446, 450, 66 L.Ed.2d 358 (1980).

2. Appellant claims that only the 214 acres have been taken by the city of San Diego. Throughout this opinion, "the property" and any similar phrase refers to this smaller portion of the 412 acres owned by appellant.

3. Apparently other portions of the 412-acre parcel have been developed to some extent, and some parts sold.

4. The city had classified 116 acres as M–1A (industrial) and 112 acres as A–1–1 (agricultural). The latter classification was reserved for "undeveloped areas not yet ready for urbanization and awaiting development, those areas where agricultural usage may be reasonably expected to persist or areas designated as open space in the general plan." San Diego Ordinance No. 8706 (New Series) § 101.0404 (1962), reproduced in Brief for Appellees C–1. A small amount of the land was zoned for residential development. (These figures total more than 214 acres. When the California courts described the zoning of the property, they did not distinguish between the 214 acres that allegedly were taken and 15 other acres that the trial court found had been damaged by the severance.)

Several events that occurred in 1973 gave rise to this litigation. First, the San Diego City Council rezoned parts of the property. It changed 39 acres from industrial to agricultural, and increased the minimum lot size in some of the agricultural acres from 1 acre to 10 acres. The Council recommended, however, that 50 acres of the agricultural land be considered for industrial development upon the submission of specific development plans.

Second, the city, pursuant to Cal.Gov't Code Ann. § 65563 (West Supp.1981), established an open-space plan. This statute required each California city and county to adopt a plan "for the comprehensive and long-range preservation and conservation of open-space land within its jurisdiction." The plan adopted by the city of San Diego placed appellant's property among the city's open-space areas, which it defined as "any urban land or water surface that is essentially open or natural in character, and which has appreciable utility for park and recreation purposes, conservation of land, water or other natural resources or historic or scenic purposes." App. 159. The plan acknowledged appellant's intention to construct a nuclear power plant on the property, stating that such a plant would not necessarily be incompatible with the open-space designation.[5] The plan proposed, however, that the city acquire the property to preserve it as parkland.

Third, the City Council proposed a bond issue in order to obtain funds to acquire open-space lands. The Council identified appellant's land as among those properties to be acquired with the proceeds of the bond issue. The proposition, however, failed to win the voters' approval. The open-space plan has remained in effect, but the city has made no attempt to acquire appellant's property.

On August 15, 1974, appellant instituted this action in the Superior Court for the County of San Diego against the city and a number of its officials. It alleged that the city had taken its property without just compensation, in violation of the Constitutions of the United States and California. Appellant's theory was that the city had deprived it of the entire beneficial use of the property through the rezoning and the adoption of the open-space plan. It alleged that the city followed a policy of refusing to approve any development that was inconsistent with the plan, and that the only beneficial use of the property was as an industrial park, a use that would be inconsistent with the open-space designation.[6] The city disputed this allegation, arguing that appellant had never asked its approval for any development plan for the property. It also contended that, as a charter city, it was not bound by the open-space

---

5. The portion of the plan that discussed the Los Penasquitos Lagoon area stated: "[T]he San Diego Gas & Electric Company has a large (240 acre) ownership which it intends to utilize as the location of a nuclear power plant sometime in the 1980's. * * * [S]uch a facility, if sensitively designed and sited, could be compatible with open space preservation in this subsystem; however, a number of approvals and clearances must be obtained prior

to the plant's construction becoming a reality." App. 160.

6. Appellant abandoned its plan to construct a nuclear power plant after the discovery of an off-shore fault that rendered the project unfeasible. Tr. 73. Its witnesses acknowledged that only about 150 acres were usable as an industrial park, and that 1.25 million cubic yards of fill would be needed to undertake such a development. Id., at 711, 905.

plan, even if appellant's proposed development would be inconsistent, with the plan, citing Cal.Gov't Code Ann. §§ 65700, 65803 (West 1966 and Supp.1981).

Appellant sought damages of $6,150,000 in inverse condemnation, as well as mandamus and declaratory relief. Prior to trial, the court dismissed the mandamus claim, holding that "mandamus is not the proper remedy to challenge the validity of a legislative act." Clerk's Tr. 42. After a nonjury trial on the issue of liability, the court granted judgment for appellant, finding that:

"29. [Due to the] continuing course of conduct of the defendant City culminating in June of 1973, and, in particular, the designation of substantially all of the subject property as open space *   *   *, plaintiff has been deprived of all practical, beneficial or economic use of the property designated as open space, and has further suffered severance damage with respect to the balance of the subject property.

"30. No development could proceed on the property designated as open space unless it was consistent with open space. In light of the particular characteristics of the said property, there exists no practical, beneficial or economic use of the said property designated as open space which is consistent with open space.

"31. Since June 19, 1973, the property designated as open space has been devoted to use by the public as open space.

"32. Following the actions of the defendant City in June of 1973, it would have been totally impractical and futile for plaintiff to have applied to defendant City for the approval of any development of the property designated as open space or the remainder of the subject property.

"33. Since the actions of the defendant City in June of 1973, the property designated as open space and the remainder of the larger parcel is unmarketable in that no other person would be willing to purchase the property, and the property has at most a nominal fair market value." App. 41–42.

The court concluded that these findings established that the city had taken the property and that just compensation was required by the Constitutions of both the United States and California. A subsequent jury trial on the question of damages resulted in a judgment for appellant for over $3 million.

On appeal, the California Court of Appeal, Fourth District, affirmed. App. to Juris., Statement B–1; see 146 Cal.Rptr. 103 (1978). It held that neither a change in zoning nor the adoption of an open-space plan automatically entitled a property owner to compensation for any resulting diminution in the value of the property. In this case, however, the record revealed that the city followed the policy of enacting and enforcing zoning ordinances that were consistent with its open-space plan. The Court of Appeal also found that the evidence supported the conclusion that industrial use was the only feasible use for the property and that the city would have denied any application for industrial development because it would be incompatible with the open-space designation. Appellant's failure to present a plan for developing the property therefore did not preclude an award of damages in its favor. The Court of Appeal, with one judge dissenting, denied the city's petition for rehearing. See 146 Cal.Rptr., at 118.

The Supreme Court of California, however, on July 13, 1978, granted the city's petition for a hearing. This action automatically vacated the Court of Appeal's decision, depriving it of all effect. Knouse v. Nimocks, 8 Cal.2d 482, 483–484, 66 P.2d 438 (1937). See also Cal.Rules of Court 976(d) and 977 (West 1981). Before the hearing, the Supreme Court in June 1979 retransferred the case to the Court of Appeal for reconsideration in light of the intervening decision in Agins v. City of Tiburon, 24 Cal.3d 266, 157 Cal.Rptr. 372, 598 P.2d 25 (1979), aff'd, 447 U.S. 255, 100 S.Ct. 2138, 65 L.Ed.2d 106 (1980). The California court in *Agins* held that an owner who is deprived of substantially all beneficial use of his land by a zoning regulation is not entitled to an award of damages in an inverse condemnation proceeding. Rather, his exclusive remedy is invalidation of the regulation in an action for mandamus or declaratory relief.[7] *Agins* also held that the plaintiffs in that case were not entitled to such relief because the zoning ordinance at issue permitted the building of up to five residences on their property. Therefore, the court held, it did not deprive those plaintiffs of substantially all reasonable use of their land.[8]

7. Contrary to the dissent's argument, the California Supreme Court's *Agins* decision did not hold that a zoning ordinance never could be a "taking" and thus never could violate the Just Compensation Clause. It simply *limited the remedy* available for any such violation to non-monetary relief. Immediately following the passage quoted by the dissent, *post*, at 1298, that court stated:

"This conclusion is supported by a leading authority (1 Nichols, Eminent Domain (3d rev. ed. 1978) Nature and Origin of Power, § 1.42(1), pp. 1–116—1–121), who expresses his view in this manner: 'Not only is an actual physical appropriation, under an attempted exercise of the police power, in practical effect an exercise of the power of eminent domain, but if regulative legislation is so unreasonable or arbitrary, as virtually to deprive a person of the complete use and enjoyment of his property, it comes within the purview of the law of eminent domain. *Such legislation is an invalid exercise of the police power since it is clearly unreasonable and arbitrary. It is invalid as an exercise of the power of eminent domain since no provision is made for compensation.*'" 24 Cal.3d, at 272, 157 Cal.Rptr. at 375, 598 P.2d, at 28. (Emphasis added by the California court). See also *id.*, at 273–274, 157 Cal.Rptr., at 375, 598 P.2d, at 29:

"While acknowledging the power of government to preserve and improve the quali-

ty of life for its citizens through the regulation of the use of private land, we cannot countenance the service of this legitimate need through the uncompensated destruction of private property rights." And see id. at 276, 157 Cal.Rptr., at 377, 598 P.2d, at 30:

" 'Determining that a particular land-use control requires compensation is an appropriate function of the judiciary. * * * But it seems a usurpation of legislative power for a court to force compensation,' " quoting Note, Inverse Condemnation: Its Availability in Challenging the Validity of a Zoning Ordinance, 26 Stan.L.Rev. 1439, 1451 (1974).

When *Agins* was appealed here, we unanimously agreed that "[t]he State Supreme Court determined that the appellants could not recover damages for inverse condemnation even if the zoning ordinances constituted a taking. The court stated that only mandamus and declaratory judgment are remedies available to such a landowner." 447 U.S., at 263, 100 S.Ct., at 2142. We believe, therefore, that it is the dissent that "fundamentally mischaracterizes," *post*, at 1296, the California ruling.

8. This Court's affirmance of the California court's judgment in *Agins* was on the ground that there was no taking. 447 U.S., at 263, 100 S.Ct., at 2142.

When the present case was retransferred, the Court of Appeal, in an unpublished opinion, reversed the judgment of the Superior Court. App. 63. It relied upon the California decision in *Agins* and held that appellant could not recover compensation through inverse condemnation. It, however, did not invalidate either the zoning ordinance or the open-space plan. Instead, it held that factual disputes precluded such relief on the present state of the record:

"[Appellant] complains it has been denied all use of its land which is zoned for agriculture and manufacturing but lies within the open space area of the general plan. It has not made application to use or improve the property nor has it asked [the] City what development might be permitted. Even assuming no use is acceptable to the City, [appellant's] complaint deals with the alleged overzealous use of the police power by [the] City. Its remedy is mandamus or declaratory relief, not inverse condemnation. [Appellant] did in its complaint seek these remedies asserting that [the] City had arbitrarily exercised its police power by enacting an unconstitutional zoning law and general plan element or by applying the zoning and general plan unconstitutionally. However, on the present record these are disputed fact issues not covered by the trial court in its findings and conclusions. They can be dealt with anew should [appellant] elect to retry the case." App. 66.

The Supreme Court of California denied further review. App. to Juris., Statement I–1. Appellant appealed to this Court, arguing that the Fifth and Fourteenth Amendments require that compensation be paid whenever private property is taken for public use. Appellant takes issue with the California Supreme Court's holding in *Agins* that its remedy is limited to invalidation of the ordinance in a proceeding for mandamus or declaratory relief. We postponed consideration of our jurisdiction until the hearing on the merits. 447 U.S. 919, 100 S.Ct. 3008, 65 L.Ed.2d 1111 (1980). We now conclude that the appeal must be dismissed because of the absence of a final judgment.[9]

II

In *Agins*, the California Supreme Court held that mandamus or declaratory relief is available whenever a zoning regulation is claimed to effect an uncompensated taking in violation of the Fifth and Fourteenth Amendments. The Court of Appeal's failure, therefore, to award such relief in this case clearly indicates its conclusion that the record does not support appellant's claim that an uncompensated taking has occurred.[10] Because the court found that the record presented "disputed fact issues not covered by the trial court in its findings and conclu-

---

9. Title 28 U.S.C.A. § 1257 grants jurisdiction to this Court to review only "[f]inal judgments or decrees rendered by the highest court of a State in which a decision could be had." Because the finality requirement of § 1257 applies to this Court's review of state-court judgments both by appeal and by certiorari, we do not address the city's contention that, inasmuch as the Court of Appeal did not uphold any statute against a constitutional challenge, this is not a proper appeal under § 1257(2).

10. We recognize that this is inconsistent with the Court of Appeal's first ruling in this case, but, as has been noted, that decision was deprived of all effect by the Supreme Court's order granting a hearing.

The dissent's statement that the Court of Appeal "concluded as a matter of law

sions," App. 66,[11] it held that mandamus and declaratory relief would be available "should [appellant] elect to retry the case." Ibid. While this phrase appears to us to be somewhat ambiguous, we read it as meaning that appellant is to have an opportunity on remand to convince the trial court to resolve the disputed issues in its favor. We do not believe that the Court of Appeal was holding that judgment *must* be entered for the city. It certainly did not so direct. This indicates that appellant is free to pursue its quest for relief in the Superior Court. The logical course of action for an appellate court that finds unresolved factual disputes in the record is to remand the case for the resolution of those disputes. We therefore conclude that the Court of Appeal's decision contemplates further proceedings in the trial court.[12]

*　*　*

Justice REHNQUIST, concurring. If I were satisfied that this appeal was from a "final judgment or decree" of the California Court of Appeal, as that term is used in 28 U.S.C. § 1257, I would have little difficulty in agreeing with much of what is said in the dissenting opinion of Justice BRENNAN. Indeed, the Court's opinion notes, that "the federal constitutional aspects of that issue are not to be cast aside lightly. *　*　*" Ante, p. 1294.

that no Fifth Amendment 'taking' had occurred," *post*, at 1300, is premised upon its misreading of the Agins opinion. See n. 8, supra. The Court of Appeal simply refused to award appellant the only remedy held to be available for a "taking" because there were disputed factual issues to be resolved.

11. Although its initial opinion affirmed the trial court's finding that any application by appellant to develop the property would have been rejected, it is clear that the Court of Appeal reconsidered that finding in the light of *Agins*. In *Agins*, the California Supreme Court held that landowners who had not "made application to use or improve their property" following the passage of a zoning ordinance and had not "sought or received any definitive statement as to how many dwelling units they could build on their land," 24 Cal.3d, at 271, 157 Cal.Rptr., at 374, 598 P.2d at 27, had not shown that the ordinance took their property without just compensation, since it permitted up to five residences to be built on the plaintiffs' property. We agreed that no violation of the Fifth and Fourteenth Amendments had been shown, since the landowners were "free to pursue their reasonable investment, expectations by submitting a development plan to local officials." 447 U.S., at 262, 100 S.Ct., at 2142.

In this case, city witnesses testified that some development of appellant's property would be consistent with the open-space plan. App. 134–135, 140, 149–150. In-

deed, the plan holds out the possibility that a nuclear power plant could be built on the site, see n. 5, *supra*, and the witnesses testified that other forms of industrial development might be permitted as well. App. 140, 149–150. The trial court's opinion does not explain why it concluded in light of this evidence that any attempt to obtain the city's permission for development of the property would be futile.

When the Court of Appeal reconsidered its decision in light of *Agins*, we believe that its reference to "disputed fact issues not covered by the trial court in its findings," App. 66, referred to this controversy. Its opinion states that damages would be unavailable "[e]ven assuming no use is acceptable to the City." Ibid. The Court of Appeal declined to award mandamus or declaratory relief because it could not make this "assumption" in light of the factual disputes.

12. Appellant's counsel shares this view:

"QUESTION: Mr. Goebel, your second and third cause of action in your complaint were petitions for mandate and the relief prayed in paragraph 3 of your complaint was that the Court order the City of San Diego to set aside the rezoning and to set aside the adoption of the open space element of its general plan. As I understand it, on remand, the trial court may grant that relief, theoretically.

"MR. GOEBEL: That's correct, Your Honor." Tr. of Oral Arg. 18.

*   *   *

[But] I would feel much better able to formulate federal constitutional principles of damages for land-use regulation which amounts to a taking of land under the Eminent Domain Clause of the Fifth Amendment if I knew what disposition the California courts finally made of this case. Because I do not, and cannot at this stage of the litigation, know that, I join the opinion of the Court today in which the appeal is dismissed for want of a final judgment.

Justice BRENNAN, with whom Justice STEWART, Justice MARSHALL, and Justice POWELL join, dissenting.*

Title 28 U.S.C. § 1257 limits this Court's jurisdiction to review judgments of state courts to "[f]inal judgments or decrees rendered by the highest court of a State in which a decision could be had." The Court today dismisses this appeal on the ground that the Court of Appeal of California, Fourth District, failed to decide the federal question whether a "taking" of appellant's property had occurred, and therefore had not entered a final judgment or decree on that question appealable under § 1257. Because the Court's conclusion fundamentally mischaracterizes the holding and judgment of the Court of Appeal, I respectfully dissent from the Court's dismissal and reach the merits of appellant's claim.

*   *   *

III

The Just Compensation Clause of the Fifth Amendment made applicable to the States through the Fourteenth Amendment,   *   *   * states in clear and unequivocal terms: "[N]or shall private property be taken for public use, without just compensation." The question presented on the merits in this case is whether a government entity must pay just compensation when a police power regulation has effected a "taking" of "private property" for "public use" within the meaning of that constitutional provision. Implicit in this question is the corollary issue whether a government entity's exercise of its regulatory police power can ever effect a "taking" within the meaning of the Just Compensation Clause.

A

As explained in Part II, supra, the California courts have held that a city's exercise of its police power, however arbitrary or excessive, cannot as a matter of federal constitutional law constitute a "taking" within the meaning of the Fifth Amendment. This holding flatly contradicts clear precedents of this Court. For example, in last Term's Agins v. City of Tiburon, 447 U.S. 255, 260, 100 S.Ct. 2138, 2141, 65 L.Ed.2d 106 (1980), the Court noted that "[t]he application of a general zoning law to particular property effects a taking if the ordinance does not substan-

---

* Those parts of the dissent dealing with the jurisdictional issue have been omitted, along with the pertinent footnotes.

tially advance legitimate state interests * * * or [if it] denies an owner economically viable use of his land." Applying that principle, the Court examined whether the Tiburon zoning ordinance effected a "taking" of the Agins' property, concluding that it did not have such an effect. Id., at 262–263, 100 S.Ct., at 2142–2143.

In Penn Central Transp. Co. v. New York City, 438 U.S. 104, 98 S.Ct. 2646, 57 L.Ed.2d 631 (1978), the Court analyzed "whether the restrictions imposed by New York City's [Landmarks Preservation] law upon appellants' exploitation of the [Grand Central] Terminal site effect a 'taking' of appellants' property within the meaning of the Fifth Amendment." Id., at 122, 98 S.Ct., at 2658. Canvassing the appropriate inquiries necessary to determine whether a particular restriction effected a "taking," the Court identified the "economic impact of the regulation on the claimant" and the "character of the governmental action" as particularly relevant considerations. Id., at 124, 98 S.Ct., at 2659; see id., at 130–131, 98 S.Ct., at 2662. Although the Court ultimately concluded that application of New York's Landmarks Law did not effect a "taking" of the railroad property, it did so only after deciding that "[t]he restrictions imposed are substantially related to the promotion of the general welfare and not only permit reasonable beneficial use of the landmark site but also afford appellants opportunities further to enhance not only the Terminal site proper but also other properties." Id., at 138, 98 S.Ct., at 2666 (footnote omitted).

The constitutionality of a local ordinance regulating dredging and pit excavating on a property was addressed in Goldblatt v. Town of Hempstead, 369 U.S. 590, 82 S.Ct. 987, 8 L.Ed.2d 130 (1962). After observing that an otherwise valid zoning ordinance that deprives the owner of the most beneficial use of his property would not be unconstitutional, id., at 592, 82 S.Ct., at 989, the Court cautioned: "That is not to say, however, that governmental action in the form of regulation cannot be so onerous as to constitute a taking which constitutionally requires compensation," id., at 594, 82 S.Ct., at 990. On many other occasions, the Court has recognized in passing the vitality of the general principle that a regulation can effect a Fifth Amendment "taking." * * *

The principle applied in all these cases has its source in Justice Holmes' opinion for the Court in Pennsylvania Coal Co. v. Mahon, 260 U.S. 393, 415, 43 S.Ct. 158, 160, 67 L.Ed. 322 (1922), in which he stated: "The general rule at least is, that while property may be regulated to a certain extent, if regulation goes too far it will be recognized as a taking." [13] The determination of a "taking" is "a question of degree—and therefore cannot be disposed of by general propositions." Id., at 416,

---

13. One interpretation of the *Pennsylvania Coal* opinion insists that the word "taking" was used "metaphorically," and that the "gravamen of the constitutional challenge to the regulatory measure was that it was an invalid exercise of the police power under the due process clause, and the [case was] decided under that rubric." Fred F. French Investing Co. v. City of New York, 39 N.Y.2d, at 594, 385 N.Y.S.2d, at 9, 350 N.E.2d, at 385; see also Brief for Appellees, at 37–38. In addition to tampering with the express language of the opinion, this view ignores the coal company's repeated claim before the Court that the Pennsylvania statute took its property without just compensation. Brief for Pennsylvania Coal Company, at 7–8, 16, 19–20, 21, 24, 28–33; Brief for the Mahons, at 73.

43 S.Ct., at 160.[14] While acknowledging that "[g]overnment hardly could go on if to some extent values incident to property could not be diminished without paying for every such change in the general law," id., at 413, 43 S.Ct., at 159, the Court rejected the proposition that police power restrictions could never be recognized as a Fifth Amendment "taking." [15] Indeed, the Court concluded that the Pennsylvania statute forbidding the mining of coal that would cause the subsidence of any house effected a "taking." Id., at 414–416, 43 S.Ct., at 159.[16]

B

Not only does the holding of the California Court of Appeal contradict precedents of this Court, but it also fails to recognize the essential

14. More recent Supreme Court cases have emphasized this aspect of "taking" analysis, commenting that the Court has been unable to develop any "set formula to determine where regulation ends and taking begins," Goldblatt v. Town of Hempstead, 369 U.S. 590, 594, 82 S.Ct. 987, 990, 8 L.Ed.2d 130 (1962), and that "[it] calls as much for the exercise of judgment as for the application of logic," Andrus v. Allard, 444 U.S. 51, 65, 100 S.Ct. 318, 326, 62 L.Ed. 2d 210 (1979). See Penn Central Transp. Co. v. New York City, 438 U.S., at 124, 98 S.Ct., at 2659 ("ad hoc, factual inquiries"); United States v. Central Eureka Mining Co., 357 U.S. 155, 168, 78 S.Ct. 1097, 1104, 2 L.Ed.2d 1228 (1958) ("question properly turning upon the particular circumstances of each case").

One distinguished commentator has characterized the attempt to differentiate "regulation" from "taking" as "the most haunting jurisprudential problem in the field of contemporary land-use law * * * one that may be the lawyer's equivalent of the physicist's hunt for the quark." C. Haar, Land-Use Planning 766 (3d ed. 1976). See generally id., at 766–777; Berger, A Policy Analysis of the Taking Problem, 49 N.Y.U.L.Rev. 165 (1974); Michelman, Property, Utility, and Fairness: Comments on the Ethical Foundations of "Just Compensation" Law, 80 Harv.L.Rev. 1165 (1967); Sax, Takings and the Police Power, 74 Yale L.J. 36 (1964). Another has described a 30-year series of Court opinions resulting from this case-by-case approach as a "crazy-quilt pattern." Dunham, Griggs v. Allegheny County in Perspective: Thirty Years of Supreme Court Expropriation Law, 1962 S.Ct.Rev. 63.

15. Justice Brandeis, in dissent, argued the absolute position that a "restriction imposed to protect the public health, safety or morals from dangers threatened is not a taking." 260 U.S., at 417, 43 S.Ct., at 161. In partial reliance on Justice Brandeis' dissent, one report urges that the Court over-

rule the *Pennsylvania Coal* case and hold that "a regulation of the use of land, if reasonably related to a valid public purpose, can never constitute a taking." F. Bosselman, D. Callies, & J. Banta, The Taking Issue 238–255 (1973).

16. The California Supreme Court, in its opinion in Agins v. City of Tiburon, 24 Cal.3d, at 274, 157 Cal.Rptr., at 376, 598 P.2d, at 29, interpreted Justice Holmes' use of the word "taking" to "indicate the *limit* by which the acknowledged social goal of land control could be achieved by regulation rather than by eminent domain." (Emphasis added.) I find such a reading unpersuasive. The Court specifically indicated that a "regulation [that] goes too far * * * *will be recognized as a taking*," and that this determination is *"a question of degree."* Pennsylvania Coal Co. v. Mahon, supra, 260 U.S., at 415–416, 43 S.Ct., at 160 (emphasis added). Clearly, then, the Court contemplated that a regulation could cross the boundary surrounding valid police power exercise and become a Fifth Amendment "taking."

The California court further argued that the Court in *Pennsylvania Coal* "did not attempt * * * to transmute the illegal governmental infringement into an exercise of eminent domain and the possibility of compensation was not even considered." Agins v. City of Tiburon, supra, at 274, 157 Cal.Rptr., at 376, 598 P.2d, at 29. This overlooks the factual posture in Pennsylvania Coal, where the *homeowner*, not the *coal company*, brought an *injunction* action to prevent the company "from mining under their property in such a way as to remove the supports and cause a subsidence of the surface and of their house." Pennsylvania Coal Co. v. Mahon, supra, at 412, 43 S.Ct., at 159. Because no one asked for an award of just compensation, there was no reason for the Court to consider it. The company only sought reversal of the Pennsylvania Supreme Court's decree that enjoined it from mining coal, and this Court granted that request.

similarity of regulatory "takings" and other "takings." The typical "taking" occurs when a government entity formally condemns a landowner's property and obtains the fee simple pursuant to its sovereign power of eminent domain. See, e.g., Berman v. Parker, 348 U.S. 26, 33, 75 S.Ct. 98, 102, 99 L.Ed. 27 (1954). However, a "taking" may also occur without a formal condemnation proceeding or transfer of fee simple. This Court long ago recognized that

> "[i]t would be a very curious and unsatisfactory result, if in construing [the Just Compensation Clause] * * * it shall be held that if the government refrains from the absolute conversion of real property to the uses of the public it can destroy its value entirely, can inflict irreparable and permanent injury to any extent, can, in effect, subject it to total destruction without making any compensation, because, in the narrowest sense of that word, it is not *taken* for the public use." Pumpelly v. Green Bay Co., 13 Wall. 166, 177–178, 20 L.Ed. 557 (1872) (emphasis in original). * * *

In service of this principle, the Court frequently has found "takings" outside the context of formal condemnation proceedings or transfer of fee simple, in cases where government action benefiting the public resulted in destruction of the use and enjoyment of private property. E.g., Kaiser Aetna v. United States, 444 U.S., at 178–180, 100 S.Ct., at 392 (navigational servitude allowing public right of access); United States v. Dickinson, 331 U.S. 745, 750–751, 67 S.Ct. 1382, 1385, 91 L.Ed. 1789 (1947) (property flooded because of Government dam project); United States v. Causby, 328 U.S. 256, 261–262, 66 S.Ct. 1062, 1065, 90 L.Ed. 1206 (1946) (frequent low altitude flights of Army and Navy aircraft over property); Pennsylvania Coal Co. v. Mahon, 260 U.S., at 414–416, 43 S.Ct., at 159 (state regulation forbidding mining of coal).

Police power regulations such as zoning ordinances and other landuse restrictions can destroy the use and enjoyment of property in order to promote the public good just as effectively as formal condemnation or physical invasion of property.[17] From the property owner's point of view, it may matter little whether his land is condemned or flooded, or whether it is restricted by regulation to use in its natural state, if the effect in both cases is to deprive him of all beneficial use of it. From the government's point of view, the benefits flowing to the public from preservation of open space through regulation may be equally great as from creating a wildlife refuge through formal condemnation or increasing electricity production through a dam project that floods private property. Appellees implicitly posit the distinction that the government *intends* to take property through condemnation or physical invasion whereas it does not through police power regulations. See Brief for Appellees 43. But "the Constitution measures a taking of property not

---

17. In the instant case, for example, appellant contended that the city's actions "denied in all practical effect any possible beneficial or economical use of the subject property." Complaint ¶ 15, App. 11. Although the Court of Appeal's first opinion has no legal effect, see n. 8, supra, the court did observe that the city's objective was "to have the property remain unused, undisturbed and in its natural state so open space and scenic vistas may be preserved. In this sense the property is being 'used' by the public. * * *" App. 60.

by what a State says, or by what it intends, but by what it *does*." Hughes v. Washington, 389 U.S. 290, 298, 88 S.Ct. 438, 443, 19 L.Ed.2d 530 (1967) (STEWART, J., concurring) (emphasis in original).   *   *   * It is only logical, then, that government action other than acquisition of title, occupancy, or physical invasion can be a "taking," and therefore a *de facto* exercise of the power of eminent domain, where the effects completely deprive the owner of all or most of his interest in the property.   *   *   *

IV

Having determined that property may be "taken for public use" by police power regulation within the meaning of the Just Compensation Clause of the Fifth Amendment, the question remains whether a government entity may constitutionally deny payment of just compensation to the property owner and limit his remedy to mere invalidation of the regulation instead. Appellant argues that it is entitled to the full fair market value of the property. Appellees argue that invalidation of the regulation is sufficient without payment of monetary compensation. In my view, once a court establishes that there was a regulatory "taking," the Constitution demands that the government entity pay just compensation for the period commencing on the date the regulation first effected the "taking," and ending on the date the government entity chooses to rescind or otherwise amend [18] the regulation.[19] This interpretation, I believe, is supported by the express words and purpose of the Just Compensation Clause, as well as by cases of this Court construing it.

The language of the Fifth Amendment prohibits the "tak[ing]" of private property for "public use" without payment of "just compensation." As soon as private property has been taken, whether through formal condemnation proceedings, occupancy, physical invasion, or regulation, the landowner has *already* suffered a constitutional violation, and " 'the self-executing character of the constitutional provision with respect to compensation,' " United States v. Clarke, 445 U.S. 253, 257, 100 S.Ct. 1127, 1130, 63 L.Ed.2d 373 (1980), quoting 6 J. Sackman, Nichols' Law of Eminent Domain § 25.41 (rev. 3d ed. 1980), is triggered. This Court has consistently recognized that the just compensation requirement in the Fifth Amendment is not precatory: once there is a "taking," compensation *must* be awarded. In Jacobs v. United States, 290 U.S. 13, 54 S.Ct. 26, 78 L.Ed. 142 (1933), for example, a Government dam project creating intermittent overflows onto petitioners' property resulted in the "taking" of a servitude. Petitioners brought suit against the Government to recover just compensation for the partial

---

18. Under this rule, a government entity is entitled to amend the offending regulation so that it no longer effects a "taking." It may also choose formally to condemn the property.

19. *Amicus* suggests that the California Supreme Court has not conclusively decided the issue whether interim damages might be awarded to compensate a landowner for economic loss sustained prior to invalidation of the zoning ordinance. Brief for United States as *Amicus Curiae* 23, and n. 24. But since the California courts fail to concede that a regulation can effect a "taking," any award of interim damages would not be justified or determined, as constitutionally required, under the Just Compensation Clause.

"taking." Commenting on the nature of the landowners' action, the Court observed:

"The suits were based on the right to recover just compensation for property taken by the United States for public use in the exercise of its power of eminent domain. That right was guaranteed by the Constitution. The fact that condemnation proceedings were not instituted and that the right was asserted in suits by the owners did not change the essential nature of the claim. The form of the remedy did not qualify the right. It rested upon the Fifth Amendment. Statutory recognition was not necessary. A promise to pay was not necessary. Such a promise was implied because of the duty to pay imposed by the Amendment." Id., at 16, 54 S.Ct., at 27.

See also Griggs v. Allegheny County, 369 U.S. 84, 84–85, 88–90, 82 S.Ct. 531, 533, 7 L.Ed.2d 585 (1962); United States v. Causby, 328 U.S., at 268, 66 S.Ct., at 1069.[20] Invalidation unaccompanied by payment of damages would hardly compensate the landowner for any economic loss suffered during the time his property was taken.[21]

Moreover, mere invalidation would fall far short of fulfilling the fundamental purpose of the Just Compensation Clause. That guarantee was designed to bar the government from forcing some individuals to bear burdens which, in all fairness, should be borne by the public as a whole. * * * When one person is asked to assume more than a fair share of the public burden, the payment of just compensation operates

20. *Amici* suggest that the Court's awards of just compensation in cases involving the United States were premised either on a "theory of implied promise to pay . . . or [on] congressional authorization [to pay] under the Tucker Act, 28 U.S.C. 1346(a)." Brief for United States as *Amicus Curiae* 27; see Brief for the National Trust for Historic Preservation et al. as *Amici Curiae* 7–8. This suggestion mischaracterizes the import of our cases. As the Court has noted:

"But whether the theory * * * be that there was a taking under the Fifth Amendment, and that therefore the Tucker Act may be invoked because it is a claim founded upon the Constitution, or that there was an implied promise by the Government to pay for it, is immaterial. In either event, the claim traces back to the prohibition of the Fifth Amendment, 'nor shall private property be taken for public use, without just compensation.' The Constitution is 'intended to preserve practical and substantial rights, not to maintain theories.'" United States v. Dickinson, 331 U.S. 745, 748, 67 S.Ct. 1382, 1384, 91 L.Ed. 1789 (1947).

21. The instant litigation is a good case in point. The trial court, on April 9, 1976, found that the city's actions effected a "taking" of appellant's property on June 19, 1973. If true, then appellant has been deprived of all beneficial use of its proper-

ty in violation of the Just Compensation Clause for the past seven years.

Invalidation hardly prevents enactment of subsequent unconstitutional regulations by the government entity. At the 1974 annual conference of the National Institute of Municipal Law Officers in California, a California City Attorney gave fellow City Attorneys the following advice:

"IF ALL ELSE FAILS, MERELY AMEND THE REGULATION AND START OVER AGAIN.

"If legal preventive maintenance does not work, and you still receive a claim attacking the land use regulation, or if you try the case and lose, don't worry about it. All is not lost. One of the extra 'goodies' contained in the recent [California] Supreme Court case of Selby v. City of San Buenaventura, 10 C.3d 110, [109 Cal.Rptr. 799, 514 P.2d 111] appears to allow the City to change the regulation in question, even after trial and judgment, make it more reasonable, more restrictive, or whatever, and everybody starts over again. * * * See how easy it is to be a City Attorney. Sometimes you can lose the battle and still win the war. Good luck." Longtin, Avoiding and Defending Constitutional Attacks on Land Use Regulations (Including Inverse Condemnation), in 38B NIMLO Municipal Law Review 192–193 (1975) (emphasis in original).

to redistribute that economic cost from the individual to the public at large. * * * Because police power regulations must be substantially related to the advancement of the public health, safety, morals, or general welfare, see Village of Euclid v. Ambler Realty Co., 272 U.S. 365, 395, 47 S.Ct. 114, 121, 71 L.Ed. 303 (1926), it is axiomatic that the public receives a benefit while the offending regulation is in effect.[22] If the regulation denies the private property owner the use and enjoyment of his land and is found to effect a "taking," it is only fair that the public bear the cost of benefits received during the interim period between application of the regulation and the government entity's rescission of it. The payment of just compensation serves to place the landowner in the same position monetarily as he would have occupied if his property had not been taken. * * *

The fact that a regulatory "taking" may be temporary, by virtue of the government's power to rescind or amend the regulation, does not make it any less of a constitutional "taking." Nothing in the Just Compensation Clause suggests that "takings" must be permanent and irrevocable. Nor does the temporary reversible quality of a regulatory "taking" render compensation for the time of the "taking" any less obligatory. This Court more than once has recognized that temporary reversible "takings" should be analyzed according to the same constitutional framework applied to permanent irreversible "takings." For example, in United States v. Causby, supra, at 258–259, 66 S.Ct., at 1064, the United States had executed a lease to use an airport for a one-year term "ending June 30, 1942, with a provision for renewals until June 30, 1967, or six months after the end of the national emergency, whichever [was] the earlier." The Court held that the frequent low-level flights of Army and Navy airplanes over respondents' chicken farm, located near the airport, effected a "taking" of an easement on respondents' property. 328 U.S., at 266–267, 66 S.Ct., at 1068. However, because the flights could be discontinued by the Government at any time, the Court remanded the case to the Court of Claims: "Since on this record *it is not clear whether the easement taken is a permanent or a temporary one*, it would be premature for us to consider whether the amount of the award made by the Court of Claims was proper." Id., at 268, 66 S.Ct., at 1069 (emphasis added). In other cases where the Government has taken only temporary use of a building, land, or equipment, the Court has not hesitated to determine the appropriate measure of just compensation. See Kimball Laundry Co. v. United States, 338 U.S. 1, 6, 69 S.Ct. 1434, 1438, 93 L.Ed. 1765 (1949); United States v. Petty Motor Co., 327 U.S. 372, 374–375, 66 S.Ct. 596, 598, 90 L.Ed. 729 (1946); United States v. General Motors Corp., 323 U.S., at 374–375, 65 S.Ct., at 358.

---

22. A different case may arise where a police power regulation is not enacted in furtherance of the public health, safety, morals, or general welfare so that there may be no "public use." Although the government entity may not be forced to pay just compensation under the Fifth Amendment, the landowner may nevertheless have a damages cause of action under 42 U.S.C. § 1983 for a Fourteenth Amendment due process violation.

But contrary to appellant's claim that San Diego must formally condemn its property and pay full fair market value, nothing in the Just Compensation Clause empowers a court to order a government entity to condemn the property and pay its full fair market value, where the "taking" already effected is temporary and reversible and the government wants to halt the "taking." Just as the government may cancel condemnation proceedings before passage of title, see 6 J. Sackman, Nichols' Law of Eminent Domain § 24.113, p. 24–21 (rev. 3d ed. 1980), or abandon property it has temporarily occupied or invaded, see United States v. Dow, 357 U.S. 17, 26, 78 S.Ct. 1039, 1046, 2 L.Ed.2d 1109 (1958), it must have the same power to rescind a regulatory "taking." As the Court has noted: "[A]n abandonment does not prejudice the property owner. It merely results in an alteration of the property interest taken—from full ownership to one of temporary use and occupation. * * * In such cases compensation would be measured by the principles normally governing the taking of a right to use property temporarily." Id. * * *

The constitutional rule I propose requires that, once a court finds a police power regulation has effected a "taking," the government entity must pay just compensation for the period commencing on the date the regulation first effected the "taking," and ending on the date the government entity chooses to rescind or otherwise amend the regulation.[23] Ordinary principles determining the proper measure of just compensation, regularly applied in cases of permanent and temporary "takings" involving formal condemnation proceedings, occupations, and physical invasions, should provide guidance to the courts in the award of compensation for a regulatory "taking." As a starting point, the value of the property taken may be ascertained as of the date of the "taking." * * * The government must inform the court of its intentions vis-à-vis the regulation with sufficient clarity to guarantee a correct assessment of the just compensation award. Should the government decide immediately to revoke or otherwise amend the regulation, it would be liable for payment of compensation only for the interim during which the regulation effected a "taking."[24] Rules of valuation already developed for temporary "takings" may be particularly useful to the courts in their quest for assessing the proper measure of monetary relief in cases of revocation or amendment, * * * although additional rules

---

23. Contrary to the suggestion of *amici*, see, e.g., Brief for the National Trust for Historic Preservation et al. as *Amici Curiae* 13–16, this is not a case involving implication of a damages remedy—The words of the Just Compensation Clause are express.

24. See generally D. Hagman & Misczynski, Windfalls for Wipeouts 296–297 (1978); Bosselman, The Third Alternative in Zoning Litigation, 17 Zoning Digest 113, 114–119 (1965). The general notion of compensating landowners for regulations which go too far has received much atten-

tion in land-use planning literature. See, e.g., Costonis, "Fair" Compensation and the Accommodation Power: Antidotes for the Taking Impasse in Land Use Controversies, 75 Colum.L.Rev. 1021 (1975); R. Babcock, The Zoning Game 168–172 (1966); Krasnowiecki & Paul, The Preservation of Open Space in Metropolitan Areas, 110 U.Pa.L.Rev. 179, 198–239 (1961). See also American Law Institute, A Model Land Development Code §§ 5–303, 5–304, pp. 202–207 (1975); Town and Country Planning Act, 1947, 10 & 11 Geo. 6, ch. 51, § 19.

may need to be developed. * * * Alternatively the government may choose formally to condemn the property, or otherwise to continue the offending regulation: in either case the action must be sustained by proper measures of just compensation. * * *

It should be noted that the Constitution does not embody any specific procedure or form of remedy that the States must adopt: "The Fifth Amendment expresses a principle of fairness and not a technical rule of procedure enshrining old or new niceties regarding 'causes of action'— when they are born, whether they proliferate, and when they die." United States v. Dickinson, 331 U.S., at 748, 67 S.Ct., at 1384. Cf. United States v. Memphis Cotton Oil Co., 288 U.S. 62, 67–69, 53 S.Ct. 278, 280, 77 L.Ed. 619 (1933). The States should be free to experiment in the implementation of this rule, provided that their chosen procedures and remedies comport with the fundamental constitutional command. See generally Hill, The Bill of Rights and the Supervisory Power, 69 Colum. L.Rev. 181, 191–193 (1969). The only constitutional requirement is that the landowner must be able meaningfully to challenge a regulation that allegedly effects a "taking," and recover just compensation if it does so. He may not be forced to resort to piecemeal litigation or otherwise unfair procedures in order to receive his due. * * *

V

In Agins v. City of Tiburon, * * * the California Supreme Court was "persuaded by various policy considerations to the view that inverse condemnation is an inappropriate and undesirable remedy in cases in which unconstitutional regulation is alleged." In particular, the court cited "the need for preserving a degree of freedom in land-use planning function, and the inhibiting financial force which inheres in the inverse condemnation remedy," in reaching its conclusion. Id., at 276, 157 Cal.Rptr., at 377, 598 P.2d at 31. But the applicability of express constitutional guarantees is not a matter to be determined on the basis of policy judgments made by the legislative, executive, or judicial branches.[25] Nor can the vindication of those rights depend on the expense in doing so. * * *

Because I believe that the Just Compensation Clause requires the constitutional rule outlined supra, I would vacate the judgment of the

---

25. Even if I were to concede a role for policy considerations, I am not so sure that they would militate against requiring payment of just compensation. Indeed, land-use planning commentators have suggested that the threat of financial liability for unconstitutional police power regulations would help to produce a more rational basis of decisionmaking that weighs the cost of restrictions against their benefits. Dunham, From Rural Enclosure to Re-Enclosure of Urban Land, 35 N.Y.U.L.Rev. 1238, 1253–1254 (1960). Such liability might also encourage municipalities to err on the constitutional side of police power regulations, and to develop internal rules and operating procedures to minimize overzealous regulatory attempts. Cf. Owen v. City of Independence, 445 U.S. 622, 651–652, 100 S.Ct. 1398, 1415, 63 L.Ed.2d 673 (1980). After all, a policeman must know the Constitution, then why not a planner? In any event, one may wonder as an empirical matter whether the threat of just compensation will greatly impede the efforts of planners. Cf. id., at 656, 100 S.Ct., at 1418.

California Court of Appeal, Fourth District, and remand for further proceedings not inconsistent with this opinion.[26]

Notes and Questions

1. The San Diego Gas Company never sought any permit for development of its land, nor did it seek to have the zoning regulations applicable to its land changed or to have the "open space" designation on the city's general plan changed. Indeed, the California intermediate appellate court had no occasion to consider invalidation of the zoning regulations and the "open space" designation as an alternative to awarding compensation because, as the intermediate court stated in its first opinion,

> Company did not claim the zoning ordinance or open space element were invalid in any way. Rather, it contended and presented evidence that the combination of the zoning on the property plus its inclusion in the open space element plus the City's policy of requiring consistency between zoning and the general plan plus City's overtures to purchase the land for open space had deprived it of the beneficial use of the land.

146 Cal.Rptr. 114 (1978). This suggests that the plaintiff, on the first appeal, deliberately avoided arguing that the city's land use controls were invalid and relied on the theory adopted in Eldridge v. City of Palo Alto, 57 Cal.App.3d 613, 129 Cal.Rptr. 575 (1976),—that the land use controls "were valid exercises of the state's police power and beyond constitutional or other attack, except * * * in proceedings for damages in inverse condemnation."

2. The plaintiff in the *San Diego* case seems to have changed its position several times during the protracted litigation. Having abandoned its claim that the city's land use controls were invalid on the first appeal to the California Court of Appeal, the plaintiff asserted when it filed its appeal to the United States Supreme Court that the restrictions imposed by the San Diego zoning ordinance and open space designation were "arbitrary, excessive, and unconstitutional," in addition to asserting that the "purported invalidation remedy proffered by [the] California state courts" was not "constitutionally adequate to substitute for just compensation." Then, when the case was orally argued before the United States Supreme Court on December 1, 1980, counsel for plaintiff stated, in response to questions from the bench, that the plaintiff was "merely seeking interim damages for deprivation of property without due process of law" rather than "asking for full damages for a complete taking without just compensation." 33 Land Use L. & Zoning Dig., No. 1, p. 4 (1981).

3. What do you think of Justice Brennan's statement, in an omitted footnote in his dissent, that "[t]hroughout the *Agins* opinion as well as the Court of Appeal decision below [in the *San Diego* case] are references to actions which 'deprive' the landowner of property use, indicating that the California courts were proceeding under the Due Process Clause of the Fifth and Fourteenth Amendments, and not the Just Compensation Clause"? Is it not clear that state action is directly subject only to the Fourteenth Amendment, so that constitutional challenges to local land use controls must be based on asserted violations of either the due process or equal protection clause of that amendment?

26. Because the California Court of Appeal, Fourth District, followed the instructions of the California Supreme Court and held that the city's regulation, however arbitrary or excessive, could not effect a "taking," the Court of Appeal did not address the issue whether San Diego's course of conduct *in fact* effected a "taking" of appellant's property. I would not reach that issue here, but leave it open for the Court of Appeal on remand initially to decide that question on its review of the Superior Court's judgment.

In short, is it not clear that the requirement of compensation when property is "taken for public use" is made applicable to the states only by virtue of the Fourteenth Amendment's due process clause? And does it not follow that a regulatory "taking" of private property without compensation entitles the landowner to some remedy—whether invalidation or compensation—only because such a "taking" does, in fact, "deprive" the landowner of his property "without due process of law" in violation of the Fourteenth Amendment?

4. Those who have advocated allowing the landowner to require a local government to pay the full market value of the land as compensation for a regulatory taking usually advance some or all of the following arguments:

(1) Land use regulations that result in a taking of private property should be subject to attack in the same manner as any other taking of private property for public use without payment of compensation.

(2) As long as privately owned land can be drastically restricted in its uses without cost to the public when land use regulations are held invalid, the economic impact of such regulations is not likely to be seriously considered when the decision to adopt the regulations is made.

(3) Invalidation of overly harsh land use regulations is not an adequate remedy because the local governing body can easily frustrate the "victorious" landowner by adopting slightly different regulations which still preclude any reasonable use of his property.

(4) Invalidation of overly harsh land use regulations often leaves the landowner with substantial uncompensated losses even if the ultimate result is to allow him a reasonable use of his land.

The first argument above is essentially an argument for logical symmetry of remedies in all kinds of taking cases. * * * The second argument—a policy argument—is more substantial, but it can be countered with other policy arguments, some of which are stated in the California Supreme Court's opinion in *Agins.* * * *

The third argument for the inverse condemnation remedy in regulatory taking cases is also substantial. The ability of local governments to play games with a plaintiff who has been successful in a suit to invalidate a zoning regulation presents a problem for which no completely satisfactory solution has yet been found. But recent judicial experiments in granting "definitive relief" to victorious plaintiffs in land use cases suggest that satisfactory solutions are possible, and that it is not necessary, in order to deal with the problem, to compel local governments to pay the value of a fee simple or a [permanent] restrictive easement in land they only intended to regulate.

The fourth argument for the inverse condemnation remedy originally sought by the plaintiff in *San Diego* may seem to be the strongest of all. But the problem of losses caused by harsh land use regulations while they are in force—that is, prior to judicial invalidation or legislative repeal or amendment—can be resolved by application of the rule stated in Justice Brennan's * * * [opinion], modified so as to make it clear that the courts may terminate a "temporary" regulatory taking by declaring the regulation invalid.

Cunningham, Inverse Condemnation as a Remedy for "Regulatory Takings," 8 Hastings Const.L.Q. 517, 535–37 (1981).

5. What ground is there for Justice Brennan's assertion that the prior Supreme Court cases cited in his dissent support his conclusion that, once a regulatory "taking" is found, compensation rather than mere invalidation is the constitutionally mandated remedy? Since none of the cases cited by Justice Brennan involved a claim for compensation, none of them addresses the prob-

lem; the issue in all these cases was whether the land use regulations were so restrictive as to be invalid under the Fourteenth Amendment's due process clause. Thus it is strongly arguable that the word "taking" was used only metaphorically in these cases to describe an invalid attempt by a state or local government to exercise the police power.

6. What do you think of Justice Brennan's repeated assertions that a "temporary" regulatory "taking" will continue until there is a legislative repeal or amendment of the local land use regulations which effect the "taking"? This seems to be based on the notion that such regulations are, in a sense, "valid," subject to performance of the constitutional duty to pay just compensation. But is this notion tenable? Surely a land use regulation, not purporting to be an exercise of the power of eminent domain and not accompanied by any provision for compensation, is simply invalid if it is found to amount to a *de facto* "taking." Consequently it can be argued that a court, in such a case, should simply declare the regulations invalid, thus terminating the period of the "temporary" regulatory "taking." Then, if the local government which enacted the regulation wishes to acquire either a fee simple or a lesser interest in the land, it can invoke its power of eminent domain in the normal way. Or alternatively, the local government may amend the offending regulations to make them less restrictive and more "reasonable."

7. If the courts were to adopt the suggestion advanced in the preceding Note, the monetary award for the "temporary" regulatory "taking" might properly be regarded as "damages" for a wrongful restriction of the landowner's property rights, rather than as payment for the "taking" of some kind of property interest. The late Professor Hagman was a vigorous advocate of the theory that the landowner should be awarded "damages" because, *inter alia*, this eliminates the need to define the property interest "temporarily taken." See, e.g., Hagman, Temporary or Interim Damages Awards in Land Use Control Cases, 4 Zoning & Planning Law Report 129, at 129–133 (1981). If it is objected that sovereign immunity may preclude imposition of damage liability on state and local governments for wrongful interference with property rights, there are two possible responses: (1) in many states the constitutional eminent domain provision requires compensation whenever private property is "taken or *damaged*" for public use; (2) 42 U.S.C. § 1983 clearly allows recovery of damages whenever a state "subjects, or causes to be subjected, any citizen of the United States or other person within the jurisdiction thereof to the deprivation of any rights, privileges, or immunities secured by the Constitution." It must be kept in mind, however, that Section 1983 creates no substantive rights; it merely provides a means by which redress for injury to a constitutional right may be obtained. Thus Section 1983 relief will be available only if the plaintiff shows that a land use regulation is either directed toward an improper purpose, employs an unreasonable method of achieving its purpose, or amounts to a *de facto* "taking."

8. Even prior to the *San Diego* case, a federal court approved of compensation for a "temporary" regulatory "taking." See Gordon v. City of Warren, 579 F.2d 386 (6th Cir.1978), where the court held that plaintiff had stated a cause of action under the Fourteenth Amendment for recovery of "damages resulting from a taking of private property for public use without just compensation," after the Michigan Supreme Court had invalidated a city ordinance found to constitute a "taking." Justice Brennan's dissenting opinion in *San Diego* has been relied on as establishing a new compensation requirement in two subsequent federal court cases. See Martino v. Santa Clara Valley Water District, 703 F.2d 1141 (9th Cir.1983); Hernandez v. City of Lafayette, 643 F.2d 1188 (5th Cir.1981). *Hernandez* is especially significant because it asserts that the

"taking" does not occur until the municipal governing body has had a realistic opportunity and a reasonable time to review the zoning regulations challenged as a *de facto* "taking" and to repeal or amend them. The *Hernandez* court specifically denied any temporary damages for the period when such a review is conducted, stating, on the authority of Agins v. Tiburon, that "[m]ere fluctuations in value during the process of governmental decision making, absent extraordinary delay, are 'incidents of ownership.' They cannot be considered a taking in the constitutional sense." Id. at 1200. Hagman suggests that the landowner should not be required to bring a lawsuit in order to bring to the attention of the local governing body his complaint that the land use regulations applicable to his property are too severe, but that "a claim for damages" or even "a formal letter setting forth the facts of the harsh regulation should be enough." See Hagman, op. cit. supra Note 7, at 134. Freilich argues that the property owner should be required to apply for "specific relief," and that the local governing body should then have three options: "(a) it may recognize the regulatory 'taking' (i.e., continue to apply the ordinance) and pay compensation from the date of enactment of the ordinance; (b) it may discontinue the regulation upon granting the application for specific relief, paying no compensation or damages; or (c) it may litigate the validity of the ordinance and pay interim damages only if the court finds that invalidation, injunction, or site specific relief is not an adequate remedy fully preserving the property owner's rights * * *." Freilich, Solving the "Taking" Equation, Making the Whole Equal the Sum of Its Parts, 15 Urban Lawyer 447, 482 (1983).

9. At least four state courts have now adopted the compensation requirement laid down in Justice Brennan's dissent in *San Diego*. See Burrows v. City of Keene, 121 N.H. 590, 432 A.2d 15 (1981); Scheer v. Township of Evesham, 184 N.J.Super. 11, 445 A.2d 46 (1982); Rippley v. City of Lincoln, 330 N.W.2d 505 (N.D.1983); Seuss Builders Co. v. City of Beaverton, 294 Or. 254, 656 P.2d 306 (1982) (planning designation as site for public park imposed "a present prohibition on inconsistent private uses" which amount to a *de facto* "taking"). See also Zinn v. State, 112 Wis.2d 417, 334 N.W.2d 67 (1983); Annicelli v. Town of South Kingston, ___ R.I. ___, 463 A.2d 133 (1983). But see Aptos Seascape Corp. v. County of Santa Cruz, 138 Cal.App.3d 484, 188 Cal.Rptr. 191 (1982) (denying damages and holding that the appropriate remedy was declaratory relief or mandamus). If state courts generally adopt the compensation requirement laid down in Justice Brennan's *San Diego* dissent as stating the views of a majority of the Supreme Court's members, consider the effect of such adoption on legislation such as Mass.Gen.Laws Ann. ch. 130, § 105, which provides as follows:

"Any person having a recorded interest in land affected by any * * * order [restricting or prohibiting dredging, filling, removing or otherwise altering or polluting coastal wetlands], may * * * petition the superior court to determine whether such order so restricts the use of his property as to deprive him of the practical uses thereof and is therefore an unreasonable exercise of the police power because the order constitutes the equivalent of a taking without compensation. If the court finds the order to be an unreasonable exercise of the police power, * * * the court shall enter a finding that such order shall not apply to the land of the petitioner; provided, however, that such findings shall not affect any other land than that of the petitioner. * * * The method provided by this paragraph for the determination of the issue shall be exclusive, and such issue shall not be determined in any other proceedings, nor shall any person have a right to petition for the assessment of damages * * * by reason of the adoption of any such order.

"The department of environmental management may, after a finding has been entered that such order shall not apply to certain land as provided in the preceding paragraph, take the fee or any lesser interest in such land in the name of the commonwealth by eminent domain *   *   * and hold the same for the purposes set forth in this section."

10.   What do you think of the following argument against adoption of the compensation requirement asserted in Justice Brennan's dissent in San Diego?

"One of the heightened dangers of adopting a simplistic automatic monetary compensation remedy is that courts, reluctant to impose financial burden[s] on municipalities, will simply refuse to find that anything is a 'taking.' *   *   *

"The unfortunate reality is the deterioration of the effectiveness of the inverse condemnation proceeding as a remedy for those landowners whose cases really do warrant invalidation or equitable relief. With courts more and more reluctant to find a real 'taking' because of the increased demand by plaintiffs that each 'taking' automatically triggers eminent domain and monetary awards, the vitality of inverse condemnation is waning." Freilich, Solving the "Taking" Equation: Making the Whole Equal the Sum of its Parts, 15 Urban Lawyer 447, 467–468 (1983).

11.   If Justice Brennan's views as to compensation for "taking" should ultimately prevail in the Supreme Court and/or should generally be adopted in the state courts, how are courts to determine the amount of compensation to be paid in "temporary" regulatory "taking" cases?   As one writer has pointed out,

> The traditional measure of compensation has been the value of whatever was "taken" as opposed to the damages suffered by the property owner involved. For example, in the typical situation where a permit is denied under an ordinance that is struck down as a taking, the property may well have appreciated in the interim so that the property owner suffered no damages from the delay. On the other hand, if one were to look instead at the rental value for the interim period of the delay as the measure of compensation, then compensation might be awarded.

Bonderman, Comment on San Diego Gas & Electric Co. v. City of San Diego, 33 Land Use L. & Zoning Dig., No. 5, p. 10, at p. 11 n. 3 (1981). Bonderman also suggests, Id. at p. 11, that states and municipalities may take some steps to limit their "temporary taking" liability by procedural measures, e.g., (1) adopting statutes or ordinances providing that neither attorney fees nor interest shall be added to the compensation awarded for a "temporary taking," and (2) adopting compensation rules, "akin to those for breach of contract, that would require a property owner to show that it had been injured in fact by any temporary taking."

Another writer recently explored the possible rules for determining compensation and concludes that the most likely candidates for judicial adoption are (1) rental value during the period of the "taking"; (2) value of an option for the period of the "taking"; and (3) difference between the value of the property immediately before the "taking" started and immediately after it started.   See Hagman, Temporary or Interim Damages Awards in Land Use Control Cases, 4 Zoning & Planning Law Report, 130, 140–143 (1981).

12.   In addition to the articles already cited in the preceding materials, see, on the general subject of regulatory "takings" and remedies therefor, Costonis, Presumptive and Per Se Takings: A Decisional Model for the Taking Issue, 58 N.Y.U.L.Rev. 465 (1983); Humbach, A Unifying Theory for the Just-Compensation Cases: Takings, Regulation and Public Use, 34 Rutgers L.Rev. 243 (1982). Johnson, Compensation for Invalid Land-Use Regulations, 15 Georgia L.Rev.

559 (1981); Kmiec, Regulatory Takings: The Supreme Court Runs Out of Gas in San Diego, 57 Ind.L.J. 45 (1982); Mandelker, Land Use Takings: The Compensation Issue, 8 Hastings Const.L.Q. 491 (1981); Stoebuck, Police Power, Takings and Due Process, 37 Wash. & Lee L.Rev. 1057 (1980).

13.   Two recent cases finding that "regulatory takings" resulted from state or local government action are Urbanization Versalles, Inc. v. Rivera Bros., 701 F.2d 993 (1st Cir.1983) (highway designation on "official map" amounted to a "taking"); Amen v. City of Dearborn, 718 F.2d 789 (6th Cir.1983) (local "slum clearance" practices amounted to a "taking").

Chapter 14

THE "ZONING" PROCESS: THE DYNAMICS OF CHANGE AND THE "COMPREHENSIVE PLAN"

Until after World War II, controlling land use by means of zoning regulations was generally considered to be a relatively static process. Once the original zoning ordinance was adopted, only minor changes in the regulations were anticipated. But all the early zoning enabling acts, following the pioneering New York zoning legislation and the Standard State Zoning Enabling Act, provided at least three methods for modifying or changing zoning regulations: (1) the granting of "variances" by an administrative agency known either as the zoning board of adjustment or the board of zoning appeals; (2) the granting of "special exceptions" by the same administrative agency; and (3) amendment of the zoning ordinance either by changing the text of the regulations or by changing the zoning map.

PURITAN–GREENFIELD IMPROVEMENT ASSOCIATION v. LEO

Court of Appeals of Michigan, 1967.
7 Mich.App. 659, 153 N.W.2d 162.

LEVIN, Judge. Defendant-appellant John L. Leo claims the circuit judge erred in setting aside a use variance granted by the Detroit Board of Zoning Appeals.

Leo owns a one-story, one-family dwelling at the northwest corner of Puritan avenue and Prest avenue, located in the northwest section of Detroit in an R–1 (single family residence) zoning district. On application and after hearing, the board granted Leo a variance to permit the use of the property as a dental and medical clinic (an RM–4 use) and to use the side yard for off-street parking on certain conditions.

The order of the board states that immediately to the west of the westerly boundary of Leo's property is a gasoline service station (at the corner of Puritan and Greenfield); that there was testimony Leo had not received any offers from residence-use buyers during the period of over a year the property had been listed and offered for sale; and, in the event a variance was granted, it was intended to preserve the present exterior of the building without significant alteration so that it would continue to appear to be a one-family dwelling.

The appeal board's dominant finding was:

"That the board found unnecessary hardship and practical difficulty because of the heavy traffic and the closeness to the business section immediately to the west."

The board also found that the proposed use would not alter the essential character of the neighborhood, would not be injurious to the contiguous property, would not be detrimental to the surrounding neighborhood, and would not depreciate property values.

Plaintiff-appellee, Puritan-Greenfield Improvement Association, filed a complaint with the circuit court which was treated by the court as one for superintending control. The matter was heard by the circuit judge on the record made before the board. The circuit judge reversed the decision of the board, stating *inter alia* that it had not been shown the land could not yield a reasonable return or be put to a proper economic use if used only for a purpose allowed by existing zoning and that such showing of hardship as had been made was of "self-created" hardship attributable to the character of the structure thereon.

The applicable enabling act provides for a board of zoning appeals authorized to grant a variance upon a showing of practical difficulties or unnecessary hardship. The Detroit ordinance requires evidence of special conditions and unnecessary hardship or practical difficulties.

The enabling act specifies neither a particular procedure for obtaining review of board of zoning appeals' action nor the scope of review. Review is obtained by means of an application for superintending control * * * which replaces certiorari. The minimum constitutional standard establishes the scope of review. The circuit judge and we are required by the Michigan constitution to determine whether the findings of the board and its order are authorized by law and whether they are supported by competent, material, and substantial evidence on the whole record. Const.1963, art. 6, § 28.

Although there has been a great deal of judicial effort expended in Michigan in considering challenges to the reasonableness or constitutionality of zoning as applied to individual properties, we find no Michigan appellate decisions construing the words "unnecessary hardship or practical difficulties."

The first modern zoning regulations were adopted by the city of New York and the phrase "practical difficulties or unnecessary hardship" was fashioned as the applicable standard to guide New York's board of appeals in considering applications for variances. A comparison of the relevant language of the applicable Michigan enabling act with that of the original New York city legislation shows that the Michigan provision authorizing the vesting in a board of zoning appeals of the authority to grant variances parallels the corresponding New York city provision.

It appears that most State enabling acts, and ordinances based thereon, use "unnecessary hardship" as the governing standard. In those States (like Michigan and New York) where the applicable standard is "unnecessary hardship *or* practical difficulties," the phrase "practical difficulties" has been regarded as applicable only when an area or a dimension variance is sought, and in determining whether a use variance will be granted the decisive words are "unnecessary hardship." In the light of this history, we have turned for guidance to decisions of other States applying the "unnecessary hardship" standard.

A text writer, Rathkopf, states that courts have held, variously, that a property owner seeking a variance on the ground of "unnecessary hardship" must show credible proof that the property will not yield a reasonable return if used only for a purpose allowed by the ordinance or must establish that the zoning gives rise to hardship amounting to virtual confiscation or the disadvantage must be so great as to deprive the owner of all reasonable use of the property. He concedes that the showing required "is substantially equivalent to that which would warrant a court in declaring the ordinance confiscatory, unreasonable, and unconstitutional in its application to the property involved." 2 Rathkopf, The Law of Zoning and Planning, p. 45–14.

These principles also find expression in the frequently stated generalizations that variances should be sparingly granted, that it is not sufficient to show that the property would be worth more or could be more profitably employed if the restrictions were varied to permit another use, and that the board of appeals, being without legislative power, may not in the guise of a variance amend the zoning ordinance or disregard its provisions.

The judicial attitudes so expressed could well have been influenced by the early history of the boards of zoning appeal and the need to declare more precise standards than the somewhat nebulous "unnecessary hardship." When zoning was in its infancy it was thought by some that without a board of zoning appeals the individual declarations of zoning ordinance invalidity would be so numerous it would become necessary to declare the legislation void as a whole and, thus, "the chief value of the board of appeals in zoning is in protecting the ordinance from attacks upon its constitutionality." That view of the purpose of the board of zoning appeals has been said to require a standard related to the reasonableness of the zoning:

"The hardship contemplated in this legislation has constitutional overtones, and it is the purpose of the variance to immunize zoning legislation against attack on the ground that it may in some instances operate to effect a taking of property without just compensation." R.N.R. Associates v. City of Providence Zoning Board of Review (1965), R.I., 210 A.2d 653, 654.

"It has been said that the function of a board of zoning appeals is to protect the community against usable land remaining idle and it is that purpose which gives definition to "unnecessary hardship.

"Since the main purpose of allowing variances is to prevent land from being rendered useless, 'unnecessary hardship' can best be defined as a situation where in the absence of a variance no feasible use can be made of the land." 74 Harv.Law Rev. p. 1401; quoted in State ex rel. Markdale Corporation v. Milwaukee Board of Appeals (1965), 27 Wis.2d 154, 133 N.W.2d 795, 799.

*   *   *

"An unnecessary hardship exists when all the relevant factors taken together convince that the plight of the location concerned is unique in that it cannot be put to a conforming use because of the limitations imposed upon the property by reason of it [sic] classification in a specific zone."   Peterson v. Vasak, supra, 76 N.W.2d at p. 426.

*   *   *

The New York Court of Appeals has stated:

"Before the Board may exercise its discretion and grant a [use] variance upon the ground of unnecessary hardship, the record must show that (1) the land in question cannot yield a reasonable return if used only for a purpose allowed in that zone; (2) that the plight of the owner is due to unique circumstances and not to the general conditions in the neighborhood which may reflect the unreasonableness of the zoning ordinance itself; and (3) that the use to be authorized by the variance will not alter the essential character of the locality." Otto v. Steinhilber (1939), 282 N.Y. 71, 24 N.E.2d 851.

The *Otto* definition has been adopted by other courts.   *   *   *

We find overwhelming support for the proposition—expressed in *Otto* —that the hardship must be unique or peculiar to the property for which the variance is sought.

"Difficulties or hardships shared with others go to the reasonableness of the ordinance generally and will not support a variance as to one parcel upon the ground of hardship."   *   *   *

Under these definitions even if the land cannot yield a reasonable return if used only for a purpose permitted by existing zoning, a use variance may not be granted unless the landowner's plight is due to unique circumstances and not to general conditions in the neighborhood that may reflect the unreasonableness of the zoning.

This limitation on the board's powers is related to the third limitation expressed in *Otto* —that a use authorized by a variance shall not alter the essential character of the locality.   In this connection we note that the Detroit ordinance prohibits a variance that would be contrary to the public interest or inconsistent with the spirit of the ordinance.   *   *   *

"If it [the hardship] affects a whole area, then his remedy lies in seeking an amendment to the zoning ordinance.   This is true even where the applicant's property is situated in an area where none of the properties can be put to any reasonable beneficial use owing to zoning restrictions.   It is not for the board in these circumstances to bestow liberties upon one single member of this group of property holders.   The legislature must be the body to make decisions of this sort even in cases where the most severe hardship can be shown." Pooley, Planning Zoning in the United States, op. cit. at p. 59.

*   *   *

While we have discussed the foregoing statements that the hardship must be unique and that there are limitations on a zoning appeal board's power to frame a remedy when the hardship is shared with others—such statements being so inextricably a part of judicial, text and scholarly definitions of "unnecessary hardship" that the construction of that term could not accurately be discussed without reference to those statements—we do not here express our views thereon, as it is not necessary to do so in order to decide this case. We limit our holding to that expressed in the next paragraph.

Our review of the authorities leads us to hold that a use variance should not be granted unless the board of zoning appeals can find on the basis of substantial evidence that the property cannot reasonably be used in a manner consistent with existing zoning. In *Otto* the New York Court of Appeals stated that one seeking a variance must show that the land in question cannot yield a *reasonable return* if used only for a purpose allowed in the relevant zoning district. It will be noted that we have used the word "property" (i.e., including improvements) rather than "land", reserving to a later day the decision whether we wish to adopt that aspect of the *Otto* definition. It will also be noted that our holding speaks in terms of "reasonable use" rather than "reasonable return." Whether property usable in trade or business or held for the production of income can reasonably be used for a purpose consistent with existing zoning will, no doubt, ordinarily turn on whether a reasonable return can be derived from the property as then zoned. While any property, including a single family residence, may be made to produce income if a tenant can be found therefor, it would in our opinion be unrealistic as to all properties (without regard to their varying utility) to resolve the question solely on the basis of the return that can be derived from the property.

In the case of Leo's property, we perceive the question to be whether the property can continue reasonably to be used as a single family residence. The appeal board made no determination in that regard, resting its finding of unnecessary hardship solely on the "heavy traffic and the closeness to the business section immediately to the west."

Leo's property has been used for some time as a single family residence. While the board found there was "testimony" that Leo had not received any offers from residence-use buyers during the period of over a year the property had been listed and offered for sale, the asking price for the house and adjoining lot was $38,500 in a neighborhood where, according to the only record evidence, houses generally sell for $20,000 to $25,000. There was no evidence of efforts to sell the property at any price lower than $38,500; indeed, there was no testimony at all as to the extent of the sales effort or the income that could be derived from the property as zoned. See Crossroads Recreation, Inc. v. Broz (1958), 4 N.Y.2d 39, 44, 172 N.Y.S.2d 129, 132, 149 N.E.2d 65; Forrest v. Evershed (1959), 7 N.Y.2d 256, 196 N.Y.S.2d 958, 164 N.E.2d 841; compare Jones v. DeVries, 326 Mich. 126, 137, 40 N.W.2d 317, et seq. applying the Grand Rapids ordinance.

Testimony that the house and lot could not be sold for $38,500 in a neighborhood where houses generally sell for substantially less than that amount does not, in our opinion, constitute any evidence that the property could not continue reasonably to be used as a single family residence.   *   *   *

Thus there was not only a failure to find that the property could not reasonably be used in a manner consistent with existing zoning, but, as we read the record, there was no evidence upon which such a finding could have been based. In this connection, it should be remembered that the fact that the property would be worth more if it could be used as a doctor's clinic and that the corner of Puritan and Prest has disadvantages as a place of residence does not authorize the granting of a variance. Heavy traffic is all too typical of innumerable admittedly residential streets. Adjacency to gasoline stations or other commercial development is characteristic of the end of a business or commercial district and the commencement of a residential district. "A district has to end somewhere." Real Properties, Inc. v. Board of Appeal of Boston (1946), 319 Mass. 180, 65 N.E.2d 199, 201.

It can readily be seen that unless the power of the board of zoning appeals to grant a use variance is defined by objective standards, the appeal board could [and we do not in any sense mean to suggest this would be deliberate] rezone an entire neighborhood—a lot or two lots at a time. The variance granted in response to one "hardship" may well beget or validate another claim of hardship and justify still another variance. If it is a hardship to be next to a gasoline station, it could be a hardship to be across from one, to be behind one, or diagonally across from one. If heavy traffic is a valid basis, variances might become the rule rather than the sparingly granted exception.

We do not wish to be understood as challenging the judgment of the board of zoning appeals. A doctor's office with the appearance of a single family residence on a busy street which already has other commercial uses may very well be a logical, sensible and unobjectionable use. However the question before us is not whether the board of zoning appeals has acted reasonably, but whether on the proofs and findings the board could grant a variance on the ground of unnecessary hardship. We have concluded that neither the proofs nor the findings justified the variance granted.

We have given careful consideration to the considerable number of cases we found where the result was based on the reviewing court's conclusion that the appeal board had not abused the discretion confided to it. If there is substantial evidence to support the necessary findings such a decision is, indeed, the correct one. However, there must be such evidence and such findings.

We have considered and rejected appellee's contention that a board of zoning appeals may not grant a use variance. We have also considered appellee's contention that the board's action should be reversed because the hardship alleged by Leo was "self-created." However, the hardship found by the board in this case could not be said to have been self-created—Leo neither created the traffic conditions on Puritan nor the gasoline station immediately to the west of his property.

Affirmed. Costs to appellee.

Note on Zoning Variances

The Michigan zoning enabling act, Mich.Comp.Laws § 125.585(d) provides that the zoning board of appeals, "[w]here there are practical difficulties or unnecessary hardship in the way of carrying out the strict letter of such ordinance, * * * shall have power * * * to vary or modify any of its rules, regulations or provisions relating to the construction, structural changes in, equipment, or alteration of buildings or structures, or the use of land, buildings or structures, so that the spirit of the ordinance shall be observed, public safety secured and substantial justice done." This language is derived from the New York general city zoning enabling act as amended in 1920; see N.Y.General City Law § 81(4) (Supp.1977–78). The language can ultimately be traced to an amendment of the 1916 New York City Zoning Resolution authorized by a 1917 special act which gave New York City authority to "provide that the board of appeals may determine and vary * * * application [of the zoning regulations] in harmony with their general purpose and intent and in accordance with general or specific rules therein contained." (N.Y.Laws 1917, ch. 601.) Section 7 of the Standard State Zoning Enabling Act contains generally similar language authorizing the zoning board of adjustment to "authorize * * * in specific cases such variance from the terms of the ordinance as will not be contrary to the public interest, where, owing to special conditions, a literal enforcement of the provisions of the ordinance will result in unnecessary hardship, and so that the spirit of the ordinance shall be observed and substantial justice done." The principal difference between the New York based zoning statutes and the statutes based on the Standard Act is that the latter do not include any reference to "practical difficulties" as a basis for granting a zoning variance.[1]

Otto v. Steinhilber, quoted and discussed in the principal case, is probably the most significant single decision on the standards to be applied in determining whether a variance can properly be granted in a particular case. The "unique circumstances" requirement laid down in *Steinhilber* was applied in Arverne Bay Constr. Co. v. Thatcher, supra p. 1124, where the court said, "Here the application * * * for any variation was properly refused, for the conditions which render the plaintiff's property unsuitable for residential use are general and not confined to plaintiff's property. In such case * * * the general hardship should be remedied by revision of the general regulation, not by granting the special privilege of a variation to single owners."[2]

---

1. Some zoning enabling acts are more specific than the New York zoning legislation or the Standard Act in setting out the standards for granting a variance. Cal. Gov.Code Ann. § 65906 (West Supp.1977), e.g., states that "[v]ariances shall be granted only when, because of special circumstances applicable to the property, including size, shape, topography, location or surroundings, the strict application of the zoning ordinance deprives such property of privileges enjoyed by other property in the vicinity and under identical zoning classification." Compare Mass.Gen.Laws Ann. tit. vii, c. 40A, § 15, which empowers the board of appeals to authorize a variance "where, owing to conditions especially affecting such parcel or such building but not affecting generally the zoning district in which it is located, a literal enforcement of the provisions of the ordinance or by-

law would involve substantial hardship, financial or otherwise, to the appellant, and where desirable relief may be granted without substantial detriment to the public good and without nullifying or substantially derogating from the intent or purpose of such ordinance or bylaw, but not otherwise." Both the California and Massachusetts statutes expressly authorize the board, in granting a variance, to impose protective conditions.

2. In a portion of the *Arverne Bay* opinion not reprinted herein, the court dealt with the defendant's challenge to "the right of the plaintiff to urge the invalidity of the zoning ordinance after denial of an application for a variance." The court said, *inter alia*, that "[t]he application for the favor of a variance is an appeal primarily to the discretion of the

Although the "unique circumstances" requirement laid down in *Steinhilber* has generally been adopted by courts in states other than New York, it appears that it may recently have been repudiated in the state of its origin. See dicta in Jayne Estates, Inc. v. Raynor, 22 N.Y.2d 417, 293 N.Y.S.2d 75, 239 N.E.2d 713, 717–718 (1968); Williams v. Town of Oyster Bay, 32 N.Y.2d 78, 343 N.Y.S.2d 118, 295 N.E.2d 788, 790 n. 1 (1973); and Dauernheim, Inc. v. Town of Hempstead, 33 N.Y.2d 468, 354 N.Y.S.2d 909, 310 N.E.2d 516 (1974).

So-called "use variances" have been recognized as within the authority granted to the board of adjustment (or appeals) by the zoning enabling act in the great majority of states, and the litigated cases on variances usually involve "use variances."

In several states it has been held that "use variances" may not be granted because they have the same effect as a rezoning amendment. See, e.g., Nicolai v. Bd. of Adj., 55 Ariz. 283, 101 P.2d 199 (1940); State v. Hudson, 400 S.W.2d 425 (Mo.App.1966); Clarke v. Di Dio, 226 So.2d 23 (Fla.App.1969). A recent revision of the California zoning enabling act has also prohibited the granting of "use variances"; see Cal.Gov.Code Ann. § 65906 (West Supp.1977), which contains the following provision: "A variance shall not be granted for a parcel of property which authorizes a use or activity which is not otherwise expressly authorized by the zone regulations governing the parcel of property."

As Green states in the article cited in *Puritan-Greenfield Improvement Ass'n*, supra p. 1245, a variance may not be granted on grounds of "unnecessary hardship" if the hardship is the result of the applicant's own actions. Hardship is clearly "self-inflicted" if a landowner or developer proceeds to build in willful or even accidental violation of the zoning regulations and the municipal authorities insist that the violation be corrected. Hardship is also "self-inflicted" when it is "manufactured"—e.g., where the landowner or developer has torn down a residential structure and then claims that his property cannot be profitably put to residential use because of high construction costs, or where he has deliberately carved an odd-shaped lot out of a larger tract and then claims that residential development is not feasible. Similarly, if a developer pays a premium price for land and then seeks a variance to permit more intensive development on the ground of financial hardship, the hardship has been held to be "self-inflicted." Josephson v. Autrey, 96 So.2d 784 (Fla.1957). In New York and Pennsylvania, however, the courts have repeatedly held that purchase of property with knowledge of the zoning regulations gives rise to "self-inflicted" hardship even if, arguably, the vendor could have demonstrated sufficient hardship to justify a variance. In the leading New York case the statement of this rule is clearly only a dictum, since on the facts it was a clear case of "manufactured" hardship. See Thomas v. Board of Standards & Appeals, 263 App.Div.

board. It necessarily assumes the validity of the ordinance." This appears to be true with respect to the general validity of the ordinance as a whole. But it can hardly be said that a property owner who seeks a variance on the ground that strict enforcement of a general rule restricting the use of all property within a district works such hardship upon him as to deprive him of property without due process of law "assumes the validity of the ordinance" as it applies to his property. On the other hand, if the board of adjustment (or appeals) denies a variance on the ground that the hardship does not result from "unique circumstances" but rather from general conditions in the neighborhood that make the zoning regulations unreasonable as to a number of properties, even a judicial affirmance of the board's denial of the variance, "cannot be a binding adjudication that, without such variation, enforcement of the general rule will not deprive the applicant of his property without due process of law." See Arverne Bay Constr. Co. v. Thatcher, 278 N.Y. at 226–27, 15 N.E.2d at 589 (1938). But it would seem that a judicial affirmance of the denial of a variance on the ground that the applicant failed to show sufficient hardship should be considered to be such a binding adjudication.

352, 33 N.Y.S.2d 219 (1942), reversed on other grounds, 290 N.Y. 109, 48 N.E.2d 284 (1943). But *Thomas* has been cited ever since for the proposition that hardship arising from purchase of land with notice of the zoning regulations is "self-inflicted." Such a broad rule is difficult to justify, since it results in a requirement that any landowner who has a legitimate claim to a hardship variance must himself obtain the variance before selling his property; otherwise, the purchaser will be barred from obtaining a variance and, presumably, must attempt to have the zoning regulations declared invalid as applied to his property. The broad New York and Pennsylvania rules on "self-inflicted" hardship have been adopted in several other states, including California, Florida, and Maryland. For a good brief discussion of the "self-inflicted" hardship problem, see 5 N. Williams American Land Planning Law §§ 146.01 through 146.07 (1975, Supp.1978).

There was no suggestion in *Steinhilber* that the standards for granting "area or dimension variances" were different from the standards for granting "use variances." But more recently the New York courts have held that different standards should be applied. As the Court of Appeals explained in Hoffman v. Harris, 17 N.Y.2d 138, 269 N.Y.S.2d 119, 216 N.E.2d 326 (1968):

> * * * An applicant for an area variance need not establish special hardship. * * * "A change of area may be granted on the ground of practical difficulties alone, without considering whether or not there is an unnecessary hardship." (Matter of Village of Bronxville v. Francis, 1 A.D.2d 236, 238, 150 N.Y.S.2d 906, 909, affd. 1 N.Y.2d 839, 153 N.Y.S.2d 220, 135 N.E.2d 724.)
>
> There is good reason for the distinction between use and area variances and the requirement of a higher standard of proof of hardship for the former. When the variance is one of area only, there is no change in the character of the zoned district and the neighborhood considerations are not as strong as in a use variance. For example, in *Bronxville* (supra), the question was whether a bank could make the floor area of its new building more than 1 and ½ times the area of its lot despite an ordinance limiting the total floor area of a building to 1 and ½ times the lot. There was no question of change of character of neighborhood since the bank was a proper use. In such a case, it seems fair that only practical difficulties without unique or special hardship need be proved to obtain a variance.

17 N.Y.2d at 144, 269 N.Y.S.2d at 123, 216 N.E.2d at 329–30. Unfortunately, the New York courts have not yet clearly indicated what they mean by "practical difficulties" and "area or dimension variance."

In Wilcox v. Zoning Bd. of Appeals, 17 N.Y.2d 249, 217 N.E.2d 633 (1966), the court sustained a variance allowing an increase in density for apartment construction as an "area variance." Other courts have been less lenient. In O'Neill v. Zoning Bd. of Adjustment of Philadelphia County, 434 Pa. 331, 254 A.2d 12 (1969), the property was located in an apartment zone, but the developer had obtained a variance allowing him to increase the floor space in the proposed building by two and one-half times. While conceding that it might be willing to relax its standards for "area" variances, the court held that the variance granted was not such a variance and that a change of such magnitude must be made legislatively. Hence, the variance was set aside. And in Taylor v. District of Columbia Bd. of Zoning Adjustment, 308 A.2d 230 (D.C.Ct.App. 1973), the court denied a variance from height, side yard, court, and lot occupancy requirements which would have allowed construction of 27 townhouses instead of 10 detached houses on the tract. The court said that, "while the requested variance may not be a use variance in its 'purest form,' it is a hybrid variance which would drastically alter the character of the zoned district" and could be characterized as a "use-area variance." (Id. at 233.) For a good general discussion of "practical difficulties" as the standard for "area or dimension variances," see 3 R. Anderson, American Law of Zoning §§ 14.45 through 14.51 (2d ed. 1977).

Presumably only states with statutory provisions for granting variances in cases of "practical difficulties" as well as "unnecessary hardship" are likely to adopt the New York rule as to "area or dimension variances."

Local zoning ordinances often purport to impose stricter or more specific standards for granting variances than those embodied in the enabling statutes. Since these more specific standards in many instances merely summarize judicial decisions interpreting the (usually) vague standards set out in the zoning enabling acts, one might suppose that courts would approve such ordinance provisions. But there is little support for this in the cases. Indeed, an ordinance provision that any variance granted must be the minimum variance necessary to provide the landowner with a reasonable return on his investment has been held invalid on the ground that the enabling act contained no such standard. Celentano, Inc. v. Board of Zoning Appeals, 149 Conn. 671, 184 A.2d 49 (1962); Coderre v. Zoning Bd. of Review, 102 R.I. 327, 230 A.2d 247 (1967).

As a result of lack of expertise, political influence, and—in some of the larger cities—far too heavy a case load, many zoning boards of adjustment (or appeals) have shown a regrettable tendency to ignore the standards prescribed by statute for granting variances. The two most recent empirical studies of the variance procedure both concluded that the board in the communities under study did not, in a majority of the cases, insist that the statutory requirements for variances be satisfied. See Dukeminier & Stapleton, The Zoning Board of Adjustment: A Case Study in Misrule, 50 Ky.L.J. 273 (1962); Comment, 50 Calif.L.Rev. 101 (1962). Even if the courts exercise vigilant oversight in the cases where judicial review of a board decision is sought they can do nothing about the great majority of cases where no appeal is taken. Thus the granting of variances without reference to the statutory standard may result in substantial erosion of the whole zoning plan, especially where (as is true in most states) "use variances" may be granted by the board of adjustment (or appeals).

Despite the universal criticism of the tendency of zoning boards of adjustment (or appeals) to be overwilling to modify the terms of the zoning ordinance, the American Law Institute's Model Land Development Code §§ 2–202 and 2–204 (1976) makes provision for both "use" and "area or dimension" variances, although the term "special development permit" rather than "variance" is used in the Model Code.

KOTRICH v. THE COUNTY OF DU PAGE

Illinois Supreme Court, 1960.
19 Ill.2d 181, 166 N.E.2d 601, appeal dismissed 364 U.S. 475, 81 S.Ct. 243, 5 L.Ed.2d 221.

Mr. Justice SCHAEFER delivered the opinion of the court:

This is a declaratory judgment proceeding which involves the validity of a "special use" permit granted by the defendant, the board of supervisors of Du Page County, to the defendant, Salt Creek Club, under the terms of the Du Page County zoning ordinance. The primary issues concern the statutory authority of the county to provide for "special uses" in its zoning ordinance, and, if the authority exists, the conditions that govern its exercise.

The defendant club is a not-for-profit corporation organized for social, educational, and athletic purposes. It owns the property in question, a six-acre parcel of land now zoned for R–2 single family residence use. On this land it proposes to build a clubhouse, a swimming pool, tennis courts and a parking area for use of its anticipated membership of 275 families.

The club applied to the zoning board for a special use permit under the county ordinance, to allow the construction of a private outdoor recreation center on the property. The board conducted a hearing and recommended to the county board that the special use permit be denied. Notwithstanding this recommendation, the county board passed a resolution granting the permit. The plaintiffs, who are adjacent property owners, commenced this suit in the circuit court of Du Page County to challenge the permit and the zoning ordinance under which it was granted. From a judgment sustaining the validity of the ordinance and the permit, they appeal directly to this court. The trial judge has certified that the validity of a county zoning ordinance is involved and that the public interest requires a direct appeal to this court. Ill.Rev.Stat.1959, chap. 110, par. 75.

The special use is a relatively new method of land use control. Zoning ordinances embodying this technique retain the usual residential, commercial, and industrial zones, specifying the uses permitted in each zone. For each zone, however, special uses are also established which are permitted within the zone only if approved by the zoning board or the governing legislative body. The Du Page County ordinance follows this general scheme, and it specifies private outdoor recreational facilities among the special uses which may be permitted in the R–2 single family residence zone. Among other special uses permitted in this zone are colleges and universities, public outdoor recreational centers, rest homes, hospitals and sanitariums, planned developments of not less than 40 acres, and "public service uses" such as electric and telephone substations, filtration plants, and fire and police stations.

The first contention advanced by the plaintiffs is that the County Zoning Enabling Act (Ill.Rev.Stat.1957, chap. 34, par. 152i, et seq.) does not authorize counties to employ this method. In support of this contention they argue that since the special use technique is not mentioned in the act, and indeed did not exist at the time the act was adopted in 1935, the legislature could not have intended to authorize it. Their position is that the legislature must specifically grant counties the power to adopt special use provisions, as it has done in the case of variations and amendments, and as legislatures of some other States have done.

They note also that procedural safeguards limit the exercise of administrative and legislative discretion with respect to variations and amendments. Written findings of fact must accompany every variation, and any variation rejected by the zoning board of appeals can be approved only by a three-fourths majority of the legislative body. The same extraordinary majority is required to approve any amendment if 20% of adjacent landowners object. It is argued that the legislature has thus indicated its intention that deviations from the established zoning pattern should be permitted only by the procedurally restricted methods included in the act.

Carl L. Gardner, a planning and zoning consultant, testified that the special use technique developed as a means of providing for infrequent types of land use which are necessary and desirable but which are potentially incompatible with uses usually allowed in residential, commercial and industrial zones. Such uses generally occupy a rather large tract of land. They can not be categorized in any given use zone without the danger of excluding beneficial uses or including dangerous ones. A typical example was presented in Illinois Bell Telephone Co. v. Fox, 402 Ill. 617, 85 N.E.2d 43, where this court affirmed a judgment ordering a special use permit to issue for construction of a telephone exchange in a residential district.

Instead of excluding such uses entirely from certain zones because of the harm they might cause, or, despite the potential harm, including them because of the benefits they will bring, the special use technique allows a more flexible approach. It contemplates that the county board may permit these uses when desirable and, if necessary, impose conditions designed to protect nearby property owners. This seems to be an effective method of dealing with a narrow but difficult problem of land use control. Approximately 25 municipalities and counties in Illinois have incorporated it in their zoning ordinances, and the record shows that its use is increasing.

It is true that the procedural restrictions prescribed for amendments and variations, as well as the standards prescribed for variations, evidence a legislative plan to guarantee property owners some protection from piecemeal changes in the general zoning scheme by ad hoc determinations with respect to particular pieces of property. And since granting a special use permit involves an ad hoc judgment which may affect surrounding property owners in the same way as a variation or an amendment, unlimited application of the special use technique to land uses that can readily be accommodated within the customary categories would undermine the protection contemplated by the statute. But unlimited application of the special use technique is not required to meet the problem it was designed to solve. Only those infrequent uses which are beneficial, but potentially inconsistent with normal uses in the various zones, need be included.

The statute authorizes the board of supervisors "to regulate and restrict the location and use of buildings, structures and land for trade, industry, residence and other uses which may be specified by such board, * * *; to divide the entire county * * * into districts of such number, shape, area and of such different classes, according to the use of land and buildings, * * * as may be deemed best suited to carry out the purposes of this Act; to prohibit uses, buildings or structures incompatible with the character of such districts respectively; * * *." (Ill.Rev.Stat.1957, chap. 34, par. 152i.) In our opinion, a residual category of those special uses which can not, without distortion, be included in the customary classifications, is permissible as a means of implementing the powers conferred by the statute.

Applying these criteria, we think that a private country club such as that involved in the present case may properly be classified as a special use in a single family residence zone. Such uses of land are often found in residential areas. Proximity to a club may increase the desirability of land. On the other hand, a club may also produce increased noise from bathers, tennis players, social functions and automobiles. If the parking area is not properly designed, headlights may shine in neighboring houses; if it is not large enough, members' automobiles will overflow onto neighboring streets. Increased traffic may produce safety hazards. Whether these undesirable consequences will occur depends upon the design of the club's facilities and its location within the zone. In such a case, governmental supervision of each situation is justified.

The plaintiffs also contend that the ordinance providing for special uses is invalid because it does not specify standards by which the county board of supervisors is to judge whether a special use permit should be granted. Although the ordinance does not prescribe standards in so many words, it does state that special uses are established for the purpose of providing "for the location of special classes of uses which are deemed desirable for the public welfare within a given district or districts, but which are potentially incompatible with typical uses herein permitted within them * * *." It also empowers the board of supervisors to impose "such * * * conditions as it considers necessary to protect the public health, safety and welfare." A fair reading of the ordinance shows that it contemplates that the county board will weigh the desirability of the proposed use against its potential adverse impact. Since the board of supervisors is a legislative body, precise standards to govern its determination are not required.

The plaintiffs' next contention is that since the impact of a special use is like the impact of a variation, the statutory requirement that written findings of fact must accompany a variation should be applied to special uses. They also assert, again by analogy to variations, that if the zoning board of appeals rejects a special use, a three-fourths majority of the county board of supervisors should be required to grant the permit. In the present case no finding of facts was adopted by the county board. The special use permit was granted without a three-fourths vote of the county board, although the board of zoning appeals had rejected the club's application, and had found specifically that the proposed use would be incompatible with the general character of the neighborhood and its trend of development would cause considerable depreciation of surrounding property, and would increase traffic congestion.

We recognize that because the special use may have the same impact upon neighboring property as a variation, procedural safeguards similar to those prescribed for variations might be desirable for special uses as well. But the enabling act imposes these safeguards only as to variations, and the two techniques are not identical. The scope of the special use, and its purpose, differ from those of the variation, which is designed to handle cases of practical difficulty or particular hardship to property owners created by zoning restrictions. For this court to impose upon the local legislative body, in dealing with special uses, the procedures required for variations would be to move from interpretation of the act to policy determination and implementation. This is the function not of the court, but of the General Assembly.

Furthermore, the impact of a special use may resemble that of an amendment as well as a variation. Yet the statutory procedures for amendments vary greatly from those of variations. A three-fourths vote of the county board is required if 20% of the adjacent landowners object, but no findings of fact are required since an amendment is considered a legislative act. By analogy to the plaintiffs' contention in this case, it may be argued that amendment procedures, rather than variation procedures, should be required when granting a special use permit. Which, if either, of the statutory procedures is appropriate for the new special use technique that has developed under the statute is a matter for legislative determination.

It is true that in Rosenfeld v. Zoning Board of Appeals, 19 Ill.App.2d 447, 154 N.E.2d 323, the Appellate Court set aside a special use permit in part for lack of written findings of fact, although it recognized that findings were not required by the zoning ordinance or the enabling act. In that case, however, the special use was granted by the zoning board of appeals of Chicago and review was under the Illinois Administrative Review Act. (Ill.Rev.Stat.1959, chap. 110, pars. 264–279.) Review under that act is on the record made in the administrative agency and its findings of fact are to be held *prima facie* true and correct. (Ill.Rev. Stat.1959, chap. 110, par. 274.) Orderly and efficient review procedure under the act may, therefore, require that the administrative agency make written findings. The same reasoning does not apply in the present case where the special use permit was granted by a legislative body and judicial review is had in an independent action on a new record made in court.

The plaintiffs contend, finally, that to allow the club to conduct its proposed activities under a special use permit will deprive them of their property without due process of law. They argue that the damage to their property far outweighs any public benefit the club may produce. Although an expert witness for the plaintiff testified that operation of the club would substantially depreciate the value of surrounding property, two witnesses for the defendants took the opposite view. The county board imposed several restrictions designed to protect nearby houses from excessive light and noise. We think the record shows that the county board's action was not arbitrary and did not deprive the plaintiffs of their property without due process of law.

The judgment is affirmed.

Judgment affirmed.

Mr. Chief Justice HOUSE, dissenting:

The county has only the powers delegated to it, expressly or by necessary implication. There is no specific authority granted by the county zoning enabling act for special use procedure, nor, in my opinion, can the device be justified under the general power to "regulate," "restrict" and "prohibit." How can it be said that a legislative intent was manifested to permit special use procedure when, as the majority opinion recognizes, such procedure was unknown at the date of enactment of the enabling legislation? The fact that statutory restrictions and standards are set up for amendments and variations indicates a legislative intent to the exact contrary.

I agree with the majority that it is a matter for legislative determination whether amendment, variation or other procedure is appropriate for the new special use technique. But, that determination must come from the legislature together with suitable standards fixed for application of the procedure. It should not, as here, be left without restriction to the whim of the local governing body.

In one breath the majority opinion admits that unlimited application of the special use technique would take away the guarantee to property owners which is the very vitals of zoning and in the next approves special use procedure because its unlimited application "is not required." The ingenuity of members of our profession could conceivably conjure up so many "unique" situations which would require applications of special use procedures that ad hoc determination could become the rule rather than the exception.

The Bell Telephone case (402 Ill. 617, 85 N.E.2d 43) is readily distinguishable. First, the ordinances involved are entirely different and, second, the special use device was not in question, but the issue was whether area and height restrictions in the volume district were applicable.

From the standpoint of zoning enthusiasts and administrators the special use device provides a flexible method disposing of troublesome "unique" situations. On the other hand, its use in such cases as here (recreation center) is the further limiting of the rights of ownership of property under the guise of the much tortured and misused police power.

Note on Special Exceptions and Special Use Permits

The Standard Act conferred on the zoning board of adjustment an additional power not included in the New York enabling legislation as to the zoning board of appeals. Section 7 of the Standard Act empowers the board of adjustment "[t]o hear and decide special exceptions to the terms of the ordinance upon which such board is required to pass under such ordinance." Since this language sounds something like the 1917 New York legislative authorization for the New York City governing body to empower its board of appeals to "determine and vary" the zoning regulations "in accordance with general or specific rules therein contained," it is not surprising that many courts have had difficulty in distinguishing "variances" from "special exceptions" under statutes based on the Standard Act. The distinction was apparently not yet recognized when Bassett wrote in 1940, for he discusses "variances" at length but does not mention "special exceptions." It is now generally recognized, however, that a "special exception" use is one specifically provided for in the zoning ordinance, but not authorized as a matter of right in a particular district; instead, the board of adjustment (or appeals) may authorize the "special exception" use if it finds the standards set out in the zoning ordinance for such use are satisfied. The classic judicial statement of the nature and purpose of the "special exception" is that contained in the opinion of Hall, J., in Tullo v. Millburn Township, 54 N.J. Super. 483, 490–91, 149 A.2d 620, 624–25 (App.Div.1959):

* * * The term might well be said to be a misnomer. 'Special uses' or 'special use permits' would be more accurate. The theory is that certain uses, considered by the local legislative body to be essential or desirable for the welfare of the community and its citizenry or substantial segments of it, are entirely appropriate and not essentially incompatible with the basic uses in any zone (or in certain particular zones), but not at every or any location therein or without restrictions or conditions being imposed by reason of special problems the use or its particular location in relation to neighboring properties presents from a zoning standpoint, such as traffic congestion, safety, health, noise, and the like. The enabling act therefore permits the local ordinance to require approval of the local administrative agency as to the location of such use within the zone. If the board finds compliance with the standards or requisites set forth in the ordinance, the right to the exception exists, subject to such specific safeguarding conditions as the agency may impose by reason of the nature, location and incidents of the particular use. Without intending here to be inclusive or to prescribe limits, the uses so treated are generally those serving considerable numbers of people, such as private schools, clubs, hospitals and even churches, as distinguished from governmental structures or activities on the one hand and strictly individual residences or businesses on the other. This method of zoning treatment is also frequently extended to certain unusual kinds of strictly private business or activity which, though desirable and compatible, may by their nature present peculiar zoning problems or have unduly unfavorable effect on their neighbors if not specifically regulated. Gasoline stations * * * are an example of this second category. The point is that such special uses are permissive in the particular zone under the ordinance and neither non-conforming nor akin to a variance.

In Brown Boveri, Inc. v. Township of North Brunswick, 160 N.J.Super. 179, 389 A.2d 483 (App.Div.1978), the court held that (1) since automobile showrooms were allowed only as special exceptions in Commercial C–2 districts, permission to use land for an automobile showroom could only be obtained through the special exception procedure and not by means of a use variance; and (2) such a special exception could not be granted in an industrial zone in any event, since automobile showrooms were not a permitted use in such a zone.

In his dissenting opinion in the principal case, House, C.J., said, "There is no specific authority granted by the county zoning enabling act for special use procedures." It is arguable, however, that authority can be found in Ill.Stat. Ann. ch. 34, § 3156, which empowers the county board of appeals to "hear and decide all matters referred to it or upon which it is required to pass under any * * * [county zoning] ordinance or resolution." The Du Page county zoning ordinance before the court in Kotrich apparently required applications for "special uses" to be made to the board of appeals—which under the statutory provision cited above could take affirmative action only by the "concurring vote of 4 members of a board consisting of 5 members or the concurring vote of 5 members of a board consisting of 7 members"—but also provided that the county governing body could overrule the decision of the board of appeals by a simple majority vote.

In Depue v. City of Clinton, 160 N.W.2d 860 (Iowa 1968), the court struck down a zoning ordinance provision which sought to allocate authority to approve "special uses" to the local governing body, although the ordinance also created a board of adjustment with power to grant "special exceptions." The court held (1) that the term "special exceptions" includes "special uses," and (2) that the jurisdiction conferred on the board of adjustment by the zoning enabling act is exclusive. The enabling act contained a provision as to "special exceptions" identical with § 7 of the Standard State Zoning Enabling Act. Accord, under a zoning enabling act derived from the New York general city enabling act as amended in 1920, Smith v. Building Inspector for Plymouth Township, 346 Mich. 57, 77 N.W.2d 332 (1959). Contra: Building Commissioner of Medford v. C. & H. Co., 319 Mass. 273, 65 N.E.2d 537 (1946).

In states where the enabling act follows § 7 of the Standard Act, however, some local governing bodies have provided in their zoning ordinances that the board of adjustment shall merely recommend the granting or denial of "special exceptions," and that the final decision shall be made by the governing body itself. E.g., Schmidt v. Board of Adjustment, 9 N.J. 405, 88 A.2d 607 (1952).

In addition to some confusion in terminology and with respect to the power of municipal governing bodies to authorize "special uses," "special exceptions," or (as they are sometimes called) "conditional uses," judicial review has recently centered mainly on the adequacy of the standards governing the authorization of such "special uses," "special exceptions," or "conditional uses." The following summary is drawn from the American Law Institute's Model Land Development Code, Tentative Draft No. 2, Note to § 2–207 (1970):

> * * * Mandelker's review of cases shows that 'nuisance standards'— negatively phrased standards directing that uses will not be allowed as exceptions if they create nuisance type external costs—have been approved overwhelmingly. Ordinances without any standards—simply authorizing an administrative board to issue an exception—generally have been held to delegate legislative authority invalidly. But most zoning ordinances provide general welfare standards and here judicial reaction is mixed. (Usually the ordinance allows the board to permit any of the enumerated special uses if such action would be in accord with the purposes and intent of the ordinance and be conducive to the general welfare.) Many cases sustain such standards without any critical comment. Some courts attempt to evaluate such standards and conclude that they are certain enough in view of the technological complexities of zoning administration. * * * A number of cases hold such standards unconstitutional or ultra vires. Confusingly, courts in the same jurisdiction, and even the same courts, render inconsistent opinions on similar standards in different cases. * * * The problems raised by exceptions are like those raised by variances. At base it is the fear that without somewhat concrete standards landowners will be vulnerable to discrimination. In addition, there is the desire to have policy made by a representative body and to assure neighborhood status quo. And as with variances, courts have not been able to take solace in procedural regularity because enabling acts and ordinances have not required administrative agencies to state in detail the reasons for granting or denying exceptions.*

New Jersey's recently revised zoning enabling act now requires that the local zoning ordinance provision for "special exceptions" shall contain "definite specifications and standards which shall be clearly set forth with sufficient clarity and definiteness to enable the developer to know their limit and extent." N.J.Stat.Ann. § 40:55D–67 (Supp.1978). Do you think this will effectively pro-

---

* Copyright 1970. Reprinted with the permission of The American Law Institute. The reference to "Mandelker's review of cases" is to Mandelker, Delegation of Power and Function in Zoning Administration, 1963 Wash.U.L.Q. 60.

hibit the use of "nuisance" or vague "general welfare" standards in New Jersey?

In *Kotrich* the court held that there was no need for written findings of fact when a special use permit was granted by a "legislative body," since in such case "judicial review is had in an independent action on a new record made in court." Does this make sense? Was the county governing body in *Kotrich* acting "legislatively" or "administratively"? Does it make any difference? Consider the following excerpt from Archdiocese of Portland v. County of Washington, 254 Or. 77, 458 P.2d 682, 686 (1969):

> * * * We examine the record of the proceedings before the Board [of County Commissioners] only to determine whether those proceedings were fairly conducted in accordance with the requirements of the ordinance and that there was a rational basis for the Board's decision. It is important to bear in mind that in these cases we and the trial court are reviewing the legislative action of a governmental unit engaged in carrying out a land use policy formulated by it. The basis for that action need not be found in "evidence" as we use that term in connection with the trial of cases before a court. The ordinance requires the Planning Commission to hold a public hearing on all proposed changes and the Board must also hold a public hearing on all appeals from the Planning Commission. But these public hearings are not trials and the views expressed by those who attend are evidence only in the broad sense that the Board may consider the points of view expressed at those hearings in reaching its conclusion.

Compare Tullo v. Millburn Township, 54 N.J.Super. 483, 496, 149 A.2d 620, 627–28 (App.Div.1959):

> [I]t is, of course, elementary that, similar to the case of a variance, an applicant for a special exception has the burden of producing proofs before the Board of Adjustment to establish that the ordinance and statutory standards are met and the agency must make adequate basic findings of fact from that evidence leading to the ultimate finding or conclusion. The findings need not be in legal language and the ultimate findings or conclusions need not parrot the legislative verbiage. These ultimate requisites may be deduced from what is actually said. It must be kept in mind that the administrative bodies are composed of laymen. The prescribed procedural pattern is a general and flexible one, adaptable to the particular case.

For a recent case considering in detail the requirements of procedural due process as they apply to the "special exception" or "special use permit" procedure, see Barton Contracting Co., Inc. v. City of Afton, 268 N.W.2d 712 (Minn. 1978).

Suppose a substantially undeveloped rural community zones its entire area for the existing agricultural and residential uses and then provides that most other types of land use shall be allowed only as "special exceptions" or "special uses" upon the granting of permits? Would such an ordinance violate either constitutional or statutory limitations upon governmental control of land use? See Rockhill v. Chesterfield Township, 23 N.J. 117, 128 A.2d 473 (1957). The New Jersey court held the ordinance void because it violated both constitutional and statutory zoning principles. The following excerpt gives the flavor of the opinion: "Reserving the use of the whole of the municipal area for 'normal agricultural' and residence uses, and then providing for all manner of 'special uses,' 'neighborhood' and other businesses, even 'light industrial' uses and 'other similar facilities,' placed according to local discretion without regard to districts, ruled by vague and illusive criteria, is indeed the antithesis of zoning. It makes for arbitrary and discriminatory interference with the basic right of private property, in no real sense concerned with the essential common welfare. The statute, N.J.S.A. 40:55–39, provides for regulation by districts and for exceptions and variances from the prescribed land uses under given conditions. The course taken here would flout this essential concept of district zoning according to a comprehensive plan designed to fulfill the declared statutory policy."

It can be argued, however, that an ordinance of the kind held invalid in Rockhill is well-fitted to the needs of largely rural communities which expect urban development to begin within a relatively short time. Perhaps the best analysis of this type of land-use regulation—called "reserve-special use zoning" by the author—is to be found in Editorial Note, 30 U.Cinc.L.Rev. 297 (1961), which also discusses other zoning techniques for dealing with urban development in previously undeveloped communities.

Under the heading "Special Development to Allow Compatible Uses," § 2–207 of the American Law Institute's Model Land Development Code (1976) authorizes essentially the type of broad "special use permit" technique held invalid in *Rockhill.* The Note to § 2–207 states:

> This section contains one of the Code's broadest grants of discretion to land development agencies; perhaps the widest discretion if the local government does not have a land development plan. *   *   *

> It is important to note the controls or limits on this broad grant of power: (1) The power to grant a special permit is not granted to the Land Development Agency by the Code; the governing body is enabled to grant power to the agency and until it does so, the agency has no power under this Section; (2) The agency may   *   *   *   grant a permit under this Section only if the application complies with the requirements of this Code and any additional criteria or limitations imposed by the ordinance; (3) Subsection (2) requires the permit-granting agency to comply with the statutory requirement that the permit be granted only to development that 'is likely to be compatible' with the development otherwise permitted as a matter of right under the development ordinance [on substantially all land in the vicinity of the proposed development].*

For more detail on "special exceptions," "special use permits," and "conditional uses," see 3 Anderson, American Law of Zoning §§ 15.01, 15.03 (2d ed. 1977); 3 Rathkopf, Law of Zoning and Planning ch. 54 (4th ed., 1977); 5 Williams, American Land Planning Law §§ 148.01 through 151.04 (1975; Supp. 1978). See also Mandelker, Delegation of Power and Function in Zoning Administration, 1963 Wash.U.L.Q. 69, 74–80: Green, New Trends in Zoning as Recognized by Court Decisions, 6 Inst. on Planning and Zoning 1 (1966); Bryden, Zoning: Rigid, Flexible, or Fluid?, J. of Urban Law 287 (1967).

KUEHNE v. CITY OF EAST HARTFORD

Supreme Court of Connecticut, 1950.
136 Conn. 452, 72 A.2d 474.

MALTBIE, C.J.   *   *   *   [A substantial part of the opinion is omitted.]

Main Street in East Hartford runs substantially north and south. The petitioner before the town council, Langlois, owned a piece of land on the east side of it which he had been using for growing fruit and

* Copyright 1976. Reprinted with the
permission of the American Law Institute.

vegetables, and he has had upon it a greenhouse and a roadside stand for the sale of products of the land. The premises, ever since zoning was established in East Hartford in 1927, had been in an A residence district. Langlois made an application to the town council to change to an A business district a portion of the tract fronting on Main Street for about 500 feet and extending to a depth of 150 feet. He intended, if the application was granted, to erect upon the tract a building containing six or eight stores, apparently in the nature of retail stores and small business establishments calculated to serve the needs of residents in the vicinity. Starting at a business district to the north and extending for almost three miles to the town boundary on the south, the land along Main Street and extending to a considerable depth on each side of it has been, ever since zoning was established in the town, in an A residence district, with certain exceptions hereinafter described. Seven hundred feet north of the Langlois property is a small business district lying on both sides of Main Street; the land on the east side is used for a fruit and vegetable stand, a milk bar and a garage and gas station; and the land on the west side, with an area a little larger than the Langlois tract in question, is now unoccupied. About 500 feet south of the Langlois property is another small business district in which is located a grill and restaurant, a drugstore, a cleaning and dyeing business and a large grocery and meat market. Formerly the land about the tract in question was used quite largely for agricultural purposes, but within the last few years a large residential community, comprising some one thousand houses, has grown up in the vicinity.

The application to the town council was based upon the claim that residents in the vicinity need the stores and services which could be located in the building Langlois proposed to erect. There was, for example, a petition filed with the council in support of the application signed by fifty-one of those residents which asked it to allow such a change as might be necessary to permit for their benefit a shopping center on the property. None of the signers, however, owned property on Main Street or in the immediate vicinity of the Langlois property. On the other hand, the application was opposed by the owner of property directly opposite the tract in question and by the owners of the two properties fronting on Main Street immediately south of the Langlois land.

The council voted that the application "be granted for the general welfare and the good of the town in that section." In Bartram v. Zoning Commission, 136 Conn. 89, 68 A.2d 308, we recently had before us an appeal from the granting by a zoning commission of an application to change a lot in Bridgeport even smaller than the tract here in question from a residence to a business zone, and we sustained the action of the commission. We said (p. 93): "A limitation upon the powers of zoning authorities which has been in effect ever since zoning statutes were made applicable generally to municipalities in the state is that the regulations they adopt must be made 'in accordance with a comprehensive plan.' Public Acts 1925, c. 242, § 3 (Rev.1949, § 837). 'A "comprehensive plan" means "a general plan to control and direct the use and development of property in a municipality or a large part of it by dividing it into districts according to the present and potential use of the properties." ' Bishop v. Board of Zoning Appeals, 133 Conn. 614, 618, 53 A.2d 659; State ex rel. Spiros v. Payne, 131 Conn. 647, 652, 41 A.2d 908. Action by a zoning authority which gives to a single lot or a small area privileges which are not extended to other land in the vicinity is in general against sound public policy and obnoxious to the law. It can be justified only when it is done in furtherance of a general plan properly adopted for and designed to serve the best interests of the community as a whole. The vice of spot zoning lies in the fact that it singles out for special treatment a lot or a small area in a way that does not further such a plan. Where, however, in pursuance of it, a zoning commission takes such action, its decision can be assailed only on the ground that it abused the discretion vested in it by the law. To permit business in a small area within a residence zone may fall within the scope of such a plan, and to do so, unless it amounts to unreasonable or arbitrary action, is not unlawful." It appeared in that case that the change was granted by the commission in pursuance of a policy to encourage decentralization of business in the city and to that end to permit neighborhood stores in outlying districts. It is true that we said in that opinion (p. 94) that if the commission decided, "on facts affording a sufficient basis and in the exercise of a proper discretion, that it would serve the best interests of the community as a whole to permit a use of a single lot or small area in a different way than was allowed in surrounding territory, it would not be guilty of spot zoning in any sense obnoxious to the law." We meant by that statement to emphasize the fact that the controlling test must be, not the benefit to a particular individual or group of individuals, but the good of the community as a whole, and we did not mean in any way to derogate from our previous statement that any such change can only be made if it falls within the requirements of a comprehensive plan for the use and development of property in the municipality or a large part of it. See Parsons v. Wethersfield, 135 Conn. 24, 29, 60 A.2d 771.

In the case before us it is obvious that the council looked no further than the benefit which might accrue to Langlois and those who resided in the vicinity of his property, and that they gave no consideration to the larger question as to the effect the change would have upon the general plan of zoning in the community. In fact, the controlling consideration seems to have been that Langlois intended to go ahead at once with his building rather than any consideration of the suitability of the particular lot for business uses, because there is no suggestion in the record that the council considered the fact that only some 700 feet away was a tract of land already zoned for business which, as appears from the zoning map in evidence, was more easily accessible to most of the signers of the petition than was the Langlois land.

In Strain v. Mims, 123 Conn. 275, 287, 193 A. 754, we said "One of the essential purposes of zoning regulation is to stabilize property uses." In this case it is significant that the change was opposed by the owners of three properties so situated as to be most affected by it, while those who supported it were the owner of the tract and residents who did not live in its immediate vicinity. It should also be noted that the petition they signed contained a provision that it should not be construed as supporting permission for the use of the premises as a liquor outlet, but at the hearing before the council the attorney for Langlois in effect conceded that the zoning regulations permitted such a use in an A business district; and if that is so and the change were granted, it is quite possible that the premises would be sooner or later converted to such a use.

The action of the town council in this case was not in furtherance of any general plan of zoning in the community and cannot be sustained.

*   *   *

There is error, the judgment is set aside and the case is remanded to be proceeded with according to law.

In this opinion the other judges concurred.

Notes and Questions

1. When *Kuehne* was decided, Connecticut's zoning enabling act was substantially identical with the Standard State Zoning Enabling Act. Section 5 of SSZEA provided that zoning "regulations, restrictions, and boundaries" might be "amended, supplemented, changed, modified, or repealed" by the local legislative body, subject to the notice and hearing requirements applicable to the initial enactment of a zoning ordinance, and also subject to the "20 percent protest" provision designed, according to Bassett, "to prevent easy or careless changes in the zoning regulations" and to protect property owners who have developed their land in conformity with existing zoning regulations. See E. Bassett, Zoning 38 (rev. ed. 1940). In addition, as the *Kuehne* opinion indicates, the Connecticut zoning enabling act included the SSZEA § 3 requirement that all zoning regulations "shall be made in accordance with a comprehensive plan," which has uniformly been held to be applicable to amendments of the zoning regulations. Unfortunately, however, the *Kuehne* opinion provides no clue as to the meaning of "comprehensive plan" in connection with rezoning amendments. It is fairly clear that East Hartford's governing body had not adopted any document that might be described as "a comprehensive plan" for land use in East Hartford, and the court's repetition of language from the earlier case of Bartram v. Zoning Commission makes it clear that the court did not think the rezoning amendment had to be based on any such document. In *Bartram*, the court approved a "spot zoning" amendment that changed the classification of a single small tract from "residential" to "business," largely on the basis of testimony that it was the policy of the zoning commission to "encourage decentralization of business in order to relieve traffic congestion and that, as part of that policy, it was considered desirable to permit neighborhood stores in outlying districts." In *Bartram* there was no proof either that a comprehensive land use plan—other than the existing zoning ordinance—was ever adopted, or that the local governing body had adopted any "policy" designating those "outlying districts" where "neighborhood stores" should be permitted.

2. When *Kuehne* was decided, Connecticut had a planning enabling act based on the Standard City Planning Enabling Act prepared by the United

States Department of Commerce and published in 1928, and containing language almost identical with SCPEA § 6, as follows:

Section 6. General Powers and Duties. It shall be the function and duty of the commission to make and adopt a master plan for the physical development of the municipality, including any areas outside of its boundaries which, in the commission's judgment, bear relation to the planning of such municipality. Such plan, with the accompanying maps, plats, charts, and descriptive matter shall show the commission's recommendations for the development of said territory, including, among other things, the general location, character, and extent of streets, viaducts, subways, bridges, waterways, water fronts, boulevards, parkways, playgrounds, squares, parks, aviation fields, and other public ways, grounds and open spaces, the general location of public buildings and other public property, and the general location and extent of public utilities and terminals, whether publicly or privately owned or operated, for water, light, sanitation, transportation, communication, power, and other purposes; also the removal, relocation, widening, narrowing, vacating, abadonment, change of use or extension of any of the foregoing ways, grounds, open spaces, buildings, property, utilities, or terminals; as well as a zoning plan for the control of the height, area, bulk, location, and use of buildings and premises. As the work of making the whole master plan progresses, the commission may from time to time adopt and publish a part or parts thereof, any such part to cover one or more major sections or divisions of the municipality or one or more of the aforesaid or other functional matters to be included in the plan. The commission may from time to time amend, extend, or add to the plan.

It is obvious, however, that the Connecticut case did not, in the principal case, equate the "comprehensive plan" required by the zoning enabling act with the "master plan" authorized by the planning enabling act. And the SSZEA mandate that zoning regulations "shall be made in accordance with a comprehensive plan"—which is still contained in most of the current state zoning enabling acts—has generally not been construed to require either that adoption of a "master plan" shall precede adoption of a zoning ordinance or, if a "master plan" has been adopted, that the zoning ordinance must be consistent with it. One reason for the failure of the courts to equate the "comprehensive plan" required by the zoning enabling acts with the "master plan" is simply that, in most states, zoning enabling acts were adopted and zoning ordinances enacted before planning enabling acts were adopted, and long before many municipalities adopted "master plans." Only in quite recent times have a few legislatures enacted new statutes mandating the adoption of municipal or county "master plans," "general plans," or "comprehensive" plans and requiring local zoning ordinances to be consistent with the local plan.

3. In Kozesnik v. Montgomery Township, 24 N.J. 154, 131 A.2d 1 (1957), the court said,

There has been little judicial consideration of the precise attributes of a comprehensive plan. * * * Our own decisions emphasize that its office is to prevent a capricious exercise of the legislative power resulting in haphazard or piecemeal zoning. * * * Without venturing an exact definition, it may be said for present purposes that 'plan' connotes an integrated product of a rational process and 'comprehensive' requires something beyond a piecemeal approach, both to be revealed by the ordinance considered in relation to the physical facts and the purposes authorized by R.S. 40:55-32. Such being the requirements of a comprehensive plan, no reason is perceived why we should infer the Legislature intended by necessary implication that the comprehensive plan be portrayed in some physical form outside the ordinance itself. A plan may readily be revealed in an end-product—here the zoning ordinance—and no more is required by the statute.

Absent a clear legislative mandate to the contrary, most courts have pretty much accepted the *Kozesnik* notion that "the comprehensive plan * * * may readily be revealed in * * * the zoning ordinance" itself.

4. Most state courts have accepted the view that local government units need not adopt a formal "master plan" as a prerequisite to enactment of a valid zoning ordinance, and that the "comprehensive plan" required by the zoning enabling acts need not exist in some physical form outside the zoning ordinance itself. However, a few courts have held that in the absence of a "separate and distinct" comprehensive plan—although no such plan is legally required—the presumption of validity usually accorded to zoning amendments is weakened. E.g., Forestview Homeowners Association v. County of Cook, 18 Ill.App.3d 230, 309 N.E.2d 763 (1974); Raabe v. City of Walker, 383 Mich. 165, 174 N.W.2d 789 (1970) (plan prepared by private organizations "cannot be substituted legally for a * * * master plan"). On the other hand, some courts not only refuse to require zoning consistency with a "separate and distinct" comprehensive plan but also sometimes invalidate rezoning amendments which are consistent with such a plan. E.g., Chapman v. Montgomery County, 259 Md. 641, 271 A.2d 156 (1970), where the court invalidated the rezoning of a 5.8 acre tract in a fast-growing part of the county from a rural residential to a commercial classification although the rezoning was consistent with the county comprehensive plan and was adopted to avoid an alternative not favored by the plan, the expansion of another nearby shopping center. Noting that the comprehensive plan is not to be equated in legal significance with the zoning ordinance, the court said that proof of a substantial growth in population in the neighborhood might justify rezoning to a higher residential density, but not for shopping center development. Such a decision creates obvious difficulties for the planning and zoning process.

5. The consequences of the general failure of courts to equate the zoning "comprehensive plan" with the "master plan" are summarized by Professor Haar as follows: *

> As a result of legislative failure to equate the 'comprehensive plan' of the zoning enabling act with the master plan for land use, courts have found it difficult to assign any independent meaning to the term. It appears constantly in the cases, but usually only as an alternative statement of a basically constitutional test. This situation is unfortunate. With the heavy presumption of constitutional validity that attaches to legislation purportedly under the police power, and the difficulty in judicially applying a 'reasonableness' standard, there is danger that zoning, considered as a self-contained activity rather than as a means to a broader end, may tyrannize individual property owners.
>
> * * * [T]he courts have taken a number of rather different approaches in testing zoning measures for consonance with the enabling act mandate of 'accordance with a comprehensive plan.' None of the meanings suggested—broad geographical coverage, "policy" of the planning or zoning commission, the zoning ordinance itself, the rational basis underlying the ordinance—do extreme violence to the statutory wording. But all of them share a common defect: they emphasize the question whether the zoning ordinance is a comprehensive plan, not whether it is in accordance with a com-

---

* Haar, "In Accordance With a Comprehensive Plan," 68 Harv.L.Rev. 1154, at   1156–1157, 1173 (1955). Copyright, 1955, The Harvard Law Review Association.

prehensive plan. Thus construed, the enabling act demands little more than that zoning be 'reasonable' and impartial in treatment, to satisfy the constitutional conditions for exercise of the state's police power.

6. What is the connection between the zoning enabling act's requirement that zoning regulation shall be "in accordance with a comprehensive plan" and the judicially developed concept of "spot zoning"? The author of a leading treatise on planning and zoning has observed that, while the "comprehensive plan" and "spot zoning" doctrines have developed from different sources, they are now "merely two sides of the same coin"—i.e., if a zoning change is "in accordance with a comprehensive plan" it will not be held invalid as "spot zoning," and if it constitutes "illegal spot zoning" it cannot be "in accordance with a comprehensive plan." See 1 N. Williams, American Land Planning Law § 27.01 (1975). This observation is certainly borne out by the opinions in *Kuehne* and in the next principal case, Rodgers v. Village of Tarrytown. And the cases generally bear out Williams' further contention that rezoning amendments are generally subjected—under either the "comprehensive plan" or the "spot zoning" rubric—to a threefold test: (1) are the uses allowed by the rezoning amendment compatible with the uses permitted in the surrounding area; (2) how large is the parcel that was rezoned; and (3) what was the legislative purpose in rezoning that parcel? Ibid.

RODGERS v. VILLAGE OF TARRYTOWN

New York Court of Appeals, 1951.
302 N.Y. 115, 96 N.E.2d 731.

FULD, Judge. This appeal   *   *   *   involves the validity of two amendments to the General Zoning Ordinance of the Village of Tarrytown, a suburban area in the County of Westchester, within twenty-five miles of New York City.

Some years ago, Tarrytown enacted a General Zoning Ordinance dividing the village into seven districts or zones—Residence A for single family dwellings, Residence B for two-family dwellings, Residence C for multiple dwellings and apartment houses, three business districts and an industrial zone. In 1947 and 1948, the board of trustees, the village's legislative body, passed the two amendatory ordinances here under attack.

The 1947 ordinance creates "A new district or class of zone   *   *   * [to] be called 'Residence B–B'," in which, besides one- and two-family dwellings, buildings for multiple occupancy of fifteen or fewer families were permitted. The boundaries of the new type district were not delineated in the ordinance but were to be "fixed by amendment of the official village building zone map, at such times in the future as such district or class of zone is applied to properties in this village." The village planning board was empowered to approve such amendments and, in case such approval was withheld, the board of trustees was authorized to grant it by appropriate resolution. In addition, the ordinance erected exacting standards of size and physical layouts for Residence B–B zones: a minimum of ten acres of land and a maximum building height of three stories were mandated; set-back and spacing requirements for structures were carefully prescribed; and no more than 15% of the ground area of the plot was to be occupied by buildings.

A year and a half after the 1947 amendment was enacted, defendant Elizabeth Rubin sought to have her property, consisting of about ten and a half acres in the Residence A district, placed in a Residence B–B classification. After repeated modification of her plans to meet suggestions of the village planning board, that body gave its approval, and, several months later, in December of 1948, the board of trustees, also approving, passed the second ordinance here under attack. In essence, it provides that the Residence B–B district "is hereby applied to the [Rubin] property   *   *   *   and the district or zone of said property is hereby changed to 'Residence B–B' and the official Building Zone Map of the Village of Tarrytown is hereby amended accordingly [by specifications of the various parcels involved]."

Plaintiff, who owns a residence on a six-acre plot about a hundred yards from Rubin's property, brought this action to have the two amendments declared invalid and to enjoin defendant Rubin from constructing multiple dwellings on her property. The courts below, adjudging the amendments valid and the action of the trustees proper, dismissed the complaint. We agree with their determinations.

While stability and regularity are undoubtedly essential to the operation of zoning plans, zoning is by no means static. Changed or changing conditions call for changed plans, and persons who own property in a particular zone or use district enjoy no eternally vested right to that classification if the public interest demands otherwise. Accordingly, the power of a village to amend its basic zoning ordinance in such a way as reasonably to promote the general welfare cannot be questioned. Just as clearly, decision as to how a community shall be zoned or rezoned, as to how various properties shall be classified or reclassified, rests with the local legislative body; its judgment and determination will be conclusive, beyond interference from the courts, unless shown to be arbitrary, and the burden of establishing such arbitrariness is imposed upon him who asserts it.   *   *   *

By that test, the propriety of the decision here made is not even debatable. In other words, viewing the rezoning in the case before us, as it must be viewed, in the light of the area involved and the present and reasonably foreseeable needs of the community, the conclusion is inescapable that what was done not only accorded with sound zoning principles, not only complied with every requirement of law, but was accomplished in a proper, careful and reasonable manner.

The Tarrytown board of trustees was entitled to find that there was a real need for additional housing facilities; that the creation of Residence B–B districts for garden apartment developments would prevent young families, unable to find accommodations in the village, from moving elsewhere; would attract business to the community; would lighten the tax load of the small home owner, increasingly burdened by the shrinkage of tax revenues resulting from the depreciated value of large estates and the transfer of many such estates to tax-exempt institutions; and would develop otherwise unmarketable and decaying property.

The village's zoning aim being clear, the choice of methods to accomplish it lay with the board. Two such methods were at hand. It could amend the General Zoning Ordinance so as to permit garden apartments on any plot of ten acres or more in Residence A and B zones (the zones more restricted) or it could amend that Ordinance so as to invite owners of ten or more acres, who wished to build garden apartments on their properties, to apply for a Residence B–B classification. The board chose to adopt the latter procedure. That it called for separate legislative authorization for each project presents no obstacle or drawback— and so we have already held. * * *

Nor did the board, by following the course which it did, divest itself or the planning board of power to regulate future zoning with regard to garden apartments. The mere circumstance that an owner possesses a ten-acre plot and submits plans conforming to the 1947 amendment will not entitle him, *ipso facto*, to a Residence B–B classification. It will still be for the board to decide, in the exercise of a reasonable discretion, that the *grant* of such a classification accords with the comprehensive zoning plan and benefits the village as a whole. And—while no such question is here presented—we note that the board may not arbitrarily or unreasonably *deny* applications of other owners for permission to construct garden apartments on their properties. The action of the board must in all cases be reasonable and, whether a particular application be granted or denied, recourse may be had to the courts to correct an arbitrary or capricious determination. * * *

The charge of illegal "spot zoning"—levelled at the creation of a Residence B–B district and the reclassification of defendant's property—is without substance. Defined as the process of singling out a small parcel of land for a use classification totally different from that of the surrounding area, for the benefit of the owner of such property and to the detriment of other owners * * * "spot zoning" is the very antithesis of planned zoning. If, therefore, an ordinance is enacted in accordance with a comprehensive zoning plan, it is not "spot zoning," even though it (1) singles out and affects but one small plot * * *, or (2) creates in the center of a large zone small areas or districts devoted to a different use. * * * Thus, the relevant inquiry is not whether the particular zoning under attack consists of areas fixed within larger areas of different use, but whether it was accomplished for the benefit of individual owners rather than pursuant to a comprehensive plan for the general welfare of the community. Having already noted our conclusion that the ordinances were enacted to promote a comprehensive zoning plan, it is perhaps unnecessary to add that the record negates any claim that they were designed solely for the advantage of defendant or any other particular owner. Quite apart from the circumstance that defendant did not seek the benefit of the 1947 amendment until eighteen months after its passage, the all-significant fact is that that amendment applied to the entire territory of the village and accorded each and every owner of ten or more acres identical rights and privileges. * * *

By the same token, there is no basis for the argument that "what has been done by the board of trustees" constitutes a device for "the granting of a 'variance'", opinion of Conway, J., 302 N.Y. p. 129, 96 N.E.2d 738. As we have already shown, the village's zoning aim, the statute's purpose, was not to aid the individual owner but to permit the development of the property for the general welfare of the entire community. That being so, the board of trustees followed approved procedure by changing the General Zoning Ordinance itself. * * * Accordingly, when the board was called upon to consider the reclassification of the Rubin property under the 1947 amendment, it was concerned, not with any issue of hardship, but only with the question of whether the property constituted a desirable location for a garden apartment.

We turn finally to the contention that the 1947 ordinance is invalid because, in proclaiming a Residence B–B district, it set no boundaries for the new district and made no changes on the building zone map. The short answer is that, since the ordinance merely prescribed specifications for a new use district, there was no need for it to do either the one or the other. True, until boundaries are fixed and until zoning map changes are made, no new zone actually comes into being, and neither property nor the rights of any property owner are affected. But it was not the design of the board of trustees by that enactment to bring any additional zone into being or to affect any property or rights; the ordinance merely provided the mechanics pursuant to which property owners might in the future apply for the redistricting of their property. In sum, the 1947 amendment was merely the first step in a reasoned plan of rezoning, and specifically provided for further action on the part of the board. That action was taken by the passage of the 1948 ordinance which fixed the boundaries of the newly created zone and amended the zoning map accordingly. It is indisputable that the two amendments, read together as they must be, fully complied with the requirements of the Village Law and accomplished a rezoning of village property in an unexceptionable manner.

In point of fact, there would have been no question about the validity of what was done had the board simply amended the General Zoning Ordinance so as to permit property in Residence A and Residence B zones—or, for that matter, in the other districts throughout the village—to be used for garden apartments, provided that they were built on ten-acre plots and that the other carefully planned conditions and restrictions were met. It may be conceded that, under the method which the board did adopt, no one will know, from the 1947 ordinance itself, precisely where a Residence B–B district will ultimately be located. But since such a district is simply a garden apartment development, we find nothing unusual or improper in that circumstance. The same uncertainty—as to the location of the various types of structures—would be present if a zoning ordinance were to sanction garden apartments as well as one-family homes in a Residence A district—and yet there would be no doubt as to the propriety of that procedure. * * * Consequently, to condemn the action taken by the board in effectuating a perfectly permissible zoning scheme and to strike down the ordinance designed to carry out that scheme merely because the board had employed two steps to accomplish what may be, and usually is, done in one, would be to exalt form over substance and sacrifice substance to form.

Whether it is generally desirable that garden apartments be freely mingled among private residences under all circumstances, may be arguable. In view, however, of Tarrytown's changing scene and the other substantial reasons for the board's decision, we cannot say that its action was arbitrary or illegal. While hardships may be imposed on this or that owner "cardinal is the principle that what is best for the body politic in the long run must prevail over the interests of particular individuals." Shepard v. Village of Skaneateles, * * * 300 N.Y. 115, 118, 89 N.E.2d 619, 620.

Notes and Questions

1. What advantage was there, from the point of view of Tarrytown, in using the "floating zone" amendment technique to introduce garden apartments into the village instead of simply amending the General Zoning Ordinance "so as to permit property in Residence A and Residence B zones—or, for that matter, in the other districts throughout the village—to be used for garden apartments, provided that they were built on ten-acre plots and that the other carefully planned conditions and restrictions were met"? The court may have supplied a partial answer when it said: "The mere circumstance that an owner possesses a ten-acre plot and submits plans conforming to the physical requirements prescribed by the 1947 amendment will not entitle him, *ipso facto*, to a Residence B–B classification. It will still be for the [planning] board to decide, in the exercise of a reasonable discretion, that the *grant* of such a classification accords with the comprehensive zoning plan and benefits the village as a whole." But what standards are to guide the "exercise of a reasonable discretion"? Is it enough to say, as the New York court did, that "the board may not arbitrarily or unreasonably *deny* applications of other owners for permission to construct garden apartments on their properties"?

It would appear that Tarrytown adopted the "floating zone" amendment technique, at least in part, to avoid the inevitable charge of illegal "spot zoning" if it should simply rezone individual tracts of land, upon application by landowners, so as to permit garden apartment development, without having previously established "specifications for a new use district."

2. Ordinances similar to the Tarrytown "floating zone" ordinance have been sustained in Connecticut. Miss Porter's School, Inc. v. Town Plan and Zoning Commission, 151 Conn. 425, 198 A.2d 707 (1964) (apartments); DeMeo v. Zoning Commission, 148 Conn. 68, 167 A.2d 454 (1961) (garden apartments); Clark v. Town Council, 145 Conn. 476, 144 A.2d 327 (1958) (shopping center). In Maryland an ordinance creating a kind of hybrid of the "floating zone" amendment and the "special exception" was sustained in Huff v. Board of Zoning Appeals, 214 Md. 48, 133 A.2d 83 (1957) (light manufacturing zone; decision to rezone was made by the zoning commissioner on recommendation of the planning commission, and his decision was reviewable by the board of zoning appeals). In Beall v. Montgomery County Council, 240 Md. 77, 212 A.2d 751 (1965), the Maryland court sustained the county council in rezoning 41.6 acres of land from single-family to multi-family high-rise residential use (R–H). Prior to the application for rezoning of the tract, the county council had created the

R-H classification as a "floating zone" to provide suitable sites for high density housing and to allow numerous types of commercial, recreational, and educational uses within the zone. The court held that no evidence of original mistake or changed conditions was required to justify rezoning of the tract to the new R-H classification "in view of the conclusion of the Technical Staff, adopted by the Planning Commission and the Council, that the application complied with the purposes of the R-H zone   *   *   *."

The American Law Institute's Model Land Development Code § 2–312(1)(c) (1976) authorizes "development by a special amendment   *   *   *   that permits development specified in a previously adopted ordinance as permissible upon stated criteria after approval by the local governing body." The Reporter's Note explains that this "covers what has been called 'floating zoning,' in which the ordinance provides somewhat flexible regulations for an unmapped zone, and performance standards determine whether a remapping amendment will be adopted. This is substantially the same as a special permission ordinance, except that final determination is left to the legislature rather than the [land development] agency."

3. The leading case disapproving the "floating zone" amendment technique is Eves v. Zoning Board, 401 Pa. 211, 164 A.2d 7 (1960). In that case Lower Gwynedd Township had created a "floating" limited industrial district. Detailed site development requirements were included for the new district, which could be located anywhere in the township on application and approval by the local governing body. The Pennsylvania court held, in part, that the "floating zone" amendment technique was unauthorized by the zoning enabling act, and that "the township supervisors have gone beyond their function of implementing a comprehensive plan with zoning regulations." Only the township board of appeals, said the court, was authorized to allow "deviations" from the zoning regulations, and then only through the "variance" or "special exception" procedure. The court's major objection to the "floating zone" amendment technique was stated as follows:

> Under the "flexible selective zoning" scheme here under attack, changes in the prevailing zoning regulations are to be made on a case by case basis, *   *   *   by the legislative body, without rigid statutory standards and without any scintilla of notice of potential change as in the case of special exceptions.   *   *   *   If the legislature contemplated such a novel scheme of zoning,   *   *   *   we are convinced it would have said so.   *   *   *

401 Pa. at 219–221, 164 A.2d at 12.

Eves has now been substantially qualified if not overruled by statutory changes and subsequent judicial decisions in Pennsylvania. See Donahue v. Zoning Bd. of Adjustment, 412 Pa. 332, 194 A.2d 610 (1963) ("floating zone" valid if land is actually rezoned to the new classification shortly after the "floating zone" is created); Raum v. Board of Supervisors, 20 Pa.Cmwlth. 426, 342 A.2d 450 (1975) (approving "floating zone" provision and distinguishing *Eves* on ground that adequate standards were not provided.) See also Pa.Stat. Ann. tit. 53, § 10603 (1972), authorizing the governing body to approve "conditional uses" after recommendation by the planning commission, and construed as overruling *Eves* in Russell v. Pennsylvania Township Planning Comm., 22 Pa.Cmwlth. 198, 348 A.2d 499 (Pa.Com.1975).

4. Can you see any advantage in the "floating zone" amendment technique as against the "special exception" technique as a means for "flexible" zoning? Or vice versa? Surely the "special exception" technique does not, as the court stated in *Eves*, give any greater advance notice to landowners of the possible intrusion of a new use in an area previously restricted against such use. Nor is

the expertise of the zoning board of adjustment, which normally administers the "special exception" procedure, likely to be greater than the combined expertise of the planning board and the local governing body, which usually administer the "floating zone" procedure. And it is hard to see how the standards generally held sufficient to guide the exercise of administrative discretion in "special exception" cases are really more definite than the statutory standards which govern the amending process. Moreover, the "floating zone" procedure results in a change of the zoning map to reflect the change in classification, while the "special exception" procedure does not.

5. The *Rodgers* opinion says that "[c]hanged or changing conditions call for changed plans, and persons who own property in a particular zone or use district enjoy no eternally vested right to that classification if the public interest demands otherwise." In fact, there is emphasis on "changed conditions" as a justification for rezoning amendments in many cases—cases involving "straight" rezoning amendments as well as "floating zones." It is clear that the Connecticut court gave substantial weight to the "changed conditions" mentioned in Bartram v. Zoning Commission, cited and quoted with approval in the *Kuehne* case, ante. See also Zoning Commission of Town of New Canaan v. New Canaan Building Co., 146 Conn. 170, 148 A.2d 330 (1969), where the court invalidated a zoning amendment placing property which had been in an apartment house zone for fifteen years in a single-family residence zone. Emphasizing that an essential purpose of zoning is to stabilize land uses and land values, the court said,

> * * * There is nothing in the finding to indicate a change in the character of the neighborhood which would warrant a reclassification of the area. * * * Before a zoning board rezones property, there should be proof either that there was some mistake in the original zoning or that the character of the neighborhood has changed to such an extent that a reclassification ought properly to be made. * * * Those who buy property in a zoned district have the right to expect that the classification made in the ordinance will not be changed unless a change is required for the public good.

The "change or mistake" rule laid down in *New Canaan* case has often been applied in "spot zoning" cases, and has the effect of reversing the usual presumption of validity that applies to zoning ordinances. The "change or mistake" doctrine has been applied most rigorously in Maryland, but even in Maryland the rule is not applied where the local government has enacted a comprehensive revision of a zoning ordinance or has replaced it with a entirely new ordinance. The "change or mistake" rule was expressly rejected in Levitt v. Village of Sands Point, 6 App.Div.2d 701, 174 N.Y.S.2d 283 (1958), and in Oka v. Cole, 145 So.2d 233 (Fla.1962). And in the next principal case, Fasano v. Bd. of County Commissioners, the court rejects any implication that it had previously (in Roseta v. Washington County) adopted the "change or mistake" rule.

FASANO v. BOARD OF COUNTY COMMISSIONERS OF WASHINGTON COUNTY

Supreme Court of Oregon, 1973.
264 Or. 574, 507 P.2d 23.

HOWELL, J. The plaintiffs, homeowners in Washington county, unsuccessfully opposed a zone change before the Board of County Commissioners of Washington County. Plaintiffs applied for and received a writ of review of the action of the commissioners allowing the change. The trial court found in favor of plaintiffs, disallowed the zone change, and reversed the commissioners' order. The Court of Appeals affirmed, 7 Or.App. 176, 489 P.2d 693 (1971), and this court granted review.

The defendants are the Board of County Commissioners and A.G.S. Development Company. A.G.S., the owner of 32 acres which had been zoned R–7 (Single Family Residential), applied for a zone change to P–R (Planned Residential), which allows for the construction of a mobile home park. The change failed to receive a majority vote of the Planning Commission. The Board of County Commissioners approved the change and found, among other matters, that the change allows for "increased densities and different types of housing to meet the needs of urbanization over that allowed by the existing zoning."

The trial court, relying on its interpretation of Roseta v. County of Washington, 254 Or. 161, 458 P.2d 405, 40 A.L.R.3d 364 (1969), reversed the order of the commissioners because the commissioners had not shown any change in the character of the neighborhood which would justify the rezoning. The Court of Appeals affirmed for the same reason, but added the additional ground that the defendants failed to show that the change was consistent with the comprenhensive plan for Washington county.

According to the briefs, the comprehensive plan of development for Washington county was adopted in 1959 and included classifications in the county for residential, neighborhood commercial, retail commercial, general commercial, industrial park and light industry, general and heavy industry, and agricultural areas.

The land in question, which was designated "residential" by the comprehensive plan, was zoned R–7, Single Family Residential.

Subsequent to the time the comprehensive plan was adopted, Washington county established a Planned Residential (P–R) zoning classification in 1963. The P–R classification was adopted by ordinance and provided that a planned residential unit development could be established and should include open space for utilities, access, and recreation; should not be less than 10 acres in size; and should be located in or adjacent to a residential zone. The P–R zone adopted by the 1963 ordinance is of the type known as a "floating zone," so-called because the ordinance creates a zone classification authorized for future use but not placed on the zoning map until its use at a particular location is approved by the governing body. The R–7 classification for the 32 acres continued until April 1970 when the classification was changed to P–R to permit the defendant A.G.S. to construct the mobile home park on the 32 acres involved.

The defendants argue that (1) the action of the county commissioners approving the change is presumptively valid, requiring plaintiffs to show that the commissioners acted arbitrarily in approving the zone change; (2) it was not necessary to show a change of conditions in the area before a zone change could be accomplished; and (3) the change from R–7 to P–R was in accordance with the Washington county comprehensive plan.

We granted review in this case to consider the questions—by what standards does a county commission exercise its authority to zoning matters; who has the burden of meeting those standards when a request for change of zone is made; and what is the scope of court review of such actions?

Any meaningful decision as to the proper scope of judicial review of a zoning decision must start with the characterization of the nature of that decision. The majority of jurisdictions state that a zoning ordinance is a legislative act and is thereby entitled to presumptive validity. This court made such a characterization of zoning decisions in Smith v. County of Washington, 241 Or. 380, 406 P.2d 545 (1965):

"Inasmuch as ORS 215.110 specifically grants to the governing board of the county the power to amend zoning ordinances, a challenged amendment is a legislative act and is clothed with a presumption in its favor. Jehovah's Witnesses v. Mullen et al, 214 Or. 281, 292, 330 P.2d 5, 74 A.L.R.2d 347 (1958), appeal dismissed and cert. denied, 359 U.S. 436, 79 S.Ct. 940, 3 L.Ed.2d 932 (1959)." 241 Or. at 383, 406 P.2d at 547.

However, in *Smith* an exception to the presumption was found and the zoning held invalid. Furthermore, the case cited by the *Smith* court, Jehovah's Witnesses v. Mullen et al, supra, at least at one point viewed the contested zoning in that case as an administrative as opposed to legislative act.

At this juncture we feel we would be ignoring reality to rigidly view all zoning decisions by local governing bodies as legislative acts to be accorded a full presumption of validity and shielded from less than constitutional scrutiny by the theory of separation of powers. Local and small decision groups are simply not the equivalent in all respects of state and national legislatures. There is a growing judicial recognition of this fact of life:

"It is not a part of the legislative function to grant permits, make special exceptions, or decide particular cases. Such activities are not legislative but administrative, quasi-judicial, or judicial in character. To place them in the hands of legislative bodies, whose acts as such are not judicially reviewable, is to open the door completely to arbitrary government." Ward v. Village of Skokie, 26 Ill.2d 415, 186 N.E.2d 529, 533 (1962) (Klingbiel, J., specially concurring).

The Supreme Court of Washington, in reviewing a rezoning decision, recently stated:

"Whatever descriptive characterization may be otherwise attached to the role or function of the planning commission in zoning procedures, e.g., advisory, recommendatory, investigatory, administrative or legislative, it is manifest *   *   * that it is a public agency, *   *   * a principle [sic] and statutory duty of which is to conduct public hearings in specified planning and zoning matters, enter findings of fact—often on the basis of disputed facts—and make recommendations with reasons assigned thereto. Certainly, in its role as a hearing and fact-finding tribunal, the planning commission's function more nearly than not partakes of the nature of an administrative, quasi-judicial proceeding, *   *   *."

Chrobuck v. Snohomish County, 78 Wash.2d 884, 480 P.2d 489, 495–96 (1971).

Ordinances laying down general policies without regard to a specific piece of property are usually an exercise of legislative authority, are subject to limited review, and may only be attacked upon constitutional grounds for an arbitrary abuse of authority. On the other hand, a determination whether the permissible use of a specific piece of property should be changed is usually an exercise of judicial authority and its propriety is subject to an altogether different test. An illustration of an exercise of legislative authority is the passage of the ordinance by the Washington County Commission in 1963 which provided for the formation of a planned residential classification to be located in or adjacent to any residential zone. An exercise of judicial authority is the county commissioners' determination in this particular matter to change the classification of A.G.S. Development Company's specific piece of property. The distinction is stated, as follows, in Comment, Zoning Amendments—The Product of Judicial or Quasi-Judicial Action, 33 Ohio St.L.J. 130 (1972):

" * * * Basically, this test involves the determination of whether action produces a general rule or policy which is applicable to an open class of individuals, interest, or situations, or whether it entails the application of a general rule or policy to specific individuals, interests, or situations. If the former determination is satisfied, there is legislative action; if the latter determination is satisfied, the action is judicial." 33 Ohio St.L.J. at 137.

1. We reject the proposition that judicial review of the county commissioners' determination to change the zoning of the particular property in question is limited to a determination whether the change was arbitrary and capricious.

In order to establish a standard of review, it is necessary to delineate certain basic principles relating to land use regulation.

The basic instrument for county or municipal land use planning is the "comprehensive plan." Haar, In Accordance with a Comprehensive Plan, 68 Harv.L.Rev. 1154 (1955); 1 Yokley, Zoning Law and Practice, § 3–2 (1965); 1 Rathkopf, The Law of Zoning and Planning, § 9–1 (3d ed. 1969). The plan has been described as a general plan to control and direct the use and development of property in a municipality. Nowicki v. Planning and Zoning Board, 148 Conn. 492, 172 A.2d 386, 389 (1961).

2. In Oregon the county planning commission is required by ORS 215.050 to adopt a comprehensive plan for the use of some or all of the land in the county. Under ORS 215.110(1), after the comprehensive plan has been adopted, the planning commission recommends to the governing body of the county the ordinances necessary to "carry out" the comprehensive plan. The purpose of the zoning ordinances, both under our statute and the general law of land use regulation, is to "carry out" or implement the comprehensive plan. 1 Anderson, American Law of Zoning, § 1.12 (1968). Although we are aware of the analytical distinction between zoning and planning, it is clear that under our stat-

utes the plan adopted by the planning commission and the zoning ordinances enacted by the county governing body are closely related; both are intended to be parts of a single integrated procedure for land use control. The plan embodies policy determinations and guiding principles; the zoning ordinances provide the detailed means of giving effect to those principles.

ORS 215.050 states county planning commissions "shall adopt and may from time to time revise a comprehensive plan." In a hearing of the Senate Committee on Local Government, the proponents of ORS 215.050 described its purpose as follows:

" * * * The intent here is to require a basic document, geared into population, land use, and economic forecasts, which should be the basis of any zoning or other regulations to be adopted by the county. * * * "[3]

In addition, ORS 215.055 provides:

"215.055 Standards for plan. (1) The plan and all legislation and regulations authorized by ORS 215.010 to 215.233 shall be designed to promote the public health, safety and general welfare and shall be based on the following considerations, among others: The various characteristics of the various areas in the county, the suitability of the areas for particular land uses and improvements, the land uses and improvements in the areas, trends in land improvement, density of development, property values, the needs of economic enterprises in the future development of the areas, needed access to particular sites in the areas, natural resources of the county and prospective needs for development thereof, and the public need for healthful, safe, aesthetic surroundings and conditions."

3. We believe that the state legislature has conditioned the county's power to zone upon the prerequisite that the zoning attempt to further the general welfare of the community through consciousness, in a prospective sense, of the factors mentioned above. In other words, except as noted later in this opinion, it must be proved that the change is in conformance with the comprehensive plan.

4. In proving that the change is in conformance with the comprehensive plan in this case, the proof, at a minimum, should show (1) there is a public need for a change of the kind in question, and (2) that need will be best served by changing the classification of the particular piece of property in question as compared with other available property.

In the instant case the trial court and the Court of Appeals interpreted prior decisions of this court as requiring the county commissions to show a change of conditions within the immediate neighborhood in which the change was sought since the enactment of the comprehensive plan, or a mistake in the comprehensive plan as a condition precedent to the zone change.

In Smith v. Washington County, supra, the land in question was designated residential under the comprehensive plan, and the county com-

3. Hearing on Senate Bill 129 before the Senate Committee on Local Government, 52nd Legislative Assembly, February 14, 1963.

missioners enacted an amendatory ordinance changing the classification to manufacturing. This court held that the change constituted spot zoning and was invalid. We stated:

" * * * Once a [zoning scheme] is adopted, changes in it should be made only when such changes are consistent with the over-all objectives of the plan *and in keeping with changes in the character of the area or neighborhood to be covered thereby.* * * * (Emphasis added) 241 Or. at 384, 406 P.2d at 547.

In Roseta v. Washington County, supra, the land in question was classified as residential under the comprehensive plan and had been originally zoned as R–10, Single Family Residential. The county commissioners granted a zone change to A–1, Duplex Residential. We held that the commissioners had not sustained the burden of proving that the change was consistent with the comprehensive plan and reversed the order allowing the zone change. In regard to defendants' argument that the change was consistent with the comprehensive plan because the plan designated the areas as "residential" and the term included both single family dwellings and duplex residences, we stated:

" * * * However, the ordinance established a distinction between the two types of use by classifying one area as R–10 and another area as A–1. It must be assumed that the Board had some purpose in making a distinction between these two classifications. It was for defendant to prove that this distinction was not valid or that the change in the character of the use of the * * * parcel was not inconsistent with the comprehensive plan." 254 Or. at 169, 458 P.2d 405, at 409.

The instant case should be distinguished from *Roseta* on the basis that we are involved with a floating zone which was not before the court in *Roseta.*[4]

5. However, *Roseta* should not be interpreted as establishing a rule that a physical change of circumstances within the rezoned neighborhood is the only justification for rezoning. The county governing body is directed by ORS 215.055 to consider a number of other factors when enacting zoning ordinances, and the list there does not purport to be exclusive. The important issues, as *Roseta* recognized, are compliance with the statutory directive and consideration of the proposed change in light of the comprehensive plan.

6, 7. Because the action of the commission in this instance is an exercise of judicial authority, the burden of proof should be placed, as is usual in judicial proceedings, upon the one seeking change. The more drastic the change, the greater will be the burden of showing that it is

4. Even in Maryland, the chief exponent of the change or mistake rule, the courts have not required that there be a showing of changed conditions or mistake in the original zoning as a condition precedent to granting a zone change when a floating zone is involved. Bigenho v. Montgomery County Council, 248 Md. 386, 237 A.2d 53 (1968); Bayer v. Siskind, 247 Md. 116, 230 A.2d 316 (1967); Board of County Com'rs of Howard County v. Tip-

ton, 244 Md. 77, 222 A.2d 701 (1966); Bujno v. Montgomery County Council, 243 Md. 110, 220 A.2d 126 (1966); Knudsen v. Montgomery County Council, 241 Md. 436, 217 A.2d 97 (1966); Beall v. Montgomery County Council, 240 Md. 77, 212 A.2d 751 (1965); Huff v. Board of Zoning Appeals, 214 Md. 48, 133 A.2d 83 (1957).

[The "floating zone" amendment technique is considered supra at p. 1281.]

in conformance with the comprehensive plan as implemented by the ordinance, that there is a public need for the kind of change in question, and that the need is best met by the proposal under consideration. As the degree of change increases, the burden of showing that the potential impact upon the area in question was carefully considered and weighed will also increase. If other areas have previously been designated for the particular type of development, it must be shown why it is necessary to introduce it into an area not previously contemplated and why the property owners there should bear the burden of the departure.[5]

8. Although we have said in *Roseta* that zoning changes may be justified without a showing of a mistake in the original plan or ordinance, or of changes in the physical characteristics of an affected area, any of these factors which are present in a particular case would, of course, be relevant. Their importance would depend upon the nature of the precise change under consideration.

By treating the exercise of authority by the commission in this case as the exercise of judicial rather than of legislative authority and thus enlarging the scope of review on appeal, and by placing the burden of the above level of proof upon the one seeking change, we may lay the court open to criticism by legal scholars who think it desirable that planning authorities be vested with the ability to adjust more freely to changed conditions. However, having weighed the dangers of making desirable change more difficult against the dangers of the almost irresistible pressures that can be asserted by private economic interests on local government, we believe that the latter dangers are more to be feared.

5. For example, if an area is designated by the plan as generally appropriate for residential development, the plan may also indicate that some high-density residential development within the area is to be anticipated, without specifying the exact location at which that development is to take place. The comprehensive plan might provide that its goal for residential development is to assure that residential areas are healthful, pleasant and safe places in which to live. The plan might also list the following policies which, among others, are to be pursued in achieving that goal:

1. High-density residential areas should be located close to the urban core area.

2. Residential neighborhoods should be protected from any land use activity involving an excessive level of noise, pollution or traffic volume.

3. High trip-generating multiple family units should have ready access to arterial or collector streets.

4. A variety of living areas and housing types should be provided appropriate to the needs of the special and general groups they are to serve.

5. Residential development at urban densities should be within planned sewer and water service areas and where other utilities can be adequately provided.

Under such a hypothetical plan, property originally zoned for single family dwellings might later be rezoned for duplexes, for garden apartments, or for high-rise apartment buildings. Each of these changes could be shown to be consistent with the plan. Although in addition we would require a showing that the county governing body found a bona fide need for a zone change in order to accommodate new high-density development which at least balanced the disruption shown by the challengers, that requirement would be met in most instances by a record which disclosed that the governing body had considered the facts relevant to this question and exercised its judgment in good faith. However, these changes, while all could be shown to be consistent with the plan, could be expected to have differing impacts on the surrounding area, depending on the nature of that area. As the potential impact on the area in question increases, so will the necessity to show a justification.

9. What we have said above is necessarily general, as the approach we adopt contains no absolute standards or mechanical tests. We believe, however, that it is adequate to provide meaningful guidance for local governments making zoning decisions and for trial courts called upon to review them. With future cases in mind, it is appropriate to add some brief remarks on questions of procedure. Parties at the hearing before the county governing body are entitled to an opportunity to be heard, to an opportunity to present and rebut evidence, to a tribunal which is impartial in the matter—i.e., having had no pre-hearing or ex parte contacts concerning the question at issue—and to a record made and adequate findings executed. Comment, Zoning Amendments—The Product of Judicial or Quasi-Judicial Action, 33 Ohio St.L.J. 130–143 (1972)

10, 11. When we apply the standards we have adopted to the present case, we find that the burden was not sustained before the commission. The record now before us is insufficient to ascertain whether there was a justifiable basis for the decision. The only evidence in the record, that of the staff report of the Washington County Planning Department, is too conclusory and superficial to support the zoning change. It merely states:

> "The staff finds that the requested use does conform to the residential designation of the Plan of Development. It further finds that the proposed use reflects the urbanization of the County and the necessity to provide increased densities and different types of housing to meet the needs of urbanization over that allowed by the existing zoning. * * * "

Such generalizations and conclusions, without any statement of the facts on which they are based, are insufficient to justify a change of use. Moreover, no portions of the comprehensive plan of Washington County are before us, and we feel it would be improper for us to take judicial notice of the plan without at least some reference to its specifics by counsel.

As there has not been an adequate showing that the change was in accord with the plan, or that the factors listed in ORS 215.055 were given proper consideration, the judgment is affirmed.

BRYSON, J., specially concurring.

The basic facts in this case exemplify the prohibitive cost and extended uncertainty to a homeowner when a governmental body decides to change or modify a zoning ordinance or comprehensive plan affecting such owner's real property.

This controversy has proceeded through the following steps:

1. The respondent opposed the zone change before the Washington County Planning Department and Planning Commission.

2. The County Commission, after a hearing, allowed the change.

3. The trial court reversed (disallowed the change).

4. The Court of Appeals affirmed the trial court.

5. We ordered reargument and additional briefs.

6. This court affirmed.

The principal respondent in this case, Fasano, happens to be an attorney at law, and his residence is near the proposed mobile home park of the petitioner A.G.S. No average homeowner or small business enterprise can afford a judicial process such as described above nor can a judicial system cope with or endure such a process in achieving justice. The number of such controversies is ascending.

In this case the majority opinion, in which I concur, adopts some sound rules to enable county and municipal planning commissions and governing bodies, as well as trial courts, to reach finality in decision. However, the procedure is no panacea and it is still burdensome.

It is solely within the domain of the legislative branch of government to devise a new and simplified statutory procedure to expedite finality of decision.

Notes

1. Although *Fasano* deals with a "floating zone" amendment to establish a "planned residential unit development," it has been treated in later Oregon cases as establishing a rule applicable to all amendments rezoning individual parcels of land. Treatment of the rezoning amendment in *Fasano* as "judicial" rather than "legislative" in nature made inevitable the court's rejection of the traditionally strong presumption of validity attaching to rezoning amendments considered as "legislative" acts. *Fasano* also made untenable the Oregon court's earlier holding, in Archdiocese of Portland v. County of Washington, 254 Or. 77, 458 P.2d 682 (1969), that the granting of a "conditional use permit" by the county governing body was a "legislative" act entitled to the usual strong presumption of validity. See Krisetensen v. City of Eugene Planning Commission, 24 Or.App. 131, 544 P.2d 591 (1976).

2. A 1974 survey by the Oregon Local Government Relations Division of the Executive Department of six counties and twelve cities disclosed that all had adopted comprehensive plans and zoning ordinances and were seeking to comply with the *Fasano* procedural requirements for rezoning amendments. Larger urban areas, like Eugene, Portland, and Washington County had adopted formal, rather legalistic, rules based on an opinion of the Oregon Attorney General issued in 1974. (Or., Att'y Gen.Op. No. 7062.) In Eugene and Portland, the city councils had shifted responsibility for rezoning hearings from the planning commission to a hearing examiner. This was expressly authorized by 1973 legislation stemming from *Fasano*. See Or.Rev.Stat. §§ 215.406 (for counties) and 227.165 (for cities) (1975). Other Oregon counties and cities with a large enough volume of rezoning applications were also considering shifting to the use of hearings examiners. The hearing examiner's jurisdiction in Eugene and Portland extends to rezoning amendments, special exceptions or special use permits, zoning variances, subdivision and site plan approvals, and appeals from decisions of the building inspector, in effect taking the place of both the zoning board of adjustment (or appeals) and the planning commission (or board). "The arguments made in behalf of the system include greater efficiency in the conduct of the hearing, elimination of legislative whim and caprice, greater consistency and uniformity of application of zoning laws and general plans, more time for the governing body to deal with broad land use questions, more narrowing of the key issues, promotion of the conduct of quasi-judicial

hearings such as preparation of findings of fact and conclusions of law." Curtin & Shirk, Land Use, Planning and Zoning, 9 Urban Law. 724, 740 (1977).

3. The *Fasano* doctrine has been adopted in a number of states. See Golden v. City of Overland Park, 224 Kan. 591, 584 P.2d 130 (1978); Lowe v. City of Missoula, 165 Mont. 38, 525 P.2d 551 (1974); Parkridge v. City of Seattle, 89 Wn.2d 454, 573 P.2d 359 (1978). In some of these cases the *Fasano* doctrine was applied to denials of rezoning applications rather than to approvals. The *Fasano* doctrine has been rejected in a number of states, however. See Wait v. City of Scottsdale, 127 Ariz. 107, 618 P.2d 601 (1980); Arnel Development Co. v. City of Costa Mesa, 28 Cal.3d 511, 169 Cal.Rptr. 904, 620 P.2d 565 (1980); Hall Paving Co. v. Hall County, 237 Ga. 14, 226 S.E.2d 728 (1976); Pemberton v. Montgomery County, 275 Md. 363, 340 A.2d 240 (1975); Kirk v. Tyrone Township, 398 Mich. 429, 247 N.W.2d 848 (1976); State v. City of Rochester, 268 N.W.2d 885 (Minn.1978). Cal.Gov.Code § 65301.5 (West 1983) now provides expressly that adoption of a rezoning amendment is a "legislative" act.

Colorado initially adopted the *Fasano* doctrine. Snyder v. City of Lakewood, 189 Colo. 421, 542 P.2d 371 (1975). Recently, however, *Snyder* has either been overruled or substantially modified by three companion cases, Margolis v. District Court, Wright v. City of Lakewood, and Yanz v. City of Arvada, all reported in 638 P.2d 297 (Colo.1981). In all three cases the Colorado Supreme Court held that zoning and rezoning decisions are legislative in character and therefore subject to the people's power of referendum and initiative as set forth in the Colorado constitution. Arnel v. City of Costa Mesa, supra, reached the same result.

In City of Eastlake v. Forest City Enterprises, 426 U.S. 668, 96 S.Ct. 2358, 49 L.Ed.2d 132 (1976), the court sustained an ordinance requiring a referendum, with a favorable vote of 55%, to give effect to any rezoning amendment adopted by the city council. In so holding, the court refused to override the state court's characterization of rezoning amendments as "legislative" acts.

But see Arnel Development Co. v. City of Costa Mesa, 126 Cal.App.3d 330, 178 Cal.Rptr. 723 (1981), holding that a zoning amendment enacted by initiative was arbitrary and discriminatory, and therefore invalid.

4. The *Fasano* doctrine was substantially modified in Neuberger v. City of Portland, 288 Or. 155, 603 P.2d 771 (1980), where the court held (1) that the action of the city council was "quasi-judicial" rather than "legislative" even though in rezoning a 601-acre parcel owned (apparently) by a single group of applicants, the council "necessarily was involved with the making as well as the application of policy when it considered the zoning change proposal"; and (2) that recent Oregon legislation had eliminated the *Fasano* requirement that a rezoning applicant must show (a) "public need" which (b) "will be best served by changing the classification of the particular piece of property in question as compared with other available property." With respect to point (2), the court said:

    *   *   *   [S]ince the date of the *Fasano* decision * * *   the legislature has taken a very active role in the field of land use regulation. It has required all cities as well as counties to engage in land use planning, and has created a statewide agency, the Land Conservation and Development Commission, to prescribe criteria for and to supervise local planning efforts. Since 1973, every session of the legislature has produced significant legislation dealing with local planning.

    We find * * *   no statutory or LCDC requirement that a showing of either public need or a comparison with other available property is a specific and independent prerequisite to a zoning amendment. In light of the continuous legislative and agency attention to the planning and zoning process since the *Fasano* decision, we conclude that the legislature and LCDC have not found it necessary to impose such requirements.

[However,] a comparison of the characteristics of the site under consideration with other property which is available for the proposed use may well be relevant in determining whether particular requirements of the comprehensive plan, LCDC goals or other applicable standards have or have not been met.

5. Although the American Law Institute's Model Land Development Code (1976) attempts to discourage participation by the local legislative body in day-to-day regulatory decisions and to commit such decisions to the "land development agency" created by the legislative body, § 2–312 of the Model Code provides for adoption of "special amendments" authorizing land development by the legislative body. § 2.312(4) provides as follows:

> (4) The decision of the governing body to adopt a special amendment shall be supported by findings and conclusions based upon the record as if a special development permit had been granted. In any judicial proceeding thereon, the findings and conclusions shall be those of the agency under subsection (2) unless the governing body, on the basis of the same record or a record prepared before it, makes other findings and conclusions.*

The Model Code Reporter's Note makes it clear that § 2–312 adopts the *Fasano* doctrine:

> This Section treats amendments applicable to one or a few pieces of property as if they were applications for special development permits. While the local governing body is given the power to approve or reject recommendations of the Land Development Agency concerning the adoption of special amendments, the action of the local governing body no longer carries with it an almost automatic presumption of validity but is treated under subsection (4) as an administrative decision that must be supported by findings of fact and reasons; and therefore, it may be challenged in court on less than constitutional grounds.   *   *   *

Note on Recent Legislation Requiring Adoption of Local Comprehensive Plans and Mandating Consistency Between Plan and Land Use Regulations

In recent years a number of state legislatures have enacted new statutes requiring that local zoning ordinances must be based upon, and be consistent with, a formally adopted "master," "comprehensive," or "general" plan as defined by statute. This is true, as we have already seen, in Oregon. One of the most comprehensive of the new statutes is Cal.Gov.Code §§ 65100 et seq. (West 1966, Supp.1983), from which the following excerpts are drawn.

"§ 65100.   *   *   *   By ordinance the legislative body of each county and city shall establish a planning agency. Such planning agency may be a planning department, a planning commission, or the legislative body itself, or any combination thereof. The planning agency of the county shall include a planning commission.

"§ 65101.   *   *   *   The functions of the planning agency are as follows: (a) It shall develop and maintain a general plan. (b) It shall develop such specific plans as may be necessary or desirable. (c) It shall periodically review the

---

* Copyright 1970. Reprinted with the
permission of the American Law Institute.

capital improvement program of the county or city. (d) It shall perform such other functions as the legislative body may provide.

"§ 65300.   *   *   *   Each planning agency shall prepare and the legislative body of each county and city shall adopt a comprehensive, long-term general plan for the physical development of the county or city, and of any land outside its boundaries which in the planning agency's judgment bears relation to its planning.

"§ 65300.5.   *   *   *   In construing the provisions of this article, the Legislature intends that the general plan and elements and parts thereof comprise an integrated, internally consistent and compatible statement of policies for the adopting agency.

"§ 65860.   *   *   *

"(a) County or city zoning ordinances shall be consistent with the general plan of the county or city by January 1, 1974. A zoning ordinance shall be consistent with a city or county general plan only if:

     (i) The city or county has officially adopted such a plan, and

     (ii) The various land uses authorized by the ordinance are compatible with the objectives, policies, general land uses and programs specified in such a plan.

"(b) Any resident or property owner within a city or a county, as the case may be, may bring an action in the superior court to enforce compliance with the provisions of subdivision (a).   *   *   *   Any action or proceeding taken pursuant to the provisions of this subsection must be taken within six months of January 1, 1974, or within 90 days of the enactment of any new zoning ordinance or the amendment of any existing zoning ordinance as to said amendment or amendments.

"(c) In the event that a zoning ordinance becomes inconsistent with a general plan by reason of amendment to such a plan, or to any element of such a plan, such zoning ordinance shall be amended within a reasonable time so that it is consistent with the general plan as amended."

The California consistency requirement is amplified by guidelines issued by the California Office of Planning and Research. The most recent guidelines provide that the consistency requirement is satisfied "if all aspects of [the] local action program or project will not inhibit or obstruct the attainment of * * * policies" articulated in the general plan. California General Plan Guidelines 77 (1980). For discussion of the California experience, see Catalano & DiMento, Mandating Consistency Between General Plans and Zoning Ordinances: The California Experience, 8 Nat.Resources Law 455 (1975); Netter & Vranicar, Linking Plans and Regulations: Local Responses to Consistency Laws in California (Am.Planning Assoc., Planning Advisory Service, Report No. 363); Lefcoe, California's Land Planning Requirements: The Case for Deregulation, 54 So.Cal.L.Rev. 446 (1981).

As indicated in Note 4 following Fasano v. Bd. of County Comm'rs, ante, the Oregon legislature enacted new legislation in the mid-1970s that requires all local governments (counties and municipalities) to adopt comprehensive land use plans based upon statewide planning goals formulated by a Land Conservation and Development Commission. This legislation also requires that all local zoning and other land use regulations shall be consistent with the local comprehensive plan. The Oregon planning legislation, which provides for state-level review of all local comprehensive plans and regulatory ordinances to determine whether they are consistent with the statewide planning goals, recently survived a third attempt at repeal through a statewide initiative. See 49 Planning, No. 1 (January 1983), p. 7.

Florida has also recently adopted statewide planning and consistency requirements. The Florida legislation is both more sharply focused and more extensive in scope than the California and Oregon legislation. In Florida, the consistency requirement applies to land development regulations other than zoning regulations, and requires that any "development order"—defined as "any order granting, denying, or granting with conditions an application for a development permit"—shall be consistent with the local, regional, and state comprehensive plans. Thus the Florida consistency mandate extends to any governmental action authorizing land development, including development permits under no-zoning ordinances such as subdivision control ordinances, and conditional use permits under zoning ordinances. See Fla.Stat.Ann. §§ 163.3161 to 163.3211 (Supp.1983). For a good discussion of the Florida legislation, see Mandelker, The Role of the Local Comprehensive Plan in Land Use.

For general discussion of planning and land use control consistency requirements, see J. DiMento, The Consistency Doctrine and the Limits of Planning 198.

Nevada also requires that zoning regulations "shall be made in accordance with the master plan for land use," which is "a comprehensive, long-term general plan for the physical development of the city, county or region." The "master plan" must include a "land use plan," defined as follows: "An inventory and classification of natural land types and of existing land cover and uses, and comprehensive plans for the most desirable utilization of land." See Nev. Rev.Stat. §§ 278.150, 278.160(1)(e), and 278.250(2).

The Model Code does not make adoption of a Local Land Use Development Plan under Article 3 a condition precedent to enactment of a valid "development ordinance," which is essentially a combination of zoning and subdivision control ordinances. (For a treatment of subdivision controls, see infra Chapter 14.) Indeed, adoption of a Local Land Use Development Plan is not even a prerequisite for the issuance of certain kinds of "special development permits" (essentially the same as "variances" and "special exceptions" under the Standard State Zoning Enabling Act). But adoption of such a Plan is required before the Local Land Development Agency may issue "special development permits for planned unit development (§ 2–210), and for development in specially planned areas (§ 2–211) * * *." If such a Plan has been adopted, the Local Land Development Agency "may devise other categories of special development permits that incorporate material in the Plan by reference (§ 2–212)." Model Code, Commentary to Article 2, at p. 28.

SYLVANIA ELECTRIC PRODUCTS, INC. v. CITY OF NEWTON

Massachusetts Supreme Judicial Court, 1962.
344 Mass. 428, 183 N.E.2d 118.

WHITTEMORE, J. This appeal under G.L. c. 231, § 96, and c. 185, § 15, by landowners in Newton, challenges the decision of the Land Court which held valid an amendment to the Newton zoning ordinance enacted on June 27, 1960. The amendment changed from a single residence A district to a limited manufacturing district the classification of 153.6 acres of land now of the petitioner (Sylvania) situated on the southerly side of Nahanton Street in the southerly end of the city and bounded on the west and south by a strip of land of the metropolitan district commission along the Charles River. The locus is diagonally across the river from the development of the New England Industrial Center in Needham which lies between Route 128 and the river. The limited manufacturing district classification had been added to the ordinance on September 21, 1959. One other parcel had been placed in the classification prior to the amendment.

The judge viewed the locus and its environs. His decision states facts in apparently full detail and incorporates all the exhibits.

1. The validity of the ordinance in all aspects, other than that discussed in point 2 below, is shown by the facts stated in the decision. It was not spot zoning; it did not violate the requirement of uniform classification; it was not invalidated because made after other nearby land had been for a long time classified for residences. It was an appropriate zoning reclassification of the locus in the light of the physical characteristics of the land and very substantial changes in the use of land in the vicinity. We do not reach the issue whether the judge's conclusion in respect of these points must be taken in any event because of his consideration of other facts not stated. The appellants do not contend that the amendment was invalid because fewer acres were reclassified than were described in the proposal of which statutory notice was given.

2. The principal issue is the effect of Sylvania's imposition of restrictions on the locus in connection with the enactment of the amending ordinance and of steps taken by the planning board, and others acting for the city, to cause Sylvania so to do.

In respect of this issue the judge found these facts: Sylvania on April 14, 1960, having an option to purchase a parcel containing 180 acres, inclusive of the rezoned locus, petitioned the board of aldermen (aldermen) to reclassify the parcel. On May 11, 1960, the planning board, after a public hearing held jointly with the aldermen's committee on claims and rules, reported that it had asked the city's planning consultant to review the petition and had decided to withhold action until he should report. On June 2, 1960, the board reported to the aldermen its vote to approve Sylvania's petition except that it recommended retaining in the residence A district a substantial frontage on Nahanton Street, including a parcel of about eighteen and one-half acres on the east side of the parcel adjacent to the property of the Charles River Country Club.

"Meanwhile, Sylvania, in consultation with the planning consultant * * * and members of the planning board and the claims and rules committee * * *, had agreed to certain restrictions upon its use of * * * [the locus]," [6] and had agreed to cede three acres, comprising

---

6. The minutes of the planning board meeting of May 25, 1960, after recording the approval of the petition with the exception noted in the opinion above, state as follows:

"The Planning Board also voted to send the following letter to the chairman of the Claims and Rules Committee: 'At a meet-

ing of the Planning Board held May 25, 1960, petition * * * of * * * Sylvania * * * was discussed in great detail and a modified but favorable decision was reached. This decision and a report on the petition are officially submitted in a separate communication to the Board of Aldermen. In considering the change of zone

the southeasterly tip of the parcel, to "Oak Hill Park Association" to be retained in the residence district. The restrictions, to be operative for thirty years from September 1, 1960, were set out in a draft of a deed attached to a proposed option agreement whereby Sylvania would give the city an option to purchase, within a thirty year period, for $300, a strip of land on the west and southwesterly side (the river side) of the parcel, adjacent to the land of the metropolitan district commission, containing thirty and one-half acres. By the option agreement Sylvania would agree to abide by the restrictions in the draft deed during the option term pending the city's exercise thereof. The intention would be to give the city a dominant estate capable of enforcing the restrictions. The deed was to convey the thirty and one-half acres subject to the restriction for the benefit of Sylvania's adjoining premises that for a period of fifty years no buildings or structures (other than fences) should be erected or maintained on the granted premises.

The proposed restrictions limited the floor area of all buildings to be constructed on the premises to 800,000 square feet; required that sixty per cent of the ground area, or seventy-three and nine-tenths acres, be maintained in open space not occupied by buildings, parking areas or roadways; set back the building line from forty to eighty feet; imposed a sliding scale of height restrictions; called for a buffer zone of comparable size to the three acres to be ceded to Oak Hill Park Association and adjacent thereto, on which no structures might be erected; restricted the number and type of signs and the type of lighting; limited the use of buildings to certain, but not all, of the uses permitted in a limited manufacturing district; and established a pattern for traffic in connection with construction on the premises.

On June 27, 1960, the aldermen's committee on claims and rules reported its approval of the petition as modified by the planning board in its formal vote of approval, except that the committee recommended that the strip on Nahanton Street reserved for the residence district be increased in depth from 140 to 180 feet. There was submitted to the June 27 meeting a memorandum by the planning consultant, addressed to the mayor and to the alderman who was chairman of the committee on claims and rules. This memorandum summarized "the acreage breakdown on the Sylvania site, based upon the tentative deed restrictions as of June 23, 1960," and included a sketch map of the site delineating the areas and restrictions.

Thereafter, at the June 27 meeting, the aldermen enacted the ordinance which approved Sylvania's petition as modified in accordance with its committee's recommendation "and in connection therewith passed [the] order * * * authorizing the mayor to accept the proposed option agreement."

requested by the above petition, the Planning Board respectfully suggests that the following conditions be obtained by agreement with the proper parties concerned, if the Board of Aldermen is favorably disposed to the zone request. * * *

[Items 1 to 6, specifying restrictions similar to but not identical with those agreed to and eventually imposed (see text of opinion)].'" [Footnotes are the court's but have been renumbered. Ed.]

Sylvania took title to the Nahanton Street parcel on July 6, 1960, and thereafter on that day executed the option agreement with attached form of deed. Certified copies of the ordinance of June 27, 1960, which amended the zoning ordinance and of the order which authorized the mayor to accept the option bear the indorsement "Executive Department Approved July 7, 1960." The deed form and option agreement were recorded on July 8, 1960.

In several other jurisdictions votes to rezone on the express condition that the owner impose restrictions (sometimes called "contract zoning") have been held invalid. Hartnett v. Austin, 93 So.2d 86 (Fla.). Baylis v. Mayor & City Council of Baltimore, 219 Md. 164, 148 A.2d 429. Rose v. Paape, 221 Md. 369, 157 A.2d 618. Carole Highlands Citizens Ass'n Inc. v. Board of County Commrs. of Prince George's County, 222 Md. 44, 158 A.2d 663. V.F. Zahodiakin Engr. Corp. v. Zoning Bd. of Adjustment of Summit, 8 N.J. 386, 86 A.2d 127. See Houston Petroleum Co. v. Automotive Prod. Credit Ass'n, 9 N.J. 122, 87 A.2d 319.

Rathkopf, The Law of Zoning and Planning (3d ed.) pp. 74–9, states that "The basis of such rule is that the rezoning of a particular parcel of land upon conditions not imposed by the zoning ordinance generally in the particular district into which the land has been rezoned is prima facie evidence of 'spot zoning' in its most maleficent aspect, is not in accordance with a comprehensive plan and is beyond the power of the municipality."

The only decision squarely to the contrary which has come to our attention is Church v. Islip, 8 N.Y.2d 254, 259, 203 N.Y.S.2d 866, 869, 168 N.E.2d 680, 683, which the judge in the Land Court found persuasive. The change of zone, sustained in a majority opinion by Desmond, C.J., had been voted on condition that the owners agree that the building should not occupy more than twenty-five per cent of the area, that a six foot fence be erected five feet within the boundary line, and that shrubbery be planted and maintained at fence height. The court said: "Since the Town Board could have, presumably, zoned this * * * corner for business without any restrictions, we fail to see how reasonable conditions invalidate the legislation. * * * All legislation 'by contract' is invalid in the sense that a Legislature cannot bargain away or sell its powers. But we deal here with actualities, not phrases. To meet increasing needs of Suffolk County's own population explosion, and at the same time to make as gradual and as little of an annoyance as possible the change from residence to business on the main highways, the Town Board imposes conditions. There is nothing unconstitutional about it." See Pecora v. Zoning Commn. of Trumbull, 145 Conn. 435, 441, 144 A.2d 48; Pressman v. Mayor & City Council of Baltimore, 222 Md. 330, 344–345, 160 A.2d 379.

We turn to an analysis of what was done in Newton and note that although no condition was imposed by the aldermen in their vote, the conclusion is inescapable that the option proposal was a significant inducement of the zoning amendment and the amendment induced the giving of the option.[7]

It is said that there was a purported, invalid exercise of the zoning power, for the vote operated to subject the locus not only to the restrictions of a limited manufacturing district but also to the restrictions of the option and deed form. But that is not, precisely, what happened. The induced, voluntary action of Sylvania, not the vote of the council, imposed the option restrictions; the vote reclassified land which was being subjected to those restrictions. The zoning decision was that the locus, so restricted by its owner, should be made a limited manufacturing district. That, in form, was an appropriate and untainted exercise of the zoning power.

What was done involved no action contrary to the best interest of the city and hence offensive to general public policy. It involved no extraneous consideration (as, for example, a request to give land for a park elsewhere in the city) which could impeach the enacting vote as a decision solely in respect of rezoning the locus.

We discern no aspect of spot zoning, lack of uniformity, or failure to conform to the comprehensive zoning plan. Even if the restrictions had been made a part of the zoning ordinance, they would not have created spot zoning. The site was all the land in the neighborhood which was proposed for reclassification. The private restrictions in no way made the locus less appropriate for classification as a limited manufacturing district. It is inconsequential that other areas elsewhere in the city, in, or to be put in, such a zoning district, would not have those restrictions. Requirements of uniformity and conformity to a plan do not mean that there must be identity of every relevant aspect in areas given the same zoning classification.

It does not infringe zoning principles that, in connection with a zoning amendment, land use is regulated otherwise than by the amendment. Zoning regulations, as Sylvania points out, exist unaffected by, and do not affect, deed restrictions. Vorenberg v. Bunnell, 257 Mass. 399, 159 N.E. 884, 48 A.L.R. 1431. Snow v. Van Dam, 291 Mass. 477, 197 N.E. 224. The owner of the locus could have imposed restrictions on it prior to the original filing of the petition for rezoning without effect upon the subsequent rezoning vote.

Since the private regulation was, beyond dispute, harmonious, consistent, and beneficial, no hurtful effect requires that we look behind the form of what was done.

It is pointed out that proposals for zoning change can be adopted only after notice and a hearing. G.L. c. 40A, § 6. But the option restrictions did not make the locus a different subject for rezoning from what it was when the notice was given and the hearing held. The vol-

---

7. By St.1903, c. 152, and G.L. c. 43, § 55, the mayor had ten days after June 27 to disapprove and return the ordinance with "his written objections" and if "notwithstanding such disapproval" the ordinance were again to be passed a two-thirds vote of all members would have been required. As noted, the option was executed on July 6, the executive department approval was on July 7, and the option was recorded on July 8.

untary limitations imposed on the use of the land, although relevant in considering the proposal to rezone it, did not call for a new notice and hearing. They could have no adverse effect on anyone other than Sylvania. As noted, none of these restrictions was inconsistent with the requirements for the zoning district. It is far fetched to suggest that citizens opposed to any change might have stayed away from the original hearing in expectation that the proposal would be disapproved. The imposition of these restrictions, subsequent to the hearing, is no more significant than are changes in the zoning proposal itself which are within the scope of the original proposal. Such changes do not require further notice.

It is objected that the council has not determined that the locus, unrestricted, is appropriate to be put in the limited manufacturing district. We agree that the zoning decision applied to the locus as affected by the option agreement. It was not, however, conditioned upon the validity of the option restrictions. The council made an appropriate zoning decision when it determined that the locus, subject to whatever limitations on its use the option effectively placed thereon, be put in the limited manufacturing district. Although not directly in issue, it may be noted that the restrictions appear to have been validly imposed by a sealed and recorded instrument. Sylvania is bound for thirty years even if the option is not exercised. Nothing now turns on an issue of the power of the mayor and council to pay for the dominant estate and take a deed.

The appellants urge that citizens should be able to look with confidence only to the zoning law to ascertain what are the zoning restrictions. The answer is that the option restrictions are not zoning restrictions, and all who have any interest in restrictions in the chain of title may find them of record.

The final objection is that even though the officials acted with good intent, beneficially to the city, and consistently with zoning principles, they were nevertheless making an unauthorized use of the zoning power. Unquestionably the officials let it be known that favorable rezoning depended in great likelihood on the adoption of the option restrictions. The planning board acted as a board when it suggested that "the following conditions be obtained by agreement with the proper parties concerned"; the planning consultant was acting as an adviser in respect of zoning when he submitted to the aldermen and the mayor the memorandum which summarized the proposed restrictions; and the aldermen confirmed their participation as a board by the vote which authorized the mayor to accept the proposed option agreement. This was all extra-statutory but nevertheless, proper activity, precedent to the exercise of the zoning power, not the exercise thereof. Whether the city may have the benefit of the pressures of its officials on Sylvania without adoption of the restrictions into the zoning proposal turns on the effect of the restrictions thereon. Since, as stated, the zoning proposal was not essentially changed, it was not necessary to reinitiate the amending process.

The locus was a unique site which was about to go into a specialized use.[8] It was appropriate and lawful to ask the prospective owner to take consistent action to ameliorate the effect of the pending drastic change of zoning classification.

It is, as other courts have noticed, anomalous for owners of nearby land who object to any change away from the residence district to object on the ground that, contemporaneously, ameliorating restrictions have been imposed. But, since they would be aggrieved by the purported change if it were illegal, we have considered the issue on its merits.

3. It is not necessary to consider Sylvania's appeal from the denial in the Land Court of its motion to dismiss the respondent land-owners' appeal.

Decision affirmed.

KIRK, J. I do not agree. The mutual advantages gained by Newton and Sylvania by their arrangement are not in issue. The motives of the participants are not questioned. The central thesis of this dissent is that the method used by Newton to impose restrictions on the use of land owned by Sylvania is invalid.

General Laws, c. 40A, § 2, provides in part, "For the purpose of promoting the health, safety, convenience, morals or welfare of its inhabitants, any city, except Boston, and any town, may *by a zoning ordinance or by-law* regulate and restrict the height, number of stories, and size of buildings and structures, the size and width of lots, the percentage of lot that may be occupied, the size of yards, courts and other open spaces, the density of population, and the location and use of buildings, structures and land for trade, industry, agriculture, residence or other purposes. * * *

"For any or all of such purposes a *zoning ordinance or by-law* may divide the municipality into districts of such number, shape and area as may be deemed best suited to carry out the purposes of this chapter, and within such districts it may regulate and restrict the erection, construction, reconstruction, alteration or use of buildings, and structures, or use of land * * * " (emphasis supplied).

There would seem to be no question (and it appears the majority agrees) that (1) each and every restriction imposed by the "option agreement" (contract)[9] is one which the city is empowered to impose by ordinance under c. 40A, § 2;[10] and (2) each and every restriction imposed by

---

8. Among the exhibits is "A Report on the Sylvania Science Center prepared by the Industrial Development Committee of the Newton Chamber of Commerce."

9. As the situation stands there are no deed restrictions on Sylvania's land. The restrictions derive from the collateral promises of Sylvania in the option agreement to abide by the "restrictions" in the undelivered deed attached to the option agreement. In this respect it should be noted that the duration of Newton's power to exercise the option is coterminous with the contract restrictions. It seems clear that this arrangement was made so that Newton, when (and only when) it felt it was necessary, could acquire a dominant estate for the specific enforcement of the restrictions. Until such a contingency occurs, which apparently is regarded as unlikely by both Sylvania and Newton, the restrictions exist only by virtue of the collateral promises. [Footnotes are by Kirk, J. Fn. 1 has been omitted. Ed.]

10. See paragraph 7 of the majority opinion.

the contract was imposed in order to further the purposes stated in c. 40A, § 2 and § 3.[11]

With equal certainty it should be clear that when a municipality elects to impose restrictions on the use of land for the purposes set out in c. 40A, §§ 2, 3, it must, under the express provisions of c. 40A, § 2, impose them *"by a zoning ordinance or by-law."* The attempt to impose them by contract is "beyond the authority conferred * * * [and] not in compliance with the terms and conditions governing its exercise" and therefore is invalid.

Moreover, c. 40A, § 6 (see also § 7), prescribes explicitly the procedural steps which must be taken prior to the adoption, amendment or repeal of ordinances or by-laws relating to land restrictions. Included among the steps is the requirement of public hearings before both the planning board and the city council after notice thereof has been given to the city's inhabitants so that "all interested persons shall be given an opportunity to be heard."[12] There is no similar requirement for notice or hearing when restrictions are to be imposed by a city on a parcel of land, however large, by contract. What we have, then, is not only an invalid method for imposing restrictions but an invalid method which admits the added evil of circumvention of the declared legislative requirement that interested parties be fully informed of the particulars of proposed municipal land restriction and be given an opportunity to be heard on these particulars.

The majority, however, states that the restrictions here imposed are not "zoning restrictions" and equates them with contract restrictions negotiated by private landowners for the benefit of adjoining land. I submit that this characterization will not withstand analysis. In the first place, the benefit of these contract restrictions does not run to or with any land now owned by Newton. Secondly, and more significantly, these restrictions were negotiated and agreed to by Newton and Sylvania in conjunction with, and as an integral part of, the enactment of the amendment to the Newton zoning ordinance. The amendment subjected the land to restrictions uniformly imposed on limited manufacturing districts; the contract subjected the land to additional restrictions in order, as the opinion recognizes, "to ameliorate the effect of the pending drastic change of zoning classification."

To my mind, the conclusion seems inescapable that, in truth and substance, the action of Newton was not the mere rezoning of a parcel of land which was already subject to privately negotiated contract restrictions but was, rather, one double-barrelled attempt to exercise the zoning power delegated to it by the Legislature under c. 40A, § 2. If the

---

11. General Laws c. 40A, § 3, provides: "Zoning regulations and restrictions shall be designed among other purposes to lessen congestion in the streets; to conserve health; to secure safety from fire, panic and other dangers; to provide adequate light, and air; to prevent overcrowding of land; to avoid undue concentration of population; to facilitate the adequate provision of transportation, water, sewerage, schools, parks and other public requirements; to conserve the value of land and buildings; to encourage the most appropriate use of land throughout the city or town; and to preserve and increase its amenities."

12. See changes made in these provisions by St.1962, c. 201, § 1.

phrases "zoning restrictions" and "exercise of the zoning power" have any meaning, they must include the restrictions here imposed by contract. To say, as the majority in effect says, that they are not "zoning restrictions" or do not constitute "an exercise of the zoning power" because the city imposes them by contract and not by ordinance seems to me to be a play on words and to beg the question. The purpose and effect of their imposition is the same whether they are accomplished by ordinance or contract. It is the method of imposition which is the critical issue.

Whatever the action of Newton may or may not be called, it (1) in fact results in the imposition of restrictions by a city (Newton is the party that can and would enforce these restrictions) (2) for the purposes set out in c. 40A, §§ 2, 3, (3) upon the use of land by the owner (4) by the contract method (5) which method is prohibited by the Legislature (6) which alone can prescribe the method, and (7) hence is illegal.

Although the burden of the foregoing discussion is the invalidity of the contract restrictions, it is my opinion that the amendment to the zoning ordinance is itself also invalid. Newton's use of two methods in close and complementary coordination to accomplish a single purpose, namely the regulation of use of Sylvania's land is, in fact and in substance, a single act. All indications are that, unless Newton had first obtained the additional contract restrictions, it would not have effected the "drastic change of zoning classification" by enacting the amendment. As the opinion states, the amendment and the contract were mutually induced.

The elimination of the invalid contract restrictions, here used in combination with the ordinance restrictions resulting from the amendment to accomplish a single purpose, defeats the single purpose. It also reveals the essential oneness or interdependence of the methods used. Thus viewed as one, it would seem inevitably to follow that such ordinance restrictions fall with the contract restrictions as being in excess of the power conferred in c. 40A, § 2.[13]

I would require compliance with the statute, and accordingly would reverse the decision.

Questions and Notes

1. Was the City of Newton "contractually bound" to rezone from single-family residential use to limited manufacturing use at any time prior to the council's adoption of the rezoning amendment on June 27, 1960? Was the council "contractually bound" not to repeal the rezoning amendment during the period from June 27 to July 7, 1960? Was the mayor "contractually bound" to approve the rezoning amendment on or before July 7, 1960? If the mayor had disapproved it, would the council have been "contractually bound" to override the mayor by a ⅔ vote of its entire membership? Once the rezoning amendment was approved and the option agreement and attached deed were recorded, was the City of Newton "contractually bound" to keep the classification placed on Sylvania's land by the rezoning amendment in effect so long as Sylvania or

13. Whether Newton could accomplish by a lawful exercise of its delegated power completely and precisely what it has attempted to accomplish by an unlawful exercise of power is, in my mind, an open question.

its successors in interest should use the land for an electronics manufacturing plant? If the answer to all these questions is "no," why should the procedure used in the principal case be called "contract" zoning? Was the court correct in stating that the council's rezoning decision was *not* conditioned on the validity of the option agreement and that the council "made an appropriate zoning decision when it determined that the locus, subject to *whatever* limitations on its use the option effectively placed thereon, be put in the limited manufacturing district"?

2. When did Sylvania become "contractually bound" to observe the restrictions in the deed attached to the option agreement? What was the consideration for Sylvania's agreement to these restrictions? What would be the consideration for its observance of these restrictions during the 30-year option period? If Sylvania, instead of developing the land in question, should sell it to a manufacturing company that sought to develop it in a way that would violate the deed restrictions, could the City of Newton enjoin such violation? If so, on what legal or equitable theory? Do you think the City would have been on safer ground if it had required Sylvania to convey the entire tract to the City and had then reconveyed it to Sylvania by a deed containing the agreed-upon restrictions, along with a clause making the observance of the restrictions an express condition subsequent and giving the City a right of entry for breach of condition?

3. When the plaintiffs decide to challenge the rezoning of the Sylvania tract, did they run any substantial risk that the court might hold the additional land use restrictions contained in the recorded deed to be invalid but sustain the rezoning amendment itself? Suppose that there had been no challenge by third parties in the principal case, and that Sylvania had later refused to observe the additional restrictions on the ground that they violated the statutory mandate that all zoning regulations "shall be uniform for each class or kind of buildings throughout each district"? If the court should accept this argument, should it simply hold the additional restrictions invalid, or should it hold the entire rezoning transactions void so that the land would revert to its prior zoning classification? See Comment, Contract and Conditional Zoning: A Tool for Zoning Flexibility, 23 Hastings L.J. 825, 836 (1972), observing that, where a municipality seeks to enforce the additional restrictions and the landowner resists, the courts generally sustain the restrictions or invalidate them without deciding the validity of the rezoning amendment itself. Is this a sensible approach?

4. In addition to Church v. Islip, cited in Sylvania in support of the validity of "contract" or "conditional" rezoning, see, accord, Scrutton v. County of Sacramento, 275 Cal.App.2d 412, 79 Cal.Rptr. 872 (1969); Cross v. Hall County, 238 Ga. 709, 235 S.E.2d 379 (1977); Funger v. Mayor & Council of Somerset, 244 Md. 141, 225 A.2d 168 (1966); Housing & Redevelopment Authority v. Jorgenson, 328 N.W.2d 740 (Minn.1983); Bucholz v. City of Omaha, 174 Neb. 862, 120 N.W.2d 270 (1963); Collard v. Incorporated Village of Flower Hill, 52 N.Y.2d 594, 439 N.Y.S.2d 326, 421 N.E.2d 818 (1981); Gladwyne Colony, Inc. v. Township of Lower Merion, 409 Pa. 441, 187 A.2d 549 (1963); State ex rel. Myhre v. City of Spokane, 70 Wn.2d 207, 422 P.2d 790 (1967); State ex rel. Zupancic v. Schimenz, 45 Wis.2d 22, 174 N.W.2d 533 (1970). Contra: Hartnett v. Austin, 93 So.2d 86 (Fla.1956); Cederberg v. City of Rockford, 8 Ill.App.3d 984, 291 N.E.2d 249 (1972); Carlino v. Whitpain Investors, 499 Pa. 498, 453 A.2d 1385 (1982).

The law of Pennsylvania as to "contract" or "conditional" zoning is unclear. In *Carlino*, the court refused to enforce an agreement between a landowner and the local governing body requiring the landowner to preserve a buffer area and not to construct an access road to an existing public street, in a suit by neighboring landowners against the township and the successor of the landowner who originally entered into the agreement. The rationale of the decision was that "[t]he police power of municipalities cannot be subjected to agreements which restrict or condition zoning district classifications as to particular properties"—the successor of the landowner who originally entered into the agreement having obtained a rezoning not subject to the agreement. It is not clear what the result would have been had the township been seeking to enforce the agreement. The earlier case of Gladwyne Colony, Inc. v. Twp. of Lower Merion, supra, was distinguished on the ground that the earlier cases "did not involve contractually conditioned rezoning, * * * since no special land use limitations or conditions were accepted by the property owner to secure the rezoning." (See 453 A.2d at 1387 n. 2.) In the *Gladwyne Colony* case it was alleged that a landowner gave parkland to a municipality in exchange for enactment of a rezoning amendment.

In Florida, the authority of Hartnett v. Austin, supra, has been weakened by Broward County v. Griffey, 366 So.2d 869 (Fla.App.1979), approving conditional rezoning.

5. R.I.Gen.Laws § 45–24–4.1 (1970) provides as follows:

* * * [T]he town or city council may, in approving a zone change, limit such change to one (1) of the permitted uses in the zone to which the subject land is rezoned, and impose such conditions upon the use of land as it deems necessary. The responsible city or town official shall cause the limitations so imposed to be clearly noted on the zoning map.

In Sweetman v. Town of Cumberland, 117 R.I. 134, 364 A.2d 1277 (1976), the court held that there is no conflict between this statutory provision and the general zoning "uniformity" requirement, since the authorization for "conditional" rezoning was expressly granted "notwithstanding the uniformity provision in the zoning enabling act." The court further held that the provision does not violate equal protection as permitting imposition of different conditions on parcels of land bearing the same use classification and that it does not violate due process as permitting municipal councils to impose conditions in an arbitrary and capricious manner.

6. Does the "conditional" rezoning technique, assuming it to be valid, have any advantage, from the viewpoint of a municipality, over the "special exception" technique or the "floating zone" amendment technique? Should other states adopt provisions like the Rhode Island statutory provision set out in supra, Note 5? Does it make the use of "special exceptions" and "floating zone" amendments unnecessary?

CHENEY v. VILLAGE 2 AT NEW HOPE, INC.

Pennsylvania Supreme Court, 1968.
429 Pa. 626, 241 A.2d 81.

ROBERTS, Justice. Under traditional concepts of zoning the task of determining the type, density and placement of buildings which should exist within any given zoning district devolves upon the local legislative body. In order that this body might have to speak only infrequently on the issue of municipal planning and zoning, the local legislature usually enacts detailed requirements for the type, size and location of buildings within each given zoning district, and leaves the ministerial task of enforcing these regulations to an appointed zoning administrator, with another administrative body, the zoning board of adjustment, passing on individual deviations from the strict district requirements, deviations known commonly as variances and special exceptions. At the same time, the overall rules governing the dimensions, placement, etc. of primarily public additions to ground, e.g., streets, sewers, playgrounds, are formulated by the local legislature through the passage of subdivision regulations. These regulations are enforced and applied to individual lots by an administrative body usually known as the planning commission.

This general approach to zoning fares reasonably well so long as development takes place on a lot-by-lot basis, and so long as no one cares that the overall appearance of the municipality resembles the design achieved by using a cookie cutter on a sheet of dough. However, with the increasing popularity of large scale residential developments, particularly in suburban areas, it has become apparent to many local municipalities that land can be more efficiently used, and developments more aesthetically pleasing, if zoning regulations focus on density requirements rather than on specific rules for each individual lot. Under density zoning, the legislature determines what percentage of a particular district must be devoted to open space, for example, and what percentage used for dwelling units. The task of filling in the particular district with real houses and real open spaces then falls upon the planning commission usually working in conjunction with an individual large scale developer. See Chrinko v. South Brunswick Twp., Planning Bd., 77 N.J. Super. 594, 187 A.2d 221 (1963). The ultimate goal of this so-called density or cluster concept of zoning is achieved when an entire self-contained little community is permitted to be built within a zoning district, with the rules of density controlling not only the relation of private dwellings to open space, but also the relation of homes to commercial establishments such as theaters, hotels, restaurants, and quasi-commercial uses such as schools and churches. The present controversy before this Court involves a frontal attack upon one of these zoning districts, known in the trade as a Planned Unit Development (hereinafter PUD).

Spurred by the desire of appellant developer to construct a Planned Unit Development in the Borough of New Hope, in December of 1964 Borough Council began considering the passage of a new zoning ordinance to establish a PUD district in New Hope. After extensive consultation with appellant, council referred the matter to the New Hope Planning Commission for further study. This body, approximately six months after the project idea was first proposed, formally recommended to council that a PUD district be created. Council consulted with members of the Bucks County Planning Commission on the text of the proposed ordinance, held public hearings, and finally on June 14, 1965 enacted ordinance 160 which created the PUD district, and ordinance 161 which amended the Borough zoning map, rezoning a large tract of land known as the Rauch farm from low density residential to PUD. Pursuant to the procedural requirements of ordinance 160, appellant presented plans for a Planned Unit Development on the Rauch tract to the Borough Planning Commission. These plans were approved on November 8, 1965, and accordingly four days later two building permits, known as zoning permits 68 and 69, were issued to appellant. * * * Subsequently, permit number 75 was issued. Appellees, all neighboring property owners opposing the issuance of these permits, appealed to the zoning board of adjustment. The board, after taking extensive testimony, upheld ordinances 160 and 161 and accordingly affirmed the issuance of the permits. Appellees then appealed to the Bucks County Court of Common Pleas. That tribunal took no additional testimony, but reversed the board, holding the ordinances invalid for failure to conform to a comprehensive plan and for vesting too much discretion in the New Hope Planning Commission. This Court granted certiorari under Supreme Court Rule 68½.

　　* * *

I

Approximately one year before the PUD seed was planted in New Hope, Borough Council had approved the New Hope Comprehensive Plan. This detailed land use projection clearly envisioned the Rauch tract as containing only single family dwellings of low density. The court below therefore concluded that the enactment of ordinance 160, and more specifically the placing of a PUD district on the Rauch tract by ordinance 161 was not "in accordance with a comprehensive plan," as required by the Act of February 1, 1966, P.L. (1965)—§ 3203, 53 P.S. § 48203. See also Eves v. Zoning Bd. of Adjustment, 401 Pa. 211, 164 A.2d 7 (1960).

The fallacy in the court's reasoning lies in its mistaken belief that a comprehensive plan, once established, is forever binding on the municipality and can never be amended. Cases subsequent to *Eves* have made it clear, however, that these plans may be changed by the passage of new zoning ordinances, provided the local legislature passes the new ordinance with some demonstration of sensitivity to the community as a whole, and the impact that the new ordinance will have on this community. * * *

Given this rule of law allowing post-plan zoning changes, and the presumption in favor of an ordinance's validity, we are not in a position, having reviewed the record in the present case, to say that the zoning board committed an abuse of discretion or an error of law when it concluded that ordinances 160 and 161 were properly passed. Presented as it was with evidence that the PUD district had been under consideration by council for over six months and had been specifically recommended by the borough planning commission, a body specially equipped to view proposed ordinances as they relate to the rest of the community, we hold that the board, within its sound discretion, could have concluded that council passed the ordinances with the proper overall considerations in mind. The PUD district established by ordinance 160 is not the type of use which by its very nature could have no place in the middle of a predominantly residential borough. It is not a steel mill, a fat rendering plant, or a desiccated egg factory. It is, in fact, nothing more than a miniature residential community.

Closely tied to the comprehensive plan issue is the argument raised by appellees that ordinances 160 and 161 constitute spot zoning outlawed by *Eves,* supra. Given the fact situation in *Eves,* however, as well as the post-*Eves* cases, we do not believe that there is any spot zoning here. In *Eves,* the municipality created a limited industrial district, F–1, which, by explicit legislative pronouncement, was not to be applied to any particular tract until the individual land owner requested that his own tract be so re-zoned. The obvious evil in this procedure did *not* lie in the fact that a limited industrial district might be placed in an area previously zoned, for example, residential. The evil was the *pre-ordained* uncertainty as to where the F–1 districts would crop up. The ordinance all but invited spot zoning where the legislature could respond to private entreaties from land owners and re-zone tracts F–1 without regard to the surrounding community. In *Eves,* it was almost impossible for the F–1 districts to conform to a comprehensive plan since tracts would be re-zoned on a strictly ad hoc basis.

Quite to the contrary, no such "floating zone" exists in the present case. On the very day that the PUD district was created by ordinance 160, it was brought to earth by ordinance 161; and, as discussed supra, this *was* done "in accordance with a comprehensive plan." Speaking of a similar procedure in Donahue v. Zoning Bd. of Adjustment, 412 Pa. 332, 194 A.2d 610 (1963), this Court faced squarely an attack based upon *Eves* and responded thusly:

"It was this case by case review [in *Eves*] which demonstrated the absence of a comprehensive plan and which sought to enable the Board of Supervisors [the local legislative body] to exercise powers they did not statutorily possess.

"In the instant case, the new classification was established and the zoning map amended within a very short period of time [in the case at bar, on the same day]. Under the rules of statutory construction which are likewise applicable to ordinances, these ordinances should be read together as one enactment. See Statutory Construction Act, May 28, 1937, P.L. 1019, § 62, 46 P.S. § 562, 1952. So construed, Ordinances 151 [creating new zone] and 155 [amending zoning map] do not create the 'floating zone', anchored only upon case by case application by landowners, which we struck down in *Eves.* While it is true that the change here was made upon request of a particular landowner, this does not necessarily create the evils held invalid in *Eves* where the defects were specifically created by the very terms of the ordinance. It is not unusual for a zoning change to be made on request of a landowner, and such change is not invalid if made in accordance with a comprehensive plan." 412 Pa. at 334–335, 194 A.2d at 611.

We think *Donahue* is completely controlling on the issue of alleged spot zoning and compels the conclusion that ordinances 160 and 161 do not fall on that ground. See also the excellent discussion of *Eves* and its progeny in Krasnowiecki, Legal Aspects of Planned Unit Development, Technical Bull. 52, Urban Land Institute, pp. 20–22 (1965).

II

The court below next concluded that even if the two ordinances were properly *passed*, they must fall as vesting authority in the planning commission greater than that permitted under Pennsylvania's zoning enabling legislation. More specifically, it is now contended by appellees that complete project approval by the planning commission under ordinance 160 requires that commission to encroach upon legislative territory whenever it decides where, within a particular PUD district, specific types of building should be placed.

In order to appreciate fully the arguments of counsel on both sides it is necessary to explain in some detail exactly what is permitted within a PUD district, and who decides whether a particular land owner has complied with these requirements. Admittedly the range of permissible uses within the PUD district is greater than that normally found in a traditional zoning district. Within a New Hope PUD district there may be: single family attached or detached dwellings; apartments; accessory private garages; public or private parks and recreation areas including golf courses, swimming pools, ski slopes, etc. (so long as these facilities do not produce noise, glare, odor, air pollution, etc., detrimental to existing or prospective adjacent structures); a municipal building; a school; churches; art galleries; professional offices; certain types of signs; a theatre (but not a drive-in); motels and hotels; and a restaurant. The ordinance then sets certain overall density requirements. The PUD district may have a maximum of 80% of the land devoted to residential uses, a maximum of 20% for the permitted commercial uses and enclosed recreational facilities, and must have a minimum of 20% for open spaces. The residential density shall not exceed 10 units per acre, nor shall any such unit contain more than two bedrooms. All structures within the district must not exceed maximum height standards set out in the ordinance. Finally, although there are no traditional "set back" and "side yard" requirements, ordinance 160 does require that there be 24 feet between structures, and that no townhouse structure contain more than 12 dwelling units.

The procedure to be followed by the aspiring developer reduces itself to presenting a detailed plan for his planned unit development to the planning commission, obtaining that body's approval and then securing building permits. Of course, the planning commission may not approve any development that fails to meet the requirements set forth in the ordinance as outlined above.

We begin with the observation that there is nothing in the borough zoning enabling act which would prohibit council from creating a zoning district with this many permissible uses. The applicable section of the borough code is the Act of February 1, 1966, P.L. (1965)—§ 3201, 53 P.S. § 48201. Under this section, council is given the power to regulate and restrict practically all aspects of buildings themselves, open spaces, population density, location of structures, etc., the only limitation on this power being that it be exercised so as to promote the "health, safety, morals or the general welfare" of the borough. Under the same act, section 1601, 53 P.S. § 46601, empowers council to adopt ordinances to govern the use of public areas, such as streets, parks, etc., again with the only limitation being that such ordinances create "conditions favorable to the health, safety, morals and general welfare of the citizens." Thus, if council reasonably believed that a given district could contain *all* types of structures, without *any* density requirements whatsoever, so long as this did not adversely affect health, safety and morals, such a district could be created. In fact, it is common knowledge that in many industrial and commercial districts just such a wide range of uses is permitted. Given such broad power to zone, we cannot say that New Hope Borough Council abrogated its legislative function by creating a PUD district permitting the mixture of uses outlined supra, especially given the density requirements.

We must next examine the statutory power of the borough planning commission to determine whether such an administrative body may regulate the internal development of a PUD district. The Act of February 1, 1966, P.L. (1965)—§ 1155, 53 P.S. § 46155 requires that all plans for land "laid out in building lots" be approved by the planning commission before they may be recorded. Thus, the traditional job of the commission has been to examine tract plans to determine whether they conform to the applicable borough ordinances. The ordinances most frequently interpreted and applied by the planning commission are those dealing with streets, sewers, water and gas mains, etc., i.e., the so-called public improvements. However, the statute contains no language which would prohibit the planning commission from approving plans with reference to ordinances dealing with permissible building uses as well. The primary reason that planning commissions have not traditionally interpreted this type of ordinance is that such regulations do not usually come into play until the landowner wishes to begin the actual construction of a particular building. By this time, the relevant subdivision plan has already been approved by the commission; thus the task of examining the plans for a particular structure to see whether it conforms to the regulations for the zoning district in which it will be erected devolves upon the local building inspector who issues the building permit.

However, in the case of PUD the entire development (including specific structures) is mapped out and submitted to the administrative agency at once. Accordingly, the requirements set forth in a PUD ordinance must relate not only to those areas traditionally administered by the planning commission, but also to areas traditionally administered by the building inspector. Therefore, quite logically, the job of approving a particular PUD should rest with a single municipal body. The question then is simply which one: Borough Council (a legislative body), the Planning Commission (an administrative body), or the Zoning Board of Adjustment (an administrative body)?

There is no doubt that it would be statutorily permissible for council itself to pass a PUD ordinance and simultaneous zoning map amendment so specific that no details would be left for any administrator. The ordinance could specify where each building should be placed, how large it should be, where the open spaces are located, etc. But what

would be the practical effect of such an ordinance?   One of the most
attractive features of Planned Unit Development is its flexibility; the
chance for the builder and the municipality to sit down together and
tailor a development to meet the specific needs of the community and
the requirements of the land on which it is to be built.   But all this
would be lost if the Legislature let the planning cement set before any
developer could happen upon the scene to scratch his own initials in that
cement.   Professor Krasnowiecki has accurately summed up the effect
on planned unit development of such legislative planning.   The picture,
to be sure, is not a happy one:

> "The traditional refuge of the courts, the requirement that all the
> standards be set forth in advance of application for development,
> does not offer a practical solution to the problem.   The complexity of
> pre-established regulations that would automatically dispose of any
> proposal for planned unit development, when different housing types
> and perhaps accessory commercial areas are envisaged, would be
> quite considerable.   Indeed as soon as various housing types are per-
> mitted, the regulations that would govern their design and distribu-
> tion on every possible kind of site, their relationship to each other
> and their relationship to surrounding properties must be complex un-
> less the developer's choice in terms of site, site plan, and design and
> distribution of housing is reduced close to zero.   It is not likely
> * * * that local authorities would want to adopt such a set of
> regulations."   Krasnowiecki, Planned Unit Development: A Chal-
> lenge to Established Theory and Practice of Land Use Control, 114
> U.Pa.L.Rev. 47, 71 (1965).

Left with Professor Krasnowiecki's "Hobson's choice" of no developer
leeway at all, or a staggering set of legislative regulations sufficient to
cover every idea the developer might have, it is not likely that Planned
Unit Development could thrive, or even maintain life, if the local legislature assumed totally the role of planner.

The remaining two municipal bodies which could oversee the shaping
of specific Planned Unit Developments are both administrative agencies,
the Zoning Board of Adjustment and the Planning Commission.   As this
Court views both reality and zoning enabling act, the Zoning Board of
Adjustment is not the proper body.   The Act of February 1, 1966, P.L.
(1965)—§ 3207, 53 P.S. § 48207(g) specifically sets forth the powers of a
borough zoning board of adjustment.   These powers are three in number, and only three.   The board may (1) hear and decide appeals where
there is an alleged error made by an administrator in the enforcement
of the enabling act or any ordinance enacted pursuant thereto; (2) hear
and decide special exceptions; and (3) authorize the grant of variances
from the terms of existing ordinances.   These powers in no way encompass the authority to review and approve the plan for an entire development when such plan is neither at variance with the existing ordinance
nor is a special exception to it; nor does (1) above supply the necessary
power since the board would not be reviewing an alleged administrative
error.

Moreover, from a practical standpoint, a zoning board of adjustment is, of the three bodies here under discussion, the one least equipped to handle the problem of PUD approval. Zoning boards are accustomed to focusing on one lot at a time. They traditionally examine hardship cases and unique uses proposed by landowners. As Professor Krasnowiecki has noted: "To suggest that the board is intended, or competent, to handle large scale planning and design decisions is, I think, far fetched." Technical Bulletin 52, Urban Land Institute, p. 38 (1965). We agree.

Thus, the borough planning commission remains the only other body both qualified and statutorily permitted to approve PUD. Of course, we realize that a planning commission is not authorized to engage in actual re-zoning of land. But merely because the commission here has the power to approve more than one type of building for a particular lot within the PUD district does not mean that the commission is usurping the zoning function. Indeed, it is acting in strict *accordance* with the applicable zoning ordinance, for that ordinance, No. 160, *permits* more than one type of building for a particular lot. To be sure, if the commission approved a plan for a PUD district where 30% of the land were being used commercially, *then* we would have an example of illegal re-zoning by an administrator. But no one argues in the present case that appellant's plan does not conform to the requirements of ordinance 160.

Nor is this Court sympathetic to appellees' argument that ordinance 160 permits the planning commission to grant variances and special exceptions. We fail to see how a development such as appellant's that meets every single requirement of the applicable zoning ordinance can be said to be the product of a variance or a special exception. The very essence of variances and special exceptions lies in their *departure* from ordinance requirements, not in their compliance with them. We therefore conclude that the New Hope Planning Commission has the power to approve development plans submitted to it under ordinance 160.

*   *   *

Notes on The Planned Unit Development Technique

1. **The PUD Concept.** As *Cheney* indicates, the core of the planned unit development concept is that zoning regulations for large-scale projects should "focus on density requirements rather than on specific rules for each individual lot." PUD regulations provide for the calculation of densities on a project basis and allow other adjustments based on a unified plan—adjustments not possible under traditional zoning which is geared to controlling the placement of a single structure on a single lot, with the lot as the basic regulatory unit. In order to make PUD work, it is obviously necessary to abandon, or at least substantially to modify, the traditional self-executing system of zoning regulation, under which—in theory, at least—a land developer obtains land that is zoned for the kind of development proposed and then needs only to secure a building permit from the building inspector. The PUD, on the other hand, is governed by much more general standards which are applied—inevitably with some exercise of discretion on the part of the administrative agency—when the developer proposes a specific project.

The proponents of the PUD concept usually assert that its principal advantages over the traditional zoning system are (a) improved design, (b) more useful open space, and (c) lower costs for the land developer. As we have already seen, the PUD technique permits a unified treatment of site design, without the restrictions imposed by the application of fixed minimum lot size, setback, and frontage requirements to individual lots. Freedom for the "cookie-cutter" block and lot pattern allows a reallocation of project densities, which in turn may produce more interesting project designs. Design freedom is particularly important in the development of rough or hilly terrain. The traditional zoning system seems to assume flat land, to which the block and lot pattern can be easily applied. In rough or hilly areas the developer must often resort to excessive grading to create building sites under the traditional zoning system. But PUD, by allowing a reallocation of densities, may enable the developer to leave rough terrain in its natural state without financial sacrifice. Moreover, since PUD regulations are not self-executing, they provide an opportunity for site plan review in conjunction with approval of specific PUD projects.

By increasing density in portions of the project area, PUD allows reduction or even elimination of front and side yard setback requirements, so that the land thus "saved" can be reserved as "common open space" for use by all project residents. This not only provides open space that is often more "usable" than the traditional front and side yards of individual lots, but may also help to make up for lack of adequate public open space in many communities.

Increased density and reduction of lot frontage requirements and "clustering" of structures in the developed portions of a PUD project area are also the key to reduction of the developer's costs, since the PUD project will require a smaller investment in streets, sidewalks, water mains, sewers, utility lines, and other physical improvements than a conventional subdivision. Not having to grade and prepare rough terrain for building may also produce savings to the land developer. The prospect of financial savings is no doubt the principal incentive for developers to opt in favor of PUD rather than conventional subdivision development.

2. **The PUD Legal Format: Floating Zone or Special Exception?** The PUD ordinance (No. 160) approved in *Cheney* clearly created an elaborate kind of "floating zone," and another ordinance (No. 161) was required to "bring it to earth." This technique will probably be the most satisfactory in jurisdictions where the "floating zone" technique has been approved.[14] Under a second ap-

---

14. The PUD ordinance (No. 160) clearly created a "floating zone." Immediately after Eves v. Zoning Bd. of Adjustment was decided, it could have been anticipated that the PUD technique might be rejected on the authority of *Eves.* But after Donahue v. Zoning Bd. of Adjustment was decided the "floating zone" objection was no longer tenable. In fact, *Donahue* did not really answer the *Eves* opinion's argument that "it was almost impossible for the F-1 districts there to conform to a comprehensive plan since tracts would be re-zoned on a strictly *ad hoc* basis." There is nothing in *Donahue* to suggest that the first rezoning amendment would exhaust the authority of the local governing body to "bring the floating zone to earth" by rezoning other tracts later on; but any subsequent rezonings would, of course, be done "on a strictly *ad hoc* basis." In *Che-*

ney, the court similarly does not suggest that New Hope's enactment of ordinance No. 161 exhausted its authority to create PUDs. In any case, as indicated supra p. 1286, Raum v. Board of Supervisors of Tredyffrin, 20 Pa.Cmwlth. 426, 342 A.2d 450 (1975), distinguished *Eves* on the ground that adequate standards for rezoning were not provided in the ordinance; and Russell v. Pennsylvania Township Planning Comm., 22 Pa.Cmwlth. 198, 348 A.2d 499 (1975), held that *Eves* was overruled by the enactment of Pa.Stat.Ann. tit. 53, § 10603 (1972), authorizing the local governing body to approve "conditional uses." The enactment of the model PUD act, Pa.Stat.Ann. tit. 53, § 10701 et seq. (1972), certainly removes any doubt as to the validity of the PUD technique in Pennsylvania.

proach the PUD district is included in the text of the zoning ordinance and is also initially mapped, usually as an "overlay" district with a set of mandatory requirements in addition to those applicable to the standard zoning classifications. A third approach is to provide for PUD regulations to be administered as "special exceptions" or "conditional uses."

At the time when *Cheney* was decided, Pennsylvania had no special enabling legislation on the subject of PUDs. Its zoning enabling act was substantially identical with the Standard State Zoning Enabling Act. Under zoning enabling acts based on the Standard Act, a variety of problems may arise, as *Cheney* shows. *Cheney* deals with two of these (in addition to the problem of validity of "floating zones"): (1) The "uniformity" problem, arising from the Standard Act § 2 requirement that all zoning regulations "shall be uniform for each class or kind of buildings throughout each district." (2) The problem of assigning responsibility for administering the PUD regulations as between the local governing body, the zoning board of adjustment (or appeals), and the planning commission (board).

Like the Pennsylvania court in *Cheney*, most courts have had little difficulty rejecting attacks on PUD ordinances based on lack of uniformity. The California intermediate appellate court was even more explicit in Orinda Homeowners Committee v. Board of Supervisors, 11 Cal.App.3d 768, 90 Cal.Rptr. 88 (1970):

> * * * [The zoning enabling act] provides that the regulations shall be uniform for each class or kind of building or use of land throughout the zone. It does not state that the units must be alike even as to their character, whether single family or multifamily. In conventional zoning, where apartment houses are permitted in a particular zone, single family dwellings, being regarded (whether rightly or wrongly) as a "higher" use, are also allowed. This causes no conflict with * * * [the statute].

Id. at 90–91. See also Chrinko v. South Brunswick Township Planning Bd., 77 N.J.Super. 594, 187 A.2d 221 (L.Div.1963), where the court noted that the PUD ("residential cluster") ordinance accomplished uniformity "because the option is open to all developers within a zoning district, and escapes the device that it is compulsory." Id. at 601, 187 A.2d at 225. The court also held that the PUD ordinance was not invalid because it incidentally benefited the PUD developer by reducing land improvement costs.

With respect to the problem of assigning responsibility for administering the PUD regulations as between the local governing body, the zoning board of adjustment (or appeals) and the planning commission (or board), compare *Cheney* with Prince George's County v. M & B Constr. Co., 267 Md. 338, 297 A.2d 683 (1972), and Lutz v. City of Longview, 83 Wash.2d 566, 520 P.2d 1374 (1974). In the *Prince George's County* case, amendments to both the zoning and subdivision control ordinances were adopted in order to authorize PUDs, and the court held that approval of PUDs was properly delegated to the planning commission as part of its subdivision control function. Under the ordinances PUDs were a permitted use in residential zones; single-family dwellings and townhouses were permitted in PUDs; reductions in lot size were allowed subject to a minimum lot size requirement; but existing overall densities and building bulk restrictions were to remain unchanged in PUD projects. In the *City of Longview* case the planning commission was authorized to approve PUDs under the PUD provision of the zoning ordinance, and had approved a PUD for multi-family use in a single-family district. The court held that PUD approvals could not be delegated to the planning commission in such a case because authorization of a change of use is a legislative function.

If the PUD district is mapped ("brought to earth") by a rezoning amendment and the regulatory problem is simply the application of the PUD standards to an individual PUD, it is not difficult to argue that the planning commission (or board) may carry out this function even though the Standard Zoning Enabling Act (and state zoning legislation based on it) does not expressly authorize the planning commission (board) to do so. If some element of discretion is built into the PUD administrative procedure, however—as was apparently the case in *Cheney* —delegation of the PUD administrative function to the planning commission (board) is more difficult to sustain. In this instance, the local governing body may have to share in the PUD project approval process, especially if density increases are contemplated in the PUD.

Many PUD provisions in zoning ordinances clearly contemplate that bargaining and negotiation between the land developer and the local authorities will precede a PUD project approval. In Rutland Environmental Protection Ass'n v. Knox County, 31 Ill.App.3d 82, 334 N.E.2d 215 (1975), the argument was made that this kind of bargaining was invalid as "contract zoning." The argument was rejected on the ground that, "Since the overall aims of * * * [PUD] zoning cannot be accomplished without negotiations and because conferences are indeed mandated by the regulating ordinance, the conduct of the * * * [county] cannot be read as contributing to contract zoning." Id. at 87, 334 N.E.2d at 219. See also Krasnowiecki, Legal Aspects of Planned Unit Development in Theory and Practice, in Frontiers of Planned Unit Development 99, at 102 (R. Burchell ed. 1973), suggesting that "zoning changes granted at the request of a particular applicant can be limited by ordinance to the proposal as described in the plans and oral testimony presented by the applicant in support of his request," and citing Albright v. Town of Manilus, 28 N.Y.2d 108, 320 N.Y.S.2d 50, 268 N.E.2d 785 (1971).

As previously indicated, it is possible to treat the establishment of a PUD designation on a particular tract as an exercise of the power to grant "special exceptions" or "conditional use permits." See Appeal of Moreland, 497 P.2d 1287 (Okl.1972), where the zoning ordinance required that PUDs be devoted primarily to residential uses and only secondarily to non-residential uses and that PUDs conform to the "intent and purposes" of the zoning ordinance and regional comprehensive plan, provided a set of design standards for PUDs, and delegated to the zoning board of adjustment the power to approve PUDs as "special exceptions." The delegation of power was sustained on the ground that, since the board's function was to determine whether a PUD complies with the standards contained in the ordinance, it would be acting in a quasi-judicial rather than a legislative capacity. Compare Chandler v. Kroiss, 291 Minn. 196, 190 N.W.2d 472 (1972), where the PUD ordinance authorized the local legislative body to grant special permits for PUDs. Since the PUD project under attack contemplated multi-family development in a district where such development was not permitted as of right, it was argued that a variance should have been sought. The court rejected this argument, observing that the ordinance provided for a "hybrid" procedure combining the variance and the special exception, and that, "[t]o the extent that the result of the proceeding for approval of a planned unit development thus alters the established, allowed land usages of the village, it has the same effect as would a succession of variances or rezonings." Id. at 202, 190 N.W.2d at 476.

Todd Mart, Inc. v. Town Bd. of Town of Webster, 49 App.Div.2d 12, 370 N.Y.S.2d 683 (1975), involved a PUD ordinance of the "floating zone" type. The following language in the opinion suggests that the court would not have approved an ordinance treating the designation of a tract as a PUD as a special exception or conditional use permit:

* * * The distinguishing feature between special use permits and planned unit developments is the size and significance of the proposed development. Whereas special use permits usually seek approval for a specified single use on a small parcel, such as service stations and swimming pools, the PUD is by its very nature a multi-use proposal for large scale developments such as shopping centers, planned integrated communities (new towns), or similar multi-uses on large parcels of land. It is obvious that petitioner's proposed shopping center of many large and small stores, including a department store, a supermarket, a theater and a bank, constructed on 20 acres of land has a greater impact on the body politic and the community in which it is planned than an application to convert a small parcel to a single use. A broad determination by the Town's legislative body is more appropriate for this task than an administrative determination made according to specified standards. The procedures set forth in the Town's zoning ordinance indicate that such a broad, legislative determination was intended * * *.

3. **PUD Enabling Legislation.** Although much local PUD legislation has been adopted under zoning enabling acts based on the Standard State Zoning Enabling Act, early PUD advocates drafted a model PUD act in 1964. See Babcock, Krasnowiecki & McBride, The Model State Statute, 114 U.Pa.L.Rev. 140 (1965). This model act sought to overcome limitations on the PUD technique inherent in the traditional zoning system. The model act, in general, opted for the "special exception" rather than the "floating zone" format, with a single approving agency—which could be the local governing body or any committee or commission designated by it—empowered to issue a unitary permit covering all aspects of a PUD project. Detailed procedural requirements for approval of PUDs on a case-by-case basis were provided, and the PUD project approval process was treated as "quasi-judicial" rather than "legislative." The model act also required a development plan, which was to provide the basis for continuing control over the PUD project area. Assurances against changes in public requirements after PUD project approval and assurances as to maintenance of common open spaces were included in the model act. See commentary on The Model State Statute, supra.

Despite the high quality of its draftsmanship, the 1964 model act was adopted in only six states; one of these states, New Jersey, has since repealed its PUD statute and redistributed its provisions, with modifications, throughout its land use control legislation. For examples of current statutes following the 1964 model act, see Conn.Gen.Stat. ch. 124a (1971); Pa.Stat.Ann. tit. 53, § 10701 et seq. (1972).

Additional options of the model act seem unlikely in view of the inclusion in the American Law Institute's Model Land Development Code (1976) of an authorization for PUD procedures as a form of "special development permission." Section 2–210 of the Model Land Development Code provides as follows:

(1) A development ordinance may authorize the Land Development Agency to grant special development permission for planned unit development by specifying the types or characteristics of development that may be permitted, which may differ from one part of the community to another.

(2) Special development permits may be granted for planned unit development, including combinations of land uses within the project area, and may be based on site planning criteria relating to the project as a whole

rather than to individual parcels, if the Land Development Agency finds that the development:

(a) will be consistent with a currently effective Land Development Plan; and

(b) is likely to be compatible with development permitted under the general development provisions of the ordinance on substantially all land in the vicinity of the proposed development; and

(c) will not significantly interfere with the enjoyment of other land in the vicinity.*

Why do you suppose the draftsmen of the Model Code decided to provide criteria for PUD project approvals but not to deal with any of the other problems raised by PUD projects?

4. **Use of the PUD Technique for Exclusionary Purposes.** Unlike zoning and subdivision controls, the review of PUDs usually involves a review of project design, including standards intended to preserve environmental amenities and an evaluation of the relationship of buildings to the site and to planned open spaces. Municipalities have tended to incorporate quite specific design standards in their PUD ordinances and to implement design review by having the developer submit detailed final project site plans. Preparation of site plans and getting them approved takes time and costs money. It is impossible to generalize as to whether the added costs are offset by savings in the cost of physical improvements installed on the PUD project site. But it is clear that many municipalities have used the PUD as a device for excluding low and moderate income persons. A municipality may achieve this objective by first establishing standard residential densities so low that development is impracticable, forcing all developers to apply for PUD approval in order to proceed. The municipality may then impose costly PUD approval requirements on developers— e.g., construction of schools for children expected to live in the development, or construction of off-site improvements benefitting the entire municipality—thus raising the cost of housing in PUDs and accomplishing the exclusionary purpose. It should be noted, however, that this particular exclusionary strategy was challenged and held unconstitutional in Oakwood at Madison, Inc. v. Township of Madison, 72 N.J. 481, 371 A.2d 1192 (1977), discussed in Note 2 following the *Mount Laurel* case supra, at p. 1207.

Bibliographical Note

The literature on planned unit development technique is voluminous. The most useful references are Frontiers of Planned Unit Development (R. Burcell ed. 1973), especially Krasnowiecki, Legal Aspects of Planned Unit Development in Theory and Practice, id. at 99; Mandelker, Controlling Planned Residential Developments (Am.Soc. of Planning Officials 1966); Symposium, Planned Unit Development, 114 U.Pa.L.Rev. 1–170 (1965), especially Krasnowiecki, Planned Unit Development: A Challenge to Established Theory and Practice of Land Use Control, id. at 47. See also F. Bair, Intensity Zoning: Regulating Townhouses, Apartments and Planned Developments (Am.Soc. of Planning Officials, Planning Advisory Serv.Rep. No. 314, 1976); Sternlieb, Burchell, Hughes & Listokin, Planned Unit Development Legislation: A Summary of Necessary Considerations, 7 Urban L.Ann. 71 (1974); So, Mosena & Bangs, Planned Unit Development Ordinances (Am.Soc. of Planning Officials, Planning Advisory Serv. Rep. No. 291, 1973); Aloi, Legal Problems in Planned Unit Development: Uniformity, Comprehensive Planning, Conditions, and the Floating Zone, 1 Real Estate L.J. 5 (1972).

Chapter 15

CONTROL OF LAND SUBDIVISION AND DEVELOPMENT

BLEVENS v. CITY OF MANCHESTER

Supreme Court of New Hampshire
103 N.H. 284, 170 A.2d 121 (1961)

Petition, for a declaratory judgment (RSA 491:22) seeking a decree of the court that the subdivision ordinance of the city of Manchester adopted October 7, 1958 pursuant to the enabling statute (RSA 36:19—36:29) does not apply to the plaintiffs' property acquired by a series of purchases between the years 1936 and 1956 . The ordinance imposes a penalty on persons selling a lot within a subdivision unless the plan of said subdivision has been approved by the city planning board. The ordinance which incorporates the regulations of the planning board further provides that no plan showing a subdivision will be approved unless the subdivider pays for all street grading and surfacing, curbing, sidewalks, water mains, sewers and other improvements.

Prior to the enactment of the ordinance, all of the land owned by the plaintiffs was subdivided into numbered house lots and such subdivision was approved by the city surveyor or by the city engineer, and plans showing such subdivision were filed in the Hillsborough County Registry of Deeds. The plaintiffs "have been, since 1946 to 1958, actively engaged in developing their property into a single-family residential area. A substantial number of house lots were sold and a substantial number of private homes were built on this property. All sales were made by reference to the publicly recorded plot showing subdivision of the property. * * * The Court finds that in the development of the property petitioners have expended substantial sums of money and have devoted a great deal of their own labor."

The plaintiffs excepted to findings of the Court and to the following ruling: "The Court rules that the petitioners have not acquired any vested right to continue development sales without compliance with the ordinance and that they may not proceed with the development without compliance with the ordinance." The plaintiffs' exceptions were reserved and transferred by Griffith, J. Additional facts appear in the opinion.

* * *

KENISON, Chief Justice. The power of the State to pass enabling legislation permitting municipal ordinances to regulate the subdivision of land has been sustained generally as a proper exercise of the police power. * * * "Since the subdivision of a large tract of land into a number of small building lots and the development thereof, either for residential or industrial purposes increases the value of the land in the aggregate to the subdivider and at the same time imposes new burdens upon the municipality and, if uncontrolled, upon other elements in the community, the validity of imposing a duty upon the subdivider to comply with reasonable conditions relating to location, site plan, location of and width of roads and sidewalks, the installation of necessary storm drains and sewers, and to restrictions on lot sizes so that the subdivision will conform to the local requirements for the safety, health and general welfare of the subsequent owners of the individual lots therein and of the community has been generally recognized." 2 Rathkopf, The Law of Zoning and Planning, ch. 71, § 9 (1960).

Statutes, like RSA 36:19—36:29, regulating the subdivision of land seek to promote the orderly and planned growth of relatively undeveloped areas within a municipality. * * * Planless growth and haphazard development accentuate municipal problems in the demand for streets, water and sanitary services which have a direct relation to traffic safety and health. * * * The subdivision of land has a definite economic impact upon the municipality and hence the regulation of subdivision activities has been sustained as a means by which the interests of the public and the general taxpayer may be safeguarded and protected. Since the subdivider of land creates the need for local improvements which are of special benefit to the subdivision, it is considered reasonable that he should bear the cost rather than the municipality and the general taxpayer. * * *

The plaintiffs' contention that "the police power is not involved" in this litigation cannot be accepted. The fact that the lot areas may be satisfactory to the subdivider and prospective purchasers, or that the streets and drainage are also satisfactory to them does not bar the application of the subdivision statute and the ordinance enacted pursuant to it. * * * "One of the problems that has arisen is that of seeing to it that building lots are not laid out and sold and houses put thereon without some decent minimum of street paving and without some decent safety and health minimum of water and sanitary facilities. We all know that where subdivision of land is unregulated lots are sold without paving, water, drainage, or sanitary facilities, and then later the community feels forced to protect the residents and take over the streets and in some way or other provide for the facilities. One of the ways in which law and legislation are attempting to prevent just such situations is that of requiring paving, water, and drainage facilities to be installed, up to minimum public specifications, as a condition of approval of the plat. By means, therefore, of this city planning approach and technique and these developments in modes of subdivision regulation, and evils of the inharmonious street system, overcongestion of population, and deficiency in paving and sanitation and water facilities are coming to be reduced and prevented." Bettman, City and Regional Planning Papers 74 (1946).

* * *

The subdivision ordinance is attacked on the ground it is arbitrary and discriminatory. At the corner of Fairfield Street and Blevens Drive as shown on the plaintiffs' map are four lots, Nos. 145, 219, 232 and 146. The first two are owned by individual owners, the third is admittedly not subject to the subdivision ordinance while the fourth owned by the plaintiffs is subject to the ordinance. These lots are beyond the portion of Fairfield Street which has been accepted by the city, and as shown by the plan, lot 146 is situated in an unimproved block of twelve lots wholly surrounded by unaccepted streets. If the plaintiffs must under the ordinance supply municipal services for that lot, it will in effect be beneficial to the other lots not subject to the subdivision regulation. This is the price of progress in any attempt to improve land development, subject however to any right to relief because of "practical difficulty or unnecessary hardship" as provided by RSA 36:26. It is no different from the effect of zoning generally where certain property may be zoned in one class and a contiguous property in another. The city must have a starting point for any new law or ordinance and it is not discriminatory merely because every lot of land is not regulated in the same degree. * * * The Trial Court has found that there has been no discrimination against the plaintiffs and the record supports that finding.

It is contended that the subdivision law and ordinance is unreasonable and contrary to public policy. Planning for land use has "become an accepted part of municipal law." Savage, Land Planning and Democratic Purposes, 34 Notre Dame Law, 65, 66 (1958). * * * The ordinance contemplates that a plat may be submitted for approval which covers "only a part of the subdividers entire holding," in which case a sketch of prospective future streets "of the unsubmitted part shall be furnished." A subdivider may thus avoid the expense of improving more land than will be immediately required. Both the statute and the ordinance provide for the granting in proper cases of exceptions, or variances from the literal enforcement of the regulations, to avoid "undue hardship" or "practical difficulty or unnecessary hardship." RSA 36:26. * * * Thus flexibility in applying the regulations to partially developed subdivisions is provided for. Certain lots owned by the plaintiffs were acquired by them as individual lots from a previous subdivider. As to them, the statute appears to be inapplicable. RSA 36:1, subd. VIII.

We conclude that the subdivision law (RSA 36:19—36:29) and the Manchester ordinance which conforms to this law are valid and constitutional. What was said in 1954 by a unanimous court in Berman v. Parker, 348 U.S. 26, 33, 75 S.Ct. 98, 102, 99 L.Ed. 27, is pertinent to this case: "The concept of public welfare is broad and inclusive. * * * The values it represents are spiritual as well as physical, aesthetic as well as monetary. It is within the power of the legislature to determine that the community should be beautiful as well as healthy, spacious as well as clean, well-balanced as well as carefully patrolled."

Exceptions overruled.

All concurred.

SUBDIVISION CONTROL ENABLING LEGISLATION

The focus to this point has been on zoning, the regulation of land development through the adoption of zoning ordinances specifying permitted and conditional uses of land. This Chapter considers subdivision control, a related land use control technique which applies when land is first subdivided and made available for development. The importance of subdivision control in land use regulation arises from the fact that raw land which is farmed or otherwise used for non-urban purposes is usually held in relatively large tracts. If it is to be made available for urban development it must first be subdivided into blocks and lots which are suitable for building purposes. It is this need to make land available for building in small individual units that creates the opportunity for controls over the subdivision process.

The regulation of land subdivision in the United States dates from before 1900. Indeed, the rectangular surveys of the public domain based upon the Northwest Ordinance of 1785 constituted a very rudimentary form of land-subdivision regulation. From 1844 on, so-called "town site laws" were passed to regulate the dividing of public domain land for town development purposes. But both the federal legislation dealing with surveys of public domain lands and the early state legislation with regard to land subdivision were primarily designed to assure that adequate engineering data would be supplied and that recorded plats would be as accurate as possible. As Beuscher has pointed out, "until 1925 or so, in most places in this country, the American subdivider was able to get away with murder and often did." [1] Even in 1928, the only states with significant subdivision control legislation were Michigan, New York, Ohio, Wisconsin, and Texas.

As we have seen, the United States Department of Commerce published a Standard City Planning Enabling Act of 1928. Title I of the Standard Act was concerned with "planning" in the narrow sense. Title II of the Standard Act was concerned with the control of land subdivision at the local governmental level. Title II of the Standard City Planning Enabling Act contained the following provisions:

Sec. 12. Subdivision Jurisdiction.—The territorial jurisdiction of any municipal planning commission over the subdivision of land shall include all land located in the municipality and all land lying within 5 miles of the corporate limits of the municipality and not located in any other municipality, except that, in the case of any such nonmunicipal land lying within 5 miles of more than one municipality having a planning commission, the jurisdiction of each such municipal planning commission shall terminate at a boundary line equidistant from the respective corporate limits of such municipalities. [2]

---

1. Beuscher & Wright, Cases and Materials on Land Use 263–64 (1969).

2. The municipal corporation remains the basic unit for subdivision control, as it is for zoning. But just over one-half of the states retain the Standard Act's authorization of extra-territorial subdivision control for distances ranging from one mile to six miles beyond the municipal boundaries. At least nineteen states also authorize counties to regulate land subdivision in states where municipalities have extra-territorial subdivision control power, the county's subdivision control jurisdic-

Sec. 13. Scope of Control of Subdivisions.—Whenever a planning commission shall have adopted a major street plan of the territory within its subdivision jurisdiction or part thereof, and shall have filed a certified copy of such plan in the office of the county recorder of the county in which such territory or part is located, then no plat of a subdivision of land within such territory or part shall be filed or recorded until it shall have been approved by such planning commission and such approval entered in writing on the plat by the chairman or secretary of the commission.[3]

tion usually begins where the municipality's ends. Thus in Petterson v. City of Naperville, 9 Ill.2d 233, 137 N.E.2d 371 (1956), the court said: "A consideration of the * * * statutes and their amendatory provisions reveals the clear intention of our legislature to grant to municipalities adopting an official plan exclusive control and jurisdiction over the subdivision of lands located not more than one and one-half miles beyond the corporate limits of the municipality. * * * The exercise of such extraterritorial powers by a municipality is, of course, always subject to the requirement that the ordinance passed pursuant to legislative authority constitutes a valid exercise of the police power, and bears a reasonable and substantial relation to the public health, safety or general welfare. * * * It is true that the legislature has given to counties certain powers relative to maps, plats and subdivisions. * * * However, there is nothing in these legislative provisions relative to the powers of counties which indicates that it was not the intention of the legislature to give exclusive control in those areas within one and one-half miles outside the territorial limits of a municipality to municipalities which have an official plan in effect in such territory." In some states, however, subdivisions are required to meet the requirements of both municipal and county authorities. In other states the county subdivision control agency must consider the recommendations of the municipality in some cases. And some states provide for joint municipal-county approval of subdivisions at the discretion of the two units. A few states require the approval of various state agencies in addition to approval at the local level.

The Standard Act defined "subdivision" as "the division of a lot, tract, or parcel of land into two or more lots, plats, sites, or other divisions of land for the purpose, whether immediate or future, of sale or of building development." About sixteen states retain this definition; some twelve states draw the line at either three or five or more lots—sometimes with a time limit such as "within one calendar year"; and about one-half of the states do not attempt to define "subdivision" at all. Frequently the division of land into multi-acre lots is exempted from regulation, as are subdivisions which do not involve the establishment of any new street. Cal.Gov.Code Ann. § 66424 defines "subdivision" to mean "the division of any improved or unimproved land * * * for the purpose of sale, lease or financing, whether immediate or future, except leases for agricultural land for agricultural purposes," including "a condominium project * * *."

3. The Standard City Planning Enabling Act did not require any city to create a planning commission. But it did impose upon any city planning commission, once created, "the function and duty * * * to make and adopt a master plan for the physical development of the municipality." Standard Act § 6. Thus the preparation and adoption of "a major street plan" would seem to be mandatory, since such a plan would necessarily constitute part of the "master plan." Once the planning commission has adopted "a major street plan," it clearly would be mandatory for the commission to exercise its power to control land subdivision within its jurisdiction, as provided in Standard Act § 13. In some states there are statutes making the regulation of land subdivision mandatory at the local level whether or not the local governing body has created a planning commission. See, e. g., Cal.Gov.Code Ann. §§ 66411 et seq. (Deering 1974, Supp.1978). See also the discussion of the Michigan subdivision control legislation in Cunningham, Public Control of Land Subdivision in Michigan: Description and Critique, 66 Mich.L.Rev. 3 (1966).

Some fifteen states retain the Standard Act § 13 requirement of a "major street plan of the territory within" the planning commission's jurisdiction "or part thereof" as a prerequisite to regulation of land subdivision. Some eleven states apparently require completion of a "master plan," and one state, the adoption of an "official map" as a condition precedent to land subdivision control. As we have seen California is one of the states where preparation and adoption of a "general plan" is required by statute in every local government unit. Hence it is not surprising to

Sec. 14. Subdivision Regulations.—Before exercising the powers referred to in section 13, the planning commission shall adopt regulations governing the subdivision of land within its jurisdiction. Such regulations may provide for the proper arrangement of streets in relation to other existing or planned streets and to the master plan, for adequate and convenient open spaces for traffic, utilities, access of fire-fighting apparatus, recreation, light and air, and for the avoidance of congestion of population, including minimum width and area of lots.

Such regulations may include provisions as to the extent to which streets and other ways shall be graded and improved and to which water and sewer and other utility mains, piping, or other facilities shall be installed as a condition precedent to the approval of the plat. The regulations or practice of the commission may provide for a tentative approval of the plat previous to such installation; but any such tentative approval shall be revocable and shall not be entered on the plat. In lieu of the completion of such improvements and utilities prior to the final approval of the plat, the commission may accept a bond with surety to secure to the municipality the actual construction and installation of such improvements or utilities at a time and according to specifications fixed by or in accordance with the regulations of the commission. The municipality is hereby granted the power to enforce such bond by all appropriate legal and equitable remedies.

All such regulations shall be published as provided by law for the publication of ordinances, and, before adoption, a public hearing shall be held thereon. A copy thereof shall be certified by the commission to the recorders of the counties in which the municipality and territory are located.[4]

Sec. 15. Procedure, Legal Effect of Approval of Plat.—The planning commission shall approve or disapprove a plat within 30 days after the submission thereof to it; otherwise such plat shall be deemed to have been approved, and a certificate to that effect shall be issued by the commission on demand: *Provided, however,* That the applicant for the commission's approval may waive this requirement and consent to an extension of such period. The ground of disapproval of any plat shall be stated upon the records of the commission. Any plat submitted to the commission shall contain the name and address of a person to

find that Cal.Gov.Code Ann. § 66473.5 provides that "[n]o local agency shall approve a [subdivision] map unless the legislative body shall find that the proposed subdivision, together with the provisions for its design and improvement, is consistent with the [officially adopted] general plan * * * or any specific plan adopted pursuant to" the California planning legislation.

4. Under the Standard City Planning Enabling Act, the planning commission was, in effect, both the legislative body enacting regulations and the administrative agency applying those regulations to individual applications for subdivision approval. Some of the current subdivision statutes follow the Standard Act in this respect. In other states the regulations governing land subdivision must be adopted by the local governing body in ordinance form. In some states the local governing body may reserve for itself the power to give or withhold final approval of subdivisions, with the planning commission acting only in a recommendatory capacity. The "tentative" approval procedure authorized by the Standard City Planning Enabling Act is retained in most of the current subdivision control legislation, often, however, under the designation of "conditional" or "preliminary" approval.

whom notice of a hearing shall be sent; and no plat shall be acted on by the commission without affording a hearing thereon. Notice shall be sent to the said address by registered mail of the time and place of such hearing not less than five days before the date fixed therefor. Similar notice shall be mailed to the owners of land immediately adjoining the platted land, as their names appear upon the plats in the county auditor's office and their addresses appear in the directory of the municipality or on the tax records of the municipality or county. Every plat approved by the commission shall, by virtue of such approval, be deemed to be an amendment of or an addition to or a detail of the municipal plan and a part thereof. Approval of a plat shall not be deemed to constitute or effect an acceptance by the public of any street or other open space shown upon the plat. The planning commission may, from time to time, recommend to counsel amendments of the zoning ordinance or map or additions thereto to conform to the commission's recommendations for the zoning regulation of the territory comprised within approved subdivisions. The commission shall have the power to agree with the applicant upon use, height, area or bulk requirements or restrictions governing buildings and premises within the subdivision, provided such requirements or restrictions do not authorize the violation of the then effective zoning ordinance of the municipality. Such requirements or restrictions shall be stated upon the plat prior to the approval and recording thereof and shall have the same force of law and be enforceable in the same manner and with the same sanctions and penalties and subject to the same power of amendment or repeal as though set out as a part of the zoning ordinance or map of the municipality.

Sec. 16. Penalties for Transferring Lots in Unapproved Subdivisions.—Whoever, being the owner or agent of the owner of any land located within a subdivision, transfers or sells or agrees to sell or negotiates to sell any land by reference to or exhibition of or by other use of a plat of a subdivision, before such plat has been approved by the planning commission and recorded or filed in the office of the appropriate county recorder, shall forfeit and pay a penalty of $100 for each lot or parcel so transferred or sold or agreed or negotiated to be sold; and the description of such lot or parcel by metes and bounds in the instrument of transfer or other document used in the process of selling or transferring shall not exempt the transaction from such penalties or from the remedies herein provided. The municipal corporation may enjoin such transfer or sale or agreement by action for injunction brought in any court of equity jurisdiction or may recover the said penalty by a civil action in any court of competent jurisdiction.[5]

5. Although these sanctions were clearly applicable even when the instrument of transfer described the lot by metes and bounds, the Standard Act clearly did not require a subdivider to obtain approval of his subdivision if he was willing to forego the use of a plat in selling his lots. Moreover, it would always be difficult to prove that a subdivider had actually made a lot sale by reference to an unapproved (and therefore unrecorded) plat when he conveyed the lot by metes and bounds. And the Standard Act § 18 provision forbidding acceptance or improvement of streets and authorization of water main and sewer construction would not, of course, have been a very effective weapon against subdividers who (as was common in the 1920's and 1930's) sought only to sell unimproved lots. Today, however, most subdividers are developer-builders to whom authorization of water main and sewer construction

Sec. 17. County Recorder's Duties.—A county recorder who files or records a plat of a subdivision without the approval of the planning commission as required by law shall be deemed guilty of a misdemeanor and shall be fined not less than $100 nor more than $500.

Sec. 18. Improvements in Unapproved Streets.—The municipality shall not accept, lay out, open, improve, grade, pave, curb, or light any street, or lay or authorize water mains or sewers or connections to be laid in any street, within any portion of territory for which the planning commission shall have adopted a major street plan, unless such street (a) shall have been accepted or opened as or shall otherwise have received the legal status of a public street prior to the adoption of such plan, or unless such street (b) corresponds with a street shown on the official master plan or with a street on a subdivision plat approved by the planning commission or with a street on a street plat made by and adopted by the commission. Council may, however, accept any street not shown on or not corresponding with a street on the official master plan or on an approved subdivision plat or an approved street plat, provided the ordinance or other measure accepting such street be first submitted to the municipal planning commission for its approval and, if approved by the commission, be enacted or passed by not less than a majority of the entire membership of council or, if disapproved by the commission, be enacted or passed by not less than two-thirds of the entire membership of council. A street approved by the planning commission upon submission by council, or a street accepted by a two-thirds vote after disapproval by the planning commission, shall thereupon have the status of an approved street as fully as though it had been originally shown on the official master plan or on a subdivision plat approved by the commission or had been originally platted by the commission.

Sec. 19. Erection of Buildings.—From and after the time when a planning commission shall have adopted a major street plan of the territory within its subdivision jurisdiction or part thereof, no building shall be erected on any lot within such territory or part, nor shall a building permit be issued therefor unless the street giving access to the lot upon which such building is proposed to be placed (a) shall have been accepted or opened as or shall otherwise have received the legal status of a public street prior to that time, or unless such street (b) corresponds with a street shown on the official master plan or with a street on a subdivision plat approved by the planning commission or with a street on a street plat made by and adopted by the commission or with a street accepted by council, after submission to the planning commission, by the favorable vote required in section 18 of this act. Any building erected in violation of this section shall be deemed an unlawful struc-

and the improvement and acceptance of subdivision streets are important. In some states, earlier platting statutes required recording of subdivision plats before sale of lots was permitted; in these states the Standard Act's prohibition of recording without subdivision approval always precluded sales of subdivision lots without approval of the subdivision plat by the planning commission. In other states, provisions requiring approval and recording of subdivision plats before sale of subdivision lots were added to the subdivision control statutes. And in almost all states today, municipalities refuse to issue building permits for unapproved subdivisions.

ture, and the building inspector or other appropriate official may cause it to be vacated and have it removed.

Sec. 20. Status of Existing Platting Statutes.—From and after the time when a planning commission shall have control over subdivisions as provided in section 13 of this act, the jurisdiction of the planning commission over plats shall be exclusive within the territory under its jurisdiction, and all statutory control over plats or subdivisions of land granted by other statutes shall in so far as in harmony with the provisions of this act be deemed transferred to the planning commission of such municipality, and, in so far as inconsistent with the provisions of this act, are hereby repealed.

Note on Local Subdivision Regulations and Procedures

Local subdivision regulations—whether adopted only by the local planning commission (or board) or adopted by the local governing body in ordinance form—consist of (1) a set of substantive standards for the design and improvement of subdivisions, and (2) procedures for submission, review, and approval or disapproval of subdivision plats. The following example, taken from a model subdivision control ordinance, demonstrates typical design standards for subdivision streets.[6]

4.18 Street Design

Proposed streets shall be in harmony and conformance with existing and proposed streets, as shown on the Town (City) Master Plan or Official Map. Street patterns shall give due consideration to contours and natural features. Where required by the Board, provision shall be made for the extension of the street pattern to abutting undeveloped property. Every proposed street in a subdivision shall be laid out and constructed as required by these regulations.

Where a subdivision abuts an existing street with an inadequate alignment, or right-of-way width, the subdivision plat shall include in the street dedication all land needed to meet the standards established by these regulations, and as approved by the Board.

Permanent dead end streets shall not exceed 600 feet in length, and shall terminate in a turnaround 100 feet in diameter, with a paved area 80 feet in diameter.

Temporary dead end streets, where future extension to another outlet is approved by the Board or where indicated on the plan, may exceed 600 feet in length. In such cases the full width of the right-of-way to the subdivision property line shall be dedicated to the municipality.

Except where it is impracticable, because of the character of the land, streets shall intersect so that within 75 feet of the intersection the street lines are at right angles, and the grade within 100 feet does not exceed one percent. No structure or planting shall impair corner visibility.

The plan of any proposed subdivision shall show all work required to connect and complete the improvements and utilities between the proposed street pattern and any connecting street in an existing subdivision.

---

6. Office of State Planning, State of New Hampshire, Handbook of Subdivision Practice 107–08 (1972). Comparable requirements are provided for other facilities. For another model subdivision control ordinance see R. Freilich & P. Levi, Model Subdivision Regulations: Text and Commentary (1975).

All streets shall be constructed and paved and all bridges, culverts, drainage structures, storm sewers, gutters, drainage ditches, and other improvements required by the subdivision plat and accompanying documents, shall be installed in conformance with the standards and specifications adopted by the governing body.

4.19   Classification of Streets

The classification of Town (City) streets shall be as defined in the Town (City) Master Plan or Official Map, and the classification of new streets and streets not shown on such plan shall be as determined by the Board. The following standards of design shall apply to streets maintained by the Town (City):

Classification	Minimum Pavement Width Feet	Minimum Right-of-Way Feet	Maximum Gradient Percent	Minimum Centerline Radius of Curve Feet
Arterial	44	100	5%	955
Major Collector	40	80	8	700
Minor Collector	30	60	10	400
Local Service	24	50	12	125

• The minimum gradient shall be 0.5 percent.

The Board may modify the maximum and minimum gradient for short lengths of streets where, in its judgment, existing topographic conditions or the preservation of natural features indicate that such modification will result in the best subdivision of land.

The Board may require greater width of right-of-way where, in its judgment, the demands of present or future traffic make it desirable or where topographic conditions create a need for greater width for grading.

Subdivision regulations generally prescribe fairly standardized procedures for submission, review, and approval or disapproval of subdivision plats. These procedures are, in practice, characterized by a process of negotiation between local public agencies and the subdivision developer. Usually the review procedures fall into four major stages: (1) pre-application review; (2) "tentative" or "preliminary" plat approval; (3) installation of required improvements; and (4) "final" plat approval.

Pre-application Review:

The subdivider usually prepares a preliminary sketch plan and a location map showing the relationship of the proposed subdivision to existing community facilities which would have to serve it or would have an influence on it. The preliminary sketch plan and the location map are usually reviewed by the professional planning staff and other local officials such as the municipal engineer, to determine whether the proposed subdivision fits into the comprehensive land use plan of the municipality (if any), whether it satisfies municipal design standards and subdivision improvement requirements, and whether the site is suitable from the point of view of topography, drainage, etc. The results of this review are then discussed with the subdivider, who is informed of any changes necessary to comply with the subdivision regulations and the comprehensive plan. Suggestions for improvement of the subdivision design are often made at this stage, along with suggestions as to the need for careful investigation by the subdivider of market demands and financing arrangements before proceeding further. Sometimes the local regulations prescribe the kind of pre-application review summarized here; sometimes this review is only suggested.

In some states—e.g., New Jersey—subdivision ordinances may exempt from the requirement of local municipal approval subdivisions where the number of new lots is less than a designated number or no new streets are involved, "or such other classes of subdivisions as such ordinance shall designate." In such cases a plat of the subdivision must be submitted to the mayor or the planning board chairman for certification that the subdivision is exempt before the plat can be recorded. In many municipalities, however, the ordinance requires "sketch plats" of *all* proposed subdivisions to be submitted first to a "subdivision committee" of the planning board for the purpose of classifying the subdivision as exempt or non-exempt, thus extending the "preapplication procedure" to cases where no further official action (other than formal certification by mayor or planning board chairman) is required.

"Tentative" or "Preliminary" Plat Review:

After the "pre-application review," if any, the subdivider must usually submit a "tentative" or "preliminary" plat. While the name suggests that the decision at this stage is "tentative," nothing could be further from the truth, for approval of the "tentative" or "preliminary" plat authorizes the laying out and improvement of streets, installation of water and utility lines, and the like. After expenditures have been made by the subdivider on such permanent facilities, it is not likely that any major changes will be required at a later stage in the approval process. Because the decision is so important, the subdivision regulations usually set out in considerable detail the information to be shown on or to accompany the plat. The plat must be submitted in sufficient time and with enough copies to allow consideration and recommendations by a variety of local agencies such as the municipal engineer, the public works department, the school board, the health department, the parks department, etc. Recommendations from all these agencies should be received by the planning commission or other approving body before it holds a public hearing on the proposed subdivision. The planning commission (or board) grants or denies "tentative" or "preliminary" plat approval under some subdivision control statutes. Other statutes require the local governing body or a body made up of representatives of various interested municipal departments to make the decision. Some statutes or ordinances provide for an appeal of the decision on the "tentative" or "preliminary" plat to the local governing body. Before approval is granted, there is often a good deal of discussion and negotiation between the subdivider and the approving body, and the parties may agree on modifications of the plat or the imposition of conditions on the approval to be granted.

If the subdivider is to proceed with installation of required improvements after "tentative" plat approval, he needs assurance that he will not be required to make costly modifications as a result of changes in zoning or subdivision regulations. Since 1953, the New Jersey subdivision control act has guaranteed that there will be no changes in the "general terms and conditions" upon which "preliminary" plat approval was granted for a period of three years. The current New Jersey statute continues this guarantee, specifying that "general terms and conditions" shall include, but not be limited to, "use requirements; layout and design standards for streets, curbs, and sidewalks; lot size; yard dimensions and off-tract improvements." This broad protection is qualified, however, by a further proviso that nothing in the statute "shall be construed to prevent the municipality from modifying by ordinance such general terms and conditions of preliminary plat approval as relate to public health and safety." N.J.Stat.Ann. § 40:55D–49(a) (West Supp.1982–83). Cf. Cal.Gov.Code Ann. § 66474.1 (West Supp.1983), which provides that the local plat approval agency "shall not deny approval of a final map * * * if it has previously approved a tentative map for the proposed subdivision and if it finds that the final map is in substantial compliance with the previously approved tentative map." In Youngblood v. Board of Supervisors of San Diego County, 71 Cal.App.3d 665, 139 Cal.Rptr. 741 (1977), it was held that this provision did not protect a subdivision developer against a change in allowable residential density resulting from an amendment to the applicable general plan; that the board of supervisors acted improperly in accepting a final subdivision map which was not consistent with the general plan as amended; and that mandamus could issue to compel the board to conform the zoning ordinance to the amended general plan if the board failed to rezone voluntarily within a reasonable time. The opinion contains a broad dictum that "the filing of the map whether tentative or final does not preclude the county, under its zoning powers, from changing zone uses." The implication is that building permits could properly be refused after approval of the "final" plat, on the basis of a zoning ordinance amendment. Hagman comments that, "[s]ince neither California statutes nor courts provide much protection under estoppel or vested rights doctrines, and since California courts never (hardly ever) invalidate harsh regulation, the developer has no assurance and no way of securing assurance that a project started can be completed. The problem has led to high social costs." 29 Land Use Law & Zoning Digest No. 11, p. 8, citing D. Hagman, Estoppel and Vesting in an Age of Multi-Land Use Permits (paper prepared for Southwestern Univ. Conference on Constitutional Law, Sept. 18, 1977).

Installation of Required Improvements:

When "tentative" or "preliminary" plat approval is obtained, the subdivider is authorized to proceed with the installation of utility lines, streets, and other required improvements. Indeed, the subdivider must do so before the "final" plat can be approved. Depending on the terms of the applicable subdivision control statute, the subdivider is often given several options: (1) actual construction of the improvements at his own expense; (2) posting a performance bond guaranteeing such construction within a given period; (3) petitioning the municipal governing body to construct the improvements and levy the cost against the lots in the subdivision under its usual special assessment procedures; (4) formation of a special district for local improvement with power to issue bonds and levy a special assessment for the purpose of paying off the bonds. Because of the currently common practice of marketing houses and lots rather than undeveloped building lots in a new subdivision, most current subdivision regulations authorize issuance of building permits concurrently with construction of streets, utilities, and other improvements. Many subdivision developers, in fact, prefer to complete construction of houses before installing streets, gutters, curbs, sidewalks and the like, in order to avoid wear and tear on these facilities during the construction of houses.

From an administrative viewpoint, a great deal of the responsibility for enforcement of the subdivision regulations shifts during this stage from the planning staff to the municipal engineer and other officials concerned to make sure that proper construction standards are met. Their certificates that improvements have been completed in accordance with municipal standards are usually required before the "final" plat can be submitted for approval.

"Final" Plat Review:

At any time within the "tentative" or "preliminary" approval period the subdivider may submit his "final" plat for approval if installation of required improvements has been completed and all the necessary certificates have been secured. The subdivider is usually permitted, if he wishes, to submit for final approval only part of the tract "tentatively" approved, so that he can initially build houses in part of the tract only and thus reduce the amount he must borrow for construction and the carrying charges on the construction loan. Some municipalities report that they actually require two "final" plats. The first is termed an "engineering" plat and sets out details of the construction and location of subdivision improvements. This plat is designed to provide the municipal engineer and other municipal departments with a permanent record of the location, size, and design of underground utility installations for use in their subsequent maintenance. The second is a "final" plat "for record" which shows information primarily significant in relation to land titles such as exact lot lines, street lines, utility easements, and the like. If only a single "final" plat is required, it must contain information of both kinds, often at the expense of clarity. The subdivision regulations usually provide for submission and review of the "final" plat or plats in substantially the same way as the "tentative" or "preliminary" plat. The primary concern of local authorities at this stage is to assure that the "final" plat or plats will be in conformity with the plans approved earlier and that construction of improvements has been completed in accordance with such plans. Some subdivision regulations provide for approval of the "final" plat or plats by the local governing body even if the planning commission (or board) was the approving agency for the "tentative" or "preliminary" plat.

If the subdivider has completed construction of all required improvements before "final" approval is given, and has obtained building permits for all the houses he plans to construct, he doesn't need protection against changes in the zoning or subdivision regulations as much as he does at earlier stages of development. But a subdivider may not have proceeded so far before he obtains "final" plat approval. In any case, it would seem that "final" approval should preclude for a reasonable time any substantial change in the zoning or subdivision regulations in force when "final" approval is granted. A number of the current subdivision control statutes preclude some or all changes for a specified time after "final" plat approval.[7] In the absence of such protective statutory provisions, it is clear that substantial change of position by the subdivider in reliance upon final plat approval may estop the municipality from changing the zoning or subdivision regulations applicable to the subdivision. It is equally clear that judicial relief will rarely be granted unless the subdivider has actually begun construction before the changes are made.[8]

7. E.g., N.J.Stat.Ann. § 40:55D–52(a) (West Supp.1978) (neither zoning requirements nor rights conferred on developer pursuant to preliminary plat approval shall be changed for 2 years after final plat approval); Conn.Gen.Stat.Ann. § 8–26a (1971; West Supp.1978) (no change in zoning or subdivision requirements for 5 years after final plat approval); Mass.Gen. Laws Ann. ch. 40A § 7A (1973) (zoning in effect when preliminary plan was submitted may not be changed for 7 years after approval of "definitive plan," if the latter is submitted within 7 months of preliminary plan approval); N.Y.Gen.City Law § 83–a (McKinney 1968) (no increases in minimum requirements for lot areas or front, side and back yard setbacks for 3 years if city has both a zoning ordinance and a planning board when final plat is approved; the period is 2 years if the city has

either a zoning ordinance or a planning board, but not both; and the period is 1 year if the city has neither).

8. E.g., Elsinore Property Owners Ass'n v. Morwand Homes, 286 App.Div. 1105, 146 N.Y.S.2d 78 (1955); Telimar Homes, Inc. v. Miller, 14 App.Div.2d 586, 218 N.Y.S.2d 175 (1961); Garvin v. Baker, 59 So.2d 360 (Fla.1952); Blevens v. City of Manchester, 103 N.H. 284, 170 A.2d 121 (1961). Cf. Ward v. City of New Rochelle, 20 Misc.2d 122, 197 N.Y.S.2d 64 (1959), affirmed 9 A.D.2d 911, 197 N.Y.S.2d 128 (1959) (conveyance to school district of land worth $140,000 and constituting over 20% of subdivision land held to preclude, after final plat approval, application of amendment "up-zoning" minimum lot size from 10,000 to 20,000 square feet and minimum lot frontage from 100 to 150 feet).

As is indicated in Blevens v. City of Manchester, supra, and in the street design standards set out above, local subdivision regulations generally require subdivision developers to dedicate to public use the land needed for the subdivision's internal street layout, and to install at their own expense a wide variety of street improvements such as street paving, gutters, curbs, sidewalks, water mains, sanitary and storm sewers, culverts, and other drainage structures. Although developers have sometimes argued that such requirements amount to "takings" of private property for public use without compensation, the courts have generally sustained such requirements as a reasonable exercise of the police power. See, e.g., Allen v. Stockwell, 210 Mich. 488, 178 N.W. 27 (1920) (requirement that subdividers grade and surface streets with gravel and install surface drains, concrete sidewalks, and sanitary sewers); Mefford v. City of Tulare, 102 Cal.App.2d 919, 228 P.2d 847 (1951) (sewers and water mains); Petterson v. City of Naperville, 9 Ill.2d 233, 137 N.E.2d 371 (1956) (curbs, gutters and storm drainage facilities); Deerfield Estates v. East Brunswick Twp., 60 N.J. 115, 286 A.2d 498 (1972) (water mains); Mid-Continent Builders, Inc. v. Midwest City, 539 P.2d 1377 (Okl.1975) (water mains); Crownhill Homes, Inc. v. City of San Antonio, 433 S.W.2d 448 (Tex.Civ.App.1968) (water mains).

On the whole subdivision developers have instituted few lawsuits challenging the validity of street dedication and improvement requirements in subdivision control ordinances, probably because (a) delay incident to litigation is so expensive and (b) developers want to make sure that the municipality will "accept" the subdivision streets and other improvements and thus become responsible for their maintenance. Sometimes, however, subdivision requirements have been challenged as being unreasonable as applied to specific situations. For example, it may be argued that installation of sidewalks on one side of the subdivision streets rather than on both sides is adequate in low density developments; that quality standards have been set too high, thus precluding the possibility of selling to purchasers in the lower income brackets who comprise a large majority of the prospective purchasers; or that the developer has been improperly required, at his own expense, to install oversized utility lines or drainage facilities, or to dedicate and improve streets of excessive width, designed to serve property outside his development. The courts have reached varying results when faced with such arguments. See, e.g., Ayres v. City Council of Los Angeles, 34 Cal.2d 31, 207 P.2d 1 (1949) (the court sustained requirements for (a) dedication of a 10-foot strip along one boundary of the subdivision to allow widening of an adjacent major traffic artery, and (b) dedication of an 80-foot strip through the center of the subdivision to allow extension of an existing cross-street, although the latter then had a width of only 60 feet—both pursuant to an existing plan for street widenings in the city); 181 Incorporated v. Salem County Planning Bd., 133 N.J.Super. 350, 336 A.2d 501 (L.Div.1975), modified on another ground, 140 N.J.Super. 247, 356 A.2d 34 (App.Div.1976) (required dedication of land for widening of existing county road along subdivision boundary was unconstitutional because it did not "appear that the * * * action of the developer will forthwith or in the immediate future so burden the abutting road through increased traffic" as to require its widening). See also Lake Intervale Homes, Inc. v. Parsippany-Troy Hills Township, 28 N.J. 423, 147 A.2d 28 (1958) (developer cannot be required to pay entire cost of water main extensions which will substantially benefit property not owned by him).

Several states provide, in the alternative, that a subdivider may install required improvements himself or have the improvements financed on a special assessment basis.

During the last 30 years local governments have frequently enacted subdivision regulations requiring contributions from subdivision developers in the form of land dedications for schools, parks, and other recreational facilities, or fees in lieu of dedication to be used by the municipality (or school district) to acquire school, park, and playground sites. As in the case of street and utility installation requirements, the municipality's purpose is to impose the costs of new schools, parks, and other recreational facilities—at least in part—on subdivision developers, thus avoiding the necessity of financing such facilities entirely out of general municipal (or school district) revenues.

Section 14 of the Standard City Planning Enabling Act provides that municipal subdivision regulations "may provide for * * * adequate and convenient open spaces for * * * recreation, light and air, and for avoidance of congestion of population." This .might conceivably be deemed to authorize compulsory dedication requirements for parks and other recreational facilities, but it clearly does not authorize such requirements for school sites. Just as clearly, § 14 does not authorize the exaction of fees or charges in lieu of land dedication. Since so many state subdivision control statutes are substantially based on the Standard Act, it is not surprising to find that subdivision exactions for school or recreational purposes have frequently been struck down as *ultra vires*. E.g., Rosen v. Village of Downer's Grove, 19 Ill.2d 448, 167 N.E.2d 230 (1961) (fee requirement *ultra vires*); Haugen v. Gleason, 226 Or. 99, 369 P.2d 108 (1961) (same; the court treated the fee requirement as an unauthorized tax upon subdividers); West Park Ave. v. Ocean Township, 48 N.J. 122, 224 A.2d 1 (1966) (fee requirement *ultra vires*). In Jordan v. Village of Menomonee Falls, 28 Wis.2d 608, 137 N.W.2d 442 (1965), appeal dismissed 385 U.S. 4, 87 S.Ct. 36 (1966), however, the court found authority for both dedication and fee requirements in an enabling act which empowered municipalities to condition subdivision approval on compliance with regulations designed to facilitate "*adequate provision for* transportation, water, sewerage, *schools, parks, playgrounds* and other public requirements," and making applicable to subdivisions "any of the provisions of" the enabling act itself "or * * * *other* surveying, monumenting, mapping and *approving requirements*" included in the local subdivision regulations. (Emphasis by the court.) In Jenad, Inc. v. Village of Scarsdale, 18 N.Y.2d 78, 271 N.Y.S.2d 955, 218 N.E.2d 673 (1966), the court held that the New York village zoning enabling act authorized both dedication and fee requirements, although the act contained only rather ambiguous language authorizing village planning boards to require subdivision maps to show "a park or parks suitably located for playground or other recreation purposes" and also authorizing a waiver of this requirement, "subject to appropriate conditions and guarantees," when the circumstances of a particular subdivision were such that park lands were not needed therein. The court held that "appropriate conditions and guarantees" might include a fee in lieu of dedication!

A number of states have enacted new subdivision control legislation expressly authorizing exactions for schools, parks, and playgrounds in recent years. E.g., Ariz.Rev.Stat. § 9–463.01(D) to (F) (Supp.1978) (compensation to developer required); Cal.Gov.Code Ann. §§ 66477, 66478 (West Supp.1978) (dedication and fee requirements authorized); Colo.Rev.Stat. § 30–28–133(4)(a) (1973) (same); Vt.Stat.Ann. tit. 24, § 4417(5) (1975) (dedication limited to 15 percent of plat; fees to be used to serve needs of area surrounding subdivision). The constitutionality of Cal.Gov.Code Ann. § 66477 (West Supp.1978), formerly Cal.Bus. & Prof.Code § 11546, is considered in the next principal case.

School, park, and playground exactions create constitutional problems not present in the case of road and highway exactions, even if they are not *ultra vires.* Since schools, parks, and playgrounds are community facilities enjoyed by users other than the residents of any particular subdivision, it is more difficult to find a nexus between the exaction and the benefits resulting therefrom; and it is also more difficult to conclude that the additional population brought into the community made it "necessary" to provide the new community facilities when the facilities are schools, parks, and playgrounds. Hence the line between subdivision exactions that are constitutional and those that are not is harder to draw than in the case of exactions for streets and utilities. The constitutional problem is considered in detail in the next principal case and the Notes following it.

ASSOCIATED HOME BUILDERS OF THE GREATER EAST BAY, INC. v. CITY OF WALNUT CREEK

Supreme Court of California, 1971.
4 Cal.3d 633, 94 Cal.Rptr. 630, 484 P.2d 606, appeal dismissed
404 U.S. 878, 92 S.Ct. 202, 30 L.Ed.2d 159.

MOSK, Justice. Section 11546 of the Business and Professions Code authorizes the governing body of a city or county to require that a subdivider must, as a condition to the approval of a subdivision map, dedicate land or pay fees in lieu thereof for park or recreational purposes. In this class action for declaratory and injunctive relief, Associated Home Builders of the Greater East Bay, Incorporated (hereinafter called Associated)[9] challenges the constitutionality of section 11546 as well as legislation passed by the City of Walnut Creek to implement the section. It is also asserted that the city's enactments do not comply

9. Associated is a nonprofit corporation organized for the purpose of promoting the home building industry. Some of the members own Walnut Creek land which they intend to subdivide into four or more lots under the Subdivision Map Act. (Bus. & Prof.Code, § 11500 et seq.)

[Some of the court's footnotes have been omitted and most of those retained have been renumbered.—Ed.]

with the requirements set forth in the section. The trial court found in favor of the city, and Associated appeals from the ensuing judgment.

Section 11546 of the Business and Professions Code provides:

"The governing body of a city or county may by ordinance require the dedication of land, the payment of fees in lieu thereof, or a combination of both, for park or recreational purposes as a condition to the approval of a final subdivision map, provided that:

"(a) The ordinance has been in effect for a period of 30 days prior to the filing of the tentative map of the subdivision.

"(b) The ordinance includes definite standards for determining the proportion of a subdivision to be dedicated and the amount of any fee to be paid in lieu thereof.

"(c) The land, fees, or combination thereof are to be used only for the purpose of providing park or recreational facilities to serve the subdivision.

"(d) The legislative body has adopted a general plan containing a recreational element, and the park and recreational facilities are in accordance with definite principles and standards contained therein.

"(e) The amount and location of land to be dedicated or the fees to be paid shall bear a reasonable relationship to the use of the park and recreational facilities by the future inhabitants of the subdivision.

"(f) The city or county must specify when development of the park or recreational facilities will begin.

"(g) Only the payment of fees may be required in subdivisions containing fifty (50) parcels or less.

"The provisions of this section do not apply to industrial subdivisions."

Section 10–1.516 of the Walnut Creek Municipal Code, which will be discussed infra, refers to a general park and recreational plan adopted by the city. It provides that if a park or recreational facility indicated on the general plan falls within a proposed subdivision the land must be dedicated for park use by the subdivider in a ratio (set forth in a resolution) determined by the type of residence built and the number of future occupants. Pursuant to the ratio, two and one-half acres of park or recreation land must be provided for each 1,000 new residents. If, however, no park is designated on the master plan and the subdivision is within three-fourths of a mile radius of a park or a proposed park, or the dedication of land is not feasible, the subdivider must pay a fee equal to the value of the land which he would have been required to dedicate under the formula.[10]

Section 11546 and the city's ordinance are designed to maintain and preserve open space for the recreational use of the residents of new subdivisions. The adoption of a general plan (subd. (d)) avoids the pitfall of compelling exactions from subdividers of land which may be inad-

---

10. The requirement of dedication is qualified as to subdivisions containing 50 parcels or less. In order to comply with subdivision (g) of section 11546 only the payment of fees may be required in subdivisions of such size.

equate in size or unsuitable in location or topography for the facilities necessary to serve the new residents. Under the legislative scheme, the park must be in sufficient proximity to the subdivision which contributes land to serve the future residents. Thus subdividers, providing land or its monetary equivalent, afford the means for the community to acquire a parcel of sufficient size and appropriate character, located near each subdivision which makes a contribution, to serve the general recreational needs of the new residents.

If a subdivision does not contain land designated on the master plan as a recreation area, the subdivider pays a fee which is to be used for providing park or recreational facilities to serve the subdivision. One purpose of requiring payment of a fee in lieu of dedication is to avoid penalizing the subdivider who owns land containing an area designated as park land on the master plan. It would, of course, be patently unfair and perhaps discriminatory to require such a property owner to dedicate land, while exacting no contribution from a subdivider in precisely the same position except for the fortuitous circumstance that his land does not contain an area which has been designated as park land on the plan.

Constitutionality of Section 11546

Associated's primary contention is that section 11546 violates the equal protection and due process clauses of the federal and state Constitutions in that it deprives a subdivider of his property without just compensation. It is asserted that the state is avoiding the obligation of compensation by the device of requiring the subdivider to dedicate land or pay a fee for park or recreational purposes, that such contributions are used to pay for public facilities enjoyed by all citizens of the city and only incidentally by subdivision residents, and that all taxpayers should share in the cost of these public facilities. Thus, it is asserted, the future residents of the subdivision, who will ultimately bear the burden imposed on the subdivider, will be required to pay for recreational facilities the need for which stems not from the development of any one subdivision but from the needs of the community as a whole.

In order to avoid these constitutional pitfalls, claims Associated, a dedication requirement is justified only if it can be shown that the need for additional park and recreational facilities is attributable to the increase in population stimulated by the new subdivision alone and the validity of the section may not be upheld upon the theory that all subdivisions to be built in the future will create the need for such facilities.

In Ayres v. City Council of City of Los Angeles (1949) 34 Cal.2d 31, 207 P.2d 1, we rejected similar arguments. In that case, a city imposed upon a subdivider certain conditions for the development of a residential tract, including a requirement that he dedicate a strip of land abutting a major thoroughfare bordering one side of the subdivision but from which there was no access into the subdivision. The subdivider insisted that he could be compelled to dedicate land only for streets within the subdivision to expedite the traffic flow therein and that no dedication could be required for additions to existing streets and highways. Moreover, he asserted, the city had been contemplating condemning the property for the purposes indicated in any event, the benefit to the lot owners in the tract would be relatively small compared to the benefit to the city at large, and the dedication requirement amounted, therefore, to the exercise of the power of eminent domain under the guise of subdivision map proceedings.

We held that the city was not acting in eminent domain but, rather, that a subdivider who was seeking to acquire the advantages of subdivision had the duty to comply with reasonable conditions for dedication so as to conform to the welfare of the lot owners and the general public. We held, further, that the conditions were not improper because their fulfillment would incidentally benefit the city as a whole or because future as well as immediate needs were taken into consideration and that potential as well as present population factors affecting the neighborhood could be considered in formulating the conditions imposed upon the subdivider. We do not find in *Ayres* support for the principle urged by Associated that a dedication requirement may be upheld only if the particular subdivision creates the need for dedication.

Even if it were not for the authority of *Ayres* we would have no doubt that section 11546 can be justified on the basis of a general public need for recreational facilities caused by present and future subdivisions. The elimination of open space in California is a melancholy aspect of the unprecedented population increase which has characterized our state in the last few decades. Manifestly governmental entities have the responsibility to provide park and recreation land to accommodate this human expansion despite the inexorable decrease of open space available to fulfill such need. These factors have been recognized by the recent adoption of art. XXVIII of the Constitution, which provides that it is in the best interests of the state to maintain and preserve open space lands to assure the enjoyment of natural resources and scenic beauty for the economic and social well-being of the state and its citizens. Statutes which further the underlying policy expressed in the constitutional section must be upheld whenever possible in order to effectuate its salutary purposes.

The legislative committee which recommended the enactment of section 11546 emphasized that land pressure due to increasing population has intensified the need for open space, that parks are essential for a full community life, and that local officials have been besieged by demands for more park space. (21 Assembly Interim Com.Report, Municipal and County Government (1963–1965) pp. 33–34.) The urgency of the problem in California is vividly described in other portions of the report set forth in the margin.[10a]

10a. The report states. "Concern is being expressed statewide in California that we may be in danger of ' * * * building ourselves into a cement-lumber jungle.' Land pressures have been building steadily and the rising market price of each available scrap of urban land has made land the focus of competitive interests and * * * values. Recreation experts, planning commissions and conservationists have long insisted that the provision of recreation areas in subdivisions is a necessity. They argue that healthful, productive community life depends in part on the availability of recreation and park space.

"Population congestion magnifies the need for urban open space. It is perhaps the visual impact of thousands upon thousands of houses built row on row

These problems are not confined to contemporary California. It has been estimated that by the year 2000 the metropolitan population of the United States will increase by 110 to 145 million, that 57 to 75 million of the increase will occur in areas which are now unincorporated open land encircling metropolitan centers, and that the demand for outdoor recreation will increase tenfold over the 1956 requirement. (See Zilavy, Comment, 1961 Wis.L.Rev. 310, fns. 1 and 2.) Walnut Creek is a typical growth community. Located minutes' distance by motor vehicle from the metropolitan environs of Oakland and East Bay communities, the city population rose from 9,903 in 1960 to 36,606 in 1970, an increase of more than 365 percent in a decade.

We see no persuasive reason in the face of these urgent needs caused by present and anticipated future population growth on the one hand and the disappearance of open land on the other to hold that a statute requiring the dedication of land by a subdivider may be justified only upon the ground that the particular subdivider upon whom an exaction has been imposed will, solely by the development of his subdivision, increase the need for recreational facilities to such an extent that additional land for such facilities will be required.

Associated next contends that even if it be conceded that no showing of a direct relationship between a particular subdivision and an increase in the community's recreational needs is required, nevertheless the subdivider cannot be compelled to dedicate land for such needs, or pay a fee, unless his contribution will necessarily and primarily benefit the particular subdivision. Whether or not such a direct connection is required by constitutional considerations, section 11546 provides the nexus which concerns Associated. The act requires that the land dedicated or the fees paid are to be used only for the purpose of providing park or recreational facilities to serve the subdivision (subd. (c)) [11] and (subd. (e)) that the amount and location of land or fees shall bear a reasonable relationship to the use of the facilities by the future inhabitants of the subdivision.[12]

without relief of open space which has been most responsible for stimulating burgeoning citizen interest in the problem of providing for recreation areas in subdivision developments. * * *

"Neighborhood parks are a necessary component of community life. The committee has not encountered one local official who would deny the value of the neighborhood park. Elected officials, particularly, have found themselves besieged by demands for more park space. Families who have moved to suburbia in the hope of finding escape from urban congestion have found instead that their children may there too be forced into the streets in their natural pursuit of recreation space. These people turn to the community as a whole for aid in providing the desired parks." (Fns. omitted.) (Assembly Interim Com. on Municipal and County Government, op. cit. supra, pp. 33–34.)

11. We do not deem subdivision (c) to mean that the facilities purchased with a particular contribution may only be used by the residents of the subdivision which made the contribution; rather, that the fees may not be diverted to any purpose other than for park or recreational facilities which will be available for use by those residents. Clearly, the constitutionality of the exaction is not dependent upon exclusive use of the facilities by those who will occupy the subdivision. *Ayres* teaches that the fact the public will also benefit from the use made of the land dedicated is not a ground for holding an exaction invalid.

12. Amicus curiae Sierra Club urges that the requirement of dedication or the payment of a fee may be justified under the state's police power even if the recreational facilities provided by the subdivider's contribution are not used for the spe-

Another assertion by Associated is that the only exactions imposed upon subdividers which may be valid are those directly related to the health and safety of the subdivision residents and necessary to the use and habitation of the subdivision, such as sewers, streets and drainage facilities. While it is true that such improvements are categories directly required by the health and safety of subdivision residents, it cannot be said that recreational facilities are not also related to these salutary purposes. So far as we are aware, no case has held a dedication condition invalid on the ground that, unlike sewers or streets, recreational facilities are not sufficiently related to the health and welfare of subdivision residents to justify the requirement of dedication. As shall appear hereinafter, several other jurisdictions have upheld exactions similar to those imposed by section 11546 on the ground that the influx of new residents increases the need for park and recreational facilities.

Associated next poses as an eventuality that, if the requirements of section 11546 are upheld as a valid exercise of the police power on the theory that new residents of the subdivision must pay the cost of park land needs engendered by their entry into the community, a city or county could also require contributions from a subdivider for such services as added costs of fire and police protection, the construction of a new city hall, or even a general contribution to defray the additional cost of all types of governmental services necessitated by the entry of the new residents.

This proposition overlooks the unique problem involved in utilization of raw land. Undeveloped land in a community is a limited resource which is difficult to conserve in a period of increased population pressure. The development of a new subdivision in and of itself has the counterproductive effect of consuming a substantial supply of this precious commodity, while at the same time increasing the need for park and recreational land. In terms of economics, subdivisions diminish supply and increase demand. Another answer to Associated's assertion is found in the provisions of section 11546 itself. As we have seen, the section requires that land dedicated or in-lieu fees are to be used for the recreational needs of the subdivision which renders the exaction. Since the increase in residents creates the need for additional park land and the land or fees are used for facilities for the new residents, although not to the exclusion of others, the circumstances may be distinguished

cific benefit of the future residents of the subdivision but are employed for facilities used by the general public. Ordinarily if land within the subdivision is dedicated for a park it may be assumed that those who will reside in the subdivision will make primary use of the park. The problem of connecting the facilities with the use made of them by the subdivision residents arises when a fee in lieu of dedication is required. In view of the provisions of section 11546, we need not decide in the present case whether a subdivider may be compelled to make a contribution to a park which is, for example, not conveniently located to the subdivision. Parenthetically, however, we perceive merit in the position of amicus curiae. It is difficult to see why, in the light of the need for recreational facilities described above and the increasing mobility of our population, a subdivider's fee in lieu of dedication may not be used to purchase or develop land some distance from the subdivision but which would also be available for use by subdivision residents.
* * *

from a more general or diffuse need created for such areawide services as fire and police protection.[13]

Associated claims that section 11546 constitutes a special burden upon the future inhabitants of the subdivision since the amount the subdivider must contribute will ultimately be reflected in the increased cost of homes to the future residents. It is asserted that a double tax will be imposed on the new residents because they must not only pay for the initial cost of the park but will also be required to assume property taxes which will be used for its development and maintenance.[14] Double taxation occurs only when "two taxes of the same character are imposed on the same property, for the same purpose, by the same taxing authority within the same jurisdiction during the same taxing period." (Rhyne, Municipal Law, p. 673.) Obviously the dedication or fee required of the subdivider and the property taxes paid by the later residents of the subdivision do not meet this definition. If Associated's claim were valid the prior residents of a community could also claim double taxation since their tax dollars were utilized to purchase and maintain public facilities which will be used by the newcomers who did not contribute to their aquisition.[15]

Another contention by Associated is that section 11546 arbitrarily imposes its requirements only upon subdividers whereas those who do not subdivide are free from its exactions. The example is suggested of an apartment house built on land which is not subdivided. The future occupants may live the same distance from a public park and have the same right to use the recreational facilities as the residents of a nearby subdivision, yet the builder of the apartment house is not required to contribute to park facilities because he has constructed his apartment without subdividing. This point has some arguable merit in the sense that the apartment builder, by increasing the population of an area, may add to the need for public recreational facilities to the same extent as the subdivider. However, the apartment is generally vertical, while the subdivision is horizontal. The Legislature could reasonably have assumed that an apartment house is thus ordinarily constructed upon land considerably smaller in dimension than most subdivisions and the erection of the apartments is, therefore, not decreasing the limited supply of open space to the same extent as the formation of a subdivision. This significant distinction justifies legislatively treating the builder of an

---

13. We do not imply that only those exactions from a subdivider are valid which present the special considerations set forth with regard to section 11546 but hold only that the exactions required by the section are justified by special factors not applicable to such matters as the increased cost of governmental services. * * *

14. If Associated does not actually pay the exaction but merely passes the cost on to the consumer, a question arises as to its standing in this proceeding since it suffers no detriment and is not authorized to represent the consumers who it asserts will be taxed. Rather than relying upon that

proposition, however, we prefer to decide the matter on the merits.

15. A related contention is advanced that the exaction constitutes a special assessment against the future owners of property in the subdivision who have no right to a hearing or to protest. Similar arguments were rejected in Jordan v. Village of Menomonee Falls (1965) 28 Wis.2d 608, 137 N.W.2d 442, 450, and Jenad, Inc. v. Village of Scarsdale, supra, 18 N.Y.2d 78, 271 N.Y.S.2d 955, 958, 218 N.E.2d 673. (But see Reps and Smith, Control of Urban Land Subdivision (1963) 14 Syracuse L.Rev. 405, 407 et seq.)

apartment house who does not subdivide differently than the creator of a subdivision.

Finally, Associated attacks the constitutionality of subdivision (f) of section 11546, which specifies that a city or county must state when development of park or recreational facilities will begin. It is claimed that the city could in one case postpone development for 10 years and in another begin development within a year, and that this discretion amounts to an arbitrary delegation of power to the local governmental body and a denial of due process and equal protection of the laws. Obviously, the need for park and recreational facilities will vary from one community to another and from one neighborhood to another within the same community. The city's resolution 2225 provides that improvements to the parks shall be made as the subdivision area develops and park facilities become necessary. Constitutional considerations do not require a more precise standard; the courts are available to redress any unreasonable delay in development.[16]

Many of the issues raised by Associated have been discussed in the cases and law reviews.[17] The clear weight of authority upholds the constitutionality of statutes similar to section 11546. While Illinois has held an ordinance requiring a subdivider to dedicate land for park purposes to be unconstitutional (Pioneer Trust & Savings Bank v. Village of Mount Prospect, * * * 22 Ill.2d 375, 176 N.E.2d 799, 801–802),[18] Montana has reached a contrary conclusion (Billings Properties, Inc. v.

---

16. An additional argument of Associated is that subdivision (g) is unconstitutional in that it provides only the payment of fees as opposed to dedication of land may be required for subdivisions containing 50 parcels or less. The basis of this claim appears to be that it discriminates against owners who subdivide into more than 50 parcels. It is true that the size of a parcel is not defined in section 11546 so that one subdivider may be required to dedicate land for a park because he divides his land into more than 50 parcels whereas another subdivider with the same total acreage but who subdivides into less than 50 parcels may only be required to pay a fee in lieu of dedication. However, we cannot see how this difference discriminates against the first subdivider since the value of the land taken from him and the amount of the fee exacted from the second subdivider are fixed in accordance with the same population-density formula except that the fee to be paid by a subdivider with less than 50 parcels is calculated not by the value of the land he would have been required to dedicate within his subdivision but by the value of the land in the portion of the local park required to serve the needs of the subdivision. The fact that in one case the payment is made in land whereas in another it is made in money does not appear to be significant or discriminatory.

17. See, e.g., Zilavy, Comment, supra, 1961 Wis.L.Rev. 310; Cutler, Controlling Community Growth, 1961 Wis.L.Rev. 370, 387–391; Johnston, Subdivision Control Exactions, 52 Cornell L.Q. 871; Heyman and Gilhool, Increased Community Costs, 73 Yale L.J. 1121; Reps and Smith, Control of Urban Land Subdivision, supra, 14 Syracuse L.Rev. 405; Cunningham, Subdivision Control, 66 Mich.L.Rev. 1, 28; Taylor, Subdivision Control, 13 Hastings L.J. 344, 350.

18. *Pioneer Trust* relied upon *Ayres*, interpreting it as holding that a developer may be compelled to provide the streets which are required by the activity within the subdivision but cannot be required to provide a major thoroughfare, the need for which stems from the total activity of the community. The court in *Pioneer Trust* goes on to state that in the light of this principle a dedication requirement may be upheld only if the burden cast upon the subdivider is specifically and uniquely attributable to his activity and that no such showing was made. The *Ayres* case cannot be interpreted in this manner. One commentator has written that *Pioneer Trust* completely misunderstood the holding of *Ayres*. (See Johnston, Subdivision Control Exactions, supra, 52 Cornell L.Q. 871, 907–908.)

Yellowstone County (1964), 144 Mont. 25, 394 P.2d 182). New York and Wisconsin have affirmed the validity of statutes requiring either dedication or a fee in lieu thereof (Jenad, Inc. v. Village of Scarsdale, supra, 18 N.Y.2d 78, 271 N.Y.S.2d 955, 218 N.E.2d 673; Jordan v. Village of Menomonee Falls (Wis.1965), supra, 28 Wis.2d 608, 137 N.W.2d 442). In Connecticut the dedication requirement has been upheld but the requirement that a fee be paid in lieu of dedication was struck down on the ground that its use was not confined for the benefit of the subdivision but to the contrary the fees could be utilized to purchase park land for the residents of the entire town (Aunt Hack Ridge Estates, Inc. v. Planning Commission of Danbury (1967), 27 Con.Sup. 74, 230 A.2d 45, 47).

The rationale of the cases affirming constitutionality indicate the dedication statutes are valid under the state's police power. They reason that the subdivider realizes a profit from governmental approval of a subdivision since his land is rendered more valuable by the fact of subdivision, and in return for this benefit the city may require him to dedicate a portion of his land for park purposes whenever the influx of new residents will increase the need for park and recreational facilities. (Jordan v. Village of Menomonee Falls, supra, 28 Wis.2d 608, 137 N.W.2d 442, 448; Billings Properties, Inc. v. Yellowstone County, supra, 144 Mont. 25, 394 P.2d 182, 187.) Such exactions have been compared to admittedly valid zoning regulations such as minimum lot size and setback requirements. (Jenad, Inc. v. Village of Scarsdale, supra, 18 N.Y. 2d 78, 271 N.Y.S.2d 955, 958, 218 N.E.2d 673.)

Constitutionality of Section 10–1.516 of the Walnut Creek Municipal Code

Turning from the state statute to the Municipal Code, Associated argues that the fees the subdivider must pay in lieu of dedicating land are, under the city's ordinance, determined arbitrarily and without a reasonable relationship to principles of equality. It is claimed, for example, that a subdivider who develops high-density land may be required to pay a higher fee in lieu of dedication than one who develops low-density land even though both builders may be responsible for bringing the same number of new residents into the community. This may be true because the higher-density land is frequently more valuable and the fee is measured by the amount of land required by the number of persons in the subdivision.[19]

While the owner of more valuable land which will support a greater number of living units may be required to pay a higher fee for each new resident than the owner of less valuable land with a lower density, it does not follow that there is no reasonable relationship between the use

19. Associated poses as an example a subdivider who owns 25 acres of land valued at $20,000 an acre, who divides his land into 100 lots for single family residences and one who owns 50 acres worth $10,000 each, which he divides into 100 lots, two to an acre. The city assumes four occupants to each single family home. Each subdivider brings 400 persons into the community and each must contribute one acre or its cash equivalent for park purposes under the city's formula. Therefore, the first subdivider contributes $20,000 while the second is required to contribute only $10,000 although both increase the community's population by the same number of new residents.

of the facilities by future residents and the fee charged the subdivider. It is a proper assumption that persons occupying housing in a high-density area will use the public recreational facilities more consistently than those residents in single family homes who have private yards and more open space readily at their individual disposal.

Another series of contentions made by Associated relates to assertedly indefinite and arbitrary standards and procedures set forth in the ordinance. It is urged (1) that the concept of the fair market value is too indefinite and that a subdivider would hesitate to incur the delay and expense of testing value in the courts, and (2) that the city has absolute discretion to determine that the dedication of land is not feasible and that a fee should be charged in lieu thereof. These contentions are without merit. The question of fair market value is litigated frequently in the courts and no authority cited requires a more precise definition. A subdivider need not delay his development because of a dispute over this issue. Nor can it be said, for the reasons pointed out in the margin below, that there are insufficient criteria for determining when a fee should be required in lieu of dedication.[20]

The ordinance and resolution also provide that if the subdivider designates open space for recreational areas and facilities, this reduces the demand for local recreational needs and if the subdivider gives guarantees that the land will be permanently maintained for such use the city may give credit to the subdivider, reducing the exactions required of him. Associated complains that this provision may result in unequal treatment of subdividers in that there are no reasonable standards for determining when the city will afford credit to one subdivider and deny it to another.

We note that section 11546 contains no requirement that a city reduce the dedication or fee requirement in the event a subdivider has voluntarily provided recreational areas. There is a sound basis for such omission. The Legislature has expressed a policy of encouraging cities and counties to adopt long-range master plans for the recreational needs of the community. Such a plan takes into account the overall requirements of the city's residents, present and future, including the local needs of subdivision residents. If a legislative body were required to give credit for private recreational areas furnished by a subdivider in his proposed subdivision, the viability of the master plan would be destroyed and the subdivider would be substituted for the city as the arbiter of the community's park needs. It is just this type of haphazard response to the community's recreational requirements that subdivision (d) of section 11546 was intended to allay.

While the city is not required to give credit for recreational facilities contributed by the subdivider, if it chooses to do so it must be given

---

20. Resolution 2225 provides that land dedication will be required if park land designated on the master plan is incorporated within the subdivision and if the slope, topography and geology of the site as well as its surroundings are suitable for the intended use of the park. However, if dedication is impossible, impractical, or undesirable, a fee will be required. The impracticality of dedication occurs whenever the physical characteristics of the land or its surroundings render the land within the subdivision unsuitable for park or recreational purposes.

broad discretion to assure that the proposed facilities are in keeping
with the master plan. Section 10–1.516, which provides that credit shall
be given if the facilities designated by the subdivider "satisfy the
* * * principles and standards" in the master plan, sets forth a sufficiently defined standard.

The parties are in disagreement as to whether fees in lieu of dedication may be used only for the purchase of land or whether they may
also be employed under the provisions of section 11546 to improve land
already owned by the city which serves the needs of the subdivision.[21]
Section 11546 provides that the fees may be used for "park or recreational purposes" or "park and recreational facilities."

The word "purposes" may be somewhat broader than "facilities" but
we must look to the underlying object of the legislation in interpreting
its scope. It is clear from what has been said above that the Legislature was concerned largely with the maintenance of open space for recreational use. We conclude that it is consistent with this purpose for
fees to be utilized either for the purchase of park or recreational land
or, if the city deems that there is sufficient land available for the subdivision's use, for improvement of the land itself as, for example, for
drainage or landscaping, but not for purposes unrelated to the acquisition and improvement of land.

The City's Ordinances and Resolutions Comply with Section 11546

On this topic a few additional matters require brief elaboration. Associated argues that the city has enacted no definite principles for park
and recreational facilities, as required by subdivision (d) of section
11546. The city's general plan indicates the location of various types of
parks and recreational facilities and there is a sufficiently detailed set
of principles and standards for the development of these facilities to
satisfy the requirements of the section.

* * *

It may come to pass, as Associated states, that subdividers will
transfer the cost of the land dedicated or the in-lieu fee to the consumers who ultimately purchase homes in the subdivision, thereby to some
extent increasing the price of houses to newcomers. While we recognize the ominous possibility that the contributions required by a city can
be deliberately set unreasonably high in order to prevent the influx of
economically depressed persons into the community, a circumstance
which would present serious social and legal problems, there is nothing
to indicate that the enactments of Walnut Creek in the present case

---

21. The parties have stipulated that if a
subdivision is located within three-fourths
of a mile from elementary school grounds
or a neighborhood or community park, the
city uses the fees provided by the subdivider for improving such recreation areas
rather than for the purchase of additional
park land. The children in the school as
well as other residents of the area use
such facilities. In the city's principles and
standards for park land it is declared that
park facilities and school sites can be more
efficiently built and operated when several
facilities are grouped and that a neighborhood park should be integrated with an elementary school to provide space for in-
door and outdoor activities. Neighborhood
parks should contain a neighborhood
center building, park area, playground,
etc., and the design should be balanced to
meet the needs of the school and the
neighborhood.

raise such a spectre. The desirability of encouraging subdividers to build low-cost housing cannot be denied and unreasonable exactions could defeat this object, but these considerations must be balanced against the phenomenon of the appallingly rapid disappearance of open areas in and around our cities. We believe section 11546 constitutes a valient attempt to solve this urgent problem, and we cannot say that its provisions or the city's enactments pursuant to the section are constitutionally deficient.

The judgment is affirmed.

Notes

1. The statutory authorization for subdivision exactions for "park or recreational purposes" sustained in *Walnut Creek*, Cal.Bus. & Prof.Code § 11546, is now Cal.Gov.Code § 66477, which is substantially identical with the provision upheld in *Walnut Creek* except for the addition, after para. (g), of the following language:

(h) Subdivisions containing less than five (5) parcels and not used for residential purposes shall be exempted from the requirements of this section; provided however, that a condition may be placed on the approval of such parcel map that if a building permit is requested for construction of a residential structure or structures on one or more of the parcels within four years the fee may be required to be paid by the owner of each such parcel as a condition to the issuance of such permit.

Land or fees required under this section shall be conveyed or paid directly to the local public agency which provides park and recreational services on a communitywide level and to the area within which the proposed development will be located, if such agency elects to accept the land or fee. The local agency accepting such land or funds shall develop the land or use the funds in the manner provided herein.

In the event park and recreational services and facilities are provided by a public agency other than a city or a county, the amount and location of land to be dedicated or fees to be paid shall be jointly determined by the city or county having jurisdiction and such public agency.

The provisions of this section do not apply to industrial subdivisions; nor do they apply to condominium projects which consist of the subdivision of airspace in an existing apartment building which is more than five years old when no new dwelling units are added, nor do they apply to parcel maps for a subdivision containing less than five (5) parcels for a shopping center containing more than 300,000 square feet of gross leaseable area and no residential development or uses.

Assuming that the California statute sustained in *Walnut Creek* was well within constitutional limits because it provided that "[t]he land, fees, or combination thereof are to be used only for the purpose of providing park or recreational facilities to serve the subdivision," how loose may the nexus between the exaction and the benefits resulting from it be?

2. In *Walnut Creek* the court met the argument that the limitation of exactions for parks and playgrounds to subdividers discriminates against subdividers—generally developers of single-family housing—as compared to apartment developers by asserting that "[t]he Legislature could reasonably have assumed that an apartment house is * * * ordinarily constructed upon land considerably smaller in dimension than most subdivisions and the erection of

the apartments is, therefore, not decreasing the limited supply of open space to the same extent as the formation of a subdivision. This significant distinction justifies legislatively treating the builder of an apartment house who does not subdivide differently than the creator of a subdivision." On the other hand, the court met the argument that "a subdivider who develops high-density land may be required to pay a higher fee in lieu of dedication than one who develops low-density land even though both builders may be responsible for bringing the same number of new residents into the community" by stating that "[i]t is a proper assumption that persons occupying housing in a high-density area will use the public recreational facilities more consistently than those residents in single family homes who have private yards and more open space readily at their individual disposal." Are the positions taken by the court on these points consistent?

3. Did the *Walnut Creek* court give adequate consideration to possible inequities as between "old" residents and "new" residents who move into subdivisions after the park dedication and fee requirements are imposed? Consider the following comment in West Park Ave. v. Ocean Township, 48 N.J. 122, 224 A.2d 1 (1966):

> But as to services which traditionally have been supported by general taxation, other considerations are evident. The dollar burden would likely be unequal if new homes were subjected to a charge in addition to the general tax rate. As to education, for example, the vacant land has contributed for years to the cost of existing educational facilities, and that land and the dwellings to be erected will continue to contribute with all other real property to the payment of bonds issued for the existing facilities and to the cost of renovating or replacing those facilities. Hence there would be an imbalance if new construction alone were to bear the capital cost of new schools while being also charged with the capital costs of schools serving other portions of the school district.

48 N.J. at 126, 224 A.2d at 4–5. See also Ellickson, Suburban Growth Controls: An Economic and Legal Analysis, 84 Yale L.J. 385, 460 (1977), arguing that "if a municipality mixes special and general revenues in financing a service, the portion financed by general revenues should presumptively be distributed equally per dwelling unit." Thus landowners forced to pay subdivision park fees, e.g., would be entitled to an offset equivalent to the benefits received by other landowners from parks financed by general revenues. Ellickson argues, generally, that the principal problem with subdivision exactions is an equal protection—fairness of treatment as among landowners—rather than a due process problem. Id. 45–89.

4. Several courts have determined the validity of subdivision exactions for park or school purposes on the basis of the test laid down in Pioneer Trust & Savings Bank v. Village of Mt. Prospect, 22 Ill.2d 375, 176 N.E.2d 799 (1961), where the court struck down compulsory dedication requirements because the record did not "establish that the need for recreational and educational facilities in the event that said subdivision plat is permitted to be filed, is one that is specifically and uniquely attributable to the addition of the subdivision and which should be cast upon the subdivider as his sole financial burden." The *Walnut Creek* opinion rejects this test, but later Illinois cases have sustained subdivision exations under it. See, e.g., Krughoff v. City of Naperville, 41 Ill. App.3d 334, 354 N.E.2d 489 (1976), upholding school and park exactions imposed by the city's subdivision control and PUD ordinances. The Naperville ordinances related the park exaction to the ultimate population of each subdivision and required "the dedication of land to be used as school sites pursuant to crite-

ria for optimum capacity, location, and site size of elementary, junior high, and senior high schools to serve the population of the development." See Platt and Malone-Merkle, Municipal Improvisation: Open Space Exactions in the Land of Pioneer Trust, 5 Urban Law. 706, 716–19 (1973), discussing the Naperville ordinances.

5.   Probably the most important case upholding subdivision exactions under the "specifically and uniquely attributable" test laid down in *Pioneer Trust* is Jordan v. Village of Menomonee Falls, 28 Wis.2d 608, 137 N.W.2d 442 (1965), appeal dismissed 385 U.S. 4, 87 S.Ct. 36 (1966), where the court said:

> We deem this to be an acceptable statement of the yardstick to be applied, provided the words "specifically and uniquely attributable to his activity" are not so restrictively applied as to cast an unreasonable burden of proof upon the municipality which has enacted the ordinance under attack. In most instances it would be impossible for the municipality to prove that the land required to be dedicated for a park or a school site was to meet a need solely attributable to the anticipated influx of people into the community to occupy this particular subdivision. On the other hand, the municipality might well be able to establish that a group of subdivisions approved over a period of several years had been responsible for bringing into the community a considerable number of people making it necessary that the land dedications required of the subdividers be utilized for school, park and recreational purposes for the benefit of such influx. In the absence of contravening evidence this would establish a reasonable basis for finding that the need for the acquisition was occasioned by the activity of the subdivider. Possible contravening evidence would be a showing that the municipality prior to the opening up of the subdivisions, acquired sufficient lands for school, park and recreational purposes to provide for future anticipated needs including such influx, or that the normal growth of the municipality would have made necessary the acquisition irrespective of the influx caused by opening up of subdivisions.

> There also may be situations, unlike the instant one, where there is no substantial influx from the outside and the proposed subdivision only fulfills a purely, local need within the community. In those situations it may be more difficult to adduce proof sufficient to sustain a land dedication requirement.

> We conclude that a required dedication of land for school, park or recreational sites as a condition for approval of the subdivision plat should be upheld as a valid exercise of police power if the evidence reasonably establishes that the municipality will be required to provide more land for schools, parks and playgrounds as a result of approval of the subdivision.

28 Wis.2d at 617, 137 N.W.2d at 447–48.

This burden of proof was held to have been satisfied by evidence that the village's population had more than doubled between 1950 and 1964, that school enrollments had more than doubled between 1958 and 1963, that forty-one subdivisions had been approved after adoption of the village's subdivision ordinance, and that a total of five dedications had been required. Moreover, the court rejected the subdividers' argument that the village's subdivision exactions could only be justified as a kind of special assessment that must satisfy the special benefits test, concluding that the general financial benefit accruing to the subdividers was sufficient to sustain the exactions. The record indicated that the subdividers' total expense for development of the subdivision in question, including the disputed "equalization fee," was $74,000, while they had sold the subdivision lots for a total of $100,000. A dissenting judge thought the fee could be sustained only as a special assessment or property tax and, on either theory, that it was invalid. The majority not only refused to treat the fee as a special assessment but also rejected the property tax characterization, stating that, "if a tax, it partakes of the nature of an excise tax and does not violate the uniformity clause found in sec. 1, art. VII of the Wisconsin constitution."

Other cases upholding subdivision exactions for schools or recreational facilities include Billings Properties, Inc. v. Yellowstone County, 144 Mont. 25, 394 P.2d 182 (1964); Jenad, Inc. v. Village of Scarsdale, 18 N.Y.2d 78, 271 N.Y.S.2d 955, 218 N.E.2d 673 (1966); Aunt Hack Ridge Estates, Inc. v. Planning Comm., 160 Conn. 109, 273 A.2d 880 (1970); and Collis v. City of Bloomington, 310 Minn. 5, 246 N.W.2d 19 (1976). Cf. Town of Longboat Key v. Lands End, Ltd., 433 So.2d 574 (Fla.App.1983).

6. Although § 14 of the Standard City Planning Enabling Act might be construed as authorizing subdivision regulations to require dedication of land for park and playground use, the statutory reference to "open spaces for * * * recreation" could also be construed simply as authorizing reservation—but *not* compulsory dedication—of subdivision land for recreational purposes. Former N.J.Stat.Ann. §§ 40:55–1.20 and –1.32 contained provisions authorizing "reservation" of recreational sites for one year, with a requirement that the subdivider be compensated if the municipality should decide to acquire such sites for public use. In Lomarch Corp. v. Mayor & Common Council of City of Englewood, 51 N.J. 108, 237 A.2d 881 (1968), N.J.Stat.Ann. 40:55–1.32 was held to be constitutional but, by implication, to require payment of compensation to the subdivider for the loss of use of the reserved land during the reservation period. The court suggested that "fair compensation" would be "the value of an 'option' to purchase the land for the year" for which the statute authorized the reservation. The recent revision of the New Jersey land use control legislation has codified *Lomarch* in the new N.J.Stat.Ann. § 40:55D–44 (West Supp.1978–79).

7. Even California requires that some compensation be paid to a subdivider when dedication of land for elementary school purposes is required under the authority of Cal.Gov.Code § 66478 (West Supp.1978), which provides (*inter alia*) as follows:

* * * * The requirement of dedication shall be imposed at the time of approval of the tentative map. If, within 30 days after the requirement of dedication is imposed by the city or county, the school district does not offer to enter into a binding commitment with the subdivider to accept the dedication, the requirement shall be automatically terminated. The required dedication may be made at any time before, concurrently with, or up to 60 days after, the filing of the final map on any portion of the subdivision. The school district shall, in the event that it accepts the dedication, repay to the subdivider or his successors the original cost to the subdivider of the dedicated land, plus a sum equal to the total of the following amounts:

(a) The cost of any improvements to the dedicated land since acquisition by the subdivider.

(b) The taxes assessed against the dedicated land from the date of the school district's offer to enter into the binding commitment to accept the dedication.

(c) Any other costs incurred by the subdivider in maintenance of such dedicated land, including interest costs incurred on any loan covering such land.

If the land is not used by the school district, as a school site, within 10 years after dedication, the subdivider shall have the option to repurchase the property from the district for the amount paid therefor.

The California statute also gives a complete exemption from the compulsory school dedication requirement to any subdivider who has owned the land being subdivided for more than 10 years prior to the filing of the tentative subdivision map.

Why should the California legislature make provision for the payment of some compensation in the event a subdivider is required to dedicate land for an elementary school site, but not when a subdivider is required to dedicate land (or pay a fee) to provide a new park or playground?

8. The American Law Institute's Model Land Development Code (1976) authorizes the land development agency to condition a special development permit on:

> (a) provision by the developer of streets, other rights-of-way, utilities, parks, and other open space, but the required provision must be of a quality and quantity no more than reasonably necessary for the proposed development; or

> (b) payment of an equivalent amount of money into a fund for the provision of streets, other rights-of-way, utilities, parks or other open space if the Land Development Agency finds that the provision thereof under paragraph (a) is not feasible; * * * †

Id., § 2–103(3). Note that schools are not included and that land dedication is the preferred alternative.

9. Imposition of governmental exactions for provision of improved streets, water mains, sanitary and storm sewerage, and open space for school or recreational purposes has historically been limited to land development involving subdivision of a tract into smaller parcels. But there is nothing in the nature of things to dictate such a limitation. Large-scale multi-family residential, commercial, or industrial development may create the need for new public facilities, just as a single-family residential subdivision does. It is rather surprising, therefore, that the development control legislation generally still requires a land subdivision to trigger the local government's power to impose exactions. The City of Newark, California recently sought partially to avoid this limitation by enacting a "license tax ordinance" imposing a tax on the business of contructing dwellings measured by the number of bedrooms in the units to be constructed. The moneys obtained from this tax were required to be deposited in a "capital outlay fund." The tax on construction of dwellings was upheld against an attack based on the theory that there was unreasonable discrimination because residential construction was taxed, overall, at a substantially higher rate than commercial and industrial construction. Associated Home Builders of Greater East Bay, Inc. v. City of Newark, 18 Cal.App.3d 107, 95 Cal.Rptr. 648 (1971).

Some municipalities have sought to avoid the limitation or exactions designed to pay for new public facilities to cases of land subdivision by levying "user" charges on any property owner who connects to the municipal water or sewer system. A major issue when such "user" charges are challenged is whether the municipality has legal authority to levy the charge, which often turns on the question whether it is really a tax which the municipality has no power to levy. If the court classifies the exaction as a "user" charge or fee rather than a tax, courts have generally not found any insurmountable constitutional barriers to their use, and have generally deferred to the local legislative decision as to the amount of the charge, subject to a loose test of reasonableness. See, e.g., Contractors and Builders Ass'n of Pinellas County v. City of Dunedin, 329 So.2d 314 (Fla.1976); Hartman v. Aurora Sanitary District, 23 Ill. 2d 109, 177 N.E.2d 214 (1961); Clarke, Inc. v. City of Bettendorf, 261 Iowa 1217, 158 N.W.2d 125 (1968); Hayes v. City of Albany, 7 Or.App. 277, 490 P.2d 1018 (1971); Weber Basin Home Builders' Association v. Roy City, 26 Utah 2d 215, 487 P.2d 866 (1971); Home Builders' Association of Greater Salt Lake v. Provo City, 28 Utah 2d 402, 503 P.2d 451 (1972); Coulter v. City of Rawlins, 662 P.2d 888 (Wyo.1983); Cherry Hills Farms v. City of Cherry Hills Village, 670 P.2d 779 (Colo.1983). See also Town of Longboat Key v. Lands End, Ltd., 433 So.2d 574 (Fla.App.1983).

In addition to the articles by Ellickson, cited supra in Note 3, and Platt & Maloney-Merkle, cited supra in Note 4, see Heyman & Gilhool, The Constitutionality of Imposing Increased Community Costs on New Suburban Residents Through Subdivision Exactions, 73 Yale L.J. 1119 (1964); Volpert, Creation and Maintenance of Open Spaces in Subdivisions, 12 U.C.L.A.L.Rev. 830 (1965); Johnston, Constitutionality of Subdivision Control Exactions: The Quest for a Rationale, 52 Cornell L.Q. 871 (1967); Harvith, Subdivision Dedication Requirements—Some Observations and an Alternative: A Special Tax on Gain from Realty, 33 Albany L.Rev. 474 (1969); Brooks, Mandatory Dedication of Land or Fees-in-lieu of Land for Parks and Schools (Am.Soc. of Planning Officials, Planning Advisory Serv.Rep. No. 266, 1971).

Chapter 16

SUBURBAN GROWTH CONTROL AND EXCLUSIONARY LAND USE CONTROLS

SECTION 1. GROWTH CONTROL TECHNIQUES

GOLDEN v. PLANNING BOARD OF TOWN OF RAMAPO

New York Court of Appeals, 1972.
30 N.Y.2d 359, 334 N.Y.S.2d 138, 285 N.E.2d 291.

SCILEPPI, Judge. Both cases arise out of the 1969 amendments to the Town of Ramapo's Zoning Ordinance. In *Golden*, petitioners, the owner of record and contract vendee, by way of a proceeding pursuant to CPLR article 78 sought an order reviewing and annulling a decision and determination of the Planning Board of the Town of Ramapo which denied their application for preliminary approval of a residential subdivision plat because of an admitted failure to secure a special permit as required by section 46–13.1 of the Town zoning ordinance prohibiting subdivision approval except where the residential developer has secured, prior to the application for plat approval, a special permit or a variance pursuant to section F of the ordinance. Special Term sustained the amendments and granted summary judgment. On appeal, the Appellate Division elected, since all necessary parties were before the court, to treat the proceeding as an action for declaratory judgment and reversed, 37 A.D.2d 236, 324 N.Y.S.2d 178.

The plaintiffs in *Rockland County Builders Association*, on the other hand, sought, in an action for declaratory judgment, to set aside the ordinance as unconstitutional and commenced the present action after the Planning Board had denied plaintiff Mildred Rhodes preliminary plat approval for her parcel of property because of a conceded failure on her part to obtain a special permit as required under the challenged ordinance. The remaining plaintiffs, Rockland County Builders Association, a membership corporation composed of builders engaged in the purchase of land and construction of residences of all types through the Town, as well as the Eldorado Developing Corporation, possessed of some 12 acres situate within the Town, apparently have never made application for approval of a plat and have never sought a special permit, as a prerequisite to such approval. Special Term, concluding that the constitutional attack was premature because of the asserted failure to exhaust administrative remedies (cf. Old Farm Road v. Town of New Castle, 26 N.Y.2d 462, 311 N.Y.S.2d 500, 259 N.E.2d 920), denied their motion for summary judgment and granted defendants' cross motion to dismiss. On appeal, the Appellate Division, 37 A.D.2d 783, 324 N.Y.S.2d 190, held that the parties were presently aggrieved and relying on *Golden*, reversed and granted plaintiffs' motion for summary judgment.

Among the complaining parties, Rockland County Builders is not a property owner and Eldorado has never sought preliminary approval of a subdivision plat. Petitioner Golden and plaintiff Rhodes have both sought plat approval and have been denied the same for failure to apply for a special permit. Though the builders are obviously not aggrieved by the recent amendments, landowners prior to gaining approval for subdivision, of necessity, would be required to apply for a special permit, which, absent certain enumerated improvements would invariably be denied. The prescription is mandatory and, were we to conclude that the standards established for the permit's issuance were unconstitutional, quite unlike the situation obtaining in Old Farm Road v. Town of New Castle, 26 N.Y.2d 462, 311 N.Y.S.2d 500, 259 N.E.2d 920, supra, the ordinance itself could admit of no constitutionally permissible construction so as to require initial administrative relief to determine whether injury has occurred (id., at p. 464, 311 N.Y.S.2d at p. 501, 259 N.E.2d at p. 920). The attack by the subdividing landowner is directed against the ordinance in its entirety, and the thrust of the petition and complaint, respectively, is that the ordinance of itself operates to destroy the value and marketability of the subject premises for residential use and thus constitutes a present invasion of the property rights of the complaining landholders. The alleged harm is thus immediate and is sufficient to raise a justiciable issue as to the validity of the subject ordinance * * *.

Experiencing the pressures of an increase in population and the ancillary problem of providing municipal facilities and services,[1] the Town of Ramapo, as early as 1964, made application for grant under section 801 of the Housing Act of 1964 (78 U.S.Stat. 769) to develop a master plan. The plan's preparation included a four-volume study of the existing land uses, public facilities, transportation, industry and commerce, housing needs and projected population trends. The proposals appearing in the studies were subsequently adopted pursuant to section

---

1. The Town's allegations that present facilities are inadequate to service increasing demands goes uncontested. We must assume, therefore, that the proposed improvements, both as to their nature and extent, reflect legitimate community needs and are not veiled efforts at exclusion (see National Land & Inv. Co. v. Easttown Twp. Bd. of Adj., 419 Pa. 504, 215 A.2d 597). In the period 1940–1968 population in the unincorporated areas of the Town increased 285.9%. Between the years of 1950–1960 the increase, again in unincorporated areas, was 130.8%; from 1960–1966 some 78.5%; and from the years 1966–1969 20.4%. In terms of real numbers, popula-tion figures compare at 58,626 as of 1966 with the largest increment of growth since the decennial census occurring in the undeveloped areas. Projected figures, assuming current land use and zoning trends, approximate a total Town population of 120,000 by 1985. Growth is expected to be heaviest in the currently undeveloped western and northern tiers of the Town, predominantly in the form of subdivision development with some apartment construction. A growth rate of some 1,000 residential units per annum has been experienced in the unincorporated areas of the Town.

272–a of the Town Law, Consol.Laws, c. 62, in July, 1966 and implemented by way of a master plan. The master plan was followed by the adoption of a comprehensive zoning ordinance. Additional sewage district and drainage studies were undertaken which culminated in the adoption of a capital budget, providing for the development of the improvements specified in the master plan within the next six years. Pursuant to section 271 of the Town Law, authorizing comprehensive planning, and as a supplement to the capital budget, the Town Board adopted a capital program which provides for the location and sequence of additional capital improvements for the 12 years following the life of the capital budget. The two plans, covering a period of 18 years, detail the capital improvements projected for maximum development and conform to the specifications set forth in the master plan, the official map and drainage plan.

Based upon these criteria, the Town subsequently adopted the subject amendments for the alleged purpose of eliminating premature subdivision and urban sprawl. Residential development is to proceed according to the provision of adequate municipal facilities and services, with the assurance that any concomitant restraint upon property use is to be of a "temporary" nature and that other private uses, including the construction of individual housing, are authorized.

The amendments did not rezone or reclassify any land into different residential or use districts,[2] but, for the purposes of implementing the proposals appearing in the comprehensive plan, consist, in the main, of additions to the definitional sections of the ordinance, section 46–3, and the adoption of a new class of "Special Permit Uses," designated "Residential Development Use." "Residential Development Use" is defined as "The erection or construction of dwellings on any vacant plots, lots or parcels of land" (§ 46–3, as amd.); and, any person who acts so as to come within that definition, "shall be deemed to be engaged in residential development which shall be a separate use classification under this

---

2. As of July, 1966, the only available figures, six residential zoning districts with varying lot size and density requirements accounted for in excess of nine tenths of the Town's unincorporated land area. Of these the RR classification (80,000 square feet minimum lot area) plus R–35 zone (35,000 square feet minimum lot area) comprise over one half of all zoned areas. The subject sites are presently zoned RR–50 (50,000 square feet minimum lot area). The reasonableness of these minimum lot requirements are not presently controverted, though we are referred to no compelling need in their behalf (see Salamar Bldrs. Corp. v. Tuttle, 29 N.Y.2d 221, 325 N.Y.S.2d 933, 275 N.E.2d 585; see also, National Land & Inv. Co. v. Easttown Twp. Bd. of Adj., 419 Pa. 504, 215 A.2d 597, supra; Concord Twp. Appeal, 439 Pa. 466, 268 A.2d 765). Under present zoning regulations, the population of the unincorporated areas could be increased by about 14,600 families (3.5 people) when all suitable vacant land is occupied. Housing values as of 1960 in the unincorporated areas range from a modest $15,000 (approx. 30%) to higher than $25,000 (25%), with the undeveloped western tier of Town showing the highest percentage of values in excess of $25,000 (41%). Significantly, for the same year only about one half of one percent of all housing units were occupied by non-white families. Efforts at adjusting this disparity are reflected in the creation of a public housing authority and the authority's proposal to construct biracial low-income family housing (see Fletcher v. Romney, 323 F.Supp. 189 [S.D.N.Y.]; Matter of Greenwald v. Town of Ramapo, 35 A.D.2d 958, 317 N.Y.S.2d 839; Matter of Farrelly v. Town of Ramapo, 35 A.D.2d 957, 317 N.Y.S.2d 837).

ordinance and subject to the requirement of obtaining a special permit from the Town Board" (§ 46–3, as amd.).

The standards for the issuance of special permits are framed in terms of the availability to the proposed subdivision plat of five essential facilities or services: specifically (1) public sanitary sewers or approved substitutes; (2) drainage facilities; (3) improved public parks or recreation facilities, including public schools; (4) State, county or town roads—major, secondary or collector; and, (5) firehouses. No special permit shall issue unless the proposed residential development has accumulated 15 development points, to be computed on a sliding scale of values assigned to the specified improvements under the statute. Subdivision is thus a function of immediate availability to the proposed plat of certain municipal improvements; the avowed purpose of the amendments being to phase residential development to the Town's ability to provide the above facilities or services.

Certain savings and remedial provisions are designed to relieve of potentially unreasonable restrictions. Thus, the board may issue special permits vesting a present right to proceed with residential development in such year as the development meets the required point minimum, but in no event later than the final year of the 18-year capital plan. The approved special use permit is fully assignable, and improvements scheduled for completion within one year from the date of an application are to be credited as though existing on the date of the application. A prospective developer may advance the date of subdivision approval by agreeing to provide those improvements which will bring the proposed plat within the number of development points required by the amendments. And applications are authorized to the "Development Easement Acquisition Commission" for a reduction of the assessed valuation. Finally, upon application to the Town Board, the development point requirements may be varied should the board determine that such a variance or modification is consistent with the on-going development plan.

The undisputed effect of these integrated efforts in land use planning and development is to provide an over-all program of orderly growth and adequate facilities through a sequential development policy commensurate with progressing availability and capacity of public facilities. While its goals are clear and its purposes undisputably laudatory, serious questions are raised as to the manner in which these ends are to be effected, not the least of which relates to their legal viability under present zoning enabling legislation, particularly sections 261 and 263 of the Town Law. The owners of the subject premises argue, and the Appellate Division has sustained the proposition, that the primary purpose of the amending ordinance is to control or regulate population growth within the Town and as such is not within the authorized objectives of the zoning enabling legislation. We disagree.

In enacting the challenged amendments, the Town Board has sought to control subdivision in all residential districts, pending the provision (public or private) at some future date of various services and facilities. A reading of the relevant statutory provisions reveals that there is no specific authorization for the "sequential" and "timing" controls adopted here. That, of course, cannot be said to end the matter, for the additional inquiry remains as to whether the challenged amendments find their basis within the perimeters of the devices authorized and purposes sanctioned under current enabling legislation. Our concern is, as it should be, with the effects of the statutory scheme taken as a whole and its role in the propagation of a viable policy of land use and planning.

Towns, cities and villages lack the power to enact and enforce zoning or other land use regulations * * *. The exercise of that power, to the extent that it is lawful, must be founded upon a legislative delegation to so proceed, and in the absence of such a grant will be held *ultra vires* and void * * *. That delegation, set forth in section 261 [3] of the Town Law, is not, however, coterminous with stated police power objectives and has been considered less inclusive traditionally. Hence, although the power to zone must be exercised under the aegis of the police power, indeed must inevitably find justification for its exercise in some aspect of the same, the recital of police power purposes in the grant, attests more to the drafters' attempts to specify a valid constitutional predicate than to detail authorized zoning purposes.[4] The latter, "legitimate zoning purposes," are incorporated in accompanying section 263 and are designed to secure safety from various calamities, to avoid undue concentration of population and to facilitate "adequate provision of transportation, water, sewerage, schools, parks and other public requirements" (Town Law, § 263). In the end, zoning properly effects, and only in the manner prescribed, those purposes detailed under section 263 of the Town Law. It may not be invoked to further the general police powers of a municipality * * *.[5]

3. Of the activities referred to and expressly sanctioned by the enabling legislation (Town Law, § 261) there would appear to be a direct correlation between population density, the demand for municipal services in the form of school, water, sanitary, police and fire protection facilities (Johnston, Land Use Control, Annual Survey of American Law [1969/70], p. 49). To the extent that the subject regulations seek to insure provision of adequate facilities, they too may be identified as forms of density controls.

4. Early legislation, based on a Standard State Zoning Enabling Act, prepared by the Department of Commerce, contemplated a minimum of flexibility and its form was dictated by widely held constitutional concerns (see Bettman, Constitutionality of Zoning, 37 Harv.L.Rev. 834; A.L.I., A Model Land Development Code, [Tent.Draft No. 1, 1968], Intro.Mem., p. xvii [hereinafter ALI, A Model Land Development Code]), not the least of which related to the scope of authorized objectives.

5. This distinction, though often unarticulated, is elemental and we have in the past held the exercise of the zoning power *ultra vires* and void where the end sought to be accomplished was not peculiar to the locality's basic land use scheme, but rather related to some general problem, incidental to the community at large (Westwood Forest Estates v. Village of South Nyack, 23 N.Y.2d 424, 428, 297 N.Y.S.2d 129, 133, 244 N.E.2d 700, 702, * * *; Udell v. Haas, 21 N.Y.2d 463, 471, 288 N.Y.S.2d 888, 895, 235 N.E.2d 897, 901; De Sena v. Gulde, 24 A.D.2d 165, 265 N.Y.S.2d 239, * * *; National Land & Inv. Co. v. Easttown Twp. Bd. of Adj., 419 Pa. 504, 526, 215 A.2d 597, supra; Delaware County Community Coll. Appeal, 435 Pa. 264, 270, 254 A.2d 641; Concord Twp. Appeal, 439 Pa. 466, 471–474, 268 A.2d 765, supra; see also, Haar, "In Accordance With a Comprehensive Plan", 68 Harv.L.Rev. 1154, 1173; 1 Rathkopf, Law of Zoning and Planning [1971 Cum.Supp.], pp. 2–9).

Even so, considering the activities enumerated by section 261 of the Town Law, and relating those powers to the authorized purposes detailed in section 263, the challenged amendments are proper zoning techniques, exercised for legitimate zoning purposes. The power to restrict and regulate conferred under section 261 includes within its grant, by way of necessary implication, the authority to direct the growth of population for the purposes indicated, within the confines of the township. It is the matrix of land use restrictions, common to each of the enumerated powers and sanctioned goals, a necessary concomitant to the municipalities' recognized authority to determine the lines along which local development shall proceed, though it may divert it from its natural course * * *.[6]

Of course, zoning historically has assumed the development of individual plats [sic] and has proven characteristically ineffective in treating with the problems attending subdivision and development of larger parcels, involving as it invariably does, the provision of adequate public services and facilities. To this end, subdivision control (Town Law, §§ 276, 277) purports to guide community development in the directions outlined here, while at the same time encouraging the provision of adequate facilities for the housing, distribution, comfort and convenience of local residents * * *. It reflects in essence, a legislative judgment that the development of unimproved areas be accompanied by provision of essential facilities * * *. And though it may not, in a definitional or conceptual sense be identified with the power to zone, it is designed to complement other land use restrictions, which, taken together, seek to implement a broader, comprehensive plan for community development * * *.

It is argued, nevertheless, that the timing controls currently in issue are not legislatively authorized since their effect is to prohibit subdivision absent precedent or concurrent action of the Town, and hence constitutes an unauthorized blanket interdiction against subdivision.

It is, indeed, true that the Planning Board is not in an absolute sense statutorily authorized to deny the right to subdivide. That is not, however, what is sought to be accomplished here. The Planning Board has the right to refuse approval of subdivision plats in the absence of those improvements specified in section 277, and the fact that it is the Town and not the subdividing owner or land developer who is required to make those improvements before the plat will be approved cannot be said to transform the scheme into an absolute prohibition any more than it would be so where it was the developer who refused to provide the facilities required for plat approval.[7] Denial of subdivision plat approv-

6. [This footnote is omitted. Eds.]

7. The difference between the ordinary situation and the situation said to subsist here resides in the fact that where plat approval is denied for want of various improvements, the developer is free to provide those improvements at his own expense. In the ordinary case where the proposed improvements will not be completed before the plat is filed the develop-

er's obligation is secured by a performance bond (Town Law, § 277; see, also, Control of Land Subdivision, Office of Planning Coordination [1968 ed.], p. 32). On the other hand, in the present case, plat approval is conditioned upon the Town's obligation to undertake improvements in roads, sewers and recreational facilities. As the Town may not be held to its program, practices do vary from year to year "and

al, invariably amounts to a prohibition against subdivision, albeit a conditional one * * *: and to say that the Planning Board lacks the authority to deny subdivision rights is to mistake the nature of our inquiry which is essentially whether development may be conditioned pending the provision by the municipality of specified services and facilities. Whether it is the municipality or the developer who is to provide the improvements, the objective is the same—to provide adequate facilities, off-site and on-site; and in either case subdivision rights are conditioned, not denied.

Undoubtedly, current zoning enabling legislation is burdened by the largely antiquated notion which deigns that the regulation of land use and development is uniquely a function of local government—that the public interest of the State is exhausted once its political subdivisions have been delegated the authority to zone * * *. While such jurisdictional allocations may well have been consistent with formerly prevailing conditions and assumptions, questions of broader public interest have commonly been ignored * * *.

Experience, over the last quarter century, however, with greater technological integration and drastic shifts in population distribution has pointed up serious defects and community autonomy in land use controls has come under increasing attack by legal commentators, and students of urban problems alike, because of its pronounced insularism and its correlative role in producing distortions in metropolitan growth patterns, and perhaps more importantly, in crippling efforts toward regional and State-wide problem solving, be it pollution, decent housing, or public transportation (ALI, A Model Land Development Code [Tent. Draft No. 2, April 24, 1970], Intro.Mem., p. xv, citing Report of National Comm. on Urban Problems [Douglas Comm.], Building the American City [1969]; see, also, New York State Planning Law Revision Study, Study Doc. No. 4 [New York State Office of Planning Coordination, Feb. 1970]).

Recognition of communal and regional interdependence, in turn, has resulted in proposals for schemes of regional and State-wide planning, in the hope that decisions would then correspond roughly to their level

fiscal needs cannot be frozen beyond review and recall" (concurring opn. Hopkins, J., 37 A.D.2d 244, 324 N.Y.S.2d 187), the "patient owner" who relied on the capital program for qualification then is said to face the prospect that the improvements will be delayed and the impediments established by the ordinance further extended by the Town's failure to adhere to its own schedule.

The reasoning, as far as it goes, cannot be challenged. Yet, in passing on the validity of the ordinance on its face, we must assume not only the Town's good faith, but its assiduous adherence to the program's scheduled implementation. We cannot, it is true, adjudicate in a vacuum and we would be remiss not to consider the substantial risk that the Town may eventually default in its obligations. Yet, those are future events, the staple of a clairvoyant, not of a court in its deliberations. The threat of default is not so imminent or likely that it would warrant our prognosticating and striking down these amendments as invalid on their face. When and if the danger should materialize, the aggrieved landowner can seek relief by way of an article 78 proceeding, declaring the ordinance unconstitutional as applied to his property. Alternatively, should it arise at some future point in time that the Town must fail in its enterprise, an action for a declaratory judgment will indeed prove the most effective vehicle for relieving property owners of what would constitute absolute prohibitions.

of impact (see, e.g., Proposed Land Use and Development Planning Law, §§ 2–102, 4–101, 4–102; ALI, A Model Land Development Code, art. 7.[8] Yet, as salutary as such proposals may be, the power to zone under current law is vested in local municipalities, and we are constrained to resolve the issues accordingly. What does become more apparent in treating with the problem, however, is that though the issues are framed in terms of the developer's due process rights, those rights cannot, realistically speaking, be viewed separately and apart from the rights of others " 'in search of a [more] comfortable place to live.' " (Concord Twp. Appeal, 439 Pa. 466, 474, n. 6, 268 A.2d 765, 768, * * *; National Land & Inv. Co. v. Easttown Twp. Bd. of Adj., 419 Pa. 504, 527–528, 215 A.2d 597, * * *; see, generally, Sager, Tight Little Islands: Exclusionary Zoning, Equal Protection and the Indigent, 21 Stan. L.Rev. 767; Roberts, Demise of Property Law, 57 Cornell L.Rev. 1).

There is, then, something inherently suspect in a scheme which, apart from its professed purposes, effects a restriction upon the free mobility of a people until sometime in the future when projected facilities are available to meet increased demands. Although zoning must include schemes designed to allow municipalities to more effectively contend with the increased demands of evolving and growing communities, under its guise, townships have been wont to try their hand at an array of exclusionary devices in the hope of avoiding the very burden which growth must inevitably bring * * *. Though the conflict engendered by such tactics is certainly real, and its implications vast, accumulated evidence, scientific and social, points circumspectly at the hazards of undirected growth and the naive, somewhat nostalgic imperative that egalitarianism is a function of growth. * * *

Of course, these problems cannot be solved by Ramapo or any single municipality, but depend upon the accommodation of widely disparate interests for their ultimate resolution. To that end, State-wide or regional control of planning would insure that interests broader than that of the municipality underlie various land use policies. Nevertheless, that should not be the only context in which growth devices such as these, aimed at population assimilation, not exclusion, will be sustained; especially where, as here, we would have no alternative but to strike the provision down in the wistful hope that the efforts of the State Office of Planning Coordination and the American Law Institute will soon bear fruit.

Hence, unless we are to ignore the plain meaning of the statutory delegation, this much is clear: phased growth is well within the ambit of existing enabling legislation. And, of course, it is no answer to point to emergent problems to buttress the conclusion that such innovative schemes are beyond the perimeters of statutory authorization. These considerations, admittedly real, to the extent which they are relevant,

---

8. Invariably, the primary responsibility for formulating and implementing zoning policy remains in the hands of local government, with provision for review at county, State and regional levels (see, e.g., Proposed Land Use and Development Planning Law, §§ 2–102, 4–101, 4–102; ALI, A Model Land Development Code, art. 7; New York State Planning Revision Study, Study Doc. No. 4 [State Office of Planning Coordination, Feb., 1970], pp. 23–52).

bear solely upon the continued viability of "localism" in land use regulation; obviously, they can neither add nor detract from the initial grant of authority, obsolescent though it may be. The answer which Ramapo has posed can by no means be termed definitive; it is, however, a first practical step toward controlled growth achieved without forsaking broader social purposes.

The evolution of more sophisticated efforts to contend with the increasing complexities of urban and suburban growth has been met by a corresponding reluctance upon the part of the judiciary to substitute its judgment as to the plan's over-all effectiveness for the considered deliberations of its progenitors * * *. Implicit in such a philosophy of judicial self-restraint is the growing awareness that matters of land use and development are peculiarly within the expertise of students of city and suburban planning, and thus well within the legislative prerogative, not lightly to be impeded * * *. To this same end, we have afforded such regulations, the usual presumption of validity attending the exercise of the police power, and have cast the burden of proving their invalidity upon the party challenging their enactment * * *. Deference in the matter of the regulations' over-all effectiveness, however, is not to be viewed as an abdication of judicial responsibility, and ours remains the function of defining the metes and bounds beyond which local regulations may not venture, regardless of their professedly beneficent purposes.

The subject ordinance is said to advance legitimate zoning purposes as it assures that each new home built in the township will have at least a minimum of public services in the categories regulated by the ordinance. The Town argues that various public facilities are presently being constructed but that for want of time and money it has been unable to provide such services and facilities at a pace commensurate with increased public need. It is urged that although the zoning power includes reasonable restrictions upon the private use of property, exacted in the hope of development according to well-laid plans, calculated to advance the public welfare of the community in the future * * *, the subject regulations go further and seek to avoid the increased responsibilities and economic burdens which time and growth must ultimately bring * * *.

It is the nature of all land use and development regulations to circumscribe the course of growth within a particular town or district and to that extent such restrictions invariably impede the forces of natural growth * * *. Where those restrictions upon the beneficial use and enjoyment of land are necessary to promote the ultimate good of the community and are within the bounds of reason, they have been sustained. "Zoning [, however,] is a means by which a governmental body can plan for the future—it may not be used as a means to deny the future" (National Land & Inv. Co. v. Easttown Twp. Bd. of Adj., 419 Pa. 504, 528, 215 A.2d 597, 610, supra). Its exercise assumes that development shall not stop at the community's threshold, but only that whatever growth there may be shall proceed along a predetermined course * * *. It is inextricably bound to the dynamics of community life and its function is to guide, not to isolate or facilitate efforts at avoiding the ordinary incidents of growth. What segregates permissible from impermissible restrictions, depends in the final analysis upon the purpose of the restrictions and their impact in terms of both the community and general public interest * * *. The line of delineation between the two is not a constant, but will be found to vary with prevailing circumstances and conditions * * *.

What we will not countenance, then, under any guise, is community efforts at immunization or exclusion. But, far from being exclusionary, the present amendments merely seek, by the implementation of sequential development and timed growth, to provide a balanced cohesive community dedicated to the efficient utilization of land. The restrictions conform to the community's considered land use policies as expressed in its comprehensive plan and represent a bona fide effort to maximize population density consistent with orderly growth. True other alternatives, such as requiring off-site improvements as a prerequisite to subdivision, may be available, but the choice as how best to proceed, in view of the difficulties attending such exactions * * *, cannot be faulted.

Perhaps even more importantly, timed growth, unlike the minimum lot requirements recently struck down by the Pennsylvania Supreme Court as exclusionary, does not impose permanent restrictions upon land use (see National Land & Inv. Co. v. Easttown Twp. Bd. of Adj., 419 Pa. 504, 215 A.2d 597, supra; Concord Twp. Appeal, 439 Pa. 466, 268 A.2d 765, supra). Its obvious purpose is to prevent premature subdivision absent essential municipal facilities and to insure continuous development commensurate with the Town's obligation to provide such facilities. They seek, not to freeze population at present levels but to maximize growth by the efficient use of land, and in so doing testify to this community's continuing role in population assimilation. In sum, Ramapo asks not that it be left alone, but only that it be allowed to prevent the kind of deterioration that has transformed well-ordered and thriving residential communities into blighted ghettos with attendant hazards to health, security and social stability—a danger not without substantial basis in fact.

We only require that communities confront the challenge of population growth with open doors. Where in grappling with that problem, the community undertakes, by imposing temporary restrictions upon development, to provide required municipal services in a rational manner, courts are rightfully reluctant to strike down such schemes. The timing controls challenged here parallel recent proposals put forth by various study groups and have their genesis in certain of the pronouncements of this and the courts of sister States (see Proposed Land Use and Development Planning Law, § 2–105, subds. 1, 2, par. [a], as proposed by Sen. No. 9028 of 1970 Legislature; ALI, A Model Land Development Code [Tent. Draft No. 2, April, 1970], §§ 2–101, 2–201, subd. [2], par. [c]; § 2–206; [Tent. Draft No. 1, April, 1968], §§ 3–101, 3–103, 3–104, 3–107, 3–108; see Westwood Forest Estates v. Village of South Nyack, 23 N.Y.2d 424, 427, 297 N.Y.S.2d 129, 132, 244 N.E.2d 700, 701, * * *; Concord Twp. Appeal, 439 Pa. 466, 475, 268 A.2d 765, supra;

National Land & Inv. Co. v. Easttown Twp. Bd. of Adj., 419 Pa. 504, 532, 215 A.2d 597, supra). While these controls are typically proposed as an adjunct of regional planning (see Proposed Land Use and Development Planning Law, arts. 3, 4; ALI, A Model Land Development Code, art. 7), the preeminent protection against their abuse resides in the mandatory on-going planning and development requirement, present here, which attends their implementation and use (see, e.g., Proposed Land Use and Development Planning Law, § 2–105).

We may assume, therefore, that the present amendments are the product of foresighted planning calculated to promote the welfare of the township. The Town has imposed temporary restrictions upon land use in residential areas while committing itself to a program of development. It has utilized its comprehensive plan to implement its timing controls and has coupled with these restrictions provisions for low and moderate income housing on a large scale. Considered as a whole, it represents both in its inception and implementation a reasonable attempt to provide for the sequential, orderly development of land in conjunction with the needs of the community, as well as individual parcels of land, while simultaneously obviating the blighted aftermath which the initial failure to provide needed facilities so often brings.

The proposed amendments have the effect of restricting development for onwards to 18 years in certain areas. Whether the subject parcels will be so restricted for the full term is not clear, for it is equally probable that the proposed facilities will be brought into these areas well before that time. Assuming, however, that the restrictions will remain outstanding for the life of the program, they still fall short of a confiscation within the meaning of the Constitution.

An ordinance which seeks to permanently restrict the use of property so that it may not be used for any reasonable purpose must be recognized as a taking: The only difference between the restriction and an outright taking in such a case "is that the restriction leaves the owner subject to the burden of payment of taxation, while outright confiscation would relieve him of that burden" (Arverne Bay Constr. Co. v. Thatcher, 278 N.Y. 222, 232, 15 N.E.2d 587, 592, * * *). An appreciably different situation obtains where the restriction constitutes a *temporary* restriction, promising that the property may be put to a profitable use within a reasonable time. The hardship of holding unproductive property for some time might be compensated for by the ultimate benefit inuring to the individual owner in the form of a substantial increase in valuation; or, for that matter, the landowner, might be compelled to chafe under the temporary restriction, without the benefit of such compensation, when that burden serves to promote the public good (cf. Arverne Bay Constr. Co. v. Thatcher, 278 N.Y. 222, 232, 15 N.E.2d 587, 592, supra).

We are reminded, however, that these restrictions threaten to burden individual parcels for as long as a full generation and that such a restriction cannot, in any context, be viewed as a temporary expedient. The Town, on the other hand, contends that the landowner is not deprived of either the best use of his land or of numerous other appropriate uses, still permitted within various residential districts, including the construction of a single-family residence, and consequently, it cannot be deemed confiscatory. Although no proof has been submitted on reduction of value, the landowners point to obvious disparity between the value of the property, if limited in use by the subject amendments and its value for residential development purposes, and argue that the diminution is so considerable that for all intents and purposes the land cannot presently or in the near future be put to profitable or beneficial use, without violation of the restrictions.

Every restriction on the use of property entails hardships for some individual owners. Those difficulties are invariably the product of police regulation and the pecuniary profits of the individual must in the long run be subordinated to the needs of the community. * * * The fact that the ordinance limits the use of, and may depreciate the value of the property will not render it unconstitutional, however, unless it can be shown that the measure is either unreasonable in terms of necessity or the diminution in value is such as to be tantamount to a confiscation. Diminution, in turn, is a relative factor and though its magnitude is an indicia of a taking, it does not of itself establish a confiscation (Pennsylvania Coal Co. v. Mahon, 260 U.S. 393, 43 S.Ct. 158, 67 L.Ed. 322; Dowsey v. Village of Kensington, 257 N.Y. 221, 177 N.E. 427, supra; Arverne Bay Constr. Co. v. Thatcher, 278 N.Y. 222, 15 N.E.2d 587, supra; cf. Westwood Forest Estates v. Village of South Nyack, 23 N.Y. 2d 424, 427, 297 N.Y.S.2d 129, 132, 244 N.E.2d 700, 701, supra).

Without a doubt restrictions upon the property in the present case are substantial in nature and duration. They are not, however, absolute. The amendments contemplate a definite term, as the development points are designed to operate for a maximum period of 18 years and during that period, the Town is committed to the construction and installation of capital improvements. The net result of the on-going development provision is that individual parcels may be committed to a residential development use prior to the expiration of the maximum period. Similarly, property owners under the terms of the amendments may elect to accelerate the date of development by installing, at their own expense, the necessary public services to bring the parcel within the required number of development points. While even the best of plans may not always be realized, in the absence of proof to the contrary, we must assume the Town will put its best effort forward in implementing the physical and fiscal timetable outlined under the plan. Should subsequent events prove this assumption unwarranted, or should the Town because of some unforeseen event fail in its primary obligation to these landowners, there will be ample opportunity to undo the restrictions upon default. For the present, at least, we are constrained to proceed upon the assumption that the program will be fully and timely implemented * * *.

Thus, unlike the situation presented in Arverne Bay Constr. Co. v. Thatcher, 278 N.Y. 222, 15 N.E.2d 587, supra, the present amendments propose restrictions of a certain duration and founded upon estimate determined by fact. Prognostication on our part in upholding the ordinance proceeds upon the presently permissible inference that within a reasonable time the subject property will be put to the desired use at an appreciated value. In the interim assessed valuations for real estate tax purposes reflect the impact of the proposed restrictions (cf. Arverne Bay Constr. Co. v. Thatcher, 278 N.Y. 222, 232, 15 N.E.2d 587, 592, supra). The proposed restraints, mitigated by the prospect of appreciated value and interim reductions in assessed value, and measured in terms of the nature and magnitude of the project undertaken, are within the limits of necessity.

In sum, where it is clear that the existing physical and financial resources of the community are inadequate to furnish the essential services and facilities which a substantial increase in population requires, there is a rational basis for "phased growth" and hence, the challenged ordinance is not violative of the Federal and State Constitutions. Accordingly, the order appealed from should be reversed and the actions remitted to Special Term for entry of a judgment declaring section 46–13.1 of the Town Ordinance constitutional.

BREITEL, Judge (dissenting). The limited powers of district zoning and subdivision regulation delegated to a municipality do not include the power to impose a moratorium on land development. Such conclusion is dictated by settled doctrine that a municipality has only those powers, and especially land use powers, delegated or necessarily implied.

But there is more involved in these cases than the arrogation of undelegated powers. Raised are vital constitutional issues, and, most important, policy issues trenching on grave domestic problems of our time, without the benefit of a legislative determination which would reflect the interests of the entire State. The policy issues relate to needed housing, planned land development under government control, and the exclusion in effect or by motive, of walled-in urban populations of the middle class and the poor. The issues are raised by a town ordinance, which, as one of the Appellate Division Justices noted below, reflect a parochial stance without regard to its impact on the region or the State, especially if it become a valid model for many other towns similarly situated.

*   *   *

It is important to note how radically the Ramapo scheme differs from those used and adopted under existing enabling acts. The zoning acts, starting from 50 years ago, based on national models, provided simply for district zoning to control population density and some planning to protect preferred uses of land, such as single-family dwellings, from other uses considered less desirable or even harmful to residential living or environmental balance. Since the beginning, in this State and elsewhere, by amendment to the enabling acts by the Legislature, provision has been made for subdivision planning and, in some instances, planned unit development, to prevent large-scale developers from dumping homes wholesale in raw land areas without private and, to some extent, public facilities essential to the use of the homes. In more recent years, since World War II, the need for a much enlarged kind of land planning has become critical. The evils of uncontrolled urban sprawl on the one hand, and the suburban and exurban pressure to exclude urban population on the other hand, have created a massive conflict, with social and economic implications of the gravest character. Throughout the nation the conflict has risen or threatened and solutions are being sought in careful, intensive examination of the problem affecting those within and those without the localities to be regulated.

    *   *   *

The urgent need to control the tempo and sequence of land development has been recognized by courts, government commissions, and commentators (see Cutler, Legal and Illegal Methods of Controlling Community Growth, 1961 Wis.L.Rev. 370; Fagin, Regulating the Timing of Urban Development, 20 Law & Contemp.Prob. 298; Report of National Commission on Urban Problems, pp. 245, 251; New York State, Office of Planning Coordination, Planning Law Revision Study, Draft Outline, pp. 13, 17). Techniques to control the rate, nature and sequence of community development are plentiful although not all are presently authorized to comport with constitutional limitations. Thus, in Albrecht Realty Co. v. Town of New Castle, 8 Misc.2d 255, 167 N.Y.S.2d 843, the Town of New Castle in Westchester County sought to control growth by placing a moratorium on the issuance of building permits for unspecified periods and with no apparent object other than controlling growth. The measure was voided because the enabling act did not authorize "a direct regulation of the rate of growth" (at p. 256, 167 N.Y.S.2d at p. 844). For another technique, in California the purchase of "development rights" or a time-limited easement by the local government reportedly has been employed. The community is saved the expense of purchasing the fee simple of the owner. It obtains flexibility by the power to release land for development while landowners are compensated. The method is also said to justify assessing or taxing the owner at a lower rate (see Cutler, op. cit., supra, at p. 394). A similar approach is followed in England and has been recently recommended by the President's National Commission on Urban Problems (Report, at p. 251; Mandelker, Notes from the English; Compensation in Town and County Planning, 49 Cal.L.Rev. 699; see, also, Ann., Zoning—With Compensation, 41 ALR3d 636).

A common technique is minimum area zoning. If it does not amount to prohibitory zoning, minimum lot requirements may be used to regulate the tempo and sequence of land development (see Matter of Josephs v. Town Bd. of Town of Clarkstown, 24 Misc.2d 366, 198 N.Y.S.2d 695). Unfortunately, however, the method is often used as an exclusionary or prohibitory device.

Finally, there is the technique sought to be exercised by Ramapo—a technique partaking somewhat of the motivation for and methods used in holding zones.

Holding zones, that is, areas reserved for future development, if legislatively authorized and carefully circumscribed, can validly and effectively implement land planning. Both the interests of localities and the broader interests of the State and its large metropolitan areas can be reconciled. Indeed, it has been suggested by the National Commission on Urban Problems that enabling legislation grant communities such power. The devising and authorization of new powers, one of which is to create holding or delayed development zones, is a chief concern of the State Office of Planning Coordination. Indeed, it plays a prominent role in its proposed legislation. Notably, in delayed development schemes limitations are invariably suggested limitations absent in the Ramapo ordinance (e.g., 3- to 5-year limits, regional and State agency review, provision for compensation). Such limitations may be essential if the delegation is to be valid constitutionally. Aside from considerations of unlimited delegation, without the standards which universally circumscribe the conduct of administrative agencies, the limitations reflect basic doctrine that even the State's zoning power is not unlimited. As observed by the Pennsylvania Supreme Court, "Zoning is a means by which a governmental body can plan for the future—it may not be used as a means to deny the future" (National Land & Inv. Co. v. Easttown Twp. Bd. of Adj., 419 Pa. 504, 215 A.2d 597, * * * at p. 528, 215 A.2d at p. 610). Again, in Concord Twp. Appeal, 439 Pa. 466, 268 A.2d 765 * * *), it observed, "Communities must deal with the problems of population growth. They may not refuse to confront the future by adopting zoning regulations that effectively restrict population to near present levels" (at p. 474, 268 A.2d at p. 768).

Either by legislation limited by decisional rule, or by decisional rule alone a limited amount of restraint in time has been held valid in controlling development, even without compensation. Thus, in the State of Washington it was suggested that the legislatively authorized right to impress "holding zones" on private property beyond the immediate reaches of present development, must be reasonably limited in its duration (State ex rel. Randall v. Snohomish County, 79 Wash.2d 619, 488 P.2d 511; see, also, Westwood Forest Estates v. Village of South Nyack, 23 N.Y.2d 424, 428–429, 297 N.Y.S.2d 129, 132–133, 244 N.E.2d 700, 702–703). Significantly, the time limitations should be brief, or reasonably fixed, and justified by emergency or statutory authorization.

* * *

By the unsupportable extrapolation from existing enabling acts, one may not usurp the unique responsibility of the Legislature, even where it has failed to act. What is worse, to do this, as a State Legislature would not, without considering the social and economic ramifications for the locality, region, and State, and without limitations essential to an intelligent delegation, is unsound as well as invalid. Moreover, to allow Ramapo's idiosyncratic solution, which would then be available to any other community like Ramapo, may end indefinitely the possibility of commanding better legislation for land planning, just because such legislation requires some diminution in the local control now exercised under the zoning acts.

There are, to be sure, the constitutional issues in the case. Some relate to the power of government to deprive the landowner of any reasonable use of his land for a period of years, up to 18 years, without compensation. These are knotty problems confronting the draftsmen of a land development code. The problems are not insuperable. The initial, principal land zoning case, Euclid v. Ambler Co., 272 U.S. 365, 47 S.Ct. 114, 71 L.Ed. 303, held rather flatly, as far back as 1926, that an owner may be made to suffer a substantial loss in the economic potential of his land without compensation. But it has always been made clear that an owner could not be deprived of all reasonable use nor could his use be postponed for more than a short time, even if only to prevent an overloading of municipal facilities * * *. Be that as it may, for many reasons these constitutional issues are better reserved for future consideration. There is little doubt that the compulsion of current interests and conflicts will require a re-examination of much legal and judicial thinking in this area. The problem, however, is not only legal. As some students of the subject have pointed out, it is not enough to regulate land development. There must be incentive to develop or else there will be little new housing except that which government could afford to build (Mandelker, The Zoning Dilemma, pp. 47–51). These are just some of the problems that the Ramapo ordinance glosses over as it attacks the problem for one town alone, a device that maybe a few more towns like Ramapo could adopt, but not all, without destroying the economy and channelling the demographic course of the State to suit their own insular interests.

At least one of the concurring opinions at the Appellate Division raised another constitutional question, namely, the power of the town to adjust tax assessments as provided in the ordinance (see concurring opn. of Mr. Justice Hopkins, 37 A.D.2d 236, 244–246, 324 N.Y.S.2d 178, 187–188). The point would be a salient one, if reached. It and the other constitutional questions need not and should not be reached because it is enough that the enabling acts do not permit the arrogation of power that the Ramapo ordinance projects.

Consequently, although the town had no power under the enabling act to adopt the ordinance in question, this does not mean that the town is not faced with a grave problem. It is. So are the many towns and villages in the State, and elsewhere in the country. But there is no doubt that the Ramapos, in isolation, cannot solve their problems alone, legally, under existing laws, or socially, politically, or economically. For the time being, the Ramapos must do what they can with district zoning and subdivision platting control. They may not declare moratoria on growth and development for as much as a generation. They may not separately or in concert impair the freedom of movement or residence of those outside their borders, even by ingenious schemes. Nor is it important whether their intention is to exclude, if that is the effect of their arrogated powers.

     * * *

A glance at other legislation in this State reveals that regional or coordinated planning is not new to the Legislature, albeit the steps thus far taken may one day be regarded as quite primitive compared with what, necessarily, is to be. Article 12–B of the General Municipal Law, Consol.Laws, c. 24, contains a congeries of provisions authorizing optional metropolitan, regional, and county planning boards. Their powers are still rather limited. Perhaps most interesting is section 239–*l* of that article which authorizes a scheme for mandatory co-ordination in counties or regions of various kinds of zoning action by the included municipalities. The legislation is significant evidence of the activity and understanding of the Legislature in land use planning, into which Ramapo would thrust itself beyond the limits now authorized by law.

A glance at history suggests that Ramapo's plan to have public services installed in advance of development is unrealistic. Richard Babcock, the distinguished practitioner in land development law, some years ago addressed himself to the natural desire of communities to stay development while they caught up with the inexorable thrust of population growth and movement. He observed eloquently that this country was built and is still being built by people who moved about, innovated, pioneered, and created industry and employment, and thereby provided both the need and the means for the public services and facilities that followed (Babcock, The Zoning Game, at pp. 149–150).

* * *

As said earlier, when the problem arose outside the State the judicial response has been the same, frustrating communities, intent on walling themselves from the mainstream of development, namely, that the effort was invalid under existing enabling acts or unconstitutional. The response * * * has * * * reflected the larger understanding that American society is at a critical crossroads in the accommodation of urbanization and suburban living, with effects that are no longer confined, bad as they are, to ethnic exclusion or "snob" zoning (see Roberts, op. cit., supra, at pp. 36–49). Ramapo would preserve its nature, delightful as that may be, but the supervening question is whether it alone may decide this or whether it must be decided by the larger community represented by the Legislature. Legally, politically, economically, and sociologically, the base for determination must be larger than that provided by the town fathers.

Accordingly, I dissent and vote to affirm the orders in both cases.

FULD, C.J., and BURKE, BERGAN and GIBSON, JJ., concur with SCILEPPI, J.

BREITEL, J., dissents and votes to affirm in a separate opinion in which JASEN, J., concurs.

In each case: Order reversed, with costs, and the case remitted to Special Term for further proceedings in accordance with the opinion herein.

Notes

1. The entire Ramapo growth control ordinance is reproduced in 24 Zoning Digest 68 (1972). As to how the Ramapo point system was developed, see Manuel, Ramapo's Managed Growth Program, 4 Planners' Notebook, No. 5, p. 1 (American Institute of Planners 1974), at p. 5:

> In attempting to arrive at a reasonable point spread within each category and at the total eligible point score of 15 which was finally incorporated into the zoning regulations, a series of extensive trial and error analysis were

performed. First of all, all existing undeveloped land areas in the unincorporated portion of the Town were mapped and the potential development capacity for each area then computed based upon existing zoning. Then a series of different overall scoring systems were tested to determine the number of lots or building units which would become eligible for approval each year, based upon the projected capital budget and capital plan. These calculations also gave the Town a measure of the probable annual rate of land consumption measured against its ultimate capacity.

In this intricate process, certain variables were fortunately held generally constant. One was the capital budget in combination with the capital plan, producing an 18 year spread for projected public improvements. The other was the concept that the Town should reach virtual development saturation at the end of the life of the capital plan, based upon the recommendation of the Town master plan.*

The opinion in *Ramapo* neglects to point out that the point system used in the Ramapo ordinance is to some extent based on the distance of the required facilities from "each separate lot or plot capable of being improved with a residential dwelling." Thus, e.g., points were given on a sliding scale for a "fire house" as follows:

Within 1 mile... 3 points
Within 2 miles.. 1 point
Further than .... 0 points

It can be argued that this distance formula is unreasonable, since fire protection is more properly measured by distance from the fire station in terms of time. See Dept. of Planning and Community Development. A Report on Population Growth in the City of Aurora [Colorado] 41 (1973), concluding that five minutes is the outer limit for safety purposes. The time it takes for a fire truck to reach a fire obviously depends on the character of the road network and the topography, and not simply on distance.

The Ramapo ordinance awarded points for drainage on the basis of the capacity of drainage systems, at points along the system, to handle peak drainage, based not on the incremental change produced by a proposed development of a tract, but on the rating given for projected complete development of all land in the area. Thus the first developer to come into an area must make drainage improvements (if he wants the maximum number of points) that will relieve the burden on future developers in the area. In light of the cases limiting subdivision exactions to those that primarily benefit a particular subdivision, is the Ramapo system for awarding drainage points valid?

It should be noted that schools were not included in the point system because they are a special district function not controlled by the town government. It was hoped, however, that school costs could be indirectly controlled by a growth management system based on other public facilities, since school system overload was a major concern of the Ramapo planners. Rather inconsistently, fire protection facilities were included in the growth control system although firehouses are not provided by the town and must be provided by special service districts formed by local residents. Moreover, the county is responsible for the construction of interceptor sewers and the town is only responsible for installation of lateral sewers.

2. The *Ramapo* decision was vigorously criticized in H. Franklin, Controlling Urban Growth—But For Whom? (Potomac Inst.1973), and Bosselman, Can the Town of Ramapo Pass a Law to Bind the Whole World? 1 Fla.St.U.L. Rev. 234 (1973). Franklin's criticism is based largely on the fact that the underlying low density zoning of Ramapo substantially limits multi-family housing to the incorporated areas within the town, which already contain most of that kind of housing, and limits fully 65 percent of all the vacant land zoned for residential use to "large lot" development, with minimum lot sizes of 25,000 to 80,000 square feet required. Only one percent of the land suitable for development is zoned for single-family houses on lots with a minimum area of 7,500 square feet, the smallest minimum provided in the zoning ordinance. Moreover, Franklin points out, no additional public housing is planned in Ramapo, no FHA-subsidized housing is under way or contemplated, and FHA subsidized single-family houses are the only forms of subsidized housing now possible in residential areas. Franklin concludes that the court's statement, in the *Ramapo* opinion, that the town "has utilized its comprehensive plan to implement its timing controls and has coupled with these restrictions provisions for low and moderate income housing on a large scale" is unfounded.

3. In March, 1983, Ramapo decided to drop the point system which was the mainspring of its growth control system. The following analysis of the reasons for the decision to abandon the point system is drawn from 49 Planning, June 1983, pp. 8–9.

The fact that a developer could obtain points on the basis of *scheduled* improvements was an essential component of the system's legal foundation; it was used to prove that the town's intent was to control growth, not to prevent it. In theory, this provision was to prevent the town from deferring improvements indefinitely, and to give developers an indication of when they might proceed.

The town had assumed that the federal government would continue to pay for sewer installation. It did not. The loss of these funds, combined with the unanticipated needs for capital improvements generated by several severe storms, forced a rationally designed, time program onto an unrealistic schedule. As a result, development, while delayed, had to be permitted to occur before the improvements were actually provided. While the system succeeded in slowing the rate of growth, temporarily lessening the impact on public facilities, it also resulted in much higher housing prices, as inflationary pressures drove up costs.

Evidence of public dissatisfaction with the point system first materialized about three years ago.   *   *   *   Recently, the program has been blamed specifically for deterring the community's economic development. When the system was adopted, the town was approving 800 dwelling units a year; current approvals are down to a fraction of that number.

Ramapo shows that a well-thought-out system of control over the timing and location of growth can withstand legal challenge. But the system's validity was predicated on its promise to provide public facilities according to an orderly schedule. When that was not done, development was delayed, but the type and pattern of development did not change. Today, as in 1964, almost all of Ramapo's housing is single-family—detached, and the location of new developments remains unaffected by the availability of improvements. We suspect that if the delays and excessive costs for processing applications were to lead to a new legal challenge, the court of appeals would probably hand down a radically different decision.

4. As Judge Breitel's dissent points out, minimum lot-size zoning may be used to regulate the tempo and sequence of land development in suburban areas. Back in the 1950's and 1960's before concerns as to "growth management" and "exclusionary zoning" had assumed great significance, the courts generally sustained relatively large minimum lot size requirements when they were challenged by land developers on due process grounds. Among the justifications offered by local governments and—usually—accepted by the courts, were the following:

(a) Preservation of the semi-rural character and appearance of suburban communities;

(b) Preservation of specific historic sites and buildings in their historic settings;

(c) Preservation for low-density development sites which, because of their topography, are not appropriate for higher density development;

(d) Provision of large enough building sites to assure a safe water supply and safe sewage disposal in areas without a public water supply and/or public sewage disposal system;

(e) Preservation of the natural capacity of the soil to absorb rainfall by limiting the area built upon, thus providing protection against flooding and soil erosion;

(f) Implementation of specific planning principles as to the proper organization of residential areas;

(g) Preservation of community identity by leaving predominantly open "green belt" areas between municipalities;

(h) Provision of some "high class" low density residential areas to balance residential development with small, low-cost houses; and

(i) Protection of the value of houses previously constructed on large lots against depreciation that would result "if sections here and there are developed with smaller lots."

In his *Ramapo* dissent, however, Judge Breitel was talking about high minimum lot-size requirements imposed in order to create temporary "holding zones" in areas to be rezoned later for smaller lot sizes in accordance with some scheme of "growth management." One of the most interesting cases on "holding zones" is Steel Hill Development, Inc. v. Town of Sanbornton, 469 F.2d 956 (1st Cir.1972). Sanbornton, in New Hampshire, "is a tiny town * * * with a year-round population of approximately 1,000 persons living in some 330 regular homes" bordering Lake Winnisquam, "within easy reach of Lake Winnipisaukee" and affording "simple access to most New Hampshire ski areas." In the Steel Hill Development case, the U.S. Court of Appeals upheld, against attack on statutory, "due process," and "equal protection" grounds, a rezoning amendment which placed approximately 70% of a developer's land in a "Forest Conservation District" where the minimum lot size was 6 acres, and 30% of its land in an "Agricultural District" where the minimum lot size was 3 acres. The effect of this rezoning was to block the developer's proposed development of 500 to 515 family units on a 510 acre tract—a development which would have doubled the town's population. The court recognized that it was "caught up in the environmental revolution" and that the case at bar required "the resolution of conflicting economic, environmental, and human values." The validity of the 3 acre lot minimums was apparently conceded on the appeal. After a good deal of soul searching the Court of Appeals sustained the 6 acre lot minimums in the "Forest Conservation District." The court said:

* * * We recognize, as within the general welfare, concerns relating to the construction and integration of hundreds of new homes which would have an irreversible effect on the area's ecological balance, destroy scenic values, decrease open space, significantly change the rural character of this small town, pose substantial financial burdens on the town for police, fire, sewer, and road service, and open the way for tides of weekend 'visitors' who would own second homes. If the federal government itself has thought these concerns to be within the general welfare, * * * we cannot say that Sanbornton cannot similarly consider such values and reflect them in its zoning ordinance. * * *

Yet, though it may be proper for Sanbornton to consider the foregoing factors, we think that the town has done so in a most crude manner. We are disturbed by the admission here that there was never any professional or scientific study made as to why six, rather than four or eight, acres was reasonable to protect the values cherished by the people of Sanbornton. On reviewing the record, we have serious worries whether the basic motivation of the town meeting was not simply to keep outsiders, provided they wished to come in quantity, out of the town. We cannot think that expansion of population, even a very substantial one, seasonal or permanent, is by itself a legitimate basis for permissible objection. Were we to adjudicate this as a restriction for all time, and were the evidence of pressure from land-deprived and land-seeking outsiders more real, we might well come to a different conclusion. Where there is natural population growth it has to go somewhere, unwelcome as it may be, and in that case we do not think it should be channeled by the happenstance of what town gets its veto in first. But, at this time of uncertainty as to the right balance between ecological and population pressures, we cannot help but feel that the town's ordinance, which severely restricts development, may properly stand for the present as a legitimate stop-gap measure.

* * * The zoning ordinance here in question has been in existence less than two years. Hopefully, Sanbornton has begun or soon will begin to plan with more precision for the future, taking advantage of numerous federal or state grants for which it might qualify. * * * Thus, while we affirm the district court's determination at the present time, we recognize that this is a very special case which cannot be read as evidencing a general approval of six-acre zoning and that this requirement may well not indefinitely stand without more homework by the concerned parties.

Id. at 961–62.

CONSTRUCTION INDUSTRY ASSOCIATION OF SONO-MA COUNTY v. CITY OF PETALUMA

United States Court of Appeals, 9th Circuit, 1975.
522 F.2d 897, cert. denied 424 U.S. 934, 96 S.Ct. 1148, 47 L.Ed.2d 342, 1976.

OPINION

Before BARNES and CHOY, Circuit Judges and EAST, District Judge.

CHOY, Circuit Judge:

The City of Petaluma (the City) appeals from a district court decision voiding as unconstitutional certain aspects of its five-year housing and zoning plan. We reverse.

Statement of Facts

The City is located in southern Sonoma County, about 40 miles north of San Francisco. In the 1950's and 1960's, Petaluma was a relatively self-sufficient town. It experienced a steady population growth from 10,315 in 1950 to 24,870 in 1970. Eventually, the City was drawn into the Bay Area metropolitan housing market as people working in San Francisco and San Rafael became willing to commute longer distances to secure relatively inexpensive housing available there. By November 1972, according to unofficial figures, Petaluma's population was at 30,500, a dramatic increase of almost 25 per cent in little over two years.

The increase in the City's population, not surprisingly, is reflected in the increase in the number of its housing units. From 1964 to 1971, the following number of residential housing units were completed:

1964	270	1968	379
1965	440	1969	358
1966	321	1970	591
1967	234	1971	891

In 1970 and 1971, the years of the most rapid growth, demand for housing in the City was even greater than above indicated. Taking 1970 and 1971 together, builders won approval of a total of 2000 permits although only 1482 were actually completed by the end of 1971.

Alarmed by the accelerated rate of growth in 1970 and 1971, the demand for even more housing, and the sprawl of the City eastward, the City adopted a temporary freeze on development in early 1971. The construction and zoning change moratorium was intended to give the City Council and the City planners an opportunity to study the housing and zoning situation and to develop short and long range plans. The Council made specific findings with respect to housing patterns and availability in Petaluma, including the following: That from 1960–1970 housing had been in almost unvarying 6000 square-foot lots laid out in regular grid patterns; that there was a density of approximately 4.5 housing units per acre in the single-family home areas; that during 1960–1970, 88 per cent of housing permits issued were for single-family detached homes; that in 1970, 83 per cent of Petaluma's housing was single-family dwellings; that the bulk of recent development (largely single-family homes) occurred in the eastern portion of the City, causing a large deficiency in moderately priced multi-family and apartment units on the east side.

To correct the imbalance between single-family and multi-family dwellings, curb the sprawl of the City on the east, and retard the accelerating growth of the City, the Council in 1972 adopted several resolutions, which collectively are called the "Petaluma Plan" (the Plan).

The Plan, on its face limited to a five-year period (1972–1977),[9] fixes a housing development growth rate not to exceed 500 dwelling units per

9. The district court found that although the Plan is ostensibly limited to a five-year period, official attempts have been made to perpetuate the Plan beyond

year.[10] Each dwelling unit represents approximately three people. The 500-unit figure is somewhat misleading, however, because it applies only to housing units (hereinafter referred to as "development-units") that are part of projects involving five units or more. Thus, the 500-unit figure does not reflect any housing and population growth due to construction of single-family homes or even four-unit apartment buildings not part of any larger project.

The Plan also positions a 200 foot wide "greenbelt" around the City,[11] to serve as a boundary for urban expansion for at least five years, and with respect to the east and north sides of the City, for perhaps ten to fifteen years. One of the most innovative features of the Plan is the Residential Development Control System which provides procedures and criteria for the award of the annual 500 development-unit permits. At the heart of the allocation procedure is an intricate point system, whereby a builder accumulates points for conformity by his projects with the City's general plan and environmental design plans, for good architectural design, and for providing low and moderate income dwelling units and various recreational facilities. The Plan further directs that allocations of building permits are to be divided as evenly as feasible between the west and east sections of the City and between single-family dwellings and multiple residential units (including rental units),[12] that the sections of the City closest to the center are to be developed first in order to cause "infilling" of vacant area, and that 8 to 12 per cent of the housing units approved be for low and moderate income persons.

In a provision of the Plan, intended to maintain the close-in rural space outside and surrounding Petaluma, the City solicited Sonoma County to establish stringent subdivision and appropriate acreage parcel controls for the areas outside the urban extension line of the City and to limit severely further residential infilling.

1977. Such attempts include the urban extension line (see text infra) and the agreement to purchase from the Sonoma County Water Agency only 9.8 million gallons of water per day through the year 1990. This flow is sufficient to support a population of 55,000. If the City were to grow at a rate of about 500 housing units per year (approximately three persons per unit), the City would reach a population of 55,000 about the year 1990. The 55,000 figure was mentioned by City officials as the projected optimal (and maximum) size of Petaluma. See, e.g., R.T. at 135–43, 145–46.

[Some of the court's footnotes have been omitted and others have been renumbered.—Ed.]

10. The allotment for each year is not an inflexible limitation. The Plan does provide for a 10 percent variance (50 units) below or above the 500 unit annual figure, but the expectation of the Council is that not more than 2500 units will be constructed during the five-year period.

11. At some points this urban extension line is about one-quarter of a mile beyond the present City limits.

12. By providing for the increase of multi-family dwellings (including townhouses as well as rental apartments), the Plan allows increased density. Whereas, during the years just preceding the Plan, housing density was about 4.5 units per acre, under the Plan single-family housing will consist of not only low (4.5 units per acre) but also medium density (4.5 to 10 units per acre). And multi-family housing, to comprise about half of the housing under the Plan, will be built at a density of 10 or more units per acre.

Purpose of the Plan

The purpose of the Plan is much disputed in this case. According to general statements in the Plan itself, the Plan was devised to ensure that "development in the next five years, will take place in a reasonable, orderly, attractive manner, rather than in a completely haphazard and unattractive manner." The controversial 500-unit limitation on residential development-units was adopted by the City "[i]n order to protect its small town character and surrounding open space." [13] The other features of the Plan were designed to encourage an east-west balance in development, to provide for variety in densities and building types and wide ranges in prices and rents, to ensure infilling of close-in vacant areas, and to prevent the sprawl of the City to the east and north. The Construction Industry Association of Sonoma County (the Association) argues and the district court found, however, that the Plan was primarily enacted "to limit Petaluma's demographic and market growth rate in housing and in the immigration of new residents." Construction Industry Assn. v. City of Petaluma, 375 F.Supp. 574, 576 (N.D.Cal.1974).

Market Demand and Effect of the Plan

In 1970 and 1971, housing permits were allotted at the rate of 1000 annually, and there was no indication that without some governmental control on growth consumer demand would subside or even remain at the 1000-unit per year level. Thus, if Petaluma had imposed a flat 500-unit limitation on *all* residential housing, the effect of the Plan would clearly be to retard to a substantial degree the natural growth rate of the City. Petaluma, however, did not apply the 500-unit limitation across the board, but instead exempted all projects of four units or less. Because appellees failed to introduce any evidence whatsoever as to the number of exempt units expected to be built during the five-year period, the effect of the 500 *development-unit* limitation on the natural growth in housing is uncertain. For purposes of this decision, however, we will assume that the 500 development-unit growth rate is in fact below the reasonably anticipated market demand for such units and that absent the Petaluma Plan, the City would grow at a faster rate.

According to undisputed expert testimony at trial, if the Plan (limiting housing starts to approximately 6 per cent of existing housing stock each year) were to be adopted by municipalities throughout the region, the impact on the housing market would be substantial. For the decade 1970 to 1980, the shortfall in needed housing in the region would be about 105,000 units (or 25 per cent of the units needed). Further, the aggregate effect of a proliferation of the Plan throughout the San Francisco region would be a decline in regional housing stock quality, a loss of the mobility of current and prospective residents and a deterioration in the quality and choice of housing available to income earners with

---

13. After the appellees initiated this suit, the City attempted to show that the Plan was implemented to prevent the overtaxing of available water and sewage facilities. We find it unnecessary, however, to consider the claim that sewage and water problems justified implementation of the Plan.

real incomes of $14,000 per year or less. If, however, the Plan were considered by itself and with respect to Petaluma only, there is no evidence to suggest that there would be a deterioration in the quality and choice of housing available there to persons in the lower and middle income brackets. Actually, the Plan increases the availability of multi-family units (owner-occupied and rental units) and low-income units which were rarely constructed in the pre-Plan days.

Court Proceedings

Two landowners (the Landowners) and the Association instituted this suit under 28 U.S.C.A. §§ 1331, 1343 and 42 U.S.C.A. § 1983 against the City and its officers and council members, claiming that the Petaluma Plan was unconstitutional. The district court ruled that certain aspects of the Plan unconstitutionally denied the right to travel insofar as they tended "to limit the natural population growth of the area." 375 F.Supp., at 588. The court enjoined the City and its agents from implementing the unconstitutional elements of the Plan, but the order was stayed by Justice Douglas pending this appeal.

*   *   *

Standing

The City also challenges the standing of the Association and the Landowners to maintain the suit. The standing requirement raises the threshold question in every federal case whether plaintiff has made out a "case or controversy" between himself and the defendant within the meaning of Article III of the Constitution. In order to satisfy the constitutional requirement that courts decide only cases or controversies and to ensure the requisite concreteness of facts and adverseness of parties, plaintiff must show that he has a "personal stake in the outcome of the controversy," Baker v. Carr, 369 U.S. 186, 204, 82 S.Ct. 691, 703, 7 L.Ed.2d 663 (1962), or that he has suffered "some threatened or actual injury resulting from the putatively illegal action." S. v. D., 410 U.S. 614, 617, 93 S.Ct. 1146, 1148, 35 L.Ed.2d 536 (1973). Further, the plaintiff must satisfy the additional court-imposed standing requirement that the "interest sought to be protected by the complainant is arguably within the zone of interests to be protected or regulated by the statute or constitutional guarantee in question." Association of Data Processing Service Organizations, Inc. v. Camp, 397 U.S. 150, 153, 90 S.Ct. 827, 830, 25 L.Ed.2d 184 (1970). A corollary to the "zone of interest" requirement is the well-recognized general rule that "even when the plaintiff has alleged injury sufficient to meet the 'case or controversy' requirement, * * * the plaintiff generally must assert his own legal rights and interests, and cannot rest his claim to relief on the legal rights or interests of third parties." Warth v. Seldin, 422 U.S. 490, 499, 95 S.Ct. 2197, 2205, 45 L.Ed.2d 343 (1975).

Appellees easily satisfy the "injury in fact" standing requirement. The Association alleges it has suffered in its own right monetary damages due to lost revenues. Sonoma County builders contribute dues to the Association in a sum proportionate to the amount of business the builders do in the area. Thus, in a very real sense a restriction on building in Petaluma causes economic injury to the Association.

The two Landowners also have already suffered or are threatened with a direct injury. It is their position that the Petaluma Plan operated of itself, to adversely affect the value and marketability of their land for residential uses, and such an allegation is sufficient to show that they have a personal stake in the outcome of the controversy. * * *

Although appellees have suffered or are threatened with direct personal injury, the "zone of interest" requirement poses a huge stumbling block to their attempt to show standing. The primary federal claim upon which this suit is based—the right to travel or migrate—is a claim asserted not on the appellees' own behalf, but on behalf of a group of unknown third parties allegedly excluded from living in Petaluma. Although individual builders, the Association, and the Landowners are admittedly adversely affected by the Petaluma Plan, their economic interests are undisputedly outside the zone of interest to be protected by any purported constitutional right to travel. Accordingly, appellees' right to travel claim "falls squarely within the prudential standing rule that normally bars litigants from asserting the rights or legal interests of others in order to obtain relief from injury to themselves." Warth v. Seldin, 422 U.S. at 509, 95 S.Ct. at 2210.

There are several exceptions to this general rule, but plaintiffs do not fall within any of them. Congress may grant standing by statute to persons who might otherwise lack standing, id., but here no statute expressly or by clear implication grants to persons in appellees' position a right of action based on third parties' right to travel. On several occasions, the Supreme Court has granted standing to persons whom a criminal statute directly affected to challenge the statute on the ground that if enforced it would infringe the rights of third parties. * * * No comparison, however, may be fairly drawn between appellees and the doctors facing criminal sanctions in [Doe v. Bolton, 410 U.S. 179, 93 S.Ct. 739, 35 L.Ed.2d 201 (1973), and Griswold v. Connecticut, 381 U.S. 479, 85 S.Ct. 1678, 14 L.Ed.2d 510 (1965)] * * *. Nor do appellees allege that the Petaluma Plan precludes or otherwise adversely affects a relationship existing between them and the persons whose rights allegedly have been violated. * * * The only connection between any of the appellees and any of the persons who purportedly are excluded from Petaluma is the possibility that but for the Plan they would be parties to a purchase-sale agreement. There exists no special, on-going relationship between appellees and those whose rights allegedly are violated which militates in favor of granting standing. * * * Nor have the Association and the Landowners shown that their prosecution of the suit is necessary to ensure protection of the rights asserted. Assuming arguendo that the constitutional right to travel applies to this case, those individuals whose mobility is impaired may bring suit on their own behalf and on behalf of those similarly situated. Although Warth v. Seldin denied standing to a group of low-income and minority-group plaintiffs, challenging exclusionary zoning practices, the case is no bar to a suit against the City brought by a proper group of plaintiffs. The

Court in Warth v. Seldin left open the federal court doors for plaintiffs who have some interest in a particular housing project and who, but for the restrictive zoning ordinances, would be able to reside in the community.

Although we conclude that appellees lack standing to assert the rights of third parties, they nonetheless have standing to maintain claims based on violations of rights personal to them. Accordingly, appellees have standing to challenge the Petaluma Plan on the grounds asserted in their complaint that the Plan is arbitrary and thus violative of their due process rights guaranteed by the Fourteenth Amendment and that the Plan poses an unreasonable burden on interstate commerce. * * * The fact that one of the Landowners' property lies wholly outside the present City boundaries and that the other's property lies mostly outside the boundaries is no bar to their challenging the City's Plan which has a direct, intended and immediate effect on the property. * * *

Other Challenges to the Plan

Although the district court rested its decision solely on the right to travel claim, all the facts and legal conclusions necessary to resolve appellees' other claims are part of the record. Thus, in order to promote judicial economy, we now dispose of the other challenges to the Plan. * * *

Substantive Due Process

Appellees claim that the Plan is arbitrary and unreasonable and, thus, violative of the due process clause of the Fourteenth Amendment. According to appellees, the Plan is nothing more than an exclusionary zoning device,[14] designed solely to insulate Petaluma from the urban complex in which it finds itself. The Association and the Landowners reject, as falling outside the scope of any legitimate governmental interest, the City's avowed purposes in implementing the Plan—the preservation of Petaluma's small town character and the avoidance of the social and environmental problems caused by an uncontrolled growth rate.

In attacking the validity of the Plan, appellees rely heavily on the district court's finding that the express purpose and the actual effect of the Plan is to exclude substantial numbers of people who would otherwise elect to move to the City. 375 F.Supp. at 581. The existence of an exclusionary purpose and effect reflects, however, only one side of the

---

14. "Exclusionary zoning" is a phrase popularly used to describe suburban zoning regulations which have the effect, if not also the purpose, of preventing the migration of low and middle-income persons. Since a large percentage of racial minorities fall within the low and middle income brackets, exclusionary zoning regulations may also effectively wall out racial minorities. * * *

Most court challenges to and comment upon so-called exclusionary zoning focus on such traditional zoning devices as height limitations, minimum square footage and minimum lot size requirements, and the prohibition of multi-family dwellings or mobile homes. The Petaluma Plan is unique in that although it assertedly slows the growth rate it replaces the past pattern of single-family detached homes with an assortment of housing units, varying in price and design.

zoning regulation. Practically all zoning restrictions have as a purpose and effect the *exclusion* of some activity or type of structure or a certain density of inhabitants. And in reviewing the reasonableness of a zoning ordinance, our inquiry does not terminate with a finding that it is for an exclusionary purpose.[15] We must determine further whether the *exclusion* bears any rational relationship to a *legitimate state interest.* If it does not, then the zoning regulation is invalid. If, on the other hand, a legitimate state interest is furthered by the zoning regulation, we must defer to the legislative act. Being neither a super legislature nor a zoning board of appeal, a federal court is without authority to weigh and reappraise the factors considered or ignored by the legislative body in passing the challenged zoning regulation.[16] The reasonableness, not the wisdom, of the Petaluma Plan is at issue in this suit.

It is well settled that zoning regulations "must find their justification in some aspect of the police power, asserted for the public welfare." Village of Euclid v. Ambler Realty Co., 272 U.S. 365, 387, 47 S.Ct. 114, 118, 71 L.Ed. 303 (1926). The concept of the public welfare, however, is not limited to the regulation of noxious activities or dangerous structures. As the Court stated in Berman v. Parker, 348 U.S. 26, 33, 75 S.Ct. 98, 102, 99 L.Ed. 27 (1954):

> The concept of the public welfare is broad and inclusive. The values it represents are spiritual as well as physical, aesthetic as well as monetary. It is within the power of the legislature to determine that the community should be beautiful as well as healthy, spacious as well as clean, well-balanced as well as carefully patrolled.

(citations omitted). Accord, Village of Belle Terre v. Boraas, 416 U.S. 1, 6, 9, 94 S.Ct. 1536, 39 L.Ed.2d 797 (1974).

In determining whether the City's interest in preserving its small town character and in avoiding uncontrolled and rapid growth falls within the broad concept of "public welfare," we are considerably assisted by two recent cases. Belle Terre, supra, and Ybarra v. City of Town of Los Altos Hills, 503 F.2d 250 (9th Cir.1974), each of which upheld as not unreasonable a zoning regulation much more restrictive than the Petaluma Plan, are dispositive of the due process issue in this case.

In *Belle Terre* the Supreme Court rejected numerous challenges[17] to a village's restricting land use to one-family dwellings excluding lodging houses, boarding houses, fraternity houses or multiple-dwelling houses.

---

15. Our inquiry here is not unlike that involved in a case alleging denial of equal protection of the laws. The mere showing of some discrimination by the state is not sufficient to prove an invasion of one's constitutional rights. Most legislation to some extent discriminates between various classes of persons, business enterprises, or other entities. However, absent a suspect classification or invasion of fundamental rights, equal protection rights are violated only where the classification does not bear a rational relationship to a legitimate state interest. See Ybarra v. City of Town of Los Altos Hills, 503 F.2d 250, 254 (9th Cir. 1974).

16. Appellees' brief is unnecessarily oversize (125 pages) mainly because it is rife with quotations from writers on regional planning, economic regulation and sociological policies and themes. These types of considerations are more appropriate for legislative bodies than for courts.

17. The plaintiffs in Belle Terre claimed *inter alia* that the ordinance interfered with a person's right to travel and

By absolutely prohibiting the construction of or conversion of a building to other than single-family dwelling, the village ensured that it would never grow, if at all, much larger than its population of 700 living in 220 residences. Nonetheless, the Court found that the prohibition of boarding houses and other multi-family dwellings was reasonable and within the public welfare because such dwellings present urban problems such as the occupation of a given space by more people, the increase in traffic and parked cars and the noise that comes with increased crowds. According to the Court,

> A quiet place where yards are wide, people few, and motor vehicles restricted are legitimate guidelines in a land-use project addressed to family needs. This goal is a permissible one within Berman v. Parker, supra. The police power is not confined to elimination of filth, stench, and unhealthy places. It is ample to lay out zones where family values, youth values, and the blessings of quiet seclusion, and clean air make the area a sanctuary for people.

416 U.S. at 9, 94 S.Ct. at 1541. While dissenting from the majority opinion in *Belle Terre* on the ground that the regulation unreasonably burdened the exercise of First Amendment associational rights, Mr. Justice Marshall concurred in the Court's express holding that a local entity's zoning power is extremely broad:

> [L]ocal zoning authorities may properly act in furtherance of the objectives asserted to be served by the ordinance at issue here: *restricting uncontrolled growth*, solving traffic problems, keeping rental costs at a reasonable level, and making the community attractive to families. The police power which provides the justification for zoning is not narrowly confined. And, it is appropriate that we afford zoning authorities *considerable latitude in choosing the means by which to implement such purposes.*

416 U.S. at 13–14, 94 S.Ct. at 1543 (Marshall, J., dissenting) (emphasis added) (citations omitted).

Following the *Belle Terre* decision, this court in *Los Altos Hills* had an opportunity to review a zoning ordinance providing that a housing lot shall contain not less than one acre and that no lot shall be occupied by more than one primary dwelling unit. The ordinance as a practical matter prevented poor people from living in Los Altos Hills and restricted the density, and thus the population. of the town. This court, nonetheless, found that the ordinance was rationally related to a legitimate governmental interest—*the preservation of the town's rural environment*—and, thus, did not violate the equal protection clause of the Fourteenth Amendment. 503 F.2d at 254.

Both the Belle Terre ordinance and the Los Altos Hills regulation had the purpose and effect of permanently restricting growth; nonethe-

---

right to migrate to and settle within a state.

The Supreme Court held that since the ordinance was not aimed at transients, there was no infringement of anyone's right to travel. 416 U.S. at 7, 94 S.Ct.

1536. Although due to appellees' lack of standing we do not reach today the right to travel issue, we note that the Petaluma Plan is not aimed at transients, nor does it penalize those who have recently exercised their right to travel. * * *

less, the court in each case upheld the particular law before it on the ground that the regulation served a legitimate governmental interest falling within the concept of the public welfare; the preservation of quiet family neighborhoods (Belle Terre) and the preservation of a rural environment (Los Altos Hills). Even less restrictive or exclusionary than the above zoning ordinances is the Petaluma Plan which, unlike those ordinances, does not freeze the population at present or near-present levels.[18] Further, unlike the Los Altos Hills ordinance and the various zoning regulations struck down by state courts in recent years, the Petaluma Plan does not have the undesirable effect of walling out any particular income class nor any racial minority group.[19]

Although we assume that some persons desirous of living in Petaluma will be excluded under the housing permit limitation and that, thus, the Plan may frustrate some legitimate regional housing needs, the Plan is not arbitrary or unreasonable. We agree with appellees that unlike the situation in the past most municipalities today are neither isolated nor wholly independent from neighboring municipalities and that, consequently, unilateral land use decisions by one local entity affect the needs and resources of an entire region. * * * It does not necessarily follow, however, that the *due process* rights of builders and landowners are violated merely because a local entity exercises in its own self-interest the police power lawfully delegated to it by the state. * * * If the present system of delegated zoning power does not effectively serve the state interest in furthering the general welfare of the region or entire state, it is the state legislature's and not the federal courts' role to intervene and adjust the system. As stated supra, the federal court is not a super zoning board and should not be called on to mark the point at which legitimate local interests in promoting the welfare of the community are outweighed by legitimate regional interests. * * *

We conclude therefore that under *Belle Terre* and *Los Altos Hills* the concept of the public welfare is sufficiently broad to uphold Petaluma's desire to preserve its small town character, its open spaces and

---

18. Under the Petaluma Plan, the population is expected to increase at the rate of about 1500 persons annually. This rate approximates the rate of growth in the 1960's and represents about a 6 per cent increase per year over the present population.

19. Although appellees have attempted to align their business interests in attacking the Plan with legitimate housing needs of the urban poor and racial minorities, the Association has not alleged nor can it allege, based on the record in this case, that the Plan has the purpose and effect of excluding poor persons and racial minorities. Contrary to the picture painted by appellees, the Petaluma Plan is "inclusionary" to the extent that it offers new opportunities, previously unavailable, to minorities

and low and moderate-income persons. Under the pre-Plan system single family, middle-income housing dominated the Petaluma market, and as a result low and moderate income persons were unable to secure housing in the area. The Plan radically changes the previous building pattern and requires that housing permits be evenly divided between single-family and multi-family units, and that approximately eight to twelve per cent of the units be constructed specifically for low and moderate income persons.

In stark contrast, each of the exclusionary zoning regulations invalidated by state courts in recent years impeded the ability of low and moderate income persons to purchase or rent housing in the locality. * * *

low density of population, and to grow at an orderly and deliberate pace.[20]

Commerce Clause

The district court found that housing in Petaluma and the surrounding areas is produced substantially through goods and services in interstate commerce and that curtailment of residential growth in Petaluma will cause serious dislocation to commerce. 375 F.Supp. at 577, 579. Our ruling today, however, that the Petaluma Plan represents a reasonable and legitimate exercise of the police power obviates the necessity of remanding the case for consideration of appellees' claim that the Plan unreasonably burdens interstate commerce.

It is well settled that a state regulation validly based on the police power does not impermissibly burden interstate commerce where the regulation neither discriminates against interstate commerce nor operates to disrupt its required uniformity.   *   *   *

Consequently, since the local regulation here is rationally related to the social and environmental welfare of the community and does not discriminate against interstate commerce or operate to disrupt its required uniformity, appellees' claim that the Plan unreasonably burdens commerce must fail.

Reversed.

Notes

1. Some additional aspects of the Petaluma plan, not covered in the court's opinion, are set out in McGivern, Putting a Speed Limit on Growth, 38 Planning 263 (1972). (McGivern is the Petaluma planning director.) McGivern notes that the city was divided by a freeway into an older western section and a newer eastern section where most of the recent growth had occurred. Part of the purpose of the plan was to redistribute future growth more equally between these two sections. The quotas are "to be established on a geographic basis (east, central, and west) [and] are based on the actual number of single-family and multifamily units proposed in the housing element of the Petaluma General Plan.   *   *   * The council may also require that between 8 and 12 per cent of each year's total quota shall be low- to moderate-income housing as defined by the housing element of the plan." Id. at 265.

The Residential Development Evaluation System is utilized to determine which developers will receive the annual quota of allowable dwelling units, and

---

20. Our decision upholding the Plan as not in violation of the appellees' due process rights should not be read as a permanent endorsement of the Plan. In a few years the City itself for good reason may abandon the Plan or the state may decide to alter its laws delegating its zoning power to the local authorities; or to meet legitimate regional needs, regional zoning authorities may be established.   *   *   * To be sure, housing needs in metropolitan areas like the San Francisco Bay Area are pressing and the needs are not being met by present methods of supplying housing. However, the federal court is not the proper forum for resolving these problems. The controversy stirred up by the present litigation, as indicated by the number and variety of *amici* on each side, and the complex economic, political and social factors involved in this case are compelling evidence that resolution of the important housing and environmental issues raised here is exclusively the domain of the legislature.

is based on a point system similar to Ramapo's. From zero to five points are awarded for each of the following public facilities factors:

1. the capacity of the water system to provide for the needs of the proposed development without system extensions beyond those normally installed by the developer;

2. the capacity of the sanitary sewers to dispose of the wastes of the proposed development without system extensions beyond those normally installed by the developer;

3. the capacity of the drainage facilities to adequately dispose of the surface runoff of the proposed development without system extensions beyond those normally installed by the developer;

4. the ability of the Fire Department of the city to provide fire protection according to the established response standards of the city without necessity of establishing a new station or requiring addition of major equipment to an existing station;

5. the capacity of the appropriate school to absorb the children expected to inhabit a proposed development without necessitating adding double sessions or other unusual scheduling or classroom overcrowding;

6. the capacity of major street linkage to provide for the needs of the proposed development without substantially altering existing traffic patterns or overloading the existing street system, and the availability of other public facilities (such as parks and playgrounds) to meet the additional demands for vital public services without extension of services beyond those provided by the developer.

It is reported that the evaluation system was utilized to require substantial contributions from developers for citywide facilities such as water, sewer, drainage, and fire protection.

The second review category is based on quality of design and contribution to public welfare and amenity. Developers are assigned from zero to 10 points on each of the following:

1. site and architectural design quality which may be indicated by the harmony of the proposed buildings in terms of size, height, color, and location with respect to existing neighboring development;

2. site and architectural design quality which may be indicated by the amount and character of landscaping and screening;

3. site and architectural design quality which may be indicated by the arrangement of the site for efficiency of circulation, on- and off-site traffic safety, privacy, etc.;

4. the provision of public and/or private usable open space and/or pathways along the Petaluma River or any creek;

5. contributions to and extensions of existing systems of foot or bicycle paths, equestrian trails, and the greenbelt provided for in the Environmental Design Plan;

6. the provision of needed public facilities such as critical linkages in the major street system, school rooms, or other vital public facilities;

7. the extent to which the proposed development accomplishes an orderly and contiguous extension of existing development as agaisnt "leap frog" development;

8. the provision of units to meet the city's policy goal of 8 per cent to 12 per cent low- and moderate-income dwelling units annually.

The city's development policy also contains the following stated objectives:

- redress a deficiency in multi-family units in Petaluma and insure "a variety of densities and building types and, thus wide ranges of rents". [An attempt was also made to lower housing prices by zoning for compact housing types, such as townhouses.]

- Strengthen and rehabilitate the Central Business District to continue as the principal commercial center in Southern Sonoma County" by severely limiting thoroughfare commercial zoning on the fringe.

2. The federal District Court opinion in Petaluma, 375 F.Supp. 574 (N.D. Cal.1974), had adopted a "growth center" theory which in part supported its holding that the Petaluma plan was unconstitutional. This theory had been developed by economic consultants to the plaintiffs; see Gruen, The Economics of Petaluma: Unconstitutional Regional Socio-Economic Impacts in II Management and Control 173. The District Court expressed the growth center theory as follows:

Growth throughout a metropolitan region takes place unevenly in certain "growth centers," areas having unused capacity which can be tapped or the ability to augment capacity to serve new residents.

(1) Petaluma is such a growth center for the San Francisco metropolitan region.

(2) Such centers serve, among other things, as residential centers for people who work elsewhere in the center cities complex, in other suburbs or in other job centers.

(3) Residential growth in such centers, though larger than in some other cities in the region, is not disproportionately larger in the sense that market, economic, demographic and other forces within the region dictate that growth shall occur in substantial part in growth centers.

(4) If such growth centers curtail residential growth to less than demographic and market rates, as has been attempted in the present case, serious and damaging dislocation will occur in the housing market, the commerce it represents, and in the travel and settlement of people in need and in search of housing. Even in cities in the region that do not qualify as "growth centers," the same exclusion of residential growth would lead to substantially the same adverse consequences, if the exclusion were region-wide.

Id. at 579. The court then noted that the growth that should occur in growth centers could not occur elsewhere. Front-end public facilities costs would be too high in new towns, facilities were not available in rural areas and would have to be provided later at great cost, and growth in older inner cities presented massive redevelopment problems that had not yet been solved. Id. at 579–80. Does a federal court have a constitutional basis for applying such a theory in considering local growth management programs? A state court? For additional discussion of the Petaluma plan see II Management and Control 121–210.

3. In explaining the "right to travel" rationale of its decision, the District Court noted that if the Petaluma quota plan were to proliferate throughout the region there would be a serious shortfall in needed housing. As a result, "Interstate, intrastate and foreign travel would be seriously inhibited, as people trying to move into the region found housing either economically unavailable or simply nonexistent in reasonable quality." 375 F.Supp. at 580–81. The right to travel doctrine has not fared well in the land use controls context in recent decisions. In CEEED v. California Coastal Zone Conservation Commission, 43

Cal.App.3d 306, 118 Cal.Rptr. 315, 333 (1974), in dealing with the permit program of the interim California coastal act, the court said:

"It does not follow, however, that all regulations affecting travel, however indirect or inconsequential, constitute invasions of the fundamental right. The right may be invoked if the regulations 'unreasonably burden or restrict' the freedom of movement. * * * In a particular case the question is whether the travel inhibited is of sufficient importance to individual liberty to give rise to a constitutional violation. * * * Thus far the United States Supreme Court has invoked the right to travel only in cases involving invidious discrimination, durational residence requirements or direct restrictions on interstate or foreign travel. * * *

"We fail to see how the Coastal Initiative interferes with fundamental right to travel. It is not discriminatory; it imposes no durational residence requirement; it exacts no penalty for exercising the right to travel or to select one's place of residence. In short, it has no chilling effect on an individual's freedom of movement. To paraphrase the language of our Supreme Court * * * plaintiffs are stretching their case mightily to bring it within the scope of the fundamental right to travel."

For additional discussion of the right to travel doctrine as it affects land use controls see Note, Municipal Self-Determination: Must Local Control of Growth Yield to Travel Rights?, 17 Ariz.L.Rev. 145 (1975); Note, The Right to Travel and Community Growth Controls, 12 Harv.J.Legis. 244 (1975).

4. Variants of the Petaluma "point system" to control municipal growth have been adopted in a number of other cities. For example, in November 1976 the voters of Boulder, Colorado, adopted an initiative proposal which limited the construction of new dwelling units to 450 per year. In 1977 the Boulder City Council adopted the following criteria to be used in allocating dwelling units among competing developers:

(a) Development proposals may receive a maximum of 30 points or a minimum of − 30 points on the basis of the availability of ten specified public services and facilities, plus a miscellany of other public, quasi-public, and private facilities.

(b) Development proposals may receive up to 20 points for provision of low and moderate income housing.

(c) Development proposals may receive up to 20 points for the mitigation of hazards and adverse environmental impacts, and conservation of natural resources and sensitive areas.

(d) Development proposals may receive up to 30 points on the basis of design and compatibility with surrounding developments. (Rev.Code of City of Boulder, Colorado, §§ 37–1301 to 37–1308.)

The Boulder ordinance specifically defines the standard for allocating points under each criterion; the planning staff makes a recommended point allocation which is either ratified or modified by the Planning Board at a public hearing. Under the Petaluma ordinance, on the other hand, the criteria are stated quite generally; members of the Residential Development Evaluation Board allocate points by private ballot, and these allocations are then averaged to determine a development proposal's final point "score."

Both the Petaluma and the Boulder "point systems" are superimposed on the normal zoning and subdivision controls. Their purpose is to regulate the rate of growth and encourage better quality development. They do not attempt to regulate use, density, bulk, or design and engineering as do the traditional zoning and subdivision controls.

5. For an analysis of growth controls which takes into account the competitive positions of the suburban units imposing such controls in the housing market, see Ellickson, Suburban Growth Controls: An Economic and Legal Analysis, 86 Yale L.J. 385, 425–35 (1977). For a brief general discussion of the use of "point systems" either as ancillary or as primary land use controls, see Wickersham, Reform of Discretionary Land Use Decision-Making: Point Systems and Beyond, 1 Zoning & Planning Law Report 65 (1978).

6. The New Hampshire Supreme Court recently held that a general police power ordinance establishing a limit on the number of building permits that might be issued each year was invalid because it did not comply with the zoning enabling act. After noting that it is not clear in New Hampshire which growth control measures may be enacted under the general police power of a municipality and which must comply with the zoning enabling act, the court held that the ordinance in question should have complied with the enabling act because it established "a definite and detailed scheme of control" and substantially restricted the use of land throughout the town. The court said, "When such ordinances become a substitute for a zoning plan, the purpose and effect of the zoning enabling legislation is defeated." But the court upheld an interim zoning ordinance amendment designed to give the town a maximum of two years in which to develop a phased growth plan. Beck v. Town of Raymond, 118 N.H. 793, 394 A.2d 847 (1978).

SECTION 2.   EXCLUSIONARY LAND USE CONTROLS

A.   ECONOMIC EXCLUSION: STATE JUDICIAL AND LEGISLATIVE RESPONSES

In the past decade and a half, "exclusionary" land use controls have been a major target of those who would like to "open up" the suburban portions of our metropolitan areas to settlement by low- and moderate-income persons. The "exclusionary" effect of the land use controls which have been challenged in the state courts is primarily economic rather than racial, although exclusion of low- and moderate-income persons obviously has a disproportionate impact on racial minorities because a higher proportion of such minorities fall into the low- and moderate-income categories. Norman Williams lists six principal "exclusionary zoning techniques: (1) total or near-total exclusion of multi-family dwellings; (2) tight limits on the number of bedrooms in multi-family dwellings; (3) total or near-total exclusion of mobile homes; (4) minimum floor space requirements for single-family dwellings; (5) minimum lot area requirements for single-family dwellings; and (6) minimum lot frontage requirements for single-family dwellings. 2 N. Williams, American Land Planning Law chs. 62–65 (1974, Supp.1983). It seems clear that the first three techniques have the most significant exclusionary effects. Under present housing market conditions the most promising possibilities for new low- and moderate-income housing lie in multifamily dwellings and mobile homes. The last three techniques apply only to single family detached dwellings and are probably less significant in terms of exclusion than the first three techniques. Of these last three techniques, minimum floor space requirements seem to be the most exclusionary. Unless minimum floor space requirements are set very low, they necessarily increase the cost of single family detached dwellings beyond the minimum that a free market in housing would produce. High minimum lot width requirements may also have a significant effect on the cost of single family housing, since the cost of street improvements normally required by subdivision control ordinances—e.g., street paving, sanitary sewers, and storm sewers—is substantial. Indeed, it has often been asserted that suburban communities have deliberately imposed "cost generating" subdivision control requirements—i.e., requirements that substantially increase the cost of surburban land development—in order to keep out low income persons rather than to protect public health, safety or general welfare.

Most of the "exclusionary zoning" litigation has occurred in three highly urbanized middle Atlantic states, New York, New Jersey, and Pennsylvania. The New Jersey courts have taken the lead, and have developed the most comprehensive new legal doctrines and remedial techniques to deal with the "exclusionary zoning" problem. The leading case is Southern Burlington County N.A.A.C.P. v. Township of Mount Laurel, which has twice been before the New Jersey Supreme Court. In its first opinion, reported in 67 N.J. 151, and 336 A.2d 713 (1975), the Court set out the major features of the Mount Laurel zoning ordinance as follows:

"Under the present ordinance, 29.2% of all the land in the township, or 4,121 acres, is zoned for industry. *   *   * At the time of trial no more than 100 acres *   *   * were actually occupied by industrial users. *   *   * The rest of the land so zoned has remained undeveloped. *   *   * [I]t appeared clear that *   *   * much more land has been so zoned than the reasonable potential for industrial *   *   * expansion warrants. At the same time, however, the land cannot be used for residential development.

"The amount land zoned for retail business use under the general ordinance is relatively small—169 acres, or 1.2% of the total *   *   *.

"The balance of the land area, almost 10,000 acres, has been developed until recently in the conventional form of major subdivisions. The general ordinance provides for four residential zones, designated R–1, R–1D, R–2 and R–3. All permit only single-family, detached dwellings, one house per lot *   *   *.

"The general ordinance requirements, while not as restrictive as those in many similar municipalities, nonetheless realistically allow only homes within the financial reach of persons of at least middle income.

*   *   *

"A variation from conventional development has recently occurred in some parts of Mount Laurel *   *   * by the use of the land use regulation device known as 'planned unit development' (PUD). *   *   *

"While multi-family housing in the form of rental garden, medium rise and high rise apartments and attached townhouses is for the first time provided for, as well as single-family detached dwellings for sale, it is not designed to accommodate and is beyond the financial reach of low and moderate income families, especially those with young children. * * *"

In its first *Mount Laurel* opinion the New Jersey Supreme Court laid down a new *"Mount Laurel* doctrine," as is explained in the second *Mount Laurel* opinion reprinted as the next principal case, and held the Mount Laurel zoning ordinance invalid to the extent that it was inconsistent with the new doctrine. The new doctrine, requiring every "developing community" in New Jersey to affirmatively afford a "realistic opportunity for the construction of its fair share of the present and prospective regional need for low and moderate income housing," was expressly based on Article I, para. 1 of the New Jersey Constitution, which provides:

"All persons are by nature free and independent, and have certain natural and unalienable rights, among which are those of enjoying and defending life and liberty, *of acquiring, possessing, and protecting property*, and of pursuing and obtaining safety and happiness." (Emphasis added.)

The Court reasoned that this constitutional provision guarantees "substantive due process and equal protection of the laws," and hence requires that all local zoning regulations be designed to promote the welfare of all economic groups within the state, not just middle and upper-income persons. Since the Court relied exclusively on the New Jersey Constitution, Mount Laurel Township's attempt to obtain review of the case in the United States was obviously doomed to failure. The appeal was dismissed and the petition for certiorari denied, 423 U.S. 808, 96 S.Ct. 18, 46 L.Ed.2d 28.

SOUTHERN BURLINGTON COUNTY N.A.A.C.P. v. MOUNT LAUREL TOWNSHIP

Supreme Court of New Jersey, 1983.
92 N.J. 158, 456 A.2d 390.

The opinion of the Court was delivered by WILENTZ, C.J.

This is the return, eight years later, of Southern Burlington County, N.A.A.C.P. v. Township of Mount Laurel, 67 N.J. 151, 336 A.2d 713 (1975) (Mount Laurel I). We set forth in that case, for the first time, the doctrine requiring that municipalities' land use regulations provide a realistic opportunity for low and moderate income housing. The doctrine has become famous. The *Mount Laurel* case itself threatens to become infamous. After all this time, ten years after the trial court's initial order invalidating its zoning ordinance, Mount Laurel remains afflicted with a blatantly exclusionary ordinance. Papered over with studies, rationalized by hired experts, the ordinance at its core is true to nothing but Mount Laurel's determination to exclude the poor. Mount Laurel is not alone; we believe that there is widespread non-compliance with the constitutional mandate of our original opinion in this case.

To the best of our ability, we shall not allow it to continue. This Court is more firmly committed to the original *Mount Laurel* doctrine than ever, and we are determined, within appropriate judicial bounds, to make it work. The obligation is to provide a realistic opportunity for housing, not litigation. We have learned from experience, however, that unless a strong judicial hand is used, *Mount Laurel* will not result in housing, but in paper, process, witnesses, trials and appeals. We intend by this decision to strengthen it, clarify it, and make it easier for public officials, including judges, to apply it.

This case is accompanied by five others, heard together and decided in this opinion.[1] All involve questions arising from the *Mount Laurel* doctrine. They demonstrate the need to put some steel into that doctrine. The deficiencies in its application range from uncertainty and inconsistency at the trial level to inflexible review criteria at the appellate level. The waste of judicial energy involved at every level is substantial and is matched only by the often needless expenditure of talent on the part of lawyers and experts. The length and complexity of trials is often outrageous, and the expense of litigation is so high that a real question develops whether the municipality can afford to defend or the plaintiffs can afford to sue.

There is another side to the story. We believe, both through the representations of counsel and from our own research and experience, that the doctrine has done some good, indeed, perhaps substantial good. We have tried to make the doctrine clearer for we believe that most municipal officials will in good faith strive to fulfill their constitutional

1. The six cases are Southern Burlington County N.A.A.C.P. v. Township of Mount Laurel, decided below at 161 N.J. Super. 317, 391 A.2d 935 (Law Div.1978) (Mount Laurel II), and directly certified by this Court; three other trial court judgments directly certified: Urban League of Essex Co. v. Township of Mahwah, Docket No. L–17112–71 (Law Div. Mar. 8, 1979) (unreported); Glenview Development Co. v. Franklin Township, 164 N.J.Super. 563, 397 A.2d 384 (Law Div.1978); and Caputo v. Township of Chester, Docket No. L–42857–74 (Law Div. Oct. 4, 1978) (unreported); and two trial court judgments that were reversed by the Appellate Division: Urban League of Greater New Brunswick v. Borough of Carteret, 142 N.J.Super. 11, 359 A.2d 526 (Ch.Div.1976), rev'd, 170 N.J.Super. 461, 406 A.2d 1322 (App.Div.1979); and Round Valley, Inc. v. Township of Clinton, Docket No. L–29710–74 (Feb. 24, 1978) (unreported), rev'd, 173 N.J.Super. 45, 413 A.2d 356 (App.Div.1980).

Because these cases raised many similar issues concerning the *Mount Laurel* doctrine, they were argued together and have been disposed of in this single opinion.

We would prefer that our opinion took less time and less space. The subject is complex, highly controversial, and obviously of great importance. We have not one, but six cases before us that raise practically all of the major questions involved in the *Mount Laurel* doctrine; furthermore we have dealt with other questions that, strictly speaking, might not be necessary for resolving these cases, since we thought it important to settle them as well. Unfortunately, as the history of the *Mount Laurel* doctrine proves, the clear resolution of issues of this kind requires extensive time and extensive discussion.

In the event changes have occurred since trial of these cases (including amendments to the relevant municipal ordinances) that render any part of our remand inappropriate, applications for revision may be made to the trial court, but only in conformance with today's rulings. Where such applications are based on ordinance amendments, the trial court should make certain that relitigation of the case based on those amendments does not result in unwarranted delay. While we recognize the legitimacy of the municipal interest in having these amendments considered on remand, the circumstances may indicate, on balance, that vindication of the constitutional obligation requires that compliance with *Mount Laurel* be determined on the basis of the prior ordinances, and that ordinance revisions be made pursuant to a remedial order of the trial court in accordance with this opinion. See Kruvant v. Mayor & Council Twp. of Cedar Grove, 82 N.J. 435, 414 A.2d 9 (1980), discussed infra at 466–467.

duty. There are a number of municipalities around the State that have responded to our decisions by amending their zoning ordinances to provide realistic opportunities for the construction of low and moderate income housing.[2] Further, many other municipalities have at least recognized their obligation to provide such opportunities in their ordinances and master plans. Finally, state and county government agencies have responded by preparing regional housing plans that help both the courts and municipalities themselves carry out the *Mount Laurel* mandate. Still, we are far from where we had hoped to be and nowhere near where we should be with regard to the administration of the doctrine in our courts.

These six cases not only afford the opportunity for, but demonstrate the necessity of reexamining the *Mount Laurel* doctrine. We do so here. The doctrine is right but its administration has been ineffective.

A brief statement of the cases may be helpful at this point. *Mount Laurel II* results from the remand by this Court of the original *Mount Laurel* case. The municipality rezoned, purportedly pursuant to our instructions, a plenary trial was held, and the trial court found that the rezoning constituted a bona fide attempt by Mount Laurel to provide a realistic opportunity for the construction of its fair share of the regional lower income housing need. Reading our cases at that time (1978) as requiring no more, the trial court dismissed the complaint of the N.A. A.C.P. and other plaintiffs but granted relief in the form of a builder's remedy, to a developer-intervenor who had attacked the total prohibition against mobile homes. Plaintiffs' appeal of the trial court's ruling sustaining the ordinance in all other respects was directly certified by this Court, as ultimately was defendant's appeal from the grant of a builder's remedy allowing construction of mobile homes. We reverse and remand to determine Mount Laurel's fair share of the regional need and for further proceedings to revise its ordinance; we affirm the grant of the builder's remedy.

*   *   *

[The Court's statement of the five companion cases is omitted.]

This opinion is divided into three sections. Section I contains a brief history of the *Mount Laurel* doctrine with a discussion of the major implementation problems addressed in this opinion; a statement of the constitutional basis for the doctrine and the appropriate scope of the judicial power to enforce it; and a summary of the more significant rulings in today's opinion. In Section II, we resolve the substantive issues raised by the six cases before us and set forth the obligations imposed upon municipalities and trial courts by the *Mount Laurel* doctrine. Finally, in Section III we apply these rulings to dispose of the six cases themselves.

---

2. For a listing of these municipalities and a discussion of their inclusionary zoning ordinances, see Department of Commu-nity Affairs, Housing Handbook for New Jersey Municipalities 12–16 (1976) (Housing Handbook).

I.

Background

A. *History of the Mount Laurel Doctrine*

In *Mount Laurel I*, this Court held that a zoning ordinance that contravened the general welfare was unconstitutional. We pointed out that a developing municipality violated that constitutional mandate by excluding housing for lower income people; that it would satisfy that constitutional obligation by affirmatively affording a realistic opportunity for the construction of its fair share of the present and prospective regional need for low and moderate income housing. 67 N.J. at 174, 336 A.2d 713.[3] This is the core of the *Mount Laurel* doctrine. Although the Court set forth important guidelines for implementing the doctrine, their application to particular cases was complex, and the resolution of many questions left uncertain. Was it a "developing" municipality? What was the "region," and how was it to be determined? How was the "fair share" to be calculated within that region? Precisely what must that municipality to do to "affirmatively afford" an opportunity for the construction of lower income housing? Other questions were similarly troublesome. When should a court order the granting of a building permit (i.e., a builder's remedy) to a plaintiff-developer who has successfully challenged a zoning ordinance on *Mount Laurel* grounds? How should courts deal with the complicated procedural aspects of *Mount Laurel* litigation, such as the appointment of experts and masters, the joinder of defendant municipalities, and the problem of interlocutory appeals? These have been the principal questions that New Jersey courts have faced in attempting to implement the *Mount Laurel* mandate, and the principal questions dealt with in this opinion. We begin by examining how some of these questions have been dealt with up to now.

Two years after *Mount Laurel I*, in Oakwood at Madison, Inc. v. Township of Madison, 72 N.J. 481, 371 A.2d 1192 (1977), this Court once again faced the exclusionary zoning issue. We ruled that "fair share" allocations need not be "precise" or based on "specific formulae" to win judicial approval. Id. at 498–99, 371 A.2d 1192. Instead, the Court explained, a court should look to the "substance" of a challenged zoning ordinance and the *"bona fide* efforts" of a municipality to remove exclu-

---

3. Several other state courts have held that municipalities have an obligation to consider regional needs in their zoning decisions. See, e.g., Surrick v. Zoning Bd. of Providence Twp., 476 Pa. 182, 382 A.2d 105, 108–10 (Pa.1977); Associated Home Builders v. Livermore, 18 Cal.3d 582, 599–601, 557 P.2d 473, 483, 135 Cal.Rptr. 41, 51 (Cal.1976); Berenson v. Town of New Castle, 38 N.Y.2d 102, 378 N.Y.S.2d 672, 341 N.E.2d 236, 242 (N.Y.1975), aff'd as modified, 67 A.D.2d 506, 415 N.Y.S.2d 669 (App.Div.1979), enforced sub nom. Blitz and Locker v. Town of New Castle, * * * [34 Land Use Law & Zoning Di-

gest, June 1982, p. 17 (N.Y.Sup.Ct., Westchester Cty., Case No. 13063/80]; see also Manatee County v. Estech Gen. Chem. Corp., 402 So.2d 1251 (Fla.Dist.Ct.App. 1981). None of these decisions, however, requires municipalities to provide their fair share of low and moderate income housing needs. For a general discussion of the case law in this area, see Blumstein, "A Prolegomenon to Growth Management and Exclusionary Zoning Issues," 43 Law & Contemp. Prob. 5 (Spring 1979); Note, Developments in the Law-Zoning, 91 Harv.L. Rev. 1427, 1635–59 (1978).

sionary barriers in order to determine whether that municipality had met its *Mount Laurel* burden.

With regard to the definition of the "region" from which fair share allocations were to be made, the majority cited with approval the trial court's formulation of a region as the " 'area from which, in view of available employment and transportation, the population of the township would be drawn, absent invalidly exclusionary zoning.' " Id. at 537, 371 A.2d 1192; quoting Oakwood at Madison, Inc. v. Township of Madison, 128 N.J.Super. 438, 441, 320 A.2d 223 (Law.Div.1974). We distinguished this very general standard for determining region from the situation with which we would be confronted if a state planning body promulgated a plan that divided the whole state into regions.

Madison also addressed the nature of a municipality's "affirmative" duty to encourage the construction of lower income housing. The Court reaffirmed that affected municipalities must provide realistic opportunities for their fair share of lower income housing, and required the municipality to provide density bonuses for the construction of multi-bedroom units, while reserving judgment, however, on other affirmative measures. 72 N.J. at 517–18, 371 A.2d 1192 (a density bonus allows the developer to build more units per acre if certain kinds of units are included in the project).

An important aspect of the Court's decision was the award of a builder's remedy to the plaintiff-developer. The Court emphasized that the plaintiff, for "six years" and through "two trials and on this extended appeal," had "borne the stress and expense of this public interest litigation." Id. at 549–50, 371 A.2d 1192. The Court admonished, however, that this kind of remedy should "ordinarily be rare." Id. at 551–52 n. 50, 371 A.2d 1192.

Finally, the Court introduced the important concept of "least cost" housing, i.e., housing built at the least cost possible, even though not inexpensive enough for lower income occupancy. Recognizing that even with subsidies and affirmative devices some municipalities simply might not be able to provide a realistic opportunity for the construction of lower income housing, the Court held that under those and *only* those circumstances such municipalities could meet their obligation with "least cost" housing. Id. at 512–13, 371 A.2d 1192.

Later in the same year that *Madison* was decided, the Court determined which municipalities were subject to the *Mount Laurel* fair share obligation. Pascack Ass'n, Ltd. v. Washington Twp., 74 N.J. 470, 379 A.2d 6 (1977); Fobe Associates v. Demarest, 74 N.J. 519, 379 A.2d 31 (1977). In *Pascack*, the Court held that "fully developed, single-family residential" communities such as Washington Township did not have any *Mount Laurel* obligation. This holding was reaffirmed in *Fobe* where the Court upheld the decision of the Demarest Board of Adjustment denying a variance sought for multi-family housing given the fact that a "developed" municipality like Demarest did not have a *Mount Laurel* obligation.[4]

4. Home Builders League v. Township of Berlin, 81 N.J. 127, 405 A.2d 381 (1979), rounds out this Court's involvement with the *Mount Laurel* doctrine since 1975. In

B. *Constitutional Basis for Mount Laurel and the Judicial Role*

The constitutional basis for the *Mount Laurel* doctrine remains the same. The constitutional power to zone, delegated to the municipalities subject to legislation, is but one portion of the police power and, as such, must be exercised for the general welfare. When the exercise of that power by a municipality affects something as fundamental as housing, the general welfare includes more than the welfare of that municipality and its citizens: it also includes the general welfare—in this case the housing needs—of those residing outside of the municipality but within the region that contributes to the housing demand within the municipality. Municipal land use regulations that conflict with the general welfare thus defined abuse the police power and are unconstitutional. In particular, those regulations that do not provide the requisite opportunity for a fair share of the region's need for low and moderate income housing conflict with the general welfare and violate the state constitutional requirements of substantive due process and equal protection. Mount Laurel I, 67 N.J. at 174 and 181, 336 A.2d 713.

That is the constitutional rationale for the *Mount Laurel* doctrine. The doctrine is a corollary of the constitutional obligation to zone only in furtherance of the general welfare. The doctrine provides a method of satisfying that obligation when the zoning in question affects housing.

It would be useful to remind ourselves that the doctrine does not arise from some theoretical analysis of our Constitution, but rather from underlying concepts of fundamental fairness in the exercise of governmental power. The basis for the constitutional obligation is simple: the State controls the use of land, *all* of the land. In exercising that control it cannot favor rich over poor. It cannot legislatively set

Berlin, the Court invalidated minimum floor area requirements (or "any other factor, such as frontage or lot size") for residential dwellings that were unrelated to the number of occupants living in a dwelling. Id. at 130, 405 A.2d 381. The Court upheld the trial court's determination that such requirements were *per se* exclusionary under *Mount Laurel.*

Six of the most important lower court decisions in this area are now before us. Other important lower court rulings reported in this area include: In re Egg Harbor Associates, 185 N.J.Super. 507, 449 A.2d 1324 (App.Div.), certif. granted, 91 N.J. 552, 453 A.2d 868 (1982) (sustaining, partly on *Mount Laurel* grounds, Department of Environmental Protection regulation imposing fair share housing obligation on developer in coastal area). Rowe v. Township of Pittsgrove, 172 N.J.Super. 209, 411 A.2d 720 (App.Div.1980) (holding that *Mount Laurel* did not require a municipality to relocate within the same municipality persons displaced through building code enforcement); Swiss Village Assocs. v. Township of Wayne, 162 N.J.

Super. 138, 392 A.2d 596 (App.Div.1978) (upholding a municipality's refusal to provide for high-rise developments in its zoning ordinance); Castroll v. Township of Franklin, 161 N.J.Super. 190, 391 A.2d 544 (App.Div.1978) (upholding the denial of a variance for a multi-family dwelling project where the developer claimed that multi-family housing, even for "median income" households, inherently serves the public interest); Nigito v. Borough of Closter, 142 N.J.Super. 1, 359 A.2d 521 (App.Div.1976) (upholding a municipality's denial of a use variance for a garden apartment complex, in part on the ground that the municipality was "developed" and therefore outside the ambit of *Mount Laurel*); Segal v. Borough of Wenonah, 134 N.J.Super. 421, 341 A.2d 667 (App.Div. 1975) (finding the defendant municipality to have no *Mount Laurel* obligation); Montgomery Assocs. v. Township of Montgomery, 149 N.J.Super. 536, 374 A.2d 86 (Law Div.1977) (holding that the *Mount Laurel* doctrine does not bar a municipality that has met its fair municipality for lower income housing).

aside dilapidated housing in urban ghettos for the poor and decent housing elsewhere for everyone else. The government that controls this land represents everyone. While the State may not have the ability to eliminate poverty, it cannot use that condition as the basis for imposing further disadvantages. And the same applies to the municipality, to which this control over land has been constitutionally delegated.

The clarity of the constitutional obligation is seen most simply by imagining what this state could be like were this claim never to be recognized and enforced: poor people forever zoned out of substantial areas of the state, not because housing could not be built for them but because they are not wanted; poor people forced to live in urban slums forever not because suburbia, developing rural areas, fully developed residential sections, seashore resorts, and other attractive locations could not accommodate them, but simply because they are not wanted. It is a vision not only at variance with the requirement that the zoning power be used for the general welfare but with all concepts of fundamental fairness and decency that underpin many constitutional obligations.[5]

5. Unfortunately, this unpleasant "vision" is to a large extent already with us, as can be seen by comparing the poverty and decay of Newark and Camden with the prosperity of many of their suburban neighbors. For a discussion of these urban-suburban disparities in New Jersey, see "Recession in Jersey: 'Dire' or 'Mild,'" The New York Times, June 28, 1982, at B1, col. 3. As many commentators ranging from law review writers to national commissions have maintained a major cause of this urban-suburban inequality has been suburban exclusionary zoning (by which we mean zoning whose purpose or effect is to keep poor people out of a community). See, e.g., Note, "Developments in the Law—Zoning," 91 Harv.L.Rev. 1427, 1624–35 (1978); A. Downs, Opening up the Suburbs (1973); Rubinowitz, Exclusionary Zoning: A Wrong in Search of a Remedy, 6 U.Mich.J.L. Ref. 625 (1973); Report of the National Advisory Commission on Civil Disorders 1 (U.S.Gov't Printing Office, 1968) (citing suburban exclusion as one of the principal causes making America "two societies, one black, one white—separate and unequal"). For a discussion of the impact of exclusionary zoning in New Jersey in particular, see M. Danielson, The Politics of Exclusion 40–43, 190 (1976). See also N.J. Department of Community Affairs, State Development Guide, Plan 84–85 (1980) (noting the "ultimately self-destructive division between affluent suburban areas and depressed inner cities").

As these commentators document, since World War II there has been a great movement of commerce, industry, and people out of the inner cities and into the suburbs. At the same time, however, exclusionary zoning made these suburbs largely inaccessible to lower income households. Beside depriving the urban poor of an opportunity to share in the suburban development, this exclusion also increased the relative concentration of poor in the cities and thereby hastened the flight of business and the middle class to the suburbs. A vicious cycle set in as increased business and middle class flight led to more urban decay, and more urban decay led to more flight, etc.

The provision of lower income housing in the suburbs may help to relieve cities of what has become an overwhelming fiscal and social burden. It may also make jobs more accessible for the unemployed poor. Deconcentration of the urban poor will presumably make cities more attractive for businesses and upper income residents to return to. For an in-depth discussion of the relationship between ending exclusionary zoning and the revitalization of our inner cities, see Downs, "Why Improving the Inner City Requires Opening up the Suburbs," in A. Downs, Opening up the Suburbs 115–30 (1973). See also the Community Development Act of 1974, in which Congress found that a "significant" cause of our nation's urban crisis is "the concentration of persons of lower income in central cities," 42 U.S.C. 5301(a)(1) (1977), and called for the "reduction of the isolation of income groups within communities" and the "spatial deconcentration of housing opportunities for persons of lower income," 42 U.S.C. 5301(c)(6) (1977); and the 1968 Report for Action of the Governor's Select Commission on Civil Disorder at 64–65.

Subject to the clear obligation to preserve open space and prime agricultural land, a builder in New Jersey who finds it economically feasible to provide decent housing for lower income groups will no longer find it governmentally impossible. Builders may not be able to build just where they want—our parks, farms, and conservation areas are not a land bank for housing speculators. But if sound planning of an area allows the rich and middle class to live there, it must also realistically and practically allow the poor. And if the area will accommodate factories, it must also find space for workers. The specific location of such housing will of course continue to depend on sound municipal land use planning.

While *Mount Laurel I* discussed the need for "an appropriate variety and choice of housing," 67 N.J. 179, 336 A.2d 713, the specific constitutional obligation addressed there, as well as in our opinion here, is that relating to low and moderate income housing. Id. All that we say here concerns that category alone; the doctrine as we interpret it has no present applicability to other kinds of housing. See Pascack, 74 N.J. at 480, 379 A.2d 6. It is obvious that eight years after *Mount Laurel I* the need for satisfaction of this doctrine is greater than ever. Upper and middle income groups may search with increasing difficulty for housing within their means; for low and moderate income people, there is nothing to search for.[6]

No one has challenged the *Mount Laurel* doctrine on these appeals. Nevertheless, a brief reminder of the judicial role in this sensitive area is appropriate, since powerful reasons suggest, and we agree, that the matter is better left to the Legislature. We act first and foremost because the Constitution of our State requires protection of the interests involved and because the Legislature has not protected them. We recognize the social and economic controversy (and its political conse-

---

Cities, while most directly affected, are not the sole victims of exclusionary zoning. The damage done by urban blight and decay is in no way confined to those who must remain in our cities. It affects all of us. Violent crime and drug abuse spawned in urban slums do not remain within city limits, they spread out to the suburbs and infect those living there. Efforts to combat these diseases require expenditures of public dollars that drain all taxpayers, urban and suburban alike. The continuing disintegration of our cities encourages business and industry to leave New Jersey altogether, resulting in a drain of jobs and dollars from our economy. In some, the decline of our cities and the increasing economic segregation of our population are not just isolated problems for those left behind in the cities, but a disease threatening us all. Zoning ordinances that either encourage this process or ratify its results are not promoting our general welfare, they are destroying it.

6. See, e.g., S. Seidel, Housing Costs and Government Regulations 9–14 (1978)

(Housing Costs) (documenting that over the last decade housing costs have far outpaced average income increases, particularly for lower income households); "Finding the House You Can Afford," The New York Times, Apr. 4, 1982, § 8, at 1, col. 2 ("affordable houses" in this region are "usually available only to families with incomes well in excess of $20,000 a year"); "Housing Is Called Big Issue," The New York Times, Apr. 12, 1981, Ell, at 38, col. 1 (reporting a statement by a New Jersey Department of Community Affairs spokesman that the average new home price in New Jersey is now $75,000, a price that only one in twenty families can afford); "Home of Future: Size Will Shrink But Not the Price," The New York Times, Jan. 25, 1981, § 1, at 20, col. 1. The importance of affordable, decent housing for individuals and families is, of course, undeniable. See, e.g., C. Hartman, Housing and Social Policy 1–5 (1975).

quences) that has resulted in relatively little legislative action in this field. We understand the enormous difficulty of achieving a political consensus that might lead to significant legislation enforcing the constitutional mandate better than we can, legislation that might completely remove this Court from those controversies. But enforcement of constitutional rights cannot await a supporting political consensus. So while we have always preferred legislative to judicial action in this field, we shall continue—until the Legislature acts—to do our best to uphold the constitutional obligation that underlies the *Mount Laurel* doctrine. That is our duty. We may not build houses, but we do enforce the Constitution.[7]

We note that there has been some legislative initiative in this field. We look forward to more. The new Municipal Land Use Law explicitly recognizes the obligations of municipalities to zone with regional consequences in mind, N.J.S.A. 40:55D–28(d); it also recognizes the work of the Division of State and Regional Planning in the Department of Community Affairs (DCA), in creating the State Development Guide Plan (1980) (SDGP), which plays an important part in our decisions today. Our deference to these legislative and executive initiatives can be regarded as a clear signal of our readiness to defer further to more substantial actions.

The judicial role, however, which could decrease as a result of legislative and executive action, necessarily will expand to the extent that we remain virtually alone in this field. In the absence of adequate legislative and executive help, we must give meaning to the constitutional doctrine in the cases before us through our own devices, even if they are relatively less suitable. That is the basic explanation of our decisions today.

C. *Summary of Rulings*

Our rulings today have several purposes. First, we intend to encourage voluntary compliance with the constitutional obligation by defining it more clearly. We believe that the use of the State Development Guide Plan and the confinement of all *Mount Laurel* litigation to

---

7. In New Jersey, it has traditionally been the judiciary, and not the Legislature, that has remedied substantive abuses of the zoning power by municipalities. A review of zoning litigation and legislation since the enactment of the zoning enabling statute in the 1920's shows that the Legislature has confined itself largely to regulating the procedural aspects of zoning. The judiciary has at the same time invalidated or modified zoning ordinances that violated constitutional rights or failed to serve the general welfare. See, e.g., Lusardi v. Curtis Point Property Ass'n, 86 N.J. 217, 430 A.2d 881 (1981) (invalidating a municipal ordinance to the extent it conflicted with the State's policy for recreational use of beachfront property); State v. Baker, 81 N.J. 99, 405 A.2d 368 (1979); (overturning zoning prohibiting more than four unrelated individuals from sharing a single housing unit); Katobimar Realty Co. v. Webster, 20 N.J. 114, 118 A.2d 824 (1955) (holding that a municipality could not bar all retail commercial uses in an industrial zone); DeMott Homes v. Margate City, 136 N.J.L. 330, 56 A.2d 423 (Sup.Ct. 1947), aff'd o.b., 136 N.J.L. 639, 57 A.2d 388 (E. & A.1948) (holding that a municipality could not bar two family homes in a seashore area). Although the complexity and political sensitivity of the issue now before us make it especially appropriate for legislative resolution, we have no choice, absent that resolution, but to exercise our traditional constitutional duty to end an abuse of the zoning power.

[From this point in the opinion many of the court's footnotes are omitted; those retained have been renumbered. Eds.]

a small group of judges, selected by the Chief Justice with the approval of the Court, will tend to serve that purpose. Second, we hope to simplify litigation in this area. While we are not overly optimistic, we think that the remedial use of the SDGP may achieve that purpose, given the significance accorded it in this opinion. Third, the decisions are intended to increase substantially the effectiveness of the judicial remedy. In most cases, upon determination that the municipality has not fulfilled its constitutional obligation, the trial court will retain jurisdiction, order an immediate revision of the ordinance (including, if necessary, supervision of the revision through a court appointed master), and require the use of effective affirmative planning and zoning devices. The long delays of interminable appellate review will be discouraged, if not completely ended, and the opportunity for low and moderate income housing found in the new ordinance will be as realistic as judicial remedies can make it. We hope to achieve all of these purposes while preserving the fundamental legitimate control of municipalities over their own zoning and, indeed, their destiny.

The following is a summary of the more significant rulings of these cases:

(1) *Every* municipality's land use regulations should provide a realistic opportunity for decent housing for at least some part of its resident poor who now occupy dilapidated housing. The zoning power is no more abused by keeping out the region's poor than by forcing out the resident poor. In other words, each municipality must provide a realistic opportunity for decent housing for its indigenous poor except where they represent a disproportionately large segment of the population as compared with the rest of the region. This is the case in many of our urban areas.

(2) The existence of a municipal obligation to provide a realistic opportunity for a fair share of the region's present and prospective low and moderate income housing need will no longer be determined by whether or not a municipality is "developing." The obligation extends, instead, to every municipality, any portion of which is designated by the State, through the SDGP as a "growth area." This obligation, imposed as a remedial measure, does not extend to those areas where the SDGP discourages growth—namely, open spaces, rural areas, prime farmland, conservation areas, limited growth areas, parts of the Pinelands and certain Coastal Zone areas. The SDGP represents the conscious determination of the State, through the executive and legislative branches, on how best to plan its future. It appropriately serves as a judicial remedial tool. The obligation to encourage lower income housing, therefore, will hereafter depend on rational long-range land use planning (incorporated into the SDGP) rather than upon the sheer economic forces that have dictated whether a municipality is "developing." Moreover, the fact that a municipality is fully developed does not eliminate this obligation although, obviously, it may affect the extent of the obligation and the timing of its satisfaction. The remedial obligation of municipalities that consist of both "growth areas" and other areas may be reduced based on many factors, as compared to a municipality completely within a "growth area."

There shall be a heavy burden on any party seeking to vary the foregoing remedial consequences of the SDGP designations.

(3) *Mount Laurel* litigation will ordinarily include proof of the municipality's fair share of low and moderate income housing in terms of the number of units needed immediately, as well as the number needed for a reasonable period of time in the future. "Numberless" resolution of the issue based upon a conclusion that the ordinance provides a realistic opportunity for *some* low and moderate income housing will be insufficient. Plaintiffs, however, will still be able to prove a *prima facie* case, without proving the precise fair share of the municipality, by proving that the zoning ordinance is substantially affected by restrictive devices, that proof creating a presumption that the ordinance is invalid.

The municipal obligation to provide a realistic opportunity for low and moderate income housing is not satisfied by a good faith attempt. The housing opportunity provided must, in fact, be the substantial equivalent of the fair share.

(4) Any future *Mount Laurel* litigation shall be assigned only to those judges selected by the Chief Justice with the approval of the Supreme Court. The initial group shall consist of three judges, the number to be increased or decreased hereafter by the Chief Justice with the Court's approval. The Chief Justice shall define the area of the State for which each of the three judges is responsible: any *Mount Laurel* case challenging the land use ordinance of a municipality included in that area shall be assigned to that judge.

Since the same judge will hear and decide all *Mount Laurel* cases within a particular area and only three judges will do so in the entire state, we believe that over a period of time a consistent pattern of regions will emerge. Consistency is more likely as well in determinations of regional housing needs and allocations of fair share to municipalities within the region. Along with this consistency will come the predictability needed to give full effect to the *Mount Laurel* doctrine. While determinations of region and regional housing need will not be conclusive as to any municipality not a party to the litigation, they shall be given presumptive validity in subsequent litigation involving any municipality included in a previously determined region.

The Chief Justice will analyze all pending *Mount Laurel* litigation to determine which, if any, should be transferred to one of the three *Mount Laurel* judges. As for the cases pending before us, given the knowledge acquired by the judges of the particular facts of the case, each will be remanded to the judge who heard the matter below with the exception of Round Valley, Inc. v. Clinton and Urban League of Greater New Brunswick v. Carteret, since neither of the judges who determined those matters remains on the trial bench.

(5) The municipal obligation to provide a realistic opportunity for the construction of its fair share of low and moderate income housing [8] may

---

8. "Moderate income families" are those whose incomes are no greater than 80 percent and no less than 50 percent of the median income of the area, with adjust- | ments for smaller and larger families. "Low income families" are those whose incomes do not exceed 50 percent of the median income of the area, with adjustments

require more than the elimination of unnecessary cost-producing requirements and restrictions. Affirmative governmental devices should be used to make that opportunity realistic, including lower-income density bonuses and mandatory set-asides. Furthermore, the municipality should cooperate with the developer's attempts to obtain federal subsidies. For instance, where federal subsidies depend on the municipality providing certain municipal tax treatment allowed by state statutes for lower income housing, the municipality should make a good faith effort to provide it. Mobile homes may not be prohibited, unless there is solid proof that sound planning in a particular municipality requires such prohibition.

(6) The lower income regional housing need is comprised of both low and moderate income housing. A municipality's fair share should include both in such proportion as reflects consideration of all relevant

for smaller and larger families. See 42 U.S.C. § 1437a(b)(2) (1982 Supp.), in which these definitions are used to define income standards for the Section 8 housing subsidy program. Our phraseology differs from that in the Section 8 program, which defines "lower income families" as analogous to our moderate income families, and "very low income families" as analogous to our "low income." 42 U.S.C. § 1437a(b) (2) (1982 Supp.).

Since the median family income rises steadily with inflation, the precise monetary definition of low and moderate income will be constantly changing. At any particular time, an interested municipality, developer, or judge can find out what low and moderate income levels are in the area ("area" being defined as a Standard Metropolitan Statistical Area (SMSA)) by asking the regional office of the Department of Housing and Urban Development in either Camden or Newark. Although we suggest use of this statutory definition in order to simplify matters for municipalities and for the courts, we are not foreclosing the argument that in particular cases another definition may be more reasonable.

When we refer in this opinion to housing being "affordable" by lower income families ("lower" meaning "low and moderate") we mean that the family pays no more than 25 percent of its income for such housing, the 25 percent figure being widely accepted in the relevant literature. See, e.g., Housing Costs, supra at 417 n. 6, at 12; C. Hartman, supra at 417 n. 6, at 4; A. Downs, Opening up the Suburbs 47 (1973). (Note, however, that the federal government in 1981 adjusted its calculations of the maximum amount of rent supplements payable to low-income tenants, estimating that no more than 30 percent of a tenant's income, rather than 25 percent, should be paid for housing. See 12 U.S.C. § 1701s(d)

(1982).) As noted supra at 417 n. 6, the median price of a home now is around $75,000, and the annual income needed to support monthly payments is in the $24,000–$37,000 range depending on interest rates. The New York Times, Oct. 17, 1982, Real Estate Section. The article assumes the home-buyer devotes 32 percent of gross income to housing expenses.

We note that in 1970, when low and moderate income for a family of four ranged up to $8,567 per year, the proportion of lower income families in New Jersey was 39.4 percent (a total of about 800,000 households). See Department of Community Affairs, Revised Statewide Housing Allocation Report 9 (1978) (HAR). The Department assumed that, at least until 1990, there would be a "continuation of current socio-economic trends," meaning that the proportion of lower income families would stay at 39.4 percent. Id. at 8. We see no reason to dispute this assumption. Based on this assumption, and on population forecasts through 1990, the HAR projected a 300,232 growth in the number of lower income households through 1990. Id. at 9. It is important to note here that this final number is based upon a DCA assumption that the average household size would be 2.71 persons per household in 1990. Id. If, as many planners now predict and as the 1980 census figures indicate, the average household size in 1990 is significantly smaller than 2.71, and if that average holds true for lower income families, the number of new lower income households in 1990 would be concomitantly larger. We also note that the number of lower income households projected for 1990, since it is based on overall population projections, presumably includes lower income households expected to be moving into New Jersey from other states.

factors, including the porportion of low and moderate income housing that make up the regional need.

(7) Providing a realistic opportunity for the construction of least-cost housing will satisfy a municipality's *Mount Laurel* obligation if, and only if, it cannot otherwise be satisfied. In other words, it is only after *all* alternatives have been explored, *all* affirmative devices considered, including, where appropriate, a reasonable period of time to determine whether low and moderate income housing is produced, only when everything has been considered and tried in order to produce a realistic opportunity for low and moderate income housing that least-cost housing will provide an adequate substitute. Least-cost housing means what it says, namely, housing that can be produced at the lowest possible price consistent with minimal standards of health and safety.

(8) Builder's remedies will be afforded to plaintiffs in *Mount Laurel* litigation where appropriate, on a case-by-case basis. Where the plaintiff has acted in good faith, attempted to obtain relief without litigation, and thereafter vindicates the constitutional obligation in *Mount Laurel*-type litigation, ordinarily a builder's remedy will be granted, provided that the proposed project includes an appropriate portion of low and moderate income housing, and provided further that it is located and designed in accordance with sound zoning and planning concepts, including its environmental impact.

(9) The judiciary should manage *Mount Laurel* litigation to dispose of a case in all of its aspects with one trial and one appeal, unless substantial considerations indicate some other course. This means that in most cases after a determination of invalidity, and prior to final judgment and possible appeal, the municipality will be required to rezone, preserving its contention that the trial court's adjudication was incorrect. If an appeal is taken, all facets of the litigation will be considered by the appellate court including both the correctness of the lower court's determination of invalidity, the scope of remedies imposed on the municipality, and the validity of the ordinance adopted after the judgment of invalidity. The grant or denial of a stay will depend upon the circumstances of each case. The trial court will appoint a master to assist in formulating and implementing a proper remedy whenever that course seems desirable.

(10) The *Mount Laurel* obligation to meet the prospective lower income housing need of the region is, by definition, one that is met year after year in the future, throughout the years of the particular projection used in calculating prospective need. In this sense the affirmative obligation to provide a realistic opportunity to construct a fair share of lower income housing is met by a "phase-in" over those years; it need not be provided immediately. Nevertheless there may be circumstances in which the obligation requires zoning that will provide an immediate opportunity—for instance, zoning to meet the region's present lower income housing need. In some cases, the provision of such a realistic opportunity might result in the immediate construction of lower income housing in such quantity as would radically transform the municipality overnight. Trial courts shall have the discretion, under those circum-

stances, to moderate the impact of such housing by allowing even the present need to be phased in over a period of years. Such power, however, should be exercised sparingly. The same power may be exercised in the satisfaction of prospective need, equally sparingly, and with special care to assure that such further postponement will not significantly dilute the *Mount Laurel* obligation.

We reassure all concerned that *Mount Laurel* is not designed to sweep away all land use restrictions or leave our open spaces and natural resources prey to speculators. Municipalities consisting largely of conservation, agricultural, or environmentally sensitive areas will not be required to grow because of *Mount Laurel*. No forests or small towns need be paved over and covered with high-rise apartments as a result of today's decision.

As for those municipalities that may have to make adjustments in their lifestyles to provide for their fair share of low and moderate income housing, they should remember that they are not being required to provide more than their *fair* share. No one community need be concerned that it will be radically transformed by a deluge of low and moderate income developments. Nor should any community conclude that its residents will move to other suburbs as a result of this decision, for those "other suburbs" may very well be required to do their part to provide the same housing. Finally, once a community has satisfied its fair share obligation, the *Mount Laurel* doctrine will not restrict other measures, including large-lot and open area zoning, that would maintain its beauty and communal character.

Many of these points will be discussed later in this opinion. We mention them now only to reassure all concerned that any changes brought about by this opinion need not be drastic or destructive. Our scenic and rural areas will remain essentially scenic and rural, and our suburban communities will retain their basic suburban character. But there will be *some* change, as there must be if the constitutional rights of our lower income citizens are ever to be protected. That change will be much less painful for us than the status quo has been for them.

*   *   *

[Most of the remainder of the court's long and detailed opinion has been omitted, but some of the highlights are set out below.]

*   *   * [W]e have decided not to make the SDGP the absolute determinant of the locus of the *Mount Laurel* obligation. Our reluctance to give it conclusive effect is based on the fact that while it has the legitimacy of legislative authorization, the Legislature has neither explicitly authorized its use for *Mount Laurel* purposes nor mandated that the actual use of land, as permitted in zoning ordinances, conform to the SDGP. Given these circumstances, we deem it prudent to allow parties to attempt to persuade the trial court, in a particular case, that the SDGP should not determine whether the *Mount Laurel* doctrine applies to the particular municipality involved in the case. While we believe important policy considerations are involved in our decision not to make the SDGP conclusive, we think it even more important to point out that

it will be the unusual case that concludes the locus of the *Mount Laurel* obligation is different from that found in the SDGP. Subject to those cases, we hold that henceforth, only those municipalities containing "growth areas" as shown on the concept map of the SDGP (or any official revision thereof) shall be subject to the *Mount Laurel* prospective need obligation.[9]

Any party in *Mount Laurel* litigation seeking a ruling that varies the locus of the *Mount Laurel* obligation from the SDGP growth areas will have to prove one of the following: (1) accepting the premises of the SDGP, the conclusion that the municipality includes any growth area, or as much growth area as is shown on the concept map, is arbitrary and capricious, or, alternatively, the conclusion that the municipality does *not* contain any growth area whatsoever is arbitrary and capricious; (2) since the preparation of the concept map (or any revision thereof) the municipality has undergone a significant transformation that renders the SDGP's characterization of it inappropriate, admitting that at the time of the preparation of the SDGP and the concept map (or any revision thereof) the classification of the municipality was correct; or (3) (and this exception shall apply only if the concept map is not revised before January 1, 1985) subsequent to the date of this decision the municipality, containing no "growth area," encourages or allows commercial, residential or industrial development or, if it contains some "growth area," encourages or allows development outside of that area.

The foregoing exceptions will allow a party to have the court impose a *Mount Laurel* obligation on a municipality that has no growth area as shown on the concept map, or to impose a greater *Mount Laurel* obligation by, in effect, proving that the growth area should be enlarged, or, conversely, to relieve a municipality from any *Mount Laurel* obligation even though the concept map shows it as including a "growth area," or to diminish the obligation by proving that the "growth area" shown on the concept map should be cut down.

*   *   *

The restriction of *Mount Laurel* litigation to three judges should simplify and perhaps, in time, substantially eliminate the issues of "region" and "regional need" from litigation. Of the three major issues in this area, their determination is most susceptible to judicial treatment.
*   *   *

---

9. The developing/non-developing distinction is therefore no longer relevant and the conclusion that fully developed municipalities have no *Mount Laurel* obligation is no longer valid. See Pascack Ass'n Ltd. v. Washington Twp., 74 N.J. 470, 379 A.2d 6 (1977), and Fobe v. Demarest, 74 N.J. 519, 379 A.2d 31 (1977). The application of the *Mount Laurel* doctrine to fully developed municipalities will undoubtedly pose difficult problems. We note only that sound land use planning and *Mount Laurel* should remain compatible both at the state and municipal level, and that, in particular, where fully developed municipalities are involved, great care may be required to assure that the benefit of *Mount Laurel* is not offset by damage to legitimate zoning and planning objectives. The *Mount Laurel* doctrine should ordinarily be able to be accommodated, for example, without placing lower income housing projects in the middle of long-settled middle or upper income sections of a town. A satisfactory resolution of the occasionally conflicting interests may at times require creativity and cooperation.

We anticipate that after several cases have been tried before each judge, a regional pattern for the area for which he or she is responsible will emerge. Ultimately a regional pattern for the entire state will be established, as will a fairly consistent determination of regional needs on both an area and statewide basis. Given that only three judges are involved, it is also not unreasonable to assume that the method for determining that municipality's fair share of the regional need will be consistent within the judge's area and tend to promote consistency throughout the state.

The determination of region and regional need by any of these judges shall be presumptively valid as to all municipalities included in the region unless the judge hearing the matter indicates otherwise for reasons stated in his or her decision. Given the importance of these determinations, municipalities not named as parties may attempt to intervene or the court may require their joinder if, all things considered, it is thought advisable that such a municipality be bound by the determination even though such joinder may complicate the litigation. The extent of such litigation, whether non-party municipalities should be allowed to participate, and whether they should be joined as parties, shall all be within the discretion of the court, who will be better able to balance the various considerations involved. While it is possible that many municipalities may seek to enter such litigation, we believe that as a practical matter most will be content to abide by litigation in which others are involved.

* * *

As for fair share, however, we offer some suggestions.[10] Formulas that accord substantial weight to employment opportunities in the municipality, especially new employment accompanied by substantial ratables, shall be favored; formulas that have the effect of tying prospective lower income housing needs to the present proportion of lower income residents to the total population of a municipality shall be disfavored; formulas that have the effect of unreasonably diminishing the share because of a municipality's successful exclusion of lower income housing in the past shall be disfavored.

In determining fair share, the court should decide the proportion between low and moderate income housing unless there are substantial reasons not to do so. The provisions and devices needed to produce moderate income housing may fall short of those needed for lower. Since there are two fairly distinct lower income housing needs, an effort must be made to meet both.

* * *

In order to meet their *Mount Laurel* obligations, municipalities, at the very least, must remove all municipally created barriers to the con-

10. As a practical matter, there are already statewide growth plans that may be of help; for instance, those developed by the Department of Environmental Protection that deal with water, sewers and air. Many of the master plans formulated by county planning boards discuss fair share. In addition, the Departments of Transportation and Energy have master plans with population projections. All of these sources can be used to generate hard numbers that could be used in allocating a fair share.

struction of their fair share of lower income housing. Thus, to the extent necessary to meet their prospective fair share and provide for their indigenous poor (and, in some cases, a portion of the region's poor), municipalities must remove zoning and subdivision restrictions and exactions that are not necessary to protect health and safety.[11]

It may be difficult for a municipality to determine how to balance the need to reduce the costs of its regulations against the need to adequately protect health and safety, just as it may be difficult for a court to determine when a municipality has reduced these costs enough. There are, however, relatively objective guides that can help both the municipality and the court. Particularly helpful, though in no way conclusive as to what the minimum standards should be in a particular community, are the Department of Housing and Urban Development's Minimum Property Standards and the suggestions as to minimum zoning and subdivision standards made by the Rutgers Center for Urban Policy Research in Housing Costs, supra at 417 n. 6. With these and other such guides, plus specific evidence submitted by the parties, we believe that a court can determine whether municipally-imposed housing costs have been sufficiently reduced.

* 　 * 　 *

Despite the emphasis in *Mount Laurel I* on the *affirmative* nature of the fair share obligation, 67 N.J. at 174, 336 A.2d 713, the obligation has been sometimes construed (after *Madison*) as requiring in effect no more than a theoretical, rather than realistic, opportunity. As noted later, the alleged realistic opportunity for lower income housing in *Mount Laurel II* is provided through three zones owned entirely by three individuals. There is absolutely no assurance that there is anything realistic in this "opportunity": the individuals may, for many different reasons, simply not desire to build lower income housing. They may not want to build any housing at all, they may want to use the land for industry, for business, or just leave it vacant. It was never intended in *Mount Laurel I* that this awesome constitutional obligation, designed to give the poor a fair chance for housing, be satisfied by meaningless amendments to zoning or other ordinances. "Affirmative," in the *Mount Laurel* rule, suggests that the *municipality* is going to do something, and "realistic opportunity" suggests that what it is going to do will make it *realistically* possible for lower income housing to be built. Satisfaction of the *Mount Laurel* doctrine cannot depend on the inclination of developers to help the poor. It has to depend on affirmative inducements to make the opportunity real.

---

11. For analyses of the extent to which municipal restrictions and exactions increase the cost of housing in New Jersey, see Mount Laurel I, 67 N.J. at 161–73, 184, 336 A.2d 713; Housing Costs, supra at 417 n. 6, at 188 (documenting that in 1972 the selling price of a new single family home could be reduced from $57,618 to $33,843 if the lot size and frontage requirements were reduced from 43,500 square feet and 200 feet to 12,000 square feet and 80 feet respectively); Final Report of the Assembly, reporting the results of a U.S. Department of Housing and Urban Development Study which showed that in a HUD project in Pittsburgh costs were reduced by 24 percent through the utilization of modern materials, the expedition of approval times, and the reduction of the cost of municipal improvements.

It is equally unrealistic, even where the land is owned by a developer eager to build, simply to rezone that land to permit the construction of lower income housing if the construction of other housing is permitted on the same land and the latter is more profitable than lower income housing. One of the new zones in Mount Laurel provides a good example. The developer there intends to build housing out of the reach of the lower income group. After creation of the new zone, he still is allowed to build such housing but now has the "opportunity" to build lower income housing to the extent of 10 percent of the units. There is absolutely no reason why he should take advantage of this opportunity if, as seems apparent, his present housing plans will result in a higher profit. There is simply no inducement, no reason, nothing affirmative, that makes this opportunity "realistic." For an opportunity to be "realistic" it must be one that is at least sensible for someone to use.

Therefore, unless removal of restrictive barriers will, without more, afford a realistic opportunity for the construction of the municipality's fair share of the region's lower income housing need, affirmative measures will be required.[12]

There are two basic types of affirmative measures that a municipality can use to make the opportunity for lower income housing realistic: (1) encouraging or requiring the use of available state or federal housing subsidies, and (2) providing incentives for or requiring private developers to set aside a portion of their developments for lower income housing. Which, if either, of these devices will be necessary in any particular municipality to assure compliance with the constitutional mandate will be initially up to the municipality itself. Where necessary, the trial court overseeing compliance may require their use.

* * *

12. In determining whether the removal of barriers, without more, will suffice, or whether affirmative devices are necessary, the trial court will undoubtedly consider the realities of the situation. It is often difficult for a court to assure itself that the municipally generated barriers to lower income housing have truly been removed. For example, provision of a relatively small area where low cost multi-family housing *could* be built—the most common technique used to zone for lower income housing—ordinarily does not result in such housing *actually* being built. This is true because when land available for multifamily housing is made artificially scarce by zoning, that land will almost surely be preempted by more profitable high-cost apartments and townhouses. See Housing Handbook, supra at 411 n. 2, at 5; Mallach, "Do Lawsuits Build Housing?: The Implications of Exclusionary Zoning Litigation," 6 Rut.-Cam.L.Rev. 653, 662 (1975). See also Madison, supra, 72 N.J. at 519, 371 A.2d 1192 (recognizing the need to "overzone" for lower cost housing in order to achieve "any likelihood" of its

actually being built). Also, communities that desire to keep out lower income housing have many means at their disposal in the complex local housing approval process to make it likely that the housing built in zones presumably "available" for lower income housing is not in fact low cost. Mallach, supra, at 662; Housing Costs, supra at 417 n. 6, at 134. In many cases, the only way for courts to ensure that municipalities with fair share obligations do not, directly or indirectly, hinder the construction of lower income housing is to require affirmative measures encouraging the construction of such housing.

Mount Laurel I made it clear that municipalities had to do more than simply refrain from adopting "regulations or policies which thwart or preclude" a realistic opportunity to build lower income housing, 67 N.J. at 180, 336 A.2d 713; additionally its obligation was "affirmatively to plan and provide, by its land use regulations, the reasonable opportunity * * *" for such housing. Id. at 179, 336 A.2d 713.

On occasion, what is needed to obtain a subsidy may be as simple as a "resolution of need" stating that "there is a need for moderate income housing" in the municipality. N.J.S.A. 55:14J–6(b). In addition to the "resolution of need," the most important federal program for providing lower income housing subsidies (the section 8 low and moderate income housing program; 42 U.S.C. § 1437f (1982 Supp.)) requires in New Jersey, as a practical matter, that the municipality grant tax abatements to developers. See N.J.S.A. 55:14J–8(f).

*   *   *

There are several inclusionary zoning techniques that municipalities must use if they cannot otherwise assure the construction of their fair share of lower income housing. Although we will discuss some of them here, we in no way intend our list to be exhaustive; municipalities and trial courts are encouraged to create other devices and methods for meeting fair share obligations.[13]

The most commonly used inclusionary zoning techniques are incentive zoning and mandatory set-asides. The former involves offering economic incentives to a developer through the relaxation of various restrictions of an ordinance (typically density limits) in exchange for the construction of certain amounts of low and moderate income units. The latter, a mandatory set-aside, is basically a requirement that developers include a minimum amount of lower income housing in their projects.

(i) *Incentive Zoning*

Incentive zoning is usually accomplished either through a sliding scale density bonus that increases the permitted density as the amount of lower income housing provided is increased, or through a set bonus for participation in a lower income housing program. See Fox & Davis, 3 Hastings Const.L.Q. 1015, 1060–62 (1977).

Incentive zoning leaves a developer free to build only upper income housing if it so chooses. Fox and Davis, in their survey of municipalities using inclusionary devices, found that while developers sometimes profited through density bonuses, they were usually reluctant to cooperate with incentive zoning programs; and that therefore those municipalities that relied exclusively on such programs were not very successful in actually providing lower income housing. Id. at 1067.[14]

---

13. For useful discussions of how inclusionary techniques have been utilized in New Jersey municipalities see the Housing Handbook, supra at 411 n. 2 and Department of Community Affairs, The Princeton Housing Proposal: A Strategy to Achieve Balanced Housing without Government Subsidy (1977) (Housing Proposal). See also Oakwood at Madison, Inc. v. Township of Madison, 72 N.J. 481, 611–16, 371 A.2d 1192 (1977) (Pashman, J., concurring and dissenting); Fox & Davis, "Density Bonus Zoning to Provide Low and Moderate Cost Housing," 3 Hastings Const.L.Q. 1015 (1977); Kleven, "Inclusionary Ordinances—Policy and Legal Issues in Requiring Private Developers to Build Low

Cost Housing," 21 U.C.L.A.L.Rev. 1432 (1974); H. Franklin, D. Falk, A. Levin, In Zoning: A Guide for Policy Makers on Inclusionary Land Use Programs (1974).

14. See Fox & Davis, supra at 445 N. 28, 3 Hastings Const.L.Q. at 1028 (reporting the results of a Stanford University Study which provides such evidence). Also, Real Estate Research Corporation (RERC), after conducting an economic feasibility study for the proposed Princeton mandatory set-aside program, concluded that the program could be devised in such a way as to assure an adequate profit for developers. Housing Proposal, supra at 445 n. 28 at 13–26 (1977). In particular,

Sole reliance on "incentive" techniques (or, indeed, reliance exclusively on any one affirmative device) may prove in a particular case to be insufficient to achieve compliance with the constitutional mandate.

(ii) *Mandatory Set-Asides*

A more effective inclusionary device that municipalities must use if they cannot otherwise meet their fair share obligations is the mandatory set-aside.[15] According to the Department of Community Affairs, as of 1976 there were six municipalities in New Jersey with mandatory set-aside programs, which varied from a requirement that 5 percent of developments in a certain zone be composed of low and moderate income units (Cherry Hill, Camden County) to a requirement that between 15 and 25 percent of all PUDs be reserved for low and moderate income housing (East Windsor, Mercer County). Housing Handbook, supra at 411 n. 2 at 12–16.[16] Apparently, judging from the Handbook itself and from responses to our inquiries at oral argument, lower income housing is in fact being built pursuant to these mandatory requirements.

The use of mandatory set-asides is not without its problems: dealing with the scarcity of federal subsidies, maintaining the rent or sales price of lower income units at lower income levels over time, and assuring developers an adequate return on their investments. Fox and Davis found that the scarcity of federal subsidies has greatly undermined the effectiveness of mandatory set-asides where they are triggered only when a developer is able to obtain such subsidies. Fox & Davis, supra, 3 Hastings Const.L.Q. at 1065–66. Where practical, a municipality should use mandatory set-asides even where subsidies are not available.

RERC recommended that developers not be required to provide more than 34 percent of their units for lower income people, with at most 14 percent for low income, id. at 17; and that the lower income requirment be met in stages, ideally three stages of 5 year periods, id. at 18. The RERC conclusions were based upon a Princeton Plan under which land zoned for low density development would be rezoned for higher densities (with a mandatory lower income set aside) only *after* a developer bought it. This would, according to the framers of the Plan, permit developers to realize significant increases in land value. Id. at 13–15.

omy, generally parallel increases in the median income of lower income families. They would not ordinarily result in rentals beyond the lower income range. As for confiscation, the builder who undertakes a project that includes a mandatory set-aside voluntarily assumes the financial burden if there is any of that condition. There may very well be no "subsidy" in the sense of either the landlord or other tenants bearing some burden for the benefit of the lower income units: those units may be priced low not because someone else is subsidizing the price, but because of realistic considerations of cost, amenities, and therefore underlying values.

15. Mandatory set-asides do not give rise to the legal issues treated in Property Owners Ass'n of N. Bergen v. Twp. of N. Bergen, 74 N.J. 327, 378 A.2d 25 (1977). We held in that case that rent control ordinances that exempted units occupied by senior citizens from future rent increases were confiscatory as to the landlord, unfair as to the tenants, and unconstitutional on both grounds. No one suggests here that units created by mandatory set-asides be exempt thereafter from rent increases under a rent control ordinance. Such increases, one aspect of an inflationary econ-

16. A similar requirement is now being enforced by the Department of Environmental Protection in reviewing development proposals in the State's protected coastal areas. In a recent Department opinion, a developer in Egg Harbor Township was ordered to provide 20 percent of its units for lower income families in order to receive Department approval for its development. The regulation was sustained in the Appellate Division. See In re Egg Harbor Associates, 185 N.J.Super. 507, 449 A.2d 1324 (App.Div.) certif. granted, 91 N.J. 552, 453 A.2d 868 (1982).

Mandatory set-asides can be rendered ineffective if a developer builds all its conventional units first and then reneges on the obligation to build the lower income units. To avoid this problem, municipalities and courts should require that a developer phase-in the lower income units as the development progresses. That is, if a developer is required to set aside 20 percent of a development for lower income units, 20 percent of *each* stage of the development should be lower income, to the extent this is practical.

In addition to the mechanisms we have just described, municipalities and trial courts must consider such other affirmative devices as zoning substantial areas for mobile homes and for other types of low cost housing and establishing maximum square footage zones, i.e., zones where the developers cannot build units with *more* than a certain footage or build anything other than lower income housing or housing that includes a specified portion of lower income housing. In some cases, a realistic opportunity to provide the municipality's fair share may require over-zoning, i.e., zoning to allow for *more* than the fair share if it is likely, as it usually is, that not all of the property made available for lower income housing will actually result in such housing.

Although several of the defendants concede that simply removing restrictions and exactions is unlikely to result in the construction of lower income housing, they maintain that requiring the municipality to use affirmative measures is beyond the scope of the courts' authority. We disagree. * * *

The specific contentions are that inclusionary measures amount to a taking without just compensation and an impermissible socio-economic use of the zoning power, one not substantially related to the use of land. Reliance is placed to some extent on Board of Supervisors v. DeGroff Enterprises, Inc., 214 Va. 235, 198 S.E.2d 600 (1973), to that effect. We disagree with that decision. We now resolve the matter that we left open in Madison, 72 N.J. at 518–19, 371 A.2d 1192. We hold that where the *Mount Laurel* obligation cannot be satisfied by removal of restrictive barriers, inclusionary devices such as density bonuses and mandatory set-asides keyed to the construction of lower income housing, are constitutional and within the zoning power of a municipality.

* * *

The contention that generally these devices are beyond the municipal power because they are "socio-economic" is particularly inappropriate. The very basis for the constitutional obligation underlying *Mount Laurel* is a belief, fundamental, that excluding a class of citizens from housing on an economic basis (one that substantially corresponds to a socio-economic basis) distinctly disserves the general welfare. That premise is essential to the conclusion that such zoning ordinances are an abuse of the zoning power and are therefore unconstitutional.

It is nonsense to single out inclusionary zoning (providing a realistic opportunity for the construction of lower income housing) and label it "socio-economic" if that is meant to imply that other aspects of zoning are not. Detached single family residential zones, high-rise multi-family zones of any kind, factory zones, "clean" research and development zones, recreational, open space, conservation, and agricultural zones, regional shopping mall zones, indeed practically any significant kind of zoning now used, has a substantial socio-economic impact and, in some cases, a socio-economic motivation. It would be ironic if inclusionary zoning to encourage the construction of lower income housing were ruled beyond the power of a municipality because it is "socio-economic" when its need has arisen from the socio-economic zoning of the past that excluded it.

* * *

We find the distinction between the exercise of the zoning power that is "directly tied to the physical use of the property," Madison, 72 N.J. at 517, 371 A.2d 1192, and its exercise tied to the income level of those who use the property artificial in connection with the *Mount Laurel* obligation, although it obviously troubled us in *Madison*.[17] The prohibition of this kind of affirmative device seems unfair when we have for so long allowed large lot single family residence districts, a form of zoning keyed, in effect, to income levels. The constitutional obligation itself is not to build three bedroom units, or single family residences on very small lots, or high-rise multi-family apartments, but rather to provide through the zoning ordinance a realistic opportunity to construct *lower income housing*. All of the physical uses are simply a means to this end. We see no reason why the municipality cannot exercise its zoning power to achieve that end directly rather than through a mass of detailed regulations governing the "physical use" of land, the sole purpose of which is to provide housing within the reach of lower income families. We know of no governmental purpose relating to zoning that is served by requiring a municipality to ingeniously design detailed land use regulations, purporting to be "directly tied to the physical use of the property," but actually aimed at accommodating lower income families, while not allowing it directly to require developers to construct lower income units. Indirection of this kind has no more virtue where its goal is to acheive that which is permitted—indeed, constitutionally mandated—than it has in achieving that which is prohibited.

* * *

As the cost of ordinary housing skyrockets for purchasers and renters, mobile homes become increasingly important as a source of low cost housing. The evidence clearly supports a finding that mobile homes are significantly less expensive than site-built housing. See Leg-

---

17. In any event the relationship of lower income units to "the physical use of the land" (i.e., their mandatory inclusion as part of a multi-family project) appears as substantial as the relationship of units for the elderly to a mobile home district. See Weymouth, 80 N.J. 6, 364 A.2d 1016 (1976). The inclusion of some lower income units in a multi-family housing project that may also house families with other income levels may be socially beneficial and an economic prerequisite to the creation of lower income units.

This problem does not arise when a municipality wants to create upper income housing since the physical requirements of the zoning district ("directly tied to the land") combined with housing market forces are sufficient. The *explicit* requirement of lower income units in a zoning provision may be necessary if the municipality's social goals are to prevail over neutral market forces. Zoning does not require that land be used for maximum profitability, and on occasion the goals of zoning may require something less.

islature's Mobile Home Study Commission, Report and Recommendations (1980) (finding that while it would take a household income of at least $21,000 to afford a medium priced site-built home in 1979, an income of $11,700 would be sufficient for a family to afford a mobile home and lot); Housing Handbook, supra, at 32. We agree fully with the finding of Judge Wood in *Mount Laurel II* that mobile homes are "economically available for persons of low and moderate income." 161 N.J.Super. at 357, 391 A.2d 935. Therefore, subject to the qualifications noted hereafter, we rule that municipalities that cannot otherwise meet their fair share obligations must provide zoning for low-cost mobile homes [18] as an affirmative device in their zoning ordinances.

* * *

There may be municipalities where special conditions such as extremely high land costs make it impossible for the fair share obligation to be met even after all excessive restrictions and exactions, *i.e.*, those not essential for safety and health, have been removed and all affirmative measures have been attempted. In such cases, *and only in such cases*, the *Mount Laurel* obligation can be met by supplementing whatever lower income housing can be built with enough "least cost" housing to satisfy the fair share. * * *

* * *

It is important for us to emphasize here that unless it meets the stringent "least cost" requirements set out above, middle income housing will not satisfy the *Mount Laurel* obligation. This is so dispite claims by some defendant-municipalities that the provision of such middle income housing will allow less expensive housing to "filter down" to lower income families. The problem with this theory is that the housing that has been built and is now being built in suburbs such as Mount Laurel is rapidly *appreciating* in value so that none of *it* will "filter down" to poor people. Instead, if the only housing constructed in municipalities like Mount Laurel continues to be middle and upper income, the only "filter down" effect that will occur will be that housing on the fringes of our inner cities will "filter down" to the poor as more of the middle class leave for suburbs, thereby exacerating the economic segregation of our cities and suburbs. See A. Downs, supra at 421 n. 8, at 9–12. Only if municipalities like Mount Laurel begin now to build lower income or least cost housing will some part of *their* housing stock ever "filter down" to New Jersey's poorer families. See Madison, 72 N.J. at 513–14 & n. 22, 371 A.2d 1192.

E. *Judicial Remedies*

If a trial court determines that a municipality has not met its *Mount Laurel* obligation, it shall order the municipality to revise its zoning or-

---

18. Not all mobile homes are low-cost. Many mobile homes are beyond the reach of even middle income households. However, the important point is that mobile homes apparently can be built that are affordable—without subsidy—by lower income families. Thus, a municipality that is not able, even with mandatory set-asides or other affirmative devices, to provide its fair share of lower income housing with site-built units may be able to meet its obligation by providing zoning for mobile homes and requiring developers in such zones to construct a certain number of lower income units.

dinance within a set time period to comply with the constitutional mandate; if the municipality fails adequately to revise its ordinance within that time, the court shall implement the remedies for noncompliance outlined below; and if plaintiff is a developer, the court shall determine whether a builder's remedy should be granted.

1. *Builder's Remedy*

Builder's remedies have been one of many controversial aspects of the *Mount Laurel* doctrine. Plaintiffs, particularly plaintiff-developers, maintain that these remedies are (i) essential to maintain a significant level of *Mount Laurel* litigation, and the only effective method to date of enforcing compliance; (ii) required by principles of fairness to compensate developers who have invested substantial time and resources in pursuing such litigation; and (iii) the most likely means of ensuring that lower income housing is actually built. Defendant municipalities contend that even if a plaintiff-developer obtains a judgment that a particular municipality has not complied with *Mount Laurel,* that municipality, and not the developer, should be allowed to determine how and where its fair share obligation will be met.

In *Madison,* this Court, while granting a builder's remedy to the plaintiff appeared to discourage such remedies in the future by stating that "such relief will ordinarily be rare." 72 N.J. at 551–52 n. 50, 371 A.2d 1192. Experience since *Madison,* however, has demonstrated to us that builder's remedies must be made more readily available to achieve compliance with *Mount Laurel.* We hold that where a developer succeeds in *Mount Laurel* litigation and proposes a project providing a substantial amount of lower income housing,[19] a builder's remedy should be granted unless the municipality establishes that because of environmental or other substantial planning concerns, the plaintiff's proposed project is clearly contrary to sound land use planning. We emphasize that the builder's remedy should not be denied solely because the municipality prefers some other location for lower income housing, even it it is in fact a better site. Nor is it essential that considerable funds be invested or that the litigation be intensive.

Other problems concerning builder's remedies require discussion. Care must be taken to make certain that *Mount Laurel* is not used as an unintended bargaining chip in a builder's negotiations with the municipality, and that the courts not be used as the enforcer for the builder's threat to bring *Mount Laurel* litigation if municipal approvals for projects containing no lower income housing are not forthcoming.

---

19. What is "substantial" in a particular case will be for the trial court to decide. The court should consider such factors as the size of the plaintiff's proposed project, the percentage of the project to be devoted to lower income housing (20 percent appears to us to be a reasonable minimum), what proportion of the defendant municipality's fair share allocation would be provided by the project, and the extent to which the remaining housing in the project can be categorized as "least cost." The balance of the project will presumably include middle and upper income housing. Economically integrated housing may be better for all concerned in various ways. Furthermore, the middle and upper income units may be necessary to render the project profitable. If builder's remedies cannot be profitable, the incentive for builders to enforce *Mount Laurel* is lost.

Proof of such threats shall be sufficient to defeat *Mount Laurel* litigation by that developer.

It is within the power of trial courts to adjust the timing of builder's remedies so as to cushion the impact of these developments on municipalities where that impact would otherwise cause a sudden and radical transformation of the municipality. This adjustment is analogous to the phasing-in of the satisfaction of present and prospective need mentioned in Ruling 10, *supra* at 420.

The trial court (and the master, if one is appointed) should make sure that the municipal planning board is closely involved in the formulation of the builder's remedy. This does not mean that the planning board should be permitted to delay or hinder the project or to reduce the amount of lower income housing required. However, with this caveat, the trial court and master should make as much use as they can of the planning board's expertise and experience so that the proposed project is suitable for the municipality.

*   *   *

2. *Revision of the Zoning Ordinance: the Master*

If the trial court determines that a municipality's zoning ordinance does not satisfy its *Mount Laurel* obligation, it shall order the defendant to revise it. Unless it is clear that the requisite realistic opportunity can be otherwise provided, the trial court should direct the municipality to incorporate in that new ordinance the affirmative devices discussed above most likely to lead to the construction of lower income housing. The trial court shall order the revision to be completed within 90 days of its original judgment against the municipality. For good cause shown, a municipality may be granted in extension of that time period.

To facilitate this revision, the trial court may appoint a special master to assist municipal officials in developing constitutional zoning and land use regulations.[20] The use of such special masters, sometimes called "hybrid" masters is not uncommon in litigation resulting in some form of institutional change.[21] See, e.g., T. Eisenberg & S. Yeazell, "The Ordinary and the Extraordinary in Institutional Litigation," 93 Harv.L.Rev. 465 (1980); T. Mayo, "Exclusionary Zoning, Remedies, and the Expansive Role of the Court in Public Law Litigation," 31 Syracuse

---

20. Prior to the commencement of the master's service, the trial court should determine the method, amount and other details of compensation. The master's compensation shall be paid in its entirety by the municipality, and is due upon entry of final judgment. Partial payments may be directed to be made in the court's discretion as the master's work progresses. See R. 4:41–2.

21. In United States v. City of Parma, 661 F.2d 562, reh. den., 669 F.2d 1100 (6th Cir.1981), the court reversed the trial court's appointment of a special master to oversee implementation of a broad range of remedies ordered to correct the defendant's violations of the Fair Housing Act,

42 U.S.C. §§ 3601 to 3619. The court relied heavily on the testimony of plaintiff United States' chief witness on remedies, who stated that no master was needed. It also implicitly concluded that the requirements for appointing a master found in the Federal Rules of Civil Procedure were not met.

That rule is more limited than our own. The federal rule directs that a master be appointed only if, among other things, "some exceptional condition requires it." F.R.Civ.P. 53(b). Our own rule provides for appointment of a master "upon approval by the Chief Justice * * * or under extraordinary circumstances." R. 4:41–1.

L.Rev. 755 (1980); "Special Project—The Remedial Process in Institutional Reform Litigation," 78 Colum.L.Rev. 784, 794 (1978); Berger, "Away from the Court House and Into the Field: The Odyssey of a Special Master," 78 Colum.L.Rev. 707 (1978); "The *Wyatt* Case: Implementation of a Judicial Decree Ordering Institutional Change," 84 Yale L.J. 1338, 1344 (1975). These impartial experts use their skills to help the parties formulate a remedy that will comply with the trial court's order and supply information that the parties may not have available to them. 78 Colum.L.Rev. at 794. They differ from traditional masters, whose roles are usually limited to serving as fact-finders and supervising procedural tasks, *id.* at 805, in that special masters work with the parties to devise a remedy that will meet with the court's approval. Id. at 805–06; 84 Yale L.J. at 1344.

While the appointment of a master is discretionary, we believe that such appointment is desirable in many cases where the court orders a revision of the land use regulations, especially if that revision is substantial. We do not view the appointment of a master as punitive in the least; it is not designed to settle scores with recalcitrant municipalities. The point here is that we intend that the appointment of masters be viewed by the court as a readily available device, one to be liberally used. In our view the master is of potential help to all concerned: to the municipality, to the plaintiffs, to the court and counsel. He or she is an expert, a negotiator, a mediator, and a catalyst—a person who will help the municipality select from the innumerable combinations of actions that could satisfy the constitutional obligation, the one that gives appropriate weight to the many conflicting interests involved, the one that satisfies not only the Constitution but, to some extent, the parties as well.

*   *   *

This form of supervision is neither as intrusive nor as novel as it might seem. It is not overly intrusive since the municipality itself develops the ordinance with the advice and assistance of the special master and the participation of the other parties. 78 Colum.L.Rev. at 809. The final result, of course, is subject to the trial court's approval. Id. Nor is it especially novel. In addition to the increasing use of special masters in the implementation of remedies in institutional litigation, courts necessarily intrude into parties' affairs in all litigation—that is the very nature of a lawsuit and its consequences. Such intrusions have traditionally taken the form of supervising a party's business, whether as a result of bankruptcy, probate, or corporate litigation; compelling parties to appear as witnesses to testify, which may entail considerable disruption of those persons' lives and affairs; creating special tribunals; and in many other ways becoming involved itself with the lives and activities of the parties. 93 Harv.L.Rev. at 474–92. We have however become accustomed to seeing courts and their delegates function in those "traditional" roles and therefore do not object to their activities, while the use of special masters is a relatively new remedial device.

*   *   *

The master will work closely not only with the governing body but with all those connected with the litigation, including plaintiffs, the board of adjustment, planning board and interested developers. He or she will assist all parties in discussing and negotiating the requirements of the new regulations, the use of affirmative devices, and other activities designed to conform to the *Mount Laurel* obligation. The parties will presumably give the master's suggestions great weight, since the revised ordinance will be submitted to the master for his or her review and recommendations prior to its submission to the court. During the course of the revision process, the master will report periodically to the court on the progress of the revision process. At the end of the 90 day period, on notice to all the parties, the revised ordinance will be presented in open court and the master will inform the court under oath, and subject to cross-examination, whether, in his or her opinion, that ordinance conforms with the trial court's judgment. That opinion, however, is not binding on the trial court. The master's powers are limited to rendering opinions, proposing findings, issuing recommendations, and assisting the court in other similar ways as it may direct.[22]   *   *   *

The municipality may elect to revise its land use regulations and implement affirmative remedies "under protest." If so, it may file an appeal when the trial court enters final judgment of compliance. Until that time there shall be no right of appeal, as the trial court's determination of fair share and non-compliance is interlocutory. Stay of the effectiveness of an ordinance that is the basis for a judgment of compliance where the ordinance was adopted "under protest" shall be determined in accordance with the usual rules. Proceedings as ordered herein (including the obligation of the municipality to revise its zoning ordinance with the assistance of the special master) will continue despite the pendency of any attempted interlocutory appeals by the municipality.

3. *Remedies for Non-Compliance*

If within the time allotted by the trial court a revised zoning ordinance is submitted by the defendant municipality that meets the municipality's *Mount Laurel* obligations, the trial court shall issue a judgment of compliance. If the revised ordinance does not meet the constitutional requirements, or if no revised ordinance is submitted within the time allotted, the trial court may issue such orders as are appropriate, including any one or more of the following:

(1) that the municipality adopt such resolutions and ordinances, including particular amendments to its zoning ordinance, and other land use regulations, as will enable it to meet its *Mount Laurel* obligations;

(2) that certain types of projects or construction as may be specified by the trial court be delayed within the municipality until its ordinance is satisfactorily revised, or until all or part of its fair share

---

22. Given the sensitive nature of the function, the master should not communicate privately with the court.

of lower income housing is constructed and/or firm commitments for its construction have been made by responsible developers;

(3) that the zoning ordinance and other land use regulations of the municipality be deemed void in whole or in part so as to relax or eliminate building and use restrictions in all or selected portions of the municipality (the court may condition this remedy upon failure of the municipality to adopt resolutions or ordinances mentioned in (1) above); and

(4) that particular applications to construct housing that includes lower income units be approved by the municipality, or any officer, board, agency, authority (independent or otherwise) or division thereof.

In determining remedies for non-compliance, the trial court may use the assistance and advice of a master subject to the guidelines set forth above.

The remedies permitted herein upon judgment of non-compliance go beyond what had previously been allowed by this Court in *Mount Laurel* cases. They were clearly anticipated by the Court, however, in *Madison*, where we explicitly approved and adopted remedies far beyond our actions in *Mount Laurel I.*

* * *

We adhere to the belief that where conventional remedies are adequate to vindicate a right, they should be employed, that it is unwise to devise remedies that partake more of administrative and legislative than of judicial power where traditional remedies will do. Judicial legitimacy may be at risk if we take action resembling traditional executive or legislative models; but it may be even more at risk through failure to take such action if that is the only way to enforce the Constitution.[23]

In short, there being a constitutional obligation, we are not willing to allow it to be disregarded and rendered meaningless by declaring that we are powerless to apply any remedies other than those conventionally used. We intend no discourse on the history of judicial remedies, but suspect that that which we deem "conventional" was devised because it seemed perfectly adequate in view of the obligation it addressed. We suspect that the same history would show that as obligations were recognized that could not be satisfied through such conventional remedies, the courts devised further remedies, and indeed the history of Chancery is as much a history of remedy as it is of obligation. The process of remedial development has not yet been frozen.

* * *

23. Some of the remedies approved here, while different in tenor from that which is ordinary, are really no more intrusive than that which is conventional. A "conventional" remedy might include a declaration that the entire zoning ordinance is void, yet it is hard to imagine a more intrusive remedy. The entire municipality remains unzoned. Anyone can build whatever is desired. That total absence of regulation is more radical than the attempt to persuade the municipality to rezone through the use of a master, or the temporary prohibition of certain kinds of construction, or indeed even the ordering of an amendment: these at least retain intact a substantial portion of the municipality's regulations.

When the court orders that an ordinance be amended, it does very little different from ordering that a variance be granted, actions taken by our courts in New Jersey for many years. It does very little different from declaring that a zoning ordinance is invalid on equal protection grounds, the effect of that often being not simply to allow a plaintiff to use his property in a manner not permitted by the ordinance, but to give the same right to an entire class. The ordinance is effectively amended to permit a use explicitly excluded, or in some cases to exclude one explicitly permitted. Sometimes the action of the court comes even closer to ordering, indeed declaring, that an ordinance has been changed, see West Point Island Ass'n v. Township Committee of Dover Twp., 54 N.J. 339, 255 A.2d 237 (1969), where this Court, in effect, affirmed the decision of a trial court ordering a municipality to take certain action, which action could be taken only by the adoption of a resolution that the municipality had not adopted. As noted above, we did not hesitate, in *Madison*, to order amendment of the municipal zoning ordinance. Similarly, in Lusardi v. Curtis Point Property Owners Ass'n, 86 N.J. 217, 430 A.2d 881 (1981), relying on the judiciary's power to regulate zoning in the public interest, we effectively modified an ordinance that conflicted with the state's policy of affording recreational opportunities on the Atlantic seafront for as many citizens as possible.

The scope of remedies authorized by this opinion is similar to those used in a rapidly growing area of the law commonly referred to as "institutional litigation" or "public law litigation." [24] While it may not have been appropriate at the time of *Mount Laurel* to employ those remedies, regularly used in such public law litigation, we clearly recognized "the further extent of judicial power in the field" by citing the lower court's decision in *Pascack*, 131 N.J.Super. 195, 329 A.2d 89 (Law Div.1974), a case in which the panoply of remedies appropriate in institutional litigation was used. What we said in *Mount Laurel* in reference to remedy eight years ago was that such remedies were "not ap-

---

24. These cases have involved school desegregation, prison, overcrowding, reapportionment and, significantly, housing. In them the courts, and they are usually federal courts, have found that the scope of a particular constitutional obligation, and the resistance to its vindication, are such as to require much more active judicial involvement in the remedial stage of litigation than is conventional if the constitutional obligation is to be satisfied. Federal district courts have retained particular school desegregation disputes for many years, fashioning remedies year after year as the circumstances seem to require; in some, they have actually taken over school districts, administered prisons, hospitals, and other institutions, ordered housing authorities to build housing in certain areas, in some cases even outside of the municipality involved. The authorities, both case and comment, are unanimous in their conclusion that exclusionary zoning cases fall within this category, that they are "institutional litigation" or "public law litigation" for the purpose of determining what kinds of procedures, including remedies, are appropriate. T. Mayo, "Exclusionary Zoning, Remedies, and the Expansive Role of the Court in Public Law Litigation," 31 Syracuse L.Rev. 755, 775 (1980); McDougall, "The Judicial Struggle Against Exclusionary Zoning: The New Jersey Paradigm," 14 Harv.C.R.C.L.L.Rev. 625, 647–54 (1979); Jennings, "The Chancellor's Foot Begins to Kick: Judicial Remedies in Public Law Cases and the Need for Procedural Reforms," 83 Dick.L.Rev. 217, 218 n. 9 (1979); "Developments-Zoning," 91 Harv.L.Rev. 1427, 1694–1708 (1978); "The Inadequacy of Judicial Remedies in Cases of Exclusionary Zoning," 74 Mich.L.Rev. 760, 768 (1976); "The Mount Laurel Case, A Consideration of Remedies," 37 U.Pitt.L.Rev. 442, 452–58 (1975); Rabinowitz, "Exclusionary Zoning: A Wrong in Search of a Remedy," 6 U.Mich.J.L.Ref. 625, 634–43 (1973).

propriate at this time, particularly in view of the advanced view of zoning law as applied to housing laid down by this opinion * * *." 67 N.J. at 192, 336 A.2d 713. That view is no longer "advanced," at least not in this state. It is eight years old. Our warning to Mount Laurel—and to all other municipalities—that if they do "not perform as we expect, further judicial action may be sought . . . ", *id.* at 192, 336 A.2d 713, will seem hollow indeed if the best we can do to satisfy the constitutional obligation is to issue orders, judgments and injunctions that assure never-ending litigation but fail to assure constitutional vindication.

4. *Summary of the Remedial Stage*

The remedies authorized today are intended to achieve compliance with the Constitution and the *Mount Laurel* obligations without interminable trials and appeals. Municipalities will not be able to appeal a trial court's determination that its ordinance is invalid, wait several years for adjudication of that appeal, and then, if unsuccessful, adopt another inadequate ordinance followed by more litigation and subsequent appeals. We intend by our remedy to conclude in one proceeding, with a single appeal, all questions involved. There will be either a judgment of compliance (from which a municipality that acted "under protest" may appeal with or without stays) signifying the trial court's conclusions that there are land use regulations and affirmative devices in place conforming to the constitutional obligation; or there will be a judgment containing one or more of many orders available in the event of non-compliance along with the action of the municipality conforming to such orders. On appeal, the appellate court will have before it everything needed to determine fully the issues.

* * *

We intend to administer the *Mount Laurel* doctrine effectively. It is complex. Its administration is important not simply to those seeking lower income housing, but to the municipalities as well. We have no desire to deprive municipalities of their right to litigate each and every determination affecting their interests, but we believe that the present procedures, allowing numerous appeals, retrials, and ordinarily resulting in substantial delay in meeting the obligation, do not strike the proper balance. While we cannot totally satisfy both the plaintiffs' and defendants' interests, we think the procedures required above come closer than those that have existed in the past to achieving a just balance of all the policies involved.

That balance also requires modification of the role of *res judicata* in these cases. Judicial determinations of compliance with the fair share obligation or of invalidity are not binding under ordinary rules of *res judicata* since circumstances obviously change. In *Mount Laurel* cases, however, judgments of compliance should provide that measure of finality suggested in the Municipal Land Use Law, which requires the reexamination and amendment of land use regulations every six years. Compliance judgments in these cases therefore shall have *res judicata* effect, despite changed circumstances, for a period of six years, the period to begin with the entry of the judgment by the trial court.[25] In this way, municipalities can enjoy the repose that the *res judicata* doctrine intends, free of litigious interference with the normal planning process.

Notes and Questions

1. In *Mount Laurel II*, reprinted above, was the New Jersey Supreme Court adjudicating or legislating? Will the three judges appointed to handle all future "Mount Laurel" litigation perform an adjudicative or an administrative function?

2. The New Jersey State Development Guide Plan (SDGP) was originally published in preliminary draft form in September, 1977. The court said that "[t]he remedial use * * * of the SDGP as the primary standard to determine the locus of the *Mount Laurel* obligation * * * is the kind of use of the SDGP contemplated by the Legislature in various statutes, and by the plan itself." But the court conceded that "the Legislature has neither explicitly authorized its use for *Mount Laurel* purposes nor mandated that the actual use of land, as permitted in zoning ordinances, conform to the SDGP." In fact, it appears that the SDGP was primarily designed as a guide to state capital expenditures. Critics have asserted that the SDGP is already out of date; that, by and large, it designates as "growth areas" subject to the *"Mount Laurel* obligation those communities where substantial growth has occurred during the past decade, thus exempting from the court's "affirmative action" mandates those communities that have most successfully limited growth in the past by means of "exclusionary" land use controls; that there is no assurance that "growth areas" shown on the SDGP maps are designated as "growth areas" on other statewide plans such as those of the New Jersey Department of Environmental Protection; and that it is questionable whether there is a consensus in New Jersey on the goals of the SDGP.[26] The New Jersey court obviously wants the SDGP to be kept current and viable, but of the 60 planners who worked on the original plan in the 1970's, only three remain on the staff of the state planning agency. A recent critical assessment of *Mount Laurel II* reaches the following pessimistic conclusion: [27]

"* * * Now that *Mount Laurel II* has made the SDGP the test by which to determine the municipalities that have to provide for a fair share of regional housing needs for low- and moderate-income persons, there is every likelihood that political pressures will become insurmountable for 'objective' planning principles to prevail in any revision of the study. There will be political pressures on officials of state government to retain or alter the 'area' designations. The future character and amenities of municipalities and the future land values of undeveloped real estate will be in issue, and the stakes will be high. Proposed revision of the SDGP will become a political hot potato. There is every likelihood that the new standard adopted by the court to resolve the dilemma of the developing municipality in January 1983 will be allowed to expire on January 1, 1985."

3. The New Jersey Supreme Court may have hoped that its *Mount Laurel II* opinion would rouse the state legislature to deal with the state's housing problems. The legislature's response, to date, can hardly be what the court

25. A substantial transformation of the municipality, however, may trigger a valid *Mount Laurel* claim before the six years have expired.

26. See 35 Land Use Law & Zoning Digest, March 1983, pp. 3–12; Planning and Law Division, American Planning Association, Newsletter, May 1983, pp. 1–7.

27. Rose, The *Mount Laurel II* Decision: Is it Based on Wishful Thinking?, 12 Real Est.L.J. 115, 130 (1983).

expected. A resolution introduced in the New Jersey Senate in May, 1983, is designed to block the court's "inclusionary zoning" mandate by an amendment to the New Jersey Constitution reaffirming each municipality's right to self-government through exercise of its zoning and planning powers and providing that local land use decisions cannot be changed by the courts, the governor, or the legislature. The co-sponsors of the resolution think the Court "went too far" when it required municipalities to seek housing subsidies and ordered mandatory "set-asides." An opposing resolution, introduced at the same time, would empower the Legislative Oversight Committee to investigate the contradictory reaction of the governor's office to *Mount Laurel II.*

4. The best critical discussion of *Mount Laurel II* will be found in Rose, The Mount Laurel II Decision: Is It Based on Wishful Thinking?, 12 Real Est.L.J. 115 (1983). Rose concludes as follows.[28]

The Mount Laurel II decision is a strong and determined statement by the New Jersey Supreme Court of its belief in the fundamental principle protected by the state constitution, that every person has the right to move freely within the state and to live where he believes opportunities of employment, safety, and the pursuit of happiness exist. * * *

These are noble ideals and cannot be faulted. The weakness of the decision may emerge in time, not from its ethical principles, but from the economic and political assumptions on which it rests. It remains to be seen whether *new* housing can be built that meets minimum standards of safety and health and is affordable by low-income persons; it remains to be seen whether there is any realistic prospect of a sufficient commitment by the American people of a portion of our national resources for anything more than a token amount of subsidized low-income housing; it remains to be seen whether the net effect of the decision will result in anything more than an acceleration of the movement of upwardly mobile middle-income families from the central cities to the suburbs, creating an even greater exacerbation of the problem of the deteriorating central cities; it remains to be seen whether municipal officials representing embattled suburban citizens seeking to protect their own quest for safety, security, and happiness will accede to the authority of the three judges and their appointed 'masters'; it remains to be seen whether the principles of sound state land-use planning will prevail against the political forces directed by a fearful and threatened suburban citizenry. * * *

Note on Judicial Treatment of Exclusionary Land Use Controls in Other States

As the New Jersey Supreme Court pointed out in *Mount Laurel II*, several other state courts have held that municipalities have an obligation to consider regional housing needs in their zoning decisions. The most important decisions are those of the New York and Pennsylvania courts.

The New York Cases: In Berenson v. Town of New Castle, 38 N.Y.2d 102, 378 N.Y.S.2d 672, 341 N.E.2d 236 (1975), plaintiffs challenged the entire zoning ordinance of the Town of New Castle on the ground that it completely excluded multiple family housing developments. The Court of Appeals laid down a two-tiered doctrine under which the Town Board was held obligated (a) to provide a properly balanced and well-ordered plan for the community which would meet its present and future needs, and (b) to consider the needs of residents of Westchester County and the larger New York metropolitan region for multi-family

---

28. Id. at 136.

housing in New Castle in order to be near their employment or for a variety of other economic or social reasons. But the high court stopped far short of the "fair share" doctrine enunciated in *Mount Laurel*, expressly declaring that there is no municipal obligation to provide for local or regional needs if those needs are already being met by other nearby communities.

On remand of the *Berenson* case, the trial judge found (a) that the zoning ordinance did not provide a properly balanced and well-ordered plan to meet the present and future needs of New Castle, (b) that regional needs for multi-family housing were not being met by other nearby communities, and hence (c) that the New Castle ordinance was exclusionary and invalid. The trial judge also ordered the town (a) to develop a policy statement indicating its willingness to encourage the construction of multi-family housing and to assist in meeting the regional housing goals of Westchester County; (b) to amend its zoning ordinance to meet the need for multi-family housing; and (c) to rezone the plaintiff's land so as to permit multi-family housing at a designated maximum density and to issue a building permit upon compliance by plaintiff with the revised zoning regulations.

The trial court's judgment was affirmed in part and reversed in part by the intermediate appellate court. Specifically, the trial court's order mandating a specific allowable density and directing issuance of a building permit was reversed. Berenson v. Town of New Castle, 67 App.Div.2d 506, 415 N.Y.S.2d 669 (1979). Subsequently, the Westchester County legislative body established a comprehensive plan for regional development, and New Castle amended its zoning ordinance so as to set up a series of multi-family districts based on density, and also to create floating zones called "designed developments." The trial court then reviewed the amended ordinance and held it valid, concluding that it satisfied both of the requirements laid down by the Court of Appeals. Since the town's amended ordinance would allow construction of 8.5% of all the multi-family housing needed in the region, as specified in the county plan, the ordinance "clearly meets New Castle's regional responsibilities." Blitz v. Town of New Castle, 34 Land Use Law & Zoning Digest, June 1982, p. 17 (N.Y.Sup.Ct., Westchester County, Case No. 13063/80). On appeal, the judgment was affirmed. 94 A.D.2d 92, 463 N.Y.S.2d 832 (1983).

Kurzius, Inc. v. Inc. Village of Upper Bronxville, 51 N.Y.2d 338, 434 N.Y.S.2d 180, 414 N.E.2d 680 (1981), clarified the *Berenson* holding to some extent. In *Kurzius*, the court said that a zoning ordinance alleged to be "exclusionary" is still entitled to the traditional presumption of validity unless it shows on its face that it was designed to achieve an improper purpose, and that this presumption can be rebutted only by showing that the ordinance was, in fact, designed to achieve an improper purpose or "without proper regard to local and regional housing needs" and with an "exclusionary" effect. On the facts in *Kurzius*, the court held that a five-acre minimum lot size requirement "within a coherent area characterized by estate-type development * * * and generally bounded by properties developed on a large lot basis" was valid. The court said that large-lot zoning may have legitimate purposes such as the preservation of open space, and found insufficient proof of either improper purpose of "exclusionary" effect—i.e., "no proof that persons of low or moderate incomes were foreclosed from housing in the general region because of the unavailability of improperly zoned land."

For an interesting recent case holding that a town's multi-family zoning practices did not violate the *Berenson* doctrine, see Suffolk Housing Services v. Town of Brookhaven, 35 Land Use Law & Zoning Digest 17 (Sup.Ct.1982). The court found the first *Berenson* requirement was satisfied because the zoning ordinance provided for multi-family districts within the town boundaries, and that the second *Berenson* requirement was satisfied because Brookhaven had issued permits for three-fifths of the existing multi-family units and 38 per cent of the existing publically subsidized housing in the county. The court rejected plaintiff's contention that the town's failure to map areas for multi-family development except in response to specific applications for rezoning did not violate either due process or equal protection guarantees. But the court also put the town on notice that it must "act more affirmatively" in the future to obtain financial aid for low- and moderate-income housing, stating that failure to do so would result in a reevaluation of the constitutionality of Brookhaven's zoning policies.

The Pennsylvania Cases: Pennsylvania, like New Jersey and New York, has in recent years invalidated local zoning ordinances as unconstitutionally "exclusionary" of low- and moderate-income persons.

In Township of Williston v. Chesterdale Farms, 462 Pa. 445, 341 A.2d 466 (1975), the Pennsylvania Supreme Court seemed to adopt the New Jersey "fair share" rule as laid down in *Mount Laurel I*. But in Surrick v. Zoning Hearing Board, 476 Pa. 182, 382 A.2d 105 (1977), the Court said that the "fair share" rule was only a "general precept" and then proceeded to apply a substantive due process test: "whether the zoning formulas fashioned by [local government] entities reflect a balanced and weighted consideration of the many factors that bear upon local and regional housing needs and development." The Court also said that, if a trial court determines that a particular municipality is a logical place for high density housing because it is part of a growing metropolitan area and has land available for such development, the court should apply an "exclusionary impact" test to determine whether the zoning ordinance before the court denies substantive due process. Thus a zoning ordinance that zones a disproportionately small part of the municipal area for multi-family housing may be invalid although it does not totally exclude such development. On the facts, the Court held that its "fair share" requirement was not satisfied by a suburban zoning ordinance that almost totally excluded multi-family dwellings. Consequently, it ordered that "zoning approval for appellant's land be granted and that a building permit be issued conditional upon appellant's compliance with the administrative requirements of the zoning ordinance and other reasonable controls and regulations which are consistent with this opinion."

The "builder's remedy" granted in *Surrick* is the remedy generally granted by Pennsylvania courts when a local zoning ordinance is found to be "exclusionary," provided the site is suitable for the proposed development and adequate public facilities are available at the site.

The Pennsylvania intermediate appeals court has generally adhered to the *Surrick* doctrine. See, e.g., In re Appeal of Elocin, Inc., 66 Pa.Cmwlth. 28, 443 A.2d 1333 (1982), holding that a township had failed to provide its "fair share" of land for multi-family dwellings where all the vacant land was zoned for single-family dwellings. Since the township was only five miles from Philadelphia, it was a logical area for additional development and population growth. It was not immune from its "fair share" requirement by virtue of the fact that 96 percent of its land was already developed, in view of the further fact that only five percent of the township's existing housing was composed of multi-family dwellings. Since the trial court never reached the issue of the reasonableness of Elocin's proposed plan for apartment construction, the case was remanded with instructions to examine Elocin's plan and to fashion a remedy that would allow construction of multi-family dwellings in the township.

Other Jurisdictions: There is language in some Michigan court opinions indicating that "exclusionary" zoning may be invalid in Michigan. See Kropf v.

City of Sterling Heights, 391 Mich. 139, 155–156, 215 N.W.2d 179, 185 (1974). The Michigan Supreme Court rejected the "preferred use" rationale relied upon by the intermediate appeals court in striking down zoning regulations that totally excluded mobile homes from a community; but the court said that, "[o]n its face, an ordinance which *totally* excludes from a municipality a use recognized by the constitution or other laws of this state as legitimate also carries with it a strong taint of unlawful discrimination and a denial of equal protection of the law as to the excluded use." Presumably this language might apply to exclusion of housing for low- and/or moderate income persons.

The California Supreme Court recently adverted to "the conflict * * * between [s]uburban residents who seek to overcome problems of inadequate schools and public facilities" and who "may assert a vital interest in limiting immigration to their community," and "[o]utsiders searching for a place to live in the face of a growing shortage of adequate housing, and hoping to share in the perceived benefits of suburban life, [who] may present a countervailing interest opposing barriers to immigration." See Assoc. Home Builders v. City of Livermore, 18 Cal.2d 582, 608–609, 135 Cal.Rptr. 41, 56, 557 P.2d 473, 488, 94 A.L.R.3d 1038 (1976). But the attack on "exclusionary" land use controls has centered in the state legislature in California.

Note on "Inclusionary" State Legislation

In *Mount Laurel II*, reprinted above, the New Jersey Supreme Court devoted part of its opinion to "Inclusionary Zoning Devices," which it further subdivided into "Incentive Zoning" and "Mandatory Set-Asides." A few states, without judicial pressure, have adopted legislation requiring local governments to enact "inclusionary" land use control ordinances. California and Oregon have adopted such legislation in recent years. Massachusetts, on the other hand, has set up a state agency with the power to override local decisions denying approval to federal or state-subsidized low or moderate-income housing projects.

As we have seen,[29] Oregon has adopted statewide land use planning and control legislation requiring all local governments to adopt both comprehensive plans and implementing land use regulations that comply with state goals with respect to "matters of statewide concern" and with planning goals promulgated by the Oregon Land Conservation and Development Commission. The statute expressly declares that "availability of housing for persons of lower, middle and fixed income is a matter of statewide concern,"[30] and further provides that "[w]hen a need has been shown for housing within an urban growth boundary at particular price ranges and rent levels, needed housing shall be permitted in a zone of sufficient buildable land to satisfy that need."[31] And the statute defines "needed housing" as "housing that includes, but is not limited to, attached and detached single family housing for both owner and renter occupancy and manufactured homes * * * located in either mobile home parks or subdivisions."[32]

In order to carry out their statutory duties, Oregon local governments must determine and seek to meet housing needs at all income levels, but in doing so, they may determine how to designate "buildable lands"[33] and may provide for needed housing either by "as of right" zoning or by means of flexible zoning procedures such as floating zones and conditional use permits. Standards for

29. Ante Chapter 14, Section 1, Note 4 following Fasano v. Board of County Commissioners.

30. Ore.Rev.Stat. § 197.307(1).

31. Id. § 197.307(2).

32. Id. § 197.303.

33. "Buildable lands" are "lands in urban or urbanizable areas that are suitable, available and necessary for residential uses." Ore.Rev.Stat. § 197.295(1).

such flexible procedures must be "clear and objective" and may not have the effect, either singly or in combination, "of discouraging the needed housing types through unreasonable cost or delay." [34]

California's statutory scheme is more complicated than Oregon's. The California comprehensive planning legislation requires inclusion of a "housing element" and a "housing program" in municipal and county comprehensive plans, which are themselves required.[35] The "housing element" of the local comprehensive plan must include an "assessment of housing needs and an inventory of resources and constraints relevant to the meeting of these needs." [36] The analysis of housing need "shall include the locality's share of the regional housing need,"[37] and the statute specifies the criteria for distribution of the regional housing need, which is to be determined by regional councils of government or, where such councils do not exist, by the state housing and community development department:

> [T]he distribution of regional housing needs shall, based upon available data, take into consideration market demand for housing employment opportunities, the availability of suitable sites and public facilities, commuting patterns, type and tenure of housing need, and the housing needs of farm-workers. The distribution shall seek to avoid further impaction of localities with relatively high proportions of lower income households.[38]

The California planning and zoning legislation also prohibits discrimination against low- and moderate-income and governmentally assisted or subsidized housing,[39] requires local governments to "zone sufficient vacant land for residential use with appropriate standards * * * to meet housing needs as identified in the general plan," [40] provides that manufactured housing (including mobile homes) is a permitted use in single-family residence districts (subject to nondiscriminatory building and land use regulations),[41] and further provides that a local ordinance "directly" restricting building permits or buildable lots is "presumed to have an impact on the supply of residential lots available in the municipality and the surrounding area" so as to impose on the local government the burden of justifying such restrictions.[42] And, finally, the California legislation provides for a twenty-five percent "density bonus" or alternative incentives for residential developers who provide at least twenty-five percent of their dwelling units for low- and/or moderate-income households.[43]

In response to enactment of the California "inclusionary zoning" legislation, at least twenty-two local government units have adopted "inclusionary zoning" ordinances [44] which share the following features: [45] (1) inclusionary requirements apply only to new developments of a certain size and to certain types of new housing; (2) mandatory set-asides are substantial, ranging from ten to thirty-three percent; (3) the set-asides are initially "subsidized" by the land developer in the form of below-market rents or sale prices, aided in some cases by federal rent subsidies under the so-called Section 8 program; (4) density bonuses are provided to offset the loss incurred by the developer on below-market

---

34. Ore.Rev.Stat. § 197.307(4).

35. Cal.Gov.Code Ann. §§ 65583–65589.

36. Id. § 65583(a).

37. Id. § 65583(a)(1).

38. Id. § 65584.

39. Id. § 65008.

40. Id. § 65913.1.

41. Id. § 65852.2. Id. § 65852.7 makes a "mobile home park" a "permitted use"

on all land planned and zoned for residential land use as designated by the applicable general plan, subject to the local government's right to "require a use permit."

42. Cal.Evidence Code Ann. § 669.5.

43. Cal.Gov.Code Ann. §§ 65915–65918.

44. See Ellickson, The Irony of "Inclusionary" Zoning, 54 So.Cal.L.Rev. 1167, 1169 (1981).

45. See id. at 1171–1181.

rentals or sales—i.e., the developer is allowed to build more units than the applicable zoning ordinance would ordinarily allow; (5) although nominally designed to benefit low- and moderate-income households, the "inclusionary zoning" ordinances mainly benefit "households one would identify in ordinary language as middle class"; (6) "[q]ueues and lotteries are generally used to select the few beneficiaries from the many applicants who find their way into the pool of eligibles"; (7) resale prices and rentals chargeable when a unit is sublet or rented to a new tenant are generally controlled in order to keep the subsidized units available to "low- and moderate-income"—i.e., middle class—households.

The Orange County, California, "inclusionary zoning" program has now provided a basis for approval of at least 5,767 units of "affordable housing"—roughly half the total of such units approved under "inclusionary zoning" programs throughout California.[46] A recent study of the Orange County program [47] concludes that, notwithstanding current problems, "inclusionary zoning" programs such as Orange County's serve as a deterrent to the unintended exclusionary effect of many local land use controls and provide increased opportunities to individuals earning a moderate income to purchase a home. It should be noted, however, that the Orange County Board has recently been considering proposed modifications of its "inclusionary" zoning ordinance, at least partly in response to increasingly heavy criticism from land developers.

The most thorough study of California's "inclusionary zoning" programs, published in 1981, reaches the following negative conclusion: [48]

> Inclusionary zoning, as usually practiced, is a misguided undertaking that is likely to aggravate the housing crisis it has ostensibly been designed to help solve. As a program of income redistribution, inclusionary zoning makes no sense. Although nominally aimed at benefiting low- and moderate-income families, almost all inclusionary units have in fact been bestowed on families in the middle third of the state's income distribution. Because only a small percentage (at most) of the members of the class of eligibles can hope soon to obtain units, inclusionists must resort to lotteries and queues to select the few lucky beneficiaries of handsome housing grants.

> Government distribution of massive subsidies to a few arbitrarily selected members of the middle class might be defensible if this redistribution produced important benefits to the larger society. The only possible social gains from inclusionary zoning are the intangible benefits flowing from the economic integration of new buildings and subdivisions. Yet even the social critics who have pushed most strongly for greater residential mobility doubt that economic integration at the block and building level is in the interest of members of any income group. Moreover, inclusionary zoning as currently practiced will have only a trivial effect on the amount of economic integration in residential neighborhoods.

> The costs of inclusionary zoning, by contract, are large and tangible. Inclusionary zoning involves in-kind housing subsidies, a method increasingly viewed as one of the most inefficient forms of income redistribution. Inclusionary zoning can also constitute a double tax on new housing construction—first, through the burden of its exactions; and second, through the 'undesirable' social environment it may force on new housing projects. In the sorts of housing markets in which inclusionary zoning has been prac-

46. Bozung, A Positive Response to Growth Control Plans: The Orange County Inclusionary Housing Program, 9 Pepperdine L.Rev. 819, 830 (1982).

47. Bozung, article supra note 18.

48. Ellickson, supra note 16, at 1215.

ticed, this double tax is likely to push up housing prices across the board, often to the net injury of the moderate-income households inclusionary zoning was supposed to help. * * *

The Massachusetts "anti-snob zoning" law [49] proceeds on a different principle than the Oregon and California legislation. The Massachusetts statute authorizes a qualified developer to apply to a local board of appeals for approval of a subsidized low- or moderate-income housing project. The board may issue a comprehensive permit for the project, deny approval, or issue a permit subject to conditions.[50] The statutory standard for local board decisions is that proposed projects are to be approved if they are "consistent with local needs." [51] But the statute further provides that the local board need not approve a project if (1) "low or moderate income housing exists which is in excess of ten per cent of the [municipality's] housing units reported in the latest decennial census" or (2) such housing exists "on sites comprising one and one half per cent or more of the total land area zoned for residential, commercial or industrial use" or (3) "the application before the [local] board would result in the commencement of construction of such housing on sites comprising more than three-tenths of one per cent of such land area or ten acres, whichever is larger, in any one calendar year."[52] These qualifications substantially limit the impact of the Massachusetts law.

When a local housing board of appeals denies approval to a proposed low and/or moderate income housing project or imposes unacceptable conditions on approval, the developer may appeal to the state Housing Appeals Committee.[53] If the Committee finds, in case of a denial, that the local board's decision was "unreasonable and not consistent with local needs," it must vacate the local board's decision and order issuance of a comprehensive permit for the proposed project.[54] And if, in the case of a conditional approval, the Committee finds that the local board's decision was "not consistent with local needs" and that the conditions imposed by the local board were "uneconomic," the Committee "shall order such board to modify or remove any such condition * * * so as to make the proposal no longer uneconomic." [55]

The Massachusetts Housing Appeals Committee cannot find the local board's action in denying or imposing conditions on approval of a proposed project inconsistent with local needs if the statutory conditions for board denial of project approval are satisfied.[56] If they are not satisfied, the Committee must balance the regional need for low- and moderate-income housing against the municipality's interest in enforcing its zoning and building regulations.[57] The Committee may find the conditions imposed on project approval to be "uneconomic" if, where the developer is a public agency or nonprofit corporation, it cannot build or operate the project without "financial loss" or, where the developer is a limited dividend corporation, it cannot "realize a reasonable return on the construction or operation of the project within the [rental] limits set by the subsidizing agency." [58]

The Massachusetts "anti-snob zoning" law was sustained in Board of Appeals of Hanover v. Housing Appeals Committee,[59] as against attack on the grounds that it violated the state Home Rule statute if construed to authorize

49. Mass.Gen.Laws Ann. ch. 40B, §§ 20–23.

50. Id. c. 40B, § 21.

51. Id. c. 40B, § 23.

52. Id. c. 40B, § 20.

53. Id. c. 40B, § 22.

54. Id. c. 40B, § 23.

55. Ibid.

56. Ibid.

57. Ibid.

58. Ibid.

59. 363 Mass. 339, 294 N.E.2d 393 (1973).

the Committee to override local zoning regulations, that it constituted an improper delegation of power without adequate standards, and that it authorized illegal "spot zoning." Subsequent decisions have placed some restrictions on the Committee's power, however. For example, a municipality's decision to acquire for conservation purposes a tract of land as to which an appeal was pending has been held not subject to Committee review,[60] and it has been held that the Committee may not authorize noncompliance with the state building code.[61]

B. RACIAL EXCLUSION: FEDERAL JUDICIAL RESPONSES

The principal federal restraints on state governmental action—and therefore on local zoning regulations—are the Due Process and Equal Protection Clauses of the Fourteenth Amendment. Federal court suits challenging local zoning regulations as "exclusionary" have generally relied on the Equal Protection Clause. Some of the recent cases have also relied on the Fair Housing Act, 42 U.S.C.A. §§ 3601 et seq., and it now appears that the Fair Housing Act will probably provide a sounder basis for "exclusionary zoning" challenges than does the Equal Protection Clause. An "equal protection" challenge faces two important obstacles:

(a) Since James v. Valtierra, 402 U.S. 137, 91 S.Ct. 1331, 28 L.Ed.2d 678 (1971), it has been clear that "discrimination against the poor" does not violate the Equal Protection Clause and that "exclusionary zoning" can be attacked on "equal protection" grounds only by showing that it directly or indirectly results in racial rather than mere economic discrimination.

(b) It is also clear that allegedly racially discriminatory land use controls can be attacked in the federal courts on "equal protection" grounds only by private developers or low-income housing sponsors who can show that concrete, viable housing projects are blocked by the local land use regulations. See Warth v. Seldin, 422 U.S. 490, 95 S.Ct. 2197, 45 L.Ed.2d 343 (1975). The following summary of the *Seldin* opinion is taken from the syllabus prepared by the official Reporter.

This action for declaratory and injunctive relief and damages was brought by certain of the petitioners against respondent town of Penfield (a suburb of Rochester, N.Y.), and respondent members of Penfield's Zoning, Planning, and Town Boards, claiming that the town's zoning ordinance, by its terms and as enforced, effectively excluded persons of low and moderate income from living in the town, in violation of petitioners' constitutional rights and of 42 U.S.C.A. §§ 1981, 1982, and 1983. Petitioners consist of both the original plaintiffs—(1) Metro-Act of Rochester, a not-for-profit corporation among whose purposes is fostering action to alleviate the housing shortage for low- and moderate-income persons in the Rochester area; (2) several individual Rochester taxpayers; and (3) several Rochester area residents with low or moderate incomes who are also members of minority racial or ethnic groups— and Rochester Home Builders Association (Home Builders), embracing a

---

60. Town of Chelmsford v. DiBiase, 370 Mass. 90, 345 N.E.2d 373 (1976).

61. Board of Appeals v. Housing Appeals Committee, 4 Mass.App.Ct. 676, 357 N.E.2d 936 (1976).

number of residential construction firms in the Rochester area, which unsuccessfully sought to intervene as a party-plaintiff, and the Housing Council in the Monroe County Area (Housing Council), a not-for-profit corporation consisting of a number of organizations interested in housing problems, which was unsuccessfully sought to be added as a party-plaintiff. The District Court dismissed the complaint on the ground, *inter alia*, that petitioners lacked standing to prosecute the action, and the Court of Appeals affirmed. *Held:* Whether the rules of standing are considered as aspects of the constitutional requirement that a plaintiff must make out a "case or controversy" within the meaning of Art. III, or, apart from such requirement, as prudential limitations on the courts' role in resolving disputes involving "generalized grievances" or third parties' legal rights or interests, none of the petitioners has met the threshold requirement of such rules that to have standing a complainant must clearly allege facts demonstrating that he is a proper party to invoke judicial resolution of the dispute and the exercise of the court's remedial powers.

(a) As to petitioner Rochester residents who assert standing as persons of low or moderate income and, coincidentally, as members of minority racial or ethnic groups, the facts alleged fail to support an actionable causal relationship between Penfield's zoning practices and these petitioners' alleged injury. A plaintiff who seeks to challenge exclusionary zoning practices must allege specific, concrete facts demonstrating that such practices harm *him*, and that he personally would benefit in a tangible way from the court's intervention. Here, these petitioners rely on little more than the remote possibility, unsubstantiated by allegations of fact, that their situation might have been better had respondents acted otherwise, and might improve were the court to afford relief.

(b) With respect to petitioners who assert standing on the basis of their status as Rochester taxpayers, claiming that they are suffering economic injury through increased taxes resulting from Penfield's zoning practices having forced Rochester to provide more tax-abated low- or moderate-cost housing than it otherwise would have done, the line of causation between Penfield's actions and such injury is not apparent. But even assuming that these petitioners could establish that the zoning practices harm them, the basis of their claim is that the practices violate the constitutional and statutory rights of third parties—persons of low- and moderate-income who allegedly are excluded from Penfield. Hence, their claim falls squarely within the prudential standing rule that normally bars litigants from asserting the rights or legal interests of others in order to obtain relief from injury to themselves.

(c) Petitioner Metro-Act's claims to standing as a Rochester taxpayer and on behalf of its members who are Rochester taxpayers or persons of low or moderate income, are precluded for the reasons applying to the denial of standing to the individual petitioner Rochester taxpayers and persons of low and moderate income. In addition, with respect to Metro-Act's claim to standing because 9% of its membership is composed of Penfield residents, prudential considerations strongly counsel against according such residents or Metro-Act standing, where the complaint is that they have been harmed indirectly by the exclusion of others, thus attempting in the absence of a showing of any exception allowing such a claim, to raise the putative rights of third parties. Trafficante v. Metropolitan Life Ins., 409 U.S. 205, 93 S.Ct. 364 (1972), distinguished.   *   *   *

(d) Petitioner Home Builders, which alleges no monetary injury to itself, has no standing to claim damages on behalf of its members since whatever injury may have been suffered is peculiar to the individual member concerned, thus requiring individualized proof of both the fact and extent of injury and individual awards. Nor does Home Builders have standing to claim prospective relief, absent any allegation of facts sufficient to show the existence of any injury to members of sufficient immediacy to warrant judicial intervention.   *   *   *

(e) Petitioner Housing Council has no standing, where the complaint and record do not indicate that any of its members, with one exception, has made any effect involving Penfield has taken any steps toward building there, or had any dealings with respondents. With respect to the one exception, this petitioner averred no basis for inferring that an earlier controversy between it and respondents remained a live, concrete dispute.   *   *   *

VILLAGE OF ARLINGTON HEIGHTS v. METROPOLITAN HOUSING DEVELOPMENT CORP.

Supreme Court of the United States, 1977.
429 U.S. 252, 97 S.Ct. 555, 50 L.Ed.2d 450.

Mr. Justice POWELL delivered the opinion of the Court.

In 1971 respondent Metropolitan Housing Development Corporation (MHDC) applied to petitioner, the Village of Arlington Heights, Ill., for the rezoning of a 15-acre parcel from single-family to multiple-family classification. Using federal financial assistance, MHDC planned to build 190 clustered townhouse units for low and moderate income tenants. The Village denied the rezoning request. MHDC, joined by other plaintiffs who are also respondents here, brought suit in the United States District Court for the Northern District of Illinois.[62] They alleged that the denial was racially discriminatory and that it violated *inter alia*, the Fourteenth Amendment and the Fair Housing Act of 1968, 42 U.S.C.A. § 3601 et seq. Following a bench trial the District Court entered judgment for the Village, 373 F.Supp. 208 (1974), and respondents appealed. The Court of Appeals for the Seventh Circuit reversed, finding that the "ultimate effect" of the denial was racially discriminatory, and that the refusal to rezone therefore violated the Fourteenth Amendment, 517 F.2d 409 (1975). We granted the Village's petition for

---

62. Respondents named as defendants both the Village and a number of its officials, sued in their official capacity. The latter were the Mayor, the Village Manager, the Director of Building and Zoning, and the entire Village Board of Trustees. For convenience, we will occasionally refer to all the petitioners collectively as "the Village."

certiorari, 423 U.S. 1030, 96 S.Ct. 560, 46 L.Ed.2d 404 (1975), and now reverse.

I

Arlington Heights is a suburb of Chicago, located about 26 miles northwest of the downtown Loop area. Most of the land in Arlington Heights is zoned for detached single-family homes, and this is in fact the prevailing land use. The Village experienced substantial growth during the 1960's, but, like other communities in northwest Cook County, its population of racial minority groups remained quite low. According to the 1970 census, only 27 of the Village's 64,000 residents were black.

The Clerics of St. Viator, a religious order (the Order), own an 80-acre parcel just east of the center of Arlington Heights. Part of the site is occupied by the Viatorian high school, and part by the Order's three-story novitiate building, which houses dormitories and a Montessori school. Much of the site, however, remains vacant. Since 1959, when the Village first adopted a zoning ordinance, all the land surrounding the Viatorian property has been zoned R–3, a single-family specification with relatively small minimum lot size requirements. On three sides of the Viatorian land there are single-family homes just across a street; to the east the Viatorian property directly adjoins the back yards of other single-family homes.

The Order decided in 1970 to devote some of its land to low and moderate income housing. Investigation revealed that the most expeditious way to build such housing was to work through a nonprofit developer experienced in the use of federal housing subsidies under § 236 of the National Housing Act, 12 U.S.C.A. § 1715z–1.[63]

MHDC is such a developer. It was organized in 1968 by several prominent Chicago citizens for the purpose of building low and moderate income housing throughout the Chicago area. In 1970 MHDC was in the process of building one § 236 development near Arlington Heights and already had provided some federally assisted housing on a smaller scale in other parts of the Chicago area.

---

63. Section 236 provides for "interest reduction payments" to owners of rental housing projects which meet the Act's requirements, if the savings are passed on to the tenants in accordance with a rather complex formula. Qualifying owners effectively pay one percent interest on money borrowed to construct, rehabilitate or purchase their properties. (Section 236 has been amended frequently in minor respects since this litigation began. See 12 U.S.C.A. § 1715z–1, and the Housing Authorization Act of 1976, Pub.L. No. 94–375, § 4, 90 Stat. 1070.)

New commitments under § 236 were suspended in 1973 by executive decision, and they have not been revived. Projects which formerly could claim § 236 assistance, however, will now generally be eligible for aid under § 8 of the Housing and Community Development Act of 1974, 42 U.S.C.A. § 1437f, as amended by Housing Authorization Act of 1976, Pub.L. No. 94–375, § 2, 90 Stat. 1068. Under the § 8 program, the Department of Housing and Urban Development contracts to pay the owner of the housing units a sum which will make up the difference between a fair market rent for the area and the amount contributed by the low-income tenant. The eligible tenant family pays between 15 and 25% of its gross income for rent. Respondents indicated at oral argument that, despite the demise of the § 236 program, construction of the MHDC project could proceed under § 8 if zoning clearance is now granted.

After some negotiation, MHDC and the Order entered into a 99-year lease and an accompanying agreement of sale covering a 15-acre site, in the southeast corner of the Viatorian property. MHDC became the lessee immediately, but the sale agreement was contingent upon MHDC's securing zoning clearances from the Village and § 236 housing assistance from the Federal Government. If MHDC proved unsuccessful in securing either, both the lease and the contract of sale would lapse. The agreement established a bargain purchase price of $300,000, low enough to comply with federal limitations governing land acquisition costs for § 236 housing.

MHDC engaged an architect and proceeded with the project, to be known as Lincoln Green. The plans called for 20 two-story buildings with a total of 190 units, each unit having its own private entrance from outside. One hundred of the units would have a single bedroom, thought likely to attract elderly citizens. The remainder would have two, three or four bedrooms. A large portion of the site would remain open, with shrubs and trees to screen the homes abutting the property to the east.

The planned development did not conform to the Village's zoning ordinance and could not be built unless Arlington Heights rezoned the parcel to R–5, its multiple-family housing classification. Accordingly MHDC filed with the Village Plan Commission a petition for rezoning, accompanied by supporting materials describing the development and specifying that it would be subsidized under § 236. The materials made clear that one requirement under § 236 is an affirmative marketing plan designed to assure that a subsidized development is racially integrated. MHDC also submitted studies demonstrating the need for housing of this type and analyzing the probable impact of the development. To prepare for the hearings before the Plan Commission and to assure compliance with the Village building code, fire regulations, and related requirements, MHDC consulted with the Village staff for preliminary review of the development. The parties have stipulated that every change recommended during such consultations was incorporated into the plans.

During the Spring of 1971, the Plan Commission considered the proposal at a series of three public meetings, which drew large crowds. Although many of those attending were quite vocal and demonstrative in opposition to Lincoln Green, a number of individuals and representatives of community groups spoke in support of rezoning. Some of the comments, both from opponents and supporters, addressed what was referred to as the "social issue"—the desirability or undesirability of introducing at this location in Arlington Heights low and moderate income housing, housing that would probably be racially integrated.

Many of the opponents, however, focused on the zoning aspects of the petition, stressing two arguments. First, the area always had been zoned single-family, and the neighboring citizens had built or purchased there in reliance on that classification. Rezoning threatened to cause a measurable drop in property value for neighboring sites. Second, the Village's apartment policy, adopted by the Village Board in 1962 and amended in 1970, called for R–5 zoning primarily to serve as a buffer between single-family development and land uses thought incompatible, such as commercial or manufacturing districts. Lincoln Green did not meet this requirement, as it adjoined no commercial or manufacturing district.

At the close of the third meeting, the Plan Commission adopted a motion to recommend to the Village's Board of Trustees that it deny the request. The motion stated: "While the need for low and moderate income housing may exist in Arlington Heights or its environs, the Plan Commission would be derelict in recommending it at the proposed location." Two members voted against the motion and submitted a minority report, stressing that in their view the change to accommodate Lincoln Green represented "good zoning." The Village Board met on September 28, 1971, to consider MHDC's request and the recommendation of the Plan Commission. After a public hearing, the Board denied the rezoning by a 6–1 vote.

The following June MHDC and three Negro individuals filed this lawsuit against the Village, seeking declaratory and injunctive relief.[64] A second nonprofit corporation and an individual of Mexican-American descent intervened as plaintiffs. The trial resulted in a judgment for petitioners. Assuming that MHDC had standing to bring the suit,[65] the District Court held that the petitioners were not motivated by racial discrimination or intent to discriminate against low income groups when they denied rezoning, but rather by a desire "to protect property values and the integrity of the Village's zoning plan." 373 F.Supp., at 211. The District Court concluded also that the denial would not have a racially discriminatory effect.

A divided Court of Appeals reversed. It first approved the District Court's finding that the defendants were motivated by a concern for the integrity of the zoning plan, rather than by racial discrimination. Deciding whether their refusal to rezone would have discriminatory effects was more complex. The court observed that the refusal would have a disproportionate impact on blacks. Based upon family income, blacks constituted 40% of those Chicago area residents who were eligible to become tenants of Lincoln Green, although they comprised a far lower percentage of total area population. The court reasoned, however, that under our decision in James v. Valtierra, 402 U.S. 137, 91 S.Ct. 1331, 28 L.Ed.2d 678 (1971), such a disparity in racial impact alone does not call for strict scrutiny of a municipality's decision that prevents the construction of the low-cost housing.[66]

64. The individual plaintiffs sought certification of the action as a class action pursuant to Fed.Rule Civ.Proc. 23 but the District Court declined to certify. 373 F.Supp., at 209.

65. A different district judge had heard early motions in the case. He had sustained the complaint against a motion to dismiss for lack of standing, and the judge who finally decided the case said he found "no need to re-examine [the predecessor judge's] conclusions" in this respect. 373 F.Supp. at 209.

66. Nor is there reason to subject the Village's action to more stringent review simply because it involves respondents' interest in securing housing. Lindsey v. Normet, 405 U.S. 56, 73–74, 92 S.Ct. 862, 874, 31 L.Ed.2d 36 (1972). See generally San Antonio Independent School District v. Rodriguez, 411 U.S. 1, 18–39, 93 S.Ct. 1278, 1288–1300, 36 L.Ed.2d 16 (1973).

There was another level to the court's analysis of allegedly discriminatory results. Invoking language from Kennedy Park Homes Association v. City of Lackawanna, 436 F.2d 108, 112 (C.A.2 1970), cert. denied, 401 U.S. 1010, 91 S.Ct. 1256, 28 L.Ed.2d 546 (1970), the Court of Appeals ruled that the denial of rezoning must be examined in light of its "historical context and ultimate effect." [67] Northwest Cook County was enjoying rapid growth in employment opportunities and population, but it continued to exhibit a high degree of residential segregation. The court held that Arlington Heights could not simply ignore this problem. Indeed, it found that the Village had been "exploiting" the situation by allowing itself to become a nearly all white community. 517 F.2d at 414. The Village had no other current plans for building low and moderate income housing, and no other R–5 parcels in the Village were available to MHDC at an economically feasible price.

Against this background, the Court of Appeals ruled that the denial of the Lincoln Green proposal had racially discriminatory effects and could be tolerated only if it served compelling interests. Neither the buffer policy nor the desire to protect property values met this exacting standard. The court therefore concluded that the denial violated the Equal Protection Clause of the Fourteenth Amendment.

II

At the outset, petitioners challenge the respondents' standing to bring the suit. It is not clear that this challenge was pressed in the Court of Appeals, but since our jurisdiction to decide the case is implicated * * * (plurality opinion), we shall consider it.

In Warth v. Seldin, 422 U.S. 490, 95 S.Ct. 2197, 45 L.Ed.2d 343 (1975), a case similar in some respects to this one, we reviewed the constitutional limitations and prudential considerations that guide a court in determining a party's standing, and we need not repeat that discussion here. The essence of the standing question, in its constitutional dimension, "is whether the plaintiff has 'alleged such a personal stake in the outcome of the controversy' [as] to warrant *his* invocation of federal-court jurisdiction and to justify exercise of the court's remedial powers on his behalf." Id., at 498–499, 95 S.Ct. at 2205, quoting Baker v. Carr, 369 U.S. 186, 204, 82 S.Ct. 691, 703, 7 L.Ed.2d 663 (1962). The plaintiff must show that he himself is injured by the challenged action of the defendant. The injury may be indirect, see United States v. SCRAP, 412 U.S. 669, 688, 93 S.Ct. 2405, 2416, 37 L.Ed.2d 254 (1973), but the complaint must indicate that the injury is indeed fairly traceable to the defendant's acts or omissions. * * *

A

Here there can be little doubt that MHDC meets the constitutional standing requirements. The challenged action of the petitioners stands as an absolute barrier to constructing the housing MHDC had contract-

---

67. This language apparently derived from our decision in Reitman v. Mulkey, 387 U.S. 369, 373, 87 S.Ct. 1627, 1629, 18 L.Ed.2d 830 (1967) (quoting from the opinion of the California Supreme Court in the case then under review).

ed to place on the Viatorian site. If MHDC secures the injunctive relief it seeks, that barrier will be removed. An injunction would not, of course, guarantee that Lincoln Green will be built. MHDC would still have to secure financing, qualify for federal subsidies,[68] and carry through with construction. But all housing developments are subject to some extent to similar uncertainties. When a project is as detailed and specific as Lincoln Green, a court is not required to engage in undue speculation as a predicate for finding that the plaintiff has the requisite personal stake in the controversy. MHDC has shown an injury to itself that is "likely to be redressed by a favorable decision." Simon v. Eastern Kentucky Welfare Rights Org., 426 U.S., at 38, 96 S.Ct., at 1924.

Petitioners suggest that the suspension of the § 236 housing assistance program makes it impossible for MHDC to carry out its proposed project and therefore deprives MHDC of standing. The District Court also expressed doubts about MHDC's position in the case in light of the suspension. 373 F.Supp., at 211. Whether termination of all available assistance programs would preclude standing is not a matter we need to decide, in view of the current likelihood that subsidies may be secured under § 8 of the Housing and Community Development Act of 1974. See n. 2, supra.

Petitioners nonetheless appear to argue that MHDC lacks standing because it has suffered no economic injury. MHDC, they point out, is not the owner of the property in question. Its contract of purchase is contingent upon securing rezoning.[69] MHDC owes the owners nothing if rezoning is denied.

We cannot accept petitioners' argument. In the first place, it is inaccurate to say that MHDC suffers no economic injury from a refusal to rezone, despite the contingency provisions in its contract. MHDC has expended thousands of dollars on the plans for Lincoln Green and on the studies submitted to the Village in support of the petition for rezoning. Unless rezoning is granted many of these plans and studies will be worthless even if MHDC finds another site at an equally attractive price.

---

68. Petitioners suggest that the suspension of the § 236 housing assistance program makes it impossible for MHDC to carry out its proposed project and therefore deprives MHDC of standing. The District Court also expressed doubts about MHDC's position in the case in light of the suspension. 373 F.Supp., at 211. Whether termination of all available assistance programs would preclude standing is not a matter we need to decide, in view of the current likelihood that subsidies may be secured under § 8 of the Housing and Community Development Act of 1974. See n. 2, supra.

69. Petitioners contend that MHDC lacks standing to pursue its claim here because a contract purchaser whose contract is contingent upon rezoning cannot contest a zoning decision in the Illinois courts. Under the law of Illinois, only the owner of the property has standing to pursue such an action. Clark Oil & Refining Corp. v. City of Evanston, 23 Ill.2d 48, 177 N.E.2d 191 (1961); but see Solomon v. City of Evanston, 29 Ill.App.3d 782, 331 N.E.2d 380 (1975).

State law of standing, however, does not govern such determinations in the federal courts. The constitutional and prudential considerations canvassed at length in Warth v. Seldin, 422 U.S. 490, 95 S.Ct. 2197, 45 L.Ed.2d 343 (1975), respond to concerns that are peculiarly federal in nature. Illinois may choose to close its courts to applicants for rezoning unless they have an interest more direct than MHDC's, but this choice does not necessarily disqualify MHDC from seeking relief in federal courts for an asserted injury to its federal rights.

Petitioners' argument also misconceives our standing requirements. It has long been clear that economic injury is not the only kind of injury that can support a plaintiff's standing. * * * MHDC is a nonprofit corporation. Its interest in building Lincoln Green stems not from a desire for economic gain, but rather from an interest in making suitable low-cost housing available in areas where such housing is scarce. This is not mere abstract concern about a problem of general interest. * * * The specific project MHDC intends to build, whether or not it will generate profits, provides that "essential dimension of specificity" that informs judicial decision-making. * * *

Clearly MHDC has met the constitutional requirements and it therefore has standing to assert its own rights. Foremost among them is MHDC's right to be free of arbitrary or irrational zoning actions. See Euclid v. Ambler Realty Co., 272 U.S. 365, 47 S.Ct. 114, 71 L.Ed. 303 (1926); Nectow v. Cambridge, 277 U.S. 183, 48 S.Ct. 447, 72 L.Ed. 842 (1928); Village of Belle Terre v. Boraas, 416 U.S. 1, 94 S.Ct. 1536, 39 L.Ed.2d 797 (1974). But the heart of this litigation has never been the claim that the Village's decision fails the generous *Euclid* test, recently reaffirmed in *Belle Terre*. Instead it has been the claim that the Village's refusal to rezone discriminates against racial minorities in violation of the Fourteenth Amendment. As a corporation, MHDC has no racial identity and cannot be the direct target of the petitioners' alleged discrimination. In the ordinary case, a party is denied standing to assert the rights of third persons. Warth v. Seldin, 422 U.S., at 499, 95 S.Ct., at 2205. But we need not decide whether the circumstances of this case would justify departure from that prudential limitation and permit MHDC to assert the constitutional rights of its prospective minority tenants. * * * For we have at least one individual plaintiff who has demonstrated standing to assert these rights as his own.[70]

Respondent Ransom, a Negro, works at the Honeywell factory in Arlington Heights and lives approximately 20 miles away in Evanston in a 5-room house with his mother and his son. The complaint alleged that he seeks and would qualify for the housing MHDC wants to build in Arlington Heights. Ransom testified at trial that if Lincoln Green were built he would probably move there, since it is closer to his job.

The injury Ransom asserts is that his quest for housing nearer his employment has been thwarted by official action that is racially discriminatory. If a court grants the relief he seeks, there is at least a "substantial probability," Warth v. Seldin, 422 U.S., at 504, 95 S.Ct., at 2208, that the Lincoln Green project will materialize, affording Ransom the housing opportunity he desires in Arlington Heights. His is not a generalized grievance. Instead, as we suggested in *Warth*, id., at 507, 508, n. 18, 95 S.Ct., at 2210, it focuses on a particular project and is not dependent on speculation about the possible actions of third parties not before the court. * * * Unlike the individual plaintiffs in *Warth*, Ransom has adequately averred an "actionable causal relationship" between Arlington Heights' zoning practices and his asserted injury.

---

70. Because of the presence of this plaintiff, we need not consider whether the other individual and corporate plaintiffs have standing to maintain the suit.

Warth v. Seldin, 422 U.S., at 507, 95 S.Ct., at 2209. We therefore proceed to the merits.

III

Our decision last Term in Washington v. Davis, 426 U.S. 229, 96 S.Ct. 2040, 48 L.Ed.2d 597 (1976), made it clear that official action will not be held unconstitutional solely because it results in a racially disproportionate impact. "Disproportionate impact is not irrelevant, but it is not the sole touchstone of an invidious racial discrimination." Id., at 242, 96 S.Ct., at 2049. Proof of racially discriminatory intent or purpose is required to show a violation of the Equal Protection Clause. Although some contrary indications may be drawn from some of our cases,[71] the holding in *Davis* reaffirmed a principle well established in a variety of contexts. * * *

Davis does not require a plaintiff to prove that the challenged action rested solely on racially discriminatory purposes. Rarely can it be said that a legislature or administrative body operating under a broad mandate made a decision motivated solely by a single concern, or even that a particular purpose was the "dominant" or "primary" one.[72] In fact, it is because legislators and administrators are properly concerned with balancing numerous competing considerations that courts refrain from reviewing the merits of their decisions, absent a showing of arbitrariness or irrationality. But racial discrimination is not just another competing consideration. Where there is a proof that a discriminatory purpose has been a motivating factor in the decision, this judicial deference is no longer justified.[73]

Determining whether invidious discriminatory purpose was a motivating factor demands a sensitive inquiry into such circumstantial and direct evidence of intent as may be available. The impact of the official action—whether it "bears more heavily on one race than another." Washington v. Davis, 426 U.S., at 242, 96 S.Ct., at 2049—may provide an important starting point. Sometimes a clear pattern, unexplainable on grounds other than race, emerges from the effect of the state action even when the governing legislation appears neutral on its face. Yick Wo v. Hopkins, 118 U.S. 356, 6 S.Ct. 1064, 30 L.Ed. 220 (1886); Guinn v. United States, 238 U.S. 347, 35 S.Ct. 926, 59 L.Ed. 1340 (1915); Lane v. Wilson, 307 U.S. 268, 59 S.Ct. 872, 83 L.Ed. 1281 (1939); Gomillion v. Lightfoot, 364 U.S. 339, 81 S.Ct. 125, 5 L.Ed.2d 110 (1960). The evidentiary inquiry is then relatively easy.[74] But such cases are rare. Absent

71. [This footnote is omitted.]

72. In McGinnis v. Royster, 410 U.S. 263, 276–277, 93 S.Ct. 1055, 1063, 35 L.Ed. 2d 282 (1973), in a somewhat different context, we observed:

"The search for legislative purpose is often elusive enough, Palmer v. Thompson, 403 U.S. 217, 91 S.Ct. 1940, 29 L.Ed.2d 438 (1971), without a requirement that primacy be ascertained. Legislation is frequently multipurposed: the removal of even a 'subordinate' purpose may shift altogether the

consensus of legislative judgment supporting the statute."

73. For a scholarly discussion of legislative motivation, see Brest, Palmer v. Thompson: An Approach to the Problem of Unconstitutional Legislative Motive, 1971, Sup.Ct.Rev. 95, 116–118.

74. Several of our jury selection cases fall into this category. Because of the nature of the jury selection task, however, we have permitted a finding of constitutional violation even when the statistical

a pattern as stark as that in *Gomillion* or *Yick Wo*, impact alone is not determinative,[75] and the Court must look to other evidence. [76]

The historical background of the decision is one evidentiary source, particularly if it reveals a series of official actions taken for invidious purposes. * * * The specific sequence of events leading up the challenged decision also may shed some light on the decisionmaker's purposes. * * * For example, if the property involved here always had been zoned R–5 but suddenly was changed to R–3 when the town learned of MHDC's plans to erect integrated housing,[77] we would have a far different case. Departures from the normal procedural sequence also might afford evidence that improper purposes are playing a role. Substantive departures too may be relevant, particularly if the factors usually considered important by the decisionmaker strongly favor a decision contrary to the one reached.[78]

The legislative or administrative history may be highly relevant, especially where there are contemporary statements by members of the decisionmaking body, minutes of its meetings, or reports. In some extraordinary instances the members might be called to the stand at trial to testify concerning the purpose of the official action, although even then such testimony frequently will be barred by privilege. See Tenney v. Brandhove, 341 U.S. 367, 71 S.Ct. 783, 95 L.Ed. 1019 (1951); United States v. Nixon, 418 U.S. 683, 705, 94 S.Ct. 3090, 3106, 41 L.Ed.2d 1039 (1974); 8 Wigmore, Evidence § 2371 (McNaughton rev.ed.1961).[79]

---

pattern does not approach the extremes of *Yick Wo* or *Gomillion.* See, e.g., Turner v. Fouche, 396 U.S. 346, 359, 90 S.Ct. 532, 539, 24 L.Ed.2d 567 (1970); Sims v. Georgia, 389 U.S. 404, 407, 88 S.Ct. 523, 525, 19 L.Ed.2d 634 (1967).

75. This is not to say that a consistent pattern of official racial discrimination is a necessary predicate to a violation of the equal protection clause. A single invidiously discriminatory governmental act—in the exercise of the zoning power as elsewhere—would not necessarily be immunized by the absence of such discrimination in the making of other comparable decisions. See City of Richmond v. United States, 422 U.S. 358, 378, 95 S.Ct. 2296, 2307, 45 L.Ed.2d 245 (1975).

76. In many instances, to recognize the limited probative value of disproportionate impact is merely to acknowledge the "heterogeneity" of the nation's population. Jefferson v. Hackney, 406 U.S. 535, 548, 92 S.Ct. 1724, 1732, 32 L.Ed.2d 285 (1972); see also Washington v. Davis, 426 U.S., at 248, 96 S.Ct., at 2051.

77. See, e.g., Progress Development Corp. v. Mitchell, 286 F.2d 222 (C.A.7 1961) (park board allegedly condemned plaintiffs' land for a park upon learning that the homes plaintiffs were erecting there would be sold under a marketing plan designed to assure integration); Kennedy Park Homes Association, Inc. v. City of

Lackawanna, 436 F.2d 108 (C.A.2 1970), cert. denied, 401 U.S. 1010, 91 S.Ct. 1256, 28 L.Ed.2d 546 (1971) (town declared moratorium on new subdivisions and rezoned area for park land shortly after learning of plaintiffs' plans to build low income housing). To the extent that the decision in *Kennedy Park Homes* rested solely on a finding of discriminatory impact, we have indicated our disagreement. Washington v. Davis, 426 U.S., at 244–245, 96 S.Ct., at 2050.

78. See Dailey v. City of Lawton, 425 F.2d 1037 (C.A.10 1970). The plaintiffs in *Dailey* planned to build low income housing on the site of a former school that they had purchased. The city refused to rezone the land from PF, its public facilities classification, to R–4, high-density residential. All the surrounding area was zoned R–4, and both the present and the former planning director for the city testified that there was no reason "from a zoning standpoint" why the land should not be classified R–4. Based on this and other evidence, the Court of Appeals ruled that "the record sustains the [District Court's] holding of racial motivation and of arbitrary and unreasonable action." Id., at 1040.

79. This Court has recognized, ever since Fletcher v. Peck, 6 Cranch 87, 130–131, 3 L.Ed. 162 (1810), that judicial inquiries into legislative or executive motivation represent a substantial intrusion into

The foregoing summary identifies, without purporting to be exhaustive, subjects of proper inquiry in determining whether racially discriminatory intent existed. With these in mind, we now address the case before us.

IV

This case was tried in the District Court and reviewed in the Court of Appeals before our decision in Washington v. Davis, supra. The respondents proceeded on the erroneous theory that the Village's refusal to rezone carried a racially discriminatory effect and was, without more, unconstitutional. But both courts below understood that at least part of their function was to examine the purpose underlying the decision. In making its findings on this issue, the District Court noted that some of the opponents of Lincoln Green who spoke at the various hearings might have been motivated by opposition to minority groups. The court held, however, that the evidence "does not warrant the conclusion that this motivated the defendants." 373 F.Supp., at 211.

On appeal the Court of Appeals focused primarily on respondents' claim that the Village's buffer policy had not been consistently applied and was being invoked with a strictness here that could only demonstrate some other underlying motive. The court concluded that the buffer policy, though not always applied with perfect consistency, had on several occasions formed the basis for the Board's decision to deny other rezoning proposals. "The evidence does not necessitate a finding that Arlington Heights administered this policy in a discriminatory manner." 517 F.2d, at 412. The Court of Appeals therefore approved the District Court's findings concerning the Village's purposes in denying rezoning to MHDC.

We also have reviewed the evidence. The impact of the Village's decision does arguably bear more heavily on racial minorities. Minorities comprise 18% of the Chicago area population, and 40% of the income groups said to be eligible for Lincoln Green. But there is little about the sequence of events leading up to the decision that would spark suspicion. The area around the Viatorian property has been zoned R–3 since 1959, the year when Arlington Heights first adopted a zoning map. Single-family homes surround the 80-acre site, and the Village is undeniably committed to single-family homes as its dominant residential land use. The rezoning request progressed according to the usual procedures.[80] The Plan Commission even scheduled two addition-

the workings of other branches of government. Placing a decisionmaker on the stand is therefore "usually to be avoided." Citizens to Preserve Overton Park v. Volpe, 401 U.S. 402, 420, 91 S.Ct. 814, 825, 28 L.Ed.2d 136 (1971). The problems involved have prompted a good deal of scholarly commentary. See Tussman & tenBroek, The Equal Protection of the Laws, 37 Calif.L.Rev. 341, 356–361 (1949); A. Bickel, The Least Dangerous Branch, 208–221 (1962); Ely, Legislative and Administrative Motivation in Constitutional

Law, 79 Yale L.J. 1205 (1970); Brest, supra, n. 8.

80. Respondents have made much of one apparent procedural departure. The parties stipulated that the Village Planner, the staff member whose primary responsibility covered zoning and planning matters, was never asked for his written or oral opinion of the rezoning request. The omission does seem curious, but respondents failed to prove at trial what role the Planner customarily played in rezoning de-

al hearings, at least in part to accommodate MHDC and permit it to supplement its presentation with answers to questions generated at the first hearing.

The statements by the Plan Commission and Village Board members, as reflected in the official minutes, focused almost exclusively on the zoning aspects of the MHDC petition, and the zoning factors on which they relied are not novel criteria in the Village's rezoning decisions. There is no reason to doubt that there has been reliance by some neighboring property owners on the maintenance of single-family zoning in the vicinity. The Village originally adopted its buffer policy long before MHDC entered the picture and has applied the policy too consistently for us to infer discriminatory purpose from its application in this case. Finally, MHDC called one member of the Village Board to the stand at trial. Nothing in her testimony supports an inference of invidious purpose.[81]

In sum, the evidence does not warrant overturning the concurrent findings of both courts below. Respondents simply failed to carry their burden of proving that discriminatory purpose was a motivating factor in the Village's decision.[82] This conclusion ends the constitutional inquiry. The Court of Appeals' further finding that the Village's decision carried a discriminatory "ultimate effect" is without independent constitutional significance.

V

Respondents' complaint also alleged that the refusal to rezone violated the Fair Housing Act, 42 U.S.C.A. § 3601 et seq. They continue to urge here that a zoning decision made by a public body may, and that petitioners' action did, violate § 3604 or § 3617. The Court of Appeals, however, proceeding in a somewhat unorthodox fashion, did not decide the statutory question. We remand the case for further consideration of respondents' statutory claims.

Reversed and remanded.

cisions, or whether his opinion would be relevant to respondents' claims.

81. Respondents complain that the District Court unduly limited their efforts to prove that the Village Board acted for discriminatory purposes, since it forbade questioning Board members about their motivation at the time they cast their votes. We perceive no abuse of discretion in the circumstances of this case, even if such an inquiry into motivation would otherwise have been proper. See n. 18, supra. Respondents were allowed, both during the discovery phase and at trial, to question Board members fully about materials and information available to them at the time of decision. In light of respondents' repeated insistence that it was effect and not motivation which would make out a constitutional violation, the District Court's action was not improper.

82. Proof that the decision by the Village was motivated in part by a racially discriminatory purpose would not necessarily have required invalidation of the challenged decision. Such proof would, however, have shifted to the Village the burden of establishing that the same decision would have resulted even had the impermissible purpose not been considered. If this were established, the complaining party in a case of this kind no longer fairly could attribute the injury complained of to improper consideration of a discriminatory purpose. In such circumstances, there would be no justification for judicial interference with the challenged decision. But in this case respondents failed to make the required threshold showing. See Mt. Healthy City School Dist. Bd. of Education v. Doyle, 429 U.S. 274, 97 S.Ct. 568, 50 L.Ed.2d 471.

[Justice Stevens took no part in the decision. An opinion by Justice Marshall, concurred in by Justice Brennan, concurring in part and dissenting in part, is omitted. A dissenting opinion by Justice White is also omitted.]

METROPOLITAN HOUSING DEVELOPMENT CORP. v. VILLAGE OF ARLINGTON HEIGHTS

United States Court of Appeals, 7th Circuit, 1977.
558 F.2d 1283, cert. denied 434 U.S. 1025, 98 S.Ct. 752, 54 L.Ed.2d 772 (1978).

Before FAIRCHILD, Chief Judge, and SWYGERT and SPRECHER, Circuit Judges.

SWYGERT, Circuit Judge.

In this case plaintiffs seek to compel defendant, the Village of Arlington Heights, Illinois ("the Village"), to rezone plaintiffs' property to permit the construction of federally financed low-cost housing. Plaintiffs contend that defendant's refusal to rezone the property was racially discriminatory. The Supreme Court has determined that defendant's action did not violate the Equal Protection Clause. The remaining issue is whether the refusal to rezone was illegal under the Fair Housing Act, 42 U.S.C.A. §§ 3601 et seq. We hold that under the circumstances of this case defendant has a statutory obligation to refrain from zoning policies that effectively foreclose the construction of any low-cost housing within its corporate boundaries, and remand the case to the district court for a determination of whether defendant has done so.

* * *

II

The Fair Housing Act, 42 U.S.C.A. §§ 3601 et seq., was enacted as Title VIII of the Civil Rights Act of 1968. Plaintiffs contend that the Village's refusal to rezone violated two of the Act's provisions. The first is 42 U.S.C.A. § 3604(a), which provides in part that "it shall be unlawful * * * [t]o make unavailable or deny * * * a dwelling to any person because of race, color, religion, or national origin." The second is 42 U.S.C.A. § 3617, which states:

It shall be unlawful to coerce, intimidate, threaten, or interfere with any person in the exercise or enjoyment of, or on account of his having exercised or enjoyed, or on account of his having aided or encouraged any other person in the exercise or enjoyment of, any right granted or protected by section 3603, 3604, 3605, or 3606 of this title. This section may be enforced by appropriate civil action.

* * *

III

In determining whether the Village's failure to rezone violated the Fair Housing Act, it is important to note that the Supreme Court's decision does not require us to change our previous conclusion that the Village's action had a racially discriminatory effect. What the Court held is that under the Equal Protection Clause that conclusion is irrelevant.

We reaffirm our earlier holding that the Village's refusal to rezone had a discriminatory effect. The construction of Lincoln Green would create a substantial number of federally subsidized low-cost housing units which are not presently available in Arlington Heights. Because a greater number of black people than white people in the Chicago metropolitan area satisfy the income requirements for federally subsidized housing, the Village's refusal to permit MHDC to construct the project had a greater impact on black people than on white people. Moreover, Arlington Heights remains almost totally white in a metropolitan area with a significant percentage of black people. Since Lincoln Green would have to be racially integrated in order to qualify for federal subsidization, the Village's action in preventing the project from being built had the effect of perpetuating segregation in Arlington Heights.

The basic question we must answer is whether the Village's action violated sections 3604(a) or 3617 because it had discriminatory effects when that action was taken without discriminatory intent. Since the violation of section 3617 alleged in this case depends upon a finding that the Village interfered with rights granted or protected by section 3604(a),[83] we can confine our inquiry to whether the refusal to rezone made unavailable or denied a dwelling to any person because of race within the meaning of section 3604(a). In resolving this issue we must addresss ourselves to two preliminary subissues: first, whether a finding that an action has a discriminatory effect, without a concomitant finding that the action was taken with discriminatory intent, is ever enough to support the conclusion that the action violated section 3604(a); and, if so, under what factual circumstances will it be enough?

A

The major obstacle to concluding that action taken without discriminatory intent can violate section 3604(a) is the phrase "because of race" contained in the statutory provision. The narrow view of the phrase is that a party cannot commit an act "because of race" unless he intends to discriminate between races. By hypothesis, this approach would excuse the Village from liability because it acted without discriminatory intent. The broad view is that a party commits an act "because of race" whenever the natural and foreseeable consequence of that act is to discriminate between races, regardless of his intent. Under this statistical, effect-oriented view of causality, the Village could be liable

83. One court has held that a violation of section 3617 can be established without first establishing a violation of sections 3603, 3604, 3605, or 3606 because to interpret section 3617 otherwise would make it superfluous. Laufman v. Oakley Bldg. & Loan Co., 408 F.Supp. 489, 497–98 (S.D. Ohio 1976). We decline to decide whether section 3617 can ever be violated by conduct that does not violate any of the four earlier sections. We do hold, however, that under the circumstances of this case, where the conduct that allegedly violated section 3617 is the same conduct that allegedly violated section 3604(a) and was engaged in by the same party, the validity of the section 3617 claim depends upon whether the failure to rezone violated section 3604(a). [Some of the court's footnotes have been omitted; those reprinted have all been renumbered. Eds.]

since the natural and foreseeable consequence of this failure to rezone was to adversely affect black people seeking low-cost housing and to perpetuate segregation in Arlington Heights.

The Supreme Court adopted the narrow view for equal protection purposes in Washington v. Davis, and defendant argues that that decision should bind us in this case as well. However, *Washington* undercuts more than it supports defendant's position. In that case, the Court created a dichotomy between the Equal Protection Clause and Title VII of the Civil Rights Act of 1964, 42 U.S.C.A. §§ 2000e et seq. Although the Court announced its new intent requirement for equal protection cases, it reaffirmed the viability of Griggs v. Duke Power Co., 401 U.S. 424, 91 S.Ct. 849, 28 L.Ed.2d 158 (1971), in which it had previously held that an employment practice that produced a racially discriminatory effect was invalid under Title VII unless it was shown to be job-related. 426 U.S. at 238–39, 246–48, 96 S.Ct. 2040. Thus, a prima facie case of employment discrimination can still be established under Title VII by statistical evidence of discriminatory impact, without a showing of discriminatory intent. United States v. City of Chicago, 549 F.2d 415, 435 (7th Cir.1977).

Defendant asserts that Title VII is distinguishable from the Fair Housing Act because Congress in Title VII mandated a more probing standard of review than it did under the Fair Housing Act. An examination of the two statutes, however, does not indicate Congress intended that proof of discriminatory intent was unnecessary under one but necessary under the other. Section 703(h) of Title VII, codified at 42 U.S.C.A. § 2000e–2(h), states in relevant part:

> [N]or shall it be an unlawful practice for an employer to give and to act upon the results of any professionally developed ability test provided that such test, its administration or action upon the results is not designed, intended or used to discriminate because of race, color, religion, sex or national origin.

The Supreme Court in *Griggs* held that this provision did not sanction all employment tests administered without discriminatory intent, in spite of the "because of race" language that it contains. Rather, the Court looked to the general congressional purpose in enacting Title VII—which was to achieve equality of employment opportunities—and interpreted section 703(h) in a broad fashion in order to effectuate that purpose.[84] 401 U.S. at 429–36, 91 S.Ct. 849.

The purpose of Congress in enacting the Fair Housing Act was "to provide, within constitutional limitations, for fair housing throughout

84. The Court did not directly construe the "because of race" language in section 703(h). Instead, it held that "any professionally developed ability test" only included tests that were job-related. 401 U.S. at 436, 91 S.Ct. 849, 854. By reading the statutory language in this manner the Court rendered the second half of the provision superfluous since a job-related test would never be "designed, intended or used to discriminate because of race."

The important point to be derived from *Griggs* is that the Court did not find the "because of race" language to be an obstacle to its ultimate holding that intent was not required under Title VII. It looked to the broad purposes underlying the Act rather than attempting to discern the meaning of this provision from its plain language.

the United States." 42 U.S.C.A. § 3601. The Second Circuit has observed that the Act was intended to promote "open, integrated residential housing patterns and to prevent the increase of segregation, in ghettos, of racial groups whose lack of opportunities the Act was designed to combat." Otero v. New York City Housing Authority, 484 F.2d 1122, 1134 (2d Cir.1973). Other courts have responded to the congressional statement of policy by holding that the Act must be interpreted broadly. See, e.g., Trafficante v. Metropolitan Life Ins. Co., 409 U.S. 205, 93 S.Ct. 364, 34 L.Ed.2d 415 (1972); Mayers v. Ridley, 151 U.S. App.D.C. 45, 465 F.2d 630, 632–35 (en banc) (Wright, J., concurring); Laufman v. Oakley Bldg. & Loan Co., 408 F.Supp. 489 (S.D.Ohio 1976); United States v. City of Parma, [1973] Equal Opportunity in Housing Rptr. (Prentice-Hall) ¶ 13,616 (N.D.Ohio 1973). See also Linmark Associates, Inc. v. Township of Willingboro, 431 U.S. 85, 93–94, 97 S.Ct. 1614, 1619, 52 L.Ed.2d 155 (1977) (recognizing that "Congress has made a strong national commitment to promoting integrated housing"); Griffin v. Breckinridge, 403 U.S. 88, 97, 91 S.Ct. 1790, 29 L.Ed.2d 338 (1971) (Supreme Court has interpreted civil rights statutes broadly).

In light of the declaration of congressional intent provided by section 3601 and the need to construe the Act expansively in order to implement that goal, we decline to take a narrow view of the phrase "because of race" contained in section 3604(a). Conduct that has the necessary and foreseeable consequence of perpetuating segregation can be as deleterious as purposefully discriminatory conduct in frustrating the national commitment "to replace the ghettos 'by truly integrated and balanced living patterns.'" Trafficante, 409 U.S. at 211, 93 S.Ct. at 368, citing 114 Cong.Rec. 3422 (remarks of Sen. Mondale). Moreover, a requirement that the plaintiff prove discriminatory intent before relief can be granted under the statute is often a burden that is impossible to satisfy. "[I]ntent, motive and purpose are elusive subjective concepts," Hawkins v. Town of Shaw, 461 F.2d 1171, 1172 (5th Cir.1972) (en banc) (per curiam), and attempts to discern the intent of an entity such as a municipality are at best problematic. See Hart v. Community School Board of Education, 512 F.2d 37, 50 (2d Cir.1975); Note, Reading the Mind of the School Board: Segregative Intent and the De Facto/De Jure Distinction, 86 Yale L.J. 317, 322–26 (1976). A strict focus on intent permits racial discrimination to go unpunished in the absence of evidence of overt bigotry. As overtly bigoted behavior has become more unfashionable, evidence of intent has become harder to find. But this does not mean that racial discrimination has disappeared. We cannot agree that Congress in enacting the Fair Housing Act intended to permit municipalities to systematically deprive minorities of housing opportunities simply because those municipalities act discreetly. See Brest, The Supreme Court, 1975 Term—Foreword: In Defense of the Antidiscrimination Principle, 90 Harv.L.Rev. 1, 28–29 (1976).

We therefore hold that at least under some circumstances a violation of section 3604(a) can be established by a showing of discriminatory effect without a showing of discriminatory intent. A number of courts have agreed. Smith v. Anchor Bldg. Corp., 536 F.2d 231 (8th Cir.1976);

United States v. City of Black Jack, 508 F.2d 1179, 1183 (8th Cir.1974), cert. denied, 422 U.S. 1042, 95 S.Ct. 2656, 45 L.Ed.2d 694 (1975); Kennedy Park Homes Assoc., Inc. v. City of Lackawanna, 436 F.2d 108, 114 (2d Cir.1970) (dictum), cert. denied, 401 U.S. 1010, 91 S.Ct. 1256, 28 L.Ed.2d 546 (1971); Resident Advisory Board v. Rizzo, 425 F.Supp. 987, 1021–24 (E.D.Pa.1976).

B

Plaintiffs contend that once a racially discriminatory effect is shown a violation of section 3604(a) is necessarily established. We decline to extend the reach of the Fair Housing Act this far. Although we agree that a showing of discriminatory intent is not required under section 3604(a), we refuse to conclude that every action which produces discriminatory effects is illegal. Such a per se rule would go beyond the intent of Congress and would lead courts into untenable results in specific cases. See Brest, Foreword, 90 Harv.L.Rev. at 29. Rather, the courts must use their discretion in deciding whether, given the particular circumstances of each case, relief should be granted under the statute.

We turn now to determining under what circumstances conduct that produces a discriminatory impact but which was taken without discriminatory intent will violate section 3604(a). Four critical factors are discernible from previous cases. They are: (1) how strong is the plaintiff's showing of discriminatory effect; (2) is there some evidence of discriminatory intent, though not enough to satisfy the constitutional standard of Washington v. Davis; (3) what is the defendant's interest in taking the action complained of; and (4) does the plaintiff seek to compel the defendant to affirmatively provide housing for members of minority groups or merely to restrain the defendant from interfering with individual property owners who wish to provide such housing? We shall examine each of these factors separately.

1. There are two kinds of racially discriminatory effects which a facially neutral decision about housing can produce. The first occurs when that decision has a greater adverse impact on one racial group than on another. The second is the effect which the decision has on the community involved; if it perpetuates segregation and thereby prevents interracial association it will be considered invidious under the Fair Housing Act independently of the extent to which it produces a disparate effect on different racial groups. See *Trafficante*, 409 U.S. at 209–10, 93 S.Ct. 364.

In this case the discriminatory effect in the first sense was relatively weak. It is true that the Village's refusal to rezone had an adverse impact on a significantly greater percentage of the nonwhite people in the Chicago area than of the white people in that area. But it is also true that the class disadvantaged by the Village's action was not predominantly nonwhite, because sixty percent of the people in the Chicago area eligible for federal housing subsidization in 1970 were white. The argument for *racial* discrimination is therefore not as strong as it would be if all or most of the group adversely affected was nonwhite. Compare Resident Advisory Board v. Rizzo, 425 F.Supp. 987, 1018 (E.D.

Pa.1976), in which plaintiffs sought to compel the construction of public housing in a predominantly white neighborhood of Philadelphia. Since ninety-five percent of the individuals on the waiting list for public housing in Philadelphia were members of minority groups, the failure to build public housing had a much greater adverse effect on nonwhite prople than on white people.

The fact that the conduct complained of adversely affected white as well as nonwhite people, however, is not by itself an obstacle to relief under the Fair Housing Act. See United States v. City of Black Jack, 508 F.2d 1179 (8th Cir.1974), cert. denied, 422 U.S. 1042, 95 S.Ct. 2656, 45 L.Ed.2d 694 (1975); Kennedy Park Homes Assoc., Inc. v. City of Lackawanna, 436 F.2d 108 (2d Cir.1970), cert. denied, 401 U.S. 1010, 91 S.Ct. 1256, 28 L.Ed.2d 546 (1971). In both of these cases, local zoning ordinances prevented the construction of low-income housing projects which would not have been limited to nonwhite people. Both courts nonetheless found a racially discriminatory effect.

What was present in *Black Jack* and *Kennedy Park* was a strong argument supporting racially discriminatory impact in the second sense. In each case the municipality or section of the municipality in which the preposed project was to be built was overwhelmingly white.[85] Moreover, in each case construction of low-cost housing was effectively precluded throughout the municipality or section of the municipality which was rigidly segregated.[86] Thus, the effect of the municipal action in both cases was to foreclose the possibility of ending racial segregation in housing within those municipalities.

It is unclear in this case whether the Village's refusal to rezone would necessarily perpetuate segregated housing in Arlington Heights. The Village remains overwhelmingly white at the present time,[87] and the construction of Lincoln Green would be a significant step toward integrating the community. The Village asserts, however, that there is a substantial amount of land within its corporate limits which is properly zoned for multiple family dwellings and on which it would have no objection to the construction of a low-cost housing project. Plaintiffs reply that all other sites within the Village limits are unsuitable under

---

85. The area of St. Louis County which included the City of Black Jack was approximately ninety-nine percent white. 508 F.2d at 1183.

The City of Lackawanna has three wards. 98.9 percent of Lackawanna's nonwhite citizens lived in the First Ward, and they constituted 35.4 percent of that ward's population. The Third Ward, where the proposed project was to be built, had 12,229 residents, of whom twenty-nine were black. 436 F.2d at 110, 318 F.Supp. at 674.

86. In *Black Jack*, the city had enacted a zoning ordinance prohibiting the construction of new multiple family dwellings. 508 F.2d at 1183. In *Kennedy Park*, the city imposed a moratorium on the construction of new subdivisions, a category into which the proposed project fell. 436 F.2d at 111.

87. Defendant asserts that the minority population of Arlington Heights has grown substantially since 1970. It contends that a special census in 1976 showed a black population of 200 and a total nonwhite population of 848. Defendant does not inform us what the total population of the Village now is, but even assuming that it has remained the same since 1970 and that defendant's statements about the 1976 census are accurate, Arlington Heights would be approximately ninety-nine percent white. We find these numbers to be evidence of "overwhelming" racial segregation.

federal guidelines governing subsidized housing. The district court never resolved this issue.

2. The second factor which appears to have been important in previous Fair Housing Act cases which focused on the discriminatory effect of the defendant's conduct was the presence of some evidence of discriminatory intent. In three cases this evidence was insufficient to independently support the relief which the plaintiff sought. See Smith v. Anchor Bldg. Corp., 536 F.2d 231 (8th Cir.1976); *Black Jack*, 508 F.2d at 1185 n. 3; Resident Advisory Board v. Rizzo, 425 F.Supp. at 1021–25 (E.D.Pa.1976).[88] In another case the court found the defendant liable on both a discriminatory intent and a discriminatory impact theory. See *Kennedy Park*, 436 F.2d at 112–14, aff'g, 318 F.Supp. at 694–95.

These courts did not address the role that evidence of intent ought to play in determining whether liability should be imposed because of discriminatory impact. But it is evident that the equitable argument for relief is stronger when there is some direct evidence that the defendant purposefully discriminated against members of minority groups because that evidence supports the inference that the defendant is a wrongdoer. Thus, the absence of any such evidence in this case is a factor buttressing the Village's contention that relief should be denied.

We conclude, however, that this criterion is the least important of the four factors that we are examining. By hypothesis, we are dealing with a situation in which the evidence of intent constitutes an insufficient basis on which to ground relief. If we were to place great emphasis on partial evidence of purposeful discrimination we would be relying on an inference—that the defendant is a wrongdoer—which is at best conjectural. In addition, the problems associated with requiring conclusive proof of discriminatory intent which we earlier discussed remain troublesome in any attempt to weigh partial evidence of intent.

The difficulties which arise from taking account of partial evidence of intent can be illuminated by comparing this case to *Black Jack*. In *Black Jack* plaintiffs proposed to build a low-cost integrated housing project in an overwhelmingly white unincorporated area of St. Louis County. The residents of the area blocked the construction of the project by incorporating the area into a city and then enacting a zoning ordinance prohibiting the construction of new multiple family dwellings. The court referred to evidence that opposition to the project was expressed in racial terms by the leaders of the incorporation movement and by the zoning commissioners themselves. 508 F.2d at 1185 n. 3. Moreover, the fact that the zoning ordinance was not enacted until after plans for the project were revealed is further evidence of discriminatory intent which is absent from the case at bar.

It is undeniable that this partial evidence of discriminatory intent undermined the equitable position of the city of Black Jack. In cases such as these, which place broad national goals in conflict with heretofore established local prerogatives, courts must take account of the facts

88. In *Rizzo* some of the defendants were found liable without a finding of discriminatory intent while other defendants were held liable on both an intent and an impact theory.

particular to each case. But too much reliance on this evidence would be unfounded. The bigoted comments of a few citizens, even those with power, should not invalidate action which in fact has a legitimate basis. See Washington v. Davis, 426 U.S. at 253, 96 S.Ct. 2040 (Stevens, J., concurring). If the goal of most of the residents of Black Jack was to protect local property values rather than to exclude black people, it would be unfair to substantially distinguish between Black Jack and Arlington Heights. Nor is it clear that Black Jack acted with more discriminatory intent than Arlington Heights because Black Jack's zoning ordinance was enacted in reaction to a proposed integrated development while Arlington Heights' zoning ordinance was enacted years in advance of the plans to build Lincoln Green. If the effect of a zoning scheme is to perpetuate segregated housing,[89] neither common sense nor the rationale of the Fair Housing Act dictates that the preclusion of minorities in advance should be favored over the preclusion of minorities in reaction to a plan which would create integration.

3. The third factor which we find to be important is the interest of the defendant in taking the action which produces a discriminatory impact. If the defendant is a private individual or a group of private individuals seeking to protect private rights, the courts cannot be overly solicitous when the effect is to perpetuate segregated housing. See Smith v. Anchor Bldg. Corp., 536 F.2d 231 (8th Cir.1976). Similarly, if the defendant is a governmental body acting outside the scope of its authority or abusing its power, it is not entitled to the deference which courts must pay to legitimate governmental action. See *Kennedy Park*, 436 F.2d at 113–14. *Cf.* United Farmworkers of Florida Housing Project, Inc. v. City of Delray Beach, 493 F.2d 799, 808–09 (5th Cir.1974) (decided on equal protection grounds). On the other hand, if the defendant is a governmental body acting within the ambit of legitimately derived authority, we will less readily find that its action violates the Fair Housing Act. See Joseph Skillken & Co. v. City of Toledo, 528 F.2d 867, 876–77 (6th Cir.1975), vacated and remanded, 429 U.S. 1068, 97 S.Ct. 800, 50 L.Ed.2d 786 (1977).

In this case the Village was acting within the scope of the authority to zone granted it by Illinois law. See Ill.Rev.Stat. Ch. 24, §§ 11–13–1 et seq. Moreover, municipalities are traditionally afforded wide discretion in zoning. Village of Belle Terre v. Boraas, 416 U.S. 1, 94 S.Ct. 1536, 39 L.Ed.2d 797 (1974). Therefore, this factor weakens plaintiffs' case for relief.

4. The final criterion which will inform the exercise of our discretion is the nature of the relief which the plaintiff seeks. The courts ought to be more reluctant to grant relief when the plaintiff seeks to compel the defendant to construct integrated housing or take affirmative steps to ensure that integrated housing is built than when the plaintiff is attempting to build integrated housing on his own land and mere-

---

89. As we have already noted, it is unclear from the record whether the effect of the Village's zoning scheme, combined with its refusal to rezone the land in question, is to preclude the construction of low- cost housing in Arlington Heights and therefore to perpetuate segregated housing. There was no question about the discriminatory effect of the zoning ordinance in *Black Jack*.

ly seeks to enjoin the defendant from interfering with that construction. To require a defendant to appropriate money, utilize his land for a particular purpose, or take other affirmative steps toward integrated housing is a massive judicial intrusion on private autonomy. By contrast, the courts are far more willing to prohibit even nonintentional action by the state which interferes with an individual's plan to use his own land to provide integrated housing. See Shelley v. Kraemer, 334 U.S. 1, 68 S.Ct. 836, 92 L.Ed. 1161 (1948). The Second Circuit has explicitly relied on the distinction between requiring affirmative action on the part of the defendant and preventing the defendant from interfering with the plaintiff's attempt to build integrated housing in deciding whether to grant relief under the Fair Housing Act. Compare Citizens Committee for Faraday Wood v. Lindsay, 507 F.2d 1065, 1069 (2d Cir.1974), cert. denied, 421 U.S. 948, 95 S.Ct. 1679, 44 L.Ed.2d 102 (1975), and Acevedo v. Nassau County, 500 F.2d 1078, 1081 (2d Cir.1974), with *Kennedy Park*, supra. See also Joseph Skillken & Co. v. City of Toledo, 528 F.2d at 878.

This factor favors plaintiffs in this case. They own the land on which Lincoln Green would be built and do not seek any affirmative help from the Village in aid of the project's construction. Rather, they seek to enjoin the Village from interfering with their plans to dedicate their land to furthering the congressionally sanctioned goal of integrated housing.

C

Anaylsis of the four factors that we have enumerated reveals that this is a close case. The Village is acting pursuant to a legitimate grant of authority and there is no evidence that its refusal to rezone was the result of intentional racial discrimination. On the other hand, plaintiffs are seeking to effectuate the national goal of integrated housing withing Arlington Heights and are asking nothing more of the Village than that they be allowed to pursue that objective. Whether the Village's refusal to rezone has a strong discriminatory impact because it effectively assures that Arlington Heights will remain a segregated community is unclear from the record.

In our judgment the resolution of this case turns on clarification of the discriminatory effect of the Village's zoning decision. We hold that, if there is no land other than plaintiffs' property within Arlington Heights which is both properly zoned and suitable for federally subsidized low-cost housing, the Village's refusal to rezone constituted a violation of section 3604(a). Accordingly, we remand the case to the district court for a determination of this question subject to the guidelines which we shall lay down. Since the Village's zoning powers must give way to the Fair Housing Act,[90] the district court should grant plaintiffs the relief they request if it finds that the Act has been violated.[91]

---

90. See 72 U.S.C.A. § 3615.

91. We note that Lincoln Green would conform with the standard set by the Village's multiple family zoning classification.

We need not reach the question of whether plaintiffs would have been entitled to relief if Lincoln Green had been out of conformance with the Village's multiple family

We realize that, even assuming that plaintiffs are able to show a strong discriminatory effect, only two of the four criteria on which we have focused point toward the granting of relief. As we have already noted, however, the factor of whether there is some evidence of discriminatory intent should be partially discounted. Moreover, if we are to liberally construe the Fair Housing Act, we must decide close cases in favor of integrated housing.

IV

We shall now describe the procedure which the district court should follow on remand.

The district court must first determine whether this case is moot. The original federal subsidy for Lincoln Green was to be obtained pursuant to section 236 of the National Housing Act, 12 U.S.C.A. § 1715z–1. In 1973, however, the Government suspended new commitments for section 236 payments. Therefore, Lincoln Green can only be built if plaintiffs can obtain another subsidy.

Plaintiffs contended before the Supreme Court that alternative subsidization would be available under section 8 of the United States Housing Act of 1937, 42 U.S.C.A. § 1437f. They carry the burden of proving this assertion in the district court.

Plaintiffs must also demonstrate to the district court that Lincoln Green would be racially integrated. They had previously discharged this burden by relying on the requirement of racial integration imposed by section 236. Since section 236 is no longer applicable, plaintiffs must either show that section 8 imposes a similar requirement or otherwise satisfy the court that the tenants of the project would be substantially nonwhite.

Assuming that section 8 funds are available, the district court must then determine whether there is any land in Arlington Heights that is both zoned R–5 and suitable for federally subsidized low-cost housing. The decision as to whether a parcel of land is "suitable" will be greatly simplified by section 8 itself. Section 8(e) sets out restrictions on subsidies granted under section 8, and section 8(e)(3) states: "[t]he construction or substantial rehabilitation of dwelling units to be assisted under this section shall be eligible for financing with mortgages insured under the National Housing Act." The National Housing Act, 12 U.S.C.A. § 1713(c)(3), provides upper limits on the cost of mortgages for housing which is eligible for mortgage insurance. The district court should use these upper limits as guidelines in determining whether the cost of a parcel of land would prohibit the construction of low-cost housing.[92]

zoning classification as well as its single family zoning classification.

92. The court will still have some discretion because the statutory limits on mortgage costs cover the combined cost of land and the construction of housing while the court will only be considering the variable of land costs. However, the court should be able to obtain objective evidence of the cost of constructing a development such as Lincoln Green aside from the cost of land. By treating the cost of construction as a constant, the court will be in a position to determine whether the cost of a parcel of land, when added to that constant, exceeds the statutory limits.

The court should also take account of any other requirements imposed by federal law.

In conducting its inquiry, the district court should place on defendant the burden of identifying a parcel of land within Arlington Heights which is both properly zoned and suitable for low-cost housing under federal standards.[93] If defendant fails to satisfy this burden, the district court should conclude that the Village's refusal to rezone effectively precluded plaintiffs from constructing low-cost housing within Arlington Heights,[94] and should grant plaintiffs the relief they seek.

The cause is remanded for further proceedings consistent with this opinion. Pursuant to Circuit Rule 18, the cause should be heard on remand by a new district judge.

FAIRCHILD, Chief Judge, concurring.

With all respect, I do not subscribe to all the principles and analytical steps described in the opinion prepared for the court by Judge Swygert.

The ultimate question is whether the refusal of the zoning change made a dwelling unavailable to plaintiff Ransom (and others) because of race. If it did, the refusal was unlawful under 42 U.S.C.A. § 3604(a).

After trial, the district court found that the Village has 60 tracts zoned for R–5 use and some of it is still vacant and available to plaintiff. The proof showed nine undeveloped tracts in excess of 15 acres, zoned R–5. It was not established whether or not these were suitable for low-cost housing under federal standards. A preliminary question arises as to why plaintiffs should have a second chance at this element of the case. I am satisfied that the mandate of the Supreme Court for further consideration of plaintiffs' statutory claim is a reason for affording a second inquiry in this area. The majority's answer appears to be that the Village has the burden on this issue. It seems to be, however, that traditional principles apply and burden should be allocated to plaintiffs.

Arlington Heights is a community of substantial size (64,000 in 1970). It seems clear that housing there is presently almost totally confined to white persons. The substantial percentage of minority persons in the whole metropolitan community and the fact that minority persons are employed in Arlington Heights render it improbable that existing housing segregation there can represent free choice among persons who might reasonably consider living there. Zoning is appropriate for regulating the location of land use within a community. With exceptions,

---

93. The concurrence argues that plaintiffs ought to bear the burden on this issue. Allocating the burden in this fashion, however, would compel plaintiffs to attempt the almost impossible task of proving a negative. It is far easier for defendant to show that a single parcel of land which is suitable does exist than for plaintiffs to show that no suitable land exists.

94. Defendant asserts that it has fulfilled any obligation with respect to low and moderate-income housing because it is committed to building one hundred fifty units of such housing in the next three years. We disagree. Even assuming that defendant's assertion is accurate and that the commitment will be carried out, Arlington Heights would remain highly segregated. The Village's plan, though laudable, cannot excuse its interference with the plans of individual landowners who are trying to build integrated housing and lessen that segregation.

which are rare in this context, it is not appropriate for total exclusion. If on remand it be demonstrated that no suitable site with proper zoning is available, I can accept the conclusion that the denial of a change in zoning was, in the circumstances of this case, unlawful under 42 U.S. C.A. § 3604(a).

Notes

1. Instead of rezoning the original project site or other vacant land in the Village of Arlington Heights, the Village annexed and rezoned an unincorporated area as a site for the proposed low-income housing project. Metropolitan Housing Development Corporation agreed to construct its project on the newly annexed land, and the agreement was embodied in a consent decree. 469 F.Supp. 836 (E.D.Ill.1979).

2. In Dailey v. City of Lawton, 425 F.2d 1037 (10th Cir.1970), the court said (*inter alia*):

> The appellants point out that the race issue was not discussed at any of the public meetings and that there was no evidence of racial prejudice on the part of any city official. If proof of a civil right violation depends on an open statement by an official of an intent to discriminate, the Fourteenth Amendment offers little solace to those seeking its protection. In our opinion it is enough for the complaining parties to show that the local officials are effectuating the discriminatory designs of private individuals. * * *

> The appellants argue that a finding of discriminatory intent is barred because the project was opposed on the grounds of over-crowding the neighborhood, the local schools, and the recreational facilities and the overburdening of the local fire fighting capabilities. The testimony in this regard was vague and general. No school, fire, recreational, traffic or other official testified in support of the appellants' claims. The racial prejudice alleged and established by the plaintiffs must be met by something more than bald, conclusory assertions that the action was taken for other than discriminatory reasons. * * *

The 10th Circuit also said that failure to show racial prejudice on the part of the local officials would not have been fatal but on this point the Supreme Court's opinion in *Arlington Heights*, supra, is contra and overrules *Dailey*. Insofar as the *Kennedy Park* case, discussed in the 7th Circuit's opinion in *Arlington Heights*, supra, allows a conclusion that the Fourteenth Amendment has been violated without a finding of racially discriminatory intent, it was also overruled by *Arlington Heights*.

3. The Black Jack, Missouri litigation, referred to in the principal case, grew out of an attempt to construct a federally subsidized multifamily housing project in an unincorporated area outside St. Louis. The Inter-religious Center for Urban Affairs, Inc. (ICUA) had contracted to buy the necessary land and had then assigned its contract rights to Park View Heights Corporation to use as a site for the housing project. After financial, legal, and organization plans were completed, citizens in the area of the proposed project petitioned for incorporation of the area. After incorporation the new city council adopted a zoning ordinance which prohibited construction of any new multifamily housing. ICUA, Parkview, and eight individuals desiring to live in the proposed housing project brought suit to challenge the validity of the ordinance. The plaintiffs charged that the zoning ordinance was adopted specifically to stop construction of the housing project, whose sponsors had promised that it would be racially integrated, and that this violated the plaintiffs' rights under the Thirteenth and

Fourteenth Amendments. The defendant city sought to justify its adoption of the prohibition against multifamily housing construction on the grounds that prior construction of apartment developments in the area had already caused serious overcrowding in the schools, had overburdened the local roads, and had overburdened local taxpayers because apartments do not pay their "fair share" of property taxes. The District Court dismissed the action on the grounds that ICUA and Parkview did not have "standing" to raise the constitutional issues and that the controversy was not yet "ripe" for adjudication. The Court of Appeals disagreed with the District Court on both of these points and remanded the case for trial on the merits. 467 F.2d 1208 (8th Cir.1972).

While the *Park View Heights* case was in litigation, the United States also brought a suit against Black Jack to invalidate the zoning ordinance insofar as it excluded multifamily housing. This suit alleged that the Black Jack zoning resulted in racial discrimination in violation of the Fair Housing Act of 1968, 42 U.S.C.A. §§ 3601 et seq. (1976). The trial judge found that the exclusion of multifamily housing was not racially motivated and dismissed the suit. 372 F.Supp. 319 (E.D.Mo.1974). On appeal, however, the Court of Appeals reversed, holding that effect rather than motive was the touchstone in making out a case of racial discrimination under the Fair Housing Act; that since the Black Jack ordinance was shown to have a racially discriminatory effect, it could only be justified by a showing of compelling governmental interest; and that the asserted governmental interests in road and traffic control, prevention of school overcrowding, and devaluation of adjacent single-family homes did not rise to the level of a compelling governmental interest where there was no factual basis for the assertion that such interests were furthered by the ordinance. United States v. City of Black Jack, 508 F.2d 1179 (8th Cir.1974), cert. denied, 412 U.S. 1042 (1975).

On remand from the 1975 Court of Appeals decision in *Park View*, the District Court awarded compensatory damages and entered a decree invalidating the Black Jack zoning ordinance, but refused to enter a decree for the additional relief sought by plaintiffs—an injunction requiring the city to take affirmative measures within a reasonable time to provide multi-racial, moderate-income housing equal in amount to that which would have been constructed in the first phase of their project had it not been blocked by Black Jack's exclusionary zoning ordinance. The plaintiffs also suggested a number of "inclusionary" zoning measures, such as density bonuses and the waiver of restrictive building and zoning requirements. The city resisted, claiming that, although intervening economic factors such as increased construction costs had made the construction of the Park View project impossible, invalidation of the Black Jack zoning ordinance provided adequate relief because it restored plaintiffs to the legal position they held prior to enactment of the zoning ordinance.

The Court of Appeals reversed the District Court's decision on the affirmative relief issue and remanded the case for consideration of the appropriate affirmative relief to be granted. Park View Heights Corp. v. City of Black Jack, 605 F.2d 1033 (8th Cir.1979). The Court of Appeals said, *inter alia*, that the District Court should consider the City's duty to seek out and make land sites available for purchase by the plaintiff class that are properly zoned and so located with reference to public facilities and services as to meet established criteria for low and moderate income family housing. Id. at 1040.

4. Joseph Skillken & Co. v. City of Toledo, 528 F.2d 867 (6th Cir.1975) involved facts rather similar to those in *Arlington Heights*. The city's refusal to rezone a tract of land to permit construction of low-rent housing was alleged to violate plaintiffs' rights under the Civil Rights Act of 1964, the Fair Housing

Act, and the 14th Amendment. The District Court held that there was sufficient evidence to prove that the city's actions were racially motivated and that no compelling governmental interest was promoted by such actions. In reversing, the 6th Circuit displayed a great deal of hostility toward the idea that refusal to rezone could violate any federally protected rights of the plaintiffs. The court said (*inter alia*):

> The zoning laws in the present case are not inherently suspect. To apply the compelling state interest test would virtually invalidate all forms of state legislation where people are affected differently. * * *

> Members of the City Council did not cause nor create the concentration of black people in Toledo, and they are under no legal obligation to deconcentrate the area or to change the zoning laws to bring about deconcentration. * * *

> Nor do we regard the refusal of the City Council to rezone * * * as obstructing the rights of minorities to housing, upon which an inference of discrimination 'in effect' may be drawn * * *.

> * * *

> We live in a free society. The time has not yet arrived for the courts to strike down state zoning laws which are neutral on their face and valid when passed, in order to permit the construction at public expense of large numbers of low cost public housing units in a neighborhood where they do not belong, and where the property owners, relying on the zoning laws, have spent large sums of money to build fine homes for the enjoyment of their families.

> A federal court ought not to exercise state legislative functions. It is without power to do so, and furthermore it has not developed proficiency in that field.

The United States Supreme Court vacated the judgment of the 6th Circuit in *Skillken* and remanded for further consideration of the case in light of the Supreme Court's decision in *Arlington Heights* and Washington v. Davis. See 429 U.S. 1068, 97 S.Ct. 800 (1977). On remand, the 6th Circuit adhered to its original opinion. See 558 F.2d 350 (6th Cir.1977).

UNITED STATES v. CITY OF PARMA

United States Court of Appeals, 6th Circuit, 1981.
661 F.2d 562.

Before LIVELY, KEITH and MERRITT, Circuit Judges.

LIVELY, Circuit Judge. This is an appeal from the final decision of the district court in an action under the Fair Housing Act of 1968, Pub. L. 90–284, Title VIII, § 801 et seq., 42 U.S.C. § 3601 et seq. (Title VIII or the Act). The district court found that the City of Parma had engaged in a number of acts which had the purpose and effect of maintaining Parma as a segregated community in violation of the Act. A broad remedial order was entered.

I.

A.

The Attorney General filed the present action in the United States District Court for the Northern District of Ohio on April 27, 1973 seeking to enjoin Parma from violating the Act.[95] Such an action by the Attorney General is authorized by § 813 of the Act, 42 U.S.C. § 3613 [96] if the conditions of that section are met. Parma filed a counterclaim in which it requested that a three-judge court be convened; this request was denied. Thereafter the defendant filed a motion for summary judgment, which was denied by the district court in an order which identified three material issues of fact in dispute:

1. Whether Parma's virtually all-white character occurred adventitiously as a result of unrestricted free choice in the market place as defendant contends or whether it resulted from deliberate discrimination which was caused or perpetuated by defendant's conduct;

2. Whether successive decisions by defendant City of Parma or by and through its officials which resulted in the exclusion of various types of federally subsidized and potentially integrated housing had the purpose or effect of making housing unavailable to persons because of race; and

3. Whether Forest City's proposal to construct Parmatown Woods was rejected solely on nondiscriminatory grounds, as Parma contends, or was treated less favorably than other proposals, wholly or partially because of the actual or anticipated race of some of the prospective residents.

United States v. City of Parma, 471 F.Supp. 453, 454–55 (N.D.Ohio 1979).

B.

Following a trial on the issue of liability the district court concluded that the record established Parma's violation of the Act in a series of actions which had both the purpose and effect of maintaining Parma as a virtually all-white community. United States v. City of Parma, Ohio, 494 F.Supp. 1049 (N.D.Ohio 1980). The court made two initial findings:

> An extreme condition of racial segregation exists in the Cleveland metropolitan area.

95. Initially, the case was consolidated with a suit filed under the Act by several individuals and the NAACP. The complaint of the individuals and the NAACP was subsequently dismissed for lack of standing, absence of a justiciable controversy and untimeliness. *Cornelius v. City of Parma*, 374 F.Supp. 730 (N.D.Ohio), *vacated and remanded*, 506 F.2d 1400 (6th Cir.1974), *vacated and remanded*, 422 U.S. 1052, 95 S.Ct. 2673, 45 L.Ed.2d 705, *remanded for dismissal*, 521 F.2d 1401 (6th Cir.1975), *cert. denied*, 424 U.S. 955, 96 S.Ct. 1430, 47 L.Ed.2d 360 (1976).

96. § 3613. Enforcement by the Attorney General; issues of general public importance; civil action; Federal jurisdiction; complaint; preventive relief

(a) Whenever the Attorney General has reasonable cause to believe that any person or group of persons is engaged in a pattern or practice of resistance to the full enjoyment of any of the rights granted by this subchapter, or that any group of persons has been denied any of the rights granted by this subchapter and such denial raises an issue of general public importance, he may bring a civil action in any appropriate United States district court by filing with it a complaint setting forth the facts and requesting such preventive relief, including an application for a permanent or temporary injunction, restraining order, or other order against the person or persons responsible for such pattern or practice or denial of rights, as he deems necessary to insure the full enjoyment of the rights granted by this subchapter.

Id. at 1055; and

The proposition that the Cleveland metropolitan area and Parma became racially segregated solely as a result of associational preferences and economics, and not because of racial discrimination, is refuted overwhelmingly by the evidence in this case.

Id. at 1057. The court then made nine findings on the causes of the "dual housing market" which is found to exist in the Cleveland metropolitan area. In addition to private activities such as discriminatory acts of real estate dealers, "red lining" by lenders and insurers and refusals to list or sell by private owners, the court found that policies of the Federal Housing Administration and the Veterans Administration, particularly with respect to restrictive covenants, and site and tenant selection practices of the Cuyahoga Metropolitan Housing Authority (CMHA) had contributed to and maintained a black ghetto on the east side of Cleveland. Id. at 1057–59.

Parma, the largest suburb of Cleveland, lies west of the Cuyahoga River. According to the 1970 census, Parma had a population of 100,216 of whom 50 were black. The same census disclosed that metropolitan Cleveland had a population of 2,064,194 of whom 332,614 were black. Thus while the metropolitan area had a black population of 16%, Parma's was a small fraction of one per cent. The largest concentration of black residents was in the east side of the City of Cleveland and in a few eastern suburbs. The district court rejected Parma's two explanations for the segregated condition of the Cleveland area—associational preference and economic factors. In doing so, the court considered expert testimony from both parties and concluded that the experts produced by the government supported their conclusions better than those who testified for the City. Id. at 1059–65.

The district court then considered the evidence which the government had introduced to prove that Parma had followed racially exclusionary policies and practices. This evidence included testimony that Parma had a reputation and image of being the Cleveland suburb most hostile to blacks and statements of elected officials of Parma which were either overtly racist or were found to have racist meanings. These findings were cited as the backdrop against which the government challenged five specific actions or series of actions in this lawsuit:

A) Parma's refusal to enact a fair housing resolution welcoming "all persons of goodwill";

B) Parma's general opposition to all forms of public and low-income housing;

C) Parma's denial of building permits for a privately-sponsored low-income housing development—Parmatown Woods;

D) Parma's enactment and application of four land use ordinances which impose height, parking and voter approval limitations on housing developments; and

E) Parma's refusal to submit an adequate housing assistance plan in connection with its application for Community Development Block Grant Funds.

Id. at 1066. Each of these actions of the defendant was then discussed at length.

The district court concluded that the rejection by the Parma City Council of a "weak resolution" of welcome in the face of intense local opposition was a symbol of the official attitude and "sent out the message that black people of goodwill were not welcome." Id. at 1068. In reaching this conclusion the court rejected the mayor's testimony that he opposed the resolution only because it was superfluous in view of state law which provided for fair housing.

The district court reviewed the history of public housing in the Cleveland metropolitan area and noted that most of the conventional public housing in the area had been built inside Cleveland. A severe shortage of public housing was found to exist in the area, and this shortage was attributed directly to the exclusion of such housing from the suburbs. Parma was found to have a genuine need for public housing. Moreover, more than 1300 families living inside Cleveland and eligible for public housing had expressed an interest in moving to Parma. Parma had refused to participate in programs of the CMHA which would have brought low-income housing to the City. The district court determined that Parma's failure to seek and provide low-income housing was based on a desire to keep minorities out of the community and concluded that "Parma's opposition to any form of public or low-income housing has had an acute and foreseeable segregative effect on this virtually all-white city." Id. at 1072. The court again rejected explanations for the City's actions put forward by the mayor in his testimony.

One of the acts which precipitated the citizens' suit was Parma's rejection of a proposal by a private builder to construct a federally subsidized multiple-family housing project to be called Parmatown Woods. Building permits for Parmatown Woods were denied after review by Parma officials. The stated reason for the denial was the developer's failure to comply with Parma's land use ordinances. The court found that Parma had not required strict compliance with all its ordinances and procedures in at least four other instances involving apartment projects, one a "luxury" multi-family development by the same organization which proposed to build Parmatown Woods. The court detailed the widespread opposition to Parmatown Woods revealed by the evidence and concluded that it was racially motivated. It was during pendency of the Parmatown Woods proposal that both the mayor and the president of the city council were found to have made public racist statements. Id. at 1079–80.

The district court stated its ultimate finding with respect to the Parmatown Woods denial as follows:

> The Court finds that an important reason for the denial of the building permits was the fear that blacks would live in Parmatown Woods. This fear resulted in deviations from standard procedure and substantive norms and rendered impracticable, if not impossible, compliance with the land-use ordinances.

Id. at 1074. The developers abandoned Parmatown Woods and built a similar project in a village adjacent to Parma.

The day before the Parmatown Woods application was rejected the voters of Parma adopted two land use ordinances by referendum. One ordinance limited all future residential structures to a height of 35 feet (Parmatown Woods, with 10 floors, would have been much higher) and the other required voter approval for the development, construction or acquisition of a subsidized housing project by a public body or participation by individuals or non-public bodies in any federal rent subsidy program. The initiative petitions which resulted in placing these ordinances on the ballot were circulated during the period when the Parmatown Woods proposal was being debated publicly. The court recognized that there had been opposition to high-rise construction in Parma for some time and that many residents opposed such construction for non-racial reasons. Nevertheless, the court found persuasive evidence to indicate that racial considerations were involved in the passage of both ordinances, and that their effect was to "make the construction of any public or low-income housing very difficult." Id. at 1088.

The government contended that two other Parma ordinances have a racially exclusionary effect. One requires 2½ parking spaces per dwelling unit and the other requires voter approval for any change in the zoning code or in existing land uses. The latter ordinance was adopted after this lawsuit was filed. Finding that the parking space requirement is abnormally high and that the voter approval requirement for zoning changes adds costly delay to the process of obtaining clearance to construct low-income housing, the court concluded that the effect of the ordinances was to perpetuate housing segregation. The court found, however, that there was no showing that either of these ordinances was adopted for the purpose of excluding minorities. Id. at 1089.

Parma applied for funds under the Community Development Block Grant program (CDBG) which is designed to bring federal funds for housing and community development to local governments. The Parma application was rejected by HUD because the City did not submit an adequate "housing assistance plan." In rejecting the application HUD found Parma's goal of "zero" for housing assistance to low-income persons to be inconsistent with demonstrated needs. The district court rejected explanations for the City's refusal to correct the deficiency in the application. In doing so the court made credibility determinations. The finding on the issue of CDBG funds was stated thus:

"The receipt of CDBG funds would have helped the City of Parma to provide an equal opportunity in housing for all races (Tr. 715). By rejecting the funds, Parma assured that it would continue to be an almost totally segregated community. The Court finds that Parma's submission of an inadequate CDBG application and its refusal to amend that application were intended to foreclose, and in fact have foreclosed, housing opportunities that would otherwise have been made available to all low-income persons, including blacks."

Id. at 1094.

In light of its findings of fact the district court concluded that a violation of the Act by Parma had been established:

"The Court, after considering the evidence in its entirety, is convinced that Parma engaged in a pattern and practice of resistance to the full enjoyment of the rights granted by Sections 804(a) and 817 of the Fair Housing Act by following a consistent policy of making housing unavailable to black persons. The Court also finds that the City's actions denied the rights secured by Sections 804(a) and 817 to groups of persons. The Court's findings are based on both a standard of racially discriminatory intent and a standard of racially discriminatory effect. *See* pp. 1052–1055, supra. Under either standard, Parma's actions amounted to violations of provisions of the Fair Housing Act which forbid discrimination in housing on the basis of race.

"The Court specifically finds that the rejection of the fair housing resolution, the consistent refusal to sign a cooperation agreement with CMHA, the adamant and long-standing opposition to any form of public or low-income housing, the denial of the building permit for Parmatown Woods, the passage of the 35-foot height restriction ordinance, the passage of the ordinance requiring voter approval for low-income housing, and the refusal to submit an adequate housing assistance plan in the Community Block Development Grant application, individually and collectively, were motivated by a racially discriminatory and exclusionary intent. The purpose of these actions, the Court finds, was to exclude blacks from residing in Parma and to maintain the segregated 'character' of the City. These actions, individually and collectively, also violated the Fair Housing Act by denying to blacks, Parma residents, and prospective low-income housing developers rights secured by Sections 804(a) and 817."

Id. at 1095–96.

In reaching these conclusions the district court considered the public statements of elected city officials, the open hostility to low-income housing exhibited by residents and officials alike and departures from normal practices by subordinate city employees in handling the Parmatown Woods application.

C.

The district court entered a separate remedial order following submissions by the parties and a hearing. United States v. City of Parma, 504 F.Supp. 913 (N.D.Ohio 1980). The "comprehensive remedial plan" formulated by the court, id. at 916, contains a general injunction against discrimination in housing by the City and a number of affirmative requirements. The general provision permanently enjoined the City, its officers, etc. from:

1. Engaging in any conduct having the purpose or effect of perpetuating or promoting racial residential segregation or of denying or abridging the right of any person to equal housing opportunity on account of race, color, religion, sex or national origin;

2.   Discriminating against any person or group of persons on account of race, color, religion, sex or national origin in connection with the planning, development, construction, acquisition, financing, operation or approval of any low-income or public housing units;

3.   Interfering with any person in the exercise of his right to secure equal housing opportunity for himself or for others; and

4.   Taking any action which in any way denies or makes unavailable housing to persons on the basis of race, color, religion, sex or national origin.

Id. at 918.

The defendant was additionally ordered to: (1) establish a mandatory fair housing educational program for all city officials and employees involved in carrying out the terms of the remedial order; (2) enact a resolution welcoming persons of all races, creeds and colors to reside in Parma and setting forth its policy of nondiscrimination in housing; (3) undertake a comprehensive program of newspaper advertising to promote Parma as an equal housing opportunity community and to make copies of the liability opinion and remedial order available, free of charge; (4) take "whatever action is necessary in order to allow the construction of public housing in the City," id. at 922; (5) adopt a plan for use of an existing "Section 8" housing program; (6) take required steps for submitting an acceptable application for CDBG funds; (7) "make all efforts necessary to ensure that at least 133 units of low and moderate-income housing are provided annually in Parma. This number is a threshold beyond which Parma must strive to go in providing new housing opportunities in the City. This is so because, in addition to addressing its current needs, Parma must address those low-income housing needs which have been in existence since at least 1968 but which have been ignored by Parma for racial reasons. This Court can require no less in carrying out its obligations in this action." Id. at 923 (footnote omitted).

In addition to the foregoing affirmative requirements the order contained provisions which invalidated the ordinance which required all low-income housing proposals to be submitted in a referendum and limited the other three ordinances in question so that they will not apply to hinder any development of low or moderate-income housing in Parma. The order also provided for the establishment of a fair housing committee within city government with specified functions and an evaluation committee to be appointed by the district court. Finally, the district court appointed a special master to see that the provisions of the order are carried out in an orderly manner. Seven "powers and functions" of the special master were set out in the order:

1.   The Special Master shall oversee the formulation, by the Fair Housing and Evaluation Committees, of the remedial procedures to carry out the provisions of this Order. He shall evaluate the sufficiency as well as the practicability of these procedures in light of the purposes which they are intended to serve;

2. The Special Master shall be available, during the formulation process, on a regular basis, to give advice to and to serve as an arbitrator of possible disputes between the parties and/or Committees. All questions which the parties and/or Committees may have concerning this Order and their duties thereunder shall be directed first to the Special Master. Questions which cannot be resolved by the Special Master may be addressed directly to the Court;

3. The Special Master shall prepare and submit to the Court recommendations concerning the remedial plan prepared pursuant to this Order, together with any revisions or alternative plans which he deems necessary to carry out the Court's mandate in this action;

4. The Special Master may conduct such hearings and investigations as he deems necessary to the performance of his duties;

5. The Special Master may utilize the services, when necessary, of experts in various fields in performing his duties under this Order. The Special Master and such experts shall have complete and unrestricted access to the records of defendant City of Parma. They shall have free access to all Parma employees and staff. They shall be given notice of and free access to all meetings, public or private, at which this Order and the remedial plan to be formulated hereunder are to be discussed. The Special Master shall determine the time and place of all meetings except those regularly scheduled governmental meetings whose time and place have been established by State law, local ordinance, or long-standing custom or tradition. Meetings set by the Special Master shall have precedence over all other business of the City. The Special Master shall preside over those parts of every meeting he attends which are, in his judgment, related to these Remedial Orders. The Special Master may bring official reporters to record and then to transcribe the minutes of said meetings, executive or otherwise. Records of executive sessions shall be held in confidence by the Special Master, his advisers, and the reporters, unless otherwise ordered by the Court. It is the intention of the Court that the Special Master's access to private meetings shall be interpreted broadly to include, for example, executive sessions and councilmanic caucuses;

6. With the consent of the attorneys for both parties, the Special Master may, as the need arises, contact and confer with the attorneys for the respective parties. If counsel for one party does not so consent, the Special Master may order a meeting with both parties;

7. The Special Master shall oversee the implementation of the ultimate remedial plan for this litigation and report to the Court, on a regular basis, concerning Parma's progress under this Order. Such report may contain recommendations, if necessary, concerning action to be taken by Parma to improve compliance with the remedial plan.

Id. at 925.

II

A.

In this appeal Parma contests virtually every conclusion of the district court, though it does not claim explicitly that any subsidiary findings upon which those conclusions are based are clearly erroneous.

* * *

B.

Some of the claimed errors refer either to jurisdiction of the court or to procedural matters.

* * *

2. Parma also asserts that the district court lacked subject matter jurisdiction because none of the provisions of the Act apply to governmental activities of municipalities. The City argues that neither the language of the Act nor its legislative history indicates a congressional intent to have it apply to municipalities.

We have examined the references to legislative history cited by both parties and find the history inconclusive. This is not surprising since Title VIII was added to the 1968 Civil Rights Act as a floor amendment. Thus, there is no committee report upon which to rely. While it appears to be true, as the City claims, that the Act was aimed primarily at the real estate industry, the legislative history does not establish with certainty that its operative provisions were not intended to be applied more broadly.

Turning to the language of the Act, it is apparent that its purposes were broadly stated. Section 801, 42 U.S.C. § 3601, states, "It is the policy of the United States to provide, within constitutional limitations, for fair housing throughout the United States." Many of the operative provisions of the Act are contained in § 804, 42 U.S.C. § 3604:

§ 3604. Discrimination in the sale or rental of housing

As made applicable by section 3603 of this title and except as exempted by sections 3603(b) and 3607 of this title, it shall be unlawful—

(a) To refuse to sell or rent after the making of a bona fide offer, or to refuse to negotiate for the sale or rental of, or otherwise make unavailable or deny, a dwelling to any person because of race, color, religion, sex, or national origin.

(b) To discriminate against any person in the terms, conditions, or privileges of sale or rental of a dwelling, or in the provision of services or facilities in connection therewith, because of race, color, religion, sex or national origin.

(c) To make, print, or publish, or cause to be made, printed, or published any notice, statement, or advertisement, with respect to the sale or rental of a dwelling that indicates any preference, limitation, or discrimination based on race, color, religion, sex, or national origin, or an intention to make any such preference, limitation, or discrimination.

(d) To represent to any person because of race, color, religion, sex, or national origin that any dwelling is not available for inspection, sale, or rental when such dwelling is in fact so available.

(e) For profit, to induce or attempt to induce any person to sell or rent any dwelling by representations regarding the entry or prospective entry into the neighborhood of a person or persons of a particular race, color, religion, sex, or national origin.

Parma contends that the use of "person" in the Act indicates an intent to reach only private transactions and practices in the real estate business. If Congress had intended to include municipalities, it is argued, it would have done so by specifying local governmental activities. The government answers that discriminatory acts of municipalities in the field of housing are proscribed by the language in § 804(a), "or otherwise make unavailable or deny, a dwelling to any person because of race, color, religion, sex, or national origin." It argues that the acts of Parma which the district court found to violate the Act did "otherwise make unavailable or deny" dwellings to black residents of the Cleveland area who need low-cost housing.[97] Given the broadly stated purpose of the Act and the fact that § 813 authorizes suit against the "person or persons" responsible for violations, the government argues that the Act reaches discrimination in housing regardless of the identity or nature of its perpetrator. It points out that "person" has been held to include municipalities in other civil rights acts. See Monell v. New York Dept. of Social Services, 436 U.S. 658, 98 S.Ct. 2018, 56 L.Ed.2d 611 (1978).

The courts of appeals which have considered the question of whether a city may be sued under the Act have answered in the affirmative. See United States v. City of Black Jack, Missouri, 508 F.2d 1179, 1183–84 (8th Cir.1974), cert. denied, 422 U.S. 1042, 95 S.Ct. 2656, 45 L.Ed.2d 694 (1975), where the issue was squarely decided. The same answer to the question is implicit in the decisions in Resident Advisory Board v. Rizzo, 564 F.2d 126 (3d Cir.1977), cert. denied, 435 U.S. 908, 98 S.Ct. 1457, 55 L.Ed.2d 499 (1978), and Kennedy Park Homes Ass'n v. City of Lackawanna, 436 F.2d 108 (2d Cir.1970), cert. denied, 401 U.S. 1010, 91 S.Ct. 1256, 28 L.Ed.2d 546 (1971). Furthermore, in Village of Arlington Heights v. Metropolitan Housing Dev. Corp. [Arlington Heights I], 429 U.S. 252, 271, 97 S.Ct. 555, 566, 50 L.Ed.2d 450 (1977), the Supreme Court, following a finding that the intent necessary to establish a constitutional violation had not been proven, remanded for de-

---

97. In addition to claiming that the City's actions violated § 804(a), the government asserts that denial of the building application for Parmatown Woods violated § 817, 42 U.S.C. § 3617:

§ 3617. Interference, coercion, or intimidation; enforcement by civil action

It shall be unlawful to coerce, intimidate, threaten or interfere with any person in the exercise or enjoyment of, or on ac-

count of his having exercised or enjoyed, or on account of his having aided or encouraged any other person in the exercise or enjoyment of, any right granted or protected by section 3603, 3604, 3605, or 3606 of this title. This section may be enforced by appropriate civil action.

The district court found violations of both § 804 and § 817.

termination of whether "a zoning decision made by a public body may, and that petitioners' [the village's] action did, violate § 3604 or § 3617." Upon remand the court of appeals found that a zoning decision of a public body can, and in the Arlington Heights case, most likely did violate the Act. The Supreme Court denied certiorari following the remand decision. Metropolitan Housing Dev. Corp. v. Village of Arlington Heights [Arlington Heights II], 558 F.2d 1283, 1290 (7th Cir.1977), cert. denied, 434 U.S. 1025, 98 S.Ct. 752, 54 L.Ed.2d 772 (1978).

In agreement with the courts which have applied Title VIII to municipalities we conclude that the comprehensive purpose of the Act would be diluted if it were held to apply only to the actions of private individuals and entities. No intent to so restrict it may be gleaned from the language of the Act. On the other hand, § 815, 42 U.S.C. § 3615, provides in part "any law of a State, a political subdivision, or other such jurisdiction that purports to require or permit any action that would be a discriminatory housing practice under this subchapter shall to that extent be invalid." This provision is not self-executing, and would require legal action against the offending state or political subdivision for its enforcement. We believe it was the intent of Congress to provide for actions against states and political subdivisions for violation of § 804, § 817 and § 813 as well.

*   *   *

C.

The substantive contentions of the City are divided into three arguments, exclusive of those which deal directly with remedy.

1. The City argues that if the Fair Housing Act purports to apply to governmental activities of municipalities, it is unconstitutional. Support for this argument, it is claimed, is found in National League of Cities v. Usery, 426 U.S. 833, 96 S.Ct. 2465, 49 L.Ed.2d 245 (1976). In that case the Supreme Court held that the Tenth Amendment prevents Congress from exercising its powers under the Commerce Clause "to directly displace the States' freedom to structure integral operations in areas of traditional governmental functions * * *." Id. at 852, 96 S.Ct. at 2474. The holding in National League of Cities does not control the present case. The Fair Housing Act was not enacted pursuant to the Commerce Clause. Rather it was based on authority of § 2 of the Thirteenth Amendment. United States v. City of Black Jack, supra, 508 F.2d at 1184; United States v. Bob Lawrence Realty, Inc., 474 F.2d 115, 120–21 (5th Cir.), cert. denied, 414 U.S. 826, 94 S.Ct. 131, 38 L.Ed.2d 59 (1973). In Fitzpatrick v. Bitzer, 427 U.S. 445, 456, 96 S.Ct. 2666, 2671, 49 L.Ed.2d 614 (1976), the Supreme Court, speaking through Justice Rehnquist, stated "We think that Congress may, in determining what is 'appropriate legislation' for the purpose of enforcing the provisions of the Fourteenth Amendment, provide for private suits against States or state officials which are constitutionally impermissible in other contexts." (Citations and footnote omitted). The Thirteenth and Fourteenth Amendments were adopted following the Civil War and both were intended to limit the authority of the states. Id. at 453–55, 96

S.Ct. at 2670–2671. Congress acted within its constitutional authority in making Title VIII applicable to the states and their political subdivisions.

2. The City also contends that the district court erred in failing to follow the established law of this circuit. Two decisions of this court are relied upon principally: Mahaley v. Cuyahoga Metropolitan Housing Authority, 500 F.2d 1087 (6th Cir.1974), cert. denied, 419 U.S. 1108, 95 S.Ct. 781, 42 L.Ed.2d 805 (1975), and Joseph Skillken & Co. v. City of Toledo, 528 F.2d 867 (6th Cir.1975), vacated and remanded, 429 U.S. 1068, 97 S.Ct. 800, 50 L.Ed.2d 786, decision adhered to, 558 F.2d 350 (6th Cir.), cert. denied, 434 U.S. 985, 98 S.Ct. 611, 54 L.Ed.2d 479 (1977). While there is language in the opinions in the above cases which supports some of the arguments of Parma, particularly with respect to the scope of the remedy, the holdings of the cases are not controlling here. *Mahaley* was a suit under the Housing Act of 1937, not the Fair Housing Act of 1968. The two statutes are quite different in their purposes and structures. The 1937 Act was not concerned primarily with ending discrimination in housing—the clear purpose of the 1968 Act. The holding of this court in *Skillken* was based on a finding that no racial discrimination was shown to have been involved in the city's refusal to grant a rezoning request and that Toledo was not racially segregated. We hold that on the record before us the district court did not err in reaching a contrary conclusion in the present case. More important for present purposes is the fact that in *Skillken* this court did not base its holdings on a construction of Title VIII. In fact, the Fair Housing Act is not mentioned in any of the dispositive language of the opinion. We find the Supreme Court's decisions in James v. Valtierra, 402 U.S. 137, 91 S.Ct. 1331, 28 L.Ed.2d 678 (1971) and City of Eastlake v. Forest City Enterprises, Inc., 426 U.S. 668, 96 S.Ct. 2358, 49 L.Ed.2d 132 (1976), cited by Parma in support of this argument to be equally inapposite.

3. Parma next argues that "the government did not sustain its heavy burden of proving its clear entitlement to an injunction, and the district court erred in determining liability under the Fair Housing Act * * *." Thus, the City asserts that none of the five grounds relied upon by the district court in granting relief furnishes a valid basis for its judgment.

(a.) The failure of the city council to adopt a resolution welcoming all persons of goodwill to Parma had only symbolic value, as the district court conceded. Certainly this failure alone would not have supported a finding of intent to exclude minorities from the City. However, there was ample testimony that Parma already had a reputation among black residents of the Cleveland area of hostility to racial minorities. Given the context in which the council debate and vote took place, we cannot hold that the district court erred in concluding that this event constituted part of a pattern or practice of official conduct which violated the Fair Housing Act.

(b.) The district court held that Parma unlawfully rejected public and low-income housing. Parma argues that it was not required to promote low-income or public housing. Two decisions are cited for the proposition that an action against a municipality for declining to include low-income or publicly financed housing in development plans fails to state a claim upon which relief may be granted. See Acevedo v. Nassau County, N.Y., 500 F.2d 1078 (2d Cir.1974); Citizens Comm. for Faraday Wood v. Lindsay, 507 F.2d 1065 (2d Cir.1974), cert. denied, 421 U.S. 948, 95 S.Ct. 1679, 44 L.Ed.2d 102 (1975). Neither of these cases was brought by the Attorney General on the basis of a pattern or practice of discrimination. Further, there was no finding of discriminatory intent in the action of either local government. Finally, the actual holding in *Faraday Wood* was a narrow one—"that a city cannot be compelled to build and finance a specific housing project designated, in part, to aid low-income families or any specified group of its citizens simply because it started to plan such a project." 507 F.2d at 1071. Since the district court did not order Parma to build or finance a specific project this holding has no relevance to the present case.

The district court rejected Parma's explanation for failing to seek low and moderate-income publicly financed housing—that the CMHA was inept and the City did not want to deal with it. There was evidence of a number of programs in which Parma could have participated without becoming involved with the CMHA. The evidence of a need for such housing, both among Parma's residents and others in the greater Cleveland area who would consider moving to Parma, was unrebutted. The evidence supported the district court's conclusion that this failure of the City was part of a pattern or practice of discrimination and resulted in large part from a decision to maintain Parma as a virtually all-white community. There is no requirement that such intent be the sole basis of official action, if it is a motivating factor. Arlington Heights I, supra, 429 U.S. 252, 265–66, 97 S.Ct. 555, 563–564.

(c.) The rejection of the Parmatown Woods project was justified, the City contends, because the developer failed to comply with some of the requirements for a building permit. This is technically correct. However, the evidence was clear that strict compliance was not required for other multiple-family developments. The deviations from customary practices in the case of Parmatown Woods consisted of a requirement of unusually strict adherence to the provisions of the Parma Planning and Zoning Code and a departure from the City's normal practice of accommodation with developers through informal negotiations. Departure from normal procedural requirements was identified by the Supreme Court in *Arlington Heights I*, supra, as a factor to be considered in seeking to learn the intent of a public body. Id. at 267, 97 S.Ct. at 564. The contrast between procedures followed in handling the application of Parmatown Woods and those of Parmatown Gardens and Parmatown Towers, two other multiple-family developments, was particularly striking. Informality and cooperation with the developer (the same developer in each case) were the essence of the attitude of Parma officers and employees in processing the Parmatown Tower and Gardens projects to successful conclusion. Significantly, neither was for low or moderate-income families. The same attitude appears to have prevailed with respect to Parmatown Woods in its early stages. Difficulties began to appear only after Parma residents and officials voiced questions about the development's occupancy and when it was made clear by HUD officials that residents in that project could not be limited to senior citizens or to Parma residents. The district court could properly conclude that the difficulties experienced with the Parmatown Woods project resulted from an intent to exclude minorities. This is particularly so in view of the public statements of two of the highest elected officials which occurred during the period when the application was pending.

(d.) We believe Parma's refusal to complete an acceptable application for CDBG funds presents the clearest evidence of the City's attitude. The very application form which was rejected for failure to include an adequate housing assistance plan revealed the need for low-income housing. The City wanted federal funds. The mayor's testimony is clear on this point. It is equally clear that the City decided to forego such funds for community development rather than accept federally assisted housing as part of the package. Of course, there is no general requirement that any community participate in the block grant program. However, in the context of this case, where a desire and need for federal development funds was admitted and no believable explanation for failure to pursue them was given, the district court was justified in finding that the reason for the city's failure to do so was rooted in an intent to exclude minorities which was part of the pattern or practice charged.

(e.) Parma contends that the district court erred in finding support for its conclusion that the City violated the Act in the four land use ordinances adopted by the City. The district court decided that no discriminatory motive was involved in enactment of the ordinances requiring 2½ parking spaces per residential unit and requiring a voter referendum for zoning changes. However, the court found that both had a discriminatory impact. On the other hand, the court determined that the ordinances prescribing height limitations for buildings and requiring voter referendum approval for public or subsidized housing were motivated, at least in part, by a desire to exclude minorities. The general right of local communities to control land use by zoning ordinances and regulations is not an issue in this case. The Supreme Court has upheld this municipal authority against a variety of challenges over the years. See, e.g., Village of Euclid v. Ambler Realty Co., 272 U.S. 365, 47 S.Ct. 114, 71 L.Ed. 303 (1926); Village of Belle Terre v. Boraas, 416 U.S. 1, 94 S.Ct. 1536, 39 L.Ed.2d 797 (1974). However, zoning decisions which have a racially discriminatory effect have been held to violate the Fair Housing Act. *City of Black Jack*, supra; see *Arlington Heights II*, supra. It was not impermissible to hold that Parma's zoning decisions were part of "a pattern or practice of resistance to the full enjoyment" of rights granted by the Fair Housing Act.

The findings of the district court on mixed questions of law and fact and its conclusion that Parma has violated the Act are amply supported by the record. We find no departure from proper legal standards in the determination of Parma's liability. The remedial order will be dealt with separately.

III

A.

With respect to remedy, Parma asserts that the district court exceeded its authority in "appointing a special master, restructuring Parma's municipal government, supplanting elected officials and depriving its citizens of their cherished right to vote in referendum." In the district court's own words, it formulated a "comprehensive remedial plan" in this case. 504 F.Supp. at 916. Though the plan is comprehensive, and in some respects unique, the question for this court to decide is whether it is a suitable remedy for the violation which was found to exist. As in cases of constitutional violations, courts must carefully tailor the remedy in cases of statutory violations, limiting it to relief necessary to correct the violations. Resident Advisory Board v. Rizzo, supra, 564 F.2d at 149. The breadth of the remedial order does not, in itself, indicate that a court has exceeded its authority. As Chief Justice Burger wrote for the Supreme Court in Swann v. Charlotte-Mecklenburg Board of Education, 402 U.S. 1, 15, 91 S.Ct. 1267, 1276, 28 L.Ed.2d 554 (1971):

> Once a right and a violation have been shown, the scope of a district court's equitable powers to remedy past wrongs is broad, for breadth and flexibility are inherent in equitable remedies.

> "The essence of equity jurisdiction has been the power of the Chancellor to do equity and to mould each decree to the necessities of the particular case. Flexibility rather than rigidity has distinguished it. The qualities of mercy and practicality have made equity the instrument for nice adjustment and reconciliation between the public interest and private needs as well as between competing private claims." Hecht Co. v. Bowles, 321 U.S. 321, 329–330, 64 S.Ct. 587, 591–592 (1944), cited in Brown, II, [Brown v. Bd. of Ed.] supra, 349 U.S. [294] at 300, 75 S.Ct. [753] at 756 [99 L.Ed. 1083].

B.

Our examination of the remedial order leads to the conclusion that most of its provisions do represent a tailoring of relief to correct the statutory violations found by the district court. Injunctive relief is specifically authorized by section 813 of the Act and has been granted in cases involving violations by municipalities. E.g., Park View Heights Corp. v. City of Black Jack, 605 F.2d 1033, 1038 (8th Cir.1979), cert. denied, 445 U.S. 905, 100 S.Ct. 1081, 63 L.Ed.2d 321 (1980). The four-part injunction entered by the district court does no more than prohibit activities of a type which the court has found to violate the Act by making housing in Parma unavailable to persons because of race. The district court did not abuse its discretion in granting this relief.

C.

The affirmative provisions of the remedial order are not as unusual as Parma suggests in its brief. Most, if not all of those provisions have been incorporated in decrees of various courts which have decided Fair

Housing Act cases. What is unusual is to find such a wide range of affirmative requirements in a case where the defendant is a political entity. It is common in pattern or practice suits against private defendants to require educational programs for employees and advertising programs to advise the public of the nondiscriminatory policies which will be followed. E.g., United States v. Youritan Construction Co., 370 F.Supp. 643, 652 (N.D.Cal.1973), aff'd in pertinent part, 509 F.2d 623 (9th Cir.1975); United States v. Long, 537 F.2d 1151, 1152 (4th Cir.1975), cert. denied, 429 U.S. 871, 97 S.Ct. 185, 50 L.Ed.2d 151 (1976); United States v. Warwick Mobile Homes Estates, Inc., 558 F.2d 194, 196 (4th Cir.1977). We can see no objection to requiring an educational program to acquaint those officials and employees of the City who are responsible for carrying out the terms of the remedial order of their obligations thereunder. With respect to the requirement of advertising, we have found no case where a similar requirement has been imposed upon a city or other political entity. Unlike realtors and lenders, a city does not ordinarily carry on an advertising program to promote its activities. Nevertheless, on uncontradicted evidence, Parma's reputation as a closed community was found to be widespread in the Cleveland area. The advertising campaign ordered by the court, if of reasonable duration, should correct this image without imposing too great a burden on the City. However, this advertising material may only reflect the official attitude of the City as an equal opportunity housing community. It may not claim to reflect the private attitudes of the citizens of Parma, as suggested by the order. Private attitudes and opinions are not subject to official control.[98] The requirement that Parma adopt a welcoming resolution is relatively innocuous and fits in with the advertising campaign which we have approved.

The requirements that the City take whatever action may be necessary to permit construction of public housing, adopt a plan to utilize an existing section 8 program and take required steps for submitting an acceptable application for CDBG funds are reasonable. All respond to the needs of Parma as found by the district court and reflect evidence at the remedial hearing concerning the best means of correcting the violations found to exist. However, if the City should adopt a feasible plan to meet its needs for such housing without resort to programs specified in the order, it is to have this flexibility. The order is affirmed as written with this understanding.

The court affirms and strongly endorses the requirement that a fair housing committee be established within city government. This was described by a highly qualified witness, Paul Davidoff, as a major compo-

---

98. The dissent appears to overlook the limitations which we have placed on the City's duty to advertise. The only concern of this court is with the official actions of the City and its representatives. To the extent these official acts and statements have created a reasonable perception that Parma is officially committed to remaining a community where racial minorities have no opportunity to reside, it was a proper element of the remedy to require that pub-licity be given to the changed official policy. The dissent refers with emphasis, to a statement in the district court remedial order that the community be informed that discriminatory practices no longer reflect the attitude of the citizens of Parma. This portion of the district court's order was not approved, and our opinion makes it clear that only the official acts and policies of the City are to be the subject of advertising.

nent of the remedial plan offered by the government. If this committee is thoughtfully constituted and functions in the manner envisioned by Mr. Davidoff, much of the tension and resentment which is evident among Parma residents and officials will be dissipated. This committee offers the best hope for a harmonious solution to the problems which this lawsuit has identified.

The requirement that Parma make all efforts to ensure that at least 133 units of low and moderate-income housing are provided each year is premature. Though this figure was suggested by a government witness, the same witness testified immediately thereafter that the fair housing committee might find that a different number of units is required. In setting the 133-unit requirement the district court merely established a threshold figure and recognized that the ultimate burden of providing low and moderate-income housing in Parma "may indeed lie with the housing development community" rather than the City itself. 504 F.Supp. at 923. The City must take all necessary steps to see that the housing needs as described in the remedial order are met in a timely fashion. However, we believe that no particular number should be required at this time, but that a goal of meeting the need for such housing within a reasonable time should be established by the committee. Accordingly, the provision fixing a specific number of units is vacated.

The district court invalidated only one ordinance, the one requiring all proposals for low-income housing to be submitted to a voter referendum. The court found that this ordinance was racially motivated and that its effect would be to make it impossible to attract any such housing. Though invalidation of an ordinance is a strong remedy, it is not beyond the power of a court where necessary to correct a violation. E.g., Park View Heights Corp. v. City of Black Jack, supra, 605 F.2d at 1038. We affirm this portion of the order along with the provision which permits the other three ordinances in question to remain in force except as they apply to low or moderate-income housing. This provision tailors the relief to the violation, and intrudes as little as possible into the authority of the City.

With the exceptions noted we find no abuse of discretion in the provisions of the remedial order discussed to this point, and those provisions are affirmed.

D.

As has been stated, the district court appointed a special master with specified powers and functions. This action was taken by the court upon its own motion. No government witness suggested a need for such an appointment and there was no provision for a special master in the proposed plan initially submitted by the government. The district judge stated that a special master is necessary for the resolution of the litigation to go forward in an orderly fashion. We find no support for this conclusion in the record. The government's chief witness on remedy, Mr. Davidoff, emphasized the necessity of getting the community of Parma involved in the task of making it a city where equal opportunity in housing would be a reality. He ascribed paramount importance to a local fair housing committee authorized to develop, monitor and implement the court's orders in this case. Davidoff stated that the "first principle" of planning a solution to a situation such as Parma's is that solutions take time. A different Parma cannot be created immediately by court order. The second principle, he testified "is that of giving maximum freedom to the local jurisdiction to develop its own solution, to try to not take away the basic rights that inhere in local government to develop its plans for its future growth." The imposition of a special master would appear antithetical to the recommendations of this witness. Mr. Davidoff said, "I think that the plan is in Parma's hands, at least in the first stage, according to my set of recommendations." Since the court largely adopted this witness's set of recommendations in its remedial order we can discern no reason for departing from the underlying philosophy of those recommendations which is to give Parma the first opportunity to correct the conditions which were found to violate the Act.

We can understand the district court's apprehension that too much of its judicial time will be taken up with administering details of the plan. We believe, however, that the court will be able to oversee implementation of the plan by working through the fair housing committee and the evaluation committee as suggested by Mr. Davidoff and as provided for in the remedial order.

The appointment of a special master to oversee implementation of a court order by a municipality is an extraordinary remedy. We do not believe that such an appointment would represent the least intrusive method of achieving the government's stated goal in this case of making Parma a community which will offer low-income persons and members of minority groups some choice as to where they will live. The order appointing a special master is reversed.

The partial stay heretofore entered by this court, 644 F.2d 887, is dissolved. The judgment of the district court is affirmed in part and reversed in part as indicated in this opinion.

[Merritt, Circuit Judge, filed an opinion in which he dissented in part from the Court's opinion because he thought the order requiring the Parma city officials, on behalf of the City, "to affirm a particular belief, to express and 'promote' a particular racial 'attitude' or political viewpoint—that discriminatory practices * * * no longer reflect the attitude of the city and its citizens"—violated the City's First Amendment rights.]

Notes and Questions

1. Because the suit in the principal case was brought by the United States under the Fair Housing Act, it was unnecessary to show that a particular housing project had been blocked by Parma's zoning regulations. The "standing" issue could not arise.

2. Contrast the attitude of the Court of Appeals panel that decided the *City of Parma* case with that of the panel that decided the *Skillken* case, discussed in Note 3 following the Arlington Heights case. Does the Court persua-

sively distinguish the two cases:? The *Skillken* opinion, in its very first paragraph, indicates that case was "brought under 42 U.S.C.A. §§ 1401 et seq., §§ 1981–1983, 2000d et seq., and §§ 3610 et seq." See 528 F.Supp. 867, 879 (1975). 42 U.S.C.A. §§ 3601 et seq. is, of course the same Fair Housing Act upon which the suit in the *City of Parma* case was based.

3. See Clients' Council v. Pierce, 711 F.2d 1406 (8th Cir. 1983) (HUD held liable for purposeful racial housing discrimination in violation of the Fifth Amendment and Title VIII of the Civil Rights Act of 1968; case remanded with directions to fashion an effective remedy directing HUD to issue orders requiring Texarkana Housing Authority to desegregate all of its housing projects).

*

Index

---

†